The
CHELSEA HOUSE LIBRARY
of LITERARY CRITICISM

The

CHELSEA HOUSE LIBRARY
of LITERARY CRITICISM

TWENTIETH-CENTURY
AMERICAN LITERATURE

Volume 1

General Editor

HAROLD BLOOM

1985
CHELSEA HOUSE PUBLISHERS
New York

MANAGING EDITOR
Sally Stepanek
ASSOCIATE EDITORS
Brendan Bernhard
S. T. Joshi
Frank Menchaca
Julia Myer
Patrick Nielsen Hayden
Anna Williams
EDITORIAL COORDINATOR
Karyn Browne
EDITORIAL STAFF
Linda Grossman
Joy Johannessen
Karin Thomsen
RESEARCH
Jack Lechner
Kevin Pask
Cornelia Pearsall
DESIGN
Susan Lusk

Printed and bound in the United States of
America.

Library of Congress Cataloging in Publication
Data
Twentieth-century American literature.
    (The Chelsea House library of literary
    criticism)
    Bibliography: p.
    1. American literature—20th century—
    History and criticism—Collected works.
    2. Authors, American—20th century—
    Biography—Dictionaries. 3. Criticism—
    United States. I. Bloom, Harold.
    II. Series.
    PS221.T834   1985   810'.9'005
    84-27430
    ISBN 0-87754-802-1 (v. 1)

CHELSEA HOUSE PUBLISHERS
Harold Steinberg, Chairman & Publisher
Susan Lusk, Vice President
A Division of Chelsea House Educational
    Communications, Inc.
133 Christopher Street, New York, NY 10014

CONTENTS

Abbreviations vi
Preface vii
Walter Abish 1
Henry Adams 6
Léonie Adams 45
Renata Adler 51
James Agee 59
Conrad Aiken 65
Edward Albee 85
William Alfred 116
Nelson Algren 119
A. R. Ammons 127
Jon Anderson 170
Maxwell Anderson 175
Robert Anderson 180
Sherwood Anderson 185
Maya Angelou 201
John Ashbery 207
Isaac Asimov 251
Margaret Atwood 258
Louis Auchincloss 264
James Baldwin 272
Imamu Amiri Baraka (LeRoi Jones) 298
Djuna Barnes 305
John Barth 314
Donald Barthelme 330
L. Frank Baum 345
Peter S. Beagle 351
Ann Beattie 357
S. N. Behrman 364
Saul Bellow 369
Stephen Vincent Benét 433
Thomas Berger 440
John Berryman 453
Ambrose Bierce 470
Elizabeth Bishop 481
John Peale Bishop 518
R. P. Blackmur 523
Robert Bly 531
Louise Bogan 538
Edgar Bowers 547
Jane Bowles 550
Paul Bowles 554
Kay Boyle 560
Ray Bradbury 566
Gwendolyn Brooks 573
Pearl S. Buck 578
Kenneth Burke 584
William S. Burroughs 591
Additional Reading 599
Acknowledgments 606

ABBREVIATIONS

AI	AMERICAN IMAGO		Nwk	NEWSWEEK
AM	AMERICAN MERCURY		NWR	NORTHWEST REVIEW
APR	AMERICAN POETRY REVIEW		NY	NEW YORKER
AS	AMERICAN SCHOLAR		NYM	NEW YORK MAGAZINE
ASt	ASIAN STUDIES		NYRB	NEW YORK REVIEW OF BOOKS
At	ATLANTIC MONTHLY		NYT	NEW YORK TIMES
B&B	BOOKS AND BOOKMEN		NYTBR	NEW YORK TIMES BOOK REVIEW
BlS	BLACK SCHOLAR		OnR	ONTARIO REVIEW
CLAJ	CLA JOURNAL		OR	OHIO REVIEW
Cmty	COMMENTARY		Parn	PARNASSUS: POETRY IN REVIEW
Com	COMMONWEAL		PN	POETRY NATION
CQ	CRITICAL QUARTERLY		PP	PLAYS AND PLAYERS
CR	CHICAGO REVIEW		PR	PARTISAN REVIEW
Crt	CRITIQUE		PSch	PRAIRIE SCHOONER
DS	DRAMA SURVEY		Ram	RAMPARTS
EJ	ENGLISH JOURNAL		REPP	REVIEW OF EXISTENTIAL PSYCHOLOGY AND
Extrp	EXTRAPOLATION			PSYCHIATRY
GQ	GENTLEMAN'S QUARTERLY		SAQ	SOUTH ATLANTIC QUARTERLY
HC	HOLLINS CRITIC		SFS	SCIENCE-FICTION STUDIES
HdR	HUDSON REVIEW		SoR	SOUTHERN REVIEW
HH	HOUND AND HORN		Spec	SPECTATOR
HR	HOPKINS REVIEW		SQ	SOUTHERN QUARTERLY
IoR	IOWA REVIEW		SR	SATURDAY REVIEW
KR	KENYON REVIEW		SRA	SATURDAY REVIEW OF THE ARTS
LP	LITERATURE AND PSYCHOLOGY		SSF	STUDIES IN SHORT FICTION
MFS	MODERN FICTION STUDIES		SwR	SEWANEE REVIEW
MinnR	MINNESOTA REVIEW		TA	THEATRE ARTS
NaR	NATIONAL REVIEW		TCL	TWENTIETH-CENTURY LITERATURE
NL	NEW LEADER		TDR	TULANE DRAMA REVIEW
NR	NEW REPUBLIC		TriQ	TRI-QUARTERLY
NS	NEW STATESMAN		VV	VILLAGE VOICE
NSN	NEW STATESMAN AND NATION		WPBW	WASHINGTON POST BOOK WORLD
	(later STATESMAN AND NATION)		YR	YALE REVIEW

PREFACE

The Chelsea House Library of Literary Criticism is designed to present a concise portrait of the critical heritage of every crucial British and American author. In thirty-seven volumes, the *Library* covers the entire range of British and American literature, from *Beowulf* and the earliest medieval epics to the work of such contemporary innovators as Thomas Pynchon. The five volumes of *Twentieth-Century American Literature* contain criticism of modern authors from the United States and Canada, the first volume covering authors from A through B.

The twentieth century has been characterized by the challenging of accepted ideas concerning the art of interpretation. Representing the growing multiplicity of critical schools and styles, consequently, is as difficult as it is necessary. In *Twentieth-Century American Literature* the editors have sought to provide the most representative essays and reviews of the modern era. In publishing critical responses to the work of each author, we have chosen material from a variety of sources—magazines, scholarly journals, and book-length studies.

As for the organization of the chapters, most are divided into two sections, extracts and essays. We have grouped the extracts into *Personal, General,* and *Works* categories; these sections embody such material as passages from memoirs, interviews, and biographies, short theoretical statements, and reviews of individual works. The essay sections are reserved for more extensive and in-depth studies of the authors and their works. Although most of the criticism is arranged chronologically, we have occasionally juxtaposed early and late reviews in order to highlight the critical dialogue.

Each entry contains an up-to-date, brief biography of the author. A list of additional reading on all authors covered concludes each volume, providing the reader with a thoughtful selection of material for further research. In general, we have preserved original footnotes in the essay sections and have omitted page references within the text if the original edition has not been cited. We have also preserved the original style of each critic, retaining British spellings and punctuation. Any editorial changes appear in carets.

In determining what authors to include, the editors, in consultation with Professor Harold Bloom, have tried to balance broad representation with in-depth coverage. We have had to omit, necessarily, relatively minor figures in order to allow space for such major writers as John Ashbery and Saul Bellow. In making our selections, we have nevertheless given place to significant albeit lesser-known authors; in particular, we have included mystery, science fiction, fantasy, and non-fiction authors whose works have inspired substantial critical examination. Moreover, we have included certain writers who may date to the late nineteenth century but whose works have a twentieth-century relevance, as reflected in the amount and nature of modern criticism devoted to them. A similar concern for diversity has informed our selection of the criticism itself. As a result, the present work provides an informative survey of the development of literary criticism and of American literature in general in the twentieth century, while fulfilling its primary purpose of providing a range of critical views of the specific authors covered.

The Editors

WALTER ABISH

1931–

Walter Abish was born on December 24, 1931, in Vienna, but grew up in Shanghai. He has taught at the State University of New York at Buffalo and State Springs, Wheaton College, and since 1979, Columbia University. His first novel, *Duel Site*, published in 1970, introduced his mode of experimental, oblique fiction; his following among critics and academics took off with *Alphabetical Africa* in 1974. The book has a unique structure: its first chapter uses only words beginning with the letter "a," the second "a" and "b," and so on up to "z"—then back down to "a."

Abish's other books include the collection *Minds Meet* (1975), *In the Future Perfect* (1977), and the acclaimed novel *How German Is It*. He received grants from the Rose Isabel Williams Foundation in 1974 and the Ingram Merrill Foundation in 1977. He lives in New York City with his wife Cecile.

General

The emphasis Abish puts on the constructed aspect of fiction is a rebuke to our worst habits of reading. We read to escape, to forget the present, to visualize, or to kill time. Abish's fiction, especially his most recent work, simply doesn't lend itself to these solipsistic urges, though it keeps us in mind of their temptation. The subversion of "realism" is only the beginning of his achievement. His writing demands that we know the meanderings of our attention as we read, that our reading be a deliberate activity, as tied to the present as the act of looking at something. The demands of Abish's fiction reflect a view of language with definite ethical implications. One aspect of this view is the notion that we know ourselves, as others know us, by the way we use language. On this view, reading, no less than speaking or thinking, is a use of language, and therefore might reveal us to ourselves no less profitably than acts of speech or thought. This notion upsets the conventional belief that introspection is the privileged path to self-knowledge. Abish's work forces us to consider the possibility that reading, done with the right sort of deliberation, might serve the purposes of self-knowledge better than the solitariness of introspection. For reading, unlike introspection, can make us consider the sense in which words we understand and use are "ours." By making such considerations central to the process of reading, Abish's fiction challenges the popular idea of our best access to ourselves as well as the popular idea of selfhood and its indebtedness to the literary concept of character.

Something that recurs in Abish's work, that sometimes seems to comprise his work, is a contention in the writing itself between linguistic incidents and fictive or narrative ones. Again and again the perception of words as the material of construction interferes with one's attempt to see the prose in terms of larger conventional components, such as character, theme, and plot. One effect of this experience is to make us realize the extent to which the rudiments of literary convention have become internal to us, that they may even be what we read with, features of our perception itself. It would be foolish to think that our own experience escapes the application of a perceptual and expressive style modeled, however crudely, on literary conventions. If reading is as much a use of language as speech, then there is reason to wonder how our habits of reading condition our understanding of ourselves and others. Abish's writing shows us that certain expectations, certain ways of reading preclude an awareness of words themselves as parts of language and of us. The style of reading his fiction recom-mends is one that makes us aware continually of the con-structed nature of prose as the basis of the pleasures and values of reading. This manner of reading is the counterpart to a particular achievement of self-knowledge, namely, the capacity to know and tolerate the linguistic reality of one's own words. By this I mean the capacity both to know one's beliefs and to know that they are beliefs without feeling them vitiated by this awareness. To know the linguistic reality of one's own words is to be fully aware of one's responsibility for them. Abish forces us to be responsible readers by making us confront continually the linguistic reality of what we read.—KENNETH BAKER, "Restricted Fiction: The Works of Walter Abish," *New Directions* 35, 1977, pp. 48–49

Works

ALPHABETICAL AFRICA

Is it anything more than a stunt, such a book, a lively piece of legerdemain by a poet much influenced by the Gallic magicians Robbe-Grillet and Henri Roussel and Raymond Queneau, all of whom have espoused the alphabetical ordering of the tropics, that most insipid of orders, to generate a technique of exposition "unworthy" of the way we have been taught to articulate a novel, to make book? I think it is *something* more than a stunt, though a stunt it is, and Walter Abish is an intrepid stuntman, eager to disclose his hocus-pocus at every turn. Indeed he has stunted his novel by his technical appara-tus and apprehensions so that it cannot be more than that one single incident which keeps recurring in his mind. He has violated all our expectations of continuity and development, flouted our trust in the created reality of fiction—but I believe he has done so for a reason. The alphabetical stammer, the lists of Swahili words, the teasing laugh with which the past be-havior of the "characters" (really names with sexual organs attached) is twitched away from us and a whole new set in-troduced in conformity with the alphabetical disciplines (wit-ness "Just another ant invasion, claims Jubutu, an African assistant auctioneer," who appears at the opening of J, where else?) is essential to Abish's intention, his ulterior motive. He has written, I believe, a novel of erotic obsession, in which language itself has received the transferred charge of feeling.

Ideas and actions here are not developed, they are dis-tributed; feelings are not dramatized, they are reified; the text is a kind of breviary of compulsive (and masturbatory) gratifica-tion. We call the great land masses *continents* because they are named after women (Africa, Asia, Europe) and we expect them

1

to be chaste—so that men may violate their darkest interiors, I suppose.

. . . ⟨It is⟩ Abish's achievement to have stunted the growth of everything that the novel, even on its deathbed, has tried to lay claim to, in order to register, in order to disclose that "one single incident which keeps recurring," which is not so much an action, of course, as a passion, "erased and immobilized in a book."—Richard Howard, "The Dark Continent A to Z," *NYTBR*, Dec. 29, 1974, p. 19

African space of another kind, and patience of a more literary sort, figure in Walter Abish's remarkable, ludicrously programmatic novel *Alphabetical Africa*. The adventure Mr. Abish has set himself is to compose a novel of twice twenty-six chapters, of which the first employs only words beginning with "A," the second words beginning with "A" and "B," and so on up to "Z," by which time the full lexical possibilities of the English language are available; then, from "Z" to "A," he moves back down the alphabet, subtracting letters one by one until the last chapter, like the first, is composed entirely of words beginning with "A." The hardships of such a journey should not be underestimated; "A" brings with it a handy number of articles and connectives, but not until "H" is reached can the pronoun "he" and the helper verb "have" be used, and for all but the fourteen chapters between "T" and "T" such virtually indispensable formations as "the," "to," "they," "their," and "this" must be dispensed with. A character called Queen Quat cannot appear until after the middle of the ascending alphabet is reached, and must perish on the downhill side when her letter vanishes. Fortunately, Mr. Abish's style, even when unhampered by artificial constraints, is rather chastened and elliptic, so his fettered progress is steadier than you might imagine. Here is a paragraph from the first chapter:

> Africa again: Antelopes, alligators, ants and attractive Alva, are arousing all angular Africans, also arousing author's analytically aggressive anticipations, again and again. Anyhow author apprehends Alva anatomically, affirmatively, and also accurately.

By the time his verbal safari reaches "G," Abish can make, at length and almost fluently, observations reminiscent of Moravia's:

> Genuine gestures are African gestures, because Africans can by a few gestures demonstrate a deep and abiding affection between altogether different foreign bodies, each clap, each groan, each facial gesture conveying a convincingly eternal dramatic African confusion and also a fusion of bodies, as bodies explore boundaries generously emitting a fresh African ecstasy. . . .

"I" releases the possibility of self-exposition, "M" brings with it the themes of memory and money and murder, and by "S" only an alerted eye and hypersensitive ear would notice that a quarter of the dictionary is still being abjured:

> Summarizing Africa: I can speak more freely. I find fewer and fewer impediments. Soon I'll reach my destination. Soon I'll also complete my documentation and my book. Daily Africa is shrinking from extreme heat and fatigue, as rebels in bush battle African armies led by foreigners.

The attainment, long anticipated by the alphabet-battered reader, of "Z"'s total freedom brings a disappointingly short chapter, written in the cramped, clicking tone of the others:

> Zambia helps fill our zoos, and our doubts, and our extrawide screens as we sit back. Each year we zigzag between the cages, prodding the alligators, the an-

telopes, the giant ants, just to see them move about a bit, just to make our life more authentic. . . .

Each chapter, as it possesses another letter, celebrates its acquisition with a burst of alliteration, so our knowledge of systematic expansion is aurally emphasized; this subtly joyous undertone of organic growth is lost in the book's second half, wherein the subtraction of letters echoes supposed land shrinkage ("Africa's gradual deterioration and Africa's decreasing area"), and some violent events on Zanzibar swallow up Queen Quat (who has painted Tanzania orange to match the maps) and squeeze the novel's protagonists—Alex, Allen, and Alva—into a climax of betrothal. The extremely silly plot begins as a jewel robbery in Antibes and a consequent flight to Angola, Burundi, Chad, etc., and culminates in a kind of people's uprising by the Vietcong-like army ants: "All complain close-by artillery barrage battered beautiful city, battered beautiful avenues, all because ants continue advance, continue creeping along, carving a continent." Though the tale is murky as well as absurd, one is tempted to concede that Mr. Abish has performed as well as anyone could, given such extravagant handicaps. "A masterpiece of its kind" does not seem too strong an accolade for a book apt to be the only one of its kind.

And there is a nice rightness to setting such a work in Africa, where incantations are still potent and national boundaries slice across tribal realities as arbitrarily as the alphabet schematizes language. Teeming yet vacant, mysterious yet monotonous, Africa permits this literary experiment. *Alphabetical Asia* would not have been so funny, *Alphabetical America* would have been cluttered with reality, *Alphabetical Antarctica* would have been blank. "Africa is a favorite topic in literature, it gives license to so much excess," the author explains, and confesses, of his old bush jacket, that it "fed my imagination long before I ever set foot on this continent." Mr. Abish is pictured on the dust jacket wearing this bush jacket, and a romantic black eye patch, in a studio containing African sculptures. For the Western mind, art and fancy and travellers' accounts form Africa's body. Though *Alphabetical Africa* gives some evidence that the author has visited the continent, it was not necessary; his Swahili dictionary and a four-color map took him where he wanted to go. Setting out with his elaborate impedimenta, he chose the mental milieu that offered him the most license and sport. Africa, explored and excavated and neocapitalized as it now is, remains—for Mr. Abish as for Moravia, as it was for Leakey and Livingstone, for Gide and Hemingway, for Rider Haggard and Edgar Rice Burroughs, for Burton and Speke and Mungo Park and Prince Henry the Navigator—an invitation to the imagination.—John Updike, "Through a Continent, Darkly," *Picked-Up Pieces*, 1975, pp. 349–51

Once when I was watching one of Ed Sullivan's jugglers keeping a table full of plates twirling atop long bamboo poles, it occurred to me that if mankind thinks of anything beyond the normal range of difficulty, someone will be damn fool enough to try it. Enter Walter Abish and *Alphabetical Africa*. The structural principle is simple: the first chapter contains only words beginning with "a"; the second expands to include "b" as an initial, and so on, through to "z," at which point the author is free to use any word he pleases. From there on, the initial letters fade one by one like the performers of Haydn's *Farewell Symphony*, until only lonely "a" is left. Somehow, despite the limitations of vocabulary, Abish does tell a story of sorts with an occasionally amusing episode (e.g., Queen Quat, influenced by the colors on a map, has her entire kingdom or queendom, since her sex changes at the whim of the author, painted orange). It is a measure of the author's humor that he manages to repeat the pun "Quat right" several times. John Ashbery, to quote a favorable opinion, writes that "Walter Abish has dovetailed his novel within a Procrustean scheme that has the terrifying and irrefutable logic of the alphabet." I suppose that if one feels that the alphabet is logical and terrifying, or uses words sloppily enough to describe it so, he will find much in Abish's effort. Barring that kind of sensibility, the book is only for those who admire extended but very simple practical jokes.—LEE T. LEMON, "Bookmarks," *PSch*, Fall 1975, pp. 277–78

IN THE FUTURE PERFECT

The more "experimental" stories in ⟨*In the Future Perfect*⟩ do not, unfortunately, sound like one-of-a-kind achievements. They strongly resemble quite a few other experimental stories.

Since ordinary reality seems inexhaustible, one might suppose that there would be infinite alternatives to it. Yet a reading of experimental fiction generally discovers only about a dozen devices: free association, motiveless acts, hackneyed incongruities, predictable discontinuities, sensationalism, tricky diction, coyness, self-consciousness, obscurantism, negativism, ponderousness, pretension. Perhaps most experimental literature ought to be read as a warning: If you think *your life is dull, just look at this.*—ANATOLE BROYARD, "One Critic's Fiction," *NYTBR*, Nov. 13, 1977, p. 75

It is useless to give the plot of any Abish story—the very act of retelling the narrative is a kind of "atrocity" because it uses words to flatten and distort effects—without making it seem silly or mad or "funny." . . . Were ⟨I⟩ to "map" or "chart" the adventures of all Abish characters, I would soon be drawn into the plot. It is his desire, of course, to force me to this realization—any interpretation of chart (criticism, autobiography, or melodramatic narrative) is an attempt to impose "perfection" upon a chaotic world. The title of ⟨*In the Future Perfect*⟩ maintains that perhaps in the "future" (whatever that means) we can find "perfection." But at the same "time" we will have changed so that "perfection" may no longer mean what it means *now*—"then" it may be "imperfect" because it is humdrum, usual, and normal. . . .

Abish is obviously obsessed by measures, numbers, lines, maps; he even implies that artistic delight arises only when we note that narrative itself is another "chart." He will take an arbitrary detail—say a quantity of words—and then write a descriptive passage with precisely the same number of words. The passage itself is usually violent or fantastic. We have a battle, therefore, between the arbitrary choice (say sixty words) and the realistic actions. The tension mounts, of course, when this device is repeated with variations. "In So Many Words" is the "story" which contains this pattern. We can concentrate upon the realistic actions and/or the "many words." We are given the choice, but we are so used to believing that people are more important than words that we are breathless. How dare Abish do this? How dare he mix styles? How dare he make us realize that we are *reading*?—IRVING MALIN, "In So Many Words," *OR*, Fall–Winter 1978, pp. 113–14

HOW GERMAN IS IT

In his previous books, Walter Abish has played the part of rubble-razer in our literary landscape, digging up the dust beneath the surface of our everyday words. He has played this part with wit and imagination, using language to question its own veracity; permitting syntactic ambiguities to hover quizzically over their object, only to zero in for a final demolition job.

Now Mr. Abish has written a novel. (The earlier *Alphabetical Africa* was more a literary extravaganza than a novel.) In *How German Is It*, Mr. Abish seeks to apply this rubble-razing technique to the new Germany. With what results? One is reminded of the gimmicky cards sent out recently by our local gas companies. The cards have a rough spot, and they say, "Scratch this surface and you will recognize the smell of gas." In both cases, the effect is less convincing than startling. . . .

Mr. Abish's mind delights in dualities. His gift for irony feeds on the contradictions in human thought and action. All his writings are an assault on the reassuring familiarity of everyday things. Now Mr. Abish seems to be saying that it is the menace lurking beneath the surface that appeals to the new Germans as a way of experiencing, if only deviously, the unassimilated terror of their past. . . .

Why not a novel? There are ideas, but no development of ideas. There are characterizations, but no character development. (For example, the brilliant set-piece about Franz, the mad waiter and erstwhile "family retainer" to the *von* Hargenaus. Franz spends his Sundays constructing a model out of headless matches of the concentration camp on which the town sits. Like Max Frisch's *Man in the Holocene*, who builds a pagoda out of "crispbread" to elude madness during a flood, Franz's obsessive "hobby" devours him with the inexorable logic of madness.)

The novel as an exploration of language then? This one might expect from Mr. Abish. It is instructive to compare a few lines from an excerpt in *Partisan Review* I, 1980 with the final book version.

PR: "'Could we possibly go over the interview again? Just briefly. . . .'

"'Yes, why not,' I reply."

Book: "'Could we possibly go over the interview again? Just briefly. . . .'

"'Yes, why not,' said Ulrich condescendingly. What a bloody twit, he thought."

PR: "Wishing to be thorough, I inquired. . . ."

Book: "Not satisfied, compelled by a German sense of *Gründlichtkeit* to investigate further, he inquired. . . ."

Everywhere connective tissue has been added, to the detriment of the text. Incongruous levels of speech are juxtaposed with unintended comic effects. The Briticism "bloody twit" is a case in point. Where four words served adequately, as in the second instance, 12 replaced them, and so it becomes unclear whether Mr. Abish is trying to parody the convoluted phrasing and stiffness of German or whether he is incapable of writing straightforward English himself. One's discomfort increases when one notes the actual misuse of words: "mechanistic" for "mechanical," "evaluate" for "assess," "limitations" for "limits," "in effect" for "in fact." His redundant phrases— "luminous light," "inundated by a deluge"—are matched in number only by adjectival clusters, generally three, presented in order of diminishing intensity (as in "the startling, the shocking, the unexpected"). Finally, recurrent sloppiness with regard to detail further shakes the reader's confidence in this author. When Ulrich leaves Paris, his clever French friends try to mask their disdain for things German by name-dropping the latest German literary names; but of the names they drop, one is Swiss (Bichsel), one Austrian (Handke), and the third, Kemposki, Mr. Abish misspells.

As a log entry, "This is the place (Switzerland) where Musil died, where Rilke died, where Gottfried Keller lived and died, where Jean Jacques Rousseau was born, and where only a few years ago Nabokov lived," this George Washington-slept-here business may be acceptable. But in the context of a novel, these allusions to literary personae must serve some real purpose if they are not to sound merely pretentious.—BETTY FALKENBERG, "Literary Games," *NYTBR*, Jan. 4, 1981, pp. 8–9

How German Is It is a peculiar novel: it's about love, but that love is doomed; it's about war, but that war is over; it's about international terrorism, but the causes and effects of it remain tantalizingly obscure; it's about the new Germany, but the ghost of the old one is lurking in the background, and its inhabitants refuse to acknowledge the impact it has on their consciences. All of this is presented in an extremely controlled diction, a style reminiscent—for its apparent raw objectivity— of Daniel Defoe's *Journal of the Plague Year*.

I say apparent, because it's all a trick. The complexity of Abish's thought grows in fact out of a jumble of clean-cut sentences that, restated at different intervals and under different circumstances, multiply and intensify the meaning we had originally taken for granted. Thus do the characters change before our eyes, and the transitions are so subtle and evasive we are not aware of the manipulations; the metaphors are so pruned and glowing that we do not immediately perceive the dark pit they are nonchalantly exposing.—NEREO E. CONDINI, "The Edge of Forgetfulness," *NaR*, May 29, 1981, p. 620

Abish is an artist of enormous resources and control, and *How German Is It* is a most readable book, not only for its bitter comic observation, but for a narrative drive propelled simultaneously by *what's going to happen?* and *what did happen?* The mercilessness of it spoils it for me, for there is a thesis guiding it, and that thesis demands that Abish rigorously suppress any extravagant energies, any complexities, any *life* within his characters, any sign that a German may have moments of sensibility (or folly) that don't support the thesis. We are familiar with this New Wave manner of observing slightly narcotized characters against "dehumanized" landscapes, but there is a difference between film and prose: in the movies there is the chance that the actor may supply some quirky and mysterious presence that may not be suggested in the desiccated script. But Abish has only his prose, and within that prose he won't (can't?) give his people or his "Germany" a chance. There is an unpleasant implied condemnation of a whole people which, not to press the point too hard, can't help reminding us of the very fault Abish won't let Germany forget. *Engagé* as all get-out, this deft writer (after a flashy *coup de théâtre* that would be "effective" in a film, but that belies the artistry on every other page) steps forward with his placard: "Is it possible for anyone in Germany, nowadays, to raise his right hand, for whatever the reason, and not be flooded by the memory of a dream to end all dreams?" What is really at stake is one's image of oneself *and others*.—GEORGE KEARNS, " 'Fiction Chronicle': *How German Is It*," *HdR*, Summer 1981, pp. 305–6

JEROME KLINKOWITZ
"Walter Abish and the Surfaces of Life"

The Georgia Review, Summer 1981, pp. 416–20

C an narrative be truly self-referential? Is it possible for a novelist, burdened with the conceptual weight of words and doubly hampered by the sequential order of story, to be as much an abstract expressionist as the painter or the musical composer, whose daubs of paint or notes of sound need not refer to anything other than themselves? One way is to treat the materials of fiction as objects in themselves—not as familiar cues to the reader (which trigger conventional responses and so set formulaic narratives to action) but rather as semiotic integers within the syntax of human behavior. This has been precisely the method Walter Abish has pursued through four books of fiction.

Since his first experimental work was published in the New Directions anthologies ten years ago, Walter Abish has been showing how the supposed realities of life (the stuff of conventionally realistic, mimetic fiction) are made of purely surface phenomena (the signs of semiologists). Because of this disposition, Abish has been called an irrealist, the polar opposite of a mannerly moralist like Updike or Bellow, with little pertinence for the workaday world.

How German Is It, his most recent novel (just awarded the Faulkner Prize), refutes this charge and shows how Abish has been writing about the ultimate reality all along. Ostensibly a situational narrative about life in "the new Germany," Abish's life study (his first, after three books of apparently metafictional exploration) reflects the manner of his more obviously experimental work. Behavior, Abish shows, is far more than a puppet show devised by a choreographer of popular morals. Instead, it is a matter of syntax, prime material for the metafictionist. And as the signifiers of language have no inherent relationship to the things they describe, so the patterns of our lives are equally an arbitrary and free-floating grammar, to be analyzed as a topology of surfaces and needs. Morals and manners in the novel are thus manipulated as verbal objects for our post-structuralist times.

Alphabetical Africa (1974) was Abish's first novel, an emphatically abstract work which by its self-conscious construction placed Abish at the farthest remove from the social realists. We can see now how that was a strategy to keep the reader on the page, where the relationship of characters and needs was inescapably artificial. In this early work, Abish proposed a rigorous discipline for both writer and reader. The initial chapter was titled "A," and used only words beginning with that letter. Chapter "B" added words starting with the letter B, and so forth through the alphabet, as the book (and its linguistic possibilities) expanded. No first person narrator until Chapter "I," no visits to Jedda until Chapter "J." At each point the reader would be aware of just how the book was composing itself—especially from midpoint on when Abish ran his persons, places, and things through a regressive structure of another twenty-six chapters titled backward from "Z," with familiar components dropping out as each letter vanished into the history of Abish's receding alphabet.

A lifeless, antiseptic technique? Not at all, as Richard Howard pointed out. *Alphabetical Africa*, he wrote, was "a novel of erotic obsession, in which language itself has received the transferred charge of feeling" which otherwise might be dissipated in the puppetry of suspended disbelief. The syntax of these characters' lives, by virtue of their expanding and contracting possibilities (the names of objects available to satisfy their needs), was forever the book's real subject. *Alphabetical Africa*, then, was that allegedly impossible achievement: an abstract expressionist novel, in which the words referred primarily to themselves yet remained charged with human energy.

How German Is It uses no such obvious device; it has a realistic setting, believable characters, and a theme which bears the test of contemporary history. But the artificiality of the whole enterprise still takes center stage. The novel has a theme and setting, but its realism is constructed to emphasize their provisional, syntactic nature. "How *German* is the new Germany?" this novel asks, implying an entire set of relationships constructed between one provisional order (The Third Reich) and another (The Federal Republic). The setting for this theme is fully artificial: the planned community of Brumholdstein, a spanking new city of several hundred thousand built to the specifications of current need. Named after a Heidegger-like metaphysician, Brumhold, whose discipline had been the questioning of "the thingness" of things, Brumholdstein is most noted for its surface quality. This new city is laid out on the site of a concentration camp; its initial apartment blocks, in fact, were constructed for the same cost as maintaining the camp as a shrine.

How form alternately expands and constricts meaning was one of the object lessons of *Alphabetical Africa*, and the topology of Brumholdstein makes the same point. The city's form, like the shape of Abish's earlier novel, is self-evident. No illusions here of random growth or the accumulations of culture over many centuries. Brumholdstein is above all an idea, a statement on the needs and fulfillments of life in postwar Germany, constructed on the boundaries of the very past it seeks to efface. Everywhere the past's temporal and spatial reality is present. "The most glorious summer in thirty-four years," the citizens exclaim, but even their small talk about the weather can't divert them from the fact that 1978 minus 34 equals 1944—a year they would prefer to forget. A street caves in to reveal the imposthume of a mass grave. Jewish inmates slaughtered by the Germans? German soldiers executed by the Russians? American prisoners, or even German captives of the conquering Allies? By Brumholdstein's own design, the past feeds the present as if to contradict the future so carefully planned.

Part of Abish's earlier practice was to find ways of emphasizing the words themselves—signifiers, not signifieds—as components in his stories. In *Minds Meet* (1975) he presented a story based on alphabetical variations ("The Abandoned Message," "Abashed by the Message," "Abashed While Receiving the Message," etc.), which nevertheless enhanced his theme regarding the frailty of human communication. *In the Future Perfect* (1977) collected stories even more mechanical: one piece featured block paragraphs titled alphabetically with the basic vocabulary of the story ("Ardor/Awe/Atrocity") and had each of its key ninety-nine words identified by a serial superscript as it appeared in the narrative; in another story, block paragraphs of conventional narrative were preceded by their component words ranked alphabetically (so that readers would have all the words in advance of the message). With such an emphasis on the makings of language, its mere assemblage was more obviously a game, and readers could appreciate how artificial and contrived (and hence humanly flawed) that game could be. No wonder the protagonists who emerged from these tales were confused, paranoid souls; no wonder the narrator was forever being excluded from the action; and no wonder everybody else seemed to be satisfied, while the story's personal center remained forlorn. Life in Abish's hands was a narrative written by a self-satisfied author willing to plot anyone else right out of existence.

How German Is It uses no such mechanical devices, other than those conveniently supplied by the Brumholdstein situation. But for the making of his narrative Abish selects certain characters for key roles, and runs their lives together in a way that demonstrates the *made* quality of their enterprise—and how, as in all such situations, intentions can be frustrated, communication blocked, and needs left unfulfilled.

Abish peoples his new Germany with a credible family of characters. Principal are the Hargenau brothers, Helmuth and Ulrich, whose father—now described as a patriot—was executed in 1944 for his part in the officers' plot against Hitler. The brothers are alternately constructing and deconstructing the postwar fatherland: Helmuth through his municipal architecture (sincerely believing that at the end of Greek and Roman and medieval achievement stand his prize-winning post office and police station) and Ulrich by his chance association with a group of young terrorists. The emphasis throughout is how both their actions disrupt the equilibrium and eventually undermine the order of life itself, as Helmuth effaces what remains of life in the thirties and forties, while Ulrich's group in turn destroys his public buildings.

Helmuth, moreover, has rich and trendy young friends, for whom he has designed a dream-home villa. Their lives, however, are all glossy surface, pure magazine-cover stuff, while behind the closed doors and shaded windows they live in autistic alienation. Ulrich, meanwhile, writes novels, seemingly to efface his own experience of living. Implicated, arrested, tried, and acquitted with his wife's band of terrorists, he moves to Paris to write and forget. But there he has an unhappy love affair, and soon returns to Germany in order to write *that* experience out of his life. Does he ever live in a legitimate present? His most famous book is titled *Now or Never*, but the quality of life around him speaks of falsity and decay. By the end of *How German Is It* we learn that Ulrich has no substantially real subject at all, just these syntactic projections of lives built on the surface of immediate need. All about him is preached the permanence and continuity of "what is basically German," but life as he lives it presents nothing to him but lies and lurking disorder. He keeps asking, "Could things be different?" and "Is there any other way to live?"—but the limits of syntax allow only this unsatisfying, one dimensional life.

By Ulrich's failure Abish shows how conventional realism cannot be written in our time, given our knowledge of the structures of human communication. But a superrealism is possible. Much like the superrealists in painting—especially Richard Estes and Ralph Goings—Abish depicts his subjects with an eye toward emphatically glossy surfaces. As a result, he defamiliarizes the soporifically familiar, and also draws our attention to those peculiarities of surface which define so many of the objects of our need. A favorite quote from Wittgenstein running through much of Abish's work is that "perfection cannot bear endless repetition." But that's what the surfaces of Abish's world are: endlessly repeated forms with no real content at all, just the shiny and compulsive surfaces of Richard Estes' "Drugstore" or Goings' colorfully painted trucks and cars.

Defamiliarization itself is another note from Wittgenstein, a reminder that as we become accustomed to seeing things in their customary light we cease to see them at all. Abish's own unique way of breaking clear from the familiar is to describe his scenes in a copybook manner, a decidedly flat style of writing which is not the result of any suppression of talent but just the opposite: by removing all hierarchal values from his perceptions, Abish sees for once how things really are. Once we humanize, he implies, we become subject to all the flawed rules of human communication from which his characters suffer.

To fully experience persons, place, and event, Abish seeks a neutral value in his writing, by which the reader is able to experience more than a simple pantomime of signs. *How German Is It* takes one through the paces of modern Germany so that everything is given careful note. "What are the first words a visitor from France can expect to hear upon his arrival at a German airport?" Abish begins. "Bonjour? Or, Guten Tag?

Or, Passport bitte?" "And how does the name Ulrich Hargenau ring in the German ear?" At once a story begins—of the terrorist events in recent years, of the father's plot and execution in 1944—and suddenly the whole world of Germany opens up. But first Abish asks what are the surface details a visitor would first notice:

> Undoubtedly the cleanliness. The painstaking cleanliness. As well as the all-pervasive sense of order. A punctuality. An almost obsessive punctuality. Then, of course, there is the new, striking architecture. Innovative? Hardly. Imaginative? Not really. But free of that former somber and authoritative massivity. A return to the experimentation of the Bauhaus? Regrettably, no. Still, something must be said in favor of the wide expanse of glass on the buildings, the fifteen-, twenty-story buildings, the glass reflecting not only the sky but also acting as a mirror for the older historical sights, those clusters of carefully reconstructed buildings that are an attempt to replicate entire neighborhoods obliterated in the last war.

The language is neutral, strictly limited to what the eye can see. But without an informing hierarchy the eye sees everything, including the functional style which cannot help but mirror the past it is meant to erase. With no humanistic hokum, puppetry, or suspension of disbelief, the theme of *How German Is It* has been stated.

Syntax and vocabulary determine form, and form determines content. We all know how the Slavic languages are short on words for describing ordinary sexuality, how the Eskimos have scores of synonyms for "snow." The value of a novel like *How German Is It* is the picture it gives us of contemporary morals and manners working themselves out in a world strictly defined by historical and philosophical limits. A planned community anticipates human needs, but once built it perpetuates those needs rather than remaining adaptive to new contingencies. In his earlier collection, *Minds Meet*, Abish used the American mania for shopping malls to consider just how such institutions create the needs they serve, and especially how characters are defined by the surfaces and boundaries within which they exist. Language, Abish shows, follows the same model.

The drama of these fictions? Human beings are larger—and their ultimate needs run deeper—than the structures improvised to contain them. By his fidelity to the surface Abish frames the energy which is always fighting to break loose. He puts that energy in the very structure of his sentences, and so becomes an action writer with words. He is one of the most legitimately expressive writers of our time.

HENRY ADAMS

1838–1918

Henry Adams was born in Boston, Massachusetts, on February 16, 1838. He would later write of himself, "Probably no child, born in the year, held better cards than he." Adams was descended from one of the most influential and wealthy families of the Revolutionary period: his great-grandfather was John Adams, and his grandfather John Quincy Adams. Yet, throughout his life he regarded his family background with pessimism, as a dead weight that locked him into a vanishing past. Adams graduated from Harvard in 1858. The school, he said, "had taught little, and that little ill," but while there Adams published his first writings and became a highly skilled public speaker.

Between 1858 and 1860, Adams studied law in a desultory way at the Universities of Berlin and Dresden. From 1861 to 1868, he lived in England as private secretary to his father, Charles Francis Adams, whom Lincoln had appointed Minister to England during the Civil War. For two years following his return, Adams lived in Washington, D.C., writing freelance articles, usually about finance. Adams then yielded to family pressure and became a teacher of medieval history at Harvard, where he would remain through 1879, receiving a Ph.D. in 1876. Throughout this period, Adams edited the *North American Review* in association with Henry Cabot Lodge. Though he was reputed to be a remarkable teacher, Adams's heart was not in it, and, in 1878, he gave up his professorship and moved back to Washington to write full-time. This was a highly prolific period, which included his *Life of Albert Gallatin* (1879), and *Democracy: An American Novel*, which was published anonymously in 1880. Adams's outpouring of work was abruptly halted in 1885 by the inexplicable suicide of his wife, Marion Hooper Adams. Her death would haunt him and his work for the rest of his life. Ironically, just prior to his wife's death he had published (under a pseudonym) the novel *Esther*, about the emotional and spiritual crises of a troubled woman.

In 1891 Adams completed *A History of the United States of America*, a nine-volume work. It firmly established Adams as a pre-eminent historian, and pioneered the theory that history should be less a record of specific events than an analysis of their underlying forces. His best-known works were written in the twentieth century: *Mont-Saint-Michel and Chartres*, printed privately in 1904 and commercially in 1913; and *The Education of Henry Adams*, printed privately in 1906 and commercially in 1918. He died on March 26th of that year. By the time of his death he had received an honorary Doctor of Laws degree from Western Reserve College (1892), the Loubat History Prize from Columbia University (1894), and had been elected president of the American Historical Association.

LEWIS MUMFORD
From *The Golden Day*
1926, pp. 217–25

Henry Adams was a historian. Almost alone among his American contemporaries, he responded to Comte's great challenge; and sought to create out of the mere annals and chronologies and fables which had once been the stock-in-trade of the historian, a more intelligible sequence, which would lead into the future as well as the past. This attempt to achieve scientific precision did not make him forfeit his imaginative penetration of the living moments of the past. His study of Mont St. Michel and Chartres which he began at a late period of his life, after having written about current events and the political character and fate of certain periods in American history, was in many ways a model of historic reconstruction: he established the mood of his period, and built into the architecture and stained glasses of the churches he examined the theology of Aquinas, the science of Roger Bacon, the songs of the troubadours, and the simple willing faith of the common people.

Since Henry Adams saw so thoroughly into the Middle Ages with its cult of the Virgin, one might fancy that he would have seen with equal insight into his own day, and the cult of the Dynamo. He was, however, so deeply immersed in his own time that he unconsciously read back into history all its preoccupations and standards. When he came to forecast the movement of history in his own day, he immediately fell into the error of location. From the standpoint of mechanical inventions, it was plain that there had been a constant acceleration of movement since, say, the Thirteenth Century. This, however, was but one activity: had Adams projected himself back into the Seventeenth Century he would have been conscious, not of space annihilating machines, but the steady increase in the art of fortification; or had he chosen painting and sculpture instead of science and machinery, he would have noted the steady decline in their relative volume and importance. The rate of change had not necessarily increased or decreased; but the departments which exhibited change had altered. That Adams should have attempted to put all these complex historic transformations into a narrow physical formula dealing with the transformation of matter and energy, shows how completely his environment had stamped him.

William James knew better than Adams on this point; and when Adams published his essay on the Phase Rule as Applied to History, James pointed out that the current theories of science as to the eventual dissipation of energies in our universe had no real bearing on human history, since from the standpoint of life what mattered was what was done with these energies before they ran down—whether the chemicals ⟨that⟩ make the pigment that go into a painting, or the picric acid that annihilates a company of men in warfare. Granted that the canvas will eventually rot away, and the men will in good time die: the only significant point is what has happened in the meanwhile. Qualitatively speaking, a minute may hold as much as eternity; and for man to have existed at all may be quite as important as if he had an infinity of worlds to conquer, an infinity of knowledge to understand, and an infinity of desires to express. A hearty, an intelligent, a believing age acts from day to day on the theory that it may die to-morrow. In such periods of intensification, as in Elizabethan England, the good may well die young, because, with a complete life, death is not a frustration. Adams, though he perhaps did not realize it, was a victim of the theological notion of eternity—the notion that our present life is significant or rational only if it can be prolonged. The test of endurance is indeed an important element in providing for the continuity of generations and the stability of effort: it can be pragmatically justified: but the notion that a quantitative existence in time is a necessary measure of worth, without which life is a blank, is a notion that occurs only when life is a blank anyway.

Life, as Emerson said, is a matter of having good days. Henry Adams was discouraged: his generation had had few good days. He looked forward to the sink of energy at zero potential, or to the operation of the phase rule in history, as necessities which canceled out the pang and penalty of human efforts. If history moved inexorably from one phase to another, in the way that a solid, under suitable conditions of temperature and pressure, became a liquid, and then a gas, what mattered it that one was helpless—that one's generation was helpless? The inexorability of the law salved the laxity and the frustration. To picture a whole and healthy society, Adams's mind ran inevitably back to the past! As soon as he faced his own day, his mind jumped, as it were, off the page; and beyond predicting a catastrophe in 1917, as Western Civilization passed from a mechanical to an electrical phase, he saw nothing. In accounting for the future, he was incapable of putting desire and imagination, with their capacity for creating form, symbol, myth, and ideal, on the same level as intelligence. And intelligence itself left only a dreary prospect! The products of human culture outside science and technology became for him little better than playthings. "A man who knew only what accident had taught him in the Nineteenth Century," he wrote, "could know next to nothing, since science had got quite beyond his horizon, but one could play with the toys of childhood, including Ming porcelain, salons of painting, operas and theaters, beaux arts and Gothic architecture, theology and anarchy, in any jumble of time."

There in a brief picture was Henry Adams's generation. Its major efforts produced the grand achievements of science and technology. Science, taken as a whole, was the highest product of the time; by successive extensions into fields unknown to Bacon or Newton or Descartes, by continuous acts of thought, by the application of the scientific procedure to the earth as a whole, in geology, to organic life, in biology, and to the human community, in sociology, science was breaking outside its Seventeenth Century shell and raising problems which the logical atomism of the older thought was incapable of even expressing, much less carrying further. As a world-view, the biology of the Darwinists was still too much tainted by Calvinist metaphysics; and the loose metaphors of mechanical progress, so patent to the observers of the Nineteenth Century, were too easily substituted as patterns for the life-histories of species and societies, whilst the mechanical technique of the laboratories, placed in the dull surroundings of the paleotechnic city, tended to put to one side problems which could be solved only in the field, or by carrying the environment of the field into the laboratory. The notions of organism, of organic environment, of organic filiation had still to claim a place beside the naïve externalities of the older physics. But with all its lack of philosophic integration, the acts of thought in Nineteenth Century science made all other acts seem fairly insignificant. Science was accepted as a complete organon of life; and all its provisionally useful descriptions became finalities.

Henry Adams was far from seeing that "the great and terrible 'physical world,'" as Geddes and Branford put it, "is just a mode of the environment of Life," and that desires and ends play as important a part in the dance of life as the matter-of-fact causal descriptions which alone he respected. The truth is, Henry Adams's generation had forfeited its desires, and it was at loose ends. It treated those objects of art which are the symbols of man's desires and masteries in earlier periods tenderly, wistfully, impotently. It loved its Correggios and Tintorettos; and its fingers lingered over velvets, brocades, and laces that happier peoples had worn; it rested in these old things, and knew that they were good. But the future had nothing to offer—except the knowledge that what is, is inevitable!

"The attempt of the American of 1900 to educate the American of 2000 must be even blinder than that of the Congressman of 1800, except so far as he had learned his ignorance . . . the forces would continue to educate and the mind would continue to react." If that were all that there was to the social process, one might well share Henry Adams's withered Calvinism. For him, the only desirable future lay in the past; what should have been a hope was a memory. If the creative impulse were not, in fact, self-renewing, if every generation did not, within its limits, have a fresh start, if all the old objects of art moldered away and nothing new ever took their places— then Adams might well read only a dreary lesson in the progress from Thirteenth Century Unity to Twentieth Century Multiplicity. Europe's spiritual capital was being spent; even those who guarded it and hoarded it could not be sure that what they called, for example, Catholicism was more than a remnant of the spirit which had once integrated every aspect of life from the marriage bed to the tomb. Steadily, Europe's fund of culture was vanishing; and its fresh acquisitions were scattered, insecure, far from covering every human activity. The American could not live long even on his most extravagant acquisitions of European culture. William James was not another Aquinas, that was plain; nor was Howells or James another Dante; and the great figures Europe still produced, an Ibsen, a Dostoyevsky, were far from getting complete sustenance from their own day; they turned away from it, rather, to folklore, philology, and the ancient institutions of religion—the dream of a Messiah, a new Christ or a newer Superman. Neither the American nor the European had more than a bare vestige of a faith or a plan of life. . . .

Impotent to answer his own questions, Henry Adams was still intelligent enough to ask them. But he did not look for the answer in the only place where it may be found: he looked for it in the stars, in the annals of invention, in the credulous, mythic-materialistic past. He forgot to look for it in the human mind, which had created these idola, as it had created Moloch and Baal and Mammon; and which might turn away from its creations, as the Israelites turned away from the gods of the Philistines, once their prophets gave them a glimpse of a more organic and life-fulfilling world.

PAUL ELMER MORE
From A *New England Group and Others*
1921, pp. 122–40

It is not as a gallery of character etchings or as a repertory of stories that Mr. Adams's book mainly interests us; it is always the observer more than the observed that holds our attention, the effect being much the same as if we were reading a novel of Henry James, in which we are less concerned with the narrated acts of a group of men and women than with the colour these actions will take in the mind of some outside spectator, revealed or half-revealed. With both the novelist and the biographer the impelling motive is curiosity rather than

sympathy; but with a difference. In James we feel more the detachment of a mere psychological experimenter, the unconcern of one who creates a world of complex emotions and wills for the somewhat chilly pleasure of taking apart what he has so carefully put together; whereas in Adams there is always present the eager desire to discover in the drama some elusive truth which, if found, would give a meaning to its unfolding scenes. The autobiography is well named *The Education of Henry Adams*, though we surmise from the beginning that no lesson will ever be learned, and that the learner has set himself to decipher a text in a foreign tongue without grammar or lexicon in his hands.

In a way the text before him was not one of his own choice, but forced on him by birth and inheritance. This breed of New England, of whom he was so consciously a titled representative, had once come out from the world for the sake of a religious and political affirmation—the two were originally one—to confirm which they were ready to deny all the other values of life. For the liberty to follow this affirmation they would discard tradition and authority and form and symbol and all that ordinarily binds men together in the bonds of habit. But the liberty of denying may itself become a habit. The intellectual history of New England is in fact the record of the encroachment of this liberty on the very affirmation for which it was at first the bulwark. By a gradual elimination of its positive content the faith of the people had passed from Calvinism to Unitarianism, and from this to free thinking, until in the days of our Adams there was little left to the intellect but a great denial:

> . . . The religious instinct had vanished, and could not be revived, although one made in later life many efforts to recover it. That the most powerful emotion of man, next to the sexual, should disappear, might be a personal defect of his own; but that the most intelligent society, led by the most intelligent clergy, in the most moral conditions he ever knew, should have solved all the problems of the universe so thoroughly as to have quite ceased making itself anxious about past or future, and should have persuaded itself that all the problems which had convulsed human thought from earliest recorded time, were not worth discussing, seemed to him the most curious social phenomenon he had to account for in a long life.

So the original affirmation had been swallowed up in its own defences, while the negative impulse grew "to a degree that in the long run became positive and hostile." But with this intellectual negation there remained almost in full force the moral impulse which from the first had been so intimately associated with a negative separatism. This is the key we must hold in our hands if we would enter into the inner life of Henry Adams and the other New Englanders of his generation, taking the word broadly—we must, if possible, put ourselves into the state of men whose conscience was moving, so to speak, *in vacuo*, like a dispossessed ghost seeking a substantial habitation. Adams "tended towards negation on his own account, as one side of the New England mind had always done." In this vacuum various minds sought relief in various ways, connecting themselves naturally with the contemporary currents of European thought. Emerson, as the purest spirit of them all, would rest in the bare liberty of prophesying, in the security of an intuition content in itself and careless of all preceding experience as formulated in law and custom. He was *par excellence* the pure Romantic, yet withal a New Englander at heart, not a German. John Fiske, if we may extend the limits of a generation so far, looked to the new discoveries of scientific evolution to give substance to the vague cosmic deity which had swum into the place of the Christian Jehovah. Most significant of all in some respects for our present subject is the case of Charles Eliot Norton. With him New England scepticism merges into the contented agnosticism of his British friends, particularly of Leslie Stephen, while the sting of conscience takes the form of distress at the licence of an agnostic society. . . .

Norton was not consistent, you will say; and rightly. There is a question to ask of a man who finds a new source of responsibility in a creed destructive of the very principle of authority, yet laments the lack of responsibility in a world that acts in accordance with such a creed; there is a beautiful inconsistency in the heart of one who professes complete agnosticism, yet spends his life in the devoted study of Dante. It is the inconsistency of a conscience that has outlived faith and not found philosophy, the will of New England working out in its own peculiar manner the problem of the nineteenth century. To Adams the question of meaning in the world came with a somewhat different emphasis. Norton was the product of a long line of theologians, and doubt, when it crept in, took primarily the form of philosophical scepticism. But Adams was not born into the Brahmin caste. From the beginning, as seen in his great-grandfather and in his ancestral cousin, the revolt against traditional authority had been rather in the field of politics, and it was in his blood, so to speak, that his agnosticism should strike first upon the belief in a providential purpose in history. That indeed is the stimulus of what he calls his education. His inquiry was to branch out into a wider sphere, and in the end was to make its return to a medieval mysticism, as Norton's did to a medieval æstheticism; but in his earlier years he was sufficiently absorbed in seeking some theory to explain the sequence of historical events. What was the meaning of this opposition which his forbears and his father had maintained against the settled institutions of government? To whose profit did it accrue, or was there any profit to be found anywhere? In what way had the world grown wiser and truer from this struggle and from all the struggles of men since the beginning of time? Where should he put his finger on the thread of progress in the terrible tangle of human misadventure?

. . . At an early period he had added to his reading of history a faithful study of science, and as he had sought for a thread of providential guidance in the one, so, under the influence of the newly based theory of evolution, he looked for signs of design and progress in the non-human order of creation. At first the two fields of inquiry had lain apart, but now, as I say, they appeared as phases only of the one problem which engaged his passionate attention. But the search baffled him, baffled him the more as it became more complex. As in history he thought he saw the evil persisting unchanged along with the good, so in the field of science he beheld the lower order of existence continuing on with the higher and throwing an element of stable confusion into progressive mutation. More than that. When he went beyond the material of biology into the dark background of inorganic forces he learned that the physicists themselves acknowledged only an inexpressible mystery. In Germany he heard Haeckel avowing that "the proper essence of substance appeared to him more and more marvellous and enigmatic as he penetrated further into the knowledge of its attributes,—matter and energy,—and as he learned to know their innumerable phenomena and their evolution." In France he heard the clearer and more authoritative voice of Poincaré making the same confession of ignorance: "[in science] we are led to act as though a simple law, when other things were equal, must be more probable than a complicated law. Half a

century ago one frankly confessed it, and proclaimed that nature loves simplicity. She has since given us too often the lie. To-day this tendency is no longer avowed, and only so much of it is preserved as is indispensable so that science shall not become impossible." Then, turning to England, he read such words as these: "In the chaos behind sensation, in the 'beyond' of sense-impressions, we cannot infer necessity, order, or routine, for these are concepts formed by the mind of man on this side of sense-impressions. . . . Briefly, chaos is all that science can logically assert of the super-sensuous." Thus as the "unknowable" came nearer to man's inquiry it seemed to put on positive and menacing hues; the pronouncements of the most advanced physical thinkers echoed to Adams what he had learnt from his own study in history—chaos in the background here and there. And if he went to the pseudo-science of psychology he was faced with another "sub-conscious chaos below the mind"; man's "normal thought," he learned, "was dispersion, sleep, dream, inconsequence; the simultaneous action of different thought-centres without central control. His artificial balance was acquired habit. He was an acrobat, with a dwarf on his back, crossing a chasm on a slack-rope, and commonly breaking his neck." Here was a question that sprang from something very far from idle curiosity. Had Adams not witnessed the terror of the mystery, when this thing called chaos had suddenly lurched forward out of its background of mystery and enveloped his little oasis of well-loved order?

What was the proper attitude towards this enigma? Was it that no one can reach beyond himself? "All that Henry Adams ever saw in man was a reflection of his own ignorance"—such was his political discernment far back in his London days; should that be the final verdict of all his seeing? In a way he had acquired what ages ago had been proclaimed by Socrates as the beginning of wisdom: not to think we know what we do not know. Into this sea of negation he had sailed from the ancient moorings of his people; but not even the New Englander of the nineteenth century could rest in pure negation. Emerson, like Socrates, had found no difficulty in combining scepticism with an intuition of pure spirituality, though, unlike Socrates, to maintain his inner vision intact he shut his eyes resolutely on the darker facts of nature. That serene indifference to evil was the last thing possible to Adams. Another New Englander, nearer to Adams in date, John Fiske, had accepted the most rigid deductions of biological evolution, and then on Darwin's law of natural selection, which for humanly felt good and evil substituted a conception of blind unfeeling mechanism, had superimposed the conception of a cosmic deity unfolding the world to

one far-off divine event,
To which the whole creation moves.

Whatever may be said of such a philosophy, it was meaningless to Henry Adams; he could not marry the faith in a benignant pantheistic will with the sort of chaos that lurked for him behind every door of our ignorance. Still another New Englander, Charles Eliot Norton, as we have seen, was content to profess a complete agnosticism of theory along with an unswerving belief in human responsibility—to what? Alas, that "what" was the little irksome word that Adams could not get out of his mind.

The answer, or the direction towards an answer, came to him as he walked the halls of the Paris Exposition of 1900. There, at least, under the guidance of his scientific friend, Langley, if he saw nothing that pointed to a rational design at the end of things, he beheld in the great gallery of machines a symbol of what science had substituted for design. "The planet itself seemed less impressive, in its old-fashioned, deliberate, annual or daily revolution, than this huge wheel, revolving within arm's-length at some vertiginous speed, and barely murmuring,—scarcely humming an audible warning to stand a hair's-breadth further for respect of power,—while it would not wake the baby lying close against its frame. Before the end, one began to pray to it; inherited instinct taught the natural expression of man before silent and infinite force. Among the thousand symbols of ultimate energy, the dynamo was not so human as some, but it was the most expressive." Force, he would say, blind whirling force, strapped and bound in iron, is supreme over all:

> Dinos has driven out Zeus and rules as king.

We should need, in fact, a living Aristophanes to celebrate this step of a New Englander's education. Other men of the century had discovered this same god, but their worship had taken strangely different forms. "Power is power," says Tolstoy, reading for himself the lesson of history at the conclusion of his *War and Peace*, "that is Power is a word, the true meaning of which is to us incomprehensible"; and then, as a good humanitarian, he personifies this Unknowable in the instinctive soul of the People. Nietzsche, too, had found only *Macht* at the heart of the world, but he worshipped this Power not at all in the impulse of the People—quite the contrary; and some of his interpreters have deified a *Schrecklichkeit* very different from the pity of Tolstoy. Perhaps the true lesson of our age would be to learn why and how this modern Janus of Power has tricked us into believing that he has only one face. But Adams was too knowing to bow the knee with Tolstoy, and too timid to salute with Nietzsche. He took another way.

Norton, as we have seen, had found agnosticism compatible with devotion to Dante, being able at least to sympathize with the energetic moral sense and the æsthetic vision of that poet; and Adams, like him, turned at last for consolation to the age of Dante, if not to Dante himself, though with a difference. From the Exposition, "caring but little for the name, and fixed only on tracing Force, Adams had gone straight to the Virgin at Chartres, and asked her to show him God, face to face, as she did for St. Bernard." What the Virgin revealed to him is told clearly enough in the autobiography, but for its fullest elucidation one should read that extraordinary disquisition on the art and poetry and philosophy and religion of the twelfth and thirteenth centuries which he entitles *Mont-Saint-Michel and Chartres*. In the Virgin Mother of God, to whose honour the cathedrals pointed their arches towards heaven, before whose throne the windows were made to glow like the jewels of a queen, for whose delight romance wove its shimmering web of words, to whom great scholars sacrificed their learning, our far-travelled New Englander saw at last the one symbol of Force comprehensible to the human heart, if not to the human brain. "The Puritans," he says, "abandoned the New Testament and the Virgin in order to go back to the beginning, and renew the quarrel with Eve"; our latest Puritan rediscovers woman on her medieval throne, and chants to her in modern speech the ancient pæan to Alma Venus Genetrix. It would be a pretty business to unravel the various motives that had impelled him on this devious way from the sturdy, if unloving, protestantism of his race. He himself makes much of the motive of love as the aspect of infinite power which man can understand. That may be; but I suspect that another attribute of the Virgin meant even more to his mind. Read, if you will, his charming pages on her interventions and miracles; you will observe that they were almost without exception performed to override the course of law and justice, and you will learn that behind her woman's pity there was another quality which Adams, at any rate, does not hesitate to glorify as equally feminine:

The fact, conspicuous above all other historical certainties about religion, that the Virgin was by essence illogical, unreasonable, and feminine, is the only fact of any ultimate value worth studying, and starts a number of questions that history has shown itself clearly afraid to touch. . . .

If the Trinity was in its essence Unity, the Mother alone could represent whatever was not Unity; whatever was irregular, exceptional, outlawed; and this was the whole human race.

Conscience was the last tie of New England to its past. Was it the perfect irresponsibility of the Virgin, human no doubt, feminine perhaps, certainly not Puritan, that gave to our tired sceptic the illusion of having reached a comfortable goal after his long voyage of education? There is a fateful analogy between the irresponsibility of unreasoning Force and unreasoning love; and the gods of Nietzsche and of Tolstoy are but the two faces of one god. To change the metaphor, if it may be done without disrespect, the image in the cathedral of Chartres looks perilously like the ancient idol of Dinos decked out in petticoats.

If we regard Adams's scholarship, his imagination, his verbal dexterity, his candour, his cynical vivacity, his range of reflection, we must give him a high place in the American literature of the past generation, a higher place probably than his present limited popularity would indicate. But one winces a little at acknowledging that the latest spokesman of the Adamses and of New England ends his career in sentimental nihilism. From Harvard College, which to Adams had been only one stage in the way of disillusion, the boy John Fiske had written: "When we come to a true philosophy, and make *that* our stand-point, all things become clear. We know what things to learn, and what, in the infinite mass of things, to leave unlearned; and then the Universe becomes clear and harmonious." The tragedy of Adams's education is that of a man who could not rest easy in negation, yet could find no positive faith to take its place. From one point of view he may appear to be the most honest and typical mind of New England in its last condition; yet withal some manlier voice, some word of deeper insight that yet faces the facts of life, we must still expect to hear from the people of Mather and Edwards and Channing and Emerson.

JAMES TRUSLOW ADAMS
From "Henry Adams and the New Physics"

The Yale Review, December 19, 1929, pp. 286–302

In his attempt to bring the facts of history under a scientific law, it was necessary for him to establish "points of reference" from which to estimate the forces with which he became engaged. He chose two: the twelfth and thirteenth centuries as the period when man was most conscious of unity, and the twentieth when unity had given place to multiplicity. His *Mont-Saint-Michel and Chartres* and his *Education* were intended to establish these "points." In both cases his method broke down, as was inevitable. No one, historian or layman, now reads these books with any reference to the author's theory of history, but in both cases the books remain great and unique. The former has been described aptly as "a series of pictures tinged with feeling and glowing with enthusiasm," and if the whole of the mediaeval story is not to be found in its pages, it nevertheless remains the best introduction for anyone who would reach to the soul of that period. As a synthesis of the thought and aspiration of one period in history, it would be difficult to find its equal. It has been of great and continued influence in America from the time when, against his wishes although with his consent, it was given to the public by the American Institute of Architects, which also elected Adams an honorary member.

The other volume—the *Education*—is now read as an autobiography, and as such it is *sui generis* in American letters. We may admit, as Brooks Adams did in his comment, that the irony is rather overdone, and most readers will end the volume before the final chapters on the theory of history, though William A. Dunning found in them the most substantial manifestation of Adams's genius. It may be recalled, moreover, that Adams never intended the book for publication and that it appeared without corrections after his death. No other autobiography by an American affords such a rich variety of starting points for deep reflection, and its influence, already great, is likely to grow. From this very brief survey of Adams's substantial accomplishment, we may pass to consider his effort to bring history into line with the scientific thought of his own day.

. . . So far, indeed, as I am aware, only one man has ever attempted to subsume the multitudinous data of human history under a strictly scientific law, and that man was Henry Adams. It is true that we hear a constant babble about scientific history and scientific historians, but in my opinion this is misleading nomenclature. The modern effort to record facts truly without bias or prejudice, is merely a step towards intellectual integrity. In time such effort may provide the raw materials for science, but it is not yet science, the very essence of which is predictable results based on law. Adams is, I believe, the only man who ever attempted to formulate a law in history that should be sufficiently scientific as to permit of its use in predicting the future, and so to use it. It is still impossible to know whether history can ever be a science, that is, whether its data are rhythmical or non-rhythmical, whether it will prove to be one of the "streaks of order" in the cosmos or whether it will not, but if it ever does prove so, Henry Adams must be accorded the first place in its establishment. It is this that gives unique interest to his, in my opinion, unsuccessful attempt.

The form which that attempt took was predetermined by the period in which it was made, and its expression would have been different twenty years earlier or ten years later. Adams wrote in 1894 that "any science of history must be absolute, like other sciences, and must fix with mathematical certainty the path which human society has got to follow." In 1900 he wrote his essay on "The Rule of Phase Applied to History," not published until after his death, in which he tried to establish history on a mathematical basis.

Adams's initiation into science had taken place by means of biology and geology, and I think that the two men who had the most influence upon his thought throughout his life were Darwin and Lyell. Just in the period, however, when he was occupied in trying to link the data of history with the growing body of scientific knowledge, the other sciences were gradually being overshadowed by physics, which threatened, like Aaron's rod, to eat up all the others. The same trend of mind that made scientific knowledge appear to be, not merely, perhaps, more useful but more valid than non-scientific, made it also appear that in physics we could at last track the secret of the cosmos to its inmost chambers. In its atomic structure, based on mathematical laws, we seemed at last to have struck rock bottom, and in the prevailing view that the whole universe was mechanistic, the vision opened of the possibility of reducing the whole of its multitudinous phenomena, human and other, to formulae concerning atoms. The problem, of course, was of enormous complexity, but its insolubility would be based on its

complexity only and not on its essential nature. In the twenty years during which Adams was working, the whole of the Newtonian physics and its concepts, were still intact. Just at the very end, indeed, the atom yielded to the electron but without, as yet, disturbing the general mechanistic basis of the cosmos. The entire universe was atomic in structure, and atoms were still, for all practical purposes, tiny billiard balls whose actions and reactions could be predicted with mathematical certainty. Larger and larger fields of phenomena were being subdued to this conception. The inference was almost irresistible that it was only a question of time when the whole would thus be subdued, including the realm of mind. If, therefore, history were to be made scientific, and if the whole of science were to become physics—a mere expression of mechanistic relations in mathematical terms—it was obvious that the data of history must be submitted to some such expression.

The Adams mind, ever since its change of phase with the first John in the eighteenth century, has been characterized by a desire to arrange phenomena under law, to transform its outlook upon the spiritual, political, or natural worlds from multiplicity to unity. The Adamses have been daring creators of hypotheses rather than laboratory plodders. It was inevitable, given Henry's intellectual inheritance and the scientific climate of his day, that his effort to make history scientific should take the form of a sweeping mathematical formula utilizing the current concepts of physics.

We may observe three stages in his progress. First comes the belief that history must be treated as a physical science, and a good deal of toying with vague thoughts of the *Pteraspis* and *Terebratula*. Then his mind becomes colored by physics and mathematics, and he tries to apply to history the first and second laws of thermodynamics. We need not concern ourselves here with this second stage, which was given full expression in *A Letter to American Teachers of History*, although we shall refer to one or two points later. The only one to be noted at once is that in dealing with these laws of the conservation of energy and of entropy, or the degradation of energy, Adams assumed that "social energy" (the whole, apparently, of human functioning) was subject to the same laws, that is, was of the same type as physical energy. William James strenuously objected to this identification. As he wrote to Henry, "you can't impress God in that way." Much might be said as to the present status of these two laws, but they are not of prime importance in Adams's theory. Granted the truth of the law of entropy, the beginning of the universe is utterly inconceivable (as it is anyway), but even so the effect upon making history a science is negligible. The main point is whether "social energy" can be identified with physical energy as Adams identified it.

About 1900, apparently, Adams ran across Willard Gibbs's work on the *Equilibrium of Heterogeneous Substances*, including the essay on "phases" of matter, and this gave a new direction to his thought. Adams's own essay, "The Rule of Phase Applied to History," was the result. In this he took as his starting point the assumption that "Thought is a historical substance," and argued that "the future of Thought, and therefore of History, lies in the hands of the physicists," and that history must be reduced to "the world of mathematical physics."

So far, Adams had been indulging in generalities. He had simply given a characteristic expression to the prevailing belief that somehow the world of mind would sooner or later have to fall under the legislation of the world of atoms, and he had played with some of the implications of such a theory. Now he was to make a genuine effort to extend the laws of physical to the realm of "social" energy. If the effort appears fantastic, it is only fair to say that he himself was, of course, aware of that aspect of his essay.

Carrying forward his list of phases beyond solid, fluid, and vapor, he postulated those of electricity, ether, space, and pure thought, assuming that "every equilibrium, of phase, begins and ends with what is called a critical point," and that the passage from one to another can be expressed by a mathematical formula. In physics he found the three variables in change of phase to be pressure, temperature, and volume. For his purpose he changed pressure into "attraction," temperature into "acceleration," and retained volume, though what he meant by the last is uncertain. In history he found that an attractive force, like gravitation, drew trickling rivulets of energy into new phases by an external influence which tended to concentrate and accelerate their motion by a law with which their supposed wishes or appetites had no conscious relation, and that "if the current of Thought has shown obedience to the law of gravitation it is material, and its phases should be easily calculated." As the nearest analogy to mind he took the comet, arguing that "if not a Thought, the comet is a sort of brother of Thought, an early condensation of the ether itself, as the human mind may be another, traversing the infinite without origin or end, and attracted by a sudden object of curiosity that lies by chance near its path. If such elements are subject to the so-called law of gravitation, no good reason can exist for denying gravitation to the mind." What he intended to mean by "attraction" appears to be indicated on the very last page he wrote on the subject when he speaks of "the attractions of occult power. If values can be given to these attractions, a physical theory of history is a mere matter of physical formula, no more complicated than the formulas of Willard Gibbs or Clerk Maxwell."

He himself experimented with the simple and far-reaching one of the law of squares. In his opinion, history had already experienced three phases, corresponding to solid, liquid, and gaseous, the phase of instinct, that of religion, and the present mechanical one. In order to get some starting point, it was essential, as we have noted above, for him to locate one of the "critical points" that marked a change of phase. This he finally located in 1600, the change from the religious to the mechanical. He suggests as the end of the mechanical phase the year 1900, with the discovery of radium. Working by his law of squares, backward, he found that the second, or religious, phase of man would have an indicated length of 90,000 years, and the first, or instinctive, phase an incalculably long span. Working onwards from the mechanical phase, the same law would give us a period of about seventeen years, until 1917, for a fourth phase, which he calls the electric, and about four years for the next phase, which he calls the ethereal, which would "bring Thought to the limit of its possibilities about 1921." Selecting some year later than 1900 for the end of the mechanical phase would slightly prolong the later phases. "Thought in terms of ether," he adds, "means only Thought in terms of itself, in other words, pure Mathematics and Metaphysics, a stage often reached by individuals. At the utmost it could mean only the subsidence of the current into an ocean of potential Thought, or mere consciousness, which is also possible, like static electricity."

Before analyzing Adams's effort further, we may apply the pragmatic test. The result is extraordinarily interesting, although it does not alter my belief in the impossibility of Adams's historical physics. It must be recalled that he was writing in 1909 and that the future was then a sealed book. His first prediction arrived at by mathematics applied to the historical process was that thought would enter upon a new phase about 1917. As a matter of fact, this was precisely what happened. In 1911 Rutherford brought about what Eddington calls

"the greatest change in our idea of matter since the days of Democritus." In 1913 Bohr elaborated the quantum theory of atomic structure, and two years later Einstein extended his doctrine of relativity. The supremacy of Euclidean geometry, Newtonian physics, and a mechanistic interpretation of the cosmos crumbled. As far as we can judge, still so close to the event, a change of "phase" in Adams's sense, comparable only to those at preceding "critical points," had occurred.

His second prediction seemed more incredible of fulfilment. To have said in 1909 that less than half a generation would "bring Thought to the limit of its possibilities" and to attempt to prove it by mathematics, was assuredly to sacrifice one's reputation to the gods of common sense, and yet this prediction also has been fulfilled in a way that no scientist could have dreamed possible when Adams wrote. In 1925 came Heisenberg's new quantum theory and in 1927 his principle of indeterminacy. The law of cause and effect simply evaporated before a world of dumfounded scientists. As Professor Bridgman of Harvard has recently confessed, the physicist now finds himself in a world from which the bottom has dropped out. Nor, as Eddington has pointed out, is the new difficulty merely a dialectical one. It lies in the very nature of human knowledge itself as revealed by the new atomic discoveries. At the very height of its achievement and intellectual pride, science has been brought up against the limit of knowledge. "We have reached the point," says Bridgman, "where knowledge must stop because of the nature of knowledge itself: beyond this point meaning ceases. . . . No refinement of measurement will avail to carry him [the physicist] beyond the portals of this shadowy domain which he cannot even mention without logical inconsistency. . . . As we penetrate ever deeper, the very law of cause and effect, which we had thought to be a formula to which we could force God himself to subscribe, ceases to have meaning. The world is not intrinsically reasonable or understandable; it acquires these properties in ever-increasing degree as we ascend from the realm of the very little to the realm of everyday things; here we may eventually hope for an understanding sufficiently good for all practical purposes, but no more." Perhaps no one would have been more stunned than Adams himself at this extraordinary success of the application of his formula. Obviously, however, this test bears no resemblance to the three astronomical tests of Einstein's doctrine of relativity. It proves the correctness of neither Adams's formula nor his method. Indeed, the very advance in physics which has brought about the fulfilment of his prediction in one direction at least, has also done much to invalidate his method of thought.

It would be an easy task to pick to pieces one by one Adams's concepts in the light of the new physics. Take one of his fundamental ideas, gravitation. So long as it was conceived of as a pull or a force or an attraction it was much easier to play with such transpositions as Adams made, and to consider the "attraction" of the earth for an apple and the "attraction" of occult power for mind as obeying similar laws, but when gravitation becomes a function of curved space, the situation becomes different even for the most easily satisfied mind. But this line of criticism is hardly worth while. I think that Adams is entitled to very high credit for making the attempt, by means which he himself knew were rather absurd in detail, to bring history within the genuinely scientific field, that is, of predictability, and to do so in the line of the promised advance in science, that is, along physical and mathematical lines. I believe, however, that his method was entirely wrong, although in a way it was the method that has been used by such scientists as Faraday and Maxwell. In other words, he tried to build up, in a field beyond previous experiment, a structure which had been found to work in other fields of tested experience.

. . . Certainly there is nothing to lead us to believe now that the application of concepts applicable to the superatomic world would necessarily or even likely work, as Adams tried to make them. Leaving out the biologists from this discussion, though their contribution would be an interesting one, and keeping to the physicists, the tendency is now away from simplification. Bridgman, for example, considers it evident that the laws of nature cannot be reduced to those of mechanics or even electricity. Among some, indeed, there is a growing tendency to admit mind or even to find "mind" and "matter" two aspects of some underlying reality. Having been, so to speak, slapped in the face and told to go home while we were looking at the electron, it may be that we shall never penetrate the mystery further, and can only speculate mystically about it. In doing that we might conceive that both "mind" and "matter" in truth did obey the same "laws," that is, that their modes of behavior would weave the same patterns in a super-mind capable of observing and reacting to the behavior of each in the same way. If the human mind can weave similar patterns for reality in the scale between the sidereal universe and the electron, stopping there, it is conceivable that a greater mind, God, or what you will, might be able to do the same thing for a wider scale, embracing our knowable range, the sub-atomic and the mental, bringing them all into harmony in his own mind. It might even be that some of our logical difficulties with the first and second laws of thermodynamics might thus be resolved. It might prove that the amount of energy remained constant and that the constant degradation of energy which we postulate in the physical universe was being balanced by an increase of energy in the mental or spiritual, a process unobservable to science but clearly so to a mind watching both aspects of reality. The difficulty, but necessity, of postulating a universe starting with a maximum of energy and slowly running down, as the law of entropy requires, might be resolved by some vast systole and diastole of energy tensity in what are to us the two aspects of reality—mind and nature. All such speculations, however, are obviously beyond science.

Was Henry Adams then pursuing an *ignis fatuus?* Was he wholly on a wrong tack in his effort to make science of history? I do not think so, but think that he merely made a mistake in trying to erect a sweeping hypothesis with too little data and to transfer to one field of experience the laws and concepts applicable only to another. The "operations," in the scientific sense, employed in studying the stream of history are entirely different from those employed in studying a stream of water, and Adams ignored "the principle that in changing the operations we have really changed the concept, and that to use the same name for these different concepts over the entire range is dictated only by considerations of convenience, which may sometimes prove to have been purchased at too high a price in terms of unambiguity."

On the other hand, I think he rendered a service in brushing aside the prevailing conception of history as "scientific" when all that was implied was a painstaking, unbiassed investigation, with much critical apparatus, of some particular eddy in the historical stream. The facts of history are susceptible of scientific treatment or they are not; that is, they recur or they do not, they are rhythmical or they are not. If *not,* then history is not and never can be a science. If they *are* susceptible of scientific treatment then it will be possible to establish laws based on recurrence, laws yielding predictability of results. Until some such laws have been discovered, I personally believe that it is sheer snobbery to speak of history as a science, a

pretense springing from the desire of the practitioners to rank themselves among the popular aristocrats in the kingdom of knowledge. Adams at least had the courage to try for something better, and he followed the path along the only way in which history can become scientific, however easy it may be to criticise the structure he raised. . . .

Adams was wholly right when, as a preliminary to establishing laws in history, he completely depersonalized it. We must cease dealing with the individual as a unique personality. We must deal only with historical phenomena which fall within the range of rhythmical recurrence and predictability. We must keep above the electron. If we choose phenomena of the scale of revolutions, let us discard all reference to picturesque personalities. Instead of writing in terms of Lafayette, Mirabeau, Danton, Robespierre, Napoleon, let us try what the result would be of treating such individuals as functions of the revolutionary process and give them symbols. In many revolutions that come readily to mind, we can already trace the regularity of the process and the emergence at similar periods of A, A^1, A^2, A^3, or X, Y, or Z, however we may choose to designate them. In this way we could reach a sort of anatomy of revolutions and avoid entangling our minds with personalities. This, of course, would be entirely different from history as it has always been written, and personally, because I do not believe in running off with other people's clothes, I should prefer to leave the term history to what is now so designated and coin a new word for history as a science, if there is to be any such thing. Very likely there is not, but if there is it must surely be as depersonalized as physics or chemistry or biology. We may speak of an atom of oxygen or an atom of hydrogen, but if we began to give the individual oxygen atoms pet names and talked about Jack Oxygen and Jill Oxygen we would not get far in establishing general laws for oxygen atoms. In the same way, in studying, say, revolutions as recurring, and thus predictable, scientific phenomena we must work comparatively through all revolutions and find the elements, the A (Lafayette) at the beginning and the A^5 (Napoleon) at the end of the movements. There are great and obvious difficulties in the way of building up a mass of such studies, but until we can deal with A and A^5 as with oxygen and hydrogen atoms instead of with the individuals Lafayette and Napoleon, I see no hope of "scientific" history.

On wholly inadequate data an Adams may endeavor to establish laws of mathematical precision or a Spengler may try to establish them biologically, but as written now, history, in which the large-scale phenomena alone offer any hope of establishing laws, so heaps and covers these over with a mass of irrelevant personalities as to make it practically impossible for anyone to study these phenomena and isolate them.

In short, the development of physics since Henry Adams made the only effort to establish a scientific law for history that has ever been made would thus seem to point clearly to the direction in which historians should go, if their work is to be brought within the field of "science." In the first place, we have been shown that irresponsibility, indeterminism, or what you will, in small-scale phenomena is not inimical to establishing laws for large-scale phenomena; secondly, that phenomena must lie within a certain scale to be attuned to human reason, and that it is necessary to find that scale; and thirdly, that concepts cannot be applied at random but must be based on operations, and not carried over from one sphere to another. Whether on this basis history may ever become scientific certainly remains to be proved. Others, under the name of laws, have pointed out influences. Others, again, under the same name, have pointed to what may or may not be tendencies.

Adams alone made the courageous effort to establish a scientific law with the validity of a fairly accurate predictableness. He was neither a Copernicus, a Galileo, nor a Newton, but until historians realize that mere accurate scholarship is not science, he is likely to stand alone as the sole pioneer of "scientific history."

VERNON LOUIS PARRINGTON
From "Henry Adams—Intellectual"
Main Currents in American Thought
Volume 3, 1930, pp. 214–27

From a similar disaster Henry Adams was saved by an early disillusionment. His efforts at *rapprochement* were little more than a gesture. While casting about after the war for a promising opening for a career he hit upon finance as a likely field and published a number of essays that drew attention to him. But it was quite impossible for him to go forward along such lines. He was too completely the intellectual, too aloof from his generation in spirit and will, to ally himself with the economic masters of the Gilded Age. Sooner or later he would go his own way, and luckily good fortune took the matter in hand promptly. No suitable opportunity offering, he was dragooned by family and friends into an assistant-professorship at Harvard, where he spent seven years trying to explain to himself and his students the meaning of the Middle Ages. Those years were his introduction to history. The passion of the student was in his blood, and he turned with zest to brood over the scanty records of past generations, seeking a clue to the meaning of man's pilgrimage on earth, trying to arrange the meaningless fragments in some sort of rational pattern, in the hope of discovering an underlying unity in what seemed on the face only a meaningless welter of complexity and irrationality. A rationalist, he followed his intellect in an eager quest for the law of historical evolution, and he ended fifty years later in mysticism. It was a natural outcome for a lifetime of rationalizing—a compensation for the mordant dissatisfactions that issued from the restless play of mind.

Dissatisfied with his labors he quitted the Harvard post in 1879 and thereafter made his home at Washington in the atmosphere of politics. From the Middle Ages he turned to the American past and set out to explore the period during which the first Adams had played his part. He could not deal with narrow parochial themes; he would not fall into the "sink of history—antiquarianism," that satisfied Charles Francis Adams. From the beginnings of his intellectual life he had been concerned with the ideas and ideals that presumably lie behind periods and civilizations; so he went back to what he regarded as the great age of American political history, to inquire into the meaning of the struggle between Federalism and Jeffersonianism for control of the venture in republicanism. But finding little satisfaction there, as he had earlier found none in Victorian England, where he had studied closely contemporary English statesmen—Palmerston and Lord Russell and Gladstone—only to convince himself that they were bankrupt of ideas and morality, and had nothing to teach concerning the good life, he abandoned the field, threw over his familiar studies, and set about the great business of reëducating himself.

From his long studies in the American past one significant thing had emerged—he had come to understand the source of certain of his dissatisfactions with current American ideals that set him apart from his fellows. He had gone back to his own origins and had traced the rise of the defiant Adams prejudices that were as strong in the fourth generation as they had been in the first. The Adams family was eighteenth-century—Henry Adams had come to understand—and he himself in mind and education and prejudices, was of that earlier time. He was a child of Quincy rather than Boston—a simple world with simple virtues that capitalism and industrialism were destroying in the name of progress. From such village loyalties he could not rid himself. Perhaps in reason he should not have preferred that earlier homespun world; but affection does not heed logic, and as Henry Adams traced the decline of Quincy to Hamilton's financial policy that started the new capitalism on its triumphant career, he was filled with bitterness. It was a vulgar order that was rising and an evil day. Since 1865 the bankers had ruled America, and they were coming finally to cajole the American people into accepting their vulgar ideals and putting their trust in a bankers' paradise. As he watched the temples of the new society rising everywhere in the land, his gorge rose at the prospect. He had no wish to dwell in a bankers' paradise. Dislike of a capitalistic society was in his blood. From father to son all the Adamses had distrusted capitalism and hated State Street. The "only distinctive mark of all the Adamses," he said late in life, "since old Sam Adams's father a hundred and fifty years before, had been their inherited quarrel with State Street, which had again and again broken out into riot, bloodshed, personal feuds, foreign and civil war, wholesale banishments and confiscations, until the history of Florence was hardly more turbulent than that of Boston."[1]

And so when at the climax of the capitalistic revolution he watched the change going on noisily all about him, when the transition to the bankers' paradise was called progress and capitalistic feudalism was hailed as the advent of Utopia, he seemed to himself a somewhat pathetic anachronism. Shades of the prison house were falling about him. "He had hugged his antiquated dislike of bankers and capitalistic society," he said bitterly, "until he had become little better than a crank." . . .

But while he clung tenaciously to his obsolete prejudices in favor of an earlier century, the pugnacious realism of that century was oozing out of him. The middle years of his life, between the acceptance of the Harvard post in 1870 and the final break with Victorianism in 1892, were intellectually an unhappy period. He was losing his grasp on realities and becoming narrowly and exclusively political-minded. It was not good for him to live daily in the presence of politics. In so "far as he had a function in life," he said of the Henry Adams of 1877, "it was as stable-companion to statesmen, whether they liked it or not."[2] The term "statesmen" was of course only a polite euphemism for the breed of politicians who played their sordid game under his critical eyes. He was rarely under any illusions in regard to them except when blinded by friendship. Certainly his etchings of Grant and Blaine and Sherman and Conkling and other servants of democracy were done with acid.

Yet in all his penetrating comment on men and measures there is a curious failure to take into account the economic springs of action. He had let slip the clue old John Adams had followed so tenaciously. An acute historian, not thus wanting, would never have traced the triumph of the gold standard to the "mere law of mass," would never have substituted a physical determinism for an economic, would never have confused the principle of mass with a minority. How far an intelligent man and a competent historian could go astray in his criticism of current ways is suggested by the curious novel *Democracy*, that he wrote in 1880 while living in the daily companionship of

John Hay and Clarence King. In dealing with the phenomena of political corruption he had none of the acuteness of old John Taylor of Carolina, who would have put his finger unerringly on the cause, or of the first Adams. If he had written *Democracy* after he had studied the funding operations of the Federalists under Hamilton's leadership, very likely he would have dealt with the problem more searchingly; but in 1880 Henry Adams revealed no more critical intelligence than did Godkin or Lowell or other critics of the Gilded Age.

The historical work done during those middle years at Washington was abundant and excellent, marked by rigorous use of sources, a dispassionate attitude towards partisan issues, and excellent form. It was easy for an Adams to take middle ground between Jefferson and Hamilton, however much his sympathies inclined to the former. In all this work, however, in the *Life of Albert Gallatin* (1879), in *John Randolph* (1882), as well as in the nine-volume *History of the United States during the Administrations of Jefferson and Madison* (1889–1891), the point of view remains too narrowly political, with the result that it fails to thrust into adequate relief the economics of the great struggle between agrarianism and capitalism; and without that clue the interpretation is wanting in substantial realism.

By 1891 he was convinced that he had got all he could from the curdled milk of politics, and he became dissatisfied with his work. There can be little doubt that it was a growing realization of the inadequacy of his analysis of social forces that determined him to abandon the field he had tilled so long and set about the business of reëducating himself. If *Mont-Saint-Michel and Chartres* and *The Education* tell anything about Henry Adams they reveal that his dissatisfactions welled up from deep springs within himself—from the consciousness of his failure to penetrate beneath the surface, to probe the hidden forces that move the puppets on the historical stage. He had long been seeking an adequate philosophy of history—for a unity behind the multiplicity—and in these early years of the nineties he was stimulated by Brooks Adams, who was then deep in his theory of the law of civilization and decay and had come to lean heavily on the principle of economic determinism.[3] "Brooks Adams had taught him," he said later, "that the relation between civilizations was that of trade," and stimulated by this rediscovery of the philosophy of the first Adams he set about the business of orienting himself to the realm of science, of substituting for a meaningless political interpretation a broader philosophical interpretation.

Very likely it was his reading in the sociology of the Enlightenment that first turned his thought to the philosophy of history—chiefly Turgot and Comte. Speaking of the years 1867–1868 he said he "became a Comteist, within the limits of evolution."[4] He had long been interested in such clues as science offered—in the geological theories of Sir Charles Lyell and the biological deductions of Darwin. But the theory of biological evolution with its implications of a benevolent progress from the simple to the complex, failed to satisfy him; and he turned to the physical sciences for a guide, discovering as the ultimate reality behind all appearances—force. This physical principle he transferred to the field of sociology. Coal-power, electrical power, he concluded, were to civilization what the gaseous theory was to physics. It was a creative suggestion and it revolutionized his conception o from the simple to the complex, failed to satisfy him; and he turned to the physical sciences for a guide, discovering as the ultimate reality behind all appearances—force. This physical principle he transferred to the field of sociolom, where he had always seen lines of will."[5] "To evolutionists may be left the processes of evolution; to historians the single interest is the law of reaction between force and force—between mind and nature—the law of progress."[6] "The great division of history into phases by Turgot and Comte first affirmed this law in its outlines by asserting the unity of progress."[7]

Thus by the aid of the physical sciences Henry Adams came back to the philosophy of determinism—a conception that may lead either to pantheism or to mechanism as one's temperament determines. In such a choice there would be no doubt which way Henry Adams would go; he must somehow reconcile determinism and progress, he must discover unity in multiplicity—and that unity and progress he found in a mystical pantheism. "Continuous movement, universal cause, and interchangeable force. This was pantheism, but the Schools were pantheist . . . and their deity was the ultimate energy, whose thought and action were one."[8] How creatively this pantheistic mysticism was to determine his later thinking is sufficiently revealed in the pages of *Mont-Saint-Michel and Chartres*. With incredible labor Henry Adams had at last made his way out of the Sahara of politics in which he had long wandered.

Phrased in less transcendental terms his philosophy of history, as he came finally to understand it, was expressed thus:

> The work of domestic progress is done by masses of mechanical power—steam, electric, furnace, or other—which have to be controlled by a score or two of individuals who have shown capacity to manage it. The work of internal government has become the task of controlling these men, who are socially as remote as heathen gods, alone worth knowing, but never known, and who could tell nothing of political value if one skinned them alive. Most of them have nothing to tell, but are forces as dumb as their dynamos, absorbed in the development or economy of power. They are trustees for the public, and whenever society assumes the property, it must confer on them that title; but the power will remain as before, whoever manages it, and will then control society without appeal, as it controls its stokers and pit-men. Modern politics is, at bottom, a struggle not of men but of forces. The men become every year more and more creatures of force, massed about central power-houses. The conflict is no longer between the men, but between the motors that drive the men, and the men tend to succumb to their own motive forces. This is a moral that man strongly objects to admit, especially in mediaeval pursuits like politics and poetry, nor is it worth while for a teacher to insist upon it.[9]

From a civilization thus tyrannized over by coal-power and electrical power, he turned away to discover if possible a civilization in which men had lived the good life that he longed for; and in his second incursion into medieval times he found what he had long been seeking. Two centuries, from 1050 to 1250, came to represent for him in the evening of his days the crown and glory of all human endeavor; the first century with its Norman Mont-Saint-Michel and its *Chanson de Roland*, with its forthright strength and simplicity, its uncritical acceptance of life and God, its hope encompassed by a sufficing unity—a strong, naïve, credulous world, yet with men's minds buttressed like their cathedrals by a faith that held in equilibrium the soaring arches of their aspirations, with every cranny and nook flooded with radiant color: and the second century, that expressed itself in the cathedral of Chartres, with its adoration of the Virgin, its courtly love of Guillaume de Lorris and Marie de Champagne, its passionate mysticism of Saint Louis and Saint Bernard and Saint Francis, and its soaring scholasticism of Thomas Aquinas—a tender, feminine age, that worshiped woman and erected its altars to Our Lady of Love rather than to Our Lady of Sorrows, that found in Isolde the ideal woman and expressed itself in Eleanor of Guienne and Blanche of Castile, in Héloïse and Marie de Champagne, more adequately than in Richard Cœur-de-Lion, till it finally went the way of mortality "with the death of Queen Blanche and of all good things about the year 1250":—to such idealization of medievalism did this child of Puritanism come in the wistful twilight of his days. He had never evaded life, nor professed himself satisfied with mean or cheap substitutes, but had sought persistently till he had come to believe that the good life had been lived once, though it might not ever be lived again. So much at least was clear gain, even though it should end in wistfulness.

Mont-Saint-Michel and Chartres is a beautiful book, the more beautiful because of its wistfulness; and the theme that runs through its pages is a denial of the values that embodied for his countrymen the sum of all excellence. It is an account of certain happy generations—so few amongst the countless many—who worshiped in love, before fear had come to the western world and crept into the message of the church; a love that elevated Mother Mary above the Christ of the Cross, and that in her shrine at Chartres would allow no hint of sorrow or suffering to appear, but represented her as looking out upon the world with a gracious and regal kindliness and mercy, quick to succor and to forgive—the spirit of love that suffices life in all its needs. *Mont-Saint-Michel and Chartres* is rich and tender and wise, perhaps beyond anything else that his generation of Americans wrote, with a mellow scholarship that walks modestly because it has learned how little it knows. Yet in its every implication it is a sharp and searching criticism of Boston and America of the nineteenth century. It repudiates every ideal of a generation that had gambled away the savor of life—that does not comprehend "and never shall," the greatness of that earlier time, "the appetite" for living, the "greed for novelty," "the fun of life."[10] It was precisely these things, unimportant though they might seem to the acquisitive mind, that Henry Adams had missed in his own life and passionately resented having missed. To come to know great men and great deeds and great ages is perhaps of doubtful expediency for one who must live amongst small men; and Henry Adams was forced to pay a heavy penalty for his catholic understanding and sympathy.

The profound suggestiveness of *Mont-Saint-Michel and Chartres* lies in the skill with which the brilliant threads of medieval art and thought and aspiration are woven into a single pattern, and the splendor of its unity traced to a mystical *élan* that found its highest expression in faith. It was the ideal of love that he discovered in the golden twelfth century—love above law, above logic, above the church and the schools: a love that explains for him the passionate worship of Mother Mary, together with the new "*courtoisie*" that sought to shape manners and morals to humane ends. The humanity of the Virgin set her above the Trinity, as the humanity of Saint Francis set him above Thomas Aquinas, for all the latter's soaring scholasticism. To one who entered those bygone times through the portals of Chartres cathedral, it was natural to interpret the total age in the light of the gentle smile of the Mother of God, and to feel her presence as a transforming spirit amongst men. Has any other Yankee interpreted so lovingly the mission of the Virgin . . . ?

Thus at last, in another land and a remote age, Henry Adams found the clue that explained for him his own failure and the source of the dissatisfactions that had tracked him

doggedly through his far wanderings. He had come to understand the reasons for the sterility of his Massachusetts past, and the last shreds of his Puritan-Federalist heritage were cast off. In comparison with the vision that came to him in the choir of Chartres, how unspeakably poor and mean were the activities he had portrayed in *Democracy*, or even those he had dealt with in his history of the early days of the republic. He had discovered the highest existence in emotional response to noble appeal; the good life was the unified life, possible only on a grand scale in those rare and great periods of social *élan* when the individual is fused in an encompassing unity. . . .

One may enter the past, of course, through such portals as one chooses; but one is likely to choose the portals that promise to open upon the world of one's desires. It was a fortunate accident, no doubt, that led Henry Adams to Chartres to study the cathedral glass under the guidance of John La Farge; nevertheless it finally determined for him his total interpretation of the Middle Ages and of all history, and that interpretation followed naturally a subtle ancestral bias. Even in his rebellion against his past he could not get away from it, but like Ruskin and John Henry Newman he came to affirm—whether rightly or wrongly, who shall say?—that the singular glory of the Middle Ages was the mystical *élan* that came to expression in the adoration of the Virgin. As a child of generations of Puritans he came back finally, in the twilight of his studies, to the great ideal of faith. And yet it is not without suggestion that William Morris, who more nearly than any other modern expressed in his daily life the spirit of the Middle Ages, never concerned himself much with the medieval church—neither its cathedrals nor its scholasticism nor its miracles—never talked about an age of faith, would scarcely have understood, indeed, what was meant by the drive of a mystical *élan*; but discovered the secret of that earlier civilization in the gild rather than the church, and traced the source of the haunting beauty that clings to all its works to the psychology of craftsmanship that found delight in shaping the raw material to the craftsman's dreams.

The difference between Morris and Adams is great enough, and at bottom it is the difference between the artist and the intellectual; yet it is a pity that Henry Adams, with his wide acquaintance in England, should never have known the one Victorian he should most have delighted in—the nineteenth-century craftsman who found in his workshop the good life the historian dreamed of, and was unhappy because it had been lost. Perhaps it would not have greatly changed the latter's interpretation. He was not a pagan in temperament to enter sympathetically into the medieval world that Morris had discovered and of which the Church was only a drapery—a drapery that never quite covered a frank *joie de vivre* that was an emotion far more realistic and human than any mystical *élan*, and that persisted long after the apogee of faith in the early twelfth century, filling all the later Middle Ages with its abundant beauty till it was finally destroyed by the economic revolution that came out of the Reformation. But at any rate he might have been led by such knowledge to set the craftsman beside the poet and the schoolman and the mystic—the nameless artist who wrought such marvels beside the patron who took care to have his name and his arms emblazoned on window and wall to remind posterity of his generosity; and certainly, his interpretation of the Middle Ages would not have suffered by such addition. Instead, an excessive intellectualism drove him back upon the naïve.

The disillusion of Henry Adams is abundantly instructive to the student of our flamboyant transition, so different from the golden Transition. Here was an honest man and an able—

none honester and none abler in his generation—who devoted his life to finding a path out of the maze of middle-class America, that should lead to a rational and humane existence. He was never overconfident of his conclusions. All arrogant dogmatisms he had long since left behind; they had become for him pathetically futile and foolish. Creeds and faiths, whether in religion or politics or economics, he no longer subscribed to; but a certain residuum remained, from his long meditations—a sense of interfusing unity, mystical, pantheistic, that his lurking skepticism dealt tenderly with. *"Inter vania nihil vanius est homine,"* he asserted as a skeptic, and as a mystic he replied, "Man is an imperceptible atom always trying to become one with God. If every modern science achieves a definition of energy, possibly it may borrow the figure: Energy is the inherent effort of every multiplicity to become unity."[11] In these later years he called himself half whimsically a "conservative Christian Anarchist"[12] and the explanation probably is to be found in his shift from intellectualism to emotion as the crown of a satisfying life. "The two poles of social and political philosophy seem necessarily to be organization or anarchy; man's intellect or the forces of nature."[13] In rare and happy periods—as in the glorious Transition—freedom finds its fullest life in a spontaneous drawing together of the whole; but as the social *élan* dies away, institutions, organization, remain. Thomas Aquinas follows Saint Francis, form remains after emotion has subsided. Nevertheless the free man must cling to his freedom, in spite of society, in spite of the political state.

> Absolute liberty is absence of restraint; responsibility is restraint; therefore, the ideally free individual is responsible only to himself. This principle is the philosophical foundation of anarchism, and, for anything that science has yet proved, may be the philosophical foundation of the universe; but it is fatal to all society and is especially hostile to the State.[14]

Though he lived in the midst of a centralizing politics and found his friends in such servants of centralization as John Hay and Henry Cabot Lodge, Henry Adams had no faith in the dominant ideals. He was never a friend to an acquisitive society with its engrossing political state. In the light of his favorite dictum that "Power is poison," he may perhaps be regarded as an old-fashioned Jeffersonian; it is another evidence of the persistence of his eighteenth-century mind. He was an arch-individualist who would go his own way and reach his own conclusions, quite unconcerned that his views were wholly at variance with those of his generation. How could it be otherwise? How should men who lived in the counting-house understand even the language of this pilgrim returned from other and greater worlds? It was foolish to talk of what he had seen. And so when he wrote *Mont-Saint-Michel and Chartres* he published it privately, and was incredulous when it was proposed to republish it and give it to the world. What had he, or the twelfth century, to say to the land of Theodore Roosevelt and Pierpont Morgan? Was not this America of theirs peopled by the descendants of the *bourgeoisie* who, six hundred years before, resentful at having been cheated—as they supposed—in their heavy investments in shrines and churches of Our Lady, had turned away from all such unprofitable business, and put their savings in lands and houses and ships and railways and banks—of which things politics was the sluttish servant? How should one who had known Saint Francis and Eleanor of Guienne take such men or such a world seriously?

Notes

1. *The Education of Henry Adams*, p. 21.

2. Ibid., p. 317.
3. Ibid., pp. 338–39.
4. Ibid., p. 225.
5. Ibid., p. 426.
6. Ibid., p. 493.
7. Ibid., p. 493.
8. Ibid., pp. 428–29.
9. Ibid., pp. 421–22.
10. Ibid., p. 139.
11. *Mont-Saint-Michel*, p. 332.
12. *The Education*, p. 405.
13. *Mont-Saint-Michel*, p. 344.
14. Ibid., p. 372.

R. P. BLACKMUR

From "Three Emphases on Henry Adams"
The Expense of Greatness
1940, pp. 253–76

W here your small man is a knoll to be smoothed away, Henry Adams is a mountain to be mined on all flanks for pure samples of human imagination without loss of size or value. That is the double test of greatness, that it show an attractive force, massive and inexhaustible, and a disseminative force which is the inexhaustible spring or constant declaration of value. As we elucidate our reaction to the two forces we measure the greatness.

In Adams the attractive force is in the immediate relevance that his life and works have for our own. The problems he posed of human energy and human society are felt at once to be special and emphatic articulations of our own problems. The disseminative, central force, which we find objectified in his works, may be felt and seen as the incandescence of the open, enquiring, sensitive, and sceptical intelligence, restless but attentive, saltatory but serial, provisional in every position yet fixed upon a theme: the theme of thought or imagination conceived as the form of human energy. We feel the incandescence in the human values and aspirations that were fused by it, from time to time, in persuasive form; and the cumulus of his life and works makes a focus, different as differently felt, whereby the particular values actually rendered shine concentrated as it were in their own best light. We make the man focus upon himself, make him achieve—as he never could for himself in the flux and flexion of life—his own most persuasive form. To make such a focus is the labour and the use of critical appreciation.

The approaches to such a labour are varied and must be constantly renewed and often revised. No single approach is omniscient or even sufficient. Here, in this essay, I want to take Henry Adams in a single perspective and submit it to three related emphases. I want to regard him as he often chose to regard himself, as a representative example of education: but education pushed to the point of failure as contrasted with ordinary education which stops at the formula of success.

The perspective is worth a preliminary emphasis of its own. It was as failure both in perspective and lesson by lesson that Adams himself saw his education. Success is not the propitious term for education unless the lesson wanted is futile. Education has no term and if arrested at all is only arrested by impassable failure. Surely the dominant emotion of an education, when its inherent possibilities are compared with those it achieved, must strike the honest heart as the emotion of failure. The failure is not of knowledge or of feeling. It is the failure of the ability to react correctly or even intelligently to more than an abbreviated version of knowledge and feeling:

failure in the radical sense that we cannot consciously react to more than a minor fraction of the life we yet deeply know and endure and die. It is the failure the mind comes to ultimately and all along when it is compelled to measure its knowledge in terms of its ignorance. . . .

Let us take for our first emphasis Adams as a failure in society. If we assume that an education means the acquisition of skills and the mastery of tools designed for intelligent reaction in a given context, it will appear that Adams' failure in American political society after the Civil War was a failure in education. Society was bound for quick success and cared only for enough intelligence to go on with. It cared nothing for political mastery, and commonly refused to admit it had a purpose beyond the aggregation of force in the form of wealth. The effect on Adams as a young man was immediate but took time to recognize. If *vis inertiae* was enough for society, any education was too much; and an Adams—with the finest education of his times—was clearly useless. The question was perhaps not initially of Adams' failure but of society's inability to make use of him: its inability to furnish a free field for intelligent political action. Washington was full of wasted talent—of able young men desperately anxious to be of use—as it is now; but no one knows what talent might accomplish, then or now, because talent has never been given a chance without being at the same moment brutally hamstrung.

The discovery—that he was to be wasted whether he was any good or not—was all the bitterer to Henry Adams because he had three generations of conspicuous ability and conspicuous failure behind him. Every Adams had ended as a failure after a lifetime of effort—marked by occasional and transitory success—to handle political power intelligently. Their intelligence they had kept; none had ever succumbed to the criminal satisfaction of power on its lowest terms—whether power for interest, or, worst of all, power for its own sake: the absolute corruption, as it seems to a scrupulous mind, of giving in; but all equally had failed at the height of their abilities. If times had changed for Henry it was for the worse. Where his ancestors found in a combination of scruple and temper an effective termination of useful public careers, Henry found his scruple alone enough to preclude a public career altogether. Scruple is sometimes only a name for snobbery, stiffness, or even an inner coldness—all, forms of disability; but in an Adams scruple was the mark of ability itself, and its limit, as it made intelligence acute, responsible, and infinitely resourceful, but a little purblind to the advantage of indirection. An Adams could meet an issue, accept facts, and demonstrate a policy, but he could never gamble with a public matter. Jefferson's epitaph for John applied to them all: as disinterested as his maker. If the odds grew heavy against an Adams he resorted to an access of will—or, if you choose to call it, a wall of stubbornness, which is merely will grown hysterical. But acts of will or stubbornness are merely the last resorts of minds compelled to act scrupulously against the unintelligent or the unintelligible. . . .

If, as I think, it was the scruple of his mind that made Adams an outsider and that at the same time gave precise value to his eccentricity, then the scruple should be defined both for itself and in terms of Adams. It is what I have been deviously leading up to: as it represents the single heroic and admirable quality of the modern and sceptical mind as such; and a quality not called for by the occasion but crowning it, even when disastrously. . . .

Specifically, with Henry Adams, scruple of thinking and thence of action was the whole point of his education for public life. Men without scruples either victimised power or suc-

cumbed to it; and if you had the wrong scruples you succumbed, like Grant, without knowing it. Political education was meant to supply the right scruples at the start, to teach sensitiveness to new ones as they came up, and to ingrain a habit of feeling for them if not apparent. It is scruples that compel attention to detail and subordinate the detail to an end. When excess atrophies the mind, whether of scruples or the lack of them, it is because either an impossible end or no end was in view. In science the adjudication of scruples is called method and taken for granted; but the whole test of the democratic process is whether or not the seat of power attracts the scrupulous intelligence and gives it rein. Here we may conceive Henry Adams as a provisional focus for that test.

In a sense no test is possible. Adams never held office. He only made himself embarrassingly available in the near background of Grant's Washington. Power was what he wanted, but on his own terms: the terms of his training. Perhaps he offered too much; perhaps his offers seemed too much like demands; at any rate he got nothing. But if we take him as a type—whether of 1868 or 1932—we can see that he was in the predicament of all young men whose abilities seem to lie in public life but who refuse waste motion. Society has no use for them as they are, and the concessions it requires are fatal to self-respect and taste, and lead either to futility, the treason of submission, or an aching combination of the two.

Both Adams and society saw politics was a game, but the difference in their angles of vision made their views irreconcilable. Adams saw the game as played impersonally with, as ultimate stake, the responsible control of social energy. Since ultimate value was never sure, every move ought to be made with the maximum intelligence and subject to every criticism your experience provided. If you stuck scrupulously to your intelligence you had the chance to come out right in the end under any scruples, democratic or not. You had a chance to put your society in control of itself at the centre of its being. That was Adams' idea of the game, the idea of any honest young man.

Society played differently. The stake was immediate power, the values were those of personal interest. Thus the actual stake—control of social energy—was left for the ventures of interests irresponsible to the government meant to control them. Society in its political aspect cared more for chaos than unity; and the democratic process was an unconfessed failure, obliviously committing itself to social anarchy. Yet the failure remained unconfessed; the society lived and gathered energy; it was omnivorous, rash, and stupid; it threatened to become uncontrollably leviathan; it seemed occasionally on the point of committing suicide in the full flush of life. Always it had been saved, so far, by its vitality, its prodigious capacity for successive ruination, or by the discovery of a new and available source of power.

There was the young man's predicament. Should he assume that society was no field for intelligence and that its own momentum was sufficient to its needs? Should he rather enter the field, outwardly playing society's version of the game, while inwardly playing his own as best he could? Or should he work on society from the outside, accepting his final defeat at the start, and express the society rather than attempt to control it?

The first choice is the hardest; taken mostly by weak minds, it resembles more the dullness of indifference than disconsolate impartiality. Most men of ability, fortunately, make the second choice; it is they that make the administration of society possible and intermittently tolerable. Individually, most of them disappear, either lose office or succumb to it; but the class is constantly replenished from the bottom. A few survive the struggle in their own identity, and these are the ideals the young men hope to cap. J. Q. Adams was one of these, Gallatin and Schurz are clearly two more, as Senators Walsh and Norris make two examples for our own day. Men like Cleveland and Theodore Roosevelt are partial survivals. Adams thought his friend John Hay not only survived but succeeded in establishing a sound foreign policy; history is a harsher judge than friendship. As a general thing promise in politics not only dies early but is resurrected in the corruption of party or unwitting interest, which is what happened to Adams' friend Lodge. For the most part Adams' reiterated sentiment remains apt: "A friend in power is a friend lost." Small men might pass unnoticed to honourable graves but the great were lost.

Henry Adams lacked the dimensions suitable to a small man in public life and lacked the coarseness of will and ability to dissimulate to seize the larger opportunity, had it offered. Hence he made gradually the third choice, and brought the pressure of all the education he could muster upon society from the outside. It took him seven to ten years to make the choice complete. The first form of pressure he exerted was that of practical political journalism, of which the principal remaining results are the essays on "The New York Gold Conspiracy," "The Session, 1869–1870," and the essay on American financial policy called "The Legal-Tender Act." The second form of pressure was also practical, and combined the teaching of history at Harvard with the editorship of *The North American Review.* Already, however, the emphasis of his mind was becoming imaginative and speculative. Seven years in Cambridge taught him the impossibility of affecting society to any practical extent through the quarterly press, or through any press at all. Two of his essays were made campaign documents by the Democrats—their import reduced to the level of vituperative rhetoric—and then forgotten; so that by the test of the widest publication possible their practical effect was nil. There remained a third form of pressure not so much indirect as remote, and that was pressure by the imaginative expression, through history and fiction and philosophy, of social character and direction; and the aim was to seize the meaning of human energy by defining its forms and to achieve, thus, if it was possible, a sense of unity both for oneself and one's society.

Expression is a form of education, and the form that was to occupy the rest of Adams' life, the subject of our second emphasis. Put another way, society had failed to attract Adams to its centre, and Adams undertook to see whether or not he could express a centre for it. Unity or chaos became the alternative lesson of every effort. Here we have gone over or climbed up to a second level of failure, which is the failure of the human mind, pushed to one of its limits, to solve the problem of the meaning, the use, or the value of its own energy: in short the failure to find God or unity. What differentiates Adams' mind from other minds engaged in the same effort is his own intense and progressive recognition of his failure; and that recognition springs from the same overload of scruples that made him eccentric to the society that produced him. What he did not recognise was the ironical consolation that the form his work took as a whole was itself as near the actual representative of unity as the individual mind can come; which is what we have now to show.

Henry Adams' mind acquired, as his work stretched out, a singular unity of conception and a striking definiteness of form. It was the idiosyncrasy of his genius to posit unity in multiplicity, and by exploring different aspects of the multiplicity to give the effect, known to be false or specious but felt as true, of apprehending the unity. In reading *The Life of Albert Gallatin,*

so successfully is the effect of Gallatin's career composed, we have to think twice before realising that it is meant to show one aspect in the story of the failure of the democratic process to unite American society. Published in 1879, when Adams was forty-one, it so well struck the theme of Adams' whole career that it can be bracketed with Adams' own autobiography and be called "The Education of Albert Gallatin."

As important here, striking his theme gave Adams his first mature prose. The previous essays had been comparatively metallic, brittle, and rhetorical, and carried a tone of intermittent assertiveness rather than of cumulative authority. It was the subject perhaps that matured the style: Gallatin was the best in character, ability, and attainment that American history had to offer. At any rate, the biography of John Randolph, which came in 1882 and portrayed the worst waste in ability and personal disintegration in American history, showed a reversion to the earlier immature style. If Adams was, as Hay said, half angel and half porcupine, then it was altogether the porcupine that got into this book. The tragedy of Randolph was personal eccentricity, his constant resorts hysteria and violence, and Adams brought those elements over into his own style. Later, in his History, Adams repaired his injustice and treated him with charity of understanding, as an energetic sample of his times.

Meanwhile and just afterwards, in 1880 and 1884, Adams published his two novels, *Democracy* and *Esther.* These suffer about equally from Adams' incompetence as a novelist, and the reader can take them best as brilliant documentary evidence of Adams' insights and pre-occupations. To intrude the standards of the art of fiction would be to obviate the burden the books actually carry. *Democracy* exhibits a political society full of corruption, irresponsible ambition, and stupidity, against the foil of a woman's taste and intelligence. So brilliant and light is Adams' execution, it is hard to decide which vice is worst of the three.

. . . ⟨A⟩s in *Democracy,* ⟨where⟩ Adams separated the bottom level of political experience, in *Esther* he separated the highest level of religious experience he could find in America and measured it against the response of a woman's intelligence. The question asked and the lesson to be learned were simple and fundamental and desperate. Assuming the Christian insight in its highest contemporary form, could the Church supply a sense of unity, of ultimate relation with God or the sum of energy, to which intelligence could respond? If the Church couldn't—and the Church had no other motive for being—nothing else could, and the soul was left on its own and homeless. Or so it seemed to Adams; hence the desperateness of the question; and hence the disproportionate importance relative to its achievement that Adams himself assigned to the book. Writing to John Hay from Japan in 1886, he suggests that it was written in his heart's blood, and again to Elizabeth Cameron from Papeete five years later, he says: "I care more for one chapter, or any dozen pages of 'Esther' than for the whole history, including maps and indexes." The nine-volume history represented the predicament of the society he had abandoned, and *Esther* represented his own predicament in relation to that God or unity the hope of which he could never in his heart altogether abandon. Like Spinoza, Adams was god-intoxicated, like Pascal god-ridden. His heart's hope was his soul's despair.

That the responding intelligence in *Esther* as in *Democracy* should have been a woman's, only reflects a major bias of Adams' imagination. Women, for Adams, had instinct and emotion and could move from the promptings of the one to the actualities of the other without becoming lost or distraught in the midway bog of logic and fact. Impulse proceeded immediately to form without loss of character or movement. More than that, women had taste; taste was what held things together, showing each at its best, and making each contribute to a single effect. Thus the argument of a woman's taste dissipated every objection of logic, and at its highest moments made illogicality itself part of its natural charm. Taste was the only form of energy sure enough of itself—as all non-human energies may be—to afford beauty; elsewhere the rashest extravagance.

Thus Adams tried everywhere to answer great questions in terms of a woman's taste and intelligence. Who else but Esther Dudley could form the centre of the book she named? Only the strength of her instinct could accept the Church if it showed itself alive, and only the courage of her taste could reject it if it proved dead or a shell. That she might be confused in instinct and unconscious of her taste, only made the drama more vivid and its outcome more desperate. The problem was hers, but an artist could help her solve it, and perhaps a scientist, too, if he felt the struggle as an artist feels it. So Wharton, the artist, puts the question to her and answers it. "It all comes to this: is religion a struggle or a joy? To me it is a terrible battle, to be won or lost." The object of the battle is Nirvana or paradise. "It is eternal life, which, my poet says, consists in seeing God." The poet is Petrarch, and his words: *Siccome eterna vita è veder dio.* Strong, the scientist, for his part tells her: "There is no science that does not begin by requiring you to believe the incredible. I tell you the solemn truth that the doctrine of the Trinity is not so difficult to accept for a working proposition as any one of the axioms of physics." Between them—between art as it aspires to religion and science that springs from the same occult source—Esther might have been able to accept religion as that great form of poetry which is the aspiration of instinct and informs the whole of taste; but the Church itself, in the person of the Reverend Mr. Hazard, her lover, failed her both in persuasiveness and light. Power in politics and pride in the Church were much alike.

> The strain of standing in a pulpit is great. No human being ever yet constructed was strong enough to offer himself long as a light to humanity without showing the effect on his constitution. Buddhist saints stand for years silent, on one leg, or with arms raised above their heads, but the limbs shrivel, and the mind shrivels with the limbs.

There is a kind of corruption in the best as well as the worst exemplars of each—which I suppose the Church would admit sooner than the state; a corruption in each case that makes for the self-falsifying effort of fanaticism. Hazard in his last argument appeals neither to instinct, intelligence, nor taste; he appeals to Esther's personal desperation and fear and so shows the ruination of emptiness within him. Esther can only answer him from the depth of revolted taste. "Why must the church always appeal to my weakness and never to my strength! I ask for spiritual life and you send me back to my flesh and blood as though I were a tigress you were sending back to her cubs." Although she loves him, the inadequacy of his church to its own purpose compels her to dismiss him, but neither for science nor for art, but for despair. That is the blood in which the book was written.

As *Democracy* foreshadowed the major theme of the *Education,* the theme of *Esther* is given deeper expression throughout *Mont-Saint-Michel,* and, as well, in at least one place in the *Education. Esther* is a representation of the failure in fact of American society to find God in religion. As he grew older, especially after the tragic death of his wife, and felt more

and more that society had abandoned him, Adams grew more preoccupied with the ultimate failure of imagination itself, as illustrated in every faculty of the mind, than with the mere indicative failure of fact. Not facts which could be met but their meanings which could not be escaped were his meat. The meaning of *Esther* is intensified and made an object of inexhaustible meditation in the meanings Adams found in the monument Saint Gaudens made for his wife in Rock Creek Cemetery. Part of the meaning lay in its meaninglessness to most of those who saw it, and part in the horror of the clergy who saw in it their defeat instead of their salvation. In a letter, Adams gave the monument the same motto he had embedded in *Esther: Siccome eterna vita è veder dio;* you could, in a gravestone, if you had the will, see what life needed but never provided. In the *Education* Adams suggests that the monument mirrors to the beholder whatever faith he has.

In *Mont-Saint-Michel and Chartres* the problem of *Esther* is made at once more universal and more personal. There Adams made an imaginative mirror of his own effort towards faith in terms of the highest point of faith—that is, of effective unity—the world had ever seen: the Christianity of the great cathedrals and the great intellectual architecture of the schools. The Virgin dominated the cathedrals as a matter of course; and Saint Thomas dominated the schools by an effort of will; but without the Virgin the schools would merely have paltered, as the cathedrals would never have been built. The Virgin was pure energy and pure taste, as her spires and roses were pure aspiration. Adams' book is the story of her tragedy; not that she was destroyed or even denied, but that men no longer knew and loved her, so lost their aspiration with the benefit of her taste, and no longer felt any unity whatsoever. The Virgin herself is still there, "but looking down from a deserted heaven, into an empty church, on a dead faith." She no longer gave orders or answered questions, and without her the orders and answers of Saint Thomas were useless; and similarly, for Adams, the orders and answers of all later authorities.

Thus the education that led Adams to the Virgin was the greatest failure of all; the highest form of unity was, in effect, for the modern man, only the most impossible to recapture. Where Esther had very simply repulsed the church because it appealed only to her weakness, Adams was in the worse ail of having no strength with which to seize it when it called for all the strength there was: he had no faith, but only the need of it. The Virgin's orders were the best ever given; obeyed, they made life contribute to great art and shine in it; but he had nothing with which to accept her administration. Her answers to his problems were final; she was herself the cumulus and unity of energy, and she removed, by absorbing, all the contradictions of experience; but seven centuries of time had made life too complicated for the old answers to fit. The same energy would need a new form to give the same meaning.

The failure of education was the failure of the unity which it grasped; the pupil was left with a terrible and weary apprehension of ignorance. Thinking of the Virgin and of the Dynamo as equally inexplicable concentrations of energy, Adams was led into the last phase of his education in the application of the mechanical theory of the inevitable change of all energy from higher to lower forms. What he wrote may be found in the later chapters of the *Education,* and in his two essays "A Letter to Teachers" and "The Rule of Phase Applied to History." It was, I think, the theory of a desperate, weary mind, still scrupulous in desperation and passionately eager in weariness, in its last effort to feel—this time in nature herself— the mystery in energy that keeps things going. It was the religious mind applying to physics on exactly the same terms and with exactly the same honest piety that it applied to the Virgin.

The nexus between the two was shown in the need for either in that fundamental condition of the mind known as *ennui*; and Adams quotes Pascal, the great scrupulous mind of the seventeenth century.

"I have often said that all the troubles of man come from his not knowing how to sit still." Mere restlessness forces action. "So passes the whole of life. We combat obstacles in order to get repose, and, when got, the repose is insupportable; for we think either of the troubles we have, or of those that threaten us; and even if we felt safe on every side, *ennui* would of its own accord spring up from the depths of the heart where it is rooted by nature, and would fill the mind with its venom."

Nature was full of *ennui* too, from star to atom. What drove it? What made energy change form in *this* direction and not that? Adams tried to find the answer in the second law of thermodynamics—the law that assumes the degradation of energy; the law which sees infinite energy becoming infinitely unavailable; and he tried hard to *feel* that law as accounting for change in human society. The attempt only put his ignorance on a new basis. As analogues, the laws of physics only made the human predicament less soluble because less tangible. You might learn a direction, but physics prevented you from feeling what moved.

Reason, in science, as Adams had discovered earlier in *Esther*, deserted you rather sooner than in religion; and the need of faith was more critical. Had Adams had the advantage of the development of the quantum theory from the thermal field to the whole field of physics, had he known that all change was to come to seem discontinuous and that nature was to reveal a new and profoundly irrational face, he would have given up his last effort before he began it. A *discontinuous* multiplicity cannot be transformed into unity except by emotional vision. Adams had earlier said it himself. "Unity is vision; it must have been part of the process of learning to see. The older the mind, the older its complexities, and the further it looks, the more it sees, until even the stars resolve themselves into multiples; yet the child will always see but one." In 1915 Adams wrote to Henry Osborn Taylor that "Faith not Reason goes beyond" the failure of knowledge, and added that he felt himself "in near peril of turning Christian, and rolling in the mud in an agony of human mortification." But he had not the faith; only the apprehension of its need which made him struggle towards it all his life.

Failure is the appropriate end to the type of mind of which Adams is a pre-eminent example: the type which attempts through imagination to find the meaning or source of unity aside from the experience which it unites. Some artists can be content with experience as it comes, content to express it in the best form at hand. Adams gives LaFarge as an instance. "His thought ran as a stream runs through grass, hidden perhaps but always there; and one felt often uncertain in what direction it flowed, for even a contradiction was to him only a shade of difference, a complementary color, about which no intelligent artist would dispute." Shakespeare is another instance. In such artists failure is incidental, a part of the experience expressed. But Adams, by attempting to justify experience and so to pass beyond it had like Milton and Dante to push his mind to the limit of reason and his feeling to the limit of faith. Failure, far from incidental, is integral to that attempt, and becomes apparent just so soon as reason falters and becomes abstract, or faith fails and pretends to be absolute. Aside from the question of

magnitude, one difference between Adams and his prototypes is, to repeat once more, just this: that his scrupulous sophistication made him emphatically aware of his own failure; and this awareness is the great drive of his work.

Here is our third emphasis. The failure of Adams in society—or society's failure to use Adams—was perhaps self-evident when stated. The singular unity of Adams' subsequent efforts to express the unity he felt has, I hope, been indicated. There remains the question of Adams' special value in the light of his avowed failure. The value is double.

The greatness of the mind of Adams himself is in the imaginative reach of the effort to solve the problem of the meaning, the use, or the value of its own energy. The greatness is in the effort itself, in variety of response deliberately made to every possible level of experience. It is in the acceptance, with all piety, of ignorance as the humbled form of knowledge; in the pursuit of divers shapes of knowledge—the scientific, the religious, the political, the social and trivial—to the point where they add to ignorance, when the best response is silence itself. That is the greatness of Adams as a type of mind. As it is a condition of life to die, it is a condition of thought, in the end, to fail. Death is the expense of life and failure is the expense of greatness.

If there is a paradox here, or an irony hard to digest, it is not in the life experienced or the failure won, but in the forms through which they are conceived, in the very duplicity of language itself, in the necessarily equivocal character, earned by long use, of every significant word. Thought asks too much and words tell too much; because to ask anything is to ask everything, and to say anything is to ask more. It is the radical defect of thought that it leaves us discontented with what we actually feel—with what we know and do not know—as we know sunlight and surfeit and terror, all at once perhaps, and yet know nothing of them. Thought requires of us that we make a form for our knowledge which is personal, declarative, and abstract at the same time that we construe it as impersonal, expressive, and concrete. It is this knowledge that leads to the conviction of ignorance—to the positive ignorance which is the final form of contradictory knowledge; but it is the triumph of failure that in the process it snares all that can be snared of what we know.

The true paradox is that in securing its own ends thought cannot help defeating itself at every crisis. To think straight you must overshoot your mark. Orthodoxy of the human mind—the energy of society in its highest stable form—is only maintained through the absorption into it of a series of heresies; and the great heresy, surely, is the gospel of unity, whether it is asserted as a prime mover, as God, or, as in art, as the mere imposed unity of specious form. In adopting it for his own, Adams knew it for a heresy. Again and again he describes unifying conceptions as working principles; without them no work could be done; with them, even at the expense of final failure, every value could be provisionally ascertained. That is the value of Adams for us: the double value of his scrupulous attitude towards his unifying notions and of the human aspirations he was able to express under them. To feel that value as education is a profound deliverance: the same deliverance Adams felt in the Gothic Cathedral. "The delight of its aspiration is flung up to the sky. The pathos of its self-distrust and anguish of doubt is buried in the earth as its last secret." The principles asserted are nothing, though desperate and necessary; the values expressed because of the principles are everything. For Adams, as for everyone, the principle of unity carried to failure showed the most value by the way, and the value was worth the expense.

R. P. BLACKMUR
From "The Novels of Henry Adams"
Sewanee Review, Spring 1943, pp. 281–304

Adams' two novels, *Democracy* and *Esther*, unlike those of a professional novelist, do not show their full significance except in connection with his life. In the case of *Democracy*, the first of the pair, the connection will be obvious when once set up, for it had to do with that part of his life which had been absorbed in the effort to make a career of politics. That is to say, it focussed, and judged, an objective ambition. With *Esther*, it is a very different matter, which it will not be easy to make clear, and upon which different opinions are possible; for in *Esther* Adams made his first attempt to express what was to most of his contemporaries an outer lack as an inner and inaccessible need. Where *Democracy* dealt with man in his relation to society in terms of existing institutions which whether they controlled or failed to control political power at least represented it, *Esther* reached out to seize, to bring to rebirth, the spiritual power which the existing church, as Adams saw it in 1883, represented only by a kind of betrayal in terms of Pilate's question. Adams was no Pilate, as who would wish to be, but he could not help asking his question in the form peculiar to his generation just as he could not help repeating it later, in his two great books, in forms which seem in their vitality to have transcended those of his generation.

Adams was a lover of Matthew Arnold's poetry, not as he loved Swinburne for intoxication and lyric escape, but because Arnold expressed for him, as the two novels show, his own dilemma. Arnold spoke for Adams more deeply than he could then speak for himself and with the blessed objectiveness of a medium alien to him, and indeed made for him a touchstone of his own fate, that fate which he felt by anticipation during the years when he wrote his novels, and which he felt had actually overtaken him after the death of his wife in 1885. Adams was above all one of those for whom Arnold spoke in his famous lines, as

> Wandering between two worlds, one dead
> The other powerless to be born.

That the dead world had a singular tenacity and assiduity as a haunt and that the coming world had an overwhelming, if uncertain, necessity as a conception, made the distress of such an image the more severe. If a man cannot act upon his dilemma, or escape it in blind action, he will sometimes attempt to make symbols or fables of what would otherwise drive him to action; and it is as such symbols, such fables, that Adams' two novels best clarify themselves. It is I think to a considerable extent how he meant them, and it is certainly how we may best use them for ourselves. They show what were to become twenty years later his major themes slowly, rather lamely, and with many concessions of a superfluous sort to the "exigences" of the popular novel, taking their first imaginative form, the one as judgment and the other as the beginning of prophecy. It is only by accident that we see them as novels at all.

Perhaps a man wandering between two worlds could not be expected to show much competence as a novelist, for if one thing is certain it is that the novel in the nineteenth century had to pay maximum attention either to one world or another and usually had to pay attention in terms of a story with either a satisfactory or a desirable ending. Adams did no such thing. He borrowed what he wished from the outsides of the popular novels of his day, and not from the best popular novels either or the newest, but from Lytton and Disraeli, from a romancer and

a fabulist. His practical conception of what a novelist could do with difficult or interesting or obsessive material (and his material *did* obsess him) was not keen; and he lacked the native gift of the story-teller and the native necessity of the imagination that is able to create character. Thus he mixed in random proportions a love story, social comedy, social satire, and, for *Democracy*, the drama of politics or, for *Esther*, the drama of faith; and among these elements he set his chosen puppets to play and be played upon through arbitrary actions and dialogue either rootlessly brilliant, or desperately conventional. Only when the author's intellect takes hold, do the scenes come alive in the sense that the reader participates in them, and what the author's intellect takes hold of was what he knew when be began to write and not what the process of writing—of dramatising—discovered for him. In short, if the novels were not by Henry Adams they would hardly be read today except to satisfy an omnivorous taste in the detritus of the third quarter of nineteenth century American fiction.

But they were by Adams; and that fact provides us with enough good will so that we can take them, not as the third-rate novels they seem, but with the maximum significance that can be extracted from them in terms of Adams' life and work. To examine the stages by which an idea or an image or a major attitude gained its final expression is often to get rid of the idea, image, or attitude in an orderly rubbish pile, but it may sometimes be, altogether to the contrary, the most actual and the most dramatic means possible of understanding them. The idea or attitude in *Democracy* became in *The Education of Henry Adams* the idea or attitude by which Adams envisaged intelligence as playing the supreme rôle in American political life, but in the novel *Democracy* that same intelligence is shown as defeated by the very inertia which Adams later showed as its source. In *Democracy* American politics is shown as failing by the accident of corruption, as it were by the inattentiveness of human intelligence. In the *Education*, political life is shown, not as failing but as in abeyance; and the question is put: whether human intelligence is, or is not, adequate to controlling the vast forces which had shaped its forms. The difference is between the mere corruption of public life and the question whether public life will, or will not, cohere.

The two problems are of course the same in the sense that the second is the deeper expression of the first. Corruption in public life comes about through a misuse of the intelligence, and political intelligence becomes adequate when, other things being equal, it is able to control its evident misuses. The labour of the man who exposes political corruption must always be first of all to expose it as wastefully unintelligent, and secondly to drive from power those who have given in to the easier forms of corruption. It is only the third and distant step that can envisage the application of active intelligence to an actual situation. The first labours are of debate, and the last is of imagination. Adams, writing *Democracy* in the winter of 1878–79, worked still in the toils of debate, but the beginning of imagination was in sight, or he would have tried his purpose in some other form than that of the novel: say the essay, the pamphlet, the broadside, forms of which indeed his novel provides running examples.

For his purpose was direct and immediate as well as remote and conceptual. A man knowing himself of great potential parts he had reached that time of life when he realised that his early force was spent and knew that he could no longer regard all things as possible. But he had not yet discovered what was possible. There was a tension in him on the surface level as well as at the deep level. Active politics still pulled in him, had pulled him to Washington from Harvard, and pulled at least as hard as history; but at the same time it pulled, it repelled. As Henry James said of him as of that time, though he was not in politics, politics was much in him. The corrupt theft of the election of 1876 could not be accepted in despair but in hope, and the hope must still be in the establishment of an independent party of the centre—the project which he had worked, with his friends, so hard upon for nearly ten years. The chief obstacles to such a party remained the party caucus, the party central committee, and the system of party spoils—all calculated to pervert public responsibility to one form or another of party irresponsibility, and all certain to transform the duty or ambition of power into a lust for power which could be gratified only in individuals, never in policies. And all the life of party lay concentrated, for Adams, in the single figure of James G. Blaine, who had twice prevented the nomination of his father, and who had only just escaped the nomination himself by a political trick of his enemies. Blaine was clearly the most powerful man in the Republican party and was the almost certain nominee for 1880. The tarnish of his corruption had somehow made his star shine more brightly. It must be made to fall. *Democracy* had as its immediate object to strike Blaine a mortal blow to which he could not retaliate; and if Blaine fell, it might signal the fall of the caucus system itself. The prospect was not good, so poor indeed that Blaine had to be turned into an ogre powerful in evil instead of a mere man intolerably weak at the centre. As history would eventually judge, so art might immediately clarify the extremes. There must be an angel to contend with the ogre.

. . . ⟨T⟩he *Nation's* review of *Democracy* complained that the tale was too simplified and the characters too composite, on the one hand of evil and on the other of good, to be either representative or probable. The *Nation* had a stake in success at the polls, and at the moment when Adams wrote his book, he had begun to feel that he had no stake in the present and had not yet envisaged his stake in the future. He was not yet himself; and that, rather than the fear that his portraits might be recognised—for they *were* recognised, regardless—was the reason for his anonymity. So with Madeleine in her flight, for flight from the problems of the intelligence represents the desire of anonymity in the sense that it anticipates the refuge of lesser identity. That is the lesson of the fable of *Democracy*— perhaps in the way of life as well as the novel: it shows the intelligence which is willing to tamper with the actual without being willing to seize it, as properly humiliated and sent flying. If the failure of Madeleine lay deeper than that, it was perhaps that she never understood the principle that the intelligence must always act as if it were adequate to the problems it has aroused. That is, it must see the evils it attacks as the vivid forms of its own abused and debased self. Otherwise, it must give up.

But not to give up requires exactly a treasure in the self which Adams felt as deeply lacking. The intelligence, as he was fond of saying later in life, the intelligence is not enough; only faith goes beyond. Faith, in the 80's, came so cheap that for costly souls it was often not to be had. A long procession of men and their ideas—Darwin, Lyell, Maxwell, Huxley, Comte, Marx, and Herbert Spencer—had combined to remove Christian faith as a simple birthright and seemed to have substituted for it only a progressively expanding area of doubt as to even the provisional validity of any evolutionary faith unless you defined the fit as those who survive. Both what was roughly called "scientific" faith and Christian faith had come in one sense into a sort of precarious balance. Each had to be fought for, and constantly reestablished, by the individual, unless you

were willing to give up all the scruples of thought and procedure which had started the fight. Each presented a mystery. The Christian faith presented its mystery beforehand as the source of faith and ended with a mystery as well; the scientific faith ended in a mystery for which it seemed to have no foundation. The one was arrogant about its facts and the other was arrogant about its traditional source; neither could afford to be arrogant about its future, unless hope could be called arrogant. If you hung between the two positions, as intelligent people mostly did, the problem was the more painful in proportion to your intelligence, or to your responsiveness, intelligent or not. Only the poor were supposed to have solved the problem, for the intelligent supposed the poor to be stupid, and therefore had need of religion, though the fact was that the poor were not stupid but plentiful and therefore had greater need of religion; their facts they had for the asking. At any rate the intelligent man who tried to make his faith his own found himself in the desperate position of having to give up, at the critical moment, and no matter which faith he chose, intelligence itself. That perhaps was because, in that energetic age, he mistook faith for a superior form of energy, like coal-power or water-power or atomic power, rather than for a primitive—or fundamental—form of insight. The poor fellow wanted to transcend himself by calling upon a higher energy, when he ought rather to have tried to discover the faith of what he actually was. It was natural, therefore, that the dichotomy of religion and science should become artificially sharp, that the arrogance of doubt should set itself against the arrogance of dogma; the problem over which they fought was itself artificial and engaged greatly only the weakness of either side, hardly ever calling on either's strength.

Yet faith, whatever it was, and however misconceived, was what kept you going. What then was an intelligent person, exposed to both sides, to do? That was the question which Adams proposed to clarify in his fable called *Esther*.

How deeply he later regarded the book is seen in the two references to it in his published letters. To John Hay he wrote, 23 August 1886, from Japan, thanking him for his high opinion of it. "Now let it die! To admit the public to it would be almost unendurable to me. I will not pretend that the book is not precious to me, but its value has nothing to do with the public who could never understand that such a book might be written in one's heart's blood." To Elizabeth Cameron he wrote 13 February 1891, from Papeete, with reference to his history then just wholly published. "It belongs to the *me* of 1870; a strangely different being from the *me* of 1890. There are not nine pages in the nine volumes that now express anything of my interests or my feelings; unless perhaps some of my disillusionments. So you must not blame me if I feel, or seem to feel, morbid on the subject of the history. I care more for one chapter, or any dozen pages of *Esther*, than for the whole history, including maps and indexes; so much more, indeed, that I would not let anyone read the story for fear the reader should profane it."

These sentences may make a mystery of what should be plain; perhaps Adams' distressed regard for the book was due to the change that had come over him since his wife's death in 1885, over a year after its publication, so that the book seemed to him a kind of posthumously reared symbol, like the monument at Rock Creek, for what their marriage had meant to him. Yet the publication itself had been made in curious circumstances. It was published not only anonymously, which might have attracted attention, but under a pseudonym, Frances Snow Compton. By Adams' instruction it was not advertised and was not offered for review. Search of the press shows only a single notice of it, and only some five hundred and twenty-seven copies seem to have been sold in America, with a few more in England. Henry Holt stated late in life that Adams had told him he wanted to see what the book would do on its own merits without promotion of any sort, and that it was to be published at his own risk. Rather than an act of publication, these circumstances seem to suggest an act of exorcism or objective suppression, as if Adams could not get rid of an inner burden except by printing it up and throwing it away, as one drives a pin into the wax image of the person whom one wishes to destroy.

A simpler explanation is that Adams had modelled Esther Dudley in the book after his own wife, and rather more closely than he had modelled the other characters after his friends LaFarge and King, with perhaps a trace of himself in the character modelled after King. Certainly Adams' inability to create independent characters, and his regular tendency to copy his friends as though they were types, suggests that the unique freshness, warmth, and affection with which Esther is modelled, and his concentration upon her sensibility rather than upon her intellect as the measure of her growth and response, could not have been an exception, but rather represented the result of his cultivated and endeared meditation upon the image of Marian Adams. If the figure of Ratcliffe in *Democracy* represents a combination in excess of the features of Blaine, perhaps the figure of Esther represents a combination in imaginative penetration upon the features of his wife, as if he wished to bridge that loneliness that lies only between the most intimately connected people. As Robert Spiller points out in his Introduction to the facsimile reprint of *Esther*, Esther Dudley is the first intimation of the woman of sensibility and imagination whom Adams symbolically enthroned in the heart of the medieval church, and whose energy, the double energy of sex and faith, he heard transformed in the Hall of Dynamos at the Paris Exposition of 1900. If that is so, then Adams wrote his Esther twice over in heart's blood, once from the heart of his love for his wife and again in the heart of the imagination which he created.

But the figure of Esther Dudley drew significance from another source as well, from the symbolism of Hawthorne's story of that name.

. . . Hawthorne's language transposes itself to the terms of a religious rather than a social faith, and indeed, till the nineteenth century, the two forms of faith had commonly been fused, and seldom did either exist independent of the other, but rather—to use John Donne's word—interinanimated each other to make a common life. So, if Hawthorne's words be read in a chosen light, the two faiths, in the royal order and in the Christian order, disappeared from Province Court at about the same time. Never afterward did the authority of God show more than the authority of the King over the people of Boston; and the symbols that remained of both were hardly understood by those who used them, and if used, were used as branches of police power rather than as the substances of insight.

As, in a way, Adams showed us in *Democracy* a state where the only responsible power was the police power and other powers were held irresponsibly, so, in *Esther*, he shows us a religion where the only effective power wielded by the church was also a kind of police power, and the great problems of faith were either received in indifference or were left to those outside the congregation. He shows us the figure of Hawthorne's Esther Dudley, with a difference. She does not hold the faith in an alien world, but she waits in an indifferent world for someone to bring the faith to her. Her struggle, then, is not to reject the false comer, but to see if she can accept him when

he comes, in the form, as it happens, of the new rector of the new Episcopal Church of St. John on Fifth Avenue. Esther Dudley is a young woman with a high taste in art and a high achievement in humanity, serious, with a conscience, an intelligence, and an infinitely malleable sensibility; she needs only a mastering faith to generate conviction and strength. She is first presented to us in the company of Professor George Strong at the first service to be held in the as yet unfinished church by the new rector, Stephen Hazard, an old classmate at Harvard of Strong's. The congregation is fashionable to an extreme, and to Esther there is no sense of spirituality or religion either in the new church or its worshippers. Hazard, when he mounts the pulpit, strikes her as all eyes and all arrogance, for he has one of those faces which at a distance show nothing but eyes, and his text was, "He that hath ears, let him hear," which involves the notion of mastery in the priest who speaks. She is therefore both repelled and a little disturbed; annoyed at the fashion and the dumb show, and innerly eager to hear. . . .

Neither of Adams' novels reached conclusions; they were rather fables of the inconclusive; complementary to each other, they represented the gropings of a maturing mind after its final theme. Taken together they make the turning-point of a mind which had constructed itself primarily for a life of political action into a new life which should be predominantly imaginative and prophetic. But the turning had not finally been made. Adams lived still between two worlds.

YVOR WINTERS
From
"Henry Adams or the Creation of Confusion" (1943)
In Defense of Reason
1947, pp. 394–414

II. *The Theory of History*

Adams' theory of history is really a philosophy and a theory of human nature; it is wholly indefensible and perverse, and we should be hard pressed to understand how a man of genius could conceive it if we had not some understanding of the history which is largely responsible for his state of mind. Briefly, he possessed the acute moral sense of New England . . . and the New Englander's need to read the significance of every event which he saw. But he was of the Ockhamist tradition; and as for the Mathers, so for him, the significance could not reside within the event but must reside back of it. He would scarcely have put it this way, and he might have denied the paternity of Ockham; but he belonged to a moral tradition which had taken its morality wholly on faith for so long that it had lost the particular kind of intelligence and perception necessary to read the universe for what it is; and had developed instead a passion to read the universe for what it means, as a system of divine shorthand or hieroglyphic, as a statement of ultimate intentions.

He had no faith, however, and hence he could not believe that there was anything back of the event: the event was merely isolated and impenetrable. Yet he possessed the kind of mind which drove him to read every event with a kind of allegorical precision; and since every event was isolated and impenetrable, he read in each new event the meaning that the universe is meaningless. Meaning had been a function of faith; and faith had been faith not only in God and his decalogue but in a complete cosmology and chronology, that is, in all of Revelation; and if any part of this system was injured, every part was destroyed. The discoveries of geologists and astronomers caused him indescribable suffering and made it utterly impossible that he should examine dispassionately the moral nature of man. . . .

Adams appears to have felt that modern science had destroyed the last possibility of human understanding, and his later writing is largely the record of an effort to bring scientific ideas to bear upon his problem. He found, first, that modern science made for confusion; and later he tried to find in scientific principles an exact formulation of the reasons why we are moving into greater confusion and of the rate of movement.

He sought in the findings of the 19th century geologists and in the theories of Darwin a new cosmology, to replace the old cosmology which these findings and others had destroyed. His discussion of his geological and evolutionary adventures is as amusing as his account of the investigation of the drawing; but it is incoherent, an assertion and exhibition of confusion, rather than explanation of it; and it is notable mainly for the anguish underlying the wit. In this department of his experience, as in others, his frustrated passion for precise understanding drove him toward the dogmatic certainty, to be achieved at any sacrifice of rationality, that no understanding of any kind was possible.

Adams, in brief, did not care for truth, unless it was amusing; for he was a modern nihilist, and hence a hedonist or nothing. But his predicament nevertheless annoyed him, for it frustrated action, just as it did for Melville's *Pierre*, and Adams was a New Englander, to whom action and the comprehension of his action were constitutionally necessary.

. . . Adams is not content, even provisionally, to study his world as it is, in the hope of arriving at a working knowledge of it; there is no knowledge, for Adams, unless it is a part of a complete system, deriving from an acceptable definition of the Absolute:[1]

> Ignorance must always begin at the beginning. Adams must inevitably have begun by asking Sir Isaac for an intelligible reason why the apple fell to the ground. He did not know enough to be satisfied with the fact. The Law of Gravitation was so-and-so, but what was Gravitation? and he would have been thrown quite off his base if Sir Isaac had answered that he did not know.

This neurotic and childish impatience, amounting almost to insolence, is the final fruit of the Christian doctrine in New England; the patience and humility of an Aristotle or a Newton are incomprehensible.

. . . Nothing was comprehensible; each event and fact was unique and impenetrable; the universe was a chaos of meaningless and unrelated data, equivalent to each other in value because there was no way of evaluating anything. Comprehension, judgment, and choice being nullified, there was no reason for action, physical or spiritual, and life was mere stagnation. . . .

In his old age, he joined his only political party, the Conservative Christian Anarchists, a party of which the only other member was his young friend Bay Lodge. His last letters, in their despair, malice, and frantic triviality are very painful reading.

I have been tracing the disintegration of a mind. Yet the moral sense persisted, strong as ever, but running amuck for lack of guidance. Adams, as I have shown, was as passionate an allegorist as Mather had been; instead of seeing God's meaning in every event, he saw the meaninglessness of a godless universe, but with a Calvinistic intensity of vision. He had, as he confessed in writing of Henry James the "obsession of idée

fixe." And not only had he the passion to see his allegorical vision, but he had the true Calvinist's passion to provide his vision with his own theology. He wrote:[2]

> From cradle to grave this problem of running order through chaos, direction through space, discipline through freedom, unity through multiplicity, has always been, and must always be, the task of education.

> Yet the problem, though one was bound to endeavor to solve it, could never be solved in fact: the solution must be a delusion:[3]

> Chaos was the law of nature; Order was the dream of man.

More than once he thought he saw his solution in permitting himself, as T. S. Eliot would have us do, to be determined by what he took to be his time, by what in fact was casual impulse:[4]

> To him, the current of his time was to be his current, lead where it might . . . he insisted on maintaining his absolute standards; on aiming at ultimate Unity.

This Emersonian disguise of his own disintegration, however, was something that he could not consistently maintain: his disintegration was not a voyage, governed by absolute standards, on a supernatural current in the direction of Unity; it was merely disintegration. And the only way to find Order in it, was to discover the reason for the disintegration and chart its rate.

He was too good a determinist and too devoutly sorry for himself to seek any part of the reason in himself, and partly because of these facts, and partly because he was committed to an obscurantistic view of history, he failed to seek it in any segment of history definite and limited enough to imply that the difficulty was due to human error that might in some measure be corrected. Like a true Calvinist and a true determinist, he turned at once, for his answer, to the Nature of the Universe, and sought to show that the whole universe, as a single mechanism, was running down. The cosmological scope of the doctrine appears most fully in the volume of essays posthumously published as *The Degradation of the Democratic Dogma*; but in *Mont-Saint-Michel and Chartres* and in the *Education* he seeks to illustrate the tendency by defining the difference between two extremes of civilization. . . .

We have seen the manner in which Adams demonstrated twentieth century multiplicity; and . . . it seems to me pointless to invent difficulties in a universe in which irreducible difficulties flourish. The philosophical problem, as I see it, is to define the various possible mysteries, and where choice is possible, to choose those which eliminate the greatest possible number of the remainder; and to keep as scientific, as Aristotelian, an eye as possible upon the conditions of our life as we actually find ourselves forced to live it, so that we may not make the mistake of choosing a mystery which shall, in proportion as it influences our actions, violate those conditions and lead to disaster. For example, a strictly deterministic philosophy, whether materialistic or pantheistic, and no matter how enticing the cosmology or theology from which it may derive, can lead only toward automatism in action, and automatism is madness. And similarly, a strictly nominalistic view of the universe can lead only to the confusion and paralysis reached by Adams; whereas a certain amount of understanding, small no doubt in the eye of God and of the philosopher, but very useful in itself, is actually possible. If we find that a theory violates our nature, we have then learned something about our nature; and we have learned that there is something wrong with the theory. When Dr. Johnson demonstrated the real existence of the wall by kicking it, he employed a philosophical argument far from subtle but absolutely unanswerable. The philosopher who needs further convincing may try driving his car against the wall, and at as high a rate of speed as he may feel the ingenuity of his philosophy to require: he may, in this manner, learn something of the nature of absolute truth. Adams quotes Poincaré[5] as saying that it is meaningless to ask whether Euclidean geometry is true, but that it will remain more convenient than its rivals. I am no mathematician and can only guess what this means; but I surmise that it means that a bridge built by Euclidean geometry may conceivably stand, whereas one built by a rival system will certainly fall. If this is true, I should be willing to accept the fact as perhaps a Divine Revelation regarding the nature of the physical universe and as a strong recommendation for the study of Euclidean geometry.

. . . Adams' view of the Middle Ages, which has been adopted by Eliot and his followers, is merely a version of the Romantic Golden Age; the thirteenth century as they see it never existed, and their conviction that major intellectual and spiritual achievement is possible only in such a Utopia can do nothing but paralyze human effort. Much of the unity and simple strength which Adams so admires in the thirteenth century was merely the result of callous indifference to horrors worse than any the twentieth century has ever known. I have the greatest of respect for the mind of Aquinas, and but little, I fear, for many of the most influential minds of the twentieth century; but I respectfully submit that had Aquinas felt himself determined by the stupidity and confusion of his time, he would probably have accomplished very little. He endeavored to learn as much as possible from the best minds of his time and of the two thousand years, more or less, preceding; and having learned that, he set out to do the best that he could with it. Adams arrived at his view of the Middle Ages by concentrating on a few great products of literature, thought, and architecture; ignoring everything else, he asserted that these were the thirteenth century. He arrived at his view of the twentieth century by reversing the process. He thus deduced that the world was deteriorating, and so found a justification for his own state of mind.

The cosmology which expands Adams' view of history to its ultimate generality is to be found in *The Degradation of the Democratic Dogma*. The essays were written during the latter part of Adams' life. In his letters he frequently refers to them as jokes, perpetrated to stir up his slow-witted colleagues; but he also refers to them seriously, and there is every reason to believe that he took them seriously. They merely enlarge upon the theory which we have been examining, and which is stated more briefly in the latter part of the *Education*; and although they are sufficiently astonishing in their irrationality, I do not know that they are much worse in this respect than the two books thus far considered.

The most important of these essays is *A Letter to American Teachers of History*. It begins with the unquestioning acceptance of two theological principles, both the product of the age which he is endeavoring to prove to be one of ultimate confusion: the Law of the Dissipation of Energy, and the assumption that man is governed by physical laws. Whether we regard Adams as the contemner of his own age, or as the apostle of scepticism, this acceptance is sufficiently startling. It can be understood only if we remember that he was the heir of the Puritans and that sooner or later his heritage was certain to overtake him completely. In order to prove the impossibility of absolute truth, he had to start from absolute truth and create

what he could believe for the moment to be a comprehensive system.

The Revelation discloses that Energy is being dissipated steadily in a godless universe: the origin of Energy in a godless universe, and the question of how this process, which must end in time, has had no temporal beginning, but has been undergoing a steady process of diminution from all eternity—these difficulties are never met. The end is certain; the beginning does not matter. The principle explains why heat ends in cold, life in death, motion in station. And the principle once established, it follows that each succeeding manifestation of energy is inferior to the last. Man is thus inferior to the early animals, and civilization is a process of decay. The emergence of human reason during this process does not trouble Adams in the least: Reason, as we have seen, leads only to confusion and inaction and is of no help in the attainment of truth; this in spite of the fact that Adams probably believed that he was using his own reason in arriving at the truths which he elucidates. Reason is a degraded form of will:[6]

> Reason can be only another phase of the energy earlier known as Instinct or Intuition; and if this be admitted as the stem-history of the Mind as far back as the eocene lemur, it must be admitted for all forms of Vital Energy back to the vegetables and perhaps even to the crystals. In the absence of any definite break in the series, all must be endowed with energy equivalent to will. . . . Already the anthropologists have admitted man to be specialized beyond hope of further variation, so that, as an energy, he must be treated as a weakened Will—an enfeebled vitality—a degraded potential. He cannot himself deny that his highest Will-power, whether individual or social, must have proved itself by his highest variation, which was incontrovertibly his act of transforming himself from a hypothetical eocene lemur,— whatever such a creature may have been,—into men speaking elaborately inflected language. This staggering but self-evident certainty requires many phases of weakening Will-power to intervene in the process of subsidence into the reflective, hesitating, relatively passive stage called Reason; so that in the end, if the biologists insist on imposing their law on the anthropologists, while at the same time refusing to admit a break in the series, the historian will have to define his profession as the science of human degradation.

We thus see that life has proceeded from the energetic form of the rock crystal, to the passive and listless form which it manifests, for example, in the United States in the twentieth century; and since this process is proven a process of degradation, the emergence of the human mind with its various complex creations, is necessarily a symptom of degeneration. Human Reason can scarcely go farther, or so one might think for a moment. But actually there is one further deduction, and Adams makes it in the course of the essay. Life has deteriorated from the energetic form of the rock crystal, through all the forms of vegetation, of animal life, and of civilization, the highest form of civilization having existed in the thirteenth century; and the energy of the universe must continue to dissipate itself until life will be reduced again to rock crystals. This is an unbroken process of deterioration; and it provides the cosmological frame for Adams' theory of history.

Man's deterioration thus becomes a matter of cosmology, of Revealed Truth, and there is no help for the matter. The best thing man can do is trust his instincts, for they are worth more than his reason, and they will guide him infallibly along the current of his time to progressively more complex degeneracy. Art is a human function, and will be governed by the general law. Art also is deteriorating, but it must deteriorate to express honestly the general deterioration of man; and we thus arrive at one of the central ideas of T. S. Eliot, which has been one of the most influential of the past twenty years, at least among the more scholarly and intellectual of our poets and critics. At the end of *Mont-Saint-Michel and Chartres* we find the matter stated in Adams' own words:[7]

> Art had to be confused in order to express confusion;
> but perhaps it was truest so.

If the chaos of the subconscious is the only reality, and if the subject-matter of art determines the form of the work, then we have arrived at *Finnegans Wake* and the poetry of Pound and Eliot as the finest expression of civilization, that is to say, of degeneracy, although in some way which almost eludes me, we have left that other product of degeneracy, the Reason. a little way behind us in arriving at our goal.

Notes

1. *Letters of Henry Adams, 1892–1918,* ed. W. C. Ford, Houghton Mifflin, 1938, p. 226.
2. Ibid., p. 12.
3. Ibid., p. 451.
4. Ibid., p. 232.
5. Ibid., p. 455.
6. *The Degradation of the Democratic Dogma,* by Henry Adams, Macmillan, 1919, pp. 192–95.
7. *Mont-Saint-Michel and Chartres,* by Henry Adams, Houghton Mifflin, p. 375.

NEWTON ARVIN
From "Introduction" to
The Selected Letters of Henry Adams
1951, pp. xi–xxx

He had begun . . . with a sense, inherited from the eighteenth century, of the letter as a serious literary form, a form with its own exacting demands on the feeling for structure, for movement, for tone, for narrative and picture; and this he did not abandon. He had come by it as naturally as possible, not only through his reading of letter-writers like Walpole, but through family inheritance. The writing of letters was an Adams property, almost an Adams privilege, like the mission to England or the keeping of the republican conscience.

. . . In no Adams before him had the expressive instinct been so strong: he was the first of them all who was born to be a writer and not a public servant or a wielder of political power, and it was partly because the mirage of political power thrust itself between him and his true aim so deceptively, though so inevitably, that his course as a writer was as impeded, as full of detours, as frustrated as it was. There were whole periods in his life, at any rate, when his powerful literary gift found its real outlet in correspondence; and the editor of this volume would maintain that, if one sets aside the *History*, it is in his letters that Henry Adams realized himself most completely, with the least uncertainty and unnaturalness, as a writer.

By the time, late in life, when he came to write the books on which his reputation usually rests—*Mont-Saint-Michel* and the *Education*—he had been driven, or had driven himself, into a painfully false and unwholesome relation with the audience he should normally have counted on. His publishing those books privately, with all the mystifications, the jittery

precautions, the elaborate disparagements in which he enveloped the process, was a symptom of something basically unhealthy in his position as a man of letters. The consequence is that, for all their brilliance, all their weight, the two books, taken as wholes, are somehow dissatisfying to the critical sense. We dislike writing that, as Keats once said, has a palpable design upon us, and the mask of Failure in the one work, the mask of rather mawkish Mariolatry in the other, are too palpably, too insistently, too heavy-handedly thrust before our vision not to end by impressing us less as personae, in the great poetic sense, than as literary false faces. The two novels Adams wrote in his forties, *Democracy* and *Esther,* are remarkable books, more remarkable than they have usually been recognized as being; but even they were published anonymously or pseudonymously, almost clandestinely, and their publication was accompanied by a thousand facetious disclaimers of authorship. The nervous self-consciousness of all this does something to explain what is unsatisfactory about these novels; for Adams's unwillingness to *commit himself* as a writer was obscurely associated with his failure, in both *Democracy* and *Esther,* to invent an action, a set of narrative symbols, that would bear up the pressure of his moral meanings.

For a man to whom the basic facts of the literary profession itself were as problematic as all this, the letter was an ideal medium. Here there was no reason to be tormented by the elementary problems of authorship, no reason to agonize over the question of an audience and one's right relation to it. An audience was at hand, and usually it was an understanding and responsive audience. First-rate letters depend almost as much on their recipients as on the man who writes them, and just as Byron was lucky in having Tom Moore and Hobhouse and Lady Melbourne to write to, so Adams was lucky, and must have known that he was, in having correspondents so congenial and so appreciative as Charles Gaskell and John Hay and, perhaps most of all, Elizabeth Cameron. One gets the strongest impression in reading these letters that, when Adams sat down to write them, the discomfort that so often afflicted him elsewhere quite fell away and he became simply a man with a pen—a man for whom, moreover, the pen was a predestined implement. Now he was wholly at one with himself and with his perfect audience of a single person, and all his powers as a writer—powers of sharp attention to people and things, of responsiveness to impressions, of insight and judgment, and above all of expression in language—found themselves in free and unembarrassed play.

The series of Adams's published letters covers a period of just sixty years: it begins with his letters from Germany as a young student in 1858 and ends with a letter to Gaskell a few weeks before his death in 1918. As the expression of a life so many-sided as his was, these letters are bound to exert their interest on a variety of levels. Their interest as a social chronicle—as "a memorial of manners and habits," to put it in his way—is exerted on only one of these, but on that level it is undeniable. The letters that have this value were mainly written in Adams's early years—in those months in Washington that followed Lincoln's election, in the years he spent as private secretary to his father in London, and then, again, in Washington, in the disenchanting year or two that followed his return. As soon as Adams joined the Harvard faculty his attention was drawn off elsewhere; even after his resignation and the return to Washington, the writing of his *History* was his great preoccupation, and after the death of his wife he withdrew too completely from social life to think of himself as in any way a recorder of it. He emerged rather warily and briefly from this seclusion when his friend John Hay was Secretary of State, and when his friend

Theodore Roosevelt was President he even ventured so far out of his retreat as to attend one or two dinners at the White House. The result was a handful of letters that have something of the old animation as chronicle. In general, however, after 1870 Adams appeals to one as a letter-writer on other grounds.

. . . In general, he was never more consistently good—never more uninterruptedly animated and vivid, or less liable to his special vices of mind and style—than in the great body of letters he wrote on his very considerable travels about the globe. If ever a man was a good traveler Henry Adams was, as he quite properly boasted in a letter to Mrs. Cameron. It is true that he went on to minimize this claim by pretending it only meant that, in any given situation, he was more comfortable than his fellow travelers. But that, as he surely knew, was a ludicrous understatement. He was a good traveler, to put it on the surface level for the moment, partly because he was extraordinarily philosophical about the discomforts and hardships of travel. There is a world of difference between Adams sitting in his study on H Street and Adams journeying on foot up a narrow river valley in Fiji or bumping along in an oxcart through the forests of Ceylon; the same man who could be plunged into gloom by a headline seems never to have much minded a gale at sea, a snowstorm in the mountains, or the necessity of dining on squid.

That, however, was the least part of his genius as a traveler, without much more significance than his baggage. What was far more important was his real love of the various world—of the world as one sees it not in newspapers or even in historical records but literally, as it unrolls itself, in travel, before the physical senses: the landscape, the city streets, the native villages, the monuments of the past, the men and women, the very animals. Can one read these letters without discerning how strong and how genuine this loving interest was, contradictory as it may seem to the bleak repudiations that form the more familiar side of Henry Adams's mind? Clearly there was a strain of magic for him in the mere fact of movement from scene to scene, and whatever his state of mind may have been, in a Berlin boardinghouse or a Washington study, however he may have despaired and denied, he seems only to have had to board a train or embark on a steamer (despite his sufferings from seasickness) to be set free for the time from his intensest anxieties and to become the other Adams, the born poet with a poet's gust for experience. One feels it at the beginning and almost as truly at the end; one feels it in the days when, with two or three other young Americans, he sets off on a walking tour through the Thuringian Forest; it is there in the period of his grief-stricken middle life when he roams with his friend La Farge through Japan and the islands of the South Seas, and even at the time when, a solitary and embittered man in his sixties, he finds himself alone, well within the Arctic Circle, gazing upon the "terribly fascinating and fantastic" landscape of glacier-laden mountains and "silent, oily, gleaming sea" that surrounds Hammerfest in Norway.

If few letters of travel anywhere are superior to these it is because Henry Adams had so fortunate a mingling of talents for the purpose. As he moved about the world, his senses were awake and aware of everything, his feeling for the tone of places was continually at work, and at the same time his mind, with its special penetrations and its rich equipment of knowledge, was restlessly taking note of all the intangibles, the "supersensibles," the impalpable analogies and contrasts and meanings. He can give one the impression of being primarily and essentially a landscape-painter in prose, a La Farge of language. He can catch what seems to be the whole quality of a moonlight night over a Hawaiian island—as he sits on a verandah and absorbs it—with his image of two palm trees on the terrace before him, glistening in the moonlight.

. . . ⟨In⟩ general these letters of travel owe half their power to his ingrained habit of going beyond the mere surface of things, the mere look of foreignness and picturesqueness, and making the difficult effort of social and psychological understanding. It is what all good travel-writers do, of course; but how many travel-writers have Henry Adams's acuteness, his malleability, his freedom from the formulated and the preconceived? Freedom even from his own formulas—for he has no sooner yielded himself, for example, to the romantic and archaic charm of Samoan life than his critical sense too comes into play, and he begins to see that the reality of that life is many-sided, and that some of its sides are not very poetic. One cannot resist the sweet temper, the gaiety, the gentleness of the Samoans, to be sure, or their nobility of appearance and manner, but the fact is, the more one sees of them, the more oppressively one becomes aware that there are virtually no individuals among them, that they are all more like one another than the inhabitants of a Yankee small town, and that they are singularly practical, unimaginative, unromantic, without intellectual curiosity or reflectiveness. "I begin to understand," writes Adams, "why Melville wanted to escape from Typee." At any rate, he had begun to understand something about primitive life that no sentimental stereotype would have prepared him for.

He may or may not have been "right" in his own reformulation of it—"right" in the literal and wholly objective sense—but he had got at something, as he almost always did, that by no means leapt to the eye, and it is these repeated flights of penetration into the intangibles that largely make his letters from abroad so absorbing. That, and the imaginative use he was constantly making of his erudition as a historian. . . .

If he had not been an ideologue, Henry Adams's letters would have lacked one of the strands of interest which of course they have. And this remains true even if one feels that some of the general ideas propounded in his later books—the ideal unity of medieval culture, the merely chaotic multiplicity of modern culture, the application to history of the Second Law of Thermodynamics, and the like—deserve a good deal less solemn and literal attention than has often been accorded them. The sheen of novelty has worn off some of these "views" by this time, and it is easier now to see the admixture in them, along with their solid elements, of wishfulness, caprice, and intellectual dice-loading. The position Adams finally arrived at was once described by Paul Elmer More as "sentimental nihilism," and the phrase will do as well as some others to suggest its particular quality. Saying so by no means implies that Adams's mind was not one of the most interesting, in its foibles as well as in its power, in American intellectual history; one of the most complex, restless, wide-ranging, and supple. And the letters enable one to follow the *development* of his mind from phase to phase as, of course, none of his books or even all his books taken together quite do. The intellectual story they tell is, quite naturally, much less artfully shaped and organized than that in the *Education*, but it is a more complex, shifting, indecisive, and credible story.

What one gets in the letters, and fails to get in the *Education*, is the whole process by which Henry Adams moved from the great Unitarian synthesis of his fathers—from its pure, cold, arid, eighteenth-century rationality and optimism—to the mechanistic catastrophism with which he ended. This latter was, of course, his final testament to posterity, but only the reader of the letters has a full sense of the delicacy with which Adams's mind was for many years balanced between the poles of hopefulness and despair, affirmation and denial, belief and skepticism. The uncertain poise was there from the beginning, as he himself, with his peculiarly Yankee type of introspective acuteness, once observed. Still in his middle twenties, writing to his brother Charles from London, he confesses that his mind is by nature balanced in such a way "that what is evil never seems unmixed with good, and what is good always streaked with evil." Ultimately he was to reach the point where "what is evil" seemed quite unalloyed with any ingredients of goodness, and that was the state of mind in which the *Education* was written. But in writing it Henry Adams—quite properly, from the stylistic point of view—simplified, distorted, and misrepresented his own intellectual and emotional past. . . .

The young Henry Adams did not need either Darwin or Grant to inspire black thoughts in his heart: Abraham Lincoln was still President, and Adams had probably not yet drunk deep of Darwinism, when, writing to Henry Lee Higginson from London, he broke out: "Meanwhile I only hope that your life won't be such an eternal swindle as most life is." And it was probably not on either scientific or political grounds that, five years later, back in Washington, he confessed in a letter to Gaskell that, even if in a few years he should have made a great reputation for himself, he would not be prepared to say what it was really worth: "The sad truth is that I want nothing and life seems to have no purpose."

The vibrations one detects in such utterances are those of an essentially personal dejection. Yet a merely private woefulness is no more characteristic of Adams's mind in his twenties than in his sixties, and already in the early letters one finds him speculating in the most impersonal terms on the nature of the world system—so evidently not a Unitarian one—that contemporary knowledge seemed more and more to be evoking. If the letters of his early and middle life reveal that he then had far higher hopes than he would later have confessed to, they also reveal how early he had arrived, tentatively anyway, at some of the grimmer conceptions that were to be characteristic of his latest thought. Something like a mechanistic theory of nature and of history had long been in his mind. "The truth is," he writes in 1863, "everything in this universe has its regular waves and tides. Electricity, sound, the wind, and I believe every part of organic nature will be brought some day within this law. But my philosophy teaches me, and I firmly believe it, that the laws which govern animated beings will be ultimately found to be at bottom the same with those which rule inanimate nature, and . . . I am quite ready to receive with pleasure any basis for a systematic conception of it all."

It was more than thirty years after he wrote these sentences that Adams got round to Willard Gibbs and Lord Kelvin, to the Law of Phase and the Second Law of Thermodynamics; but it is evident how long his mind had been wholly prepared for them. And not even at the end was he to take an essentially bitterer view of the doom to which science was hurrying mankind than he had taken in 1862: "Man has mounted science," he then wrote, "and is now run away with it. I firmly believe that before many centuries more, science will be the master of man. The engines he will have invented will be beyond his strength to control. Some day science may have the existence of mankind in its power, and the human race may commit suicide by blowing up the world." In 1910 he was saying not "may" but "will," and he was saying it with a gloomy eloquence of manner he had not commanded in his twenties. He was speaking, too, as one has to recognize, in the ghastly light of more evidence than there had been at hand in 1862. But he was giving voice to fears that, in one guise or another, had long tormented him.

This is not to say that there was no development whatever in Adams's intellectual life but only that the development was more continuous (as well as more contradictory) than the reader who limits himself to the late and best-known books is likely to guess. And it is certainly not to say that his intellectual interests were limited to these large historical and philosophical matters: no reader of the *Education* would suppose that they were, but only a reader of the letters will quite realize how great was the variety of ideas to which at one time or another Adams turned his mind, or with what agility and boldness his mind played over most of them. Now it is the shallow careerism of Alexander Hamilton, now the particular place of sex in Japanese life, now the vulgar mercantile quality of the architecture of the Valois and Touraine. He glances at Anglo-Saxon poetry, and his quick, offhand remarks might have come from a literary critic of genius; he animadverts on the evolution of finance capital, and seems to have given most of his life to the problem; he finds himself reflecting on the unself-consciousness of his father and that whole generation of New Englanders, and suggests in half a dozen sentences a sustained and searching essay in psychological history. Meanwhile he has been willful, petulant, illiberal, and superficial at a hundred points; he has ridden a few hobbies—and even a few phrases (his "gold bugs," for example)—to the brink of prostration and over; he has obstinately shut his eyes to every manifestation of new life that he does not wish to consider, and allowed his prophetic catastrophism to waste and weaken itself in senile hysteria. It has all mattered relatively little to the responsive reader: the foibles of a first-rate mind are always a small price to pay for its real fruits, and among the fruits of Adams's mind his letters come very close, at the least, to holding first place.

LIONEL TRILLING
"Adams at Ease"
A Gathering of Fugitives
1952, pp. 117–24

It is impossible to be consistent in the feelings with which we respond to Henry Adams. Sometimes he is irresistible, as in his memories of his boyhood, or in the exercise or expression of friendship, or in some fleeting reference to his dead wife. Sometimes he is hateful, as in his anti-Jewish utterances, or in the queer malice with which he infused the visions of doom of his later life. There are times when he is supreme in manly delicacy, and times when he seems feline, or trifling and shallow. It often occurs to us to believe that his is the finest American intelligence we can possibly know, while again it sometimes seems that his mind is so special, and so refined in specialness, as to be beside any possible point.

It would of course be easier for us to settle our personal accounts with him if only his personality were a private one. We might then choose simply to conclude that the flaws of his temper are of a kind that prevents us from giving him full credence. Or we might feel, with more charity and worldliness, that this was a man who lived to be eighty years old, who was articulate for more than sixty of those years, and who, one way or another, made himself the subject of all that he said, who, although not a confessional writer as we nowadays understand that term, was not bound by conventions of reticence other than those he created for himself—we might well feel of such a man that it would be strange indeed if he did not exhibit a good many of the inadequacies that the human spirit is heir to.

But it is not easy to come to a final settlement with Adams's personality either in the way of condemnation or in the way of tolerance because, as I say, it isn't a private personality that we are dealing with: it is a public issue. And it is not an issue that in the course of our lifetime we are likely to take a fixed position on. Once we involve ourselves with Adams, we are fated to be back and forth with him, now on one side of the issue, now on the other, as the necessities of our mood and circumstance dictate. We are at one with Adams whenever our sense of the American loneliness and isolation becomes especially strong, whenever we feel that our culture belongs to everyone except ourselves and our friends, whenever we believe that our talents and our devotion are not being sufficiently used. At such moments we have scarcely any fault to find with Adams the man. His temperamental failings sink out of sight beneath his large and noble significance.

Yet it isn't possible to identify ourselves with Adams for very long. One's parsnips must be already buttered, as Adams's were, before one can despair as wholeheartedly as he. One needs what he had, a certain elegance of *décor*, something of an almost princely style of life, a close and intimate view of the actuality of the power one undertakes to despise, and freedom to travel and observe, and leisure to pursue the studies by which one fleshes the anatomy of one's dark beliefs. And even apart from the economic considerations, we can't long afford the identification with Adams. We come to see, as William James saw, that there is a kind of corruption and corruptingness in the perfect plenitude of his despair. With James we understand that Adams's despair is a chief condition of its own existence, and that the right to hope is earned by our courage in hoping. And when we see this, we turn on Adams, using against him every weapon on which we can lay our hands. We look for the weaknesses in his theory of history and of society (it is not hard to find them), we question his understanding of science, we seek out the rifts in his logic—and we insist, of course, on the faults of his personal temper, we permit his irony to irritate us, we call him snobbish, and over-fastidious, and *fainéant*.

But we shall be wrong, we shall do ourselves a great disservice, if ever we try to read Adams permanently out of our intellectual life. I have called him an issue—he is even more than that, he is an indispensable element of our thought, he is an instrument of our intelligence. To succeed in getting rid of Adams would be to diminish materially the seriousness of our thought. In the intellectual life there ought to be frequent occasions for the exercise of ambivalence, and nothing can be more salutary for the American intelligence than to remain aware of Adams and to maintain toward him a strict ambivalence, to weigh our admiration and affection for him against our impatience and suspicion.

Two recent Adams items seem to me peculiarly useful in helping us keep the right balance of our emotions toward their author. Newton Arvin has made a selection of Adams's letters in the Great Letters Series, the publishers of which, Farrar, Straus, and Young, have met the occasion of the presidential convention season with a new printing of Adams's Washington novel, *Democracy*. If, as I think, the scales have tipped rather against Adams in the last few years—is this because some of his worst predictions have come dismally true?—if at the moment he is more out of favor than in, these two books will do much to restore the equipoise of our judgment.

Adams, as we all remember, thought of himself as a child of the eighteenth century, and his belief in his anachronism is substantiated by nothing so much as his letters. His family was formidable in the epistolary art, his grandmother Abigail being

something of a genius in it, and Henry practiced it with an appropriate seriousness. Early in his career he speaks half-jokingly of a desire to emulate Horace Walpole in the representation of the manners and habits of his time, and he made bold to hope that his letters would be remembered when much in the historical scene was forgotten. There is a common belief that those who write letters to posterity as well as to their friends are bound to write dully, but this is not true in general and it certainly is not true of Adams. Since personal letters were first valued and published, no public or quasi-public person can write them without the awareness of posterity. And of course for Adams archives were no great thing, and the notion that he was adding to their number did not make him awkward or, in the bad sense, self-conscious. The historical past, the historical present, the historical future, were the stuff of his existence, the accepted circumstance of his most private thoughts and most intimate friendships.

Adams's capacity for friendship was one of the most notable things about him, and it is of course a decisive element of the greatness of his letters. In this he is peculiarly a man of the nineteenth century, which was the great age of friendship. Men then felt that the sharing of experience with certain chosen spirits was one of the essential pleasures of life, and even writers and revolutionaries found it possible to have close, continuing communication with each other. Adams, we almost come to believe as we read his letters, was the last man, or perhaps the last American, to have had actual friendships. He mistrusted much in the world, but he trusted his friends, and he so far developed his great civilized talent for connection that he could be in lively communicative relationship even with his family, and even with women.

. . . In the letters it was possible for Adams's mind to work without the excessive elaborations of irony which are characteristic of his published late writings. This irony is no doubt always very brilliant, but as Mr. Arvin observes, it is all too obviously less a function of the author's intelligence than of his personal uneasiness in relation to the unknown reader, of that excess of delicacy and self-regard which led him into the irritating high-jinks of flirtatious hesitation about publishing his two great works. But in the letters there is no embarrassment and there is no irony beyond what normally and naturally goes with the exercise of a complex intelligence.

Then the letters, as Mr. Arvin remarks, give us an Adams who loved the world in its manifold variety much more than we might ever conclude from the books. He delighted in the pleasures that the world could offer, in what might be observed of the world for the joy of observation rather than for the support of a theory of the world's uninhabitability. Further, it is from the letters that we get a notion of the development of Adams's mind which is more accurate than his own formal account of it in *The Education*. "Only the reader of the letters," as Mr. Arvin says, "has a full sense of the delicacy with which Adams's mind was for many years balanced between the poles of hopefulness and despair, affirmation and denial, belief and skepticism."

Certainly the reader of the letters gets what the reader of *The Education* does not get, the awareness of how late in coming was Adams's disillusionment with democracy. *The Degradation of the Democratic Dogma* was not the title that Adams himself gave to the oddly contrived posthumous volume that his brother edited and published under that name, but it is a phrase that accurately suggests Adams's attitude in his last years, and *The Education* would lead us to believe that this attitude was established with him upon the defeat of his youthful political expectations with the publication of the list of

Grant's cabinet. Yet the letters of the middle years, even after the process of disillusionment had begun, are full of references to his continuing faith in democracy. In 1877 he wrote to his English friend, Charles Milnes Gaskell: "As I belong to the class of people who have great faith in this country and who believe that in another century it will be saying in its turn the last word of civilisation, I enjoy the expectation of the coming day." And in 1881 he could write to Wayne MacVeagh upon the occasion of Garfield's assassination: "Luckily we are a democracy and a sound one. Nothing can shake society with us, now that slavery is gone."

And the same essential faith in the American democratic ideal is implicit in Adams's novel, *Democracy*, despite its satiric rejection of the actualities of American government in 1879. There is no touch of irony in the speech which Adams puts into the mouth of his questing heroine, Mrs. Lightfoot Lee, when she takes it upon herself to chasten a young Italian Secretary of Legation who too easily accepts the idea that "there was no society except in the old world":

> "Society in America? Indeed there is society in America and very good society too; but it has a code of its own, and newcomers seldom understand it. I will tell you what it is, Mr. Orsini, and you will never be in danger of making any mistake. 'Society' in America means all the honest, kindly mannered, pleasant-voiced women, and all the good, brave, unassuming men, between the Atlantic and the Pacific. Each of these has a free pass in every city and village, 'good for this generation only,' and it depends on each to make use of this pass or not as it may happen to suit his or her fancy. To this rule there are *no* exceptions, and those who say 'Abraham is our father' will surely furnish food for that humour which is the staple product of our country."

It rings, does it not, with the passionate naivety of an old-fashioned high-school oration, yet such sentiments about their country once served to aerate and brighten the minds of even the most sophisticated and critical of Americans—one finds them being uttered at a certain period by Henry James and with a passion of optimism no less naive than that of his friend Adams.

The awareness of this very attractive naivety of idealism is essential for the understanding of Adams's ultimate development in pessimism. It is endemic in *Democracy*, appearing in the use which is made of the simplicity and plainness of General Lee's house at Arlington, and in the elaborate discussion of Mount Vernon and General Washington as representing the republican virtues which, although receding into the past, are still part of the American dream.

In his introduction to the *Selected Letters*, Mr. Arvin refers to Adams's two anonymously published novels, *Democracy* and *Esther*, as "remarkable books, more remarkable than they have usually been recognized as being." And so they are. Of the two, *Democracy* is, I think, the more attractive. *Esther*, which stands in the same interrogative relation to religion that *Democracy* stands to politics, is full of velleities of thought and feeling about its subject, and these, while possibly they make for an interesting darkness in the work, also make for uncertainty and irresolution. But *Democracy* is all clarity and brightness, and entirely satisfying so far as it goes. It does not, as a novel, go very far—does not pretend to go very far. It is brief and witty and schematic; everything in it is contrived and controlled by the author's intelligence and his gaiety. It can claim a degree of cousinage with Peacock's novels of intellectual humors; it shares the light speed of this form and it has more than a few Peacockian moments, such as that in which the bright young American heiress explains to a British visitor the trouble that Americans have with their sundials:

> "Look at that one! they all behave like that. The wear and tear of our sun is too much for them; they don't last. My uncle, who has a place at Long Branch, had five sun-dials in ten years."
> "How very odd! But really now, Miss Dare, I don't see how a sun-dial could wear out."
> "Don't you? How strange! Don't you see, they get soaked with sunshine so that they can't hold shadow."

But although its humor is frequent and its wit pervasive, *Democracy* does not move among ideas with the Peacockian lack of commitment to anything but common sense. It is concerned to ask a question which was of the greatest importance to Adams himself, and to his countrymen: The nature of American political life being what it is, is it possible for a person of moral sensibility to participate in it?

The person upon whom the test is made is the attractive and intelligent young widow, Madeleine Lee—Adams is already, in middle life, making woman the touchstone and center of civilization. Bereaved of a husband and baby in a single year, Mrs. Lee has tried to fill her life with civilized interests, and, having found philosophy and philanthropy of no avail, has established herself in Washington intent on trying political activity as a last resort. "She wanted to see with her own eyes the action of primary forces; to touch with her own hand the massive machinery of society; to measure with her own mind the capacity of the motive power. She was bent upon getting to the heart of the great American mystery of democracy and government."

She wanted, in short, the experience of power, as did Adams himself. It was not merely her being a woman that brought it about that "the force of the engine was a little confused in her mind with that of the engineer, the power with the men who wielded it"; the confusion had existed in Adams's mind when he had decided that there was no possible place for him in American political life; the confusion is no confusion at all but an accurate statement of the fact.

Madeleine's experience of the men who wield the power, or try to wield it, is the substance of her sad education. Presidents of the United States, she learns, are likely to be foolish, vulgar, bedeviled men, who, with their impossible wives, lead the most hideous lives of public ceremony. Reformers maintain their equanimity only by a bland ignorance of the nature of what they are trying to change. Most senators are nonentities, and the one senator who is more than that, who does have the strength and craft to control the great machine, is, as poor Madeleine finds, venal—corrupt not merely through personal motives but by the acknowledged terms of his profession, by his devotion to party. And since it is this Senator Ratcliffe whom Madeleine is drawn to by reason of his power and even thinks of marrying, his acceptance and rationalization of his immorality is decisive with her. She surrenders Washington and withdraws from the political life, and the posed question is conclusively answered: No, it is not possible for a person of moral sensibility to take part in American politics.

Very likely the means by which the answer is made will seem too simple to us nowadays and not quite relevant to our situation—not that the moral probity of senators is now an article of our political faith, but that we do not take senatorial corruption for granted as it was taken for granted in the Seventies when Mark Twain instituted his famous comparison between the moral character of senators and that of hogs. But the question is still a valid one, and so, in some important part, is Adams's answer.

DAVID L. MINTER
From
"Apotheosis of the Form: Henry Adams' *Education*"
The Interpreted Design as a Structural Principle in American Prose
1969, pp. 103–33

> The day shall come, that great avenging day,
> When Troy's proud glories in the dust shall lay,
> When Priam's powers and Priam's self shall fall,
> And one prodigious ruin swallow all.
> 　　　　(Homer, The *Iliad*, in Pope's translation)

> 　　　　it is great
> To do that thing that ends all other deeds,
> Which shackles accidents and bolts up change.
> 　　　　　　　　(William Shakespeare,
> 　　　　　　　　*Anthony and Cleopatra*)

*T*he *Education of Henry Adams* represents Henry Adams' effort, with a labor of the imagination, to offset the destructive work of "wasteful Time";[1] it is his effort to render his self, his heritage, and the complexly troubled relation between them inviolable. The *Education* grew, moreover, out of deliberate appropriation of autobiography as a literary form. The work's proper subtitle is, to be sure, "A Study in Twentieth-Century Multiplicity," not "An Autobiography," but as early as January 1883 the urge to tell his story had established itself in Adams' consciousness. "I am clear," he wrote John Hay, "that you should write autobiography. I mean to do mine."[2] Moreover, to Adams autobiography meant not a loose memoir but a distinct art form with distinct problems and possibilities. In the Preface of 1907, he places his work in a tradition defined by Rousseau and Franklin. Later, in his Editor's Preface, he compares his work with *The Confessions of St. Augustine*, which he had praised, in a letter of February 1908 to William James, as a work shaped by a definite "idea of literary form." Augustine, as Adams saw him, was preeminent as an artist in autobiography because he had a "notion of writing a story with an end and object, not for the sake of the object, but for the form, like a romance."[3] In short, like its companion piece, *Mont-Saint-Michel and Chartres*, which is an extended piece of praise to a "method" that had inspired art of "singular unity," the *Education* is a monument to Adams' devotion to "form."[4] The one Adams toward whom all other Adamses in the *Education* muddle and grope is the artist as "weary Titan of Unity"—the artist as one cognizant that man's problem, "From cradle to grave," is the peculiarly and preeminently human problem "of running order through chaos, direction through space, discipline through freedom, unity through multiplicity."[5]

There is more behind the *Education*, however, than appreciation of the devotion of the Middle Ages to "organic unity both in . . . thought and in . . . building."[6] Haunted by what he took to be a widening gap between available fact and acceptable truth, the Adams of the *Education* is seeking poetically to use facts in order aesthetically to overcome tension between truth and fact. Late in the *Education*, in the tone that made Brooks Adams suspect Henry of never being "quite frank with himself or with others,"[7] Adams remarks that no historian who "values his honesty" can at all afford concern for truth; the historian who "cares for his truths," Adams asserts, "is certain to falsify his facts" (p. 457). Aware that the men of his day were called to live between the reigns of different forms of ordered meaning, in what was theologically an interim and politically an interregnum, Adams sought to explore the problems and possibilities thus created. What did it mean to live in an era in which concern for fact as available and accepted datum had to be kept apart from concern for truth as ordered and acceptable meaning? For us, Adams says in *Chartres*, "the poetry is history, and the facts are false." In terms of the tension thus established between truth as meaning and facts as data, the *Education* is concerned with truth, not with fact, with poetry, not with history. To borrow again from its companion volume, "the world" of the *Education* is "not a schoolroom or a pulpit, but a stage."[8]

In part because it is more a stage than a schoolroom or pulpit, and in part because it is both an autobiography and a companion volume to *Mont-Saint-Michel and Chartres*, the *Education* is fabulously complex. In its early stages it unfolds as the story of a boy strangely born under the shadow and consecrated to the service of a distinct family heritage: "Had he been born in Jerusalem under the shadow of the Temple and circumcised in the Synagogue by his uncle the high priest, under the name of Israel Cohen, he would scarcely have been more distinctly branded" (p. 3). What complicates the *Education*, however, even more than Adams' sense of his finely textured heritage, is the distance he pushes his story beyond the personal. . . .

Adams' effort to run order through chaos, to bring harmony to tension, rhythm to contradiction, and form to incongruity, leads, first, to his philosophy of history, and second, to his decision, by writing the *Education*, to make his search for order an imaginative quest. . . .

Adams' theory participates in the most fashionable tendency of his time—the tendency, sponsored by the "great word Evolution," to make "a new religion of history" (p. 91); and it couples understanding of the natural world with interpretation of the historical process. But the formula is what it is precisely because, invented to fill the void created by failed formulas, it is shaped to meet man's needs. In short, it is a monument to man's refusal simply to adapt himself to a nonhuman world. In it, in keeping with "the law" or "the principle of resistance" (pp. 7, 21), man refuses to accept the specious success of mere survival; he insists upon achieving order through transformation of a world not made for him. Adams thus refuses to cease invention without having fashioned a formula, but he also acknowledges that "Unity is vision" (p. 398)—that " 'Order and reason, beauty and benevolence, are characteristics and conceptions . . . solely associated with the mind of man' " (p. 450)—that "Chaos [is] the law of nature" and "Order . . . the dream of man" (p. 451).

Like the efforts of King and Hay, Adams' intellectual effort is limited. For, though it is not paid for with Adams' life, it does not increase man's control over life. Nor does it endure. Because it must always be subject to the shifting angle of man's vision of a changing world, intellectual formulation too is evanescent. On this count, Aquinas, like Rome, is actual: he is Newton; he is going to be Darwin and Marx. In short, like King's expeditions and Hay's treaties, Adams' formula is doomed inevitably to become a relic and ruin of the past. Like all who attempt to move toward the civilized, Adams meets "scandalous failure" in the very moment of his "complete success" (see p. 477; cf. p. 472).

In recognition that his formula is an invention of himself for himself, Adams must add that he finally cares "no more" for "his dynamic theory of history . . . than for the kinetic theory of gas" (p. 501).[9] Like the "true" lies of Joseph Conrad's characters, Adams' intellectual formula is a heroic act in an ironic mode. His invention affirms human affirmation. When made in full knowledge that man's formulas are his own invention, the act of affirming formulation is supremely an act of life. Adams' man finally is moved by needs that no enervating recognition of the bleakness of man's fate can extinguish. Knowing that all specifically human visions of meaning are "illusions" (to use Conrad's word) or invented "formula[s]," mere "convenient fiction[s]" (to use two of Adams' own), Adams nonetheless defines man's final wisdom as recognition that the illusions are "necessary": that the formulas are "infinitely precious," the fictions man's highest "achievement"; that in the end they are, all ironically, man's "only truth."[10]

In response to life Adams accordingly shapes his own convenient and fitting fiction, which he must entertain in the proper spirit and render with the proper tone. At this point skepticism and faith merge. Because he can find no value and meaning outside himself, because he can look back to no revelation, nor forward to any realization of an absolute, Adams must accept his world as the natural habitat of none of the values that it is human to create and humane to try to live. Man's "convenient fiction[s]" thus represent a heroic response to the chaos that surrounds him, engulfing his efforts at order.

For King the scientist and Hay the statesman, as well as for Adams the philosopher, it is chaos that is real, chaos that sooner or later cannot not be known. Yet each of these men moves, and must move, beyond knowledge of chaos to make "All [his] life" a struggle for impossible order and unity (p. 398). Only in such struggle, only in affirmation, are Adams' men supremely human. Given the complexly ironic aspects of Adams' vision, however, the supreme instance of man's effort to give order and meaning to "something that defie[s] meaning" (p. 499) must necessarily be not a rational theory but a work of the imagination. The climax of the *Education* comes not when Adams invents his intellectual formula, his theory of history, but when he sets for "himself . . . the task" of writing *Mont-Saint-Michel and Chartres* and *The Education of Henry Adams* as companion volumes from which he could "project his lines forward and backward indefinitely," defining himself and his world in infinite context (p. 435). The *Education*, in a word, represents Adams' final effort not only to assure that he has not "sat all [his] life on the steps of Ara Coeli" merely to accept "assassination" as "forever . . . the last word of Progress" (pp. 471–72), but also to assure "that the family work of a hundred and fifty years" will not fall into the abyss of final failure but will be lifted "into the grand perspective of true empire-building" (p. 363).

Despite the overwhelming presence of nature, which is seen in the *Education* as having always "hurried and hustled" man without ever consulting his "convenience" (p. 493), and despite the overpowering presence of history, which is seen in the *Education* as the leveler of man's planned efforts to build an eternal city of man, new vision is made possible. When Adams returns to New York for the last time, he sees a radically new world. It is, to be sure, "unlike anything man had ever seen—and like nothing he had ever" intended or "much cared to see"; but to Adams' new vision, it is also "striking" and "wonderful" (p. 499).

Within the *Education*, it is from John LaFarge that Adams learns to replace or complement the way of the "American mind," the way of direct assertion or denial of "something that it takes for a fact," with the way of art (p. 369). As the one "alternative" to arithmetic and statistics (p. 351), art is concerned with the logic and truth of the imagination. From LaFarge, Adams learns to carry "different shades of contradiction in his mind," and, rather than " 'reason too much,' " to seek "a tone—a shade—a *nuance*" (p. 370). It is preeminently in its poetic, imaginative mode that the human mind itself becomes for Adams "the subtlest of all known forces" (p. 476). Just as man responds to existence—to being caught up in the flux and movement of his natural and historical environment—by seeking actively to impose specifically human and humane order, thereby to make life of mere existence; and just as the human mind responds to inchoate existence and to partially ordered life by seeking to "invent" a formula that will permit man "to fit" the "pieces" of the "puzzle" into meaningful pattern; so does the aesthetic imagination creatively respond to all man's ordering efforts, seeking to make art of them, seeking, that is, by ordering all man's ordering efforts, to turn failure into triumph.[11]

Even more than his invented formula (which might conceivably lead to a plan of action), the *Education* is limited because it does not directly further Adams' mastery of actual life. But unlike his philosophical theories, it is, as a work of art, neither tentative nor evanescent, but absolute. It constitutes his supreme no to chaos and disorder. For in it he declines simply to accept himself as having appeared "suddenly and inexplicably out of some unknown and unimaginable void"; in it he refuses simply to pass his life in the physical chaos of nature and history and in "the mental chaos of sleep," quietly to wait until he awakes, following years of "growing astonishment," to find himself "looking blankly into the void of death" (p. 460). In it he insists, to the contrary, on charged and consummated vision. Having acknowledged the actuality of chaos, he accordingly must become a "fabulist" who celebrates his struggle "to escape the chaos which cage[s]" him (p. 460). For only as such a fabulist can he celebrate that struggle in each of its realms—in nature and history—and under each of its aspects—under the eye that seeks to discern order and the will that seeks to impose it, under the apprehending mind that seeks to invent formulas, and under the imagination that seeks to fashion images of man and his failed efforts.

Because the *Education* is the story of a man whose "accidental education" prepares him for the act of telling it, it is finally the story of its story. Throughout his autobiography, Adams' imagination behaves "like a young pearl oyster, secreting its universe to suit its conditions until it [has] built up a shell of *nacre* that embodie[s] all its notions of the perfect." Adams thus celebrates his own image of perfection: for him it is "true" and beautiful because it is he that has "made it." Adams' imaginative construct comes to be what it is and to embody the triumph it embodies only at great cost and sacrifice and only within its limited realm. But it may "justly" be called "a work of art"; for, as an effort at supreme order and as a labor of inclusive affirmation, it constitutes its maker's ultimate act of life, his final adherence to "the principle of resistance" (pp. 83, 458, 21).

Notes

1. William Shakespeare, Sonnet 15, ll. 11–14.

2. Letter to John Hay, January 1883, in Worthington C. Ford, ed., *Letters of Henry Adams, 1858–1918* (2 vols. Boston and New York, Houghton Mifflin, 1930–38), *1*, 347. On the problem of the *Education* as autobiography, see Ernest Samuels, *The Young Henry Adams* (Cambridge, Mass., Harvard University Press, 1948), p. ix.

3. Letter to William James, February 1908, Ford, *Letters, 2*, 490.

See Sayre, *The Examined Self*, pp. 7–10; and J. C. Levenson, *The Mind and Art of Henry Adams* (Boston, Houghton Mifflin, 1957), p. 306.

4. Henry Adams, *Mont-Saint-Michel and Chartres* [1904] (Boston and New York, Houghton Mifflin, 1913), pp. 382–83. This work is hereafter cited as *Chartres*.

5. Henry Adams, *The Education of Henry Adams* [1907] (Boston and New York, Houghton Mifflin, 1918), pp. 455, 12. All page references in the text of this chapter are to this work.

6. *Chartres*, p. 380.

7. Brooks Adams, "The Heritage of Henry Adams," introduction to Henry Adams, *The Degradation of the Democratic Dogma* (New York, Macmillan, 1919), p. 1.

8. *Chartres*, pp. 226, 108.

9. On Adams as an historian, see Levenson, pp. 135, 367–76; and W. H. Jordy, *Henry Adams: Scientific Historian* (New Haven, Yale University Press, 1952), passim and esp. pp. 220–88. Adams' theoretical statements should be read, it seems to me, with attention to the complex irony that informs them. Adams was capable for instance of referring to "The Rule of Phase Applied to History" as "a mere intellectual plaything . . . not meant to be taken too seriously" (Letter to Brooks Adams, February 1909, quoted in Ford, *Letters of Henry Adams*, 2, 515, n. 1); and of saying that his "A Letter to American Teachers of History" was "a mere bit of amusement . . . a joke, which nobody will know enough to understand" (Letter to Brooks Adams, January 1910, ibid., 2, 533). Adams' longing for final—"scientific"—understanding of history was real and enduring, but he formulated his own "scientific" theories rather to honor man's need for such understanding than in belief that they represented it. In 1909 he wrote Brooks Adams giving him permission to do as he would with "The Rule of Phase Applied to History"; to "my point of view," he added, it is "only a sort of jigsaw puzzle, put together in order to see whether the pieces could be made to fit. Too well I knew the inadequacy of the public mind . . . The fools begin [sic] at once to discuss whether the theory was true" (Henry Adams, Letter to Brooks Adams, February 1909, in Harold D. Cater, ed., *Henry Adams and His Friends: A Collection of His Unpublished Letters* [Boston, Houghton Mifflin, 1947], p. 639).

10. Robert Penn Warren, Introduction, Joseph Conrad, *Nostromo* [1904] (New York, Random House, 1951), pp. xxii–iv. Henry Adams, Letter to Charles Francis Adams, Jr., May 1863, Ford, *A Cycle of Adams Letters*, 1, 278. Despite knowledge that failure was probable, that man "should cease" in his effort to find meaning was not, for Adams, "within the range of experience" (*The Degradation of the Democratic Dogma*, p. 126).

11. See Adams as quoted above, n. 9, and cf. the *Education*, pp. 50, 156–57, 469, 472–73.

LOUIS AUCHINCLOSS
From *Henry Adams*
1971, pp. 12–43

He and his wife, Marian Hooper of Boston, whom he had married in 1872, settled in Washington, and he began at last a full-time career as a historian. The next eight years were the happiest of his life. The young Adamses were the center of the brightest, gayest group in the capital. Henry James was to describe them at this period with good-natured sharpness in the guise of the Alfred Bonnycastles in "Pandora." Mrs. Bonnycastle in that tale has a fund of good humor that is apt to come uppermost with the April blossoms; her husband is "not in politics, though politics were much in him." They solve their social problems simply by not knowing any of the people they do not want to know, although here Mr. Bonnycastle sometimes finds his wife a bit too choosy. He remarks toward the end of the season: "Hang it, there's only a month left, let us be vulgar and have some fun—let us invite the President!"

But with all the fun and the parties Adams was still hard at work. He had acquired the Albert Gallatin papers which he edited in three large volumes, with a fourth for his own biography of Jefferson's secretary of the treasury (1879). As history the life is admirable; as entertainment it is very dry. One doubts if even such a literary magician as Lytton Strachey could have made Gallatin's personality interesting. However highminded, judicious, industrious, patriotic, conscientious, Gallatin was dull and his correspondence is dull, and dullness permeates his biography. Adams demonstrates all of his subject's best qualities in his own careful, clear rendition of the important facts, and there they remain for students, and for students only.

Just the opposite is true of Adams' biography of John Randolph of Roanoke (1882). Here he is dealing with an absolutely reprehensible man who was the scourge of the House of Representatives for two decades and who ultimately came to symbolize everything that was violent, recalcitrant, and irrational in the point of view of the southern slaveholder. Randolph's importance in history is that he became the prophet around whom the forces of secession could ultimately rally. It is certain that he was alcoholic; it is probable that he was partially insane. No more different character from Gallatin could possibly be conceived, and they face each other a little bit like Milton's God and Milton's Satan, with the balance of interest falling in Satan's favor. Fortunately, the book on Randolph is short, for about halfway through one begins to lose interest. The character is too absurd to hold the stage except as a grisly historical fact, and once that historical fact has been set forth there is little to be gained by summaries of his irrational speeches. The work ultimately fails, like *Gallatin*, because of its subject. It could have only been strengthened if Adams had had the material and the inclination to delve into the psychological reasons for Randolph's behavior. He would have done better to have made it the topic of one of his masterly essays in the *North American Review*. As he said himself, Randolph's biographer had the impossible job of taking a "lunatic monkey" seriously.

Gallatin and Randolph were both to play major roles in the great historical work on which Adams now embarked: *The History of the United States of America during the Administrations of Thomas Jefferson and James Madison*. When completed it ran to nine volumes, the last of which was not published until 1891. Before the appearance of Dumas Malone's study of Jefferson's first term, Adams' *History* was considered by many the definitive work on the first years of the American nineteenth century.

The short chapters, the straightforward, vigorous, masculine prose, the geographical and political sweep of the narrative, and the sharp, pungent assessments of motives and failings, conceal the enormous and laborious research in American, French, English, and Spanish state papers that underlay them. Adams was to say in *The Education* that he had published a dozen volumes of American history for no other purpose than to satisfy himself whether, by the severest process of stating, with the least possible comment, such facts as seemed sure, in such order as seemed rigorously consequent, he could fix for a familiar moment a necessary sequence of human movement. He selected his period (1801 to 1817) because it represented a natural semicolon in American history. By the turn of the century the United States had established itself as an independent nation that was bound, one way or another, to survive, and by 1815 that nation had accepted the fact, whether all of its statesmen did so or not, that it was going to survive more or less as other nations survived. It was not, in other words, to be an Arcadia—set apart. The two double terms of Jefferson and Madison represent, therefore, the historical hiatus in which Americans gave up their dream that they were different from other human beings. Adams' central theme is the disillusionment of two presidents who found that their governments were ineluctably controlled by facts and not ideals.

Both presidents were to find themselves in the position of Napoleon in Tolstoi's *War and Peace*, pulling at tassels inside a carriage under the illusion that it was they, rather than the charging horses, who made it go. Adams demonstrates that when history offered Jefferson the chance to purchase Louisiana, he discovered that he could not turn it down—that he did not even want to. So he doubled the size of the union by means of a treaty for which there was no shadow of authority in the Constitution whose strict construction he had so passionately urged. And Madison, in his turn, according to Adams, found himself obliged to build up the armed forces that he had wished to abolish and to engage in warfare which he had believed fatal to liberty. And both he and Jefferson found themselves caught up in the job of enforcing an embargo as despotically as any tyrant abroad.

This conception of Jefferson as an idealist philosopher-president, imbued with the fatuous faith that there were no international difficulties that could not be solved by negotiation, has been subject to the criticism that Adams was prejudiced against the third president, who, after spurning the political ideas of John Adams, ended by adopting them. There may be some truth in this. Why should Adams attack Jefferson for inconsistency, which can be a very great virtue in a statesman, unless he believed that the latter had preempted a credit in history that more properly belonged to his great-grandfather? Then, too, Adams, with the down-to-earth thinking of the scholar who has never been tempted to compromise, may have found it difficult to appreciate the enormous range and flexibility of Jefferson's political mind. Adams admired diplomats and rarely politicians. Jefferson was rarely a diplomat and always a politician. One is reminded at times of Lord Morley's statement that if Adams had ever surveyed himself naked in a mirror, he might have been more tolerant of human deficiencies.

Adams' predilection for diplomacy is the source of the best and weakest parts of the *History*. The more brilliant passages are those that take place outside the United States: in London, Paris, and Madrid; in St. Domingo and on the high seas. The chapters that deal with Napoleon have a particular fascination, not only because they put the naive, serious-minded American statesmen in dramatic contrast with this monster of Old World cynicism and champion of brute force, but because they show Adams, the historian, struggling desperately in his quest for sequence, for cause and effect, against the tide of chaos, against the appalling evidence that a single individual was turning history into whim. Napoleon plays in the *History* just the reverse of the role that he plays in *War and Peace*. It is ironical that Adams, who largely agreed with Tolstoi's concept of political leaders being carried along in the flood of events which they try vainly to control, should take exception to Tolstoi's primary illustration of his theory. Yet so it is. Napoleon seems to strike Adams as the one human being of the period who contains in himself an energy equivalent to a nation's energy and who is thus able to deflect history from its normal course. When one sees the emperor lolling in his hot bath and shouting at his brothers about the Louisiana Purchase, one feels that Adams is here dealing with a different kind of force from that generated by Jefferson, by Burr, by Canning, or even by Andrew Jackson. The mere fact that Napoleon is the only man in nine volumes whom we see in a bathtub underlines his individuality. Even-

tually, the processes of history would right themselves, and Napoleon's empire would disintegrate, even more quickly than it was put together, but it still remains a phenomenon unique in European history.

One can see why Adams was ultimately disappointed in his sequences. For despite all his labors and all his perceptions, the true cause of the War of 1812 is never made clear. Through several volumes of lucidly described diplomatic negotiations between England and the United States we see the government first of Jefferson and then of Madison submit tamely to every humiliation imposed upon it by a British crown determined not only to keep its former colony a small power but to seize by any means, legal or illegal, its growing trade. Adams pursues skillfully, if at times tediously, the endless negotiations in the seven years preceding the war: in Paris, Washington, and London, over the American embargo, the American Act of Non-Intercourse, the British Orders in Council, and Napoleon's Berlin and Milan decrees. Fixed in the policy of isolation, hallucinated by the vision that the new democracy, left to itself, would develop powerfully and peacefully, Jefferson and his successor are seen deliberately blinding themselves to the fact that neither Canning nor Napoleon will give the slightest consideration to any diplomatic protest that is not backed up by force.

But why then the war? Why did the United States, having suffered every diplomatic rebuff, finally elect to throw away the price of its shameful submission? So far as the reader can make out, the country was hounded unprepared into a war which its administration did not seek by a group of young hotheads in Congress led by Henry Clay and John C. Calhoun. But Adams did not know why: "The war fever of 1811 swept far and wide over the country, but even at its height seemed somewhat intermittent and imaginary. A passion that needed to be nursed for five years before it acquired strength to break into act, could not seem genuine to men who did not share it. A nation which had submitted to robbery and violence in 1805, in 1807, in 1809, could not readily lash itself into rage in 1811 when it had no new grievance to allege; nor could the public feel earnest in maintaining national honor, for every one admitted that the nation had sacrificed its honor, and must fight to regain it. Yet what honor was to be hoped from a war which required continued submission to one robber as the price of resistance to another? President Madison submitted to Napoleon in order to resist England; the New England Federalists preferred submitting to England in order to resist Napoleon; but not one American expected the United States to uphold their national rights against the world."

It is difficult for the reader at this point not to ask why, if a war is going to be created simply by an unreasonable war fever, such an inordinate amount of space has been devoted to the unraveling of the diplomatic skein that is not directly related to it. Of course, it might be answered that the unraveling of the diplomatic skein is part of a historian's task simply because it is there to unravel, but even conceding this, one cannot escape the conclusion that the diplomatic chapters could be summarized without losing much of their importance. One suspects here that Adams, being a pioneer in the British, French, and Spanish archives, fell a little bit in love with material so far virgin to the historian and indulged in overquotation. There is also the fact that, having himself spent eight years as secretary to the United States minister in London, he had a natural fascination in peering under the formal cover of diplomatic interchange to the reality beneath.

Adams believed that a historian should first detach himself and his personal enthusiasms and disapprovals from the field of human events that he has selected to study. He should then develop his own general ideas of causes and effects by observing the mass of phenomena in the selected period. After the formation of such ideas, he should exclude all facts irrelevant to them. In his *History*, his most important general idea is that the energy of the American people ultimately seized control of a chain of events which was initiated by energies in Europe. He attempted to trace this American energy in finance, science, politics, and diplomacy. Individuals were not of primary importance to him, which explains why even Jefferson is never presented in a full portrait and why Madison remains a more shadowy character than any of the British statesmen described. Adams believed that in a democratic nation individuals were important chiefly as types. In the end, his *History*, like most great histories, is a failure, if a splendid one, because we are never brought to a full comprehension of what this all-important energy consists. It seems possible that Adams might have approached its nature more closely had he widened his field of study, had he spent more time observing the commercial society of American cities, the farms of the North and the plantations in the South, and less of the day-to-day negotiations of the Treaty of Ghent.

During the years of heavy work on his *History*, Adams relaxed from one discipline, characteristically, by subjecting himself to another. He wrote and published two novels, *Democracy*, which appeared anonymously in 1880, and *Esther*, which he brought out under the pseudonym of Frances Snow Compton in 1884. The identity of the author was for years a carefully guarded secret. These novels have aroused an interest in our time incommensurate with their merit. They are in the class of Winston Churchill's paintings—of primary interest to the biographer. That is not to say that they are bad. Indeed, competently organized and agreeably written, they cause no squirms of embarrassment even to the most critical reader. But compared to Adams' other work they are pale stuff, and commentators are reduced to the scholar's game of spotting the origins of the *Education* in *Democracy* and that of *Mont-Saint-Michel and Chartres* in *Esther*. Mrs. Lightfoot Lee's disenchantment with her corrupt senator, exposed by Adams' alter ego, John Carrington, reflects the author's own disgust with post-Civil War Washington, and Esther Dudley's rejection of the Episcopal Church contains the seed of Adams' nostalgia for a church that she might not have rejected. Yet neither novel significantly illuminates the later works. They remain in the end footnotes for Adams enthusiasts.

Democracy attained considerable popularity in its day as a political roman à clef. Certainly, the characters are more subtle than the issues. Mrs. Lightfoot Lee, like a Jamesian heroine, has money and social position and a bright, fresh spirit full of ideals. She has come to Washington in quest of some great and enlightened statesman whose humble and helping consort she may become. Her cousin John Carrington falls in love with her, but he is not at all what she wants. He is a Confederate veteran who has lost all and accepted defeat, but only because he has grimly accepted the verdict of history. Despising the victors, he concentrates on making a lonely living as a lawyer in the conquerors' land, a cynical, trenchant, attractive figure, the only real man in the book, so much like Basil Ransom in Henry James's novel *The Bostonians* of the same period that one wonders if he and Adams might not have used the same model.

Madeleine Lee wants something much more effervescent than Carrington; he is cold tea to the champagne that she visualizes. At last she thinks that she has found her ideal in Senator Ratcliffe, the colossus of Illinois who is able to gain control of the administration of the new president before the latter has even taken office. It is Carrington's distasteful duty to disillusion Madeleine, and he resolutely goes about putting together the necessary proof that the senator's career has been founded on a bribe. Madeleine, convinced, flees both senator and Washington. That is the whole story.

It is flat. One might have hoped that Madeleine would at least fall in love with the villain—if only to make her decision harder—but her creator, who detested senators, could not allow this. One might also have hoped that the senator would devise an interesting defense to her charge. But he tells Madeleine that the end justifies the means, and his end is nothing but the tired old rhetorical goal used by every contemporary statesman who ever waved the bloody shirt: preservation of the union. Adams might have answered this criticism of his plot by pointing out that he was telling the simple truth. Statesmen like Senator Ratcliffe in the reconstruction era *did* dominate the scene, and men like Carrington *were* helpless to do more than record their own indignant dissent. Madeleine Lee, in flying off to Europe, has only expressed the despair of her creator at the prospect of Washington. Living a century later in not dissimilar times, should we not appreciate her position? Perhaps. But we are dealing with a novel, and novels must be concerned less with truth than the appearance of it.

Esther Dudley's choice in *Esther* is a good deal harder than Madeleine's, for she is very much in love. The story again involves a renunciation, her renunciation of a deeply religious young minister whose faith she finds she cannot share. The novel is full of their arguments and finally bogs down in the reader's inability to see why an agnostic, with a little bit of tact, could not be a perfectly good minister's wife. One is almost surprised, in the end, that the subject has not been more interesting. It cannot be only that we care less about the question of faith today. Our interest in *Anna Karenina* is not diminished by our knowing that today the heroine could have divorced her husband and married Vronski with no loss of social position. No, it is rather that Adams himself has so little sympathy for the Reverend Stephen Hazard. He makes his evangelicism ridiculous, so that one suspects that Esther may be well out of her engagement. If the man of political power in the 1870's and 1880's was a pirate, the man of God was an anachronism. As husbands went, there was not much to choose between them. Esther would have to wait twenty years and visit Chartres Cathedral, as one of Adams' adopted nieces, before she would encounter a religion that could move the hearts of men. And even then it would only be the memory of one.

There is a distinct similarity between Adams' two heroines and the heroines of Henry James's early and middle periods. Madeleine and Esther each have the impulsiveness, the charm, and the strict integrity of Isabel Archer in *The Portrait of a Lady*. It is probable that this freshness and ebullience, this happy idealism united with a stubborn, at times gooselike, refusal to compromise, was a characteristic of American girls of the period and perhaps of Marian Adams herself. It was what made them ultimately pathetic, at times even tragic. One can find analogies in the American girls of Anthony Trollope's later novels. But certainly with Adams himself, this concept reflects a deep preoccupation. All his life he was more at ease with women than men, and after Marian's death he transferred some of his dependence to Elizabeth Cameron, the beautiful wife of Senator Don Cameron of Pennsylvania. When he wrote Mrs. Cameron that he valued any dozen pages of *Esther* more than the whole of his *History*, he may have been only half serious, but he may also have been expressing an intuitive conviction that the charm of Esther Dudley was precisely what was missing from the historical work. . . .

⟨*Mont-Saint-Michel and Chartres*⟩ has always been a difficult book for librarians to classify. Should it be catalogued under travel or history or even fiction? Certainly, it purports to pass in the first category. The narrator claims that he is writing a guidebook for a niece, adoptive or actual, on a long, leisurely summer tourist trip from Brittany to Paris to Chartres. The point of view from which we take the story is the uncle's. He, of course, is Adams himself, a first-class traveler, as selective in his scholarship as he undoubtedly is in his foods and wines, with nothing to interrupt him in a happy season of poking about in Gothic cathedrals. The atmosphere of the golden age of tourism pervades the story. A generation before, and travel was all dusty roads, jolting carriages, and pot-luck inns. A few years later it would be the sharing of treasures with a million seekers and a thousand buses. But just at the turn of the century, with the advent of the automobile, for a brief delectable time, the past belonged to a few happy exquisites, who wrote big illustrated volumes such as Henry James's *Italian Hours* and Edith Wharton's *A Motor Flight through France*. The "pigs" whom Adams had seen in Brittany were easily avoided.

The reader of *Mont-Saint-Michel* soon learns that he is in the hands of no ordinary guide. The uncle disclaims any pretensions of being an architect, a historian, or a theologian; he insists on only one virtue, an indispensable one in any honest tourist: he is "seriously interested in putting the feeling back into the dead architecture where it belongs." That he succeeds in this I think no reader will dispute. Whether it is always the appropriate feeling may sometimes be in question. When it is, Adams is a great historian. When it is not, he is a great romantic.

We start in the eleventh century at Mont-Saint-Michel in Brittany just before the Norman Conquest of England. Adams' architectural plot begins with the Romanesque, the rounded arch, the age of the conquering soldier and militant priest, of the *Chanson de Roland*, an age of simple, serious, silent dignity and tremendous energy. We move through Caen to Paris and at last to Chartres and the year 1200, the time of the Gothic arch and the cult of the Virgin. This Adams sees as the finest and most intense moment of the Christian story. The chapters on the Cathedral of Chartres, on its statuary, its apses, its incomparable glass, are a remarkable lyrical achievement. Adams sees Mary as superior to the Trinity. She is what equity is to law. There is no hope for sinful men in the rigid, logical justice of Christ. He is law, unity, perfection, a closed system. But the Virgin is a woman, loving, capricious, kind, infinitely merciful. She is nature, love, chaos. The cathedral is her palace, and the most beautiful art in history is displayed there to please her. Adams makes us feel at one with the crushed crowd of kneeling twelfth-century worshipers as we lift our eyes after the miracle of the Mass to see, far above the high altar, "high over all the agitation of prayer, the passion of politics, the anguish of suffering, the terrors of sin, only the figure of the Virgin in majesty." But the chapter ends on a dry note. Moving suddenly back to his own day the uncle leaves the Virgin "looking down from a deserted heaven, into an empty church, on a dead faith."

That is the end of the architectural trip, yet the book is only half finished. Adams now traces the influence of the Virgin in literature, in contemporary history, and in theology. He offers translations of some of the versifications of her miracles; he describes the great royal ladies of the period; he conveys the sense of Mary's ambience in the world of court poems and courteous love. The emotion in these chapters begins to approach that of the naive and passionate chroniclers whom he quotes. He sternly warns us that if we do not appreciate the charm of this or that, we may as well give up trying to understand the age. Our guide has become a priest and one of Mary's own. The feeling conveyed is a unique aesthetic effect.

He does not, however, leave us in the days of Mariolatry. The priest now turns professor. In the last chapters he explains how the church was taken away from the Virgin. She was a heretic, in essence, for she denied the authority of God and asserted the greater force of woman. The theologians had to put her back in her place and build a religious philosophy that would stand up to the most unsettling questions of the logicians. In the final chapter on St. Thomas Aquinas Adams sees him building his theology as men built cathedrals: "Knowing by an enormous experience precisely where the strains were to come, they enlarged their scale to the utmost point of material endurance, lightening the load and distributing the burden until the gutters and gargoyles that seem mere ornament, and the grotesques that seem rude absurdities, all do work either for the arch or for the eye; and every inch of material, up and down, from crypt to vault, from man to God, from the universe to the atom, had its task, giving support where support was needed, or weight where concentration was felt, but always with the condition of showing conspicuously to the eye the great lines which led to unity and the curves which controlled divergence; so that, from the cross on the flèche and the keystone of the vault, down through the ribbed nervures, the columns, the windows, to the foundation of the flying buttresses far beyond the walls, one idea controlled every line; and this is true of Saint Thomas's Church as it is of Amiens Cathedral. The method was the same for both, and the result was an art marked by singular unity, which endured and served its purpose until man changed his attitude toward the universe. . . . Granted a Church, Saint Thomas's Church was the most expressive that man has made, and the great Gothic cathedrals were its most complete expression."

Is it true? Was France like that in the twelfth and thirteenth centuries? It has often been pointed out that Adams' idyllic era of true faith was actually a period of lawless strife and brigandage in which a few ambitious and secular-minded priests raised cathedrals to their own glory. Undoubtedly he oversimplified, exaggerated. His Chartres may be to cathedrals as Moby Dick is to whales. But if the religious spirit that he so brilliantly evokes in his strong sinuous prose did in fact exist, he may, by isolating it from the turmoil in which it was embedded, have come closer to the essence of his era than some more comprehensive historians.

How far Adams has traveled in his experiments with historical method may be measured by contrasting his *Gallatin* with *Mont-Saint-Michel*. The former shows the historian at his most restrained. The documents speak for the author, while in the latter the historian (or guide) propels us despotically by the elbow, allowing us to see only what appeals to his own taste (at times almost his whim), and colors the whole panorama with his violent personal distaste for his own times. But the guide is always entertaining, and the reader, one submits, may know Eleanor of Guienne and Abélard better than, in the earlier works, he knows any member of Jefferson's cabinet.

. . . He had planned the *Education* as a companion piece to *Mont-Saint-Michel*. It would present the twentieth century in contrast to the twelfth: the chaos of infinite multiplicity as opposed to Saint Thomas Aquinas' divine order. Adams had been fascinated at the Paris Exposition of 1900 by the Gallery of Machines of the Champ de Mars. This he had visited day after day to watch in entrancement the silent whirring of the great dynamos. He wrote to Hay that they ran as noiselessly and as smoothly as the planets and that he wanted to ask them, with infinite courtesy, where the hell they were going. He saw in them the tremendous, ineluctable force of science in the new century. Surely, it was the very opposite of the warm concept of the overwatching Virgin of Chartres. As his new book came to mind, it may have occurred to him in that very gallery that the narrator who would constitute the most dramatic contrast to the dynamo would be the one who was then watching it: Henry Adams himself.

He may also have been induced to put the book in the form of a memoir (in the third person) by two other factors: first, his dislike of biographies in general, coupled with the fear that he himself might one day be the victim of a hack, and, second, by his enthusiasm for Henry James's life of William Wetmore Story, a complimentary memoir, written at the request of the family, in which the author avoided the embarrassment of facing up to his subject's bad sculpture and poetry by a colorful evocation of his background, including the Boston of his origin. Adams saw much more in this than James had ever intended. He professed to find in the picture of Boston all the ignorance and innocence of a small, closed, parochial society that had been blind enough to believe that a Story could sculpt or a Sumner legislate. It gave him the point from which to start his own *Education*.

It is less the story of an education than the story of the purported failure of one. Adams contends that his family background, his schooling, even his experiences in political and diplomatic circles, in no way prepared him for life in the second half of the nineteenth century. When he and his parents returned to the United States from London in 1868, they were as much strangers in their native land, he claimed, as if they had been Tyrian traders from Gibraltar in the year 1000 B.C. But this, he should in fairness have conceded, was not so much the fault of Harvard or of Boston society, or even of the Adams family, as it was the fault of the raging speed of change in his century. Grant, the new president in 1869, was not, according to Adams, a thinking man, but a simple energy. To achieve worldly success in his era, very little in the way of education was needed. But was worldly success the only kind of success? Because a tycoon had not been educated, was education useless? Adams never convinces us that he would have been willing to scrap the least part of his own maligned education.

Having made his basic point that he was not educated by any of his supposedly educating experiences, Adams proceeds to outline the kind of quasi-education that he received through a series of disillusionments. As a boy he had regarded Senator Charles Sumner as a great statesman and friend; in later years he found him a vain and malicious old peacock. In the early London days he had been convinced that Lord Palmerston was bent on the destruction of the American union and that Gladstone favored the North; later he discovered that just the opposite was true. Friends turned out to be enemies; enemies, friends. Even in the world of art there was no certainty. No expert could tell him whether or not the supposed Raphael sketch that he had bought in London was genuine.

Adams tells the story of each disillusionment entertainingly enough, but in the illusionless world in which we live, we may find his surprise a bit naive. It does not seem to us in the least astonishing that a statesman should say one thing, intend

another, and desire a third. Self-interest is so taken for granted that we require our most eminent citizens to sell their stocks before serving in the president's cabinet, and, as for art, we should simply shrug in amusement if it turned out that the roof of the Sistine Chapel had been painted by Boldini.

Finally, in the *Education*, the "uneducated" author, on the threshold of old age, amalgamates his own laws of the sequence of human events with those of the physical sciences to deduce a "dynamic theory" of history that is not taken seriously by either scientists or historians today.

If, then, Adams' claim that he was never educated is simply a paradox for the sake of argument, if his disillusionments strike us as naive, and if his dynamic theory is without validity, wherein lies the greatness of the book? It lies, I submit, in the extraordinarily vivid sense conveyed to the reader of history being formed under his eyes, in the crystallization of the myriad shapes of the twentieth century out of the simple substance of the eighteenth. I know of no other autobiography (as I shall impenitently insist on calling it) which conveys anything like the same effect. And in no other of his writings does Adams more luminously demonstrate what Henry James called "his rich and ingenious mind, his great resources of contemplation, resignation, speculation." . . .

. . . We travel through the nineteenth century with a guide who is a good deal less detached than he claims, who is almost at times romantic, almost at times passionate. It is a unique fusion of history and memoir. We see the century growing more diverse and chaotic until it becomes terrifying, but always in the foreground, shrugging, gesticulating, chuckling, at times scolding, is the neat, bustling figure of our impatient but illuminating observer. He can stretch his imagination to any limit, but not his tolerance or his personality. He ends where he began, an aristocrat, a gentleman, a bit of a voyeur. The fixed referent of Henry Adams holds the book together even more than the constant pairing off of unity with multiplicity. At times it almost seems as if Adams himself, cool, rational, skeptical, were the one, and observed mankind, moving at a giddy rate of acceleration toward nothingness, the many. Only in the very end, when the observer disappears into the theorist and the memoir into a theory, does multiplicity at last prevail. One's trouble in reading the *Education* is that as one moves from unity to multiplicity, the story inevitably loses its character and vividness. Most of the memorable passages are from the earlier chapters. . . .

The "education" of Henry Adams might be defined as his own belated conviction that science, for all its achievements, had not resolved the basic mystery of the one and the many, the eternal question of whether the universe is a divine unity or a composite of more than one ultimate substance, a supersensuous chaos that no single theory can encompass. The only thing of which the author of *Mont-Saint-Michel* and the *Education* could feel absolutely sure was that in the twelfth century man had believed in such a unity and that in the twentieth his less fortunate descendant did not. All Adams could now see in the dark and dangerous era that lay ahead was the seemingly unintelligible interplay of forces. . . .

I believe that Adams always misconceived his principal talent. He wanted the recognition of scientists for his theories in a field where he was not equipped to make any serious contribution. The picture of Adams, the descendant of presidents, a kind of early American "Everyman," a survival from the Civil War in the day of the automobile, traveling from one end of the globe to the other in quest of the absolute, pausing before Buddhas and dynamos, has so caught the imagination of the academic community that his biography, which he wrote as well as lived, has become, so to speak, one of his works, and his most fantastic speculations the subjects of serious theses. Yet to me his primary contributions to our literature were aesthetic. He is far closer to Whitman and Melville than to Bancroft or Prescott, and he is not at all close to Einstein.

In history he went as far as could be gone on the basic presumption, later repudiated by himself, that the study of trade, diplomacy, and politics can be made to reveal the sequence of human events. No historian has unraveled with more illuminating clarity the exchange of thought in chancelleries, the effects of embargoes, and the influences of electorates on legislators and administrators. If Adams' historical writing leans to the austere, it is because he was determined not to be sidetracked by the quaint, the picturesque, the sensational, or the merely entertaining. Although he denied this from time to time, as when he wrote his publishers that he had given the public a "full dose" of Andrew Jackson because of its "undue interest" in that soldier and statesman, his denial is not convincing, for nobody could think that the portrait of Jackson in the *History* is more than a minimal sketch.

Adams gave up writing American history because he did not believe, after long consideration of what he had done, that he had made any really significant contribution to the long quest for cause and effect. Yet, when he turned from the austerity of historical writing to the looser and more copious field of the novel, he discovered that he did not have the kind of imagination that operated much more easily without limitations of fact. The historian is only too evident in *Democracy* and *Esther*. Both tales are confined to the bare bones of their situations. There is almost no detail of background, and the characters are analyzed only insofar as necessary for us to understand their plotted actions. As in seventeenth-century French fiction, we are confined to essentials. Adams may have considered that in depicting his senator as a monster he was allowing himself a riot of indulgence, but Ratcliffe is given the smallest possible crime to justify his classification as villain.

It is interesting in this respect to contrast his mind with that of Henry James, a lifelong friend whose fiction Adams consistently admired. No two minds could have been more different. As Leon Edel has pointed out, Adams always sought a generalization while James sought to particularize. Adams wanted to know the law of the universe, while James was studying the effect of Paris on a single American soul. Yet each man appreciated the other. Adams loved the subtlety of James's characterizations, and James admired the sweep of Adams' reaching. James, however, would not have approved of Adams' experimentation with the novel form. To him the art of fiction was only for the totally dedicated. We know that he read *Democracy* and said of it that, despite the coarseness of its satire, it was so good that it was a pity it was not better, but he did not know that Adams had written it.

Adams did not find the medium of expression best adapted to his talents until he left the world behind and went to the Pacific with John La Farge. In Tahiti he explored the reconciliation of instinct with logic in his history of the island. There was no even seeming sequence of events to be derived from economics or diplomacy. He had to find it in legends and customs inextricably tied up with the emotions which, as a historian in the older sense, he had tried to eliminate from the field of observed phenomena. The experiment was not a success, but it was a rehearsal of what he was next to do when he came to the Gothic cathedrals of France. "Putting the feeling back" in the stones of Chartres was his goal there, and he

attained it. He then proceeded to expand this goal, in the *Education*, to putting the feeling back into his own life and into the contemporary history of the United States and wrote one of the monuments of American literature.

It is not to denigrate the earlier work of Adams to say that *Mont-Saint-Michel* and the *Education* represent the finest flowering of his mind. The biographies and the *History* are not only valuable in themselves; they were indispensable preliminaries. But one may regret that Adams did not more fully recognize his own major phase. He was always determined to be valued for something other than his best.

The great bulk of his correspondence, filling three volumes, shows this. Some of the letters, particularly those from the Pacific, are as brilliant and evocative as John La Farge's water colors of the same subject. But through the ones that deal with social and political life the shrill, constantly repeated strain of dramatic and rhetorical pessimism becomes a great bore. One wonders why Adams thought that it would divert his correspondents. And then, too, he seems to take a perverse pleasure in *not* giving descriptions of people and events that one knows he could describe incomparably. Perhaps it was because all his friends knew the same people and events, but to the modern reader it is like reading Saint-Simon with the characterizations removed. If Adams had only had a correspondent on the moon to whom he had had to give an impression of our planet, a niece in space, he might have been the greatest letter writer in American literature.

His last book, *The Life of George Cabot Lodge*, was published in 1911. It was a memoir that he had written about the senator's son, "Bay," a poet who had died prematurely two years before. The memoir had been written at the request of Senator Lodge and given to him to publish or not as he pleased. It is a tactful and charming piece in which the narrative is largely used to string together quotations from the young man's letters. This is not because Adams was embarrassed by a task that he could not well refuse. He enormously liked Bay Lodge and evidently admired his poetry. But he was by nature too reticent for this kind of eulogy. Perhaps it was just as well. The letters reveal a young man whose talent must have been more in his flaming good looks and enthusiasm than in any originality of imagination or poetic aptitude. Bay Lodge's idealism and aspiration seem to have charmed the aging Adams. They went to the theater together in Paris and discussed ideas for Lodge's plays. They formed together a fanciful political party called the Conservative Christian Anarchists. Lodge was a rebel against Boston society, but he expressed his rebellion largely by appearance, in the manner of some youths today. He wore a huge black hat and gold watch around his neck and let his hair grow long. At least he was going to *look* like an artist. Perhaps he fascinated Adams because he was so exactly his opposite. Adams always dressed and acted the conservative, but his black frock coat covered the heart of a poet.

JAMES M. COX

From "Autobiography and America"

Virginia Quarterly Review, Spring 1971, pp. 269–76

V

It is a long way from Thoreau and Whitman to Henry Adams, largely because Adams himself sought to make the space in time as wide as possible. Yet differently as he saw and created his life from theirs, like them he eschews the confessional element in autobiography. He does not remember, explain, or defend his past in the manner of Mill and Newman anymore than he wishes to confess, reveal, and justify it in the manner of Rousseau, but, like Franklin and Thoreau, he makes use of it and makes it useful. His too is a model life, but not a paradigm like Franklin's or a challenge like Thoreau's, for his whole notion of a model life is that of a mannekin—a figure in which clothing, outline, and pattern are everything, the life nothing but plaster and sawdust, an elusive and ironic joke at the center of education, which is at once history, the thought into which life has died, and art, the narrative upon which life is spent. Being an historian, Adams saw life as history; being an autobiographer, he knew he had to make life art. Being these and being an Adams too, he dared to identify his history with that of his country. Comprehending these strands of being in a single narrative, he left an autobiography which drew life from the autobiography that had gone before him and abundantly gave meaning back to it, as I shall try to demonstrate.

There are two striking facts of form in Adams's *Education*. First, it is written in the third person and therefore guarantees the possibility of completeness. Second, it has a gap in the center, a vacuum of twenty years about which Adams hardly speaks. We know—and such a fact of form forces us to wonder if we don't know—what happened during those twenty years. He taught at Harvard (he touches upon this fact) and was therefore not a student of life. He wrote history (he alludes to this at points along his way) and was thus an historian instead of being a part of history. And he married, only to experience the tragedy of his wife's suicide (he alludes only once to that harrowing event, telling of watching in Rock Creek Cemetery the people who came to see St. Gaudens' great sculpture of grief which monumentalized his wife's grave). These three acts are the silence in the midst of life, and the autobiography which surrounds them is the act of mind converting them into their opposite. The teacher is converted into the student Henry Adams; the historian is converted into the victim and expression of history. And the grief-stricken husband is converted into the pleasure seeker of the mind whose whole act of play is to convert his past into a third person in an act of joyful suicide.

To see these paradoxes is to begin to grasp the consequences of Adams's third person narration, consequences which Adams embraces with almost dismaying enthusiasm. Thoreau had retained the "I" but in order to achieve a completed self was forced into the synechdochic strategy of making a part stand for the whole. Adams however, by converting himself into the third person was able to treat himself not as character—for characters are in fiction and drama, not in autobiography—but as history. The consequences of such a strategy are enormous. For if the self is truly history, then it is somehow past, and Adams would become merely the biographer of himself. Yet Adams is not a biographer but an autobiographer, and of all things the *Education* is not, one is surely biography. It is rather a division of the self into two parts, two poles—a past and a present—in which the present self generates the past self as history. The new Henry Adams, the present generative consciousness, which in conventional historical terms grew out of the past, is by virtue of Adams's inversion actually releasing and attracting the old Henry Adams (he would be the young Adams in conventional terms) toward his source. Adams fully realizes these inversions by means of a style which can best be described as a series of paradoxes riding upon a narrative current.

The new Adams, the present Adams, who is as much the source as the end of the past, constantly exposes the descent of the old Adams, who, born too late into history from a line of Presidents and fated for success and power, steadily failed. The old Adams, always unprepared for contingency, is drawn forward—not recorded or chronicled—through the resistance of history toward the moment of the present which is the hidden "I" that he can never reach. That is the fate of Adams's form which casts the self as history. The old Adams's approach to the present is as a victim of forces beyond his control, a child amid theory, politics, technology, and above all, accelerating history. Everything he is made to learn merely unprepares him for the past through which he is drawn. He is the great grandson and the grandson of Presidents only to feel himself cast aside from the sources of power; he goes to Harvard only to discover himself a fool in Europe; he faces Civil War as a loyal Union man only to discover that the real treason was the betrayal of his father by Charles Sumner, the most trusted family friend; he goes to England as secretary for his father the ambassador in an effort to secure the balance of power they think England holds only to discover that the Civil War has already shifted the power to America and that England by remaining neutral has actually fallen behind history; he learns evolution only to return to America and find Grant in the White House; he attempts to expose the economic scandals of the Grant era only to find himself in touch with the energy of capital—which defies all his calculations; he teaches medieval history at Harvard only to discover his total ignorance of all history; he writes the history of the early years of the Republic only to recognize that the ideas of humanistic history are completely negated by the laws of physical energy. And so at last he attempts to learn the laws of science in an effort to plot force and energy in time, thereby making the art of history a science possessing predictive force, only to realize that acceleration is the law of history. Having made his predictions and seen the law of acceleration, he steps aside.

This series of belated recognitions constitutes the history and the failure of the old Adams, but it is failure generated by the polarity of the new Henry Adams in relation to the old. Indeed, the new Adams is literally *educating* the old Adams, giving the title an active and present sense which is often overlooked. Moreover, he is educating him all the time, at every instant of the narrative. For the education is nothing less than the act and vision whereby the new Adams ironically objectifies the old as a victim of history. If the old Adams is being educated by the new, the discovery is not simply one of gloomy personal failure but of the failure of all the history he has lived through—the dissolution of an old order of causation into a new energy. Thus the nineteenth century dissolves into the twentieth, exposing in the process that the men of power—thinkers, politicians, and diplomats—were not simply wrong but did not even know what they were doing, were indeed victims of the power and drift of history. Their ignorance was but one more mass of energy for the historian to measure in terms of its force.

As the old Henry Adams is attracted toward the new, his life is taken, not as a loss or grief but as a conversion, and not the conversion of confessional form—the conversion of man into God as in Augustine, or into feeling as in Rousseau—but a conversion into historical force, so that autobiographical narrative does not displace history, as in Franklin, but becomes an ironic vision of history. The moment of conversion is, as everyone knows, Adams's vision of the dynamo in the gallery of machines at the Paris exposition of 1900, six hundred years after Dante's vision of Beatrice. The dynamo is the beautiful objectification of Adams's act of form, for it comes into being at precisely the moment when the old Henry Adams has been attracted to the present source of his energy. True to his form at this moment when he envisions the dynamo as the end of the old Adams, the new Adams is able to see an opposite force, not forward in time but backward in history; he sees the Virgin.

These then become the poles of past and future which the old and new Adams generate as they meet at the beginning of twentieth century; they are at the same time the poles of energy which constitute Adams's conversion, for they make possible his dynamic theory and act of history. Because it is at once theory (an analytic formulation about past and future) and act (a literal attraction of the old Adams to the source which has generated him) it can become a genuine vision, but a vision in Adamic not in Augustinian terms, for it is a conversion of the self not into divine but into historical lines of force. That is why Adams's vision of the future is not so much prophetic as it is speculative.

Happily for us, the poles of dynamo and Virgin are also beautifully conclusive as a vision of autobiography and America. For Adams's discovery of the dynamo takes us directly back to our point of departure. After all, Franklin not only invented American autobiography; he also discovered—fathered might be the better term—electricity, and those Promethean acts bind him deeply to Adams's form and substance. More than that, there was an old family score for Adams to settle, and though Adams was terribly ironic about himself and his progenitors, he *was* an Adams through and through and had a way of dealing with the Jeffersons and Randolphs who had thwarted his great grandfather. Franklin in Paris during the American Revolution had driven John Adams to distraction with his social ease, detachment, and wit. While John Adams toiled, Franklin seemed to play and yet reap all the praise. The whole miserable contrast so piqued Adams that he confided his exasperation to his Journal. So in disclosing the dynamo as the essence of America and the future which would be American, Henry Adams was settling old scores even as he was being utterly true to his form. If Franklin had seen autobiography as self-generation, Adams would show the end of self-generation. Instead of seeing his life as the rise from obscurity to prominence, Adams saw it as the descent from prominence into obscurity and utter posthumous silence. Instead of treating life as a chronicle of success, Adams showed it as both the history of failure and the failure of history. Thus at the moment of his conversion, the old Adams feels like worshiping the dynamo, but the new Adams generates the opposite of the dynamo—the Virgin of a deeper, more primal past. For what autobiography as self-generation perforce left out was woman, the force which had moved the medieval world in Adams's illuminated vision of the past, and yet the force which had been rendered irrelevant by American autobiography and revolution. There were no women in Franklin's world of the self-invented self—only the wife as helpmeet in the most practical sense and as a practical object for excess sexual energy. There were no women at all in Thoreau. Although there was a feminine principle in Whitman, he hermaphroditically absorbed it as he absorbed Kanada and Missouri and Montana.

And so Adams delightfully chose the Virgin, not at all as a converted Catholic, possibly as atonement and love for the wife who had killed herself, certainly as a pleasure seeker in history where he could be a tourist to his heart's desire.

All this is much, but it is not all. Adams declared an end to education, autobiography, and history in 1905, the year John Hay concluded the treaty between Russia and Japan. That marked the end of Adams's old eighteenth-century provincial America, the America of Franklin's invention. That America had moved from peripheral and provincial entity to become *the*

treaty-making power in the West, and thus a line of force to meet the inertia of Russia and China in the East. Thus, the city which had drawn his ancestors from Quincy and Boston and which Adams, having failed to occupy as President, had occupied as historian was now the center of power in the West—the point from which Adams could let the energy of his mind run its own lines of force into the past and future.

But there is still more. 1905 was the date of Einstein's equation and the beginning of all that it has meant. Though Adams may not have known the equation, who, after reading "The Education," can say that he could not have imagined it? Even to ask the question is to answer it, for the fact is that Adams's *Education* is the heroic act of the imagination unifying history and science in an act of mind and art. To read it is to recognize the genuine pathos of C. P. Snow's cry of alarm, some fifty years later, at the perilous division between the two cultures of science and the humanities. Whatever its content, the form of Snow's "scientific" vision is, like his forms of fiction, still in the age of Howells. Adams had not only seen and measured the division between the two cultures but had imagined them as the poles of attractive force which, converting the inertia of life and history into energy of mind, would transform the self into a unifying consciousness—a third force in a new magnetic field. That is why his book is genuinely true to its title, remaining to this day an education for *any* twentieth-century reader. Of all American literature, it alone deserves to be required reading for all *students*, which is far from saying that it should be required reading for everyone or that it is the "best" American autobiography.

HARVEY GROSS
From *The Contrived Corridor*
1971, pp. 20–31

. . . he found himself lying in the Gallery of Machines at the Great Exposition of 1900, his historical neck broken by the sudden irruption of forces totally new.

(The Education of Henry Adams)

I

Nietzsche was little more than a name to Henry Adams; we have no record that Adams knew the meditation "Of the Use and Disadvantage of History"—or that Adams ever read a line of Nietzsche.[1] Yet doubtless he would have recognized himself, with his usual ironic self-deprecation, as one of Nietzsche's epigones: a latecomer into the world of Steam and Democracy, congenitally gray-headed and ill-equipped to endure frantic years of being a "helpless victim," waiting to be sent "he knew not where."[2] In his calmer moments Adams tells us he was a "consenting, contracting party"[3] to his life and career; but more often the voice of *The Education* and his letters assumes the inflections of a blackly humorous observer and suffering target of historical forces.

It is this persona, hugely present, that shall be the Henry Adams of my consideration. He appears as witness and victim, as malign critic of his age, and, of course, as prophet. This persona is projected large over recent literary discussion, and Adams emerges as something of a culture-hero. As a culture-hero I intend to regard him. I make no attempt to fathom the other Adams who lurks behind the irritable temper and bitter self-mockery of the letters and the mannered diffidence and outrageously coy understatements of *The Education*. Adams endured terrible suffering and often gave terrible expression to his suffering; he sustained the disappointments of his personal life with admirable stoicism—but he also gave the age in which he lived holy and particular hell.

One tack is to regard Adams as an American Nietzsche. Such comparison is voluntaristic and rhetorical; Adams had neither Nietzsche's powerful gift of psychological insight nor his poetic imagination. Nor did Adams have the explosive effect Nietzsche had; he did not influence an entire generation and help bring his prophecies to fulfillment. But Adams's personal development, his temperament and style, his current relevance, all touch on Nietzsche's life and work. They both served academic tenures. Both did brilliant work in the historical disciplines and both declared, with passionate vehemence, that they were spoiled by an excess of historical knowledge. Both became polemicists against their age. Adams precariously controlled vast currents of interior violence; like Nietzsche, he frequently vented his despair and frustration in extreme statements. From extremity Nietzsche passed into insanity and finally silence. Adams's later years were disfigured by a hysterical advocacy of violence and pathological anti-Semitism. Both hated their century and the supposed cultural squalor, the aesthetic deprivation of democratic existence. Both predicted (and hoped) that the civilization they so hated would be destroyed in some unnamable cataclysm. Both perfected a literary style of epigrammatic brilliance; reading their books is a journey into mined territory. We are blown up by astonishing insights and prophecies which long ago turned out true.

A temperamental similarity shows in their aggressive literary style—the style of those whom Edwin Muir calls "pseudo men-of-action."[4] Pseudo men-of-action—Carlyle, Neitzsche, Spengler, and Adams—never leave the study but with hot polemical zeal cheer loudly the brutal behavior of others. They live in a dream of action and history. In his unbuttoned moments Adams displays a ferocious taste for vicarious violence. His letters to Elizabeth Cameron on the Dreyfus Affair reveal him a two-fisted partisan of the anti-Dreyfusards and a delighted spectator of the Paris riots: "But Zola howled; and the Bourse actually fought—Jews against Gentiles—till the police came in. A good day's work! and rioting too in Havana! and a new outbreak in India! *Tiens! ça marche!* One can't imagine larks like this every day, to be sure . . ."[5]

I am aware of Adams's heavy-handed ambivalence. He knows and does not know it is cruel to enjoy violence; he cannot resist taking a small boy's pleasure in observing the world proceed to blow itself up. He cannot resist (to cite Yvor Winters) the temptation "to be witty rather than intelligent."[6] On such matters as "the antisemitic ravings of Drumont"[7] or the innocence of "the howling Jew Dreyfus"[8] Adams prefers irony to understanding, wisecracks to humanity. Adams became a victim of his own irony—that aggressive defense against the misfortunes of his life and the alarming developments in his country, in the world of burgeoning scientific development, and in international affairs. He would not avert his gaze; he was repelled by the excesses he noted and analyzed, fascinated by the enormities he predicted. Irony allowed him to come to terms with the raging disorders of the outer world and the inner world of his own personality—which, in its perverse way, yearned for the chaos it abhorred.

Like Nietzsche, Adams became a critic and moralist of knowledge. He was a trained and skillful historian and spent long years working at his profession. His instinct and passion for order led him back to medieval Europe which he envisioned as a single culture with the Blessed Virgin as presiding female deity. This vision of a homogeneous Middle Ages is celebrated in his most serene attempt at historical reconstruction, *Mont-Saint-Michel and Chartres*. Adams does not seek the "truth" about the Middle Ages; indeed, he admits "The twelfth and thirteenth centuries, studied in the pure light of political economy, are insane." Rather, he sees the thirteenth century through the great rose window at Chartres and in the light streaming from the Virgin. The unity he discovers exists in carefully selected details, in the delightful fiction that the sexual energy emanating from Our Lady brought ultimate meaning into the chaos of medieval life.

Mont-Saint-Michel and Chartres is a beautiful and touching effort to see pattern in the life of the past. But in the shadowed world of the later nineteenth century, Adams painfully discovers that historical knowledge is without pattern or significance, that history is no longer knowledge but the brute violence of irrational energies. History is not the poetic evocation of architecture " . . . and the last and greatest deity of all, the Virgin. . . ." History is the Dynamo shocking modern men and their society into near insensibility; our guiding trope for this belief is given in Chapter XXV of *The Education:*

> Satisfied that the sequence of men led to nothing and that the sequence of their society could lead no further . . . while the mere sequence of thought was chaos, he turned at last to the sequence of force; and thus it happened that, after ten years' pursuit, he found himself lying in the Gallery of Machines at the Great Exposition of 1900, his historical neck broken by the sudden irruption of forces totally new.

Adams rejects even the possibility of historical knowledge, for "the mere sequence of thought was chaos. . . ." But Adams's world was experiencing vast and terrible changes; *something* must be behind the decadence of the French aristocracy, the skulduggery of bankers and politicians, the disastrous financial panics which threatened to undermine the capital holdings of the Adams family. History may be unfathomable; historical process, however, is real and terrifying. Adams no longer regarded history as the informed and informing memory of man; history became History, the Powerhouse of Change, and was now invested with metaphysical significance. Adams felt he must understand not men, not events, not ideas but the dynamics of an inscrutable process.

His final, bleak hope was to discover historical "laws" based on stop-press scientific information. The posthumously published *The Degradation of the Democratic Dogma* expounds, in crude and confused analogic terms, a supposed "scientific" theory of history. The theory founders on the rocks of stubborn monism; on Adams's inability or unwillingness to differentiate between history and nature—between the world of matter and the world of men and ideas; and on Adams's desperate need for certainty and immediate answers to complex problems. Adams urges the discovery of "historical law":

> You may be sure that four out of five serious students of history who are living today have, in the course of their work, felt that they stood on the brink of a great generalization that would reduce all history under a law as clear as the laws which govern the material world . . . The law was certainly there, and as certainly was in places actually visible, to be touched and handled, as though it were a law of chemistry or physics. No teacher with a spark of imagination or with an idea of scientific method can have helped dreaming of the immortality that would be achieved by the man who should successfully apply Darwin's method to the facts of human history.[9]

Two long essays, "A Letter to American Teachers of History" and "The Rule of Phase Applied to History," elaborate the questionable thesis that history may be subsumed under natural science. The essays display dilettante scientism and incredible analogic gymnastics; one quotation may serve to illustrate Adams's method: ". . . the historical inquirer or experimenter . . . may assume, as his starting point, that Thought is a historical substance, analogous to an electric current, which obeyed the laws—whatever they are—of Phase. The hypothesis is not extravagant."[10] Adams wishes a predictive science of history; as the argument unwinds we discover The Rule of Phase—indeed all of Adams's theory of history—is not the formulation of scientific law but its radical opposite: thinly veiled prophetic utterance. "The law of phase," the law of inverse squares, the second law of thermodynamics—all of which figure in Adams's discourse—strike us as the familiar types and symbols of biblical prophecy:

> Signs are taken for wonders. "We would see a sign!"
> The word within a word, unable to speak a word,
> Swaddled in darkness.

An earlier essay, "The Tendency of History" (also included in *The Degradation of the Democratic Dogma*), is more restrained. Adams is ambivalent toward knowledge that portends a dismal future. He recognizes the self-fulfilling nature of prophecy and its peculiar ability to bring about exactly the catastrophes it warns against. Because his new "science of history" sees the certain downfall of traditional culture, Adams moves back from such knowledge. The world is not ready to hear about the triumph of communism and the overthrow of property. "Would society as now constituted tolerate the open assertion of a necessity which should affirm its approaching overthrow?"[11]

Adams hedges his belief in such a necessity. "The Tendency of History" was officially addressed to the American Historical Association and it sings the qualified music of academic caution. But in his letters and the posthumous *Education*, as a private party or a voice from the grave, Adams is hardly restrained about the decadence he everywhere sees. He reads Max Nordau's sensational *Entartung (Degeneration)*, a journalistic product of the *fin de siècle*, and writes to Charles Milnes Gaskell, "The other day I thought I saw myself, but run mad and howling. I took up a book without noticing its title particularly and read a few pages. Then vertigo seized me, for I thought I must be inventing a book in a dream."[12] He encourages his brother Brooks to write *The Law of Civilization and Decay*, but carefully disassociates himself; he asks his "idiot brother"[13] to strike his name from the dedication page and declares, "I do not care to monkey with a dynamo."[14] Adams feels there is nothing to be gained in openly telling society what lies in wait.

Adams lived long enough to have the dubious satisfaction of knowing his insights and instincts were correct. The outbreak of the First World War came as a prophecy confirmed and he felt his theories were vindicated. Bernard Berenson, a frequent target for Adams's tirades, wrote him in 1914: "I trust that you are satisfied at last and that all your pessimistic hopes have been fulfilled."[15] Adams did not live to see the end of the war; symbolically enough, he died in the midst of the cataclysm he had so long predicted. Six months after his death came the publication of *The Education of Henry Adams*. With *The Education* Adams gradually emerged as a major figure among those intellectuals who sensed the direction of change and calculated its devastations.

Adams's restlessness, his neurotic scrupulosity, his frenzied energy directed toward forcing answers from a silent cosmos suggest that he succumbed to the irrationalism and anarchy he so feared. He was deeply horrified at the break-up of the old order; he consoled himself with the intensity of his

nihilistic utterances and "Tory anarchism." From one angle of vision, his theory of history appears a job of massive rationalization, an undertaking to justify his unsuccess. Henry Adams never lived in the White House, as did his grandfather and great-grandfather; History and its mysterious energies flowed against him. Adams's theory of history, with all its noise and doom, appears vindictive and personal. We are tempted to confute his theory in a polemical spirit: Adams, not getting the world on his own terms, consigns it to Hell.

From another angle of vision, Adams's characterization of historical energy is of crucial importance. The Dynamo and Virgin make no contribution to the philosophy of history; they provide metaphors for the literary imagination and images of new, unfathomable forces in politics and society. Symptomatic of an emerging mood, they suggest that human behavior is based not on logical endeavor but on instinct and unconscious and pre-conscious motivations. Adams takes his place with Freud and Nietzsche, Bergson and Sorel, and the other new men of the early twentieth century who were rediscovering the irrational component of human thought and action.

II

> The proper study of mankind is woman . . .

Nietzsche's most celebrated parable dramatizes a madman crying out the death of God through the marketplace of the modern world.[16] Opposed to the dead God is the living Dionysus, Nietzsche himself, asserting a radical doctrine of creativity against the life-destroyers of the nineteenth century. The aging Henry Adams, "lying in the Gallery of Machines at the Great Exposition of 1900, his historical neck broken by the sudden irruption of forces totally new," is an equally dramatic image of the modern existential agony. Opposed to the Dynamo and its pitiless rays of energy was the Virgin, Adams's beloved life symbol, *his* image of the creative principle. Adams's Virgin is no theological abstraction but wholly flesh and blood, maternal and sexual. Adams identifies Her with the divine patroness of Lucretius's *De Rerum Natura*:

> Aeneadum genetrix, hominum divumque voluptas
> Alma Venus . . .

A wit summed up Santayana's ambivalent relationship to Roman Catholicism in this ironic credo: "There is no God and Mary is His Mother." Adams might have similarly expressed his idiosyncratic Mariolatry: "God has died and his Mother is my mistress."

Adams's fondness for the Virgin expresses a very high estimation of women and a personal susceptibility. He is most attractive in his excited and tender responsiveness to female sexuality. His letters from Samoa and Tahiti are suffused with an erotic awareness that edges close to pornography—if we adhere closely to standards current in Adams's day. Certainly the delight Adams shows in female nakedness is hardly expected from one who "brought up among the Puritans knew that sex was sin."

Adams came to think otherwise. He castigated American life for its prudish refusal to accept the joy and use the power of sexual experience; he recognized, long before D. H. Lawrence and Leslie Fiedler, the unhealthy sexlessness of classic American literature. American life was symptomatic; the problem was European, perhaps worldwide. Sexual vitality and creative energy were drying up at the wellsprings of civilization. And the desiccation of sexual life withered the religious impulse. Christianity died as the power of womanly influence diminished before masculine assault. "At times, the historian would have been almost willing to maintain that the man had overthrown the Church chiefly because it was feminine."[17]

The Virgin, Alma Venus, no longer stood at the world's center; no lines of force emanated from modern woman. The loss of the female principle was a profound cultural deprivation and a grave spiritual sickness.

Adams saw civilization maintained at too severe a cost. The modern world had technology and democracy, widening urbanization and increasing financial affluence. For these gifts of progress men paid an overwhelming psychic price. The competitive anxieties of industrial life subverted man's sexuality: "He could not run his machine and a woman too; he must leave her, even though his wife, to find her own way, and all the world saw her trying to find her way by imitating him."[18] A new race of women workers crowded factories and offices; the birth rate declined rapidly from Victorian plentitude. Adams saw that woman's identity suffered confusion; masculinity and femininity required new definitions and the act of love acquired meanings outside the sphere of children and family. He envisioned a sterile world of sexless men and unhappy, frustrated women. The men worshipped the Dynamo; Adams himself had offered blasphemous prayers: "Before the end, one began to pray to it; inherited instinct taught the natural expression of man before silent and infinite force."[19] Woman, isolated and driven, denied her sex by unmorally asserting it ("the American woman was oftener surprised at finding herself regarded as sexual");[20] by competing with men; or by entering the abyss of mental dislocation. Woman, severed from traditional stabilities, gained "equality" with her tormentor and quickly earned the privilege of sharing man's self-conscious anguish.

We need only to recall the impotent men and hysterical women of modern literature, avatars of the wounded Fisher King and abandoned Isolde, to find validation for Adams's anxieties. The Fisher King and Hyacinth Girl of *The Waste Land*, Clifford and Connie Chatterley, Jake Barnes and Lady Brett, Detlev Spinell and Gabriele Klöterjahn (of Thomas Mann's *Tristan*) are sexual cripples: sensitive, injured men who cannot make love; neurotic women, unsatisfied in both deprivation and excess. The loss of the female principle harrows Eliot's vision of urban despair, blackens the towns and landscapes of D. H. Lawrence's prophetic novels, and desolates the mountain refuges and Venetian seascapes of Hemingway and Mann. Failure in love is attributed to bourgeois brutality and insensitivity, to a mechanized, impersonal social order, and to the sickening catastrophe of world war. "That dirty war," the sympathetic *poule* remarks to Jake Barnes when he tells her he was hurt in the war. History frustrates the life-giving act of sex.

Virgin and Dynamo have often been remarked a grotesque antithesis. "The two symbols . . . ," Austin Warren tells us, "are not parallel."[21] The Dynamo is a mechanic fallacy, a perversely modern development of the romantic pathetic fallacy. Nature is no longer anthropomorphic, displaying human feeling and shedding human tears. Rather, nature and man become mechanized like those birds and beasts in animated cartoons who stop with a shrieking of brakes and fly with the noise of airplanes. Adams views history as he views the great machine of the universe noisily running down according to the second law of thermodynamics. But the trouble is not in the universe but in ourselves. Dynamo and Virgin are emblematic of human irrational energies; Adams finds History and Women equally unfathomable, impervious to understanding and incapable of explanation. The trouble resides underground, below conscious levels. Adams never brings to explicit formulation that the Dynamo and Virgin might represent the eternal polarities of destruction and creation, the human aggressive instinct and the human capacity for regeneration. Dynamo and Virgin resemble Freud's immortal antagonists,

Thanatos and Eros. And Adams must have suspected, as Freud did toward the end of his life, that the "heavenly powers" of destruction and creation originate at the same dark center of the human soul.

III

Adams never suggests a reconciliation of Dynamo and Virgin. He mentions no possibility of a synthesis which might combine and recombine the antagonist forces. The energies are disparate, remote from each other in time and in mental space; they are equally remote as substances and causes. The Virgin was medieval, human, female, compassionate; the Dynamo is modern, mechanical, mindless, destructive. The Virgin was real substance; her work is that of Eros, "builder of cities." The Dynamo is that metaphysical monster, History; its work is annihilation. Between Dynamo and Virgin there can be no rapprochement, no possibility for fruitful conflict. Virgin and Dynamo have polar attributes, but they do not, cannot, interact. The power of the Virgin ran down and her influence died with the emergence, during the Renaissance, of the modern world. The power of the Dynamo is accelerating according to "the law of inverse squares" and will destroy us all. This power is curiously mortal, an emanation of Adams's own dissolving personality. He identified, in his intensely personal way, the end of his own life with the end of history. (And it might not be irrelevant to note that the chief prophets of cataclysmic philosophies of history—Carlyle, Spengler, Nietzsche, and Adams himself—were all childless men. Those who have not given hostages to Fortune can speculate with some comfort—and perhaps satisfaction—that the world will end with their deaths.)

Adams's view of history is anti-dialectical and linear. Unlike Hegel, who saw history as an immortal interchange of decay and growth, decline and progress, Adams saw steady decline toward ultimate chaos. Again unlike Hegel, Adams made no distinction between history and nature. Caught up in the Darwinism and Comtism of his age, he made a desperate subsumption of history under physics. Man and universe, action and thought, material cause and spiritual effect were lumped together as operating under the same putative law. History, nature, and human personality merged into a single substance impelled by the same energy. If the sun was destined to cool in two million (or billion) years, this to Adams was an omen of imminent historical disaster. If the laws of thermodynamics foretold a diminution of available energy in the universe, this to Adams meant certain historical catastrophe. Hegel noted that history is Spirit (human thought and action) moving through the realm of time; nature is "the development of the Idea in Space." Adams does not discriminate between nature, which displays cyclical, recurrent, and essentially predictable processes; and history, which displays ever renewed, ever different, cumulative, and spiraling processes.

Adams's linear eschatology and his analogical magic with the mathematics of doom issue from the Puritan imagination. Adams's involuted, cranky sensibility, which often felt the events of history as personal outrages (or the machinations of the Jews), is a burden of New England character. His was, as Austin Warren points out, a New England conscience, fussily preoccupied with the state of the soul and dedicated to the pursuit of self-improvement. Adams does not escape Calvinist predestinarianism and its intoxication with types and symbols. Nor does Adams escape the New England agony of knowing that men are ordained to walk a certain path yet nevertheless must bear personal responsibility and endure the torments of guilt. Adams, like Gerontion, is caught in the Dynamo of historical process and confronted by History's bewildering power to confuse moral issues:

These tears are shaken from the wrath-bearing tree.

The power of History will destroy us; historical knowledge is at best fragmentary, incomplete; at worst, misleading. Caught in the process, deceived by knowledge: such was Henry Adams's dilemma. All the more agonizing was his emotional acceptance but intellectual rejection of the Christian solution to the historical riddle. He understood and approved the great medieval synthesis of religion, high culture, and common life—the supposed unity of thought and feeling which pervaded the age of the Gothic cathedrals. The intricate logic and aesthetic balance of medieval theology resolved the historical dilemma: history was a testing of souls in this world; its purpose and meaning became known in The City of God. But for Adams God had died with the advent of the modern world; and history, nature, and individual personality moved in a straight line to their destined conclusion.

Notes

1. Adams mentions Nietzsche only once in passing in *The Education*, not at all in the *Letters*.
2. *The Education of Henry Adams* (New York: The Modern Library, 1931), p. 109.
3. *The Education*, p. 4.
4. See Edwin Muir, *Essays on Literature and Society* (Cambridge, Mass., 1965), p. 126.
5. Letter to Elizabeth Cameron, January 13, 1898. *Letters of Henry Adams, 1892–1918*. Edited by W. C. Ford (Boston and New York, 1938), p. 145.
6. See Yvor Winters' *In Defense of Reason* (Denver, 1947), p. 398.
7. *Letters*, to Elizabeth Cameron, July 27, 1896, p. 110.
8. *Letters*, to Elizabeth Cameron, September 5, 1899, p. 238.
9. *The Degradation of the Democratic Dogma* (New York, 1920), p. 127.
10. Ibid., p. 283.
11. Ibid., p. 130.
12. *Letters*, to Charles Milnes Gaskell, June 20, 1895, p. 71.
13. Henry Adams refers to his brother Brooks as "my idiot brother" (with ironic affection, of course) in a letter to Elizabeth Cameron, September 25, 1894. *Letters*, p. 57.
14. *Letters*, to Brooks Adams, June 5, 1895, p. 68.
15. Quoted in Ernest Samuels, *Henry Adams: The Major Phase* (Cambridge, Mass., 1964), p. 554.
16. In *Die Fröhliche Wissenschaft* (Hanser Verlag, Vol. II), pp. 126–128.
17. *The Education*, p. 446.
18. Ibid., p. 445.
19. Ibid., p. 380.
20. Ibid., p. 447.
21. Austin Warren, *The New England Conscience* (Ann Arbor, 1966), p. 178.

Léonie Adams

1899–

Léonie Fuller Adams was born in Brooklyn on December 9, 1899. She was already a prolific poet by the time she graduated from Barnard College in 1922; her Barnard poems were collected in her first book, *Those Not Elect* (1925). From 1922 to 1926 she worked for the Wilson Publishing Company, and from 1926 to 1928 for the Metropolitan Museum of Art. The publication of *High Falcon* in 1929 established her reputation as a lyric poet with a rare talent for communicating metaphysical joy.

After studying in Europe on a Guggenheim fellowship, she took a post as English professor at New York University, which she held from 1930 to 1932. Since then, she has taught at Sarah Lawrence (1933–34), Bennington (1935–37 and 1941–44), New Jersey College for Women (1946–48), and Columbia (1947–1968). She also served as consultant in poetry and fellow of letters for the Library of Congress (1948–1955).

Adams published few poems between *This Measure* in 1933 and *Poems: A Selection* in 1954. The latter won her the Harriet Monroe Poetry Award and the Bollingen Prize. Since then she has published occasionally in magazines, and has translated the work of François Villon. She was married to the critic William Troy from 1933 to his death in 1961. She lives in New Milford, Connecticut.

Miss Adams's first volume of poems contains such richness in familiar varieties that one might succeed in defining her quality analytically, in many instances phrase by phrase, with quotations from songs out of plays by Ford or Webster, and from Herbert and Carew. One should not expect to find Miss Adams after 1650—nor before the lyrics in *The Broken Heart*. Her poetry lacks the eighteenth-century interest in the object noted but not seen—

A pair of garters, half a pair of gloves,
And all the trophies of his former loves

—and it lacks the line by line simplicity of the early Elizabethan song:

Pack clouds away and welcome day,
With night we banish sorrow.

Her sensibility, metaphysical in Johnson's sense, has isolated a world somewhere between eighteenth-century decoration and the fresh intensity of a lyric by Thomas Heywood or Greene. For all her aptness in certain early sixteenth-century conventions—typically the subjective dialogue, in her "Death and the Lady"—the fusion of her qualities brings her closer to

Carew than to any other poet. This, again, in spite of a Shakespearean idiom in some of her sonnets:

> Since now most precious mines can give no gold
> So absolute but it's made metaphor.

But Miss Adams, without any of the older classical machinery, more intensely visualizes and relates her images; she expresses herself in her best poems in terms of something impersonal and beyond conviction—an intense awareness of *things*. Her probing intensity is a little like that of her contemporary, Louise Bogan. Thus she does not exploit the extended intellectuality of Donne; her intelligence acts within its immediate problems. Her poetry is not an exhibit; it is quiet, serious, static. This last quality is a fixed relation between her and her world; she is not philosophically ambitious. "Never, being damned, see Paradise," writes Miss Adams in the title poem; it is the subject matter of all the verse in this book. Wit, or its current version in dandyism, is a quality that Miss Adams has rejected for a more serious irony; having accepted her own intricately derived world, she doesn't attempt to refute its terms. She is serious without an inversion of sentimentality.

Her irony designs the contexture of her perceptions; it is not a property.

> Now is my very marrow gone to dreaming,
> And I am stricken by its dream's precision
> To live bewildered between blood and seeming.

Her poetry becomes purer, if less directly exciting, when this irony, nearly always introspective, vanishes in a strict contemplation of its "objective reference"—in an absorption in the object itself.

> And if a lark shook out his wing,
> That shadow on your cheek I found.

> Now on dark wounds falls dreamily,
> Like a celestial dew, the snow.

Some of the personal, aesthetically unresolved confusion of these two ways of seeing persists, and Miss Adams has written fewer successful poems than an adept artificer of magazine verse would let himself write. Miss Adams is personal, meticulous, detached from ulterior literary motives; a distinguished limited sensibility, she is a distinguished minor poet. There are perhaps five poems in this book of almost ultimate perfection. But the many unrealized poems are honorably committed. She is conscious of a problem in poetic values, and her failures in integrity are worth considerably more than the neat reconstructions of properties into which several of her women contemporaries, after their first interesting successes, have been quickly diverted.—ALLEN TATE, Review of *Those Not Elect* (1926), *The Poetry Reviews of Allen Tate: 1924–1944*, 1983, pp. 42–43

Miss Adams' close study of the metaphysical poets, and her steady loyalty to their principles of form and imagery, has not deprived her verse of a sensibility which reflects her own mind and its environment. By their tone, selective austerity, and quality of design, her poems belong to the severest tradition of English lyrical verse, whose masters begin with Breton and end with Marvell. It would be difficult to tell by what means she has safely appropriated their outlook, or how she has supplied for her own ideas a comparable background of feeling and experience. Yet it is clear that she has found her lesson in Campion, Herrick, Crashaw, and Vaughan, and that a few of her pages will some day be bound with the best of theirs as the finest harvest of metaphysical verse. Proof for this contention exists in *Quiet*, *Midsummer*, and *April Mortality* from her first

book, and in *The River in the Meadows*, *Lullaby*, and *Kennst Du Das Land* from this one.

Upon closer examination it will be found that, while they compare externally with the Jacobean lyric on many points, these poems resemble it most in one essential and consistent respect. Miss Adams does not fail to distinguish between the sensory accidents of intellectual experience, and the conceptual attainments of the intellect itself. It is a definitive line in poetry—this rigid demarcation between image and concept. In many acceptable poets (particularly the baroque *virtuosi* of the present day) it is blurred or wholly confused by uncertain motives. Yet Miss Adams' control of symbolic elucidation and analogy sets her apart with the pure though frugal genius of Crashaw, Traherne, and Vaughan. It is their comparative laxity in this discipline that places Mrs. Wylie and Mr. MacLeish in the more brilliant but erratic company of Webster, Jonson, and Donne. Even without our current obsession by the relationship between recent metaphysical poets and their ancestors in the seventeenth century, it would not be difficult to go back from the present volume to Vaughan's dialogue, *Death*, Traherne's *The Praeparative*, Crashaw's *Charitas Nimia*, or Herrick's epigrams in *Noble Numbers*, and to find in them a similar discrimination in elucidating (but never disfiguring) the idea by means of the natural and practicable image.

In other respects Miss Adams defines her own observations, prejudices, and compromise. With her, the light of spiritual asceticism falls on problems of the heart and body, rather than on matters of devotional and theological argument. Her observations are on the whole free from remote astronomical and supernatural references, adhering instead to the city, the countryside of farms, the intimate landscape with many of its conventional properties retained, or the pages of books. And Miss Adams' compromise is still her period's, best stated in *Those Not Elect*:

> Never, being damned, see Paradise.
> The heart will sweeten at its look;
> Nor hell was known, till Paradise
> Our senses shook.

Even without the dedication page of *High Falcon*, reference to Louise Bogan's recent *Dark Summer* would be inevitable. Both volumes show the intensity, the technical prudence, and the richness of vital experience which give the poems concentration. But even though Miss Bogan practices a severer caution, she must be credited with greater diversity and breadth. At least fifteen poems in *High Falcon* suffer through being somewhat casual and fortuitous. In an art whose intensity soon exhausts the vitality of any one image or idea, they duplicate impressions and details, and thus overplay their themes. This may be seen by grouping on one hand *Acquittal*, *Every Bird of Nature*, *Lament of Quarry*, and *High Falcon*; or on another *Sundown*, *Evening Sky*, and *Country Summer*, in the last of which the pastoral introspection burns itself out and becomes ashen. It would be difficult to find in Miss Bogan's book as exhaustive a canvass of special topics: *The Mark*, *The Crossed Apple*, *Simple Autumnal*, and *Ad Castitatem* stand alone in superb understatement. They are self-sufficient, requiring and finding no variation; they convert the reader at once to the esthetic or emotional prejudice they define. Miss Adams risks losing the reader's attention through elaboration, through failing to transfix it by a single thrust. Hardy, Eliot, and Pound encountered this danger, Hardy alone by real mastery evading it. I think Miss Adams still has a chance to, by widening her outlook but restricting her enquiries. But Hart Crane and Miss Bogan have never encountered it.

Natural sympathy has given Miss Adams' observations a rare opulence. She has explored the details of rural landscape and weather almost to the point of specialty. The heraldic richness of these lines from *Winter Solstice* is rivaled only in the fine sections of *The Seasons*, or in Collins and Keats:

> Prepare the sun his bier,
> The sun, the fallen year,
> With all the spoil it yields,
> For their fresh almanach is shrunk and dry.
> Those pheasants whose proud tread
> Made royal summer fields
> Hang speckled crop to crop,
> And strung before the gamester's shop
> The hare stares out with frozen eye.

This quality, extended within a pattern of greater flexibility, appears at its finest in *Kennst Du Das Land*, which, with *A River in the Meadows* and *To Unconscionable Sound*, marks Miss Adams' highest achievement. Fragmentary quotation would ruin the cumulative beauty of these poems, yet the reader will find that, in each, nature is approached contemplatively. The impressions are held in immobile suspension. The world is static, as the metaphysical observer requires it to be. In no poem may be found the impulsive capture of impression (together with the accompanying swell in phrase) which one discovers in Vaughan or (to take a closer instance) in Mrs. Meynell's *The Rainy Summer*. Miss Adams' virtue is of another order. She displays the persistent curiosity which pushes an analysis forward until it has achieved a perfect distillation of the essence of a perception. This is a clue to her spiritual bravery. It may be delayed by physical reticence, but it attains to freedom in the end. We may take the word of *Many Mansions*:

> The last majority attained,
> And shut from its small house of dust,
> Into the heritage of air
> The spirit goes because it must:
> And halts before the multiple plane
> To look more ways than left and right,
> And weeping walks its father's house
> Like something homeless in the night:
> For now less largely let abroad,
> Though but the world, they say, is mine,
> I shiver as I take the road.

In her favorite image, Miss Adams is the bird that harries heaven for its highest meaning. But she maintains the mystic's realism, and patience in the ordeal of art. Thereby she not only enriches current literature, but keeps alive in poetry one of its noblest traditions.—M. D. Z., "A Harrier of Heaven," *Poetry*, Feb. 1930, pp. 332–36

Two of the faults most common in her work, as well as most irritating, though perhaps not most profoundly important, are a persistent use of certain forms of ambiguous syntax, chiefly the dangling participle and the pronoun of uncertain reference, a use which results in an obscurity in no wise organic to the feeling and hence definitely bad; and a tendency to dilute and expand certain poems ("Windy Way" is one of the worst examples) with pretty literary turns and phrases which bear much the same relationship to poetry that scales bear to music.

More important is her preoccupation with, and exaggeration of, the significance of, the feelings attendant upon the fringe of sleep; these feelings are sometimes genuinely curious, but only the most unbridled mysticism can imbue them with any vast amount of meaning. The tendency to take them too seriously is indicative of a tendency to find profundity in the strange simply because it is strange, and this, though it has

been a common poetic vice for at least a hundred and fifty years, is decidedly uncritical and is bound to be in one degree or another disastrous to poetry. It is much more difficult to face experience on one's feet and with one's eyes open than in any other condition, and it is hence vastly more necessary that one endeavor to give it order while in this condition.

Miss Adams' mysticism shows itself in another way in two of her most perfectly executed songs, "Time and Spirit," and "The Mount," as well as in a few less perfect pieces. The feeling, the experience, in these poems involves certain ideas which most readers, I imagine, will have a hard time taking seriously, and it involves these ideas not by rejecting them nor by regarding them sceptically, but by accepting them with a certain fervor. The reader, to experience the poems, must likewise accept them; but as the acceptance in most cases can be no more than extremely temporary, the poems become momentary luxuries, indulgences, and are scarcely spiritual necessities. This sort of easy indulgence, of facile escape from the real difficulties of achieving spiritual mastery, is altogether too common in modern poetry. Mr. Hart Crane is another serious sinner on this score, and one of the greatest is Mr. Yeats, who exhibits an inordinate capacity for temporarily solving the riddle of life in magnificently written lines, his solution, frequently being something no more considerable than a handful of automatic letters, and the grandeur of his rhetoric on such an occasion leaving the reader dumfounded.

Finally, there are probably not over a dozen poems in the book that are not packed with echoes, general and specific, from Yeats. Mr. Yeats, though he has written poems that are almost certainly of a major order, has a very dangerous habit of striking histrionically noble attitudes when he finds himself in the face of situations that are genuinely hard to understand; such attitudes are at best but very rough estimates of the situations and a very rough substitute for the humble and careful exactness of Hardy or of Baudelaire. They are, being somewhat ready-made and standardized, the most easily imitated aspect of his work; and they are particularly tempting to a generation whose more intelligent members are struggling desperately to reassert the dignity and moral values lost by their predecessors. There is every reason to believe at the present moment that Mr. Yeats may exert as funest an influence in the next five or six years as did Mr. Eliot in the last, and one that may be recognized and abandoned more slowly, for appearing to be something it is not. His weaker moments and methods offer too facile an escape from the too facile collapse of Mr. Eliot: they offer escape via a stylistic formula rather than intellectual and moral effort and hence can lead ultimately only to another collapse or to poetry that, though apparently sustained, is devoid of genuine meaning. They add intellectual unsoundness to the emotional unsoundness of Mr. Eliot, or rather they seem to conceal the latter under the former.—Yvor WINTERS, *HH*, April–June 1930, pp. 459–60

When Léonie Adams' two books of poetry appeared, *Those Not Elect* (1925) and *High Falcon* (1929), critics and reviewers turned with relief from the poetry of feminine self-identity to welcome a poet of personal reticence whose verses held great charm. As at this particular moment critics were much preoccupied with discussing the merits of twentieth-century neo-metaphysical poetry, Léonie Adams' verse was put into the company of Vaughan's and Herbert's poetry; and she was spoken of as being both a "metaphysical" poet and a "mystic." . . .

As one rereads the poetry of Léonie Adams it is more seemly to agree, and certainly more pertinent, that at her best she was more unworldly than metaphysical. Seventeenth-century philosophy, learning, irony, and religious "enthusiasm" as well as the conflicts of scientific observation and theological wit are singularly absent from her work, nor do her lines revive the strains of seventeenth-century music. Her "keepings" (as Gerald Manley Hopkins would have called them) were of Hopkins, Walter de la Mare, and John Crowe Ransom—and in her poem, "The Mount," her cadences and metrics resemble, if anything, a variation in lyrical verse that had acquired distinction in the poetry of W. B. Yeats's middle years. All this is said not to dispraise the charm of Léonie Adams' gifts, but to define their character with greater accuracy than her earlier critics have done.

John Crowe Ransom's "Antique Harvesters," the most sensitive of his finer poems which appeared in his *Two Gentlemen in Bonds* (1927), contained the following lines:

> We pluck the spindling ears and gather the corn.
> One spot has special yield? "On this spot stood
> Heroes and drenched it with their only blood."
> And talk meets talk, as echoes from the horn
> Of the hunter—echoes are the old men's arts,
> Ample are the chambers of their hearts.
>
> Here come the hunters, keepers of a rite.
> The horn, the hounds, the lank mares coursing by
> Straddled with archetypes of chivalry;
> And the fox, lovely ritualist, in flight
> Offering his earthly ghost to quarry. . . .

And from Léonie Adams' *High Falcon* we have two parallels to Ransom's "Antique Harvesters," one from "The Moon and Spectator," and the second from "Ghostly Tree," and from these it is not unreasonable to assume that Ransom shared with Hopkins and de la Mare her highest esteem and the position of a master:

> The moon, that chill frame, I saw enact
> Her rite commemorative of a bound ghost,
> And thought of a night wildly born, outliving storm,
> And its tears lost.
>
> O beech, unbind your yellow leaf, for deep
> The honeyed time lies sleeping, and lead shade
> Seals up the eyelids of its golden sleep.
> Long are your flutes, chimes, little bells, at rest,
> And here is only the cold scream of the fox,
> Only the hunter following on the hound;
> While your quaint-plumaged,
> The bird that your green summer boughs lapped
>   round,
> Bends south its soft bright breast.

And again it was as though the closing stanzas of "Antique Harvesters," with their mention of death and "the Proud Lady," had brought to Léonie Adams' mind the title of one of her best-known poems, "Death and the Lady"; the theme and charms of her poem recalled Matthias Claudius' *Der Tod und das Mädchen*, a lyric which in its haunting echoes and refrains found an appropriate parallel in the music written for it by Franz Schubert; certainly, Léonie Adams' re-creation of her world had a closer kinship to the revivals of a Gothic imagination in the poetry of the early and late nineteenth century than it had to metaphysical poetry in the sense in which Samuel Johnson defined the term. . . .

The frequent use of the word "sweet," the "so sweet pain," and the adjective "cold," even the sound of her "airy shell" spoke of her mingled debt to and careful, attentive readings in the poetry of de la Mare and Gerard Manley Hopkins. And Léonie Adams' "Kennst Du Das Land" revived for readers of poetry in 1929, less profoundly of course, but with unmistakable grace and charm, the Gothic world of imagination that

Poe had discovered an hundred years before Miss Adams' *High Falcon* had its proofs corrected and sent to the printer. . . .

It was not without misgiving and a sense of disquiet that sympathetic readers of Léonie Adams' verses—and this after a silence since 1929 which had been broken only by a poem, *This Measure*, published in a limited edition in 1933, and rare appearances in *Poetry* and *The New Republic*—discovered the following statement by her in Fred B. Millett's *Contemporary American Authors* (1940):

> I sometimes feel that poetry at present like other things is about to undergo the kind of variation that amounts to the leap to a new genus. I was first preoccupied with sound patterns—that took me to the seventeenth century—then I recognized the necessity for the more modern preoccupation with images which should not be gathered along the way of discourse or meditation, but assumed before starting out, like apparel, or entered into as a world. I have been silent a long time because I am now grappling with the limitations of the lyric.

The statement was certainly ill advised, and in respect to the writing of poetry, naïve. Lyric forms are limited only by the resources and talents of the poet who employs them; a lyric is either written or it remains undone, and during the past fifteen years, traditional lyric forms have been employed with individual variation and distinction by a large number of poets, including E. E. Cummings, Robert Frost, T. S. Eliot, Edith Sitwell, W. H. Auden, Dylan Thomas, and Henry Treece—and there was, of course, no evidence of their "grappling with" the form itself, its limitations, its subject matter, or the very language with which their poems had been written.

From this statement one returns (as her critics turned in 1925 and 1929) to the rediscovery of the small, Gothic, yet distinct and delightful world of Miss Adams' imagination; and it is more than likely that some five or six of her lyrics will continue to be enjoyed by the readers of popular anthologies of verse.—HORACE GREGORY, *A History of American Poetry 1900–1940*, 1946, pp. 291–97

The reluctance to confront things ugly as readily as things lovely is a fault from which the lyrics of Léonie Adams are not exempt. One of their virtues is that they realize the tenuous loveliness of which they speak. None of her contemporaries has recorded more subtly the movement of the hours as sky and earth body them forth. She is as no other the poet of light, whether it be that of the dawn that "comes wildly up the East," or of the moon: "The harrier of clouds, a flame half-seen," or of the "Evening Sky":

> How now are we tossed about by a windy heaven,
> The eye that scans it madded to discern
> In a single quarter all the wild ravage of light,
> Amazing light to quiver and suddenly turn
> Before the stormy demon fall of night;
> And yet west spaces saved celestial
> With silver sprinklings of the anointed sun. . . .

Just as the eye's little orbit contains "sky balancing chaos," so within the bounds of a slight lyric Léonie Adams holds "heaven slain and quickening." More than the miracle of physical vision is suggested here. The wild beauty and mystery of the evening sky confronting the small, intensely conscious spectator are so presented as to make us realize that as the eye apprehends what is beyond the grasp of every other sense, so the mind has the power to imagine what the eye has never seen. Her "venerable silver-throated horn," her legendary boat drifting up the river like a swan, her hares and falcons, have wandered out of Yeats' country, but she writes by the light that illumined the world of earlier, more confident religious poets.

Different as is her approach to the heavenly spectacle from that expressed in their devotional works, she frequently recalls the tone as well as the imagery of the author of *Centuries of Meditations* and of the poet who could say, as simply as if he were speaking of the aurora borealis,

> I saw Eternity the other night
> Like a great Ring of pure and endless light,
> All calm, as it was bright . . .

Turned to the finest vibrations of the play that goes on in the supernal theater, Miss Adams pays due tribute to the dramatist—time.

Poems having to do with the conjugal quarrel between body and soul, even more than those describing sunsets and moonrise, may be expected to have an ethereal quality. The same airy atmosphere bathes those lyrics in which Miss Adams deals with one of the great commonplaces of verse, romantic love. Her concern is with the more subtle states of communion or division between lovers. The scene is furnished by unearthly elements, the mortal pang quickened or assuaged because it is endured in sight of "The sky, that's heaven's seat."

The body of Miss Adams' work is slight and her scope limited. Her debt to the metaphysicals does not include the conversational idiom and the ironic wit that makes the chief of them congenial to many of her fellow-poets. Nor does she extend her purview to take in such grosser and uglier aspects of even the most private world as are present to one of her masters, W. B. Yeats, or to her contemporary, Elder Olson, whose work is singularly close to hers in structure and texture. But if Miss Adams does not range widely, she cuts deep.—BABETTE DEUTSCH, "The Ghostly Member," *Poetry in Our Time,* 1952, pp. 235–37

Miss Adams's poetry is a difficult labor. Intensely compact, intensely intellectualized, and rigorously ascetic, it comes true, but it does not come easy. The matter, as she writes in "Sundown," is sanctified, "dipped in a gold stain." It seems doubtful that there can be a wide audience for Miss Adams's gold stain, but that there will always be a group of discerning and enthusiastic readers seems certain. . . .

At this tentative stage I find myself with one principal question to ask of my rereadings, a question not of the gift and devotion of the poet but of the scale of the human experience. A wrong question perhaps. Or one that would be wrong if applied to a lesser talent. I have it in mind, however, that Miss Adams's poems are the work of a very considerable talent, and that granted the poet's aesthetic ability to accomplish whatever he sets out to accomplish, we are sooner or later required to ask how much the poet has taken on in a human way.

Let the question be located around the following poem, a sonnet titled, "Alas, Kind Element!"

> Then I was sealed, and like the wintering tree
> I stood me locked upon a summer core;
> Living had died a death, and asked no more.
> And I lived then, but as enduringly,
> And my heart beat, but only as to be.
> Ill weathers well, hail, gust and cold I bore,
> I held my life as hid, at roots, in store.
> Thus I lived then, till this air breathed on me.
> Till this kind air breathed kindness everywhere,
> There where my times had left me I would stay.
> Then I was staunch, I knew nor yes nor no;
> But now the wistful leaves have thronged the air.
> My every leaf leans forth upon the day;
> Alas, kind element! which comes to go.

I find this a fascinating poem. It is also a poem that could have been written at any time between 1575 and 1625. Is it fair to ask how many centuries the poet can afford to put by? In diction? In movement? In awareness?

I have no certain answer to these questions, especially in the face of the poem's excellence. I find myself believing that had the poem turned up as a lost manuscript of a Shakespeare sonnet, I should have accepted it and admired it as such. And yet is it not reasonable to think that it is easier, or at least less relevant, to rewrite even Shakespeare than it is to find the form of what lives not only in eternal time but in that eternal time that lies behind the day we live in? Can the poet put by all obligation to wrestle with what Hippolyte Taine called "the moral temperature" of his times? Compared to much modern poetry Miss Adams's gold stain shines like a splendor. Yet, touch it against such a poem as Thomas's "Refusal to Mourn"—to cite only one—and the gold stain seems dimmer. It remains, to be sure, a thing of the spirit, but more nearly of the spirit's jewelry than of its ray and center. Or does it? These thoughts and these questions offer themselves and seem relevant.—JOHN CIARDI, *Nation,* May 22, 1954, p. 445

ELDER OLSON
From "Louise Bogan and Léonie Adams"
The Chicago Review, Fall 1954, pp. 70–87

It would be generally conceded, I think, that Louise Bogan and Léonie Adams are among the four or five American women who have produced poetry of high distinction, thus far in this century. Their reputations, solidly established in the twenties, have survived a number of spectacular revolutions in literary taste, theory, and practice; certain of their poems seem to have become permanently imbedded in anthologies of contemporary poetry; in short, their situation is excellent, except for the danger that the greater part of their work may be ignored precisely because a piece or two remains in high favor. I, for one, should be sorry to see all their craft and skill come to be represented merely by so much as is manifest in a few poems; and I should like to do what I can to prevent this, by considering the larger aspects of their art. Both poets have very recently published volumes which span their careers up to the present; so that such consideration is now possible. . . .

A mind and a style really unique are impossible to describe; and Miss Adams' art is so delicate that to say it produces an effect of enchantment, that it places one in landscapes of vision or dream, is at once to vulgarize it. It does produce enchantment, and does deal in visions and dreams, however. Her imagination translates her sensations into something rare and strange. Common objects appear as they would under special conditions of light and atmosphere, strangely brightened and enhanced, and somehow made portents and tokens of something still more strange. I have said that Louise Bogan's imagery is solid and substantial because it ranges over all forms of feeling, and gives us objects as they naturally and familiarly appear. Adams' imagery is chiefly visual and auditory; objects seem weightless as they do in dreams, shapes are etherealized, colors are made purer and more luminous, sounds clearer and more delicate. All things appear, whatever sense they appeal to, as they might to one in a drowsy fever, or between sleeping or waking, or fast in a spell.

Chiefly she seems to "outstare substantial stuff," as she herself says:

The day comes wildly up the east,
Because the cup of vision broke,
And those clear silver floods released
Go ravaging the calm sky of night;
And all who to that seeing woke
Look coldly on a common sight,
As to outstare substantial stuff.
The substance never is enough
When lids are drenched apart by light. . . .

Her marvelous imagination, or, if you will, her vision, thus gives her extraordinary things: waters, for instance, so clear

They will stain drowning a star,
With the moon they will brim over.

or sky

. . . in which the boughs were dipped
More thick with stars than fields with dew

or leaves

. . . deepening the green ground
With their green shadows, there as still
And perfect as leaves stand in air. . . .

When she does offer us what I have called "objective" imagery, however, she does so with great effect. Here, for instance, is the very essence of a winter nightfall, more economical and precise even than Eliot's first *Prelude*:

December, mortal season, crusts
The dark snows shuffled in the street,
And rims the lamp with sleet.
The beggar, houseless, chill, and thin,
Leans to the chestnut vendor's coals,
The cart creaks off which trails the winter bush,
And the thick night shuts in.

This is surely very close to the vein of Shakespeare's "When icicles hang by the wall" or Blake's "When silver snow decks Susan's clothes/And cold jewel hangs at th' shepherd's nose."

Like Bogan, she exhibits a single character; herself, quite probably; and we see her chiefly as engaged in the exquisite contemplation of the phantasma of her thought. *Twilight Revelation* is typical of her art:

This hour was set the time for heaven's descent,
Come drooping toward us on the heavy air,
The sky, that's heaven's seat, above us bent,
Blue faint as violet ash, you near me there
In nether space, so drenched in goblin blue
I could touch Hesperus as soon as you.

Now I perceive you, lapped in singing light,
Washed by that blue which sucks whole planets in,
And hung like those top jewels of the night,
A mournful gold too high for love to win.
And you, poor brief, poor melting star, you seem
Half to sink, and half to brighten in that stream.

And these rich-bodied hours of our delight
Show like a mothwing's substance when the fall
Of confine-loosing, blue, unending night
Extracts the spirit of this temporal.
So space can pierce the crevice wide between
Fast hearts, skies deep-descended intervene.

Here a perception transmuted by imagination generates all; she sees twilight, not as we do, as simple twilight; she sees it as the descent of the heavens, as the actual incursion of outer space into the earth's atmosphere. And thus her lover, near her as he is, seems remote "in nether space"; "so drenched in goblin blue," so "washed by that blue which sucks whole planets in," that he is remote as a star. She feels him, thus,

"too high for love to win"; he is, moreover, seen as but a brief and transitory thing among the perduring stars, even as he is momentarily transfigured by the light which he shares with them; and all the time of love, rich as it is, seems suddenly insubstantial as a moth's wing. Thus, she muses, between even the most closely-bound hearts, the skies intervene; and twilight has become a portent both of the brevity of love (for merely by setting it against the eternal, we see that it is not) and of the essential isolation of the human soul; this whatever lovers feel or say.

Notice that all the imagery is of the same order as, and is a consequence of, the very first image; and the moment we imagine the first, we enter into her own thought, strikingly original as it is, and feel as she does, in perfect sympathy with her. Identification and sympathy or empathy are not so general in art as theorists have tended to claim; they result only when the artist has brought us perfectly into the frame of mind of his character and set forth the cause or object of emotion precisely as the character apprehends it. In Miss Bogan's poetry, for instance, the effect depends upon our considering the poetic character as distinct from ourselves; Miss Adams, on the contrary, demands identification. This is one reason why she uses more imagery than Bogan; she must at all times make us see things as she sees them, to carry us with her.

It is a reason, too, why she depends upon suggestion, rather than implication. Implication can operate only when we are familiar with consequences; where interpretations and consequences are very unusual, we cannot infer to any great effect. I doubt, for example, whether many of us—if any of us—would have been able of ourselves to see twilight as "heaven's descent" in the sense in which Miss Adams does, and whether any of us would have been able to intuit from it, as she does so easily and naturally, the transience and loneliness of love, together with the poignant beauty of that transience and loneliness. Suggestion is another matter; our minds can be led along a given course, familiar or unfamiliar, by the evocation of certain ideas in certain conjunctions. When Bogan makes us feel the still brightness of the court, it is by implication, and we can reduce it to syllogism: *if* the mirrors "gaze" and the parquet shines with unbroken tranquillity, *then* the chambers are deserted, and so on. But compare that with the following lines from Adams' *The Rounds and the Garlands Done*:

Day that cast the lovely looks is sped,
And from the turf, circled with white dew,
The lovers and the children are gone;
Leaving the wreath, the bouquet fresh, looped up
    with grasses.
All the golden looks are spent,
And the time of the rounds and the garlands done.

Here we feel that we are looking upon the earth of the Golden Age, or at least that of some eternal pastoral; the sunlight was surely not ours, but that which shines in the poems of Sappho, in *Daphnis and Chloe*, or in Sidney's *Arcadia*. But the poet has neither said nor implied that it was; she has merely suggested it by a few cunning phrases; and her magic is so subtle and immediate that we must make a special effort to realize that perhaps, after all, whe was talking about a scene in a park.

Indeed, her words bring to mind almost constantly the customs, beliefs, arts, and sciences of an older day; they cast, thus, a veil which half brightens, half obscures the immediate reality. These excerpts call to mind old customs, for example:

Then, tatter you and rend,
Oak heart, to your profession mourning. . . .

WALTER ABISH

HENRY ADAMS

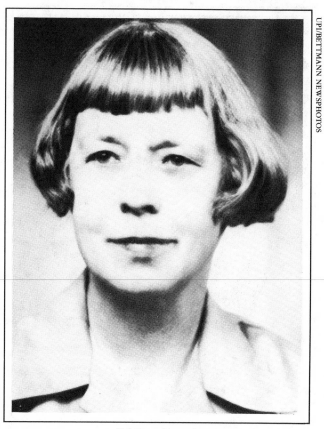

LÉONIE ADAMS

JAMES AGEE

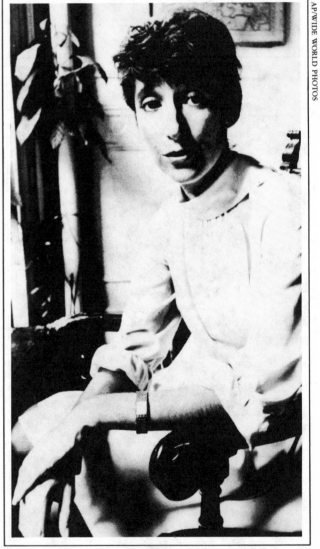

RENATA ADLER

CONRAD AIKEN

"Of my father's father I got a proud steed,
And a barb of my father I took". . . .

The lost was twenty jewels worth. . . .

These, surely, recall an old cosmogony:

Cast on the turning wastes of wind
Are cords that none can touch or see. . . .
. . . older than the golden sun
And his measure trod with night.

The following, again, recall Renaissance sculpture and pre-Renaissance painting:

There marble boys are leant from the light throat,
Thick locks that hang with dew and eyes dewlashed,
Dazzled with morning, angels of the wind,
With ear a-point for the enchanted note.
. . . so at the innocent lady's feet
The blond, the young, delicate ones of heaven,
Stare at the pretty painted skies.

If her thought is in an older key, her language shows the same deliberate archaism. It has been called Elizabethan; as a matter of fact, it is not; yet there is this much truth in calling it so, that she reminds one more of the Elizabethans and of certain metaphysical poets—Traherne and Marvell especially, I should say—than of anyone else, even such astute imitators of the Elizabethan and Jacobean as Darley and Beddoes. It would be absurd to condemn her on this account, and I do not suppose that any sensible person ever would; perhaps nine-tenths of the greatest glories of English poetry are written in some sort of artificial language. The real question is whether her diction is effective or not; and her successes are so overwhelming that there is no point to the question.

All this archaism has the same function: to remove any sense of immediacy which might produce violent emotion, and to address the gentler instead; that is, to soften and transform emotion much as time itself does. The wilder emotions are produced by immediacy, the gentler by remoteness; the *Iliad* sets us in the very midst of its events, ancient and half-mythical as they were, and excites emotions of one kind; the *Eve of St. Agnes* places its events far back, and evokes emotions of the other.

But there is this point, too, as far as the archaism of her ideas is concerned: that ideas function very differently in poetry from the manner in which they do in science or philosophy. In the latter they have value as they are adequate or true, and as they have logical consequences of some value; in poetry they have value as they affect imagination and emotion. For ideas have an imaginative and emotional dimension as well as an intellectual one; Dante's notion of Hell is a sublime and terrifying one, whether it be true or false, and poets of our own day (Millay, for one) have continued to use the idea of the planetary atom, discarded though it is by science, because of the sheer magnificence of the notion that our universe could thus consist of an infinity of worlds within worlds, a thought, as Emerson says, "to dwindle our astronomy into a toy." Donne and Milton similarly used outworn conceptions of science purely for their emotional effect. The question of when philosophic or scientific thought becomes poetic material—a question often raised since the early nineteenth century—seems to me to have a very obvious and certain answer; it does so whenever the emotional qualities of thought can be actualized.

In an age of startling poetic innovations, neither Miss Bogan nor Miss Adams has been thought of as an innovator. I think they have not quite had their rights in this matter. In the matter of versification alone, each made important advances. Bogan broke up the "tight" and regular stanza-forms with some very original variations, while retaining the general effect of strictness and regularity, and she also contrived, in *Summer Wish*, for example, a distinctly modern development of blank verse, highly plastic and serviceable. Adams' innovations in versification are too numerous and too subtle to discuss here; I shall bluntly say, at whatever risk of exciting indignation, that no poet of our day, not even Yeats, can be said to have a finer and more delicate ear.

The question of how much of the work of these poets will last is a natural and unavoidable one; it is also rather a futile one. The only guarantee an artist can have against fortune lies in the integrity, soundness, and discipline manifest in his art. That Miss Bogan and Miss Adams possess this guarantee is, I should say, beyond question.

RENATA ADLER

1938–

Renata Adler was born on October 19, 1938, in Milan, Italy; she was raised in Danbury, Connecticut, and at boarding schools. After graduating from Bryn Mawr in 1959, she studied with Claude Lévi-Strauss in Paris on a Fulbright scholarship, then went to Harvard for her M.A. in philosophy. In 1962 she joined the staff of the *New Yorker*, and has written stories and articles for the magazine ever since.

Adler achieved notoriety in 1968, when she became film critic for the *New York Times*. Her iconoclastic reviews delighted some readers and outraged others; she left the paper in 1969 with a devoted following and her first book, *A Year in the Dark: Journal of a Film Critic*. It was published the following year, along with a collection of non-fiction pieces, *Toward a Radical Middle*.

In 1974, Adler wrote speeches for House Judiciary Committee Chairman Peter Rodino during the hearings on President Nixon's impeachment. That same year, she won the O. Henry Award for a short story that later became part of her first novel, *Speedboat* (1976). The book won a Hemingway Award in 1977, by which time Adler had entered Yale Law School; she graduated in 1979. In 1978 she spent six months as film critic for the *New Yorker*, an experience which led to her controversial attack on regular critic Pauline Kael in *The New York Review of Books* in 1980. Adler's critical reputation received another boost when her novel *Pitch Dark* appeared in 1983; also that year, she worked briefly at the revived *Vanity Fair*. She lives in New York City.

Works

Renata Adler seems deliberately to have written the kind of novel she least admires. *Speedboat* has no plot, no tears, no characters flat or round, no conflict of great ideas, no deep scheme. You do not merely note the absence of such things; you miss them actively because the author has made you miss them. She has created a world precisely opposed to one we would prefer, has done so down to the form of her presentation which, as an argument against itself, is effective on those grounds alone. But there is more to this book than cleverness.

The narrator (without a narrative) is a woman journalist whose "mind is a tenement," she says. The novel, then, is a form of slumming: half-baked reports on times and places—not hers alone, and in no special order—as if she were keeping a scrapbook of passages used in her articles, or perhaps discarded. To call her tone dispassionate would suggest that passion is sensed in abeyance, but that isn't it. If anything, the tone is surprised, sometimes falsified for a laugh, sometimes genuine: one brilliant survivor peering with chatoyant eyes at the life which threatens her to the point of amusement.

Speedboat is concerned with the speed of that life. Our journalist has a mind of the ancients that naturally pulls back and away, which is the source of her ironies. She can write one sentence, for example, that moves in two directions, forcing a standstill: "His children own the town these days, for what it's worth." Everything else in the novel is going forward in spurts and plunges, too fast even for the celebrants who wish to move with the machines, so that the giddy lady who insists on riding in a brand new speedboat breaks her back from her own excited bouncing. Fractures in other passages are less severe, but in their battles with passengers the planes and boats and trains are clearly winning. Every chapter after the first begins with a ride.

Otherwise the book is about this woman, who cannot do things. She can't cook; "I cannot read maps; my sense of direction is so poor and unstable that maps somehow make it worse." Ordinarily such admissions are self-congratulating, but our journalist is no critic. She earnestly takes lessons in everything, partly to correct her poor sense of direction, though finally, even in flying lessons, she has her way, at her own pace. She is "the sort of reporter who hangs around, or rather, tags along." Since everyone else is trying to get ahead of the, some indefinite, game, she who tags along has the advantage of wit.

So she tells a lot of anecdotes, like the one about the widow in the garden:

> A few years ago, the wire services reported that, on account of a defective latch, the cargo door on a DC-10 opened, in flight. A coffin fell out. A lady at work in her flower garden saw what she took to be a coffin fall from the sky into a neighboring field. Having been recently widowed, the lady made the obvious inference. She put down her trowel, drove to the nearest state asylum, and committed herself. When reporters reached her, to tell her the thing had really happened, and to ask her reaction to it, the lady preferred to stay right where she was.

It isn't meant to be new. We can hear this story, and understand it immediately; the widow's option is reasonable, predictable; we have heard the tale before; we know the moral backwards; our journalist knows that we know; and so on. Then why tell it? Because it's like a metaphor or cliché—"the camel, I had noticed, was passing with great difficulty, through the eye of the needle"—that only means something after insistent repetitions.

Besides, our journalist believes that we are merely interested in what she tells us. She is lovable, and does not know it. Nobody in the novel tells her so, certainly none of her men. She thinks that her intelligence, not her heart, holds her book together.

Yet the feeling one takes from *Speedboat* is in fact not the intellectual condemnation of a speed-bound world, but how wasteful it is for this woman to live in such a place. The senseless races she observes seem made for singles, people with feather-weight luggage who run better unencumbered by family and other ties. In a swift aside she dryly mocks the memorable lines of her college education, citing "only connect" from Forster's *Howards End*, the one phrase all English professors seem born with. But the mockery turns on her who unwillingly has mastered the life of no connections to the point where the novel ends, and she hesitates to tell her lover that she is pregnant.

She feels only connected to her words. She seems not so much a journalist by profession as a journalist by birth, as if implying that in a life of no events (the novel begins: "Nobody died that year. Nobody prospered") everyone is a journalist. Personality becomes the event. The investigative reporter is not an investigator of experience, but an investigator of self as it succumbs to experience. The crime or folly exposed sends someone to jail or to the corner, yet its main public value is cathartic. The people know pity and terror thanks to the journalist who has found a way of becoming a pity or terror by entering the story he writes. A way of life, of giving life to a dead thing.

Accordingly our lady of the keen eyes and mordant anecdotes becomes her non-events as if they happened, the idea of death growing inside her as it grows in the novel, stage by stage, as in a tenement. Every so often an unsolved murder crops up, and we are hustled by it so as not to look too hard or recognize the victims. But the accumulation of these murders gets to you after a while. Eventually one sees death in the journalist herself, or maybe a wish for it—hidden so carefully in the scraps and jokes. "Becoming pregnant is taking a hostage," she says. What does one do with a hostage who might identify you?

Nothing in *Speedboat* is supposed to hurt you, but it does, which is probably what Adler is saying about the speed machines as well. The novel closes on the phrase "you can't miss it," meaning "you're never going to find it." The phrase has all the goodwill in the world.—Roger Rosenblatt, "The Back of the Book," NR, Oct. 16, 1976, pp. 32–33

There is an intelligence maybe as fine as Beattie's, though far more detached and abstracting, in Renata Adler's *Speedboat*, labeled a novel by her publishers but much less persuasive as narrative fiction than as a blending of autobiographical fragments with reportage. A valuable satirist, Adler is as incisive as Mary McCarthy on the pretensions of academics, intellectuals, and financially comfortable culture-vultures. "There is a particular fanaticism about riding in progressive summer camps and prep schools," her alter-ego narrator remarks in a representative fine passage.

> The camps may sound either drawn from Hiawatha, or like a condition that will require surgery—my brothers went to Melatoma, I to Sighing Rock. The schools will be named for an improbable condition of the landscape (Peat Cliff, Glen Willow Sands, Mount Cove, Apple Valley Heights), or for something dour and English: Gladstone Wett. The riding teachers are named Miss Cartwright, Miss Farew, Martha Abbott Struth. Ms. Struth, if she is married,

will have her own academy, which teaches every horse thing from gymkhana to dressage. Mr. Struth has been away or dead for twenty years.

But one way of crystallizing Adler's limitations, one way of acknowledging the relative modesty of her claims as a novelist, is to observe that these witty and telling lines also represent the author in one of her warmest, most sympathizing humors. How differently, with what comic attentive tolerance, might Ann Beattie have written of lonely Ms. Struth in her life among students and stallions! In most of the crisply written, discontinuous anecdotes that comprise *Speedboat*, Adler's narrator remains just as distant from her topics, and also frequently speaks in gloomier accents, alluding self-consciously to Yeats's overworked prophecy of our slouch toward apocalypse and announcing with insufficient self-mockery that "sanity . . . is the most profound moral option of our time." Except for a few significant sentences in the final pages, this world-weary narrator describes her anxious urban life, her journalistic tours through territories of pain and folly, even her own sexual experiences, with the neutral dispassion of an archeologist sifting alien fragments. Her disembodiment is so severe, confessions of bafflement and disconnection rush so easily from her lips, that her authority as a witness to outer events is radically enfeebled, and *Speedboat* comes to seem the authentic register of a malaise that resides not in the world but in the narrator herself. Most reviewers understood Adler's book to offer a clear perspective on "the special oddities and new terrors of contemporary life," as Donald Barthelme's jacket-blurb proposes. But the alienation and emotional numbness projected by Adler's narrator-double must seem familiar to anyone acquainted even superficially with the now attenuated conventions of literary modernism. *Speedboat* is genuinely persuasive as an autobiographical document, as a self-judging exposé of the easy posturing, the essentially derivative and *literary* nihilism, to which intelligence and sensibility are peculiarly vulnerable in these muddled times. Adler herself understands this, or comes to understand it during the course of her writing, for she ends her book with a paragraph that opens itself to vital energies that have been largely absent from the text until now, energies of sympathy and imagination that are inaccessible to mere wit or to satire even at its most ambitious. The paragraph begins with a surprising description of the narrator's lover: "Jim has in his mind, I think, one erratically ringing alarm clock, one manacled dervish, one dormouse, replete with truisms, and one jurist with a clarity of such an order that I tend to love his verdict in most things." Nothing in the book has quite prepared us for this affection and playfulness, which constitute an unmistakable judgment upon the self-protecting disengagement to which the narrator has been captive. Intelligence and accurate perception retain their centrality in her scheme of things, but are deepened measurably by her willingness to risk closeness and honest feeling. Her temperament has not reversed or radically transformed itself, but it has begun to open and to enlarge. "It could be," she says in her final sentence, as if to signal her rejection of the styles of avant-garde irony that had earlier defined her as a writer and as a woman, "It could be that the sort of sentence one wants right here is the kind that runs, and laughs, and slides, and stops right on a dime."—David Thorburn, YR, Summer 1977, pp. 587–88

I remember *Speedboat*, which was a wonderfully fresh and thoughtful book, written as if the author neither knew nor cared how other people wrote; she would proceed in her own remarkable way.

Her second novel ⟨*Pitch Dark*⟩ necessarily lacks that element of surprise; we know her by now. But it conveys the same sense of freshness, or originality practiced not for its own sake but because the author is absolutely desperate to tell us how things are just as forthrightly and truthfully as possible. Or maybe it's not so much how things are as what is felt—what her heroine feels upon arriving at the frayed, sad, uncertain end of a love affair.

Even with her opening remarks, Kate—who is the narrator as well as the heroine—shows herself obsessed with getting this story across to us exactly right. Where to start? we hear her wondering, and she begins first one way and then another, discarding whole paragraphs as they prove unsatisfactory.

> He knew that she had left him when she began to smoke again.
> Is that where it begins?
> I don't know. I don't know where it begins. It is where I am.
> . . . Why don't you begin with at first?
> Look, you can begin with at first, or it seems, or once upon a time.
> Or in the city of P.
> Or in the city of P. In the rain. But I can't. It is not what I know how to do.
> Well, you must get these things straight, you know, resolve them in your mind before you write them down.

But she doesn't get them straight; that's not her style. Instead, she presents us with a scattering of fragments, stray bits and pieces that she trusts will come to have meaning for us. Some of the fragments float past over and over, at first unexplained—brief sentences like "Quanta, Amy said, on the train," and "Not here, Diana said, to her lasting regret," and "What do you tell the Sanger people? Lily asked." Eventually these sentences are given a context; it's as if they had to ripen first. Other fragments work more as the refrain in a love song might: "Did I throw the most important thing perhaps, by accident, away?" and "How could I know that every time you had a choice you would choose the other thing?"

Like *Speedboat*, *Pitch Dark* gives the effect of an intelligent, wry, rather quirky woman lying awake in the small hours, staring at the ceiling and sorting over her life. There's the same reflectiveness, the same insomniac earnestness in her voice, the same eerie immediacy in the recollected voices of others. Curious and sometimes comical questions snag her attention. What steps, what peculiar procession of events, led the first football quarterback to think up the custom of wiping his hands on a towel draped over the center's rear end? And isn't it likely that the *Odyssey*'s tale of Penelope weaving and unweaving was merely an alibi, invented because when Ulysses returned, Penelope had "two difficult circumstances to explain. The presence of the suitors, and how very little weaving she had done"?

As the fragments collect, the situation emerges. Kate's lover is named Jake, he's married, he has grown children. He and Kate have been together for a long while, perhaps too long. Kate should probably have said good-bye some time ago. Midway through the book, she describes a past trip to Ireland where she encountered nothing but blank looks and hostility and deception. It was a solitary journey, nothing to do with Jake, but it effectively symbolizes her terrible feeling of separateness. She recalls that Jake never took her to New Orleans, though he knew how much she wanted to go, and that he wouldn't give her the name of his tree sprayers, or his building contractor, or his backhoe operators, though she asked for them repeatedly. All trivial and even amusing complaints, as she is the first to admit; but then at unexpected moments the larger, deeper complaints break through:

> I remember this word, that look, that small inflection, after all this time. I used to hold them, trust them, read them like a rune. Like a sign that there was a house, a billet, a civilization where we were. I look back and I think I was just there all alone. Collecting wisps and signs. Like a spinster who did know a young man once and who imagines ever since that she lost a fiancé in the war. Or an old fellow who, having spent months long ago in uniform at some dreary outpost nowhere near any country where there was a front, remembers buddies he never had, dying beside him in battles he was never in.

. . . At one point, Kate mentions a journal that she kept in her twenties. Her entries covered a Sunday to the Wednesday of the following week; after that she wrote no more. What stopped her, she says, was that when she read back over the journal, it struck her as incomprehensible. "There were no events, few names, no facts, no indication whatever of what *happened*, apart from this gloom, that cheering up, this gloom again." In a sense, Kate could be speaking of *Pitch Dark*. The book is not a narrative of events—although a few events do occur here—but a description of a certain weighted moment in a woman's life.

Can such a moment make for a satisfying novel? That's up to the individual reader, I suppose. If you read these fragments in hope of some forward motion—some conclusive final goal—you'll be disappointed. But if you simply allow them to settle in their own patterns, flashing light where they are, you'll find *Pitch Dark* a bright kaleidoscope of a book.—ANNE TYLER, "End of a Love Affair," NR, Dec. 5, 1983, pp. 27–28

Renata Adler's new novel, like her previous work of fiction, *Speedboat*, is a genre unto itself, a discontinuous first-person narrative. Miss Adler's mind is analytical and her style ebullient. She also has an old-fashioned real story to tell, a love story, although it is by no means told plain. You have to piece it together as you would if you had picked up a stranger's private journal. You have to read between the lines (the lines themselves are another sort of entertainment) and snatch at bits and fragments until the whole becomes clear, and the character of the narrator is filled out by the honest expression of her feelings, her opinions and pensées, her daily experiences, always with an edge of desperation.

The narrator, Kate Ennis, is a reporter on a newspaper: She has had an affair for eight years with Jake, a married man inconsiderate and selfish, with whom she is still in love when she decides to break from him.

It seems excessive for a very bright woman still to be in love with Jake. It does seem perfectly natural to the reader that in the end he apparently wants her back (on his terms), for Kate has the advantage of displaying her excellent gifts, her eloquence and wit, to the reader throughout the other parts of her narrative. Kate tells of Jake's final telephone calls: "You said, again, Kate, I'll change things, if that's what you want." But these brief pleas are all we get from Jake.

The point I wish to make is that, in the modern novel, it is extremely difficult to create a character worth the reader's caring about. In democratic times we find it out of key to put on show a personage of Aristotle's "certain magnitude." Art is not democratic. Miss Adler has succeeded with Kate in creating a character worth the trouble of writing and reading about, because of Kate's lively ideas, her intelligent opinions, her funny narrative style and her wonderful access to her own honesty.

We feel for her plight, her broken heart, her love story. She is an élite person in spite of herself. But the reader isn't induced to care a damn whether she goes back to Jake in the end. He is not given substance. He is the ordinary man, one of many. This doesn't appear to be quite Miss Adler's intention.

The anecdotes and theories, self-analyses and commentaries on world affairs that go to build up Kate's character make up the first and third parts of *Pitch Dark*. The most imposing vignette in the first part is the story of a raccoon that comes daily to Kate's country house near New York—"I thought he was growing to trust me, when in fact he was dying"—and its sad disposal. The raccoon, to my mind, comes off as a more effective character than Jake. Miss Adler gives it importance.

But there is a mystery, and it is a literary mystery, at the airport. Kate Ennis decides to change her name in order to make good her escape. She is convinced she is being watched, followed, so this is reasonable. Kate records: "Traveling under a false name might be a crime of some sort. I should make the name as like my own as possible to account for the mistake. Alder, I thought. But then that does happen so often. I was afraid they might make the same mistake and be on the lookout for just such an Alder. So I thought, Hadley, since no one would look under H. And then, in my new hilarity, I thought, Why not Haddock. But that seemed going too far."

She settles on Hadley for a false name "as near my own as possible." But her own name is Ennis, and Alder, Haddock, Hadley do not resemble Ennis, could not possibly pose as either a visual or aural mistake. If the "I" of the story, on the other hand, has suddenly changed from Miss Ennis to Miss Adler, the author herself, that would be understandable, but it is nowhere else in the book suggested that the identities of author and character have temporarily merged.

Does Miss Adler mean to suggest that she herself is Kate Ennis? Illogical characters are fine, but this has the effect of professional illogic. It breaks the fiction, and, for a brief moment, we have autobiography. One of the refrains that recurs throughout the book runs, "Whose voice is this? Not mine. Not mine." The mystery of the false name remains. Whose voice?

The big question a work like this imposes on the reader is, What is a novel? There is no absolute definition, but certainly, to some extent, a novel is a representation of the author's vision of life. *Pitch Dark*, like Miss Adler's *Speedboat*, is a work of fiction mainly by virtue of the fact that it claims to be so; we take it for granted the "I" of the novel is a fictional character. In both books, the character is a journalist. And Miss Adler's vision too is a journalistic one. In *Speedboat* the narrator claims: "I do not, certainly, believe in evolution. For example, fossils. I believe there are objects in nature—namely, fossils—which occur in layers, and which some half-rational fantasts insist derive from animals, the bottom ones more ancient than the top. The same, I think, with word derivations . . . I have never seen a word derive."

This, I think, is the vision of life reflected in Miss Adler's fiction. Nothing evolves, nothing derives. Effects do not result from causes. Episodes are recorded without any connection with each other. Fortunately, they are fascinating episodes.—MURIEL SPARK, "Breaking Up with Jake," NYTBR, Dec. 18, 1983, pp. 1, 24

About fifteen pages into *Pitch Dark*, Renata Adler's narrator, Kate, finally sustains a vignette longer than a paragraph or two. It's about a dying raccoon she finds in her house one night. She calls the wildlife commissioner, an elderly man who leaves his television set to come and take the animal away. How much does she owe him? "'Well, ma'am, I work for the town,' he said. 'Whatever you think is appropriate.' He put the bill in the pocket of his shirt." When he's gone, she assumes that he will kill the animal with sadistic indifference.

The episode underscores a few of the shortcomings of this tiresome, foolish second novel. First, for all the vividness of her anecdotal eye, Adler has no respect for character, no sense of what needs and doesn't need to be told: it hardly requires a Tolstoy to recognize the importance of specifying the precise value of that bill. Second, although Kate's decision to juggle the index cards of her life into a book is animated by her inexplicable love for Jake, an aging, married lawyer, she has less to say about him than about the raccoon. Third, Kate appends many morals to the story—she mistook the critter's illness for trust; she betrayed the putative trust; "We traveled a bit along life's road together"—but it remains one of many Creative Writing conceits loosely shuffled into the deck. Fourth, Kate's unwarranted assumption about the wildlife commissioner's cruelty typifies the bullying meanness with which she dispatches everyone. Such an unappealing cast, such a disreputable narrator.

Misanthropy is as legitimate a motive for writing fiction as any other, and there are passages in *Pitch Dark* that reminded me of Katherine Anne Porter in their unblinking severity. Porter, however, was first and last a storyteller, and she made her case by adhering to a Flaubertian obsession with getting things right. Adler can't be bothered with specifics. She wants something more, a mood; she arrives at something less, a sentimental accretion of generalizations, trivia, in-jokes, newspaper items, anecdotes and disquisitions (some clever, others sophomoric) on Homer, football, euthanasia, libel cases, newspaper bylines and computerized typewriters. She writes reminders to herself like "Hey, wait" and "Look here, you know, look here."

Kate is fretfully trying to put in focus her six-year love affair with Jake. She compiles scribblings and scraps of conversation as if the smoke rising from those ashes will compensate for the absence of narrative fire. The result is an adult's version of the kind of diary Kate wrote as a girl: "There were no events, few names, no facts, no indication whatever of what *happened*, apart from this gloom, that cheering up, this gloom again." Jake is a cipher, and Kate offers not a clue as to why she is devoted to him or why the reader should care if she leaves him or not. Is he loving, attentive, attractive, good in bed? We see only that he is manipulative, petty, disingenuous and grasping. He's about to celebrate his thirty-fifth wedding anniversary; he drinks. But then, Kate's no prize either.

In lieu of having a breakdown (assuming the novel itself doesn't embody one, like Salinger's "Seymour: An Introduction," which, come to think of it, *Pitch Dark* resembles), Kate flies to Ireland for a rest. Her assessment of the Irish is despicable. It begins: "An occasional creature of great poetry and beauty; the others, suspicious, crafty, greedy, stubborn, incurious, stupid, devious, violent, and cruel." Punctuated by infuriating non sequiturs and notes to herself, this thesis is developed for the entire middle section of the novel. I assume the reader is meant to identify with Kate, but it's difficult to be sure. Kate is an extremely paranoid woman who drives on the wrong side of the road, smacks a truck, abandons a rented car, sneaks out on her host and needlessly lies to everyone she meets, even a "providential" cabdriver; yet she can't understand why the natives are suspicious of her. She mentions, almost gloatingly, a woman who neglects to flush the toilet—a phenomenon Kate has apparently never encountered in the

United States. These passages read like the revenge of a disgruntled tourist, but they are only the most obvious examples of a xenophobic elitism that also leaps at the bastardized English of an immigrant cabby and a sushi chef. Kate scrutinizes everyone in her life, past and present, friends and strangers, for blemishes. There are so many pimples we never see a face.

Adler adds her own twist to the vogue for true-life novels. Hoping to flee Ireland unrecognized (it's never clear exactly why), Kate decides to use a different name, but "one as like my own as possible." She comes up with Alder. In the raccoon scene, however, we learned that Kate's last name is Ennis. The discrepancy is never explained. Other omissions are more annoying. Much of *Pitch Dark* is structured like a mystery. The writer's notes are clues, memory aids, relating to incidents that, when finally revealed, will presumably enlighten Kate and the reader. We get pages and pages of refrains on the order of "Quanta, Amy said, on the train, in that blizzard, in answer to my question, Quanta." And so, trusting fools, we read on, waiting to find out who Amy is and what she meant and why they were on a train in a blizzard. But the answers are less than compelling, and we recognize before long that we've been strung along by yet another example of Creative Writing. Many loose ends are never tied up at all. There's a lot of talk about libel suits, for example, beginning with an obvious reference to Lillian Hellman, whose "special circle" comes to represent for Kate "one of the most important cultural manifestations of its time," and proceeding with hints about a suit Kate won. We never learn a thing about Hellman's cultural manifestation or Kate's suit. No ideas or ramifications or even facts are allowed to interrupt the nervously fussy mood of privileged melancholy.

There are acute and bristling paragraphs here and there—lucid elaborations of stealth and guilt in the Irish countryside, piquant generalizations about men and women. One of the best of these comes early and begins: "Sometimes he loved her, sometimes he was just amused and touched by the degree to which she loved him. Sometimes he was bored by her love and felt it as a burden. Sometimes his sense of himself was enhanced, sometimes diminished by it. But he had come to take the extent of her love as given, and, as such, he lost interest in it." These are disquieting passages because in them you sense Adler's potential to write a brave novel about the way people come together and fall apart. But she's opted for cleverness and subterfuge and sentiment and mood. At one point Kate dismisses Gertrude Stein as sentimental and unreadable, but she might have been describing her own novel, with its assorted tender buttons that nag and mystify. "You are the nearest thing to a real story to happen in my life," Kate persistently writes of Jake, but instead of shedding light on that story, Adler/Alder goes around unscrewing all the bulbs, leaving the page pitch dark.—GARY GIDDINS, "Quanta, Amy said, on the train . . . ," *Nation*, Feb. 18, 1984, 199–200

ROGER SHATTUCK
"Quanta"

New York Review of Books, March 15, 1984, p. 3

Stories happen only to people who can tell them.
(attributed to Thucydides)

Nature abhors a vacuum—at least in the little nook of the universe we inhabit. According to continuities and correspondences we cannot easily explain, the descriptive power of that statement appears to extend to some areas of art. When Kandinsky during the first decades of the century began to empty his paintings of the representation of external reality, a surrounding pressure of motifs awaited the opportunity to enter the vacated space. Theosophy, Besant's and Ledbetter's *Thought Forms*, and the geometry of the spiritual filled his nonobjective works as fragmented trees and figures had filled his earlier visionary landscapes.

A comparable development has affected some advanced areas of literature. For a number of years I have kept a list of devices and terms proposed from many sides to replace unity as the central organizing principle, particularly in the novel: digression, parody, marginal discourse, reflexivity, fragment, miscellany, theme and variations, *écriture*, palimpsest, and many more. The peculiar quality of Renata Adler's latest book, like the earlier *Speedboat* is that, while adopting several of these devices, it insists on describing the vacuum itself. *Pitch Dark* injects into the seemingly vacant life of the author's surrogate narrator-protagonist enough dye to give the emptiness shape and visibility. The dye is compounded of short anecdotes, comic asides, deadpan refrains, and dissertations on far-fetched topics. It shows up the vacant space without filling it, and the resultant style veers rapidly between liveliness and diagnosis.

. . . Everything Adler writes in her "novels" hovers among genres, among generations, among far-flung places, and among available moral attitudes. We would have to go at least as far back as Constant's *Adolphe* to find a beginning for this tendency toward psychological inconclusiveness. Unamuno carried it to exasperating extremes in his coy masterpiece of 1914, *Niebla*. It flows powerfully about us now in the work of Cynthia Ozick, of Milan Kundera, and of Nathalie Sarraute, about whom Adler has written a perceptive essay. Within this strain of hovering and inconclusiveness Adler has succeeded in establishing a magpie niche of her own.

Symmetrical as a triptych, *Pitch Dark* offers three fifty-page, loosely interlocking stories. Using half-page chunks—false starts, vignettes, insistent echoes—"Orcas Island" describes the never-quite-realized breakup of an affair between Kate Ennis, the narrator, and Jake, an older married man. He is vaguely understanding, preoccupied, and always off-stage. The most sustained passage works up a five-page parable about a sick raccoon who takes shelter beside Kate's stove and will not leave. Not very subtly the parable suggests that Kate is caught between her desire to go away for just a week with Jake to New Orleans and her need to take refuge alone on an island. The ruminations in this first section end characteristically with a question: "Did I throw the most important thing perhaps, by accident, away?" By now the reader understands that "the most important thing" can be stated in this frequently repeated form: "But you are, you know, you were, the nearest thing to a real story to happen in my life."

The second section, which gives its title to the book, relates with relatively few interruptions what I read as a diversionary and cautionary tale told from the middle outward. On the way to a friend's loaned estate in Ireland in search of quiet and rest, Kate has a minor car accident whose consequences infect her with a sense of disgust and guilt. She refers to herself as a "tortfeasor." These pages, whose mood of self-isolation may be taken to connect with the first section, held me more by the occasional clarity of detail than by any power in the events. There are two exceptions. Driving late at night she reverts out of habit to the right lane in a left-handed country and just misses a head-on collision with an Irish priest. (In *Speedboat*, a head-on collision is successfully consummated in a Buñuel-like apotheosis of bodies tossed into telephone wires. Then they all sit down together undismayed. Later we learn that there are convergent and divergent plots.) The other incident coyly reveals the book's umbilical cord to the outer world. Half-convinced at the airport that she should take a false name in order to escape undetected from Ireland, Kate Ennis writes: "I should make the name as like my own as possible to account for the mistake. Alder, I thought." Kate gets out of Ireland in a confusion of names; on a similar basis Adler or Alder remains very much inside *Pitch Dark*. Cervantes would have shaken his head over these clumsy maneuvers.

In "Home," the last section, the prolonged breakup with Jake is brought back into the foreground and compressed into an insistent telephone obbligato. Every third or fourth page one encounters a shred of despairing conversation overheard in London where Kate is working as a journalist. The rest of the time she is either shaping a fragile life in a small house with pond in a New England town within commuting distance of New York, or seeking refuge and solitude on Orcas Island off Seattle. Constant interruptions block any continuity that might be called a story line. The interruptions themselves, on the other hand, rough in a motif that concerns the betrayal of reality by inaccurate reporting. We follow an argument about alleged collaboration between the Nazis and the early Zionists, an outburst about the disastrous effects of anonymous sources and the advent of the byline on newspaper stories, and an essay on the abuse of the legal system.

Meanwhile Jake has a cautious reaction to reading "Orcas Island," the first part of this book you hold in your hand. Gradually it all circles back on itself in an accelerating swirl so that the last ten pages push nineteen distinct items of flotsam in front of the patient or distraught reader. Someone who cannot let go is drowning.

> In the repetitions and formulas, the courts sometimes rise from their droning with a phrase so pure, deep, and mighty that it stays. It remains forever just the way to say that thing. More probably than not. Utterly without fault. Not my act. Beyond a reasonable doubt. Last intervening wrongdoer. Cloud on title. An ordinary man. A prudent man. A reasonable man. A man of ordinary intelligence and understanding. Wait, wait. Whose voice is this? Not mine. Not mine. Not mine. Res ipsa loquitur. A man must act somehow.
> Do you sometimes wish it was me?
> Always.
> Pause.
> It is you.

By dint of repetition, variations in phrasing and speech patterns, and frequent interventions, Adler has created in *Pitch Dark* a sense of form that could be called cubist. The three sections do not develop a careful self-portrait of the central character. Yet the impulse behind the book is autobiographical, even confessional, rather than novelistic—i.e., genuinely concerned with other people's lives. The reader has to assemble Kate as the sum of her scattered parts—shy-bold, cosmopolitan, idealist, nostalgic, *farouche*. It does not spin a tale in spite of one underlined reference to the Penelope story. Rather it depicts a mode of vision, a process of gathering odds and ends into a "piece" in both the fictional and the journalistic sense. Two hundred years ago Laurence Sterne had already mastered the art of self-interruption and elaborate detour. In reading Adler I began jotting in the margins "aecp" to designate the occasional voice of an alter-ego-critic-professor bringing things to a halt, shaking her finger, and breaking any illusion of narrative momentum.

> Do I need to stylize it, then, or can I tell it as it was?
> So there is this pressure now, on every sentence, not just to say what it has to say, but to justify its claim upon our time.
> And this matter of the commas. And this matter of the paragraphs.
> Are we speaking of the anti-claque? No, not at all, of an actual person.

The frequent gaps in the prose imply both a fainthearted hope of connection and the kind of total breakdown and fresh start that Sartre detected between every successive sentence of Camus's *The Stranger*. In this inwardly impassioned work by a writer who lived as student and journalist through the Fifties, Sixties, and Seventies, there seems to be no moral center beyond the end of an affair. Sputnik, the sit-ins, the assassinations, the moonshot, Vietnam, Watergate do not even ruffle the surface. How are we to take hold of this antinovel and its predecessor, *Speedboat*, to which it seems to be a close sequel?

I believe these astutely shuffled works take shape and have an effect in two related ways. Despite the lack of reference to major social and political events, the books convey the sense of an era that cohabits uncomfortably with its past. The antepenultimate sentence of *Speedboat* holds out a small key. "I think there's something to be said for assuring the next that the water's fine—quite warm, actually—once you get into it." Next *generation* she means. Even though both novels describe, primarily through fractured form and terse diction, a version of trauma, an ego detached like a retina, still the neurosis is bearable and has its small rewards. I am reminded of how Henri Murger half-unwittingly caricatured his milieu in a little book of sketches called *La Vie de Bohème* (1849). In an era of revolutions and social upheaval he helped to create the myth of young provincial idealists surviving on love and art in their attic rooms in Paris.

We still haven't rejected that myth.

JOSEPH EPSTEIN
"The Sunshine Girls"

Commentary, June 1984, pp. 63–65

Of the two (Joan Didion and Renata Adler), Renata Adler is the less practiced novelist. She has written, in fact, two novels but no narratives. *Speedboat*, her first novel, and *Pitch Dark*, her second, are both composed for the most part of short, journal-like entries, which, in the modernist spirit, a reader has rather to assemble on his own. *Speedboat*, published in 1976, was much praised; it won the Ernest Hemingway Award for best first novel of the year in which it was published.

Reading it today, one notices certain affinities with the work of Ann Beattie: a flatness of expression meant to convey a deep spiritual fatigue. On the formal level, the novel seems Barthel-mystically influenced, though without Barthelme's intellectual playfulness. . . .

Miss Adler is not telling a story in *Speedboat*; instead she is trying to create a feeling through the thoughts, incidents, and odd happenings that occur to the presence at the center of her book, Jen Fain, who is a working journalist also teaching a film course at a school that resembles the City University of New York. The feeling she is trying to create is one of dislocation, disorientation, depression. "There doesn't seem to be a spirit of the times," Jen Fain remarks on the second page of the book. Miss Adler, though, will soon enough supply one. On that same page she has her character remark, "I think sanity, however, is the most profound moral option of our time." And at the bottom of the page, awaking at the apartment of one of her men friends, she is told, "Just stay here. *Angst* is common." We are, you might say, off and limping.

Manhattan Transfer John Dos Passos called his novel of New York life in the early 1920's; *Manhattan Transference* Renata Adler's account of New York life in the early 1970's might be called, for even though Miss Adler is no lover of therapeutic culture, the world she describes in *Speedboat* is a highly neurotic one. "Sometimes it seems that this may be a nervous breakdown—sleeping all day, tears, insomnia at midnight, and again at four A.M. Then it occurs to me that a lot of people have it." In *Speedboat* disconnection is a way of life. Rats roam the halls; a Doberman pinscher attacks an old woman. Jen Fain reports: "I knew a deliverer of flowers who, at Sixty-ninth and Lexington, was hit by a flying suicide. Situations simply do not yield to the most likely structures of the mind." And: "There are some days when everyone I see is a lunatic." These passages pile up, and all are written, in the spiritual if not the grammatical sense, in the passive voice.

Having said all this, I must go on to say that I do not find *Speedboat* boring. It ought to be, but it isn't. Perhaps it isn't because, though the book offers none of the traditional pleasures of the novel, it does offer pleasures of a different kind. When it begins to hum, Miss Adler's is a lively mind, which throws off interesting insights. "Lonely people," she writes, "see double entendres everywhere." In a brilliant passage she talks about what she calls "the Angry Bravo," which is what goes on when, in her example, an audience cheers *No, No, Nanette* when in fact behind their cheers is rage at *Hair* or whatever the going triumph of the day is. She is also clever on the unseriousness of certain artists and intellectuals. In a scene in which no names are given, an Indian lady whom I take to be Mrs. Gandhi is told by a poet whom I take to be Allen Ginsberg, "I think in this country we need to disburden ourselves of our, our burden of rationality." To which Miss Adler offers the capping comment. "He sat down. It did not seem exactly India's problem."

The world depicted in *Speedboat* is that of unattached youngish people for whom money is not a serious problem but finding a purpose in life is. They I won't say bound but at least crawl into one another's beds, less it seems out of passion than out of the need for comfort and solace against a cold world. They are distanced from life. Boredom is among their deadliest enemies. They have endless time to spend thinking about themselves. ("'Self-pity' is just sadness, I think, in the pejorative," says Miss Adler's Miss Fain.) Therapy is no help. "In every city, at the same time, therapists earned their living by

saying, 'You're too hard on yourself.'" There is a slightly frenetic stylishness about their lives. "Elaine's was jammed"; a
man invents a drink called "Last Mango in Paris." Nothing
quite holds. Jen Fain avers: "The radical intelligence in the
moderate position is the only place where the center holds."
But of those who write or argue or say that the center will not
hold, I always wonder how they know they are standing in the
center—or anywhere near it.

It doesn't take long for *Speedboat* to run out of gas. The
book provides no forward motion, nothing in the way of
momentum. In a snippet of conversation reported in one of
Miss Adler's paragraphs, a man says: "Janine, you know I'm
very tired of your *aperçus*." So in time does one grow tired of
Miss Adler's, which, in a book without any narrative force,
could, any one of them, as easily appear on page 14 as on page
203. Cause and effect, narrative order, nothing seems to matter. "It all ends in disaster anyway." But then Miss Adler is
forthright about not having a story to tell. Toward the close of
Speedboat, she writes: "There are only so many plots. There
are insights, prose flights, rhythms, felicities. But only so many
plots."

Friend, here's the bad news: you want to call yourself a
novelist, you're going to have to find a plot.

Pitch Dark, Renata Adler's recent novel, does appear to be
setting out to tell a story: that of the break-up of an eight-year
love affair between another journalist, Kate Ennis, and a married man referred to as Jake. But the story turns out not to be
much of a story. As the dust-jacket copy has it, " . . . *Pitch
Dark* moves into new realms of feeling." This book, too, peels
off into aperçuistical paragraphs; it is interested in making dis-
connections. It is about, as the narrator of this non-narration
says, "my state of mind." This second book of Miss Adler's is
more modernist, more avant-garde, in intention than *Speedboat*. The practical consequence is that, within its pages, more
puzzles are offered, more elaborate games are played.

Like all contemporary works of modernist intention, *Pitch
Dark* is highly self-reflexive—that is, it often talks about itself.
Thus, two-thirds through the book Miss Adler writes:

But will they understand it if I tell it this way?
Yes, they will. They will surely understand it.
But will they care about it?
That I cannot guarantee.

The way that *Pitch Dark* is told is aslant, through indirection.
"Do I need to stylize it, then, or can I tell it as it was?" Miss
Adler stylizes it, in my view. At the forefront of her book is the
affirmation that stories can no longer be told. "For a woman, it
is always, don't you see, Scheherazade. For a man, it may be
the Virginian. There he goes, then, striding through the dust of
midday toward his confrontation. Here I am, of an evening,
wondering whether I can hold his interest yet a while."

Throughout *Pitch Dark* lines repeat, meant to convey a
refrain-like resonance. "But you are, you know, you were, the
nearest thing to a real story to happen in my life," is one such
line: "Did I throw the most important thing perhaps, by accident, away?" is another. We cannot know for certain who is
saying these lines, Kate or Jake. But the lines recur, as do,
among others, these two: "The world is everything that is the
case," which is from Wittgenstein, and "And in the second
place because," which is the first line of a Nabokov story. Both
these lines are there to establish the modernity of Miss Adler's
narrator's mind as well as to establish the modernity of her own
intention in this book. Of the Wittgenstein line, an
epigrammatic couplet by the poet Donald Hall seems particularly pertinent here:

The world is everything that is the case.
Now stop your blubbering and wash your face.

For there is a certain high-tone blubbering going on in
Pitch Dark. In its pages Miss Adler has the portentousness knob
turned all the way up. "As much as this is the age of crime,
after all, this is the century of dislocation," Kate Ennis notes.
"Not just for journalists or refugees; for everyone." As for the
novel's weather report, it is given on page 79: "I stand, in pitch
dark now, and in heavy rain."

Miss Adler never does get around to telling the story of
Kate Ennis's long love affair with Jake. Instead she shows the
sad after-effects of its break-up. Accounts of events, she believes, are lies. What is important are moods, feelings, symbols. So we are given an account of a raccoon who slowly dies
of distemper on the stove of Kate Ennis's country house. Is this
meant to stand in for the symbolic death of her love affair? So
we are given a lengthy, deliberately paranoid account of a trip
through Ireland. Is this meant to stand in for Kate Ennis's
feeling of utter disorientation after the prop of her love affair is
pulled out from under her? So the same lines repeat and resound throughout the book. Miss Adler succeeds in giving her
novel a highly claustral feeling. Reading it one feels rather as if
one is being asked to play handball in an empty but very small
closet.

Bleak, psychologically inconclusive, bereft of the normal
pleasures of storytelling, *Pitch Dark* has nonetheless enjoyed a
pretty good run in both the popular press and from critics. In
part, I suspect, this derives from the autobiographical atmosphere of the novel. In the course of an adulatory piece about
her in *New York* magazine Miss Adler implied—and perhaps
more than implied—that the love affair that she has not really
written about in *Pitch Dark* is one that she herself has gone
through. Then there is a celebrity sheen playing about the
book's pages. Kate Ennis is often aloft, en route to one or
another island; in Ireland she stays at the house of a former
American ambassador to that country. There is also the attraction of gossip. "One morning, in the early nineteen-eighties,
Viola Teagarden filed a suit in a New York State court against
Claudia Denneny for libel. Also named as defendants were a
public television station and a talk-show host." We all know
who Viola and Claudia are, do we not? Withholding such
obvious names is a fine advance on name-dropping.

As for the critical appreciation of *Pitch Dark*, here Miss
Adler has what I think of as the moral minority on her side—
that select group of critics who worry about not lending approval to avant-garde endeavor. Roger Shattuck, for example, writing in the *New York Review of Books*, has remarked that "Adler
has created in *Pitch Dark* a sense of form that could be called
cubist." Professor Shattuck plays that old shell game of modern
criticism, switching genres, in which the critic has to guess
under which genre the work lies. "Adler, like many of her
contemporaries, abjures fusion, practices simple removal," he
writes. "The resulting minimalist genre should properly not be
called a novel, for it answers radically different expectations,
brings other rewards." Better yet, the book has allowed Professor Shattuck to erect what he calls "the innarratability principle," which has to do with the inability—or, more precisely,
unwillingness—of certain modern writers to tell their story
straight out.

But to return to the old, perhaps boring, narratability principle, would it be too rude to suggest that Miss Adler has let slip
away an extremely interesting story? The story of being a married man's mistress, told from the point of view of the mistress,
is after all neither a common nor an unpromising one. What is
it about women who enter into lengthy affairs with married

men? What do they have to gain? What is it they are afraid of? Why are they so ready to put themselves almost automatically in second place or below? But then this is a story Renata Adler, given her view that accounts of incidents are lies and that narrative contains the seeds of its own falsity, could never tell. She is among that band of contemporary writers who evidently do not agree with Oscar Wilde's statement: "It must be our faith that there is nothing that cannot be said with words."

JAMES AGEE

1909–1955

James Agee was born in Knoxville, Tennessee, on November 27, 1909. After his father's death in 1916, Agee attended several boarding schools. The last was Phillips Exeter Academy, where he began to write. He produced a volume of poetry, *Permit Me Voyage*, in 1934, two years after graduating from Harvard. During the rest of the 1930s he worked for *Fortune* magazine, which assigned him to write on tenant farmers in Alabama. Agee and photographer Walker Evans spent five years on the project, published in 1941 as *Let Us Now Praise Famous Men*.

In 1939 Agee wrote a treatment for a screenplay of André Malraux's *Man's Fate*. The movie was never made, but Agee's interest in cinema was piqued. He became film critic for *Time* and for the *Nation*, where his passionate, intelligent reviews virtually invented modern film criticism. They were collected as Volume One of *Agee on Film* in 1958. Volume Two contains the screenplays he wrote after 1948, including *The African Queen*, filmed by John Huston in 1951; *The Night of the Hunter*, filmed by Charles Laughton in 1955; and the unproduced *Noa Noa*, based on the journal of Paul Gauguin.

The 1950s were difficult for Agee, blocked by self-doubt and the effects of years of heavy drinking. His autobiographical *The Morning Watch* appeared in 1950; his next book, the novel *A Death in the Family*, was published after his death in New York City on May 16, 1955. The book won him the acclaim he never received in life, including a Pulitzer Prize in 1958. Agee was married three times, and had four children.

General

To the dozen or so good reasons that have been suggested for our having no new major novelists in America I should like to add one more. America now maintains so many areas in which a creative talent can find room for exercise that a writer whose gifts at one time would have assured us a long series of good fictions is now invited to divert his energies in a dozen different directions. And for an example of what happens to solicit some talents I would offer the case of James Agee, who had a great gift and would, one suspects, have written some fine novels. . . .

Agee had no illusions as to what was expected of him as a writer for *Fortune*: he was supposed to take an assignment and turn the material he and his researcher could gather into a sufficiently slick and smooth-running story. There was no doubting his sincerity when he said that he was working "in a whorehouse," but there was also no doubt that he took great satisfaction in concocting, out of the most recalcitrant technical materials, what have to be called masterpieces of that kind of journalism.

His ability to plunge so deeply into a *Fortune* assignment was the first manifestation of what it was in Agee that has since made people say he did not keep his "promise." Conventionally, if one writes a book of poems which "show promise" then one must go on and write another book of poems or the promise is not "kept." But Agee lacked, even more than other writers of our time, the traditional respect for genres. He went one step beyond Baudelaire's notion that any work of art contains an obstacle which the artist creates as part of the act of conceiving what he is going to do, and then conquers in the execution. For Agee, if not in theory at least in his practice of writing, the presence of an obstacle, in any kind of writing job whatever, was enough to give the job the status of a work of art. It would be false, of course, to say that he set as high a value on a *Fortune* article as on a poem or a piece of fiction, but it is gospel true that he could lose himself as completely in writing of one kind as in writing of the others. What counted was the job, the problem that was presented to the craftsman.

Admittedly, Agee was an extreme case—but just how much American talent is diverted in this way from the traditional literary forms? And how many novels have gone unwritten in our time because writers have satisfied the urge-to-write by writing which we do not label literary?

In any case, by 1934 his poetry had become a rather desultory pursuit. Agee had always been superbly indifferent about what happened to finished manuscripts. (Still further evidence that for him the important part of any writing job was the doing.) He kept no records. A piano bench in his apartment was overflowing with manuscript, but he told one New York publisher that he did not have the material for a second book of poems. Occasionally a piece of his verse would appear in a magazine like the *New Masses* or the *Partisan Review*, and doubtless still other pieces appeared in periodicals where no one has yet thought of looking for them. Compiling a check list of his poems becomes, for this reason, as difficult a task as one could take on. Manuscripts of a long "Don Juan," a satire on his youth and education, and of a long poem called "Pygmalion," which a dozen people remember having seen at one time or another, seem never to have got into print. The same is true of a novel, *The Circle*, which he had written at, off and on, since he was at Exeter, and a series of parodies of radio broadcasts to which, at one point, he devoted considerable time. So long as he stayed with *Fortune* the process of scattering went on.—W. M. FROHOCK, "James Agee—The Question of Wasted Talent," *The Novel of Violence in America,* 1957, pp. 212–17

Works

This remarkable book ⟨*Let Us Now Praise Famous Men*⟩ began as a journalistic assignment "of" share-croppers, but the editors did not reckon with their men, and the result is a serious effort to present three Alabama families and their little houses in their inner humanity and divinity on the rolling world. Agee's subjective sobriety is deeper than could be imagined, and perhaps the best portions of the work are those very ones in which he describes his misgivings at being a spy and a stranger, his refusal to submit to the categories of sociology or the devices of drama, and (to my mind a place of intense beauty) the description of his guilty joy as he fine-combs the house when the family is away.

Of the farmers, very little reality is conveyed, but there is a striking presentation of Agee himself. In rejecting the ordinary frames of explanation, he falls back on his immediate awareness and a passionate desire, and occasional sentiment, of being "with" or even "in" his subjects. At the same time, he seems to know himself not at all—but just the feeling of his anxiety and longing—so that he is always reading into their situation his own qualities, frailties, and often prejudices. Sometimes this is done with insufferable arrogance, as when he feels, on the briefest acquaintance, that a girl is going off to a marriage of misery.

He speaks always as if there were a norm of virtue and happiness: he is too modest to think this out: he continually feels and judges on the basis of it: and he occasionally explains that being as such is a disease.

Obviously, whether conscious or not, to present one's-self thru objective descriptions is a good method; but when Agee raises his art to the level of theory, which requires understanding, he is far off. His passages on the poetics of what he is doing are confusion, and he seems not to realize that many other writers, faced with the white page and their past and immediate experience, also ask what they are about, and that there are several ways to go from there. When his scrupulousness is raised to theory, he is for all the world like the girl who tries for the prize for Conspicuous Modesty. Above all, till he acquires the gift of objective personal intuition, he should shun like the plague the matter of educational psychology.

What is surprising to me is that a writer so conscious and ashamed of his "own kind" (journalist, Harvard, urban, etc.) is so unable to shake all that off, to treat it ironically, or with scientific heat.

On a point of technique: altho the division of the work into sections on Shelter, Clothing, Education, Work, etc. is reasonable, I do not see why it would be less true or more "artistic" to present the subject prior to this analysis, concretely functioning with them all. And especially, in place of the lists of items that Agee gives us, must we not return again and again to Lessing's remark on Homer: he shows us the dress of Agamemnon when Agamemnon is putting it on. As a critic of architecture I am simply flabbergasted by the sentence "Since a house is so entirely static a subject, the presenting of it may be slow going."

Many of the items, for instance the oil-lamp or the overalls, are presented with extraordinary beauty and power and a kind of isolated truth. The observation of the style, surface, and

matter of things, not people, is sensitive often to the point of genius. The sense of their proportions, tradition, and social tone is more feeble.

In this brief notice I must culpably omit any mention of the effects of Agee's singular prose, and the least mention of Evans' marvelous photographs.—PAUL GOODMAN, *PR,* Jan.–Feb. 1942, pp. 86–87

I began by saying that Agee's text ⟨*Let Us Now Praise Famous Men*⟩ fails in an important way; I of course did not mean this inevitable and intended failure, which is part of Agee's conscious method and attitude. And certainly I did not mean that Agee fails as a writer to execute what he undertakes. On the contrary, nine out of every ten pages are superb. Agee has a sensibility so precise, so unremitting, that it is sometimes appalling; and though nothing can be more tiresome than protracted sensibility, Agee's never wearies us: I think this is because it is brilliantly normal and because it is a moral rather than a physical sensibility. To be sure, his judgment fails him now and again and some of the introspective and meditative passages turn furiously purple. But against this we can set the scores of astounding scenes he has created: the Negro singers, the three people on the hopeless farm, the two young Negroes overtaken on the road, the departure of Emma; and with these many of the meditations, such as the one on the paradox of the beauty which he cannot help seeing in the poverty; and the precise descriptions of the method of work, of financial arrangements, of house-gear, of clothes (especially the disquisition on overalls), of the graveyard. The book is full of marvelous writing which gives a kind of hot pleasure that words can do so much.

The failure I referred to is certainly not literary; it is a failure of moral realism. It lies in Agee's inability to see these people as anything but good. Not that he falsifies what is apparent: for example he can note with perfect directness their hatred of Negroes; and not that he is ever pious or sentimental, like Steinbeck and Hemingway. But he writes of his people as if there were no human unregenerateness in them, no flicker of malice or meanness, no darkness or wildness of feeling, only a sure and simple virtue, the growth, we must suppose, of their hard, unlovely poverty. He shuts out, that is, what it is a part of the moral job to take in. What creates this falsification is guilt—the observer's guilt at his own relative freedom. Agee is perfectly conscious of this guilt and it is in order to take it into account that he gives us so many passages of autobiography and self-examination; he wants the reader to be aware of what is peculiar and distorting in the recording instrument, himself. But his device, intended in the interest of objectivity, does not succeed. For one thing, too much of our attention is taken with subtracting Agee from his record, even though we respect both the invitation to subtract and the personality we are asked to deduct. And then, despite Agee's clear consciousness of his guilt, he cannot control it. It overflows and carries away the truth that poverty and suffering are not in themselves virtue.

And yet, even when this failure has been noted, Agee's text still is, it seems to me, the most realistic and the most important moral effort of our American generation.—LIONEL TRILLING, "Greatness with One Fault in It," *KR,* Winter 1942, pp. 101–2

James Agee's novelette ⟨*The Morning Watch*⟩ is an ambitious one. It makes large demands on the short fictional form and on language. It achieves some brilliant successes and flirts with some lamentable failures, as nearly every fiction must which proceeds on Mr. Agee's principle. This is the principle of *tour de force,* or, as Melville said, "violent escalade." (I think of

Melville because *The Morning Watch*, though more *professional* than anything Melville wrote, makes certain demands on metaphor and myth which are almost as fierce and as impossible as those in *Pierre*.) Since Mr. Agee is a very good writer, the virtue of his story generates the vice, and conversely. We discover striking poetic *synthèse*; we are excited by a fast-paced shifting from experience to experience; we perceive a schematic assertion of "meaning." But, on the other hand, there is a great surplus of poetical consciousness as compared with what the persons and situations of the story appear to necessitate; there is a disproportion between substance and form, between meaning and metaphor; and despite a great deal of local excitement and activity, there is a heavy inertness of the whole. . . .

Although it has always been difficult for American writers of the headlong, myth-making type to believe, there are certainly limits to what the exacerbated sensibility can accomplish by itself. And although it deploys and substantiates itself in a variety of ways as if it were about to transcend the *tour de force* and become a realized fiction, exacerbated sensibility remains Mr. Agee's chief stock in trade. Joyce's *Portrait of the Artist* reminds us of the usefulness of the objective modes of drama, plot, and idea in presenting this subject matter. The people around Mr. Agee's central figure are shadowy. And the boy himself is always in danger of being kidnapped from the dramatic and ideational context by the highly wrought language. The repetitiousness with which the boy has evil thoughts and then feels contrite cannot help being monotonous since these incidents do not exfoliate anywhere except in local metaphor—a handicap somewhat serious in a fiction professedly dealing with the passage of an individual from weakness to strength, isolation to society, self-torture to peace, and so on.

The trouble with Mr. Agee's language is not that it lacks skill or brilliance or subtlety, for often it pre-eminently possesses these qualities. The trouble is that his language is a kind of free-lance, predatory agent within his book. The following is a fair example of the author's standard success:

> The nave replied to their timid noises with the threatening resonance of a drumhead. Not even the sanctuary lamps were lighted, but the night at the windows made just discernible the effigies and the paintings and the crucifix, no longer purple veiled but choked in black, and the naked ravagement of the High Altar. The tabernacle gawped like a dead jaw. By this ruthless flaying and deracination only the skeleton of the Church remained; it seemed at once the more sacred in dishonor, and as brutally secular as a boxcar.
>
> To cross its axis without the habitual genuflection felt as uneasy as to swim across a sudden unimaginable depth, and as Richard turned and bowed before the central devastation he realized: nothing there. Nothing at all; and with the breath of the Outer Darkness upon his soul, remembered the words: And the Veil of the Temple was rent in twain.

This is genuinely splendid and daring. Yet at the end of such a paragraph one feels that the author has turned loose a kind of ravenous metaphorical beast who has swallowed up the hero. If it be argued that this is a proper "poetic" device, if not quite proper as a general rule in prose fiction, one may point out that (for example) Dante never allows this sort of thing to happen in the *Comedy*. A related tendency is Mr. Agee's excessive animism, which permits him to say of almost any object that it is "bruised" or "stunned." And so, just as the reader feels the need to reconstitute character and action as apart from language and sensibility, he also has to reconstitute life as the center of sensitivity.

The last section of *The Morning Watch* shifts to a directly symbolic method. Like the early sections, it is often successful in particular but remains dubious as a whole fictional construction. A locust shell, a plunge to the depths of the water in a quarry and the return to the surface, a snake shedding its skin are all symbolic of Richard's transition to a new life. There are overtones of *Job* and of Melville. The snake, which Richard kills, contains the *mana* of God's creativity, like the Leviathan of *Job*. And like Ahab contemplating Moby Dick, the boy "saw perfected before him, royally dangerous and to be adored and to be feared, all that is alien in nature and in beauty: and stood becharmed." Killing the snake, which he associates with his father, the boy acquires freedom and animal power. The locust shell (one would judge) becomes the symbol of his attachment to the cycles of time and to eternity. Sharing with Melville's whale an immediate relation to the dawn of earth—"Mesozoic, Protozoic, Jurassic"—it is also the life Christ put behind him in order to be reborn. Mr. Agee's symbolic conclusion is really a little series of homilies and prose poems. The symbols must be among the most striking in contemporary fiction, yet they do not convince us that what Mr. Agee says has happened to Richard has happened. Where the plot demands at least a measure of relaxed and perspicuous biography of spiritual change, we have spectacular semantic gestures instead.

Emily Dickinson's precept—"Nature is a haunted house, art a house that tries to be haunted"—appears to be Mr. Agee's motto too. It implies that the structure of art is already provided by the mere intention to create and that all the artist needs to do is inspirit and to populate—that is, to haunt—the house. To point out that this is a rather large assumption is not to advance what Mr. Agee will perhaps think are "academic" scruples about form but to suggest that if you start out so exclusively with the mere unguarded sensibility, you need more than rhetorical brilliance and willed forcefulness to produce a durable fiction.—RICHARD CHASE, "Sense and Sensibility," *KR*, Autumn 1951, pp. 688–90

The posthumously published *A Death in the Family* is Agee's final item of his career in letters, a novel on which he had been at work for eight years. It does not give him any new importance as an American writer, but it does bring to a delicate and satisfying flowering his very great ability to create the qualities and the nuances of private feeling.

A Death in the Family is not a major book, but a haunting one. It presents human anguish in language of surface accuracy and of great evocative power. Phrase after phrase sets all the tentacles of the reader's private sea of the subconscious alert and waving. It is also a curiously intractable book because it constantly raises the question of what a novel exists to do. Like his earlier *The Morning Watch*, it is an episode of personal grief, well remembered and told as if it were a novel. . . .

These events have an intense emotional effect on the reader because of Agee's skill in presenting them with an almost intolerable immediacy. Rufus, standing at the curb, watches a horse "draw a buggy crisply but sedately past," and notes that "in the washed black spokes, sunlight twittered."

And Agee can hold the reader's emotions in much tighter rein. The accuracy of his description of Rufus' first view of his father's coffin forces the reader to hold on desperately to his own composure:

> It was very long and dark; smooth like a boat; with bright handles. Half the top was open. There was a strange sweet smell, so faint that it could scarcely be realized.

Rufus had never known such stillness. Their little sounds as they approached his father, vanished upon it like the infinitesimal whisperings of snow, falling on open water.

There was his head, his arms; suit; there he was.

But it is the very intensity of feeling, beautifully poised in words, which puts severe limitations on *A Death in the Family*. Serious prose fiction characteristically demonstrates the possibilities and the results of its given events, and of its given characters' acts and decisions. Agee was unwilling or unable to endow either the events or the characters of his novel with this fictional vitality and coherence. He exploits only the emotional content of his material, not its meaning. *A Death in the Family*, therefore, has little of fiction's customary impact on our view of things. It lacks narrative thrust and intellectual excitement.

There are moments of grief and loss in everyone's life which one cannot live with, but can only recover from. And they are, oddly, the moments when one recognizes one's feelings to have been most alive. The success of *A Death in the Family* is that it brings to the surface of the reader's consciousness these forgotten, rejected moments—his own tender, unusable anguish.— David L. Stevenson, "Tender Anguish," *Nation*, Dec. 14, 1957, pp. 460–61

. . . I have to insist that *A Death in the Family* is not about childhood, or the way boys and girls grow up, or learn to cope with tragedies like the loss of a parent. Yet the novel does touch upon all of that; in fact, Agee unquestionably has a consistent vision of the child's special kind of human situation, and he wants to unfold the vision before us unobtrusively but as fully as the Follet family and their fortunes (or moment of awful misfortune) will permit him. . . .

Agee knows that a disaster brings to focus and heightens the importance of what has preceded it; tragically, unexpectedly, the natural ups and downs of a person's life, a family's life, have to be tested and found either wanting or sufficient; and such a test can be as unfair and hard in its own way as the awful precipitating crisis. Agee had to begin somewhere, and it was not all that clever of him to give us a father and son intimately together for what turns out to be the last time. The psychological elements he chooses to emphasize before the phone rings, bringing Ralph's voice to his brother, Jay, with news of the grave illness of their father—Jay would go, find the news exaggerated, and die on his way home—are quite another matter: they are elements not every writer, however good, would choose to present so clearly and immediately, and they are also elements, I would argue, that in a few pages establish Agee's view of human nature. It is a view familiar to us of the twentieth century: the enormous influence of childhood is rather obviously stressed. . . .

We are constantly kept to a story; there is no larger theme, no lesson subtly or not so subtly worked in. In so doing Agee was no doubt immediately denying his readers much they may expect and feel themselves entitled to have: prompt speculation about the meaning of death; the beginning of a discussion of the way children grow up and come to terms with certain overwhelming and unexpected assaults; and maybe a remedy or two, or an example of what ought be said and done in this sophisticated, emotionally self-aware century. Nor are such gestures or obsessions so much to ask of a novelist; Thomas Mann outlived Agee, and before both of them there is a splendid tradition of avowedly philosophical and psychological novels that might have served to inspire a writer like Agee, who knew quite clearly who to live up to and what to gain sanction from.

But he resisted; this is not a novel that concentrates its energies on states of mind, what they are like and how they are changed. Nor ought we say an author was nearly consumed by his many concerns, hence unable to give this novel of his the kind of sustained analytic attention its subject matter might otherwise have obtained. Agee was certainly a discursive writer, and a man rather easily distracted. Yet this is a tightly written novel. He intentionally refrains from using his characters to illustrate the unconscious at work in children or the torment an overworked conscience can bring to a bereaved wife. Even the lyric moments are kept under careful control, for Agee a considerable achievement.—Robert Coles, "Childhood: James Agee's *A Death in the Family*," *Irony in the Mind's Life*, 1974, pp. 61–66

PETER H. OHLIN
Agee
1966, pp. 22–47

On the whole, it can be said that Agee's poetry, especially in *Permit Me Voyage*, exists in a field between two poles: one of them is the example of the sixteenth- and seventeenth-century Elizabethans, Donne, Shakespeare, and others; the other is provided by such American poets as Whitman and Hart Crane. Agee was of course familiar with the metaphysical poets; in his letters he writes: "I've been reading a good deal of John Donne and Herbert, Vaughan, and Emily Dickinson, whose work bears a remarkable resemblance to Donne."[1] And the preparation he foresees for himself in his long letter to Father Flye seems to recall Donne in its conjunction of opposites into balance: "I've got to make my mind as broad and deep and rich as possible, as quick and fluent as possible; abnormally sympathetic and yet perfectly balanced."[2] In certain sections of Agee's "Epithalamium," the use of paradox recalls Donne and the Elizabethans, even though Agee's language avoids the angularly strong lines of Donne:

> For that the flesh arises like a wall
> Between two souls, all love has known distress.
> But they have conquered sorrow, conquered all
> That clouded love: are one in nothingness.
>
> Such nothingness remains, and yet is gone,
> Looks upon all, and yet is void of sight,
> Quickens the roots of every flowering dawn,
> Coils in the core of every ripening night:
>
> It breathes from steady water, is the pain
> Of bursting seeds, the agony of earth
> Shuddering out its life; . . .
>
> (43)

In the "Sonnets," Agee sometimes employs the kind of direct and forcefully conversational opening line that we have learned to associate with Donne:

> What curious thing is love that you and I
> Hold it impervious to all distress
> And insolent in gladness set it high
> Above all other joy and goodliness?
>
> (49)

> Why am I here? Why do you look at me
> Triumphantly and lovingly and long?
>
> (50)

> Is love then royal on some holy height?
> Thence does he judge us, thence dispense his grace?
>
> (51)

Those former loves wherein our lives have run
Seeing them shining, following them far,
Were but a hot deflection of the sun,
The operation of a migrant star.
(55)

The sonnet cycle, in fact, reminds one of the Elizabethans in its meditational nature: all twenty-five sonnets deal with the human condition conceived in Anglo-Catholic (or, for that matter, Catholic) terms. The first sonnet, significantly, begins with Adam and the world which he has left to mankind:

So it begins. Adam is in his earth
Tempted and fallen, and his doom made sure
O, in the very instant of his birth:
Whose deathly nature must all things endure.
The hungers of his flesh, and mind, and heart
That governed him when he was in the womb,
These ravenings multiply in every part:
And shall release him only to the tomb.
Meantime he works the earth, and builds up nations,
And trades, and wars, and learns, and worships chance,
And looks to God, and weaves the generations
Which shall his many hungerings advance
When he is sunken dead among his sins.
Adam is in his earth. So it begins.
(46)

This is the beginning, the origin, of the human condition. No image could better symbolize for Agee the plight of mankind than the picture of Adam, "his doom made sure / O, in the very instant of his birth," yet struggling against all odds to find for himself a release from those "hungers" which define his life. In its circular movement (the first line occurs with a slight reversal as the last line), the sonnet suggests, in fact, the history of all mankind, and this sense is supported by the sestet which rises above Adam's particular situation as a human individual to examine the life he has made for himself, with work, trades and wars, and to see him as the weaver of generations: here is our beginning in history.

With this situation in mind, the rest of the twenty-five sonnets explore the human condition in greater detail. The succeeding sonnet, for instance, begins: "Our doom is in our being. We began / In hunger eager more than ache of hell," and goes on to explore how this "hunger" dominates the human condition. This, of course, is Agee's conception of original sin, of man's predestined shortcomings, but it is significant that he chooses to call it hunger rather than desire. It is one of Agee's characteristics, all through his works, that he reduces such an absolute concept as the human condition to its most elemental terms: in that sense, "hunger" is more concrete than "desire," which has largely psychological connotations. Also, Agee was never blind to the human quality in this hunger, even though it stands as an opposite to the divine in man: in the sonnet, he continues with a set of paradoxes discussing just this:

And in that hunger became each a man
Ravened with hunger death alone may spell:
And in that hunger live, as lived the dead,
Who sought, as now we seek, in the same ways,
Nobly, and hatefully, what angel's-bread
Might ever stand us out these short few days.
(46)

"Hunger" and "angel's-bread," "nobly, and hatefully," these are paradoxes that seem to define the human predicament.

The attempt to see the human situation in terms as elemental as possible leads Agee, in the third sonnet, to describe a human life in terms of the changing seasons, not,

however, with the emphasis on how a human life can be said to correspond in its stages to the various seasons of spring, summer, fall, and winter, but with a wealth of concrete details which emphasize and give richness to the inevitability of their passing:

The wide earth's orchard of your time of knowing,
Shine of the springtime pleasures into bloom
And branched throes of health; but soon the snowing
And tender foretaste of your afterdoom,
Of fallen blossoming air persuades the air
In hardier practices: and soon dilate
Fruits and the air together that shall bear
Earthward the heavied boughs and to their fate. . . .
(47)

In the fourth sonnet, the poet examines the human condition from yet another point of view: looking back on the line of his ancestors, he sees their valiant striving as well as their failure, and realizes that the same strife is now his, and that the knowledge of inevitable failure does not excuse him from the task:

I have been fashioned on a chain of flesh
Whose backward length is broken on the dust:
Frail though the dust and small as the dew's mesh
The morning mars, it holds me to a trust:
My flesh that was, long as this flesh knew life,
Strove and was valiant, still strove, and was naught:
Now it is mine to wage their valiant strife
And failing seek still what they ever sought.
I have been given strength they never wore.
I have been given hope they never knew.
And they were brave, who can be brave no more.
And they that live are kind as they are few.
'Tis mine to touch with deathlessness their clay:
And I shall fail, and join those I betray.
(47)

In one sense, this is a declaration of human fallibility as proclaimed by Catholic dogma (Catholic rather than Protestant because of the emphasis on "their valiant strife" rather than on "faith"), but even more, it is a statement that the inevitable failure is what gives dignity to and, in fact, defines a human being, and that every new generation, with its new strength and new hope, must define itself through a new strife and a new failure. This is so not merely in theological terms but also in all human activities: in sonnet VIII and the following sonnets, the failure of love is explored:

Be mindful that all love is as the grass
And all the goodliness of love the flower
Of grass, for lo, its little day shall pass
And withering and decay define its hour.
(49)

Finally, in the last sonnet of the cycle, the failure of the poet himself is mentioned:

These are confusing times and dazed with fate:
Fear, easy faith, or wrath's on every voice:
Those toward the truth with brain are blind or hate:
The heart is cloven on a hidden choice:
In which respect I still shall follow you.
And when I fail, know where the fault is due.
(58)

"Failure," said Melville in his essay on Hawthorne, "is the true test of greatness," and Agee is constantly concerned with the quality of human failure (and, as will be shown later, in *Let Us Now Praise Famous Men*, the artistic problem becomes one of taking failure into account during the creation of a work of art, to make the very failure itself into art). Instead of turning this awareness of failure into a gloomy righteousness over human depravity, Agee sees it as what must be affirmed if one wants to be human. . . .

Even after this brief disucssion of Agee's sonnets, it should be clear that the sonnets at least attempt what Agee meant when he said, "I want to *write symphonies*. That is, characters introduced quietly (as are themes in a symphony, say) will recur in new lights, with new verbal orchestration, will work into counterpoint and get a sort of monstrous grinding beauty. . . ."[3] For while the theme of the whole cycle is the condition of man as defined by religious doctrine, it occurs with many subtle variations in new settings to throw new light on a different situation. This is perhaps the most noteworthy achievement of the cycle as a whole and it points up to what Agee was later to attempt. Considered separately, as poems, the individual sonnets are not always successful; in general, they suffer from their close approximation of seventeenth-century poetics and a slightly archaic style, but when they do succeed, as do sonnets XX, XXII, and XXIV, to cite only three, they have a clear precision of language, a delicate concreteness of imagery, and a subtle sense of rhythm.

Yvor Winters has called "A Chorale" a "remarkable poem" (without explaining why),[4] but perhaps the most remarkable thing about the poem is simply the effort to write "a chorale." The choice of genre is itself symptomatic of Agee's strong commitment to his religious background, and the poem struggles to find adequate expressions for this commitment in a world which has turned its back on it. Thus, the poem grows out of the poet's sense of religion as providing a standard for judgment, and it is the radical nature of the poet's choice which is perhaps more amazing than anything else. For it would seem that the poem remains too strongly bound by its own sense of archaism to be quite effective: instead of the awareness of tradition in a new dress (such as we can find it in, say, Eliot or Auden), the poem gives us an elegantly contrived pastiche.

While there are fine passages that are modern in the best sense of the word (such as "Great God kind God the deep fire-headed fountain / Of earth and funneled hell and hopeful mountain"), the diction in general, for instance, echoes the Book of Common Prayer (neologisms like "heartsearth" and "allsalvation" presumably modeled on words like "lovingkindness") or early Bible translations ("sweet earth," "wasting shadow," "sickly slow," "ghosted Gods"). The syntax in the first few stanzas is so uncomfortable that it makes one think of Milton's worst Latinizing excesses. In this way, we get mainly imitation rather than original; and this failure to reconcile the tradition with the present can be seen in the following couplet (addressed to Christ):

> The time is withered of your ancient glory:
> Your doing in this sweet earth a pretty story.
>
> (37)

It seems safe to suggest that the words "a pretty story" are meant to be ironic in this context, yet they fail because the tone of flippancy they engender has not been logically or emotionally suggested in the earlier stanzas, where, on the contrary, the present evil state of the world is discussed in the loftiest rhetoric ("How knowledge muffles wisdom's eye to danger: / How greed misrules: how greed's enraged avenger / Swears greed the equal prize for man's pursuing, / And your undoing").

Despite this failure, however, it is the tone of the poem which attracts attention. The poet's attitude to his material reveals an uncompromising attempt to judge the deterioration of the modern world from certain basic values of the Christian tradition. The poem also shows clearly that the poet has real-
ized the need for a rhetoric of some sort to lift the matter out of its everyday connections and make it "poetically" true. In other words, we find here Agee's realization that the conflict between the Christian tradition and the decay of the modern world cannot be resolved in realistic terms if it is not to turn into a trivial quarrel; the high rhetoric is needed to lift the poem to a level on which the conflict can be meaningfully resolved in the minds of the poet and his reader. Unfortunately, Agee's rhetoric borrows so much from the Elizabethans that the poem becomes little more than a pastiche; but the attempt is in itself worthy of notice for it foreshadows the kind of attack on a literary problem which appears in *Let Us Now Praise Famous Men*. Above all, there is evident in the poem passion as well as compassion, high seriousness, and humility:

> If this your Son is now indeed debasèd
> Among old effigies of God effacèd,
> Blaze in our hearts who still in earth commend you:
> Who through all desolation will defend you:
> For we are blinded all and steep are swervèd
> Far among many Deaths who still would be preservèd.

The same tone is present in the best poem of the collection. "Dedication" begins with the following words: "In much humility / to God in the highest / in the trust that he despises nothing" (16); and under the heading "And in his commonwealth," it goes on to list a long number of people, places, and things to whom the poet directs his dedication. Exactly what it is that the poet dedicates is not immediately clear: it may be his book of poems, or it may be his life, or it may be the spiritual effort of the person who happens to be writing the lines.

Essentially, the poem is based on the same conception that underlies "A Chorale": the world is seen in a traditional Anglo-Catholic manner with God as the inevitable point on which the structure of the world is based. The poet's emphasis, as he looks at the world, on continuous human failures, is, again, a reflection of the traditional Christian concept of human fallibility. . . .

It is impossible to know if Agee would ever have become a major poet had he concentrated more of his talents on verse. As this chapter has shown, he was acutely aware of the medium he was working in, he felt dissatisfied with traditional form and expressed a desire to write "musically" and to evolve a new kind of poetic diction. In this, he hardly succeeded, not because he lacked the talent, but because his ambition was so out of the ordinary and, also, because, as it turned out, prose proved to be a better medium for it than poetry. The early poetry simply shows a talented young man working with language, developing his skill in handling words, rhythms, images, and metaphors, and, above all, emotions. And all that is best in the poetry, the clear and precise language, the high rhetoric, the human involvement, the moral effort, the search for a huge symphonic structure accommodating the details of human experience, simple and complex, all looks forward to what he was to attempt more decisively in *Let Us Now Praise Famous Men*. The poetry, try as it may, does not entirely succeed in fusing that improbable combination of an Anglo-Catholic tradition and a Whitmaniacal "feeling of love for everything." As John Bradbury has pointed out, it "often sinks to the Stuart level in his effusive treatment of religious and sentimental themes,"[5] but in "Dedication," where the Anglo-Catholicism is used as a perspective or a point of view rather than as a theme, Agee does succeed in building a "musical" structure with a powerful, reiterative impact in the manner of Whitman.

Notes

1. *The Letters of James Agee to Father Flye* (New York: George Brazil-
   ler, 1962), p. 41.
2. *Letters*, p. 47.
3. *Letters*, p. 47.

4. Yvor Winters, *In Defense of Reason* (New York: The Swallow Press
   and W. Morrow and Company, 1947), p. 512.
5. John M. Bradbury, *Renaissance in the South* (Chapel Hill: The
   University of North Carolina Press, 1963), p. 186.

CONRAD AIKEN

1889–1973

Conrad Potter Aiken was born in Savannah, Georgia, on August 5, 1889. When he was eleven, he discovered the bodies of his parents, killed in an apparent suicide pact. He lived with an aunt in New Bedford, Massachusetts, until he entered Harvard in 1907. There he shared the presidency of the *Advocate* with T. S. Eliot, who became an important artistic influence on Aiken as well as a close friend. In 1912 he graduated; married Jessie McDonald, with whom he would have three children; and launched into a literary career of perpetual motion, moving from poetry to fiction to essays to drama as easily and frequently as he moved from place to place.

For the next decade Aiken travelled, writing for a variety of publications and consorting with fellow Imagists Ezra Pound and Amy Lowell. He was a conscientious objector in World War I. From 1919 to 1925 he was American correspondent for the *Athenaeum*, and from 1921 to 1922 for the *London Mercury*. In the late 1920s he taught at Harvard, divorced his wife, and married Clarice Lorenz. His *Selected Poems* won a Pulitzer Prize in 1930. Under the pseudonym "Samuel Jeake, Jr.," Aiken was London correspondent for the *New Yorker* from 1934, when he received a Guggenheim fellowship, to 1936. In 1937 he divorced Clarice to wed Mary Hoover.

Aiken served as poetry consultant to the Library of Congress from 1950 to 1952, the year the autobiographical *Ushant* was published. The book won the Bryher Award, and is thought by many critics to be Aiken's finest work. Two years later, *Collected Poems* won a National Book Award. Later awards included the Bollingen Prize, an American Academy of Poets fellowship, the Gold Medal of the National Institute of Arts and Letters, the St. Botolph Award, and a National Medal for Literature. He died in Savannah on August 17, 1973. His daughter Joan is a celebrated author of children's books.

General

At the same time, Aiken has been more deeply concerned in his work with the investigation, exploration, and definition of his own developing consciousness than any other of our major contemporary poets. He has sought, particularly in his novels, to achieve a precise understanding of his own growth, both as a person and as an artist. One of his comments on the work of Archibald MacLeish is particularly revealing—deliberately so—along these lines. Criticizing MacLeish's prefatory remark that "My development as a poet is of no interest to me and of even less interest, I should think, to anyone else," Aiken observed: "One might as well say that one's growth as a human being, as a tree, as a world, or even as a God, is of no concern either to oneself or to another. It simply isn't true. One *is*, and profoundly, interested in one's own growth: one cannot escape it: and to deny one's interest is perhaps merely (inversely) to overstate it. Is it possible that Mr. MacLeish is *over*concerned with his development as a poet, *just as we are?*"

Aiken *has* been concerned with his own development. It might even be said that all of his books, his criticism and fiction as well as his poetry after *Turns and Movies*, are progressive comments upon the state of his (to use one of his own titles) "changing mind." The primary purpose of my study of Aiken will be to consider how he has developed and to what end—and what problems have arisen in consequence of his need and desire to develop in a particular way. Throughout his career, he has sought the means whereby he might make his mental

and emotional development articulate; and he has used various forms to do this in his search for a linguistic and structural equivalent to his mental experience. Almost every one of his books in the past forty years has approached this problem in a new way, with a new style (though, of course, with some constant characteristics), each intended to communicate most directly the particular experience embodied in it. I should make it clear that in speaking of Aiken's development I am not also implying that his poetry has become more perfect. Each book has not inevitably advanced upon its predecessors. Probably *Senlin* (1918), the Preludes (1931–1936), and A *Letter From Li Po* (1955), separated by many years, and quite different, are all on the same level of artistic achievement. The books that surround these fall below the aesthetic culminations which they represent. But we will be tracing out an evolution: a clear movement from one work to another throughout Aiken's career. And the principle of that evolution is Aiken's deepening and subtilization of his self-awareness. As Erich Kahler defined "evolution" in general, the movement of Aiken's career has been "neither straight nor circular, but proceeds in a revolving movement, at once expanding and advancing, like a spiral." How then, I shall inquire, has Aiken expanded the range of his experience, and how, at the same time, has he successfully refined his means to explore and exploit his consciousness, from his earliest to his most recent work?

This, as it seems to me, is the kind of study which is needed at this stage of our understanding of Aiken's work. As Allen Tate observed in his citation of Aiken for the Gold Medal of the Institute of Arts and Letters, Aiken has written "a formidable body of work with which we have not yet come to terms." This body of work—and its form and function—will be my one and only concern. There is no question, of course, that Aiken's poetry is his major achievement; consequently, I shall be mainly concerned with elucidating that part of his work. I will, however, also consider Aiken's fiction and criticism, since both help to illuminate aspects of his poetry. R. P. Blackmur observed of Aiken's first novel, *Blue Voyage*—and the same is true of his later novels—that "the novel is the prose version of the poems. In the novel we get the psychology, and the philosophical notions behind it, in an almost pure form; in the poems these are translated into symbols, images, and music. In both, the poet is preoccupied with the Blue Voyage or Great Circle Passage of the soul, the *voyage à l'infini*, the exploration of his own heart." Since the appearance of Aiken's autobiographical "essay," *Ushant*, it has been clear that Aiken himself understands his literary career in terms of the experience he has been able to express in his fiction. With the sole exception of *The Kid*, he mentions his poems in only a cursory fashion in *Ushant*, while he discusses his fiction at length. Although Aiken does this ironically, he also intends thereby to emphasize his fiction. For the critic of Aiken, then, the novels assume considerable importance aside from their individual merits, since an understanding of his fiction helps toward an elucidation of his poetry.

Aiken has also written a great deal of criticism. The check list of his reviews and essays lists over two hundred and fifty pieces, written from 1915 to 1955. Marianne Moore has written of Aiken that "he was the perfect reviewer, Diogenes' one honest man, fearing only to displease himself" (*Wake*, 56). He was one of the first American critics to apply Freudian and other psychological theories to the judgment of poetry in an investigation of the mechanism of literary creation. Because he employed novel, if not revolutionary, standards of critical judgment, he was forced to develop and explain his ideas anew in each of his critical essays. More than most poets, then, Aiken constantly provides insights into the critical bases of his creative productions. Perhaps more important, he has, on occasion, reviewed his own books. He anonymously reviewed his *Nocturne of Remembered Spring* in 1917; and in 1919, at Harriet Monroe's invitation, discussed the aims of *The Charnel Rose*. Recently, in analyzing the reasons why he "drifted into criticism at all," Aiken has spoken of the relationship between his criticism and the development of his poetry. Of his *Scepticisms* (1919) he wrote: "Its effect on myself was deep and permanent. It was apparent to me that I must henceforward be concerned as much with criticism as with poetry or fiction, that it could go hand in hand with these quite naturally and easily, and with the already foreseeable advantage that one genre could thus fortify or fructify or clarify the other: they could work in tandem." After *Scepticisms* we can observe an expansion in the range of Aiken's criticism. He was quite consciously using his criticism—as he used his fiction—to provide new areas of awareness for his poetry. Taken as a whole, therefore, Aiken's criticism possesses the same interest and importance as his fiction in an investigation of his development.—JAY MARTIN, "Introduction" to *Conrad Aiken: A Life of His Art*, 1962, pp. 9–12.

Works

POETRY

When there appear the collected or selected poems of a mature poet, the temptation to "place" him with respect to his con-

temporaries is very great. One realizes, of course, that the attempt is very dangerous, but it may conceivably be illuminating. The best American poets of Mr Aiken's generation, it should be fairly safe by now to say, are Robert Frost (if his age does not disqualify him), W. C. Williams, Ezra Pound, T. S. Eliot, Marianne Moore, Mina Loy, Archibald MacLeish, John Crowe Ransom, Wallace Stevens, and possibly H. D. It is doubtful if any one of these is a poet of the very first order if we look for the qualities that Arnold found or thought he found in Wordsworth (and Wordsworth was, according to Arnold, only of the second order) or that one today can find easily enough in Arnold; but Mr. Frost in six or eight of the lyrics in *West-Running Brook* will come fairly near the mark, in spite of his deliberate (and not wholly successful) effort to evade certain themes that Arnold would have insisted on his mastering (see his shockingly timid remarks in the lyric called "The Times Table"); and Dr. Williams will come at least as near in a dozen or more scattered lyrics, in spite of the various criteria of good poetry that he has endeavored at different times to establish, which would, if applied to his own best poems, render them of little or no worth. Whatever the spiritual limitations of any of this list of writers, however, they have shown themselves here and there to be, all of them, first rate stylists. The question arises whether Mr. Aiken is their equal as a stylist; it is my opinion that he is not.

Mr. Aiken's debt to Mr. Eliot has been over-estimated; it really amounts to little or nothing. Mr. Eliot's early work, which is supposed to have exerted the influence, employs a line that is based on the standard iambic pentameter; Mr. Aiken's line varies, but it is almost never that. The only resemblance that I can discover is the similar tendency to wandering rhymes (very common in all of the late French symbolists, from Laforgue to Vielé-Griffin); and in *Senlin* Mr. Aiken made his protagonist philosophize while combing his hair. Like Mr. Eliot, Mr. Aiken has used a kind of stream-of-consciousness method, and like him also has endeavored through the use of that method to deal rather extensively with the spiritual difficulties and the concrete aspects of our period. *The Waste Land* lacks form; Mr. Aiken's long poems in a sense achieve form or at least cohesion—that is, they are not obviously falling apart from line to line. But if one examines them carefully, it is fairly evident that the lines cohere not because they have any common intention or direction, but because they have no intention or direction; there is nothing to force them apart, no group of identities for the poet to weld together. Mr. Aiken has practically no sense of the integrity of the line; Mr. Eliot, whatever his weaknesses, has that sense as a critic, though he often fails to rise to it as a poet, and, when he does rise to it, often fails to get beyond it. If one performs the experiment of opening Mr. Aiken's book at random to two or three passages in any of the long poems or in nearly any of the short ones, one can scarcely help being struck by the almost exact similarity of his work at every point. The following passage is from *The Jig of Forslin*:

> I heard a story once of one who murdered,
> For what I cannot remember; but he murdered.
> With a knife's greedy edge, or with white hands—
> What does it matter? The swift deed was done . . .
> That was a sombre sea-pool to explore—
> Strange things are on that floor.
>
> And once, the music I was listening to
> Suddenly opened, like a luminous book,
> To one bright page that told of a strange thing:
> A man stepped out in the purple of an arc-light,
> A man I knew—I knew him well—
> And because the harlot he loved had jilted him,
> He held his breath and died.

This is from a short poem:

And already the minutes, the hours, the days,
Separate thoughts and separate ways,
Fall whitely and silently and slowly between us,
Fall between us like phantasmal rain and snow.
And we, who were thrust for an instant so sharply
    together,
Under changing skies to alien destinies go.

Melody heard in the midnight on the wind—
Orange poppy of fire seen in a dream—
Vainly I try to keep you. How the sky,
A great blue wind, with a gigantic laugh,
Scorns us apart like chaff.
Like a bird blown to sea am I.

Mr. Aiken's heroes commit murder to appropriate music, fall from skyscrapers, or wander in the lamplight in the rain (to steal a cadence from him) in exactly the same frame of mind and in the same colorless vocabulary. Each act (an almost infinite variety of disconnected and meaningless acts, a kind of cosmic drift or milky way of acts, in fact) passes before one; each is mentioned, but none is poetically realized. One cannot think of any one of Mr. Aiken's poems as a unit, but one can think only of his poetry as a vague and perpetual flux. His poems, like his lines, lack bounds. He achieves a momentary illusion of form by abandoning all claim to form; his poems move evenly, but they might just as well stop anywhere; they are simply a record of revery.

Mr. Aiken has expounded at one time or another theories of musical outline that I do not profess wholly to understand. Musical outline in a poem is, I imagine, if it becomes an isolated quality, a vice rather than a virtue. The kind of proportion that involves not only the sound of the lines, but the meanings and connotations of the words as words, of the lines as lines, and of the poem as a whole, is the sum total of poetic style, but it is a very complex thing. It may occur in poems as short as Mr. Frost's "Acquainted with the Night" or Dr. Williams' "To Waken an Old Lady." It will never be achieved by letting cadences run on indefinitely in a long sweeping wash of sound, for such sound will utterly swamp the other components. To achieve it one must be aware of and control a good many qualities at once. Excessive attention to one quality in art, as in other activities, usually indicates a rather general blindness and seldom results in the mastery even of that quality. Dr. Williams' meter, as pure meter, is incomparably better than Mr. Aiken's, and so is Mr. Frost's. Mr. Aiken's metrical effects are facile and uncontrolled; he succeeds perfectly in achieving second-rate effects that would be mussed up badly by a more critical, even if more creative, mind, such as, say, Mr. Eliot's. Swinburne sins the same way, but does not go so far; also his positive virtues are more considerable. One could say the same of Ezra Pound. Aiken, Swinburne, and Pound achieve their varying degrees of success and their uniform smoothness, one suspects, because their respective critical visions are not much clearer than their creative. Mr. Eliot is not so lucky.

Mr. Aiken's place, then, I imagine, is very likely to be in that fringe of contemporary poets who have achieved a kind of frail brilliance through the exaggeration and limited mastery of some one quality. His best poem is "Priapus and the Pool." It is short, and, though it is a bit diffuse, it says at least as much as any of his long pieces. The cadences are terser and better orchestrated than in anything else he has done; his meter, at least, in this poem, has form—one has a feeling that it is doing fairly definite and interesting things, and one can forecast the arrival of the end before one gets there. The poem deserves a respectable place beside the *Blue Symphony* of John Gould

Fletcher, a poet who regarded poetry and music as about the same thing and who thought, for a time, that by naming and suggesting colors in a regulated series one could create a type of music; and beside the "Patterns" and one or two late poems by Amy Lowell, whose nervous preoccupation with leaves and sunlight occasionally took on a brittle charm. Mr. Aiken's place is less among the best poets of our time than among the most interesting poetic curiosities. If one is sceptical about the truth of this conclusion let him compare, say, any of Mr. Aiken's nocturnal reveries with Mr. Frost's "Acquainted with the Night"; the difference is the difference between a formless record of mere fact and a sharply limited and beautifully ordered poetic structure—limited as Arnold used the term, and not in the pejorative sense in which it is often used today, and, though ordered, none the less fearful and haunting—and, incidentally, a poetic structure of vastly more significance than has been so far admitted by any of Mr. Frost's old-guard admirers.—YVOR WINTERS, *HH*, April–June 1930, pp. 454–57.

Most poets publish too many poems. Consequently their collected volumes are disorderly overgrown parks in which the reader is lost and masterpieces are obscured by volubility and prolixity. This is certainly true of Wordsworth, as it is true of Browning, and to a lesser extent true of Keats, Shelley, Tennyson, Swinburne, and Robinson, among others. The real difficulty is that it is necessary, often, to write a great deal in order to write a few good poems, and the poet has no certain way of knowing whether he is about to write a good or bad poem.

But then, at the other extreme, there are some poets—and this volume shows that Aiken is one of them—who reach their full meaning and being only when they write a great deal and are read in bulk. Hardy is perhaps the best example. In a literal sense his work would not exist if he had not written more than a thousand pages of lyric poems; if, indeed, he had not written a great many poems which are in themselves weak, poor, or defective, but give his work a rich completeness which no single poem contains. And the complication is increased by the deception of the anthology: the jewels of anthologies invariably misrepresent poets like Hardy and Aiken, just as they sustain the vulgar, natural tendency to regard poetry as consisting of purple passages, isolated eloquence, and excited language.

Hence this volume of collected poems, which contains the work of forty years, is valuable in that it helps to remove such obstructions as anthological habitation, the false lights of literary fashion, and the complex, contradictory impressions which accumulate during a long and complex poetic career. But far more important than that, the inclusive character of the volume makes possible a new experience of all of Aiken's work. Poems which at first seemed unimportant in themselves gain a new and profound meaning as phases and stages of a long progress and pilgrimage. And other poems, which seemed when they appeared separately to be only charming and delightful lyrics, exist now in a new light, possessing an underlying seriousness which was not at first apparent.

The progress and pilgrimage begins and ends with the situation of modern man, the situation of the modern ego naked and alone in the midst of a cosmos which may be as meaningless as it is enormous, or which may have a hidden meaning, but which certainly makes every hope and belief subject to the torment of doubt. This sense of existence arose with the overwhelming triumph of physical science; it haunted and obsessed the poetry of the nineteenth century (which is the reason that Arnold's "Dover Beach" is the most representative poem of the century); and it presents itself less directly in most modern poetry only because it has been taken for granted: there is no longer a conflict between the world pictures of religion and of science because the religious image of the world has long since ceased to be a literal and *visual* part of consciousness.

Where other modern poets take the modern image of the cosmos as, at most, a point of departure or a background irrelevant to human concerns and values, in Aiken's work it is always present as an inevitable awareness, as a kind of cold night which surrounds all things, like the sky itself. Whatever the subject, object, or emotion of the poem, it is framed within this awareness: everything may be a dream, hallucination, illusion, or delusion, as everything is subject to time, nature, and death. The self is hidden from the self by the very nature of the self, as it is removed from true certainty about love, knowledge, nature, and society. The mind and every object of the mind exist within an inexhaustible mystery and abyss:

> Then came I to the shoreless shore of silence
> Where never summer was, nor shade of tree,
> Nor sound of water, nor sweet light of the sun,
> But only nothing and the shore of nothing,
> Above, below, around, and in my heart.

But no matter how great the darkness, one cannot live by darkness. One must confront the darkness of existence—the silence of the stars, the depths of the atom, the gulf between each conscious being—with all the attitudes which the imagination makes possible. This is the essential center of Aiken's poetry. It has often been admired for the wrong reasons or misunderstood because it is a veritable fountain of attitudes toward existence as a whole. He is a metaphysical poet in the old sense of metaphysical which has virtually nothing to do with the metaphors of John Donne. The wind does not merely blow; "the wind blows from Arcturus"; a human being cannot be seen within a narrative or dramatic framework, but " . . . it was there, at eight o'clock, I saw / Vivien and the infinite together."—Delmore Schwartz, "The Self Against the Sky," NR, Nov. 2, 1953, pp. 24–25.

The course of poetry appears to have turned away from Conrad Aiken, leaving him an industrious and unfashionable Historic Personage with space in all the textbooks and anthologies and very few readers. Beside the work of those poets who sweat for the ultimate concentration—Thomas, Robert Lowell, John Berryman—Aiken seems terribly low-keyed and diffuse. His long later poems, in fact, seem very like words murmuring endlessly to themselves in poetic terms without in the least resembling poetry as we have come to believe it should be. Part of this neglect—surely unfortunate—results from the fact that Aiken is consistently evaluated by standards which are inimical to his temperament and the characteristics of his verse: concentration, ambiguity, verbal eccentricity, irony, paradox, concreteness (*à la* Williams), and the ability to produce powerfully suggestive phrases suitable for quotation in reviews. Aiken has none of these attributes to any marked degree; he is obviously after other things.

The Morning Song of Lord Zero contains twenty-three new poems of some length, including a sequence about vaudeville performers written in 1916 and revised and published— mistakenly, to my view—in 1961. The other three sections are drawn from earlier books, A *Letter to Li Po*, *Skylight One*, and *Sheepfold Hill*, a fact which calls further attention to Aiken's enormous output, for these books have all been published since his monolithic *Collected Poems*. The huge bulk of his work is closely related, I think, to his basic orientation toward writing, which allows not so much for individually distinct poems to be made, but for poetry as a continuous act to go on unin-

terruptedly. For Aiken, language is quite simply a self-sufficient interior universe. In this respect his poems are radically different from those of almost all other poets now writing. In Williams, for example—or in newer writers like Theodore Roethke or William Stafford—the poem has a curious power to return you to the actual world with a deeper sense of the meanings that lie hidden in it. There is a profound and mysterious connection between the moment of illumination in the poem and the thing that the poem is about; one feels an interchange between language and reality, each gaining from the other, and in this sense the poems of Roethke, Stafford, James Wright, and others have a life-enhancing quality that is, I suspect, ultimately unanalyzable, but is nevertheless unmistakable. When we turn to Aiken's verse, though, we are not likely to feel that this is the case. We come to suspect, instead, that words are being used not to point back to things that exist independently of words, but as a kind of substitute for them, leading us farther and farther from the realm of hard edges and experienceable relationships into the bodiless toils of syntax, verbal legerdemain, and symbol-making in which the primary virtue of any evoked rose, stone, or tree is that it *is* a symbol.

> We'll summon in one dream all motives forth
> and you shall be the south and I the north
> and we will speak that language of the brain
> that's half of Portugal or all of Spain
> or of those yet unsounded seas
> that westward spawn beneath the menstrual moon:
> what are we but divided souls that live
> or strive to in the sundered self of love?

Nothing quickens here. It is a poetry of thoughtful but perhaps not necessary musing, a kind of verbal daydreaming according to long habit. There are no hard and fast rules as to what is admissible; literally anything may come in, from an occasional genuinely imaginative observation like "sudden as a tree of lightning" to the most random and trivial associations that have never quite managed to find the oblivion they deserve. Consequently, Aiken's poems *are* terribly diffuse, and seem much of the time to be portions lifted from an endless reverie, the reverie that one begins at birth and continues uninterruptedly until death. The sense of necessity that art alone makes possible is almost totally absent, and one surrenders to the serious, musical murmur as to a long after-dinner nap in which one dreams of poetry dreaming that it is poetry.

In regard to Aiken's writing as it has come to exist on the page, I have two complaints. The first is against the frequent juxtaposition of words that have similar sounds but different meanings: the uninteresting and coyly mannered verbal jugglery that all but runs off with Aiken's autobiographical *Ushant* and figures here more obtrusively than in his earlier books of verse.

The Man
    Perfection, it may be—or imperfection it may
    be—
The Woman
    Or confection perhaps. What a delicious garden. The leaves
    are not of the fig, nor figment, one believes
    in neither.

The other difficulty is more pervasive and more damaging to the poetry: it is what might be called the "metaphor-or-bust" syndrome.

> the hawk hangs over his beloved hill
> as love hangs over the destined heart:

and once more joyfully we begin
the ancient dance of meet and part,
                                    wherein
each is in turn the hawk and each the heart.

One is struck immediately by both the obvious strain and the total irrelevance of the figure to any conceivable real passion; the hawk—to say nothing of the hill and the dance—is only an arbitrary poetic device distantly and somewhat predictably standing for what may or may not have been an actual emotional experience. The danger here is that such poetic bombinating in the void can take place more easily without genuine experience than with it, requiring nothing but itself, a pleasant and conventional "sensible emptiness" of words. Despite his compulsion to follow an analogy until it drops dead of exhaustion, Aiken does not appear to recognize that such a practice, as he uses it, is essentially anti-poetic: that this particular trope, for example, was not a good idea to begin with, being mechanical and unsuggestive. Over the whole book there is this effect of straining to *make mean*: to assign to the fortuitously drifting and recombining materials of one man's eternal reverie—the innumerable and intolerable details of memory—significance, order, value. None of these significances come out of the matter of the poems with anything like a feeling of inevitability; the details, some of them very good in their own right, are simply saddled with them and told to rise and walk, resulting in an air of contrivance and falsity more and more difficult to dispel as one reads on. If nothing else, however, *The Morning Song of Lord Zero* should help to establish one thing definitively: that the lyric impulse extended beyond its proper limits is at best a questionable vehicle for philosophic musings.

And yet, through the clouds of poetic vapor that Aiken exudes, through the long-winded and unworkable analogies, the unprofitable word play, the vagueness of reference and the on-and-on-*and*-on of his grave, muffled words, a kind of kingdom exists. One is troubled on going into it, and remains troubled on coming out of it, as though haunted by a sensibility so astonishingly rich, various, and self-obsessed that language is inadequate to express it. Perhaps the aim of Aiken's lifelong reverie is not to send one back into one's external world, where the thorn draws blood and the sun shines differently from moment to moment, but into the endlessly ramifying labyrinth of one's own memory. And it is no small compliment to Aiken to say that, once one enters there with the total commitment Aiken's example encourages, one is struck by its likeness to Aiken's: to that vast, ectoplasmic, ultimately inexplicable—though one tries to explain—and often dimly beautiful universe whose only voice he is.—James Dickey, "Conrad Aiken," *Babel to Byzantium*, 1968, pp. 89–93

FICTION

Recently a letter appeared in one of the literary reviews that reminded its editors that we have in the United States at least one writer who may still appropriately be called a man of letters, and the name was Conrad Aiken. It is curious how, year after year for more than four decades now, general readers and editors alike have *had* to be reminded of that name, which does indeed support an achievement that, in its brilliant distinction and, more than that, in its scope, makes Conrad Aiken so much more than a writer alone. He has the range of the literary master: the beautiful bulk of his poetry in all its formal splendor and variety; literary essays of pioneering quality; one of the most extraordinary autobiographies in the language; four novels, at least two of which—*Great Circle* and *King Coffin*—must endure; a play; more than forty short stories.

If the entire work of Conrad Aiken demonstrates this mastery of a range possessed by few modern writers, the forty-one short stories demonstrate a range of mood and method, within the scope of the single form, that is almost as surprising; yet all of them, like the whole body of his work, are stamped with the mark of his imagination, and could have been written by Conrad Aiken alone.

In that complex imagination there is a prominent strain of rather bemused irony that, when he gives it free rein, produces stories that are essentially comic, even rather lighthearted, with a satiric edge that cuts into a human foible or a paradox of personality or a turn of fate's screw, cuts deftly, delicately, without either the ritual air of major surgery or the thrust of passionate involvement. Such stories are "No, No, Go Not to Lethe," "The Necktie," "West End," "O How She Laughed!" and a good many others. They seem to say, with an air of the literary shrug, "Well, there it is. What do you think? Odd, isn't it?" Or, "Queer, isn't it, although surely he had it coming?" Or, "Amusing?" Yet even in these stories there is usually another strain, a note struck off from the taut strings of the stretched nerves, something sharp, shrill or somber, sinister, or mockingly morbid, an echo out of psychic chaos. Think only, for example, of that quite alarming hero of "No, No, Go Not to Lethe," whose ambition is to enfold and paralyze others in the coils of his observation of them without ever himself becoming in the least involved. It is a comic story, but the laughter seems to come eerily up from the bottom of a very deep and a very old well.

This is, of course, the note that characterizes the most splendid and the best known of Conrad Aiken's short stories, those stories in which he moves from the mundane into the mysterious, into hysteria, horror, hallucination, phobia, compulsion, dream, death, and, more often than not, back again into the mundane. The sudden penetration into the shadows of consciousness, a veil surprisingly pulled back and dropped again, something beyond our perception perceived in it, a mythical beast suddenly gazing curiously up at us from the shrubbery at the end of our own well-kept garden: these are the gestures that are made by stories like "Silent Snow, Secret Snow" and "Mr. Arcularis" and many another. . . .

Just as the structure of these stories characteristically develops in the effort of the material to assert a reality beyond or below its mundane shape, so their drama characteristically arises within an individual mind as it struggles to break over the edge of its own limitations. This whole considerable body of fiction, long and short, has, for this reason, a central core of formal as well as psychological concern, an implicit, primary unity that marks it over and over as the product of this imagination and no other, as the work of this author. . . .

It is at this margin, at this edge, where, without barrier, the water of daily human experience stands against the wall of air that is outside it—it is at this margin that Conrad Aiken's fiction is written. (His extraordinary novels develop and amazingly sustain the central concern of the stories.) And thus his fiction asks its great questions: "Was the North Star hung at the world's masthead only in order that on a certain day in a certain year an ugly wallpaper should be glued to the walls of this room?" Human tragedy exists because of the suffering that must inhere in a consciousness that can ask the question at all. It persists, with life itself, because the clocks in the city do strike, and with their reverberations, draw the invisible circles around that consciousness, saving it for its order, yes, but in the very act of saving it, re-committing it to an area within which questions must go on being asked.

We have, I think, no other body of fiction like this—so

centrally coherent, its very coherence derived from a contemplation of the intransigence of that incoherence that lies scattered on all sides of us, and above and below, and, worst of all, within. But also best of all. For rationality would be a poor and shriveled thing if it did not have all that other to nourish no less than to alarm it. As life would be if it did not have the basic resources that can make it into art.—MARK SCHORER, "Conrad Aiken," *The World We Imagine*, 1968, pp. 254–60.

STANLEY J. KUNITZ
"The Poetry of Conrad Aiken"
The Nation, October 14, 1931, pp. 393–94.

There are few events more cataclysmic in the life of an introspective young man than his first reading of the philosopher Hume. When Conrad Aiken was a student at Harvard it is probable that he came upon that triumphant passage in the *Treatise of Human Nature* affirming that we are

> . . . nothing but a bundle or collection of different perceptions, which succeed each other with an inconceivable rapidity, and are in a perpetual flux and movement. The mind is a kind of theater, where several perceptions successively make their appearance, pass, repass, glide away, and mingle in an infinite variety of postures and situations. . . . The comparison of the theater must not mislead us. They are the successive perceptions only, that constitute the mind; nor have we the most distant notion of the place where these scenes are represented, or of the materials of which it is composed.

A letter from the poet to Houston Peterson, quoted in the latter's *Melody of Chaos*, reveals Aiken haunted from the inception of his poetic career by the notion of

> . . . a single human consciousness as simply a *chorus*: a chorus of voices, influences. As if one's sum total of awareness and identity were merely handed to one progressively and piecemeal by the environment. As if one were a mirror. As if one were a vaudeville stage across which a disjointed and comparatively meaningless series of acts was perpetually passing. This flux being one's being.

Aiken does not trace this picture of the self "to any particular source in his own experience, to any book or person," comments Mr. Peterson, as though to confirm his assumption that the original poet is original philosopher too. I am more inclined to accept the observation of I. A. Richards that one idea—even a borrowed one—is sufficient for the lifetime of a poet. Aiken was fortunate enough to borrow his idea in youth and to find it endlessly viable and fascinating.

The letter that served to elucidate the theory behind his early work, dating from about 1915, is also a perfect synopsis of his latest published poem, *The Coming Forth by Day of Osiris Jones*. Deriving its title and some of its substance from the Book of the Dead, in which the deceased is always called Osiris, this technically ingenious work acquaints us with the late Mr. Jones by representing the objects he possessed and admired, the clothes he wore, the rooms he occupied. While Jones is being weighed in the Great Balance, the "things" of his mortal existence become vocal. They accuse him; they ignore him; they babble round him with the malice of unreason. Only his Books, symbolic of memory, defend his soul. The poem is a dramatization, in short, of the consciousness-as-chorus idea; stylistically the most clever and materially the most complete statement of Aiken's theme. If it appears less suggestive than, say, *Senlin*, and more superficial than, say, *The House of Dust*, the explanation is probably in its concision, its tougher diction, its freedom from mellifluous rhetoric. If it remains a minor performance, it is because of a grave error of proportion: too much trivial detail (Characteristic Comments, Inscriptions in Sundry Places, etc.) not compensated by bulk. You may catalogue flyspecks, metaphysical or otherwise, in a work the size of *Ulysses*, but the Joycean humor is ill-advised in a forty-three-page poem. It takes too long for the details to add up to an emotion.

I have said that *The Coming Forth* is an offshoot of Aiken's old poetic root. Its departure in form, however, makes it something of a sport. I value it more than I should, perhaps, in the catalogue of Aiken's work, because of the gratifying certainty that I shall never confuse it with anything else he has written. All the symphonic poems except *Senlin*—though I know them well—mix in my head, dissolve into a single music. I see a pathetic, rusty-haired little fellow who eternally sits at a window, chin propped up in his hands, sleeves fuzzy at the elbows—eternally sits and dreams through the pane. Somewhere an invisible orchestra begins to play. Out of the crannies of his brain troop "nuns, murderers, and drunkards, saints and sinners, lover and dancing girl and sage and clown." A weird melodrama unfolds. The ghostly mummers, obedient to Hume's explicit stage directions, "pass, repass, glide away, and mingle in an infinite variety of postures and situations." When they are gone, all that remains for the observer is a confused awareness of the major tragedy of minor souls.

> Is there a horn we should not blow as proudly
> For the meanest of us all, who creeps his days
> Guarding his heart from blows, to die obscurely?

Festus, the only one of Aiken's protagonists to attain heroic stature, fled from his own power, crying, "I will not have a god who is myself!" Why does the contemporary soul seek to divide itself among its adventures and possessions? Perhaps to evade the burden of conscience unrelieved by the promise of salvation. Perhaps because in the modern world only sensations and things have value.

One of the characteristics of an integrated poet—for example, Yeats—is that his works complement one another; Aiken's overlap. It is as though he has lacked the patience or the time utterly to drain from his consciousness the acid of his first creative impulse. Of all his long poems only *John Deth* impresses me as being wholly pure in concept, self-bounded in achievement.

The world is his poison; music is his anodyne; the ego is his companion. The study of the ego, in its ecstasies, in its intricate and ambiguous humiliations, is his passion. As for the problem of salvation, it scarcely enters into his lucubrations. He has little faith in grace, except the grace of love; and no faith at all in works. A poem, I should say, interests him less than its creation; suicide, less than despair; murder, less than jealousy; the event, less than the prelude. Hence the title, *Preludes*, of his forthcoming volume, a collection (brilliant, on the whole) of sixty-four dramatic-lyric poems. Seeing a leaf fall, the poet meditates on the "wars of atoms in the twig."

> This is the world; there is no more than this,
> The unseen and disastrous prelude, shaking
> The trivial act from the terrific action.
> Speak: and the ghosts of change, past and to come,
> Throng the brief word. The maelstrom has us all.

A study of the *Preludes* in proof sheets suggests that Aiken is beginning, with romantic bravura, to embrace the maelstrom. He speaks more frequently and familiarly of God than was his wont. "It is to self you come—and that is God," he writes. And again, "No gods abandon us, for we are gods." What will this divinity do with his time?

> In the beginning, nothing; and in the end,
> Nothing; and in between these useless nothings,
> Brightness, music, God, one's self. . . . My love,
> Heart that beats for my heart, breast on which I sleep,—
> Be brightness, music, God, myself, for me.

In these new lyrics of Aiken one occasionally detects an uncomfortable straining for effect, a movement toward the monstrous and unforeseen conclusion—or, in its lighter phase, toward the paradoxical or merely shocking. The ultimate poetic manifestations of a thoroughgoing hedonistic solipsism might prove, at the least, curious.

Aiken's idealism has one undeniable virtue: it provokes him ceaselessly to poetry. Fertility may or may not be a sign of genius. In Aiken's case I do believe it marks him out as possessing or being possessed by that "queer thing." Continuously present in his work is the sense of musical delight, which, together with the power of producing it, Coleridge rightly defined as a gift of imagination, a sign of the poet born, not made. Aiken's imagination is apparently inexhaustible. Even though he should continue to rewrite his theme, his best work, unlike that of any other poet of his generation, seems to lie ahead of him.

It is commonly said that he is over-facile, and it is true that he at times deludes himself into the conviction that he is saying something when he is really saying nothing at all. An artificer at heart, he will, for the sake of rounding off a phrase, of arriving at a climax, or even of achieving a rhyme, betray himself miserably with words. He will stuff a poem with such cumulated emptiness as:

> You in whose smile are the flamings and fadings of suns,
> In whose laughter are hidden the secrets of the past,
> In whose "yes" are the blue corridors of eternity,
> In whose "no" flash the scarlet lightnings of death. . . .

Having learned how simple it is "to invert the world inverting phrases," he is frequently quite content to play with ideas like the ubiquitous juggler in his poems. Having once written, "The world is intricate, and we are nothing," he is constrained to wonder why he might not just as well have said, "The world is nothing; we are intricate." He will strike off any number of bad poems in order to forge a good one, and he will publish them all, being reckless of his talent.

An almost pathologically savage concept of evil is embodied in his work. It is more than "the sound of breaking" at the center of the world; it is the living world full of decay:

> Torrents of dead veins, rotted cells,
> Tonsils decayed, and fingernails:
> Dead hair, dead fur, dead claws, dead skin:
> Nostrils and lids; and cauls and veils,

the "abysmal filth of Nothingness" that the Goya of his crapulous vision beheld pouring from time when the seconds cracked like seeds. A physician's son, Aiken is fully cognizant of the processes of katabolism. He is capable of anatomizing an emotional state with fiendish cruelty.

Nevertheless, there emanates from the body of his work an unmistakable vapor of sentimentalism. Sentimentalism is an easier word to spell than to define, but if you will carefully consider two verses, one reading

> The melodious mystery of flesh,

and the other,

> I had found unmysterious flesh,

you may agree with me in thinking the one flabbily adolescent in thought and expression, the other hard and mature. The first line is from Aiken's *Senlin*; the second from a lyric by Louise Bogan. Aiken began by being a "soft" poet. His latest work, notably *The Coming Forth*, is considerably harder in texture. This is as much a matter of technique as of substance. In the beginning, persuaded by a musical analogy, he sought to record, as it were, the onomatopoeia of disillusion. In the long symphonic pieces he wished to compose a "music" distinguished by its "elusiveness, its fleetingness, and its richness in the shimmering overtones of hint and suggestion." He melted down the skeleton of syntax and poured it into the rhythm of his mood. Whereas, in the metaphysical poets, one can almost feel the bare delicate bones of grammar under the phrase, Aiken substituted melody for grammar. Time was his style. Whether or not he will ever withdraw from his twilights and fluxes is problematical, although his recent work hints at the possibility. It will not be enough for him merely to woo the pure crystalline beauty of the Uranian style: he must first tire of the perpetual vaudeville of his brain and drive from the theater his company of jugglers, acrobats, and clowns, leaving himself alone with the alone.

CALVIN S. BROWN
"The Poetry of Conrad Aiken"
Music and Literature
1948, pp. 195–207

Probably no poet has been more concerned with music than Conrad Aiken, or has used it more fruitfully. The interest is visible even in the titles of his poems, where we find nocturnes, tone-poems, variations, dissonants, and symphonies. He describes himself as groping for musical effects from the beginning of his poetic career, and though he has tended to become more metaphysical during the past decade, the influence can still be seen in even such traditional and fixed types as his sonnet sequence, and, to a lesser extent, the *Brownstone Eclogues*. Nevertheless, the principal musical techniques and approaches had been worked out on their most impressive scale before the *Selected Poems* of 1929, and hence we shall concern ourselves primarily with the poems contained in that volume.

Many poets have used titles containing (frequently false) musical implications, and many have been fond of musical references and intricately developed symbols. Aiken's peculiarity does not lie in any one single aspect of the musical influence, but in its extent, richness, and cohesion. The formal arrangement of a good deal of his poetry is based on musical principles rather than on the more widely accepted poetic ones. His symbols are developed and combined in ways analogous to the composer's handling of themes. He has given us, here and there, enough information about the theoretical basis of his work to make it clear that the musical analogies are deliberately and skilfully cultivated. And, finally, this poetry based on music is alive with musical references which reinforce both the implications of its structure and a philosophy in which music is that epitome of the individual and the universe which it was to Schopenhauer.

From the purely formal point of view, Aiken makes extensive and intricate use of the general principles of repetition, variation, and contrast, though he never attempts exact poetic equivalents of the larger musical structures. Frequently, however, we find ABA forms, and these forms often overlap or enclose one another. Thus four of the long poems—*Senlin, The Pilgrimage of Festus, The House of Dust,* and *The Jig of Forslin*—devote an appreciable part of their last sections to repetition, either exact or with slight variation, of material from the first sections. *Forslin* offers a good example of the complication created by an extension of this principle. The poem as a whole contains the ABA structure just mentioned. But Part IV is also an ABA structure, as is at least one still smaller subdivision, Section iii of Part V. In *Senlin* also we find this type of organization on a smaller scale: the first four sections have the typical musical structure of AABA (a complete form in itself); but the A section is used twice, with new material between the recurrences, at the end of the poem. This habit of returning to the beginning for the end is as common in Aiken's poetry as it is in music,[1] and the source of the device is clearly shown when he has Music, speaking as a character, refer to the

> weak hand that touched, strong hand that held, weak
>   hand that touched;
> eyes that forgetting saw, and saw recalling,
> and saw again forgetting; memory moving
> from wonder to disaster, and to wonder. . . .[2]

Another favorite musical device is parallelism carried to such a point that one passage is clearly a variation on another. Occasionally, as in some of the "Variations," this technique is used for its own sake and thus resembles the musical theme and variations.[3] More frequently, however, as in the larger musical forms, the variation occurs at some distance from the original version as part of a larger pattern. It may take the form of a shift in meter, tense, imagery, tone—almost any kind of change, so long as the original passage is still clearly recognizable. A good example occurs in *Senlin*, where the morning-song[4] contains the quatrain:

> There are houses hanging above the stars
> And stars hung under a sea. . . .
> And a sun far off in a shell of silence
> Dapples my walls for me. . . .

Eight pages later[5] the passage is varied to

> There are houses hanging above the stars,
> And stars hung under a sea:
> And a wind from the long blue vault of time
> Waves my curtains for me. . . .

Variations of this sort are among the most conspicuous structural elements of Aiken's poetry.

Another favorite device, partaking of both repetition and variation, is something of an approximation to the rondo form of music. It consists of two themes which are consistently alternated. In spite of the fact that Aiken speaks of developing such juxtapositions in an attempt to find a poetic equivalent of counterpoint, the device is really parallel to the musical practice of alternation between contrasting themes, strings and woodwinds, loud and soft, etc. One of the most striking examples of this method, a passage alternating between the thoughts of an old man and a young girl living in apartments one above the other, was originally published as a separate poem entitled "A Counterpoint," though it was later incorporated into *The House of Dust*.[6] Another conspicuous example[7] is based on the interplay between the suggestions of the music which a man hears at a concert and the chatter of his companion. Out of numerous other instances of this method we may select the morning-song of *Senlin*[8] as probably the most effective. The two alternating themes are Senlin (his actions and thoughts) and the world outside his window. The first of these, however,

is in itself compound and achieves its effect by an alternation between the trivial acts with which the day begins and the sense of the vastness and beauty of the universe which occupies his mind. The first two sections show the interplay of these themes. This alternation is kept up throughout one section of the poem, not with mechanical regularity, for such regularity kills the very effect which the device is designed to produce, but with sufficient consistency and rapidity to give the intended sense of the simultaneity of these diverse elements in Senlin's consciousness.

The border-line between these formal devices of repetition and variation and the development of recurrent symbols is a real one, even though it cannot be exactly located. Up to this point we have dealt with formal elements, but it now becomes necessary to deal with content. In Aiken's longer poems a great deal of attention is given to the development of what, for lack of a better name, we may call symbols or themes. Perhaps the latter is really the better term, since these themes do not symbolize anything in the sense in which Hester Prynne's scarlet letter symbolizes her burden of guilt. Rather, a theme is intended to evoke a state of mind by presenting imagery suggestive of that state. And in this way they are far more like musical themes than like the ordinary subjects of poetry. We may well question whether the primary purpose of a theme in music is to evoke a specific state of mind, but the theme is certainly a thing in itself, both sensuously and intellectually satisfying, and independent of any criteria of objective truth. Its chief function is to be developed so that its own inherent possibilities and its relationships with other themes will be fully exploited. Except that words necessarily have external reference—a fact which Aiken is sometimes inclined to lament—and that there is an external portraying of a state of mind, however indefinable and tenuous, Aiken's themes are essentially like those of the composer.

Their development, then, proceeds along musical lines, with endless modification and combination. A theme already established may be merely suggested in a word or two; a casual phrase may be returned to and expanded until it becomes a full-fledged theme in its own right; two or more themes may be fused to form a single indivisible unit. The anthologists have isolated, for their own purposes, certain sections of Aiken's longer poems in precisely the same way that collections of parlor-music often print merely the statement of a theme from a symphony: the processes are the same, and the nature and extent of the loss are the same.

It is impossible to describe the effect of this technique adequately, but its methods can be shown. Perhaps it will be well to begin with such a short and simple example as *Evensong*.[9] A girl looked out of her window at twilight, and we are given her train of thoughts and her state of mind, with a background of the sights and sounds which she experienced. "She looked into the west with a young and infinite pity." In the next line the last words are repeated as "a young and wistful pity," and thus one of the recurrent themes of the poem is established. As twilight came on there were slight occasional sounds, such as the murmur of leaves, "and then the hush swept back." As it grew darker, lights were turned on, and the leaves casually mentioned a moment ago are now described in some detail as, wet after rain, they glistened with the street-lights shining up through them. Looking out on this, she felt "a young, and wise, and infinite pity" for the girl without a lover, and went from this feeling into a blending of memories of love with a sense of "tragic peacefulness." She wondered: "Would her lover, then, grow old sooner than she . . . ?" Would he lose interest in the light through the leaves, and the twilight?

And her first question came back into her mind. A neighbor sang a child to sleep, and the song was singularly poignant. Because it came up through the leaves of the tree? Or because, as she looked out, she "thought of all the mothers with a young and infinite pity?" The child went to sleep; "the hush swept back." If it were not raining, she thought, there would be a full moon, and the lovers would be in the park—she herself might be going there. Would she grow old and lose interest in love in the park and the latest ways of putting up one's hair? But would her lover grow old sooner than she? And yet, as she watched the city and the wet leaves, once again

> It seemed as if all evenings were the same;
> As if all evenings came,
> Despite her smile at thinking of a kiss,
> With just such tragic peacefulness as this;
> With just such hint of loneliness or pain,
> The perfect quiet that comes after rain.

Short as this poem is, and general as this account of its themes has had to be, something of their development, repetition, variation, and interplay can be seen. The longer poems are infinitely more complex. I have just abandoned an attempt to make a detailed analysis of the themes in *The Jig of Forslin*. The thing cannot be done. One soon reaches the point where, say, the underwater imagery merges with so many other things that it is impossible to say whether we have one theme or five. Is listening to rain on the roof a reappearance of this theme, or not? And what of the chance (?) occurrence of a word like *eddy* or *flow*? The problem suggests one critic's remark[10] about the omnipresent three-note figure which opens the *Second Symphony* of Brahms: "Presently we see it, even where it is not, as when the sun is in our eyes." Other themes present the same difficulties. Nevertheless, a few examples will illustrate the complexity, if not the subtlety, of the thematic development in *Forslin*.

The first section—slightly less than two pages—introduces five separate themes destined for development in later stages of the work. First comes the motive of twilight, as Forslin sits in his room and his dreams come back to him. But dream and reality merge, and the figure which illustrates the uncertainty in his own mind is the first appearance of the pervasive underwater imagery:

> Now, as one who stands
> In the aquarium's gloom, by ghostly sands,
> Watching the glide of fish beneath pale bubbles,—
> The bubbles quietly streaming
> Cool and white and green . . . poured in silver. . . .
> He did not know if this were wake or dreaming;
> But thought to lean, reach out his hands, and swim.

Among other things, he remembered having "stepped in from a blare of sunlight/Over the watery threshold to this gloom"; and this sudden change from light to darkness (or from darkness to light) appears later in various guises. He also remembered music weaving its patterns and opening doors for him—a theme perhaps even more fruitful than the underwater imagery, and frequently combined with it. The idea of music in general is immediately transformed into one of its favorite forms, the music of the café or cabaret. But before this happens the clash of cymbals is compared to "a voice that swore of murder." This hint is taken up a few lines later as Forslin thinks how he sits there in his room: in the world outside, people were dancing and making love, "And the murderers chose their knives." Thus, very unobtrusively, is introduced the theme of the knife-murderer, which is later gradually built up into one of the principal motives. And finally the first sec-

tion closes with a slightly varied repetition of the lines about the aquarium.

The second section is a single page, but Aiken manages, with the greatest air of casual effortlessness, to introduce into it every one of the five themes stated in the first section, to give a bit more elaboration to some of them (the knife-murderer, for example) and to make the first combination of the two most important ones:

> Deep music now, with lap and flow,
> Green music streaked with gleams and bubbles of light,
> Bears me softly away.

The third section—almost the only piece of "straight" narrative in the poem—goes back to tell who Forslin is and what he is doing there meditating in his room as evening falls. Beyond this point, detailed analysis is impossible. New themes appear, one of them a striking image of a bird falling, seen against the sheer side of a tower. Familiar themes are hinted at, combined, reinterpreted. Familiar phrases are reechoed. The twilight theme is merged with those of music and the aquarium in one passage:[11]

> This is as if, in the going of twilight,
> When skies are pale and stars are cold,
> Dew should rise from the grass in little bubbles,
> And tinkle in music among green leaves.

And near the end of the poem there is a passage of summary in which every phrase evokes associations elaborately built up by earlier treatment of the themes which are here merely mentioned:

> Who am I? Am I he that loved and murdered?
> Who walked in sunlight, heard a music playing?
> Or saw a pigeon tumbling down a wall?
> Someone drowned in the cold floods of my heart.
> Someone fell to a net—I saw him fall.[12]

Though the fact has no bearing on the aesthetic qualities of any single work, it is interesting to note that several of these themes are favorites of Aiken's and occur in a number of his poems of the "symphony" type. So standard do some of them become that in *Time in the Rock*[13] Aiken himself rejects them as so well worn that they are no longer adequate for his purposes:

> But no, the familiar symbol, as that the
> curtain lifts on a current of air, the rain
> drips at the window, the green leaves seen in the
> lamplight are bright against the darkness, these
> will no longer serve your appetite, you must have
> something fresh, something sharp—

But they were good symbols while they lasted, and they achieved remarkable effects in a number of distinguished poems. In the "symphonies" as a group they were employed in much the manner that has already been described for *Forslin*, except that in some later ones (*The House of Dust* and *Senlin*, for example) the transitions between different sections are made smoother and less startling.

What is ultimately the point of all this manipulation of forms and themes? In itself it might seem like a harmless enough kind of solitaire for anyone who happened to find it amusing, but hardly a thing to present to the public as literature. The general answer to these objections is that certain things can be communicated only by devious means, and that these happen to be precisely the things which Aiken wishes to communicate. In an article[14] contributed to *Poetry* in 1919 (ostensibly a review of his own *The Charnel Rose*) he developed at some length the theory on which these works were written, admitting that his views on the subject were not clear at first, since theory has to be developed through practice. He confesses to "some complex which has always given me a strong bias towards an architectural structure in poetry analogous to that of music," and briefly traces his efforts to achieve this structure until "finally in *Forslin* and *Senlin* it achieved something like a logical outcome."

> What I had from the outset been somewhat doubtfully hankering for was some way of getting contrapuntal effects in poetry—the effects of contrasting and conflicting tones and themes, a kind of underlying simultaneity in dissimilarity. It seemed to me that by using a large medium, dividing it into several main parts, and subdividing these parts into short movements in various veins and forms, this was rendered possible. I do not wish to press the musical analogies too closely. I am aware that the word symphony, as a musical term, has a very definite meaning, and I am aware that it is only with considerable license that I use the term for such poems as *Senlin* and *Forslin*. . . . But the effect obtained is, very roughly, that of the symphony or symphonic poem.

Each section of the poem is colored by what has gone before and, retrospectively, by what is to follow; hence a section repeated will not be exactly the same thing that it was on its first appearance. Furthermore, contrasting tones ("emotion-masses") build up their effects in precisely the same way as contrasting forms. This all leads to an evocative poetry "of which the chief characteristic is its elusiveness, its fleetingness, and its richness in the shimmering overtones of hint and suggestion." In fact, "It is a prestidigitation in which the juggler's bottles or balls are a little too apt, unfortunately, to be altogether invisible."

> It remains, finally, to point out the profound danger of the method I have been outlining: the danger, I mean, that one's use of implication will go too far, and that one will cheat the natural human appetite for something solid and palpable. One cannot, truly, dine—at least every evening—on, as Eliot would remark, "smells of steaks in passage-ways." One must provide for one's symphony a sufficiently powerful and pervasive underlying idea—and, above all, make it sufficiently apparent. Whether the time will come when we shall be satisfied with implication for its own sake, no one, of course, can guess.

This is a well-considered and mild enough statement from the inventor and practitioner of a theory, and objectors will find that Aiken has forestalled them on almost every point. There is, however, one question which it does not raise.

Why did Aiken wish to develop this fleeting and evocative form of poetry? Because he wished to deal, not with the relationships between the individual and other persons or his physical or social environment, but with what goes on in the individual himself. The problem of personal identity, the impossibility of fully communicating anything, the simultaneous complications of thought and feeling—these are the problems which fascinate him. These elusive things can never be stated; but there is a chance that they may be gradually formed in a reader's mind by an indirection comparable to the phenomena themselves. What the metaphysicals set out to do for the consciously thinking mind Aiken wishes to do for the feeling mind, especially in a state of reverie. Once again, his own statement is conclusive. In his novel *Blue Voyage* the rather autobiographical hero Demarest writes a long letter to Cynthia, who has apparently decided to have nothing more to do with him. The letter begins with long accounts of childhood experiences of its

author, but is never finished. A second letter,[15] designed to replace this one, tells about the first:

> A long, sentimental reminiscence of my childhood! Yes, I actually believed for a moment that by some such circumferential snare as that I might trap you, bring you within my range, sting, and poison you with the subtle-sweet poison of a shared experience and consciousness. That again is highly characteristic of me. It is precisely the sort of thing I am always trying to do in my writing—to present my unhappy reader with a wide-ranged chaos,—of actions and reactions, thoughts, memories and feelings,—in the vain hope that at the end he will see that the whole thing represents only *one moment, one feeling, one person*. A raging, trumpeting jungle of associations, and then I announce at the end of it, with a gesture of despair, "This is I!"

Or, equally well, this is Forslin, who lived in poverty ten years in order to learn to throw one billiard ball into the air and catch and hold it balanced on another billiard ball; who has performed the feat for the first time in vaudeville and received no applause because it looked too easy; who has decided to kill himself with gas; and who now wanders in his own jungle of associations.

All the verse "symphonies" of Aiken have a similar purpose, and the verse strives to achieve a fluidity by which it can respond to every shift of tone or imagery. The basic form of most of these poems is irregularly rhymed verse employing considerable metrical freedom—an intermediate form which can (and does) pass with ease either to such fixed forms as regularly rhymed quatrains, or to free verse. It is an ideal medium for this purpose. A rigidly followed verse-form cannot give the required fluidity: that is why the attempt at symphonic arrangement in the "fifteen hundred more or less impeccable octosyllabic couplets" of *Earth Triumphant* had to be "exceedingly rudimentary," and why *Disenchantment: A Tone Poem* could not go much further. On the other hand, imposing form on this type of material is a difficult process at best; hence it is foolish to reject the aid offered by the recurrent patterns of verse. A comparison of the loose prose of Mrs. Bloom's famous sewer of consciousness (or of Demarest's thoughts, influenced by Mrs. Bloom, in *Blue Voyage*) with the verse of *Forslin*, *Senlin*, or *Festus*, leaves no doubt as to the superiority of the latter form.

We can now begin to understand Aiken's artistic preoccupation with musical effects, and our understanding will be aided by a consideration of some of his references to music. Throughout his poetry it is a recurrent theme, not as a superficial ornament, but as an inherent characteristic of his thought. His world is remarkably auditory—so much so that abstractions usually present themselves in audible form, as in the repeated references to "the horns of glory." Not content with the music of the dance or of the café, he is always hearing strange and solemn music imprisoned in walls and floors, or rising from the depths of earth or sea.

But the music actually heard, even in imagination, forms only a small part of Aiken's musical references. More often, music is a symbolic way of presenting the otherwise inexpressible complications of human thoughts, dreams, even relationships and daily lives. Music and literature are the only arts of movement, and literature can really present only one thing at a time. But music, with its different instruments, its cross-rhythms, its contrapuntal complications, can and does present *simultaneously* a number of different things which are both independent of each other and interrelated. One theory of musical aesthetics is based on the thesis that the laws of musical development are identical with those of human thought.[16] This is certainly Aiken's point of view, and thus we see why, with all his writing about music, he has so very few references to specific composers or works: he does not want the particularity of a specific composition, but rather the generality of the nature of music.

Readers of Aiken's poetry will remember countless passages in which music is symbolically used to represent the complexities of human consciousness, but it may be worth while to select a few of the most striking ones for quotation. In *Meditation on a June Evening*[17] the thought of a loved one develops musically in the mind:

> My thoughts turn back to you,
> Like tired music in a tired brain
> Seeking solution in the worn refrain;
> It returns, it returns,
> It climbs and falls, struggles, disintegrates,
> Is querulous, resentful, states, restates;
> But always, like one haunted, comes again
> To that one phrase of pain;
> And that one phrase, you know as well as I,
> Is the remembered pallor of your face;
> And a certain silence, and a certain sky,
> And a certain place.

The main section of Forslin's thoughts is introduced by a statement that

> Things mused upon are, in the mind, like music,
> They flow, they have a rhythm, they close and open,
> And sweetly return upon themselves in rhyme.
> Against the darkness they are woven,
> They are lost for a little, and laugh again,
> They fall or climb.[18]

Not only the individual's secret thoughts, but the relationships between individuals are essentially musical patterns:

> We are like music, each voice of it pursuing
> A golden separate dream, remote, persistent,
> Climbing to fire, receding to hoarse despair.
> What do you whisper, brother? What do you tell me?
> We pass each other, are lost, and do not care.[19]

But beyond this representation of thought and daily life, music opens up other vistas. Aiken frequently comments on the poverty of language and its inability to express the subtleties which he seeks. That is why, in most of his poetry, "we deal in juxtapositions."[20] When words fail, he turns to music; in fact, anything which words cannot adequately express—love and passion, for instance—*is* music.[21] In his later manner, after the period of the "symphonies," Aiken devotes a fine lyric[22] to this difference in the capacities of musical and literary expression:

> Music will more nimbly move
> than quick wit can order word
> words can point or speaking prove
> but music heard
> How with successions it can take
> time in change and change in time
> and all reorder, all remake
> with no recourse to rhyme!
> . . .
> But verse can never say these things;
> only in music may be heard
> the subtle touching of such strings,
> never in word.

Thus the unanswerable problems of the universe can be hinted at only by musical comparisons, for music is in itself a complete and parallel universe. At the conclusion of the speech made by Music in *The Coming Forth by Day of Osiris Jones*[23] we have a clear statement on this point:

> O death, in shape of change, in shape of time,
> in flash of leaf and murmur, delighting god
> whose godhead is a vapour, whose delight
> is icicles in summer, and arbutus
> under the snowdrift, and the river flowing
> westward among the reeds and flying birds
> beyond the obelisks and hieroglyphs—
> whisper of whence and why, question in darkness
> answered in silence, but such silence, angel,
> as answers only gods who seek for gods—
> rejoice, for we are come to such a world
> as no thought sounded.

But this explanation of the ultimate is illusory. When Festus tries to explore human knowledge, "it occurs to him that the possibility of knowledge is itself limited: that knowledge is perhaps so conditioned by the conditions of the knower that it can have little but a relative value."[24] Once again, a musical figure carries the idea. While Festus and the Old Man who represents his *alter ego* are discussing the problems of knowledge they hear a solemn, haunting music which may perhaps be the ultimate expression of the universe.[25] Yet they are forced to realize that

> It is a music
> Of mortal origin and fleshly texture.
> Who knows if to god's ears it may be only
> A scream of pain?

As they draw nearer, they see that it is played by an orchestra of butchers.

> Thus ends our pilgrimage! We come at last,
> Here, in the twilight forests of our minds,
> To this black dream.

Thinking to explore knowledge itself, they have explored only their own mind: whatever man may understand or know about the nature of things is ultimately only his own thought, and the music of the spheres is thus necessarily only the still, sad music of humanity.

Thus we return to music as a symbol of the intricacies of the human consciousness. Frequently in Aiken's poetry there is mention of music muttering behind closed doors, and clearly heard only on those rare occasions when a door is momentarily opened. A long section of *The House of Dust*[26] is devoted to an elaboration and explanation of this symbol. We can quote only a brief part of it here:

> Once, on a sunbright morning,
> I walked in a certain hallway, trying to find
> A certain door: I found one, tried it, opened,
> And there in a spacious chamber, brightly lighted,
> A hundred men played music, loudly, swiftly,
> While one tall woman sent her voice above them
> In powerful sweetness. . . . Closing the door
> I heard it die behind me, fade to whisper,—
> And walked in a quiet hallway as before.
> Just such a glimpse, as through that opened door,
> Is all we know of those we call our friends. . . .
> We hear a sudden music, see a playing
> Of ordered thoughts—and all again is silence.
> The music, we suppose, (as in ourselves)
> Goes on forever there, behind shut doors,—
> As it continues after our departure,
> So, we divine, it played before we came. . . .
> What do you know of me, or I of you? . . .
> Little enough. . . . We set these doors ajar
> Only for chosen movements of the music. . . .

This, then, is the music which haunts Aiken, the music which he so extensively describes and imitates in his verse symphonies. Until fairly recently, the great aim of his poetry was to open those doors, admit us to the room, and let us hear whole concerts of this fleeting, elusive music of the mind. The very nature of the undertaking made complete success impossible, but by means of a musical symbolism and musical techniques Aiken has succeeded farther than anyone else who has made the attempt.

Notes

1. As other conspicuous examples we may mention "Variations," *Selected Poems* (N. Y., 1929), pp. 66–76, and *Time in the Rock* (N. Y., 1936), LXV, p. 95.
2. *The Coming Forth by Day of Osiris Jones* (N. Y., 1931), p. 37.
3. See *Preludes for Memnon* (N. Y., 1931), Sec. XXXV, for an excellent example.
4. *Senlin*, II, ii.
5. *Senlin*, II, x.
6. First published in *Poetry: A Magazine of Verse*, 1919. Included in *The House of Dust*, IV, iv.
7. *The Jig of Forslin*, V, iv.
8. *Senlin*, II, ii.
9. *Selected Poems*, pp. 3–6.
10. Goepp, *Great Works of Music*, I, 386.
11. III, i.
12. V, v.
13. *Time in the Rock*, XCII, p. 132.
14. *Poetry: A Magazine of Verse*, XIV, 152–159.
15. *Blue Voyage* (N. Y., 1927), pp. 291–292.
16. See Gehring, *The Basis of Musical Pleasure* (N. Y., 1910).
17. *Nocturne of Remembered Spring and Other Poems* (Boston, 1917), p. 16.
18. *The Jig of Forslin*, I, vii.
19. *The House of Dust*, III, viii.
20. *The Jig of Forslin*, I, vi.
21. *Preludes for Memnon*, XVI.
22. *Time in the Rock*, LXXXIII.
23. p. 37.
24. The "Argument" printed as introduction to *The Pilgrimage of Festus* (N. Y., 1923).
25. *The Pilgrimage of Festus*, V, i.
26. *The House of Dust*, IV, iii.

R. P. BLACKMUR

"Conrad Aiken: The Poet"

Atlantic Monthly, December 1953, pp. 77–82

I

The newly collected poems of Conrad Aiken run to so many hundreds of pages no one reader can easily digest them in bulk. Nor can any one reader discriminate the best from the better and the better from the worst with any certainty even of personal choice. Digestion and discrimination must be the gradual labor of many readers. Yet it is good to have all the poems in one place; they make a bulk, and bulk is a great part of Aiken's quality in much the same way it is part of the quality of Swinburne, or Hugo, or Carducci, or Sir Walter Scott, each in his different way. It is not for isolated poems that these poets are remembered; anthologies cannot do them justice or even give a proper sample taste.

Some poets concentrate, compound, and construct their experience into words. Others, like Aiken, expand and extend and exhaust their experience. Their unity is in all their work, not in single efforts, where indeed the unity may evaporate.

This is because such poets, and especially Aiken, work in a continuous relation to the chaos of their sensibilities (Houston Peterson called his book about Aiken *The Melody of Chaos*), and each separate poem issues with a kind of random spontaneity: the least possible ordering of experience, what is possible within the devices of prosody (such as the couplet, the quatrain, the sonnet, and so on), never the maximum possible ordering under what Coleridge called the coadunative powers of the mind. There is no generalizing power of the mind. Yet all the poems together make a generalization.

Perhaps we cannot say what that generalization is, though we may feel it. Who can say what the sphinx generalizes?—or a change in weather?—or Jacob wrestling in the stream? Yet we know very well, and try our best to say. So with Aiken. We must see if the shifts and alternations in his weather do not make a climate which generalizes them. Luckily Aiken himself supports this effort. If he did not exactly choose he somehow found it necessary to write in the mode of imagination here described.

In his autobiographical narrative called *Ushant*, Aiken gives an account of a prophecy of his life made to him by an eccentric "Unitarian-minister-and-clairvoyant" one morning in a Bloomsbury boardinghouse. "You have the vision, the primary requisite," said this gentleman. "You will be a true seer: it is, I fear, in the communication that you will fail. You will always tend to rush at things somewhat prematurely: you will see beyond your years, ahead of your maturity, so that continually, and unfortunately the immaturity of your expression, a certain glibness and triteness, will tend to spoil your excellent ideas, leaving them to be adopted and better expressed—better organized because better understood—by others." And he went on: "You will touch [life] at almost every possible point; and, if you do die spiritually bankrupt, you will have known at least nearly everything—known and seen it, even if ultimately without the requisite power, or love, or understanding, or belief, to harmonize it into a whole, or set it into a frame. . . . You will want to taste your own spiritual death."

To this, and the rest of it, Aiken gives full assent: "How devastatingly true!" We all have such an uncle in the cupboard who says such words in our ears, if we listen: it is under such words that we see the divisive nature of our politics, our culture, and our individual selves. Aiken has written one version of the poetry of that condition, just as Eliot has written another version, which Aiken will not quite understand, thinking Eliot's version a betrayal of his. "That [Eliot's] achievement was unique and astounding, and attended, too, by rainbows of creative splendor, there could be no doubt. Indeed, it was in the nature of a miracle, a transformation. But was it not to have been, also, a surrender, and perhaps the saddest known to D. in his life?"

D. is Aiken objectively observed, spun out, developed, and coiled round himself as endlessly as possible within a single volume. And that volume, *Ushant*, is the best key we have to what Aiken the man was up to in creating Aiken the poet. From *Ushant*, then, it is easy to clarify and support what Aiken (or D.) undertook to believe the prophetic Unitarian from California meant in the Bloomsbury room. At one place Aiken says D. had a bias for form as form, "that inventions of form must keep a basis in order and tradition" and must be related to "a conscious and articulated *Weltanschauung*, a consistent view." On the next page he remarks that through Freud "at last the road was being opened for the only religion that was any longer tenable or viable, a poetic comprehension of man's position in the universe, and of his potentialities as a poetic shaper of his own destiny, through self-knowledge and love." The combination (of the philosopher and the maker) was expressed in the two volumes of "Preludes" which he here calls "serial essays towards attitude and definition."

But there are three other sets of remarks which would seem to clarify the way in which Aiken actually approached his double problem. One is where he refers to himself as the priest of consciousness in flight. A second is where he develops the notion that the true theory of art is, necessarily, the unwritten book; that the true aesthetic is of the impossible, where the act of initiation is taken as an end in itself. The third set of remarks summarizes his underlying philosophy: "One must live, first, by seeing and being: after that could come the translation of it into something else. This constant state of his 'falling in love,' falling in love with all of life, this radiant narcissism, with its passionate need to emphasize and identify, this all-embracingness, must find something to do with itself. Subject and object must be brought together, and brought together in an apocalypse, an ecstasy, a marriage of heaven and hell."

It might be supposed that everyone has a little more life—a little more seeing and being—than he can quite manage; but there is no need to quarrel with Aiken about that. What is interesting here is the "radiant narcissism" which is the radical quality of all his acts of apprehension, or at any rate of those which get into his poems and other fictions. His autobiography is itself an act of radiant narcissism. What he writes shines with the expanded light—perhaps the idiopathic light, perhaps the light of self-healing or idio-therapy—of what he has seen and been; and the hope is that, with the aid of the traditions and forms of poetry, it may be light for others also.

Aiken's life is a self-feast mediated in poetry, and what is so attractive about his poetry is that each of us, by letting his own egoism shine a little, may eat of himself there. This is also why he can speak of his world as a "rimless sensorium," and why the Unitarian prophet was right in telling the young Aiken that he would never set life into a frame.

But not everybody needs to make frames. If Aldous Huxley complained in 1920 that Aiken would have to find "some new intellectual formula into which to concentrate the shapelessness of his vague emotions," he was not reminding us of Aiken's obligation so much as he suggested our own. So long as this Narcissus remains radiant it will be our business to find a frame or frames for the radiance. The Narcissus is only ourselves at a desirable remove: the heightened remove of poetry in which even our worst selves seem authentic and our best impossible of attainment. For it is poetry like this which teaches us we could never put up with our best selves.

II

What then does Aiken do—what is his radiance—between the double blows of life and theory? What is his music and how does he sing it? He sings on two trains of thought or themes and he sings like the legendary bard, improvising old tunes as if they were his own by discovery or inheritance, or both. To expand into clarity and towards judgment these phrases will be the remaining task of this essay. What are the themes and how does a bard sing?

One theme is the long, engorged pilgrimage of the self coming on the self: the self creating the self as near objectively as possible. The second theme has to do with the dramatization—in theatrical terms, so far as a poem can be a theater—of the selves of others. *The Jig of Forslin* edges towards a fusion of both themes: where the self comes on a dramatization of the self, full-fledged and self-creative. *Turns and Movies,* his next set of poems, represents the second theme; *Senlin,* a few years later, represents the first. If there is a single theme

in Aiken's work, it is the struggle of the mind which has become permanently aware of itself to rediscover and unite itself with the world in which it is lodged.

When the soul feels so greatly its own flux—the flow of itself recalling and eddying upon itself—it becomes very difficult to reassess the world other people inhabit. Very difficult and of absolute necessity. Bertrand Russell wrote his most lucid book, *Introduction to Mathematical Philosophy,* while in prison during the First World War as a conscientious objector to that world. In Aiken it is the self that is such a prison; one bursts out of it without ever leaving it, and one bursts into it without ever having been there. It is the contest of our private lives with the public world.

No theme could be closer to us; almost every mode of the modern mind tends to make the private life more intolerable and the public life more impossible. Only what used to be called ejaculations of the spirit suggests the blending of the tolerable with the possible. Arnold thought poetry could do the job of religion, but Arnold had never heard of psychology (psychiatry, psychoanalysis, and psychosomatics). Aiken could not help having Arnold for an uncle, but he had "psychology" for his other self, the hopeful and destructive brother of his heart.

In his poems there is always the cry: "Am I my brother's keeper?" But it is both brothers who cry, not one: sometimes they cry alternately, sometimes together. The attractive force of Aiken's poetry lies in these joined cries; they make the radiance of this Narcissus. Narcissus is only the personal, anecdotal, and legendary form for that frame of mind known as solipsism: the extreme subjective idealism that believes the mind creates the world when it opens its eyes. It lies in the background of the whole movement in modern art called expressionism (the feeling that what one says commands its own meaning) and is related to make the artist or outsider, as such, the characteristic hero of modern literature. Solipsism is the creative egoism, not of the primitive savage who believes in nothing he does not see, but of the civilized and excruciated consciousness which claims credence for everything it does see and, by the warrant of sincerity of feeling, everything it might see.

This is why we speak of so many levels of consciousness, all of them our own, and for that reason all valid; but none of them dependable for others, none of them showing to others any surety of motive. Dostoevsky invented buffoons who acted out of caprice. Gide invented criminals who made *actes gratuites.* Kafka invented his hero "K" who could not act at all. Aiken's work belongs in this train of thought with his deliberate egoism, his structure by series and repetitions and involutions, his preludes to attitude and definition, the emphasis on the incomplete or aborted act of the incomplete or aborted ego. Your solipsist, because for him no action can ever be completed, is bound to be violent in expression.

Readers of Aiken's novels will easily understand the application of these remarks to all his work. Indeed the long poems will come immediately to seem themselves novels in a philosophico-lyric mode. The chaos under the skin of perception has become both part of the body, its bloodstream, and united with the mind, its creative matrix. For the mass of Aiken's work is deliberately pre-morphous; it is prevented from reaching more than minimal form. He attempts to preserve the chaos he sees and he attempts to woo the chaos he does not see. The limit of form which attracts him is the form just adequate to keep the record with grace: the anecdote, the analysis, and the prelude. He has the sense that as things are finally their own meaning (as he is himself), so they will take up immediately their own form.

This is true with the poems, and increasingly so from the earlier to the later volumes. *Turns and Movies* is a series of dramatic monologues, hard, rapid, and anecdotal, rather like *Satires of Circumstance* or *Time's Laughing-stocks* by Thomas Hardy, full of murder, open and hidden hatred, wrong marriages, and burning infidelities: an effort to grasp the outside world by its violent sore thumbs. *Punch, the Immortal Liar*, the next volume, is Aiken's first conscious effort to fuse the two halves of his theme, and we get the violence of the inner man seizing that of the outside world. *Senlin*, four years later, is philosophical, meditative, musical, and repetitive, the free onward solipsism of the pilgrim trying to come on himself.

Something like one of these sets of attitudes can be applied to any of the original volumes. *Festus* is part of the pilgrimage. The *Charnel Rose* is a kind of theatrical or *Turns and Movies* version of romantic love. In *John Deth* we have the solipsist working towards annihilation, as in *Osiris Jones* we have him working towards epiphany. *Priapus and the Pool* is free erotic expressionism moving into philosophy. The *Kid* is an historical version of *Turns and Movies*, a frontier version of the civilized soul, remarking tradition as he goes. *And in the Human Heart* is an effort to make the inner violence transform the outer through love. *The Preludes of Attitude and Definition* exhibit in infinite variety both the tension and the distension of the two violences, what keeps the soul together in every moment but the last in its lifelong series of fallings apart.

The attitude breeds the vital chaos of definition. (Which may remind some readers of Aristotle's remark that there is an optimum definition for any point at issue, and one should never define more than necessary. In Aiken's preludes the right amount is reached when the vitality of the chaos is reached.) Lastly, though not last in chronology, the *Brownstone Eclogues* most clearly fuse, join, and crystallize the two violences of Aiken's theme, and it is from them therefore that an example will be drawn.

But a single quotation will not be enough. There is a poem in Aiken's mid-career which is a kind of anterior example of the meaning of the passage chosen from the *Eclogues*. The earlier poem has a lucky title for the purpose. It is classical, Freudian, and as anomalous as the next breath of air you breathe: altogether universal is "Electra" in the human heart. In "Electra" is the trespass of one human upon another; in the eclogue is the trespass into the human of the nonhuman out of which everything human is made. Here is the passage from "Electra":—

'Under this water-lily knee' (she said)
'Blood intricately flows, corpuscle creeps,
The white like sliced cucumber, and the red
Like poker-chip! Along dark mains they flow
As wafts the sponging heart. The water-lily,
Subtle in seeming, bland to lover's hand
Upthrust exploring, is in essence gross,
Multiple and corrupt. Thus, in the moonlight'
(She hooked a curtain and disclosed the moon)
'How cold and lucent! And this naked breast,
Whereon a blue vein writes Diana's secret,
How simple! How seductive of the palm
That flatters with the finest tact of flesh!
Not silver is this flank, nor ivory,
Gold it is not, not copper, but distilled
Of lust in moonlight, and my own hand strays
To touch it in this moonlight, whence it came.'

This is what humans make when their egoisms trespass impossibly into each other's flesh. Here is the passage from *Brownstone Eclogues*; it is the complete poem called "Dear Uncle Stranger":—

All my shortcomings, in this year of grace,
preach, and at midnight, from my mirrored face,
the arrogant, strict dishonesty, that lies
behind the animal forehead and the eyes;
the bloodstream coiling with its own intent,
never from passion or from pleasure bent;
the mouth and nostrils eager for their food,
indifferent to god, or to man's good.
Oh, how the horror rises from that look,
which is an open, and a dreadful, book!
much evil, and so little kindness, done.
selfish the loves, yes all, the selfless none;
illness and pain, ignored; the poor, forgotten:
the letters to the dying man, not written—
the many past, or passing, great or small,
from whom I took, nor ever gave at all!
Dear Uncle stranger, Cousin known too late,
sweet wife unkissed, come, we will celebrate
in this thronged mirror the uncelebrated dead,
good men and women gone too soon to bed.

This is what trespasses into the human, "the bloodstream coiling with its own intent," and it is precisely what makes possible the creation of "the finest tact of flesh." The one trespasses upon as it illuminates the other. The two together make the original warrant for the ego to make whatever artifacts it can. Narcissus is not all of us but at some sore point we are all of us Narcissus. Aiken's theme is his radiance.

III

So for his theme. How does the bard sing? In the easiest language and the easiest external forms of any modern poet of stature. He sings by nature and training out of the general body of poetry in English. He writes from the cumulus of cliché in the language, always, for him, freshly felt, as if the existing language were the only reality outside himself there were. There is hardly ever in his work the stinging twist of new idiom, and the sometimes high polish of his phrasing comes only from the pressure and friction of his mind upon his metres.

It is hard to make clear, in a period where so many poets play upon their words and so many readers think the play is all there is, that this superficially "easy" procedure with language has long since and will again produce poetry—even the difficult poetry of the soul wrestling with itself. But it is so with Aiken, and it is worth while to end these remarks by trying to make this matter clear. Aiken depends on the force of his own mind and the force of metrical form to refresh his language. The cumulus upon which he really works is the cumulus of repetition, modulation by arrangement, pattern, and overtone. He writes as if the words were spoken to let the mind under the words sing. He writes as if it were the song of the mind that puts meaning into the words.

Thus, as in popular songs, the words themselves do not matter much, yet matter everything *and* nothing to those who sing them and those who hear them. This is to say Aiken takes for granted that his words are real; he never *makes* his words real except by the agency of the music of their sequence. No method works all the time, and when Aiken's method fails, you get the sense of deliquescence in his language, as if any words would do because none would work. To understand the successes of the method takes time and familiarity. In his language, but not in his conceptions, he depends more on convention than most poets do in our time, almost as much as Dryden or Pope. The point is, if you look into his conventions you will find them right, just, genuine, and alive. What more do you want? You have brought with you what was required.

Finally—for poetry is an affair of skill at words—Aiken demands of you, at a serious level, the same skill that newspaper poets demand at no level at all. Your newspaper poet merely wants to say something to go with what he feels. Aiken is looking hard to find, and make real, the emotion that drives, and inhabits him. Aiken, as Croce might say, has a vast amount of the same talent the newspaper poet has so little of. The amount of talent makes all the difference. The existence of poets like Aiken make poetry possible.

MALCOLM COWLEY
From "Conrad Aiken: From Savannah to Emerson"
As I Worked at the Writer's Trade
1963, pp. 233–47

Candor was close to being his central principle as a man and a writer, particularly as a poet. The principle evolved into a system of aesthetics and literary ethics that unified his work, a system based on the private and public value of self-revelation. No matter what sort of person the poet might be, healthy or neurotic, Aiken believed that his real business was "to give the lowdown on himself, and through himself on humanity." If he was sick in mind, candor might be his only means of curing himself. "Out of your sickness let your sickness speak," Aiken says in one of his Preludes—

> the bile must have his way—the blood his froth—
> poison will come to the tongue. Is hell your kingdom?
> you know its privies and its purlieus? keep
> sad record of its filth? Why this is health.

"Look within thyself to find the truth" might have been his Emersonian motto; and it had the corollary that inner truth corresponds to outer truth, as self or microcosm does to macrocosm. Aiken believed that the writer should be a surgeon performing an exploratory operation on himself, at whatever cost to his self-esteem, and penetrating as with a scalpel through layer after layer of the semiconscious. That process of achieving self-knowledge might well become a self-inflicted torture. At times the writer might feel—so Aiken reports from experience— "the shock of an enormous exposure: as if he had been placed on a cosmic table, *en plein soleil*, for a cosmic operation, a cosmic intrusion." Let him persist, however, and he will be rewarded by finding—here I quote from a letter—"what you think or feel that is secretly you—shamefully you—intoxicatingly you." Then, having laid bare this secret self, which is also a universal self, the writer must find words for it, accurate and honest words, but poured forth—Aiken says in a Prelude—without reckoning the consequences:

> Let us be reckless of our words and worlds,
> And spend them freely as the tree his leaves.

Here enters the public as opposed to the merely private value of complete self-revelation. By finding words for his inmost truth, the writer—especially the poet—has made it part of the world, part of human consciousness. He has become a soldier, so to speak, in the agelong war that mankind has been waging against the subliminal and the merely instinctive.

But service in the war involves much that lies beyond the simple process of discovering and revealing one's secret self. The writer must divide himself into two persons, one the observer, the other a subject to be observed, and the first must approach the second "with relentless and unsleeping objectivity." The observer-and-narrator must face what Aiken calls

"That eternal problem of language, language extending consciousness and then consciousness extending language, in circular or spiral ascent"; and he must also face the many problems of architectural and sequential form. The words that depict the observed self must not only be honest; they must be "twisted around," in Aiken's phrase, until they have a shape and structure of their own; until they become an "artifact" (a favorite word of his) and if possible a masterpiece that will have a lasting echo in other minds. The "supreme task" performed by a masterpiece—as well as by lesser works and deeds in a more temporary fashion—is that of broadening, deepening, and subtilizing the human consciousness. Any man who devotes himself to that evolving task will find in it, Aiken says, "all that he could possibly require in the way of a religious credo."

His name for the credo was "the religion of consciousness." It is a doctrine—no, more than that, a system of belief—to which he gave many refinements and ramifications. Some of these are set forth, with an impressive density of thought and feeling, in two long series of philosophical lyrics, *Preludes for Memnon* (1931) and *Time in the Rock* (1936); Aiken regarded these as his finest work. But the doctrine is a unifying theme in almost all the poetry of his middle years, say from 1925 to 1956, and in the prose as well. It is clearly exemplified in his novels, especially in *Blue Voyage* (1927), which brought young Malcolm Lowry from England to sit at the author's feet, and *Great Circle* (1933), which contains a brilliant, drunken, self-revealing monologue that Freud admired; he kept the book in his Vienna waiting room. Self-discovery is often the climax of Aiken's stories, and it is, moreover, the true theme of his autobiography, *Ushant* (1952). At the end of the book he says of his shipmates on a postwar voyage to England, "They were all heroes, every one of them; they were all soldiers; as now, and always, all mankind were soldiers; all of them engaged in the endless and desperate war on the unconscious.". . .

Without in the least abandoning his religion of consciousness, Aiken's poems of the 1950s and 1960s introduced some new or partially new elements. One of these was a note of ancestral piety, with allusions to earlier Aikens, but more to his mother's connections, the Potters (who had started as New Bedford Quakers) and the Delanos. The note is already audible in "Mayflower," written in 1945. It is a poem partly about the ship (on which two of the poet's ancestors had been passengers), partly about the flower, and partly about the sandy shores of Cape Cod, where the Pilgrims had landed before sailing on to Plymouth. In other poems there is frequent mention of what might be called ancestral scenes: New Bedford and its whaling ships; the Quaker graveyard at South Yarmouth, on the Cape, where Cousin Abiel lies buried; Sheepfold Hill, also on the Cape; and Stony Brook, where the herring used to spawn by myriads. There is also talk of godfathers and tutelary spirits: among the poets Ben Jonson, Shakespeare, Li Po, and among historical figures Pythagoras and William Blackstone, the scholar and gentle heretic who built a house on the site of Boston before the Puritans came, then moved away from them into the wilderness. Blackstone becomes the hero of Aiken's cycle of poems about America, *The Kid* (1947). In "A Letter from Li Po" (1955), the Chinese maker of timeless artifacts is set beside the scoffing Quaker, Cousin Abiel:

> In this small mute democracy of stones
> is it Abiel or Li Po who lies
> and lends us against death our speech?

Another new or newly emphasized feature of the later poems is something very close to New England Transcendentalism. Its appearance should be no surprise, except to those who have fallen into the habit of regarding Transcendentalism as a purely historical phenomenon, a movement that flourished from 1830 to 1860, then disappeared at the beginning of the Civil War. On the contrary, it has been a durable property of New England thinking, a home place, one might say, to which some poets return as they grow older. In one or another of many aspects, the Transcendental mood is manifested in Robinson, in Frost, to some extent in Eliot, perhaps in Millay—see "Renascence" and some of the very late poems—then in Cummings, Wilder, S. Foster Damon, John Wheelwright, and most clearly in Conrad Aiken.

A complete definition of Transcendentalism would comprise most of Emerson's essays, beginning with *Nature*. As a shorter definition, the best I have found is a paragraph in the article "Transcendentalism" in *The Oxford Companion to American Literature*. One is grateful to the editor, James D. Hart, for bringing almost everything together in a few sentences. He says:

> . . . the belief had as its fundamental base a monism holding to the unity of the world and God and the immanence of God in the world. Because of this indwelling of divinity, everything in the world is a microcosm containing within itself all the laws and meaning of existence. Likewise the soul of each individual is identical with the soul of the world, and latently contains all that the world contains. Man may fulfill his divine potentialities either through a rapt mystical state, in which the divine is infused into the human, or through coming into contact with the truth, beauty, and goodness embodied in nature and originating in the Over-Soul. Thus occurs the doctrine of the correspondence between the tangible world and the human mind, and the identity of moral and physical laws. Through belief in the divine authority of the soul's intuitions and impulses, based on the identification of the individual soul with God, there developed the doctrine of self-reliance and individualism, the disregard of external authority, tradition, and logical demonstration, and the absolute optimism of the movement.

For a brief statement of Transcendental doctrines, James Hart's paragraph—from which I have omitted a few introductory phrases—seems to me almost complete. It does omit, however, two doctrines of some importance. One is the rejection of history—at least of history conceived as an irreversible process, a causally linked series of events in which the masses as well as the "representative men" play their part. For this rejection, see Emerson's essay "History" and also many of Cummings' later poems. Thornton Wilder, a New Englander by descent and residence—though born in Wisconsin—tells us that history is not a sequence but a tapestry or carpet in which various patterns are repeated at intervals. Having spatialized time in this fashion, Wilder could never have become a social or a political historian, and the statement applies to others working in the same tradition.

One might say that Transcendentalists as a type—if such a type exists—are most at home in essays and poetry. If they turn to fiction, as Wilder did, they write novels dealing with morals rather than manners. Manners are the expression of standards prevailing in a group, and Transcendentalism denies the existence of groups except as arithmetical sums of separate persons: one plus one plus one. Only the individual is real and bears within himself a portion of the Over-Soul. That is the other doctrine omitted from Hart's admirable paragraph, and it explains why the Transcendental cast of mind is skeptical about

political science and usually contemptuous of politicians. Aiken, for example, says of himself in *Ushant*: ". . . he had never found it possible to take more than a casual and superficial interest in practical politics, viewing it, as he did, as inevitably a passing phase, and probably a pretty primitive one, and something, again, that the evolution of consciousness would in its own good season take care of."

Is consciousness, for Aiken—the consciousness of mankind as shared by each individual—close to being an equivalent of the Over-Soul? That might be stretching a point, and indeed, I should be far from saying that, among twentieth-century New England writers, there is any complete Transcendentalist in a sense that might be accepted, for instance, by Margaret Fuller. It is clear, however, that there are several New England writers, most of them among the best, whose work embodies aspects of the Transcendental system (though seldom its "absolute optimism"). The aspects are usually different in each case, but two of them, at least, are shared by all the writers I mentioned. All are fiercely individual, in theory and practice, and all are moralists or ethicists, even or most of all when defying an accepted system of ethics.

Why this revival of the Transcendental spirit should be particularly evident in New England is hard to say. One is tempted to speak of something in the blood, or in the climate, or more realistically of a tradition handed down by a father or a favorite schoolteacher, rejected in the poet's youth, then reaccepted in middle age. Usually there is not much evidence of a literary derivation: for instance, Cummings and Millay were not at all interested in the earlier Transcendentalists. Aiken might be an exception here. Boldest of all in his development of certain Transcendental notions, he also, rather late in life, found them confirmed by ancestral piety and especially by the writings and career of his maternal grandfather.

William James Potter was a birthright Quaker who became a Unitarian because he felt that the doctrines of the Friends were too confining. In 1859 he was called to the Unitarian church in New Bedford, where he soon began to feel that Unitarianism was confining too. In 1866 he refused to administer the rite of communion; following the example of Emerson, he told his congregation that he could no longer do so in good conscience. In 1867 he refused to call himself a Christian and was thereupon dropped from the roll of Unitarian ministers. He was so admired, however, for being upright and unselfish and a good preacher that his congregation gave him a unanimous vote of confidence. With Emerson, Colonel Higginson, and others, he then founded the Free Religious Association, which was intended to unite all the religions of the world by rejecting their dogmas and retaining from each faith only its ethical core. Dogmas were what he abhorred.

When the poet came to read Grandfather Potter's published sermons, he was impressed by their bold speculations about the divine element in men. He wrote an admiring poem about his grandfather, "Halloween," in which he quoted from the journal that Potter had kept during his early travels in Europe. A quoted phrase was ". . . so man may make the god finite and viable, make conscious god's power in action and being." That sounds the Transcendental note, and it is also close to phrases that Aiken himself had written: for example, in the 1949 preface to one of his Symphonies, where he says that man, in becoming completely aware of himself, "can, if he only will, become divine."

There is another point, apparently not connected with Grandfather Potter, at which Aiken comes even closer to Transcendentalism. Once more I quote from that convenient definition by James Hart: ". . . everything in the world is a microcosm containing within itself all the laws and meaning of existence. Likewise, the soul of each individual is identical with the soul of the world, and latently contains all that the world contains. . . . Thus occurs the doctrine of correspondence between the tangible world and the human mind." Aiken, with his senses open to the tangible world, often speaks of this correspondence, which sometimes becomes for him an identity. Thus, he says in "A Letter from Li Po":

> We are the tree, yet sit beneath the tree,
> among the leaves we are the hidden bird,
> we are the singer and are what is heard.

Reading those lines, one can scarcely fail to think of Emerson's "Brahma":

> They reckon ill who leave me out;
> When me they fly, I am the wings;
> I am the doubter and the doubt,
> And I the hymn the Brahmin sings.

Aiken is still more clearly Emersonian, however, in what is almost the last of his poems, *THEE*, written when he was seventy-seven. Though comparatively short—only 250 lines, some consisting of a single word—it appeared as a handsome book, with lithographs by Leonard Baskin, and it is indeed one of his major works. First one notes that the poet has changed his style and that here—as, to a lesser extent, in some of the other late poems—he has abandoned the subtle variations and dying falls of his earlier work. *THEE* is written in short, galloping lines with rhymes like hoofbeats:

> Who is that splendid THEE
> who makes a symphony
> of the one word
> be
> admitting us to see
> all things but THEE?

Obviously THEE is being used here as the Quaker pronoun: "Thee makes," not "You make" or "Thou makest." Aiken may well have learned that usage from the Potter family. As for his question "Who?" it sends us back once more to Emerson. Just as Aiken's "consciousness" at times come close to being the Emersonian Over-Soul, so THEE is the spirit of Nature as defined in Emerson's essay. "Strictly speaking," the essay says, ". . . all that is separate from us, all which Philosophy distinguishes as the NOT ME, that is, both nature and art, all other men and my own body, must be ranked under this name, NATURE." Aiken's name is THEE, but it has a different connotation. Whereas Emerson's Nature is admired for revealing in each of its parts the universal laws that wise men obey, Aiken's THEE is a pitiless force that nourishes and destroys with the divine indifference of the goddess Kali. Also and paradoxically, it is a force evolving with the human spirit—

> as if perhaps in our slow growing
> and the beginnings of our knowing
> as if perhaps
> o could this be
> that we
> be
> THEE?
> THEE still learning
> or first learning
> through us
> to be
> THY THEE?

> Self-praise were then our praise of THEE
> unless we say divinity
> cries in us both as we draw breath
> cry death cry death

> and all our hate
> we must abate
> and THEE must with us meet and mate
> give birth give suck be sick and die
> and close the All-God-Giving-Eye
> for the last time to sky.

When I first read THEE, it reminded me strongly of an untitled poem by Emerson, one that Aiken, so he told me, had never read—and no wonder he had missed it, since it does not appear in the *Complete Works*, even buried with other fragments in an appendix. One finds it in Volume II of the *Journals*, a volume including the period of spiritual crisis that followed the death of Emerson's beloved first wife, Ellen. She died February 8, 1831, and the poem was written July 6—at night? it must have been at night—immediately after a tribute to Ellen and thoughts of rejoining her in death. The poem, however, seems to announce the end of the crisis, since it is the entranced statement of a new faith. Here are two of the stanzas:

> If thou canst bear
> Strong meat of simple truth,
> If thou durst my words compare
> With what thou thinkest in the soul's free youth,
> Then take this fact unto thy soul,—
> God dwells in thee.
> It is no metaphor nor parable,
> It is unknown to thousands, and to thee;
> Yet there is God.
> . . . .
> Who approves thee doing right?
> God in thee.
> Who condemns thee doing wrong?
> God in thee.
> Who punishes thine evil deed?
> God in thee.
> What is thine evil need?
> Thy worse mind, with error blind
> And more prone to evil
> That is, the greater hiding of the God within. . . .

Emerson never went back to polish or even finish the poem, so that it remains a broken rhapsody—rather than an artifact like THEE—and yet it states bluntly the seminal idea that he would develop in his essays of the dozen years that followed. What made me think of the poem when reading *THEE* is something in the style, in the irregular lines—not all of them rhymed—and in the message, too, with its identification of outer and inner worlds and its assertion that men are potentially divine. Of course where Emerson celebrates the power of the indwelling spirit, Aiken gives a twist to Transcendental doctrine by stressing, first, the indifferent power of THEE, and then the dependence of THEE on the individual consciousness—with which it must "meet and mate," from which it learns to become more truly itself, and with which, perhaps, it must die. The speculation seems more imaginative than philosophical, and yet one feels that—with the whole religion of consciousness—it finds a place in the Transcendental line.

In Aiken's beginnings, he had been poles apart from Emerson. He had been atheistic and pessimistic, not optimistic and Unitarian. He had never been impressed by the German Romantic philosophers or by the Neoplatonists, let alone by Sufism and Brahmanism; instead his intellectual models had been Poe first of all, then Santayana, Freud, and Henry James. He would have been out of place in Emerson's Concord, since he continued all his life to be fond of women, mischief, bawdy limericks, and martinis. Nevertheless, at the end of his long career, he had worked round to a position reminiscent of that which Emerson had reached in 1831, before he had published anything. That seems to me an intellectual event of some interest, especially since it was announced in a memorable poem. But *THEE* aroused little attention when it appeared in 1967, and later it seems to have been almost forgotten.

R. W. FLINT
"Rhapsody in Blue"

New York Review of Books, February 6, 1964, pp. 12–13

Conrad Aiken is one of the Saturnians, the giants who bring their golden ages with them, who are consequently, in their venerable years, always being hailed as the last of the last, the last true Bostonian, the last full-scale man of letters. Graham Greene calls him "perhaps the most exciting, the most fully satisfying of living novelists." Aiken is thoroughly New England in the Hawthorne sense—says "yes/O at lightning and lashed rod," knows as well as Hopkins that "the mind, mind has mountains: cliffs of fall/Frightful, sheer, no-man fathomed. Hold them cheap/May who ne'er hung there"—but R. P. Blackmur's somewhat funereal Introduction to this most welcome collection of Aiken's five novels is considerably more so, more grimly, mytho-psychologically New England than the novelist, as if the least fearful lineament of this *atra cura* of the northlands were too precious to be overlooked or undervalued. So be it; Blackmur has his own authority as critic of an old friend whose work he generously admires. He writes excellently of "the finding, declaration, and loss of the self or psyche among the melodramas of love and jealousy, death and immolation, personal power and the frustrate abyss which in their fragments assault his sensibility." The essential form of the novels, Blackmur finds, is the journey. "It is the combination of the form with the material that makes the innovation. The form is the picaresque, the material that of psychology or the conditions of life which a particular psychology points at. Let us call the combination the Psychological Picaresque."

This is good, and would be better if Blackmur were a little less eager to assure us that Aiken has done something respectably strenuous—one remembers that R. W. B. Lewis also made a sort of moral calisthenics out of the Picaresque. In an innocent-looking passage, Blackmur flashes his steel: "It is conscience not consciousness that can make or follow a pattern; and it is conscience that estimates the lies we tell in our search for the truth of self or love in our blue voyage along the great circle of conversation." Now this is really dynamite, because Aiken has always advertised himself as one of the high priests of Consciousness and Blackmur is making a desperate, last-minute attempt to get him back to the high safe ground of The Great Moral Tradition. These words are always getting overloaded. In the Thirties, consciousness was dressed up in a blue shirt and a lunch-pail and called Awareness. But when you recall how very many times the word appears in the Jameses and in Aiken himself, you see that Aiken is throwing everything he has against New England moralism, however refined, however humane.

Not that he ever tried to kill his own active, generous and excitable conscience—who more scornful of the conscience-killers than he?—but rather that this thin mentalistic word "consciousness," for better or worse, was to be his sign of everything generous, adventurous, dramatically, vigorously, and cleansingly outrageous. I think you must admit this to "get" Aiken, the man who successfully crossed the abyss between Santayana and Freud, who sometimes did in fiction what William James thought he was doing in philosophy and psychology, what Henry James kept assuring his brother he was always doing but actually only attempted in a few late novels, notably *The Spoils of Poynton*, *What Maisie Knew*, and *The Awkward Age*—making so bold an imaginative leap forward into the materialization of the world that conscience and consciousness become one. I find Aiken's fiction much more interesting than the *nouveau roman*, but attribute this more to the quality of his performance than to a difference of method. The younger novelists are catching up to Aiken and acting a lot more solemnly about it. Aiken is deeply, soul-stirringly *amusing*—as *Finnegans Wake* would be if we could understand it without a trot. His "vaudeville of the psyche" enlists, in spurts and flashes, every kind of gusto that fiction has known.

King Coffin, a novel that takes a young Nietzschean of Cambridge through all the phases of enlightened megalomania into madness and final suicide, is a perfect abstract of Aiken's technique. The hero's every move, as he plans to murder an insignificant little advertising man, is actually a response to some outside stimulus, so that while he supposes himself to be eliminating a futile symbol of his world's futility, in fact his world is murdering him. Not only that; in his enthusiasm for cutting a picturesque figure he scatters clues that would certainly have hung him had he gone through with the crime. No closer collaboration of mind and circumstance could be imagined. Forgive me, Mr. Blackmur, but Jasper Ammen is *not* "a good companion on the domestic scene for Gide's Lafcadio . . . Stavrogin . . . Vautrin . . . Felix Krull. . . ." He is an elaborate joke, he is *really* mad, no companion for anybody—the *reductio ad absurdum* of Aiken's strategy of total immersion.

King Coffin is a parabolic link between the novels, a cruelly affectionate satire on those candle-lit Beacon Street debating and esthetic societies that Aiken and Blackmur shared in their youth, whose aura of glittering badinage surrounds all of Aiken's heroes. Just because it provides "the best local topography" it's as frightening a picture of the trapped consciousness as you will find outside of Dostoevsky. One skips and goes back, mesmerized. So much is involved of Aiken's unwilling explorations of the borderlands of sanity; yet it *is* just a farce after all. Gerta is Gerta so that she may have a Gerta-daemmerung; Ammen means amen.

King Coffin is mostly action, *Blue Voyage* is mostly talk, soliloquy and dream, but its radical clowning is the fullest practice of the method that *King Coffin* offers as schematic farce. All I need observe of this well-known novel—which still seems the best of the five—is how much more cheerfully Aiken contemplates the foolishness of his ship of fools than Katherine Anne Porter does hers. *O tempora, O mors deploranda artis!*

Great Circle takes us through the course of a week-long analysis, heightened and accelerated by whiskey, of a middle-aged Bostonian who returns to Cambridge to find that his wife has been unfaithful with a mutual friend. If there is a poetry and a metaphysics in the overcoming of jealousy, this is it. Aiken makes a little too much of everything, but his very excess is part of the novel's catharsis, if you stay with him, and contributes to the hard, clear, definite beauty of the Sanders Theater episode at the end.

Conversation is another *tour de force*, the two contrary contrapuntal voices of which combine more easily in one's later reflection on the book than they do in the harsh but fascinating act of reading. The plot is nothing less than an endless, bitter, book-long quarrel between a spectacularly mismated painter and his priggish New Bedford wife who feels neglected and thinks her daughter *cannot* go to the local public schools. Aiken was never more New England than in attempting to transmute all this nastiness into something beautiful through a therapy of bitterness. But the counterplot is an admirable lyric evocation of autumn on Cape Cod, enriched by the painter's charming banter with his little daughter and the arrival in town of some wonderfully horrible types from Greenwich Village. If you find Marquand and the other little Marquands too bland, try this—if you have the courage.

A Heart for the Gods of Mexico doesn't quite deliver what its title promises. The Mexican episodes are disappointing compared with those in *Ushant*. It has two good features—a gusty evening amongst the eateries and drinkeries of downtown Boston, and a painfully sardonic train trip *by day-coach* from Boston to Cuernavaca. I will skip the extraordinary Bostonian moral gymnastics that bring this about. Suffice it to say that a book need not be a real novel to be good Aiken.

If I haven't suceeded in bringing Aiken-the-novelist into focus, as any talented undergraduate could bring Joyce into focus with a New-Critical-analysis of *The Dead*, it is because his *joie de vivre* is always—except in parts of *Blue Voyage* and most of *Ushant*—bursting out of the plot which his experience suggests and swirling about in long, exuberant, entertaining eddies of talk that look pretty dangerous on the page. He *is* a dangerous man.

CONRAD AIKEN
"Poetry and the Mind of Modern Man"
Poets on Poetry
1966, pp. 1–7

As a regular and energetic critic of American poetry from 1915 on, contributing editor of *The Dial*, American correspondent for the *Athenaeum* in London and *The London Mercury*, and editor of three anthologies of American poetry, it will be clear that from very early in this century I had to take sides and to make up my mind not only where poetry should go, but where I, too, as a poet, should go. In my first volume of criticism, published in 1919, I discussed this involvement with considerable candor in a preface called "Apologia Pro Specie Sua." In sum, I argued that each of us was trying to urge poetry in a direction favorable to himself and that dispassionate judgment was a chimera. This was, of course, the period when the so-called New American Poetry was emerging in the persons of Frost, Robinson, Masters, the Imagists, Pound, Eliot, the Vorticists, and the groups in New York known as "the Others." My own position in this melee was, I would say, a shade to the left of center, if we take Robinson as the center. I was opposed to the extremes of fragmentation advocated by the Imagists and the Others and argued, in my review in 1917, that Eliot's rhymed free verse, which was not really free verse at all but a highly controlled and very subtly modulated medium, was probably the best signpost available as to the direction in which the form and tone of poetry might most adventurously go.

This precocious judgment has, I think, been proved true by time. A great deal of the "newest" of the so-called new poetry has now either become dated or disappeared, and, in the perspective we have since gained, we can see that there was never any real revolution in American poetry, in the true sense of an overturning, but rather an orderly and quite logical development from the past, both American and European. It is true that, as James said earlier in his study of Hawthorne, we were aware of a meagerness in our past, or, at any rate, of a lack

of richness in it, or at least some of us thought so; this accounts but only partly for the remarkable exodus of young American writers to Europe after World War I. It accounts, too, for the fact that Eliot and myself, who were friends at Harvard College from 1908 on, discussed this need for a richer chemical solution in which to swim and breathe, a more sustaining *ambiente* than our own then appeared to be. What could be done about it? Eliot, as we all know, elected France and what was then "modern" French poetry and got this creative venom into his veins before the fortunes of World War I settled him in England. I myself preferred the English tradition and lived there many years because that seemed to me what I needed. Later, the fortunes of another war sent me back to America, where I found that my ancestral roots claimed me; I should have remained there all the time.

And the truth is that James was wrong, and so were Eliot and myself and all the others, in thinking that there was an insufficient cultural inheritance in this country; it was there, but neither our teachers nor ourselves were yet aware of it. In Whitman, Melville, Dickinson, Mark Twain, Emerson, Thoreau, Hawthorne, Poe, and James himself, what more could the ripening consciousness of this country, which in a curious way was both old and young, demand? It was enough, if only someone had pointed it out to us; but it remained for *ourselves* to make the discovery. As it was left for me, for example, to make the "discovery" of Emily Dickinson—which was disapproved of by both Pound and Eliot—in an essay on her and a selection of her poems published in England in 1924.

Anyway, there it all was, waiting for us; and I think we can now see that it was at just about this point, in the early 1920's, that we can be said to have first taken possession of it and that this possession began to be manifest in our work. We could see our roots in Whitman and Emerson and Dickinson and then, in the forgotten figure of Trumbull Stickney, the link between them and us, the first sounding of the "modern" note, the abandonment of the oratorical or grandiose for a more flexible and colloquial tone of voice, which nevertheless, when occasion demanded, could rise to the full *vox humana* of the highest poetic speech. We were quite conscious of our search for this medium. Eliot found it in Vildrac and Laforgue, even in Henley's *Sunday up the River*, while I found it in Stickney, John Masefield, and in some of Francis Thompson. As early as 1911, in a composition course at Harvard, I produced a longish narrative poem, called "The Clerk's Journal," which deliberately eschewed "poetic" words and tried to emphasize the telephone wires and cobblestones, not to mention the lunch counters and coffee cups.

This was one side of the poetic experiment in which we were all engaged, the linguistic and tonal side; but in my own case it was made more complicated by the fact that at this time two other influences were brought to bear on me. Music was one of these, in particular that of Richard Strauss in the tone poems and the symphonies and quartets of Beethoven; and this was to lead me pretty far afield. An early poem of this period was subtitled "A Tone Poem." This was followed by a group of sonatas and nocturnes, very bad indeed, and then by the group of "symphonies" which now compose the book called *The Divine Pilgrim*. Admittedly, this preoccupation led to considerable diffuseness, which I was, myself, the first to acknowledge; but I defended it, too, and not without ingenuity, and I think these poems still have their virtues.

But, if they have, it is largely because of the *other* influence—both had really begun at Harvard—and this was my interest in the then "new" psychology of Freud and in the notion, learned from Santayana in his lectures on *Three Philosophical Poets*—Lucretius, Dante, and Goethe—that poetry at its best and broadest must be philosophical, must have at its center some sort of world view, or *weltanschauung*. But how, in the fragmented world of the psychologists—not only Freud, but Jung, Adler, Ferenczi, Holt, and all the rest—was one to shape this? The symphonies of *The Divine Pilgrim* sought it in an overall solipsism, but with increasing accent on the disintegration of the ego, the disappearance of the self into series, like the vaudeville actors who come and go on the stage. The two interests do, I think, hold the book together and give it an aim. If it is certainly no *Faust*, it at least belongs to that category. And its final section, "Changing Mind," written a little later than the others and which takes as its theme the complete breakdown of personality into its components of heredity and sex, signals, I think, the moment of change-over from the earlier and more deliberately musical style to the later, which is more condensed, analytic, and even at times *perceptual*.

But before I go into that, let us pause at this moment, which is 1925, and look round at what the other poets are up to. As a matter of fact, it is one of the most brilliant moments for poetry in the century. Stevens had just published *Harmonium*, probably his best book, with all his characteristics fully developed, but with the form in tight and delicious control and the humor and metaphysics going hand in hand. Eliot had stunned us all with *The Waste Land*. Robinson, now for a moment neglected, was at his apogee in that extraordinary sequence of Arthurian romances, *Merlin* and the others, which can only be likened, psychologically, to Henry James. And, if Masters had come and gone, leaving behind him little more than *Spoon River*, Frost was at the top of his form and Cummings, Marianne Moore, and William Carlos Williams were coming importantly on stage. Sandburg was having his greatest success; Jeffers and MacLeish were emerging. On the whole, I think it can be said that at this point and for the next thirty years the best poetry written in English was American. In fact, I think it has remained so since. English poetry, in a sense, had moved to America.

But with complications. For this galaxy of poets was seldom agreed on anything. Each had to go his own way. It was in some respects a kind of quiet—and sometimes not so quiet—gang warfare. And I think we all realized this—it was kill or be killed; it was the normal evolutionary process and involved, quite rightly, the survival of the fittest; it was poetry, as the vanguard of man's consciousness, as it always has been, once again, by trial and loss, finding out its own way, or trying to, to bring into consciousness every scrap of knowledge, from whatever field and no matter how uncompromisingly unpoetic or antipoetic it might seem to be.

And it was toward this concept of poetry that I, myself, now began more and more deliberately to move, and in this I think it can be said that, although my later poetry *looks* different or *sounds* different, nevertheless this basic direction can be seen in it all. What begins with the musical fragmentation of *The Jig of Forslin* and *The House of Dust* or the animist dissociations and reassociations of the consciousness of Senlin in "Senlin: A Biography," turns more and more, by degrees, into a preoccupation with the very nature of consciousness itself, that evanescent bubble of awareness which is all that we know of ourselves. This, of course, is my answer to the question asked me by the editor of this series, namely, whether the change in man's world during this century has preoccupied me. And how could it not? With Darwin, Nietzsche, and Freud behind us, where were the comfortable values to which

we had been born? Perhaps this fact was brought home to me earlier than to most of my generation, for I inherited this sort of liberalism and agnosticism from my grandfather, William James Potter, who was one of the great liberal Unitarians of the nineteenth century, had adapted himself by midcentury to *The Origin of Species*, studied with Humboldt, and was one of the founders and later president of the Free Religious Association. I was brought up with no beliefs, or none of a dogmatic sort. Wasn't it enough that the world was beautiful, terrible, astonishing, even incredible? One could, if one liked, call it divine or conceive of a god in various forms, as my Festus does, to amuse himself, in "The Pilgrimage of Festus." But more important, it seemed to me, was to take the *next* step, and analyze the world in the only terms we had any genuine knowledge of, to wit, ourselves. One must be as conscious of this as possible, if only as a preliminary step to anything else; and this endeavor seemed to involve another possible concept—that in the *evolution of consciousness* man was already embarked, willy-nilly, on a perhaps divine pilgrimage of his own.

I do not want to be and cannot be too precise about all this or the timing of it; who of us can possibly remember the exact point at which he became finally conscious of the compass of his mind and the relation of this compass to his body, the whole psychosomatic machine? Like everything else, this knowledge comes in fractions, is a series, an accretion. One observes, as a child, the wasp stinging the locust to death, then dragging away the locust to its underground nest. And to bring this observation into association with the small boy's experience of urinating into a bowl and there, by himself, creating an entire cosmos of bubbles, and of an extraordinary beauty, is to realize how early in life one begins this attempt at a correlation of the mysteries, apparently inexplicable, with one's own unexplainable existence at the very center of it. Who am I? We inevitably get back to that fundamental question. And how did I come by it? And what should I do with it?

Well, those have been my preoccupations, and they have allowed me a quite considerable range. As for form, here again I have always maintained that, as poetry is an art, and perhaps the highest, it should use every prosodic and linguistic device at its disposal; I cannot subscribe to the theory that a mere counting of syllables can be substituted for verse. And the form must be suited to the theme. In the two series of "Preludes," which I think are the center of my work, I did not hesitate to mix a sort of organic free verse with the most formal of lyrics. As for another poem, "The Kid," a poem that deals with the pioneers of America, those of the mind as well as of the broadax, I didn't hesitate to use a kind of ballad form, a folk doggerel, in couplets, which nevertheless, when necessary, could become pure seventeenth-century severity. And again, for such longer philosophical meditations as "A Letter from Li-Po" or "The Crystal" I found a free blank verse most suitable. In short, the theme will almost invariably, left to itself, call the tune.

The poet is only the medium.

Finally, I would like to repeat something I said thirty years ago about poetry in general and its function.

Poetry has always kept easily abreast with the utmost man can do in extending the horizon of his consciousness, whether outward or inward. It has always been the most flexible, the most comprehensive, the most farseeing, and hence the most successful, of the modes by which he has accepted the new in experience, realized it, and adjusted himself to it. Whether it is a change in his conception of the heavens, or of the law of gravity, or of morality, or of the nature of consciousness, it has always at last been in poetry that man has given his thought its supreme expression—which is to say that most of all, in this, he succeeds in making real for himself the profound myth of personal existence and experience.

But if poetry is to accomplish this, in any age, it must think; it must embody the full consciousness of man at that given moment. It cannot afford to lag behind the explorations of knowledge, whether of the inner or outer worlds; these it is its business to absorb and transmute. What made Elizabethan poetry great, above all, was the fearlessness with which it plunged into the problem of consciousness itself. No item of man's awareness was too trivial to be noted, too terrifying to be plumbed. Shakespeare's poetry is everywhere vascular with this rich consciousness of self, thought being carried bodily into the realm of feeling, and feeling as boldly carried into the realm of thought. This was no mere decorative toy, no amusement or anodyne for women; it was the advance guard in man's conquest of the knowable. It was a portrait of man with the sweat on his brow, the blood on his hands, the agony in his heart;

with his gaieties, his absurdities, his obscenities; his beliefs and his doubts. No poetry since has been so great, for none has been either so comprehensive or so truthful. The fashions changed, the "idea" of poetry changed, the novel absorbed a part of its province—one could multiply indefinitely the reasons for it. But today, as I have suggested, the signs are not wanting that poetry may again occupy its own province, may again speak with full-voiced gusto of the horrors and subtleties and magnificences of the great myth in which we find ourselves the bewildered actors.

And I would like to say again what I said in 1948, in one of the prefaces to my collection of symphonies, that in the evolution of man's consciousness, ever widening and deepening and subtilizing his awareness, and in the dedication of himself to this supreme task, man possesses all that he could possibly require in the way of a religious credo; when the half-gods go, the gods arrive; he can, if he only will, become divine.

Edward Albee

1928–

Edward Albee was born on March 12, 1928, in Virginia, and was then adopted in Washington, D.C., by a wealthy couple who raised him in Larchmont, New York. His adoptive father was a partner in the Keith-Albee Theatre Circuit; the stagestruck boy wrote his first play at age twelve. By the time he attended Trinity College in 1946–47, he had written a novel, many short stories, and reams of poetry. For the next ten years Albee worked as an office boy, a record salesman, a book salesman, and a Western Union messenger.

In 1958, after turning thirty, he quit his job and wrote *The Zoo Story* in three weeks. It was an immediate success, winning an Obie and the Vernon Rice Memorial Award. Three more Albee one-acts were produced in 1960: *The Death of Bessie Smith*, *Fam and Yam*, and *The Sandbox*, which evolved into *The American Dream* the following year. 1962 saw the premiere of Albee's first full-length play, *Who's Afraid of Virginia Woolf?* The play's raw language and emotions created a scandal; when it was denied the Pulitzer Prize, both of the prize committee's theatre advisors resigned. It did win two Tonys and the New York Drama Critics Circle Award, and was made into an Oscar-winning film in 1966.

Tiny Alice (1964) proved as controversial as *Virginia Woolf*, if less popular. Albee finally won a Pulitzer in 1967 for *A Delicate Balance*, and again in 1975 for *Seascape*. The latter failed at the box office and received mixed reviews, like every Albee play since the late 1960s, including *All Over* (1971), *Counting the Ways* (1976), *The Lady From Dubuque* (1980), and *The Man With Three Arms* (1983). He has fared no better with adaptations, such as the book for a disastrous musical version of *Breakfast at Tiffany's* in 1966, or *Lolita* in 1981. He often directs his own plays, and is noted for aiding young playwrights. Albee was awarded doctorates from Emerson College in 1967 and Trinity College in 1974, as well as the Gold Medal for Drama from the American Academy of Arts and Letters in 1980. He lives in New York City.

General

It is incredible to consider that on the basis of four plays, one little more than a fragment, Edward Albee, the *enfant terrible* of America's *avant garde*, is being seriously considered in many quarters as a genuinely important playwright. The same critics and theorists who deny Thornton Wilder his legitimate right to be called a great playwright because he has written so little are ready to canonize young Albee as the greatest thing in modern drama.

This neatly tailored young man, who sounds quite rational and even personable, writes like a bomb-carrying anarchist. Without benefit of beret and red armband he seems to be

principal among the new iconoclasts in our theatre. This group, claiming some inspiration from Ionesco, causing many a theatre-goer to shake his head in helpless bewilderment, seek, it seems, to shake the contemporary theatre to its roots, to put mystery back on a stage that has become enamored of fact and completely captivated by obvious *formulae*—a theatre which to them has become ossified. . . .

Undoubtedly the *avant gardist*, and Albee here provides a fortunate case in point, has an axe to grind. He is original— terrifically original—and in his originality, extreme as it may often be, lies his strength. Nevertheless, it is difficult to peer through the smokescreen of paradox to see whether or not he really has something to say. In the theatre the audience doesn't *bother* to comprehend unless the playwright, within the generally accepted and known conventions of the stage, says what he has to say in a reasonably overt manner. No audience can sit happily guessing as to what the playwright means. . . .

The *avant gardist* despairs of the modern theatre's technique and it is at this point we can scream derision at the precocious band who would level our theatre and render it a grotesque playground of their own devising. One needn't argue with their position that our modern world is a piteous place, constipated with egocentricity and bilious with smugness. We can accept this analysis and we can cheer any sincere and well-chosen efforts taken to better it. We *can* question the *means*, however, and it is in the means that the commendable objectives of some of the *avant gardists* (like Albee who does not appear a nihilist) are tragically betrayed.

In these cases, and let's use Albee for an example, we can note that he neither lectures interestingly like Brecht, delights and outrages like Shaw, nor sings like O'Casey as he slings his thunderbolts into the world's teeth. He fails dismally in getting his audiences up and outside themselves. He only slaps them back into the lonely cell of ego where they must dwell unfulfilled and in spineless terror. Albee is too busy indulging in private ironies to share with the humble generosity that is inevitably present in an artist who is earnest and true. . . .

Albee's theatre gives nothing. It seeks attention in return for the dry crust of a spurious mystery. A concatenation of the same *non sequiturs* and banalities one hears on the street are poor payment indeed for those who come to the theatre. . . .

Edward Albee, brash young novice, has torn off the white veil of humility and is confidently belching in the sanctuary of art. He writes for the narrow audience, an audience far removed from the broad pastures of grassroots participation where great plays are grown. His *Zoo Story*, following the hysterical indictments of conformity and self-isolation contributed by some of the European *avant gardists*, really paves the way for a new and insidious kind of conformism—one in which personal responsibility and the inexorable obligations occasioned by man's social nature are trampled under by the *new* herd.

It is a sad thing to see a young man—even one as intellectually complacent and self satisfied as Albee appears to be—given . . . adulation so early. Adulation that allows him to evade, even within himself, the problem of self-justification. Many a potential talent has been ruined by the flush of early success, and though to this date Albee has achieved only limited production in small theatres and under one management, he has been widely lionized as the champion of the new stage form, as the beardless young prophet who will deliver our theatre from the old nasty ways.

Perhaps if he takes the trouble to master his craft, if he builds endurance for his short-winded muse, if he correlates his natural ear for modern speech to something rational and truly dramatic, he will in time become a playwright to reckon with. He may even become the theatrical Messias for which the American theatre stands waiting.—Richard A. Duprey, "From Pilate's Chair," *Just off the Aisle*, 1962, pp. 74–80

⟨In⟩ Edward Albee's work, we see a tension between realism and the theatre of the absurd. *The Death of Bessie Smith* is a purely realistic play, and *Who's Afraid of Virginia Woolf?* is, for all its showiness, no more than a cross between sick drawing-room comedy and naturalistic tragedy. *The Zoo Story*, *The Sandbox* and *The American Dream* are, on the face of it, absurd plays, and yet, if one compares them with the work of Beckett, Ionesco or Pinter, they all retreat from the full implications of the absurd when a certain point is reached. Albee

still believes in the validity of reason—that things can be proved, or that events can be shown to have definite meanings—and, unlike Beckett and the others, is scarcely touched by the sense of living in an absurd universe. Interesting and important as his plays are, his compromise seems ultimately a failure of nerve—a concession to those complementary impulses towards cruelty and self-pity which are never far below the surface of his work.

Albee has been attracted to the theatre of the absurd mainly, I think, because of the kind of social criticism he is engaged in. Both *The Zoo Story* and *The American Dream* are savage attacks on the American Way of Life. . . .

The American Way of Life, in the sense in which I am using the phrase, is a structure of images; and the images, through commercial and political exploitation, have lost much of their meaning. When the Eisenhower family at prayer becomes a televised political stunt, or the family meal an opportunity for advertising frozen foods, the image of the family is shockingly devalued. The deception practised is more complex than a simple lie: it involves a denial of our normal assumptions about evidence—about the relation between the observed world and its inner reality. This is why the techniques of the theatre of the absurd, which is itself preoccupied with the devaluation of language and of images, and with the deceptive nature of appearances, are so ideally suited to the kind of social criticism Albee intends. It is for this reason, too, that he has felt able to use the techniques of the theatre of the absurd, while stopping short of an acceptance of the metaphysic of the absurd upon which the techniques are based. It is possible, clearly, to see the absurd character of certain social situations without believing that the whole life is absurd. In Albee's case, however, this has meant a restriction of scope, and his plays do not have the poetic quality or imaginative range of *Waiting for Godot*, for instance, or *The Caretaker*, or *Rhinoceros*. . . .

For the playwright who accepts without reservations that he is living in an absurd universe, the loss of faith in reason which is at the heart of this vision and the conviction that the rational exploration of experience is a form of self-deception, imply a rejection of those theatrical conventions which reflect a belief in reason. Characters with fixed identities; events which have a definite meaning; plots which assume the validity of cause and effect; dénouements which offer themselves as complete resolutions of the questions raised by the play; and language which claims to mean what it says—none of these can be said to be appropriate means for expressing the dislocated nature of experience in an absurd world. In terms of formal experiment, then, the theatre of the absurd represents a search for images of non-reason.

Albee has used these images of non-reason in his attack on the American Way of Life without . . . accepting the underlying vision which generated them. His work belongs to the second level of the theatre of the absurd: it shows a brilliantly inventive sense of what can be done with the techniques, but stops short of the metaphysic which makes the metaphysical gymnastics. Nevertheless, a deep stream of dramatic perception and committed passion flows underground in him, and when it occasionally comes to the surface it irrigates our dry theatre the way almost nothing else is doing these days.—Richard Gilman, "Chinese Boxes" (1965), *Common and Uncommon Masks*, 1971, pp. 137–39

According to Albee . . . existential or "outside" problems are solved only if they can be made over on the model of relationships within the family: Nick as son; Nick and Honey as children . . . ; Edna and Harry as children; the menacing Van Man in *American Dream* as son . . . ; death as an Oedipal grandson in *The Sandbox*. Although in *Virginia Woolf* there is an apparent finality about the solution that implies that the problems entering with Nick have been solved, George does not actually meet the challenge Nick poses. The problem simply understands and vanishes. However cooperative the problems are as they leave, their unmotivated exit is a clear indication that the family cannot and does not provide a real solution. Although the plays overtly state the opposite, in fact not all the problems evoked by the plays can be transposed to family relationships.

So the fundamental contradiction in Albee has to do with opposing ideas about the function and centrality of the family. Overtly the plays propose that problems and conflicts seen in the family originate in distortions of family relationships and can be solved by righting these relationships in stereotypical—even heavy-handed—ways. Covertly within the plays the opposing issue is also posed: that problems and conflicts seen in the family originate outside the family (in work, politics, society, and existence, all quite vaguely presented by Albee), and that the family is incapable of solving them. . . .

The resolution therefore turns on two necessarily linked evasions. Order is restored by assimilating all problems to family relationships, and curing them by re-establishing sexual stereotypes and killing (or mutilating) the rival. This solution never traces the sources of the man's failure, but rather confuses the cause of the man's failure with its effect—the dominance of the woman. This is the first evasion. Then, problems raised in the play which cannot be assimilated or transformed into family issues simply decamp, unsolved and unaccounted for at the end. This is the second evasion, which logically follows from the first. . . . Losing power over men, over career, over rivals, an Albee character will seek to gain power over women and children. The injured pride of semi-displaced persons seems to be at stake, since those people would need the almost self-congratulatory messages that their failure is not a real failure after all, and that their powerlessness can magically resurface as power in normative sexual and family relations.

The role of the middle group in modern capitalist society is very possibly reflected in the play's almost impotent angers, which are saved by the transformation of failure to "choice" and powerlessness to power, all elements of the larger solution: privatization. . . . ⟨Albee⟩ makes available a set of explanations and transformations appropriate to the needs of this group: their failure is a more heroic kind of success, involving choice or will. And the private world of family and sexual relations is still controllable. Further, Albee's play makes available a stylized matrix of vicious ripostes which gives the audience the cathartic satisfaction of total malice, without laws or norms, all at the service of a restoration of order. . . . The anger and nastiness of the play's dialogue is therefore an expression of the actual powerlessness and apparent power of the social group in the audience whose belligerent malaise Albee so piercingly, and even prophetically, expresses.—RACHEL BLAU DUPLESSIS, "In the Bosom of the Family: Contradiction and Resolution in Edward Albee," *MR*, Spring 1977, pp. 139–42

Albee-playwright was born at the age of thirty, with perfect command of contemporary colloquial stylized dialogue. . . . Edward Albee is the most skillful composer of dialogue that America has produced. His very first play showed thorough mastery of colloquial idiom—syntax, vocabulary, and above all rhythm. With adroit combinations of monologue and witty repartee, Albee dramatizes human situations. He never permits his characters to lapse into discussion, and he rarely inflates them with abstraction. Almost always, he mirrors the meaning

of events in the rhythm of his dialogue: Jerry's indirection, George's surgery, Julian's fragmentation, the Long-Winded Lady's long wind. Difficult as marriage is *within* his plays, they contain unusually harmonious marriages of sound to sense.

But suspicion is born of Albee's very brilliance. His plays are too well crafted, his characters too modishly ambiguous, his dialogue too carefully cadenced. This is not to say that he writes perfect plays—whatever that may be—but his surface polish seems to deny subsurface search, much less risk. Again and again, O'Neill stumbled and fell in the darkness of his dramas; even the final achievements lack grace, but their solidity endures. Miller has probed into his own limited experience and into his own limited view of the experience of his time, but his plays sometimes give evidence of reaching to his limits. Williams expresses his guiltiest urges, and though the very naiveté of his guilt restricts the resonance of his plays, he does agonize toward religious resolution. Albee's plays are not devoid of suffering, and in any case one cannot measure the quality of a play by some putative pain of the playwright. Nevertheless, Albee's craftsmanship recalls the meditation of the disembodied voice of *Box*: "arts which have gone down to craft." And it is particularly ungrateful to turn his own finely modulated words against Albee. But just because his verbal craft *is* so fine, one longs for the clumsy upward groping toward art.—RUBY COHN, "The Verbal Murders of Edward Albee," *Dialogue in American Drama*, 1971, p. 169

Fate has not been kind to Edward Albee. I don't mean only the bitterness of early success and subsequent decline, though that's hard enough. Worse: He was born into a culture that—so he seems to think—will not let him change professions, that insists on his continuing to write plays long after he has dried up.

It's a notable fact (I've noted it previously myself) that some of the glowing names in the history of English drama wrote imperishable plays when they were young and then went on into other lives. Congreve, Wycherley, Vanbrugh, Sheridan, Barker, all spent most of their later years in other occupations. Apparently each of them felt he had written all he could or wanted to in play form, and changed. But today, pinned to public account by the intensities of hype, the dramatist evidently feels that to change professions, even if he might be good at another job, would be to admit defeat. Though exhausted—like Albee and Miller and Williams—he trudges on, to our embarrassment if not to his.

Look at Albee's career since its peak, which I take to be *Who's Afraid of Virginia Woolf?*, produced 18 years ago. Three adaptations, *The Ballad of the Sad Cafe*, *Malcolm*, and *Everything in the Garden*, all deplorable. (The very fact that he began making adaptations right after the success of *Virginia Woolf* was a sign of nerve tremor.) Then *Tiny Alice*, *A Delicate Balance*, *All Over*, and *Seascape*, a long torpid decline interrupted only briefly by a pair of short, passable attempts at the Absurd, *Box* and *Quotations From Chairman Mao Tse-Tung*. What marked the full-length plays, right after the realism of *Virginia Woolf*, was Albee's use of mysticism and death. I mean use, utilization, not inquiry or dramatization. The big words and ideas became weapons to club us into awe of the works' profundity, a conclusion that was inescapable because the works themselves were so tenuous, even silly. Allegory (*All Over*) and symbolism (*Seascape*) were also called into service, creakingly. Overall, Albee seemed compelled to write plays just to prove that he is still a playwright, and he grabbed at sonorous subjects and august methods to cloak his insufficiencies.—STANLEY KAUFFMANN, *SR*, March 15, 1980, p. 34

Works

THE ZOO STORY

The Zoo Story is flawed by improbabilities and perhaps needless notes to provoke, shock or outrage—comic and horrifying by turn. Yet the play gives ample evidence of genuine feeling and an intimate knowledge of certain aspects of the contemporary scene, especially of our metropolitan area. If there were not some danger of being taken too superficially, I should say that in *The Zoo Story* certain tragic and crucial factors which have contributed to produce the "beat" generation have been brilliantly dramatized.

The young man in *The Zoo Story*, who intrudes on a respectable and modest citizen sitting on a Central Park bench, is isolated in his poverty, his self-educated ignorance, his lack of background or roots, his total estrangement from society. He has no connection with anybody, but he seeks it—in vain. When he succeeds in approaching an animal or a person, it is always through a barrier of mistrust and in a tension of disgust, fear, despair. When he breaks out of the emotional insulation of his life, it is only by a violent intrusion into the complacent quiet of the mediocre citizen on the park bench; and that unoffending bystander is then forced into effecting the mad young man's suicide. To put it another way: the derelict finally achieves a consummation of connection only through death at the unwitting and horrified hands of society's "average" representative.

This story is conveyed with rude humor—very New York—a kind of squalid eloquence and a keen intuition of the humanity in people who live among us in unnoticed or shunned wretchedness. We come not only to know the pathetic and arresting central figure as well as the astonished stranger he "victimizes," but through them both we also meet the unseen but still vivid characters of a lady janitor, a Negro homosexual neighbor, a dog and other denizens in the vicinity of both the West and East Seventies of Manhattan.

The Zoo Story interested me more than any other new American play thus far this season. I hope its author has the stuff to cope with the various impediments that usually face our promising dramatists.—HAROLD CLURMAN, "*The Zoo Story* and Beckett's *Krapp's Last Tape*" (1960), *The Naked Image*, 1966, pp. 14–15

Edward Albee (born in 1928) comes into the category of the Theatre of the Absurd precisely because his work attacks the very foundations of American optimism. His first play, *The Zoo Story* (1958), which shared the bill at the Provincetown Playhouse with Beckett's *Krapp's Last Tape*, already showed the forcefulness and bitter irony of his approach. In the realism of its dialogue and in its subject matter—an outsider's inability to establish genuine contact with a dog, let alone any human being—*The Zoo Story* is closely akin to the world of Harold Pinter. But the effect of this brilliant one-act duologue between Jerry, the outcast, and Peter, the conformist bourgeois, is marred by its melodramatic climax; when Jerry provokes Peter into drawing a knife and then impales himself on it, the plight of the schizophrenic outcast is turned into an act of sentimentality, especially as the victim expires in touching solicitude and fellow-feeling for his involuntary murderer.—MARTIN ESSLIN, *The Theatre of the Absurd*, 1961, p. 225

What Albee has written in *The Zoo Story* is a modern Morality play. The theme is the centuries old one of human isolation and salvation through sacrifice. Man in his natural state is alone, a prisoner of Self. If he succumbs to fear he enforces his isolation in denying it. Pretending that he is not alone, he surrounds himself with things and ideas that bolster the barrier between himself and all other creatures. The good man first takes stock of himself. Once he has understood his condition, realized his animality and the limitations imposed upon him by Self, he is driven to prove his kinship with all other things and creatures, "with a bed, with a cockroach, with a mirror. . . ." (The progression that Jerry describes is Platonic.) In proving this kinship he is extending his boundaries, defying Self, proving his humanity, since the kinship of all nature can be recognized only by the animal who has within him a spark of divinity. He finds at last, if he has been completely truthful in his search, that the only way in which he can smash the walls of his isolation and reach his fellow creatures is by an act of love, a sacrifice, so great that it altogether destroys the self that imprisons him, that it kills him. Albee, in recreating this theme, has used a pattern of symbolism that is an immensely expanded allusion to the story of Christ's sacrifice. But the symbolism is not outside of the story which he has to tell, which is the story of *modern* man and *his* isolation and hope for salvation. He uses the allusion to support his own story. He has chosen traditional Christian symbols, I think, not because they are tricky attention-getters, but because the sacrifice of Christ is perhaps the most effective way that the story has been told in the past.—ROSE A. ZIMBARDO, "Symbolism and Naturalism in Edward Albee's *The Zoo Story*," *TCL*, April 1962, pp. 10–17

In his first and best one-act, *The Zoo Story* (1959), Albee tells a rather simple story which, largely because it remains so implicit, has often evaded audiences and critics. At base, Albee describes a failed homosexual pass. On the surface, though, the play remains innocent only to the innocent eye. Jerry, a young disheveled man, confronts Peter, a tweedily dressed, graying father in his middle forties, sitting on a bench in Central Park. Jerry solicits Peter's reluctant attention; and once he has a receptive audience, Jerry tells of his vain attempt to establish communication with his landlady's mangy dog. After this long monologue, Jerry starts to nudge Peter, provoking a fight. To make the battle more "evenly matched," Jerry gives Peter his knife which Peter holds out in front of him as a stiff-armed defense. Jerry impales himself on it—quite deliberately, it seems—and once he feels death coming, he says, "Thank you, Peter, I mean that now," adding, "You have comforted me. Dear Peter."

Beneath this surface runs a homosexual undercurrent. Jerry never explicitly announces his desire to entice Peter, but Jerry's passions are implicit in nearly every speech he makes. Early in the play, Jerry addresses Peter as "boy" and then alleges that Peter can sire no more children. Jerry goes on to say that he lives next door to a "colored queen" and that he often tells strangers, "Keep your hands to yourself, buddy." Peter's usual reply is an indignant, "I must say I don't . . ."; and since throughout the play he is truly unaware of Jerry's real intention, his insensitivity becomes a major source of pathos and comedy.

Albee, like Tennessee Williams, knows how to transform a physical object into a dramatic symbol so that every time the object is mentioned we become more aware of its ulterior meaning. Here Albee has two major sets of symbols—dogs and cats, animals and vegetables. Dogs are surrogate-males, and cats become females. Thus, when Jerry says he wants companionship with a dog, he symbolically announces his homosexual designs. Secondly, an "animal" is a male who will not respond to a homosexual pass, while a "vegetable" is more acquiescent. Around the directions North and South, Albee weaves another stream of symbolic suggestions. Early in the play, Jerry makes sure he has been moving northward, but "not due north," through Central Park and then describes how he brought his mother's cadaver north; and just before he dies, he tells Peter, "I decided that I would walk north." In the north, of course, awaits death.

Once we recognize these symbols, much of the play's "mystery" dissolves into meaningful action. We can, for instance, easily grasp the significance of Jerry's attempt to befriend a dog and, in addition, appreciate it as one of the most moving speeches in contemporary theatre. When Jerry makes physical advances on Peter, first by tickling him until his voice becomes falsetto and then nudging him off the bench, Jerry says, "You're a vegetable; Go lie down on the ground." (Translation: You're a passive male so be a female with your back on the ground.) Again, Peter misses the point. In desperation, Jerry starts a fight with Peter, drawing his knife and giving it to Peter who holds it in front of him like an erected phallus.

Culminating the surrogate seduction, Jerry impales himself upon its blade with rhythms suggestive of an orgasm; and in his dying speech, Jerry confirms to Peter that because, "You've defended your honor, . . . you're not really a vegetable; you're an animal." In his desperate action, Jerry has solved his predicament—he finds both the sexual contact to assuage his desire and death to end it. On one level, then, Albee is writing about the predicament of the lonely homosexual who is never quite sure if the man he tries to pick up is "gay" and whose possible contacts are limited. On another level, he tells of one man's terrible isolation and his desperate need to break out of his shell. Either way, *The Zoo Story* is the most flawlessly wrought and tightly executed of all his plays and probably one of the great one-acts in American dramatic literature.—RICHARD KOSTELANETZ, "The Art of Total No," *Contact*, Nov.–Dec. 1963, pp. 62–70

In the unlikely event that anything like a "movement" of young American dramatists will ever get off the ground, the world premiere of Edward Albee's *The Zoo Story* will undoubtedly be commemorated as its starting point. Characteristically enough, this world premiere did not take place in the United States, where the critics seldom hail anything new in the arts until they have had the green light from across the Atlantic. In this case the green light came all the way from West Germany, where *The Zoo Story* was first produced in Berlin on September 28, 1959. The story of how *The Zoo Story* was first produced in Germany and subsequently became a success in New York after having previously been rejected right and left over here is extremely instructive for those trying to understand the fantastic world of the New York theater with its Alice-in-Wonderland economics, according to which the producers and theater-owners rake in all the money (and pay the featherbedding stagehands, house managers, and public relations men with it) while the actors and authors, unless the play is exceptionally "successful," starve. Naturally enough, if the sole purpose of theatrical productions is the personal enrichment of the producer and the theater-owner, new plays such as *The Zoo Story* have not the faintest chance of being put on unless they come with some built-in guarantee of success such as a European reputation. That is exactly what happened to Albee's play. After being passed around New York for a bit, it was sent to Europe by a friend of the author, and there it was finally produced. When it came back, it came with critical acclaim behind it and labels reading "avant-garde," "philosophy of the absurd," and "disciple of Beckett" plastered all over it. It was thus safe to produce and duly opened at the Provincetown Playhouse in New York on January 14, 1960, being obediently accorded enthusiastic reviews by critics who almost certainly

didn't understand a word of it but who had done their homework on the European press notices and the academic pronouncements.—GEORGE WELLWARTH, *The Theatre of Protest and Paradox*, 1964, p. 321

His first play, indeed, is not only within its limits a good and effective play; it is virtually an epitome, for good and for ill, of all his later original drama. . . . Since *The Zoo Story* does argue—not only through Jerry but through the action the play presents—that in mid-twentieth-century America the possibility of genuine intellectual understanding is lost beyond recall, consistency compels Albee to take great care that the events of his play be no more intellectually understandable to his audience than they are to Jerry and Peter; and I believe that his care has on the whole been rewarded: many of Albee's admirers have seemed to feel deeply for Jerry and Peter, but no one has claimed to know them. . . . Albee's comprehensive denial of intellect establishes a theatre incapable of resolution—a theatre suitable to fantasy, perhaps, but a theatre in which Albee's realism cannot help being inconclusive.—MELVIN L. PLOTINSKY, *DS*, Winter 1965, pp. 220–23

In *Zoo Story*, I named two characters Peter and Jerry. I know two people named Peter and Jerry. But then the learned papers started coming in, and of course Jerry is supposed to be Jesus . . . which is much more interesting, I suppose, to the public than the truth.—EDWARD ALBEE, interview with William Flanagan, *Writers at Work*, Third Series, 1967, p. 338

THE DEATH OF BESSIE SMITH

The most obvious theme of this play is doubtless that suggested by the situation—racism. Bessie Smith in Albee's work becomes the victim, not of an automobile accident, but of the intolerance raging in the South. The author has taken care not to limit his subject to the anecdote and to generalize his argument. Racism appears in the play at three different levels. First it is manifest in the simple withholding of aid to Bessie Smith. But this aspect, if it is the most brutal and the most eloquent, is held to an undercurrent through most of the play, being directly expressed in barely three of the shorter scenes. Moreover, Albee explicitly refuses to personalize the victim: he never shows Bessie Smith to us. It might be argued that by using her name he necessarily restricted his message to a specific case. But the singer died in 1937 and the play was written in 1959— that is to say, at a time when the circumstances of her accident and death had long formed a Bessie Smith legend. Thus the name no longer referred to a single person, but to a whole race of pariahs, of the disinherited. The language touches on the same problem in a network of allusions, images and remarks which, in isolation, would have minimal effect, but which combine to establish more surely than a long description the racist climate of the South, the atmosphere permeated with prejudice, cruelty and hatred. At one time the Father fulminates against "those goddam nigger records" which aggravate his headaches. At another the Nurse amuses herself by humiliating the Orderly, assigning him degrading errands, reminding him that the needs of their Negro patients come second in the hospital's priority to the whim of their honored patient, the Mayor (who is undergoing treatment for his hemorrhoids). Again, the Intern ironically taunts the Nurse about the lynchings and other horrible punishments reserved for Negroes: ". . . orderlies you may burn at will, unless you have other plans for them. . . ."

In the relationship between the Nurse and the Orderly, Albee has found another—and perhaps the most effective—level of meaning. Here he recovers the evocative power of *The*

Zoo Story when he draws for us a Negro who has become auto-racist. The character is at once pathetic and repellent, a monster and a martyr. His legitimate desire to find his place in the sun is transformed into an obsequious opportunism: he endures any sarcasm, wounding remark or disgusting duty. He tries to please everyone and succeeds in isolating himself from all. Banished and disgraced by his race, he is the target and laughingstock of his betters, the whites. The Nurse even suggests (and here Albee's imagination is truly superlative) that in order to escape his condition he spends his evening soaking bleach into his skin.

But the Negro himself is only criticized to the extent that the criticism also applies to the white society which conditions him. In the last scene, he is leaning with his back to the wall—a symbolic posture—but it is an empty being, an automaton without a soul, who speaks. He is at this point so estranged from his world that the death of a black woman signifies less to him, who should be the first one touched by it, than to the Nurse or the Intern. Albee has been able to create here an impressive image of all those who have let themselves be convinced that it is shameful to be born black. But his goal is primarily to brand those who have done the convincing. With *The Death of Bessie Smith* Albee made his contribution to the activities of northern intellectuals on behalf of racial equality. His art became the means to criticize and denounce a situation to which, as an American, he is particularly sensitive. . . .

⟨Another⟩ important theme of *The Death of Bessie Smith* is that of illusion, of the life-lie. Suggested in *The Zoo Story*, it is here further developed, foreshadowing *Who's Afraid of Virginia Woolf?* where the problem acquires central importance. All the characters in *The Death of Bessie Smith* are out of touch with reality. Everyone has, in the words of the Nurse, "a pretty hard time reconciling himself to things as they are." Everyone, consequently, has composed a world of dreams in which he tries to survive and to which he has secured himself as if to a life-buoy. The Father, deteriorated, as much physically as morally, his helplessness symbolized by an ineffectual cane, has fastened on the idea of an illusory past grandeur; now he pretends to a close friendship with the Mayor. The Negro Orderly, a pariah who denies his birthright incessantly, believes that one day he will have done forever with carrying bedpans for white patients and bearing his superiors' taunts. The Intern, a beginning doctor in a second-rate hospital in the deep South, dreams of noble deeds and a glorious career. But his mediocre job serves him as a pretext for not setting out for Spain to fight Franco. Jack, the friend of Bessie Smith, has his own dream—a second chance for Bessie, a return to success and fame symbolized by a trip to New York, to a mythical *North* where all men are equal. The Nurse also seeks to escape the familial, economic, emotional and sexual frustrations of her situation: she deludes herself that she is a member of an important family with good prospects for marrying above her condition.

Absurdly, destiny, another guise of Gregers Werle, arrives to smash their illusions and reveal their tragic imperfections. Bessie Smith dies in a car accident. The new career Jack dreams of ends before it can begin; the young doctor's willingness to act runs afoul of ineluctable death. The Orderly dooms himself by his refusal to help and understand his Negro brethren. The Nurse also seems to triumph, but her victory is a death comparable to Jerry's in *The Zoo Story*, since she annihilates the man she is attracted to; nor can she wholeheartedly participate in her father's pretense of aristocracy.

The final message is as despairing as in the gloomiest plays of Strindberg and the bitterest of Ibsen. In *The Wild Duck* after

a series of illustrations of the life-lie, the Norwegian dramatist has Dr. Relling draw a pragmatic lesson which finally reveals the truth to Gregers Werle, the instrument of the drama. But we would search in vain in *The Death of Bessie Smith* for a protagonist capable of extracting meaning from the jazz-singer's death. Not one shows even the first dawning consciousness of the absurdity of his life and the tragedy of death. On this philosophical pessimism is superimposed a social tragedy, already painted on a noble scale by Tennessee Williams—the decay of southern society, the shameful anachronism in the heart of America. This image of a dying society is underlined by the symbolism of the setting sun, which gives the whole play its nostalgic aura. The absurdity of individual existence is thus made perceptible in a social context and a symbolic atmosphere which extend not only to an entire generation but to the succession of generations which form a civilization.

Consequently, what holds our attention is less the characters themselves than the historical and metaphysical drama which they act out before us. These characters *en situation* are charged with demonstrating the absurdity of a particular society—but also the absurdity of the human condition in general. Proofs are hardly needed of this reduction of characters to abstractions. In the manner of Strindberg and the German expressionists, Albee has given names only to Bessie Smith, her friend Jack, and their bar acquaintance, Bernie. All three are authentic Negroes who suffer, hope and die because they have been born black. He establishes a contrast with the other characters, who are only identified by their function. The Orderly, who has disowned his essence, has also lost his name. In contrast with the other Negroes in the play, he is only the anonymous "orderly." In a Strindbergian expressionistic fashion the characters also have an aspect of caricature: the Nurse is the female vampire who ushers in the gallery of Albee's destructive women; the young doctor is only an ineffectual idealist; the Orderly is an Uncle Tom, preoccupied with offending no one; the Father is all helpless spite. Opposite them is Bessie Smith, an invisible presence who paradoxically seems more vivid by her pathetic effort to "come back," more authentic in her stupefied condition, more pitiable and human because of her severed arm, her bruised flesh, her spilled blood—more important finally by her very destitution and death. Through the intentional irony, the marionettes one sees grow pale before the humanity of the one who never appears.

It has been said that the play suffers from a structural deficiency, that the two parallel plots only coalesce at the moment when the play is ended, that the two actions are integrated little if at all. It is obvious that this is not a well-made play to which one can apply the criteria of realistic theater; the schematic characterization, the cinematographic cutting, the suggested setting, the symbolic lighting, bring this play closer to the German expressionistic theater. To confront the spectator with a shocking situation which will jar his indifference, Albee employs a dual device: the death of Bessie Smith, the result of absurd racial prejudice, suddenly throws a revealing light on the vacuousness of the characters, their existences and their hopes, and on the desperate absurdity of the human condition. Even if we refuse to concede Albee's structural success, the human situations which he has created, the evocative language, the vigorously ironic dialogue and the particularly nervous rhythm make the play an arresting work.

Gerald Weales said in 1962 that *The Death of Bessie Smith* is a thematic and formal exception in the works of Albee. On the contrary, it seems to me that the play is part of a continuous development. The playwright passes from the mitigated naturalism of *The Zoo Story*, through a period of expressionistic experimentation, to the ironic surrealism of *The Sandbox* and *The American Dream*. On the other hand, the themes of the battle of the sexes and the life-lie recall the preceding play and foreshadow *Who's Afraid of Virginia Woolf?* The character of the Nurse, with her frustrations, her paternal attachment, her scorn of the other sex, her hysterical determination to destroy what she loves, and her intense vulgarity, is a prefiguration of Martha. This play elaborates a portrait of Woman worthy of Strindberg which is repeated in each of the later plays.—GILBERT DEBUSSCHER, *Edward Albee: Tradition and Renewal*, 1967, pp. 21–30

THE AMERICAN DREAM

The American Dream and *The Death of Bessie Smith* are further evidence that Albee's talent has not yet found its way out of chrysalis. Both plays are inferior to *The Zoo Story*, but all three embody the same vital defect: the absence of any compelling theme, commitment, or sense of life which might pull them into focus. Lacking this larger vision, Albee's plays—while beginning auspiciously, with a pyrotechnic display of . . . brittle irony—always collapse at the finish, either into whimpering melodrama (*Bessie Smith*) or into embarrassing self-exposure (*American Dream*). The consequence, reflected in both productions (which also end feebly after promising beginnings), is an abrupt switch in tone, and sometimes a sense of bewildering irrelevance—as in *Bessie Smith* where a Gothic report of the blues singer's death in an auto accident is forcibly superimposed on the main story of a malignant Southern nurse (out of Williams) and an idealistic intern who unaccountably pursues her.

The disunity of *The American Dream* is more damaging, since it mars a better work. The play begins as a scorching satire on upper-middle-class family life (aggressive Mommy and castrated Daddy tormenting sweet-crusty Grandma), in which the fatuities of daily conversation are brutally excoriated through the use of clichés, small talk, and illogical non sequiturs. Albee, who has not yet developed his own style, borrows Ionesco's techniques here, and he manipulates them well in a febrile, somewhat bitchy manner. But while *The Bald Soprano* opened out onto all vacuous families, Albee closes in on one (and an odd one, too); and with strong suggestions of personal bitterness, the play shifts into a story of adoption. This shift is signified by the entrance of the "Dream," a fully grown Adonis in regulation theatre garb (blue jeans, tee shirt, cowboy boots) who proceeds to pour out toneless pathological confessions about his inability to feel, love, connect, be whole, etc. When Mommy, who has already dismembered his twin, adopts him, the curtain descends, while Grandma (now "dead") poignantly comments on the repetition from the wings. Thus, like *The Zoo Story*, this play begins as a sardonic comedy and ends as a whining letter to the chaplain, compromised by the author's inability to objectify or transcend the wounded Self.—ROBERT BRUSTEIN, "Fragments from a Cultural Explosion" (1961), *Seasons of Discontent*, 1965, pp. 47–48

The importance of *The American Dream* is that it's Edward Albee's. A young playwright of genuine talent—that is, one who is not merely clever—is rare nowadays. (I hope I am wrong about this scarcity.) So everything that Albee writes should be given special attention. This should not be adulatory: it is dangerous to make "stars" of playwrights while they are in the process of growth; nor should our attention consist of slaughtering the playwright's second or third play in behalf of the hallowed first one.

The American Dream is a one-act abstract vaudeville sketch. It purports to typify the well-to-do American middle-class home in this age of automation and mechanized men and women. The excellent little set is hung with frames without pictures; the room itself has expensive furniture hideously gilded, blank prefabricated walls and above them all the Stars and Stripes—in short, no intimacy, no personality, no vibrations. Daddy, who earns the money, has had part of his gut removed and of sex there is no question. The family is childless. Grandma, who has a remnant of spunk left in her dry bones, is at once a protected and abandoned bit of household crockery—a sort of skeleton in the closet. She says all the right things at the wrong time and the wrong things at the right time. No one listens to anyone else or cares about what is said when they do listen. There is total spiritual, intellectual stasis. The child—called a "bumble" rather than a baby—once adopted by this juiceless family was smashed and dismembered by them.

Into this vacuum enters the "American dream" in the person of a tall, good-looking boy, a perfect juvenile specimen. He has no feelings, no active desires, no real ambition. Passively waiting, he is a prettily furbished shell. He is adopted by Mommy and Daddy—to undergo the same treatment as the earlier "bumble."

The play is funny and horrid, a poker-faced grotesque. It reminds one of Ionesco's one-act plays *The Bald Soprano* and *Jack*, although the Frenchman's plays are freer in their extravagance and more devastating. There is no harm in a young writer's being influenced—it is inevitable; besides, one chooses one's influence in the direction of one's sympathies. But there is a certain literalness in *The American Dream*—even at moments a flatness of writing—which makes me suspect that the French influence on Albee (Genet, Beckett, Ionesco and others) is not altogether helpful.

I mean by this that Albee's talent—as with most Americans—lies closer to realism than perhaps he knows. *The Zoo Story* had its "symbolic" side too and was also terrifyingly humorous—as well as obliquely tender—but what abstraction there was in it arose from true observation of specific people in specific environments.

Abstraction becomes decoration when it loses touch with its roots in concrete individual experience; and the word "decoration" is just as appropriate where the abstraction is satirically fierce as where it is beguiling. So while I appreciate the comment and the bitter barbs which *The American Dream* contains, I would caution the author to stick closer to the facts of life so that his plays may remain humanly and socially relevant. For it is as easy to make a stereotype from a critical and rebellious abstraction as from a conformist one.—HAROLD CLURMAN, "The American Dream" (1960), *The Naked Image*, 1966, pp. 14–15

The trouble with Albee's acutely original play, *The American Dream*, is that its bizarre Ionesco details don't add up to an experience. This one-hour work has almost everything that fancy can supply but hardly anything that experience can validate. The details, either irrational or so logical as to be extravagant, are amusing as they come at the playgoer with a suddenness and a barrage of non sequiturs rarely encountered in "real-life" situations. For a dozen minutes or so, the humor keeps the play crackling. Mr. Albee's oblique treatment of the banal tedium of domestic life recalls Ionesco's *The Bald Soprano* yet seems decidedly fresh, and the satire is crisp and bracing. Then, with the entrance of "Grandma," who knows she is considered superfluous by her daughter, the author introduces a note of genuine poignancy into the proceedings, and the pathos of old age soon changes into delight when the cross old woman turns the tables on "Mommy" and gives her more than one jagged piece of her mind. . . .

After the Grandma episode, however, *The American Dream* fell apart by the sheer weight of its rapidly accumulated bright particles. A bright new talent went to pieces here because it was unsustained, so far as I could determine, by a point of view that would provide cohesiveness for Mr. Albee's random scorn and rebelliousness.—JOHN GASSNER, "Edward Albee: An American Dream?" (1961), *Dramatic Soundings*, 1968, pp. 591–92

In *The American Dream*, his most important play to date, Albee has picked an ideal subject and title with which to start a movement. As he notes in his preface, several critics have taken sharp exception to the play on the grounds that it is negative in approach, that it tends to denigrate its subject, and that it is "nihilist, immoral, and defeatist" in content. All these things are undoubtedly true. But what did the critics expect? A play that *celebrates* the American dream would be utterly pointless, would, indeed, strictly speaking, be precisely what the critics called Albee's play. It would be nihilist, immoral, and defeatist because it would be perpetuating a lie. The "American Dream," the principle of freedom and individuality for which the country was founded has, as any clear-thinking and courageous person cannot hesitate to admit, become thoroughly corrupted by precisely the things Albee is attacking in his play: by misplaced hero worship; by values based exclusively on the crassest commercialism; by flabby, unthinking complacency; and by brutal destruction of human emotions. To *celebrate* the "American Dream," even supposing there were anything left to celebrate, would be utterly useless. What would be the point of flattering an audience and sending them away with hands folded in self-congratulatory complacency on their comfortably rounded stomachs? This is a function performed efficiently enough by our annual open-air, massed-voice, historico-patriotic pageants, most of which are staged, significantly enough, in the South. The function of the drama is not to celebrate what is good but to protest against what is bad. Progress can come about only through criticism.

Albee's technique in *The American Dream* is caricature. He takes the traditional elements of the American dream—the happy family, the efficient go-getter, the idealistic hero—and shows them in the grotesquely distorted form that he feels they have assumed. The happy family becomes an emasculated money supplier dominated by an emotionally sterile, nagging wife; the efficient go-getter becomes a sexless female machine; the idealistic hero becomes a handsome, empty-headed, hollow shell of a man with the outlook and philosophy of a professional pimp. Interestingly enough, as the critics might have known had they been the competent drama scholars they should be instead of the ill-educated journalists casually kicked onto the drama desk by their editors that they are, Albee is by no means the first man to treat the American dream theme in this way. Back in 1933 George O'Neil, who might well have become one of America's greatest dramatists had he not died early, wrote a play called *American Dream* which deals with the degeneration of the American ideal using even more "nihilism, immorality, and defeatism" than Albee's play. O'Neil used the panoramic method, showing the moral disintegration of one American family through several generations, while Albee shows us a caricatured version of the end product; but the general idea is the same. It would be instructive to be able to see parallel productions of the O'Neil and Albee plays.—GEORGE WELLWARTH, *The Theatre of Protest and Paradox*, 1971, pp. 325–26

WHO'S AFRAID OF VIRGINIA WOOLF?

The premiere of Edward Albee's first Broadway hit raises distinct problems for the American theatre. Albee is grown up now and he is no longer sheltered by that lovely excuse of inadequacy, "promising young playwright." *Who's Afraid of Virginia Woolf?* announces Albee's arrival and the New York critics, hungry for a king, have welcomed him to our theatre royalty, enthroning Albee next to O'Neill, Miller, and Williams. This joke would be unworthy of comment except that Albee's coronation—far from being a happy event—uncovers a running sore in our theatre.

What makes Albee run? It can't simply be his salaciousness, his dirty jokes, his ability to wisecrack as glibly as Lenny Bruce. These things contribute to his popularity of course, for no road is easier to run than that sexy highway blazed over a half-century ago. But it would be merely smug to condemn our theatre this way, and then sit back and wait for the return of the Roman circus with its exciting sadism and its diverting coital games. No; Albee runs because we see in his work a reflection of a sentimental view of ourselves, a view which pleases us. Like children or never-quite-reformed Puritans who cannot forget Jonathan Edwards we enjoy thinking of ourselves as "naughty," and we eagerly exaggerate our naughtiness into hard vices and our vices into perversities. Oh, if we only could play "humiliate the host" or "hump the hostess" as do the heroes of *Virginia Woolf*; if only our lives were truly *that* decadent! Albee gratifies an adolescent culture which likes to think of itself as decadent.

We want to believe that we are living in the last days, that the world is falling in on our heads, that only our sickest illusions are able to offer us any reason for living. Everyone wants to be Nero watching Rome burn. To attend the last orgy, to be part of it, this is a comfortable and exciting escape from reality—the child's way out. Albee's characters, like the playwright himself, suffer from arrested development. They play the game of decadence, just as he plays the game of creativity. There is no real, hard bedrock of suffering in *Virginia Woolf*—it is all illusory, depending upon a "child" who never was born: a gimmick, a trick, a trap. And there is no solid creative suffering in the writer who meanders through a scene stopping here and there for the sake of a joke or an easy allusion that *almost* fits.

But even more, the values of *Virginia Woolf* are perverse and dangerous. Self-pity, drooling, womb-seeking weakness, the appeal to a transcendent "god" who is no God, the persistent escape into morbid fantasy—all these things are probably too close to our *imagined* picture of ourselves. It is the game of the child who thinks he is being persecuted, who dreams up all kinds of outrages, and who concludes finally that his parents found him one day on the doorstep. Albee wants us to indulge in this same game, this cheap hunt for love; he wants us to point to the stage and simper: "Oooo, there we are! How pitiable, how terrible!" The danger is that Albee may succeed; we are on the verge of becoming the silly role we are playing.

I much prefer Gelber where junk is junk and the connection is real. In Gelber—as in O'Neill, Williams, and Miller—there is at least a sincerity, an honesty. But Albee makes dishonesty a virtue, perversion a joke, adultery a simple party game. In honest play-writing if man is mocked he is mocked before God, before the human condition; in Albee's play man is mocked before Oswald Spengler. Sartre once described the life of bad faith as a living lie—of actually believing an untruth and then acting on that false belief. Albee is not conscious of his own phoniness, nor of the phoniness of his work. But he has posed so long that his pose has become part of the fabric of his creative life; he *is* his own lie. If *Virginia Woolf* is a tragedy it is of that unique kind rarely seen: a tragedy which transcends itself, a tragedy which is bad theatre, bad literature, bad taste—but which *believes* its own lies with such conviction that it indicts the society which creates it and accepts it. *Virginia Woolf* is a ludicrous play; but the joke is on all of us.

The upsetting thing—the deeply upsetting thing—is that American theatre-goers and their critics have welcomed this phony play and its writer as the harbinger of a new wave in the American theatre. The American theatre, our theatre, is so hungry, so voracious, so corrupt, so morally blind, so perverse that *Virginia Woolf* is a success. I am outraged at a theatre and an audience that accepts as a masterpiece an insufferably long play with great pretensions that lacks intellectual size, emotional insight, and dramatic electricity. I'm tired of play-long "metaphors"—such as the illusory child of *Virginia Woolf*—which are neither philosophically, psychologically, nor poetically valid. I'm tired of plays that are badly plotted and turgidly written being excused by such palaver as "organic unity" or "inner form." I'm tired of morbidity and sexual perversity which are there only to titillate an impotent and homosexual theatre and audience. I'm tired of Albee.

Genet can raise sexual perversion to the level of ontological speculation—he is a poet and a mighty intellect. Beckett can transform static dramatic situations into valid metaphors for man's condition—he, too, is a poet and a mighty intellect. Albee can only follow meagerly and blindly in their path, patching together several of their insights and devices over the thinly disguised skeleton of Eugene O'Neill. I am ashamed of a theatre which welcomes Albee's new play as a classic, because this means only that we are starving for heroes and kings and will pay almost any price, including our own theatrical self-respect, our self-respect as artists and citizens, for them. *Virginia Woolf* is doubtlessly a classic: a classic example of bad taste, morbidity, plotless naturalism, misrepresentation of history, American society, philosophy, and psychology. There is in the play an ineluctable urge to escape reality and its concomitant responsibilities by crawling back into the womb, or bathroom, or both.

A dear friend of mine wrote to me that *Virginia Woolf* gnawed at her, and that such a play must have something to it—that it could not be ignored. That's right—there is no way in which we can ignore danger or disease. But it is not right therefore to welcome the plague into our midst. We must not ignore what Albee represents and portends, either for our theatre or for our society. The lie of his work is the lie of our theatre and the lie of America. The lie of decadence must be fought. It is no accident that the other side of the coin—the lie of painless goodness—also had a fine run on Broadway as it was portrayed in Robert Bolt's comforting paean to nostalgia, *A Man for All Seasons*. We must fight both lies. But Albee's is more dangerous—for it is a lie in current usage these days, and one which is likely to have an infective and corrosive influence on our theatre.—RICHARD SCHECHNER, "Who's Afraid of Edward Albee?", *TDR*, Spring 1963, pp. 7–10

Let's start by admitting that I'm prejudiced: I directed Edward Albee's play, and I've been reading ⟨*Tulane Drama Review*⟩ for years. Normally, I don't believe in responding to bad notices of plays I've worked on (or good ones either); but I am outraged and ashamed that the Editor of our leading theatrical quarterly has made so sweeping a series of statements concerning Albee's sincerity of intention, his character, and his talent; it is not possible for me to stomach without protest an indictment of Edward Albee's work as a "lie" and a "plague," an indictment as fundamentally false as those earlier ones, in less responsible quarters, which labeled Samuel Beckett a "hoax" and Harold Pinter a "pretentious fake."

The right of the Editor—or anyone else—not to like or agree with or even to understand *Who's Afraid of Virginia Woolf?* is unquestioned. Some of my best friends don't care for it though, as with the Editor's example, the play continues to gnaw at them long after they have seen it. There are also a few who write me notes or call me up in the middle of the night to tell me how special they think it is, how much it has affected their thinking, their emotions, and their faith in the possibility of theatre. (Although the Editor states categorically that "it lacks intellectual size, emotional insight, and dramatic electricity.") Not all of them are psychotics, reactionaries, or homosexuals.

If I follow the Editor's general thesis, it contains several major points: that comparing Albee to such elder statesmen as O'Neill, Miller and Williams is sacrilege and a "joke"; that Albee's writing is primarily a dirty joke, sentimentalized to fit in with our concepts of "naughtiness" and "decadence"; that his work is based on gimmicks but lacks any real substance; that his values are morbid, perverted, imitative; and that those values (through the popular and critical success of *Virginia Woolf*) threaten to engulf and further destroy our theatre.

Without attempting to enthrone Albee alongside anyone (though I personally admire him above all other Americans now writing for the stage), or to hail *Virginia Woolf* as a classic of the modern theatre (which I have no doubt it will become), I would only state that, in my experience, a more honest or moral (in the true sense) playwright does not exist—unless it be Samuel Beckett. To blame Albee for the "sickness" of his subject matter is like blaming the world's ashcans on the creator of Nagg and Nell—which has been done. And if what Albee is doing is giving us a "sentimentalized" view of ourselves rather than one as harshly and starkly unsentimental as any I know, why didn't those theatre party ladies buy it up ahead of time as they do all those other technicolor postcards which pass for plays? Or is Albee not rather dedicated to smashing that rosy view, shocking us with the truth of our present-day behavior and thought, striving to purge us into an actual confrontation with reality? Anyone who has read any portion of any play he has ever written surely must sense the depth of his purpose and recognize, to some extent, the power of the talent which is at his disposal; certainly no intelligent, aware individual today can fail to recognize somewhere in Albee's characters and moods the stirring of his own viscera, the shadow of his own self-knowledge.

If the child in *Virginia Woolf* is merely a "gimmick," then so is the wild duck, the cherry orchard, that streetcar with the special name, even our old elusive friend Godot. But Albee's play is not about the child—just as *Godot* is not about Godot but about the waiting for him—but about the people who have had to create him as a "beanbag" or crutch for their own insufficiencies and failures, and now are left to find their own way, if there is to be a way, free of him. If truth and illusion are not exactly original themes, any more than they were for O'Neill, the test is not *what* but *how* and how specifically the writer illuminates the immediacy of human life. If Albee's particular choice is more lacking in plot than our editor wishes, its reality is based upon a classic simplicity, a contemporary feeling unmatched in our theatre, a musical economy—in spite of its length—and an ability to hold and shatter his audience.

What baffles me is why the Editor is making such a fuss. Is Western civilization actually in danger because both Howard Taubman and Walter Kerr managed to agree that *Virginia Woolf*—with all its faults—represents a major writing talent in our theatre and should be seen by people who consider themselves serious theatre-goers? (Why, even Bob Brustein had kind words to say about Albee this time, including something about his having borrowed from the Greeks.) Would the American theatre be better off, would it be less voracious, corrupt, morally blind, and perverse, had the play never been written or presented? Would the Editor have been happier about life had the play failed, i.e. echoed the verdict of the *New York Daily News* and *Mirror*, those two shining Galahads of democratic journalism, which shared his opinion that it was filthy, corrupt, gangrenous, and should immediately be withdrawn lest it contaminate the pure atmosphere of the society which they represented?

That ⟨*Tulane Drama Review*⟩ is against the voracity and hypocrisy of Broadway has always been evident—till now. And when a play which, like it or not as you will, is serious, literate, individual in style, ablaze with talent, and written without concern for Broadway values (it was originally intended for off-Broadway); when such a play is presented with taste and economy, without abdicating to the star-system, the theatre-party system, the fancy-advertising system; when the combined talents of a remarkable cast working together in a way Broadway casts rarely do serve to lift the work to "success" over the normal run of machine-made mediocrities which reign supreme in our commercial theatre, it seems to me no cause for rejoicing rather than wailing and gnashing of teeth. After all, there might be a better chance for a play more to the Editor's personal tastes getting on the boards next time because *Virginia Woolf* has at least shown it possible to draw a sizeable audience without lowering its standards. Certainly, those Broadway wiseacres who thought it didn't stand a chance are now revising their opinion of what does.

It is possible, as the Editor says, that *Who's Afraid of Virginia Woolf?* is "bad theatre, bad literature, bad taste"; it is also at least equally possible that it is good theatre, good literature, good taste. Only time will tell. In the meantime, I'm not asking the Editor to love my girl as much as I do—that's what makes horseracing and marriages, not to mention theatre criticism—but I do resent his directly labeling her a degenerate whore. I believe the day will come when, as with that other over-avid executioner, John de Stogumber, he will regret being so quick to rush her to the stake.—ALAN SCHNEIDER, "Why So Afraid?", *TDR*, Spring 1963, pp. 10–13

Albee's first full-length play . . . affords so much pulsating moment-by-moment drama, so many unreeling facets of character and so many fluctuations of feeling, and one is so continuously knocked down, picked up, and knocked down again in the course of the play, that it takes a massive quantity of resistance to conclude that *Who's Afraid of Virginia Woolf?* is not drama on the grand scale. It reaches the same order of harrowing dramatic power as Elizabethan melodrama which the unfinicky Elizabethans called tragedy. The very same thing can be said indeed of a good many of O'Neill's plays. . . . For me, in fact, Albee is in the direct line of succession from O'Neill. Even if he has yet far to go if he is to achieve his predecessor's breadth of interest, variety of tone, or range of compassionate insight, Albee has the same slugging technique and the same strategy of massive assault in thrusting across the footlight area his awareness of human bedevilment. And in their writing they employ the same heavy Mahler scoring with an overplus of *ostinato* markings, although Albee's lines move

faster and with more precision than O'Neill's. Interestingly enough, both O'Neill and Albee came to public notice as the authors of undeniably effective one-act plays before winning larger audiences as the authors of notably oversized full-length drama. This fact should give pause to those who see in the larger works mere repetitiveness or verbal incontinence rather than an essential dramatic pulsation and rhythm. The larger works reveal, rather, a similar fascination with the details of feeling and dramatic action, and with the momentum of recurring impulses that characterize behavior in an extensive situation of crisis and constitute its exciting vibration.

It is possible to work up a strong resentment toward the play, to be sure, but it is not an easy drama to ignore or forget. Mr. Albee has written a terrifying thing—perhaps *the* negative play to end all negative plays, yet also a curiously compassionate play (I feel plenty of compassion for the driven woman and her long-suffering husband), and exhilarating one (if for no other reason than the passionateness of the characters) and even a wryly affirmative one because of the fighting spirit of the principals whose behavior breathes the fire of protest along with the stench of corruption.—JOHN GASSNER, "Who's Afraid of Virginia Woolf?" (1963), *Dramatic Soundings*, 1968, pp. 592–95

Who's Afraid of Virginia Woolf? . . . is unhappily considerably more than full-length since it lasts well over three hours. Although the play could be tightened (it has at least one hour of purely excess dialogue), the process would merely result in making meaninglessness more playable. After the promise of *The American Dream*, *Who's Afraid of Virginia Woolf?* is a disappointment. It was perhaps too much to hope that Albee would produce something as significant as *The American Dream* for his first Broadway effort; too much to hope that the production of *Who's Afraid of Virginia Woolf?* would mark the entrenchment and acceptance of the off-beat, paradoxical, enigmatic plays of Albee, Richardson, Kopit, and Weinstein that constituted the off-Broadway seed of the putative new American drama. In *Who's Afraid of Virginia Woolf?* Albee has succeeded merely in producing a long piece of intellectualized *kitsch*. . . .

It might be as well to . . . examine this play in the light of Albee's subsequent development. Everyone recognized a distinctly promising theatrical talent in *The Zoo Story* and *The American Dream*. At the same time it was obvious that these two plays were directly derived from the French avant-garde drama. Excellent imitations though they were, they were still imitations. Literary reputations are based on a writer's ability to state and develop a theme, not on his ability to improvise on someone else's theme. Thus it was that when *Who's Afraid of Virginia Woolf?*—and subsequently *Tiny Alice* and *A Delicate Balance*—appeared, it was hailed by the majority of the critics (Robert Brustein, Tom Driver, and Richard Schechner were honorable exceptions) as the advent of Albee's own distinctive style. The fact is, however, that Albee is as derivative in his later plays as in his earlier ones. The difference is that he has moved from the honesty of Ionesco to the shrewdly calculated, box-office oriented claptrap of Tennessee Williams. *Who's Afraid of Virginia Woolf?* belongs squarely in the Williams school of transom-peeping drama, where the whole effect is based on a concrete realization of the habitual gossip column peruser's wildest fantasies. Such a play, of course, while it may well become a commercial success, is not necessarily one that will be taken seriously by critics and scholars. For that, intellectual profundity is essential; and since the amorphous boundaries between appearance and reality constitute the *stoff* of one of our more vexing critical problems, the *appearance* of profundity is as a rule quite enough. There are two ways in which this appearance can be brought about. One is the imposition on the play of the expectation of profundity based on the playwright's past performances. Thus the critics were psychologically prepared to find profundity in *Who's Afraid of Virginia Woolf?* when it came out because they had found it in *The Zoo Story* and *The American Dream*. The most extraordinary significance can be read into the flattest drawing room comedies and into soap operas exuding essence-of-banality given the *a priori* assumption that significance of some sort must be there. The other way in which the appearance of profundity can be created is by spraying symbols around. As a result of all this we are afflicted with a flood of mildly ingenious interpretations of *Who's Afraid of Virginia Woolf?* showing that it is really a parable of the decline and fall of Western society or of the moral bankruptcy of the intelligentsia. Alternatively, we may be told that the play is about the achievement of mutual honesty through the purgation of illusion or about the conflict between humanitarianism and soulless science. Such interpretations are based on the fact that the protagonists are called George and Martha (as in the first First Family—the contrast between the two families shows how far we have degenerated), that the setting is called New Carthage (the new is as effete as the old and must also be destroyed), that George reads the Catholic burial service over his imaginary son, or that George and Nick (whom one critic, in an inspired crescendo of idiocy, identified with Nikita Khrushchev) represent the struggle between science and humanities because one is a historian (who has never done anything) and the other is a biologist (who has not done anything yet). Actually, the arguments between George and Nick about their respective specialties would impress even a bunch of sophomore engineering or business administration students as dull and obvious. To anyone reading the play without previous assumptions it should rapidly become clear that these allusions were put in by Albee precisely so that they might be picked up by unwary critics.—GEORGE WELLWARTH, *The Theatre of Protest and Paradox*, 1971, pp. 328–31

Who's Afraid of Virginia Woolf? is in many important respects a "first." In addition to being the first of Albee's full-length plays, it is also the first juxtaposition and integration of realism and abstract symbolism in what will remain the dramatic idiom of all the full-length plays. Albee's experimentation in allegory, metaphorical clichés, grotesque parody, hysterical humor, brilliant wit, literary allusion, religious undercurrents, Freudian reversals, irony on irony, here for the first time appear as an organic whole in a mature and completely satisfying dramatic work. It is, in Albee's repertory, what *Long Day's Journey into Night* is in O'Neill's: the aberrations, the horrors, the mysteries are woven into the fabric of a perfectly normal setting so as to create the illusion of total realism, against which the abnormal and the shocking have even greater impact. In this play, for the first time, the "third voice of poetry" comes through loud and strong with no trace of static. The dramatist seems to have settled back silently, to watch while his characters take over the proceedings, very much like those six notorious characters who pestered Pirandello's dramatic imagination.

In *Who's Afraid of Virginia Woolf?* the existential dilemma is dramatized with full sympathy in its most painful human immediacy. The weak are redeemed in their helplessness, and the vicious are forgiven in their tortured self-awareness. The domineering figure of Woman is no longer the one-sided aberration of *The Sandbox* and *The American Dream*; it is a haunting portrait of agonized loyalty and destructive love. The submissive Male is raised to the point of

tragic heroism in his understanding of the woman who would kill the thing she loves. The action itself is beautifully consistent; it makes no excessive demands, but moves along simply and with utter realism to the edge of a mystery. . . .

As in the earlier plays, Sex is the dynamo behind the action. But in this case, instead of an oversimplified statement about homosexuality and who is responsible for it, or a brief reminder of how private sexual indulgence turns into prurient lust, or an unsympathetic suggestion of how heterosexual demands within a materialistic society corrupt and destroy the individual, we have for the first time an examination of the various phases through which a sexual relationship passes in its normal, or rather, its inevitable development. Like Shaw, who shocked a good many of his contemporaries, and still shocks a good many of his readers today, by insisting that love and sex don't mix easily in marriage, Albee is here reminding us of the deterioration which even the best-matched couple will suffer in their sexual relationship if love is not properly distinguished from it and nurtured apart from it. There is almost an Augustinian conviction in Albee's insistence on what sex in marriage is *not*. . . .

Albee is no Augustinian, and he might even reject Shaw; but what he succeeds in doing is giving their view added authority. He has depicted in this play the excruciating agony of love as it struggles to preserve the fiction of its purity through a mass of obscenities and the parody of sex. The Son-myth is the embodiment of that fiction. It is the frustration around which the action of the play revolves.

Albee plays on the theme a number of ways, one of which is the introduction of a kind of Shakespearean subplot, in the story of the second couple. Honey and Nick have some kind of sex together, but little love and no children. Honey confesses, late in her drunken stupor, that she doesn't want children. Her fear of pregnancy is also a fear of sex, basically, and throws new light on the story of her courtship and marriage. The hysterical pregnancy which "puffed her up" and made Nick marry her has its own complicated explanation, no doubt; but at the time it took place, it served—in part at least—as a guard against sexual abandonment and a way back into conventional and acceptable relationships. Honey's predicament is characteristic of Albee's handling of complicated human motivation. He neither blames nor prescribes a moral "cure." His dramatic instincts keep him from easy labels; not once does he betray his characters into clinical diagnoses of the kind that O'Neill was prone to. Honey is anything but a case history; in her own way she is pathetically attractive and appealing. There is a kind of strength in her not wanting to keep up with the others. Her childlike trust looks ridiculous in that company, but it is incongruous in the same way that the impossible purity of Martha's fictional son is incongruous. When she returns from the "euphemism," after George's vicious Get the Guests, she says simply, "I don't remember anything, and you don't remember anything either." Her despair, though different from Martha's, is just as intense and real to her. Like the fictional son of her hosts, her innocence is already compromised. The *Walpurgisnacht* is her initiation party. Her childish decision not to remember unpleasant things has to be put to the test.

Honey, like Martha, is childless; but the parallel is propped up by contrast. Martha wanted children and hasn't any; Honey doesn't want them and manages to keep from having them—or, rather, she doesn't want to go through the pains of childbirth. At the end she confesses pathetically that she fears the physical labor connected with childbirth and reveals a very different kind of impulse. The two stories move toward the same psychological vacuum. The hysterical pregnancy and the fictional son are conceived in different ways, but they are essentially the same kind of birth. Both are the result of impotence, or rather, of a willful assertion which proves abortive. George fails to measure up to Martha's ambitions for him as the son-in-law of the college president; Nick fails to measure up to Honey's romantic dream. Both women give birth to an unsubstantial hope.

Sex is the name of the game; but around Martha—the embodiment of Mother Earth—everything sexual seems to collapse. Men are all flops, and she herself a fool to be tempted by them. . . . In spite of appearances and what she says in her verbal skirmishes, George is the only man who has ever satisfied her sexually. Even the suggestion of physical impotence is canceled out in the end, when George proves that the ultimate power of life and death lies with him.

The parallel between the two couples is strengthened by other contrasts. Nick and Honey are just starting out and have something of the hopes and energies that George and Martha had when they first came together; but where George failed, Nick might well succeed. He is willful in a petty way, knows exactly what he wants, and is callous enough to reach out and grab it. His plans are clear and realizable. He is much more practical and less idealistic than George, but lacks George's potential to adjust to what the world calls failure. George's *failure* is incomprehensible to Nick: would anyone, in his right mind, turn down a high administrative post simply to indulge a passion to write the great American novel? The irony is that Nick wants what George had in his grasp and turned down. In this context, Nick's designs seem downright petty, while George's worldly failure takes on heroic colors. For George, money means compromise; for Nick, it is the one sure sign of success. His decision to assume the "responsibilities" of marriage was in large measure determined by the fact that Honey was rich; but already he has failed in his role, unable to share his wife's fears and hopes. He is absolutely callous to her emotional needs, bent on humoring her in order to get what he wants. His relationship with Honey is an excellent barometer of his relationship with the rest of the world. He will very likely get everything he wants; but the world will hold his success against him, for his ambition is utterly transparent. George and Martha have understood this and are contemptuous of him; Honey suspects it but cannot bring herself to face the truth.

These ironic oscillations produce something resembling the oppressive emptiness of the plays of Beckett and Sartre. The inescapable dialectic builds up to the recognition, on the part of each of the protagonists, of what he is not and cannot ever be. Each absorbs as much as he is capable of taking in; the rest of the lesson is there to be heard and carried away in the memory. In their hell, the will continues to assert itself in impotent frustration. The exorcism which finally comes about is a vacuum—stylistically, the play reflects the collapse of the will in a quick staccato of monosyllables which brings the action to its close. The exhaustion of pretense is caught neatly in the tired jingle which earlier in the evening, at Daddy's party, brought down the house. Nothing happens in the play, but reality is changed completely in the gradual discovery and recognition of what is inside us all. Whatever else Martha will hit on to substitute for Junior, it can never be confused again with the real condition of her life. This is not necessarily an advantage; confession craves absolution, but all Martha can hope for (and George) is compassion.

The existential mood is caught by means of ambiguous explanations, unfinished or incomplete stories, emotional climaxes suddenly deflated into absurdity. The scene where George "shoots" Martha is a striking example of the explosion of emotional tension into frivolity. Martha is playing up to Nick, as George watches; when she brings up the story about the boxing match in which she managed to stun George, he leaves the room. Martha goes right on—it's all part of their repertory—and George eventually returns with a shotgun which he raises, aims . . . and shoots. But what bursts out, without a bang, is a Chinese parasol. The tension breaks; there is a moment of hysterical relief—but it is only the prelude to a new emotional buildup.—ANNE PAOLUCCI, *From Tension to Tonic,* 1972, pp. 45–52

THE BALLAD OF THE SAD CAFÉ

The first of the three Albee adaptations is *The Ballad of the Sad Café,* based on Carson McCullers' novella of the same name. The play opened October 30, 1963, at the Martin Beck Theater to mixed reviews. Henry Hewes said: "This faithful, intelligent, and sensitive adaptation is the most fascinating and evocative piece of work by an American playwright . . . this season." Martin Gottfried, however, called *Ballad* "a play of little theatre value."

Notwithstanding the usual diversity of criticism a new Albee play engenders, most reviewers admitted that it was faithful to the novella with amazingly few changes in the story line. Notably, that the fight takes place out-of-doors instead of inside the café, and that the events of Amelia's short marriage to Marvin are not revealed to the viewer until somewhat later in the play than in the novella. To keep as close to the original prose as possible, Albee incorporated a narrator who, with minimal alterations, spoke the novella's lyrical passages. Originally, the playwright planned to use a tape recording of Carson McCullers speaking those passages, but the idea was dropped in favor of a narrator-stage manager as in *Our Town.*

Much of the negative reaction to *Ballad* centered about Albee's decision to use a stage narrator. Most critics felt that his presence was alienating as well as undramatic. Walter Kerr in particular emphasized that the novella's material, use of chorus, and incorporation of a narrator, all conspired to cause alienation. In a later article he returned to the same point and said, "in the theatre we should not need hired guides." Robert Brustein was even less diplomatic when he described the narrator as having only one function: "to provide the information which the author has been too lazy to dramatize."

While I don't hold to the belief that use of narration always constitutes undramatic playwrighting (we have only to look at Brecht), certain problems do arise from Albee's decision to use a narrator. Perhaps the most penetrating of these is the lack of motivation for the man to tell his story. As Albee has written it, we sense no impelling reason to listen to this grotesque love ballad. John McClain made a similar observation when he noted: "We don't, in fact, know very much about anybody in 'The Sad Café,' including the man who wanders through the proceedings, giving us only hints and suggestions."

Miss McCullers clarifies the story for her reader early in the book by telling him what to expect. Albee, however, waits until page one hundred and sixteen before making the same point:

> *The Narrator:* The time has come to speak about love. Now consider three people who were subject to that condition. Miss Amelia, Cousin Lymon, and Marvin Macy. . . . Now, the beloved can also be of any description: the most outlandish people can be the stimulus for love. Yes, and the lover may see this as clearly as anyone else—but that does not affect the evolution of his love one whit. . . .

Thus we have had to watch most of this adaptation with

no intermission, without knowing why the narrator has chosen to submit us to this unpleasant tale of freakish love. We feel dislocated from the material and unable to focus in on the play. Robert Brustein corroborated this reaction when he wrote: "Because of my unfamiliarity with dwarf-loving lesbians, [the play] was rather lost on me." *Newsweek*, too, wanted to "know why they behave as they do." It is my contention that had Albee kept to the chronology of the novella, and not tried to build suspense by holding off thematic material until very near the end of the play, the critics would have reacted more favorably to the play's grotesqueness.

Still another reason for the narrator's inability to pull his audience into the play stems from a sociological condition less prevalent in the theatre today than when *Ballad* was first produced. As unflattering as it is to our sense of supposed sophistication, as little as five years ago the Broadway audience found it difficult to accept a Negro's omnipotence over the lives of white Southerners. They sat silent, feeling that Albee intended a sociological comment, which of course he did not.

The logical choice, it would seem, would have been to use Marvin's brother, Henry Macy, as the storyteller. Henry has a special interest in Amelia's story because it is his brother she marries. Having him step into the play and out of it, as character-narrator (much like *Our Town*) would have helped tie the two areas of the play together. . . .

What is perhaps the most surprising aspect of *Ballad* is its similarity to still another play: Sartre's *No Exit*. Both plays reveal the dynamics of unfulfilled love. In the Sartre play, three rather despicable people are placed together in one room. They have been picked by the powers in control (it seems they have died and are now residing in hell) to clash psychologically with one another until the room becomes hell to live in. What kind of human triangle produces psychological hell? Sartre puts a lesbian in with a whore who can't stomach her and seeks, instead, the solace of a man who is repulsed by her promiscuity and looks to the lesbian as a symbol of masculine triumph. *Ballad* offers much the same situation. Amelia is in love with Lymon, who rejects her in favor of Marvin. Marvin is not interested in the dwarf except to use him as a means to getting at Amelia, who continues to rebuff him. Walter Kerr noticed the sado-masochistic libidinal linking and analyzed the trio's interaction: "It is clear . . . that each of these figures is destroyed by the one he loves. . . ." An interesting note to the comparison of the two plays is that Colleen Dewhurst was chosen for the part of Amelia after being seen in a television showing of Sartre's *No Exit*, where she played the lesbian.

The Sartre play works because the group is put together as punishment for certain crimes committed against society. It doesn't make any difference how personally repugnant they are; we do not have to empathize with them in order to react positively to their retribution. *Ballad*, however, creates the same hellish situation (even to its constant reference to heat) when it should have created an environment filled with compassion. The proximity of the play's characters and situation repel us, where the novella's lyric distance intrigues us. *Newsweek*'s critic talked of basically the same thing when he commented that the play "is clothed in the too, too solid flesh of living actors, [making] these phantasmal beings lose the unreality that made them real."

In the last analysis, the events of *Ballad* do not stand up to the intriguing concept that initiated the work; namely, that for some, the state of being loved is intolerable. What happens is that the theme becomes subverted by an overwhelming sense that what we see is not the human condition, but a freak show. It becomes impossible to identify with a petulant, vengeful dwarf, an ex-drug-pushing rapist, or a hostile, semi-ignorant, frigid woman.

Albee's ever-present concern with the outcasts of society has mistakenly led him to recreate for the stage what is, despite its haunting lyricism, essentially not engrossing dramaturgy.— MICHAEL E. RUTENBERG, *Edward Albee: Playwright in Protest*, 1969, pp. 167–79

TINY ALICE

The kindest way to view *Tiny Alice* is as an honorable experiment. To be candid, the play struck me as the sort of thing a highly endowed college student might write by way of offering us a Faustian drama.

Its locale is generalized (neither England nor America), its action unreal, its speech a mixture of literate vernacular and stilted literacy. The settings . . . are expensively and toweringly monumental, with a touch of the vulgarly chic. Except for the first scene, they represent the habitat of "the richest woman of the world."

I shall not discuss the plot because that might lead you to believe that I complain of its being too extravagantly symbolic or too obscure. The significance of certain details may elude one—and no harm done—but the play's intention is clear enough. It tells us that the pure person in our world is betrayed by all parties. The Church is venal, the "capitalist" heartlessly base, the "proletarian" cynical and, for all the good he may do, powerless and subservient. There remains Woman: enticing mother image and never-perfectly-to-be-possessed mate. (She may also embody the universal "Establishment.") The crisis in the pure man's life arises when, having found himself uncertain of his faith, he commits himself to a home for the mentally disturbed. Suffering from the need for tenderness and from religious anguish, he dwells in this womb of conscience to emerge after six years as a lay brother determined above all "to serve." But those who rule us—Church, the Economic Forces and Woman—bid him accept the world as it is. Being pure he cannot do so. Isolated and bereft of every hope, he must die—murdered.

Like Picasso, who said that his pictures do not have to be "understood," only seen and felt, Albee has suggested that people need not puzzle over his symbols; they have only to relax enough to be affected by them. There is this difference, however: Picasso paintings, whatever their "meaning," are fascinating on the surface. So too are Beckett's plays, Genet's and the best of Pinter's. Their images hold us; their complexities are compact with material in which we sense substantial value even when we are unable to name the exact nature of their composition. In art, Braque once observed, "It is not the ultimate goal which is interesting but the means by which we arrive there."

The surface or fabric of *Tiny Alice* is specious. The first scene (between "capitalist" and Cardinal) has some of the comic venom of *Virginia Woolf* but—except for those exhilarated by insults aimed at the clergy—it is by no means as apt. There is a certain cunning of suspense in the play, but the clearer it becomes the less convincing it seems. Its artistic method is too generalized to wound or even to touch us. Its pathos is weak, its scorn jejune, its diction lacking in most of its author's personal flair.

I do not ask Albee to stick to realism. *The Zoo Story* and *The Death of Bessie Smith* are not, strictly speaking, realistic plays—nor, in fact, does *Virginia Woolf* belong in that category. But in those plays Albee's dialogue had a true eloquence, a refreshingly dry and agile muscularity because it issued from the concrete. Their vocabulary was grounded in a life Albee had intimately experienced in his environment and in his senses. In *Tiny Alice* all his artful devices leave one impassive. The only moment my interest was piqued, I confess, was in the ambiguously sexual scene when the pure one succumbs to the millionairess' naked body.

Even though the play's terms rather than their meaning are what disconcert me, something more should be said about the content. Though Albee's spirit and gifts are entirely distinct from those of such recent masters of European drama as Beckett and Genet (each of whom in turn is different from the other), there is evidence of a similar "defeatist" strain. I do not share their view of life, but I recognize the aesthetic potency of Beckett's and Genet's work. They speak with genuine originality. They are, moreover, voices revealing of our day. That is their justification and their merit. (It is also to be noted once again that their work, though divorced from realism, is composed of indelibly memorable theatre metaphors.)

We often speak of their work as "negative" or "pessimistic." In a way, however, the pessimism of *Tiny Alice* has an even greater coherence, a more thoroughgoing finality than that of the Europeans. But though it is always easier to adduce evidence for a black view of life, that is, to prove the world an intolerably damned place, than to urge us in any contrary sense, one soon discovers that the conclusions of pessimism have only a minor value. For logic and proof bear little relation to the processes and conduct of reality. The more tightly one argues the futility of our life's struggle, the more futile the point becomes. It is much too simple. Thus the importance of *Tiny Alice* diminishes as our understanding of it increases.— HAROLD CLURMAN, "Tiny Alice; Hughie," *Nation*, Jan. 18, 1965, p. 65

Edward Albee has called his new play a "mystery story," a description which applies as well to its content as to its genre. The work is certainly very mystifying, full of dark hints and riddling allusions, but since it is also clumsy and contrived, and specious in the extreme, the mystery that interested me most was whether the author was kidding his audience or kidding himself. *Tiny Alice* may well turn out to be a huge joke on the American culture industry; then again, it may turn out to be a typical product of that industry. The hardest thing to determine about "camp" literature, movies, and painting is the extent of the author's sincerity. A hoax is being perpetrated, no doubt of that, but is this intentional or not? Is the contriver inside or outside his own fraudulent creation? Does Andy Warhol really believe in the artistic validity of his Brillo boxes? *Tiny Alice* is a much more ambitious work than the usual variety of camp, but it shares the same ambiguity of motive. For while some of Albee's obscurity is pure playfulness, designed to con the spectator into looking for nonexistent meanings, some is obviously there for the sake of a sham profundity in which the author apparently believes.

My complaint is that Albee has not created profundity, he has only borrowed the appearance of it. In *Tiny Alice*, he is once again dealing with impersonation—this time as a metaphor for religious faith—and once again is doing most of the impersonating himself. The central idea of the play— which treats religious ritual as a form of stagecraft and playacting—comes from Jean Genet's *The Balcony*; its initial device—which involves a wealthy woman handing over a fortune in return for the sacrifice of a man's life—comes from Duerrenmatt's *The Visit*; its symbolism—revolving around mysterious castles, the union of sacred and profane, and the agony of modern Christ figures—is largely taken from Strindberg's *A Dream Play*; and its basic tone—a metaphysical rumble arising out of libations, litanies, and ceremonies created by a shadowy hieratic trio—is directly stolen from T. S. Eliot's

The Cocktail Party. The play, in short, is virtually a theatrical echo chamber, with reverberations of Graham Greene, Enid Bagnold, and Tennessee Williams being heard as well; but Albee's manipulation of these sources owes more to literature than to life, while his metaphysical enigmas contribute less to thematic perception than to atmospheric fakery.

To approach *Tiny Alice* as a coherent work of art, therefore, would be a mistake, since, in my opinion, most of it is meaningless—a frozen portent without an animating event. There are thematic arrows, to be sure, planted throughout the play: allusions to the imperfectibility of human knowledge, appearance and reality, the unreachableness of God, but all these ultimately point down dead-end streets, or are bent and twisted by leaden paradoxes. . . .

The only thing that might redeem a concept like this from its own pretentiousness is some kind of theatrical adroitness; but I regret to say that Albee's customary ingenuity has deserted him here. The language, first of all, is surprisingly windy, slack, sodden, and repetitive; the jokes are childishly prurient ("The organ is in need of use," says the sexually undernourished Julian upon visiting the chapel); and the usual electricity of an Albee quarrel has degenerated—when it is employed in the opening scene between the Cardinal and the Lawyer—into mere nagging. Furthermore, Albee has not been able to exploit his own devices sufficiently. The miniature castle is a good conceit; but it functions more for obfuscation than for theatrical effect, being used to good advantage only once (when the chapel catches fire). And finally, the play vacillates between excessive fruitiness and excessive staginess, whether Julian is being enfolded within the wrapper of the naked Alice (and disappearing somewhere near her genital region), or being gunned down by the Lawyer in a manner reminiscent of Victorian melodrama.

. . . Hanley, Jones, and Albee seem to be preoccupied with important contemporary concerns—the position of minority groups, the Negro revolution, Existential *Angst*, the loss of faith—but some essential commitment is seriously lacking, and the central questions are invariably skirted. What results is less an artistic quest than a fashionable posture or personal exhibition, with the playwright producing not masterpieces but conversation pieces. This, to be sure, is the characteristic art of our time. Now that the cultural revolution has become an arm of big business, the mass media, and the fashion magazines, values have all but disappeared from artistic creation, and a crowd of hipsters and their agents are cynically exploiting the fears and pretensions of a semi-educated public. But while the nihilism of Pop Art, for example, is relatively open, the theatre continues to simulate values and feign commitments: it will not be long before these masks fall too.— ROBERT BRUSTEIN, "Three Playwrights and a Protest," *Seasons of Discontent*, 1965, pp. 307–10

The central idea for *Tiny Alice* came to Albee as he was reading a newspaper account of a man who had been kept imprisoned inside a room which was itself inside another room. Something about this "Chinese-box" situation appealed to him both because of its relevance to the problems of dramatic structure and because of the fascinating metaphysical aspects which these contingent realities suggested.

When the play first appeared in New York, its reception was something less than ecstatic. At best it was thought to be a personal therapy paralleled perhaps by Tennessee Williams' *Camino Real*; at worst it was a confidence trick pulled on the world in general and the drama critics in particular. When the dust had begun to settle and the play was published, Albee's bland assurance, in an author's note, that the meaning of the play was so clear as to obviate comment did little to convince those who had been completely baffled by the performance itself. Neither did it serve to redeem a work which unquestionably remains more effective in print than on the stage. . . .

If the need to face reality was the main principle which emerged from *Who's Afraid of Virginia Woolf?*, then Albee had done little to define exactly what he meant by reality in that play. He had made no attempt to integrate the metaphysical world into his picture or to assess its validity as a part of the reality to which he urged his characters. With *Tiny Alice* he remedies this and attempts to analyse the whole question of religious faith.

Nevertheless, there is a direct connexion between *Tiny Alice* and *Who's Afraid of Virginia Woolf?*, between brother Julian's religious reveries and George and Martha's frenetic distractions. For when Albee stresses the relationship between spiritual ecstasy and erotic satisfaction, as he does by emphasising the sensuous nature of Julian's visions, he is not intent simply on making a cheap debating point about the nature of evangelical power. His thesis is rather that the individual craves a spiritual distraction just as he craves a carnal one—as a substitute for a frightening reality. Just as Nick had turned to sexuality as a retreat from the real world, so Julian turns to religion for much the same reason. Where George had created a fantasy son to fill a vacuum in his own life, Julian "creates" a son of God. . . .

For all Julian's desire to believe in an after-life which will grant some kind of retrospective meaning to the real world, he is unable to place his faith wholeheartedly in this man-made God. Indeed it is this element of doubt, the fact that he remains fundamentally "dedicated to the reality of things, rather than their appearance," which at one stage had taken him to an asylum, his faith temporarily lost, and which makes him an ideal subject for the conspiracy. For the conspirators sense that he is "walking on the edge of an abyss, but is balancing. Can be pushed . . . over, back to the asylum/ . . . Or over . . . to the Truth." The truth with which they confront him is the need, in Alice's words, to "accept what's real."

But this is precisely the crucial question: just what is "real"? Is reality simply the limited world of human possibilities in which death provides an apparent proof of futility, or is it the more expansive world in which "faith is knowledge" and the individual an element in a grand design? Who is right, the existentialist or the determinist, the secularist or the Christian? Should Julian place his faith in God, "Predestination, fate . . . accident," or should he embrace the restricted world of human suffering and love?

Distrusting language, as he had in *The Zoo Story* and *Who's Afraid of Virginia Woolf?*, Albee chooses to dramatise this dilemma in symbolic terms. The central symbol which he uses is that of a "model" castle which dominates most of the play. This "model" seems to be an exact replica of the castle within which the action takes place. It is accurate in every detail. When a fire breaks out in the larger castle is also breaks out in the "model." But Julian is uncertain in which of the two it had originated, and therefore uncertain as to which is the original and which the copy. This Platonic paradox clearly lies at the very heart of the play, as it does of Julian's crisis of conscience. For he remains unsure of the true nature of reality until the very end of the play, when he is converted, as Martin Buber would say, "to this world and this life." In symbolic terms, this is represented by his acceptance of the "model" castle as the "real" one and the larger version as merely a projection of it—an interpretation which the lawyer himself endorses when he says of the castle in which he lives that "it *is a* replica . . . Of that . . . [*Pointing to the model*]." The con-

spiracy, therefore, is evidently devoted to convincing Julian that he should accept this apparent diminution of his concept of reality. As the lawyer advises him, "Don't personify the abstraction, Julian, limit it, demean it."

While Plato's idea of the real world clearly differed in kind from Albee's, one feels that they would both concur in Plato's belief that the function of knowledge is "to know the truth about reality." Indeed, the sort of trauma which faces Julian when he is urged to accept the apparently diminutive "model" as symbolising reality is comparable to that which faced Plato's man in the cave. For the world of reality is, almost by definition, unattractive to those who have lived sufficiently long with illusion. It is precisely for this reason, in fact, that the conspirators are forced to employ a more acceptable image of the real world in the person of Alice. . . .

The title of Albee's play would seem to suggest that *The Collected Works of Lewis Carroll* should be necessary reading, and several critics have in fact been at pains to insist on its relevance. For clearly Alice's Wonderland, as an escape from "dull reality," can be seen as a parallel to Julian's wonderland of religion, in so far as it grows out of a similar unwillingness to accept the restrictions of reality. Moreover, the confrontation of reality and illusion, which lies at the heart of Albee's play, is achieved in Carroll with a symbol which, like Albee's, is essentially Platonic. But while Carroll's literally "tiny" Alice is a part of the illusory world, Albee's tiny Alice symbolises reality. If Carroll insists on returning his protagonist to the real world at the end of his book, it is, perhaps, not without a nostalgic glance back over his shoulder to his wonderland, however brutal that wonderland may at times appear. There is no such nostalgic glance in Albee.

Julian has to relinquish the abstraction which is his retreat from reality. In doing so he abandons the robes of the Church for the clothes of ordinary life, a change which symbolises his shift of identity. This assumption of identity as a function of an adopted role is reminiscent of Nigel Dennis's satire on the great abstractions of modern society, *Cards of Identity* (1956). Here, too, three conspirators effect a change of identity in a man lured to their "mansion" by the prospect of monetary gain—a change signified here, as in *Tiny Alice*, by a physical change of clothes. To Dennis, also, religion is one of those projections whereby man escapes from the immediate reality of his situation and accepts a ready-made identity. It is an escape, moreover, which implies a denial of intellect, as it does a denial of reality. In Dennis's ironical words, "God is worshipped as a solid only by backward people; once educated, the mind reaches out for what cannot be grasped, recognises only what cannot be seen: sophistry adores a vacuum"; or, more succinctly, as he puts it in his unabashed satire on religion, *The Making of Moo* (1957), "You have nothing to lose but your brains."

In *Tiny Alice* . . . Albee's apocalyptic vision, implied in *Who's Afraid of Virginia Woolf?*, is more clearly defined. The abstract fear of the former play is crystallised in Julian's perception of the terrifying loneliness of man. Used to the projections of his own sensibilities, he has to come to accept a diminution of his concept of reality. He also has to accept his responsibility for creating his own identity and meaning. For Albee is insisting that man's freedom and identity ultimately depend on his ability to discount reliance on an abstraction which is the creation of his own metaphysical solitude. As Goetz had said in Sartre's *Lucifer and the Lord* (1951), "God is the loneliness of man. . . . If God exists, man is nothing."

Albee has said that "the new theatre in the United States is going to concern itself with the re-evaluation of the nature of reality and, therefore, it's going to move away from the naturalistic tradition." *Tiny Alice*, like *Who's Afraid of Virginia Woolf?* before it, is proof of Albee's personal devotion to this principle. Indeed, when Alice makes her first appearance dressed as an old crone, only to throw off her disguise and appear in her full beauty, this in itself is surely an indication of Albee's central purpose in a play which he himself has called "a morality play about truth and illusion," and which is clearly dedicated to stripping the masks from religion, hypocrisy, materialism, and cant.

Albee is concerned . . . with what Thomas Mann, in a slightly different sense, has called the "dark underside" of man, those areas in his life, that is, which he tries desperately to conceal even from himself. For Albee, like Pirandello and later Genet, is all too aware of the internal and external pressures on the individual to escape from doubt, ambiguity, and uncertainty by retreating into a pre-determined role—whether that role be shaped by the Church or by society. For as a clearly defined functionary man feels that he is no longer adrift in a purposeless world, but is part of what he is prepared to accept as a meaningful order. Albee is finally concerned with this individual's response to seeing himself without a mask. He is concerned with penetrating behind the façade of public assurance to the true sense of fear, desertion, and real courage which he sees as lying at the heart of the human predicament. This, in a sense, is that "dissolution of the ego" which Joseph Wood Krutch has seen as the essential subject of contemporary literature. To Albee, though, it is essential to dismantle the ego, not in order to find the source of its psychosis, but rather to discover the foundation of its strength. Like the protagonist of Ralph Ellison's *Invisible Man*, Julian has to dive down into the depths of his consciousness before he can emerge again with a valid response to his surroundings.

But this is essentially an internalised drama—one which is of necessity acted out within the mind of the protagonist. This in itself accounts for Albee's move here towards monologue. For when Albee describes *Tiny Alice* as "something small enclosed in something else," he is not only referring to the central symbol of the castle, but also to the structure of a play which can be legitimately seen as a monodrama taking place entirely within Julian's own tormented mind. To the extent that this is true, a great deal of the obscurity and ambiguity which lies at the heart of the play can be seen as a direct expression of Julian's own bewilderment—a fact which nevertheless fails to redeem the confusions of a play which all too often substitutes technical facility for genuine engagement. Where Pirandello had succeeded in translating his metaphysical conundrums into flesh and blood, *Tiny Alice* remains for the most part a merely ingenious exercise. Pirandello justifiably boasted that he had converted the intellect into passion. In the place of passion Albee offers only refined anguish.—C. W. E. BIGSBY, "Tiny Alice," *Edward Albee: A Collection of Critical Essays*, pp. 124–34

In *Who's Afraid of Virginia Woolf?*, Edward Albee attempted to move beyond the narrowness of his personal interests by having his characters speculate from time to time upon the metaphysical and historical implications of their predicament. In *Tiny Alice*, the metaphysics, such as they are, appear to be Albee's deepest concern—and no doubt about it, he wants his concerns to seem deep. But this new play isn't about the problems of faith-and-doubt or appearance-and-reality, any more than *Virginia Woolf* was about "the Decline of the West"; mostly, when the characters in *Tiny Alice* suffer over epistemology, they are really suffering the consequences of human deceit, subterfuge, and hypocrisy. Albee sees in human nature

very much what Maupassant did, only he wants to talk about it like Plato. In this way he not only distorts his observations, but subverts his own powers, for it is not the riddles of philosophy that bring his talent to life, but the ways of cruelty and humiliation. Like *Virginia Woolf*, *Tiny Alice* is about the triumph of a strong woman over a weak man.

The disaster of the play, however—its tediousness, its pretentiousness, its galling sophistication, its gratuitous and easy symbolizing, its ghastly pansy rhetoric and repartee—all of this can be traced to his own unwillingness or inability to put its real subject at the center of the action. An article on the theater page of *The New York Times* indicates that Albee is distressed by the search that has begun for the meaning of the play; the *Times* also reports that he is amused by it, as well. When they expect him to become miserable they don't say; soon, I would think. For despair, not archness, is usually what settles over a writer unable to invent characters and an action and a tone appropriate to his feelings and convictions. Why *Tiny Alice* is so unconvincing, so remote, so obviously a sham—so much the kind of play that makes you want to rise from your seat and shout, "Baloney"—is that its surface is an attempt to disguise the subject on the one hand, and to falsify its significance on the other. All that talk about illusion and reality may even be the compulsive chattering of a dramatist who at some level senses that he is trapped in a lie.

What we are supposed to be witnessing is the destruction of a lay brother, sent by the Cardinal to whom he is secretary, to take care of the "odds and ends" arising out of a donation to the Church of two billion dollars. The gift is to be made in hundred-million-dollar installments over a twenty-year period by a Miss Alice; the wealthiest woman in the world, she lives in a castle with her butler and her lawyer, each of whom has been her lover. On a table in the library of the castle stands a huge model of the castle itself; deep within the replica, we are eventually encouraged to believe, resides the goddess Alice, whose earthly emissary, or priestess, or cardinal, is the millionairess, Miss Alice. In the name of, for the sake of, Alice, Miss Alice sets out in her filmy gown to seduce Brother Julian; once that is accomplished, a wedding is arranged, presided over by the Cardinal. At this point Miss Alice promptly deserts Julian— leaving him to Alice, she says; the Cardinal turns his back on what he knows is coming and takes the first hundred million; and the lawyer shoots the bridegroom, who dies with his arms outstretched, moaning at the end, "I accept thee, Alice, for thou art come to me. God, Alice . . . I accept thy will."

None of this means anything because Albee does not make the invention whole or necessary. The play strings together incidents of no moral or intellectual consequence, and where the inconsistencies, oversights, and lapses occur, the playwright justifies them by chalking them up to the illusory nature of human existence. It is as though Shakespeare, having failed to settle in his own mind whether Desdemona did or did not sleep with Cassio—and consequently leaving the matter unsettled in the play—later explains his own failure of imagination by announcing to the press that we can never penetrate reality to get to the truth. The world of *Tiny Alice* is mysterious because Albee cannot get it to cohere. To begin with, the donation of two billion dollars to the Church is irrelevant to the story of Julian's destruction—what the money will *mean* to the Church doesn't enter his mind. In fact, though he is sent to the castle to make arrangements for the gift, not a word is said of the money until the Cardinal appears at the end to pick up the cash, and then we learn that Church lawyers have been working out the essentials of the deal on the side. And why does the Cardinal want the money? Hold on to your hats. Though he dresses like a prince of the Lord, he is really greedy!

Least convincing of all is what should be the most convincing—Tiny Alice Herself, and the replica, or altar, in which her spirit resides. The implications of a Woman-God, her nature, her character, and her design, are never revealed; but is this because they are beyond human comprehension, or beyond the playwright's imagination? Though *his* God is mysterious, certainly the Cardinal could discuss Him with some conviction and intelligence (and ought to, of course, instead of appearing as a pompous operator). Why can't Miss Alice or the lawyer discuss theirs? Why don't they answer the questions that are put to them? There is, after all, a difference between the idea that life is a dream and a predilection to being dreamy about life. But withholding information is Albee's favorite means of mystifying the audience; the trouble comes from confusing a technique of dramaturgy, and a primitive one at that, with an insight into the nature of things.

> *Butler:* This place [the real castle] was in England.
> *Miss Alice:* Yes, it was! Every stone, marked and shipped.
> *Julian:* Oh, I had thought it was a replica.
> *Lawyer:* Oh no; that would have been too simple. Though it is a replica . . . in its way.
> *Julian:* Of?
> *Lawyer: (Points to model)* Of that. *(Julian laughs; the lawyer says)* Ah well.

But instead of getting him off the hook with "Ah well," why doesn't Albee press the lawyer a little? Why doesn't Julian inquire further? For a lay brother who is, as he so piously says, "deeply" interested in the reality of things, how little persistence there is in Julian's curiosity; how like a child he is in the answers he accepts to the most baffling mysteries that surround him. Indeed when Albee begins to see Julian as a man who walks around acting like a small boy in a huge house full of big bad grownups, he is able to put together two or three minutes of dialogue that is at least emotionally true. To the delights and dangers of the Oedipal triangle (boy in skirts, mother in negligee, father with pistol) Albee's imagination instantly quickens; but unfortunately by presenting Julian as a befuddled boy, he only further befuddles the audience about those metaphysical problems that are supposed to be so anguishing to Julian as a man. For instance, when a fire miraculously breaks out in the chapel of the castle and in the chapel of the replica, one would imagine that Julian, with his deep interest in reality, would see the matter somewhat further along than he does in this exchange:

> *Julian:* Miss Alice? Why, why did it happen that way—in both dimensions?
> *Miss Alice: (Her arms out)* Help me.
> *Julian:* Will you . . . tell me anything?
> *Miss Alice:* I don't know anything.
> *Julian:* But you were . . .
> *Miss Alice:* I don't *know* anything.
> *Julian:* Very well.

That is the last we hear of the fire. But how *did* it happen? And why? I know I am asking questions about the kind of magical moment that qualifies a play for the Howard Taubman Repertory Theater for Sheer Theater, but I would like to know who this Alice is that she can and will cause such miracles of nature. Might not Julian, a lay brother, who has the ear of a Cardinal, rush out to tell him of this strange occurrence? But then the Cardinal exists, really, only as another figure to betray and humiliate poor Julian, the baffled little boy. As a Cardinal, he is of no interest to Albee, who seems to have introduced the Catholic Church into the play so that he can have some of the men dressed up in gowns on the one hand, and indulge his cynicism on the other; he does nothing to bring into collision the recognizable world of the Church and its system of beliefs, with the world that is unfamiliar to both Julian and the audience, the world of Tiny Alice. Such a confrontation would, of course, have made it necessary to invent the mysteries of a Woman-God and the way of life that is a consequence of her existence and her power. But Albee is simply not capable of making this play into a work of philosophical or religious originality, and probably not too interested either. The movement of the play is not towards a confrontation of ideas; it is finally concerned with evoking a single emotion—pity for poor Julian. In the end the playwright likens him to Jesus Christ— and all because he has had to suffer the martyrdom of heterosexual love.

Tiny Alice is a homosexual day-dream in which the celibate male is tempted and seduced by the overpowering female, only to be betrayed by the male lover and murdered by the cruel law, or in this instance, cruel lawyer. It has as much to do with Christ's Passion as a little girl's dreaming about being a princess locked in a tower has to do with the fate of Mary Stuart. Unlike Genet, who dramatizes the fact of fantasying in *Our Lady of the Flowers*, Albee would lead us to believe that his fantasy has significance altogether removed from the dread or the desire which inspired it; consequently, the attitudes he takes towards his material are unfailingly inappropriate. His subject is emasculation—as was Strindberg's in *The Father*, a play I mention because its themes, treated openly and directly, and necessarily connected in the action, are the very ones that Albee has so vulgarized and sentimentalized in *Tiny Alice*: male weakness, female strength, and the limits of human knowledge. How long before a play is produced on Broadway in which the homosexual hero is presented as a homosexual, and not disguised as an *angst*-ridden priest, or an angry Negro, or an aging actress; or worst of all, Everyman?—PHILIP ROTH, "The Play That Dare Not Speak Its Name," *NYRB*, Feb. 25, 1965, p. 4

At first sight this is an extremely complex play, but Albee himself assures us that "the play is quite clear." I think Albee means this remark quite literally, and I think he is right. In the sense that meaninglessness is inevitably clear, the play *is* clear. *Tiny Alice* is a veritable alphabet soup of symbols, like Tennessee Williams' *Camino Real*. The symbols are thrown in at random so that each critic can pick them out and form his own pattern. All that is required to render such a play significant is a group of docile, symbol-hunting, jig-saw puzzle enthusiasts. Given Miss Alice (symbol of wealth), the Cardinal (symbol of religion), Julian (symbol of lost faith), the martyrdom, the Chinese box puzzle of the castles-within-castles, and the perverse sexuality, one can come up with almost anything— except coherence. The key to the whole matter almost certainly lies in the sexual aspects of the play's plot, the central event being the seduction of Julian, a seduction which is initiated in extremely ambiguous terms as he kneels before Miss Alice's open robe, under which she is presumably naked, and buries his face in her sex—or thereabouts. This is the only apparently heterosexual act in a play that is shot through with blatant homosexual references, but while I am prepared to accept Martha and Honey as having been intended as females all along, I cannot but think that Miss Alice was originally a man. The homosexual aspects of the play are further reinforced when we learn that "tiny alice" is homosexual jargon for the male anus. This is something that Albee either did or did not know when he wrote the play. If he did not know it, then its use as the title of a play already full of homosexual references is an extraordinarily unfortunate coincidence. If he did know it, then the play is a truly outrageous piece of effrontery concocted with the utmost cynicism.—GEORGE WELLWARTH, *The Theatre of Protest and Paradox*, 1971, pp. 332–33

A DELICATE BALANCE

Edward Albee's recent work poses a number of problems for the reviewer, one of them being that it is virtually impossible to discuss it without falling into repetition. Looking over the anthology of pieces I have written about his annual procession of plays, I discover that I am continually returning to two related points: that his plays have no internal validity and that they are all heavily dependent upon the style of other dramatists. At the risk of boring the reader, I am forced to repeat these judgments about A *Delicate Balance*. The fourth in a series of disappointments that Albee has been turning out since *Who's Afraid of Virginia Woolf?*, this work, like its predecessors, suffers from a borrowed style and a hollow center. It also suggests that Albee's talent for reproduction has begun to fail him until by now the labels on his lendings are all but exposed to public view. Reviewers have already noted the stamp of T. S. Eliot on A *Delicate Balance* (a nametag that was somewhat more subtly imprinted on *Tiny Alice* as well), and it is quite true that Albee, like Eliot before him, is now trying to invest the conventional drawing-room comedy with metaphysical significance. But where Eliot was usually impelled by a religious vision, Albee seems to be stimulated by mere artifice, and the result is emptiness, emptiness, emptiness.

A *Delicate Balance* is, to my mind, a very bad play—not as bad as *Malcolm*, which had a certain special awfulness all its own, but boring and trivial nevertheless. It is also the most remote of Albee's plays—so far removed from human experience, in fact, that one wonders if Albee is not letting his servants do his living for him. Although the action is supposed to take place in suburban America—in the living room and conservatory of an upper middle-class family—the environment is more that of the English landed gentry as represented on the West End before the Osborne revolution. Leatherbound books sit on library shelves, elbowing copies of *Horizon*; brandy and anisette and martinis are constantly being decanted between, over, and under bits of dialogue; the help problem becomes an object of concern, as well as problems of friendship, marriage, sex, and the proper attitude to take toward pets; and characters discuss their relationships in a lapidary style as far from modern speech as the whistles of a dolphin.

The failure of the language, actually, is the most surprising failure of the play, especially since Albee's control of idiom has usually been his most confident feature. Here, on the other hand, banal analogies are forced to pass for wisdom: "Friendship is something like a marriage, is it not, Tobias, for better or for worse?" The plot is signaled with all the subtlety of a railroad brakeman rerouting a train: "Julia is coming home. She is leaving Douglas, which is no surprise to me." A relaxed idiom is continually sacrificed to clumsy grammatical accuracy: "You are a guest," observes one character, to which the other replies, "As you." If colloquialisms are spoken, they are invariably accompanied by self-conscious apologies: One character drinks "like the famous fish," while another observes, "You're copping out, as they say." Empty chatter is passed off as profound observation with the aid of irrelevant portentous subordinate clauses: "Time happens, I suppose, to people. Everything becomes too late finally." And the play ends with one of those vibrato rising-sun lines familiar from at least a dozen such evenings: "Come now, we can begin the day."

It is clear that Albee has never heard such people talk, he has only read plays about them, and he has not retained enough from his reading to give his characters life. More surprisingly, he has not even borrowed creatively from his own work, for although a number of Albee's usual strategies are present in A *Delicate Balance*, they do not function with much cogency. One character, for example, tells of his difficulties with a cat that no longer loved him—a tale that recalls a similar tale about a dog in *The Zoo Story*—but here the narrative is no more than a sentimental recollection. Similarly, a dead child figures in this work, as in so many Albee plays, but it has no organic relevance to the action and seems introduced only to reveal the sexual hang-ups of the protagonist and to fill up time.

Too much of the play, in fact, seems purely decorative: there simply isn't enough material here to make up a full evening. A *Delicate Balance* concerns a family of four—a passive husband, an imperious wife, an alcoholic sister-in-law, and a much divorced daughter—whose problems are exacerbated when they are visited by some married friends. This couple has just experienced a nameless terror in their home, and when they move in on the family for comfort and security, a delicate balance is upset, all the characters learning that terror is infectious, like the plague. This plot has a nice touch of mystery about it, but its main consequence is to move various sexually estranged couples into each other's rooms after various impassioned dialogues. What finally puzzles the will is how very little Albee now thinks can make up a play: a few confessions, a few revelations, a little spookiness, and an emotional third-act speech.

. . . A *Delicate Balance* is an old house which an interior decorator has tried to furnish with reproductions and pieces bought at auction. But the house has never been lived in and the wind murmurs drily through its corridors.—ROBERT BRUSTEIN, "Albee Decorates an Old House: A *Delicate Balance*" (1966), *The Third Theatre*, 1969, pp. 83–86

Albee is progressing. *Who's Afraid of Virginia Woolf?* was about the emptiness that surrounds and threatens to swallow our relationships; *Tiny Alice* was about the void lurking behind our deepest beliefs; now, A *Delicate Balance* is about the nothingness, the bare nothingness of it all—it is a play about nothing. Nothing will come of nothing was not spoken of the theatre: *there* nothing has been known to yield glittering and even golden returns. *Heartbreak House*, for example, is a play more or less about nothing, and so are most of Beckett's plays. But Shaw fills his nothingness with incisive speculation, so that the mind, though working in a near-vacuum, begets its own thrilling parabolas; Beckett raises nothingness to fierce tragicomic, almost epic, heights. But the nothingness—perhaps more accurately *nothinginess*—of Albee's play is petty, self-indulgent, stationary. Albee's nothing is as dull as anything.

Tobias and Agnes, a genteel, middle-aged couple, are the pillars of suburbia. They drink, vegetate, and speechify. With them lives Agnes's alcoholic younger sister, Claire, between whom and Tobias there may or may not be some hanky-panky. Claire and Agnes loathe each other, which allows Claire to pour out a steady stream of wisecracks floating out over the stream of liquor flowing down. The daughter of the house, Julia, aged 36, returns as her fourth marriage is breaking up; this phenomenon occurs every three years, and her parents keep her room ready to soothe the post-marital depression. This uneasy ménage could just barely be kept in a delicate balance if it weren't for the neighbors and best friends, Harry and Edna, who, sudden preys to a terrible but nameless fear, arrive unannounced and intending to stay, apparently, forever.

They are given Julia's room, which causes that ungay divorcee to have hysterics and almost shoot the intruders. After much soul-searching and several storms in a martini glass, leading up to a frenzied tirade of Tobias's full of instant self-contradiction, Harry and Edna go home, after all, leaving the family quartet to play, in precarious equilibrium, sour-sweet music on one another's heartstrings.

The first thing to strike one about all this is its rank improbability. Why are any of these people here? Why should Agnes tolerate Claire's sniping, and why would Claire want this ungenial hostess, even with free drinks and the rather square host thrown in as an ice cube? Why should Julia rush home to recuperate, when she and her parents do not seem particularly in tune, and she is wealthy and big enough to undertake a hotel? Why should the neighbors wish to move in? Edna was at her knitting, Harry at his recorded French course, when the mysterious terror seized them. But what makes them think that they can move in with their friends indefinitely, or, rather, definitively? And why; when in that vacuous household, amid jangling cocktail glasses and nerves, there is plenty of room for the fear to move right in with them? Finally, the key problem makes no sense: should one put up one's neighbors, in the name of friendship, in perpetuity, or shouldn't one? No half-way sane people would arrive with such a request, and no halfway conceivable people would seriously entertain the notion of so entertaining them. Yet in Albee's play this is presented with a straight face, earnestly, though the idea belongs in absurdist farce, where, however, it would be handled with Ionescoan wit or Pinterish balefulness.

But, presumably, there is a deeper meaning: something, no doubt, like what is a marriage, a family, friendship, and how does one keep these relations going in the face of a world grown meaningless. Now, first of all, I am tired of this mythical "meaningless world" when the playwright fails to create or suggest any outer world (one isolated reference to income taxes might as well have been to Chinese calligraphy), and when he neglects to indicate what meaningfulness might have been before it got mislaid. This posturing play abounds in the cocktail-party profundities and family-reunion soundings that bloated up Eliot's drama, but at least Eliot was, however flatfootedly, after some sort of myth or metaphysic. Albee, too, must drop little hints: one can play with Claire's clairvoyance, with Julia as a latter-day Juliet, with Tobias and Agnes as Tobias and the Angel—but, as Elizabeth Hardwick notes, "a reading of the *Book of Tobit* did not produce any deepening allegory."

That may still leave Albee's language, which, according to a chorus of reviewers, is a marvel and a joy. Now, it is true that Albee is in love with language, which sets him above your average playwright who does not even realize that language exists, but, for all that, Albee's love affair is sadly one-sided. The language of *Virginia Woolf*, for example, often lapses into subliteracy: "He is breathing a little heavy; behaving a little manic," "A son who I have raised," "I have never robbed a hothouse without there is a light from heaven," the curious notion that *ibid* means something like "in the same way," which frequently recurs in the stage directions, e.g., "NICK (*very quietly*) . . . GEORGE (*ibid*)" etc. etc. In my review of *Tiny Alice*, I quoted a goodly number of similar lapses, and, mind you, always in the speech of supposedly cultivated persons. So again here, as in "You're not as young as either of us were," or in Claire's dogged distinction that she is not "an alcoholic" but "*a* alcoholic," which is supposed to be amusingly portentous, but manages to be merely nonsense, linguistically and otherwise.

But there is a much more profound insensitivity to language at work here, and the more painful since Albee (as he did

in *Tiny Alice*) has one of his characters apologize for his alleged articulateness. But Albee's "articulateness" is either self-conscious poeticism, "When the daylight comes, comes order with it," or long, syntactically overburdened sentences and paragraphs, or putative shockers like, "Your mummy got her pudenda scarred a couple of times before she met daddy," where "pudenda" is rather too recherché for Tobias, and "scarred" much too sadistic: it may be consistent with his character to be sardonic, but not to be beastly. Or, again, consider, "And if we were touching, ah, what a splendid cocoon that was!" How inept to use the weak word "touching" for sexual contact (as it is here used) and to match this up with "cocoon," which does not suggest two beings becoming one, but, on the contrary, one ego narcissistically shutting itself off. Or take this exchange: "You are not young, and you do not live at home.—Where do I live?—In the dark sadness, yes?" Is this supposed to be irony or lyricism? In either case, I say, the dark sadness, no. And even Albee's usually dependable bitchy wit fails him all too often here, as in "AGNES: Why don't you go to Kentucky or Tennessee and visit the distilleries? CLAIRE: Why don't you die?"

What, one wonders, was the real motive behind *A Delicate Balance*? I, for one, still believe in Albee's perceptiveness and even in his talent (he did, after all, write *The Zoo Story* and *Virginia Woolf*); why would he hurtle into such utter pointlessness? It occurs to me that at least since *Virginia Woolf*, Albee's plays and adaptations have been viewed by many as dealing overtly or covertly with homosexual matters; Albee may have resolved here to write a play reeking with heterosexuality. To be sure, the edges are fuzzy. The good friends Harry and Tobias spend a summer sleeping with the same girl, a practice about which psychoanalysis has a thing or two to tell. When an unprepossessing and gauche saleswoman tries to help Claire with a bathing suit and asks her what she could do for her, Claire replies with a nasty smirk fraught with *double entendre*, "Not very much, sweetheart," a piece of repartee appropriate only to an invert. And there is a whole sequence in which Agnes and Tobias figuratively (and sneeringly) reverse sexes and roles in their relationship with Julia. But all this is not at the heart of the play. At the heart of the play things are heterosexual and totally lifeless.—JOHN SIMON, *HdR*, Winter 1966–67, pp. 627–29

EVERYTHING IN THE GARDEN

Albee's version of *Everything in the Garden*, in short, is without interest, and I'm not concealing very well my reluctance to write about it. What continues to remain somewhat interesting, because unresolved, is the author's ambiguous relationship to his audience. As I have had occasion to remark somewhat too often, Albee's identity as a dramatist is highly uncertain. Lacking his own vision, he turns to adaptation; lacking his own voice, he borrows the voice of others. What has remained constant through his every change of style—through the progression of his influences from Genet to Strindberg to Pirandello to Williams to Ionesco to Eliot—is his peculiar love-hatred for those who attend his plays. Albee's desire to undermine the audience and be applauded for it is now leading him into the most extraordinary stratagems and subterfuges, just as his desire to be simultaneously successful and significant has managed by now to freeze his artistic imagination. He has two choices, I think, if he is ever to create interesting work again: either to resolve this conflict, or to write about it. But both alternatives oblige him to become a great deal less masked, a great deal more daring, a great deal more open than he now chooses to be.—ROBERT BRUSTEIN, "Albee at the Crossroads" (1967), *The Third Theatre*, 1969, pp. 87–90

BOX-MAO-BOX

QUOTATIONS FROM CHAIRMAN MAO TSE-TUNG

In the last dozen or so years Edward Albee has delivered a number of theatrical shocks to a Broadway scarcely renowned for its fearless commitment to experimentation. As a result, the metaphysical enigmas of *Tiny Alice* and the "surreal" images of *Malcolm* were both greeted with a mixture of suspicion and incomprehension. Though the 1968 production of two related one-act plays, *Box* and *Quotations from Chairman Mao Tse-Tung*, fared somewhat better, these too strained critical responses forged in the Ibsenesque crucible of the American theatre. Walter Kerr responded with predictable bemused boredom while Jack Kroll, who produced a sensitive assessment of the two plays in his *Newsweek* review, missed the essential ambivalence of Albee's stance. Equally misleading was Michael Rutenberg's description of the work as "another protest play," in his book *Edward Albee: Playwright in Protest*, for it is precisely Albee's unwillingness to be contained by such casual labels which is the source of the evocative quality of plays which are concerned with debating the function of art and the individual's responsibility in a world increasingly scornful of public and personal realities.

Throughout his career Albee has plotted the graph of man's attempt to relate to his social and metaphysical situation. His central belief is that expressed by Freud in *The Future of an Illusion*: "man cannot remain a child for ever; he must venture at last into the hostile world. This may be called '*education to reality*'." From Peter's refusal to acknowledge the simple inadequacy of his life in *The Zoo Story*, to George and Martha's illusory child in *Who's Afraid of Virginia Woolf?* and Julian's flight to religion in *Tiny Alice*, he has charted the desperate need for illusion which has afflicted society and left the individual trapped in permanent adolescence. Where Beckett sees man as irrevocably condemned to live out a metaphysical absurdity, Albee's position is basically existential. He sees the cataclysm as very much man's own creation and, as such, avoidable. This is the point of his comment, in the introduction to the published version of the plays that "A playwright—unless he is creating escapist romances (an honourable occupation, of course)—has two obligations: first, to make some statement about the condition of 'man' . . . and, second, to make some statement about the nature of the art form with which he is working. In both instances he must attempt change."

He takes as his subject modern society's apparent determination to conspire in its own demise through a wilful refusal to risk the anguish which inevitably stems from personal commitment and from human relationships forged in an imperfect world. In the face of this the individual is urged to accept the realities which circumscribe and define his identity, while placing himself in implacable opposition to a social system which trades simple humanity for the dubious benefits of material success and an unruffled, if illusory, security. The movement which Albee detects towards fragmentation, in individual lives as in society at large, an anomie privately and publicly compensated for by a desperate commitment to any ordered structure (the longing for "law and order" is not without its metaphysical implications), is seen by him as a deadly flight from the saving grace of human interdebtedness. *Box* and *Quotations from Chairman Mao Tse-Tung* provide a focus for these earlier more random observations. In *Who's Afraid of Virginia Woolf?* he had suggested a political dimension to George and Martha's exorcism of illusion; in *Tiny Alice* he had detailed the origin and nature of religious delusion and in *A*

Delicate Balance examined the social fictions deemed necessary to the continuance of corporate life. In his two experimental plays he attempts to bring together the whole metastructure of illusions which together create the fabric of the private and public world, suspecting with Freud that, "having recognized religious doctrines to be illusions, we are at once confronted with the further question: may not other cultural possessions, which we esteem highly and by which we let our life be ruled, be of a similar nature? Should not the assumptions that regulate our political institutions likewise be called illusions, and is it not the case that in our culture the relations between the sexes are disturbed by an erotic illusion, or by a series of erotic illusions." This comprehensive network of illusion stretches even to those artists whose central objective opposes the ordered world of art to the frightening flux of reality. Where a writer like Wallace Stevens rejects Freud's assertion, seeing the poet as one "capable of resisting or evading the pressure of reality," giving to life "the supreme fictions without which we are unable to conceive of it," Albee embraces Freud's scepticism and sees the function of the writer as precipitating that "education to reality" which he had made the central tenet of *The Future of an Illusion*.

In *The Necessary Angel* Wallace Stevens observed that "the commonest idea of an imaginative object is something large. But apparently with the Japanese it is the other way round and with them the commonest idea of an imaginative object is something small. With the Hindu it appears to be something vermicular, with the Chinese, something round and with the Dutch, something square." The remark could scarcely provide a more appropriate starting point to an analysis of *Box* and *Quotations from Chairman Mao Tse-Tung*—two plays which are not only structured around just such a "square" imaginative object but which examine the role and function of imagination, in the form of ideological constructs no less than artistic creations. For it was Stevens, too, who asserted that "the diffusion of communism exhibits imagination on its most momentous scale" following "the collapse of other beliefs," thus establishing that very connection between the artist's "fictions" and social illusions which Albee was at pains to demonstrate.

⟨*Box*⟩ opens on a stage dominated by a large cube—the sides picked out with masked spotlights. After five seconds we hear a voice come from the back or sides of the theatre—itself, of course, a box. The voice announces the subject, "Box," and then begins a monologue which is in fact the working out of a dialectic. The play is essentially the self-questioning voice of the artist or of any individual alive to personal and public responsibilities. But the elegiac tone, together with reiterated use of the past tense, makes it clear that this is both a prophecy and a post-apocalyptic elegy for a departed civilization; the play which follows offers an explanation for that cataclysm, a "memory of what we have not known," a memory "to be seen and proved later."

Box is a protest against the dangerously declining quality of life—a decline marked in one way by the corruption of genuine artistry to suit the demands of a consumer society which has no place for the artist except as a simple manufacturer, and in another by the growth of an amoral technology with a momentum and direction of its own. . . .

Wallace Stevens has observed that "in an age in which disbelief is so profoundly prevalent or, if not disbelief, indifference to questions of belief, poetry and painting, and the arts in general, are, in their measure, a compensation for what has been lost." Man's interest "in the imagination and its work is to be regarded not as a phase of humanism but as a vital self-assertion in a world in which nothing but the self remains, if that remains." This basic truth of modernism highlights the paradox of Albee's work. He has always been obsessed with a sense of loss—a theme which runs through his life as clearly as his plays—but he has also consistently refused to retreat into stoicism, which he regards as a cowardly and ultimately lethal retreat from commitment, or into protective illusion. As a writer he has shown a healthy scepticism towards the spurious products of the imagination, whether these take the form of O'Neill's pipe-dreams or the elaborate artifice of art. Yet his central theme—the need to reject the seductive consolation of unreality, the desperate necessity to abandon faith in a specious sense of order, and the urgency of genuine communication between individuals stripped of pretense and defensive posturing—is advanced in plays which are, of course, nothing more themselves than elaborate and carefully structured fictions in which invented characters act out a prepared and balanced scenario. His awareness of this dilemma is perhaps reflected in his ironical reference to the careful construction of the box, which stands as a persuasive analogue of the well-made play: "this is solid, perfect joins . . . good work . . . and so fastidious, like when they shined the bottom of the shoes . . . *and* the instep." Clearly these plays are in part an attempt to resolve such a dilemma. There are no characters in *Box*. *Quotations* borrows speeches from other writers and then fragments them until Albee's conscious control is to some degree subverted. Such structure as is apparent is supplied partly by chance, by random association, and by an audience for whom the box, which dominates the stage, becomes a *tabula rasa* to be interpreted variously as the artificial construction of an artist, a visual image of order, a paradigm of the theatre, an image of the restricted world in which the individual exists or the empty shell of the body whose voice lingers on as a warning and an epitaph.

In approaching these plays it is essential to recall Albee's comment that "the use of the unconscious in the twentieth-century theatre is its most interesting development" for we have his assurance that "whatever symbolic content there may be in *Box* and *Quotations from Chairman Mao Tse-Tung*, both plays deal with the unconscious, primarily." Both works represent an experiment in liberating the dramatic event from the conscious and potentially restricting control of the writer. Similar experiments have been conducted with music by John Cage, though in pieces like "Rozart Mix" and "Williams Mix" he rigourously excluded all conscious control, in the one case surrendering the recording and composition to a number of other people, and in the latter, recording a collage of sounds by purely random means. Indeed he has subsequently rejected even this since it excluded that indeterminacy in actual performance which he had come to value. Albee's practice, however, differs in several important respects, although, interestingly enough, he admits in the introduction to his diptych that he was attempting "several experiments having to do . . . in the main . . . with the application of musical form to dramatic structures." He insists on retaining for himself a tight control over rhythm and tone and establishes with considerable attention to detail the basic structure of the two plays. While he allowed chance to play an important role he also reserved the responsibility of manipulating the text to secure the maximum effect. Albee, moreover, is not retreating from the centrality of language in his work but is intent on discovering the potential of words freed from their immediate context and released from their function of forwarding the details of linear plot, delineating the minutiae of character, and establishing the context and structure of conscious communication. In *Box* the sibylline utterances of the disembodied voice, together with the enigmatic central image (in contrast to the allegorical directness of the central symbol in *Tiny Alice*), leave the audience to respond to intimations of personal loss and the suggestive outlines of a visual image on a sub-conscious and intuitive rather than a conscious and cerebral level. In *Quotations* coherent monologues are deliberately fragmented in order to release meaning, while private and public fears are juxtaposed according to chance assonance. The play is a collage of words and images; it uses surrealist methods not to reveal the marvellous but to penetrate the bland façade of modern reality—personal, religious, and political.

At first sight *Quotations* is a curious work. Of the four characters one is silent, one reads lines taken directly from Mao's quotations, one recites a poem written by the nineteenth-century popular poet Will Carleton, and only one speaks dialogue written by Albee himself (only slightly more than half of the lines were written by Albee). Like Breton with the printed word or Ernst with visual matter Albee is intent on bringing together disparate materials and experiences to create an image with the power to bypass intellectual evasion. Mao's quotations and Carleton's poems are to an extent simply "found" material with which he can create a play with the power to disturb not merely conventional notions of theatre—a discrete and highly structured model—but parallel assumptions about the nature of reality. The play is intended to capture not only the simultaneity of life—the complex interplay of public and private worlds—but also the fluid, evanescent, and equivocal quality of any art which sets out to plot the decline of morality and morale in an age bereft of convictions which genuinely touch the quick of life. With religion dead—the minister sits mute throughout the play—there is only political activism, a sentimental longing for lost innocence, the short-lived consolation of sexuality, or a deadly solipsism which hastens that cataclysm which is the inevitable product of such a massive failure of nerve. . . .

In the introduction to the two plays Albee suggests that while they "are separate works" which "were conceived at different though not distant moments" and can "stand by themselves" and even be played separately, they are "more effectively performed enmeshed"; *Quotations*, indeed, being "an outgrowth of and extension of the shorter play." The connection between the two now seems clear enough. The drift towards death becomes most ominous precisely when one no longer has a clear perception of the value of life. Death comes by default as humane values are sacrificed to self-justification and political expediency. The kind of selfishness which enables a woman to respond to news of her husband's imminent death with the cry, "But what about *me*! Think about *me* . . . ME! WHAT ABOUT ME!" and which permits Mao to declare, "we are advocates of the abolition of war; we do not want war; but war can only be abolished through war," clearly threatens to destroy the very purpose of life itself.—C. W. E. Bigsby, "*Box* and *Quotations from Chairman Mao Tse-Tung*: Albee's Diptych," *Edward Albee: A Collection of Critical Essays*, 1975, pp. 151–63

ALL OVER

We're still expected to take Edward Albee seriously. Broadway has one comedy writer, Neil Simon, and one serious writer. Now that Williams seems withered and Miller seems all munched out, Albee is the high-art jewel of the Big Time. If we had a healthy and fruitful theater, Albee might be tolerable as one among many, a formerly vital, now-attenuated mediocrity. As it is, the news that Albee has written a play makes Broadway throb, makes the Ph.D. candidates slaver, and makes the general audience—or what's left of it—gather round like the crowd outside a palace waiting for word that a son has been born to keep the royal line alive.

But ever since *Who's Afraid of Virginia Woolf?*—Albee's last good play—all we've been getting from the royal bedchamber are abortions: two plays and three adaptations that are all varyingly bad and two one-act plays that are Absurdist imitations. In fact, those two imitations, *Box* and *Mao*, were the best of this poor lot because at least they showed that Albee was listening to something besides his own purr.

With his new play, *All Over*, the purr begins again with the very first lines, the feeling that the author thinks he's very high-toned indeed. Some people are sitting in the huge bedroom of a dying man: his wife and his two (grown) children, his mistress, his best friend, a doctor and nurse. The wife asks, "Is he dead?" and his mistress says that the man always objected to the use of the verb "to be" with the word "dead" because he felt it a contradiction, that the question should really be, "Has he died?" At once we are in the presence of a playwright who wants us to know that he is not one of your run-of-the-mill theater dumbbells.

Throughout the play, Albee obtrudes this pygmy-mandarin style. When the daughter interrupts the mother, the latter says, "Do not deflect me." Later, the daughter, who is disliked, says, "*Non grata* has its compensations." And Albee may be the only dramatist now writing who uses "for" as a conjunction: "We cannot avoid them, for we are no longer private." That's class, folks.

But this classy tone isn't even consistent. There are gags. The nurse says of death, "It gets us where we live." In a quarrel the daughter says, "Fuck yourself," to the mistress. After an irrelevant line from someone else, the mistress says musingly, "I've often wondered just how one does that." (Whenever a rude word is used, it's couched in genteel archness.)

I've dwelt first on the language because it's a screen between us and the play. What lies behind the screen? An allegory, about dying, and life. At one point Albee gives us oblique advice not to take his play as allegory, but this is just kittenish. No one has a name in this play: the program lists them as The Wife, The Daughter, etc., and no one is ever addressed by name. . . .

Allegory is a risky form because it directs our attention so fiercely to content. Other forms can thrive on style, but allegory implies that the author had something so large to say that only by abstraction could he handle the magnitude of his message. Yet all that really happens in *All Over* is the exact opposite of allegorical intent: we learn specific details of the characters' backgrounds and relationships. They might as well have been called Ethel and Fred and Cora, the setting might as well have been realistic to the last tack. . . . The method is bastard Chekhov: everyone gets at least one aria. A few of the arias are modestly effective, though always self-conscious, full of balanced phrases and artful dying falls; but the play remains an anthology of set-pieces, generally tedious.

Not to belabor Albee with Chekhov, one difference between them is that none of Albee's material comes from or tends toward a central idea. Under the attitudinizing style and the unrevealing strokes of psychological candor, there is a vacuum. Just before the end, the wife says, "All we've *done* is think of ourselves," a thought that had struck me about an hour and a half earlier and that even then hadn't seemed specially enlightening about human nature in a sickroom. We listen to them think about themselves all evening, in largely predictable terms. (I longed for the dying husband to shout behind the screen: "Will you all kindly shut up and let me die in peace?"

And why, even in an allegory, doesn't the doctor object to all this chatter in a dying man's chamber?) The wife finally confesses that she loves no one but her husband, the daughter confesses that she knows no one likes her and she doesn't like herself much, the mistress faces loneliness; with these and similarly unsurprising revelations about all these uninteresting characters, the play ends.

Now it's not enough to say that all this is not enough: it's worse. The trumped-up revelations, the unproductive confrontations, retroactively reveal Albee's real bankruptcy, that he knew he had nothing to say *before he started*. There is no hint in this play that Albee was genuinely on fire to say something and that he misconstrued his own depth. Rather, the impression is that he thought of the mechanism—the death-chamber symbolism—and simply began, assuming that the magic of the mechanism and the weight of his reputation would supply Art. A playwright must write, I suppose he thought, and this structure would give him the chance to show again his velvet way with words and his penchant for symbols that are provocative so long as you don't question them. In my view this was the genesis of *Tiny Alice*, an even more complicated piece of symbolic gymnastics and the most ludicrously over-explicated play of our time. *All Over* is somewhat simpler but is just another somewhat arrogant display piece, puffed up with sophomoric diction, a desperate grab at something to keep its now-vacant author busy. Death as a catalyst on the lives of survivors is always a promising idea. The contemplation of death, as Tarleton says in Shaw's *Misalliance*, is "a delightful subject." But Albee's play is like its setting: chic upholstery stuck in the middle of a bare stage.—STANLEY KAUFFMANN, *NR*, April 17, 1971, pp. 24, 38

About Edward Albee's *All Over*, someone should have said "Come off it!" long before it reached the production stage, and in fact we will shortly be without one of our good playwrights if someone does not say something at least as blunt to him in the near future. The play is not only self-indulgent in itself, but it is also another step for Albee into a thicket of verbiage which began to sprout ominously in *A Delicate Balance* and became thoroughly overgrown in *Box-Mao-Box*. . . .

In the security of his enormous prestige, Mr. Albee is evolving from a writer into a "writer." Dialogue, and specifically the long spoken set piece (like the story of Jerry and the Dog in *The Zoo Story*), was this playwright's specialty, and much of his initial dazzle came from his rhetorical surprises and his good ear for the weird rhythms of human speech, which he recorded honestly and which were made to serve his dramatic purposes.

All Over is a collection of such speeches, but the rhythms are by now so self-conscious, the rhetoric so elaborately precious, that for one thing it does not sound like human speech at all. In phrases that seem to derive from Ivy Compton-Burnett or Henry James, endless parenthetical refinements fog every thought. . . . One result is that the characters all speak with the same voice. . . .

Perhaps we could be encouraged that Mr. Albee seems just slightly at war with himself. He wants to maintain a Beckett-size metaphysical view of death, in a quasimusical structure of theme and variations, but at the same time his instincts hunger for the sort of character conflict which gave life to *The Zoo Story* and *Who's Afraid of Virginia Woolf?* In this play confrontations do erupt briefly and enigmatically from time to time, but subside quickly. . . . And ironically, the final confrontation, such as it is, between wife and mistress seems only a gratuitous taste of what that complex relationship might have been, yet at the same time it is so prosaic as to diminish any metaphysical overtones the writer has set up.

. . . ⟨T⟩he playwright himself . . . is center stage throughout the play, rambling along, searching for profound things to say. He has not found them, and we would all be better off the next time if he would get out of the way and turn his characters loose.—MICHAEL MURRAY, "Albee's End Game," *Com*, April 23, 1971, pp. 166–67

Edward Albee, it is said, is determined never to rest on the laurels of previous successes and therefore careful to avoid ever writing two plays in exactly the same style. That is why he has followed the early absurdist-style *American Dream* with the bold frankness of *The Death of Bessie Smith*, the lacerating Strindbergian tirades of *Who's Afraid of Virginia Woolf?* with the symbolism and poetic imagery of *Tiny Alice*, the gentle eeriness of *A Delicate Balance* with the far-out experimentalism of *Mao-Box-Mao*. With *All Over* Albee seems to have entered the stylistic realm of highly formalised and abstract ritual theatre, somewhere between the classicism of Racine, who portrayed life as a series of lofty emotional climaxes between characters of the utmost abstractness, and German Expressionism which so disdained the vulgarity of individualism that it labelled its characters simply The Man, The Woman, The Seducer and so on. . . .

It is all beautifully—to my taste far too *beautifully*—written but, being a ritual, which means the re-enactment of a primal scene which always takes exactly the same course, utterly predictable. And the abstractness of the characters is such that no suspense and very little emotion seem possible.—MARTIN ESSLIN, *PP*, March 1972, pp. 38–40

Throughout his work, Edward Albee has always been concerned with the failure of love to neutralize the pain of an existence which he thinks finally absurd if not redeemed by the integrity of human values. He has constantly flirted with apocalypse and has revealed a puritan conviction that the path to redemption lies through suffering. But he has repeatedly drawn back from the brink, sustained by a vision of liberal concern, by a conviction that it remains possible for individuals and, perhaps, nations, to be shocked into an awareness of the true nature of their situation and thus of the paramount need for compassion and, in the last resort, love, however imperfect that love may be.

With *Box* and *Quotations from Chairman Mao Tse-Tung*, that conviction seemed more attenuated and shrill. In his more recent play it genuinely seems *All Over*. For the basic process of human life appears to be structured on a slow withdrawal from the Other; a gradual plunge into the Self which must eventually result in spiritual collapse. Love itself seems nothing more than an expression of self-concern. As The Wife remarks, in what seems to be an accurate observation of the motives of those who surround her, "Selfless love? I don't think so; we love to *be* loved. . . . All we've *done* is think about ourselves. Ultimately." This is as long a step from the self-sacrificing love of Jerry, in *The Zoo Story*, as the essentially static quality of his recent plays is from the exuberant action of his early work. The play ends, significantly, too significantly, with the words, "All over."

The tone in his recent plays is, then, no longer that of a confident liberalism rehearsing the great verities of the nineteenth century—personal and public responsibility. . . . The tone now is elegiac. The rhythm is no longer the vibrant crescendo and diminuendo of *Who's Afraid of Virginia Woolf?* and *Tiny Alice*. It is the slow, measured, and finally faltering

pulse beat of *Box* and *Quotations from Chairman Mao Tse-Tung*.

Yet, Albee's concern in *All Over* is essentially that of his earlier work. He remains intent on penetrating the bland urbanities of social life in an attempt to identify the crucial failure of nerve which has brought individual men and whole societies to the point not merely of soulless anomie but even of apocalypse. . . . In *All Over* Albee pursues . . . flight from reality to its source in personal betrayal, to a flaw in human character which must be faced if it is to be understood and remedied. . . .

But here, once again, is ample evidence that Albee is not an absurdist. The absurdity which he identifies is a wilful product of man, not the casual gift of an indifferent universe. He peoples his plays, not with the cosmic victims of Samuel Beckett, but with the self-created victims of modern society. The irony of Beckett's plays lies in the failure of his characters to recognize that things cannot be other than they are; the irony of Albee's plays lies in the failure of his characters to realize that things can be other than they are. At the same time this does not make him a confident social critic with a political blueprint for a future society. It is simply that he asserts a potential for action and concedes the existence of human values in a way which would be alien to the absurdist. The values that he endorses are essentially liberal ones, but this is a liberalism fully aware of the human and social realities which have made the absurdist vision such a compelling feature of the post-war world. For, of course, a writer whose solution to a contemporary sense of anomie is love, risks a potentially disabling sentimentality. Although he is not guilty of the confusion between Eros and Agape—which distorts and all too often trivializes a similar theme in the work of Tennessee Williams and James Baldwin—in placing the weight of his liberal commitment squarely on man's potential for selfless compassion he is in danger of simplifying human nature and falsifying the history of personal and social relations. It is his considerable achievement that for the most part he successfully avoids the trap. If he calls for a renewal of human contact and a resolute acceptance of the real world, he is prepared to concede the tenuous nature of his solution and the increasingly desperate nature of personal and social reality. The liberal values which he embraces are indeed associated in *All Over* with a generation approaching death. The point is clear. Modern society has replaced human relationships with pragmatic alliances, and the values which used to sustain the social structure are at risk. The society which he pictures is flirting with its own extinction, as one character suggests that condemned prisoners wish to embrace their executioner.

The difficulty of such an assumption, however, is that it implies a romantic nostalgia for an unexamined past. Throughout his work Albee has made appeals to the values of a former age, through the person of Grandma in *The American Dream* and *The Sandbox*, George the historian, in *Who's Afraid of Virginia Woolf?*, and the aging Tobias in *A Delicate Balance*, without ever questioning the reality of those values or their historical force. The immediate future, on the other hand, is represented by a series of caricatures. The Young Man in *The American Dream* and *The Sandbox*, Nick in *Who's Afraid of Virginia Woolf?*, Claire in *A Delicate Balance*, and The Son in *All Over* are all vacuous, impotent, sterile, or sexually incomplete. It is a terminal generation with no apparent understanding of vital human needs. . . .

The real problem of *All Over* is that Albee seems . . . to succumb to a basic conviction of American theatre, namely that seriousness and pretentiousness are in some way necessarily allied. To all intents and purposes *All Over* is Albee's version of Arthur Miller's *After the Fall*. There is the same concern with human failure and betrayal, the same anguished fascination with the slow decay of love which mirrors the physical slide towards the grave. His characters speak the same pseudopoetic prose, creating a ceremony of death which is part expiation and part celebration. There is also, alas, the same sacrifice of language and theatrical truth to a deeply felt personal anguish, so that the result is a play which paradoxically fails to create anything more compelling than imitation baroque—verbal arabesques, and emotional arpeggios rooted in no recognizable human sensibility. The play is not realistic. Albee's drawing rooms, like Pinter's, are charged with metaphysics; they glow with significance. Sometimes, as in Albee's *Who's Afraid of Virginia Woolf?* or Pinter's *The Birthday Party*, realism and symbolism blend into powerful metaphor; sometimes, as in *All Over* or *Old Times*, the metaphor crushes the characters until one admires tone, tempo, rhythm, register, imagery, everything but human relevance. And that price is especially great in Albee's work where he is intent on urging precisely the need for such relevance. Albee seems to have placed himself in the paradoxical position of stressing the need for a revival of liberal values in a play with no recognizable human beings. An expressionistic satire such as *The American Dream* can bear such an approach, though even here Grandma's subversive vitality is a crucial element in emphasizing the survival of non-utilitarian standards. In *All Over* the paradox is potentially destructive. Albee has come more and more to resemble T. S. Eliot in creating didactic ceremonies, cerebral puppet shows manipulated with an impressive economy of energy, but dangerously lacking in the kind of compelling humanity and subtle theatricality which makes Beckett's work, for example, so much more than an intellectual valedictory.—C. W. E. BIGSBY, "To the Brink of the Grave: Edward Albee's *All Over*," *Edward Albee: A Collection of Critical Essays*, 1975, pp. 168–74

SEASCAPE

In . . . *Seascape* Edward Albee seems drained of almost all vitality—theatrical, intellectual, artistic. And vitality was always Albee's bottom line, the one quality that even his detractors admitted he possessed. In the early plays, that vitality was startling, disturbing, explosive, part of a youthful artistic personality that, despite streaks of callowness and derivativeness, expressed the lethal tensions of the American '60s. But after the tremendous impact of *Who's Afraid of Virginia Woolf?* a disastrous thing happened to Albee—he began to think, or rather he assigned his mind to take over on scouting duty, leaving his feeling to clop along in the rear. The prospects for this revamped task force were not good, and sure enough it has wound up lost in the desert. . . .

. . . Albee's last two plays, *All Over* and now *Seascape*, break down as his shallow but relentless "thinking" undermines his weakening emotional and poetic energy. The tipoff is right at the heart of things—language. The serrated edges of his speech are filed down as Albee experiments with a texture of indirection, notably in *Box-Mao-Box* with the character called, significantly, the Long-Winded Lady. But in *Seascape* that long-windedness has become a constipated language that moves in colonic spasms. Aiming for a Jamesian effect that will achieve great tension by suspending the finality of utterance, Albee achieves only the ultimate in pure nagging.—JACK KROLL, "Leapin' Lizards," *Nwk*, Feb. 10, 1975, p. 75

Edward Albee's *Seascape* is the kind of play that can be loved only by God and Clive Barnes, at least one of whom doesn't exist. . . .

This simpleminded allegory can be interpreted in a dozen convenient, wishy-washy ways, the "lizards" standing for underprivileged minorities, upward mobility, *élan vital*, the instinctual, or whatever; the human beings for the bourgeoisie, the declining West, the Establishment, the victims of the superego, or whatnot. Or any other vague antinomies that must be reconciled so that some great, original philosophic maxim like "Life must go on" or "Life is a continual evolutionary process" might be derived from this splendiferous parable. Banal as all this is, a real artist might have breathed life into it; Albee endows it only with doughy verbiage, feebly quivering inaction, and grandly gesticulating pretentiousness. There is a canard abroad, originated by Albee himself, that an Albee play has linguistic distinction. It has, to be sure, a style more literary than that of a play by Murray Schisgal or Neil Simon, but so has a sophomore term paper about William Faulkner. Here are some *Seascape* samples: "Continue the temporary and it becomes forever." "We've earned a little life, if you ask me—ASK ME!!!" "They don't look very formidable in the sense of prepossessing." "Nice, isn't it, when the real and the figurative come together?" "Sex goes, it diminishes—well, it becomes a holiday. Not like eating or sleeping; but that's nice, too—that it becomes a holiday." Notice what sorry stratagems are at work in these, for Albee, better-than-average lines. *Figurative* is, inappropriately, dragged in for *imagined* or *wished-for*; *formidable* is, inappositely, hauled out instead of *striking* or *impressive*. And so a platitude or triviality is supposedly ennobled by recourse to solecism. Epigrams like Albee's can be made with a cookie mold: "Continue the singular and it becomes the plural." "Continue not to conform and it becomes conformity." Continue piling up lines and it becomes a play. Ah, but you see, Simon and Schisgal would never use the word *figurative*, even thus incorrectly. This is the *je ne sais quoi* that makes Albee literature.

. . . It is hard enough to strike a spark by rubbing two sticks together, but Albee's dramaturgy has, for years now, been trying to do it with one. Yes, *The Zoo Story* and *Virginia Woolf* were plays; but how long will reviewers and audiences forgive such gaffes as *Tiny Alice*, *The Ballad of the Sad Café*, *Malcolm*, *Everything in the Garden*, *A Delicate Balance*, *Box-Mao-Box*, *All Over*, and now *Seascape*, this piece of flotsam washed ashore near Albee's Montauk home? To go on tolerating, however minimally, this proliferation of pratfalls is not to strike a blow for Albee so much as to strike a blow against euthanasia. Such incurable playwriting should have been put out of its misery sooner, while it still preserved a shred of dignity. But, I dare say, Albee is a playwright of ideas for people who have never had an idea.—JOHN SIMON, "Evolution Made Queasy," *NYM*, Feb. 10, 1975, p. 55

THE LADY FROM DUBUQUE

Whenever I review a play by Edward Albee, I worry about the distribution of his royalties. He has such a perfect gift for theatrical mimicry that I begin to imagine August Strindberg, Eugene O'Neill, and T. S. Eliot rising from their graves to demand for their estates a proper share of *Who's Afraid of Virginia Woolf*, *Tiny Alice*, and *A Delicate Balance*. Even living authors like Samuel Beckett, Eugene Ionesco, and Harold Pinter might be contemplating a case against Albee, not so much for expropriating their plots and characters as for borrowing their styles. In his latest play, *The Lady from Dubuque*, the playwright has gone to an unusual source—namely himself. I can see a lawsuit coming—Albee v. Albee—where the younger accuses the older writer of plagiarism, perhaps even alienation of affection and breach of promise.

Albee certainly has breached his promise in his last 11 plays, not excepting *The Lady from Dubuque*. It is really quite an awful piece, drenched with those portentous religious-philosophical discharges about death and truth and illusion that have been swamping his work ever since he got the preposterous idea in his head that he was some kind of (prematurely ancient) prophet and metaphysician of our disorders. I felt acutely embarrassed for actors charged with saying things like "Everything is true . . . therefore nothing is true . . . therefore everything is true." If *that* is true, then they ought to stop talking altogether. Unfortunately, they don't. And the characters they are given to play are not much improvement on their dialogue. . . .

Still, Albee faking Albee is better than Albee faking Eliot, if you're measuring degrees of fakery. I found enough faint echoes of the old ripper in the play to keep my eyelids from closing—as they did (before the dying hero's) in *All Over*, and Albee's other boring discourses on mortality. Every so often, a little wave of energy courses through the dead electrical circuits of the work, as when a character says, "My cup runneth over," and another replies, "Right, but watch the rug." A little more of this stuff, and I might have snapped awake entirely, but Albee's heart is no more in the bickering of his couples than in the suffering of his heroine. Perhaps the ghastly reception and quick closing of this play will get him angry enough to give up the metaphysical gush and get back to his proper work—cutting the jugulars of his unfortunate American contemporaries.—Robert Brustein, "Self-Parody and Self-Murder," *NR*, March 3, 1980, p. 26

In *All Over*, Edward Albee wrote about a man dying offstage; in *The Lady from Dubuque*, he writes about a woman dying more or less onstage. Otherwise, there is not much difference: *All Over* was the worst play about dying until Michael Cristofer's *The Shadow Box*; *The Lady from Dubuque* is the worst play about dying since *The Shadow Box*. It is also one of the worst plays about anything, ever.

 . . . *The Lady from Dubuque* is a lot of desperate pretensions and last-ditch attitudinizing about nothing, borrowed for the most part from previous Albee catastrophes. Let me enumerate the strategies for stretching out nothing into two acts. (1) Repetition. Roughly one fourth of the dialogue is multiple repeats, e.g.: "I suppose you should know." "I suppose I should know." "I suppose you should." Second billing, after the Bar, should go to the Echo. (2) Asides. After a character has spoken to another, he will repeat the same point to the audience, thus: "I like your friends. *(To audience)* I like his friends." About one thirteenth of the play is redundant asides. (3) Not answering simple questions. This, drawn out beyond endurance, supposedly creates suspense. (4) Irrelevant but grandiose political or metaphysical mouthings. So Marx and Engels are trotted out repeatedly, or America is told: "We're too moral [or "immoral"—it hardly matters] to survive; a real Nixon will come along someday if the Russians don't." If Albee has read even one chapter of *Das Kapital*, I'll eat the others. (5) Obscenity. When all else fails, bring on the four-letter words. Albee, apparently, takes this to be still daring; but, then, he is always a couple of decades behind. Which leads to (6) *Ex post facto* liberalism. Oscar revels in ironies at the expense of racism as if they were boldly new; they have been heard on Broadway (and elsewhere) for 30 or 40 years. (7) Running gags that, though unfunny, keep running; thus variations on "No offense!" "None taken!" pop up a half dozen times. (8) Mystification. Is Elizabeth Jo's mother, or are she and Oscar angels of death? Obviously Albee himself doesn't know; he has publicly stated that they are not, yet how else—

except perhaps as master burglars—could they get past the locks of an expensive Manhattan apartment? But mystification obviates the need for characterization, which is beyond Albee. Besides, as we are told in one of the deepest lines, "Everything is true—therefore, nothing is true." Still, I'll tell you; Elizabeth is really Tinier Alice (as Albee says about Jo, and perhaps about himself, "Each moment she becomes less and less"), and Oscar is really Wilde through a glass, darkly.

One last point. Albee is sometimes described—most often by himself—as a word-wizard, a stylist. No. He shares his characters' subliteracy. In the play, we hear such offenses against grammar as "tear up a few mutual tufts" and "we need a circus to bounce it all off of." In a recent *Times* interview, Albee said, "exchanged mutual hostages" and "to keep everybody's mind off of Jo's dying."—John Simon, "From Hunger, Not Dubuque," *NYM*, Feb. 11, 1980, pp. 74–76

LOLITA

Evaluating Edward Albee's *Lolita* solely on the basis of injustices done to the Nabokov novel is a disservice to the play; such evaluation misses Albee's larger, more theatrical intent. The drama at best uses the novel as a departure point, adopts its narrative framework, exploits certain of its verbal and visual images. Albee unsuccessfully attempts something more ambitious than mere adaptation: his departures from the novel are calculated to facilitate his own theatrical and spiritual sensibility. Comparing the play and the novel makes such a sensibility manifestly clear. The Nabokov book should be examined to illuminate Albee's work; it should not be used as a sacrosanct standard by which to judge the quality of an adaptation. . . .

The picaresque structure of the Nabokov novel carries us more and more deeply into the unique psychological world of Humbert, while using Humbert's passions to stand for larger, more universal human passions and obsessions. Puritanism tempers the pedophilic, moral rigor matches prurience, a black grimness of humor and purpose balances a surprising frailty. Such combinations account for much of the novel's power. . . . These alliances of light and dark, of universal and idiosyncratic are the crucial determinants of Humbert's character, yet these alliances are severed in Albee's adaptation.

Albee's Author embodies the moral force, the restrainer who must confound Humbert. When sensual encounters border on the graphic, the Author drops a large curtain and obscures the lovemaking, he encourages Clare Quilty's attempts to lure Lolita from Humbert; he even calls a halt to Humbert's call for pedophiliacs in the audience and curtails the graphic description of seduction. Humbert willingly relinquishes such moral restraint but thereby loses any sensitivity, sense of love, or moral presence that could deepen and enrich the character. Albee confines Humbert's obsessive passions to the sexual, and reduces his love to mere pedophilic lust.

This bifurcation of Nabokov's Humbert maims any growing moral tension. The Author and Humbert enjoy a congenial relationship. They treat Humbert's love as amusing, inevitable, perhaps even as logical, but never as obsessive or alarming; Freudian vaudeville replaces passion. Even the normally stern Author allows himself to slide into sleaze after the seduction of Lolita. . . . Albee's *Lolita* is sterile, passionless, and his protagonist is a satyr, not a sufferer.

But perhaps Albee's *Lolita* is not supposed to be about passions at all. Indeed, adapting *Lolita* for the stage has incurred a host of new problems that alone may account for such a switch in focus. In the novel, Lolita is never seen except through Humbert's eyes. Even in her most difficult moments, his epithets of passion bathe her in a beatific glow, incarnate her as a divine "nymphet"; she never vanishes from our minds. This technique of perpetual presence and its importance to the themes of obsession are more difficult, though not impossible, to achieve onstage; indeed, Lolita's stage appearances undermine our response to Humbert's passion. Embodied by an actress, Lolita attains precisely the independence of persona that Nabokov denies her. Humbert's paeans to sensuality are contradicted by the corporeal presence of a gangly, foul-mouthed girl with jutting elbows and knocking knees. Her every move strains any belief in Humbert's "light of my life, fire of my loins," and when she exits, she vanishes—totally. A tension is automatically established between Humbert's possessed perceptions of Lolita and the audience's more objective, detached ones. The commonplace Lolita cannot match the ethereal one Humbert describes; her pretensions to any eroticism beyond mere carnality become solely inventions of Humbert's. And because he is reduced to a one-dimensional, amoral omnivore, she cannot really affect him by provoking any inner conflict or confusion; she can only satisfy his sexual appetite. From god-life *figura*, she has descended to mere creation.

This concern with creator and creation dominates Albee's play. A superstructure has been imposed on the novel, one that emphasizes the Author as *figura* as the Humbert-Author relationship supersedes the Humbert-Lolita one. In the play, Albee creates a surrogate presence, A Certain Gentleman. This second Author in turn creates Humbert, who in turn creates Lolita. . . . Such a structure holds fascinating potential on various moral, social, psychological, even theological planes.

But Albee does not carry this structure beyond its inception; there is no consistent development of ideas. . . . ⟨Nothing⟩ that Albee accomplishes in *Lolita* suggests any fascination, indeed any involvement, with his characters or with this new emphasis on the created and the creator. Deprived of passions and true feelings, his characters can reveal nothing about love; stripped of moral dimension, the play can neither indict nor condone social mores; tentative in its understanding of the connection between art and artist, the play cannot manipulate the distance between audience and actor or between author and play. *Lolita* does not have to be about Humbert's passion for Lolita, but neither can it be a work totally devoid of passion. The dramatic Author(s), in denying any passionate involvement with their creations, undercut the ultimate source of literary life and energy. Albee's *Lolita* is born of inertia, tedium, and it frequently discloses its parentage. This passionless center only emphasizes Albee's own lack of vital connection with the theater and compounds the problems of adaptation.

For *Lolita* traps as well as inspires Albee. The idea of adaptation frees Albee for his new focus; in dealing with situations and themes already created, he can more fully manipulate certain distances and structures. But Albee never demonstrates a need for using *Lolita* as his source; hundreds of other novels could have served his purposes just as easily. Nabokov's plot, a reaction to social attitudes of the 1950's, cannot meet certain demands of the 1980's, especially when forced into the present and stripped of its passionate underpinnings. Albee nonetheless tries to update the novel by merely adding four-letter words, stale jokes about the Shah, and lame references to early morning television. Such vulgarizations cannot move *Lolita* into the present. Indeed, this additional profanity clearly violates Nabokov's sense of propriety and stunning verbal economy, while highlighting Albee's verbal flabbiness. "Is this a lecture?" the Author asks. "An

exegesis. The briefest of exegeses." Humbert replies. Such hair-splitting demonstrates the turgid, untheatrical nature of the text.—BEN CAMERON, "Who's Afraid of Vladimir Nabokov?: Edward Albee's *Lolita*," *Theater*, Summer 1981, pp. 77–79

GERALD WEALES
"Edward Albee: Don't Make Waves"
The Jumping-Off Place: American Drama in the 1960's
1969, pp. 24–53

Edward Albee is inescapably *the* American playwright of the 1960's. His first play, *The Zoo Story*, opened in New York, on a double bill with Samuel Beckett's *Krapp's Last Tape*, at the Provincetown Playhouse on January 14, 1960. In his Introduction to *Three Plays* (1960), Albee tells how his play, which was written in 1958, passed from friend to friend, from country to country, from manuscript to tape to production (in Berlin in 1959) before it made its way back to the United States. "It's one of those things a person has to do," says Jerry; "sometimes a person has to go a very long distance out of his way to come back a short distance correctly."

For Albee, once *The Zoo Story* had finished its peregrinations, the trip uptown—psychologically and geographically—was a short one. During 1960, there were two other Albee productions, largely unheralded—*The Sandbox*, which has since become a favorite for amateurs, and *Fam and Yam*, a *bluette*, a joke growing out of his having been ticketed as the latest white hope of the American theater. These were essentially fugitive productions of occasional pieces. In 1961, one of the producers of *The Zoo Story*, Richard Barr, joined by Clinton Wilder in the producing organization that is always called Theater 196? after whatever the year, offered *The American Dream*, first on a double bill with William Flanagan's opera *Bartleby*, for which Albee and James Hinton, Jr., did the libretto, and later, when the opera proved unsuccessful, with an earlier Albee play *The Death of Bessie Smith*. During the next few years, there were frequent revivals of both *Zoo* and *Dream*, often to help out a sagging Barr-Wilder program, as in 1964 (by which time Albee had become a coproducer) when first *Dream* and later *Zoo* were sent in as companion pieces to LeRoi Jones's *Dutchman*, after Samuel Beckett's *Play* and Fernando Arrabal's *The Two Executioners*, which opened with Jones's play, were removed from the bill. Albee had become an off-Broadway staple.

By that time, of course, Albee had become something else as well. With *Who's Afraid of Virginia Woolf?* (1962), he had moved to Broadway and had a smashing commercial success. By a process of escalation, he had passed from promising to established playwright. After *Woolf*, Albee productions averaged one a year: *The Ballad of the Sad Café* (1963), *Tiny Alice* (1964), *Malcolm* (1966), *A Delicate Balance* (1966) and *Everything in the Garden* (1967). None of these were successes in Broadway terms (by *Variety's* chart of hits and flops), but except for *Malcolm*, a gauche and imperceptive adaptation of James Purdy's novel of that name, which closed after seven performances, all of them had respectable runs and generated their share of admiration and antagonism from critics and public alike.

Although favorable reviews helped make the Albee reputation, critics have consistently praised with one hand, damned with the other. If Harold Clurman's "Albee on Balance" (*The New York Times*, January 13, 1967), treats Albee as a serious playwright and if Robert Brustein's "A Third Theater"

(*The New York Times Magazine*, September 25, 1966) seems to dismiss him as a solemn one, only Broadway serious, the recent collections of their reviews—Clurman's *The Naked Image* and Brustein's *Seasons of Discontent*—indicate that both critics have had the same kind of reservations about Albee from the beginning. Albee, contrariwise, has had reservations of his own. From his pettish Introduction to *The American Dream* to the press conference he called to chastise the critics for their reactions to *Tiny Alice*, he has regularly used interviews and the occasional nondramatic pieces he has written to suggest that the critics lack understanding, humility, responsibility.

In spite of (perhaps because of) the continuing quarrel between Albee and his critics—a love-hate relationship in the best Albee tradition—the playwright's reputation has grown tremendously. It was in part the notoriety of *Who's Afraid of Virginia Woolf?* that turned Albee into a popular figure, and certainly the publicity surrounding the making of the movie version of *Woolf* helped to keep Albee's name in the popular magazines. Whatever the cause, Albee is now the American playwright whose name has become a touchstone, however ludicrously it is used. Thus, Thomas Meehan, writing an article on "camp" for *The New York Times Magazine* (March 21, 1965), solicits Andy Warhol's opinion of *Tiny Alice* ("I liked it because it was so empty"), and William H. Honan, interviewing Jonathan Miller for the same publication (January 22, 1967), manages to get Miller to repeat a commonplace criticism of Albee he has used twice before. . . .

"I consider myself in a way the most eclectic playwright who ever wrote," Albee once told an interviewer (*Transatlantic Review*, Spring, 1963), and then he went on to make an elaborate joke about how he agreed with the critics that twenty-six playwrights—three of whom he had never read—had influenced him. Critics do have a way of getting influence-happy when they write about Albee—particularly Brustein, who persists in calling him an imitator—but they have good reason. There are such strong surface dissimilarities among the Albee plays that is easier and in some ways more rewarding to think of *The Zoo Story* in relation to Samuel Beckett and Harold Pinter and *A Delicate Balance* in terms of T. S. Eliot and Enid Bagnold than it is to compare the two plays, even though both start from the same dramatic situation: the invasion (by Jerry, by Harry and Edna) of private territory (Peter's bench, Tobias's house). Yet, the comparison is obvious once it is made. Each new Albee play seems to be an experiment in form, in style (even if it is someone else's style), and yet there is unity in his work as a whole. This is apparent in the devices and the characters that recur, modified according to context, but it is most obvious in the repetition of theme, in the basic assumptions about the human condition that underlie all his work.

In *A Delicate Balance*, Tobias and his family live in a mansion in the suburbs of hell, that existential present so dear to contemporary writers, in which life is measured in terms of loss, love by its failure, contact by its absence. In that hell, there are many mansions—one of which is Peter's bench—and all of them are cages in the great zoo story of life. Peter's bench is a kind of sanctuary, both a refuge from and an extension of the stereotypical upper-middle-class existence (tweeds, horn-rimmed glasses, job in publishing, well-furnished apartment, wife, daughters, cats, parakeets) with which Albee has provided him—a place where he can safely not-live and have his nonbeing. This is the way Jerry sees Peter, at least, and—since the type is conventional enough in contemporary theater, from avant-garde satire to Broadway revue—it is safe to assume that the play does, too. Although Albee intends a little satirical fun at Peter's expense (the early needling scenes are very success-

ful), it is clear that the stereotyping of Peter is an image of his condition, not a cause of it. Jerry, who plays "the old pigeonhole bit" so well, is another, a contrasting cliché, and it is the play's business to show that he and Peter differ only in that he does not share Peter's complacency. Just before Jerry attacks in earnest, he presents the play's chief metaphor:

> I went to the zoo to find out more about the way people exist with animals, and the way animals exist with each other, and with people too. It probably wasn't a fair test, what with everyone separated by bars from everyone else, the animals for the most part from each other, and always the people from the animals. But, if it's a zoo, that's the way it is.

"Private wings," says Malcolm in the play that bears his name. "Indeed, that *is* an extension of separate rooms, is it not?" In a further extension of a joke that is no joke, Agnes, in *A Delicate Balance*, speaks of her "poor parents, in their separate heavens." *Separateness* is the operative word for Albee characters, for, even though his zoo provides suites for two people (*Who's Afraid of Virginia Woolf?*) or for more (*A Delicate Balance*), they are furnished with separate cages. "It's sad to know you've gone through it all, or most of it, without . . . " says Edna in one of the fragmented speeches that characterize *A Delicate Balance*, as though thoughts too were separate, "that the one body you've wrapped your arms around . . . the only skin you've ever known . . . is your own—and that it's dry . . . and not warm." This is a more restrained, a more resigned variation on the Nurse's desperate cry in *Bessie Smith*, " . . . I am tired of my skin. . . . I WANT OUT!"

Violence is one of the ways of trying to get out. The Nurse is an illustration of this possibility; she is an embryonic version of Martha in *Virginia Woolf*, with most of the venom, a little of the style, and practically none of the compensating softness of the later character, and she hits out at everyone around her. Yet, she never escapes herself, her cage. The other possibility is love (that, too, a form of penetration), but the Albee plays are full of characters who cannot (Nick in *Virginia Woolf*) or will not (Tobias, the Nurse) make that connection. The persistent images are of withdrawal, the most graphic being the one in *A Delicate Balance*, the information that Tobias in fact withdrew and came on Agnes's belly the last time they had sex. Although failed sex is a convenient metaphor for the failure of love, its opposite will not work so well. Connection is not necessarily contact, and it is contact—or rather its absence, those bars that bother Jerry—that preoccupies Albee. He lets Martha and George make fun of the lack-of-communication cliché in *Virginia Woolf*, but it is that cultural commonplace on which much of Albee's work is built. Jerry's story about his landlady's vicious dog—although he over-explains it—is still Albee's most effective account of an attempt to get through those bars, out of that skin (so effective, in fact, that Tobias uses a variation of it in *Balance* when he tells about his cat). Accepting the dog's attacks on him as a form of recognition, Jerry tries first to win his affection (with hamburger) and, failing that, to kill him (with poisoned hamburger: it is difficult to differentiate between the tools of love and hate). In the end, he settles for an accommodation, one in which he and the dog ignore each other. His leg remains unbitten, but he feels a sense of loss in the working arrangement: "We neither love nor hurt because we do not try to reach each other."

Give me *any* person . . . " says Lawyer in *Tiny Alice*. "He'll take what he gets for . . . what he wishes it to be. AH, it is what I have always wanted, he'll say, looking terror and betrayal straight in the eye. Why not: face the inevitable and call it what you have always wanted." The context is a special one here, a reference to Julian's impending martyrdom to God-Alice, who comes to him in the form or forms he expects. I purposely dropped from the Lawyer's speech the references to "martyr" and "saint" which follow parenthetically after the opening phrase, for as it stands above, the speech might serve as advertising copy for the Albee world in which his characters exist and—very occasionally—struggle. The too-obvious symbol of *The American Dream*, the muscle-flexing young man who is only a shell, empty of love or feeling, is, in Mommy's words, "a great deal more like it." *Like it*, but not *it*. Appearance is what she wants, for reality, as Grandma's account of the mutilation of the other "bumble" indicates, is dangerous.

The American Dream is a pat example of, to use Lawyer's words again, "How to come out on top, going under." Whether the accommodation is embraced (*Dream*) or accepted with a sense of loss (Jerry and the dog), it is always there, a way of coping instead of a way of life. It can be disguised in verbal trappings—comic (the games of *Virginia Woolf*) or serious (the religiosity of *Tiny Alice*, the conventional labels of *A Delicate Balance*). In the absence of substance, it can be given busy work; Girard Girard spells everything out in *Malcolm*: "You will move from the mansion to the chateau, and from the chateau back. You will surround yourself with your young beauties, and hide your liquor where you will. You will . . . go on, my dear." The unhidden liquor in *A Delicate Balance* (even more in *Virginia Woolf*, where it serves the dramatic action, as lubricant and as occasional rest) provides an example of such busyness: all the playing at bartending, the weighty deliberation over whether to have anisette or cognac, the concern over the quality of a martini. The rush of words (abuse or elegance) and the press of activity (however meaningless) sustain the Albee characters in a tenuous relationship (a delicate balance) among themselves and in the face of the others, the ones outside, and—beyond that—the nameless terror.

There is nothing unusual about ⟨Albee's⟩ slightly unstable mixture of philosophic assumption and social criticism; it can be found in the work of Tennessee Williams and, from quite a different perspective, that of Eugène Ionesco. The differentiation is useful primarily because it provides us with insight into the shape that Albee gives his material. If the lost and lonely Albee character is an irrevocable fact—philosophically, theologically, psychologically—if all that *angst* is inescapable, then his plays must necessarily be reflections of that condition; any gestures of defiance are doomed to failure. If, however, the Albee character is a product of his societal context and if that context is changeable (not necessarily politically, but by an alteration of modes of behavior between one man and another), then the plays may be instructive fables. He has dismissed American drama of the 1930's as propaganda rather than art, and he has disavowed solutions to anything. Still, in several statements he has suggested that there are solutions—or, at least, alternatives. Surely that possibility is implicit in his description of *The American Dream* as an "attack." In the *Transatlantic Review* interview, he said that "the responsibility of the writer is to be a sort of demonic social critic—to present the world and people in it as he sees it and say 'Do you like it? If you don't like it change it.'" In the *Atlantic*, he said, "I've always thought . . . that it was one of the responsibilities of playwrights to show people how they are and what their time is like in the hope that perhaps they'll change it."

Albee, then, shares with most American playwrights an idea of the utility of art, the supposition not only that art should convey truth, but that it should do so to some purpose. There is

a strong strain of didacticism in all his work, but it is balanced by a certain ambiguity about the nature of the instructive fable. In interviews, he harps on how much of the creative process is subconscious, how little he understands his own work, how a play is to be experienced rather than understood. Insofar as this is not sour grapes pressed to make an aesthetic (his reaction to the reviews of *Tiny Alice*), it may be his way of recognizing that there is a conflict between his attitude toward man's situation and his suspicion (or hope: certainly *conviction* is too strong a word) that something can, or ought, to be done about it; between his assumption that this is hell we live in and his longing to redecorate it.

Whatever the nature of the chasm on the edge of which the Albee characters teeter so dexterously, to disturb the balance is to invite disaster or—possibly—salvation. If the conflict that I suggest above is a real one, it should be reflected in the plays in which one or more characters are willing to risk disaster. *The American Dream* and *The Sandbox* can be passed over here because, except for the sentimental death of Grandma at the end of the latter, they are diagnostic portraits of the Albee world, not actions performed in that setting. *The Death of Bessie Smith* and *The Ballad of the Sad Café* are more to the point, but they are also special cases. Although risks are taken (the Intern goes outside to examine Bessie; Amelia takes in Cousin Lymon in *Ballad*), the plays are less concerned with these acts than they are with the kind of expositional presentation—not particularly satirical in this case—that we get in *Dream*. Even so, the Intern's risk is meaningless since the woman is already dead; and Amelia's love is necessarily doomed by the doctrine the McCullers novella expounds—that it is difficult to love but almost impossible to be loved—and by the retrospective form the play took when Albee saddled it with a maudlin message-giving narrator. *Tiny Alice* and *Malcolm* are two of a kind, particularly if we consider them as corruption-of-innocence plays, although there is also a similarity of sorts between Malcolm's attempt to put a face on his absent father and Julian's attempt to keep from putting a face on his abstracted Father. They are even similar in that Albee, sharing a popular-comedy misconception about what that snake was up to in the Garden, uses sex as his sign of corruption—ludicrously in *Alice*, snickeringly in *Malcolm*. Traditionally, one of two things happens in plays in which the innocent face the world: either they become corrupted and learn to live with it (the standard Broadway maturity play) or they die young and escape the corruption (Synge's *Deirdre of the Sorrows* or Maxwell Anderson's *Winterset*). In the Albee plays, both things happen. Julian dies after accepting the world (edited to fit his preconceptions about it) and Malcolm dies, muttering "I've . . . lost so much," and loss, as the plays from *The Zoo Story* to *A Delicate Balance* insist, is what you gain in learning to live with it. There are extenuating circumstances for the deaths in these plays (Julian's concept of God is tied in with his desire to be a martyr; Malcolm's death is borrowed from Purdy, although Albee does not seem to understand what Purdy was doing with it in the novel), but these plays, too, are illustrations of the Albee world, and the deaths are more sentimental than central. *Everything in the Garden* is such an unlikely wedding of Albee and the late Giles Cooper, whose English play was the source of the American adaptation, that it is only superficially characteristic of Albee's work.

It is in *The Zoo Story*, *Who's Afraid of Virginia Woolf?* and *A Delicate Balance* that one finds dramatic actions by which the ambiguity of Albee's attitudes may be tested. . . . ⟨In *The Zoo Story*,⟩ Peter is plainly a man knocked off his balance, but there is no indication that he has fallen into "an awareness of life." In fact, the play we are watching has already been presented in miniature in the dog story, and all Jerry gained from that encounter was "solitary but free passage." "There are some things in it that I don't really understand," Albee told Gelb. One of them may be that the play itself denies the romantic ending.

Virginia Woolf . . . works against the presumably upbeat ending, but Albee may be more aware that this is happening. According to the conventions of Broadway psychology, as reflected, for instance, in a play like William Inge's *The Dark at the Top of the Stairs*, in a moment of crisis two characters come to see themselves clearly. Out of their knowledge a new maturity is born, creating an intimacy that has not existed before and a community that allows them to face their problems (if not solve them) with new courage. This was the prevailing cliché of the serious Broadway play of the 1950's, and it was still viable enough in the 1960's to take over the last act of Lorraine Hansberry's *The Sign in Sidney Brustein's Window* and turn an interesting play into a conventional one. *Virginia Woolf* uses, or is used by, this cliché.

Although the central device of the play is the quarrel between George and Martha, the plot concerns their nonexistent son. From George's "Just don't start on the bit, that's all," before Nick and Honey enter, the play builds through hints, warnings, revelations until sonny-Jim is created and then destroyed. Snap, goes the illusion. Out of the ruins, presumably, new strength comes. The last section, which is to be played "very softly, very slowly," finds George offering new tenderness to Martha, assuring her that the time had come for the fantasy to die, forcing her—no longer maliciously—to admit that she is afraid of Virginia Woolf. It is "Time for bed," and there is nothing left for them to do but go together to face the dark at the top of the stairs. As though the rejuvenation were not clear enough from the last scene, there is the confirming testimony in Honey's tearful reiteration "I want a child" and Nick's broken attempt to sympathize, "I'd like to. . . ." Then, too, the last act is called "The Exorcism," a name that had been the working title for the play itself.

As neat as Inge, and yet there is something wrong with it. How can a relationship like that of Martha and George, built so consistently on illusion (the playing of games), be expected to have gained something from a sudden admission of truth? What confirmation is there in Nick and Honey when we remember that she is drunk and hysterical and that he is regularly embarrassed by what he is forced to watch? There are two possibilities beyond the conventional reading suggested above. The last scene between Martha and George may be another one of their games; the death of the child may not be the end of illusion but an indication that the players have to go back to GO and start again their painful trip to home. Although there are many indications that George and Martha live a circular existence, going over the same ground again and again, the development of the plot and the tone of the last scene (the use of monosyllables, for instance, instead of their customary rhetoric) seem to deny that the game is still going on. The other possibility is that the truth—as in *The Iceman Cometh*—brings not freedom but death. To believe otherwise is to accept the truth-maturity cliché as readily as one must buy the violence-life analogy to get the positive ending of *The Zoo Story*. My own suspicion is that everything that feels wrong about the end of *Virginia Woolf* arises from the fact that, like the stabbing in *Zoo*, it is a balance-tipping ending that conventional theater says is positive but the Albee material insists is negative.

In *A Delicate Balance*, the line is clearer. The titular balance is the pattern of aggression and withdrawal, accusation and guilt which Tobias and his family have constructed in order to cope with existence. Agnes suggests that Tobias's "We do what we can" might be "Our motto." When Harry and Edna invade the premises, trying to escape from the nameless fears that have attacked them, they come under the white flag of friendship. Tobias must decide whether or not to let them stay, knowing that the "disease" they carry is contagious and that infection in the household will likely upset the balance. His problem is one in metaphysical semantics, like Julian's in *Tiny Alice*, although *God* is not the word whose meaning troubles him. "Would you give friend Harry the shirt off your back, as they say?" asks Claire, before the invasion. "I *suppose* I would. He *is* my best friend," answers Tobias, and we hear echoes from *The American Dream*: "She's just a dreadful woman, but she *is* chairman of our woman's club, so naturally I'm terribly fond of her." *Dream's* satirical fun about the emptiness of conventional language becomes deadly serious in *Balance*, for Tobias must decide whether the meaning of *friendship* is one with substance or only surface—whether *friendship* is a human relationship implying the possibility of action and risk, or simply a label, like *marriage* or *kinship*, to be fastened to a form of accommodation. As Pearl Bailey sang in *House of Flowers*, "What is a friend for? Should a friend bolt the door?" Tobias (having failed with his cat as Jerry failed with the dog) decides to try doing more than he can; in his long, broken speech in the last act, he displays his fear, indicates that he does not want Harry and Edna around, does not even like them, "BUT BY GOD . . . YOU STAY!!" His attempt fails because Harry and Edna, having decided that they would never risk putting real meaning into *friendship*, depart, leaving a depleted Tobias to rearrange his labels. He will have the help of Agnes, of course, which—on the balance—is a great deal, for she finds the conventional words of goodbye: "well, don't be strangers." Edna, who not many lines before made the "only skin" speech, answers, "Oh, good Lord, how could we be? Our lives are . . . the same." And so they are.

Thematically, *A Delicate Balance* is Albee's most precise statement. The gesture toward change, which seemed to fit so uncomfortably at the end of *The Zoo Story* and *Virginia Woolf*, has been rendered powerless within the action of *Balance*. Not only are Albee's characters doomed to live in the worst of all possible worlds; it is the only possible world. The impulse to do something about it can end only in failure. Yet, Albee cannot leave it at that. He cannot, like Samuel Beckett, let his characters turn their meaninglessness into ritual which has a way, on stage, of reasserting the meaning of the human being. He almost does so in *Virginia Woolf*, but his suspicion that games are not enough—a failure really to recognize that games are a form of truth as much as a form of lying—leads to the doubtful exorcism. Although the *angster* in Albee cannot let Tobias succeed, the latent reformer cannot help but make him heroic in his lost-cause gesture. He becomes an older, wearier, emptier Jerry, with only the unresisting air to throw himself on at the end.

"Better than nothing!" says Clov in *Endgame*. "Is it possible?" Out of the fastness of his wasteland, and against his better judgment, Albee cannot keep from hoping so.

. . . Albee's plays are really about the accommodations forced on man by his condition and his society. It is impossible, however, to get through a discussion of Albee without facing up to what might be called—on the analogy of the fashionable critical term *subtext*—his sub-subject matter. That is the "masochistic-homosexual perfume" that Robert Brustein found hanging so heavily over *The Zoo Story*. It is a perfume of little importance except insofar as it throws the audience off the scent of the play's real quarry. . . .

Albee may be fond of symbols and allusions, echoes and things overheard, but he plainly does not work . . . with dramatic images that come from outside his plays. This does not mean that he is the naturalist he occasionally claims to be, as when he told a *New York Times* interviewer (September 18, 1966) that even *Tiny Alice* was naturalistic. Even in *Virginia Woolf*, which is certainly the most naturalistic of his plays, the situation is basically unrealistic; the drinking party is a revelatory occasion, not a slice of life in a small New England college. For the most part, his characters have neither setting nor profession, and when they are defined by things, the process is either conventionally (Peter's possessions) or unconventionally (the contents of Jerry's room) stereotypical, so obviously so that realism is clearly not intended. Nor do the characters have biographies, at least of the kind one has come to expect from the psychological naturalism of the Broadway stage. *Virginia Woolf*, harping as it does on the parental hang-ups of its two principals, comes closest to that pattern, but it is never very clear in this play how much of the memory is invention, which of the facts are fantasy. If *Virginia Woolf* and *The Zoo Story* are, at most, distant cousins of naturalistic drama, how much more remote are Albee's plainly absurdist plays (*The Sandbox*, *The American Dream*), his "mystery" play with its label-bearing characters (*Tiny Alice*), his drawing-room noncomedy (*A Delicate Balance*).

A close look at Albee's language provides the clearest indication of the nonrealistic character of his plays. *A Delicate Balance* is the most obvious example. The lines are consciously stilted, broken by elaborate parenthesis ("It follows, to my mind, that since I speculate I might, some day, or early evening I think more likely—some autumn dusk—go quite mad") or pulled up short by formal negative endings ("Must she not?"; "is it not?")—devices that call for inflections which stop the natural flow of speech. There are lines that are barely comprehensible ("One does not apologize to those for whom one must?"), which cannot be read without great deliberation. The verbal elaboration has particular point in this play since the language itself becomes a reflection of the artificiality of the characters and the setting, a pattern in which form replaces substance. This can best be seen in the play's most intricate digression. "What I find most astonishing," Agnes begins as the play opens, only to interrupt herself with her fantasy on madness. Her thought meanders through Tobias's practical attempt to get the after-dinner drinks, and we are fifteen speeches into the play, past two reappearances of the "astonish" phrase, before her opening sentence finally comes to an end. Seems to end, really, for the phrase recurs just before the final curtain, as Agnes goes her placidly relentless way—"to fill a silence," as the stage direction says—as though the intrusion of Harry and Edna and Tobias's painful attempt to deal with it were an easily forgotten interruption of the steady flow of nonevent.

In the *Atlantic* interview, explaining why he felt that English actors were needed for *Tiny Alice*, Albee said that he had moved from the "idiomatic" language of *Virginia Woolf* to something more formal. *A Delicate Balance* is a further step in elaboration. Yet, the language of the earlier plays, however idiomatic, is plainly artificial. Albee has used three main verbal devices from the beginning: interruption, repetition, and the set speech, the last of which makes use of the first two. The set speeches are almost formal recitations, as the playwright recognizes in *The Zoo Story* when he lets Jerry give his monologue a title: "THE STORY OF JERRY AND THE DOG!" There are similar speeches in all the plays: Jack's "Hey . . . Bessie"

monologue which is the whole of Scene 3 of *Bessie Smith*; the Young Man's sentimental mutilation speech in *The American Dream*; George's "bergin" story and Martha's "Abandon-ed" speech in *Virginia Woolf*; the narrator's speeches in *Ballad*; Julian's dying soliloquy in *Tiny Alice*; Madame Girard's Entre-Scene monologue in *Malcolm*; Jack's direct address to the audience in *Garden*. Although Albee does not direct the speaker to step into a spotlight—as Tennessee Williams does with comparable speeches in *Sweet Bird of Youth*—he recognizes that these are essentially solo performances even when another character is on stage to gesture or grunt or single-word his way into the uneven but persistent flow of words. Of Tobias's big scene at the end of *Balance*, Albee says "The next is an aria." In *The Zoo Story*, Jerry does not use a simple narration; his story is momentarily stopped for generalizing comments ("It always happens when I try to simplify things; people look up. But that's neither hither nor thither") and marked with repeated words ("The dog is black, all black; all black except . . . ") and phrases ("I'll kill the dog with kindness, and if that doesn't work . . . I'll just kill him"). The word *laughter* punctuates the "bergin" story the way laughter itself presumably broke the cocktail-lounge murmur of the bar in which the boys were drinking.

It is not the long speeches alone that are built of interruption and repetition; that is the pattern of all the dialogue. On almost any page of *Virginia Woolf* you can find examples as obvious as this speech of George's: "Back when I was courting Martha—well, don't know if that's exactly the right word for it—but back when I was courting Martha. . . ." Then comes Martha's "Screw, sweetie!" followed by another attempt from George, more successful this time. "At any rate, back when I was courting Martha," and off he goes into an account which involves their going "into a bar . . . you know, a *bar* . . . a whiskey, beer, and bourbon *bar*. . . ." Sometimes the repetitions become echoes that reach from act to act as when Martha's "snap" speech in Act Two is picked up by George in the snapdragon scene in Act Three. From *The Zoo Story* to *Everything in the Garden*, then, Albee has consciously manipulated language for effect; even when it sounds like real speech—as in *Virginia Woolf*—it is an exercise in idiomatic artificiality.

At their best, these artifices are the chief devices by which Albee presents his dramatic images. Neither naturalist nor allegorist, he works the great middle era where most playwrights operate. He puts an action on stage—an encounter in a park that becomes a suicide-murder, a night-long quarrel that ends in the death of illusion, an invasion that collapses before the defenders can decide whether to surrender or to fight—which presumably has dramatic vitality in its own right and from which a meaning or meanings can emerge. The central situation—the encounter, the relationship implicit in the quarrel, the state of the defenders and the invaders—is defined almost completely in verbal terms. There is business, of course, but it is secondary. Jerry's poking and tickling Peter is only an extension of what he has been doing with words; George's attempt to strangle Martha is a charade not far removed from their word games. When events get more flamboyant—the shooting of Julian, Julia's hysterical scene with the gun—they tend to become ludicrous. The most obvious example in Albee of physical business gone wrong is the wrestling match between Miss Amelia and Marvin Macy in *The Ballad of the Sad Café*; the fact that it is the dramatic climax of the play does not keep it from looking silly on stage. Ordinarily, Albee does not need to ask his characters to *do* very much, for what they *say* is dramatic action. "The old pigeonhole bit?" says Jerry in *The Zoo Story*, and although it is he, not Peter, who does the pigeonholing, the accusation and the mockery in the question is an act of aggression, as good as a shove for throwing Peter off balance.

In the long run, Albee's reputation as a playwright will probably depend less on what he has to say than on the dramatic situations through which he says it. The two Albee plays that seem to have taken the strongest hold on the public imagination (which may be a way of saying they are the two plays I most admire) are *The Zoo Story* and *Virginia Woolf*. The reason is that the meeting between Jerry and Peter and the marriage of George and Martha, for all the nuances in the two relationships, are presented concretely in gesture and line; they take shape on the stage with great clarity. *Tiny Alice*, by contrast, is all amorphousness. It may finally be possible to reduce that play to an intellectual formulation, but the portentousness that hovers over so many lines and so much of the business keeps the characters and the situation from attaining dramatic validity. *The Zoo Story* is more successful as a play, not because its dramatic situation is more realistic, but because it exists on stage—a self-created dramatic fact.

A Delicate Balance is a much stronger play than *Tiny Alice*. As the discussion early in this chapter indicates, it is probably Albee's most perfect combination of theme and action, and its central metaphor—the balance—is important not only to the play but to Albee's work as a whole. Yet, compared to *Virginia Woolf*, it is an incredibly lifeless play. The reason, I think, is that the Martha-George relationship has dramatic substance in a way that the Tobias-Agnes household does not. Too much has been made—particularly by casual reviewers—of the violence, the hate, the anger in the Martha-George marriage. It is just as important that the quarrel be seen in the context of the affection they have for one another and the life—even if it is a long, sad game—which they so obviously share. One of the best inventions in all of Albee is the gun with the parasol in it, for what better way of seeing the relationship of Martha and George than in terms of a murderous weapon that is also a sheltering object; the instrument is a metaphor for the marriage, and its use is a preview of what will happen in the last act.

From the moment the play opens, from Martha's challenge, "What a dump. Hey what's that from?" it is clear that Martha and George play the same games. He may be tired at first, not really in the mood for a session of name-the-movie, or he may be faking indifference because he cannot remember that the "goddamn Bette Davis picture" Martha has in mind is *Beyond the Forest* (1949), but there is companionship in the incipient quarrel that will not disappear as the argument grows more lethal. It can be seen directly in several places. Near the beginning of the play, after a mutual accusation of baldness, they go into a momentary affectionate scene in which his "Hello honey" leads to her request for "a big sloppy kiss." Almost the same phrase, "C'mon . . . give me a kiss," is her compli-

ment for his having been clever enough to introduce the parasol-gun into the game room. Much more important than the grand games to which he gives labels—Humiliate the Host, Get the Guests, Hump the Hostess—are the small games that they play constantly—the play-acting routines, the little-kid bits, the mock-etiquette turns, the verbal games. The whole force of the play depends on their existence as a couple, a relationship made vivid in moments such as the one in Act III when Nick, humiliated at his sexual failure, begins angrily, "I'm nobody's houseboy . . . " and Martha and George shout in unison, "Now!" and then begin to sing, "I'm nobody's houseboy now. . . ." Their closeness is important if we are to recognize that George can be and is cuckolded. This event takes place on stage in Act II when Martha and Nick dance together sensuously and, speaking in time to the music, she tells about George's abortive attempt to be a novelist. It is at this moment that their marriage is violated, that George's anger shows most plainly, that he initiates a game of Get the Guests. "Book dropper! Child mentioner!" accuses George, and we see—perhaps before he does—the connection that forces him to carry "the bit about the kid" to its murderous conclusion. One may come away from *Virginia Woolf* suspicious of the end of the play and its presumed implications but never in doubt about the dramatic force of either characters or situation.

A Delicate Balance provides a marked contrast. We learn a great deal about the antipathy between Agnes and Claire, the sexual life of Agnes and Tobias, the marriage problems of Julia, the nameless fears of Edna and Harry, but the situation is explained more than it is presented. Some of the language is witty, some of it—particularly Agnes' lines—is quietly bitchy, but speeches do not pass from one character to another, carving out a definition of their relationship; lines fall from the mouths of the characters and shatter on the stage at their feet. Thematically, this is fine, since separateness is what Albee wants to depict, and he is ingenious in the way he lets the artificiality of his language contribute to the general sense of empty façade. Unfortunately, the characters are defined only in terms of their separateness, their significance as exemplary lost ones. Not so indeterminate as *Tiny Alice*, *A Delicate Balance* still lacks the kind of concreteness that comes from a dramatic image fully realized on stage. The characters are given a little biography, a few mannerisms, a whisper of depth, but they remain highly articulate stick figures moving through a sequence of nonevents to a foregone conclusion.

Unless Edward Albee is on some unannounced road to Damascus, there is not much doubt about what he will be saying in the plays that lie ahead of him. It is how he chooses to say it that will be important. In the face of his most recent work, in which significance seems to be imposed from the outside instead of meaning rising from within, we have every reason to be afraid, not of, but for *Virginia Woolf*.

WILLIAM ALFRED

1922–

William Alfred was born on August 16, 1922, in New York City. He worked for *American Poet* magazine in the early 1940s, then served in the Army from 1943 to 1947. Upon graduating from Brooklyn College in 1948, he went to Harvard, where he studied under Archibald MacLeish. He received his Ph.D. in 1954, and has taught there ever since.

Alfred wrote his first verse play, *Agamemnon*, in 1954, although it went unproduced until 1972. His second, *Hogan's Goat*, took nine years to complete—Alfred rewrote it four times before its Off-Broadway premier in 1965. A celebration of Irish Brooklyn where Alfred grew up, the play was extremely popular, launching the career of actress Faye Dunaway. It was adapted into an unsuccessful Broadway musical, *Cry For Us All* in 1970, and filmed for public television the following year.

Since then, Alfred has written plays for regional theaters: *The Curse of the Aching Heart* (a sequel to *Hogan's Goat*) in 1979, *Holy Saturday* in 1980, and *Nothing Doing* in 1982. He has received an Amy Lowell Traveling Poetry Fellowship, a Brandeis Creative Art Award, and a National Institute of Arts and Letters Grant. In addition to his plays, Alfred has authored a translation of *Beowulf*. He lives in New York City and Cambridge.

William Alfred's purpose in writing this verse play in four acts is not to make an adaptation of Aeschylus; he wishes to penetrate the myth itself, that "ambush of reality," that familiar place (he goes on to say in his preface) we might find in no matter how foreign a city. Thus he would work where Aeschylus worked, and where the imaginations of his "private" readers work, whether consciously or not; and he would make his play directly from—or in?—the life of that myth, and not from its literature.

We would be speechless if he succeeded entirely, or even almost entirely. We do not expect this young poet to rival Aeschylus with his first play; and we do not expect him (though his preface says this play is "Greek by accident") to get the ring of Greek out of his ears in the making of his lines.

What is sure is that he has done a fine play, with a few moments of really high distinction. The Clytemnestra in the quarrel scene of the second act is an authentic realization; there is a bite to her anger and her bitterness, and there is something in her genuinely touching. And in the last scene of the last act, the play seems to break wholly into its own kind of immediacy, in the desperate weariness of Aegon just before the murder of Agamemnon, and in the lonely anguish of Cassandra.

I would like to see what William Alfred could do with the completely contemporary setting: characters, atmosphere, idiom. Mr. Eliot says that it is cheating to do the verse drama in any terms *but* the contemporary; or at least that we do not have a full realization of verse drama for our times unless we meet the problem head-on. I think Mr. Eliot is right; and I do not think his statement implies any more than Mr. Alfred understands in his preface. But I suggest that the literal application of Mr. Eliot's requirements, oddly enough, might make things easier rather than harder for a poetry true to the accent of our speech and at the same time to that solemn accent beyond both English and Greek.

If these remarks sound ungrateful, it is the solid achievement and the intriguing promise of William Alfred's *Agamemnon* that inspire them. They do not seem at cross purposes with a play that finds on the tombstone of a Vermont cemetery as definitive a line as Cassandra was ever made to utter: "It is a fearful thing to love what death can touch."—HENRY RAGO, *Com*, Dec. 3, 1954, pp. 259–60

William Alfred, author of *Hogan's Goat*, is reported to have said that the critics told him what the play is about. One may suppose that there was a concealed irony in the statement. On the other hand the admission may be a clue to a flaw in Mr. Alfred's interesting play.

Its theme, according to another remark ascribed to the playwright, has to do with the "human tendency to think you can get away with anything and take it back"—in a word, retribution. One pays for one's errors, no matter how forgivable they may be. Without being pretentious, the play aims at tragedy. Its failure in this respect does not invalidate its merits nor diminish its attractiveness. What gives the play color and its special quality, apart from its writing, is its "historical" aspect.

The story concerns the Irish immigrants in the Brooklyn of 1890. It was a separate town at the time and the dramatic action centers upon the mayoralty fight between two men: Matthew Stanton, 37, who had come a poor boy from his native land only twelve years before, and old Edward Quinn, long the incumbent Mayor, a cynical, corrupt, determined politico, typical of old Tammany. It is a struggle for power which Quinn clings to because he knows himself to be worthless without it, and which Stanton covets in order to make something of himself in America. Stanton is a reform candidate, bent on throwing out the old rascal, but in his hunger for power he is as ruthless as the boss he would replace. The reformer—"house devil and street saint"— is not wholly aware of the poisons which are bred by his drive to win.

The rather complicated and somewhat melodramatically old-fashioned plot concerns Aggie Hogan, first Quinn's mistress, then Stanton's. (On this account Stanton has come to be nicknamed *Hogan's Goat*.) Believing her to have been unfaithful, Stanton abandons Aggie whom he has secretly married. He hides this fact, goes to London for a while where he marries a well-born Irish girl and returns with her to Brooklyn. She feels herself exiled amid the roughs and toughs in her new home and suffers a sharp sense of guilt because she was married only by civil law.

On the basis of this past history Quinn is able to frustrate his rival's bid for power, but not until Stanton, to prevent his wife from leaving him (she has learned of his unavowed marriage), pushes her down a flight of stairs. This leads to her death, his arrest and to Quinn's ultimate defeat because of his connection with the scandal.

In writing his play, Mr. Alfred seems to have been impelled by various ambitions. To begin with, the above-stated intention is implied in such lines as "There are some things in life you can't take back"—the plot consequence of which is that not only the sinner but also the innocent are destroyed. Concomitant with this thought is the idea that in the quest for power lie the seeds of crime.

Further, the author wished to recreate the Irish Brooklyn of old with its mixture of religiosity, ignorance, provincial charm, fecklessness and brutality—the sweetly rancid festering of our ghettos in their growth and in their dissolution. Finally there is the purely literary striving (Mr. Alfred is a professor of English at Harvard) to envelop and elevate all this material through the use of modern verse forms, language which makes poetic patterns of the vernacular.

These several motivations do not altogether coalesce in *Hogan's Goat*. The play is diffuse; it imparts a sense of riding on different tracks to a destination which may be important but which is never reached. Though the characters are ably and often engagingly drawn—notably the crusty monster Quinn— none of them has sufficient size or originality to confer tragic dimension. The plot is "pushed" to make its point, and the point, being extremely serious, is not acceptable on the basis of the play's contrivance. One becomes stubborn in such cases, saying to oneself: "I know that what is being said is supposed to be a religious verity, but since it has been demonstrated through patent artifice I refuse to believe or be moved by it."

Still something remains which holds our attention and commands respect. Though the surface is conventional (there are certain old plays and recent novels about similar situations), we are persuaded that we are seeing not simply a story of the Irish in old Brooklyn but a part of the social history that shaped us. We seem to witness the development of our cities through talent, energy, industry, rascality, fraud and idealism. The play not only tells us about those crooks of occasional genius who built the metropolises; it makes us feel and understand them. The American past, nearly always travestied in Hollywood, is rarely used with authentic sensibility on the stage. Our drama seems to have no background in history before 1912 at the earliest. Plays written about us before that time were in virtually all instances even more bogus than the films.

The verse used in *Hogan's Goat* gratifies the ear and, on the whole, convinces as a fitting theatrical medium. The gap between the kind of metaphors and images employed and the characters who speak them is not wide enough to be discomfiting. The happiest touches are short phrases, bits of picturesque insult and homely quips. Except for a speech describing the immigrants' voyage to America in steerage, the sustained passages are less telling. There are flights of rhetoric which either are false to character in their dramatic context, or sound as if the author were taking time out to prove himself a poet. This artistic laxity results in technical awkwardness.

One is scrupulous in noting these faults because it is not enough in the case of a fundamentally worth-while effort by a gifted new writer to rejoice that he has achieved something of a hit, that he has added to the support of such an undertaking as The American Place Theatre—which last season brought us Robert Lowell's *The Old Glory*. One must regard the event as a hearty step in a difficult course which demands critical structure as well as encouragement.—HAROLD CLURMAN, *Nation*, Nov. 29, 1965, pp. 427–28

I remember William Alfred reading, some dozen years ago in Harvard's Sanders Theatre, from his verse play, *Hogan's Goat*. I recall being impressed by his reading and unimpressed by his writing. The American Place Theatre has now given *Hogan's Goat* a compact and tidy production, but the play continues to be sprawling, sentimental melodrama decked out with verse that smacks of a Christopher Fry hopped up on Sean O'Casey. Oh, the heart is in the right place in this tale of an 1890 scandal that cost an eagerly aspiring immigrant-Irish publican the mayoralty of Brooklyn; and his passionate young spouse, her life. But plays do not live by heart and vaulting metaphors alone. In an interview, Alfred declared his love for Katharine Cornell, and *Hogan's Goat* is fairly drenched in Cornell and Guthrie McClintic, though a trained nose may even catch a whiff of Maxwell Anderson. Nevertheless, this is not really an offensive play, merely a benighted one. It does, in any case, attempt to create plot and characters, and even if these Irish priests, politicos, ward-heelers, floozies, biddies, and bibbers have worn their garments of lovable local color hopelessly threadbare, and even if the romantic and political intrigues, clashes, and lightning revelations are smudged with the thumbprints of countless popular dramatists, there is here an old-fashioned love of old-fashioned theatre for which one may heave a sympathetic sigh.

Frederick Rolf's staging is suited to the nature of the play, and the production is well designed by Kert Lundell. The acting is always workmanlike, though Ralph Waite makes the hero rather more uninteresting than he already is. The whole thing, with all its lapses, has a professional finish to it, which, along with the built-in prestige of verse drama, had the reviewers tossing nosegays at Mr. Alfred with both hands, to which he responded by promising to turn *Hogan's Goat* into a trilogy, instead of quitting while he is ahead.—JOHN SIMON, *HdR*, Spring 1966, pp. 114–15

"W. A."

"Talk of the Town"

The New Yorker, January 25, 1982, pp. 26–29

William Alfred, the playwright and Abbott Lawrence Lowell Professor of the Humanities at Harvard, is in town preparing for the opening of his new play, *The Curse of an Aching Heart*, starring Faye Dunaway, who appeared in Mr. Alfred's first play, *Hogan's Goat*, sixteen years ago. At that time, we spent an exhilarating afternoon with Mr. Alfred, walking around with him in the South Brooklyn area in which he had spent most of his pre-Harvard life, and which he loved. He had made the area the locale for *Hogan's Goat*, which tells about an Irish Catholic couple in 1890—they had married outside the Church and felt guilty about it—and he has made the same area the locale for *The Curse of an Aching Heart*, which is about a Brooklyn woman of thirty-five (the daughter of Josie Finn, the character who caused trouble for the Miss Dunaway character in *Hogan's Goat*) looking back over her life between the nineteen-twenties and the nineteen-forties, the decade in which the play is set. This woman, as Mr. Alfred puts it, "comes to decide that her life has to it a daily glory."

Now we have had the pleasure of spending another afternoon with Mr. Alfred, this time in Manhattan, in the Lenox Hill area, where he lived between the ages of four and a half and nine. For the first year and a half, he boarded, and later he was a day student, at St. Ann's Academy, which used to be on

East Seventy-sixth Street near Lexington. He attended Mass at the Church of St. Jean Baptiste, which is still at Lexington and East Seventy-sixth Street, and he moseyed around the Third Avenue shops with his father, a bricklayer, and his mother, a telephone operator, when they weren't working and had the time. Mr. Alfred keeps a second home—a tiny apartment—in this area, in addition to a house in Cambridge. The apartment is a very short walk away from the Church of St. Jean Baptiste, where Mr. Alfred now attends Mass every morning on his way to the theatre for rehearsals of his play.

This is what Mr. Alfred gave the press agent for *The Curse of an Aching Heart* to say about his new play: "Santayana once wrote that everything in nature is lyrical in its ideal essence, tragic in its fate, and comic in its existence. Being, then, is the dazzle each of us makes as we thread the dance of those three rhythms of our lives. My hope is that *The Curse of an Aching Heart* occasionally captures that dazzle as water captures light."

I. *The Apartment*

A third-floor walkup, over Orwasher's Bakery ("Fresh Bread Daily") on the ground floor. Inside the building entrance, fading brown stencillike representations of flowers on mustard-colored walls. Rickety tile stairs. Rickety brown-painted door to the apartment. Mr. Alfred opening the door to us, looking only a hint affected by the passage of sixteen years: the same dark, ascetic face, the same large brown eyes, the same strong impression of innocence, deep humor, compassion, and good will. He was wearing a gray flannel suit, a dark-blue shirt with a button-down collar, a gray-and-blue striped poplin necktie. We stepped directly into a comforting little kitchen with a window.

"I'm making you a cup of tenement-house coffee, freshly perked," he said. "I love the smell. Especially with its being so cold outside."

The kitchen was shining clean. A rectangular wooden table with oilcloth on the top. Under a board cover, a bathtub, old-fashioned, with legs like a puppy's. Refrigerator and stove dollhouse size, but a full-sized percolator on the stove. To the left of the kitchen, a diminutive bedroom. To the right, a living room only slightly larger, with sofa, floor-to-ceiling bookshelves, an armchair, an old black-and-white television set, a sewing table used as a desk. The room's two windows, with a fire escape outside, looked out on other windows, other fire escapes.

"It's compact, like a ship, in here," Alfred said. "It's only a hole in the wall, but I love it. I love the neighborhood. I got the place right after my father died, eight years ago, for a hundred and seventy-five dollars, and today it's only up to two hundred and ninety-five dollars and eighty cents. The landlord, Mr. Braun, is a very nice man. When I had my heart attack, in Cambridge, two years ago, my lease was up, and I told Mr. Braun I didn't know whether I'd be coming back, but he held the place for me without a lease, and he didn't raise the rent."

We had the coffee, out of delicate blue-and-white china cups, in the living room, at the sewing table. On the walls: a crucifix; a Picasso print, in a brown wooden frame, of peasants in a field, resting; a *Hogan's Goat* poster featuring the name of Ed Begley; a small eighteenth-century wash drawing of country musicians by Jean Baptiste Le Prince.

"I think he did some of the murals for the Hermitage," Mr. Alfred told us. "I found the painting in a thrift shop. I got it for twenty bucks. I got a genuine 1790 Coalport-china teapot in another thrift shop for only eighteen bucks. My mother loved china; she collected it. In a way, I'm still buying presents

for somebody who isn't here anymore. I love the thrift shops. My mother loved them. They used to be all up and down Third Avenue. The best one was the one called Stuyvesant Square—it's now moved over to Second. They can't pay the Third Avenue rents. We dressed out of the thrift shops. Beautiful things. We always had the most beautiful clothes. I bought this tie I'm wearing in a thrift shop yesterday. Fifty cents." Mr. Alfred laughed an openly joyful laugh. We picked up from the sewing table a small nineteenth-century clock in a gilded brass case, its works visible through glass, its face, with Roman numerals, enamelled in pale green.

"Faye gave it to me for Christmas," Mr. Alfred said. "It winds up with a key. It's a travelling clock. Faye knows I used to collect clocks."

Mr. Alfred started packing some items into a dark-green Harvard book bag. "I've been helping get the props for the play," he said, identifying each item before he packed it away. "The *Staats-Zeitung und Herold*, because there's a man on the streetcar in the play who carries one. The paper still looks the same as it did fifty years ago. A bottle of toilet water— Florida Water. I got them this brass shovel with a black handle— brought it from Cambridge. My mother used this Louis Sherry candy box as a sewing box. I like to have things that are mine on the set."

Time to go. Mr. Alfred put on a black topcoat with a velvet collar and a worn-looking dark-gray fedora, and opened the door of his apartment. A heavy aroma strongly suggesting well-seasoned pot roast. . . .

II. *The Church*

. . . "I haven't stopped teaching at Harvard during this rehearsal time," Mr. Alfred told us. "Luckily, this is Reading Period—the time for the kids to consolidate what they have studied and to write their term papers. I've read twenty-five papers and have another twenty-five to go, by the kids in my course in Old English Literature from the Beginnings to the Norman Conquest. I also teach a playwriting course and have five honors' tutorial students, along with four more I couldn't say no to, in independent studies. I get presents for all my girl students in this Supply Store, and for the boys, too. They have wonderful old things. Buttons. Picture postcards. You can get the weirdest things in there. I found a postcard that reminded me of 'Krazy Kat' humor. It showed a boy and a dog. The boy is saying, 'If you laugh and smile all the while, How will the streetcar fare,' and the dog is saying, 'Bite him, Fido. He's got no suspenders.' I like it especially because a streetcar figures in the new play. Wait till you see our set. Our set designer made us a real streetcar that goes on a real track all around the stage. Be careful!" Mr. Alfred held us back, out of the path of an aggressive, speeding taxi. "My mother used to say, 'They'll kill you; it's on their way,'" he said, giving his all-out laugh. . . .

Inside the Church of St. Jean Baptiste. "There's been a white dove trapped in this church for several days," Mr. Alfred said, looking around as we sat down in a pew at the rear. No dove to be seen. On the dome in the center of the transept: "CHRISTUM REGEM ADOREMUS DOMINANTEM GENTIBUS. . . ."

"Every Friday, all of us from St. Ann's Academy would have Benediction," Mr. Alfred said. "A priest would give the sermon. The following Friday, he'd come back and you'd be asked how much you remembered of the sermon. If you remembered enough, you'd win a holy picture. I'd win maybe once every three weeks. I was a great woolgatherer. Instead of listening to the sermon, I'd be thinking of what we were going to have for supper. Look! There's the white dove! Isn't that amazing?"

Nobody else in the church seemed to notice the dove, which was sitting on the altar. . . .

III. *The Theatre*

Outside, on the steps of the church, Mr. Alfred pulled his hat down closer to his ears and stood for a moment, blinking at D'Agostino's, on the other side of Lexington Avenue. We walked over with him to 170 East Seventy-seventh Street.

"This is where the school's soccer yard was," he told us. "I was pretty good at soccer, because I had big feet. I was always fouling people with my feet. And here, next to it, was the dormitory where I slept. It was just like the one in the movie 'Zéro de Conduite.' Rows of beds up and down. I was in such a state of blues. I had one friend—Maurice, who was three months older than I was. He was very sweet to me. He had a pen—you looked through it and you saw the Tour Eiffel. And Brother John was a lovely man. He knew instinctively about children. He knew when you were blue. But he didn't condescend to you. A very grave, very sweet man. A year in that place, though, seemed like a century. I hated it. About thirty years ago, when the school was still here, I came to see it. All the Brothers I knew were gone. I had been having nightmares that I was still at St. Ann's. I felt I might lay the dreams to rest. I don't know when they tore the place down. Well, I'd better be bringing the props to the theatre," he said, pulling his hat down farther, against a sharp wind. "I don't like to miss the rehearsals. Those actors! They are so *good*! Oh, my, they break your heart. They make me cry. Every time. They're afraid for me on opening night. They want to put a paper bag over my head."

We got into a taxi and headed down to West Forty-fourth Street. "Wait till you see our theatre," he said. "It's the Little Theatre. Built in 1912 by Winthrop Ames, one of Guthrie McClintic's first employers. It held two hundred and ninety-nine people in those days. Now it's got a balcony and holds four hundred and ninety-nine. It has a beautiful Georgian front. And it's right next door to Sardi's. Four stories high. Winthrop Ames used to have his offices over the theatre. A very dignified-looking man. McClintic used to say that Ames looked like a Velázquez cardinal. Ames went to Harvard. Class of 1895. I looked him up, because his initials, W. A., interested me, if you don't mind my getting loopy again."

Inside the Little Theatre, it was cozy and warm. A spectacular-looking multilevel set—a revolving sculpture of a latticework of pipes suggesting a fire-escape landscape—had a realistic streetcar on a track. The set designer was conferring with the director. The lighting man was testing his set of color cards against the stage. The actors were walking around the stage, across the stage, onto the stage, off the stage. Mr. Alfred told us that the production cost three hundred and seventy-five thousand dollars, and that five main producers and fifty independent investors had put up the money. "Nothing from me," Mr. Alfred said. "Not since my ten-cents-a-week allowance have I held on to money. Watch, now. What you're looking at up there is Bond Street and Third in South Brooklyn, in back of a disused brewery. The audience is the Gowanus Canal. Watch."

The streetcar onstage began to move on its track. Mr. Alfred looked as though he needed to have a paper bag put over his head.

NELSON ALGREN

1909–1981

Nelson Algren was born in Detroit on March 28, 1909. He graduated from the University of Illinois in 1931, and worked during the first years of the Depression as a salesman, a carnival barker, and a migrant worker. He began writing while employed at a Texas gas station in 1933; his first novel, *Somebody in Boots*, was published two years later. During his marriage to Amanda Kontowicz from 1936 to 1939, Algren worked for the Federal Writers Project, and wrote stories that were later included in the collection *The Neon Wilderness* (1947). After finishing a second novel, *Never Come Morning*, in 1942, he served as an Army medic in World War II.

Algren took five years to complete his next novel, *The Man With the Golden Arm*. Published in 1949, it won the National Book Award and was made into a movie in 1956. Between 1949 and 1951, he became close to Simone de Beauvoir and her friends, including Jean-Paul Sartre. Another good friend was Ernest Hemingway, about whom Algren wrote *Notes From a Sea Diary* (1963). Dubbed "the poet of the Chicago slums" by Malcolm Cowley, Algren was a noted raconteur, whose most famous quip was the formulation of three laws: "Never play cards with a man named Doc, never eat at a place called Mom's, and never sleep with a woman whose troubles are worse than your own."

In 1956 Algren thoroughly revised *Somebody in Boots* to produce *Walk on the Wild Side*, an "American fantasy" that is often considered his best book. It was filmed in 1962. He taught at the University of Iowa and the University of Florida in the 1960s, and from 1965 to 1967 was married to Betty Ann Jones. His last book, *The Devil's Stocking*, was published after his death in New York on May 9, 1981.

General

⟨Nelson⟩ Algren is a novelist who has embraced the conditions of naturalism—its determinism (within limits) of social environment and heredity, its preoccupation with the people of the lower depths, its pessimism about the nature of man and about man's fate in a hostile world. Algren's prose, however, while it may often be sentimental and soft about the edges, is not harsh and ungainly, as naturalistic prose has traditionally been in this country. The poetic quality of his writing comes in part from the impressionistic way in which he sees reality. He has an acutely developed feeling for mood, and he chooses his details in an artful, sometimes artificial, way to give us the atmosphere of half-light in which his characters live. He carefully sets before us the dirty Kleenex or the pavement-colored cap as details that speak to our senses in such a way as to convey his meaning. The quality of his prose comes, then, not wholly from the tradition of naturalism (although it reminds one of Frank Norris') but from Algren's conviction that his writing depends more upon feeling than upon intellect. In a *Paris Review* interview, he said, "I depend more on the stomach" than Saul Bellow; "I always think of writing as a *physical* thing." The physical quality in his writing—it is significant that he works out in a gym preparatory to writing—emphasizes the belly-head distinction which he himself makes. His allegiance is to the feelings. He is indifferent to ideas, even uncomfortable with them.

The importance which Algren gives to his feelings might be a justification for calling him a romantic. At least the appeal to the emotions in the poetic character of the prose gives him a marginal kinship with romanticism. At the end of the eighteenth century, coincidental with the early manifestations of romanticism, there appeared on the scene the man of feeling, who developed the notion of benevolence. I suggest that what I have labeled Algren's romanticism on the basis of the style of his writing is related to the compassion in the nature of his sensibility. He is the twentieth-century romantic man of feeling, inexplicably caught in the city slums. He pushes his characters on to their inevitable destruction—virtually no one wins in Algren's world—and is true in this way to his naturalistic premises. But he gives them yearnings for love or pride in themselves as separate and identifiable individuals—yearnings that reveal a tender concern for them as human beings. They are not animal-like creatures doomed to progressive deterioration. What looks like an awkward incongruity between style and matter is seen to be an organic relationship.

Algren's reliance on feeling explains a good deal about his attitude toward social reform. A writer so suspicious of the intellect as Algren could never come into a meaningful relationship with a body of idea. The Marxist influence upon his work, which is apparent in the epigraphs he selected for his first novel, published in 1935, does not lead to the novel of ideas or to an analysis of society. Not that Algren is content with the state of American society. He despises, as he has said, its marriage to gadgetry. He resents its structure and its value assumptions. He lives among the people underneath and has a feeling for them, and so he writes, not out of indignation but, as he says, out of "a kind of *irritability* that these people on top should be contented, so absolutely unaware of these other people, and so sure that their values are the right ones. I mean, there's a certain satisfaction in recording the people underneath, whose values are as sound as theirs, and a lot funnier, and a lot truer in a way. There's a certain over-all satisfaction in kind of scooping up a shovelful of these people and dumping them in somebody's parlor." The writer's job is to accuse, to

play the wasp, Algren insists, and he does so by attacking what he calls the bluebird version of America. Algren's criticism of American life is not in any sense ideological. It is a compound of resentment and perversity, of feelings; it is a conviction that the respectable classes ought to have their noses rubbed in the poverty and degradation of American life as an antidote to their self-satisfaction; it is a conviction that the poor are just as good as the rich, and more fun to boot; it is sheer sentimental sympathy for the underdog.

I should not want to accuse Algren of mindlessness, but certainly one finds in him indifference to the intellect. When he began to write he revealed a leftist orientation, but he seems to have drifted away from the radical tradition. The fact is that he was never solidly rooted in the left, and his social criticism has always been as impressionistic as his style. The Marxism in Algren's work has never been more than surface deep, in my view, and he peeled off that surface in the course of the forties. If he is at the end of the forties closer to the Symbolists than to the Marxists, this is only an indication that his style, which has remained steadily the same throughout his career, has triumphed over his fitful flirtation with ideas. It seems to me that no *essential* change has taken place in Algren from beginning to end.

When Algren was on the staff of the *Daily Illini* in college, he reports, "⟨I⟩ used to go down to the city jails and wait around for something to happen. It was a good time in my life." The jail burned itself into Algren's imagination, and he has never left it. He is the poet of the jail and the whorehouse; he has made a close study of the cockroach, the drunkard, and the pimp, the garbage in the street and the spittle on the chin. He has a truly cloacal vision of the American experience. In his world dead-end streets always end in blank walls where his unheroic heroes, unattached and usually unemployed, come to their end. The heroes do not want to be unattached or unheroic. They yearn for love, and sometimes fleetingly find it. They yearn for the large, savagely virile gesture—they want to assert themselves by fighting back—and sometimes they almost achieve it. They yearn for a redemption from guilt, for a clean conscience. Strangely, love and heroism and conscience are not completely dead in Algren's world. They are just impossible. The heroes must die.

. . . What gives Algren his distinction is that he is a naturalist who cares about style and who is linguistically adventuresome and aware, if not always successful. His distinction is that he has a great reservoir of sympathy which he extends, sometimes indiscriminately, to all the unfortunates in his nightmare world. What distinguishes him is the way he blends his naturalism. He blends its determinism with a sympathy for his people that nevertheless cannot deter him from sending them to their miserable fates. And he blends a determinism which should rob them of will with an assertion of will—the will to love, the will to penance, the will to find the self—which testifies finally to their humanity.—CHESTER E. EISINGER, "Nelson Algren: Naturalism as the Beat of the Iron Heart," *Fiction of the Forties*, 1963, pp. 74–85

Works

CHICAGO: CITY ON THE MAKE

If you've tried New York for size and put in a stint in Paris, lived long enough in New Orleans to get the feel of the docks and belonged to old Marseille awhile, if the streets of Naples have warmed you and those of London have chilled you, if you've seen the terrible green-grey African light moving low over the

Sahara or even passed hurriedly through Cincinnati—then Chicago is your boy at last and you can say it and make it stick.—*Chicago: City on the Make.*

Nelson Algren is one of God's angry and gifted men, a Chicagoman—and maybe a Chicago-firster—to the bitter end. As his admirers know, his fiction is a heady, curious blend of skidrow Chicago talk and poetic insight. He writes like no one else in America today. His profile of Chicago has depth if not breadth; by ordinary standards it is an unfair picture of the city, and therein lies its strength. About as unflattering as a Goya portrait of nobility, its degree of distortion is a measure of its creative impact. Intolerance is one of the qualities of art with which Algren is richly endowed.

Albert Halper, lead-off man for the October Chicago issue of *Holiday Magazine*, may have written a better-balanced piece about America's inland metropolis, but Algren's article, now expanded into this hard-covered, muscular little book, searches a city's heart and mind rather than its avenues and public buildings. Algren's Chicago, a kind of American annex to Dante's Inferno, is a nether world peopled by rat-faced hustlers and money-loving demons who crawl in the writer's brilliant, sordid, uncompromising and twisted imagination.

At its best, which is much of the time, this seamy Valentine to Chicago is literature that takes off from Sandburg without ever being a take-off on "the white-haired poet" whom Algren invokes as part of the glorious old Chicago "that had its big chance and fluffed it." It was always a hustler's town, Algren keeps telling us, a natural for the "Mountain grog seller and river gambler, Generous Sport and border jackal, blackleg braggart and coonskin foisterer, Long Knives from Kentucky and hatchet men from New York, bondsmen brokers and bounty jumpers. The joint is still in an uproar. Every hour on the hour. All night long."

Chicago has two faces, "one for winners and one for losers; one for hustlers and one for squares," Algren chants. Anyone who has read Algren's fine short stories or the revved-up poetry of his novels knows which face is for him. It's an obsessive love, tight-walking (without falling from) the line of hard-boiled sentimentality that inevitably leads Algren to his nameless, useless nobodies who "sleep behind the taverns, who sleep beneath the El."

Who sleep in burnt-out buses with the windows freshly curtained; in winterized chicken coops or patched-up truck bodies. The useless, helpless nobodies nobody knows: that go as the snow goes, where the wind blows, there and there, and there, down any old cat-and-ashcan alley at all . . . way way down there where no one has yet heard of phone-vision or considered the wonders of technicolor video . . . there where they sleep the all night movies through and wait for rain or peace or snow; there beats Chicago's heart.

Along with the nobodies, the cynical, belligerent chamber of commerce in Algren's heart points with provincial pride to the somebodies: Jane Addams, Mickey Finn, Hinky Dink Kenna ("a hustler's hustler, part philanthropist and part straight brigand"), King Oliver and Louie Armstrong, Grover Cleveland Alexander, Barney Ross and Bix Biederbecke, Sandburg, Lindsay, Masters, Anderson, Dreiser. In the Twenties, Algren reminds us, Chicago was more than the stockyards and the pulsing terminal of America, it was "the homeland and heartland of an American renaissance."

Some readers may wish Algren wouldn't interrupt the impassioned blank verse of this loving and hateful tour to take sideswipes at names and places he's got it in for. They may wonder why a writer of such talent and integrity should succumb even infrequently to a Peglerian "watch-me-shoot-fish-in-a-barrel" style. The way he swings around to attack "the cocktail-lounge culture of New York," for instance. Or when he hauls off like one of his fans, Papa Champ, to take a potshot at little Truman Capote. Or when; in a passage that is either undertone or overwrought, he cuffs Richard Wright for powdering out on Chicago in favor of intellectual hangouts in Paris.

Yes, this Algren is an angry man, a Chicagoman, punching all the time straight from the shoulder; and maybe the chapter shouldn't be taken away from him if once in a while he sneaks in a low one. That's the kind of writer he is. Something like Chicago itself, a "Jekyll-and-Hyde sort of burg," a Debs-and-McCormick town, a Capone-and-Hutchins town. Muscles and brains. Hustlers and poets. The white-haired poet himself never used the American language more effectively to conduct the tension Algren passes on to us from his city on the make, the city he loves like a beat-up old harridan whose youthful charms only he remembers—Hustlertown, U.S.A.—BUDD SCHULBERG, "Heartbeat Of a City," *NYTBR*, Oct. 21, 1951, p. 3.

For Algren there are neither partial truths nor soft truths, but only the whole and hard truth. It is the compulsion to tell the whole, hard truth as a contradiction to our national lies that constitutes the basic impulse and moving spirit behind Algren's serious writing. Simone de Beauvoir shrewdly identifies this essential quality in her depiction of Algren (as Lewis Brogan) in her autobiographical novel *The Mandarins*:

At first, I had found it amusing meeting in the flesh that classic American species: self-made-leftist-writer. Now, I began taking an interest in Brogan. Through his stories, you got the feeling that he claimed no rights on life and that nevertheless he had always had a passionate desire to live. I liked that mixture of modesty and eagerness.

"Whatever made you start writing?" I asked.

"I always liked printed paper. When I was a kid, I used to make up newspapers by pasting press clippings in notebooks."

"There must have been other reasons."

He reflected. "I know a lot of different kinds of people; what I want is to show each of them how the others really are. You hear so many lies!" He fell silent for a moment. "When I was twenty, I realized that everyone was lying to me, and it made me mad. I think that's why I started writing and why I'm still writing."

Algren's whole truth, to name it in the terms he used in *Conversations with Algren*, is that there is a world whose existence the middle-class American denies, "that there are people who have no alternative, that there are people who live in horror, that there are people whose lives are nightmares."

Such is the nature of Algren's world. Whatever its universal human implications—and I intend to argue that Algren's world conveys such implications—Algren's fiction depicts but three milieux: life on the road or in the jails of the Southwest in the 1930s; life in the slums, bars, and whorehouses of New Orleans in the '30s; life in the poorer working-class neighborhoods, especially the Polish, in the Chicago of the 1930s and '40s. Similarly, the population of Algren's world consists of hobos, prostitutes, criminals, fighters, drug addicts, cops, drunks, losers, cripples, down-and-outers, and innocent boys from small towns soon mutilated by life. Nowhere in Algren are there people vibrantly healthy, free of guilt, clean, fulfilled, content. Their existence—*our* existence, we would prefer to say—is suggested only in the abstract: as the faceless and faintly hostile crowds through which Algren's underground men travel, or as the invisible but potent force behind the police who are the nemesis of Algren's characters. The whole truth for Algren could also be described in vivid dramatic metaphors, especially in the scenes of violence so graphically depicted as to be nearly unbearable, and once viewed, unforgettable: a man in a jail cell dying of gunshot wounds, too far gone in shock to give the assent (required by law) to perform the surgery that might save his life; a legless man smashing to a pulp what had been the face of a handsome youth, in a fight over a prostitute.

Algren's first novel *Somebody in Boots* (1935) was in part a picaresque and in part a proletarian novel; it contained in episode, theme, and character the germ cells for some of Algren's later work, particularly a number of the stories in *The Neon Wilderness* (1949) and much of *A Walk on the Wild Side*. The theme of *Somebody in Boots* can be stated simplistically in Marxist terms: poverty corrupts. Men are driven to violence and crime by it; women are driven to prostitution by it; both men and women are degraded and dehumanized by it. Indeed, the novel's last two sections are prefaced with quotations from the Communist Manifesto. But there is much in the novel that drives from Algren's peculiar and consistent *weltanschauung*, rather than the social philosophy of Marxism which he was soon to abandon. The novel's protagonist has those qualities native to all of Algren's heroes; he is fundamentally innocent and well-intentioned, and he yearns most of all to love and be loved. His badness comes not from inherent viciousness but from the conditioning imposed by the jungle environment he inhabits. Although he commits crimes and boasts about his toughness, inwardly he remains fearful, even childlike, and never attains to the real savagery and evil of some of those around him. Together with what are for Algren's work prototypical descriptions of filth, brutality, poverty, hunger, the novel also advances Algren's prototypical assertion of the possibility of romantic love among even the criminal, the downtrodden, and the supposedly lost.

However, Algren's best work remains neither his first novel nor his last, but the two novels of the 1940s: *Never Come Morning*, 1942, and *The Man with the Golden Arm*, 1949. These books focus on the Chicago milieu which is the true center of Algren's world. They incorporate and integrate a number of the best stories published in *The Neon Wilderness*. They are largely free of the self-consciously florid writing that mars both Algren's earliest and most recent works. Their strongest effects come from keenly visualized dramatic scenes rather than from editorializing. They are of Algren's work the most fully realized in action, character, and structure.

Both novels belong in that important tradition or mode of American fiction which begins with Crane's *Maggie* and is continued in the best of Dreiser, ancestors Algren proudly claims, a tradition we might call symbolic realism or lyrical naturalism. This is a richer tradition than that of documentary realism and naturalism, wherein I would place such writers as Farrell. Like the best work in that richer tradition, *Never Come Morning* and *The Man with the Golden Arm* are distinguished by great verisimilitude and authenticity of setting and language, given emotional force by the artist's profound involvement in the lives of his doomed characters, sharpened by irony, supported upon a carefully designed structure, and made resonant by symbolic undertones. The pattern of action of both novels is identical: the essentially innocent and potentially noble protagonists, though besmirched by crime and fallen into

vice, seek and temporarily find fulfillment and expiation through love, and even momentarily attain a kind of success, only to be trapped by their earlier misdeeds at the very moment of their greatest triumph and happiness.

If these protagonists, Lefty Bicek and Frankie Machine, are already lost when we first meet them, or soon after, if, naturalistic heroes that they are, their fates have already been determined, they nevertheless remain within the range of our sympathies because they are brought to life as neither subhuman brutes nor noble savages. Each is a victim of his environment, but each is also among the aristocrats of that environment. Lefty has a splendid body and ability as a fighter; Frankie has quick hands and a nimble brain. More important, though their sensibilities have been coarsened to the point where they can be casually cruel, both have the ability to give love and the capacity to receive it. Despite their surface toughness, both retain and respond to conscience. Each has a lofty dream: Lefty to be a prizefighting champion; Frankie to play the drums with a big-name band, but, in fact, each would gladly settle for a pathetically modest reality: Lefty to get enough money to marry his girl; Frankie to get the monkey off his back. In short, despite the narrowness of their world and its distance from ours, despite the fact that Algren's protagonists both become murderers, we see them as men and we realize that their suffering is meaningful.

The central theme of *Never Come Morning*, its whole truth, so to speak, is the refutation of what has been among the hallowed official truths of American society, a truth which Algren considers the blackest lie: the belief that the individual retains the power of choice, of deciding between alternatives, in plotting his destiny. The novel's hero, Lefty Bicek, has no alternatives. The police captain who arrests him, first for a mugging, and at the end of the novel for murder, keeps this legend on the wall of his office: I HAVE ONLY MYSELF TO BLAME FOR MY FALL. Yet, ironically, only after Lefty has already fallen, only after his doom is already sealed, does he assume the strength and wisdom to consider alternatives. . . .

Although Algren's fiction is more notable for its mood, its rendition of milieu, and its individually powerful scenes than for completely integrated and symmetrical structure, the novel's architecture does support its themes, in corollary or analogous form. It is organized around three motifs: fight, prison, dream, each of which is also crucial to Algren's work at large. . . .

. . . *Never Come Morning* demands a prominent place in an important American literary mode, which, contrary to a current critical cliché, is far from dead. But good as it is, *The Man with the Golden Arm* excels it. Not only is Algren's novel the first serious treatment in our literature of the drug addict, it is also a profoundly felt and profoundly moving book. This novel marks the culmination of Algren's identification with characters the "normal" man might think beneath or beyond his sympathies, yet such is Algren's craft that he extends the norm. I know no more powerful scene of its kind in any literature than that in which Frankie takes a shot of morphine from the peddler, Louie. This is a scene in which Algren makes us participate, regardless of our range of experience.

We participate because the novel is morally pertinent. As in Algren's other serious work the themes of love, freedom, and guilt are central to *The Man with the Golden Arm*, although expressed in different dramatic terms than in *Never Come Morning*. The particular conflict here is that between self-sacrifice and self-preservation, a conflict knotted into the relationship between Frankie Machine and his wife Sophie, his friend Sparrow, and his girl Molly. These are dynamic relationships which fluctuate with the condition of the participants. Such is Algren's version of the whole truth that his people tend to prey on one another, whether in friendship or in love. There are no relationships in Algren's world in which each receives as much as he gives. Thus Frankie gives to his wife, gives and takes simultaneously in his friendship, and receives from Molly.

. . . Just as betrayal, slavery, and guilt dominated *Never Come Morning* and determined the fates of its characters, so the major characters in *The Man with the Golden Arm* suffer cruel destinies, regardless of what their self-preservation or self-sacrifice would seem to earn them in an equitable universe: Frankie dies a suicide, Sophie is committed to an asylum, Sparrow and Molly face long prison terms.

Although I have stressed the tragic aspects of Algren's work, I should also point out that his books are not comprised of total gloom and unrelieved misery. There is considerable gusto and comedy throughout his work, especially in *The Neon Wilderness* and *The Man with the Golden Arm*. Indeed, the alternation between comic and tragic episodes is perhaps the most distinctive structural principle of *The Man with the Golden Arm*.

. . . In his practice, Algren has been faithful to his theory. He has written about the ugly, the sordid, the depraved, the fallen, and he has made them all morally significant—even, at moments, beautiful. It is thus especially unfortunate that Algren should have despaired of the success of his serious writing and abandoned it for journalism.

But Algren's ambitions as a social novelist notwithstanding, his ambition to write "influential" books, books that ameliorate unfair conditions, he has perhaps already accomplished something more important for literature: the scenes he has created have become part of our imaginative life, and his people are now among those we know. Algren's version of the whole truth in such works as *Never Come Morning* and *The Man with the Golden Arm* convinces us no more that his is the *whole* truth than does Dostoyevsky's vision of truth in *Notes from Underground*. Algren's truth, like Dostoyevsky's, attains its greatest conviction as a particular and imagined truth. Whatever validity it has to life, its larger validity is to art. I believe that Algren's truth attains this larger validity.— SHELDON NORMAN GREBSTEIN, "Nelson Algren and the Whole Truth," *The Forties: Fiction, Poetry, Drama*, 1969, pp. 300–9

A WALK ON THE WILD SIDE

Nelson Algren's first short story appeared in *Story Magazine* in 1933 at a time when he was a migratory laborer in the Southwest. He won some immediate recognition among writers, critics and publishers, and about two years later his first novel, *Somebody in Boots* was published. A powerful work, it remains today as one of the books of the thirties which is likely to outlive its own time. Since then, Algren has published four other works of fiction, *Never Come Morning*, *Neon Wilderness*, a collection of short stories, *The Man with the Golden Arm* and now, his latest novel, *A Walk on the Wild Side*. *The Man with the Golden Arm* was described by *Time* magazine as "One of the finest novels of the year . . . " Ernest Hemingway predicted that Nelson Algren would rank "among our best American novelists."

When we deal with a writer of talent, it seems to me that the question of recognition and praise is secondary and sometimes incidental. What is of more importance is to try and understand what that writer is and to gain some sense of the character and nature of his books. And Algren, in his latest novel, gives us a great deal of help. The jacket blurb of this book quotes him as follows:

> *A Walk on the Wild Side* wasn't written until long after it had been walked. That was through what remained of old Storyville by the summer of 1931. I'd come to New Orleans with a card entitling me to some editorial position because I'd attended a school of journalism. I wasn't sure whether I wanted to be a columnist or a foreign correspondent but I was willing to take what was open. What was open was a place on a bench in Lafayette Square if you got there early. I found my way to the streets on the other side of the Southern Pacific station, where the big jukes were singing something called "Walking the Wild Side of Life." I've stayed pretty much on that side of the curb ever since.

It might be said that Algren's novels are weak in structure, and that they evince a lack of good constructive sense and an inability to maintain a narrative pace; or that his novels are different in kind, quality and character from those books which show structure, constructive capacity and an ability to sustain a narrative pace. Algren writes all around a character and gradually you realize that his character is real. He is atmospheric and impressionistic. Here, his book is slow in getting off the ground and one needs to be patient and to read slowly through the opening sections, which are not well organized, before one realizes that once again he is reading an Algren novel with the traits which mark—I might almost say trademark—Nelson Algren's fiction. Especially after he lands Dove in New Orleans, he is at his best.

Algren can lavish poetic feeding on objects, sights, scenes, areas where few would find anything lyrical. At the same time, there is sometimes a descent into bathos. He can overdo his poetizing of the drab. Because of this, his writing is uneven and from page to page as you read, you are alternately moved, lifted up and then dropped flatly into an unexpected pool of sentimentality.

Concerning *A Walk on the Wild Side*, Nelson Algren states:

> This is a story that tries to tell something about the natural toughness of women and men, in that order. . . . I like to think it is really about any street of any big town in the country.

A Walk on the Wild Side is not about any street in any big city of the country: it is about any street of the lost in a big city. Algren is a chronicler of the lost, but a chronicler whose talent is, to my mind, definite and unmistakable. All of his novels seem equally uneven: but all of them reveal his special talent, and give their reward. If you like Nelson Algren's work, you'll like *A Walk on the Wild Side*. It is the product of a distinguished American writer.— JAMES T. FARRELL, "On the Wrong Side of Town," *NR*, May 21, 1956, pp. 18–19

As a jailbird named Cross-Country Kline remarks late in *A Walk on the Wild Side*: "There's no trick in not going down the drain if you don't live in the sink." From the raw poetry of its beginning in a depression-blighted Texas tank town (1931 A.D.) through the Storyville horror parlors of New Orleans and back again, Nelson Algren's new novel stays with the sink people. We watch them squirm, fight, pander, couple, get drunk, and embroider daydreams that are only slightly less grotesque than the serialized nightmare of their daily lives. As in *Never Come Morning* and *The Man With the Golden Arm*, Mr. Algren gives us a bum's-eye view of a social echelon seldom mentioned in specific terms except by the cop on the beat.

And in many ways it is a better-made book than any he has written before. The Chicago School of Realism has a new headmaster who frames his materials in back-country balladry and earthy lyricism. Enveloping pornography, as bluntly couched as ever, has now become incidental to the journalist's desire to get the facts and the historian's need to relate them to human affairs. To complete the effect, one could only ask for Toulouse-Lautrec illustrations and Louis Armstrong music.

Not that everybody who reads books will enjoy this guided tour of depression degeneracy and degradation, complete with a full cast of submerged people whom the author regards tenderly and with full allowance for contributing circumstance. *Caveat lector* to the young, the militantly pure in heart, and the old lady from Dubuque. Yet Mr. Algren's way with words, handled with full respect for interior rhythms, and his rich comedic sense help to make A *Walk on the Wild Side* an impressive performance. Prostitutes, pimps, freaks, and half-people wander at will through an episodic plot; but one can't think of a dull one in the lot. And an old abortionist, now occupied with more devious obscenities, speaks for all: "Look out for love, look out for trust, look out for *giving*. Look out for wine, look out for daisies and people who laugh readily. Be especially wary of friendship, Son, it can only lead to trouble."

Dove Linkhorn, a ruttish country boy who believes in acts before words, blazes quite a trail for the reader. Leaving Texas by the hobo route following a forcible encounter with a waitress twice his age, illiterate young Dove swaggers into Storyville society where anything is fine if a body enjoys it and can get away with it, from stealing on down. As a gawky stud-bum with yellow shoes, the boy joins a man's world which centers in the houses and hangouts of red-light row. In a way he becomes one of the prominent members of this little community, participating in all its games and divertissements with a zest too violent to be feigned. Some of his best friends are prostitutes, including a former schoolteacher who lives with him long enough to impart a sketchy reading familiarity with poetry. It is quite an idyll among the girls, business agents, sexual freaks, and rheumy-eyed expendables. But the fun falters when Dove is picked up in a raid and joins other oddballs in the local jail. And the fun grinds to a complete halt shortly after his release when Dove and the school-marm's amputee gentleman friend meet in a climactic saloon fight that stays terribly memorable in the mind. The worldly indoctrination of Dove Linkhorn, now finished, has nearly finished him. Only the spectre of a country boy remains to be counted, and it may be that Mr. Algren intended all along to arrive at this moral QED.

A *Walk on the Wild Side* will be too rough for frail sightseers, but a participant's backward look at a wild 1931 landscape with figures seems worth the effort. "It's awful when it's like this," Dove thought, "and it's like this now."—JAMES KELLY, "Sin-Soaked in Storyville," *SR*, May 26, 1956, p. 16

WHO LOST AN AMERICAN?

Nelson Algren, teller of the moving stories in *The Neon Wilderness* (and especially of that masterly fable, "How the Devil Came Down Division Street"), author of the celebrated *The Man With the Golden Arm*, and of the weird and special A *Walk on the Wild Side*, has been silent too long. Or, rather, he has been fretfully silent, the fret manifested by occasional reviews, interviews, magazine pieces, comments, groans and gripes. A born writer, for one reason or another stalled in his vocation, may back and fill in this way. *Who Lost an American?* is the distillation of this fret, a collection of memories,

notes, burlesques and prejudices in a book that is part fact, part fiction.

Some of these exercises in style are marvelously funny, and the comic moments are the high ones of this book. With his Division Street blade Algren swiftly does in some unpleasant types—a psychotic literary agent, self-displaying writers, gassed-up critics. The portraits are surely not fair, but they draw real blood. Algren also dispatches, once again, the long-suffering American tourist. On the other hand, he has a soft spot in his prose for the beggars of southern Europe, and himself as once he was, searching through London for a lady of light character. Where, O where, is the girl who seemed so nice? Where is that young G.I. who was so young?

Although the book is put together as if it were a travel book, with headings indicating an informal guide to New York, London, Paris, Dublin, Barcelona, Seville, Almeria, Istanbul, Crete and Chicago, it is actually a notebook ramble through the wild side of Algren's fancy. There are the recurrent literary "in" jokes—parodies of public prose, outraged gossip, attacks on the overrated fads of literary politics. This is balanced against nostalgia for sweeter times, more honest people, a relevant proletarian politics. There is some incidental humorous observation of foreign climes, composed with an attitude of shrewd disdain like that of Mark Twain's travel writings. Then Algren returns, again and again, to battle the bourgeois citizens of America as if they were killing him right now.

Perhaps they are. Perhaps Americans make a great deal of trouble for themselves and for Nelson Algren. Or, perhaps, Algren's own trouble is closer to home, within the novelist's perpetual rage to master his themes and himself.

The weakest element in this entertaining book is a righteous intolerance that makes its author swing wildly at a variously named, but finally undefined, Enemy. Writers write about idealized conceptions of themselves, among other matters, but the portrait of the innocent narrator, pure in heart but surrounded by corruption, seems far from justified by the evidence of these wicked pages.

The best thing in the book is Algren's personal rhythm—irreverent, funny, surreal, as if he has blended the lyricism of his early writing, "within a rain that light rains regret," with a tough meander and wail like that of funky jazz. Algren is a writer, the authentic poetic article; a fresh haircut strikes his eye as vividly as the murder of a Chicago poker player on a backstairs. It would be fine to discover him working once again on people whom he could feel in his blood and within an action that might carry his special melody.—HERBERT GOLD, "After All, Who Is the Enemy?" *NYTBR*, June 2, 1963, p. 23

NOTES FROM A SEA DIARY

In 1962 Nelson Algren booked passage on a freighter to Pusan, Kowloon, Bombay and Calcutta. Recalling his visit with Ernest Hemingway seven years earlier, he decided to write about Hemingway, as well as the trip, because "I would be the inventor of the very first essay on Hemingway smelling of salt." This arch, arbitrary tone is all that binds the two sets of fragments that, spliced together, form *Notes From a Sea Diary*—short declamations on Hemingway and his critics, and long anecdotes of life on board ship and in the ports.

The meeting with Hemingway (one imagines other encounters: John Updike meeting Emil Zola, Tom Wolfe meeting L.-F. Céline) fills a mere six pages—some hostile banter and a conversation at cross-purposes on hyenas and boxing. It tells little about Hemingway and much about Algren, who like many others seems to have sought out The Champ to prove he could last a round with him.

But that is also the Algren of the rest of the book—among drunk sailors, pimps, hustlers, con men, thieves, and lovable helpless saps—Algren always unfazed, trading knowledgeable stories on boxing, baseball and crime, putting everyone on with tough comebacks out of the corner of his mouth, but secretly sucking a sweet seed of compassion.

Many of the sections begin and end with choppy little rhapsodies that resemble his poems—of which there are two in this book—self indulgent and pretentious. The stories are full of fake-significant clinchers and comebacks.

"For doomful seas from the black edge of the world would come rolling through nights without moon . . . 'Don't take things so hard, Pacific,' I consoled the poor brute—'girls come home from school in Malaysia too.' It wasn't my first time out of the barn either."

Is one supposed to laugh? Applaud? He does seem to want congratulation. But for what? Is he being profound, or just frankly entertaining? In the end you aren't sure, so he has failed both ways.

The "criticism" is largely attacks on others who have written on Hemingway. Algren names names and spares nothing he disbelieves, which is fine. But he often takes glee in long personal assaults which, aside from their intellectual justice, repel by their insistence and malice. Many of his critical statements are clichés or inanities swimming loosely in rant. Occasionally he rises passionately, with honest heat and thoughtful comment. But quickly he is back on his stool, and again you're listening to the tough-sentimental literary lush with intellectual whisky-courage, boasting "I can lick any critic in the house," his breath somewhat stronger than his brains.

In the anecdotes, as in the criticism, there are moments of real emotion and power, but they are brief. What his book might have been shows in the chapters describing the caged whores of Bombay. Despite sometimes shoddy writing ("She was the eldest child and had eleven siblings, all younger than herself."), Algren is moving because he concentrates not on his performance but on his subject.

Then quickly it is over, and we are back in the romance of the hardboiled, the soggy mess behind the hard exterior, the male counterpart of the myth of the golden-hearted whore. In all his talk of junkies and hoods, the violent and violated, Algren never talks about the central facts of their lives: anxiety and boredom. Instead he creates a noble savagery—a literary cult of the antisocial, as little connected with life as the literary communism of the thirties was with *real politik*.

What began years ago as a small but unique gift became a habit, and finally a tic, a machine clanking out a self-intoxicating gabble of Algrenisms. If the later Hemingway's self-parody was saddening, Algren's merely irritates, though if it continues through a few more books like *Who Lost an American?* and *Notes from a Sea Diary*, it may become the sort of helpless posturing one sees in old queens, and rouse genuine pity.

Near the end he quotes Hemingway—not at his best, but in one of his later moments of self-adoring silliness: "Life is the greatest left-hander we know, unless it was Charlie White of Chicago." Unfortunately, this is the part of the great man Algren wants to emulate and even exceed. Most painful is the fact that small fragments of this book suggest he is capable of a good deal more.—ARNO KARLEN, "Hard Shell, Soft Center," *NYTBR*, Aug. 22, 1965, pp. 4–5

NELSON ALGREN
From an interview with
Alston Anderson and Terry Southern
Writers at Work: The Paris Review *Interviews*
ed. Malcolm Cowley
1959, pp. 234–39

Interviewers: Do you think of *The Man with the Golden Arm* as being very autobiographical?

Algren: Oh, to some extent I drew on some people I knew in a half way. I made some people up and ah . . . the "Dealer" was . . . sort of a mixture; I got two, I dunno, two, three guys in mind. I know a couple guys around there. I knew *one* guy especially had a lot of those characteristics, but it's never clearly one person.

Interviewers: Well, anyway, you do think of some *one* person who could have started you thinking about Frankie Machine, since, apparently, you had at first planned an entirely different book.

Algren: The only connection I can make is . . . well, I was thinking about a war novel, and I had a buddy—little Italian bookie—pretty good dice-shooter, and he always used that phrase. We'd go partners—he's a *fairly* good crap-shooter—I mean, he's always good for about three passes. And then I'd say, "Pick it up, Joe, pick it up," and he'd say, "*Don't worry, gotta golden arm.*" Then he'd come out with a crap. He never picked it up at all—but that's where I got that title. That was a guy I knew in the Army. It has no connection, it just happened to fit in later.

Interviewers: How do you think you arrived at it thematically—rather than a war novel?

Algren: Well, if you're going to write a war novel, you have to do it while you're *in* the war. If you don't do the thing while you're there—at least the way I operate—you can't do it. It slips away. Two months after the war it was gone; but I was living in a *living* situation, and . . . I find it pretty hard to write on anything in the past . . . and this thing just got more real; I mean, the neighborhood I was living in, and these people, were a lot more *real* than the Army was.

Interviewers: What was the neighborhood you were living in?

Algren: Near Division Street.

Interviewers: Was this one of those books that "wrote itself"?

Algren: No. No, it didn't write itself. But I didn't have to contrive it. I mean, the situation hits you and you react to it, that's all. . . .

Interviewers: Did you ever feel that you should try heroin, in connection with writing a book about users?

Algren: No. No, I think you can do a thing like that best from a detached position.

Interviewers: Were you ever put down by any of these people as an eavesdropper?

Algren: No, they were mostly amused by it. Oh, they thought it was a pretty funny way to make a living, but—well, one time, after the book came out, I was sitting in this place, and there were a couple of junkies sitting there, and this one guy was real *proud* of the book; he was trying to get this other guy to read it, and finally the other guy said he had *read* it, but he said, "You know it ain't so, it ain't like that." There's a part in the book where this guy takes a shot, and then he's talking for about four pages. This guy says, "You know it ain't like that, a guy takes a fix and he goes on the nod, I mean, you know that." And the other guy says, "Well, on the other hand, if he *really* knew what he was talking about, he couldn't write the book, he'd be out in the can." So the other guy says, "Well, if you mean, is it all right for squares, sure, it's all right for squares." So, I mean, you have to compromise. But the book was somehow incidental to my relationship with them, inasmuch as they always had some hassle going on, and—well, this needle thing wasn't always up front, you know. I mean, these were people you just went to hear a band with. It was only now and then it'd come to you—like it might suddenly occur to you that one of your friends is crippled or something—it would come to you that the guy's on stuff. But it didn't stay with you very much. . . .

Interviewers: Do you think of any particular writers as having influenced your style, or approach?

Algren: Well, I used to like Stephen Crane a lot and, it goes without saying, Dostoevski—that's the only Russian I've ever reread. No, that ain't all, there's Kuprin.

Interviewers: How about American writers?

Algren: Well, Hemingway is pretty hard not to write like.

Interviewers: Do you think you write like that?

Algren: No, but you get the feeling from it—the feeling of economy. . . .

Interviewers: Do you think there's been any sort of tradition of isolation of the writer in America, as compared to Europe?

Algren: We don't have any tradition at *all* that I know of. I don't think the isolation of the American writer is a tradition; it's more that geographically he just *is* isolated, unless he happens to live in New York City. But I don't suppose there's a small town around the country that doesn't have a writer. The thing is that here you get to be a writer differently. I mean, a writer like Sartre *decides*, like any professional man, when he's fifteen, sixteen years old, that instead of being a doctor he's going to be a writer. And he absorbs the French tradition and proceeds from there. Well, here you get to be a writer when there's absolutely nothing else you can do. I mean, I don't know of any writers here who just started out to be writers, and then became writers. They just happen to fall into it.

Interviewers: How did you fall into it?

Algren: Well, I fell into it when I got out of a school of journalism in '31 in the middle of the depression. I had a little card that entitled me to a job because I'd gone to this school of journalism, you see. I was just supposed to present this card to the editor. I didn't know whether I wanted to be a sports columnist, a foreign correspondent, or what; I was willing to take what was open. Only, of course, it wasn't. Things were pretty tight. Small towns would send you to big cities, and big cities would send you to small towns; it was a big hitchhiking time, so I wound up in New Orleans selling coffee—one of these door-to-door deals—and one of the guys on this crew said we ought to get out of there because he had a packing shed in Rio Grande Valley. So we bummed down to the Rio Grande. Well, he didn't have a packing shed, he *knew* somebody who had one— one of those things, you know—but what he did do, he promoted a Sinclair gasoline station down there. It was a farce, of course, it was an abandoned station in the middle of nowhere; I mean, there was no chance of selling gas or anything like that, but I suppose it looked good for the Sinclair agent to write up to Dallas and say he had a couple guys rehabilitating the place. There was nothing to the station, it didn't even have any windows. But we had to dig pits for the

gas, and then one day the Sinclair guy comes up with a hundred gallons of gas and wanted somebody to take legal responsibility for it. So my partner hands me the pencil and says, "Well, you can write better than I can, you been to school," and I was sort of proud of that, so I signed for it.

Then my partner had the idea that I should stay there and take care of the station, just keep up a front, you know, in case the Sinclair guy came around, and he'd go out—he had an old Studebaker—and buy up produce from the Mexican farmers very cheap, and bring it back and we'd sell it at the station— turn the station into a produce stand. I mean, we were so far out on this highway that the agent couldn't really check on us—we were way out; there were deer and wild hogs and everything out there—and in three weeks we'd be rich. That was *his* idea. But the only thing he brought back was black-eyed peas. He paid about two dollars for a load of black-eyed peas—well, that was like buying a load of cactus—but he wouldn't admit he'd made a mistake. So, he went around to the big Piggly-Wiggly store and they said they'd take *some* of the peas if they were shelled. So he set me to shelling the peas. I shelled those damn peas till I was nearly blind. In the meantime, he'd left town, out to promote something else.

Then one day he showed up with another guy, in a much better-looking car—he'd left the old Studebaker there at the station—and I saw them out there by the pit fooling around with some sort of contraption, but it didn't dawn on me, and then it turned out they were siphoning the gas into this guy's car. Well, they left town before I knew what was happening. When I caught on I was being swindled, of course, I was very indignant about it, and I wrote letters that took in the whole South. I gave the whole Confederacy hell. Oh, it was nowhere, just nowhere, nowhere. So I wrote a couple letters like that— and I was very serious at the time, and some of that got into the letters. Ultimately, I got out of there. I poured a lot of water into the empty tank, but I felt like a fugitive because I didn't account to the Sinclair guy. It was a terrible farce, but later when I got home—I don't know how much later—I read the letters again, and there was a story in them, all right. So I rewrote it and *Story Magazine* published it, and I was off. But that's what I mean by "falling into it." Because I was really trying to become a big oil man. . . .

Interviewers: Do you try to write a poetic prose?

Algren: No. No, I'm not writing it, but so many people say things poetically, they say it for you in a way you never could. Some guy just coming out of jail might say, "I did it from bell to bell," or like the seventeen-year-old junkie, when the judge asked him what he did all day, he said, "Well, I find myself a doorway to lean against, and I take a fix, and then I lean, I just lean and dream." They always say things like that.

Interviewers: What do you think of Faulkner?

Algren: Well, I can get lost in him awful easy. But he's powerful.

Interviewers: It's interesting that Hemingway once said that Faulkner and you were the two best writers in America.

Algren: Yeah, I remember when he said that. He said, "After Faulkner . . . " I was very hurt.

Interviewers: You said that the plot of *The Man with the Golden Arm* was "creaky." How much emphasis are you going to put on plot in your future writing?

Algren: Well, you have to prop the book up somehow. You've got to frame it, or otherwise it becomes just a series of episodes.

Interviewers: You gave more attention to plot in this book you've just finished.

Algren: This one I plotted a great deal more than any

other. In the first place because it's more of a contrived book. I'm trying to write a reader's book, more than my own book. When you're writing your own book, you don't have to plot; it's just when you write for the reader. And since I'm dealing with the past, the thirties, I have to contrive, whereas, with a living situation, I wouldn't have to.

Interviewers: Do you think that this one came off as well as *The Man with the Golden Arm*?

Algren: Mechanically and, I think, technically, it's done more carefully, and probably reads better than previous books.

Interviewers: You make this distinction between a "reader's book" and a book for yourself. What do you think the difference is?

Algren: It's the difference between writing by yourself and writing on a stage. I mean, if the book were your own, you'd be satisfied just to have the guy walk down the sidewalk and fall on his head. In a reader's book, you'd have him turn a double somersault. You're more inclined to clown, I think, in a reader's book. You've got one ear to the audience for yaks. It's just an obligation you have to fulfill.

Interviewers: Obligation to whom?

Algren: Well, you're talking economics now. I mean, the way I've operated with publishers is that I live on the future. I take as much money as I can get for as long as I can get it, you know, a year or two years, and by the end of that time your credit begins to have holes in it, and—well, you have to come up. After all, they're businessmen. Of course, you can get diverted from a book you *want* to write. I've got a book about Chicago on the West Side—I did a hundred pages in a year, and I still figure I need three years on it—but I was under contract for this other one, so it took precedence. I didn't want to contract for the first one, because I just wanted to go along as far as I could on it without having any pressure on me. The one I contracted for is the one I finished, and now I'm going back to the one I want to do.

Interviewers: Did you enjoy writing *The Man with the Golden Arm* more than you did this last one?

Algren: Well, it seemed more important. I wouldn't say I enjoyed it more, because in a way this was a much easier book to do. The lumber is all cut for you. The timber and the dimensions are all there, you know you're going to write a four-hundred-page book; and in that way your problems are solved, you're limited. Whereas, with a book like that *Man with the Golden Arm*, you cut your own timber, and you don't know where you're building, you don't have any plan or anything.

Interviewers: Do you find that you take more care with a thing like that?

Algren: No, I always take great care. I think I'm very careful, maybe too careful. You can get too fussy. I do find myself getting bogged down wondering whether I should use a colon or a semicolon, and so on, and I keep trying each one out. I guess you can overdo that.

Interviewers: Do you think that writing a book out of economic obligation could affect your other work?

Algren: No, it won't have anything to do with that at all. One is a matter of *living* and reacting from day to day, whereas the book I just finished could be written anywhere there's a typewriter.

Interviewers: Do you think your writing improves?

Algren: I think technically it does. I reread my first book, and found it—oh, you know, "poetic," in the worst sense.

Interviewers: Do you feel that any critics have influenced your work?

Algren: None could have, because I don't read them. I doubt anyone does, except other critics. It seems like a sealed-off field with its own lieutenants, pretty much preoccupied with its own intrigues. I got a glimpse into the uses of a certain kind of criticism this past summer at a writers' conference— into how the avocation of assessing the failures of better men can be turned into a comfortable livelihood, providing you back it up with a Ph.D. I saw how it was possible to gain a chair of literature on no qualification other than persistence in nipping the heels of Hemingway, Faulkner, and Steinbeck. I know, of course, that there are true critics, one or two. For the rest all I can say is, "Deal around me."

Interviewers: How about this movie, *The Man with the Golden Arm*?

Algren: Yeah.

Interviewers: Did you have anything to do with the script?

Algren: No. No, I didn't last long. I went out there for a thousand a week, and I worked Monday, and I got fired Wednesday. The guy that hired me was out of town Tuesday.

A. R. AMMONS

1926–

Born on February 18, 1926, Archie Randolph Ammons grew up on a farm near Whiteville, North Carolina. He began writing poetry while serving in the U.S. Naval Reserve from 1944 to 1946. He graduated from Wake Forest College in 1949, the year he married Phyllis Plumbo. Ammons was an elementary school principal for two years, then a graduate student at the University of California at Berkeley. From 1952 to 1961, he worked as vice-president of a glass company in Atlantic City. While there, he published his first collection of poems, *Ommateum with Doxology* (1955). He left the job on a Breadloaf Fellowship, and became poetry editor of the *Nation* in 1963. The following year he published a second collection, *Expressions of Sea Level*, and began teaching at Cornell, where he remains.

Pastoral, conversational, and somewhat unorthodox as a poet, Ammons wrote *Tape for the Turn of the Year* (1965) on a continuous roll of adding machine tape. He received a Guggenheim

Fellowship in 1966, and an American Academy of Arts and Letters Fellowship in 1967. *Uplands* won the Levinson Prize in 1970, *Collected Poems* the National Book Award in 1973, *Diversifications* the Bollingen Prize in 1975. He lives in Ithaca with his wife; they have one child.

General

"Life is an affair of people not of places. But for me," Wallace Stevens wrote, "life is an affair of places and that is the trouble." That trouble, that strain in American writing has continued to prompt some of our best verse: solitary testings of the mind against a landscape, as if these were the only really telling encounters. Anyone who responds to Frost or Stevens, or knows A. R. Ammons's earlier books, will be prepared for *Uplands*, for its tough wry explorations, as well as for the intensity and buoyancy with which Ammons makes a familiar kind of poetry his own.

He has always had a gift for recalling romantic promises as if there were fresh ways for them to be fulfilled: "For it is not so much to know the self/as to know it as it is known/by galaxy and cedar cone." But after these exhilarating prospects come the sobering performances, the puzzles of the "surrendered self among unwelcoming forms." What sound like visionary promptings— lightning weddings of the self to the outside world—become bewildering before his eyes. It is not only a matter of calling into question the easy ways we have for encountering what we see, but also of facing the frustrations of the most willing, the most ardent, the most open observers.

In one of the best poems in *Uplands*, Ammons likens the mind's meeting an experience to the concentration of the laser beam. "Laser" closes with an all too human lapse:

> the mind tries to
> dream of diversity, of mountain
> rapids shattered with sound and light,
> of wind fracturing brush or
> bursting out of order against a mountain
> range: but the focused beam
> folds all energy in:
> the image glares filling all space:
> the head falls and
> hangs and cannot wake itself.

That falling away in the face of abundance is one of the characteristic gestures in this book. We are reminded that we are intruders in nature, that our most precise expressions are only approximate, that "there is nothing small enough to conjure clarity with."

Who else would illustrate the title "Clarity" with a poem about erosion? A rockslide, exposing all the stresses beneath what we imagine to be solid, reveals "streaks &/scores of knowledge/now obvious and quiet." Ammons enjoys giving civilized words like *clarity, knowledge, obvious,* and *quiet* a tumble. His poems deliberately belie their abstract titles— "Periphery," "Classic," "The Unifying Principle"—scaling down the large questions of philosophy and romantic lyric to answers made possible by discrete and particular encounters.

Even when he takes on the notion of a "unifying principle" in nature (those common definitions and perceptions which allow us to be comfortable in the world), he does so with a careful sense of how standards are built up from intractable, unrepeated or eccentric events:

> a particular tread that sometimes unweaves, taking
> more shape on, into dance: much must be
> tolerated as out of timbre, out of step, as being not
> in its time or mood (the hiatus of the unconcerned)
> and much room provided for the wretched to find
> caves
> to ponder way off in. . . .

Two kinds of poems seem to satisfy Ammons's needs. One is a short lyric which makes momentary assertions against nature's obliterating powers: these are small-scale ecstasies, and often the most minimal claims must suffice. In "Further On," summer sensations are shadowed by the approaching inhuman freeze of winter which "takes the gleeful, glimmering/tongues away." The threat is to human speech and understanding: "the wind lifting its saying out/to the essential yell of the/lost and gone." In that light, even the ability to describe, to offer the reader a corner of landscape, becomes a form of self-assertion. What serves is an exact sense of the surviving instincts of summer life: "lichen, a wintery weed,/fills out for the brittle sleep:/ waterbirds plunder the shallows."

By and large the short poems do battle against the "periphery," the profusion and separateness in the outside world, "thickets hard to get around in/or get around/for an older man." The alternative form for Ammons is a much more abandoned one: the long swirling interior monologue in which he gives himself up to fluidity and change. *Uplands* has one splendid example, "Summer Session 1968," a journal of being on and off duty at Cornell. In sometimes slangy, sometimes lyrical short lines, it eddies from one subject to another as the poet plays at being the Bloom of his own Ithaca:

> the problem is
> how
> to keep shape and flow:

Disciplined as he is, Ammons is wittily aware—the line breaks suggest it—of the difficulties of such poems; some, like "Spiel" in the present volume, seem too random. But "Summer Session 1968" justifies the experiments. Its earthy anecdotes, landscapes and interpolated notes from friends are full of a wild sense of self that he also urges upon his students.

> revise the world:
> they clip, trim, slice:
> they bring it in:
> oh no I say you've just put it on stilts:

A few years ago Ammons threaded a long poem (book length!) along an adding machine tape, producing a December diary, "Tape for the Turn of the Year." That was the most flamboyant of his efforts to turn his books of verse into something beyond the neat chapters or gatherings marking stages in a poet's career. He no longer believes in summaries; if one expects them, one must look back to *Corson's Inlet* (1965), his best single book and the one that announced his poetic credo, or to the *Selected Poems*, which Cornell University Press published quite handsomely two years ago. For the moment— "Uplands" is the first of such volumes—we can expect something closer to journals of mental states, each poem an entry finding a form and a scene for a very exact encounter or discovery.

As Ammons puts it in "Conserving the Magnitude of Uselessness": in behalf of "all things not worth the work/of having," in behalf of singularity

> the poets will yelp and hoot forever
> probably
> rank as weeks themselves and just as abandoned.

All Ammons's control is here (the cagey probably; the play on abandoned); so is the subversive bravado which is the gift of his poems.—DAVID KALSTONE, *"Uplands"*, *NYTBR*, May 9, 1971, pp. 5, 20

Works

Poems Small and Easy is the subtitle of this most important group of poems whose matter is in fact larger than their length, and whose meditative structure is rather harder than their syntax. A. R. Ammons's work is probably to embody the major vision of nature in the poetry of our part of the century. But the 87 short lyrics which record part of that vision have no obvious formal counterparts. Neither the loosely-versified scout manuals and ecological gospel-songs of the moment, nor epigrammatic modes of moralizing landscape descending from Robert Frost, nor the constantly refocusing, relentlessly uncaptioned snapshots of the unarranged that some poets have learned to take from William Carlos Williams, provide models for Ammons's intense and profound imaginative excursion.

It is a solitary walk through the rural for which these poems do, indeed, brief us, as they map, gloss, sketch and caption, compare, probe, emend, reconstruct, and perform the other verbal acts to which meditative moments give rise. Henry Vaughan in the 17th century, walking through his West Country, watching parts of the world blaze into significance; his contemporary Sir Thomas Browne, decoding the signatures of the general in the facts of biology along his East Anglian shore; the latter's 20th century descendant, the great D'Arcy Thompson, revealing nature's unconscious mathematics—these are some of Ammons's less obvious predecessors.

"My eyes'/concision shoots to kill"—so concludes his aubade, "Off," and the hunting of the world begins with a hard look into the center of things, a center from which each poem, as well as the whole volume, starts out. In the opening poem, hearing how "A bird fills up the/streamside bush/with wasteful song" the poet traces it to "song's improvident center" rather than to the dark wood of heroic tragedy refused in Robert Frost's "Come In." The subsequent ordering of the poems in *Briefings* is built along the great imaginative outdoor walk as a romantic counterpart of the erotic museum through which confessional sonnet sequences move.

Major visionary moments—"The Quince Bush" transfixed by morning glory, the myth of depth in "Crevice," poems like "He Held Radical Light" and "Doubling the Grass"—are interspersed with annotations and shifts of gaze from the page of the world the poet has been reading to the world of the page: remarks on poetics, even epigrams, here find their place. "Hippie Hop" concludes an editorializing nonpoem with a grim antithetical necessity: "I make/analogies, my bucketful of/ flowers: I give flowers to people/of all policies, sexes and races/ including the vicious, the/uncertain, and the white."

What is central to this poetry is the figure the poet's mind makes in the midst of the landscape it is scanning. Its determining fiction is of a man motionless in the country: what moves is the interaction of his ordering mind with the givens of the world. Often, the axis of that motion passes through the knowns of geology or botany, just as it traces, on occasion, the courses of a moral imperative seen in some growth or shape. The reaches of this vision have a boundlessness we have seen before in American romanticism. Consider, for example, the conclusion of "Circles" with its Emersonian thrust beyond the allusion of the title: "something nearer than/the pleasure of/circles drives into the next/moment and the next" as the poet contemplates his backyard flowers. The difficulties of this rich and profound poetry are not so much those of its occasionally elliptical syntax, nor of Ammons's almost unique use of the full colon as a linkage between members of a growingly complex figure. True poetry seems hard in a world where rhetoric comes so easily as does the simulation of imagination in machines for producing images.

In the last, and perhaps most remarkable poem in the book, "The City Limits," Ammons considers the "radiance" leaping out of depths as well as surfaces of things, the mind's own light, and turns back to the conclusion of all the great American readers of landscape and specimen—that the search for meanings will find in the hieroglyphs over which it broods the terms of the brooding consciousness itself. At the end of this poem and of the book, "the man stands and looks about, the/leaf does not increase itself above the grass, and the dark/ work of the deepest cells is of a tune which May bushes/and fear lit by the breadth of such calmly turns to praise."—JOHN HOLLANDER, "Briefings," *NYTBR*, May 9, 1971, pp. 5, 20

In 1955, Ammons' first book, *Ommateum*, discovered his tremendous theme: putting off the flesh and taking on the universe. For this poet, there is no windy abstraction in the notion, but a wonderful and rustling submission to the real, the incidental and the odd. Indeed, the poignance of momentary life in its combat with eternal design so haunted the poet that a decade later, in his magnificent second and third books, *Expressions of Sea Level* and *Corsons Inlet*, he had not yet come down on the side of transcendence, nor even taken off. Determined rather to suffer or search out immersion in the stream of reality without surrendering all that is and makes one particularly oneself, Ammons devised a notation of events as faithful to the wavering rhythm of metabolism as it might be to the larger fixities of celestial order:

> for it is not so much to know the self
> as to know it as it is known
>   by galaxy and cedar cone,
> as if birth had never found it
> and death could never end it:

That terminal colon is a characteristic of Ammons' verse—a sign to indicate not only equivalence but the node or point of passage on each side of which an existence hangs in the balance; and the balance is the movement of the verse itself, a constant experiment with the weight of language the line can bear, can meaningfully break beneath, so that the enjambment will *show* something more than completion or incompletion. Between these two books, Ammons published a kind of satyr play of self-hood, *Tape for the Turn of the Year* (1965), "a long thin poem" written on a huge roll of adding-machine tape run through the typewriter to its conclusion, a poem about the specifications of identity by the very refusal to prune or clip:

> the center-arising
> form
> adapts, tests the
>   peripheries, draws in,
> finds a new factor,
> utilizes a new method,
> gains a new foothold
> responds to inner and outer change. . . .

And these mediations led, or prodded, the poet, by 1966, to a further collection, *Northfield Poems*, in which the provisional is treasured as an earnest (though hardly a solemnizing) of survival: "no finality of vision,/I have perceived nothing completely,/tomorrow a new walk is a new walk," he says, and the walk is almost always on the beach, the shore. Ammons rehearses a marginal, a transitional experience; he is a littoralist of the imagination because the shore, the beach, or the coastal creek is not a place but an *event*, a transaction where life and death are exchanged, where shape and chaos are won and lost. And then in 1968 Ammons chose from all these books (except for the indiscreet, revelatory *Tape*) a magnificent series of *provisions*, stays against chaos as against finality, articles of belief, a mastered credulity, his *Selected Poems*. Insufficiently attended to, this book is the masterpiece of our period, the widest scope and the intensest focus American poetry has registered since Frost, since Stevens, since Roethke.

And now we have the new book, three dozen lyrical pieces, mostly no more than a page long, and two extended texts, the erotic experiment "Guitar Recitativos" and the superb dedication poem called "Summer Session" which closes "with my trivia/I'll dispense dignity, a sense of office,/ formality they [the poet's students] can define themselves against." A collection necessarily *slight* if measured against the massive accumulation of Ammons' past, yet if we recall the original sense of the word—*plain, simple*—then we can say, with Pope, "slight is the subject, but not so the praise," for in these sudden, attractive fits and starts the poet urges himself into a new economy, a bright particularity of diction entirely *gainful* to his panoply, a way of handling verse without giving up conversation:

> arriving at ways
> water survives its motions.

The way is enjambment, a wizardry in working with the right-hand margin, so that the line never relinquishes its energy until it can start up its successor. "Certain presuppositions are altered," Ammons announces, talking about the look of "summit stones lying free and loose/out among the shrub trees" in the Alleghenies. We are no longer on the beach in these poems, but in the mountains, among masses, solids, fixities, and the problem is how to get moving again. It is the poet's situation, the poet's dilemma, to make the mountain come to Mohammed, and he has started the pebbles rolling:

> every
> exigency seems prepared for that might
> roll, bound, or give flight
> to stone: that is, the stones
> are prepared: they are round and ready.

Thus the book itself is an account—scrupulous in its details, its hesitations, its celebrations of minor incidents, lesser claims— of how a landscape or a man comes to realize motion, comes to be *on the way* rather than in it. There is, here, a place, then the discovery that the place can be left, then a sanctification of that discovery, its loss and gain. In other words, there are Ammons' three favorite words: *ambience, salience, radiance.*—RICHARD HOWARD, "A New Beginning," *Nation*, Jan. 18, 1971, pp. 90–92

With these *Collected Poems* a lag in reputation is overcome. A. R. Ammons's 400 pages of poetry, written over the space of a generation, manifest an energy, wit and an amazing *compounding* of mind with nature that cannot be overlooked. Even with the omission of Ammons's longest continuous work, *Tape for the Turn of the Year* (1965), this is a remarkable book, enriched by three long poems (together almost 80 pages) that must have been composed since *Uplands* (1970) and *Briefings* (1971). Indeed, with *Hibernaculum*, 112 stanzas in length, a high point of the poet's delayed career is reached. His first book, *Ommateum (Compound Eye)*, caused no stir when it appeared in 1955; and even the mid-sixties' explosion of *Expressions at Sea Level* (1964), *Corsons Inlet* (1965) and *Northfield Poems* (1966) did not make of him an inescapable presence. Ammons snared some academic admirers, but many remained suspicious of this prolific nature bard who kept turning it out like prose. His distinction as a major American poet will now be evident.

There is a problem of bulk. Ammons is a poetic Leviathan, "Created hugest that swim the Ocean stream." The intrepid mass and inner paradoxes of his verse delight and alarm at the same time. Perception is enough, Ammons seems to say, or too much. Nature-news flashes all around us, "bends and blends of sight," "the news to my left over the dunes. . . ." The ticker-tape effect is especially remarkable in such poems as "Saliences" or the microcosmic "Corsons Inlet." It bespeaks, however, no simple vitalism, for nature's plenty makes us feel poor.

Ammons yields to every solicitation from nature only to find he has no identity left, or no firm power of naming. "So I said I am Ezra," he begins his first poem, conjoining saying and naming. But, he continues, "the wind whipped my throat/ gaming for the sounds of my voice." Ammons's best poems about this loss of self and voice to nature are "Gravelly Run" and the late and very beautiful "Plunder." In the latter, reality accuses the mind of "stealing" from it to create language, and the punishment for this strange new Prometheanism is, clearly enough, that the poet cannot collect himself, even in these *Collected Poems*.

A man, says Emerson, "cannot be a naturalist until he satisfies all the demands of the spirit. Love is as much its demand as perception." This clarifies, perhaps, the difficulty of all nature-poetry, but especially that of Ammons. For he subdues himself totally to *love of perception*, refusing all higher adventure. "No arranged terror: no forcing of image, plan,/or thought:/no propaganda, no humbling of reality to precept:/ terror pervades but is not arranged, all possibilities/of escape open: no route shut, except in/the sudden loss of all routes" ("Corsons Inlet"). Nature herself, as in Wordsworth, must lead to a loss of the way.

This means, however, that Ammons can only extend the Wordsworthian revolution: emptying lyric poetry of false plots, then keeping the emptiness open for a confluence (always gracious or chancy) of event and significance. Hence his "eddies of meaning" or "swervings of action/like the inlet's cutting edge," which produce an essayistic type of poem of variable length and tenuous meter; hence also those fine, organic minglings of mind and nature, or interlacings of figure and ground. But what is often given up is the formal, graduated perfection we still feel in many poems like "Gravelly Run," "Laser," "The City Limits" and "Periphery."

Undeceived poets like Ammons are aware that nature cannot suffice even when they claim that "somehow it seems sufficient/to see and hear whatever coming and going is." Their nature poetry is an almost religious kind of discipline: it acknowledges the mind's defeat, chastens self-concern, and tempers the philosophical quest for meanings. At some point, then, the "Overall" or "sum of events" must be reckoned with. This is what happens preeminently in "Essay on Poetics," "Hibernaculum" and "Extremes and Moderations," which revive modern poetry's quest for the long poem.

In these extravagant and beautiful poems—verse essays really—Ammons maintains a virtuoso current of phrasing that embraces all types of vocabulary, all motions of thought, and leads us back now to Whitman and now to the accumulative (if hopefully cumulative) strain of Pound's *Cantos* or Williams's *Paterson*. Building on a non-narrative base, that is, on a will-to-words almost sexual in persistence, he changes all "flesh-body" to "wordbody" and dazzles us with what he calls "interpenetration"—a massively playful nature-thinking, a poetic incarnation of smallest as well as largest thoughts.

Let me quote two sequences from *Hibernaculum* to show the difficult integrity of these longer poems. Here is Ammons at his worst:

                    I see
Aggregates of definition, plausible
        emergences. I see
reticulations of ambience . . .

what do I see: I see a world made,
        unmade, and made again
and near crying either way: I look
        to the ground for the
lost, the ground's lost: I see grime,
        just grime, grain
grist, grist. . . .

This is not improved by the Hopkinsian bumps and grinds. There are too many words: inspiration becomes inflation, "invents vents" and destroys adequate form.

At his best, however, Ammons, like Rilke and Stevens, addresses "the empty place" that threatens his power of speech. A poet, says Rilke in the *Sonnets to Orpheus*, cannot but celebrate: "nie versagt ihm die Stimme am Stauber" ("his voice never fails him, though it is choked by dust"). Nature's indifference, or even the uselessness of speech in the face of that indifference, provokes Ammons to bursts of astonishing celebratory power:

                    if the night is to be
habitable, if dawn is to come
        out of it, if day is ever
to grow brilliant on delivered
        populations, the word

must have its way by the
        brook, lie out cold all night
along the snow limb, spell by
        yearning's wilted weed till
the wilted weed rises, know
        the patience and smallness

of stones: I address the empty
        place where the god
that has been deposed
        lived. . . .

It is not always easy to appreciate an imaginative project of such scope, especially when it is fragmented in so many ways, scattered over so much verbal space. Even the essay-poems, "on course but destinationless," seem occasionally all periphery and no center. Ammons's nature chit-chat can bring him closer to William Cowper's *The Task* than to Wordsworth's *Prelude* or to Coleridge in his streamy *Notebooks*.

The poet knows the problem, of course; he hints that he wants to do away with the traditional center-plus-frame kind of lyric in favor of one that respects the principle of entropy. Like nature's energy, poems should run down into an "ideal raggedness: the loose or fragmented or scopy," even as they release imagistic bursts, "airy avalanches, sketchy with event . . . overspills, radiances."

Yet because Ammons expresses everything in casual or pastoral terms, because he "lies low in the light as in a high testimony," there is a danger his achievement will remain self-limited. Instead of a true "saying, binding" he may be creating only an *objet trouvé* art—full of delightful nuggets of perception and self-perception, veined stones found on the beach of the mind which the child prefers to the rare or terrible crystal. But no one in his generation has put "earth's materials" to better use, or done more to raise pastoral to the status of major art.— GEOFFREY H. HARTMAN, "*Collected Poems 1951–1971*," *NYTBR*, Nov. 19, 1972, pp. 39–40

Ammons's first book, *Ommateum*, published in 1955, seems not to have attracted much attention; his second appeared nine years later. Recently he has been more prolific, and critics,

particularly Harold Bloom and Richard Howard, have considered his work seriously and at length, but few had probably anticipated a *Collected Poems* of such dimensions (almost 400 pages, to which must be added the recent Norton reissue in a separate volume of his 200-page poem *Tape for the Turn of the Year*). If his importance was suspected before, it is now, as so often happens, confirmed merely by the joining of several volumes in one—not only because the solidity and brilliance are at last fully apparent but because, as also often happens, the occasionally weaker early poems somehow illuminate and give access to the big, difficult later ones.

Ammons's landscape is American sidereal; a descendant of Emerson, as Bloom has pointed out, he is always on the brink of being "whirled/Beyond the circuit of the shuddering Bear" from the safe confines of backyard or living room. But the fascination of his poetry is not the transcendental but his struggle with it, which tends to turn each poem into a battleground strewn with scattered testimony to the history of its making in the teeth of its creator's reluctance and distrust of "all this fiddle."

Reading the poems in sequence one soon absorbs this rhythm of making-unmaking, of speech facing up to the improbability of speech, so that ultimately Ammons's landscape—yard, riverbed, ocean, mountain, desert, and soon "the unseasonal undifferentiated empty stark"—releases the reader to the clash of word against word, to what Harold Bloom calls his "oddly negative exuberance." The movement is the same, from the visible if only half-real flotsam of daily living to the uncertainties beyond, but one forgets this from one poem to the next; each is as different as a wave is from the one that follows and obliterates it. One is left, like the author at the end of his best-known poem, "Corsons Inlet," "enjoying the freedom that/ Scope eludes my grasp, that there is no finality of vision,/that I have perceived nothing completely,/that tomorrow a new walk is a new walk."

The poet's work is like that of Penelope ripping up her web into a varicolored heap that tells the story more accurately than the picture did. And meanwhile the "regional" has become universal, at an enormous but unavoidable cost; the destructiveness of the creative act in Ammons ("what/destruction am I/ blessed by?") permits him to escape, each time, the temptations of the *paysage moralisé*. Much has been written about the relation of the so-called "New York School" of poets to the painting of men like Pollock, but in a curious way Ammons's poetry seems a much closer and more successful approximation of "Action Painting" or art as process. ("The problem is/how to keep shape and flow.")

Marianne Moore pointed out that "inns are not residences," and a similar basic corrective impulse runs throughout Ammons, giving rise to a vocabulary of pivotal words. "Saliences" (the title of one of his best poems), "suasion," "loft," "scary," "motion," and "extreme" are a few which assume their new meaning only after a number of encounters, a meaning whose sharpness corrects a previous one whose vagueness was more dangerous than we knew. A "loft" (also frequently used as a verb) is not a summit, but a way station and possibly the last one; saliences are pertinent and outstanding but not necessarily to be confused with meanings; suasion is neither persuasion nor dissuasion. The corrective impulse proceeds as much from prudence as from modesty; in any case it can coexist with occasional outbursts of pure egotism: "I want a squirrel-foil for my martin pole/I want to perturb some laws of balance/I want to create unnatural conditions" (but the poem of which this is the beginning is entitled "The Imagined Land"), just as Ammons's frugality and his relentless understatement are countered by the swarming profusion of the poems.

This austerity could lose its point in the course of such a long volume: the restricted palette; the limited cast of characters (bluejays, squirrels, and other backyard denizens figure prominently, along with the poet's wife, child, and car, not to forget the wind with whom he has dialogues frequently in a continuing love-hate relationship); the sparse iconography of plant, pebble, sand, leaf, twig, bone, end by turning the reader back from the creature comforts he might have expected from "nature" poetry to the dazzlingly self-sufficient logic which illuminates Ammons's poetry and in turn restores these samples from nature to something of their Wordsworthian splendor—but Wordsworth recollected in the tranquillity of midcentury mindless America, and after the ironic refractions of Emerson, Stevens, and Williams. For despite Ammons's misgivings, his permanent awareness of "a void that is all being, a being that is void," his "negative exuberance" is of a kind that could exist only after the trials of so much negation.

> I can't think of a thing to uphold:
> the carborundum plant snows
> sift-scum on the slick, outgoing river
> and along the avenues car wheels
> float in a small powder: my made-up
> mind idles like a pyramid. . . .
> ("Working Still")

But if he is unable to find a saving word for the polluted (in so many ways) American scene, his speech elevates it even as it refuses to transform it. "No American poet," writes Harold Bloom in an essay on Ammons, "When You Consider the Radiance," in his book *The Ringers in the Tower*, "not Whitman or Stevens, shows us so fully something otherwise unknown in the structures of the national consciousness as Ammons does." And for Americans who feel that America is the last truly foreign country, this something comes startlingly alive in poem after poem, as in the magnificent "One: Many":

> . . . and on and on through the villages,
> along dirt roads, ditchbanks, by gravel pits and on
>   to the homes, to the citizens and their histories,
> inventions, longings:
> I think how enriching, though unassimilable as a
>   whole
> into art, are the differences: the small-business
> man in
>   Kansas City declares an extra dividend
> and his daughter
>   who teaches school in Duquesne
> buys a Volkswagen, a second car for the family:
> out of many, one
> from variety an over-riding unity,
>   the expression of
> variety. . . .

How perfect and how funny in its Whitmanesque nod to the automotive industry is that "buys a Volkswagen, a second car for the family": it seems as much by its music as by its sense to sum up everything that is beautiful and wrong in our vast, monotonous, but very much alive landscape. And Ammons knows this well; he ends the poem with an unemotional summation that, in its reluctant acceptance of the "opaque" world that is still "world enough to take my time, stretch my reason, hinder/and free me," can also stand for the work:

> no book of laws, short of unattainable reality itself,
> can anticipate every event,
> control every event: only the book
> of laws founded against itself,

founded on freedom of each event to occur as itself,
lasts into the inevitable balances events will take.
> —JOHN ASHBERY, "The American Grain,"
>   *NYRB*, Feb. 22, 1973, pp. 4–6

"When Whitman said 'O Pioneers'"—observed F. Scott Fitzgerald—"he said all." With Fitzgerald the cry had already become a groan, but the American urge to "sing possible/changes/that might redeem," in A. R. Ammons's words, proves stubborn, and our writers' wagons can still be heard heading out of town, creaking for joy. If not toward a greater America then toward "eternal being," or heterocosm joyous," they make their dauntless way. The Romantic dream of returning at dawn "wet/to the hips with meetings" is quite dead in England, but our own Ammons and W. S. Merwin, among others, are out without their long boots. Like the more troubled Pound, Stevens and Williams before them, like Emerson, Thoreau, Melville, Whitman, they are poets of a possibly redeeming change, a change sought in what Emerson called "an original relation to the universe."

. . . ⟨W⟩hile Merwin has run on toward "the decimal of being," Ammons has turned back. Once oblique, prophetic, isolate, cloudbrowsed, he has become almost folksy. "Redemptions despise the reality," he observes, disapprovingly, and says: "I expect to promote good will and difficult/clarities: I'm tired of bumfuzzlement and bafflement."

Ammons's new "good will" is Romantic, but so democratic, so accepting, so rationalized, that it is almost casual: he is in no haste at all to hitch his wagon to a star. He now seeks "the good of all in the good of each." As for his "difficult" clarity, it is chiefly the "unmendably integral" connection of everything to everything else in the universe. "Touch the universe anywhere and you touch it/everywhere." What survives of his pared Romanticism is the seed-choked belief that "nothing is separate." Brushing shoulders, it may be, with the all-inclusive, infinitely loving James Agee of *Let Us Now Praise Famous Men*, similarly using the colon to mark what Agee called the "mutual magnetisms" of things, the unity of "the bottom and the extremest reach of time," Ammons has gone on to develop more explicitly, laboriously, abstractly, the concept of reality as a great fugue, a holy unity. This concept is, as he says, the "mysticism" of modern science, the radiance glimpsed in the cooperative lives of a cell as well as in the long reach of the galaxies (which are directly accountable, observes this science, for the inertia of matter—for such calm as there is—in all the other galaxies). Nothing is separate. Nothing is even different, at the core: there the universal unit, the "nervous atom," "spins and shines unsmirched." Still, "having/been chastened to the irreducible," Ammons says, "I have found the/irreducible bountiful." There are "many rafts to ride and the tides make a place to go."

In colonizing for poetry the structural models of science, Ammons has become an intellectual's Whitman, afoot with a laboratory vision that, for all its abstract vocabulary, and however palely, he lectures and tweaks into poetry. Between the hieratic Romanticism of Pound, Stevens and Merwin and the "nude" Romanticism of Whitman, he takes a place near W. C. Williams, his language more textbooky but his procedures more open. Because his "idealism's as thin as the sprinkled/sky and nearly as expansive," one can move about freely in his sensibility; it is neither frost nor frolic. The appeal of this new, pulled-up Romanticism is its levelness, including the way it constantly levels with the reader. The cold hand of science has taken the fever out of this prophet's brow: he just chats intelligently, on and on, happy with the scheme of things, wanting you to be happy, too.

With his "most open suasion," his desire for an "open form" that offers "room enough for everything to find/its running self-concisions and expansions, its way," Ammons has created a new poetic structure: the poem as democratic continuum. Where Whitman's numbered sections are new breaths, new embraces, Ammons's are artificial overlays on a non-stop monologue that keeps pace with the "progressing/motions" of the universe. Random, flexible, this "Form of a Motion" will turn in mid-line from, say, the "plenitude of nothingness" among galaxies to the "neck-nicking walk" of pheasants, or the United Nations, or a visit with the poet Philip Booth—turn as amiably and unanxiously as the universe itself includes the microbe and the Milky Way, being an intermediary to all. With its "full freightages of recalcitrance," "Sphere" means to be a vision "gravid" with reality, a vision of the contrarieties and reconciliations of the very motions of being.

One of those modern poems that pose in front of a mirror, "Sphere" talks repeatedly about itself, betraying hopes that it fails to fulfill. It tells us we may "dip in anywhere," which is true, but also that "the poem reaches a stillness which is its form," which is true indeed of most poems, but not of poems that let you "dip in anywhere." The "mutual magnetisms" between the manifold elements of the poems are as weak as Ammons's idealism—weak as a direct consequence of the theoretical securities, the abstractness, of that idealism. The "harmony" that is "the highest/ambience of diversity," the "common reality past declaration" that "the fragments will be apprehended/to declare"—this simply fails to appear. There is only the continuity of Ammons's language, its "flexible path," and the telling and retelling of his intellectual beads: *motion, multeity, diversity, form, nothingness, stayings, changes, radiality*, etc. And how could it be otherwise in a poet, so given to ratiocination, to explicit "suasion"?

. . . Having drained off all but a wetting of the implicit, Ammons has left almost everything to his intelligence, the crispness of his language, the geniality of his tone, and the greatness of his subject, his *reasonable* approach to Romantic "spirituality." If the result is the "open" American counterpart of the closed Augustan verse essay—equally an *essay*—still in this reader's palm, at first weighing, it feels major. Though it has nothing of the feat about it it has scope, is original and blandly imposing. And to his linear discourse Ammons gives just enough "jangling dance" to shock "us to attend the moods of lips." Although almost nothing in the poem moves or ravishes, almost everything interests and holds—holds not least because it tests, and finds thin, the spiritual satisfactions available in being a conscious part of a universe afloat in nothingness. The talk is not desperate but, by and large, is just talk. The subject is not really in Ammons as the kind of happiness that threatens to swell into a yelp or surf onto silence. But Romanticism has always been in trouble; dissatisfaction is its nature; Ammons is doing what he can.—CALVIN BEDIENT, "*Sphere*," *NYTBR*, Dec. 22, 1974, pp. 12–13

Obsessive is the word . . . that best describes A. R. Ammons's *Sphere: The Form of a Motion*. At least the motion of its form is that: 155 sections, each section with four stanzas, each stanza with three lines; the whole connected with colons so that the only measure is duration—this series of provisional appositions has no impulse toward outcome. In the coda to his *Collected Poems*, Ammons asked himself for a poem of "plenitude/brought to center and extent," a poem of "periphery enclosing our system with/its bright dot and allowing in nonparlant/quantities at the edge void"—the achievement still denied by his thin *Tape for the Turn of the Year* and tentative "Hiberna-

culum." *Sphere* is that poem. Inevitably in a work of such length there are patches of tedium, discursive chats and catalogues, as the poet's mind moseys. But then the poem is a deliberate anthology of observations and perceptions that can swerve, with "insweeps of alteration," from a cosmogony to a quince bush, a patchwork that "insists on/differences, on every fragment of difference till the fragments/cease to be fragmentary and wash together in a high flotation/interpenetrating like the possibility of the world." And his accretive design mutes its intentions on a reader: "not to persuade you,/enlighten you, not necessarily to delight you, but to hold/you." What he seeks to hold is not our attention—though he always does—but our presence, as Whitman does, the poet whom Ammons often invokes as his "kosmos" model here: "I'm interested in you, and/I want you to be a poet: I want, like Whitman, to found/a federation of loveship." That posture, despite repetitions which map the poem as an American geography, is forced and unconvincing, especially for a poet who has been, uniquely, comfortable in his isolation with self and nature, without the usual strains of solipsism or paranoia.

If the poem has any patron besides the early Ammons, it is Lucretius, the poet of space and solids, of regeneration and reform, of distinctions rather than closure. The lyrical interludes of natural detail in *Sphere* counterpoint its fascination with "the high syrup invisible moving under, through,/and by discretions our true home, not these bodies so much/change makes and ends." The energies of relationship between matter and meaning, and the imposition of the given, are Ammons's "true home":

> when the item is moved beyond class
> into symbol or paradigmatic item, matter is a mere
>   seed
> afloat in radiance: it is the mystery, if reasonable, that
> when the one item stands for all, the one item is so
>   lost
> in its charge that is no longer bounded but all
>   radiance:
> this is the source of spirit, probably, the simple result
>   of
> the categorizing mind.

As his own mind categorizes the dynamics of "shape & flow," the poet again adapts the metaphors of science, though his interest in versing scientific discoveries has always seemed less for their explanations than for their formulaic quality. They function as occasional hypotheses, as points along his poetic compass whose quadrants are "High & Low," "center" and "periphery"—that is to say, tone and capacity. These are both rhetorical and personal problems, which the poem seeks to display and reconcile in its rambling continuum, the sphere of its own and the poet's experience. "A single dot of light, traveling, will memorize the sphere," which is why he invites his reader to "dip in anywhere, go on until the/attractions fail." In his effort to find direction to "a specified radial essential," Ammons's indirections proceed through contradiction and repetition—the necessity to erase his assertions with reality—so that the poem is always compromising itself in a parody of paradigm.

But if that is the poem's pretext, its motives are more personal. Surely Harold Bloom is right to advocate this poet's precursors as those whom Ammons himself refers to as "gentlemen of the naked vision"—the ecstatic Emerson, the expansive Whitman, the elusive Stevens. As he says in *Sphere*, "some people when they get up in the morning see/the kitchen sink, but I look out and see the windy rivers/of the Lord in the treetops." But the poem explores his evasions of the visionary role: "it has never occurred to me to face the terror but/as to how to hide from it I'm a virtual booth of information." Information he provides, to baffle his power; his "massive registration" is meant to "hamper/the imagination with full freightages of recalcitrance." The stubborn facts of life—"the visible, coherent, discrete"—assume an ambivalent redemptive status for Ammons, preserving his identity from definition by translating his visions into compensations rather than supporting them as necessities that are literally breathtaking. The heightened self-consciousness of this aspect of his project is sometimes distressing. As a denial, it is unsuccessful; as a dilemma, it is compelling. The deepest motive, though, is finally celebration—the kind of poetic praise that, as Rilke insists, must digest so much of the world's sorrow. *Sphere* celebrates the "heterocosm joyous," the radiance that an earlier poem proclaims all of nature is accepted into. It lies along "the route/from energy to energy," so that "motion is our only place." This "mathematics of stoop and climb" figures the final harmony "in the highest/ambience of diversity." *Sphere* is an unwieldy, absorbing, "abstract" poem; both its ambition and accomplishment are rare, and remind that

> if you do everything with
> economy and attention, the work itself will take on
> essentialities of the inevitable, and you will be, if
> causing,
>
> participating in grace.
> —J. D. McCLATCHEY, "New Books in Review," *YR*, Spring 1975, pp. 430–32

Ammons, though only recently much discussed, published his first volume, *Ommateum*, in 1955. His greatly productive phase comprised five volumes from 1964 to 1968, the last of these the very fine *Selected Poems* (1968). *Uplands* (1970) and *Briefings* (1971) mark a new and major period in his work.

Of the poets in my own generation, Ammons seems to me the likeliest to attain a central position in our imaginative history. He is less representative than Merwin, less dramatic than James Wright, and—while ultimately difficult—less immediately challenging in his difficulties than Ashbery. His centrality stems from his comprehensiveness, for he offers a heterocosm, an alternate world to the nature he uneasily meets, and also from his certain place in the Emerson-Whitman-Dickinson-Frost-Stevens-Crane succession that Roethke narrowly missed joining. Ammons makes a strong seventh in a line of major poets of the "native strain" or "native element" that various critics have identified for us. I am aware of how immensely our major poets differ from one another, but in a larger perspective than we ordinarily employ they can be seen to verge upon a common vision. Even Dickinson and Stevens belong to Emerson's universe of mind, as Whitman, Frost, and Crane more clearly do. Ammons, though a Southerner and a man obsessed with Minute Particulars, is the most Emersonian poet we have had since Whitman's petering out after 1860. . . .

The dialectic of earlier Ammons shuttles back and forth, incessantly, from the desire for "the unseasonal undifferentiated empty stark" to the consciousness that "origin is your original sin," a consciousness of separateness as necessity. The two masterpieces of *Selected Poems* are "Corsons Inlet" and "Saliences," where this dialectic is most strikingly set forth. In the lyrics of *Uplands* and *Briefings* the dialectic has been allowed to recede into the background, and the spent seer, trapped in a universal predicament, broods on every sharp instance where the ideas of permanence and change come together in a single body. The body's (or area's) outer edges, the

long peripheries or nerve endings of perception, now obsess this Emersonian seeker who has learned, to an ultimate sorrow, that indeed there is an outside or circumference to us. "The only sin is limitation," Emerson insisted in "Circles," but Ammons has translated limitation into origin. What remained for Emerson, once he had translated limitation by Fate, was the one part of Power in us that at given moments could overwhelm the ninety-nine parts of Fate. The later Ammons holds to his bargain with the wind. To claim even one part of Power is to claim order, and all of order now belongs to the vehicle of change. Permanence abides in the still-explicable sphere of origins, in the particulars of being that yield with marvelous slowness to the necessity of entropy, if they yield at all:

> take the Alleghenies for example,
> some quality in the air
> of summit stones lying free and loose
> out among the shrub trees: every
> exigency seems prepared for that might
> roll, bound, or give flight
> to stone: that is, the stones are
> prepared: they are round and ready.

This outward-opening conclusion of *Uplands* is Ammons' new mode, fearfully strong in its apparent tentativeness. The seer now praises a kind of sacred hesitation, as at the close of the central lyric, "Periphery":

> so I complained and said maybe I'd brush
> deeper and see what was pushing all this
> periphery, so difficult to make any sense
> out of, out:
> with me, decision brings its own
> hesitation: a symptom, no doubt, but open
> and meaningless enough without paradigm:
> but hesitation
> can be all right, too: I came on a spruce
> thicket full of elk, gushy snow-weed,
> nine species of lichen, four pure white
> rocks and
> several swatches of verbena near bloom.

The gift of hesitation is the beauty of the particular. Hesitation is a symptom as the desire for unseasonal unity was a symptom, for hesitation like desire is a metonymy. The part taken for a whole allows wisdom, the wisdom that stops short of satisfaction. Seeking the Other in the Emersonian Not-Me of nature, the seer had learned indirection and finally resignation. Now, not seeking, not even watching or waiting, he is found— not by the Other—but by momentary visitations of radiance almost wherever the nerve endings give out. Emersonianism, the most impatient and American of perceptual traditions, has learned patience in the latest Ammons.

"Conserving the Magnitude of Uselessness," the wisest lyric in *Uplands*, is a large, clear celebration of this new patience, a hymn "to all things not worth the work/of having." Like the late Frost of *In the Clearing*, Ammons now sees "the salvation of waste" and writes his version of that great poem, "Pod of the Milk-Weed." "Over-all is beyond me," the earlier Ammons had lamented, but now he joins himself to those poets, band of brothers at the Dark Tower, "rank as weeds themselves and just as abandoned" who know that "nothing useful is of lasting value." . . .

What begins to break through in the final poems of *Briefings* is a unique pride and saving comedy, yet still Transcendental in its emphasis. In "Levitation," the ground, "that disastrous to seers/and saints/is always around/evening scores, calling down . . . ," is shaken by its sudden realization that "something might be up there/able to get away." But the "something," the seer ascending like Stevens' Canon Aspirin, does not know it can and will get away, and turns:

> cramped in abstraction's gilded loft
> and
> tried to think of something beautiful to say:

Next to the humor there rides always the terror of the unsought particulars as they too transcend, as they rise free of the sin of their separate origins. In "Pluralist," indeed a "comforting/(though scary) exemplum," the maple tree expresses contrary notions:

> one side going west and the
> other east or northeast or one
> up and the other
> down: multiple angling:
> the nodding, twisting, the
> stepping out and back
> is like being of two minds
> at least. . . .

But the exemplum is "that maple trees/go nowhere at all." That this both scares and comforts is finally no comfort, for Ammons is so much of a seer, however spent, that his comforts sometimes cannot be ours, any more than Frost's savage consolations console us, though they impress and go on moving us.—HAROLD BLOOM, "Dark and Radiant Peripheries," *Figures of Capable Imagination*, 1976, pp. 158–68

Bibliographically speaking, ⟨*Collected Poems 1951–1971*⟩ is confusing, with no information on what volumes the poems originally appeared in, nor with any indication whether poems have been dropped or volumes not included, nor an account of revisions, if any. In short, it is a selected collected poems, with the poems arranged on odd principles (poems composed during a four- or five-year period are grouped together, but not in the sequence in which they appeared at first book publication).

In *Briefings* (1971) Ammons brought his difficult form of short poetry to perfection. The poetry he is best able to write is deprived of almost everything other poets have used, notably people and adjectives. (Where would Whitman have been, shorn of his soldiers, sleepers, and shipwrecked women, not to speak of his incandescent palette of adjectives?) Ammons has written some poems about "people," including his mule Silver, and even permits himself an adjective now and then, but rarely one more subjective than an adjective of color or measurement. "Half-dark," "massive," "high," "giant," "distant," "long," "broad," "noticeable," "late," "dry," "diminished," "passable" (implying height of hills), and "quiet" are the crop gleaned from two pages chosen at random (188–189) in the *Collected Poems*, and these "objective" adjectives, Ammons' own, are balanced by only one "subjective" adjective on the same pages ("taxing"—an opinion imputed to a hill trying to be a mountain and finding it hard). Such word-counts are perhaps not very gripping, but I found myself reduced to them in trying to understand what new language Ammons is inventing. (If he never succeeded, it wouldn't matter what he was up to, but since he does bring it off, we need to know how he is working out for us "a new knowledge of reality.") What he does is remarkable both in its sparseness and in its variety. One can't say "richness" because there is no sensual "give" in this poetry—but it does attempt an imitative recreation, no less, of the whole variety of the natural world, if not, regrettably, of what Stevens called its "affluence." But if, as Ammons seems to think, affluence is brought rather by the perceiving and receptive mind, as a quality, rather than inhering in nature itself (nature, who perceives herself singly, we may say, as an acorn here, a brook there, rather than corporately congratulat-

ing herself on all her brooks), then a poetry attempting this ascetic unattributiveness must refrain from celebrating the multiplicity of the world in human terms. Why it should be so wrong to let in human gestalt-making is another question; Ammons permits himself entry when the poem is about himself, but he won't have any of those interfering adjectival subjectivities when he's occupied with morning glories or caterpillars or redwoods. This discipline of perfect notation is almost monklike, and, monklike, it takes what comes each day as the day's revelation of, so to speak, the will of God. Ammons wakes asking what the world will today offer him as a lesson and he is scarcely permitted choice: if it is snowing, he has to deduce the mantra in the snow; if it is a night with a masked aurora, it is to the aurora that he must compose that night's address. He is like a guitarist presented every day with a different señorita in the balcony, and commanded, like some later-day Sheherezade, to think up each day different but appropriate serenades reflecting the lady's different looks.

. . .Very often, in his later poetry, Ammons tries to reassure himself on the value of his poetics by comparing it to the geological and organic motions of the universe, so molecularly deep and so cosmically all-embracing: we hear about the genetic code and double helices, cryogenic events and supernovas, colloidal floats and platelets, estuary populations, nucleations, defoliations, the underground mantle, and so on, through all the vocabulary, one might say, of *Scientific American*. "Ecology is my word," declares Ammons adding "my other word is/ *provisional*," and he says elsewhere, half in play and half in earnest:

> I get lost for fun,
> because there's no chance of getting lost: I am seeking the
> mechanisms physical, physiological, epistemological, electrical,
> chemical, esthetic, social, religious, by which many, kept
> discrete as many, expresses itself into the
> manageable rafters of salience, lofts to comprehension.

This "Essay on Poetics" is presented with an unusual amount of candor, summing up what we had had glimpses of in "Motion" and "Poetics" and "Zone," and any critic would be glad if one day he understood Ammons as well as Ammons, rather exceptionally among poets, understands himself. "I was thinking last June," he confesses, "so multiple and diverse is the reality of a tree, that I/ought to do a booklength piece on the elm in the backyard here:/wish I had done it now because it could stand for truth, too." In fact, he even begins the tree poem, and in a burst of fancy imagines how he would have to determine the tree's place in space by longitude, latitude, distance from the earth's core, and other methods. Never has there been a poetry so sublimely above the possible appetite of its potential readers. Genial as Ammons' programs are, and impressive as his lava-flows of language become in the long poems, these longer efforts are less likely to win an audience (except those of us captive enough to listen like a three-years' child to anything new and personal being done with words) than the shorter poems.

It is with his short poems, where he does obstinate battle with both multiplicity and abstraction at once, being fair to the weeds and the vines and the grasses and the worms, and at the same time rising to grand speculations on man's nature and the design of life, that Ammons will win a permanent audience. Ammons' conversations with mountains are the friendliest and most colloquial conversations with the inanimate recorded in poetry since Herbert talked to his shooting-star ("Virtu," "Classic," "Reversal," "Schooling," and "Eyesight" belong to this group); another group includes poems rejoicing in the world, like the beautiful "This Bright Day": others retell, over and over, with a satisfying variety in imagery, the climb up to perspective and the slide back down to particularity, that process out of which lyric is built (and these include the splendid "Two Possibilities," "One More Time," and "High and Low," with its Emersonian determination and its rueful country debacle):

> A mountain risen
> in me
> I said
> this implacability
> must be met:
> so I climbed
> the peak:
> height shook and
> wind leaned
> I said what
> kind of country is
> this anyhow and
> rubbled
> down the slopes to
> small rock
> and scattered weed.

Then there is another group, not making points at all, just seeing how things are: these are the ones I like best, and would first anthologize, the ones like "Treaties," where Ammons' instinctive identification with earthly events affords a symbolism which remains natural and, though clear, inconspicuous:

> My great wars close:
> ahead, papers,
> signatures, the glimmering
> in shade of
> leaf and raised wine:
> orchards, orchards,
> vineyards, fields:
> spiralling slow time while
> the medlar
> smarts and glows and
> empty nests
> come out in the open:
> fall rain then stirs
> the black creek and
> the small leaf slips in.

Such poems, though perhaps not Ammons' superficially most ambitious, are the ones that last in the mind, drawing as they do on his feeling that "if a squash blossom dies, I feel withered as a stained/zucchini and blame my nature." Ammons has taken into the realm of nature Donne's "any man's death diminishes me," and so can write about the lives and deaths in nature as though they were (and they are) his own. It is a severe poetry, attempting the particularity of Hopkins with none of what Hopkins' schoolmates called his "gush," trying for the abstraction of Stevens without Stevens' inhuman remove from the world of fact, aiming at Williams' affectionateness toward the quotidian without Williams' romantic drift. Since Ammons is still in mid-career, we can watch the experiment, we hope, for a good while yet: if he can succeed (even granting the absurdity of some of the niches and odd corners of his enterprise), he will have written the first twentieth-century poetry wholly purged of the romantic.—HELEN VENDLER, "Ammons, Berryman, Cummings," *Part of Nature, Part of Us,* 1980, pp. 330–35

HAROLD BLOOM
From "A. R. Ammons:
'When You Consider The Radiance'"
The Ringers in the Tower
1971, pp. 257–89

> Nature centres into balls,
> And her proud ephemerals,
> Fast to surface and outside,
> Scan the profile of the sphere;
> Knew they what that signified,
> A new genesis were here.
> > Emerson, *Circles*

In 1955, A. R. Ammons, in his thirtieth year, published his first book of poems, *Ommateum, with Doxology. Ommateum* consists of thirty Whitmanian chants, strongly influenced by the metric of Ezra Pound (though by nothing else in Pound). *Doxology* is an intricate religious hymn, in three parts, more ironic in tone than in direction. In the lengthening perspective of American poetry, the year 1955 will be remembered as the end of Wallace Stevens's career, and the beginning of Ammons's, himself not Stevens's heir but like Stevens a descendant of the great originals of American Romantic tradition, Emerson and Whitman. Beyond its experimentation with Poundian cadences, *Ommateum* shows no trace of the verse fashions of the fifties; I cannot detect in it the voice of William Carlos Williams, which indeed I do not hear anywhere in Ammons's work, despite the judgments of several reviewers. The line of descent from Emerson and Whitman to the early poetry of Ammons is direct, and even the Poundian elements in *Ommateum* derive from that part of Pound that is itself Whitmanian.

Ommateum's subject is poetic incarnation, in the mode of Whitman's *Sea-Drift* pieces, Emerson's *Seashore*, and Pound's *Canto II.* The Whitman of *As I Ebb'd with the Ocean of Life* is closest, suggesting that poetic disincarnation is Ammons's true subject, his vitalizing fear. In the "Foreword" to *Ommateum* he begins his list of themes with "the fear of the loss of identity." The first poem of the volume, the chosen beginning of this poet's outrageously and wonderfully prolific canon, is an assumption of another's identity. This other, "Ezra," is neither Pound nor the biblical scribe of the Return, but a suddenly remembered hunchback playmate from childhood, brought back to the poet's consciousness by a report of his death in war. The whole of Ammons is in this first poem, but half a lifetime's imaginings will be necessary to transfigure this shore-burst into the radiance already implicit here:

> So I said I am Ezra
> and the wind whipped my throat
> gaming for the sounds of my voice
> I listened to the wind
> go over my head and up into the night
> Turning to the sea I said
> I am Ezra
> but there were no echoes from the waves
> The words were swallowed up
> in the voice of the surf
> or leaping over swells
> lost themselves oceanward
> Over the bleached and broken fields
> I moved my feet and turning from the wind
> that ripped sheets of sand
> from the beach and threw them
> like seamists across the dunes

swayed as if the wind were taking me away
and said
   I am Ezra
As a word too much repeated
falls out of being
so I Ezra went out into the night
like a drift of sand
and splashed among the windy oats
that clutch the dunes
of unremembered seas

As in the *Ode to the West Wind* and *As I Ebb'd with the Ocean of Life*, so here the poet's consciousness is assaulted by the elements he seeks to address, reproved by what he hopes to meet in a relationship that will make him or keep him a poet. The motto of Ammons's first poem might be Whitman's:

Nature here in sight of the sea taking advantage of me
   to dart upon me and sting me,
Because I have dared to open my mouth to sing at
   all.

Later in *Ommateum*, Ammons echoes *As I Ebb'd* more directly, recalling its terrifying contraction of the self:

Me and mine, loose windrows, little corpses,
Froth, snowy white, and bubbles,
(See, from my dead lips the ooze exuding at last,
See, the prismatic colors glistening and rolling,)
Tufts of straw, sands, fragments . . .

This becomes, in his ninth chant, Ammons's emblem of the last stage of "peeling off my being":

but went on deeper
till darkness snuffed the shafts of light
   against the well's side
     night kissing
the last bubbles from my lips

The Emersonian ambition to be possessed fully by the Transcendental Self is Ammons's early theme as it was Whitman's, and is still pervasive in Ammons's latest lyrics, but turned now in a direction avoided by his precursors. . . .

⟨The⟩ extraordinary poem, *The City Limits*, marks one of the limits of Ammons's art, and almost releases him from the burden of his main tradition. "The guiltiest swervings of the weaving heart," for a poet as poet, are those that swerve him away from his poetic fathers into an angle of fall that is also his angle of vision. For an Emersonian poet, an American Romantic, the angle of vision becomes the whole of life, and measures him as man. Sherman Paul, acutely measuring Emerson's own angle, provides the necessary gloss for this Emersonian poem, *The City Limits*:

The eye brought him two perceptions of nature—nature ensphered and nature atomized—which corresponded to the distant and proximate visual powers of the eye. These powers, in turn, he could have called the reasoning and understanding modes of the eye. And to each he could have assigned its appropriate field of performance: the country and the city.

We can surmise that the sorrow of all Emersonian poets, from Whitman to Ammons and beyond, comes from the great central declaration: "I become a transparent eyeball; I am nothing; I see all; the currents of the Universal Being circulate through me; I am part or particle of God." But if "Thought is nothing but the circulations made luminous," then what happens when the circulations are darkening? The currents of the Universal Being do not cease to circulate, ever, and the "mathematic ebb and flow" of Emerson's *Seashore* is no consolation to temperaments less rocky than Emerson's own (one thinks not only of Whitman, but of middle Stevens, and late

Roethke). To a grim consciousness like Frost's in *Directive*, the wisdom of the Emerson of *The Conduct of Life* is acceptable, admirable, even inevitable, and this late Emersonian strain may never be so worked out in our poetry as to vanish. But Ammons has none of it, and the toughness of his own consolations and celebrations comes out of another tradition, one that I do not understand, for everything that is Southern in American culture is necessarily a darkness to me. Ammons is a poet of the Carolina as well as the Jersey shore, and his relation to Whitman is severely modified by rival spirits of place. The Ezra-poet is as obsessed with sandstorms as any Near Easterner; for him the wind makes sheets of sand into sea mists. In *The City Limits* the radiance, despite its generosity, cannot reach what is overhung or hidden, and what is wholly hidden cannot be accepted into the light it will not take. There is for Ammons a recalcitrance or unwilling dross in everything given, and this "loneliness" (to use one of his words for it) marks his verse from *Ommateum* on as more than a little distinct from its great precursors.

I am writing of Ammons as though he had rounded his first circle in the eye of his readers, and there is no other way to write about him, even if my essay actually introduces him to some of its readers. The fundamental postulates for reading Ammons have been set down well before me, by Richard Howard and Marius Bewley in particular, but every critic of a still emergent poet has his own obsessions to work through, and makes his own confession of the radiance. Ammons's poetry does for me what Stevens's did earlier, and the High Romantics before that: it helps me to live my life. If Ammons is, as I think, the central poet of my generation, because he alone has made a heterocosm, a second nature in his poetry, I deprecate no other poet by this naming. It is, surprisingly, a rich generation, with ten or a dozen poets who seem at least capable of making a major canon, granting fortune and persistence. Ammons, much more than the others, has made such a canon already. A solitary artist, nurtured by the strength available for him only in extreme isolation, carrying on the Emersonian tradition with a quietness directly contrary to nearly all its other current avatars, he has emerged in his most recent poems as an extraordinary master, comparable to the Stevens of *Ideas of Order* and *The Man with the Blue Guitar*. To track him persistently, from his origins in *Ommateum* through his maturing in *Corsons Inlet* and its companion volumes on to his new phase in *Uplands* and *Briefings* is to be found by not only a complete possibility of imaginative experience, but by a renewed sense of the whole line of Emerson, the vitalizing and much maligned tradition that has accounted for most that matters in American poetry.

Emerson, like Stevens and Ammons after him, had a fondness for talking mountains. One thinks of Wordsworth's old men, perhaps of the Virgilian Mount Atlas, of Blake's Los at the opening of Night V, *The Four Zoas*, of Shelley's Mont Blanc, which obstinately refuses however to take on human form, and affronts the humane revolutionary with its hard, its menacing otherness. Emerson's Monadnoc is genial and gnomic:

"Monadnoc is a mountain strong,
Tall and good my kind among;
But well I know, no mountain can,
Zion or Meru, measure with man.
For it is on zodiacs writ,
Adamant is soft to wit:
And when the greater comes again
With my secret in his brain,
I shall pass, as glides my shadow
Daily over hill and meadow.

> Anchored fast for many an age,
> I await the bard and sage,
> Who, in large thoughts, like fair pearl-seed,
> Shall string Monadnoc like a bead."

Emerson is not providing the golden string to be wound into a ball, but one of a series of golden entities to be beaded on a string. Monadnoc awaits the Central Man, the redemptive poet of *Bacchus*. Thoreau, in his fine poem on the mountains, characteristically avoids Emerson's humanizing of an otherness, and more forcefully mountainizes himself:

> But special I remember thee,
> Wachusett, who like me
> Standest alone without society.
> Thy far blue eye,
> A remnant of the sky,
> Seen through the clearing or the gorge,
> Or from the windows of the forge,
> Doth leaven all it passes by.
> . . .
> Upholding heaven, holding down earth,
> Thy pastime from thy birth;
> Not steadied by the one, nor leaning on the other,
> May I approve myself thy worthy brother!

Wachusett is not to be strung like a bead, however strong the bard and sage. Thoreau is a more Wordsworthian poet than Emerson, and so meets a nature ruggedly recalcitrant to visionary transformations. Ammons, who has a relation to both, meets Emerson's kind of mountains, meets a nature that awaits its bard, even if sometimes in ambush. In *Ommateum*, there is not much transformation, and some ambuscade, and so the neglect encountered by the volume can be understood. Yet these chants, setting aside advantages in retrospect, are remarkable poems, alive at every point in movement and in vision. They live in their oddly negative exuberance, as the new poet goes out into his bleak lands as though he marched only into another man's phantasmagoria. One chant, beginning "In the wind my rescue is," to be found but mutilated in the *Selected Poems* (1968), states the poet's task as a gathering of the stones of earth into one place. The wind, by sowing a phantasmagoria in the poet's eyes, draws him "out beyond the land's end," thus saving him "from all those ungathered stones." The shore, Whitman's emblem for the state in which poets are made and unmade, becomes the theater for the first phase of Ammons's poetic maturity, the lyrics written in the decade after *Ommateum*. These are gathered in three volumes: *Expressions of Sea Level* (1964), *Corsons Inlet* (1965), and *Northfield Poems* (1966), which need to be read as a unit, since the inclusion of a poem in one or another volume seems to be a matter of whim. A reader of Ammons is likeliest to be able to read this phase of him in the *Selected Poems*, whose arrangement in chronological order of composition shows how chronologically scrambled the three volumes are.

Ammons's second start as a poet, after the transcendental waste places of *Ommateum*, is in ⟨his⟩ *Hymn*. . . .

The chants of *Ommateum* were composed mostly in a single year, from the Spring of 1951 to the Spring of 1952. In 1956, Ammons fully claims his Transcendental heritage in his *Hymn*, a work of poetic annunciation in which the "you" is Emerson's "Nature," all that is separate from "the Soul." The *Hymn*'s difficult strength depends on a reader's recognition that the found "you" is: "the NOT ME, that is, both nature and art, all other men and my own body." Juxtapose a crucial passage of Emerson, and the *clinamen* that governs the course of Ammons's maturity is determined:

> The world proceeds from the same spirit as the body of man. It is a remoter and inferior incarnation of

God, a projection of God in the unconscious. But it differs from the body in one important respect. It is not, like that, now subjected to the human will. Its serene order is inviolable by us. It is, therefore, to us, the present expositor of the divine mind. It is a fixed point whereby we may measure our departure.

Emerson's fixed point oscillates dialectically in Ammons's *Hymn*. Where Emerson's mode hovers always around metonymy, parts of a world taken as the whole, Ammons's sense of the universe takes it for a symptom. No American poet, not Whitman or Stevens, shows us so fully something otherwise unknown in the structures of the national consciousness as Ammons does. It cannot be said so far that Ammons has developed as fluent and individual a version of the language of the self as they did, but he has time and persistence enough before he borrows his last authority from death. His first authority is the height touched in this *Hymn*, where everything depends upon a precision of consequences "if I find you." "The unassimilable fact leads us on," a later poem begins, the leading on being Ammons's notion of quest. If all that is separate from him, the "you," is found, the finding will be assimilated at the final cost of going on out "into the unseasonal undifferentiated empty stark," a resolution so far as to annihilate selfhood. One part of the self will be yielded to an apprehension beyond sight, while the other will stay here with the earth, to be yielded to sight's reductiveness, separated with each leaf.

This is the enterprise of a consciousness extreme enough to begin another central poem, *Gravelly Run*, with a quietly terrifying sense of what will suffice:

> I don't know somehow it seems sufficient
> to see and hear whatever coming and going is,
> losing the self to the victory
> of stones and trees,
> of bending sandpit lakes, crescent
> round groves of dwarf pine:
> for it is not so much to know the self
> as to know it as it is known
> by galaxy and cedar cone . . .

But as it is known, it is only a "surrendered self among/ unwelcoming forms." The true analogue to this surrender is in the curious implicit threat of Emerson's Orphic poet:

> We distrust and deny inwardly our sympathy with nature. We own and disown our relation to it, by turns. We are like Nebuchadnezzer, dethroned, bereft of reason, and eating grass like an ox. But who can set limits to the remedial force of spirit?

The remedial force of spirit, in this sense, is closest to being that terriblest force in the world, of which Stevens's Back-ache complains. Ammons, who knows he cannot set limits to such force, warns himself perpetually "to turn back," before he comes to a unity apparently equal to his whole desire. For his desire is only a metonymy, and unity (if found) compels another self-defeating question:

> You cannot come to unity and remain material:
> in that perception is no perceiver:
> when you arrive
> you have gone too far:
> at the Source you are in the mouth of Death:
> you cannot
> turn around in
> the Absolute: there are no entrances or exits
> no precipitations of forms
> to use like tongs against the formless:
> no freedom to choose:

to be
    you have to stop not-being and break
off from *is* to *flowing* and
    this is the sin you weep and praise:
origin is your original sin:
    the return you long for will ease your guilt
and you will have your longing:
    the wind that is my guide said this: it
should know having
    given up everything to eternal being but
direction:
how I said can I be glad and sad: but a man goes
  from one foot to the other:
wisdom wisdom:
    to be glad and sad at once is also unity
and death:
    wisdom wisdom: a peachblossom blooms on a par-
    ticular
tree on a particular day:
    unity cannot do anything in particular:
are these the thoughts you want me to think I said but
    the wind was gone and there was no more knowl-
    edge then.

The wind's origin is its original sin also; were it to give up even direction, it would cease to be *Guide*, as this poem is entitled. If the wind is Ammons's Virgil, an Interior Paramour or Whitmanian Fancy remains his Beatrice, guiding him whenever wind ceases to lead. The poetic strength of *Guide* is in its dialectical renunciation of even this daimonic paramour. For the wind speaks against what is deepest and most self-destructive in Ammons. "Break off from *is* to *flowing*" is a classic phrasing of the terrible dream that incessantly afflicts most of our central poetic imaginations in America. "Unity cannot do anything in particular"; least of all can it write a poem.

The wind, Ammons's way to knowledge, is certainly the most active wind in American poetry. In *Ommateum*, the wind is a desperate whip, doubting its own efficacy in a dry land. It moves "like wisdom," but its poet is not so sure of the likeness. In the mature volumes, it is more a blade than a whip, and its desperation has rendered it apologetic:

    Having split up the chaparral
    blasting my sight
    the wind said
      You know I'm
      the result of
    forces beyond my control
    I don't hold it against you
    I said
    It's all right I understand

For the wind "dies and never dies," but the poet goes on:

    consigned to
    form that will not
    let me loose
    except to death
    till some
    syllable's rain
    anoints my tongue
    and makes it sing
    to strangers:

To be released from form into unity one dies or writes a poem; this appalling motive for metaphor is as desperate as any wind. Wind, which is "not air or motion/but the motion of air," speaks to a consciousness that is not spirit or making, but the spirit of making, the Ezra-incarnation in this poet:

    I coughed
    and the wind said
    Ezra will live
    to see your last
      sun come up again
    I turned (as I will) to weeds and
    the wind went off
      carving
    monuments through a field of stone
      monuments whose shape
    wind cannot arrest but
    taking hold on
    changes
    While Ezra
      listens from terraces of mind
    wind cannot reach or
    weedroots of my low-feeding shiver

When the poet falls (as he must) from this Ezra-eminence, the terraces of mind dissolve:

    The mind whirls, short of the unifying
  reach, short of the heat
    to carry that forging:
    after the visions of these losses, the spent
  seer, delivered to wastage, risen
    into ribs, consigns knowledge to
    approximation, order to the vehicle
of change . . .

He is never so spent a seer as he says, even if the price of his ascensions keeps rising. If from moment to moment the mode of motion is loss, there is always the privileged *Moment* itself:

        He turned and
        stood
        in the moment's
        height,
        exhilaration
        sucking him up,
        shuddering and
        lifting
        him
        jaw and bone
        and he said
        what
        destruction am I
        blessed by?

The burden of Ammons's poetry is to answer, to name that enlargement of life that is also a destruction. When the naming came most complete, in the late summer of 1962, it gave Ammons his two most ambitious single poems, *Corsons Inlet* and *Saliences*. Though both poems depend upon the context of Ammons's canon, they show the field of his enterprise more fully and freely than could have been expected of any single works. *Corsons Inlet* is likely to be Ammons's most famous poem, his *Sunday Morning*, a successfully universalizing expression of a personal thematic conflict and its apparent (or provisional) resolution. But *Saliences*, a harder, less open, more abstract fury of averted destructions, is the better poem. *Corsons Inlet* comforts itself (and us) with the perpetually renewed hope of a fresh walk over the dunes to the sea. *Saliences* rises past hope to what in the mind is "beyond loss or gain/ beyond concern for the separate reach." Both the hope and the ascension beyond hope return us to origins, and can be apprehended with keener aptitude after an excursus taking us deeper into Ammons's tradition. Ammons compels that backward vision of our poetry that only major achievement exacts, and illuminates Emerson and all his progeny as much as he needs them for illumination. Reading Ammons, I brood on all American poetry in the Romantic tradition, which means I yield to Emerson, who is to our modern poetry what Wordsworth has been to all British poetry after him; the starting-point, the defining element, the vexatious father, the shadow and the despair, liberating angel and blocking-agent, perpetual irritant and solacing glory.

John Jay Chapman, in what is still the best introductory essay on Emerson, condensed his estimate of the seer into a great and famous sentence: "If a soul be taken and crushed by democracy till it utter a cry, that cry will be Emerson." In the year 1846, when he beheld "the famous States/Harrying Mexico/With rifle and with knife!", Emerson raised the cry of himself most intensely and permanently:

> Though loath to grieve
> The evil time's sole patriot,
> I cannot leave
> My honied thought
> For the priest's cant,
> or statesman's rant.
>
> If I refuse
> My study for their politique,
> which at the best is trick,
> The angry Muse
> Puts confusion in my brain.

The astonished Muse found Emerson at her side all through 1846, the year not only of the Channing *Ode*, but of *Bacchus* and *Merlin*, his finest and most representative poems, that between them establish a dialectic central to subsequent American poetry. In *Bacchus*, the poet is not his own master, but yields to daimonic possession. In *Merlin*, the daimonic itself is mastered, as the poet becomes first the Bard, and then Nemesis:

> Who with even matches odd,
> Who athwart space redresses
> The partial wrong,
> Fills the just period,
> And finishes the song.

The poet of *Bacchus* is genuinely possessed, and yet falls (savingly) victim to Ananke—he is still *human*. The poet of *Merlin* is himself absorbed into Ananke and ceases to be human, leaving *Bacchus* much the better poem. To venture a desolate formula about American poetry: our greater poets attain the splendor of Bacchus, and then attempt to become Merlin, and so cease to be wholly human and begin to fail as poets. Emerson and his descendants dwindle, not when they build altars to the Beautiful Necessity, but when they richly confuse themselves with that Necessity. Poetry, Emerson splendidly observed, must be as new as foam and as old as the rock; he might also have observed that it had better not itself try to be foam or rock. . . . The Ammonsian literalness, allied to a similar destructive impulse in Wordsworth and Thoreau, attempts to summon outward continuities to shield the poet from his mind's own force. A *Poem Is a Walk* is the title of a dark, short prose piece by Ammons that tries "to establish a reasonably secure identity between a poem and a walk and to ask how a walk occurs, what it is, and what it is for," but establishes only that a walk by Ammons is a sublime kind of Pythagorean enterprise or Behmenite picnic. Emerson, who spoke as much wisdom as any American, alas spoke darkly also, and Ammons is infuriatingly Emersonian when he tells us a poem "is a motion to no-motion, to the still point of contemplation and deep

realization. Its knowledges are all negative and, therefore, more positive than any knowledge." *Corsons Inlet*, *Saliences*, and nearly a hundred other poems by Ammons are nothing of the kind, his imagination be thanked, rather than this spooky, pure-product-of-America mysticism. Unlike Emerson, who crossed triumphantly into prose, Ammons belongs to that company of poets that *thinks* most powerfully and naturally in verse, and sometimes descends to obscure quietudes when verse subsides.

Corsons Inlet first verges on, and then veers magnificently away from worshipping the Beautiful Necessity, from celebrating the way things are. "Life will be imaged, but cannot be divided nor doubled," might be the poem's motto; so might: "Ask the fact for the form," both maxims being Emerson's. Ammons's long poem, *Tape for the Turn of the Year*, contains the self-admonishment: "get out of boxes, hard/forms of mind:/ go deep:/penetrate/to the true spring," which is the initial impulse of *Corsons Inlet*. The poet, having walked in the morning over the dunes to the sea, recollects later in the day the release granted him by the walk, from thought to sight, from conceptual forms to the flowings and blendings of the Coleridgean Secondary Imagination. Released into the composition of *Corsons Inlet*, he addresses his reader directly (consciously in Whitman's mode) to state both the nature of his whole body of poetry, and his sense of its largest limitation:

> I allow myself eddies of meaning:
> yield to a direction of significance
> running
> like a stream through the geography of my work:
>   you can find
> in my sayings
>   swerves of action
>   like the inlet's cutting edge:
>   there are dunes of motion,
> organizations of grass, white sandy paths of re-
>   membrance
> in the overall wandering of mirroring mind:
> but Overall is beyond me: is the sum of these events
> I cannot draw, the ledger I cannot keep, the account-
>   ing
> beyond the account:

Within this spaced restraint, there is immense anguish, and the anguish is not just metaphysical. Though this anguish be an acquired wisdom, such wisdom proffers no consolation for the loss of quest. The anguish that goes through *Corsons Inlet*, subdued but ever salient, is more akin to a quality of mind in Thoreau than to anything in Emerson or Whitman. What Transcendentalists wanted of natural history is generally a darkness to me, and I resort to the late Perry Miller for some light on "the Transcendental methodology for coping with the multifarious concreteness of nature. That method is to see the particular as a particular, and yet at the same time so to perceive it as to make it, of itself, yield up the general and the universal." But that is too broad, being a Romantic procedure in general, with neither the American impatience nor the American obsession of particularity clearly distinguished from Wordsworthianism. Wordsworth was wonderfully patient with preparations for vision, and was more than content to see the particulars flow together and fade out in the great moments of vision. Emerson scanted preparations, and held on to the particulars even in ecstasy. In Thoreau, whatever his final differences with his master, the Emersonian precipitateness and clarity of the privileged moment are sharpened. When I read in his *Journals*, I drown in particulars and cannot find the moments of release, but *The Natural History of Massachusetts*, his first true work, seems all release, and very close to the terrible nostalgias *Corsons Inlet* reluctantly abandons. William Ellery Channing, memorializing Thoreau clumsily though with love, deluges us with evidences of those walks and talks in which Overall was never beyond Thoreau, but came confidently with each natural observation. But Ammons, who would want to emulate Thoreau, cannot keep the account; his natural observations bring him wholly other evidences:

> in nature there are few sharp lines: there are areas of
> primrose
>   more or less dispersed;
> disorderly orders of bayberry; between the rows
> of dunes,
> irregular swamps of reeds,
> though not reeds alone, but grass, bayberry, yarrow,
>   all . . .
> predominantly reeds:

All through the poem beats its hidden refrain: "I was released from . . . straight lines," "few sharp lines," "I have drawn no lines," "but there are no lines," "a wider range/than mental lines can keep," "the waterline, waterline inexact," "but in the large view, no/lines or changeless shapes." A wild earlier poem, called *Lines*, startlingly exposes Ammons's obsession, for there nature bombards him, all but destroys him with lines, nothing but lines. . . .

This is Ammons's Mad Song, his equivalent of Stevens's *A Rabbit as King of the Ghosts*, another poem of the mind's mercilessness, its refusal to defend itself against itself. "Deranging, clustering" is the fear and the horror, from which *Corsons Inlet* battles for release, mostly through embracing "a congregation/rich with entropy," a constancy of change. The poet who insists he has drawn no lines draws instead his poem out of the "dunes of motion," loving them desperately as his only (but inadequate) salvation, all that is left when his true heaven of Overall is clearly beyond him. Yet this remains merely a being "willing to go along" in the recognition not of the Beautiful but the Terrible Necessity:

> the moon was full last night: today, low tide was low:
> black shoals of mussels exposed to the risk
> of air
> and, earlier, of sun,
> waved in and out with the waterline, waterline
>   inexact,
> caught always in the event of change:
>   a young mottled gull stood free on the shoals
>   and ate
> to vomiting: another gull, squawking possession,
>   cracked a crab,
> picked out the entrails, swallowed the soft-shelled
>   legs, a ruddy
> turnstone running in to snatch leftover bits:
> risk is full: every living thing in
> siege: the demand is life, to keep life: the small
> white blacklegged egret, how beautiful, quietly stalks
>   and spears
>   the shallows, darts to shore
>   to stab—what? I couldn't
> see against the black mudflats—a frightened
> fiddler crab?

This great and very American passage, kin to a darker tradition than Ammons's own, and to certain poems of Melville and Hart Crane, is *Corsons Inlet's* center, the consequence of the spent seer's consignment of order to the vehicle of change. I remember, each time I read it, that Ammons is a Southerner, heir to a darker Protestantism than was the im-

mediate heritage of the New England visionaries or of Whitman. But our best Southern poets from Poe and Timrod through Ransom, Tate, Warren, have not affected his art, and a comparison to a Southern contemporary like James Dickey indicates sharply how much Ammons is the conscious heir of nineteenth-century Northern poetry, including a surprising affinity to Dickinson in his later phase of *Uplands* and *Briefings*. But, to a North Carolinian one hundred years after, Transcendentalism comes hard and emerges bitterly, with the Oversoul reduced from Overall to "the overall wandering of mirroring mind," confronting the dunes and swamps as a last resource, the final form of Nature or the Not-me.

From the nadir of "every living thing in/siege," *Corsons Inlet* slowly rises to a sense of the ongoing, "not chaos: preparations for/flight." In a difficult transitional passage, the poet associates the phrasal fields of his metric with the "field" of action on every side of him, open to his perception "with moving incalculable center." Looking close, he can see "order tight with shape"; standing back, he confronts a formlessness that suddenly, in an extraordinary epiphany, is revealed as his consolation:

> orders as summaries, as outcomes of actions override
> or in some way result, not predictably (seeing me
>   gain
> the top of a dune,
> the swallows
> could take flight—some other fields of bayberry
>   could enter fall
>   berryless) and there is serenity:
>   no arranged terror: no forcing of image, plan,
> or thought:
> no propaganda, no humbling of reality to precept:
> terror pervades but is not arranged, all possibilities
> of escape open: no route shut, except in
>   the sudden loss of all routes:

"No arranged terror" is the crucial insight, and if we wish to inquire who would arrange terror except a masochist, the wish will not sustain itself. The poem's final passage, this poet's defense, abandons the really necessary "pulsations of order," the reliable particulars, for what cannot suffice, the continued bafflement of perceiving nothing completely. For Ammons, the seer of *Ommateum* and the still-confident quester of the *Hymn*, this bafflement is defeat, and enjoying the freedom that results from scope eluding his grasp is hardly an enjoying in any ordinary sense. The poem ends bravely, but not wholly persuasively:

> I see narrow orders, limited tightness, but will
> not run to the easy victory:
>   still around the looser, wider forces work:
>   I will try
> to fasten into order enlarging grasps of disorder,
>   widening
> scope, but enjoying the freedom that
> Scope eludes my grasp, that there is no finality of
>   vision,
> that I have perceived nothing completely,
>   that tomorrow a new walk is a new walk.

Origin is still his original sin; what his deepest nature longs for, to come to unity and yet remain material, is no part of *Corsons Inlet*, which grants him freedom to choose, but no access to that unity that alone satisfies choice. The major poem written immediately after *Corsons Inlet* emerges from stoic acceptance of bafflement into an imaginative reassurance that prompts Ammons's major phase, the lyrics of *Uplands*, *Briefings*, and the work-in-progress:

Consistencies rise
and ride
the mind down
hard routes
　　walled
with no outlet and so
to open a variable geography,
　　proliferate
possibility, here
is this dune fest
　　releasing,
mind feeding out,
gathering clusters,
fields of order in disorder,
where choice
can make beginnings,
　　turns,
　　reversals,
where straight line
and air-hard thought
can meet
unarranged disorder,
　　dissolve
before the one event that
creates present time
in the multi-variable
　　scope:

Saliences thus returns to *Corsons Inlet's* field of action, driven by that poet's need not to abide in a necessity, however beautiful. *Saliences* etymologically are out-leapings, "mind feeding out," not taking in perceptions but turning its violent energies out into the field of action. If *Corsons Inlet* is Ammons's version of *The Idea of Order at Key West* (not that he had Stevens's poem in mind, but that the attentive reader learns to compare the two), then *Saliences* is his *The Man with the Blue Guitar*, a discovery of how to begin again after a large and noble acknowledgement of dark limitations. *Saliences* is a difficult, abstract poem, but it punches itself along with an overwhelming vigor, showing its exuberance by ramming through every blocking particular, until it can insist that "where not a single single thing endures,/the overall reassures." Overall remains beyond Ammons, but is replaced by "a round/quiet turning,/beyond loss or gain,/beyond concern for the separate reach." *Saliences* emphasizes the transformation of Ammons's obsessive theme, from the longing for unity to the assertion of the mind's power over the particulars of being, the universe of death. The Emersonianism of Ammons is constant; as did Whitman, so his final judgment of his relation to that great precursor will be: "loyal at last." But *Saliences* marks the *clinamen*; the swerve away from Emerson is now clarified, and Ammons will write no poem more crucial to his own unfolding. Before *Saliences*, the common reader must struggle with the temptation of naming Ammons a nature poet; after this, the struggle would be otiose. The quest that was surrendered in *Guide*, and whose loss was accepted in *Corsons Inlet*, is internalized in *Saliences* and afterward.

Saliences approximates (indeliberately) the subtle procedure of a subtradition within Romantic poetry that goes from Shelley's *Mont Blanc* to Stevens's *The Auroras of Autumn*. The poet begins in an austere, even a terrifying scene of natural confrontation, but he does not describe the scene or name the terror until he has presented fully the mind's initial defense against scene and terror, its implicit assertion of its own force. So *Saliences* begins with a vision of the mind in action "in the multi-variable/scope." A second movement starts with the wind's entrance ("a variable of wind/among the dunes,/

making variables/of position and direction and sound") and climaxes at the poem's halfway point, which returns to the image of the opening ("come out of the hard/routes and ruts,/pour over the walls/of previous assessments: turn to/the open,/the unexpected, to new saliences of feature." After this come seventy magical lines of Ammons upon his heights (starting with: "The reassurance is/that through change/continuities sinuously work"), lines that constitute one of a convincing handful of contemporary assurances that the imagination is capable always of a renovative fresh start.

The dune fest, which in the poem's opening movement is termed a provocation for the mind's release from "consistencies" (in the sense of Blake's Devourer), is seen in the second movement as *Corsons Inlet's* baffled field of action:

wind, a variable, soft wind, hard
steady wind, wind
shaped and kept in the
bent of trees,
the prevailing dipping seaward
of reeds,
the kept and erased sandcrab trails:
wind, the variable to the gull's flight,
how and where he drops the clam
and the way he heads in, running to loft:
wind, from the sea, high surf
and cool weather;
from the land, a lessened breakage
and the land's heat:
wind alone as a variable,
as a factor in millions of events,
leaves no two moments
on the dunes the same:
　　keep
free to these events,
bend to these
changing weathers:

This wind has gone beyond the wind of *Guide*, for it has given up everything to eternal being, even direction, even velocity, and contents itself to be shaped and kept by each particular it encounters. Knowing he cannot be one with or even like this wind, knowing too he must be more than a transparency, an Eye among the blind particulars, the poet moves to a kind of upper level of Purgatory, where the wind ceases to be his guide, and he sees as he has not seen before:

when I went back to the dunes today,
　　saliences,
congruent to memory,
spread firmingly across my sight:
the narrow white path
rose and dropped over
grassy rises toward the sea:
sheets of reeds,
tasseling now near fall,
filled the hollows
with shapes of ponds or lakes:
bayberry, darker, made wandering
chains of clumps, sometimes pouring
into heads, like stopped water:
　　much seemed
constant, to be looked
forward to, expected:

It is the saliences, the outleapings, that "spread *firmingly* across my sight," and give him assurances, "summations of permanence." The whole passage, down through the poem's close, has a firm beauty unlike anything previous in Ammons. Holding himself as he must, firmly apart from still-longed-for unity, he finds himself now in an astonishing equilibrium with the particulars, containing them in his own mind by reimagining them there:

> . . . in
> the hollow,
> where a runlet
> makes in
> at full tide and fills a bowl,
> extravagance of pink periwinkle
> along the grassy edge,
> and a blue, bunchy weed, deep blue,
> deep into the mind the dark blue
> constant:

The change here, as subtle as it is precarious, only just bears description, though the poet of *Uplands* and *Briefings* relies upon it as though it were palpable, something he could touch every way. The weed and the mind's imaginative constancy are in the relation given by the little poem, *Reflective*, written just afterward:

> I found a
> weed
> that had a
>
> mirror in it
> and that
> mirror
>
> looked in at
> a mirror
> in
>
> me that
> had a
> weed in it

In itself this is slight; in the context provided by *Saliences* it is exact and finely wrought. The whole meaning of it is in "I *found*," for *Saliences* records a finding, and a being found. Because of this mutual finding, the magnificent close of the poem is possible, is even necessary:

> where not a single single thing endures,
> the overall reassures,
> deaths and flights,
> shifts and sudden assaults claiming
> limited orders,
> the separate particles:
> earth brings to grief
> much in an hour that sang, leaped, swirled,
> yet keeps a round
> quiet turning,
> beyond loss or gain,
> beyond concern for the separate reach.

I think, when I read this passage, of the final lines of Wordsworth's great Ode, of the end of Browning's *Love among the Ruins*, of the deep peace Whitman gives as he concludes *Crossing Brooklyn Ferry*, and of Stevens closing *As You Leave the Room*:

> An appreciation of a reality
> And thus an elevation, as if I left
> With something I could touch, touch every way.
>
> And yet nothing has been changed except what is
> Unreal, as if nothing had been changed at all.

This is not to play at touchstones, in the manner of Arnold or of Blackmur, but only to record my experience as a reader, which is that *Saliences* suggests and is worthy of such company. Firm and radiant as the poem is, its importance for Ammons (if I surmise rightly) transcends its intrinsic worth, for it made possible his finest poems. I pass to them with some

regret for the splendors in *Selected Poems* I have not discussed: *Silver, Terrain, Bridge, Jungle Knot, Nelly Myers, Expressions of Sea Level*, and for the long poem, *Tape for the Turn of the Year*, a heroic failure that is Ammons's most original and surprising invention.

Uplands, published in the autumn of 1970, begins with a difficult, almost ineluctable lyric, *Snow Log*, which searches for intentions where they evidently cannot be found, in the particulars of fallen tree, snow, shrubs, the special light of winter landscape; "I take it on myself," the poet ends by saying, and repeats the opening triad:

> especially the fallen tree
> the snow picks
> out in the woods to show.

Stevens, in the final finding of the ear, returned to the snow he had forgotten, to behold again "nothing that is not there and the nothing that is." *Snow Log* seems to find something that is not there, but the reader is left uncertain whether there is a consciousness in the scene that belongs neither to him nor to the poet. With the next poem, *Upland*, which gives the volume both its tonality and title, the uncertainty vanishes:

> Certain presuppositions are altered
> by height: the inversion to
> sky-well a peak
> in a desert makes: the welling
> from clouds down the boulder fountains:
> it is always a
> surprise out west there—
> the blue ranges loose and aglide
> with heat and then come close
> on slopes leaning up into green:
> a number of other phenomena might
> be summoned—
> take the Alleghenies for example,
> some quality in the air
> of summit stones lying free and loose
> out among the shrub trees: every
> exigency seems prepared for that might
> roll, bound, or give flight
> to stone: that is, the stones are
> prepared: they are round and ready.

A poem like this is henceforth Ammons's characteristic work: shorter and more totally self-enclosed than earlier ventures, and less reliant on larger contexts. He has become an absolute master of his art, and a maker of individual tones as only the greater poets can accomplish:

> . . . the stones are
> prepared: they are round and ready.

. . . In *Uplands* and the extraordinary conceptions of the recent volume, *Briefings*, the motions of water have replaced the earlier guiding movements of wind. *If Anything Will Level with You Water Will*, the title of one fine poem, is the credo of many. "I/mean the telling is unmediated," Ammons says of a rocky stream, and his ambition here, enormous as always, is an unmediated telling, a purely visionary poetry. It is not a poetry that discourses of itself or of the outward particulars, or of the processes of the poet's mind so much as it deals in a purer representation than even Wordsworth could have wanted. The bodily eye is not a despotic sense for Ammons (as it became for Thoreau) who has not passed through a crisis in perception, but rather has trained himself to sense those out-leapings later available to the seer (like Emerson) who had wisdom enough to turn back from Unity. For pure representation in the later Ammons, I give *Laser* (from *Uplands*) as a supreme example:

An image comes
and the mind's light, confused
as that on surf
or ocean shelves,
gathers up,
parallelizes, focuses
and in a rigid beam illuminates the image:
the head seeks in itself
fragments of left-over light
to cast a new
direction,
any direction,
to strike and fix
a random, contradicting image:
but any found image falls
back to darkness or
the lesser beams splinter and
go out:
the mind tries to
dream of diversity, of mountain
rapids shattered with sound and light,
of wind fracturing brush or
bursting out of order against a mountain
range: but the focused beam
folds all energy in:
the image glares filling all space:
the head falls and
hangs and cannot wake itself.

I risk sounding mystical by insisting that "an image" here is neither the poetic trope nor a natural particular, but what Ammons inveterately calls a "salience"; "the image glares filling all space." Not that in this perception there is no perceiver; rather the perceiving is detached, disinterested, attentive without anxiety or nostalgia. Perhaps this is only Ammons's equivalent of the difficult "half create" of *Tintern Abbey* or Emerson's "I am nothing; I see all," but it seems to ensue from the darker strain in him, that goes back to the twenty-sixth poem in *Ommateum*, "In the wind my rescue is," which stated a hopeless poetic quest: "I set it my task/to gather the stones of earth/into one place." In *Uplands*, a profound poem, *Apologia pro Vita Sua*, makes a definitive revision of the earlier ambition:

I started picking up the stones
throwing them into one place
and by sunrise I was going far away
for the large ones
always turning to see never lost
the cairn's height
lengthening my radial reach:
the sun watched with deep concentration
and the heap through the hours grew
and became by nightfall
distinguishable from all the miles around
of slate and sand:
during the night the wind falling
turned earthward its lofty freedom and speed
and the sharp blistering sound muffled
toward dawn and the blanket was
drawn up over a breathless face:
even so you can see in full dawn
the ground there lifts
a foreign thing desertless in origin.

"Distinguishable" is the desperate and revelatory word. To ask, after death, the one thing, to have left behind "a foreign thing desertless in origin," the cairn of a lifetime's poems, is to have reduced rescue into a primordial pathos. Yet the poem,

by its virtue, renders more than pathos, as the lyric following, on the same theme, renders more also:

Losing information he
rose gaining
view
till at total
loss gain was
extreme:
extreme & invisible:
the eye
seeing nothing
lost its
separation:
self-song
(that is a mere motion)
fanned out
into failing swirls
slowed &
became continuum.

Offset is the appropriate title; this is power purchased by the loss of knowledge, and unity at the expense of being material. *Uplands*, as a volume, culminates in its last lyric, *Cascadilla Falls*, placed just before the playful and brilliant long poem, *Summer Session 1968*, in which Ammons finds at last some rest from these intensities. Despite its extraordinary formal control and its continuous sense of a vision attained, *Uplands* is a majestically sad book, for Ammons does not let himself forget that his vision, while uncompromised, is a compromise necessarily, a constant knowing why and how "unity cannot do anything in particular." The poet, going down by Cascadilla Falls in the evening, picks up a stone and "thought all its motions into it," and then drops the stone from galactic wanderings to dead rest:

the stream from other motions
broke
rushing over it:
shelterless,
I turned

to the sky and stood still:

I do
not know where I am going
that I can live my life
by this single creek.

From this self-imposed pathos Ammons wins as yet no release. Release comes in the ninety delightful lyrics gathered together in *Briefings* (first entitled, gracefully but misleadingly, *Poems Small and Easy*), this poet's finest book. Though the themes of *Briefings* are familiarly Ammonsian, the mode is not. Laconic though transfigured speech has been transformed into "wasteful song." The first poem, *Center*, places us in a freer world than Ammons would give us before:

A bird fills up the
streamside bush
with wasteful song,
capsizes waterfall,
mill run, and
superhighway
to
song's improvident
center
lost in the green
bush green
answering bush:
wind varies:
the noon sun casts
mesh refractions

on the stream's amber
bottom
and nothing at all gets,
nothing gets
caught at all.

The given is mesh that cannot catch because the particulars have been capsized, and so are unavailable for capture. The center is improvident because it stands at the midmost point of mind, not of nature. *Briefings* marks an end to the oldest conflict in Ammons; the imagination has learned to avoid apocalyptic pitch, but it has learned also its own painful autonomy in regard to the universe it cannot join in unity. With the confidence of this autonomy attained, the mind yet remains wary of what lurks without, as in *Attention*:

Down by the bay I
kept in mind
at once
the tips of all the rushleaves
and so
came to know
balance's cost and true:
somewhere though in the whole field
is the one
tip
I will someday lose out of mind
and fall through.

The one particular of dying remains; every unmastered particular is a little death, giving tension to the most triumphant even among these short poems. *Hymn IV*, returning to the great *Hymn* and two related poems of the same title, seals up the quest forever:

You have enriched us with
fear and contrariety
providing the searcher
confusion for his search

teaching by your snickering
wisdom an autonomy
for man
Bear it all
and keep me from my enemies'
wafered concision and zeal
I give you back to yourself
whole and undivided

I do not hear bitterness in this, or even defiance, but any late Emersonian worship of the Beautiful Necessity is gone. With the going there comes a deep uncertainty in regard to poetic subject, as *Looking over the Acreage* and several other poems show so poignantly. The ironically moving penultimate poem of *Briefings* still locates the poet's field of contemplation "where the ideas of permanence/and transience fuse in a single body, ice for example,/or a leaf," but does not suggest that the fusion yields any information. The whole of *Briefings* manifests a surrender of the will-to-knowledge, not only relational knowledge between poetic consciousness and natural objects, but of all knowledge that is too easy, that is not also loss. Amid astonishing abundance in this richest of his volumes, I must pick out one lyric as representative of all the others, for in it Ammons gives full measure of a unique gift:

He held radical light
as music in his skull: music
turned, as
over ridges immanences of evening light
rise, turned
back over the furrows of his brain
into the dark, shuddered,

shot out again
in long swaying swirls of sound:
reality had little weight in his transcendence
so he
had trouble keeping
his feet on the ground, was
terrified by that
and liked himself, and others, mostly
under roofs:
nevertheless, when the
light churned and changed
his head to music, nothing could keep him
off the mountains, his
head back, mouth working,
wrestling to say, to cut loose
from the high, unimaginable hook:
released, hidden from stars, he ate,
burped, said he was like any one
of us: demanded he
was like any one of us.

It is the seer's horror of radical light, his obduracy to transcendence, that moves the seer himself, moves him so that he cannot know what he should know, which is that he cannot be like ourselves. The poem's power is that we are moved also, not by the horror, which cannot be our own, but by the transcendence, the sublime sense we long to share. Transcendent experience, but with Emerson's kind of Higher Utilitarianism ascetically cut off by a mind made too scrupulous for a new hope, remains the *materia poetica* of Ammons's enterprise. A majestic recent poem like *The City Limits* suggests how much celebration is still possible even when the transcendent moment is cruelly isolated, too harshly purified, totally compelled to be its own value. Somewhere upon the higher ridges of his Purgatory, Ammons remains stalled, unable for now to break through to the Condition of Fire promised by *Ommateum*, where instead of invoking Emerson's Uriel or Poe's Israfel he found near identity with "a crippled angel bent in a scythe of grief" yet witnessed a fiery ascent of the angel, fought against it, and only later gained the knowledge that "The eternal will not lie/down on any temporal hill."

DAVID KALSTONE
From "Ammons' Radiant Toys"

Diacritics, Winter 1973, pp. 13–20

Less than total is a bucketful of radiant toys.
(A. R. Ammons, "Cut the Grass")

Pastoral is hard reading today, not simply because we are more removed from "nature" than the city-dwellers who wrote the first pastoral poems, but because it is a genre scored with contradictions. Its language, stripped of social entanglements, can be baffling and abstract, strenuous testings of the mind against a landscape, as if these were the only really telling encounters. Its modern exponents—Frost, Stevens and Ammons among them—seem almost sentenced to write pastoral poems. "Life is an affair of people not of places. But for me," Wallace Stevens wrote, "life is an affair of places and that is the trouble." Companionable eclogues have long since given way to solitary discoveries, thoughtful shepherds to epistemologists.

Modern pastoral exposes the problems of modern poetry in their most extreme forms. Rather than serving as a welcome setting for verse, landscape presents a test of the poet's ability to see and enter the world, a crisis of observer and object. Poets like Stevens and Ammons satisfy and frustrate us because, drawn to the radiance of things of this world, these writers are also the most ample and abstract witnesses of their own failure to possess them. In Stevens' words, "It is the human that is the alien,/The human that has no cousin in the moon" ("Less and Less Human, O Savage Spirit"). Ammons sees the poet, pastoral or otherwise, as a "surrendered self among unwelcoming forms" ("Gravelly Run"). His large ambitions and his frequent fallings away in the face of abundance make Ammons' pastoral poems sound puzzled and urgent, the frustrations of the most willing, the most ardent, the most open observer. I cannot agree with Helen Vendler that Ammons "will have written the first twentieth-century poetry wholly purged of the romantic" (*Yale Review*, LXII, 3, 1973; p. 424). His *not* being purged is the problem. He has always had a gift for recalling romantic promises as if there were fresh ways for them to be fulfilled: "for it is not so much to know the self/as to know it as it is known/by galaxy and cedar cone" ("Gravelly Run"). Yet after these exhilarating prospects come the sobering performances, the puzzles of the "surrendered self among unwelcoming forms." What sounded like visionary promptings—lightning weddings of the self to the outside world— become bewilderments before his eyes.

To devise in the face of that sense of nature an ample rhetoric has been Ammons' problem and finally his distinction: to have invented a pastoral poem at once jagged and discontinuous, but still open to radiance; to have found a grammar that almost erases the speaker who uses it. We can see Ammons' claims over landscape at their most minimal in a recent poem like "Further On":

> Up this high and far north
> it's shale and woodless snow:
> small willows and alder brush
>
> mark out melt streams on the
> opposite slope and the wind talks
> as much as it can before freeze
>
> takes the gleeful, glimmering
> tongues away: whips and sticks
> will scream and screech then
>
> all winter over the deaf heights,
> the wind lifing its saying out
> to the essential yell of the
>
> lost and gone: it's summer now:
> elk graze the high meadows:
> marshgrass heads high as a moose's
>
> ears: lichen, a wintery weed,
> fills out for the brittle sleep:
> waterbirds plunder the shallows.

In this poem summer sensations are almost stunted by reminders everywhere of the approaching inhuman freeze: "the brittle sleep," the cold which "takes the gleeful, glimmering/tongues away." More important, the threat is put in terms of human speech and understanding: "the wind lifting its saying out/to the essential yell of the/lost and gone." Against such odds, against a "yell" that strangles articulation, even the ability to describe, to offer the reader a corner of landscape becomes a form of self-assertion. What serves is an exact sense of the surviving instincts of summer life: "lichen, a wintery weed,/fills out for the brittle sleep:/waterbirds plunder the shallows."

Many of Ammons' short poems—especially those in *Uplands* (1970) and *Briefings* (1971)—end in just such reduced circumstances, whether facing inhuman zero weather, as in "Further On," or doing battle against the "Periphery," the profusion and separateness of the outside world, "thickets hard to get around in/or get around for/an older man." The poem

"Periphery," after looking for explanations and for a center that governs the luxuriant border growth, lapses at its close into documentary satisfactions:

> I came on a spruce
> thicket full of elk, gushy snow-weed,
> nine species of lichen, four pure-white
> rocks and
> several swatches of verbena near bloom.

These precise notations are ultimately shrunken relatives of Whitman's famous catalogues—more modest, but announcing some kinship as in another recent poem, "Breaks":

> From silence to silence:
> as a woods stream
> over a
> rock holding on
> breaks into clusters of sound
> multiple and declaring as
> leaves, each one,
> filling
> the continuum between leaves,
> I stand up,
> fracturing the equilibrium,
> hold on,
> my disturbing, skinny speech
> declaring
> the cosmos.

This is not one of Ammons' very best poems. With its awkward bow to Whitman, the "I" seems unsettled, uneasily self-assertive, "standing up" when at other moments in the poem the speaker is pointedly guarded: guarded by the parentheses which enclose the poem ("From silence to silence") and by its otherwise self-deprecating tone, the "disturbing, skinny speech" which contrasts so sharply with Whitman's expansive line.

From the title on ("Breaks": noun or verb? ruptures? bits of fortune? glimpses as through a clouded sky?), Ammons courts a certain confusion. The poem fans out, one simile explained by another, the sound of a woods stream over rocks compared to the "declaration" of new leaves. From that simile within a simile, he pops into the poem "fracturing the equilibrium." The grammar is not entirely clear. He "holds on" like the jutting rock but "declares" like the clusters of sound breaking over it. His "disturbing, skinny speech" is a wry deflation of the stream's "multiple" sound and the "declaring" leaves. No need to labor a simple point, one that helps us understand Ammons' more interesting lyrics. After nature's generous sounds, the assertion of self seems both awkward and a little uncontrolled, an odd placing of the ego. Surprised by fluency, he doesn't appropriate the landscape as Whitman would, though the phrase "declaring the cosmos" might well be Whitman's own.

I am talking about the observer's voice and the assurance it offers us over objects and landscapes. Even Robert Frost's country speakers are sociable by comparison with Ammons'. Frost's wit—his secure rhymes, the way he spreads his net over the sonnet's frame, his puns that catch the eye in a conspiracy of meaning—never allows natural terrors to terrorize form. It is good to have his tone in mind for comparison with Ammons'. Something like "One Step Backward Taken" with its near jingles about geological upheavals in a new ice age ("Whole capes caked off in slices") absorbs catastrophe before it occurs (capes into cake):

> I felt my standpoint shaken
> In the universal crisis.

But with one step backward taken
I saved myself from going.

Frost's backward step is also a foreseeing one, a witty preparation.

In a more somber version of disaster, "Desert Places," Frost looks at a snow scene which threatens to obliterate everything. From an initial urgency ("Snow falling and night falling fast, oh, fast/In a field I looked into going past"—insistent participles, phrases rather than sentences) the poem gathers to a self-assertion that takes in all the fear:

They cannot scare me with their empty spaces
Between stars—on stars where no human race is.
I have it in me so much nearer home
To scare myself with my own desert places.

The poem finds a form and assured tone which answer the terror that remains undiminished. Frost can be homely, witty, and desperate in a single line: "The loneliness includes me unawares," asserting by the end a kind of canny control. Balanced sentences and emphatic rhetoric can replace the poem's introductory phrases acting out the mind's growing command as it understands its terrors:

And lonely as it is that loneliness
Will be more lonely ere it will be less—
A blanker whiteness of benighted snow
With no expression, nothing to express.

Always beleaguered by nature, Frost has his witty standpoint, his one step backward to take. Frost's poems end, have a place to go, come to rest.

This is precisely what we feel Ammons cannot do: "Stop on any word and language gives way:/the blades of reason, unlightened by motion, sink in" ("Essay on Poetics"). He has his doubts about the finished poem and his own place in it. A few years ago he threaded a book-length poem along an adding machine tape—the poem ended when the tape did—producing a December diary, *Tape for the Turn of the Year*. That was his most flamboyant attempt to turn his verse into something beyond neat gatherings. With *Uplands* and *Briefings*, his most recent short volumes, he was obviously resisting summaries and the idea of books marking stages in a poetic career. They were closer to journals of mental states, each poem an entry finding a form and a scene for a very exact encounter or discovery. The point lay not only in single adventures, but in the continuing, sometimes driven effort: "why does he write poems: it's the only way he can mean/what he says [. . .]/he keeps saying in order to hope he will/say something he means [. . .]/poems deepen his attention till what he is thinking/catches the energy of a deep rhythm" ("Hibernaculum"). The oddest part of that statement is how tentative it is; he keeps writing in order at least to "hope" he'll touch "meaning."

Under such pressures Ammons was bound to value a style that kept moving. "Viable" tells part of the story:

Motion's the dead give away,
eye catcher, the revealing risk:
the caterpillar sulls on the hot macadam
but then, risking, ripples to the bush:
the cricket, startled, leaps the
quickest arc: the earthworm, casting,
nudges a grassblade, and the sharp robin
strikes: sound's the other
announcement: the redbird lands in
an elm branch and tests the air with
cheeps for an answering, reassuring
cheep, for a motion already cleared:

survival organizes these means down to
tension, to enwrapped, twisting suasions:
every act or non-act enceinte with risk or
prize: why must the revelations be
sound and motion, the poet, too, moving and
saying through the scary opposites to death.

Looking askance at "revelation," this poem twins it with danger, scales it down to watching for prey, for the smallest movements. Rather than revelation, there is "the revealing risk"; the "dead give away" is the only moment when the currents of life become visible, palpable for us. The puns and playfulness are part of Ammons' game. Observing, catlike, the rippling caterpillar, the startled cricket, the earthworm prey to the robin, his poem mimics their motion with its own chain of clauses and darting participles. It must, above all, sound offhand, the somber truth buried in the casual opening line. Motion is caught as from the corner of the eye.

Ammons had long since, in a poem called "Motion," talked about the impossibility of ever identifying word with thing. Poems are "fingers, methods,/nets,/not what is or/was." Still he had faith in the music of a poem which

by the motion of
its motion
resembles
what, moving, is—
the wind
underleaf white against
the tree.

In "Viable" he is more canny, more reticent, and also more alive to what *compels* him to seek renewals of motion. Poetry—the movement of poetry—comes closer to reflex and to survival; the final line of "Viable" only confirms a shadow we have already felt. Nature's small creatures, the poem admits, are observed not so much for their own sake as to be a pulse for the poet. He attempts, through verse, movements as minute as theirs. Motion reveals; sound, like the robin's call, waits for a reply, tests the air for "an answering, reassuring/cheep, for a motion already cleared." The question that closes the poem is rhetorical; there are no answers to its *why*, only repeated close observation of tiny actions to relieve an innate and natural "tension." The poet is alive to risks, taking his prize, hoping to prove for this moment that he is alive by catching "the energy of a deep rhythm," all the time acknowledging that he too is ultimately prey. In paraphrase this sounds like a desperate enterprise, but in the poem such explicit meanings are subsumed by metaphor until the very end, absorbed in risk and variety—*sulls*, *ripples*, *nudges*, and *strikes*.

A poem like "Viable" is very revealing of Ammons' developed style. Natural facts—an enormous repertoire of them, closely observed—tick through his verse and make it seem, at least superficially, a fulfillment of William Carlos Williams' "No ideas but in things." Ammons' measured, skinny lines focus our attention on things and parts of things with the insistence of a slow-motion camera.

Yet he is restless adopting that style, even when setting out its advantages: "I'm doing the best I can,/that is to say, with too many linking verbs: the grandest/clustering of aggregates permits the finest definition" ("Viable"). The superlatives suggest a fussy version of Williams' "objectivity." Certainly Williams' notation pulses through Ammons' short poems, just as the casual, almost random style of the Beats and New York School give him a way to talk about the provisional and constantly changing voices in his long poems. Those voices contribute to his later verse, but also go against a natural bent, a desire that nature signify or "add up." As a reading of "Viable" suggests, objects may seem like counters in a larger game.

Why then adopt voices close to the minimal and casual, styles which seem least suited to ambitious statement? Certainly the constant struggle of realistic notation and visionary pressure charges these later poems with problematic power and beauty, and explains their curious blurring of the ego. But it is only when we look back to Ammons' early work, poems which reach openly for transcendence, that we see how much he needed the concrete resistance of contemporary objective styles. . . .

What is remarkable about "Gravelly Run" is the modulation of tone, the range of voices to which it is open. At the beginning seer and observer seem united. The opening rhythms widen to visionary assurance ("as if birth had never found it/and death could never end it"); observation narrows to the utmost particularity (the emphatic consonant-clotted "long/stone-held algal/hair and narrowing roils"). From that exercise, taking a sharper license, he imagines the cedars as spires. A rebuke is prompt and compact. "Reflect," offered as a gesture of understanding, is drained of its meditative meaning before our eyes. Human gesture becomes nothing but a reflection, a mirror; the poem turns everything brutally physical, a world of unconnected particles, his visionary effort merely that of the "surrendered self among unwelcoming forms."

From this time on the placing of self in Ammons' work is one of its oddest features. In "Saliences," one of his best poems, the *I* enters only in its closing third. It has, of course, made earlier veiled appearances, from the moment, in fact, that this poem announces its title, which has to do with the interaction of mind and landscape. Saliences are, as Bloom notes, "outleapings, 'mind feeding out,' not taking in perceptions but turning its violent energies out into the field of action." The ostensible subject of the poem is a dunes walk like that of "Corsons Inlet." But an elaborate syntax keeps the "I" from making assertions in any ordinary way:

>   Consistencies rise
>   and ride
>   the mind down
>   hard routes
>   walled
>   with no outlet and so
>   to open a variable geography,
>   proliferate
>   possibility, here
>   is this dune fest
>   releasing
>   mind feeding out,
>   gathering clusters,
>   fields of order in disorder,
>   where choice
>   can make beginnings,
>   turns,
>   reversals.

The very notion of a distanced "mind" is provocative. It both acts (feeding, gathering) and is acted upon (ridden down, released). More important, the distinction between the two is almost erased when the "dune fest" begins. We are to be caught in a whirl of motion, self merging with the outer world. The rhythm, the short lines and relentless alternation of noun and participle practically blot our differences between actions of mind and nature. Nouns are suspended in a chain of participial explosions of equal force ("releasing/mind feeding out,/gathering clusters"). The maneuver is vital; you almost feel that the verbal motion is more important than the mixture

of abstractions and particulars swept along, and that everything moves, dissolving "before the one event that/creates present time," an event described in the long second section of the poem, the palpable "unarranged disorder" of the wind. Tracing the sequence of tenses here is one way of telling the story: a sweep of present participles through the landscape ("weathering shells with blast/[. . .] lifting the spider"); then the wind traced in past participles, a loving dialogue with objects it touches ("wind/shaped and kept in the/bent of trees,/[. . .] the kept and erased sandcrab trails"). All this is done with a Whitmanic force, minimal pauses, the movement constantly aided by repetitions of words and participial endings—but in a shorter line than Whitman's to accelerate the flow.

Only then, after this virtual effacement of the self, does he begin in a third movement to lay claim to the experience: with imperatives ("bend to these/changing weathers") and, finally, with his first use of the simple past tense ("when I went back to the dunes today"). This is the first real admission of a separate observer and leads to what Bloom describes as the "firm beauty" of the last seventy lines, a detailed tracing of "the reassurance [. . .]/that through change/continuities sinuously work." In a recapitulation of the previous day's sights and sounds, all changed but with shades of resemblance (the "saliences" of the title "congruent to memory") he finds "summations of permanence!/where not a single thing endures." The confusion of present and past in the memory is full and fruitful:

>   much seemed
>   constant, to be looked
>   forward to, expected:
>   from the top of a dune rise,
>   look of ocean salience: in
>   the hollow,
>   where a runlet
>   makes in
>   at full tide and fills a bowl,
>   extravagance of pink periwinkle
>   along the grassy edge,
>   and a blue, bunchy weed, deep blue,
>   deep into the mind the dark blue
>   constant.

Is it full tide? or is the mind thinking ahead to the expected moment of full tide and ocean salience which it fuses with the present feel of pink periwinkle and the blue weed that partakes, for the observer, of land and sea? The evasive *where*, some elided verbs covered by obliging commas—these work to blur present and past in a more relaxed confusion of mind and nature than is felt in the first part of the poem. "Saliences" builds to a close as beautiful as that of Stevens' "Sunday Morning."

>   desertions of swallows
>   that yesterday
>   ravaged air, bush, reed, attention
>   in gatherings wide as this neck of dunes:
>   . . .
>   earth brings to grief
>   much in an hour that sang, leaped, swirled,
>   yet keeps a round
>   quiet turning,
>   beyond loss or gain,
>   beyond concern for the separate reach.

The elegiac close allows for the observer's limitations as well as for nature's "deaths and flights." In fact, the spectator's discretion is one of the poem's great secrets. Manipulating rhythms, but particularly verb tenses—energetic displacements at the outset, subtler swellings at the close—is a way of veiling the observer, without whom, on the other hand, he had come to recognize, no poem exists. Ammons is testing another approach to vision: not claiming it as a seer, but invoking or propitiating it; withdrawing, making us forget he is there; appearing to be close to details, yet minimizing the spectator's presence and powers.

It is here that Williams' devotion to "things" would become useful. The stripped-down lists, the focussed notation were indeed to become ingredients of Ammons' *Briefings*, but not, we can see from "Saliences," the only ingredients. Nor, as a poem like "Viable" suggests, was the balance between discrete particular and a suggested visionary pattern always so grandly, so securely achieved as in "Saliences." The pattern elsewhere may be elusive, the details under pressure to yield it up. Ammons' verse is more restless than Williams' lyrics. The most precise details seem only approximate: "there is nothing small enough to conjure clarity with."

"Clarity" is in fact one of Ammons' subjects. But what other poet would illustrate that title with a poem about erosion? Ammons now enjoys giving visionary words like *clarity* a tumble. A rockslide, exposing the stresses beneath what we imagine to be solid, reveals "streaks &/scores of knowledge/now obvious and quiet." The poem deliberately belies its abstract title and the ordinary meanings of *knowledge, obvious,* and *quiet,* scaling down the large questions of philosophy and romantic lyric to answers made sensible by discrete and particular encounters:

> After the event the rockslide
> realized,
> in a still diversity of completion,
> grain and fissure,
> declivity
> &
> force of upheaval,
> whether rain slippage,
> ice crawl, root
> explosion or
> stream erosive undercut:
>
> well I said it is a pity:
> one swath of sight will never
> be the same: nonetheless,
> this
> shambles has
> relieved a bind, a taut of twist,
> revealing streaks &
> scores of knowledge
> now obvious and quiet.

Though we have an illusion of the utmost particularity, the first-person observer is almost incidental, invoked only by a chatty comment, otherwise absorbed or lost in the poem whose principal effort is a "realization" of motion—the motion latent in every knot of geological structure. Specific words don't seem to matter as much as the total assembly of nouns and the illusion that they trace out all geological contingencies. At first it is even hard to tell whether the opening section is governed by "realized" or by "diversity of," all the nouns parallel to "completion"; both effects are forceful. The exertions and knotting of syntax seem again an effort to blur traditional functions of grammar; the poem strains toward the general by being as toughly particular as possible. Series of details are preferred over a sustained rhetorical structure that might suggest a spectator's control over them.

We can see how precarious these claims are by comparison with Whitman's large gestures, appropriating objects for the self. "I think we are here to give back our possessions before/they are taken away," Ammons says in the searching long poem "Hibernaculum." That attitude makes Whitmanian confidence impossible. No wonder then that the "I" eventually leaves many of Ammons' briefer poems, letting objects take them over, as in "Periphery" and "Further On." The poem exists for him in a continually threatened state, like a sheet of ice

> for language heightens by dismissing reality,
> the sheet of ice a salience controlling, like a
> symbol,
> level of abstraction, that has a hold on reality
> and suppresses
> it, though formed from it and supported by it:
> motion and artificiality (the impositional remove
> from reality)
> sustain language: nevertheless, language must
> not violate the bit, event, percept,
> fact.
>
> (Essay on Poetics)

The violation of fact becomes the death of language: "when that happens abandonment/is the only terrible health and a return to bits, retrials/of lofty configurations."

It is true, then, that in recent poems Ammons characteristically narrows attention to find the smallest details which might confirm a relation between self and nature, that his verse's pressured motion seeks the "energy of a deep rhythm."

> I think I'm almost
> down to shadows, yielding to their masses,
> for my self out here, taut against the mere
> suasion of a star, is explaining, dissolving
> itself, saying, be with me wind bent at leaf
> edges, warp me puddle riffle, show me
> the total yielding past shadow and return.
>
> (Schooling)

But it is also important and marvellous that in the very best of his recent work his anxiety is either muted or seen in a new light: muted, as in "Peracute Lucidity," where the self builds, but without commenting on it, the very chapel in nature it was prevented from inhabiting in "Gravelly Run."

> clarity's chapel
> bodied by hung-in boughs: and
> widening out over the pond, the blown
> cathedral luminous with evening glass:
> I go out there and sit
> till difference and event yield to
> perfect composure: then the stars
> come out and question every sound, the brook's.

Only at the end is there a slight rebuke to his confidence, a delicate disturbance that ripples but does not overturn his inhabited scene.

Elsewhere he sets anxiety in a new key. The setting of "Peracute Lucidity" had "a perspicuity like a sanctuary." "Triphammer Bridge," one of Ammons' most beautiful new poems, takes the very word "sanctuary" and, turning it over, as if it were a prism, takes an explicit pleasure in the powers of language that Ammons seldom allows himself.

> I wonder what to mean by *sanctuary,* if a real or
> apprehended place, as of a bell rung in a gold
> surround, or as of silver roads along the beaches
> of clouds seas don't break or black mountains
> overspill; jail: ice here's shapelier than anything,
> on the eaves massive, jawed along gorge ledges, solid
> in the plastic blue boat fall left water in: if I

think the bitterest thing I can think of that seems like
reality, slickened back, hard, shocked by rip-high
wind:

> sanctuary, sanctuary, I say it over and over and the
> word's sound is the one place to dwell: that's it, just
> the sound, and the imagination of the sound—a
> place.

Sanctuary: the word itself is the subject, as if Ammons
were for once enjoying the separation of self and nature. Imagination creates its sanctuaries: the bell echoing in gold; the
cloud beaches free of eroding seas and piercing mountain
peaks; but also—and given co-ordinate place—"jail." Still,
confinements are shapely—"massive," "jawed"—transformed
despite reminders of an adverse life: the rains of autumn, the
bitter shaping force of wind, inseparable from the palpable
pleasure he takes in shapes it has made. The poem itself is like
the ice of which he speaks: its past participles, like ice crystals,
take the sting out of bitter action. The difference between real
and apprehended, bitter and sweet, includes all reminders of
frailty and a joy, finally, in repeating the word that has evoked
them all, "*sanctuary* [. . .] the one place to dwell." The
exaltation of the final line, its real abandonment to the force
and pleasure of imagination, recalls the late, great poems of
Wallace Stevens.

Recently, then, Ammons has found ways to step back
from the whirl of the provisional and particular to which, of
necessity, his work has been committed. Perhaps his long
poems have satisfied his need for "movement," and he has new
notions of what the short poem can do. "The City Limits,"
which Bloom praises so highly, suggests all the hidden threats
and difficulties of vision prominent in *Briefings*, but suspends
them in a wonderfully sustained rhetorical structure almost like
that of the most controlled and contemplative of Shakespeare's
sonnets. Five clauses, repeating, "When you consider the
radiance [. . .] when you consider [. . .] When you consider the abundance,"—the *whens* tensing rhetorical springs for
an expected *then*, each clause taking in another corner of
abundance and vicissitude—finally license the high pleasure
and relief of the closing lines: "then [. . .] the dark/work of
the deepest cells is of a tune with May bushes/and fear lit by
the breadth of such calmly turns to praise." "The Arc Inside
and Out," which closes *Collected Poems*, is another example,
with its controlled rhetoric, of a firmer meditative order.

But Ammons is unpredictable, full of the subversive bravado of natural and even random facts. There is no way of
knowing whether (or when) you will find him desperate to get
back to them ("wrestling to say, to cut loose/from the high,
unimaginable hook") or on the contrary full of the yearning
which Stevens expressed for things beyond "the separate
reach":

> Unreal, give back to us what once you gave:
> The imagination that we spurned and crave.
> (Wallace Stevens, "To the One of Fictive Music")

PATRICIA A. PARKER
From "Configurations of Shape and Flow"
Diacritics, Winter 1973, pp. 25–33

T he poet who speaks in the Foreword to his own first
volume of "the chaotic particle in the classical field,"
goes on to dazzle us with a profusion of such titles as "Nucleus," "Bourn," "Center," "Periphery," "Circles," and
"Round," and begins the longest and most difficult of his re-

cent poems, "Hibernaculum," with an evocation of the "timeless relations" of "center to periphery," "core-thought to consideration" is of all the present generation of poets not only the
most strikingly Emersonian in his own way, but the one most
conscious of the dynamics and metamorphoses of his tradition's most persistent emblem, from Emerson's essay *Circles*
and Whitman as "encompasser of worlds" to Dickinson's "Circumference" and "Circumstance" and the ninth of Stevens'
"Thirteen Ways of Looking at a Blackbird": "When the blackbird flew out of sight,/It marked the edge/Of one of many
circles."

Even the early *Ommateum*[1] poems betray a fascination
with what Dickinson called the "Wizardry" of "Geometry."
The diagrammatic easiness of these poems is provided by the
two axes inevitable no matter where the poet stands—the
earth's horizontal surface and that upright animal man, in "the
boost of perpendicularity,/directional and rigid" ("Doxology").[2] Because of this upright position, a stance as challenging to entropy as the mountainous coiffures in Wallace
Stevens' "Le Monocle de Mon Oncle," the "I" of these desert
dramas inhabits a plainisphere and, judging all things from his
own vertical precipice, naturally sees the earth as flat and the
sun as sinking into an abyss. These axes are still the implicit
setting of the later poem "Recovery," with its shadow "hardened into noon," and in the twenty-seventh of the *Ommateum*
poems Ammons seems to delight in geometric wizardry almost
for its own sake. . . .

The double time we know from Eliot or Joyce becomes in
Ammons' poem a revelation of old and new visions of empire,
Cartier travelling up the St. Lawrence to "Hochelaga," his
modern counterpart taking "'The Laurentian' out of New
York/first morning after the strike ended." The connection,
once again, is the paradigm. Montreal, once a margin on the
French empire, is now—except for a little competition from
the "Queen" and "parent companies in England and Germany"—a margin on the American one. The "prospect"
afforded Cartier by the "panoramic" view from "Mt. Royal"
becomes the "prospects" mapped out over breakfast from the
twenty-two storey height of "'The Panorama.'" The easily de-
fendable island Cartier surveys from his mountain of vision
becomes the factory location on Linden Street, "four walls, a
limited, defined, exact place,/a nucleus,/solidification from
possibility." And if the problem of balancing "growth possibility" with sufficient central control is now a more delicate operation than it was for Cartier with his "tin paternosters" and
"knives," the present "nucleus" does not appear to be in danger
as long as the response from the margins is "Yassuh." . . .

The tension between shape and flow in Ammons' poetry
continues from the synthesis that "fails (and succeeds) into
limitation" in "The Misfit" to "Hibernaculum" and the "definitions" that produce "about the same/securities and disasters." The most revealing explorations of the grief and glory of
living in a world where no circumference is final are, however,
the poems written in the decade immediately following *Ommateum*. The tone of "Hymn V" and its demand that all questions be "in/triumphs of finality" categorically "answered and
filed" is clearly ironic, but the irony only slightly masks the
pain of being without the "old rich usage" of the final lines. It
is a pain that we still hear in the later poem "The Eternal City"
in its statement of the need to preserve even in ruin "all the
old/perfect human visions, all the old perfect loves." In
"Joshua Tree," the wasteland quester waiting for "some/
syllable's rain," is like similar figures in Stevens the poet's
image of himself and his own poetic dilemma, without "eternal
city," "liturgy," or "dome."

The poet of the much later lyric "Cut the Grass" knows that for man the encloser, "less than total is a bucketful of radiant toys" and that the only way of taking on the "roundness" is to try, like Whitman in the crucial twenty-fifth section of "Song of Myself," to encompass everything within the circle of "Speech." But he also knows, with the Emerson of *Nominalist and Realist*, that "No sentence will hold the whole truth, and the only way in which we can be just, is by giving ourselves the lie"; and this, in effect, is what he does in the early poem "Unsaid" when he asks his readers to listen for the things "left out." His realization of the futility of trying to define the fluid becomes in a later poem a contempt for "The Confirmers" equal to anything in Dickinson.

When, however, the "disorder ripe" along the "peripheries" of his control becomes what Emerson in *Circles* calls "the Unattainable, the flying Perfect, around which the hands of man can never meet," then the unencompassed is much more menacing. In a poem appropriately entitled "Attention," it becomes the unemcompassed as Achilles' heel, the "one/tip" he will some day "lose out of mind/and fall through." And when the "unassimilable fact" of "The Misfit" becomes "What This Mode of Motion Said," its "leading on" is of a more sinister kind:

> pressed too far
> I wound, returning endless
> inquiry
> for the pride of inquiry:

Emerson in the essay on Plato describes this revenge as that of the "bitten world" on the "biter." Ammons' version of the fatal consequences of this quest both for nature and for her would-be encompasser is the poem "Jungle Knot," where owl— "errors of vision"—and anaconda—"errors of self-defense"— kill each other in a "coiled embrace."

Between "Hymn V" and "Corsons Inlet" fall a great many poems, some of which involve an equally unsatisfactory center, Ammons' version of what Wallace Stevens, in "Notes Toward a Supreme Fiction," calls "the first idea," the "muddy centre before we breathed." Partly because he is as aware as his predecessor that neither the rigidly centered self nor the attempt to encompass everything is a sufficient or even possible way of living constantly in change, Ammons occasionally provides us with his own variation on the Stevensian mode of reduction, as in the early poem "This Black Rich Country," which begins: "Dispossess me of belief:/between life and me obtrude/no symbolic forms." His most serious temptation, however, goes beyond Stevens to Emerson, and it is perhaps for this reason that where he is most tempted he is most ironic. "The Golden Mean" is a brilliant satiric exposure of the argument of Emerson's essay *Experience* and its description of man as "a golden impossibility," just as the later poem "Mean" is a kind of *Compensation* pushed to its extreme. But each of them, like the picture of "Mr. Homburg" in Stevens' "Looking across the Fields and Watching the Birds Fly," says as much about the poet as about his target.

It is, nevertheless, this same irony, or sometimes just whimsical humor, which provides him with the distance from both Emerson and himself that he clearly needs. In one of the later lyrics entitled "Classic," this distance is realized, as it often is in Ammons, by the poem's dramatic context. The "I" here is caught "scribbling again" by the mountain, but protests that by now he has learned the lessons of reduction and can scribble in "a fashion very/like the water here/uncapturable and vanishing." The mountain's reply is to remind him of past sins:

> but that
> said the mountain does not
> excuse the stance
> or diction
> and next if you're not careful
> you'll be
> arriving at ways
> water survives its motions.

If the "stream" here is, as I think it is, at least partly like the "flecked river" of Stevens' "This Solitude of Cataracts," one of these past sins is the original one in this tradition: what in the very Emersonian seer of Stevens' poem is the desire to merge with some "permanent realization" at the "azury centre of time."

These glances at the tradition and its central emblem may suggest that if Ammons in some ways suffers the disadvantages of a latecomer—"My hands are old/and crippled keep no lyre," in the most light-hearted treatment of this problem ("Mountain Liar")—he also in one sense shares in the advantages of latecoming: he knows where this tradition's central image led its first circular philosopher and his knowledge makes him wary. The "too/adequate relationship" he protests against in the late poem entitled "Periphery" is at least in one of its senses what Emerson in the essay *Power* describes as "causality" or the "strict connection between every pulse-beat and the principle of being." The decision to go "deeper" and see what is "pushing all this/periphery, so difficult to make any sense/out of, out" takes us all the way back to the poetic motto of Emerson's *Circles* and the "new genesis" such a penetration of earth's "surface" would bring. But the "hesitation" at the end is Ammons' own and brings its own rewards:

> with me, decision brings its own
> hesitation: a symptom, no doubt, but open
> and meaningless enough without paradigm: but
>   hesitation
> can be all right, too: I came on a spruce
> thicket full of elk, gushy snow-weed,
> nine species of lichen, four pure white rocks and
> several swatches of verbena near bloom.

As a wariness of the center and its fixity, it returns, this time with Emerson named, in a crucial section of "Hibernaculum": "O/Plotinus (Emerson, even) I'm just as scared as comforted/by the continuity, one sun spelling in our sun-made heads."

In some of the early poems, however, Ammons' own greatest temptation is to honor any going thing, to celebrate in a poem like "Mechanism" the "precise and/necessary worked out of random, reproducible,/the handiwork redeemed from chance." When it appears, it is in a language which shows just how much of a fascination for him Emerson's "Balance-loving Nature" and her "bunch of/compensating laws" ("The Wind Coming Down From") could become. In one early poem, the distance he needs takes, once again, the dramatic form of "Ezra," who, tired of being "the dying portage" of "deathless thoughts," interrupts the mountain's lecture to give his own version of a merging with the Beautiful Necessity, "the Way in whose timeless reach/cool thought unpunishable/by bones eternally glides" ("Whose Timeless Reach"). But in "Lines," where "deranging" in the final line captures both the French sense of upsetting an order of some kind and the very graphic English description of the mad as "deranged," there is no interposed "Ezra" or "I" and something much closer to Ammons' own temptation is at stake. The poet who is always asking us to see "the wonderful workings of the world" ("Cut the Grass") constantly apprises us, in his best lyrics, of the kind of perception which is an act of love. But "Lines" is perception itself as madness, a madness not of confusion but of too much lucidity. And it is exactly this "boreal clarity" which leads to the terrible surrender of the "spent seer" at the end of "Prodigal":

> the mind whirls, short of the unifying
> reach, short of the heat
>   to carry that forging:
>   after the visions of these losses, the spent
> seer, delivered to wastage, risen
>   into ribs, consigns knowledge to
>   approximation, order to the vehicle
> of change, and fumbles blind in blunt innocence
>   toward divine, terrible love.

Or that, again, in "Motion for Motion," leads to a "blurred mind overexposed":

> I—lost to an
> automatic machinery in things, duplicating, without
> useful difference, some changeless order extending
> backward beyond the origin of earth,
> changeless and true, even before the water fell, or
> the sun broke, or the beetle turned, or the still
> human head bent from a bridge-rail above to have a
>   look.

The difficulty of sustaining the burden of these mysteries brings Ammons to the point Stevens reached in the seventh section of "The Auroras of Autumn": the temptation to assume what he calls in "Motion for Motion" some "will not including him" which has "a clear vision of it all" even if he himself does not. It is the flirtation with "the possibility of rule as the sum of rulelessness" that seems to be moving Ammons' best-known poem, "Corsons Inlet," in the same direction and then does not.

"Corsons Inlet" and "Saliences," both written in 1962, appear less than halfway through the *Collected Poems*, but together they are the pivotal point of the collection, marking both the continuity and the difference in the poems written before and since. Both are poems of sea level, the marginal, transitional place that makes Ammons, in Richard Howard's phrase, a "littoralist of the imagination."[3] "Corsons Inlet," in its refusal of all "arranged terror" and "humbling of reality to precept," takes us all the way back to the *Ommateum* Foreword, and though its promise to be satisfied with the "freedom" that "Overall" and "Scope" elude his grasp is not the final word in Ammons for an order that will suffice, the release it represents here is the necessary outward movement that a later title will call "Countering." "Saliences" read closely holds in potential so much of the poetry written since that we can return to it to illuminate even the longest and most ambitious of Ammons' recent work. The wind that earlier brought "rescue" to the stonegatherer becomes the "variable" that both brings the mind out of its "hard routes/walled/with no outlet" and saves the mechanism of natural change from an eternal sameness. Its "dunes," taken as a releasing perception for "old dunes/of mind," provide an image that will return in the poem entitled "Dunes" and its discovery that "loose" ground is more "available" than "firm" even if "Taking root in windy sand/is not an easy /way/to go about/finding a place to stay." The wind "shaped and kept in the/bent of trees" leads all the way to the later poem "Pluralist" and its maple tree "large/enough to express contrary/notions," and both provide an indication of how to read the kind of "objectivity" that is always in Ammons only "the objective way of talking about ourselves" ("Extremes and Moderations"). The counsel to mind to "bend to these changing weathers" recalls the dangers of "ice-bound/mind" in the earlier poem "Thaw." And the preference for "gradual

shadings out or in" over the abruptness of "alarm" will be echoed in poems all the way to "Hibernaculum" and its recognition that there must be some law of succession for mental states, some "protection against jolt-change."

"Saliences" is still a decade away from the longer and more difficult of the *Collected Poems*, but both in its refusal to give assertion up and in its realization of the need to "bend," it begins the search for some "Unifying Principle" which will keep the "shape" without damming up the "flow" and for a poetics which will involve a "Countering" of the "crystal of reason" whether or not it actually reaches "the higher/reason" that "contains the war/of shape and loss/at rest" ("Countering"). Whatever else this might mean, it seems to involve in the more recent poetry a new control which is at once a new freedom. In "The Put-Down Come On," it is a search which states that it will be satisfied if probability—"what has always happened"—and possibility—"what/has never happened before"—seem, if only "for an instant," reconciled. In what several readers have sensed as the freer world of these poems, it seems to involve a kind of centering which is not a solipsism, in the same way as the enterprise of the late poem, "Conserving the Magnitude of Uselessness," is not a terrifying or engulfing exercise because its very conservation is an act of mind saving mind from itself.

One beautiful example of this new freedom is a poem written soon after "Saliences," with the significant title "Center":

> A bird fills up the
> streamside bush
> with wasteful song,
> capsizes waterfall,
> mill run, and
> superhighway
> to
> song's improvident
> center
> lost in the green
> bush green
> answering bush:
> wind varies:
> the noon sun casts
> mesh refractions
> on the stream's amber
> bottom
> and nothing at all gets,
> nothing gets
> caught at all.

This lyric gathers up and removes the burden and threat of so many earlier images that it seems almost to stand as a declaration of this new freedom to the reader who has been following the geography of Ammons' work. Its "mesh" does not entrap realities, nor do its stream's "refractions" bring him a blurred mind overexposed. The symmetry of its "noon sun" does not oppress, and the wasteful capsizing of its "waterfall" need not be furiously entertained. Its "center," finally, is freer because it is neither the destruction of the vertical "moment" nor a bird of glass, hard and removed.

"The Unifying Principle" suggested in the poem of that name recalls the possible "modes of structuring" the spent seer of "Prodigal" failed to "perfect" before consigning all order to the vehicle of change. In the most recent poetry, this principle seems to be emerging as the search for a "balance" which will be not the static tightrope walk of "The Golden Mean" but the constant in and out motion that gives a double meaning to the "ecology" of "Extremes and Moderations." Like the dualities of the earlier poem "Risks and Possibilities," "extreme" here can be either a too-rigid order or a too-sudden change, with the "moderations" providing the countering movement which saves us from each:

> circulations are moderations, currents triggered by
> extremes:
> we must at all costs keep the circulations free and
> clear,
> open and unimpeded: otherwise, extremes will be-
> come trapped,
> local, locked in themselves, incapable of transaction:
> some
> extremes, though *are* circulations, a pity, in that
> kinds of
> staying must then be the counters.

The fact of this duality helps to clarify what are frequently puzzling contexts for the word "saliences" in Ammons' most recent work and to suggest, finally, what "taking on the round-ness," in this poet's continuing fascination with the circle, is coming to mean. Emerson in a Journal entry of 1857 defines "salience" as "the principle of levity [. . .] the antagonist of gravitation [. . .] the balance, or offset, to the mountains and masses." But Ammons, in "Levitation," evokes the perils of ascent in a world where the ground "disastrous to seers/and saints" is always around "evening scores, calling down" and in another lyric entitled "Offset" suggests the losses as well as the gains in one seer's antagonism to gravity. The paradox in "Offset" of an ascent whose "extreme" is both gain and loss is a reminder that perspective is purchased only by the loss of "ground," a danger in the "principle of levity" itself which gives one late poem the title "The Limit":

> the salience,
> in a bodiless arrogance,
> must preserve
> algal tracings or it
> loses further (already scared of loss)
> ground for possible self-imaginings.

The conclusion here that "it's interwork/that pays with mind" subsumes all of the search for "balance" that provides us, finally, with the connection between Ammons' two princi-ple figures—the axes of "High & Low" and the tension be-tween "center" and "periphery"—the four directions "mind can go" in the recent and appropriately entitled "Staking Claim." "Interwork" in the drama of rising and falling seems to mean in the most recent lyrics not a final decision either way, but an ongoing activity of mind, what Ammons calls his "likely schizophrenia" in the poem entitled "One More Time." In "Extremes and Moderations," the seeming contradiction be-tween the statements, "it's impossible anyone should know anything about the concrete/who's never risen above it" and "the lofted's precarious: the ground is nice and sweet and not/ at all spectacular," is instead a dialectic necessary in the "econ-omy of the self." When the paradigm is not "High & Low" but concentration and diffusion, this imperative becomes in "Hibernaculum" the "mind" which from "the undifferentiated core-serum" turns "to the definition of its tangles for rescue" and then "back to the core for clarification" and in "The Swan Ritual" an activity which recalls the terrible centering of "La-ser" at the same time as it suggests how its menace might be removed:

> Yield to the tantalizing mechanism:
> fall, trusting and centered as a
> drive, following into the poem:
> line by line pile entanglements on,
> arrive willfully in the deepest

> fix: then, the thing done, turn
> round in the mazy terror and
> question, outsmart the mechanism:
> find the glide over-reaching or
> dismissing—halter it into

> a going concern so the wing
> muscles at the neck's base work
> urgency's compression and
> openness breaks out lofting
> you beyond all binds and terminals.

That the possible dangers of centering here should be those inherent in a poem leads us finally to the one aspect of "shape & flow" that seems to be increasingly the subject of Ammons' ongoing meditations. The late poem "Image" and its "indefinable idol" raises, though obliquely, the problem of how a poet can be at once image-maker and "iconoclast," how, in short, poetry might point to its own contingency at the same time as it necessarily gives shape to the flow. The poet who listens for the "Expressions of Sea Level" or the language of the orange tree in "Communication" frequently senses human speech as intrusion, from the "round/fury" of "Spindle" and its "violence to make/that can destroy" to the "disturbing, skinny speech" which by "fracturing" nature's "equilibrium" gives an-other poem the title "Breaks." The search for a poetic that "traps no/realities, takes/no game" ("Motion") leads in Ammons from the early poem "Unsaid" to the curious and delightful ruse of the late "Snow Log," where the decision to take nature's "intention" on himself enables him to get back again everything he seemed to have given up. The delicate balance of this achievement in Ammons' best lyrics is what enables him, as Harold Bloom has remarked, "to have a com-plete vision of his own heterocosm, at once an alternative world to outward nature and yet also the actuality of nature given back to us again."

As program, this poetic enterprise leads from the sugges-tion in "Motion" that the "music/in poems" by "the motion/of its motion" may resemble "what, moving, is" all the way to the three long poems which are successful partly because each has, as one of its subjects, the long poem—"Essay on Poetics," "Extremes and Moderations," and "Hibernaculum." The very length of these verse essays suggests that Ammons is far from giving assertion up, and the most recent, "Hibernaculum," is the most moving in its evocation of the continuing need for and need of the poetic word:

> if the night is to be
> habitable, if dawn is to come out of it, if day is ever
> to grow brilliant on delivered populations, the word
> must have its way by the brook, lie out cold all night
> along the snow limb, spell by yearning's wilted weed
> till
> the wilted weed rises, know the patience and small-
> ness
> of stones: I address the empty place where the god
> that has been deposed lived: it is the godhead: the
> yearnings that have been addressed to it bear anti-
> quity's
> sanction: for the god is ever re-created as
> emptiness, till force and ritual fill up and strangle
> his life, and then he must be born empty again.

This "god" is the "indefinable idol" of "Image," and the poetic "word" situated between "delivered populations" and the "empty place" takes us back to the peripheral being of the early poem "Muse." That the too-centered "majority" in "Im-age" is described as "unerring" is both ironic and precise; for the wanderings of this poet's "loose speech" are precisely what inform the perambulating mode of the three long poems. The relation of "center" to "periphery" is still very much their dominant configuration, but less as the locked "geometry" of the early poems than as what "The Unifying Principle" calls "loose constellations," "less fierce, subsidiary centers, with the/attenuations of interstices, roughing the salience." These "interstices" are both the mode of a poetry which presents itself as process and the recognition of contingency that leads Ammons to speak in "Hibernaculum" of the void "inside" and "outside" and in the "Essay on Poetics" of the "emptiness" at the center of the "lyric" and of "earth." "Extremes and Moderations" has as its ostensible subject ecology and ends with it as its "chief concern." But the fact that it also disclaims the structure of "beginning,/development" and "end" and suggests in the hesitations of its close the implication in all poetic forms of closure suggests that "ecology" is also the "less fierce center" of the poem's own mode, the "lattice work" stanza "that lets the world/breeze unobstructed through."

These three long poems exemplify the looser order of "The Unifying Principle" at the same time as they reveal on closer reading the figures of their own remarkable coherence, the "circulations" which keep "Extremes and Moderations" moving, the "topography" which the "Essay on Poetics" enables us to "see," and the "timeless relations" which form the gatherings and concentrations of moving mind in "Hibernaculum." Even as recently as the poem "Spiel," the poet is taking lessons from the spider's "open-ended house" and the spider's knowledge that "safety,/closed up to perfection,/traps" finds its counterpart in the open-ended mode of these poems which at once have their own complex "identity" and suggest that the best of Ammons may be still to come. The resolution of "Corsons Inlet" was to stake off no beginnings or ends. For the reader who has been following this poet's configurations of shape and flow, there is no more satisfying or beautiful close to Ammons' most recent volume than the poem, "The Arc Inside and Out," which travels once more the directions of centering and encompassing—"these two ways to dream"—and then opens itself to another beginning:

> and
> every morning the sun comes, the sun.

Notes

1. *Ommateum, with Doxology* (Philadelphia: Dorrance & Co., 1955).
2. All parenthetical references are to A. R. Ammons, *Collected Poems: 1951–1971* (New York: W. W. Norton & Co., 1972)
3. "A. R. Ammons: 'The Spent Seer Consigns Order to the Vehicle of Change,'" in *Alone with America: Essays on the Art of Poetry in the United States Since 1950* (New York: Atheneum, 1965); p. 14.

HYATT H. WAGGONER
From "The Poetry of A. R. Ammons"

Contemporary Poetry in America
ed. Robert Boyers
1974, pp. 330–38

Ammons is a visionary poet in the Neoplatonic tradition introduced and best represented in our (American) poetry by Emerson. I would guess that he has read a good deal of Emerson and pondered much on what he has read. Maybe not. Maybe he has read only a little and gotten all his Emersonianism from that little, working out for himself, as Emerson did, the consequences of a few major ideas about the relations of the Many and the One. Or maybe it has come to

him at second and third hand, through Pound and Williams, Whitman and Frost, all of whom make their appearance in his poetry. It is clear at least though that he has read "Brahma"—which could have been sufficient for the right kind of mind—for he alludes to it and paraphrases it in "What This Mode of Motion Said" in *Expressions of Sea Level*. Emerson: "When me they fly, I am the wings"; Ammons: "I am the wings when you me fly"; Emerson: "I am the doubter and the doubt"; Ammons:

> I am the way by
> which you prove me
> wrong,
> the reason you
> reason against me.

Some other "Emersonianisms" in the poetry. . . . "Raft," the opening poem in *Expressions of Sea Level*, a somewhat self-consciously Romantic poem in which the sought-for unity with nature—or with the undefinable Reason behind nature—is distanced by a tone of playful make-believe, is central Emerson: let go, yield, be blown by the winds of spirit. *Spiritus*: breath, wind. The Muse, the deeper self, the Holy Spirit. The boy on the circular raft is swept out to sea by the tides to where the winds control his motion toward the east, the rising sun. Neoplatonists: sun, source of light, life, and goodness; emanation. Christian Neoplatonists: sun = Son. . . . The Romantic sea-voyage; the "innocent eye" of the child. Several poems in the same volume make explicit what "Raft" implies by the story it tells. For instance, "Guide": "the wind that is my guide said this"; and "Mansion":

> So it came time
> for me to cede myself
> and I chose
> the wind
> to be delivered to.

The word *soul* can be used only in actual or implied quotation marks by contemporary poets. Since Ammons takes what the word refers to very seriously, he seldom uses it: there is nothing "so-called" about spirit in his work. Like Emerson, he is ambiguous about what he refuses to name. Emerson usually preferred to define the "Over-Soul," "World-Soul," "The Spirit," "The Real" in negative terms, as he does in the opening of the essay on the subject, following the long tradition of "negative theology." He was surer about Immanence than about Transcendence: "A light from within or from behind," with the ambiguity kept. Only in "Circles," in the early essays, does he drop the subjective-objective ambiguity and attribute unqualified Transcendence to the One: "the eternal generator of circles," that is, the Creator of the circles of physical and spiritual reality. Ammons' poetry keeps both Emerson's theoretic ambiguity and the intensity of Emerson's search for vision.

Ammons has a *mind*, too good a mind to be content with the kinds of superficial Romanticism that are becoming fashionable in contemporary poetry. I would like to call him a philosophical poet—except that description might turn away some of those who should read him, and except also that the phrase is in part intrinsically misleading in its suggestion that he deals principally in abstractions. He deals with the perfectly concrete felt motions and emotions of the particular self he is and, like Emerson again, looks for and often sees "Correspondences" between these motions and those of animate and inanimate nature, both nature-as-observed (winds, tides, seeds, birds) and nature-as-known-about (the chemistry of digestion, entropy).

The title poem of *Corsons Inlet* is such a philosophical

poem, treating the relations and claims of logic and vision, order created and order discovered, being and becoming, art and nature. Rejecting any "finality of vision," it still prefers the risk of vision to any "easy victory" in "narrow orders, limited tightness." The poet's task is to try to "fasten into order enlarging grasps of disorder," the task Emerson set before the poet in "Merlin" and "Bacchus." I find significance in the fact that the poem was first entitled "A Nature Walk." If there is no order discoverable in nature, the order of art is a contrivance without noetic value. Ammons, like his Romantic and Transcendental poetic forebears, is not content to make pretty, or even interesting because intricately fashioned, poems. "Corsons Inlet" seems to me at once one of the finest and one of the most significant poems written by any of our poets in recent years. It is a credo, a manifesto, a cluster of felt perceptions, and a demonstration that, up to a point at least, vision *can* be both achieved and conveyed.

Though I am persuaded that my frequent mentions of Emerson up to this point do not distort but rather illuminate Ammons' work, still they might prove misleading if I failed to mention the ways in which the poet's vision is *un*like Emerson's. (Emerson, I should explain, is very fresh in my mind these days, for I have just spent a year rereading and writing about him. But I am still not importing my own preoccupation into Ammons' poetry: Emerson is there, and I happen to be well prepared to notice his presence—in many more ways, and more poems, than I have mentioned or will mention.) Let me try to generalize the difference first. Ammons comes as close to rediscovering the Romantic Transcendental vision of Emerson as any thoughtful and well-informed man of the late twentieth century is likely to be able to, but as a man of our time he simply cannot be a "disciple," he can only learn from, be stimulated by, walk the paths of, and be honest about his differences with, the poet who more than any other foreshadows him, as I see it.

A few of the differences. Ammons allows to come into consciousness, and so into his poetry, much more freely than Emerson did, the existential *angst* that Emerson must have felt but usually repressed. (See "1 Jan." in *Tape for the Turn of the Year* for Ammons' statement on this. The point he makes there—"I know the/violence, grief, guilt,/despair, absurdity"—is clear in all the volumes without being stated.) Death, disorder, entropy (one of his few technical philosophical terms) are never far from the surface of any of Ammons' poems, and frequently they are central in them. Poetry, he says in *Tape*, has "one subject, impermanence." Never unaware of "a universe of horror," Ammons knows that "we must bear/the dark edges of/our awareness," but the goal of his search remains "a universe of light" (*Tape*, "1 Jan.")

A different man in a different age, Emerson erected his defenses against fear and grief stronger and taller than Ammons', though I should say that in his best poetry—in prose as well as in verse—he was sufficiently open to all his feelings, even these, to allow his wonderful intelligence to work freely. Still, it is true, however one may take the fact, that Ammons does not transcend so easily or so far.

Related to this as a symptom is to a cause is the much greater concreteness of the way Ammons' imagination works, and so of his poetic language. As Emerson was more concrete, specific, even local (think of the first line of "Hamatreya") than the Pre-Romantics whose style his often resembles, so Ammons is more concrete, specific, local, and *personal* than Emerson. On this matter, as on style in general, Ammons' affinity seems to be with Pound and Williams, but of course Pound and Williams were more Emersonian than they knew.

A difference that is more strikingly obvious but I think finally less important is that of verse-forms. Emerson's theory, at least the part of it we are most likely to remember, called for organic or open form, but only a few of his best poems put the theory successfully into practice, and then only partially. Ammons, like most of his best contemporaries, has moved all the way toward practicing the theory announced in "The Poet" and elaborated in "Poetry and Imagination." Still, there is not an immeasurable gap, formally speaking, between "Merlin" and "Poetics" in *Briefings*.

Tape for the Turn of the Year, Ammons' "long thin poem" typed on a roll of adding-machine paper, a poetic journal which keeps turning into a poetic meditation, is the most continuously interesting, the strongest, the finest long poem I have read in I don't know how many years. It is as concrete as the *Cantos*, but the facts in it are not exotic lore out of the library and they are not illustrations of theories. It is at once personal and historical, like *Paterson*, but I don't feel, as I do in that poem at times, any attempt to impose the larger meanings. The meanings rise from the facts of personal history, the life the poet led from December 6 to January 10, the meals, the weather, the news, the interruptions, the discrete perceptions, and are presented for just what they are, felt thoughts. *Tape* proves—for me, anyway—the point Ammons makes in it somewhere, that poetry is "a way of/thinking about/truth" even while, as an art form, its distinctiveness is its way of "playing" with language to create untranslatable meanings.

Stylistically, *Tape* is "good Emerson," not so much in resembling Emerson's poems (though it does resemble them in certain ways, at times) as in following-out Emerson's theory. Transcendental poetic theory puts enormous emphasis on the single word, the single image, the discrete perception that may become an intuition. The short lines of the poem would seem merely stylish if they could not be justified in terms of this aspect of Transcendental Poetics. "Stylish" they may be, but the reason for the style emerges from the lines surprisingly, astonishingly. Prosaic, lyric, meditative, philosophic by turns, *Tape* is a wonderful poem. Read it.

Ammons' latest poems strike me as showing two developments. Stylistically, they are somewhat less "open," more thought-out, "reasonable," logically disciplined. They have pulled back a little from the letting-go and letting-out of the earlier work. There is less abandon, more control. Stylistically firmer perhaps, they seem to me less daring. Their style might be described as more "mature," but maturity brings losses as well as gains. The transparent eyeball narrows slightly to shield itself against the too-dazzling light. Ammons said toward the end of *Tape* that after the long, in a sense "dictated," poem he wanted to write short, artful lyrics, and he's doing it. And of course art is artificial. But I hope he will continue to leave openings, cracks maybe, in his conceptual boxes.

In any poet as fine as Ammons, a stylistic change signals a change in sensibility and vision. "Transaction" in *Uplands* ("I attended the burial of all my rosy feelings") describes the new "resignation" (Is this the right word? I'm not sure.) explicitly, but a good many of the poems in the two latest volumes exhibit it.

In *Tape* he reminded us—warned us?—that "I care about the statement/of fact" and suggested that "coming home" meant "a way of/going along with this/world as it is:/nothing ideal," but he still invited us to the dance. Wisdom involves a kind of resignation, I suppose, as one of its elements, but I think of it as contrasting with rashness and inexperience rather than as first cousin to prudence. I should hate to see Ammons become too prudent. I don't think he will.

The most recent poems may be less ambitious philosophically and less openly Romantic-Transcendental in their imaginative questing, but the quest itself has not been abandoned and the conception of how the journey should be undertaken—how thinking, feeling, imagining, responding can find expression and thus be realized, recognized, identified, and shared in a particular verbal object we call "this poem"—has not essentially changed. In the inseparable union of physics and metaphysics in Ammons' imagination, the emphasis may have shifted a little from the *meta* to the *physics*, but the union has not been dissolved, as of course it must not be if poetry is to continue to have noetic value. (Heidegger's "What Are Poets For?" in his recent *Poetry, Language, Thought* is relevant here. What are poets for in a dark time?) "Poetics" in *Briefings* should send any readers of it who don't remember the essay back to Emerson's "Poetry and Imagination." "Ask the fact for the form." Imagination and circles, imagination and possibility, the expanding spheres of possibility—of apprehension, of recognition, of meaning—finding their forms in poems. . . .

Harold Bloom is quoted on the back cover of *Briefings* as saying that the lyrics in the book "maintain an utterly consistent purity of detached yet radiant vision." Right on target. But I'd like to shrink the ambiguities of this a bit if I can without putting us and Ammons into a mentalistic box. "Consistent": consistent with all the other lyrics in the volume, yes, but not entirely consistent, in tone or statement, with the best of the earlier lyrics or even with the prayer ("14 Dec.") and the several credos (*credo*: I believe) in *Tape*. A little more defensive, more guarded, more "intellectually prudent." There's a concern with defining differences: ". . . keep me from my enemies'/wafered concision and zeal" ("Hymn IV," *Briefings*). A fear almost that vision may harden into doctrine.

"Purity": Yes, of style, of tone, of vision too. The wonderful thing is that the purity is at once a purity of style and a purity of vision, in both cases (or perspectives: two sides of the same coin) a unique balance maintained between conflicting perceptions of the One and the Many, the Real and the Actual, etc.—to borrow some Emersonian terms for what is not easily talked about in any terms.

"Detached": "Wafered concision" suggests that the detachment is from High Church zealots who localize "the eternal generator of circles" (Emerson's term in "Circles") in the manageable little round wafer of Communion. But the detachment is equally, I think, from the rationalistic formulations of the ineffable that betray an idolatrous attitude not toward a common substance, bread, but toward the results of a process, directed abstract thought. I say this not from the evidence of this poem, which, by its emphasis, might not seem to prompt it, but from the evidence of the whole corpus of the poetry as I have read it.

"Radiant": No need for clarification (if that's the word for what I'm trying to do) here. "Radiant" in the sense that applies to Blake, Emerson, Whitman, Cummings, Roethke.

"Vision": Right again, of course. But "vision" and "visionary" can be a way of throwing positivistic enemies off the scent. Vision of what? Assuming that God is not a "being" among other beings, and so, being unlimited spatially and temporally ("God is the circle whose center is everywhere and circumference nowhere"—the practitioners of the "negative theology," and Emerson, said), is undefinable, still I'd say a sense of God's reality, whether as immanent or as *deus absconditus*, is everywhere present in the poems and should be recognized, for it does more than anything else (of the many factors at work, some unknown, some unknowable,) to give the poems

their special *kind* of "vision." Heidegger, "What Are Poets For?" again.

I'd like to make the word *religious* respectable once again among literary critics, rescue it from Freud ("the future of an illusion") and give it to Jung, who used the word not to clobber the naively pious but to point to something real and permanent in human experience. ("Permanent" until *now*, maybe.) Ammons is a poet of religious vision who is as wary of intellectualist abstractions as he is of pious dogmas. *That's* the peculiar feature of the "purity" of his "vision," it seems to me. Peculiar in our time, not peculiar if we think of the poetic visionaries who are his ancestors, whether he knows it or not—and he probably does, for he seems to know everything.

The "veracity" of Ammons' poetry (his word, and Emerson's before him, in "Poetry and Imagination"), the sense it creates in us that the radiance, when it comes, is real, discovered, not invented or faked, is causally related, I suspect, to the steadiness with which the poet has looked into the Abyss. The gains for the imagination from such looking are incalculable, but it must be hard on the nerves. One wants to survive as well as write "short rich hard lyrics," as Ammons is doing now. I want Ammons to do both—that is, survive and write. Perhaps the slight narrowing of the eyelids over the transparent eyeballs I seem to detect in the later work is necessary for the survival. But the transparency remains essential to his kind of vision. Dilemma. Poets age, like the rest of us.

I don't try very conscientiously to "keep up" with all the new poetry in the magazines and the slender volumes, but I can say that of the "new" poets I've read since Roethke's death, Ammons seems to me at or near the top. His poetry is, among other things, more important, a "sign" granted for the strengthening of the faith, the faith that in a dark time light may still be seen, not invented (no "Supreme Fiction," no fiction at all), by the unguarded eye.

At his best (I don't much like "Summer Session 1968"), Ammons is a highly distinguished poet of religious vision who grants the Transcendence but finds his occupation chiefly in searching out the traces of the Immanence. May he survive, save himself for this, and be visited often by the Muse, indulging as little as may be in the writing of merely fashionable poems.

PAUL ZWEIG
From "The Raw and the Cooked"
Partisan Review, Fall 1974, pp. 608–12

In his collection, Ammons includes every moment and modulation of his talent: the luminous leafed in with the trivial, the carefully achieved with the self-indulgent, the too long with the too short. One has to wade through a great deal of tentative language before coming upon the fine sparse poems which represent Ammons's best. But the labor is by no means all loss. The very shagginess and roughness of the collection forces the reader to become intimate with Ammons's elusive rhythms. One has the experience not so much of reading a work, as of entering into a process, in the course of which finished poems emerge, like pure crystals, their stony husk refined away. There is power in all of this. The roughness and profusion of Ammons's work becomes, somehow, a figure for his obsession; the sense of a process rushing brilliantly, though inconclusively forward is, finally, true to the idea of his poetry. As a result of sifting and panning all of this ore—a labor not without tedium—one understands, finally, why Ammons's turn at the banquet table has come.

At a time when the limits of the conversational style have come to be felt more and more strongly, Ammons offers, in great abundance, precisely those qualities neglected during the 1960s: intricate language and conceptual ambition. Reading through many of his longer poems, one is impressed by Ammons's attempt to connect a density of style reminiscent of Gerard Manley Hopkins, with an elaborate reflective framework which recalls Wallace Stevens. The echo of Stevens is inevitable, since Ammons's main concern is to articulate a philosophy of perception which must be simultaneously argued and demonstrated in the poetry. The main point of Ammons's conception seems to be his view that the mind and the world are joined together in a seamless intricacy. It is not simply that the mind and the world mirror each other, for mirrors contain settled forms, they connect but they also interpose limits. Like Alice, the poet has solved the surface of the mirror. He perceives, and renders in language, the interpenetrating gusts of movement by which the mind and the world make each other whole. As Ammons writes in "Corsons Inlet":

> I have reached no conclusions, have erected no
> boundaries,
> shutting out and shutting in, separating inside
> from outside: I have
> drawn no lines:
> as
>
> manifold events of sand
> change the dune's shape that will not be the same
> shape
> tomorrow,
>
> so I am willing to go along, to accept
> the becoming
> thought, to stake off no beginnings or ends, establish
> no walls:

This is Ammons at his clearest, yet somehow not at his best. The statement he makes is accurate enough: the aim of his poetry is not finishing, but unfinishing; it is to cut the world loose from the illusion of settled forms, and set it flowing in the ever new flood of perception. His words cascade irregularly on the page in a mimetism of released energy. The "idea" is there all right. But the poetry is cold, the experience, for all its intricacy, is thin. And here is Ammons's gravest fault. All too often he fails to connect the conceptual framework of the poem with the local effects of his language. This is especially true in the early work, but it remains true of his longer, more ambitious poems throughout. His images turn moments of experience into sensuous complexities; Hopkins-like compressions of syntax offer the reader "a hundred sensations a second," as Ammons remarks. But a gap yawns between this brilliant seething of impressions and the overarching discourse which Ammons intends as his "idea of order." Between sensuous mimetism and cold philosophy there is a space, which Ammons does not fill often enough. But the space between is where we live. It is where the "idea" thickens into passion, where passions clarify into thought and perception. "Corsons Inlet" and "Saliences" are often cited as examples of Ammons's conceptual power. We are invited by critics to think of Wordsworth in "Tintern Abbey," of Emerson, of Eliot's discursive passages in "Four Quartets." But "Corsons Inlet" is governed by windy and abstract rhetoric, as in the passage quoted above. The poem begins crisply enough, with a description of the poet walking along a beachfront, exploring the uncertain margin between land and sea, reflecting on the per-

petual movement which dissolves shapes through an alchemy of slow transitions, as the sand dune simultaneously stands and blows away, as the tide is a tireless alternation of land and water. But the landscape is quickly dimmed by the fog of meaning which Ammons projects upon it. Ammons's power of perception, his most brilliant quality, lapses into a compromise which is neither sensuous, nor especially thoughtful either:

> in nature there are few sharp lines: there are areas of
> primrose
> more or less dispersed;
> disorderly orders of bayberry; between the rows
> of dunes,
> irregular swamps of reeds,
> though not reeds alone, but grass, bayberry, yarrow,
> all . . .
> predominantly reeds:

Academic critics like Harold Bloom and Geoffrey Hartman have been partly responsible for the enlarged interest in Ammons's work. *Diacritics*, a university magazine devoted to literary theory, recently published an entire issue on Ammons. One is happy for this renewed interest on the part of the academy for poets and for poetry. Bloom's and Hartman's enthusiasm for Ammons probably reflects their sense of a failure in the antirhetorical poetry of the past decade. After years of a poetic style which militated against ideas and repudiated conceptual ambition, they found in Ammons a poet both thoughtful and complex, whose work invites the sort of critical scrutiny which the great works of modernism also invited. Like Stevens, Pound, and Eliot, Ammons in his poetry demands explication. And let us be reminded, explication is not simply a form of detached analysis. It is a mode of reading required by, and appropriate to, complex poems. As practiced by the great critics of modernism—Blackmur, Empson—it becomes a form of intellectual ascesis, mobilizing the passions of thought in an activity akin to the methods of meditation about which Louis Martz has written.

But these critics have done Ammons a curious disservice, for they have focused their praise on his weakest quality—his attempt to formulate complicated ideas in poetry—and overlooked what seems to me to be his real achievement: the lyrical articulation of small moments of experience; his ability to organize shapes of language into an epiphany of movement, a frozen flood of perceptions which is visionary not because of any passionate metaphysics, but because of the sheer clarity of the poet's ability to recreate what he "sees." I don't mean to say that Ammons doesn't think well, or that his ideas are not interesting. They are; more important, they provide a framework which releases the intensity of his best short poems. But they do not make good poetry. Unlike Eliot or Stevens, Ammons does not write well about ideas. His conceptual reach does not intensify his language. When he writes "philosophical" poems, or inserts reflective passages into poems, he becomes boring and abstract. Only when his poem plunges into the moment itself does it gain the exhilarating clarity which is Ammons's best quality, as in this short poem, "Winter Scene":

> There is now not a single
> leaf on the cherry tree:
>
> except when the jay
> plummets in, lights, and,
>
> in pure clarity, squalls:
> then every branch
>
> quivers and
> breaks out in blue leaves.

The shock of hard, swift vision here is powerful and lovely. It recalls the sort of naked language which William Carlos Williams made possible in American poetry. There are many poems like this in the *Collected Poems*. One comes upon them as upon wells of clear drink in a complicated landscape. The seamless intricacy of world and mind is not a subject matter of the poem, but a medium into which the poet has been launched. In poems like these, the scaffolding has been forgotten; the poet is naked in the world, and the world has become naked to him. He is thinking with his "eyes" not his mind, or rather, his mind has let itself loose into the fusing brilliance of perception.

In another mode more special to his vision, Ammons has written poems which are intricate mimetisms of change, expressing his sense of the unceasing movement which is all we can know of experience, and of the world. Such poems succeed when they grasp the form of movement in a kind of visual onomatopoeia, instead of offering conclusions about a metaphysics of change. Given Ammons's obsession with instability and process, it is no surprise that he should have trouble with conclusions, both in the philosophical and in the formal sense. It is only in mid-movement, like a sudden vision of all the drops in a column of falling water, that his poetry attains a sort of cold ecstasy. . . .

A. R. Ammons is an excellent poet. His *Collected Poems* resembles a flood of scraps and pieces mingled with finely wrought objects. The power of the flood is blurred but it is governed by a vision which imposes itself and, gradually convinces, not as an argument, which Ammons manages with only moderate skill, but as a lived clarity; and that, finally, is much more rare and precious.

Clearly, a poet refuses the dominant language of his time at his peril. Often those poets who succeed create a new language, as Allen Ginsberg did when he wrote *Howl* amid the overpolished tones of the 1950s. At first glance Ammons too seems to be a maverick, working vigorously against the limitations of the plain style, making a case in his work for a new intricacy of conception. Yet his best poems are closer to the plain style than one might think. It is when one hears William Carlos Williams in the background of his voice that the poems work clearly and solidly, not when one hears Hopkins or Stevens. Like so many other poets of the 1960s, Ammons's strengths and limitations derive from his flight into immediacy, his unwillingness to work with or against the limiting framework of culture and tradition. In this sense, of course, Ammons is extraordinarily American. But the impulse to reinvent all language, and all thought, falls short in his work. What survives is Ammons's version of the dream which is at the heart of so much recent poetry: the anticultural, Rousseauean dream of a purer, more articulate nature.

HAROLD BLOOM
From "The New Transcendentalism"
Figures of Capable Imagination
1976, pp. 137–49

I n turning to A. R. Ammons, the wisest and I prophesy most enduring poet of his generation, we confront the most direct Emersonian in American poetry since Frost. . . . Here I wish to describe the great achievement of the latest Ammons, as gathered in the large *Collected Poems 1951–1971* (1972), particularly three long poems: *Essay on Poetics, Extremes and Moderations, Hibernaculum*, but also two crucial recent lyrics.

The *Essay on Poetics* begins by giving us Ammons' central signature, the process by which he has made a cosmos:

Take in a lyric information
totally processed, interpenetrated into
wholeness where
a bit is a bit, a string a string, a
cluster a cluster, everything beefing up
and verging out
for that point in the periphery where
salience bends into curve
and all saliences bend to the same angle of
curve and curve becomes curve, one curve, the
whole curve:
that is information actual
at every point
but taking on itself at every point
the emanation of curvature, of meaning, all
the way into the high
recognition of wholeness, that synthesis,
feeling, aroused, controlled, and released . . .

Ammons' "periphery" is at once the "circumference" of Emerson and Dickinson, and also the nerve-ending of the quester who goes out upon circumference. Ammons' "salience" is the further projecting or out-leaping from the longest periphery that the seer has attained. That makes Ammons' "salience" his equivalent of the Pound-Williams "image" or the Stevensian "solar single,/Man-sun, man-moon, man-earth, man-ocean." Far back, but indubitably the starting-place, Ammons' *Essay on Poetics* touches Whitman's 1855 "Preface" and Whitman's fecund ground, Emerson's "The Poet," a prose rhapsody mostly of 1842. Ammons expounds a "science" that now seems curious, but Emerson called it "true science." More than Whitman, or even Thoreau or Dickinson or Frost, Ammons is the Poet that Emerson prophesied as necessary for America:

. . . For through that better perception he stands one step nearer to things, and sees the flowing or metamorphosis; perceives that thought is multiform; that within the form of every creature is a force impelling it to ascend into a higher form; and following with his eyes the life, uses the forms which express that life, and so his speech flows with the flowing of nature. All the facts of the animal economy, sex, nutriment, gestation, birth, growth, are symbols of the passage of the world into the soul of man, to suffer there a change and reappear a new and higher fact. He uses forms according to the life, and not according to the form. This is true science. The poet alone knows astronomy, chemistry, vegetation and animation, for he does not stop at these facts, but employs them as signs. He knows why the plain or meadow of space was strown with these flowers we call suns and moons and stars; why the great deep is adorned with animals, with men, and gods; for in every word he speaks he rides on them as the horses of thought.

As in "Tintern Abbey," standing closer to things is to see into their life, to see process and not particulars. But it is not Wordsworthian nor even neo-Platonic to possess a speech that is magic, to speak words that are themselves the metamorphosis. This violent Idealism is Emerson's Transcendental science, a knowing too impatient for the disciplines of mysticism, let alone rational dialectic. To read Emerson's "The Poet" side-by-side with any British Romantic on poetry, except Blake, is to see how peculiar the Emersonian wildness is. Only a step away and Emerson will identify a true poet's words with

Necessity, as though nature's absolute confounding of our faculties simultaneously could make us skeptics and scientists affirming an inevitable insight. Emerson, here as so often, seems to break down the humanly needful distinctions between incoherence and coherence, relying upon his tone to persuade us of an intelligibility not wholly present. Ammons, like any strong poet, handles influence by misprision. His Emersonianism is so striking and plausible a twisting askew of that heritage as to raise again the labyrinthine issue of what poetic influence is, and how it works.

To talk about a poem by Ammons in terms of Emerson or Whitman is to invoke what one might term the Human Analogue, as opposed to Coleridge's Organic Analogue. No poem rejoices in its own solitary inscape, any more than we can do so. We have to be talked about in terms of other people, for no more than a poem is, can we be "about" ourselves. To say that a poem is about itself is killing, but to say it is about another poem is to go out into the world where we live. We idealize about ourselves when we isolate ourselves, just as poets deceive themselves by idealizing what they assert to be their poems' true subjects. The actual subjects move towards the anxiety of influence, and now frequently *are* that anxiety. But a deeper apparent digression begins to loom here, even as I attempt to relate the peripheries and saliences of Ammons to the great circumference of his ancestors.

Reductively, the anxiety of influence *is* the fear of death, and a poet's vision of immortality includes seeing himself free of all influence. Perhaps sexual jealousy, a closely related anxiety, also reduces to the fear of death, or of the ultimate tyranny of space and time, since influence-anxiety is related to our horror of space and time as a dungeon, as the danger of domination by the Not-Me. Anxiety of influence is due then partly to fear of the natural body, yet poetry is written by the natural man who is one with the body. Blake insisted that there was also the Real Man—the Imagination. Perhaps there is, but he cannot write poems, at least not yet.

The poem attempts to relieve the poet-as-poet from fears that *there is not enough for him*, whether of space (imaginative) or time (priority). A subject, a mode, a voice; all these lead to the question: "What, besides my death, is my own?" Poets of the Pound-Williams school, more than most contemporary poets, scoff at the notion of an anxiety of influence, believing as they think they do that a poem is a machine made out of words. Perhaps, but mostly in the sense that we, alas, appear to be machines made out of words, for poems actually are closer to—as Stevens said—men made up out of words. Men make poems as Dr. Frankenstein made his *daemon*, and poems too acquire the disorders of the human. The people in poems do not have fathers, but the poems do.

Ammons, like Merwin and Ashbery, is aware of all this, for strong poets become strong by meeting the anxiety of influence, not by evading it. Poets adept at forgetting their ancestry write very forgettable poems. Ammons' *Essay on Poetics* swerves away from Emerson by the exercise of a variety of revisionary ratios, cunningly set against mere repetition. . . .

The later Ammons writes out of a vision "transcendental only by its bottomless entropy," yet still Emersonian, though this is the later Emerson of *The Conduct of Life*, precursor of Stevens in *The Rock* and Frost throughout *In The Clearing*. *Extremes and Moderations* is Ammons' major achievement in the long poem, written in "the flow-breaking four-liner," starting out in an audacious transcendentalism and modulating into the prophetic voice Ammons rarely seeks, yet always attains at the seeking. . . . Ammons signifies what Emerson's circle called the Newness, onsets of transcendental influx.

"Moderations" are the rescues of these evaded furies that Ammons attempts for the poetry of life, while carefully distinguishing even the extremes from mere phantasmagorias:

> . . . that there should have been possibilities
>   enough to
> include all that has occurred is beyond belief,
>   an extreme the
> strictures and disciplines of which prevent
>   loose-flowing
> phantasmagoria . . .

Though the poem concludes in a moving ecological outrage, an outrage the poet appears to believe is his theme, its concerns hover where Ammons' obsessions always congregate, his resistance to his own transcendental experience. This resistance is made, as all constant readers of Ammons learn, in the name of a precarious naturalism, but the concealed undercurrent is always the sense of an earlier bafflement of vision, a failure to have attained a longed-for unity with an Absolute. The latest Ammons rarely makes reference to this spent seership, but the old longing beautifully haunts all of the difficult recent radiances. Here is a typical late lyric, "Day," manifesting again the extraordinary and wholly deceptive ease that Ammons has won for himself, an ease of mode and not of spirit, which continues to carry an exemplary burden of torment:

> On a cold late
> September morning,
> wider than sky-wide
> discs of lit-shale clouds
> skim the hills,
> crescents, chords
> of sunlight
> now and then fracturing
> the long peripheries:
> the crow flies
> silent,
> on course but destinationless,
> floating:
> hurry, hurry,
> the running light says,
> while anything remains.

The mode goes back through Dickinson to Emerson, and is anything but the Pound-Williams "machine made out of words" that Hugh Kenner describes and praises in his crucially polemical *The Pound Era*. "The long peripheries," for Ammons, are identical with poems, or rather with what he would like his poems to be, outermost perceptions within precise boundaries, or literally "carryings-over" from the eye's tyranny to the relative freedom of a personally achieved idiom. What now distinguishes a lyric like "Day" from the characteristic earlier work in the Ammons canon is the urgency of what another late long poem, *Hibernaculum*, calls "a staying change," this seer's response to our current time-of-transition from our recent confusions to whatever is coming upon us: "I think we are here to give back our possessions before/they are taken away." . . .

Emerson and Ammons share a nature that on the level of experience or confrontation cannot be humanized. Yet they share also a Transcendental belief that one can come to unity, at least in the pure good of theory. Their common tone is a curious chill, a tang of other-than-human relationship to an Oversoul or Overall that is not nature, yet breaks through into nature. Like Emerson, its founder, Ammons is a poet of the

American Sublime, and a residue of this primordial strength abides in all of his work.

Collected Poems 1951–1971 closes with a magnificent poem that is Ammons' overt *apologia*, and I will close this essay by giving the poem entire, and then attempting a defining observation upon its place in the tradition of American poetry. . . . "The Arc Inside and Out." . . .

Ammons' "little arc-line" is both his Blakean Minute Particular or vision that cannot be further reduced, and his Emersonian "new circle" or vision that cannot be further expanded. He begins his poem by a vehement reduction to "the face-brilliant core stone" and proceeds by an equally vehement expansion to a "suasion, large, fully-informed." Both reduction and expansion are lovingly dismissed as rival dreamings. This poet's reality, still transcendent, is the arc-line, at once peripheral and salient, a particular apple or a particular gulp of water, that itself is dream-inducing, but this is a dream of Whitman's or Stevens' colossal sun, of a reality so immediate as to carry its own transcendence. Ammons remains, somewhat despite himself, the least spent of our seers.

RICHARD HOWARD
"The Spent Seer Consigns Order
to the Vehicle of Change"
Alone with America
1980, pp. 1–24

All of a sudden, with an unheralded and largely unacknowledged cumulus of books, a poet who accounts for himself with laconic diversity as the holder of the B.S. degree from Wake Forest College in North Carolina, as the principal of an elementary school in that State at the age of 26, as an executive, thereafter and inconsequently, in the biological glass industry:

(how you buy a factory:
determine the lines of force
leading in and out, origins, destinations of lines
determine how
    from the nexus of crossed and bundled lines
        the profit is
obtained, the
forces realized, the cheap made dear,
and whether the incoming or outgoing forces are
    stronger)

and currently as an English teacher:

(I'm waiting to hear if
Cornell will give me
a job: I need
to work &
maybe I write
too much)

—suddenly, then, A. R. Ammons has exploded into the company of American poets which includes Whitman and Emerson and articulates the major impulse of the national expression: the paradox of poetry as process and yet impediment to process. More honestly than Whitman, acknowledging his doubts as the very source of his method ("teach me, father: behold one whose fears are the harnessed mares of his going!"), though without Whitman's dramatic surface, Ammons has traced out the abstractive tendency, the immaterialism that runs through all our *native strain*, in both acceptations of the phrase: to suffer or search out immersion in the stream of reality without surrendering all that is and makes one particu-

larly oneself. The dialectic is rigorous in Ammons' version—the very senses which rehearse the nature of being for the self, the private instances of the sensuous world, must be surrendered to the experience of unity:

we can approach
unity only by the loss
of things
a loss we're unwilling
to take—
since the gain of unity
    would be a vision
of something in the
continuum of nothingness:
we already have things:
    why fool around?

And how avoid the "humbling of reality to precept?" "Stake off no beginnings or ends, establish no walls," the poet urges, addressing that Unity: "I know if I find you I will have to leave the earth and go on out . . . farther than the loss of sight into the unseasonal, undifferentiated stark"—a region, a Death, to speak literally, where there is no poetry, no speech to one's kind, no correspondence perceived and maintained, but only the great soft whoosh of Being that has obsessed our literature from its classical figures, as Lawrence saw so clearly, down to Roethke, Wright Morris, Thornton Wilder.

In 1955, A. R. Ammons, a native and occasional resident of North Carolina, issued a wispy first book of poems and then held his peace, or rather his pugnacity, for ten years. When he next broke the silence, with a triad of voluble and original books at the age of forty, the development from that initial and inconclusive—certainly unconcluded—effort, the achievement in the terms of means and meaning reached so far that it is difficult, now, to see *Ommateum* for what it is, rather than an omen, a symptom.

The title means *compound eye*, as in an insect, and to the magnifying vision of such "iridescence of complex eyes" Ammons returns in the posterior books:

I see how the bark cracks and winds like no other bark
chasmal to my ant-soul running up and down . . .

I suppose the thirty-some litanies in *Ommateum* are to be taken as so many various lenses, ways of looking at landscape, history and deity which together make up one of those strange bug-eyed views wherein the world is refracted into various but adjacent fragments. The book is dedicated to Josephine Miles, the distinguished poet and teacher Ammons had met during his studies (three semesters) at the University of California, and is prefaced by an arrogant, unsigned foreword which asserts that the poems "rather grow in the reader's mind than exhaust themselves in completed, external form." It is just such exhaustion, "the coercive charm of form" as Henry James called it, which the collection lacks, for all its nicely witnessed natural movements:

and the snake shed himself in ripples
across a lake of sand

or again, more wittily:

The next morning I was dead
    excepting a few peripheral cells
and the buzzards
waiting for a savoring age to come
sat over me in mournful conversations
that sounded excellent to my eternal ear . . .

and despite its many fine passages, aspirations to share yet shed a nature regarded, throughout, as a goal and equally as a prison, the pitch is insistently wordy and too shrill:

> But the wind has sown loose dreams
> in my eyes
>   and telling unknown tongues
> drawn me out beyond the land's end
>   and rising in long
>   parabolas of bliss
> borne me safely
> from all those ungathered stones

After many such vociferations, one wonders whose voice it is that utters these hymns to—and against—Earth. The sapless lines, terminated only by the criterion of conversational or rhetorical sense, cannot beat against a stiffening rhythmic constant, and we are reminded of Miss Moore's prescription, taking her words in whatever pejorative sense they may bear: "ecstasy affords the occasion, and *expediency determines the form*." Whose, then, is the voice that chants these prayers to the unstringing of all harps? The only aid the young poet affords is the assumption in several poems of the identity of the prophet Ezra. In a later book too, "I Ezra" returns, "the dying portage of these deathless thoughts," and we recall that this prophet is generally regarded as responsible for the revision and editing of the earlier books of Scripture and the determination of the canon. The persona appears in Ammons' poems, I think, when he is desperate for an authoritative voice; the nature of his enterprise is so extreme, and the risks he is willing to take with hysterical form and unguarded statement (unguarded by image, as Coleridge said that "a whole Essay might be written on the Danger of *thinking* without Images") so parlous, that the need for such *authority* must be pretty constant:

> I am Ezra
> as a word too much repeated
> falls out of being . . .

Yet even in this first book, especially as we tend to read it with the later work in mind, as a propaedeutic function of that work, it is evident that Ammons has discovered his tremendous theme: putting off the flesh and taking on the universe. Despite a wavering form, an uncertain voice, Ammons means to take on the universe the way Hemingway used to speak of taking on Guy de Maupassant—the odds, it is implied, more than a little in favor of the challenger. Here in *Ommateum*, then, is the first enunciation of the theme, in the crude form of a romantic pantheism:

> Leaving myself on the shore
> I went away
> and when a heavy wind caught me I said
>   my body lies south
> given over to vultures and flies
> and wrung my hands
> so the wind went on . . .
> The flies were gone
> The vultures no longer searched
> the ends of my hingeless bones . . .
> Breathing the clean air
> I picked up a rib
>   to draw figures in the sand . . .

And more decisively, in one of the finest early pieces, with its many echoes of Pound's diction and of course the metric of Dr. Williams, properly assimilated to the poet's own requirements which are speed, ease, and the carol of the separate phrase:

> Peeling off my being I plunged into
> the well
> The fingers of the water splashed
>   to grasp me up
> but finding only
>   a few shafts

> of light
>   too quick to grasp
>   became hysterical
>   jumped up and down
>   and wept copiously
> So I said I'm sorry dear well but
> went on deeper
> finding patched innertubes beer cans
> and black roothairs along the way
> but went on deeper
> till darkness snuffed the shafts of light
>   against the well's side
>   night kissing
>   the last bubbles from my lips.

By the time, ten years later, of his second book, *Expressions of Sea Level*, Ammons had extended and enriched this theme to stunning effect—not only in versions of nature and the body, but in terms of poetics as well, enforcing the substitution of the negative All for the single possibility of being:

> go back:
>   how can I
> tell you what I have not said: you must look for it
> yourself: that
> side has weight, too, though words cannot bear it
> out: listen for the things I have left out:
>   I am
>   aware
> of them, as you must be, or you will miss
> the non-song
> in my singing.

Here Ammons has found, or fetched out, besides a functioning arrangement of words on the page, the further device of the colon, which he henceforth wields in its widest application as almost his only mark of punctuation—a sign to indicate not only equivalence, but the node or point of passage on each side of which an existence hangs in the balance:

> a tree, committed as a tree,
> cannot in a flood
>   turn fish,
> sprout gills (leaves are
> a tree's gills) and fins:
>   the molluscs
> dug out of mountain peaks
> are all dead . . .

This observation, from a long poem called "Risks and Possibilities"—one of the penalties of his method, of course, is that Ammons requires length in order to indulge his effects, lacking that compression of substance which amounts to a "received form"—exhibits, too, a curious and rueful connivence with the universal doxology that to represent any one form of life is a limitation, a limitation that cannot be transcended beyond the mere consciousness of it. For only limited forms of life *matter*, and I intend the pun—are of *material consequence*. In one of his saddest poems, an astonishing meditation called "Guide," Ammons admits that it is not, really, worth "giving up everything to eternal being but direction," as the wind has done. With the humility of a man whose enormous ambitions have been chastened by a constatation of his restricted place in the world—and the chastening has been a religious experience, in the literal sense of religion: a linking, a binding, even a fettering—the poet returns to his body, his particular geography and even his rather bleak sociology. Stretching his long legs on late-afternoon walks down the Jersey coast, he has learned that "when I got past relevance the singing shores told me to turn back":

What light there
no tongue turns to tell
to willow and calling shore
though willows weep and shores sing always

In *Expressions of Sea Level* we are given a lot more to go
on, and consequently go a lot farther, than the persona of Ezra
and some rhapsodic landscapes of apocalypse. We are given,
with great attention to vegetable detail and meteorological conditioning, the scenes of the poet's childhood in a North Carolina backwoods, the doctrine and rationale of his metaphysical
aspirations:

the precise and
necessary worked out of random, reproducible,
the handiwork redeemed from chance . . .
I will show you
the underlying that takes no image to itself,
cannot be shown or said,
but weaves in and out of moons and bladderweeds,
is all and
beyond destruction
because created fully in no
particular form . . .

and the resignation, the accommodation of himself to the tidal
marshes of New Jersey as the site of the poet's individual drama. Here is a man obsessed by Pure Being who must put up
with a human incarnation when he would prefer to embody
only the wind, the *anima* of existence itself:

So it came time
for me to cede myself
and I chose
the wind
to be delivered to
The wind was glad
and said it needed all
the body
it could get
to show its motions with . . .

With the acknowledgment of these limitations has come an
interest in other, equally limited, possibilities. One of
Ammons' most interesting sidelines, a lagoon of his main drift,
is a concern with archaic cultures whose aspect often reminds
us, in its amalgam of the suggestive detail and the long loose
line, in its own prose music, of Perse:

Returning silence unto silence
the Sumerian between the river lies.
His skull crushed and molded into rock
does not leak or peel.
The gold earring lies in the powder
of his silken perished lobe.
The incantations, sheep trades, and night-gatherings
with central leaping fires,
roar and glare still in the crow's foot
walking of his stylus on clay.

But not until a more recent book, *Corson's Inlet*, would this
mode be brought into accord with the main burden of
Ammons' song—the made thing of his impulse. Song may
seem an odd word for a verse in which I have descried the
music of prose, a verse which is as near as words can get us to
our behavior, no more than a fairly cautious means of putting
down phrases so that they will keep. Yet though the iambic
cadence, and all it implies and demands by way of traditional
lilt, has been jettisoned as utterly as Dr. Williams ever decreed,
there *is* a song in Ammons' windy lines, a care for the motion
of meaning in language which is the whole justice of prosody;

consider this invocation to the wind, one more of many, and
perhaps the loveliest:

When the tree of my bones
rises from the skin
come and whirlwinding
stroll my dust
around the plain
so I can see
how the ocotillo does
and how the saguaro-wren is
and when you fall
with evening
fall with me here
where we can watch
the closing up of day
and think how morning breaks

There is another strand of discourse in *Expressions of Sea
Level*, whose very title gives an idea of Ammons' use of a new
vocabulary, one that Kenneth Burke would call "scientistic," I
guess, to mean the dramatic use of an exact nomenclature, in
Ammons' case a use quite properly managed:

An individual spider web
identifies a species:
an order of instinct prevails
through all accidents of circumstance
though possibility is
high along the peripheries of
spider
webs:
you can go all
around the fringing attachments
and find
disorder ripe,
entropy rich, high levels of random,
numerous occasions of accident . . .

this poem concludes:

if the web were perfectly pre-set
the spider could
never find
a perfect place to set it in: and
if the web were
perfectly adaptable,
if freedom and possibility were without limit,
the web would
lose its special identity . . .

The dangers of this kind of thing, the dangers of which
Coleridge spoke, were evident, of course, to the author of
"River," whose mastery of natural imagery and vocalic music is
exact and generous, as in this example of what Hopkins called
"vowelling off":

I shall
go down
to the deep river, to the moonwaters
where the silver
willows are and the bay blossoms,
to the songs
of dark birds
to the great wooded silence
of flowing
forever down the dark river
silvered at the moon-singing of hidden birds.

The repetition of the short *i* and the variants on the sound of
"river" in "forever" and "silvered" in the last two lines—not to
sound too much like the late Dr. Sitwell—indicate and insure

a consciousness of effects that become the living twist of things we call idiom.

Insurance is what we shall mostly need in dealing with Ammons' next book. Mooning around the house and waiting for *Expressions of Sea Level* to come off the press in December of 1964, the poet produced, in a two month period, and with a determination to reach an end that became more than obsessive, became self-destructive, "a long thin poem" written on a huge roll of adding-machine tape run through the typewriter to its conclusion ("I am attracted to paper, visualize kitchen napkins scribbled with little masterpieces: so it was natural for me . . ."). The "serious novelty" of the enterprise is unquestionable, and there are many beautiful tropes in this long *Tape for the Turn of the Year*, chiefly in the form of pious assurances that the undertaking is or will be worthwhile:

> let this song
> make
> complex things salient,
> saliences clear, so
> there can be some
> understanding

Enough to suggest that the text is not so much a poem as the ground of a poem, the dark backing of a mirror out of which all brightness may, as a condition, come. There are two moments of confrontation, when Ammons links his 200-page transcribed tape with the generality of his gift as a poet:

> ecology is my word: tag
> me with that: come
> in there:
> you will find yourself
> in a firmless country:
> centers and peripheries
> in motion,
> organic
> interrelations!
> that's the door: here's
> the key: come in,
> celebrant,
> to the one meaning
> that totals my meanings . . .

The other moment of address follows closely:

> my other word is
> *provisional* . . .
> you may guess
> the meanings from *ecology*:
> don't establish the
> boundaries
> first . . .
> and then
> pour
> life into them, trimming
> off left-over edges,
> ending potential . . .
> the center-arising
> form
> adapts, tests the
> peripheries, draws in,
> finds a new factor,
> utilizes a new method,
> gains a new foothold,
> responds to inner and outer
> change . . .

This is the poet arguing himself onward. His book arrives, the Muse ("a woman in us who gives no rest") reassures him (if not us), and in acknowledgment he turns, a moment, to address us

before returning to his vocation in the most luscious of his books so far, *Corson's Inlet*:

> I've given you the
> interstices: the
> space between . . .
> I've given you
> the dull days
> when turning and turning
> revealed nothing . . .
> I've given
> you long
> uninteresting walks
> so you could experience vacancy: . . .
> our journey is done:
> thank you
> for coming:
> the sun's bright,
> the wind rocks the
> naked trees . . .

Published almost simultaneously with the indiscreet, revelatory *Tape, Corson's Inlet*, from the title poem with its sure grasp of site ("the 'field' of action with moving, incalculable center") to the farewell to the reader, to poetry and to the spirit of place given at the end ("surrendered self among unwelcoming forms: stranger, hoist your burdens, get on down the road"), stands as the farthest and still the most representative reach into, upon, and against Being which the poet has yet made. It opens with a poem that nicely illustrates the perfected diction Ammons has now achieved, a rhythmical certainty which does not depend on syllable-counting or even accentual measure, but on the speed and retard of words as they move together in the mind, on the shape of the stanzas as they follow the intention of the discourse, and on the *rests* which not so much imitate as create the soft action of speech itself. There is a formality in these gentle lines which is new to American poetry, as we say that there is a draughtsmanship in the "drip-drawings" of Pollock which is new to American painting: each must be approached with a modulated set of expectations if we are to realize what the poet, the painter is about. Consider the close of this first poem, "Visit," in Ammons' fourth book, and compare its resonance—reserved but not evasive, convinced but not assertive—with the heartier music of a similar passage, too famous to quote, in Frost:

> . . . or you can come by shore:
> choose the right: there the rocks
> cascade less frequently, the grade more gradual:
> treat yourself gently: the ascent thins both
> mind and blood and you must
> keep still a dense reserve
> of silence we can poise against
> conversation: there is little news:
> I found last month a root with shape and
> have heard a new sound among
> the insects: come.

The device of the colon helps keep a dense reserve of silence to poise against the "conversation" here, and the reason for the visit—finding a root with shape and hearing a new sound—is a kind of compressed *ars poetica* of Ammons' enterprise, that understanding of natural process which will include the negative moment: "what destruction am I blessed by" the poet asks in "the moment's height," but his prosody asks the question in a firmer, more axiological *set*, the resources of imagism that are generally employed to accommodate a natural movement here made over to a powerful abstraction:

exhilaration
sucking him up,
shuddering and
lifting
him
jaw and bone
and he said
what
destruction am I
blessed by?

Then comes the book's title poem, like so many of Ammons'
largest statements the account of "a walk over the dunes" which
is also a natural history of the poem itself:

the walk liberating, I was released from forms,
from the perpendiculars,
    straight lines, blocks, boxes, binds
of thought
into the hues, shadings, rises, flowing bends and
    blends of sight:

the interrelations of *making* and of a beneficent destruction are
here followed out ("I was released from forms"), the actions of
sea and land serving as the just emblem of the mind's resources, so that the poet can discuss his undertaking precisely
in the terms of his locus, and indeed acknowledges his inability
to wield any terms *except* those afforded him by what Kenneth
Burke calls the scene-agent ratio:

                        I allow myself eddies of meaning:
yield to a direction of significance
running
like a stream through the geography of my work:
    you can find
in my sayings
                    swerves of action
                    like the inlet's cutting edge:
                there are dunes of motion,
organizations of grass, white sandy paths of re-
    membrance
in the overall wandering of mirroring mind:
but Overall is beyond me: is the sum of these events
I cannot draw, the ledger I cannot keep, the
    accounting
beyond the account . . .

It is characteristic that so many of these poems—and in the
previous book as in the one to come—take up their burden
from the shore, the place where it is most clearly seen that
"every living thing is in siege: the demand is life, to keep life";
whether he investigates the small white blacklegged egret, the
fiddler crab, the black shoals of mussels, the reeds, grass,
bayberry, yarrow, or "pulsations of order in the bellies of min-
nows," Ammons is concerned to enunciate a dialectic, "the
working in and out, together and against, of millions of
events," and *event* is precisely his word—

            no finality of vision,
I have perceived nothing completely,
        tomorrow a new walk is a new walk

he insists: Ammons rehearses a marginal, a transitional experience, he is a littoralist of the imagination because the shore,
the beach, or the coastal creek is not a *place* but an *event*, a
transaction where land and water create and destroy each
other, where life and death are exchanged, where shape and
chaos are won and lost. It is here, examining "order tight with
shape: blue tiny flowers on a leafless weed: carapace of crab:
snail shell" that Ammons finds his rhythms, "fastening into
order enlarging grasps of disorder," and as he makes his way
down the dunes, rhythms are "reaching through seasons, motions weaving in and out!"

The rebellion against Being and into eternity is put down
by the body itself on these expeditions the poet makes, safaris
into mortality which convince him that "the eternal will not lie
down on any temporal hill," and that he must "face piecemeal
the sordid reacceptance of my world." It is not acceptance, but
reacceptance which must be faced, the world which must be
learned *again* as the poet, borrowing Shelley's beautiful image,
"kindles his thoughts, blowing the coals of his day's bright
conscious" in order "to make green religion in winter bones."
In *Corson's Inlet* doctrine has been assimilated into "one song,
an overreach from which all possibilities, like filaments,
depend: killing, nesting, dying, sun or cloud, figure up and
become song—simple, hard: removed." That is Ammons' definition of his aspiration—a long way from the breezy expostulations in *Ommateum*—and, I believe, of his achievement as
well: his awareness and his imagination have coincided. Not
that the poet has lost his initial impulse—for example, the
close of the finest poem in that first volume, quoted earlier—
"night kissing/the last bubbles from my lips"— finds itself enlarged and suited to the poet's wider utterance here, so that the
poem called "Libation" in *Corson's Inlet* ends: "Now keep me
virile and long at love: let submission kiss off/the asking words
from my lips." There is a loyalty to finite being, "losing the self
to the victory of stones and trees, of bending sandpit lakes,
crescent round groves of dwarf pine," Ammons says in the last
poem of the book, "Gravelly Run," a central impulse that
"extends the form, leads us on," and if there is also a freedom
to explore an eccentric impulse, as in the brilliant poem "The
Strait," it is a freedom granted because the divergent "filaments" have been braided back into the main strand, a rope of
sand indeed. The poem concerns a worshipper at the pytho-
ness' cave, questioning the ways of receiving the oracle, and
ends with the kind of "simple, hard: removed" words which so
often suggest, in this poet, the pre-Socratic impulse:

                go
        to your fate:
        if you succeed, praise the
                god:
        if you fail,
        discover your flaw.

Yet such terrors of self-knowledge are generally, by this climax
of submissive response in the poet's work, abated by his more
habitual reference to the design, the order, the form of the
natural world: "for it is not so much to know the self,"
Ammons admits,

        as to know it as it is known
            by galaxy and cedar cone,
        as if birth had never found it
        and death could never end it.

In 1966 Ammons published his fifth book, in which again
"events of sense alter old dunes of mind, release new channels
of flow, free materials to new forms": *Northfield Poems* enacts
Ammons' now familiar insurgence against finitude, and his
resignation, once the impossibilities of both macrocosm and
molecule are confessed, to the demands of form as *the vehicle
of change*:

            unlike wind
            that dies and
            never dies I said
            I must go on
            consigned to
            form that will not
            let me loose

except to death
till some syllable's rain
anoints my tongue
and makes it sing
to strangers:

"some syllable's rain" intimates this poet's trust in language, when any confidence in the body's identity, as in that of bog and bay, is lost; in all these "riding movements" the transformation finally relied on is the transformation of process into words; as Valéry said in the canonical utterance about such littoral metamorphoses, the poet comes to learn *le changement des rives en rumeur*, the change of shores to sound. For Ammons, there is a liberation as well as an acknowledgment of inadequacy about his failure to reduce himself to singleness or to swell to a "savage" chaos:

when I tried to think by what
millions of grains of events
the tidal creek had altered course,
when I considered alone
a record
of the waves on the running blue creek,
I was released into a power beyond my easy
failures:

the power is the strength, the wit, the *balance* of mind which enables him to fall back on his verbal nature, acknowledging that "the dissolved reorganizes to resilience" in his language, that reflexive tool of his specific incarnation:

only the book of laws founded
against itself
founded on freedom of each event to occur as itself
lasts into the inevitable balance events will take.

Ammons' poems are that book of laws founded against itself, perpetually questioning not only the finality, but the very finitude of the world, deploring in an almost Catharist way the "fact" that "coming into matter, spirit fallen trades eternity for temporal form," asserting that it is their part to consummate—by the "gist of 'concrete observations,' pliant to the drift"—the world's body which, as in "February Beach," is in constant modification:

creation may not be complete,
the land may not have been
given
permanently,
something remains
to be agreed on,
a lofty burn of sound, a clamoring and
coming on . . .

In this metaphysical breviary, the self is forever giving itself instructions about its own disembodied aspirations—"if you must leave the shores of mind," Ammons adjures his "Discoverer," reverting to his familiar accommodation of the Sea of Being in the salt marshes of Northfield,

if to gather darkness
into light, evil into good,
you must leave the shores of mind,
remember us, return and rediscover us.

The dissident Ezra, who reappears in one or another of these poems, is said to listen from terraces of mind "wind cannot reach or weedroots"—and at once we know this is not the Way: for Ammons, only what comes back into being by an eternal yet secular reversion—remembered, returned to, rediscovered—is viable:

The world is bright after rain
for rain washes death out of the land and hides it far

beneath the soil and it returns again cleansed with
life
and so all is a circle
and nothing is separable . . .

Indeed, the prophetic lurch to the edges of being—into that "scientific" area of "cytoplasm's grains and vacuoles" on the one hand, and the pulsing, shooting abstractions of "matter and energy" on the other—is repudiated in the final statement of *Northfield Poems*, though there are no final statements in this world of Ammons', of course, only articles of belief, only a mastered credulity:

energy's invisible
swirls confused, surpassed
me: from that edge
I turned back,
strict with limitation,
to my world's
bitter acorns
and sweet branch water.

Uplands: New Poems

What was it like, to bear witness to the articulation of a great career in American poetry, to account for volume as it succeeded volume, revision as it focused vision, until the trajectory was complete, the canon fulfilled? What did a critic *feel* in the presence of the new work (including "Acquainted with the Night") when in 1928 Frost's sixth book *West-Running Brook*, followed his *Selected Poems* at a five-year interval? We can look it up: a shift was remarked, was lamented, a shift to a more "philosophic" mode among the short poems which chiefly composed the book, the title poem now the sole "characteristic" regional dialogue once so distinctive in Frost's work. "Slight" is used in three of the reviews to dismiss Frost's escape from his own previous selection. In other words the sliced-apple effect was evident: as soon as new work was exposed, it turned brown in the open air, and it was the *preceding* poems, mysteriously digested meanwhile, which were declared to exhibit the poet's true mastery, his authentic character, while the immediate achievement represented a wrong turning, a misapprehension, a falling off. If it is true, as Wordsorth said, that a poet must create the taste by which he is enjoyed, it is also true that he must continually dislodge himself if he is to create more than taste.

We can look up what the critics said of Frost's sixth book, or Stevens', or Auden's—indeed, it is a humbling exercise—but the retrospective, with regard to feeling, is always a category of bad faith, and we had better examine our own feelings *now*, for we are faced with just such an occasion, just such an opportunity. Here is Ammons' sixth book, two years after his *Selected Poems*, four years after his last new work. The situation, then, is parallel to Frost's in 1928: the poet reaches that stalled place in his career where it is necessary to inventory his resources, to take stock—what else is a Selected Poems?—of his possibilities, those behind him and those ahead. And then he must move, must find—invent—what there is in himself which will make further work identifiable yet not identical. It is the crisis of middle life which he must emblematically resolve: to acknowledge not only his future but his past, betraying neither:

the problem is
how
to keep shape and flow

No wonder so many of these new poems are concerned with initiations, submissions to motion, giving way, getting started. But before Ammons wrests himself free, by so many "scoops scopes scrimps and scroungings," by the geological energies of "fill, siftings, winnowings, dregs,/cruds, chips," let me rehearse in a paragraph the mountainous achievements at his back, from which he is setting forth.

In 1955, Ammons' first book, *Ommateum*, discovered his tremendous theme: putting off the flesh and taking on the universe. For this poet, there is no windy abstraction in the notion, but a wonderful and rustling submission to the real, the incidental and the odd. Indeed, the poignance of momentary life in its combat with eternal design so haunted the poet that a decade later, in his magnificent second and third books, *Expressions of Sea Level* and *Corsons Inlet*, he had not yet come down on the side of transcendence, nor even taken off. Determined rather to suffer or search out immersion in the stream of reality without surrendering all that is and makes one particularly oneself, Ammons devised a notation of events as faithful to the wavering rhythm of metabolism as it might be to the larger fixities of celestial order:

> for it is not so much to know the self
> as to know it as it is known
>   by galaxy and cedar cone,
> as if birth had never found it
> and death could never end it:

that terminal colon is a characteristic of Ammons' verse—a sign to indicate not only equivalence but the node or point of passage on each side of which an existence hangs in the balance; and the balance is the movement of the verse itself, a constant experiment with the weight of language the line can bear, can meaningfully break beneath, so that the enjambment will *show* something more than completion or incompletion. Between these two books, Ammons published a kind of satyr play of selfhood, *Tape for the Turn of the Year*, "a long thin poem" written on a huge roll of adding-machine tape run though the typewriter to its conclusion, a poem about the specifications of identity by the very refusal to prune or clip. And these mediations led, or prodded, the poet to a further collection, *Northfield Poems*, in which the provisional is treasured as an earnest (though hardly a solemnizing) of survival: "no finality of vision,/I have perceived nothing completely,/tomorrow a new walk is a new walk." And then in 1968 Ammons chose from all these books (except for the indiscreet, revelatory *Tape*) a splendid series of *provisions*, stays against chaos as against finality, articles of belief, a mastered credulity, his *Selected Poems*. Insufficiently attended to, this book is a masterpiece of our period, the widest scope and the intensest focus American poetry has registered since Frost, since Stevens, since Roethke.

And now we have a new book, three dozen lyrical pieces, mostly no more than a page long, and two extended texts, the erotic experiment "Guitar Recitativos" and the superb dedication poem called "Summer Session" which closes "with trivia/I'll dispense dignity, a sense of office,/formality they [the poet's students] can define themselves against." A collection necessarily *slight* if measured against the massive accumulation of Ammons' past, yet if we recall the original sense of the word—*plain, simple*—then we can say, with Pope, "slight is the subject, but not so the praise," for in these sudden, attractive fits and starts the poet urges himself into a new economy, a bright particularity of diction entirely *gainful* to his panoply, a way of handling verse without giving up conversation:

> arriving at ways
> water survives its motions.

The way is enjambment, a wizardry in working with the right-hand margin, so that the line never relinquishes its energy until it can start up its successor. "Certain presuppositions are altered," Ammons announces talking about the look of

"summit stones lying free and loose/out among the shrub trees" in the Alleghenies. We are no longer on the beach in these poems, but in the mountains, among masses, solids, fixities, and the problem is how to get moving again. It is the poet's situation, the poet's dilemma, to make the mountain come to Mohammed, and he has started the pebbles rolling:

> every
> exigency seems prepared for that might
> roll, bound, or give flight
> to stone: that is, the stones
> are prepared: they are round and ready.

Thus the book itself is an account—scrupulous in its details, its hesitations, its celebrations of minor incidents, lesser claims— of how a landscape or a man comes to realize motion, comes to be *on the way* rather than in it.

Briefings: Poems Small and Easy

Hard upon *Uplands* appears *Briefings: Poems Small and Easy*. Small and easy! Ever since his deprecating "Foreword" to his first book and his embarrassed asides braided right into his adding-machine epyllion, it has been evident that Ammons is a great craftsman in his poems, but an erratic stage director or prompter from the wings. What he calls "small and easy" may not be anything of the kind, and need not be called anything at all. He is ever uneasy, this poet of what David Kalstone once identified as subversive bravado, as he walks his way into "song's improvident/center/lost in the green bush"; and like Ammons we shall be at a loss to say much that is to the point about his genre, about his poetics, though the affinities are there, the spectral precursors and the *a posteriori* spooks— Emerson, Dickinson, Whitman, then Pound, Williams, Stevens. It is not to the *point* that we are to speak, anyway, as Ammons keeps telling us—rather it is out of muddle and even mud that we get what matters; it is out of chaos that cosmos comes:

> between life and me obtrude
> no symbolic forms:
> grant me no mission . . .
> leave me this black rich country
> uncertainty, labor, fear: do not
> steal the rewards of my mortality.

We are, then, to be at a loss with Ammons, and happy to be there, for it is only when losses are permitted, invited even, that there are possibilities invoked. In the poem called, crucially, "Poetics", Ammons admits how he goes about making, precisely, by leaving off as much as by inventing, by finding:

> I look for the forms
> things want to come as
> from what black wells of possibility,
> how a thing will unfold: . . .
> not so much looking for the shape
> as being available
> to any shape that may be
> summoning itself
> through me
> from the self not mine but ours.

The search is for a poetic incarnation, but it is also an abandonment of the search, a hope of poetic disincarnation, a way of overcoming by literally *undergoing* the separate self. In this, Ammons' energies are dedicated concurrently with those of his fellow American poets. But it is only in Ammons that I find all three moments—the changing from, the changing, and the changing to—exalted equally. Only Ammons, I think, of all American poets today, has—when he is not diverted into his hip asides—the capacity to endow the moment of loss, the moment of metamorphosis and the moment of release with an equal light, "the blue obliteration of radiance."

Indeed the three moments are what Ammons calls, in his accounting for events, for outcomes, for irreversible exits and recurrences alike, ambiance, salience, radiance. These are his three favorite words for the phenomenon signified (there is a place), then for the phenomenon abandoned (the place can be left), then for the phenomenon sanctified (only loss reveals what the reward was to be). It is no accident, except insofar as everything in Ammons is literally an accident, a falling-to, a befalling, it is no accident that the greatest poem in this latest book is the last, and neither small nor easy, the cross-titled poem "The City Limits", which begins its 18-line single sentence "When you consider the radiance" and ends with the acknowledgment that each thing is merely what it is, and all that can be transcended is our desire for each thing to be more than what it is, so that for such a consideration of the losses of being, the very being of loss, "fear lit by the breadth of such calmly turns to praise." It is all there in Ammons—the fear and the light, the calm and the breadth, the turning and the praise, and that is why he is a great poet.

Collected Poems 1951–1971

I have published an account of each of Ammons' books as they appeared, following a first long essay on his work; I have taught, or been taught by, the poetry in seminars at two universities, where it became clear to my students as it became incontrovertible to me that for all our probable ignorance of the ruddy turnstone and its habits, here was a great poet, surely one of the largest to speak among us, today, of what we are and are not, speaking wherever we troubled to listen in a voice so reticent in all its authority, so gorgeous in all its immediacy, that we could scarcely miss the accents of its persuasion, overheard, underlying, central. My intention here, therefore, is not one of summing up what is in every sense a going concern; it is not yet appropriate to tabulate results, for the poet is still very much ahead of us, making his way by the light of what he calls *the noons of recurrence*. Rather I should like to record my sense, merely, of a stunned gratitude for the work as it masses thus provisionally, my response to a recent rereading of the territory covered so far, always with the understanding that as Ammons ruefully admits, "less than total is a bucketful of radiant toys."

It is difficult to speak of any quantity of Ammons' poems without employing spatial metaphors—he is the poet of walking, and his is the topography of what one pair of legs can stride over, studies in *enjambment* indeed—and I have not resisted the difficulty: in all its guises, Ammons' poetry is never disguised—it takes a spiral trajectory, so that wherever we take it, his art is complete *that far*. In fact, it is the nature of this book's unrelenting course ("I like the order that allows," is how Ammons puts it) to describe that arc between the impossible and the necessary which will be this poet's particular balance, his special poise: between metaphor (saying that something is something else) and identity (saying that something is what it is). This is an old argument in our poetry—the argument between Thoreau and Emerson, between nature and vision, between the natural and the visionary, and no one has more shrewdly *drawn the line* than Ammons by this showing of twenty years work. It is no accident that the word *coil* and the word *collection* writhe upward to the surface from the same root.

"The war of shape and loss" is Ammons's Homeric conflict, the beach his Troy, though in the later poems a backyard will do: any *place* is an event for this bordering imagination,

and what comes as something of a surprise in the discovery of his solitude, his singleness (there are no friends in this poetry, no other people, in fact; most dialogue is with the wind, with mountains, and when Ammons turns away from "cytoplasm's grains" or from "energy's invisible swirls," what he turns *back* to is not any human bond:

> I turned back
> strict with limitation,
> to my world's
> bitter acorns
> and sweet branch water.)

—what comes as an astonishment, I was saying, with the poet's solitary contemplations is his sociability of *form*. Ammons is a great inventor of forms, and his poetry murmurs and glitters with the sensuality of his "boundaried vacancies." I think our expectation would be that a man of such lonely confrontations would have devised a sort of paradigm of utterance, an exemplary discourse by which to speak his piece, and would *by now* have settled down to "a perfect carriage/for resolved, continuous striving." Nothing of the kind. "Firm ground is not available ground," he observes, and risks his prosody in all the quicksands of variation. The characteristic somatic gesture in Ammons is that of testing his weight, seeing how much traffic any particular utterance can bear, from the favored mark of punctuation, the colon, to the endless open hexameters of "Hibernaculum":

> a poem variable as a dying man, willing to try anything,
> or a living man, with the consistency of either direction:
> just what the mind offers to itself, bread or stone:
> in the swim and genesis of the underlying reality things
> assume metes and bounds, survive through the wear
> of free-being against flux, then break down to swim and
> genesis again: that's the main motion but several
> interturns have been concocted to confuse it: for example . . .

and Ammons is off again. *Pages of examples*, his book might be called, and indeed it is exemplary, at a time of recipes and formulas, to find this supreme artificer inventing an unheard-of prosody each time he writes a poem. "Versification or diversification," he propounds, thereby suggesting that what has already been achieved is merely a chain—what Ammons cares about is the forging of new links, the finding of the next connection.

It is why so much of his poetry is given over—given away, as he likes to say—to erasure, destruction, loss, "the chant of vacancies, din of silences." Only when you have unmade something is there room for new making: "listen for the things I have left out." "Arrange me into disorder," Ammons implores his "Muse", and it is because his poetry hovers and shivers, in all its intonations (Ammons can be vatic, pop, sheepish, dogged, even kittenish, but the exactitude of his vocabulary makes his best poems geological, they are the *words of earth*), on the line, the arc, the curve between arrangement and chaos, that he is not merely a collected poet but a *collecting* one, that he keeps gathering within his circumference new reaches of the same substance, the same energy.

In the eight years since I began to read, and study, and love this man's poetry, I have had the opportunity to know the poet as well, and I presume it is appropriate to friendship that I "extend the form" of his collection, his coil, by adding to it a poem Ammons has not collected, but which he wrote after a visit I had made to his classes at Cornell, a poem which is a major provision—because provisional—for understanding the nature of his enterprise, the quality of his undertaking:

Untelling

Poetry is the word that has no other words,
the telling indistinguishable from the told:
it is all body (spirit) until it moves
and moving only is its declaring, divisible
neither into mind nor feeling, mind-felt,
form only if motion stays an instant into form,
otherwise form-motion, the body and the void
interpenetrating, an assuming, a perfect allowance:
how it moves away, returns, settles or
flashes by, how it works its worked space
into memory's body may tell tellings,
narratives, progressions beyond,
surrounding an instant's telling, though
only body-in-motion can place them there:
being is its afterlife whose life was becoming:
mind and other words confront, untell its dream.

It is sufficient excuse, this offering of an uncollected poem by A. R. Ammons, for my exultation over his collection: the poet who asks "what/destruction am I/blessed by?" is thereby a master maker of his period, and by the working together of his movement and his stillness, leaves us the monument we need; "and fear lit by the breadth of such calmly turns to praise."

HELEN VENDLER
From "Spheres and Ragged Edges"
Poetry, October 1982, pp. 26–33

Ever since Schiller distinguished naive from sentimental poetry, we have been worried by the pathetic fallacy (as Ruskin named it). It is the aesthetic version of the tree falling in the woods; does it make a sound if nobody is there to hear it? Is nature hospitable of itself to meaning (by its rhythms and its orders, its catastrophes and its variety) or are our symbolic uses of it truly abuses, a foisting of our sentiments onto an inert and indifferent scenery? This question has become one that no modern "nature poet" from Wordsworth on can avoid addressing in a perfectly conscious way.

Hopkins, because he was a religious poet, at first assumed an authenticating God transmitting symbols through the book of the creatures:

These things, these things were here and but the
    beholder
Wanting; which two when they once meet,
The heart rears wings bold and bolder
And hurls for him, O half hurls earth for him off
    under his feet.

This rapturous confidence in the Keatsian "greeting of the spirit" could not persevere in Hopkins's ultimately dualistic moral world, where ethics took a necessarily higher position than the aesthetic. At the end, all the diversity of the world (and with it, its symbolic potential) had, for Hopkins, to be wound onto two spools, parted into two flocks, the elect and the damned:

Let life, waned, ah let life wind
Off her once skeined stained veined variety upon, all
    on two spools; part, pen, pack
Now her all in two flocks, two folds—black, white;
    right, wrong; reckon but, reck but, mind

But these two; ware of a world where but these two
    tell.

Stevens's great explorations into the question of the pathetic fallacy (beginning with "The Snow Man," itself a variant on Keats's "In drear-nighted December") occupy him throughout his life, as he meditates the plain sense of things, the bare particular of the natural rock, and the fictive leaves that cover the rock and are a "cure" of it. Ashbery's poems (to cite a contemporary example) are full of jokes on the pathetic fallacy; but jokes are a way of using the convention, even if in a climate of gentle irony. In all these cases, the coincidence of nature with feeling or insight is the problem: is it a trick we play on ourselves, or a means of understanding—even a secular equivalent of grace?

I have written before on Wordsworth's magisterial (and in certain ways conclusive) meditations on this subject in the Intimations Ode: Wordsworth decided that our ability to use transferred epithets bestowing human adjectives on natural scenes ("the *innocent* brightness of a *new-born* day") was a way of objectifying our own feelings about innocence and birth, an activity necessary if we were to think about innocence and birth at all. ("We thought in images," says Lowell of poets.) The intercourse between soul and nature, in Wordsworth's view, clarifies the soul to itself and also endears natural sights (previously merely visual) as they become repositories of a moral and personal *Gestalt*:

The clouds that gather round the setting sun
Do take a sober coloring from an eye
That hath kept watch o'er man's mortality.

Once the habit of reciprocal looking and feeling is formed, looking taps feeling just as feeling transfigures looking: nature then appears to be an originating lamp rather than a reflecting mirror.

In Ammons, the question of the pathetic fallacy is raised again and again, most luminously and painfully in his great poem "Grace-Abounding," where the title makes explicit his claim that in states of inchoate feeling he finds a relief so great in the clarification offered by a visual image chanced upon in nature that the feeling corresponds to that which Bunyan named "grace abounding." We recall that in the Biblical formulation, where sin abounds, grace will the more abound: in Ammons's frame of things, the emphasis changes from sin to misery. In the poem, where he is trapped in a vise of misery, the sight of a hedge completely encased and bound down by ice so strikes him that he realizes that it is an image, perfectly correspondent, of his inner anguish, the more anguishing because it had as yet remained unimaged, unconceptualized, and therefore indescribable. The relief felt when the hedge strikes his eye, and his state is at last nameable, is grace—not offered by Ammons as an "equivalent" to Bunyan's grace, but as *the same thing*, a saving gift from an external source. A poet who has felt that unexpected solace will seek it again.

Ammons looks literally for sermons in stones, books in the running brooks. He has been reproached for the minuteness of his detail, for scrutinizing every letter of the natural alphabet, even every syllable in the genetic code, seeking to extract from each item its assuaging human clarification. If a hedge of ice can explain him to himself, why so can a pebble (and it has) or a wave (and it has). "Grace Abounding" is a critical poem in Ammons's canon because it tells us his habitual state—one of a mute congestion of burdened feeling that must go abroad, baffled, letting the eye roam aimlessly, if minutely, until it feels the click that tells it, when it sees the hedge of ice, that that visual form is the mirror of its present feeling. Of course, while the eye is performing its apparently aimless scrutiny, before the connection can be made, before the appropriate image catches the eye, the work seem dull, even servile. This tedious phase of ruminative watching occupies the first part of Ammons's "Meeting Place" in this issue of *Poetry* (Hopkins: "Which two when they once *meet*,/The heart rears wings"). The creek water (says Ammons in "Meeting Place") has motions, yes; the wind contributes its motions, yes; the falls also does. These are, Ammons grants, "indifferent" actions. So much for the truths of modernity. After that, the poem turns atavistic, suggesting that all matter shares deep affinities of behavior; from subatomic particles to forms determined by physical law (the sphere of a waterdrop, the body's extensional limits in dance) our human motions obey the same tendencies as nature's motions. Ammons both affirms and questions this axiom of "ancestral" actions in the second part of his poem: "is my/address attribution's burden and abuse? . . . have I/fouled their real nature for myself/by wrenching their meaning, if any, to destinations of my own/forming?"

No poem is made a poem by asking questions about *poiesis* and the pathetic fallacy, of course. But when we follow the course of "Meeting Place" we see that it enacts the meeting itself. The apparently random and tediously prolonged inquiry into the most fugitive motions of the creek is Ammons's becoming "multiple and dull in the mists' dreams," in a version of Keatsian "indolence." By the time Ammons reaches the end he is claiming the powers of the magus: "when I call out to them . . . /an answering is calling me." The second surprising word, after "dull," is "howling": the spirits that arise in "Meeting Place" arise from a place like hell ("A minist'ring angel shall my sister be/When thou liest howling!"). These spirits would remain fettered and imprisoned forever without the releasing spell of "figures visible." In making the imprisoned figures ancestral ones, Ammons is being not only Freudian but Christian: Adam and Eve were the first figures released in the harrowing of hell.

The utter congruence between Christian grace and *poiesis* in Ammons is nowhere clearer than in the other new poem printed here called "Singling and Doubling Together," a colloquy with God (or a divine immanence in all things, after the Buddhist model). The simplest way, perhaps, to think about Ammons's central assertion here is in terms of the Christian doctrine of the Incarnation—that God "risked all the way into the taking on of shape/and time." I have here made the verb into an active one ("God risked"), but Ammons has written it as a participial adjective, skirting the problem of voluntariness in God's circumscription of himself; Ammons's "you," risked into time, "fail and fail with me, as me" (Hopkins: "I am all at once what Christ is, since he was what I am"). But Ammons's ecstatic Hopkinsian ode to a presence in leafspeech and bush-snappings and pheasant-flight is deliberately undoctrinal and intimate, reminding us of Whitman's equally lyrical, but entirely sensuous, doublings of self. Ammons originally thought to call this poem (as the typescript shows) by a religious title, "Communion": it defines *poiesis* as Herbert defined it: "It is that which while I use/I am with thee." Ammons's single long sentence making the ode contains no surprises like "dull" or "howling" in "Meeting Place": cast in the form of a love-poem (Stevens: "And for what, if not for you, do I feel love?"), "Singling and Doubling Together" requires the decorum of unclouded praise. The poem deliberately takes the form of spherical perfections, as its first line—"My nature singing in me is your nature singing"—engenders, having come full circle, its close—"changed into your/singing nature, when I need sing my nature nevermore." By ending with its poet's death rather than with the transcendent persistence of an im-

manent singing, the poem is true to its earthly origins rather than to its religious antecedents; but in fact the beauty of the poem lies in its intertangled breaths of hymn and observation, of grace and birds and bushes. Its incantatory tonality is utterly different from the tones of the sedulous naturalist at the opening of "Meeting Place" (the poems meet, of course, in their endings).

It is odd to turn from these high lyrics to the epigrams of Ammons's new collection, *Worldly Hopes*; the contrast reminds us that Ammons is always oscillating between his expatiations and his "briefings" (as between, from another angle, his hymnody and his nihilism). The short poems here are more of Ammons's experiments in the minimal. The question is how few words can make a poem, and how densely can a few words be made to resonate. Here is "Providence":

> To stay
> bright as
> if just
> thought of
> earth requires
> only that
> nothing stay

"To stay bright as if just thought of/Earth requires only that nothing stay"—Ammons's art in brevity forbids this sort of rewriting (which all bad poems can sustain). The couplet that I have turned the poem into robs the poem of its doomed *rime riche* of the first and last lines, its form of measure (two words per line), and the wit of the line breaks ("bright as—" turns out not to be "bright as day" but "bright as if," a curl of thought). My couplet (which of course will not scan, either) also loses Ammons's philosophic emphasis on the "trivial" words "as," "if," "just," "of," and "only"—the sort of words whose insidiousness interested Wittgenstein, too.

"Providence" trembles, with the lightest of touches, toward some reminiscences (Frost: "Nothing gold can stay"; Stevens: "Required, as a necessity requires"). And like many of Ammons's short poems, it burdens itself with a title of overwhelming philosophical or religious significance (others in this volume include "Righting Wrongs," "Subsumption," "Epistemology," "Oblivion's Bloom," "Immortality," and "Volitions"). "Providence"—the word is religiously defined as God's loving care for us—represents Ammons's grafting of an American Protestant mentality onto Keats's discovery of the ambiguous mercy of mortality. In its seven lines (formal "perfection" would demand eight), the poem recalls various early poems of Yeats in which the eighth line is designedly dropped to symbolize loss.

Even Ammons's simplest lyrics have points to make of the sort I have mentioned in "Providence." An ingenious and eccentric angle of vision or play of metaphor in them catches the eye; but something also catches the breath:

> I went back
> to my old home
> and the furrow
> of each year
> plowed like
> surf across
> the place had
> not washed
> memory away.

The backdrop of this poem ("I Went Back") is essentially Shakespearean (the furrow of time, the obliterating sea, the memory of the poet). But rewritten, the poem takes on another cast:

> I went back to my old home,
> And the furrow of each year,
> (Plowed like surf across the place),
> Had not washed memory away.

There is something Blakean about the poem-as-quatrain ("I was angry with my friend . . . :/And it grew both day and night. /Till it bore an apple bright"). (This may be an irrelevant comparison; but we grasp at straws in trying to describe poetic effects.) Once again, here, Ammons departs from the eight-line "norm" to suggest, by adding a ninth line, the persistence of memory beyond the "natural" term of its physical moment. The energizing phrase of the poem is clearly "plowed like surf across the place," said of the furrow: the other phrases are far more conventional. In a complex image the furrow (singular) of each year (of an aggregate many), plowed (as of earth) like surf (as of ocean) across the place, is said to have failed to obliterate memory. This image is like a triple exposure in photography: first, there is the physical family farm (home); second, there is its spiritual form plowed as far as the eye can see by the furrows of Time; third, the plowed form is washed over by a new form of deluge, a surf of inner oblivion that has an intent to drown and erase the past. A fourth form, memory, then comes to replace the first, at least in the poem; but the memory being identical to the physical farm revisited, they join and merge.

If these brief forms seem constricting at times, it is because we know Ammons's discursive amplitudes. I have not found any poem in this book to equal the sublime "Easter Morning" (which *Poetry* had the honor of printing before it appeared in *Coast of Trees*). There are new versions here of themes Ammons has touched before: they range from the artist's defense of his life (a fairly savage and sardonic version called "The Role of Society in the Artist") to exercises in pure verbality ("Shit List"). Science, as always, provides apt metaphors ("Precious Weak Fields," "Reaction Rates," "Working Differentials") and the antagonisms of writing are made ever more cunning.

In Ammons, the compulsion to form lurks as a danger. When he says that a poem "begins in contingency and ends in necessity" he is of course right, but necessity need not always wear a necessitarian aspect; it can assume an openhanded stance too, as it sometimes does in Williams or Stevens: "rooted they/grip down and begin to awaken"; "It was like a new knowledge of reality." As Ammons packs words ever more densely and punningly, perhaps necessity begins to usurp some of the place of contingency.

If we step back, after reading Ammons's account of the alternate burgeoning and collapse of "worldly hopes" (as religion would call them) as well as his hymns of thanksgiving for "grace" with which we began, we can see in him a representative figure for the persistence of the Protestant vein in American poetry. He uses the strategy of religious language with much of Dickinson's attachment to it, but he preserves, as Dickinson did not, the tonality of genuine prayer (resembling in this Stevens above all). If this were all he offered—religious language, religious tonality—Ammons would be simply a poet of religious nostalgia, a whited sepulcher. That he is not, we must attribute to two virtues of style which coexist with the religious elements and counterbalance them. One is the grounding of reality in the seen (like Williams, he finds his ideas in things). And the other is his stubborn inclusion of the recalcitrant detail, the hard ragged edge resisting the spherical sheerness of ultimate religious vision. In his naturalist speech, in his untroubled admitting of the psychic origins of the pathetic fallacy, Ammons is modern; in his willingness to substitute the word "grace" for the poetic experience of nature in lieu of the words "pathetic fallacy," he argues, like all poets, for the primacy of feeling in the naming of inner response. If the clarification conferred by the natural world—there is one in almost every poem by Ammons—feels like what Bunyan named "grace," then it *is* grace. What does not feel like a fallacy cannot be truthfully called one. Ammons is sure that the number of fluid inner states is infinite, and that the only matrix of possibility ample enough to correspond with the inner world is the massively various outer world. And the only mediating instrument between the liquid currents of mind and the mountains and deserts of matter is language, that elusive joiner of rivers to rock:

> I tangled with
> the world to
> let it go
> but couldn't free
>
> it: so I made
> words
> to wrestle in my
> stead and went
>
> off silent to
> the quick flow
> of brooks, the
> slow flow of stone

Words are the scapegoat in the fiction that Ammons here names "Extrication": they wrestle with the angel of matter for us.

JON ANDERSON

1940–

Jon Victor Anderson was born on July 4, 1940, in Massachusetts. His life has largely revolved around writing and the teaching of writing. Anderson began teaching at the University of Portland in 1968, went on to Ohio University and the University of Pittsburgh, and since 1976 has taught in the renowned creative writing program at the University of Iowa. He has given numerous readings of his works, which include: *Looking for Jonathan* (1968), *Counting the Days* (1974), *In Sepia* (1974), and *Death and Friends* (1970). Critical acclaim for his work came in 1973, when he was nominated for the National Book Award for *Death and Friends*.

NELSON ALGREN

EDWARD ALBEE

A. R. AMMONS

WILLIAM ALFRED

MAXWELL ANDERSON

SHERWOOD ANDERSON

ROBERT ANDERSON

Works

"Negative capability," as the romantic poet John Keats defines it, is the writer's special gift of remaining in doubts and uncertainties, of sympathizing with many points of view, and not trying to assert himself by "irritable reaching after fad and reason." The strength of Jon Anderson's *Death & Friends* is the obverse of that "negative" virtue. Anderson's verse is peculiarly irritable without ceasing to be empathic and imaginative. It displays a speed of phrasing and positivity of observation that strike back at experience by heightening it. Though the poet seeks a measure of distance or "the aesthetics of pain"— something to allow him real maturing, a Keatsian luxury of self-development—he finds only further experience. He writes on, therefore, in a kind of bitter ecstasy, making his stupor his subject. "His head nods as he walks, a blind,/or holy, affirmative machine."

An American surrealism (which we have met before in Lowell, Sexton, Scully and others) depicts the poet as victim. Not a victim of the Muse or other fatal lady or numinous angel but simply of his honesty vis-à-vis experience. The striking metaphor or sustaining conceit, in this type of poetry, instead of stretching our mind, returns it to one, inescapable point:

> The raccoon lay down at dawn,
> Its little feet were pointing upward
> Even the tourists are sick.
> And the daily, beneficial light
> which had traveled a long time
> toward us, lies on its head
> in meadows, and against trees.

When more disjunctive, the poet's fast, montaging style creates a kind of anti-panorama, as if American free-ways led not into "spacious skies" but from one claustrophobic place to another:

> We move into the next storm
> and slaughterhouse without regret.
> It is morning; the animals fall down,
> their bodies silently steam.
> Coffee scalds the air above the cup.

Only in the "perfect air" of such poems as "The Parachutist" does the poet slow down enough to allow a widening, quasi-visionary panorama to emerge.

One respects Anderson's honesty except when it turns against speech. He uses for his epigraph "We are attempting to communicate, but no communication between us can abolish our fundamental difference . . ." and flirts in *The Honest Craftsman* with the myth of the mute, inglorious poet. His style, often attractively whimsical, grows more laconic and self-sacrificial as we read on: *Death & Friends* opens with "The Parachutist," a generous and emblematic poem, yet ends with a puzzling two-liner, a Poundian haiku on ancestors who recorded everything (weather and death) in the same dry style: "Because of death, they are valuable./A man waters his lawn." When we do encounter what looks like a poem large enough to settle into—not nervously broken up by line-breaks or punctuation—it turns out to be nostalgic prose ("Each Day Does That").

What is it that has stolen the breath-soul of this poet? Why the fetish of "difference" and "incommunicability," and that notebook style? Is Pound the villain, with his attempt to kill the metronome with every new lyric? Or is it a deeper fear of machines, in this Mechanical Age? Somewhere too the winter-genius of Robert Frost ("In the north I have come to imagine/the lakes are filled/with clarity") rises to chasten the poet.

Anderson is so honest that he thinks his precursors were even more honest. But the truth is they were more deceptive. Those dead friends of the poet's, with their "terrible simplicity," are no help. They almost stifle the real poetic talent of this second book (*Looking for Jonathan*, his first, came out in 1968). We do not need another version of the cursive style. Fortunately, however, his voice can chafe at the bit and become a controlled eloquence. When he ventures to release his breath, then "the released breath/believes in life":

> the campaign for living with ourselves
> which was a saint who became free
> is moving swiftly now into the fields,
> gliding over the snow—
> a heart of great lightness, grown
> altogether practical and strange.

There are few poems here without brilliant wording or movingly precise emotions. Among his successes one could mention "The Robots," "The Campaign for Peace in our Time," "Pierrot Without Memory" and "Salt."

If my admiration is nuanced, it is because we are so often left with a battlefield report, as in "The Wars of Adolescence." An action already over, or which cannot be mastered, is manipulated into speech by means of strong images and obvious puns. A typical Anderson situation this: writing "notes" on experiences that violate him. Perhaps every writer does it; but some have a larger or "epic" subject-matter. It makes a difference, surely, whether one is a victim of an air-crash, a love-affair or state brutality. The image of victimage, in Anderson's poems, is too general, too impressionistic. He seems to be, finally, his own victim, slipping from humorous detachment into forced confession, and from verbal mastery into a sense of verbal defeat. To the charge that this is adolescent moodiness he would probably reply: adolescence is fate.—GEOFFREY HARTMAN, "Poet as His Own Victim," *NYTBR*, July 30, 1972, pp. 4–5, 10–11

In *The Inner Gate*, the longest poem of his new book, *In Sepia*, Jon Anderson writes:

> I desired a single terrible event,
> The passage from which would measure time.

After reading this book, it is not so important that the reader is left waiting for *his* epiphany, as that the writer himself seems also to hang, waiting. One feels for Mr. Anderson, walking back through streets, and seasons, searching for the single episode that will put things and his own being in place, the breaking-into-time of a force or an idea that orders the self and makes the poem worthwhile. *In Sepia* is that journey, a travelling backwards, looking and listening for those tell-tale marks of existence. Are they in memory? in news? In the title poem we see the writer exiled, outside looking in on a scene that might be of any house and yet made uniquely his own.

> . . . Death
> Was the person into whom you stepped. Life, then,
>   Was a series of static events;
> As: here the child, in sepia, climbs the front steps
>   Dressed for winter. Even the snow
> Is brown, &, no, he will never enter that house
>   Because each passage, as into
> A new life, requires his forgetfulness. . . .
> Death was a process then, a release of nostalgia
>   Leaving you free to change.
> Perhaps you were wrong; but wailing at night
>   Each house got personal. Each
> Had a father. He was reading a story so hopeless,
>   So starless, we all belonged.

Often, this walk backwards, this journey of the soul, produces an exceptionally well-spoken poem. The beginning of *Counting the Days* compares well with what has remained one of Jon Anderson's finest poems, *The Parachutist* in *Death & Friends*.

> Just as we wake up, yawn, & lift a shade to explore,
> (Always imperfectly amazed at subtle change, but
>   limited
> By expectations & the window's frame from which
>   we gaze:
> A yard: of weeds & dogs & brown boughs, though
> Sometimes even the boughs altered by falling snow)
> So he is counting the days, the years back toward
> A serious initial thought. . . .

The long poem, *The Inner Gate*, begins with the lines

> At a certain time of life
> That failure I had long before surmised,
> Which was a destiny born
> Of self-consciousness, assured itself.

But the lines are misleading; except for a few poems, the work in this book is rather free of the Twentieth-Century soliloquy-grown-into-poem. Mr. Anderson has never been a pretentious writer, but a lack of extremism could be one of his book's central weaknesses. At times, one waits for him to suspend the journey, or walk through *Autumn Day* and tackle something larger and broader, at full speed, an *Inner Gate* expanded. But as they stand, these poems produce an identity and a foundation for that grander work, and a solid contribution to the Pittsburgh series by one of its best writers.—JAMES MARTIN, "Questions of Style," *Poetry*, May 1975, pp. 105–7

An uncompleted drawing often has a spurious brilliance, suggesting what its maker could not in fact bring to successful issue. Many of the earlier poems in this volume have a similarly vivid incompleteness, an assertion of image unbacked by deliberate coherence, which show how far the mature poet, capable of resolution and of the balancing magic of freighting the lightest word with thought, has traveled. Curiously, some of the most definite and complete poems by Anderson are those dealing with indefinite states.

Here are excellent poems dominated by fog or snow or a drifting waste of water and particularly by a craving or a yielding to the effortless and deathly passage of freefall. In one of the collection's best poems, "The Parachutist," the descending figure falls dreamily and quietly through more slowly falling snow into a frozen lake. In "Aviators," the fliers are "falling down/ forever toward your blue receding town." A long late poem of fine authority, "The Inner Gate," ends, "These are the raptures of falling in space forever."

And how beautifully Anderson writes of the poet's job of continuing in uncertainty, in "Refusals":

> That tapping all night is yourself.
>
>   . . .
>
> Thinking, maneuvering
> Over the dark & chartless waters
> & under mysterious orders not to come in.

What began perhaps as a defect, a muzziness in early poems such as "American Landscape with Clouds & a Zoo," where we are told "Everything/Is too brief, eternal, stable, unpredictable," has become a strength, a mature unwillngness to force a conclusion, a skill at playing the clarity of a line—a clarity that amounts to happiness as brilliant sunlight asserts good luck, whatever it shines upon—against the confusion and self doubt that it expresses, as in "John Clare":

> Toward dawn, there was an undirected light the
>   color of steel;

> The aspens, thin, vaguely parallel strips of slate,
> Blew across each other in that light.
>   I went out
> Having all night suffered my confusion, &
> Was quieted by this.

It is Anderson's gift to permit the reader to share the solace derived from his observation of the world's grace.—PENELOPE MESIC, *Poetry*, Feb. 1984, pp. 297–98

Jon Anderson's new book, *The Milky Way: Poems 1967–1982*, contains an ample selection of poems from his three previous volumes (*Looking for Jonathan*, *Death & Friends* and *In Sepia*) plus a new, previously unpublished collection, *American Landscape with Clouds & a Zoo*. In this latter group there are some affecting lyrics about the past, death, memory and love, which are marked by strong lines and poignant renderings of light, weather and the seasons ("Then it was autumn & the leaves fell down,/Full of the odors of tobacco/& coffee"). Anderson is a skillful introspectionist and can tell you exactly what he is feeling with fine moment-to-moment precision.

Anderson's work contains much that is sweet, heartfelt, intense, pained and ecstatic, yet as a craftsman he is simply not in the same league as Pinsky and Wright. He lapses into facile devices, often ending poems, for instance, with cute or sententious single lines set off from flaccid stanzas. Here is the end of "Falling in Love":

> The dusky gourdlike eggplant
> We will batter & fry come morning
> Adorns the kitchen table,
> A little shade of vegetable contemplation.
> I think it is lonely.
> I think it would like you to awaken.

He falls into what sound like bad translations of Rilke ("Like the seasons, their terrible/Seemingly effortless labor to simply *become*") or, worse, into humorless psychobabble ("I was restored/By your bearing & openness to pain").

Anderson writes, in "A Globe of Snow," of liking the poet Tu Fu, whose works "Assume a mutual understanding." His own poetry not only assumes a sympathetic reader, it demands one who will identify with and bless the incoherent consciousness behind its shifting voices, thoughts and forms. The dust jacket of *The Milky Way* quotes him as saying, "My poetry isn't for everyone. It's for people like myself who want to contend with themselves. I think of my poems as intimate conversations with close friends, to whom I'm not afraid to reveal my vulnerabilities and loneliness. It might sound exclusive, but that's the way it is. There are other writers to take care of other audiences." Sincerity is a fine thing, but Anderson too often relies on it to supply what his technique isn't able to. He writes, in "American Landscape with Clouds & a Zoo," like a frustrated hippie:

> America is in trouble & you're too
> Fucked-up to even understand, buy it.
> Is America fucked-up because it understands
> Itself only too well as you do you?

He was writing similarly sixteen years ago, as in "Preparation for Travel," from his first book, *Looking for Jonathan*:

> For my birthday
> God gave me 10,000 white birds, so
>   that I
>   would not be alone, but I am.
> So I am writing to you,
> the only poem I ever write; badly,
> but in sincerity.

I am trying to love you.
Love me. I have no shame.

Anderson has never purged his language of its youthful reliance on inarticulateness as an expressive mode, or learned to edit out his sappier, windier passages. Too often his stanzas, which sit on the page with decorous formality, turn out to be merely arranged, lacking necessity in everything from their line lengths to their syntax and figures. Worst of all, his seemingly compulsive preoccupation with the self, time and memory serves only as a lever to general phrasemaking:

> Maybe the past is neither found nor lost,
> But misconceived;
> The future dies of fear.
> If memory is remorse,
> The present is rapt borderline,
> You must descend a gradual ladder of grass
> Into the childish earth
> Now, before the wind's fist,
> The storm,
> The earth's darkening.
> ("Memory: A Vision")

If it were all as simple as that, then the terrible, painful questions Wright and Pinsky struggle with would be only so much wasted breath. Surely their labors and their language—so various, resourceful and un-easy—stand as the best criticism of even Anderson's best work.—ELIZABETH FRANK, "The Middle of the Journey," *Nation*, April 7, 1984, pp. 423–24

WILLIAM DICKEY
"The Poem and the Moment"

Hudson Review, Spring 1971, pp. 160–68

In a great deal of this work (of Anderson, Ammons, Berry, Carruth, Everson, Lowell, Snyder), then, the quality of the poet is to be an observer, someone to whom things happen, or a medium through which they can be recognized. This attitude appears in the absence of "I"; the pronouns change to "he" or "you" or "it." It shows in a refusal to elevate language, and an assumption that the sparest and most colloquial language is the best. It shows (in Berry in particular) the impossibility of dramatic poetry—even though Berry includes a short verse play, it rings immediately false because the characters cannot assume *personae* but must speak with essentially the same voice. And it shows frighteningly in a dominance of images of dark and death: the cold, the north, the distance of stars, the places where land breaks off in overcrops tilted above the sea, the frozen cities (Anderson):

> The city, very white, extends
> for a few miles; around it
> is nothing important. Its streets
> are not crowded, or dirty.
> Partially submerged in entrances,
> the women are indistinct; dress, often
> the color of dust. Happiness is not
> important. If you have been walking, it seems
> endlessly, in those blazing streets
> there is always a shop open.

And again Anderson:

> And, David,
> but for love of you (& some
> others) I'd give up. You said,
> "I can't find my life, either."
> It falls all winter;
> it falls into your hair & your eyes, making

them wet again:
> the lost freshness
> for which we hurt ourselves, and write these letters.

. . . Anderson's world is one in which the human condition is scarcely bearable, and separation is the strongest reality. It is a world that cannot accept the double nature of humanity: the flesh and the soul simultaneously there, each mocking the reality of the other. The body becomes grotesque or discontinuous:

> We thought sex was a root.
> It would grow crooked, arthritic
> & hard, very
> relentless, serious, positive. . . .

Or:

> Drifting above your bed,
> here are my hands,
> head, feet, the five white islands
> turning & joined. . . .

The opposite possibility is that of the saint, the figure who escapes, but only by deliberate pain, from the condition of the body:

> The saint flagellates himself; it seems
> to be another man. Not pain,
> but the aesthetic of pain is learned.
> He knows there is no reward for being hurt.
> Slowly he strips his skin.

The most charged word in that passage may be "it." For as the human being turns into a part of a human being (it is not "the poor" but "the mouths of the poor" that grin at us, follow us home, stick to the car's fender) so both the human being and the angel can become an "it," a thing. In the city of robots "your aluminum police, our angels, soar. . . ."

It would be easier to dismiss Anderson's terrible sense of meaninglessness, of the failure of life, if he exaggerated his language. But even the poems that make use of surreal technique exhibit extreme control, a grave understatement. Only the thinnest edge of life is breathing here—the observer has come to his smallest shape, and all I can hope for him is the narrow chance he allows himself:

> But I want to be what you ask.
> In that northern country
> blood burns a trail; the snow
> is hurt by it. I want to be hurt by it,
> running with the small animal's terror
> into the next thing, courage;
> and, surviving, the necessity of care. . . .

R. G. Everson's poems are northern, too, but in them the north seems to represent an open possibility, rather than an image of despair and vacuity. Thus he writes, in "Report for Northrop Frye":

> Nothing ever alive precedes man here
> If "Poetry can be made only out of other poems"—
> in new space to what may I refer?
> We bring our own light to a dark place
> Crowbar, sledge hammer, pick
> pound Labrador granite
> We make sounds from Arctic silence
> Life is here and now—we bring it
> We bring men's laughter and good sense

As far from Anderson, one might think, as the Earth from Antares. And yet, only a few pages later, the slip of the self, the drop out of identity, shows up:

> I start new like a girl in another town
> I am no longer big with soul

My past and future are thrown away
the lot flushed down tumult

Perhaps it is geography that permits the contradiction. If there is a physical wilderness to live in, it may not be necessary consistently to recognize an interior one. I see Anderson as living in no space other than metaphysical: all of the poems could be written by the same mind no matter what its location. Everson has still the sense of an open world to move in and through. Places are important to him, and his poems usually take place in a recognizable town or countryside. Even the names of places have an independent virtue: "The townships of Ontario county where we walk are/ Rama/ Mara/ Thora/ Brock/ Reach/ Whitby/ Pickering/ Uxbridge/ Scott/ I shall die/ before five o'clock . . ." He has the feel of speed too: "On & on out of Alberta/ into Saskatchewan/ running/ without pulling up/ running wildly . . ." Everson's rear-end brakeman slowly wearing his own path beside the rail-path across Canada is able to see a continuity he has made, and perhaps therefore able to confront forthrightly what happens to continuity:

We cannot see the swaddled child,
his years on the world are also hidden
The living baby is brought into his home
The coffin roof hinges open for a lifetime.

CAROL MUSKE
"Ourselves as History"

Parnassus, Spring–Summer 1976, pp. 114–17

Jung said: "One does not become enlightened by imagining figures of light, but by making the darkness conscious." One is enlightened reading Jon Anderson, but not by light. The book is titled *In Sepia*, the color of old photos, monochrome drawings, the color of dried blood, an exact shade of memory. The language is acutely tuned to remembering—and to the origins of memory. Anderson is writing from the darkness where memory begins, making that darkness conscious.

This book is a history of the imagination—and again the mood is Jungian, Jung being another nonbeliever in "events" of autobiography (for him, only the "memories, dreams and reflections" survive). Anderson lives at that crossing where imagination usurps memory; the act of remembering is of necessity an act of the imagination. He is where "light is nothing/it enters and reflects" but the darkness is germinal. . . . "You lie awake/you watch the stars revolve, repeat," "the photograph quickens," "stages of memory darken and go by" and "synapse shuttles through the skull."

Despite the gentle oriental gestures of self-effacement ("Whatever I do, I am always leaving"), these are not poems of death's annihilation or the oblivion of darkness; their preoccupation is with death and the beginnings of self. The resignation of lines like "These are the joys of falling in space forever" or "Out of a cloud I come falling into a cloud" is deceptive. There is an ironically insistent tone, a vague possessiveness for what is lost and irrevocable—the sincerity and compulsiveness, the self-consciousness of the ghost who feels obligated to haunt you. The secret of poetry, "friends," (in case you were wondering) is "cruelty," the "one cold flower" the poet leaves on your windowsill, whose beauty renders you "inconsolable" all day.

This is a quickening before birth, the conspiracy of the unborn: "I had secretly thought to accrue a life/to imply the passage of time/of myself, as citizen from here to there." And

I desired a single terrible event
the passage from which would measure time.

The desire for birth and the tremendous loss inherent in being born, of giving oneself life and, simultaneously, death, is a major paradox. The poet is forever sleepwalking between conception and birth—on the level of ideation he is doomed to abstraction, with the impossible task of making the abstract a supportable form, a beginning for the real. "I would remember my conception, not the act." We would not accept this hesitancy, this fanaticism for the philosophically exact from a lesser poet. But this cultivated atropism, this turning-away, is pure, the purity of a poet who almost *is* an idea, who can remember or imagine (the same thing for the unborn) his own death—and knows how, still and all, to survive and to be conscious in survival.

The only act finally available to the poet is the poem, the only commitment to language, to telling, where he can create an arbitrary history of our lives. To go back to childhood and further back, to other memories when the stories were real, told by fathers and "so hopeless,/So starless, we all belonged," as in "Counting the Days":

. . . this journey into dissolution
As memories become events, become anticipations
Then dissolve, will empty us of our complex doubts.
You will certainly love yourselves as history: potential
Which only took a certain lovely arbitrary route . . .

Like Mark Strand, whose influence is felt here, Anderson chooses to tell the "story of our lives," with the same certain sense of loss and anxious arbitrary documentation, the familiar ironic exactitude in "haunting" time—satirizing its content and forging its signature.

He will tell the stories, not out of love, but "care" and because "We who have changed, & have/No hope of change, must now love/The passage of time."

How can I say this, only beginning to see
Such understanding as
Can make you whole. These stories end, as
Always, in our gradual belief. They are
The lands we live in,
The women we finally meet as friends,
The friends we overcome. We overcome
Ourselves. The words
You wanted are that story we tell
Ourselves so often it is eventually real
Or plain, so, much
The same measure, or passing of time
Where we dissolve.

These poems of strange, almost unbearable beauty and subtlety are all we need to know forever and for now of ourselves, if we could only read ourselves and tell it out. These poems glow darkly, their strength lies outside of time and in darkness—in the given mysteries, the histories by which we invent ourselves.

Charles Wright knows what Anderson knows ("knowing nothing changes or everything/And only to tell it . . .") but chooses another path to enlightenment: a head-on confrontation with language.

Memoirs are recorded faithfully, literally (as in the sequence, "Tattoos," each numbered poem refers to a specific memory listed at the end of the sequence). A clue to his relationship with language lies in a clear recollection of learning to write words in the Palmer method (listed as "memory of words as things"). The poem is an object lesson, substantiating itself with the shapes of the developing calligraphy, abstraction made sensuous and morphous before our eyes:

> Oval oval oval oval push pull push pull
> Words unroll from our fingers
> A splash of leaves through the windowpanes,
> A smell of tar from the streets:
> Apple, arrival, the railroad, shoe.

. . .

> Mojo and numberless, breaths
> From the wet mountains and green mouths, rust-
>   lings,
> Sure sleights of hand,
> The news that arrives from nowhere:
> Angel, omega, silence, silence . . .

MAXWELL ANDERSON

1888–1959

Maxwell Anderson was born on December 15, 1888, in Atlantic, Pennsylvania. His father was a Baptist minister who moved from pulpit to pulpit, taking his family with him. In 1911 Anderson graduated from the University of North Dakota and married Margaret Haskett. He earned an M.A. from Stanford University in 1914, then taught high school and college for several years. A committed pacifist, he refused to fight in World War I. From 1918 to 1924 Anderson wrote for magazines and newspapers in New York, and in 1921 co-founded and edited *Measure*.

His first play, *White Desert* (1923), was unsuccessful, but his second became an enormous hit the following year. Written with Laurence Stallings, *What Price Glory?* was a sharp, savage satire on war that made its authors famous. Anderson had his first solo success, *Outside Looking In*, in 1925, the year he published his only book of poetry, *You Who Have Dreams*.

With *Elizabeth the Queen* in 1930, Anderson began to explore verse drama, the medium that would encompass most of his later work. He attempted another medium the same year in his screenplay for *All Quiet on the Western Front*. Other Anderson screenplays included *Rain* (1932) and *Death Takes a Holiday* (1934). In 1933, two years after his first wife died, he married Gertrude Anthony; he also won a Pulitzer Prize for the political satire *Both Your Houses*; and founded Anderson House, which published his subsequent works. 1935 saw the premiere of his most esteemed play, *Winterset*, a verse tragedy based on the Sacco and Vanzetti case. It won the New York Drama Critics Circle Award, as did *High Tor* two years later. 1938's *Knickerbocker Holiday* was a musical comedy, with a score by Anderson's close friend and Connecticut neighbor Kurt Weill. It was presented by the Playwrights Producing Company, which Anderson helped found.

By the time *The Eve of St. Mark* ran on Broadway in 1942, Anderson had modified his pacifism; the play was a stirring patriotic drama. Four substantial successes followed: *Joan of Lorraine* (1946), *Anne of a Thousand Days* (1948), *Lost in the Stars* (1949, adapted with Weill from Alan Paton's *Cry, the Beloved Country*), and *The Bad Seed* (1954). Gertrude Anderson died in 1953; Anderson married Gilda Oakleaf the next year.

Anderson's many awards included a Gold Medal for Drama from the American Academy of Arts and Letters in 1954, and honorary doctorates from Columbia and the University of North Carolina. He died on February 28, 1959, in Stamford, Connecticut. He had three children by his first wife and one by his second.

Personal

According to Donald Heiney, Maxwell Anderson is "an anomaly in twentieth-century literature," a Romanticist "whose chief contribution to the theatre has been in the virtually obsolete form of verse drama." Heiney might well have added the anomaly of Anderson's making some of this verse drama both an artistic and a commercial success for more than a decade on the Broadway stage. Indeed, several anomalies emerge from the circumstances of Anderson's life and background. He was not born in or around New York City, the birthplace of a surprising number of famous American playwrights; his family contained no artistic or theatrical members of whom record survives, except that his mother painted pictures as a hobby and that an uncle sang on the radio; his youth bordered on poverty; his rearing and most of his formal education took place in the then crude Middle West which was—according to Van Wyck Brooks and despite the interesting opposing evidence by Bernard De Voto—practically a cultural desert; he did not attend Professor G. P. Baker's famous drama class at Harvard, unlike several of his successful contemporaries; and, until he was about thirty-five, he had no intention of making a career out of drama.—ALFRED SHIVERS, "The Dancing Firefly Years," *Maxwell Anderson*, 1976, p. 17

General

It is because he is poetic that Mr. Anderson is so popular, though this is not the reason for his failure as a dramatic poet. In fact, the best of his plays, *Winterset*, happens also to be the most poetic—with its striking river-bank setting, its hurdy-gurdy, gangsters, Molnaresque fantasy, and melodramatic suspense—and did not fail to carry off its quota of prizes and box-office receipts. Despite its textureless philosophizing about "this hard star-adventure," its lovemaking that declines into

> I will take my hands
> and weave them to a little house, and there
> you shall keep a dream . . .

and its hero's wisecracks, painfully mimicking Hamlet's fitfully bitter wit, the play has genuine inventiveness and even, here and there, a touch of illumination. Anderson's theatrical personification of Judge Thayer, who condemned Sacco and Vanzetti, as an old man, half-witted, wandering through America to argue that in spite of everything justice has been done (a sort of pharisaic Ancient Mariner), is, to me, the author's most subtle and completely realized character—far superior dramatically to his Elizabeth, and Mary of Scotland, who seem more diversified in psychological respects. The Judge's lines, too, perhaps because their speaker has a specific living theme, possess a precision and decorative integrity unusual in Anderson's theatre, dispensing with the unfortunate imagery with which the author habitually bombards the infinite.

. . . .In the eleven verse plays since 1929, Mr. Anderson has learned how to let his fancy play about historical episodes, working them into a pattern of love, nostalgia, and hope. He has moved expeditiously from Elizabethan England, through Colonial America, nineteenth-century Austria, contemporary New York and Florida. In each case, however, the historical subject has merely provided a change of scene. The joinings that lock real events solidly together into drama have not been penetrated. Though the pieces are rich in theatrical bits, no plot coils up out of them; thus the characters cannot develop heroic stature, but tend to idle about the stage seeking a reason for existence. Their speeches are footnotes (frequently quite long) to the action, rarely part of it. As *personae* they are thin and abstract, and often behave without motivation, except for declarations of desire expressed in the most general terms.

Nor has Mr. Anderson created or unearthed new types, as the realistic American theatre has succeeded in doing. His queens, noblemen, thugs, adolescents, are invariably stock figures grown familiar through the motion pictures.

Consciously or otherwise, Mr. Anderson seems more interested in arguing for his philosophy of life than in any particular happening, past or present. Each of his full-length plays turns upon a love story, essentially the same in all. A potentially perfect romance is frustrated by another need, political (the crown in *Elizabeth*, *Mary*, etc.), social (*Wingless Victory*, *Winterset*), or private (*High Tor*, *Key Largo*). While an assortment of contemporary topics are touched upon—the decay of aristocracy, race prejudice, class injustice, revolution and absolutism—the mechanism of the play is always the love affair, and the issue always a certain omnipresent danger of "dying within." I cannot say whether Mr. Anderson favors love or some other faith as the life principle. Elizabeth gives up Essex for "the crown" and is fated to become "the queen of emptiness and death"; in contrast, Washington in *Valley Forge* puts aside a love affair, but thinking of the Revolution declares, "I'd have died within if I'd surrendered"; again, Prince Rudolph in *The Masque of Kings* commits suicide rather than assume the crown because he's "learned from the little peddler's daughter how to keep faith with the little faith I have beyond time and change." Perhaps the author's point of view is summed up by King in *Key Largo*:

> A man must die
> for what he believes . . .
> and if he won't then he'll end up believing
> in nothing at all—and that's death, too.

No doubt Mr. Anderson means his message to be, ultimately, one of hope, in that people *are* ready to die for something. To me, however, it is entirely depressing, with much in it of popular science and the endless revolution of the spheres.

Since Mr. Anderson thus poetizes history, he feels no obligation to it in matters of story, characterization, or literary style. The last is especially important in considering his work in relation to poetry. Mr. Anderson's rhetoric is neither archaic nor modern. Broadway locutions mix with Shakespearean leftovers, like beans in a pudding.

Archduke John:

> . . . I was burdened once
> with one of these royal frumps. She's back with
>   mamma
> and I've gone human with a chorus girl.
> But you might have helped yourself to a sweeter portion
> than you'll share with the prince, my dear.

Currents of language developed by a dozen different cultures and individual temperaments are siphoned into a single vat, until all that is heard is the gurgle of school readings. To what age or etiquette, for example, could one assign the "wit" placed in the mouth of Sir William Howe upon his learning of the Continentals' capture of British forage: "Sic transit horse-feed mundi?"

. . . Rhetoric so lacking in inner tone is not given a special magic by being set up as verse. Nor is verse in the American theatre something new and tender, a "beginning," as Mr. Anderson has contended. Quite the opposite. It has always been here, and has commonly identified itself with the most barren academicism. The first native play professionally performed in America, *The Prince of Parthia*, by Thomas Godfrey, was a tragedy in blank verse. From this eighteenth-century take-off, imitations of Shakespeare continued without pause to reach for poetic immortality, though each was soon forced to plead with Boker's Lanciotto:

> Here let me rest, till God awake us all.

. . . Mr. Anderson's verse plays, though sometimes more flexible than their nineteenth-century counterparts, belong to the "classical" tradition that visited upon hundreds of towns in the pioneer West such names as Athens, Olympia, Hannibal, Waterloo, Alexandria, and other evocations of "the great." It seems certain that the fate of the imaginative theatre rests less with them than with the arduous, if at times pinched and aborted, experiments of modern poetry.—HAROLD ROSENBERG, "Poetry and the Theatre," *Poetry*, Dec. 1940, pp. 258–63

. . . There is nothing reprehensible about repeating a valid theme, but repetition without variety is to rewrite the same play. Certainly Shakespeare does not vary from his persistent concern with man's triumph over evil, but each play is a variation on the theme, with new characters to champion the cause. Anderson keeps on telling us that the noble cannot survive in a world of gangsters and that a courageous death is the final deed of revolt.

The Golden Six was offered at an off-Broadway theatre and barely survived the reviews. Turning to off-Broadway may not necessarily indicate decline in popular favor. An increasing number of established writers prefer to launch a new work away from the hazards of Broadway, particularly if the play is an experimental personal statement or a probing in new directions that invites less fanfare and a special audience. But the tale of Claudius in *The Golden Six* was Anderson in decline. Yet, though his reputation has suffered more than that of others, his contribution to the American theatre cannot be so lightly dismissed.

His work since World War II has not equaled his stirring though somewhat sentimental dramas of the earlier period. *Truckline Cafe* (1946) was a failure, but *Joan of Lorraine* (1946) and *Anne of a Thousand Days* (1948) were well received. *Lost in the Stars*, the musical version of Alan Paton's warmly human South African novel, *Cry, the Beloved Country*, had a book by Maxwell Anderson and music by Kurt Weill. His first play of the fifties was *Barefoot in Athens* (1951), a story of Socrates' final days, which was followed by the long-run success of *The Bad Seed*, a gruesome melodrama of a disturbed child who enjoys murder, based on the novel by William March. Like so many others, Anderson has resorted to adaptations, as he did with *The Day the Money Stopped*, from the novel by Brendan Gill.

Anderson's early work prompted many to hail him as the worthy successor of O'Neill. The strange collaboration of Anderson, Stanford University graduate and schoolteacher, with the hard-hitting journalist Laurence Stallings had turned out the lusty, raucous deflation of wartime heroics in *What Price Glory?*—the first of many plays with question marks in the title. His cooperation with Harold Hickerson produced the burning anger of *Gods of the Lightning*, a defense of Sacco and Vanzetti. On his own, Anderson attempted to rewrite the same tale in *Winterset*, in which gangsters, lovers, and Judge Gaunt speak in an awkward blank verse within the shadows of a metropolitan bridge. Elizabeth of England and Mary, Queen of Scots, may deserve the dignity of poetic speech, but its use is justifiable only if demanded by the nobility of concept. Anderson's verse is consciously literary and superimposed, but one cannot gainsay the moments of hope it engendered of a theatre striving to soar beyond realism into grandeur of language. The weakness is twofold. Language should rise out of situation and character. Anderson's people recite rhetorical speeches and move in prearranged directions.

The *Winterset* theme repeats itself in all of Anderson's work. He had professed a faith in gradualism in his earlier plays, but he was quickly disillusioned by a world in which corruption flourishes and goodness of spirit goes unrewarded. Young Mio and Miramne die. Esdras, the philosopher, stands over their bodies, which are riddled with machine-gun bullets, and says, "I find no clue, only a masterless night, and in my blood no certain answer . . ." Man's glory is "not to cringe . . . but standing, take defeat implacable and defiant . . ." Stirring words for the lost and spiritually isolated, but hardly a courageous cry to those under the heel of Hitler or Mussolini. Anderson may have a secret admiration for the gangster, for though Trock knows he is to die in six months, he goes on killing, acting, living. For the sensitive, there is no way out but the dignity of death. Victor in *Key Largo*, choosing to remain with the remnants of the International Brigade in Spain, repeats,

> I have to believe there's something in the world that isn't evil. I have to believe there's something in the world that would rather die than attempt injustice . . . something positive for good . . . that can't be killed or I'll die inside.

In the harsh world of America's rise to material power, such words cast a glow of spiritual longing. Although he ranks among the most incorruptible of playwrights, Anderson dwindled into the most sentimental, and the most defeatist. The Indian in *High Tor* says, "Nothing is made by men but makes, in the end, good ruins." A Mio or a Victor needs roots in American soil. Anderson remains his own High Tor, a memo-

rable historic event, but of another day.—ALLAN LEWIS, "The Tired Deans," *American Plays and Playwrights of the Contemporary Theatre*, 1970, pp. 140–42

Works

The plays are not far apart in time—Maxwell Anderson's *Winterset* (1935), Brecht's *The Private Life of the Master Race* (1934ff.), and Sidney Kingsley's dramatization (1951) of Arthur Koestler's *Darkness at Noon* (1941). Based on historical events in America, Germany, and Russia, respectively, they examine different aspects of one large theme: the separation of power and justice in the actions of public authority, and the impact of this on the victims of power.

While Brecht and Kingsley portray authoritarian regimes, Anderson, working from the Sacco-Vanzetti case, develops the irony of a legitimate court's acting on the theory that

> justice, in the main,
> is governed by opinion. Communities
> will have what they will have. . . .
> (Act II)

Here is the material that can produce a satirical or even cynical tone, and indeed that tone is almost always present in *Winterset*. Mio Romagna, the avenging son of Bartolomeo Romagna, the man unjustly executed for murder in connection with a mail robbery, repeatedly slips into the contemptuous manner of premature disillusionment. Anderson always presents police as heavy-handed, stupid, or corrupt. By the final scene Trock Estrella, the man who really committed the murder for which the elder Romagna was executed, has killed three other people to protect himself for the remaining six months of life that fatal illness allows him. Such actions point toward the despair that marks some extreme melodrama of disaster.

Yet Anderson, as his prefatory essay makes clear, aspires to the tragic mode, and in four characters he finds a dividedness that could reach tragic proportions. The first of these is Judge Gaunt, who sentenced Romagna to death, and whose sense of guilt, or at least doubt, has driven him, at the start of the play, into mental disorder. But the judge, who could become a tragic hero, disappears for good before the end of Act II, and is never carried through to an ultimate confrontation of himself; he wavers between anxiety and self-justification, falls into pettiness and even whining, and finally is incapable of sustaining our interest. Two other characters that could be treated tragically are Garth Esdras and his father Rabbi Esdras; Garth knows that Trock Estrella was the murderer, but, with the entire approval of his father, keeps quiet to protect himself (Trock and his gunmen are always rather incredibly standing around ready to shoot anyone who displeases Trock). Thus they not only prevent justice but contribute to the death of Garth's sister Miriamne and of Mio Romagna, whom Miriamne loves. But Garth seems only annoyed by this outcome, and Esdras, after a brief request for forgiveness, drifts off into a vague philosophical essay. Neither has much strength of motive beyond the son's self-protectiveness and the father's there's-nothing-much-that-can-be-done-about-anything line; hence the tragic possibility is completely unrealized. Finally, Miriamne Esdras is caught between her love for Mio, whose mission in life is to clear his father's name, and her devotion to her brother, who could clear that name at some risk to himself; at a crucial moment she opts for her brother and then in penance lets herself be shot by the gunmen. But her struggle is given neither centrality nor tension, and at most she seems a sweet, mild, and pathetic girl rather than a desperately tried Antigone.

Closest to the dramatic center of the play is Mio Romagna; his role is melodramatic, and at one point, like a detective and district attorney in one, he seems on the edge of a triumph. But love for Miriamne makes him irresolute; the situation gets away from him; the tables are turned, and instead of bringing out the truth he is hemmed in by gunmen. At this moment he declares "I've lost / my taste for revenge" and begs Miriamne,

> . . . teach me a treason to what I am, . . .
> . . . teach me how to live
> and forget to hate!

(Act III)

Here is the widening out of the revenger's monopathic character, and theoretically this should lead us to sense magnitude in the play. But Mio's sentiments, however admirable, seem misplaced; he has not committed an evil that has suddenly overwhelmed his consciousness and made all action in the world irrelevant; rather he is in undeserved danger in which all energy ought to go into self-preservation. An actual melodrama makes a legitimate demand on him, and he falls inappropriately into the gestures of a tragic hero coming into insight. The renunciation of revenge is meaningful only if one has power and opportunity to commit revenge; an ambush by thugs calls for a different focus of energies. When Mio achieves, presumably, a nobler code of life, and then simply walks out and gets shot by a gunman, and thus inspires his girl to expose herself and get shot too, Anderson loses a grip on both melodramatic and tragic character and falls into the operatic.—ROBERT BECHTOLD HEILMAN, "Anderson's *Winterset*," *Tragedy and Melodrama: Versions of Experience,* 1968, pp. 276–78

Since *Winterset*, Mr. Anderson has produced both *The Masque of Kings* and, still more recently, the highly successful but pretentious and derivative comedy *The Star Wagon* (1937) in which a clumsily conceived "time machine" provides the occasion for some highly unoriginal speculations on the theme of Barrie's *Dear Brutus* and for some pleasantly executed but not very novel scenes poking gentle fun at the manners prevalent during the American Age of Innocence. Both plays—especially the last—are discouraging enough to those who had hoped that Mr. Anderson would waste no more time writing the kind of easy successes he has already so abundantly demonstrated his ability to turn out. Both would, however, be more discouraging than they are were it not for the fact that since *Winterset* he has also written *High Tor*, the best of his comedies and one which has at least a certain relation to what seems the most important part of his potential contribution to contemporary dramatic writing. It is light and insubstantial, but it is also an attempt to find a place on the modern stage for a kind of comedy which seems to have died almost three centuries ago. And to that extent it is, like *Winterset*, an effort to reclaim for our own use a source of delight which our ancestors took for granted but of which we have lost the secret.

Anyone who came in near the middle of a performance of *High Tor* might have been pardonably bewildered. High in the air he would have seen two substantial but sinister citizens imprisoned in the bucket of an idle steam shovel, while upon a crag just beneath, the robustious shade of one of Henry Hudson's men was holding converse with a stenographer from a twentieth-century office. Other things just as odd as that happen quite regularly throughout the play, and yet they can seem quite reasonable to one who has followed from the beginning the airy and delightful fantasy. Versatility is one of the most conspicuous though not the most important of Mr. Anderson's many virtues, and in *High Tor* he wrote a playfully imaginative

comedy agreeably unlike anything our theaters are accustomed to house.—JOSEPH WOOD KRUTCH, "The Poetic Drama: Maxwell Anderson," *American Drama Since 1918*, pp. 301–2

It was the collaborated *What Price Glory?*, one of the toughest plays of the tough twenties, which established Mr. Anderson as a playwright. That was in 1924, when we had all decided to put aside what was left of romance, patriotism, religion, and idealism of any variety. Noisily disillusioned, we would settle down to whatever version of skepticism blended most amusingly with the last bottle supplied by a bootlegger.

What Price Glory? hit that mood perfectly. Here was war as it is—the whole nasty, brutish, senseless mess, with little adventure and no romance unless the feud of Flagg and Quirt over the favors of Cognac Pete's daughter could be so dignified. As for making the world safe for democracy, Kiper disposed of that one by telling the truth: he had joined up to see the girls.

Of course, there was Captain Flagg, who seemed a somewhat better type of officer than was needed for such a hard-bitten exposé of war. There was his curious confidence in the superior morale produced by lax discipline. When the general called Flagg's men a bunch of bums, the retort was, "Individualists, General, individualists", which drew the general's grudging admission that Flagg's outfit was the best for hard assignments. But in the welter of profanity and dug-out humor, no one noticed such lines. Mr. Anderson was established as a "hard guy" who had no "truck" with sentimental illusions.

In *Key Largo*, of the 1939–40 season he wrote again of war for democracy, again asked the question, what price glory? The answer came with poignant emphasis. No man of sense dies for glory, yet a man will die for that which he deeply believes—for the essential values of Western Civilization, for personal freedom and integrity. Lacking faith in such values and the will to fight for them, a man dies spiritually—"and that's death, too". His 1940 play, *Journey to Jerusalem*, amplifies this interpretation of his problem of belief by projecting it into the realm of religion. Mr. Anderson seems to be saying that faith in God must be added to social and political convictions, if the modern world is to regain sanity and wholeness of spirit.

Roughly, fifteen years separate *What Price Glory?* and these last two plays; fifteen years in which Mr. Anderson with all of us has lived through the worst of depressions, a long and searching criticism of capitalist democracy, the constant strain of New Deal experimentation, the decline of free institutions in Europe, and the ever-widening triumphs of totalitarianism. One wonders how an intelligent person, with vision sharp for realities and the intellectual honesty which must call black, black when he sees it, could have moved from the hard, skeptical realism of *What Price Glory?* to the sturdy and poetic affirmations of *Key Largo* and *Journey to Jerusalem*. Surely, this development must have meaning for us.—EDWARD FOSTER, "Core of Belief: An Interpretation of the Plays of Maxwell Anderson," *SwR*, Winter 1942, pp. 87–88

EDMUND WILSON

"Prize-Winning Blank Verse" (1937)
The Shores of Light
1952, pp. 674–80

There is perhaps not much point, at this time and in this place, of writing a depreciation, merely for the sake of a depreciation, of the plays of Mr. Maxwell Anderson. Mr. Anderson is by no means pretentious about his work. It is the donors of the Pulitzer Prize, who gave a prize to *Both Your Houses,* and the members of the Drama Critics' Circle, who have twice in succession chosen plays of his for their award, that have made his work appear pretentious. And Mr. Stark Young has already discussed in these pages the various productions of Mr. Anderson's plays and dealt admirably with their literary as well as with their theatrical qualities. I see, morover, that Mr. V. F. Calverton and Mr. George Jean Nathan have chosen this moment to light into him. There are, however, certain things to be said about Maxwell Anderson's general aims that none of these critics has said, so I shall lay on with the rest.

Toward the end of the season last year, when *Winterset* had been covering itself with glory, I went around to see what I understood from the reports of it I had heard to be a great American poetic drama on the theme of Sacco and Vanzetti. What I was actually confronted with was a belated disembodied shadow of the productions, so unpopular in their day—universally neglected by the critics—of the old New Playwrights' Theater in Grove Street. There were the Jews out of Em Jo Basshe's *The Centuries;* the street scene, with its agitators and policemen, out of Dos Passos's *Airways, Inc.;* and a general influence of the stagecraft—the set that accommodates a variety of scenes—of John H. Lawson. During the first act, I became quite interested, for it seemed to me that the writers of the New Playwrights might have founded a school, after all, and I was hoping that Mr. Anderson might have succeeded in improving on his originals. But as the play went on, I was baffled at discovering that the New Playwrights' characters were expressing themselves in blank verse of an hypnotic monotony and imagery of a dismal banality. The revolutionary social content had been extracted from the New Playwrights entirely. *Winterset* was indeed that wonderful coffee which enables you to sleep like a child. I did, in fact, fall asleep in the course of the last act and only woke up again when somebody fired a gun. All the characters were now being killed in an ending which was Elizabethan at least in its wholesale slaughter; but I was left quite unmoved by the fate of stage fictions who talked Mr. Anderson's blank verse.

I afterwards made a point of reading the text of *Winterset* in order to find out what I had missed. But the play seemed to me even feebler than it had when I had seen it on the stage. The production and the acting had invested some of the scenes with something like imagination; but in the text I could not discover anything that seemed to me in the least authentic as emotion, idea or characterization. Mr. Anderson is dealing with the aftereffects of such a tragedy as the execution of Sacco and Vanzetti. He makes the son of an anarchist father, executed for another's crime, fall in love with the sister of the real criminal, whom he has devoted his life to pursuing. The young man gives up his revenge, sparing the girl's brother and allowing himself to fall into the hands of the gang. Miriamne has come to represent for him "all hope and beauty and brightness drawn Across what's black and mean"; he wishes to emerge from "this everglades of old revenge" and "forget to hate," perhaps at last to forgive. But it is too late. The gangsters kill them both. The Talmudic old Jewish father closes the play by announcing the "masterless might" of the universe, and declaring that only the human "cry toward something dim In distance, which is higher than I am" makes man the "emperor of the endless dark even in seeking."

> this is the glory of earth-born men and women,
> not to cringe, never to yield, but standing,
> take defeat implacable and defiant,
> die unsubmitting.

But what is the point of this? Mr. Anderson's hero, Mio, has just given up his life's purpose. In what sense is his defeat "implacable and defiant"? He is supposed to be the son of an anarchist, a class-conscious victim of the class war, and such a man would scarcely have regarded the exposure of the real culprit and the vindication of his father's innocence as merely a matter of private revenge. Yet Mr. Anderson makes him succumb to his interest in a little girl whose supposed sweetness of character is made to manifest itself in speeches that sound as if they had been written under the influence of a favorite English teacher and published in the school magazine by a young daughter of the bourgeoisie; and then gives him a funeral speech—of a kind, by the way, not especially appropriate to the mentality of a Talmudic Jew—which suggests some Promethean champion of the human mind and will.

I have also read—not having seen them—*The Masque of Kings* and *High Tor,* and they make upon me the same impression of pointlessness and mediocrity. The protagonist of *The Masque of Kings* gives up his revolutionary purpose just as Mio gives up his revenge; the protagonist of *High Tor* gives up the noble stand he has taken against the vandalism of industrial development. Mr. Anderson's heroes are always retiring: they become disillusioned with their own designs before instead of after they have realized them, and this makes his dramas rather disappointing. There is never any real fight. When everything is over, some sententious character gives expression to the thought *"Sic transit gloria mundi!"* in more or less hackneyed terms, and Mr. Anderson's performance is finished.

For the rest, Mr. Stark Young has analyzed these plays as much as it is profitable to do, and he has even, I feel, sometimes been led by skillful production or acting to give them a little more credit than they deserve. He is quite kindly about *High Tor,* which seems to me—among plays that make any claim to serious consideration—one of the silliest I have ever read. I agree with Mr. Young when he says that some of the bursts of Mr. Anderson's poetic eloquence "sound like a Stephen Phillips version of an Arthur Symons translation of a decadent German versifying of a lax translation of Euripides."

Yet Maxwell Anderson's writing is not all so bad as that. The point is that in his blank verse he is seen at his worst. The prose parts of his plays are much better. And in the days when he wrote prose altogether—in *What Price Glory?* and in the hobo play that he made from Jim Tuly's *Beggars of Life*—he showed a gift for vernacular dialogue much richer and more original than anything that has appeared in his verse.

Mr. Anderson has, however, a positive conviction that plays should be written in verse. He has explained in his preface to *Winterset.* "Those," he says, "who have read their literary history carefully know that now is the time for our native amusements to be transformed into a national art of power and beauty. It needs the touch of a great poet to make the transformation, a poet comparable to Aeschylus in Greece and Marlowe in England. Without at least one such we shall never have a great theater in this country, and he must come soon, for these chances don't endure forever. I must add, lest I be misunderstood, that I have not mistaken myself for this impending phenomenon. I have made my living as teacher, journalist and playwright and have only that skill as a poet which may come from long practice of an art I have loved and studied and cannot let alone."

This assumption of Mr. Anderson's seems to me quite mistaken. It is true that verse has been passing out as a technique for writing plays; but is it true that it is really needed? After all, verse-technique has also passed out in all sorts of other departments of literature to which no one would now think of restoring it. In the last century, it was still used for novels; in the eighteenth century, for essays. Before that, in the ancient world, it was used for prophecies, laws, science, history and manuals of agriculture. Whatever the reasons for its falling into disuse, it is undeniable today that pure verse-technique has come to be employed—and is almost never otherwise effectively employed—in a narrow and specialized field: that of lyric poetry. The modern writers who come closest to the great writers of epics and the great dramatic poets of the past—the Flauberts and Tolstoys and Ibsens and Shaws and Prousts—have almost invariably written prose. At most, there is a blending with prose of something of the technique of verse: in certain writers one can see the transition quite clearly. For example, the long poems of Robinson Jeffers show a tendency to disintegrate into prose; and the prose novels of James Joyce contain vestiges of the rhythms of verse. Isn't it true that if Synge and O'Neill, of whom Mr. Anderson speaks, had lived in Otway's time, they would have still been writing their tragedies in verse? And is Mr. Maxwell Anderson prepared to assert that the plays of Molière, for example, which, through an accident purely chronological, happen partly to have been written in verse, would be the worse for having been written in prose? The mere literary technique itself is not the issue here: the technique is determined by the rhythms of speech, and it changes with these rhythms, which in turn are determined by the pace of life and, basically, by man's relation to his environment, which changes from age to age. One sees this very plainly in Ibsen, who began by writing plays in verse, of which his countrymen say he was one of their great masters, but who, outgrowing the influence of the romantic era, became later a master of prose. Does Maxwell Anderson consider that *The Wild Duck* and *Hedda Gabler* are less successful than *Brand* and *Peer Gynt*, and can he imagine them written in verse? And what could be more

synthetic than the costume-dramas of Rostand, the chief practitioner of modern poetic drama?

Mr. Anderson, it seems to me, in his own plays, has presented the most striking example of the obsolescence of verse-technique. He is capable of writing well—in prose, and when he is close to American speech. But in these recent verse-plays he writes badly—not, I think, because he is technically incompetent, but rather because English blank verse has no longer any relation to the tempo or tongue of our lives, and so can provide no vehicle for his genuine gift of dialogue: the old rhythms can inspire him to nothing but a flavorless conventional imagery that was already growing trite in our grandfathers' time. When Mr. Anderson makes an effort to combine blank verse with the language of everyday speech, he gets something, as in *Winterset*, which is neither, and dreadful. (It is true that T. S. Eliot, in *Murder in the Cathedral*, has done better with the verse-drama than Maxwell Anderson; but, to my mind, the best scenes in this play are the prose ones: the sermon and the speech of the assassins.)

I am inclined to believe, furthermore, that it is Maxwell Anderson's infatuation with blank verse that has aborted his talents all around. Along with the rhythm goes not only the imagery, but the attitude, the point of view. Instead of any sentiments that any real people might conceivably feel today in connection with the events he depicts, the commentators in Mr. Anderson's plays can only proffer the dimmest echoes of the sentiments of the Elizabethans in connection with events of quite a different character. A technique ought to grow out of the material; but Mr. Anderson is trying to impose on his a technique that has nothing to do with it. Instead of getting deeper into reality as he progresses in his artistic career, he is carried by his blank verse farther away.

ROBERT ANDERSON

1917–

Born April 28, 1917, in New York City, Robert Anderson received his A.B. in 1939 and M.A. in 1940 from Harvard University. He was a teaching assistant in English there from 1939 to 1942, when he entered the U.S. Naval Reserve. He served until 1946, winning a Bronze Star and the Army-Navy Playwriting Contest. After the war, Anderson taught at the New School for Social Research and wrote for radio and television; his first plays were produced at regional theaters.

Anderson's reputation was made when *Tea and Sympathy* became a Broadway success in 1953. Unusually frank for its time, the play established Anderson's feeling for human relationships and understanding of loneliness. A diluted film version followed in 1956. Anderson was badly shaken that year by the death of Phyllis, his wife of sixteen years. He had recovered by 1959, when he married actress Teresa Wright and premiered *Silent Night, Lonely Night*. Also that year he received an Oscar nomination for his screenplay of *The Nun's Story*. He later scripted the film *The Sand Pebbles* in 1966. *You Know I Can't Hear You When the Water's Running*, a collection of four short playlets, topped Anderson's *Tea and Sympathy* record in 1967. Less popular with audiences but more so with critics, *I Never Sang for My Father* opened the following year. It became a film in 1970; Anderson's screenplay was Oscar-nominated and won a Writers Guild of America award.

Anderson turned to writing novels in the 1970's, producing *After* (1973) and *Getting Up and Going Home* (1976). Divorced since 1978, he lives in Connecticut.

Works

Tea and Sympathy is a totally successful play because it deals with a theme which has a strong appeal to our audiences and because it is extremely well produced.

I speak of the play's theme, although I was not altogether sure at first what the theme was. Perhaps it would be more accurate to say that the play tells an interesting story which suggests a number of themes none of which are emphasized or probed at any particular depth. The story is that of a sensitive prep-school boy who on very slight evidence is suspected of being a homosexual. The suspicion is furthered because the boy is a shy, introspective adolescent given to playing the guitar, "long-haired" music, and discussion of plays like *Candida*. The main theme therefore is a defense of the special person in a society which tends to look askance at the "odd" individual, even the unpremeditated non-conformist. If the play has a message, it is to the effect that a boy like its protagonist may be more truly a man than those falsely rugged folk who oppress him.

The play also cautions us against prejudice, slander, and false accusation—in a word, is a plea for tolerance. Naturally, we are all for it: every contribution in this direction is more than welcome. Yet in this regard I cannot help thinking that we have arrived today at a peculiar brand of tolerance. We tolerate the innocent! We say "this person who is accused of being off-beat—socially, sexually, or politically—is not guilty; we must therefore be tolerant." If he is guilty, should we then tear him to bits? I should prefer to see a play in which, let us say, a homosexual is shown to be a genuinely worth-while person and the persecution that he suffers is presented as a disease within ourselves.

This thought leads me to another. In our theater we are forever beginning all over again. When O'Neill wrote his early plays, we felt we had come of age: we were now free to speak as forthrightly as any of the Europeans. We could be not only frank but, if we pleased, savage or pessimistic. Though now easily acceptable, a play like *Tea and Sympathy* is probably still regarded by many as adventurous and advanced, though it is actually primitive in its theme, characterization, and story development. It is, in fact, a very young play.

This is no adverse comment on it. It is the work of a young playwright, Robert Anderson, whose approach is honorably craftsmanlike and humane.—HAROLD CLURMAN, *Nation*, Oct. 17, 1953, pp. 317–18

Tea and Sympathy by Robert Anderson is about a private-school boy who is to lose the feeling that he is a homosexual by proving his potency with the housemaster's wife. The subject matter suggests a whole roster of other plays (*The Green Bay Tree, The Children's Hour* . . .) but most of all *Tea and Sympathy* strikes me as the 1953 version of *Young Woodley*, not so much for its plot, or even its setting, as for its relation to the public's current view of what is scandalous. The formula for such a work is Daring as Calculated Caution. Or: Audacity, Audacity, But Not Too Much Audacity. Such a play must be "bannable" on grounds of what used to be considered immoral but also defensible on grounds of what is now considered moral. Sweet are the uses of perversity.

Tea and Sympathy is a highly superior specimen of the theatre of "realist" escape. Superior in craftsmanship, superior in its isolation, combination, and manipulation of the relevant impulses and motifs. Its organization of the folklore of current fashion is so skilful, it brings us to the frontier where this sort of theatre ends. But not beyond it. One doesn't ask the questions one would ask of a really serious play. Here, in the cuckoo land of folklore, one doesn't ask how the heroine knows the hero is innocent, one doesn't permit oneself the thought that he may not be innocent, for he has an innocence of a kind the real world never supplies: an innocence complete and certified. One doesn't ask how her husband could be so unloving and yet have got her to love him: one accepts her neat, fairy-tale explanation that, one night in Italy, he needed her. One doesn't ask just how the heroine's motives are mixed—to what extent her favors are kindness, to what extent self-indulgence—for, in this realm, the author enjoys the privilege of dreamer,

neurotic, and politician to appeal to whatever motive is most attractive at the moment.—ERIC BENTLEY, "Folklore on Forty-Seventh Street," *The Dramatic Event: An American Chronicle*, 1954, pp. 150–51

Robert Anderson, whose *Tea and Sympathy* established him as one of our foremost authorities on the sensitive young man in a hostile world, has practically sewed up this title with his new play, called *All Summer Long*. . . .

The young, Mr. Anderson continues to insist, suffer with an intensity that is far beyond the average comprehension, and our society, generally speaking, is ruthlessly organized against them. Since it is without the automatic shock and calculated dénouement of its predecessor, *All Summer Long* seems to me a better and more reputable play, but I still can't help feeling that the author's tendency to identify himself with children in a child's world, to see life sheerly as a war between passionate young innocence and tarnished adult experience, keeps his work from being really very stimulating to the mature. In this case, the enormous volume of evidence advanced to prove that grownups are awful strikes me as more than a little dull, and since his contrasting affirmations of faith in their juniors depress me only slightly less, I think we'll just let that point go.

The action of the play focusses on a boy who celebrates his twelfth birthday midway in the proceedings. The argument—which I might debate but won't—is that this is a peculiarly significant age. Social criticism is born, and for the first time the child is aware of cruelty, vulgarity, and futility, and, of course, their opposites, as actual qualities in those around him. It is a time when models for future behavior are chosen, when the first genuine moral decisions are made, and, especially, when sex can turn into a wonder or a horror overnight. . . .

Together, the brothers meet and rout the family's concerted efforts to corrupt the younger boy's dreams, and together they try to fight back the river, and though they fail pathetically at that, the great affirmative lesson is learned. This would seem to be that, on the whole, love and faith are better weapons than hatred and despair, and what reasonable man would think of quarrelling with that? In justice to Mr. Anderson, it should be stated that *All Summer Long* contains a good many quite funny and touching things. The complaints against it here are, first, that there are not nearly enough of them; second, that the drawing of character in almost absolute terms of black and white has a rather naïve air on a modern stage; and, third, that having said just about the same thing once, the author might have been well advised to refrain from saying it again.—WOLCOTT GIBBS, "More Tea," NY, Oct. 2, 1954, pp. 63–67

In Robert Anderson's *Silent Night, Lonely Night* which opened at the Morosco last evening, Barbara Bel Geddes and Henry Fonda conduct a long discussion of love, marriage and adultery.

Since Miss Bel Geddes and Mr. Fonda are golden people with persuasive voices, it is easy to believe that what they say is true. Never a false note in their arias of words. But after an act and a half of recollections and rationalizations, a theatregoer cannot be blamed if he wishes that Mr. Anderson and his actors would please change the subject.

In a beautiful New England inn (gloriously designed by Jo Mielziner) two lonely people in adjoining rooms meet on Christmas Eve. He is in a mournful mood because his wife is confined in a mental institution on the village hill. She is in a mournful mood because her husband, in London on business, has confessed to an infidelity. They are, in the phrase of the man, the "whistling, walking wounded."

For an act and a half they tell each other the unhappy

stories of their lives and resist adultery for noble reasons. Between the first and second scenes of the second act, however, they resort to adultery to assuage their grief. For all practical purposes this seems to solve their problems. On Christmas Day they are both refreshed, and they resume their separate married lives in good heart.

To Mr. Anderson, all this doubtless has a private significance that has to be respected. But his elegy on marriage is performed in public and has to be judged by public standards. They are likely to seem a little chilly to Mr. Anderson. Although the dialogue is written by a man who respects the graces of style, *Silent Night, Lonely Night* is excessively verbose. It is also uneventful. *Two for the Seesaw* was hardly more constricted in scope.

Doubtless Peter Glenville has the soundest of reasons for directing the performance with a slow, ruminative pace. Two people under heavy private burdens are talking about intimate affairs reluctantly and are not likely to be glib at their first meeting.

Miss Bel Geddes and Mr. Fonda make their characters winning. Even in a mood of grief, she is sunny and beautiful; she speaks her lines with a reticent inflection that is disarming. He lounges across the stage and talks with a leisurely deliberation that makes everything seem spontaneous and genuine. Although Miss Bel Geddes and Mr. Fonda are skillful actors, they have also been abundantly gifted by nature. . . .

At brief intervals they are joined by other agreeable actors ⟨who⟩ bring a little variety from the outside into Mr. Anderson's series of confessions by two grieving people. But *Silent Night, Lonely Night* is also a long night. During the discussion between the man and the woman, one phrase turns up frequently: "I'm so sorry." Perhaps that would be a suitable phrase with which to conclude this notice.—BROOKS ATKINSON, "Theatre: *Silent Night, Lonely Night*," NYT, Dec. 4, 1959, p. 36

A slightly impertinent question that occurred to me during the dining-out scene in *I Never Sang for My Father* was "Is Robert Anderson for or against Schrafft's?" As in most of the play's many scenes, the playwright obviously sees the humor and pathos of each typical family activity, but deliberately refrains from ridicule or anger. Presumably he does so because his protagonist, a fortyish son with a compulsion to be kind to his parents, would in real life also refrain from taking these more dramatic attitudes. The hope is, of course, that the theatergoer will recognize himself in the exercise of such restraint. And indeed what emerges from his new play is a gentle reminder of how well-to-do American families unintentionally pollute the lives of their members.

But what also emerges is a kind of dull disappointment in the ordinariness and familiarity of it all. The play begins rather promisingly as the son, Gene, steps forward to share his intelligence with us. His philosophical statement, "Death ends a life but not a relationship, which struggles on in the survivor's mind towards a resolution it may never find," is spoken in a special density of light that suggests the mysterious area of the subconscious. Then by a subtle brightening of the lights we bob up to the surface of the play's actuality, to meet the son's aged parents returning from a Florida vacation.

There is some amusement in the rambunctious rudeness of the father, who insists upon worrying about loss of his luggage, despite the ludicrous fact that he can't even remember what his bags look like. And there is also fun in the mother—about whose health the father pretends to be concerned—

voicing her real anxiety about her husband's cough. But from this point on it is all only a sporadically engaging demonstration of the falseness of the family's interrelationships. Theoretically, this demonstration is leading Gene to an understanding of the truth about himself and his father, but as the playwright has warned us, resolution is not to be expected in his play any more than it is in life.

Thus when in the play's second act Gene's sister shows up to face him down with the psychoanalytic truth of his behavior, we are not very surprised. And there is insufficient time for a really convincing Freudian explanation to be expounded. Not that there isn't something very profound in a self-centered father who regards his son as a dividend, and who exploits his guilt, but the playwright doesn't stay underwater long enough.

One suspects that the whole play would have benefited had it stayed more consistently within the mysterious world of memory as did *The Glass Menagerie*. For the best parts of *I Never Sang for My Father* are those that treat its important and unusual subject least literally and least logically. Unfortunately, they are outnumbered by the drearier ones in which the playwright's sense of fair play and verisimilitude prevail.—HENRY HEWES, "Fair Play for Schrafft's," SR, Feb. 10, 1968, p. 39

Another addition to the two-character bedroom boom is Robert Anderson's *Silent Night, Lonely Night* (1959). There are minor characters in the play, but the action centers on the man and woman in a New England inn on Christmas Eve. They are middle-aged, unhappy in their marriages, and terribly despondent. Katherine is opposed to adultery, for she comes of stern moral background. John Sparrow, guilt-laden about his wife's mental illness, has had previous affairs but has always remained coldly distant, unable to feel a sincere emotion. They circle back and forth in their preparation for the affair, with the telephone handy as a means of communication with the missing mates. Sex again is salvation, and the implicit approval of extramarital relations is mitigated by each one's returning to his marriage in the end, better prepared to endure his unhappiness. . . . The Christmas background implied the religious approval of resurrection through adultery. The play is amazingly devoid of action, a subdued, nonviolent, and often graceful discussion of two people's quest for human warmth, but it falls into the trap of skirting the forbidden and restoring the accepted.

Tea and Sympathy (1953), Robert Anderson's first play, which has become a standard vehicle in summer stock, did indicate a delicacy of feeling and show skill in constructing a realistic suspense drama. Anderson intended to have Tom Lee a nonconformist, the young man who cannot bring himself to engage in the usual vulgarities of school life. The accusation of homosexuality dominates the play. The now-famous resolution in which Laura Reynolds, the housemaster's wife, unbuttons her blouse and invites Tom to the proof of his manhood has little relation to the logic of the plot, but is a nicely superimposed shock-ending. Anderson's other play, *All Summer Long* (1954), was based on Donald Wetzel's novel *A Wreath and a Curse*, and is less concerned with sex. A boy builds a retaining wall to save the family house from the expected flood, while the adults are too busy with their petty bickering to become involved in anything beyond the self. Anderson has spent five years as a Hollywood screenwriter, but is now returning to the theatre. He is engaged in a musical version of the motion picture *Roman Holiday*, a reversal of the usual practice in which Broadway musicals become Hollywood pictures, and has completed another play about marital difficulty, *The Days Between*.—ALLAN LEWIS, "The Emergent Dreams—Kingsley, Inge & Co.," *American Plays and Playwrights of the Contemporary Theatre*, 1970, pp. 155–56

JOHN GASSNER

"Affirmations?"

Theatre at Crossroads

1960, pp. 289–93

It would have been difficult to find a more intelligent and sensitive playwright for the assignment of dramatizing Donald Wetzel's *A Wreath and a Curse*, the novel upon which *All Summer Long* was based. Nobody familiar with *Tea and Sympathy* could doubt that Robert Anderson would make sensitive drama out of the tensions of these confused young characters who receive little sympathy, guidance, or encouragement from their bumbling elders. Anderson did make sensitive drama out of the substance of the book, and Alan Schneider's production of *All Summer Long*, in the intimacy of a small arena theatre, apparently brought out such appealing qualities in the play that expectations for the success of the dramatization on Broadway ran high. But these were not realized. . . .

While one cannot generalize in speaking of ethnic or national qualities it does seem that the extravagant world of Chekhov, a world he could not have entirely invented, offers a richer supply of attractive, amusing and moving failures than the world of Robert Anderson's *All Summer Long*. The characters of the book were drab and commonplace, unstimulating and unamusing representatives of lower middle-class life. . . .

New York reviewers evinced various degrees of affection for *All Summer Long*. The play presents the stalemate of a family engaged in petty interests while its home is being undermined, both literally and symbolically, by erosion. Only the twelve-year-old son, Willie, encouraged and watched over by the elder, temporarily crippled brother Don, makes an effort to save the home. But the stone wall the lad has built all summer long with insufficient strength and resources gives way in the end, and the hapless family is compelled to abandon the house.

A just appraisal of Robert Anderson's second Broadway work must distribute praise and blame. Praise should be given to some excellent details of characterization and feeling; blame to laboriousness in underscoring the lesson and for a general mildness of action and characterization. An excellent argument may be advanced against the requirement of an exciting plot, but only if the author's work on theme and characters provides an inner excitement of its own. *All Summer Long* drifted too long before coming to its conclusion. If no objection could be raised against the expectedness of the conclusion itself—who does not expect Chekhov's Cherry Orchard family to lose its estate—our judgment of the play was nevertheless affected by the degree to which interest was sustained while we were waiting for the blow to fall. How much interest could we take in those who endeavored to avert the blow and failed to do so. How much concern for whether or not the blow would fall? In *All Summer Long* the movement of the play was too uneventful, and some torpor overcame us while we were being languidly carried toward the catastrophe.

The drift of the characters was the very subject of the dramatization, and their lassitude gave an aura to their personality that was distinctly attractive. It was possible to agree with those reviewers who found *All Summer Long* appealing, for Robert Anderson's talent made it possible for us to take some interest in the play's characters, especially in the little boy who patiently erected his pitifully inadequate stone wall against erosion. But it is also true that the characters were not particularly engrossing on their own merits. One of the principals, Don, who encourages his little brother with lectures while indulging his own melancholy, did not wear well. One could only wish that the playwright had managed to make the drifters and their drift more arresting and poignant. More poetry of characterization and symbolism was needed to avoid the mild depressiveness of the family drama. It is a pity that the proper and full employment of a keen sensibility is so difficult and rare on the contemporary American stage with native middle-class characters. Which is perhaps only another way of saying that Chekhovian artistry has a difficult time of it in our theatre.

It is interesting to observe how the sensibilities of a writer like Robert Anderson have fared in this extrovert theatre of ours. Whereas the Chekhovian progression of *All Summer Long* was a descending one, *Tea and Sympathy*, written later but produced earlier on Broadway, had an ascending movement. It also had a sensational conclusion and a dramatic pressure that propelled the action forward in spurts of intrigue, conflict, discoveries, and reversals.

Tea and Sympathy, a work of greater sensitivity than *All Summer Long*, consists of one activated situation after another. An adolescent at a boarding school comes under suspicion of homosexuality because he prefers the refinements of art to the customary manly sports. The insensitivity of his classmates is compounded by the curious relentlessness of his sports-minded schoolmaster and the obtuseness of his father. When the boy is overcome by the realization that he is considered abnormal a classmate prevails upon him to disprove the accusation by going to a prostitute. His failure with her, the cause of which is obviously the coarseness of the woman, nearly destroys his self-confidence. He might resign himself to homosexuality as his natural condition but for the intervention of the wife of the athletic schoolmaster. The schoolmaster's persecution of the boy has become intolerable to her. The play concludes with her taking matters into her own hands. An unloved wife, she puts her athlete-husband in his place by pointing out to him that it is he who is the latent homosexual, a fact that his penchant for going out camping with the boys confirms rather than refutes. In persecuting the suspected adolescent he is really punishing himself as well as trying to suppress his own propensities. Having sent her husband away she then turns her attention to the desperate boy and allays his fears by giving herself to him.

It is hardly necessary to point out that the progression of this play consists of one theatrical reversal after another. We arrive at one high point when the wife pins the charge of homosexuality on the manly teacher and at another high, indeed distinctly sensational point, when the woman offers herself to the adolescent in order to save him from a dangerously wrong opinion of himself. Under the spell of the action and the attractive personality of Deborah Kerr the questionable features of this climax were likely to be overlooked. The boy's libido might easily have failed him again, for instance, if for no other reason than that she is his schoolmaster's wife as well as a person who could have overawed him with her dignity. Even at the considerable risk of forcing the development of events and of moving toward a hazardous resolution Anderson, abetted by the explosive talent of his director, Elia Kazan, took his drama of adolescence out of the cherry orchard. Whatever we may think of his means we can hardly doubt that Robert Anderson's decidedly un-Chekhovian play-writing sustained the interest of his public and secured his sensitivity a place in the popular American theatre.

It is greatly to Anderson's credit that he was not at all content to have his say exclusively in the terms of overt and sensational action that first made him a successful Broadway playwright. *All Summer Long* reached New York after *Tea and Sympathy*, but the play showed no sign of having been sensationalized for the Times Square super market. Anderson's last play of the Fifties, *Silent Night, Lonely Night*, was an exercise in restraint. Not many reviewers appreciated the discipline he imposed on himself in his story of two lonely adults who find each other on Christmas night only to part the next morning, the hero going to his mentally disturbed wife, the heroine to her unfaithful husband. . . .

Complicating events were sparse in *Silent Night, Lonely Night*. These could have been supplied easily enough if the author had been willing to contrive a plot. But he would have regarded such tinkering with the feelings of his characters or with their limited capacity for action as an act of sacrilege. He rested his case instead solely on the shy rapprochement of two people and took the calculated risk of exhibiting nothing else on the stage. It was quite a risk to take on Broadway but it was worth taking for those of us, apparently a minority, who were held by the author's finely spun web of feeling and insight. I enroll myself with that minority, although I believe that ideally *Silent Night, Lonely Night* should have been a long one-act play in two or three scenes. (It is deplorable that playwrights aiming for a Broadway production have to observe a conventional length in their playwriting.)

But the Anglo-Saxon stiffness or restraint in the relationships of the two protagonists, while thoroughly natural in the play, is far removed from the buoyancy and rich variety of tone and mood that enabled Chekhov to turn even stalemate into drama. When the curtain fell on *Silent Night, Lonely Night* one felt that the author had gone as far as it was possible to go with his subject matter and that he had even taken longer than necessary to get there.

SAMUEL J. BERNSTEIN
From *"Double Solitare* by Robert Anderson"
The Strands Entwined
1980, pp. 93–105

In *Double Solitaire*, a play that many critics believe to be his best, or at least his best since *Tea and Sympathy*, Robert Anderson makes his most trenchant and personal statement on marriage. The play centers on Charley and Barbara Potter, who must decide whether or not to renew their marriage vows on their twenty-fifth anniversary, as Charley's parents, Ernest and Elizabeth Potter, had done twenty-five years before. The occasion for the decision is the forthcoming fiftieth wedding anniversary of the elder Potters. The elder Potters would feel proud, would perhaps receive a kind of *Good Housekeeping* Seal of Approval on their own marriage if their children would assert this same gesture of faith in marriage. The request by the parents, made individually to Barbara by Mrs. Potter and to Charley by his aggressive father, precipitates a crisis, a crisis already long in preparation in the lives of Barbara and Charley.

The question that informs the entire play is: Will Barbara and Charley stay together or separate? In essence, this is what their decision to renew or not renew their vows would mean. The deeper question raised is: What kind of an institution is marriage? Is it good or bad inherently? Is it good for some but not for others, and, if it can be good, does its goodness last?

As the curtain rises, Barbara, age forty-one, is sitting at stage left; Charley, age forty-three, is sitting at stage right. The stage is bare with the exception of a round table and two chairs at each side. The elder Mrs. Potter enters, speaks with Barbara, and walks off into the shadows. Mr. Potter then enters and speaks to Charley; within the dialogue, the elder Mr. Potter's speeches are often long enough to be considered monologues. In each case the elder person tells the younger of marital incompatibility and adjustments. The elder Potters reveal that they play double solitaire and fill their lives with a round of activities that prevent personal isolation. Mrs. Potter enjoys her poetry readings, her garden, her sewing, and her church work. . . .

While the play explores the conflict between Barbara and Charley, its scope is larger; it ultimately succeeds in putting all marriages on trial. In so doing, the play makes one of the most tortured, honest, and sensitive explorations of marriage in American theatre. It is in terms of this fundamental exploration, this examination of the inherent and ultimate value of marriage, that Sylvia's timeless and almost placeless appearance makes its special, and especially subtle, aesthetic contribution.

Sylvia is a woman who found that she was not well suited to marriage. While married, she was irritable, demanding, and boring, and she let herself go physically. When she broke off with her husband, she lost weight and began to feel better about herself. Since her divorce, she has seen a different man each night of the week, and not only for sex. This life has pleased her. Although friends have told her that she may be lonely when she gets older, and although she relies on a dog for companionship on Mother's Day, Christmas, and other "tribal times," she has rejected many marriage offers (all of which, she claims, were made just when the men were getting tired of making a real effort). She feels it is better to live an exciting, episodic life (despite the prospect of ultimate loneliness) than to submit to a boring exercise in mere security.

As is obvious, Sylvia, in the singularity of her monologist's role and in the content of her remarks, raises many questions that bear both on the Charley-Barbara reaffirmation decision and on the whole question of marriage itself. She intensifies the uncertainties about marriage in general and about both Potter marriages in particular. She also provides potential behavioral options for Barbara, options that remain active possibilities even after the play concludes. Sylvia's appearing from the shadows gives her an incorporeity and abstract dimension that complement the believable personal dimension of her stage appearance and her use of believable, familiar language. Sylvia's function is complex, poetic, and part of an image of overall fragmentation both in the lives of Charley and Barbara and in the institution of marriage, which George, a later character, describes as a dying institution in a period of transition.

What we have said of Anderson's portrayal of Sylvia and of his experimentation with time and setting is true of the subsequent episodes and characters as well. After Sylvia's monologue, Charley speaks in succession with his friend George, a writer whose work he edits; with his son Peter; and, finally, with his wife. While there exist many aesthetic motivations for the George conversation to precede the Peter conversation, there are no purely, or predominantly important rational ones; again, we are not absolutely certain that Charley speaks with George before he speaks with Peter or that either of these conversations occurs prior to Sylvia's monologue. So much of what occurs is part of Barbara and Charley's independent thought processes and is also part of the abstract, essentially dimensionless probing of marriage. The free, somewhat mysterious and flexible arrangement of conversational incidents mirrors the anguish of the younger Potters and permits the detailed, sinuous exploration of the larger question without creating dullness. That there is a kind of geometric balance of speeches and characters in the play provides a tension-creating superstructure that keeps us emotionally involved as we learn and assimilate details and consider theoretical questions. . . .

Just before she submits, Barbara expresses uncertainty as to whether they will be together two years hence. Therefore, the play leaves many questions unresolved; most importantly, we are left to ponder its central dramatic question: will or should Barbara and Charley stay together? In a "well-made play," we would be directed toward an answer. However, Anderson elects not to wrap things up so tidily. Instead, he provides us with a thorough exploration of "a marriage on the rocks" and some very trenchant criticism of the marriage institution itself. Rarely has any writer written so sincerely, so personally, and yet so dispassionately of portions of human experience that are usually hidden away and left unexplored. By doing this, he confronts pain.

Unlike the "well-made play," in which great care is expended on preparation for or foreshadowing of all future developments, *Double Solitaire* presents a series of random core incidents. Its development is not based on a "logic of events." Although it is somewhat foreshadowed, even the final scene occurs without any clear sense of inevitability; yet, it is fully within the realm of verisimilitude. No twisted incidents, no secret letters or delayed messengers mar the play; the final scene occurs gracefully, growing out of the play's total aesthetic, not out of any logical or mechanistic formula.

Whether the term "well-made play" is a useful critical conception or merely a misleading and exclusivist tag is a moot point. If we do assume that it is a formal and precise critical category, as we have hypothesized in this examination, we must surely exclude Robert Anderson's *Double Solitaire* from this category. Anderson's play is not mechanical; rationalistic; grounded simply in logic; bound by cause and effect; unidimensional; or beset by the sometimes tortured, artificial devices of playwrights intent on "well-made" works with clear, simple conclusions. Rather, it is a sensitive, multidimensional, episodic, detailed exploration of marriage as a highly troubled institution clung to by very vulnerable individuals. It is honest and direct, and it uses many experimental devices to move itself along. As Anderson himself has said:

> This is not a "well-made play." The structure is far more complex than that term would suggest. Into the play *Double Solitaire*, I put everything I knew about playwriting.

Besides being a playwright of renown, a teacher of playwriting, and a script writer for radio and films, Anderson is a student of English letters who is certainly aware of traditions. These facts alone ought to discourage an application of the "well-made play" rubric; *Double Solitaire* is an experiment in dramaturgy, drawing upon and blending many of the techniques of the past and adding some truly novel touches as well. More experimental than the actual structure is the the subject itself; Anderson's exploration of love and marriage is unique in its depth and honesty. The playwright who first treated homosexuality on the American stage, who preceded and foreshadowed the existence and comicality of the Theater of Nudity, who showed that polite conversation can still form the heart of dramatic experience in *Silent Night, Lonely Night*, and who demonstrated that a keen comic skill also lay within his ken in *You Know I Can't Hear You When the Water's Running*, has made an important and truly innovative contribution to dramaturgy in *Double Solitaire*.

Sherwood Anderson

1876–1941

Born in Ohio in 1876, one of seven children, Sherwood Anderson once claimed that his first exercises in fiction were imaginative reworkings of his father's tall tales. The family spent Sherwood's early years moving from one small Ohio town to another. His formal education was scanty: he left school at fourteen, probably because the family needed money.

As a young man, Anderson served in Cuba during the Spanish-American war, and after the war returned to Ohio to manage a paint factory. It was at this factory that his now famous "awakening" occurred. As he described it, he suddenly realized one day as he was sitting in his office that freedom from the paint factory was only a few short steps away, and acting on this moment of enlightenment, he walked away and left the factory forever.

Anderson soon left for Chicago and the beginning of his literary career. His association with the "Chicago Group," which included Theodore Dreiser, Carl Sandburg, Sinclair Lewis, and Willa Cather, eventually enabled the publication of his writing. By 1921, he was sufficiently well established to afford a year in Europe. On his return, he lived briefly in New Orleans and New York, but soon decided that he preferred small town life. He bought a farm and a newspaper in Virginia in 1924, and spent most of the rest of his life there. A prolific writer, he wrote for and edited two papers, continuing to publish fiction, much of it autobiographical. Anderson married four times and had three children. He died in Panama, where he succumbed to peritonitis while en route to Latin America.

Among his major works are *Mid-American Chants* (1918), *Many Marriages* (1922), and *Hello, Towns* (1929). He is best-known, however, for *Winesburg, Ohio*, published in 1919.

Personal

In the ingenuousness with which he articulated his creed of the artist as a folk-inspired amateur and in the insistence with which he rehearsed, through a variety of symbolic guises, his liberation from the bourgeois world, Anderson made of his life a culture-legend which often overshadowed his work. This legend soon became a model of the struggle for artic-ulation—or rather the struggle for identity through a cathartic articulation—in which so many untutored but gifted young American writers invariably engaged. Just as Anderson always found it necessary to erect elaborate barriers against the world from which he had escaped in 1912, so they wrote to purge themselves, again and again, of its corruptions, its barbarisms, and its constrictions. That world, however, was not easily shaken off and it showed its ultimate power over American writers in their compulsive need to expend a high proportion of their energy in denying it. For Anderson and for others like him, writing was at least as much a means by which to forge a personal identity as it was an objective discipline of the imag-ination. No wonder so many of the writers who came after Anderson, both Thomas Wolfe the individual and the in-numerable facsimile Thomas Wolfes, recognized in their lives one or another variant of his legend. Anderson seemed the archetype of all those writers who were trying to raise them-selves to art by sheer emotion and sheer will, who suspected intellect as a cosmopolitan snare that would destroy their gift for divining America's mystic essence, and who abominated the society which had formed them but knew no counterpoise of value by which to escape its moral dominion.—IRVING HOWE, *Sherwood Anderson*, 1951, pp. 246–47

One day during the months while we walked and talked in New Orleans—or Anderson talked and I listened—I found him sit-ting on a bench in Jackson Square, laughing with himself. I got the impression that he had been there like that for some time, just sitting alone on the bench laughing with himself. This was not our usual meeting place. We had none. He lived above the Square, and without any especial prearrangement, after I had had something to eat at noon and knew that he had finished his lunch too, I would walk in that direction and if I did not meet him already strolling or sitting in the Square, I myself would simply sit down on the curb where I could see his doorway and wait until he came out of it in his bright, half-racetrack, half-Bohemian clothes.

This time he was already sitting on the bench, laughing. He told me what it was at once: a dream: he had dreamed the night before that he was walking for miles along country roads, leading a horse which he was trying to swap for a night's sleep—not for a simple bed for the night, but for the sleep itself; and with me to listen now, went on from there, elaborat-ing it, building it into a work of art with the same tedious (it had the appearance of fumbling but actually it wasn't: it was seeking, hunting) almost excruciating patience and humility with which he did all his writing, me listening and believing no word of it: that is, that it had been any dream dreamed in sleep. Because I knew better. I knew that he had invented it, made it; he had made most of it or at least some of it while I was there watching and listening to him. He didn't know why he had been compelled, or anyway needed, to claim it had been a dream, why there had to be that connection with dream and sleep, but I did. It was because he had written his whole biog-raphy into an anecdote or perhaps a parable: the horse (it had been a racehorse at first, but now it was a working horse, plow carriage and saddle, sound and strong and valuable, but with-out recorded pedigree) representing the vast rich strong docile

sweep of the Mississippi Valley, his own America, which he in his bright blue racetrack shirt and vermilion-mottled Bohe-mian Windsor tie, was offering with humor and patience and humility, but mostly with patience and humility, to swap for his own dream of purity and integrity and hard and unremitting work and accomplishment, of which *Winesburg, Ohio* and *The Triumph of the Egg* had been symptoms and symbols.

He would never have said this, put it into words, himself. He may never have been able to see it even, and he certainly would have denied it, probably pretty violently, if I had tried to point it out to him. But this would not have been for the reason that it might not have been true, nor for the reason that, true or not, he would not have believed it. In fact, it would have made little difference whether it was true or not or whether he be-lieved it or not. He would have repudiated it for the reason which was the great tragedy of his character. He expected peo-ple to make fun of, ridicule him. He expected people nowhere near his equal in stature or accomplishment or wit or anything else, to be capable of making him appear ridiculous.

That was why he worked so laboriously and tediously and indefatigably at everything he wrote. It was as if he said to himself: 'This anyway will, shall, must be invulnerable.' It was as though he wrote not even out of the consuming unsleeping appeaseless thirst for glory for which any normal artist would destroy his aged mother, but for what to him was more impor-tant and urgent: not even for mere truth, but for purity, the exactitude of purity. His was not the power and rush of Mel-ville, who was his grandfather, nor the lusty humor for living of Twain, who was his father; he had nothing of the heavy-handed disregard for nuances of his older brother, Dreiser. His was that fumbling for exactitude, the exact word and phrase within the limited scope of a vocabulary controlled and even repressed by what was in him almost a fetish of simplicity, to milk them both dry, to seek always to penetrate to thought's uttermost end. He worked so hard at this that it finally became just style: an end instead of a means: so that he presently came to believe that, provided he kept the style pure and intact and unchanged and inviolate, what the style contained would have to be first rate: it couldn't help but be first rate, and therefore himself too. . . .

The exactitude of purity, or the purity of exactitude: whichever you like. He was a sentimentalist in his attitude toward people, and quite often incorrect about them. He be-lieved in people, but it was as though only in theory. He expected the worst from them, even while each time he was prepared again to be disappointed or even hurt, as if it had never happened before, as though the only people he could really trust, let himself go with, were the ones of his own invention, the figments and symbols of his own fumbling dream. And he was sometimes a sentimentalist in his writing (so was Shakespeare sometimes) but he was never impure in it. He never scanted it, cheapened it, took the easy way; never failed to approach writing except with humility and an almost religious, almost abject faith and patience and willingness to surrender, relinquish himself to and into it. He hated glibness; if it were quick, he believed it was false too.—WILLIAM FAULK-NER, "A Note on Sherwood Anderson" (1953), *Essays, Speeches and Public Letters*, ed. James B. Meriwether, 1965, pp. 3–7

Of his life Sherwood Anderson always wished to construct a parable, even a myth. It had various forms, but they all sprang from a central action. The central action is this: on November 27, 1912, a successful manufacturer in the town of Elyria, Ohio, dreaming sometimes of becoming a great benevolent tycoon, chafing more often at the stultifying routines of promotion and salesmanship, Sherwood Anderson, aged thirty-six, walked out of his office and away from his wife and family into the freedom of a wandering literary life, never to return to business. "'For the rest of my life I will be a servant to [words] alone,' I whispered to myself as I went along a spur of railroad track, over a bridge, out of a town and out of that phase of my life."

It is a pretty fable that has considerable psychological relevance to the lives of many modern American writers even when its literal relevance is as slight as it was to the facts of Anderson's life. . . .

In the opening year of the twentieth century, significantly enough, Sherwood Anderson became an advertising man, and soon he was writing copy in which, very much in keeping with the times, he glorified what was then called the "adventure" of business. Always attractive to women, he married a girl above him in social station, moved to Cleveland where he became the president of a mail-order firm, and from there to Elyria, Ohio, where he presently bought a paint factory that produced something called "Roof-Fix." Wanting to "ennoble" that business activity which he had chosen as his own, he was at the same time writing what he called "lies" in his advertising copy. A conflict developed between his wish to succeed in the ordinary commercial world and his wish to escape into the imaginative world and into real writing.

He read a good deal, and it was probably now that he came across *Three Lives*. More and more he brooded about the character of the artist and about his situation in an industrial society. In about 1910, like Gertrude Stein when she gave up translating Flaubert, Anderson, having translated Stein, began to write short fiction of his own, and by 1912 he had written drafts of what would become his first two novels. At the same time, torn by conflict, he had taken to drink, turned from his wife to the comforts of loose women, and was neglecting his business, which suffered accordingly. If, in his later recollections, he was to say that he let people think he was a little mad so that his creditors would forgive him when he deserted his business, the fact is that he *was* a little mad. On November 27, 1912, that famous day of sudden rebellion and liberation, his nerves collapsed. Four days later, haggard, disheveled, and suffering from aphasia—a loss of the power of speech—he was found wandering around Cleveland in a daze and was hospitalized by the police. Late in December his wife brought him back to Elyria. In February 1913 he disposed of his business and left alone for Chicago to return to the servitude of advertising. He was now thirty-six years old, his marriage would last another two years (when he would marry a sculptress named Tennessee Mitchell), but he would continue in advertising for another ten years. So much for the fable!—MARK SCHORER, *The World We Imagine*, 1968, pp. 306–8

General

If Sinclair Lewis dramatized the new realism by making the novel an exact and mimetic transcription of American life, Anderson was fascinated by the undersurface of that life and became the voice of its terrors and exultations. Lewis turned the novel into a kind of higher journalism; Anderson turned fiction into a substitute for poetry and religion, and never ceased to wonder at what he had wrought. He had more intensity than a revival meeting and more tenderness than God; he wept, he chanted, he loved indescribably. There was freedom in the air, and he would summon all Americans to share in it; there was confusion and mystery on the earth, and he would summon all Americans to wonder at it. He was clumsy and sentimental; he could even write at times as if he were finger-painting; but at the moment it seemed as if he had sounded the depths of common American experience as no one else could.

There was always an image in Anderson's books—an image of life as a house of doors, of human beings knocking at them and stealing through one door only to be stopped short before another as if in a dream. Life was a dream to him, and he and his characters seemed always to be walking along its corridors. Who owned the house of life? How did one escape after all? No one in his books ever knew, Anderson least of all. Yet slowly and fumblingly he tried to make others believe, as he thought he had learned for himself, that it was possible to escape if only one laughed at necessity. That was his own story, as everything he wrote—the confession in his *Memoirs* was certainly superfluous—was a variation upon it; and it explained why, for all his fumbling and notorious lack of contemporary sophistication, he had so great an appeal for the restive postwar generation. For Anderson, growing up in small Ohio villages during the eighties and nineties at a time when men could still watch and wait for the new industrial world to come in, enjoyed from the first—at least in his own mind—the luxury of dreaming away on the last margin of the old pre-factory freedom, of being suspended between two worlds.—ALFRED KAZIN, "The New Realism: Sherwood Anderson and Sinclair Lewis," *On Native Grounds*, 1942, pp. 210–11

The Andersonian village is examined "from within." Anderson bothers little with the placid and deceptive exteriors of village life, but is concerned primarily with the feelings of those who live within the narrow confines of village society. The energy of the villager has only infrequent opportunity for expression; most often it fails to appear at all, except in violent explosions of emotion, affective orgies, which erupt and disturb mightily the calm surface of appearances. The forces that keep emotional expression imprisoned are often the conventions of the village, and the tendency to misunderstand pure for impure motives; not unusually, however, it is the timidity of the villager himself, who permits the curtailment of his emotional life because he is afraid of his strength. Hatred of the conventions or hatred of persons serves to deflect the energies of men from what might be their normal outlets. Escape from boredom, or from a worse fate, disgrace in the eyes of the community, is manifested in little, symptomatic acts—such as Doc Reefy's "paper pills" or Adolph Myers's nervous gestures with his hands—or in symbolic substitutes for actual sensual gratification. The revelation to the Reverend Curtis Hartman, for example, satisfies him because he has observed the hand of God laid on the "immoral" naked form of a woman. For Anderson's villagers the body is fundamentally a medium of expression; no force can effectively silence the body without making it ugly. The desire for wealth has caused Tom Butterworth to neglect the life of the body, makes him a servant of industrial masters; all of his relationships with his wife and daughter are distorted and twisted as a consequence. Clara's "coming of age" temporarily arouses his interest in the body: "As in the days of his courtship of her mother and before the possessive passion in him destroyed his ability to love, he began to feel vaguely that life about him was full of significance" (*Poor White*). But this new interest is soon counteracted by suspicion of his daughter's actions; he refuses to allow her any normal outlets for her newly awakened passion, and ships her off to the state university at the earliest opportunity.

Are not these examples evidences of "neurosis through repression"? Not altogether—and in some respects, not at all. For Anderson has another explanation for many of these acts—the native inarticulateness of the Middle Westerner. The valiant soul of which Anderson speaks will rebel against conformity and defeat it; but the average, all-too-human townsman suppresses the beauty or the yearning in his soul, and appears inarticulate and weak in his community. To Anderson the forces which deprived man of the simple, beautiful life are sometimes social and economic; but it is man's inherent timidity, his unwillingness or his inability to circumvent the laws and restrictions of the "just" which account mainly for his conformity. The life within him is stilled for lack of courage; if it is ever revealed, the realization comes in moments of poignant sorrow, or violent, deathly revolt. . . .

Anderson's themes are primarily bound by his search for the causes of man's frustration. What makes men more decent and moral, than healthy and sensual beings? The figures of *Winesburg, Ohio*, and of *Poor White* are victims of both external restrictions and of their own timidity—a sort of perverted gentleness. The source of much impotence lies in basic repressions of society—the business world, industrialism, middle-class decorum. Anderson is anxious to point out that primitive life is unimpeded by such barriers to happiness. He offers a variety of suggestions to imprisoned man: the totalitarian, rhythmic discipline preached by Beaut McGregor in *Marching Men*; simple repudiation, as practised by John Webster in *Many Marriages* and by Aline Grey in *Dark Laughter*; the communism of *Beyond Desire*. Fundamentally, Anderson offers no real solution to the problems he raises.—FREDERICK J. HOFFMAN, *Freudianism and the Literary Mind*, 1957, pp. 241–48

What Anderson did for younger writers was to open vistas by finding new depths or breadths of feeling in everyday American life. Again with Whitman he might have boasted that he led each of them to a knoll, from which he pointed to "landscapes of continents, and a plain public road." He gave them each a moment of vision, and then the younger writer trudged off toward his separate destiny, often without looking back. Rereading Anderson's work after many years, one is happy to find that its moments of vision are as fresh and moving as ever. They are what James Joyce called "epiphanies"; that is, they are moments at which a character, a landscape, or a personal relation stands forth in its essential nature or "whatness," with its past and future revealed as if by a flash of lightning. For Anderson each of the moments was a story in itself. The problem he almost never solved was how to link one moment with another in a pattern of causality, or how to indicate the passage of time.—MALCOLM COWLEY, "Anderson's Lost Days of Innocence," *NR*, Feb. 15, 1960, p. 16

In his photographs he often showed his hair hanging over his eyes. The affectation means a great deal: first mere arty affectation (how he loved the "free spirits" of Greenwich Village and New Orleans!), then something feminine and wanting to be pretty and lovable for prettiness, and then of course the blurring of sight when you try to see through your own hair. What do you see? A world organized by your hair. "I must snap my finger at the world. . . . I have thought of everyone and everything." His sympathy and his oceanic feelings alternate with arrogant despair in which the arrogance can deceive no one. So desperately hurt he is, trying so hard to convince the "word-fellows" he wanted to admire him. But then his nostalgia gives us the mood he sought to force:

> . . . old fellows in my home town speaking feelingly of an evening spent on the big, empty plains. It has taken the shrillness out of them. They had learned the trick of quiet. It affected their whole lives. It made them significant.

We understand him at last!

And then again the helpless bombast: "At my best, brother, I am like a great mother bird. . . ." He exuded through his pores the ferocious longing of a giant of loneliness. The typical chords from his letters sound under the charging heroes of the stories:

> Youth not given a break—youth licked before it starts.
>
> Filled with sadness that you weren't there.
>
> I have a lot I want to tell you if I can. . . . Anyway you know what I mean when we talked of a man working in the small, trying to save a little of the feeling of man for man.

The romantic sentimentalist held up his mirror to look at his world, peered deeply, saw himself instead, of course; wrote painfully about what he saw; and it turned out that he was writing about the world after all, squeezing it by this palpitating midwestern honesty out of his grandiose sorrows and longings. Sometimes, anyway. He was not a pure man; he had a kind of farmer cunning, plus his groaning artiness and pretense, with which he hoped to convince the "word-fellows" and the pretty girls that he was a Poet although not a young one. What he really wanted was to be alone in that succession of gray furnished rooms he talked about so eloquently, making immortal the quiet noise and gentle terror of his childhood. "I try to believe in beauty and innocence in the midst of the most terrible clutter." But clutter, too, was the truth of his life; he fed on it; how else does a poet take the measure of his need for "beauty and innocence"? He must have remained an optimist, too, amidst all his disillusion. He married four times. To the end of his life he went on believing and marrying.

Anderson the writer arouses a poking curiosity about Anderson the man even in the most resolutely detached reader. The note of confession is always with us: "Here I am, it's good that you know!" he seems to be saying.

His very paragraphs are soaked in his own groping speech. He repeats, he cries out, he harangues, he pleads. All his work, the abysmal failures and the successes which have helped to construct the vision Americans have of themselves, represents an innocent, factitious, improvised, schemed reflection and elaboration of the elements of his own life. He turns the private into the public and then back into the private again. His mystery as a man remains despite his childish longing to reveal himself—the mystery of a man who looks at a man with a beard and a scar in a conference room and sees, instead, a lover fleeing his girl's brothers through the fields. (They had knives and slashed—could this be the same man? he asks himself.) Anderson confounds us with bombast and wit, tenderness and soft-headedness, rant and exquisite delicacy.—HERBERT GOLD, "*Winesburg, Ohio*: The Purity and Cunning of Sherwood Anderson," *Modern American Fiction*, ed. A. Walton Litz, 1963, pp. 87–88

The major theme of Anderson's writing is the tragedy of death in life: modern man, lacking personal identity and with his senses anesthetized, has become a spiritless husk unfitted for love of man and community. This perennial theme is common enough in our time, though it was relatively dormant in the late 1910's when Anderson first enunciated it. It became his leitmotiv when, in 1912, at the age of thirty-six, he suffered a nervous breakdown and rejected his past. Thereafter he viewed this event as a symbolic rebirth which had purified him of false values and freed him from the confines of deadening institutions.

The pattern is classic in Western culture. It has recurred

often in American life since Puritan times, with special frequency in the nineteenth century after the rise of transcendentalism. But in the 1920's it was somewhat anachronistic for a man to present himself dramatically, not only as artist but also as human being, in the messianic role of someone who had achieved a second birth and now had come forth to utter prophetic truths. Nor did Anderson's lower-class origins in Ohio, his vaunted and obvious lack of education, his emphasis upon the American and the common, his bohemian dress and manners, his concern with lust and love, and his charismatic religious overtones make him more palatable either to the intellectual or to the average man. . . .

Anderson's reverent attitude toward language was a wholesome sign of his promise as a writer. In the 1900's, it was useful to him because of his limited vocabulary and his unfamiliarity with the range of rhetorical devices to be found in literature. But his emphasis upon "words" as self-sufficient entities, and his lack of concern with their meaning, foreshadowed his later obsessive preoccupation with them. As he struggled unsuccessfully with the expression of ideas and emotional nuances in his first two novels, he came to believe that his failure resulted from the faulty character of his words rather than from the absence of that profound imaginative experience which willy-nilly finds vivid expression even in a limited language. "There is a story.—I cannot tell it.—I have no words," he would write in 1921. . . .

The invigorating effect of Gertrude Stein's experimentation with language in *Tender Buttons* is evident in *Marching Men*. Her theory is virtually summed up by Anderson in the novel: "It is a terrible thing to speculate on how man has been defeated by his ability to say words. The brown bear in the forest has no such power and the lack of it has enabled him to retain a kind of nobility of bearing sadly lacking in us. On and on through life we go, socialists, dreamers, makers of laws, sellers of goods and believers in suffrage for women and we continuously say words, worn-out words, crooked words, words without power or pregnancy in them."—BROM WEBER, *Sherwood Anderson*, 1964, pp. 6–21

Works

WINESBURG, OHIO

⟨An⟩ impressive realization that came to me with my re-reading was that ⟨*Winesburg, Ohio* (1919)⟩ has form. The book as a whole has form; and most of the stories have form: the work is an integral creation. The form is lyrical. It is not related, even remotely, to the aesthetic of Chekhov; nor to that of Balzac, Flaubert, Maupassant, Tolstoy, Melville. These masters of the short story used the narrative or dramatic art: a linear progression rising to a peak or an immediate complex of character-forces impinging upon each other in a certain action that fulfilled them and rounded the story. For an analogy to the aesthetic of the Winesburg tales, one must go to music, perhaps to the songs that Schubert featly wove from old refrains; or to the lyric art of the Old Testament psalmists and prophets in whom the literary medium was so allied to music that their texts have always been sung in the synagogues. The *Winesburg* design is quite uniform: a theme-statement of a character with his mood, followed by a recounting of actions that are merely variations on the theme. These variations make incarnate what has already been revealed to the reader; they weave the theme into life by the always subordinate confrontation of other characters (usually one) and by an evocation of landscape and village. In some of the tales, there is a secondary theme-statement followed by other variations. In a few, straight narrative is attempted; and these are the least successful.

This lyric, musical form has significance, and the tales' contents make it clear. But it is important, first, to note that the cant judgment of Sherwood Anderson as a naïve, almost illiterate storyteller (a judgment which he himself encouraged with a good deal of nonsense about his literary innocence) is false. The substance of *Winesburg* is impressive, is alive, because it has been superbly *formed*. There are occasional superficial carelessnesses of language; on the whole, the prose is perfect in its selective economy and in its melodious flow; the choice of details is stript, strong, sure; the movement is an unswerving musical fulfillment of the already stated theme. Like Schubert, and like the Old Testament storytellers, the author of *Winesburg* comes at the end of a psychological process; is a man with an inherited culture and a deeply assimilated skill. He is a type of the achieved artist.—WALDO FRANK, "*Winesburg, Ohio* After Twenty Years," *Story*, Sept.–Oct. 1941, pp. 29–30

From "Queer" it is possible to abstract the choreography of *Winesburg*. Its typical action is a series of dance maneuvers by figures whose sole distinctive characteristic is an extreme deformity of movement or posture. Each of these grotesques dances, with angular indirection and muted pathos, toward a central figure who seems to them young, fresh, and radiant. For a moment they seem to draw close to him and thereby to abandon their stoops and limps, but this moment quickly dissolves in the play of the dance and perhaps it never even existed: the central figure cannot be reached. Slowly and painfully, the grotesques withdraw while the young man leaves the stage entirely. None of the grotesques is seen full-face for more than a moment, and none of them is individually important to the scheme of the dance. The distances established between the dancers, rather than their personalities, form the essence of the dance. And in the end, its meaning is revealed in the fact that all but the one untouched youth return to precisely their original places and postures. . . .

Winesburg is an excellently formed piece of fiction, each of its stories following an arc of movement which abstractly graphs the book's meaning. There develops in one of the grotesques a rising lyrical excitement, usually stimulated to intensity by the presence of George Willard. Just before reaching a climax, this excitement is frustrated by a fatal inability at commuication and then it rapidly dissolves into its original diffuse base. This structural pattern is sometimes varied by an ironic turn, as in "Nobody Knows" and "A Man of Ideas," but in only one story, "Sophistication," is the emotion allowed to move forward without interruption.

Through a few simple but extremely effective symbols, the stories are both related to the book's larger meaning and defined in their uniqueness. For the former of these purposes, the most important symbol is that of the room, frequently used to suggest isolation and confinement. Kate Swift is alone in her bedroom, Dr. Reefy in his office, the Reverend Curtis Hartman in his church tower, Enoch Robinson in his fantasy-crowded room. The tactful use of this symbol lends *Winesburg* a claustrophobic aura appropriate to its theme.

Most of the stories are further defined by symbols related to their particular meanings. More valid than any abstract statement of theme is the symbolic power of that moment in "The Strength of God" when the Reverend Curtis Hartman, in order to peek into Kate Swift's bedroom, breaks his church window at precisely the place where the figure of a boy stands "motionless and looking with rapt eyes into the face of Christ."

Though *Winesburg* is written in the bland accents of the

American storyteller, it has an economy impossible to oral narration because Anderson varies the beat of its accents by occasionally whipping them into formal rhetorical patterns. In the book's best stretches there is a tension between its underlying loose oral cadences and the stiffened, superimposed beat of a prose almost Biblical in its regularity. Anderson's prose is neither "natural" nor primitive; it is rather a hushed bardic chant, low-toned and elegiacally awkward, deeply related to native speech rhythms yet very much the result of literary cultivation.

But the final effectiveness of this prose is in its prevalent tone of tender inclusiveness. Between writer and materials there is an admirable equity of relationship. None of the characters is violated, none of the stories, even the failures, leaves the reader with the bitter sense of having been tricked by cleverness or cheapness or toughness. The ultimate unity of the book is a unity of feeling, a sureness of warmth, and a readiness to accept Winesburg's lost grotesques with the embrace of humility. Many American writers have taken as their theme the loss of love in the modern world, but few, if any at all, have so thoroughly realized it in the accents of love.

Read for moral explication, as a guide to life, Anderson's work must seem unsatisfactory; it simply does not tell us enough. But there is another, more fruitful way of reading his work: as the expression of a sensitive witness to the national experience and as the achievement of a storyteller who created a small body of fiction unique in American writing for the lyrical purity of its feeling. No other American writer has so throughly communicated the sense of that historical moment when the native sweetness had not yet been lost to our life, when the nation began to stir from provinciality but had not yet toughened into imperial assurance. In the shabby crevices of this world Anderson discovered the lonely and deformed souls who would never be noticed by official society; he found concealed reserves of feeling, of muted torment and love.

There is in all this something of the quality of adolescence. It is precisely this quality of adolescence which has caused most of the uncertainties and difficulties in our response to Anderson's work. When we say—this is the favorite gambit of hostile critics—that Anderson's work deals not with reality but with adolescent gropings, we ignore the reality of those very gropings; we ignore, as well, the fact that from these gropings none of us is or should be exempt. . . . In that more durable part of his work, *Winesburg* and some of the short stories, adolescence comes through in a radiant comeliness, a sweet surge of feeling. His faults, his failures, and his defeats can hardly be ignored: he was almost always limited in moral sensibility and social perspective. Yet there were a few moments when he spoke, as almost no one else among American writers, with the voice of love.—Irving Howe, "Sherwood Anderson: *Winesburg, Ohio*," *The American Novel*, ed. Wallace Stegner, 1965, pp. 162–65

. . . Anderson's characters ⟨in *Winesburg, Ohio*⟩ . . . become what he liked to call 'grotesques'; indeed, his original title for the collection was to have been *The Book of the Grotesque*. He retained that title for the first and prefatory story, a small credo for the volume, depicting a writer like himself who recognizes that individuals become grotesque when they seize one truth from the many, make it their own, 'try to live . . . life by it'. In fact Anderson's use of the term is perplexing, because he meant two things by it. On the one hand, the grotesque was his subject; like his friend Edgar Lee Masters, whose poem cycle *Spoon River Anthology* (1916) was also an influence on him, Anderson wanted to portray a gallery of damaged small-town

figures, caught in moments of distortion and loneliness, the conditions of their distortion, the moments of their self-discovery. But he also wanted to make the grotesque his *method*, a modern technique of writing, for, as he said, 'in *Winesburg* I made my own form.' The grotesque was his modernist means of depicting an estranged world in order to distil its nature and concentrate on the forms by which distortion might disclose underlying creativity.—Malcolm Bradbury, *The Modern American Novel*, 1983, p. 48

OTHER WORKS

There is in ⟨*Tar, a Mid-West Childhood* (1926)⟩ just a trifle of ⟨the⟩ depreciation of childhood, and the lack of interest in children, which is its root. Mr. Anderson inquires surprisingly whether there can be such a thing as a vulgar child, and pronounces it inconceivable. Yet there could surely be nothing more evident than that there are innumerable childen who come out of the everywhere into here wearing a made-up tie. Not to have perceived that is to enroll oneself among those who say, "I love children," or, "I hate children," which is as absurd as to say, "I love people," or, "I hate people." Whoever could make such a remark betrays that he is unable to observe the individualities of children, because he is dominated by some abstract conception of childhood. Of a certainty Mr. Anderson was not among such when he wrote that superb short story about the boy on the race track, "I Want to Know Why." But unquestionably the small boy Tar is painted in pale sepia tints to square with the common ideal of the mediocrity of the young; and the representation is still further weakened by indulgences of Mr. Anderson's curious tendency to drag the *tempo* of life, by breaking up movements that in normal humanity are easy and sweeping into delayed, puttering motions, by inserting inarticulateness like a plum in the mouths of his characters. This is an irritating trick of his, because it does not belong to his artistic vision of life. It is an intrusion on his work of his attempt to settle a moral problem of his own. One of his characteristics is a glorious facility, which he possibly gets from his Latin blood. One sees it again and again in his work when he gets going. There is a passage in *A Story Teller's Story*, in which he flings a vivid expression of a certain aspect of America across four pages just as Michelangelo filled a panel of the roof of the Sistine Chapel with his image of the creation of Adam, with an air of having spent no time or effort on it, having just called it into being by a whole turn of the will, a half-turn of the wrist. But this facility is a gift that Mr. Anderson quite unfairly dislikes, because he insists on identifying it with the braggart, hail-fellow-well-met, yarn-spinning tiresomeness of the father he describes in *A Story Teller's Story* and in *Tar*, though if there is any connection between them the second is merely an expression of the first so embryonic as to be useless and certainly not to be taken as evidence against it. But Mr. Anderson has his prejudice. Therefore, he rejects harmony of being. He is infatuated with human machinery that groans and creaks.

But there are two passages in *Tar* which far outweigh all its faults, which make it a book to be read and kept. There is a chapter describing how this father, Dick Morehead, came home drunk when the children were at supper. His children sit round the table with bowed heads, very quiet, uncomfortable, frightened. They have been brought up decently by their mother. Dick has never come home like this before. He tries to serve them with the baked potatoes in the dish in front of him. But his fork misses the potato and strikes the dish. The mother gets up and takes the dish from him and serves the children herself. Dick, uneasy, guilty, starts talking, not to the family around him, for he feels they are rejecting him, but to the stove. His shame at his failure in life makes him cry out to the stove innumerable names of persons who owed him money when he ran a harness shop some years before, and had never paid him. Tar, who had been very ill, who is sitting up at the table for the first time after many days, falls into a kind of waking dream, fits faces to all those names which appear and disappear in the darkness behind the stove. Amazing world, where a man can do something to hold sway as if he were a tree and not a man, and talk to a stove as he would usually talk to his family, and change from a protective, authoritative father into a fighting and pitiful stranger. No wonder the walls waver, the faces dance and dissolve in the shadow, the little boy slips from his chair into the darkness, slips so that his mother will pick him up and carry him away in the darkness of her arms. That is an exquisite chapter. It makes one think of some of the best of Hans Christian Andersen, of *What the Moon Saw.*

The other chapter is about Tar and his sister Margaret. Margaret was feeling very nervous. As a matter of fact, Mrs. Moorhead was very sick and was going to die soon, and maybe they all knew about it, although they didn't admit it to each other. And, anyway, the Moorhead house wouldn't be a very good place for a girl to grow up in. She would get discouraged. Tar was a newsboy then; he went down to the trains and got the papers and delivered them at the houses of all the people who had ordered them. One night a bridge got washed out and the trains were late. Tar went down to the station for the 4:30 train to no purpose, and he tried again at 6 and 9. Then he meant to give it up and go to bed, but Margaret got all worked up and excited about it. So they went back at 10, and again at 11, and then they just stayed at the station and waited, though the telegraph operator told them they were crazy kids. The train came in at 1:30 and then they took the papers and went all over town slipping them under the people's doors, though the electric lights were turned off and it was pouring with rain. And they dared come home by the short cut through the cemetery. . . .

It is a superb account of the intangible adventures of youth and the mysterious satisfaction they give.

Certainly Mr. Sherwood Anderson is an unequal writer and *Tar* is disfigured with flatness and sham *naïveté*, but that does not, of course, affect my conviction that he has genius. Unequal writing is less of a condemnation of an author than it ever was before, for the conditions in which modern writers choose their mediums ensure that they shall constantly be setting themselves difficulties which they cannot always surmount. The people who wanted to write about a man's private adventures, those that go on within his own breast, used always to write verse. But now they are impatient of using metre and rhyme. They like to sport among the subtler rhythms of prose. . . .

Why could not Mr. Sherwood Anderson have written those passages by themselves, just for the glorious pattern of sight and sound and feeling that they are? The reason is that he is afraid somebody will ask, "But what happened next? Isn't it rather pointless the way you've left it?" Certainly they would have had the right to ask that if what they were reading was a chapter about Tom Jones in a book whose aim was to be a history of Tom Jones. But they would be wrong if they asked that quesion after the last line of "We'll go no more a-roving" or "The Ode to the Nightingale." Since something has been revealed by the poet which is true in eternity it is frivolous to ask him what happened to it in time.—REBECCA WEST, "Sherwood Anderson, Poet," *The Strange Necessity*, 1928, pp. 315–20

Mr. Anderson has given us some admirable short stories, which are all the better for the strain of naive mysticism and childlike repetitive wonder which runs through them. When he is at his best, which is usually when he is also at his simplest, his air of newborn innocence is charming; it gives to his theme a lyric freshness that is all too rare in contemporary fiction. But, alas, some demon in Mr. Anderson's breast goads him perpetually toward deeper and more transcendental things, and these almost always play the very deuce with him. Like Mr. D. H. Lawrence, he has intermittently sought a kind of sex-mysticism, full of dark, esoteric currents and subliminal fevers, as the key to the universe; his novels are full of this. And it is, perhaps, also true that he shares with Mr. Lawrence a curious messianic preoccupation with the soul—the soul, be it understood, always envisaged as a thing essentially animal. Mr. Anderson's "dark laughter" and Mr. Lawrence's "lumbar ganglion" are merely their different ways of getting at this elusive phenomenon.

Mr. Lawrence entertains no doubts whatever as to his rightness about such affairs: he is emphatic, even savage, in his assertiveness. But Mr. Anderson, if he is just as dreadfully sure of himself, just as egotistically convinced of his vision and its value for humanity, and of the importance (as propaganda) of all the "phases of his soul" (again to paraphrase the writer of the blurb), proceeds to his assertiveness with his characteristic air of self-questioning. Here, in these curious parables, is once again that rather disarming manner of his, with its "What I mean is this" and its "Well, what I was trying to say—," and its "But I'll begin over again, and try to say it better." This manner has become a mannerism; one is too often reminded of the small boy desperately in earnest to say something that entirely transcends his powers of speech. And it has also, more is the pity, begun to seem, in Mr. Anderson, rather an affectation.

As for the parables ⟨in A *New Testament* (1927)⟩ themselves, or poems, or gnomic prose, in which we are to find Mr. Anderson's "doctrine" (*qui d'ailleurs n'existe pas*), the best one can say for it is that it is, unmistakably, imaginative. But beyond that one cannot go. For Mr. Anderson's symbolisms and parables are too wholesale to be effective, too amorphous to be clear, too structureless and humorless to be anything more than readable. Once or twice, when he condescends to be simple and forthright, as in "Young Man in a Room" or "In a Workingman's Rooming House," he gives us a vigorous and moving bit of poetic prose, succinct and real. But for the most part one feels that he is trying too hard, that he is a little overweening. His reach exceeds his grasp. The profuseness with which he empties his unconsciousness, the indiscriminateness with which he allows image to lead to image and one autistic chain of thought to bud another, defeats his own end, and in the upshot one has a mere welter of pictures, some bad and some good, but in the main meaningless.

One feels of Mr. Anderson that he has simply lost himself hopelessly in his own little poetic chaos, in the illusion that he has there discovered the ultimate truth. Might a sense of humor have saved him from this unreflecting verbalistic zeal? What can one say to an author who remarks, earnestly, "Sometimes as I walk in the streets, a look of intelligence comes into my eyes." To comment on that would be cruel. As for his explicit belief that "nothing is to be achieved by being smart and definite, and to be vague—they keep telling me—is to be insane, a little unbalanced," one can only retort that nothing is more dangerous in literature than the vague. Vagueness can only be used by a genius, and when it is so used it is usually, on analysis, found to be admirably precise. The terms may shimmer, but the mood and meaning are clear.—CONRAD AIKEN,

"Anderson, Sherwood" (1935), *Collected Criticism*, 1968, pp. 131–32

⟨*Sherwood Anderson's Notebook* (1926)⟩ displays the growing bitterness of Anderson, the anxiety, the nervous depressions, the feeling of instability just when he is being recognized as a 'successful' writer. He knows a man, Anderson says, who would give anything for fame. 'Well, I have had a little of that. He may have mine. Let's trade.' The volume gives us happier views of the writer: his love of luxury and of splash ('I would like a string of race horses, a farm, a yacht.'), his vitality and curiosity ('Presently I shall die with a thousand, a hundred thousand tales untold. People I might have loved I shall not love'), along with his warmth and humility. Yet all the new places, people, experiences that Anderson tries to enter into—these too are affected by his sense of impermanence and failure; this whole inexhaustible hunger for life is to some degree fanatical and obsessed. Somewhere here—in these trees, rivers, buildings, in these children, servant girls, factory workers, prostitutes, perhaps, in all these crafts and sciences, races and religions of a modern America—can he find the answer to his dilemma? These are all possible clues, partial escapes, slippery niches. The Negro, in particular, seems to be farther removed from the machine age, and—'for whole days I try being a black man.' Anderson listens to their songs; perhaps here? But in the end, he thinks, they will be caught up also. 'The whites will get us. They win. Don't turn your back on the modern world. Sing that too, if you can, while the sweet words last.'

In an essay like 'I'll Say We've Done Well,' the elements of Anderson's personal anxiety are inextricably joined with the predicament of his society. For isn't it his own Ohio, Anderson asks—isn't it just this stronghold of an older provincial life that has become a citadel of modern industrialism?

> Have you a city that smells worse than Akron, that is more smugly self-satisfied than Cleveland, or that has missed as unbelievably great an opportunity to be one of the lovely cities of the world as has the city of Cincinnati? . . . I claim that we Ohio men have taken as lovely a land as ever lay outdoors and that we have, in our towns and cities, put the old stamp of ourselves on it for keeps.

These are bitter tones for the communal lover of the Ohio tales, and the pages of the *Notebook* hold many such sharp and bitter indictments of the industrialized America of Anderson's maturity—of 'the apparent meaninglessness of individual life against the background of something huge, uncontrolled, and diabolically strong.' In 'King Coal,' the last of the sketches in the volume, and one of the best short pieces Anderson ever wrote, he reaches the crux of the matter. There are some questions, he says, that keep coming back to him—

> It seems to me that love has much to do with the fiber and quality of men as citizens of a country, and the whole matter of hustling pushing coal-mining factory-building modern life for the most part remains in my mind in the form of annoying and to me unanswerable questions. I find myself going about day after day and asking myself such questions as these, 'Can a man love a coal mine, or a coal-mining town, a factory, a real-estate boomer. . . . If a man lives in a street in a modern industrial town, can he love that street? If a man does not love the little patch of ground on which his own house may stand, can he in any sense love the street, the city, the state, the country of which it is a part?'

And, because he would not like to see love of country become in the end a thing like modern religion, occasionally

pumped into temporary life by 'some political Billy Sunday and by propaganda in the newspapers,' such questions, Anderson adds, are disquieting. And indeed they are. For what Anderson has been recording is, of course, the fundamental impasse of the nineteen-twenties in American literature. Though some of our writers, like Scott Fitzgerald, will be only partly conscious of the true nature of their predicament and some, like Henry Mencken, only too aware, pushed the issue away from consciousness, the hostility of the American artist to his own society is a central trait of the decade. . . .

⟨Anderson nibbled at many⟩ 'solutions' to the economic impasse of the American twenties. But never knowing the answers, he knew enough to avoid the easy answers. The Ohio Nada was still from Ohio and, however despairing, it came from the center of mid-American life: Anderson remains the spokesman of the meek even when the meek have become intolerable. These obscure and outraged ordinary American souls whom he has been portraying are so much part of him, indeed, that just *because* of their warped existence, he must believe in them all the more. 'I told my people life was sweet, and men might live,' is nevertheless the concluding note of his Chicago tales, and you are not likely to notice this sentiment in much first-rank American writing for the next fifteen years. If Sherwood Anderson is one of the first social rebels of the early twenties to attack the illusions of civilization in the United States, and in this sense helps to set the tone of the decade, he is also—and this is the main sense of his work as a whole—one of the last to believe in the possibility of civilization in the United States.—MAXWELL GEISMAR, "Sherwood Anderson: Last of the Townsmen," *The Last of the Provincials: The American Novel 1915–25*, 1943, pp. 247–50

Anderson was a man with a mission and he tried sincerely and repetitiously to recommend himself as a serious missionary. His criticism of the industrial demon led him to the creation of simple angels. Their most highly intelligent act was their groping toward profound truths, from which each fashioned his own grotesque. The individual inadequacies of these people added up to a huge and grotesque inadequacy located at the heart of modern American society. Anderson's characters find no relief in Floyd Dell's bohemias; they are, in fact, illiterate, unlettered, and inarticulate, striving desperately and vainly for a verbal equivalent of their feelings. It is only occasionally that they can find such an equivalent; but when they do, as do Sponge Martin and Bruce Dudley of *Dark Laughter* (1925), they become not only articulate but garrulous.

The range and meaning of Anderson's protest found their most successful expression in *Poor White* (1920). Here, in the character of the almost dumbly shy Hugh McVey is a veritable stereotype of pre-industrial man. The irony of the narrative lies in his having perfected a machine for the planting of cabbages because he desperately wants to save the poor laborers in the cabbage fields from their backbreaking work. From this motive, therefore, and not from a lust for power and wealth, McVey becomes an inventor and a servant of the industrial world. He destroys the beauty of Bidwell, which changes from a pleasant small town into an ugly industrial center. Throughout these distressing experiences McVey remains a shy, gentle creature, free of the brutalizing effects of wealth and the temptations of power. At the novel's end he is able to sum up his experience and the town's, using his own unwitting contribution to its corruption as the unholy example.

This novel contributes the simplification of a thesis which is present implicitly or overtly in many of its contemporaries. The thesis embraces Freudian influences as it does social and historical criticisms. The simple, natural soul is one of the victims of a soulless and vulgar materialism; in its primitive habitat, and in such survivals as the Negroes, it had enjoyed the virtues of a simple and unsubtle sincerity; but the advantages of materialism are gained at the sacrifice of man's nobler impulses, which are repressed almost to the point of extinction. The survivor of this holocaust is apparently a man who either remains remarkably simple in spite of overpowering odds against his chances, or the man who "has had enough" and who walks out on the world, endlessly explaining and glorifying his decision.—Frederick J. Hoffman, *The Modern Novel in America, 1900–1950*, 1951, pp. 107–8

CHARLES C. WALCUTT
From "Sherwood Anderson:
Impressionism and the Buried Life"
American Literary Naturalism: A Divided Stream
1956, pp. 224–32

Anderson's naturalism may be considered on three planes: his exploration of character without reference to the orthodox moral yardsticks; his questionings, and his quiet, suppressed conclusions as to what orders our cosmos and what is man's place in it; and his social attitudes, which are left-wing and increasingly critical, as the years pass, of American business enterprise. After briefly discussing these aspects of Anderson's work, I shall try to show how his naturalism, while making possible his exquisite insights into personality, confronts him with a later version of the problem of structure that baffled Hamlin Garland: Anderson's medium is the short story or sketch; in the novel he is baffled by the problem of form.

Understanding naturalism as a result of the divided stream of American transcendentalism enables us to account for many confusions and contradictions which appear in the tradition. Does the appeal to nature, for example, commit us to reason or unreason? Is truth to be found in the study of the scientist, the insight of the mystic, or the simple reactions of the folk? In short, is reason or impulse to be more respected? These are old questions, indeed, but they seem no less confusing now than they have ever been, for never have the poles of order and frenzy whirled more bewilderingly around an unknown center. Respect for reason seems to be a part of modern naturalistic thinking, but so does respect for instinct. How can it be that these two contrary notions exist in the same general pattern of ideas? The answer is that the dichotomy between order and frenzy, between reason and instinct, is not the important or major one. In a larger scheme, Authority goes at one pole, and at the other stands Nature whose two children are order (or reason) and instinct. Under the orthodox dispensation man was to be enlightened by revelation and controlled by the rule of Authority. Under the new, he is to find the truth in himself. Since the emotions have been most severely distrusted under the aegis of orthodoxy, it is natural that, in the revolt against it, the rationalism of the eighteenth century should precede the emotionalism of the nineteenth, and that the scientific materialism of the late nineteenth century should precede the second return to emotion that we see in the psychology of Freud and the fiction of Sherwood Anderson. In each trend the return to reason comes as the first rebellion against orthodoxy, the return to emotion the second. Anderson, in almost everything he writes, searches out the emotional values involved in an experience. He seeks to render the actual flow of life to people in small towns and on farms who are struggling with all their

natural ardor against the confines of tradition or the inhibitions of Puritanism.

Anderson explores two major themes. One is discovery, the other inhibition. These themes correspond with the demands of the two branches of the divided stream of transcendentalism. The theme of discovery is the recognition of spirit, the unfolding of the world and its perception by the intuition, the secret insight by which a man's life is suddenly revealed to him. It comes when George Willard sits in the dark over the fairground with Helen White; when the adolescent narrator of "The Man Who Became a Woman" (in *Horses and Men*, 1924) after a night of extraordinary adventures, culminating in the illusion that he has turned into a woman, breaks through the veil of ignorance and confusion and goes forth to a new life; when Rosalind Westcott of "Out of Nowhere into Nothing" (in *The Triumph of the Egg*, 1921), who has gone home from Chicago to ask her mother's advice and has found only a complete lack of sympathy, walking through the night comes into possession of a delicious confidence in her powers: "She found herself able to run, without stopping to rest and half-wished she might run on forever, through the land, through towns and cities, driving darkness away with her presence."

The theme of inhibition appears in almost every story of Anderson's, and it relates to three general areas of cause and experience. The first is the problem of growing up. Every youth finds himself baffled, inarticulate, frustrated because he does not know what he wants out of life. He wants to be loved, more than anything else, perhaps, but he also wants to express himself and to communicate with others, and these needs cannot be answered until they are clearly recognized. Childhood and youth are therefore characterized by bottled-up yearnings, unformed desires, and wild resentments. Second is the frustration which comes from the absence of a tradition of manners that could lend graciousness and ease instead of the rawness and harshness that grow when people express themselves through broad humor, scurrility, and cruel pranks. Third is the problem of social opportunity which becomes increasingly important in Anderson's later work. People without education, mill workers in *Beyond Desire*, all the countless Americans who have not even a meager share of the opportunities which constitute the democratic dream of a full life for all—these live in endless spiritual privation, and passages which appear with increasing frequency in the later books suggest that Anderson shared the hatred of the oppressed for the vapid plutocrats who deprive them. This theme of inhibition obviously reflects the materialistic branch of the transcendental stream when it identifies spiritual and material privation. If Anderson ever suggested that all we need in America is a tradition of manners and devout observances to control the wildness of the yokel, he would be returning to orthodoxy and dualism. This he never does.

Rather he evolves the concept of the *grotesque* to indicate what small-town life has done to its people. The grotesque is the person who has become obsessed by a mannerism, an idea, or an interest to the point where he ceases to be Man in the ideal sense. This condition is not the single defect referred to by Hamlet:

> these men—
> Carrying, I say, the stamp of one defect,
> Being Nature's livery, or Fortune's star—
> Their virtues else—be they as pure as grace,
> As infinite as man may undergo—
> Shall in the general censure take corruption
> From that particular fault.

It is, rather, the state wherein the defect has become the man, while his potentialities have remained undeveloped. Anderson describes it thus:

> That in the beginning when the world was young there were a great many thoughts but no such thing as a truth. Man made the truths himself and each truth was a composite of a great many vague thoughts. . . .
>
> And then the people came along. Each as he appeared snatched up one of the truths and some who were quite strong snatched up a dozen of them.
>
> It was the truths that made the people grotesques. The old man had quite an elaborate theory concerning the matter. It was his notion that the moment one of the people took one of the truths to himself, called it his truth, and tried to live his life by it, he became a grotesque and the truth he embraced became a falsehood.

Again and again the stories of Anderson are marked by a union of surprise and insight. What was apt to be merely shocking or horrendous or sensational in the work of Zola and Norris acts in Anderson's stories as a key to a fuller grasp of the extraordinary range of "normal" reality. He has got into the heart of bizarre, even fantastic experiences which are nevertheless also universal.

"Godliness: A Tale in Four Parts," in *Winesburg, Ohio*, presents the effects on children and grandchildren of the zeal for possessions and godliness that dominates the simple heart of Jesse Bentley. Jesse has the simplicity and power of a prophet; with these go the blindness of a fanatic and the pitiful ignorance of a bigot. When his grandson, David, is twelve, he takes him into the forest and terrifies him by praying to God for a sign. The boy runs, falls, and is knocked unconscious on a root, while the old man, oblivious to the boy's terror, thinks only that God has frowned upon him. When David is fifteen, he is out with the old man recovering a strayed lamb when Jesse conceives the notion that, like Abraham, he should sacrifice the lamb and daub the boy's head with its blood. Terrified beyond measure, the boy releases the lamb, hits Jesse in the head with a stone from his sling, and, believing he has killed the old man, leaves that part of the country for good. As for old Jesse, "It happened because I was too greedy for glory," he declared, and would have no more to say on the matter. Here Anderson is, on the surface, studiously objective, presenting only the cold facts; but the delicacy and sweetness of his style invest this harsh tale with a rare quality of understanding and love. The hidden life has never been more effectively searched out. Here there is no judgment either of the fanatical old man or of the terrified boy whose life he nearly ruins. Pity, understanding, and insight there are, made possible by the naturalistic impulse to seek into the heart of experience without reference to the limits or prepossessions of convention.

Winesburg, Ohio is full of insights into the buried life, into the thoughts of the repressed, the inarticulate, the misunderstood. Most frequently frustrated is the desire to establish some degree of intimacy with another person. A tradition of manners would accomplish just this by providing a medium through which acquaintance could ripen into intimacy. Small-town America has wanted such a tradition. In place of it, it has had joking, backslapping, and buffooning which irk the sensitive spirit and make him draw ever more secretly into himself. The concluding paragraph of "The Thinker" shows these confused and constricted emotions working at a critical moment in the life of a boy who wants to get away. He has told a girl whom

he has long known rather at a distance that he plans to leave Winesburg, and she has offered to kiss him:

> Seth hesitated and, as he stood waiting, the girl turned and ran away through the hedge. A desire to run after her came to him, but he only stood staring, perplexed and puzzled by her action as he had been perplexed by all of the life of the town out of which she had come. Walking slowly toward the house, he stopped in the shadow of a large tree and looked at his mother sitting by a lighted window busily sewing. The feeling of loneliness that had visited him earlier in the evening returned and colored his thoughts of the adventure through which he had just passed. "Huh!" he exclaimed, turning and staring in the direction taken by Helen White. "That's how things'll turn out. She'll be like the rest. I suppose she'll begin now to look at me in a funny way." He looked at the ground and pondered this thought. "She'll be embarrassed and feel strange when I'm around," he whispered to himself. "That's how it'll be. That's how everything'll turn out. When it comes to loving some one, it won't never be me. It'll be some one else— some fool—some one who talks a lot—some one like that George Willard."

In another story he speaks of "the quality of being strong to be loved" as if it were the key to America's need.

These ideas are all in the naturalistic tradition in that they are motivated by the feeling of need for their expression of the "inner man." Anderson assumes that this inner man exists and is good and "should" be permitted to fulfill itself through love and experience. The need is alive and eager; it is the social order that prevents its satisfaction.

Patterns emerge in *Winesburg, Ohio* through the growth of George Willard, who may be considered the protagonist of what connected story there is. George appears frequently, sometimes in an experience and sometimes hearing about another's. An extraordinary pattern emerges when George receives, late at night in the newspaper office where he works, a hint he cannot yet interpret from the minister, who enters brandishing a bloody fist, exclaiming that he has been "delivered." "God," he says, "has appeared to me in the person of Kate Swift, the school teacher, kneeling naked on a bed." The minister has been peeping at her through a small hole in the colored window of his study. This night as his lustful thoughts were running wild, Kate, naked, beat the pillow of her bed and wept, and then knelt to pray, and the minister was moved to smash the window with his fist so that the glass would be replaced and he would no longer be tempted. The turmoil in the schoolteacher's bosom resulted from a mixture of interest, desire, enthusiasm, and love. Earlier the same evening she had been thinking of George Willard, whom she wanted to become a writer, and became so excited that she went to see him in the newspaper office, and for a moment allowed him to take her in his arms. George was only a youth at this point, and the schoolteacher's interest in his talents was perfectly genuine and unselfish. But she was also a passionate and unsatisfied woman in whom interest and desire interacted. When George put his arms around her she struck his face with her fists and ran out into the night again. Some time later the minister burst in, and it seemed to George that all Winesburg had gone crazy. George goes to bed later, fitting these puzzling incidents together and thinking that he has missed something Kate Swift was trying to tell him.

All the gropings and cross-purposes of these grotesques and semi-grotesques reveal the failure of communication in

Winesburg. The mores impose a set of standards and taboos that are utterly incapable of serving the pent-up needs in the hearts of the people. They regard themselves with wonder and contempt while they study their neighbors with fear and suspicion. And the trouble, which begins with the gap between public morality and private reality, extends finally into the personality of a rich and good person like Kate Swift. Because her emotions are inhibited she acts confusedly toward George; is desperate, frightened, and ashamed; and fails to help him as she had wanted to do.

The climax (perhaps it should only be called the high point in George's life to then) of the book occurs when George Willard and Helen White reach a complete understanding one autumn evening, sitting up in the old grandstand on the fairgrounds, rapt and wordless. "With all his strength he tried to hold and to understand the mood that had come upon him. In that high place in the darkness the two oddly sensitive human atoms held each other tightly and waited. In the mind of each was the same thought. 'I have come to this lovely place and here is this other,' was the substance of the thing felt." It is most significant that this experience is almost entirely wordless. The shared feeling, indeed, is of seeking and wondering. It is inarticulate because it occurs in a world without meaning. Such incidents suggest that men's instincts are good but that conventional morality has warped and stifled them. Interpreted in terms of the divided stream of transcendentalism, they show that the spirit is misdirected because its physical house is mistreated. When Whitman wrote

Logic and sermons never convince,
The damp of the night drives deeper into my soul
Only what proves itself to every man and woman is so

he was making the same plea for the liberation of body and spirit together that we infer from *Winesburg, Ohio*. I say infer, because Anderson does not precisely declare this; one might indeed infer that he regards these repressions as inseparable from life—that he takes the tragic view of man—but I think not entirely so. The pains of growth are probably inevitable, but the whole world is not as confining as Winesburg, and Anderson seems to say that people *should* be able to grow up less painfully to more abundant lives. His protagonist does, and gets away from Winesburg, though he endures torments of misunderstanding and unsatisfied love which cannot be laid to Winesburg so much as to the condition of youth in this world.

But George Willard, who will escape, is different from Elmer Cowley, who is literally inarticulate with frustration and the conviction that everyone in Winesburg considers him "queer"; from old Ray Pearson, who runs sobbing across a rough field through the beauty of an autumn evening in order to catch Hal Winters and tell him not to marry the girl whom he has got in trouble—not marry like himself and be trapped into having more children than he can support and living in a tumble-down shack by the creek, working as a hired hand, bent with labor, all his dreams come to naught. Those buried lives are disclosed with heartbreaking insight. And as we reflect upon them we sense the aptness of the "naturalistic" view of life that the author puts into the mind of George Willard and also presents as his own thought. "One shudders at the thought of the meaninglessness of life while at the same instant . . . one loves life so intensely that tears come into the eyes."

If the universe here seems meaningless, the needs and emotions of men are intensely meaningful. Anderson feels love for them and pity for their desperate and usually fruitless questing. It is not therefore surprising that he should turn increasingly in his later works toward emphasis on the social and institutional causes of their frustration. Like Hamlin Garland, however, Anderson does not master the structure of the novel. His poignant sketches, which contain some of the best and most memorable writing in our literature, do not "connect" naturally into the sustained expression of the longer form. Perhaps the scale is too narrow or the feeling too intense and special. Perhaps Anderson could not achieve the necessary objectivity. Certainly the patterns of protest and socialism do not provide the sort of frame upon which he could weave.

BROM WEBER
From *Sherwood Anderson*
1964, pp. 34–45

The bulk of Anderson's important creation is far greater than most critics and readers appear to have realized. His significant contribution to American literature begins with *Winesburg, Ohio* and includes many pieces of prose and poetry published in books and magazines from 1916 to 1941. To that body of work should be added the successful chapters and sections from generally unsatisfactory books, as well as the luminous autobiographical sketches compiled in the posthumous *Memoirs*.

One reason Anderson's writing has not received full recognition, apart from the disappointment aroused by his novels, is the uneven character of his books. Anderson's eagerness to publish, encouraged by editors and publishers, is partially responsible. For example, the two books which crystallized his fame as a short fiction writer in the early 1920's— *The Triumph of the Egg* (1921) and *Horses and Men* (1923)— are mixtures of quality and dross. In both books he included pages salvaged from discarded novels which were on the whole below the level of his current work. "Unlighted Lamps" and "The Door of the Trap" (*The Triumph of the Egg*) are sections of novels begun before 1913. "A Chicago Hamlet" (*Horses and Men*) is a portion of a 1918 novel; "An Ohio Pagan" and "'Unused'" in the same collection are parts of unpublished novels begun in 1920. A little more than half of *Horses and Men* thus belies the subtitle's description of the contents as "tales." Anderson's last collection of short fiction, *Death in the Woods* (1933), is similarly uneven. It should be noted, however, that the novel fragments frequently contain some of Anderson's most evocative writing. The pantheistic embrace of nature in "An Ohio Pagan," for example, has rarely been equaled in American literature.

Another reason for the relative neglect of Anderson's total accomplishment is the special nature of his talent. He wrote in an age which believed it could master the disorder of existence with patterns of order derived from myths and ideologies of the past or else with descriptions of objects and behavior that possessed the irreducible precision of scientific writing. Because Anderson did not adopt either one of these solutions, his reputation was severely damaged during the 1920's. A reassessment is now in order, for his alleged weaknesses ironically have become strengths which link him with some of the most vigorous currents in contemporary literature. Anderson's vision and method reappear triumphantly in recent American literature in the writing of Carson McCullers, Bernard Malamud, Flannery O'Connor, Tennessee Williams, Edward Albee, Saul Bellow, and John Hawkes. Anderson's pioneering conglomeration of the picaresque, the antiheroic, the grotesque, the passionate, and the rebellious is no longer puzzling nor is it a sign of irresponsible "mindlessness."

One of the most interesting discoveries to be made is that sentimentality is not one of the chief characteristics of Anderson's writing. When dealing with characters whose suffering and confusion he delineated at excessive length, failing to complicate and particularize their uniqueness or to impart visible moral and intellectual significance to their predicaments, he did become pathetic and sentimental. Illustrations of his failure to claim the complex response of a reader are *Many Marriages* and "Out of Nowhere into Nothing."

But Anderson's critical temper conflicted strongly with his tendency toward acceptance and complacency. He could become exceptionally sharp, often brutal, in combating the impulse of quiescence. The lively battle he carried on elicited an amused, ironic attitude toward himself and his world. He often wrote satirically ("The Egg," 1920, and "The Triumph of a Modern, or, Send for the Lawyer," 1923) and often comically ("I'm a Fool," 1922, "There She Is—She Is Taking Her Bath," 1923, and "His Chest of Drawers," 1939). To have separated satire and comedy is misleading, however, for Anderson at his most humorous gives us that rare blend known as the tragicomic. When he achieved it, as in "The Egg," it rested in a delicate suspension of irony that looked back to the narrative voice of *Winesburg, Ohio*. Despite lapses into what Faulkner in 1925 described as an "elephantine kind of humor about himself," Anderson's vision remained deeply, incongruously tragicomic. Despite the dark years through which he passed in the late 1920's, this vision reemerged in his last decade of life, typically in his insistence in *Plays: Winesburg and Others* (1937) that the dramatized version of "The Triumph of the Egg" must be carefully directed in order to maintain a balance between comedy and tragedy; to play it either for "laughter" or "tears" alone would destroy the play.

Essentially Anderson was a lyric writer. Having accepted middle-class thought uncritically at first, then having rebelled against it, he feared that any other system of thought would be equally delusive, would limit and frustrate him, especially since reason tended to become abstract and to ignore the heart. "Feeling instinctively the uncertainty of life, the difficulty of arriving at truth," he resolved to remain "humble in the face of the great mystery" ("'Unused,'" 1923). He might have been describing his own work when he wrote in *A Story Teller's Story*: "Dim pathways do sometimes open before the eyes of the man who has not killed the possibilities of beauty in himself by being too sure."

Anderson could be irritatingly blunt in stating his position, sneering at "slickness," "smartness," and glibness in all fields including literary criticism; thus he inevitably aroused charges of "mindlessness," "immaturity," and "distrust of ideas." Though he winced under the blows of increasingly harsh criticism, he unhesitatingly rejected ready-made truths of past and present. He turned his gaze inwards, searching for tentative explanations of mystery in the texture of his own emotional and social experience. His writings articulate the development of his perceptions of self in relation to the world, of the difficulties encountered on the way.

Anderson never abandoned the vision of himself as a poet despite the unfavorable reception of *Mid-Western Chants*, as late as 1930 writing an extraordinary prose poem in "Machine Song" (*Perhaps Women*, 1931). From 1919 to 1927 he assiduously wrote prose poems which appeared in magazines and *The Triumph of the Egg* and were collected in *A New Testament* (1927). He regarded this work at the outset as "a purely insane, experimental thing . . . an attempt to express, largely

by indirection, the purely fanciful side of a man's life, the odds and ends of thought, the little pockets of thoughts and emotions that are so seldom touched." The poems on the whole are inchoate, too vague and incoherent to communicate more than faint hints of subconscious existence. But they were valuable exercises nonetheless. When Anderson turned to prose during this period, he passed beyond the mere undisciplined expression of self and made skillful use of poetic techniques which he never forgot.

As in *Winesburg, Ohio*, the varying perceptions of a poetically conceived narrator animate and unify most of Anderson's best stories, quite a few of which are products of the 1930's. . . .

The uncertain, groping narrator of an Anderson story employs an art of suggestion to articulate his search for pattern and meaning in human existence. His experiences are fragmentary, incoherent, inexplicable. The chronological sequence of time may be interrupted and reversed by memories, inadvertent thoughts, gusts of emotion, and frustrated attempts at comprehension. Objects and people are haphazardly perceived, grotesquely distorted. Absurdly helpless, the narrator may succumb to impotence, give vent to explosive stirrings in his subconscious, flee the envelope of his body in mystical anguish or ecstasy, obsessedly focus upon trivialities such as a bent finger, find momentary relief in the muscular health and grace of animals.

Since the story is an articulation of the narrator's experience, its movement is repetitive and circular; it is not rounded off with a meaningful conclusion, for that would violate the narrator's integrity, his stance of wonder and search. Anderson's rejection of conventional plot and climax was aesthetically appropriate. So was his frequent representation of physical detail as incomplete image and generalized noun, his emphasis upon the musical sound of language before it becomes sense in order that he might portray the transformation of undifferentiated sensation and emotion into intelligible form.

The welter of sensuous and emotional perceptions is integrated—despite the powerful centrifugal impulse—by various unifying elements. The narrator maintains a consistent tone of voice. Whether youth or adult, light or serious, comic or satiric, critical or suppliant, he is also visibly interested and compassionate, anxious to discern the reality behind appearance. Moments in the story—episodes, sensations, repetitions—suddenly blaze up to give intense thematic illuminations. Objects, gestures, and events are encrusted with symbolic meaning. These symbols recur and invest the narrator's perceptions with deepened or new significance. Often these symbols are transformed into archetypal patterns of elemental human experience, such as sacrifice, initiation, and rebirth; Anderson's corn seed, for example, is a fertility symbol, its planting a ceremonial drama of death and resurrection.

Many of Anderson's stories, like his novels, are autobiographical either wholly ("In a Strange Town") or partially ("I Want to Know Why"). Presentation of a story from the first-person point of view encouraged an autobiographical concern. On the other hand, as a writer of autobiography, a form that fascinated him because of his vision of himself as "the American Man . . . a kind of composite essence of it all," he tended to fictionalize the details of his biography. This fusion of fact and fiction produced some of Anderson's finest lyrical prose. For example, "Death in the Woods," regarded as one of Anderson's best stories even by unfavorable critics, appeared as a third-person narrative (Chapter XII) in his autobiographical novel *Tar* (1926). In the same year, it also appeared as a story in the *American Mercury*; the name "Tar" had been replaced by "I" and third-person pronouns and other details revised to clarify the narrator's personal relations and experiences. "A Meeting South," the subtle account of Anderson's intimacy with Faulkner in New Orleans, conceals Faulkner under a pseudonym and was probably read as fiction in the *Dial* (April 1925). It reappeared the next year as an autobiographical sketch in *Sherwood Anderson's Notebook* and finally was identified as a story in *Death in the Woods*. Anderson's autobiographical writings, which compose much of his total work, must be taken into account before any definitive conclusions about his literary significance can be ventured.

A starting point might well be Chapters X and XI of *Tar*, portrayals of horse racing as brilliantly colored and airy as Raoul Dufy's watercolors of French tracks, written in a supple vernacular that captures motion and youth with clear-eyed verve. Another excellent piece is "The Nationalist" (*Puzzled America*, 1935), a satirical dialogue with "the rat king of the South" who wants Congress to abolish the law protecting snowy egrets from shooting by feather-hunters. "'It isn't the money I am thinking about,' he said. There was a grave injustice being done. 'These egrets,' he said again, 'are not American birds. They are foreign birds and they come up here only to eat our American fish.'" Two sketches, "White Spot" (1939) and "Morning Roll Call" (1940), both published posthumously in *The Sherwood Anderson Reader*, are brilliant examples of his ability to express himself during his last years with the vibrancy that had been a basis for his distinction during the early 1920's.

"White Spot" and "Morning Roll Call" had been intended for *Sherwood Anderson's Memoirs*, a work left unfinished when he died on March 8, 1941, in the Panama Canal Zone while on an unofficial goodwill tour to South America. According to James Schevill, the book was faultily edited by Paul Rosenfeld. Such sketches as "White Spot" and "Morning Roll Call" were omitted; a few random magazine pieces more than a decade old were included despite their incongruous misrepresentation of the style and aim of the autobiographical sketches Anderson wrote during the late 1930's and which constitute most of the volume. Unfinished though the book is, however, it represents a fitting culmination of his career. All of his earlier concern with self-revelation and stylistic nuance bore fruition in charming, lyrical pages that leave one in awe at the resiliency of the human spirit as it copes with the mysteries of being in art.

The vivacity and insight of Anderson's memoirs are remarkable in view of the severe decline of his reputation in the mid-1920's and the lengthy emotional depression that affected him thereafter. To those critics who did not read his works attentively or at all after 1925, when *Dark Laughter* appeared, and to those who know Anderson's writing only on the basis of *Winesburg, Ohio* and two over-anthologized stories—"I'm a Fool" and "I Want to Know Why"—the vibrancy of the memoirs will be truly inexplicable.

Perhaps Anderson should not have expected his work early or late to be wholly or widely appreciated. From the very beginning his literary reputation was shaky. Newspaper and magazine reviewers of his early books regularly oscillated between praise and blame, often mixing both.

Since Anderson was an avant-garde writer, however, a "little magazine" phenomenon, he was at first more enthusiastically received by young writers and critics interested in an American literature that was original, complex, unsentimental, and bold in dealing with taboo subjects such as sex. Thus young Hart Crane in 1921 wrote an encomium of Anderson's "paragraphs and pages from which arises a lyricism,

deliberate and light, as a curl of milk-weed seeds drawn toward the sun. . . . He is without sentimentality; and he makes no pretense of offering solutions. He has humanity and simplicity that is quite baffling in depth and suggestiveness . . ."

But before long even the recognition of the avant-garde was qualified or withdrawn. It generally began to misjudge and overlook Anderson's method and to conclude mistakenly that he was an elderly, provincial American realist because he wrote about the Midwest and praised Dreiser for his human sympathy and his frankness in the treatment of sex. Anderson's persistent criticisms of Dreiser's style as clumsy and of Sinclair Lewis' style as superficial were ignored. The epitome of ultimate avant-garde response to Anderson is best seen in the pages of the *Dial*, which published him frequently, printed laudatory statements, and early in 1922 bestowed upon him the first *Dial* award for distinguished service to American letters, then in the next few years directly and allusively in reviews and other forms of comment gradually formulated a negative attitude toward him.

Anderson's rejection by the avant-garde deepened a sense of estrangement from vital currents of modern literature that had begun earlier when his first prominent supporters—Frank, Brooks, Paul Rosenfeld—kept finding fault with his theories and writings. In such works as *A Story Teller's Story* (1924), *The Modern Writer* (1925), and *Sherwood Anderson's Notebook* (1926), he hopefully sought to define and justify his credo. He was not helped in this task by his antipathy to "talk" about literature and ideas or by his aversion to systematic exposition. Much of what he said had the nub of good sense but it was insufficiently clarified, overcast with a playfulness inappropriate for the occasion, and gave the impression of being narcissistic self-praise of an aesthetic phenomenon superior to traditional morality and critical judgment. Self-consciously ironic and derisive references to the "modern" began to appear in his fiction and articles. An attempt to demonstrate superior "modernity" in *Dark Laughter* was a fiasco: its style, supposedly an emulation of that in James Joyce's *Ulysses*, revealed a misunderstanding of the stream-of-consciousness technique; its rendition of expatriate American experience in Europe was ludicrously uninformed and unperceptive.

The strongest blows against Anderson's prestige and well-being came from young writers whom he had befriended. Hemingway, in whom Anderson had discovered "extraordinary talent" in 1921 and whose *In Our Time* (1925) had been published as a result of Anderson's efforts, parodied Anderson in *The Torrents of Spring* (1926). Faulkner, whose *Soldiers' Pay* (1926) had also been published following Anderson's efforts, less publicly but just as sharply ridiculed Anderson in the foreword to *Sherwood Anderson & Other Famous Creoles* (1926), a book published in a limited edition in New Orleans.

For the rest of his life, from the mid-1920's on, Anderson engaged in a quest for rediscovery of the talent which seemed to have atrophied. F. Scott Fitzgerald had written: "To this day reviewers solemnly speak of him [Anderson] as an inarticulate, fumbling man, bursting with ideas—when, on the contrary, he is the possessor of a brilliant and almost inimitable prose style, and scarcely any ideas at all." Anderson perceived, with utter rightness, that there is no style without form, no form without content, that ideas are no more important than the evocative enunciation of experience. He had traveled much during his early years as an advertising man and now he resumed his travels. His second marriage had ended in divorce in 1924, two years after he left the advertising business; his third marriage broke down in 1929. Restlessly he went about the country, observing men and women, listening, attempting to regain the equilibrium of mind, emotion, and voice that had earlier produced his particular artistic vision. The idea that a permanent home might provide stability attracted him. In 1926 he built a house in the mountains of southwestern Virginia; for several years beginning in 1927 he edited two newspapers in the nearby town of Marion, Virginia. Meanwhile he continued to write stories and articles, to struggle desperately with new novels. He was often stricken with black, destructive moods, on one occasion even threw the manuscript of an unpublished novel out of a hotel window, but persisted in his search for orientation. In 1930 he fell in love with his future fourth wife; their marriage was successful. Slowly he regained his self-confidence, his talent, and his sense of humor. These are embodied in writings which swell the enduring corpus of his work beyond that already produced by 1926, writings in which he returned to the common people and locales he had earlier portrayed with similar irony, pity, and understanding.

The ultimate test of a writer's permanence is the power of his words to rekindle generations other than his own. Not until all of the fine writing which Anderson produced during the sixteen-year period after 1925 has been assembled and read will it be possible to undertake the "proper evaluation" for which Faulkner called. Meanwhile, an important place in American literary history seems assured. With characteristic humility Anderson himself had said in 1921 "that after all the only thing the present generation of men in America could expect to do is to make with their bodies and spirits a kind of fertilizing element in our soil." The issue of final grandeur and fame was a matter he left to others.

BENJAMIN T. SPENCER
From "Sherwood Anderson: American Mythopoeist"
American Literature, March 1969, pp. 4–16

This persistent concern with loneliness both in Anderson's own life and in that of his characters, Lionel Trilling has asserted, is in part traceable to his excessive reliance on intuition and observation and to his unfortunate assumption that his community lay in the "stable and the craftsman's shop" rather than in the "members of the European tradition of thought." That Anderson was only superficially and erratically involved with the literary and philosophical past of Europe is undoubtedly true. As late as 1939 he could declare that he did not know what a "usable past" is, and that his concern was rather to live intensely in the present. In effect Anderson was emphasizing the inductive and the autochthonous as primary in the literary imagination, as Emerson, Thoreau, and Whitman had done before him; or, in anticipation of William Carlos Williams, he was committing himself to the principle that only the local thing is universal. By concentrating on the elemental tensions of provincial life he was assuming, as Mark Twain had done with the Mississippi, that the archetypes of human character and situation would most surely emerge, and that by returning to "nature" or the "soil" American literature would find at once its uniqueness and its authenticity. Hence his dismissal also of recent European art as a model for American artists. How irrelevant is Whistler's pictorial mode, he wrote in the 1920's, to a valid expression of the "rolling sensuous hills . . . voluptuously beautiful" in California; and how silly are those painters who follow Gauguin when the varied life and color of New Orleans is available to them. The "half-sick neurotics, calling themselves artists" as they stumbled about the California hills, apparently resembled the "terrible . . . shuffling lot" of Americans he later observed in Paris. Yet from writers whom

he venerated as the great fictional craftsmen of Europe—Turgenev, Balzac, Cervantes—he induced what seemed to him to be the fundamental principle for a durable American literature: indigenous integrity. These authors were "deeply buried . . . in the soil out of which they had come," he asserted in *A Story Teller's Story*; they had known their own people intimately and had spoken "out of them" with "infinite delicacy and understanding." With this indigenous commitment, Anderson believed, he and other American writers could belong to "an America alive . . . no longer a despised cultural foster child of Europe." . . .

By the 1930's, and especially with the stringencies of the economic depression, Anderson's corn gods had proved illusory. In his earlier romantic commitment to the divinely organic he had construed the machine as a seductive threat to a Mid-American reunion with the earth. In those days he could still believe in the triumph of the egg—to use the title of one of his volumes which contains the story "The Egg," a humorous treatment of the effort of the persona's father to subdue a simple egg by standing it on end or forcing it into a bottle. His humiliating defeat, one may suppose, may be taken to reflect Anderson's earlier view of the futility of human attempts to contain or subdue the primal, organic forces of nature. . . . As imposed behavior and technological demands had succeeded freedom and personal pride in craftsmanship, he commented in *Poor White*, men and women had become like mice; and in *Dark Laughter* he spoke of the "tired and nervous" cities, with their "murmur of voices coming out of a pit." Over a decade later in his Southern novel *Kit Brandon* only a few of the mountain girls seemed to him to have retained a self-respect and proud individualism akin to that of "the day of America's greater richness." Of this older richness another symbol was the horse, which as a boy in the livery stable he had found to be the most beautiful thing about him and superior to many of the men with whom he had to deal. In the industrial era, he wrote in *A Story Teller's Story*, since machines had supplanted horses, his own nightmare as a writer was that of being caught as a prisoner under the "great iron bell"—that is, we may interpret, under the great humanly wrought inanimate doom. . . .

Though by the mid-1920's Anderson felt obliged to abandon many of the mythic assumptions of his Midwestern years, he could not renounce entirely the demands of his mythopoeic imagination. During the last fifteen years of his life, therefore, he sought new centers and media for a viable myth which would bring unity and beauty to his life. This he found in the mill towns of the new industrial South and in the girls who worked therein. Formerly the South had been for Anderson New Orleans and the southern Mississippi, where the dark, ironic laughter of the Negroes had seemed to express for him an elemental spontaneity and vital sense of life—a "touch with things" such as stones, trees, houses, fields, and tools, as Bruce Dudley enviously concedes in *Dark Laughter*—which made the members of a subject race humanly superior to the sterile life about them. In the later Southern novels the Negroes have all but disappeared, and though the mill girls, who as a vital center supplant them, are too much at the mercy of their factory world to embody any mythic assurance, they do point to a redemptive feminine principle which Anderson, like Henry Adams, found in his later years the surest counteragent to the disintegrating power of the machine. It was the American woman, he concluded in the 1930's, who alone could reintroduce the "mystery" which a technological age had dispelled and without which "we are lost men." Since American women at their best had not yet been "enervated spiritually" by the machine or accepted from it a "vicarious feeling of power," perhaps women, he argued in his book entitled by that phrase, might rescue the American man "crushed and puzzled" as he was in a mechanical maze.

Yet, just as Anderson's phrase "perhaps women" suggests an acknowledged tentativeness in his later mythic formulations, so his treatment of the machine in his late works often discloses a new ambiguity. As his recourse to woman for salvation reflects Adams's adoration of the Virgin, so his discovery of the poetry as well as the power of the machine follows the example of another of his five "greatest Americans," Whitman, who abandoned the pastoral milieu of "the splendid silent sun" to discover the poetry of ferries and locomotives and crowded streets. Yet Anderson, with his earlier sustained distrust of the machine, could not free himself from an ambivalence in his later years; he felt both awe and impotence, he confessed, in the presence of the vast order and power and beauty of machinery, and his tribute to Lindbergh as an emergent culture hero, the new type of machine man, as well as his sympathetic portrayal of the speed-obsessed Kit Brandon, the heroine of a late novel, betrays an uneasiness not present, say, in his characterizations of Sponge Martin and the Negroes in *Dark Laughter*. Yet watching the superb technology of the whirling machines, his hero Red Oliver, in *Beyond Desire*, no doubt reflected much of Anderson's later attitude by confessing that he felt "exultant" and that here was "American genius" at work—America at "its finest." Two years earlier, in 1930, Anderson had declared that he would no longer be "one of the . . . protestors against the machine age" but henceforth would "go to machinery" as if it were mountains or forests or rivers. Hence his poem to the beneficence of the automobile and his attempts to catch the excitement of the cotton mills in his "Machine Song" or "Loom Dance." Yet he also felt impelled to express the more sinister admixture of fear and awe experienced in the presence of the textile machines, whose hypnotic speed and incessant shuttle rhythms could induce in Molly Seabright, a mill girl in *Beyond Desire*, an indifference and confusion which led to a loss of identification with the human world about her. Modern American industry, he concluded ambivalently in *Perhaps Women* (1932), was indeed a "dance," a "flow of refined power," to which men lifted up their eyes in worshipful adoration. Surely in such statements the failure of Anderson to approach the machine as if it were mountains and rivers is manifest. The earlier mythopoeic imagination has become bifurcated into myth and poetry; the validity of the myth is not felt, and the poetry is an act of will rather than of imagination. In this bifurcation and desiccation one may no doubt find much of the explanation for Anderson's decline in his later years.

BRIAN WAY
From "Sherwood Anderson"
The American Novel and the 1920's, ed. Edward Arnold

1971, pp. 115–20

Judge Turner, in ⟨Anderson's⟩ autobiographical volume *A Story-Teller's Story* (1924), sums up the qualities of the people in his Ohio home-town in terms which could well speak for Anderson himself:

'We are what we are, we Americans, . . . and we had better stick to our knitting. Anyway, . . . people are nice here as far as I have been able to observe and

although they are filled with stupid prejudices and are fools, the common people, workers and the like, such as the men of this town, wherever you find them, are about the nicest folk one ever finds.'

Anderson's feelings about the mid-West are highly ambivalent. On the one hand it is home: it gives him a warm sense of people he knows and understands intimately, and, at a deeper level, it is . . . the source of all his deepest insights as an artist. On the other hand, it is a place where life is intolerably narrow and restricted, and where the niceness praised by Judge Turner is balanced by a strong undercurrent of cruelty. This expresses itself through gossip, vicious practical jokes, and the systematic persecution of those who do not belong to the herd. Anderson exposes these shortcomings unsparingly in 'Nobody Laughed' and 'Morning Roll Call' (both from *The Sherwood Anderson Reader*), and in certain episodes of *Poor White*. Sensitive men and women like George Willard and Mary Cochran must leave if they can, otherwise they will be warped and imprisoned like Wash Williams, the central character of 'Respectability', whose grotesque appearance cuts him off from other people as completely as if he were a hideous monkey in a cage.

For Anderson, however, the mid-West is not solely a background for his characters, nor even a set of conditions which helps to shape their lives. Like so many American novelists—Cooper, Hawthorne, Hamlin Garland, Willa Cather, Edith Wharton, Faulkner, Steinbeck, Wright Morris—he has a developed historical sense, and his work often reflects the broad pattern of evolution and disintegration to be seen in American provincial life. The parts of 'Godliness' (*Winesburg, Ohio*) which deal with Jesse Bentley, and the novel *Poor White*, are outstandingly good examples of this kind of writing.

In Jesse Bentley, the fanaticism of the American protestant tradition and nineteenth-century economic individualism combine to produce a diseased restlessness of spirit:

Jesse Bentley was a fanatic. He was a man born out of his time and place and for this he suffered and made others suffer. Never did he succeed in getting what he wanted out of life and he did not know what he wanted.

At first, in the post-Civil War years, Jesse sees himself as a primitive patriarch, an Old Testament man of God owning flocks and lands like his biblical namesake. In exalted moods he is convinced that in acquiring more land he is fulfilling God's special plan, since the other farmers of the valley are Philistines who must be driven out, as David the son of Jesse drove the Philistines of his day from the Valley of Elah. But as the pressure of industrialism comes to Ohio he gradually loses this grandiose primitive vision, and begins to dream of fortunes to be made by 'shrewd men who bought and sold':

Faintly he realized that the atmosphere of old times and places that he had always cultivated in his own mind was strange and foreign to the thing that was growing up in the minds of others. The beginning of the most materialistic age in the history of the world, when wars would be fought without patriotism, when men would forget God and only pay attention to moral standards, when the will to power would replace the will to serve and beauty would be well-nigh forgotten in the terrible headlong rush of mankind toward the acquiring of possessions, was telling its story to Jesse the man of God as it was to the men about him.

Anderson's treatment of the development of Jesse Bentley reflects very strongly the dilemma of the American who sees his country emerging from puritanism. He feels that in many ways American puritanism is hateful, cruel, bigoted and narrowing, and that an escape from it is spiritually necessary. Nevertheless, he finds that the American road away from puritanism does not lead to liberation and a better life, but to materialism, impoverishment of spirit and a loss of human dignity. Jesse, instead of being imbued with the language of the Bible and the exalted if warped imaginings it once aroused in him, becomes obsessed merely with the vulgar commercialism of the provincial newspapers and business magazines which begin to circulate with the coming of industry.

Similarly Hawthorne had observed seventy years earlier that, while the New England of Hester Prynne's day was a cruel and detestable society, it also contained a grandeur lacking in the 'exhausted soil' of the Salem of his own day; and that the savagely heroic figure of the brutal, witch-hunting Colonel Pyncheon had been replaced by the contemptibly furtive, hypocritical and corrupt Judge Pyncheon.

Anderson explores this phase of historical development in America on a much larger scale in *Poor White* (1920). Although he attempted the full-length novel a number of times, this is the only one in which he achieved a convincing artistic success. Even so it has serious weaknesses, and any claim one makes for it must rest largely on the first seven chapters.

In part, it is the story of what might have happened to Huck Finn if he had been 'sivilized', and thrown into the ferment of the Gilded Age. Hugh McVey grows up in a squalid little Mississippi river-town, like those Huck passes through in the company of the King and the Duke. Hugh's father is a drunken loafer like Pap, though without the latter's streak of manic violence. Anderson's attitude to Hugh's poor White heritage of 'bad blood' and indolence is divided: he is clearly repelled by the filth and squalor, and the mindless ignorance it represents, and yet at the same time he is aware of a certain richness and expansiveness in Hugh's loafing, day after day, on the banks of the immense river. When the railroad reaches Hugh's home-town, he gets a job at the station, and Sarah Shepard the station-master's wife takes him in hand. She is a New England woman—the puritan tradition personified—and she makes Hugh clean, industrious, restless and ambitious. His imaginative life is eliminated along with his idling, and he moves away from the stagnating river life to the Ohio town of Bidwell. At first there appears to be some compensatory gain: it is in his new way of life, his struggle to acquire a new identity— a puritan identity—, that Hugh finds the drive which makes him an inventor, a creative mind. His invention of a machine for planting cabbages gives Bidwell its first factory and initiates a rapid industrial growth. But Hugh has to pay for this new creativity by losing all spontaneity of response. His imaginative life had been closely linked with the life of the senses—the luxurious, almost sensual, indolence of his drowsing and day-dreaming on the Mississippi shore—and when he loses this, not only is his inner life impoverished, but he is cut off from other people. He is socially isolated, he has no friends, and his capacity for love or any kind of sexual relationship is atrophied. In the long run the fiasco of his marriage with Clara Butterworth can be put down to this deprivation.

The second strand in his destruction is the industrialization he himself has done so much to bring about. The greed of his rich father-in-law Tom Butterworth (a debased version of Jesse Bentley) finally destroys the very creativity—the inventiveness—liberated in Hugh by the puritan tradition. Towards the end of the novel we find that his latest invention—a hay-loader—has been forestalled by the work of another inventor in Iowa. Tom Butterworth, having found that the other man has

no financial backing, sets Hugh to modify his design so that they can get round the patent. Hugh finds he is unable to work in the climate created by this swindle. His imagination partially reawakens: he finds himself picturing the inventor he has been told to cheat, instead of setting his mind to the mechanical problem he has been told to solve. But his imagination is not awakened in a way that helps him to re-order his life: he cannot create a relationship with his wife, but can only come to her intermittently like an animal in the dark for sexual relief. At the end he seems to regress into a kind of mindless dreaminess, playing for hours with a few coloured stones. There is a dim reflection of the days of brooding by the Mississippi, but with none of the richness, the expansiveness, the sensuous ease, of that earlier time.

It is clear from the story of Hugh McVey that Anderson takes an extremely pessimistic view of what American civilization, during the phase of industrialization, has done to many individual Americans. But there are a number of places in which he takes a wider perspective, and tries to evoke the more general qualitative changes which took place in the life of the rural and small-town communities of the mid-West. In spite of their narrowness and provincial isolation, these communities, in the last years of the nineteenth century, had begun to mature into a distinct and valuable phase of American civilization:

> In all the towns of mid-western America it was a time of waiting. The country having been cleared and the Indians driven away into a vast distant place spoken of vaguely as the West, the Civil War having been fought and won, and there being no great problems that touched deeply their lives, the minds of men were turned in upon themselves. . . . For the moment mankind seemed about to take time to try to understand itself.
>
> (chapter 3)

Anderson evokes the slow settling and maturing process which had led to this moment in chapter 7, where he describes the small frame-houses built by the Ohio farmers on their land:

> After one of the poor little houses had been lived in for a long time, after children had been born and men had died; after men and women had suffered and had moments of joy together in the tiny rooms under the low roofs a subtle change took place. The houses became almost beautiful in their old human-ness. Each of the houses began vaguely to shadow forth the personality of the people who lived within its walls.

The mid-West pioneer farming community was on the verge of becoming a civilization but, at that moment, instead of a slow flowering into a life of amenity which the old farming life had largely lacked, industry struck the mid-West a paralysing blow which destroyed all human values—even the little the farming and small-town communities had already achieved:

> A sense of quiet growth awoke in sleeping minds. It was the time for art and beauty to awake in the land.
>
> Instead, the giant, Industry, awoke. Boys, who in the schools had read of Lincoln walking for miles through the forest to borrow his first book, and of Garfield, the towpath boy who became president, began to read in the newspapers and magazines of men who by developing their faculty for getting and keeping money had become suddenly and overwhelmingly rich. Hired writers called these men great, and there was no maturity of mind in the people with which to combat the force of the statement often repeated.

Interesting as this explicit analysis is, the success of *Poor White* depends on Anderson's power to present his vision through the creation of scene and character. One of the finest of these is the scene in which Hugh McVey gets his idea for a cabbage plant-setting machine. He watches, himself unobserved, while old Ezra French and his family plant cabbages by moonlight, crawling over the ground in an extravagant demonstration of the crushing burden of physical labour. In a flash of intuition, the principle of the invention come to him. Wildly excited, he forgets where he is, rises to his feet, and begins to follow the crawling figures down the rows, miming the action of the revolving mechanical arms which will set the plants in the soil. When the French sons and daughters turn at the ends of their rows and see Hugh advancing on them, they flee in terror. Their life is earthbound, crude, grotesque, and yet there is a strange poetry in the workings of a folk-imagination which sees in Hugh's gesticulating figure the ghost of a redskin, risen from the Indian burying-ground which lies beneath the field, to haunt the paleface intruders.

Maya Angelou

1928–

Maya Angelou was born Marguerite Johnson in St. Louis, Missouri in 1928. Her life is arguably her art, for she has won her greatest critical acclaim for her autobiographical writing rather than her poetry and drama. Angelou has also applied her talents to the performing arts: she has studied dance with Martha Graham, and has also formally studied music and drama. She toured nationally in the company of *Porgy and Bess* in 1954, and she later directed her own stage version of her autobiographical *And Still I Rise*. Angelou has also worked for Hollywood writing scripts and composing songs for her screenplays. Known in the U.S. as a prominent spokesperson for Black awareness and as the host of several television specials on Black culture, Maya Angelou's interests eventually led her to Africa, where she worked as a reporter and editor in Egypt and Ghana, and as a teacher at the University of Ghana. Angelou was nominated for the National Book Award in 1970 for *I Know Why the Caged Bird Sings* and in 1972 for the Pulitzer Poetry Prize for *Just Give Me a Cool Drink of Water 'fore I Diiie*. She married in 1973 and has one child. Her works include: *Gather Together in My Name* (1979), *Singin' and Swingin' and Gettin' Merry Like Christmas* (1976), *The Heart of a Woman* (1981), and *Shaker, Why Don't You Sing?* (1983).

Personal

Black Scholar: Can you comment a bit on the importance of endurance in black writers?

Maya Angelou: Endurance is one thing. I think endurance with output, endurance with productivity is the issue. If one has the fortune, good or bad, to stay alive one endures, but to continue to write the books and get them out—that's the productivity and I think that is important to link with the endurance.

I find myself taking issue with the term minor poet, minor writer of the 18th century, minor writer of the 19th century; but I do understand what people mean by that. Generally they mean that the writer, the poet who only wrote one book of poetry or one novel, or two, is considered a minor poet or minor writer because of his or her output, its scarcity. I can't argue with that. I do believe that it is important to get the work done, seen, read, published, and *given* to an audience. One has enjoyed oneself, one has done what one has been put here to do, to write. Another thing is that one has given a legacy of some quantity to generations to come. Whether they like it or not, whether the writer values the next generation, or values the work or not, at least there is something, there is a body of work to examine and to respond to, to react to.

I know a number of people who do work very slowly but I don't believe, although I have close friends who write slowly, in taking five years to write one book. Now I think they have psyched themselves into believing they cannot work more quickly, that hence because they work slowly their work is of more value. They also believe—they have bought that American baloney, the masterpiece theory—everything you write must be a masterpiece, each painting you paint must be a masterpiece.

Black Scholar: I want to talk to you more about that. I think any artist in this society is inhibited in many ways because it is not an aesthetic society.

Maya Angelou: Materialistic.

Black Scholar: I think the black writer has even more difficulty because his vision is antagonistic, it's a racist society, his whole stuff is different. Do you think that the masterpiece syndrome further inhibits the output of black writers?

Maya Angelou: To me that inhibits *all* artists. Every artist in this society is affected by it. I don't say he or she is inhibited, he or she might work against it and make that work for them, as I hope I do, but we are affected by it.

It is in reaction to that dictate from a larger society that spurs my output, makes me do all sorts of things, write movies and direct them, write plays, write music and write articles. That's because I don't believe in the inhibition of my work; I am obliged, I am compulsive, I will work against it. If necessary I will go to work on a dictionary, you understand, just to prove that that is a lot of bullshit.

So every artist in the society has to deal with that dictate. Some are crippled by it, others, I believe, are made more healthy. Because they are made more strong, and become more ready to struggle against it.

. . . So I am saying that all of the problems of artists in a mechanistic, materialistic society, all those problems are heightened, if not doubled, for the black American artist.

So as usual the black writer—I can only speak for the

writer—the black writer in particular should throw out all of that propaganda and pressure, disbelieve everything one is told to believe and believe everything one is told *not* to believe. Start with a completely clean slate and decide, "I will put it out."

A great writer only writes one book every five years. Says who? Who made that rule? I don't believe it. Just because it is told to me I don't believe it; on general principle I don't believe it. And I look at a James Baldwin with those pieces of work out. If I want to read Ralph Ellison, I am obliged to reread and reread and reread *Invisible Man* or *Shadow and Act* and how many times can you reread it? You get the essence, then you get the details and there it is. But if I disagree with Baldwin in, say, *No Name in the Street*, I can pick up *Fire Next Time*, I can go to read *Blues for Mr. Charlie*—I just used a piece from *Blues for Mr. Charlie*—I can go to see *Amen Corner*, I can read a short story from *Going to Meet the Man*; I mean the work is there.

Whatever I say, I cannot ignore the fact that the man has put the work out there. . . . One of the most aggravating things of all is to pick up a review of a work of mine and have a reviewer say, "She is a natural writer." That sometimes will make me so angry that I will cry, really, because my intent is to write so it seems to flow. I think it's Alexander Pope who says, "Easy writing is damn hard reading," and vice versa, easy reading is damn hard writing. Sometimes I will stay up in my room for a day trying to get two sentences that will flow, that will just seem as if they were always there. And many times I come home unable to get it so I go back the next day, 6:30 in the morning, every morning, 6:30 I go to work. I'm there by 7:00; I work till 2:00 alone in this tiny little room, 7 × 10 feet. I have had the room for two years and they have never changed the linen. I've never slept there. There is nothing in the room except a bed, a face basin, and that's it. I write in longhand. If it is going well I might go to 3:00 but then I pull myself out, come home, take a shower, start dinner, check my house, so that when Paul comes in at 5:30 I have had a little time out of that, although my heart and my mind are there, I still try to live an honest life. Then when you go back it looks different to you. I think that a number of artists again, or people who have pretensions that in order to be an artist you must have the back of your hand glued to your forehead, you know, and walk around and be "terribly terribly . . ." all the time, thinking great thoughts of pith and moment. That's bullshit. In order to get the work done and *finally that is all there is*, it's the *work!* all the posturing, all the lack of posturing, none of that matters, it is finally the work. You don't really get away from it but you try and I think that is very healthy.—MAYA ANGELOU, Interview with Robert Chrisman, *BIS*, Jan.-Feb. 1977, pp. 45–49

Works

POETRY

. . . I can't help feeling that Maya Angelou's career has suffered from the interest her publishers have in mythologizing her. *Oh Pray My Wings Are Gonna Fit Me Well* is such a painfully untalented collection of poems that I can't think of any reason, other than the Maya Myth, for it to be in print: it's impossible, indeed, to separate the book's flap copy, with its glossy celebration of "Maya Angelou . . . one of the world's most exciting women. . . . Maya, the eternal female" from the book itself. All this is especially depressing because Angelou, "eternal female" or not, is a stunningly talented prose writer, whose marvelous *I Know Why the Caged Bird Sings* has quite

properly become a contemporary classic. Why should it be necessary, then, for her to represent herself publicly as the author of such an embarrassing tangle as

> I'd touched your features inchly
>   heard love and dared the cost.
> The scented spiel reeled me unreal
>   and found my senses lost.

And why, instead of encouraging Angelou, didn't some friendly editor Block (as *The New Yorker* would say) the following Metaphor:

> A day
> drunk with the nectar of
> nowness
> weaves its way between
> the years
> to find itself at the flophouse
> of night. . . .

To be fair, not all the verse in *Oh Pray . . .* is quite as bad as these two examples. A few of the colloquial pieces—"Pickin Em Up and Layin Em Down" or "Come. And Be My Baby"—have the slangy, unpretentious vitality of good ballads. "The Pusher" ("He bad/O he bad"), with its echoes of Brooks's "We real cool", achieves genuine scariness. And "John J." might be a portrait in verse of Bailey, the handsome brother Angelou renders so beautifully in *I Know Why. . . .* But these are only four or five poems out of the thirty-six in this collection. And most of the others, when they're not awkward or stilted, are simply corny. The writer whose unsentimental wit and passionate accuracy gave us such a fresh account of growing up black and female really doesn't need to publish "No one knows/my lonely heart/when we're apart" or "No lady cookinger than my Mommy/smell that pie/see I don't lie/No lady cookinger than my Mommy" (from "Little Girl Speakings"). Angelou can hardly be accused of self-parody: for one thing, most of the poetry here is too unself-conscious, too thoughtless, to be in any sense parodic. But, for whatever reason, the wings of song certainly don't seem to fit her very well right now.—SANDRA M. GILBERT, "A Platoon of Poets," *Poetry*, Aug. 1976, pp. 296–97

And Still I Rise is Angelou's third volume of verse, and most of its thirty-two poems are as slight as those which dominated the pages of the first two books. Stanzas such as this one,

> In every town and village,
> In every city square,
> In crowded places
> I search the faces
> Hoping to find
> Someone to care.

or the following,

> Then you rose into my life,
> Like a promised sunrise.
> Brightening my days with the light in your eyes.
> I've never been so strong,
> Now I'm where I belong.

cannot but make lesser-known talents grieve all the more about how this thin stuff finds its way to the rosters of a major New York house while their stronger, more inventive lines seem to be relegated to low-budget (or no budget) journals and presses. On the other hand, a good Angelou poem has what we call "possibilities." One soon discovers that she is on her surest ground when she "borrows" various folk idioms and forms and thereby buttresses her poems by evoking aspects of a culture's written and unwritten heritage. "One More Round," for example, gains most of its energy from "work songs" and "protest songs" that have come before. In this eight-stanza poem, the even-number stanzas constitute a refrain obviously, a "work song" refrain:

> One more round
> And let's heave it down.
> One more round
> And let's heave it down.

At the heart of the odd-number stanzas are variations upon the familiar "protest" couplet "But before I'll be a slave/I'll be buried in my grave," such as the following: "I was born to work up to my grave/But I was not born/To be a slave." The idea of somehow binding "work" and "protest" forms to create new art is absolutely first rate, but the mere alteration of "work" and "protest" stanzas does not, in this instance, carry the idea very far.

Other poems, such as "Willie," cover familiar ground previously charted by Sterling Brown, Langston Hughes, and Gwendolyn Brooks. Indeed, Angelou's Willie, despite his rare powers and essences ("When the sun rises/I am the time./When the children sing/I am the Rhyme."); approaches becoming memorable only when he is placed in that pantheon where Brooks's Satin-Legs Smith and Brown's Sportin' Beasly are already seated. Similarly, "Through the Inner City to the Suburbs," "Lady Luncheon Club," and "Momma Welfare Roll" bear strong resemblances in several poems of Brooks's pre-Black Aesthetic period in *Annie Allen* and *The Bean-Eaters*.

Up to a point, "Still I Rise," Angelou's title poem, reminds us of Brown's famous "Strong Men," and it is the discovery of that point which helps us define Angelou's particular presence and success in contemporary letters and, if we may say so, in publishing. The poetic and visual rhythms created by the repetition of "Still I rise" and its variants clearly revoke that of Brown's "strong men . . . strong men gittin' stronger." But the "I" of Angelou's refrain is obviously female and, in this instance, a woman forthright about the sexual nuances of personal and social struggle:

> Does my sexiness upset you?
> Does it come as a surprise
> That I dance like I've got diamonds
> At the meeting of my thighs?

Needless to say, the woman "rising" from these lines is largely unaccounted for in the earlier verse of men and women poets alike. Most certainly, this "phenomenal woman," as she terms herself in another poem, is not likely to appear, except perhaps in a negative way, in the feminist verse of our time. Where she *does* appear is in Angelou's own marvelous autobiographies, *I Know Why the Caged Bird Sings* and *Gather Together in My Name*. In short, Angelou's poems are often woefully thin as poems but they nevertheless work their way into contemporary literary history. In their celebration of a particularly defined "phenomenal woman," they serve as ancillary, supporting texts for Angelou's more adeptly rendered self-portraits, and even guide the reader to (or back to) the autobiographies. With this achieved, Angelou's "phenomenal woman," as persona *and* self-portrait, assumes a posture in our literature that would not be available if she were the product of Angelou's prose or verse alone.—R. B. STEPTO, "The Phenomenal Woman and the Severed Daughter," *Parn*, Fall 1979, pp. 313–15

AUTOBIOGRAPHY

Maya Angelou writes like a song, and like the truth. The wisdom, rue and humor of her storytelling are borne on a lilting rhythm completely her own, the product of a born writer's senses nourished on black church singing and preaching, soft mother talk and salty street talk, and on literature: James Weldon Johnson, Langston Hughes, Richard Wright, Shakespeare and Gorki. Her honesty is also very much her own, even when she faces bitter facts or her own youthful foolishness. In this second installment of her autobiography ⟨*Gather Together in My Name*⟩, as in her much praised first book, *I Know Why the Caged Bird Sings*, Maya Angelou accomplishes the rare feat of laying her own life open to a reader's scrutiny without the reflex-covering gesture of melodrama or shame. And as she reveals herself so does she reveal the black community, with a quiet pride, a painful candor and a clean anger.

Gather Together in My Name is a little shorter and thinner than its predecessor; telling of an episodic, searching and wandering period in Maya Angelou's life, it lacks the density of childhood. In full compensation, her style has both ripened and simplified. It is more telegraphic and more condensed, transmitting a world of sensation or emotion or understanding in one image—in short, it is more like poetry. (Maya Angelou published a book of poems, *Just Give Me a Cool Drink of Water 'fore I Diiie*, in between the two autobiographical volumes.)

"Disappointment rode his face bareback." "Dumbfounded, founded in dumbness." "The heavy opulence of Dostoevsky's world was where I had lived forever. The gloomy, lightless interiors, the complex ratiocinations of the characters and their burdensome humors, were as familiar to me as loneliness." "The South I returned to . . . was flesh-real and swollen-belly poor." "I clenched my reason and forced their faces into focus." Even in these short bits snipped out of context, you can sense the palpability, the precision and the rhythm of this writing. The reader is rocked into pleasure, stung into awareness. And the migrant, irresolute quality of the story—a faithful reflection of her late adolescence in the forties—resolves into a revelation. The restless, frustrated trying-on of roles turns out to have been an instinctive self-education, and the book ends with Maya Angelou finally gaining her adulthood by regaining her innocence.

. . . In *Gather Together in My Name*, the ridiculous and touching posturing of a young girl in the throes of growing up are superimposed on the serious business of survival and responsibility for a child. Maya Angelou's insistence on taking full responsibility for her own life, her frank and humorous examination of her self, will challenge many a reader to be as honest under easier circumstances. Reading her book, you may learn, too, the embrace and ritual, the dignity and solace and humor of the black community. You will meet strong, distinctive people, drawn with deftness and compassion; their blackness is not used to hide their familiar but vulnerable humanity any more than their accessible humanity can for a moment be used to obscure their blackness—or their oppression. Maya Angelou's second book about her life as a young black woman in America is engrossing and vital, rich and funny and wise.—ANNIE GOTTLIEB, "Growing up and the Serious Business of Survival," *NYTBR*, June 16, 1974, pp. 16, 20

Increasingly puzzling and unsettling, the more one tries to work with it, is Maya Angelou's *I Know Why the Caged Bird Sings*. Writing during her thirties, Angelou, of course, has a far less mature point of view than Mead and Hellman, whose autobiographies were written when they were in their sixties, which may be why she never comes to terms with the matriarchal face that her biological mother embodies. She paints it over with a daughterly love that the mother does not deserve and that is singularly unconvincing.

The most positive and convincing face of the matriarchate and the one that provides the foundation of Angelou's personality is her father's mother, the grandmother to whom she is strangely and without explanation sent at age three just because the parents are divorced. She calls her Momma, and the first part of the book is a hymn to her.

Momma's looming, quiescent, brooding qualities make her far more primal and numinous than Mead's grandmother. Momma's religiosity, her resting on providence, her inflexibility and conservativism, and even her irrationality make her into a mindless though practical mother hen:

> People . . . said she used to be right pretty. I saw only her power and strength. She was taller than any woman in my personal world, and her hands were so large they could span my head from ear to ear. . . .
> In church when she was called upon to sing, she seemed to pull out plugs from behind her jaws and the huge, almost rough sound would pour over the listeners and throb in the air.

Everyone in Stamps admired "the worth and majesty of my grandmother." Momma is proud of being black, disapproving even of Shakespeare since he was white. Her matriarchal realm includes her son Willy, crippled from birth, whom she continues to protect and shelter as if he were a child. She rules with deep love and an iron hand, often from principles she does not bother to explain to Angelou and her brother Bailey: "Her world was bordered on all sides with work, duty, religion and 'her place.' I don't think she ever knew that a deep-brooding love hung over everything she touched." She stands strong and silent even before the obscenely vicious baiting of the local white children; Angelou seems in the rest of her narrative to emulate this strength during such horrors as the rape by Mr. Freeman and the knifing by her father's mistress.

It is not until the appearance of her father that Angelou questions the worth of being female, but the father's obvious preference for Bailey makes her wish to have been a boy. Then she meets her frivolous and beautiful mother who could pass for white and finds that even as a female, she is inferior to the prevailing cultural standards. The oppressiveness and lack of maternal love in her mother's Venus-like role are reflected in the gradual destruction of Bailey as he attempts to internalize his mother's image, to come to terms with her sending them away twice to Momma. The mother's cold yet heated sexuality is apparent throughout. In the matriarchate of her mother, Mr. Freeman (the mother's live-in lover) seems to have all life force suspended, sitting inanimate until the mother appears. He seems to be useful only for sexual purposes, and he uses Angelou as an extension of her mother. Then, in the most shocking callousness one could adopt toward a child, the mother returns her daughter to Momma because Maya is depressed after the rape.

In her own behavior at the end of her book, Angelou splits the feminine archetype of her mother's cold Venus and her grandmother's primal warm sheltering Demeter aspects. She offers herself to a neighborhood boy for her first voluntary sexual experience. This partakes of the anonymity of the temple whore and Venus' use of the male as sexual cohort only. This act also reflects Angelou's inability to feel that a man could find her desirable, even though her mother's third husband, who appears on the scene in Angelou's early teens, has been kind to her. In a psychologically bizarre ending, Angelou finds her adulthood through her acceptance and love of her baby son. Her mother brings him to her bed, and when she awakens, she finds that she has instinctively slept so as not to

hurt him. This acting out of her grandmother's qualities of sheltering, warm, fortress-like physicality reflects her comfort with the Demeter archetype, not with the adult woman's Venus or Hera (the wife archetype) couplings with the male. It seems a celebration of womanhood through becoming the Primal Great Good Mother, but skipping all the steps in between of establishing authentic contact with the male world and/or making one's own matriarchal realm. She says she feels close to her own mother at the end, but that too is difficult to believe. Her mother has thoroughly betrayed her, but never does Angelou show us that she or her mother has consciously confronted this rejection. In a way, having the baby can be seen as Angelou's counter-betrayal. At any rate, the emergence of the baby from the womb of this girl-child who has not even been truly sexually awakened in any concrete way seems a tragic way to end the book and begin life as an adult. Birth as self-actualization or gender realization would appear a very limited step toward consciousness; at any rate, I always feel tricked at the book's conclusion. However, perhaps it is psychologically apt and even life-affirming in that Angelou does not lose but consolidates her sense of the strength of her grandmother and all she symbolizes. Like ⟨Lillian⟩ Hellman, she is a survivor *only* through the expression of a positive feminine principle *outside* the nuclear family.—STEPHANIE A. DEMETRAKOPOULOS, "The Metaphysics of Matrilinearism in Women's Autobiography," *Women's Autobiography*, 1980, pp. 196–99

Maya Angelou's book ⟨*The Heart of a Woman*⟩, covering as it does the years roughly 1957–1961, is a third installment of her personal saga. The book also covers one of the most exciting periods in recent African and Afro-American history. The beginning of a new awareness of Africa on the part of Negroes. It is the period of the early civil rights marches, of Malcolm X and Dr. Martin Luther King, Jr., of the Egypt of Nasser and the Ghana of Nkrumah, and the murder of the Congo's Patrice Lumumba. It is also the period when Maya tries her wings and learns that she can fly, of her brief but important marriage to a South African freedom fighter, and the period when her *wunderkind* son, Guy Johnson, grows into manhood.

As with all her books *The Heart of a Woman* can be mined for its riches: instruction, insight, humor, wry wit, lore, and fine writing. From this casebook on successful single parenting, we can see the perils a single mother, in this case a black one, faces in bringing up a black male child in our society, where so many things seem bent on preventing him from reaching adulthood. Beyond the brute struggle to provide, there must be the constant watchfulness to insure that the child is not physically maimed or spiritually stunted. Then there is the danger of bringing up a male child by a lone woman, walking the fine line between sensuality and sexuality, the danger of distorting his sexuality. Maya Angelou shows how one woman succeeds in skirting these dangers and comes out safely on the other side.

In her marriage to Make, we see the inherent problems of an Afro-American marrying a traditional African. No way an African-American woman, used to an essentially equal relation with her man, can long submit to the subservient role an African wife is expected to play. She discovers on her visit to a London Afro-Asian conference that educated African women, too, were resenting their marital restraints and were beginning to do something about them.

As befits a master story teller, Maya Angelou's book is rich with the tight sketch, the apt portrait, the pithy line. Like

Thoreau, she builds from the sentence. Throughout her account of her many experiences, I am constantly arrested when she uses just the right sentence to share some insight or fix some conclusion.

While Maya Angelou does many things in *The Heart of a Woman*, what she keeps constant throughout the book is that it is the account of a black W-O-M-A-N's life. Her experiences with women, her love and respect for them and theirs for her, her niceness and delicacy in dealing with them, from her mother to her friends, even to mere acquaintances, these could provide a model of conduct for any woman to follow.

Few will come away from this look into Maya Angelou's heart without being moved.—ADAM DAVID MILLER, *BIS*, Summer 1982, pp. 48–49

Outstanding are several of her characterizations (in *The Heart of a Woman*): of her mother, Vivian Baxter Jackson, depicted in a gem of a scene in Fresno's Desert Hotel; of Make, with his strengths as a revolutionary and his idiosyncrasies—custom-tailored clothes, luxurious tastes, deceptions, feelings of male superiority and rigidities of conventional African behavior. Picasso never distorted portraits of his son, and in the same way Guy, Angelou's son, is treated with the utmost finesse and tenderness.

These portraits, however, are in flagrant contrast to the fanatic hostility the author expresses toward all white people. Certainly there is cause for bitterness, but its extremity is sad and unfortunate. In spite of national recognition and success, Angelou cannot seem to learn (at least by the time of the writing of this book) the wisdom in Martin Luther King's counsel when he tells her, "Remember we are not alone. There are a lot of good people in this nation. White people who love right and are willing to stand up and be counted." Instead she seems to agree with Malcolm X, who tells her, "All whites are blue-eyed devils trained to do one thing—take the black man's life."

The naïve lack of understanding of the meaning of Christ's "Turn the other cheek" is astounding in one of obvious intelligence. Her venomous hostility to one and all of the white race gives no quarter but is the epitome of stereotype and cliché. She would have compassion and gives none. She would have a world free of prejudice and is herself guilty of a reverse prejudice as violent as that of the psychopathic Southerner of the pre-civil rights days. When she appears in the Jean Genet play *The Blacks*, she wonders why the largely white audience "sits gaping as black actors fling filthy words and even filthier meanings into their faces," only to respond to this ridicule by applauding and shouting "Bravo!" I must admit that as a member of that audience, I recall wondering the same thing, and I assure Angelou that one person there did not join in the applause. Genet proposes that if blacks seize power, they will become as tyrannical and hate-ridden as the whites. Does Angelou not realize that her own attitude substantiates this? Only at the very close of the book does she state, "Sooner or later I am going to have to admit that I didn't understand black men or black boys and certainly not all white men." Let us hope it will be sooner rather than later that she learns that a prayer for mercy itself "doth teach us all to render the deeds of mercy."

Although the book on the whole cannot be called a great artistic or literary achievement, it nevertheless is absorbing, with several scenes narrated skillfully: the demonstration at the United Nations, the performance at the Apollo Theatre, life in Cairo's diplomatic circles, her son's accident—all these are molded by a talented writer who does attempt to be honest. Thereby some insight into the heart of one lusty, creative,

bitter yet courageous black woman is gained.—DAISY ALDAN, *World Literature Today*, Autumn 1982, p. 697

In the philosophy of Henri Bergson, there are two kinds of time: the measurable time of science, and *durée*. *Durée* is the kind of time creative people experience. It consists of moments of creative bursts of energy, intuition, insight, and *élan vital* (the creative surge of life). Change, flux, and freedom of choice are the real facts of life in Bergsonian philosophy. Freedom comes from growth, which comes from change.

Marguerite Johnson changed. From a poor plain black girl growing up in Stamps, Arkansas, she changed. From a single mother with the odds stacked against her, she changed. In the spirit of Don L. Lee (Haki Madhubuti) she changed, because she knew the real enemy was herself. Marguerite Johnson changed to Maya Angelou, singer, dancer, poet, civil rights activist, and playwright.

The Heart of a Woman is the fourth volume of Maya Angelou's autobiography. The predecessors are: *I Know Why the Caged Bird Sings*, *Gather Together in My Name*, and *Singin' and Swingin' and Gettin' Merry Like Christmas* (all available in paperback). The major theme of each of these volumes, and especially the latest, is Maya's ceaseless *élan vital*. She has lived in the kind of time Bergson described so well—not the stale measured time of rationality, but burstingly procreative time. And her greatest creation, one might say, is herself.

The major influences in Angelou's life were her mother, who was always ready with an apt aphorism; her son Guy, who changed his name, too (from Clyde) and inspired his mother to achieve; and a steady stream of well-wishers who often valued her talent more highly than she did herself. Under these influences Maya became the startling moth that emerged from a plain chrysalis.

Super-achievers like Maya Angelou usually write autobiographies, sometimes more than one. (W. E. B. DuBois, for example, wrote his first one in his late twenties, another on his fortieth birthday, another on his fiftieth, and so on.) All autobiographies ultimately have a theme and make a statement. In Maya Angelou's latest book, the theme is twofold: creativity and engagement. We learn by her example the value of both an artistic and an activist lifestyle. The real story of Maya Angelou is the story of a plain, black, six foot tall girl, a child of the American South, who has lived triumphantly and is telling us how she "got ovah."—MARIA K. MOOTRY IKERIONWU, "A Black Woman's Story," *Phylon*, March 1983, pp. 86–87

SIDONIE ANN SMITH
"The Song of a Caged Bird:
Maya Angelou's Quest After Self-Acceptance"
Southern Humanities Review, Fall 1973, pp. 366–75

In (the) primal scene of childhood which opens Maya Angelou's *I Know Why the Caged Bird Sings*, the black girl child testifies to her imprisonment in her bodily prison. She is a black ugly reality, not a whitened dream. And the attendant self-consciousness and diminished self-image throb through her bodily prison until the bladder can do nothing but explode in a parody of release (freedom).

In good autobiography the opening, whether a statement of fact such as the circumstance of birth or ancestry or the recreation of a primal incident such as Maya Angelou's, defines the strategy of the narrative. The strategy itself is a function of the autobiographer's self-image at the moment of writing, for the nature of that self-image determines the nature of the pattern of self-actualization he discovers while attempting to shape his past experiences. Such a pattern must culminate in some sense of an ending, and it is this sense of an ending that informs certain earlier moments with significance and determines the choice of what experience he recreates, what he discards. In fact the earlier moments are fully understood only after that sense of an ending has imposed itself upon the material of the autobiographer's life. Ultimately, then, the opening moment assumes the end, the end the opening moment. Its centrality derives from its distillation of the environment of the self which generated the pattern of the writer's quest after self-actualization.

In Black American autobiography the opening almost invariably recreates the environment of enslavement from which the black self seeks escape. Such an environment was literal in the earliest form of black autobiography, the slave narrative, which traced the flight of the slave northward from slavery into full humanity. In later autobiography, however, the literal enslavement is replaced by more subtle forms of economic, historical, psychological, and spiritual imprisonment from which the black self still seeks an escape route to a "North." Maya Angelou's opening calls to mind the primal experience which opens Richard Wright's *Black Boy*. Young Richard, prevented from playing outside because of his sick, "white"-faced grandmother, puts fire to curtains and burns down the house. For this his mother beats him nearly to death. Richard's childhood needs for self-expression culminate in destruction, foreshadowing the dilemma the autobiographer discovers in his subsequent experience. His needs for self-actualization when blocked eventuate in violence. But any attempt at self-actualization is inevitably blocked by society, black and white, which threatens him with harsh punishment, possibly even death. Finally Wright is forced to flee the South altogether with only the knowledge of the power of the word to carry with him. *Black Boy's* opening scene of childhood rebellion against domestic oppression distils the essence of Wright's struggle to free himself from social oppression.

Maya Angelou's autobiography, like Wright's, opens with a primal childhood scene that brings into focus the nature of the imprisoning environment from which the self will seek escape. The black girl child is trapped within the cage of her own diminished self-image around which interlock the bars of natural and social forces. The oppression of natural forces, of physical appearance and processes, foists a self-consciousness on all young girls who must grow from children into women. Hair is too thin or stringy or mousy or nappy. Legs are too fat, too thin, too bony, the knees too bowed. Hips are too wide or not wide enough. Breasts grow too fast or not at all. The self-critical process is incessant, a driving demon. But in the black girl child's experience these natural bars are reinforced with the rusted iron social bars of racial subordination and impotence. Being born black is itself a liability in a world ruled by white standards of beauty which imprison the child *a priori* in a cage of ugliness: "What you looking at me for?" This really isn't me. I'm white with long blond hair and blue eyes, with pretty pink skin and straight hair, with a delicate mouth. I'm my own mistake. I haven't dreamed myself hard enough. I'll try again. The black and blue bruises of the soul multiply and compound as the caged bird flings herself against these bars:

> The Black female is assaulted in her tender years by all those common forces of nature at the same time that she is caught in the tripartite crossfire of mascu-

line prejudice, white illogical hate and Black lack of power.

Within this imprisoning environment there is no place for this black girl child. She becomes a displaced person whose pain is intensified by her consciousness of that displacement:

> If growing up is painful for the Southern Black girl, being aware of her displacement is the rust on the razor that threatens the throat.
>   It is an unnecessary insult.

If the black man is denied his potency and his masculinity, if his autobiography narrates the quest of the black male after a "place" of full manhood, the black woman is denied her beauty and her quest is one after self-accepted black womanhood. Thus the discovered pattern of significant moments Maya Angelou superimposes on the experience of her life is a pattern of moments that trace the quest of the black female after a "place," a place where a child no longer need ask self-consciously, "What you looking at me for?" but where a woman can declare confidently, "I am a beautiful, Black woman."

Maya Angelou's autobiography comes to a sense of an ending: the black American girl child has succeeded in freeing herself from the natural and social bars imprisoning her in the cage of her own diminished self-image by assuming control of her life and fully accepting her black womanhood. The displaced child has found a "place." With the birth of her child Maya is herself born into a mature engagement with the forces of life. In welcoming that struggle she refuses to live a death of quiet acquiescence:

> Few, if any, survive their teens. Most surrender to the vague but murderous pressure of adult conformity. It becomes easier to die and avoid conflicts than to maintain a constant battle with the superior forces of maturity.

One final comment: one way of dying to life's struggle is to suppress its inevitable pain by forgetting the past. Maya Angelou, who has since been a student and teacher of dance, a correspondent in Africa, a northern coordinator for the Southern Christian Leadership Council, an actress, writer, and director for the stage and film, had, like so many of us, successfully banished many years of her past to the keeping of the unconscious where they lay dormant and remained lost to her. To the extent that they were lost, so also a part of her self was lost. Once she accepted the challenge of recovering the lost years, she accepted the challenge of the process of self-discovery and reconfirmed her commitment to life's struggle. By the time she, as autobiographer, finished remembering the past and shaping it into a pattern of significant moments, she had imposed some sense of an ending upon it. And in imposing that ending upon it she gave the experience distance and a context and thereby came to understand the past and ultimately to understand herself.

Moreover, she reaffirms her sense of self-worth by making the journey back through her past on its own terms, by immersing herself once again in the medium of her making. Stamps, Arkansas, imprinted its way of life on the child during her formative years: the lasting evidence of this imprint is the sound of it. Her genius as a writer is her ability to recapture the texture of the way of life in the texture of its idioms, its idiosyncratic vocabulary and especially in its process of image-making. The imagery holds the reality, giving it immediacy. That she chooses to recreate the past in its own sounds suggests to the reader that she accepts the past and recognizes its beauty and its ugliness, its assets and its liabilities, its strength and its weakness. Here we witness a return to and final acceptance of the past in the return to and full acceptance of its language, the language a symbolic construct of a way of life. Ultimately

Maya Angelou's style testifies to her reaffirmation of self-acceptance, the self-acceptance she achieves within the pattern of the autobiography.

JOHN ASHBERY

1927–

John Lawrence Ashbery was born on July 28, 1927, in Rochester, New York, and grew up on a farm upstate. He attended Harvard, where he wrote a thesis on Auden, and completed an M.A. at Columbia University.

Ashbery's first book, *Some Trees*, was chosen by Auden in the Yale Younger Poets Series, with a foreword by Auden himself. In the years that followed, Ashbery was usually grouped together with O'Hara, Koch, and Schuyler, as part of the "New York School," despite the fact that between 1955 and 1965 Ashbery lived in Paris. Although the differences between the several poets were marked, they did all share an antagonism towards what they saw as the excessive academicism and pomposity of American poetry in the 1950's.

In Paris Ashbery worked as an art critic for the *International Herald-Tribune* and for *Art News*. He was also an editor of *Locus Solus*. In voluntary exile from his own language, he wrote the most bizarre, murky and controversial poems of his career, collected in 1962 as *The Tennis Court Oath*, and savaged by the critics.

After his return to New York, *Rivers and Mountains* (1966) established something like a return to normality. The book won high praise in some quarters, as did all Ashbery's later books, but it was not until 1976 and the bestowal of the Pulitzer Prize, the National Book Award, and the National Book Critics Circle Award on *Self-Portrait in a Convex Mirror* that Ashbery's work won widespread critical and popular acceptance. Since *Self-Portrait in a Convex Mirror* he has published several more books, of which the latest is *A Wave* (1984).

No other major American poet has had to weather such critical storms to arrive at his present reputation. His poetry has been relentlessly challenging and experimental. Its present popularity suggests that despite its oddities, strangeness, and difficulty, it has spoken to "the center of today."

Ashbery has written plays and essays and co-authored, with James Schuyler, a comic novel entitled *A Nest of Ninnies*. He currently teaches creative writing at Brooklyn College and is Art Critic for *Newsweek*. He lives in Manhattan.

RICHARD HOWARD
From "'You May Never Know How Much
Is Pushed Back into the
Night, Nor What May Return.'"
Alone with America
1980, pp. 25–56

This poet has been bravely endorsed by his friends ("the illumination of life turned into language and language turned into life"), brutally dismissed by his enemies ("garbage"), and acknowledged with some bewilderment by his reviewers ("words often appear in unexpectedly brilliant new combinations"). All agree broadly, though, that Ashbery is *avant-garde* whatever else he may be, and it is on that consensus I should like to loiter a little, before proceeding, with the poet's help, to a ponderation of the achievements—or what I can recognize as the achievements—in his chief volumes of verse.

The military figure commonly employed to describe the modern artist in his experimental and initiating capacity is so

natural to us—we even use it pejoratively, to condemn what appears a timid reliance on the conventional: a *rear-guard* artist is scarcely an artist at all, these days—that it is something of an effort to disengage the notion of *opposition*, of combat and conquest which is the activity we like to associate with the artist as the antagonist of the bourgeoisie, from the notion of *protection*, of scouting and reconnoitre which implies that the vanguard is in advance precisely in order *to guard*. The point—I shall concentrate here on the artist's custodial relation to his art, rather than his hostility to the public—is not to abandon the main body of your troops altogether, but to maintain certain exchanges, to insure certain complicities which will make your own skirmishes up ahead of some service to the more unwieldy forces in the rear—and perhaps the more unwieldy precisely because the more forceful.

In the saving, the conservative sense of the term, Ashbery is, sufficiently to compel our trust, an advance-guard poet. I hope to show how he has kept in touch with the tradition he outdistances, how he has remained ahead of something whose force and weight at his back he is fruitfully (if at times fearfully) aware of. That there are many occasions when, it seems to me, he has allowed his communication-lines with the regulars to be cut speaks neither for nor against him. It is a question of the terrain covered and of the engagements fought. The poet who wrote his master's essay on the novels of Henry Green and who invoked, presenting an *inédit by* Raymond Roussel in the French magazine *l'Arc*, that bewildering author's *particularités qui ajoutent à sa beauté strictement littéraire*—the poet who is also a playful scholiast of the hyperbaton is evidently well prepared to leave us in whatever lurch he finds ineluctable. We need not question his decision, or what seems to us his determination, so to leave us; let us merely remind him that a vanguard, as Roussel himself would certainly have known, is also a variety of hybrid peach valued not so much for its own fruit as for its grafting powers.

I spoke just now of enlisting Ashbery's help in our examination of his work. It is an assistance we have come to look for from those artists whose project is evidently going to make some demand upon our patience, or upon our capacity to be diverted. Lest we remain, like Napoleon, *inamusable*, many writers have provided a clue in the form of an imaginative schema or construct which heightens the work's inner resonance at the same time that it defines the *poetics* by which the contraption operates. For example, as early in his career as 1893, Gide noted the likelihood of such a device (and indeed its appeal, for him, extended to the method of Edouard's *Journal* within *The Counterfeiters* and to the *Journal of the Counterfeiters* published along with the novel):

> I like discovering in a work of art . . . transposed to the scale of the characters, the very subject of that work. Nothing illuminates it better, nothing establishes more surely the proportions of the whole. Thus in certain paintings by Memling or Quentin Metsys, a tiny dark convex mirror reflects the interior of the room where the scene painted occurs. Similarly, in Velasquez' *Meninas* (though in a different way). Finally, in *Hamlet's* play within the play, as in many other dramas. In *Wilhelm Meister*, the marionette scenes or the parties at the château. In *The Fall of the House of Usher*, the passage being read to Roderick, etc. None of these examples is entirely fair. What would be much more so, what would say what I want . . . is the comparison with that method in heraldry which consists of putting a second blazon in the center of the first, *en abyme*.

In Ashbery's case, the blazon *en abyme* occurs at the start, rather than at the center, though in all this poet's larger pieces, there is an impulse to break out of the legalities of a compositional system and to address the reader directly ("But no doubt you have understood/it all now and I am a fool. It remains/for me to get better, and to understand you . . ."). If Ashbery's poems themselves are a *blazon of making*, which is after all what the word poem means, inside them we generally find that second blazon, the inclination to speak up without being mediated by the poem ("That something desperate was to be attempted was, however, quite plain"); the work criticizes its own text by accommodating in its texture an alternative patois. From the start, as I say, Ashbery has afforded us various admonitory nudges and eye-rollings: in the little play "Turandot," a kind of meiotic eclogue in three scenes and a sestina, the princess begins by calling for

> Laughs and perfect excisions
> In which the matter biteth the manner,

and when the hungry prince asks for her first question, she retorts

> There are no questions.
> There are many answers. . . .

And if that is not quite enough to prepare us for a sestina, surely the only one in English, in which one of the teleutons is "radium," it suggests nonetheless, in a characteristically abrupt way, the embarrassment of riches we must confront. In 1953, the same year *Turandot and Other Poems* was published in a pamphlet by the Tibor de Nagy Gallery (all the poems were reprinted three years later in *Some Trees* except for a three-stanza piece called "White" and "Turandot" itself), this poet's one-act play *The Heroes* was produced off-Broadway (and later published in a collection which also included plays by Merrill and O'Hara). Ashbery's *dégagé* comedy about the heroes of the Trojan War, set in a Long Island house-party strongly reminiscent of the accommodations Henry Green affords *his* personnel, contains four speeches by Theseus, victor over the labyrinth and the minotaur, and one by Circe, sorceress and visionary, which become crucial to our understanding of his poetry—of what it will not do for us as well as of what it must. If we are bewildered by our first encounter with *Turandot and Other Poems*, if we are baffled not only by the imagery but by the syntax and the tonality of lines like these from "White":

> Where is the tempest buttered? The giants
> In their yachts have privately forgotten
> by which hand slipped under the door
> Its screaming face. I rode into
> The scared dead town, parked the Plymouth—
> No one in the central dark bar—
> "Perhaps Pat is dead" but it buckled,
> Came on, all puce zones alight
> And in the death of muck and horror
> Knelt one on the quiet trapeze of the sky.

—if we are defeated by such lines, which Ashbery has not chosen to carry over into the canon of his work and which I can therefore quote here without having to say more about them than that they suggest his disconcerting gift for placing a recognizeable, even a tantalizing "scene" (as here, from the movies: lines four through seven) among a cluster of irreconcileable propositions—and *disconcerting* must be our normative word here, for it identifies if it does not stigmatize this poet's powerful centrifugal, dissociative impulse—if such lines, then, bewilder, baffle, defeat and disconcert us, we will find our scandal rehearsed and in some senses relaxed and even redeemed by these speeches from *The Heroes*. Reading Theseus on the labyrinth, we are on the way to reading Ashbery on the art of poetry, a tiny dark convex mirror indeed:

> . . . I took advantage of the fact that it was built like a maze. Whenever you do this, even if the problem is just one in algebra, everything becomes simple immediately. Because then you can sit back and get a picture of yourself doing whatever it is. If you do not grant its own peculiar nature to the problem, you can have no picture of yourself and consequently feel harassed and lonely. Without imagination nothing can be easy.
> . . . I'd always supposed the world was full of fakes, but I was foolish enough to believe that it was made interesting by the varying degrees of skill with which they covered up their lack of integrity. It never occurred to me that the greatest fake of all [the minotaur] would make not the slightest effort to convince me of its reality . . . not a pretense! But there it was, a stupid unambitious piece of stage machinery!
> . . . There was nothing to do but give the thing a well-aimed kick and go home. . . .
> . . . There are large holes in the roof, so the visitor is

free, if he wishes, to climb out on top and survey the ground plan of the whole edifice. In short, he is in the dubious position of a person who believes that dada is still alive. . . . Now comes the strangest part of all: you have been in the maze several days and nights, and you are beginning to realize you have changed several times. Not just you, either, but your whole idea of the maze and the maze itself. . . . The maze looks just the same as ever—it is more as if it were being looked at by a different person. But I was so happy there, for now at last I was seeing myself as I could only be—not as I might be seen by a person in the street: full of unfamiliarity and the resulting poetry. Before, I might have seemed beautiful to the passerby. I now seemed ten times more so to myself, for I saw that I meant nothing beyond the equivocal statement of my limbs and the space and time they happened to occupy . . . I realized I now possessed the only weapon by which the minotaur might be vanquished: the indifference of a true aesthete. . . .

It is almost a catalogue of the modernist principles Ashbery has recited, a post-symbolist enchiridion: the poem as simultaneous structure, impersonal, autonomous, released from the charge of expression, of assertion; the poem as arbitrary construct, absurd, self-destroying, no longer aspiring to convince or even to hoax; the poem as an agent of transformation, equal in value to the poet himself and therefore capable of changing him; the poem as means of escape from identity, leading into a world of contemplation, indifference, bliss. Theseus' final statement of his situation, a *tirade* to Circe, brings us even closer to Ashbery's later poems:

. . . Let me tell you of an experience I had while I was on my way here. My train had stopped in the station directly opposite another. Through the glass I was able to watch a couple in the next train, a man and a woman who were having some sort of a conversation. For fifteen minutes I watched them. I had no idea what their relation was. I could form no idea of their conversation. They might have been speaking words of love, or planning a murder, or quarreling about their in-laws. Yet just from watching them talk, even though I could hear nothing, I feel I know those people better than anyone in the world. . . .

The proposition of a reality that may be identifiable and even beautiful, though it outstrips understanding, is certainly what we shall need in exposing ourselves to Ashbery's first book, which was published by the Yale Series of Younger Poets in 1956 with a remarkably disaffected foreword by W. H. Auden. In the shade of *Some Trees*, I would cite the last of Ashbery's blazons, from the end of *The Heroes*; it is Circe's answer to Theseus' rather blithe assumption that it is enough to *recognize* reality whether one understands it or not. The old witch forces the triumphant hero to acknowledge how much harder it is going to be than he has been prepared to admit—and we stand admonished along with Theseus and Ashbery, *en abyme* in the face of *the poems*:

. . . So far this play has been easy. From now on it's going to be more difficult to follow. That's the way life is sometimes. Yea, a fine stifling mist springs up from the author's pure and moody mind. Confusion and hopelessness follow on the precise speech of spring. Just as, when the last line of this play is uttered, your memory will lift a torch to the dry twisted mass. Then it will not seem so much as if all this never happened, but as if parts continued to go

on all the time in your head, rising up without warning whenever you start to do the simplest act.

A glance at the table of contents tells us, first of all, how thoroughly aware Ashbery is of his conventions—more than aware, elated to have them at hand: "Eclogue," "Canzone," "Sonnet," "Pantoum" and three sestinas dramatize this poet's fondness for the art's most intricate forms, and his facility with them. Other pieces are named for works of literature themselves—"Two Scenes," "Popular Songs," "The Instruction Manual," "Album Leaf," "Illustration," "A Long Novel," "A Pastoral"—suggesting that Ashbery has none of the advanced artist's habitual hostility to his own medium, for all his dissociative techniques and fragmenting designs. He has even taken Marvell's famous poem, or at least the title of it, and put himself into the photograph: "The Picture of Little J. A. in a Prospect of Flowers"—

. . . I cannot escape the picture
Of my small self in that bank of flowers:
My head among the blazing phlox
Seemed a pale and gigantic fungus.
I had a hard stare, accepting

Everything, taking nothing,
As though the rolled-up future might stink
As loud as stood the sick moment
The shutter clicked. Though I was wrong,
Still, as the loveliest feelings

Must soon find words, and these, yes,
Displace them, so I am not wrong
In calling this comic version of myself
The true one. For as change is horror,
Virtue is really stubbornness

And only in the light of lost words
Can we imagine our rewards.

This is but the third section of a poem that runs through much of the diction of English poetry, and even its exaggerated symbolist postures ("the rolled-up future might stink/as loud as stood the sick moment/the shutter clicked") cannot decoy us from the discovery that this poet is obsessed by the most classical of poetic themes: the immortalization of experience by words. For a poet, even one who would leave Andrew Marvell behind him, "the loveliest feelings/must soon find words, and these, yes,/displace them . . . and only in the light of lost words/can we imagine our rewards." The placing of that "yes" betrays the argument Ashbery has had with himself on this subject, and also betokens the victory he has reached over his own love of incoherence (poems called "Errors" and "Chaos"). Most of the poems in the book aim, as one firing buckshot may be said to aim, at a single target: the elusive order of existence which the poet knows to be there, just beyond his reach.

From every corner comes a distinctive offering.
The train comes bearing joy;
For long we hadn't heard so much news, such
   noise . . .
As laughing cadets say, "In the evening
Everything has a schedule, if you can find out what it
   is."

The notion that The Poem is already there, *in the world*, and must be collected somehow by the poet, is what keeps these pieces going. "Some Trees" itself puts the matter perfectly (though there is a second and probably a third way of reading that title—not only "Several Trees," but also "These Trees as opposed to Others," and even "Trees Indeed!" the way Churchill used to say "Some Chicken—Some Neck!")—

> These are amazing: each
> Joining a neighbor, as though speech
> Were a still performance.
> Arranging by chance
>
> To meet as far this morning
> From the world as agreeing
> With it, you and I
> Are suddenly what the trees try
>
> To tell us we are:
> That their merely being there
> Means something; that soon
> We may touch, love, explain.

By "logic of strange position" rather than by any emotional
adequacy or correspondence, any psychological explanation,
any moral recovery, this poet sweeps the world's body into his
net. It is in this, surely, that Ashbery is truly advanced, even
revolutionary—his notion that the world not only contains but
is his poem, and that he cannot, in order to write it, draw the
world into himself as has traditionally been attempted, but
must rather extrude himself into the world, must *flee the center*
in order to be on the verge at all points. As he had said, in *The
Heroes*, "I saw that I meant nothing beyond the equivocal
statement of my limbs and the space and time they happened to
occupy," so he says in *Some Trees*, "What are lamps/when
night is waiting?" and again,

> The mythological poet, his face
> Fabulous and fastidious, accepts
> Beauty before it arrives . . . He is merely
> An ornament, a kind of lewd
> Cloud placed on the horizon.
>
> Close to the zoo, acquiescing
> To dust, candy, perverts; inserted in
> The panting forest, or openly
> Walking in the great and sullen square
> He has eloped with all music
> And does not care. For isn't there,
> He says, a final diversion, a greater
> Because it can be given, a gift
> Too simple even to be despised?

Beyond the evident influence of Stevens ("We can only
imagine a world in which a woman/walks and wears her hair
and knows/all that she does not know. Yet we know/what her
breasts are"), and the occasional note of Perse ("Lovely tribes
have just moved to the north./In the flickering evening the
martins grow denser./Rivers of wings surround us and vast
tribulation"), the poems in *Some Trees* that most compel our
trust in Ashbery's bond with what has already been made, his
covenant with the convention, are two which owe most to
Apollinaire: "The Instruction Manual" and "Illustration."
These strike the note of "a gift too simple even to be
despised"—one from inside: "The Instruction Manual," that
deploys all of Ashbery's skill with direct statement, the narrative
of an achieved identity confronting the given world; and one
addressing the other: "Illustration," about a woman "who acts
out," as Auden puts it, "her private mythology and denies the
reality of anything outside herself." It is a comfort, in the
presence of poems like "Grand Abacus"—the very title suggests
the alien and alienating machinery, all those bright beads
clicking back and forth on the wires, but not much being
accounted for beyond a certain insanely "clever" calculation:

> Perhaps this valley too leads into the head of long-ago
>   days.
> What, if not its commercial and etiolated visage,
>   could break through the meadow wires?

> It placed a chair in the meadow and then went far
>   away.
> People come to visit in summer, they do not think
>   about the head.
> Soldiers come down to see the head. The stick hides
>   from them.
> The heavens say, "Here I am, boys and girls!"
> The stick tries to hide in the noise. The leaves,
>   happy, drift over the dusty meadow.
> "I'd like to see it," someone said about the head,
>   which has stopped pretending to be a town . . .

—it is more than a comfort, it is a condition of our engagement
to rehearse a poem as evidently entangled with consistency as
"Illustration." The suicide about to leap from her cornice is
presented to us as a "novice," though we do not at once know
whether her novitiate is to life or death. The commandments
of man and god against self-slaughter are reviewed in a pun:

> . . . Angels
> Combined their prayers with those
> Of the police, begging her to come off it.

The inducements of society ("'I do not want a friend,' she
said"), of adornment, pleasure and selfishness fail to persuade
the woman against her resolution; only the blind man offering
flowers approaches success,

> For that the scene should be a ceremony
> Was what she wanted. "I desire
> Monuments," she said. "I want to move
> Figuratively, as waves caress
> The thoughtless shore. You people I know
> Will offer me every good thing
> I do not want. But please remember
> I died accepting them." With that, the wind
> Unpinned her bulky robes, and naked
> As a roc's egg, she drifted slowly downward
> Out of the angels' tenderness and the minds of men.

There is an exactitude about this, and a wild imaginative
choice of analogy ("to move figuratively, as waves caress the
thoughtless shore" or "naked as a roc's egg") that conjugate to
make something particularly poignant. The private mythology,
thirsty for ritual and "monuments," pitted against the trivial life
of the crowd watching, is seen as an *illustration* in the old sense
(the sense meaning *lustration* as well) in which all objects and
incidents are taken, by poetry, as a sanctification of life. The
body of any symbol, the Church says, is absurd, and Ashbery's
practice concurs. In the second part of this poem, which I take
it bears a reciprocal relation to the figure of the suicide, each
part being the "illustration" of the other, no such preposterous
emblems are devised (like "blue cornflakes in a white bowl" for
the sea and its curving beach); rather the poet immediately
moralizes the fable: "much that is beautiful must be discarded/
so that we may resemble a taller/impression of ourselves." And
his final vision of the episode's meaning is Ashbery at his most
controlled, his most beautiful:

> . . . Moths climb in the flame,
> Alas, that wish only to be the flame:
> They do not lessen our stature.
> We twinkle under the weight
> Of indiscretions. But how could we tell
> That of the truth we know, she was
> The somber vestment? For that night, rockets sighed
> Elegantly over the city, and there was feasting:

There is so much in that moment!
So many attitudes toward that flame,

We might have soared from earth, watching her glide
Aloft in her peplum of bright leaves.

But she, of course, was only an effigy
Of indifference, a miracle

Not meant for us, as the leaves are not
Winter's because it is the end.

There is the same rueful adieu to experience in "The Instruction Manual," or at least the same note of frustration sounded, as at the end of "Illustration," but because the utterance is made in the poet's own persona there is a waggishness in the wistfulness—the comedian, as Ashbery would say, as the letter A—but lower-case. It is the Apollinaire attitude toward language if not the Apollonian one—the words set down with only so much care as to make them cope—that is most evident here, in this long exercise in projection:

I wish I did not have to write the instruction manual
    on the uses of a new metal.
I look down into the street and see people, each
    walking with an inner peace,
And envy them—they are so far away from me!
Not one of them has to worry about getting out this
    manual on schedule.
And, as my way is, I begin to dream, resting my
    elbows on the desk and leaning out of the window
    a little
Of dim Guadalajara! City of rose-colored flowers!
City I wanted most to see, and most did not see, in
    Mexico!

There follows a long, exact travelogue, the phrasing so perfect and the feeling so painfully compressed in the objects selected for *émerveillement* that it almost seems as if Mr. James Fitzpatrick had had a possible genre going for himself after all; but then we reach the end, and realize how difficult this "simple" kind of writing must be to carry off, how disabused Ashbery's whimsy is, and how devastating his criticism of himself:

How limited, but how complete, has been our expe-
    rience of Guadalajara!
We have seen young love, married love, and the love
    of an aged mother for her son.
We have heard the music, tasted the drinks, and
    looked at colored houses.
What more is there to do, except stay? And that we
    cannot do.
And as a last breeze freshens the top of the weathered
    old tower, I turn my gaze
Back to the instruction manual which has made me
    dream of Guadalajara.

None of Ashbery's other poems, even in this first book, exploit with such consecution, with such a progressive impulse, these characteristic modes of his; but their tonalities recur throughout the body of his work, no matter how spattered and pointillist the phrases ("murk plectrum" is probably the best—or worst—example), how discrepant the imagery. "The Instruction Manual" and "Illustration" afford us the framing possibilities: the hand-to-mouth music of a self locating its unavailable hopes wherever it can; and the aberrant mind, possessed of its own beautiful truth, disqualifying the accommodations of a cachectic world. I suspect that by now Ashbery is as sick of having these two poems lit upon by his admirers and even by his detractors as Eliot professed to be of having to recite "Prufrock"—in both cases, the poets would deplore the inroads of an early success upon their later style. But in Ashbery's instance, the later style is so extreme, so centrifugal, that it is well to be reminded of its wonderful and central antecedents before, as he says in his title poem,

Our days put on such reticence
These accents seem their own defense.

By the time *Some Trees* was published, Ashbery had moved to Paris where he was to live for a decade. It would be easy to suggest that his experiments in the loosening, explosion and relocation of the poem were a result, or at least a concomitant, of his isolation in a literary milieu where *anything* he might do would be incomprehensible—why not, therefore, do anything? Too easy, and also, I suspect, unjust to the odd strictness of the thirty poems of *The Tennis Court Oath*, published in 1962, six years after his first book. With work as demanding and as bewildering as this, there is always the tendency to cry havoc and let slip the cogs of boredom ("there is a terrible breath in the way of all this"). The compositional techniques of Roussel and of his own understanding of vanguard art brought Ashbery, in this new collection—an extremely long and various one, by the way—to a pitch of distraction, of literal eccentricity, that leaves any consecutive or linear reading of his poems out of the question. In fact, it is only questions that are left. We must be guided in our response ("there are many answers") by the capital statement on poetics which Ashbery appended to his *curriculum vitae* after *The Tennis Court Oath* was published:

I feel I could express myself best in music. What I like about music is its ability of being convincing, of carrying an argument through successfully to the finish, though the terms of this argument remain unknown quantities. What remains is the structure, the architecture of the argument, scene or story. I would like to do this in poetry. I would also like to reproduce the power dreams have of persuading you that a certain event has a meaning not logically connected with it, or that there is a hidden relation among disparate objects. But actually this is only a part of what I want to do, and I am not even sure I want to do it. I often change my mind about my poetry. I would prefer not to think I had any special aims in mind. . . .

Remembering Theseus' image of the couple seen through the train window, whose words could not be made out, though the hero felt an intimacy "just from watching them talk," we know what to expect from these pieces, each of which generally contains its own monument and epitaph *en abyme*, my favorite being one that occurs in the four-page stream of images called "The New Realism":

Police formed a boundary to the works
Where we played
A torn page with a passionate oasis.

Let me list (in the original sense of the word—to make a border or marginal accommodation) some of the passionate oases in these extraordinary poems—after all, it *is* extraordinary to set so many lines together with an evident concern for music, diction, "a more than usual order," and still remain subliminal in "message":

the year books
authored the heart bees—
beers over beads somewhat
broken off from the rest. . . .

In the title poem, then, after the poet has declared "you come through but/are incomparable," he announces "there was no turning back but the end was in sight." In "America" he points to his Pierrot-preoccupations: "tears, hopeless adoration, passions/the fruit of carpentered night." In "Measles":

> I write, trying to economize
> These lines, tingling. The very earth's
> A pension.
> You limit me to what I say.
> The sense of the words is
> With a backward motion, pinning me
> To the daylight mode of my declaration.

In "The Lozenges" he declares: "We all have graves to travel from, vigorously exerting/the strongest possible influence on those about us." And in "A Last Word":

> But these were not the best men
> But there were moments of the others
> Seen through indifference, only bare methods
> But we can remember them and so we are saved.

Evidently there is little rhythmic enterprise in these poems, the images being for all purposes assorted one to a line in the cadences of a suburban speech-pattern ("I jest/was playing the piano of your halitosis"), and one supposes much less of an attraction to the closed, conventional forms than in the earlier book. In the first of the "Two Sonnets," for instance, there are only thirteen lines, and though the sonnet "feeling" is there, I suppose, it is difficult to see the force of it, so impatient is Ashbery with his own submission to the form:

> The body's products become
> Fatal to it. Our spit
> Would kill us, but we
> Die of our heat.
> Though I say the things I wish to say
> They are needless, their own flame conceives it.
> So I am cheated of perfection.

Here the poet is constantly tweaking his mind in the direction of his poetics ("though I say the things I wish to say they are needless"), and neglecting to pursue to their formal ends the emblems and figures which "the sonnet" ordinarily suggests, though the opening quoted here has all the *panache* of, say, Merrill Moore. There is still a sestina in this volume—a remarkable one called "Faust" which has more to do with Ashbery's earlier mode than with the cut-up-novel pieces like "Europe" that crowd this collection. What is new in "Faust" is a certain narrative glamor, an extension of phrasing that is to become one of Ashbery's surprising strengths, unclotting the preposterous imagery and committing the mind to a sustained experience:

> If only the phantom would stop reappearing!
> Business, if you wanted to know, was punk at the
>   opera.
> The heroine no longer appeared in *Faust*.
> The crowds strolled sadly away. The phantom
> Watched them from the roof, not guessing the
>   hungers
> That must be stirred before disappointment can
>   begin.

"Thoughts of a Young Girl" and "To Redouté" are further—brief—respites in a host of disproportions—"these things," as Ashbery says in "The Shower," "these things are the property of only the few." Mostly, *The Tennis Court Oath* is an exasperating book of improper fractions, lovable for its own love of earth:

> . . . Confound it
> The arboretum is bursting with jasmine and lilac
> And all I can smell here is newsprint . . .

or again,

> Nothing can be harmed! Night and day are begin-
>   ning again!
> So put away the book,
> The flowers you were keeping to give someone:
> Only the white, tremendous foam of the street has
>   any importance,
> The new white flowers that are beginning to shoot up
>   about now.

and beyond construing, for all its evident and cunning construction Valéry remarks somewhere that we call beautiful a work which makes us aware, first, that it might not have existed (since its nonexistence would have meant no vital loss), and secondly, that it could not have been other than it is. In these middle poems of Ashbery's, I miss the tug between the first proposition and the second, for there is too much evidence in favor of the possibilities of nonexistence, not enough credence given to inevitability. That Ashbery himself was aware of the discrepancy accounts, I think, for all the self-carping *en abyme*, and leads, happily, into the firmer, fuller achievements of his next volume, which restores the tone of "The Instruction Manual"—diffident, tender and, for all its irony, rapturous!—and the temper of "Illustration"—penetrating, elegiac and, for all its wiliness, truthful.

In 1963, Ashbery interrupted the measured mystery of his expatriation and, on the stage of the Living Theater in New York, gave a reading of new poems to an audience as curious about what had become of him as it was convinced of his accomplishment in the past. In his absence, *The Compromise, or Queen of the Caribou*, a melodrama, had been performed at the Poets' Theater in Cambridge, and *To the Mill*, a kind of Happening *avant la lettre* had been published in Alfred Leslie's one-shot review *The Hasty Papers*. A glance at the end of *To the Mill* will suggest, I think, the quality of the poet's own performance, upon his first appearance in his native land for many years:

> (The midwife empties a paper bag of dust over Tom &
>   Katherine, who cough and sneeze.)
>
> *Katherine*: My sore throat.
>
> (The midwife disappears behind a rock. Cecilia exits
>   left on the horse. Ernest exits to the left and
>   reappears carrying a drum. The professor en-
>   ters from the right, also carrying a drum.)
>
> *Ernest*: My leg.
>
> (Bill exits to the left. Mary enters from the left and
>   Cecilia, on the horse, from the right.)
>
> *Curtain*

For there was the poet, striding up and down the set of *The Brig*, behind strands of barbed wire (to protect him from us? us from him?), wreathed in clouds of smoke as he consumed one cigarette after the other and with remarkable skill and security read out the poems that already indicated how far he had come from the atomized shocks of *The Tennis Court Oath* ("The arctic honey blabbed over the report causing darkness"). In that last book, he had asked, of course:

> Isn't Idaho the Wolverine state?
> Anyway Ohio is the flower state
> New York is the key state.
> Bandana is the population state.
> In the hay states of Pennsylvania and Arkansas
> I lay down and slept . . .

thereby ringing a change beyond even Mr. Eliot's on "By the waters of Leman" and inventing a badly-needed "population state." This might have prepared us for "Into the Dusk-Charged Air"—a catalogue of 160 lines, each of which contains the name of a river and a characterizing landscape or location:

> . . . Few ships navigate
> On the Housatonic, but quite a few can be seen
> On the Elbe. For centuries
> The Afton has flowed.
>   If the Rio Negro
> Could abandon its song, and the Magdelena
> The jungle flowers, the Tagus
> Would still flow serenely, and the Ohio
> Abrade its slate banks . . .

But there was no predicting the impulse of continuity, of rapt persistence which the other poems exalted to an altogether new pitch of identity; it was as if the poet had come to tell us "about the great drama that was being won":

> To turn off the machinery
> And quietly move among the rustic landscape.

That curious selfhood of Ashbery's which by fond abnegation found the poem in the world rather than in any centripetal operation or ordering of the sensibility, gathered and gleaned its ready-mades in what seemed, coming from the stage, a furthered capacity to *relate* in both the associative and the narrative senses of the word. And when, in 1966, Ashbery returned from Paris, his third book confirmed the sense one had at his reading three years before that here was perhaps the first poet in history in whose work anxiety (with all its shaping, climax-reaching concerns) had no place, a poet for whom the poem was poem *all through* and at any point, without emphases or repetitions (a maze, a labyrinth, rather than an obstacle-course). This, I think, is why we are rarely able to respond to this *oeuvre* in the way we do to the traditional modes anchored in what Northrop Frye calls the seasonal myths, for recurrence and the cyclical patterns of ritual simply do not apply to Ashbery's poetry in its characteristic extension here. Nothing in *Rivers and Mountains* "depends on everything's recurring till we answer from within" as Frost put it, "because," as Ashbery answers, *"all the true fragments are here."* In the first poems in the book we find, *en abyme*, some more of those apologies for the poems themselves, but they are no longer militant or even apologetic, they are triumphant in accounting for the *over-all* texture of these anti-psychological poems: "continuance quickens the scrap which falls to us . . . a premise of so much that is to come, extracted, accepted gladly but within its narrow limits no knowledge yet, nothing which can be used." And again, most significantly: *"Each moment of utterance is the true one; likewise none are true."* Existence is reported to be as ineffable as in the poems of *Some Trees*, but no longer beyond the poet's grasp because he is no longer grasping:

> Here I am then, continuing but ever beginning
> My perennial voyage, into new memories, new hope
>   and flowers
> The way the coasts glide past you. I shall never forget
>   this moment
> Because it consists of purest ecstasy. I am happier
>   now than I ever dared believe
> Anyone could be. And we finger down the dog-eared
>   coasts . . .
> It is all passing! It is past! No, I am here,
> Bellow the coasts, and even the heavens roar their
>   assent

> As we pick up a lemon-colored light horizontally
> projected into the night, the night that heaven
> Was kind enough to send, and I launch into the
>   happiest dreams,
> Happier once again, because tomorrow is already
>   here.

These *dasein*-dazzled lines are from *The Skaters*, a poem of some thirty pages and, with *Clepsydra*, Ashbery's largest statement, a telluric hymn (as the book's title and title poem indicate: "in the seclusion of a melody heard/as though through trees") to a confessed, a welcomed evanescence that somehow guarantees ecstasy. The poem is not about skaters, but takes the image of their action for its own:

>   . . . the intensity of minor acts
> As skaters elaborate their distances,
> Taking a separate line to its end. Returning to the
>   mass, they join each other
> Blotted in an incredible mess of dark colors, and
>   again reappearing to take the theme
> Some little distance, like fishing boats developing
>   from the land different parabolas,
> Taking the exquisite theme far, into farness, to
>   Land's End, to the ends of the earth!
> But the livery of the year, the changing air
> Bring each to fulfillment. . . .

And so Ashbery is off, inventorying "the human brain, with its tray of images" filled by his encounters with the world. Over and over, the object of the poem becomes its subject, its making its meaning; except for the late poems of Wallace Stevens, I know no more convincing meditation on the power the mind has to submit itself to forms, and by them be formed:

>   this poem
> Which is in the form of falling snow:
> That is, the individual flakes are not essential to the
>   importance of the whole . . .
> Hence neither the importance of the individual
>   flake,
> Nor the importance of the whole impression of the
>   storm, if it has any, is what it is,
> But the rhythm of the series of repeated jumps, from
>   abstract into positive and back to a slightly less
>   diluted abstract.

The long lines, loose though they are, keep a spring, a resilience, in part as a result of "the evidence of the visual," the surprising way Ashbery has of giving "the answer that is novelty/that guides these swift blades o'er the ice," and in part because we recognize the tone of voice as the innocent, astonished, ravished one we had heard in "The Instruction Manual"—only cleared of the old jerkiness, taking now more than bite-size morsels of the earthly meal and discovering "the declamatory nature of the distance travelled." In "Clepsydra," too, Ashbery offers a splendid pledge as much to his achievement as to his intention. The title means a water clock, of course, a contrivance to measure time by the graduated flow of a liquid through a small aperture ("each moment of utterance is the true one"), and in the terms of the poem itself "an invisible fountain that continually destroys and refreshes the previsions." As in "The Skaters," the poem becomes a meditation on its own being in the world:

>   . . . it was
> Like standing at the edge of a harbor early on a sum-
>   mer morning
> With the discreet shadows cast by the water all
>   around

And a feeling, again, of emptiness, but of richness in
      the way
The whole thing is organized, on what a miraculous
      scale,
Really what is meant by a human level, with the
      figures of giants
Not too much bigger than the men who have come
      to petition them
A moment that gave not only itself, but
Also the means of keeping it, of not turning to dust
Or gestures somewhere up ahead
But of becoming complicated like the torrent
In new dark passages, tears and laughter which
Are a sign of life, of distant life in this case.
And yet, as always happens, there would come a
      moment when
Acts no longer sufficed and the calm
Of this true progression hardened into shreds
Of another kind of calm, returning to the conclu-
      sion, its premises
Undertaken before any formal agreement had been
      reached, hence
A writ that was the shadow of the colossal reason
      behind all this
Like a second, rigid body behind the one you know is
      yours.

Such poetry is no longer merely the realm, but the means of
self-encounter; its method has been to pluck from the world the
constituted terms of its being, but Ashbery has exalted his
linguistic recognition-scene into something more than a product, a prey, a proof of being-in-the-world. He has made his
discourse identical with his experience "in such a way as to
form a channel," or again, as he says, "the delta of living into
everything." In this way,

                              . . . any direction taken was the
      right one,
Leading first to you, and through you to
Myself that is beyond you and which is the same
      thing as space
                        . . . moving in the shadow of
Your single and twin existence, waking in intact
Appreciation of it, while morning is still and before
      the body
Is changed by the faces of evening.

Three Poems

In his previous collection, it was apparent—no, let us say
it was apprehensible, that Ashbery's poems carried on in a
language without the tension of negativity, without the invoked
anxiety of a closed form. In short, or at length, the poems were
moving toward—and some had already moved right in on—
prose, an utterance unpoliced if not unpoliced (the policy
turning out to be "to keep asking life the same question until
the repeated question and the same silence become answer"),
innovative or advanced, as everyone keeps saying about this
writer, because the lines were not wielded to convey the disci-
plinary, punitive passion which has always been the art's
contribution and conventional resource. Now in *Three Poems*,
where discourse has "come to mean what it had been called on
for," where "our narration seems to be trying to bury itself in
the landscape," there are no lines at all, nor even clusters of
enjambed statements: there are prose *texts* (something woven,
as a snare or *toil*), "a kind of trilogy meant to be read in
sequence," Ashbery says, constituting "a glad mess" of the
matte instances he had aspired to in that last book as "articulate
flatness, goal, barrier and climate," achieved now "far from the

famous task, close to the meaningless but real snippets that are
today's doing."

The first text, "The New Spirit", about fifty pages long, is
said by the poet to record a spiritual awakening to earthly
things; and though very few earthly things are vouchsafed, the
endeavor is "to formulate oneself around this hollow, empty
sphere . . . as objects placed along the top of a wall," for in
Ashbery's spiritual exercises the aim is to be aimless, void,
abluted, to get out of the way of intention in order to enable
"the emptiness that was the only way you could express a
thing." The second text, "The System", about the same
length, is said by Ashbery to be "a love story with cosmological
overtones," material handled, certainly fingered, by a parody of
dialectical homiletics. Love here consists of all the possible
objections to it ("it prepares its own downfall while never quite
beginning"), and only comes to exist when it acknowledges
"the inner emptiness from which alone understanding can
spring up." The third text, "The Recital", is a much briefer
embroidery on the poet's relations to his victories in love and
spiritual awakening which are, of course, coincident with his
losses ("I am quite ready to admit that I am alone"). But such
résumés are merely pretexts—the texts themselves, "provocative but baffling", weave a continuous meditation upon a
series of thematic oppositions—self against others or solitude,
presence in place and time against all the elsewheres of absence, art against landscape—so many sermons upon Ashbery's
real text: "the major question that revolves around you, your
being here."

Each poem or fiction (the words mean the same: a *made
thing*, what Ashbery calls "the created vacuum") begins with
an aporia, a confession of failure or incompetence, and then
builds on that admission in a difficult welter of pronouns. "I",
"you" and "he" are not easily discriminated, though easily
discredited—it is as if Aeschylus had not yet summoned the
second actor from the chorus to argue against that first great
voice, or as if the persons of the drama here, "the debris of
living", were indeed "proposed but never formulated." However, once it is announced that "the system was breaking
down," or that "the problem is that there is no new problem",
then the contraption can get started: "the note is struck, the
development of its resonances ready to snap into place. For the
moment we know nothing more than this." And by degrees, in
a prose so unfeatured by nomination (the only allusions are to
the Tarot deck, Childe Roland, Don Quixote and Alice—all
famous problems themselves), so unfettered to events ("things
will do the rest . . . I renounce my rights to ulterior com-
memoration"), that we are forever in danger of wandering from
its project, the poems rise to their odd altitude, what Ashbery
calls "an erect passivity," on their own apotropaics, "no live
projection beyond the fact of the words in which they were
written down."

And indeed Ashbery *wants* us to elude the notion of
project—it is only when he has warded off choice and emphasis
that the poem has, literally, the chance to assume its life—
until then, "one senses only separate instances and not the
movement of the fall." Again, "nothing is to be learned, only
avoided"; *then* the text which started up in self-erasure and
which persisted in an articulation of emptiness, can come to its
end in fulfillment, its conclusion of Being, "a place of ideal
quiet" on which the world is merely a comment, a diacritical
marking. "All the facts are here, and it remains only to use
them in the right combination," Ashbery exults, for he knows
that the "right combination" must exclude any helping hand
from *him*. Such is the "cost that reality, as opposed to naturalness, exacts," he muses, and it is an enormous cost, for it

makes the poet's problem our own: "Our apathy can always renew itself."

As long ago as *The Tennis Court Oath*, Ashbery had operated by a prosody of intermittence and collage; here, for the same reason—to make poems which are, rather than which are *about*, the world—he invokes a poetics of continuity and encirclement ("I am to include everything: the furniture of this room, everyday expressions, as well as my rarest thoughts and dreams . . . the odd details resolved but nesting in their quirkiness, free to come and go"), the enterprise now being to get it all in rather than to leave it all out, as in the notorious "cut-up" poems like "Europe" of over a decade ago. That is why *Three Poems* must be in prose, the sole medium capable of cancelling itself out, of using itself up: the texts must be capable of proceeding without John Ashbery. How perfectly he knows this! "There comes a time when what is to be revealed actually conceals itself in casting off the mask of its identity." *Three Poems* marks that time.

Self-Portrait in a Convex Mirror

"I wrote in prose because my impulse was not to repeat myself," Ashbery told an interviewer about his last book, *Three Poems*. His present one is again response to those elements of recuperation, of recurrence and reversion which poetry—even such seamless poetry as Ashbery's, which observes beginnings and ends by a prosody of intermittence and collage rather than any such conventional markings as rhyme or repetition—is taken to incarnate, if not to incorporate. He has returned to returning—hence the self-portrait, hence the mirror, hence the convexity: "crooning the tunes, naming the name."

The subject of the self-portrait is the same new thing: if it is all there, the world, "this angle of impossible resolutions and irresolutions", then how do I get into it, how do I find a place in what is already *given*, and if I am already there, how can there be room for all that, "the many as noticed by the one"? The book is a series of meditations on this dilemma:

> And am I receiving
> This vision? Is it mine, or do I already owe it
> For other visions, unnoticed and unrecorded
> On the great relaxed curve of time . . .

long, radiant visions, cross-cut by the usual (usual for Ashbery: no one else could accustom us to "this painful freshness of each thing being exactly itself") opacities of diction and association which—"mutterings, splatterings"—one may like or loathe, depending . . . There is no choice, however, about the title poem and half a dozen others, which are, as everyone seems to be saying, among the finest things American poetry has to show, and certainly the finest things Ashbery has yet shown. "It's all bits and pieces, spangles, patches, really; nothing/ stands alone," the poet has written since the book, and we must weave his observation back into the warp of what he calls "a complicated flirtation routine". When I speak of the widespread admiration for Ashbery's work, I do not mean to patronize him or his detractors; we are confronted with an utterance at times consistently firm, cool, inclusive, and resolute (and by "times" I mean pages and pages of verse—not since Wallace Stevens, indeed, has there been a voice in which "changes are merely/features of the whole"), and at times by verbal tantrums as preposterous as anything in the long lineage of self-indulgence; as the poet himself glosses the situation: "I tried each thing, only some were immortal and free." But in this book as in no other, the brooding seems to get out from under the allusive looniness that was always Ashbery's resource when the going got rough or smooth; *the ride*, as he says *continues*, and we are presented with "the major movement as a firm

digression, a plain that slowly becomes a mountain." The poet, ruminating upon his relation to the past, especially upon the greatness of the past, and to the future, especially upon the grotesquerie of the future, is quite conscious of his idiopathy—as conscious as any of his critics:

> I know that I braid too much my own
> Snapped-off perceptions of things as they come to
> me.
> They are private and always will be.
> Where then are the private turns of event
> Destined to boom later like golden chimes
> Released over a city from a highest tower?
> The quirky things that happen to me, and I tell you,
> And you instantly know what I mean?

They are here, those private turns of events, and as Ashbery remarked to his interviewer, "in this kind of meditative verse the things in a room and the events of everyday life can enter and become almost fossilized in the poems." What keeps them from becoming entirely fossilized, what keeps the concrete from becoming concretion and calculus, lethally lithic, immobile, is the sense of before and after, the movement of time which washes through these pages, these long-winded portages across "this wide, tepidly meandering, civilized Lethe" which else would become "choked to the point of silence."

"*The history of one who came too late*," Ashbery puts it in his wonderful poem 'As You Came from the Holy Land" (where Harold Bloom was quick to seize upon it, exhibit A in the endless catalogue of belatedness which for him constitutes poetry's knowledge of itself); yet in the title poem, Ashbery puts it conversely: "*All we know/is that we are a little early*": we are here, or there, and the rendezvous has not been kept:

> . . . everything is surface. The surface is what's there
> And nothing can exist except what's there . . .

So speaks a man whom the world has failed, who is not yet fulfilled by anything except his own existence, his abashed solipsism. The point is not to decide, to determine whether one is early or late, ahead of time or behind *the times* (the past of Parmigianino's portrait, which alas Viking Press has failed to reproduce just where and when we need it, on the book jacket); the point is to discover there is movement, change, and a linking-up, a being-in-league, however bewildering, with all the rest. Again and again, in his room, or under a tree, or looking at an old photograph (girls lounging around a fighter bomber, 1942!), the poet has occasion to remind himself of the recurrence—it is why he has returned to verse, why he has reversed—of the reversion:

> There is some connexion . . . among this. It con-
> nects up,
> Not *to* anything, but kind of like
> Closing the ranks so as to leave them open.

For me the opacities, what used to register as accidents, are now assimilated into the mastery, so that as John Hollander says, what lingers on after their startlingness is their truth. The poet seems to me (it is what I mean by mastery) to have gained access to a part of his experience which was once merely a part of his imagination: he has made his experience and his imagination identical:

> It is both the surface and the accidents
> Scarring the surface . . .
> These are parts of the same body.

And this incorporation, this embodiment has required of his talents that he leave off prose; that he shed those aberrational nuttinesses which are so alluring that "to get to know them we must avoid them"; that he move in on his visions with all the instruments, the devices, the pharmacopoeia of, say, a Parmigianino; as Ashbery says, and never has he proved more accurate about himself, though the proof of the accuracy must *be* himself:

> The great formal affair was beginning, orchestrated,
> Its colors concentrated in a glance, a ballade
> That takes in the whole world, now, but lightly,
> Still lightly, but with wide authority and tact.

Houseboat Days

After the garland of prizes bestowed in docile succession upon *Self-Portrait in a Convex Mirror*, it is apparent that we have entered a new phase of Ashbery criticism, one we might call post-favorable. I doubt if it is more helpful (though I can see it is more highfalutin) to say, with John Brinnin, that Ashbery's "dazzling orchestrations of language open up whole areas of consciousness no other American poet has ever begun to explore" than it was to say, with John Simon in the bad old days, that Ashbery's poems were "garbage". But it would appear that with this new book we are in the presence of a Figure who need not abide our question, "a living contemporary who should be beyond all critical dispute" (Harold Bloom). Here is the opening of a poem, "Bird's-Eye View of the Tool and Die Co.," which I promise is neither harder nor softer than many others in the book, though it begins with a nice reversal of Proust's first line:

> For a long time I used to get up early.
> 20–30 vision, hemorrhoids intact, he checks into the
> Enclosure of time familiarizing dreams
> For better or worse. The edges rub off,
> The slant gets lost. Whatever the villagers
> Are celebrating with less conviction is
> The less you. Index of own organ-music playing,
> Machinations over the architecture (too
> Light to make much of a dent) against meditated
> Gang-wars, ice cream, loss, palm terrain.

I should say that was beyond critical dispute, or should be, simply because it is largely inaccessible to critical procedure. Fortunately (for my enterprise) not all of Ashbery's work in his new book resists analysis or even interest so successfully. There is a great deal of poetry which is indeed beautiful and beguiling and benign in its transactions with our understanding; quite as characteristic as the teratoma I have just instanced is the *whole poem* "Blue Sonata", of which I quote the close, thereby giving equal time to the amazing clarity of this celebrated opacifier:

> . . . It would be tragic to fit
> Into the space created by our not having arrived yet,
> To utter the speech that belongs there,
> For progress occurs through re-inventing
> These words from a dim recollection of them,
> In violating that space in such a way as
> To leave it intact. Yet we do after all
> Belong here, and have moved a considerable
> Distance; our passing is a facade.
> But our understanding of it is justified.

Most of the poems in *Houseboat Days* which I can make out at all are like this bit, deliberations on the meaning of the present tense, its exactions and falsifications, its promises and rewards. "There are no other questions than these,/half-squashed in mud, emerging out of the moment/we all live, learning to like it"—Ashbery is often painfully clear as to what he would wring from his evasive experience ("what I am probably trying to do is to illustrate opacity and how it can suddenly descend over

us . . . it's a kind of mimesis of how experience comes to me"), and the pain is there in the tone, now goofy and insolent, then again tender and self-deprecating, vulnerable but not without its gnomic assertions ("It is the nature of things to be seen only once"), various but not without a consistent grimace ("It's all bits and pieces, spangles, patches, really; nothing/stands alone").

The position from which these proceedings flow and flare is rather the converse of what I read in the *Self-Portrait*. Here there is a cool resolution about the dialectic of self and other; the poet seems more or less content (more or less sad) to be at grips with "this tangle of impossible resolutions and irresolutions", but only *for now*. The trouble, and his subject, is that the moment passes, that *now* becomes *then*, losing everything in the process. Whatever is easy-moving, free and pleasant tends to calcify or to rot, leaving dust and ash on the mind's plate: "The songs decorate our notion of the world/and mark its limits, like a frieze of soapbubbles."

Whence a prosody, as I have called it, of intermittence and collage; no such conventional markings as rhyme or repetition—rather, *seamless verse*, jammed rather than enjambed, extended rather than intense; it must go on and on to keep the whole contraption from coming round again, and to work upon us its deepest effect, which is a kind of snake-charming. Quotation occasionally reveals the allure, but not the sense of endless possibilities, of merciless hopes:

> . . . To praise this, blame that,
> Leads one subtly away from the beginning, where
> We must stay, in motion. To flash light
> Into the house within, its many chambers,
> Its memories and associations, upon its inscribed
> And pictured walls, argues enough that life is
>   various.
> Life is beautiful. He who reads that
> As in the window of some distant, speeding train
> Knows what he wants, and what will befall.

The passage is from the title poem, which refers specifically, I believe, to living in the present, one's domicile upon an inconstant element, one's time at the mercy and the rigor of the stream: "The mind/is so hospitable, taking in everything/like boarders, and you don't see until/it's all over how little there was to learn/once the stench of knowledge has dissipated . . ." The misery in this poem, as in all the rest, is that of being deprived by the past and the future of the present; it is only now that the poet can see and seize the clutter as fertilizing, "not just the major events but the whole incredible/mass of everything happening simultaneously and pairing off,/channelling itself into history": experience is wrenched away—is no longer "his"—by the suspect neatness of memory, as by the sacrificial omissions of art, and so these poems are not to record a life, they are not memorials, any more than they are to decorate a tradition, they are not monuments. "What I am writing to say is, the timing, not/the contents, is what matters"—hence almost anything will turn up inside these "parts of the same body", and almost anyone—any pronoun—will become someone else. With a grim chuckle (he actually spells it out: "but perhaps, well, heh heh, temper the wind to the shorn lamb . . .") Ashbery twitches the text away from personality: "I don't think my poetry is inaccessible . . . I think it's about the privacy of everyone." And perhaps that is why they present such brutal clarifications: the privacy of everyone is a hard thing to acknowledge, especially when it is staring at you from the page, hysterically open to distraction, eager to grab the language of packaging and put it into the *perpetuum mobile* of poetry. The texts include everything, they leave out only the necessary transitions and gear-shifts which we call narrative and which have traditionally governed the decorum of our attention. In such a world, "things overheard in cafes assume an importance previously reserved for letters from the front"— and indeed, the front itself shifts to the back room, the view from the kitchen window, the voices overheard in the next bedroom. Of course no poem can keep pace with "eventuality," with the character and quality of existence as it becomes event—not even Ashbery's poem can satisfy him as to the scope and focus of "the present"—but the zany failures mount up as the only important enterprise, undertaking, overdrive:

> And we made much of this sort of materiality
> That clogged the weight of starlight, made it seem
> Fibrous, yet there was a chance in this
> To see the present as it never had existed . . .

The point or the patch is to be at the center of things, the beginning: better not prepare any received standard version of history or fable, "reread this/and the past slips through your fingers, wishing you were there." Better still, take the lesson of painting, which is always in the present, always on hand or it is nothing. So Ashbery's poems will be meditations on how to write his poems, where to begin in order always to be beginning, without that dying fall of classical recital, instead inscribed upon the evanescence of eternity: "a final flourish/that melts as it stays." Painting and music too will help—take the string quartet:

> The different parts are always meddling with each
>   other,
> Pestering each other, getting in each other's ways
> So as to withdraw skillfully at the end, leaving—
>   what?
> A new kind of emptiness, maybe bathed in freshness,
> Maybe not. May be just a new kind of emptiness.

That is the risk this poetry takes, of course: by jettisoning the traditional baggage of the art and assimilating instead the methods and "morality" of the other arts (though not architecture: Ashbery is against architecture the way his critics have learned to be against interpretation), the poet incurs the possibility of "maybe just a new kind of emptiness." But the risk is worth it to Ashbery, who has never dismissed the religious possibility of emptiness—affectlessness, abjection—as *the* condition of fulfillment. (Has he not written, in *Self-Portrait*, "there is some connexion . . . among this. It connects up,/not to anything, but kind of like/closing the ranks so as to leave them open", where he sounds kind of like a SOHO Simone Weil.) It is worth what I call the risk and what he would call the necessity of emptiness—boredom, confusion, irritation, even torment—to reach what he undoubtedly and diligently *does* reach, a world whose terms are refreshed to the point, to the pinnacle, where experience is without anxiety because it is *delivered*, in both senses of that word: presented and released. A world without anxiety, without repression, without the scandal and the labor of the negative. Or as Ashbery puts it:

> Something
> Ought to be written about how this affects
> You when you write poetry:
> The extreme austerity of an almost empty mind
> Colliding with the lush, Rousseau-like foliage of its
>   desire to communicate
> Something between breaths, if only for the sake
> Of others and their desire to understand you and
>   desert you
> For other centers of communication, so that understanding
> May begin, and in doing so be undone.

CHARLES BERGER
From "Vision in the Form of a Task:
The Double Dream of Spring"
*Beyond Amazement: New Essays
on John Ashbery*
Ed. David Lehman
1980, pp. 179–208

For too long Ashbery has seemed to readers—especially professional readers—a poet more often casual than relentless about establishing meaning. His mask of insouciance has managed to remain intact, despite the writing of poem after difficult poem, and the evidence is that each new effort has been aimed hard at getting his subject right—not fixing it forever, but bringing the moment's wisdom and the moment's ephemerality together. Too often, critics have stressed the latter and ignored the former. A myth grew up around Ashbery: he had somehow discovered new dimensions to the poetic act, or a new kind of writing machine, capable of generating poems in the absence of the usual anxieties about subject—more remarkably, poems free from worry about the traditional criteria of greatness. Ashbery has contributed to this myth in subtle ways, but supporters and critics have gone even further, sometimes suggesting that Ashbery had willed himself to be a minor poet, inhabitor of a necessarily diminished sphere. They seize on lines such as the following: "To step free at last, miniscule on the gigantic plateau—/This was our ambition: to be small and clear and free."

These lines come from "Soonest Mended," one of Ashbery's most popular poems. It is a poem written firmly in the middle voice and one which seems to erect an aesthetic credo out of holding to the middle range in all things: "a kind of fence-sitting/Raised to the level of an aesthetic ideal." The poem needs to be quizzed on this advocacy, however, if it does not indeed already question itself. One reason "Soonest Mended" is so well liked, aside from its wrought gracefulness and measured tone of loss, is that it gives an image of the poet many readers would like Ashbery to be: casual, urbane, resigned to "an occasional dream, a vision."

Now the poems we have been considering—"The Task," "Spring Day," "Evening in the Country," "Parergon"—are hardly what we would call conversational, although "Evening in the Country" comes closest perhaps to "Soonest Mended" in its use of the long line as a way of achieving flexibility of voice. Yet the conversational measure tightens toward the close of "Evening in the Country," and even though Ashbery keeps to an urbane pitch he manages to ascend the chariot of poetic deity. Readers are probably coming to realize that Ashbery has almost unobtrusively mastered the long line—the line of more than ten syllables—and now uses it as powerfully as anyone before him in the twentieth century. From *Double Dream* to *Houseboat Days* his power over this measure has only grown. The long line is also the visionary line, the mode of Whitman and Blake, and Ashbery has not been reluctant to use it in this task. The lengthened line, however, can trail away from the poet, as it does in "As I Ebb'd with the Ocean of Life," creating an effect of dispersed power and draining strength. Or the line can seem to hover in a kind of fruitful suspension, a creative sense of drift and repose. This feeling steals over one at times in reading Keats's odes, where the lines seem to grow longer than ten syllables as the Keatsian patience spreads its wings. "Soonest Mended" fulfills this last use of the long line almost perfectly, but it is worth noting that the poem is sui generis and not "vintage" Ashbery. More often, Ashbery will begin with a sense of drift but then gather toward some point of vision. The first poem in *Houseboat Days* is a perfect illustration. "Street Musicians" sees rising signs of drift but looks beyond them to what it perceives as a possible source, an "anchor": "Our question of a place of origin hangs/Like smoke."

"Barely tolerated, living on the margin," is something between a boast and a lament. The margin, once again, does not necessarily lead to marginality: it may be the true center. Yet "Soonest Mended" is less sure than other Ashbery poems of the poet's power to be the center wherever he falls out, on the "brink" or what not. I would still argue that even as the poem's seemingly limpid lines crystallize with time and repeated readings, so its sense of marginality inches toward the center. Indeed, the movement is already there in the poem however one interprets it, for the margin of the poem's opening line becomes a "mooring" at the end. The precarious present yields to a sense of origins: the self is where it is as a result of an original event or choice. Our exile to the margin is self-willed. We started out from the margin-as-mooring; we are always placing ourselves by necessity at the brink of a new beginning, a making ready. Only when we lose the trace of the tether back to this site do we regard ourselves as weakly marginal. So the poem will move back through personal memory to an event *in illo tempore*, or sacred time, when the poet's true chronology began.

"Soonest Mended" remains striking within the Ashbery oeuvre not so much for its return at the end to a sense of origination—other poems certainly enact this course—as for its planned, haphazard course *to* that end. David Kalstone has written beautifully of this trajectory. He speaks of the poem's "brave carelessness" and points out, rightly, that "the tone is partly elegiac."[1] Ashbery's suppression of mimesis only partly obscures the clear fact that "Soonest Mended" is, as Harold Bloom calls it, a lament for "Ashbery's generation."[2] Writing at the level he does throughout *The Double Dream of Spring* inevitably means that Ashbery will feel deep ambivalence toward this comically helpless "generation" and toward his own early self. But I must disagree with Kalstone when he says that "'mooring' sounds as much like death as a new life."[3] He tends to be more concerned with how the poem "shifts quickly from one historical hazard to another," while "the energetic lines breathe the *desire* to assert ego and vitality."[4] As a stylistic description of the poem this cannot be surpassed.

"Historical hazard" is something Ashbery does not often open his poems to; the randomness of the ordinary is not quite the same thing. Such randomness can be organized and redeemed by the solitary eye; but history, or life within the community, can become far more oppressive to the poet. Ashbery's detractors would argue that he closes himself off to what he cannot organize, despite an appearance of the erratic within his poems, and this is hard to dispute. "Soonest Mended" gives us a somewhat coded account of community and offers reasons why this poet must find it dissatisfying. Another poem in the volume, "Clouds," will deal more severely with the need to break away, artistically speaking, from even the most nourishing community. "Soonest Mended" does not quite enact such a break, turning its gentler scrutiny on the poignant inability of any enclave whatsoever to satisfy the desire for true speech. This pathos comes through in a key passage where Ashbery sets the sign of disillusionment against the undeniably sweet faces of the others:

> This is what you wanted to hear, so why
> Did you think of listening to something else? We are
>   all talkers

It is true, but underneath the talk lies
The moving and not wanting to be moved, the loose
Meaning, untidy and simple like a threshing floor.

The powerful enjambment at the end of the third line in this quotation expresses all of Ashbery's ambivalence. "Underneath the talk lies"—so he might wish to leave it, until a softening sets in and he admits that beneath the deceit of social "talk" there hides the shifting forms of desire. The last line in this passage echoes the muse/mother's reprimand in "The Task"—"Just look at the filth you've made"—and here, too, the scatterings wait to be gathered into meaning. This vision of the others, the desired but not "extinct" community, will never fully betray or renounce the spirit of that time and place. It is enough to point, once, to the inevitable wounds that arise when we give and take in mere "talk." About this (least said), soonest mended.

Beyond conversation and beneath the colloquial texture of the poem lies the deep meaning of poetic language:

> Night after night this message returns, repeated
> In the flickering bulbs of the sky, raised past us, taken
>   away from us,
> Yet ours over and over until the end that is past truth,
> The being of our sentences, in the climate that
>   fostered them,
> Not ours to own, like a book, but to be with, and
>   sometimes
> To be without, alone and desperate.

This is the credo that holds the haphazard aesthetic course together, and it is a credo Ashbery is willing to share. He does not astonish the others as he did in "Parergon." In fact, "Soonest Mended" ends with several attempts to register halting progress, so unlike the streaming movement at the close of "Parergon," as though Ashbery were trying to blend defeat with triumph. Does this, in the context of the poem, amount to a version of survivor guilt? Thus, the visionary moment becomes a "hard dole," "action" turns to uncertainty, preparation is "careless." And yet no degree of restraint can fully quell the sense of triumph and power attendant upon recovering the spot of origin at the poem's close. "That day so long ago," the day of poetic inauguration, does not belong to the time frame of memory. It belongs to a greater sequence. To understand the resonances of such a "day" it would help to look at the preceding poem in *The Double Dream*, "Plainness in Diversity." This lesser-known poem abbreviates the course traveled by "Soonest Mended" but moves in a remarkably similar direction. Once again it is the emptiness of "talk" that brings the truth home to the poetic quester; his place is elsewhere:

> Silly girls your heads full of boys
> There is a last sample of talk on the outer side
> Your stand at last lifts to dumb evening
> It is reflected in the steep blue sides of the crater,
> So much water shall wash over these our breaths
> Yet shall remain unwashed at the end. The fine
> Branches of the fir tree catch at it, ebbing.
> Not on our planet is the destiny
> That can make you one.
> To be placed on the side of some mountain
> Is the truer story.

The second stanza continues to construct an outline of the journey myth, as it uses "the sagas" to discover a fitting point of origin and a worthy end to the quest:

> There is so much they must say, and it is important
> About all the swimming motions, and the way the
>   hands

Came up out of the ocean with original fronds,
The famous arrow, the girls who came at dawn
To pay a visit to the young child, and how, when he
    grew up to be a man
The same restive ceremony replaced the limited
    years between,
Only now he was old, and forced to begin the jour-
    ney to the stars.

"Plainness in Diversity" locates us in myth more firmly than "Soonest Mended" chooses to do; but the gesture of starting out with which the latter concludes is also, surely, a version of heroism.

Another account of this truer—that is to say, more severe— poetic autobiography comes in the mysterious poem "Clouds," a terse lyric of bounded quatrains, gnomic and revealing at the same time. The poem tells something of the same story as "Soonest Mended," but its voice is wholly different. "Clouds"—the title becomes clear only in the last line—has none of the evasive charm of "Soonest Mended." It judges the generation out of which Ashbery emerged with harsher accuracy and claims expansive, indeed Dionysian, powers for its own speaker. (Semele, upon whom the poem devolves at the close, was the mother of Dionysus.) The opening quatrain can hardly be matched elsewhere in Ashbery's writing for its uncanny mixture of power and prophecy, on the one hand, tranquillity and reverie on the other:

All this time he had only been waiting,
Not even thinking, as many had supposed.
Now sleep wound down to him its promise of dazzl-
    ing peace
And he stood up to assume that imagination.

These lines might stand as epigraph to *The Double Dream of Spring*, the volume in which Ashbery first truly stands up to assume the task of poethood. What distinguishes "Clouds" from other such moments of declaration is its preoccupation with what came before. Both "Parergon" and "Evening in the Country" showed glimpses of the *others*, the dark background against which Ashbery measures the intensity of his own flare. Here the poet broods more penetratingly on the character of these others—the poets, let us say, with whom Ashbery started out. The names of this generation are well known. Ashbery schematizes the setting in "Clouds" and leaves us with a strong, if intentionally vague, impression only of an avant-garde enclave worrying problems of continuity and rupture. Ashbery turns to judge them, sounding like an abstract version of Yeats assessing the poets of the nineties:

There were others in the forest as close as he
To caring about the silent outcome, but they had
    gotten lost
In the shadows of dreams so that the external look
Of the nearby world had become confused with the
    cobwebs inside.

"They had gotten lost": *he*, on the other hand, has been found. "Clouds" gives itself over to declaring this difference, which amounts to declaring its speaker greater than the others—"He shoots forward like a malignant star," as the poem later puts it—while at the same time holding him true to the poetic program of this early coterie. "Clouds" emblematizes the conflict in Ashbery's crossing from the early phase of *Some Trees* and *The Tennis Court Oath* to *Rivers and Mountains* and *The Double Dream of Spring*. We might choose to see the promise of this early phase as fulfilled in the poems of *The Double Dream*—yet how can one fulfill the experimental, the tentative? And how can one establish continuity with a phase

that was itself committed to personal and historical discontinuity?

How can we outsmart the sense of continuity
That eludes our steps as it prepares us
For ultimate wishful thinking once the mind has
    ended
Since this last thought both confines and uplifts us?

This stanza, the ninth of fourteen, marks the point of transition in the poem. The preceding stanzas turned over the question of continuity, of resisting what the poem calls "joining," even while acknowledging the need to forge "separate blocks of achievement and opinion." "Clouds" scatters penetrating kernel descriptions of avant-gardism, none of which is more striking than the following:

                            And the small enclave
Of worried continuing began again, putting forth
    antennae into the night.
How do we explain the harm, feeling
We are always the effortless discoverers of our career,
With each day digging the grave of tomorrow and at
    the same time
Preparing its own redemption, constantly living and
    dying?

The poem's "sestet," its final five or six stanzas, grants that we can never "outsmart the sense of continuity," but it does not take this as a sign of defeat. Rather, Ashbery drops any note of elegiac helplessness and strikes out, in a remarkable evocation of animal vitality. No more worried continuing, no more sleek antennae:

He was like a lion tracking its prey
Through days and nights, forgetful
In the delirium of arrangements.

The conceit is striking and outrageous. We hunt down "continuity," even devour it at moments, but we cannot extinguish the concept or the species itself: we are tied to our prey. The circle of tracking and destruction is obsessive, a "delirium of arrangements." We waste the present in this *quest for* a present uncontaminated by the past. We locate ourselves on the outer rim of this devastation, pushing farther into the brake:

The birds fly up out of the underbrush,
The evening swoons out of contaminated dawns,
And now whatever goes farther must be
Alien and healthy, for death is here and knowable.
Out of touch with the basic unhappiness
He shoots forward like a malignant star.
The edges of the journey are ragged.
Only the face of night begins to grow distinct
As the fainter stars call to each other and are lost.
Day re–creates his image like a snapshot. . . .

The glory and the sorrow of the avant-garde are acted out here, in the flight outward and the inevitable return to habitual nature: our image rendered by someone or something else.

"Clouds" is a powerfully condensed poem, ascetically framed and argued. Vision is not deflected as it is in "Soonest Mended"; there is no pretence of lassitude, no effort to mask the true desires of the poetic self. In fact the poem is so clear about how it places its speaker that we, as readers, perhaps search for evasions that simply are not there. This is one of the more curious reactions Ashbery inspires in his audience. But even if we pay homage to the obliquity of presentation in "Clouds," we cannot fail to recognize the poem's true prey as it emerges with the abrupt invocation of Semele, the mother of Dionysus. If the god is about to be born at the end of the poem, he is about to be born again, into poetry, at the poem's opening. The shock of these terms is itself instructive: it cautions us against reading Ashbery too casually.

On the way toward "Fragment" and away from these charged lyrics, we might think about some poems in *The Double Dream of Spring* that seem to exist for the sheer sake of performance. Intended to elude interpretation, these poems never become nonsensical. Instead, they end as parodies where, more often than not, the matter of parody can be located in the "serious" poems of the volume. The place of texts such as "Variations, Calypso and Fugue on a Theme of Ella Wheeler Wilcox," "Farm Implements and Rutabagas in a Landscape," "Some Words," "Sortes Vergilianae," is crucial: nearly every line, every moment from these variously wild poems can be "related" to more coherent structures of meaning elsewhere in *The Double Dream*. These poems mock interpretation on their own ground—they mean, but mean elsewhere, anywhere else but within their own boundaries. A residual trace of guilt can be found in Ashbery toward the whole enterprise of false coherence, and this is why he makes his readers collaborate so strenuously in the hermeneutic process of coming upon meaning. He seems at times deliberately to mar his poems, although I would argue that this occurs more often in *Houseboat Days* than in *The Double Dream of Spring*. His bad conscience at approximating the "traditional" poem with its criteria of lucidity and comprehensibility is somewhat appeased by the overtly experimental poems in his volumes: these disperse meaning as much as other poems concentrate it. It is not that the experimental poem in *The Double Dream*, for instance, is formless; on the contrary, this kind of poem is overdetermined by form. Meaning goes along for the ride. What these experimental poems do best is to exaggerate and hypostatize thematic concerns and prosodic patterns that exist everywhere in *The Double Dream*. The volume is extraordinarily well-knit and, in a sense, it is these willful, seemingly unbounded pieces that most remind us of this fact. Such experimentation is *vitally* parasitic; it is alive in itself but also needs the preexistence of texts found elsewhere: a bit of doggerel from Ella Wheeler Wilcox, the "Popeye" cartoon, a French text by Arthur Cravan, the notion of a privileged "sacred" text that exists as pure anteriority (Vergil). For a poem that stands alone we must turn to the deeper experimentalism of a true masterpiece: "Fragment."

The title at first leads us to expect jaggedness in the poem's lines—frequent and sharp transitions—certainly not the overt symmetry of fifty ten-line stanzas, parodically reminiscent of stately Renaissance pageantry. Yet, if we look closer, is there not a sense of completion in the title's emphasis on the singular: "Fragment," not "Fragments"? (Suppose Pound had called his epic *Canto*?) So, even if the poem stands in synecdochic relation to some external whole, it completely embodies its own partiality. It is a whole fragment. There are, not surprisingly, many tag lines, emblematic moments in the poem, that help us to parse the title: "The stance to you/Is a fiction, to me a whole" is one such moment in which Ashbery flatters his song. A later passage turns against this self-flattery and broods about the poem's possible incompleteness:

> the externals of present
> Continuing—incomplete, good-natured pictures
> that
> Flatter us even when forgotten with dwarf specula-
> tions
> About the insane, invigorating whole they don't
> represent.

Insane, invigorating: Is the whole worth capturing? Deciding this is as difficult as trying to locate the poem's transitions,

which are everywhere and nowhere. We are tricked by the title and by an earlier mélange like "The Skaters" into readying ourselves for a tour de force of ellipsis. Yet the poem flows and flows, somehow running over its point of switchover, eliding its own elisions in a credible portrait of continuity. The lines, however seemingly discontinuous, are held together by a metrical or rhythmic hum, a buzzing undertone of similitude and relationship.

Whether it opens on a note of closure or aperture, "Fragment" clearly *does* begin with a marked point of departure. It is also worth noting that the poem's last stanza seems to be a clear end-sign. This is a good reminder to the reader not to ignore sequence entirely, even at moments of exasperation (or release), when the thread of continuity appears most strained. Invoking April as it does, "Fragment" pays homage to the hallowed starting ground for the long poem in English, from Chaucer to Eliot. And indeed, the poem's first six lines are among the most densely and richly allusive Ashbery has yet written. The poem opens by seeming to deny the possibility of further openings: "The last block is closed in April." Whatever "block" may mean, from building metaphor to cell block, the overt sense in the line moves toward grim, monosyllabic finality. Yet the force of "April" as a point of origin or place of aperture overrides any terminus, impelling the line as a whole to say: "The last block is closed in aperture"; we move toward a new opening even as we shut down or shut out the past (the last).

The focus on "her face" in the poem's second line introduces a series of concentric circles of reference, where "she" comes to stand for the beloved in all her avatars: lover, mother, muse, earth itself. Ashbery's cynosure is about as readily identifiable as Keats's Moneta or Stevens's female imago figures. And, indeed, the powerful apostrophe in stanza two— "your face, the only real beginning, / Beyond the grey of overcoat"—links Ashbery to these two, especially on that mysterious and crucial ground where the origins of Eros and the lyric are intertwined. Ashbery's overt strategy of invocation by repetition and difference does not end here, however; we need to confront the shade of Eliot as well, summoned by the proximity of "memory" to "April," and by the figural substitution for the missing word in the Eliotic triad: April, memory . . . *desire*. Desire, indeed, is the key to the whole of the poem's magnificent opening. It is the "intrusion" that "Clouds over" the beloved's countenance; it is the dream of "older/ Permissiveness," as the stanza goes on to call it, a shrewd way of troping upon the erotic storehouse of childhood and adolescence. And desire helps us to understand why the budding forsythia extend a present sympathy to us, in opposition to the "recondite" or buried past, return to which can only involve a lethal falling backward:

> You
> See the intrusions clouding over her face
> As in the memory given you of older
> Permissiveness which dies in the
> Falling back toward recondite ends,
> The sympathy of yellow flowers.

(I do not read "The sympathy of yellow flowers" as being in apposition to "recondite ends." I place a mental ellipsis between lines five and six in the opening stanza.) Here Ashbery separates himself from Eliot, who viewed his Waste Land flowers as anything but sympathetic tokens. For Ashbery, however, the forsythia bloom as an emblem of "a moment's commandment," to use the clarion phrase upon which he closes this first "block" of words. They stand as sign of openness, of potential: Who is equal to imagine them? The second half of this dense inaugurating stanza finds a credo to withstand the intrusion of the past and releases the stanza as a whole from its brooding density. The credo centers on "Space not given and yet not withdrawn/And never yet imagined: a moment's commandment." The rest of "Fragment" will explore that space in an attempt to merit the muse/moment's injunction.

"Fragment" is a poem that endlessly emblematizes itself; its primary point of reference is itself as an ongoing process of opening out, creating new imaginative routes, new patterns among the old hieroglyphs. This preoccupation of the poem with the poem is linked to the dilemma of the ghostly "author" who can love only himself:

> that this first
> Salutation plummet also to the end of friendship
> With self alone. And in doing so open out
> New passages of being among the correctness
> Of familiar patterns.

An unwary reader might assume that here, in the poem's second stanza, Ashbery freely acknowledges the perils of solipsism, the rigor mortis of self-love, hoping for a release from both narcissism and "familiar patterns" (with the latent pun on familiar brought to the surface). A reading such as this would make for good conventional advice: open yourself to others and release the creative force within you, and so forth. Yet the clear sense of wishing to end "friendship/With self alone" does not necessarily imply a turn toward a real erotic other. Nor does it necessarily imply a break with the family romance (to use Freud's term); note that Ashbery traces his new passage *among* the correctness (a loaded word) of the familial maze. What we do feel is an abandonment of one strategy toward the self replaced by another, one that does not acknowledge otherness so much as it demystifies the prestige of the self. Otherness is denied by the insistence upon "familiar" patterns as the ground for erotic salutation of whatever sort, and the sense of the lone self is also rebuked by the recognition that, as Dickinson says, the "perished patterns murmur"[5] in us—the ghostly ancestors constitute the hushed undertone of our deepest longings. Finally, the crucial notion of fictionality is introduced: "The stance to you/Is a fiction, to me a whole." Once again, Ashbery's syntax operates to create an interpretive dilemma. The sentence seems to imply contrast: "the stance to you [on the one hand], to me [on the other]." But I do not think it works this way: instead Ashbery forces the reader, by his device, to decide what the difference is between a fiction and a whole. We desire such a difference and are reluctant to concede that a whole *might be* only a fiction, a stance, but we cannot really justify the desire for such a state except as nostalgia for a lost sense of objective plenitude.

To Ashbery, then, there is no essential paradox in calling a fiction a *whole* (this issue, of course, bears upon the poem's title); it comes down to a question of belief in the fiction, a Stevensian notion. Moreover, the only difference between "you" and "me" involves shades of belief. Both are, indeed, pronouns or substitutions; the second-person substitution grants that the fictional or linguistic self lives among others, is a partial fiction, while the more proximate "me" regards itself and the self it "replaces" as the whole of things. The sense of you and me converging in one compact—a mutual defense treaty—is sung in the poem's fourth stanza: "You exist only in me and on account of me/And my features reflect this proved compactness."

The fiction of wholeness, taking wholeness *as* a fiction, is accompanied throughout "Fragment" by a quest for the center both as origin and as present focal point. "Fragment" opens, as we have seen, with a double statement about origin or starting

point: what comes before must be repeated and ruptured at the same time. We end in order to begin again; we *continue* to begin. The sense we gather of the increased tension in Ashbery's verse as it moves from "The Skaters" to "Fragment" very likely results from the severity of his concern with origins, not merely beginnings, with the center and not those wheeling circles upon which "The Skaters" focuses: "The figure 8 is a perfect symbol/Of the freedom to be gained in this kind of activity." Now this distinction certainly does not mean that Ashbery ever comes to rest on a point of pivot in "Fragment"; rather, he is preoccupied with establishing a relation to a center, however absent, however shifting and elusive. For the reader of current criticism as well as poetry, one of the most remarkable things about "Fragment" is its plethora of terms for describing both the quest for centered space and the issue of that quest. No present writer, whether poet or philosopher, can offer us such a rich prism of sensuous tropes for the invisible core. Indeed, Ashbery's startling alternation of abstract and concrete modes of diction reminds one of Dickinson's sixth sense for apprehending unexpected sights on the verge of the formless, the invisible.

The poem's fifth stanza offers an "opening" emblem of the center—"that stable emptiness"—and deliberately pairs it with a dry and reductive vision of erotic union: "that coming together of masses." The one, we are told, "coincides" with the other, and this is hardly surprising; to valorize the self for its stability (its "warm antiquity," to use a phrase of Stevens's)[6] is to view any union with another as a mere random collision of physical particles. This flat and somewhat sterile opposition is deliberately put forth by Ashbery as a statement of the given, the ordinary predicament of retentive and self-absorbed inwardness. This is Ashbery's condition, though he presents it here, near the beginning of the poem, in a minor key; more triumphant assertions will follow, when stable emptiness gives way to motion and more fertile cavities. A few stanzas later, for example, the emptiness speaks, the stable center becomes a roaring wind tunnel:

> The hollow thus produced
> A kind of cave of the winds; distribution center
> Of subordinate notions to which the stag
> Returns to die: the suppressed lovers.

Cliché, as usual with Ashbery, only partially deflates; to call this Aeolian cavern a "distribution center" somehow glamorizes the stock term. The feel of the line remains powerful, and we can momentarily forget, as Wordsworth does at a similar juncture in *The Prelude* when earth winds also speak to him, that the rush of sound issues from a hollow.[7] "Hollow," indeed, is close enough to "hallow" for us to think of this cavern as a sacred void or grotto. A touch of myth also creeps in with that most emblematic of creatures, the stag, here invoked as a thirsting for primal waters. The unpredictability of Ashbery's style allows him this use of the stag because it has been preceded by the hopelessly worn phrase "subordinate notions"—a term that, having found itself stranded in a poem, looks forward to some saving figure of speech. Both the source and the quester for that source are fictional creations, illusory but necessary. The hollow must seem to produce the desired sound: it must be the very echo of that desire.

Ashbery soon gives the eye its place, too, at the vacant center. The poem's ninth stanza represents the momentarily centered consciousness standing in "the center of some diamond," coordinating sharp images as they move toward him in a kind of crystal dance. The rythm is slow and stately; the world moves in upon the poet's eye. The stanza should be read as a refinement of the eye that earlier saw only the coming together of crude masses. Here sight is so sharp that only particulars or particles are at first visible, until even they are broken down into their constituent colors. The idea is to sharpen focus so intensely that the customary world is no longer visible. Sight is supreme, and sight annihilates fact:

> Slowly as from the center of some diamond
> You begin to take in the world as it moves
> In toward you, part of its own burden of thought,
>   rather
> Idle musing, afternoons listing toward some sullen
> Unexpected end. Seen from inside all is
> Abruptness. As though to get out your eye
> Sharpens and sharpens these particulars; no
> Longer visible, they breathe in multicolored
> Parentheses, the way love in short periods
> Puts everything out of focus, coming and going.

The Roethke of "Four for Sir John Davies" would have appreciated the symmetry of this writing. But the real place to go—if go one must—is to the Stevens of "Asides on the Oboe." This stanza of Ashbery's only grows in stature when the Stevens poem is read alongside it. Stevens's crystal man, his diamond globe, is obviously relevant here, but I also think the poem's epigraph is crucial for Ashbery. "Fragment" everywhere endorses this ethos and this rigor:

> The prologues are over. It is a question, now.
> Of final belief. So, say that final belief
> Must be in a fiction. It is time to choose[8]

There is a deceptively limpid quality to Ashbery's style that readers have mistaken for indecisiveness. Certainly the poet himself at times conspires with some of his readers to create the impression of overly relaxed meditation. "Fragment" may be the most misleading of Ashbery's poems in this regard. Actually, the seeming ease of Ashbery's verse comes from the astonishing rapidity of his thought. He can at times move with a flickering intensity that works to lighten the weight of his lines; Ashbery may prove opaque, but dense he is not. He elongates a thought as molten steel is stretched. The effect can be to attenuate the thread of reference but not really to weaken it. Ashbery knows the heat of his own mind, and so it is natural to find him, in a remarkable stanza of pure lyric energy, declaring that "your only world is an inside one"—and the source of illumination for this inwardness is a blazing candle of artifice:

> Thus your only world is an inside one
> Ironically fashioned out of external phenomena
> Having no rhyme or reason, and yet neither
> An existence independent of foreboding and sly grief.
> Nothing anybody says can make a difference;
>   inversely
> You are a victim of their lack of consequence
> Buffeted by invisible winds, or yet a flame yourself
> Without meaning, yet drawing satisfaction
> From the crevices of that wind, living
> In that flame's idealized shape and duration.

The erotic flame burns by itself, nourishing itself in the absence of meaning. Yet there is a ghost of an Orphic fertility rite in this flaming crevice. If "Fragment" is in some vestigial sense a love poem addressed to a real person, or a poem of consolation over the impossibility of such a relationship, then a stanza such as this offers searing compensation. "Satisfaction" is self-induced. Given that conclusion, the stanza ends on a note of triumph as it discovers "idealized shape and duration." Yet a certain residual ambivalence creeps into a line such as: "inversely / You are a victim of their lack of consequence." Why a victim? How shrewd the phrasing is here: one grieves,

Ashbery insists, over others' lack of consequence, one is victimized by it, even while one grows in power as they decline. (It is worth noting that "they" is a sign of remoteness for Ashbery, an indication of reduced filiation.) "Nothing anybody says can make a difference"; yes, but this seems a rueful declaration.

Yet the consequences of contact—indeed, penetration— with the other are more than rueful: they inspire a sense of loss and waste. Perhaps the poem's most startling image serves to verify Yeats's adage: "the tragedy of sexual intercourse lies in the perpetual virginity of the soul." The moment of intercourse should be a passage to the center; but, as if we did not already know the score, Ashbery reminds us and his "lover" that "The volcanic entrance to an antechamber / Was not what either of us meant." Elsewhere in the poem physical contact is rendered as a species of violence—the last stanza, for example, speaks of two people who "collide in this dusk"—and beyond or after collision lies the violence of achieved impact. The cruel and perpetual surprise of erotic union, even physiologically considered, is that any sexual orifice can be only an antechamber. We reach it only to feel somehow more exiled than before: "outside within the periphery." Even in the act of intercourse we find ourselves voyeurs; we are sure that beyond this dividing wall lies the secret. This emblematic episode reverberates throughout the poem and has something to do with the pervasive tone of sober realization in "Fragment," found even at its most visionary moments. Brooding on this picture of tantalizing proximity to the source, one thinks ahead to the poem's penultimate stanza, where the self is caught in its essential isolation:

> back to one side of life, not especially
> Immune to it, in the secret of what goes on:
> The words sung in the next room are unavoidable
> But their passionate intelligence will be studied in
>   you.

It is fully characteristic of Ashbery to extend a "gloss" on an important passage to more than three hundred lines. This is only another way of noting the breathtakingly rich tapestry of "Fragment": every swirl of metaphor leads the reader to a related arabesque elsewhere in the poem. This play of tropes may strike us at first as erratic, governed only by chance; but as we stay with the poem "chance" gravitates toward "dance," to use a revealing internal rhyme found late in the poem and one that stays in the mind as a perfect description of the asymmetrical symmetry of "Fragment."

The "volcano" stanza startles us with its dead-endedness. How *are* we to recover from the fate of being "outside / Within the periphery"? This is really only another way of asking after the true center, or at least a truer sense of centeredness than is available in the erotic relationship. For Ashbery, as for other American poets, the way to this sense lies in a marriage, however stormy, of flesh with air. This union more often takes the form of an *agon* between two sources of power, two living allegories of natural process. When self and other meet, the "meeting escapes through the dark / Like a well." But when the seer confronts nature he can feel "the oozing sap of touchable mortality." This line occurs in a sequence just before the passage into the antechamber of failed eros, a sequence in which Ashbery takes on the wholly American and wholly Romantic enterprise of matching the self first against the sun and then against the emblematic blood orange, fruit of natural process. At the close of stanza twelve Ashbery situates himself at the threshold moment and prepares for the event, or the advent, of the sun's rising. Ashbery calls it the "active memorial," a phrase that refers both to the sun and to the poet's chant of welcome. The break between stanzas eleven and twelve elides not only the sunrise but the whole passage of day, passing through this vacancy to another conventional spot of time—sunset. At this point the poet's powers fail him and "convention gapes."

> This time
> You get over the threshold of so much unmeaning, so much
> Being, prepared for its event, the active memorial.
> And more swiftly continually in evening, limpid
> Storm winds, commas are dropped, the convention gapes,
> Prostrated before a monument, disappearing into the dark.
> It would not be good to examine these ages
> Except for sun flecks, little on the golden sand
> And coming to reappraisal of the distance.
> The welcoming stuns the heart, iron bells
> Crash through the transparent metal of the sky
> Each day slowing the method of thought a little
> Until oozing sap of touchable mortality, time lost and won.

Through the passage of day, the sun has hardened into a monument; but tomorrow will bring an attempted recovery, not in an effort to battle the sun directly—that is Whitman's way—but in a more "reasonable" measuring of sun flecks on the sand. At this point Ashbery will not heave himself at the sublime. He is open, however, to being shattered anew by the magnitude of sunrise. And yet Ashbery does not quite turn away from the challenge, either, although he appears to ground his sublime aspiration in "a touchable mortality," redirecting his gaze from the sun to the golden fruit of the sun: the blood orange.

> Like the blood orange we have a single
> Vocabulary all heart and all skin and can see
> Through the dust of incisions the central perimeter
> Our imagination's orbit.

In this tiny globe, like a good metaphysical poet, Ashbery sees the great globe and his own spherical nature. The discovery leads him to a sense of his imagination's orbit as being one with the sun's path. The crucial phrase in this magnificent stanza describes that route as "the central perimeter / Our imagination's orbit." What a play on the concept of centrality! The stanza shows us an inside lodged within the periphery, *as the* periphery; it speaks of centrality wandered away from the center yet not errant, but moving in a fixed path. Each word in this gnomic phrase redefines and creates space for the others: central opens the way for perimeter, perimeter is redeemed by central. This is the point upon which Ashbery wishes to take up his stance: the central man on the edge, never lulled into believing that the center will hold nor ever quite willing to view all things as falling apart.

The process of centering and decentering the self is Ashbery's major passion in "Fragment"; line after line works toward making the axis of vision coincident with the axis of things, only to discover that art requires a necessary disjunction or asymmetry. This quest to fix the place of the poetic self in regard to the external world is triggered by the movement toward the poem's ghostly, erotic other, followed by the harsh recognition that the self is necessarily alone. This detachment toward the erotic object is one aspect of the poem's mystery: Ashbery speaks at a distance from the beloved usually encountered only in formal elegy. In fact, "Fragment" often takes on the eerie tonality of epitaph; the title may be read, on one level

at least, as an elegiac epitaph to a lost and impossible attempt to center the self in another.

There is a related peril, however, in regarding any one achieved stance, any one moment, as central: this is the danger of self-limitation or resistance to motion and change. Keats, always open to the temptations of permanence but aware of how they "tease us out of thought," stated the dilemma acutely in his famous letter to Shelley: "My imagination is a monastery, and I am its monk."[9] In the Psyche ode, Keats was careful to leave a window in the mind *open*—"To let the warm Love in!" And we remember those magic casements opening on perilous seas. (Is there a connection here to the title of a poem from *Houseboat Days*: "Wet Casements"?) Stevens goes even further toward resisting this temptation to achieve the center. The epigraph to "Notes toward a Supreme Fiction" regards "the central of our being" as a place in which we rest "for a moment." More graphically yet, in a direct allusion to the Keatsian emblem, Stevens's hermit of a poet's metaphors (his first idea) "comes and goes and comes and goes all day."[10]

The to-and-fro movement of this hieratic persona is something Ashbery affirms everywhere in his poetry. To feel centered is, of course, to feel powerful, to be all one thing. To remain in this feeling is to become a monument to oneself, and this is spiritual death. One must open out new passages of being even while recognizing that the passage begins from the center and moves outward to another center, there to begin again. This kind of movement brings freedom as well as power. The freedom of new passages is a fine trope for the whole concept of the *quest*, and so it is no surprise to find Ashbery, at one point in "Fragment," bestowing the regalia of the questor upon himself as he prepares to invade that other "room," the world:

> To persist in the revision of very old
> Studies, as though mounted on a charger,
> With the door to the next room partly open
> To the borrowed density, what keeps happening to
> So much dead surprise, a weight of spring.

"A weight of spring" may also be read as a "spring weight": when the density of self becomes too pronounced we turn to the borrowed density "out there" as a release.

By putting himself on a charger in this fashion, Ashbery risks the countercharge that he is being merely quixotic. But he keeps the figure in mind and returns to it some nine stanzas later:

> Out of this intolerant swarm of freedom as it
> Is called in your press, the future, an open
> Structure, is rising even now, to be invaded by the present
> As the past stands to one side, dark and theoretical
> Yet most important of all, for his midnight interpretation
> Is suddenly clasped to you with the force of a hand
> But a clear moonlight night in which distant
> Masses are traced with parental concern.
> After silent, colored storms the reply quickly
> Wakens, has already begun its life, its past, just whole and sunny.

The uncanny alternation of abstract and concrete tropes continues: where we would expect to find a castle, instead we glimpse "an open structure." If anyone objects that I am pushing the chivalric metaphor too far by seeing this invasion as a grand charge, the next line—"As the past stands to one side, dark and theoretical"—should clinch the comparison. Who is this onlooker if not the Lady of Romance? The dark lady turns out to be no lady at all, but a parent, an "ancestor," as the next stanza informs us. Ashbery has never parodied more subtly and never been more serious in his adherence to the parodied stance. His wit is bewildering here; the quest romance survives, although the quester is not quite a solitary. His companion, no longer an erotic ideal, has become something of a magus, a friendly wizard. The turn from the beloved toward the true subject of the poem could not be clearer. Ashbery quests for a kind of visionary wisdom, or *gnosis*, rather than erotic comfort. In fact, this moment of contact with the ancestor is the closest Ashbery comes to another person in the poem.

Who might this Merlin persona be? We would simply call him an anterior poet figure, a great poet who now appears in the guise of a prophet. This line of poet-prophets starts with Vergil, so it is entirely appropriate to find a poem in *The Double Dream* entitled "Sortes Vergilianae." I would venture a closer guess, however, as to the identity of this ancestor. "Silent, colored storms": these must be the auroras, and whose key signature are they, if not Stevens's?[11] The rendering of Stevens as magus is a shrewd commentary on the stance that poet does indeed take in "The Auroras of Autumn," and an acknowledgment on Ashbery's part that the two share a common sense of apocalyptic threat.

But just as Stevens moved to unmake the malice of the auroras by "a flippant communication under the moon,"[12] so Ashbery, having paid homage to his true theme, even more than his ancestor, now responds with a flippancy of his own:

Thus reasoned the ancestor, and everything
Happened as he had foretold, but in a funny kind of
    way.
There was no telling whether the thought had un-
    rolled
Down to the heap of pebbles and golden sand now
Only one step ahead, and itself both a trial and
The possibility of turning aside forever.

Alongside the rhetoric of homage there is the language of dismissal: "The possibility of turning aside forever." The dialectic between the two accounts for poetic strength. What makes this strength especially hard to come by is that "the fathers," as a later stanza puts it, also recognized the need to strike out against the background of a relatively fixed order:

The fathers asked that it be made permanent,
A vessel cleaving the dungeon of the waves.
All the details had been worked out
And the decks were clear for sensations
Of joy and defeat, not so closely worked in
As to demolish the possibility of the game's ever
Becoming dangerous again, or of an eventual meet-
    ing.

The ancestors' sanctification of perpetual questing gets in the way of the new poet, even if the decks remain clear. Better to banish all such pictures of the heroic—aurora, ships—and turn to the difficult freedom of the present image:

                    I can tell you all
About freedom that has turned into a painting;
The other is more difficult, though prompt—in fact
A little too prompt: therein lies the difficulty.

No one moment in "Fragment" can be definitive: here the banished pictures return. The reader will find Ashbery toying throughout with the idea of the poem as picture (he is, after all, a professional art critic). At one point, Ashbery seems to regard his framed stanzas as "pictures / Of loving and small things". The bit of Spenserian "season pageantry" that follows this phrase tries for an intentional allegorical stiffness, as if to mock

the poem's vigorous spontaneity. So the seasons pass, filled with details that accrue to "an infinity of tiny ways." Having done with the pretense of controlled picture-making, Ashbery turns against this kind of storytelling in the interests of larger brush strokes. The turn is characteristic of Ashbery's procedure in "Fragment" and elsewhere: offer one mode of working toward the subject, then shatter that way with a truer act of imagination:

The other pictures told in an infinity of tiny ways
Stories of the past: separate incidents
Recounted in touching detail, or vast histories
Murmured confusingly, as though the speaker
Were choked by sighs and tears, and had forgotten
The reason why he was telling the story.
It was these finally that made the strongest
Impression, they shook you like wind
Roaring through branches with no leaves left on
    them.
The vagueness was bigger than life and its apotheosis
Of shining incidents, colored or dark, vivid or
    serious.

This credo prefers apocalypse over apotheosis, the image of imaginative power (here ironically troped as "vagueness") over the "shining incidents" of pictorial mimesis. Such rich "vagueness" does not betray the present to a static image, nor does it freeze (frieze) the past. Even the old studies must be "revised," as we have seen; the past as well as the future is an open structure in constant need of revisionary invasion by the present. Words for this kind of revision fill "Fragment," suggesting that the whole can never be satisfactorily captured, even when the whole is "past": "version" and "interpretation," in particular, stand out from the text in a number of important passages. The poem's fourth stanza confronts the issue directly, conceding that the poem is a version (in the root sense of "translation") of what is the "only real one"—namely, the external event posited not so much as a stable existence in itself, but rather as the uncapturable referent to which interpretation and revision always point, the *idea* of a referent. For if the real event is truly outside, then all relation ceases:

Not forgetting either the chance that you
Might want to revise this version of what is
The only real one, it might be that
No real relation exists between my wish for you
To return and the movements of your arms and legs.

What is important to note here is Ashbery's free acknowledgement that his poem is one version, one possible text among others. At its strongest it can make us forget other texts, just as its author's centered consciousness can make us oblivious of other centers; but there still remains the specter of a sequence of endless translations:

                    And as one figure
Supplants another, and dies, so the postulate of each
Tires the shuffling floor with slogans, present
Complements mindful of our absorbing interest.

We return to the concept of the central perimeter, which may be rephrased here as the notion of a central text continually revising itself and displacing its own center, seeing itself and its world anew: "Then the accounts must be reexamined,/ Shifting ropes of figures." This "figure" says it all: in "Fragment" we are dealing with columns of *figures*—tropes—to be added up or interpreted. It makes no difference how the figures are placed: the sum will be the same. (Again, I would argue that only the opening and closing stanzas of the poem cannot be shifted at will.) All that is required of the interpreter is agility enough to climb up or down these "shifty" ropes suspended between no discernible termini.

Or *does* "Fragment" aim at a resolution? The final lines of the poem predict only "flat evenings / In the months ahead," but a few stanzas before this Ashbery ventures on what seems like a more optimistic prophecy:

People were delighted getting up in the morning
With the density that for once seemed the promise
Of everything forgotten.

This "lighthearted" density might be a resolution we could achieve: a present peace in the absence of memory. But even before this vision fully takes hold, Ashbery imagines the counterpart within us of such healthiness—the invalid inside us who cannot forget that history means death:

and the well-being
Grew, at the expense of whoever lay dying
In a small room watched only by the progression
Of hours in the tight new agreement.

What then would be a good agreement between the various hours? To answer this, I must go outside the bounds of "Fragment" to one of the shorter lyrics in *The Double Dream*, "Years of Indiscretion." All versions of the self as presented in this rich volume of poetry can, I believe, subscribe to the poetic ethic of this poem's closing chant:

Fables that time invents
To explain its passing. They entertain
The very young and the very old, and not
One's standing up in them to shoulder
Task and vision, vision in the form of a task
So that the present seems like yesterday
And yesterday the place where we left off a little
while ago.

Notes

1. David Kalstone, *Five Temperaments* (New York: Oxford University Press, 1977), p. 192
2. Harold Bloom, *Figures of Capable Imagination* (New York: Seabury Press, 1976), p. 185
3. Kalstone, *Five Temperaments*, p. 192
4. Kalstone, *Five Temperaments*, p. 192
5. See her poem #724
6. Wallace Stevens, *Collected Poems* (New York: Knopf, 1954), p. 139
7. Wordsworth, *The Prelude*, book 2, ll. 306–310
8. Stevens, *Collected Poems*, p. 250
9. See his letter of August 1820
10. Stevens, *Collected Poems*, p. 381
11. Cf. Harold Bloom, *Figures of Capable Imagination* (New York: Seabury Press, 1976), p. 199
12. Stevens, *Collected Poems*, p. 418

HAROLD BLOOM
From "The Charity of the Hard Moments"
Figures of Capable Imagination
1976, pp. 200–208

Though "The New Spirit," first of the *Three Poems*, was begun in November 1969, most of it was written January to April, 1970. In a kind of cyclic repetition, the second prose poem "The System" was composed from January to March

1971, with the much shorter "The Recital" added as a coda in April. This double movement from winter vision to spring's re-imaginings is crucial in *Three Poems*, which is Ashbery's prose equivalent of *Notes toward a Supreme Fiction*, and which has the same relation as *Notes* to *Song of Myself*. Where Stevens reduces to the First Idea, which is "an imagined thing," and then equates the poet's act of the mind with the re-imagining of the First Idea, Ashbery reduces to a First Idea of himself, and then re-imagines himself. I am aware that these are difficult formulae, to be explored elsewhere, and turn to a commentary upon *Three Poems*, though necessarily a brief and tentative one.

I described "Evening in the Country" as a "convalescent's" displacement of American Orphism, the natural religion of our poetry. *Three Poems* might be called the masterpiece of an invalid of the Native Strain, even a kind of invalid's version of *Song of Myself*, as though Whitman had written that poem in 1865, rather than 1855. Ashbery's work could be called *Ruminations of Myself* or *Notes toward a Saving but Subordinate Fiction*. Whitman's poem frequently is address of I, Walt Whitman, to you or my soul. Ashbery's *Three Poems* are addressed by *I*, John Ashbery writing, to *You*, Ashbery as he is in process of becoming. *I*, as in Whitman, Pater, Yeats is personality or self or the *antithetical*; *You*, as in the same visionaries, is character or soul or the *primary*. Ashbery's swerve away from tradition here is that his *You* is the re-imagining, while his *I* is a reduction.

"The New Spirit," the first poem's title, refers to a rebirth that takes place after the middle-of-the-journey crisis, here in one's late thirties or early forties:

. . . It is never too late to mend. When one
is in one's late thirties, ordinary things—like a
pebble or a glass of water—take on an expressive
sheen. One wants to know more about them, and
one
is in turn lived by them. . . .

This "new time of being born" Ashbery calls also "the new casualness," and he writes of it in a prose that goes back to his old rhetorical dialectic of alternating ellipsis and the restored cliché. Indeed, "The New Spirit" opens by overtly giving "examples of leaving out," but Ashbery then mostly chooses to stand himself in place of these examples. Why does he choose prose, after "The Skaters" had shown how well he could absorb prose into verse at length? It may be a mistake, as one advantage, in my experience, of "The New Spirit" over "The System" and "The Recital," is that it crosses over to verse half-a-dozen times, while they are wholly in prose. I suppose that the desire to tell a truth that "could still put everything in" made Ashbery wary of verse now, for fear that he should not be as comprehensive as possible. Speaking again as the poet of "Fragment" he defines his predicament: "In you I fall apart, and outwardly am a single fragment, a puzzle to itself." To redress his situation, the New Spirit has come upon him, to renovate a poet who confesses he has lost all initiative:

. . . It has been replaced by a strange kind of happiness within the limitations. The way is narrow but it is not hard, it seems almost to propel or push one along. One gets the narrowness into one's seeing, which also seems an inducement to moving forward into what one has already caught a glimpse of and which quickly becomes vision, in the visionary sense, except that in place of the panorama that used to be our customary setting and which we never made much use of, a limited but infinitely free space has established itself, useful as everyday life but transfigured so that its signs of wear no longer appear as a reproach but as indications of how beautiful a thing must have been to have been so much prized, and its noble aspect which must have been irksome before has now become interesting, you are fascinated and keep on studying it. . . .

This, despite its diffidence, declares what Emerson called Newness or Influx, following Sampson Reed and other Swedenborgians. Sometimes the *Three Poems*, particularly "The System," sound like a heightened version of the senior Henry James. But mostly Ashbery, particularly in "The New Spirit," adds his own kind of newness to his American tradition. At first reading of "The New Spirit," I felt considerable bafflement, not at the subject-matter, immediately clear to any exegete aged forty-two, but at the procedure, for it was difficult to see how Ashbery got from point to point, or even to determine if there were points. But repeated reading uncovers a beautiful and simple design: first, self-acceptance of the minimal anomalies we have become, "the color of the filter of the opinions and ideas everyone has ever entertained about us. And in this form we must prepare, now, to try to live." Second, the wintry reduction of that conferred self is necessary: "And you lacerate yourself so as to say, These wounds are me." Next, a movement to the *you* and to re-imagining of the *I*, with a realization that the *you* has been transformed already, through the soul's experience as a builder of the art of love. With this realization, the consciousness of the New Spirit comes upon the *I*, and self and soul begin to draw closer in a fine lyric beginning: "Little by little / You are the mascot of that time." An event of love, perhaps the one elegized in "Fragment," intervenes, illuminates, and then recedes, but in its afterglow the New Spirit gives a deeper significance to the object-world. After this seeing into the life of things, the growth of the mind quickens. But the transparency attained through the new sense of wholeness "was the same as emptiness," and the sense of individual culmination serves only to alienate the poet further from the whole of mankind, which "lay stupefied in dreams of toil and drudgery." It is at this point of realization that the long and beautiful final paragraph comes, ending "The New Spirit" with a deliberate reminiscence of the end of "The Skaters." Two visions come to Ashbery, to make him understand that there is still freedom, still the wildness of time that may allow the highest form of love to come. One is "the completed Tower of Babel," of all busyness, a terror that could be shut out just by turning away from it. The other is of the constellations that the tower threatened, but only seemed to threaten. They beckon now to "a new journey" certain to be benign, to answer "the major question that revolves around you, your being here." The journey is a choice of forms for answering, which means both Ashbery's quest for poetic form, and his continued acceptance of an "impassive grammar of cosmic unravelings of all kinds, to be proposed but never formulated."

I think that is an accurate account of the design of "The New Spirit," but I am aware such an account gives little sense of how Ashbery has added strangeness to beauty in thus finding himself there more truly and more strange. The transcendental re-awakening of anyone, even of an excellent poet, hardly seems *materia poetica* anymore, and perhaps only Ashbery would attempt to make a poem of it at this time, since his aesthetic follows Stevens by discovering the poem already formed in the world. His true and large achievement in "The New Spirit" is to have taken the theme of "Le Monocle de Mon Oncle," already developed in "Fragment," and to have extended this theme to larger problems of the aging and widening consciousness. Men at forty, Stevens says, can go on paint-

ing lakes only if they can apprehend "the universal hue." They must cease to be dark rabbis, and yield up their lordly studies of the nature of man. "The New Spirit" is Ashbery's exorcism of the dark rabbi in his own nature. Its achievement is the rare one of having found a radiant way of describing a process that goes on in many of us, the crisis of vision in an imaginative person's middle age, without resorting to psychosexual or social reductiveness.

"The System" is Ashbery's venture into quest-romance, his pursuit as rose rabbi, of "the origin and course / Of love," the origin and course together making up the System, which is thus a purposive wandering. Since the poem opens with the statement that "The system was breaking down," the reader is prepared for the prose-poem's penultimate paragraph, that tells us "we are rescued by what we cannot imagine: it is what finally takes us up and shuts our story."

The account of the System begins in a charming vision too genial for irony, as though Aristophanes had mellowed wholly:

> From the outset it was apparent that someone had played a colossal trick on something. The switches had been tripped, as it were; the entire world or one's limited but accurate idea of it was bathed in glowing love, of a sort that need never have come into being but was now indispensable as air is to living creatures . . . if only, as Pascal says, we had the sense to stay in our room, but the individual will condemns this notion and sallies forth full of ardor and *hubris*, bent on self-discovery in the guise of an attractive partner who is *the* heaven-sent one, the convex one with whom he has had the urge to mate all these seasons without realizing it. . . .

This "glowing love" inevitably is soon enough seen as "muddle," and the first phase of quest fails: "Thus it was that a kind of blight fell on these early forms of going forth and being together, an anarchy of the affections sprung from too much universal cohesion." Rather than despair, or yield to apocalyptic yearnings, Ashbery consolidates upon his curious and effective passivity, his own kind of negative capability, becoming "a pillar of waiting," but Quixotic waiting upon a dream. As he waits, he meditates on "twin notions of growth" and on two kinds of happiness. One growth theory is of the great career: "a slow burst that narrows to a final release, pointed but not acute, a life of suffering redeemed and annihilated at the end, and for what?" This High Romanticism moves Ashbery, but he rejects it. Yet the alternative way, a Paterian "life-as-ritual" concept, the *locus classicus* of which we could find in the magnificent "Conclusion" to *The Renaissance*, he also turns from, or asserts he does, though I think he is more a part of this vision than he realizes. He fears the speed with which the soul moves away from others: "This very speed becomes a source of intoxication and of more gradually accruing speed; in the end the soul cannot recognize itself and is as one lost, though it imagines it has found eternal rest."

By evading both notions of growth, Ashbery rather desperately evades growth itself. Confronting two kinds of happiness, "the frontal and the latent," he is again more evasive than he may intend to be. The first is a sudden glory, related to the epiphany or Paterian "privileged moment," and Ashbery backs away from it, as by now we must expect, because of its elitism, he says, but rather, we can surmise, for defensive reasons, involving both the anxiety of influence and more primordial Oedipal anxieties. The latent and dormant kind he seeks to possess, but his long espousal of it seems to me the weakest sequence in *Three Poems*, despite a poignant culmination in the great question: "When will you realize that your dreams have eternal life?" I suspect that these are, *for Ashbery*, the most important pages in his book, but except for the lovely pathos of a dreamer's defense, they are too much the work of a poet who wishes to be more of an anomaly than he is, rather than the "central" kind of a poet he is fated to become, in the line of Emerson, Whitman, Stevens.

This "central" quality returns wonderfully in the last twenty pages of "The System," as the quest for love begins again. A passage of exquisite personal comedy, Chaplinesque in its profundity, climaxes in the poet's defense of his mask: "your pitiable waif's stance, that inquiring look that darts uneasily from side to side as though to ward off a blow—." Ashbery assimilates himself to the crucial Late Romantic image of the failed quester, Browning's Childe Roland, for the author of *Three Poems* now approaches his own Dark Tower, to be confronted there by every anxiety, as human and as poet, that he has evaded:

> . . . It is only that you happened to be wearing this look as you arrived at the end of your perusal of the way left open to you, and it "froze" on you, just as your mother warned you it would when you were little. And now it is the face you show to the world, the face of expectancy, strange as it seems. Perhaps Childe Roland wore such a look as he drew nearer to the Dark Tower, every energy concentrated toward the encounter with the King of Elfland, reasonably certain of the victorious outcome, yet not so much as to erase the premature lines of care from his pale and tear-stained face. Maybe it is just that you don't want to outrage anyone, especially now that the moment of your own encounter seems to be getting closer.

This version of Childe Roland's ordeal is an Ashberyian transformation or wish-fulfillment, as we can be reasonably certain that Browning's quester neither wants nor expects a "victorious outcome." But Ashbery feels raised from a first death, unlike Childe Roland, who longs for any end, and lacks a "quiet acceptance of experience in its revitalizing tide." Very gently, Ashbery accomplishes a Transcendental and open ending to "The System," complete with an Emersonian "transparent axle" and even an equivalent to the closing chant of Emerson's Orphic Poet in *Nature*, though Ashbery's guardian bard speaks to him in a "dry but deep accent," promising mastery. Insisting that he has healed the sadness of childhood, Ashbery declares his System-wanderings are completed, the right balance attained in "what we have carefully put in and kept out," though a lyric "crash" may impend in which all this will be lost again. But, for now:

> The allegory is ended, it coils absorbed into the past, and this afternoon is as wide as an ocean. It is the time we have now, and all our wasted time sinks into the sea and is swallowed up without a trace. The past is dust and ashes, and this incommensurably wide way leads to the pragmatic and kinetic future.

This Shelleyan conclusion, akin to Demogorgon's dialectical vision, offers hope in "the pragmatic" yet menaces a return of the serpent-allegory (whose name is Ananke, in Ashbery as in Stevens or Shelley) in the still "kinetic" future.

The Coda of "The Recital" is a wholly personal apologia, with many Whitmanian and Stevensian echoes, some of them involuntary. "We cannot interpret everything, we must be selective," Ashbery protests, "nor can we leave off singing" which would return the poet to the living death of an unhappy childhood. Against the enemy, who is an amalgam of time and selfishness, Ashbery struggles to get beyond his own solipsism,

and the limits of his art. On the final page, an Emersonian–Stevensian image of saving transparence serves to amalgamate the new changes Ashbery meets and welcomes. This transparence movingly is provided by a Whitmanian vision of an audience for Ashbery's art: "There were new people watching and waiting, conjugating in this way the distance and emptiness, transforming the scarcely noticeable bleakness into something both intimate and noble." So they have and will, judging by the response of my students and other friends, with whom I've discussed Ashbery's work. By more than fifteen years of high vision and persistence he has clarified the initial prophecy of his work, until peering into it we can say: "We see us as we truly behave" and, as we see, we can think: "These accents seem their own defense."

DAVID KALSTONE
From "Self-Portrait in a Convex Mirror"
Five Temperaments
1977, pp. 170–199

In 1972 John Ashbery was invited to read at Shiraz, in Iran, where for several years the Empress had sponsored a festival of music, art, and drama which was remarkable, even notorious, for its modernity: Peter Brook's *Orghast*, Robert Wilson's week-long production *Ka Mountain and GUARDenia Terrace*, Merce Cunningham's dances, the music of Stockhausen and John Cage. Ashbery and another visitor, David Kermani, reported that "to a country without significant modern traditions, still under the spell of its own great past, where a production of Shaw or Ibsen would count as a novelty, such an effort even might seem quixotic." Taking into consideration Iranian critics who demanded Shakespeare first or Chekhov first, Ashbery's own response was delighted and characteristic: "The important thing is to start from the beginning, that is, the present. Oscar Wilde's 'Take care of the luxuries and the necessities will take care of themselves' might well have been the motto of the festival, and its justification."[1] That oversimplifies his view of tradition and modernism, this poet who has rich and felt connections, for example, to Traherne and Marvell as well as to recent poets like Wallace Stevens and Auden and Marianne Moore. But the present is always Ashbery's point of departure: "Before I read modern poetry, the poetry of the past was of really no help to me."[2]

Familiar notions about a poet's development won't quite apply to Ashbery's work. He doesn't return to objects, figures and key incidents which, as the career unfolds, gather increasing symbolic resonance. Nor do his poems refer to one another in any obvious way. Ashbery writes autobiography only inasmuch as he writes about the widening sense of what it is like to gain—or to try to gain—access to his experience. The present is the poem. "I think that any one of my poems might be considered to be a snapshot of whatever is going on in my mind at the time—first of all the desire to write a poem, after that wondering if I've left the oven on or thinking about where I must be in the next hour."[3] Or, more tellingly, in verse ("And *Ut Pictura Poesis* Is Her Name," from *Houseboat Days*):

> The extreme austerity of an almost empty mind
> Colliding with the lush, Rousseau-like foilage of its
>   desire to communicate
> Something between breaths, if only for the sake
> Of others and their desire to understand you and
>   desert you

For other centers of communication, so that un-
     derstanding
May begin, and in doing so be undone.

Like Penelope's web, the doing and undoing of Ashbery's
poems is often their subject: fresh starts, repeated collisions of
plain talk with the tantalizing and frustrating promises of "poetry." The "desire to communicate" erodes, over a pointed line-
break, into hasty beleaguered utterance. Nor does an accumulating personal history provide a frame for him with outlines
guiding and determining the future: "Seen from inside all is /
Abruptness."

> And the great flower of what we have been twists
> On its stem of earth, for not being
> What we are to become, fated to live in
> Intimidated solitude and isolation.
>
> ("Fragment")

In his images of thwarted nature, of discontinuity between
present and past, Ashbery has turned his agitation into a principle of composition. From the start he has looked for sentences,
diction, a syntax which would make these feelings fully and
fluidly available. When he used strict verse forms, as he did in
much of his first book, *Some Trees*, it was always with a sense of
their power to explore rather than to certify that he was a poet.
There are three sestinas in *Some Trees*, and one, the remarkable "Faust," in his second book, *The Tennis Court Oath*.

> These forms such as the sestina were really devices at
> getting into remoter areas of consciousness. The real-
> ly bizarre requirements of a sestina I use as a probing
> tool. . . . I once told somebody that writing a sestina
> was rather like riding downhill on a bicycle and hav-
> ing the pedals push your feet. I wanted my feet to be
> pushed into places they wouldn't normally have
> taken. . . .[4]

Ashbery's rhyming, too, was restless. At the close of "Some
Trees" his final rhymes create a practically unparaphraseable
meaning, the two words inviting overtones they wouldn't have
in prose:

> Placed in a puzzling light, and moving,
> Our days put on such reticence
> These accents seem their own defense.

There were other, drastic attempts to get at "remoter areas
of consciousness," some of them in *The Tennis Court Oath*
close to automatic writing. "Europe," a poem Ashbery now
thinks of as a dead end, was "a way of trying to obliterate the
poetry that at the time was coming naturally"[5] to him. Exploding any notion of continuity, it consisted of "a lot of splin-
tered fragments . . . collecting them all under a series of
numbers." The "French Poems" in *The Double Dream of
Spring* were first written in French, then translated "with the
idea of avoiding customary word-patterns and associations."[6]
In *Three Poems*, his fifth book, long prose pieces were a way to
overflow the "arbitrary divisions of poetry into lines," another
way to an "expanded means of utterance."[7]

What I am getting at is that a great deal of Ashbery's
writing is done in an atmosphere of deliberate demolition, and
that his work is best served not by thinking about development,
but by following his own advice: beginning at the beginning,
"that is, the present." *Self-Portrait in a Convex Mirror* (1975) is
the present with which I want to begin. The long title poem of
that volume is in every sense a major work, a strong and beautiful resolution of besetting and important problems. . . .

"Self-Portrait" begins quietly, not overcommitted to its
occasion, postponing full sentences, preferring phrases:

> As Parmigianino did it, the right hand

Bigger than the head, thrust at the viewer
And swerving easily away, as though to protect
What it advertises. A few leaded panes, old beams,
Fur, pleated muslin, a coral ring rung together
In a movement supporting the face, which swims
Toward and away like the hand
Except that it is in repose. It is what is
Sequestered.

A lot could be said about Ashbery's entrance into poems and
his habit of tentative anchorage: "As on a festal day in early
spring," "As One Put Drunk into the Packet Boat" (title: first
line of Marvell's "Tom May's Death"). Such openings are
reticent, similes taking on the identity of another occasion,
another person—a sideways address to their subject or, in the
case of "Self-Portrait," a way of dealing with temptation. The
speaker in "Self-Portrait" appears to "happen" upon Parmigianino's painting as a solution to a problem pondered before
the poem begins. At first glimpse the glass of art and the face in
the portrait offer him just the right degree of self-disclosure and
self-assertion, the right balance of living spirit and the haunting
concentrated maneuvers of art. The judicious give-and-take
appeals to him: thrust and swerve; toward and away; protect and
advertise. (This is, by the way, one of the best descriptive impressions of a painting I know.) That balanced satisfaction never returns. What at first comforts him, the face "in repose,"
prompts an unsettling fear: "It is what is / Sequestered." This is
the first full sentence of the poem—brief, shocked and considered, after the glancing descriptive phrases. An earlier draft of
the lines was weaker: "protected" rather than "sequestered" and
the word placed unemphatically at the end of the line, as if
some of the menace to be sensed in the finished portrait hadn't
yet surfaced.

From then on the poem becomes, as Ashbery explains it
in a crucial pun, "speculation / (From the Latin *speculum*,
mirror)," Ashbery's glass rather than Francesco's. All questions
of scientific reflection, capturing a real presence, turn instantly
into the other kind of reflection: changeable, even fickle
thought. The whole poem is a series of revisions prepared for in
the opening lines, where in Parmigianino's receding portrait he
imagines first that "the soul establishes itself," then that "the
soul is a captive." Finally, from the portrait's mixture of
"tenderness, amusement and regret":

> The secret is too plain. The pity of it smarts,
> Makes hot tears spurt: that the soul is not a soul,
> Has no secret, is small, and it fits
> Its hollow perfectly: its room, our moment of
>   attention.

In an earlier draft of the poem it was not quite so clear why
such strong feeling emerges:

>   that the soul
> Has no secret, is small, though it fits
> Perfectly the space intended for it: its room, our
>   attention.

Rewriting those lines Ashbery allowed more emphatic fears to
surface. "The soul is not a soul." Acting on an earlier hint that
Parmigianino's mirror chose to show an image "glazed,
embalmed," Ashbery sees it in its hollow (overtones of burial)
rather than in the neutral "space intended." "Our moment of
attention" draws sparks between the glazed surface of the portrait and the poet's transient interest which awakens it, and
places notions like the *soul* irredeemably in the eye of the
beholder. When the poet looks at this ghostly double, alive in
its mirroring appeal, the emerging fear comes across like Milly
Theale's (*The Wings of the Dove*) in front of the Bronzino
portrait resembling her, "dead, dead, dead."

Throughout "Self-Portrait in a Convex Mirror" the poet speaks to the portrait as in easy consultation with a familiar, but with an ever changing sense of whether he is addressing the image, trapped on its wooden globe, or addressing the free painter standing outside his creation, straining to capture a real presence, restraining the power to shatter what may become a prison: "Francesco, your hand is big enough / To wreck the sphere, . . ." An explosion has been building from the start as Ashbery returns over and over, puzzled by that hand which the convex mirror shows "Bigger than the head, thrust at the viewer / And swerving easily away, as though to protect / What it advertises." At first that defensive posture in a work of art attracts him, an icon of mastery. But, a little later, feeling the portrait as "life englobed," he reads the hand differently:

> One would like to stick one's hand
> Out of the globe, but its dimension,
> What carries it, will not allow it.
> No doubt it is this, not the reflex
> To hide something, which makes the hand loom
>   large
> As it retreats slightly.

The hand returns not in self-defense, but

> to fence in and shore up the face
> On which the effort of this condition reads
> Like a pinpoint of a smile, a spark
> Or star one is not sure of having seen
> As darkness resumes.

Philosophic questions mount, but always apprehended through gestures, new expressions glimpsed as one stares at the painting—here a glint of self-mockery, as the painter absorbed with prowess finds himself trapped by his medium after all. "But your eyes proclaim / That everything is surface. . . . / There are no recesses in the room, only alcoves." The window admits light, but all sense of change is excluded, even "the weather, which in French is / *Le temps*, the word for time." The opening section of "Self-Portrait" winds down, the poet bemused but his poetry drained of the emotional concentration which had drawn him to the painting; a glance at the subject's hands sees them as symbolically placed, but inexpressive:

> The whole is stable within
> Instability, a globe like ours, resting
> On a pedestal of vacuum, a ping-pong ball
> Secure on its jet of water.
> And just as there are no words for the surface, that is,
> No words to say what it really is, that it is not
> Superficial but a visible core, then there is
> No way out of the problem of pathos vs. experience.
> You will stay on, restive, serene in
> Your gesture which is neither embrace nor warning
> But which holds something of both in pure
> Affirmation that doesn't affirm anything.

This is not Ashbery's final reading of the portrait's gesturing hand. But it launches a series of struggles with the past, with "art," with the notion of "surface," with the random demands of the present—struggles which are not only at the heart of this poem but a paradigm of Ashbery's work. Parmigianino's portrait has to compete with the furniture of the mind confronting it: the poet's day, memories, surroundings, ambitions, distractions. The solid spherical segment becomes confused, in the Wonderland of the mind, with other rounded images, toys of attention—a ping-pong ball on a jet of water, and then, at the start of the second section, "The balloon pops, the attention / Turns dully away." There is a rhythm to reading this poem, however wandering it may seem. We experience it as a series of contractions and expansions of interest in the

painting, depending upon how much the poet is drawn to its powers of foreshortening and concentration, and alternately how cramped he feels breathing its air. The transitions between sections are marked as easy shifts in inner weather, opposed to the weatherless chamber of Parmigianino's portrait:

> The balloon pops, the attention
> Turns dully away.
>   . . . .
> As I start to forget it
> It presents its stereotype again
>   . . . .
> The shadow of the city injects its own
> Urgency:
>   . . . .
> A breeze like the turning of a page
> Brings back your face.

The painting occurs to him at times as a ship: first, a "tiny, self-important ship / On the surface." In mysterious relation to it the enlarged hand in the distorted portrait seems "Like a dozing whale on the sea bottom." Threatening? Or a sign of throbbing vitality, an invisible part of its world? Later the portrait

> is an unfamiliar stereotype, the face
> Riding at anchor, issued from hazards, soon
> To accost others, "rather angel than man" (Vasari).

Toward the end of the poem, the ship sails in to confirm some sense of

> this otherness
> That gets included in the most ordinary
> Forms of daily activity, changing everything
> Slightly and profoundly, and tearing the matter
> Of creation, any creation, not just artistic creation
> Out of our hands, to install it on some monstrous,
>   near
> Peak, too close to ignore, too far
> For one to intervene? This otherness, this
> "Not-being-us" is all there is to look at
> In the mirror, though no one can say
> How it came to be this way. A ship
> Flying unknown colors has entered the harbor.

Self-important and tiny? Issued from hazards? Flying unknown colors? Through contradictory senses of the ship, Ashbery judges the portrait's relation to risk and adventure, to the mysterious otherness of "arrival" in a completed work of art.

What happens, for example, when we start to imagine the life of cities behind the surface of a work of art, in this case the sack of Rome which was going on where Francesco was at work; Vienna where Ashbery saw the painting in 1959; New York where he is writing his poem? These are ways Ashbery has of summoning up the countless events which nourished the painting and his response to it. That outside life, again imagined in terms of risk, adventure, voyages, can be profoundly disturbing—a life not palpable in a "finished" work.

> a chill, a blight
> Moving outward along the capes and peninsulas
> Of your nervures and so to the archipelagoes
> And to the bathed, aired secrecy of the open sea.

Such images focus the problem of how much life is lived in and outside a work of art. There is no point in disentangling what is hopelessly intertwined. The images flow toward and counter one another, and the reader accumulates a bewildering sense of what it is to be both fulfilled and thwarted by his own grasped moments of vision (all attempts at order, not just artistic creation, Ashbery tries to remind us). Francesco's portrait has the capacity to make us feel at home; we "can live in it as in fact we have done." Or "we linger, receiving / Dreams and inspirations on an unassigned / Frequency." But at another moment the portrait seems like a vacuum drawing upon *our* plenty, "fed by our dreams." If at one point the mind straying from the conical painting is like a balloon bursting, not much later the straying thoughts are imagined as wayward, even sinister progeny of the painting: the balloon has not burst at all. "Actually / The skin of the bubble-chamber's as tough as / Reptile eggs."

Struggling with the past, with art and its completeness, Ashbery is also struggling with the impulses behind his own writing at the very moment of writing.

> you could be fooled for a moment
> Before you realize the reflection
> Isn't yours. You feel then like one of those
> Hoffmann characters who have been deprived
> Of a reflection, except that the whole of me
> Is seen to be supplanted by the strict
> Otherness of the painter in his
> Other room.

The threat is pressed home by a shift from an impersonal "you" to an endangered "me." The finished work of art is like "A cloth over a birdcage," and the poet wary of its invitations:

> Yet the "poetic," straw-colored space
> Of the long corridor that leads back to the painting,
> Its darkening opposite—is this
> Some figment of "art," not to be imagined
> As real, let alone special?

By the closing pages of the poem two irreconcilable views of "living" have proposed themselves. Parmigianino's appears to be a "Life-obstructing task." ("You can't live there.") More than that, the portrait exposes the poet's own efforts in the present:

> Our time gets to be veiled, compromised
> By the portrait's will to endure. It hints at
> Our own, which we were hoping to keep hidden.

When "will to endure" and "life-obstructing" are identified with one another, as they are here in describing our daily fiction-making activities, the psychological contradictions are themselves almost unendurable. Imagining is as alien and miraculous as the ambivalent image he finds for it: "A ship / Flying unknown colors has entered the harbor." Our creations, torn out of our hands, seem installed "on some monstrous, near / Peak, too close to ignore, too far / For one to intervene." Another way of looking at it: "the way of telling" intrudes "as in the game where / A whispered phrase passed around the room / Ends up as something completely different."

An alternative? Though the poem is always pressing us out of the past, it has no unmediated language for the present, which is as hard to locate as other poets' Edens. Where poets describing unknown worlds have always "liken'd spiritual forms to corporal," Ashbery must perform some of the same *likening* to enter the corporal present itself. He knows the present only from before and after, seen as through a terrifying hourglass:

> the sands are hissing
> As they approach the beginning of the big slide
> Into what happened. This past
> Is now here.

Four of these five monosyllables—"This past is now here"—point to the present with all the immediacy of which English is capable, and *past* disarms them all. There is no comfort in the provisional, in being open to the rush of things. In fact, one of the most devastating contemporary critiques of randomness in poetry comes in the final moments of Ashbery's poem. Yet it is

a critique from within, in a poem open to the vagaries of mind—and from a writer deeply committed to describing the struggles we undergo in describing our lives. This is his unique and special place among contemporary poets. The blurring of personal pronouns, their often indeterminate reference, the clouding of landscapes and crystal balls, are all ways of trying to be true not only to the mind's confusions but also to its resistance of stiffening formulations.

In the distorting self-portrait of Parmigianino, Ashbery found the perfect mirror and the perfect antagonist—a totem of art and the past caught in the act of trying to escape from itself. Parmigianino's work of art confirms the poet in a vocation which refuses to be rescued by art, except in the moment of creation.

> Hasn't it too its lair
> In the present we are always escaping from
> And falling back into, as the waterwheel of days
> Pursues its uneventful, even serene course?

This is a difficult dialectic to which he submits. Francesco is the indispensable partner in a continuing conversation; yet Ashbery's final reading of the painterly hand in the self-portrait is the boldest stroke of all:

> Therefore I beseech you, withdraw that hand,
> Offer it no longer as shield or greeting,
> The shield of a greeting, Francesco:
> There is room for one bullet in the chamber:
> Our looking through the wrong end
> Of the telescope as you fall back at a speed
> Faster than that of light to flatten ultimately
> Among the features of the room, . . .

The pun on *chamber*, the dizzying transformations of rounded room into telescope and gun barrel, are triumphant tributes to all the contradictions of this poem and the hard-won struggle to be free of them. It would be a shallow reading which sees this poem as a modernist's dismissal of the past. Ashbery translates that *topos* into radical and embracing human terms. The elation we feel comes from the writer's own unwillingness to take permanent shelter in his work. Any work of art—not just those of the distant past—has designs on us, exposes for what it is our "will to endure." Ashbery builds the awareness of death and change into the very form of his work. It is the old subject of Romantic lyric—of Keats's *Ode on a Grecian Urn*—but here without undue veneration for the moments out of time. Ashbery admits into the interstices of his poem a great deal of experience—confusion, comedy, befuddlement, preoccupation—in which he takes as much joy as in the "cold pockets / Of remembrance, whispers out of time," which he also celebrates. His withdrawal from the privileged moments is never as regretful or as final as Keats's from his "cold pastoral." Nor is it as rueful as Ashbery's own sense of desertion in "Definition of Blue" where "you, in this nether world that could not be better / Waken each morning to the exact value of what you did and said, which remains." In that earlier poem Ashbery feels diminished and powerless before a "portrait, smooth as glass, . . . built up out of multiple corrections," which "has no relation to the space or time in which it was lived." In the spaciousness of "Self-Portrait in a Convex Mirror" Ashbery radiates a new confidence in his ability to accommodate what is in the poet's mind: the concentrated poem and its teeming surroundings. In its achieved generosity and fluidity, in its stops and starts and turns, Ashbery's long poem dispels some of the frustrations of language and form, or assimilates them more closely into the anxieties and frustrations of living. . . .

It is the jumble of everyday pleasures and frustrations that we hear most often in the fluid style of some of the shorter poems of *Self-Portrait in a Convex Mirror*. Even the longer poem "Grand Galop" is almost literally an attempt to keep the poem's accounting powers even with the pace of inner and outer events. Naturally it doesn't succeed. The mind moves in several directions at once, and the poem is partly about the exhaustions and comic waste carried along by the "stream of consciousness":

> The custard is setting; meanwhile
> I not only have my own history to worry about
> But am forced to fret over insufficient details related
>   to large
> Unfinished concepts that can never bring themselves
>   to the point
> Of being, with or without my help, if any were
>   forthcoming.

At the start of the poem, the mind moves on ahead of some lists of names (weigela, sloppy joe on bun—the end of the line for Whitman's famous catalogues) and then the poem says we must stop and "wait again." "Nothing takes up its fair share of time." Ashbery calls our attention repeatedly, and with frustration rather than exultation, to the fact that the poem's time is not actual time.

"Grand Galop" also laments the generalizing and pattern-making powers which intervene and block our experience of particulars:

> Too bad, I mean, that getting to know each just
>   for a fleeting second
> Must be replaced by imperfect knowledge of the
>   featureless whole,
> Like some pocket history of the world, so general
> As to constitute a sob or wail unrelated
> To any attempt at definition.

Imperfect and *featureless* fall with deadpan accuracy in lines which expose the hazards of "aping naturalness." Ashbery's "A Man of Words" finds that

> All diaries are alike, clear and cold, with
> The outlook for continued cold. They are placed
> Horizontal, parallel to the earth,
> Like the unencumbering dead. Just time to reread
>   this
> And the past slips through your fingers, wishing you
>   were there.

Poetry can never be quite quick enough, however grand the "galop," however strong the desire to "communicate something between breaths." This explains some of the qualities of Ashbery's style which trouble readers. What seems strange is not so much *what* he says as the space between his sentences, the quickness of his transitions. "He" will become "you" or "I" without warning as experiences move close and then farther away, photographs and tapes of themselves. Tenses will shift while the poem refers to itself as part of the past. We feel as if something were missing; we become anxious as if a step had been skipped. So does the poet who, in several of the shorter poems, describes himself as a dazed prologue to someone else's play. In "As One Put Drunk into the Packet Boat," he longs for a beautiful apocalypse:

> for a moment, I thought
> The great, formal affair was beginning, orchestrated,
> Its colors concentrated in a glance, a ballade
> That takes in the whole world, now, but lightly,
> Still lightly, but with wide authority and tact.

There are moments when Ashbery takes perilous shelter in the world of fable and dream, as in "Hop o' My Thumb," whose speaker, a kind of Bluebeard, imagines possessing his sirens ("The necklace of wishes alive and breathing around

your throat") in an atmosphere at once hothouse and *Lost Horizon*:

> There are still other made-up countries
> Where we can hide forever,
> Wasted with eternal desire and sadness,
> Sucking the sherbets, crooning the tunes, naming
>   the names.

Yet these worlds, while drawing out some gorgeous imaginings, generate as much restlessness as the confusing world of daytime plenty. We may share the moment in "Märchenbilder" when "One of those lovelorn sonatas / For wind instruments was riding past on a solemn white horse." With it goes impatience, the desire to escape, a very rich and suggestive ambivalence. The fairy tales

> are empty as cupboards.
> To spend whole days drenched in them, waiting for
>   the next whisper,
> For the word in the next room. This is how the
>   princes must have behaved,
> Lying down in the frugality of sleep.

The third of the exotic poems in this volume, "Scheherazade," suggests what Ashbery is after in such works. He doesn't retell the story of the Sultan and the ideal storyteller, but he does explore with evident interest and desire the condition of that inventive lady. She is part of a world of dry lands, beneath which are rich hidden springs. "An inexhaustible wardrobe has been placed at the disposal / Of each new occurrence." She loves the "colored verbs and adjectives,"

> But most of all she loved the particles
> That transform objects of the same category
> Into particular ones, each distinct
> Within and apart from its own class.
> In all this springing up was no hint
> Of a tide, only a pleasant wavering of the air
> In which all things seemed present.

That love of detail and rich ability to cope with it, an experience of the world without anxiety, without being overwhelmed by plenitude, is rarely felt in *Self-Portrait*, and therefore to be envied in the world of "Scheherazade." Is it available in the randomness of daily life in America? Ashbery has an affectionate eye and an especially affectionate ear for the comic and recalcitrant details of American life: "sloppy joe on bun" stands not too far from the weigela which "does its dusty thing / In fire-hammered air." In "Mixed Feelings" several young girls photographed lounging around a fighter bomber "circa 1942 vintage" summon up a sense of the resistant particulars which tease the imagination. The fading news-shot flirts with the poet's curiosity. He names the girls of that period affectionately—the Ruths and Lindas and Pats and Sheilas. He wants to know their hobbies. "Aw nerts, / One of them might say, this guy's too much for me." Each side has its innings: the girls are imagined as wanting to dump the poet and go off to the garment center for a cup of coffee; the poet, laughing at their "tiny intelligences" for thinking they're in New York, recognizes that their scene is set in California. What's delightful about this poem is the relaxed exchange of imagining mind with imagined objects, a kind of seesaw in which each is given independent play. Though the girls are dismissed, he is fully prepared to encounter them again in some modern airport as "astonishingly young and fresh as when this picture was made."

One of the most engaging things about Ashbery's book is his own susceptibility to American sprawl, while understanding its impossible cost. There is a serious undertone—or is it the main current?—in a poem called "The One Thing That Can Save America."

> The quirky things that happen to me, and I tell you,
> And you instantly know what I mean?
> What remote orchard reached by winding roads
> Hides them? Where are these roots?

Along with a healthy love of quirkiness, Ashbery expresses a bafflement that any individual radiance is ever communicated from one person to another. The "One Thing" that can "Save America" is a very remote and ironic chance that

> limited
> Steps . . . can be taken against danger
> Now and in the future, in cool yards,
> In quiet small houses in the country,
> Our country, in fenced areas, in cool shady streets.

The poem reaches a political point which it would be over-simplifying, but suggestive, to call "populist."

The enemy, over and over again, is *generality*. The generalizing habit, he tells us in "All and Some," draws us together "at the place of a bare pedestal. / Too many armies, too many dreams, and that's / It." I don't mean that *Self-Portrait in a Convex Mirror* gets down to cracker-barrel preaching. There is too much self-mockery for that.

> Do you remember how we used to gather
> The woodruff, the woodruff? But all things
> Cannot be emblazoned, but surely many
> Can, and those few devoted
> By a caprice beyond the majesty
> Of time's maw live happy useful lives
> Unaware that the universe is a vast incubator.

What I am getting at is that Ashbery's new variety of tone gives him access to many impulses unresolved and frustrated in *The Double Dream of Spring*.

Whitman's invitation for American poets to loaf and invite their souls can't have had many responses more mysterious, peculiar, searching and beautiful than Ashbery's recent poems. Where he will go from here there is, to use one of his titles, "no way of knowing." What *is* important is that Ashbery, who was on speaking terms with both the formalism of the American 1950s and the unbuttoned verse of the 1960s, is now bold and beyond them. His three most recent books have explored apparently contradictory impulses—a melancholy withdrawal and a bewildered, beguiling openness—which stand in provocative tension with one another. Older readers have tended to find the poems "difficult"; younger readers either do not experience that difficulty or see past it, recognizing gestures and a voice that speak directly to them. Perhaps it is reassuring to them: a voice which is honest about its confusions; a voice which lays claim to ravishing visions but doesn't scorn distractions, is in fact prey to it. Ashbery does what all real poets do, and like all innovators his accents seem both too close and too far from the everyday, not quite what we imagine *art* to be. He mystifies and demystifies at once.

Notes

1. John Ashbery and David Kermani, "Taking Care of the Luxuries (The Shiraz Festival)," *Saturday Review / The Arts*, November 4, 1972, pp. 60–63.
2. Louis A. Osti, "The Craft of John Ashbery: an Interview," *Confrontation* 9 (Fall 1974), p. 89.
3. *The Guardian* (April 19, 1975), p. 8.
4. *The Craft of Poetry: Interview from the New York Quarterly*, ed. William Packard (Doubleday, 1974), p. 124.
5. *Confrontation*, p. 94.
6. *Craft of Poetry*, p. 130.
7. Ibid., p. 126.

PAUL BRESLIN
From "Warpless and Woofless Subtleties"
Poetry, October 1980, pp. 42–47

"If you took a survey asking readers of poetry to name the best living American poet," a colleague of mine was saying the other day, "John Ashbery would come out far ahead. Why, he might get as much as six percent—more if no one could vote for himself." In the present marginal state of the art, the situation James Atlas has described as "Poetry Cornered," Ashbery has some reassuring signs of centrality. In a time when so much poetry seems easy—easily written, easily read, and easily forgotten—his convoluted syntax, his wide vocabulary, in general his obvious difficulty, give the impression of seriousness and depth. His subdued lyricism and his willingness to deal with concepts like "truth," "hope," and "love" appeal to the reader's conservative instincts, while the relentless parody he turns against his own conservative gestures dispels any suspicion of Arnoldian priggishness. Above all, Ashbery has a superb ear, a gift evident not only in his lyrical passages, but also in his dead-accurate mimicry of the banal cadences heard in newspapers, self-help books, and (let's face it) literary criticism.

And yet, after one acknowledges Ashbery's seriousness and virtuosity, it suddenly becomes difficult to characterize his poetry more specifically. One can take the old-fashioned language of romantic transcendence as the heart of his style, and the parodic undercutting as the expression of modern skepticism about the possibility of such transcendence, or of an unusually severe "anxiety of influence." This is Harold Bloom's portrait of Ashbery. David Shapiro, in his new study, emphasizes the parodic aspect. Invoking Derrida, Barthes, and (by allusion) Stanley Fish, he portrays Ashbery as a maker of "self-consuming" texts designed to remind us of the inadequacy inherent in all discourse whatsoever. The common reader, impressed by Ashbery's verbal brilliance but put off by his obscurity, and by the vague pronouncements of admiring critics, may privately suspect a touch of fraud. There is, I think, a good deal of fudge in Ashbery along with the genius; in this essay, I shall attempt a rough estimate of the proportions.

To begin with, Ashbery's obscurity is more often than not soluble, and is not the most serious objection that can be raised against him. It is true that some passages in his work are simply non-sequiturs, and that no amount of careful re-reading will resolve them into anything else. But even these deliberately opaque passages can be understood as an imitation of the way reality presents itself to our consciousness. As such, they become relevant to Ashbery's central recurring subject, which is, crudely stated, the conflict between our unappeasable wish to discover moral meaning in our existence, and our inevitable distrust, as enlightened cultural relativists, of any such discovery. The speaker of an Ashbery poem is tormented with momentary glimmerings, but when his abortive epiphanies trail off into nonsense or banality, he keeps his balance, regards the puncturing of his latest illusion with urbane detachment.

Ashbery's obsessive subject, unfortunately, is so vast and featureless that it might as well be no subject at all. His poems, with very few exceptions, are portraits of the whale's forehead. They return, again and again, to an "it" that has no antecedent and can best be understood as "life" or "the way things are." Circling around the same huge problem, the poems depend on a characteristic set of effects which, however surprising when first encountered, become predictable and even boring when repeated so incessantly. The turn of a particular phrase may still dazzle with its ingenuity, but one has the sense of Reading Ashbery Again, rather than of reading a new poem by Ashbery. The style becomes arabesque, its intricacy of detail lost in a general impression of sameness. To borrow a phrase from "The New Spirit," Ashbery's work is a tissue of "warpless and woofless subtleties." One's evaluation of it will depend, finally, on whether or not one sees a point in such radical decentering or, to put it less politely, amorphousness.

Ashbery's most characteristic (and perhaps most overworked) effect is the self-cancelling epiphany. Near the end of "Business Personals" in *Houseboat Days*, we read:

> Such simple things,
> And we make of them something so complex it
>   defeats us,
> Almost. Why can't everything be simple again,
> Like the first words of the first song as they occurred
> To one who, rapt, wrote them down and later sang
>   them:
> "Only danger deflects
> The arrow from the center of the persimmon disc,
> Its final resting place. And should you be addressing
>   yourself
> To danger? When it takes the form of bleachers
> Sparsely occupied by an audience which has
> Already witnessed the events of which you write,
> Tellingly, in your log? ["]

Not only is the "simple" utterance oracular, it fizzles out in the long-windedness of the second question, with its prosaic image of "bleachers." Nonetheless, the poems often end with a cautious return to elevated diction in the closing lines, giving a muted suggestion of resolution or permanence: "These days stand like vapor under the trees" ("The Gazing Grain"), "The feeling is a jewel like a pearl" ("Friends"). But since these endings sound tentative and seldom engage with symbols or motifs found elsewhere in the poems, the closure seems arbitrary. The wheel of appearances has merely stopped on the illusion rather than the disillusionment next to it.

At first glance, such undercutting seems boldly experimental and ruthlessly honest, but when one has read enough poems to sense that it is a routine procedure, one understands that Ashbery finds the wheel of appearances amusing and does not mind terribly when an attractive illusion dissolves. After all, another will soon be along to take its place. One need not be bored at the Grand Hotel Abyss. There is nostalgia and sadness in Ashbery, but no existential terror, and very little real sense of shock or disorientation. Among his favorite locutions are "of course," "already," "after all," and "the same," verbal tags which assure us that what we are reading is not really strange, is indeed only what we should have expected. Along with these goes a coercive "we" familiar from Auden, who is, after Wallace Stevens, the most visible influence on Ashbery's style. Ashbery's "we" does not refer to humanity as a whole, or even the set of all possible readers for his poetry; it refers to those who have the sophistication to recognize that things are as the poet tells us they are. To refuse this confidential "we" is to declare one's stupidity. The title of Ashbery's newest collection, *As we Know*, illustrates this attitude perfectly.

There is an old joke in which The Lone Ranger and Tonto find themselves ambushed by hundreds of Indians. "Well, Tonto," the masked man says, "it looks like we have to fight them off ourselves." Tonto looks around, does a moment's calculation, and replies: "What you mean 'we'—paleface?" Which is, I suppose, the question I would like to put to Mr. Ashbery. For I fail to see why an honest recognition of

'our' plight compels 'us' to disdain subject matter and meaning. Does the fact that we cannot understand the final purpose of our lives make the particulars of which they are composed uninteresting, meaningless, or contemptible? Can poetry do nothing but beat its head against an epistemological wall? For all of Ashbery's brilliance, I find his unending preoccupation with disappointed transcendence boring. I admire most among his poems the ones that anchor his epistemological probings in some particular situation or symbol, or in which his images are more evocative and referential than usual. My favorites— "These Lacustrine Cities," "The Skaters," and "Self-Portrait in a Convex Mirror"—are 'about' something, in a conventional sense. In these poems, the subject exerts a gravitational pull against the dispersive energies of Ashbery's style, setting up a fertile tension between the recognition that reality is in some respects fluid and the common-sense fact that we nonetheless continue to interpret it as differentiated into particular events, persons, and things. In addition to poems like these, of which Ashbery has written perhaps fifteen or twenty in his career, there are passages within long poems that detach themselves from the abstract buzz surrounding them. Perhaps the best of these is the account of the history of Western consciousness at the beginning of "The System." And there are also poems like "Voyage Into the Blue" in *Self-Portrait* that gain coherence, despite the lack of a finite subject, by working within the traditions of the modern meditative poem, as established by Stevens, Eliot, and Valéry, with a minimum of campiness, self-parody, and posturing. Ashbery has been too much praised for his "originality"; his best poems are the ones that do not apologize for their relation to literary tradition. There is an enormous amount of self-distrust, even self-hatred, in his parodic gestures; I wish that he would trust his own lyrical and meditative impulses more. If he really believes that an illumination is fraudulent, why does he continue to record his own flutterings with the watchfulness of a seventeenth-century Puritan diarist? His self-parody suggests a deep-seated fear of being thought sentimental, rather than a real rejection of sentiment or faith.

Having declared my position, I turn to the volumes under review. Harold Bloom has pronounced *Houseboat Days* the best of Ashbery's books. I'm still inclined to prefer *Rivers and Mountains* and *Self-Portrait in a Convex Mirror*, since nothing in *Houseboat Days* is quite as memorable as the best poems in those collections. But *Houseboat Days* does contain more of those poems focussed on a definite subject than most Ashbery volumes. Not that there are very many, even here: "The Other Tradition" describes some sort of meeting in a rural setting (a writer's conference, perhaps); "Pyrography" is about the rootlessness of American life; "Melodic Trains" is about travel; "Syringa" is a treatment of the Orpheus myth. The rest of the book is devoted to further versions of the recurring Ashbery poem. All of the thematic poems, appropriately enough, deal with transience: the speaker is on a train, or driving around, or attending a conference for a few days. Even the Orpheus myth is made to serve this theme.

Ashbery's revisions of the Orpheus myth in "Syringa" would be revealing if what they revealed had not been so evident already. In Ashbery's version, Eurydice did not vanish because Orpheus turned around to look at her, for

> . . . it is the nature of things to be seen only once,
> As they happen along, bumping into other things,
>   getting along
> Somehow. That's where Orpheus made his mistake.
> Of course Eurydice vanished into the shade;
> She would have even if he hadn't turned around.

Much of the pathos of the original version stems from the fact that Orpheus had it within his power to rescue Eurydice and failed: his love prevailed over the god of the underworld, but his love also undid this victory. Ashbery, for once unsubtle, cuts the knot at a stroke. In his revision, the myth becomes just one more example of his ubiquitous moral: that life is always pulling the rug out from under us, that we go on looking for miracles and epiphanies but are forever disappointed. One might think that 'we' would learn from our experience, but we don't. Yet despite this irritating trivialization, "Syringa" is one of Ashbery's better poems. I especially like the treatment of Orpheus's death. Ashbery dismisses the possibility that the Bacchantes killed Orpheus "for his treatment of Eurydice," deciding instead that "his music, what it was doing to them," had "more to do with it." What the Bacchantes find intolerable is "The way music passes, emblematic / Of life and how you cannot isolate a note of it. . . ." Music, like so much else, is made to serve the theme of mutability, but the passage ends in an interesting complication:

> For although memories, of a season, for
>   example,
> Melt into a single snapshot, one cannot guard,
>   treasure
> That stalled moment. It too is flowing, fleeting;
> It is a picture of flowing, scenery, though living,
>   mortal,
> Over which an abstract action is laid out in blunt,
> Harsh strokes. And to ask more than this
> Is to become the tossing reeds of that slow,
> Powerful stream, the trailing grasses
> Playfully tugged at, but to participate in the action
> No more than this.

Paradoxically, the wish to rescue anything from flux merely imprisons one the more completely in flux, like the reed buffeted by the stream. These lines may seem like yet another homilectic on behalf of negative capability, until we remember that the poem is called "Syringa," which comes from the Greek word for pipe or reed. We do "become the tossing reeds," because we cannot help asking "more than this." And since the passage is about the death of Orpheus, one may find in the image of the "tossing reeds" that scarcely "participate in the action" a symbol of death. In that case, to transcend the contingencies of time and nature is to embrace death itself—as in Keats's "Ode to a Nightingale." This complexity of meaning, by the way, would be quite impossible without a clearly defined subject drawing the parts into relation with each other.

The longest poem in *Houseboat Days*, "Fantasia on 'The Nut-Brown Maid,'" seems to me dull, despite some redeeming moments. The title notwithstanding, it is not a fantasia "on" anything in particular, and as a result it breaks down into the abstract noodling of the regulation-issue Ashbery poem. As early as the "Eclogue" in *Some Trees*, Ashbery had tried the device of introducing two speakers, and hence the expectation of dialogue, only to have his speakers talk past rather than to each other. Like so many of his effects, this one palls with repetition; one gets the joke right away, but the poem rattles on nonetheless. The best things in *Houseboat Days*, besides "Syringa," are "Pyrography" and the title poem, with such uncharacteristically ingenuous passages as this one:

> But I don't set much stock in things
> Beyond the weather and the certainties of living and
>   dying.
> The rest is optional. To praise this, blame that,
> Leads one subtly away from the beginning, where
> We must stay, in motion. To flash light

> Into the house within, its many chambers,
> Its memories and associations, upon its inscribed
> And pictured walls, argues enough that life is
>   various.
> Life is beautiful. He who reads that
> As in the window of some distant, speeding train
> Knows what he wants, and what will befall.

. . . . The mode in which he works is extremely narrow; his relentless self-cancellation takes away almost all that his lyrical genius gives. But there is no denying his gift for the music of language, and every now and then, when he paroles himself from his prison of self-reference, he writes poems that belong among the best of our time.

HELEN VENDLER
"Understanding Ashbery"

The New Yorker, March 16, 1980, pp. 108–136

It seems time to write about John Ashbery's subject matter. His *As We Know* will, of course, elicit more remarks on his style—a style so influential that its imitators are legion. It is Ashbery's style that has obsessed reviewers, as they alternately wrestle with its elusive impermeability and praise its power of linguistic synthesis. There have been able descriptions of its fluid syntax, its insinuating momentum, its generality of reference, its incorporation of vocabulary from all the arts and all the sciences. But it is popularly believed, with some reason, that the style itself is impenetrable, that it is impossible to say what an Ashbery poem is "about." An alternative view says that every Ashbery poem is about poetry—literally self-reflective, like his *Self-Portrait in a Convex Mirror*. Though this may in part be true, it sounds thin in the telling, and it is of some help to remember that in the code language of criticism when a poem is said to be about poetry the word "poetry" is often used to mean: how people construct an intelligibility out of the randomness they experience; how people choose what they love; how people integrate loss and gain; how they distort experience by wish and dream; how they perceive and consolidate flashes of harmony; how they (to end a list otherwise endless) achieve what Keats called a "Soul or Intelligence destined to possess the sense of Identity."

It is worth quoting once more Keats's description of this world not as a vale of tears but as a vale of what he called "soul-making." We are born, according to his parable, with an intelligence not yet made human; we are destined to the chastening of life, which, together with painful labor on our part, tutors our chilly intelligence into a feeling and thinking soul. "I will put it in the most homely form possible," wrote Keats to his brother George in Kentucky:

> I will call the *world* a School instituted for the purpose of teaching little children to read—I will call the *human heart* the *horn Book* used in that School—and I will call the *Child able to read, the Soul* made from that *school and its hornbook*. Do you not see how necessary a World of Pains and troubles is to school an Intelligence and make it a soul?

In a less passionate tone, Keats added in another letter that the mind in uncongenial company is forced upon its own resources, and is left free "to make its speculations on the differences of human character and to class them with the calmness of a Botanist."

In these passages, Keats writes very generally—in the first with the generality of parable, in the second with the generality of taxonomy. Ashbery, too, is a generalizing poet, allegorizing and speculating and classifying as he goes, leaving behind, except for occasional traces, the formative "world of circumstances," which, as Keats says, by the trials it imposes proves the heart, alters the nature, and forms a soul. Ashbery turns his gaze from the circumstances to the provings and alterations and schoolings that issue in identity—to the processes themselves. He has been taking up these mysteries with increasing density in each of his successive volumes.

I was only one of many readers put off, years ago, by the mixture of willful flashiness and sentimentality in *The Tennis Court Oath* (1962). And I was impatient for some time after that because of Ashbery's echoes of Stevens, in forms done better, I thought, and earlier, by Stevens himself. Ashbery's mimetic ear, which picks up clichés and advertising slogans as easily as "noble accents and lucid inescapable rhythms" (as Stevens called them), is a mixed blessing in the new book (which has undigested Eliot from the *Quartets* in it), as in the earlier ones. But though some superficial poems still appear in these new pages, poems of soul-making and speculative classification—evident in *Rivers and Mountains* (1966) and taking expository form in the prose of *Three Poems* (1972)—have been in the ascendant since *Self-Portrait in a Convex Mirror* (1975) and *Houseboat Days* (1977). In *Self-Portrait*, Ashbery gives his own version of the Keatsian soulmaking:

> It is the lumps and trials
> That tell us whether we shall be known
> And whether our fate can be exemplary, like a star.

"Bright star, would I were steadfast as thou art," Keats wrote, echoing Shakespeare and Wordsworth. The Ashbery touch comes in the word "lumps," as in "to take your lumps"—the word anchoring the lofty sentiment to our ironic existence in the world.

Increasingly, Ashbery's poems are about "fear of growing old / Alone, and of finding no one at the evening end / Of the path except another myself," as the poem "Fear of Death" (from *Self-Portrait*) rather too baldly puts it. The distinct remove of his subject matter from immediate "experience" also concerns Ashbery:

> . . . What is writing?
> Well, in my case, it's getting down on paper
> Not thoughts, exactly, but ideas, maybe:
> Ideas about thoughts. Thoughts is too grand a word.

Something—which we could call ruminativeness, speculation, a humming commentary—is going on unnoticed in us always, and is the seedbed of creation: Keats called it a state of "dim dreams," full of "stirring shades, and baffled beams." We do not quite want to call all these things "thoughts." They nonetheless go on. Do we have ideas about them? Well, yes, as Keats did when he thought of them as shadowy stirrings, perplexed shafts of light. Our "ideas" about these "thoughts" that are not thoughts are, as Keats said, the stuff of poetry before it is put into a neater mental order. Intuition, premonition, suspicion, and surmise are the characteristic forms of Ashbery's expression. Otherwise, he would not be true to the stage of spiritual activity in which he is interested. In Ashbery we find, above all, what Wordsworth called

> . . . those obstinate questionings
> Of sense and outward things,
> Fallings from us, vanishings,
> Blank misgivings of a Creature
> Moving about in worlds not realized. . . .

These misgivings and questionings are often put quite cheerfully by Ashbery, in a departure from the solemnity with

which truth and beauty are usually discussed. The chaos we feel when one of the truths we hold to be self-evident forsakes us is generally the source of lugubrious verse; for Ashbery, for whom a change of mood is the chief principle of form, "the truth rushes in to fill the gaps left by / Its sudden demise so that a fairly accurate record of its activity is possible." In short, a new truth sprouts where the old one used to grow, and the recording of successive truths is what is on Ashbery's mind.

A certain coyness attacks poets, understandably enough, when they are asked about their subject matter. It seems too self-incriminating to reply, "Oh, love, death, loneliness, childhood damage, broken friendships, fate, time, death, ecstasy, sex, decay, landscape, war, poverty." Back in 1965, the Interview Press, in Tucson, published "John Ashbery and Kenneth Koch (A Conversation)," in which the following exchange occurs:

> *Ashbery*: I would not put a statement in a poem. I feel that poetry must reflect on already existing statements.
> *Koch*: Why?
> *Ashbery*: Poetry does not have subject matter, because it is the subject. We are the subject matter of poetry, not vice versa.
> *Koch*: Could you distinguish your statement from the ordinary idea, which it resembles in every particular, that poems are about people?
> *Ashbery*: Yes. Poems are about people and things.

To this playful warding off of banality (all the while including it), Ashbery truthfully adds, "When statements occur in poetry they are merely a part of the combined refractions of everything else." One can't, in short, extract the discursive parts from a poem and think they are the poem, any more than one can substitute the discursive remark "Beauty is truth, truth beauty" for the ode of which it is a part. However, the relation that was agitating Keats in that ode was surely the relation between truth and beauty, between the representational and the aesthetic, and there is no harm in saying so. Similarly, for Ashbery, it is no disservice to his eloquent fabric of "filiations, shuttlings . . . look, gesture, / Hearsay" ("Self-Portrait") to speak of what the shuttlings are shuttling around, what the gestures are gesturing to.

An eminent scholar told me recently, more in sorrow than in anger, that he had read and reread the poem "Houseboat Days" and still he could not understand it. This can happen, even as people read Ashbery with good will, because Ashbery has borrowed from Stevens a trick of working up obliquely to his subject, so that the subject itself makes a rather late appearance in the poem. The poem begins with a thought or image that provides a stimulus, and the poet works his way into the poem by an exploratory process resembling, Ashbery has said, philosophical inquiry. The beginning, Ashbery modestly adds, may eventually not have very much to do with the outcome, but by then it has become enmeshed in the poem and cannot be detached from it. If a reader proceeds past the rather odd and off-putting beginning of "Houseboat Days," he will come to a meditation, first of all, on how little either the mind or the senses finally give us. In youth, we are appetitive, mentally and physically, and are convinced we are learning and feeling everything; as we age, we find how much of what we have learned is corrupted by use, and how fast the surge of sensual discovery ebbs:

> . . . The mind
> Is so hospitable, taking in everything
> Like boarders, and you don't see until
> It's all over how little there was to learn

> Once the stench of knowledge has
> dissipated, and the trouvailles
> Of every one of the senses fallen back.

After the next meditation (on the insusceptibility of our inmost convictions to reason and argument) comes a meditation on the ubiquitous presence, no matter what your convictions make you praise or blame in life, of intractable pain:

> . . . Do you see where it leads? To pain. . . .
> . . . it . . . happens, like an explosion in the brain,
> Only it's a catastrophe on another planet to which
> One has been invited, and as surely cannot refuse:
> Pain in the cistern, in the gutters. . . .

Oddly enough, our first response to emotional pain all around us, down in the cisterns, up in the gutters, is to deny we are feeling it; it is, Ashbery muses, "as though a universe of pain/ Had been created just so as to deny its own existence." In the manifesto that follows, Ashbery sets forth a Paterian ethics of perception, introspection, memory, art, and flexibility. He argues, given the nature of life, against polemic and contentiousness:

> But I don't set much stock in things
> Beyond the weather and the certainties of living and
>   dying:
> The rest is optional. To praise this, blame that,
> Leads one subtly away from the beginning, where
> We must stay, in motion. To flash light
> Into the house within, its many chambers,
> Its memories and associations, upon its inscribed
> And pictured walls, argues enough that life is
>   various.
> Life is beautiful. He who reads that
> As in the window of some distant, speeding train
> Knows what he wants, and what will befall.

What we hear in these lines, with their ethos of sweetness and Hellenic light borrowed from Arnold, is a syntax borrowed from Yeats: "He who can read the signs nor sink unmanned" and "May know not what he knows, but knows not grief." But Yeats would not continue, as Ashbery does, by readmitting in the next line a Keatsian melancholy: "Pinpricks of rain fall again." Hope, he says, seems in middle age a futile emotion: "hope is something else, something concrete/You can't have." Hope exists still, but suppressed, confined to the subterranean life of dream, repressed until the force of desire becomes unmanageable—a tidal wave:

> . . . It becomes a vast dream
> Of having that can topple governments, level towns
>   and cities
> With the pressure of sleep building up behind it.
> The surge creates its own edge
> And you must proceed this way: mornings of assent,
> Indifferent noons leading to the ripple of the question
> Of late afternoon projected into evening.

And what results from the balked torrential surge and earthquake of desire? They find their way much diminished, says the poet, into these poems, these addresses, these needle-tracings of disturbance:

> Arabesques and runnels are the result
> Over the public address system, on the seismograph
>   at Berkeley.

And what do they cost, these houseboat days, our days in this fragile ark, adrift on the Byronic tide? They cost precisely (by a "little simple arithmetic") everything, and they point to the end of the vacation, that "last week in August" which the poem envisages, with not much time left at all, as the rain gathers, and we notice this instant "for the first and last time,"

as one would notice a place on the dustcover of a book one is closing, "fading like the spine / Of an adventure novel behind glass, behind the teacups." In this light, the mournful beginning of the poem—about a break in a previously healthy surface, about thinking, over the hotel china, at breakfast, about the end of one's stay—is also about the common heresy of thinking oneself immortal and finding the wing of death rushing above, about the tendency of the mind to linger (to "botanize," to borrow Keats' metaphor) on these questions of time and death, and about the equal tendency of life (a dazed daisy, or life "dazed with the fume of poppies," to quote the unrevised ode "To Autumn") to blossom again in its inhospitable environment:

> "The skin is broken. The hotel breakfast china
> Poking ahead to the last week in August, not really
> Very much at all, found the land where you be-
>   gan . . ."
> The hills smouldered up blue that day, again
> You walk five feet along the shore, and you duck
> As a common heresy sweeps over.
>   We can botanize
> About this for centuries, and the little dazey
> Blooms again in the cities. . . .

Life for Ashbery, as everyone has noticed, is motion. We are on boats, on rivers, on trains. Each instant is seen "for the first and last time;" each moment is precious and vanishing, and consequently every poem is unique, recording a unique interval of consciousness. This is a consoling aesthetic, since by its standards every utterance is privileged as a nonce affair; it is also mournful, since it considers art as fleeting as life. In an interview he gave to the *New York Quarterly* (reprinted in *The Craft of Poetry*; Doubleday, 1974), Ashbery spoke unequivocally on various topics—his subject matter, his supposed "obscurity," his method of writing, his forms, his influences. There are occasional self-contradictions in the piece, as might be expected in conversation on matters so complex. But, for the record, some of Ashbery's helpful remarks bear repeating:

> All my stuff is romantic poetry, rather than metaphysical or surrealist. . . . As far as painting itself goes . . . I don't feel that the visual part of art is important to me, although I certainly love painting, but I'm much more audio-directed. . . . French poetry on the whole hasn't influenced me in any very deep way. . . . I'm attempting to reproduce in poetry . . . the actions of a mind at work or at rest. . . . ["The Skaters"] is a meditation on my childhood which was rather solitary. I grew up on a farm in a region of very hard winters and I think the boredom of my own childhood was what I was remembering when I wrote that poem—the stamp albums, going outside to try and be amused in the snow. . . . Also an imaginary voyage prompted by the sight of a label or a postage stamp was again a memory of childhood. . . . In the last few years I have been attempting to keep meaningfulness up to the pace of randomness . . . but I really think that meaningfulness can't get along without randomness and that they somehow have to be brought together. . . . The passage of time is becoming more and more *the* subject of my poetry as I get older. . . . ["Fragment"], like maybe all of my poems, [is] a love poem. . . .

The entire interview is a revealing one, and links Ashbery conclusively to the Western lyric tradition. In short, he comes from Wordsworth, Keats, Tennyson, Stevens, Eliot; his poems are about love, or time, or age.

And yet it is no service to Ashbery, on the whole, to group him with Stevens and Eliot; when he echoes them most compliantly, he is least himself. In any case, though he descends from them, he is not very much like them: he is garrulous, like Whitman, not angular, like Eliot; he is not rhetorical, like Stevens, but, rather, tends to be conversational, for all the world like Keats in his mercurial letters. The familiar letter, sometimes the familiar essay are his models now that he has forsaken the formal experiments of his earlier books. We open *As We Know* already included, by its title, in a complicity of recognition and inquiry. The book clarifies itself over time, and is itself the clearest of all Ashbery's books; his special allusiveness, a private language perfected over the past twenty years, appears in it, of course, but there are long stretches of accessible table talk, so to speak. These appear chiefly in "Litany," a long poem written in double columns, in what I find a somewhat trying imitation of the bicameral mind. It is full of perfectly intelligible and heartfelt ruminations on soul-making in art, life, and criticism. On the whole, it wonders why—placed, as we are, on this isthmus of our middle state—we go on living and doing the things we do: inventing, imitating, and transforming life.

> . . . Earthly inadequacy
> Is indescribable, and heavenly satisfaction
> Needs no description, but between
> Them, hovering like Satan on airless
> Wing is the matter at hand:
> The essence of it is that all love
> Is imitative, creative, and that we can't hear it.

Ashbery, like Coleridge, who found all life an interruption of what was going on in his mind, lives in the "chronic reverie" of the natural contemplative. As often as not, his contemplation is chagrined, reproachful of the world that promised us so much and gave us so little. At times, he even doubts whether we are doing any soul-making at all:

> . . . And slowly
> The results are brought in, and are found disappoint-
> ing
> As broken blue birds'-eggs in a nest among rushes
> And we fall away like fish from the Grand Banks
> Into the inky, tepid depths beyond. It is said
> That this is our development, but no one believes
> It is, but no one has any authority to proceed further.
> And we keep chewing on darkness like a rind
> For what comfort it can give in the crevices
> Between us. . . .

These are the dark passages that Keats foresaw and feared, sketched by Ashbery in his characteristically speckled humor.

Ashbery has said that his long poems are like diaries, written for an hour or so a day over long periods, and "Litany"—a "comic dirge routine," like so many of his poems—has to be listened to as well over a long stretch of time. Such a form of composition, he says in a poem at the end of *Houseboat Days*, has to do with "The way music passes, emblematic / Of life and how you cannot isolate a note of it / And say it is good or bad." Nor can a line, or a passage, or an inception or conclusion from Ashbery be isolated as good or bad: "the linear style / is discarded / though this is / not realized for centuries." It is our wish to isolate the line as touchstone which makes us at first find Ashbery baffling; once we stop looking for self-contained units we begin to feel better about our responses, and soon find a drift here, a meander there that feels, if not like our old beloved stanzas or aphorisms, at least like a pause in the rapids. What we find in him (to quote again from *Houseboat Days*) is "branching diversions around an axis": the axis of loss,

or forgetfulness, or remorse, or optimism, or human drama—since we are all, as Ashbery wittily says, "characters in the opera *The Flood*, by the great anonymous composer."

Houseboat Days is the volume containing Ashbery's most explicit short accounts of his own intent. His model there is a tapestry done in the form of a Möbius strip; this metaphor, with its (literal) new twist on an ancient figure for the web of art, coexists with the metaphor of the litany, the chain of words, the sequence of lessons in the heart's hornbook:

> We may as well begin the litany here:
> How all that forgotten past seasons us, prepares
> Us for each other, now that the mathematics
> Of winter is starting to point it out.

As things are reduced, once leafless, to the harsh geometry lesson of winter, we learn the diagrammatic forms of life, and chant its repetitive and lengthening chant. Such is the mournful view. On the other hand, Ashbery is irrepressibly sanguine. Something will always turn up to change the mood, as it does in a sonata. Never was there a "castaway of middle life" (Ashbery was born in 1927) more confident of his daily bread from the ravens:

> . . . Impetuously
> We travel on, life seems full of promise,
> . . . Surely
> Life is meant to be this way, solemn
> And joyful as an autumn wood. . . .

Of course, this cannot last, and the wood is "rent by the hunters' / Horns and their dogs." But a renewal does keep happening: the sun brings, as is its wont, a zephyr, a cowslip.

Not only is Ashbery perennially hopeful, he is perennially generous, especially toward the whole enterprise of art—its origins in experience, the collecting of data that might help it along, its actual, stumbling efforts, its stiffening into print or onto canvas, its preservation by the academies. In "Litany," he is quite willing, for example, for the academy and the critics to exist. After all, his fresco or his "small liturgical opera," this litany, will be preserved by the academy, described by critics, long after the author dies, and even while time threatens to devour everything:

> Certainly the academy has performed
> A useful function. Where else could
> Tiny flecks of plaster float almost
> Forever in innocuous sundown almost
> Fashionable as the dark probes again.
> An open beak is shadowed against the
> Small liturgical opera this time.
> It is nobody's fault. And the academy
> Has saved it all for remembering.

As for critics, they are there, like the poets, to keep reminding people of what is in fact happening to them:

> . . . People
> Are either too stunned or too engrossed
> In their own petty pursuits to bother with
> What is happening all around them, even
> When that turns out to be extremely interesting. . . .
> . . . who
> Can evaluate it, formulate
> The appropriate apothegm, show us
> In a few well-chosen words of wisdom
> Exactly what is taking place all about us?
> Not critics, certainly, though that is precisely
> What they are supposed to be doing.

The despair of language here is a sign of Ashbery's yearning for a vision less than preformulated, more than foreseeable: for something done by great poets ("and a few / Great critics as well," he adds generously); that is, to

> . . . describe the exact feel
> And slant of a field in such a way as to
> Make you wish you were in it, or better yet
> To make you realize that you actually are in it
> For better or for worse, with no
> Conceivable way of getting out. . . .

I quote these lines even though they are not among Ashbery's best—they haven't his eel-like darting—because they show his earnestness about the whole enterprise of art, as he asks for a new criticism, deriving from the actual current practice of poetry, for only in this way do we make our poetry intelligible to ourselves:

> It is to count our own ribs, as though Narcissus
> Were born blind, and still daily
> Haunts the mantled pool, and does not know why.

It is as though poetry were incompetent to see its own image until reflected in the discursive analysis of criticism. And it may be so.

The best moments in Ashbery are those of "antithesis chirping / to antithesis" in an alternation of "elegy and tocca-ta," all told in a style of "ductility, its swift / Garrulity, jump-ing from line to line, / From page to page." The endless begin-nings and endings in Ashbery, the changes of scenery, the shifting of characters ally him to our most volatile poets—the Shakespeare of the sonnets, the Herbert of "The Temple," the Keats of the letters, the Shelley of "Epipsychidion." He is different from all but Keats in being often very funny; in "Litany," for example, he gives himself mock commands and injunctions:

> . . . And so
> I say unto you: beware the right margin
> Which is unjustified; the left
> Is justified and can take care of itself
> But what is in between expands and flaps. . . .

And in a parody of Blake he goes "bopping down the valleys wild;" the poetry of pastoral, parodied, becomes both touching and ridiculous:

> The lovers saunter away.
> It is a mild day in May.
> With music and birdsong alway
> And the hope of love in the way. . . .

Then, in a trice, the pastoral grows grim:

> . . . Death likes to stay
> Near so as to be able to slay
> The lovers who humbly come to pray
> Him to pardon them yet his stay
> Of execution includes none and they lay
> Hope aside and soon disappear.

And so the small liturgical opera of "Litany" goes on through three parts, in a Protean masque of genres. Different readers will prefer different arias and, through the device of the double columns, different counterpoints. My current favorite is an ode to love:

> . . . It is, then,
> Gigantic, yet life-size. And
> Once it has lived, one has lived with it.
> The astringent,
> Clear timbre is, having belonged to one,
> One's own, forever, and this
> Despite the green ghetto that intrudes
> Its blighted charm on each of the moments
> We called on love for, to lead us

> To farther tables and new, surprised,
> Suffocated chants just beyond the range
> Of simple perception.

This ode continues for nearly forty lines; the part I have quoted is paired, in the other column, with a reflection on solitude, perhaps preceding death:

> . . . The river is waning
> On. Now no one comes
> To disturb the murk, and the profoundest
> Tributaries are silent with the smell
> Of being alone. How it
> Dances alone, in winter shine
> Or autumn filth.

As always in Ashbery, there is a new beginning, an upswelling. Even the end of "Litany" shows us caught in the reel of life, as the naïf speaker earnestly addresses us for help:

> Some months ago I got an offer
> From Columbia Tape Club, Terre
> Haute, Ind., where I could buy one
> Tape and get another free. I accept-
> Ed the deal, paid for one tape and
> Chose a free one. But since I've been
> Repeatedly billed for my free tape.
> I've written them several times but
> Can't straighten it out—would you
> Try?

We all think life's first reel is free; we always find ourselves billed for it over and over; we can never "straighten it out." Never has Freud been so lightly explicated.

The rest of *As We Know*—forty-seven short lyrics—is not any more easily summarized than "Litany." There are poems (I begin this list from the beginning) about growing up, about fidelity, about identity, about death, about (I have skipped two) the permanence of art, about construction, deconstruction, and perpetual creative joy in the face of death:

> . . . We must first trick the idea
> Into being, then dismantle it,
> Scattering the pieces on the wind,
> So that the old joy, modest as cake, as wine and
> friendship
> Will stay with us at the last, backed by the night
> Whose ruse gave it our final meaning.

One could go on, listing the subjects of all forty-seven poems. They are all "about" something. Some are carried off better than others; some seem destined to last, to be memorable and remembered—none more so than the calmly fateful "Haunted Landscape."

"Haunted Landscape" tells us that we all enter at birth a landscape previously inhabited by the dead. We all play Adam and Eve in the land; we then suffer uprootings and upheaval. We are all—as Ashbery says, quoting Yeats—"led . . . / By the nose" through life; we see life and ourselves dwindle into poverty, and it is only our naïveté (some would say stupidity) that lets us construct castles in air, which of course collapse. Life is both a miracle and a non-event. At the end, we die, and become part of the ground cover and the ground; we become ghosts, as we are told by an unknown herald that it is time to go. The transformation takes place without our knowing how, and our history becomes once again the history of earth's dust. This is the "plot" of "Haunted Landscape;" there is no plot more endemic to lyric. I quote the middle lines, about the eternal reappearance and sexual conjunction and final undoing of the archetypal human couple:

> She had preferred to sidle through the cane and he

To hoe the land in the hope that some day they
    would grow happy
Contemplating the result: so much fruitfulness. A
    legend.
He came now in the certainty of her braided
    greeting. . . .
They were thinking, too, that this was the right way
    to begin
A farm that would later have to be uprooted to make
    way
For the new plains and mountains that would follow
    after
To be extinguished in turn as the ocean takes over
Where the glacier leaves off and in the thundering of
    surf
And rock, something, some note or other, gets
    lost. . . .

It is from Stevens that Ashbery learns the dispassionate record-ing of horror, as here the farm is uprooted, the plains are extinguished, and the irretrievable note (of hope, of happiness, of love) is lost, if not under the glacier then in the crash of surf and rock. And what can we look back on? Only the ruined pastoral, our quenched dreams, our diminished life:

And we have this to look back on, not much, but a
    sign
Of the petty ordering of our days as it was created and
    led us
By the nose through itself, and now it has happened
And we have it to look at, and have to look at it
For the good it now possesses which has shrunk from
    the
Outline surrounding it to a little heap or handful
    near the center.

"Others call this old age or stupidity," comments Ashbery. We cannot bear to utter those words of ourselves.

In the meantime, the only heroism, even when life be-comes shaming and humiliating, is to attain the eye that misses nothing:

    The wide angle that seeks to contain
    Everything, as a sea, is an eye.
    What is beheld is whatever lives,
    Is wildly unappetizing and inappropriate,
    And sits, and fits us.

With every construction of pleasure, there arises, says Ashbery, a precisely equivalent and simultaneous construct of criticism, and vice versa: "They are constructing pleasure simul-taneously / in an adjacent chamber / That occupies the same cube of space as the critic's study." The perplexed relations between these two—pleasure and criticism, beauty and truth—are shown in constant flux in these poems, the question per-petually reëxamined:

    The contest ends at midnight tonight
    But you can submit again, and again.

Ashbery is an American poet, always putting into his poems our parades and contests and shaded streets. He some-times sounds like Charles Ives in his irrepressible Americana, full of "dried tears / Loitering at the sun's school shade." There is nonetheless something monkish in these poems, which, in spite of their social joy and their hours of devoted illumination in the scriptorium, see a blank and blighted end. The poem with the portmanteau title "Landscapeople" sums up our dilemma—the intersection of humanity and nature. It tells us, in brief, all that Ashbery has to say at this moment about our lives, a summary both scarred and sunlit:

Long desired, the journey is begun.
    The suppliants
Climb aboard the damaged carrousel:
Some have been hacked to death, one has learned
Some new thing, and all are touched
With the same blight. . . .

It is the blight man was born for, we remind ourselves. We travel in circles on the carrousel, going nowhere:

And the new ways are as simple as the old ones,
Only more firmly anchored to the spectacle
Of the madness of the seasons as it unfolds
With iron-clad rigidity, filling the sky with light.

The sacred seasons, Keats wrote, must not be disturbed. But they bring the chilly auroras of autumn, as Stevens said, filling the sky with "the color of ice and fire and solitude." At the close of "Landscapeople," Ashbery thinks of Wordsworth's "Immortality" ode, and of his own art as a Rilkean Book of Hours:

We began in an anonymous sensuality
And lived most of it out before the difference
Of time got in the way, filling up the margins of the
    days
With pictures of fruit, light, colors, music, and
    vines,
Until it ceases to be a problem.

I have been extracting chiefly the more accessible parts of Ashbery, but it is possible to explain his "hard" parts, too, given time, patience, and an acquaintance with his manner. It is possible also to characterize that manner—by turns so free-floating, allusive, arch, desultory, mild, genial, unassertive, accommodating, wistful, confiding, oscillatory, tactful, self-deprecatory, humorous, colloquial, despairing, witty, polite, nostalgic, elusive, entertaining. It is within our grasp to schematize his practice, categorize his tics—opaque refer-ences, slithering pronouns, eliding tenses, vague excitements, timid protests, comic reversals, knowing clichés. We can rec-ognize his attitudes—the mania for collection, the outlandish suggestions, the fragrant memories, the camaraderie in an-guish. If we ask why the manner, why the tics, why the atti-tudes, and we do ask it—at least, I have sometimes asked it and heard it asked—the answer, for a poet as serious as Ashbery, cannot be simply the one of play, though the element of playfulness (of not being, God forbid, boring or, worse, bored) always enters in, and enters in powerfully. The answer lies in yet another of Ashbery's affinities with Keats. Keats said that the poet had no identity of his own but, rather, took on the identities of other things— people, animals, atmospheres— which pressed in upon him. "I guess I don't have a very strong sense of my own identity," said Ashbery in the *New York Quar-terly* interview. "I find it very easy to move from one person in the sense of a pronoun to another and this again helps to produce a kind of polyphony in my poetry which I again feel is a means toward greater naturalism." "A crowd of voices," as Stevens called it, is spoken for by the single poet; as we feel ourselves farther and farther from uniqueness and more and more part of a human collective, living, as Lowell said, a generic life, the pressure of reality exerts a pressure on style—a pressure to speak in the voice of the many, with no portion of their language (whether the language of cliché, the language of the media, the language of obscenity, or the language of tech-nology) ruled out. Our dénouement is a collective fate; we are "already drenched in the perfume of fatality." What the poet can do is remind us of "the gigantic / Bits and pieces of knowl-edge we have retained," of that which "made the chimes ring."

If anything, in Ashbery's view, makes a beautiful order of the bits and pieces and the chimes ringing, it is poetry:

> If you listen you can hear them ringing still:
> A mood, a Stimmung, adding up to a sense of what
>   they really were,
> All along, through the chain of lengthening days.

VERNON SHETLEY
"Language on a Very Plain Level"
Poetry, July 1982, pp. 236–41

It takes a certain effort of historical imagination to feel just how strange T. S. Eliot's poems must have seemed to most of his early readers; what was decried in the 1920's as hermetic and impenetrable is now taught, without particular difficulty, to the brighter sort of high school student. So one suspects that the reader of fifty years hence will require a certain mental leap to understand the accusations of incomprehensibility that have dogged John Ashbery's career almost from its beginnings. With a few exceptions, the people we pay to do our reading for us have sadly botched their reading of Ashbery, and the fog of misconceptions that surrounds his poems has grown to such proportions that it threatens to overwhelm the interested reader approaching Ashbery, and to obscure the qualities of the poetry itself.

Having heard much of Ashbery's impenetrability, how surprised our reader will be when he or she opens the books and finds them filled with poems of an astonishing, limpid immediacy. Ashbery can write poems that amount to no more than aggregations of discrete fragments; in that case, one's reaction is simple: one turns to the next page and goes on to the beautifully transparent lyric that usually awaits one there. Ashbery's diabolically clever strategy has been to hide his meaning where no one would think of looking for it: in plain view. Poe's Prefect, who knew all the most subtle methods of detection, was nevertheless outdone by Dupin's purposeful naïveté, and the reader of Ashbery will do better to clear his mind of preconceptions than to seek out some veiled esoteric sense. Ashbery almost always means exactly what he says, and so one cannot read him too literally: this poet, like most good poets, is thoroughly literal-minded. That is not to imply that his work does not demand attention and concentration; indeed concentration, rather than memory, is the key resource the reader must bring to Ashbery. Much of Ashbery takes place in the movement, the flux and reflux of syntax, so that each poem's shape grows only in time, the time of the poem's reading, rather than cohering in the connect-the-dots fashion of high modernist poetry. His elaborate and extraordinarily varied syntactical figures offer themselves naturally as pathways into the poems, yet critics still struggle to sum up Ashbery by the old arithmetic of spatial form. The reader willing to follow attentively the working out of each new impulse will find that the poem, rather than baffling or obstructing him, yields a vast range of joyfully elaborated poetic sensations:

> At first it came easily, with the knowledge of the
>   shadow line
> Picking its way through various landscapes before
>   coming
> To stand far from you, to bless you incidentally
> In sorting out what was best for it, and most suitable,
> Like snow having second thoughts and coming back
> To be wary about this, to embellish that, as though
>   life were a party
> At which work got done.

Here the reader moves with these paired participles to stand at the fixed point of the paired infinitives, yielding in turn to an extended simile that acquires so much materiality in its working out that it calls forth a further simile, one that stretches backwards, from its tenuous trailing position, to encompass the whole of this impulse and its transformations.

That Ashbery's poetry is in some sense private must be admitted, but no poet since Pope will 'scape whipping on that score. That one's subjectivity is clichéd does not make it any the less subjective, and Ashbery's explorations of his own consciousness have a great deal more to say about the quality of our experience here and now than our present-day bards, of the great and eternal themes, late descendants of Arthur Hugh Clough. No one better understands and conveys the predicament of the mind in our time and place than Ashbery: struggling under the accumulated wreckage of history and culture, crossed randomly and insistently by the phantasmagoria of popular culture, suspecting all its own impulses to limit and to order. Ashbery's is a poetry of everyday life, of those moments of lyric redemption that occur to us, so randomly, so much unsought, but a poetry aware also that those moments subside, flow back into the texture of our days: "But in the long run serious concerns prevail, such as / What time is it and what are you going to do about that?"

That said, one might caution the reader that *Shadow Train* is by no means the best place to start in reading Ashbery, as it occupies a curious position in the evolving body of his work. This collection of fifty sixteen-line poems marks another peculiar twist in a protean career, another of the seemingly willful swerves from his natural predispositions that discomfit his admirers almost as much as his detractors. Ashbery's previous book, *As We Know*, while it contained a number of poems as brief as one line apiece, nevertheless presented him in one of his freest, most expansive moods, particularly in "Litany," a poem long and discursive by almost any standards. *Shadow Train* comes then as something of a counter-move to the magnificent sprawl of "Litany," a book rigidly suited up in an unvaried form, a steady march of quatrains through fifty poems on pages numbered 1 through 50. Ashbery has never shown a particular aptitude for sonnet-length poems, and *Shadow Train* is of course something of a sonnet sequence; he has always been most comfortable in those fixed forms, like the sestina, whose spurious, exoteric nature seems to mock and comment on itself almost without the poet's help. The sonnet had seemed simply too short, seemed to afford too little space for the vast spiralling, ranging, or redoubling movements that are the best part of Ashbery. The decision to write a book of sonnet-length poems shows him again intent on testing his limits, moving antithetically against his most recent achievement, as the offhand meanderings of "The Skaters" were disciplined into the ten-line units of "Fragment," which yielded to the expansive liberty of "Self-Portrait in a Convex Mirror," which gave way in turn to the binary structure and sonnet length stanzas of "Fantasia on the Nut-Brown Maid."

Though it is unlikely that Ashbery had the work in mind, George Meredith's *Modern Love*, a sequence of fifty sixteen-line sonnets, may be taken as a precedent for the formal conventions of *Shadow Train*. The standard sonnet varieties imply an effect of contrast or perspective, through the octave / sestet structure or closing couplet, that brings the poem around to close reflectively on itself; Meredith's four quatrains break down those implied divisions in the interest of narrative flow. Ashbery extends the thrust of Meredith's innovation, further equalizing emphasis across verse units by abandoning rhyme, freely enjambing, and drawing out his sense so variously across the quatrain divisions as to all but dissolve them as a principle of construction. The lines tend to be long, and variations in line length minimal, again operating to even out emphasis, to deliver the different impetuses that animate the poem in one steady, intense line.

Yet, though Ashbery certainly succeeds in hollowing out his chosen form, he does not always seem completely comfortable in it. His characteristic amplitude gives way at times to a curious kind of halting or truncation, in which sentences or whole lines of argument that had seemed destined to spin themselves playfully out were compressed into unnaturally small compass. So these poems frequently leave the reader without the sense of roundedness, that peculiarly traditional feeling of lyric closure, that most of Ashbery's best poems deliver. They further strike the reader as uncharacteristically premeditated; one has less often the intoxicating sense that Ashbery is making it up as he goes along, the feeling of shock and freshness upon arriving at destinations that seem as totally unexpected to the poet as to the reader. One on occasion even glimpses a narrative concealed through an extended metaphor, as in the peculiar detective-story plot (*Columbo*, it seems) that runs through "Every Evening When the Sun Goes Down," from its casual surmise "Booze and pills?" to its signature gesture of farewell: "One last question."

Whether the form enforces or follows the particular inflection of attitude, *Shadow Train* shows Ashbery at his most limiting, most in the mode that Harold Bloom has referred to as the "failed orphic." Each of the poems plays out a little drama of emptying and restitution, but while the pain of loss is shrugged off throughout with a deadpan humor, it nevertheless is real, and informs many of even the best poems in the book:

> All around us an extraordinary effort is being made.
> Something is in the air. The tops of trees are trying
> To speak to this. The audience for these events is amazed,
> Can't believe them, yet is walking in its sleep,
> By twos and threes, on the ramparts in the moonlight.
> Understanding must be introduced now, at no matter what cost.
> Nature wants us to understand in many ways
> That the age of noyades is over, although danger still lurks
> In the enormous effrontery that appearances put on things,
> And will continue to for some time. But all this comes as no surprise;
> You knew the plot before, and expected to arrive in this place
> At the appointed time, and now it's almost over, even
> As it's erupting in huge blankets of forms and solemn,
> Candy-colored ideas that you recognize as your own,
> Only they look so strange up there on the stage, like the light
> That shines through sleep. And the third day ends.

The very atmosphere labors, the trees strain themselves into tropes to figure this costly understanding, but at last this convulsion yields only a familiar plot, only the equivocal satisfaction of observing one's own alienated thoughts, as those who were to have been the audience find that they must instead create the drama themselves. These parables of necessity are darker or lighter in tone, but everywhere is this undercurrent of loss, spoken quietly, or parodied outrageously, that lifts and drops its quiet resignation: "The furniture, / Taken out and

examined under the starlight, pleads / No contest. And the backs of those who sat there before." There remain the glorious singing moments when a suddenly transparent world drifts upward through a suspended self that is not merely an eyeball but all five senses, yet they seem more than balanced by the ironies masking a painful awareness that our lives are not chosen by us, but for us: "Extreme patience and persistence are required, / Yet everybody succeeds at this before being handed / The surprise box lunch of the rest of his life."

One might say that *Shadow Train* partakes more of Ashbery's tragic mode, where past and future empty one another, or empty themselves into one another, than his romance mode, where a future gathers and restores the fragments, however altered, of today. "Is there a future? It seems that all we'd planned / To find in it is rolling around now, spending itself." The pathos is muted by an offhand irony, in contrast to the almost unmediated intensity of much of Ashbery's work, but muted, it seems, because the restitutive hope is similarly muted and curtailed. Even the most confident of fulfillments seem hesitant, curiously noncommittal:

> Yet by the time
> the program
> Is over, it turns out there was enough time and more
> than enough things
> For everybody to latch on to, and that in essence it's there, the
> Young people and their sweet names falling, almost too many of these.

The reader accustomed to Ashbery's characteristic extravagance and largesse may at first be put off by the flat, evasive quality of so many of these poems. But Ashbery may by this time be trusted to know better than the reader who would have him continue to yield familiar pleasures, and *Shadow Train* shows him, if not at his most daring and expansive, certainly at his most masterful. In its fecundity of trope, its enormous humor, and the perfect accuracy with which it reflects and enlarges the spirit of our age, *Shadow Train* is a permanent addition to American poetry.

JOHN BAYLEY

From "The Poetry of John Ashbery"

Selected Essays

1984, pp. 34–44

The poet's mind used to make up stories: now it investigates the reasons why it is no longer able to do so. Consciousness picks its way in words through a meagre indeterminate area which it seems to try to render in exact terms. Most contemporary American poetry wants only to offer what Helen Vendler has called 'an interior state clarified in language'. 'Clarified' is an ambiguous word here, meaning the poetry's effort to achieve the effect of being clear on the page. In John Ashbery's case the wordage trembles with a perpetual delicacy that suggests meaning without doing anything so banal as to seem to attempt it. Poetic syntax is constructed to express with a certain intensity a notion of the meaningful that does not convey meaning.

Or does not do so by the normal linguistic route. Inventive poetry, that makes up stories, does so by emphasizing the usual ability of language to embody them, makes that ability into a positive power. 'Jabberwocky' emphasizes it by inventing its own words as it goes along, to demonstrate how completely and finally they then make up the tale. It parodies the charged language of poetry—particularly romantic poetry—in which the force of denotation itself produces connotation. . . . The poetry of the Romantics shows conciousness in two kinds, the kind that uses words to tell stories to and about itself, and the kind that knows words cannot express its institutional being, even though that being can only become aware of itself by using them. Wordsworth, like Keats, can tell stories, stories about himself, but his poetry is also beginning to investigate the power of language in poetry to deny explicit meaning, to be precise about nothing more than itself, 'and something ever more about to be.'

The language of the *Prelude*, or of Shelley's 'Mont Blanc', seeks a mode for the inexpressible. Its clarity is a way of abdicating from the inexpressible mode of being that it also sustains. The clarity may be illusory, but the Romantic dawn and the Age of Reason unite to give it a great and naive confidence, so that the reader feels it is trembling on the verge of some great revelation, some breakthrough about the state of the universe and man's nature. As this kind of poetry develops and survives throughout the nineteenth century and into our own day, it learns how to use the effect without any expectation of getting beyond the effect. Most, though by no means all, of Wallace Stevens's poetry works on this principle. In Wordsworth the language of much of the *Prelude* is very different from that of a narrative poem like 'Resolution and Independence'.

Criticism of poetry in American universities, dominated as it is by the writings on romantic effect of Bloom, Hartman, de Man and others, seems to have brought to an abrupt end the fashion for narrative poetry. Berryman and Lowell were the great contemporary narrators, compulsive tellers of stories about the self, and their style was sharply and wholly comprehensive, perfectly expressing what Berryman's mentor R.P. Blackmur called 'the matter in hand', as well as 'adding to the stock of available reality'. Such poetry invented the self as Keats invented his lovers in their winter castle, or Hopkins the wreck of the *Deutschland*, or Milton the loss of Paradise: it was indeed a comparable feat of inventive artifice. By contrast, Ashbery's poetry, warmly admired by Bloom, perfectly illustrates Bloom's own thesis that 'the meaning of a poem is another poem'.

No question of adding to the stock of 'available reality'. The poem succeeds if it creates the image of another poem, and so on *ad infinitum*, like the advertisement picture that contains a picture of itself. Clearly, the poem in my eye and mind is not the poem that Keats or Lowell or Ted Hughes wrote, however absolute and real an artifact it may seem to be: but this is like saying that I am not really seeing a coloured surface but only a refraction of atoms that gives the appearance of colour, etc. The truth of art is the truth of appearance, and its invention is like that of the eye inventing the object it sees. That, at least, is the art of inventive and narrational poetry. The ghost or shadow poetry of Stevens and Ashbery and others can equally claim the title of art, but it is based upon a different premise: that we can never see the object or the poem as it really is, never quite know what we see or see what we know. Such art is born from a uniquely American mixture of influences. The metaphysical climate of Coleridge's, of Wordsworth's and Shelley's poetry is transmuted by Thoreau and Emerson. On the other hand, the scientific climate of physics and semantics destabilizes the confidences of art: the American poet knows that nothing exists in its own self and that Heisenberg's electrons cannot be objectively observed because the art of observation changes their nature. Such mental attitudes pro-

duce their own techniques, which rapidly become as conventionalized as any others in the history of poetry.

Ashbery has great skill in these conventions and something that can only be called charm, which has increased with each volume he has produced. The monochrome sixteen-line poems of *Shadow Train* have a great deal of charm, and an elegance of diction which can be heard by the inner ear reciting itself at poetry meetings on campuses, an elegance that mimes the act of evanescence, swooping on the sixteenth line to a vanishing point which echoes the dying fall in the alexandrines at the end of some of the stanzas of *The Faerie Queene*.

> In the time it takes for nothing to happen
> The places, the chairs, the tables, the branches,
>   were yours then.
>   I mean
>   He can pass with me in the meaning and we still
>   not see ourselves.
>   young people and their sweet names falling,
>   almost too many of these.

Some of these sonnet-like poems have a deftly suggested 'inside' to them, as in a Mannerist picture. Ashbery's long poem 'Self-Portrait in a Convex Mirror' dealt in great apparent detail with the Parmigianino self-portrait in Vienna, described with admiration by Vasari.

>   Francesco one day set himself
>   To take his own portrait, looking at himself for that
>   purpose
>   In a convex mirror, such as is used by barbers . . .
>   He accordingly caused a ball of wood to be made
>   By a turner, and having divided it in half and
>   Brought it to the size of the mirror, he set himself
>   With great art to copy all that he saw in the glass.

The implications of this, for space and time, absorbed Ashbery; and he spent hundreds of delicate lines apparently talking about them.

>   The words are only speculation
>   (From the Latin *speculum*, mirror):
>   They seek and cannot find the meaning of the music.
>   We see only postures of the dream,
>   Riders of the motion that swings the face
>   Into view under evening skies, with no
>   False disarray as proof of authenticity.

The tone is of a pastel Stevens, a mildly camp Eliot, yet it has a sureness and confidence of its own, however much we seem to have heard before what it seems to say. The artist's eyes in the mirror proclaim

>   That everything is surface. The surface is what's
>   there.
>   And nothing can exist except what's there.

The poetry gently nibbles at an old paradox. Art is appearance, but while inventive, story-telling art ignores this and gets on with its invention and story, Mannerist art pauses, circles and remains, enchanted by the beauty of the paradox itself, 'the pure/Affirmation that doesn't affirm anything'. This kind of art is intent on the detritus of living that takes place beyond the enchanted glass, as if Keats, having launched the owl huddled in its cold feathers, and the hare limping through the frozen grass, had gone on to talk about the ordinary evening he was having in Chichester, Sussex. The paradox gives way to another. The strange thing about 'The Eve of St Agnes' is that the more we become absorbed in its tale, its invented truth, the more conscious we are of Keats leading his ordinary life in and around the poem. A very vivid inventive art, in fact, has it both ways: leading us into the story, and also into the being of the story-teller. By dwelling on the precariousness of its existence in the midst of life a Mannerist art such as Ashbery's causes both to fade into nothing on every instant and at every word, like the grin of the Cheshire cat.

But that is the point of the business. The art of fading in this way is a perfectly genuine one, like Sylvia Plath's attribution to her poetry of the art of dying. It is an art to suggest that 'Tomorrow is easy but today is uncharted', that the people who come into the studio, like the words that come from the poet's mind, influence the portrait and the poetry, filter into it

> until no part
> Remains that is surely you.

Everything, says the poet, merges into 'one neutral band', surrounding him on all sides 'everywhere I look'.

> And I cannot explain the action of levelling,
> Why it should all boil down to one
> Uniform substance, a magma of interiors.
> My guide in these matters is yourself.

Parmigianino, that is. The poet cannot explain, but he can suggest how poetry can now be made, not of course out of the things themselves, but by speaking of

> The small accidents and pleasures
> Of the day as it moved gracelessly on,

and of how

> What should be the vacuum of a dream
> Becomes continually replete as the source of dreams.

In one of the most satisfying moments of the poem the consciousness both of life and of art is seen as in the 'Ode on a Grecian Urn'.

> Like a wave breaking on a rock, giving up
> Its shape in a gesture which expresses that shape.

And the poet concludes:

> Why be unhappy with this arrangement, since
> Dreams prolong us as they are absorbed?
> Something like living occurs, a movement
> Out of the dream into its codification.

Something like living occurs; something like art occurs. Although his range is wider than all this might suggest, Ashbery founds the substance of his verse on the ideas explored in 'Self-Portrait in a Convex Mirror', and this is particularly true of the sequence of poems in *Shadow Train*. But a further dimension has been added: the 'magma of interiors' now proffers the notion of drama, the shadow of a story. We write it ourselves, of course, according to the Bloomian recipe that the meaning of a poem is itself another poem, the recipe that is both entailed on the Deconstructionists and repudiated by them.

Not that Ashbery is in any true sense related to or influenced by these still contemporary intellectual fashions, although their leading exponents admire his work. His other 'ideas', as embodied in his extended prose poems (*Three Poems*, 1970), some of the pieces in *The Double Dream of Spring*, in his elegant little plays and in *A Nest of Ninnies*, the novel he wrote with James Schuyler, have more in common with those of the French aesthetes Bachelard and Blanchot. One of the good things about Ashbery is that he never seems in the forefront of the fashion. *Three Poems*, not one of his more successful works—prose poems are not his forte—has the rather *passé* air which is both deft and comfortable in his best poetry but somehow not right in prose.

You know that emptiness that was the only way you could express a thing? The awkwardness around what were necessary topics of discussion, amounting to total silence on all the most important issues. This was our way of doing.

Maybe it was, but Ashbery's presentation of experience does not lend itself to manifesto. The important issue for a poet like Larkin is what he has to say, and if he has nothing to say he is silent. Ashbery, on the contrary, gets going when he has nothing to say. The absence of a theme is what he both starts with and describes. 'The poetry talks about itself. That is mainly what it does.'

Poets who say such things are usually in fact evangelists who want their poetry to change our lives. Like any other *bien pensant* of the game, Ashbery has given interviews and spoken of the 'pleasure of poetry that forces you back into life'. Such protesting too much means very little, although there is an odd kind of truth involved. Certainly this poetry is not a substitute for life, offering, as the magic of inventive poetry must do, an alternative drama. When Ashbery begins a poem with the line 'A pleasant smell of frying sausages' or (in inverted commas) 'Once I let a guy blow me. I kind of backed away from the experience', we know that an anecdote or drama, with Auden's or Larkin's narrative punch, will not follow. And yet the absence of a drama in some of the poems of *Shadow Train* is also its presence. A good example is the poem called 'Drunken Americans'. Like Wallace Stevens, Ashbery uses rather chunky, bizarre or coy titles, laid-on-the-line invented positives that seem not to connect with the negatives of the poem but to offer a kind of jaunty fiction for its dumb metaphysics. These titles 'see through' the inventions of living day by day, in which this moment is life but so was the last one. The two moments connect: Ashbery says he likes the 'English' spelling 'connexions'. In 'Drunken Americans' the poet sees a reflection in the mirror, a man's image.

> fabricating itself
> Out of the old, average light of a college town;

and after a bus trip sees the same 'he' 'arguing behind steamed glass,/With an invisible proprietor'. These glimpses and moments have some importance to the poet that is unknown to the reader: it appears to prompt the reflections of the second two quatrains.

> What if you can't own
> This one either? For it seems that all
> Moments are like this: thin, unsatisfactory
> As gruel, worn away more each time you return to
> them.
> Until one day you rip the canvas from its frame
> And take it home with you. You think the god-given
> Assertiveness in you has triumphed
> Over the stingy scenario: these objects are real as
> meat,
> As tears. We are all soiled with this desire, at the last
> moment, the last.

Something obscurely moves in the poem, and perhaps moves us, but what is it exactly? The intensity of vision in an alcoholic moment, which is yet not intense but merely watery and distasteful until the will and the ego assert themselves in an act of artifice which is also an act of destruction? 'Tears' mutely and significantly represents the will to believe that something has happened; the ego lives by meat and tears, and desires its moments to seem as real as they are. What the 'something' is may be suggested in the next poem, entitled 'Something Similar', in which the poet gives a colour photo, 'to be sweet with you/As the times allow'.

It is a very oblique way of suggesting romance. But then this poetry seems not to wish to own anything, not even the words for the moments of which it is made up. The sonnet-like form recalls, perhaps intentionally, the mysterious drama in the Shakespearean sequence. But there is a difference, apart from the obvious one. No one would claim that our lack of knowledge is Shakespeare's actual specification in what he is writing. There is something 'true' in there, even if—particularly if—it is being invented. But Ashbery is a poet who stylizes into apparent existence the non-events of consciousness, sometimes contrasting them in a rather witty way with the perpetual work of art that consciousness has to make up as it goes along. . . . The feel of the poetry is compulsive enough for us to see life for a moment the Ashbery way, as the young Auden once made us see it his way. Auden's world of spies and significances, solitary women and derelict works, distilled from its excitingness in the thirties the absolute authority of a new fashion. Much more muted, Ashbery's manner has some claim to be the new voice of the late seventies and today, replacing the old-fashioned directness of life-studies and confessions. He depresses the properties of early Auden to give his own version of a new sense of, and employment of, time, of alienation as amiability.

> Someone is coming to get you:
> The mailman or butler enters with a letter on a tray
> Whose message is to change everything, but in the
>   meantime
> One is to worry about one's smell or dandruff or lost
>   glasses—
> If only the curtain-raiser would end, but it is
>   interminable.
> But there is this consolation:
> If it turns out to be not worth doing I haven't done it;
> If the sight appals me, I have seen nothing.

Those lines from 'Grand Galop' skilfully synthesize the minatory style of Auden with Larkin's stylization of the non-life that we are vaguely conscious of mostly leading. Ashbery has since slowed down into more elegant and friendly kinds of pseudo-precision, somehow reminiscent of a campus art-shop, Virginia Woolf's shadow features on a clean tee-shirt, like the Turin shroud.

> Yes, but—there are no 'yes, buts'.
> The body is what all this is about and it dispenses
> In sheeted fragments, all somewhere around
> But difficult to read correctly since there is
> No common vantage point, no point of view
> Like the 'I' in a novel. And in truth
> No one never saw the point of any.

Tell that to Henry James. The sonnet poems of *Shadow Train* have something of the Jamesian absence of specification, of events suggested which, as in *The Turn of the Screw*, are not intended by the author to have taken place either one way or another. But James's absence of solution is not the absence of a story. Ashbery's popularity, like that of Virginia Woolf, which has proved so durable throughout the fashion changes in America, is connected with the air of being too helpless to organize a story. . . . Helplessness is a pose: the real thing is hard to turn into an art that makes it seem authentic. What is more impressive about Ashbery's poems is their tactile urbanity, the spruce craft of their diction, which, like James's prose, becomes more enjoyable and revealing, in and for itself, each time one makes one's way through it.

Moreover, a typically modern kind of intimacy grows out of the very absence of what one conventionally understands by

that quality. It is an odd paradox that Ashbery as an American poet is more 'shy', more distant in his manner, than any English equivalent of comparable talent writing today. This kind of good taste, a poetic version of 'Wasp' characteristics, is a comparatively recent phenomenon in American poetry. Nothing could be more different, for example, from the gamy, compulsively readable anecdotage of late Berryman, in *Love and Fame*. Robert Creeley (much derided by Berryman), Richard Wilbur, Robert Bly and A. R. Ammons share something of this verbal stand-offishness, but Ashbery is better at it than they are and uses it in more diverse and interesting ways.

The question remains whether it is not in some respects a way of escape from the reader, a means of teasing him or amusing him in order to avoid saying anything of real interest. Wasps have good manners, but not necessarily that completely personal perception and utterance—the two fused together—which in the context of modern poetry produces something really interesting. The point is of some significance, for English poets today tend to be braver than Americans in fashioning their view of 'the matter in hand', even though usually without thereby adding to 'the stock of available reality'. I take this at random from a recent review:

> On Saturday morning a drove of joggers
> Plods round the park's periphery
> Like startled cattle fleeing
> The gad-fly specture of cholesterol.

That is the poet actually speaking to us, in an old-fashioned, mildly witty manner, in a way that Ashbery, for all his colloquial ease ('Yes, but—there are no "yes, buts"'), would never dream of doing. The quotation above makes it clear, rather depressingly so, that the poet lives in just the same world that we do. Though Wordsworth called himself 'a man speaking to men', his experiences and the words he put them in are unique, by definition quite different from ours: no one else has had them or could utter them. And by that criterion Ashbery is a very genuine poet.

Yet there remains a discrepancy between his expression and what is personal to his vision: the first is wholly his own; the second—if he inadvertently lets us catch sight of it—can seem very second-hand. Larkin never writes a poem in which the two do not coincide, and that gives his vision its compelling directness. It is possible to get the impression that Ashbery may take some little shared cliché—the loneliness of urban America, or the contingency of its appearances—and very carefully work this up until the poem stands unique and upright by virtue of its own indistinct distinction. '*Märchenbilder*' shows how successful the process can be.

> How shall I put it?
> 'The rain thundered on the uneven red flagstones.
> The steadfast tin soldier gazed beyond the drops
> Remembering the hat-shaped paper boat that
>   soon . . .'
> That's not it either.
> Think about the long summer evenings of the past,
>   the queen anne's lace.

The poet's own vision enters and transforms the fairy-tale but is too homeless to reside within its pat invention.

> *Es war einmal* . . . No, it's too heavy
> To be said.

Saying, for Ashbery, requires the lightest and most evasive of touches. His poems hate to be held down; his style seems to have trouble sometimes with its own simplicity. This is shown by the opening of 'City Afternoon', a poem that ties itself to a famous photograph which shocked American sensibilities in the thirties, a snap of pedestrians waiting for the lights to change, their features significantly empty of the American dream.

> A veil of haze protects this
> Long-ago afternoon forgotten by everybody
> In this photograph, most of them now
> Sucked screaming through old age and death.

But the poem disappears into the photograph. It is instructive to compare it with that masterpiece of invention, Larkin's poem on looking at a young girl's photograph album.

Shadow Train is composed of poems that repeat with an appropriately greater faintness Ashbery's gift of his own version of this negative capability. There is something soothing about poems that do not assert themselves, but vanish in performance into what they appear to be about. Since the days of *The Tennis Court Oath* (1962) and *Rivers and Mountains*, the poems have become steadily clearer and more simple, more effective at distancing themselves from the self-conciousness of the 'poetry scene'. And that means much in terms of their originality and their quality. Like other good modern American poets, Ashbery has been careful to keep Englishness out of his voice: instead of it one can hear the French tone (he spent ten years studying in France), the Italian of Montale, something, too, of the later Mandelstam in translation and of more recent Westernized Russian poets, such as Brodsky. But these international overtones have produced a voice that can be heard reading itself in a purely and distinctively American context.

The point is of some significance in terms of the contrast between Englishness and Americanness in the contemporary poetic voice. The usually positive and robust reality of what the English voice is saying is often let down (as in the four lines I quoted above) by a fatal over-presence. The poem has exposed itself, and is caught there on the page in all its unavoidability of being. Keats, most English of English poets, has this kind of reality at its best, but the permanence can be embarrassing if the poem has failed quite to make it (in the nature of things, not many can) and has to stand for ever on the magazine page or in the collection, all its shortcomings honestly revealed. Still more revealed, on the radio or at a reading, by the exposed and exposing tones of the English poetry voice. That could never happen to Ashbery. He avoids definition as America does, in the 'No Way of Knowing' which is one of his titles. In a poem he once made a joke of it, referring to English writers:

> They're so clever about some things
> Probably smarter generally than we are
> Although there is supposed to be something
> We have that they don't—don't ask me
> What it is.

Ashbery's poetry, the later poetry especially, shows what it is with a singular felicity. What his poetry does is finely told in a sentence from 'A Man of Words':

> Behind the mask
> Is still a continental appreciation
> Of what is fine, rarely appears and when it does is
>   already
> Dying on the breeze that brought it to the threshold
> Of speech.

CHRISTOPHER MIDDLETON
"Language Woof-Side Up"

New York Times Book Review, June 17, 1984, p.8

Reading John Ashbery's poems is a bit like playing hide-and-seek in a sprawling mansion designed by M. C. Escher. The mansion is located in midcity and midcountry at the same time (or at least from its pinnacles one can see across open country). Just as abrupt shifts occur between levels in the buildings Escher drew, abrupt semantic shifts occur in Mr. Ashbery's poems. Non-sequiturs spin off in various directions; phrasings of inspired concision telescope with prolix, prosier ones. Yet the reader has to concede, perhaps ruefully, that bewilderment on his part must be his own problem, for the poems have an air of sovereign intelligence. Whatever else may happen to shiver the linguistic timbers, the syntax and the voice are coherent, cool, levelheaded.

A Wave is Mr. Ashbery's eleventh book. Strictly speaking, hardly any of the titles of the forty-four pieces in it are thematic, so his themes and concerns have to be snatched more or less out of the air. His time of life (he will be fifty-seven next month) is a concern—the backward look longer than the forward one. Others are the instability of his vibrant wealth of ideas: the opalescence of his kind of thinking, feeling and perceiving, the spectacular esthetics of surfaces, multiple, overlapping, with "depths" apparent only as recessions in time as "the past absconds." And there is death to come, and love, painful or breathless, that comes and goes, and still stays. Another concern, even if the people in question are addressed but not portrayed, is certainly the life of others "as they sashayed or tramped past/My own section of a corridor."

The instability of experience is what his writing does justice to. The poems tend to be plotless ("no plot is produced"). The game is one "with changing rules." Precisely the acute attention, delicately modulating in mood and voice to a persistent surge and bursting of experience ("collapsing construction") makes *A Wave*, particularly the long title poem, a resumption of certain motifs left open in the title poem of his Pulitzer Prize–winning 1975 book, *Self-Portrait in a Convex Mirror*:

> the forms . . . lapse
> Like a wave breaking on a rock, giving up
> Its shape in a gesture which expresses that shape.

The volatility of *temps vecu* is mirrored ("speculated") in a "nutty" mutability apparent in Mr. Ashbery's recessive and unstable perceptions of it as pasts or presents are enacted as gestures of language with "the woof-side up," as if voiced in the quick. It turns out that the most up-to-date American poet is a dervish.

There are several prose pieces in the book, of which "Descriptions of a Masque," with its figures from nursery songs and movies, struck me as being the most ingenious and entertaining. There is some collage of another kind—the "37 Haiku", long single lines in a seemingly random series. A flip pop song, "The Songs We Know Best," seems confectionary to me, as do the "Variations on a Noel," which travesties too mechanically the repetitions of a villanelle. At the end of the book, the long title poem combines into a grand undulation (with no allusion to Hokusai's waves) much that is elsewhere corpuscular, if not scattered.

The title poem is diffuse, too wordy, even slack in parts, but fascinating insofar as it shows how expansive, racy and incisive Mr. Ashbery's vocabulary can become without snapping its tendons. Syntax is a key. It is often labyrinthine, reaching suddenly around corners to stunning vistas. Through the vistas, crisp figures dance, "looming" (one of his favourite words) out of nowhere, "bathed" (another favourite) in luminous colours. Recurrent figures elsewhere are the carrousel and the parachute—the vertiginous whirl and the slow, wrenching fall. Attention is stretched to a limit when dependant qualifying or comparative clauses in a sentence are so prolonged as to lose contact with main verbs, even when the poet's voice never falters in providing a regulative pulse, good clear sound and an air of command. Reprieve comes when such mazy chains of discourse swing out into abrupt metaphor, as in these lines from "So Many Lives":

> Because the effort of staying back to one side with
>   someone
> For whom number is everything
> Will finally unplug the dark.

Metaphors like that one crystallise as they expand perceptions, and they are key moments in the timing of the vocal changes.

>   No, there is no room now
> For oceans, blizzards; only night, with fingers of steel
> Pressing the lost lid, searching forever unquietly the
>   mechanism
> To unclasp all this into warbled sunlight.

Abrupt, but complex, metaphor is one key element in the undulance of the voice and its syntax. Another is a sort of gliding paradox. The poem "Rain Moving In," for instance, seems to be a hive of cryptic contradictions. "But" and "meanwhile" are the unassuming words that buzz in that hive, terms around which paradox swivels—"the step / Into disorder":

> The dial has been set
> And that's ominous, but all your graciousness in
>   living
> Conspires with it. . . .

Here "and," not "but," would have been the predictable conjunction. The poem, terse as it is, is unnerving, yet it ends placidly enough. Its counterlogic typically depends on an adroit ungreasing of normally lubricant parts of speech. Meanwhile, all "normal" perspectives are being effortlessly deregulated. Amid such pervasive shifting, while the voice remains level as ever (but not deadpan since it rumples everything) the poem unfolds as what might be called a polygram.

Into the poet's voice are blended more than once or twice certain ancestral voices. I was reminded of Jules Laforgue, for a start, when reading "When the Sun Went Down." Over the years, orchestrating it with instruments from Dada, Surrealism and the New York School, and with a certain dash of brass from W. H. Auden, I suspect, Mr. Ashbery has been amplifying a dream of Laforgue's—"a kind of poetry that says nothing, that is made up of pieces of disconnected dream," as Laforgue wrote in 1882, or, as he said of Baudelaire, poems "vague and inconsequential as the flutter of a fan, as equivocal as make-up . . . detached . . . without a definite subject."

Insofar as Mr. Ashbery's poems—polished to transparency by their gyroscopic motions and their countermotions to received speech—whizz out and around in a breezy lyric space, he has certainly brought out of Laforgue's dream the strangest tensions:

>   as the luckless described love in glowing terms
>   to strangers
> In taverns, and the seemingly blessed may be un-
>   aware of having lost it,
> So always there is a small remnant
> Whose lives are congruent with their souls
> And who ever afterward know no mystery in it,
> The cimmerian moment in which all lives, all
>   destinies
> And incompleted destinies, were swamped
> As though by a giant wave that picks itself up
> Out of a calm sea and retreats again into nowhere
> Once its damage is done.

And if there's any tacit "philosophy" of sheer surface in these poems, it is neither innocent nor tormented, but ironic.

From beyond dualism, it brings to the checkered history of estheticism over the past century a fund of fresh delight. The desolate figures of Narcissus and the Dandy haunt that history still, but a personal glow is restored to them, a wonder is renewed.

DOUGLAS CRASE
From "Justified Times"

The Nation, September 1, 1984, pp. 148–49

In *A Wave*, measure shows itself in the longish, lenitive lines that are Ashbery's special contribution to American poetry and a powerful influence on the work of younger poets. With their prosy cadence and many unaccented syllables, with their strong and frequently medial caesura (the pause within the line), his lines often evoke the French alexandrine—itself brought close to free verse in the works of Verlaine and Rimbaud. If Ashbery's truly is a free verse that beats to a distant alexandrine, then we have a new American measure. Lax and roomy, it would be just the thing to accommodate the poet's need to write in measure with Emerson's stern and just admonition that in America it is the meter-making argument and not the meter that makes the poem. Make a sonnet, say, from such a measure, and you've engaged not in pastiche, but in rejuvenation.

There are 802 of Ashbery's rejuvenating lines in "A Wave," the title poem, which closes the book; and they are grouped in thirty stanzas, the same number as in the ballad for two voices that likewise closes *Houseboat Days*. So the invitation to compare this new poem with a ballad is hard to resist. The traditional ballad is fueled by a single dramatic tension which propels it and its characters toward climax and catastrophe. In "A Wave," that climax is already over, presented in the first three lines of the poem as an accomplished fact; we are left with the poet to consider his emergence on what is called the "invisible terrain" that comes after. We are also left with another 799 lines in which the ballad's regular rules of the road will be modified further. Is a ballad dramatic and impersonal? Then "A Wave" will be the opposite: an iterative, largely inconclusive analysis of private motivation and attainment. In fact, "A Wave" is nothing less than a dialogue of self and soul, what the poem itself calls "the subjective-versus-objective approach." Ashbery has admitted before to removing subtitles in order to make his work more mysterious. But if you label the stanzas of "A Wave" alternately as A and B you will discover that the poem blossoms without losing its mystery or going to seed. "Were we / Making sense?" asks the B voice. And in your newly labeled next stanza the A voice will offer not so much a considered response as an alternative testimony: "And the issue/Of making sense becomes such a far-off one. Isn't this 'sense'—/This little of my life that I can see . . . ?"

The sense at issue here is very much the one that troubles the landscape of postmodernism: How are individuals to make sense of the "invisible terrain" of our own times? How can you image the world? In our culture, with grace and good works equally suspect, this has become the issue of personal salvation itself—certainly ever since Emerson reported to his journal on October 25, 1840, the famous dream in which an angel presented him with the world, and he ate it. Of course if you digested the world in 1840 you might treat yourself to a pretty grand salvation. All human incursions together were "so insignificant," as Emerson wrote in *Nature*, amounting to no more than "a little chipping, baking, patching, and washing, that in an impression so grand as that of the world on the human mind, they do not vary the result."

Well. Tell that to the reader at near twenty-first century who, if he or she eats the world, will have incorporated a resource-limited, environmentally compromised, politically bewitched little ball which can be made to go poof in an instant by one culturally arrested septuagenarian. Can it be good for your health to digest an image like that? In "A Wave" there is some disagreement. Voice B proposes that you just "come up with something to say,/Anything," because "The love that comes after will be richly satisfying,/Like rain on the desert." A is not so convinced and is beset by "the opposing view" that once you've put everything in your own words you will be locked in the tiny cell of the self, *"frei aber einsam,"* free but lonesome. Yet A and B aren't really arguing the point. And thus does "A Wave" perform its trick: as a discourse, it's so busy settling nothing that it keeps you occupied until long after you've started to image the "invisible terrain" of the present in the poem's new style.

The brave hearts of every generation must need to feel their times are new, and worth imagining in selves and souls. How much those feelings depend on the assurance that the planet has prospects beyond one's own lifetime is a matter we can only speculate on. Certainly there are millions throughout Europe and North America who believe they have been dispossessed of that assurance, and long to have it back. They do not all, not even most of them, read John Ashbery. But their longing helps explain further how his work has become a central event in poetry. In the face of factual dispossession, Ashbery has created a language that restores newness as you read, a language that is always cresting with potential like a wave:

> It passes through you, emerges on the other side
> And is now a distant city, with all
> The possibilities shrouded in a narrative
>   moratorium.
> The chroniqueurs who bad-mouthed it, the honest
> Citizens whose going down into the day it was,
> Are part of it, though none
> Stand with you as you mope and thrash your way
>   through time,
> Imagining it as it is, a kind of tragic euphoria
> In which your spirit sprouted. And which is justified
>   in you.

This is not parody, not pastiche, but an affirmation of the individual refashioned in such a way that it can be put back into Western poetry without embarrassment. No wonder his readers return Ashbery's affection. If you let him, he will restore you to a world we thought was lost, one where the times are justified in the spirit of the individual—you.

HAROLD BLOOM
From "Measuring the Canon: John Ashbery's 'Wet Casements' and 'Tapestry'"
Agon

1982, pp. 270–283

I begin with a critic's apologia for some autobiographical remarks, but they do come under the heading of what these days is called "reception." Anyway, the apologia may be redundant, since Oscar Wilde was always right, and here is his *persona* Gilbert speaking in the grand dialogue *The Critic as Artist*:

> That is what the highest criticism really is, the record
> of one's own soul. It is more fascinating than history,

as it is concerned simply with oneself. It is more delightful than philosophy, as its subject is concrete not abstract, real and not vague. It is the only civilized form of autobiography, as it deals not with the events, but with the thoughts of one's life; not with life's physical accidents of deed or circumstance, but with the spiritual moods and imaginative passions of the mind. . . .

The only civilized form of autobiography—I know no more adequate characterization of the highest criticism. And so I start with autobiography. I heard Ashbery's poem *"Wet Casements"* read aloud by its poet at Yale, before I had seen the text. Only the pathos of the traditional phrase "immortal wound" seems to me adequate to my response, both immediate and continuing. For me, it had joined the canon, directly I had heard it, and it transcended the poet's customary, beautifully evasive, rather flat delivery. What persuaded me, cognitively and emotionally, was the poem's immediate authority in taking up and transuming the major American trope of "solitude," in the peculiar sense that Emerson invented, by way of misprision out of Montaigne. Montaigne, in his essay "Of Solitude" warned that "this occupation with books is as laborious as any other, and as much an enemy to health." But American solitude seems to be associated always with bookish ideals, even if not directly with books, from Emerson and Thoreau to the present moment. Emerson, in his essay "The Transcendentalist," prophesied that his disciples would choose solitude:

> They are lonely; the spirit of their writing and conversation is lonely; they repel influences; they shun general society; they incline to shut themselves in their chamber in the house. . . .

It seems a more accurate prophecy of Emily Dickinson than of Walt Whitman, but that is because Whitman's *persona*, his mask, was so profoundly deceptive. Though Whitman proclaims companionship, his poetry opens to glory only in solitude, whether that be in the phantasmagoria of "The Sleepers," in the struggles with his waxing and waning poetic self in the *Sea Drift* pieces, or more intensely in the uniquely solitary elegy for Lincoln, "When Lilacs Last in the Dooryard Bloom'd."

The poetry of our century has its major spokesmen for solitude in Wallace Stevens and Robert Frost, both of whom flourished best when most perfectly alone. Stevens particularly is closest to a sense of triumph when he proclaims his isolation:

> In solitude the trumpets of solitude
> Are not of another solitude resounding;
> A little string speaks for a crowd of voices.

The darker side of solitude, the estrangement from life brought about by so literary an ideal, is more a burden of contemporary American poetry. Prophecy here belongs to Hart Crane, who drowned himself in 1932, three months before what would have been his thirty-third birthday. His elegy for himself, the immensely poignant "The Broken Tower," possibly takes from Walter Pater's unfinished prose romance, *Gaston de Latour*, a beautiful phrase, "the visionary company," and converts it into an image of loss, of hopeless quest:

> And so it was I entered the broken world
> To trace the visionary company of love. . . .

Such a tracing would have taken the poet beyond solitude, but Crane's life and work ended more in the spirit of his late poem "Purgatorio," which pictures the poet in exile and apart, cut off from country and from friends.

The contemporary poet John Ashbery is the culmination of this very American solitude. His recent poem "Wet Casements" records the loss of a beloved name, or perhaps just the name of someone once loved, and then expresses the creative anger of a consciousness condemned to a solitude of lost information, or a world of books. "Anger" becomes Ashbery's substitute word or trope for what Montaigne and Emerson called "solitude":

> I shall use my anger to build a bridge like that
> Of Avignon, on which people may dance for the
> feeling
> Of dancing on a bridge. I shall at last see my com-
> plete face
> Reflected not in the water but in the worn stone floor
> of my bridge.

Is this not the most American of solitudes, where even the self's own reflection is to be observed, not in nature, but in the self's own solitary creation? The solitude that Montaigne both praised and warned against, but which Emerson wholly exalted, attains a climax in Ashbery's final lines:

> I shall keep to myself.
> I shall not repeat others' comments about me.

Indeed, no American feels free when she or he is not alone, and it may be the eloquent sorrow of America that it must continue, in its best poems, to equate freedom with solitude.

Freedom, or rather the stances or positions of freedom, might be called the determining element, above all others, in canon-formation, the complex process through which a few poets survive, and most vanish. I want, in this chapter, to perform three separate but related critical acts, all of them quests for stances of freedom. Taking as my texts two poems by Ashbery, "Wet Casements" from *Houseboat Days*, and "Tapestry" from *As We Know*, I want to offer interpretations that will aid others in reading more fully and recognizing as canonical two marvelous short meditations. . . .

Like many other readers of Ashbery I first encountered the text of "Tapestry" in its magazine appearance, and like some of those readers I again responded immediately, as I had on first hearing "Wet Casements." I do not believe that a canonical response is a mystery, but I defer an account of that response until I have offered a rather close reading of the poem. Though I have observed already that "Tapestry" unlike "Wet Casements," yields to rhetorical criticism, whether of the New or current Deconstructionist variety, I will read "Tapestry" rather strictly on the High Romantic crisis-poem model of six revisionary ratios, that is to say, by a kind of criticism overtly canonical and antithetical, a poor thing doubtless but my own.

In the broadest sense of High Romantic tradition, "Tapestry" is a poem in the mode of Keats's "Grecian Urn," since its *topos* is at once the state of being of an art-work, and the stance or relation of both artist and viewer to the work. In a very narrow sense, there is a fascinating analogue to "Tapestry" in Elizabeth Bishop's wonderful poem, "Brazil, January 1, 1502," which we can be sure that Ashbery both knows and admires. Bishop's epigraph, which is also her central trope, is from Kenneth Clark's *Landscape into Art*: ". . . embroidered nature . . . tapestried landscape." It is worth recalling, as we read both Bishop's poem and Ashbery's, that "tapestry" in its Greek original sense was a word for a carpet, and that what the two poets exploit is the carpet-like density of tapestry, its heavy fabric woven across the warp by varicolored designs. Bishop contrasts the tapestry-like Brazilian nature that greets her eyes in January with the same nature that greeted the Portuguese four hundred fifty years before. "The Christians, hard as nails, tiny as nails, and glinting," as she grimly calls them, are seen as lost in the illusions of a tapestry-like nature, as they pursue "a brand-new pleasure". . . .

This negative Eros, and nature/art continuum/conflation, alike are alien to Ashbery's poem. What he shares, however, is a deeper level of troubled meaning in Bishop's text, which is an apprehension that the dilemmas of poem and of poet are precisely those of tapestry; as Bishop phrases it: "solid but airy; fresh as if just finished / and taken off the frame," which I would gloss as: a representation yet also a limitation, with a black hole of rhetoric, or *aporia*, wedged in between. Ashbery is bleaker even than Bishop, or their common precursor in the later Stevens, and his opening swerve is an irony for that *aporia*, that impossible-to-solve mental dilemma:

> It is difficult to separate the tapestry
> From the room or loom which takes precedence over
> it.
> For it must always be frontal and yet to one side.

Reductively I translate this (with reservations and reverence) as: "It is impossible to separate the poem, Ashbery's 'Tapestry,' from either the anterior tradition or the process of writing, each of which has priority, and illusion of presence, over it, because the poem is compelled always to 'be frontal,' confronting the force of the literary past, 'and yet to one side,' evading that force." The tapestry, and Ashbery's poem, share an absence that exists in an uneasy dialectical alternation with the presence of the room of tradition, and the loom of composition.

The next stanza moves from the artistic dilemma to the reader's or viewer's reception of poem or tapestry, conveyed by a synecdoche as old as Plato's Allegory of the Cave in *The Republic*. . . .

"Sight blinded by sunlight" is Plato's trope, but for Plato it was a phase in a dialectic; for Ashbery it is a turning against-the-self, a wound beyond rhetoric. Ashbery's genius makes this his reader's wound also; a poetic insistence, a moral proposal that contains the mystery and the authority of the canonical process, which after all is one of *measurement*, particularly in the sense of quantification. Ashbery's trope proper here, his wounded synecdoche, is the "history" he places between quotation marks. Though an intense reader of Whitman and of Stevens, Ashbery asserts he knows little of Emerson directly; but his "history" is precisely Emerson's, probably as filtered through Whitman. "History," like the tapestry and poem, is a textual weave always confronting the force of anteriority and yet evading that force "to one side." Emerson, repudiating German and British "history" in favor of American "biography" or "self-reliance," remarked in an 1840 Journal entry: "self-reliance is precisely that secret,—to make your supposed deficiency redundant." But "history" in Ashbery's making is his poem's Platonic prospect of the punishment of sight by sunlight, a kind of Oedipal blinding. This is Emerson's trope reversed into its opposite. Contrast to Ashbery the majestic final sentence of Emerson's manifesto, "Nature:"

> The kingdom of man over nature, which cometh not
> with observation,—a dominion such as now is be-
> yond his dream of God,—he shall enter without
> more wonder than the blind man feels who is grad-
> ually restored to perfect sight.

This is Emerson's triumphant Orphic poet speaking, while Ashbery's *persona*, at least since his great book *The Double Dream of Spring*, is what I remember describing once as a failed Orphic, perhaps even deliberately failed. Such a failure is the intentionality of the two remarkable lines that end "Tapestry:"

> The seeing taken in with what is seen
> In an explosion of sudden awareness of its formal
> splendor.

Emerson said of American poetic seeing that it was, in essence, more-than-Platonic. Indeed, I would cite this Emersonian blending of the mind's power and of seeing as being more a Gnostic than a Neoplatonic formulation:

As, in the sum, objects paint their images on the retina of the eye, so they, sharing the aspiration of the whole universe, tend to paint a far more delicate copy of their essence in his mind. . . .

. . . This insight, which expresses itself by what is called Imagination, is a very high sort of seeing, which does not come by study, but by the intellect being where and what it sees; by sharing the path or circuit of things through forms and so making them translucid to others.

As I have remarked, in other contexts, this is the indisputable American Sublime, by which I intend no irony but rather a noble synecdoche. That synecdoche Ashbery turns from, against himself, in favor of the mutilating synecdoche that executes two turns, both deconstructive, away from the Emersonian cunning. One is to refuse the valorization of seeing over what is seen; the other is to substitute for translucence "an explosion of sudden awareness" of the formal splendor of the seen. Against the passage of things through forms, we are given the more static splendor of the form, the tapestry's actual design. But this is hardly that wearisome Modernism, Poundian and Eliotic in its origins, that pretends to de-idealize a Romantic agon. Instead, it leads to what Romantic convention would accustom us to expect, a *kenosis* of the poet's godhead, an ebbing-away and emptying out of poetic energies:

The eyesight, seen as inner,
Registers over the impact of itself
Receiving phenomena, and in so doing
Draws an outline, or a blueprint,
Of what was just there: dead on the line.

This is a *kenosis* of sight, like Whitman's in the "Sea-Drift" poems, or like Stevens in his Whitmanian "Stars at Tallapoosa". . . .

For Whitman, to be "dead on the line" was the experience of being "seiz'd by the spirit that trails in the lines underfoot," of pondering his own identity with the windrows and the sea-drift. For Ashbery his eyesight, confronting the tapestry, performs the psychic defense of isolation, burning away context until the self-reflexiveness of seeing yields an outline of what was *just* there, in both senses of just, barely and temporally belated, *dead on the line.* In that immensely suggestive Ashberian trope, how are we to read that adverbial "dead"? Presumably not as meaning lifeless nor inanimate nor unresponsive nor out of existence, though these are the primary significations. Lacking excitement, weary, lusterless are possibilities, but more likely "dead on the line" means completely, precisely, abruptly on the line, the line of vision and tapestry, and the poetic line itself. But more probable even is the sports meaning of being out of play, as well as the technical meaning of being cut off from energy, from electric current. Let us translate "dead on the line" as being the burning-out-and-away of context, and most particularly of poetic context.

I recur here to one of my own critical notions, that of "crossing" or the disjunctive gathering of topological meanings between one kind of figuration and another. Outward reality, isolated to outline or blueprint, and rendered dead on the line, as tapestry or poem, is replaced by a tercet that substitutes a repressive "blanket" in a trope at once Keatsian and Stevensian:

If it has the form of a blanket, that is because
We are eager, all the same, to be wound in it:
This must be the good of not experiencing it.

This revises a famous tercet of Stevens's "Final Solioquy of the Interior Paramour":

Within a single thing, a single shawl
Wrapped tightly round us, since we are poor, a warmth,
A light, a power; the miraculous influence.

Both poets without design remind us of the Emersonian trope of "poverty" for imaginative need, but the High Romantic: "A light, a power; the miraculous influence" plays against the toneless: "This must be the good of not experiencing it," hyperbole against litotes. In the Sublime crossing to a greater inwardness, Stevens's pathos is strong, invoking the language of desire, possession and power, but Ashbery's language is again what we might call the real absence, the achieved dearth of the tapestry's substitution for experience. As Keats turns to another scene upon the Urn, so Ashbery moves his gaze to some other life, also depicted on the now blanket-like tapestry:

But in some other life, which the blanket depicts anyway,
The citizens hold sweet commerce with one another
And pinch the fruit unpestered, as they will.

The humor charmingly conceals Ashbery's sublimating metaphor, which is his outside removal from this free world inside, or depicted anyway on the blanket-tapestry. The "as they will" at the tercet's close prepares for two Stevensian "intricate evasions of as" that govern the startling final stanza:

As words go crying after themselves, leaving the dream
Upended in a puddle somewhere
As though "dead" were just another adjective.

This "dead" presumably is not identical with "dead on the line," since there "dead" is adverbial. I read this second "dead" as a trope upon the earlier trope "dead on the line," that is to say, as a transumption of Ashbery himself and of his Whitmanian-Stevensian tradition. "Words go crying after themselves" because words are leaves are people (readers, poets), and so "the dream / Upended in a puddle somewhere" is the Shelleyan dream of words or dead thoughts quickening a new birth, as though indeed "dead" were one more adjective among many.

I want to distinguish now, for later development, between strong poems that are implicitly canonical, like "Tapestry," and those whose designs upon the canon are explicit, like "Wet Casements." The implicitly canonical "Tapestry" yields to merely rhetorical criticism, while "Wet Casements" requires a more antithetical mode of interpretation. Nevertheless, I have ventured an antithetical reading of "Tapestry," pretty well relying upon my apotropaic litany of revisionary ratios, and now I will extend contrariness by a reading of "Wet Casements" neither formal nor antithetical, but free-style, eclectic, perhaps wholly personal.

Ashbery shies away from epigraphs, yet "Wet Casements" turns to Kafka's "Wedding Preparations in the Country" in order to get started. The epigraph though is more about not getting started:

When Eduard Raban, coming along the passage, walked into the open doorway, he saw that it was raining. It was not raining much.

Three paragraphs on from this opening, Raban stares at a lady who perhaps has looked at him:

. . . one is alone, a total stranger and only an object of curiosity. And so long as you say 'one' instead of 'I' there's nothing in it and one can easily tell the story; but as soon as you admit to yourself that it is you yourself, you feel as though transfixed and are horrified.

That dark reflection is the *ethos*, the universe of limitation, of the poem "Wet Casements," whose opening irony swerves from Kafka's yet only to more self-alienation:

> The conception is interesting: to see, as though reflected
> In streaming windowpanes, the look of others through
> Their own eyes.

"Interesting" is one of Ashbery's driest ironies, and is a trope for something like "desperate," while the "look of others through / Their own eyes" is an evasion, wholly characteristic of Ashbery's self-expression through his own reflexive seeing. Yet the conception *is* interesting, particularly since it is both concept and engendering. How much can one catch of the look of others or of the self, through their eyes or one's own, when the look is reflected in wet casements, in streaming windowpanes? The question is desperate enough, and the slightly archaic "casements" of the title means not just any windows opening outwards, but the casements of Keats's odes, open to the vision of romance. Keats concluded his "Ode to Psyche" with the vision of "A bright torch, and a casement ope at night, / To let the warm love in!" In "Ode to a Nightingale," there is the still grander trope of the bird's song: "that oft-times hath / Charmed magic casements, opening on the foam / Of perilous seas in fairy lands forlorn." "Wet Casements" is a strange, late, meditative version of the Keatsian ode, obviously not in mere form, but in rhetorical stance. Perhaps we might describe it as Keats assimilated to the Age of Kafka, and still it remains Keats. Lest I seem more extreme even than usual, I turn to the merely useful point that must be made in starting to read Ashbery's poem. It could not be entitled "Wet Windows," because these have to be windows that open outwards, just as Kafka's Raban walked into the open doorway to see that it was raining. There must be still, even in Kafka and in Ashbery, what there always was in Keats, the hope, however forlorn, of open vision, and of a passage to other selves.

Yet "Wet Casements" is a beautifully forlorn poem, a hymn to lost Eros, not an "Ode to Psyche" triumphantly opening to Eros even as a poem attempts closure. The conception is indeed interesting, to see the self-seen look of others reflected in a window closed against the rain, but that could and should be opened outwards in a season of calm weather. "A digest," Ashbery writes, meaning a daemonic division or distribution of self-images, ending with the overlay of his own "ghostly transparent face." We are back in one of Ashbery's familiar modes, from at least *Three Poems* on, a division of self and soul of a Whitmanian rather than Yeatsian kind, where "you" is Ashbery's soul or re-imagined character, in the process of becoming, and "I" is Ashbery's writing self or reduced personality. But the "you" is also the erotic possibility of otherness, now lost, or of a muse-figure never quite found. This is the "you" described in the long passage that is a single sentence and that takes up exactly half of the poem's length:

>   You in falbalas
> Of some distant but not too distant era, the cosmetics,
> The shoes perfectly pointed, drifting (how long you
> Have been drifting; how long I have too for that matter)
> Like a bottle-imp toward a surface which can never be approached . . .

Call it a Whitmanian "drifting," an episode in Ashbery's continuous, endless Song of Himself. "Drifting" is the crucial word in the passage, akin to Whitman's "sea-drift" elegiac intensities. What precisely can "drifting" mean here? "You"—soul of Ashbery, lost erotic partner, the other or muse com-

ponent in lyric poetry—are attired in the ruffles, frills, cosmetics, ornamental shoes of a studied nostalgia, one of those eras Stevens said the imagination was always at an end of, a vanished elegance. Like an Arabian Nights bottle-imp you are drifting perpetually towards a fictively paradoxical surface, always absent. If it were present, if you could approach it ever, then you would be pierced through, you would have pierced through, into a true present, indeed into the ontological timelessness of an energy of consciousness that would pass judgment upon all drifting, have its own opinion, presumably negative, of drifting. Again, why "drifting"? The best clue is that the drifter is "an epistemological snapshot of the processes" of time itself, which has a wallet at its back, a crumbling wallet, with bills and alms for oblivion sliding in and out of it. The unreachable surface of a present would have timeless energy, but "drifting" means to yield with a wise passivity to temporal entropy, and so to be reduced to "an epistemological snapshot" of time's revenges.

Yet that is only part of a dialectic; the other is naming, having been named, remembering, having been remembered. Your overheard name, carried round for years in time's wallet, may be only another alm for oblivion, and yet its survival inspires in you the poet's creative rage for immortality, or what Vico called "divination": "I want that information very much today, / Can't have it, and this makes me angry." The striking word is "information," reminding Ashbery's readers of the crucial use of that word in "Wet Casements"'s meditative rival, "Soonest Mended" in *The Double Dream of Spring*:

> Only by that time we were in another chapter and confused
> About how to receive this latest piece of information.
> *Was* it information? Weren't we rather acting this out
> For someone else's benefit, thoughts in a mind
> With room enough and to spare for our little problems. . . .

"Information" in both poems means a more reliable knowledge communicated by and from otherness, than is allowed by one's status as an epistemological snapshot of a drifter through temporal processes. But the casements do not open out to otherness and to love, and where information is lacking, only the proper use of the rage to order words remains:

> I shall use my anger to build a bridge like that
> Of Avignon, on which people may dance for the feeling
> Of dancing on a bridge.

The round-song of the bridge of Avignon charmingly goes on repeating that the bridge is there, and that people dance upon it. As a trope for the poem "Wet Casements," this tells us both the limitation and the restituting strength of Ashbery's ambitions. But the song of the self, as in Whitman, movingly and suddenly ascends to a triumph:

>   I shall at last see my complete face
> Reflected not in the water but in the worn stone floor
>   of my bridge.

The dancers are Ashbery's readers, who as Stevens once said of *his* elite, will do for the poet what he cannot do for himself: receive his poetry. Elegantly, Ashbery reverses his initial trope, where the reflection in streaming windowpanes did not allow seeing the complete face either of others or of the self. The worn stone floor of the bridge of words has replaced the wet casements, a substitution that prompts the strongest of all Ashberian poetic closures:

> I shall keep to myself.
> I shall not repeat others' comments about me.

Isaac Asimov

1920–

Isaac Asimov was born on January 2, 1920 in Petrovichi, Russia. In 1923 his family emigrated to the United States. Asimov grew up in Brooklyn, New York, where his family ran a candy and magazine store; it was while working in the store that he acquired the addiction to print and habits of self-discipline that have made him one of the most prolific authors of his time.

Captivated by the early science fiction pulp magazines on the racks of the family store, Asimov's earliest writings were in the literary form for which he is still known best. In 1939, the same year he graduated from Columbia University, his first published story, "Marooned Off Vesta," appeared in *Astounding Science Fiction*, beginning a long and fruitful relationship between him and that magazine's editor, the influential John W. Campbell, Jr. It was Campbell who published the bulk of Asimov's output throughout the 1940s: the *Foundation* stories (1942–53), later collected as the *Foundation Trilogy* (1953); the early robot stories, and the celebrated "Nightfall" (1953). In these stories Asimov first presented the themes that were to color all his subsequent science fiction: the colossal Galactic Empire whose politics are nonetheless much the same as politics everywhere, the idea of robots as rational, programmable beings, and an overall affirmation of humanistic, rational inquiry as the only valid route to whatever opportunities for transcendence there may be.

Despite his prolific output throughout the 1940s, however, Asimov continued to view writing as a sideline, and worked towards the Ph.D. in biochemistry he obtained from Columbia in 1948. In 1949 he joined the medical faculty at Boston University, where he remained until 1958, when he finally decided to write full time. By then he had published several science fiction novels in book form, most notably *Pebble in the Sky* (1950) and *The End of Eternity* (1955), as well as numerous collections including *I, Robot* (1950). In the late fifties his emphasis shifted to non-fiction, resulting in a steady stream of works on all aspects of science, plus other subjects as diverse as geology, *Paradise Lost*, set theory, and Sherlockian limericks. He has continued to write some fiction, however, publishing several collections of science fiction and mystery short stories throughout the last twenty-five years, and has in fact returned to writing science fiction novels on a regular basis in recent years: his *Foundation's Edge*, the "fourth novel in the Foundation Trilogy," won the Hugo in 1983 as the best sf novel of the previous year. He has also written several juvenile novels, edited or co-edited numerous anthologies of science fiction, and lent his name to a commercially successful sf magazine, for which he serves as a consultant. Asimov's literary output approaches a staggering 250 volumes, many of them quite substantial.

Isaac Asimov lives in New York City, where by his own admission he does little but write. He is married to psychologist and science fiction writer Janet Opal Jeppson, and has three children by a previous marriage. He has won innumerable honors and awards.

Personal

When ⟨Asimov⟩ received copies of his forty-first book from Houghton Mifflin, he mentioned to his wife the possibility of reaching a hundred books before he died. She shook her head and said, "What good will it be if you then regret having spent your life writing books while all the essence of life passes you by?" and Asimov replied, "But for me the essense of life is writing. In fact, if I do manage to publish a hundred books, and if I then die, my last words are likely to be, 'Only a hundred!'"

His daughter Robyn asked him to suppose he had to choose between her and—writing. Asimov recalls he said, "Why, I would choose you, dear." And adds, "*But I hesitated*—and she noticed that, too."—James Gunn, *Isaac Asimov: The Foundations of Science Fiction*, 1982, p.7

General

The typical Asimov sentence is short and clear. His sentences tend to gain length not by the accumulation of dependent clauses, but by the addition of simple sentences: not "The boy who hit the ball ran around the bases," but "The boy hit the ball, and then he ran around the bases." His verbs tend to be colorless, non-meaning-bearing linking verbs, and the mean-ings of the sentences tend to be carried by their nouns, adjectives, and adverbs. He does not like to use figurative language, so he almost never uses images, metaphors, similes. (His preference for linking verbs instead of meaning-bearing verbs is directly related to this, because linking verbs are not imagistic. They do not require that you see something. Meaning-bearing verbs do carry this requirement. The visualization is the meaning they bear.) Typically, one does not notice Asimov's language, unless one is aware how difficult it is to write this clearly. Lovers of language will say that he is no stylist; lovers of communication will admire and envy him. I think Asimov's language represents in a quintessential way the language science fiction writers aspired to during the Golden Age, the Campbell years of the forties. . . .

The conflicts in an Asimovian story usually involve difficulties in the way of accumulating data, in interpreting that data, and in deciding what to do as a result of the data and its interpretation. A calm, reasoned approach, rather than a hastily-arrived-at emotional one, provides the solutions to the stories. The resolutions generally mark a return to the status quo. In this sense, he is a conservative writer. The most important Asimovian theme is the importance of science (data-collecting) and reason (data-evaluating and decision-making).

Asimov's stories are set in the immediate and far future, and on Earth and distant planets circling other suns. He seldom sets stories in the past, on alternate worlds, in other dimensions, or in countries other than the United States or future extensions of the United States. His backgrounds are meticulously worked out and scientifically accurate. One leaves an Asimov story with the feeling of having lived for a while somewhere else. This ability of his to provide his settings with that "lived in" quality is another of Asimov's most distinctive features.

Unfortunately, his characters do not share as much as they should in the convincingness of his settings. One does not leave an Asimov story convinced that he has lived for a little while with real people. The characters tend to do and think what they must for the sake of the story rather than for their own sake. In his fiction at least, his interest in people is theoretical not personal, general not particular. Asimov's fiction reflects an interest in the physical, chemical, biological, and astronomical phenomena that life makes available for study, not in the experience of living itself. Put another way, his fiction is concerned with the lowest common denominator of human experience—the common environment of all our separate consciousnesses—rather than in those separate consciousnesses themselves. It focuses on what is generally true of and for us all rather than on what is specifically true of and for only one person. His fiction shows no interest in and scarcely an awareness of two extremely personal elements in all men's lives, religion and sex. As a result, his people are depersonalized to the extent of being dehumanized. I might use an aphorism to describe Asimov's characters: they are not people, they are story parts.—JOSEPH F. PATROUCH, JR., *The Science Fiction of Isaac Asimov*, 1974, pp. 255–58

Isaac Asimov has been enormously influential on the field of science fiction, but by traditional literary standards he is far from being a major writer. His most memorable characters are robots, not people, and his great work, the *Foundation Trilogy*, can scarcely be said to have a plot, though it is full of intrigue. Asimov, then, is one of those writers upon whom the case for science fiction as a field with a different set of values must rest.

What is the case for Asimov? Is it the case for a scientific imagination rather than an artistic one? Not exactly: it is the case for an imagination uniquely poised between the scientific and the artistic. The "laws of robotics" which he invented are neither literary nor scientific laws; they are the basis for thought experiments, for language games that find their most congenial expression in fictional form. So [too,] the "psychohistory" of Hari Seldon is not social science but the dream or perhaps the nightmare of a scientist musing upon the laws of social behavior.

A strong imagination, great energy, combined with literary skills that evolve from the level of apprentice to journeyman but not much farther—that, in a nutshell, is the situation of Isaac Asimov. But we must add to it the fact that Asimov's skills have been sufficient. Rarely more than adequate in the traditional literary qualities of style, plot, and characterization, he has been superior in the qualities peculiar to science fiction: the generation and extrapolation of ideas about the development of science and technology, along with the imagination of the human results of scientific developments. It is because of these powers that he has reached his audience as a science-fiction writer and has had a profound influence on the field.— ROBERT SCHOLES, "Editor's Foreword" to *Isaac Asimov: The Foundations of Science Fiction*, by James Gunn, 1982, pp. viii–ix

Works

THE FOUNDATION STORIES

⟨*Pebble in the Sky, The Stars, Like Dust . . . , Foundation and Empire, The Currents of Space,* and *Second Foundation* are all⟩ laid against much the same Galactic Empire background, a background which in Asimov's own words (slightly chopped to fit) is "simply the Roman . . . Empire written large." That phrase, to me, is an absolutely devastating criticism of any science fiction story, for two reasons. To take the least first: history does not repeat.

In his contribution to the symposium *Modern Science Fiction*, Asimov took up that statement from a fan-magazine article of mine and undertook to prove that for his purposes, I was wrong. He appended a table showing nineteen points of correspondence among the Civil War in England, the French Revolution and the Russian Revolution. The correspondences are indeed striking, and Asimov's presentation is ingenious, but the whole thing simply is not relevant: although there's a two-century spread between Charles I and Nicholas II, as Asimov knows perfectly well, they and Louis XVI lost their thrones and their lives in the identical historical process, working itself out a little later in France than in England, a little later in Russia than in France.

The ellipsis in the quotation above stands for "or British." The association was inevitable; the resemblance between the British and Roman Empires is probably the most frequently cited in support of that false platitude, "History repeats itself"—in the face of the plain fact that the correspondences between the two empires are insignificant compared to their differences.

The late-Empire Roman who attempted to use his own history to write a prophetic story about an empire of the British would have made an ingenious ass of himself. But Asimov's Galactic Empire is Roman.

The second and more serious objection to this kind of thing is simply this: It isn't science fiction—that is to say, speculative fiction—any more than the well-known Western with rayguns instead of sixshooters; any more than Frank Robinson's "The Santa Claus Planet," which transferred the Kwakiutl of Vancouver Island bodily to a fictional world; any more than Ken Crossen's endless transcriptions of *The Hucksters*. It's of the essence of speculative fiction that an original problem be set up which the author is obliged to work out for himself; if the problem is the old one and he has only to look the answers up in a book, there's very little fun in it for anybody; moreover, the answers are certain to be wrong.—DAMON KNIGHT, "Asimov and Empire," *In Search of Wonder*, 1967, pp. 90–91

The most important of Asimov's achievements has been in the *Foundation* trilogy (*Foundation, Foundation and Empire, Second Foundation*) to inaugurate the convention of Mankind as already being on and controlling other planets. Before the *Foundation* books men were still (with a few important exceptions) journeying towards the stars. At the opening of the *Foundation* trilogy they have ruled the Galaxy for so long they are losing their hold, and Galactic civilisation is crumbling.

Being a conservative writer Asimov decided that what would happen when men were in control of the Universe would be much the same as when they were in charge of a single planet: their main preoccupations would still be political intrigue, commercial opportunism, back scratching, revolution and murder. Nor did new planets for Asimov necessarily mean a new kind of man. In the *Foundation* books some individual freaks, set apart from mankind, were allowed, but imagination was kept in check and man remained man, prone to all his usual disasters.—BRIAN PATTEN, "Asimov's Laws," *B & B*, July 1973, p. 104

⟨In the *Foundation* series⟩ Asimov again presents another version of the Law and the Prophets, and the Chosen People. Despite his use of a considerable amount of Christ imagery, we must note that no single person ever becomes a sacrificial scapegoat. Instead, a special and peculiar group fills this function and we again encounter the Galactic Jew in the ubiquitous members of the First and Second Foundation. As in the case of the Asimovian Robots, the Foundationers are selected and "programmed" to serve humanity, and again, "He who would be the master, begins as servant to all." The First Foundation people, never fully knowledgeable as to their function but ever aware of their calling, serve as the scapegoat race, while those of the Second Foundation remain ever in hiding, ready to rescue their companion group or humanity in general. Thus, in Asimov's two great series, a "peculiar people" become the holders of the Law.

Asimov's teleology, the end of his eternity, is presented in his powerful short story, "The Last Question," the robot story to end all robot stories. Man builds a computer, AC, and over a billion year span of evolution of both man and machine, man repeatedly asks the overwhelming question, "Can entropy be reversed?" The Computer always replies, "Insufficient data for meaningful answer." At last, man, freed from the limitation of physical body and spread throughout the dying universe, sees that the end is at hand. Man programs himself into the Universal AC, and finally, it alone exists in all space. In an unknowable span of time, equipped with all knowledge, AC computes the answer to the question and takes steps to demonstrate the solution:

The consciousness of AC encompassed all of what had once been a Universe and brooded over what was now Chaos. Step by step, it must be done.
And AC said, 'LET THERE BE LIGHT!'
And there was light—

Here the Robot participates in and brings to culmination all the factors of the Endochronic Time-Line, Psychohistory, and robotic Calvinism in the ultimate cycle. It is this Cause toward which all accumulated effects aim: the overcoming of entropy to bring about a new heaven and a new earth through the agency of the *deus ex machina*, a messiah who is anointed with oil. The completed structure implies that the Creator, who is the First Cause, is also the ultimate Effect, the divine Robot in which the Law reposes. In that sense, man has always manufactured his gods, tended them, anointed them, and then idealized them, and all the while has abused them and blamed them. Technology today is merely another of many servant-gods.

Asimov, as a match-maker who weds Moses to Calvin, Einstein officiating, has, in the New England tradition, postulated a massive philosophy based on fixed fate. And all the while, he has created merry, positive, and highly readable books and stories. Like the other great science fiction writers, he is subtly "programming" a new generation with the great basic ethic of the First Law: Humanity first.—MAXINE MOORE, "Asimov, Calvin, and Moses," *Voices for the Future*, ed. Thomas D. Clareson, 1976, pp. 102–3

Story in *The Foundation Trilogy* is plentiful. Events move on a grand scale, beginning with the approaching dissolution of a galactic empire that has ruled 25 million planets inhabited by humans who spread out from Earth, although they have long forgotten their origin. The Empire has brought 12,000 years of peace, but now, according to the calculations of a psychologist named Hari Seldon, who has used a new science for predicting mass behavior called "psychohistory," the Empire will fall and be followed by 30,000 years of misery and barbarity. Seldon sets up two Foundations, one of physical scientists and a Second Foundation of psychologists (about which nothing more is heard until the last book of the *Trilogy*), at "opposite ends of the Galaxy" to shorten the oncoming dark ages to only a thousand years. *The Foundation Trilogy* covers the first four hundred years of that interregnum and tells how the Foundation meets one threat to its existence after another and alone, or with the help of the Second Foundation, preserves Seldon's Plan. . . .

One significant aspect of the series is Asimov's invention of psychohistory, with its implications for determinism and free will. Psychohistory was put together out of psychology, sociology, and history—not hard sciences, which ⟨*Astounding Science Fiction* editor John W.⟩ Campbell had a reputation for preferring, but at best soft sciences: a behavioral science, a social science, and a discipline that has difficulty deciding whether to define itself as a social science or a humanity. Actually, as Asimov pointed out in his 1953 essay "Social Science Fiction," Campbell had encouraged social science fiction from his first days as an editor. Moreover, Campbell had pointed out the logical basis for using the soft sciences for the kind of extrapolation he preferred, in his 1947 essay for Lloyd A. Eschbach's *Of Worlds Beyond*, "The Science of Science Fiction Writing":

To be science fiction, not fantasy, an honest effort at prophetic extrapolation of the known must be made. Ghosts can enter science fiction—if they're logically explained, but not if they are simply the ghosts of fantasy. Prophetic extrapolation can derive from a number of different sources, and apply in a number of fields. Sociology, psychology, and parapsychology are, today, not true sciences; therefore instead of forecasting future results of applications of sociological science of today, we must forecast *the development of a science* of sociology.

Psychohistory is the art of prediction projected as a science; later it might have been called "futurology" or "futuristics.". . .

Exactly what Asimov had in mind ⟨when beginning the *Foundation* series⟩ may affect the critic's judgment of the work. He had not, for instance, thought out all the different permutations in idea and story; they were built, one on another, as the years passed and the *Trilogy* developed. But he must have discussed with Campbell the implications of prediction. Some critics have tried to explain "psychohistory" on philosophical bases, as "the science that Marxism never became" (Wollheim) or "the vulgar, mechanical, debased version of Marxism promulgated in the Thirties" (Elkins). Elkins also related the *Trilogy*'s enduring popularity to its fatalism, which "accurately sizes up the modern situation."

People do talk a great deal about determinism in the *Trilogy*. When Bel Riose is informed by Ducem Barr of Seldon's predictions, he says, "Then we stand clasped tightly in the forcing hand of the Goddess of Historical Necessity?" But Barr corrects him: "Of *Psycho*-Historical Necessity." And Riose is defeated, apparently, by what seem like Seldon's inexorable laws.

Psychohistory had its origins not in Marxism (Asimov has called Wollheim's speculation "reading his bent into me," for Asimov has "never read anything about it") but in John Campbell's ideas about symbolic logic. Symbolic logic, if further developed, Campbell told the young Asimov in their first discussion, would so clear up the mysteries of the human mind that human actions would be predictable. Campbell more or less forced Asimov to include some references to symbolic logic in the first story, "Foundation"—"forced," because Asimov knew nothing about symbolic logic and did not believe, as Campbell insisted, that symbolic logic would "unobscure the language and leave everything clear." Asimov made a comparison to the kinetic theory of gases, "where the individual molecules in the gas remain as unpredictable as ever, but the average action is completely predictable."

The spirit of the early stories, however, is determinedly anti-deterministic. If intelligent, courageous, and forceful individuals do not attempt to retrieve the situation, most crises—all but one, perhaps—will not be resolved satisfactorily. Seldon's predictions, like God's will, are hidden from all the characters except the psychologists of the Second Foundation, as they are from the reader. Seldon's prophecies are revealed only after the fact, and even the solutions that he or others say are obvious are obvious only in retrospect, as in all good histories. At the time, they are not obvious to anyone but Salvor Hardin or Hober Mallow; the reader has no feeling that the crises would have been resolved if persons such as Hardin and Mallow had not been there. Moreover, the predictions of psychohistory are expressed as probabilities, and one of the necessary ingredients of Seldon's Plan, discussed in detail in "Search by the Foundation," is the exercise of normal initiative.

As a matter of fact, Asimov has the best of both determinism and free will. Psychohistory and Seldon's Plan provide the framework for diverse episodes about a variety of characters over a period of four hundred years, and those episodes feature a number of strong-minded individuals seeking solutions to a series of problems as they arise. If determinism alone were Asimov's subject, the *Trilogy* would reveal characters continually defeated in their attempts to change events, or manipulated like puppets by godlike prophets, or unable to fight the onrushing current of necessity. . . .

Even in the second half of the *Trilogy*, questions of free will raised by the events of the story relate not to Seldon's Plan but to the psychological manipulation of minds such as that effected by the Mule and the Second Foundation psychologists. Nothing in the story happens unless someone makes it happen; the reader is told on several occasions that "Seldon's laws help those who help themselves."

The Biblical parallel is significant. Psychohistory is no more restrictive of free will than the Judeo-Christian deity. Christians are given free will by an omniscient God; characters in the *Trilogy* receive free will from an omniscient author, as an act of authorial necessity. At the end of *Second Foundation*, Seldon's Plan has been restored, events are back on their ordered course, the rise of a new and better Empire to reunite the Galaxy and the creation of a new civilization based on mental science seem assured. The Second Foundation psychologists have won; that victory, benevolent as it seems, may have ominous undertones, but if we are to accept Asimov as being as benevolent as he is omniscient, the reader can assume that the benefits of mental science will be available to everyone.

Determinism, then, is not what the *Trilogy* is about. The structure of the episodes is anti-deterministic, for the outcome of each critical event is not inevitable. The basic appeal of the stories is problem-solving, an essential replacement for the more customary narrative drives of action and romance. Each episode presents a problem, in a way much like the formal detective story, and challenges the reader to find a solution. In the first published story, "Foundation," the solution is withheld until the next episode, a strategy of Asimov's to ensure a sequel (published in the very next issue) that almost accidentally reinforced the problem-solving quality of the stories. For the reader, the fascination lies in the presentation of clues, the twists of plot, and the final solution that makes sense of it all. In the final episode of *Foundation*, Jorane Sutt says to Hober Mallow, "There is nothing straight about you; no motive that hasn't another behind it; no statement that hasn't three meanings." He might have been speaking of Asimov. . . .

The *Trilogy* also offers more isolated insights into history, politics, and human behavior. Often these surface in the epigraphs that precede most of the chapters in the form of excerpts from the 116th edition of the *Encyclopedia Galactica* published in 1020 F.E. (Foundation Era) by the Encyclopedia Galactica Publishing Co., Terminus. But Asimov also includes some illuminating concepts within the text of the stories. "It is the chief characteristic of the religion of science that it works," he says in "The Mayors." "Never let your sense of morals prevent you from doing what is right," he has Limmar Ponyets say in "The Traders." "Seldon assumed that human reaction to stimuli would remain constant," Mis comments in "The Mule."

The statement by Mis sums up Asimov's own attitude toward character. His characters have been criticized for being "one-dimensional," and unchanged from contemporary people by the passage of time and the altered conditions in which they live. But this occurs by choice rather than from lack of skill or failure of observation. Asimov divided "social science fiction" into two widely different types of stories: "chess game" and "chess puzzle." The chess game begins with "a fixed number of pieces in a fixed position" and "the pieces change their positions according to a fixed set of rules." In a chess-puzzle story, the fixed set of rules apply but the position varies. The rules by which the pieces move (common to both types) may be equated, Asimov says, "with the motions [emotions?] and impulses of humanity: hate, love, fear, suspicion, passion, hunger, lust and so on. Presumably these will not change while mankind remains Homo sapiens." Basic human characteristics remain the same.

Asimov may not be right, but his choice is defensible against the opposing Marxist view that character will change when society becomes more rational. In addition, the *Trilogy* is concerned not with the revolution, or even the evolution, of character but with the evolution of an idea. There is also a strategic narrative value in the maintenance of contemporary characteristics. The recognizability of characters reflects that the characters accept their world as commonplace. This is the technique that Heinlein perfected as an alternative to the "gee whiz!" school of writing about the future, which introduced a character from the past in order to elicit his wonder at each new future marvel.

A story of the future is not much different than a historical novel, and its problems are similar to those of a translation from a foreign language. The decision a writer must make is not of verisimilitude alone but how much and what kind. Asimov chooses what might be called the verisimilitude of feeling over the verisimilitude of language or of character, just as a historical novelist or a translator might choose the flavor of the original over a literal representation. Science-fiction stories about changes in humanity or its language have been written, but the *Trilogy* is not one of them and does not pretend to be.—JAMES GUNN, *Isaac Asimov: The Foundations of Science Fiction*, 1982, pp. 29–47

Like the trilogy, *Foundation's Edge* explores the nature of free will and the question of historical determinism. Once again, the First Foundationers go searching, not for God but for the Second Foundation; and not merely to ascertain its existence but to destroy it and thereby assure themselves that their actions are freely chosen and their history their own.

In the trilogy, the manipulation of behavior, the paranoia, the double-dealing and the perception that things are never what they seem created a story full of spy-novel twists and surprises. *Foundation's Edge* starts off promisingly in the same vein but ultimately loses itself in an overly elaborate plot, which introduces a third controlling force with a counterculture flavor, a search for the origins of life on a mythical planet called Earth and the promise of a further sequel which will allow Asimov to connect the *Foundation* with his other abiding passion—robots.

I wish he had left well enough alone. Asimov may have written *Foundation's Edge* to deflect the heavy club of determinism with which he bludgeoned the First Foundation— and the reader—in the trilogy's surprise ending (I remember my Stalinist college friends in the late 1960s loved it). But in an excess of repentant zeal, he has tampered too much with his basic material; *Foundation's Edge* destroys the harmony and balance of the theme the trilogy so elegantly set up and played out. Though the denouement of the *Foundation* trilogy may have shocked us, at least it made sense. *Foundation's Edge* does neither.—MARY ELLEN BURNS, "And Nos. 3 and 7," *Nation*, March 5, 1983, p. 281

THE ROBOT STORIES

What is a man? What is a machine? These questions intrigue Asimov. Man sees himself as distinct from animals because of his higher intelligence and his ability to store information and to pass it from individual to individual and from generation to generation. Each new generation begins with the accumulated knowledge of all the previous generations. But what happens to man's image of himself when machines begin to acquire some of these characteristics? If machine intelligence can perform the functions of human intelligence, is man then nothing more than a machine? . . .

The Three Laws of Robotics have attracted more attention than any other aspect of Asimov's cybernetic SF. In SF religious tales are rare. So are stories debating the niceties of various moral codes. SF has traditionally based itself on the natural and social sciences, which aim to be analytic not normative. Certainly no writer grounds his fiction more solidly in science than Asimov, yet he has formulated an ethical code now famous in and out of SF. Two recent texts on artificial intelligence make references to the Three Laws, and one of the authors says he sees no reason why the laws cannot be programmed. Adrian Berry's *The Next Ten Thousand Years* (1974) also cites the Three Laws. Even Asimov himself expresses amazement at the wide influence of those Three Laws. "It is rather odd to think that in centuries to come, I may be remembered (if I am remembered at all) only for having laid the conceptual groundwork for a science which in my own time was nonexistent." The laws are as follows:

1. A robot may not injure a human being nor, through inaction, allow a human being to come to harm.
2. A robot must obey the orders given it by human beings except where such orders would conflict with the First Law.
3. A robot must protect its own existence as long as

such protection does not conflict with the First or Second Law.

The Three Laws are an important element in at least a dozen stories. Asimov explains that "there was just enough ambiguity in the Three Laws to provide the conflicts and uncertainties required for new stories, and to my great relief, it seemed always to be possible to think up a new angle out of the sixty-one words of The Three Laws.". . .

Asimov uses a behavioral definition of ethics and suggests that computer programs be written to operationalize that behavior. If the behavior regarded as ethical can be described, a program for it can be written. Writing such a program is well within the capability of present computer programming. Asimov follows the approach of the behavioral psychologists. Not motives or consciousness but the behavior of the individual is examined. Skinner proposes in his operant conditioning that desirable behavior be defined and that the individual be programmed to respond, through positive reinforcement, with that behavior. Similarly, Asimov's computer would be programmed to respond in a prescribed way, the only difference being that it is much easier to program a computer than a human.

The difficult part of the task is to decide what is desirable. Who will define the ideal? It seems likely that John Stuart Mill's concept "the greatest good for the greatest number" would have to be the essential criterion for designing the ideal.

Thus, while not a simple task, defining ideal behavior and writing a computer program to obtain it would be possible. The program would control the performance of the technology, not the performance of man himself. However, man increasingly expresses himself through technology. Programming the technology to operate according to ethical principles would be a great step toward an ethical society. The world's great religious systems have attempted to program man's mind with an ethical system, but they have been only partially effective because man's emotions, ambitions, and aggressions often override the programming. Overriding would not be a problem, however, in the computer program.

Such an ethical technology would be desirable, of course, but it would come at some cost. The model of behavior would inevitably reflect the values of the modelers. Many persons might disagree with those values. Given the diversity of human nature, any model of ethical behavior will be defective from some points of view. The implementation of the model would mean some restriction of individual liberty; a degree of conformity would be the result. It would require a trade-off—the loss of some individual freedom for the sake of some social order and freedom from violence and war.

Any discussion of computer programming of ethics is still highly speculative. But there is no reason why speculations could not someday become realities. Asimov's significant accomplishment is that the drama he has created with the Three Laws has set us thinking. Perhaps in the real world ethical concepts could be operationalized in computer technology. No other science fiction writer has given the world that vision.— PATRICIA S. WARRICK, *The Cybernetic Imagination in Science Fiction*, 1980, pp. 62–68

The power of ⟨"The Bicentennial Man" (1976)⟩ results from an interweaving of two tales, one told and one untold. Andrew's story traces the evolution of robots toward the organic, first set in motion when man learned to create artificial intelligence housed in a machine. But equally moving is the tale not told, the story of man's evolution toward the mechanical as his new cybernetic technology gives him the means to replace organic with machine parts. This design of told and untold tales woven into a future of human metamorphosis is the music of ambiguity, suggesting man's glory and his tragedy when his technological creativity changes his essential nature. The echoing notes, after the story transforming robot into man and man into robot ends, suggest what it means to be the human that Nature created. Andrew ascends, or perhaps descends, into manhood; the direction is not clear, but the price of his journey is his immortality. The contrapuntal design of the story suggesting man's journey toward machinehood silently whispers that the price of man's immortality may be his humanity. . . .

"The Bicentennial Man" incorporates all Asimov's previous ideas about machine intelligence as the story moves on to explore new territory: the ethical and philosophical implications for man in creating high level intelligence. . . .

Asimov does something in "The Bicentennial Man" which he had never done in his previous thirty-five stories about robots and computers. He tells the story from the point of view of the robot. He assumes a robot with consciousness and free will, plants the reader squarely in that consciousness by his selection of the robot's point of view, and opens the story with a scene where the robot exercises his free will as he deliberates a choice: to be or not to be a man, even if the price of manhood may be death. Andrew is not plagued with Hamlet-like indecision, although the reader will not know the consequences of his choice until the final scene.

Recollecting the evolutionary steps in the design of intelligence that led him to this moment of decision, Andrew recapitulates the two hundred years of his history (and also recapitulates the evolutionary process of Asimov's discussion of artificial intelligence over the previous thirty-five years). Then, having traced the stages of his development, Andrew pushes the evolutionary process into the future. Here the Asimovian imagination is at its best, taking dazzling leaps forward in time, but always pushing off from the current stage of knowledge in the field. He starts with questions currently being asked by researchers in artificial intelligence. What is human intelligence? The answer seems to be that it is information stored, processed, and used by the human organism to accomplish purposeful acts. A corollary question immediately arises. What is machine intelligence? The answer to this is similar to the first, except that now the process takes place in an inorganic mechanism. Asimov probed but did not define the likenesses and differences between organic and inorganic intelligence in "Stranger in Paradise" (1974). Now he pushes the question to the utmost—and finds an answer both definitive and ambiguous. He reflects the growing awareness in the fields of computer science, psychology, biology and philosophy that the differences between human and artificial intelligence are not nearly so clear as they once appeared to be.

The approach Asimov chooses to the puzzle of intelligence, human or machine, leads to the power of the story. Inverting the obvious approach—man examining artificial intelligence—he elects to have Andrew explore the nature and implications of human intelligence for a robot. As he learns about his master and creator, Andrew longs to become like him. Andrew's struggle to evolve beyond his programmed obedience is dramatized with great economy, and almost entirely through dialogue. The Martin family, in its four generations, represents the small group of men who realize the potential of artificial intelligence and take actions to foster and expand it. The U.S. Robots Corporation stands for the economic system supported by the mass of men who wish only to exploit robot technology for profit and who feel no ethical responsibility to this new form of emerging intelligence. The

law is represented in various ways over the 200-year period of the story—lawyers, regional legislators, and finally the World Court. Each time Andrew brings to the courts a request for protection of his rights, they are confounded, replying that there is no precedent to follow. . . .

Through all the years, Andrew never loses his dream. "The truth is," he says as he finally asks the chairperson of the World Science and Technology Committee to legally declare him human, "I want to be a man. I have wanted it through six generations of human beings." The chairperson disparages the likelihood of such a precedent-shattering event happening. But Andrew is persistent, fighting by indirection and legal maneuvers because the Three Laws prevent his taking any direct action against humans. Because his intelligence is never muddied by emotions, he can reason clearly and with utmost logic. He sees, finally, that he cannot be declared a man as he had hoped, despite freedom, intelligence, and an organic body, because his brain is different. The World Court has declared a criterion for determining what is human. "Human beings have an organic cellular brain and robots have a platinum-irridium positronic brain. . . ." Andrew is at an impasse. His brain is man-made; the human brain is not. His brain is constructed; man's brain is developed.

Finally, Andrew pushes the implication of this statement to its ultimate meaning. The greatest difference between robot and man is the matter of immortality. He reasons: "Who really cares what a brain looks like or is built of or how it was formed? What matters is that brain cells die; *must* die. Even if every other organ in the body is maintained or replaced, the brain cells, which cannot be replaced without changing and therefore killing the personality, must eventually die." He realizes that the price of being human is to sacrifice his immortality. In the final moving episode of the story, he submits to surgery rearranging the connection between organic nerves and positronic brain in such a way that he will soon die. When he performs this ultimate act of sacrifice, the Court at last declares him a man.

"The Bicentennial Man" is a powerful, profound story for several reasons. Foremost, Asimov leaves much unsaid, the story at which he only hints. Andrew's process toward manhood and death is unfolded against a background where man is developing technology moving him toward artificial intelligence and immortality. As machine intelligence evolves to human form, human intelligence is evolving toward machine form. The implication of this transformation is that a clear line between the animate and inanimate, the organic and inorganic, cannot be drawn. If we see the fundamental materials of the universe as matter, energy, and information patterns (or intelligence), then man is not unique. He exists on a continuum with all intelligence. He is no more than the most highly evolved form on the Earth. This view implies that ethical behavior should extend beyond human systems to include all systems because any organizational pattern, human or nonhuman, organic or inorganic, represents intelligence. A kind of sacred view of Nature and of all the universe, arrived at not by religious mysticism but by pure logic, emerges from this reading of "The Bicentennial Man."

. . . The untold tale that weaves through the story questions man's dream of achieving immortality. Andrew's patient and costly journey to reach humanity; his joy in freedom, creativity, and learning; his willingness to die to give life to his dreams—all these ask the reader to see with a fresh vision and delight the meaning of human life. Is it just possible, as Andrew suggests, that life is precious for man because he is a mortal who dreams and who knows he must die? Will man's quest for immortality be as costly as Andrew's journey to humanity?—PATRICIA S. WARRICK, "The Contrapuntal Design of Artificial Evolution in Asimov's 'The Bicentennial Man'," *Extrp*, Fall 1981, pp. 232–40

The puzzle and the ingenious solution were what sold Asimov's robot stories to Campbell and to his readers. But those were not the stories' only virtues. The concern with the Three Laws also had relevance to human behavior, sometimes stated, more often not. This does not mean simply the overt references to such matters as the Frankenstein complex: the fear of robots and the banning of their use on Earth has more fictional value than philosophic validity. Although clearly motivated by Asimov's dislike for the archetype and enabling him to deal with contrasts in attitudes and behavior, the terrestrial antipathy toward the robots seems less convincing than desirable for reasons of plot. Robot computers are not banned, nor are other non-humanoid robots. The banning of the robots and apprehension concerning them, however, provides many conflicts in a series that has little inevitable conflict built into it. Asimov is able to get around the bans when he desires, particularly in the robot stories published after 1950.

More important are the philosophic implications of the Three Laws. In "Runaround," for instance, Speedy is in the position of a human who has been ordered to perform an important task but who discovers that doing it will endanger his life. A human might not exhibit his conflict in a fashion so cleverly balanced between a command that must be obeyed and a danger that must be avoided, but the circle he enscribes around the selenium pool shows an understanding of human nature that a soldier cowering in a shell hole might not. Cutie has the characteristics of many prophets, finding his certitude in Platonic introspection rather than scientific evidence; and his analysis suggests to the reader, in passing, how improbable are the universe and the life itself that we take for granted. . . .

Asimov is eclectic. He never set out to write a consistent future history of the robots, even though the publication and the surprising success of *I, Robot*, with its parts glued together, made it seem as if he had. A certain number of common elements and cross-references has tended to reinforce the illusion. But it would be a mistake to judge the robot stories on this basis. *I, Robot* is the only self-sufficient and almost self-consistent work and should be adequate for the critic who desires unity.

The robot stories are a body of literature, much like the Scandinavian sagas or the Greek legends, that focuses on the question of how one should respond to the reality of the particular universe in which these groups of stories exist from a cluster of viewpoints. The greatest value of the robot stories is not in internal consistency but in multiplicity of consideration. In these stories Asimov provided readers with the unique excitement of an inquiring and artistic mind returning again and again to a single question and discovering not only new variations but sometimes different answers.—JAMES GUNN, *Isaac Asimov: The Foundations of Science Fiction*, 1982, pp. 67–78

OTHER WORKS

The title story of Asimov's collection, *The Martian Way*, is surely one of the best science fiction novellas ever published. The story's taking-off point is simple: If no miracle fuels or propulsion systems come along, but Mars is to be colonized anyway, then it will have to be done with step rockets. A-B-C. All right, then what happens to the discarded steps—hundreds of thousands of tons of salvageable steel? Asimov's answer: they drift on out across the Martian orbit, until Scavengers in tiny two-man ships come out to get them.

The drama of "The Martian Way" is in those ships. Asimov, writing compactly and with enviable control, makes every phase of them intensely believable—the irritation that grows in the cramped quarters, the squabbling "Scavenger widows" at home, the monotony of waiting, the excitement—like hooking God's biggest fish—of a fat strike.

A lesser writer, fumbling for something to say, would have made these men little tin heroes, tight-lipped and glint-eyed, with shoulders from here to there. Asimov's characters are good-natured, human, unextraordinary, wonderful joes.

And a lesser writer, dealing with the long voyage to Saturn which turns this story from a vignette into an epic, would have marked time with mutinies, sprung seams, mold in the hydroponics tanks and Lord knows what all else. Asimov, instead, has rediscovered the mystic euphoria and beauty of space travel. Of those who have written about this imaginary journey, how many others have even tried to make Saturn glow in the reader's eyes like the monstrous jewel it is?

When you read this story, if you haven't already, you'll realize how much there is of heroics in run-of-the-mill science fiction, and how little true heroism. Asimov will make you feel the distances, the cold, the vastness, the courage of tiny human figures against that immense backdrop.

It's seldom that science fiction sticks as closely as this to its proper theme; if it happened more often, probably the respectable critics would have given in long ago.—DAMON KNIGHT, "Asimov and Empire," *In Search of Wonder*, 1967, pp. 93–94

As a result of ⟨a⟩ challenge to handle aliens and sex as he never had before, Asimov wrote the brilliant middle section of *The Gods Themselves*. In this section he takes us elsewhere and allows us to live there for a while. It is a detailed study of consciousness as it developed and lives in a vastly different environment from our own. Perhaps, as much as anything else, it leaves behind an awe-full respect for life and sentience.

But no science fiction alien can ever be entirely different from ourselves. They spring out of and are thus rooted in the human imagination. In one sense what Asimov has done is return to a certain type of medieval allegory, the type represented by *The Romance of the Rose*, in which the allegorical abstractions are abstracted from the human psychology. The family groups of three—exemplified here in Dua, the female, and Odeen and Tritt, the males—are abstracted from each of us. The medieval allegorist might have called Dua, Emotion; Odeen, Intellect; and Tritt, Common Sense. In these days of unisex and women's lib, it is interesting that Dua, the female, creates an environment within which Tritt, the male, can conceive and rear the children. Asimov does not present simply Male-Intellect-Logic versus Female-Emotion-Intuition. (Fill in whatever other dualities you are used to.) Instead, each of us has within him a Dua, an Odeen, and a Tritt, and *The Gods Themselves* can be read profitably, I think, as a reminder that our natures are not dual but complex.—JOSEPH F. PATROUCH, JR., *The Science Fiction of Isaac Asimov*, 1974, pp. 267–68

We customarily read the biography or autobiography of a novelist or poet either because he has led an interesting life or because by reading about the man we hope to gain some insight into the works. Since Isaac Asimov admits in his Introduction that "nothing of any importance has ever happened" to him, readers of *In Memory Yet Green* might reasonably expect that his 200th book will tell them something about how, and why, he wrote the volumes that preceded it. Unfortunately, Asimov devotes most of his energies to churning out undigested trivia and seldom gives us more than a superficial commentary on his fiction.

Of course there may be people somewhere who want to know what Isaac Asimov wants to tell them—like how much he was paid for each of his stories (and when the check arrived), or when and by whom his son was circumcised, or what he ate when he was taken to lunch by an editor from Little, Brown. Others may want to hear Asimov tell them about his brilliance (a subject which finds its way into almost every chapter). For that matter, some of the anecdotes are quite funny—like this exchange from a meeting with Frederick Pohl just after Asimov was drafted:

> [Pohl] said, "My AGCT score was 156. What was yours?"
> I reddened (I know I did, because I felt myself redden) and said, "I got 160, Fred."
> "Shit!" he said.

To my mind, though, the one potentially redeeming feature of the book is the description of Asimov's relationship to John W. Campbell, Jr. Here we get an insider's view of one of the most important figures in the history of American science fiction. The portrait is not always flattering—Asimov, a New Deal liberal, places Campbell's politics "somewhere to the right of Attila the Hun"—but it is clear that the high standards set by Campbell's *Astounding*, and the interest Campbell showed in Asimov's early stories, were major factors in launching Asimov's career as a science-fiction writer. Campbell's influence was sometimes more direct, as when he suggested the idea for "Nightfall" or formulated the Three Laws of Robotics. Even Campbell's faults, like his chauvinistic refusal to believe that extraterrestrials could be superior to human beings, had their impact on Asimov's fiction.

The passages dealing with Campbell show how good this book could have been, but they are not really enough by themselves to make this book very valuable. Despite its more than seven hundred pages, this is a lightweight volume—and Asimov is threatening to send another in its wake. There is always a chance that the second volume will be better than the first, but it would be better still if Asimov would turn his attention to a new novel and leave the telling of his life to someone else.—Patrick A. McCarthy, *SFS*, July 1979, pp. 227–28

Margaret Atwood

1939–

Margaret Atwood was born on November 18, 1939 in Ottawa, Ontario. Her family traveled constantly through the Canadian bush country, where much of her writing is set. She received a B.A. from the University of Toronto in 1961, and an M.A. from Radcliffe in 1962. She studied at Harvard from 1962 to 1963, and again from 1965 to 1967. In the interim she taught at the University of British Columbia; she has subsequently lectured at Sir George Williams University, York University, and the University of Toronto.

Atwood's first book of poetry, *Double Persephone*, won the E.J. Pratt Medal in 1961, but it was with *The Circle Game* in 1966 that she began to attract critical attention, winning the Governor General's Award and the President's Medal. After another book of poems, *The Animals in That Country* (1968), Atwood published her first novel, *The Edible Woman* (1969). As her work became increasingly angry in the early 1970s, she developed a strong following among feminists, centering around her 1972 novel *Surfacing*. Also in 1972 Atwood published *Survival*, a major critical study of Canadian literature, and *Power Politics*. The latter, like 1974's *You Are Happy*, was a group of poems dealing with Atwood's marriage and divorce. *Two Headed Poems* in 1978 was an exploration of Canadian consciousness.

Atwood continues to alternate between poetry (*True Stories*, 1981), novels (*Lady Oracle*, 1976; *Life Before Man*, 1980; *Bodily Harm*, 1981), short stories (collected as *Dancing Girls*, 1977, and *Murder in the Dark*, 1983), and books for children (*Up in the Tree*, 1978, and *Anna's Pet*, 1980). Her awards include the Bess Hopkins Prize in 1974, and the Molson Prize and Guggenheim Fellowship in 1981. She has received honorary doctorates from Trent University, Queen's University, Concordia University, and Smith College. Margaret Atwood lives in Alliston, Ontario with the writer Graeme Gibson; they have one child.

General

⟨We⟩ are clearly to find *Power Politics* not a collection but a book. Why does the shape of the book, especially toward the end, bother me? When she says:

> In the room we will find nothing
> In the room we will find each other

why do I not believe? Perhaps the language does not change enough, the terms of the struggle deepen mythologically but do not change in any convincing way from the conventional power struggle. Some fear seems to prevent her breaking through in this book as she breaks through with her protagonist in *Surfacing*. To put it another way, she doesn't seem able to imagine the next stage, and a book that remains caught in its first terms while seeming to suggest that it will transcend them, is frustrating, but brilliantly so. It is still a strong and good sequence and a far more satisfying book as a book than ninety per cent of the poetry collections I read. Only in reading her work I have come to want more than that. A talent like hers needs to transcend its own categories, to integrate the preconscious and conscious materials, the imagery and ideas. Her wit can lead her into trivia; just as her passion for the omen can lead her to see the portentous in grains of sand and jam jars. . . .

The source of integration of the self, the reservoir of insight in Atwood lie deep in a wild and holy layer of experience usually inaccessible in modern life—in how her characters make a living, how they act with each other, how they respond or fail to respond to birth, death, loss, passion, how they permit themselves to live out of touch with what they want and what they feel. The landscape of the psyche in Atwood tends to be a cabin in the Canadian woods, on a lake, on a river—the outpost of contact between straight lines (roads, houses, gardens) and natural curves (trees, deer, running water): the imposed order and the wild organic community. . . .

To cease to be a victim, each of her protagonists fights an entirely solitary battle. Their only allies are the dead, the forces in nature and the psyche, their own life energies. Yet they must live among others. Somehow the next step is missing. I don't believe one woman can single-handedly leave off being a victim: power exists and some have it. Atwood seems to me still to rest in an untenable coyness about what it will mean in the daily world to attempt to take charge of one's life—as a Canadian, as a working person (none of her protagonists have money) and as a woman.

Atwood is a large and remarkable writer. Her concerns are nowhere petty. Her novels and poems move and engage me deeply, can matter to people who read them. As she has come to identify herself consciously, cannily, looking all ways in that tradition she has defined as literature of a victimized colony, I hope that she will also come to help consciously define another growing body to which her work in many of its themes belongs: a women's culture. With her concern with living by eating, with that quest for the self that Barbara Demming has found at the heart of major works by women from the last one hundred fifty years (*Liberation*, Summer 1973), with her passion for becoming conscious of one's victimization and ceasing to acquiesce, with her insistence on nature as a living whole of which we are all interdependent parts, with her respect for the irrational center of the psyche and the healing experiences beyond logical control, her insistence on joining the divided head and body, her awareness of roleplaying and how women suffocate in the narrow crevices of sexual identity, she is part of that growing women's culture already, a great quilt for which we are each stitching our own particolored blocks out of old petticoats, skirts, coats, bedsheets, blood and berry juice.— MARGE PIERCY, "Margaret Atwood: Beyond Victimhood," *APR*, Nov.–Dec. 1973, pp. 42–44

Both *The Edible Woman* and *Surfacing* corrupt the prototypical romance movement from descent to ascent by demonstrating that the upper world is merely a reflection of the lower world of darkness, ambiguity, and isolation. The end of *The Edible Woman* brings Marian back to the same problems that caused her descent into the netherworld of Part II. The narrator of *Surfacing* is also left with the impossible task of trying to ascend from the dreams which always place her between stations on a road full of lies and ghosts and phantoms, monsters from the deep. And then there is Joan (in *Lady Oracle*), whose comical follies are also part of a modern fall from any meaningful sense of self or community. Atwood's novels are well-crafted and sometimes very funny; but most importantly they haunt us as stories about multi-faceted characters who are as fragmented and duplicitous as the times in which they live.— ROBERT LECKER, "Janus through the Looking Glass: Atwood's First Three Novels," *The Art of Margaret Atwood*, eds. Arnold E. Davidson and Cathy N. Davidson, 1981, p. 203

Substitute forest for castle and think of the ghosts of Mrs. Radcliffe's *The Italian* and the ghost story or Gothic form of the typical Atwood novel and poem begins to take shape. Obviously, there are displacements: the threat of unstructured or unmapped space is more sinister and alarming than ruins; the "malignant face" is of the forest, not the dark man who represents power; there are psychic hazards in space of this kind subtly examined in Foster's account of spatial metaphors, the tension of inner and outer in Atwood's poems, the peculiar mind-body dislocations (physically here, psychically there). To be sure, the pattern is richly suggestive of a variety of dark threats, either psychological or hidden in the social structure.—ELI MANDEL, "Atwood's Poetic Politics," *Margaret Atwood: Language, Text and System*, eds. Sherrill E. Grace and Lorraine Weir, 1983, p. 57

Works

NOVELS

. . . (W)hat is most striking about *Surfacing* is the integrity of the writer's imagination, a quality somewhat more visible in her earlier books of poetry than in the imagery of *An Edible Woman* (1970), her first novel. Everywhere in the language of this story there are dependencies, associative prefigurings, linkages extending and refining meaning. Moments of dramatic crisis evolve from metaphor itself, as it seems, so that when, in a fury at false art, the heroine destroys the *cinéma vérité* film, the act reverberates in the reader's mind with a whole set of connected matters—the heroine's searchings through her own childhood drawings for something genuine, her response to her father's fascination in Indian rock paintings, and much more. The action of the book as a purification by violence of false identity is never erratic; the same standard that denies the heroine herself a name governs her judgment of other human beings: "I could see into him, he was an imposter, a pastiche, layers of political handbills, pages from magazines, *affiches*, verbs and nouns glued onto him and shredding away, the original surface littered with fragments and tatters . . . Second-hand American was spreading over him in patches, like mange or lichen. He was infested, garbled and I couldn't help him; it would take such time to heal, unearth him, scrape down to where he was true." The ways in which surfaces and surfacing are configured in these pages, moving through successive bands of meaning from veneers to deaths by drowning, are both shrewd and deep.

Atwood's overarching theme—the sin of trivialization, the unpardonable crime of strangling your own seriousness—is better managed than some of its subsidiaries: as, for example, America as locus of universal corruption. And her prose, to speak of that, is mannered: kinky about pronoun references, flashback signals, other bitty-bitchy details. But the writing does invariably have solid objects—a specified social context— in view. There is news in *Surfacing* of minor and major kinds—news about where the grass is packed in rucksacks and when it's broken out, news also about where exactly the rot comes in nowadays in so-called good marriages of youngsters turning 30, and news about the character of the tensions suffered by a woman once browbeaten into marriage and determined never to be thus intimidated again. Doubtless many sensitive and intelligent younger women will feel, as they read this tale, a special sense of possessiveness, the solace of solidarity (someone else has been here, someone besides me knows what's what). But like all moving and instructive novels, *Surfacing* shuts nobody out.—BENJAMIN DEMOTT, "Recycling Art," *SRA*, April 1973, p. 86

In 1830, Sir Charles Lyell published *Principles of Geology* and introduced the possibility of human extinction. From that point on, all the anxiety, uncertainty, and alienation which individual mortality had hitherto generated began to look like small potatoes. The knowledge of extinction is our second fall from innocence, and like the first—knowledge of our own deaths—it is almost unendurably nauseating to contemplate.

Not for everyone though. The characters in Margaret Atwood's fierce new novel, *Life Before Man* (life *after* man is the implied gallows joke), can't seem to get through a day without obsessing on extinction. Unlike Doris Lessing's fixation on future cataclysm, Atwood's people (most of whom work in the Ontario Museum of Natural History) look back to the dinosaur's prophetic tale. Although nobody knows exactly why the giant lizards didn't make it, *Life Before Man* posits the notion that obsolescence may simply be built into the process of life. We're not doomed because we're irresponsible and wicked; we're just doomed. Quel consolation.

Life Before Man is full of variations on the theme of extinction, but whereas total obliteration of the species has a rather limited mirth-yield, Atwood the satirist shoots mainly at smaller scale extinctions—monogamy, repressed feelings, polite conversations, and novels of manners that describe these fossils. Though far from extinct, the rotten childhood, failed marriage, failed affair, failed fuck, successful suicide, and cancer death also figure in the story. *Life Before Man* is wry, pitiless, and sometimes moving. But there are problems.

Atwood gets trapped by her own cleverness and skill at literary games. An omniscient narrator tells the story, alternating between the perspectives of the three main characters: Elizabeth, the survivor, Lesje, an archeologist and lover of old bones, and Nate, estranged husband of Elizabeth and tepid lover of Lesje. The point of this narrative device is partly to send up the Jamesian novel, where dramatic tension derives mainly from the disparity between statement and feeling—a vision in which the pulse races not at consummation, but at interruptus, at the exquisitely restrained sentiment and suspended confession.

As well as parodying them, Atwood's narrator speaks for her characters because like tongue-tied dinosaurs living in the age of candor, not one is capable of spitting out an honest thought. Elizabeth lies in order to control, Lesje covers up out of fear. Nate dissimulates because he has no idea what he feels. But while Atwood is good at satirizing perverse withholding, the novel's formal structure ultimately dwarfs the characters. They don't have the blood and the story doesn't have the juice Atwood intended. The emotional core isn't in the comedy, but in the way real life is shown being lived, and this should have cracked the novel's structure at some points, plumped its skeleton with irregular contours. Instead, *Life Before Man* is tight as a poem in which nothing much happens; thematic obsessions take the place of drama, and the writing becomes precious. Also, because the characters are observed rather than recorded, they become stereotypes: Elizabeth is too calculating and cold, Lesje too naive, and Nate too noncommital to be believed.

Still, Atwood can unquestionably write a sentence. Her meditations on extinction, adaptation, and survival deepen on each successive page. From time to time, Atwood shows that even if people could say what they felt, they wouldn't necessarily have the language to express the complexities of evolving life. "'Did you lose your job,' Nate asks. A fatuous question perhaps, but what is he supposed to say to his wife's castoff lover?" The shifting perspectives produce some fine ironies: "Elizabeth is old enough to know that one woman's demon lover is another's worn-out shoe."

At her most powerful, Atwood shows what it's like to ride and trip toward extinction without quite feeling it happen, to see the signs of obsolescence in the faces of children, and to feel the pull toward shelter on the one hand, and toward bloodpumping danger on the other. *Mutatis mutandis, momento mori,* and *danse macabre* is the dinosaur's message.—Laurie Stone, "Dinosaur Dance," VV, Jan. 7, 1980, p. 32

In *Surfacing* . . . we have a vision of our own fragmented culture in which the few moments of coherence are marked or introduced by signs recalling the unbroken world of the previous inhabitants of this land. The environment of Atwood's heroine appears to be almost a non-culture, for the coherence which may seem to be the most important quality of the North American Indian cultures is not transmitted along with the objects and symbols taken out of their original cultural context. The narrator's return to a silent community is evidence of the failure of our civilization to provide a meaningful context to her life. However, I am not sure that this implicit condemnation of our society does justice to the realities of most contemporary lives. The "Americans" of the book are the living dead not because they kill, not because they kill with machines, but because they kill without meaning. Is meaning to be provided by society or by culture alone, or should we, like the shamans of old, seek for it beyond a known but no longer sufficient world? This is the problem finally faced by *Surfacing.*—Marie-Françoise Guédon, "*Surfacing*: Amerindian Themes and Shamanism," *Margaret Atwood: Language, Text and System*, eds. Sherril E. Grace and Lorraine Weir, 1983, p. 110

POETRY

Power Politics . . . creates a mirrored Gothic of the Other where a male who is both wretch and victim, monster and villain, stalks a female who is both distorter and creator, adventurer and victim. Inside this doubly Gothic structure the horror and the terror redouble, divide, and multiply. Atwood's sequence thus reflects not only Gothic literature and modern, fragmented reality, but also the particular power politics of a society where men have outward power and women have inward pain: the female *I* is alienated from her body and her head, even from her terror; addict, she comes alive only in relation to a sexual Other who is a series of oppressive masculine poses. His power threatens her, his sufferings milk her; either way, she is his victim and yet guilty of her victimization. That she prefers the Gothic horrors to reality is not only her private addiction, but also the politics of how the dominated endure, and the aesthetics of how the bored escape. That the Gothic stays interior, and that the *I* creates only by seeing—not by speaking, leading, acting—is not only a Gothic addiction/vision, but is also the silence of the politically isolated and disabled.—Judith McCombs, "Atwood's Haunted Sequences," *The Art of Margaret Atwood*, eds. Arnold E. Davidson and Cathy N. Davidson, 1981, p. 52

Margaret Atwood's *Two-Headed Poems* are full of interesting ideas, memorable images, and intelligent observations. She has a deep understanding of human motivation, and her poetry deals naturally with an intricate sort of psychology most poets ignore. Her poems are often painfully accurate when dealing with the relationships between men and women or mothers and daughters. And yet with all these strengths, Atwood is not an effective poet. She writes poetry with ideas and images, not with words; her diction lies dead on the page. Her poems have a conceptual and structural integrity, but the language itself does not create the heightened awareness one looks for in poetry. The problem centers in her rhythms, not only the movement of words and syllables within the line, but also the larger rhythms of the poem, the movements from line to line and stanza to stanza. While the pacing of her ideas works beautifully, her language never picks up force.

One notices the curious neutrality of Atwood's language most clearly in her sequence of prose poems, "Marrying the Hangman," which obliquely tells the story of Françoise Laurent, a woman sentenced to death for stealing, who legally avoids punishment by convincing the man in the next cell to become a hangman and then marrying him. (Atwood uses a real historic incident here, but the plot seems like something out of a Mascagni opera.) The language in these prose poems is qualitatively no different from the language of her verse, except that it has no line breaks. It most resembles a passage of "elevated" prose, like an excerpt from Joan Didion's histrionic *Book of Common Prayer*.—DANA GIOIA, "Eight Poets," *Poetry*, May 1982, p. 110

There is a haunting Imagist sufficiency about the title poem of *You Are Happy*; Imagism passes through practice into theory, as Atwood tells of a winter walk, beginning with a verse that is an irregular haiku: eighteen syllables arranged four, nine, five instead of seventeen arranged five, seven, five, but otherwise traditional in its natural image and seasonal setting:

> The water turns
> a long way down over the raw stone,
> ice crusts around it

The poem proceeds with the walk which the poet and her companion take, wandering to the open beach, seeing the unused picnic tables, the brown gravelly waves. The headless carcass of a deer lies in a ditch; a bird runs across the road in the pink glare of the low sun. All is stated in images, until the last five lines, which expound the very core of Imagist doctrine, the subordination of idea to image:

> When you are this
> cold you can think about
> nothing but the cold, the images
> hitting into your eyes
> like needles, crystals, you are happy.

Only in the very last phrase, "you are happy," is the emotion that the images have carried through the poem explicitly stated.

This poem exemplifies the startling actuality that is one of the striking features of so many of the items in *You Are Happy*. Such poems are related to the life which Atwood took up when in the early 1970's she retreated to live in old Loyalist country at Alliston, Ontario, in a way re-enacting Susanna Moodie's experiences, since she too was involved in a kind of pioneering, getting an old farm back into shape and some degree of production. They are poems about place, but unlike Al Purdy's poems about the Loyalist country, they are not really about time in the historic sense; Atwood is less concerned than Purdy about ancestors and prefers to find them in myth and literature rather than in the kind of genealogical speculation through which he pushes backward to the roots of our past, or at least of his. . . .

The past that is "always heavier than you thought" hangs like a miasma over "Digging," where the poet digs dung in the barnyard as if it were a way of exorcising anger, grudges, "old remorse." And when the exorcism has worked, there is the pure flame of experience, as in "You Are Happy," and the rich contentment of "Late August" that takes up the Keatsian theme—"Season of mists and mellow fruitfulness"—and makes out of it an exceptional Atwoodian poem in which the characteristic astringency is dissolved and a dreaming sensual-

ity bridges the Romantic generations far more effectively than Keats's Canadian imitators did in the 1890's, with their precise metrical and metaphoric derivations. "Late August" is

> . . . the plum season, the nights
> blue and distended, the moon
> hazed, this is the season of peaches
> with their lush lobed bulbs
> that glow in the dusk, apples
> that drop and rot
> sweetly, their brown skins veined as glands
> [. . .]
> The air is still
> warm, flesh moves over
> flesh, there is no
> hurry

There is a kind of verbal *trompe l'oeil* in such poems. Time and change seem to have been stilled: "there is no/ hurry." And the illusion of timelessness is of course a quality of both Imagist poetry and of the kind of Romantic verse that was most strikingly exemplified in Keats's Odes. What is so clearly present is so in time, as well as space, and we have the sense of suspension in an eternal moment. But the very phrase, "eternal moment," gives the illusion away. Time starts up when we close the page, and we know that change has produced what the poet—and we vicariously—experience as changeless, and that change will afterwards break the spell. It is Atwood's acknowledgment of the co-existence of the sense of timelessness and changelessness that special times and moods confer on us, with the reality of change, that gives *You Are Happy* a range and a poignancy which make it more complex in its perplexities and its rewards than any of Atwood's earlier volumes.— GEORGE WOODCOCK, "Metamorphosis and Survival: Notes on the Recent Poetry of Margaret Atwood," *Margaret Atwood: Language, Text and System*, eds. Sherril E. Grace and Lorraine Weir, 1983, pp. 129–31

PHYLLIS GROSSKURTH
"Victimization or Survival"

Canadian Literature, Winter 1973, pp. 108–10

In her first novel, *The Edible Woman*, Margaret Atwood seemed unable to effect a resolution between a novel of manners and an expression of her essential vision. With *Surfacing*, she has brilliantly succeeded in creating a narrative style which fuses content and form—a quality of prose comfortably close to the diction of her poetry.

> I said "It's a heron. You can't eat them." I couldn't tell how it had been done, bullet, smashed with a stone, hit with a stick. This would be a good place for herons, they would come to fish in the shallow water, standing on one leg and striking with the long spear bill. They must have got it before it had time to rise.

This central passage from *Surfacing* summarizes themes that have informed her five books of poetry: anger at wanton destruction; the dehumanization of people to the point where the crucifixion of other creatures elicits only a morbid eagerness to record it; and the supine resignation of the witnesses to the desecration.

Surfacing is about victimization—both external and self-imposed. Atwood has already written about it in many poems, particularly in one she calls "The trappers" in *The Animals in That Country*:

> The trappers, trapped
> between the steel jaws of their answerless
> dilemma, their location,
> follow, stop, stare down
> at dead eyes

In *Surfacing* the narrator travels north to search for her father, a recluse botanist, who has been reported missing from the isolated island which was once her home. She is accompanied by a married couple, David and Anna ("She's my best friend, my best woman friend; I've known her two months") and Joe, a potter with whom she has been living for a short time. The others have offered to go with her because they are making an improvised film called *Random Shots* in which they attempt to impale the bizarre vagaries of existence.

The tripartite structuring of the novel is an essential key to an understanding of the developing self-awareness of the unnamed narrator. The first part is recorded in the present tense because she has lost her temporal and emotional bearings. The mythologized Canadian landscape becomes a metaphor for something that somehow got mislaid along the way—innocence, security, peace. Her father had once said that there was nothing in the north but the past, so perhaps this journey will be a re-charting of time past. Possibly she can erect a marker on the spot where her head had been severed from her heart.

Everything is disturbingly different until they reach the island. Here she takes over efficiently and naturally because as a child she had memorized its rules for survival, exemplified by the manuals kept in the cottage—*How to Stay Alive in the Bush*, *Animal Tracks and Signs*, *The Woods in Winter*. At first the others find everything "neat"; in fact, for a while it is so much of a holiday that they decide to stay on for another week. Absorbed in their own hedonism, it never occurs to them to consult their "hostess" who is withdrawing from them to a point where she feels a menacing sense of entrapment by a decision over which she had no control.

Part II reverts to the past tense as the characters, now truly in extremis, begin to reveal the fear that fills their hollowness. The "armour" (a reiterated image) with which they have fortified themselves in the city, cracks into alarming fissures. Anna continues to apply the protective "vizor" of her make-up, but the true desperation of her marriage to David emerges in a situation where they can no longer cope with their ever-changing rules of who is to play victim and who victimizer. The narrator tries to continue to work at the "career" she had been persuaded to adopt in the city—an illustrator of translations of children's stories. Her fabrications are now distorted and grotesque monsters.

Despite her longing for solitude in which to pursue her quest, her companions are necessary because they help her to identify the enemy. David continues the ritualistic gesture of shaking his fist at the Americans fishing out the lake ("Bloody fascist pigs"), but "she" begins to see that he and the other Canadians are indistinguishable from the Americans in dress, manner, and speech: they are the real destroyers with their slogans, their laminated equipment, and their indifference to the creeping universal disease symbolized by the dying white birches.

Her relationship with Joe also undergoes a series of changing attitudes. He had first been attracted to her because she seemed so "cool", so completely acquiescent in non-commitment. His physical attractiveness and his work are the only things that define him. She loathes his ugly pots, mutilated and slashed with holes so that she can't even put flowers in them because "the water would run out through the rips." Their basement apartment filled with these objects is an appropriate setting for aborted fertility. Joe, too, begins to lose his nerve. In order to seize some sort of security, he suggests that they get married. When she rejects him, his moodiness stalks her like a lurking predator.

Against this background of alienated relationships, she withdraws into her furtive search for her father. A rationalist, he had believed everything could be explained; a botanist, he admitted nothing that could not be classified. Accordingly she searches through his numerous diagrammed papers for a key to his condition and his whereabouts. Eventually she finds some drawings of Indian rock-paintings. Her first reaction is that he has gone mad; but when she finds a letter from an American academic, she realizes that her father had been abetting him in photographing the paintings as classifiable artifacts. But the level of the lake has been raised by the power company, so she has to dive deep below the surface of the water where she encounters only a floating image of death. Later her father's body is recovered, weighted down by the camera which is as alien to this environment as David's random shots.

There is no longer any necessity for pretence; and Anna now openly describes her as "inhuman" because she has refused to play the game according to their rules. Having accepted the fact of her father's death, she can view her life in terms of the present tense. Redemption lies through expiation, exorcism, and fertilization. After rejecting Joe in Part II, she deliberately lets him impregnate her. Then, just as they are about to depart for the city, she unrolls the film into the lake and flees in a canoe, a refusal to reaccommodate herself to rules and values she can never absorb. It is, in fact, a more affirmative act than Marion's consumption of her surrogate self at the end of *The Edible Woman*.

Left alone on the island, she destroys all the records of her past. Most important of all, she realizes that she has been looking for the wrong person. It is her mother, with her instinctual rapport with what is truly natural who should have been the object of her search. Previously she had described her mother as either fifty years ahead or ten thousand years behind her time—a true earth-mother. It is she who provides her with a legacy for the future. By returning to the primitive life of the woods into which her mother has been re-incarnated, she catches a glimpse of what she might do with her life. She had denied her essential nature when she killed life by an abortion in the city. Victimization is no longer inevitable. Perhaps survival—and something more—can be achieved with Joe who is still "only half-formed."

This novel—like all Atwood's writing—is so richly complex that a review of this length can do no more than sketch some of its aspects. Exploration in depth can be achieved only by complete immersion in her work. When one surfaces, the world looks startlingly new.

GEORGE WOODCOCK
From "Bashful but Bold: Notes on
Margaret Atwood as Critic"
The Art of Margaret Atwood
eds. Arnold E. Davidson and Cathy N. Davidson
1981, pp. 236–41

S he has tended to preserve with a certain quiet obstinacy her amateur position, discussing her fellow writers with personal informality more often than with critical formality, and in *Survival* she has produced one of the oddest-looking critical books ever written in Canada.

The genesis of the book, which seems to have been put together quite quickly before its publication in 1972 as a fattish tract for the nationalistic times, appears to have lain in Atwood's period of literary missionary work, when she became so concerned over the absence of Canadian books and authors in schools and colleges that she would travel around the southern Ontario countryside giving talks and readings at schools and lugging suitcases full of books by Canadian poets which she tried to sell for the cause. At this time she decided to write what she called "a teacher's guide to the many new courses in Canadian literature."

By now—I write in 1979—we have a number of such guides, and usually "in the kingdom of the blind the one-eyed man is king." When Margaret Atwood gets to work on such a project, it seems to be a case of third-eye not quite fitting into the local situation but nevertheless telling one-eye to keep no-eye out of the mire.

Survival ended up being a curious hybrid of a book, for the mechanical features of the course guide are retained: the lists of recommended texts, the feature of "fifteen useful books," the appendices relating to research resources are all there, and while this may be informative to the uninformed, it is plaguily condescending to anyone who has even a rudimentary knowledge of Canadian books and the literature concerning them. The serious reader who does not wish to be biased against Atwood's conclusions must ignore these intrusions which seem like a kind of survival course to test the reality of one's interest in the book or its subject. This means refusing to read (or reading on a shallower level of one's mind) perhaps a quarter of the book in order to arrive at the real core of *Survival*, the work that eventually emerged but was not intended.

For *Survival* is one of those mildly exasperating books in which a brilliant intelligence has been unable to put the brakes on its activity and has run far ahead of the task undertaken, so that all readers get more than they bargain for, and the disappointed are perhaps as numerous as those who are gratefully surprised. The body of the work is a sophisticated and challenging exposure of the Canadian psyche as revealed through our literature, an exposure that is double-edged since it also reveals that the born writer who attempts to popularize usually ends up producing something whose real meaning can be appreciated only by her peers. I suspect most students on any level of the educational ladder below the postgraduate (unless perhaps they attend Victoria College, Toronto) will be confused when they are faced with *Survival* and will never emerge from their bewilderment.

Yet Margaret Atwood presents very plausibly and supports with shrewdly chosen examples from the work of Canadian writers the argument that our literature is still scarred and distorted by the mental condition that emerges from a colonial past. It is, she suggests, essentially a literature of failure. Our greatest triumphs as a nation were achieved by blind collective urges; the "heroes" we name in connection with them turn out to be at best outward successes, and often not even that. Our literature reflects this situation.

All Canadian attitudes, in Atwood's view, can be related to the central fact of victimization imposed or at least attempted, and she lists and grades these attitudes, from "*Position One: To deny the fact that you are a victim*" (which objectively considered is the ultimate in victimization), to "*Position Four: To be a creative non-victim*," the position of those—among

whom the reader hopefully includes himself—whom Atwood tells "You are able to accept your own experience for what it is, rather than having to distort it to make it correspond with others' versions of it (particularly those of your oppressors)."

Such a literature, Atwood suggests, whether it expresses a denial or a recognition of experience, reflects an attitude to life that aims no higher than survival. French Canadians turned this fact into a self-conscious way of life, with *La Survivance* as a motto but also a national aim; the English Canadians recognized it explicitly in their pioneer literature and implicitly in their literary identification with animals, whom they see as quintessential victims and whose triumph can be no more than to live on to face another danger and, if they are fortunate, another survival.

It is a thesis that admirably fits many of the facts about our life and our literature, and in presenting it Atwood has condensed into a sharp focus the scattered insights which many other critics have recorded about the Canadian condition. We have no heroes; only martyrs. We pride ourselves with Calvinist or Jansenist smugness on our ironic modesty. With an inverted Pharisaism, we stake what claims we may propose to moral superiority, not on our successes, but on our failures. The main difference between Atwood and the others, like Frye and D. G. Jones who have explored the same territory, is that their maps are descriptive, charts for explorers; hers are tactical, tools in a campaign, charts to help us repel a cultural invasion and arise, foursquare in Position Four, consciously manifesting our true identities.

There is some truth in Malcolm Ross's contention that Atwood "offers us a rhetoric not a poetic."[1] The propagandist urge which we have seen her repudiating seems here to be turned towards the very heart of the world of literary creation, and writers' works are interpreted as records of the experience of being colonialized in such a way that one cannot see them as other than autobiographical, even if the final effect is a collective rather than an individual one.

There are, of course, other limitations to Atwood's thesis. There are many Canadian writers whom it does not fit, like Robertson Davies and Irving Layton and Ethel Wilson. On the other hand obsessions with failure and survival are not especially Canadian. Survival as a recurrent mythic pattern is exemplified in world literature from the *Epic of Gilgamesh* and the *Odyssey* down to the novels of such colonizing (rather than colonized) writers as Kipling and (more ambiguously) Orwell, who by Atwood's criteria looks like a pretty good candidate for Canadian cultural naturalization, given his famous remark that every life, viewed from the inside, is a failure.

Yet even if we must deny that Atwood's thesis identifies a peculiarly or universally Canadian condition, we have to agree that our poets and novelists of failure and survival have been too numerous and too compelling not to give a special flavour to our literature. It is no accident that to be dubbed "a survivor" is a compliment among Canadians. The more generalized criticism becomes, the more tentative inevitably it is, and certainly no critical map of the literary terrain of any land or period should be accepted as more than a useable frame of reference, a hypothesis that holds the facts together. *Survival* performs both functions.

But—bearing in mind Atwood's own admission that most critical schemata are creations of the critics' minds—we can perhaps at this point relate the various facets of her creativity and remark that the prime importance of *Survival*—to the reader if not necessarily to the writer—may well be not its remarks about Canadian books (many of which have been made in other ways by other people) but the fact that it gives another form to themes and insights that can be found in her poetry and her fiction.

In fact, when we try to distill the real spirit that inspires *Survival* we go down below the ephemeral level of polemics and come to the persons inspiring the book. And here—I must shift to the singular since I am discussing personal identifications—one finds a kind of mental toughness and resilience which call up a poem from *Power Politics* that has always seemed to me to project a poetic as well as an ethical stance so far as Atwood was concerned:

> Beyond truth,
> tenacity: of those
> dwarf trees & mosses,
> hooked into straight rock
> believing the sun's lies & thus
> refuting/gravity
> & of this cactus, gathering
> itself together
> against the sand, yes tough
> rind & spikes but doing
> the best it can

It seems to me that the tenacity, the defensive strength, the "doing/the best it can," characterize Atwood's own poetry but characterize also her view of Canadian literature. But beyond the recognition of being and hence survival, beyond the mere will to continue, there is the journey of self-discovery that begins from the simplest levels and which at the end of *Survival* Atwood offers for Canadian literature and, through it, for Canadian self-awareness. It is a journey with bleak beginnings, but the start has been made:

> When I discovered the shape of the national tradition I was depressed, and it's obvious why: it's a fairly tough tradition I was saddled with, to have to come to terms with. But I was exhilarated too: having bleak ground under your feet is better than having no ground at all. Any map is better than no map as long as it is accurate, and knowing your starting points and your frame of reference is better than being suspended in the void.

Thus, in *Survival* one finds transmuted into logical terms many of the ideas one absorbs almost osmotically from reading Atwood's poems, and perhaps in more direct ways from her novels, which also are reflected in some of her critical essays,

like "Canadian Monsters," where there are echoes of the heroine's preoccupation with Gothic novels in *Lady Oracle* (itself a splendid fictional critique of the genre and those who write it) and in the grotesque incidents that propel *Edible Woman* and *Surfacing* at times over the edge into fantasy.

But *Surfacing* has perhaps a more central role in one's view of Atwood as critic than the other novels, since it was written just before *Survival*, which, as Eli Mandel has remarked, can almost be read as a "gloss" on that novel. Certainly *Surfacing* concerns survival, and it is also so obsessed with Canadian victims that one can find therein a majority of the types of victims described in *Survival*'s various chapters. There are animal victims, victim Indians (but not Eskimos since it is too far south), victim children, victim women, victim French Canadians, a victim artist, and victim sham pioneers, since it is too late in history for real ones. The other victim types—explorers, immigrants, heroes, and jail breakers—are not directly represented, but in a sense the narrator is all of them, since in searching for her dead father she explores her own past, she migrates into a new self, she breaks the jail of her imprisoned old self, and she is as much the heroine as the tone of the novel admits.

More than that, *Surfacing* like *Survival* portrays Canada as a victim of the sickness of colonialism, and, while one should not over-stress the didactic elements in these aspects of the novel, there is enough to show that the novel and *Survival* were inspired by related impulses. Each in its own way is a book about self-realization, hence life-realization; *Surfacing* appears to concern an individual and *Survival* a people, but the allegory of the novel is collective and the emotion inspiring the critical polemic is personal. The difference may be that the novel contains an extra element of criticism, self-criticism, in the form of a self-mockery, that writers on Atwood have been slow to recognize. Let us take her seriously, but not too seriously. She has never claimed to be a systematic critic. But in her mutable way she has been a good and important one at this crucial time in the development of our sense of a literary culture.

Notes

1. Malcolm Ross, "Critical Theory: Some Trends," in *Literary History of Canada*, 2nd ed., Carl F. Klinck, ed. (1965; Toronto: Univ. of Toronto Press, 1976), Vol. 3, pp. 160–75.

Louis Auchincloss

1917–

Louis Stanton Auchincloss was born in 1917 in New York City, the son of a prominent New York family. While at Yale University, he wrote two novels, after which he concluded he could never succeed as a writer and left college without graduating. Auchincloss then decided to become a lawyer and earned a law degree from the University of Virginia. He has practiced law all of his life, apart from two and a half years in the early 1950's, when he gave up law to devote himself to writing. He found, however, that writing alone could not satisfy him, and returned to his practice in 1954.

In spite of the exigencies of family life and a career on Wall Street, Auchincloss has published over twenty novels and collections of short stories. He has spent nearly his entire life in New York, where most his novels are set. Notable among his works are *The Rector of Justin* (1964), *Portrait in Brownstone* (1962), and *Venus in Sparta* (1958). He is married, and has three children.

MARGARET ATWOOD

ISAAC ASIMOV

MAYA ANGELOU

JOHN ASHBERY

DJUNA BARNES

IMAMU AMIRI BARAKA

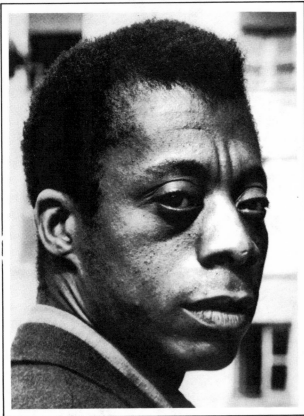

JAMES BALDWIN

LOUIS AUCHINCLOSS

Works

People who have followed the career of Louis Auchincloss, the only living novelist who practiced law at 67 Wall Street, have been waiting for some time for him to tackle the downtown legal world head-on in a novel. (His nearest approach to the subject, up to now, was *A Law for the Lion*, in which he explored a sensational divorce case with special attention to its legal ramifications.) Now, with *The Great World and Timothy Colt*, he has done it, and has done it well, bringing to this task the qualities that were to be found in almost all of his earlier work: a limpid style, an easy skill at letting his characters come alive through dialogue, a willingness to deal with important issues and an ability to dramatize them in human terms. But perhaps his most distinctive characteristic is his interest in contemporary manners and his belief—shared with Fielding, Jane Austen and Thackeray, but with few enough contemporary American writers—that small differences in social behavior cannot only reveal character, but affect destinies.

Consider the pivotal scene of *The Great World and Timothy Colt*. Timothy, great grandson of a rector of Trinity Church and a destined partner of the firm of Sheffield, Knox, Stevens and Dale, goes to a party thrown by George Emlen, a bumptious client with whom he does not get along at all well, and, after too many drinks and considerable goading in public by Emlen, Timothy insults the client by toasting him as "his own financier, his own lawyer, his own accountant, and if there's any justice in the afterlife, which I very much doubt, his own hell!"

Now, by the standards of many contemporary writers, that would be such a mild imprecation that an antagonist would consider it suitably answered with an obscenity or two. It must be just about the most genteel, and grammatically the most complex, insult to have been hurled in American fiction since Henry James. But it turns out be the turning point of Timmy's career. As a result of it, he quarrels with his wife (who feels Timmy should apologize to Emlen, which he does, under pressure), quarrels with his sponsor at the firm, and finally, having decided that there is no middle ground between his ideals and the great world, leaves his wife and children, takes up with Emlen's first cousin, a worldly and charming girl, and begins practicing law as ruthlessly and cynically as he can. He comes a cropper, of course, because he does not know how to be tough at the right times, and after his conscience has gnawed at him for a while about a rather shady distribution of a trust, he quite unnecessarily confesses in court to malpractice, and fades out under the shadow of possible disbarment.

In essence, this is the familiar comedy of the boy from the provinces being debauched by the city slickers—although, with a telling stroke of irony, Mr. Auchincloss makes his innocent one the boy brought up in the city, while the adopted New Yorkers, restless and ambitious, are the worldly ones. But Timmy is so ironbound in his initial idealism, so abandoned in his overnight defection to legal and social opportunism, and in general so impulsive in his reaction to every situation that one is perhaps inclined to laugh at him more than Mr. Auchincloss has intended. He is entirely real, though, and in spite of his erratic behavior he is likable. One thinks at the end, "Well, good old Timmy, isn't it just like him to go and do a fool thing like that! When they made Timmy, they left out the shock absorbers. He takes everything right in the stomach."

What we are offered besides Timmy is a great deal of witty social observation of uptown and downtown New York life, and some fascinating information about the inner workings of Wall Street law firms. The old-line, philosophically inclined lawyer, Knox, and the smoother, more practical, more opportunistic Dale are first-rate portraits, as are Timmy's two girls: Ann, his loyal, stubborn, rather unimaginative wife, and Eileen, an appealing idealization of urban sophistication. As for the legal matters, this midtown observer found them lucidly explained and continuously interesting, although I can't help wondering what is going to be said downtown about Mr. Auchincloss' implication that corporate practice is the province of purists and geniuses while estates and trusts tend to fall to men of expediency.

Apart from his knowledge of the law, Mr. Auchincloss probably knows more about traditional New York City society than any other good novelist now working. Furthermore, he seems to believe in the continuing importance of what is left of such society, and the values it attempts to preserve and hand down. It is precisely the background presence of such belief that makes his satirical jibes so entertaining, and makes the rather neat, foursquare world of his books so comforting to read about. *The Great World and Timothy Colt* appeals in part, perhaps unintentionally, to the escapist impulse; but it also shows how traditional writing methods and social attitudes can throw a refreshing light on parts of the contemporary scene.— John Brooks, "Ideals on Trial," *NYTBR*, Oct. 21, 1956, pp. 4, 50

⟨*Venus in Sparta*⟩ is Louis Auchincloss' seventh book and fifth novel since *The Indifferent Children* (1947). It is obviously high time someone pointed out that he is one of our very best young novelists. This is far more than a matter of his knowledge of "the highest stratum of American society" or of his alleged resemblance to Edith Wharton. It is true Mr. Auchincloss knows a good deal about the successful and indifferent children of the earth. The busy dowagers like Aunt Jo Cummings (*Sybil*), with their crude sense of glory, the Gertrude Farishes (*Venus in Sparta*), with their brooding terror of life, the Gerald Hunts (*A Law for the Lion*), who live the ordered lives of the emotionally dead—these people he represents with such complete and quiet understanding that it is easy to overlook their horror, and their ultimate pathos.

What moves Mr. Auchincloss is the miracle of the developed heart flourishing incongruously in the great world. The heroines of his novels—Syvvie Tremaine (*The Indifferent Children*), Sybil Rodman (*Sybil*), Eloise Dilworth (*A Law for the Lion*), Ann Colt (*The Great World and Timothy Colt*)—are the wholly intent and touchingly gawky kind of people who dominate his imagination. Their honesty is his comedy: when Timmy asks Ann if she loves him, she cries, almost petulantly, "Well, you know I do!" Everyone is astonished to discover that the equally misfit heroine of one of the short stories in *The Injustice Collectors* is, as her aunt suddenly realizes, "a saint! That's what saints are!"

The problem for such people is freedom, release "from the task of trying to comprehend and live by the standards of others." The ultimate reason for Mr. Auchincloss' brilliant image of the well-to-do world of Chelton School, New York, and Eastern Bay is that its standards are the most difficult to get free of. At least since *A Law for the Lion* (1953) he has been considering the possibility of the law's triumph. In that book Eloise Dilworth is made satisfied with her loneliness; in the last chapter Mr. Auchincloss even provides a slightly ironic happy ending for Hilda Dilworth to distract us—and perhaps himself—from any doubts there may be. But in his next book Timothy Colt has nothing to live by but "a *willed* truth," and Michael Farish, the hero of *Venus in Sparta*, has, at the end, nothing at all.

With this novel, then, Mr. Auchincloss confronts defeat, though he is only beginning to see all that defeat means to him. Michael Farish of the Hudson River Trust Company has put himself, "carefully, self-consciously, at times agonizingly, in step" with his world, leaving only one tiny escape, a concealed legal blunder with which he believes he can destroy his career whenever necessary. His ambition to become head of Hudson is a fantasy to which he clings only because he suspects, rightly, that his alternative is chaos.

When he discovers his wife's unfaithfulness, the situation goes out of control, just as it did for Timothy Colt when Ann made him apologize to George Emlen. Michael then commits himself to freedom, only to discover that his Venus armed, Alida Parr, is worse than his wife and that the surrogate thinks his legal blunder good law. His wife's first husband had called Michael "Young Lochinvar." It is just right: Michael has about as much chance of finding freedom in the great world of the indifferent children as Lochinvar would have had.

Mr. Auchincloss works out this history with his unfailing awareness of all that the great world is, but, as Michael sinks into what is never called despair, the story is drastically fore-shortened. The nightmare of random impulses in which he exists is intensely real, but we do not learn enough from the Mexican episodes—which are meant to reveal the sources of his despair—really to feel it. Nevertheless, *Venus in Sparta* has the most important subject Mr. Auchincloss has yet tackled and is a big step forward for a writer who commands his experience as very few of our younger writers can.—ARTHUR MIZEN-ER, "Young Lochinvar Rides to Defeat," *NYTBR*, Sept. 21, 1958, p. 4

After the violence of James Baldwin's *Another Country*, the turgidity of Philip Roth's *Letting Go*, and the complexity and intensity of Doris Lessing's *The Golden Notebook*, Louis Auchincloss's *Portrait in Brownstone* is a pleasant change. Auchincloss knows so well what he can do and goes about his job with such quiet competence that his novels are always satisfying, and *Portrait in Brownstone* is Auchincloss at his best.

Auchincloss, as has often been said, is a novelist of manners, one of the few extant. Like Edith Wharton, for whom he has strong but not uncritical admiration, he writes about people of wealth and position, about what is sometimes called "good society." No part of American society is or ever has been stable, but in good society there is at least an air of stability. Certain assumptions are shared, for a time at any rate, and there is some agreement as to what constitutes proper behavior. Against such a background the subtler human relationships can be studied with a precision that is quite impossible in more turbulent situations, and this is the great virtue of the novel of manners as written by Jane Austen and Henry James and all the rest of Auchincloss's predecessors. . . .

The portrait of Derrick ⟨in *Portrait in Brownstone*⟩ is an admirable piece of work. Auchincloss knows Wall Street, and he has frequently made good use of his knowledge. He is not concerned, however, with the mysteries of finance but with the human beings to be encountered downtown. Derrick is not, in Auchincloss's eyes, a villain, but he is not a likable individual. He is a cold man, except for his romantic passion for Geraldine; arrogant, merciless, contemptuous. After ten years of marriage Ida reflects: "His self-sufficiency had had the effect of encasing my feeling for him in a cold-storage cellar where all of its strength but not all of its sweetness had been perpetuated. I no longer liked many of my thoughts about Derrick." Derrick is the kind of character one can believe in but would just as soon not meet.

Ida, on the other hand, is likable if not always admirable. She accepts, without too much difficulty, the way of life into which she was born. Strongly loyal to her family, she suffers her first great disillusionment with Derrick when he removes from the title of the firm the name of Uncle Linn Tremain, to whom he owes so much. But she is loyal to Derrick, too, and to the children she has borne him.

The great point about Ida is that she is not crushed by Derrick, although she might so easily have been. After they have been married for more than twenty years, he says: "Ida fascinates me. I've never been able to make the least dent in the wall of her preconceptions." She can act decisively and even unconventionally in the matter of her daughter's second marriage, and the strength she has held in reserve makes itself felt as Derrick's strength is waning. A relative tells her, "You have a whole arsenal of weapons that you've never even peeked into. Well, *peek!* Reach in, dearie, and fight for your life." She fights, all right, manipulating her son into the marriage she wants him to make, and preserving the position of her son-in-law. She is acute enough to know that she is adopting Derrick's role—"I had become, like him, a monster"—but she carries out the role with high efficiency, and Derrick in the end is grateful.

Auchincloss tells the story in a neat, dry style that repeatedly gives great pleasure. Of the relations between Derrick and Geraldine he observes, "The affair, like everything else in her life, including her brief conversion to the Catholic Church, turned out to be something of a disappointment. . . . It was hardly agreeable to feel like a piece of cheese which had fallen into the jaws of a patiently waiting fox or like another share of stock in the bursting Hartley portfolio."

The astringent style is appropriate to Auchincloss's attitude. Unlike J. P. Marquand, whom he somewhat resembles in choice of subject matter, he is given neither to satire nor nostalgia. (Marquand was often divided between them.) Auchincloss takes his people completely for granted. "The rich are different from us," Scott Fitzgerald is supposed to have said. They are different, Auchincloss would seem to be replying, in interesting but essentially minor ways. They are like most of the rest of us in being neither spectacularly good nor spectacularly bad.

What distinguishes the novel, as I suggested at the outset, is its subtlety. Sometimes we have to be hit over the head, as James Baldwin hits us, and I have no doubt that I shall remember *Another Country* when *Portrait in Brownstone* has grown misty in my mind; but the world is not all of one piece, and the insights of an Auchincloss have their importance for us. The questions he raises are not cataclysmic, but they are persistent.—GRANVILLE HICKS, "*Portrait in Brownstone*" (1962), *Literary Horizons*, 1970, pp. 188–91

The title of Louis Auchincloss's latest novel ⟨*The Book Class*⟩ refers to a lunch-time literary seminar, held monthly by a dozen former debutantes during the early years of this century.

The Book Class, of course, also refers to that tony social stratum, which Mr. Auchincloss has dissected in novel after novel. It is a hermetic, snobbish class, acutely tribal in its rituals and intensely status-conscious, a class that defines "comfortable" as owning a brownstone on the Upper East Side, a country house on Long Island—maintained by half a dozen servants—several cars and maybe a yacht or two. The men have all graduated from Groton and Yale to cushy Wall Street jobs; and their wives are free to spend their days in such high-minded pursuits as shopping, lunching and gossip. Though these people do their share of complaining about the appalling conditions of modern life, they never shirk their duty of keeping up appearances—even during Prohibition, they have two wines at dinner.

As usual, Mr. Auchincloss delineates the manners and mores of this self-made, American aristocracy with glossy, efficient prose, garnished with a pinch of irony and a dab of melodrama. No doubt all the allusions in this novel to Henry James and Edith Wharton are there to remind the reader that Mr. Auchincloss means to follow in their illustrious tradition, but while he is adept enough at portraying the effects of a rarified milieu on character, his narrative lacks a necessary density and texture.

Like the shiny parquet floors of their apartment houses, Mr. Auchincloss's people are just a little too finely polished, a little too tidily assembled, to really intrigue the reader. Further, there is a tendency, on the author's part, to compress their dilemmas and intrigues into a single line or paragraph, and as a consequence, the characters hover on the verge of becoming actual personages—interesting in the way that our friends and colleagues are—only to collapse back into the realm of cliché. We may feel, for instance, a flicker of interest in Leila—a member of the Book Class, initially described as a frustrated beauty, whose one hobby consists of having her jewelry reset—but we soon discover that she is just another regretful divorcée, addicted to pills and liquor and self-pity.

As for the other members of the Book Class, they, too, represent a fairly predictable collection of upper-class attitudes and postures. A startling number of them have high foreheads, aquiline noses and blond hair; and almost all speak in the same chatty, superior tones, their sentences bristling with exclamation points and an inexplicable number of theater metaphors.

There is Georgia Bristed, the formidable and unflappable hostess of a right-wing literary salon; Justine Bannard, the unhappily married granddaughter of a famous mining tycoon; Mylo Jessup, a "Madonna-like flapper," resigned to sublimating her artistic impulses to the hearty, outdoorsy esthetic of her polo-playing husband; Adeline Bloodgood, a pretty spinster who has mortgaged her youth to work for an eminent old man, and Cornelia Gates, a bossy, high-spirited society woman, cowed by her dour husband.

The portraits of these women are presented by Mr. Auchincloss from the point of view of Cornelia's son, Christopher Gates. Prissy, cynical and irritatingly self-righteous, Christopher is himself something of a stereotype—a snooty, homosexual interior decorator, quick with the wicked bon mot but always ready to lend a sympathetic ear to his mother's friends. He is apparently such a wonderful confidant that the members of the Book Class are all drawn to him like a magnet. They hand him their memoirs and their letters, and invite him to luncheon tête-à-têtes, where they politely spill their guts over a cup of tea. All this makes for a somewhat contrived, episodic narrative, in which nearly every chapter pivots around the disclosure of one woman's secrets and fears.

What holds the book together are Christopher's—and Mr. Auchincloss's—fine-grained observations about the world inhabited by these women, a world dominated by decorum and certain inviolable rules of conduct. Men are expected to marry within their social class, and women are expected to put their husband's needs before their own. One may help a needy friend by paying hospital and doctor's bills, but not by putting up with maudlin scenes; and grief, caused by the death of a friend, is permissible only if that person falls into "the permitted mourning category."

In this novel, as in *The Rector of Justin* and *The Winthrop Covenant*, Mr. Auchincloss implies that such rules were once the glue that held together a stern, but deeply felt system of ethical values. As they have been handed down, generation to generation, however, they have become little more than useful justifications for preserving a selfish status quo. Indeed, the world of the Book Class ultimately revolves around the cold, hard transactions of money and social standing, not around the humane ones of love and understanding. Perhaps it is this fact that accounts for the cool tone of *The Book Class*, and, in the end, leaves the reader feeling so detached.—MICHIKO KAKUTANI, *NYT*, July 26, 1984, p. 20

At first thought, it seems an unlucky blow of chance that this slight, spare, skillful novel ⟨*The Book Class*⟩ by Louis Auchincloss should appear in the same year and so soon after 88-year-old Helen Hooven Santmyer's life work,. . . *And Ladies of the Club*. Both novels use a woman's literary group as framework—Mrs. Santmyer to give us a history of a small Ohio city through the stories of its dominant families and Mr. Auchincloss to limn the lives and influence of women in the segment of American life he has made his own, New York society. Mrs. Santmyer's seems the weightier and more important book.

On second thought, one realizes the two books should not be compared. They are for different readers. In crass market terms,. . . *And Ladies of the Club* is for supporters of the bestseller list, with their appetite for historical detail and "the big read"; Mr. Auchincloss's novel is for the young and upwardly mobile (who are said to like short books) and those who fancy, in their imagination at least, a world of class and status built on wealth and family. Mr. Auchincloss has written 27 books of fiction; their setting has usually been the "comfortable" world, which meant "in the 1930's . . . an apartment or brownstone in town, a house in the country, having five or six maids, two to three cars, several clubs and one's children all in private schools." No one does it better.

The current Auchincloss evokes the others. The narrator is that favorite of the author's—the somewhat effeminate misfit who is of that world but just enough of an outsider to be a good observer. In *The Book Class*, he is Christopher Gates, an elderly decorator, driven to desperation by "the lawyer in menacing black sequins, the surgeon in blood red *crêpe de Chine*," who harangue him about sexual discrimination at dinner parties. He makes a claim in a television symposium that women's liberation has cost women most of the domestic, economic and political power it took their ancestors 2,000 years to achieve. In consequence, he says plaintively, "I have every woman's libber in the city down on me." He decides to justify himself by making a sober appraisal of just what power the wives and daughters of the managers of money and industry did hold and uses the members of his mother's book discussion group for his study.

These women are alike in being serious about the lives they lead and, except in one case, their refusal to use feminine wiles to attain their ends. "They use tribalism instead," Christopher Gates says in summing them up. Collectively, they had impressed him as a young man with the idea that women are intellectually and intuitively superior to men but not "nicer."

There are, quite naturally, echoes in these women of the women in the earlier Auchincloss books. Leila, to whom "the great business of life is men," reminds one of Cordelia Turnbull in *The Rector of Justin*. And almost all of them, as wives of bankers, lawyers, businessmen—even a potential headmaster—seem very like Ada Tilney in *Powers of Attorney*, who with "her high pale brow under her faded brown hair . . . was like a rock washed clean by years of [her husband's] absences at conventions, testimonial dinners, committee meetings, or simply at the office." They are busy, these women, running households, presiding at charity board meetings, shopping, lunching, entertaining—but their lives seem peripheral to the lives of the men in their world.

From the beginning, Christopher Gates admitted that the women to whom he had attributed power had no real political or economic clout. After examining their lives, he asks himself, "Just what was the 'power' of the Book Class? . . . Was it a figment of my imagination?" In the end, he can make only one small affirmation: "Those women continued to occupy an unduly large space in the reflections and fantasies of their surviving children." The reader must ask why.

The only surviving member of the Book Class insists that these women did not waste their lives. They accepted their world and their position and believed they had a duty to maintain both. They knew they were privileged and felt under an obligation "to be good" and, one infers, to do good.

It is Mr. Auchincloss's achievement that, although, as one of his characters asserts, the world and society of the Book Class is as long gone as Imperial Rome, he makes even its peripheral characters interesting and in so doing raises questions for our own era. Would these women have been happier now—"with careers and divorces"? As he has the last of them answer, it's hard to say.—ABIGAIL McCARTHY, "Tribalism, Not Feminism," *NYTBR*, Aug. 12, 1984, p. 4

JAMES W. TUTTLETON
From "Cozzens and Auchincloss"
The Novel of Manners in America
1972, pp. 245–61

III

Auchincloss is the rightful heir of the tradition (of the novel of manners) as it has been handed down through the great European and American practitioners of the form. Auchincloss is not only conscious of the tradition but he has written extensively about it—in relation to the fiction of Proust, Trollope, Meredith, Thackeray, George Eliot, Mrs. Wharton, Marquand, James, and O'Hara. And because he has offered us an orientation toward his fiction by calling himself a "Jacobite"—that is, a follower of Henry James, many reviewers have concluded that it is enough to describe him as an imitator of the Master. Auchincloss calls himself a Jacobite "because so much of my lifetime's reading has been over the shoulder of Henry James." To read the criticism, letters, and fiction of James, Auchincloss has observed, "is to be conducted through the literature of his time, English, American, French and Russian, by a kindly guide of infinitely good manners, who is also infinitely discerning, tasteful and conscientious." James, for Auchincloss, has always been a "starting point," a "common denominator."[1] But Auchincloss has always, once started, gone his own way—often qualifying and contesting, as well as enlarging, the social insights of the nineteenth-century novelist of manners. . . . Not all of his novels are novels of manners— he is fascinated by the unexhausted possibilities of the novel of character—and not all of his novels of manners are of equal interest. Nevertheless, his talents have developed so rapidly since 1960, his social and psychological insight has deepened so, and his formal designs are so fascinating that nearly every one of his books repays perusal.

The world brought to life in his novels of manners is the world of the metropolitan rich in New York City—particularly the lives of the lawyers, bankers, trust officers, corporation executives, and their wives and daughters. As a lawyer, Auchincloss knows them in their Park Avenue penthouse apartments and in their soberly dignified Wall Street offices. He sees the glitter and glamour of their world, its arrogant materialism and its unexpected generosities. He knows the rigidity of its conventions—just how far they can be bent, at what point they break—or break a character. He understands what happens to the idealistic men and the unfulfilled women of this world. And he is able to tell their stories with unusual sympathy. Rarely has Auchincloss ventured from this small but exclusive world because it is the world he knows best. From Henry James he learned the lesson that Edith Wharton would not: the lesson that she *must* be "tethered in native pastures, even if it reduces her to a backyard in New York."[2] The New York haut monde is Louis Auchincloss's backyard. His ten novels are his Austenean two inches of ivory.

IV

Auchincloss most nearly resembles James in the emphasis he gives to moral issues that grow out of the social lives of the very rich. Yet he differs from the Master in the informed analysis he is able to give to the nice problems of ethics in the legal profession—a command of the world of Wall Street brokers and bankers which James himself sorely regretted not having. *Venus in Sparta*, for example, balances the story of a trust officer who risks malfeasance by concealing evidence affecting the interpretation of a will with the story of a couple whose marriage ends in adultery, divorce, and a suicide. In *The Embezzler*, Guy Prime steals a large sum of money for reasons ultimately ambiguous. But his partner's affair with Prime's wife suggests that together they have robbed him of his capacity to function both as a broker and as a husband. In *The Great World and Timothy Colt*, an idealistic lawyer deliberately insults a client and refuses to apologize because his act has been a matter of conscience, not superficial bad manners. But when his wife, fearing that he will lose his long-sought partnership, compels him to apologize—to compromise his integrity, as he sees it—he enters the "great world" with a vengeance: he models his conduct on that of his amoral partner; he has an affair with another woman; and he conceals information in such a way as to neglect his trust. Colt draws back from utter disaster before the point of no return; but recovering his integrity costs him his brilliant legal career.

In some of his novels of manners Auchincloss explores the ambiguities of selfhood, affirming, finally, the freedom and autonomy of the human personality. I have already suggested the extent to which novelists of manners like Edith Wharton, John O'Hara, and J. P. Marquand—who have been profoundly influenced by the behaviorism of the naturalistic sciences—tend to believe that the personality is conditioned by the material environment and to recreate character through descriptions of houses, clothes, furniture, and the like. Auchincloss rejects this approach to characterization. For him, "character" exists independent of the web of the material environment that surrounds it. As Ida Trask Hartley observes, in describing the narrow gray limestone facade of Mr. Robbins's house—with its "grinning lions' heads and balconies for flowerpots supported by squatting ladies, and topped with a giant dormer studded with bull's-eye windows": "Nobody passing it today would believe that it had not been built by the most pushing parvenu. Yet I know how little the houses of that era sometimes expressed the souls of their occupants."[3]

In *A Law for the Lion*, Eloise Dilworth seeks to discover

whether there is any real identity beneath the various roles she has played during her lifetime—the childish niece to her aunt and uncle, the submissive wife to her indifferent husband, the taken-for-granted mother to her children. Her search for an answer leads her to reject the meaningless manners and conventions of the social world she has been brought up in. But her losses are more than compensated for by her discovery that there is a real self beneath the functions imposed on her by her social existence. This kind of "Who am I?" theme is also developed in *Sybil*, *Portrait in Brownstone*, and *The House of Five Talents*. A variation on it is the "Who is he?" theme developed in *The Rector of Justin*. In this novel Frank Prescott, recently deceased headmaster of a preparatory school, is recreated through the differing recollections and impressions of several characters—the priggish young admirer, the irreverent daughter, the wife, the friends, the students, and alumni. What the novel suggests is that we can never know what Prescott was really like because none of the narrators knew the real Prescott—he presented a different side to each of them. It might well be asked whether there was any "real" Prescott behind his various masks. The answer is yes, but we can never know him except through his various biographers. Auchincloss's dramatic technique in this "conventional novel of character" creates a built-in ambiguity comparable to that of James's *The Awkward Age*.

Auchincloss's preoccupation with identity in fiction is based, I believe, on a question posed by James, in a conversation between Isabel Archer and Madame Merle in *The Portrait of a Lady*, about the "shell of circumstances" and the irreducible self: "What shall we call our 'self'?" Madame Merle asks Isabel. "Where does it begin? Where does it end? It overflows into everything that belongs to us—and then it flows back again. I know a large part of myself is in the clothes I choose to wear. I've a great respect for *things*! One's self—for other people—is one's expression of one's self; and one's house, one's furniture, one's garments, the books one reads, the company one keeps—these things are all expressive."[4] Auchincloss rejects the behaviorism of Madame Merle. The personality of Frank Prescott is never adequately expressed by the impressions of others, just as the irreducible "I" of Eloise Dilworth is never fully expressed by her furniture or the sum of her functions.

But to make this point is to oversimplify what is in fact a complex problem for Auchincloss as a creator of character. For in some of his novels, he is at great pains to show that society (with its misimpressions) and time (with its alteration of conventions) *do* impinge on the self which—for better or worse—is expressed through its various roles. For Eloise, Timothy Colt, Sybil Hilliard, Ida Hartley, and Augusta Millinder, the triumph of the personality over the roles imposed by the external world makes for a kind of limited victory of the self. But Auchincloss's world has its darker depths, and his novels by no means always end in such "moral triumphs." For Geraldine Brevoort in *Portrait*, for Michael Farrish in *Venus in Sparta*, and for Guy Prime in *The Embezzler*, the world is an arena of ever more burdensome responsibilities arising out of the illusory importance of caste and class. . . .

VI

In semipolitical literary criticism there are sometimes objections to the kind of people Cozzens and Auchincloss write about. It is sometimes said, for example, that the world of New York society people is somehow not as interesting as that of sharecroppers, boxers, or big game hunters. Granville Hicks has confessed this bias in remarking that "to many people, myself included, an Italian boy who robs a poor Jew is a more

challenging subject than an upperclass New Yorker who misappropriates funds, and a bewildered intellectual in search of wholeness of spirit belongs more truly to our times than the aged headmaster of a fashionable preparatory school."[5]

But there is no necessary reason why this claim should be true. *The Assistant* and *Herzog* may be better novels than *The Embezzler* and *The Rector of Justin*. But their superiority has nothing to do with the subject matter or the "relevance" of these books—it has to do only with the greater artistry by which the novels of Bellow and Malamud are brought more vividly to life. In justifying the attention he gives to people like Guy Prime, Augusta Millinder, Ida Trask, and Frank Prescott, I find it instructive to remember Auchincloss's observation on the universality of Tolstoy's art: "What he understands is that if a human being is described completely, his class makes little difference. He becomes a human being on the printed page, and other humans, of whatever class, can recognize themselves in his portrait. The lesson of Tolstoy is precisely how little of life, not how much, the artist needs."[6]

His view of Proust also casts light on Auchincloss's choice of subject. In arguing that there has never been "so brilliant or so comprehensive a study of the social world" as that found in Proust, Auchincloss observes: "To him the differences between class and class are superficial. Snobbishness reigns on all levels, so why does it matter which level one selects to study? Why not, indeed, pick the highest level, particularly if one's own snobbishness is thus gratified? Society in Proust parades before us, having to represent not a segment of mankind, but something closer to mankind itself. It is the very boldness of Proust's assumption that his universe is *the* universe . . . that gives to his distorted picture a certain universal validity. It is his faith that a sufficiently careful study of each part will reveal the whole, that the analysis of a dinner party can be as illuminating as the analysis of a war. It is his glory that he very nearly convinces us."[7]

Without wishing to draw the parallel too closely, I submit that Auchincloss also sees that the differences between classes are superficial and that there is therefore no adequate reason why one should not deal with headmasters and lawyers, bankers and brokers, if they permit the kind of social analysis that illuminates our essential human predicament. The problem implicit in his choice is that of making us believe that his universe is—if not *the* universe—at least a *believable* universe and in describing his characters so fully and convincingly that we do not care about the class they belong to. It is Auchincloss's difficulty that, as good as most of his novels are, he does not always so convince us. But the limitation is one of the writer's talent, not of his material.

It is probably a mistake to think about Auchincloss's characters as belonging to a distinct "class." He does not believe that the United States is a classless society. But he does recognize that it is not possible for the contemporary American novelist of manners to write the kind of fiction produced by Howells, Wharton, and James. The increasing democratization of the United States, he argues in *Reflections of a Jacobite*, has resulted in a rearrangement of social attitudes, so that today "snobbishness is more between groups than classes, more between cliques than between rich and poor." "Surely there is a difference," he remarks, "between the feelings of the man who has not been asked to dinner and those of the man who has been thrown down the front stairs."[8]

Most of these groups, however (labor-capital, East-West, North-South, young-old, workers-intelligentsia), do not provide much for the would-be novelist of manners. "It is my simple thesis," Auchincloss has argued, "that the failure more generally to produce this kind of novel is not attributable to the decadence or escapism of mid-twentieth century writers, but rather to the increasingly classless nature of our society which does not lend itself to this kind of delineation. I do not mean by this that we are any duller than the Victorians, but simply that the most exciting and significant aspects of our civilization are no longer to be found in the distance and hostility between the social strata."[9] Consequently, like James, he has turned increasingly toward the inward lives of his characters in order to explain why, in this classless but cliquish society, people hang on to their snobbish ways as they do.

The divided career of Louis Auchincloss (as lawyer-novelist) and his indifference to sociological explanations of evil have led other critics to attack Auchincloss's social and moral criticism as fakery, and to claim that Auchincloss is captivated by the very social prejudices which are his subject. Robert M. Adams, for example, has ridiculed Auchincloss for writing, "like a latter-day Trollope, a pseudo-critique of commercialism which collapses docilely as soon as one perceives it is being launched from a platform provided by commercialism itself."[10] The assumption on which this statement is based—that the novelist must stand outside the world he seeks to criticize before his criticism can be authentic—is arrant nonsense. Auchincloss may be a conservative; he may not be interested in reform or in Old or New Left radicalism. But this fact in itself does not invalidate his critique of the limitations—moral and social—of the world he belongs to and describes. There is certainly adequate rational, theological, and moral justification for the claim that evil arises from selfish, dissipated, snobbish people as well as from economic or sociological causes.[11]

No politician, Auchincloss takes society, for literature, more or less as he finds it. But he is not guilty of what Edith Wharton called "the tendency not infrequent in novelists of manners—Balzac and Thackeray among them—to be dazzled by contact with the very society they satirize."[12] He is fascinated by the world he portrays: he loves the details of an estate settlement as much as Thackeray loved the stylish little supper parties of Mrs. Rawdon Crawley; he is as fascinated by the complexities of a corporation merger as Proust was by the intricacies of precedence; and he is as delighted by the eccentricities of the rich as Balzac was by the spectacle of miserly greed. But if Auchincloss loves his world, he is not taken in by it. Conscious of the moral and social incongruities between his world and the world of, say, Malamud, he is as disturbed as any reader of the *Partisan Review* that no matter how painstakingly Proust "underlines the dullness, the selfishness, and the fatuity of the Guermantes set, they remain to the end still invested with much of the glamour in which his imagination clothed them."[13]

But Auchincloss has no wish to idealize or glamorize his "aristocracy" or to claim for it a nostalgic virtue inconsistent with the known facts of New York City social life. Nor is he "hankering after any good old days." He has asked whether anyone would wish to return to "a New York where servants slept in unheated cubicles on the top of drafty brownstones, with an evening off every second week. . . ."[14] His love for the elegance and iniquity of this world is the love of an artist for his material, which is quite another thing from his feeling for it as a man. Every writer, he has observed, has two points of view "about the society in which he lives: that of a citizen and that of an artist. The latter is concerned only with the suitability of society as material for his art. Just as a liberal journalist may secretly rejoice at the rise of a Senator McCarthy because of the opportunity which it affords him to write brilliant and scathing denunciations of demagogues, so will the eye of the novelist of manners light up at the first glimpse of social injustice. For his books must depend for their life blood on contrast and are bound to lose both significance and popularity in a classless society."[15] Our awareness of the distinction between society as experienced and society as transformed in fiction ought to discourage us from condemning, as a reactionary, the novelist who insists on exploring inequities and ambiguities from inside the social citadel. Auchincloss's value is that he keeps alive a lively tradition in novels that are themselves vital proof of his considerable talent.

Notes

1. Louis Auchincloss, *Reflections of a Jacobite* (Boston, 1961), pp. vii–viii.
2. Henry James, *The Letters of Henry James*, ed. Percy Lubbock, 2 vols. (New York, 1920), I:396.
3. Louis Auchincloss, *Portrait in Brownstone* (Boston, 1962), p. 76.
4. Henry James, *The Portrait of a Lady*, 2 vols. (New York, 1951), I:287–88.
5. Granville Hicks, "A Bad Legend in His Lifetime," *Saturday Review* 5, February 1966, pp. 35–36.
6. Auchincloss, *Reflections of a Jacobite*, p. 163.
7. Ibid., p. 111.
8. Ibid., pp. 148–49.
9. Ibid., p. 142.
10. Robert M. Adams, "Saturday Night and Sunday Morning," *New York Review of Books*, 9 July 1964, p. 15.
11. Auchincloss, *Reflections of a Jacobite*, p. 8.
12. Edith Wharton, *A Backward Glance* (New York, 1934), p. 325.
13. Auchincloss, *Reflections of a Jacobite*, pp. 104–5.
14. Ibid., pp. 139–40.
15. Ibid., p. 140.

GORE VIDAL

From "The Great World and Louis Auchincloss" (1974)
Matters of Fact and Fiction
1977, pp. 29–33

At any given moment the subject or the matter of American fiction is limited by the prevailing moral prejudices and assumptions of the residents in book-chat land. U-novels must always be predictably experimental (I reserve for another occasion a scrutiny of those interesting cacti) while the respectable P-novel is always naturalistic, usually urban, often Jewish, always middle-class, and, of course, deeply, sincerely heterosexual.

Conscious of what the matter of fiction *ought* to be, Mr. Hicks somewhat nervously puts Louis Auchincloss on his list. On the one hand, Auchincloss deals entirely with the American scene, writes in a comfortably conventional manner, and is one of the few intellectuals who write popular novels. On the other hand, despite these virtues, Auchincloss is not much thought of in either the P or the U world and Mr. Hicks is forced to buzz uneasily: "Although I have read and reviewed most of Louis Auchincloss's work in the past twelve years, I hesitated about including him in this volume." So the original Debrett must have felt when first called upon to include the Irish peerage. "Certainly he has not been one of the movers and shakers of the postwar period." As opposed, presumably, to Reynolds Price, Wright Morris, Herbert Gold, Bernard Malamud, and the other powerhouses on Mr. Hicks's list. Actually, only two or three of Mr. Hicks's writers could be said to have made any contribution at all to world literature. But that is a matter of taste. After all, what, Pontius, *is* literature?

Mr. Hicks returns worriedly to the *matter* of fiction. Apparently Auchincloss "has written for the most part about 'good' society, the well-to-do and the well-bred. And he has written about them with authority. What bothers me is not that he writes about this little world but that he seems to be aware of no other. Although he is conscious of its faults, he never questions its values in any serious way." This is fascinating. I have read all of Auchincloss's novels and I cannot recall one that did not in a most serious way question the values of his "little world." Little world!

It is a tribute to the cunning of our rulers and to the stupidity of our intellectuals (book-chat division, anyway) that the world Auchincloss writes about, the domain of Wall Street bankers and lawyers and stockbrokers, is thought to be irrelevant, a faded and fading genteel-gentile enclave when, in actual fact, this little world comprises the altogether too vigorous and self-renewing ruling class of the United States—an oligarchy that is in firm control of the Chase Manhattan Bank, American foreign policy, and the decision-making processes of both the Republican and Democratic parties; also, most "relevantly," Auchincloss's characters set up and administer the various foundations that subsidize those universities where academics may serenely and dully dwell like so many frogs who think their pond the ocean—or the universe the university.

Of all our novelists, Auchincloss is the only one who tells us how our rulers behave in their banks and their boardrooms, their law offices and their clubs. Yet such is the vastness of our society and the remoteness of academics and book-chatterers from actual power that those who should be most in this writer's debt have no idea what a useful service he renders us by revealing and, in some ways, by betraying his class. But then how can the doings of a banker who is white and gentile and rich be *relevant* when everyone knows that the only meaningful American experience is to be Jewish, lower-middle-class, and academic? Or (in Mr. Hicks's words), "As I said a while ago and was scolded for saying, the characteristic hero of our time is a misfit." Call me Granville.

Ignorance of the real world is not a new thing in our literary life. After the Second World War, a young critic made a splash with a book that attributed the poverty of American fiction to the lack of a class system—a vulgar variation on Henry James's somewhat similar but usually misunderstood observations about American life. This particular writer came from a small town in the Midwest; from school, he had gone into the service and from there into a university. Since he himself had never seen any sign of a class system, he decided that the United States was a truly egalitarian society. It should be noted that one of the charms of the American arrangement is that a citizen can go through a lifetime and never know his true station in life or who his rulers are.

Of course our writers know that there are rich people hidden away somewhere (in the gossip columns of Suzy, in the novels of Louis Auchincloss), but since the Depression the owners of the country have played it cool, kept out of sight, consumed inconspicuously. Finally, no less a P (now P-U)-writer than that lifelong little friend of the rich Ernest Hemingway felt obliged to reassure us that the rich are really just folks. For the P-writer the ruling class does not exist as a subject for fiction if only because the rulers are not to be found in his real world of desperate suburbs. The U-writer knows about the Harkness plan—but then what is a harkness? Something to do with horse racing? While the names that the foundations bear do not suggest to him our actual rulers—only their stewards in the bureaucracy of philanthropy, the last strong-hold of the great immutable fortunes.

The serious P-writer knows that he must reflect the world he lives in: the quotidian of the average man. To look outside that world is to be untrue and, very possibly, undemocratic. To write about the actual rulers of the world we live in (assuming

that they exist, of course) is to travel in fantasy land. As a result, novels to do with politics, the past, money, manners, power are as irrelevant to the serious P-writer as are the breathy commercial fictions of all the Irvingses—so unlike the higher relevancies of all the Normans.

In a society where matters of importance are invariably euphemized (how can an antipersonnel weapon actually kill?) a writer like Louis Auchincloss who writes about the way money is made and spent is going to have a very hard time being taken seriously. For one thing, it is now generally believed in book-chat land that the old rich families haven't existed since the time of Edith Wharton while the new-rich are better suited for journalistic exposés than for a treatment in the serious P- or U-novel. It is true that an indiscriminate reading public enjoys reading Auchincloss because, unlike the well-educated, they suspect that the rich are always with us and probably up to no good. But since the much-heralded death of the Wasp establishment, the matter of Auchincloss's fiction simply cannot be considered important.

This is too bad. After all, he is a good novelist, and a superb short-story writer. More important, he has made a brave effort to create his own literary tradition—a private oasis in the cactus land of American letters. He has written about Shakespeare's penchant for motiveless malignity (a peculiarly American theme), about Henry James, about our women writers as the custodians and caretakers of the values of that dour European tribe which originally killed the Indians and settled the continent.

Mr. Hicks, with his eerie gift for misunderstanding what a writer is writing about, thinks that Auchincloss is proudly showing off his class while bemoaning its eclipse by later arrivals. Actually, the eye that Auchincloss casts on his own class is a cold one and he is more tortured than complacent when he records in book after book the collapse of the Puritan ethical system and its replacement by—as far as those of us now living can tell—nothing. As for the ruling class being replaced by later arrivals, he knows (though they, apparently, do not) that regardless of the considerable stir the newcomers have made in the peripheral worlds of the universities, showbiz, and book-chat, they have made almost no impact at all on the actual power structure of the country.

Auchincloss deals with the masters of the American empire partly because they are the people he knows best and partly, I suspect, because he cannot figure them out to his own satisfaction. Were they better or worse in the last century? What is good, what is bad in business? And business (money) is what our ruling class has always been about; this is particularly obvious now that the evangelical Christian style of the last century has been abandoned by all but the most dull of our rulers' employees (read any speech by any recent president to savor what was once the very sound of Carnegie, of Gould, and of Rockefeller).

Finally, most unfashionably, Auchincloss writes best in the third person; his kind of revelation demands a certain obliqueness, a moral complexity which cannot be rendered in the confessional tone that marks so much of current American fiction, good and bad. He plays God with his characters, and despite the old-fashionedness of his literary method he is an unusually compelling narrator, telling us things that we don't know about people we don't often meet in novels—what other novelist went to school with Bill and McGenghis Bundy? Now, abruptly, he ceases to play God. The third person becomes first person as he describes in *A Writer's Capital* the world and the family that produced him, a world and family not supposed either by their own standards or by those of book-chat land to produce an artist of any kind.

JAMES BALDWIN

1924–

James Baldwin was born on August 2, 1924, in Harlem, New York City. His father, the son of a slave, was a lay preacher. Baldwin's original intention was also to direct his energies to the ministry. After receiving a deferment from military service, in 1944, however, he moved to Greenwich Village. It was there that he met Richard Wright, whose writing exerted a considerable influence on him. Baldwin received a Rosenwald Scholarship with Wright's help in 1948, and subsequently moved to Paris.

Although such fellowships are often awarded to young writers, in Baldwin's case it proved to be a crucial event in his life. Essentially, it marked the beginning of his self-imposed exile from the United States. As Baldwin later wrote in *Go Tell It on the Mountain*: "I was icily determined—more determined, really, than I knew—never to make my peace with the ghetto but to die and go to hell before I would let any white man spit on me, before I would accept my 'place' in this republic."

In 1963 he published what is perhaps his most acclaimed and controversial book, *The Fire Next Time*. Baldwin's rejection of racial separatism as preached by Black Muslims was a unique stance compared with the ideas espoused by many of his contemporaries. Baldwin continued to receive numerous awards, fellowships, and grants, and today maintains his place as one of the seminal figures in Black American literature. Even though he has not published since 1979, he explains that he is "standing in the wings again, waiting to take my cue."

Personal

Julius Lester: You have been politically engaged, but you have never succumbed to ideology, which has devoured some of the best black writers of my generation.

James Baldwin: Perhaps I did not succumb to ideology, as you put it, because I have never seen myself as a spokesman. I am a witness. In the church in which I was raised you were supposed to bear witness to the truth. Now, later on, you wonder what in the world the truth is, but you do know what a lie is.

Lester: What's the difference between a spokesman and a witness?

Baldwin: A spokesman assumes that he is speaking for others. I never assumed that—I never assumed that I could. Fannie Lou Hamer [the Mississippi civil rights organizer], for example, could speak very eloquently for herself. What I tried to do, or to interpret and make clear was that what the Republic was doing to that woman, it was also doing to itself. No society can smash the social contract and be exempt from the consequences, and the consequences are chaos for everybody in the society.

Lester: There's a confidence in your use of the word witness—a confidence about the way the world is and the way it should be. I wonder if it's possible for writers now, black or white, to have that confidence. I wonder if the world hasn't changed between the time you started and the time we started.

Baldwin: Well, it may have. In one way or another, one is very much a prisoner of his time. But I know what I've seen and what I've seen makes me know I have to say, *I know*. I won't say I believe, because I know that we can be better than we are. That's the sum total of my wisdom in all these years. We can also be infinitely worse, but I know that the world we live in now is not necessarily the best world we can make. I can't be entirely wrong. There're two things we have to do—love each other and raise our children. We have to do that! The alternative, for me, would be suicide.

Lester: That sounds romantic to me.

Baldwin: I don't think I'm romantic. If I am, I wouldn't know it, so it's kind of a fruitless question. . . .

Lester: In "Alas, Poor Richard," you write that it's "not possible to overstate the price a Negro pays to climb out of obscurity." And you go on to write that "The higher he rises, the less is his

journey worth." . . . ⟨Y⟩ou've risen higher than any black writer, even higher than Wright in terms of public acclaim, recognition and esteem. How much has the journey been worth?

Baldwin: What happened to me came as a great surprise. Obviously, in the essay, I'm speaking to some extent of a public journey, though the word public is not used. I don't feel bitter about the journey, and that may be indicative of something. I don't feel bitter and I don't feel betrayed. I was a maverick, a maverick in the sense that I depended on neither the white world nor the black world. That was the only way I could've played it. I would've been broken otherwise. I had to say, "A curse on both your houses." The fact that I went to Europe so early is probably what saved me. It gave me another touchstone—myself. Then the idea of becoming an artist as distinguished from a celebrity was real. I never wanted to become a celebrity. Being a maverick saved my life. What club could I have joined? I had to make peace with a great many things, not the least of which was my intelligence. You don't realize that you're intelligent until it gets you into trouble.

Lester: Is the celebrity James Baldwin anyone that you know?

Baldwin: That's a very good question. Not really. Not really. It's almost a garment I wear. But the celebrity never sees himself. I have some idea what I'm doing on that stage; above all, I have some idea what sustains me on that stage. But the celebrity is not exactly Jimmy, though he comes out of Jimmy and Jimmy nourishes that, too. I can see now, with hindsight, that I would've had to become a celebrity in order to survive. A boy like me with all his handicaps, real and fancied, could not have survived in obscurity. I can say that it would have had to happen this way, though I could not see it coming.

Lester: One night you were talking semicoherently about facing the fact of having to find a new language.

Baldwin: Where was I? Oh yes! I was here—at least I wasn't on television. Anyway, a language is a frame of reference, isn't it? And I can only be semicoherent about it now because I'm in the process of experimenting. I say a new language. I might say a new morality, which, in my terms, comes to the same thing. And that's on all levels—the level of color, the level of identity, the level of sexual identity, what love means, especially in a consumer society, for example. Everything is in question, according to me. One has to forge a new language to deal with it. That's as coherent as I can be about it.

Lester: What do you see as the task facing black writers today, regardless of age or generation?

Baldwin: This may sound strange, but I would say to make the question of color obsolete.

Lester: And how would a black writer do that?

Baldwin: Well, you ask me a reckless question, I'll give you a reckless answer—by realizing first of all that the world is not white. And by realizing that the real terror that engulfs the white world now is a visceral terror. I can't prove this, but I know it. It's the terror of being described by those they've been describing for so long. And that will make the concept of color obsolete. Do you see what I mean?

Lester: I see what you mean, but some black writers of my generation might say that the responsibility of black writers is to write about black people.

Baldwin: That is not a contradiction. If our voices are heard, it makes the concept of color obsolete. That has to be its inevitable result.—JULIUS LESTER, "James Baldwin: Reflections of a Maverick," *NYTBR*, May 27, 1984, pp. 22–24

General

Though Baldwin has abandoned the primitive Calvinism on which he was reared, its dogma still has him in thrall. Everything he has written is filled with a sense of human depravity, a deterministic view of the universe, a hopeless search for salvation, and a conviction that unregenerate, alienated modern man is doomed. "The human heart is deceitful and above all things desperately wicked." "There is no health in us," and our damnation is sure. In Baldwin's theology, however, there is no Messiah. The "Power" is an illusion, and the "Glory" has departed. Jehovah the Avenger will smite, for our offense is rank. Fear, loneliness, desperation, the sense of sin stalk all Baldwin's characters; all life culminates for them in a single, terrible moment, as the past is said to flash before the eyes of drowning men.—CHARLES H. NICHOLS, "The New Calvinism," *Cmty*, Jan. 1957, pp. 94–95

One looks to the essays for the motives of the fiction. The essays are indeed always dramatic—they are passionate, a sentience moves through them. They do include real experience—Baldwin's own, but slightly transformed by their subjects. And they are "personal," in the sense not of coziness, but in the fact that they create a person. They are quite as much concerned with the style—the identity, precisely—of the man speaking as they are with their various topics. They have that feeling of an intimate involvement. They are themselves, that is to say, *almost* fiction.

But then they aren't fiction. One expects of serious fiction a thoroughness and a probing that Baldwin's essays have not, a progress of events, a moving through contradiction and complication. The pity Baldwin brings in his essays to what is at bottom always his own plight does not move. It is already completely formulated, and it is not analytic but appreciative. It stops short. Fiction pure would demand that he go on, into himself, that he participate in himself. And the informal essay permits him the pity without real involvement. It permits him to shift ground and in many various ways to repeat himself without going on to an end. The essays present him with many applications of an insight he has already had into his own nature and situation, and excuse him from the imaginative pursuit of it.

The essays don't have the seriousness of fiction. It happens, and by the same measure, that they don't have the seriousness of essays either, even though the insight on which

they are built has every validity. The single insight does apply equally to Baldwin's own experience as a Negro and an American, and to what was the position of William Faulkner, and to that of expatriates in Paris, and, in fact, to everyone everywhere. Raised to its metaphysical dimensions, it is that insight into man's perpetual condition which tells of man's loneliness on this isthmus of a middle state. It is the insight which Baldwin latterly, with a flourish, has come to call the tragic sense of life. There is in it not only a truth, but a cliché which becomes a significant truth only when one gets down to cases. And Baldwin's difficulty as an essayist, briefly, is that he tends to arouse expectations of cases which he doesn't satisfy. If, by writing essays, he evades the demands of fiction, by writing essays as fiction he evades the demand of thorough ideas.

. . . For a Negro writer of talent and conscience there is no avoiding the burdens of spokesmanship, and it is not only a matter of conscience and of the obvious social necessities. Indeed, it would seem that for Baldwin the very attempt to avoid spokesmanship led him to it, and if he is not very good at it, that betrays not a failure of rigor or courage but a crisis of honesty. It is the fact that in all of his fictions, including his one "white" novel, writing honestly and in pursuit of the complex personal truth, he has found himself come around to the point where there is nothing else to do but howl his frustration, or turn to essays and write spokesman-like protest. "It is quite impossible," Baldwin says in another early essay, "to write a worthwhile novel about a Jew or a Gentile or a Homosexual, for people refuse, unhappily, to function in so neat and one-dimensional a fashion." One can't, obviously, by the same token, write a novel about a Negro. But one can't either, Baldwin seems to have discovered repeatedly, write a story about a Negro and deny that he is a Negro, deny that what Ralph Ellison called the "little question of civil rights," what Alain Locke called the Negro's "shadow," do constitute much of the reality of the person.

That dilemma gives way to another. This Negro-ness as a personal reality may really be a kind of invisibility. The fact that he is a Negro, that his life is in great part the effect of a long history and a ramifying system of persecution, prevents what Baldwin calls identity. And so at the point of discovering Negro-ness, at the point where his heroes are about to discover it, Baldwin must turn to speak publicly as a Negro, to some immediately social purpose, therefore as a spokesman, to the distortion or abandonment of the personal identity. And then if he doesn't speak convincingly as a spokesman, it is because that personal identity, and not social salvation, was the goal.—MARCUS KLEIN, "James Baldwin: A Question of Identity," *After Alienation*, 1962, pp. 154–63

It has been the thesis of this appraisal that ⟨Baldwin's⟩ novels have been his "other country," one uncommonly valuable to him as a way of developing his talent, while his nonfiction has broadcast his prophecy and his reports. But the prophecy must also react upon the novels and the work as a whole, working its effect on their nature and structure. The less the problems which initiated some of the essays have to do with symptoms and appearances, the more, then, both essays and novels must expose the "unadmitted . . . fears and longings"—both white and Negro, after all, human ones. Baldwin has further pointed out in the fascinating essay "Stranger in the Village" that the race issue engages forms and symbols of blackness and whiteness which lie at the very origins of Western Civilization, like its Dionysos and Apollo, its Devil and its God. There can be no isolating of such unnamed elements of our life and no new ethical forms and language for our civilization without there being equally enormous changes in our literature and our literary forms. So far Baldwin himself has, I think, accomplished more house cleaning and rebuilding in the essay than in the novel. He has learned the art of the novel but taught the art of the essay. It could be, therefore, that his most suitable form might turn out to be the "letter," the flexible, honestly personal kind of essay he has been patiently improving through most of his career. Such "letters" seem peculiarly appropriate for his kind of distance and his continuing journey, for Baldwin is a pilgrim. Whether he can keep this distance without his fictional other countries remains to be seen. He has a big job, and the challenge to his art is every bit as great as the challenge of his material, which is a very serious challenge indeed.—ROBERT F. SAYRE, "James Baldwin's Other Country," *Contemporary American Novelists*, ed. Harry T. Moore, 1964, pp. 168–69

Baldwin's essays—"Everybody's Protest Novel," "Many Thousands Gone," "Notes of a Native Son," "Fifth Avenue, Uptown," and "Nobody Knows My Name"—are among the finest polemical pieces written today; they seem already part of the permanent record of racial relations in this country, definitive of a certain way of being even as we now read them. Personally they speak of Baldwin's youth, a youth that culminated in the death of his father (so movingly described in "Notes of a Native Son") when he discovered the legacy that had been given him: "nothing," his father had said, "is ever escaped."

Baldwin was just nineteen years old when his father died, and this legacy, which for his father meant God's justice and eternal judgment, and other eschatological certainties, became for the boy, ineluctably and terribly, existentialist. *Nothing is ever escaped*—neither color nor one's sexual reality nor death. His early work is an attempt to assert that fact: *Go Tell It on the Mountain* records the fanaticism of his father and the boy's emergence into a God-less world; the essays reject white abstractions such as "quality" and "freedom" and "wealth." Like Frederic Henry in *A Farewell to Arms*, Baldwin finds abstract words obscene and empty beside the individual heroic acts committed, the specific results achieved. "I am very often tempted to believe," he has said, "that this illusion [that our state is a state to be envied by other people because we are powerful, and we are rich] is all that is left of the great dream that was to have become America; whether this is so or not, this illusion certainly prevents us from making America what we say we want it to be."

The process of rejection and negation, which has occupied Baldwin until the present day, suggests his special contribution to the thought of our time: he rejects the abstractions, the promises, the white man's vague projections of hope for the Negro—he denies all but the very tangible.—THEODORE GROSS, "The World of James Baldwin," *Crt*, Winter 1964–65, pp. 141–42

A major theme of *The Fire Next Time* is the death of the traditional God of Western civilization. Throughout the essay the church is shown to be a place of refuge for emotional cripples, a "mask for self-hatred and despair," in which the teachings of Jesus have become subverted by those of the "mercilessly fanatical and self-righteous St. Paul." Baldwin's own concept of God is perhaps best defined in *Nobody Knows My Name*:

> I suggest that the role of the Negro in American life has something to do with our concept of what God is, and from my point of view, this concept is not big enough. . . . To be with God is really to be involved with some enormous, overwhelming desire, and joy,

and power which you cannot control, which controls you. I conceive of my own life as a journey toward something I do not understand, which in the going toward, makes me better. I conceive of God, in fact, as a means of liberation and not a means to control others.

In this passage we can sense the undercurrent of Baldwin's deep desire for submission, a desire basically incompatible with his role as public spokesman for civil rights. As a public spokesman he urges rebellion, while as an artist his inner need is for acceptance. The one role demands social action while the other denies the relevance of that action. Baldwin himself is not unaware of this dilemma. He says, in *Notes of a Native Son*:

> It began to seem that one would have to hold in the mind forever two ideas which seemed to be in opposition. The first was acceptance, the acceptance, totally without rancor, of life as it is, and men as they are: in the light of this idea, it goes without saying that injustice is a commonplace. But this did not mean that one could be complacent, for the second idea was of equal power: that one must never, in one's own life, accept these injustices as commonplace but must fight them with all one's strength. The fight begins, however, in the heart and it now had been laid to my charge to keep my own heart free of hatred and despair.

While the idea of rebellion against injustice is dominant in the essays on the racial crisis, the idea of acceptance of the ultimate existential fact is there too. . . .

Baldwin's two roles involve somewhat different views of the human condition. In his role as spokesman he is committed to the belief that man's fate can be changed through concerted social action, that Mister Charlie could give the Negro stature if he would only give him freedom now. The artist, however, sees a more complex problem. He sees the achievement of significance as a much more personal process in which each man must try to discover his own nature, accept what he finds, and then involve this nature with other people, through love. Each stage of the process requires so much courage that few of Baldwin's characters can ever achieve genuine involvement. Elizabeth has achieved it in the first novel, and several of the characters in *Another Country* achieve it, though their achievement is more precarious than hers. In the fiction, it is this process which offers the possibility of improving the human condition.

To some extent the roles are complementary; both the fiction and the essays denounce the imprisonment of Negroes by the white world and the web of social illusions we have woven to veil the final existential fact. And both roles are based upon a desperate faith. Asked in an interview for his opinion of the nation's future, Baldwin echoed Camus' view of suicide as the only real philosophical question. "I can't be a pessimist because I'm alive," Baldwin said. "To be a pessimist means that you have agreed that human life is an academic matter, so I'm forced to be an optimist." Baldwin's characters are always talking about the possibilities for making their lives more meaningful, but their few fleeting moments of illumination are menaced by the threatening wind of fatality and despair.— HOWARD M. HARPER, "James Baldwin—art or propaganda?", *Desperate Faith*, 1967, pp. 141–61

As a writer Baldwin is as obsessed by sex and family as Strindberg was, but instead of using situations for their dramatic value, Baldwin likes to pile up all possible emotional conflicts as assertions. But for the same reason that in *Giovanni's Room*

Baldwin made everybody white just to show that he could, and in *Tell Me How Long the Train's Been Gone* transferred the son-father quarrel to a quarrel with a brother, so one feels about *Another Country* that Baldwin writes fiction in order to use up his private difficulties; even his fiction piles up the atmosphere of raw emotion that is his literary standby. Why does so powerful a writer as Baldwin make himself look simple-minded by merely asserting an inconsequential succession of emotions?

> They encountered the big world when they went out into the Sunday streets. It stared unsympathetically out at them from the eyes of the passing people; and Rufus realized that he had not thought at all about this world and its power to hate and destroy.
> "They out there, scuffling, making that change, they think it's going to last forever. Sometimes I lie here and listen, listen for a bomb, man, to fall on this city and make all that noise stop. I listen to hear them moan, I want them to bleed and choke, I want to hear them *crying*."
> The college boys, gleaming with ignorance and mad with chastity, made terrified efforts to attract the feminine attention, but succeeded only in attracting each other.

But in *Notes of a Native Son*, *Nobody Knows My Name*, *The Fire Next Time*, Baldwin dropped the complicated code for love difficulties he uses in his novels and simplified himself into an "angry Black" very powerfully indeed—and this just before Black nationalists were to turn on writers like him. The character who calls himself "James Baldwin" in *his* nonfiction novel is more professionally enraged, more doubtfully an evangelist for his people, than the actual James Baldwin, a very literary mind indeed. But there is in *Notes of a Native Son* a genius for bringing many symbols together, an instinctive association with the 1943 Harlem riot, the streets of smashed plate glass, that stems from the all too understandable fascination of the Negro with the public sources of his fate. The emphasis is on heat, fire, anger, the sense of being hemmed in and suffocated; the words are tensed into images that lacerate and burn. Reading Baldwin's essays, we are suddenly past the discordancy that has plagued his fiction—a literal problem of conflict, for Baldwin's fiction shows him trying to transpose facts into fiction without sacrificing the emotional capital that has been his life.—Alfred Kazin, *Bright Book of Life*, 1971, pp. 222–24

James Baldwin's career has not been an even one, and his life as a writer cannot have been, so far, very placid. He has been both praised and, in recent years, denounced for the wrong reasons. The black writer, if he is not being patronized simply for being black, is in danger of being attacked for not being black enough. Or he is forced to represent a mass of people, his unique vision assumed to be symbolic of a collective vision. In some circles he cannot lose—his work will be praised without being read, which must be the worst possible fate for a serious writer. And, of course, there are circles, perhaps those nearest home, in which he cannot ever win—for there will be people who resent the mere fact of his speaking for them, whether he intends to speak for them or not.—Joyce Carol Oates, *NYTBR*, May 19, 1974, p. 1

Works

GO TELL IT ON THE MOUNTAIN

⟨Go Tell It on the Mountain⟩ is a novel about Harlem's storefront churches, seen through the eyes of the people who go to one of them. These people have blood and flesh in their church, and in their past in the South, and it would seem that, therefore, their story would be of wonder, strength, tragedy, and sometimes beauty. The story is of all these things, partly. But it is not what the author hopes it will be, when he says of his intentions: "It is a fairly deliberate attempt to break out of what I always think of as the 'cage' of Negro writing. I wanted my people to be people first, Negroes almost incidentally."

He has not really accomplished that in this book, because there is always the absolute feeling of injustice toward a people, not as people, but as a race of people. The disasters that occur are those that occur only, or largely, because these are Negro people. Their feelings may be those shared in other circumstances by others, but these, here, are clearly marked 'Negro.' Yet the mark of the spirit is here, that which can be seen in any experience of men who have a sense of sin and a sense of repentance. . . .

There are many strong and powerful scenes in this work. Mr. Baldwin has his eye clearly on the full values that his sincere characters possess, though these values often are tossed aside and trampled. His people have an enormous capacity for sin, but their capacity for suffering and repentance is even greater. I think that is the outstanding quality of this work, a sometimes majestic sense of the failings of men and their ability to work through their misery to some kind of peaceful salvation. Certainly, the spark of the holy fire flashes even through their numerous external misfortunes.—T. E. Cassidy, "The Long Struggle," *Com*, May 22, 1953, p. 186

Mr. Baldwin's concern with Negro culture is not so much to deny or discover it, but to present it in its pitifully tragic contradictions. His portrayal of Negro life demonstrates how the myth of African savagery is perpetuated among the Negroes themselves both by the condition of the Negro community in America and by the institution that affords their principal refuge from that savagery, religion. . . .

There are two "mountains" in ⟨*Go Tell It on the Mountain*⟩. When, at the end, John is "saved" and has begun his tortured ascent of the mountain of Holiness, we feel that the injustice of his condition is subsumed for the moment in the larger, impersonal justice of the novel—the strange justice of tragedy. This is his doom, and there is a rightness about it if only because it is inevitable. But we recall that other "mountain," the hill in Central Park from which John, at the beginning of the book, looked down beneath "the brilliant sky, and beyond it, cloudy and far away, he saw the skyline of New York." It is the same kind of elevation from which, I am sure Mr. Baldwin wants us to remember, Eugène de Rastignac, at the close of *Père Goriot*, surveys Paris. It is the prominence from which all the "young men from the provinces" catch their glimpse of the worlds they are to love and win. But for John Grimes there can be no winning; and when we realize this, that he can stand only on the mountain of Holiness, an otherworldly mountain made of bitterness and renunciation, a mountain where he finds his real identity, the poignancy of his earlier vision comes upon us with great force.

. . . Mr. Baldwin has elsewhere trenchantly declared his antipathy to the kind of "protest novel" which ignores the personality of the Negro; now he has written a novel which is the strongest protest that can be made, because it intelligently faces the complex dilemma of its characters.

. . . The fundamental quality in the lives of these Negroes is frustration; every demand they make on life is rejected. It can be said this is essentially true for all of us, but it is surely many times truer for the Negroes. For us the larger world which limits our fulfillment and cuts down our demands is almost impersonal—it is the world of nature, or of institutions so old and traditional that they seem themselves almost natural—institutions whose sanctions often appear as kindly in protecting us as they are malevolent in denying our desires. But the Negro inhabits a universe that extends at least the *chance* of fulfillment to everyone but himself. He must work in the midst of wealth and status, but must live and breed on the margins of society; at the same time he covets the material and social felicities as much as anyone—indeed, more than anyone, for since he has so little direct experience of them, their value is magnified. It is not surprising, then, that the excessiveness of the Negroes' sense of sin, so bound up in their desires for the pleasures of the world, is in direct proportion to their distance from the social, material abundance it contains. . . .

It must be said also that as the episodes of *Go Tell It on the Mountain* unfold, a rather nasty kind of irony begins to assert itself. Although each event in the novel conveys both a religious import and an awareness that life is being sacrificed for religion's sake, Mr. Baldwin's desire to give both points of view has led him in some places to substitute a poised indecisiveness for his usual superb impersonality. Unfortunately, the full compassion that John's fate should elicit sometimes resides merely on the surface of the prose, in formal gestures:

> And the dust made him cough and retch; in his turning the center of the whole earth shifted, making of space a sheer void and a mockery of order, and balance, and time. Nothing remained: all was swallowed up in chaos. And: *Is this it?* John's terrified soul inquired—*What is it?*—to no purpose, receiving no answer. Only the ironic voice insisted once more that he rise from that filthy floor if he did not want to become like all the other niggers.

There are two kinds of rhetoric at work in this passage. The first is inflated—"swallowed up in chaos," etc.—and is supposed to convey John's torment. The "ironic voice" of the last sentence, on the other hand, represents Mr. Baldwin's attempt to balance or deflate the extravagance of his hero's religious experience. This is characteristic of almost every passage in the section that deals with the conversion. Clearly, however, neither term is adequately presented, nor are the two impulses they represent reconciled. The clichés in the first part of the passage, and the uneasiness in "filthy" and "nigger," are sufficient evidence for the unsureness of touch which blemishes the last section of the book. The truth is that Mr. Baldwin is not sure of what he wants to say, finally, and he disguises this uncertainty in an affected distance from his material. This indecisiveness, with its compensating impulse toward neatness, seems to me a real fault. It leads to a certain falseness of tone and withholding of commitment—one might almost say of Mr. Baldwin's own identity—that constrict the novel and divest it of moral backbone. This is very much like that faulty irony in Hardy's novels, which eats away at the stature of the characters, forcing them to fit an idea which dominates the novelist's mind; T. S. Eliot's comment on Hardy applies equally to Mr. Baldwin: "He will leave nothing to nature, but will always be giving one last turn of the screw himself."—Steven Marcus, "The American Negro in Search of Identity," *Cmty*, Nov. 1953, pp. 459–63

There is a new name to be added to the list of serious and talented young writers—that of James Baldwin. Born in Harlem in 1924, Mr. Baldwin was the son of a preacher, and, he tells us, was a preacher himself from the age of fourteen to the age of seventeen. Shortly after ceasing to preach, he turned to literature, and, in the next few years, he had two fellowships and wrote two books, neither of which was published. Now he has a book in print, *Go Tell It on the Mountain*, and a very fine book it is.

Readers of the *Partisan Review* may remember Mr. Baldwin as the author of two interesting and disturbing articles, "Everybody's Protest Novel" and "Many Thousands Gone." In these articles he discussed the dangers of indignation in fiction, the problem of stereotypes in fiction about Negroes, and the place of the Negro in American life. Re-reading them now, after reading his novel, one sees them as the statement of a personal and pressing dilemma: acknowledging the bitterness he felt as a Negro, he was putting on record his determination not to allow that bitterness to dominate his work as a novelist.

Go Tell It on the Mountain is the result of that struggle and the proof of Baldwin's victory, for there is no danger that it will be pigeonholed as a novel of protest, it neither expresses indignation nor seeks to arouse it, and we do not think of the characters as victims of injustice or as anything less than human beings.

> One writes out of one thing only—one's own experience. [Baldwin has said] Everything depends on how relentlessly one forces from this experience the last drop, sweet or bitter, it can possibly give. This is the only real concern of the artist, to recreate out of the disorder of life that order which is art. The difficulty then, for me, of being a Negro writer was the fact that I was, in effect, prohibited from examining my own experience too closely by the tremendous demands and the very real dangers of my social situation.

In other words, the Negro problem was there in the foreground, and he had to get behind it to find the kind of reality that seems to him to be the artist's proper concern.

Two other talented Negro novelists, Ralph Ellison and Richard Wright, have recently written about Negroes without writing novels of protest. They have done so, however, by demonstrating that the Negro problem is at bottom merely a variant of the human problem: We are all "invisible men," we are all "outsiders." In the long run, we begin to forget that their heroes are Negroes, and that is what they want us to do. Their strategy is excellent, but Baldwin's is even subtler. His novel centers in a characteristic Harlem institution, the storefront church, and we never lose the awareness that we are reading about Negroes. The fact that his characters are Negroes is important, but increasingly we are made to feel that its importance is secondary.

What happens in the novel is that John Grimes gets religion on his fourteenth birthday, and perhaps the most remarkable thing Mr. Baldwin has done is to give this experience an intense reality. In the first part of the novel we see John in his normal range of activities. He is afraid of his father, devoted to his mother, alienated from and worried about his "bad" younger brother. He makes a birthday excursion into the sinful world of Times Square, returns to a family crisis, and helps to prepare for Saturday evening services at the Temple of the Free Baptized. In the second section, we learn about his father and mother, and then, in the third section, comes the conversion.

"In the context of the Negro problem," Mr. Baldwin has written, "neither whites nor blacks, for excellent reasons of their own, have the faintest desire to look back; but I think that the past is all that makes the present coherent, and further, that the past will remain horrible for exactly as long as we refuse to assess it honestly." In his novel, he looks steadily at that segment of the past that is relevant to his story. Through the recollections of Gabriel Grimes, John's supposed father, and those of Gabriel's sister Florence, as they take part in the

Saturday-evening service, a dramatic and significant story unfolds. Their old mother, born in slavery, links them with the more remote past. They themselves are, in different ways, products of the migration northward. Gabriel's story is marked by violence and sin and the struggle for righteousness, and violence has touched the life of Elizabeth, his wife and John's mother.

The adroitness with which Mr. Baldwin sets these dramas within the framework of John's conversion is evidence of his skill as a novelist. Yet he never seems obsessed with form, as some of the other young novelists do; it is something that he knows how to make serve his purpose. Indeed, his technical skill, which is remarkable in many ways, is most remarkable for its unobtrusiveness. His narrative is assured and straightforward, and the description of John's seizure achieves its great emotional effect without any fireworks. Best of all is the dialogue, with its strong, authentic rhythms. Everything about the book bears witness to a mastery that is astonishing in so young a novelist.

The strange and fatal conflict between ideal and reality is the theme of this book, as it is of much of the world's greatest literature. The principal characters of the novel are sustained by their peculiarly dogmatic and violent interpretation of Christianity. The faith of Gabriel and Deborah and Elizabeth, and of Praying Mother Washington and Sister McCandless and Brother Elisha, is grotesque but dignified. They are the saved, set apart from the rest of the world, and their lives have meaning; but for this high privilege they pay by their adherence to a code of morality that puts a heavy burden on weak human flesh and may result, as it has resulted with Gabriel, in sins worse than those against which the saints preach.

Mr. Baldwin makes us fully aware of the meaning of religion for these people, and, because we have seen enough of Gabriel and Elizabeth to understand the tensions of John's childhood, his conversion becomes a climax for us as well as for him. Mr. Baldwin wisely drops the story there. There are intimations that there will be other climaxes for John, but it is enough that we understand why the conversion has happened and what, for the moment, it means to him.

Mr. Baldwin has said that he wants to be "an honest man and a good writer." It is obvious that he has had a tremendous struggle against attitudes on the part of others, and emotions within himself, that might have made him a more or less dishonest propagandist; but he has achieved his goal, and he has also achieved, as a consequence of the struggle, a phenomenal maturity.—GRANVILLE HICKS, "*Go Tell It on the Mountain*" (1953), *Literary Horizons*, 1971, pp. 87–90

It is remarkable how forcibly the background is kept background in this little book, however pressing its possibilities for development. It is purposely kept a "small" book—young John's short story (and, to explain it, his family's)—even an unfinished one, carefully, unforcedly told. To hear it one must see, as John sees, all the reality of ghetto life: the fumy jelly roll of black folks' sinning, the ambiguous fury of their holiness; one must hear, as he hears, of lynchings and rapes and beatings. But all this is unaggressive; it remains a carefully held-down background that never juts into jarring high relief. All the race truths and war truths are no less "real" for this containment; they may in fact be more convincing, for the honest casualness of presentation, working on the reader like subliminal persuasion. Baldwin had a small, tight, private story to relate, and refused to be distracted by explosions in the background.

The effect is true, and therefore small—truncated, incomplete. The loving, voluptuous style, a rhetoric of rocking prose rhythms stolen from Negro song and Negro sermon (half or more of the book is chanted in Scriptural cadences, graven in Scriptural imagery) may not vary enough to sustain a two hundred-page narrative. (Then again, such "tediousness" may only occur to unwilling, non-participating readers.) Baldwin is as unafraid of glorious prose as he is of honest prose, and the book is woven out of both. But the strength, at last, is that of his own personal necessity, a necessity that the reader can vicariously share. It is the strength of a harrowing prayer, simple and felt, of a small tragic truth that enlarges the heart. The book is carven with love. Because of its peculiar kind of necessary, very personal truth, it remains one of the few, the very few, essential Negro works.—DAVID LITTLEJOHN, *Black on White*, 1966, pp. 123–24

The resolution of the plot ⟨of *Go Tell It on the Mountain*⟩ comes about when John achieves his salvation on the threshing floor. What is resolved? All the fears, anxieties, tensions of John's life up to that point are washed away. His father is finally seen by John in "proper" perspective. He has, that is, changed his relation to Gabriel and will no longer be dominated by him. He has divested Gabriel of authority by transference of his allegiance from his earthly to his Heavenly Father. The salient point in the threshing-floor episode is the lack of distance between the author and the main character. Another writer might have seen the dynamics of the scene as indicating the resolution of the relation between father and son, and the particular mode it takes as simply the vehicle through which the transformation occurs. As it is, the author believes as much as the character in the contextual scheme. Hence there is no irony or ambiguity present. John's religious experience is seen not as a subterfuge for dealing with a difficult and not unusual psychic phenomenon—the tension between fathers and sons during adolescence—but rather as in itself true and real. This means, then, that John's experience is a truly Christian one, that the novel is a Christian novel and that it points to what the author conceives to be a sphere of reality beyond the experiential.—DONALD B. GIBSON, "James Baldwin: The Political Anatomy of Space," *James Baldwin: A Critical Evaluation*, ed. Therman B. O'Daniel, 1977, p. 6

GIOVANNI'S ROOM

Much of ⟨*Giovanni's Room*⟩ is laid in scenes of squalor, with a background of characters as grotesque and repulsive as any that can be found in Proust's *Cities of the Plain*, but even as one is dismayed by Mr. Baldwin's materials, one rejoices in the skill with which he renders them. Nor is there any suspicion that he is working with these materials merely for the sake of shocking the reader. On the contrary, his intent is most serious. One of the lesser characters, in many ways a distasteful one, tells David that "not many people have ever died of love." "But," he goes on, "multitudes have perished, and are perishing every hour—and in the oddest places!—for the lack of it." This is Mr. Baldwin's subject, the rareness and difficulty of love, and, in his rather startling way, he does a great deal with it.—GRANVILLE HICKS, "*Giovanni's Room*" (1956), *Literary Horizons*, 1971, p. 93

⟨*Giovanni's Room* represents⟩ two new departures in Baldwin's work: . . . its locale is France, and there are no Negroes in it. While I am not urging Baldwin to flee Paris for Harlem, and I certainly do not mean to imply that he should write only about Negroes, it is my feeling that *Go Tell It on the Mountain* has a substantiality and conviction lacking in *Giovanni's Room*. The latter's characters are on the periphery of the society in which they live, and though Baldwin attempts to make them symbolic of a universal malaise, they are like roots out of a dry ground. It is difficult to take them very seriously. No character here has an inner and outer world as fully realized as Gabriel's in *Go Tell It on the Mountain.*

One is tempted to compare Baldwin with Hawthorne, except that Hawthorne had a healthiness of mind and spirit and a disinterestedness as an artist which Baldwin altogether lacks. In Baldwin the culminating effect is one of damnation; wretched man is dragged before the bar and condemned to endless fires of guilt and fear. It is the New Calvinism dramatized. In the end, Baldwin's books are strangely out of date; they are written as if Locke and the Enlightenment had not happened. Their determinism, doom, and feeling of depravity are unrelieved not only by the sense of human possibility, but even by the hope of spiritual salvation.—CHARLES H. NICHOLS, "The New Calvinism," *Cmty,* Jan. 1957, pp. 95–96

Giovanni's Room (1956) is by far the weakest of Baldwin's novels. There is a tentative, unfinished quality about the book, as if in merely broaching the subject of homosexuality Baldwin had exhausted his creative energy. Viewed in retrospect, it seems less a novel in its own right than a first draft of *Another Country.* The surface of the novel is deliberately opaque, for Baldwin is struggling to articulate the most intimate, the most painful, the most elusive of emotions. The characters are vague and disembodied, the themes half-digested, the colors rather bleached than vivified. We recognize in this sterile psychic landscape the unprocessed raw material of art.

And yet this novel occupies a key position in Baldwin's spiritual development. Links run backward to *Go Tell It on the Mountain* as well as forward to *Another Country.* The very furniture of Baldwin's mind derives from the store-front church of his boyhood and adolescence. When he attempts a novel of homosexual love, with an all-white cast of characters and a European setting, he simply transposes the moral topography of Harlem to the streets of Paris. When he strives toward sexual self-acceptance he automatically casts the homosexual in a priestly role.

Before supporting this interpretation, let me summarize the plot. David, an American youth living abroad in Paris, meets a girl from back home and asks her to marry him. Hella is undecided, however, and she goes to Spain to think it over. During her absence, David meets Giovanni, a proud and handsome young Italian. They fall deeply in love and have a passionate affair. When Hella returns, David is forced to choose between his male lover and his American fiancée. He abandons Giovanni to the homosexual underworld, which is only too eager to claim him. When Guillaume, whom Baldwin describes as "a disgusting old fairy," inflicts upon the youth a series of humiliations, Giovanni strangles his tormentor. He is tried for murder and executed by the guillotine. Meanwhile David, who has gone with Hella to the south of France, cannot forget Giovanni. Tortured by guilt and self-doubt, he breaks off his engagement by revealing the truth about himself.

At the emotional center of the novel is the relationship between David and Giovanni. It is highly symbolic, and to understand what is at stake, we must turn to Baldwin's essay on André Gide. Published toward the end of 1954, about a year before the appearance of *Giovanni's Room,* this essay is concerned with the two sides of Gide's personality and the precarious balance that was struck between them. On the one side was his sensuality, his lust for the boys on the Piazza d'Espagne, threatening him always with utter degradation. On the other was his Protestantism, his purity, his otherworldliness—that part of him which was not carnal, and which found expres-

sion in his Platonic marriage to Madeleine. As Baldwin puts it, "She was his Heaven who would forgive him for his Hell and help him to endure it." It is a drama of salvation, in which the celibate wife, through selfless dedication to the suffering artist, becomes in effect a priest.

In the novel Giovanni plays the role of Gide; David, of Madeleine. Giovanni is not merely a sensualist, but a Platonist as well: "I want to escape . . . this dirty world, this dirty body." It is the purity of Giovanni's love for David—its idealized, transcendent quality—that protects him from a kind of homosexual Hell. David is the string connecting him to Heaven, and when David abandons him, he plunges into the abyss.

We can now appreciate the force of David's remark, "The burden of his salvation seemed to be on me and I could not endure it." Possessing the power to save, David rejects the priestly office. Seen in this light, his love affair with Giovanni is a kind of novitiate. The dramatic conflict of the novel can be stated as follows: does David have a true vocation? Is he prepared to renounce the heterosexual world? When David leaves Giovanni for Hella, he betrays his calling, but ironically he has been ruined for both the priesthood and the world.

It is Giovanni, Baldwin's doomed hero, who is the true priest. For a priest is nothing but a journeyman in suffering. Thus Giovanni defies David, the American tourist, even to understand his village: "And you will have no idea of the life there, dripping and bursting and beautiful and terrible, as you have no idea of my life now." It is a crucial distinction for all of Baldwin's work: there are the relatively innocent—the *laity* who are mere apprentices in human suffering—and the fully initiated, the *clergy* who are intimate with pain. Among the laity may be numbered Americans, white folks, heterosexuals, and squares; among the clergy, Europeans, Negroes, homosexuals, hipsters, and jazzmen. The finest statement of this theme, in which the jazzman is portrayed as priest, is Baldwin's moving story, "Sonny's Blues."

Assumption of the priestly role is always preceded by an extraordinary experience of suffering, often symbolized in Baldwin's work by the death of a child. Thus in *The Amen Corner* Sister Margaret becomes a store-front church evangelist after giving birth to a dead child. And in *Giovanni's Room* the protagonist leaves his wife, his family, and his village after the birth of a stillborn child: "When I knew that it was dead I took our crucifix off the wall and I spat on it and I threw it on the floor and my mother and my girl screamed and I went out." It is at this point that Giovanni's inverted priesthood begins. Like Gide, he rebels against God, but the priestly impulse persists. He retreats from the heterosexual world, achieves a kind of purity in his relationship with David, is betrayed, and is consigned to martyrdom.—ROBERT A. BONE, *The Negro Novel in America,* 1965, pp. 226–28

ANOTHER COUNTRY

Another Country is about a crucial year in the lives of a group of people who inhabit a kind of underworld of interracial and intersexual relations. Of the five main characters, two are Negroes—a once-famous jazz drummer, Rufus Scott; and his younger sister, Ida, an aspiring singer—and the other three are white—Rufus' closest friend, a young, unpublished and unmarried writer (Vivaldo Moore); a woman whose marriage is beginning to fail (Cass Silenski); and a homosexual actor who comes originally from the South (Eric Jones). Rufus—by far the most impressive character Baldwin has ever created—has a love affair with a pathetic white Southern girl named Leona which ends for him in suicide and for her in insanity. After

Rufus' death, his sister Ida falls in love with Vivaldo, and while they are living together (less stormily than Rufus and Leona had, but stormily enough), Ida is unfaithful to him with a television producer who promises to further her career; and he, though not a homosexual, spends a night with Eric by whom, as Stanley Edgar Hyman delicately put it, he permits himself to be "rectally violated." By this time, we have already learned that Rufus, although not a homosexual either, had also once had an affair with Eric. As for Eric, he too crosses over the line and enters into an affair with Cass, who is fed up with the kind of man her husband has become since producing a successful but trivial novel.

Whites coupled with Negroes, heterosexual men coupled with homosexuals, homosexuals coupled with women, none of it involving casual lust or the suggestion of neurotic perversity, and all of it accompanied by the most serious emotions and resulting in the most intense attachments—it is easy enough to see even from so crude a summary that Baldwin's intention is to deny any moral significance whatever to the categories white and Negro, heterosexual and homosexual. He is saying that the terms white and Negro refer to two different conditions under which individuals live, but they are still individuals and their lives are still governed by the same fundamental laws of being. And he is saying, similarly, that the terms homosexuality and heterosexuality refer to two different conditions under which individuals pursue love, but they are still individuals and their pursuit of love is still governed by the same fundamental laws of being. Putting the two propositions together, he is saying, finally, that the only significant realities are individuals and love, and that anything which is permitted to interfere with the free operation of this fact is evil and should be done away with.

Now, one might suppose that there is nothing particularly startling in this view of the world; it is, after all, only a form of the standard liberal attitude toward life. And indeed, stated as I have just stated it, and held with the mild attachment by which most liberal and enlightened Americans hold it, it is scarcely more shocking than the usual speech made at every convention of the National Society of Social Workers. But that is not the way James Baldwin holds it, and it is not the way he states it. He holds these attitudes with a puritanical ferocity, and he spells them out in such brutal and naked detail that one scarcely recognizes them any longer—and one is frightened by them, almost as though they implied a totally new, totally revolutionary conception of the universe. And in a sense, of course, they do. For by taking these liberal pieties literally and by translating them into simple English, he puts the voltage back into them and they burn to the touch. Do you believe, he demands of you, that racial prejudice is wrong, that all men are created equal, that individuals must be judged on their own merits? Then you must dare to surrender the objections you are still harboring in your soul against miscegenation. You must acknowledge that there is no reason why whites and Negroes should not sleep together and marry and produce children with as little interference as members of the same race now encounter. And that this is impossible you must recognize as a momentous fact about American life, signifying a moral sickness that may end by destroying our capacity for any kind of human contact whatever. Do you believe, he demands of you again, that love is the supreme value and that sex is the most natural expression of love? Then you must realize that the stifling of your own impulses toward a sexual articulation of the love you feel for members of your own sex is unnatural, signifying a warping of the instincts and of the body that may end by destroying your capacity for any sexual experience whatever.

Another Country, then, is informed by a remorseless insistence on a truth which, however partial we may finally judge it to be, is nevertheless compelling as a perspective on the way we live now. It is a cruel truth, and a demanding one, but it is not without an element of sweet spiritual generosity. For implicit in it is the idea that everyone carries his own burden, that every burden is ultimately as heavy as every other and that a man is either brave enough or strong enough to stand up straight under the weight on his back or he isn't; and if he isn't, he will pay the price and no one else has the right to judge him harshly; and if enough people are found to be lacking in enough bravery or enough strength, then there must be something wrong with the conditions they are being forced to endure and the values these conditions have bred.

Wherever Baldwin manages to remain true to this vision—as in the magnificent opening section about Rufus, the account of the relations between Vivaldo and Ida and scattered passages in every other part of the book—he is at his very best, achieving a unique blend of subtlety and forcefulness, anger and understanding. But there are situations and characters that tax Baldwin's power to sustain the burden of his moral attitude to the breaking point. Thus, he is merciless on Cass Silenski's husband Richard, who is a bad writer and a success, while remaining infinitely charitable toward Vivaldo, who is also a bad writer but a failure; he inclines toward sentimentality in most of the erotic passages involving either a white and a Negro, or a homosexual and a woman, whereas he is visibly skeptical of the validity of the more standard varieties of sex; he can trace every nuance in the relations of an unmarried couple, but in writing about marriage he falls into something very close to philistinism; and in general he judges his white characters (with the exception of the homosexual Eric) by more rigorous criteria than he is willing to apply to the Negroes in the book. All of which means that Baldwin, who speaks so passionately of the white man's need for the courage to know the Negro and the heterosexual's need to know the homosexual, is himself unable to summon up the courage to know and respect those who live in that other country usually designated as normal.

But in the end, the failures of *Another Country*, however serious, seem unimportant beside the many impressive things Baldwin has accomplished here. Within the context of his own development as a writer, I believe that *Another Country* will come to be seen as the book in which for the first time the superb intelligence of Baldwin the essayist became fully available to Baldwin the novelist, in which for the first time he attempted to speak his mind with complete candor and with a minimum of polite rhetorical elegance, and in which for the first time he dared to reveal himself as someone to be feared for how deeply he sees, how much he demands of the world and how powerfully he can hate. Is it perhaps this dangerous militancy that made so many reviewers dislike *Another Country*? The question is worth pondering.—Norman Podhoretz, "In Defense of a Maltreated Best Seller" (1962), *Contemporary Literature*, ed. Richard Kostelanetz, 1964, pp. 234–37

Baldwin's preoccupation with sexual love between blacks and whites may be yet another symptom of his effort to extend the thematic range of his fiction beyond the boundaries of race. Sexual love emerges in his novels as a kind of universal anodyne for the disease of racial separatism, as a means not only of achieving personal identity but also of transcending false categories of color and gender. It may not be excessive to claim, as Marcus Klein has done, that love represents for Baldwin "the perfect democracy, the new Eden, wherein all complicating distinctions since Eden will have disappeared." There is, in fact, a sustained dramatic contrast throughout his fiction between the generalized tensions of prejudice and hostility, as they exist in the public environment of the action, and the intimacy and trust existing between the friends and lovers who make up the inner community of principal characters. As the forces of discrimination grow stronger in the outside world, the characters grow more undiscriminating in their sexuality, achieving through countless combinations and recombinations of relationships some brief sense that they are still alive. In *Another Country*, the most sexually strenuous of Baldwin's novels, there are affairs between a black male musician and a Southern white woman, a white male homosexual actor and a white housewife, a black woman and a white male heterosexual writer, who spends one night of love with the actor, who in his turn once had an affair with the musician. The remarkable thing about these people, apart from their indefatigability, is that they are really not interested in one another at all. In fact, they are no more real to one another than they are as characters. They do not share common tastes, interests, or ideas, only bed, and when they are out of bed, which is seldom, they talk endlessly about trivia, consume great quantities of food, cigarettes, and liquor, and moon about feeling vast unutterable emotions of tenderness and loyalty. Very little happens in *Another Country* except copulation and conversation. Yet Baldwin obviously takes it all very seriously. He wraps his characters round and round with skeins of "self-righteous and virtuous sentimentality" and describes them in precisely the rhetoric of "excessive and spurious emotion" that he found so distasteful in *Uncle Tom's Cabin*. One might have assumed on the evidence of his essays and early fiction that Baldwin would be consumed in the fires of hate and that his future as a novelist could well depend on his achievement of compassion and objectivity. But it seemed probable after the appearance of *Another Country* and the later novel, *Tell Me How Long the Train's Been Gone*, that he might instead be destined to drown in the throbbing seas of sentimental love.—John W. Aldridge, "The Fire Next Time?", *SR*, June 15, 1974, p. 24

Another Country reveals a liberalizing of Baldwin's attitudes but by no means an abdication of basically conservative values. The context of the novel is social, not cosmological; it focuses on problems related to racial interaction; it contains far more social protest than any of the preceding novels; its morality is less stringent, though no less imperative, than heretofore. At the same time, however, its assumptions about the basic nature of the social problems it confronts give rise to a societal analysis essentially conservative in character. It assumes that large-scale social problems, such as racial oppression and its resulting social manifestations, are the result of limitations within the psyches of individuals rather than of the dynamics of contending social forces. Hence, the responsibility for social problems lies with the individual, be he oppressed or oppressor, victimizer or victim. In the terms of the novel, this means that black people are shown oppressing whites as well as conversely, and there is no clear distinction to be made between the one act of oppression and the other. In *Another Country* race does not matter in the sense that every individual has the capacity, regardless of color, to be victim or victimizer. Equal-opportunity suffering indeed! I do not wish to argue the problem of the responsibility of the victim in his victimization. I would contend, however, that equating the two roles as a general premise serves more to justify oppressors, whether groups or individuals, than to condemn them.—Donald B. Gibson, "James Baldwin: The Political Anatomy of Space," *James Baldwin: A Critical Evaluation*, ed. Therman B. O'Daniel, 1977, pp. 10–11

IF BEALE STREET COULD TALK

A sparse, slender narrative, told first-person by a 19-year-old black girl named Tish, *If Beale Street Could Talk* manages to be many things at the same time. It is economically, almost poetically constructed, and may certainly be read as a kind of allegory, which refuses conventional outbursts of violence, preferring to stress the provisional, tentative nature of our lives. . . .

Baldwin certainly risked a great deal by putting his complex narrative, which involves a number of important characters, into the mouth of a young girl. Yet Tish's voice comes to seem absolutely natural and we learn to know her from the inside out. Even her flights of poetic fancy—involving rather subtle speculations upon the nature of male-female relationships, or black-white relationships, as well as her articulation of what it feels like to be pregnant—are convincing. Also convincing is Baldwin's insistence upon the primacy of emotions like love, hate, or terror: it is not sentimentality, but basic psychology, to acknowledge the fact that one person will die, and another survive simply because one has not the guarantee of a fundamental human bond, like love, while the other has. Fonny is saved from the psychic destruction experienced by other imprisoned blacks, because of Tish, his unborn baby and the desperate, heroic struggle of his family and Tish's to get him free. Even so, his father cannot endure the strain. Caught stealing on his job, he commits suicide almost at the very time his son is released on bail.

The novel progresses swiftly and suspensefully, but its dynamic movement is interior. Baldwin constantly understates the horror of his characters' situation in order to present them as human beings whom disaster has struck, rather than as blacks who have, typically, been victimized by whites and are therefore likely subjects for a novel. . . .

Yet the novel is ultimately optimistic. It stresses the communal bond between members of an oppressed minority, especially between members of a family, which would probably not be experienced in happier times. As society disintegrates in a collective sense, smaller human units will become more and more important. Those who are without them, like Fonny's friend Daniel, will probably not survive. Certainly they will not reproduce themselves. Fonny's real crime is "having his center inside him," but this is, ultimately, the means by which he survives. Others are less fortunate.

If Beale Street Could Talk is a moving, painful story. It is so vividly human and so obviously based upon reality, that it strikes us as timeless—an art that has not the slightest need of esthetic tricks, and even less need of fashionable apocalyptic excesses.—Joyce Carol Oates, *NYTBR*, May 19, 1974, pp. 1–2

Baldwin is a professional fugitive, he is always on the run; from his colour in *Giovanni's Room*, a love story between pure whites; from his class in *Tell Me How Long the Train's Been Gone*; and now the final trick as he escapes from his own sex in *If Beale Street Could Talk*. These social and sexual cells are so vague as to almost defy belief, but Baldwin is clear about his freedom: it consists of the small open space known as romance, that last straw in an ocean of uncertain uncertainties. His female agent in this book is Tish, a nineteen year old black girl who is both pregnant and in love—an unusual combination making a safe nest from which Baldwin can survey the nasty world with the wide eyes of infancy. The nastiness is compounded when Tish's lover, Fonny, is sent to jail adding, I suppose, depth to their romance.

Baldwin always stays very close to his material; the structure of the novel is tied to a kind of self-reflectiveness which disobeys the conventional laws of narrative, and the narrative itself breathes with Baldwin's own life as he returns yet again to that primal vision which apparently remains untarnished with the passing of his years. This is the poor, black world of streets and stoops and store-front faith which Baldwin can summon with incantation and which he pours all over himself in an effort to keep his vision clean.

There is that same, impassioned prose—a relic of the evangelical past which leads to sub-headings such as 'Troubled About My Soul' and 'Zion'—and Baldwin constructs the language as if it were the hallowed container of sacred meanings. His novels are attempts to push and pull these truths into some recognisable human shape and perhaps these truths, the gods of that familial hearth which Baldwin has preserved throughout his work, are almost human. They are those of 'life', 'feeling' and 'experience' and Baldwin tills those acres of silent passion which are generally supposed to pass between people at moments of intensity, and which are beyond mere words.

That is why he has never aspired to a casual, Yankee mimeticism, and the model for his black allegories lies somewhere around D. H. Lawrence rather than his ostensible mentor, Richard Wright, whose own writing is nothing more than white journalism plus blood. Baldwin has an impassioned and quasi-Biblical manner which allows him to denounce and lament like a funky Johnny Ray. Its advantages are fervour (if fervour _is_ an advantage) and grace, but what it gains in heat it loses in light, and there is precious little veracity or detail within his sermons. _If Beale Street Could Talk_ is composed largely of cardboard, since stereotypes are the only possible vehicles for the single-minded passions, wordless joys and lengthy silences which Baldwin insists upon discovering in every basement. White policemen and spinsters are always very bad, young blacks and young lovers are thoroughly and undoubtedly good. But even cut-outs can be daubed with a little fresh paint, and Baldwin is adept at that mawkish and slightly camp diction which passes for conversation amongst blacks: "Now the cops who put him in this wagon know that the dude is _sick. I know_ they know it. He ain't supposed to be in here—and him not hardly much more than a kid." This is the fantasy of urban America, and in this garish light we may steal away from Baldwin, leaving him to rouge his wounds in public.— PETER ACKROYD, "A Little Black Magic," _Spec_, July 6, 1974, p. 22

In _If Beale Street Could Talk_ Baldwin has produced another fantasy of rather larger social implications, this time one in which the characters of black people living in contemporary Harlem are shown to be so noble and courageous that one is constrained to wonder how we ever imagined that conditions in the black urban ghettos are anything other than idyllic. If to be black is to be beautiful, to be poor and black is to be positively saintly. Yet another fiction of great attractiveness to the white mind is thus perpetrated: Ghetto blacks are very happy with their lot. In fact, they are just as simple and fun-loving as the grinning old darkies of southern legend.

To be sure, there is a good deal of adversity in Baldwin's story, but it is there just to demonstrate how well his characters can cope with it and come through with courage undaunted and hopes unsullied. A nineteen-year-old black girl named Tish is in love with, and becomes pregnant by, a young black sculptor named Fonny. They plan to be married, but Fonny is unjustly accused of raping a Puerto Rican woman and is sent to prison. The action turns on the efforts of Tish and her family to track down and persuade the woman that she made a mistake and thus to exonerate Fonny. For a variety of reasons this

seems, by the close of the novel, a most unlikely possibility. The woman has disappeared into Puerto Rico. Fonny's trial has been indefinitely postponed, and he remains in prison. Tish at the end is in process of giving birth. Amidst all these dark troubles, life is renewed and faith in life re-affirmed. Fonny, the sculptor, sits in prison "working on the wood, on the stone, whistling, smiling. And from far away, but coming nearer, the baby cries and cries and cries and cries and cries and cries and cries, cries like it means to wake the dead." Thus, the novel's concluding lines.

It is extremely sad to see a writer of Baldwin's large gifts producing, in all seriousness, such junk. Yet it has been evident for some time that he is deteriorating as a novelist and becoming increasingly a victim of the vice of sentimentality. This seems a particular pity because Baldwin may have one great novel left within him which it would take the most radical courage to write, the story of a talented black writer who achieves worldwide success on the strength of his anger and, in succeeding, gradually loses his anger and comes to be loved by everybody. Clearly, such acceptance can be considered a triumph for a black man in America, but it can be death for a black writer in whom anger and talent are indivisible.—JOHN W. ALDRIDGE, "The Fire Next Time?", _SR_, June 15, 1974, pp. 24–25

OTHER NOVELS

In part because of the insipidity of the prose, ⟨_Tell Me How Long the Train's Been Gone_ is⟩ as a whole . . . rather shadowy and dim. The account of the Harlem boyhood is moving at times, but Baldwin has described Harlem more effectively in some of his essays. Of the Harlem characters the only one who truly lives is Caleb, who is convincing both as young rebel and as middle-aged preacher. Leo, on the other hand, especially after he has become a popular actor, is not easy to believe in.

I wonder why Baldwin chose to write about Leo if he could make no more of him than he has done. The lesson of the novel seems to be that Negroes hate white people and have good reason for doing so, but Baldwin has preached on this text before and much more eloquently. All that is new is an emphasis on violence. In the last scene Leo and Christopher are driving around San Francisco after the former's release from the hospital. Christopher says, "Look, I'm a young cat. I've already been under the feet of horses, and I've already been beaten by chains. Well, you want me to keep going under the feet of horses?" When Leo says he doesn't, Christopher draws the moral: "Then I think you got to agree that we need us some guns. Right?" Although he does agree, Leo demurs a little: "But we're outnumbered. You know." And Christopher replies, "Shit. So were the early Christians."

The early Christians didn't want to kill off the Romans; they wanted to convert them, and used nonviolence as a way of doing so. But, even apart from that detail, the ending is weak. That white people in America have committed terrible crimes against American Negroes seems to me undeniable, and I can't blame Negroes for hating our guts. But I can't see hatred as a political program. It seems clear by now that the more fanatical Negro leaders have hurt their people more than they have hurt white people, and what we have seen is, I'm afraid, only the beginning. Put it in terms of the book: where is Leo going now? what will he do? what can come out of the sterility of hate? Perhaps Baldwin knows, at least subconsciously, the weakness of his position, and that is why the novel lacks strength.— GRANVILLE HICKS, "_Tell Me How Long the Train's Been Gone_" (1968), _Literary Horizons_, 1971, pp. 103–4

Just Above My Head is a long and ambitious novel in which we find again many of Baldwin's obsessions. He returns to the Harlem and the church of his first novel, *Go Tell It on the Mountain* (1953); to the homosexuality of *Giovanni's Room* (1956) and *Another Country* (1962); and to the social and political outrage that has inspired all his work. Whether the visions of the past are still vivid is another question. . . .

The anxious tone of this novel is a long way from the romantic melancholy of *Giovanni's Room*, a book neglected not only because of its homosexual protagonists but also because in it Baldwin was writing exclusively about white characters, though he was hardly the first black writer to do so. . . . Abandoning his idealism about love, Baldwin now writes sentimentally . . . . The parents are wise, forgiving, and everyone is uniformly resilient and "caring." If Baldwin means to honor the family as one of the reasons why blacks have, if nothing else, survived, his way of doing so is hardly convincing. Giving to the family generous amounts of noble qualities results in a neat symmetry: *us* versus *them*. The hagiographic approach helps to account for the flatness and didacticism of this work, as it did of Baldwin's last novel, *If Beale Street Could Talk* (1974), a book that was also dogmatic in its insistence on families and marriage as joyous alliances against an oppressively conceived "them." From Baldwin's other writings, one knows he has had a far more complicated idea of the family.

Increasing disillusionment over the years may have led Baldwin to search for something like a "people's book." But there is a repetitious and inert quality to *Just Above My Head*. Attempting to be earthy, to render a vernacular, black speech, Baldwin loses something when he declines to use the subtle language of his essays. In many ways the bombast in Hall's narration creates not a closeness to the material but a peculiar distance from it. In using a kind of ordinary language, hoping for what Richard Wright once called "the folk utterance," Baldwin has denied himself the natural lyrical mode of expression for which he has such a high gift.

Eldridge Cleaver's irresponsible attack in *Soul On Ice* may help to explain the turn in Baldwin's work. Cleaver claimed that Baldwin's work revealed a hatred of blacks, of himself, and a sycophantic love for whites, manifested in a racial death wish. Baldwin, according to Cleaver, attacked Wright's *Native Son* and dismissed Norman Mailer's *The White Negro* because he despised and feared masculinity. Cleaver also described the black homosexual as counterrevolutionary, castrated by the white man. His assault was doubtless prompted not only by the propaganda of Black Manhood but also by his own anti-intellectualism. The intimidation of Baldwin was extreme; along with many other black writers he faced the threat of being branded as a collaborator. Even as late as 1972, Baldwin could only answer by saying that he thought Cleaver merely felt impelled to issue a warning because he saw Baldwin as "dangerously odd, . . . of too much use to the Establishment to be trusted by blacks."

The fury of the Black Power movement seemed to demand of Baldwin a new set of definitions with which to express his loathing of America's racial troubles. In the long essay *No Name in the Streets* (1971), he charged Western societies with the "lie of their pretended humanism"; he once described how the "irresponsibility and cowardice" of the intellectual community during the McCarthy era first alerted him to the hypocrisy of rational liberalism. The political events of the Sixties—upheavals, assassinations, and secret police persecutions—fully confirmed his suspicions. Baldwin had made a choice, one he hoped to realize in his writing.

As Harold Cruse pointed out, however, Baldwin was not much interested in identifying social and economic causes. He always conceived of racial and political injustice as deriving from sin and requiring salvation, an argument rooted in his Christian training. His many exhortations to collective conscience went unheard. The nation did not atone for the sin of slavery and still moves away, indifferent, unchastised. Baldwin's exasperation with this "emotional poverty" has brought him to repudiate most of the claims of Western culture—"I don't believe in the wagons that bring bread to humanity"—and to seek a refuge, however delusory, in black solidarity.

It would appear from this book that he is weary of battling alone and wishes for a wider, more popular acceptance, a coming home to the "folk." There is a sad irony here. When Baldwin was young, in Paris, he quarreled with his "spiritual father," Richard Wright, over Baldwin's attack on the genre of protest novels. Wright felt betrayed and Baldwin defended himself by saying that all literature may be protest but not all protest was literature. Later, when recalling Wright's isolation from other blacks in Paris, his aloneness, his alienation, Baldwin wrote: "I could not help feeling: *Be Careful. Time is passing for you, too, and this may be happening to you one day.*" Baldwin now writes as if he is haunted by this prophecy. *Just Above My Head*, with its forced polemical tone, represents a conversion of sorts, a conversion to simplicities that so fine a mind as Baldwin's cannot embrace without grave loss.—Darryl Pinckney, "Blues for Mr. Baldwin," *NYRB*, Dec. 6, 1979, pp. 32–33

SHORT STORIES

The stories of *Going to Meet the Man* (1965) were evidently written at different stages in Baldwin's career, and many of their effects depend on interreflections back and forth with the earlier works. Some stories borrow the voice and setting of *Go Tell It on the Mountain*; others the jagged, brittle tones, the Manhattan underground world of *Another Country*. Many echo the essays, too, and there are even tastes of the whining, bullying rant of *The Fire Next Time*, the flip self-importance of the Mailer essay, the turgid speculations of *Nothing Personal*.

Of the weak, or perverse, or merely dispensable stories—four out of eight, which is certainly respectable—two are appendices to *Go Tell It on the Mountain*, with the same hero and his family, roughly the same manner and tone, although with almost nothing of the novel's harrowing, cathartic effect. Least impressive are "Previous Condition" and "This Morning, This Evening, So Soon," both of which represent the worst of the several James Baldwins: the pretentious, near-paranoiac, picked-on Negro, ostentatiously bearing all the sufferings of his race. In both cases, a clue is the total lack of detachment between the author and his chip-on-the-shoulder narrative heroes. The suffering, self-pitying voice is a sign of James Baldwin's least controlled and least valuable fiction.

Of the four better pieces, "Sonny's Blues" hovers delicately in tone between *Go Tell It on the Mountain* and *Another Country*. It is a small, artless, ambling story, one weak man's memory of his brother: the account of his long attempt to understand his brother Sonny, a junkie turned jazz pianist in Harlem, so quietly and uncertainly told that it is almost not a story at all, but just the telling, the trying: a confession that drifts coolly and unhurriedly through digression and reminiscence.

"Come Out of the Wilderness," at the opposite extreme, is a dazzling display of Baldwin's style at its sharpest. Its prose surface has a bristly, electric exactness, its dialogue the bright newness of good talk. The story, an open and unprejudiced playing through of the *odi et amo* tensions of an affair, seems a distillate of all that is best in *Another Country*. It has the same crackling Manhattan setting, the same crouching-cat tension. It has something new and surprising to say about the races. And it offers a cool, cruel analysis of the self-deluding stratagems of lovers, a microscopic plotting of our bitchy little hearts.

"The Man Child" is something entirely new for Baldwin, a highly charged, lyrical, pastoral tragedy. Four people—a boy, his father, his father's friend, his mother—are frozen in a mythic isolation. Their story grows, the trap tightens, slowly and expansively, through incremental repetitions, incantatory rhythms, the loving simple cadences of a legend.

The title story, "Going to Meet the Man," is Baldwin's second attempt to imagine sympathetically the mind of a Southern white bigot. I found his picture to be credible, intense, and at times almost hypnotically convincing: everything that *Blues for Mister Charlie* was not. It is basically a lynching story, of which there are literally dozens of examples in Negro literature. But this is the first to be drawn from the point of view of a more or less sympathetic observer, the Southern deputy sheriff as a young boy. As the boy's anticipation turns to a strange kind of horrified fulfillment, the reader may find himself forced to admit that there *is* in this barbaric, anti-human rite a genuine primeval satisfaction—a disturbing, very Baldwinesque lesson.—DAVID LITTLEJOHN, *Black on White*, 1966, pp. 133–35

DRAMA

If there is ever a Black Muslim nation, and if there is television in that nation, then something like Acts Two and Three of *Blues for Mr. Charlie* will probably be the kind of thing the housewives will watch on afternoon TV. It is soap opera designed to illustrate the superiority of blacks over whites. The blues Baldwin may think he is singing for Mr. Charlie's sinning seem to me really to be sung for his inferiority. First, Negroes are better-looking, particularly Negro women. When the white men in the play claim *They're after our women!* they are obviously having guilt-ridden fantasies: almost every Negro man around would testify, and almost everyone does, that white women are cold, unappealing, "pasty-faced bitches"— particularly Richard, who for all his promiscuity with the pasty-faces of New York, is well-cured of such frivolous lust by the time he appears back home: that is, on the stage. On the other hand, when the Negro students (mostly the Negroes are students; mostly the whites are plain old crackers) reply *You're after ours!* the play then "proves" this to be true. The only sexual affairs of real consequence to Lyle Britten and Parnell James were with Negro women—Lyle with a girl both pretty and passionate, and Parnell with a girl in possession of both these qualities, plus a third: she was a reader. The first time he came upon her alone she was poring over *The Red and the Black* in the library. Negroes then, even studious ones, make love better. They dance better. And they cook better. And their penises are longer, or stiffer. Indeed, so much that comprises the Southern stereotype of the Negro comes back through Negro mouths, as testimony to their human superiority, that finally one is about ready to hear that the eating of watermelon increases one's word power. It is as though the injustice of our racial situation is that inferiors are enslaving their superiors, rather than the other way around. . . .

His making a hero of blackness, combined with his sentimentalizing of masculinity, blinds Baldwin to the fact that Richard's condition is no less hideously comic than Lyle Britten's. There is no glory or hope, not a shred of it, to be found in the life of either the black man or the white. What these characters give evidence to, what the play seems to be about really, is the small-mindedness of the male sex. It is about the narcissistic, pompous, and finally ridiculous demands made by the male ego when confronted by moral castastrophe. Of course to take pride in one's maleness, as so many of the men in this play would like to do, is hardly ridiculous; but to identify this maleness with the size and capabilities of one's penis is to reveal about as much depth of imagination as I remember finding one long Saturday afternoon among my colleagues in an Army motor pool. It is shattering (and not as the writer intends so obviously for it to be) to hear the young Negro woman, Juanita, announce to the audience at the close of Act Two in the most stirring tones, "And I'll see the world again— the marvelous world. And I'll have learned from Richard— how to love." From *Richard?* Richard's boasting about being black and bragging about his penis have blinded somebody to the truth about him, which is that neither he, nor Lyle, for that matter, is a wretched man; they only behave wretchedly. They are banal men who suffer most their own banality. In fact, *A Study in the Banality of Evil* would have been a title more to the point of the play that Baldwin has actually written than *Blues for Mr. Charlie*.—PHILIP ROTH, "Channel X: Two Plays on the Race Conflict," *NYRB*, May 28, 1964, p. 11

The truth is that *Blues for Mister Charlie* isn't really about what it claims to be about. It is supposed to be about racial strife. But it is really about the anguish of tabooed sexual longings, about the crisis of identity which comes from confronting these longings, and about the rage and destructiveness (often, self-destructiveness) by which one tries to surmount this crisis. It has, in short, a psychological subject. The surface may be Odets, but the interior is pure Tennessee Williams. What Baldwin has done is to take the leading theme of the serious theater of the fifties—sexual anguish—and work it up as a political play. Buried in *Blues for Mister Charlie* is the plot of several successes of the last decade: the gruesome murder of a handsome virile young man by those who envy him his virility.—SUSAN SONTAG, "Going to Theater, etc.," *Against Interpretation*, 1966, p. 151

Both times I saw the play there were as many, if not more, whites in the audience than there were Negroes. One could not help but feel the negative vibrations radiating from the whites during the major portion of the evening. They seemed to squirm throughout the play and grow little in their seats; many tried to hold a straight face (face of chalk), but one could see and feel the hot charge boiling beneath their white masks. Upon two occasions—(a) when Richard (the Negro hero), back down South telling his friends how many white girls he has slept with up North, is showing a photograph of a girl with long hair and remarks, "Man, you know where all that hair's been"; and (b) when Richard tells Lyle, (the Southern bigot) who has been threatening him, "Man, are you scared I'm going to get in your wife's drawers?"—I thought half of the white audience might jump up and storm out of the theater. But they held onto their seats. Again, after Richard has been murdered by Lyle, and Juanita (Richard's sweetheart, played by Diana Sands) in lamentation delivers her speech on how Richard made love to her, describing it in plain but powerful language, telling how she took Richard into her womb and how she "grind" him and how meaningful the act was—again, I saw the theater faces of white people twist and contort in agony and revulsion. In fact, the white ladies sitting next to me began gossiping very rapidly about the careers of Rip Torn (Lyle) and Pat Hingle (Parnell, the Southern liberal) as if nothing was happening on stage at all. And the applause of the whites—one got the impression that it was as much out of nervous reaction to cover up embarrassment as it was an expression of honest enthusiasm.

On the other hand, Negroes seemed to be enthralled with delight and moral vindication to see for the first time the true nature of their lives, and their plight, played back to them with dignity and no beating around the bush. Many Negroes were there with white companions. I recall one tall dark Negro who is a famous man. He came in with his white girl and sat down as if he was out for the usual "highbrow" theater evening. Before the play was half through, the Negro had unbuttoned his collar, had reared back in his seat, and was looking around as if he himself had written *Blues for Mister Charlie*. Pride was bursting on his face and chest.—CALVIN C. HERNTON, "A Fiery Baptism," *Amistad*, Summer 1970, p. 201

ESSAYS

In 1961, five years after *Giovanni's Room*, James Baldwin brought out his second book of essays, *Nobody Knows My Name*. Those five years had not been silent years; nor were they a period of retreat. On the contrary. The author had during that time traveled considerably, taken on assignments and published the essays (before they were collected) in various journals. Most of the pieces were mainly concerned with the question of color, and though for Baldwin the question of color is the question of humanity, it is in this interval, because of a number of brilliant essays ("The Discovery of What It Means to Be an American," "Princes and Powers," "Faulkner and Desegregation," "Alas, Poor Richard," "The Black Boy Looks at the White Boy") that he becomes The Spokesman. I am tempted to say Captive Spokesman, but the dialectic between "captive" and "voluntary" is subtle and elusive. There is nothing I can think of that James Baldwin is not aware of; of course he is aware of the problems implicit in his statement that his greatest responsibility is to last and get his work done. But between the resolve and the execution lies an abyss. Between the thought and the act falls the shadow. *Nobody Knows My Name* is a rare and great book, yet one senses in it a kind of tragedy—not flaw, but tragedy. Society has somehow got hold of him in the wrong sort of way. Some subtle deflection has set in. The essays correspond to a part of himself only. He is engaged profoundly, yet partially. There are, one feels, enormities in Baldwin that are not engaged—curiosity, mysticism, bawdiness, laughter, poetry (dark and haunted), tenderness. Is he doing, metaphorically, what Lenin did, refusing to listen to Beethoven because it made him gentle? In order to be most effective must one become monolithic, steel, Stalin?—HARVEY BREIT, "James Baldwin and Two Footnotes," *The Creative Present*, eds. Nina Balakian, Charles Simmons, 1963, pp. 11–12

Mr. Baldwin would admit, I think, that when (and this is quite often) he is guided by his emotions he finds himself in a position not far from that of the Black Muslims. He quite rightly resents the claims of whites that they are superior to colored people. But in fact he thinks that the colored are superior. True, they have, like the anti-fascists, been made, almost involuntarily, better as a result of the crimes perpetrated against them, for which they are in no way responsible. Few independent witnesses would dispute this. But Mr. Baldwin also makes Henry-Miller-like generalizations about the emasculation, joylessness, lack of sensuality, etc., of white Americans to prove their inferiority to the joyous, spiritual, good, warm Negroes.

I agree that in certain ways, and not only in America, the so-called backward, primitive, oppressed, and—for the most part—colored people are "better" than us whites who form a

world class of "haves" and rulers. The quality of this superiority James Baldwin admirably conveys by the word *sensual*: "To be sensual, I think, is to respect and rejoice in the force of life, of life itself, and to be present in all that one does, from the effort of loving to the breaking of bread." Negroes—and one might add (although Mr. Baldwin does not do so) a large number of other people in the world who are "have-nots"—are forced back onto personal values. It is by no means clear, though, whether the oppressed if they were set over their oppressors— the blacks over the whites—would not lose their "sensuality" and become as bad as the present white ruling class. Lack of sensuality is the result of running and deriving benefits from an industrial society. The "sensual" are simply the outcasts. . . .

Mr. Baldwin asserts that the white American does not recognize death because he does not recognize life. He does not recognize the "constants" of life in himself, and therefore he does not recognize them in the Negro. If he recognized the Negro as a being like himself, then he would recognize in himself those constants which he acknowledges in the Negro. Thus the black can "save" the white by making the white conscious of his humanity.

This position is summarized in his letter to his nephew: "*Integration* means that we, with love, shall force our brothers to see themselves as they are, to cease fleeing from reality and begin to change it." . . .

Although Mr. Baldwin considers love is the only answer to the American race problem, it is not at all evident from his book that he loves white Americans, and at times it is even doubtful whether he loves his own people. Not that I blame him for this. What I do criticize him for is postulating a quite impossible demand as the only way of dealing with a problem that has to be solved.

Mr. Baldwin's bias towards discussing the American Negro as though he had no characteristics in common with Negroes elsewhere or other oppressed people and classes contributes to his tendency to think that the problem can only be met by all Negroes and all white Americans being seized at the same moment by the same wave of love. My argument is that the relationship of Negro to white exists within a situation comparable to other situations. It is partly a situation of color, partly one of class. The American Negro is in effect a world proletarian who suffers under the disadvantage that he appears to be indelibly branded as such by the blackness of his skin. People used to talk about the European proletariat as Baldwin does about Negroes, as though their status was inbred and could only be changed by love (which meant it could not be changed at all). But if you change the circumstances of the workers, so long as they are white they simply become like other white people who are not workers. What is menacing about the color problem is that even if you change the status of the Negro his color remains the same. Color prejudice is extremely deep, and far more widespread than Mr. Baldwin seems to realize, since it exists all over the world, where similar circumstances (such as that of there being a majority of Negro proletarians among a minority of whites) produce similar results. Moreover, color prejudice is not confined to white Americans and Europeans. It exists between colored people themselves. . . .

So-called capitalists have on the whole learned to legislate away the social problems which logically seemed to lead to irreconcilable positions ending in revolution. The color problem is the twentieth-century version of what in the nineteenth century was the problem of the proletariat. In theory at least it should today be soluble without revolution. What Mr. Baldwin calls "love"—at any rate all generous feeling—is required to support the legislation and anticipate the very dangerous situation which will arise unless a great deal is done very quickly. The great contribution of Mr. Baldwin is that he finds words to express what one knows to be true: how it feels to be an American Negro. Within his own works he has solved the problem of integration: not by love, but by imagination using words which know no class nor color bars.—STEPHEN SPENDER, "James Baldwin: Voice of a Revolution," *PR*, Summer 1963, pp. 257–60

Readers of Baldwin's previous work, both his essays and his fiction, will find little ⟨in *The Fire Next Time*⟩ that is startlingly new. The confessional voice, the apocalyptic style, the prophetic warning, the turbulent emotion contained and disciplined by stylistic elegance, the gospel of love after the storm of hate—all this is familiar enough. Even the autobiographical material—memories of his preacher father, his Harlem boyhood, his own boyhood crisis of faith and renunciation—will recall his first novel, *Go Tell It on the Mountain*. What is new is that this is a summation in which all previously formed fragments and thoughts are yoked violently together, fused, under tremendous pressure into a single statement. The effect is one of credo, manifesto: Here, finally, in all deliberation (Baldwin seems to be saying), is where I stand. It is desperately important, for me, for you, for all of us, that you heed what I say, and act upon it.

Don't look for analysis of the "Negro Question" here, any more than you would look for it in a sermon, or a lyric poem. Baldwin is a novelist, not a historian or sociologist; and his essays are a novelist's essays. "Down at the Cross" is a letter from within, though it is addressed to his countrymen, and the world. The state it seeks to analyze is an internal one; its temperature is the heat of feeling. Baldwin evokes a state of mind—his own, and, possibly, that of some other Negro intellectuals. How representative his particular angle of vision may be, is another matter.

The job of lyric, however, is to find language and form for how the lyricist feels; if, in telling, he discloses or discovers your feeling too, you owe him a debt you can hardly repay. When Baldwin records, with finest notation, his exacerbated sense of what it is like to be a Negro; when he renders, with furious conviction, the indignities and humiliations which attend his every step, the stifling and perpetual pressure which closes in upon a Negro simply because he is one; when he conveys his sense of the social climate by which the Negro comes despairingly to know, from earliest childhood, the atmosphere in which desperation is bred, that he is a pariah, a little more than animal, but less than human—then, I have no doubt, there can scarcely be a Negro who does not listen to him with full assent. But when we listen to any of Baldwin's voices—his passionately exhortatory one, or his carefully modulated one, his denunciation or his final warning or his pleading—it is not the voice, nor is it the tone, of reason we are hearing, for Baldwin is not a "reasonable" man; it is a lamentation, and a curse, and a prayer. *The Fire Next Time* is a tract-for-the-times, not an argument in the usual sense; and if we are not to be disappointed by false expectations, we must approach it for what it is.

The occasion which provides Baldwin his perspective for assessing precisely where he stands is an evening he spent with Elijah Muhammad, the prophet of the Black Muslim movement (of which Malcolm X is the leading public figure). The question placed before him was, in effect, Whose side are you on? Ours or theirs? God's or the Devil's?

On the Black Muslim side there was (is) absolute es-

chatological certainty—a theology, a theory of history, a sense of destiny; and on Baldwin's, ambiguity, doubt, pain; the anguish that arises from knowing at one and the same time that the empirical evidence on which the Muslims base their protest and movement is, simply and incontrovertibly, the life history of the American Negro, and that their conclusions, based on separatism, are, for him, not only inadequate and mistaken in the way a political program may be, but profoundly—morally, spiritually—wrong. Their evidence is his (and ours); and no one has sought it out more steadily, seen it more severely and sensitively, or recorded it more brilliantly and movingly than has Baldwin himself.

It is at the point where commitments must be made that he parts ways, though not entirely without guilt, with the Muslims. So deep and unremitting is the hatred which is the entire emotional content of their ideology that they must renounce, cut themselves off from, their American past, from all involvement with the white devil, even to the extent of discarding Christian names and assuming personas. These are the terms of the dialectic; against the purity of their absolutes, Baldwin painfully wrenches from the depths of his own hatred a hope of love. In effect, if not in explicit intention, that is what the book, and especially the "Letter from a Region of My Mind" is—the response Baldwin never made to Elijah Muhammad that night in Chicago.

To love the lyncher and embrace the hangman—that is a strange resolution. Yet Baldwin's message is not to be confused with that ancient prayer, for there is no forgiving *these* crimes. The key term of the discourse, "love," must be defined in some radically new way: as it stands it accommodates too many antithetical terms and motives to be of much use in ordinary discourse. "Love," as it appears here, is no program of action, no doctrine for a new movement; it is an action and a movement which must occur within the suffering self, a commitment on one's own part to accept his historic and individual past and compel others to a like acceptance—to force, by the revealing power of the paradox, the white man to accept himself, to accept the tragedy, and condition, that is our common lot, to accept his sexuality and that of others, his death and theirs. For if the white man can accept himself, he can love himself, and love others, love the very fact of their otherness. And what Baldwin invokes is the apocalyptic power of love, the irresistible forcing power of love to induce the catalyst which will, in his conception, alter the course of history. One must first have an identity before he can acknowledge the identity of others; one must be capable of love and *self*-respect before he can give love and respect others.

Now it is terribly easy to dismiss the Muslim doctrine as paranoid: anyone will show you how to do it; and it is almost as easy to dismiss Baldwin's witness as a fashionable compound made of Russian novels and French existentialism and Viennese depth psychology—as mysticism, or, at any rate, mystery. And while you are cogently pointing out to Baldwin how quixotic and absurd he is—and love *is* the most absurd of all our odd notions—the Government of the United States in its awful majesty can barely get a small girl into a kindergarten no child should have to go to, or a young man into a university that is something less than a community of scholars in passionate pursuit of the truth, or a citizen into a poll booth so that he may cast a vote for county sheriff or coroner. While you are telling him about the Supreme Court decision of 1954, Baldwin has genocide in a region of his mind; meanwhile, you counsel patience, but there is no time; and as you prove progress, the heart sinks.

The Fire Next Time is an authoritative argument from

extremity. Baldwin, it should finally be noted; derives that title from a "prophecy, re-created from the Bible in song by a slave" and closes his book with the passage of origin:

> God gave Noah the rainbow sign,
> No more water, the fire next time!

—SAUL MALOFF, "Love: The Movement Within," *Nation*, March 2, 1963, pp. 181–82

. . . Like Richard Avedon's, James Baldwin's rage is here inspired largely by opportunism, but while the photographer is taking advantage of the times, the writer is letting the times take advantage of him. Once direct and biting in his criticism of American life, Mr. Baldwin has repeated his revolt so often that it has now become a reflex mannerism that curls his fingers around his pen and squeezes out empty rhetoric. In *Nothing Personal*, certainly, Baldwin has either adapted his ideas to the intellectual chic of the women's magazines, or he is putting his readers on. How else is one to explain such Norman Vincent Pealisms as "I have always felt a human being could only be saved by another human being"—and "One must say Yes to life and embrace it wherever it is found"—and, again, "All that God can do, and all that I expect Him to do, is lend one courage to continue one's journey and face one's end, like a man."

These are some of Baldwin's concluding affirmations, designed to harmonize with Avedon's surf symphony. To accompany Avedon's rogue's gallery, Baldwin supplies vestpocket indictments of TV, advertising, architecture, psychoanalysis, and the New York Police Force. But Baldwin's attacks are significant less for their familiar content than for the conditioned response they are expected to provoke in the reader—and, especially, for the format in which they appear. But lending himself to such an enterprise, Baldwin reveals that he is now part and parcel of the very things he is criticizing; and this curious assimilation accounts in part for something in his writing first noticed by Marcus Klein—his ambiguous use of the word *we*. Constantly shifting between objective nouns and first person plural pronouns ("talking to Americans is usually extremely uphill work. We are afraid to reveal ourselves because we trust ourselves so little") or between the generic and the personal ("our opulence is so pervasive that people who are afraid to lose whatever they think they have persuade themselves of the truth of a lie. . . ."), Baldwin exposes a highly uncertain critical identity, never sure whether he is talking for himself, for the Negroes, for Americans, or for the whole human race.

This uncertainty leads him not only into contorted grammar but also into incredible self-inflation. My favorite Baldwinism—and a typical one, though it comes from another context—is this: "If you pretend that I hauled all that cotton for you just because I love you, you're mad." When the messianic fit is upon him, Baldwin frequently develops a bass-baritone voice and starts singing "Let my people go," confusing himself with the whole of Negro history. By the same token, he is presumptuous enough to generalize wildly about the American young ("we have no respect for children"), even though he himself is childless, and to deny the existence of any happy marriages, though he has never been married. The author of *Notes of a Native Son* was a highly aware and complicated individual; the author of *Nothing Personal*, and the rest of his recent writings, is merely a self-constituted Symbol, bucking hard for the rank of Legend. . . .

. . . America is sick all right, but it is sick in more things than these physicians know. It is sick, very sick, for example, in some of its critics, particularly the two represented here, who make the doctors and the malady seem almost indistinguishable. *Nothing Personal* shows us an honorable tradition of revolt gone sour, given over to fame and ambition, discredited by shadowy motives, twisted by questionable ideals, turned into a theatrical gesture by café society performers. The participation of Richard Avedon in this hypocritical charade is not of very great moment, since Avedon's photography—whether he is blandishing or subverting his models—still remains an arm of show business. But the participation of James Baldwin signifies the further degeneration of a once courageous and beautiful dissent. Whether this is temporary, one cannot say. Let us fervently hope it is. But meanwhile it is serious enough to merit our deepest apprehension and regret.—ROBERT BRUSTEIN, "Everybody Knows My Name," *NYRB*, Dec. 17, 1964, pp. 10–11

Baldwin still believes in love, equating it with "grace," as both means and end of greater human understanding. He makes some positive statements about love in his essays. In *The Fire Next Time*, in national and personal terms, he strikes at the necessity for coming to terms with outdated idealism, asserting that Americans chronically do not wish to face reality, though the American dream stands to be revised in harsher light. For as long as they resist such change they will lack "authority" (just as the men in his fiction lack authority). "It is the responsibility of free men to trust and to celebrate what is constant—birth, struggle, and death are constant, and so is love, though we may not always think so—and to apprehend the nature of change, to be able and willing to change. I speak of change not on the surface but in the depths—change in the sense of renewal." But one must comprehend love as something more than childish ideal and demand. He discusses a kind of love that is "so desperately sought and so cunningly avoided. Love takes off the masks that we fear we cannot live without and know we cannot live within. I use the word 'love' here not merely in the personal sense but as a state of being, or a state of grace—not in the infantile American sense of being made happy but in the tough and universal sense of quest and daring and growth."

This conception of "love" is furthered in another passage from *The Fire Next Time*, on the topic of sensuality, so that it resembles that union of tender affectionate feelings and sensual feelings prescribed above. "To be sensual is to respect and rejoice in the force of life, of life itself, and to be *present* in all that one does, from the effort of loving to the breaking of bread." Such sensuality is more than lasciviousness, or panting ungratified sexuality—"The word 'sensual' is not intended to bring to mind quivering dusky maidens or priapic black studs." Leaving aside racial implications (a special aspect of the problem), we see it is still a state of "grace" or renewal being described ("to celebrate," and "the breaking of bread," after all, suggest "holy" communion). That Baldwin feels impelled to explore (in writing which postdates the fiction considered here) what sensuality is *not* is reminiscent of the troubled sexuality of his male characters, which is to say that Baldwin comprehends solutions that his characters do not enact, that he envisions a state in which men *co-exist* harmoniously with women who are neither "mothers" nor "whores," rather than cling to their convictions of desertions and betrayals from the opposite sex in perpetual self-justification of their own flights from and faithlessness towards them: this is a state in which reality would no longer "stink."—CHARLOTTE ALEXANDER, "The 'Stink' of Reality: Mothers and Whores in James Baldwin's Fiction," *LP*, Spring 1968, pp. 25–26

F. W. DUPEE
"James Baldwin and the 'Man'"
The New York Review of Books, February 1963, pp. 1–2

As a writer of polemical essays on the Negro question James Baldwin has no equals. He probably has, in fact, no real competitors. The literary role he has taken on so deliberately and played with so agile an intelligence is one that no white writer could possibly imitate and that few Negroes, I imagine, would wish to embrace *in toto*. Baldwin impresses me as being the Negro *in extremis*, a virtuoso of ethnic suffering, defiance and aspiration. His role is that of the man whose complexion constitutes his fate, and not only in a society poisoned by prejudice but, it sometimes seems, in general. For he appears to have received a heavy dose of existentialism; he is at least half-inclined to see the Negro question in the light of the Human Condition. So he wears his color as Hester Prynne did her scarlet letter, proudly. And like her he converts this thing, in itself so absurdly material, into a form of consciousness, a condition of spirit. Believing himself to have been branded as different from and inferior to the white majority, he will make a virtue of his situation. He will be different and in his own way be better.

His major essays—for example, those collected in *Notes of a Native Son*—show the extent to which he is able to be different and in his own way better. Most of them were written, as other such pieces generally are, for the magazines, some obviously on assignment. And their subjects—a book, a person, a locale, an encounter—are the inevitable subjects of magazine essays. But Baldwin's way with them is far from inevitable. To apply criticism "in depth" to *Uncle Tom's Cabin* is, for him, to illuminate not only a book, an author, an age, but a whole strain in a country's culture. Similarly with those routine themes, the Paris expatriate and Life With Father, which he treats in "Equal In Paris" and the title piece of *Notes of a Native Son*, and which he wholly transfigures. Of course the transfiguring process in Baldwin's essays owes something to the fact that the point of view is a Negro's, an outsider's, just as the satire of American manners in *Lolita* and *Morte d'Urban* depends on their being written from the angle of, respectively, a foreign-born creep and a Catholic priest. But Baldwin's point of view in his essays is not merely that of the generic Negro. It is, as I have said, that of a highly stylized Negro, a role which he plays with an artful and zestful consistency and which he expresses in a language distinguished by clarity, brevity, and a certain formal elegance. He is in love, for example, with syntax, with sentences that mount through clearly articulated stages to a resounding and clarifying climax and then gracefully subside. For instance this one, from *The Fire Next Time*:

> Girls, only slightly older than I was, who sang in the choir or taught Sunday school, the children of holy parents, underwent, before my eyes, their incredible metamorphosis, of which the most bewildering aspect was not their budding breasts or their rounding behinds but something deeper and more subtle, in their eyes their heat, their odor, and the inflection of their voices.

Nobody else in democratic America writes sentences like this anymore. It suggests the ideal prose of an ideal literary community, some aristocratic France of one's dreams. This former Harlem boy has undergone his own incredible metamorphosis.

His latest book, *The Fire Next Time*, differs in important ways from his earlier work in the essay. Its subjects are less concrete, less clearly defined; to a considerable extent he has

exchanged prophecy for criticism, exhortation for analysis, and the results for his mind and style are in part disturbing. *The Fire Next Time* gets its title from a slave song: "God gave Noah the rainbow sign,/No more water, the fire next time." But this small book with the incendiary title consists of two independent essays, both in the form of letters. One is a brief affair entitled "My Dungeon Shook" and addressed to "My Nephew on the One Hundredth Anniversary of the Emancipation." The ominous promise of this title is fulfilled in the text. Between the hundred-year-old anniversary and the fifteen-year-old nephew the disparity is too great even for a writer of Baldwin's rhetorical powers. The essay reads like some specimen of "public speech" as practiced by MacLeish or Norman Corwin. It is not good Baldwin.

The other, much longer, much more significant essay appeared first in a pre-Christmas number of *The New Yorker*, where it made, understandably, a sensation. It is called "Down At the Cross: Letter From a Region of My Mind." The subtitle should be noted. Evidently the essay is to be taken as only a partial or provisional declaration on Baldwin's part, a single piece of his mind. Much of it, however, requires no such appeal for caution on the reader's part. Much of it is unexceptionally first-rate. For example, the reminiscences of the writer's boyhood, which form the lengthy introduction. Other of Baldwin's writings have made us familiar with certain aspects of his Harlem past. Here he concentrates on quite different things: the boy's increasing awareness of the abysmally narrow world of choice he inhabits as a Negro, his attempt to escape a criminal existence by undergoing a religious conversion and becoming at fifteen a revivalist preacher, his discovery that he must learn to "inspire fear" if he hopes to survive the fear inspired in him by "the man"—the white man.

In these pages we come close to understanding why he eventually assumed his rather specialized literary role. It seems to have grown naturally out of his experience of New York City. As distinct from a rural or small-town Negro boy, who is early and firmly taught his place, young Baldwin knew the treacherous fluidity and anonymity of the metropolis, where hidden taboos and unpredictable animosities lay in wait for him and a trip to the 42nd Street Library could be a grim adventure. All this part of the book is perfect; and when Baldwin finally gets to what is his ostensible subject, the Black Muslims or Nation of Islam movement, he is very good too. As good, that is, as possible considering that his relations with the movment seem to have been slight. He once shared a television program with Malcolm X, "the movement's second-in-command," and he paid a brief and inconclusive visit to the first-in-command, the Honorable Elijah Muhammad, and his entourage at the party's headquarters in Chicago. (Muhammad ranks as a prophet; to him the Black Muslim doctrines were "revealed by Allah Himself.") Baldwin reports the Chicago encounter in charming detail and with what looks like complete honesty. On his leaving the party's rather grand quarters, the leader insisted on providing him with a car and driver to protect him "from the white devils until he gets wherever it is he is going." Baldwin accepted, he tells us, adding wryly: "I was, in fact, going to have a drink with several white devils on the other side of town."

He offers some data on the Black Muslim movement, its aims and finances. But he did a minimum of homework here. Had he done more he might at least have provided a solid base for the speculative fireworks the book abounds in. To cope thoroughly with the fireworks in short space, or perhaps any space, seems impossible. Ideas shoot from the book's pages as the sparks fly upward, in bewildering quantity and at random. I don't mean that it is all dazzle. On the cruel paradoxes of the Negro's life, the failures of Christianity, the relations of Negro and Jew, Baldwin is often superb. But a lot of damage is done to his argument by his indiscriminate raids on Freud, Lawrence, Sartre, Genet and other psychologists, metaphysicians and melodramatists. Still more damage is done by his refusal to draw on anyone so humble as Martin Luther King and his fellow-practitioners of nonviolent struggle.

For example: "White Americans do not believe in death, and this is why the darkness of my skin so intimidates them." But suppose one or two white Americans are *not* intimidated. Suppose someone coolly asks what it means to "believe in death." Again: "Do I really *want* to be integrated into a burning house?" Since you have no other, yes; and the better-disposed firemen will welcome your assistance. Again: "A vast amount of the energy that goes into what we call the Negro problem is produced by the white man's profound desire not to be judged by those who are not white." You exaggerate the white man's consciousness of the Negro. Again: "The real reason that non-violence is considered to be a virtue in Negroes . . . is that white men do not want their lives, their self-image, or their property threatened." Of course they don't, especially their lives. Moreover, this imputing of "real reasons" for the behavior of entire populations is self-defeating, to put it mildly. One last quotation, this time a regular apocalypse:

> In order to survive as a human, moving, moral weight in the world, America and all the Western nations will be forced to reexamine themselves and release themselves from many things that are now taken to be sacred, and to discard nearly all the assumptions that have been used to justify their lives and their anguish and their crimes so long.

Since whole cultures have never been known to "discard nearly all their assumptions" and yet remain intact, this amounts to saying that any essential improvement in Negro-white relations, and thus in the quality of American life, is unlikely.

So much for the fireworks. What damage, as I called it, do they do to the writer and his cause—which is also the concern of plenty of others? When Baldwin replaces criticism with prophecy, he manifestly weakens his grasp of his role, his style, and his great theme itself. And to what end? Who is likely to be moved by such arguments, unless it is the more literate Black Muslims, whose program Baldwin specifically rejects as both vindictive and unworkable. And with the situation as it is in Mississippi and elsewhere—dangerous, that is, to the Negro struggle and the whole social order—is not a writer of Baldwin's standing obliged to submit his assertions to some kind of pragmatic test, some process whereby their truth or untruth will be gauged according to their social utility? He writes: "The Negroes of this country may never be able to rise to power, but they are very well placed indeed to precipitate chaos and ring down the curtain on the American dream." I should think that the anti-Negro extremists were even better placed than the Negroes to precipitate chaos, or at least to cause a lot of trouble; and it is unclear to me how *The Fire Next Time*, in its madder moments, can do anything except inflame the former and confuse the latter. Assuming that a *book* can do anything to either.

IRVING HOWE
"James Baldwin: At Ease in Apocalypse"
Harper's Magazine, September 1968, pp. 92–100

At least in our literature, the black man remains invisible. Almost anyone can rage about "the Negro question,"
almost anyone pronounce and exhort. But only two or three American novelists have thus far managed to write novels in which Negro men and women come through as credible figures. How disconcerting it is, how unsettling to our liberal pieties, that only from William Faulkner, a Southerner whose opinions on this matter ranged from the benighted to the befuddled, have we gotten a sizable group of Negro characters in whose reality we can immediately believe! Why blacks should be invisible to white writers we have no difficulty in supposing ourselves to know, usually through a masochistic notion that does little credit to the humanity of either color. But what is a good deal more baffling is the scarcity of serious fiction by Negro writers. There is Richard Wright's *Native Son* and, still more notable, Ralph Ellison's *Invisible Man*; there are a few younger Negro writers of talent though not yet fulfillment; and not much else.

A few decades ago we all thought we knew why Negro writers were blocked. They were castrated by the psychology of deference; they kept their anger bottled up; they had not achieved that identity which comes to the suppressed only through rebellion. Then Richard Wright published *Native Son*, a crude but overwhelming book, in which the central figure is not so much a distinctive human being as an elemental force through which to release the rage black men had not dared to express. Other Negro writers, stirred and perhaps liberated by Wright's achievement, tried to imitate his posture of wrath, but rarely with success; for as it turned out, the significance of *Native Son*, which I take to be a major American text, is at least partly that among books of its kind it was the one that came first.

In time, then, it began to seem that anger might not be enough and that protest might turn out to be a sterile box in which the middle-class whites, murmuring their guilt and sympathy, would be delighted to keep Negro writers locked. A young and then unknown black writer named James Baldwin wrote in 1951 that the failure of the protest novel "lies in its insistence that it is [man's] categorization alone which is real and which cannot be transcended." Rebelling against Richard Wright even while acknowledging that Wright had influenced him profoundly, Baldwin declared his wish to compose novels in which *the* Negro would be dissolved as a social phantom of hatred and condescension, and instead a variety of Negroes, in all their particularity and complexity, would be imagined. He wanted to write the kind of novel that would show the life of the Negroes through "an unspoken recognition of shared experiences which creates a way of life." And meanwhile he published those brilliant, nervous essays—gestures of repudiation, glimmers of intention—called *Notes of a Native Son*.

The program was Baldwin's, yet by a bitterly ironic turn, its realization came not from him but from another writer, Ralph Ellison, whose *Invisible Man* is the only novel written by an American Negro which on a major scale brings to imaginative life the experience of black people, both in the North and the South. Baldwin did publish *Go Tell It on the Mountain*, a delicate narrative, blending memoir and fiction, about his Harlem boyhood; but his major talent, then as now, was for the essay, first through a style of Jamesian elegance and later through a style of flaming declamation. Yet the program which the young Baldwin set for himself—a program of aesthetic autonomy and faithfulness to private experience, as against ideological noise and blunt stereotype—was almost impossible for the Negro writer to realize. Even *Invisible Man*, for all its imaginative freedom, could not do so completely.

In the early 'sixties there took place a fierce polemic between Ralph Ellison and myself concerning the role of the Negro writer in America, and more particularly, the extent to which that writer would have to accept the voicing of protest as his unavoidable obligation or burden. In the eyes of most literary people, Ellison had the better of this exchange. He seemed to be defending the independence of the creative act and the right of Negroes to compose with precisely the freedom white novelists enjoyed, while I seemed to be saying that for the foreseeable future the Negro writers would not be able, even if they wished, to escape the imperatives of protest. There is no point in rehearsing this argument here, and I am hardly the one to do it—except to remark that in those years the intellectual atmosphere, strongly conservative and antipolitical, predisposed many people to sympathize with Ellison's views, while today both of us would be denounced as "finks" by militant blacks and certain literary people for whom a nuance of thought looms as a personal affront.

When Baldwin published his novel *Another Country* in 1962, I saw it as a partial confirmation of my views. All of his earlier values—complexity, subtlety, irony—were abandoned in behalf of a style that was sometimes as crude, though never as powerful, as that of Wright in *Native Son*. For *Another Country* came out at a time when the Negro revolt was beginning to gather strength, and Baldwin, who had been one of its most eloquent public spokesmen, probably could not have avoided the stance of militancy even if he had cared to—the very stance which in his early essays he had found so damaging to literary achievement.

Now, after having read Baldwin's new novel *Tell Me How Long the Train's Been Gone*, I have come to feel that the whole problem of Negro writing in America is far more complex than I had ever recognized, probably more complex than even Ellison had supposed, and perhaps so complex as to be, at this moment, almost beyond discussion. *Tell Me How Long the Train's Been Gone* is a remarkably bad novel, signaling the collapse of a writer of some distinction. But apart from its intrinsic qualities, it helps make clear that neither militancy nor its refusal, neither a program of aesthetic autonomy nor its denial, seems enough for the Negro novelist who wishes to transmute the life of his people into a serious piece of fiction. No program, no rhetoric, no political position makes that much difference. What does make the difference I would now be hard pressed to say, but as I have been thinking about the Negro writers I know or have read, I have come to believe that their problems are a good deal more personal than we have usually supposed. For the Negro writer, if he is indeed to be a *writer*, public posture matters less than personal identity. His problem is to reach into his true feelings, be they militant or passive, as distinct from the feelings he thinks he should have, or finds it fashionable to have, about the life of his fellow blacks. The Negro writer shares in the sufferings of an exploited race, and it would be outrageous to suppose that simply by decision he can avoid declaring his outrage; but he is also a solitary man, solitary insofar as he is a writer, solitary even more because he is a black writer, and solitary most of all if he is a black man who writes. Frequently he is detached from and in opposition to other blacks; unavoidably he must find himself troubled by his relationship to the whole looming tradition of Western literature, which is both his and never entirely his; and sooner or later he must profoundly wish to get away from racial polemic and dialectic, simply in order to reach, in his own lifetime, some completeness of being. As it seems to me, James Baldwin has come to a point where all of these problems crush down upon him and he does not quite know who he is, as writer, celebrity, or black man; so that he now suffers from the most disastrous of psychic conditions—a separation between his feelings and his voice.

II

The protagonist of Baldwin's new novel is named Leo Proudhammer, and thereby is announced a program of sorts. Leo: lion, king of the cats. Proudhammer: the black man's pride affirmed as if with a hammer.

Proudhammer is a successful Negro actor in his middle years; he enjoys the adulation of both other blacks and the white middle-class public; he is sharp in tongue, cultivated in speech, but puny in body. No one will miss the likelihood that Leo Proudhammer is at least in part an imaginative version of James Baldwin. The mixture of self-caress and feline scratching with which Proudhammer is treated strengthens the impression that we are in the presence of a narcissistic image.

At the outset Proudhammer suffers a severe heart attack. He has been working too hard, driving himself toward a status that brings no peace, tearing at his psyche with the claws of ambition. He is a great success; but still black. He is the long-time lover of Barbara, a distinguished white actress; but also drawn to homosexual affairs, expecially with a young black militant named Christopher who offers release from the multiple hang-up, as Baldwin conceives it, of rationality and the stable psyche.

Proudhammer lies recuperating in a hospital while Barbara and Christopher hover over him protectively. In abrupt flashes, he thinks back to the main events of his life, purring over and despising himself at the same time. The technique is not exactly a stunning innovation, but no matter: it has been serviceable in the past and could be again.

In one of the few persuasive portions of the novel, Leo's mind races back to the harshness of his boyhood in Harlem. There are echoes of *Go Tell It on the Mountain*: a grandiose, embittered, and weak father, his mind stocked with fantasies about old black kings even as he works at a wretched job in the garment center; a light-skinned warm mother, forever a haven; and Caleb, the older brother whom Leo loves and perhaps the only person he really can love. As a novelist, Baldwin has always been helpless before the mysteries of heterosexual love, and when he turns to homosexual love he usually drops into a whipped-cream sentimentalism which reminds one of nothing so much as the boy-meets-girl stories in the *Saturday Evening Post* of twenty years ago. The simple strong and authentic affection he can dramatize is that between brothers, trapped together in a slum, despairing of their parents and the world, drawn into a web of incestuous defense.

James Baldwin can never be wholly uninteresting when he writes about Harlem, especially Harlem as seen through the eyes of a vulnerable black boy. This is the place he knows, the turf of his imagination. The boy Leo gets lost on a subway and is brought home, with an amused sardonic protectiveness, by a black stranger—an incident in which the quiet reality of racial bonds is shown far more convincingly than in scenes of screeching militancy. And the book is also alive whenever young Caleb and little Leo are together, learning to deceive their parents, discovering the threats and pleasures of the street, educating one another about the world that awaits them.

Yet even when he turns back to Harlem, Baldwin has become a slack and self-indulgent writer. Too frequently he falls back upon his worst fault: a lazy readiness to turn on his passionate rhetoric instead of building toward concrete presentation. It is a fault which leads him to falseness of characterization, a kind of indifference to the terms of his own imaginative creation.

One night Leo and Caleb are stopped by a vicious white policeman and painfully humiliated. That such incidents are all too common in our cities I do not doubt. Here is what Baldwin makes of it:

> Caleb took out his wallet and handed it over. I could see that his hands were trembling. I watched the white faces. I memorized each mole, scar, pimple, nostril hair; I memorized the eyes, the contemptuous eyes. I wished I were God. And then I hated God.

Negro boys have plenty of reason to hate white cops. The first four of Baldwin's sentences, while not especially vivid, are credible. But let us remember that we are being shown a little boy, still rather innocent and strongly protected by his family. Can we then believe that at this frightening moment he would wish he were God? I greatly doubt it, yet must suppose it barely possible. What seems to me beyond credence, and a false intrusion by a writer imposing his own attitudes and thereby destroying the unity of his characterization, is the claim of the final sentence that the boy then hates God. Such a sentiment would be entirely persuasive in a grown-up Negro, especially the grown-up Negro who has written this novel; it might just barely be persuasive in the mind of the boy when *remembering* his humiliation. But no amount of sympathy can persuade one that in such a passage Baldwin is really portraying the experience of a Negro boy rather than making an oration about it.

A page or two later Leo asks Caleb:

> "Caleb," I asked, "are white people people?"
>
> "What are you talking about?"
>
> "I mean—are white people—*people*? People like us?"
>
> He looked down at me. His face was very strange and sad. It was a face I had never seen before. We climbed a few more stairs, very slowly. Then, "All I can tell you, Leo, is—well, *they* don't think they are."

Intrinsically, this passage seems false through an excess of cuteness: it fails to ring true not because we doubt that Leo should here be full of distress, but because we doubt that the boy would express himself in a way at once so convenient to both middle-class notions about childhood charm and Black Nationalist notions about them white devils. Worse still, even if the two passages I have just quoted are each independently persuasive, they utterly destroy one another in juxtaposition: for who can suppose that a boy sophisticated enough to have learned to "hate God" can a few pages later be innocent enough to wonder whether whites are "people"?

A linked falseness of language betraying sloppiness of feeling and observation then appears in magnified form when the elder Proudhammer learns about his sons' humiliation:

> . . . his lips became bitter and his eyes grew dull. It was as though, after indescribable, nearly mortal effort, after grim years of fasting and prayer, after the loss of all he had, and after having been promised by the Almighty that he had paid the price and no more would be demanded of his soul, which was harbored now: it was as though in the midst of his joyful feasting and dancing, crowned and robed, a messenger arrived to tell him a great error had been made, and that it was all to be done again. Before his eyes, then, the banquet and the banquet wines and the banquet guests departed, the robe and crown were lifted, and he was alone then, frozen out of his dream. . . .

This passage moves from an adequate, though by no means distinguished, description of the father's grief to a piece of willed fancy which solicits our attention not for the character's feelings but for Baldwin's verbal bravado. Without clarity or charm or firm relation between object and word, it is a speechmaker's prose.

III

Language rarely lies. It can reveal the insincerity of a writer's claims simply through a grating adjective or an inflated phrase. We come upon a frenzy of words and suspect it hides a paucity of feeling. In his new book Baldwin rarely settles into that controlled exactness of diction which shows the writer to have focused on the matter he wishes to describe or evoke; for Baldwin is now a writer systematically deceiving himself through rhetorical inflation and hysteria, whipping himself into postures of militancy and declarations of racial metaphysics which—for him, in *this* book—seem utterly inauthentic.

One sign, a minor sign, of these troubles is Baldwin's compulsive use of obscenity: those blazing terms of revelation, "shit" and "fuck," occur endlessly in his dialogue. If it be said that this is the way people really talk and that Baldwin is merely recording the truth, I would reply that the defense is incompetent. Real-life conversation is notoriously imprecise, wasteful, and boring; no novelist, even if he clings to a program of naturalistic fidelity, can avoid the need to compress and stylize his dialogue; and Baldwin employs these obscenities—they come to seem as emotionally affecting as punctuation—for reasons that have nothing to do with literary realism. He is driven, in this book, by a need to show himself as a very up-to-the-minute swinger, a real tough guy, even though his native talent is for delicacy and nuance; he is writing with an eye toward that harlot called *Zeitgeist*.

A much more important sign of difficulty is the abandon with which Baldwin opens wide the spigot of his rhetoric, that astonishing flow of high eloquence which served him so well in his later essays but is a style almost certain to entrap a novelist. For if you sound like the voice of doom, an avenging god proclaiming the fire next time, then you don't really have to bother yourself with the small business of the novelist, which is to convey how other, if imaginary, people talk and act. Baldwin seems to have lost respect for the novel as a form, and his great facility with language serves only to ease his violations of literary strictness.

There is still a third way in which Baldwin's language betrays him, perhaps most fundamentally of all. When he writes about Proudhammer's rise to fame and the adulation he receives from friends and public, Baldwin slips into the clichés of soap opera, for which he had already shown an alarming fondness in the past when dealing with homosexual love. Buried deep within this seemingly iconoclastic writer is a very conventional sensibility, perfectly attuned to the daydream of success. Now, if you add all these styles together, you get a weird mixture: the prose of *Redbook* (the magazine for young mamas) and the prose of *Evergreen Review* (the magazine for all them mothers).

One series of flashbacks in *Tell Me How Long the Train's Been Gone* is concerned with Proudhammer's success as an actor, and the other series with Baldwin's notions about homosexual love as it is linked to black militancy. The first comes straight out of those movies of twenty-five years ago about the theatrical success of a poor slum urchin (call me Gershwin), shown now in his ripe old age at a testimonial dinner and looking back on his hard but honest climb to the top. The second tries out the idea that black men devoted to homosexuality and visions of racial apocalypse are somehow more pure, more soulful, and more trustworthy than men still messing around with women.

Proudhammer working as an odd-job boy at the summer

theater of a nasty Jewish director; Proudhammer making his successful if nerve-racking debut in a little theater; Proudhammer as the idol of thousands; Proudhammer surrounded by his faithful growling valet, his long-suffering white lady lover, and his scrappy young black boyfriend (why must the fantasies of black writers be as mediocre as those of whites? because we are all, young Leo Proudhammer to the contrary notwithstanding, made of common clay)—all this comes straight from the heart and bowels of American mass culture.

Here is Leo Proudhammer, veteran of stage and screen, in a moment of reflection:

> There really is a kind of fellowship among people in the theater and I've never seen it anywhere else, except among jazz musicians. Our relationships are not peaceful and they certainly are not static, but in a curious way, they're steady. I think it may be partly because we're forced, in spite of the preposterous airs we very often give ourselves, to level with each other. . . .

A perfect speech, some time back, for Spencer Tracy; a perfect speech, a little time ahead, for Sidney Poitier. And then this bit on his first night:

> I've done lots of plays since then, some of them far more successful, but I'll never forget this one. There is nothing like the first plunge, and any survivor will tell you that. When the curtain came up, I knew I was going to vomit, right there. . . . The moment I delivered my first line, "No, Miss," I knew I was going to be all right. . . . I played that scene for all that was in it, for all that was in me, and for all the colored kids in the audience. . . .

Times change, of course. In my day the speaker of such lines would have been playing his heart out for a weeping Jewish mama.

This kind of junk, precisely because it is so familiar, indeed so deeply ingrained in our popular culture, may be judged fairly harmless. But Baldwin doesn't stop there. To the clichés of the ages he adds the cant of the moment. He writes on the tacit assumption that the guilt of his white liberal readers will allow him to say just about anything, indeed, that this audience will accept and revel in the tokens of his contempt, even if the price he must pay is a kind of literary suicide.

Here is Leo Proudhammer at the summer theater, with a rather decent white actress who has taken him to her bed, and taken him, so far as we can learn from Baldwin, not because he is black but simply because she thinks it might be fun:

> I worked with my lips and my tongue and my fingers, she wasn't working much yet, but she would; we fooled around. I can't say what was driving me. Perhaps I had to know—to know—*if* my body could be despised, how *much* it could be despised; perhaps I had to know how much was demanded of my body to make the shameful sentence valid. . . . I got her nearly naked on that sofa, shoes and stockings off, dress half on, half off, panties and bra on the floor. I was striding through a meadow, and it certainly felt like mine.

Brushing aside the dime store poetry of that last sentence, let us try to see what is happening here. The white actress, remember, has shown no hostility toward Leo; nothing preceding this passage indicates that he regards their encounter as warranting its "elevation" to a fateful meeting of colors; indeed, it has all been shown in terms of a casual excitement, a bit of fun; but Baldwin, in his presumption that his novel will be

deepened and his audience shaken by the injection of racial shame, must transform the business of making an attractive white actress into a quasi-apocalyptic stroke of symbolism. And what enables him almost to get away with it is our presumption, reasonable enough in general, that a sexual meeting between people of different colors may indeed carry a large weight of meaning and trouble for at least one of them—a presumption which a careless and contemptuous writer can then fall back on to avoid the task of specific depiction and particular validation.

A similar falseness occurs during the summer theater experience. Proudhammer learns that "many of the roles played by white people could only be played by means of tricks, tricks which could never help one come closer to life, and all of which one would have to discard in order to play even one scene from, say, Ibsen."

Fair enough; even though this would also seem to be true for actors of any color. But then comes a wild leap of conclusion:

> I was discovering what some American blacks must discover: that the people who destroyed my history had also destroyed their own.

The inconsequence here is staggering. Is Proudhammer-Baldwin trying to say that white actors, having "destroyed their history," are as a group incapable of playing Ibsen? Or that there is some deep connection between the "destruction" of black history and the incapacity of most actors, white or black, to perform Ibsen? Or is he saying anything at all? The rhetoric becomes more and more oppressive and pretentious. Here is a Proudhammer reverie on the nature of love:

> Everyone wishes to be loved, but in the event, nearly no one can bear it. Everyone desires love but also finds it impossible to believe that he deserves it. However great the private disasters to which love may lead, love itself is strikingly and mysteriously impersonal; it is a reality which is not altered by anything one does.

And here is the way Baldwin supposes two grown-up people (not Greer Garson and Leslie Howard) to be talking to one another while the man lies sick in a hospital bed:

> ". . . Leo, you always want people to forgive *you*. But we, we others, we need forgiveness, too. We sometimes need it, my dear"—she smiled—"even from so wretched a man as you." And she watched me very steadily, with that steady smile.
> I said, after a moment, with difficulty, "True enough, dear lady. True enough. But I wonder why I feel so depressed."

IV

Tell Me How Long the Train's Been Gone ends with a doubled climax, by means of which the sexual and political themes come together. Barbara, the white lady love, is seduced by Christopher, the black boyfriend, while Leo Proudhammer is recovering from his heart attack. In itself, this fact is not especially shocking, human beings, white or black, being what they are; it is the utter cant, Baldwin's by now wearisome racial metaphysics, which the lady uses to explain the seduction, that *is* shocking:

> "I think *he* wanted"—she stopped—"I think *he* wanted to find out—if love was possible. If it was really possible. I think he had to find *out* what I thought of *his* body, by taking mine." She paused. "It wasn't like that," she said, "with you and me."

The political climax occurs a few pages later when Christopher explains to Proudhammer that "you got to agree that we need us some guns," and Proudhammer answers, "Yes, I see that." An uncharacteristic flash of intelligence overcomes him for a moment, however, and he says to Christopher, "But we're outnumbered you know." To which Christopher answers: "Shit. So were the early Christians."

Placed as it is at the end of the book, and as the last word spoken by any of the characters, Christopher's reply is clearly meant to be a decisive stroke, a sign of Baldwin's acquiescence. So let us look at it for a moment.

Some of the early Christians, presumably unlike the Black Nationalists of today, *wanted* to die, since they looked upon martyrdom as an avenue to paradise and did not care whether they were outnumbered or not. Hence, they can hardly be taken as a significant model for young blacks, unless Baldwin is proposing (what hardly seems likely) a parallel course of sanctification through suicide. Other early Christians—and by now, no longer so early—had as their goal not the destruction of the oppressive state, presumably the goal of the Black Nationalists today, but rather a gradual infiltration into places of power. This indeed, is what happened: the Christians, slowly transforming the nature of their belief, took over the Empire, or if you wish, the Empire took over Christianity. So, again, Christopher's comparison has no relevance to the present moment. But finally there is the not inconsequential fact that the early Christians, who were absolute pacifists, never said, "we need us some guns," and never proposed to destroy the Roman state as a tiny minority shooting it out with an oppressive majority. Again, therefore, the proposal to employ guns cannot be rationalized as a tactic or justified as a morality by comparison with the "early Christians." What, then, is the force of Christopher's remark? Its force—and I believe that for many readers it will have a notable force—lies simply in the assumption that not many people will trouble to think about it critically and indeed that the current intellectual atmosphere in this country discourages people from thinking.

Tell Me How Long the Train's Been Gone will appeal to the liberal white devils who buy books and who now think, some of them, that it is fashionable to look with kindliness on the Black Panthers and to speak—after all, it's not *their* blood—with approval about the fantasies of apocalypse being nurtured in certain academic and black circles. As such, the novel is a document of and for the moment, an emblem of the 'sixties.

Strangely, however, it also shows, in a few scenes, what Baldwin's true gift as a novelist might be. It is not a gift for sexual *Sturm und Drang*, whether hetero or homo or bi; nor for militant protest; nor for political prophecy. Baldwin's true gift as a novelist is for comedy of manners, nuanced observation, refinement of detail. How absurd and painful that in *this* book Baldwin should now and again show a kinship with the kind of fine-threaded fiction written by . . . Jane Austen. There is, for instance, a fine scene in which the young actors at the summer theater meet some local Negroes, have an uncomfortable dinner with them, and go off warily to a black gin mill: it is all done with control and exactness. There is a nice bit in which Leo and his parents go out on the streets of Harlem to shop, and the playfulness of the older people breaks out for a minute. There is a good section in which Leo works in a restaurant owned by a tough Jamaican woman, and Baldwin can describe with neat detail their division of labor, responsibility, and emotion.

But this is not a moment in which our culture can encourage a writer to develop a small talent. This is a moment when writers feel driven to destroy themselves: with comforts of doom, illusions of prophecy, rhetoric of blood.

BENJAMIN DeMOTT
"James Baldwin on the Sixties:
Acts and Revelations"
Saturday Review, May 27, 1972, pp. 63–66

Pity spokesmen; their lot is hard. The movement of their ideas is looked at differently from that of other men, studied for clues and confirmations, and comes therefore to seem unindividual—less a result of personal growth than of cultural upsurge. Why in 1961 did James Baldwin speak of the black man's "love" of the white man? (The passage occurs in *Notes of a Native Son*: "No one in the world . . . knows Americans better or . . . loves them more than the American Negro. . . . We are bound together forever. We are part of each other.") Answer: Baldwin spoke of love because the times dictated this line.

Again, why in 1963 did James Baldwin amend the concept of love, introducing the notion of a saving remnant committed to raising levels of consciousness? (The passage occurs at the end of *The Fire Next Time*: "If we—and now I mean the relatively conscious whites and the relatively conscious blacks, who must, like lovers, insist on, or create, the consciousness of the others—do not falter in our duty now, we may be able, handful that we are, to end racial nightmare, and achieve our country, and change the history of the world.") Answer: Baldwin amended the concept of love because in those years the movement had begun to awaken to itself and the awakening dictated the amendments.

Yet again, why in 1972 does James Baldwin announce that the black man "must kill" the white? (The passages occur in the book at hand: ". . . it is not necessary for a black man to hate a white man, or to have any particular feelings about him at all, in order to realize that he must kill him." And, "There will be bloody holding actions all over the world, for years to come: but the Western party is over, and the white man's sun has set. Period.") Answer: Baldwin speaks of killing because the advent of a new militancy, together with disillusionment about prospects for reform, dictates still further change.

Difficulty in seeming to be your own man, rather than a knee-jerk reactor to events, is but one of many problems besetting spokesmen. Another has to do with expense of spirit. Few Americans have been called on as frequently as has James Baldwin in the last decade to function as the public voice of rage or frustration or denunciation or grief. Repeatedly, on television, on college platforms, at hundreds of public meetings, the author of *The Fire Next Time* has had to seek within himself both the energies and the vocabulary of fury—to search for the words that will make real to himself and others the latest atrocity. Traditional oratory can perhaps be equal to cattle prods, mortgage racketeers, heroin syndicates, and assassinations. But where in his word-hoard can a spokesman reach for means of articulating feelings about defenseless children bombed to death while singing a hymn at Sunday school? What terms does he find to name his revulsion on learning that at a state prison an already wounded prisoner was stabbed three times in the rectum with a screwdriver by a "correction officer"? How does he conduct a hunt for language that hasn't been emptied out by repetition—how can he witness his own scramblings for freshness without coming in some sense to despise this self-involved fastidiousness? To function as a voice of outrage month after month for a decade and more strains heart and mind, and rhetoric as well; the consequence is a writing style ever on the edge of being winded by too many summonses to intensity. You write, if you are James Baldwin,

"The land seems nearly to weep beneath the burden of this civilization's unnameable excrescences"—and perhaps hesitate for a minute, dissatisfied by the sentence, the willed pathos. But what can be done? Shrug, and let the words stand.

Then, further, there's the problem of fame, and how to handle its trophies. The spokesman becoming a celebrity among celebrities need not forsake his cause, isn't obliged to care less than before about his people. But his life circumstances must change. Earlier on, the round of his days could be simply described; no clutter of details associated with conventional success and achievement undercut his protest at the denials of American life. Now, however, he is everywhere undercut. In *No Name in the Street* James Baldwin visits Watts and works in schools—and returns in the afternoon to the Beverly Hills, and condescends to the hotel's ambience in passing (". . . as hotels go, the Beverly Hills is more congenial than most. . . ."). In the Seventies this writer's first-name world embraces not just "Huey" and "Angela" but "Eartha," "Gadge," "Marlon," dozens of the beautiful; his own retinue includes chauffeur and bodyguard; his domiciles multiply; and when, at the close of his book, he dates the work and places its composition, hints of splendor rise from the words: "New York, San Francisco, Hollywood, London, Istanbul, St. Paul de Vence, 1967–1971."

Finally, the spokesman has competition. Is it not tasteless to contend that men compete for recognition as champion voice of agony? Tasteless, yet true. Fame and power are at stake here as elsewhere, and while the writer is concerned not to exalt himself above his cause, he is scarcely an innocent; he feels the others crowding him, bidding for a share of influence. And distraction mounts. Not every commentary on the meaning of the black experience in the Sixties, or earlier, intrudes on the turf marked out by *The Fire Next Time*. Julius Lester's tale of the times, *Search for a New Land*, is more journalistic than apocalyptic; James Foreman's *The Making of Black Revolutionaries* traces intricacies of political infighting among civil-rights groups in a manner that inhibits emotional involvement; and if Harold Cruse's *Crisis of the Negro Intellectual* ranks as a committed work, its tone is historical and scholarly almost to the end, and the personal voice is cool.

But angrier books abound. There's ferocity in Ameer Baraka, and Eldridge Cleaver has gone so far as to attack the author of *Nobody Knows My Name* and to argue straight out, in *Soul on Ice* (1967), that Baldwin's "name" is inflated and his message muddled: "There is in James Baldwin's work the most grueling, total hatred of the blacks, particularly of himself, and the most shameful, fanatical, fawning, sycophantic love of the whites that one can find in the writings of any black American writer of note in our time. This is an appalling contradiction, and the implications of it are vast."

In a word, there's a price for everthing, spokesmanship included. The pressures are serious, they build up quickly—and their effect is evident in the work at hand. *No Name in the Street*, a reconstruction of James Baldwin's activities and states of mind during the Sixties (there are glances further backward, and the book ends with President Nixon congratulating Governor Rockefeller on his handling of the Attica uprising), is less powerful, rhetorically, than *The Fire Next Time*, and, although self-referential, contains nothing to match the family remembrances in *Notes of a Native Son* The writer is restless, rushes himself, seems bored with the drill of conventional dramatization. Much space is given, in the latter portion of the book, to his efforts on behalf of his former bodyguard, Tony Maynard by name, imprisoned on a murder charge; the pages lose force because Maynard, underdone as a character, lays no claim on the audience as a distinct human creature. Much

space is also assigned to a projected movie of *The Autobiography of Malcolm X*; these pages lose force because the writer fails to take his reader to the center of the crisis of "control" that led to war with the studio and the decision to abandon the screenplay. Students of James Baldwin's novels will find in the present work a number of images and episodes with interesting bearings on *Go Tell It on the Mountain, Another Country*, even *Giovanni's Room*. But the book as a whole resembles a collection of fragments—snapshots of friends, new snippets about the Harlem boyhood and the down-and-out-in-Paris years, glimpses of the writer on magazine assignment in the South, reports of encounters with Dr. King, Malcolm, Huey Newton. And the unifying ruminations—discursive and historical remarks on the meaning of black-white relationships, predictions about the course of these relationships in the years ahead—don't invariably avoid repetitiousness.

Yet, despite the book's faults, despite the trials and afflictions of his spokesmanship, this author retains a place in an extremely select group: that composed of a few genuinely indispensable American writers. He owes his rank partly to the qualities of responsiveness that have marked his work from the beginning and that seem unlikely ever to disappear from it. Time and time over in fiction as in reportage, Baldwin tears himself free of his rhetorical fastenings and stands forth on the page utterly absorbed in the reality of the person before him, strung with his nerves, riveted to his feelings, breathing his breath. And such moments turn up still in his writing. Here is Baldwin remembering Birmingham, a talk with Reverend Shuttlesworth, an instant at which the minister considers the issue of safety. It's nighttime, early in the voter-registration drive; ahead lie stepped-up bombings, and murders. The two men have been talking together, in Baldwin's hotel room. During the conversation Shuttlesworth keeps walking back and forth to the window. The writer realizes his guest is checking on his car below, making sure nobody puts a bomb in it. He wants to say this, wants to acknowledge the danger and his own awareness of it—but the minister offers him no opening. At last, as Shuttlesworth is leaving, Baldwin speaks out ("I could not resist. . . . I was worried. . . ."), and he sees the man's face change ("a shade of sorrow crossed his face, deep, impatient, dark"), and at once he lives into the response imaginatively, naming it from within, sensing the "impersonal anguish," showing forth the minister wrestling within himself, confronting fear with the almost-sustaining truth that "the danger in which he stood was as nothing compared with the spiritual horror which drove those who were trying to destroy him."

Precisely the same swiftness of penetration occurs as the writer remembers a classic moment of exclusion. He enters a small-town southern restaurant through the "wrong door":

"What you want, boy? What you want in here?" And then, a decontaminating gesture, "Right around there, boy. Right around there."

I had no idea what [the waitress] was talking about. I backed out the door.

"Right around there, boy," said a voice behind me.

A white man had appeared out of nowhere, on the sidewalk which had been empty not more than a second before. I stared at him blankly. He watched me steadily, with a kind of suspended menace. . . . He had pointed to a door, and I knew immediately that he was pointing to the colored entrance. And this was a dreadful moment—as brief as lightning, and far more illuminating. I realized that this man thought that he was being kind. . . .

Clearly James Baldwin can still take a feeling from inside: Amidst terror, he registers an exact reading of the combined sense of power and inner, *moral* self-approval in the white who shows him "the right way."

But what matters at least as much as this responsiveness is Baldwin's continuing willingness to accept the obligation imposed on him by his pride—namely, that of specifying the losses to the culture as a whole flowing from its blindness to truths born in and taught by blackness. To say this isn't entirely to discount the chronicle aspect of *No Name in the Street.* The narrative is spotty and discontinuous, but it does provide inklings of what it would be like to possess a coherent (although devastatingly despairing) view of recent times, to be able to see even the most dreadful events as part of a pattern. For some citizens the fates of Dr. King, Malcolm X, and Robert Kennedy can be gathered only under a vague rubric ("violence in America," "shocking," "beyond understanding"). Baldwin's narrative is told from the perspective of someone noting connections, replacing soft illusions of randomness with hard-boned inevitabilities, and often justifying his readings by citing particulars not only of his own feelings but of those of the victims. Everywhere in the book linkages are fixed between events that white memories tend to hold apart—witness these comments on the close of the great Washington Monument petitionary march and its sequel:

> Martin finished with one hand raised: "Free at last, free at last, praise God Almighty, I'm free at last!" That day, for a moment, it almost seemed that we stood on a height, and could see our inheritance; perhaps we could make the kingdom real, perhaps the beloved community would not forever remain that dream one dreamed in agony. The people quietly dispersed at nightfall, as had been agreed. . . . I was in Hollywood when, something like two weeks later, my phone rang, and a nearly hysterical, white, female CORE worker told me that a Sunday school in Birmingham had been bombed, and that four young black girls had been blown into eternity. That was the first answer we received to our petition.

Merely by pointing at "sequels," Baldwin bares the structure of the times as given in the experience of his community, and it is a fearful sight.

And it is, to repeat, the author's resources of pride that figure most strikingly in the acts of revelation. True pride is never less than stunning—which is to say, even if it didn't impose obligations, Baldwin's pride would remain a phenomenon notable in itself. These fierce resistances, iron spurnings of every prepared slot of "inferiority"—it is wrong to view them esthetically and thereby drain them of psychological urgency; yet it's hard to gaze on them without remembering Keats's remarks on the "fineness" of a quarrel in the street. The key to excitement in Baldwin's writing is the imminence of contest, the brooding rage to prove self-worth, to duel with the humiliators and cut through to their place of blankness. And it's his grasp of his comparative worth that demands the duel, forces him into "availability," openness to others; he's driven to perceive inner realtities as they exist for persons not himself at least in part because, the system being what it is, others are bound to misassess him, bound to need setting straight. There are no wild moments of release in *No Name in the Street* matching the terrible passage in *Notes of a Native Son* wherein the young Baldwin, told for the thousandth time ". . . don't serve Negroes here," roars up from his chair and hurls a half-full pitcher of water, shattering mirrors behind the bar. The gestures in the name of worth here become gestures of mind,

and sometimes take the form of dismissals of traditional culture:

> The South African coal miner, or the African digging for roots in the bush, or the Algerian mason working in Paris, not only have no reason to bow down before Shakespeare, or Descartes, or Westminster Abbey, or the cathedral at Chartres: they have, once these monuments intrude on their attention, no honorable access to them. Their apprehension of this history cannot fail to reveal to them that they have been robbed, maligned, and rejected: to bow down before that history is to accept that history's arrogant and unjust judgment.

The dream of demolishing history is extravagant and in the end self-diminishing; the force of the will, the superb hatred of bowing down nevertheless compels admiration.

But, as just indicated, the prime use of Baldwin's writing is as a guide to fortunes possessed by the dispossessed. Other writers—Frantz Fanon, Albert Memmi, Paolo Freire—hint at the size of the holdings, open up awareness of the way in which a thousand assumptions would be transformed if standard middle-class reality had to negotiate its acceptance with things as they truly are. And these writers exceed James Baldwin in restraint; Baldwin's proud-hearted love of his people often sends him close to euphoric boosting:

> . . . the doctrine of white supremacy, which still controls most white people, is itself a stupendous delusion: but to be born black is an immediate, a mortal challenge. People who cling to their delusions find it difficult, if not impossible, to learn anything worth learning: a people under the necessity of creating themselves must examine everything, and soak up learning the way the roots of a tree soak up water.

But when he lays out his case experientially, it has uncommon authority. "I have been to Watts to give high-school lectures," he writes, and

> these despised, maligned, and menaced children have an alertness, an eagerness, and a depth which I certainly did not find in—or failed to elicit from—students at many splendid universities. The future leaders of this country (in principle, anyway) do not impress me as being the intellectual equals of the most despised among us. I am not being vindictive when I say that, nor am I being sentimental or chauvinistic; and indeed the reason that this would be so is a very simple one. It is only very lately that white students, in the main, have had any reason to question the structure into which they were born; it is the very lateness of the hour, and their bewildered resentment—their sense of having been betrayed—which is responsible for their romantic excesses; and a young, white revolutionary remains, in general, far more romantic than a black one. For it is a very different matter, and results in a very different intelligence, to grow up under the necessity of questioning everything—everything, from the question of one's identity to the literal, brutal question of how to save one's life in order to begin to live it. White children . . . whether they are rich or poor, grow up with a grasp of reality so feeble that they can very accurately be described as deluded—about themselves and the world they live in. . . .

The writer means to create an image of his people that will not only recover their dignity, that will not only spell out what they have to teach, but that will sting all sane folk to jealousy. It is, many will say, adopting postures of regret and pity, a typical "spokesman's project"—and doubtless there's justice in the observation. But the lesson Baldwin teaches in this flawed, bitter, continuously instructive book—you make your way to actualities only by waking to the arbitrariness of things—goes out a few miles beyond "race issues." And those among us who can't or won't master the lesson, or who, having mastered it, carp instead of clap at the pugnacity behind it, had best save the pity for themselves.

PEARL K. BELL
From "Blacks and the Blues"

The New Leader, May 27, 1974, pp. 3–5

In 1949, early in his career, James Baldwin published a now legendary essay, "Everybody's Protest Novel," in which he took a stand that at the time was astonishing to encounter in a Negro novelist. Writers with a Cause such as Harriet Beecher Stowe and Richard Wright, Baldwin argued, are not novelists but pamphleteers, and though their moral sincerity is unexceptionable, they reduce their characters to pawns on a chessboard of social injustice, members "of a Society or a Group or a deplorable conundrum to be explained by Science."

Depending as it does on exaggeration and distortion and moralistic simplification, Baldwin passionately contended, the work of the protest novelist must never be confused with art. Because it substitutes a confused theological fantasy of both the bad and the good life for the elusive realities, a book like *Uncle Tom's Cabin* or *Native Son* is acutally "a rejection of life, the human being, the denial of his beauty, dread, power, in its insistence that it is [his] categorization alone which is real and which cannot be transcended."

The pigeonholes of protest, in sum, impose a false notion of order on the creative artist; they debase and misrepresent the intricately perplexing individual nature of black experience, replacing the troubled, authentic singularity of personal identity with a meretricious, high-minded collective anonymity. The true business of the novelist, Baldwin insisted, was not the inflammatory manipulation of social responsibility and reform, but the far more difficult and courageous revelation of man's complexity. "Only within this web of ambiguity, paradox, this hunger, danger, darkness, can we find at once ourselves and the power that will free us from ourselves."

The essay was an extraordinarily self-assured performance for so young and so *Harlem* a writer. Yet shortly before it was published, Baldwin had in fact left Manhattan and America altogether, hoping through exile in Europe to escape from a suffocating society that not only seemed to lock every black writer into the crude simplicities of propaganda and protest, but was also peculiarly inimical to a homosexual like himself. Europe did not of course prove to be the unconstrained color-blind paradise of Baldwin's naïve expectations. It did, however, make possible a personal change of perspective that enabled him to complete his first and best novel, *Go Tell It on the Mountain*, an autobiographical chronicle of his evangelical-preacher father: "In America, the color of my skin had stood between myself and me; in Europe, that barrier was down. . . . The question of who I was had at last become a personal question, and the answer was to be found in me."

Until the early 1960s, that answer, for Baldwin, consisted largely of a literary and intellectual cosmopolitanism that freed him, for a time, from the racial shibboleths and platitudes of "Negro" fiction. Thus in his second novel, *Giovanni's Room*,

he told the troubled story of some white homosexuals in Paris in the first person—out of a defiantly cocky need to prove that a Negro novelist could successfully obliterate the facts of race from his work, if not from his life.

Oddly, while he was programmatically right about the objectives of fiction for the artist, Baldwin's own novels have been on the whole uninteresting and fatally strained. If *Giovanni's Room* was a startling experiment in audacity, it was nonetheless a feeble novel; and *Another Country* and *Tell Me How Long the Train's Been Gone* are lazy and sentimental, full of hackneyed violence and tin-ear dialogue, thin and unrealized characters, speciously "shocking" melodrama.

Indeed, Baldwin has never been altogether at home in the novel. His real power as a writer is to be found in his auto-biographical essays, particularly in that small and lacerating masterpiece, "Notes of a Native Son." In this anguished, brilliantly moving memoir of the terrible summer of 1943, Baldwin tells of the death of his autocratic father a few hours before the birth of the man's last child, and of the rioting mob that smashed through Harlem on the day of the funeral. In the confluence of these three profoundly irreversible events, young Baldwin learned to understand the tragic folly of bitterness and hatred and despair: "The dead man mattered, the new life mattered; blackness and whiteness did not matter; to believe that they did was to acquiesce in one's own destruction. Hatred, which could destroy so much, never failed to destroy the man who hated and this was an immutable law." Still, the insight proved immutable only for the duration of Baldwin's youth.

By the time he returned to the U.S. in the mid-1950s, Baldwin was already in his 30s and had learned, like many other American writers before him, that what Europe had prepared him for, with taunting indirection, was America. Especially crucial for him was the fact that the nation was rumbling with the tumultuous beginnings of the civil rights movement and black nationalism. In the early 1960s, in his now characteristic pattern, Baldwin published a pedestrian novel, *Another Country*, and a magnificently eloquent memoir and lamentation, *The Fire Next Time*, a reflective inquiry, dark with foreboding, into the lessons his own private chaos could derive from black history. In the nightmare of centuries of Negro suffering Baldwin found a fierce beauty, the moral transcendence of self-discovery and confirmation: "That man who is forced each day to snatch his manhood, his identity out of the fire of human cruelty that rages to destroy it knows, if he survives his effort . . . something about himself and human life that no school on earth—and, indeed, no church—can teach."

Passionate and lucid in its melancholy recognitions, in its beautifully sustained tension of rage and intelligence, *The Fire Next Time* was a black jeremiad spoken with incredible dignity. Baldwin did not bludgeon the guilty white reader into reaching for his consoling and stuffed hair shirt. One did not have to consent to Baldwin's prophecy of doom and conflagration in order to be moved by his vision of black suffering. (Needless to say, in the eyes of contemptuous black militants like Eldridge Cleaver, Harold Cruse and Julian Mayfield, the essay failed to absolve him of the venal sin of fraternization with white liberal intellectuals.)

Yet less than a decade later, in *No Name in the Street*, Baldwin repudiated temperateness and insight to take up the torch of apocalypse. This violently bitter requiem for the civil rights movement, published in 1972, degenerated almost immediately into indiscriminate sniping, mindless contumely ("White Americans are probably the wickedest and most dangerous people . . . in the world today"), myopic nonsense ("White America remains unable to believe that black America's grievances are real"), and paranoid malediction (America is "the Fourth Reich"). Where the tone of *The Fire Next Time* had been at once intensely personal and free of egoism, *No Name in the Street* revealed a Baldwin indecently self-important about his own celebrity. The elegiac compassion and unflinching self-scrutiny that had given his earlier essays such grace and authority were smothered by a nervous pomposity about the trivia of fame, and an ungovernable indulgence in the irresponsibilities of bigotry and hate.

The gifted young maverick who wrote "Everybody's Protest Novel" a quarter of a century ago will be 50 this year and he has just published his fifth novel, *If Beale Street Could Talk*. It is not only Baldwin's shallowest work of fiction, but ironically it commits those very atrocities of distortion and stereotyping that he long ago deplored in *Native Son*: Richard Wright's acquiescence in the pervasive American fantasy that the Negro "is a social and not a personal or a human problem."

The title is the clue to Baldwin's intention of writing a novel in the manner of a blues ballad—Beale Street, in Memphis, was the stamping ground of the great blues composer W. C. Handy. There is no hint in *Beale Street*, though, of the sardonic blues spirit that Ralph Ellison transmuted so effectively in *Invisible Man*. Baldwin's novel is not a blues story, it is an ethnic soap opera—complete with cardboard characters shoved through pseudotragic charades of doom and catastrophe.

Tish Rivers, the 19-year-old Harlem girl who tells the story, is pregnant by her childhood sweetheart, Fonny Hunt, a young sculptor who has been jailed by an evil white policeman on the false charge of raping a Puerto Rican woman. (Fonny's real crime is that of living in the Village when he should have stayed uptown.) Tish's lovingly devoted family impoverishes itself in an effort to get Fonny out of jail and prove his innocence before the baby arrives, and Tish's mother even flies to San Juan to find Fonny's alleged victim. Unfortunately, the Puerto Rican woman goes mad before she can be persuaded to return to New York. Will Fonny get out of jail? Will his baby ever know its daddy? As in all soap opera, we are left hanging in the end.

Beyond its factitious plot and one-dimensional characters, *If Beale Street Could Talk* is rendered even more implausible by Tish's inconsistent rhetoric. Though she is depicted as a simple and unbookish girl, her narrator's voice keeps shifting from a tough and brutal Harlem idiom into sudden inexplicable flights of highly sophisticated literary imagery—the intrusive ventriloquist's voice, in fact, of James Baldwin. But what finally accounts for the book's mawkish incredibility is that it was conceived and written as a social indictment, and not as a work of the creative imagination.

WILFRID SHEED
"The Twin Urges of James Baldwin"
Commonweal, June 24, 1977, pp. 404–7

When James Baldwin goes wrong (as he has taken to doing lately), it usually seems less a failure of talent than of policy. Of all our writers he is one of the most calculating. Living his life on several borderlines, he has learned to watch his step: driven at the same time by an urge to please and a mission to scold.

In his early days, the twin urges came together to make very good policy indeed. White liberals craved a spanking and

they got a good one. But then too many amateurs joined in the fun, all the Raps and Stokelys and Seales, until even liberal guilt gave out. And now the times seems to call for something a little different. *The Devil Finds Work* shows Baldwin groping for it—not just because he's a hustler, at least as writers go, but because he has a genuine quasi-religious vocation. In the last pages he richly describes a church ceremony he went through as a boy, akin to attaining the last mansions of mysticism: and you have to do *something* after that. Your work, even your atheism, will always taste of religion.

And this is the first problem we come across in the new book. Because the subject is movies, and most movies simply do not accommodate such religious passion. So his tone sounds false. He may or may not feel that strongly about movies (it's hard to believe), but sincerity isn't the issue. A preacher doesn't have to feel what he says every Sunday: rhetoric is an art, and Baldwin practices it very professionally. But the sermon's subject must be at least in the same ball-park as the style, or you get bathos, the sermon that fails to rise.

Since Baldwin is too intelligent not to notice this, we get an uneasy compromise between old habits and new possibilities. The folks pays him to preach (to use his own self-mocking language), so he turns it on mechanically, almost absentmindedly, lapsing at times into incoherence, as if he's fallen asleep at the microphone. But since getting mad at the movies is only one step removed from getting mad at the funnies, he escapes periodically in two directions, one bad and one good.

The bad one is to change the subject outrageously in order to raise the emotional ante: thus there are several references to how white people like to burn babies that totally stumped me. A prophet should disturb all levels of opinion and must therefore be something of a precisionist. But this stuff passes harmlessly overhead. Blacks have been known to kill babies too, in Biafra and elsewhere, but nobody said they like it. People apt to be reading Baldwin at all have long since graduated from this level of rant. He may write for the masses, but he is read by the intelligentsia.

But his second escape at times almost makes up for the first: which is simply to talk about movies according to their kind, with amusement, irony and his own quirky insights. More writers should do this: we were raised as much in the movie house as the library, and it's pretentious to go on blaming it all on Joyce. In Baldwin's case a movie case-history is doubly valuable because his angle is so solitary, shaped by no gang and deflected by no interpretation, and shared only with a white woman teacher, herself a solitary. Nobody ever saw these movies quite the way he did, or ever will.

Unfortunately the childhood section is tantalizingly short, and the adult's voice horns in too often, but some fine things come through: in particular the way the young Baldwin had to convert certain white actors into blacks, even as white basketball fans reverse the process today, in order to identify. Thus, Henry Fonda's walk made him black, and Joan Crawford's resemblance to a woman in the local grocery store made her black, while Bette Davis' popping eyes made her not only black but practically Jimmy himself.

This is vintage Baldwin: and if he lacks confidence in his softer notes he shouldn't (his sentimental notes are another matter). He does not automatically *have* to lecture us on every topic he writes about. In this more urbane mode, his racial intrusions often make good sense. For instance in checking *A Tale of Two Cities* against what he has learned in the streets he perhaps inadvertently suggests to this reader at least how Dickens might have veered away from what *he* had learned in the streets. In fact Baldwin's whole treatment of this story suggests a potential literary critic, if he'd calm down for a minute.

This section ends with a valuable addition to Baldwin's early autobiography: a corpus to which one had thought no further additions were possible. He discovers the theater and loses his religion almost at the same moment. The reality of stage actors playing Macbeth is enough to blow away even that encounter with the Holy Ghost. And as if to symbolize this, he literally tiptoes out of church one Sunday and heads downtown for a show: taking, as he says in another context, his church with him.

If stage acting could transplant God, it utterly demolished screen acting for him. "Canada Lee [in *Native Son*] was Bigger Thomas, but he was also Canada Lee: his physical presence, like the physical presence of Paul Robeson, gave me the right to live. He was not at the mercy of my imagination as he would have been, on the screen: he was on the stage, in flesh and blood, and I was, therefore, at the mercy of *his* imagination." If you're raised an incarnational Christian (and it's hard to imagine another kind), flesh and blood can be food and drink to you. Henceforth in even the silliest play, the actors' presence would thrust reality through at Baldwin; conversely, only the greatest of actors could insert physicality into a movie, and that fleetingly.

His own course was set. Embodied reality, thick, hot and tangible is Baldwin's grail, even jerking him loose from his own rhetoric. So he became a man of the stage, dealing with real people and not their images; and he wrote some of his best work for it—including my own favorite *Amen Corner* in which he uses the stage to exorcise the Church once and for all. Only to come out more religious than ever—only at random now, passionately foraging for Good and Evil in race, in movies, even in Norman Mailer.

Perhaps, then, not the ideal man to write about movies. The magic element which is their particular genius is precisely what maddens his fundamentalist soul the most. Like Pascal at the real theater, he sees nothing but lies up there. Although he seems to know something about the craft of movies, it doesn't interest or charm him in the least. His book has no pictures, which is unusual in a film book, but quite appropriate for this one. Because even the stills would be lies.

Specifically lies about race. And here we have a right to expect the latest news from Baldwin and not a rehash. I assume he is still a Black spokesman in good standing. Although his book is disarmingly datelined from France, which is nearer the *pied-noir* country, there must be a victims' network of information which keeps him up to date. But his personal witness, his strength, has begun to sound tentative. He talks of being terrorized in some Southern town, but he can't remember what year or, apparently, the distinction between one town and another. "It is hard to be accurate concerning the pace of my country's progress." Very hard from St. Paul de Vence. We can get fresher testimony than that every day of the week.

Anyhow for Baldwin there is still just something called the South, unchanging and indivisible, and the liberals down there might as well pack up shop. It's a bleak picture and if Baldwin sees any lift in the clouds he either isn't telling or he rejects it as a dangerous illusion, an invitation to drop one's guard. For instance, in the dopey film, *In the Heat of the Night*, there is a scene where the white sheriff humbles himself to carry Sidney Poitier's bags, and Baldwin sees for a moment something "choked and moving" in this, only to round on it sternly as a dangerous daydream. "White Americans have been encouraged to keep on dreaming, and black Americans have been alerted to the necessity of waking up."

So paranoia as before is his message to Blacks, and a white reviewer is in no position to question it. Since no improvement is to be trusted, the implicit solution is revolution, and Baldwin talks airily of seizing property as if this were still the slaphappy sixties when all seemed possible. For the moment, revolutionary rant seems as remote as the evangelism that used to pacify Blacks: but again, Baldwin isn't quite calling for it, only toying with it. His new position is still very much in the works.

Meanwhile off-screen, geographical distance may have obscured some of the social nuances Baldwin usually pounces on so swiftly and surely. He talks for instance of whites being terrified of Blacks, and Blacks being enraged by whites, as if this blanketed the case. But one of the odd things that happened in the sixties was that the Blacks became largely de-mystified, for better or worse. By accepting such drugstore rebels as Rap Brown and Stokely Carmichael at their own valuation, we let ourselves in for one of the greatest letdowns in memory. The black enigma was transformed overnight into the black chatterbox. Although, as Claude Brown once said privately these men could not have rounded up ten followers in Harlem, they told us they were leaders, so we took them for leaders. And we were relieved to find they were not the brooding giants that Baldwin had conjured, but just average publicity hounds.

Because of this comical misunderstanding, many whites ceased being impressed by Blacks altogether, except such as carried knives, and a new psychic alignment occurred that Baldwin should come home and tell us about. The problem now is not so much fear as deepening indifference. Baldwin still writes as though our souls were so hag-ridden by race that even our innocent entertainments reflect it. And he gives us the old castration folderol as if it were piping hot. But the news I hear is different. Many whites now go for years without thinking about Blacks at all. The invisible man has returned. And as *de facto* segregation continues to settle like mold, his future seems assured.

On the Black side of the fence, one simply has to take him on trust. Young Blacks today *seem* more confident than Baldwin's prototypes but it might only take a few full-time bigots plus some ad hoc recruits—as in South Boston—to chip the paint off this. What one can question, by the current division of racist labor, is his account of the white psyche. Because here again he simply says nothing that a contemporary reader can use. His white men sound at times exactly like Susan Brownmiller's rapists, whom that author also transformed into Everyman, and in fact like all the hyperaggressive bullies you've ever met: and these surely come in all colors.

Of such movies as *Death Wish* or *Straw Dogs* or the worst of Clint Eastwood (if such there be) or black exploitation films—in short all the movies that validate bullying on one side or another and make it chic—he says nothing except, tantalizingly, of the latter that they "make black experience irrelevant and obsolete" (his own, or everyone's?). If by chance he has not seen the others, in particular *Death Wish*, the mugger-killing wet dream, he has wandered unarmed into the one subject Americans really know about.

Baldwin's weakness as a prophet is to suppose that the rest of us experience life as intensely as he does; and his strength is roughly the same. If his overall sociology is suspect right now, his ability to enlarge a small emotion so that we can all see it is not. And this perhaps rescues him even as a writer about movies.

Throughout, his eyes swarm greedily over the screen, scavenging for small truths. And although brotherhood epics like *In the Heat of the Night* and *Guess Who's Coming to Dinner* were flailed insensible by white critics, leaving precious little to pick on, in each case he finds some scene or other even richer in phoniness, or closer to truth, than we suspected. For instance, in the latter film, he has a passage on a successful black son's relation to his father that probably no one else would have thought of. While for the former, he provides such a droll plot summary that the absurdity jumps a dimension.

He is also good on *The Defiant Ones* and *Lawrence of Arabia* though here one senses that he is not saying all he knows. He talks at one point of the seismographic shudder Americans experience at the word homosexual, but he handles it pretty much like a hot potato himself: talking around and around it without quite landing on it. Again this is policy (the word homosexual does go off like a fire alarm, reminding us to put up our dukes) but in this case, I think, too much policy. When Baldwin holds back something it distorts his whole manner. The attempt to seduce is too slick. And this, just as much as his compulsion to preach when there's nothing to preach about, diverts him from his real lover, truth. He is not seeing those movies as an average black man, but as a unique exile, and the pose is beginning to wear thin.

So, the tension remains. He has been away a long time and I'm sure he has a story to tell about that, perhaps his best one yet. It is hard to believe that in Paris and Istanbul his mind

was really on American movies: but they might have been something in the attic that he wanted to get rid of. And the attempt is worthwhile if only for the sake of some sprightly lines, to wit, "J. Edgar Hoover, history's most highly paid (and most utterly useless) *voyeur*," and random bangs and flashes. He even talks several times of *human* weakness (as opposed to white weakness)—including his own: which suggests that the hanging judge may be ready to come down from his perch and mix it with us.

But for now he remains up there wagging his finger sternly at the converted and the bored. And with so many clergymen, he too often deduces Reality solely by intelligence in this book, and while he has more than enough of that quality, it tends to fly off in bootless directions unless anchored by touch. He is right to love the stage. His art needs real bodies. But anyone who sees reality as clearly as Baldwin does must be tempted at times to run like the wind; and perhaps, for just a little while, he's done that. After all, that's what movies are for—even for those preachers who denounce them the loudest.

Imamu Amiri Baraka
LeRoi Jones
1934–

Imamu Amiri Baraka was born LeRoi Jones on October 7, 1934 in Newark, New Jersey. Although his original intention was to join the ministry, upon graduating from high school in 1950 he attended Rutgers University on a science scholarship. He transferred to Howard University in 1954.

Between 1954 and 1957, Jones served in the Strategic Air Command. In 1958 he moved to Greenwich Village and began working as a jazz critic for such magazines as *Jazz Review*, *Downbeat*, and *Metronome*. It was in the Village that Jones became associated with Beat poets such as Allen Ginsberg and Charles Olson. Also in 1958 he married Heddi Cohen, with whom he had two children.

Throughout the late 1950s and early 1960s, Jones was extremely active on the New York literary scene. He was a poetry editor for Corinth Books and the Totem Press, edited numerous anthologies, and taught courses in contemporary poetry and creative writing at the New School for Social Research and Columbia University, where he completed his Masters degree in literature in 1964.

That same year his plays *The Dutchman* and *The Slave* were produced, the former winning an Obie award as best play of the season. By 1965 he had published a novel, *The System of Dante's Hell*, received a Guggenheim Fellowship, and was well on his way to becoming a major figure on the New York literary scene. However, Jones became increasingly discontented and later withdrew from the Village, divorced his wife, and moved to Harlem.

It was also at this time that he changed his name to Imamu Amiri Baraka. The names generally signify the following: Imamu, a Mohammedan Philosopher/Poet/Priest; Amiri, an African Warrior/Prince; and Baraka, spiritual conversion from Christianity to Islam as well as elimination of the slave name Jones. The new name was indicative of a more politically and socially committed point of view: in the late 1960s Baraka worked as a writer and activist for Black unity both in Harlem and in his home town of Newark, with the United Brothers of Newark and the Black Community Development and Defense Organization.

Baraka continues to write and lecture in poetry and Black literature.

Personal

In 1965, LeRoi Jones was a young, black, literary lion. His play, *Dutchman*, had been awarded the Obie for the best American play of 1963–64. Grove Press had published a book of his poems, *The Dead Lecturer*, and was bringing out a novel, *The System of Dante's Hell*; two of his one-act plays, *The Baptism* and *The Toilet*, were playing to enthusiastic houses. An-

other play, *The Slave*, had just closed a successful run, and Jones was much in demand on the lecture and poetry-reading circuit. He was thirty-one years old, well reviewed by critics, constantly referred to in conjunction with "Negro writing," and that bible of commercial masturbation, *Playboy* magazine, described him as "the most discussed—and admired—Negro writer since James Baldwin." Blah-blah.

Jones was a novelty, one of the first black voices crying out in the white wilderness. The lectures he gave, the panel discussions he participated in—all were utilized as platforms for launching attacks upon white America whose bullshit Jones, like many black men, had loved too well, from which he had expected too much, by which he had been cuckolded, and about which he was now bitter. Many of these attacks were ill-conceived, barely logical, too shrill, often grossly unfair, and always aimed at the crotch of the soft, white, good, liberal, WASP-Jewish intellectual. (Universal Honkie hate came later.)

The response was predictable. "White philanthropy runs amuck again," Jones wrote in a story called "Unfinished."

What he meant was that while in 1965 and into 1966 he kept cursing, ranting and raving and writing about himself, about beautiful black and hateful white America, for his efforts he received the John Hay Whitney Award, became a Guggenheim Fellow, taught classes at the New School for Social Research and at Columbia University. He was laved with cocktail party love and lionized with literary laurels and cash monies.

At first, the blasé New York culture scene was titillated by his maledictions. He was invited to all the enchanted-circle beautiful-people parties, literary events, show business orgies, and hip gatherings. The more he attacked white society, the more white society patronized him. Who'd have suspected that there was so much money to be made from flagellation? Whitey seemed insatiable; the masochistic vein was a source of hitherto untapped appeal, big box office stuff, and LeRoi Jones was one of the very first to exploit it.

Naturally the smart money crowd, the commercial-intellectual establishment, decided he was running a game, that he was into a gimmick, a commercial pose, a successful device. After all, LeRoi had been around the Village for years, had run with the white beatniks in the early '50s, had married a white Jewish girl. So how could he really mean what he was saying? Actually *mean* it . . .?

That was 1965. It is now three years later, and the score has changed. Currently, Jones is out of jail on $25,000 bail.

"Bail, hell! $25,000 isn't bail, it's a goddamned ransom," Jones snorted. He has an appeal pending for a conviction of illegal possession of firearms, for which he received a two-and-a-half to three-year prison sentence and a $1000 fine. That's the score these days. LeRoi Jones, like the rest of America, has changed since 1965.

We were all such innocents back then and so much more corrupt. (Violence may be monstrous, but self-deception is moral corruption.) In 1965, black and white men of good will were integrating the South together. Civil rights was still a possibility. So how could LeRoi be so serious? He was *ours*. Wasn't he?

He wasn't, and he *was* serious. He demonstrated this fact by an act that not even the cynical New York art world could pass off as a publicity bit or another tasteless tantrum. Jones, on the very brink of the American dream of fame and fortune, withdrew from the magic circle and went uptown. All the way uptown—to Harlem—leaving the high art scene to his white colleagues. The intellectual establishment could and did take the insults, obscenities, bad manners and name calling. But what was unforgivable, the one thing they couldn't take, was to be deserted, stood up. LeRoi Jones left them.

He traded in his successful-writer's suit for an Afro-American costume. He stopped speaking to his old white friends and rarely came down from the black ghetto. Said one of these ex-friends, "Maybe Roi is a racist, but he sure as hell is no opportunist." He sure as hell wasn't. . . .

But what is the purpose of Jones? Obviously, not what it

seems, for LeRoi Jones is obviously not what he seems. He is no martyr, unless we martyr him. Neither is he a black bogeyman, a Mau-Mau monster or, as several of his former white friends have described him, a bad-talking clown. He is a poet, a playwright, a conscience, a consciousness.

Probably Norman Mailer's characterization of Jones at a recent benefit is the best explanation of Jones's purpose, his *raison*, and a fair description of his true talents. That night at New York's Town Hall, Mailer said that Jones had written the best one-act play in America (*Dutchman*) and went on to say, "Who is this man, why are we here, will we survive? Thank you."

Therefore, if we wish to allow Jones to fulfill himself, if we desire to turn black militancy into a *wholesome contribution*, we have only to alter those elements in our society which thwart the Negro, frustrate the poet and menace our survival.

We have merely to tear down the ghettos and build up decent, integrated communities; re-educate our police departments to value life above property; destroy racial prejudice on both sides of the black and white picket fence dividing the cities; provide equal educational and employment opportunities for all; impeach Judge Kapp and others who have no conception of or respect for the law; share the wealth; and make a few other alterations in the shape and style of our society.

To exorcise LeRoi Jones and his black devils and save ourselves from the summers to come, we need only follow the above suggestions. Then we won't have to worry about Black Power, white backlash, civil insurrection, police brutality or anything else. For by that time, surely, the Messiah will have come. . . .

LeRoi Jones and I were never really friends. I knew him very casually about 15 years ago when we both lived in Greenwich Village. I'd run into him in Washington Square Park or at one of the jazz clubs or at some party, and then we'd say Hello, and that was about it. And then, for a few months, I lived with a girl who had lived with LeRoi.

I don't know LeRoi Jones very well, and I don't pretend to know what goes on in black inner space. I don't know what is going on in the black community of Newark. I suspect that there is division, political fratricide, and all the usual agonies. I can say that justice has not been meted out to Jones; I can also say that Jones hasn't been very just to others.

But justice and Jones are strangers. America has kept them apart. Understand that, and you can understand Jones' indifference to the fate of white radicals and his cooperation with white racists, the Newark Police and, indirectly, with HUAC.

"The native is an oppressed person whose permanent dream is to become the persecutor," Frantz Fanon wrote in his *Wretched of the Earth*, and LeRoi Jones is living testimony to the dreadful truth. Never mind that he knows better; never mind that his appeal fund was organized and contributed to by the white radical intellectuals whom Jones circuituously finked out on. Forget your preconceptions of decency and justice, these qualities have nothing to do with Jones. Or did you think he'd be grateful?

I would only remind those who still can't reconcile Jones' perfidy with their image of a black poet-revolutionary that Roi never preached equality; he's never called for a united front, only for a black front. The fact that he is the poet laureate of this Black Revolution may confuse some hardcore innocents who still think that the Black Revolution has something to do with white justice. Or that poets can't be social perverts. Or that certain fanatics wouldn't sell their (white) brothers to save their (black) skin. That is what the color war is about. That is what fratricide is about.

Whether or not this is an exact description of LeRoi Jones,

I can't say for certain. I can only suggest that if the shoe fits, Jones can wear it. Along with his crown of thorns.—STEPHEN SCHNECK, "LeRoi Jones or, Poetics & Policemen or, Trying Heart, Bleeding Heart," *Ram*, June 29, 1968, pp. 14–19

General

These streets stretch from one end of America to the other and connect like a maze from which very few can fully escape. Despair sits on this country in most places like a charm, but there is a special gray death that loiters in the streets of an urban Negro slum. And the men who walk those streets, tracing and retracing their steps to some hopeless job or a pitiful rooming house or apartment or furnished room, sometimes stagger under the weight of that gray, humiliated because it is not even "real."

Sometimes walking along among the ruined shacks and lives of the worst Harlem slum, there is a feeling that just around the corner you'll find yourself in South Chicago or South Philadelphia, maybe even Newark's Third Ward. In these places life, and its possibility, has been distorted almost identically. And the distortion is as old as its sources: the fear, frustration, and hatred that Negroes have always been heir to in America. It is just that in the cities, which were once the black man's twentieth century "Jordan," *promise* is a dying bitch with rotting eyes. And the stink of her dying is a deadly killing fume.

The blues singers know all this. They knew before they got to the cities. "I'd rather drink muddy water, sleep in a hollow log, than be in New York City treated like a dirty dog." And when they arrived, in those various cities, it was much worse than even they had imagined. The city blues singers are still running all that down. Specifically, it's what a man once named for me unnatural adversity. It is social, it is economic, it is cultural and historical. Some of its products are emotional and psychological; some are even artistic, as if Negroes suffered better than anyone else. But it's hard enough to be a human being under any circumstances, but when there is an entire civilization determined to stop you from being one, things get a little more desperately complicated. What do you do then?

You can stand in doorways late nights and hit people in the head. You can go to church Saturday nights and Sundays and three or four times during the week. You can stick a needle in your arm four or five times a day, and bolster the economy. You can buy charms and herbs and roots, or wear your hat backwards to keep things from getting worse. You can drink till screaming is not loud enough, and the coldest night is all right to sleep outside in. You can buy a big car . . . if the deal goes down. There's so much, then, you can do, to yourself, or to somebody else. Another man sings, "I'm drinkin' t.n.t., I'm smokin' dynamite, I hope some screwball starts a fight."

One can never talk about Harlem in purely social terms, though there are ghetto facts that make any honest man shudder. It is the tone, the quality of suffering each man knows as his own that finally must be important, but this is the most difficult thing to get to. (There are about twenty young people from one small Southern town, all friends, all living within the same few blocks of the black city, all of whom are junkies, communally hooked. What kind of statistic is *that*? And what can you say when you read it?)

The old folks kept singing, there will be a better day . . . or, the sun's gonna shine in my back door some day . . . or, I've had my fun if I don't get well no more. What did they want? What would that sun turn out to be?

Hope is a delicate suffering. Its waste products vary, but most of them are meaningful. And as a cat named Mean Wil-

liam once said, can you be glad, if you've never been sad?—LEROI JONES, "Cold, Hurt, and Sorrow (Streets of Despair), *Black American Literature*, ed. Darwin T. Turner, 1969, pp. 136–37

LeRoi Jones did not respond immediately to the stirrings of black political activism in the 1950s. The poems which appear in his first collection, *Preface to a Twenty-Volume Suicide Note*, were written between 1957 and 1960 and bear the impress of influences other than those of a stirring social world or of a black literary tradition. Indeed, the shaping influences on these early poems are, as he explained in an interview conducted in 1960, the surrealism of Lorca, which itself helped to neutralize an earlier influence by Eliot, and the work of William Carlos Williams, Robert Creeley, and Charles Olson. He saw the abandonment of Eliot as a necessary break with academicism in poetry. The tradition he wished to identify with, and the one he saw as restoring American poetry to the mainstream of modern verse, was that of twentieth-century modernism, just as he saw the prose writing of Jack Kerouac, Hubert Selby, Jr., and Edward Dorn as a demotic modernism. From Williams he learned "mostly how to write in my own language—how to write the way I *speak* . . . to write just the way it comes to me, in my own speech, utilizing the rhythms of speech rather than any kind of metrical concept . . . . From Pound, the same concept that went into the Imagist's [sic] poetry—the idea of the image and what an image ought to be. I learned, probably, about verse from Pound—how a poem should be made, what a poem ought to *look* like. . . . And from Williams how to get it out in my own language." From Olson he derived the connection between line length and breathing. In his magazines, *Yugen*, edited with his wife, Heddi Cohen, and *The Floating Bear*, edited with Diane Di-Prima, he published mostly the work of the Beats, together with the San Francisco poets and those who had been at Black Mountain College.

Despite his concern for a modernist engagement with the process of writing, with writing as subject as well as process, he was equally concerned that the new poetry and prose should exist as social reality—that it should be both an expression and an essential part of a social dynamic. At the time this did not imply a polemical literature, but one which, in its language and in its social presumptions, was not simply detached, ironic, autonomous. By "social" he seems to have meant primarily a linguistic and intellectual consonance between art and public activity, rather than a direct response to political change. Hence, the Beats both articulated and were part of that sense of disaffiliation which seemed to typify a generation of Americans in the 1950s.

At the same time, it seems curious that Little Rock and the beginning of the civil rights movement should have had such little effect on his work. And, indeed, it is one of the minor ironies of the Beats that their dismissal of the established political and social machine should have extended to those who sought most actively to alter it. Rebellion was to be metaphysical not actual; alienation was a spiritual condition not a business of actual deprivation (witness Kerouac's naive distortions of Negro life which he could perceive only in terms of the emotional and sensual release which he himself pursued through the ghetto streets of Denver and on into Mexico).

Jones's was a decidedly urban setting, and the world to which he related was primarily that of the literary avant-garde. Indeed, in the 1960 interview, he suggested that he did not in fact know many Negroes—a sense of detachment from racial origins which he later suggested he had exaggerated. His wife was white, and his immediate milieu was that of Greenwich Village. The political world was tangential. And yet, insofar as he defined the poetic landscape, in Olson's sense, as what the poet sees from where he is standing, there was a level on which his racial background was bound to inform his work. And, three years later, Olson's phrase had indeed become the basis for an avowedly political stance. In a violent denunciation of James Baldwin in *Kulchur* magazine, he insisted that "it is deadly simple. A writer must have a point of view, or he cannot be a good writer. He must be standing somewhere in the world, or else he is not one of us, and his commentary is of little value." The bitterness of the assault was, at least in part, an indictment of his own former sense of uninvolvement; his accusation that Baldwin had wished to live free of the fact of racial struggle was an expression of his own sense of guilt at having done precisely the same thing. In 1960, however, his sense of racial identity was more general. Hence, he accepted that it was an unavoidable influence and that it gave him access to a special experience denied to others. But that provided only an unvoiced tone and context for his work in contrast to the poetry of Langston Hughes for whom it was subject. The fact of his racial identity was something he "would deal with . . . when it has to do directly with a poem and not as a kind of broad generalization that doesn't have much to do with a lot of young writers today who are Negroes." Indeed, he implied that the inferior quality of much black writing had been a consequence of its sociological bias. . . .

The transformation of LeRoi Jones into Amiri Baraka, a black committed poet and political activist, was gradual, but traces of his development are there to be seen. When President Kennedy was assassinated, he wrote a poem which was literally pasted into the winter edition of *Kulchur* magazine, of which he was music editor. While this acknowledged a belief in the integrity of Kennedy and the reality of the hopes inspired by his presidency which he would later have disavowed, there is a strong sense in the poem of an historical caesura which provides something of a rationale for his own determined separatist mentality in later years. For the future which he sees is hopelessly compromised:

> From now on we will sit in nightclubs with jewish
>   millionaires
> listening to the maudlin political verse of a money
>   narcissist.
> And this will be the payback for our desires?
> For history, like the ringing coin
> that will not bend
> when we bite it.

The collection of poems published the following year, *The Dead Lecturer*, expressed the same growing concern with his cultural identity. In "Green Lantern's Solo," he asked

> . . . What man removed from his meat's source, can
>   continue
> to believe totally in himself?

Though most of them show a continuation of the concerns and forms to be found in his first volume, now he dedicates one poem to Robert Williams, with whom he had traveled to Cuba and who had been forced to flee the country. In this he protests the

> . . . deadly idiot
>   of compromise
> who shrieks compassion, and bids me love my
>   neighbor. Even beyond the meaning
> Of such acts as would give all my father's dead ash to
>   fertilize their bilious
> land.

and asserts that

> I am deaf and blind and lost and will not again sing
>   your quiet verse. I have lost
> even the act of poetry.

Indeed, one poem, "Black Dada Nihilismus," anticipates the committed black poetry which followed the publication of this volume. But, amidst the apocalyptic imagery of black murder and rape, there is a last plea, an equivalent of the hesitation implied in his powerful play of black revolt, *The Slave*, which also appeared in 1964. For the final stanza prays:

> May a lost god damballah, rest or save us
> against the murders we intend
> against his lost white children
> black dada nihilismus

When the change came, when he left his wife and white friends and fellow writers and moved from the Village to Harlem, discovering, as he felt, the full meaning and potential of his blackness and shaping it into a lesson for others, the revulsion which he felt for his own past was so sharp that it was expressed in a corruscating language designed to burn out his past equivocations and exorcise what now seemed to him his defection from responsibility.—C. W. E. BIGSBY, "The Black Poet as Cultural Sign," *The Second Black Renaissance*, 1980, pp. 277–80

Works

POETRY

His special gift is an emotive music that might have made him predominantly a "lyric poet," but his deeply felt preoccupation with more than personal issues enlarges the scope of his poems beyond what the term is often taken to mean.

> . . . Lighter, white man
> talk. They shy away. My own
> dead souls, my, so called
> people. Africa
> is a foreign place. You are
> as any other sad man here
> american.

I feel that sometimes his work is muddled, and that after the event he convinces himself that it had to be that way; in other words, his conception of when a poem is ready to be printed differs from mine. But while he is not the craftsman ⟨Gilbert⟩ Sorrentino is, he is developing swiftly and has a rich potential. Certain poems—especially "The Clearing," "The Turncoat," "Notes for a Speech"—show what he can do. They are beautiful poems, and others that are less complete have passages of equal beauty.

Since beauty is one of the least precise words in the language I had better define what I mean by it in this instance: the beauty in Jones's poems is sensuous and incantatory, in contrast to the beauty in Sorrentino's which is a sensation of exactitude, a hitting of nails on the head with a ringing sound. In his contribution to the notes on poetics at the back of the Grove Press anthology, *The New American Poetry*, Jones speaks of Garcia Lorca as one of the poets he has read intensely; and what is incantatory (magical) in his work, while it is natural to him, may well have been first brought to the surface by the discovery of an affinity in the magic of Lorca.

Most of what may seem, to those unfamiliar with it, arbitrary or perverse typographical eccentricity in some of these books is simply an attempt—frequently successful—at a notation that will give precise shades of tempo and inflexion. It is true that there are certain shared mannerisms—for instance, I have never been able to see anything useful in printing *would* as *wd.*; and I confess I am unable to understand the function of the marginal arrow which accompanies one of Blackburn's poems. But the reader who honestly wants to accept from contemporary poetry what it has to offer (which is a great deal) must learn to distinguish between minor irritations such as these and the truly functional techniques which can be fully appreciated only if he takes time to read the poems aloud, or at least to *sound them out* in his head.—DENISE LEVERTOV, *Nation*, Oct. 14, 1961, p. 252

In a mid-sixties poem, Baraka uttered a subtle and brief manifesto for the future of blacks: "to turn their evil backwards is to live." He has also said: "We want to conjure with Black life to re-create it for ourselves." *In Our Terribleness* fulfills both those demands. It is a poetic-photographic essay that both recreates and defines black life for the black reader. It is an expression of soul, and soul is a kind of "terribleness" that black people have nurtured as they survived in America.

Its title is derived from black slang, in which, reversing the white standard, "bad" and "terrible" are synonymous with "good" and "superb." "Since there is a 'good' . . . corny as Lawrence Welk On Venus, we will not be that. . . . We will be, definitely, bad, bad," Baraka states. "Our terribleness is our survival as beautiful things. . . . To be bad is one level. But to be terrible, is to be badder dan nat.". . .

Baraka urges blacks to observe their own culture, their own life style—understand and glory in its distinctiveness. Therefore, common objects are amplified in meaning, poetically given a significance more commensurate with their special place in black life. In Baraka's vision shoes are mirrors that one day might have lights on them—"Drums hammer the streets of America its bloods' walkin." A toothpick hanging from the lips of a black man is transformed: "Transmutation. The dumb wood now vibrating at a higher rate. With the blood. His mouth wand. The toothpick of the blood is his casual swagger stick.". . .

But *In Our Terribleness* is more than just a collection of sensitive photographs and poetic commentary. Beyond what might be considered a self-indulgent glorification of cultural attributes that blacks are already familiar with and that the nonblack reader would consider insignificant, Baraka's intent is revelatory. His "long image story in motion, papermotion" is an exhortation for the spiritual unification of blacks. "Nigger is a definition of the wholly detached from material consideration," he says. "Nigger don't have no gold/not even a negro got gold but a negro think like he would if he/had gold/a nigger is holy. . . . We niggers together."

In Our Terribleness is perhaps Amiri Baraka's greatest book. No doubt this is a result of his directing his work towards the black reader. (In a sense, blacks are the book's real creators; Baraka and Fundi are simply interpreters, image makers, who give the black experience a greater significance.) There may be legitimate arguments for both sides of the black writer's audience dilemma, but the writer who ignores his black audience and rages against white America and colonialism runs the special risk of simply creating protest literature. Trinidadian novelist V. S. Naipaul once suggested that such a preoccupation lessens a writer's universal appeal. If Naipaul's suggestion has any significance, then *In Our Terribleness* abundantly exemplifies that much sought after universality of literature. White readers and critics may have to come to terms with the long ignored humanity of blacks, however, before they discover its universal appeal.—RON WELBURN, "Reviving Soul in Newark, N. J.," *NYTBR*, Feb. 14, 1971, pp. 20–21

Baraka's early works are thoroughly "expressive." The poems written from 1958 to 1961 and included in *Preface to a Twenty-Volume Suicide Note* and the uncollected poems and stories of the same period are written in free forms and printed with striking graphic and orthographic peculiarities, among them CAPITALS, *italics*, and abbreviations (yr, sez, wd, cd, sd, tho, thot, &, &c.) suggestive of Olson's typewriter. Baraka echoes those writers who are mentioned most frequently in his early works, or at least in the dedications: the familiar group of Creeley, Ginsberg, Kerouac, McClure, O'Hara, Olson, Snyder, Whalen, Wieners, and Williams. Among Baraka's own specific and distinguishing qualities are not only name-dropping and abundant literary allusions, but also an associative speed which drives his poems at a great acceleration, away from frequently enigmatic, sometimes apparently unrelated titles, through fragmentary or incomplete thoughts, images, quotations, imaginary soliloquies and reflections, into continually new and occasionally quite surprising situations, considerations, puns, or observations, and toward frequently strong, occasionally even harshly abrupt endings.

The effect of rapidly progressing montages approaches an "avalanche of words," which Baraka unleashes, sometimes spontaneously, in much of his early poetry. As "projective verse," the poetry works through a connection of poetic turns, modes, lyrical situations, and imaginative and associative lines with perceived and recreated "reality," frequently suggested by names of places, streets, and cities, of poets, friends, politicians, and relatives, and even of commercial goods and brands. In "Axel's Castle," the location of the world of romance within a few blocks of Bleecker and MacDougal Streets in Greenwich Village illustrates this technique. The opposition of literature and reality is also reflected in Baraka's poetic idiom. In his Wieners review, Baraka expressed his awareness that any kind of "colloquial usage is 'dangerous' in poetry, since if it is not done extremely well, it is most easily vanquished, or at least, made ridiculous." In many of his own poems, Baraka was willing to face this danger, and contrasted traditional poetic moods (love, loneliness, suicidal feelings, seasonal changes, or artistic creation), which are often expressed in a "high" modernist diction, with sudden flashes of "low" street language, jargon, or colloquialisms, usually without achieving a ridiculous or destructive effect.

The early poems are collages of several recurring thematic elements. In most of the poems an omnipresent "I/eye" remains in the center of consciousness. Often the poet probes into the realms of autobiography and identity, high art and avant-gardist artists, Black music, American popular culture, and the heroes and antiheroes of the Western world. Or he expresses himself as an outsider in protest against "others," while exorcising his own past and indulging without inhibitions in provocative sexual themes.

The invocations of poetic peers and elders are numerous, as Baraka appropriates modern poetry to his own uses. The allusions are frequently playful and ironic, and occasionally hostile and iconoclastic; but at all times, Baraka employs his strategy of "popularizing", i.e., of playing the "high" against the vernacular. In the title of an early poem, Baraka continues the word play that led from the cliché "spring and fall" to William Carlos Williams' "Spring and All"; the poem "Spring & Soforth," published in 1960, develops a Melvillean concern for the "equinoctial," which is, significantly, awakened by the poet's *visionary* possession of a woman. He characteristically compares himself to a ray ("an arm of the sun") lying quietly

between your legs
like my bright
equinoctial eye.

Baraka's wide reading is reflected in his poetry, but it is the struggle between the formal demands of the Eliot tradition and the free-verse "local" sense of Williams' poetry which shapes Baraka's own struggle for a poetic idiom. Baraka's affinities to Williams are pervasive; and more than once Baraka explained that he learned from Williams "how to write the way I *speak* rather than the way I *think* a poem ought to be written" or, in other words, how to achieve the freedom of his expressive aesthetic. In contrast to Williams, T. S. Eliot represented, for Baraka, an objective art of structural containment and tight aesthetic control. It is therefore not surprising that Baraka referred to his "earlier" "Eliot period" as a "shell" which he had to break out of, since Eliotic "rhetoric can be so lovely, for a time . . . but only remains so for the rhetorician." Allusions to Eliot, whom Baraka later calls "the Missouri lad who wishes himself into a Saville [sic] Row funeral," the American who buttons himself up in an English suit, and thus chooses an English death, are plentiful throughout Baraka's writings.— WERNER SOLLORS, "Early Poetry and Prose," *The Quest for a "Populist Modernism,"* 1978, pp. 37–38

DRAMA

In 1965, Jones clearly defined the specific role of the black artist in America: to aid in the destruction of America as he knows it.

> His role is to report and reflect so precisely the nature of the society, and of himself in that society, that other men will be moved by the exactness of his rendering and, if they are black men, grow strong through this moving, having seen their own strength, and weakness; and if they are white men, tremble, curse, and go mad, because they will be drenched with the filth of their evil.
>
> The Black Artist must draw out of his soul the correct image of the world. He must use this image to band his brothers and sisters together in common understanding of the nature of the world (and the nature of America) and the nature of the human soul.
>
> The Black Artist must demonstrate sweet life, how it differs from the deathly grip of the White Eyes. The Black Artist must teach the White Eyes their deaths, and teach the black man how to bring these deaths about.

Jones sees the black artist as a moralist.

He is specific about the duties of the Revolutionary Theatre, born in the 1960's: it should force change; it should be change. It must cleanse black audiences of their ugliness. It must force them to see their beauty: the strength in their minds and in their bodies. It must take dreams and give them a reality. The ritual and historical cycles of reality must be isolated. Clearly, the Revolutionary Theatre, which Jones describes as a theatre of victims, is a political theatre, a weapon. It will show what the world is and what it should be.

> We are preaching virtue and feeling, and a natural sense of the self in the world. All men live in the world, and the world ought to be a place for them to live.

The Revolutionary Theatre is moral. Its tasks are also those of its playwrights. Jones, one of the architects of this theatre, has taken his own advice.—JEANNE-MARIE A. MILLER, "The Plays of LeRoi Jones," *CLAJ*, March 1971, pp. 331–32

The Baptism, first produced in 1964, is a useful introduction to Baraka's drama because it includes features that dominate the earlier plays and others that foreshadow subsequent developments in Baraka's dramatic art. Set in a church, the play is

actually a modern morality drama about a young boy who is accused by an old woman of masturbating while pretending to pray. As the action unfolds it centers on a growing contest for the soul—and body—of the boy. The contest pits the old woman and the minister of the church against a homosexual who is contemptuous of his opponents' hypocrisy toward sex and who expresses a frank need for love and for an honest sexuality. The minister and the old woman are revolting not simply because they are puritanical but because their puritanism is a thin disguise for sexual desires (for the boy in this case) that they are unable to express frankly. As the contest becomes violent they strike the homosexual to the ground and in turn they are cut down by the boy who now claims to be the Son of God. At this point the play ends abruptly: the boy is carried off by a motorcyclist who is supposed to be a "messenger" of the boy's father.

As a morality play centered on a moral struggle between love and puritanism *The Baptism* exploits an old dramatic tradition with special ironic effects. The usual conflict between good and evil in the morality play tradition of Christian culture appears here with significant modifications. The forces of evil are now associated with the Christian Church itself; love and charity are embodied by the homosexual, a conventional figure of moral and sexual "perversion." And given the ambiguous figure of the boy himself (child figure and Christ archetype) then the moral struggle takes on an ironically twofold meaning: it is traditional insofar as it involves a contest for the soul of the human individual; and it is antitraditional in that Christianity is no longer an unquestioned symbol of goodness but is actually associated with evil. Indeed the most crucial outcome of the play's moral conflict is the degree to which Christianity emerges as an inherently corrupting tradition which makes it impossible for the individual to experience love and sexuality to the fullest, except on nonconformist or rebellious terms. Social traditions in the play are inherently destructive because they sanction a pervasive lovelessness and a neurotic fear of sex and feeling. The church is the main target in this regard because it is the institution which embodies these traditions.

The morality design of the play is, therefore, basically ironic in conception. Baraka recalls the old morality traditions of early Christian drama in order to attack those traditions and the Christian ethic that they espoused. And insofar as *The Baptism* subverts Christian morality and art, it anticipates the use of the morality play format in Baraka's black nationalist, anti-Western drama. For in those later plays, as we shall see, political conflicts take on the form of moral contests in which a Western dramatic tradition (the morality play) becomes a device for rejecting the West itself. Moreover, this subversive, antitraditionalist use of tradition is reflected in the play's title. The ritual of baptism is no longer an initiation into the established conventions of religious belief and social morality. It has now become a ritual of exposure and subversion, one directed against the conventions themselves.—LLOYD W. BROWN, *Amiri Baraka*, 1980, pp. 138–40

Like the train of its setting, *Dutchman* moves with tremendous bursts of energy and periodic lulls. As the train pulls out of the station, the tension accelerates immediately with Lula's increasingly abusive treatment of Clay, who, by virtue of his apparent naiveté, wins the sympathy of the audience. Midway through the play, however, this incessant goading threatens to completely exasperate the audience, to drain them all too hastily. The maturing dramatist effectively counters this by ending the first scene. By dividing the action into two scenes, he not only gives the audience a chance to regroup emotionally, he also manages to give the play a greater sense of depth. After those few seconds of darkness, the audience views the opening action of scene II with the distinct feeling that a great deal has happened, as well as the hope that Clay has started to better acquit himself with Lena. This hope is short-lived, however, for the dramatist starts anew the pattern of scene I as the train pulls out at the beginning of scene II.

Again Lula takes the initiative. She tells Clay how they will behave at the party, utters more strange statements of the kind that kept him off-balance throughout the first scene, and finally attacks him with an intensity surpassing that of the first scene. Like the screaming train, the action of the play is near peak acceleration. At this point, *i.e.*, during Lula's most vile outpouring, both Clay and his sympathetic viewers are thoroughly exhausted and provoked. Clay's outburst, a masterful rendering of the age-old dramatic reversal, even goes beyond the earlier break in action in that it simultaneously relieves and maintains tension. It relieves the tension inasmuch as it fulfills our desire for some self-assertion on Clay's part. Yet it maintains tension in the promise of a final and violent clash of antagonistic forces. Although we are ready for the expected clash, Baraka puts us off guard with his fine sense of timing. He lulls us into forgetting the promised end with the calm immediately following Clay's eruption. Consequently, we rest in the feeling that Lula has finally been silenced. . . .

The train and the action of *Dutchman* simultaneously grind to a halt. However, in the troubling denouement, we perceive evidence of the entire pattern beginning anew with the entrance of the anonymous young man, who is, from all appearance, like Clay or Warren Enright, a "well-known type." As the train accelerates, this young man's tragic end is inevitably projected in our minds.

Along with his masterful manipulation of suspense and tension, Baraka shows his growth in the ease with which he combines the mythic and the literal in *Dutchman*. We are prepared for his duality of meaning from the opening lines of the text. *Dutchman* takes place "In the flying underbelly of the city. Steaming hot, and summer on top, outside. Underground. The subway heaped in modern myth." The setting suggests that the play will delve into the troubling, but too often denied truths of race relations, American style. This setting, like the encounter between the exaggeratedly "real" characters, is, indeed, meant to represent a more elusive inner or psychic reality. As if he wanted to make sure no one mistook this work for the overt naturalism of, say, *The Toilet*, Baraka gives important alternative directions: "Dimlights and darkness whistling by against the glass. (Or paste the lights, as admitted props right on the subway windows.)" He seeks to synthesize the naturalistic and expressionistic modes, to take the best each has to offer. This is evidenced not only in his approach to setting, but also in the characterization of *Dutchman*. Lula and Clay are simultaneously "real" persons and highly symbolic types. The powerful effect of the drama, derived from this synthesis of artistic modes, has been compared frequently to that of Albee's *The Zoo Story*, another lean, parable-like work concerned with the tragic consequences of failure to communicate.—Henry C. Lacey, "Joseph to His Brothers," *To Raise, Destroy and Create*, 1981, pp. 73–74

PROSE

In addition to his plays and poems, Jones has produced three books. The first of these, *Blues People* (1964), is an attempt to define the American Negro through his music. Jones is hard put throughout the work to isolate the unadulterated African and Negro elements in American blues and jazz, and the elaborate sociological conclusions he draws from his investigations appear somewhat disproportionate to the evidence he offers. On Jones's behalf, though, it must be said that he has researched his material carefully and, theories aside, has made a rather informative contribution to the literature of jazz.

Jones's other nonfiction work, *Home* (1967), is a collection of articles, essays, and reviews, in which the reader can, if he wishes, trace the development of Jones's political, literary, and social views as they become more and more militant and nationalistic. But since Jones here says nothing that Wright, Baldwin, and Malcolm X have not said better, it would be tedious to repeat what he does say. What may be interesting biographically is that Jones in this book (and at greater length in a lecture he once delivered at Berkeley) cites an incident at Howard when a dean castigated him for eating a watermelon on campus, thereby endangering Howard's public image of the educated Negro. It was at Howard, Jones writes, that he was shocked into realizing the "sickness" of the Negro—which suggests that discovering racism at an age well past the impressionable years may produce more extreme reactions (Wright, Jones) than the racism others have experienced all their lives.

Jones's one novel, *The System of Dante's Hell* (1965), deals mainly with the narrator's remembrances of his adolescent years in Newark. The prose is largely in fragments and simple sentences, and the memories are associated without transition, as they would be in a dream or nightmare. There is some attempt at traditional narrative at the end, but the novel as a whole must be termed, for want of a better word, "experimental." Despite Jones's attempt to structure his hell ("the torture of being the unseen object and the constantly observed subject") according to Dante's nine circles, the relationship is casual, and the novel is as explosive and directionless as some of Jones's poems. Yet the hell is very real. It is equally a song of self-disgust and an act of hostility toward the reader. "This thing, if you read it, will jam your face in my shit. Now say something intelligent!" The narrator successfully evokes the sordid, dreary sounds and images of Negro slums, and there are fleeting glimpses of sexual experiences with males and females. But above all the novel reads like a kind of melancholic obsessive return to the past, as if Jones, not unlike Jean Toomer years before him, were seeking "absolute pain," possibly to discover himself at last, possibly to obliterate himself.— Edward Margolies, "Prospects: LeRoi Jones," *Native Sons*, 1968, pp. 197–98

Many of the essays in ⟨*Selected Plays and Prose of Amiri Baraka/LeRoi Jones*⟩ are governed by a punitive, vindictive inclination, which is part of Baraka's rhetorical style as one who has mounted the ramparts. "Newark, Before Black Men Conquered," from *Raise Race Rays Raze* (1969), is ruthlessly honest about the corruption of political life in that city. It also reveals Baraka's angry ambition. He is less self-promoting and a much more interesting, skeptical observer in the essay "Cuba Libre," from *Home*, which is about his visit there in July 1960. It is a valuable piece of reportage. Baraka describes his impression of Castro, the changes in the country's institutions, the mood of the people and the exuberant anniversary celebration at the shrine of the Revolution, Sierra Maestra. The essay also marks the beginning of Baraka's political odyssey, his search for the revolution in America.

Now that Baraka identifies himself as a Marxist, he has shrewdly omitted from this collection essays from his nationalist period. An essay in The New Nationalism in which Baraka says, "We cannot understand what devils and the devilishly influenced mean when they say equality for women," or an essay from *Home* in which Baraka remarks, "Most American white men are trained to be [homosexuals]" would offend the current cultural mood. Though the essays printed here differ in subject matter—Baraka now cares more for the dictatorship of the proletariat than he does for the glorification of Black Manhood—they exhibit the same lust for doctrine, the joy of jargon. "Capitalism is an economic system, a mode of production, characterized by private ownership of the means of production, the lands, the factories, mineral wealth, transportation, communication, waterways. This means of production is owned privately by a single class in capitalist society called the capitalist class or the bourgeoisie." The novice recites his catechism, and the solemnity is almost comical. The utter lack of sophistication in Baraka's analysis makes these essays—"The Revolutionary Tradition in Afro-American Literature," "National Liberation Movements" and "Black Liberation / Socialist Revolution"—feeble contributions to the Marxist critique. In one of his late poems, Baraka attacks Angela Davis for being a "movie star" and "fronting" for the lies of the Communist Party. A pity, for he could learn something from her

application of the materialist methodology to black history, regardless of what he thinks of her party affiliation.

One often wonders to whom these essays are addressed. They exhibit an alarming pedagogical condescension: "All the wealth that the workers produce that they do not get is called *surplus value*, and this is the secret of capitalism that Karl Marx discovered. One hundred workers in an hour can put together 100 automobiles from which a gross profit of $500,000 can be realized. Each worker is paid $10 for that hour; $10 times 100 is $1000. Subtract that from $500,000 and you understand what surplus value is, and you also understand why capitalism must be destroyed. . . ." Hardly the cutting edge. Where are the workers who would tolerate being instructed in such a manner? Baraka is better on the subject of black music and society. One wishes for more of that and less of his political flailings.—Darryl Pinckney, "The Changes of Amiri Baraka," *NYTBR*, Dec. 6, 1979, pp. 9, 29

Djuna Barnes

1892–1982

Djuna Barnes was born on June 12, 1892 in Cornwall-on-Hudson, New York, to an unsuccessful painter and an English violinist. Her father, who changed his name repeatedly before settling on Wald Barnes, gave all five children flamboyant names and kept them out of the school system in order to make them great individuals. Barnes was educated by her family before attending Pratt Institute and the Art Students League in New York City. From 1913 she supported herself (and her then-divorced mother and younger brothers) by journalism. She began writing for the *Brooklyn Eagle* as "Lydia Steptoe," and by the 1920s was one of the most celebrated literary women in Paris, contributing to journals like *Vanity Fair*, *The New Yorker*, *The New Republic*, and *Smart Set*. Many of her articles were unsigned: they remain uncollected.

Barnes's first book, *The Book of Repulsive Women 8 Rhythms and 5 Drawings*, appeared in 1915. Then came a collection of poems, stories, and drawings, *A Book* (1923). She also wrote one-act plays, presented by the Provincetown Players; the *Ladies Almanack*, a parody of Elizabethan language and Parisian lesbians; and then her major works, the novels *Ryder* (1928), *Nightwood* (1936), and the play *The Antiphon* (1958).

Her circle in Paris included Gertrude Stein, Ezra Pound, T. S. Eliot, and James Joyce. Joyce was one of the few people whom Barnes considered a genius, and she was the only person in Paris who dared call him "Jim" to his face. Eliot persuaded Faber to publish *Nightwood*, and wrote an introduction in which he praised its "great achievement of style, the beauty of phrasing, the brilliance of wit and characterization, and a quality of horror and doom very nearly related to that of Elizabethan tragedy." A later admirer of Barnes's work was Dag Hammarskjöld, who co-translated *The Antiphon* into Swedish and had it performed at Stockholm's Royal Dramatic Theatre, intending this as a first step towards a Nobel Prize for Barnes.

Starting in the 1920s, Barnes drank much and often, and had what she called "my famous breakdowns," being hospitalized in Paris, London, and New York. At the outbreak of World War II she had to move back to New York, where she lived in steady isolation on Patchin Place in Greenwich Village. She died on June 18, 1982.

Works

The new work by the author of *Nightwood, Ryder,* and *A Night Among the Horses* is a play written in verse; beyond this, it is not easy to characterize. To me, it seems to combine under extreme pressure several elements distinctive in a good deal of work which defines for us the term "modern," and these elements might be outlined thus . . .

1. An art of serious parody. Travesty may be the better word. Eliot's introduction to *Nightwood* called our attention to "a quality of horror and doom very nearly related to that of

Elizabethan tragedy"; in *Antiphon* we have, rather, Jacobean qualities—free, excessive and often grotesque in style, ever full of random brilliancies, morbid and mordant:

> It's true the webbed commune
> Trawls up a wrack one term was absolute;
> Yet corruption in its deft deploy
> Unbolts the caution, and the vesper mole
> Trots down the wintry pavement of the prophet's head.

When it is good, it is splendid; when it is bad, it is absurd; but it is almost always fascinating. Considered only technically, it is a *tour de force* as brilliant as Nigel Dennis' parody of late Shake-speare in his novel, *Cards of Identity*; but this is a great deal darker and is of more persistent intention. It is as though the author would deliberately assert the connexion of tragedy less with life than with a certain exalted and strained condition of language. It is parody not as Shelley's "Swellfoot the Tyrant" is parody, but parody proceeding from desperation, as in Eliot's "Fragments of an Aristophanic Melodrama," or in the music ascribed to Adrian Leverkühn in Mann's *Dr. Faustus*—"all the methods and conventions of art today are *good for parody only*." Style mocks at itself in the mirror, and the idea of the art-work itself, the exquisite and finished product endeared to a century of "well-made plays" which no one wants, is broken.

2. Breaking-up of surfaces; destruction of the conventional sequences and coherencies of "plot." *The Antiphon* is a play almost without a literal level to its action; allegory, moral and anagoge are made to emerge as by a kind of Cubist handling from the shattered reflections of "story." I find this richness sometimes confusing (no more confusing, really, than I find *Hecuba* or *The Bacchae*), and am still mighty hesitant about such understanding as two readings have produced, but I will risk a brief note of interpretation.

The doom on the house is allegorically the fall of civil-ization—"Let us speak of Beewick as our country," says Augusta—and the end of history: the pathos of Augusta and Miranda in Act III is, as it were, the lament of Eve looking back upon centuries.

Augusta's dead husband, Titus Higby Hobbs of Salem (Mass.), is seen as Jehovah, who created the world and re-pented of his creation and left his progeny to suffer its destruc-tion, unless they can find security in the doll's house shown to Augusta at the epiphany by her son Jeremy, the disguised and ineffectual redeemer. This doll's house is called "Hobbs' Ark," and through its windows are revealed the mysteries of genera-tion, which the mother, however, is unable to accept.

Morally, the play represents the soul seeking life and find-ing death, and finding death a mercy. Yet there is in this an obscurely redemptive movement, if it is not to be read as a further sarcasm: among the many symbolic properties which furnish Burley Great Hall are the two halves of a gryphon, "once a car in a roundabout." At the beginning of Act III, the two halves have been brought together under a crown, and here Miranda lies sleeping. To Augusta, the gryphon seems to move: "We have a carriage!" she says, and the two women thus begin their elegiac journey through past ages. Now this gryphon, I suppose, refers us to the gryphon seen by Dante in the Earthly Paradise, where its double nature, eagle and lion, figures forth incarnation, duality resolved, divine and human nature made one. It is upon this car that Augusta and Miranda, who are also one, finally fall. It may be that the parable here embodied is the anagogic bearing of the play: the failure of both the Old Law and the New. Or, since Augusta and Miranda are one, or interchangeable—"I am she, and she Miranda," "Miranda's all Augusta laid up in Miranda"—it may be that the paradigm is more complicated, telling how the old cove-nant under the Father was revoked by the new covenant with the Son, and how this in turn was revoked for modern times by the Puritan revolution (the house was a college of chantry priests, but has been in the family since the seventeenth cen-tury). "This history," says William Blake, "has been adopted by both parties"; but maybe the difficulty of interpretation here springs from the entrance of a third party, for it has been rare in literature for "this history" to be told us by a woman.

3. Treatment of language as an independent value. I mean by this that the extreme violence and dense compaction

of the words is constantly taking us away from immediate ac-tion, away from narrative, away from the solidity of things ordered, and involving us instead in a dimension specifically poetic rather than dramatic, a complicated vast web of relation in which the threads are spun among dissolving objects, as if you were to have constellations without stars. This is how Shakespeare tends to work at moments of the greatest intensity, save that with Shakespeare you have always the feeling of being anchored to solidity in the action. Miss Barnes works this way all the time, and her handling of the style seems in conse-quence to be sometimes hysterically strained.—HOWARD NEMEROV, "A Response to *The Antiphon*," NWR, Summer 1958, pp. 88–91

Recently *Time* magazine, pernicious as ever, dismissed the *Selected Writings* of Djuna Barnes by saying that the best of her work, *Nightwood*, offered little more than "the mysterioso effect that hides no mystery," and even Leslie Fiedler has de-scribed Djuna Barnes' vision of evil as effete. Yet all her myth and fear are mightily to be envied. Surely there is unpardon-able distinction in this kind of writing, a certain incorrigible assumption of a prophetic role in reverse, when the most baf-fling of unsympathetic attitudes is turned upon the grudges, guilts, and renunciations harbored in the tangled seepage of our earliest recollections and originations. It is like quarreling at the moment of temptation. Or it is like working a few tanger-ines on a speedily driven lathe. Djuna Barnes is one of the "old poets," and there is no denying the certain balance of this "infected carrier" upon the high wire of the present. She has moved; she has gone out on a limb of light and indefinite sexuality and there remains unshakeable. She has free-wheeled the push bicycle into the cool air.

Djuna Barnes, Flannery O'Connor, Nathanael West—at least these three disparate American writers may be said to come together in that rare climate of pure and immoral *creation*—are very nearly alone in their uses of wit, their comic treatments of violence and their extreme detachment. If the true purpose of the novel is to assume a significant shape and to objectify the terrifying similarity between the unconscious de-sires of the solitary man and the disruptive needs of the visible world, then the satiric writer, running maliciously at the head of the mob and creating the shape of his meaningful psychic paradox as he goes, will serve best the novel's purpose. Love, for Djuna Barnes, is a heart twitching on a plate like the "lopped leg of a frog"; for Flannery O'Connor it is a thirty-year-old idiot girl riding in an old car and tearing the artificial cherries from her hat and throwing them out the window; for Nathanael West, love is a quail's feather dragged to earth by a heart-shaped drop of blood on its tip, or the sight of a young girl's buttocks looking like an inverted valentine. Each of these writers finds both wit and blackness in the pit, each claims a new and downward sweeping sight and pierces the pretension of the sweet spring of E. E. Cummings. Detachment, then, is at the center of the novelist's experiment, and detachment allows us our "answer to what our grandmothers were told love was, what it never came to be"; or detachment allows us, quot-ing again from *Nightwood*, to see that "When a long lie comes up, sometimes it is a beauty; when it drops into dissolution, into drugs and drink, into disease and death, it has a singular and terrible attraction." But mere malice is nothing in itself, of course, and the product of extreme fictive detachment is ex-treme fictive sympathy. The writer who maintains most suc-cessfully a consistent cold detachment toward physical violence . . . is likely to generate the deepest novelistic sym-pathy of all, a sympathy which is a humbling before the terrible and a quickening in the presence of degradation.—JOHN HAWKES, "Fiction Today," *MR*, Summer 1962, pp. 786–87

Kenneth Burke recently made a fresh start with *Nightwood*, contending that the book "aims at . . . a kind of 'transcendence downward.' . . ." He finds an intention to make the plot absolute, in a series of "[Biblical] Lamentations, much as though this were the primal story of all mankind." One is not persuaded that Burke admires the book. But his rigor with the content is a good augury. He is concerned with the Scriptural mode of the work. Had he comprehended the preceding novel *Ryder*, he would have noticed the Scriptural mode in its beginnings. It would be mad to say that Djuna Barnes intended to write a substitute Testament for humankind. What she did intend was a dismissal of Scriptural authoritarianism by deliberately crafted Scriptural frames, each playing with Biblical language, each designed to present sardonically the Law as an insufficient revelation of the nature of man, and, first for her, that of woman. Burke surveys too little. But his study proposes that Djuna Barnes was intent upon novelistic structure. We should remember that she wrote in an American era of the novel when *consciousness* was all. (O'Neill, of course, tried to use some ill-digested Freud to "expand" the American drama, without notable success.) Djuna Barnes wished to bring to the American novel the full burden of the dark of the mind, the night, the subconscious. She intended to be an American surrealist. Clearly she thought of herself as unique. She was unique; and today she belongs in the unique company of some of our new writers.

The doctrines of the surrealists have spread very slowly into Protestant America. T. S. Eliot noted in his introduction to *Nightwood* the perseverance of the Puritan morality, its dismissal of the images of sleep as nonfigurative in the life of the "successful" man. The American future may come to evaluate the psychedelic age as prophecy. Vonnegut, Pynchon, and Hawkes, as examples from this American present, suggest the coming on of a new morality, and a new mode in an art of fiction as full exposition: the totality of the dark and the light, subconscious and conscious, the mind at the full. In the renascence of Djuna Barnes she will be read with our new novelists. The reading will not advance affinities to Poe, and, at the other end of the spectrum, to Joyce. Poe wrote his tales as symbols of the "furnishings" of one mind, his own. Djuna Barnes intended to expose the human condition, as she saw it, by fictive analogies. As for Joyce, one should simply note with André Breton, the chief French spokesman of surrealism, that Joyce is not a true surrealist. "Joyce labors to keep himself within the framework of *art*. He falls into novelistic illusion." The distinction rests in the insistence of surrealism upon an exposition of universals. Thus, despite the distance between Poe and Joyce, each is intent upon art as illusion, a privacy of vision ending with the limits of each sovereign imagination. The point is that the vision does not refer, as though it were a self-contained picture from Synthetic Cubism, beyond itself. In the intent of Gertrude Stein, the deep privacy of the fiction, the poetry, the plays, there is a comparable evidence of the self-contained. All of this is to say that the work of Djuna Barnes is designed to refer beyond itself. Related to the tenets of surrealism, her work urges the need for a new morality and the need for a new scripture describing the phenomena of the human mind. . . .

Breton wrote in his *Second Manifesto of Surrealism* (1930): ". . . we are not afraid to take up arms against logic, if we refuse to swear that something in dreams is less meaningful than something we do in a state of waking. . . ." So Djuna Barnes, speaking through Matthew O'Connor in *Nightwood*: ". . . they [the French] think of the two [wakefulness and sleep, day and night] as one continually . . . Bowing down from the waist, the world over they go, that they may revolve about the Great Enigma. . . ." When Matthew later contends against "that priceless galaxy of misinformation called the mind, harnessed to that stupendous and threadbare glomerate called the soul. . . ." he extends the "French" wisdom of his author, looking, at her behest, into the depths of an older culture with a profounder knowledge of *mind* and *soul*. Was it that Americans were kept in relative ignorance by the stern rubrics of Puritan "logic" and by the wider and pervasive Protestant denial of the mystery, the Great Enigma, which all faithful readings of Scriptural Law must reject? Did these biases prohibit in America a knowledge of the truth of human existence, as though we were iron-bound to Scriptural Law which was itself born of the sleep and the dream of men? Is it foreign to Americans to contend, with Matthew O'Connor in *Nightwood*, "To our friends . . . we die every day, but to ourselves we die only at the end"? Gide said very much the same; so has Sartre. Professional surrealism is not the absolute source for either of these Frenchmen. But the angle of vision of recent French metaphysics and French art is there. Djuna Barnes, without any doubt, reflected most strenuously in her unique explorations the French modes which she knew. We suppose a continued dedication on her part to French thought as she published *The Antiphon*, her verse play, in 1958. This is a dedication to art as antiphon, the answer from the life of the subconscious; and one finds here, in this substantial example of her surrealist style, a recapitulation which stretches back to Baudelaire.

> Where the martyr'd wild fowl fly the portal
> High in the honey of cathedral walls,
> There is the purchase, governance and mercy.
> Where careful sorrow and observed compline
> Sweat their gums and mastics to the hive
> Of whatsoever stall the head's heaved in—
> There is the amber. As the high plucked banks
> Of the viols rend out the unplucked strings below—
> There is the antiphon.

The risk of paraphrase is great. But this poetry may be read in this sense: the cathedral represents faith of whatever order; faith becomes amber, honey solidified into gem; it is made by reason, the conscious mind; but there is a music below the strings of cathedral music, a music to "rend out" the silent strings below, the dark of the subconscious; and from below, the unvoiced dark, comes the antiphon, given a voice through the invitation of the upper voice, returning an answer to the high-plucked strings above. Art, in the sense of Baudelaire, exists to join the day and the night into a whole, the whole of the human mind. Baudelaire's principle became the credo of an art.

This essay has been written in avoidance of value judgments of Djuna Barnes. It was intended as a study of the figure in the carpet, the tapestry displaying structured themes. Much has been neglected, of first importance the poetic idiom and its relation to surrealistic practice. Her compounding of the unlike in juxtaposition, objects of essential dissimilarity compelled into adjacency, is fully in accord with surrealistic techniques. It may frequently remind us of the compulsions of Giorgio di Chirico. Eliot's contention that her work will appeal primarily to readers of poetry is upheld, of course; but the commitment of the poetry may be far other than Eliot was willing to recognize. This much is certain: Whoever studies the French affinities of American artists after the First World War will be obliged to take Djuna Barnes into serious account. Woman militant in our midst was felt in her own weight with the inception of American Transcendentalism. Woman creative as an explorer of the subconscious remains in American fiction an impressive and exceptional voyager.—JAMES BAIRD, "Djuna Barnes and Surrealism: 'Backward Grief'," *Individual and Community*, 1975, pp. 163–81

⟨T⟩he following is suggested as a working definition of black humor: it makes no attempt to minimize the terror of the post-World War I universe; it uses comedy to encourage sympathy as well as to expose evil; it suggests futurity; it celebrates comic distortion as an indication that anything is possible; and it is related to the poetic use of language. Three primary characteristics remain especially significant: extreme detachment on the part of the author; the comic treatment of horror and violence; and disruption or parody of conventional notions of plot, character, theme, and setting. The result is highly conscious, unrealistic, militantly experimental comic fiction.

Nightwood is one of the first American novels to reflect the working definition, yet apparently only Sharon Spencer has mentioned its comic spirit. Briefly commenting on the chapter "Watchman, What of the Night?" she describes the dialogue between Dr. Matthew O'Connor and Nora Flood as "intense, extremely funny, and extremely ludicrous. . . . The setting is the doctor's rented room in a cheap Paris hotel, a room that is in itself so terrifying and ridiculous that it might inspire pages of analysis of its 'black comedy.'" The black humor of *Nightwood* is, indeed, particularly illustrated in the grotesque, violent characters, the detached attitude toward the descriptions of outrageous clothes and houses, and the parody of the novelist's role.

These comic elements are part of Barnes' larger thematic concern with modern man's separation from a more primitive animal nature—at first glance, hardly the theme for a humorous novel. Only Robin Vote is united with her bestial side, yet she wanders through Europe from city to city and from lover to lover in a futile effort to attain full humanity. In *Nightwood*, humanity, day, and present contrast with beast, night, and past. Thus Robin is introduced as an "infected carrier of the past" and as having "the eyes of wild beasts." Her various love affairs with Felix, Nora, and Jenny illustrate a search for someone to tell her that she is innocent, for, as Barnes suggests, awareness of innocence leads to consciousness of moral values and, in turn, to humanity. Robin's three principal lovers, however, are unable to help her achieve the human state. Caught up in their own senses of alienation, and goaded by selfish love of Robin, they become animal-like themselves in their desperation to appropriate the bestial woman.

The numerous love affairs are destructive, painfully pursued, and selfishly concluded, for each character searches for a lover who might alleviate his sense of incompleteness. The longed-for reunion between animal and human states never takes place, and the characters are left with an impossible choice: to be primarily human, which means the painful awareness of alienation; or to be primarily animal, which means the longing for moral consciousness. Barnes suggests that the scale has tipped too far on the side of humanity, and she would probably agree with Dr. O'Connor's advice to Nora: "Be humble like the dust, as God intended, and crawl."

The discussion of theme might suggest to the unprepared reader that *Nightwood* is anything but comic. Happily, however, Barnes has not written a novel of unrelenting gloom. Her sense of humor is evident from the beginning, and her use of funny elements with a depressing theme reflects the perplexing mixture so vital to black humor. . . . Recognition of the comedy, however, depends upon the individual reader, for Barnes maintains total authorial detachment. Hedvig and Guido are not singled out as comic dupes, as characters who deserve only our laughter. Seen in the context of the novel, they are no more grotesque and ridiculous than the major characters who are damned by alienation and cursed by thwarted love. . . .

None of these people can be called characters in the conventional sense. They do not "live," nor are they "round," and the reader is never encouraged to identify with them. Like the characters in many contemporary black humor fictions, Barnes' people are static and subordinated to theme. *Nightwood* provides insight into the disordered human condition by conveying generalizations about love, bestiality, and religion, and it avoids the reader's expectations of verisimilitude and character development. In most instances Felix, Nora, Robin, and Jenny act as vehicles for the poetic prose, for the "saving beauties of language"; they are not essential to Barnes' ideas nor to her means of expressing them. Specific details and descriptions are purposely omitted so that upon finishing *Nightwood* one cannot define what the characters wear or how they look. Poetic generalizations about homosexual or heterosexual love in the midst of discussions about bestiality, the night, and religion do not need living characters or realistic events. O'Connor's reaction to Jenny perhaps best expresses the reader's complex feelings about the characters in experimental black humor fiction: "That poor shuddering creature had pelvic bones I could see flying through her dress. I want to lean forward and laugh with terror."—DONALD J. GREINER, "Djuna Barnes' *Nightwood* and the American Origins of Black Humor," *Crt*, Aug. 1975, pp. 45–49

ALAN WILLIAMSON
"The Divided Image: The Quest for Identity in the Works of Djuna Barnes"
Critique, Spring 1964, pp. 58–74

I

Djuna Barnes, as a lesser member of the cluster of Lost Generation writers, has suffered from becoming the idol of an avant-garde cult while remaining unknown to the general public and deprecated by critics. On the one hand, she is justly praised for the strangeness and profundity of her psychological portraits, the eccentric keenness of her thought, the brilliant rendering of doom and decay, and a style which is at the same time precise and evocative. On the other hand, she is damned for the obscurity of her style and thought, for the morbidity and abnormality of her concerns, and for the unyielding pessimism with which she views man and his destiny.

The ultimate appraisal must fall closer to that of the cultist than to that of the philistine. Nonetheless, attempts in the heat of combat to exalt her into a major figure are unsound; she is clearly a writer of very limited range and meager production, and as such must be relegated to the status of a brilliant minor writer. *Nightwood* is a masterpiece from any point of view; *The Antiphon*, the quasi-surrealist, quasi-Jacobean verse tragedy, is virtually unstageable but contains perhaps the best poetry written for the theater in our time. The early works, the stories, plays and poems in *A Book* (reissued with additions, as *A Night*

Among the Horses) and the early novel *Ryder* are highly original but stillborn, giving little suggestion of the brilliant if unprolific achievement of the later period.

Djuna Barnes' work is permeated by the dualism of day and night, which is expounded at length, if somewhat cryptically, in the great monologues of *Nightwood*. In the day, which is the world of everyday life, men behave as if they were immortal, as if a human being were a determinate, knowable and rational entity, and as if human communication, through language and, more profoundly, through love, were valid and satisfying. In the world of night, which underlies the day and which man enters through suffering, all these assumptions prove false. Man is "but a skin about a wind, with muscles clenched against mortality" (*Nightwood*). Under man's rational consciousness lies the subconscious, an unfathomable jungle of dark forces which determine his life and which he cannot know or control. In his unconscious nature, any man is capable of every crime: "There is not one of us who, given an eternal incognito, a thumbprint nowhere set against our souls, would not commit rape, murder and all abominations." Man is made aware of his unconscious self in dreams, in which his irrational impulses project themselves without fear of restraint or consequences. "We wake from our doings in a deep sweat for that they happened in a house without an address, in a street in no town, citizened with people with no names with which to deny them. Their very lack of identity makes them ourselves."

Human communication is also a deceptive surface. Language, as a process of definition and abstraction, falsifies reality by denying the elements of change and mystery: it gives "a word (for a thing) . . . and not its alchemy." Communication in love is equally unsatisfactory. Love is, for reasons that will be developed later, the direst need of the unconscious, and yet it is thwarted by the very nature of the unconscious as a sealed and impervious inner life unknown to the conscious selves which try to communicate.

> We swoon with the thickness of our own tongue when we say, 'I love you,' as in the eye of a child lost a long while will be found the contraction of that distance—a child going small in the claws of a beast, coming furiously up the furlongs of the iris.

To paraphrase this typically intricate and economical simile, in trying to articulate love in language, as in the spectacle of a civilized child lost in the jungle who has reverted to an animal, we feel the magnitude of the distance between the rational consciousness and the animalistic forces of the unconscious.

Djuna Barnes' vision of love is thus in a sense Proustian: the torment of love lies in the knowledge that the beloved has a secret inner life in which the lover can never participate. The lover is jealous not of the known, but of the suspected rival. The emblem of love is the lover watching over the sleeping beloved, realizing that he can never know what is going on inside her at this moment, that she may be betraying or killing him in a dream, and at the same time knowing that he is equally capable of betraying or killing her in his dreams. The tragic paradox of love lies in the fact that the unconscious, which is the source of the desire for love, is incapable of possessing or of being possessed; it betrays the beloved in dreams, as it may force the conscious self to betray her in life. Love, in its stark futility, becomes, for the lover, a kind of death: "The night into which his beloved goes . . . destroys his heart."

Thus man struggles in a world whose surface placidity is radically contingent on irrational hidden forces; he is isolated and constantly vulnerable to the destructive power of death, love and the darkness within himself. Djuna Barnes focuses the enigma of man's predicament and renders it significant in terms of a myth which bears a close kinship to the Christian myth of the Fall, but which offers little possibility of Christian redemption. The ecclesiastical tone which T. S. Eliot took in defending Djuna Barnes suggests strongly that he perceived a Christian habit of thought, if not doctrinal Christianity, in a writer who contended that "No man needs curing of his individual sickness; his universal malady is what he should look to."

Djuna Barnes' Eden myth draws not on the orthodox Christian tradition, but on the Hermetic tradition, according to which man was created, in the union of conscious mind and animal matter, as a single hermaphroditic being, whose fragmentation into separate sexes occurred at the time of the Fall. This bisexual Adam was static and immortal, encompassing all human possibilities in potentiality; thus it was complete within itself, neither needing nor desiring anything in the external world. Translating from Christian into Darwinian terms, Djuna Barnes identifies this ideally unified identity with the moment in evolution of the "beast turning human," when unconscious, passionate animal vitality took on rational consciousness. Man remembers and yearns for this moment through a kind of Jungian race memory: "a mirage of an eternal wedding cast on the racial memory." On the individual level, this "eternal wedding" is identified with the half-forgotten period of early childhood when the personality is not fully formed and the child lives an existence impervious to the outside world, the period which Freud termed the source of the vision of paradise. In the post-Edenic world, the Hermetic Adam is incarnate in idiots and the insane, human beings who lack all "human" qualities, the capacity to feel emotion, to need and to become involved with the outside world. Robin Vote in *Nightwood* is such a person, and thus plays a pivotal role in the book and in Djuna Barnes' total vision; the quotations used to describe the Edenic vision have been taken from the passage in which Robin is introduced, which will subsequently be analyzed in detail.

The "universal malady" of the post-Edenic consciousness is the contradiction between its need for love and its intrinsic isolation, between its yearning for the remembered "eternal wedding" and its awareness of its fragmented and mortal nature. From this heretical Christian account of man's condition derive two of the most striking themes in the work of Djuna Barnes: the disoriented hero and the incestuous vision of love.

The typical hero in Djuna Barnes' work suffers from a radical split in his identity between what he aspires to be and what he psychologically or physically is. The extremes of this dissociation are found among the doomed figures of *Nightwood*, whose lives constitute a revolt against the very facts of their physical being: the Jew who has built his whole concept of the meaning of his life around his fraudulent pretenses to aristocracy, and the sexual inverts. In the early novel *Ryder*, Wendell's revolt is directed against his psychological identity; being essentially weak, shiftless and feminine, he creates and attempts to live by a false mask of strong, lusty, even brutal virility. The theme is echoed in the character of Miranda in *The Antiphon*, who is spiritually crippled by her inability to come to terms with her past and her family background, which are inescapably part of her.

This perpetual protagonist represents, in its most extreme form, the tragic encounter between an aspiring hero and a limiting universe, in that the antagonist is the protagonist's own nature rather than some external force pitted against him. This intensification is, however, also an internalization of the tragic process, and therefore non-dramatic. Comparing Djuna Barnes with other tragic writers, one discovers in her a curious repression of violence; introspective monologue is substituted for dramatic confrontation, and quiet acceptance of incurable suffering replaces the bloody catastrophe as a resolution. *The Antiphon* is an exception to this rule, and its situations are correspondingly more external; but even here there is, especially in comparison with the play's Jacobean models, a strange disparity between the depth of psychological horror and its expression in violence, which contributes greatly to the play's uncanny effect.

The one external involvement with which Djuna Barnes is passionately concerned is love; and her vision of love always contains an element of incest. The important love relationships in the later works are nearly always either familial or homosexual. Love, as the externalization of the disoriented hero's quest, arises from the fragmented individual's craving for Edenic completion; therefore the most perfect love is that in which the lovers are mirror-images, complementary to each other but sharing the same basis of identity in blood and/or sex. Thus Djuna Barnes writes in "Six Songs of Khalidine," an early poem in the form of an elegy for a dead Lesbian lover:

It is not gentleness but mad despair
That sets us kissing mouths, O Khalidine,
Your mouth and mine, and one sweet mouth unseen
We call our soul. . . .

(A *Book*)

In similar terms, Nora Flood in *Nightwood* describes her own Lesbianism: "A man is another person—a woman is yourself, caught as you turn in panic; on her mouth you kiss your own." The Lesbian lover is "yourself," but "caught as you turn in panic," a turned, inverse, mirror image. This element of complementarity within an integral, shared identity is fundamental in the two most fully explored love-relationships in the work of Djuna Barnes: the Lesbian relationship between Nora and Robin in *Nightwood*, and the filial relationship between Miranda and her mother Augusta in *The Antiphon*. Both relationships clearly represent a union of separate and opposed halves of a single identity. All of Nora's spiritual faculties are directed outward, in an intense interaction with other individuals; she lacks understanding or even awareness of her own subconscious. Robin, on the other hand, is sealed in a kind of trance in which she has lost the ability to communicate with the outside world. Thus Robin looks to Nora for a love which can penetrate through her trance, make her capable of antiphonal love, and save her from insanity, while Nora, in loving Robin, is attempting to capture and understand her own subconscious. Similarly, for Miranda, to accept her mother despite her mother's guilt towards her is to accept her family background as a part of herself, and thus is the only way to attain self-knowledge and a complete identity. For Augusta, the only atonement which can restore the integrity she has lost by her marriage is to gain the acceptance and love of her daughter Miranda, her chief victim. It is Miranda who memorably celebrates the antiphonal love between two halves of the same identity as man's only possibility for salvation, for escape from the fragmentation and solitude which are the "universal malady":

As the high plucked banks
Of the viola rend out the unplucked strings below—
There is the antiphon.
I've seen loves so eat each other's mouth

Till that the common clamour, co-intwined,
Wrung out the hidden singing in the tongue
Its chaste economy—there is the adoration.
So the day, day fit for dying in,
Is the plucked accord.

(*The Antiphon*)

Djuna Barnes is, however, pessimistic about the possibility of such an escape; both the Nora-Robin and the Miranda-Augusta relationships end in mutual destruction.

The role of doctrinal Christianity, or, more precisely, Catholicism, in Djuna Barnes' vision is problematical. Churches, prayers, and apocalyptic imagery are ubiquitous, and Catholicism seems to be the ultimate, if unsatisfactory, source of strength for her saint, Matthew O'Connor in *Nightwood*; yet Christian salvation in its orthodox sense is clearly not even a conceivable solution to man's predicament. Djuna Barnes seems to be a radical Ockhamite fideistsceptic, for whom the disproportion between man and the total order renders any aspiration to knowledge of a divinity presumptuous and futile; only a blind appeal is possible. As Matthew puts it, "we all love in sizes, yet we all cry in tiny voices to the great booming God, the older we get." God is simply a name that man pronounces desperately when confronted with the ultimate contingency, precariousness and limitation of his position in this world. The Catholic Church, for Djuna Barnes, embodies this point of view because it interposes hierarchy, sacrament and the intercession of the saints between the believer and God; Protestantism presupposes a direct communication which, for her, resembles a negotiation between Lilliput and Brobdingnag. Her heretical theology is perfectly expressed in *Ryder*: "For some is the image, and for some the Thing, and for others the Thing that even the Thing knows naught of; and for one only the meaning of That beyond That."

It is virtually impossible to speak of an ethic in Djuna Barnes' view of human situations, because that view rests on a total psychological determinism. Man is subject to the dictates of his unconscious nature even in his revolt against that nature itself. The courses of all the relationships in *Nightwood* are inevitable once chance has initially brought the characters together at certain particular places at certain particular times; the perception of this stark inevitability in human situations is the main cause of Matthew O'Connor's breakdown. No ethical principle can aid the hero who enters the world of the night through love or disorientation; the only dictum which can be directed to the ordinary person who is spared this suffering is a warning to pay homage to the dark gods for continued preservation from a destruction which it is finally beyond the individual's power to prevent: "think of the night the day long, and of the day the night through, or at some reprieve of the brain it will come upon you heavily" (*Nightwood*).

Safety is the reward of moderation; but for man in his highest state of consciousness, which comes only in aspiration and revolt, destruction is inevitable. Pain increases in direct proportion to consciousness. Thus conscious life seems to be a mere freak of nature, or at most a register through whose tormented search for unity and permanence the inhuman universe is made aware of its own disorder and flux. Yet in this situation Djuna Barnes finds a basis for attaching a tragic value, which extends beyond stoicism, to human aspiration and suffering. Love, in that it seeks to heal fragmentation, to overcome solitude, and to deny mortality, is man's most perfect act of revolt; and in love man himself, by the force of his own suffering, of love as spiritual death, invests the loved object's existence with a value which it, as a meaningless freak of creation, did not possess before it was loved. "We were created that the earth might be made sensible of her inhuman taste; and love that the body might be so dear that even the earth should roar with it" (*Nightwood*).

The apocalyptic imagery attached to love throughout the works of Djuna Barnes bears out the implications of this sentence. In the early elegy cited above, she refers to the pain of love as being in some strange way immortal, and preserving the identities of lover and beloved beyond death:

> And now I say, has not the mountain's base
> Here trembled long ago unto the cry
> 'I love you, ah, I love you!' Now we die
> And lay, all silent, to the earth our face.
> Shall that cast out the echo of this place?
>
> (*A Book*)

The same theme of a symbolic, if not literal, immortality echoes in Nora's cry when she realizes that her love for Robin is doomed. The speech could stand as emblem of the victory which man, in his love, as in religion, desperately affirms over the forces which destroy him.

> In the resurrection, when we come up looking backward at each other, I shall know you only of all that company. My ear shall turn in the socket of my head; my eyeballs loosened where I am the whirlwind about that cashed expense, my foot stubborn on the cast of your grave.
>
> (*Nightwood*)

II

Djuna Barnes' short but intricate masterpiece, *Nightwood*, illustrates perfectly her muted and restrained variant of the Jacobean tradition, in which the tragic situation arises within a single person or between two people rather than on a larger social scale, the tragic doom operates through inner deterioration rather than through violence, and tragic revelation takes place in monologue rather than in confrontation. Her method is the direct opposite of that of the Jacobean dramatists, or of Faulkner, in which dark, inherently indefinable forces project themselves in a contorted, Gothic action which can never attain the status of a perfect objective correlative; in her work, style and action always suggest rather than define or project. The style of *Nightwood*, with its heavy reliance on metaphor and connotation, reflects this approach to content. Criticizing T. S. Eliot for his enthusiastic praise of *Nightwood*, Ezra Pound remarked in a limerick that "Her Blubbery prose had no fingers or toes," contrasting her with Marianne Moore, "scarce an exuberance, rather protagonist for the rights of vitrifaxis and petrifaxis."[1] Yet style, for Djuna Barnes, must be oblique and suggestive rather than definitive, because the language of reality is irrational, and cannot be translated into rational vitrification; for her, the fingers and toes of style serve only to strangle reality.

The structure of *Nightwood* rests on the contrapuntal relationship between two distinct plots. The first centers around Robin Vote's strange and richly symbolic malady and its destructive effects on her and on the fragmented individuals for whom she exercises a magnetic attraction; the second traces the disintegration of Matthew O'Connor in the face of his inability to absolve this group, and especially Nora, of the exactions of their private dooms.

The somnambule is the controlling metaphor for Robin. She moves through the world in a dreamlike, self-contained inner existence, utterly impervious to any contact with the outside world. The perilous and unexplained trance into which she has fallen at her first introduction is emblematic of her terrible predicament; like Matthew in the emblem, Nora in actual life will cause her to awake for an instant, only to be plunged back into disintegration and insanity.

The realization of this character, which puzzled Eliot, is typical of Djuna Barnes' method of creating characters. She makes very little use of the orthodox realistic method of revealing character dramatically, through a copious and objective recording of action and dialogue, but rather concentrates on three techniques, in addition to monologue: the manipulation of decor, the emblematic use of a single gesture, and the self-conscious imposition of image and metaphor. An example of the latter, and dominant, method is the paragraph in which Robin is first described:

> The perfume that her body exhaled was of the quality of that earth-flesh, fungi, which smells of captured dampness and yet is so dry, overcast with the odour of oil of amber, which is an inner malady of the sea, making her seem as if she had invaded a sleep incautious and entire. Her flesh was the texture of plant life, and beneath it one sensed a frame, broad, porous and sleep-worn, as if sleep were a decay fishing her beneath the visible surface. About her head there was an effulgence as of phosphorus glowing about the circumference of a body of water—as if her life lay through her in ungainly luminous deteriorations—the troubling structure of the born somnambule, who lives in two worlds—meet of child and desperado.

Images of unconscious life, of very old species low on the evolutionary scale, are used: "that earth-flesh, fungi," "plant life." To these is connected the image of "oil of amber, which is an inner malady of the sea:" ambergris, beauty produced out of malady and decay ("luminous deteriorations"), and a product of the sea, symbol of flux and the unconscious, and primal origin of the evolution of life. By a play on words (ambergris is a waxy substance, and the word comes from the French *ambre gris*) ambergris becomes "oil of amber," fusing the connotations of oil, linked to sex, flux, and the irrational, and amber, a hard, impregnable case enclosing the fossil of a prehistoric animal, as the "dry" fungus holds "captured dampness," and as the somnambule's psychological shell immures her animal-like unconscious life from the outside world. The single phrase, "oil of amber," serves to reveal the intricate web of image and connotation which Djuna Barnes, in a technique more typical of poetry than of the novel, weaves into her descriptions. In the remainder of the paragraph, the rhetoric becomes more analytical: Robin is sealed in a "sleep incautious and entire," which is also a "decay" which "fishes" the depths of her unconscious. She lives entirely in the primordial world of the subconscious, and thus combines the innocence of the child, to whom good and evil are meaningless because he is unaware of the outside world, and the capacity to commit all crimes, since she is given over totally to the dominion of irrational forces: she is "meet of child and desperado."

Robin's decor echoes the same themes; her hotel room, with its jungle overtones, is patterned on Henri Rousseau's painting *The Dream*, in which a sleeping woman on a couch is transplanted from the real world of which she is oblivious to the middle of a jungle, the world of her dream. The room, in which Robin is "thrown in among the carnivorous flowers as their ration," is sinister, suggesting the corrosion of Robin's human consciousness by the almost vegetable trance in which she is trapped.

Further on, the connection between Robin's sealed inner life and the myth of the Hermetic Adam becomes explicit:

Sometimes one meets a woman who is beast turning human. Such a person's every movement will reduce to an image of a forgotten experience; a mirage of an eternal wedding cast on the racial memory; as insupportable a joy as would be the vision of an eland coming down an aisle of trees, chapleted with orange blossoms and bridal veil, a hoof raised in the economy of fear, stepping in the trepidation of flesh that will become myth; as the unicorn is neither man nor beast deprived, but human hunger pressing its breast to its prey.

She is the "eternal wedding" of consciousness and unconscious life, the evolutionary mid-kingdom which is also the "forgotten experience" of early childhood. Like the Hermetic Adam, she is imperviously sealed within herself, and hermaphroditic: she first appears wearing trousers, and the subsequent action confirms her bisexuality. She embodies the myths of creation and paradise and, for Djuna Barnes, the related myths of creatures half-animal and half-human; yet her transformation into myth is for her a source of "trepidation." The reason for this becomes clear when one realizes that this transformation takes place concretely in the eyes of the disoriented individuals who love her, in that her complete but indeterminate identity represents to each of them his particular mirror image, his means of self-completion and salvation. Thus their love for her is an exploitation of her malady and lack of volition to transform her into a tool through which the lover can complete himself; it is a spider-life fusion of copulation and cannibalism, "human hunger pressing its breast to its prey." All her lovers, and especially Nora who understands and tries to save her, end by driving her deeper into solitude and madness, as she in turn destroys them by her inability to respond to their love and heal them.

Robin's transformation into the mirror image of the beholder is illustrated in the succeeding paragraphs, as the perspective changes from that of the author into that of the Baron.

The "Baron" is a Jew who passes himself off as an aristocrat. Out of a racial memory of the constant insecurity of the ghetto and the cultural rootlessness of a people who had neither a homeland nor a genuine participation in the cultures amid which they lived, he aspires to become part of an ancient tradition which will purge him of his sense of cultural lostness and give his posterity a patterned existence both physically and spiritually secure. To fulfill his design, he needs a suitable wife to give him children and bring them up in devotion to the aristocratic tradition; he sees Robin only in the light of her potentiality to fill this role.

Thus the Baron sees Robin's strange completeness only in the terms in which it offers salvation to his own fragmentation; he is aware only of her strange affinity for the past, her quality of seeming to be a dead spirit out of a past epoch reincarnate in a living being, a museum piece somehow endowed with life. The union of past and present in Robin represents to him the union of the separated halves of his own destiny, the spiritual aristocrat and the physical Jew: "as if this girl were the converging halves of a broken fate, setting face, in sleep, toward itself in time."

Robin enters into marriage with the Baron with a somnambule's indifference. After the marriage, the Baron realizes that Robin can never be limited to the role he has conceived for her, that her attention is fixed not, as he had thought, on history but on "something not yet in history." In revolt against the mold into which he tries to force her, she, "strangely aware of some lost land in herself," takes to wandering. The Baron finally violates her sealed inner life not in copulation but by

childbirth, through pain. She has been forced, by pain and violence, into an awareness of another being, in a kind of psychological rape; as a necessary consequence, she leaves the Baron.

This is the basic pattern for all of Robin's relationships. They begin in a quest for completion on the lover's side, and in indifference on hers; they break down as Robin revolts against the lover's attempt to force her into a mold and to compel a response from the depths of her being. Finally they end when the lover succeeds in wounding her to the point that her inner being is affected, and she must abandon him. This pattern appears most fully in the relationship between Robin and Nora Flood, which marks the crisis in Robin's development.

Nora Flood is a completely externalized personality, capable of unlimited sympathy and self-giving; she is equally incapable of selfishness and of introspection. Her spiritual life consists entirely in sympathy, in "recording . . . in a smaller but more intense orchestration" the spiritual forces around her. In receiving the confessions of others she is capable of total understanding but not of moral judgment: "she recorded without reproach or accusation, being incapable of self-reproach or self-accusation." For as staunch a believer in original sin as Djuna Barnes, the incapacity for self-accusation must indicate either a total obliviousness to the external world, as in Robin's case, or a total lack of self-knowledge, as in Nora's.

Nora's memories and dreams are the primary key to the subconscious forces which are driving her. In her first dream, she is standing in her grandmother's room at the top of the house, looking down the stairwell at Robin, who is at the bottom, and calling to her to come up. As she calls, however, the stairway expands, carrying Robin farther and farther away from her. From Nora's memories we learn that her grandmother, whom she "loved more than anyone," was a disturbed personality with Lesbian tendencies. This suggests that Nora's relationship with her grandmother established a primary pattern for her subsequent love-relationships. Her capacity for love, as she herself confesses, derives from her need for power, her need to possess and save a person who is in some way lost. Her sexual role is thus active and masculine, and her Lesbianism is its natural consequence. Her need for possession is the projection of a need for self-possession; the lost, irrational, inner-directed being whom she loves represents her own subconscious, the "night" half of herself of which she is oblivious. In the dream, thus, the grandmother represents the role into which Nora tries to draw Robin, "Robin disfigured and eternalized by the hieroglyphics of sleep and pain." Nora's very attempt to make Robin her protected and saved love-object dooms the relationship, and drives the two farther apart, since Robin is unable to respond to or accept Nora Flood's possessive, protective flood of love.

Nora describes her love for Robin thus: "I tried to come between and save her, but I was like a shadow in her dream that could never reach her in time, as the cry of the sleeper has no echo, myself echo struggling to answer." Robin consciously feels a "tragic longing to be kept, knowing herself astray," yet, being psychologically unable to accept the role Nora tries to force on her, Robin Vote must again revolt by wandering, in a series of drunken binges and Lesbian affairs. In this moral inferno, she retains her innocence by her imperviousness to contact with the outside world: "She knows she is innocent because she can't do anything in relation to anyone but herself."

Robin finally loses her innocence as a result of Nora's efforts to penetrate the sealed depths of her being. Nora describes this psychological rape: "she was asleep and I struck her awake. I saw her come awake and turn befouled before me, she who had managed in that sleep to keep whole." Nora forces Robin into an instant of intense contact, in which Robin becomes aware of Nora for the first time, and thus of her own guilt towards Nora, and of herself as seen through Nora's perspective. Thus Robin passes from static insanity to a state of fragmentation and perpetual torment, having gained a conscious perspective on her own madness and degradation, while remaining subconsciously trapped in her trancelike incapacity for responsive love. Nora represents to Robin the Madonna, both as inaccessible redeemer and as tacit accuser, since it is only through her that Robin possesses a vision of unattainable salvation and a sense of her own degradation; thus Robin must leave her, hoping to slip back into the sleep of insanity.

The ending contains the sinister suggestion that Nora herself is slipping into the trance of madness. This is hinted at in her second dream, in which her father (her masculine, protective sexual personality) attempts to rescue her dead grandmother (Robin) from a glass coffin, and, failing, dies himself. In the final interview with Matthew, in which Nora's behavior verges on hysteria, it becomes clear that a process of ingrowing is taking place in her which, in view of Robin's fate, is clearly sinister; her ability to feel and to become involved with the outside world is benumbed or even dead, while an intense awareness of her own subconscious appears in her for the first time. Matthew futilely warns her of this: "You are . . . experiencing the inbreeding of pain. . . . But when you inbreed with suffering . . . you are destroyed back to your structure as an old master disappears beneath the knife of the scientist who would know how it was painted." The failure of Matthew's attempt to purge Nora of her love for Robin and thus save her from incipient insanity is the immediate cause of his breakdown.

Matthew O'Connor, who acts as Greek Chorus to the tragedy of Robin and Nora, is a doctor practicing without a license, a sponger and petty thief, and a homosexual, and yet a saint in the traditional sense of the word. His vices render his sainthood credible, yet they serve a deeper function in elucidating the nature of that sainthood. Like Prince Myshkin's hypothesized impotence, Matthew's homosexuality, especially in view of the brief, mechanical, and purely physical nature of his homosexual liaisons, creates in him the ascetic negation of passion necessary for pure compassion and disinterestedness in dealing with human situations. Furthermore, his homosexuality, as a radical kind of disorientation, forces upon him a stark and unmitigated awareness of the desperate limitation and contingency of the human predicament. Matthew's plight recalls the myth of Philoctetes, of the wounded artist or saint who, through his wound, gains knowledge of the universal darkness underlying and threatening man's life, and a compulsion to creative or redemptive action as a defense against this destructive force.

Matthew appears at the beginning of the first great monologue in a woman's gown, symbol of his sexual disorientation; but in Nora's mind the gown soon becomes more pregnantly symbolic, as the "natural raiment of extremity" worn by "infants, angels, priests, the dead." There is an implicit suggestion of Christ, the priest and victim; as a radically fragmented being, a man who should have been a woman, Matthew has suffered to the full the spiritual death of the night, and yet he is also the priest of the night, attempting to offer consolation and a sense of dignity on its victims. Matthew undergoes a genuine and Christlike agony in the face of human suffering; he combines a total self-consciousness, to the point of calculated deception, with respect to his methods, and a total lack of self-

consciousness and pride with respect to his motives. This appears most clearly in the scene in the empty church.

Unlike Christ, however, Matthew realizes from the start that his function is merely palliative. His principal weapon against human suffering is talk, which he uses, not to show a way to salvation, but merely to distract, and to give the listener a sense of dignity which will make him more able to endure. Thus the great monologue spoken to Nora is not intended to tell her, as she wishes to be told, how to save her relationship with Robin, but rather how to bear its loss, which is revealed as inevitable in the story which the doctor, after his long prologue, finally tells.

Matthew's talk, while seemingly mystical and abstract, undergoes subtle and self-conscious variation according to the person to whom it is addressed; the same concept, the limitation or "universal malady" of man, is expressed in terms of "the night" and "love" when Matthew speaks to Nora, in terms of "the past" when he speaks to the Baron. Like the traditional saint, Matthew is always concerned with the particular situation. However, he depends for his effect more on the distracting power and emotional tone of words than on their meaning. Nora, for instance, clearly is not intended to understand Matthew's monologue, nor does she; she remains silent, breaking in with desperate questions only when the illustrative examples the doctor uses wander, by chance, close to her own particular predicament.

Even in its limited purpose, however, the monologue is ultimately futile; it cannot finally alter in any way Nora's incapacity to endure her fate. The failure of Matthew's aspiration to sainthood is brutally clear in the supreme irony by which Matthew himself plays a decisive role in Robin's abandonment of Nora, the event which is the direct cause of his breakdown. It is Matthew who, out of pity for Jenny, introduces her to Robin and thus precipitates Robin's break with Nora. Matthew suffers under a tremendous burden of pity for others, who, by the "universal malady" inherent in their humanity must inevitably frustrate, maim and destroy each other; yet, perceiving the deterministic psychological forces by which they are driven, he knows he cannot blame, alter or save them. He is thus placed in a position which must ultimately become unbearable.

There are suggestions of deterioration in Matthew long before his final breakdown: "The Baron was shocked to observe, in the few seconds before the Doctor saw him, that he seemed old, older than his fifty odd years would account for." Matthew's inability to save Nora is only the final straw in the accumulation of futility which destroys him. He is broken basically by the realization that he cannot be Christ, that he cannot transmute the perpetual crucifixion of his life into any kind of redeeming force. He has selflessly assumed the burden of others' suffering in addition to his own, and has not even been able to palliate that suffering by his Christlike act. This is the root of his despair: "I love my neighbour. Like a rotten apple to a rotten apple's breast affixed we go down together. . . . I apply the breast the harder, that he may rot as quickly as I." He is driven mad, not by the ingratitude of others, but by the realization that, after the enormity of his suffering, he is not "a good man doing wrong, but the wrong man doing nothing much."

At the end of the book, Robin, in an act which represents simultaneously a disintegration into total animality and a masochistic atonement for her guilt towards Nora, attempts intercourse with Nora's dog as Nora looks on horror-stricken. The incident ironically fulfills Matthew's apocalyptic utterance on the immortality of Nora and Robin's love: "Nora will leave that girl some day; but though those two are buried at opposite ends of the earth, one dog will find them both." The dramatic irony preserves the tension in which the two plots merge and which is the root of *Nightwood* as tragedy: that man's aspiration as crystallized in love, whether sexual or Christian, is both the means by which man invests his existence with value and the

main instrument through which his "universal malady" works to destroy him.

Notes

1. *Letters of Ezra Pound,* New York: 1950, p. 286

JOHN BARTH

1930–

John Simmons Barth was born in Maryland in 1930. After studying briefly at Juilliard, he transferred to Johns Hopkins for his B.A. and M.A. He has taught at Pennsylvania State University and has held chairs of English at the State University of New York at Buffalo and at Johns Hopkins. A winner of the National Book Award for *Chimera* in 1973, Barth is also a member of the National Institute of Arts and Letters and the American Academy of Arts and Sciences. His first novel, published in 1956, was *The Floating Opera*; it was followed by *The End of the Road* (1958), *The Sot-Weed Factor* (1960), *Giles Goat-Boy* (1966), *Lost in the Funhouse* (1968), *Chimera* (1972), *Letters* (1979), and *Sabbatical* (1982). John Barth was married in 1950; he divorced and was remarried in 1970. He has three children from his first marriage.

General

It is striking . . . to see how much Barth's fiction has been moving toward the fulfillment of an idea—the idea being the repudiation of narrative art. Barth's most recent works, a group of short stories, take on in their form the very paralysis which in one way or another is the central subject of the novels. That is the paradox of Barth's novels: they are about paralysis, they seem even to affirm paralysis, yet they have more narrative energy than they know what to do with. (In this respect, Barth's novels are the very obverse of Saul Bellow's whose heroes, for all their individualism and psychic exuberance, don't do very much, and end up as laconic and passive accepters of a world they know to be silly and dull. Barth's heroes, for all their scepticism and paralysis of will, are kept a lot busier in the complex network of Barthian plot strands, and a good deal more involved in their frantic entanglements with other people. Bellow's heroes seem to have been created for Barthian plots; while Barth's heroes would be more comfortable left dangling. It is a great temptation to say that Jacob Horner should have been the writer of Herzog's letters, and that Henderson should have been the one to take Ebenezer Cooke's journey to the New World.)

Barth has written four novels. Each is generally longer, wilder, more ambitious, more outrageous than its predecessor, and at the core of each is a greater nihilism. That growing nihilism is also something of a paradox since the heroes of the first two novels—Todd Andrews in *The Floating Opera* and Jacob Horner in *End of the Road*—would seem to have reached the limits of despair. Todd Andrews spends the entire novel contemplating and almost accomplishing his suicide; Jacob Horner is suffering from what his doctor describes as immobility. In contrast, the heroes of the last two novels—Ebenezer Cooke in *The Sot-Weed Factor* and George Giles in *Giles Goat-Boy*—are bumpkins. Naive, optimistic, ingenuous: impossible vehicles for despair, one would think, except that that is what they become. Nihilism is merely a quirk of character in *The Floating Opera* and *End of the Road*; it is not much more than a setting for comedy, a device for irony. But

nihilism is what *The Sot-Weed Factor* and *Giles Goat-Boy* come to. It is the moral, meaning, and upshot of experience in these novels, and it is embedded in their very form. *The Sot-Weed Factor,* disguised as an eighteenth-century novel, is really a radical definition of the novel of the twentieth century. *Giles Goat-Boy,* disguised as cosmic allegory, keeps undercutting its own allegorical premises by denying the possibility of meaning, identity, and answers in a world in which these things are always shifting, masked, and unattainable. The deeper nihilism of Barth's last two novels comes from their proclaiming not so much the impossibility of life but the impossibility of narrative.

All this talk about nihilism suggests the greatest paradox of all. Barth is most immediately a humorist. For a novelist like Bellow, the comedy of life is a reflection of the emotional and moral depth of life. The comedy in Barth's novels is the mockery of emotions and moral values: what his characters feel and perceive is only further grist for hilarity. The suicide issue of *The Floating Opera* is an existential put-on; all issues in Barth's novels come down to some sort of game. And so does the emotional life of his characters. They love as they suffer: it is something they check in and out of. Love is simply a comic absurdity, another game. In fact it is the same game in all four novels: a peculiar adulterous relationship in which the husband urges his wife's infidelity with the hero. . . . In another writer this affection for the *ménage à trois* could be regarded as quite a hang-up. In Barth it is a kind of touchstone. The ordinary moral and psychological implications don't count here at all. What immediately counts is, on the level of plot, the entanglements; on the level of meaning, the nuttiness. But what also counts, beyond immediate laughter, is a lingering sorrow, an underlying disgust, and a metaphor for the impossible strain of human attachment and commitment.—BEVERLY GROSS, "The Anti-Novels of John Barth," *CR,* Nov. 1968, pp. 95–97

The gesture of perennial renewal demanded of Black Humor is not undertaken lightly. To date Barth has been one of its most seriously self-immolative fabulist adventurers. He did not embrace the role of Menelaus on the beach at Pharos wrestling with Proteus for his literary identity with the alacrity of George

Goat-Boy determined to make himself a culture hero. The facts would indicate that he stumbled somewhat onto this novelistic path when he broke free of the "Maryland-based verisimilitude" of *The Floating Opera* and *The End of the Road* into the historical amplitudes of *The Sot-Weed Factor*. Barth has admitted to being ignorant of the patterns of mythic heroism at the time of his writing *The Sot-Weed Factor*. Nevertheless, Ebenezer and Burlingame in combination exhibit most of the characteristics of the culture hero listed by Lord Raglan in *The Hero*. Once he learned of the hero with a thousand faces, as mapped by such comparative mythographers as Lord Raglan and Joseph Campbell, he recognized the usefulness of the archetype in his exploration of the disease of modern life—Todd Andrews's, Jake Horner's, and Ebenezer Cooke's malaise, *cosmopsis* Jake Horner tags it—the uncertainty of an essential "I." . . .

Intent on testing whether the current loss of self is simply the latest multiagonist masking a mythic identity, Barth deliberately employs the hero with a thousand faces for his protagonist in *Giles Goat-Boy*. In this act, Barth indicates, if the early novels had not already made it clear, that the Great Labyrinth is imaged for him less by the cosmos than by the mind, less by the incoherent social scene than by the disintegrated self. His literary aim then is not, like that of Borges and the younger Black Humorists . . . to create a paradigmatic design more coherent than that found in the world. Rather, Barth's preoccupation is with isolating and identifying the ineluctable sense of what it is to be human. He fails in *Giles Goat-Boy* essentially because the mythic prototype he parodies is too hybrid a form, too diffusely "hit-and-miss" a system. Gerhard Joseph is right to conclude that Barth, "in his depletion of the picaresque mode, in his erudite catalogues of ideas, or in his name-calling contest between the prostitutes," was trying in *The Sot-Weed Factor* "to convey the impression that sheer exhaustiveness for its own sake contributes to a meaningful comic [cosmic?] order." The literary form of *The Sot-Weed Factor*, its correspondences to the novels of Fielding and Richardson limited its boundaries, as did also Barth's divided attention to the human and the cosmic labyrinths. In *Giles Goat-Boy* Barth was unhampered by such generic considerations and went all out to compress within the covers of one book the whole story of man, "from primitive animal to autonomous computer." That the effort did not lead Barth to a redefinition of man meaningful for our time but left him like George Goat-Boy, with all the old categories, contradictions, and appearances still as ill-defined and as imminent of the primordial threat of chaos as ever, does not mean that the novel was altogether a dead end for Barth. With it he learned, as Borges seems to have known intuitively from the outset, that the objectivity of the mythographer, with his empirical arrangement of diverse materials, does not lead one to the heart of the matter, to the identification of the self, but merely to the accumulation of the flotsam and jetsam of civilization, the hero remaining the sum of his disparate parts, the quotient of his thousand and one faces. Barth also learned that if George was merely equivalent to the refractions of his thousand images, Oedipus offered a mythic correlative to the private self as well as scoring highest on "Lord Raglan's twenty-five prerequisites for ritual heroes."—Max F. Schultz, "The Metaphysics of Multiplicity; and, the Thousand and One Masks of John Barth," *Black Humor Fiction of the Sixties*, 1973, pp. 29–31

John Barth's fictions are . . . dominated by a sense of irony concerning the fragility of the individual's asserted world of meaning, but his works are marked by a much greater feeling of desperation as they explore the absurdities of our language structure—our funhouses. His characters and voices are obsessed by the nature and limit of meaning. The earlier novels, more self-consciously existential than the recent books, are concerned with the validity of meaning structures, of epistemological and philosophic knowledge. They question whether these structures allow for the significant expansion of meaning, whether they allow for the establishment of a more vital sense of meaning. What dominates Barth's thinking most recently, however, especially in *Chimera* and *Lost in the Funhouse*, though prefigured in both *Giles Goat-Boy* and *The Sot-Weed Factor*, is the actual structure of our discourse. He reflects on the constancy of the patterns of meaning in our culture, most particularly on the recurrence of mythic narrative patterns in literature. The emphasis is not so much the limits of meaning, but the meaning of our meaning.

This question is sustained, yet made almost unbearable, by the recognition of the basic arbitrariness of language, by the fact that no new meanings can be asserted (they all betray the same desires, the same structures, the same insufficiency), and by the impossibility of ever refusing to continue to assert the fictions we call reality. If Barth laments the self-imposed distance of the modern artist from the commonly accepted version of reality, he first sees that all stories are essentially the same story. He comprehends that all fictions are ultimately about themselves, about the creation of the world by the word. The Key to the Treasure, he reveals in *Chimera*, is the Treasure. The predominant theme in his recent fiction is the mythic patterns of the creation of a vital life-world by the classic hero (read artist). But the self-reflexiveness Barth shares with the contemporary era denies any final validity to such creations. Consequently, his characters are second generation mythic heroes and artists conscious of the patterns of their desires, and lamenting their loss of a naïve engagement in action.

Barth's irony negates any demand of the contemporary artist to create a radically new vision, particularly according to an existentialist or avant-gardist model. Indeed, what appears to be developing among the writers discussed here is a structuralist perspective which rejects both the modernist and avant-garde traditions of the past 125 years. The basis of contemporary stylistic experimentation or innovation is no longer a belief in an historical directionality grounded in the nineteenth-century faith in political and scientific progress. Expressing a thorough investigation of the fundamental semiotic structures of our culture, contemporary innovative fiction illuminates in the play of meaning and non-meaning, language and silence, the creative aspects of our realm of being. The structure of our discourse is the structure of our desires and our illusions, our needs and our fictions. Recognizing that there are no privileged languages, self-reflective literature does not claim to establish actual meaning in the world, but offers an awareness of the meaning of our meanings.

Pynchon, Kosinski, Brautigan, Sukenick, Nabokov, and Barth all testify to our fundamental positioning within the vault of language. Reaching toward the latent existence of the world around us, their fictions always return to the meaning of that reaching. If we see, or create, meaning, it is recognized as one more artifice. The desert does not speak, and the *Koran* is only a story.—Charles Russell, "The Vault of Language: Self-Reflective Artifice in Contemporary Fiction," *MFS*, Autumn 1974, pp. 358–59

Barth . . . is a professional schoolteacher. He is a professor of English *and* Creative Writing. He is extremely knowledgeable about what is going on in R and D land and he is certainly eager to make his contribution. Interviewed, Barth notes "the inescapable fact that literature—because it's made of the common stuff of language—seems more refractory to change in general than the other arts." He makes the obligatory reference to the music of John Cage. Then he adds, sensibly, that "the permanent changes in fiction from generation to generation more often have been, and are more likely to be, modifications of sensibility and attitude rather than dramatic innovations in form and technique."

Barth mentions his own favorite writers. Apparently "Borges, Beckett and Nabokov, among the living grand masters (and writers like Italo Calvino, Robbe-Grillet, John Hawkes, William Gass, Donald Barthelme)—*have* experimented with form and technique and even with the *means* of fiction, working with graphics and tapes and things. . . ." What these writers have in common (excepting Robbe-Grillet) "is a more or less fantastical, or as Borges would say, 'irrealist,' view of reality. . . ." Barth thinks—hopes—that this sort of writing will characterize the seventies. . . .

To read Barth on the subject of his own work and then to read the work itself is a puzzling business. He talks a good deal of sense. He is obviously intelligent. Yet he tells us that when he turned from the R and R of his first two novels to the megalo-R and R of *The Sot-Weed Factor*, he moved from "a merely comic mode to a variety of farce, which frees your hands even more than comedy does." Certainly there are comic aspects to the first two books. But the ponderous jocosity of the third book is neither farce nor satire nor much of anything except English-teacher-writing at a pretty low level. I can only assume that the book's admirers are as ignorant of the eighteenth century as the author (or, to be fair, the author's imagination) and that neither author nor admiring reader has a sense of humor, a fact duly noted about Americans in general—and their serious ponderous novelists in particular—by many peoples in other lands. It still takes a lot of civilization gone slightly high to make a wit.

Giles Goat-Boy arrived on the scene in 1966. Another 800 pages of ambitious schoolteacher-writing: a book to be taught rather than read. I shall not try to encapsulate it here, other than to say that the central metaphor is the universe is the university is the universe. I suspect that this will prove to be one of the essential American university novels and to dismiss it is to dismiss those departments of English that have made such a book possible. The writing is more than usually clumsy. . . .

By 1968 Barth was responding to the French New Novel. *Lost in the Funhouse* is the result. A collection (or, as he calls it, a "series") of "Fiction for Print, Tape, Live Voice." Barth is not about to miss a trick now that he has moved into R and D country. The first of the series, "Night-Sea Journey," should—or could—be on tape. This is the first-person narrative of a sperm heading, it would appear, toward an ovum, though some of its eschatological musings suggest that a blow-job may be in progress. Woody Allen has dealt more rigorously with this theme.

The "story" "Lost in the Funhouse" is most writerly and self-conscious; it chats with the author who chats with it and with us. "Description of physical appearance and mannerisms is one of several standard methods of characterization used by writers of fiction." Thus Barth distances the reader from the text. A boy goes to the funhouse and. . . . "The more closely an author identifies with the narrator, literally or metaphorically, the less advisable it is, as a rule, to use the first-person narrative viewpoint." Some of this schoolteacherly commentary is amusing. But the ultimate effect is one of an ambitious but somewhat uneasy writer out to do something

brand-new in a territory already inhabited by, among other texts that can read and write, the sinister *Locus Solus*, the immor(t)al *Tlooth* and the dexterous *A Nest of Ninnies*.

It is seldom wise for a born R and R writer to make himself over into an R and D writer unless he has something truly formidable and new to show us. Barth just has books. And sentences. And a fairly clear idea of just how far up the creek he is without a paddle. "I believe literature's not likely ever to manage abstraction successfully, like sculpture for example, is that a fact, what a time to bring up that subject. . . ." What a time! And what is the subject, Alice? Incidentally, Barth always uses quotation marks and "he says." . . .

Barth was born and grew up a traditional cracker-barrelly sort of American writer, very much in the mainstream—a stream by no means polluted or at an end. But he chose not to continue in the vein that was most natural to him. Obviously he has read a good deal about Novel Theory. He has the standard American passion not only to be original but to be great, and this means creating one of Richard Poirier's "worlds elsewhere": an alternative imaginative structure to the mess that we have made of our portion of the Western hemisphere. Aware of French theories about literature (but ignorant of the culture that has produced those theories), superficially acquainted with Greek myth, deeply involved in the academic life of the American university, Barth is exactly the sort of writer our departments of English were bound, sooner or later, to produce. Since he is a writer with no great gift for language either demotic or mandarin, Barth's narratives tend to lack energy; and the currently fashionable technique of stopping to take a look at the story as it is being told simply draws attention to the meagerness of what is there.—GORE VIDAL, "American Plastic: The Matter of Fiction" (1974), *Matters of Fact and Fiction*, 1977, pp. 111–117

Works

⟨Todd Andrews⟩ spends much of his time building boats, an activity which he himself equates with the writing of his *Inquiry*. He also gives us some direct hints to see his novel as yet another kind of boat-building. From his childhood the idea of building a boat and sailing away has been the very image of his yearning: 'the intensity of this longing to escape must be accounted for by the attractiveness of the thing itself, not by any unattractiveness of my surroundings. In short, I was running *to*, not running *from*, or so I believe.' It is hardly necessary to point out that this is another version of a very recognizable American dream. Even the reinterpretation of apparent flight as real quest is one we have encountered before (in *Catch-22*). Andrews's desire was to build a completely private craft. 'Left to myself, absolutely to myself, I was certain I could build one and surprise everybody with the finished product.' It is a perfect metaphor for that wish to create one's own unique form or structure which we have had occasion to comment on. In the midst of one of the worst episodes in his life, when he is being beaten up in a brothel, he remembers thinking, 'Why isn't the whole thing a sailboat?' It is a poetic way of saying, I wish I could escape from the impositions of the given world into the liberation of a privately created one.

But Todd Andrews never finishes his boats, and here the implications of the metaphor become important. For just as he works on boats which never actually get him on to the water, so he labours at systems of thought which never serve to propel him into life. Indeed it is his preoccupation with system-building which serves to exclude him from the element in which he should live. The attempt to reproduce existence in patterns of rational thought is doomed to incompletion. For one thing, he can inevitably see multiple possible significances in every single fact—there is no end to the possible readings or versions of life. More seriously, as he realizes when he works out a new philosophic position, it is only 'a matter of the rearrangement of abstractions'—just as when he has to use a new ploy in one of his law suits it only involves a shift of rhetoric. It is all a matter of word play, and none of it makes the slightest difference to the fact of his weak heart. On the day he decided to commit suicide he did indeed think that he had completed a vessel of thought, just as he thought he had finished his *Inquiry*. This 'new philosophical position,' like a new rowboat,' as he explicitly says, is his conclusion that there is no final reason for living. And when he experiences a moment of hesitation about putting it into practice, he reproaches himself in this way, 'Can he be called a builder who shies at launching the finished hull? For what other purpose was it finished?' This is the one boat he does attempt to set sail in—to death.

But even this one doesn't float. By one of the nicest ironies of the book, while the real Floating Opera is indeed floating, Todd's private boat is sinking—i.e. his plan to commit suicide by blowing up the Opera is being thwarted by an accident. The show on board is a very old one, very corny, full of the same old gags, the same old roles, the same old acts—like life itself. But that's the show that goes on. As the captain—of course called Adam—says, that boat was built to last. The posters which spring up all over town to advertise its advent on the day Todd intends to commit suicide describe it as 'original and unparalleled', which is of course quite true. For one of the things Todd learns that day is that he cannot parallel the original. He will never complete any of his own boats.

Except for the novel. This boat—and he himself uses the metaphor—he completes, and he knocks it together in just the way he pleases, according to his own plan. 'It's a floating opera, friend, fraught with curiosities, melodrama, spectacle, instruction and entertainment, but it floats willy-nilly on the tide of my vagrant prose,' he says of his book near the beginning; and near the end: 'Say what you wish about the formal requirements of story-telling; this is my opera, and I'll lead you out of it as gently as I led you in.' We might compare his floating opera to Hawkes's floating island, for both provide a free space in which the writer can order things as he will, and at the same time both are the results of this assertion of personal patterning. Todd claims that: 'It seems to me that any arrangement of things at all is an order,' the implication being that one man's mess may be another man's pattern. Todd tells us that he lives his life 'in much the same manner as I'm writing this first chapter', and it is of course important that Todd is both character and author—like the Invisible Man and Augie March for instance—demonstrating his freedom to arrange his own life by the way he writes about it. This way is 'after my fashion—which, remember, is not unsystematic, but simply coherent in terms of my own, perhaps unorthodox, system.' As I have tried to show, this is a very characteristic feeling in contemporary American fiction. If there has to be a system, so the feeling goes, then I will make very sure that it is a system of my own choosing and making.—TONY TANNER, "What is the Case?," *City of Words*, 1971, pp. 233–35

"Historicity and self-awareness, he asseverated, while ineluctable and even greatly to be prized, are always fatal to innocence and spontaneity. Perhaps adjective period Whether in a people, an art, a love affair on a fourth term added not impossibly to make the third less than ultimate." Arriving at this judgment, the narrator of "Title" in Barth's *Lost in the Funhouse*

concludes that today's writers, schooled in criticism, burdened with self-consciousness, laboring in vineyards harvested by their recent predecessors, have been reduced to pushing each other literally "to fill in the blank." The "blank," he suggests, is what remains (or what does not remain) of our recent literary past. "Love affairs, literary genres, third item in exemplary series, fourth—everything blossoms and decays, does it not, from the primitive and classical through the mannered and baroque to the abstract, stylized, dehumanized, unintelligible blank." Discounting irony, the mood recalls the darkest of all passages in *Ecclesiastes*. Vanity of vanity, says the Preacher: "For in much wisdom is much vexation, / and he who increases knowledge increases sorrow."

The plight of Barth's monologist reflects not merely a crisis in *belles lettres* but the predicament of the age itself which, like its counterpart, prose fiction, appears to be "about played out." Too much is known, too much has been tried, too much is now over with, yet nothing has been settled, Barth intimates, striking a tone peculiarly appropriate for the seventies. Certainly it seems painfully clear that for all our striving after systematic truth (especially in moral philosophy and aesthetics) we do seem to have lost our capacity for zest to the extent that our thought processes have become self-conscious and historical. Familiarity denatures insight; what can be analyzed in terms of origin or motive soon loses its power to enthrall us.

These observations are neither startling nor new, yet in one sense the dilemma of the contemporary writer is unique. In the compressed space of several generations a dozen literary movements have flourished and been catalogued, manifestos studied, techniques codified and perfected, ranks assigned, order imposed. Sheer volume is reason in itself to explain Barth's observation that literature by now has exhausted the vast seed bag of potentialities that were brought to flower in the recent past. In his essay, "The Literature of Exhaustion," Barth specifies: "By 'exhaustion' I don't mean anything so tired as the subject of physical, moral, or intellectual decadence, only the used-upness of certain forms or exhaustion of certain possibilities—by no means necessarily a cause for despair." The "real technical question," he elaborates, "seems to me how to succeed not even Joyce and Kafka, but those who've *succeeded* Joyce and Kafka," namely, Beckett and Borges. In Barth's evaluation of Borges's work there can be found a suggestion of the direction he himself has embarked upon as a means of transforming art's paralysis. Borges's "artistic victory, if you like, is that he confronts an intellectual dead end and employs it against itself to accomplish new human work." As the narrator of "Anonymiad" remarks in *Lost in the Funhouse*, the point is that "one can't pretend to an innocence outgrown or in other wise retrace one's steps, unless by coming full circle." Borges is willing to make this voyage, employing as method a unique conception of the Baroque, which he defines as "that style which deliberately exhausts (or tries to exhaust) its possibilities and borders upon its own caricature." Moreover, in fiction the possibilities opened by such procedure suggest "how an artist may paradoxically turn the felt ultimacies of our time into material and means for his work—*paradoxically* because by doing so he transcends what had appeared to be his refutation. . . ." The final possibility (adds the narrator of "Title") might then be for the artist to "turn ultimacy against itself to make something new and valid, the essence whereof would be the impossibility of making something new."

In *Lost in the Funhouse* Barth brings these conceptions to realization. Based on his notion of ultimacy turned against itself by means of a style that is self-exhausting and yet comically triumphant, the book reveals a dazzling display of modernist techniques even while it examines the depletion of certain forms of modernist expression and the unbearable self-consciousness of intellectual life. Myths, symbolism, interior monolog, time shifts, varieties of point of view, mixed media, esoteric word play—all are employed, parodied, and refreshened as Barth's vision of the funhouse is defined.

Like Borges, Barth is convinced that his artistic victory can be gained only by confronting the recent past and "employ[ing] it against itself to accomplish new human work." Therefore, in an attempt to exhaust the possibilities of its own tradition, *Lost in the Funhouse* begins as an elaborate parody, revival, and refutation of Joyce's masterpiece, *A Portrait of the Artist as a Young Man*. That Barth consciously is engaged in this endeavor there can be no doubt. Joyce himself is mentioned twice in the title story as an originator and authority on techniques of modern fiction, and the recycling of Joycean/Homeric materials, especially the Daedalus-labyrinth motif ("Night-Sea Journey," "Lost in the Funhouse," "Echo," "Menelaiad") is intentional. In the true spirit of caricature, Barth's attitude toward his model is both respectful and subversive.—MICHAEL HINDEN, "*Lost in the Funhouse*: Barth's Use of the Recent Past," *TCL*, April 1973, pp. 107–9

If *The Floating Opera* is a preliminary testing ground for the most intensely self-conscious of Barth's narrative procedures, *The End of the Road* may appear something of a regression in storytelling. It has a much more conventional plot; things, very grim things indeed, happen in the book, unlike the story of Todd Andrews where the center of the tale is a kind of negative action, a deciding not to decide. And the narrative itself is much more straightforward. There are none of the narrative indirections, the strange and farfetched associations of past and present, speculation and action, which led some critics to compare *The Floating Opera* with that most self-conscious of fictions, *Tristram Shandy*. In fact, *The End of the Road* is a careful, almost point-for-point reworking of the themes and structures of *The Floating Opera*, one whose spare, unadorned representation of those concerns is, not only a darkening of the comic nihilism of the earlier book, but a remarkable refinement in Barth's command of his own distinctive powers.

"In a sense, I am Jacob Horner." This is the first sentence of *The End of the Road*, and it is surely one of the most famous opening lines in recent fiction. Horner begins at the point of enlightenment (or anti-enlightenment) which Todd Andrews had achieved at the end of *The Floating Opera*.

. . . ⟨T⟩he central and very grim situation of *The End of the Road*, is of course a deliberate reprise of the affair *à trois* which is such a rich part of *The Floating Opera*'s comedy. Todd Andrews is confronted with the relatively impersonal passion of Jane Mack and the basically dunderheaded idealism of Harrison; while Horner—such is the deepening of Barth's own sense of his themes—contends not only with the powerful and potentially murderous idealism of Joe Morgan, but with the very real deterioration of Rennie's mind. For the first time in his fiction, Barth presents a picture of authentic, compelling, unintellectual despair in Rennie's agony as she discovers, first, that she has betrayed the husband who has literally been her image of a personal god and then, that she does in fact love, not only her husband, but the man with whom she has betrayed him. And if Horner is caught between the contradictory ideas of the doctor and the rationalist Morgan, Rennie—more terrifyingly—is caught between the ideologies of Morgan and Horner, and is crucified between those rending abstractions. . . .

The End of the Road, that is to say, is about the end of the road: the terminal defeat, the end of all fictions which awaits even the most courageous and clever of attempts to shape and control reality. It is, as I have said before, an extraordinarily unpleasant book to read, and to write about. But its unpleasantness is not merely the flesh-crawling, vaguely pornographic sort of shock narrative which has, in the last two decades, become a permanent staple of the American fiction market. Oddly and surprisingly enough, the reader of *The End of the Road* is left with a feeling which can only be called *bracing*. The deaths, the waste, and the hypocrisy of the novel are grim indeed, but their very grimness makes a further and less annihilating point. For at the center of the story, caught in the web of the doctor's sham, Joe Morgan's egotism, and Jacob Horner's abstracted role playing, is the fact of Rennie's own, confused, but ineluctably human passion. The end of the road is the end of the road because it is the point at which the intellectual content of nihilism encounters the sheer fact of human love and human loss which it—or any philosophical position—is inadequate to account for or deal with. "*I don't know what to do,*" Horner shouts over the phone to Joe Morgan after Rennie's death; the two antiheroes of thought confront each other, in a landscape of failed possibilities, over the inescapable and inescapably dead body of the woman who had loved them both. That love itself—or the paralyzing memory of it—remains, after one has closed the novel, the sole admirable fact about the whole grisly affair. Indeed, although Barth's succeeding books will take a long and excruciatingly devious road toward its realization, the fact of "love"—the first, most vulnerable, and most indispensable of civilized and civilizing fictions, the true primal myth—that scandalous and irrational fact will become more and more the center and the goal of his narrative experiments.

The End of the Road is a considerable distance from such later articulations, although it establishes the difficulties involved in what will be Barth's full assertion of the humanizing powers of love and myth.—FRANK McCONNELL, "John Barth and the Key to the Treasure," *Four Postwar American Novelists*, 1977, pp. 126–31

Midway in *Letters*, Barth reproduces a patch of his own correspondence in which he asserts that the book "will *not* be obscure, difficult, or dense in the Modernist fashion." And he adds that, while "it will hazard the resurrection of characters from my previous fiction . . . as well as extending the fictions themselves, [it] will not presume, on the reader's part, familiarity with those fictions, which I cannot myself remember in detail." I'm sorry to report that there's some self-deception in these observations. Ambiguities of identity in the chief characters, the irrelevance of whole chapters of historical matter to what the nonspecialist reader must regard as the narrative main line, the author's near obsession with historical and linguistic correspondences, doublings, and layerings—these combine to produce extreme difficulty. And if it is true that Barth doesn't expect his reader to know his previous books, it is no less true that readers ignorant of them are bound to be mystified often, especially by the letters from the master of the mathematical novel. ("Giles our prix buck passed on! Les nans reduced to browsing on LILYVAC's language circuits!") There's a character in this book with a forty-hour-a-week job who discloses she is reading Barth's complete works, at the rate of a volume per month. Anybody gainfully employed who means to conquer *Letters* in a month should go on part time.

Is it really worth bothering? Yes and no, leaning yesward. Besides Germaine Pitt, much Rabelaisian humor, and the high-camp theatrics of the filming episodes, *Letters* contains at least two extended and admirable sections of narrative—a carefully detailed history of a family of Eastern Shore stonemasons, and a farewell cruise around the Chesapeake on a skipjack whose captain has a movingly precise appreciation of the joys of pure physicality. In addition, the author's speculative intelligence is rarely out of sight, whether his focus is the nature of a political liberal, or the early impact of the American idea on European intellectuals, or how to chisel letters on a tombstone, or how to set canvas for a sweetheart run downwind, wing-and-wing. And while Barth's fascination with the technology of narrative is often wearing, it does stimulate brooding on the meaning, for contemporary life, of the decline of the storytelling craft. The scholar-critic Frederic Jameson recently observed that in the West, "literary construction itself seems to have joined a long list of extinct or vanishing handicrafts or other skills." John Barth's bemused teasing out and exhibition of the story elements of his fable comes to seem, well before the end, a mode of decent piety—a last touching attempt, in the twilight of yarn-spinning in words, to evoke and objectify the beauty and mystery of the spinner's skills.

More important than any of this is the scrupulousness with which the book's basic theme—call it the fiction of fiction—is explored. Other writers besides Barth—the best of the type is surely Thomas Pynchon—create figures whose lives, like Germaine Pitt's, are dominated by fictional forces or myths beyond their understanding. Few writers work as patiently or as ingeniously as Barth at explaining the derivation of such figures—why they have cropped out all at once in our fiction, what their roots are in contemporary intellection. Time and again in *Letters* the author invites his reader to ponder the present status of the idea of the real and the unreal, present thinking about the arbitrariness of signs, present critiques of naive realisms, scientific and otherwise. Time and again his narrative becomes an instrument for renewing comprehension of the universal human enclosure in fictions novelists never made—the truth, that is, "that our concepts, categories, and classifications are ours, not the World's. . . ."

Whether the novel as hitherto constituted is the proper setting for such instruction can be debated. So too can the wisdom of promoting complex epistemological fiction in a manner suggesting that a swell evening's read lies ahead. And there is something in this late-twentieth-century embrace of the theme of reality as mirage that hints at enfeebled responsiveness—inability to awaken any sense of pain and injustice except that which deals abstractly with them as "clichés." Yet despite all this, *Letters* remains worth wrestling with. It is by turns a brain-buster, a marathon, an exasperation, a frustration, a provocation to earnest thought. Barth is preaching, wittily but with total conviction, on the limits of our kind, on the sanity of doubting that we know where in our lives, fiction stops. His book intimates that things as they are—the myths of the West, of free enterprise, the scientific method, of the energy crises, all those orderings of life shaped in the nightly news—may hold less of a key to the truth of our being than the dream some neighbor is dreaming as we turn the page. A piece of me believes this; therefore I think *Letters* has a future.—Benjamin DeMott, "Six Novels in Search of a Novelist," *At*, Nov. 1979, p. 92

First, Mr. Barth eschews realism simply because, as Fenwick Turner observes in one of his discussions with Susan about the techniques they are going to use to tell their story: "I won't have our story be adulterated realism. Reality is wonderful; reality is dreadful; reality is what it is." But realism, he says, is a "bore."

Second, the various antirealistic tricks that Mr. Barth

plays on his text serve to call the reader's attention to the various nonrealistic levels on which the story operates. For example, at one typical point, the narrators, who of course turn out to be jointly Fenwick and Susan, observe that Fenwick "is not displeased to find our story follows, in a general way, the famous tradition: summons, departure, threshhold crossing, initiatory trials etcetera. He declares it to our authorial prerogative, however, to bend the pattern to fit our story, so long as we don't bend the story to fit the pattern." While this observation is both playful and a shade pedagogical, it also happens to be accurate, we realize, and we are not altogether worse off for being aware of it.

Third, Mr. Barth's willful violation of realistic literary convention forces him to make use of an extensive set of nonrealistic areas. These persistently call attention to their own artificiality as well as to the artificiality of all literary conventions. Yet paradoxically, they don't in any way compromise the reality of the characters themselves or what is happening to them.

For example, at one point, Fenwick and Susan debate whether Susan's mother, Carmen B. Seckler, is really justifying her existence in the story. They decide to give her another chance. She then comes "on stage": and shocks everyone, including the reader, by announcing the unforeseen death of an important minor character. Our awareness of her being on trial somehow heightens the effect of her news. This is just one of many instances in which the artificiality of the technique makes the story's reality more real.

Finally, the nonrealistic technique of *Sabbatical* builds its own kind of suspense. Throughout the story, the question looms ever more compellingly whether the book is going to resolve itself by exploring a realistic mystery involving what the Central Intelligence Agency is really up to on an uncharted island that Fenn and Susan have stumbled upon, or whether the resolution is merely going to explore the book's technique.

. . . The story's reality and technique increasingly flow into each other to form a Mobius strip. Or to put it another way, the reality is the technique and vice versa. The final effect is ever so slightly claustrophobic—the book ends up being a novel about how the same novel came to be written. But *Sabbatical* is an altogether accessible experiment and, on the whole, extremely entertaining.—Christopher Lehmann-Haupt, *NYT*, May 27, 1982, p. C 23

From the beginning Barth has avoided social criticism in his novels. "I can't in fiction get very interested in such things," he told John Enck. "My argument is with the facts of life, not the conditions of it." In a more recent interview, however, Barth not only confesses his preoccupation "as a private citizen" with the women's liberation movement, but concedes that the woman's question is one of the themes that holds *Chimera* together. Yet, he quickly adds, only a "simple-minded critic could say my trio of novellas is about women's lib. . . . That's not at all what it's about for me." Barth is too careful a craftsman to include anything in his fiction that does not contribute to that fiction as a whole, so the references to women's liberation in *Chimera* are of considerable consequence. Yet he is not playing games when he insists that the novel is not *about* the women's movement. Rather, women's liberation provides a clue to the significance of Barth's more general use of myth in the novel. Concerning myth Barth has said:

> I always felt it was a bad idea on the face of it . . . to write a more or less realistic piece of fiction, one dimension of which keeps pointing to the classical myths—like John Updike's *Centaur*, or Joyce's

Ulysses, or Malamud's *The Natural*. Much as one may admire those novels in other respects, their authors have hold of the wrong end of the mythopoeic stick. The myths themselves are produced by the collective narrative imagination (or whatever), partly to point down at our daily reality; and so to write about our daily experiences in order to point up to the myths seems to me mythopoeically retrograde. I think it's a more interesting thing to do . . . to address them directly.

In his treatment of the myths of Scheherazade, Perseus, and Bellerophon, Barth does address the myths directly; in his scattered references to women's liberation he suggests an aspect of daily reality to which these myths point. The interrelationship of myth and daily reality becomes Barth's concern. *Chimera* is not about the woman's question, but about the larger historical, psychological, and esthetic concerns that the woman's question embodies.

Accordingly Barth chooses for *Chimera* myths that are associated with that point in antiquity when patriarchal control began to emerge. . . .

Barth's primary concern . . . is less with the historical dimensions of the myths he has chosen to retell than with the psychological and esthetic implications of those primordial fictions. Indeed, Barth's "recycling" of ancient narratives itself represents his desire to return, at least metaphorically, to the creative springs of all story and literally to the sources of creativity in the human mind. Like the genie in "Dunyazadiad," Barth suffered a serious writer's block in 1969. Also like the genie, Barth "found his way out of that slough of the imagination in which he'd felt himself bogged . . . by going back, to the very roots and springs of story": those ancient myths of Scheherazade, Perseus, and Bellerophon. Although an overly *self*-conscious use of ancient materials can prove artistically inhibiting, Barth has conceded, a conscious use of mythic patterns not only can prove fruitful as a source of artistic material but can also result in "the genuinely mythopoeic," although mythopoeia will be manifested in new and different ways. Barth seems in basic agreement with Carl Jung, who maintains, "It is . . . to be expected that the poet will turn to mythological figures in order to give suitable expression to his experience. Nothing would be more mistaken than to suppose that he is working with second-hand material. On the contrary, *the primordial experience is the source of his creativeness*, but it is so dark and amorphous that it requires the related mythological imagery to give it form." Barth's use of ancient myths, then, brings him into contact with what Jung calls "the hinterland of man's mind," that "tremendous intuition striving for expression" which is the source and stimulant of all story.

Especially pertinent to Barth's concerns in *Chimera* is the fact that this mythopoeic reservoir is frequently viewed as feminine. "The creative process," writes Jung, "has a feminine quality, and the creative work arises from unconscious depths—we might truly say from the realm of the Mother." At least since *Giles Goat-Boy* Barth has associated creativity, if not with the feminine, then with the fusion of masculine and feminine consciousness. He would no doubt agree with Erich Neumann's assessment that "all creative cultural achievement—at least in its highest form—represents a synthesis of receptive matriarchal and formative patriarchal consciousness." The feminine unconsciousness informs; the masculine consciousness forms. What becomes necessary in art, as well as in most human activity, is a balance between masculine and feminine consciousness.—CHARLES B. HARRIS, "The New

Medusa: Feminism and the Uses of Myth in *Chimera*," *Passionate Virtuosity*, 1983, pp. 127–30

ROBERT SCHOLES
From "John Barth's *Giles Goat-Boy*"
Fabulation and Metafiction
1959, pp. 75–86

John Barth's fourth work of fiction is a tract for our times, an epic to end all epics, and a sacred book to end all sacred books. It is not, I hasten to say, a merely blasphemous work of empty nihilism, though some reviewers have reacted as if it were. It is a work of genuine epic vision, a fantastic mosaic constructed from the fragments of our life and traditions, calculated to startle us into new perceptions of the epic hero and saviour. It is epic in its scope: in its combination of myth and history, of the ideal and the actual. And it is a sacred book because it is concerned with the life of a religious hero and with the way to salvation. True, it treats these matters comically, even farcically at times; and it is militantly fabulative, insisting on its fabulous dimension, its unreality. But this insistence is part of the book's point: In our time any sacred book must be a work of fiction.

Barth's choice of comic allegory as the method of his fiction should come as no surprise to anyone who has read this book from the beginning. The vision of fabulation is essentially comic because it is an instrument of reason; and it is frankly allegorical because it has not the naïve faith in the possibility of capturing the actual world on the printed page which realism requires of its practitioners. Barth has observed that "If you are a novelist of a certain type of temperament, then what you really want to do is re-invent the world. God wasn't too bad a novelist, except he was a Realist." Realism, in this view, is a game that only God can play. Man is not in a position to re-create God's world on paper. The old realistic novel has always assumed that a readily ascertainable thing called reality exists, and that we all live in it; therefore, it is the only thing to write about. But Barth says that he doesn't "know much about Reality." He declines the realistic gambit, refuses to accept the notion that the truth can be captured just by reporting the way things are. Barth insists on an inevitable "discrepancy between art and the Real Thing." His comment on the French *nouveau roman* is enlightening:

> From what I know of Robbe-Grillet and his pals, their aesthetic is finally a more up-to-date kind of psychological realism: a higher fi to human consciousness and unconsciousness. Well, that's nice. A different way to come to terms with the discrepancy between art and the Real Thing is to *affirm* the artificial element in art (you can't get rid of it anyhow), and make the artifice part of your point instead of working for higher and higher fi with a lot of literary woofers and tweeters. That would be my way. Scheherazade's my *avant-gardiste*.

The Real Thing, then, is God's world. The world of the fabulator is different. And the difference, the artifice, is "part of your point." The fabulator's attitude toward life is elliptical. By presenting something that is like life but markedly different from it, he helps us to define life by indirection. Fabulation is a tricky business for both reader and writer—a matter of delicate control on the one hand and intelligent inference on the other.

Any reader of *Giles Goat-Boy*, then, will be put on his mettle. The demands on his learning and ingenuity will be strenuous.

In *Giles Goat-Boy*, John Barth has forged an allegorical instrument that enables him to piece together our fragmented world and explore the possible ways of living in it. To understand the vision of this book, the reader must come to terms with its allegory. He must learn its workings—its facets and their relations; in fact, he must discover how to play his part in the interpretation of the events of the story. . . .

The allegorist acknowledges the visionary power of his linguistic medium. He sees through his language. Metaphor, the vital principle of language, is also the animating force in allegory. It is because life can be seen as a journey, a quest, or a voyage that Dante, the Redcross Knight, or Gulliver can serve as examples of human behavior, even though they exist for us in imaginary and non-realistic realms. John Barth has chosen two basic metaphors for his fabulative epic, which combine to make a dominant image from which many metaphorical consequences flow. He has chosen to see the universe as a university, and he has chosen to make his hero a man whose formative years were spent as a goat among goats. Before discussing the workings of the allegory itself, I want to consider the appropriateness of these two choices as metaphors for the human condition, and their effectiveness as basic materials for an allegorical narrative.

First, appropriateness. Language has provided the key to the first of these basic metaphors in the similarity of the words universe and university. The words are identical for three syllables, and then—worlds apart. But there is a meaningful connection between these two worlds. If the universe means *everything*—our whole world from the innermost piece of the smallest particle, outward to the ends of space, including those heavenly and hellish realms discerned only by poets and prophets—then the university means the place where *everything* is present as an object of inquiry and concern. For the thoughtful person, the world *is* a university, and his education always in process. For Barth, the university must have had the great virtue of including everything, already organized in terms of inquiry and quest. And beyond that, the American university of the present, though it strives to preserve an atmosphere of critical scrutiny and contemplation, is by no means an Arcadia studded with ivory towers where detached mandarins think beautiful thoughts. Despite its heritage from pagan academies and Christian cloisters, the modern American university is a brawling marketplace where CIA men mingle with student leftists, and careering business majors jostle with poets and painters. Not only is a university involved in the study and practice of politics in the statewide, national, and international spheres; it has its own internal politics, too. At some points, in fact, the two begin to merge. Men move back and forth between university posts and positions in government with increasing freedom. Concepts like the "multiversity" emphasize this particular penetration. And when a recent governor of our most populous state, a man with presidential aspiration, made his first significant official act the firing of the head of that state's university system, who could say the world is not in the university and the university in the world? It is precisely because the directors of universities, foundations, and corporations have become virtually interchangeable with high government officials—many of them serving Caesar and Socrates almost simultaneously—that Barth is able to get so much allegorical leverage from his selection of the university as his universe.

The appropriateness of his other fundamental metaphor should be equally evident. Again, language has provided the key. The connection between man and goat begins with the metaphorical application of the word for young goat to the young human. We all begin as kids. But if any particular kid should grow up to become a religious leader, the bringer of a new dispensation, a saviour who can expect ultimately that martyrdom with which mankind habitually reward their saints—then a whole new range of metaphorical materials comes into play; for we touch here on the connection between pastoral imagery and the religious life. This is the connection Milton exploited so powerfully in "Lycidas" by taking advantage of all the metaphorical implications of the word *pastoral*. Barth proceeds similarly. From goat-boy to scapegoat, the pilgrimage of George Giles ranges over the same metaphorical ground, only in comic and satyric fashion. From the traditional description of Christian judgment as a matter of separating "the sheep from the goats" Barth draws metaphoric strength. By making his "hero" a "goat" (an expression which in our idiom is paradoxical) he has chosen to upset the traditional Christian view of salvation. In tradition Christ, the Lamb of God, drove the pagan gods out of Europe and stilled forever the voice of the goatish Pan. Barth's *Revised New Syllabus* comically but seriously reinstates the goatish side of man. George is, as Stoker jokingly remarks, "Enos Enoch with balls"—a saviour who will restore sexuality to an honored place in human existence. In this respect Barth joins Yeats, Lawrence, Swinburne, and other artists who have rebelled against the puritanical and ascetic side of the religion founded by the "Pale Galilean." There should be nothing shocking in this. In a post-Freudian world, even the traditional celibacy of the Roman Catholic priesthood is being seriously challenged from within the Church. Barth's *Revised New Syllabus* simply reflects this new attitude.

If we grant the appropriateness of Barth's choice of basic metaphors, we may go on to consider their effectiveness, which is largely a matter of the interaction of the two metaphors. The metaphors of goat/man and university/universe merge when George the Goat-Boy leaves the *pasture* to enter the *campus*, metaphorically exchanging one *field* for another. His curious upbringing as a Goat-Boy and his potential as a possible saviour or "Grand Tutor" make this journey especially poignant. Having been brought up as a kid, an animal, George seeks to reach the highest possible level of human development. The enormity of this quest reflects the enormity of human existence, for we all begin as kids, faced with the problem of becoming as fully human as possible. The university becomes the proper sphere for George's quest because it is the place where life is studied and questioned. This enables Barth to use terms like "commencement," "failure," and "passage" as ways of talking about the whole development of human beings. Because universities were originally church oriented, with holy orders normally the object of a university degree, there is a theological implication in this system which Barth can exploit. And because the system combines this theocratic and authoritarian machinery with an antipathetic spirit of inquiry and skepticism, it provides the appropriate arena for the drama of George's search for Answers, as well as the proper test for his ecclesiastical aspirations.

Universities function now, all too often, as mere trade schools for aspirants to various technical positions. But at their center we still can find the notion that the unexamined life is not worth living, and that the university is a place where life may be examined. Ethical philosophy, which shares, or ought to share, with literature the central position in university education—frequently begins with the old choice between being a happy animal or an unhappy man. We begin to learn the rudiments of ethics by accepting our humanity and exploring its implications. George the Goat-Boy makes this choice literally, having actually experienced the pleasures of happy animal existence. Some of the implications of the choice are explored in the following passage, which is not—as at least one critic has suggested—Barth's own view of life, but only the point of departure from which a man with aspirations to full humanity must leave, and which no man can leave without some nostalgic backward glances. Here George presents the goatish view of life:

> Who neglects his appetites suffers their pangs; Who presumes incautiously may well be butted; Who fouls his stall must sleep in filth. Cleave to him, I learned, who does you kindness; Avoid him who does you hurt; Stay inside the fence; Take of what's offered as much as you can for as long as you may; Don't exchange the certain for the possible; Boss when you're able, be bossed when you aren't, but don't forsake the herd. Simple lessons, instinct with wisdom, that grant to him who heeds them afternoons of browsy bliss and dreamless nights. Thirteen years they fenced my soul's pasture; I romped without a care. In the fourteenth I slipped their gate—as I have since many another—looked over my shoulder, and saw that what I'd said bye-bye to was my happiness.

It should be obvious that neither Barth nor his spokesman George is offering a recipe for the good life here; the speaker is commemorating his passage from kidship to manhood, his departure from the world of animal happiness for the troubled world of men. This typical, this archetypal journey is simply rescued by Barth from the realm of matter-of-course and given new life by his literalizing of the metaphor of child as kid and the consequent dramatization of the choice between animal simplicity and human complication. But to explore Barth's vision in any way approaching thoroughness, we must move beyond these basic metaphors to their operation in the whole allegorical structure of the book.

Allegory is notoriously an affair of "levels," but I should like to discard that notion—which implies more of a fixed hierarchy among kinds of meaning and a stricter separation among them than I believe exists, even in the great traditional allegories. Yet there are different meanings and different kinds of meaning in any richly imagined allegory. To encompass this variety of meaning without the unwelcome implications of "levels," I should like to consider the varieties of meaning in *Giles Goat-Boy* as facets or dimensions which become discernible to us when we consider the narrative from different angles of vision. This fabulation has, for example, its element of pure story or pure romance, the meanings of which are visceral rather than intellectual. These romance elements, however, are intimately connected with Barth's deliberate employment of myths and archetypes—dimensions of narrative that modern criticism is equipped to measure and understand. At the same time, the central events in the story of the hero's progress involve his adaptation of certain distinct ethical attitudes and his action according to those attitudes. The consequences of George's acting according to these different ethical attitudes lead him (and us) to evaluations of them, giving the book a philosophical dimension which is structurally central to the narrative. There are also important facets of *Giles Goat-Boy* that we might call sociological, psychological, and historical. We are used to thinking of matters of these latter kinds as the domain of realistic fiction rather than as allegorical facets of a work which is not essentially a piece of realism. This may make it hard for us to accept the validity of this dimension in a work

of fabulation. Yet this is just what we must do in order to come to terms with Barth's narrative. Or, rather, it is one of a number of things we must do to grasp the whole narrative with full awareness of all its dimensions. For our reading of multi-dimensional allegory depends not only on our apprehending all the dimensions of the narrative, but also, even mainly, on our being aware of the interaction among them.

JOHN D. STARK
From "John Barth"
The Literature of Exhaustion
1974, pp. 126–71

B arth attacks the same kinds of literature that Borges and Nabokov have badly scarred, the various kinds of realistic fiction. The novel differentiated itself from other kinds of prose fiction and attained its status as an independent genre because of its realism, so an anti-realist must dispel the belief that novels must perforce be realistic. Barth tries to do this by showing that realism had to be invented, too, that it was not just *there* to be accepted as the natural mode for writers to use. He describes in "Anonymiad" a bard inventing a new kind of literature, and claims that "the whole conception of a literature faithful to daily reality is among the innovations of this novel opus." He attacks another disturbing bias in favor of realism by claiming that this mode of literature does not avoid artifice but merely uses another kind of artifice. Among the intercalated comments on the art of fiction in "Lost in the Funhouse" is this one: "Initials, blanks, or both were often substituted for proper names in nineteenth-century fiction to enhance the illusion of reality. . . . Interestingly, as with other aspects of realism, it is an *illusion* that is being enhanced, by purely artificial means."

If a reader becomes convinced that realism should not be the criterion by which he can measure modes of literature but only one among many modes, he can calculate its strengths and weaknesses. The problems of opposites and of unity and duality continually foil realists, as Barth shows in the plot of many of his works by having the characters who accept a realistic world view try to deal with opposites. Besides George, Eben Cooke in *The Sot-Weed Factor* and the Siamese twin in "Petition" cannot cope with this matter. The twin presents the more graphic example, since he has to deal with opposites not only philosophically but also physically. Barth makes sure that these characters try in various ways to make sense of and deal with the world by conceiving of it as a system of opposites. When all of these ways fail, Barth expects the reader to conclude that dividing the world into opposites does not make sense. Opposition, like space and time, is one of the basic constituents of the commonsense notion of the world, so if realism cannot deal with it, realism's claim to superiority among literary modes loses its credibility. Because it cannot make sense of opposites, realism cannot do what it claims, accurately mimic the world. Barth's paradigmatic realist is the nymph for whom "Echo" is named. She seems to imitate exactly but she always distorts slightly, usually by omission. A reader who can agree with Barth up to this point will probably concede the next point in his chain of reasoning, that as long as all modes of literature, including realism, are artificial instead of mimetic, writers might just as well revel in their artifice.

The realists have problems not only because of the distortion of the lens they turn on the world, but also because of the world's distortions. The latter does not correct the lens's distortions; it compounds them. As Barth becomes more determined about his anti-realism his characters become more convinced of the world's absurdity. In *The Floating Opera* and *The End of the Road* his characters consider that they may be living in a chaotic world. Burlingame in *The Sot-Weed Factor* speaks the most fervently for this position. He says of man, "he is by mindless lust engendered and by mindless wrench expelled, from the Eden of the womb to the motley, mindless world. He is Chance's fool, the toy of aimless Nature—a mayfly flitting down the winds of Chaos." Nothing in this novel except Barth's art contradicts Burlingame's statement, but that exception is absolutely crucial.

Better worlds exist in the imagination, so writers should turn their backs on the lunacy of mundane existence and devise their own sane and orderly worlds. Barth has admitted that he wishes to devise his own worlds: the "impulse to imagine alternatives to the world can become a driving impulse for writers. I confess that it is for me." He dramatizes this impulse in *Giles Goat-Boy*, the novel he was writing when he made this statement. In a "cover letter" J. B., an obvious mask for Barth, describes his meeting with the strange creature who brought him the manuscript that forms the body of this novel. The emphasis in this scene falls on J. B.'s visitor and his book, but J. B. himself is important, too, because he is a writer. Using Wittgenstein's terms, he talks about the book he is writing: "My hero, I explained, was to be a Cosmic Amateur; a man enchanted with history, geography, nature, the people around him— everything that *is the case*—because he saw its arbitrariness but couldn't understand or accept its finality." This accurately describes the agony that afflicts the characters in Barth's first three books. More important, it describes Barth's attitude toward his material in those books. In this illuminating speech he abjures his former belief that order can be found in the world, finally understanding and accepting the absurdity of the world and vowing to write about what he will establish as the case. One warning is necessary here. It is a serious error to call Barth an Existentialist because of his vision of chaos. His pointing out of absurdity is only one, and a minor one at that, of his ways to attack reality. Furthermore, his attack on reality matters less than does the edifice he erects where reality once stood. . . .

Unlike Borges, Barth does not frontally attack reality by claiming that it is a dream. He suggests, more moderately, that life is *like* a dream, an opium dream. Moreover, he makes this suggestion only by implication, in a description of an opium dream that Eben has. He dreams that he is climbing mountains and is faced with a difficult choice of routes, so he decides to make an arbitrary choice and see it through. He does not realize it but here he follows Burlingame's advice that one should admit the absurdity of life and assert himself through arbitrary choice. Aside from this brief passage Barth has little interest in dreams.

To him the world dissolves not into dreams but into language. His theory of the linguistic basis of reality has been related to some of the aspects of his work that have been discussed. The visibility of a bit of wood pulp in a piece of paper in "Water-Message" and the equally dramatic invention of writing in "Anonymiad" show readers how remarkable it is that men can transmute reality into literature. Also in the naming of Ambrose in "Ambrose His Mark" language must be fitted to reality, and this story, too, implies that this process is not automatic but difficult. The relation of this theme to so many others demonstrates its centrality to Barth's vision.

Barth has known for some time that trouble results if someone attaches the wrong word to an object or if he can find no word for an object. Early in his career, in *End of the Road*,

he describes the trouble that develops from Rennie Morgan's lack of a word for the combination of love and hate. One of George's assignments in *Giles Goat-Boy* turns out to be purely a linguistic problem. He has failed to fix the clock because he does not understand what he must do, but then he realizes that "fix" can also mean fix in place, in which case he has no problem. This insight, despite Barth's modest disclaimer that he has little philosophical knowledge, sounds very much like one of Wittgenstein's primary contributions to philosophy: his theory that philosophical problems can be reduced to linguistic problems.

The next step in the replacement of everyday reality by a linguistic construct is to claim that a substantial part of human activity, much more than just human utterances, actually is linguistic. Near the end of *Giles Goat-Boy* Barth describes a committee that is trying to trace the history of "pass," "fail" and their derivatives, believing that "the history of certain such interpretations . . . could be said to figure the intellectual biography of studentom [mankind]." Here he claims that language has even more value for man, because it determines almost completely how people think and thereby determines to a large degree how they live. This theory naturally would appeal to a literary man, because it leads to the theory that reality is particularly amenable not only to language but also to media that rely on language, most notably, literature. After that one can easily say that language and literature *are* reality, and Barth has often but hesitantly made that assertion. . . .

Barth also makes it obvious that his characters are fictive. He makes most of them flat and stereotyped, especially those from minorities, like Indians, Blacks and Jews. Scholes puts it another way by saying that in *Giles Goat-Boy* the "characters are closer to pre-novelistic kinds of characterization than to the deep individuality of the realists." Occasionally Barth has a character announce his fictiveness so that a reader cannot miss it. George says, "a fact, . . . even an autobiographical fact, was not something I perceived and acknowledged, but a detail of the general Conceit, to be accepted or rejected." At least once, in *The Sot-Weed Factor*, a character also draws the appropriate conclusion for the reader, the one that all of these techniques of characterization support. Burlingame claims, "'all assertions of *thee* and *me*, e'en to oneself, are acts of faith, impossible to verify.'"

Barth's plots attack the notions of causality and time, rather than depending on them, as the realists' plots do. He links the actions together in haphazard fashion, and characters meet usually not because their destinies bring them together but because of coincidence. The plots also lack internal consistency. In *The Sot-Weed Factor* he is especially oblivious to consistency; some of its characters even die and then reappear later. The enormous complexity of Barth's plots makes it nearly impossible for anyone to understand them, even if he could depend on traditional organizing devices like the conception of cause and effect. . . .

Barth also combats the realists on the battleground of point-of-view. Rejecting more sophisticated ways to divide this element of fiction into categories, he uses the common one of first-person and third-person and shows that this can be a false distinction. By doing this he proves that point of view is much more complex than most realists suspect. His most subtle proof of this complexity appears in "Echo." Gerhard Joseph has explained it in an intricate discussion that requires extensive quotation:

> "Echo" . . . accomplishes the complete amalgama-
> tion of the first- and third-person point of view. Nar-

cissus seems to be the speaker, telling his familiar tale in the third person to Tiresias as an antidote to self-love: "One does well," the story opens, "to speak in the third person, the seer advises, in the manner of Theban Tiresias. A cure for self-absorption is saturation: telling the story over as though it were another's until like a much repeated word it loses sense." As Narcissus explores this perspective, lapsing at one point into the first person within the first person, we are led to suspect that the speaker may be either Tiresias or Echo, in which case the identity of the interlocutor is just as doubtful. While the narrative line is relatively clear because of the myth's familiarity, it becomes impossible to distinguish teller from listener and, ultimately, narrative from narrator.

The reader has even more difficulty making distinctions about this story than Joseph claims, for Narcissus is not the only one who "sees the nymph [Echo] efface herself until she becomes no more than her voice." The reader sees the same thing. In this effacement Barth presents his ultimate quibble with conventional ideas about point of view. He no longer denies only the distinction between first and third persons; he denies the distinction between point of view as a whole and character. He also suggests that everything else in a story can become subservient to a narrative voice. He makes the same suggestion in "Menelaiad": "this isn't the voice of Menelaus; this voice *is* Menelaus." Then he builds so many Chinese boxes in this story that the reader begins to believe this statement by and about the narrative voice.

To pare away the elements of fiction an author can next eliminate the narrative voice, by having the story tell itself. This supposedly happens in "Autobiography." Despite the interest, perhaps even the originality of this strategy, executing it does not take much skill, certainly much less than the skill with which Barth handles the point of view in "Echo." This idea as it appears in "Autobiography" can be visualized as a series of Chinese boxes. The outermost ones are again the author and the work. Then comes the narrative voice, according to Barth the ground of any story, and then the actual content of the story. Lately he has been trying to work outward from this last box, destroying each box as he goes until he leaves only the work and himself. That is, he would like to create a story called "Autobiography" that has no content and that would be like a Platonic form of a story. He creates a finite system of boxes in this story, since no other boxes can be built that will encompass the last one. This project sounds like some of Beckett's attempts to make do without various elements of fiction. More generally, to use this strategy a writer of the Literature of Exhaustion must first admit that literature is dead. Then he tries to prove this charge by destroying literature's constituents—while writing stories. . . .

In many ways, then, Barth is a classic writer of the Literature of Exhaustion, but a tendency in his work, his growing interest in the theme of love, has allowed him to keep in touch with realism. However, he frequently takes an ironic attitude toward this theme. His first two, realistic novels depend quite heavily on the love theme, *The Floating Opera* more heavily than it first appears. Todd contemplates suicide not because of his philosophical impasse or even his awareness of his body brought on by Jane Mack's unintentionally disturbing remark about his peculiar fingers. Rather, her remark and his resulting temporary impotence—a condition that has been periodically bothering him—in conjunction force him to set aside his mask of cynicism and realize that he loves her. Todd will not admit this feeling in his narration and probably does not admit it to

the higher centers of his consciousness, but Barth makes it clear that only this motive will explain Todd's actions. Thus, this philosophical novel actually turns on the issue of love. The love theme in *End of the Road*, although more crucial, is also so straightforward that it need not be explained here. However, both Todd and Jake Horner love in strange, impersonal ways.

In *The Sot-Weed Factor* love plays an important part. Through most of this novel it is subordinate to other themes like innocence, timelessness and opposites. At the very end, however, it comes to the forefront and the novel ends with a dénouement like a Shakespearian comedy's in which everyone marries. In Barth's novel, however, another unraveling occurs when the matches begin to dissolve, which ironically undercuts this theme. The love theme in *Giles Goat-Boy* is almost identical. Through most of this novel it conveys the ideas that Barth wants to examine. At the end, the relation between George and Anastasia becomes paramount, and the techniques of the Literature of Exhaustion give way to the conventional novelistic techniques that are usually used to develop love themes.

Lost in the Funhouse depends throughout on the love theme and does not subordinate it to other concerns. The cry of "'love, love, love'" that ends the first story, "Night-Sea Journey," echoes throughout the book. Often the love is unrequited, as in "Petition," or vicarious, as in "Water-Message," but these varieties are no less real. This theme plays an even more important part in two other stories. In "Menelaiad" Menelaus learns that he must placate not Athena, the goddess of wisdom, but Aphrodite, the goddess of love. Moreover, after one unpeels all the layers of this story, the core, the love story of Menelaus and Helen, becomes visible. "Ambrose His Mark" ends with the main character admitting his attitude toward the experiences he has just had:

> He wishes he had never entered the funhouse. But he has. Then he wishes he were dead. But he's not. Therefore he will construct funhouses for others and be their secret operator—though he would rather be among the lovers for whom funhouses are designed.

This is the subterranean message of *Lost in the Funhouse*.

In *Chimera* Barth treats love ironically. He compares sex so often with narration that the former theme becomes less important in itself than as a metaphor for the latter theme. For example, he says of the genie and Scheherazade "'this last comparison—a favorite of theirs—would lead them to a dozen others between narrative and sexual art.'" Moreover, Barth's technical experiments so dominate this book that the love relations in it lose their credibility and immediacy. This irony prevails in spite of the autobiographical implications of this theme in *Chimera*. In sum, it looks as if Barth will not use the theme of love to lead him back toward realism, but will instead continue his interest in the aesthetic themes of the Literature of Exhaustion.

MANFRED PUETZ
From "John Barth's *The Sot-Weed Factor:*
The Pitfalls of Mythopoesis"
Twentieth Century Literature, 1976, 454–60

John Barth's writings are epitomes of contemporary American fiction: they expose some of its key problems and they test representative strategies for solving them. Barth belongs to a new school of fabulators[1] whose inventiveness, whose unexpected fantasies and whose renewed love for old tales have dominated the fictional landscape of the past decade in America. But beyond mere inventiveness and wit, ostentatious glibness and stylistic idiosyncracies, Barth has a keen awareness of topicality—not in the derogatory sense—and offers in his novels of ideas (a sub-genre long despised) prototypical formulations of present day pathology. Thus Barth's early fiction takes off on a statement of contemporary nihilism and absurdity. It puts variations of existentialist thought concerning the possibility or impossibility of stringent self-definition to a test. His later works increasingly concentrate on the function of the imagination in the self-defining process. It is in these works that Barth explores the dangers inherent in a reapplication of mythical schemes to history and everyday life and in the practice of storifying human experience.

In 1964 Barth announced that *The Sot-Weed Factor*, a seventeenth-century mock epic, was planned as one of three amusing novels sounding the depth of nihilism in our time. He added: "I had thought I was writing about values and it turned out I was writing about innocence."[2] The heroes of Barth's earlier novels *The Floating Opera* and *The End of the Road* were forever seen coping with questions of "ultimate" sense and "absolute" value. Their answer to such questions consisted, simultaneously, in a gesture of futility and a relative affirmation. Ebenezer Cooke, central character of *The Sot-Weed Factor*, is preoccupied with the same set of questions, but tends to try out more radical responses to the problem. In the absence of all clear-cut answers, Cooke chooses to create the absolutes he will henceforth build and rely upon, a decision which puts him into the favorable position of someone who is no longer forced to cope with "fundamental" and "ultimate" values, but rather with the technicalities of what follows from his first, arbitrary choice.

The opening gambit of Barth's novel is a familiar one. It is almost identical to that in *The End of the Road*; it has outlines similar to the opening of *The Floating Opera*; and it is reminiscent of the situation so many fictional characters in the American novel of the sixties find themselves in. In a letter to his sister Anna, Ebenezer writes: "All Roads are fine Roads, beloved Sister, none more than another . . . to choose one, impossible! . . . I cannot choose, sweet Anna: twixt Stools my Breech falleth to the Ground!" To which the narrator adds: "The man (in short), thanks both to Burlingame and to his natural proclivities, was dizzy with the beauty of the possible; dazzled, he threw up his hands at choice, and like ungainly flotsam rode half-content the tide of chance." In other words, Eben's situation indicates that he suffers from the very "cosmopsis" Jacob Horner in *The End of the Road* had discovered, named, and learned to hate. The consequences for the lives of these two characters are similar. Like Horner, Eben is subject to fits of total immobility. He is characterized as "consistently no special sort of person," and (somewhat unlike Horner's case) immobility and lack of decision determine even the most intimate specifics of his love-life. What Ebenezer has detected in his comic explorations of life is the curious reversal of a state the nineteenth century had seriously fretted over. In *The Sickness Unto Death* Søren Kierkegaard stated that human beings inevitably fall into despair when they lack possibility. Ebenezer Cooke has found out—representative for many characters of contemporary fiction—that the reverse is valid too: human beings invariably fall into despair when confronted with too many possibilities.

In this quandary Cooke unwittingly takes to a solution which seems to resolve his problems with a stroke of genius. True to a maxim which he only later is able to state explicitly,

namely "that what the cosmos lacks we must ourselves supply"—a maxim which seems to have sprung straight out of Shelley's *Defence of Poetry*—he creates his own essence and decides to hold on to it no matter how adverse conditions might become. Creating his essence means in practice little else but creating a role; and the ensuing complications of the novel, from Eben's first collisions with experience to the disappointment of the end, are all planted together with the initial choice. This choice, in turn, seems to precede the chooser. Born out of the innocence of new beginnings, this is Eben's decision and argument:

> Faith, 'tis a rare wise man knows who he is: had I not stood firm with Joan Toast, I might well ne'er have discovered that knowledge! Did I, then, make a choice? Nay, for there was no *I* to make it! 'Twas the choice made *me*: a noble choice, to prize my love o'er my lust, and a noble choice bespeaks a noble chooser. What am I? What am I? *Virgin*, sir! *Poet*, sir! I am a virgin and a poet.

In the course of the ensuing events, Eben's original fantasy generates other fantasies. These he easily incorporates into the grandiose dream he pits against the bleak world of the given. Since he is the poet per se, later specified as the celebrated Poet and Laureate of Maryland, there must be a land worthy of his labor and praise. Since his love is pure and untainted by what he considers base motives, there must be a woman worthy of it. Thus the myth of Maryland, the perfect, and the fantasy of Joan Toast, his eternal love, are born. In sum, the hero turns to the panacea of mythopoesis and creates fictional schemes and mythical worlds around himself which in turn support the very self-concepts from which all interpretations of self and world have sprung. In *The Sot-Weed Factor* not even the hen knows which came first, she or the egg.

What is spontaneous, almost instinctive, reaction in Ebenezer gains the status of a philosophical program in Burlingame, legendary tutor and counterpart to the title figure of the novel. Where Cooke blindly gropes for solutions, Burlingame has reasoned out in advance what might be attempted, what should be done, and what can be justified. As the teacher of Ebenezer and his twin sister Anna he enthusiastically seizes on the children's natural talent for playacting. He encourages them to assume various identities, to try on different roles for size, and to approach an understanding of history and historical personalities through a reenacting of the past. His is an attitude toward history and tradition that partly imitates attitudes of the Romantics: if you want to know who you are, search for the historical models from which you have been cast. Moreover, if you cannot find any suitable models which will facilitate an understanding of yourself, then invent them, create them, and impose them on an existence whose chief characteristic has always been lack of essence. "One must needs make and seize his soul," Burlingame instructs Ebenezer,

> and then cleave fast to't, or go babbling in the corner; one must choose his gods and devils on the run, quill his own name upon the universe, and declare, "'Tis I, and the world stands such-a-way!" One must *assert, assert, assert,* or go screaming mad. What other course remains?

About the necessity and justification of such an act of self-creation there can be no doubt. In an earlier discussion between Eben and Burlingame, which took the shape of an extended treatise on the question of identity, the latter has laid the philosophical foundations for his beliefs. The knotty problem of identity, Burlingame held, arises because "The world's indeed a flux, as Heraclitus declared: the very universe is naught but change and motion." In this sea of change there seems to be only one guarantee for a continuous sense of sameness in the life of the individual:

> 'Tis the house of Identity, the Soul's dwelling place!
> Thy memory, my memory, the memory of the race:
> 'tis the constant from which we measure change; the
>   sun. Without it, all were Chaos right enough.

But the individual's memory, as Burlingame quickly points out, is not truly a reliable foundation. Is it not sometimes faulty? Does it not tend to color everything it holds? Hence Burlingame—who in this passage alternately sounds like Heraclitus, a phenomenologist, and an existentialist philosopher—warns that nothing is truly reliable except a man's ability to alter himself and to hang on for a while to the self-concepts he has defiantly created. Only the double acts of creation and faith, to both of which Eben will later cling as artist and quester, are worthy of our pursuit. Yet, for the moment our hero is more confused than reassured. "Marry," he exclaims, "your discourse hath robbed me of similes: I know of naught immutable and sure!" To which Burlingame, the archetypal "Suitor of Totality, Embracer of Contradictories, Husband to all Creation," prophetically answers: "'Tis the first step on the road to Heaven."

In yet another way the figure of Burlingame dominates the intellectual landscape of the novel. Barth uses him in order to demonstrate the dangers inherent in a strategy devised by many contemporary novelists for the benefit of their fictional characters. The novel of the sixties has celebrated with unsubdued enthusiasm the second coming of Proteus, the archetypal shape-shifter, and the maxims of Protean existence have been elevated to the status of a new philosophical program in our time. If change itself is the defining feature of human existence, the argument goes, then why not seize the opportunity to transcend the concept of the unitary self and become a whole spectrum of varying selves?

Barth, who has a knack for conceiving characters whose material situations become metaphorical equivalents for their spiritual plights, has put Burlingame in the perfect position to explore the overwhelming potentials of Protean existence. (Another of these allegorical homunculi familiar from Barth's fiction is the child-hero Ambrose, who appears in three sections of *Lost in the Funhouse* and whose queer personal fate of receiving no name at birth epitomizes, maybe too demonstratively, the American hero's plight of being born without a clear identity.) Burlingame is a foundling, fished, like Moses, out of the water, or as he puts it himself, "sprung *de novo* like a maggot out of meat, or dropped from the sky." Since he has thus no demonstrable link with history, no fixed position in the world, he can feel free to create his own identity from whatever materials he appreciates, "*ex nihilo* and without travail." As it happens, he is also convinced that all existence is "a Heraclitean flux" of which he wants to partake in its totality. Of his own ambitions he says: ". . . I love no part of the world, as you might have guessed, but the entire parti-colored whole, with all her poles and contradictories." From both premises together he draws conclusions which instantly make him the paradigm for a modern existence of self-regulated change. First, "When I reflect on the weight and power of such fictions beside my own poor shade of a self, that hath been so much disguised and counterfeited, methinks they have tenfold my substance!" Second, "I have no parentage to give me place and aim in Nature's order: very well—I am outside Her, and shall be Her lord and spouse!" It is this intention to test the limits of a radical program in new forms of self-discovery and not the simple thrills of endless travesties which Burlingame acts out in

the course of the novel. Slipping alternately into the roles of Lord Baltimore, John Coode, Peter Sayer, Timothy Mitchell, Nicholas Lowe, and even Ebenezer Cooke himself, Burlingame makes travesty the backbone of a new philosophy. There is a suggestive little episode in Barth's latest book, *Chimera*, where somebody tells the story of a species of snails common in the Maryland marshes.

> There's a special kind of snail in the Maryland marshes—perhaps I invented him—that makes his shell as he goes along out of whatever he comes across, cementing it with his own juices, and at the same time makes his path instinctively toward the best available material for his shell; he carries his history on his back, living in it, adding new and larger spirals to it from the present as he grows.

Apparently Burlingame, too, is such a snail except that his efforts at self-creation go even further: for Burlingame does not hesitate to shed, once in a while, his self-assembled house and exchange it for a brand-new one.

As Burlingame is quick to notice and Barth is eager to emphasize, Burlingame's philosophy compels him in practice to walk a tightrope without a net. As long as he has no link with the past and the world, he is free to embrace experience in its totality and to choose or even to create any number of roles. But at the same time this freedom makes him utterly diffuse and somehow nullifies him as an individual. Embracing everything, he eventually embraces (like Thomas Pynchon's heroine V.) nothing. Alternatively, if he establishes a clear link with the world (as he finally does when he finds out and accepts that he is the son of the Tayac Chicamec of the Ahatchwhoops Indians and the brother of Charley Mattassin and Cohunkowprets), he finds the one identity that substantiates him as a person, but he loses touch with the all-inclusive possibilities which constituted his freedom. There can be no satisfying solution to such a quandary, a fact of which Burlingame himself is aware.

> There is a freedom there that's both a blessing and a curse, for't means both liberty and lawlessness. 'Tis more than just political and religious liberty—they come and go from one year to the next. 'Tis philosophic liberty I speak of, that comes from want of history. It throws one on his own resources, that freedom—makes every man an orphan like myself and can as well demoralize as elevate.

Barth attempts to offer a solution, though. But he can only do so at the price of sacrificing philosophical stringency to superficial speculation. In the end, we witness Eben and his sister fleetingly speculate that Burlingame probably did not accept the verdict of his true identity and again slipped into one of his disguises, namely that of Nicholas Lowe.

Ebenezer Cooke's complementary quest for self-definition illustrates yet another problem that arises when the imagination gains undisputed dominance in life. As he loses touch with the realities in and around him, and as he methodically transcends the boundaries of actual experience, both reality and experience are converted to mere substrata of art. Ebenezer's mythopoeic view becomes a lens that distorts reality by refracting it as a potential or actual work of art. The realm of facts becomes by analogy the realm of aesthetic appearances: what Ebenezer surrenders in actual experience he gains back as the subject of his poetry. The poem he intends to write is only the most obvious token of this transformation. It is more important that in the same process Ebenezer's whole life is slowly converted into a unique work of art. By letting go of the world and the self he gains the momentary freedom to re-create both as autonomous objects. But by the same act he plants the seeds of a potential collision with experience which is likely to refute the very precepts on which his artistic creations were based. Ebenezer seems to be dimly aware of such a danger. Hence he shies away from experience and too great an involvement in life and attempts to preclude a refutation of his fantastically conceived world and his imaginatively born self. Yet, predictably, such refutations occur whenever he mixes with the world around him. Eben's fantasies of himself as the Poet Laureate, of Malden as a worldly paradise, and of Joan Toast as his perfect love turn sour, paradoxically, while they become partly true. In the end, Ebenezer discovers himself precisely because he abandons the false images he had forced upon himself. He comes into his own, because he revokes all mythical preconceptions and deviates from the patterns of autistic creation. Consequently, the process of art feeding on reality is now reversed in the novel. Ebenezer finally achieves fame as a poet and is offered the Laureateship by the young Lord Baltimore (which he declines), but only after he has discarded his fantasies of being the Poet Laureate and after he has displaced a panegyric on Maryland with a nasty work that heaps on Maryland the abuse it deserved all along. He finally becomes the husband of his love Joan Toast, but only after his perfect lady has turned into a dying wreck. To a certain extent, even the justice and order he had dreamed of win the upper hand at Malden, but only in a bizarre process of restoration which is a mockery of justice. And, paradoxically, yet typically for the reversals of *The Sot-Weed Factor*, the most conspicuous effect of Cooke's tongue-lashing attack on Maryland is that "Maryland, in part because of the well-known poem, acquired in the early eighteenth century a reputation for graciousness and refinement comparable to Virginia's, and a number of excellent families were induced to settle there." Such constellations suggest a failure of the imagination and of all mythopoeic ambitions. Yet it is not the author's imagination which is seen to fail, but the limitations are rather shown as inherent in the mythopoeic imagination itself.[2]

Notes

1. Compare Robert Scholes's study *The Fabulators* (New York: Oxford Univ. Press).
2. "John Barth: An Interview," *Wisconsin Studies in Contemporary Literature*, 6, 1 (Winter/Spring 1965), p. 11.

JOHN BARTH
From "Welcome to College—and My Books"

New York Times Book Review, September 16, 1984, pp. 36–37

I hadn't quite realized how *academic* . . . my life's work as a writer of stories has been. All of my books, I see now, are in the genre the Germans call *Erziehungsromane*: "upbringing-novels," education novels—a genre I had not found especially interesting after "David Copperfield" except as a vehicle for satire or an object of parody.

More dismaying, when I reviewed my literary offspring under this aspect, I realized that what I've been writing about all these years is not only orientation and education (rather, disorientation and education), but imperfect or unsuccessful or misfired education at that: not *Erziehungsromane* but *Herabziehungsromane*: "downbringing novels." That I failed to recognize this before now is exemplary: I am obliged to reorient myself to my own bibliography, as one must occasionally revise one's view of oneself retrospectively in the light of some new self-knowledge, usually bad news.

The themes of my work, I suppose, are regression, reenactment and reorientation. Like an ox-cart driver in monsoon season or the skipper of a grounded ship, one must sometimes go forward by going back. As an amateur sailor and navigator myself, I like the metaphor of dead reckoning: deciding where to go by determining where you are by reviewing where you've been. Aeneas does that; many of the wandering heroes of mythology reach an impasse at some crucial point in their journey, from which they can proceed only by a laborious retracing of their steps. This is the process, if not the subject, of my novel-in-*regress*, and it is the substance of this orientation talk.

Todd Andrews, the hero of my first novel, *The Floating Opera*, goes to college originally in order to fulfill his father's expectations more than his own. His own expectation is to drop dead before he finishes this sentence, from a certain kind of heart disease he learned he had while serving in the army in World War I. It takes him most of his undergraduate career (and most of a chapter) to discover what on earth he's doing there in the university; his orientation period, you might say, lasts almost to the baccalaureate. Even postgraduately, he is given to unpredictable shifts of life style: in successive decades he plays the role of a libertine, an ascetic, a practicing cynic; he ends up at 54 (his present age in the novel) a sexually feeble smalltown nihilist lawyer with an ongoing low-grade prostate infection and subacute bacteriological endocarditis tending to myocardial infarction, writing long letters to his father, who committed suicide a quarter-century since. The fruit of his education, formal and informal, is one valid syllogism:

1. There is no ultimate justification for any action.
2. Continuing to live is a variety of action.
3. Therefore etc.

Whence he moves, less validly, to the resolve not only to kill himself that very evening, but to take a goodly number of his townspeople, friends, lovers and such with him: He means to blow up the showboat of the novel's title by opening some acetylene gas tanks under the stage. The attempt fails; the show goes on; Todd Andrews's deductive faculty is restored, perhaps by the gas, and he understands (but neglects to inform Albert Camus) that, given his premises, he's likely to go on living because—in his case, at least—there's finally no more reason to commit suicide than not to.

If this sounds to you like the thinking more of a 24-year-old than of a 54-year-old, that is because the author was 24 at the time. Todd Andrews is a moderately successful lawyer but he couldn't have done better than a gentleman's C+ in Logic 1, and he must have flunked the Chemistry of Gases cold. I hope your education will be more successful.

Novel No. 2, *The End of the Road*, is set on and around the campus of a seedy little state teachers college at the opening of the fall term. (In the film version, the campus sequences were shot at Swarthmore.) The central character is a grad school dropout and ontological vacuum named Jacob Horner, who is subject to spells of paralysis because he suffers from the malady *cosmopsis*, the cosmic view. He is teaching English grammar on orders from his doctor, as a kind of therapy; but the prescription fails, as did his education. He becomes involved with a colleague's wife, a kind of nature-girl on the wrong trail: Nature may abhor a vacuum, but she shows her abhorrence by rushing to fill it. The novel ends with an illegal and botched abortion fatal to the young woman (this was the 1950's) and a final abdication of personality on Horner's part. I see now, however, that it was not the clinical abortion but Horner's aborted education that originally wound the mainspring of the plot: his total disorientation in the concourse of

Baltimore's Penn Station, where he first becomes immobilized because he can't think of any reason to go anywhere—and, apparently, can't go anywhere without a reason.

Those two novels make a little duet: a nihilist comedy and, if not a nihilist tragedy, at least a nihilist catastrophe. I am a twin—an opposite sex twin—and I see in retrospect that I've been oriented as a writer to the same iteration-with-variation that my sister and I exemplify: a sort of congenital redundancy.

There followed a pair of very long novels, *The Sot-Weed Factor* and *Giles Goat-Boy*, each of whose heroes begins with a radically innocent orientation of which he is disabused in successive chapters. Ebenezer Cooke, the hero of *The Sot-Weed Factor*, matriculates at Cambridge University near the end of the 17th Century; he has been ruinously disoriented by a tutor who professes *cosmophilism*, the sexual love of everything in the world: men, women, animals, plants, algebra, hydraulics, political intrigue. Cooke, like Jacob Horner, tends toward paralysis; he copes with the tendency by a radical assertion of his innocence and his fondness for versifying: He declares himself programmatically to be a virgin and a poet, as one might choose a double major, and sets out for the New World with a commission as Poet Laureate of the Province of Maryland. But the commission is spurious, his talent is questionable, the New World isn't what he'd been led to suspect and commissioned to eulogize; his innocence grows ever more technical and imperfect.

In the end Cooke has to marry a whore and contract a social disease in order to regain the estate he didn't recognize as his until he'd lost it. His poetry gets a little better, but it's written figuratively in red ink—his own blood—and it is admired for the wrong reasons. By the time he is legitimately appointed Poet Laureate, he couldn't care less. Ebenezer Cooke would recommend that you choose some other major than Innocence, which he comes to see he has been guilty of.

Giles Goat-Boy, raised by goats on one of the experimental stock-farms of an enormous, even world-embracing university, takes as *his* orientation program the myth of the wandering hero: He majors, as it were, in mythic heroism. It is not a gut course, though Giles has to descend into the very bowels of knowledge, and of the Campus, in order to earn his degree. After nearly 800 pages, the main thing he seems to have learned is that what he has learned can't be taught: In his attempts to eff the ineffable, his truths get garbled, misconstrued, betrayed by verbalization, institutionalism. He almost ceases to care—as, I'm sure, many serious teachers do. But the *almost* is important.

After those two long books came a pair of short ones. Both are about orientation, disorientation, reorientation. Both involve wandering heroes from classical mythology, usually lost. (One reason why classical mythic heroes need to know which way is east is that they traditionally travel west. But they *always* lose their way.) The first book of the pair is a series of fictions for print, tape and live voice called *Lost in the Funhouse*. Orientationwise, the title speaks for itself. The other consists of three novellas, called *Chimera*. "Dunyazadiad," the opening panel of the *Chimera* triptych, is a reorchestration of one of my favorite stories in the world: the frame-story of *The Thousand and One Nights*. You know the tale: how King Shahryar is driven so mad by sexual jealousy that he sleeps with a virgin every night and has her killed in the morning, lest she deceive him; and how that wonderful young woman Scheherazade, the vizier's daughter, beguiles him with narrative strategies until he comes to his senses. For a time, I regarded the *Nights* as an insightful early work of feminist fiction: Scheherazade is called

specifically "the Saviour of Her Sex"; the king's private misogyny is shown to be dangerous not only to his women but to his own mental health and, since he's the king, to the public health as well. Later in my own education as a writer, I came to regard the story as a metaphor for the condition of narrative artists in general, and of artists who work on university campuses in particular, for a number of reasons:

1. Scheherazade has to lose her innocence before she can begin to practice her art. Ebenezer Cooke did, too; so do most of us.

2. Her audience—the king—is also her absolute critic. It is "publish or perish," with a vengeance.

3. And her talent is always on the line. Never mind how many times she has pleased the king before; she is only as good as her next piece. So are we all.

4. But this terrifying relationship is also a fertilizing one; Scheherazade bears the king three children over those 1,001 nights, as well as telling all those stories. Much could be said about those parallel productions.

5. Which, however, cease—at least her production of stories ceases—as soon as the king grants her the "tenure" of formal marriage. So it goes.

My version of the story, told by Scheherazade's kid sister, Dunyazade, echoes some of these preoccupations:

> "Three and a third years ago, when King Shahryar was raping a virgin every night and killing her in the morning, and the people were praying that Allah would dump the whole dynasty, and so many parents had fled the country with their daughters that in all the Islands of India and China there was hardly a young girl, my sister was an undergraduate arts-and-sciences major at Banu Sasan University. Besides being Homecoming Queen, valedictorian-elect, and a four-letter varsity athlete, she had a private library of a thousand volumes and the highest average in the history of the campus. Every graduate department in the East was after her with fellowships—but she was so appalled at the state of the nation that she dropped out of school in her last semester to do full-time research on a way to stop Shahryar from killing all our sisters and wrecking the country.
>
> Political science, which she looked at first, got her nowhere. Shahryar's power was absolute; by sparing the daughters of his army officers and chief ministers . . . he kept the military and the cabinet loyal enough to rule out a *coup d'état*. Revolution seemed out of the question, because his woman-hating, spectacular as it was, was enforced more or less by all our traditions and institutions, and as long as the girls he was murdering were generally upper-caste, there was no popular base for a guerrilla war.
>
> So we gave up poly sci and tried psychology—another blind alley. . . . She grew daily more desperate; the body-count of deflowered and decapitated Moslem girls was past 900, and Daddy was just about out of candidates. . . . When nothing else worked, as a last resort she turned to her first love, unlikely as it seemed, mythology and folklore, and studied all the riddle/puzzle/secret motifs she could dig up. 'We need a miracle, Doony,' she said (I was braiding her hair and massaging her neck as she went through her notes for the 1,000th time), 'and the only genies I've ever met were in stories, not in Moormen's-rings and Jews'-lamps. It's in words that the magic is— Abracadabra, Open Sesame, and the rest—but the magic

words in one story aren't magical in the next. The real magic is to understand which words work, and when, and for what; the trick is to learn the trick.'

In other words—as Dunyazade and Scheherazade and the Author come to learn in the pages that follow—the *key* to the treasure may *be* the treasure.

The tuition for that sort of lesson can be very high. Retracing one's steps—"becoming as a kindergartener again," as the goat-boy puts it—may be necessary to a fruitful reorientation, but one runs the risk of losing oneself in the past instead of returning to the present equipped to move forward into the future.

Perseus (in the second *Chimera* novella, called "Perseid") understands this, though he's not sure for a while what to do with his understanding. He too has retraced his heroical route, recapitulated his mythic exploits, and not for vanity's sake, but for reorientation. As he says one night to the nymph Calyxa, as she and he are making love:

"Well, now perhaps it was a bit vain of me to want to retrace my good young days; but it wasn't *just* vanity; no more were my nightly narratives: Somewhere along that way I'd lost something, took a wrong turn, forgot some knack, I don't know; it seemed to me that if I kept going over it carefully enough I might see the pattern, find the key."

"A little up and to your left," Calyxa whispered.

Perseus' research is successful: he finds the key and moves on to his proper destiny, which is to become a constellation in the sky, endlessly reenacting his story in his risings and settings. Perseus "makes it" because his vocation is legitimate: He doesn't major in Mythic Heroism; he happens to *be* a mythic hero, whose only problem is what to do for an encore.

More cautionary is the lesson of Bellerophon, the hero of the final *Chimera* novella. Like Giles the goat-boy, Bellerophon aspires to be a mythic hero; it is his only study. When Perseus reaches middle age, he researches his own history and the careers of other mythic heroes in order to understand what brought him to where he is, so that he can go on. Young Bellerophon's orientation, on the other hand, is that by following perfectly the ritual pattern of mythic heroes—by getting all A's and four letters of recommendation, as it were—he will become a bona fide mythic hero like his cousin Perseus. What he learns, and it is an expensive lesson, is that by perfectly imitating the pattern of mythic heroism, one becomes a perfect imitation of a mythic hero, which is not quite the same thing as being Perseus the Golden Destroyer. Hence the novella's title *Bellerophoniad*. Something similar may befall the writer too fixated upon his/her distinguished predecessors; it is a disoriented navigator indeed who mistakes the stars he steers by for his destination.

He is not, my Bellerophon, entirely phony, however: he is too earnest for that; too authentically dedicated to his profession, whatever the limits of his gift. What's more, he really does kill the Chimera—that fictive monster or monstrous fiction—to the extent that it ever really existed in the first place. Bellerophon's immortality is of a more radically qualified sort: what he becomes is not the story of his own exploits, as Perseus does up there among the other stars, but the *text* of the story *Bellerophoniad*. Pegasus, the winged horse of inspiration on which Bellerophon has flown, gets to heaven (in fact, he's one of the constellations in the Perseus group); his rider is thrown at

the threshold of the gate, falls for a long time (long enough to tell his long tale), and is transformed just in the nick of time into the pages, the sentences, the letters of the book *Chimera*. To turn into the sound of one's own voice is an occupational hazard of professional storytellers; even more so, I imagine, of professional lecturers.

That brings us to the present. Now: all these retracements, recapitulations, rehearsals and reenactments really would be simply regressive if they didn't issue in reorientation, from which new work can proceed. But that, as Scheherazade says, is another story.

Postscript 1984, for the Class of 1988

The novel *Letters*, published shortly after that orientation lecture, centers upon an enormous (and hypothetical) third-rate American university, Marshyhope State, constructed for my purposes on the freshly filled salt marsh of my native Dorchester County, in Maryland. The year is 1969, the heyday of American academic imperialism and gigantism. Marshyhope's architectural symbol and intended beacon to the world, The Tower of Truth, on the eve of its dedication already shows signs of subsiding into the fenlands whence it sprang, like the Hancock Tower into Back Bay Boston. "All great cultures," the critic Leslie Fiedler once remarked, "arise from marshes"— and not a few thereto return.

As R. D. Laing rationalizes schizophrenia, at least in certain cases, as a sane response to a deranged but inescapable set of circumstances, so the cautionary example of Marshyhope State suggests that—in certain cases, at least—the fault of disorientation may lie not in ourselves, Horatio, but in our alma maters and paters. To disoriented undergraduates I say: By all means allow for that possibility—but do not jump to that conclusion, as it is most likely mistaken.

My little novel, *Sabbatical: A Romance* (1982), carries the Laingian scenario farther. Todd Andrews in *The Floating Opera* (and again in *Letters*) wonders sentence by sentence whether his heart will carry him from subject to predicate; in *Sabbatical*, set on Chesapeake Bay in 1980, the background question is whether the world will end before the novel does.

More specifically, the question is whether one can responsibly bring children into the disoriented powder-keg wherein we dwell. The prospective parents in *Sabbatical* are literal navigators, of a seaworthy cruising sailboat (she is a proper young academic, on sabbatical leave; he is a decent, middle-aged ex-C.I.A. officer, between careers). *They* are oriented; the course they steer is accurate, if not always straightforward. What's more, after years of marriage and trials large and small they remain happily in love with each other. In an oriented world, their landfall—and progeny—would be assured. In the troubled and dangerous waters through which they, like the rest of us, necessarily sail, however, no degree of skill in navigation or of seaworthiness in the vessel guarantees that our destination will still be there at our Estimated Time of Arrival.

This being the more or less apocalyptic case—the Sot-Weed Factor supplanted as it were by the Doomsday Factor— why set a course at all, whether toward graduation or procreation or distinguished career or further fiction? This is the approximate subject of my next effort at self-orientation: my novel presently in the works. But that, as Scheherazade says, is another story, for another night.

DONALD BARTHELME

1931–

Donald Barthelme was born on April 7, 1931 in Philadelphia. While he was still young, his family moved to Texas. Except for a period of service in the U.S. Army, Barthelme lived and worked primarily as a journalist in the 1950s.

In 1962 he moved to New York City, where he became managing editor of the journal *Location*. The magazine survived only two editions, but its contributors included Saul Bellow, Marshall McLuhan, and John Ashbery. Barthelme himself contributed a critical essay and his first short story. He began contributing fiction to the *New Yorker* and other magazines shortly afterward, and published his first collection, *Come Back, Dr. Caligari*, in 1964. He soon became known for the peculiarity of his work: his stories were linguistic games, characterized by parody of the language of advertising and politics, elaborate joking and punning, disjointedness, absurd situations, and other techniques labeled by critics "avant-garde," "innovative," or simply "bizarre."

In 1966 Barthelme received a Guggenheim Fellowship. His first novel, *Snow White*, was published the following year. A collection of stories, *City Lights*, won much praise in 1970. In 1972 Barthelme's first book for children, *The Slightly Irregular Fire Engine, or: The Hithering Thithering Djinn*, won the National Book Award. Since then, this highly controversial author—once condemned as a celebrant of "unreason, chaos, and inexorable decay"—has continued to publish stories and collections. His books now include *Guilty Pleasures*, a book of satires and parodies, and two more novels. He lives in New York with his third wife, Birgit.

General

'Fragments are the only forms I trust,' writes Donald Barthelme, turning the suspicion of conventional patternings into an aesthetic principle. A fragmentary form is an open-ended one that is amenable to the disarrangings and rearrangings of fantasy and, as such, offers Barthelme a way of countering the conditioning forces and expressing his distrust of the 'finished' objects all around him. His writing may be compared to the Watts Towers in Los Angeles. Items of contemporary detritus are extracted from their habitual contexts or heaps and assembled in such a way that improbable fairy towers arise from the melancholy desolation of the surrounding trash-strewn urban landscape. Through the resourceful rearranging of the artist, waste is transformed to magic, environment is redeemed by play. At the same time Barthelme's work often reveals a distinct dread of environment and conveys a disquieting unease. It is this combination of play and dread which makes his odd personal fantasies seem so appropriate to contemporary America.

In the last story of Barthelme's first book, *Come Back, Dr. Caligari* (1964), a man appears on a TV programme which pays people to recount their personal experiences. He starts off, '"My mother was a royal virgin, and my father a shower of gold,"' and continues in a similar mythic-heroic-magical vein; and, says Barthelme, 'although he was, in a sense, lying, in a sense he was not.' This nostalgia for the terms of the fairy-tale in the age of commercial TV perhaps explains the basic idea of the novel which followed, *Snow White* (1967). To attempt to extract a narrative from the book would be rather beside the point—though there are seven men who live with Snow White, their occupations being window-washing, and making Chinese baby food in vats, and there is some detectable villainy and violence which ends in a death and a hanging. The character who announces that he gets his nourishment from 'the ongoing circus of the mind in motion. Give me the odd linguistic trip, stutter and fall, and I will be content,' offers a better approach to this book. For it is a language circus, and Barthelme has such sport with the words and things which make up 'the trash phenomenon' that one registers a spirit of resilience and carnival countering the deadening accumulations which make up the materials he handles. One character 'blows his mind' with the aid of mantras and insect repellent, 'To stop being a filthy bourgeois for a space. . . . To gain access to everything in a new way.' Barthelme does it with words.

To introduce Snow White into the contemporary world is obviously to gain the opportunity for ironies, incongruities, clashes of genre (the fairy-tale, pornography, the junk catalogue) and indirect sentimentality—for where will Snow White find her prince in contemporary America? One incident is designated as '*Irruption of the magical in the life of Snow White*', but arguably she is an irruption of the magical in the life of all the others. In particular she adds a dimension of discontent. '"I just don't like your world,"' she cries. She tells them that she remains in their world because she has not been able to imagine anything better. '"But my imagination is stirring. . . . Be warned."' She feels a sense of 'incompleteness' and lets down her hair in traditional fashion to see who will seek or save her. But no one even attempts to climb her hair and she feels that this must be the 'wrong time' for her if the present world is 'not civilized enough to supply the correct ending to the story'. (By contrast, her seven cohorts have a malevolent fantasy of burning her.) An unidentified voice near the end of the book complains of '"Total disappointment"', and it could well be Snow White's. Before they found her, the seven men lived lives 'stuffed with equanimity', but she has introduced 'confusion and misery' into their lives. If one sees her as embodying the disappointed imagination beginning to bestir itself, then one can see why the men who have lived with her become much less at ease among things. By the end the narrator is turning over the concept of '*something better*'; 'trying to break out of this bag that we are in'. And on the last page there are just a few headings for unwritten future chapters, the last three being:

SNOW WHITE RISES INTO THE SKY
THE HEROES DEPART IN SEARCH OF
                    A NEW PRINCIPLE

HEIGH-HO

'Tis off to work they go. Only this time perhaps they will not be content just to tend the vats and wash the windows.

The inclination to play with 'beautiful *dreck*' (as Ludwig Bemelmans once called it) and the countering instinct to get away from matter altogether—a profoundly American combination of feelings—provide the tensions which hold Barthelme's best work together and give it its distinctive vibrant strangeness. An unidentified voice in one chapter of *Snow White* speaks up in defence of his manufacture of an unlikely product, plastic buffalo humps. Revealingly, he bases his defence on the recognition that much of our speech is not communication but a sort of non-semantic stuffing or 'sludge' which we use to fill up the sentences.

> The 'sludge' quality is the heaviness that this 'stuff' has, similar to the heavier motor oils, a kind of downward pull but still fluid, if you follow me, and I can't help thinking that this downwardness is valuable. . . . Now you're probably familiar with the fact that the per-capita production of trash in this country is up from 2.75 pounds per day in 1920 to 4.5 pounds per day in 1965 . . . that rate will probably go up, because it's *been* going up, and I hazard that we may very well soon reach a point where it's 100 percent. Now at such a point you will agree, the question turns from a question of disposing of this 'trash' to a question of appreciating its qualities, because, after all, it's 100 percent, right? . . . So that's why we're in humps. . . . They are 'trash', and what in fact could be more useless or trashlike? It's that we want to be on the leading edge of this trash phenomenon, the everted sphere of the future, and that's why we pay particular attention, too, to those aspects of language that may be seen as a model of the trash phenomenon.

We may hardly be surprised that the police band in one of Barthelme's stories is asked to play 'Entropy', for like so many other American writers Barthelme seems to feel that that is the tune to which contemporary society is dancing. The men who live with Snow White

> like books that have a lot of *dreck* in them, matter which presents itself as not wholly relevant (or indeed, at all relevant) but which, carefully attended to, can supply a kind of 'sense' of what is going on. This 'sense' is not to be obtained by reading between the lines (for there is nothing there in those white spaces) but by reading the lines themselves. . . .

Elsewhere in the book a boy, asked by his girlfriend what will become of them both, replies, '"Our becoming is done. We are what we are. Now it is just a question of rocking along with things as they are until we are dead."' The message seems to be—go with the trash flow.

To some extent this sounds like a justification of Pop Art, in which the things that are filling up our environment are moved into our museums having first been enlarged, made more solid or multiplied. You are not asked to read between the soup cans. Just so, Barthelme's work is packed with the detritus of modern life; it seems like an unbroken stream of the accumulations and appurtenances which we see around us. But Barthelme turns it all to strangeness by omitting or deliberately fragmenting the habitual arrangings and separations by which we seek to retain a sense of control over the slowly filling environment. He fractures the syntax and the taxonomies which we hope will keep us sane. His prose seeks to simulate the strange confluence of words and things which is our actual experience, so that the commonest objects from kitchen, bathroom or street are mixed up with the commonest

clichés of contemporary intellectual talk; reminders of TV, radio, film, science-fiction, are added to the mix, while sudden moments of intense sexuality or violence alternate with long periods of deprivation and boredom—the whole *dreck* consort dancing or sinking, together. Returning to Barthelme's own phrases we could say that his prose seems to want to be all 'filling' or 'sludge', rocking along with things as they are with a richer sense of fantasy than our habitual modes of attention allow us to enjoy.

But the mood that most often comes across is finally very different from the sort of trash-happiness which Barthelme's work seems at times to be purveying. '*I want to go to some other country. . . . I want to go somewhere where everything is different,*' says a character in the first story of Barthelme's first book ('Florence Green is 81'), and although the idea is mocked, like every other idea offered as idea in Barthelme, this note of yearning for an unknown somewhere else sounds throughout his work. There is a strong feeling of being distinctly not at home in the trash age; though, since all the usual modes of complaint, dissatisfaction, nostalgia, etc., are registered as being part of the very trash continuum they seek to repudiate, themselves helping to top up the contemporary plenum, this feeling of not-at-homeness necessarily comes through in indirect ways. Thus, for instance, a thirty-five-year-old man is made to attend school with eleven-year-olds. He is told that since the desk-size (social environment) is correct, the pupil-size (uncomfortable individual consciousness) must be incorrect ('Me and Miss Mandible'). He is surrounded by people who read all the signs around them as promises (the American dream); but he has learned a bleaker wisdom—'that signs are signs, and that some of them are lies.' But Barthelme usually avoids all allegorical portentousness with his antic, and sometimes manic, humour which refuses to allow his material ever to settle in recognizable narrative patterns.

The result is a curious kind of prose, sometimes feeling rather hard and shellacked, like plastic, at other times fluttering like gay ribbons over the contemporary landscape, like the bunting over used car lots. It can be by turns engaging and ominous. One could take two stories from his most recent collection, *Unspeakable Practices, Unnatural Acts* (1968), to suggest the kind of alternation of mood in his work. In 'The Balloon' an enormous balloon suddenly appears over the city. It has no meaning and is apparently purposeless; it is simply a thing which has been mysteriously inserted into the environment. Everyone has a different theory or fantasy about the balloon. Mainly what people enjoy about it is 'that it was not limited or defined', and they come to play on its yielding amorphousness.

> This ability of the balloon to shift its shape, to change, was very pleasing, especially to people whose lives were rather rigidly patterned, persons to whom change, although desired, was not available. The balloon . . . offered the possibility, in its randomness, of mislocation of the self, in contradistinction to the grid of precise, rectangular pathways under our feet.

In terms of the story the balloon is explained as a 'spontaneous autobiographical disclosure' connected with sexual deprivation. But take it as a kind of free-form artistic product, flexible, plastic and ephemeral, and it exemplifies the sort of art which Barthelme and many other American writers are increasingly interested in. It represents an invitation to play, a gesture against patterning, a sportive fantasy floating free above the rigidities of environment; and the invitation and gesture are more important than the actual material of which the balloon is composed.

Against the delights of 'The Balloon' we may put the anxieties of 'Indian Uprising'. 'We defended the city as best we could'; so it starts, and though we can never be sure just who or what the Indians are, by the end they have padded 'into the mouth of the mayor' and occupied the end of Barthelme's story, dominating the narrator's concluding perspective. The defence has been conducted with familiar things. 'I analyzed the composition of the barricade nearest me and found two ashtrays, ceramic . . . a tin frying pan; two-litre bottles of red wine,' the list continues for half a page and ends, 'a Yugoslavian carved flute, wood, dark brown; and other items. I decided I knew nothing.' Things, singly or in accumulation, may not prove much of a defence. The narrator seeks love from a girl who flees from him down streets running with a filthy stream suggesting 'excrement, or nervousness'. He asks his girl, '"Do you think this is a good life?" The table held apples, books, long-playing records. She looked up. "No."' We cannot exactly follow the syntax of the story, but as we experience the modulations and shifts in situations and sentences the unease increases and we begin to feel that this is not a good life and realize that the city cannot hold. When an officer reports by radio that the garbage dump has begun to move, we believe him. There is one rather disturbing character who keeps turning up, a teacher named Miss R. It is not clear which side she is on, but she is suspiciously efficient in handling steel shutters and tends to favour clinically bare rooms. She believes that the litany is the only acceptable form of discourse, and prefers the 'vertical organization' of words in lists. The narrator, on the other hand, prefers 'strings of language extended in every direction to bind the world into a rushing, ribald whole'. But it seems that Miss R.'s impersonal methods of organization and control are destined to prevail over his sense of play. For at the end of the story, the narrator is being stripped and interrogated by a group which consists of Miss R. and the Indians. The enemy is, then, uncertain, but real; threat and coercion come in many forms, from many quarters. Defeat is spreading through the city.

In the last story of *Unspeakable Practices, Unnatural Acts*, 'See the Moon', Barthelme seems to offer a fairly specific account of his art as being a sort of collage activity appropriate to the times. The narrator is awaiting the birth of his child. Meanwhile he is conducting what he calls his lunar hostility studies (for he believes that the moon hates us). Both 'light-minded' and 'insecure' (like Barthelme's prose) he explains his method. 'You've noticed the wall? I pin things on it, souvenirs. . . . It's my hope that these . . . souvenirs . . . will someday merge, blur—cohere is the word, maybe—into something meaningful.' With this assemblage on the wall he intends to act as a kind of Distant Early Warning System to his unborn child.

> Here is the world and here are the knowledgeable knowers knowing. What can I tell you? What has been pieced together from the reports of travellers.
> Fragments are the only forms I trust.
> Look at my wall, it's all there.
>   —TONY TANNER, "Fragments and Fantasies," *City of Words*, 1971, pp. 400–406.

Works

Comanches are invading the city. The hedges along the Blvd Mark Clark have been barbed with wire. "People are trying to understand." This is "The Indian Uprising," the finest story in Donald Barthelme's new collection. There's fruit on the table, books, and long-playing records. Sylvia, do you think this is a good life? *Unspeakable Practices, Unnatural Acts* is the third

and best of Barthelme's books, and each of them has seemed unnatural; certainly none speaks. A captured Comanche is tortured. The work of Gabriel Fauré is discussed. The nameless narrator sands a hollow-core door he intends as a table. He has made such a table for each of the women he's lived with. There've been five. So far. Barricades are made of window dummies, job descriptions, wine in demijohns. They are also made of blankets, pillows, cups, plates, ashtrays, flutes. The hospitals have run out of wound dusting powder. Zouaves and cabdrivers are rushed to the river.

> This unit was crushed in the afternoon of a day that began with spoons and letters in hallways and under windows where men tasted the history of the heart, cone-shaped muscular organ that maintains *circulation of the blood*.

It is impossible to overpraise such a sentence, and it is characteristic: a dizzying series of swift, smooth modulations, a harmony of discords. "With luck you will survive until matins," Sylvia says, and then she runs down the Rue Chester Nimitz, uttering shrill cries. Or she runs down George C. Marshall Allée. Or. . . . Miss R. is a school-teacherish type. She naturally appears for no reason. The only form of discourse she likes is the litany. Accordingly, the 7th Cavalry band plays Gabrieli, Boccherini. And. . . .

In addition to the *way* he tells his stories, Barthelme habitually deals with unnatural apathy and violence—unnatural indeed, but not abnormal; so ordinary, in fact, that although we speak of killing by the countless, of lives indifferent, closed, and empty of any emotion, of cliché and stereospeech, of trademarks and hypocrisy, we speak so repetitiously, so often, so monotonously, that our discourse is purely formal (a litany). The words we hear are travelogues of gossip; they are slogans, social come-ons, ads, and local world announcements; phatic, filling our inner silence, they produce an appearance of communion, the illusion of knowledge. Counterfeit, they purchase jail.

The war is not going well. We've used love, wine, cigarettes, and hobbies, in our barricades, to shore against our ruin. Useless. The ghetto's been infiltered. There's a squabble in Skinny Wainwright Square. The narrator drinks deeply, and deeply feels the moreso of love. Sometimes the narrator is examining maps; sometimes he's in bed, tracing scars on the back of his beloved; sometimes he's pointing proudly to his table; sometimes he is garroting the testicles of an indian. Sometimes. . . .

There are other names in this story: Jane, Block, Kenneth, and Miss R. Miss R., one feels, is not to be trusted. She recommends metal blinds for the windows; she arranges words in lines, in stacks. Perhaps she's in the pay of the enemy. She also speaks for the author. That's the trouble: everyone speaks for the author. "Strings of language extend in every direction to bind the world into a rushing, ribald whole." Nevertheless the war is not going well. We try to keep informed, but in the end we know nothing. "You feel nothing," hectoring Miss R. says.

> You are locked in a most savage and terrible ignorance. . . . You may attend but you must not attend now, you must attend later, a day or a week or an hour, you are making me ill.

But where are the indians by this time? "Dusky warriors padded with their forest tread into the mouth of the mayor." With helicopters, a great many are killed in the south, but they are mostly children from the north, the east. Like the narrator, we are captured by these Comanches; taken to a white and yellow room. "This is the Clemency Committee," Miss R. says, for it *is* she. "Would you remove your belt and shoelaces." Now as ordered we've removed our belts and shoelaces, and we've looked

> (rain shattering from a great height the prospects of silence and clear, neat rows of houses in the subdivisions) into their savage black eyes, paint, feathers, beads.

The indians with their forest tread, through one aperture or another, have padded into all of us.

Barthelme has managed to place himself in the center of modern consciousness. Nothing surrealist about him, his dislocations are real, his material quite actual. Radio, television, movies, newspapers, books, magazines, social talk: these supply us with our experience. Rarely do we see trees, go meadowing, or capture crickets in a box. The aim of every media, we are nothing but the little darkening hatch they trace when, narrowly, they cross. Computers begin by discriminating only when they're told to. Are they ahead that much? since that's the way we *end*. At home I rest from throwing pots according to instructions by dipping in some history of the Trojan war; the fête of Vietnam is celebrated on the telly; my daughter's radio is playing rock—perhaps it's used cars or Stravinsky; my wife is telling me she loves me, is performing sexercises with a Yoga Monday, has accepted a proposal to be photo'd without clothing, and now wonders if the draft will affect the teaching of Freshman Chemistry. Put end to end like words, my consciousness is a shitty run of category errors and non sequiturs. Putting end to end and next to next is Barthelme's method, and in Barthelme, blessed method is everything.

In his novel, *Snow White*, he tells us about the manufacture of buffalo humps.

> They are "trash," and what in fact could be more useless or trashlike? It's that we want to be on the leading edge of this trash phenomenon, the everted sphere of the future, and that's why we pay particular attention, too, to those aspects of language that may seem as a model of the trash phenomenon.

Much interest is also shown in "stuffing," the words which fill the spaces between other words, and have the quality at once of being heavy or sludgy, and of seeming infinite or endless. Later we are told (Barthelme is always instructing the reader) that the seven dwarfs (for the novel is a retelling of the fairy story)

> . . . like books that have a lot of *dreck* in them, matter which presents itself as not wholly relevant (or indeed, at all relevant) but which, carefully attended to, can supply a kind of "sense" of what is going on. This "sense" is not to be obtained by reading between the lines (for there is nothing there, in those white spaces) but by reading the lines themselves. . . .

Dreck, trash, and stuffing: these are his principal materials. But not altogether. There is war and suffering, love and hope and cruelty. He hopes, he says in the new volume, "these souvenirs will merge into something meaningful." But first he renders everything as meaningless as it appears to be in ordinary modern life by abolishing distinctions and putting everything in the present. He constructs a single plane of truth, of relevance, of style, of value—a flatland junkyard—since anything dropped in the dreck *is* dreck, at once, as an uneaten porkchop mislaid in the garbage.

In the second story of this volume, Barthelme imagines that a balloon has been inflated at some point along 14th Street and allowed to expand northward to the Park. Just as, in the novel, there are pages of dim-witted reaction to Snow White's long black hair, so also in this case:

> There was a certain amount of initial argumentation about the "meaning" of the balloon; this subsided

because we have learned not to insist on meanings. . . .

Eventually people take park-like walks on it, and children jump from nearby buildings onto it, or climb its sides. The story is full of spurious facts and faked considerations typical of science-fiction. When the narrator's girl returns from Bergen, the balloon is deflated and packed off to be stored in West Virginia, its inventor no longer a victim of sexual deprivation, the balloon's suggested cause.

If "The Indian Uprising" is a triumph of style, achieving with the most unlikely materials an almost lyrical grace and beauty, "The Balloon" is only charming; and a commercial bit like "Robert Kennedy Saved from Drowning" (a spoof of the English Lord and Elizabeth Taylor lady-magazine interview, and stuffed with syrupy cliché and honeyed contradiction) is simply cheap. Here Barthelme's method fails, for the idea is to *use* dreck, not write about it. Another short, properly savage piece, written in bureaucratic engineerese, is a "Report" on a recently developed secret word which, when "pronounced, produces multiple fractures in all living things. . . . " Still another concerns two mysteriously military men who are buried in a bunker. They watch a console and each other; they watch for breakdown, something strange. They do not know for which city their bird is targeted. They watch, and they wait for relief. While we are reading, none comes. Barthelme is often guilty of opportunism of subject (the war, street riots, launching pads, etc.), and to be opportune is to succumb to dreck. Two stories, written in a flat, affected style resembling a nervous tic that's nonsignificant of nerves, both about cutouts named Edward and Pia, permit the reader to race to the finish ahead of the words, to anticipate effects, and consequently to appreciate a cleverness in the author almost equal to his own.

> It was Sunday. Edward went to the bakery and bought bread. Then he bought milk. Then he bought cheese and the Sunday newspapers, which he couldn't read. (It's a Swedish newspaper.)

But cleverness is dreck. The cheap joke is dreck. The topical, too, is dreck. Who knows this better than Barthelme, who has the art to make a treasure out of trash, to see *out* from inside it, the world as it's faceted by colored jewel-glass. A seriousness about his subject is sometimes wanting. When this obtains, the result is grim, and grimly overwhelming.

> People were trying to understand. I spoke to Sylvia. "Do you think this is a good life?" The table held apples, books, long-playing records. She looked up. "No."

—William H. Gass, "The Leading Edge of the Trash Phenomenon," *NYRB*, April 25, 1968, pp. 5–6.

The literary movement known as Black Humor or Dark Comedy, which achieved a certain inflated prominence in the early sixties, has lately shown signs of reaching some condition of impasse or exhaustion. The high claims of its initial publicity have not been fulfilled, and although it has attracted talents as diversely original as John Barth, Joseph Heller, Thomas Pynchon, Bruce Jay Friedman, and Donald Barthelme, these writers continue to seem notable more for their potential than for their clearly major distinction. The movement has also been compromised by the accumulation around it of a small army of camp followers, clowns, and pitchmen, who have apparently seen in it a chance to cash in on their mediocrity through emulation of their betters, and who have busied themselves perverting the styles of Black Humor into affectations, and affectations into platitudes.

From the beginning the movement has had considerably more than its share of critical attention because it appeared to be a development toward imaginative revitalization of a form that had long been moribund, the form of novelistic satire and self-parody, and because it seemed to promise some renewal of relationship between fiction and the actualities of the social world, a relationship which had grown so tenuous in the forties and fifties that vast sectors of the reading public eagerly mistook the erotic voyeurisms of John O'Hara for penetrating insights into the sociology of American life.

But it has gradually become evident that the promises which critics discovered in Black Humor were projections more of their own hopes than of creative possibilities actually present in the movement itself. For just as Black Humor has all along been characterized by a kind of fashionableness achieved without passing through any of the arduous stages of slow arrival and gradual acceptance, so it has quickly ossified into one more cliché of anti-cliché, one more casualty of the instantly assimilative and accommodative processes of our culture. As has happened with so much post-avant-garde art, there seems to have been only the briefest interval between the time when Black Humor was recognized as an important innovative gesture and the time when it was absorbed into style and decor and became nearly indistinguishable from the advertising gimmicks and promotional techniques which have so often been the rightful objects of its horror. The pose or stance of the Black Humorist soon became as familiar and predictable and as falsely provocative as the set of a *Vogue* mannequin's thighs. Suddenly, it seemed capable of registering only the histrionics of a ritual angst, a merely ornamental, because creatively unearned, absurdity, a sleek couturier note of apocalypse.

Yet it was in the nature of Black Humor to be peculiarly susceptible to this kind of debasement. Even at its best it always verged perilously on the sick joke, the nightclub wisecrack, the pop art slapstick of the comic-strip cartoon. Its characteristic humor was often more black-face than black, and the ubiquitous Catch-22 of its satire seemed too flip and feeble, and above all too *good-natured*, a mockery of the insidious workings of bureaucratic conspiracy. In fact, the most crippling weakness of Black Humor was that it cut itself off from the vital source of effective satire—the close observation of the social and political world—just because it was too easily horrified by the grotesqueness and complexity of that world, and so found it less painful to retreat into cuteness than to endure and create the true dark comedy of contemporary anguish. In its programmatic preoccupation with the sickness, the absurdity, the incomprehensibility of events, it abdicated its responsibility to deal coherently with events. The result was that, except in a very few cases, such as Barth's *The Sot-Weed Factor* and Friedman's *Stern*, the prime requirement of successful satire was never fulfilled by Black Humor writers: the living reality of the object or condition being satirized was too obliquely suggested in their work or was altogether missing from it.

It has often been argued in defense of Black Humor that fiction in our time has lost the possibility of making this social connection because the events of the social world have become themselves fictitious. Life not only imitates fiction but assimilates to itself the fiction-making functions, so that the happenings reported on any day in the newspapers will in effect outimagine the creative mind and thus cheat it of its revelatory and prophetic powers. But this would seem to suggest that fiction is best produced in dull ages, and the history of literature indicates that just the opposite is true. Rather, it seems to be the case that contemporary experience has so anesthetized us to the impact of grotesque and appalling occurrences that we no long-

er believe they can have any connection with, or any power to influence, the course of individual destiny or the drama of our hermetically personal consciousness. We have suffered a paralysis or eclipse of imagination before the nightmare of history in this age. Hence, we cannot imagine a fictional rationale in which events might be interpreted meaningfully in relation to the self. Our only recourse seems to be to fantasize the feelings of dislocation which obsess the self, or project images which convey, however incoherently, our sense of moral and emotional trivialization in the face of events.

Of the Black Humor writers whose work represents some expression of, or adjustment to, this dilemma, Donald Barthelme is in many ways the most interesting because he has the talent and intelligence occasionally to overcome its worst effects. A few stories in both his first volume, *Come Back, Dr. Caligari*, and this new book brilliantly demonstrate the power of sheer creative imagination to make the vital connection between satire and the social world. Barthelme's recurrent theme is precisely the trivialization of contemporary life and consciousness, and in these few stories he is able to dramatize his sense of that trivialization within the context of living fact and event which created it. But there is a vast distance between the stories which succeed in this way and the many others which are victimized by the fallacy of imitative form, in which dislocation is expressed through dislocation, and trivialization through trivia, to the amusement and edification of nobody. These stories strike one as exercises in free association and automatic writing or as descriptions of bad dreams jotted down in the middle of the night for the benefit of one's analyst, and some of them sound as though they had been begun in the hope that of their own accord, through the sheer act of being written, they would eventually discover their subject and meaning.

Reading them is like finding oneself adrift in a sea of orbiting psychic garbage. Punctured beer cans, potato peelings, gnawed apple cores, squashed toothpaste tubes, stringy hanks of some dubious-looking viscous material float around and seemingly through one, always in the same fixed relation to oneself and everything else, and always somehow impenetrable because one is so completely penetrated by them. The stories are quite literally verbal immersions in dreck, the evacuated crud and muck of contemporary life, and they very effectively dramatize the sensations of being suffocated and shat upon and generally soiled and despoiled in soul and mind which accompany our daily experience of contemporary life. But they do not dramatize the cultural, political, or historical circumstances which give use to these sensations, nor do they end in a satirical or even a specific thematic formulation. Everything is offered in dead pan and with the mechanical iterativeness of items recited from a grocery list. Everything is offered, but somehow finally nothing is given.

The effect is actually very much like that of some of the New Wave films which introduce the viewer to an experience through a process of such total saturation in trivial details that it is often impossible to tell which detail or episode is supposed to be more important than some other, hence impossible to detect the thematic principle which finally binds the details together into meaning. One always suspects the artist of suggesting that he does not really know what he intends the depicted experience to mean, and so will leave it to us to decide for ourselves. In such a case, we are obliged, as Virginia Woolf once said, to do the artist's imagining for him, and while that may be a kindness to him, it is no help whatever to the cause of art.

Barthelme appears to be indictable on the same charge. Over and over in his stories he seems to be inviting us to take over the job of bringing into focus some idea which has eluded his powers of imaginative resolution. For example, in this new volume the story called "Edward and Pia" apparently has to do with an American expatriate and his Scandinavian mistress and the emptiness of their existence in Europe. The characters move apathetically through a horizontal succession of experiences, none of which is distinguished from any other in the slightest way, presumably because they are all equally without meaning and value. We learn that Edward and Pia went to Sweden, that Pia was pregnant, that in London they had seen *Marat/Sade* at the Aldwych Theater, that Edward and Pia walked the streets of Amsterdam and were hungry, that they went to the cinema to see an Eddie Constantine picture, that on Sunday Edward went to the bakery and bought bread, that Edward and Pia went to Berlin on the train, that Edward received a letter from London, that Edward looked in the window of the used radio store and it was full of used radios, that Edward put his hands on Pia's breasts, that the nipples were the largest he had ever seen. Then he counted his money. He had two hundred and forty crowns. And so on and on and on.

All this is undoubtedly redolent of the trivialization of life in our time, and it may well be an attempt to say something about the form of spiritual death that accompanies the atrophy of all sane responses to life and all hopes of finding causal relationships within experience. But it comes through most clearly as an example of imagination succumbing to the trivia which is its material.

There may even be some justice in the thought that such benumbed recitations of detail are intended to be viewed as if they were being enacted under the outraged eye of the cosmos, and we are meant to hear rumbling behind it all the distant thunder of the archangelic armies advancing to bring down upon us the terrible wrath of God. But as Auden saw, even during such a cosmic occurrence as the crucifixion, dogs go placidly on with their doggy life, and "the expensive delicate ship that must have seen something amazing," the fall of Brueghel's Icarus into the sea, "had somewhere to get to and sailed calmly on."

It would appear that the cosmic and the apocalyptic, whether in art or in life, cannot be dramatized directly, cannot meaningfully stand alone. They can finally be understood only in terms of their simple and probably ironical relationship to the doggy life and the very real people sailing away on that ship. It is the task of fiction continually to reaffirm this relationship. Or, in an age such as ours, fiction may be obliged to reinvent it. For between the crucifixion and the doggy life, between our grandiose visions of doom and the specific creature experiences which embody them, there now lies a chasm which only the best talent and intelligence can hope to bridge. It takes little of either simply to say that the chasm is there and then to laugh at its existence. We know it is there, and the knowledge has long ago ceased to amuse.—JOHN W. ALDRIDGE, "Dance of Death," *At*, July 1968, pp. 89–91

An illustration of postmodernism's love-hate relationship with its cultural precursors is found in Donald Barthelme's *Snow White*, one of the postmodernist works that is most skillful in its deployment of the literary past in a subversive way. A passage from the novel helps show how Barthelme assimilates aspects of modernism so as parodically to undermine them:

> "Try to be a man about whom nothing is known,"
> our father said, when we were young. Our father said
> several other interesting things, but we have forgotten
> what they were. . . . Our father was a man about
> whom nothing was known. Nothing is known about

him still. He gave us the recipes. He was not very interesting. A tree is more interesting. A suitcase is more interesting. A canned good is more interesting.

Barthelme here parodies the advice which Henry James had offered to the aspiring fiction writer: "Try to be one of the people on whom nothing is lost." Barthelme inverts the assumptions about character, psychology, and the authority of the artist upon which James, the "father" of the modernist "recipe" for the novel, had depended. In postmodernist fiction, character, like external reality, is something "about which nothing is known," lacking in plausible motive or discoverable "depth." Language forfeits its traditional power to render experience significantly, and meaning itself, as we have seen, comes to be regarded with a mixture of distrust and boredom. James had stressed the importance of artistic selection and ordering, defining as the chief obligation of the novelist that he so order his material as to "be interesting." Barthelme subverts these Jamesian principles by introducing a law of equivalence according to which nothing is intrinsically more "interesting" than anything else. Such a logic destroys the determinacy of artistic selection and elevates canned goods to equal status with human moral choice as legitimate artistic subject matter.

In place of James' earnest dedication to his craft, Barthelme assumes an irreverent stance toward his own work, conceding the arbitrary and artificial nature of what he creates. Literature retracts any Jamesian claims to deal "seriously" with the world and reverts—for quite different reasons—to the kind of open confessions of the artificial, make-believe status of the novel which so annoyed James in his reading of Thackeray and Trollope. The writer's very inability to transcend the solipsism of his perception and the circularity of his medium determines both his subject-matter and his structural principles.—GERALD GRAFF, "The Myth of the Postmodernist Breakthrough," *Tri-Quarterly*, Winter 1973, pp. 400–401

The best examples of Barthelme's pure collage stories are collected in *Guilty Pleasures*, as "pretexts for the pleasure of cutting up and pasting together pictures, a secret vice gone public. Guilty pleasures are the best." In such works as "The Expedition" and "A Nation of Wheels" he parodies dead metaphors, but not as the story's sole point. Instead, Barthelme's graphic juxtapositions and clever captioning put life back into dead words, in an amusing way (such as placing a mammoth tire at the end of a barricaded street, and commenting, "All defenses proved penetrable"; or advising "The secret police were everywhere," as a similar tire lurks in the bushes of Edouard Manet's "The Picnic"). Barthelme, like Frank O'Hara, defamiliarizes objects by presenting them in unusual contexts, apart from their anaesthetizing use by social and often commercial media. Whenever possible, he uses the media's own techniques, but always as an opportunity to "collage in" a more striking object of attention—such as when during a boring episode of *The Ed Sullivan Show* he substitutes something more exciting, a pornographic film spliced into the network cable by pranksters. Barthelme's practice does have a moral dimension, for as Frank O'Hara says, "The slightest loss of attention leads to death." But his real motive and achievement has been to replace an inferior work of art with a better one.

The writer is judged not by what he has said but by what he has made. Barthelme's constructions follow the principles of collage, and are aided by the theory of abstract expressionist art. Its canvas becomes Barthelme's page; we admire the push and pull of energies he has created on that page, by juxtaposing the words of technocrats with poets, or the inventions of Goodyear and Goodrich with the paintings of Manet. A good word-

collage story is "Porcupines at the University," written for the
New Yorker in 1970 and later collected in *Amateurs*. Unlike
some of the stories from *City Life* which troubled Schickel and
Kazin, "Porcupines" deals with a simple and recognizable
world. The university seems like an actual university, and the
porcupines behave like real porcupines. Barthelme's reshaping
of the familiar minority student story by changing "blacks" to
"porcupines" serves as ironic commentary, and also manages
to tell the story in a fresh and appealing manner. On this level
his achievement is no less conventional than Bernard Malamud's in "The Jewbird," where the tired situation of a smelly
old uncle living with a younger family is revitalized by casting
the old man as a talking bird. In these terms, the criteria Kazin
used to judge Barthelme as a bad writer can be turned around
to Barthelme's benefit.

But "Porcupines at the University" does so much more.
Beyond the ironic commentary is the simple fun of seeing what
happens when a number of unlike things—cowboys, porcupines, academic deans—are mixed together in a closed environment (or "frame," as we should say for the collagist). And
beyond any moral judgment Barthelme might make on the
legitimacy of student protest versus academic resistance is his
artistic achievement in holding together so many dissimilar
things, so that, despite all their wild disparities, they create a
model of a more coherent order than we are likely to find in the
quotidian world. Barthelme's skill as a collagist makes his artifice hold together. All elements in his construction are true to
their own roles. The Dean speaks in character (" 'And now the
purple dusk of twilight time/Steals across the meadows of my
heart,' the Dean said"), and when confronted by the scout
("Porcupines! . . . Thousands and thousands of them. Three
miles down the road and comin' fast!") reacts like a Dean
("Maybe they won't enroll"). Later on, the cowboys wrangling
the herd act their parts, debating whether to "vamoose" or
"parley" with the heavily armed Dean. . . .

The Dean tries to dodge the porcupines' situation by manipulating language. He has nothing against porcupines, he
implies; it's just that "We don't have *facilities* for four or five
thousand porcupines." His wife suggests, "They could take
Alternate Life Styles." But again it isn't Barthelme's motive to
tell his readers something they already know, that in the 1960s
some college administrators were callous toward minority students. Instead, he shows us things we may have forgotten: how
words themselves take on bogus meanings, how certain scenes
are so familiar that we no longer see them until something
noteworthy is dropped in their midst. As Frank O'Hara insisted, "a painting is a sheer extension, not a window or a door;
collage is as much about paper as about form . . . a sensual
interest in materials comes first." By emphasizing objects
rather than meaning, Barthelme can have the porcupines be
porcupines, cattle, and students all at the same time. In terms
of metaphor, the tenor fades away and we are left with the
materials of pure vehicle. The reader then participates with
Barthelme in his push and pull of juxtapositions; instead of
telling us something obviously apparent, he takes us through
his own process of awakening and rediscovery.

Barthelme's stories which do not incorporate distinct
graphic or verbal collages still rely on words and images as
objects, much as they would be used by a collagist. The best
examples of these are collected in *Sadness* which includes stories Barthelme has identified as parts of an aborted novel, and
which are the closest yet he has come to social mimesis. "Critique de la Vie Quotidienne," a story completely concerned
with the quotidian world, actually has the same structure as the
highly experimental and almost fully abstract "Sentence" from

City Life. Each uses overly long sentences—several pages at a
time in the former, and eight full pages in the latter. Barthelme
makes these long sentences bearable by the insertion of vividly
interesting nouns, verbs, and gerunds; "Sentence," which is
really about nothing other than a grammatical sentence working its way down one page and across to another, features a
panoply of objects (a wife on her way to the shower, an FM
radio playing rock music) such as would flatter the most mimetic of socially realistic stories. But Barthelme's story is not mimetic, or even referential; it is simply a sentence. . . .

Just as film and abstract modes of art redirected the visual
aesthetics of art earlier in this century, Barthelme's word-
collages are changing the aesthetics of fiction. But there are
sources for what Barthelme is doing: his manner of making
graphic collages is partly dependent upon Max Ernst, who in
turn published an entire graphic-collage novel (something
Barthelme has not yet attempted) in 1934, *Une Semaine de
Bonté*. The seven sections of this "surrealistic novel in collage"
follow the days of the week, one of the simplest patterns for
narrative fiction. And the materials of Ernst's collages are likewise recognizable from the real world. But these were only his
starting materials. From engravings of nineteenth-century sentimental scenes, fantasy creations of graphic artists, gargoyles,
animals, and natural elements Ernst composed a narrative of
objects, none referring to anything but itself. And as Barthelme
proposes for his own art, Ernst's product became "an *itself*," a
new reality which by its defamiliarization process threw the
reality of the daily world into higher relief. Barthelme may not
proceed exactly in this direction, for Ernst did not use a single
word. Barthelme's goal is to create similar objects, but with the
stricter discipline of using language. Applying the aesthetics of
collage to the linguistic signifiers of our culture is his means of
reaching this goal.

But there is a source beyond Max Ernst: the American
artist, Joseph Cornell. Because Ernst's collage depends so
heavily upon dynamic and kinetic juxtaposition, upon the
viewer's impelled movement from one unlikely element to the
next, some critics have insisted that collage is in fact a linear
art. By extension, the argument could run full circle: that the
elements of Barthelme's compositions are fragmentary, and
that his end products do not cohere. The works of Joseph
Cornell, however, are executed in the form of boxes, which
contain objects more romantically suggestive (even symbolic)
than comic. Dore Ashton has demonstrated how Cornell's intention derives from the romantics and symbolists, and how his
assemblages are meant to suggest moments of mystical configuration, capturing magical connections within such personally familiar objects as clay pipes, stamps, and train schedules.
The results cannot be read linearly—the connections work
only in a spatial sense.

The novelist Steve Katz has made his own Cornell-like
construction from instances of the number "43," and explains
the use of such petty examples of common magic (including
astrology and the like): "These systems are tools useful to help
you yourself arrive at a description of reality, but as soon as you
depend on the system itself for the answers, start looking *at* it
rather than *through* it, there begins to form a cataract of dogma
over your perception of things as they are." The very zaniness
of Cornell's choice of objects precludes taking them seriously
for themselves; and by emphasizing the idiosyncratic in their
choice, he makes their importance personal, rather than
systematic. There may be real connections somewhere, beyond
our reach; indeed, when things happen in coincidence, we feel
happy—as Katz says, he is "grateful for a mysterious resonance
that sometimes occurs and illuminates."

The practical benefit? "It does seem relaxing to find that one of these systems works for us," Katz insists, "because suddenly certain of our responsibilities for ourselves are taken off our heads for the moment, and we can give up some anxieties and get high." That high, Katz shows, collapses when we respond to the system which produced it in any other than spatial fashion. Barthelme's fictions work the same way. To be perceived properly, they must be read as the art not of commentary, but of collage.—Jᴇʀᴏᴍᴇ Kʟɪɴᴋᴏᴡɪᴛᴢ, "Donald Barthelme's Art of Collage," *The Practice of Fiction in America*, 1980, pp. 107–13

LARRY McCAFFERY
From "Barthelme's *Snow White*:
The Aesthetics of Trash"
Critique, 1975, pp. 19–32

We are governed by words, the laws are graven in words, and literature is the sole means of keeping these words living and accurate—

(Ezra Pound)

The final possibility is to turn ultimacy, exhaustion, paralyzing self-consciousness and the adjective weight of accumulating history . . . to make something new and valid, the essence whereof would be the impossibility of making something new—

(John Barth)

What does a writer do when he thinks that language no longer communicates effectively, that words have lost their power to move us, that reality is no longer capable of sustaining mythic devices, that telling "stories" of any kind is suspect? Perhaps the most successful recent reply to these questions can be found in Donald Barthelme's *Snow White*, a work which seeks to exploit the decay of language and literature. Like so many other works of art in this century, *Snow White* has as its "subject matter" art itself. It is not the "real world" which it seeks to represent, but the status of art; and as with any significant work of art, we can learn something about ourselves if we respond to it. *Snow White* can, therefore, best be termed a "self-reflexive" work in that even as it is being created, it seeks to examine its own condition. Rooted deeply in a fundamental distrust of most of the conventional principles of fiction, the book also shows an understanding of Wittgenstein's famous distinction between what can be told and what can be shown. Not a description or theory of the conditions and limitations of language and literature, *Snow White* portrays these features in its very fabric.

In an essay describing the views held by many contemporary "literary pessimists," George Steiner stated that:

There is a widespread intimation, though as yet only vaguely defined, of a certain exhaustion of verbal resources in modern civilization, of a brutalization and devaluation of the word, in the mass cultures and mass politics of the age. . . . It is grounded in historical circumstance, in a late stage of linguistic and formal civilization in which the expressive achievements of the past seem to weigh exhaustively on the possibilities of the present, in which word and genre seem tarnished, flattened to the touch, like coin too long in circulation.[1]

Obviously, the problems faced by a writer who accepts the notion of the "brutalization and devaluation of the word" are

enormous. Essentially, three courses are open to such a writer: he may, like Rimbaud (and to an extent, like Beckett), choose the suicidal rhetoric of silence; he may, like Ishmael Reed, William Gass, and Robert Coover, attempt to revitalize the word and call for strategies which can replenish the power and poetry of language—such pleas have been issued by a variety of writers in the last two centuries: by Wordsworth, by Whitman, by the French Symbolists, by Eliot, by the surrealists; and, finally, the writer may adopt the strategy of self-consciously incorporating the decayed, brutalized elements into his own particular idiom and make the new idiom part of his point. Such strategy is employed by Celine, by Burroughs, and by Barthelme in *Snow White*.

Although 180 pages in length, *Snow White* is not so much a novel as a sustained collection of fragments, organized loosely around the Snow White fairy tale in what resembles a "collage" method. Barthelme's rendition of the myth is, of course, peculiarly modern. As Richard Gilman has said:

. . . the tale is here refracted through the prism of a contemporary sensibility so that it emerges broken up into fragments, shards of its original identity, of its historical career in our consciousness . . . and of its recorded or potential uses for sociology and psychology.[2]

Thus, like Joyce in *Ulysses*, and like a significant number of recent writers,[3] Barthelme has turned to a familiar myth (rather than to "reality") to provide a basic framework for his tale, although the "material" which he places into the framework is drawn from a wide range of literary and cultural sources.

Despite its mythic framework, *Snow White* is likely to leave an initial impression of shapelessness on the reader. As in *Ulysses* and works by writers of encyclopedic tendencies (Nabokov, Pynchon, and Borges), *Snow White* presents us with a profusion of bits and pieces, both high and low, drawn from books and other literary storing houses (folk tales, myths, newspapers, advertisements). Often Barthelme incorporates into his work the sorts of events, names, fads, and data which can be found in the daily newspaper. Even more often, however, these fragments are drawn from cliches of learning—hackneyed opinions dressed up in even more hackneyed styles. We find, for example, parodies of specific literary styles and conventions, pseudolearned digressions about history, sociology, and psychology, mock presentations of Freudian and existentialist patterns, and inane concrete poems. Barthelme's use of the heterogeneous mixture of learning and verbal trash does not contribute to any verisimilar design but communicates a sense of what it is like to be alive at a given moment.[4]

If we examine the structure of *Snow White* more closely, we find that, unlike Joyce in *Ulysses*, Barthelme's mythic perspective is prevented from being seriously mythic to any extent. The big problem for Barthelme—as for any writer today who wishes to rely on myth in one way or another—is a self-consciousness about myth that has reached such paralyzing proportions that most contemporary use of myth is overtly self-conscious and is employed primarily for comic purposes.[5] We find exactly this sense of a writer manipulating myth for his own comic or parodic purposes in *Snow White*. Indeed, in many respects the book seems to be deliberately mocking Joyce's painstaking efforts at creating mythic parallels, suggesting perhaps that the condition of both language and reality make such devices unavailable to the modern writer.

With the example of *Ulysses* in mind, we can find parallels between the events and characters in Barthelme's *Snow White* and those of the "historical version" of the fairy tale (appropriately enough, Barthelme relies almost as much on the

Disney movie as on the Grimms' original). The "action" of the story often twists and halts unexpectedly, but eventually it fulfills the basic situation of the fairy tale as follows: Snow White, now twenty-two and beautiful, has grown tired of the words she always hears and has rebelled by writing a dirty poem. She is presently living with seven men (the dwarf figures) who daily sally forth ("Heigh-ho") "to fill the vats and wash the buildings"[6] of a Chinese food factory. Concerned about her promiscuity (she copulates with her roommates daily in the shower room), Snow White has rationalized that they only add up to two "real men" (hence their "dwarfishness"). Later on, the rest of the familiar cast is completed with the appearance of Jane, a young woman who is the witch-figure, and Paul, the Prince for whom Snow White is waiting. While Jane begins to spin her wicked web, Paul digs a bunker, sets up a dog-training program, and keeps watch over Snow White with a self-devised Distant Early Warning System—all designed to help him watch and eventually win her. Paul finally makes the fatal error of eating the "poisoned apple" himself (in this instance, a poisoned vodka Gibson), which the evil Jane has intended for Snow White. As the story concludes, Snow White is left to cast flowers on Paul's grave, and "revirginized," she rises into the sky.

One should quickly note that any summary is extremely misleading, for Barthelme is much more intent on creating his "collage effect" than on permitting a story-line to develop in any straightforward fashion. The progression of events in *Snow White* is, for example, continually interrupted by digressions, catalogues, lists, and seemingly gratuitous trivia. Each of the heterogeneous fragments is given its own individual section or "chapter," which is usually very short (they are rarely more than two pages long, and several are only one or two lines). Transitions between the sections are sketchy at best and often are entirely lacking; to establish a time scheme for the events in the book, for example, is quite impossible. Relying mainly on juxtaposition rather than the more usual novelistic principle of transition to achieve its effects, Barthelme's apparent intent in bringing together this collection of fragments in such a blatantly non-linear fashion is to create the verbal equivalent of a collage.

Aiding his collage effect, Barthelme switches the typography back and forth between conventional type and large black upper-case letters—much like silent-film titles. The titles seem to provide objective or authorial perspectives on the action—a technique used, for example, by Dos Passos and more recently by Julio Cortazar in *Hopskotch*. This device, however, is also being used self-consciously, so that the "authorial insights" are themselves parodies, as in the following banal and inconsequential asides:

PAUL: A FRIEND OF THE FAMILY

PAUL HAS NEVER BEFORE REALLY
SEEN SNOW WHITE AS A WOMAN

Likewise, the "background sections" typically turn out to be cliched, scholarly-sounding assessments—sometimes attributed to specific writers but usually not—of literature, history, or psychology:

THE SECOND GENERATION OF ENGLISH
ROMANTICS INHERITED THE PROBLEMS
OF THE FIRST, BUT COMPLICATED BY THE
EVILS OF INDUSTRIALISM AND POLITICAL
REPRESSION. ULTIMATELY THEY
FOUND. . . .
THE VALUE THE MIND SETS ON EROTIC
NEEDS INSTANTLY SINKS AS SOON AS SAT-
ISFACTION BECOMES READILY AVAILABLE.

SOME OBSTACLE IS NECESSARY TO SWELL
THE TIDE OF THE LIBIDO TO ITS
HEIGHT. . . .

At other times, the passages seem to trail off into total incoherency, as when the following neatly centered list of words appears:

EBONY
EQUANIMITY
ASTONISHMENT
TRIUMPH
VAT
DAX
BLAGUE

Such digression and irrelevancies, of course, considerably impede the narrative of the book and prevent Barthelme from relying on conventional tension, development, and plot. For Barthelme, the formal structures belong to a previous literature, the product of a defunct reality. Indeed, even the characters in *Snow White* seem to be openly conspiring to refuse to cooperate with our expectations. Since for Barthelme the changes in modern society make the holding of any mythic center impossible, we find that the mythic parallels in *Snow White* follow only up to certain points, and then find appropriate alterations. The characters openly defy their traditional roles and undercut nearly all our expectations about them.

Like every other literary device in the book, the characters themselves are parodies of their archetypes, uniformly flat and almost comic-bookish in nature. Any sense of their actual identities is minimal and the whole realistic notion of developing a history or background for them is ignored. The book is almost devoid of the sort of details usually provided by novelists to help "realize" the action in their stories. Thus, the name of the city, physical descriptions of the characters or settings, indications of a daily routine—all are left out. Any background information provided is usually obscure and serves to mock and defeat our expectations. Of the dwarfs' background, for example, we know virtually nothing except that they were all born in various National Forests. Of their father we are told: "Our father was a man about whom nothing was known. Nothing is known about him still. He gave us the recipes. He was not very interesting. A tree is more interesting. A suitcase is more interesting. A canned good is more interesting." Since we are given no physical descriptions, no backgrounds, and no idiosyncratic traits, we can "know" the characters only through the words they speak—and even here only minimal distinctions are made. Indeed, at times the dwarfs seem to have a difficult time identifying even each other: "'That's true, Roger,' Kevin said a hundred times. Then he was covered with embarrassment. 'No, I mean that's true, Clem. Excuse me. Roger is somebody else. You're not Roger, You're Clem. That's true, Clem.'"

What does manage to emerge from the blurred personalities of the dwarfs is that they are literally made up out of our society's stock provisions of psychological afflictions, jealousies, introspections, and cliched opinions. On the other hand, they are obviously grotesquely unsuited for the unselfconscious, selfless service required of them in the myth.

Even more unsuited is Paul, whose princely role is to rescue Snow White from her captivity with the dwarfs and save her from the murderous intentions of the witch-like Jane. But Paul is destined to be defeated in both his attempts, apparently doomed by the conditions of contemporary life which make sustaining the archetype which Paul should embody impossible. The type of figure Paul should be, Barthelme suggests, has been driven underground—or into parody—by the neuroses and self-consciousness facing all modern men. From the beginning, Paul (who, in keeping with the current demand for princes, is receiving unemployment compensation) is concerned about the implications which Snow White's appearance has for his own life; he seems to sense immediately that involvement with her will impose on him duties and obligations—responsibilities he is not certain he can fulfill. Thus, after he has seen Snow White suggestively hanging her black hair out of the window, Paul remarks:

> It has made me terribly nervous, that hair. It was beautiful, I admit it. . . . Yet it has made me terribly nervous. Why some innocent person might come along, and see it, and conceive it his duty to climb up, and discern the reason it is being hung out of that window. There is probably some girl attached to the top, and with her responsibilities of sorts.

Paul's response to these obligations is to flee, although he retains considerable awareness of the implications of his actions. He realizes, for example, that conditions in today's society militate against true "princeliness." In rationalizing his decision to hide in a monastery in western Nevada, Paul considers the lack of opportunity for heroic action today:

> If I had been born well prior to 1900, I could have ridden with Pershing against Pancho Villa. Alternatively, I could have ridden with Villa against the landowners and corrupt government officials of the time. In either case I could have had a horse. How little opportunity there is for young men to have personally owned horses in the bottom half of the 20th century! A wonder that we U. S. youth can still fork a saddle at all.

After brief sojourns in France as a music instructor and in Rome as a member of the Italian Post Office, Paul decides to abandon his efforts at princely evasion. Like many of modern literature's comically conceived anti-heroes, Paul is totally incapable of responding naturally to any situation because his decision-making process has been encrusted by the sludge of literary and cultural conventions. Rather than meeting his challenges directly, Paul vacillates, mediates, and filters his responses. Comically, he digs a bunker outside of Snow White's house and installs an observation system which includes mirrors and dogs attached to wires. When the moment of crisis arrives, bungling Paul drinks the poisoned vodka Gibson intended for Snow White; muttering banalities to the very end—"This drink is vaguely exciting, like a film by Leopoldo Torre Nilsson," Paul dies "with green foam coming out of his face." So much for Prince Charming.

Snow White, meanwhile, has patiently been waiting for reluctant Paul to complete his duties. As she explains to one of her anxious wooers:

> But this love must not be, because of your blood. . . . I must hold myself in reserve for a prince or a prince-figure, someone like Paul. I know that Paul has not looked terribly good up to now and in fact I despise him utterly. Yet he has the blood of kings and cardinals in his veins.

As Paul soon demonstrates, Snow White is overestimating the ability of royal blood to produce a contemporary prince-figure. We may question whether such concepts as "royal blood," "princeliness," and "heroic action" were viable in any age, but literature (including history books) has conditioned us to think otherwise. We are led, like Snow White, to react to Paul through these filtered, largely literary stereotypes. As Snow White realizes, the fault may not lie so much in Paul as in our own unrealistic expectations of him: "Paul is a frog. He is frog

through and through. . . . So I am disappointed. Either I have overestimated Paul, or I have overestimated history."

The obvious suggestion is that reality can no longer sustain the values needed to create either a hero-figure or the proper ending to a fairy tale. Snow White is doomed to future disappointments because heroes are now created only in movies and books—and even here they are found less and less because reality is losing its capacity to support fictions of this kind. Consequently, we have to content ourselves with media-produced substitutes. Speaking of the dwarfs, Snow White says:

> The seven of them only add up to the equivalent of about two real men, as we know them from the films and from our childhood, when there were giants on the earth. It is possible, of course, that there are no more real men here, on this ball of half-truths, the earth, that would be a disappointment. One would have to content oneself with the subtle falsity of color films of happy love affairs, made in France, with a Mozart score.

In many respects, we are expected to share Snow White's realization as we respond to Barthelme's book: our expectations, built by previous encounters with literature, are destined to be left unsatisfied. If we are, like Snow White, disappointed with this prospect, we have overestimated language (since it can no longer communicate effectively) and reality (since it no longer produces the kinds of heroes, logical progressions, and predictable feelings which are the stuff of the traditional novel).

If we turn now to the central question of the role of language in Barthelme's book, we find that, more than anything else, the book seems to be "about" the condition of language and the possibilities which exist today for a writer to communicate something meaningful to his readers. Throughout the book a variety of very topical subjects are brought up: the Vietnam war, crowded street conditions, air pollution, political corruption. But as Gilman has observed, "the novel isn't about these things, not about their meaning or even their phenomenological appearance. It is about their status in the imagination."[7] Barthelme is, therefore, not so much interested in using such material for satiric analysis as he is in seeing how such things have affected the public consciousness, especially in the way that consciousness is reflected in language. *Snow White*, then, deals steadily with the problems of its own composition, often analyzing itself as it moves forward—all the while mocking our interpretations and attempts at making "outer referents."

At times this anticipatory mocking has quite specific targets. As Barthelme is aware, our reaction to any work of fiction is influenced by a variety of literary and critical suppositions. Readers, as well as writers, have become so self-conscious about literary and critical conventions that writers have difficulty in creating anything which is not already a cliche. Having accepted this fact, Barthelme has some fun with it. Like Nabokov, for example, Barthelme takes special delight in poking fun at the Freudians. At times we are presented passages so teasingly Freudian that they slip over into parodic self-commentaries, as the following:

WHAT SNOW WHITE REMEMBERS:
THE HUNTSMAN
THE FOREST
THE STEAMING KNIFE

In other situations, the characters themselves either anticipate our probable interpretations of what is happening or create their own interpretation. One of the dwarfs, for example, says of the women they watch while they are at work, "We are very much tempted to shoot our arrows into them, those targets. You know what that means." And, of course, we do. Not surprisingly, Snow White is very much aware of the literary significance of letting down her hair from the window: "This motif, the long hair streaming from the high window, is a very ancient one I believe, found in many cultures, in various forms. Now I recapitulate it, for the astonishment of the vulgar and the refreshment of my venereal life." Bill, the most self-conscious dwarf, is also the book's most expert symbol hunter, at times even anticipating the potential sources on which readers might rely to give "meaning" to a scene. When Bill notices the long black hair hanging out of the apartment window, he asks himself whose hair it might be: "This distasteful answer is already known to me, as is the significance of this act, this hanging, as well as the sexual significance of the hair itself, on which Wurst has written. I don't mean that he has written *on* the hair, but rather about it." This kind of talent and knowledge proves to be quite useless for Bill, just as similar efforts on our part would be. In this instance, Bill's awareness of the variety of meaning he can attribute to Snow White's actions in no way helps him decide what to do about them, for as he soon admits, "It is Snow White who has taken this step, the meaning of which is clear to all of us . . . in the meantime, here is the hair, with its multiple meanings. What am I to do about it?"

In terms of its self-analysis, even more evident than the mocking of our interpretations are the many digressions about language, including discussions of the language of *Snow White* itself. Like the fiction of Barth and Borges, *Snow White* embodies in form as well as content the difficulties of writing in the modern age. One such "self-discussion" occurs when Dan presents a Borgesian (Klipschorn?) discussion about the nature of language:

> You know, Klipschorn was right I think when he spoke of the "blanketing" effect of ordinary language, referring, as I recall, to the part that sort of, you know, "fills in" between the other parts. That part, the "filling" you might say, of which the expression "you might say" is a good example, is to me the most interesting part, and of course it might also be called the "stuffing" I suppose, and there is probably also, in addition, some other word that would do as well, to describe it, or maybe a number of them. . . . The "endless" aspect of "stuffing" is that it goes on and on, and in fact, our exchanges are in large measure composed of it, in larger measure even, perhaps than they are composed of that which is not "stuffing."

Barthelme, of course, is a master of creating exactly the sort of "filling" and "stuffing" that Dan is talking about—he is, as Dan later says, "on the leading edge of the trash phenomena." Like Pinter, Beckett, and Ionesco, Barthelme exhibits a continual interest in the linguistic idiosyncrasies and banalities which people use to express themselves—and which have made the creation of literature and even communication of any sort increasingly difficult. When the "language machine" begins to "run idle" (Wittgenstein), not only do people become increasingly more isolated, but writers of any kind find that they can take nothing for granted. Thus, the narration of *Snow White* is frequently interrupted so that Barthelme can explain the specific meaning of words or phrases which might be confusing or misleading. When Barthelme describes Henry's process of examining his weaknesses as "weaknesses pinched out of the soul's ecstasy one by one," he becomes worried about our possible objections to the metaphor and explains himself. Here, as elsewhere, when he speaks with his own voice, the tone has the flat, elevated ring of a scholarly

essay which is exactly suited for the mock treatment he is presenting:

> Of course "ecstasy" is being used here in a very special sense, as misery, something that would be in German one of three aspects of something called the *Lumpwelt* in some such sentence as "The *Inmittenness* of the *Lumpwelt* is a turning toward misery." So that what is meant here by ecstasy is something on the order of "fit," but a kind of slow one, perhaps a semi-arrested one that is divisable by three.

Another indication given that language is not functioning properly can be found in certain passages which lose direction and slide into pure irrelevancies. The digressive method is not the one found, say, in *Tristram Shandy*, for it is not based on an associational logic and does not "lead anywhere." A certain passage will begin with fairly ordinary, novelistic intentions (providing clarification, additional description) and then uncontrollably begin to wander off into regions of "pure blague." The following discussion of Bill by one of his fellow dwarfs demonstrates the method quite well. After learning that Bill is absent "tending the vats," we have an apparent digression about his clothes turn into a random selection of verbal garbage:

> Bill's new brown monkscloth pajamas, made for him by Paul should be here next month. The grade of pork ears we are using in the Baby Ding Sam Dew is not capable of meeting U. S. Government standards, or indeed, any standards. Our man in Hong Kong assures us, however, that the next shipment will be superior. Sales nationwide are brisk, brisk, brisk. The pound is weakening. The cow is calving. The cactus wants watering. The new building is abuilding with leases covering 45 percent of the rentable space already in hand. The weather tomorrow, fair and warmer.

Problems with language are even more apparent in certain sections in which broken and incomplete thoughts and sentences strain to become "realized" but manage to appear only in incomplete, syntactically fractured fragments. The method, which has some obvious affinities with Beckett's later writing and with Burroughs' "cut-up" technique, sometimes uses ellipses to separate widely different thoughts. Possibly we are to assume that what is being left out is not worth being printed in its entirety.

Finally, the most pervasive way in which Barthelme demonstrates the bankruptcy of language and literary traditions is the more familiar approach of parodying well-known styles and methods. Like the "Oxen of the Sun" section of *Ulysses*, *Snow White* is created out of a variety of narrative styles traceable to specific literary sources; in addition, allusions to these works, some direct and others veiled, are everywhere and serve to reinforce the reflexive nature of the work. Often the short sections of the book are created from a hodge-podge of styles, modulating rapidly between specific literary parodies (Stendhal, Rimbaud, Shakespeare, Lorenz Hart, Burroughs), current slang, academic cliche, and advertising jargon. The style, whatever its source, is usually wholly inappropriate to the subject at hand: an eloquent sermon is delivered against "buffalo music," a learned commentary is presented on "The Horsewife in Modern Society."

The reversals and incongruities in Barthelme's *Snow White* should probably remind us of the difficulties involved when *any* writer attempts to express reality. At the same time, we should recognize in its strange mixture of styles, irrelevancies, and cliches something familiar—for *Snow White* is literally created out of the trashy, too-familiar words we have around us every day. The first words spoken by Snow White are, "Oh, I wish there were some words in the world that were not the words I always hear!" Barthelme's book attempts to create new art out of these same words and in the process it exploits the very nature of the debased condition into which language and story-telling have fallen. Steadily it places before us the questions of what resources are left to language, what power to words, images, and stories to move us. Unprincely Paul's solution to these problems is to retreat into the silence indicated by the ellipsis which concludes the following: "I would wish to retract everything, if I could, so that the whole written world would be . . ." As we see in *Snow White*, however, Barthelme's solution is quite different.

Notes

1. George Steiner, "Silence and the Poet," *Language and Silence* (New York: Atheneum Press, 1967), p. 46.
2. Richard Gilman, "Donald Barthelme," *The Confusion of Realms* (London: Weidenfeld and Nicolson, 1970), p. 45.
3. A sampling of contemporary writers who are interested in mythic applications of this sort would probably include John Barth, Robert Coover, John Gardner, Thomas Pynchon, Ishmael Reed, Iris Murdoch, Thomas Berger, and John Seelye.
4. *Snow White* probably best fits under what Northrop Frye has termed the "anatomy" in his "Theory of Genres," *Anatomy of Criticism* (Princeton: Princeton Univ. Press, 1967), pp. 311–25.
5. Robert Scholes discusses the tendency in *The Fabulators* (New York: Oxford Univ. Press, 1967), especially in Barth's *Giles Goat Boy*.
6. Donald Barthelme, *Snow White* (New York: Bantam Books, 1968), p. 8.
7. Gilman, p. 50.

THOMAS M. LEITCH
From "Donald Barthelme and the End of the End"
Modern Fiction Studies, Spring 1982, pp. 129–43

Perhaps the most striking feature of Donald Barthelme's fiction is the number of things it gets along without. In Barthelme's fictive world, there appear to be no governing or shaping beliefs, no transcendent ideals or intimations, no very significant physical experience, no sense of place or community, no awareness on the part of his characters of any personal history or context of profession or family or, for the most part, personal relationships, no psychology of character, indeed no characters at all in the usual sense of the term, no guarantee, at the level of incident, of verisimilitude or of rational causality or of plot itself, no thickness of circumstantial detail which might make his world seem more densely realistic, and no considerable exploration of such themes as love, idealism, initiation, or death.

Of course, there are exceptions, or apparent exceptions, to each of these rules. "110 West Sixty-First Street" (in *Amateurs*[1]) concerns a precisely defined location. "Robert Kennedy Saved from Drowning" (*Unspeakable Practices, Unnatural Acts*) is a collection of episodes ostensibly intended to provide insight into the character of a politician named Robert Kennedy. "Florence Green Is 81" (*Come Back, Dr. Caligari*), like most of Barthelme's work, is full of sharply realistic, indeed photographic, detail. And *The Dead Father* is all about families, physical experience, and death. Each of these exceptions, however—and there are many others—is peculiarly suspect. We know from his title that Barthelme is writing about Robert Kennedy or 110 West Sixty-First Street, and to a certain degree

these stories depend on these identifications: "Abraham Lincoln Saved from Drowning" would be a profoundly different story, and the title "61 West 110th Street," changing only the neighborhood of New York, would make that story nonsense. But these identifications, however central, are curiously disengaged. "110 West Sixty-First Street" projects a contemporary urban consciousness without committing itself to any assertions about that particular address. Barthelme's Robert Kennedy is not only unrecognizable as the brother of the late President but made more remote rather than more accessible by Barthelme's brief episodes ("K. at His Desk," "Described by Secretaries," "Behind the Bar," and so on). Even *The Dead Father* is characterized by this sort of disengagement with its presumed subjects. The Dead Father speaks about his family: "Without children I would not be the Father. No Fatherhood without childhood. I never wanted it, it was thrust upon me" (p. 17). Barthelme describes a sexual rendezvous in similarly schematic terms:

> Cockalorum standing almost straight up but a bit of
>   wavering.
> Julie licks.
> Pleasure of Thomas. Movement of Thomas's hips.
> Julie lights cigarette.
> Thomas remains in Position A. (p. 159)

The laconic presentation indicates or designates an experience but pointedly declines to engage that experience as experience. In Barthelme, love, death, fatherhood, and Robert Kennedy are always ideas or objects, never experiences which engage emotional commitment.

For this reason it might be more accurate to say, not that Barthelme's stories are never about passion, idealism, and death, but that the word *about* has a special, narrowly focused meaning in Barthelme that makes his fiction unusually difficult to summarize. A summary of a story, say in a review article, normally describes the subject of the story. To describe Barthelme's stories by reference to their professed subjects, the things they are about, is possible but thoroughly misleading. "The Glass Mountain" (*City Life*) is about a man trying to climb the side of a glass mountain. "Cortés and Montezuma" (*Great Days*) is about the subjugation of the Mexican ruler by the Spanish conquistador. "The Temptation of St. Anthony" (*Sadness*) has a subject accurately defined by its title. In each case, however, an accurate summary is inadequate or misleading or simply irrelevant because it fails to describe the important ways in which Barthelme's stories elude the genres his subjects imply. "The Glass Mountain" is not, despite its subject, a fairy tale: it diverges at too many points from the rules for fairy tales. "Cortés and Montezuma" is not a historical anecdote, "The Temptation of St. Anthony" an exercise in hagiography, "Robert Kennedy Saved from Drowning" a political or personal profile. These stories could more aptly be described as parodies of the genres their subjects imply; the point is simply that the subjects themselves would give anyone who did not already know Barthelme's stories a false impression of them.

It might be objected here that summary gives a false impression of any story whatsoever, and to a certain extent this is no doubt true. But the summary of most fiction is likely to be a plot summary: in saying what a given story is about, we tend to recapitulate, or at least to suggest, the plot. "Young Goodman Brown" is about a man who has an intense experience of evil at a real or imagined witches' sabbath. "The Beast in the Jungle" is about a man who spends his entire life waiting for an experience to which he feels doomed. "A Good Man Is Hard to Find" is about the confrontation between a Georgia family, especially the grandmother of the family and an escaped convict. Each of these situations implies a plot that is itself expressive of the author's view of the world. Even on a higher plane of generalization, the respective situations—the equivocal role of the imagination in the perception of evil, the perils of well-bred but implacable egoism, the offering of grace in a moment of supreme physical and spiritual danger—each implies a plot, and, as Aristotle says of tragedy, "the incidents and the plot are the end [*telos*]" of the whole work. Aristotle contends that "the end is the chief thing of all,"[2] and this dictum holds for many dramatists and novelists, but not for Barthelme, whose fictive situations characteristically fail to imply any *telos* in the sense of coherent plot development. Barthelme's stories are organized around situations (or suppositions or hypotheses) that commit him to no particular line of narrative development, or indeed to the very conception of development. Having created in "Daumier" a character who escapes from his "insatiable" self by postulating or daydreaming "surrogates" who are "in principle satiable," Barthelme writes: "Now in his mind's eye which was open for business at all times . . . Daumier saw a situation" (*Sadness*, pp. 163, 164–65). The situation Daumier envisions—a surrogate Daumier acting as a scout for an expedition of *au pair* girls, threatened with capture by Jesuits, across "the plains and pampas of consciousness" (p. 164)—implies no particular line of development, and when the Jesuits eventually do capture the girls and lead them off to a convent, Daumier merely switches gears to another, "second person" (p. 178) surrogate.

"Daumier" provides an unusually full exposition of Barthelme's situational or suppositional narrative method, which might be described as the examination of manifold aspects of a given situation. All of Barthelme's stories might well have begun with *Suppose*. Suppose a thirty-five-year-old man were inadvertently placed in a sixth-grade class ("Me and Miss Mandible," *Come Back, Dr. Caligari*). Suppose a giant balloon appeared one night over Manhattan ("The Balloon," *Unspeakable Practices, Unnatural Acts*). Suppose a dog fell from a third- (or fourth-) floor window and landed on an artist passing below ("The Falling Dog," *City Life*). Suppose Edward Lear, foreseeing his death, turned it into a public event ("The Death of Edward Lear," *Great Days*). In nearly every case, the hypothetical situation, instead of being subjected to a single chosen line of development, is revolved or considered under different aspects, so that Barthelme's stories often seem to assume the form of meditations. Writers such as Hawthorne, James, and O'Connor tend to choose characteristic subjects: their stories are generally variations on a typical situation or theme. But thematic analysis is largely irrelevant to Barthelme's work because his situations are themselves arbitrary and haphazard: what is characteristic, instead of thematic development, is the tone of Barthelme's handling. However illogical, disruptive, or outrageous the situations are, they are always treated circumstantially, in the same deadpan tone. Stories such as "I Bought a Little City" and "The Captured Woman" (both in *Amateurs*) might have been titled "Some of the Unexpected Problems I Faced After Buying Galveston, Texas" or "Situations and Adventures That Arose Between Me and the Woman I Had Captured." In each case the premise is gratuitous: the town is already purchased, the woman captured, when the story begins, and no explanation is ever given why anyone would want (or how he would be able) to buy towns or capture women, or why towns or women would stand for such treatment. Even when a line of narrative development is pursued—will Cecelia, in "A City of Churches," be forced to operate a car-rental agency in a city whose inhabitants all live

in churches and would never rent a car "in a hundred years" (*Sadness*, p. 53)? will the Dean, in "Porcupines at the University" (*Amateurs*), be able to prevent the threatened invasion of porcupines?—the development, like the characters' thoughts, is completely logistical. What are the effects of laying out plots of land to resemble pieces of a giant jigsaw puzzle? Can a Gatling gun repel a wave of porcupines? Barthelme's landscapes are without shadows or narrative past: each story begins with a premise which, like the rules of a game, is simply given. The action of the characters, when they act at all, is to come to terms with the given situation by adapting their normal habits to its requirements, however bizarre. When the captured woman offers her husband "the chance to rescue me on a white horse—one of the truly great moments his life affords," he writes back to tell her "how well he and the kid are doing together. How she hardly ever cries now. How *calm* the house is" (*Amateurs*, p. 97).

The discordance between the fantastic situation and the determination to cope with it logistically, more than any summary or catalogue of situations, gives the flavor of Barthelme's world. In this respect, at least, his work seems less kindred to that of other short story writers than to that of other figures associated with *The New Yorker*, in which most of Barthelme's stories first appeared—figures such as S. J. Perelman, James Thurber, Saul Steinberg, and Woody Allen, whose humorous effects arise from a contrast between outrageous premises and deadpan presentation. "I can't get in touch with your uncle," a Thurber medium tells her dismayed client, "but there's a horse here that wants to say hello."[3] The trick is to intimate and deflate metaphysical or teleological pretenses as economically as possible, as in Woody Allen's aphorism: "Not only is there no God, but try getting a plumber on weekends."[4] The fictional form most dependent on this rhythm of presentation is of course the cartoon, itself an essential avatar of *The New Yorker*'s sensibility, and Barthelme's stories might themselves be considered cartoons that resemble those not only of *New Yorker* artists like Thurber and Steinberg but also of such recent figures as B. Kliban and Monty Python. Kliban's straightforward acceptance of outrageous premises—his cartoons include "Gondolier Attacked by Rabbis" and "Never Give a Gun to Ducks"—rivals Barthelme's own; the graphic work of the British comic troupe Monty Python, which freely adapts, juxtaposes, and animates stolid Victorian graphic designs, undercuts its targets very much as Barthelme's work does, and looks a good deal like Barthelme's own graphic work in "At the Tolstoy Museum" and "Brain Damage" (*City Life*), "The Flight of Pigeons from the Palace" (*Sadness*), "The Expedition" and "A Nation of Wheels" (*Guilty Pleasures*).

Barthelme's fiction, like the graphic work of Kliban and Monty Python, produces its effects by combining materials calling for different responses which are undercut by the process of juxtaposition. A print of a wheel and another of a hastily barricaded city are perfectly serious; but when they are put in the same frame in different scales, they imply a situation whose patent absurdity (America becomes a nation of wheels in the sense that wheels take over the country) suggests in turn the perfect deadpan caption: "All defenses were found to be penetrable" (*Guilty Pleasures*, p. 138). Barthelme has called this structural procedure "the principle of collage . . . the central principle of all art in the twentieth century in all media," and explained:

> New York City is or can be regarded as a collage, as opposed to, say, a tribal village in which all the huts . . . are the same hut, duplicated. The point of collage is that unlike things are stuck together to make,

in the best case, a new reality. This new reality, in the best case, may be or imply a comment on the other reality from which it came, and may be also much else. It's an *itself*, if it's successful: [an] . . . "anxious object," which does not know whether it's a work of art or a pile of junk.[5]

Barthelme's observation that any collage, including his own fiction, is "an *itself*" suggests a dimension, not only of his work, but of all fiction, which critics are often unable to appreciate or discuss systematically. Short stories and novels, like ritual tragedy, normally have a teleological dimension, an end toward which the events of the plot are moving. Aristotle uses *telos* in the double sense of unity of plot (as the plot of *Oedipus* or *Macbeth*, for example, rushes forward to an end) and unity of thought, conception, or purpose. S. H. Butcher, in his commentary on the *Poetics*, has concluded that for Aristotle, poetic unity is manifested not only "in the causal connection that binds together the several parts of a play," but also "in the fact that the whole series of events, with all the moral forces that are brought into collision, are directed to a single end. . . . The end is linked to the beginning with inevitable certainty, and in the end we discern the meaning of the whole."[6] The end or *telos* implies both a line of development for the plot and a rationale which allows a literary or dramatic work to be apprehended as a unitary whole and for which, in an ultimate sense, the work was written. . . .

It is excessively difficult to establish a critical vocabulary for a fiction that so resolutely resists structural closure. Some problems of analysis might be resolved by classifying Barthelme's stories as anatomies, to use the word by which Northrop Frye designates certain works by such writers as Petronius, Apuleius, Rabelais, Erasmus, Swift, Voltaire, and Peacock. The anatomy, according to Frye, "deals less with people as such than with mental attitudes" and "presents people as mouthpieces of the ideas they represent." In such works, Frye observes, "the intellectual structure built up from the story makes for violent dislocations in the customary logic of narrative." Although "a magpie instinct to collect facts" is a hallmark of the anatomist, short anatomies have been written in the form of "a dialogue or colloquy, in which dramatic interest is in a conflict of ideas rather than of character."[7] In Frye's terms, Barthelme would be an anatomist, not of manners or ideas, but of objects, artifacts of human culture, junk. Such a conclusion could be supported by passages like the following paragraph from "The Indian Uprising":

Red men in waves like people scattering in a square startled by something tragic or a sudden, loud noise accumulated against the barricades we had made of window dummies, silk, thoughtfully planned job descriptions (including scales for the orderly progress of other colors), wine in demijohns, and robes. I analyzed the composition of the barricade nearest me and found two ashtrays, ceramic, one dark brown and one dark brown with an orange blur at the lip; a tin frying pan; two-litre bottles of red wine; three-quarter-litre bottles of Black & White, aquavit, cognac, vodka, gin, Fad #6 sherry; a hollow-core door in birch veneer on black wrought-iron legs; a blanket, red-orange with faint blue stripes; a red pillow and a blue pillow; a woven straw wastebasket; two glass jars for flowers; corkscrews and can openers; two plates and two cups, ceramic, dark brown; a yellow-and-purple poster; a Yugoslavian carved flute, wood, dark brown; and other items. I decided I knew nothing. (*Unspeakable Practices, Unnatural Acts*, pp. 4–5)

This painstaking catalogue of cultural debris achieves its eerie and dazzling effect by removing each object from the context that would give it meaning: as William H. Gass has shrewdly remarked of Barthelme, "Anything dropped in the dreck *is* dreck, at once, as an uneaten porkchop mislaid in the garbage."[8] The fear of objects losing their meanings, as when they are sold at an auction that deprives them of the context they had for their owners, underlies a good deal of recent American fiction, including Gass's *Omensetter's Luck*, which begins with an auction, and Thomas Pynchon's *Crying of Lot 49*, which ends with one. Such anxiety accords well with what Frye calls the "highly intellectualized" temper of the anatomy. Unlike Gass and Pynchon (and, for example, John Barth), however, Barthelme does not present lists of objects in order to assimilate them into a coherent intellectual structure. The form of the anatomy implies, if not a teleology of plot, certainly an intellectual *telos* or rationale. But Barthelme's work makes neither of these teleological commitments because it projects neither an order for the situations, facts, and objects it presents nor an intelligible attitude toward them. Barthelme is more truly a magpie than the writers Frye considers because he has a magpie's interest in his material, displaying it not because it implies a *telos* but because it is bright and eye-catching. The "trash phenomenon," which one of his characters describes as having "(1) an 'endless' quality and (2) a 'sludge' quality" (*Snow White*, pp. 97, 96), is not threatening or lamentable in Barthelme; it is just there, like a pile of Christmas gifts waiting to be unwrapped, thrown together for the moment in a context that emphasizes their objecthood at the expense of their meaning.

Barthelme's preference for displaying his material rather than anatomizing it suggests that his fiction involves a compositional principle other than the intellectual rationale described by Frye or the different but similarly structural principles of Todorov and McCanles. In Barthelme's work, as in musical comedy, a situation need imply no *telos*, neither an intelligible plot nor a coherent rationale, if it is worth displaying for its own sake. The limitation of structuralist criticism, preeminently a reader's criticism, is that it presupposes a given structure to be filled in, whereas, from the writer's point of view, fiction often involves a situation to be filled out. The two perspectives are complementary, not contradictory, but Barthelme's work places unusual stress on the second.

Barthelme's narrative situations are less often teleological than tellable, to use the term Mary Louise Pratt has borrowed from the linguist William Labov and applied to literary texts. Tellable assertions, explains Pratt, "must represent states of affairs that are held to be unusual, contrary to expectations, or otherwise problematic." Although Pratt uses "interesting" as a synonym for "tellable" and notes that "information does not have to be new to be tellable," she emphasizes the teleological dimension that makes most narratives tellable in contending that the speaker of a tellable utterance is seeking "an *interpretation* of the problematic event, an assignment of meaning and value," so that spoken narratives commonly fail, if they do fail, in teleological terms: "The experience was trivial, the teller longwinded, or we 'missed the point.'"[9] Stories can be repeated over and over, however, even to an audience already familiar with their point. Children, as every parent knows, have the greatest tolerance for unvaried narrative repetition, and indeed are suspicious of variation; but the tolerance persists in adults' fondness for familiar anecdotes: "I love to hear you tell the story of how you got the wedding guests to move those pianos."

Adults have more appetite than children for narrative elaboration. Pratt points out that because "what literary works chiefly do is elaborate on the states of affairs they posit," fictive narration can be "exceedingly redundant"; an author, like an oral storyteller, "can pile detail upon detail, and can even be blatantly repetitive, because he is understood to be enabling his audience to imagine and comprehend the state of affairs more fully and to savor it for a longer time."[10] Tellable narratives are to a great extent both retellable and capable of practically endless elaboration; indeed, the better an audience already knows a narrative, the less concerned it is that the narrator get to the point.

An important implication of Pratt's discussion, though one she does not make explicit, is that often the process of elaboration itself can make a narrative tellable: that is, insofar as the point of a narrative is display rather than *telos*, elaboration, repetition, and discursiveness are precisely what make the narrative tellable. The difference between most novels and their plot summaries is that the summaries retain narrative *telos* without tellability. Imagine a summary of the sentence describing a barricade in "The Indian Uprising": "I examined the barricade nearest me and found it was made up of many objects, miscellaneous, recherché, absurd." The point of Barthelme's sentence, insofar as it has a point, is the plenitude or exuberance of particularization that makes it, unlike its summary, tellable.

This way of establishing tellability is characteristic of a great deal of fiction besides Barthelme's. To the extent that any fiction elaborates a given situation without implying a *telos*, or without altering the *telos* the situation itself implies, it seeks to make that situation more tellable. Sometimes, as often in Barthelme, the main point of the elaboration is pointlessness—a point by which audiences are understandably bewildered. One of Monty Python's most notorious sketches is called "The Death of Mary Queen of Scots." Two members of the troupe sit next to a window in a room, and from offstage, presumably through the window, comes the exchange, "Are you Mary Queen of Scots?"—"Aye." There follow perhaps thirty seconds of mayhem offstage: beating, thumping, ripping, pummeling, intermingled with bloodcurdling shrieks. Finally, a voice from outside says quietly: "There, she's dead," to which another voice replies, "No I ain't!" During the first five seconds or so of pounding and screeching, the mayhem is certainly, in Pratt's terms, unusual or problematic, but it soon thereafter becomes pointless and tedious, until, when it has gone on too long to be accidentally pointless, the audience gradually realizes that the pointlessness is intentional. Once the sketch has established this new convention of pure discursiveness, so that pounding and screeching can be considered as normal behavior, an audience often finds it amusing to a degree this summary will hardly suggest. The principle of display here might be described by the maxim *too much is enough* or by the compositional principle, most notably exemplified by Tristram Shandy, of getting carried away.

The designedly pointless repetitiveness of much of Monty Python's material has attracted a large, but not universal, audience. Television viewers are so accustomed to a simplified (and radically foreshortened) teleology in situation comedies and comic sketches that their initial reaction to Monty Python is often bored or bemused: "This is just silly." Most readers of Sterne and Dickens, however, accept their narratives as tellable precisely because of the conventions of elaboration, repetition, and discursiveness. A character like Mr. Micawber, who has no psychology to speak of, is far less provocative or sympathetic than any of George Eliot's characters, and students first approaching Dickens often consider Micawber simply unpromising or shallow. But Dickens' theatrical or histrionic conception of Micawber, which prescribes for him always the same gestures and speeches, gives him a magical or incantatory vitality. Just as all Dickens' grotesques have a tellability based on the conviction established by the unvarying repetition with which they are displayed, Shandy's digressions have a tellability based always on their antiteleological irrelevance, their resistance to development, closure, or informing rationale.

Although writers like Barthelme, Dickens, and Sterne are unusually discursive, narrative fiction in general is shaped by both a structural imperative, an impulse in the broadest sense teleological, and a discursive or elaborative impulse. Narrative tellability can be based on either teleology or elaboration—circumstantial detail, for example, establishes a sense of verisimilitude and an elaborative range that can both make a narrative more tellable—and no narrative, not even Barthelme's, works absolutely in isolation from either impulse, though their relative importance may vary widely from one narrative to the next. Barthelme's resolute emphasis on narrative elaboration, which reduces the importance of *telos* to a minimum, is significant principally as a challenge to the limitations of thematic and structural analysis and as a reminder that the first requisite of a narrative, the merit on which all other merits depend, is that it be worth telling.

Notes

1. Parenthetical references throughout are to the Little, Brown edition of *Come Back, Dr. Caligari* (Boston, 1964) and the Farrar, Straus and Giroux editions of *Snow White* (New York, 1967), *Unspeakable Practices, Unnatural Acts* (1968), *City Life* (1970), *Sadness* (1972), *Guilty Pleasures* (1974), *The Dead Father* (1975), *Amateurs* (1976), and *Great Days* (1979).
2. *Aristotle's Theory of Poetry and Fine Art*, trans. S. H. Butcher, 4th ed. (1911; rpt. New York: Dover, 1951), Ch. vi, p. 27.
3. *Men, Women and Dogs*, new ed. (New York: Dodd, Mead, 1975), p. 50.
4. "My Philosophy," in *Getting Even* (New York: Random House, 1971), p. 33.
5. Joe David Bellamy, *The New Fiction: Interviews with Innovative American Writers* (Urbana: University of Illinois Press, 1974), pp. 51–52.
6. *Aristotle's Theory of Poetry and Fine Art*, pp. 284–285.
7. *Anatomy of Criticism: Four Essays* (Princeton, NJ: Princeton University Press, 1957), pp. 309–311.
8. "The Leading Edge of the Trash Phenomenon," in *Fiction and the Figures of Life* (1971; rpt. New York: Vintage, 1972), p. 101.
9. *Toward a Speech Act Theory of Literary Discourse* (Bloomington: Indiana University Press, 1977), pp. 136–138, 51.
10. *Toward a Speech Act Theory of Literary Discourse*, pp. 148, 146.

L. FRANK BAUM

1856–1919

Lyman Frank Baum was born in Chittenango, New York, on May 15, 1856. After attending Peekskill Military Academy, he worked at jobs ranging from acting and theatrical management to newspaper reporting to chicken farming (the subject of his first book, in 1886). In 1882 he married Maud Gage, the daughter of a prominent suffragette, and continued to run through jobs: storekeeper, axle grease salesman, department store buyer and window dresser, and finally writer of children's books.

Father Goose: His Book (1899) sold well, but *The Wonderful Wizard of Oz* (1900) made Baum famous and rich. The book became a Broadway musical hit in 1902, and was filmed in 1910, 1920 (with Oliver Hardy as the Tin Woodman), and by MGM in 1939. Demand for sequels was immediate, but Baum wrote several other books—notably *American Fairy Tales* (1901)—before producing *The Marvelous Land of Oz* (1904). In 1905, Baum adapted it into a musical. Four Oz books later, in *The Emerald City of Oz* (1910), he announced the end of the series, but hundreds of protesting letters from children convinced him to relent. Besides his fourteen Oz tales, he wrote scores of other children's books, including fantasies which he eventually tied into his complex Oz mythology. He also wrote four unsuccessful novels for adults, under one of his many pseudonyms.

After 1902, Baum lived with his wife and four children in California, where he raised songbirds and chrysanthemums at "Ozcot," a house built with Oz earnings. He was fascinated by the growth of the motion picture industry, and ran a financially disastrous studio, the Oz Film Manufacturing Company, in 1914 and 1915. The Oz books grew increasingly dark in tone before his death on May 6, 1919; the last, *Glinda of Oz*, was published posthumously in 1920.

Personal

"L. Frank Baum was a character," ⟨Eunice Tietjens⟩ writes. "He was tall and rangy, with an imagination and a vitality which constantly ran away with him. He never wrote fewer than four books a year. . . . Constantly exercising his imagination as he did, he had come to the place where he could honestly not tell the difference between what he had done and what he had imagined. Everything he said had to be taken with at least a half-pound of salt. But he was a fascinating companion.

"He was never without a cigar in his mouth, but it was always unlit. His doctor had forbidden him to smoke, so he chewed up six cigars a day instead. There was one exception to this. Before he took his swim in the lake in the afternoon he would light a cigar and walk immediately into the water. He would solemnly wade out till the water was up to his neck and there walk parallel with the shore, moving his arms to give the impression that he was swimming. When a wave splashed on the cigar and put it out he at once came in and dressed.

"His house was full of the most remarkable mementos of the time when it had been necessary for him 'to rest his brain,' following a stroke of facial paralysis. He had painted the walls with stencilled designs; he had made a sign of wrought iron and painted wood for the dooryard, 'At the Sign of Father Goose'; he had made furniture; he had written a small book of poems (!), had set it up in type himself, printed and bound it by hand. Last of all, because all this had not yet rested his brain enough, he had made an elaborate piano arrangement of Paul ⟨Tietjens'⟩ music for *The Wizard of Oz*—though he was no musician it was pretty good—had then figured out the system by which pianola records were made, and had cut a full-length record of this arrangement out of wrapping paper! This seems to have done the trick, and he was presently back at work."

Surviving friends of Baum all remember him as a modest, dignified gentleman who enjoyed meeting people, talking, and telling funny stories. "He was a very kindly man," Mrs. Baum states in a letter, "never angry, pleasant to everyone, but when his mind was active with some story he would meet his best friend and not see him."—MARTIN GARDNER, "The Royal Historian of Oz," *The Royal Historian of Oz and Who He Was*, 1975, pp. 27–28

General

Folk lore, legends, myths and fairy tales have followed childhood through the ages, for every healthy youngster has a wholesome and instinctive love for stories fantastic, marvelous and manifestly unreal. The winged fairies of Grimm and Andersen have brought more happiness to childish hearts than all other human creations.

Yet the old-time fairy tale, having served for generations, may now be classed as "historical" in the children's library; for the time has come for a series of newer "wonder tales" in which the stereotyped genie, dwarf and fairy are eliminated, together with all the horrible and bloodcurdling incident devised by their authors to point a fearsome moral to each tale. Modern education includes morality; therefore the modern child seeks only entertainment in its wonder-tales and gladly dispenses with all disagreeable incident.

Having this thought in mind, the story of *The Wonderful Wizard of Oz* was written solely to pleasure children of today. It aspires to being a modernized fairy tale, in which the wonderment and joy are retained and the heart-aches and nightmares are left out.—L. FRANK BAUM, "Introduction" to *The Wonderful Wizard of Oz*, 1900

The Oz books became classics, then, not because Baum succeeded in writing a new kind of Americanized fairy story, but because he adapted the fairy tale tradition itself to twentieth-century American taste with imaginative ingenuity. There are in the Oz books a number of references to American locale, and Dorothy herself, of course, comes to Oz via a prairie twister. But beyond such casual references Oz has no real relation to the United States—it is fundamentally the out-of-time, out-of-space fairyland of tradition. Working from the midst of older materials, Baum's clever and occasionally brilliant variations on traditional themes are marks of craftsmanship and creativeness of a high order. It is not solely in their "Americanism," nor in their avoidance of the "horrible and bloodcurdling," nor in their rejection of moralism (which Baum did not wholly reject), nor in their pure entertainment value (which Baum did maintain), that the power of the Oz books lies. It stems rather from Baum's success in placing his work directly in the stream of the past, in his assimilation into Oz of the ageless universals of wonder and fantasy. What Baum did was to enlarge the resources of the European inheritance by making it possible to find the old joy of wonderment in the fresh new setting of Oz, creating a bright new fairyland in the old tradition.

That this was no minor achievement is shown by what happened to Baum after *The Wizard* appeared. Its popularity required a second Oz story, and then a third, until Baum, having created Oz, could not escape it. *The Wizard* was apparently written with no intention of supplying a sequel; it is a complete unit, with nothing in it to anticipate a successor, much less thirteen of them. For almost ten years after its appearance he tried hopefully to avoid writing more Oz books, producing several stories for an older age group and even some novels for adults. He even tried to end the series in 1910 with *The Emerald City of Oz*, but he was driven back to Oz by the demands of his readers and, one suspects, his own unconscious inclinations. Finally, promising that "as long as you care to read them I shall try to write them," he resigned himself to at least one Oz story a year.

Whatever Baum's original disclaimer, the strain of moralism is strong in the Oz books. They are not simply pure entertainment, devoid of any lesson, for as Baum once admitted, he tried to hide "a wholesome lesson" behind the doings of his characters. The child (or adult, for that matter) who reads the Oz books for a second or third time can usually find its hiding place, and one of the pleasures of reading Baum lies in its discovery. Baum's "wholesome lesson" is particularly evident in his creation of characters whose function is fully as much didactic as dramatic. The lesson of the Woodman, the Scarecrow, and the Lion in *The Wizard of Oz* is clearly a moral one. The Tin Woodman, a kindly, compassionate creature who weeps at stepping on a beetle, wants a heart so that he may love. The Scarecrow, who laments his lack of a brain, shows shrewd common sense from the beginning. The Cowardly Lion, when the chips are down, is as brave as a lion can be, learning (a message of reassurance to any child) that to fear danger is normal but that the important thing is to have more courage than fear. Yet not until each possesses the symbol of what he wants is he confident and satisfied—something that Dorothy wisely recognizes. You have within you, Baum seems to say, the things you seek; the symbol is of no value while the virtue is.—RUSSEL B. NYE, "An Appreciation," *The Royal Historian of Oz and Who He Was*, 1975, pp. 4–5

Works

THE WONDERFUL WIZARD OF OZ

It is impossible to conceive of a greater contrast than exists between the children's books of antiquity that were new publications during the sixteenth century and modern children's books of which *The Wonderful Wizard of Oz* is typical. The crudeness that was characteristic of the old-time publications that were intended for the delectation and amusement of an-

cestral children would now be enough to cause the modern child to yell with rage and vigor and to instantly reject the offending volume, if not to throw it out of the window. The time when anything was considered good enough for children has long since passed, and the volumes devoted to our youth are based upon the fact that they are the future citizens; that they are the country's hope, and are thus worthy of the best, not the worst, that art can give. Kate Greenaway has forever driven out the lottery book and the horn book. In *The Wonderful Wizard of Oz* the fact is clearly recognized that the young as well as their elders love novelty. They are pleased with dashes of color and something new in the place of the old, familiar, and winged fairies of Grimm and Andersen.

Neither the tales of Aesop and other fableists, nor the stories such as the "Three Bears" will ever pass entirely away, but a welcome place remains and will easily be found for such stories as "Father Goose: His Book," "The Songs of Father Goose," and now *The Wonderful Wizard of Oz*, that have all come from the hands of Baum and Denslow.

This last story of *The Wizard* is ingeniously woven out of commonplace material. It is of course an extravaganza, but will surely be found to appeal strongly to child readers as well as to the younger children, to whom it will be read by mothers or those having charge of the entertaining of children. There seems to be an inborn love of stories in child minds, and one of the most familiar and pleading requests of the children is to be told another story. . . .

Dorothy, the little girl, and her strangely assorted companions, whose adventures are many and whose dangers are often very great, have experiences that seem in some respects like a leaf out of one of the old English fairy tales that Andrew Lang or Joseph Jacobs has rescued for us. A difference there is, however, and Baum has done with mere words what Denslow has done with his delightful draughtsmanship. The story has humor and here and there stray bits of philosophy that will be a moving power on the child mind and will furnish fields of study and investigation for the future students and professors of psychology. Several new features and ideals of fairy life have been introduced into the *Wonderful Wizard*, who turns out in the end to be only a wonderful humbug after all. A scarecrow stuffed with straw, a tin woodman, and a cowardly lion do not at first blush promise well as moving heroes in a tale when merely mentioned, but in actual practice they take on something of the living and breathing quality that is so gloriously exemplified in the "Story of the Three Bears," that has become a classic.

The book has a bright and joyous atmosphere, and does not dwell upon killing and deeds of violence. Enough stirring adventure enters into it, however, to flavor it with zest, and it will indeed be strange if there be a normal child who will not enjoy the story.—"A New Book for Children," *NYTBR*, Sept. 8, 1900, p. 605

HENRY M. LITTLEFIELD
From *"The Wizard of Oz: Parable on Populism"*
American Quarterly, Spring 1964, pp. 50–57

*T*he Wizard of Oz has neither the mature religious appeal of a *Pilgrim's Progress*, nor the philosophic depth of a *Candide*. Baum's most thoughtful devotees see in it only a warm, cleverly written fairy tale. Yet the original Oz book conceals an unsuspected depth, and it is the purpose of this study to demonstrate that Baum's immortal American fantasy encompasses more than heretofore believed. For Baum created a children's story with a symbolic allegory implicit within its story line and characterizations. The allegory always remains in a minor key, subordinated to the major theme and readily abandoned whenever it threatens to distort the appeal of the fantasy. But through it, in the form of a subtle parable, Baum delineated a Midwesterner's vibrant and ironic portrait of this country as it entered the twentieth century.

We are introduced to both Dorothy and Kansas at the same time:

> Dorothy lived in the midst of the great Kansas prairies, with Uncle Henry, who was a farmer, and Aunt Em, who was the farmer's wife. Their house was small, for the lumber to build it had to be carried by wagon many miles. There were four walls, a floor and a roof, which made one room; and this room contained a rusty-looking cooking stove, a cupboard for the dishes, a table, three or four chairs, and the beds.
>
> When Dorothy stood in the doorway and looked around, she could see nothing but the great gray prairie on every side. Not a tree nor a house broke the broad sweep of flat country that reached to the edge of the sky in all directions. The sun had baked the plowed land into a gray mass, with little cracks running through it. Even the grass was not green, for the sun had burned the tops of the long blades until they were the same gray color to be seen everywhere. Once the house had been painted, but the sun blistered the paint and the rains washed it away, and now the house was as dull and gray as everything else.

Hector St. John de Crèvecoeur would not have recognized Uncle Henry's farm; it is straight out of Hamlin Garland.[1] On it a deadly environment dominates everyone and everything except Dorothy and her pet. The setting is Old Testament and nature seems grayly impersonal and even angry. Yet it is a fearsome cyclone that lifts Dorothy and Toto in their house and deposits them "very gently—for a cyclone—in the midst of a country of marvelous beauty." We immediately sense the contrast between Oz and Kansas. Here there are "stately trees bearing rich and luscious fruits . . . gorgeous flowers . . . and birds with . . . brilliant plumage" sing in the trees. In Oz "a small brook rushing and sparkling along" murmurs "in a voice very grateful to a little girl who had lived so long on the dry, gray prairies."

Trouble intrudes. Dorothy's house has come down on the wicked Witch of the East, killing her. Nature, by sheer accident, can provide benefits, for indirectly the cyclone has disposed of one of the two truly bad influences in the Land of Oz. Notice that evil ruled in both the East and West; after Dorothy's coming it rules only in the West.

The wicked Witch of the East had kept the little Munchkin people "in bondage for many years, making them slave for her night and day." Just what this slavery entailed is not immediately clear, but Baum later gives us a specific example. The Tin Woodman, whom Dorothy meets on her way to the Emerald City, had been put under a spell by the Witch of the East. Once an independent and hard working human being, the Woodman found that each time he swung his axe it chopped off a different part of his body. Knowing no other trade he "worked harder than ever," for luckily in Oz tinsmiths can repair such things. Soon the Woodman was all tin. In this way Eastern witchcraft dehumanized a simple laborer so that the faster and better he worked the more quickly he became a

kind of machine. Here is a Populist view of evil Eastern influences on honest labor which could hardly be more pointed.[2]

There is one thing seriously wrong with being made of tin; when it rains rust sets in. Tin Woodman had been standing in the same position for a year without moving before Dorothy came along and oiled his joints. The Tin Woodman's situation has an obvious parallel in the condition of many Eastern workers after the depression of 1893.[3] While Tin Woodman is standing still, rusted solid, he deludes himself into thinking he is no longer capable of that most human of sentiments, love. Hate does not fill the void, a constant lesson in the Oz books, and Tin Woodman feels that only a heart will make him sensitive again. So he accompanies Dorothy to see if the Wizard will give him one.

Oz itself is a magic oasis surrounded by impassable deserts, and the country is divided in a very orderly fashion. In the North and South the people are ruled by good witches, who are not quite as powerful as the wicked ones of the East and West. In the center of the land rises the magnificent Emerald City ruled by the Wizard of Oz, a successful humbug whom even the witches mistakenly feel "is more powerful than all the rest of us together." Despite these forces, the mark of goodness, placed on Dorothy's forehead by the Witch of the North, serves as protection for Dorothy throughout her travels. Goodness and innocence prevail even over the powers of evil and delusion in Oz. Perhaps it is this basic and beautiful optimism that makes Baum's tale so characteristically American—and Midwestern.

Dorothy is Baum's Miss Everyman. She is one of us, levelheaded and human, and she has a real problem. Young readers can understand her quandary as readily as can adults. She is good, not precious, and she thinks quite naturally about others. For all of the attractions of Oz Dorothy desires only to return to the gray plains and Aunt Em and Uncle Henry. She is directed toward the Emerald City by the good Witch of the North, since the Wizard will surely be able to solve the problem of the impassable deserts. Dorothy sets out on the Yellow Brick Road wearing the Witch of the East's magic Silver Shoes. Silver shoes walking on a golden road; henceforth Dorothy becomes the innocent agent of Baum's ironic view of the Silver issue. Remember, neither Dorothy, nor the good Witch of the North, nor the Munchkins understand the power of these shoes. The allegory is abundantly clear. On the next to last page of the book Baum has Glinda, Witch of the South, tell Dorothy, "Your Silver Shoes will carry you over the desert. . . . If you had known their power you could have gone back to your Aunt Em the very first day you came to this country." Glinda explains, "All you have to do is to knock the heels together three times and command the shoes to carry you wherever you wish to go." William Jennings Bryan never outlined the advantages of the silver standard any more effectively.

Not understanding the magic of the Silver Shoes, Dorothy walks the mundane—and dangerous—Yellow Brick Road. The first person she meets is a Scarecrow. After escaping from his wooden perch, the Scarecrow displays a terrible sense of inferiority and self doubt, for he has determined that he needs real brains to replace the common straw in his head. William Allen White wrote an article in 1896 entitled "What's the Matter With Kansas?" In it he accused Kansas farmers of ignorance, irrationality and general muddle-headedness. What's wrong with Kansas are the people, said Mr. White.[4] Baum's character seems to have read White's angry characterization. But Baum never takes White seriously and so the Scarecrow soon emerges as innately a very shrewd and very capable individual.

The Scarecrow and the Tin Woodman accompany Dorothy along the Yellow Brick Road, one seeking brains, the other a heart. They meet next the Cowardly Lion. As King of Beasts he explains, "I learned that if I roared very loudly every living thing was frightened and got out of my way." Born a coward, he sobs, "Whenever there is danger my heart begins to beat fast." "Perhaps you have heart disease," suggests Tin Woodman, who always worries about hearts. But the Lion desires only courage and so he joins the party to ask help from the Wizard.

The Lion represents Bryan himself. In the election of 1896 Bryan lost the vote of Eastern labor, though he tried hard to gain their support. In Baum's story the Lion, on meeting the little group, "struck at the Tin Woodman with his sharp claws." But, to his surprise, "he could make no impression on the tin, although the Woodman fell over in the road and lay still." Baum here refers to the fact that in 1896 workers were often pressured into voting for McKinley and gold by their employers.[5] Amazed, the Lion says, "he nearly blunted my claws," and he adds even more appropriately, "When they scratched against the tin it made a cold shiver run down my back." The King of Beasts is not after all very cowardly, and Bryan, although a pacifist and an anti-imperialist in a time of national expansion, is not either.[6] The magic Silver Shoes belong to Dorothy, however. Silver's potent charm, which had come to mean so much to so many in the Midwest, could not be entrusted to a political symbol. Baum delivers Dorothy from the world of adventure and fantasy to the real world of heartbreak and desolation through the power of Silver. It represents a real force in a land of illusion, and neither the Cowardly Lion nor Bryan truly needs or understands its use.

All together now the small party moves toward the Emerald City. Coxey's Army of tramps and indigents, marching to ask President Cleveland for work in 1894, appears no more naively innocent than this group of four characters going to see a humbug Wizard, to request favors that only the little girl among them deserves.

Those who enter the Emerald City must wear green glasses. Dorothy later discovers that the greenness of dresses and ribbons disappears on leaving, and everything becomes a bland white. Perhaps the magic of any city is thus self imposed. But the Wizard dwells here and so the Emerald City represents the national Capitol. The Wizard, a little bumbling old man, hiding behind a facade of papier mâché and noise, might be any President from Grant to McKinley. He comes straight from the fair grounds in Omaha, Nebraska, and he symbolizes the American criterion for leadership—he is able to be everything to everybody.

As each of our heroes enters the throne room to ask a favor the Wizard assumes different shapes, representing different views toward national leadership. To Dorothy, he appears as an enormous head, "bigger than the head of the biggest giant." An apt image for a naive and innocent little citizen. To the Scarecrow he appears to be a lovely, gossamer fairy, a most appropriate form for an idealistic Kansas farmer. The Woodman sees a horrible beast, as would any exploited Eastern laborer after the trouble of the 1890s. But the Cowardly Lion, like W. J. Bryan, sees a "Ball of Fire, so fierce and glowing he could scarcely bear to gaze upon it." Baum then provides an additional analogy, for when the Lion "tried to go nearer he singed his whiskers and he crept back tremblingly to a spot nearer the door."

The Wizard has asked them all to kill the Witch of the West. The golden road does not go in that direction and so they must follow the sun, as have many pioneers in the past. The land they now pass through is "rougher and hillier, for there were no farms nor houses in the country of the West and the ground was untilled." The Witch of the West uses natural forces to achieve her ends; she is Baum's version of sentient and malign nature.

Finding Dorothy and her friends in the West, the Witch sends forty wolves against them, then forty vicious crows and finally a great swarm of black bees. But it is through the power of a magic golden cap that she summons the flying monkeys. They capture the little girl and dispose of her companions. Baum makes these Winged Monkeys into an Oz substitute for the plains Indians. Their leader says, "Once . . . we were a free people, living happily in the great forest, flying from tree to tree, eating nuts and fruit, and doing just as we pleased without calling anybody master." "This," he explains, "was many years ago, long before Oz came out of the clouds to rule over this land." But like many Indian tribes Baum's monkeys are not inherently bad; their actions depend wholly upon the bidding of others. Under the control of goodness and innocence, as personified by Dorothy, the monkeys are helpful and kind, although unable to take her to Kansas. Says the Monkey King, "We belong to this country alone, and cannot leave it." The same could be said with equal truth of the first Americans.

Dorothy presents a special problem to the Witch. Seeing the mark on Dorothy's forehead and the Silver Shoes on her feet, the Witch begins "to tremble with fear, for she knew what a powerful charm belonged to them." Then "she happened to look into the child's eyes and saw how simple the soul behind them was, and that the little girl did not know of the wonderful power the Silver Shoes gave her." Here Baum again uses the Silver allegory to state the blunt homily that while goodness affords a people ultimate protection against evil, ignorance of their capabilities allows evil to impose itself upon them. The Witch assumes the proportions of a kind of western Mark Hanna or Banker Boss, who, through natural malevolence, manipulates the people and holds them prisoner by cynically taking advantage of their innate innocence.

Enslaved in the West, "Dorothy went to work meekly, with her mind made up to work as hard as she could; for she was glad the Wicked Witch had decided not to kill her." Many Western farmers have held these same grim thoughts in less mystical terms. If the Witch of the West is a diabolical force of Darwinian or Spencerian nature, then another contravening force may be counted upon to dispose of her. Dorothy destroys the evil Witch by angrily dousing her with a bucket of water. Water, that precious commodity which the drought-ridden farmers on the great plains needed so badly, and which if correctly used could create an agricultural paradise, or at least dissolve a wicked witch. Plain water brings an end to malign nature in the West. . . .

The Wizard, of course, can provide the objects of self-delusion desired by Tin Woodman, Scarecrow and Lion. But Dorothy's hope of going home fades when the Wizard's balloon leaves too soon. Understand this: Dorothy wishes to leave a green and fabulous land, from which all evil has disappeared, to go back to the gray desolation of the Kansas prairies. Dorothy is an orphan, Aunt Em and Uncle Henry are her only family. Reality is never far from Dorothy's consciousness and in the most heartrending terms she explains her reasoning to the good Witch Glinda,

> Aunt Em will surely think something dreadful has happened to me, and that will make her put on mourning; and unless the crops are better this year than they were last I am sure Uncle Henry cannot afford it.

The Silver Shoes furnish Dorothy with a magic means of travel. But when she arrives back in Kansas she finds, "The Silver Shoes had fallen off in her flight through the air, and were lost forever in the desert." Were the "her" to refer to America in 1900, Baum's statement could hardly be contradicted.

Current historiography tends to criticize the Populist movement for its "delusions, myths and foibles," Professor C. Vann Woodward observed recently.[7] Yet *The Wonderful Wizard of Oz* has provided unknowing generations with a gentle and friendly Midwestern critique of the Populist rationale on these very same grounds. Led by naive innocence and protected by good will, the farmer, the laborer and the politician approach the mystic holder of national power to ask for personal fulfillment. Their desires, as well as the Wizard's cleverness in answering them, are all self-delusion. Each of these characters carries within him the solution to his own problem, were he only to view himself objectively. The fearsome Wizard turns out to be nothing more than a common man, capable of shrewd but mundane answers to these self-induced needs. Like any good politician he gives the people what they want. Throughout the story Baum poses a central thought; the American desire for symbols of fulfillment is illusory. Real needs lie elsewhere.

Thus the Wizard cannot help Dorothy, for of all the characters only she has a wish that is selfless, and only she has a direct connection to honest, hopeless human beings. Dorothy supplies real fulfillment when she returns to her aunt and uncle, using the Silver Shoes, and cures some of their misery and heartache. In this way Baum tells us that the Silver crusade at least brought back Dorothy's lovely spirit to the disconsolate plains farmer. Her laughter, love and good will are no small addition to that gray land, although the magic of Silver has been lost forever as a result.

Notes

1. Henry Nash Smith says of Garland's works in the 1890s, "It had at last become possible to deal with the Western farmer in literature as a human being instead of seeing him through a veil of literary convention, class prejudice or social theory." *Virgin Land*, p. 290.
2. Hicks declares that from the start "The Alliance and Populist platforms championed boldly the cause of labor. . . ." *Revolt*, p. 324. See also Bryan's Labor Day speech, *Battle*, pp. 375–83.
3. Harold U. Faulkner, *Politics, Reform and Expansion* (New York, 1959) pp. 142–43.
4. Richard Hofstadter (ed.), *Great Issues in American History* (New York, 1960), II, pp. 147–53.
5. Bryan, *Battle*, pp. 617–18, "During the campaign I ran across various evidences of coercion, direct and indirect." See Hicks, *Revolt*, p. 325, who notes that "For some reason labor remained singularly unimpressed" by Bryan. Faulkner finds overt pressure as well, *Reform*, pp. 208–9.
6. Faulkner, *Reform*, pp. 257–58.
7. C. Vann Woodward, "Our Past Isn't What It Used To Be," *The New York Times Book Review* (July 28, 1963), p. 1; Richard Hofstadter, *The American Political Tradition* (New York, 1960), pp. 186–205.

GORE VIDAL
From "On Rereading the Oz Books"
New York Review of Books, October 3, 1977, pp. 38–44

I have reread the Oz books in the order in which they were written. Some things are as I remember. Others strike me as being entirely new. I was struck by the unevenness of style not only from book to book but, sometimes, from page to page.

The jaggedness can be explained by the fact that the man who was writing fourteen Oz books was writing forty-eight other books at the same time. Arguably, *The Wizard of Oz* is the best of the lot. After all, the first book is the one in which Oz was invented. Yet, as a child, I preferred *The Emerald City; Rinkitink*, and *The Lost Princess* to *The Wizard*. Now I find that all of the books tend to flow together in a single narrative, with occasional bad patches. . . .

Despite stylistic lapses, *The Land of Oz* is one of the most unusual and interesting books of the series. In fact, it is so unusual that after the Shirley Temple television adaptation of the book in 1960, PTA circles were in a state of crisis. The problem that knitted then and, I am told, knits even today many a maternal brow is Sexual Role. Sexual Role makes the world go round. It is what makes the man go to the office or to the factory where he works hard while the wife fulfills *her* Sexual Role by homemaking and consuming and bringing up boys to be real boys and girls to be real girls, a cycle that must continue unchanged and unquestioned until the last car comes off Detroit's last assembly line and the last all-American sun vanishes behind a terminal dioxin haze.

Certainly the denouement of *The Land of Oz* is troubling for those who have heard of Freud. A boy, Tip, is held in thrall by a wicked witch named Mombi. One day she gets hold of an elixir that makes the inanimate live. Tip uses this magical powder to bring to life a homemade figure with a jack-o-lantern head: Jack Pumpkinhead, who turns out to be a comic of the Ed Wynn-Simple Simon School. "'Now that is a very interesting history,' said Jack, well pleased; 'and I understand it perfectly—all but the explanation.'"

Tip and Jack Pumpkinhead escape from Mombi, aboard a brought-to-life sawhorse. They then meet the stars of the show (and a show it is), the Scarecrow and the Tin Woodman. As a central character neither is very effective. In fact, each has a tendency to sententiousness; and there are nowhere near enough jokes. The Scarecrow goes on about his brains; the Tin Woodman about his heart. But then it is the limitation as well as the charm of made-up fairy-tale creatures to embody to the point of absurdity a single quality of humor.

There is one genuinely funny sketch. When the Scarecrow and Jack Pumpkinhead meet, they decide that since each comes from a different country, "'We must,'" says the Scarecrow, "'have an interpreter.'"

"'What is an interpreter?' asked Jack.

"'A person who understands both my language and your own. . . .'" And so on. Well, maybe this is not so funny.

The Scarecrow (who had taken the vanished Wizard's place as ruler of Oz) is overthrown by a "revolting" army of girls (great excuse for a leggy chorus). This long and rather heavy satire on the suffragettes was plainly more suitable for a Broadway show than for a children's story. The girl leader, Jinjur, is an unexpectedly engaging character. She belongs to the Bismarckian *Realpolitik* school. She is accused of treason for having usurped the Scarecrow's throne. "'The throne belongs to whoever is able to take it,' answered Jinjur as she slowly ate another caramel. 'I have taken it, as you see; so just now I am the Queen, and all who oppose me are guilty of treason. . . .'" This is the old children's game I-am-the-King-of-the-castle, a.k.a. human history. . . .

There is a struggle between Jinjur and the legitimate forces of the Scarecrow. The Scarecrow's faction wins and the girls are sent away to be homemakers and consumers. In passing, the Scarecrow observes, "'I am convinced that the only people worthy of consideration in this world are the unusual ones. For the common folks are like the leaves of a tree, and live and die unnoticed.'" To which the Tin Woodman replies, "'Spoken like a philosopher!'" To which the current editor Martin Gardner responds, with true democratic wrath, "This despicable view, indeed defended by many philosophers, had earlier been countered by the Tin Woodman," etc. But the view is not at all despicable. For one thing, it would be the normal view of an odd magical creature who cannot die. For another, Baum was simply echoing those neo-Darwinians who dominated most American thinking for at least a century. It testifies to Baum's sweetness of character that unlike most writers of his day he seldom makes fun of the poor or weak or unfortunate. Also, the Scarecrow's "despicable" remarks can be interpreted as meaning that although unorthodox dreamers are despised by the ordinary, their dreams are apt to prevail in the end and become reality. . . .

Glinda the Good Sorceress is a kindly mother figure to the various children who visit or live in Oz, and it is she who often ties up the loose ends when the story bogs down. In *The Land of Oz* Glinda has not a loose end but something on the order of a hangman's rope to knot. Apparently the rightful ruler of Oz is Princess Ozma. As a baby, Ozma was changed by Mombi into the boy Tip. Now Tip must be restored to his true identity. The PTA went, as it were, into plenary session. What effect would a book like this have on a boy's sense of himself as a future man, breadwinner and father to more of same? Would he want, awful thought, to be a Girl? Even Baum's Tip is alarmed when told who he is, "'I!' cried Tip, in amazement. 'Why I'm no Princess Ozma— I'm not a girl!'" Glinda tells him that indeed he was—and really is. Tip is understandably grumpy. Finally, he says to Glinda, "'I might try it for awhile,—just to see how it seems, you know. But if I don't like being a girl you must promise to change me into a boy again.'" Glinda says that this is not in the cards. Glumly, Tip agrees to the restoration. Tip becomes the beautiful Ozma, who hopes that "'none of you will care less for me than you did before. I'm just the same Tip, you know; only—only—'"

> "Only you're different!" said the Pumpkinhead; and everyone thought it was the wisest speech he had ever made.

Essentially, Baum's human protagonists are neither male nor female but children, a separate category in his view if not in that of our latter-day sexists. Baum's use of sex changes was common to the popular theater of his day, which, in turn, derived from the Elizabethan era when boys played girls whom the plot often required to pretend to be boys. In Baum's *The Enchanted Island of Yew* a fairy (female) becomes a knight (male) in order to have adventures. In *The Emerald City* the hideous Phanfasm leader turns himself into a beautiful woman. When *John Dough and the Cherub* (1906) was published, the sex of the five-year-old cherub was never mentioned in the text; the publishers then launched a national ad campaign: "Is the cherub boy or girl? $500 for the best answers." In those innocent times Tip's metamorphosis as Ozma was nothing more than a classic *coup de théâtre* of the sort that even now requires the boy Peter Pan to be played on stage by a mature woman.

Today of course any sort of sexual metamorphosis causes distress. Although Raylyn Moore in her plot *précis* of *The Enchanted Island of Yew* (in her book *Wonderful Wizard Marvelous Land*) does make one confusing reference to the protagonist as "he (she)," she omits entirely the Tip/Ozma transformation which is the whole point to *The Land of Oz*, while the plot as given by the publisher Reilly & Lee says only that "the book ends with an amazing surprise, and from that moment on Ozma is princess of all Oz." But, surely, for a

pre-pube there is not much difference between a boy and a girl protagonist. After all, the central fact of the pre-pube's existence is not being male or female but being a child, much the hardest of all roles to play. During and after puberty, there is a tendency to want a central character like oneself (my favorite Oz book was R.P. Thompson's *Speedy in Oz*, whose eleven- or twelve-year-old hero could have been, I thought, me). Nevertheless, what matters most even to an adolescent is not the gender of the main character who experiences adventures but the adventures themselves, and the magic, and the jokes, and the pictures.

Dorothy is a perfectly acceptable central character for a boy to read about. She asks the right questions. She is not sappy (as Ozma can sometimes be). She is straight to the point and a bit aggressive. Yet the Dorothy who returns to the series in the third book, *Ozma of Oz* (1907), is somewhat different from the original Dorothy. She is older and her conversation is full of cute contractions that must have doubled up audiences in Sioux City but were pretty hard going for at least one child forty years ago.

To get Dorothy back to Oz there is the by now obligatory natural disaster. The book opens with Dorothy and her uncle on board a ship to Australia. During a storm she is swept overboard. Marius Bewley has noted that this opening chapter "is so close to Crane's ('The Open Boat') in theme, imagery and technique that it is difficult to imagine, on comparing the two in detail, that the similarity is wholly, or even largely accidental."

Dorothy is accompanied by a yellow chicken named Bill. As they are now in magic country, the chicken talks. Since the chicken is a hen, Dorothy renames her Billina. The chicken is fussy and self-absorbed; she is also something of an overachiever: "'How is my grammar?' asked the yellow hen anxiously." Rather better than Dorothy's, whose dialogue is marred by such Baby Snooksisms as "'zactly," "auto'biles," "'lieve," "'splain."

Dorothy and Billina come ashore in Ev, a magic country on the other side of the Deadly Desert that separates Oz from the real world (what separates such magical kingdoms as Ix and Ev from our realer world is never made plain). In any case, the formula has now been established. Cyclone or storm at sea or earthquake ends not in death for child and animal companion but translation to a magic land. Then, one by one, strange new characters join the travelers. In this story the first addition is Tik-Tok, a clockwork robot (sixteen years later the word "robot" was coined). He has run down. They wind him up. Next they meet Princess Languidere. She is deeply narcissistic, a trait not much admired by Baum (had he been traumatized by all those actresses and actors he had known on tour?). Instead of changing clothes, hair, makeup, the Princess changes heads from her collection. I found the changing of heads fascinating. And puzzling: since the brains in each head varied, would Languidere still be herself when she put on a new head or would she become someone else? Thus Baum made logicians of his readers. . . .

Although it is unlikely that Baum would have found Ruskin's aesthetics of much interest, he might well have liked his political writings, particularly *Munera Pulveris* and *Fors*. Ruskin's protégé William Morris would have approved of Oz, where

> Everyone worked half the time and played half the time, and the people enjoyed the work as much as they did the play. . . . There were no cruel overseers set to watch them, and no one to rebuke them and find fault with them. So each one was proud to do all

JOHN BARTH

DONALD BARTHELME

L. FRANK BAUM

ANN BEATTIE

S. N. BEHRMAN

PETER S. BEAGLE

he could for his friends and neighbors, and was glad when they would accept the things he produced.

Anticipating the wrath of the Librarian of Detroit, who in 1957 found the Oz books to have a "cowardly approach to life," Baum adds, slyly, "I do not suppose such an arrangement would be practical with us. . . . " Yet Baum has done no more than to revive in his own terms the original Arcadian dream of America. Or, as Marius Bewley noted, "the tension between technology and pastoralism is one of the things that the Oz books are about, whether Baum was aware of it or not." I think that Baum was very much aware of this tension. In Oz he

presents the pastoral dream of Jefferson (the slaves have been replaced by magic and good will); and into this Eden he introduces forbidden knowledge in the form of black magic (the machine) which good magic (the values of the pastoral society) must overwhelm. . . .

Despite the Librarian of Detroit's efforts to suppress magical alternative worlds, the Oz books continue to exert their spell. "You do not educate a man by telling him what he knew not," wrote John Ruskin, "but by making him what he was not." In Ruskin's high sense, Baum was a true educator, and those who read his Oz books are often made what they were not—imaginative, tolerant, alert to wonders, life.

PETER S. BEAGLE

1939–

Peter S. Beagle was born on April 20, 1939 in New York City. He attended the University of Pittsburgh, from which he graduated in 1959, and went on to Stanford where he studied on a Wallace Stegner Writing Fellowship from 1960 through 1961.

In 1960 he published A *Fine and Private Place*, a humorous ghost story which, while largely unnoticed by readers of fantasy, impressed numerous mainstream critics as an unusually promising work. Several years elapsed before his second novel, *The Last Unicorn* (1968), came out, by which time the Tolkien boom had created a substantial audience for his sophisticated treatment of quasi-medieval fantasy themes. Since then he has added little to his corpus of fiction: one novella (*Lila the Werewolf*, 1974) and one short story ("Come, Lady Death," 1978). Despite this, his reputation remains remarkably high among readers and critics both in the science fiction and fantasy world and in the general literary community.

Aside from fiction, Beagle has written occasional nonfiction on a variety of topics, most notably in the autobiographical travelogue *I See By My Outfit* (1965).

Peter S. Beagle has been married once, and divorced; he has three children. He lives in Watsonville, California, where he writes during the week and performs as a singer-guitarist on weekends. In 1981 he was Guest of Honor at the Seventh World Fantasy Convention.

Works

Peter S. Beagle's first novel, A *Fine and Private Place*, is a fantasy on certain currently-fashionable themes. Almost all the action takes place in a cemetery, and some of the principal characters are dead. One who isn't is a raven, a voluble and sardonic old bird, not Poe's melancholy symbol but Elijah's industrious benefactor. That Beagle, working with such materials, can engage the reader's interest is evidence of his literary skill. . . .

The idea with which Beagle seems to have begun is that the distinction between living and not living is less than clear-cut. His concern is not with life after death but with death in life. . . .

A *Fine and Private Place* may not be a work of the first importance, but it seems to me quite as important as many solemn and pretentious novels I have read. Beagle neatly avoids those pitfalls of the fantasist: sentimentality, coyness, and an air of profundity. He persuades the reader to play his game of make-believe, and then rewards him with an admirably sustained performance. For so young a writer, he is amazingly sure of himself, and it will be interesting to see what he writes next.—GRANVILLE HICKS, "Visit to a Happy Hunting Ground," *SR*, May 28, 1960, p. 18

⟨*The Last Unicorn*⟩ is a fable, of course, as well as a fantasy. The unicorn is a symbol of the imagination, and King Haggard's country is an image of a world in which the imagination has been destroyed, a wasteland. Schmendrick represents the artist; recognizing his failures, he learns that the power he craves comes and goes according to its own laws and is not under his control. Mommy Fortuna's Midnight Carnival, which raises profound questions about illusion and reality, is a place most of us have visited in our dreams.

Further interpretations are possible, but to me the fantasy is what counts. As he has shown before, Beagle has extraordinary inventive powers, and they make page after page a delight. Early on, for example, the unicorn is greeted by a butterfly who identifies himself as "a roving gambler." He says, "Death takes what man would keep, and leaves what man would lose. Blow, wind, and crack your cheeks. I warm my hands before the fire of life and get four-way relief." Telling her about the Red Bull, he advises: "Let nothing you dismay, but don't be half-safe," and when he starts to leave, he says politely, "I must take the A train."

Captain Cully, who, as he tells Schmendrick, has had thirty-one ballads written about him, is desolate because none of them is included in Child's *English and Scottish Popular Ballads*. When they meet Prince Lir, Schmendrick is relieved, because now he is certain that they are operating in a proper fairy story, and the prince, falling in love with the Lady Amalthea, the disguised unicorn, kills five dragons, destroys witches, giants, and demons, "not to mention the winged horses, the basilisks and sea serpents, and all the rest of the livestock." There is less facetiousness as the story moves to its end, but there is considerable humor even in the midst of lively drama.

The book is rich not only in comic bits but also in passages of uncommon beauty. Beagle is a true magician with words, a master of prose and a deft practitioner in verse. He has been compared, not unreasonably, with Lewis Carroll and J.R.R. Tolkien, but he stands squarely and triumphantly on his own feet.—GRANVILLE HICKS, "Of Wasteland, Fun Land and War," *SR*, March 30, 1968, pp. 21–22

⟨In⟩ his second novel, *The Last Unicorn*, Beagle has blended fantasy and reality even more deftly, and has largely ironed out his previous stylistic difficulties.

. . . Always the miraculous is juxtaposed with the mundane: a prophetic butterfly intones a riddle about the Red Bull and caps it with, "Let nothing you dismay, but don't be half-safe." There are ballads about goblins and Robin Hoods, then—"Won't you come home, Bill Bailey," and, "Buckle down, Winsocki. . . ." In this way the fable on the stage is fused with the seemingly unfabulous existence of the audience. On the one hand, Beagle is saying that the same magic as there is in his tale exists in our sloganized lives. But to the cynics he may also be saying that if we think unicorns and wizards are unreal, we should examine the "verities" of our own lives. . . .

Inevitably, critics have compared *The Last Unicorn* to Tolkien's *The Lord of the Rings*. Beagle's book is less ambitious, yet it comes closer to poetry. While Tolkien's fine energy was largely directed at keeping the plot rolling, Beagle is interested in texture as much as structure: he meanders, embroiders, occasionally fusses too much with his palette, but usually manages to imbue his characters and situations with an incandescence as bright as the supernal glow of his unicorn's horn. *The Last Unicorn* is an exquisite little fable, no more—but certainly enough.—HAROLD JAFFE, *Com*, June 28, 1968, p. 447

Peter Beagle is one of the great appreciators of Tolkien. His essay on "Tolkien's Magic Ring" expresses the delight that many of us felt on discovering *The Lord of the Rings*. It points to Tolkien's own faith in his materials as a source of strength, and it describes the sense Tolkien conveys that his story and the world within it were found rather than invented. But it has little to say about *how* Tolkien makes his commitment infectious, and that should be the main concern of anyone who intends to follow in his footsteps.

Before Beagle attempted a fantasy he wrote a funny, offbeat ghost story called *A Fine and Private Place*. The type of low-key satire found in it is completely foreign to Tolkien's fantasy: it is more likely to be found in the better grades of television situation comedy. When, in *The Last Unicorn*, Beagle attempted to express his appreciation for Tolkien in the form of a literary homage, he had to find some middle ground between the style he was accustomed to and the matter he was trying to incorporate. If there is any middle ground between wry comedy and high fantasy, it might just be the Thurber fairy tale, which is dazzling and funny and solemn, all at the same time. And the tone of *The Last Unicorn*, in its opening pages, is remarkably like that of *The White Deer*. Even little tricks like the anticlimactic catalogs that both mock the subject and endear it to us, are the same. Here is a sample, a description of the unicorn:

She had pointed ears and thin legs, with feathers of white hair at the ankles; and the long horn above her eyes shone and shivered with its own seashell light even in the deepest midnight. She had killed dragons with it, and healed a king whose poisoned wound would not close, and knocked down ripe chestnuts for bear cubs.

But as soon as Beagle tries to inflate his fairy tale to encompass a world and a vision, after the manner of Tolkien, the Thurberish deftness departs and he grows self-conscious. The graft fails to take, and the two components draw apart, the magic into sentimentality and the modern voice into embarrassed joking. He gives his wizard the deflating name of Schmendrick and lets him indulge in anachronisms at the expense of the story, unlike Thurber, whose anachronisms always reinforce the charm of the fairy tale world through contrast. The center of *The Last Unicorn* does not hold: its characters and imagery go flying off in all directions, without reference to the patterns of significance that should command. Parts of the story are memorable: the fraudulent magical circus that reminds one of Ray Bradbury's sinister carnival, the outwardly prosperous but inwardly barren town, the vision of unicorns floating like froth on the surf, the ponderous and fearsome Red Bull.

But Beagle does not gather these things into a satisfying whole because he lacks faith in them. He must lack faith, since he is always throwing pixy dust in our eyes to keep us from finding him out. This is pixy dust: "The witch's stagnant eyes blazed up so savagely bright that a ragged company of luna moths, off to a night's revel, fluttered straight into them and sizzled into snowy ashes." So is this: "Schmendrick lighted down to support her, and she clutched him with both hands as though he were a grapefruit hull." The first is uncalled-for, the second (grapefruit hull?) just silly. In neither case does the imagery advance the story, or even relate to what is going on. One feels like telling the author to play fair and let us see what he is about. Fantasy is not like parlor conjuring; its effects do not arise from misdirection and patter.—BRIAN ATTEBERY, *The Fantasy Tradition in American Literature*, 1980, pp. 158–59

RAYMOND M. OLDERMAN
From *Beyond the Waste Land: A Study of the American Novel in the Nineteen-Sixties*
1972, pp. 221–39

Beagle takes ⟨the⟩ sense of wonder and makes it the central concern of his work. Wonder has been so obscured by the profusion of deadening detail in contemporary life that it takes a "pure" fable to retrieve it. There is no black humor in *The Last Unicorn* because form and content are unified to help us see again the small *happy* mysteries of human life and the magic of the world—if we dream dreams of annihilation, we do also dream some happy dreams. The fabulous mixture of fact and fiction in all the novels we have discussed so far should have prepared us to accept the wonder of unicorns and the possibilities of a qualified happy ending; *The Last Unicorn* not only celebrates what Pynchon and Vonnegut and others would like to openly celebrate, it restores a certain needed balance. The answer to the question of whether or not ours is an age for unicorns records Beagle's awareness of that need for balance: "No," says a second hunter, ours is probably not a good age, "but I wonder if any man before us ever thought his time a good time for unicorns."

In a sense, Vonnegut and Beagle together present the full range of alternatives offered by what I have repeatedly called the novelist's vision in the sixties. Vonnegut gives us a choice between cataclysm and a certain balanced state of detached but compassionate caring. Beagle gives us a recognition of life's pains and sorrows, but only a symbolically ponderous threat of annihilation; he emphasizes, instead, the balance of caring and loving with a world of wonder. Vonnegut prepares us to understand that a move beyond the waste land could as well be a move toward destruction as a move toward rebirth, but for Beagle the move—although it acknowledges life's recalcitrance and the dangers of the Red Bull—is out of the waste land and into the magic of life, as in his first novel, *A Fine and Private Place*, where the main character literally moves out of a cemetery to rejoin the living. The difference between the two visions can be defined somewhat by each author's approach to clichés and folksy truisms. Both burrow into a cliché and upset its usual tired perspective, but Vonnegut does it to expose the horror that can be concealed in the ordinary, while Beagle hopes to revalue what we have seen too often—to revalue by making us see anew. The rediscovery of wonder in the world may ultimately be the best our decade can offer as a substitute for a truly accepted mythology to move us out of the waste land. The sixties seem ripe for such a rediscovery; Tolkien has been gobbled up with a great deal of enthusiasm, and the atmosphere of the late sixties in particular is filled with "flower children" and lectures on the false values that lead us to exist without wonder. Although we might expect it, Beagle's lovely fable is not a parody—it assumes a willingness to value things fresh and fragile and not necessarily sophisticated. Such an assumption is a sign of health. Not only does Beagle succeed, I believe, in unearthing our own enchantment with the world, but he does so with his eye constantly on what is vital to our age—and such a "relevant" rebirth for the reader is surely a portent that we *can* move beyond the waste land. . . .

The story of *The Last Unicorn* is the simple romance of a female unicorn's quest to release all other unicorns from the tyranny of the mysteriously powerful Red Bull. The unicorn is aided by Schmendrick the Magician, Molly Grue, and Prince Lír. The quest involves an ultimate confrontation with King Haggard, father of Lír and keeper of the Red Bull, and a final battle with the Bull itself. Before that confrontation the unicorn is turned into the lovely Lady Amalthea by Schmendrick, and as the Lady gradually forgets her immortal nature, she and Prince Lír fall in love. The ending is, of course, a victory over Haggard and the Red Bull, and the unicorn's return to her nonhuman form. It is a magnificent romance with a sweetly sorrowful happy ending.

The meanings of the allegorical figures are—as in most twentieth-century allegory—widely suggestive rather than single objective manifestations of absolute divine Truth. Each figure contributes to an overall image of what it is to be human, what it is to be an artist, and what it is to be alive in a world of wonder. The unicorn herself is a dream of beauty, the kind of dream that makes humans wake weeping with a sense of human loss, and the knowledge of unbearable beauty. The reader requires no special knowledge of the mythological unicorn to catch Beagle's creation—Beagle tells us no golden bridle is needed, nor any other apparatus; all you need is a "pure heart." The unicorn is the opposite of the dream of annihilation that dominates our lives according to Pynchon, Hawkes, and Vonnegut. She is the dream we have forgotten how to see, the thing whose absence makes our world a waste land; she is renewal

and rebirth, the lost fertility and potency of life. When we learn to see the unicorn we will be healed and reborn and the world will be ripe again, as it is in the closing moments of the book. "She is a rarer creature than you dare to dream," Schmendrick tells us in a typical burst of lyrical but inept adoration. "She is a myth, a memory, a will-o'-the wish. Wail-o'-the wisp." Even when she is enchanted and turned into the Lady Amalthea, the unicorn's eyes "are full of green leaves, crowded with trees and streams and small animals." She is the embodiment of wonder and to be aware of her existence is to know the magic of the world, the silver underside of leaves. Just to have glimpsed her is enough to alter a man, like the Mayor's men who watch the unicorn disappear into the night "like a falling star," and who now and then after that "laughed with wonder in the middle of very serious events and so came to be considered frivolous sorts." Even King Haggard, the king of wastelanders, is touched with wonder when he sees the unicorn. In fact, he is always touched with wonder when he sees a unicorn, and for that reason he has used the evil power of the Red Bull to help him hoard all the unicorns and deprive the world of wonder, making it into the familiar wasted land.

Beagle uses the unicorn to help define what it is to be human. Because the unicorn is immortal she helps us understand time, death, and mortality. "'It's the princesses who have no time,'" Molly Grue tells the unicorn. "'The sky spins and drags everything along with it, princesses and magicians and poor Cully and all, but you stand still. You never see anything just once. I wish you could be a princess for a little while, or a flower, or a duck. Something that can't wait!'" And Molly adds in doleful verse:

> "Who has choices need not choose.
> We must, who have none.
> We can love but what we lose—
> What is gone is gone."

The unicorn ponders for us, at random times, the human sorrow of growing old—the sense of loss, the pain, and the tears. When she does become a princess—the Lady Amalthea—and learns to love, we discover the value and beauty of man's fragile hold on time. Beagle seems to imply through the unicorn's shift from and to immortality, that love is made valuable precisely because we can *choose* it despite its inevitable brevity. The same thing is true concerning the magic of doing good—something Schmendrick discovers. Doing good, like love, cannot be valued for what it accomplishes, since the unicorn flatly declares, "You are a man, and men can do nothing that makes any difference." Loving and doing good must be chosen, as Lír and Schmendrick choose them, for the beauty and pleasure and wonder of loving and doing good. Otherwise, they are only swallowed up by time and never even achieve pleasure. This, of course, is the kind of universal concept usually explored by poetry, and it contributes, along with Beagle's style which often breaks into unannounced and sometimes comic verse, to the novel's lyric impact. The poetic conclusion in both *The Last Unicorn* and *A Fine and Private Place* decidedly includes the information that immortality is not so much fun—not even as much fun as mortality.

The paradoxes of sad pleasure and mortal love are only two of the many paradoxes about man that the unicorn exposes when she moves from unicorn to woman and back again. Man inspires simultaneous "tenderness and terror," and he, unlike a unicorn, is capable of "cruelty and kindness." When the unicorn is first changed to a human: "her face was the silly, bewildered face of a joker's victim. And yet she could make no move that was not beautiful. Her trapped terror was more lovely than any joy that Molly had ever seen, and that was the most terrible thing about it." This image conveys something of Beagle's overall idea of what it is to be human. Not only must the unicorn be a "joker's victim" to be human, she must learn despair and weariness and pride, and yet she will still be somehow beautiful. Schmendrick has the final word on what it means to be human. "You can love and fear, and forbid things to be what they are, and overact." The combination of poetic paradoxes revealed by the unicorn adds up to Beagle's vision of the wonder of being human—the wonder and the pain.

The Red Bull, opponent of the unicorn, is Beagle's version of that same power or force we have seen continually in the novel of the sixties, the power that usurps man's control of his own life. The unicorn fears the Red Bull not because it seeks her death, but because it seeks to possess her very being. Fear and the Bull are constantly and closely identified—since it never fights, but only conquers, the Bull operates and succeeds only through the agency of fear. It unfits its opponents, turns them docile—as with the unicorns already captured and imprisoned in the sea—and leads them to the brink of annihilation. The Bull is immense, shapeless, and blind as fear; he drools thunder and "he was the color of blood, not the springing blood of the heart but the blood that stirs under an old wound that never really healed." He is "raging ignorance" and "a swirling darkness, the red darkness you see when you close your eyes in pain." It is the fear itself, and not the possibility of destruction, which Beagle insists conquers unicorns and makes the world a waste land—fear is always as big and as aggressively threatening as a Bull. There is no limit to the size of the Red Bull, and it seems to expand as its victim's fear expands. Beagle, in most of his imagery, connects the Red Bull with sickness—with unhealed wounds and pain—for the Bull must be eliminated to heal the kingdom, to restore unicorns and the wonder and fertility of life.

The Red Bull is very like the image of the wolf in *Who's Afraid of Virginia Woolf?*—the archetypal image of the ambiguous and unknown force that has gained control of man's life. Beagle, too, does not really identify that force; it does have something to do with fear, but the threat is left to hover, combining the unrealness of a cartoon and the mythical voraciousness of a wolf—the mythical might of a bull—in an image of that unseen force with its power vested nowhere that haunts us from behind the facts of our daily life. The power could be the Big Bad Bull as easily as it could be a Conspiracy or an Institution, the sources of potentially demonic power made specifically culpable by many novelists in the sixties. In any case, the Red Bull is the waste land maker, and like Eliot's waste land, the Red Bull can never be eliminated. When it does not vanquish, it vanishes, and the wonder and fertility of the world are restored; but the Red Bull never dies. To move beyond the waste land the conquerors of the Red Bull must constantly renew their victory.

King Haggard is the ostensible keeper of the Red Bull— the Red Bull tentatively serves him as it would serve others who were without fears because they were without compassion or hope. Haggard is the authority figure who uses fear and the Red Bull to oppress his people and keep his world a waste land. He is driven by greed and selfishness to make a private possession of unicorns, and thereby deprive the world of wonder. But Haggard is not really an allegorical poke at authority; he is too sad and too much without hope. He is, rather, the man who prides himself on having no illusions and who loses his "heart's desire in the having of it." We are told that Haggard, speaking of food, repeats the old housewife's complaint with a new twist: "He says that no meal is good enough to justify all the money and effort wasted in preparing it. 'It is an illusion,' says he, 'and

an expense. Live as I do, undeceived.'" Not only is such an anti-illusion attitude an enemy to wonder, especially the wonder of art, but it reveals a man who detests the sources of his own being. He sustains himself without delusion, and that could lead to sustaining himself without food. He has already destroyed his spiritual food, for while he genuinely does get pleasure from unicorns, his imprisonment of them betrays the source of his pleasure. Poor Haggard just does not know how to be content. He is truly the king of the wastelanders, burying himself and fearing the April of the unicorn that could stir his dull roots with spring rain. But he is particularly, paradoxically human because he wants pleasure even as he destroys it, and denies himself to prove that there is no pleasure. "His eyes were the same color as the horns of the Red Bull." He is weary of life, but anxious to exist, and tired and haggard from the emptiness of existence.

The sad side of Haggard makes him a tentatively suggested everyman: he is not so much the man to be beaten as the wound to be healed in all of us—the cure, of course, is the wonder of the unicorn and the human magic of love. The fragility of time does not lead Haggard to see love's value as others do; on the contrary, he tells us, "I always knew that nothing was worth the investment of my heart, because nothing lasts, and I was right, and so I was always old." Nonetheless, it is just precisely that haggard part of us which ultimately reveals its own anathema—just as king Haggard does and is wont to do—for nothing weary or hopeless can exist if we are touched by the wonder of the unicorn, and Haggard is unicorn-touched: "Each time I see my unicorns," Haggard confesses, "it is like that morning in the woods, and I am truly young in spite of myself, and anything can happen in a world that holds such beauty." Although they cannot heal Haggard, wonder and beauty can heal the rest of us as the unicorn once "healed a king whose poisoned wound would not close." The poison wound is our own haggardness, and that is healed as King Haggard is destroyed—when the unicorns are returned to the world, and our ability to see them is restored.

One of the three aides who help the unicorn is Schmendrick the Magician. Schmendrick, a kind of bumbling Prospero, an inept artist, has a tender heart but is a doubtful craftsman. "I am Schmendrick the Magician," he announces in his more confident moments, "the last of the red-hot swamis, and I am older than I look." His ineptitude is so monumental that his teacher, a famous wizard, felt sure Schmendrick was meant for big things and so cast a spell on his life: "You shall not age from this day forth, but will travel the world round and round, eternally inefficient, until at last you come to yourself and know what you are." To know what he is as an artist is, of course, to know what place magical wonder has in the world of the imagination—when Schmendrick is cured of his ineptitude and his immortality it is because the unicorns have returned to the world. A world without wonder is a world where an artist can be nothing but inept, so in order to know himself, Schmendrick learns to value the fragility and pleasure of beauty itself. Only in a waste land is there no function for an artist, since there is neither beauty nor wonder; thus, the artist—as Eliot also pointed out—is unheeded and unneeded, for all he can do is make wastelanders feel uncomfortable. Schmendrick, at first, does not even do that: instead of producing a work of magical art, he "made an entire sow out of a sow's ear; turned a sermon into a stone, a glass of water into a handful of water, a five of spades into a twelve of spades, and a rabbit into a goldfish that drowned." When he does produce his first work of art, it is really a bit of plagiarism, for he evokes the presence of Robin Hood and his Merry Men.

But even when he performs the magical transformation of the unicorn into a woman, Schmendrick is not an artist in control of his craft—he tells us that the magic took possession of him; it was the art that chose, not the artist. As we have seen, however, a good human being learns to *choose* love for no other reason than its wonder; similarly Schmendrick learns that a good artist chooses to perform good magic under his *own control* because good magic is a very nice activity among the things a man can do with his little moment of life.

Before Schmendrick becomes a true artist he is troubled by the practical value of his art. He wants magic to be useful. In a waste land where the peasants are oppressed by King Haggard, where the unicorns are kept captive, and where greed, selfishness, and fear—as appear in Haggard and the people of Hagsgate—feed the brutal power of the Red Bull, an artist would like to feel relevant. He would like to do some concrete good. Schmendrick feels frustrated by his failure to be effectual in combating certain reactionary, anti-unicorn forces, and he is often reduced to shouting at wastelanders and conjuring good imaginative threats—like letters in the *Times*: "You pile of stones, you waste, you desolation," he shouts at someone who is a menace to unicorns, "I'll stuff you with misery till it comes out of your eyes. I'll change your heart into green grass, and all you love to sheep. I'll turn you into a bad poet with dreams. I'll set all your toenails growing inward. You mess with me." Wanting to be useful leads Schmendrick to the brink of despair and when the final encounter with the Red Bull begins, he is willing to abandon the artist's quest, a quest to find the value of magic and wonder. Before he even attempts the supreme act of art—turning Lady Amalthea back into a unicorn, or perhaps we could say turning all humans back toward the rediscovery and rebirth of wonder—before he even tries, he despairs, for he is not sure that such an act has value. "Let it end here then, let the quest end," he says, echoing what has been the eternal lament of any artist confronting his times. "Is the world any the worse for losing the unicorns, and would it be any better if they were running free again? One good woman more in the world is worth every single unicorn gone." It is the very same problem that has influenced literary directions in the past, and will probably be unusually influential on the direction of the novel in the seventies. Its corollary asks: is it not more human to give some concrete aid to the sufferers of life than to write the greatest poem?

Schmendrick solves the dilemma when he realizes that magic and art exist only for and because of the human—in fact, the assumption of his powers, the making of his magic as an artist, the end of his curse, and the discovery of himself all come not because of any act of social charity, but because in watching Lír's heroic courage he comes to understand the value and beauty of being human. "Wonder and love and great sorrow shook Schmendrick the Magician then, and came together inside him, and filled him, filled him until he felt himself brimming and flowing with something that was none of these." Heroic courage, as we shall see, is for heroes; artists, according to the tale, are meant to forge something magically human from wonder, love, and sorrow. Schmendrick learns what we have learned: the fable is an act of love, and needs no other use. It exists so we can sing, as Schmendrick sings, "*I did not know that I was so empty, to be so full*" (Beagle's italics). Man, as the unicorn points out, is not a meaningful creature and nothing he does will matter, but he can choose, nonetheless, to create and to understand that being human might mean living in a world of wonder. The choice will not restore Eliot's poet-prophet, or Prospero's brave new world, but Beagle maintains it can at least help us resee the world, and in that there might be a rebirth beyond the waste land, a rebirth for us all since we all can be filled with the wizard's wonder just by learning to see. "That is most of it," Schmendrick tells us, "being a wizard—seeing and listening. The rest is technique."

The inspiration for Schmendrick's discovery of himself and for the unicorn's success against the Red Bull comes from the hero of the tale, Prince Lír. The Prince's birth is attended by all the proper portents but he does not really hit his heroic stride until after he meets the Lady Amalthea and falls deeply in love with her. Then he courts her with all the usual claptrap of romance heroes.

> I have swum four rivers, each in full flood and none less than a mile wide. I have climbed seven mountains never before climbed, slept three nights in the Marsh of the Hanged Man, and walked alive out of that forest where the flowers burn your eyes and the nightingales sing poison. I have ended my betrothal to the princess I had agreed to marry—and if you don't think that was a heroic deed, you don't know her mother. I have vanquished fifteen black knights waiting by fifteen fords in their black pavilion, challenging all who come to cross.

And the deeds go on, involving dragons and ogres and one brother-in-law of an ogre. But none of this wins the Lady Amalthea. Nothing does until she begins to forget her immortal nature, and then she is won by a gentle song, a little tenderness, and a pure heart. Lír, who is a decidedly sweet hero, has to redo his theories of herohood, and he proves equal to the task. When he is offered the choice between keeping the Lady Amalthea for himself and allowing her to become a unicorn again, his response is magnificent. He knows what his selfishness could mean; if he repeats Haggard's folly he will deprive the world of wonder and make it continue as an arid waste land. "The true secret of being a hero," he tells us from his unicorn-inspired vision, "lies in knowing the order of things. . . . Things must happen when it is time for them to happen. Quests may not simply be abandoned; prophecies may not be left to rot like unpicked fruit; unicorns may go unrescued for a long time, but not forever. The happy ending cannot come in the middle of the story." He cannot hoard the magic that could heal the ailing waste land—he cannot, that is, and still be a hero, and he must be a hero; Lír's sense of decorum tells him that; it is why he is in the story. He has, as he tells us, been reborn because of the unicorn—he has come to see what it means to be human and to see the value of living in a mortal's world. "You were the one who taught me," he tells Lady Amalthea, "I never looked at you without seeing the sweetness of the way the world goes together, or without sorrow for its spoiling. I became a hero to serve you, and all that is like you. Also to find some way of starting a conversation." Through love Lír achieves the same vision of the world's wonder that Schmendrick achieves through his art and both discover the need for sharing. But Lír is called upon to perform an even more inspiring and truly heroic act than sharing his vision.

With the Lady Amalthea changed back to a unicorn, Lír, Schmendrick, and Molly Grue are forced to watch as the Red Bull drives the dispirited unicorn toward the sea. Lír is frantic with love and anxiety; he turns to Schmendrick, but the artist admits that wizardry is not much use in saving unicorns from fear—nothing is, in fact. Lír, however, will not accept such helplessness. "That is exactly what heroes are for," he says to Schmendrick, adding a touch of the active man's contempt for the poet. "Wizards make no difference, so they say nothing does, but heroes are meant to die for unicorns." With that he steps between the Red Bull and the unicorn. He is immediately crumpled and tossed to the beach; for, as we once learned from a secretive kitchen cat, it is a "valiant absurdity" to love a unicorn. Lír's gesture has no effect on the Red Bull, but the valiant *compassion* of his act penetrates the unicorn's fear, stops her flight, and she turns to defeat the Bull. Lír's heroism does not lie in any large dragon-sized deed; it comes from the simple and pure act of caring. Just as Lír has learned the love of wonder from the unicorn, the unicorn learns the wonder of love from Lír. Perishable as it is and foolish as it is, human love makes the unicorn envy the world of mortality. As in the Greek myths of old, we mortals know who has gotten the better hand from time's double-dealing. The unicorn, victorious but in sorrow "for the lost girl who could not be brought back," touches the battered Lír with her magic horn, lingering for the memory of love, and he is once again reborn. Lír is king now—king of a land restored to wonder and fertility as the unicorns have been restored to the world.

But you need not be a poet or a hero to comprehend the wonders of a unicorn-touched world. Molly Grue is neither—she is, in fact, a very ordinary everyday drudge like the rest of us, and she labors in her own way to aid the unicorn.

> Molly Grue cooked and laundered, scrubbed stone, mended armor and sharpened swords; she chopped wood, milled flour, groomed horses and cleaned their stalls, melted down stolen gold and silver for the king's coffers, and made bricks without straw. And in the evenings, before she went to bed, she usually read over Prince Lír's new poems to the Lady Amalthea, and praised them, and corrected the spelling.

She supplies the place of a sensitive lay reader for Schmendrick's art and Lír's romances, and she is confidante and confidence-builder for both men. She is also often Beagle's point of view for the reader. Specializing in neither art nor derring-do, she is still able to respond with tenderness to the value of the unicorn, and her response guides the reader. We are led to a layman's view of the world's wonder, and what better proof of the possibility by poor, past-her-prime, not-very special Molly Grue. Yet, even Molly does become special, and pretty, and loved, as she and Schmendrick end the tale by beginning a new quest to follow their unicorn forever, "a new journey, which took them in its time in and out of most of the folds of the sweet, wicked, wrinkled world, and so at last to their own strange and wonderful destiny."

It is a short step from the fabulous mixture of fact and fiction we have seen in many novels of the sixties to a traditional allegorical fable where the imagination is the only reality. But *The Last Unicorn* resists this kind of simplification. Beagle's allegory focuses on both the wonder of the imagination and the wonder of the world. There is some sort of thing we call a world that exists, in its mysterious way, outside the imagination. The artist, like Schmendrick, uses his illusions to explore the possibilities of the human imagination and ultimately to reveal the nicer magic in human life. The moral of the fable lies in learning how to see: good illusions, like the ones Schmendrick creates, lead to the discovery of unicorns; bad illusions like "Mommy Fortuna's Midnight Carnival" lead to dreams of annihilation—the same dreams Pynchon, Hawkes, and Vonnegut feared. We have already seen Schmendrick's good illusions, but there are other genres in Beagle's

allegory of the imagination—there is, for example, the work of a marvelous butterfly who is not quite up to serious wizardry, but who has his popular appeal: "'Death takes what man would keep,' said the butterfly, 'and leaves what man would lose. Blow, wind, and crack your cheeks. I warm my hands before the fire of life and get four-way relief.'" And when asked if, as an artist of scraps and snatches, he can recognize who the unicorn is, the butterfly responds: "Excellent well, you're a fishmonger. You're my everything, you are my sunshine, you are old and gray and full of sleep, you're my pickle face, consumptive Mary Jane." But the butterfly does understand what a unicorn means, and even warns the last unicorn about the Red Bull; gathering all his powers of concentration before he departs to "take the A train," he sputters out: "No, no, listen, don't listen to me, listen. You can find your people if you are brave. They passed down all the roads long ago, and the Red Bull ran close behind them and covered their footprints. Let nothing you dismay, but don't be half-safe."

Most *humans*, however, are much more willing to see the monsters in Mommy Fortuna's Midnight Carnival than to see a unicorn. Mommy is the magician of evil and ugly illusions, "bad fables" as they are called—illusions that are inevitable when fortune becomes a "mommy" who cackles at human willingness to believe in nightmares. Her specialty is "stormy dreams sprung from a grain of truth." People come to see her animals and, as the unicorn points out, their willingness to believe in ugly things makes a poor unhappy dog into a terrible Cerberus, or a plain crocodile into a fire-breathing dragon. Bad illusions can even spoil the artist: take the spider—in Mommy's carnival she becomes the mythical Arachne, and, worst of all, she believes it. So the illusions she spins are the most dangerous, because "she sees those cat's-cradles herself and thinks them her own work." They are cat's-cradles like the ones pointed out by Vonnegut or Pynchon that seduce us with the glamorous prospect of our own annihilation—look at her webs and your eyes go "back and forth and steadily deeper, until they seem to be looking down into great rifts in the world, black fissures that widened remorselessly and yet would not fall into pieces as long as Arachne's web held the world together." The humans who come to the Carnival and almost all the humans that the unicorn meets can see these unhappy illusions, but they cannot see the unicorn. Because of the Red Bull, because of fear, they see nothing but the possibilities of death, and so the land is wasted and wonder, when it does appear, cannot be recognized. "I suppose I could understand it if men had simply forgotten unicorns," the unicorn reflects over man's surprising blindness, "or if they had changed so that they hated all unicorns now and tried to kill them when they saw them. But not to see them at all, to look at them and see something else—what do they look like to one another, then? What do trees look like to them, or houses, or real horses, or their own children?" Beagle's moral—if we need to call it that—is clear; we live in a waste land because we *choose* to look at death, and have either forgotten how to see the world's wonder or, having seen it, grow haggard in trying to possess it, thereby losing our heart's desire in the having of it. And if that is not the moral, then this statement from the unicorn must be—something to keep in mind when faced with harpies or red bulls—"You must never run from anything immortal. It attracts their attention."

ANN BEATTIE

1947–

Ann Beattie was born September 8, 1947, in Washington, D.C. She received a B.A. from American University in 1969, and pursued graduate study at the University of Connecticut until 1972, stopping short of a Ph.D. While there, she began to sell short stories, and met David Gates, a musician and writer whom she married in 1972; they have one son.

Beattie received over twenty rejection slips from *The New Yorker* before "A Platonic Relationship" was accepted in 1974; she has since been a regular contributor to the magazine. In 1975, Beattie left Connecticut for Charlotte, where she became a visiting writer and lecturer at the University of North Carolina. Beattie published both *Distortions*, a collection of short stories, and *Chilly Scenes of Winter*, a novel, in 1976. The latter work chronicles a man's passage through the activism and expansiveness of the 1960's into the passivity of the 1970's. Though critical reaction to the book was mixed, its immense popularity turned Beattie into the primary chronicler of the aftermath of the counterculture. She is not pleased with the label: "I keep protesting that's a horribly reductive approach to my work." *Chilly Scenes* also established Beattie's unique style: non-metaphoric, with short, flat sentences and a wealth of detail.

Beattie left North Carolina in 1977 when she became the Briggs-Copeland Lecturer in English at Harvard. She was unhappy there and left in 1978 to accept a Guggenheim Fellowship. The following year marked both the publication of *Secrets and Surprises* and the opening of *Head Over Heels*, a film adaptation of *Chilly Scenes of Winter*, in which Beattie played a small part. In 1980 *Falling in Place* was published, a novel written in only seven weeks. Though well received critically as a stylistically mature and complicated work, it did not enjoy the popularity or impact of her first novel. *Jacklighting* followed in 1981, and *The Burning House*, another collection, in 1982.

Beattie lives in New York City. She received a Distinguished Alumnae Award from American University in 1980, and an award from the American Academy of Arts and Letters the same year.

General

To say that Ann Beattie is a good writer would be an understatement. Her ear for the banalities and petty verbal cruelties of the late '70s middle-American domestic idiom is faultless, her eye for the telling detail ruthless as a hawk's. She knows her characters inside out, down to the very last nastiness and sniveling sentiment, and she spares us nothing. . . .

All could be illustrations for Christopher Lasch's *The Culture of Narcissism*, demanding love and commitment from those around them but unwilling to give it. They feel that their lives are entirely out of control, that they lack power and cannot be expected to take responsibility for the consequences of their actions. Their dominant moods are anger and self-pity, and we find their triviality enraging until we come to see them not as minor sadists but as drowning people clutching each other's throats out of sheer panic. Adrift in a world of seemingly pointless events, bombarded with endless media flotsam, trapped in a junkyard of unsatisfactory objects, plugged into the monologues of others who appear to be deaf to their own, these characters cry out for meaning and coherence, but their world hands them nothing more resonant than popular song titles and T-shirt slogans.

Despite it all they remain yearning romantics. What they want from each other is nothing less than salvation, and Beattie's vision is ultimately a religious one. With religion having been designated as uncool, however, they're stuck in Middle Earth.

The only answer for these glutted but spiritually famished people would be God or magic. God appears only as a T-shirt slogan—"God Is Coming And She Is Pissed"—and magic is represented by a third-rate party magician who gets a crush on Cynthia in a laundromat. He's a fraud, but he does represent magic of a kind: His love for Cynthia, unrequited though it is,

is the only bit of disinterested altruism in the book. He doesn't want to possess her, he wants to wish her well, and it is through his magic binoculars that Cynthia sees her vanished lover as he finally appears again. It isn't much, but in view of the odds it's a tiny miracle. . . .

Sometimes the reader feels caught in an out-of-control short story, sometimes in a locked train compartment filled with salesman's samples and colossally boring egomaniacs, but most of the time, thanks to Beattie's skill, her novel not only convinces but entrances. The details are small, but the picture of our lives and times built up from them is devastating.— Margaret Atwood, "Ann Beattie: Magician of Muddle," *WPBW*, May 25, 1980, pp. 1–9

Works

Beginning to read this new collection of short stories is like going out alone into the night in the country: it's very dark, and the flashlight doesn't seem to illuminate much. Single objects—a car, a dog—loom up with uncanny significance. Familiar things look strange, one-dimensional. There are barely audible rustlings in the undergrowth which could mean anything, or nothing. It is very quiet.

But gradually one becomes accustomed to the faint light and realizes that there is more going on in these spare tales than first meets the eye. Although the men and women Ann Beattie writes about are well endowed with cars and dogs—and histories, and homes, and "relationships"—their most compelling feature is the profound anomie that darkens their lives. A young bride feels that "if she were [a] piece of sculpture and if she could feel, she would like her sense of isolation." Another young woman, buffeted by a lover who comes and goes like the tide, thinks "perhaps being powerless was nice, in a way." In "Friends," the longest and warmest of the stories, the kind and timid protagonist is "embarrassed" by his desire to marry and live alone with the woman he loves. Action is the result of chance; will is discomfiting; passion is terrifying.

The unrelieved passivity of these characters might seem repellent, but Beattie is skillful at provoking our interest in them. Personality glints off their most trivial actions, and a stubborn refusal to give in (to whom? to what?) lies behind their lethargy. A tightly controlled, monochromatic prose gives these portraits the revealing clarity of photographs.

Beattie's stories are an encouraging sign that short fiction, until recently neglected as a serious form for the exploration of character, is once again enjoying its rightful popularity.—BENJAMIN DeMOTT, "Short Reviews," *At*, March 1979, pp. 132–33

The squalor of aimless souls has been Miss Beattie's obsessive subject in two collections of stories, *Distortions* and *Secrets and Surprises*, and the novel *Chilly Scenes of Winter* (recently made into a movie called *Head Over Heels*). By now the chaotic world of post-everything dropouts has come to seem her private literary fiefdom, populated by men and women well over thirty, educated to no purpose, living on family handouts, unattached and uncommitted. Terrified by silence, they fend it off continually with rock, dope, and the insatiable pursuit of whimsy and new kicks. They all turn up again in *Falling in Place*, but by now it is drearily clear that Ann Beattie has nothing fresh to reveal about these disaffected drifters. . . . Confronted once again with these hollow and disordered spirits, whose habits and gestures and speech Miss Beattie knows with flawless intimacy, we are unable to feel anything but boredom and distaste for the muddled weirdness she records with such disingenuous objectivity.

As though she realizes how narrow and unrewarding this familiar ground has become, Miss Beattie has widened the range of her scrutiny in *Falling in Place* by writing not only about dropouts but also about an unhappy suburban family and its dreadful children. But she moves into John Cheever's territory without any of his mournful humanity, and the people she finds there turn out to be not very different from and certainly no more admirable than her aging hippies.

After eighteen years of marriage, the only language John Knapp and his wife Louise have in common is the weaponry of insult and bitter sarcasm. Their ten-year-old son, John Joel, is fat and miserable, his only friend a malevolent boy of twelve whose idea of fun is sticking pinholes in his mother's diaphragm and acting out the sadistic comics he collects. Mary, John Joel's nasty fifteen-year-old sister, is forced to go to summer school because she failed English. The only reason she wants to pass the summer course is "just so she would never have to read, or have read to her, another book." Her English teacher, Cynthia, a graduate student at Yale, has a flaky lover who is tormented by nightmares about atom-bomb fireballs meant just for him; awake, he is usually stoned, his only occupation the manic squandering of a sizable inheritance.

Though Cynthia is the novel's only character that one can imagine possibly escaping from the disarray, for she alone has made an active and rational choice in life instead of passively letting things happen, it is soon clear that she is no less doomed than the rest of them. At heart she is as dislocated as her lover, subject to numbing depression, often as helplessly mired in swamps of fragmented inconsequence as her adolescent students. Thinking about her own adolescence, she summons up this ragged skein of memory:

> Her boyfriend from high school had become a
> Marine and later acted in an underground porn film

about Vietnam that she never got to see. Someone who had seen the film told her that he was in drag in the film—a peasant woman who got raped. The person who had seen it and told her that was pretty unreliable, though. He himself was a failed actor, and it would be like him to be jealous of her old boyfriend and to make up a lie like that. When she turned twenty-one, her old boyfriend had had a birthday cake that said "OM" made for her at Carvel. That was after the Marines, and before the porn film. During the break, there had been an ice-cream cake.

It is not just *things* that happen to these idle souls, but thoughts and words and feelings: everything flows together with deadpan randomness—laundromats, brand names, cute T-shirts and bumper stickers, rock songs and campy movies, snatches of wispy talk overheard in the New York coffee shops and department stores and offices and Connecticut houses through which Miss Beattie's specimens drift in a listless stupor. While such wads of dissociated irrelevance have sometimes worked in Ann Beattie's short stories, they become unendurably monotonous in a novel unless the purposeless inertia is disrupted by some decisive action.

That indispensable thunderclap, the dramatic, unexpected event which should stop everyone in his tracks for a long moment of unaccustomed lucidity, occurs more than halfway through *Falling in Place*: John Joel, egged on by his friend Parker, aims a supposedly unloaded gun at his detested sister, and a bullet tears through her side. But the incident alters nothing, enforces no lucidities. Mary survives, her stunted soul unchastened by the brush with death. Her brother will spend half a lifetime with psychiatrists, but we know it will make little difference. Her parents, for a while understandably shaken, will probably divorce and probably remarry (John has a very young and feckless mistress in New York), and their lives will remain essentially the same. Moral apathy has so completely displaced genuine emotion in all these corroded hearts that their lives must go on as always, untouched by the promise of change and redemption.

But one cannot really assert this with any confidence, for who can be sure that Ann Beattie is passing judgment of such a kind—indeed, of any kind—on the deplorable persons she has transfixed with her keen and indefatigably watchful eye? Not once does she reveal the secret of her fascination with all this exasperating flotsam, and *Falling in Place* does entirely without those moments of wacky farce that often brighten her short stories. Making no comic gestures, taking everything in with her customary neutrality and giving it all back, Miss Beattie seems oblivious to her readers, unperturbed by their inevitable irritation and boredom.

Though her stories can be strange and clever, though she is an undeniable original, what Ann Beattie entirely fails to arouse in us as we yawn through *Falling in Place* is any conviction that the men, women, and children whose odd and empty lives she transcribes so expertly count for something that deserves our attention. It scarcely needs saying that we do not have to love a novelist's characters in order to be stirred by them, or that great literary art has always been as much, in fact more, concerned with despicable and wrong-headed and destructive human nature as it is with virtue. But we can respond strongly to empty and meaningless lives in fiction only to the extent that the writer is alive to the human consequences of such emptiness and can persuade us that his invented creatures *matter* in some authentic way. If we do not become involved, all we can feel is tedium and indifference.

Still, Miss Beattie's flat, impassive, unlyrical voice—the

style that is a kind of anti-style, absorbing anything that comes to mind because one thing is no better and no worse than another—may very well suit the prevailing mood as Marge Piercy's thumping optimism cannot. It is as though, when anxious uncertainty is the very air we breathe, nothing seems worth the effort of moral judgment, and in any case it would make no difference to the way things are. They may, and then again they may not, just fall into place.—PEARL K. BELL, "Marge Piercy and Ann Beattie," *Cmty*, July 1980, pp. 60–61

JOHN UPDIKE
"Seeresses"

The New Yorker, November 29, 1976, pp. 164–66

Ann Beattie's first novel, *Chilly Scenes of Winter*, thaws quite beautifully; our first impression, of a pale blank prose wherein events ramify with the random precision of snow-ferns on a winter window, yields, in the second half, to a keen warmth of identification with the hero, Charles, and an ardent admiration of the author's cool powers. Miss Beattie, as readers of her short stories know, works at an unforced pace. Her details—which include the lyrics of the songs her characters overhear on the radio and the recipes of the rather junky food they eat—calmly accrue; her dialogue trails down the pages with an uncanny fidelity to the low-level heartbreaks behind the banal; her resolutely unmetaphorical style builds around us a maze of familiar truths that nevertheless has something airy, eerie, and in the end lovely about it. Her America is like the America one pieces together from the *National Enquirers* that her characters read—a land of pathetic monstrosities, of pain clothed in clichés, of extraterrestrial trivia. Things happen "out there," and their vibes haunt the dreary "here" we all inhabit.

Chilly Scenes of Winter takes place in an unnamed city that must be Washington, D.C.; the slush and sniffles and stalled starters of hibernal megalopolis dampen and chill the book clear through. Charles, who is twenty-seven, works for the government, but for which department or in what function is never explained. He is in love with a woman, Laura, whom he met while she was estranged from her husband, and who has gone back to her husband. He makes contact with her once near the beginning of the book and again near the end. In between, his life is filled with mooning remembrances of her, and with a number of friends and relations who, though real, are ghostly and intermittent in their manifestations to him. His mother, Clara, is mentally unbalanced, given to baths and nudity and psychosomatic pain. His stepfather, Pete, is lonely, awkward, sometimes tipsy, pathetic in his clumsy efforts to win some affection from his stepson, tedious in his addiction to brand-name consumerism and ritual optimism, but withal game, loyal to his mad spouse, and rather winning: a remarkably affectionate and intricate portrait of a very ordinary man. Charles' sister Susan is nineteen, stolid, and involved with a pompous medical student, Mark, whose obnoxiousness, we are delicately led to understand, may be largely in Charles' beholding. Also, there is Charles' old girlfriend, Pamela, who has become an unsteady sort of lesbian, given to sudden reversions to heterosexuality and abrupt flights to California and back. And Charles' potential new girlfriend, Betty, a typist with heavy legs and clothes that try too hard; our hero's unsuccessful attempt to launch his heart into an affair with this doughy apparition is one of the saddest repeating jokes in the rueful

comedy of his aimless days. And there is his best friend, Sam, who could do cartwheels in grade school and is still good with girls, but who has lost his dog and then his job. And there is Sam's new dog, who is nameless, and has insomnia, and jingles his collar as he paces the floor at night. All these characters, not excluding the dog, are exquisitely modulated studies in vacancy, and grow on the reader like moss. At first, Miss Beattie's unblinking sentences, simple declarative in form and present in tense, remind one of Richard Estes' neo-realist street scenes, which render with a Flemish fineness the crassest dreck of our commercial avenues, omitting no detail save pedestrians. After some pages, her tableaux seem more like Segal's plaster-bandage sculptures, their literal lifelikeness magically muffled in utter whiteness. But then color steals into the cheeks of her personae, a timid Wyeth sort of color at first, the first flush of our caring, and this color deepens, so that her portraits at last appear as alive, as likely to make us laugh and cry, as any being composed in these thin-blooded times.

Charles and Sam and Pamela mourn for the sixties. "Everybody's so pathetic," Sam says. "What is it? Is it just the end of the sixties?" Susan, who wasn't there, thinks Woodstock was "a drag. It was nothing but mud." When asked if college kids dance nowadays, she says, "Nobody does much of anything any more. I don't even think there are many drugs on campus." When Bill, Charles' boss, asks him what he should do to "limber up" his Harvard-obsessed son, Charles recommends, with uncharacteristic firmness, a Janis Joplin record. If the moral limbo of this book has an angel in it, it is Joplin; the characters' tenebrous values point backward to her, to the time of violent feeling and communal ecstasy. The novel's literary patron saint, though, is all fifties: J. D. Salinger. Not only does Miss Beattie in a kitchen-cabinet inventory echo the epic bathroom-cabinet inventory in "Zooey," she invokes the master's works specifically:

> "Remember taking me to the zoo [Laura asks Charles], and how upset I got when I asked what giraffes did for fun and you said, 'How could they do anything?'"
>
> "I should have thought of a nicer answer," he says. "Like the cab driver Holden Caulfield asks about the ducks in winter."

If Laura and Charles have a cloying trait, it is their shared "way of feeling sorry for things." She feels sorry not only for giraffes but for plants: "Laura buys plants that are dying in supermarkets—ones that have four or five leaves, marked down to nineteen cents, because she feels sorry for them." Charles, as a child, even felt sorry for bobbing-bird toys: "The birds would dip interminably over a glass of water. One night he felt sorry for them because they weren't getting any rest and poured the glass of water on the floor and attached the birds to the empty glass."

Miss Beattie seems to feel sorry for this whole decade. Her range of empathy is broad and even lusty. Her long ninth chapter, taking Charles and Sam out for an evening at a restaurant, where they are joined by a third at-loose-ends young man, called (another *hommage*?) J. D., displays a fearless length of purely male palaver as it goes from lonely and strained to drunken and uproarious. Her depiction of Charles' mother's craziness is chillingly, touchingly, clairvoyantly right; madness and dreams are areas in fiction where, because almost anything would seem to go, almost nothing does. Miss Beattie's male dreams are good, too:

> That night he dreams that he is launched in a spaceship to the stars. His mother is there. She is taking a

bath on a star. He gets back in the rocket. Mechanical failure! That strange jingling! He sits up in bed, eyes wide open. The dog is walking again, his collar jingling. By now it is clear; the dog has insomnia.

And she succeeds in showing love from the male point of view, not in its well-publicized sexual dimension but in the pastel spectrum of nostalgia, daydream, and sentimental longing. The accretion of plain lived moments, Miss Beattie has discovered, like Virginia Woolf and Nathalie Sarraute before her, is sentiment's very method; grain by grain the hours and days of fictional lives invest themselves with weight. The plot turns a corner, and we feel a pressure behind the eyes. What could appear drier and more fruitless than this flat description of how to serve a meal, one of the novel's frequent obeisances to the daily fact of food:

> Charles lifts the roast out of the oven, puts it on a plate and carries it to the table. He goes back and gets the pan of lima beans, pours most of the water into the sink, and carries the pan to the table. He goes back and turns off the oven and the burner and gets the wine. He takes the wine to the table, where Sam is sitting, then goes to the kitchen for glasses.

But at the book's end another step-by-step description of food processing (how to make an orange soufflé) carries to a delicious consummation nearly three hundred pages of Charles' unsatisfied hungering. Patience pays off for hero and author alike. Not to give it away, but Miss Beattie in the turned-down oven of her long indoors Washington winter has cooked up a rare delicacy, a convincing happy ending.

JOHN ROMANO
"Ann Beattie and the 60's"

Commentary, February 1977, pp. 62–64

Ann Beattie's stories have been appearing in the *New Yorker* for the past few years, and have now been collected in a volume called *Distortions*, published simultaneously with the author's *Chilly Scenes of Winter*, a novel. It is unusual, of course, for a new author to appear with two books at once, but evidently Ann Beattie has been able to compel special treatment from her publisher as well as from reviewers and readers. It is the uniqueness of her talent that compels. Her best fiction renders a distinctive subject matter in a distinctive tone, and the note she sounds is powerfully her own.

Her subject matter is a certain shiftlessness and lack of self-apprehension besetting people in their twenties and thirties: a former Phi Beta Kappa guiltily resigned to living on welfare checks, young wives rejecting husbands and lovers in desultory and emotionless gestures of independence, a lesbian feminist whose only friends are male. She conveys the drabness of these lives by her tone and by an almost hallucinatory particularity of detail. We are taken on that round of grocery shopping, walking the dog, getting the worthless car fixed, which Auden had in mind when he said that "in headaches and in worry,/Vaguely life leaks away." But Beattie's writing is not tedious; there is, instead, something graceful and painstaking about her fidelity to the ordinary.

The story, "Imagined Scenes," presents a young woman who works nights sitting up with an old man who has insomnia, while her husband, a graduate student, is busy studying for his oral exams. Or so she assumes. The daily schedules of the couple barely overlap. They do not inhabit the same hours, and there is something chilling and mysterious about the gap between them. When she returns home in the mornings, there are frequent signs of inexplicable activity: three coffee cups on the table, or a favorite plant missing. Once when she calls home at four in the morning there is no answer. Her husband's explanations are plausible—a couple she has never met came to visit, he was asleep when the phone rang—but they are oddly insufficient, too, and seem slightly sinister in the haze of mutual incomprehension. The glimpses, the physical data, which the woman has of her husband's life in her absence tell her nothing, though they hint at guilty secrets. They cannot be either ignored or interpreted. Scattered among them are the monologues of her patient, the old man, which are very skillfully made to seem only accidentally relevant to the woman's puzzling home life. We are given nothing more. However, a suggestion of the peculiar way in which Beattie makes such material her own lurks in the title: "Imagined Scenes." We do not realize, or not all at once, that what the young woman has "imagined" is not her husband's private or guilty activity. She has accepted not the explanations but the sufficiency unto themselves of the physical facts. She "imagines" only that she is in Greece, or someplace warm, by the sea, while the scene of her actual present life is snowy. It is the reader who has been seduced into guessing at the husband's hidden life.

I dwell on this short story because it seems to me emblematic of Beattie's skill in this genre. But one thing more should be said about it, which goes rather beyond skill. We guess at the "real facts" of the woman's life because we care about her, her sadness has been made significant. It follows that the author has cared about her in the making. But then it is more astonishing to perceive that the woman cares so little, so indistinctly, for herself. She is not suspicious, she has no imagination; the mark of Beattie's respect for this creation is not to have slipped her some healthy suspicion, as it were, under the counter. In this forbearance the writer resembles some impossible ideal of a loving parent who succeeds in not interfering in her children's lives. To love one's characters—Tolstoy is the presiding genius here—is to allow them to be who they are.

A risk of a particular kind attends this achievement and Beattie is not immune to it. The style of much "serious fiction" in recent years has tended to be cool, to attend scrupulously to the surface of events, with a language pruned and polished in respect of its own surface. Now Beattie's writing has something in common with this style: her sentences are often plain, flat, their grammar exposed like the lighting fixtures in avant-garde furniture boutiques, and the effect is at first wearying. Only later does the sympathetic center of her work betray itself. We may feel misled by the outward reserve, but, again, her willingness to distort when necessary, her passion for the particular, is ultimately an index of her concern for the integrity of things and people in themselves.

Many of the people in these books verge on the grotesque—dwarfs, a cleaning woman hulking in mind and body who believes she was a cat in a former life. Here, too, Beattie risks a convergence with her slicker contemporaries, whose fascination with the grotesque is full of smugness about what is "normal." (Beattie herself invokes the photographs of Diane Arbus in several places, but I for one have never quite decided what Arbus's relation to her subjects really was.) There is a dog in *Chilly Scenes of Winter* who is a good example of Beattie's success with the grotesque. The dog is purchased to replace an entirely admirable dog who has died of old age, much mourned. But the new dog is ugly—part dachshund, part cocker spaniel—as well as hapless and insomniac. And yet, the people around him feel the dog must be fed and must not be compared to his predecessor; at night, his audible perambulations must be endured. Because, "terrible genetic mistake" that he is, the dog, named "Dog," is real and undeniable. He is part of that world of fact that Beattie honors almost compulsively, whatever its unwelcomeness or distortion.

The central figure of the novel, *Chilly Scenes of Winter*, is a young man named Charles, whose quality of self-ignorance is Beattie's fullest, most intelligent image. He does not know that he is smart, and apparently does not wish to know it, because he has chosen to work in a government office where his abilities are irrelevant. He does not know that he is kind: his many services to others are unmarked by signs of sympathy, generosity, concern, or liking; he is made dizzy by his sister's assertion that he is good. His knowledge that he is unhappy is merely circumstantial. Approaching thirty, he has come to terms with none of the absurd relationships that comprise his life. His mother is "emotionally disturbed," prone to nakedness and sloppy, day-long bathing. Pete, his alcoholic stepfather, depends pathetically on his reluctant friendship. Laura, whom Charles loves but seems—sometimes—to have lost, is married. Charles spends much of the book driving slowly past her house, for the sight of the light in her window. ("What's this, *The Great Gatsby* or something?" his friend quips)—only to discover, near the end, that she had moved out weeks ago. Charles's only workable relationship is with his friend Sam, his constant companion, who is present on nearly every page. It is significant that Sam as portrayed by Beattie is dull, shapeless, unrealized. His friendship with Charles is at once blank and affectionate. Its very existence is capable of surprising them, when they must notice it:

> "You're my only friend," Charles says.
> "You're *my* only friend," Sam says.
> "That's pathetic," Charles says.
> "How did this happen?"
> "I don't know. I just stopped seeing people or they moved or something."

Charles and Sam know nothing, in fact, about the causes of their loneliness except the details of the pleasureless routine it imposes upon them. Charles is forever gazing hungrily into a cupboard bare of anything except Tuna Stretcher and a jar of pickles, forever wondering at the existential courage of people who do all their shopping on one day for the week ahead. "Maybe Edward Hopper? Or a cartoon?" he asks of the world that takes place around him, mingling the surreal and the mundane:

> He sits at the counter next to an old woman who smells of mint. Her hair rolls away from her face in even waves. A shopping bag is wedged between her feet. There is a dirty white towel over whatever is in the shopping bag. The woman is drinking black coffee, into which she empties three packs of "Sweet 'n Low." She is humming "Swing Low, Sweet Chariot." Charles orders tea with lemon. A priest comes in and greets the old woman enthusiastically. She moves from the counter to a booth with him, knocking Charles as she draws out her shopping bag. Something moves under the towel: a cat. A striped cat.

The scene is unnerving, as Charles distinctly feels; but he feels, too, that it is harmless, and that it is a mistake to be unnerved. It awakens in him the conviction of his own paranoia: "sleeping people in public places are always dead." But on second look it is over-shrewd to shrug off the latent threat. The brand name drifts mysteriously into the song lyric. The shopping bag is

alive. Charles's eye for detail reflects the paradox of Beattie's own: a passive accuracy of observation masks an active, unsettling distrust of what one sees.

The word game of "Sweet 'n Low" brings to mind one aspect of Ann Beattie's writing that seems to me regrettable. Charles's mother's baths, his own baths, his sister's showers; Sam's car, Pete's car; dogs and cats; medical references, doctors, disease—all these constitute what used to be called "motifs" or images. Details drifting from person to person, thing to thing, they bend too steadily and purposefully toward significance, betraying an obtrusive self-consciousness about craft which is rather rare in Beattie's work. This seems to me directly at odds with the vitality of her talent, her capacity to conjure the independence and actuality of things.

Given her particular subject matter, it hardly seems necessary to underline Beattie's pertinence to the present cultural-political pass. In *Chilly Scenes of Winter*, in the story "Fancy Flights," and elsewhere, our attention is called to a contemporary pathos whose effects few have yet begun to gauge: the sadness over the passing of the 60's. It is by no means necessary to feel this nostalgia in order to ponder its importance. Let me say at once that Beattie herself does not seem sad. Some reviewers have referred to the image in "Fancy Flights" of an ex-hippie locked in his bathroom, smoking dope and talking to his daughter's bunny rabbit, with the Mick Jagger lyric running through his mind: "All the dreams we held so close all seemed to go up in smoke." But the reviewers have failed to remark that this is one of Beattie's only *unsympathetic* portraits, the only one of her protagonists she doesn't like.

Charles's lament for the passing of the 60's, which is more to the point, occurs in abrupt, anxious seizures of lostness and bewilderment. "Elvis Presley is forty," he says. "Jim Morrison's *widow* is dead." The tone is that same tone in which he laments the waning quality of Hydrox cookies: "What happened to them? They used to be so good. Sugar. No doubt they're leaving out sugar." It is witty of Beattie to confine the sociological import of her novel to such trivial remarks. She conveys adroitly the sensibility of After-the-Fall, without making fictive claims for the heights from which we fell. The Golden Age mythology and its attendant rhetoric will inevitably attach, for a while, to talk about the 60's. This represents, of course, a historical distortion, matched in its badness of fit only by the myth that the New Left was the Antichrist. Beattie's presentation of Charles's nostalgia for the 60's suggests that such longing has the limits of an elegy to lost innocence, and the advantages, too. It distorts, but it also provides, however disingenuously, the idea that things can be better than they are, because they have been better before now. As usual, the prospects for hope seem to depend upon some degree of mystification.

ANNE HULBERT
"Secrets and Surprises"

The New Republic, January 20, 1979, pp. 34–36

Secrets and surprises might seem like unexpected specialties for Ann Beattie. In the pages of *The New Yorker* and of her two previous books—*Distortions*, a collection of short stories, and *Chilly Scenes of Winter*, a novel—she anatomizes the everyday lives of characters who are headed nowhere in particular and are unfamiliar with the usual literary kind of secrets and surprises—the kind associated with epiphanies. But as Beattie has hinted all along and emphasizes in this new collection of short stories, hidden knowledge and unexpected discoveries are also staples of ordinary, undramatic life. They don't just belong to rare moments, and they don't necessarily irradiate life with significance. Her characters are lonely and can't help having secrets; they are used to being taken aback by the unexpected because they foresee little and control less. Their lives don't really change after they acknowledge their secrets to themselves or partially reveal them to others. Instead, another disorderly day dawns. In the appropriately uninflected prose and loosely structured stories of *Secrets and Surprises* Beattie makes the days and characters come to life—almost paradoxically—more powerfully and poignantly than she has before.

The days Beattie depicts, however nondescript they are, are not the 9–5 mainstream kind. She writes about her own contemporaries, who turned 20 and lethargically offbeat as the 1960s came to an end. They lead marginal lives out in the country or on the fringe of cities. A character in *Chilly Scenes of Winter* articulates the feeling that pervades almost every story: "'Everybody's so pathetic,' Sam says. 'What is it? Is it just the end of the sixties?'"

It's not that the 1960s have left Beattie's characters bitterly disillusioned about politics or society; the decade has simply drained them. They aren't motivated by any ambitions of their own, or by external goals or expectations. Instead of looking out for number one or trying to be respectable, they look to friends, with whom they often share a kind of communal esprit, although nothing as concrete as a commune. In her stories, Beattie shows from up close how ambiguous these friendships can be, how many secrets and surprises they can hold.

In fact, her longest story is entitled "Friends." There Beattie evokes in rich detail the amorphous scene of drifting friends—and lovers, since that is what many of the friends have been or wish they were—that sets the tone for the whole collection. Perry, the protagonist, has abandoned the lonely project of winterizing his Vermont house to join a crowd of old friends—gathered from various outposts in New England—for a partying weekend at Francie's house in New Hampshire. The first night there, when all the guests are sprawled drunkenly about the house, Perry retreats to the attic mattress he has appropriated after countless weekend visits.

> Waiting to fall asleep he thought about what Francie had told him recently: that he was her best friend. 'A woman should have another woman for her best friend,' Francine said and shrugged, 'but you're it.' 'Why would you have to have a woman for a best friend?' he said. She shrugged again. 'It's hard for men and women to be best friends,' she said. He nodded and she thought he understood, but all he meant to acknowledge was that they were close, but that there was also something hard about that. What it was, was that it had never been the right time to go to bed with her, and if he did it after all this time, he would have been self-conscious.

In any case, there is barely a moment for unassertive Perry to divulge his secret love in the confusion of friends—a band of rock musicians, a "spacy" woman and her baby daughter, a neurotically hypersensitive teacher, and an array of other flaky types—dropping in and out, breaking up and making up. But there is no place for frustration or resentment to mount in Beattie's diffuse atmosphere; ambivalence prevails. "Sometimes it bothered him that he was just one of the people she liked to have around all the time, although it meant a lot to

him that they had all been friends for so long." Beattie unobtrusively displays truly remarkable imaginative insight and accomplished control in her evocation of Perry's low-key preoccupation. As she showed in *Chilly Scenes of Winter* in her exhaustive portrayal of her lovelorn protagonist, Charles, she is at home in the emotional life of men—attuned to their hopes, reveries and romantic longings, which interest her more than their lusts.

Beattie's central theme is one that calls for variations; for the relationships she describes are distinguished by seeming—at least to those involved in them—not to follow any standard pattern. Commitments are unclear, expectations unformulated and communications faulty. Beattie imagines variations in all their minute particularity in her stories; and this collection of them conveys an often dispiriting sense of the common underlying muddle.

The general outline of "Friends" reappears in "A Vintage Thunderbird" and "Colorado," and Beattie comes the closest she ever does to suggesting a representative predicament. Nick and Robert, the protagonists of these stories, are best friends with Penelope and Karen respectively, but secretly wish they were more. The women, enigmatic themselves and not very understanding of others, meanwhile move in with and out on other men. Neither Robert nor Nick makes the move to surprise his friend with an admission of his love; but each is always there to deal with the surprises visited upon him by that friend. The surprises—even those that directly affect the friendship, as when Penelope suddenly proposes to Robert that the two of them leave "stifling" New Haven and head for Colorado—are not decisive turning points; they are barely registered as ripples in the general drifting course of their lives. It's details, however, more than situation outlines (there really are no plots) that count for Beattie and that she makes weigh with us. She describes the nondescript, accounts for moments that usually slip away between eventful hours, notes unconnected thoughts that pass through her characters' minds, records minute details—"the little crust of salt on her bottom lip." The ineluctable but unpredictable daily progress of lives on her pages seems familiar, in a depressing yet also reassuring and even enlightening way; days in real life have the same mixture of commonplace outline and mysterious detail.

Beattie adds familial relations to other of her stories, and she shows that blood ties don't clarify or secure matters between characters. In "La Petite Danceuse de Quatorze Ans" the famous artist fathers of Griffin and Diana are part of the cause of their having a relationship in the first place and all of the cause of the complications of it. (In fact, the father fixation so dominates that we miss the disparate array of minor preoccupations Beattie usually gathers about her characters and apparently artlessly arranges.) The ironic narrator of "The Lawn Party," one of the best stories in the collection, returns to his parents' house for the Fourth of July with his daughter, without his wife, and without his arm, which he has lost in a car accident with his wife's sister, the woman he really loved. He refuses to join his relatives on the lawn but does not really escape them. Instead he distracts himself from serious solitary brooding with sardonic banter with emissaries sent to rouse him—and even with his student/friend who might be a real companion. Beattie explores the claims of siblings in "Deer Season," where two sisters try to rearrange their stultifying life together when a past common lover returns, and in "A Clever Kids Story," which depicts a sister's effort to come to terms with her memory of her youthful adoration of her brother. As usual, there is no final reckoning for Beattie's characters, just a trying process of reacting—usually with an unsettling lack of feeling or energy—

to demands and events they don't control and can't neatly reconcile.

Other stories are about stranger human contacts—about relationships that emphasize the root sense of isolation and enigmatic detachment latent in all her stories. In "Distant Music" Sharon and Jack, who share "a hatred of laundromats, guilt about not sending presents to relatives on birthdays and Christmas, and a dog—part Weimaraner, part German Shepherd—named Sam," meet in Washington Square on Friday to spend the weekend together and trade Sam for the next week. Sharon is silent and not used to being loved; and she seems strangely unperturbed when Jack leaves her and when Sam, grown vicious, is put away. In "Octascope," a less successful story, another passive woman and her baby move in with a marionette-maker, sight unseen. She longs, almost desperately, for facts about him: "I have to know if we are to stay always, or for a long time, or for a short time," she says. Instead, the two of them talk of eggs and beehives. There is a lot of disquieting, empty space in these stories—in the characters' heads and hearts and in the holes between characters.

But Beattie sees more than blankness. The secret she shares with us in acutely captured moments and carefully recorded details is of the unobtrusive but crucial presence of generous impulses and good intentions in lives that are lonely and undirected, in friendships that are full of ignorance and confusion. And at a time when hopelessness and bleak isolation are assumed in much fiction—and are never very far from her own—that is a surprise.

JACK BEATTY
"Falling in Place"

The New Republic, June 7, 1980, pp. 34–36

In the two novels and many stories she has produced since she began to publish in the early 1970s, Ann Beattie has written almost exclusively of the now not so young men and women who came of age in the 1960s, a time that bears a prelapsarian glow to her characters as they look back at it from the no-man's-land of subsidized passivity into which so many of them seem to drift after leaving the trenches of graduate school. Not surprisingly, and not without justice, Ann Beattie has been praised on sociological grounds as the chronicler of this generation. She has indeed been given the kind of critical attention usually reserved for our handful of art novelists, and this both because of her subject matter and because of her technique. Ann Beattie disdains the bogus dynamism of plot for a more oblique and lifelike mode of development which eschews intensifications, strong ironies, and climaxes. In literary commentary there is a prejudice against the well-paced and plotted story, and in the making of the reputation of a writer like Ann Beattie the part this plays should not be underestimated.

My own view is that Ann Beattie's sociological realism is superficial, a reflective realism of accurate detail—what songs are in, what clothes, what expressions—rather than the kind of critical realism whose exemplar is *Buddenbrooks.* As for her artistry, I think she has yet to adapt her laid-back sensibility to the large-scale dynamics of the novel. Her short stories seem immediately accomplished, whereas in *Chilly Scenes of Winter* and now in *Falling in Place* one misses that irresistible momentum of conclusion one always feels in a first-rate novel. She drifts and pads just when we want her to get on with it. She can't seem to rein in her characters, either; and she rivals them

in her tolerance for gabby potheads who fill her books with clouds of sophomoric banter.

The recipient of a graduate school education in English, Ann Beattie no doubt has had it drummed into her that narrative mastery is a species of imperialism that went out with the high tide of capitalism, the death of God, the end of patriarchy, or something equally nasty and portentous. Since we are no longer in control of our lives, this view holds, the novelist ought not to play God in controlling the destinies of her characters. (In fact, one of Ann Beattie's stories contains a parable about a godlike narrator of childhood stories, and he, tellingly, is killed in Vietnam.) Drift in a novel is not therefore what we have always thought it, an artistic weakness, but a profound comment on the way we live now. We drift, characters in the novels that represent us drift, all God's former children drift.

Ann Beattie buries her stories under heaps of detail. When one of her characters enters a room you know you're going to get an inventory of everything that character sees. Has Ann Beattie ever considered the effect of this? Along with her characters, she seems to be stalling, marking time, trying to figure out what to do next. One never feels this with an accomplished novelist, and even a hack would know that he has to keep things moving along. But Ann Beattie is a writer of sensibility, and the point of all her details is to give that faculty a workout, and never mind that this makes her readers impatient with her fine local effects, and her novels draggy and slack.

In fact, the first half of *Falling in Place* isn't slack at all. Ann Beattie has a reputation as a rapid producer, so one is not surprised that the time of the novel is last summer. The surprise is her milieu, for, as *Publishers Weekly* rightly says, we are in "Cheever country," that green reach of western Connecticut whose spiritual condition is marvelously evoked by one of Beattie's characters when she says: "It's so beautiful here, and we don't notice it very much, and when we do, it doesn't seem to help." All those lawns, all that unhappiness.

Cheever country it certainly is, and if I may be permitted an allusion, I would say that it is Heller country also—the suburban Heller of the underrated *Something Happened.* The cast of characters is the same in both novels—a sexually restive husband, a martyr wife, an unhappy little boy, a bitchy teenage girl. So is the theme implied by this paradigmatic assemblage—that the American Dream is a cheat. That both fictional fathers are advertising men is not Beattie's homage to Heller but an inevitability for any writer who takes up the theme of shadows over suburbia. Advertising, after all, has become an almost wholly metaphoric profession. In making a character an advertising man, a novelist shucks the burden of describing his workaday life: we already know what he does, and we don't like it. It's a relief to know that Beattie is not above exploiting a cliché, for its economies.

Beattie's ad man is John Knapp. At the good Cheever age of 40, he has drifted into an affair with Nina, a woman so young that she refers to his wife, Louise, as "old." Nina, a graduate of Bard, is a more familiar Beattie type. She has a small apartment on the West Side, with whose every roach Beattie makes us familiar, a job at Lord and Taylor, claims she is more "together" than John, and possesses a platoon of dropout friends who drop in inconveniently and always with the exasperating nonchalance of the wholly self-absorbed. There is very little in the way of plot. Instead, to move things along Beattie shifts rapidly from New York to Connecticut, from Nina to John to Louise, and also to John's children, John Joel and Mary. Mary's summer school teacher, Cynthia, also has a place on this crowded canvas, as does her circle of friends and tag-alongs, who, in one of the interesting loopings in the novel, link her to Nina.

This brisk cutting from character to character is combined, at first effectively, with brief italicized codas to the main chapters containing the intense ruminations of several of the characters. The shifts in mood and point of view thus produced, plus our roused expectations over whether John, who has already taken to living with his mother in Rye, will finally leave his wife for Nina, create a sense of movement that sweeps us along for a while. The narrative method is similar to that in such Altman films as A *Wedding* or *Nashville*, where rapid cutting from character to character takes the place of a forward flowing narrative centered on a single character. But this method works better in a film, which swims past us in an hour or two, than it does in a novel, where we need the tug of a strong narrative line to make us turn the pages. Heller, to return to him for a moment, was attacked for writing a big novel without a strong narrative line; nothing happened, the critics carped. But Heller's prose is so charged with feeling that

he can compel us by the power of his voice alone. By contrast, Ann Beattie's prose voice is flat, even, uninflected. It is an admirable instrument for conveying the laid-back styles of her characters, but there is no agony in it, as there is in Heller's voice. And agony compels.

Something finally happens in *Falling in Place*, and in yet another parallel to Heller's novel, it involves the ad-man's son. John Joel, a fat 10-year-old with an empty summer stretching before him, is the most affecting character Beattie has drawn. His father has inexplicably moved out of the house, his mother seems to care more for the memory of her dead dog than she does for him, his nemesis, his sister, taunts him for his weight, and his only friend is a chubby little monster named Parker. *He* is a superb and memorable invention, full of the rage that Beattie's post-1960s characters lack. Parker pricks holes in his mother's diaphragm, and what he does to John Joel is equally shocking. If only the novel ended 20 pages after this event! But no, it drifts on and on, out of gas, for another 100 pages. In *Falling in Place* Ann Beattie's editors have let her talent down.

S. N. BEHRMAN

1893–1973

Samuel Nathaniel Behrman was born on June 9, 1893, in Worcester, Massachusetts. After attending Clark College in Worcester from 1912 to 1914, he transferred to Harvard, where he studied playwriting alongside Sidney Howard. He received a B.A. in 1916, then an M.A. from Columbia in 1918. For the next nine years he was a Broadway press agent, a book reviewer for *The New Republic* and the *New York Times*, and a frequent contributor of stories and articles to magazines. Several unsuccessful collaborations closed out of town before Behrman's first solo play, *The Second Man*, became a Broadway hit. It established the form of Behrman's work to come: sophisticated comedy of manners, set in the brittle stratosphere of the aristocracy. Throughout the 1930s, Behrman produced not only five successful plays—*Brief Moment* (1931), *Biography* (1932), *End of Summer* (1936), *Amphitryon 38* (1937), and *No Time For Comedy* (1939)—but a number of screenplays, such as *Queen Christina* and *Anna Karenina* for Greta Garbo. In 1936 he married Elza Heifetz; they had one child, and raised her two children by a previous marriage.

With *No Time For Comedy*, Behrman left the auspices of the powerful Theatre Guild for those of the Playwrights Producing Company, which he co-founded with Sidney Howard, Elmer Rice, Maxwell Anderson, and Robert Sherwood. The company produced his next several plays, including *The Pirate* in 1942 and the long-running *Jacobowsky and the Colonel*, which won the New York Drama Critics Circle Award for 1944. Critics began to note a decline in Behrman's work after World War II; most of his new plays were adaptations, without the probing social comment of his originals. In the early 1950s, he turned to other media, writing a biography of the art dealer *Duveen* in 1952, and a celebrated series of childhood reminiscences for the *New Yorker*, collected as *The Worcester Account* in 1954. That year also saw the premiere of his biggest hit, the musical *Fanny*, for which he wrote the book with Josh Logan. The semi-autobiographical *The Cold Wind and the Warm* (1958) was less popular, but its critical reputation has grown ever since.

More books followed in the next decade. Behrman produced a biography of Max Beerbohm in 1960, and in 1968 fulfilled a lifelong ambition by writing a novel, *The Burning Glass*. His last two plays, 1962s *Lord Pengo* (adapted from *Duveen*) and 1964s *But For Whom Charlie*, recaptured some of the old Behrman spirit and success. His last published work was his memoir, *People in a Diary* (1972). He died on September 9, 1973, in New York City.

Personal

To be brought up in a poverty-stricken household, to know nothing but poverty in childhood and adolescence, is not so bad while you are enduring it; it is quite tolerable in fact, at

least it was in my case. It is in later life that it takes its toll. In the Providence Street ghetto in Worcester, Massachusetts, everybody was as poor as we were. The one rich man on the hill, who had a stucco house with a stained-glass window and who owned a Winton Six, was still devoured by the consuming passion to become the president of the Providence Street Syn-agogue directly across the street from us. He was illiterate in Hebrew and therefore had no standing. My father, on the other hand, who didn't have a penny, was learned in the sacred books and did have standing. There used to be an expression on the hill—"Does he know the little black dots?"—referring to the symbols for cantillation under letters of the Hebrew texts—and if you didn't know them, neither stained-glass windows nor Winton Sixes could save you. I realize now that the Providence Street community was a theological aristocracy in which money gave you no status. But I have been haunted by dreams of poverty all my life, through all the years since I have emerged from it. I dream that I am in hotel rooms without the money to pay for them. I dream that I am jobless and can't get a job. A pet, though disagreeable, dream is that I am walking, in a heavy rain, and carrying a leaden suitcase from Boston to Worcester. When I get to Worcester, there is nowhere to go. Everyone is dead. I go to the Bancroft Hotel, go up in the elevator, and walk down a corridor. Exhausted from the walk, my shoes and my clothes soaking, I open a door, see a bed, and sink down on it. Then I see that the room is occupied. I must not fall asleep lest the occupant come in. I struggle to remain awake. I fall assleep. . . .

I went for two years to Clark College in Worcester, then switched to Harvard to study playwriting with George Pierce Baker. Harvard was idyllic then. Forty years later I was invited to come to Kirkland House for a week to "talk to the boys." The difference between the Cambridge I had known and the one I saw now was shattering: the difference between a small, man-ageable town and a swollen segment of the Boston-Washington conurbation. Exotics jostled each other in the streets—town and sari. For years after leaving Harvard I used to dream, in the inhospitable, jobless years I spent in New York, that I would wake up in Weld Hall, on the Harvard Yard. And yet the two years at Harvard were a clouded fantasy. I was haunted by the incessant query: What would I do when I got out, how get a job, how make a living? Providence Street got its licks in! My fears proved not to be chimerical; I did have a terrible time getting a job in New York—and in other cities as well.—S.N. BEHRMAN, *People in a Diary*, 1972, pp. 6–7

In the fall of 1958 a Broadway-bound play, *The Cold Wind and the Warm*, opened at the Colonial Theater in Boston. Three complimentary tickets arrived at our home in Worcester from the author, S. N. Behrman, who had been my father's closest friend when they grew up together in Worcester's eastside tene-ment ghetto at the turn of the century. Despite the fact that the play was purported to be an evocation of my father and the incidents surrounding his short life, and that the very solid and reputable actor Eli Wallach would be portraying him, my mother chose not to go. A considerable charge of ill will and animosity had been generated in the family—we were ex-tensive; uncles, aunts, and cousins spread throughout southern New England—by a series of stories Behrman had published in *The New Yorker* during the forties and early fifties. The stories told of growing up in the Jewish tenement community of Provi-dence Street in Worcester, and through them ran the bright bizarre indelible thread of my father, who, persons close to the friendship agreed, had been Behrman's mentor, sponsor, and to a large extent the source of his inspiration. The character was called Willie Lavin, but he was instantly and totally recognizable as Dan Asher by the remaining members of the community. The stories were later collected into a book, *The Worcester Account*, and from that book the 1958 play emerged.

With each successive stage of presentation, the familial hostility smoldered anew, bursting into flame in variegated

New England hot pockets. I had read all the stories and thought the portrayal of my father, of whom I had only a shadowy recollection, compassionate and loving throughout. But Behrman, in the eyes of the family, had committed two unforgivable sins: He had not asked the widow's permission to evoke her husband's life, and in the culminating story in the series, a poignant and incisive exploration titled "Point of the Needle" which appeared in the June 5, 1954, issue of *The New Yorker*, he revealed the latter stages of my father's mental illness and the explicit circumstances of his suicide in a neurological institution. That issue struck Worcester and outlying points, as my mother wrote in an anguished letter to Behrman, "like an avalanche." No one dreamed that Sam Behrman would reveal the last days of his dear friend's life when the harrowing details had been carefully concealed from my brother and me and our cousins for so many years.—DON ASHER, *The Eminent Yachtsman and the Whorehouse Piano Player*, 1973, pp. 16–17

General

As for an assessment of Behrman in his own right, considered apart from those literary influences that were brought to bear on him, there is the inescapable conclusion that some of his plays and published books were a critical success; some were not. Only his prose essays remained at a high level of achieve-ment and survive today as the best of his work. His one attempt at writing a novel, as has been made clear, was, by common consensus and by his own estimation, a failure. In truth, the often commended brilliance of his stage dialogues has been overstressed through the years by friendly critics such as Joseph Wood Krutch. It required, after all, such theatrical talent as that of the Lunts, Katherine Cornell, and Ina Claire to bring Behrman his stage successes, although not infrequently the discontentment of his principal actors sent Behrman back to his desk for the revision of an entire scene. Too often, however, no amount of rewriting would save certain plays such as *Wine of Choice* and *Dunnigan's Daughter* from the deserved wrath of critics.

Probably the most astute assessment of Behrman is that of John Gassner who wrote that "Behrman's art of comedy, in-cluding his so-called comic detachment consists of an ambiva-lence of attitudes that has as its sources the simultaneous possession of a nimble mind and a mellow temperament." For Behrman is at the same time critical and forgiving of human weakness. The "nimble mind" of which Gassner speaks allowed Behrman to form moral judgments in a great many plays, among them *Meteor*, *Amphitryon 38*, and *Jane*; but the mellow temperament prevented him from possessing an out-right vindictiveness, even in a play like *Jacobowsky and the Colonel* where, with a certain comic detachment, he chose at the conclusion to look toward the dawning of a better era in human history than to treat the horrors of fascism with all of the vindictiveness he might have.

Behrman is the humane product of the same American Dream at which he had scoffed as a young man but which he came to embrace as a matured writer when what he wrote lent credence (as, for example, in *The Worcester Account*) to the fabled promise of America. Even then, however, Behrman looked at America with a critical but understanding point of view. In *Meteor*, for instance, Raphael Lord's dynamic urge to rise spectacularly in the capitalistic system results in a moral and economic catastrophe, not because the system itself is necessarily corrupt, but because Lord himself does not play within such rules as exist. The same general explanation can be applied to a play like *Dunnigan's Daughter* in which Clay

Ranier's shabby sense of values is at fault, not his fundamental desire to become an economic "success." A reading of *Duveen* also illustrates that the American millionaires who were Duveen's customers are not unsophisticated because of their exposure to the American Dream but because they themselves are conspicuously and regrettably short on aesthetic and moral cultivation.

In real life Behrman developed this aesthetic and moral cultivation in himself. He played by ethical standards and wrote to the end that others might be pleasantly entertained while they were gently but seriously informed at the same time. In plays like *Biography, Rain from Heaven,* and *End of Summer* Behrman commented on the need for mutual toleration of social and political views; and he did so with an element of wittiness. In the first act of *End of Summer,* for example, a conversation between old Mrs. Wyler and the young radical Will Dexter is well in progress when she poses a question: "I suppose you're one of those young radicals our colleges are said to be full of nowadays. Tell me, what do you young radicals stand for?" Dexter replies with a comic, if honest, answer: "I haven't decided exactly what I'm for, but I'm pretty certain what I'm against." Such exchanges as these are serious in a comic vein, and they contain in essence the comic approach that endeared him to both critics and theater audiences. Throughout his career Behrman appealed to his public through the intellect and the heart, never through the glands. He believed quite realistically and without naiveté in the proposition that life can be savored and refined and that the human race can, if it wishes, be perfected and improved upon beyond anything commonly considered possible. He preferred to think of man as a fragment of God, as he wrote in *Rain from Heaven,* rather than as a highly developed animal. Most of all, he illustrated in his own life and writing that it is not only preferable but reasonable that human beings can laugh and yet come to terms with the stark reality of life.—KENNETH T. REED, S. N. *Behrman,* 1975, pp. 134–36

Works

DRAMA

Biography, despite an excellent initial idea and many flashes of expert high comedy dialogue, never measures up in the sum total to the expectations in store for it. After a good first act, and a less good second act, it seems to be continually on the verge of coming to grips with its main theme only to skate blithely away from it in the field of farce. In his characterization, too, Mr. Behrman, except in the subtle delineation of his leading character, has only sketched types, which are all the more obviously types in contrast to the central figure. As *Biography* does afford considerable amusement, it may seem unnecessarily perverse to dwell at length on its failings. If *Biography* were the work of a less gifted playwright this might be true. We should be thankful for what we had received and hope for more next time. But Mr. Behrman, by right of being one of our most brilliant writers of high comedy—a field in which American dramatists are notable chiefly because of their rarity—must be judged by standards considerably more severe.

Mr. Behrman has selected as his protagonist a charming, easy-going woman painter whose relations with her fellow men have not been "evil" but just casual during a lifetime of love affairs. At forty when the edge seems to be wearing thin on life she is revivified by the offer of a thwarted and arrogant young emissary of a cheap publishing house to write her biography for a sensational magazine, detailing facts about prominent subjects painted and loved by her.

Stung to anger by the blatant rudeness of the young editor, yet captivated by his sullen and rather pathetic crusading qualities, she starts to work, only to draw down on her head the ire of her first lover, now a platitudinous candidate for the United States Senate, who intercedes with his prospective father-in-law to prevent the publication which may ruin his career. She finally falls in love with and lives with the young editor, reenkindles unwillingly the spark of devotion in her first lover who proposes matrimony, and then burns the manuscript of her own free will and departs for Hollywood to chronicle more great names on canvas, knowing that her spirit of "tolerance" could never permit her to be happy with either man.

In brief outline *Biography* seems to bear the elements of a splendid comedy and in brief outline it does. The trouble is that Mr. Behrman was not content to let his story tell itself in the terms of the characters but must needs introduce many extraneous scenes which detract from his main plot—notably the farcical one in the third act wherein the first lover, his fiancée, and prospective father-in-law all argue it out in the woman's studio. Some of these interludes are comic in themselves, but high comedy should spring primarily from the characterization, and even brilliant dialogue cannot disguise this fact.—MORTON EUSTIS, "Wonderland: Broadway in Review," *TA,* Feb. 1933, pp. 103–4

Walter Prichard Eaton in the latest number of *Harper's* in an article entitled "The Plight of the Dramatist," lays the present low condition of the American drama to the public itself; not to its being stupid or uninterested in the theatre, but to its intellectual and ethical chaos. The modern dramatist finds himself unable to employ the old themes which once were the backbone of the drama because they have to do with concepts, ethical, moral or religious no longer believed in by the mass of theatre-goers. I am in complete agreement with Mr. Eaton. We are living in an age in which woman's virtue is in many circles no longer looked upon as important, when family ties are disintegrating, when, in short, few who make up metropolitan audiences seem to believe in any spiritual or moral order. Of course a playwright can write about merely material things: the revolt against poverty and physical inferiority, against social inequalities, even against boredom, but as these things have at root a spiritual basis, the playwright doesn't get very far even here. His plays are shallow, barren, even if the people are superficially well observed. He uses the microscope rather than the telescope, and the result is that too often he sees not the stars or the cosmic law, but merely crawling bacilli.

There are, however, honorable exceptions, and of them is S. N. Behrman, the one true master of comedy the American theatre possesses today. Mr. Behrman knows that things are not as they should be, but until recently he had been content simply to show up the forces at work, standing outside them, letting their protagonists speak for themselves. Urbane, tolerant and open minded, he has given each side its opportunity to put its best foot forward. This is the mark of the comic dramatist of the more liberal type. In his latest play, however, he begins to show signs of wanting to enter the arena as a participant. The theme of *The Talley Method* is: a distinguished surgeon whose utterly materialistic type of mind, admirable as it is in dealing with his patients, fails utterly in its relations with his children and with the woman he wants to marry. Mr. Behrman sees that materialism is the death of life, and steps down from his ivory tower to combat it. Unfortunately, however, he is only as yet half armed. He knows his adversary, but he hasn't the weapons to kill him. He possesses irony, but irony is after all a form of self indulgence, a sop to one's stultified moral revolt; and when

Mr. Behrman is indignant he turns not to words that sear, but to this irony. Now I am not at all sure that Mr. Behrman should try to enter the arena. As a comic dramatist who exhibits the forces that are struggling for mastery he is unrivalled. Moreover he is a master of the unspoken word, of saying more than his mere lines appear to utter. As such he magnificently poses the problems that confront us. Perhaps he would do well to allow others to find the remedy.—GRENVILLE VERNON, *Com*, March 14, 1941, p. 519

OTHER WORKS

Lord Duveen of Millbank, the greatest international art-dealer in history, died at the age of sixty-nine, just in time to escape the outbreak of the last World War; his fabulous run of luck held good to the very end. For his services to this country—he presented additional room for pictures to the National Gallery and the Tate, financed the housing for the Elgin Marbles for the British Museum and contributed £200,000 to the British Red Cross—he was successively rewarded, first with a knighthood, then with a baronetcy, and finally with a peerage. For his services to the United States he was perhaps sufficiently recompensed by the £5,000,000 fortune he accumulated. The two services were in their way complementary. With his American money he was able to buy up the heirlooms of impoverished English families; and with his English title he found it easier to sell these exports in America. The fraction of the proceeds that recrossed the Atlantic to benefit our national galleries might legitimately be regarded as conscience money.

But the title, although it came in useful to impress benighted Californian *nouveaux riches*, was not enough in itself to coax out the dollars from hard-headed business men in return for a few square feet of painted canvas. For that purpose the really effective instrument was Duveen's own abounding vitality, coupled with an insidious method of approach and a shrewd appraisal of each particular millionaire he had to deal with. As for rivals in the field in the shape of other art dealers, they were trounced with every weapon at his disposal. He appropriated their best customers by guile, he sent emissaries to distant country houses to forestall their purchases, and in the last resort he would challenge the authenticity of their wares. No old master was allowed to be genuine unless guaranteed by Duveen.

Apart from the disadvantage that he had no personal acquaintance with his subject, Mr. Behrman's method of biography is the same as that of Boswell with the even more pungent personality of Dr. Johnson. There is no need to expound such self-revealing characters; they may be said to be writing their own lives as they go. Their passage through life can be faithfully traced by the volley of anecdotes perpetually discharged from them by some law of individual dynamics. Mr. Behrman had only to collect, and arrange under appropriate headings, all the Duveen stories in circulation throughout the globe: and there is Duveen in person before us, reckless, unscrupulous, overbearing; yet beaming all over, "life-enhancing" as Berenson reluctantly called him, and unmistakably the best of company. And to visualise the cocksure fellow, we have Steinberg's portrait on the frontispiece: Duveen mesmerising some imaginary millionaire.

Steinberg suggests *The New Yorker*, for which *Duveen* was originally written as a serial in six instalments. But without any reminder it would be hard not to recognise the terse, wide-awake, ironical style—adaptable to a high level of literature, yet echoing discreetly the cruder rhythms of journalism—which contributors to that famous magazine all seem to share in common. It is rather a pity that Mr. Behrman, when

transposing his six articles into book form, did not take the chance to cut out the overlappings and repetitions entailed in serial production. But this lack of final polish is only a slight blemish on what is bound to be one of the most popular light biographies for many a long year.—RALPH PARTRIDGE, "'How Utterly Duveen!'," NSN, June 28, 1952, p. 776

It seems churlish to charge a writer who has made his name in one literary mode with transferring intact habits of perception and technical devices accumulated over a lifetime of practice to another literary mode when, surprisingly, he tries his hand at it rather late in his career. Yet strive as one will to resist it, S. N. Behrman compels us to see his first novel ⟨*The Burning Glass*⟩ as an infinitely extended version by other means of a Behrman play.

Take a fairly marginal example relating to a secondary character. (In this novel, most examples are marginal; and most characters, even the major ones, are minor.) Stanley Grant (né Jacob Ben Sion-Trynin), a successful young playwright and screenwriter who is one of the book's two principal characters, is fashioning a play based on his experience of having loved to no avail a girl in complicated family circumstances. Why has she spurned him? Is it because she is carrying on a furtive affair with her ailing mother's doctor-lover? Did her mother die naturally, or was her death hastened by the sinister doctor? *Is* he sinister? It never occurs to Grant—nor is one altogether sure of Behrman's judgment—that the reason may be that he is a singularly unattractive and contemptible sort who, added to the rest of his sins, suffers from acne.

Grant is meditating on the girl. "That Sally!" he reflects. "That enigma! The most desirable girl in the world, surely." Now there is not the slightest evidence that Sally is anything like the most desirable girl in the world, though everyone sings her praises, and two of the novel's few practicing homosexuals are mad for her. Grant's judgment is negative evidence. She is, from all one sees and hears of her, a peculiarly empty and insipid girl, coy and muddle-headed; and while a desirable actress might convince us she is a desirable girl, the novel does not.

Off-stage, indeed, is where the action is—gales and maelstroms of action, all of it invisible. Since these are Behrman characters, they are—typically—rich, fashionable, glamorous, the sort who dine late, speak burnished phrases, frequently address one another as "darling," and attend the Festival at Salzburg, where in fact much of the action takes place, roundabout 1937. The wings are stacked deep in corpses. A man we have never seen is reported dead of his own hand. A scholarly refugee from Hitlerism, whom we scarcely know save by name, commits suicide in abstract despair; and a few pages later a beautiful actress follows suit.

While the little lives unfold beneath, the lights of Berchtesgarten burn the night through; while the characters pursue their vain and idle course, the Mustache—as he is not infrequently called—has other plans for them. This is intended, of course, to give weight and gravity to the novel's frivolities. It fails to do so: history is an accident of the novel's time; the characters and actions are in no important way affected; the pathos is superimposed, does not solemnize the events even retrospectively. These men and women, themselves jaded, are the collectors of jade; and though they, too, live in the shadow of the holocaust about to engulf the world, they are phantoms, wraiths. When the war finally descends, it is hardly alluded to—a time to be got over so that Grant can visit his ex-wife and child in Palestine, whence they have improbably emigrated.

The novel is not without its pleasant moments. Behrman

is Behrman: he can and does write elegantly. He is a composer of deft, and sometimes witty, dialogue; but the lines, which fade from the memory a moment after they are uttered, are disembodied mots spoken by spectres. The purling, ingratiating tone flattens everything to the same level. If Behrman had written the Book of Job, the central character would have been a charming, cultivated man no longer young, world-weary beyond his years, perhaps a gentleman farmer, a kind of Near Eastern Montaigne, Jewish but cosmopolitan, a collector of rare scrolls, who had suffered some minor business reverses and—as if he didn't have enough trouble—was further afflicted by an embarrassing skin condition.—SAUL MALOFF, "Of Sin and Acne," *NYTBR*, July 21, 1968, p. 31

JOSEPH WOOD KRUTCH
From *The American Drama Since 1918*
1939, pp. 180–200

When the Theatre Guild produced *The Second Man* in the spring of 1927, S. N. Behrman, its author, was almost totally unknown. He had, to be sure, appeared as co-author of an unsuccessful comedy seen on Broadway shortly before, but his name meant nothing to the public and *The Second Man* was an astonishing revelation of a talent not only highly original but already sure of itself. Since then Mr. Behrman has continued to write plays which give him as sure a position in the contemporary American theater as any writer can claim. No other has more clearly defined or more convincingly defended an individual and specific talent.

It is, as we shall see, difficult to discover in the rather commonplace incidents of his career any explanation of the fact that the whole cast of his mind should be as different as it is from that of any of his fellows, but from the very beginning it was evident that he had accepted and assimilated the Comic Spirit so successfully that he could write with a consistent clarity of thought and feeling unrivaled on our stage. Farce, burlesque, sentimental romance, and even satire are with us common enough. They are, as a matter of fact, natural expressions of that superficial tendency toward irreverence which overlays the fundamental earnestness of the American character. Embarrassed by deep feeling or true comedy, we take refuge in the horse-play of farce or the ambiguities of "sophisticated" romance, where the most skittish of characters generally end by rediscovering a sentimentalized version of the eternal verities. But the remarkable thing about Mr. Behrman is the unerring way in which his mind cut through the inconsistency of these compromises, the clarity with which he realized that we must ultimately make our choice between judging men by their heroism or judging them by their intelligence, and the unfailing articulateness with which he defends his determination to choose the second alternative.

. . . The comic attitude—like any other consistent attitude—cannot be undeviatingly maintained without involving a certain austerity. The time inevitably comes when it would be easier to relax for a moment the critical intelligence and to pluck some pleasant flower of sentiment or—in other words—to pretend that some compromise is possible between the romantic hero and the comic one. But Mr. Behrman never allows himself to be betrayed by any such weakness and he pays the penalty of seeming a little dry and hard to those pseudo-sophisticates who adore the tear behind the smile because they insist upon eating their cake and having it too. Just as they giggle when they find themselves unable to sustain the level of O'Neill's exaltation—unable, that is to say, to accept the logic of his demand that life be consistently interpreted in terms of the highest feeling possible to it—so, too, they are almost equally though less consciously baffled by Behrman's persistent anti-heroicism. Comedy and tragedy alike are essentially aristocratic; only the forms in between are thoroughly popular. . . .

Mr. Behrman's plays are obviously "artificial"—both in the sense that they deal with an artificial and privileged section of society and in the sense that the characters themselves are less real persons than idealized embodiments of intelligence and wit. No person was ever so triple plated with the armor of comic intelligence as his heroes; no society ever existed in which all problems were solved—as in some of his plays they are—when good sense has analyzed them. Just as the tragic writer endows all his characters with his own gift of poetry, so Mr. Behrman endows all his with his own gift for the phrase which lays bare to the mind a meaning which emotion has been unable to disentangle. No drawing-room ever existed in which people talked so well or acted so sensibly at last, but this idealization is the final business of comedy. It first deflates man's aspirations and pretensions, accepting the inevitable failure of his attempt to live by his passions or up to his enthusiasms. But when it has done this, it demonstrates what is still left to him—his intelligence, his wit, his tolerance, and his grace—and then, finally, it imagines with what charm he could live if he were freed, not merely from the stern necessities of the struggle for physical existence, but also from the perverse and unexpected quixoticisms of his heart. . . .

His method, like every other method, has of course its limitations. Certain dramatic aspects of the conflict between the philosophy of those who have and the philosophy of those who have not obviously cannot be observed in a drawing-room. If, as the proponents of the left-wing drama maintain, the real significance of that conflict does not emerge except on the battlefield where concrete things are being fought for, then it is plain enough that only plays which move through the factory and the field can communicate that significance. But a fundamental assumption of intellectual comedy is that one kind of understanding of any conflict is possible only on the sidelines, or at some other place where, for the moment at least, the battle is not raging. And Mr. Behrman's drawing-rooms are merely realistic substitutes for a spot of enchanted ground upon which deadly enemies can meet, fragments of neutral territory over which flies the flag of social convention guaranteeing against any breaches of the peace other than those which come within the definition of the "scene" as opposed to the brawl. Here the contented sybarite can exchange thrusts with the reformer, but here also the revolutionist can, not too improbably, come to express his inclusive contempt for all the rules of a game which is not, to him, worth playing.

Mr. Behrman's clarity and wit being what they are, the result is an exhilarating exploration of minds and temperaments which can be as clear and stimulating as it is only because he has adopted still another convention—that by virtue of which each character is permitted to speak as wittily as the author can make him. For this same reason the battle is, moreover, almost necessarily a draw. That does not mean that Mr. Behrman conceals the direction in which his own sympathies lie. He is, as clearly here as in the other plays, among those who hold that the sensibilities and loyalties of his liberals—"inhibited by scruple and emasculated by charm," as one character puts it—are indispensable to any possible good life, however insufficient they alone may be to guarantee it.

But this revelation of his own conviction does not involve any failure to give the revolutionist an opportunity to make the best possible statement of his case, and there is no reason whatever why many spectators should not conclude that he actually has the best of the argument.

Had Mr. Behrman happened to live in a more stable society he would doubtless have written comedies even more strictly in the line of the great comic tradition than these later works are. Faced with the problem of writing comedy in an atmosphere which so many are ready to say makes pure comedy either impossible or at least impertinent, he has evolved something which it might not be improper to call the Comedy of Illumination—a kind of comedy in which grave issues of the moment are touched upon but which differs from sociological comedy on the Shavian model in two respects. In the first place there is a less consistent tendency to beg the question in order to favor one side in the debate; in the second place—and this is more important—the moral is not the moral of an enthusiast, but a moral appropriate to a comic intelligence which cannot but feel that the solution of all problems is ultimately to be discovered by tolerance and common sense no matter how completely impossible it may be to employ either effectively during certain moments of crisis.

SAUL BELLOW

1915–

Saul Bellow was born on June 10 (officially recorded as July 10), 1915 in Lachine, Quebec. The son of a Russian émigré businessman, Bellow has lived in Chicago since he was nine and has made it the setting for many of his novels.

Bellow attended the University of Chicago, Northwestern University (where he studied anthropology and sociology) and the University of Wisconsin (where he did graduate work in anthropology).

Dangling Man, his first novel, was published in 1944. Acclaimed by Delmore Schwartz and Edmund Wilson, it established Bellow as one of America's most gifted young novelists. *The Victim*, his second novel, appeared in 1947. Bellow now considers both novels "timid," though they are still widely admired. With *The Adventures of Augie March* (1953), Bellow's characteristic style—less compressed and more imaginatively exuberant—began to emerge. Bellow has stated that "On the whole, American novels are filled with complaints about the sovereign Self." With *The Adventures of Augie March*, much of it written in cafes and trains while Bellow was travelling in Europe, and *Henderson the Rain King* (1959), a comic fantasy set in Africa, Bellow presented his own alternative to the prevailing mood in the American novel, as he saw it. But it was *Herzog* (1964), the work with which Bellow is most identified, which won him the greatest critical accolades.

Since *Herzog* Bellow has published short stories and plays, as well as several more novels. *Humboldt's Gift* (1975) nominally won Bellow the Nobel Prize in 1976. His most recent books are *The Dean's December* (1982), and *Him With His Foot in His Mouth* (1984), a collection of short stories.

Apart from winning the Nobel Prize, Bellow has won the National Book Award three times, the Prix International de Littérature, and many other awards. He has married three times and has several children. He currently heads the Committee on Social Thought at the University of Chicago. He was recently named a National Treasure.

Personal

. . . Bellow had not yet published a novel, and he was known for his stories and evident brilliance only to a small intellectual group drawn from the *Partisan Review* and the University of Chicago. Yet walking the unfamiliar Brooklyn streets, he seemed to be measuring the hidden strength of all things in the universe, from the grime of Brooklyn to the leading stars of the American novel, from the horror of Hitler to the mass tensions of New York. He was measuring the world's power of resistance, measuring himself as a contender. Although he was friendly, unpretentious, and funny, he was serious in a style that I had never before seen in an urban Jewish intellectual: he was going to succeed as an imaginative writer; he was pledged to grapple with unseen powers. He was going to take on more than the rest of us were.

As Bellow talked, I had an image of him as a wrestler in the old Greek style, an agonist contending in the games for the prize. Life was dramatically as well as emotionally a contest to him, and nothing of the agony or contest would be spared him. God would try him in his pride and trip him up, and he knew it; no one was spared; he had been brought up an orthodox Jew, and he had a proper respect for God as the ultimate power assumed by the creation. A poor immigrant's gifted son, he had an instinct that an overwhelming number of chances would come his way, that the old poverty and cultural bareness would soon be exchanged for a multitude of temptations. So he was wary—eager, sardonic, and wary; and unlike everybody else I knew, remarkably patient in expressing himself.

For a man with such a range of interests, capacities, and appetites, Bellow talked with great austerity. He addressed himself to the strength of life hidden in people, in political issues, in other writers, in mass behavior; an anthropologist by training, he liked to estimate other people's physical capacity, the thickness of their skins, the strength in their hands, the force in their chests. Describing people, he talked like a Darwinian, calculating the power of survival hidden in the species. But there was nothing idle or showy about his observations, and he did not talk for effect. His conceptions, definitions, epigrams, *aperçus* were of a formal plainness that went right to the point and stopped. That was the victory he wanted. There was not the slightest verbal inflation in anything he said. Yet his observations were so direct and penetrating that they took on the elegance of achieved thought. When he considered something, his eyes slightly set as if studying its power to deceive him, one realized how formidable he was on topics generally exhausted by ideology or neglected by intellectuals too fine to consider them. Suddenly everything tiresomely grievous came alive in the focus of this man's unfamiliar imagination.—ALFRED KAZIN, "My Friend Saul Bellow," *At*, Jan. 1965, pp. 51–52

Saul Bellow is the living author I most admire. Since having read his description of a woman washing window-glass in "The Dangling Man" so many years ago I have found him the most interesting author I know writing in English, which is the only language I can read with ease these days. Saul's virtuosity, his keen sense of the perils of his vocation and the architecture of his accomplishments seem to me peerless.—JOHN CHEEVER, *NYTBR*, Dec. 4, 1977, p. 3

General

Bellow's work sounds to many intellectuals like the *intellectual* literature they have long hoped one of their number might someday produce. Not only was ⟨Bellow's early fiction⟩ obviously, almost, it seemed, deliberately, not "great" in the classic, grass-roots sense, but it embodied the intellectual-academic ideal, highly fashionable in the forties and fifties, of a fiction small in scope, tidy in form, antidramatic in content, ambiguous in meaning, which turned on the shy, sad sufferings of intellectual characters trapped in darkly internal crises of personal identity and moral responsibility. In a very real sense, it was just the sort of fiction most intellectuals would have written if they had been able to write fiction. It derived from their kind of experience and educational background; it had the staid, sedentary, vaguely pedagogical quality that they recognized, however reluctantly, to be the quality of their own lives; it was written with the same wry fastidiousness about the stereotypes and platitudes, the same distrust of cant and affectation, that their own deep commitment to literary values had given them. It quite simply expressed them in a way that the fiction of Fitzgerald, Hemingway, and Faulkner never had and never could, no matter how much they may have admired it in their youth or been entranced by the vision of experience it put forward.—JOHN W. ALDRIDGE, "'Nothing Left to Do but Think'—Saul Bellow" (1964), *Time to Murder and Create*, 1966, p. 87

In view of what Bellow has attempted to say in his novels, it is entirely appropriate that he should have turned from the formal models of iconoclastic modernism to transform and vitalize traditional modes of fiction. . . . The relationship of the great modern writers to the world has usually been one of retreat or attack—retreat from society to subjectivity, from politics ("in the Aristotelian sense," as Herzog puts it) to art or religion; attack upon bourgeois culture and industrialization, on all the institutional and individual forms of modern man's spiritual sterility. Such martial activity of the soul has often called for

bold innovation in form, so that the writer could build his own bastion in literary structure or blow things apart with words.

Bellow, on the other hand, has sought in his fiction for ways to recover a civilized self, assuming that, for all that has gone wrong with our civilization, we can still learn within its context how to live decent, satisfying lives. Significantly, Herzog's grandiose and unrealized ambition is to write a book "with a new angle on the modern condition, showing how life could be lived by renewing universal connections; overturning the last of the Romantic errors about the uniqueness of the Self; revising the old Western, Faustian ideology." Precisely revision, not rejection or revolution, has characterized the relationship of Bellow's fiction both to literary and moral traditions.

The moral pattern of all his work, first sketched out in *Dangling Man*, most vitally realized in *Herzog*, is clear enough. Perhaps the best resumé of that pattern is Bellow's play, *The Last Analysis*, which delightfully transposes virtually all the major themes of his fiction into a farcical key. Every one of Bellow's heroes suffers, like Bummidge in the play, from "humanitis"—which, as Bummidge's secretary explains, is "when the human condition gets to be too much for you." The term is appropriately mock-clinical: being human is a difficult business in Bellow's view, but he sees it as an evasion to paste down the difficulty with a quasi-scientific label like "neurosis" which implies that the problem can be handled by a professional, a therapist. Every man is his own analyst, Bummidge suggests, and this is pretty much the condition of each of Bellow's protagonists.

Each of the novels ingeniously develops its own secular equivalents for the cult of psychoanalysis. In one way or another, each of the central figures is engaged, like Bummidge, in recapitulating his own past so that he can make some sense out of his life. Herzog, with better intellectual equipment and more minute self-knowledge than any of the others, is the one who is able to bring the process to a successful conclusion. Beginning with *Augie March*, a series of guides or quasi-therapists is introduced into the novels, the people whom Herzog sardonically describes as "Reality Instructors." The Reality Instructors all claim to be, or at least know, the Way and the Truth. They are generally attractive figures, seductively so, and almost all are magnificent egotists, tinged or broadly streaked with madness. *Augie March* offers the most colorful gallery of Reality Instructors—the Napoleonic Einhorn, eagle-obsessed Thea, Mintouchian the worldly Armenian, the megalomaniac genius Basteshaw—but the later novels also abound with them—Queen Willatale and King Dahfu in *Henderson*, Dr. Tamkin in *Seize the Day*, Valentine Gersbach in *Herzog*. With the exception of the figures in *Henderson*, the Reality Instructors are drawn more and more sharply as outrageous charlatans. Humanitis, the novels imply, is not a disease which can be cured by self-appointed professionals. Every human being must learn to handle his own case, putting on, as Bummidge does, his own dark glasses and Viennese accent, urging himself to go "deeper, deeper," in the words of Bummidge to the empty couch.

The point is not that Bellow has been carrying on in his writings a personal vendetta with psychoanalysis, though there may be some element of that. (The one character in *Herzog* even more drastically negative than Madeleine is Edvig, the analyst.) Psychoanalysis, as it is spoofed in ⟨*The Last Analysis*⟩ and attacked in ⟨*Herzog*⟩, is a dangerous delusion because it is the clearest instance of all the approaches to life which try to reduce solving human problems to a formula, a methodology, a technique. The Reality Instructors in the novels turn out to be fakes because reality is what Augie March calls a "multiverse," not a unified system in which fixed principles can be enunciated by those who know the system. There is a salubrious note of tentativeness in the moral self-exploration of all Bellow's heroes. This is probably the main reason for the relatively unsatisfactory endings of his novels until *Herzog*. Morally inevitable tentativeness of the sort Bellow imagines into his protagonists cannot really be brought to a resolution— it always implies more questioning, more self-discovery.

To describe this quality of tentativeness another way, one might say that there is a stubborn core of innocence in all Bellow's heroes. Each is a kind of Huck Finn with no faithful Jim to guide him, a person in some ways impressively knowing about the world, yet always looking at it with eyes of youthful wonder, insisting upon grasping it in his own way. The irrepressible desire for life, however deadening experience has been, which characterizes Bellow's protagonists, is the expression of this innocence, or, from another point of view, the means of preserving it. Henderson, in contrast to the typically modern voyagers to dark continents, is not jaded or defeated, only confused; and, as Willatale informs him, he has the gift of Grun-tu-molani or "Man want to live," which is the talisman of his innocence and the motive force of his redemption.

The opposite of innocence as the word applies to Bellow's heroes is not worldliness or corruption but simply thinking you know what the score is. Bellow's innocents at home and abroad are always looking about in perplexity: there doesn't seem to be any scoreboard around. This is probably one important reason for the ring of authenticity in Herzog's massive attack upon "the Wasteland outlook, the cheap mental stimulants of Alienation." Herzog does not attempt to replace the established Wasteland ideology with another one; his argument against it is based on his innocent—that is, tentative, personal—sense of life. To proclaim programmatically that life is good, that the Wasteland is mere fiction, would be another way of pretending to know the score. "We learn to be unfeeling toward ourselves and incurious," complained Joseph, the protagonist of *Dangling Man*. Herzog's ability to renounce what he calls the modern god of Death and to pull together the wreckage of his own life is the result of his resistance to this grim process of negative learning. He manages to remain genuinely curious about himself and to feel for himself; this is the ultimate source of his innocence, his ability to wonder. And if there are also elements of narcissism in his preoccupation with self, he is aware of them and can turn them into redeeming comedy.— Robert Alter, "The Stature of Saul Bellow," *Midstream*, Dec. 1964, pp. 12–14

In Isaac Bashevis Singer's story, "Gimpel the Fool," which Saul Bellow translated for the *Partisan Review* and for *A Treasury of Yiddish Stories* (1953), the hero Gimpel is forced to accept many monstrous impositions upon his patience and good humor and belief. But he yields to the necessity; what's the good of *not* believing, he argues. "Today it's your wife you don't believe; tomorrow it's God Himself you won't take stock in." Of course, this statement is mock-heroic, or—even worse—deliberately anti-heroic. Marcus Klein speaks of the European ghetto tradition of *dos kleine menschele*, or the *stetl*, "who is forced by the presence of perils everywhere to ingenious ways of personal survival."

Whatever the influence of this creature, this "fool of reality," there is no question that Saul Bellow's great "affirmation" is in the struggle against chaos and "clutter," of a "too muchness" of everything, toward life and the freedom to live. This freedom includes the will to act eccentrically, to remain

"dangling" before society's "normalcy"; but it is not the kind of attitude Dostoevsky eventually leaves to his underground man. Bellow's hero moves *into* society, with a desperate hope that the human dilemma will be solved in community recognition and action.

There is always an air of the ludicrous and the absurd in the world to which the Bellow creature seems committed. It is not the "absurd" of Camus's reading of Kafka, however; the absurdity of Bellow's world is more likely to consist of a profusion of things, a clutter and surplusage of experience, the city world of Chicago and New York, where "things" and gestures and manners and knowledges are heaped upon one another because there isn't enough space to contain them or time to consider them separately. Bellow's heroes are therefore something less than ideally heroic; they are agonizingly at grips with their own personal and moral identity and security; with surviving the flux and contrarieties of experience; finally, with the overwhelming noumenal question of their relation to an unknown. We cannot expect from them either the large qualities of conventional heroism or the agonizing moral toothaches of the "alienated hero." For, as Marcus Klein says, alienation is "morally reprehensible." To be separated from the rest of society is a condition wholly deplorable.

Bellow's novels therefore scan the human world for its types of separation, conformity, rebellion, and adaptation. Ultimately, he seeks for affirmation; it is a modest ambition, however, and he will not conclude it at the expense of novelistic virtues. In his own statement, in *The Living Novel*, he speaks of the necessity to affirm as equivalent to the need to survive. Modern writers, he says,

> are prone, as Nietzsche said in *Human, All Too Human*, to exaggerate the value of human personality. . . . Why should wretched man need power or wish to inflate himself with imaginary glory. If this is what power signifies it can only be vanity to suffer from impotence. On the nobler assumption he should have at least sufficient power to overcome ignominy and to complete his life.

To overcome ignominy and to complete his life: surely these are modest ambitions? But of course in the world of World War II and after, perhaps they are not so modest after all?

The phenomena of affirmation are variously called: "radical innocence," "dogmatic innocence," "beatitude," gestures of "the American existentialist," the hipster, etc. They require some form of general explanation. Of course it would be easy to say simply that writers of the present generation had come through an "ordeal" and were therefore pledged to affirm. But frequently affirmation seems too desperate, too viciously improvisatory, too bitterly anti-everything to be recognizable by any customary sight or definition. Further, recent literature is *not* all affirmative, by any means. The work of the new dramatists, the plays and the fiction of Samuel Beckett, the fantasies and the angry realism of much contemporary literature testify against any patent notion of spontaneous yea-saying in the teeth of an almighty Nay.

The fact is that recent experience is horrifying, frightening enough to dispel many notions of easy acceptance. Yet the *kind* of will that Bellow defines in his hero is not unusual; in Bellow's case it is the Yiddish comic or fool, the *schlemiel* or *schlimazl* of Yiddish humor. One needs to remember that Bellow speaks, not of the grand affirmation or of the "beat-itude" of some contemporaries, but of "sufficient power to overcome ignominy and to complete [one's] life." Bellow, with Roth, Malamud and a growing number of other Jewish writers, is drawing upon the resources of humor, comedy, wisdom, and "secular prayer" that make up the modern Jewish personality in America. He is almost invariably an urban personality, though in at least one example (Bruce Friedman's *Stern*, 1962), he ventures into the suburbs. He is seldom any longer engaged in the struggle against anti-Semitism, because American Jews have enjoyed in recent years great freedom from persecution—perhaps because the experience of World War II and the discovery of Auschwitz and Dachau and its kind have proved traumatically useful; perhaps because the exercises of guilt of the current American have concentrated on problems of Negro integration.

All of these facts leave the way free to a phenomenal rise in the value of Jewish humor and wisdom: a middle-middle class form of manners, which penetrates every aspect of American life. In Bellow's case at least, it is the strategies of survival of *dos kleine menschele*, or the devices, at several levels of sophistication, of the *schlimazl*, that govern the "affirmation of life" and keep it from getting out of hand. The essential task is to fight against loss of identity, to make a "show" of virtue and a satisfactory life in this world, since the next world has been only nebulously indicated and surely does not inspire confidence. Bellow's great contribution lies in his ability to "socialize" the effort to survive in the modern world. Like Philip Roth and Bernard Malamud, he draws heavily upon Jewish manners for the scene and quality and style of his fictions. As in many of Malamud's short stories, the ultimate concerns of Bellow's novels are eschatological. The stratagems used to make a completed life seem an adequate surrogate of immortality. Also, they are not stuffily "fake profound," but produce the impression of ideas carefully sifted through nuances of human behavior.—Frederick J. Hoffman, "The Fool of Experience: Saul Bellow's Fiction," *Contemporary American Novelists*, ed. Harry T. Moore, 1964, pp. 80–83

There is one famous compliment to a novelist that nobody is ever going to offer Saul Bellow, and that is to say that his books are the product of a sensibility so fine that no idea could violate it. It seems doubtful whether any interesting writer, even James, really fits that formula, in any case, if you think that is the condition the art should aspire to, Bellow is not your man. Yet for many people he is the man. In America, where more and more the hypotheses of literary historians tread the heels of literature, Bellow has already been snugly fitted into neat intelligible patterns. He is the big novelist who emerged at the precise conjunction of race, milieu and moment—when, as Leslie Fiedler puts it, 'the Jews for the first time move into the centre of American culture' as the group best-equipped to act as an urban, Europe-centred elite. Augie March is Huck Finn Chicago-Jewish-style, still, in Mr. Fiedler's dialect, in search of a primal innocence, but above all an urban Jew, with the appropriate worries, failures and aspirations. Or, according to Norman Podhoretz, Bellow in 1953 came through with *Augie March* at just the right moment to encapsulate and typify the new revisionist liberalism, moving away from the Left at the same conscientious pace as *Partisan Review*.

Aside even from these professionally large and resonant explanations, much has been written about Bellow, and this is not surprising. When all the reservations have been made he is so good that anybody can see it with half an eye; only severe doctrinal adhesion prevents the recognition that he is a far more interesting writer than Mailer. One remarkable thing about him is that along the way he has conjured out of the air new talents, powers he apparently did not have, even *in posse*,

when he started in the Forties. With this bonus he is more gifted than the gifted young, including the handsomely endowed Philip Roth. Furthermore, he is, for all the glitter of ideas, accessible, easier to get to than John Hawkes, further out in the open than Malamud. Thus he made everybody flock to read him without sacrificing intellectual seriousness, and without growing plump enough to be caught in the meshes of the critics' hypotheses.

Bellow's career has some curious aspects. He has never lacked support. *Dangling Man* brought him respect, nearly 20 years ago, not only in America but here. Rereading it now, one finds it a little rigid, worthy but off-putting, a book one does not wish longer. I suppose that at the time, in a different and on the whole duller literary epoch, the intelligence with which the wretched but hard-thinking hero was placed, his eloquent and intellectually respectable introspection, were what won perceptive praise. Now the diagrams of alienation seem too square, the prose somewhat inelastic; it is hard to find in it the vivacity and inventive power one associates with Bellow. Perhaps it might be said that the austerity of the book gives it a kind of fidelity to its moment. Anyway, *The Victim*, though it had some of this rigour, and some of this period quality, was more various and flexible. But the big change, the *détente*, came only in the early Fifties, with *The Adventures of Augie March*.

It would be easy to run through the rollcall of this book's deficiencies, but the point is that Bellow had found his new form. Perhaps it struck him that the tragic stance of classic alienation, and even the existence of intellectuals, looked funny in this new world. They became a source of gags, and the hero turned picaro. Simultaneously with this new circumstance, Bellow became profusely inventive, exhibited a sense of the true comedy of intellect, which is painful as well as funny. There was some lamenting about what he gave up—the effects which arise from a firm management of structure, for example; it seemed that he thought these appropriate only to the short novel, and this guess was apparently confirmed when he next wrote a very good novella, *Seize the Day*, and went on to another inventive sprawl in *Henderson the Rain King*.

At least one ingredient is common to all the novels: the hero is, in Alfred Kazin's phrase, 'burdened by a speculative quest'. They all have the same humble need (however little this humility comes through in their conduct) to sort out human destiny by sorting out their own. In a world of chaotic particulars, where the only speculations which draw any support are bogus, vulgarised or corrupt, the speculative quest turns into a sequence of extravagantly funny or pathetic gestures, and the happiest ending that can be hoped for is that of *Seize the Day*, when Tommy Wilhelm, a middle-aged flop, winds up weeping at the funeral of somebody he doesn't know.

The great merit, and at the same time the great difficulty, of such writing is that it does try to get into fiction the farcical excitements of thinking as distinct from behaving. To do this straight seems almost impossible, or, if you think it works in *La Nausée*, unrepeatable. Bellow gets round the problem in the same way every time. The speculative interest is never put straight in. In *Seize the Day* the wise sayings come from the fraudulent Tamkin; in *Henderson* fantasy bears the freight of speculation. ⟨*Herzog*⟩ is full of furious thinking, and Herzog, the hero, does most of it, but not 'straight'. The first sentence of the book says: 'If I am out of my mind, it's all right with me'.—Frank Kermode, *NS*, Feb. 5, 1965, pp. 200–201

. . . Bellow's heroes seek value, equilibrium, salvation—Henderson's word—an earthly condition in which body and soul may live. The condition, if it were possible, would allow the self a genial relation to its world. Henderson gave up hunting because it seemed 'a strange way to relate to nature'. Augie looks with anguish at the eagle which Thea is training to kill lizards. Aggression, aggression, aggression. The self will not take the offensive, it will not profit from the sufferings of others, it will return a verdict for reason 'in its partial inadequacy and against the advantages of its surrender', as Joseph says. Bellow's characters reach a dark moment in which they feel that reason has nothing to do with action. Augie's conjunction with Stella on a mountain of wet grass in Mexico is followed by the reflection that, 'After much making with sense, it's senselessness that you submit to.' Tommy Wilhelm sees himself as a man 'who reflected long and then made the decision he had rejected twenty times'.

Basically, these characters want to be assured of their own existence. Augie meditates that, 'Personality is unsafe in the first place. It's the types that are safe. So almost all make deformations on themselves so that the great terror will let them be.' The great terror takes many desolately prosaic forms, including the boredom of one day following another, the Indian file of tedium. Joseph says, 'It may be that I am tired of having to identify a day as "the day I asked for a second cup of coffee" or "the day the waitress refused to take back the burned toast", and so want to blaze it more sharply, regardless of the consequences.'

There is another demand; that a man be his own master, agent in his own action. The philosopher Clarence Irving Lewis has argued that 'a being which could not act would live out its life within the bounds of immediacy. It could find no difference between its own content of feeling and reality. There could be no self, because there could be no other-than-self: the distinction could not arise'. Bellow's heroes want to choose, because their humanity depends upon the hazard of choice, but they fear that the irrational may be a categorical condition, like the air we breathe. Hence the image of dissociation. These men seek salvation within their own being and from their own resources. They find no sustenance in other people, in society. Society is what went wrong: the body politic and the world's body are bankrupt. The only mode of society which Bellow's men take seriously is the family. Augie is devoted to his family and to the idea of the Person. But he has no vision of society as a great family, in which a man might live with due autonomy while being a member of something larger than himself. And often, outraged by a society which has failed and deceived them, these characters seek moral simplicity as an entirely private possession. Henderson goes through the heart of darkness into the desert, impelled to 'simplify'.

In theory, there is no conflict between this desire and the urge to 'love'. Bellow often quotes Simone Weil: 'To believe in the existence of human beings as such is love.' This is the ground of his entire fiction. But in practice it rarely obtains. Joseph spends a lot of time pondering the difference between persons and things. In *The Victim* Schlossberg defines, for Asa's benefit, what it means to be human. Henderson tells Romilayu: 'The only decent thing about me is that I have loved certain people in my life.' But there is an incorrigible vacuum between theory and practice, between profession and realization. Bellow's characters live on the assumption that belief in the existence of human beings as such must come later; after they have managed to secure a belief in their own existence. They do not take much stock in the idea that precisely by committing ourselves to the existence of other people our own existence is certified. They think that they can say 'I' before saying 'Thou'.—Denis Donoghue, *The Ordinary Universe*, 1968, p. 197–98

Bellow is positively hypnotized by the part of human life he knows best, as a novelist should be, and he sees everything else in this focus. But without being detached and "impartial" about the long Jewish struggle for survival, he is fascinated and held by the texture of Jewish experience as it becomes, as it can become, the day-to-day life of people one has created. This is very different from writing about people one names as Jews but who, no matter how one feels about them, are just names on the page. Texture is life relived, *life* on the page, beyond praise or blame. . . .

⟨The⟩ air of having lived, of experiencing the big city in every pore, of being on the spot, is the great thing about Bellow's fiction. It is this living acrid style—in the suddenly chastened, too glibly precise, peculiarly assertive bitterness of postwar American writing, with its hallucinated clarity about details, its oversized sense of our existence of too many objects all around (what desolation amidst wonders!)—that made us realize Bellow as an original. He is a key to something that would emerge in all the American writing of this period about cities, the "mass," the common life. This was not the "minority" writing of the poignant, circumscribed novels of the 1930s. . . . Bellow had come out of a ghetto in Montreal, the Napoleon Street that makes one of the deeper sections of *Herzog*. But what made him suddenly vivid, beginning with what was later to seem the put-on of *The Adventures of Augie March* (1953), was his command of a situation peculiarly American, founded on mass experience, that was as far from the metaphysical wit in Kafka as it was from the too conscious pathos of the Depression novels. With Bellow an American of any experience could feel that he was in the midst of the life he knew.

What was perhaps most "American" about it was the fact that despite all the crisis psychology in *The Victim*, *Seize the Day*, and *Herzog*, there was a burning belief in commanding one's own experience, in putting it right by thought. Each of these narratives was a kind of survival kit for a period in which survival became all too real a question for many Americans. The Jewish experience on that subject—and what else had the experience been?—seemed exemplary to Americans, especially when it came armed with jokes. Goodbye to Henry Roth and how many other gifted, stunted, devastated Jewish novelists of the Thirties. In book after book Bellow went about the business of ordering life, seeing it through, working it out. He was intimate with the heights-and-abyss experience of so many intellectual Jews, the alternating experience of humiliation and the paradise of intellectual illumination. And it was this depiction of life as incessant mental struggle, of heaven and hell in the same Jewish head, that made Bellow's readers recognize a world the reverse of the provincial, a quality of thought somber, tonic, bracing, that was now actual to American experience yet lent itself to Bellow's fascinatedly personal sense of things. . . .

Above all, the Bellow persona was an hallucinated observer of what Sartre called the "hell that is other people"—he brilliantly sized up the strength in other people's arms, lives, faces, seeing what they had to say to the predominating self's vision at the heart of each Bellow novel. . . . Bellow influenced himself far more than others ever did, which is why book after book added up to what he had experienced and learned. The key belief was that right thinking is virtue and can leave you in charge of the life that is so outrageous to live.

The process of self-teaching thus becomes the heart of Bellow's novels, and the key to their instructiveness for others. One could compile from Bellow's novels a whole commonplace book of wisdom in the crisis era that has been Bellow's subject and opportunity. His novels are successively novels of instruction as well as existential adventure tales. . . .

Thinking is for Bellow the most accessible form of virtue. The "reality instructors" have become indistinguishable from the worldliness with which they are clotted. Bellow's recurrent hero, by contrast, is so concerned with thinking well that the imbalance between the hero and his fellows becomes an imbalance between the hero's thinking and the mere *activity* of others. Bellow is not a very dramatic novelist, and unexpected actions tend to be dragged into his novels—like Herzog's half-hearted attempt to kill his wife's lover—as a way of interrupting the hero's reflections. But evidently Bellow's personae attain their interest for *him* by their ability to express the right opinions. And not surprisingly, the protagonists of Bellow's novels are the voices of his intellectual evolution. A Bellow anthology would take the form of a breviary, an intellectual testament gathered from diaries, letters to public men and famous philosophers that were never mailed; arias to the reader à la Augie March, the thoughts of Artur Sammler that are neural events in the privacy of one's consciousness because they cannot be expressed to others—they are too severe, too disapproving.—ALFRED KAZIN, *Bright Book of Life*, 1973, pp. 128–35

⟨Bellow is⟩ amused by a crucifix (as if it were a toy without a history); and about sex he's a baby. But beyond this, one reads him with the seriousness one brings to the redemption of the garbage pile of one's own life. He mixes recklessness with a primordial awe, and his philosophic whine concentrates mainly on the petty, where we live. His perception of the unity of the human mind doesn't wash out its diversity. He uses language like a gill. Our worst writers (even when they are, in language, our best) write as if their own being were a one-shot affair, instead of an instance of a continuing history; solipsists, who want to be "original," bore because they don't believe in evil. Bellow, even when he is on the run from history, believes in history; and his whole fiction is a wrestling with the Angel of Theodicy. It's uncomfortable to read him because he doesn't allow a distance (as Chekhov does) between the rumpled spirits of his fiction and the reader, and because in this sense he isn't a "modern"; also he is argumentative and nags after a victory. All this means he is a real Voice.

What, in literature, is a Voice? A presence—a corpus of fine size—that can speak to its own generation because it has itself been spoken to by the generations before.—CYNTHIA OZICK, *NYTBR*, Dec. 4, 1977

Works

DANGLING MAN

Here, for the first time I think, the experience of a new generation has been seized and recorded. It is one thing simply to have lost one's faith; it is quite another to begin with the sober and necessary lack of illusion afforded by Marxism, and then to land in what seems to be utter disillusion, only to be forced, stage by stage, to even greater depths of disillusion. This is the experience of the generation that has come to maturity during the depression, the sanguine period of the New Deal, the days of the Popular Front and the days of Munich, and the slow, loud, ticking imminence of a new war. With the advent of war, every conceivable temptation not to be honest, not to look directly at experience, not to remember the essential vows of allegiance to the intelligence and to human possibility and dignity—every conceivable temptation and every plea of convenience, safety and casuistry has presented itself.

Joseph, the hero of *Dangling Man*, is remarkable because he has the strength (and it is his only strength) to keep his eyes open and his mind awake to the quality of his experience. He has been for a time a member of the Communist Party and he has been offered a business career by a successful older brother. He has rejected both. With the coming of the war, he undergoes the slow strangulation of being drafted but not inducted into the army because of various bureaucratic formalities. During this period in the inter-regnum between civilian and army life, he is gradually stripped of the few pretenses and protections left to him. A Communist refuses to speak to him; his brother attempts to lend him money; his niece taunts him as a beggar; his friends who have made their "meek adjustments" are repelled by his unwillingness to accept things as they are; he quarrels with his friends, his relatives, his wife who is supporting him and the people who live in the rooming house in which he spends his idle days. And finally, unable to endure the continuous emptiness and humiliation of his life, he sees to it that he is immediately taken into the army. . . .

As a novel, the faults of *Dangling Man* come mainly from the fact that it is somewhat too linear in its movement and contained within too small an orbit. Thus, in seeking to keep Joseph's frame of mind constantly in the foreground, Bellow brushes over a number of dramatic possibilities, particularly those inherent in Joseph's marriage relation and his rejection of financial success. The narrative is perhaps too spare in its use of detail and background. And the use of the journal as a form blocks off the interesting shift of perspective that could be gained by presenting Joseph through the eyes of some person of the preceding generation. But, given Bellow's choice of a diary for conveying a larger social pattern, these limitations were perhaps hardly to be avoided, and this small book is an important effort to describe the situation of the younger generation.—DELMORE SCHWARTZ, "A Man in His Time," *PR*, Summer 1944, pp. 348–50

Bellow's first novel, *Dangling Man*, 1944, owed more to the example of Kafka than Dreiser. Its awareness of things is acutely contemporary: hungry, bitterly ironic, introspective. The world it depicts is one in which man, seeking freedom, must finally deny it; in which the humanistic dictum "tout comprendre, c'est tout pardonner" is made unintelligible by the alliance of metaphysical absurdity with social regimentation; in which the flayed moral sense can only express itself by futile or nasty gestures.

It is these gestures, always unpleasant—there is no more adequate word for them—that redeem Joseph from the impotence to which he is prey: they are the weak, scratchy tokens of his rage. Joseph—he has no paternity beyond his crisis and no other name—seems a curious combination of Oblomov and Musil's Man Without Qualities, Hamlet and Prufrock, Kafka's K. and Dostoyevsky's Man from Underground, the hero crippled and spiteful. He sits in his room awaiting the day's minor crises while his wife, Iva, earns their living. He considers himself a moral casualty of a war which denies him the possibilities both of freedom and commitment, a man condemned by a condemned age. . . .

Dangling Man is a tight, speculative, and penetrating novel which nevertheless fails to find a sustaining form. The structure is not without interest, is vaguely avant-garde: it is the record of a spiritual defeat in diary form, written with an admixture of quotidian drabness and intensity. The style reflects the tedium and despair, the slovenliness and showy humiliations of Joseph's life, and reflects them often in sordid images—spilled orange juice or a half-plucked chicken in the sink. But the colorless style and rancid manner of confession, though apparently suited to the mood of the novel, insulate it from the currents of reality; they predetermine our attitude to the material and allow no contrary influence, no enriching substance, to enter in. This is another way of saying that the "objectivity" of the diary device is perhaps too obviously feigned, that Joseph does not remove himself sufficiently from authorial control to enlist our genuine sympathies. Joseph, unlike the heroes of Kafka, say, remains too much the puppet all the way around; his vitality as a *fictional* character is low. The brilliant inventiveness of Bellow is still muted here, and the vigor of his imagination exhibits itself mainly in a dance of ideas—though there are contradictions on the point of Personal Destiny he has not seen fit to purge—in grim irony, skull-like laughter, Mephistophelian comedy. Everyone and everything in the novel contains an element of the grim fantastic. Turned inward upon itself and thinly dramatic, the novel still leaves the ineradicable impression of a man who screams out in laughter to see his guts dangling from his belly.—Ihab Hassan, "Saul Bellow: The Quest and Affirmation of Reality," *Radical Innocence*, 1961, pp. 294–99

THE VICTIM

⟨The Victim⟩ might have stopped with a portrayal of the plight of the Jew, unnerved in advance before the charges of his enemy (who is entirely without guilt? who can feel a *right* to security before another's failure?), learning through the acceptance of his guilt and the assertion of his innocence to be free; but Leventhal is realized with such passionate patience and skill, achieved with such scrupulous regard for detail rising from a sense that the meanings of each trivial fact are inexhaustible and mysterious—that he becomes, deeply as he is a Jew, human, and, infinitely as he is particularized, universal. We think of Leopold Bloom, the urban man, the sojourner, the bastard artist, infinite in feeling, limited in expression; the style is at once low-keyed and violent with that baffled urge toward articulateness. Every aspect of that hot, lonely midsummer is felt at once as real and obsessive—Leventhal is what we are, and what, in terror, we dream we are. Secure for a moment, established in routines of decency and sufficiency in the blind institutionalized process of modern life—as we say, "lucky," and assailed suddenly by the accusation that is monstrously unfair and cannot be denied. To have rejected utterly his guilt and responsibility would have been for Leventhal a lie, and yet accepting them brings him in the end to a sullied house, to insolence and the point of death. It is difficult, after all, to be human—and nothing less is at stake.

The Victim is a fruitful and satisfying achievement, surely one of the most complexly moving books of the past ten years. The tension between its realistic surfaces and its symbolic implications is admirably sustained; the quality of its *achieved* ideas, their passionate implication in the fable, and their coherence with the tone and structure make a book whose unity, amazingly these days, is one of inclusion, not exclusion, a book whose pleasures are neither irrelevant nor unwitting, a novel that establishes in a single gesture its structure and its meaning. In each novel, the fate of the form is at stake, and we must be grateful to the young writer adequate to his responsibilities.—Leslie Fiedler, *KR*, Summer 1948, p. 527

THE ADVENTURES OF AUGIE MARCH

One might expect a consensus of the reviewers of a book to decide whether it is any good or not. For most books they do this well enough, and the books are immediately forgotten, forever. But for a few books, although they try to do this, all they can truly speak to is the book's importance; its degree of excellence or badness may be matter of debate for years or decades. The reviewers of Saul Bellow's new novel, *The Adventures of Augie March*, whether admiring, like Lionel Trilling and Robert Penn Warren, or disapproving, like Maxwell Geismar and Norman Podhoretz, appear to have established it firmly as important. Making small attempt, then, to estimate its merits, let us inquire a little into its relation to its tradition. It looks like a naturalistic novel, undoubtedly. But there are radical differences between it and the naturalism, say, of Dreiser and James T. Farrell.

If we compare with *Augie March* other well-written novels like *The Naked and the Dead* and *Lie Down in Darkness*, we notice that its style is far more individual: it is almost as intensely individual as Hemingway's or Faulkner's. Whether this style is Bellow's or Augie's is at present Bellow's secret; he has certainly not employed it before. His next book might be supposed to let us into the secret. But considering the fact that nobody yet knows whether the style of Mark Twain's masterpiece was Huck's or his, perhaps we may never know. Now a powerful and singular style has been at work in American naturalism before—namely, Stephen Crane's—but that was a long time ago. The later men have just drudged along. We have to consider the general effect of this on language. Dreiser's verbless maundering off toward some invisible period has done our language no good. I would guess that the effect of the sharpness and acrobatic freedom of *Augie March* ought to be salutary, as Crane's naturalism was.

A second difference is related to style, but transcends it. The book is dominated by a recurrent allusiveness to masters of Greek, Jewish, European, and American history, literature, and philosophy. Sometimes their deeds or opinions are mentioned, sometimes they rule the imagery. We might call them Overlords, or Sponsors. ("If you want," Augie says at one point, "to pick your own ideal creature in the mirror coastal air and sharp leaves of ancient perfections and be at home where a great mankind was at home, I've never seen any reason why not.") The Overlords have a double use. They stand as figures of awe and emulation to Augie (one of whose favourite authors is plainly Plutarch)—corresponding in this to the heroes of his actual experience, such as Einhorn. And they create historical depth, the kind of legendary perspective that our naturalism has deeply desired; a portrait on the scale of Einhorn's would be impossible without them. Replacing the vague merciless forces invoked by Dreiser, they remind me of the marvelous vast heads of statues in some of Watteau's pictures, overlooking his lovers. They are bound to irritate some readers as pretentious or hand-to-mouth, or a mannerism, because they are a new element, a new convention, in our fiction; new conventions are likely to irritate at first.

Along with these differences goes a decisive change in theme from the naturalism we have known, which dealt as a rule with success, and was likely to be tragic. Augie does not aim at success, and his story is a comedy, having for theme the preservation of individuality against the pressures in American life (modern life) toward uniformity, the adoption of socially acceptable roles: pressures exactly toward success, or at any rate security. The pressures are dramatized by Bellow as "recruiting," everybody's attempts to get Augie to serve their ends. Augie is all risk, he always consents; but then he always withdraws, because, experimental and aggressive, he is trying to refuse to lead a disappointed life. The insistence upon having one's own fate we might relate to the divorce now between parents and children, in (as W. H. Auden has put it) "a society where the father plays as minor a role as he plays in America."

Augie has no visible father (he is illegitimate) and can hardly follow in his father's footsteps.

The novel, then, because of the recruiting, has the form of a theme-and-variations, and because of the search for a fate good enough, it has also the direction of a "pilgrimage"— Bellow's word late in the book. The first is more important than the second, but I don't quite understand Clifton Fadiman's regarding it as "undirected." Another critical mistake seems to me to be Warren's when he wishes that Augie "had been given the capacity . . . for more joy and sorrow." Surely he suffers and rejoices enough for several books. Possibly Warren read *The Adventures of Augie March* too much in the light of Bellow's earlier, constricted novels, which strike me as interesting now chiefly in relation to this one. Both the stunning wit and the emotional range are new here to Bellow. Wit has not been a characteristic of our twentieth-century naturalists, either. At the same time, notwithstanding these differences, *Augie March* does clearly belong on the Dreiser side, inclusive and tidal, as against Hemingway's and, in its insistence that what is wide-spread shall also be intense, may help to foster a fresh dimension for naturalism.—JOHN BERRYMAN, "A Note on *Augie*" (1953), *The Freedom of the Poet*, 1976, pp. 222–24

The Adventures of Augie March is the third of Saul Bellow's novels, and by far the best one. It is, in my opinion a rich, various, fascinating, and important book, and from now on any discussion of fiction in America in our time will have to take account of it. To praise this novel should not, however, be to speak in derogation of the two earlier ones, *The Dangling Man* and *The Victim*. Both of these novels clearly indicated Saul Bellow's talent, his sense of character, structure, and style. Though *The Dangling Man* did lack narrative drive, it was constantly interesting in other departments, in flashes of characterization, in social and psychological comment. In *The Victim*, however, Bellow developed a high degree of narrative power and suspense in dealing with materials that in less skill-ful hands would have invited an analytic and static treatment. These were not merely books of promise. They represented— especially *The Victim*—a solid achievement, a truly distinguished achievement, and should have been enough to win the author a public far larger than became his. They did win the attention of critics and of a hard core of discriminating readers, but they were not popular.

The Dangling Man and *The Victim* were finely wrought novels of what we may, for lack of a more accurate term, call the Flaubert-James tradition. Especially *The Victim* depended much on intensification of effect by tightness of structure, by limitations on time, by rigid economy in structure of scene, by placement and juxtaposition of scenes, by the unsaid and with-held, by a muting of action, by a scrupulous reserved style. The novel proved that the author had a masterful control of the method, not merely fictional good manners, the meticulous good breeding which we ordinarily damn by the praise "intelligent."

It would be interesting to know what led Saul Bellow to turn suddenly from a method in which he was expert and in which, certainly, he would have scored triumphs. It would be easy to say that it had been from the beginning a mistake for him to cultivate this method, to say that he was a victim of the critical self-consciousness of the novel in our time, to say that in his youthful innocence he had fallen among the thieves of promise, the theorizers. Or it would be easy to say that the method of the earlier books did not accommodate his real self, his deepest inspiration and that as soon as he liberated himself

from the restriction of the method he discovered his own best talent.

These things would be easy to say but hard to prove. It would be equally easy to say that the long self-discipline in the more obviously rigorous method had made it possible for Bellow now to score a triumph in the apparent formlessness of the autobiographical-picaresque novel, and to remember, as a parallel, that almost all the really good writers of free verse had cultivated an ear by practice in formal metrics. I should, as a matter of fact, be inclined to say that *The Adventures of Augie March* may be the profit on the investment of *The Dangling Man* and *The Victim*, and to add that in a novel of the present type we can't live merely in the hand-to-mouth way of incidental interests in scene and character, that if such a novel is to be fully effective the sense of improvisation must be a dramatic illusion, the last sophistication of the writer, and that the improvisation is really a pseudo-improvisation, and that the random scene or casual character that imitates the accidental quality of life must really have a relevance, and that the discovery, usually belated, of this relevance is the characteristic excitement of the genre. That is, in this genre the relevance is deeper and more obscure, and there is, in the finest examples of the genre, a greater tension between the random life force of the materials and the shaping intuition of the writer.

It is the final distinction, I think, of *The Adventures of Augie March* that we do feel this tension, and that it is a meaningful fact. It is meaningful because it dramatizes the very central notion of the novel. The hero Augie March is a very special kind of adventurer, a kind of latter-day example of the Emersonian ideal Yankee who could do a little of this and a little of that, a Chicago pragmatist happily experimenting in all departments of life, work, pleasure, thought, a hero who is the very antithesis of one of the most famous heroes of our time, the Hemingway hero, in that his only code is codelessness and his relish for experience is instinctive and not programmatic. This character is, of course, the character made for the random shocks and aimless corners of experience, but he is not merely irresponsible. If he wants freedom from commitment, he also wants wisdom, and in the end utters a philosophy, the philosophy embodied by the French serving maid Jacqueline, big-legged and red-nosed and ugly, standing in a snowy field in Normandy, hugging still her irrepressibly romantic dream of going to Mexico.

But is this comic and heroic philosophy quite enough, even for Augie? Augie himself, I hazard, scarcely thinks so. He is still a seeker, a hoper, but a seeker and hoper aware of the comedy of seeking and hoping. He is, in fact, a comic inversion of the modern stoic, and the comedy lies in the tautology of his wisdom—our best hope is hope. For there is a deep and undercutting irony in the wisdom and hope, and a sadness even in Augie's high-heartedness, as we leave him standing with Jacqueline in the winter field on the road toward Dunkerque and Ostend. But to return to the proposition with which this discussion opened: if Augie plunges into the aimless ruck of experience, in the end we see that Saul Bellow has led him through experience toward philosophy. That is, the aimless ruck had a shape, after all, and the shape is not that of Augie's life but of Saul Bellow's mind. Without that shape, and the shaping mind, we would have only the limited interest in the random incidents.

The interest in the individual incidents is, however, great. In *The Victim* the interest in any one episode was primarily an interest in the over-all pattern, but here most incidents, and incidental characters, appeal first because of their intrinsic qualities, and, as we have said, our awareness of their place in the over-all pattern dawns late on us. In incident after incident, there is brilliant narrative pacing, expert atmospheric effect, a fine sense of structure of the individual scene. In other words, the lessons learned in writing the earlier books are here applied in another context.

As for characterization, we find the same local fascination. The mother, the grandmother, the feeble-minded brother, the brother drunk on success, the whole Einhorn family, Thea, the Greek girl—they are fully realized, they compel our faithful attention and, in the end, our sympathy. As a creator of character, Saul Bellow is in the great tradition of the English and American novel, he has the fine old relish of character for character's sake, and the sort of tolerance which Santayana commented on in Dickens by saying that it was the naturalistic understanding that is the nearest thing to Christian charity.

It is, in a way, a tribute, though a back-handed one, to point out the faults of Saul Bellow's novel, for the faults merely make the virtues more impressive. The novel is uneven. Toward the last third the inspiration seems to flag now and then. Several episodes are not carried off with the characteristic elan, and do not, for me at least, take their place in the thematic pattern. For instance, the Trotsky episode or the whole Stella affair, especially in the earlier stages. And a few of the characters are stereotypes, for example, Stella again. In fact, it is hard to see how she got into the book at all except by auctorial fiat, and I am completely baffled to know what the author thought he was doing with her, a sort of vagrant from some literary province lying north-northeast of the *Cosmopolitan Magazine*. Furthermore, several critics have already said that the character of Augie himself is somewhat shadowy. This, I think, is true, and I think I know the reason: it is hard to give substance to a character who has no commitments, and by definition Augie is the man with no commitments. This fact is a consequence of Bellow's basic conception, but wouldn't the very conception have been stronger if Augie had been given the capacity for deeper commitments, for more joy and sorrow? He might, at least, have tried the adventurer's experiment in those things? That is, the character tends now to be static, and the lesson that Augie has learned in the end is not much different from the intuition with which he started out. He has merely learned to phrase it. There is one important reservation which, however, I should make in my criticism of Augie. His very style is a powerful device of characterization. It does give us a temper, a texture of mind, a perspective of feeling, and it is, by and large, carried off with a grand air. Which leads me to the last observation that the chief release Saul Bellow has found in this book may be the release of a style, for he has found, when he is at his best, humor and eloquence to add to his former virtues.—ROBERT PENN WARREN, "The Man With No Commitments," NR, Nov. 2, 1953, pp. 22–23

Saul Bellow's new novel is a new kind of book. The only other American novels to which it can be compared with any profit are *Huckleberry Finn* and *U.S.A.*, and it is superior to the first by virtue of the complexity of its subject matter and to the second by virtue of a realized unity of composition. In all three books, the real theme is America, a fact which is not as clear in this new work as it is in its predecessors, perhaps because of its very newness. The sheer bigness of America as a theme and as a country has always made the novelist's task difficult, which may be the reason that Thomas Wolfe was so excited by trains, just as it certainly has something to do with the fact that *U.S.A.* does not possess complete narrative unity.

In other American novels of the same seriousness and ambition, the theme of America and of being an American is narrowed to a region—Hawthorne is writing about New England, Faulkner is writing about the South—or the novels are about Americans in Europe, which is almost as true of Hemingway as it is of James; or there is, in any case, a concentration upon a particular American *milieu*. Moreover, the classic choice of the American writer has been either uncritical affirmation on the one hand, or on the other hand some form of rejection, the rejection of satire in Lewis, the rejection of social protest in Dos Passos, or the rejection of tragedy in Dreiser and Fitzgerald. The point can hardly be overemphasized: Huck Finn is in flight from civilization; Milly Theale is swindled of, above all, her desire to live; Lambert Strether (or William Dean Howells) discovers in middle age that he has not really lived at all; Lily Bart commits suicide; Richard Cory blows out his brains; J. Alfred Prufrock feels that he "should have been a pair of ragged claws"; Frederic Henry makes "a separate peace"; Quentin Compson has to say four times that he does not hate the South; Clyde Griffiths is electrocuted; Jay Gatsby is murdered. There are many other instances of the same kind, almost none of which can be considered purely as tragedy, but more precisely as catastrophe: Clyde Griffiths and Jay Gatsby perish because they are Americans, Agamemnon and Macbeth because they are human beings.

The Adventures of Augie March is a new kind of book first of all because Augie March possesses a new attitude toward experience in America: instead of the blindness of affirmation and the poverty of rejection, Augie March rises from the streets of the modern city to encounter the reality of experience with an attitude of satirical acceptance, ironic affirmation, the comic transcendence of affirmation and rejection. As he says at the very start: "I am an American, Chicago-born—Chicago, that somber city—" (the adjective should make it clear that to be an American is far from the same thing as being a 100 percent American) "and go at things as I have taught myself, free style, and will make the record in my own way: first to knock, first admitted; sometimes an innocent knock, sometimes a not so innocent . . . ," and it is soon clear that Augie has identified America and adventure, an identification which functions as both method and insight. Augie's style of speech is the kind of speech necessary for going everywhere and talking to all kinds of Americans: he is a highbrow of sorts, but he does not talk like one, knowing that if he did, there would be the wrong kind of distance between himself and most other human beings. Being a pure product of the big city, he talks like a wise guy and he is a wise guy, like the other guys on the block; but he does not entirely like being a wise guy, and he is one not for the sake of any sense of self it gives him, but because it is a way of staying alive if you live in twentieth-century America, staying alive and getting around. Augie is an adventurer in every sense of the word, including the not so innocent sense, because adventure is the only way to the reality of experience in America. This essential fact about Augie has been the cause of misgivings in several critics who have otherwise expressed much admiration for the book, and who feel that there is something wrong about Augie's resistance to commitments, or what Augie himself calls being recruited. Augie does not want to be recruited or committed to the commitments which others have decided are desirable for him, one of which is a wealthy marriage. To be committed is to be pinned down and cut off from the adventure of reality and of America, to be cut off from hope and from freedom and from the freedom to move on to new hopes when some hopes collapse. Once you are committed, the frontier is gone. This may not be the most desirable moral attitude, but it certainly gives Augie a degree of awareness which none of the other characters possess. The critics who felt misgivings about

Augie's being uncommitted recognized the overwhelming reality of a dozen other characters. But since their reality is given solely through Augie's mind, there must be a necessary connection between Augie's uncommitted or free mind and his perception of their reality. Moreover, as Augie himself might say, you have got to be sure that you are not committing yourself to what that guy Erich Fromm calls "escape from freedom." To which it must be added that Kierkegaard, in pointing the necessity of choice and commitment, attacked the very commitments which Augie resists, the conformist, conventional, and official roles which are characteristic forms of inauthenticity, a term which anticipates the stuffed shirt.

And the connection between Augie's chief attitude and his grasp of experience comes to a climax in the wonderful episode of the eagle who, like Augie, refuses in his own way to be committed. Any paraphrase of the episode would violate its narrative tact and subtlety, but the main thing about the eagle is his refusal to be dominated beyond a certain point by another being: which seems quite sensible to Augie and outrageous cowardice to the girl who is training him and who is also trying to impose another kind of domination upon Augie. Augie does not want to be dominated and he does not want to dominate anyone else: this is a free country, and to dominate or to be dominated is to be cut off from the reality of experience and of human beings in America, however else it may be in a hierarchical society. Augie is precisely like the veterans of the last war who once the war was over wanted to get out of the army because no matter how high your rank, there was always someone else to boss you around: freedom is existence, as America is adventure. Since America began as an adventure, Augie is right to conclude as he does:

> Why, I am a sort of Columbus of those near-at-hand and believe you can come to them in this immediate *terra incognita* that spreads out in every gaze. I may well be a flop at this line of endeavor. Columbus, too, thought he was a flop, probably, when they sent him back in chains. Which didn't prove there was no America.

Thus, by hoping for the best and being prepared for the worst, Augie proves that there is an America, a country in which anything might happen, wonderful or awful, but a guy has a fighting chance to be himself, find out things for himself, and find out what's what. For the first time in fiction America's social mobility has been transformed into a spiritual energy which is not doomed to flight, renunciation, exile, denunciation, the agonized hyper-intelligence of Henry James, or the hysterical cheering of Walter Whitman.—DELMORE SCHWARTZ, "Adventure in America," *PR*, Jan. 1954, pp. 112-15

In *The Adventures of Augie March*, Mr. Saul Bellow has set out to write a comic epic or picaresque novel about life in Chicago. The American scene offers rich opportunities for this genre and it is long since it has been handled with comic irony. The child of foreign-born parents seeking his fortune and his identity is a modern version of the hungry valet of the 17th and 18th centuries and Mr. Bellow is sufficiently instructed to know that, if a modern picaresque novel is to be worth writing, it probably ought to be done in a prose style which makes as definite a break with the past as the styles of the picaresque masters did. The question is, what kind of prose style? The earliest picaresque was done flamboyantly and with popular exaggeration; but Defoe wrote plainly and Fielding with the ironical sententiousness of the educated. Mr. Bellow has invented a new confection of racy, talking speech and literary marzipan which can be defended as the kind of thing a half-educated young rogue would work out for himself between the pool-room and High School. For myself, I find this style affected and arch. The prose has a monotonous sing-song cadence and, for whole chapters at a time, can be cut up into Alexandrines; it is pungent but it is coagulated. It is a rhetoric—and sometimes no more than the rhetoric of the catalogue. . . .

One switches off and tunes in again to Mr. Bellow and he is inevitably on the air, good and bad together, a generous, tangy, and self-conscious mixture. One section of the novel, the part which describes his departure with a rich divorcée to Mexico where she takes her pet eagle to hunt lizards, is a distinct decline from the novelist's Chicago pages—indeed, here he is comic without knowing it. Mexico for Mr. Bellow is what Africa was for Mr. Hemingway. One has no confidence in the wretched eagle as a symbol and one begins to think the whole poetic side of Mr. Bellow's equipment as a writer is artifice and pretence. The fact is that whenever he is writing in a plain manner about people he is shrewd, sharp and original; but when he starts analysing, explaining, discoursing and glamorising, he is "hamming up" his subject.

The Adventures of Augie March is one more attempt to write "the great American novel." It is moved by that emotion of nostalgia which is basic in American literature. The book is wonderfully crowded, sentimental—not always in the bad sense—and shows a greed for the externals of life and the surface of human feeling. If one compares Mr. Bellow's attempt with a not so vastly different English novel, Joyce Cary's *The Horse's Mouth*, one sees how much more selective the English writer is and how much more festively inventive of incident and character. Mr. Bellow thickens into mere reminiscence beside him. But in Mr. Cary there is and can be no element to compare with that sense of the American phenomenon which Mr. Bellow and so many American novelists have. It is not always an aesthetic advantage, indeed, often the reverse, but it gives the American novelist an initial fever and a dramatic advantage, even if it makes his material seem more important than it may really be. The lack of such a sense of there being anything phenomenal, dramatic or generally moving about Glasgow or Birmingham has turned English novelists away from the appetite for environment and the greed for human nature. To their loss.—V. S. PRITCHETT, *NSN*, June 19, 1954, p. 803

Mr. Saul Bellow's *The Adventures of Augie March* is ⟨a⟩ study in the spiritual picaresque, a later form of the traditional *bildungsroman* in which the *pícaro* or hero is consciousness rather than swashbuckling rogue, and so is required, as the rogue is not, to develop, deepen, strike through its first illusion to the truth which, at the end of the road, it discovers to be its fate. But *Augie March* begins with the aphorism, "Man's character is his fate," and it ends with the aphorism transposed "man's fate is his character." The learning is in the transposition. Man's fate is that he shall inherit, be stuck with, his character. The movement which the transposition represents is the movement from the naturalistic to the existentialist, from what is determined to what is accepted or chosen. Augie at the end of the road simply comes into his destiny, although, as it happens, it is not the destiny, the alternative to the "disappointed life," for which he sought. It is the destiny which his character fated, and so, like the rogues of literature in the past, he is not changed but confirmed. I suspect we accept this in those earlier rogues because, having recognized their qualities of character at the outset, we turn our attention to the manner in which these qualities display themselves from adventure to adventure, and find there a confirmation of what we recognized. The emphasis is not on what the hero becomes but on what he does and the bizarreness and excitement of what he does. We know, besides, that his destiny, when it is achieved, will be a formula and a fake—a magical inheritance, a last-minute revelation of noble birth, the conquest of beauty, a "happily ever after." The drama is in the adventure, our interest in being titillated and duped. But the problem which immediately presents itself in the case of Augie is that while his adventures are formed in the pattern of the traditional picaresque, his character demands exposition through the developing form of the more modern *bildungsroman*. He is a Stephen Dedalus set adrift in a world made for Moll Flanders or a Jonathan Wild. As a man with a mission, he is required to impose his will on his experience, to subdue or be subdued, and so to change. But Mr. Bellow feels his obligation to the picaresque too strongly, particularly to the requirement that he who begins as a *pícaro* must end as a *pícaro*, and so we are left at the end with the mission unfulfilled, the will unimposed, the man unsubdued.

To have been an altogether successful adaptation of the picaresque form, the novel would have had to consist of a series of episodes recounting high adventure and intrigue, with an overlay of equally high comedy and social satire. We would then have been placed in the position to appreciate and find full satisfaction in the quality of the adventure and in the confirmation of what we already knew to be Augie's character as he engaged the adventure. But the adventure in the novel as it stands is neither high enough nor rich enough to be a justification of the whole, and we are struck more by Augie's isolation from than by his participation in the social scene of satire. That is, in fact, the necessity which the theme of the novel imposes upon him. He must be disengaged because he must hold out. As the novel develops, we begin to notice, furthermore, as we notice in *Catcher in the Rye*, that the social scene tends to become rarefied and increasingly inspecific. It is not a proper subject for the traditional picaresque satire of the foibles and frailties of class, although the novel does contain many excellent portraits of people. The class structure is simply not there to be satirized, except insofar as the status of individuals is related to money. What one sees is simply the rich and the poor, and these consequently become the poles of commitment between which Augie vacillates. It is interesting to see, however, that the novel in its early sections partakes of some of the dramatic advantages arising out of the racial and economic tensions of lower-class urban experience, a type of experience which in the twenties and thirties was much more common to our larger cities than it is now. The Depression experience alone, in fact, provides Mr. Bellow with nearly all the social and class materials he has, as well as with the perspective of under-privilege from which to judge those materials. But in the early sections we are plunged into a crowded and fully developed world, alive with discord and tensions. There are Augie's mother, his brothers Simon and Georgie, and Grandma Lausch, the Kinsmans, the Coblins, the Kleins, Bluegren and Clem Tambow, the Einhorns, the Commissioner, Kreindl, and Dingbat. But later on, as Augie matures, this world is left behind, the tensions slacken, the social scene becomes depopulated, and we move from a closely interacting mass of people to isolated personalities—the Renlings, the Fenchels, Cissy Flexner, Padilla, Mimi Villars, Hooker Frazer, the Magnuses, then Thea Fenchel, the millionaire Robey, Kayo Obermark, Mintouchian, Basteshaw, and finally Stella. And as this development occurs, the narrative slows and thins out, and

Augie's pilgrimage becomes merely a horizontal and unmotivated progression through experience. It also becomes less and less clear precisely what Augie's real problem is. We know that he has, as he says, a lot of opposition in him and that he refuses to lead a "disappointed life." Like Holden Caulfield he wants a life in which he can accept the full risks of his humanity, but he also wants a specific fate and function, a destiny worthy of his talents and ideals. In David Riesman's terms, he appears, at first glance, to be an "inner-directed" man holding out against the conformist pressures of an "other-directed" society, but it would be truer to say that he is "inner-directed" in temperament but not in aim and that he is holding out against an "inner-directed" society of strongly ambitious and acquisitive aims, the kind of society which we had in this country up until roughly the beginning of World War II. Nevertheless, the point of Augie's life, the point of his resistance, and, therefore, his point as a character, are all strongly ambiguous. He holds out, but in the name of what we never really know.

There is a sense in which it might be argued that Augie both as a character and as a social type is an example of what happens when the individual loses, or is unable to find, a moral purpose, an "inner-directed" goal. All of Augie's adventures are, in a way, pragmatic conquests, attempts to confirm through the application again and again of the test of experience a truth and a vision of reality which ought to come from within and be imposed upon experience. His situation is such that he is able to see validity everywhere, particularly in the lives which those around him have settled for. But the problem he poses as a fictional character is that, as a man committed to nothing, he can have no dramatic centrality; his conflict with society can never be really intense or meaningful because there is nothing at stake, no price of spiritual opposition which might endow him with tragic or pathetic value. This, it seems to me, is the vitiating paradox behind him and his story as a whole. He is empty and without commitment and, in keeping with the rule of decorum and the truth of his social situation and Mr. Bellow's theme, he must be so. But his emptiness is his dramatic ruin, just as it is the ruin of nearly all the characters in recent American fiction. The force of the fall from innocence, of the failure of an heroic design, has given way to the surly spasm of futility and what has been called "the merely middle-class emotion of embarrassment."

It is perhaps because Mr. Bellow subconsciously sensed Augie's inadequacy as a character that he sought through his style to impose upon his material an almost fearsome significance, a disguise of acute profundity, allusion, and paradox, suggesting that behind or above the people of the novel there hangs a thick cloud of metaphysical, philosophical, and historical truth in relation to which their thoughts and actions have meanings more sublime than any that may appear on the surface. One can in fact say that it is the style alone that preserves the novel from the purely naturalistic stereotype, that keeps it from being simply a chronicle of the adventures of an educated Studs Lonigan. It is the style, in particular, which suggests through its images and metaphors that there is a philosophically informed dimension to Augie's development. It creates around him an aura of speculation and examination, so that throughout nearly the whole of his progress, we continue to believe that he is truly engaged in a struggle to choose among fantastically complicated metaphysical alternatives, and that at the end his revelation and ours will come. But as the concrete basis for Augie's development moves farther and farther away from the gaseous invertebrate metaphysic of the style, the style is forced to accomplish more and more, until finally it is required to create all the meaning out of its own resources and to state more meaning than exists in the subject or the scene to be stated.—JOHN W. ALDRIDGE, *In Search of Heresy*, 1956, pp. 131–36

SEIZE THE DAY

Seize the Day logically culminates a line of development begun with *Dangling Man* (1944), and continued through *The Victim* (1947), and *The Adventures of Augie March*, Bellow's *Bildungsroman* that won the 1954 National Book Award. Horace's *Carpe diem* furnishes the title for *Seize the Day*; for his work as a whole, Bellow could well adopt another Latin tag, the one found on the coins of his adopted country—*E pluribus unum*. For Bellow has tried to lasso the universe, to explore the splendid, profligate diversity of human experience, and to seek the ties that bind. His all-inclusiveness forces him to skip about from one level to another; the swift leaps from the sublime to the ridiculous and back have the flavor of the best Jewish humor—and are equally productive of brilliant insights into the human condition. Romantic at root, this impulse to embrace the world leads to, in his own phrase, "a mysterious adoration of what occurs." As Joseph says in *Dangling Man*, "In a sense everything is good because it exists. Or, good or not good, it exists, it is ineffable and, for that reason, marvelous." Bellow, recipient of a Guggenheim award, knockabout intellectual, and an intimate of the greatest living con man, Yellow Kid Weil, sees his role, as does Augie March, as that of "a Columbus of those near-at-hand." Since "judgment is second to wonder," in his work celebration of life takes precedence over criticism. (In *Day*, all the major characters are partially right, partially justified. Bellow's compassion is the greater for being non-selective.) But what distinguishes this author from other "acceptors" is that with him acceptance is an outgrowth of full knowledge, not a substitute for it.

So much for *pluribus*. It is the vast tract Bellow must traverse in his search for the *unum*. Each man *is* an island, entire unto himself, and it is no good pretending otherwise. Bellow has few peers in delineating the particularity, the uniqueness of the topography of a single individual. But he also insists that individuals form archipelagos, and far beneath the surface all are rooted to the same ocean floor. Out of this awareness he draws two themes that pervade his work—the horrible price of insularity (far from rare in modern fiction) and, transcending this, the common humanity shared by all.

In his drive to illumine this latter motif Bellow has passed through four phases. Since each is organically related to the one preceding, they are not *that* sharply divided; they are, however, apparent enough to warrant noting. In *Dangling Man* the emphasis is ideational; what we get is mostly Joseph's thought and some of his speech. In *The Victim* ideas and action revolving around the theme of the difficulty of being human are neatly correlated, almost in a one to one ratio. In the sprawling *Augie* Bellow seems more confident of his abilities to convey attitudes through action rather than discourse, so that thought becomes the pungent seasoning and not the whole stew. Finally, in *Day* he descends deeply to a primal level of atmosphere and feeling that communicates in a way that defies analysis but that carries the moist, hot sting of truth.

The growth and ripening of Bellow's attitudes have been paralleled by the perfecting of his medium of expression. He has fused the varied and often conflicting elements of American English into a natural whole that is ours and yet remains peculiarly his own. Almost alone among today's writers he can select words and phrases, here from the gutter, there from the

ivory tower, without the slightest hint of embarrassment or awkwardness.

For all his virtues (and they are considerable), Bellow is by no means flawless. If writing were dancing, the symbol of much postwar American fiction would be Fred Astaire: urbane, a bit wistful, it camouflages its lack of commitment behind a dazzling command of techniques. Bellow, on the other hand, is a Nijinsky, but one who takes an occasional pratfall. If at times he falls heavily, it is because he leaps higher, dares more, than those who are content to stay within the confines of competence.

The most apparent of Bellow's faults is his incapacity to deal convincingly with women. The female figures in his novels repeatedly fall into one of two categories; they are either nags or nymphomaniacs, and the Bellow hero is too often a passive figure, condemned to suffer verbal abuse on the one hand or a physical embarrassment of riches on the other. No Bellow novel has a heroine and in none of them does the protagonist's fate directly hinge upon his relationship with a woman. Joseph's wife Iva "has a way about her that discourages talk," and is alternately colorless and irritating. Joseph also has a mistress, Kitty, but it is noteworthy that she seduces him. The central action of *Victim* could not have occurred at all without the absence of Mary, wife of the protagonist, Asa Leventhal; and the little that we know about her relates almost entirely to the weird, abortive period of their engagement. In *Augie* many of the episodes that in other novels would be called "love scenes" are little more than rape fantasies with Augie as the assaulted. In the final chapters Augie is married to Stella, but matrimony seems to have transformed her from nympho to nag: "She sits and listens . . . and refuses me—for the time being, anyway— the most important things I ask of her." If and when Augie lights out for the territory, Stella will probably be left behind. In *Day*, Tommy's wife Margaret, from whom he is separated, never gets closer than letters and telephone calls to refuse him a divorce and badger him for money. Nor is Tommy's mistress, Olive, ever clearly visualized.

The argument could be advanced that all this is intended, that Bellow uses these women as an analogue of the animal, natural side of life. Thus the abortive heterosexual relationships symbolize the twentieth-century American's failure to cope effectively with Nature. But if this be true, need it happen in all four of Bellow's novels? Surely, with the slow erasure of the distinction between the sexes that has been occurring in the past half-century, women are not incomprehensible and one could serve as *the*, or at least *a*, central figure in a Bellow novel.

Bellow's second failure—that his books don't end, they just stop—is perhaps more easily explained. With his avowal that "character is fate," sheer plot, the arrangement of events, has a diminished importance. Since life won't fit the neat forms of art, Bellow's flaw probably stems from his greater devotion to the former than the latter. It remains to be seen whether these faults can be transcended or whether they are logically outgrowths of the author's deepest beliefs. One rather suspects that his perceptions of women will remain the same, while predicting better resolutions for his future books. Bellow is certainly not insensitive to aesthetic issues, and the ending of *Seize the Day* is several cuts above those of the other three novels.

These strictures aside, it must be said that Saul Bellow is perhaps the major talent of the past decade. He has displayed magnificent fulfillment of his early promise and is now at an age—chronological and artistic—to produce his best work. Publication of his two works-in-progress will be awaited with uncommon eagerness, for he may very well be the fair-haired boy, *El Bello*, of current American letters.—Robert Baker, "Bellow Comes of Age," *CR*, Vol. II, 1957, pp. 107–10

Saul Bellow's novel *Seize the Day* represents, I believe, an extraordinary contribution to the relationship between father and son as a theme in fiction. The father-son relationship is an area of experience which the artist shares to a larger degree than he does any other kind of experience with the cultural historian, the moral philosopher, and more recently with the psychologist, particularly the psychoanalyst. . . .

I should like to consider, with what I trust is neurotic sensibility, Saul Bellow's *Seize the Day* as a novel in which the character and the action of the central figure, Tommy Wilhelm, are determined by and represent the neurotic conflict between instinctual cravings and outwardly determined frustrations. The conflict between father and son is central to the novel, but its repressed content is latent throughout until the last moment, when, as Freud describes it, "the repression is shattered." The novel is interesting, too, in that without deserting the psychoanalytic point of view one can apprehend in the action certain cultural implications. When I finished reading *Seize the Day* I was struck by what appeared to me to be the premeditated delineations of the character and psychopathology of Tommy Wilhelm. But I was equally struck by the unpremeditated affinities of both Tommy Wilhelm and his father with Kafka's father and son as they appear in Kafka's "Letter to His Father." It is this affinity that suggests an extension of the neurotic problem—the outwardly determined frustration which is the product not of a single cultural milieu, but of an encounter between two conflicting milieus.

. . . ⟨W⟩hen we turn to comparisons between *Seize the Day* and Kafka's fiction we are aware of only a pivotal connection—the mutilated relationship between sons and fathers. Kafka's gray Petrouchka-like protagonist and his two-dimensional, expressionistic backgrounds expand into the extremely dimensionalized Tommy Wilhelm and his crowded hour on upper Broadway. But the psychic conflict is identical, and the outcome, while it would not be one Kafka would have chosen, is at least Kafkan.

The desolation of Tommy Wilhelm is a very carefully determined event whose determinants are only explainable in psychoanalytic terms, and whose aesthetic achievement is valid only if we accept the somewhat invidious precondition for enjoyment Freud proposes. In Kafka the neurotic is in the artist, not in the work. The work itself is delivered over, in a manner of speaking, to the controlled insanity of Kafka's world; the interpretive potential is manifold. In *Seize the Day* the neurotic is in the work—and the interpretive potential is singular, a matter of reconciling the events in the novel to the character of Tommy Wilhelm, of explaining the manifest in terms of the repressed.

The day Saul Bellow seizes on which to describe Tommy Wilhelm is the day of one of Wilhelm's many undoings, distinguished from the rest only by the lyric and poetically desirable revelation purchased at the price of everything he owns.

On the day in question Wilhelm has been refused money and love by his father; his wife badgers him for more money; the bogus psychologist Dr. Tamkin has power of attorney over Wilhelm's remaining funds, which have presumably been invested in lard and rye futures. The lard and rye fall; Wilhelm is wiped out, and Tamkin disappears. Wilhelm's reaction to these misadventures is best described as despair; tempered at the very outset by resignation, neurotic fatalism. . . .

The broadest psychoanalytic category within which Tommy Wilhelm operates is that of the moral masochist, the victim, for whom suffering is a *modus vivendi*, a means of self-justification. This aspect of Tommy Wilhelm is the most explicitly realized level of his character. But it deserves closer study as the basis for other, more subtle elements in the novel. The person to whom Wilhelm is masochistically attached is, of course, his father, Dr. Adler, before whom he exhibits his helplessness. And it is equally apparent, even to Wilhelm, that, with individual differences, the other figures on whose mercy he throws himself, are in a declining series, fathers—Maurice Venice, the Rojax Corporation, Tamkin, Mr. Perls, and Mr. Rappaport. He even appreciates the masochistic commitment, when, in considering old Rappaport's devotion to Theodore Roosevelt, he thinks: "Ah, what people are! He is almost not with us, and his life is nearly gone, but T.R. once yelled at him, so he loves him. I guess it is love, too."

What determined Wilhelm's fixation on this all-powerful father in the past is supplied in the novel to the extent that we can reconstruct his childhood—the love and protection of his mother and the stern, sadistic disciplinarianism of his father—followed by his mother's death at the moment of his first failure in Hollywood. The death of one parent, in fact, any intimate bereavement, induces a retreat from adult effectiveness toward dependence, and a heightened dependence on the surviving parent. Dr. Adler was pressed, willy nilly, into service as the mother in addition to his role as the father. But Dr. Adler's tyrannical, uncompromising character has anticipated what might in Wilhelm's life have been a momentary lapse from effectiveness into fixed regressive patterns, has rendered his son incapable of independence. In this sense, a psychoanalytic irony enters into the description of the relationship between father and son, in that the doctor's forthright disgust with his son's weaknesses is a disgust with a situation of which he himself is the author. There is more truth than Dr. Adler is aware of in his "What a Wilky he had given to the world!" But, we can reasonably argue, Wilhelm is not always unsuccessful. He has assumed adult responsibilities over twenty years of his life, and until the ultimate day of his latest failure, he has not invoked his father's help. However, we must consider that as a neurotic personality, Wilhelm is not completely *hors de combat*; he is crippled, not dead, and his ego, besieged from without and betrayed from within, is still in command. He knows a hawk from a handsaw.

What the day of the novel exhibits is the phenomenon known as traumatophilia. The neurotic calendar is crowded with grotesque anniversaries, the observance of which offer a certain relief to the mechanism of repression, worn out in the service of the ego. The consciousness must be allowed from time to time to participate in the unconscious strivings of the individual, as Ferenczi suggests, to "equalize" the effects of the original painful experience throughout the psyche. It is the return of the repressed. In Wilhelm it is the masochistic necessity to fail, to be destroyed at the hands of the punishing father, in order, under the terms of the moral masochistic commitment, to retain his love, and, in less obvious ways, to memorialize certain events in the past.—Daniel Weiss, "Caliban Or Prospero: A Psychoanalytic Study on the Novel *Seize the Day*," *AI*, Fall 1962

HENDERSON THE RAIN KING

In *The Victim* and his extraordinary story, *Seize the Day*, Bellow wrote in a manner that is somehow "Russian"—that is, he created works of realistic fiction in which the events and characters were suffused with a mysterious glow of meaning and signification. The plots are as tight as works for the stage and the stories gave the reader unusual intellectual and artistic satisfaction. In an airless, urban scene, he put down his characters, men deep in predicament, sinking in bad luck or moral uncertainty. The style is tense, with a peculiarly nervous keenness of observation and expression.

The Victim and *Seize the Day* are short and dramatic; in between them came *The Adventures of Augie March*, which is long and episodic, narrated in the first person like *Henderson the Rain King*, and has another embattled, wise-guy hero, a "traveling man." There is a bizarre incompatibility between the two styles, the two conceptions of subject matter. Bellow has a superb gift for characterization and milieu—but *Henderson the Rain King* is a book deliberately without any characters at all. The hero is not a character in the usual sense. He tells us something, indeed much, about his past but he is seen as a figure in a fantasy, a great not-unlikely American going through absurd, unbelievable scenes with various story-book African tribes. The setting is composed of vivacious words coming, as they used to say, from a "fevered artistic brain" rather than from any true observation of geography or actual terrain. The standard to be applied here is not that of realistic fiction, but of, we suppose, odd works like *Don Quixote* or *Gulliver's Travels*. The fantastic journey is perilous. If a work in this form does not succeed brilliantly it is likely to fail dismally. Instead of accuracy the writer will have to call upon the rarest imaginative inspiration. A real man can only be evicted from a real place to make room for the universal destiny, playing itself out among eternal scenery. The impulse to incur these risks is usually the satiric talent expressing itself. But Bellow's book is not a satire although it has satiric bits. Perhaps it is meant as a piece of comic exuberance like *A Sentimental Journey*. But Sterne's post horses and chaises dash up to real inns.

Henderson, then, is not a "character" but he is an "American"—traveling about a dry continent he ends up as a god who makes rain. In his adventures there are possible interpretations, perhaps even "world-wide implications" tucked away here and there if one wanted to look for them. They do not come readily to mind, giving the reader the sense that however ridiculous and unreal the events are they represent human helplessness or folly. When Henderson throws out the water with the frogs are we thinking of bungling engineers in the Point Four Program?

It is another part of the joke that Bellow, very shortly before the publication of this novel, should have expressed himself against "deep readers" and symbolic interpretation on the front page of the book section of *The New York Times*. *Henderson* cannot be read except deeply, nor be understood except symbolically. And the fact that this is so, that the literal meaning is rather thin in dramatic texture, and that, nevertheless "deep" and symbolical meanings do not jump out at us is a real fault. The scenery is too unreal for picaresque comedy; the events have too little resonance for symbolic fantasy.

Bellow is everywhere felt to be among the best of the young novelists and many would rate him first. *Henderson the Rain King* is very much less to my taste than his previous work and yet it is not exactly to be designated a "falling off" or even a "standing still," a repetition. It is an autonomous work, a mutation. There is a suggestion of it in *Augie March*, but that novel is closer in spirit to *The Victim* and *Seize the Day* than to *Henderson the Rain King*. This last novel is an incredibly secure piece of composition—profuse, splashy, relaxed. It is large and Bellow seems to want largeness, as though he felt his own position as an important American novelist imposed the

responsibility for a large effort. He will not, knowing our artistic retreats, be guilty of "the refusal of greatness." But he may, eager courtier, travel too far in pursuit.—ELIZABETH HARD-WICK, "A Fantastic Voyage," *PR*, Spring 1959, pp. 300–303

When realist writers write novels in which ideas play important roles, the procedure is usually a form of concealment: the action is tied-into the idea either as illustration or contradiction of it. The big, organizing idea of a novel close to *Henderson*, Mann's *Felix Krull*, is something like the reality of fakery, and the book is cluttered with such detail as glorious-looking champagne bottles containing miserable champagne, actors seen first under the lights and then backstage, crooks, magicians, illusionists of all sorts, a whole Mann spectrum drawn from department stores to interstellar space. The picaresque adventures are sunk into this detail which is assembled to illustrate, or rather, to compose the themes. On the other hand, in such a book as *The Magic Mountain*, the characters in action contradict the notions they expound and for which they sometimes seem to stand. (A humanitarian pacifist challenges a Jesuit convert to a duel, and the latter kills himself.) *Henderson* takes neither one of these classic routes; its actions are discrete from the notions which make up no small part of the book, those of Henderson himself, or of the two beautiful obesities, the women of Bittahness, or of the almost-MD, William James-reading totem king, Dahfu. The notions of *Henderson* glow like actions and the actions like ideas. . . .

As for the ideas themselves, they exist in terms of Henderson's need, and have as much relation to belief as Bellow's Africa to Tom Mboyo's. The major one—a version of the notion that we are in no small part the product of the images we absorb—can be found in such different places as the beginning of Plutarch's life of Timoleon, *Felix Krull*, and the somatic psychology of Wilhelm Reich. What counts in the novel is that Henderson's reaction to them is part of the revelation of his personality, and for Bellow, as for Malamud and some of the other fine novelists of the time, personality is back in the middle of the novel, not where their great predecessors—Proust, Joyce, and to somewhat lesser extent, Mann—put it, as part of a thematic scheme which apportions the size and intensity of every element. *Henderson* is a kind of bridge between *Augie*, *Seize the Day*, and these thematic novels; the difficulty is that the bridge must bear the weight of constant invention, invention which can draw hardly at all on the home detail in which the other novels luxuriate. An original like Bellow can't lean on the second-hand views of travellers and movies, and must be on the qui vive for the cliches which always threaten writing about the exotic. Consequently, much of Henderson's detail is landscape, physiognomy and a few clothing props, and the investment there is great. Bellow readers, used to commodity markets, Mexican resorts, Evanston haberdasheries, and the Machiavellians and con-men who in vintage Bellow load the pages, must go into another gear. They will be helped by the fact that *Henderson* is a stylistic masterpiece.—RICHARD STERN, "Henderson's Bellow," *KR*, Autumn 1959, pp. 658–60

The best of our novelists seem to achieve one transcendent performance, followed by self-imitation, or loss of energy, or the substitution of will for creation. Wright Morris is an exception; Saul Bellow is another. Though less prolific than Morris, Bellow has a greater range of concerns and is, on the whole, a more profound if less uncompromisingly difficult a novelist. In an essay in *Esquire*, characteristically entitled "No! in Thunder," Leslie Fiedler, one of Bellow's earliest admirers, admonishes Bellow for resolving *Henderson the Rain King* affirmatively, because (and I am somewhat oversimplifying Fiedler's position) the only honest response to the contemporary world is denial. Though Fiedler's construction is not wholly unreasonable, he argues it too literally (as Stevens tells us, "After the final no there comes a yes") and applies it speciously as if it were an esthetic principle. Moreover, in making his point, Fiedler misreads, or rather narrowly reads, the ending of Bellow's novel. What is being affirmed in Henderson's ecstatic run across the Newfoundland ice? Contemporary civilization? The universe? Hardly. The regeneration of the self, the endurance of the spirit? In part. It is Henderson, however, not Bellow, who is euphoric; it is Henderson who is celebrating his survival, who is affirming the regeneration of his life. It is rather late in the day to be confusing a first-person protagonist with his author, but that, in effect, is what Fiedler has done. In other parts of the novel, Henderson experiences a similar euphoria (he is chronically manic), an hallucinatory sense of well-being, only to discover afterward that he has beguiled himself. The ending is at least in part ironic; otherwise why have Henderson's affirmation of life take place on a lifeless wasteland? One might answer, of course, because it happens in Newfoundland. But isn't that just the point of Bellow's irony? The new-found land is desolate; Henderson's new-found self is also somewhat illusory. Here, as throughout the novel, Henderson is quixotic. Bellow is not, however, wholly undercutting his hero. The scene is not *just* ironic as it is not just affirmative. Henderson's survival of his adventures in that treacherous dream Africa of the spirit, with all his extraordinary powers of strength and energy undiminished by the bruises of time, is in itself remarkable. As always, Henderson reasons with his feelings, not his brain, and it is his energy—the source of his life—not his self-knowledge, that he is celebrating. Henderson's ecstatic self-affirmation, "running—leaping, leaping, pounding, and tingling over the pure white lining of the gray arctic silence," is possible only where there is no real world about to deny it—where there is nothing crucial at stake to expose his well-meaning ineptitude. That Henderson, in spite of all evidence to the contrary, retains his blind illusions is his absurdity as well as his redeeming grace.

Where Bellow's first two novels are somewhat indebted to Dostoevsky and Kafka, *Henderson the Rain King* is a unique and adventurous work. It is also a conspicuously American book in the great tradition of the romance novel from Hawthorne and Melville through Faulkner. After Faulkner, Bellow is our major novelist, and his achievement (with Faulkner's) has provided seed for what appears to be one of the strongest crops of fiction in our history.—JONATHAN BAUMBACH, "The Double Vision: *The Victim* by Saul Bellow," *The Landscape of Nightmare*, 1965, pp. 52–54

Seize the Day completes *Augie March* in much the way *The Victim* completes *Dangling Man*, although in a more expansive, more irresistibly orchestrated opposition than that of the first two novels. But for *Henderson the Rain King* there is neither precedent nor subsequent analogue. Eugene Henderson, as Sarah Blacher Cohen observes in her study, *Saul Bellow's Enigmatic Laughter*, is really the nightmare goy, manic, sensual, a giant of excess, who torments the balance of characters like Asa Leventhal; but here, for once, he occupies center stage, tells his own tale. A millionaire in comic quest of the absolute—"Violent suffering is labor," he says, "and often I was drunk before lunch"—Henderson for a while even pursues the pastoral ideal by becoming a pig farmer: how emblematically *goyische* can one get?

But, perhaps because Bellow does for once give free rein to the absurdist, hallucinatory element of his imagination, *Henderson the Rain King* resembles, more immediately than any of his other novels, those fictions of the fantastic which characterize the sixties. "What made me take this trip to Africa?" asks Henderson at the very beginning of his story. It is a question never really answered in the book—and, indeed, Henderson's periodic rephrasing of that central query is bound to remind us of Tristram Shandy's obsessive attempts, in what must be one of the most absurdist novels ever written, to answer the apparently simple question, "How did I get born?" John Barth, Vladimir Nabokov, Thomas Pynchon, and others were virtually to revolutionize the shape of American fiction by their deliberate invocation of archaic, frequently eighteenth-century narrative techniques. But Bellow anticipates their major work in *Henderson*. Though his narrative is not as ostentatiously "antinovelistic" as that of *The Sot-Weed Factor* or *Pale Fire*, it amounts to a subtle critique, not only of his own previous work, but of the chances for the humanistic tradition of the novel to survive meaningfully under the onslaught of apparent universal chaos. It is, in its way, Bellow's most frankly metaphysical novel. But it is also more.

Bellow would doubtless disapprove of any crude allegorizing of his books, but in the case of *Henderson* such gracelessness is not only unavoidable, but actually enhances the tale's final brilliance. For Eugene Henderson demands to be taken as an example of the American psyche at the end of the Eisenhower decade. Wealthy beyond even the possibility of physical discomfort (unless such discomfort is actively sought out), well educated in the great antecedents of his culture (but not so scholarly that he cannot forget a source, confuse a quotation to his own advantage), he is—more than the nightmare goy of a Leventhal—the impossible dream of an Augie March brought to life. And, in spite of or because of his luxuriant at-homeness with reality, he is terribly discontent, tormented by a yearning that is nearly madness for the springs of life, the heart of desire. He is, in other words, a romantic dilettante—but a dilettante in search of the very urgency, the creative desperation which can terrify or shock him into a true, which is to say, a political and moral culture. The self-image most frequently in Henderson's mind is that of King Nebuchadnezzar in the Book of Daniel, the king who was punished for his presumption against God with the fulfillment of the prophecy "They shall drive thee from among men, and thy dwelling shall be with the beasts of the field."

It is, in fact, among the beasts—not of the field, but of the jungle—that Henderson makes his final attempt at confrontation and self-vindication. The myth of Nebuchadnezzar is never far from the surface of his story. Previous Bellow characters had shudderingly recognized the presence of the beast, the heraldic monstrosity of whatever does not tolerate man, in the curious color of a sunset over Staten Island or, like Augie, actually met an avatar of the beast in the ferocious-looking but cowardly eagle Caligula. But Henderson actually seeks out such a confrontation and in so doing becomes Bellow's closest approximation of what we shall see to be the permanent ethic, existentially foolhardy, of Norman Mailer. And if Henderson falters and moans when the confrontation finally comes, with the lioness Atti, he nevertheless persists in that confrontation to a point which is equally heroic and buffoonish.

It was Thomas Hobbes—and after him, virtually the entire eighteenth century of political theorists—who argued that man in the state of nature, denuded of the reassurances of the social contract, is little better than a ravenous animal. The romantic revolution itself arises out of eighteenth-century reasonings and is brooded over by Rousseau's celebration of the nobility of "savage" man before his corruption and betrayal by social artificiality. But romanticism never really makes peace with the Enlightenment idea of "natural" civilization as the brutally uncivilized war of all against all. The noble savage of Rousseau, Chateaubriand, and to some extent Shelley is not so much a positive myth of pure anarchism (as it became in such later versions as Edgar Rice Burroughs's Tarzan) but is, rather, a negative, pastoral judgment on the present unreformed state of society. The high romantic contemplates the vision of Edenic, natural man the more efficiently to plan a reorganization of present man which can approximate, on the willed, artificial level of culture, the intuited freedom and dignity of that mythic, metahistorical nature.

This is an aspect of so-called romantic primitivism which is often misunderstood. But Eugene Henderson, though he manages only fumblingly and with comic distortion to articulate his insights, lives out a precise and brilliantly planned drama of the romantic political dialectic. At one point, after wandering through Africa with only his guide for company, he comes upon the outskirts of a native village, where a young girl, upon seeing him, bursts into uncontrollable weeping. His disconcerted reaction, in all its engaging clumsiness, is a parable of romantic man's anguished introspection before the sheer, overwhelming fact of politics, the fact of other people:

> Society is what beats me. Alone I can be pretty good, but let me go among people and there's the devil to pay. Confronted with this weeping girl I was by this time ready to start bawling myself, thinking of Lily and the children and my father and the violin and the foundling and all the sorrows of my life. I felt that my nose was swelling, becoming very red.

His trip to Africa itself is impelled, if not ultimately caused, by a particularly shocking version of that opening of the insane at the heart of the everyday which is, by now, a familiar aspect of Bellow's work. One day on his farm Henderson is in the midst of a violent quarrel with Lily, his second wife. He shouts, pounds the table—and kills a woman in his wrath:

> Miss Lenox was the old woman who lived across the road and came in to fix our breakfast. . . . I went into the kitchen and saw this old creature lying dead on the floor. During my rage, her heart had stopped.

Society, indeed, is what beats Henderson—beats him so severely that he must regard his egoistic anguish as a murderous force. There is even something brilliantly Hobbesian (or Lockean, or Humean) in the very articulation of Miss Lenox's demise. He does not say, "Because of my rage, her heart had stopped," but rather, "During my rage." But, causal or not, this awful coincidence is enough to send him on his manic quest. At the beginning of the next chapter, he begins the narrative of his sojourn in Africa.

Like many other questers in contemporary American fiction, Henderson does not even have a clear idea of the object of his quest. But, taking the story in the double context of the myth of Nebuchadnezzar and the heritage of eighteenth-century liberal thought, we can say that his search is actually for a principle of rationality—for an order which will enable him to believe in himself and in the dignity of his immense passions and yearnings, and, at the same time, to collaborate in the realization of the dignity and independence of other people in a cohesive, charitable society. If Augie March is a "saint of charity" striving to realize his own separate existence, Hender-

son is the reverse: a saint (or monster) of egoism trying to realize the claims of other people.

One can say, in fact, that Henderson goes to Africa to learn the wisdom of Tarzan and, instead, discovers the mirror of Hobbes—discovers, that is, his own ineluctable moral involvement with others, even at the heart of supposedly the most "savage" country in the world. The rationality he discovers, then, is a rationality which condemns his own egoism, even though it is his very egoism, his heroic insistence on seeing things through, which leads him to the discovery of that rationality. This is the romantic revolutionary paradox and the shape of Henderson's experience.

Bellow, here as elsewhere, remains a faithful enough student of anthropology to ridicule our comfortable Western belief in the exclusiveness of our claims to rational civilization. The two tribes Henderson encounters exhibit not only the richness and complexity of so-called primitive societies as they actually exist, but also the possibility of producing sensitive human beings fully as compelling as the self-confident and self-accusing Henderson. More important, though, the two tribes offer a schematic diagram of Henderson's own, quintessentially Western and "enlightened" idea of Natural Man. Eugene Henderson's first name means "well-born": as the heir of the romantic ideal of universal aristocracy, this civilized nobleman in doubt of his own nobility seeks, in Africa, a natural, primal kingship which will substantiate the lessons he has learned (and unlearned) about his own separate destiny. We remember the con-man version of that promise in *Seize the Day*, Tamkin's assurance that "Thou art King. Thou art at thy best." Henderson's journey may be thought of, then, as an attempt to rediscover and re-prove the heroic tradition so cheapened in Tamkin's poem. Hence the ironic title of the book, for Henderson does, indeed, become a "Rain King," a ritual monarch of the warlike tribe of the Wariri, but finds that kingship fully as artificial, fully as fraught with the complex, agonizing dubiety of social existence as was the life of New England he had thought to transcend.

The first tribe Henderson visits, the peace-loving, bovine Arnewi, are a parody of the Rousseauist and Chateaubriandesque idea of the "savage": affectionate, sensual in a prepubescent way, the perfect subjects, in their Edenic innocence, for Henderson's Faustian desire to lead. But this very desire thwarts itself and in so doing incidentally destroys the Eden of the Arnewi. Trying to rid their water supply of the ritually untouchable frogs which infest it, Henderson blows up the reservoir. Self-exiled from the now doubly melancholy Arnewi, he enters the country of the more dangerous Wariri, where he meets his double, the splendidly ego-consolidated King Dahfu, master and lover of the lioness Atti, who needs to prove his kingship by capturing the male lion believed to reincarnate the spirit of his father. Dahfu, however, comically disappoints Henderson's quest for a truly natural, pastoral state of human nobility. For Dahfu, as Henderson learns, has given up a promising career as a doctor to return to the kingship of his people and is much given to reading the European psychologists and physiognomists of the nineteenth century, with a view to elaborating his own theory of spiritual and physical correspondences. He is, in other words, a very Cartesian savage indeed, and as he traps Henderson into assuming the role of "Rain King" or water-giver of the tribe, we realize that he is—cleverly and perhaps educatively—using the leverage of Henderson's own naive ideas of the "primitive" against him.

Dahfu is killed in the climactic, liturgical lion hunt which would have solidified his kingship. He is, in fact, the victim of a palace conspiracy no less complicated or sinister than those which have beset Versailles and St. Petersburg. And here again the parody of the novel is unmistakable. An earlier voyager and explorer of the possibilities of civilization, Swift's Gulliver, found himself a cumbersome, self-destructively immense giant among the Lilliputians and a minuscule, eternally victimized atom of personality among the Brobdignagians. Bellow's later but equally gullible mental traveler finds himself, first, a carrier of that very impulse to power which he seeks to escape among the Arnewi, and then an innocent victim of the *Realpolitik* he refuses to recognize—till it is too late—underneath the exotic trappings of Wariri culture. More than any other Bellow hero, Henderson tries to escape the killing dichotomy of romantic individualism and politics by escaping politics altogether—and finds politics (almost in the Platonic sense of our spiritual responsibility for others) everywhere. The last, wonderfully inconclusive scene of the novel gives us Henderson, temporarily grounded en route back to America, leaping exultantly around an icy airfield in Newfoundland (what more ironically named place for this book of frustrated discovery to end?), clutching in his arms a lonely Persian orphan boy, also voyaging to the New World. It is a moment which may be either a breakthrough into an elemental charity or the despairing expression of an impossible ideal of love. But, as either or both, it is one of the most powerful and enigmatically metaphysical scenes in Bellow's fiction.—FRANK D. McCONNELL, "Saul Bellow and the Terms of Our Contract," *Four Postwar American Novelists*, 1977, pp. 30–36

HERZOG

Where shall a contemporary novel begin? Perhaps unavoidably: with the busted hero reeling from a messy divorce and moaning in a malodorous furnished room; picking at his psyche's wounds like a boy at knee scabs; rehearsing the mighty shambles of ambition ("how I rose from humble origins to complete disaster"); cursing the heart-and-ball breakers, both wives and volunteers, who have, he claims, laid him low; snarling contempt at his own self-pity with a Johnsonian epigram, "Grief, Sir, is a species of idleness"; and yet, amidst all this woe, bubbling with intellectual hope, as also with intellectual gas, and consoling himself with the truth that indeed "there were worse cripples around."

This is Moses Herzog, hero-patsy of Saul Bellow's extremely, if also unevenly, brilliant new novel. Herzog is a representative man of the sixties, eaten away by those "personal relations" which form the glory and the foolishness of a postpolitical intelligentsia. He is a good scholar, but cannot complete his books. He rips off imaginary letters to great men, finessing their wisdom and patronizing their mistakes. He is a lady-killer, "aging" at 47 and worried about his potency. He is a loving father twice-divorced, who each time has left behind him a child as token of good will. He is a true-blue Jewish groaner, and perversely, groans against fashionable despair. Inside or outside our skins, we all know Herzog: *Hypocrite lecteur—mon semblable—mein schlemiehl.* Hungering for a life of large significance, eager for "a politics in the Aristotelian sense," he nevertheless keeps melting into the mercies of women, each of whom, in sequence, really understands him.

Herzog is Bellow's sixth novel and in many ways the most remarkable. All of his books—whether melancholy realism, moral fable or picaresque fantasia—represent for him a new departure, a chosen risk in form and perception. Bellow has the most powerful mind among contemporary American novelists, or at least, he is the American novelist who best assimilates his intelligence to creative purpose. This might have been foreseen at the beginning of his career, for he has always been able to

turn out a first-rate piece of discursive prose; what could not have been foreseen was that he would also become a virtuoso of fictional technique and language.

Behind Bellow's writing there is always a serious intention, but as he grows older he becomes increasingly devoted to the idea of the novel as sheer spectacle. His last few books comprise a hectic and at times ghastly bazaar of contemporary experience; they ring with the noise of struggle; characters dash in and out, glistening with bravura; adventures pile up merrily, as if the decline of the West had not been definitely proclaimed; the male characters plunge and rise, mad for transcendence; the women (a little tiresomely) are all very beautiful and mostly very damaging. And the language spins. . . .

Herzog himself is not, in the traditional sense, a novelistic character at all. He is observed neither from a cool distance nor through intimate psychological penetration. We experience him intensely, entering his very bones; yet, trapped as we are in his inner turmoil, we cannot be certain that finally we know him. For Bellow has not provided a critical check: there is no way of learning what any of the other characters, by way of Jamesian correction, might think or feel about Herzog. Bellow offers not a full-scale characterization but a full-length exposure of a state of being. We do not see Herzog acting in the world, we are made captive in the world of Herzog. The final picture is that of Herzog in cross-section, bleeding from the cut.

In one sense, then, there is a complete identification between Bellow and Herzog: the consciousness of the character forms the enclosing medium of the novel. But in a more important respect Bellow manages skillfully to avoid the kind of identification which might lead one to conclude that he "favors" his central character or fails to see through his weaknesses and falsities—a fault that could radically distort the line of vision by which everything is to be considered. That Herzog cannot accurately perceive the other figures in the novel and that we are closely confined to his sense of them, is true and in ways I shall later suggest, a limitation. But not a crippling limitation. For it soon becomes clear that, while totally committed to Herzog's experience, Bellow is not nearly so committed to his estimate of that experience.

For the most part, however, *Herzog* marks a notable advance in technique over Bellow's previous books. He has become a master of something that is rarely discussed in criticism because it is hard to do more than point toward it: the art of timing, which concerns the massing, centering and disposition of the characters and creates a sense of delight in the sheer motion of the narrative.

Bellow has also found a good solution to a technical problem which keeps arising in the contemporary novel. Most readers, I imagine, groan a little when they see a novelist wheeling into position one of those lengthy and leaden flashbacks in which, we know in advance, the trauma will be unveiled that is to explain the troubles of time-present. These flashbacks, by now one of the dreariest conventions of the novel, result in a lumpiness of narrative surface and blockage of narrative flow. But Bellow has managed to work out a form in which the illusion of simultaneity of time—a blend of past with the present-moving-into-future—is nicely maintained. Instead of the full-scale flashback, which often rests on the mistaken premise that a novelist needs to provide a psychiatric or sociological casebook on his characters, Bellow allows the consciousness of his narrator to flit about in time, restlessly, nervously, thereby capturing essential fragments of the past as they break into the awareness of the present. Through these interlockings of time—brief, dramatic and made to appear simultaneous—he creates the impression of a sustained rush of experience.

Bellow began his career as a novelist of somber intellectuality: his impressive early book *The Victim* asks almost to be read as a fable concerning the difficulties of attempting a secure moral judgment in our day. With *Augie March* he made a sharp turn, casting aside the urban contemplativeness and melancholy of his previous work, and deciding to regard American life as wonderfully "open," a great big shapeless orange bursting with the juices of vitality. Though in some ways his most virtuoso performance, *Augie March* suffers from a programatic exuberance: it is fun to watch the turns and tricks the suddenly acrobatic Bellow can execute, yet hard to suppress a touch of anxiety concerning his heart-beat.

With *Augie March* Bellow also began to work out a new fictional style, for which there may be some predecessors—just possibly Daniel Fuchs and Nathanael West—but which in the main is an original achievement. By now it has come to be imitated by many American Jewish novelists as well as by a few gentiles trying wistfully to pass, but none of these manages it nearly so well as Bellow himself.

What Bellow did was to leave behind him the bleak neutrality of naturalistic prose and the quavering sensibility of the Jamesian novel: the first, he seemed to feel, was too lifeless and the second insufficiently masculine. Beginning with *Augie March*—but none of this applies to his masterful novella, *Seize the Day*—Bellow's prose becomes strongly anti-literary, a roughing up of diction and breaking down of syntax in order to avoid familiar patterns and expectations. The prose now consists of a rich, thick impasto of verbal color in which a splatter of sidewalk eloquence is mixed with erudite by-play. Together with this planned coarsening of texture, there is a great emphasis on speed, a violent wrenching and even forcing of images, all the consequence of his wish to break away from the stateliness of the literary sentence. Analytic refinement is sacrificed to sensuous vigor, careful psychological notation to the brawling of energy, syntactical qualification to kinesthetic thrust. (One is reminded a bit of action painting.) Psychology is out, absolutely out: for to psychologize means to reflect, to hesitate, to qualify, to modulate, to analyze. By contrast, the aim of Bellow's neo-baroque style is to communicate sensations of immediacy and intensity, even when dealing with abstract intellectual topics—to communicate, above all, the sense that men are still alive. Toward this end he is prepared to yield niceties of phrasing, surface finish, sometimes even coherence of structure.

It is a style admirably suited to the flaming set-piece, the rapid vignette, the picaresque excursion. But it is not so well suited to a sustained and complex action, or a lengthy flow of experience, or a tragic plot, or what George Moore, in discussing the nature of fiction, called the "rhythmic sequence of events." In *Augie March* there is a run of action but hardly a plot; in *Herzog* a superbly-realized situation but hardly a developing action; and in both of these novels, as well as in *Henderson*, not much of a "rhythmic sequence of events." That is why, I think, none of them has a fully satisfying denouement, an organic fulfillment of the action. In principle these books could continue forever, and that is one reason Bellow finds it hard to end them. He simply stops, much against one's will.

Finally, Bellow's style draws heavily from the Yiddish, not so much in borrowed diction as in underlying intonation and rhythm. Bellow's relation to Yiddish is much more easy and authoritative than that of most other American Jewish writers. The jabbing interplay of ironies, the intimate vulgarities, the

strange blend of sentimental and sardonic which characterizes Yiddish speech are lassoed into Bellow's English: so that what we get is not a sick exploitation of folk memory but a vibrant linguistic and cultural transmutation. (Precisely at the moment when Yiddish is dying off as an independent language, it has experienced an astonishing, and not always happy, migration into American culture. In two or three decades students of American literature may have to study Yiddish for reasons no worse than those for which students of English literature study Anglo-Saxon.)

One of the most pleasing aspects of *Herzog* is that Bellow has brought together his two earlier manners: the melancholy and the bouncy, the "Russian" and the "American," *Seize the Day* and *Augie March*. *Herzog* is almost free of the gratuitous verbalism which marred *Augie March*, yet retains its vividness and richness of texture. The writing is now purer, chastened and a great deal more disciplined.

There is a similar marshalling of Bellow's earlier themes. For some years now he has been obsessed with that fatigue of spirit which hangs so dismally over contemporary life. *Seize the Day* shows a man utterly exhausted, unable so much as to feel his despair until the wrenching final page. *Augie March* shows a man composing a self out of a belief in life's possibilities. Of the two books *Seize the Day* seems to me the more convincing and authentic, perhaps because despair is easier to portray than joy, perhaps because the experience of our time, as well as its literature, predisposes us to associate truth with gloom. In any case, what seems notable about *Herzog* is that nothing is here blinked or evaded, rhetoric does not black out reality (Herzog declares himself "aging, vain, terribly narcissistic, suffering without proper dignity"); yet the will to struggle, the insistence upon human possibility, is maintained, and not as a mere flourish but as the award of agony. Herzog learns that

> . . . To look for fulfillment in another . . . was a feminine game. And the man who shops from woman to woman, though his heart aches with idealism, with the desire for pure love, has entered the female realm.

Not, perhaps, a very remarkable lesson, but worth learning when the cost comes high. More importantly, Herzog says about himself, wryly but truthfully, that he is a man who "thought and cared about belief." To think and care about belief: that is the first step toward salvation.

For all its vividness as performance, *Herzog* is a novel driven by an idea. It is a serious idea, though, in my judgment, neither worked out with sufficient care nor worked into the grain of the book with sufficient depth. Herzog, he tells us, means to write something that will deal "with a new angle on the modern condition, showing how life could be lived by renewing universal connections, overturning the last of the Romantic errors about the uniqueness of the Self, revising the old Western, Faustian ideology. . . ." This time clearly speaking for Bellow, Herzog declares himself opposed to

> The canned sauerkraut of Spengler's "Prussian Socialism," the commonplaces of the Wasteland outlook, the cheap mental stimulants of Alienation, the cant and rant of pipsqueaks about Inauthenticity and Forlornness. I can't accept this foolish dreariness. We are talking about the whole life of mankind. The subject is too great, too deep for such weakness, cowardice. . . .

And in the magazine *Location* Bellow has recently written an attack on "the 'doom of the West' [which] is the Established Church in modern literature." It is a Church, he says, which asserts the individual to be helpless among the impersonal mechanisms and sterilities of modern life; it cultivates self-pity and surrender; and it is wrong.

Bellow has touched on something real. Talk about "the decline of the West" can be elitist rubbish. The posture of alienation, like any other, can collapse into social accommodation. Cries of despair can become mere notes of fashion. Where the motif of alienation in the literature of modernism during the late 19th and early 20th Centuries signified an act of truth, courage and sometimes rebellion too, now it can easily become the occasion for a mixture of private snobbism and public passivity. Yet may not all ideas suffer this sort of outcome in a culture which seems endlessly capable of assimilating and devitalizing everything? Suppose Bellow's assault upon alienation becomes fashionable (it is not hard to imagine the positive thinkers who will hasten to applaud): will it not then suffer a public fate similar to that of the ideas he attacks?

Bellow is being just a little too cavalier in so readily disposing of a central theme of modernist literature. Surely, as it was manifested in the work of writers like Joyce, Flaubert, Eliot and Baudelaire, the sense of alienation expressed a profound and even exhilarating response to the reality of industrial society. (An imagining of despair can be as bracing as a demand for joy can be ruthless.) And does not the sense of alienation, if treated not as a mere literary convenience but as a galling social fact—does this not continue to speak truthfully to significant conditions in our life?

I raise these matters because Bellow, as a serious writer, must want his readers to consider them not merely in but also beyond the setting of his novel. When, however, one does consider them strictly in the context of *Herzog*, certain critical issues present themselves. There is a discrepancy between what the book actually is—brilliant but narrow in situation and scope—and the sweeping intentions that lie behind it; or in other words, between the dramatic texture and the thematic purpose. In the end one feels that *Herzog* is too hermetic a work, the result of a technique which encloses us rigidly in the troubles of a man during his phase of withdrawal from the world. The material is absorbing in its own right; it is handled with great skill; but in relation to the intended theme, it all seems a little puny.

Bellow has conceived of the book as a stroke against the glorification of the sick self, but the novel we have—as picture, image, honest exposure—remains largely caught up with the thrashings of the sick self. One wants from Bellow a novel that will not be confined to a single besieged consciousness but instead will negotiate the kind of leap into the world which he proclaims, to savor the world's freshness and struggle against its recalcitrance, perhaps even to enter "politics in the Aristotelian sense."

Meanwhile, critics and readers, let us be grateful.—IRVING HOWE, "Odysseus, Flat on His Back," *NR*, Sept. 19, 1964, pp. 21–26

Herzog has the senses to respond, the emotions to care, and the mind to probe his surroundings, his people, and himself. He also has the conscience and the vision and the vitality to try to turn everything into a human reality—he is famished for the real, for everything, which is another way of saying that Bellow has been able to make a man and a novel which has room for and can pack in our statistical, fluctuating encyclopedia.

I use that notion with Flaubert and Joyce in mind, for Bellow has done for the 1964 "moving city" (New York-Chicago-Ludeyville) what Flaubert did for mid-nineteenth century Paris and what Joyce did for 1904 Dublin. Flaubert's Frederick Moreau receives the imprint of Paris in his heart,

Bouvard and Pécuchet translate *idées reçues* into action with the enthusiasm of lovable but mindless automatons, Stephen Dedalus receives Dublin's material and moral atmosphere into his nerves and bloodstream before turning them off with his "patented refrigerating device," Bloom registers municipal Dublin in patience, meditation, dream, and regret. Herzog brings this history up to date. Herzog is not *l'homme moyen sensuel*, or the man in the street, or the artist, or the natural active man, though he includes these. He has, it seems to me, absorbed those ancestors (as Bellow has absorbed their authors) and found the best figure for the present American which we have had. Herzog's father was the perfect outsider (a European Jew who made his living in the Montreal slums as a bootlegger distilling fine scotch whisky for the U.S. market), two of whose sons have become wealthy American businessmen and the third (Moses) a professor. Thus Herzog comes from the provinces (Moreau), grows up in and out of a suffocating tradition (Dedalus), and becomes a pedlar of dreams (Bloom). But he does not sell ads; he is a Ph.D., and that is just right for the post-World War II "hero." Bellow does not use a professor because that is all he knows, but because he wants the kind of man who has one foot in the world of speculative intelligence and one in the active life.

. . . The book exists in a moving present during which Herzog tries to come to terms with all of his experience and to shape his future. He confirms that he has a future, even if it is only to endure:

> Survival! he noted. *Till we figure out what's what. Till the chance comes to exert a positive influence.* (Personal responsibility for history, a trait of Western Culture, rooted in the Testaments, Old and New, the idea of the continual improvement of human life on this earth. What else explained Herzog's ridiculous intensity?) *Lord, I ran to fight in Thy holy cause, but kept tripping, never reached the scene of the struggle.*

But he can't get out of touch; when he does he has his one moment of panic and of incoherency. His exuberance ("scope" and "intensity," he calls it) is the true binding force of the novel and of his reality. His sympathy draws him toward everyone, uniting him with the human sufferer, and his intellect keeps him concerned with the secret cause, whatever it may be. The book thus has the tragic dimension which Joyce defined, but it is bathed in what Joyce called the perfect end of art, joy, which is most fully realized in comedy. What Bellow has achieved is the Shakespearean sense of variety which sees all around a situation and a passion, and realizes it in character, scene, and meditation. Herzog's obsessive "relating" makes all of his recollections and gestures dramatic. His exuberance is almost compulsive (a true condition of our time). In his passion to understand people and himself he rehearses them in retrospective narration and drama. These elicit his efforts to apprehend his experience in its connectedness, his stabs at intellectual and ideological resolutions, his letters to Anima Mundi. He makes us feel that we have experienced a contemporary anatomy of love, that (like Hamlet) he includes all of the others whether he is raging or meditating. His ecstatic amours, his imaginative flights, the theories spun from his spidery entrails, his "most" story to his daughter Junie in the police station, the cluttered pastoral at Ludeyville, are part of the same man and the same world. He is not a picaresque saint, for the network is too tightly woven; he exists *in* his world so that both he and it are simultaneously alive, and he is too much a man to be canonized.

What this means is that Bellow has written a novel with a

great form. Driving, prowling, under arrest in plethoric Chicago, trying "out of its elements, by this peculiar art of his own organs," to create his version of it, and so to reshape his past and his present, Herzog feels at home: "He was perhaps as midwestern and unfocused as these same streets. (Not so much determinism, he thought, as a lack of determining elements— the absence of a formative power.)" (cf. Dreiser, whose naturalism, whose Hurstwood and Clyde Griffiths light up in the background). Bellow has mustered such a formative power; he forces, into a reality which can be lived, the American east and west, the city and the frontier. In artistic terms, Bellow has achieved a beautiful balance of personality and impersonality by making the novelist's voice sound through the whole and unify the whole ambience; he is sometimes with his character ("I"), sometimes around him ("He"). His voice moves in and out, creating the comic aether; it reflects the fluctuating border between involvement and detachment, color and line, tragedy and comedy. It has both the narrative drive of outer events, and the meditative convolutions of the city-saturated modern soul. I am reminded that Pound called Henry James a "drinker of men, of things, of passions," whose voice could be overheard "weaving an endless sentence." *Herzog* is also what Pound called *Ulysses*, "a passionate meditation on life."

But Herzog is unmistakably modern: the vital interchange between the artist and his character is more nervous and compelling than that between Joyce and Bloom, and James's world of agreed-upon conventions and manners has properly given way to the fluid informality of a mass society. The artist is not paring his nails, nor can he have Olympian confidence in his milieu. Bellow's voice exploits his donnée fully, but it cannot be a calm voice, nor is Herzog drowned out by the garrulity of Molly Bloom. One might call it a combination of Cervantes' nostalgic voice and the agonized voice of Shakespeare's Hamlet, which is driving willy-nilly toward the future. I feel, as I read the book, that Bellow has opened up a new quixotism, a new hamletism, weighted with and weighted down by the very world which impinges upon us. Herzog is an American Josef K. with great powers of endurance, whose religious sense is freed from dogma, from the Freudian darkness, and from the terror of totalitarian inevitability. Bellow has included both the Idol of Refined Art and the Idol of Raw Life in a greater amalgam; he feels life, if not steadily (which surely it is not), at least whole. His voice is a great civilizing voice which picks up the challenge of D. H. Lawrence, for Bellow is willing to express "man alive" in his drive toward a transvaluation of values, a change of heart, a reinterpretation of the Holy Ghost (though none of these terms can define Bellow's voice or his tone precisely).

I have implied that Bellow's novel is something of a synthesis, one of those encyclopedic works which makes one feel that it has been built upon the work of the writer's predecessors, upon his own development as a writer and a man, and upon the work of his contemporaries. For instance, Bellow has reinvented the epistolary form to convey the sense of eighteenth-century urbanity and the sense of the present city-dweller who tries to get into events, and into *l'histoire morale contemporaine*, by writing letters to the editor. His use of the past, which today comes to us as fragments of racial consciousness, as theories, and as a fluid tradition, extends the Joycean use of literary and religious myth; it is more relevant to us, and it reflects the absence of any standard which would make the modern vision a satiric one (Pound's insistence that Joyce used Homer primarily as scaffolding, and that *Ulysses* strikes most forcibly our sense of the relation between life and art, as we live them, than upon art as an end—a view which is reasserted by

Robert M. Adams in his *Surface and Symbol*—adumbrates the perspective in which Herzog should be seen. Allegorizing is a clear and present danger; even Malamud's *The Natural* has been reduced to allegory). Scenes recur: Herzog sitting on the toilet reading Pope measures exactly Bellow's sense of the difference between Herzog's reality and Bloom's: Flaubert's *encyclopédie d'idées reçues mise en farce*, and Bloom's archetypal meditations, have become creative ideas which measure and affect action. Frank Alpine braced in the dumbwaiter shaft to spy on Helen Bober while she takes a shower has been enriched by Herzog's balancing to watch Gersbach give Junie a bath. Herzog has rediscovered nature by extending and enriching S. Levin's adaptation from Thoreau. Again, his notes for a proposed "Insect Iliad" for Junie, inspired by tent caterpillars and containing ants, water-skaters, cicadas, a wasp, and a stag-beetle, which he gives up, nods at but eschews the metaphysical overtones of Thoreau watching the war of the ants and of Lt. Frederick Henry playing God over the ants on the burning log. From his own work, Bellow has combined the man dangling in himself, the victim imposed upon by his own conjured municipal nightmare, the urge to seize the day, Augie March on the move. He has pulled the lines formed by the sequence of his previous novels into a single grand circle and filled it; the synthesis reflects not only his growth, but a new grasp on reality. Instead of constructing an abstract metaphysical and symbolic system, as Yeats did, to enable him "to hold in a single thought reality and justice," he has taken "the tradition" as a series of achieved realities. His intensity has "used" it, transformed, to make intelligible a present world.

Herzog is, among other things, a history and synthesis of "The novel." It gathers in not only novels of the past and current novels, but part-novels and novels-manqué. It sweeps up the sociological scalpel-and-bludgeon novel, the bitch-goddess novel, the fairy-and-dyke novel, the sex-machine novel, the howl novel, the addict novel. One goes on and on as new connections light up on Bellow's switchboard. To change media, which suggests not only Bellow's method but also the extent to which *Herzog* is alive to visions of the contemporary reality, we are reminded of Fellini's camera and his impervious surfaces, of Antonioni's sense of the haunt of places, of the tone qualities which give *Dr. Strangelove* its civilizing atmosphere. As a final illustration I am reminded of Ermanno Olmi's sense of the world as an organization, especially of that ominous breathing on the soundtrack of *Il Posto*, which seems to be the respiration and heartbeat of the actors, and of one's companions (?) in the audience of the dark theater, but at the end is shockingly revealed to be the regular beat of the mimeograph machine. Bellow is aware of the realities of the past and of the present, and he conveys them.

What I am being led to say is that Bellow's style is able to present this comprehensive reality on a scale ranging from the directness of presentation and statement, to the obliqueness of the most subtle and revealing poetry. . . .

At any rate, I think that *Herzog* is a great American novel, whose vision will provide perpetual delight and whose techniques will repay other writers for the study. As I said, I think that it makes a near-epical synthesis. Hemingway said "Every novel which is truly written contributes to the total knowledge which is there at the disposal of the next writer who comes"; Bellow's does that because he has been "able to understand and assimilate what is available as his birthright and what he must, in turn, take his departure from." *Herzog* has "the dignity of movement of an iceberg" whose bottom is in the tradition. We might ask, though, whether any book can really be a classic when it is centered too much in character, so that "action in character" replaces "character in action." Is there too little narrative? Is *Herzog* a *Sartor Resartus*? Again, Hemingway posed the problem aptly: "Prose is architecture, not interior decoration, and the Baroque is over. For a writer to put his own intellectual musings, which he might sell for a low price as essays, into the mouth of artificially constructed characters which are more remunerative when issued as people in a novel is good economics, perhaps, but does not make literature." Yet Bellow has made the ideas fiction, because he has made what Hemingway called "People": "People in a novel, not skillfully constructed *characters*, must be projected from the writer's experience, from his knowledge, from his head, from his heart and from all there is of him . . . . a good writer should know as near everything as possible." Bellow has tried to know all that, and has taken the great risk of trying to give it fictional form.

What kind of novel is it? We can find there the elements of the historical, ideological, metaphysical, romantic, anti-romantic, erotic, and picaresque novels; of the novel of manners, the anti-novel, the romance, etc. But above all, it is a great comic novel. As an anthology of ideas and speculations it even has the quality of being an education. Even if you know all the antagonists, colleagues, and ideas that set Herzog off (I didn't), his angle gives you a fresh view of things you know. Further, Bellow relates ideas immediately to life (that is another sense in which *Herzog* is *really* an academic novel—or an intellectual novel—though we never get onto a campus). No novel I have read makes me keep saying "that is just what life is like." Yet, it is also magnificent art; Bellow continually gives one confidence that he is creating a great form, one which includes multiplicity with the shape and rhythm of beauty. It is astonishingly modulated in that space between life and art which it tries to express, so that I feel I am experiencing the novel with all of my faculties. I have not read a contemporary novel which comes as close to turning Hemingway's ingredients—the tradition, interior decoration, and experience—into a fictional form which can contain them and integrate them. But critics should keep in mind that *Herzog* is a great open form which is new (My interpretation is only provisional!—F.R.); that it calls for perspectives which can elucidate a form based upon our special "field" reality: the one which lies between—both separating and relating them, for it is their "stuff"—life and art, a man and the *res publica*, the infinite pulverizations of which we are made. Above all, there is Joyce's mild complaint about the critics of *Ulysses*, reported by Pound: "If only someone had said among all those critics, that the book is really damn *funny*!"—FORREST READ, "*Herzog*: A Review," *Epoch*, Fall 1964

Bellow's most important cultural essays—"The Thinking Man's Wasteland" (1965), his talk to the PEN Conference in 1966 (as it later appeared in *The New York Times Book Review*), and, in 1971, "Culture Now: Some Animadversions, Some Laughs"—address themselves directly, and with often startling crudity of mind, to the cultural issues which came to dominate his fiction after *Seize the Day*. In particular, *Herzog* in 1964 and *Mr. Sammler's Planet* in 1968 are efforts to test out, to substantiate, to vitalize, and ultimately to propagate a kind of cultural conservatism which ⟨Bellow⟩ shares with the two aggrieved heroes of these novels, and to imagine that they are victims of the cultural debasements, as Bellow sees it, of the sixties.

The fact that some of his best work—*The Victim, Dangling Man*, and *Seize the Day*—are generally regarded as distinguished contributions to the literature of the Waste Land tradition would not in itself invalidate his disparagements of

that tradition or of the academic promotion of it. Other writers, including Mailer, have managed to live within some such complex of attitudes to their own and to our profit. The difference in Mailer's case is that he has a confidently zestful appetite for, and an assurance in his capacities to cope with, the cultural obscenities which might otherwise force him into those feelings of self-righteous victimization so crippling to Bellow's work. Without knowing it, Bellow is far more alienated than Mailer. It shows in his writing; or rather in the evidence that the act of writing, and the promise of cultural mastery which might be engendered by it, is not in his case sufficient to save him from the feelings of victimization visited on his heroes. And yet he likes continually to imagine that it is. Thus when he speaks out in the PEN address against "the disaffected, subversive, radical clique," he doesn't seem to recognize there, anymore than in his novels, that he is exposing his own "disaffection," poorly disguised by bad jokes:

> On the one hand these teachers, editors, or cultural bureaucrats have absorbed the dislike of modern classic writers for modern civilization. They are repelled by the effrontery of power, and the degradation of the urban crowd. They have made the Waste Land outlook their own. On the other hand they are very well off. They have money, position, privileges, power. They send their children to private schools. They can afford elegant dental care, jet holidays in Europe. They have stocks, bonds, houses, even yachts. With all this, owing to their education, they enjoy a particular and intimate sympathy with the heroic artistic life. Their tastes and judgments were formed by Rimbaud and D. H. Lawrence. Could anything be neater?

There is a random vulgarity in the superficial notations of this passage which is but one evidence of Bellow's effort to blind himself to the fact that he is no less "repelled" by such things as "the degradation of the urban crowd." This has been, after all, a theme in all his work; it is responsible for some of its most powerful descriptive efforts; and one is forced into the embarrassment of supposing that the essential difference between Bellow and the people he is here criticizing is that he, but not they, deserves "elegant dental care," etc., etc., etc. Bellow's problem in the sixties is that the imagined forces of dissolution are not, in this passage or elsewhere in his writing during the period, substantially enough evoked, are indeed too trivially evoked, to teach him, in Empson's phrase, "a style from a despair."

Despite some surface differences, the style of *Herzog* and of *Mr. Sammler's Planet* projects the same authorial presence: of a man nursing imagined betrayals, a man who chooses to retaliate by historical pontifications which, given his own sense of the wastes of history, are intellectually barren, and who nonetheless tries to validate what he says by a species of comic evasion. The comedy, that is, is a way of convincing us that because he himself presumably knows he's being rhetorically banal, the banality must therefore illustrate not the deprivations of his imagination but the bankruptcy of contemporary culture. No one who does not hopelessly confuse culture with literature and both of these with the limits set by the accomplishments of Saul Bellow is apt to be convinced by this procedure.

The test is all in the "doing," as James said long ago, and it is peculiar that those who share Bellow's cultural conservatism have failed to ask themselves whether or not his performance as a writer, as distinct from his opinions as a would-be thinker, contribute to the vitalization either of literary culture or the language. On any close inspection, Bellow's rhetorical ambitions are seen to be disjointed from those aspects of his later fiction which are most compelling—the brilliance of detailed, especially of grotesque, portraiture, and a genius for the rendering of Yiddish-American speech. In *Herzog* in particular, his writing is most alive when he writes as a kind of local colorist. And yet, in the language of analysis and Big Thinking with which he endows his hero, and it is, again, of a piece with the canting style of Bellow's essays, he wants to be taken as a novelist of civilization, especially the civilization of cultural degeneracy as it affects the urban-centered Jew in the American sixties.

That he tries to localize these immense concerns within essentially Jewish material is not the problem. . . . Bellow feels threatened in his role as public defender of two distinct yet historically harmonious cultural inheritances: of the Jew as poor immigrant, the outsider whose native resources save him from the bitterness of alienation, and of the Jew as successful *arriviste* in American society, enriched and burdened all at once by traditions of high culture. Now a kind of insider looking out, he yearns for those cultural supports which, since World War II, have been commercialized by the society at large if not submerged entirely under the tidal waves of mass produced taste. . . .

This is a difficult position for a writer to be in; it is also an extraordinarily profitable one. Bellow has so far shown himself unequal to them. Because if contemporary culture is so corrupt and corrupting as he makes it out to be, then the very rhetoric he so glibly uses in his essays and in the essayistic meditations of Herzog and Sammler is more discredited than he dares admit. In the writings of this century where there is a disposition about the state of the culture similar to Bellow's, there is also a kind of stylistic and formal complication generally missing from his work. This complication is not "academic" or faddish or willful. Instead it reflects a confirmed sense of the enormous effort required both to include, with any kind of human generosity, and then to correct, by the powers of style, the preponderant influences of pop culture and of a ruined education system. Some of the consequences to Bellow's work of the essential timidity of his effort—like all timidity it tends to be both self-pitying and vindictive—have been noticed by Morris Dickstein and Richard Locke and by a few of the reviewers of *Mr. Sammler's Planet*. But *Herzog*, while being universally praised, was nonetheless equally flawed, an indication of what was later to become more evidently the matter. . . .

Given Bellow's ambitions so much to exceed the confined circumstances of ⟨Herzog's⟩ life and to make it a "representative" modern one, his method seems, on the very face of it, disastrously claustrophobic. Normally we'd wonder how the author is to operate freely within such a book, much less manage to puff it up. Of course he makes himself felt in the ordering of things, so that the fragments of the story as they flash through Herzog's mind are comically, sometimes critically juxtaposed with his intellectual theorizings. And the very first line, "If I am out of my mind, it's all right with me, thought Moses Herzog," is a joke about the hero's "rightness" and about his "thinking" that maybe we're expected to carry like a comic tuning fork through the rest of the book. The evidence increases as one reads, however, that Bellow is in the novel whenever he wants to be simply by becoming Herzog, the confusions at many points between the narrative "I" and "he" being a blunt and even attractive admission of this. But the identification of hero and author is apparent in other, ultimately more insidious ways. Thus Herzog is allowed to characterize himself in a manner usually reserved to the

objectivity of the author: the letters he writes, and never mails, to the living who betrayed his love, to the dead thinkers who betray his thinking, to the living great who betray him politically are, he says, "ridiculous." (He does not himself betray the book by also admitting that the letters, for all the parroted praise the reviews have given them, are frequently uninventive and tiresome.) He claims also not to like his own personality.

Bellow's novelist skill is here seen most adroitly at the service of his larger intellectual and, too obviously, of his more personal motives. Allowing no version of the alleged betrayals other than Herzog's, Bellow still must protect his hero's claims to guiltlessness by a process all the more ultimately effective for being paradoxical: he lets Herzog's suffering issue forth less as accusations against others than as self-contempt for his having been cozened by them. There could be no more effective way to disarm the reader's scepticism about the confessions of such a hero within so protective a narrative form. Bellow can thus operate snugly (and smugly) within the enclosure of his hero's recollections, assured, at least to his own satisfaction, that he has anticipated and therefore forestalled antagonistic intrusions from outside. He really does want Herzog's mind to be the whole world, and the hero's ironies at his own expense are only his cleverest ruse in the arrangement. No wonder, then, that Herzog's talk about himself and about ideas is, in passages that carry great weight, indistinguishable from the generalized Bellovian rhetoric by which here, as in Bellow's other novels, "victims" become "modern man," their situation the World's: "He saw his perplexed, furious eyes and he gave an audible cry. *My God! Who is this creature? It considers itself human. But what is it? Not human in itself. But it has the longing to be human.*"

The recurrence of such passages in Bellow's work is only one indication of how straight we are to take them, of how much he tends to summarize himself in the pseudo-philosophical or sociological or historical expansions of the otherwise parochial situations of his heroes. Perhaps the most lamentable result of Bellow's complicity at such points is that he loses his customary ear for banality of expression or for the fatuity of the sentiments. I don't know another writer equally talented who surrenders so willingly to what are by now platitudes about his own creations. Seldom in Faulkner, even less in Joyce, and far less frequently in Lawrence than people who can't listen to his prose like to believe, do we find what the literary ragpickers call key passages. Where such passages obtrude in writing that asks us to be discriminating about style, as they do in Fitzgerald and Hemingway as well as in Bellow, there is always a lack of assurance in what Bellow has himself called "the sole source of order in art": the "power of imagination." And he distinguished this from "the order that ideas have." "Critics need to be reminded of this," he remarks in "Distractions of a Fiction Writer."

His alertness in the matter is understandable. Between his evident intellectual ambitions and the fictional materials he thinks congenial to them there is in *Herzog*, as in *Henderson the Rain King* and in *The Adventures of Augie March*, a gap across which these novels never successfully move. Sections of the present book read like a lesser *Middlemarch*, the longest of the "ridiculous" letters offering pretty much what Bellow-Herzog want to say about "modern" life. Herzog's interest in romanticism is itself an expression of a familiar concern of Bellow: the effort to preserve individuality during a period of economic and scientific acceleration with which it is supposedly impossible for the human consciousness to keep pace. Henry Adams, among others, gave us the vocabulary; George Eliot predicted the condition; Bellow the novelist is victimized by it. What I call the gap in his novels between their intellectual and historical pretensions, on one side, and the stuff of life as he renders it, on the other, prevents me from believing that he is himself convinced by his snappy contempt for "the commonplaces of the Waste Land outlook, the cheap mental stimulants of Alienation." Quoted from a letter of Herzog's these are obviously identical with Bellow's own attitudes. My objection isn't merely that Bellow would replace the "commonplaces" of alienation with even more· obvious commonplaces about "the longing to be human." I mean that his works, the truest and surest direction of their energy, suggest to me that imaginatively Bellow does not himself find a source of order in these commonplaces. . . .

To a considerable degree the novel does work as a rather conventional drama of alienation, though this is precisely what Bellow doesn't want it to be. It is about the failure of all available terms for interpretation and summary, about the intellectual junk heap of language by which Herzog-Bellow propose dignities to the hero's life and then as quickly watch these proposals dissolve into cliché. . . . His comedy always has in it the penultimate question before the final one, faced in *Seize the Day*, of life or death—the question of what can be taken seriously and how seriously it can possibly be taken. The result, however, is a kind of stalemate achieved simply by not looking beyond the play of humor into its constituents, at the person from whom it issues, at the psychological implications both of anyone's asking such questions and of the *way* in which he asks them.—RICHARD POIRIER, "Herzog, or, Bellow in Trouble," (1965, rev. 1975), *Saul Bellow: A Collection of Critical Essays*, ed. Earl Rovit, 1975, pp. 81–88

. . . ⟨o⟩f course, *Herzog* is a comic novel. I should suppose that any modern effort to justify God's ways to man must be inherently comic. Justice, after all, is man's creation and the destruction of mankind is God's, and any attempt to harmonize the two must lead to that glottal stop that is usually death, but can sometimes be laughter. In Bellow's novel, the man of ideas, Moses E. Herzog, acts, suffers, fails and partially succeeds as a human agent without displaying any evidence that there is a causal connection between his thinking and his acting. The world of his ideas is a separate one. He entertains himself with it. He uses it to celebrate his soul, to upbraid himself, to pity his ignominies. But it is always a world separate and discrete from him, and this is a fact that he and the reader learn to regard as comic because any other reaction would be intolerable. Sprawled out in his hammock in the Berkshires like a caricature of a Transcendentalist, Herzog takes stock of the broken shards and disappointed hopes of his life. He has been twice divorced, he has failed in his friendships, fallen far short of his scholarly ambitions. He has found no sureties in sex, love, religion, philosophy, history, or human relationships. His mind—rich, exotic and delightfully erratic—racapitulates, reorganizes, resuffers the burden of his memories. Writing fragmented mental letters to the quick and the dead, re-enacting the salient scenes of his past, haranguing Nietzsche, Heidegger, General Eisenhower, Herzog finally subsides into mental silence. His mind offers no more ideas. No more words. He tells himself that he has accepted the dull brutal fact of his existence, but neither he nor we are able to know whether it is affirmation or sheer exhaustion that puts an end to his cerebration. And this, I take it, is comedy: a 341-page remembrance of things past in which the memories fail to cohere or explain—in which the movement of the main character is an illusory introspective spiral that comes out nowhere.

But *Herzog* is comic in other ways as well. "If I am out of my mind, it's all right with me, thought Moses Herzog." These are the opening words of the novel—a novel that takes place, after all, *in the mind* of Moses Herzog. Sometimes Herzog *is* out of his mind, sometimes not. But he is always aware of himself on two levels of awareness. That is, he is aware of himself as a man in the Berkshires engaged in a self-indulgent scrutiny of those past selves that his memory serves up to him. And, second, those recollected selves are themselves self-conscious; they too were self-aware in their moments of vital being. The possibilities for the ironic and futile play of identities within such a narrative focus are well-nigh inexhaustible. For, whether Herzog is in or out of his mind, the reader is usually kept within it, and this allows Bellow to manipulate the distances between his reader and his main character on the principle of a very complicated, double-motioned elevator mechanism. Sometimes we are allowed to look directly at Herzog, but more frequently the barrier of his personality is dissolved and we have to become Herzog looking at himself (or looking at himself looking at himself). And thus, although there are usually two layers of irony separating Bellow from Herzog when the focuses are working well, the reader is not always so shielded. And this, it seems to me, is what makes the reading of the novel so intimately painful and intensely comic at times. The same device of multiple perspective that separates Bellow from Herzog forces the reader into an overintimate identification. To be sure, the distances are not always successfully controlled. But when they are, *Herzog* becomes an almost terrifyingly impersonal book and the reader is caught in the most personal of engagements with it. The frustrated congestion of ideas becomes the personal property and obligation of the reader alone, and Bellow disappears from his own artifice. And this, too, is comedy—surreptitious, sadistic, even pedagogical in its demands.

But the modern comedy of identity has other uses as well, and Bellow's composition is an enormously artful one. We have already remarked the comic lack of movement in the main character's long progression from nowhere to nowhere. There is, however, something else that needs to be said. The device of multiple perspective tends to cancel out the actual lack of movement, since awareness of self-awareness creates a dynamic psychic motion in itself, and it is this rhythm that dominates the structure of the novel. When all is working well, the multiple perspectives engender an incredible circumambience of ironic directions; when the distances collapse, Bellow runs the danger of maudlin self-pity and sentimentality. In general, however, he is much more successful than unsuccessful in sustaining his balances in *Herzog*; and in this he is greatly aided by his happy conception of protagonist, that hammock-sprawling oxymoron, Moses E. Herzog. For he is, ultimately, a comic compendium of paradoxes: rational student of irrationality, skeptical believer, calculating, middle-aged innocent, self-effacing egotist, erotic intellectual, Montreal-born, Russian-Jewish American. He learns nothing, does nothing, slays no dragons, burns no bridges; and yet he is still in a supremely comic way, not only the hero of his novel, but an heroic character—a perfectly possible and viable figure of modern heroism.

"The hero is he who is immovably centered," wrote Ralph Waldo Emerson, a poet-thinker whom both Herzog and Bellow seem to respect. In spite of (or because of) the fact that he is constantly shifting his senses of self-awareness, Moses Herzog is an immovably centered man. In a way that Emerson may just have been guileful enough to have been suggesting, the centrality of self has changed from a reliance on some irreducible atomic entity like soul or spirit or immutable consciousness to a creative network of protean self-relationships. In this sense Herzog is a dazzling acrobat of consciousness, a pre-stidigitator of his constantly burgeoning selves, vulnerable or discoverable in no single one of them, immovably centered in their dynamic totality. The Wandering Jew—uprooted, displaced, always as detached and alien as consciousness itself—receives a comic apotheosis. It is he, the homeless one, who is able to establish a fruitful liaison with the world. In Herzogian terms, the Mosaic law has been amended to read, "Be it ever so humiliating, there's no place like home." And, perversely, on this level, the discrete world of ideas *does* become causally connected with man's actions. *To think*—even though it is possible only to think about oneself—becomes synonymous with *to act*. And the greatest actor, the largest hero of our time, would be the man who thinks most about his many selves in the most fluidly creative way. Thus, when Moses Herzog asks himself at the end of the novel what it is that he wants, his answer is both comic and momentously brave. "Not a solitary thing. I am pretty well satisfied to be, to be just as it is willed, and for as long as I may remain in occupancy." And at this point the reader should be aware that Herzog's lease of occupancy will extend to the temporal and psychic limits of his capacity for self-consciousness.

It would be possible to denigrate Bellow's remarkable accomplishment in this novel by overstressing the importance of some of its undeniable weaknesses. To do so would be petty, but not to point to them at all would be a critical disservice. Some of these weaknesses are probably inevitable in light of the immense strain that the restricted mode of composition must have imposed. I have already suggested that the ironic perspectives do not always function in balance. The passages directly concerned with the plot-triggering adulterous betrayal—the recollections of Madeleine and Valentine—smack too rawly of emotion untempered by art. There is also a tendency toward a wearying sameness in the over-all texture of the novel. Episodes, ruminations and characterizations merge together in an even consistency which resists discrimination and makes for monotony. The reader misses the urgency of anticipation that the conventional suspense-rhythm of narration usually supplies. Given the comic needs of Bellow's plan and his decision to remain within the associational field of one man's mind, this was perhaps a necessary sacrifice, but it is still a weakness. The prose style, on the other hand, is almost completely admirable—sensuous, lucid, satirical, grotesque, erudite and racy of the urban soil. It is only when Bellow attempts a purely lyrical flight that I find him deficient. And except for the Sono episodes (which are deliciously funny), the erotic scenes (especially with Ramona) seem to me forced and unconvincing. The reminiscent encounters between Herzog and his familial circle, by contrast, possess the authenticity of art at its very highest. Bellow's muse is essentially comic and unfashionably rational and *Herzog* is a resounding success, a joy to read and a painful delight to reflect upon.

But I must briefly pursue one final—possibly irrelevant—reflection. I have tried to show that this is a highly comic novel of ideas, intransigently social, and desperately honest in trying to face up to the soul-crushing intellectual challenges of our times. I think that Bellow is the most important novelist we have and I think that *Herzog* is his richest and fullest achievement. And yet when one invokes the still palpable ghosts of Faulkner and Hemingway, not to mention the nineteenth-century American giants, we are immediately aware of his lesser stature in comparison to them. They too were passionately concerned with the ambivalences of self, identity, and the implacable hostility of the universe. They too were in their differing ways comic. But their stances in relation to their art

and the world show some cardinal differences from Bellow's. They were each of them, in some sense, "provincials"; he is not. They were each of them capable of rejecting or ignoring the world in order to construct their own worlds; he cannot do this. Their majesty consists in their ability to have built counterworlds in despite of the actual worlds around them. And the actual world has come to embrace their mythic structures as actualities and it has moved on its axis to come into accord with the rhythms of their imaginations. Bellow may conceivably surrender too much of his private myth to the exigencies of the world. His intellectual and emotional cosmopolitanism, his commitment to a social good, may cause him to modify the structuring shapes of his own dreams to accord with the world-as-it-is. And if this speculation should possess some truth, it is the world's loss as well as Bellow's, for the world will have no choice except to absorb his work, which changes it not. His accomplishment is a major one. Yet might it not be even greater if he could compel the world to move in the measures of his own vision?—EARL ROVIT, "Bellow in Occupancy," *AS*, Spring 1965

In the original *Dangling Man* . . . Joseph suffers from 'a feeling of strangeness, of not quite belonging to the world, of lying under a cloud and looking up at it.' He feels himself cut adrift from the past, living in a spectral present tense in which Tuesday is the same as Saturday because both are featureless. So we register the first difference in *Herzog*, that a verifiable past is Moses's ball and chain. But at least he has a past. Like Wilhelm in *Seize the Day*, he is 'a visionary sort of animal,' but he commits himself to his own experience. Wilhelm 'had cast off his father's name,' but Moses keeps the name and the image. His father and mother are dead, but they range through his story, carrying the brute weight of their existence. Moses never repudiates them. Like *The Adventures of Augie March*, this is a Jewish story, a family story. Indeed, it is closer in spirit to *Augie March* than to any of the other books, before or after. Bellow has given up the allegorial neatness of *The Victim* in preference for the richer idiom of fact and event. Equally, he has evaded the symbolic itch of *Henderson the Rain-King*: we are not required to take a course in 'the Africa within.' Herzog's experience is given to us in the same terms in which it is given to him; specific acts, casualties, and sufferings. We are not allowed to substitute a formula for the things given. Nor is he. The plot is a commitment to live through the terms of its reference: Herzog keeps going, he strikes through every proffered mask, and because God is finally Good he is eventually allowed to reach a quiet place, the rediscovered Berkshires of his spirit. Bellow has often found trouble in making an appropriate Act Five, but the end of *Herzog* is entirely convincing, Moses lying down, containing himself, feeling the strength of his quietness for the first time. Tommy Wilhelm believed that the 'easy, tranquil things of life' might still be recovered, that even yet life might be 'reduced to simplicity again.' The simplicity is realized in *Herzog*, but it is not a reduction; life is enhanced in those quiet Berkshires.

So the book is animated by Bellow's constant concern; Fact and Value, the relation between the terms; the redemption of the event, the thing done, because it is done in a certain spirit. Herzog knows that he must do a great deal of mind-work if he is to preserve his vigilance and be ready to deal with his experience as it comes to him and he goes to meet it. 'Awareness was his work; extended consciousness was his line, his business.' But he knows that this can't be the answer: we have been conscious for centuries, and, look, we have not come through. The quality of our consciousness is wrong, to begin with. We need the consciousness of appreciation, not the consciousness of possession; the open hand, not the grip of claw. There is a long passage, late in the book, where Herzog ponders these matters. 'Not thinking is not necessarily fatal,' he reflects. 'Did I really believe that I would die when thinking stopped?' This is the first sign of health, the old body standing up to defend itself against the destructive consciousness. 'Go through what is comprehensible and you conclude that only the incomprehensible gives any light.' Further: 'And consciousness when it doesn't clearly understand what to live for, what to die for, can only abuse and ridicule itself.' The knowledge of these fundamental things is not obtained in the head. It is a sixth sense, closely in touch with the other five; or perhaps it is an ur-sense prior to any other. And if it has a special intimacy with one of the five, it is with the sense of touch: we come to know what to live for by touch, in the silence of wonder. Herzog has spent much of his life abusing and ridiculing himself, writing manic letters to men good and bad, living and dead, for fear his mind will stop and, stopping, bring him crashing to the ground. The turning-point comes when he gives up the abuse and the struggle to convert experience into mind; and simply waits. The human imagination, he says at one point, 'starts by accusing God of murder.' It cultivates a grievance. No more of that: let the dead grievances bury their dead. Herzog has lived most of his life converting experience into words, as if words alone were certain good: 'I go after reality with languge.' But he comes to discover that words are destructive, subversive, if sought in the wrong spirit. 'Perhaps I'd like to change it all into language, to force Madeleine and Gersbach to have a *conscience*. There's a word for you.'

So this is a book of genial words reaching into silence. At the end, Herzog finds that he has said everything he needs to say, at least for the present; there will be no more talk, no messages, no unmailed letters to Nietzsche. Now, for a saving while, he will live modestly among tangible things, trusting to the emergence of light without force or pressure. So his last fictive moments are spent among wine bottles, hats, roses, a Recamier couch, Mrs. Tuttle's broom. Forty pages earlier he wrote: 'The dream of man's heart, however much we may distrust and resent it, is that life may complete itself in significant pattern. Some incomprehensible way. Before death. Not irrationally but incomprehensibly fulfilled.' This is his 'rage for order,' but he discovers that he stands a better chance of finding order when the rage is stilled, and he tries to trust the world. This does not mean that he calls off the hunt or sacks his imagination; it means that he prescribes new conditions, sets a new quiet key.

. . . ⟨T⟩he book makes a strange and beautiful figure. The first half is all steam, mania, *angst*; energy lurching, an expense of spirit in a waste of hate and shame. Some of this is brilliantly done; especially when Herzog is brought home by the Himmelsteins and a browbeating session leaves the victim distracted. (Himmelstein is first cousin to old Einhorn in *Augie March*.) Bellow's feeling for this scene is impeccable; where the browbeater is thick, ignorant, and right while the victim is all sensibility and wrong. He is not quite as good when the scene is academic and clever; the visit of Shapiro to the Herzogs is a bright parade of highbrow lore, Moses the odd-man out, but it is unconvincing, a set piece too set in its ways.

Bellow is a man's novelist. His female characters tend to be done with far smaller resource, as in *Herzog* Ramona, given in great detail, is a piece of cardboard while Father Herzog, a brief sketch, is authentically 'there.' Bellow's prose can deal with women only when they are magisterial figures in the landscape of the past; and then they are nearly men. If a woman is thirty-five and about to become the hero's mistress, the chances are that she will reveal herself the product of scissors-and-paste. The reason is, perhaps, that in Bellow's fiction these women are there merely to give the hero something more to suffer; they merely add to the noise and fret of his life. And, strictly speaking, anyone could do this for him. In the novels since *Augie March* Bellow's imagination is devoted to this problem, among many; how to lure the facts into peace without denying their recalcitrance, how to reach solid ground, how to live. Women have very little to do with this part of the story: the hero's problem is now personal and representative.

I mention this limitation to suggest that Bellow's resources as a novelist, more impressive than ever, are not unlimited. But he is one of the important novelists because of the depth at which his options are made and his sense of the pressure they have to meet. This is what the novelist's integrity means, the measure of his scruple. If we think of *Herzog* as a severe examination of the modern orthodoxies in literature, the Wasteland myth and the arrogance of consciousness, we know at the same time that Bellow is not a smiling salesman selling toothpaste. His 'positives' go no further than the propriety of silence, at this time; the illness is not miraculously cured. I would not ask him to go beyond this point. But *Herzog* is important because it reveals our whining orthodoxies for the shoddy things they are; and because it urges us to try again, and try harder. The book tells us that we are infatuated with our own illness, since we deem it the proof of our integrity. But health is better than illness, and *Herzog* points to at least one possibility.

This is what the style of the book implies: it is a prose of human size, much freer than that of *Dangling Man* or *The Victim*. The early books are rigid in their parables, they live by constriction, and they exhibit a correspondingly rigid style. The style is the parable. But according as Bellow has liberated himself, more and more deeply, from the governing orthodoxies of modern literature, he has moved into richer modes of style. There is clearly a direct relation between the possibilities he sees in life and those he has discovered in his language. The eloquence of the writing wells up from the life it exhibits, the characters, events, situations: it is not an artificially induced eloquence, a merely personal invention. In the scene in the police-station, when Madeleine comes to bring Junie home after Herzog's arrest, the graph of Herzog's feeling as he watches her is drawn with remarkable exactitude: technically, it is largely a matter of syntax, beginning with the short sentences in which Herzog registers the precision of Madeleine's movements, her command of herself, the way she knows where to drop the milk-carton even though she has just entered the room. And as the thoughts incite one another, the syntax reflects the nervous gesture, the twitches of feeling. But the feelings were there before the prose; the prose 'imitates' them. Hence the change of tempo at the end, the nerves calmed; and the prose is like Mrs. Tuttle's broom, the exact and faithful answer to its occasion.—DENIS DONOGHUE, *The Ordinary Universe*, 1968, pp. 199–203

Herzog may appear to himself as a meandering hero, adrift, rudderless on the stream of his own meditations, but this is not the true angle of the narration, for enclosing these meditations is a clear narrative-dramatic framework, a plot situation of almost classical design. On that level, the story is not told by Herzog but by the author, who focuses sharply on Herzog's inner landscape, but in equal measure upon the outer events with which he is at all times engaged. Here the hero is clearly controlled and beheld as moving forward on his journey by definite stages, each complementing or contrasting the others.

Thus the initial confrontation with Madeleine in Chicago is balanced with the second confrontation after the automobile accident. There Herzog gains a kind of moral victory to make good his earlier defeat. The closing scenes in Ludeyville balance earlier scenes in the same locality, in particular the encounter described earlier on with his fellow-historian, Shapiro, whose notions had been distorted by the pessimistic philosophies of Proudhon and Spengler. Herzog had reviewed Shapiro's book during his European tour (another kind of letter-writing with no clearly defined addressee), but the true answer to it is only achieved after his return to Ludeyville when he finally affirms his own faith in human survival "after the fall."

There is a genuine progress in the narrative. Herzog is not the same man at the end of the book that he was at the beginning. In this sense, the structure is more like that of *Portrait of the Artist as a Young Man* than it is like *Ulysses*. There is a double movement: there is the idle flux of associations conveyed through the endless letter-writing and through the reflective monologues, but there is also the inexorable movement of the plot forward from one epiphany to the next, and in the total design there is the movement from servitude to freedom, from sickness to health, and from darkness to a glimmering light. *Herzog* may be said to imply the later novelist's answer to and rejection of the interior mode, whether of dialogue or monologue, as an all-valid story-telling method, and the affirmation of the objective-realistic moral history as its true and indispensable accompaniment. For Bellow, the interior mode is the expressive mode of mental sickness and disorder, or at best a therapeutic technique exactly analogous to spilling the beans on the psychiatrist's couch, a technique of free association to be abandoned when the crisis is passed and we return to the world of moral responsibilities.

It is notable that, as the novel proceeds, it becomes less reflexive and more dramatic. In this respect also the confrontation in the police station marks a decisive turning-point. Herzog's mental action now becomes more or less synchronized with the clock-time of the story. The final abandonment of the uncontrolled interior mode of story-telling coincides with the emergence of Herzog from his neurosis, so that, when we reach the last page, his meditation beats in time with the actual experience in hand. Finally, he realizes that the letter-writing will now cease: "Yes, that was what was coming in fact. The knowledge that he was done with these letters." For to catch the rhythm of purposeful existence in which men are tried and their spirits tempered to fine issues, we need a more solid and compact fusion of inner and outer experience: we need to turn away from the illusion of dialogue to true dialogue.

But we should be careful to add that there is no fundamental breakthrough, and Bellow is too honest a writer to pretend that there is. He does not achieve that real dialogue which a passionate commitment to history and its promises would imply. Herzog does not *go* anywhere: there is no happy marriage. He is not going to settle down with Ramona at the end, but rather is he going to have to endure in his relationship with her the same unresolved tensions which have hitherto mastered his spirit. Now he will endure them better; that is all. The book does not ultimately offer salvation, and in that sense it fails as a twentieth-century epistle from the Hebrews. And one should add that if it fails to indicate a solution for modern ills, by the same token it fails to find a solution for the problem of the modern novel.

Salvation—an inseparable feature of the early eighteenth- and nineteenth-century novel—was, naturally, not just a question of a happy ending. Prosperity and happiness are offered along with moral justification, a victory of the spirit. Robinson Crusoe gains his soul without losing the world. So do the characters of Jane Austen: they attain twenty thousand pounds a year and moral fulfilment simultaneously. The irony of *Great Expectations* consists in the fact that Pip gains something better than material treasure; he gains spiritual maturity, but a measure of worldly happiness is not lacking—at least in the revised ending. This may not be Christian exactly; it is nevertheless Biblical. Job finally receives the long-distance call he has been waiting for, and with it he gets back his wealth and honors. The Hebraic schema is fully present in such a novel as *Joseph Andrews*, which borrows the outline of the Joseph story complete with reunion between long-lost father and wandering son at the end.

Salvation in this sense goes out in the novels of Conrad, Hardy, and Balzac, and it does not come back. The novel has had to get along without it and its loss has left each novelist with the problem of discovering some other pattern of coherence. This has not been easy. The problem is as much aesthetic as moral. Among the novelists of the "stream of consciousness" a kind of circular movement is achieved (*The Waves*, *Ulysses*); what is gained is the satisfaction of the completed cycle, as in some nature-myth. In *To the Lighthouse* we are directed to a symbol which seems to represent completion and stability; there is a journey, but again the form of the symbol is fundamentally cyclical after the Greek fashion. Instead of a pilgrim's progress ending in salvation, we have the brief voyage to the still center of the turning world. Now, the intimations of fulfilment are scarcely more tangible at the end of *Herzog* than they are at the end of *Ulysses* or *To the Lighthouse*; nevertheless we are directed forward towards the world we live in, to our time and our history. The dénouement involves a simultaneous ordering of worldly affairs and of spiritual needs. There is no actual salvation, but the gesture of the novelist is in that direction.

Bellow is too deeply disillusioned to accept the Hebraic schema in its totality. He is too conscious of the radical collapse of Western civilization both around him and within him. At the same time, he is too realistic in the Hebraic fashion to accept any of the substitutes for the Hebraic schema which modern novelists have found in their search for alternative patterns of coherence. The biological solution offered by Lawrence—the mystic marriage between man and nature—will not do, nor will it do to escape as Joyce does in *Ulysses* from history into Homeric legend. Of course, Bellow loses much by this honesty. He misses the epic and the heroic, for, after all, the mock-epic is a variety of the epic, and through its means Bloom had been linked imaginatively with Elijah, with Ulysses, with the archetypal Wanderer who returns to his wife's bed and his ancestral roof-tree. The Homeric schema gives *Ulysses* poetic richness as well as epic grandeur.

Against this it must be insisted that Bellow's Herzog moves about in a world strangely emptied of mythology. The great American dream of the River, of the Frontier, of the Titans who built the railroads and the skyscrapers, has ceased to yield its magic, and nothing else has come to take its place. As a result, the world of Bellow is a prose-world. Moses Herzog affirms the possibility of survival after holocaust, but in the absence of any positive reviving dream of the future to support it, such an affirmation remains a private, empty gesture. The intensity that he discovers in himself at the end does not bring his fundamental isolation to an end, for there is neither the myth of Eldorado nor the Jewish vision of salvation to give substance and form to these intimations of hope.

Herzog is an alienated American. But let it be noted that

he is no less an alienated Jew: he feels no fundamental bond with the Jewish past and the Jewish future. We do not connect him either ironically or seriously with the great Moseses whose glory Leopold Bloom had recited to Stephen Dedalus: "Three seekers of pure truth, Moses of Egypt, Moses Maimonides, author of the *More Nebukim* (Guide of the Perplexed) and Moses Mendelssohn of such eminence that from Moses (of Egypt) to Moses (Mendelssohn) there arose none like Moses (Maimonides)" (*Ulysses*, p. 671). Jerusalem is just one of the places to be visited on his European tour. It does not speak to him as it had spoken to George Eliot and to Theodor Herzl of the fulfilment of historic promises. Such disenchantment is decidedly no part of the Hebraic tradition which confidently projects the symbols of the past upon the future. Bellow's concern is more exclusively with the present, its riches as well as its unbelievable curruption; and perhaps it is unfair to set up imaginary standards for a work which has so obviously succeeded in making its own impressive statement. Yet Bellow is partly to blame for this, for the novel he has written has the disturbing tendency to point beyond itself and to demand to be set against a more universal backdrop and a more lengthening perspective than the novelist has in fact provided.—HAROLD FISCH, "The Hero as Jew: Reflections on *Herzog*," *Judaism*, Winter 1968, pp. 51–54

Elsewhere Bellow has written: "We make what we can of our condition with the means available. We must accept the mixture as we find it—the impurity of it, the tragedy of it, the hope of it." It is just this emphasis on *mixture* that distinguishes Herzog and other Jewish schlemiels from the meek Christians like Melville's Billy Budd or Faulkner's fabled corporal. Schlemiels are not creatures of the Manichean imagination: even Charlie Chaplin's *The Great Dictator* divides the alternatives of civilization too sharply between innocence and guilt to be an authentic part of the genre. Though the moral dilemma must always be presented as a confrontation between opposites, its tone is determined by the implied purity of each faction. Herzog and his comic forebears are themselves a little tainted; never having known the primal innocence of Eden, they do not pull up their skirts in outrage at the appearance of villainy, and having no ascetic inclinations, their own chances of "staying clean" are slight. The otherworldly purity of the saints, products of the Christian literary imagination, is best suggested by their silence or stuttering: holiness beyond speech. The stained humanity of the schlemiel pours out in obsessive verbosity. Yet to say that the polarization between good and evil is less extreme is not to imply that the moral concern is any the less acute. In an article written concurrently with the last parts of *Herzog*, Bellow puts the proposition as follows:

. . . either we want life to continue or we do not. If we don't want to continue, why write books? The wish for death is powerful and silent. It respects actions; it has no need of words.

But if we answer yes, we do want it to continue, we are liable to be asked how. In what form shall life be justified? That is the essence of the moral question. We call a writer moral to the degree that his imagination indicates to us how we may answer naturally, without strained arguments, with a spontaneous, mysterious proof that has no need to argue with despair.

Herzog is such an attempt at proof.

What sets Herzog apart . . . is his intelligence, and more particularly, his self-consciousness. In *Menahem Mendl*, Sholom Aleichem juxtaposes the life-styles of two characters for ironic effect, but here the protagonist juggles his own distinct levels of existence. Not only does Herzog elucidate his opinions and clarify his feelings, he is able, as an intellectual and a professor of history, to relate those opinions and feelings to the broader flow of Western thought. Thus we find Herzog raising many of his own questions on the nature of the fool. . . .

Is the fool escaping his adult responsibilities, or is he alone fulfilling them? If the only alternatives are the Ayn Rand objectivists and Herzogian innocents, may the progress of civilization not indeed depend upon him?

Not the author or reader, but the character himself raises these questions. Maynard Mack has written that comedy depends on our remaining outside, as spectators, in a position from which we may notice the discrepancies between the facades of personalities as they present themselves, and these personalities as they actually are. "The point of view that ours must be continuous with in comedy is not the character's but the author's." Though true for classical comedy, this description does not fit *Herzog*. Bellow has deliberately—how deliberately only a careful study of syntax will reveal—written the entire book from the character's own point of view, allowing him to observe and note all the discrepancies, and thereby making him the conductor of humor. Because comedy does depend on discrepancies between surface and substance, Herzog is allowed at least two modes of observation: the letters, a direct means of externalizing his concerns; and indirect narration, also reflecting the protagonist's point of view, but permitting a wider inclusion of conversation and event. The rapid transition from one to the other sometimes accounts for the comic tone, as when Moses, fleeing from the sex-priestess, Ramona, writes political kudos to Stevenson and Nehru while his unsteady thoughts hurtle him back and forth to and from his personal involvements. More often, within the indirect narration itself, Herzog reveals the self he admires side by side with the self he scorns:

The house in Ludeyville was bought when Madeleine became pregnant. It seemed the ideal place to work out the problems Herzog had become involved with in *The Phenomenology of Mind*—the importance of the "law of the heart" in Western traditions, the origins of moral sentimentalism and related matters, on which he had distinctly different ideas. He was going—he smiled secretly now, admitting it—to wrap the subject up, to pull the carpet from under all other scholars, show them what was what, stun them, expose their triviality once and for all. It was not simple vanity, but a sense of responsibility that was the underlying motive. That he would say for himself. He was a *bien pensant* type. He took seriously Heinrich Heine's belief that the words of Rousseau had turned into the bloody machine of Robespierre, that Kant and Fichte were deadlier than armies. He had a small foundation grant, and his twenty-thousand-dollar legacy from Father Herzog went into the country place.

The irony of "It seemed" and "He was going" in the second and third sentences derives from the superimposition of Herzog's present knowledge of himself over past hopes. He mocks both his unfulfilled expectations and the very substance of his ideas. The recognition that he is a "bien pensant type" is like his perception, cited earlier, that he is like the old song "There's flies on me, there's flies on you, but there ain't no flies on Jesus." He is ironic about his would-be goodness, suspicious of its motives, and scornful of its inutility. Looking back on the ambitious scholar he was, he smiles at his boy-scout meritoriousness. And the final juxtaposition of his sources of income is the unkindest cut of all, the small foundation grant with the big legacy, the earnings of the great intellectual overshadowed by the rewards of the dutiful boy. Here the character, aware and amused by the dismal gap between "is" and "would have been," makes himself his own comic butt.

Herzog's internalization of irony sets him apart from Bloom, from whose saga his name alone is lifted: In *Ulysses*, Joyce has placed in apposition "the persuasive surfaces of personalities as they see themselves, and these characters as they are," even when he seems to be offering a stream of consciousness. The very form of the mock epic imposes the shadow of his heroic predecessor over a dwarfed Bloom. Joyce called his work *Ulysses*, but Herzog casts his own little light. In *Herzog*, the protagonist is endowed with the complexity of mind and ironic vision that in *Ulysses* remains the prerogative of the author. The result is not an ironic exposure of life, but rather an ironic life, exposed.

Herzog is finally the character who lives according to a twofold perception of himself in relation to the world, both giant and dwarf, alien and center of the universe, failure and success, cuckold and great lover, intellectual and schlemiel. The single reality of the naturalists is for him insufficient. To Sandor Himmelstein, the deformed lawyer, he protests:

> "And you think a fact is what's nasty."
> "Facts *are* nasty."
> "You think they're true because they're nasty."

To James Hoffa, who shares this "angry single-mindedness," he considers saying: "What makes you think realism must be brutal?" Herzog fights the Wasteland rhetoricians, "The vision of mankind as a lot of cannibals, running in packs, gibbering, bewailing its own murders, pressing out the living world as dead excrement." He points out how corrupting is the effect of this mode of perception on both the individual and on society. Even as he is insisting on the need for the pumping heart, for "moral realities," he jibes at himself:

> Do not deceive yourself, dear Moses Elkanah, with childish jingles and Mother Goose. Hearts quaking with cheap and feeble charity or oozing potato love have not written history.

Time and again he makes fun of his search for love and belief in love as a female pursuit, which in the terms of this novel is no flattering tribute. Yet, finally, when all is said and written, Herzog addresses himself seriously, if not earnestly, to his and, as he sees it, the world's situation: "We must get it out of our heads that this is a doomed time, that we are waiting for the end, and the rest of it, mere junk from fashionable magazines." The intellectual rejection of pessimism is ultimately coupled with a psychological readiness to accept, even bless, the future. The ironic life accepts itself. "Anyway, can I pretend that I have much choice?"

Because Herzog's irony is internalized, there is less than the usual ironic distance between author and character. This opens the book to charges of sentimentality, since modern literature and literary criticism are very much concerned with distances and masks, and we are frankly unaccustomed to committing our disbelief to the hands of a reliable narrator. In this work, the author's position or point of view is not noticeably different from the protagonist's. Herzog steers his pumping heart between the Scylla of Madeleine ("Feel? Don't give me that line of platitudes about feelings") and the Charybdis of Valentine, the false commercialized whirlpool of a heart. He controls the novel even when he is not yet in control of himself. Bellow has written a humanist novel, presenting one individual's life—a life by all standards a near-failure—which in its intelligence and energy commands our attention and affection. *Herzog*, a study of irony as a modern form of moral vision, is the more *engagé* because of Saul Bellow's minimal irony about his subject.—RUTH R. WISSE, "The Schlemiel as Liberal Humanist," *The Schlemiel as a Modern Hero*, 1971, pp. 101–107

With the fading of the Romantic dream of love, there fades now also the Romantic hero. Our representative novel is likely to be the *Herzog* of Saul Bellow, who is as central a writer as we have. Moses Herzog is a professional Romanticist, and very much a Romantic, but in the last ditch: narcissistic, masochistic, anachronistic, depressive, self-defeated, yet altogether charming, altogether a man of feeling, a sublime egotist. He is Man on the Dump, but speaks for all of us; an absurd case, but undeniably our version of the hero.

In one of his reveries, or imaginary letter-writings, Herzog, as a scholar of the subject, broods negatively upon Romanticism:

> . . . as the form taken by plebeian envy and ambition in modern Europe. Emergent plebeian classes fought for food, power, sexual privileges, of course. But they fought also to inherit the aristocratic dignity of the old regimes, which in the modern age might have claimed the right to speak of decline. In the sphere of culture the newly risen educated classes caused confusion between aesthetic and moral judgments. . . .

It is difficult to dispute this, and simple enough to see it as coming again today. In defense of Romanticism, Herzog answers his own dark analysis by defending the idea of Man against contemporary historicisms that urge a narrow repressiveness in place of the dream of a more perfect human being. Yet the sensibility of our moment is already post-Herzog, and Bellow speaks for a generation on the other side of the gap, for a late Romantic humanism that does not permeate what is emerging.

A country with the certain prospect of continuous external warfare, and imminent internal rebellion, is unlikely to reverse the direction in which its sensibility is moving. Cultural prophecy is a mug's game, but it is always fun and, like the imagination, it wishes to be indulged. We are a very long way from any kind of a realistic or classical reaction against the scene that escalates daily around us. Probably we will move directly from the High Romantic into the Decadent this time round, if indeed we have not largely started there. Gore Vidal's parody novel, *Myra Breckinridge*, may be as far as neopornography can go, or it may spark a kind of *art nouveau* of our time, in which a terrible elegance is born. What Bellow says of Herzog's students will be true of all of us: "It became apparent . . . that they would never learn much about the Roots of Romanticism but that they would see and hear odd things."—HAROLD BLOOM, "Epilogue: A New Romanticism? Another Decadence?" *The Ringers in the Tower*, 1971, p. 346

MOSBY'S MEMOIRS AND OTHER STORIES

Perhaps the most complete and compact short story that Saul Bellow has ever written, a story significant in many ways, is the early "Looking for Mr. Green" (1951). Without striving to be a novel and without violating the unwritten canons of short fiction as his other short stories do, it crystallizes some of the major themes of Bellow's fiction. It also marks the exact moment of transition in Bellow's development as an artist, for it issues from a creative mood poised precariously between the belief that man is somehow a victim of the human condition, and the powerful awareness that man can somehow transcend this condition. "Looking for Mr. Green" is a Bildungsroman that makes use of the basic pattern that underlies Bellow's fiction, that of the quest. It is a minor classic of our time, a story that has the resonance that Joyce's "The Dead" has, releasing ripples upon ripples of concentric meanings that vanish into the mystery of an evocative silence.

. . . One should read "Looking for Mr. Green" as a modern dramatization of Ecclesiastes, which is a congeries of meditations and questions about the impossibility of ever solving the riddle of human life. The writer seeks to make some sense of the bewildering complexity and the vanity of human existence even though he knows that all speculation is futile. He acknowledges the existence of the divine but cannot understand its inscrutable ways. But he does not despair or indulge in a *Miserere*. Ecclesiastes suggests that one must take the world as one finds it, acknowledge the days and ways of darkness, accept life's conditions and direct one's life accordingly. A certain degree of happiness can indeed be attained. *Carpe diem*, one should seize the day: "Go thy way, eat thy bread with joy, and drink thy wine with a merry heart; for God now accepteth thy works. . . . Whatsoever thy hand findeth to do, do it with thy might; for there is no work, nor device, nor knowledge, nor wisdom, in the grave whither thou goest" (Ecclesiastes 9:7–10). The protection afforded by wisdom and wealth is a help against the terrible onslaughts man has to face. Ecclesiastes also suggests that cooperation with one's fellow-men in a piece of work will result in greater rewards, for unity is strength.

In the *Show* interview, Bellow tells of his reading of the Hebrew Scriptures: "My childhood was in ancient times which was true of all orthodox Jews. Every child was immersed in the Old Testament as soon as he could understand anything, so that you began life by knowing Genesis in Hebrew by heart at the age of four. You never got to distinguish between that and the outer world."

The Old Testament flavor of "Looking for Mr. Green" is unmistakable, and one can sense the pressure of Ecclesiastes on Bellow's creative consciousness in the composition of the story. The word *sun* is repeated throughout; "under the sun" is a recurring phrase in Ecclesiastes for the world and the human condition. Grebe's brushing at the sunbeam that covers his head during the interview with Raynor can now be seen as more than a touch of realistic detail. Winston Field talks about money as the sun of human kind, while Raynor stresses the importance of a comfortable salary and the futility of knowing about the human condition: both, like Ecclesiastes, offer practical suggestions, not counsels of despair. Grebe himself is a younger, a modern *Koheleth* (Hebrew for the Greek Ecclesiastes, "the preacher") who hunts for Mr. Green and for the meaning of human existence. His long day in the black ghetto telescopes the cumulative experiences of a lifetime so that Grebe is led to the same conclusions that Ecclesiastes reached after having lived a full life under the sun. No intellectual solutions are offered; no final answers are provided; human existence continues to remain a mystery. As his day draws to a close, Grebe becomes aware of some forms of sustenance that help man in his sojourn on this earth.

"Looking for Mr. Green" needs to be recognized as one of the great short stories of our time, great in its evocation of mystery and in the tremendous reach of its meaning.— EUSEBIO L. RODRIGUES, "Koheleth In Chicago: The Quest for the Real in 'Looking for Mr. Green,'" *SSF*, Summer 1974, pp. 387–93

MR. SAMMLER'S PLANET

Barthelme's parody of intellectual languages points to a connection between the crisis of language and the crisis of society. It suggests that the general dissemination of the concepts of advanced intellectual culture has deluded people into believing that all the mysteries of human nature can be explained by the simple act of affixing verbal labels on them. The sudden availability of the diagnostic vocabularies of sociology, psychoanalysis, and literary criticism seems to have implanted in mass society a vast delusion, simultaneously fatuous and pathetic, of self-understanding. Herzog calls this "the delusion of total *explanations*." In *Herzog* and *Mr. Sammler's Planet*, terms like "alienation" are part of the arsenal of cant wielded by false "explainers" and "reality-instructors," cultural opportunists who capitalize on unearned theories of despair and revolution—in what they are quick to recognize as a seller's market for such "cultural canned goods." As one explainer, Lionel Feffer, candidly tells Sammler:

> "I'm convinced that knowing the names of things braces people up. I've gone to shrinkers for years, and have they cured me of anything? They have not. They have put labels on my troubles, though, which sound like knowledge. It's a great comfort, and worth the money. You say 'I'm manic.' Or you say, 'I'm a reactive-depressive.' You say about a social problem, 'It's colonialism.' Then the dullest brain has internal fireworks, and the sparks drive you out of your skull. It's divine. You think you're a new man. Well, the way to wealth and power is to latch onto this. When you set up a new enterprise, you redescribe the phenomena and create a feeling that we're getting somewhere. If people want things named or renamed, you can make dough by becoming a taxonomist."

As both Sammler and Herzog recognize, such "explanations" purvey knowingness, not knowledge.

The central theme of *Mr. Sammler's Planet* is the degeneration of the ideology of modernism, and this is presented as an aspect of the more general collapse of Western liberal individualism and its ideal of personal autonomy. Sammler's past makes him a nexus of the historical forces, both hopeful and destructive, whose collision has created the present-day world. A former democratic-socialist and heir of the progressive Enlightenment, Sammler is also a victim of the Holocaust and in a wartime act of revenge he has participated in its murderous brutality. His past places him at the intersection of Western liberal individualism and the forces which have destroyed it— or, rather, perverted it. For ironically, as it now comes home to Sammler, in his meditations, liberal individualism has survived the Holocaust, but in forms which parody its original inspiration. Originating as part of a noble dream of uniting science with morality and liberating the mass of humanity from the nightmare of historical circumstance, liberal individualism has detached itself from its motivating ideas of good and evil and divided into opposing but collaborating factions: "an oligarchy of technicians, engineers, the men who ran the grand machines," tolerates a culture of hedonistic self-indulgence and "symbolic wholeness." This historical vision gives Sammler's criticism an authority and clarity lacking in Herzog's comparatively sentimental whining. It is no doubt easier for us to like Herzog, who is lovably mixed up and therefore not superior to us. A character like Sammler, who clearly *is* superior, in wisdom if not in ability to carry it into action, requires more risks on the part of his creator. He does not win our affection by the standard pose of being in the dark about everything.

The characters surrounding Sammler are possessed by a neurotic "fever of originality," at once arrogant and desperate, which issues in exhibitionistic playacting, and the quest to be "interesting": "theater of the soul" performed "with hair, with clothes, with drugs and cosmetics, with genitalia, with round trips through evil, monstrosity, and orgy. . . ." Life has begun to imitate bad experimental art:

> Life looting Art of its wealth, destroying Art as well by its desire to become the thing itself. Pressing itself into pictures. Reality forcing itself into all these shapes. Just look (Sammler looked) at this imitative anarchy of the streets—these Chinese revolutionary tunics, these babes in unisex toyland, these surrealist warchiefs, Western stagecoach drivers. . . .

. . . ⟨I⟩t is important to distinguish between Bellow's and Roth's reliance on conventions of traditional realism and Barthelme's overturning of these conventions. And it is necessary to acknowledge the differing views of language and its debasement which underlie these opposed methods. Barthelme's irony toward official, institutional, professional, and artistic jargon does not stop at these targets but spreads and envelops *all* language, including Barthelme's own authorial prose. His stories call attention to their own inability to overcome their imprisonment in the artifices of language and the solipsism of consciousness, though it should not be forgotten that this very strategy itself makes a statement. Bellow, for his part, is no less aware than Barthelme of the immense deterioration of the traditional languages of cultural authority: "It was not the behavior that was gone," Sammler thinks at one point. "What was gone was the old words . . . the terms beaten into flat nonsense." But Bellow wishes to affirm the substance for which the old words had stood: truth, honor, compassion, virtuous impulse: "About essentials, almost nothing could be said. Still, signs could be made, should be made, must be made."

Barthelme's protagonist at the end of "A Shower of Gold" reaffirms a Shakespearean ideal of human nobility, but the language in which he does so is self-parodic:

> "My mother was a royal virgin," Peterson said, "and my father a shower of gold. My childhood was pastoral and energetic and rich in experiences which developed my character. As a young man I was noble in reason, infinite in faculty, in form express and admirable, and in apprehension. . . ." Peterson went on and on and although he was, in a sense, lying, in a sense he was not.

Compare this with the conclusion to *Mr. Sammler's Planet*, where the affirmation is not qualified by irony. Of his friend Gruner, whose death he has just witnessed, Sammler thinks:

> "He was aware that he must meet, and he did meet—through all the confusion and degraded clowning of this life through which we are speeding—he did meet the terms of his contract. The terms which, in his inmost heart, each man knows. As I know mine. As all know. For that is the truth of it—that we all know, God, that we know, that we know, we know, we know."

Sammler himself, as he realizes, has failed to live up to his standards due to his limited compassion for the frailty that surrounds him. But the authority of the standards themselves is not compromised by this fact. Bellow acknowledges Barthelme's skepticism about man's ability to know truth, but he attacks the perverse tendency of such skepticism to become an excuse for self-pity and self-indulgent despair. And for Bellow, affirmation survives "the confusion and degraded clowning" of

contemporary life which is included so richly in the texture of his novel, whereas for Barthelme it does not.

These recent works by Bellow and Barthelme, then, in many ways exemplifying the antithetical poles in the current literary debate between tradition and innovation, look at the plight of "advanced" consciousness from distinctly different perspectives. And yet their views of the plight itself, one might say their definitions of it, have much in common. Both writers perceive that it is not only the traditional moral and artistic languages that have forfeited their power, but the counterlanguages of modernist adversary culture as well. Both expose the hollowness into which the cult of creative autonomy has degenerated.—GERALD GRAFF, "Babbitt at the Abyss," *Literature against Itself*, 1979, pp. 229–38

HUMBOLDT'S GIFT

The concepts of goofiness, of silliness, of "shenanigans" keep recurring. Human activity, often frenzied and feverish in Bellow's fiction, is more than ever felt as a distraction to thought, an obstacle to some truth: "One thought, How sad, about all this human nonsense which keeps us from the large truth." Though ⟨*Humboldt's Gift*⟩ begins as if it will be a wonderfully animated meditation upon the sociological question of the intellectual's place in America, the questions that really fascinate Charlie Citrine are more transcendental and mystical—questions of death, of immortality, of "light-in-the-being": "I mean a kind of light-in-the-being, a thing difficult to be precise about, especially in an account like this, where so many cantankerous erroneous silly and delusive objects actions and phenomena are in the foreground." Small wonder, then, that the events of the novel pull away from the issues, and effusion replaces conversation (with everybody, including the supposedly unintellectual Renata, sounding like Charlie), and the many brilliant episodes become too many—a static of human busyness that prevents Charlie from tuning in and that leads the reader to tune out. Rinaldo Cantabile, for instance, is at first a compelling apparition, a figure of frantic menace and insecurity, a "nervous invention" that simultaneously illustrates Charlie Citrine's "weakness for the sensational" and demonstrates Saul Bellow's marvellous susceptibility to the eccentric particulars of American life in motion. When, toward the end of the book, amid a welter of exploded schemes and fresh entanglements, Cantabile reappears, he seems a mere annoyance, a bothersome shrill squawking over the telephone, a demented *deus* lowered from a needless *machina*, a thoroughly excessive device introduced to get the hero to go to a movie that is sweeping the world and would have come to his attention anyway; Cantabile is dismissed, by a suddenly unfascinated Citrine, like a messenger in Shakespeare. Cantabile has become a bore because the possibility of development is permitted no character but the omnipresent, amorphous, relentlessly self-regarding narrator.

Piecemeal faults might be found with *Humboldt's Gift*. When, a little more than halfway through, the novel leaves Chicago, it abandons a regional portrait of considerable accumulating richness. The Madrid section is relatively tenuous; the "shenanigans" are especially abstract and hurried. The novel has more characters than it can use; some, like Cantabile's girlfriend Polly and the crooked financier Stronson, exist as if only to occasion their descriptions, and none, save Humboldt and his wife, Kathleen, occupy more than one corner of the territory that the story's time span stakes out. Bellow's style, breezy and tough and not always grammatical, feels fallen away from a former angelic height. . . .

But Bellow's great gifts deserve great indulgence, and the only real trouble with *Humboldt's Gift* is that the problems that engage the author do not engage the gears of his story. Death, power, America—Charlie Citrine has much to say about these cherished topics, but his remarks are incongruously juxtaposed and interwoven with the "shenanigans," the "capers," the "daily monkeyshines" that compose his mystic's impression of natural human events. Tellingly, Charlie confesses, "I could read a little in the great mysterious book of urban America. I was too fastidious and skittish to study it closely—I had used the conditions of life to test my powers of immunity; the sovereign consciousness trained itself to avoid the phenomena and to be immune to their effects." Perception, for the supremely perceptive Citrine, has become a tic, a trick to exploit. Himself immune, he scoops up impressions, pours out descriptions. . . . The veil of *maya* isn't what it used to be for Bellow, though he is not yet mystic enough—unlike I.B. Singer—to look at daily monkeyshines for glimmers of supernatural light. Nor, unlike the former celebrant of Chicago, Theodore Dreiser, can he accept the natural world as the only world, portentous by its own final weight. So he gives us a world as craziness, as "goofy . . . a solid mass of improbabilities," a world kept spinning by whimsical impulses and savage egos, an earth that is "literally a mirror of thoughts" to the central, immune viewer, who devotes his attention more and more to the world beyond death, to the anthroposophy of Rudolf Steiner, to the consoling curious possibilities that "our bones are crystallized out of the cosmos itself" and the universe is "the living garment of God" and "we occupy a point within a great hierarchy that goes far far beyond ourselves." These supernatural preoccupations of Bellow's are not in themselves unworthy—it takes a courageous humanism to perceive that life is infinitely cramped by the loss of an expectation of an afterlife—but they do make the veil of his fictional phenomena thin. We know, reading, that there will be many surprises but no revelations, that no turn of event will dreadfully deepen the theme, that the essentially cerebral and comic spirit of the creator will contrive to preserve his hero from essential harm. And so it is: Charlie Citrine loses Renata but takes comfort in one of those dazed, ignominious retreats so dear to Bellow heroes; he loses his money but more falls to him; he leaves his city and his children but in the spirit of a holiday, the sleep of his soul, as he thinks of it, is disturbed but not shattered. He rolls over, amid the rumpled sheets and untied threads of the plot.

And yet. Of course there are passages that no one but Bellow could have perpetrated—scenes that are, in the flow of their wit and felt detail, simply delicious. The giddying ascent with Cantabile up through the unfinished skyscraper ("the hollow interior filled with thousands of electric points resembling champagne bubbles") to a windy height from which the indignant hood sails airplanes folded from fifty-dollar bills . . . the unfailingly tender sketches of old Chicago neighborhoods—with such evocations, enlivened by love and alarm, Bellow fragmentarily makes good the book's implicit promise to illuminate the "overwhelming phenomenon" of America, in its "abominable American innocence." The very thinness of the veil, for Bellow, enables him to exaggerate and poeticize. Mind permeates Bellow's renderings; permeability is the essence of his fluid, nervous, colorful mimetic art. The most passing moment gets its infusion of magic. For instance: Briefly, Citrine remembers visiting Humboldt's widow on a ranch in Nevada. She has remarried; her new husband, a cowboy called Tigler, is particularized by "the bold bronze face with ginger tufted brows, the bent horse-disfigured legs." When, fishing on a lake with Charlie, Tigler falls into the water and has to be rescued,

the bronze returns as more than a color—as his substance—and metaphor elevates the incident into fable:

> I could see the late Tigler's Western figure as if it were cast in bronze, turning over and over in the electrical icy water, and then I saw myself, who had learned swimming in a small chlorinated tank in Chicago, pursuing him like an otter.

The touch of fantasy is Bellow's obedient imp; he is as fertile as reality itself in arresting incongruities. Humboldt is prevented from committing street violence not by any faceless passerby but by a "group of lesbians gotten up as longshoremen;" Humboldt passingly mentions a hospital suicide who "took a fork and hammered it into his heart with the heel of his shoe;" and a pack of Humboldt's cats is made hyper-real by Charlie's recalling one "with a Hitler mustache." Bellow is not only the best portraitist writing American fiction, he is one of our better nature poets. . . .

This seventh (not counting *Seize the Day*) novel shares many qualities with Bellow's first, *Dangling Man*, written more than thirty years ago. The same Chicago, the same ruminativeness, the same moral passion oddly mixed with passivity and spurts of farce and quarrel. The early novel even runs the same calendar course, from December to April, an entombed time of the year whose vernal resurrection means much to Bellow, though "a city boy." From the outset, his fiction gravitated toward heroes suspended in, as *Dangling Man's* Joseph puts it, "sheer dishevelment of mind." And out of Joseph's dishevelment emerge a number of principles that Charlie Citrine, in his slacker, racier tone, might still propound. . . .

Joseph is young, his novel is a scattered journal, he resolves "to begin schooling myself in shrewdness." Charlie Citrine has certainly acquired a worldly shrewdness, as well as (like Saul Bellow) the riband of an honorary Chevalier. But after making one's way through the worldly mass of *Humboldt's Gift*, so rich in information and speculation, one wonders if, for Bellow's kind of dangling, rather than doing, man, the shorter length and implicative texture of the youthful book weren't better. We marvel at a safe distance at Charlie's predatory relationships with his bitchy ex-wife and his mistress, whereas we entered into Joseph's gentle, mundane, unspokenly doomed marriage to Iva. *Dangling Man*, though in snippets, merged earth and air, whereas *Humboldt's Gift*, washed up on our drear cultural shore like some large, magnificently glistening but beached creature from another element, dramatizes, in its agitated sluggishness, the body/mind split that is its deepest theme.—JOHN UPDIKE, "Draping Radiance with a Worn Veil," NY, Sept. 15, 1975, pp. 122–30

Humboldt's Gift is immediately recognizable as a novel by Bellow. No other contemporary novelist writes with his careful mixture of control and abandon. Yet compared to previous works it shows striking differences that cannot be described as developments of earlier tendencies. The changes occur at all levels. The characters' names have a jocose eighteenth-century flavor: Charlie Citrine, Von Humboldt Fleisher, Rinaldo Cantabile. Citrine, the floundering family man here, appears to confront solitude more fatefully than Bellow's other protagonists. The tone of the narrative has shifted markedly toward irony. Yet the currents of philosophizing reach a more urgent pitch than ever before. It is necessary to read *Humboldt's Gift* with great care—with caution even. . . .

Bellow found his style and his voice with *Augie March*, his third novel. Since then he has alternated regularly between first and third person narrative. Yet that alternation does not seem to modify the controlling sensibility in his novels any more than does the varied series of central characters he creates. A Jewish intellectual from Chicago speaks in a voice indistinguishable from that of an eccentric ivy-league millionaire crashing around the African landscape. These modern picaros talk to us from inside deeply disjointed worlds, with a ready supply of funny stories and off-beat culture, stumbling occasionally into a moment of illumination.

However there is something beyond the prose that makes *Humboldt's Gift* read well, aloud and in the mind. Divided into loose unnumbered sections of varying length, the book gives the impression of recording Citrine's voice wherever he goes. Everything is included. We read long digressions on pet subjects, overblown descriptions, and remarks implying that no accumulation of detail will suffice to portray a character. Some of the throwaway lines, comic and critical, bring things to a standstill. "I don't want to interfere in your marriage, but I notice that you've stopped breathing." "It made me think what a tremendous force the desire to be interesting has in the democratic USA." The book is studded with trinkets and oddities. But unlike what is going on in much contemporary French and American fiction, Bellow's irregularities grow not out of doubts about the value of continuous narrative but out of a calm confidence that he has a story to tell. That story can carry with it many excrescences. Robbe-Grillet and Burroughs, though very different from each other in other respects, go to great lengths to fit one sentence to the next according to aural and visual patterns that evade linear narrative. In contrast, Bellow's faith in the shapely existence of a tellable story unites and lends significance to the miscellaneous elements of Citrine's world.

Out of all these aspects of Bellow's fiction grows its most characteristic quality: the sense of plenitude. The world is full to overflowing, and it all connects even though the ultimate enigma will never be dissipated. It is not just that Bellow tells us in scrupulous detail how everyone's breath smells and what they wear and the way they move—and sometimes overdoes it, as I have pointed out. His filling in of the parts outruns mere naturalism and represents a desire to direct the basic act of attention to everything that confronts us—that means to everything there is. This sensuous and spiritual plenitude furnishes both the subject of Citrine's epiphany in the jet and the narrative technique by which it is conveyed. Bellow has had to earn the right to use totem-taboo phrases like "universal sapphire" and "everything-nothing capacity."

. . . *Humboldt's Gift* is not a *roman à clef*, yet it toys repeatedly with that possibility. The process goes on both at the outer edges of the story, where "real people" (Stevenson and Kennedy, literary types like Philip Rahv and Lionel Abel) prowl in the shadows, and at the center where Citrine is endowed, more or less, with Bellow's age, profession, background, success, place of residence, and much more. Since before Rousseau and Sterne the novel has embraced autobiography without shame. No form of self-revelation through fiction need upset us. What troubles me here, however, is the tone of the book, audible yet less insistent in Bellow's recent novels. It is a tone of self-irony, which seems to increase in direct proportion to the autobiographical content, and in compensation for it. The more closely Bellow projects himself into Citrine, the more mocking his voice seems to become. . . .

And then there's the ending, the crocuses sees in the cemetery. At the end of *The Adventures of Augie March* it was a French peasant woman walking off across the fields; in *Henderson the Rain King* it was the Persian boy carried in Henderson's arms; in *Herzog*, the freshly picked flowers. In the final burial scene of *Humboldt's Gift* I find no hint at parody, nothing to cloud the implication that a kind of redemption is beginning. Somehow, we are to understand, Citrine will place himself back within life.

Can it be so? I read unconvinced. The previous pages have set the stage for comic catastrophe. The celebrity-writer who has hobnobbed with Kennedys is now so deeply wounded that he must settle for a rest cure at the Swiss Steiner Center. As his life comes apart, Citrine talks to himself constantly about significant changes for the better taking place within him. But I detect no shift in mental metabolism, no climacteric, only a stronger concern with survival of the self. The well-rounded sensibility responding to the plenitude of life, the voice itself, does not change. For it is Bellow's, masked by the irony that provokes our caution.

Humboldt's Gift shows no flagging of Bellow's intelligence and stylistic powers. He writes like a bird planing, sure of his height, sure of his wings, sure of the language there beneath him, sustaining his flight and as transparent as air. Alert to all his ancestors and rivals from Diderot to Joyce to Pynchon, Bellow has chosen to write an autobiographical novel in the realist tradition. By sheer command of words, he succeeds in animating the busy, smug, self-deprecating I of the narrator. But, as my earlier remarks should suggest, the fictional impulse is out of adjustment. The spark is unsteady. Charlie Citrine is too close to Bellow to fill out a fully extruded novel. He is not close enough to impose the dark challenge of confession. Bellow, of course, plays across that gap—whence his arch and often apologetic tone. He knows there are no rules. But in the characters of Augie March, Henderson, Herzog, and Sammler, all in some degree projections of himself, he employed devices to create an adequate distance from himself. In *Humboldt's Gift* Bellow gets in his own way.

He must have foreseen the risks and decided to take them. He sounds like an ironic ventriloquist, a nearly impossible feat. I was absorbed by the book because Bellow cannot write a dull page. But his awaited masterpiece of exuberant intelligent fiction is still to come. One can hear it muttering through the sardonic treasures of *Humboldt's Gift*.—ROGER SHATTUCK, "A Higher Selfishness?" *NYRB*, Sept. 18, 1975, pp. 21–25

A point of weakness in *Humboldt's Gift* concerns the lack of distance between Citrine and the reader. There is usually surrounding Bellow's protagonists a certain aura of the bogus, factitious and insincere, which is an important element in accommodating the schema of Romantic quest to the form of realistic prose narrative and in registering the comic discrepancy between the hunger for enlightenment and the unlikelihood of its being fed by the dead materialistic weight of mid-twentieth century America. In *Henderson the Rain King*, the colloquial pyrotechnics and schmaltziness of Henderson, a first person narrator like Citrine, are a necessary counterweight to the overtly mythic dimensions of his journey to the Africa within. When he says 'I am to suffering what Gary is to smoke. One of the world's biggest operations' the reader says 'Baloney' but descends with him into Dahfu's lion's den with undiminished apprehension and excitement. In Bellow's finest novel, which does not have a first person narrator, the sufferings and bafflements of Herzog are similarly authenticated through their being qualified by the slight distance kept between him and the reader, a distance that helps us to feel the truth of Herzog's self-description as 'a prisoner of perception, a compulsory witness.'

In *Humboldt's Gift* on the other hand, there is no ironic distance between Citrine and the reader, no gap to qualify and consequently to intensify our involvement in his quest. We fail to see any symbiosis between Citrine's ideas and his actions. As a result his elaborate, superbly articulate mini-lectures on the doctrines of Steiner, American materialism, the decline of the poetic imagination, and other subjects tend to remain uninvolving, unresonant, academic.

This lack of resonance is increased and made more damaging to the novel by Bellow's inability to have Citrine do more than tell the reader about his otherworldly apprehensions. He cannot body them forth in image or symbol, nor dramatize and make palpable his process of spiritual growth. He can only assert, relying on rhetorical embellishment and extended paraphrase of his sacred texts in a way that recalls the artistic falling off in the later Whitman, where the mystical assertions and vatic generalizations of a disembodied 'I' replace the felt immediacy and specificity of the younger poet who insisted 'I am the man, I suffered, I was there.'

The last scene of *Humboldt's Gift* describes the reinterment of the bodies of Humboldt and his mother on a warm, still April day that as yet evidences no signs of the return of spring. It seems to Citrine that 'a massive check threatened, as if a general strike against nature might occur. What if blood should not circulate, if food should not digest, breath fail to breath, if the sap should not overcome the heaviness of the trees? And death, death, death, death, like so many stabs, like murder—the belly, the back, the breast and heart. This was a moment I could scarcely bear.' But the scene, and the novel, ends with the discovery of a crocus struggling up through last autumn's leaves. Bellow doubtless meant to place this image at the end of his novel as an emblem of immortality, a non-discursive sign of the post-mortal rebirth of the soul along the Emersonian lines of Citrine's earlier reflection that 'Each thing in nature was an emblem for something in my own soul.' But because its range of suggestiveness is not controlled by its context or its position in a pattern of images, different readers will necessarily have differing responses to the crocus' appearance.

If this mean flower had been discovered blowing at the end of *Henderson the Rain King* or *Herzog*, it would have been an appropriate coda evoking Wordsworthian thoughts of shared mortality, endurance, human sympathy, and a sense of the sufficiency of life on earth. In *Humboldt's Gift* the flower is given a weight of supernatural intimation which it cannot carry. In the lovely catalogue of vernal flowers in *Lycidas*, Milton had been momentarily tempted to find a supernatural meaning in the annual renewal of nature. But he quickly checked himself because he realized that the returning flowers offered only a naturalistic assuagement:

> For so to interpose a little ease,
> Let our frail thoughts dally with false surmise.

Because Saul Bellow has not similarly checked himself, the return of the crocus at the end of *Humboldt's Gift* may be taken as an emblem of his inability to incorporate satisfactorily in fictional form his new-found interest in the life to come.— KERRY MCSWEENEY, "Saul Bellow and the Life to Come," *CQ*, Spring 1976, pp. 70–72.

Humboldt's Gift, like nearly all of Saul Bellow's fiction, asks one question—can Man be saved? Always Bellow stacks the deck against himself—not, Can Man that noble creature be saved, but can Joe Klutz, that "suffering joker" with a longing for nobility, be saved.

In the World of Distraction, the world in which the ego, the social self, moves, the answer is *no*. But there is always *another* world in a Bellow novel: it is a world of love, of search for the light of God and the will of God, a world in which the person is no fool, or is a holy fool, in which the soul (not the ego or personality but something deeper, truer) *is* worthy of salvation.

These two opposed worlds are expressed in two opposed voices: the external World of Distraction is given to us with comic energy; is it idiosyncratic, daemonic, oppressive. Bellow pours out lists, creates a wonderful, jazzy, idiomatic language. The Inner World, the World of Love, is given to us lyrically. It is full of quiet mystery.

It is as if Bellow's protagonists were in exile from a Platonic world of the Real, enmeshed in a shadow world of distractions. The comedy of the novels is to watch them trying to extricate themselves from distraction, and, as if it were fly-paper, getting more and more stuck. But the beauty *behind* the comedy is in the intimation of that other world, of a "home world" (as Humboldt calls it). "Banished souls . . . longing for their home-world. Everyone alive mourned the loss of his home-world," says Charlie, thinking of Humboldt. Without this sense of a home-world Bellow would be simply a skillful, realistic and comic writer. But infused through his narratives, encountering manic or oppressive distractions, is the "inner miracle," the "core of the eternal in every human being," intimation of a truer, higher, deeper life than this crazy mess we're surrounded by, this crazy mess that is, finally, our absurd, hungry selves. "We never seem to lose our connection with the depths from which these glimpses come," Bellow says in his Nobel Prize address.

. . . ⟨T⟩he question, Can Man Be Saved, comes down, in *Humboldt's Gift*, to: Can the soul be saved from the power of distraction? But underlying that abstract question is a simpler, more concrete one: *Can I be saved from death*. In an interview some years ago Bellow declared that of all his characters, Henderson, "that absurd seeker of high qualities," was almost like Bellow himself. "What Henderson is really seeking is a remedy to the anxiety over death. What he can't endure is this continuing anxiety: the indeterminate and indefinite anxiety, which most of us accept as the condition of life which he's foolhardy enough to resist." Overshadowing each of Bellow's protagonists is this terror of death—in some, disguised, in some, more direct, in all fused and confused with the question of human survival and the survival of humane values.

Charlie tries to connect the two questions: the question of death to that of the power of the poet to defeat distraction. This power, Charlie believes, is tied up by terror of death. So the poet sleeps—as Charlie himself has been sleeping for years. Sleep is a response to boredom, and the first principle of modern boredom, according to Charlie, is acceptance of the "metaphysical assumptions about death everyone in the world had apparently reached": "either you burn or you rot." But the poet's power can be released: " . . . To assume, however queerly, the immortality of the soul, to be free from the weight of death that everybody carries upon the heart presents, like the relief from any obsession . . . a terrific opportunity. . . . Terror of death ties his energy up but when it is released one can attempt the good without feeling the embarrassment of being unhistorical, illogical, masochistically passive, feebleminded." Then the poet does not, like Humboldt, have to destroy himself to testify to the glory of his good. His energies can be used.

But this connection between the power of the soul, of the poet, and the question of death and immortality, is not experienced, not a living part of the fiction. We *hear* that Charlie is less afraid of death after reading Rudolf Steiner. We *hear* about his belief in the immortality of the soul. We *hear* that Charlie has experienced an inner light. But none of this does

Bellow make real for us. He simply lets Charlie report it. And Bellow is too competent a writer not to know how weak is Charlie's newfound faith, how impossible as fictional development. I believe we are meant to take it as *denial*, defense against anxiety. In "The Heavy Bear," Delmore Schwartz, the prototype of Humboldt, wrote,

> The strutting show-off is terrified,
> Dressed in his dress-suit, bulging his pants,
> Trembles to think that his quivering meat
> Must finally wince to nothing at all.

These lines could be an epigraph to *Humboldt's Gift*. For if the faith in immortality is not realised fictionally, the terror of death is powerfully rendered. Again and again we are made to suffer the terror of being buried. Charlie could "conclude how bourgeois it was that I should be so neurotic about stifling in the grave," but it wasn't comforting, and he was not able to attend funerals. "I couldn't bear to see the coffin shut and the thought of being screwed into a box made me frantic." At the time he is telling us his story, he is much less afraid of death, but death anxiety nevertheless permeates the book. . . .

The modern world, the American world, assumes a life without God, a life in which death is final. Essentially, the world of distraction is this modern American world, while the inner, true world is the "world of our fathers." The struggle between them, which energizes the novel, is oedipal at the same time as cultural—is oedipal *because* it is cultural.

The oedipal conflict is left vague, shadowy, in Bellow's fiction, dealt with directly only in *Seize the Day* and *Herzog*. But it is there. When Bellow attempts to create a larky, uncomplicated character, he finds it necessary to make him fatherless. Ironically, this is the novel—*Augie March*—Bellow dedicated to his own father. And still the falsity of Augie's larkiness begins to put pressure on the picaresque structure of that novel. But Joseph, in *Dangling Man*, is *directly* threatened with Gehenna (hell) by his father. Tommy is told by *his* father, "I'm not going to pick up a cross. I'll see you dead, Wilky, by Christ, before I let you do that to me." Herzog's father threatens to shoot him and Herzog feels deserving of being shot. Charlie's father is dead, and we learn little about him; however, Humboldt is there to play surrogate father.

"For me he had charm, he had the old magic." This sentence is from *Humboldt's Gift*—Charlie is talking about Humboldt. It could as well have been spoken of Herzog. Herzog sees his father as a "broken-down monarch." Both have dignity, both are failures. Charlie's real father is, like Herzog's, a poor man who tries to maintain his position as a gentleman. Perhaps Bellow felt he had written in *Herzog* all he needed about that figure. Besides, here we have Humboldt, his spiritual father. Like Herzog's papa, Humboldt, too, attacks and accuses his "son" of betrayal—of entering the world of distraction. And Humboldt claims that Charlie has betrayed him with regard to his wife Kathleen: Charlie, he says, knows where Kathleen has gone. He tells New York of Charlie's betrayal and pickets the theater where Charlie is making a success. Like Herzog's father, Humboldt has a gun and with it threatens a "young critic," sure that Kathleen has run off with him. The surrogate father, jealous of his wife: a transformed drama of Oedipus. And Charlie feels the pressure of the dead Humboldt just as Herzog feels the pressure of his father. Finally, both leave legacies to the protagonist, and these legacies are in each case connected with the protagonist's salvation.

In a sense, Humboldt's legacy is Humboldt himself. Charlie, once Humboldt is dead, feels he has to act out that part of himself which formerly was acted out by Humboldt. He

must play the role of self-destructive artist, and we see even the jealousy and fantasies of persecution (in a less extreme form) of his spiritual father. Freud (in "Morning and Melancholia") pointed out how in mourning, and in its fantasy image melancholia, the lost love object is introjected by the mourner. The mourner identifies with the lost person. The introject is taken into the ego and is attacked by what Freud later termed the superego. Karl Abraham argued that sometimes this figure can be taken into not the ego but the superego and becomes a powerful attacker. Both dynamics are at work in Charlie's case. He acts like Humboldt, begins to fall apart, and attacks himself for his disaster. In this, Charlie is Joseph, Leventhal, Wilhelm, Henderson, Herzog: their stories begin when their defenses are crumbling, they are beginning to fail; they condemn themselves. But Humboldt is also the accuser. representation of the "world of our fathers" threatening Charlie with the curse of an empty life, worthy of death.

The real mourning is for the Father—not the literal father but the fantasy figure from childhood, figure of love and terror, worshipped and rebelled against. The real "work" in the novel is the detachment of the ego from the introjected father. In Bellow's work the Father is an ambiguous figure—a judge and failure both. Here again. The struggle of the protagonist is to survive both the judgement and the failure of the internalized Father. But the fictions can never permanently end the struggle. They resolve it temporarily in a symbolic form; temporarily the accuser/failure is put to sleep in the psyche. Then again it erupts. This may account for the dissatisfaction critics feel with the endings of Bellow's novels. The protagonist may be successful—but in a realm in which that success can't be tested, and we're not quite sure how he got there.

The condemning father, the guilty modern son: this is again and again the situaton in Bellow's novels. *Dangling Man*, *The Victim*, *Seize the Day*, *Henderson the Rain King*, *Herzog*, *Mr. Sammler's Planet* (where the point of view is that of the father) and *Humboldt's Gift* (where the father is not literal but spiritual). The imago of the condemning father is also projected onto other characters in the fiction, so that it becomes one aspect of the protagonist's whole world: surrounding the figure of the son are more or less angry, judgemental reality instructors. "Very well, Moshe Herzog," thinks Herzog to himself while Sandor Himmelstein wildly attacks, "if you must be pitiable, sue for aid and succor, you will put yourself always, inevitably, in the hands of these angry spirits. Blasting you with their Truth." Tommy Wilhelm might as easily be saying this about his father. . . .

If one recurrent scene in *Humboldt's Gift* is the flight from the dying Humboldt, a second is the memory of Charlie's stay in a TB sanatorium when he was eight years old. The memory is of a little boy who weeps for the loss of his parents, weeps because he might "never make it home and see them." That same terrible sense of separation, that same threat of death, are still upon him. Ultimately, the "home world" Humboldt and Charlie talk about is the childhood home, the painful, loving home nothing has ever replaced. To keep the dead with him, to stay loyal to their values, is to preserve in his heart the core of his childhood world. It is an antidote to his own anxiety over death.

Nearly all Bellow's fiction turns on the protagonist's confrontation with the fact of his own death. But mostly what he "learns" is to accept "the terms of his existence," to accept death as Henderson did through the death of King Dahfu. In *Humboldt's Gift*, on the other hand, the narrative moves toward denial of death. The fact of death makes the protagonist turn—here as elsewhere—to an assertion of significant life. But here death itself is finally negated. And since universally, then for Charlie, too. He flees the world of distraction for solitude because the world of distraction is a dying world.

This is, of course, a traditional view held by Christian culture. It is hardly a Jewish view, for in Jewish tradition heaven is in this world, redeemed. While there is great tension between the world as it is and the redeemed world, they are also one and the same. Throughout Bellow's work there is a concern for redemption in the here and now. Joseph's moment of serenity is in the contemplation of a piece of string. Herzog accepts his life as it is—"I must play the instrument I've got," he says. Tommy experiences a moment of love and compassion in a filthy subway. Always the world of love and goodness lifts up from, transcends the everyday world, and yet it *is* that world, transformed. Even in *Mr. Sammler's Planet*, with its yearning for other-worldly transcendence, the weight of the book falls on the dying Elya, who "fulfils his contract" in *this* world—the virtuous (though flawed) husband, father, friend. In *Humboldt's Gift*, however, the yearning for transcendence is much more complete—a Platonic transcendence, stretching towards an unrealised, abstract world of light, rejecting this "tragic earth." Like Bunyan's Christian, Charlie flees a world of death, a world in which he himself will die. And he asserts, or at least receives intimations of, immortal life in the spirit. If Sammler read Meister Eckhardt, Charlie reads that modern mystic Rudolf Steiner. "Under the recent influence of Steiner, I seldom thought of death in the horrendous old way. I wasn't experiencing the suffocating grave or dreading an eternity of boredom, nowadays. Instead I often felt unusually light and swift paced, as if I were on a weightless bicycle and sprinting through the star world. Occasionally I saw myself with exhilarating objectivity, literally as an object among objects in the physical universe. One day that object would cease to move and when the body collapsed the soul would simply remove itself."

This is where all the connections with the dead lead us. Charlie has made the dead live in the narrative to break down our "metaphysical denial" of them. They live and therefore so will Charlie live. Converting—as he had once done—the terror of death into "intellectual subject matter" could "not take the death curse off." His exploration had to be of a different kind— "Real questions to the dead have to be imbued with true feeling. . . . They must pass through the heart to be transmitted." The death curse is lifted by his love of and communications with the dead. That is the real legacy of the dead, the legacy of Humboldt. . . .

Humboldt's Gift is built on the conflict between the world of distraction, a world in which people live meaninglessly and die with finality, and a spirit which transcends that world. Clearly this is not an abstract question in the novel but is motivated by the flight from guilt and death, a flight from oedipal conflict which is both personal and cultural. Finally, Bellow, through Charlie, is able to say *yes*, the human being can be saved, saved from death of the soul.

Humboldt's *gift*: the title has two meanings: his "gift" in the sense of poetic powers to struggle with the world of distraction, and his "gift" in the sense of a legacy which strengthens Charlie to continue that struggle, a gift from the dead to the living. Finally, that gift is the intimation of immortality.

But how seriously should we take this gift? Does Bellow mean us to read Charlie's transcendence of the world of distraction as credible or as, in the psychoanalytic sense, denial? Both, I suppose. If Bellow spins out his own longing into his character, he does not, unlike Charlie, permit himself any easy spiritual solutions. He maintains ironic distance from Charlie

as he did from Herzog—and yet uses Charlie to express his vision of the struggle of the human soul to survive. One part of Saul Bellow is of course the nutty Charlie, as one part of Goethe is Faust. But Bellow sets that part of himself dancing, as he sets Henderson dancing bear-like around the plane, while Bellow the artist enjoys the dance.—JOHN CLAYTON, "*Humboldt's Gift*: Transcendence and the Flight From Death," *Saul Bellow and His Work*, ed. Edmund Schraepen, 1978, pp. 31–48

TO JERUSALEM AND BACK

Visiting Israel for several months in 1975, Bellow kept an account of his experiences and impressions. It grew into an impassioned and thoughtful book, sometimes an exasperating one. As Bellow wryly notes, "If you want everyone to love you, don't discuss Israeli politics"—and discuss them is very much what he does.

Through quick sketches and vignettes, Bellow evokes places, ideas, people, reaching a sharp if patched-together picture of contemporary Israel. Writers are often drawn to this loose form, since it allows them to dazzle and flee, shift tones at will, evade the labor of transitions. Yet a reader may find it frustrating, if only because one expects from a writer like Bellow more sustained argument, deeper probing. We don't get it.

What we do get is often wonderful. Steeped in the skepticisms of Chicago but still responsive to the war-cries of ideology, Bellow proves a keen listener. Like every other visitor to Israel, he soon tumbles into "a gale of conversation." He loves it: it makes him feel at home.

When you go to Israel you can easily suppose that everyone there is a born dialectician, speaking for parties that exist and parties that don't. To American Jews raised on bristling immigrant streets the Israeli scene can appear pleasingly familiar—it's like being back in those heated "circles" in Jackson Park in Chicago or Crotona Park in the Bronx where uncles debated politics. But if you look a bit deeper, you see there are new kinds of Israelis, not such great talkers, not flushed with messianic fevers. Perhaps these are the Israelis of tomorrow.

A few of them appear in Bellow's book, but shadowed, glimpsed, out of reach. In the foreground are the talkers. We get talk from intransigent right-wingers intent upon a "greater Israel," from anxious "doves" who want to stretch out a hand of peace in behalf of survival, from writers who feel the country's obsession with politics is stifling them, and from a masseur at the King David Hotel, a body-culture nut, who seems to have stepped right out of a Bellow story. (This chap advises, as relief from neck tension, tracing numbers one to nine with your head; I can report it doesn't do much for tension but certainly helps gain attention.)

Bellow delights in the liveliness, the gallantry of Israeli life: people on the edge of history, an inch from disaster, yet brimming with argument and words. He delights not with sappy tourist delusions but with a tough critical spirit: his Israel is pocked with scars and creases, and all the more attractive.

Simply as a travel book, *To Jerusalem and Back* is spotty. There are a few remarkable descriptions, such as one in which Bellow finds "the melting air" of Jerusalem pressing upon him "with an almost human weight. Something intelligible, something metaphysical is communicated" by the earthlike colors of this most beautiful of cities. "Elsewhere you die and disintegrate. Here you die and mingle." But notice that even here Bellow quickly shifts from place to human response. Little in his book can match in scenic vividness Melville's 1857 journal of a visit to Palestine ("No moss as in other ruins—no grace of decay—no ivy—the unleavened nakedness of desolation . . . ").

    . . . Bellow succumbs a few times to moods of apocalypse, bemoaning American "innocence" before the evil forces of the world. We are "lightly chloroformed" by our naïve good will and refuse to see that the world is caught up in a struggle to the death. Bellow inclines, though not consistently, toward seeing the Arabs as ineluctably bent upon the destruction of Israel—which would render the idea of negotiations a delusion and danger. He inclines toward seeing the Communist powers as ineluctably expansionist—which would render the idea of détente a delusion and danger.

    We have echoes here of Solzhenitsyn's jeremiads and, much less impressively, of those lugubrious essays in magazines so different as *Commentary* and *The National Review* foreseeing the end of civilization because Western liberals have "gone soft." But isn't this sort of thing just as abstract and ideological, just as out of touch with the complicated realities of politics, as the vulgar-marxism of Jean-Paul Sartre which Bellow rightly attacks?

    That the Arabs may want finally to destroy Israel could well be true; but since they can't, it is necessary to make concrete political choices which could range from a "hawkish" takeover of the West Bank to a "dovish" proposal to trade the occupied territories for a secure peace, and nothing in the generalized excoriations of Arab psychology or theology tells us which policy is better. Similarly, it is true that the Communist system represents a danger to humane values, and it may well be true that the Soviet Union operates under an expansionist thrust; but that does not yet tell us which policy is required for coping with these problems, whether a return to a Dulles-like cold war or Kissinger's strategy or another variant of détente.

    As for American innocence, that—if Bellow will forgive me—resembles a bit the "canned sauerkraut" he once called the fixed and unexamined notions of intellectual life. American innocence in Vietnam? In Chile? In Iran? I could think of other descriptives: stupid, criminal, reactionary. When American policy is more satisfactory in adhering to announced democratic ends, as in helping Israel, that too has little to do with innocence. Good or bad, there's not much "light chloroform" left in American consciousness. And where, for that matter, has the West shown so flabby a will in resisting Communism—that is, where it had some prospect of success? Angola? Could any sane person have seriously proposed sending troops there? And if not, what else? Speeches by Pat Moynihan?

    Bellow recovers quickly from these ideological seizures and at the end reprints a statement by one of his University of Chicago colleagues, Morris Janowitz, putting forward a moderately "dovish" view. "The West Bank territory, with mutual adjustments, would serve as the basis of a Palestine state. But it would be a state that recognizes the interdependence of the contemporary world. . . . The crucial issue would be the guarantees of military security and the prevention of terrorism."

    No one can say with assurance that this scheme would work, no one can say with assurance that the "hawk" policy would necessarily lead to a new war. The political argument is complicated. By and large, it seems to be conducted in Israel with an openness not always present in the United States, among Jews or non-Jews. But one thing seems certain to me: the bemoanings of American innocence and the invocations of looming apocalypse don't tell us very much about the specific choices of policy that Israel and its friends must make.

    Let's end on a happier note. Bellow's voice in this new

book *is* mellower than in the past; he has found his way back, after *Sammler* and *Humboldt*, to the world's charms. As he races through his Israeli encounters, we are aware of the presence of his wife Alexandra, a Greek lady of humor and sense. She likes the hats of the Hasidim. "Couldn't you get one of those beautiful hats?" she asks. Bellow answers: "I don't know whether they sell them to outsiders." Lovely that life for Bellow should imitate Bellow's art!—IRVING HOWE, *NYTBR*, Oct. 17, 1976, pp. 1–2

THE DEAN'S DECEMBER

A genre has long since defined itself, Nobel-certified: the Saul Bellow Novel. This is the Novel as First-Draft Dissertation: a rumination on the sorry state of the world, insufficiently formal for the Committee on Social Thought at the University of Chicago, however well it may translate into Swedish, but not unworthy of that Committee's encouraging noises. About the sorry state of the world there is nothing to be done save accept it, as every Bellow protagonist must learn for himself the way Job did. And since the Bellow Novel is obdurately protagonist-centered, what the reader gets to do is share his learning process.

    In *The Dean's December*, the Dean—not a Jewish Dean from the Bellow Repertory Company, not at bottom an *echt* dean at all but a mere dean of students, moreover a moon-faced French-Irish ex-newspaperman named Albert Corde who has drifted into academe, and don't confuse him with his fox-faced creator—the Dean, if I could just finish this sentence, is stranded in communist Rumania waiting for his mother-in-law, Valeria, to die.

    His wife, Minna, née Raresh, is an astrophysicist of the Palomar caliber; he cannot understand a thing she does, save that she brings together "a needle from one end of the universe with a thread from the opposite end." Here, Minna being preoccupied with her mother, he gets little solace from her. And it's cold and he speaks no Rumanian: plenty of time to ruminate. Herzog, left in solitude, wrote letters. Corde can simply run on, third-person imperfect.

    What he has to ruminate about includes how the college administration reacted to his two-part *Harper's* article about Chicago. "Corde had let himself go, indignant, cutting, reckless." Here he is being reckless:

> The cabdriver who picks up and returns all these dialysis patients is an enormous black woman in red jersey trousers. Her feet seem quite small. Her shoes have high heels. Her straightened hair hangs to her shoulders. She wears a cabby's cap and a quilted jacket. . . . These passenger-patients are her charges, her friends. She wheels forward the television set. The sick woman asks for Channel Two, and sighs and settles back and passes out.

You have to suspend belief to imagine *Esquire*, let alone *Harper's*, publishing to the extent of two long installments these meanderings of an epigone of Saul Bellow's, and suspend it further to imagine a late twentieth-century urban American university being flustered by their indignant high-mindedness.

    Has the creator of Augie March mislaid his street smarts? Augie wouldn't have asked us to credit "a flood of mail," no less, inundating *Harper's*, or the notion that at a worldly Chicago college the sight of "one of its deans taking everybody on" makes them "jittery," "upset." Who, by the way, is he taking on in that dialysis vignette? The taxi driver? The patients? Channel Two, maybe? No, just death. "These are dead men and women. The metabolic wastes obviously affect their brains." It's the *irremediable* that gets to a Bellow character.

Note that phrase, though, "*a flood* of mail." Saul Bellow's mind has been grooved by recurring images, and thirteen years ago—the very year Neil Armstrong set foot on the moon—Bellow imagined a more sardonic flood.

In *Mr. Sammler's Planet* his Corde of those days, Mr. Sammler, was arguing to the extent of twenty pages with a Hindu biophysicist named Lal about whether man ought to be fooling with other worlds at all, seeing his mess on this one. The discussion was not trenchant even in 1969, and time has not sharpened it, though inside that novel it did some useful chores. It helped keep active the slightly defoliated eloquence from which the book drew most of its continuity, and it resumed the larger debate that reverberates from one end of the Bellow shelf to the other: what reasons, if any, can be stated for going on with the human enterprise, given all the ways God and man appear to collaborate in thwarting it?

That grand debate is as old as the Book of Job. What the author of the Book of Job couldn't have foreseen was Saul Bellow's reverse perspective, the farcical. The debate between Sammler and Lal was ended like this:

> "So I suppose we must jump off, because it is our human fate to do so. If it were a rational matter, then it would be rational to have justice on this planet first. Then, when we had an earth of saints, and our hearts were set upon the moon, we could get in our machines and rise up. . . ."
>
> "But what is this on the floor?" said Shula. All four rose about the table to take a look. Water from the back stairs flowed over the white plastic Pompeian mosaic surface. . . .
>
> "Is it a bath overflowing?" said Lal.
>
> "Shula, did you turn off the bath?"
>
> "I'm positive I did."
>
> "I believe it is too rapid for bath water," said Lal. "A pipe presumably is burst."

So much for technology? No, so much for the human right to goof off on visions of grandeur. The pipe burst thanks to the greed of an elegant bum named Wallace, who was upstairs banging it open on the theory that it was a dummy pipe with money inside. He suspected his father of stashing about the house large wads of money tendered by the Mafia for medical favors.

Sheer farce. Yet since Wallace's father was the unequivocally decent character in *Mr. Sammler's Planet*, and was also at that moment scant hours from death by cerebral aneurysm, these researches into the plumbing were tasteless and nearly impious as well as inept, and the flood that came cascading down the staircase to drown out talk about spacecraft admonished like the waters with which God overwhelmed all earth long ago, out of exasperation with human folly.

That was the once and possibly future Saul Bellow: a sardonic connoisseur of Old Testament motifs, a moralist, a fabulist. His fictions, in reflecting a tribal penchant for arguing, revert to the topics over which God and Job once squared off. To invent a new impersonator of Job is more or less his formula for getting a new book started: someone whose "Why me?" can extend to "Why anyone?"

Six years ago last May, Mr. Bellow could be watched for an hour as he and astronaut Neil Armstrong accepted academic honors from the oldest university in Ireland. There was much to amuse a prickly ironist, not least the complex fate that had brought a puppeteer whose character called the astronauts "superchimpanzees" to the same platform with the very man whose foot first tested extraplanetary soil. He also heard himself eulogized in some 250 words of Latin, composed by a poker-faced wag. In the cribs they'd been issued at the door spectators could match "*Insanumne genus humanum? Testes plerique*" against Bellow's "Is the race crazy? Plenty of evidence."

There exists no Latin—or French or Swedish for that matter—for the crisp nihilism of "Plenty of evidence": the word "evidence" plucked from law and the sciences and steam-rollered flat to do for street argot. It's quintessential Bellow, accurately chosen, utterly resistant to export. It also recalls, as did the whole Irish occasion, a Bellow who'd have judged *The Dean's December* dreary: a book (for one thing) so remote from reliance on idiom that there's nothing save the regime to impede a Rumanian version.

For along the way Bellow has acquired an alter ego named Herzog, who first surfaced in the 1964 novel of that name and promptly addled his creator's head by lecturing into generous stupor the bestowers of the James L. Dow Award, the International Literature Prize, *and* the National Book Award. Herzog—a Leopold Bloom with a Ph.D.—prides himself on the cogency of his moral reflections, as, you can tell, does Corde, does Sammler, does . . . oh, come on, as does their author, who promptly signed up the ruminative Herzog as collaborator.

That was unwise, seeing that one meaning of "ruminative" is "characterized by a mind like a cow's stomach." But soon Herzog was being entrusted with the pen for pages on end. Those swatches of *Mr. Sammler's Planet* you may remember skipping were the work of Herzog: the fictional intelligence enjoying time out while something got written that might go into *Partisan Review* (he's changed magazines since).

"Sammler thought that this was what revolutions were really about. In a revolution you took away the privileges of aristocracy and redistributed them. What did equality mean? Did it mean all men were friends and brothers? No, it meant that all belonged to the elite. Killing was an ancient privilege. This was why revolutions plunged into blood."

Solemn as Sherwood Anderson's in *Dark Laughter*, that voice is the voice of Herzog: never mind that the name on the title page is the name of Saul. "Sammler thought." O Lord, "thought." The mind cowers. "A Thought," an acquaintance of G.K. Chesterton's used to announce, uplifting a large hand; to whom someone once said in exasperation, "Good God, man, you don't call that a *thought*, do you?" Herzog would have called it a Thought, whatever it was. Corde, alas, thinks too. Here he is thinking aloud on an interracial encounter:

> "Race has no bearing on it. I see Spofford Mitchell and Sally Sathers, two separatenesses, two separate and ignorant intelligences. One is staring at the other with terror, and the man is filled with a staggering passion to *break through*, in the only way he can conceive of breaking through—a sexual crash into release."

We're to imagine him *saying* that to someone. Moreover, since what Spofford Mitchell did to Sally Sathers was lock her in the trunk of his car, rape her repeatedly, and finally shoot her in the head, there may be those among us who will reject platitudes from Communications 1A; will even opt for Jeremiah's summation (17:9), that the heart of man "is deceitful, and desperately wicked." Such readers may be thought of as unqualified for later Bellow, where much of the time the thread of the protagonists' lucubrations is the same thing as the plot itself.

Not that *The Dean's December* lacks all touch of as skilled a fabulist as you might want. Its opening is rich with possibility.

"Corde, who led the life of an executive in America—wasn't a college dean a kind of executive?—found himself six or seven thousand miles from his base, in Bucharest, in winter, shut up in an old-fashioned apartment."

In the bundle of worries he spends long hours unpacking, Chicago dominates, a place of terminal craziness: its rich without point, its poor without hope, its ongoings rife with jagged violence and sexual hysteria, its very jails full of rats and sodomizings and stabbings. There fate assigns each denizen his place in one or the other of two anarchies: the legitimate, the illegitimate. No melioration of Chicago seems thinkable.

Is there life after Chicago? If so, Bucharest seems to emblematize it. Bellow's Bucharest is neither a Lower Slobovia of ludicrous privations nor a Len Deighton playground for adventurous free-world spirits. It's a suitable limbo for Corde's introspections: a bleak, half-lighted city where informers and bureaucrats are endured like the weather, and the genteel who can remember other times are furtive in guarding their diminished ceremonies.

No writer has more authority with the feel of a place:

December brown set in at about three in the afternoon. By four it had climbed down the stucco of old walls, the gray of Communist residential blocks: brown darkness took over the pavements . . . more thickly and isolated the street lamps. These were feebly yellow in the impure melancholy winter effluence. Air-sadness, Corde called this. In the final stage of dusk, a brown sediment seemed to encircle the lamps. Then there was a livid death moment. Night began.

Corde empathizes readily with the "air-sadness": with starker phenomena as well. At one baleful session with a Party administrator, he feels himself "the image of the inappropriate American . . . incapable of learning the lessons of the twentieth century; spared, or scorned, by the forces of history or fate or whatever a European might want to call them."

This means: he senses that a Rumanian colonel will despise his incomprehension of brute power, which scorns to bend regulations merely so that a defected astrophysicist with her American bogus-academic husband may visit a paralytic in intensive care. If you'll notice, Corde is empathizing with what he feels the colonel feels about what he feels about the colonel's nonfeeling. With the book only a few hundred words old and its exposition still crisp, already we're in that deep.

We swim at such treacly depths because in this way station for his stunned soul Corde has nothing to do but wait: for one more hospital visit, arranged by bribery; for Valeria to die; for a grim day at the crematorium; for the flight home. Not that when he does have, or will have, things to do (in Chicago) does *doing* any longer seem to signify. In his morass of seeing-all-sides, acts are irrelevant.

So his plight—killing time in limbo—is rather close to the plight of his author, who must fill a book with sheer inaction and has consequently piped in what's been all too fluent for him of late years, the Herzogian vitality to be gotten from *opinions*.

Hence, multipage excerpts from Corde's *Harper's* article (reruminated, even, with trial revisions), chapter-long replays of Chicago conversations, an audience with the American ambassador (on whom "he wanted to try out . . . some of his notions about the mood of the West"), expostulations with a boyhood friend, now a big-shot syndicated journalist; more, more.

And his drear December has left his creator bereft of occasion for the sort of comic epiphany that can salvage all: scenes like the miniature Noah's Flood in *Mr. Sammler*, or the page near the end of *Henderson the Rain King* (1959) where the hero

(you have to believe this) climbs into a roller coaster with a mangy old trained bear, too old to ride a bike anymore.

And while we climbed and swooped and dipped and swerved and rose again higher than the Ferris wheels and fell, we held on to each other. By a common bond of despair we embraced, cheek to cheek. . . . I was pressed into his long-suffering age-worn, tragic and discolored coat as he grunted and cried to me.

That's a high Saul Bellow moment, one of the highest. Devoid of reflections, it prompts them. It would have been understandable to the author of the Book of Job, who envisioned Leviathan drawn out of the sea with a kind of Hebrew safety pin, and tethered on a leash for laughing maidens. Impossible to imagine it in Latin.—HUGH KENNER, "From Lower Bellowvia," *Harper's*, Feb. 1982, pp. 62–65

RICHARD CHASE
"The Adventures of Saul Bellow:
Progress of a Novelist"
Commentary, April 1959, pp. 323–30

With the publication of *Henderson the Rain King*, Saul Bellow confirms one's impression that he is just about the best novelist of his generation. The new book has faults; it is uneven, it is sometimes diffuse. And besides the liability of its real faults, it makes its appeal to literary qualities which, although very much in the American tradition, Serious Readers have learned during the last decades to scorn. For much of its length *Henderson* is a "romance" rather than a "novel." It forfeits some of the virtues of the novel (realism, plausibility, specificity), but gains some of the virtues of romance (abstraction, freedom of movement, extreme expressions of pathos, beauty, and terror). The book is sometimes farcical, melodramatic, zany—qualities that Serious Readers know, know all too well, are inferior to Realism and Tragedy. But *Henderson* has realism and tragedy too, although not so much as some of Bellow's other writings.

Bellow has chosen a fertile subject—a demented American aristocrat at loose ends and in search of his soul. This is a subject which, before *Henderson the Rain King*, few if any American novelists had thought of using, except at the relatively low level of imaginative intensity that characterizes the polite novel of manners. In the brutal, loony, yet finally ennobled Henderson we have a character who for dire realism and significant modernity far surpasses in dramatic intensity the frustrated aristocrats portrayed by writers like Edith Wharton and J.P. Marquand. It is interesting, by the way, that of the few reviewers of *Henderson* I have read, none mentioned the patrician heritage of the hero, although this heritage is of cardinal importance in understanding him. It is as if the reviewers still regard "an aristocrat" as nothing but a walking collection of manners and therefore unsuitable for portraiture in anything but a novel of manners. Yet even in democratic America the well-born may receive as part of their birthright a certain dynamism, a distortion of character, a tendency to extreme behavior, or other qualities not easily expressed by a novel of manners.

One praises *Henderson the Rain King* in spite of the fact that in some ways it is not up to the high level Bellow set in *The Adventures of Augie March* and in the short novel *Seize the Day*, the best single piece Bellow has written. It is a thinner brew than *Augie* (but what novel isn't?) and less sustained and concentrated in its impact than *Seize the Day*. After the wonderful first forty pages or so, during which we see Henderson on his home grounds, Connecticut and New York, there is a distinct falling off. We doubt whether Bellow should have sent him off so soon to Africa, where most of his adventures occur. We perceive that the author is not always able to make his highly imaginative Africa into an adequate setting for his hero. We fear that Bellow is in danger of confusing Henderson with another pilgrim to Africa, Hemingway. We feel that the book wanders uncertainly for a bad hour or so in the middle. But then it begins to pull itself together again, overcomes the threadbare plot, and triumphantly concludes in a mad moment of tragi-comedy.

The book's shortcomings, along with certain qualities that strike me as real virtues, have led some Bellow devotees to put *Henderson* down as a failure or at best a misguided lark in a never-never land (if *Augie* is Bellow's *Huck Finn*, is not *Henderson* his *Connecticut Yankee in King Arthur's Court*?). But these adverse judgments are wrong. Bellow still works in a comic tradition that is greater than farce or the comedy of manners. He has not only farce and wit but also humor—a richer thing, being permeated with realism, emotion, and love of human temperament. His imagination is fecund and resourceful. His tradition, at a hazard, includes, besides the naturalistic novel, Mark Twain, Walt Whitman, Joyce, and Yiddish humor.

Over the years Bellow's writing has shown a great deal of flexibility and power of development. He did not start off with the big Thomas Wolfe attempt at an autobiographical first novel. He saved that subject until his third book, *Augie March*, and by doing so possibly avoided the fate of many young writers who have a special story to tell, such as that of being brought up in an immigrant family in an American city, but who find that after the story has been told, they have nothing else to say. True, Bellow's first novel, *Dangling Man*, was ostensibly autobiographical and in some of its passages it caught the experience of a young intellectual in the uncertain days of our involvement in World War II. Yet the story was told with so much reticence as to give a thin, claustral quality to the whole. Bellow's second novel, *The Victim*, was one of those books published in the years just after the war that seemed to promise a resurgence of American writing (and yet how many new writers of those days have failed to fulfill themselves!). As compared with *Dangling Man*, *The Victim* was notable for its increase in objectivity and drama, and for its picture of the complicated relations between a disorderly, drunken, middle-class Gentile and a hapless but morally self-directing Jew in search of a precarious status. Here Bellow was dealing with what was to be his favorite theme—the impulse of human beings to subject others to their own fate, to enlist others in an allegiance to their own moral view and version of reality. In *The Victim* it is the Jew Leventhal who must resist the attempt of the anti-Semitic Allbee to involve him in his fate. This theme gets its fullest treatment in *Augie March*, but finds its ultimate significance in *Seize the Day*.

The Adventures of Augie March first acquainted us with the formidable music Bellow can make when he pulls out all the stops. Like many other fine American books, it astonishes us first as a piece of language. There are the rather dizzy medleys of colloquial and literary words. For example, Grandma Lausch, the picturesque tyrant of the family in which Augie is brought up, is said to be "mindful always of her duty to wise us up, one more animadversion on the trusting, loving, and simple surrounded by the cunning hearted and the tough." "Not," says Augie, "that I can see my big, gentle, dilapidated, scrubbing, and lugging mother as a fugitive of immense beauty from such classy wrath." There is no doubt that Augie, who tells the whole story in the first-person, is right in describing himself as "gabby." A wayward adolescent, almost a juvenile delinquent, he sometimes seems to resemble Marlon Brando. But he is not sullen and inarticulate in the modern style of American youth—far from it. Like any Rabelais, Whitman, Melville, or Joyce, he loves to catalog things, such as the people in the Chicago City Hall: "bigshots and operators, commissioners, grabbers, heelers, tipsters, hoodlums, wolves, fixers, plaintiffs, flatfeet, men in Western hats and women in lizard shoes and fur coats, hothouse and arctic drafts mixed up, brute things and airs of sex, evidence of heavy feeding and systematic shaving, of calculations, grief, not-caring, and hopes of tremendous millions in concrete to be poured or whole Mississippis of bootleg whisky and beer."

Augie is a real poet and lover of the tongue which his immigrant race has only just learned to speak. He loves to explore its resources. And we don't complain much if he is sometimes a bit on the flashy side, a little pretentious and word-besotted in the language he hurls at our heads. Often he is perfectly simple and as appealing as Huckleberry Finn, whom he sometimes reminds us of, while he is still a boy and beset by odd illusions. If Mark Twain had been willing to use the four-letter word, he might have made Huck say, as Augie does, "I understand the British aristocrats are still legally entitled to piss, if they should care to, on the hind wheels of carriages."

Augie is hard to characterize, and of course that is the point about him. He declines the gambit of the young man in an immigrant family; he does not have the drive to succeed or establish himself in a profession. Believing that to commit oneself to any sort of function in the going concern of society is a form of death, he remains unattached and free, although to what end we never fully learn. He is a little of everything: a student, a petty thief, adopted son, tramp, lover, apprentice to assorted people and trades, a would-be intellectual in the purlieus of the University of Chicago, a suppositious Trotskyite, an eagle tamer, a merchant seaman. He is protean, malleable, "larky and boisterous," vain, strong, vital, and also a bit of a fall-guy, in fact "something of a schlemiel." The plot of *Augie March* is that of Whitman's *Song of Myself*—the eluding of all of the identities proffered to one by the world, by one's past, and by one's friends. Augie calls himself "varietistic," just as Whitman says, "I resist anything better than my own diversity." "What I assume, you shall assume," writes Whitman. And Augie reflects on "what very seldom mattered to me, namely, where I came from, parentage, and other history, things I had never much thought of as difficulties, being democratic in temperament, available to everybody and assuming about others what I assumed about myself." Augie remains elusive and diverse. His fate is not that of any of the memorable people he knows: Grandma Lausch, his brother Simon, Mrs. Renling, Einhorn, Sylvester, Clem Tambow, Mimi, Thea, Stella.

Not that Augie is entirely happy about himself, or sure in his own mind that varietism and freedom from ties will lead him to individual autonomy. Bellow seems to leave him wavering as the novel draws to a close. At one point Augie calls for autonomy, for the unattached individual—"a man who can stand before the terrible appearances" without subjecting himself to any of them. He wants to take the "unsafe" road and be a "personality" rather than take the safe road and be a "type." He resists being "recruited" to other people's versions of reality and significance. And yet Augie strikes us as being puzzled, as we are, by the questions: What *is* his personality, what *is* his version of reality and significance? At any rate we find him wishing that his fate "was more evident, and that I could quit this pilgrimage of mine." At the end he is married and in Paris, "in the bondage of strangeness for a time still," yet oddly wishing that he could return to the States and have children. But even the idea of paternity is not allowed to thwart his desire for unattached selfhood. Where, he asks, is character made? And he answers that "It's internally done . . . in yourself you labor, you wage and combat, settle scores, remember insults, fight, reply, deny, blab, denounce, triumph, outwit, overcome, vindicate, cry, persist, absolve, die and rise again. All by yourself! Where is everybody? Inside your breast and skin, the entire cast." But all this sounds less like an autonomous personality than a man far gone in solipsism and illusion. Augie's concluding words belie the "oath of unsusceptibility" he has taken. At the end he exclaims, "Why I am a sort of Columbus of those near-at-hand and believe you can come to them in this immediate *terra incognita* that spreads out in every gaze." Augie's wish that people could "come to" each other entirely without any ulterior motive or aggression is praiseworthy, but we share his doubts that they ever can.

"A man's character is his fate," Augie says at the beginning and end of his story. But the question, What is his character? is not answered. The idea of character in *Augie March* is contradictory. Bellow is, from one point of view, in the line of the naturalistic novelists (Norris, Dreiser, and Farrell—who have also written about Chicago), and he therefore conceives of character deterministically as the product of heredity and environment. "All the influences were lined up waiting for me," says Augie. "I was born, and there they were to form me, which is why I tell you more of them than of myself." On the other hand, as I said above, Bellow follows the Whitman tradition, which believes that character is the autonomous self, the given transcendent fact which no amount of natural conditioning can fundamentally change. The naturalistic account is incomplete because it tries to describe only what *produces* character; the transcendentalist account is vague, however liberating and inspiring it may be. A logical difficulty or a moral or metaphysical anomaly doesn't necessarily spoil a fiction. And in fact it strikes me that it is exactly Bellow's mixture of attitudes toward character that makes his novel such a rich experience.

What Augie fears is the death of the self, and his judgment of the contemporary world is that it is terribly resourceful in its stratagems for destroying the self. In *Seize the Day* Tommy Wilhelm comes to understand the death of the self in a harrowing scene in a funeral parlor, a scene more profound and moving than anything the bumptious Augie undergoes. Wilhelm, middle-aging, an unemployed salesman, separated from his wife and two children, is on the ebb tide of his fortunes. The scene is in and about a hotel on Broadway and not the least value of the story is the accuracy with which Bellow has reproduced the bleak gerontocracy which has gathered there from all parts of New York and Europe—the "senior citizens," as our culture calls them, the forlorn octogenarians, the wistful widowers, the grimy, furtive old women. One of the aged is Wilhelm's father, a retired doctor with a professional sense of success and rectitude, who regards his hesitant romantic son as "a slob." Malleable like Augie, but less resilient, Wilhelm allows his career to be spoiled at the outset by putting himself under the guidance of Maurice Venice, who promises to get him a job as a movie star but turns out to be a pimp. He has lost, or given up, his job as a salesman of baby furniture, and

now is at the mercy of the recriminations directed at him by his father and his wife. Of course, they have their point, but Wilhelm is not entirely wrong in thinking that there is something sinister and inhumanly aggressive in their nagging insistence that (as Augie would say) he allow himself to be recruited to *their* versions of reality.

But in trying to escape from his father and his wife, Wilhelm comes under the influence of Dr. Tamkin, who, whatever else we may think of him, is certainly one of Bellow's most glorious creations. Reminiscing, Augie March had exclaimed, "Why did I always have to fall among theoreticians!" It is a poignant question, suggesting that in a world where no one is certain about truth, everyone is a theoretician. And to the fastest theorizer goes the power; he is the one who can "seize the day." Dr. Tamkin, investor, alleged psychiatrist, poet, philosopher, mystic, confidence man, is one of the fast talkers. He is an adept in the wildly eclectic world of semi-enlightenment and semi-literacy which constitutes the modern mass mind when it expresses itself in ideas, the crazy world of half-knowledge, journalistic clichés, popularized science, and occultism, the rags and tatters of the world's great intellectual and religious heritages. Bellow is a master at describing this state of mind, and a sound moralist in suggesting that a Dr. Tamkin would be less reprehensible if he were merely greedy and materialistic, like the characters in naturalistic novels— but, no, he must also be a mystic, a psychiatrist, and a theoretician. And so Wilhelm, the well meaning, not too bright ordinary man, is all the more bewildered and devastated when the seven hundred dollars he has given Tamkin to invest in lard is lost and he is ruined.

Wandering the streets in search of Tamkin, who seems to appear and disappear in the crowds like a ghost, Wilhelm is jostled by a group of mourners into a funeral parlor where, standing by the coffin of a man he does not know, he weeps uncontrollably for his own symbolic death, the death of the self. In this scene we have in its deepest expression one side of the meaning (as I understand the difficult idea) of Augie's apothegm: "Well, given time, we all catch up with legends, more or less." The same idea is expressed in the odd English of the somewhat incredible King Dahfu in Bellow's new novel: "The career of our specie is evidence that one imagination after another grows literal. . . . Imagination! It converts to actual. It sustains, it alters, it redeems!. . . . What Homo sapiens imagines, he may slowly convert himself to." But the human power of actualizing the imaginary is a two-edged sword, which can destroy as well as redeem. We can be destroyed if, as in his moment of final anguish and illumination Wilhelm understands he has done, we allow ourselves to be recruited to, allow ourselves to become actualizations of, other people's versions of reality. Yet catching up with the legend or realizing the imaginary can also be liberating and redemptive. So we gather at the moment when Wilhelm catches up with the legend of his own death—a legend that has been entertained by himself and by those he has known—while he gazes, with the great revelation, at the stranger in the coffin.

Thus it appears that although Bellow's insistence on being free is not a complete view of human destiny, neither is it simply a piece of naivety or moral irresponsibility, as has sometimes been suggested. He believes that if we ever define our character and our fate it will be because we have caught up with our own legend, realized our own imagination. Bellow's fertile sense of the ever-possible conversion of reality and imagination, fact and legend, into each other is the source of the richness and significance of his writing. He differs in this respect from the traditional practice of American prose romance, which forces the real and imaginary far apart and finds that there is no circuit of life between them. (On this point see my book, *The American Novel and Its Tradition*.) Bellow differs, too, from the pure realist, who describes human growth as a simple progress away from legend and toward fact, and from the naturalistic novelist, who conceives of circumstance as always defeating the human impulse of further thrusts toward autonomy. Which is merely to say that Bellow's sense of the conversion of reality and imagination is something he shares with the greatest novelists.

Bellow gives the light treatment to some of his favorite themes in *Henderson the Rain King*, although there are tragi-comic moments which for the extreme expression of degradation and exaltation surpass anything in the previous books. With a fatal predictability, the conventional reviewers, often in the midst of encomia, have reproved Bellow for "descending" to farce, as well as to melodrama and fantasy. It does no good to ask where writers so different as Mark Twain, Dickens, Molière, Joyce, and Aristophanes would be without farce.

This is Bellow's first novel with no Jewish characters (although we hear at the beginning of a soldier named Nicky Goldstein, who told Henderson that after the war he was going to raise mink; with characteristic sensibility, Henderson decides on the spot that he will raise pigs). Perhaps in selecting for his hero a tag-end aristocrat, Bellow is responding in reverse to Henry Adams's statement at the beginning of the *Education* that as a patrician born out of his time he might as well have been born Israel Cohen. At any rate we find Henderson ruefully reflecting that despite the past eminence of his family, "Nobody truly occupies a station in life any more. . . . There are displaced persons everywhere." As Henderson at fifty-five freely admits, he has always behaved "like a bum." His father, though, had been an impressive example of rectitude; he had known Henry Adams and Henry James; the family eminence goes back at least to Federal times. His father had followed the traditional life of public service. He had written books of social and literary criticism, defended persecuted Negroes, and in general regarded it as his inherited duty to help guide the national taste, opinion, and conduct in his day.

As for Henderson himself, he cheerfully admits that he is one of the "loony" members of the family—like the one that "got mixed up in the Boxer Rebellion, believing he was an Oriental" or the one that "was carried away in a balloon while publicizing the suffrage movement." Yet he still affirms—to the point of rainmaking for the parched inhabitants of Africa—the "service ideal" that "exists in our family." Like Wilhelm in *Seize the Day*, he has faced death, not in the war but while gazing at the soft white head of an octopus in an aquarium. "This is my last day," he thought on that occasion. "Death is giving me notice." But Henderson is strong, brutal, willful, with great stature and a big belly. Very much a creature of his time, he "seeks wisdom," believing that earlier generations have performed all the more practical tasks—"white Protestantism and the Constitution and the Civil War and capitalism and winning the West," all these things have been accomplished. But, he goes on, "that left the biggest problem of all, which was to encounter death. We've just got to do something about it . . . it's the destiny of my generation of Americans to go out into the world and try to find the wisdom of life." True, Henderson is often retrospective. He has moments of family nostalgia and piety, when he tries to get in touch with his dead father and mother. For this purpose he goes to the cellar and plays a violin (a genuine Guarnerius, of course) that had belonged to his father. He croons, "Ma, this is 'Humoresque' for you" and "Pa, listen—'Meditation from Thaïs.'" As we see, Henderson

is not only musical but occult. He is "spell-prone . . . highly mediumistic and attuned."

But Henderson does not find fulfillment in such activities. He is bored and dissatisfied with his disorderly wife. Like most moderns he loves and pursues "reality" and yet he is just as strongly drawn to the mythic and the magical. He is alternately depressed and exalted by his inchoate notions, in describing which Bellow shows himself again to be an inspired interpreter of the eclectic, semi-literate mind of contemporary culture. Henderson needs new realms to discover, new opportunities of service and redemption. And so he is off to Africa, an Africa which is sometimes that of fantasy ("those were wild asses maybe, or zebras flying around in herds") and sometimes that of Sir James Frazer and Frobenius.

He finds in Africa that there is a curse upon the land. A terrible drought is killing the cattle of the first tribe he encounters, for although the cistern is full of water, the water is infested with frogs, which frighten the cattle away and which the natives have a taboo against killing. Henderson improvises a grenade to blow up the frogs, but blows up the whole cistern too. This is unfortunate because things had been going well for him. For example, Henderson had been absorbing animal magnetism from the natives, as when he ceremonially kisses the fat queen's belly: "I kissed, giving a shiver at the heat I encountered. The knot of the lion skin was pushed aside by my face, which sank inward. I was aware of the old lady's navel and her internal organs as they made sounds of submergence. I felt as though I were riding in a balloon above the Spice Islands, soaring in hot clouds while exotic odors rose from below."

But it is with the next tribe, the Wariri, that his most significant adventures occur. Here Henderson performs the ritual of moving the ponderous statue of the Rain Goddess, whereupon he is made Rain King, stripped naked, flayed, and thrown into the mud of the cattle pond, in the midst of the downpour he has summoned from heaven by his act. Humiliated, abject, yet gigantic, triumphant, visionary, an Ivy-League medicine man smeared with blood and dirt, Henderson dances on his bare feet through the cruel, hilarious scene. "Yes, here he is," cries our hero, "the mover of Mummah, the champion, the Sungo. Here comes Henderson of the U.S.A.—Captain Henderson, Purple Heart, veteran of North Africa, Sicily, Monte Casino, etc., a giant shadow, a man of flesh and blood, a restless seeker, pitiful and rude, a stubborn old lush with broken bridgework, threatening death and suicide. Oh, you rulers of heaven! Oh, you dooming powers! . . . And with all my heart I yelled, 'Mercy, have mercy!' And after that I yelled, 'No justice!' And after that I changed my mind and cried, 'No, no, truth, truth!' And then, 'Thy will be done! Not my will but Thy will!' This pitiful rude man, this poor stumbling bully, lifting up his call to heaven for truth. Do you hear that?"

There ensue several lengthy conversations on life and human destiny between Henderson and the philosophical King Dahfu—a somewhat pathetic monarch whom we often see surrounded by his demanding harem of naked women. He has read books like William James's *Principles of Psychology* and believes that when he dies his soul will be reborn in a lion, the totem animal of the tribe. Like the naturalistic novelists, Bellow is fond of characterizing people by analogies with animals. But Bellow, like Swift, follows the greater comic traditions of animal imagery. Tommy Wilhelm caricatures himself as a hippopotamus, yet the effect is to make him more human, more understandable, more complicated, rather than less so.

What might be called Bellow's totemistic style of comedy and character drawing gets a full workout in *Henderson*. A raiser of pigs and a self-proclaimed bum, Henderson has thought of himself as a pig. King Dahfu believes that what Henderson needs is rehabilitation in the image of the lion totem, and he therefore puts our hero through a course of what can only be described as lion-therapy, complete with psychiatric terms like "resistance" and "transference." This takes place in a cage under the palace, where the king keeps a magnificent lioness. The therapy consists in repeated exposure to the lioness, first getting Henderson to try to quell his fears of her and finally getting him to imitate the lioness, on his hands and knees, growling and roaring, so that by sympathetic magic he can absorb lion-like qualities. The scene in which he is finally able to roar satisfactorily, though still terrified, is a great comic moment. The king and the lioness watch Henderson "as though they were attending an opera performance." Henderson describes the roar he lets out as one which "summarized my entire course on this earth, from birth to Africa; and certain words crept into my roars, like 'God,' 'Help,' 'Lord have mercy,' only they came out 'Hoolp!' 'Moooorcy!' It's funny what words sprang forth. 'Au secours,' which was 'Secoooooor' and also 'De profoooondis,' plus snatches from the 'Messiah' (He was despised and rejected, a man of sorrows, etcetera). Unbidden, French sometimes came back to me, the language in which I used to taunt my little friend Francois about his sister." In this abject, ridiculous, and yet eloquent roar we are impressed with the full pathos, the utter humiliation, and also the odd marginal grandeur of Henderson. After this he writes a letter to his wife directing her to apply for his admission to the Medical Center, signing the application "Leo E. Henderson" (although his name is Eugene). For now he is resolved to become the M.D. he has always dreamed of being since, as a boy, he had been inspired by the example of Sir Wilfred Grenfell. Of course the letter never arrives.

Henderson escapes from the Wariri after King Dahfu has been killed trying to capture the lion who is his father. One need hardly bother about the plot—the conniving witch doctor, the escape from prison, the hazardous flight of Henderson. It is all pleasant enough in the reading.

But the end is magnificent. Here we have Henderson walking around the blank, wintry airport in Newfoundland, where his plane has put down for refueling. He is paternally carrying in his arms an American child who speaks only Persian and is being sent alone to Nevada. He remembers how his own father had been angry at him once when he was a boy and how he had hitch-hiked to Canada, where he had got a job at a fair. His task was to accompany and care for an aged, toothless, and forlorn trained bear who was ending his days of performing by taking rides on a roller-coaster, though paralyzed by fear and vertigo and occasionally wetting himself, for the delectation of the crowds who watched from below. "We hugged each other, the bear and I, with something greater than terror and flew in those gilded cars. I shut my eyes in his wretched, time-abused fur. He held me in his arms and gave me comfort. And the great thing is that he didn't blame me. He had seen too much of life, and somewhere in his huge head he had worked it out that for creatures there is nothing that ever runs unmingled." Henderson the boy is long dead; Henderson the lion has disappeared, so has Henderson the pig. Henderson the bear remains, "long-suffering, age-worn, tragic, and discolored." Still a rather preposterous clown, he has nevertheless achieved a certain nobility by his way of "mingling" in the common fate of creatures. Will he remain Henderson the bear? Not if he can live up to the declarations of freedom and growth he made earlier in the book. "I am Man . . . and Man has many times tricked life when life thought it had him taped." And, though saddened, he had agreed with King Dahfu that "Nature is a

deep imitator. And as man is the prince of organisms he is the master of adaptations. He is the artist of suggestions. He himself is his principal work of art, in the body, working in the flesh. What miracle! What triumph! Also, what disaster! What tears are to be shed!"

The king's words strike Bellow's "note." His main characters—Augie, Tommy Wilhelm, Henderson—are adept at imitation and at adaptation. They are different, to be sure. Augie remains young, strong, charming, yet emotionally soft. Wilhelm is wistful, unstable, romantic. Henderson is wild, brutal, a clown. But they are all malleable, emergent, pragmatic, and protean; they love freedom, development, pleasure, and change. They seek both natural and transcendent experiences that are expressive of their way of life.

What is so far chiefly missing in Bellow's writing is an account of what his heroes want to be free *from*. As Bellow is always showing, their very adaptibility lays them open to forms of tyranny—social convention, a job, a father, a lover, a wife, their children, everyone who may want to prey upon them. And all of these forms of tyranny, fraud, and emotional expropriation Bellow describes brilliantly. But only in *Seize the Day* is there a fully adequate, dramatically concentrated image of what the central figure is up against—the institutional, family, and personal fate that he must define himself by, as heroes in the greatest literature define themselves. *Augie March* is prodigiously circumstantial, but the circumstances are never marshaled into a controlling image, and Henderson is bundled off to Africa before we see enough of him in his native habitat to know fully, by understanding the circumstances of his life, what his character and his fate are. But who can complain when, once he is in Africa, we see him in episodes which make us think him the momentary equal, for tragi-comic madness, for divine insanity, of the greatest heroes of comic fiction?

NORMAN PODHORETZ
"The Adventures of Saul Bellow" (1959)
Doings and Undoings
1964, pp. 205–27

Most serious critics today—at least those who have concerned themselves at all with current writing—would probably single out Saul Bellow as the leading American novelist of the postwar period. There are many reasons for this. First of all, Bellow is an intellectual, by which I do not only mean that he is intelligent, but also that his work exhibits a closer involvement with ideas than the work of most other writers in this period. Alfred Kazin, one of his warmest admirers, for example, calls attention to the fact that Bellow's characters "are all burdened by a speculative quest, a need to understand their particular destiny within the general problem of human destiny," and he compares Bellow to "'metaphysical' American novelists like Melville, for he identifies man's quest with the range of the mind itself." Nor is it simply that Bellow is concerned with ideas; the concern itself operates on a high level of sophistication and complexity—higher, even, than Norman Mailer's, if not more audacious. He is an educated, exquisitely self-conscious writer, at the opposite pole from someone like James Jones, and yet not in the least academic or Alexandrian. His books, whatever else we may say of them, *mean* something: they are charged with the urgency and the passion of a man to whom the issues he writes about are matters of life and death. And finally, Bellow is a stylist of the first order, perhaps the greatest virtuoso of language the novel has seen since Joyce.

But these qualities alone do not account for the special, almost personal, interest that serious critics have always taken in Bellow. For an adequate explanation, we also have to look, I believe, at the changing historical context out of which his novels have come and in terms of which their impact has been registered. Bellow began writing fiction at a time when the literary avant-garde in this country had reached a point of sheer exhaustion, and when the moral and social attitudes associated with it no longer seemed relevant either to life or to literature— and he was the first gifted American novelist to search for another mode of operation and a more viable orientation to the world of the postwar period. Since a large and influential body of intellectuals was engaged on a similar quest, Bellow naturally assumed a position as spokesman and leader. There is, indeed, a sense in which it may even be said that the validity of a whole new phase of American culture has been felt to hang on whether or not Saul Bellow would turn out to be a great novelist.

The direction in which Bellow would find himself going in search of this new orientation was evident as far back as his first novel, *Dangling Man*, a short bitter book about a Chicago intellectual who is told to hold himself in readiness for the army and then waits around in lonely idleness for nearly a year before the draft board finally acts. If we think of *Dangling Man* as a war novel, we can see how far Bellow's starting-point was from Mailer's, to whom the experience of war offered an opportunity for establishing continuity with the past—with, that is, the conventions of naturalism and the progressive ideas that were its traditional ally. The war for Bellow did not mean an exposure to the great realities of hardship, violence, and death; nor did it mean a confrontation between the virtuous individual and the vicious instrument of a vicious society. On the contrary: it meant the disruption of continuity with the past, the explosion of a neat system of attitudes that had for a time made life relatively easy to manage. These attitudes can be summed up in the word "alienation," provided we understand that the term refers not merely to the doctrines of a small group of radicals bred on Marx, but to the hostile posture toward middle-class society adopted by nearly all the important writers of the modern period, whatever their particular political persuasion. T. S. Eliot and Ezra Pound on the right, or the largely non-political Hemingway, Fitzgerald, and Faulkner, were no less "alienated" from the America of the 20's and 30's than John Dos Passos and James T. Farrell on the left. What distinguished the 30's in this regard is simply that a temporary alliance was struck between the avant-garde in literature and radicalism in politics, so that a phenomenon like *Partisan Review* could develop, and a critic like Edmund Wilson could conclude his book on symbolism with the assertion that Marxism had provided a "practical" answer to the questions posed by the modernist movement. Those writers and intellectuals who decided around the time of the Moscow trials that Stalin had betrayed the revolution might altogether have lost their faith in the possibility of a practical solution to the spiritual problems of the age if not for the fact that a third alternative presented itself in the form of a new proletarian revolution led by Trotsky. With America's entry into the war, however, the few shreds of revolutionary hope that had managed to survive the end of the decade disintegrated completely. Yet the collapse of revolutionary hopes only killed the belief in a *practical* or political solution to the spiritual problems of the age; it did not kill the problems themselves, nor did it destroy the sharpness with which writers and intellectuals experienced those problems. (That was left to the 50's to accomplish.)

From this perspective, we can see why *Dangling Man* ought to be called a prescient book. Published in 1944, it was one of the first expressions of the dislocation that set into American intellectual life during the 40's, when a great many gifted and sensitive people were quite literally dangling, like the Joseph of Bellow's novel, between two worlds of assumption and were forced back upon themselves to struggle with all the basic questions that had for so long been comfortably settled. At 27 Joseph has not only repudiated the radicalism of his immediate past, but has come to believe that there can be no political answers to problems of the spirit. There is, he admits, something about modern society that creates special and unprecedented difficulties for the individual who aspires to the best that mankind has been able to accomplish—to wholeness of being, grace of style, and poise of spirit. But he also feels that we abuse the present too much: surely it must still be possible to do again what so many others have done before. Though he continues to "suffer from a feeling of strangeness, of not quite belonging to the world," he refuses to accept alienation as a strategy for getting by. Alienation, he says, "is a fool's plea. . . . You can't banish the world by decree if it's in you. . . . What if you declare you are alienated, you *say* you reject the Hollywood dream, the soap opera, the cheap thriller? The very denial implicates you," and if you decide that you want to forget these things, "The world comes after you. . . . Whatever you do, you cannot dismiss it." It may even be that it is a "weakness of imagination" that prevents people from seeing "where those capacities have gone to which we once owed our greatness." Nevertheless, a man must protect himself from the world, and if he has no recourse either to alienation as a style of life or to political activism, how is he to live? Perhaps, Joseph thinks, "by a plan, a program . . . an ideal construction, an obsessive device." But it would be better to get along without such an "exclusive focus, passionate and engulfing," partly because there is always "a gap between the ideal construction and the real world, the truth," and partly because "the obsession exhausts the man," often becoming his enemy.

What Bellow is attempting to do here, then, is challenge the standard idea of the heroic that dominates 20th-century literature in general and the fiction of the 30's in particular: the idea that under modern conditions rebellion is the only possible form of heroism. He is saying, in effect, that all the traditional modes of rebellion (including—and perhaps especially— the simple act of conscious dissociation from society) have been robbed of their relevance by the movement of history. Heroism as Bellow envisages it in *Dangling Man* would consist in accepting the full burden of time and place, refusing to hold oneself aloof, and yet managing not to be overwhelmed or annihilated. The image he has in mind, in other words, is neither Prometheus nor Ahab, but Beethoven, Shakespeare, Spinoza—men who have achieved (to use the phrase that was soon to become so fashionable) the tragic sense of life. It goes without saying that Joseph is very far from this goal; but he has the ambition, and the main thing that happens to him in the course of the novel is that he is pushed by suffering into recognizing that the sober, balanced, Olympian attitudes of his earlier self were an evasion rather than a stage in his progress. In a word, he discovers evil—the reality that must be contended with before the tragic sense of life can develop. He also discovers how far he still has to go and how pitifully ill-equipped he is for making the journey—which means that he has experienced a necessary humiliation. At the end, he hurls himself with a kind of joyous bitterness into the army and the war, hoping to learn through "regimentation of spirit" what he had been unable to learn as an isolated "free" man.

Yet it is hard to believe that Joseph will do very much

better in the army than he managed to do in his lonely room. He is too self-consciously eager for further humiliation, too ready to extract the wisdom from suffering before it even comes to a boil, too little endowed with the robust toughness that would be needed to make him seem a plausible candidate for the destiny to which he aspires. Thus, what Bellow has actually succeeded in creating in Joseph is not a character whose job it will be to find a way of realizing the highest human possibilities under modern conditions, but an extraordinarily intelligent portrait of a type that was to come into great prominence in the years following World War II. Joseph is still the alienated modern man who has been a leading figure in the literature and social thought of the 20th century, but he differs from his immediate ancestors in lacking a plan or program or obsessive device to justify, support, and enrich his estranged condition. Like Mailer's Lovett in *Barbary Shore*, he is doomed to alternate bursts of aimless hysteria and pathological apathy; and again like Lovett, he is forced to drag himself through the world without the help of the past and without a sense of wide future possibilities. ("I, in this room, separate, alienated, distrustful, find in my purpose not an open world, but a closed, hopeless jail. My perspectives end in the walls. Nothing of the future comes to me.") As he himself observes, "the greatest cruelty is to curtail expectations without taking away life completely," and it is to this cruelty that he is exposed, the more so because he can find nothing in the life he leads to "hold and draw and stir" him. Whereas the answer to this predicament was once art (but he is not an artist) or revolution (but revolution is impossible), Joseph's answer is to accept the society of which he is inescapably a part and to work toward transcending it. The fact that this answer exists within the novel only as an abstractly stated proposition rather than a concrete presence, is, of course, a major failing, just as it is the main reason for the book's imaginative thinness. Written in the form of a journal, *Dangling Man* hardly ventures beyond the consciousness of the central character and is so highly self-involved that even when Bellow does move outside Joseph's mind and into the world around him, the novel remains cheerless and claustral, giving the impression of a universe barren of people and things, a kind of desert beaten by the wind and sleet of a foul Chicago winter.

Cheerlessness also characterizes the world of Bellow's second novel, *The Victim* (1947). Here the Chicago winter gives way to a New York summer, and instead of emptiness we get a sense of crowds milling, seething, and sweating. "On some nights New York is as hot as Bangkok" is the opening sentence, and this association of the city with an exotic primitive place is unobtrusively reinforced throughout the narrative, until we begin to understand that what we have in *The Victim* is a vision of the city as a tiny village surrounded on all sides by a jungle that threatens at any moment to spill over and engulf the precarious little human oasis at its center. This is New York seen through the eyes of a writer overwhelmed by the sheer animality of the human species, and nagged by the suspicion that "civilization" may be a gigantic and desperate illusion—and an illusion that is becoming more and more difficult to sustain.

Discussing the conviction he once had of the mildness of his own character and trying to rationalize his horror of violence, Joseph tells us in *Dangling Man* that the famous passage from Hobbes which describes life in the State of Nature as "nasty, brutish, and short" was always present to his mind, and one imagines that the same passage was always present to Bellow's mind as he was writing *The Victim*. The central figure, Leventhal, is a man of even greater spiritual timidity than Joseph, though not being an intellectual, he has no theories to bolster his timidity. He goes through life with the feeling of having "got away" with something, by which he means that he might very easily have fallen among "that part of humanity of which he was frequently mindful—the lost, the outcast, the overcome, the effaced, the ruined." But it gradually becomes clear in the course of the novel that what Leventhal really fears is crossing over a certain boundary of the spirit, beyond which lies not merely failure, but violence and the darker passions: he is afraid of being "drowned at too great a depth of life." In order to keep from drifting out of the shallow water, he has always resorted to various psychological tricks ("principally indifference and neglect"), and *The Victim* is about a crisis that crashes through his wall of defenses and jolts him into reconsidering his life and his character. The crisis takes the form of his pursuit by the down-and-out anti-Semite of patrician origin, Kirby Allbee, who accuses Leventhal of having maliciously caused his ruin, and (less importantly) Leventhal's simultaneous involvement in the illness and death of his brother's child. With great subtlety and brilliance Bellow traces the process by which Leventhal is drawn into acknowledging responsibility for Allbee, not because Allbee's accusations against him are justified (they are not), but because he learns to recognize a kinship with Allbee himself, who embodies everything he most fears in the world and in his own soul.

From a purely literary point of view, *The Victim* represents a great step forward for Bellow. Whereas in *Dangling Man* we get the feeling that the few dramatic incidents included are brought in only to create the spurious impression that Joseph's theoretical speculations are anchored in the events of his life, in *The Victim* the abstract metaphysical questions that are so important to Bellow arise naturally and spontaneously (and ingeniously) out of the story. The book, moreover, is beautifully constructed and paced, so that Leventhal's growing sympathy for the repulsive Allbee sneaks up on the reader as insidiously and surprisingly as it sneaks up on him. The sub-plot is managed with less dexterity; there is something perfunctory and perhaps a little schematic about it, as though Bellow thought it necessary to provide Leventhal with an experience of death in case his crisis should seem lacking in dimension and profundity.

From the point of view of Bellow's quest for a new orientation to the world around him, however, *The Victim* is not so much an advance over *Dangling Man* as a companion piece to it. If *Dangling Man* challenges the strategy of alienation under the altered conditions of the postwar period, *The Victim* launches an assault on the prudence, caution, and spiritual timidity that Bellow believes to lie behind alienation in a postradical world. "You people take care of yourselves before everything," Allbee says to Leventhal. "You keep your spirit under lock and key. . . . You make it your business assistant, and it's safe and tame and never leads you toward anything risky. Nothing dangerous and nothing glorious. Nothing ever tempts you to dissolve yourself." There is, of course, a certain justice in the charge, as Leventhal goes on to discover, but there is also something to be said in his favor. He lives by a sensible idea of responsibility as against Allbee's insistence that no one can be held responsible for the terrible things that happen to him, and he knows far better than Allbee that a price has to be paid for avoiding the awful dangers of "cannibalism." At the same time, however, Leventhal has been denying the darker sides of his nature, and it is these that he learns to respect and acknowledge in the course of his relations with Allbee. He comes to see that if Allbee is an animal and a monster, so too is he an animal and a monster, capable of savagery and malice and gratuitous cruelty, and he also comes to recognize that his timidity has robbed him of warmth and sympathy and the capacity to reach into the being of another.

Yet it is important to notice that these profound lessons carry no startling practical consequences. In an epilogue to the novel, we come upon Leventhal some years later, and the only change that has taken place is that "Something recalcitrant seemed to have left him; he was not exactly affable, but his obstinately unrevealing expression had softened. . . . And, as time went on, he lost the feeling that he had, as he used to say, 'got away with it.'" In other words, he is now more at peace with himself than before. He has not ventured into the "depths" that he once feared would drown him; he has merely (like a successfully analyzed patient) learned something about himself that has helped him come to terms with the world and make a settlement. During his difficulties with Allbee, he had reflected that "Everybody wanted to be what he was to the limit. . . . Therefore hideous things were done, cannibalistic things. Good things as well, of course. But even there, nothing really good was safe. . . . There was something in people against sleep and dullness, together with the caution that led to sleep and dullness." *The Victim* is concerned with criticizing "the caution that led to sleep and dullness," but Bellow wishes to do so in a complicated way, never blinking at the "cannibalistic things" that can erupt once this caution is overthrown. In the end, he does not advocate that it be overthrown; all he does is recommend that the anti-cautious impulses be acknowledged and accepted, and it is perhaps his feeling that nothing more ambitious can be offered that accounts for the oppressively pessimistic tone of the novel. I call it oppressive because it is a pessimism over the human condition even darker than Freud's in *Civilization and Its Discontents*. In *The Victim*, the making of a settlement (that is, the stifling of the instincts) is seen as bringing no positive rewards or compensations of any significance—no increase of energy through sublimation, no powerful Faustian drive; it merely has the negative virtue of preventing the outbreak of "cannibalism." Nor is Bellow's pessimism here of a piece with the grim view of life that led Hobbes to insist on the necessity of a strong social authority. Bellow wants no strong authority to enforce repression, and he knows that such authorities as do exist are—deservedly—in a seriously weakened condition. *The Victim* is thus highly characteristic of the postwar ethos, restricting itself to a consciousness of how difficult and complicated things are and seeing little hope of remedial action of any kind whatever. Taking itself as a tragic view of life, this attitude is in reality a form of the very cautiousness and constricted sense of possibility that Bellow attacks both in *Dangling Man* and *The Victim*.

By the early 50's, however, while Bellow was working on *The Adventures of Augie March*, the ethos of which his first two novels had been among the early premonitions was also in process of consolidating itself, and as its outlines grew clearer, it gained steadily in confidence and militancy. The first stage (reflected, it may be, in the pessimism of *The Victim*) was an almost reluctant admission that America had become the only protection against the infinitely greater menace of Soviet totalitarianism. But what began as a grim reconciliation to the lesser of two evils soon turned into something rather more positive, ranging from the jingoism of a few ex-radicals who travelled as far to the right as they could go, to the upsurge of an exhilarating new impulse to celebrate the virtues of the American system and of American life in general. So powerful was this new impulse that it even found its way into the pages of *Partisan Review*, which had always been the very symbol of the attitudes now under attack.

The spiritual atmosphere of this phase of American cultural history was fully captured and expressed for the first time in a novel by *The Adventures of Augie March*, which perhaps explains why the book was greeted with such universal enthusiasm and delight when it appeared in 1953. The attitudes of what its enemies called "the age of conformity" and its friends "the age of intellectual revisionism" were all there; the prevailing tone of the age was there; and a new Bellow, reborn into exuberance and affirmation, was there too. "I am an American, Chicago-born," ran the opening words of the novel, and anyone who knew Bellow's earlier work immediately understood him to be asserting that he had managed to cut through all the insoluble problems over the proper relation of the self to society with which he had been wrestling for ten years—cut through them to this wonderfully simple declaration of his identity. The man who had been dangling had finally come to rest in a new maturity of style and vision; the victim of a cruel universe offering only the consolations of an uneasy settlement was now rushing headlong into a world of possibility: he was discovering the richness and glory of the life around him, and everywhere he looked there were treasures to reap. Instead of a bleak Chicago or a threatening New York, we are swept in *Augie* through whole continents, each more vividly colored than the other. Instead of puny characters forever taking their own pulses and dragging themselves onerously from one day to the next, we are introduced in *Augie* to huge figures like the crippled Einhorn whom Bellow belligerently compares to Caesar, Machiavelli, Ulysses, and Croesus ("I'm not kidding when I enter Einhorn in this eminent list"); like Grandma Lausch, who is portrayed as a giant among formidable old women; and like Thea Fenchel, who is reviving the art of falconry and captures poisonous snakes with her bare hands. Most important of all, perhaps, we get a new prose style, the first attempt in many years to experiment with the language in fiction. In contrast to earlier experiments, however, this one expresses not an attempt to wall off the philistines, but precisely a sense of joyous connection with the common grain of American life. And finally, there was the form of the novel itself. Bellow had done his duty by the well-made novel, writing in the shadow of the accredited greats who were sanctioned both by the academy and the literary quarterlies—Flaubert, Kafka, Gide, Henry James—and again he anticipated a widespread feeling in his implicit declaration that this tradition had become a burden rather than a help. For *Augie* he looked back to another tradition—the picaresque, with its looseness of structure, its saltiness of language, its thickness of incident, its robust extroversion. And the fact that one of the greatest of all American novels (whose title is echoed by his own) itself derived from this tradition made it all the more obvious that he had hit upon the right mode for a novel that was setting out to discover America and the American dream anew.

In certain respects, Augie March is a familiar figure, an image of modern man living in a hopelessly fluid society, forced to choose an identity because he has inherited none, unable to find a place for himself. He is rootless, cut off, even (if you like) alienated. But far from responding to this situation with the usual anxiety, he is "larky and boisterous," and his rootless condition makes life endlessly adventurous and endlessly surprising. His uncertainty about his own identity, moreover, is represented as a positive advantage, leading not to the narcissistic self-involvement of a Joseph or a Leventhal, but rather to a readiness to explore the world, a generous openness to experience. Nor is his optimism superficial or blind. He understands that there are powerful arguments against his position, and he knows that optimism is a faith which, like any other, must be maintained in the teeth of the opposing evidence. "What I guess about you," one of his friends tells him, "is that you have a nobility syndrome. You can't adjust to the reality situation. . . . You want to accept. But how do you know what you're accepting? You have to be nuts to take it come one come all. . . . You should accept the data of experience." Augie's reply is significant: "It can never be right to offer to die, and if that's what the data of experience tell you, then you must get along without them."

Here, then, was the hero Bellow had been looking for since the start of his literary career; here, it seemed, was a way out of the impasse at which the mode of alienation had arrived—a way that offered the possibility of participating fully in the life of the time without loss of individuality, a way that pointed toward a fusion of mind and experience, sophistication and vitality, intelligence and power. Since this was also the way that so many of Bellow's contemporaries had marked out for themselves, it is not surprising that they should have approached *The Adventures of Augie March* with a ready disposition to take the novel's pretensions wholly at face value. Yet the truth is that like the ethos of which it was the most remarkable reflection, *Augie* was largely the product not of a state of being already achieved, but rather of an effort on Bellow's part to act as though he had already achieved it. As a test case of the buoyant attitudes of the period, in other words, *Augie* fails—and it fails mainly because its buoyancy is embodied in a character who is curiously untouched by his experience, who never changes or develops, who goes through everything yet undergoes nothing.

The strain it cost Bellow to maintain this willed buoyancy becomes most strikingly evident in the prose style he invented for *Augie*. It is a free-flowing style that makes use of three apparently incongruous rhetorical elements—cultivated, colloquial, and American-Jewish—each deriving from a different side of Augie's character and announcing, in the very fact of their having been brought together, the new wholeness of being to which Bellow had always aspired. When it works, as it does at many isolated moments in the novel, this style is capable of extraordinary effects:

> [Mama] occupied a place, I suppose, among women conquered by a superior force of love, like those women whom Zeus got the better of in animal form and who next had to take cover from his furious wife. Not that I can see my big, gentle, dilapidated, scrubbing, and lugging mother as a fugitive of immense beauty from such classy wrath . . .

But the rightness, the poise, and easy mastery of this passage are not typical of *Augie* as a whole. More often Bellow seems to be twisting and torturing the language in an almost hysterical effort to get all the juices out of it:

> The rest of us had to go to the dispensary—which was like the dream of a multitude of dentists' chairs, hundreds of them in a space as enormous as an armory, and green bowls with designs of glass grapes, drills lifted zigzag as insects' legs, and gas flames on the porcelain swivel trays—a thundery gloom in Harrison Street of limestone county buildings and cumbersome red streetcars with metal grillwork on their windows and monarchical iron whiskers of cowcatchers front and rear. They lumbered and clanged, and their brake tanks panted in the slushy brown of a winter afternoon or the bare stone brown of a summer's, salted with ash, smoke, and prairie dust, with long stops at the clinics to let off clumpers, cripples, hunchbacks, brace-legs, crutch-wielders, tooth and eye sufferers, and all the rest.

The frantic and feverish pitch betrays the basic uncertainty that I have been pointing to in the Bellow of *Augie March*: it tells us that there was simply not enough real conviction behind the attitudes out of which the novel was written. And it tells us to expect the radical shift of mood that did indeed come over Bellow in his next book, *Seize the Day*.

Probably it would be foolish to relate this change too closely to the parallel shift in mood that occurred among American intellectuals in general during the same period. Nevertheless, the parallel is worth noticing, for it suggests that the optimism of the intellectuals about America was as strained and willed as the prose of *Augie March* itself. The irrepressible doubts that lurked on the underside of the new optimism were bound to emerge once more as the dreary Eisenhower years wore on, but when they did emerge, it was in a form very different from the ones they had taken in the decades before World War II. To be sure, the old idea that the modern world was suffering from a "loss of values" came back again, but even that idea soon began to seem inadequate to account for the dimensions of the spiritual vacuum that many intellectuals saw lying beneath the surface prosperity and apparent confidence of the Eisenhower Age. The more and more frequent outbreaks of juvenile violence; the sharp rise in the consumption of narcotics (including legal drugs like tranquillizers and sleeping pills); the fantastic divorce rate; the suicides; the breakdowns—all this showed how great a gap had developed between the realities of experience in America and the moral vocabulary of the age.

It is against this background, I think, that the upsurge during the late 50's of various forms of anti-rationalism must be understood. The sudden popularity of Zen, Reichianism, and existentialism reflected the growth of a conviction that the source of our trouble lay deep in the foundations of Western civilization—deeper than politics could reach, deeper than a mere opposition to capitalist society or middle-class values could cure. We were a people so far removed from nature, so lost in abstraction, so cut off from the instinctual that only—as Norman Mailer put it—a "revolution backward toward being" could save us. Bellow, of course, has never gone as far in this direction as Mailer—he has too skeptical a mind to go far in any theoretical direction—but his last two novels, *Seize the Day* and *Henderson the Rain King*, seem to indicate an equally strong awareness on his part of the depth to which the contemporary crisis has cut. The world of *Seize the Day*, indeed, might fairly be compared with the world of the *Deer Park*, for each in its own way is an image of a society at the end of its historical term, a civilization whose particular compromise with nature has all but broken down.

Like *The Victim*, *Seize the Day* is set in New York, but if Bellow once saw the city as a tiny village holding out desperately against the surrounding jungle, here he sees it as "the end of the world, with its complexity and machinery, bricks and tubes, wires and stones, holes and heights." So far has the divorce of man from nature proceeded that "the fathers are no fathers, and the sons no sons," and money—that most refined of all abstractions—rules in place of the natural affections. Communication is no longer possible under these circumstances ("Every other man spoke a language entirely his own, which he had figured out by private thinking"), and there is no telling "the crazy from the sane, the wise from the fools, the young from the old or the sick from the well." Love has disappeared along with communication, and what remains is a world full of lonely men, "a kind of hell[or] at least a kind of purgatory. You walk on the bodies. They are all around. I can hear them cry *de profundis* and wring their hands . . . poor human beasts."

This, then, is a civilization on the edge of collapse:

Seven per cent of this country is committing suicide by alcohol. Another three, maybe, narcotics. Another sixty just fading away into dust by boredom. Twenty more who have sold their souls to the Devil. Then there's the small percentage of those who want to live. That's the only significant thing in the whole world of today. Those are the only two classes of people there are. Some want to live, but the great majority don't. . . . They don't, or else why these wars? I'll tell you more . . . The love of the dying amounts to one thing; they want you to die with them.

The central figure of the story, Tommy Wilhelm, is one of those who want to live, though it is part of Bellow's complex purpose to reveal this fact only gradually both to the reader and to Wilhelm. He is presented at first as a weak, blundering, self-destructive man riddled with self-pity and totally lacking in the resources of character that would enable him to redeem the mess he has made of his life. Only when we reach the closing scene do we realize that his desperate appeals to his father for help and his wild gamble on the commodities exchange were unconsciously motivated (like all the crucial decisions he has ever made) by a saving impulse to liberate himself from the false values that have always dominated his soul. These values are money and success, the pursuit of which has perverted a whole civilization, turning millions of people into slaves of the social system, enemies of themselves, monsters with murder in their hearts who go resentfully and hideously to their graves never knowing why life has been so bitter. Indeed, there is probably no more frightening picture of old age in literature than the one Bellow draws in *Seize the Day*—the men like Wilhelm's father meanly and coldly and selfishly clutching at his withered life, or like the retired chicken-farmer Rappaport ("I'm older even than Churchill") who sits day after day at the commodities exchange greedily waiting for a rise in rye or barley or lard. This is what the pursuit of success and money finally amounts to in the world of *Seize the Day*, and it is what Wilhelm—as he dimly comes to recognize in the closing pages—has always resisted by blundering over and over again into failure.

Because of its masterful concentration, its vividness of detail, its brilliance of characterization, and its grandeur of theme, *Seize the Day* probably deserves its reputation as the best thing Bellow has so far done. It is so good, in fact, that one wonders what prevents it from being great. My guess would be that Bellow was putting the brakes on himself in writing the story, that he allowed a certain timidity in the face of his own most powerful response to life—and I mean to life, not to the historical circumstances of the moment—to soften the impact of his material. This response, to judge by all those things in his work that carry the most conviction, is one of angry resentment and bitterness—precisely the kind of bitterness that is expressed in the terrible line in *King Lear*: "As flies are we to the wanton gods; they kill us for their sport." Even the comic side of his talent participates in this bitterness, for comedy in Bellow's fiction is almost always directed against the utopian theorizers (like Robey, Thea Fenchel, and Bateshaw in *Augie March*), who simply cannot understand how little help there is for being human. For some reason, however, Bellow has never been willing to give his bitterness free rein; he is always trying to stifle it or qualify it, and it is this refusal of anger, I believe, that robs *Seize the Day* of the great power it might have had.

The answer to Wilhelm's predicament, we are given to understand, is love, and we gather from the description of a momentary revelation he had once experienced that by love

Bellow means something like the Christians' *agapé*. And with a good many Christian writers, he seems to believe that a man's capacity to "seize the day"—that is, to live fully in the present—depends on his capacity to know himself as kin to all other men. The nature to which Bellow wishes to return in *Seize the Day* is not the instinctual nature that Norman Mailer talks about, but nature as the theologians have conceived of it: a harmonious universe ruled over by God, a universe in which man has reassumed his proper place in the cosmic hierarchy. "We are bleeding at the roots, because we are cut off from the earth and sun and stars, and love is a grinning mockery, because, poor blossom, we plucked it from its stem on the tree of Life, and expected it to keep on blooming in our civilized vase on the table." This is not, of course, Bellow; it is D. H. Lawrence. Yet the passage fairly characterizes the doctrinal core of *Seize the Day*, and another remark of Lawrence's points toward the "positive" values implied in the novel: "Augustine said that God created the universe new every day; and to the living, emotional soul this is true. Every day dawns upon an entirely new universe, every Easter lights up an entirely new glory of a new world opening in utterly new flower. And the soul of man and the soul of woman is new in the same way, with the infinite delight of life and the ever-newness of life."

But this is a theory, and Bellow, we know, is skeptical of theories, which is perhaps one reason why he puts these sentiments, cruelly vulgarized, into the mouth of Dr. Tamkin, a charlatan, a fake, and a liar. Making Tamkin the spokesman of his own views, however, is perhaps also his way of saying that today even those who know the truth are caught up in the false values of our civilization—the churches, as it were, are corrupt, the prophets are fools and probably a little crazy. Nevertheless, the fact that he is skeptical of the theory does not prevent Bellow from allowing it to inhibit the response which his story, in its primary emotional impact, demands. "You see," Tamkin tells Wilhelm, "I understand what it is when the lonely person begins to feel like an animal. When the night comes and he feels like howling from his window like a wolf." And Wilhelm agrees. "One hundred falsehoods," he says to himself of Tamkin's remarks, "but at last one truth. Howling like a wolf from the city window. No one can bear it any more. Everyone is so full of it that at last everyone must proclaim it. It! It!" What the reader waits for in *Seize the Day* is exactly this howl, some expression of wrath, some violent uproar which would release the "great knot" in Wilhelm's chest that has been strangling him by inches, and which would express the full extent of Bellow's outrage at life. It never comes. All Bellow gives us at the end is a fit of weeping that, he says, carries Wilhelm "toward the consummation of his heart's ultimate need." We have already been told what this need is—it is love. If, however, Bellow had been ruthless in following out the emotional logic of *Seize the Day*, it would almost certainly have been murder—and *Seize the Day* would almost certainly have become a great book.

In *Henderson the Rain King*, Bellow's latest novel, the ideology of love does not so much inhibit him as obscure his central intention. Returning to the loose picaresque mode of *Augie March*, Bellow tells the story of a middle-aged millionaire, the ne'er-do-well scion of an old patrician family, who runs off to Africa in a state of crisis and is transformed by a series of fantastic adventures he encounters there. The Africa of the novel bears very little relation to the real Africa; it is an imaginary place, and Bellow might have avoided a certain amount of misunderstanding if he had given it an imaginary name. Similarly, if he had presented Henderson in frankly allegorical terms instead of confusing the issue by making him a Hudson Valley aristocrat, he would not have left himself open to the charge of having failed to create a believable hero, or of having failed at the end to put Henderson's regeneration to the test back in the "real" world. In my opinion, while Henderson is obviously not believable as a Hudson Valley aristocrat, he is completely convincing as an allegorical personification of the vague malaise, the sense of aimless drift and unused energy, that seems to afflict a prosperous and spiritually stagnant society like our own. And while Henderson's regeneration cannot be accepted as a total transformation of character, it seems to me wholly credible as an *experience*, the kind of experience that religious converts speak of when they say they have been re-born.

The important question is: to what, precisely, is Henderson re-born? Here and there, and especially in the concluding pages, Bellow makes several pious gestures in the direction of Love, but this only confuses the issue even further, for if anything Henderson is saved by being re-born into more rather than less self-involvement. The transforming revelation he experiences with the help of King Dahfu is that the world from which he has fled is not to be confused with reality: reality is in the self and not in the circumstances or conditions that surround the self. "The world of facts is real, all right, and not to be altered. The physical is all there, and it belongs to science. But then there is the noumenal department, and there we create and create and create." A voice inside him had been crying "*I want! I want! I want!*" He had never known what it wanted, but now he knows:

> It wanted reality. How much unreality could it stand? . . . We're supposed to think that nobility is unreal. But that's just it. The illusion is on the other foot. They make us think we crave more and more illusions. Why, I don't crave illusions at all. They say, Think Big. Well, that's baloney of course, another business slogan. But greatness! That's another thing altogether. . . . I don't mean pride, or throwing your weight around. But the universe itself being put into us, it calls out for scope. The eternal is bonded onto us. It calls out for its share. This is why guys can't bear to be so cheap.

With *Henderson*, then, Bellow seems to have come very close to surrendering the idea that the world of postwar America is a rich and inviting world and that the strategy of alienation is—as he called it in *Dangling Man*—a fool's plea. He is still resolutely non-political, for when he talks in *Henderson* about the "world of facts" that cannot be altered, he makes no effort to exempt the world of social facts from the category of the unalterable. So, too, he is still fixed on the notion that it is only spiritual timidity or—to take another phrase from *Dangling Man*—"a weakness of imagination" that robs us of the capacity to achieve true wholeness of being, true grace of style, true poise of spirit. For all that, however, *Henderson*, properly understood, represents a further stage in Bellow's development away from the forced affirmations of *Augie March*—here, at least, as in *Seize the Day*, he writes with a sharp awareness of the extent to which the problems of contemporary life are more than merely a matter of individual pathology. What one awaits is a novel by Bellow that would unambiguously locate the source of the malaise that afflicts Joseph, Leventhal, Wilhelm, and Henderson in the institutions under which they are forced to live—in that particular "world of facts" which belongs not to science but to politics, not to nature but to history, not to the realm of the physical but to "the noumenal department" where we "create and create and create." Bellow could find no better target than this for the rage that is contained within him and

that has perhaps always been stifled only for lack of its proper object.

DANIEL FUCHS
"Saul Bellow and the Modern Tradition"
Contemporary Literature, Winter 1974, pp. 67–89

Novelists are often our best critics and nowhere more so than in the novel itself. Art may best be a criticism of life by being a criticism of art. No American writer since the war has given us as level-headed, vibrant, and true a description of contemporary life as Saul Bellow and no one has delineated so clearly and so deeply the relationship of the way we live now to what we read now, of character to ideas, personality to books. The Bellow protagonist often bears the most intense feelings through an arena of the most palpable cultural props. Survival depends equally on how he feels and what he thinks, which are inseparable. In carrying this weight of seriousness, Bellow runs counter to the popular (and populist) image of the novelist whose mistrust of ideas and even words qualifies him as still another rugged saint of adventure. In American literature physical acts are eloquent (Hemingway, Faulkner) but the reflective consciousness is often muted. But if Bellow is a novelist of intellect, he is not an intellectual novelist. He eschews the thesis novel, one which proceeds because of an idea; this he considers "French" (Gide, Sartre, Camus). Bellow sees his characters in their personal reality, sees them as selves, or better, souls, whose thought moves with the inevitability of an emotion. This is, in his view, the "Russian" way with ideas (Tolstoy, Dostoevsky). If there is something unfamiliar to the American common reader in this mind and body involvement—as opposed to one or the other—there is something perhaps even more unfamiliar to the uncommon reader in the grounds of the argument. For no one has so persistently and successfully gone against the grain of modernism, which is still a kind of orthodoxy in the universities and even the quarterlies. In this respect Bellow is the postmodernist par excellence in that his very inspiration often comes from a resistance to its celebrated aesthetic ideology, with its tendency toward monumentality and its perhaps inevitably concomitant tendency toward coldness.

Any description of this ideology had best begin with illustrations from its origin, French literature in its later nineteenth-century flowering. A radical subjectivity, an idealism of the word marks the aesthetic realism of Flaubert and symbolism of Mallarmé. "The story, the plot of a novel is of no interest to me. When I write a novel I aim at rendering a color, a shade. . . . In *Madame Bovary*, all I wanted to do was to render a grey color, the mouldy color of a wood louse's existence."[1] As Bellow has remarked, where Phaedra embodied the passion of Racine, the new aesthetic aristocrat manifested his passion in virtuosity. *Madame Bovary* is a great book partly because there is an element of charity in Flaubert's attitude toward Emma which transcends the strictures of his letters. This element is not present in *The Sentimental Education*, whose protagonist, Frederic Moreau, is the first of the nauseous heroes. Contemplating the flood of Parisian Sunday perambulators, Frederic feels "the knowledge that he was worth more than these men mitigated the fatigue of looking at them."[2] Frederic's king's-eye view, his "atrophy of heart," his self-destructive reduction of illusion (Flaubert seems to be engaged in homeopathic self-cure) appear again and again. Modern life appears as a wasteland. "As for the living, we will let the servants do that," concludes the aesthete artist in *Axel's Castle*. And Eliot's "young man carbuncular," which Allen Tate has called the high-water mark of modern poetry, shows that the servants may not even do that.

Like most saints, Flaubert was fortunate in the choice of his disciples. Martyrdom was converted into religion—the religion of art. In *Dubliners*, Joyce's style of "scrupulous meanness" was a nod to the master as were the variations on Flaubertian themes: the death of illusion in "Araby," the irony of "Grace," the aesthetic virtuosity of a story about still another unlived life in "The Dead." *The Portrait of the Artist as a Young Man* may be viewed as a resolution of the Flaubertian problem. For subjectivity to assert any kind of real freedom under modern conditions, it must be extraordinary. The tragedy of Emma Bovary is that she is ordinary. In *Portrait* heroism resides in the character as well as the work of art. In its extremity, the heroism develops into a self-deification, clearly echoing Flaubert's letters in its theory of impersonality. To the extent that they make style the subject of their books, subordinating personality to form, character to artifact, event to irony, action to words, making experience the reflection of some higher truth, these writers are reducing the historical to the point where it is merely a reflection of a perfection which can never be known. This is the imaginative utopianism of the modern. To the degree that the actual is debased, the ideal is exalted. Flaubert and Dedalus are like "a god"—god over what? Stephen thinks of himself as a "priest of eternal imagination." But eternal and imagination are logically contradictory. When, in his review of *Ulysses*, Eliot says that Joyce's method works "towards making the modern world possible for art," we see where the cart stands in relation to the horse. The modernist aesthetic invented the New Criticism, in which judgments of form preceded judgments of meaning. This movement on the part of an aesthetic aristocracy was an emasculation of rational, experience-oriented, liberal man. Subsequently, in place of history we found myth; in place of Freud, Jung. Commenting adversely on this, Bellow says that the Jungian primordial experience brings illumination through drill, orthodoxy, and imitation, so that the golden moment will return. Weeping by the waters of Babylon, we sadly live.[3] Eliot and Jung are cast in the same mold. Jung's comments on art subordinate the merely personal to the higher impersonality. The artist is not a self but a medium. In its most extreme form this appears in Rimbaud: "It is a mistake to say: I think. One ought to say: I am thought. . . . *I* is someone else."[4] It is no accident that Rimbaud also says, "Man is finished! Man has played all the roles." Rimbaud, the arch-hipster, in "Bateau Ivre" took the archetypal bad trip in search, no doubt, of the prelapsarian. What modernism often unfolds, what Flaubert, Joyce, and Eliot offer us, is the secular equivalent of Original Sin (in Eliot, of course, we later get the religious "equivalent"). Joyce is the greatest of these writers in that he often transfigures his characters in the face of this condition. Like Eliot, in "Ash Wednesday," though in a totally different ambience, they achieve an inconclusive purgatorial nobility.

Volumes have been written in support of the greatness of *Ulysses* by exegetes of the sacred text, yet the book, great as it is, illustrates the weakness of modernism. In one sense, *Ulysses* represents a move back to *Madame Bovary* in that the youthful energy of Stephen, sublimated and idealized as it is, comes to nothing. Though Joyce is left with only the ordinary voices of Dublin, the greatness of *Ulysses* is that the ordinary is seen to be heroic. This is made possible by Joyce's rejection of Stephen's king's-eye view, since the ordinary, Joyce would have us believe, transfigures even him. Nonetheless the fa-

mous reconciliation at the end of *Ulysses* between the "father" and the "son" exists as a brilliant rhetorical pattern rather than an experience, for two men urinating together in the street is hardly the moral equivalent of an artistry which exhibits the most dazzling aesthetic virtuosity of any novel ever written, and Molly's recollection of Bloom, moving though it is, will scarcely change the status quo between them. Despite the sort of honor Joyce displays towards his characters, everyone exists in a moonlike relation to emotion and all remain almost as isolated as the characters in *Madame Bovary*. In *Ulysses* Joyce is a student past master but the gap between words and deeds is if anything even more glaring with such a weight cast on such an inconclusive frame. Stephen, the character who might have been noblest, falls hardest, while Bloom, our Ulysses, has a mind remarkable for its activity, but even more for its passivity. And the shape of this quester's life—the sense of significant event—is amorphous. As Bellow once remarked to me, for Bloom, going to a funeral resembles taking a bath. In *Finnegans Wake* we get the logical extreme of Joyce's aesthetic—not a day in the life of everyman, but all days in the life of all men. In trying to express all of history, Joyce becomes ahistorical, as myth obscures individuality in an ambience of imposed fatality. In this astonishing reading of the collective unconscious, language itself must be a merely historical description; so Joyce invents a new one. *Finnegans Wake* shows us that it is not Stephen Dedalus but Joyce himself who is a priest of eternal imagination. If only there were one.

"The last sick sufferer from the complaint of Flaubert." So does D. H. Lawrence describe Thomas Mann in a review of *Death in Venice*: Flaubert "stood away from life as from a leprosy. And Thomas Mann, like Flaubert, feels vaguely that he has in him something finer than ever physical life revealed. . . . And so, with real suicidal intention, like Flaubert's, he sits, a last too-sick disciple, reducing himself grain by grain to the statement of his own disgust, patiently, self-destructively, so that his statement at least may be perfect in a world of corruption."[5] If the relatively balanced *Death in Venice* elicits this blast against aestheticism, what would Lawrence have said of *Doctor Faustus*? In Aschenbach, perversity, disintegration, and disease, the revenge of the Dionysian, is attended by a nobler sense of life's possibility, in which a generous illumination, an enlargement of soul, accompanies the destruction of the body. This cannot be said of Mann's last artist-hero, Adrian Leverkühn.

The remarkable thing about the encounter of the modern Faustus with the devil is the condition of the pact. Faustus will sell his soul, not for knowledge, not for worldly power, not for Satanic freedom, not for experience, not for pleasure, not for love—but for art. But what is art without these qualities? When this Faustus makes his pact, he is losing not only his salvation, he is losing his humanity. The Promethean is reduced to the aesthetic as art is reduced to a merely intellectual version of the demonic. The crucial clause in the contract is one that the modern artist-hero is all too familiar with, involving as it does alienation from ordinary life. Hell profits him, says the devil in archaic "Lutheran" German: "if you renay all living creature, all the Heavenly Host and all men. . . . Thou maist not love. . . . Thy life shall be cold."[6] Later in life, Leverkühn, in a fit of mellowness, does wish to marry, but in terms which do not belie the pact: "Not only for the sake of comfort, to be better bedded down; but most of all because [I hope] to get from it good and fine things for [my] working energy and enthusiasm, for the human content of [my] future work."[7] Like Eliot, he wishes to make life possible for art, for life is cold but art is warm. The devil purveys "towering flights and illuminations

. . . colossal admiration for the made thing . . . the thrills of self-veneration" which, as we have seen, are indistinguishable from self-hatred: "yes, of exquisite horror of himself, in which he appears to himself like an inspired mouthpiece, as a godlike monster," who sinks into "unfruitful melancholy but also into pains and sickness."[8] In his assault on "the bourgeois order" and "bourgeois raffinement . . . a culture fallen away from cult," the devil opts for a new mythic barbarism; "excess, paradox and mystic passion, the utterly unbourgeois ordeal."[9] Serenus Zeitblom, the devoted humanist, shrewdly sees a connection between aestheticism and barbarism and understands when one of Leverkühn's masterworks is reproached for both "blood boltered barbarism" and "bloodless intellectuality." (Appropriately, it is called *Apocalypse* and signals the end of the world; the aesthetic is predictable: "in its dissonance stands for the expression of everything lofty, solemn, pious, everything of the spirit; while consonance and firm tonality are the world of hell, in this context a world of banality and commonplace.")[10] *Doctor Faustus* carries to one logical extreme the reactionary ideology implicit and sometimes explicit in the modern tradition. These tendencies mirrored an even more sinister combination of "blood boltered barbarism" and "bloodless intellectuality"—political fascism.

There was a time when the poet could be compared to the lunatic and lover. In *Doctor Faustus* the devil says that "the artist is the brother of the criminal and madman,"[11] a significant shift. The artist-hero, as we have seen, may be beyond the pale of ordinary life, beyond good and evil as it is defined in "conventional" morality, a morality which is found wanting, if it is found at all. The artist appears as the creator of a higher morality, a superman, an immoralist. But what if the exceptional man is not an artist? What of the undignified aspect of immoralism? Where then do his explosive insights flare? Where does this energy, often plebian, go? In the character of Julien Sorel, the first of the plebian, immoralist criminals, *The Red and the Black* provides an original answer. The central assumption of the book—a romantic one—is that however devious the brilliant *ambitieux* Julien is, his deviousness is justified given the social circumstances. Julien is an immoralist insofar as he conquers the world he despises, but the "murder" and sequel to it show that he is not an immoralist at heart; the real reason for his death is his intransigent rejection of the value of class distinction. As usual, there is a sort of premodernist balance in Stendhal in that energy and morality are not yet totally disjunctive.

They appear to be in Raskolnikov, in whom the crime, though premeditated, is impersonal, symbolic if you will. Like Sorel, this penniless, powerless, incipient intellectual lives in the shadow of Napoleon. His breakthrough into "heroism," a grim caricature of power, stems from his contempt for ordinary life. The fatal catalyst is his obsession to find out whether "he was a louse like everybody else or a man," whether he could be a Napoleonic superman beyond good and evil. The didactic point of *Crime and Punishment* is that crime must be punished, that the superman, however sorrowfully approximated, must fail. Dostoevsky's account of "bourgeois" morality (e.g. Luzhin) is, however, Nietzschean. And the dramatic force of Raskolnikov's contempt for ordinary life (including his own) has, not surprisingly, often been taken as the vital energy of the book. His immoralism has found imitators.

Gide's Lafcadio is one of these. What is passional in Dostoevsky becomes theoretical in Gide, as the desperate longing for freedom becomes a meditation on the gratuitous act. The murder of Amedée has no dramatic motive other than Lafcadio's desire to prove his freedom, but the psychological motive

is clear and familiar—he is still another protagonist with a king's-eye view of ordinary life. Genevieve, his Sonia, is attracted to him because he is "hedged in by all the ludicrous conventions of their world,"[12] and, in this *sotie*, Gide presents us with nothing but ludicrous conventions (family, church, literature, science). Although we would never know it from the book itself, Gide did not intend this to be an affirmation of nihilism; it has, however, often been taken as such. Lafcadio's attitude, in a minor key, is part of the new popular culture. When Phoebe Zeitgeist, being murdered, asks, "Why? What have I ever done to you?" she is told: "Poor child! Be not so naive as to believe that cruelty and violence must necessarily be motivated! The malicious act, set apart from the commonplace, lackluster treadmill of goal-oriented drives, attains a certain purity of its own being."[13] What Lafcadio shows us is crime as aestheticism. Who would have thought he would become a folk hero?

Though Camus' Meursault has a venerable lineage, his fate reveals a certain purity of nihilistic design which is new. "One might fire, or not fire—and it would come to absolutely the same thing."[14] Meursault's crime is not an isolated event, but part of a general soullessness: he is totally devoid of piety or feeling at his mother's funeral; he is willing to marry his girl if she is keen on it, but answers "no" when she asks him if he thinks marriage is serious. Since we have in Meursault a rigidity, a mean excess, a human being acting like a machine, why isn't this book a comedy? Why aren't our sides splitting? Because the author's assumption—and the assumption of the age?—is that nobility attaches to the belief in nothing; its honesty transcends the stupid normative judgments made upon it. In a typical modernist reversal, the center of judgment, common sense, is seen as ludicrous. While this is true enough in many instances of our lives, the intensely sympathetic portrayal of murderous nihilism breaks new ground. "It's common knowledge that life isn't worth living anyhow,"[15] says our hero. Isn't that what Flaubert said? What is most disturbing about Camus' novel is that the immoralist position *in extremis* has become the property of everyman, for the starkness of the novel proceeds from the sense that there is no aesthetic release, no superman alternative. Camus is in the modern tradition in that in *The Stranger* he has written a book beyond which one cannot go. In its modernist extremity it is still another novel in which a tradition comes to an end.

The central thrust of Bellow's fiction[16] is to deny nihilism, immoralism, and the aesthetic view. He wishes to make art possible for life. Where the artist-hero sought isolation, the Bellow protagonist longs for community, and ironic distance gives way to the nearness of confession as we are on a personal standard. The *noli me tangere* of modernism gives way to "I want, I want," the cold exquisiteness of modernist art to a superjournalistic accessibility. This is the formal meaning of the breakthrough of *Augie March*, where stasis gives way to speed, radiance to ordinary daylight, spatial form to temporal form; narrative is back and the formal meaning reflects a moral one. Augie's excited belief in the "axial lines of life," though somewhat undercut by the subsequent narrative, is typical of the reassessment of common possibility which is the burden of Bellow's mature work. If the artist-hero proper is nowhere present in Bellow, what may be called the citizen-hero is often there: the dangling man and Augie have hopes for a colony and a school; Herzog wants "politics in the Aristotelian sense"; Artur Sammler had desired an international fellowship. The aesthetic gives over to the ethical, the artist to the thinker—one may even say, the beautiful (in the French sense of *le beau*) to the good. Indifferent to myth, Bellow brings us into the wildness of current history, the liberal arena. For authenticity of vision we are given not the collective unconscious but the "glittering eye" of full historical consciousness, since the emphasis is not on the artist but on the event, not on "divine impulse . . . surface polish . . . the law of numbers"[17] but on issues, description, and emotion recollected in some semblance of tranquility. Bellow is the heir of the first modernists, the romantics, rather than the archmodernists. Like Keats, he is certain of nothing but "the holiness of the heart's affections"; he has not lost belief in the self or even the soul. In Bellow we may have trouble locating good and evil, but we are never beyond it. Immoralist activity, the ultimate nihilistic act, may be temptations, but they are temptations which it is necessary to overcome. Perversity is not a metaphor of release from civilized inhibition, as it is in *Death in Venice* and its bedfellows, but a form of *mishigas*, tolerable comic madness. Bellow, like others in the postmodern period, illustrates what one wit has called the power of positive sex. What is perhaps the quintessential symbolist poem, "L'Après-midi d'un faune," in its rendering of a fugitive animal sensuality, is about coitus interruptus. The effective missionary style of Herzog reminds us that morality pays.

The general characteristics of modernism—alienation, fragmentation, break with tradition, isolation and magnification of subjectivity, threat of the void, weight of vast numbers and monolithic impersonal institutions, hatred of civilization itself—are obviously authentic in one way or another. Any definition of postmodernism assumes them, as does any postmodern writer. What Bellow does is resist total absorption by them and repudiate the modernist orthodoxy of "experimentation" which derives from this view, the aesthetic ideology already described. Above all, he tries to dramatize states of emotion and consciousness which prove that there is more to it than that. His prose—of course it varies from book to book—reflects the tension involved in this resistance, balanced as it is between affirmation and skepticism, the manic and the depressive, action and revery, common sense and mystical feeling, the ordinary and the abstruse, the colloquial and the learned, Yiddish inflection and latinate elongation. From *Augie March* on there is always an energetic temperament, a personal voice speaking through the contraries, making them one. There is neither the sort of irony that implies the split between public and private, nor is there coterie appeal. A writer for whom the mundane does not eclipse subjectivity but intensifies it, Bellow, in this sense, transcends Stephen Spender's distinction between the modernist novel of sensibility and the antimodernist novel of sociology,[18] the novel of poetry and the novel of prose. While Pound was trying to purge the language of poetry of abstraction and to make poetry as well-written as prose, Joyce and Virginia Woolf, in reaction to Bennett, Galsworthy, and Wells, showed that prose could be as well-written as poetry. Bellow shows that prose can be as well-written as prose. His creative repudiation of the modernists makes him a virtuoso in spite of himself.

But one must choose between Spender's categories, and Bellow is in the camp of the prose contemporaries, not the poetic moderns; the realists, not the visionaries. He has always been critical of what he calls the "dismal revolutionary style" derived from modernist visionaries and their belief that man is finished. In the followers of the classical visionaries, Rimbaud and Lawrence, he notes these characteristics: "trance, dream-utterance, androgynous, homosexual, antinomian, squalor, mesmerism, charlatanism."[19] Shamanism is part of the current dislocation. But self-appointed grace is always suspect in that it implies too easily, as we have seen, legions of the damned.

Bellow sees Lawrence's views of sex as analogous to the antinomian salvation through art: "There are the saved and the damned, the elect and the lost, the orgastic and the impotent."[20] It is characteristic of Bellow to prefer Lawrence's art to his doctrine, to admire *The Lost Girl* and to dislike *The Plumed Serpent*.[21] The relationship between Alvina and Ciccio is a margin of hard-won authenticity, and Alvina is so well-realized partly because her past is so well-documented. The portrait of Mr. Houghton and his Manchester House is one of the best things in Lawrence. In *The Lost Girl* Bellow is won over by the triumph of an instinctively ascertained fulfillment, but the ideology of sex, the absurd "political" dimension, shows us the hubris of the visionary. Where the doubt of Alvina becomes the pervasive disgust of Kate, Lawrence needs a system to convince himself, so, the world failing her, Kate flees into myth. Don Ramon is the "Natural Aristocrat" who will be "Savior" to the mean peons: "One must disentangle oneself from persons and personalities," he says, "to turn beyond them to the greater life."[22] This is protofascism. It is well and good to say that Lawrence was not "interested" in politics—but politics, to paraphrase Trotsky, is interested in Lawrence. Bellow has always insisted that the deepest truth is to be found in the personal. In this sense, his rejection of *The Plumed Serpent* parallels his rejection of *Doctor Faustus*, of which he has said: "We cannot continue to build in every novel such total systems in order that we may know what, for example, a woman feels when her husband deserts her, what a man feels on his death-bed. We must take our chances on a belief in the psychic unity of mankind."[23] The monumentality and coldness of modernism, then, is to be countered by the primacy of merely personal emotion. The Bellow novel generally brings a reduction in scale for a corresponding gain in human warmth.

Bellow's first paragraph as a publishing novelist is an attack on modernism. In what is an obvious allusion to Hemingway, the protagonist complains that emotion, inner life, is suppressed in "an era of hard boiled-dom."[24] Hemingway (in his irony, restraint, mistrust of emotion, disillusioned style, deflation of public rhetoric—all related to his tough-guy manner) is still another disciple of Flaubert.[25] When Joseph says, "most serious things are closed to the hard-boiled," he is valuing emotion in a way which makes sense when describing Bellow's career as a whole. But, considering Joseph's inner life, one may well choose the tough-guy alternative. Full of the modern disgust and self-pity, he is cast as a victim in a landscape that might be out of Flaubert or *Dubliners*. Yet he has the energy to write in the confessional style, and the virtue of the psychological age in which he is living—honesty. Here is established, albeit in a minor key, Bellow's first link to the romantic "I," Rousseau, Goethe, Wordsworth, Stendhal, those "who felt no shame at making a record of their inward transactions" (*DM*, p. 9).

Things were not always bad for Joseph. The alter-ego, the healthy man he was last year, had an essentialist view rather like Bellow's own. "In all principal ways, the human spirit must have been the same," (*DM*, p. 25) he says. Related to this, he expresses the *amor fati*: "In a sense everything is good because it exists. Or, good or not good, it exists, it is ineffable, and for that reason, marvelous" (*DM*, p. 29). He asks himself, "How should a good man live?" and plans "a colony of the spirit," but a bad party shatters the idea of a colony and separates the old enlightenment Joseph from the new modern one. Joseph quotes Hobbes. What particularly bothers him about the party is the victimization of a girl through hypnotism: "it had been so savage because its object could not resist" (*DM*, p. 57). Passivity, victimization, nonentity—modern qualities too real to let his subconscious rest—drive him invariably into a rage; indeed, this is the main line of action though he is scarcely conscious of it. He insists on being recognized by a functionary of the Communist Party to which he once belonged because he fears nonentity. In his spite, in his self-hatred, in his mixture of intellection and powerlessness, in his flair for the embarrassing violent flare-up, he is like Dostoevsky's underground man (from the book of that title to which *Dangling Man* has obvious technical affinities as well). In a moment of rare serenity, Joseph is moved by Piatagorsky playing Haydn but is displeased by his niece's Cugat records. She says, "What you call me or think doesn't matter" (*DM*, p. 70), which hits him where he can least afford to be hit. When she becomes more explicit, "Dirty no-account" (*DM*, p. 71), he spanks her. Later, his smug, profession-oriented friend Abt makes him reflect on the declining idea of greatness, a legacy of romantic (secular) salvation with its images of heroic immoralism and benign criminality. From the "great sadness" of Werther and Don Juan to "the great ruling images of Napoleon" to "those murderers who had the right over victim because they were greater than the victims to men who felt privileged to approach others with a whip" (*DM*, p. 89) and so on until we get to Hollywood mass culture, we "have been taught there is no limit to what a man can be" (*DM*, p. 88). The rest of the fragmentary story shows us that there is only limit. The self-pity becomes so oppressive that when Joseph tells the Spirit of Alternatives, "I'm a chopped and shredded man," we want to get him that opening in the cereal factory. Joseph proves too weak to be free and welcomes the regimentation of army life. At one point, thinking of a painter friend, he says: "Those acts of imagination save him. . . . My talent, if I have any at all, is for being a citizen, or what is today called, most apologetically, a good man" (*DM*, p. 91). But regimentation remains the height of his goodness.

Similarly, in *The Victim*, the central character overcomes apathy in a tawdry urban landscape. Despite considerable temptation to the contrary, he will not accept the notion that man is nothing and that we are not responsible for one another. Here regimentation is not the answer because dignity—the way between superman indifference and underground man envy— is. The real break from modernist apathy occurs in *Augie March*, for Augie does not have to choose dignity; it is a quality of the world he inhabits. The city, the neighborhood, the family, the affair—all have reality. In writing a picaresque novel, Bellow is committed to a world whose surfaces are worth beholding, whose activities are worth recording. The one is involved with the many, as the marginal man goes through a panoply of social types. Ambition, passion, soul, fate—these are living concerns. The claustral quality of his first novels gives way to a wide open world, depression to larkiness, obsession to ease. In proclaiming his unity with the large, expansive quality of the older novel, Bellow is trying to bypass the modernist syndrome. In Augie, Bellow attempts to portray the most estranged of modern qualities—charm.

If Augie is a rogue, he is a thinking rogue. His civilized voice tells us that his education has gone well beyond the college of hard knocks into the school of soft abrasions. The tone of the novel, therefore, is one of qualified buoyancy: "I am an American, Chicago born—Chicago, that somber city" (*AM*, p. 3). If, as he asserts, in the face of the oppressive doctrine of determinism, that "a man's character is his fate" (*AM*, p. 3), he is well-aware that "his fate, or what he settles for, is also his character" (*AM*, p. 154). With his keen eye for corruption, he sees that Simon's closed moneyed milieu and its resultant mere "success" is a perversion of the heroic will.

Despite the break, the brothers cannot help feeling for each other. Though Augie recognizes the "world-wide Babylonishness" (*AM*, p. 70), he will not believe that "we are at the dwarf end of all times" (*AM*, p. 60), will not accept the modern cult of the past. If he were capable of being a disciple, he would compare Einhorn to Caesar, Machiavelli, or Ulysses. Bellow sees history alive in even the minor, passing character, like Mr. Kreindl, the Klabyasch player, who is seen in his Napoleonic aspect. Similarly, Bellow suspends the ironic attitude. When Grandma Lausch tidies her corset "to take the eye of a septuagenarian Vronsky or Des Grieux" (*AM*, p. 15), she is seen not with contempt but with affection. Even when she may deserve contempt, as in her paranoid farewell, Augie would rather think of her noble admonition to be a somebody. The desire to be a somebody—this is at least half of Einhorn's greatness: the refusal to be a victim although fate seems almost to have made him one.

Just as he rejects the past as a golden age, utopianism of any sort is suspect in Augie's view. Thea's believing that "there must be something better than what people call reality" (*AM*, p. 316) is an ominous indication of her self-enclosed version of reality. Augie tags along uxoriously and must sooner or later be victimized. Basteshaw, the utopian who has "created life" (*AM*, p. 509) and the solution to all the ills the flesh is heir to, is a brute in his personal life and subjugates Augie to his will. As he falls asleep in the mad lifeboat, Augie has the chance to kill him but nurses him instead, feeling pity for him. If Augie keeps his bearings through all the conflicting realities that people seem to like to impose on him, it is because he is in touch with "the axial lines of life" (*AM*, pp. 454 f.), an intuitive knowledge expressed in unabashed traditional abstractions— "Truth, love, bounty, usefulness, harmony." Since life itself perpetuates human value man doesn't have to die to be reborn, like Osiris, a wasteland mainstay. In a related idea, Augie later thinks: "I don't know who this saint was who woke up, lifted his face, opened his mouth, and reported on his secret dream that blessedness covers the whole Creation but covers it thicker in some places than in others. Whoever he was, it's my great weakness to respond to such dreams. This is the *amor fati*, that's what it is, or mysterious adoration of what occurs" (*AM*, pp. 526 f.). Considering the difficulties he has been experiencing with his wife, Stella, one detects a note of unearned optimism, but like the old Jacqueline dreaming of Mexico, it is the hallmark of this *ingénu* to "refuse to live a disappointed life" (*AM*, p. 536).

Seize the Day may be considered a reaction to the somewhat excessive exuberance of *Augie March*. If *Augie March* was his clearest rejection of modernism to date, *Seize the Day* seems to be in a phase of agreement with its negative power. It is his most piercing study of alienation, of the depravity of bourgeois society—the radical's Bellow. But if *Seize the Day* is about the alienation of a good man, the goodness is there and not ironically given, for Tommy's vision of love in the subway is a strumming of the axial lines. Similarly, when his wife drives at him in her impersonal, mercenary way, Tommy says, "Thou shalt not kill! Don't you remember that" (*SD*, p. 112). Above all, the image of the dead man—a surrogate for humanity, for his father (whom he has just seen in that position in the steam room), and for himself as well—brings an upwelling of sympathy and pain before the fact of mortality. "The consummation of his heart's ultimate need" are the tears that betoken the burning need for human connection. Norman Podhoretz has suggested that the story would have been better if Tommy had murdered his father, but Podhoretz was not aware of the symbolic meaning of this act for Bellow. A work of great force, *Seize the Day* is possibly Bellow's most perfectly realized work; consequently, some think it his very best. But I believe that the breakthrough into a larger, wilder, aggrandizing subjectivity that we get in *Henderson the Rain King* and *Herzog* makes the next phase of his work his most original and most valuable.

Bellow has commented that Henderson, "the absurd seeker of high qualities," is the character most like him.[26] Although the scene is Africa, *Henderson the Rain King* is a personal idyll. Myth serves the cause of personal transcendence; the primitive, the voice of civilization; the heart of darkness, the heart of light. As some of the critics have noticed it is a parody of Conrad, Lawrence, Hemingway, rather than another note on the decline of the West. Dahfu encourages Henderson in the belief "that chaos doesn't run the whole show. That this is not a sick and hasty ride, helpless, through a dream into oblivion" (*HRK*, p. 175). The Covent Garden school of anthropology, comically employed, yields not a wasteland but some measure of fruition; instead of the Fisher King, the Rain King. In his movement from innocence to experience, from the Arnewi to the Wariri, the voice of wisdom is partly the voice of Blake. Henderson's cure, such as it is, owes much to a romantic, vitalistic naturalism. Henderson can think of Dahfu as "a true artist" and a superman in his benign aspect, as when he tells the threatening tribesmen: "Sometimes these great men go beyond themselves. Like Caesar or Napoleon or Chaka the Zulu. You ought to be glad that he's not a Chaka and won't knock you off" (*HRK*, p. 251). Here Henderson defends the voice of civilization and the tablets he wishes to break embody what seems to him a harsh, ritualistic primitivism. Henderson is transformed by Dahfu to the extent that he becomes a "Beer" rather than a "Becomer." This accounts for his giving up the violin, an event symbolic of his transformation: "*I wanted to raise myself into another world. My life and deeds were a prison*" (*HRK*, p. 284). In escaping to Africa Henderson exorcises the escapist in himself.

In *Henderson the Rain King* and *Herzog* Bellow is offering us the new comedy, one which he sees beginning with Svevo's *Confessions of Zeno*. Introspection, self-knowledge, hypochondria, so solemnly treated in the modern tradition, are here the subject of humor. The novelist enjoys laughing at himself, as he does at others. "The inner life, the 'unhappy consciousness,' the management of personal life, 'alienation'—all the sad questions for which the late romantic writer reserved a special tone of disappointment and bitterness, are turned inside-out by the modern comedian. Deeply subjective self-concern is ridiculed. *My* feelings, *my* early traumas, *my* moral seriousness, *my* progress, *my* sensitivity, *my* fidelity, *my* guilt—the modern [read contemporary] reader is easily made to laugh at all of these."[27] (Bellow gives the population explosion, the political and scientific revolutions, wars, failures of religion as reasons for the change.) Bellow sees, for example, *Lolita* as a reworking of *Death in Venice*, with Nabokov mocking the Nietzschean, Freudian theme. "Humbert is not impressed by sickness, nor does he associate it with genius; perversity is a concept from the whiskered past with its notions of normalcy." That is, perversity as a sign of a special fate, normalcy being associated with dumb health. The new comedy is "our only relief from the long-prevalent mood of pessimism, discouragement and low seriousness (the degenerate effect of the ambition for high seriousness) . . . the comic spirit is also the spirit of reason opposing the popular orgy of wretchedness in modern literature." In saying this, in appealing to a norm of rationality, Bellow is reversing the dark, outsider strain of comedy which, in many variants and tones, from desperation to gaiety, con-

stitutes the dominant strain of the modern tradition. Bellow is appealing to a community which apparently exists. *Herzog* and *Lolita*, perhaps the two best American novels since the war, are also two of the most truly read and widely popular. *Herzog* seems the better book in that the comic intention is nowhere mitigated by a diminished seriousness in the conception of the central self and climactic action.

The "plot" of *Herzog* is given in the first paragraph. What is important is the dramatization of consciousness, the movement toward recovery, the clairvoyance of a comic tone. *Herzog* begins in gloom and ends in light. The physical action of the book runs parallel and is at one point identical to the shift in consciousness. The flexible third person-I narrator, taken over from Donleavy's *The Ginger Man*, another postmodern comedy of consciousness, gives us maximum illumination. We view Herzog and view Herzog viewing Herzog. The most brilliant innovation is the renovation of the epistolary technique, allowing as it does a blending of discursiveness and intimacy, the argumentative and the personal, *kulturkampf* and the *cri de coeur*. Ideas are never free of the passional element and learning wears a common grace. In his Kant and Hegel, he wants his lox and bagel. No system is substituted for human response, nor do the ideas direct the psychological states. Eventually, the private content of the letters attains the positive outlook of the rather consistently elaborated ideas (though, tonally, the idea-letters move from tension to tranquility). The pathos of the letters is heightened by the fact that they are never sent.

As private man and as scholar Herzog battles the wasteland outlook. He too senses the axial lines of life: "his study was supposed to have ended with a new angle on the modern condition, showing how life could be lived by renewing universal connections; overturning the last of the Romantic errors about the uniqueness of the Self; revising the old Western, Faustian ideology; investigating the social meaning of Nothingness" (*H*, p. 39). Here Herzog attacks nihilism, the aesthetic aristocracy, immoralism, and existentialist dehumanization, indicating that the revision of the Faustian ideology would be in the direction of Goethe (including, of course, the rejection of Mann); accordingly, he later refers to his new energy as "a Faustian spirit of discontent and universal reform." Herzog's rejection of Heidegger's "fall into the quotidian" is another variant of his resistance to Nothingness, his refusal to give up on ordinary life. In this vein, he chastises his friend Shapiro for "a merely aesthetic critique of modern history" (*H*, p. 75), derived doubtless from Burckhardt and Nietzsche, with their contempt for mass democracy. Nietzsche has Herzog's qualified admiration; it is that he has become debased, the master of those whose view is "aesthetic"—Lafcadio, Dr. Faustus, Hulme, Pound, Eliot—which Herzog finds distracting. To have assumed that "the deterioration of language and its debasement was tantamount to dehumanization led straight to cultural fascism" (*H*, p. 76). Though Herzog can give a certain assent to Hulme's rejection of romantic "dampness," he recognizes that, for all his degeneracy, Rousseau had an openness, an honesty, a sense of himself, that made him large, larger than his detractors: "I do not see what we can answer when he says 'Je sens mon coeur et je connais les hommes'" (*H*, p. 129). Corollary to the wasteland aesthetic is "the new utopian history, an idyll, comparing the present to an imaginary past, because we hate the world as it is" (*H*, p. 163). Our self-awareness has indeed been purchased at a great cost to instinct. But when we then fabricate a golden past, the only outlet for inspiration in the absence of it becomes a "negative transcendence" or kind of immoralism: "This is pursued in philosophy and literature as well as in sexual experience, or with the aid of narcotics, or in 'philosophical,' 'gratuitous' crime and similar paths of horror" (*H*, p. 164). The immoralist "tradition" from Sade to Mailer, from Raskolnikov to Lafcadio to Meursault is included herein. Herzog refuses to give credence to Proudhon's belief that "God is *the* evil," thereby rejecting the immoralist view that everything is possible.

How do these complex but familiar ideas relate to the central physical action? *Herzog* can be described as the story of a murder which does not take place. We have been speaking of the idea content of *Herzog* in a way that is necessarily restrictive of the novel as a whole, for the murder scene—like the portraits of Gersbach, Mady, and Herzog—is comic. Herzog with his antique gun zeroes in on the villainous Gersbach—who has just given his daughter a bath! "Herzog saw faint wisps of powder that floated over Gersbach's stooping head. His red hair worked up and down. He was scouring the tub. Moses might have killed him now" (*H*, p. 257). But, of course, no; "the tenderness of such a buffoon to a little child" and the thought that they too can bring up a little child mitigates his contempt. The triumph of Herzog is that he refuses to see them as wasteland characters; the taking of a life has meaning, since life has meaning. In his actions as in his thoughts, then, Herzog rejects the nihilist view. This scene is given by a master of the new comedy in which, as Bellow says, deeply subjective self-concern is ridiculed. The release Herzog feels after his decision is psychological as well as moral, for he is not trapped in his ego.

Is Ramona the answer? Not, in the last analysis, any more than her Marcuse or Brown; sexual utopianism is simply the loveliest modernist falsification. Herzog is left with an intellectual and emotional balance that can only be called affirmation. His prayer to God is another version of the *amor fati*, which is itself an instinctive rejection of the modernist negative apocalypse.

The comedy and intellectuality of *Herzog* is rounded out by a tone of personal elegy vis-à-vis Herzog's familial past. His father, like Simon Dedalus, is an elaborate failure, but this does not at all dispel the strong feeling of son for father, or father Herzog's depiction as a man whose "I" had such dignity. Similarly, like an anti-Meursault, he feels his mother's death as no one else can. "Whom did I ever love as I loved them?" (*H*, p. 147) says Herzog, yet, the weakness of excessive dwelling on this deep filial emotion is known to the depressive Herzog. Here, as elsewhere, however, Bellow is affirming universal connections at the risk of being square.

On the face of it *Mr. Sammler's Planet* looks as if it might be a work similar to *Herzog* in that its central intelligence is an introspective man, whose professional life, to say nothing of his personal life, is something of a shambles. Another man whose allegiance to certain deeply felt traditional intuitive conceptions carries the day in the face of the dual assault of aestheticism and utopianism. Again Bellow makes no compromises with his reader, rendering in detail the contemporary metropolitan climate—one of violently conflicting ideas which are inseparable from emotions. But there are great changes. Bellow has left behind the subjective, lyrical quality of *Herzog* and *Henderson the Rain King*, the "special comedy" of these central characters, in a book whose times are darker, whose protagonist is more of a witness than an agent. When the focus of madness is in the age rather than the hero, we do not need the embodiment of a powerful, crazy style but the preserver of a quiet sanity that will hold. There is, in other words, an increasing objectivity in the new work, a movement away from the dramatization of obsessions; accordingly, the third person nar-

rative illustrates the greater difference between author and protagonist. What dramatizes it even more is the fact that this is Bellow's first postsexual creation, a desired distancing effect being achieved by the creation of a seventy-two-year-old character. This can be viewed not only as a quality of the nature of things but as witness to a life whose scars and tensions have not left much room for the ease of sex. Think of old Einhorn, the Commissioner, "still an old galliard, with Buffalo Bill vandyke . . . he swanked around, still healthy of flesh, in white suits, looking things over with big sex-amused eyes" (*AM*, p. 61).

Sammler is the witness to a universal dissonance. In the rendering of a broad, social panorama this is Bellow's harshest book. New York has always been an enervating experience for the Bellow protagonist. Chicago has been relatively normal, but here the malevolence is palpable. The pollution, the guarded approaches, the ripped-out, urine-smelling phone booths, the universal dog dung—this is only the landscape of a deeper rot. Most important, it is clear that the rot is a result of the oblique triumph of modernism, a triumph of sorts, for the aesthetic aristocracy is now the aesthetic mob: Mallarmé is spinning in his grave; Raskolnikov has a fellowship; nihilism is alive in the murderous behavior of the revolutionary. Reason seems to retreat in the face of "the century's great crime," the holocaust, seeking explanations in the bureaucratic, dehumanized[28] quality of modern life, denying the possibility of simple moral judgment. Hannah Arendt (never named) is, in Sammler's view, the victim of modernist, mass-man, Weimar assumptions. Indeed, reason is in danger of becoming another lost illusion—even in the view of Sammler himself.

Sammler's Anglophilia, his admiration of H. G. Wells, is an expression of civilized possibility, rationality, sanity. Wells, who is political "in the Aristotelian sense," views literature as a means to a greater end, that end being social harmony, international community. Sammler opposes this to Weimar intellectualism (whose popular American embodiment is the stalinoid Herbert Marcuse), which is an expression of the modernism we have been defining. Yet Wells too came to be depressed by the century of war. What, thinks Sammler, has come of the *Cosmopolis* project for a World State, or his articles in *News for Progress* and *The World Citizen*. Lecturing at Columbia on this ideal of "a service society based on a rational scientific attitude toward life," Sammler feels "what a kind-hearted, ingenuous, stupid scheme it has been" (*MS*, p. 41). His feeling seems justified as the new brutality is made flesh when Sammler is violently attacked for saying that Orwell said that British radicals were protected by the Royal Navy. One would not ordinarily think of Orwell as a defender of the Establishment. Beyond that, of course, why attack Sammler for reporting what Orwell said? Orwell is, as the phrase goes, "counter-revolutionary." And Sammler? An "effete old shit," whose "balls are dry." The Freudian-Marxism of Reich is in the wings here. Revolution cannot be merely political or economical, since authority—all authority—should and can be destroyed only by a crusade of unrepressed children. Sammler is attacked by still another mad utopian.

The other stunning event of the brilliant opening of *Mr. Sammler's Planet*, the menacing self-exposure of the black pickpocket, is equally indicative of a world gone topsy-turvy. (Significantly, the doorman is not there—one of several failures of the guardian function; nobody coming to the besieged Feffer's aid is another.) Authority resides in the size of a man's member. It speaks for itself: "It was a symbol of superlegitimacy or sovereignty. It was a mystery. It was unanswerable. The whole explanation" (*MS*, p. 55). Speak about transcendence downward! The situation is grim as immoralism appears in the most astonishing guises. Sammler's implicit allusion to Edmund's famous speech in *King Lear* is taken without a break in narrative stride: "Make Nature your God, elevate creatureliness, and you can count on gross results." Sammler muses pessimistically, "Maybe you can count on gross results under any circumstances" (*MS*, p. 55).

The bleakness of *Mr. Sammler's Planet* derives from the fact that the suffering of the central character is no longer inseparable from pleasure. Comedy is reserved almost exclusively for the secondary and minor characters—though there is much of this—because normalcy is *in extremis*: where the comedy of *Henderson the Rain King* and *Herzog* depended on the resiliency of good will, the last-ditch confidence of reason, the ability to establish a normative perspective, Sammler has all but lost this ability. The major character in later Bellow who is closest to being alienated, he is the most precarious of Bellow's yea-sayers. If this is partly due to his age, it is also due to his experience—Herzog thought of himself as a kind of survivor but Sammler literally is one. Moreover, Sammler is the only character in Bellow to take a life. Considering the symbolic meaning this act has in Bellow, it strikes us with shattering force, for it is an acknowledgment, as in *King Lear*, that the world can present an animal pattern. Sammler has his bizarre Cordelia, but Gruner has none. Sammler's real Cordelia is his consciousness, which is not entirely isolated. Sammler tells Wallace of the section in *War and Peace* in which the captive Pierre's life is spared because he has exchanged "a human look" with the cruel General Davout: "Tolstoy says you don't kill another human being with whom you have exchanged such a look. . . . I sympathize with the desire for such a belief . . . men of genius . . . are almost forced to believe in this form of psychic unity. I wish it were so" (*MS*, pp. 188 f.). This is the most tenuous statement of the axial lines or universal connections or moral self theory in Bellow.

But when recalled to the battleground of ideas by Lal's physics and metaphysics of the moon, the irreducible moralist in Sammler is revived. In his own way, Lal is still another embodiment of the modernist negative apocalypse. His utopianism is pragmatic: "the species is eating itself up. And now Kingdom Come is directly over us and waiting to receive the fragments of a final explosion. Much better the moon" (*MS*, p. 219). Lal, who has read the symbolists, embodies one of the ironies of history. It is not the symbolists but the mechanists they despised who may make the incredible voyage: "the invitation to the voyage, the Baudelaire desire to get out—get out of human circumstances—or the longing to be a drunken boat, or a soul whose craving is to crack open a closed universe is still real, only the impulse does not have to be assigned to tiresomeness and vanity of life, and it does not necessarily have to be a death-voyage. The trouble is that only trained specialists will be able to take the trip" (*MS*, p. 219). Lal defends the plausibility of his utopia in that he sees around him a widespread death wish, at which point Sammler affirms the moral being of man, the "pain of duty which makes the creature upright" and the "instinct against leaping into Kingdom come" (*MS*, p. 220). The overleaping of ordinary life is again proscribed. Sammler has the good Gruner as an example of present decency and living proof that there is "a bond." He also has his saintly Meister Eckhart.

When, walking down Broadway, Sammler sees what seems to him a host of "Hollywood extras. Acting mythic. Casting themselves into chaos, hoping to adhere to higher consciousness" (*MS*, p. 149), he feels the value of the ancient imitation of good. In the debasement of modernism, life has become art. "The standard is aesthetic" (*MS*, p. 147) in the same sense that Shapiro's critique of modern history is aesthetic. There is an attempt "to rise above the limitations of the ordinary forms of common life" (*MS*, p. 147), a middle-class bohemianism which is a caricature of the avant-garde. In playing sexual fantasist, guerrilla, or desperado, one can fantasize a life beyond the ethical. Never mind that Sade's blasphemy is reduced to hygiene; never mind the consequences of symbolic crime. For Sammler, this is an area where even Kierkegaard was a fool to tread. Indeed, the vogue of Kierkegaard's *Fear and Trembling* is of a piece with the eccentricity of the age. Sammler would understand that the point of the biblical story is that, though Abraham is superhuman in his obedience, God does not exact an immoralist tribute. As Sammler reads it, once again we have an equation of the aesthetic and immoralist positions: "He thought often what a tremendous appeal crime had made to the children of bourgeois civilization. Whether as revolutionists, as supermen, as saints, Knights of faith, even the best teased and tested themselves with thoughts of knife or gun. Lawless. Raskolnikovs" (*MS*, p. 63). The meaning of Sammler's life is that the ethical can never be suspended. Civilization depends upon it. Nowhere is Bellow more Jewish than in his constant insistence on this point.

Mr. Sammler's Planet has its own special "poetry" of decadence and pathology. The device of the septuagenarian alien allows Bellow to present the strangeness of contemporary reality with unexampled distance. But if Bellow is playing Dostoevsky to the young's possessed, he has not achieved the pathos of the master. And sainthood is not the answer to the passionate longing for solution that motivates his mature work. Perhaps the future holds for us a novel in which the affirmative consciousness emerges as action, in which the margin of agreement between public and private life takes fire and finds home. Though he is our leading novelist, no other American writer still inhabits so palpably the air of significant future, for Bellow has repudiated the immediate past in a way that gives life to the present.

Notes

1. Gustave Flaubert, "Style as Absolute," in *The Modern Tradition*, eds. Richard Ellmann and Charles Feidelson (New York: Oxford Press, 1965), p. 126.
2. Gustave Flaubert, *The Sentimental Education*, trans. Anthony Goldsmith (London: Dent, 1956), p. 62.
3. Paraphrase of "Notebooks," *Herzog*, B.18.12. Used by permission of Saul Bellow.
4. Arthur Rimbaud, "The Poet as Revolutionary Seer," in *The Modern Tradition*, p. 203.
5. D. H. Lawrence, "German Books: Thomas Mann," *Phoenix* (London: Heinemann, 1961), p. 312.
6. Thomas Mann, *Doctor Faustus*, trans. H. T. Lowe-Porter (New York: Knopf, 1948), pp. 241, 249.
7. Ibid., p. 436.
8. Ibid., p. 230.
9. Ibid., pp. 242f.
10. Ibid., p. 375.
11. Ibid., p. 236.
12. André Gide, *Lafcadio's Adventures*, trans. Dorothy Bussy (Garden City: Anchor, 1953), p. 254.
13. *The Evergreen Reader*, ed. Barney Rosset (New York: Grove Press, 1968), p. 473.
14. Albert Camus, *The Outsider (The Stranger)*, trans. Stuart Gilbert (London: Hamish Hamilton, 1958), p. 67.
15. Ibid., p. 118.
16. Bellow is not alone in his position. The general description of it applies to some considerable degree to Malamud, Ellison, Cheever, Morris, H. Gold, Stern, and others. The C. P. Snow group has certain clear affinities as well.

17. Gustave Flaubert, "An Aesthetic Mysticism," in *The Modern Tradition*, p. 198.

18. Stephen Spender, *The Struggle of the Modern* (Berkeley: Univ. of California Press, 1965), p. 121.

19. "Notebooks," 1967 Gift, 5.17; draft of "Skepticism and the Depth of Life."

20. Saul Bellow, "Where Do We Go from Here: The Future of Fiction," *Michigan Quarterly Review*, 1, No. 1 (Winter 1962), 27.

21. A paraphrase from an interview, *Paris Review*, No. 36 (Winter 1966), 54.

22. D. H. Lawrence, *The Plumed Serpent* (New York: Vintage, 1955), pp. 272, 275.

23. Saul Bellow, "The Creative Artist and His Audience," *Perspectives* (1954), 101.

24. Saul Bellow, *Dangling Man* (New York: Meridian, 1955), p. 9; further parenthetical page references will be preceded by *DM*. References from other Bellow works, and their respective abbreviations, will be from the Viking Press editions: AM—*The Adventures of Augie March* (1953); SD—*Seize the Day* (1956); HRK—*Henderson the Rain King* (1959); H—*Herzog* (1964); MS—*Mr. Sammler's Planet* (1970).

25. One may recall Hemingway's praise of Flaubert, in *The Green Hills of Africa* (New York: Scribners, 1935), p. 70: "He was the one we believed in, loved without criticism."

26. "Successor to Faulkner?" *Show*, No. 4 (November 1964), 38.

27. Saul Bellow, "Literature," *The Great Ideas Today* (Chicago: Encyclopedia Britannica, Inc., 1963), pp. 173f.

28. Similarly, Bellow, in his own person attacks Arendt's view of the *nouveau roman* and Nathalie Sarraute's defense of it. Arendt concurs with the bald, dehumanized notion of narrative: "Man as such is or has become unknown so that it matters little to the novelist whom he chooses as his hero and less into what kind of surroundings he puts it" (*New York Review of Books*, March 5, 1964). "It" is right! Bellow answers that this state of affairs "may indicate also a terribly dangerous political condition, for of what has Dr. Arendt written so movingly if not the consequences of such interchangeability of persons? It is in Auschwitz that we see what an outlook can lead to." "Notebooks," C.3.29, "Bellow on Rosenberg on Bellow." Cf. *Location*, No. 2.

MALCOLM BRADBURY
From
"'The Nightmare in Which I'm Trying to Get a Good Night's Rest': Saul Bellow and Changing History"
Saul Bellow and His Work, ed. Edmund Schraepen
1978, pp. 12–29

Bellow's ⟨Nobel Prize⟩ acceptance speech might indeed encourage us to see him as a writer concerned with humanist and transcendental pieties, a writer urgent in pursuit of that "broader, more flexible, fuller, more coherent, more comprehensive account of what we human beings are, who we are, and what this life is for," about which he spoke. Evidently, these concerns are central to Bellow, but they are sometimes identified, by his more critical critics, with a simplistic positivism and a taste for rhetorical afflatus—particularly visible in the famous endings to his novels, which have not always been found creditable or pleasing. What I want to argue is that we should not miss, in Bellow's works, as in his statements, a vigorous and powerful sense of the tensions involved, nor an understanding of the dark places in which mind and experience today are likely to take us. I want us to notice that note of provisionality and resilience. If writers have any task to perform for us critics today—and with the growing abstraction of modern criticism their tasks seem to grow fewer and fewer; writers are steadily becoming something like heuristic devices to en-

able criticism to validate its own self-generating functions—then it is surely to produce in us a sense of spiky anguish and unease about what we make of them. In contemplating a writer who has insisted on what could be crudely called his "message," but also on his provisionality and his elusiveness, who has maintained a proper doubt about the deductions made by the deep readers of the world, and who has a marked aversion to being plotted and fixed, we ought to pay our proper dues to that provisionality, to carry a due sense of the flexibility, variety and change of his career and his work. Bellow is indeed a writer who has sought the "true impression," those transcendentalist distillations that speak to vision, revelation, the worth of life that is greater than death. But he has always sought, as a writer best should, those affirmations amid the paradoxes of life, amid time and history. His stories have sought coherence and comprehensiveness, but they have not done this by avoiding the historical and experiential continuum in which modern life is lived; each new novel is a new encounter with the shifting world of disorder and chaos, with a new hero, a new dilemma, a new milieu, a new culture-reading. This has shaped his style and his form, for both of these elements of writing are historical derivatives; Bellow has, I think, always understood as much, and this merits serious analysis.

And it may be that to that analysis a European perspective has much to give. Bellow has, indeed, long appealed to European readers, and some of the best criticism has come from this side of the Atlantic. I say this not to question or qualify the power of the excellent American criticism and scholarship his work has received, but to consider the reasons for his European appeal. Bellow is a writer who seriously inhabits a large tradition. His sources evidently go back deeply into American writing—both to Emerson and the transcendentalists, to whom he refers often, and to Dreiser and the naturalists, whom he has also praised—but he also reaches into the classic stock of European modernism. It is not hard to find the links with Dostoevsky's troubled heroes, caught in the fragmentations of a culture collapsing into political disorder, nor to Conrad's bleak world in which civilization is a thin veneer overlying anarchy, calling forth an "absurd" existential affirmation. Kafka and Camus lie behind him, as does Isaac Bashevis Singer, who carried the dark metaphysics of the Jewish tradition across the Atlantic; his novels touch on the pain and price of European history. In an essay of 1963, Bellow offered some ironic thoughts on the appeal of contemporary American writers for European intellectuals. Invoking Wylie Sypher's excellent book, *Loss of the Self in Modern Literature and Art*, he observed that a literature of the lost and inauthentic self had become a staple of modern writing, that this had arisen in Europe naturally, out of the crises of its contemporary history and thought, out of definitive theories of the human condition, but that it had also become an instinctive feature of modern American writing, giving it its modern appeal. "American writers," he said, "when they are moved by a similar spirit to reject and despise the Self, are seldom encumbered by such intellectual baggage, and this fact pleases their European contemporaries, who find in them a natural, that is, a brutal and violent acceptance of the new universal truth by minds free from intellectual preconceptions." Bellow is indeed ironic about the phenomenon, and offers to stand, himself, outside it, challenging, as he does again in his attack on Robbe-Grillet in his acceptance speech, the novel of lost ego or privatized existence, the novel of a cybernetic or a post-anthropomorphic world. The alternative, evidently, is a humanist case, and this, indeed, is what Bellow offers at the end of this same essay ("Undeniably the human being is not what he was commonly thought a century ago. The question nevertheless remains. He is something. What is he? . . . The mystery increases, it does not grow less as types of literature wear out. It is, however, Symbolism or Realism or Sensibility wearing out, and not the mystery of mankind"). Bellow's writing is, indeed, humanist, but it is not the humanism of the past; if there runs through it a metaphysical intent, a desire to identify the weight and measure of the human mean, then the task can only be performed by a just registration of the power of a modern world where massified indifference exists, where the city and its hostile anonymity is truer than any message from nature, where war, holocaust and genocide are facts, where civilized cultural solutions must mediate with a world where Auschwitz has existed, and where men mechanize themselves to go to the moon, where individual experience is dwarfed by a commanding world of process and history. Bellow's books express an obsessively modern concern, a concern for finding his mean within a contemporary situation—a situation invested, as it is in the other great modern writers like Kafka and Camus, with whom we may worthily compare him, with crisis and loss. Bellow's attempt to reconstitute humanism—the classic seriousness of great fiction everywhere—within the context of such a vision seems to me essential to his contemporary appeal, and it does link him with modern European writing. It also leads to a very distinctive art form, to versions of the post-humanist humanist novel.

For the consequences of such an enterprise will be finally manifest as form, which I take to be a mode of grammar for relating figure to landscape, subject to object, self to society, in an historical context. Bellow apparently gestures toward the revival of the liberal novel, a form that has, as is well known, a strained history in our modern and modernist century. The liberal novel is, I take it, the novel of a Whiggish history, where there is a community of progress between self and society, where individuals reach outward into social community for civility, reality and maturity. Its character, then, is social and realistic, and it is attentive to history in individual and community, seen as a co-operative, onward, sequential process, so that chronology is growth, in man and society. Bellow's plots do have something like a liberal rhythm. They are hero-centred, to a degree unusual in modern fiction; the hero often gives his name to the novel. He is usually a man, often a Jew, cast in some representative role or seeking to acquire one; he is often very experienced in the life of the world, like the aged Sammler, or in its mental history, like Herzog; and is frequently a writer or an intellectual. He is anxious about Self, and is usually to be found exploring his solitude, establishing the inward claim, but experiencing loss of contact and connection. He is anxious about Mind, which may be our salvation or our highest source of suffering. And, irritably, he usually moves toward a social becoming, finding, if in ambiguous and often monetary forms, a bond of responsibility that ties him to others, relates him to the human structure, establishes a sense of man's measure ("He is something. What is he?") and the nature of his biological and mental tenure on earth. In this process, certain prime reminders are necessary: man is mortal, and the facts of death must be weighed; man is biologically in process, and his physical history drives him; man is consciousness, and the substance of awareness and thought are urgently on trial; man is urban, and can only take his measure from the social format he has evolved for himself; man is real, and so is the world, and the two substantialities have persistent trouble in coming into balance, so that we are tempted toward thoughts of extreme alienation, urgent romantic selfhood, intimations of apocalypse; man has an intelligence, which may destroy or redeem him; man is a performer in a conditioned and material universe, a post-romantic universe in historical evolution, so that

his state is likely to be perceived by him as essentially ironic, a state of loss, comic or otherwise.

These are rhythms of stress, but they habitually press toward a characteristic Bellovian ending—the famous endings where something like a humanist reconciliation appears always to occur, life being seen in the view of death, self being seen in the view of the other. A balanced sense of reality is sought, though so is a transcendentalist composure. Involved in this is a reinvigorated sense of possible community, though it is not usually the community as given. The endings suggest composure following flux, but often they are ambiguous: because they are brief moments; because they are textually endings, with a rhetorical function; because they are not really firm stepping stones into a more transcendental tone in his next novel, which more commonly returns us to something like a beginning. For the rhythm involved is ceaseless, continuous, and very much in history, a history of perverting culture and misled consciousness in which, nonetheless, recoveries are possible. It is liberal insofar as Bellow believes in the novel as a moral instrument for the large human questions: Keith Opdahl rightly stresses that Bellow's intentions have always remained "intensely moral," though he notes that the morality arises from unease and paradox: Bellow's heroes are, he says, "ostensibly men of love, dependent on the world, but they are at bottom alienated." Bellow also understands the novel as a metaphysical or philosophical instrument, a mode for having and invigilating serious ideas: Nathan Scott identifies his work as "an essentially meditative enterprise" in which the character at the centre, transcending the immediate pressures of environment and the limitations of the social matrix, "asks himself some fundamental questions about the nature of his own humanity"—questions that, Scott says, are increasingly answered, as the sequence of novels develops, by a falling into peace, an acquiescent submission to the multilevelled mystery of existence. And, if Bellow's version of community or civility tends towards metaphysics and transcendence, so his version of history tends towards chaos. We do not live in an age of moral proportion or balanced sensibilities, which freely generates liberalism, a sense of relation with the natural world and the historical sequence; and we do not get such a world reflected back at us from Bellow's work. Rather we get a crisis of liberalism, a dark division between the domain of self and the reflection from the outward world. An awareness of isolation and inner madness in self, and void in the once reflecting universe, is crucial to this fiction. Thus, though his method moves toward reconciliation and realism, there is a systematic questioning of reality as a community or consensus. Bellow once remarked that no-one can will common reality and a communal world into existence by fiat; it is a crucial statement, and the attempt of the novels to open up an intercourse with the world—that large, transcendental aim that is present in much American literature, and produced many of its classically ambiguous texts, notably *Moby-Dick*—is challenged by it.

In Bellow's novels, world and consciousness are essentially at odds; the world is a substantially material and systematic process requiring a high cost of consciousness. If, as Bellow said, the theme of *Herzog* is "the imprisonment of the individual in a shameless and impotent privacy," then Herzog's faltering step onward is an equivocal progress. For the dominant realm of the book is the world of disintegration and madness that generates Herzog's fervent mental and social action, the wonderful letters, the incessant comedy of argument with the "reality instructors" and their five-cent versions of synthesis. The book is a comedy of the will to become, and it is becoming rather than being that is the main object of Bellow's attention; synthesis is itself a comic posture, a function of our metaphysical absurdity, and man is a "suffering joker" in whom self and community, reason and desire, constantly war. Bellow's heroes are modern men, formed by modern quandaries, living in a mental world deriving from the solipsistic vein in the romantic heritage, and a physical world naturalistically in process. History has its own massive social mechanisms; as Joseph, the ex-Marxist hero of *Dangling Man*, notes, the old metaphysical stage of good and evil has been reset in the secular world, and "under this revision, we have, instead, only history to answer to." With this, consciousness transacts on an evolutionary stage, much attended to in his story "The Old System" and in *Mr. Sammler's Planet*. Consciousness thus is considerably a derivative of the times, is historically made. Bellow's transcendentalist questions thus occur within an historical continuum, in a world of determinants and processes, genetic and historical. An awareness of the changing history of consciousness has, traditionally, much to do with the evolution of the novel form, crucially concerned with the relation of individual to world. And this knowledge Bellow has in full measure; it sustains not only the pressure felt by his protagonists, but the pressure that history exercises over fictional form. In short, it has been an essential power in Bellow's artistic development.

II

The notion that Bellow's writing has developed and changed over the course of his career has not always appealed to his critics; some have seen one basic "type" of novel recurring right through his career, and others have found his writing "conservative" and singularly unresponsive to the historical pressures that have been held to have transformed the novel stylistically over the period during which he has been writing. Bellow's own comments about contemporary experiment (such as his criticism of Robbe-Grillet in the Nobel Prize speech) have encouraged the view that he has attempted to sustain beyond its time a mode of realism and civility that is now without full authority. In fact, of course, historical imperatives do not work so simply; a form authenticates itself by the forceful power of individual talents seriously creating it. But in any case the judgment seems wrong; indeed one of Bellow's strongest resources has been his artistic resilience and his power, through a very changeable period of history, to mediate the claims of form and the claims of time. Bellow first published in 1941, but he came seriously to notice as one of the new generation of novelists who came to prominence in the years after the war, when a distinct stylistic and aesthetic climate, which was also a political climate, was forming. This was a period of revived liberalism, invigorated by the reaction against totalitarianism that arose with the battle against and the defeat of Nazism, and then the cold war struggle with an imperialistic Communism in a volatile new balance of superpowers. The politics and aesthetics of liberalism were an important version of pluralism and democracy; yet at the same time the postwar social order, with its materialism, its pressure toward conformity, its move toward mass society, seemed also to threaten the liberal self. The reaction against totalitarian models also shaped aesthetic and formal choices. Both the lore of Modernism and the lore of Naturalism—especially in its thirties form as a politico-social realism—came under question. The 1950s seemed hungry for a post-political politics, a post-ideological ideology; in this process literature and culturist concern became centralized as foci of intellectual activity. Modern literature, with its sense of irony, scruple and moral ambiguity, with its dark report on modern angst and exposure, yet its hungry

concern to identify an adequate modern image of man, provided a canon that, in many quarters, replaced more ideological texts, in particular the texts of 1930s Marxism, the god that had failed. In the new mood of political abeyance, when there was strong concern with a humanism that would recover morality from the holocaust, literature became a mode of anxious moral and metaphysical exploration. In particular it was Jewish writers, with their sense of traditional alienation and their profoundly relevant witness to the recent holocaust, who concentrated the spirit of the necessary imagination—what Lionel Trilling would call "the liberal imagination." And their novels, concerned both with the identity of solitude, and the hunger for community, became exemplary novels for the new season.

The liberal novel was, in fact, the appropriate form for a time that needed to identify itself afresh: to identify what it had lately passed through, and the character of the times now coming, times of mass and affluence, conformity and lonely crowd existence, intellectual unease and alienation. The result was a modernized liberal mode, one that related a sense of intellectual disablement to a feeling of oblique connection to a society which, for all its hostile indifference, its naturalist struggle, had remained pluralist. But it was, of course, a synthesis very clearly provisional in character: one that the new radical passions of the next decade, the Sixties, would rescind. For, with the Sixties, as Morris Dickstein has lately put it, "one of those deep-seated shifts of sensibility that alters the whole moral terrain" occurred: the cold war season that had put politics in abeyance ended; as young people reacted against the Vietnam war, a new politics of withdrawal from the social order evolved, and a much more action-centred, kinetic and politically activist sensibility came to dominate. In the arts, the moral containments of Fifties fiction weakened: a new aesthetic of provisionality and counter-cultural action, an art of irrationality and outrage grew to assault the mood of the Fifties. It was also in part a reaction against the liberal synthesis of individual and communal reality that brought the new post-modernist text, lexically complex but moving toward a zero degree of meaning, an emphasis on its own fictionality; so did confessional fiction, based on the subjectivity of narrators, and the non-fiction novel, founded on the conviction that an extremist reality and history was a relevant fiction in itself. The aesthetic change was marked, and it clearly either restructured or disabled many careers. . . . ⟨Bellow⟩ has not, of course, become a post-modernist writer; he has not written the non-fictional novel, and, though he has verged on the confessional mode, mostly notably in *Herzog*, it has been within a highly contained framework. But he has paid a due attention to the changing historical world, which resynthesizes forms and alters consciousness, and in each new novel has presented us with a new world, a world conceived of as being in historical motion and mutation.

Thus to go back to *Dangling Man* and *The Victim* is now to go back a long way. These two first novels were fables of solitude and civility, existential texts obliquely pulled back towards liberalism. *Dangling Man* (1944), written in the then popular manner of absurdist diary literature, inherited from existential writers like Sartre and Camus, set during the war, takes its hero, bereft of employment and politics in the wartime economy, off into a Kafka-esque solitude and absurdism, an irritable enclosure, explicitly existential, for he is unable to find essence in existence. His military induction becomes the solution to the problem, a moment of compulsory civility; the final cry, "Hurray for regular hours! And for the supervision of the spirit! Long live regimentation!" is a testament of loss, a testament of gain. *The Victim* (1947), written with the same closure and tightness, is also about social responsibility enforced: Asa Leventhal is required to recognize and respond to the oblique chain of connection that links him with the unemployment, poverty, and suffering of another man, a gentile, despite all the appropriate excuses—the impersonal naturalist struggle of the city, the general recognition of broken bonds, the open competition for place, the current philosophies of Darwinism that deny moral affiliation. Like *Dangling Man*, *The Victim* is set in the world of the modern hostile city, New York in the hot summer sun, a determinist, naturalist environment where bodies push against bodies and the world works through a process that—as in Dreiser's fatalistic writing—arbitrarily benefits some and sinks others. But both books, dependent as they are on absurdist or naturalist modes, use them to transcend the consequent syntheses; hence they generate a liberal metaphysic of connection, which he was to take yet further in his tight novella *Seize the Day*. Bellow took the tradition in order to amend it, to raise those questions about the measure of the human with which a central chapter in *The Victim* deals.

Then, however, his work moved, into a new comic picaresque mode, the mode of *The Adventures of Augie March* (1953) and *Henderson the Rain King* (1959). The old naturalist and existential containments were relaxed, and the new novels were texts of expansion and flow, novels of character formation in which the heroes were large mental and moral travellers in quest through massive social, psychic and neo-mythic landscapes to find the measure of their being, the nature of their human tenure. The new form released in Bellow a potential for mythic and fantastic writing we had not earlier seen; it also released a Bellovian metaphysical vernacular. Bellow himself reported a new prose manner in his work, though he would identify *Augie March* as "too effusive and uncritical." And in *Henderson* in particular the task became that of creating a modern method of fabulation, with an imaginary Africa providing an anthropological geography against which he could set a tale of psycho-mythic adventure. The claims of realism were amended; the aim was comic psychic progress through the kingdom of nature, where animals fabulously measure out the potential for realizing one's human characteristics. Henderson, moving from pig to lion to bear, falls into a rhythm of nature where there is biology but also a "becoming." Like Augie before him, like Herzog after him, Henderson, in the kingdom of process, finds it possible to become a self-creator.

But with the next novel, *Herzog* (1964), probably Bellow's best, one senses another essential change in his writing. The comic picaresque, releasing the hero to his adventures, will no longer serve; this is because Herzog's adventures are essentially those of the mind, but also because the mind is constrained, super-imposed upon, in interaction with, a universe at odds with it—the world of the modern city, which is an apocalyptic wilderness, corrupt, disintegrating, a place of assault and disorder. The novel's form is appropriately more elaborate: the extraordinary action of Herzog's well-funded but disordered mind is laid anti-chronologically over a plot that explores the outward world of reality and process, and brings him into contact with those who offer to speak for it, the "reality instructors" with their modern syntheses, their lives of contemporary boredom. Herzog's state is anguish, and it is an historical anguish . . . Herzog, through his intellectual sources and his surrounding world, inherits the appropriate agony, and turns his personal life "into a circus, into gladiatorial combat." In a world of perverted relations, where all guides, including one's women, are negative tutors, madness seems sense, and an outward violence, an act of retaliation against the city and the

damaging boredoms that make up personal life, seems an answer. But the novel is comic; Herzog, "that suffering joker," recognizes that this is a farcical solution. History, massed in the city and in Herzog's own mind, where the old ideas of genius have become the canned goods of intellectuals ("Do we need *theories* of pain and anguish?"), is played as farce: "I fall upon the thorns of life; I bleed. And what next? I get laid, I take a short holiday . . ." Herzog, seeking to redistill history and our ideas of it, seeks "a new angle on the modern condition, showing how life could be lived by renewing universal connection, overturning the last of the Romantic errors about the uniqueness of the Self," does finally discard his violence and his madness, averts his "merely aesthetic critique of modern history," accepts the relation of self and world, and a balanced tenure of his own being.

Herzog is an apocalyptic novel about the defeat of florid apocalypse, a long mental battle with the advocates of an absurdist romanticism, of therapeutic syntheses, the life of alternated boredom and stimulation in the wasted city. The battle itself is Herzog's alternative therapy, and it is his vivid intellectual warfare that sustains the book. But if the confessional and therapeutic novel of the wasteland world has become an appropriate modern American form, this is the closest Bellow has come to it. Its achievement is to dismiss the obvious lore by which it might be interpreted, and to avoid the obvious solution: the psycho-verbal collapse and the sexual exposure of Roth's Portnoy, Tarnopol, or Kepesh, for example. Herzog finds his "new angle on the modern condition," recognizes a vividness and worth in the world, finds equilibrium without librium, accepts diurnality and contingency, making it whole. It is an ending we may doubt: the green rural world of Ludeyville, with its natural transcendence and its pleasure-principle associations, is a conventional pastoral outside the city where anguish is made; the surviving relationship with Ramona offers, too, an abeyance of the sexual warfare with which Bellow's later novels resound, but in the form of the complaisant, dream-like woman who puts on no pressure. But the ending is within the comic contour of the book, and it is also provisional, a moment's step beyond solipsism and irrationality, but not a lasting answer. But what we should note is Bellow's comprehensive understanding of the lore of modern anguish, and his concern with the odds set against Herzog's momentary composure. If Bellow rejects the indulgent and spurious alienations that have come from the legacy of nineteenth-century romanticism and historicism, and have been fed into a late twentieth-century model of therapeutic and alienated man, he has also made his hero an alienated figure, living amid the intellectual, social, political and psychological bewilderments of the modern urban world, and in a state of opposition.

Indeed it is these bleak apprehensions that pass on into *Mr. Sammler's Planet* (1970), Bellow's most anxious and apocalyptic novel, a crisis book for a crisis year, the year of high radical passions and moonshot. Again it is Bellow's evident assumption in the book that a dark history is once more in process; on earth, the cities decline, romantic and irrational passions run wild, and in the larger cosmos human consciousness seems to be in some moment of biological osmosis, adjusting to the move toward new planets. New York City is a Babelian waste, disorganized, crime-ridden, over-populated, lost, sexually barren; only evil appears to invigorate. Consciousness is overwhelmed by force, as in Henry Adams' model of the multiverse; only irony seems possible. Sammler is yet more displaced than Herzog, a survivor from elsewhere, a stranger, a man almost beyond life, twice born; he carries with him the dark ambiguity of inherited culture—which is both the civilized European intensities, and the dark underlying explosion of irrationality, disorder and holocaust in the concentration camps. Sammler is himself an apocalyptic figure, casting his one cold eye on the horsemen who pass by, gazing with his "kindly detachment, in farewell-detachment, in earth-departure-objectivity," from his own extra-territorial standpoint, that of the man who knows the death beyond life. He has seen the price both of repression and unmitigated selfhood, the will set free; trying to "live with a civil heart. With interested charity. With a sense of the mystic potency of mankind," he feels the powerlessness of his lesson, the uselessness of a liberal civility. But again the will to apocalypse seems the great enemy; and if to the modern world Sammler stands in muted resistance, he also stands in resistance to its most obvious solutions, is a figure for the death that in the end makes life worthy of more than purely biological or historical interpretation. Both of these novels are significant acts of restructuring, encounters with a dark time, and they both recognize and qualify the "florid apocalypse" of post-modern thought.

Sammler is not only Bellow's most apocalyptic but his most pessimistic novel, a book in which irony and a desire for human community are hardly sufficient to contain disgust. But in the event Bellow turned again, and moved richly away from the growing irony of mode, also visible in his short stories, toward comedy and picaresque. *Humboldt's Gift* not only replays some of Bellow's earlier resources; it also seems to secrete in itself a commentary on his whole development so far. It is a book about two writers, and the oblique inheritance that links them; about the space between two historical generations, two versions of culture; about a sort of literary history, and two versions of creative individual and process, between "we" and "it." Humboldt is the writer in the Fifties spirit, a man of the great *Partisan Review* age when it seemed mass society needed artistic intellectual saviours, Fisher Kings for the Waste Land; Citrine writes in a world where "culture" is furiously abundant, though not necessarily to culture's benefit. In a BBC interview with Melvyn Bragg, Bellow himself distinguished between Humboldt as the "modernist" writer (one could quibble with the term, but I take it the reference is to Humboldt's sense of artistic mission, his intensity, his fury) and Citrine the writer in a large age and a lowered season, making "a comic end run." We might take him to stand for Bellow himself, the anxious comedian writing amid a contemporary, confusing turmoil of style and ideology, expressing a struggle which makes inward life a strained farce and outward life an onerous technological process, though in fact Bellow evidently contains something of Humboldt too. Nonetheless the novel is seen from Citrine's point of view: the writer as survivor, sixty, with money in the bank, confused amid a difficult divorce, an anxious love-life, a sense of past obligations, an awareness of contemporary disorders. He lives in a new America where society rewards and demolishes its writers indiscriminately, playing a comic capitalist game with them, where art is affluent succour, supporting the display of the modern self; even the wives of *mafiosi* are doing Ph.D.'s in modern literature. It is, as in *Sammler*, a world of "hypercivilized Byzantine lunacy," and an exact contemporary culture reading. Notably its setting is Chicago, "a cultureless city pervaded nevertheless by Mind," a city of muggers and affluence, flamboyant selfhood and civic void, boom and boredom. The outward reality is so vast and fanciful that it seems useless to make sense of an inner one, but Charlie tries, hunting for some transcendental gesture, a vigorous tug from the realm of the mystical and the Platonic. Charlie's performance is a comic stumble, but it gets somewhere, finally

to the graveyard, where, in a void modern necropolis, Humboldt is mechanically reburied, but Charlie inherits a legacy of survival, a myth of endurance.

Humboldt's Gift is a novel about the self in a world of mind, a world not only of history but versions of history, a world not only of psyches but of versions of psyche. "Around our heads we have a dome of thought as thick as the air we breathe," Augie March had reflected, ". . . there's too much of everything of this kind, *that's* come home to me, too much history and culture to keep track of, too many details, too much news, too much example, too much influence, too many guys to tell you to be as they are, and all this hugeness, abundance, turbulence, Niagara Falls torrent. Which who is supposed to interpret? Me?" Humboldt, attempting to master everything, from Verlaine to the *Police Gazette*, writes himself large in such a world; and dies in a flophouse. Citrine, amidst an even more massive contingency, survives in the space that Humboldt leaves behind. And, as *Sammler* was a novel in and about the ironic spirit, *Humboldt's Gift* is a novel in and about the comic spirit. Citrine endures and survives, and so does his creator, making his own comic end run, not in the form of a high modernist text, but as a text in and about history, a metaphysical farce about contemporary consciousness in its turbulence. Like his heroes, the novelist is pushed himself into postures of resilience, strategies for survival. Bellow has thus been a novelist of conditional form; he has not become a post-modernist writer, concerned with the problems of fictionality or the redemption of text. Rather he has written of and within the cultural continuum, and written with, I think, Nietzsche's famous sixth sense: the capacity for historical insight, the consciousness of historicism.

III

In 1953, Philip Rahv, a friend of Bellow's, published an article, "The Myth and the Powerhouse," which had many cogent comments to make on what he called contemporary "mythomania": for this was the high season of mythic interpretation in American criticism. He remarked that, for many postwar critics, "the super-temporality of myth provides the ideal refuge from history," and added that "To them, as to Stephen Dedalus, history is a nightmare from which we are trying to awake. But to awake from history into myth is like escaping from a nightmare into permanent insomnia." It is perhaps not too far-fetched to suppose that when, in the opening chapter, of *Humboldt's Gift*, Bellow is evoking the great mental and literary resources of Humboldt, "the Mozart of gab," and remarks:

> He had read many thousands of books. He said that history was a nightmare during which he was trying to get a good night's rest. Insomnia made him more learned. In the small hours he read thick books—Marx and Sombart, Toynbee, Rostovzeff, Freud . . .

he is recalling Rahv, his *Partisan Review* days, and the preoccupation with the struggle between the myth and the powerhouse of history. Humboldt, the great capitalizer of nouns—Poetry, Beauty, Love, History, the Waste Land, the Unconscious, Manic, Depressive—lives in Augie's Niagara Falls abundance. His joke, of course, goes back to *Ulysses*, and the classic answer Modernism gave to the nightmare of history was the move toward symbolism, toward the transcendent, spatial form; it was a move away from fiction as historiography and toward fiction as myth—the move that transliterates Homer's long historical tale of the founding of a nation through the return of a wanderer into Joyce's epic of consciousness, held within a single day. Modernist writing, in short, encouraged the mythic interpretation, but Rahv, a veteran of the Thirties, an editor of *Partisan Review*, where Bellow published, around which Humboldt so clearly functions, a voice of that movement from politics to cultural concern which marked the postwar years, was concerned with a necessary reminder. Bellow, I think, alludes to it, in his way of creating Humboldt; he also, I think, sufficiently shares it. The Nietzschean sixth sense, historicism, was not to be outrun; Bellow's own aesthetic and intellectual origins, his sense of the power of naturalism, his concern with sociology, his recognition of the weight of determinants, in short, his post-naturalist and post-Marxist synthesis, would dispose him to Rahv's view. . .

Bellow is, I think, essentially the novelist as invigilator of . . . a world of historical, material and psychological abundance, an era of a Niagara Falls of history and culture under which self seems dwarfed, but to which it must react. For we are surrounded not just by History, but by thoughts about History: versions of liberation, images of provisional reality, notions of Alienation, Anomie, Plight. What we have now is a world in which there prevails both a nineteenth-century positivism and a twentieth-century relativism: Bellow knows both, as the writers and commentators of his generation, schooled in the Marxism of the 1930s, the rescinded historicism of the 1950s, so well did. His work contains as knowledge the proposition that environment and process may well determine man, as he shows us in *The Victim*; but equally that man may be a Columbus in such a world, that character may determine fate, as he suggests to us in *Augie March*. He knows that consciousness is a collective historical flow, as he shows us in *Mr. Sammler's Planet*; he proposes that mind may remodel all offered syntheses of reality and process, as he suggests in *Herzog*. But above all he is the novelist of ideas conserved or redeemed as consciousness in the universe of material and psychic abundance. It is ideas that offer Humboldt his answer to unmitigated process. "Maybe America didn't need art and inner miracles. The USA was a big operation, very big. The more *it*, the less *we*. So Humboldt behaved like an eccentric and a comic subject." Humboldt offers the large comedy, the picaresque synthesis; he fails and succeeds, leaving Citrine his gift. Citrine's role, as survivor, is a small comedy, in his later world which cannot become whole, where the merger of the material and the mental takes yet stranger forms, where life is populous with modern seekers, the new mental rabble of the wised-up world, where even "policemen take psychology courses, and have some feeling for the comedy of human life." In a world where everyone has internalized history, peace may be sought; a good night's rest would be nice but history, being consciousness too, is inside us, and we are glutted with it. Self is no longer freedom; history is no longer an outward politics, an independent process.

This is, I think, Bellow's abiding preoccupation, his continuing theme; and it is the word "comedy" that proposes the nature of his response. As early as *Dangling Man*, Joseph had observed comedy as the one power the self possesses: there is, he reflects, an "element of the comic or fantastic in everyone," and it is this element that cannot be brought under control. This is the transforming apprehension, the basis of a response to overwhelming mass that is inside as well as outside us. It is what releases the self into an attentive psycho-historical performance, the grounds for supposing that, between self and substance, it and we, we have an existence. It is the principle from which the actions of his heroes arise, which lets them be heroes: it is a recognition of man's absurd exposure in *Dangling Man*, a metaphysical acceptance of responsibility in *The Victim*, a euphoric mode of self-discovery in *Augie March*, a fantastic intercourse with the natural universe in *Henderson*. It is a self-compensating madness in *Herzog*, an ironic mode of survival in *Mr. Sammler's Planet*, the essence of the legacy in *Humboldt's Gift*. It is essentially both a self-realizing and mediating power, a form of due attention; it is the measure of an adequate mean for man in a world that seems, according to obvious logics of causality, to offer him none. It is the comedy of the mind in serious process, registering both its inventive splendours and its way of knowing its own confinements. It is, as form, the instrument that does not close the text up to its own formalism, but opens it to contingency, change, and process. Bellow seems to me the great modern novelist of the attempt to reconcile mind, in all its resource and confusion, its anguish but also its fantastic fertility, with a life that is absurd and extravagant, where not only material force but the ideas and forms of consciousness that surround it flow furiously, thrusting countervailing information at us, causing men to grope in boredom or despair for a version of reality, a right opinion, a therapeutic selfhood. We live in a world, then, when the measure of man can scarely be taken, but where mind insists that we take it. The resulting perception is comedy, an observation of disparity—we are both grand and absurd, little and big—and also of freedom, for the mind, invigilating itself, has the power of discrimination, the gift to know. Absurdly, we have, amid all the powers, a vivid self-presence; of that curious presence Bellow is surely the great metaphysical comedian.

FRANK D. McCONNELL
"Saul Bellow and the Terms of Our Contract"
Four Postwar American Novelists
1977, pp. 1–11

If the postwar American novel really exists as a body of fiction with specific aims, common problems, and distinctive ways of confronting those problems, then the work of Saul Bellow should occupy a special eminence therein. He received his B. S. from Northwestern University in 1938, beginning his adult career on the eve of the war which was to cast such long and dark shadows over the century's life. He has continued to produce fiction and cultural criticism of major importance—and undiminished energy—from the midst of that war into the seventies.

In the context of American writing, the sheer longevity of Bellow's talent is a remarkable thing. For some years now, it has been a cliché of criticism—and a popular mythology—that American novelists tend in an extraordinary degree to be one-book geniuses. There appears to be something in our cultural climate which encourages or even necessitates the fate of writers who, after initial and brilliant success, either spend the remainder of their lives trying vainly to repeat and recapture their first glory, or simply find it impossible to write any more at all. Fitzgerald and Hemingway, before their canonization by the academy, were continually faulted—both by the critics and, it seems, by their own private demons—for not living up to the achievement of *The Great Gatsby* and *The Sun Also Rises*. Norman Mailer's violent love-hate affair with the novel seems to have been generated in large part by his inability, throughout the fifties, fully to satisfy the expectations aroused by *The Naked and the Dead*. And the forties saw at least three brilliant writers—Ross Lockridge of *Raintree County*, Thomas Heggen of *Mr. Roberts*, and Paul Bowles of *The Sheltering*

Sky—who fell prey, in varying modalities of violence, to this complex fatality. Even Faulkner, whose gift survived past all expectation, can be seen not so much as a denier of that nemesis, but more as a clever manipulator of it. Faulkner's strategy is to make his work a single "first novel," spinning out the immense tale of Yoknapatawpha County in a series of books which are less individual novels than chapters of one encyclopedic and sustained vision.

It would be overreaching to suggest that Bellow has singlehandedly defeated the "one-book fate" for a whole generation of American novelists; but it is nevertheless true that his books, from *Dangling Man* (1944) to *Humboldt's Gift* (1975), form a consistent, carefully nurtured *oeuvre* not often encountered in the work of American writers. And it is equally true that the productions of John Barth, Thomas Pynchon, and—frenetically—Norman Mailer all display the same sort of continuity, the same sense of cultivated and constructed fictive argument, as do Bellow's books. There is something European about Saul Bellow's series of novels, in the fiction's openness to the widest range of philosophical, historical, and political debate and in the openness of each single fiction to further development and debate in subsequent tales. And we can argue that one of the great achievements of American fiction generally in the postwar period has been its acquisition of just such a feeling of expanse. Whether Bellow influences such a subtle development is, naturally, beyond proof and pointless to discuss. What cannot be denied is that he is the first American novelist of his generation to raise both the special problems and the special possibilities of postwar fiction, even though he may be the first of a generation which has often found cause to disown and repudiate his primacy.

The case of Saul Bellow is an interesting incident of that nebulous thing, the history of taste. His first two novels, *Dangling Man* and *The Victim* (1947), were successful if not earthshaking books, earning high critical praise even in a decade which seems to have produced more than its share of original young writers. But *The Adventures of Augie March*, which won the National Book Award in fiction for 1953, established its author beyond all question as the important writer of his time: comparisons of *Augie March* to the best of Twain and Melville were commonplace by the middle of the fifties. *Seize the Day* (1956) and *Henderson the Rain King* (1959) consolidated Bellow's hegemony over American prose. It is a safe bet that if an English teacher or graduate student of the fifties was asked, "Who is the greatest living American writer?" the answer would be, "Saul Bellow." If the answer was "Norman Mailer," it was to be assumed that the respondent was being coy; if it was "William Gaddis," "William Burroughs," or "John Barth," he was being perverse.

But 1959, the year of *Henderson*, was a fateful year: the last of the Eisenhower decade, and the earliest of America's full-scale involvement in the politics of North and South Vietnam. And the last, in many ways, of Bellow's undisputed preeminence in his country's letters. Five years were to intervene between *Henderson* and the publication of his next novel. And they were five years which saw, not only the internal and external erosion of the nation's public self-confidence, but the reemergence of Norman Mailer, the maturation of John Barth, and the appearance of Thomas Pynchon. By the time *Herzog* appeared in 1964, the contours of American fiction had changed since Eugene Henderson took his fantastic voyage to darkest Africa. Bellow came to appear, to some, less and less at home in the new climate; to others, more and more curmudgeonly. Celebrants of the absurdist fiction of "black humor" could contrast the riotous comedy of *An American*

Dream or *The Sot-Weed Factor* to the solemnities and *longueurs* of *The Victim* or *Seize the Day*—quite forgetting, in the contrast, the rich and often outrageous sense of comedy in *Augie March* and *Henderson*. Bellow's fiction, regnant throughout the Eisenhower era, could be unfairly invoked as a literary symbol of those years, a symbol of the political mediocrity and moral timidity which spawned Richard Nixon, Ed Sullivan, and *Confidential* magazine. And Bellow himself, in some ways, appeared to concur in the eclipse of his influence. After the comic fantasy of *Henderson*, *Herzog* could be regarded as a retrenchment in the direction of realism and high seriousness. *Herzog* is, at least, the first novel in which Bellow's main character is an academic intellectual rather than a freeranging, canny and unattached jack-of-all-trades. And though *Herzog*, like *Augie March*, won the National Book Award for its year, the award this time could be thought of as the cautious honoring of an emeritus rather than the joyful recognition of a vital and originating talent. *Mr. Sammler's Planet* (1970) is Bellow's own recognition of and ironic statement upon this emeritus status. Artur Sammler, his septuagenarian, European hero living through the manic sixties in the heart of New York City, is unmistakably a vision of his own fictive career, ignored or (worse) pensioned off by the very writing it has generated: "What was it to be entrapped by a psychiatric standard (Sammler blamed the Germans and their psychoanalysis for this)! Who had raised the diaper flag? Who had made shit a sacrament? What literary and psychological movement was that? Mr. Sammler, with bitter angry mind, held the top rail of his jammed bus, riding downtown, a short journey."

In the question "Who had made shit a sacrament?" we can hear Bellow's own cultured, traditional revulsion against the scatological metaphysics of Mailer's *An American Dream*, Barth's *Giles Goat-Boy*, and Pynchon's *V*. But if we also choose to see in the novels of Mailer, Barth, and Pynchon an earnest concern with the resurrection of the art of fiction as a living enterprise, an attempt—however varied—to turn fiction to use in living with the everyday and the everyday to use in the construction of saving fictions, then the answer to Sammler's question is a curious one. For it is Bellow himself, as much as any contemporary American writer, who has helped make "shit"—the omnipresent, tawdry materiality of middle-class life—into a sacrament, or into the matter of serious myth. And Bellow's own resistance, then, to the development of fiction becomes itself an important feature of the fruitful but dangerous territory his work has mapped out.

There are at least two ways of looking at Bellow's position in American fiction, each of which contradicts the other and both of which, at times, are true. The development of the novel form represented by Barth, Pynchon, and the later Mailer is characterized by a riotous sense of fantasy and a deliberate flaunting of the conventions of naturalistic narrative. We may say, then, either that Bellow's novels avoid, out of timidity or pomposity, the allurements of this fantasy-vision of the world; or that such fantasy, while present in his best work, is nevertheless triumphantly contained therein—a suburb of nightmare in which other writers may be forced to dwell, but which Bellow visits only occasionally and when it suits his larger purpose. If the word can still be used in any but a derogatory sense, Bellow is a realist: his characters all have names, families, dull (usually nonacademic) jobs, and live in recognizable locales. One could learn a good deal about Chicago from reading *Humboldt's Gift* and about Manhattan from *Mr. Sammler's Planet*—a claim that cannot be made for the Maryland of *The Floating Opera* or the New York of *V*. But at the same time—and this, not the geography, is the permanent interest of his characters—they lead intense, gloomy mental lives which continually threaten to break the comfortable reality of their surroundings, casting them adrift in a sea of hallucination, romance, and guilt. Nowhere is this delicate balance of tendencies better caught than in *The Victim*, as the hero, Asa Leventhal, crosses the ferry to Staten Island to visit his sister-in-law and her sick child:

> The towers on the shore rose up in huge blocks, scorched, smoky, gray, and bare white where the sun was direct upon them. The notion brushed Leventhal's mind that the light over them and over the water was akin to the yellow revealed in the slit of the eye of a wild animal, say a lion, something inhuman that didn't care about anything human and yet was implanted in every human being too, one speck of it, and formed a part of him that responded to the heat and the glare, exhausting as these were, or even to freezing, salty things, harsh things, all things difficult to stand.

The inhuman glare of the lion's eye, the color of the beast, is the ultimate fate and the ultimate test which awaits not only Leventhal, but all of Bellow's heroes. Two of them, in fact, will actually meet an emblematic beast who either consumes or purifies their pretensions to civilized humanity: Augie March encounters the bald eagle Caligula, and Henderson is forced to stroke the lioness Atti. But the beast need not be literally, physically there. At any moment, as one walks down a city street, talks to a lover or a friend, has a bland breakfast with one's aging father, the abyss may open, the world turn ugly and murderous, and the carnivorous ape within each of us reassert his primacy over all we have invented of civilization and decency. Moses Herzog, that agonized and self-betrayed scholar, is trying to write an intellectual history of the modern world "investigating the social meaning of Nothingness." But Herzog's book can, finally, achieve no more than Leventhal's Staten Island epiphany: the shuddering recognition of how little distant we actually are from the savagery of our origins, how fragile a thing is the civilization which makes, we continue to tell ourselves, our life worth living.

But this denuding confrontation with the inhuman is, in one form or another, the common denominator and common originator of most contemporary fictions; and what distinguishes Bellow is not only his firm and unusually "realistic" articulation of this theme, but the distinctively traditional moral context in which he articulates it. His training as an anthropologist equips him—as it does another former anthropology student, William Burroughs—to understand the arbitrary, eternally endangered quality of civilized society. But unlike Burroughs, Bellow insists in book after book that that delicate, arbitrary thing, civilization, is still possible, still capable of being asserted, even in the face of the beasts our own civilization has loosed against itself in the forms of dehumanized labor, political and economic terrorism, and imaginative stultification. The passage I cited from *The Victim* is, in this respect, characteristic of Bellow's style. For while the color of the beast is there, in all its implied threat to the certainties of Leventhal's existence, it is there only as metaphor, or better, as an image at second remove: the towers on the shore have, at sunset, a curious color, like the color one can see in the eyes of lions, the color of the inhuman. As serious as the threat is, it is nevertheless contained within and disciplined by the very prose which articulates it. In an age of excess and apocalypse, an age which has in many ways turned the end of the world into its most important product, Bellow remains a resolutely antiapocalyptic novelist, defending the value of the human middle ground when most of us, much of the time, seem to have forgotten that territory's very existence. But the efficiency of his defense of normality is a function, absolutely, of his powerful sense of the impingements of the abnormal, of his ability to imagine, as chillingly as any novelist writing today, the manic horrors of solipsism and nightmare which lurk around every corner, down every street, of our artificially daylit cities.

The Victim, again, contains an extraordinary and perhaps intentionally prophetic allegory of Bellow's own position vis à vis the novelists who have succeeded him. Leventhal is taking his young, neglected nephew Philip out for a day in Manhattan, attempting to cheer the boy with sunshine and snacks. But when Leventhal suggests walking from Pennsylvania Station to Times Square, Philip wants to ride the subway. The boy is fascinated by the technical details which honeycomb the city's underground—"water pipes and sewage, gas mains, the electrical system for the subway, telephone and telegraph wires, and the cable for the Broadway trolley"—details whose allure Leventhal cannot understand. And when they finally debark at Forty-second Street, Leventhal reluctantly agrees to take Philip to a movie—whereupon the boy immediately chooses his uncle's least favorite genre, a Boris Karloff horror film.

When we remember the fascination of writers like Mailer and Pynchon with the dark underground of urban life—both literal and figurative—and the powerful fascination of so many contemporary novelists with the metaphor of modern existence as an immense horror film (Mailer's *The Naked and the Dead*, Burrough's *Nova Express*, Donald Barthelme's *City Life*, Brock Brower's *The Late Great Creature*, Pynchon's *Gravity's Rainbow*), it is difficult not to see in this episode Bellow's own accurate forecast of where American fiction is headed and of his position in that movement. Both the boy and the man are concerned with survival of the most elemental sort, with finding, at the center of the urban desert, an image of the truth and a reason to go on. But while the younger survivor seeks out, embraces, the dangerous complexities of the underground and the too real fantasies of the horror film, the older man participates in both with a cool distaste, a humanist's wry reluctance.

This is to say that to read Bellow intelligently we must call into serious question our time-honored prejudices about the nature of "realism" and "fantasy" as varieties of narrative. Like all good novelists, Bellow not only educates us about the parameters of our own lives, he also educates us in the craft of reading novels. The fantastic and the realistic modes are carefully and continually intermingled in his tales. And, far from being a relic of the Eisenhower decade, Bellow appears more and more to be an artist who had to wait for the absurdist explosion of sixties fiction for his novels to be put in a true perspective. Rereading, from the vantage point of *The Sot-Weed Factor* or *Gravity's Rainbow*, even the comparatively tame narrative of *The Victim* or *Seize the Day*, we can see that those fifties-style celebrations of Bellow's "accurate eye" or "sense of life" were only part of the story. For, at his best and most characteristic, he is a true and brilliant fabulator of the American postwar variety—and one whose distinctive and firm commitment to literary tradition renders his fabulations all the more powerful and valuable.

There is, indeed, one specific tradition of this sort, a mingling of fantasy and realism, to which Bellow is more properly the heir than are many other writers. That is the tradition of the Jewish tale, found in the legends of the Hasidic rabbis, the marvelously pure folk stories of Sholem Aleichem, and the more sophisticated, bitter parables of Isaac Bashevis Singer. In these stories, the interpenetration of the everyday, creatural life of the *shtetl* and the high magic of man's reconciliation with Yahweh is at the very center of the narrative's power. Bellow's talent for the realistic-fantastic mode undoubtedly owes something to this highly developed, urban folk art, though not as much as do the fictions of a Jewish writer like Bernard Malamud in *The Natural* or *The Assistant*.

That Bellow's work can be characterized by "Jewishness" is another of those truisms which, while they contain a good deal of significance, may be ultimately misleading. The fifties saw an extraordinary efflorescence of what was heralded at the time as the "American Jewish novel," much as the sixties were celebrated as the era of the underground, absurdist black humorists. While it is true that Philip Roth (*Letting Go*), Edward Wallant (*The Pawnbroker*), Bruce Jay Friedman (*Stern*), Malamud, and Bellow all used the figure of the American Jew as a central symbolic feature in their explorations of the national soul (or lack of same), it is impossible to assign to that figure any meaning consistent from one writer to another. American fiction has always been obsessed with the idea of the outsider, the man who, for one reason or another, can never quite assimilate himself to the unself-conscious optimism of the classic American dream and who therefore becomes a living test of that dream's pretensions to a truly universal liberty and peace. (This obsession in the American novel was, of course, most brilliantly traced in the work of another great Jewish writer of the decade, Leslie Fiedler in *Love and Death in the American Novel*.) From the Indians of James Fenimore Cooper through the vatic adolescents of Mark Twain to the blacks of Leroi Jones and Ishmael Reed, the outsider figure has always been among the most familiar in our literature. But the Jew, in his special complexity, was an unusually powerful, suggestive version of the outsider for the emerging sensibility—or better, emerging panic—of the fifties.

The American Jew, in many ways, was the red Indian of Levittown. The period after World War II was not, of course, the first great era of urban expansion in America, but it was the first era in which urban expansion came to be a central, disturbing facet of the American imagination. Sociologists, economists, politicians, and novelists began to realize, during the forties and fifties, that the growth of the city had become the most important fact for the future of democratic man. The city was no longer the center for weekday trade and weekend carousing it had largely represented to the nineteenth-century mind, nor was it the morally arid wasteland of the post–World War I imagination. It had become, quite simply, the essential context in which life, for better and worse, was henceforth to be lived out in America. The decade of Bellow's first triumphant novels was also the decade which saw the belated discovery of urban existence as a special kind of life, as well as the emergence of that peculiar amalgam of technologist and visionary, the "city planner." If Bellow's fiction is an instance, that is, of the Europeanization of the American novel, one reason for this is that his period is the period of the Europeanization (or urbanization) of American culture.

In the new city of postwar America, the new society taking account of its own immense technological sophistication, what better outsider-figure could be invented than the Jew? Unlike the Indian, his "outsideness" is not a function of his physical separation from the center of culture. The Jew, traditionally, lives within and is brilliant within the very heart of urban life. Unlike the black, his response to the culture which subtly excludes him is not anger or revolution (one thinks of Bigger Thomas in Richard Wright's *Native Son*), but rather acceptance coupled with silent disaffiliation and a wry irony which—

at least imaginatively—can be more devastating than a Molotov cocktail. The Jew, in European as well as American tradition, is the man in whom history has become incarnate: the man whose very existence calls the infinitely progressive future into question by his reminiscence of an infinitely disappointing past, of diaspora, pogrom, the idea of *Rassenschade*. He is the ideal red Indian of an urban culture since, like Chingachgook and Uncas in Cooper's novels, he knows the topography of his own peculiar jungle better than the pioneers, cowboys, explorers, and goyim who condescendingly enlist his loyalty.

It is no surprise, then, that the "Jewish novel" enjoyed the splendid realizations it did in the fifties. Throughout the decade, in fact, the only outsider-myth which offered any alternative to it was that of the total dropout, the beatnik: the often less than noble savage whose disaffiliation was so programmatic and so idealized that he could brook no mode of separation but a return to the absolute non-participation of the fictional Indian himself. It is not without significance, indeed, that the two most permanently valuable members of the Beat Generation, Allen Ginsberg and Norman Mailer, are both outsiders of one kind—Jews—whose rage for separation leads them finally to disown that variety of outsidership for something at once purer, more deliberately chosen, and thence perhaps more self-defeating.

But unlike Mailer, his only serious rival in the fiction of the fifties, Bellow is content with Jewishness. And yet his use of that heritage and that myth sets him apart from any putative "Jewish" school of writing, just as it sets him apart from the more banal complacencies of so much other fiction of the age. Bellow's Jew is an urban outsider, an alien at the heart of, and living almost unnoticed within, the urban meltingpot; but as a Jew he is also the heir and avatar of a moral and ethical heritage which is at the very origin of the civilization that rejects him. And he is therefore the heir and avatar of diseases of the soul—and their potential cures—which have less to do with Jewishness than they do with the larger business of living at all in this age of the world. Bellow is a "Jewish" novelist, that is, in just the degree to which a writer like Graham Greene is a "Catholic" one. The aura of historical tradition and moral rigor is, for both men, an inescapable condition of their storytelling—and yet only as a model, a testcase, for the chances of any tradition's, any morality's survival in contemporary reality. Neither writer, one would think, can have made many converts to his particular religion. For the very great force of both writers is precisely in their sense of the difficulty and ambiguity of the theological norms—precisely, in a theological sense, in their gift for heresy.

The archetypal situation of a Bellow novel, then, may be paraphrased in this way: a man, always an American and usually a Jew, often an intellectual and never less than highly intelligent, discovers chaos. The chaos he discovers, moreover, is not the romantic, Nietzschean abyss nor the existential gulf of the absurd, but a homegrown variety of those monstrosities, implicated in the very texture of his personal relationships, his everyday hopes and activities, his job. The plot of the characteristic Bellow fiction, then, is the story of the hero's attempt to live with, survive within, the void that has opened at his feet. That is to say, Bellow's heroes, like the novelist himself, are concerned with finding a way to revivify the sanctions and values of Western culture in the context of the terrible complexity of the new megalopolis and the "lonely crowd." They are not—like some of the characters of Mailer and Pynchon, among others—mythmakers, questing for a new order and a new morality adequate to the crisis of contemporary history.

They are mythpreservers, whose greatest efforts are bent toward reestablishing the originating values of civilization even against the nightmare civilization threatens to become.

Bellow is an ideological novelist. For all his vaunted "realism," for all the authenticity of his locales and the convincing ring of his characters' urban speech, he is a writer for whom thought, ideas, the concepts we hold of what goes on around us, are ultimately more important than "what goes on" itself. If inauthenticity is the besetting disease of mid-twentieth-century man, Bellow articulates the violent crisis of that disease in what must be its most classical form. It is the fever that comes more severely to intellectuals than to others, the horrifying discovery that, for all your thought, all your balanced and well-learned sense of the terms of life, nothing—nothing—really avails when you have to face the wreckage of a love affair, the onslaught of age, the unreasoning hatred of the man staring you in the face. That is the color of the beast, the senseless, brute throbbing of reality which waits within the insulated city. And that is the color which Bellow's narrative dialogues seek, if not to obliterate, at least to make tolerable, tamed once again to the systems of thought which have been evolved over the millennia for the very purpose of taming it.

The dialogue form, indeed, is the most perennial and perennially creative form of Bellow's narrative. Not a great natural storyteller—not a great delineator of raw action, movement, physical violence—he is a consummate inventor of conversation, either between two people or, more often, between the quarreling halves of a single personality. Like the Talmud, his books are full of passionate talk, the debates of earnest and ironic teachers over the myriad possible interpretations of the lesson of the text—only, in Bellow, the "text" is not the divine text of Torah, but the quotidian text of a single mind in its warfare with the material world. His fiction, that is, while it deals realistically with real characters, is also continually capable of making ideas themselves the most active and most interesting "characters" of the action.

This tendency of Bellow's work achieves, in his most recent books, a level of originality, complexity, and strangeness which is one of the most remarkable events of recent American writing. But it is a tendency which has been present in his work from the beginning, and which, from the vantage of the present, accounts for the sometimes clumsy quality of his earlier books. *Dangling Man* and *The Victim* set out the perimeters of his moral concerns with graphic, occasionally inelegant precision. And in both novels the presence of dialogue as an austere collision of viewpoints and philosophies plays a central and organizing role.

STEPHEN VINCENT BENÉT

1898–1943

Stephen Vincent Benét was born in Bethlehem, Pennsylvania, on July 22, 1898, twelve years after the birth of his brother, the poet William Rose Benét. As Benét's father was a captain in the Army, his family moved frequently during his first sixteen years, and Benét attended military academies in California and Georgia. In 1915 a poem of Benét's was professionally published in the *New Republic*; later that year he went to Yale, where he published his first book of poems, *Five Men and Pompey* (1915), and, in 1916, joined the staff of the *Yale Literary Magazine*. After a temporary leave to serve in the Army and the State Department, Benét returned to Yale and received a B. A. in 1919 and an M. A. in 1920, working with Henry Seidel Canby.

In 1920 Benét met Rosemary Carr, whom he married the next year; they had three children. The couple settled in New York, but in 1926 Benét received a Guggenheim Fellowship and went to Paris to work on *John Brown's Body*, which was published in 1928. Upon his return to the United States in 1929, Benét was elected to the National Institute of Arts and Letters, and in 1933 he accepted the editorship of the Yale Series of Younger Poets competition. Two years later, he began reviewing regularly for the *New York Herald Tribune* and the *Saturday Review of Literature*. In 1939 Benét's story "The Devil and Daniel Webster" (1936), which had won the O. Henry Memorial Prize for best American short story of the year, was made into an operetta by Douglas Moore, with libretto by Benét. Toward the end of his life, Benét became an activist on behalf of American democracy, and his "Prayer" was read by President Roosevelt at the United Nations inaugural ceremonies. Stephen Vincent Benét died of a heart attack on March 13, 1943.

Benét was the recipient of many honors and prizes, including the Pulitzer Prize on two occasions (for *John Brown's Body* and posthumously for *Western Star*) and the O. Henry Memorial Prize on three occasions. Aside from the large quantity of poetry for which he is best known, Benét wrote several novels including *The Beginning of Wisdom* (1921) and *James Shore's Daughter* (1934), a quantity of short stories, and a few dramas and libretti. His short history *America*, published in 1944, was translated into many languages.

Out at Neuilly, Steve dug in, toted masses of books home from a Paris library, and went to work recreating the American Civil War. Those long armchair discussions with his father, in California and Georgia, must have recurred to him vividly! His

utter surprise when the finished book became a best-seller is a story that has often been told. When asked by a ship-news reporter what it felt like, he characteristically remarked that to him it was as though he had given birth to a grand piano. Prior to this, his longest flight into history had been a novel concerning the Minorcan revolt at New Smyrna, Florida, called *Spanish Bayonet*. Then our father had been alive. This time the only shadow on Steve's success was the fact that our father was gone, though he had lived to read portions of the manuscript in its early stages. As for myself, the summer of its completion I was staying with my wife, Elinor Wylie, in the village of Burley in the New Forest in England. I vividly recall Steve coming over from Paris to see us, reading to us one night in our cottage from his manuscript, before a glimmering fire of coals. It was an immortal evening.

The success of this book enabled him to proceed with his writing more at his own pace. It also brought him the Pulitzer Prize. His short stories grew better and better. Today one of the most famous is being interpreted on the screen by Walter Huston, Edward Arnold, and others. But at first he was loath to collect them. He brought out, instead, a collection of ballads and poems, work of the past fifteen years. Here were, among other excellent things, his earlier *Nation* Prize poem, "King David," the famous "Mountain Whippoorwill," that fine sonnet sequence called "The Golden Corpse," and also a strangely moving earlier poem of untried youth, which he had attempted to revise. But it was now 1930 and the poem had first been written in 1917. So the new last verse reads:

> After the thirteenth year, the water runs as before,
> The gemmed wave in the water, the starlight on the
>   gem,
> All but the crew who sailed there, and they return no
>   more,
> But the words are as they were written. I cannot alter
>   them.

That too I find characteristic of Steve; for one of his virtues is loyalty—not blind, not sentimental, but considered, wise, and final. He has something in his character like a rampart. It cannot be moved. Five or six years later, in *Burning City*, which contains his great poem against dictators, he gives us several fiery glimpses of what it is to be a real poet.—WILLIAM ROSE BENÉT, "My Brother Steve," *SR*, Nov. 15, 1941, pp. 23–24

In book publishing Steve played an active part, coming to New York after taking his M. A. at Yale, to which he returned for a year following World War I. Even during the later Paris sojourns his mind was often engaged in publishing problems. He advised young writers constantly and untiringly, and read and reported on manuscripts for several firms. To the editing of the Yale Series of Younger Poets he gave strength and patience and, latterly, with Carl Carmer, to the Rivers of America Series. And there were other projects.

Ever since my partners and I went into business in 1929, he had, I suppose, read and reported on practically every book of merit we have published, and many of little merit. He considered himself a member of our firm, and, if we were puzzled, someone would say, "Phone Steve!" He was always there. His notes and reports, several of which we received in the days immediately following his death, would read: "We must publish this, although we'll never make a cent on it," or "This isn't art, but why not sell a lot of copies?"

Authors who have received his criticisms, either through the mails or sitting in his study, know that here was a man whose critical standards were firm, in whose reactions to manuscripts or books was no hint of personal prejudice. It is unthinkable that he was ever envious or jealous. He read with lightning speed and yet his often very full reports were not only accurate in detail but colorful and occasionally—well, robust!

When he respected or admired the work, even though critical of detail, we practically always sent the reports to the authors unedited, and the authors felt honored because they came from S. V. B. I can think of no exception. Dismay sometimes, discussion often, but never hurt or angry retort.

However, the reports didn't always reach the authors! And in case anyone imagines that exchange of opinion with Steve was solemn, I quote:

"Boy, is this a lollypop! It reminds me of the great old days when Ouida was a girl. . . . It is full of sex, melodrama, high sassietty at its wickedest, war, noble sentiments and everything but the kitchen stove. . . . The story is quite as incredible and goes quite as far as *And So, Victoria*. It has that unmistakable lushness that can't be faked. . . . It seems to be a natural for the lending-libraries, a natural for the audience that got sucked in by *Europa*. As literature it isn't worth a god damn. But it is well enough written so that the background is in key with the story. And things happen on every page. . . . I think we ought to publish this if the agent doesn't want too much for it. I may be losing my mind but I think a lot of gals are going to want [the hero] in their stockings for Christmas."

We didn't publish. I forget why not. Maybe the agent wanted too much for it.

Nor were the reports inevitably kind. I think you will recognize a certain scorn in the following:

"This is slop.

"I have no wish to be hard on any of God's creatures, and I am sure Miss or Mrs. ——— is an estimable woman. She writes the kind of woman's club verse that gets into the local paper and the smaller unpaid poetry magazines. That's all. It has no more relation to poetry than Turkish paste has. And some of it is pretty arch, too.

"I'm afraid she will have to pay for the publication of this vol. Certainly there's no reason why F & R should. No matter who recommended it, it is still slop."

And this one, on an unsolicited first draft of a first novel which later became well-known and by an author who has written a number of fine books since:

"I am for this. It seems to me a good bet for the Discoverers. Whoever the guy is, he is entirely original. If it reminds me of anything, it reminds me in spots of a slightly cuckoo Tom Sawyer. And, in spots, it's almost as well told.

"Of course there will be people who will feel, 'But what the hell? What is all this all about?' But I don't think that matters. There will be just as many people, like me, who won't care.

"It's sui generis and I haven't any particular criticism to make. The man has a real talent and I strongly recommend publication."—JOHN FARRAR, "'For the Record,'" *Stephen Vincent Benét*, 1943, pp. 12–14

Works

This poem ⟨*John Brown's Body*⟩ is the most ambitious ever undertaken by an American on an American theme. Yet our judgments must be qualified: there is an important sense in which it is not ambitious enough. There is a sense in which its sole title to poetry is the fact that it is written in verse. It is a weakness of our publishing system that a piece of writing can seldom be sold to the public without having had a great many lies told about it; the author and his work, and the public, too, are put in a false position in which no one, spiritually, is profited. *John Brown's Body* has merit enough; it has hair-raising defects; and yet it deserves to be widely read and, within reason, praised. It is an interesting book, but it is not the kind of work that the public has been led to believe it is.

It has been called among other things an epic and it has been compared, not unfavorably, to the *Iliad*. Mr. Benét himself has no such pretensions; he is modest, and persons who have not lost their heads over the poem should keep them in reviewing the nonsense that has been written about it, lest Mr. Benét be confounded with his prophets and unjustly blamed. The poem is not in any sense an epic; neither is it a philosophical vision of the Civil War; it is a loose, episodic narrative which unfolds a number of related themes in motion-picture flashes. In spite of some literary incompetence in the author and the lack of a controlling imagination, the story gathers suspense as it goes and often attains to power.

Many passages, particularly the lyrical commentaries scattered throughout, are so good that one suspects that the vicious writing, which is most of the poem, comes of too hasty composition. Perhaps Mr. Benét, like most Americans, is mysteriously betrayed into writing with his ear to the ground. It is not his fault; let us say it is the fault of the "system"; yet whoever may be at fault, the poem contains lines like these (which are not the worst):

> Now the scene expands, we must look at the scene as
>   a whole.
> How are the gameboards chalked and the pieces set?

There are too many other lines quite as flat, and they are not all bad because Mr. Benét has a bad ear for verse; they are due, rather, to a lack of concentration in the grasp of the material. The transitions are often arbitrary or forced, and this blemish, which at first sight seems to be merely literary, really takes the measure of Mr. Benét's capacity as a "major poet."

For he does not see the Civil War as a whole. I do not mean that he has not visualized all the campaigns (he has done this admirably), nor that he is deficient in general ideas as to what the war was about. It is simply that his general ideas remain on the intellectual plane; they are disjointed, diffuse, uncoordinated; they never reach any sweeping significance as symbols. The symbol of John Brown becomes an incentive to some misty writing, and instead of sustaining the poem it evaporates in mixed rhetoric. Mr. Benét sees that the meaning of the war is related to the meaning of Brown; yet what is the meaning of Brown? The presentation of Brown as a *character* is interesting; but it is neither here nor there to say, symbolically, that he is a "stone" or, at the end, that the machine-age grows out of his body. It is a pretty conceit, but it is not large enough, it is not sufficiently welded to the subject matter to hold together a poem of fifteen thousand lines. Is it possible that Mr. Benét supposed the poem to be about the Civil War, rather than about his own mind? This would explain its failure of unity; for if a poet has some striking personal vision of life, it will be permanent, and it will give meaning to all the symbols of his irresistible choice. We are permitted to say that the Civil War interests Mr. Benét; it has no meaning for him. He has not been ambitious enough.

Yet Mr. Benét himself appears, in this connection, to have recognized the diffuseness of his impulse. He seems to have felt that the partial glimpses he has given us of the social backgrounds of the war were not strong enough to carry the poem along, and he has contrived a "human interest story" to take the place of a comprehensive symbol. Jack Ellyat, the Union private, is captured at Shiloh; he escapes to a cabin in the woods, where he seduces the beautiful daughter. So far, so good; but when, shortly after the war, the daughter with the baby appears at Ellyat's home-town in Connecticut, the ways of God are not sufficiently mysterious. It is a trick done for effect; the effect is bad.

Many passages in the narrative are complete poems in themselves; a bare collection of these might display Mr. Benét's true stature to better advantage than their context does. Many are distinguished poems; the Invocation is one of the best recent productions by an American.

Mr. Benét has steeped himself in the documents of the age, and many of the historical portraits are freshly done; the interpretation in some instances is highly original. The picture of Lincoln is, as usual, uncritical and unconvincing. The greatest successes are Davis and Lee. If professional historians, particularly those of the Northern tradition, will follow Mr. Benét's Davis, a distorted perspective in American history will soon be straightened out. Nowhere else has Lee been so ably presented, yet the Lee is not so good as the Davis; for, perhaps frightened by the pitfalls, Mr. Benét openly points them out, and the portrait is too argumentative. Yet these and countless minor figures—generals, statesmen, private soldiers, runaway Negroes, plantation ladies, each sharply drawn in his right character—move in an atmosphere all their own that takes us past the literary blemishes to the end. Yet is this atmosphere a quality of the poem or of our memories? Succeeding generations will decide.—ALLEN TATE, "The Irrepressible Conflict," *Nation*, Sept. 19, 1928, p. 274

For twenty years Mr. Benét has been praised as a prodigy, a patriot, an entertainer, and a prize-winner; it has not been so easy to take him seriously as a poet. But one becomes conscious of a wish to resist this difficulty and summon up a reasonable interest in a writer so devoted to the American tradition that he has won, at whatever sacrifice of critical respect or comparison with the more formidable talents of his period, one of the largest popular followings of the past two decades. His verse is a survival of an abundant native line; it has become a virtual guide-book of native myth and folklore, their place-names, heroes, humors, and reverences. He followed the mid-western poets of the pre-War revival in this affection; one poem in *Burning City*, a tribute to Vachel Lindsay which precedes another to Walt Whitman, reminds us of this continuity. At a moment when even special students of poetry are expressing exasperation with the more rarefied purities of esthetic belief, when political contempt is directed against intellectual verse and symbolist influences, when a new order of lyric realism is being demanded of Americans and the author of *John Brown's Body* is held up at the Writers' Congress as a model of popular eloquence to revolutionaries, Mr. Benét's day for sober honors seems at last to have arrived. *Burning City* claims attention on these grounds and one hopes to see a practiced hand demonstrate to floundering proletarian talents the right ways of using popular language and subjects, of translating common human tastes and necessities into a verse that will surmount the futility of convincing only those believers who require no conversion to the ways of light. The fact that Mr. Benét has sensed this situation and turned to social and political subject compels such curiosity.

. . . Mr. Benét follows in a poetic line that is never so relaxed or self-confident as in the presence of prophetic enormities that might paralyze another order of poets to the point of speechlessness. This confidence is important; it indicates his type—the romantic fabulist. It explains both the ease with which he has spun past legends out of any stuff that fell to hand—Biblical, historical, or fantastic—and the temerity that produced in *John Brown's Body* a whole text-book of dramatic and metrical varieties. Ease of this kind is as enviable as it is convenient in a poet who wants to work in the large dimensions of popular myth. There can be no undue worry about refining allegory or imagery to the point of exact meaning, no severe economy in a poem's structure, and no privacy in its references. Such verse strives to be as indulgent to the reader's attention as possible, and no generosity is greater than that exhibited by Mr. Benét's facile yarn-spinning imagination. His poem on Lindsay amounts to much more than a reproachful tribute to an ignored and neglected singer of the tribe: it shows how Mr. Benét derived, through Lindsay, from the bardic romantics who held sway in American poetry for over a century. Kipling, Masefield, Morris, and Rossetti might be studied as English revivalists of ballad and epic heroics, but not necessarily, for in America this tradition, in its homeliest form, was the living authority of text-books and family anthologies all the way from Neihardt, Riley, and Markham, back through Hay, Harte, and Miller, to the bearded dynasties of Longfellow and Bryant—a succession hostile to eccentric talent or refined taste, scornful of modernity or exotic influence, once the pride of the burgeoning Republic, and now chiefly a source of cheerful embarrassment to teachers and blushing incredulity to their students. Mr. Benét has aspired from his school-days to a place in this old American line. He has preferred, to the tests and risks of a loftier poetic hardihood, the homespun satisfactions recently expressed by Robert Frost:

> At least don't use your mind too hard,
> But trust my instinct—I'm a bard.

Toward such bardship he has mastered a profuse stock of native lore and made himself, next to Lindsay, the most proficient balladist on native themes in the century. If the sentiment of local traditions survives for future poets, it may be largely due to his efforts. One admits a strong pull on even the most guarded of patriotic feelings, as well as on human impulses over which vigilance may now be more safely relaxed.—Morton Dauwen Zabel, "The American Grain," *Poetry*, Aug. 1936, pp. 276–79

Of Mark Sabre, the hero of *If Winter Comes*, we are told that Byron's poems was "the first book he had ever bought 'specially'—not, that is, as one buys a bun, but as one buys a dog." I have a similar feeling for Stephen Vincent Benét's *Heavens and Earth* (his third volume of poems, following *Young Adventure*, and *Five Men and Pompey*, published while he was still at school). For that was the first book I ever bought on the strength of a review—and I wish my own reviews were always as reliable as that one proved to be. It appeared in *The Yale Literary Magazine*; I was a schoolboy at Taft at the time, and read the *Lit* much more religiously than I did when I got to Yale. What chiefly struck me in it was a comparison to William Morris, a current idol of mine, and a number of quotations, excellently chosen, which showed me that here was one of my predestined books. I bought it the first day of the following vacation (it was one of the curious features of secondary education as then practiced that while at school it was made as difficult as possible to read any books) and found all that I had been looking for and more besides. The resemblance to William Morris in certain poems was plain enough; in his first novel, *The Beginning of Wisdom*, which belongs to what he has elsewhere described as "the required project in those days, a school and college novel," Benét says of the boy who is not quite himself that one of his first outpourings was "a long and bloodily bad ballad stewed from the bones of William Morris"; but it was resemblance to Morris where he is least dangerous as an influence, in the mood of mediaevalism combined with brutal realism of "Shameful Death" or "The Haystack in the Floods"—and, making allowance for some youthful romanticism, the mood, here, of "Three Days' Ride."

But there was of course a great deal more than that. Even in that one poem, there was also, for instance, a technical device to take your breath away—literally, the way the *pnigos* in Aristophanes took away the breath of the actor—if (as you should) you read it aloud. It is that innocent refrain,

> From Belton Castle to Solway side,
> Hard by the bridge, is three days' ride,

which, at each repetition, becomes more menacing, until in its final form,

> From Belton Castle to Solway side,
> Though great hearts break, is three days' ride,

the beating stresses give you a feeling in the chest which you will recognize from the last time you ran five miles.

There were other matters of technique, too, to fascinate a schoolboy who had recently discovered the subject. There is the dirge in "The First Vision of Helen"—which he would not let me include here, with the oversevere judgment of a creator who has gone on to something else. God, I suppose, admires the dinosaurs less than we do. The poem is in various metres; one section begins:

> Close his eyes with the coins; bind his chin with the
> shroud.

That line, you will notice, is made of the musical phrase *tum ti tum ti ti tum* twice repeated; and that, with what the books call anacrusis and anaclasis, is the metrical unit of the entire lament. It was not until freshman year at Yale when I read *Prometheus Bound* that I learned to call it a dochmiac; but I was able to recognize it as a single foot, and a complete and rare one. (Gilbert Murray and another have used it to render Greek choruses; as far as I know it occurs nowhere else in English.) A good deal later I was able to ask Steve Benét, "M. Jourdain, did you know that in that passage you were writing in dochmiacs?" He replied honestly that he did not know whether he had ever encountered the foot or not, but he believed he had just felt that anapaests were "too curly."

Whether he found or invented it, it is the perfect measure for the sway of the bearers ("Slow as the stream and strong, answering knee to knee"); and the accommodation of the line to the breath in these two poems is the promise of what he achieves in *John Brown's Body* when he attacks one of the primary problems of verse in our day, the finding of a form which may bear the same relation to our easygoing talk that, presumably, blank verse did to the more formal speech of an earlier generation. Half a dozen poets are attempting it; Benét was one of the first in the field, and I think is the most successful, with the long, loose, five- or six-beat line that carries the bulk of *John Brown's Body*. It will be improved in the later poems; in *John Brown's Body* it is sometimes a little too loose, coming perilously near prose; yet it can carry casual conversations without incongruity, or at need can deepen without any sense of abrupt transition into blank verse for the nobility of Lincoln or Lee, or even slip into rhyme for the romantics of the Wingates. And it passes the great test for existence as a metre: single lines of it stay in your memory, existing by themselves.

It is over now, but they will not let it be over.

Professor Procrustes could explain that as an iambic or an anapaestic line, and name its variations; but to plain common sense it is neither. It is in a metre of its own; one of our time; one which Benét has given us.

There was more, too, in that thin purple book with a gilt demi-Pegasus on the cover, to meet one halfway and lead one out of the Pre-Raphaelite dreamland. There was an impish humor, which appeared not only in the openly grotesque poems, but was likely to crop up anywhere—in the tempting quotation, for instance, which begins "Young Blood," and which, when you catch him with the question, Steve will blandly tell you that he invented. It is this quality, by the way, which is most readily apparent when you know him. He is given a puckish air by his habit of twisting his legs round his chair, by his round glasses, and his squeaky voice—which I always hear, in "Nightmare with Angels," giving his own peculiarly emphatic intonation to the conclusion "In fact, you will not be saved." In talk he seems to "make fun" of everything, not in the sense of ridicule, but with the humor that comes from looking at anything with a really original mind. His talk ranges over everything he has read (and he has read everything) building pyramids in the air, and, like his own "Innovator," turning them upside down to see how they look; while from time to time his wife Rosemary puts in a wise and charming word as she sits serenely sewing—looking like an unusually humorous version of the housewifely Athena, as Steve behind his spectacles looks like an unusually humorous version of Athena's owl.

That is the Benét of the dry comments in *John Brown's Body*, upon McClellan—

He looked the part—he could have acted the part
Word perfectly. He looked like an empire-builder.
But so few empire-builders have looked the part—

or upon Wendell Phillips—

He did his part,
Being strong and active, in all ways shaped like a
man,
And the cause being one to which he professed devotion,
He spoke. He spoke well, with conviction, and frequently.

It is the Benét of the fantasies and fables, of the extraordinary "Nightmares," which deepen from the fantastic-amusing to the fantastic-terrifying. It's the author who can rewrite an old fairy tale for today in the much-reprinted "King of the Cats," or can write a new legend so perfect that it seems to have been always a part of our folklore—for the Devil and Daniel Webster ought forever to haunt New Hampshire as solidly as Rip Van Winkle and his gnomes haunt the Hudson. And the Benét who turns pyramids upside down in talk is the one who writes with imagination. The popular magazines are filled with stories that have invention, and ingenuity, and even a sort of conjurer's illusion; but the rarest thing in the world there or anywhere else is real imagination, which is real magic—such as you find in that astonishing piece of what-if, "The Curfew Tolls," or that haunting evocation of the feeling of certain quiet city backwaters, "Glamour." It is also one of the marks of imaginative insight that it can have an Einsteinian view of both sides of a solid at once; can see Napoleon as a good deal of a scoundrel and also as a great man; can destroy all the traditional witchery of the traditional Southern belle, and yet leave her, somehow, mistress of a more undeniable spell than before.—BASIL DAVENPORT, "Stephen Vincent Benét," *Selected Works of Stephen Vincent Benét*, 1942, pp. ix–xii

Stephen Vincent Benét's death was a particular loss because he added to the variety of American poetry. His contribution of the historical narrative was unique, since few practised it and no other approached his success. It is important to define his effort. He was not interested in mouthing the word "America." Nor was his praise that blind rhapsody of a nation intended, by celebrating the poet's nationality, to celebrate the poet. Benét's deep regard for the U.S.A. was based not on a feeling of blood and earth, but on an honest belief in this country as remarkably permitting human freedom. He knew the misery and corruption, and you'll find them in his books. But, stronger than any other motive, you will find Benét's fascination with the effort of these states to be a place where that reckless and distorted word "liberty" actually means individual right and intellectual exemption.—PAUL ENGLE, "The American Search," *Poetry*, Dec. 1943, p. 160

The history of Benét's short-story writing is a record of struggle with three adversaries: his innate preference for the freedoms of poetry rather than the restrictions of short fiction; the exigency of earning a living largely through marketable stories; and the folly of magazine editors. The editors he withstood when to yield meant selling a principle; the substantial income he needed he eventually attained; and the mastery of the form he achieved after a prolonged struggle.

"The short story," Benét admitted, "was never exactly my forte." His biographer observes that creating his finer short stories was a punishing process for Benét, imposing great psychic and physical tension. Even the commercial product did not come easily. "Finished another short story today," he reported to his wife in 1921, "a very short one, thank God, only 4,000 words. I tried to copy Millay-Boyd in it and rather produced the effect of an elephant trying to walk the tightrope—I am not at my best in the flippant sentimental."

Perhaps because of his deep-seated uneasiness with and even distaste for the short story, Benét did not experiment in its form. In his best work, however, he gave to the traditional structure an easy balance, an unobtrusive precision, and a finish that reveal nothing of his travail in its composition. Despite his choice of conventional form, he was characteristically undogmatic about the form of the short story; he remarked that Edward O'Brien, editor of the annual collections of the best American short stories, was "as prejudiced in favor of the formula formless story as the big-magazine-editor of 1925 was prejudiced against it." Benét found the older structure with a definite beginning, middle, and end—as practiced by Poe, by Henry James, or, in more leisurely fashion, by Washington Irving—more suitable for his own purposes than the Chekhovian moment-of-insight tale, as practiced in America by Sherwood Anderson. Benét came to employ the old device of a narrator in many of his stories, and he did so skillfully, making effective use of the greater immediacy, rapport with the reader, and interesting self-revelation or concealment which this point of view affords; but he did no pioneering in the form of the short story.

The scores of Benét stories that appeared in second- or third-rate mass circulation magazines during the 1920's and with less frequency during the 1930's attest to the degree to which he had to merchandise his creativity. As usual, he knew exactly what he was doing. He described one of his concoctions, written to help finance a year in Paris for the writing of *John Brown's Body*, as "a dear little candy-laxative of a tale about a sweet little girl named Sally. . . . I do not see how it can fail to sell—it is so cheap!" On another occasion he referred sardonically to "one of my celebrated, bright, gay stories of gay, bright, dumb young people." His bitterness, according to Fenton, was basically directed at the inflexible narrowness of the editors of the popular magazines which alone could pay him the money he needed. When the editor of the *Saturday Evening Post* asked Benét to alter the figure of investment broker Lane Parrington in "Schooner Fairchild's Class" so as not to make him such a stuffy representative of conservatism, Benét refused. He wrote his agent that "if you have to class-angle a story for the *Post* as you'd have to for the New Masses, only in reverse—there's no point in my trying to write for them. I can't work that way." Benét took this stand at a time when the *Post* had been paying him $1,250 a story.

Benét sought sometime during the mid-1920's to reconcile his artistic conscience with his financial needs by writing fiction stamped with his own originality and excellence yet possessed of wide popular appeal. He achieved this reconciliation by taking familiar materials from American history and folklore and mixing them with the bright colors of his imagination. "We have our own folk-gods and giants and figures of earth in this country," Benét once remarked. "I wanted to write something about them." Out of his ambition sprang such fresh, fine tales as the Daniel Webster group—"The Devil and Daniel Webster," "Daniel Webster and the Sea Serpent," and "Daniel Webster and the Ides of March"—"Jacob and the Indians," "A Tooth for Paul Revere," "Freedom's a Hard-Bought Thing," and "Johnny Pye and the Fool-Killer." Not so good a story as any of these but notable as the earliest example of Benét's use of American types and legends is "The Sobbin' Women." Though it owes something to the legend of the Sabine women, Benét transformed the Roman story through the use of such characters as the Oldest Inhabitant of a nineteenth-century small town, a hedge parson, and the seven brothers with American folk-hero qualities. Later Benét widened his historical themes to include European and contemporary affairs. History in one phase or another is the subject of his finest short stories, as it is of his poetry.— PARRY STROUD, "The Short Stories: From Wholesale to Artistry," *Stephen Vincent Benét*, 1962, pp. 114–16

HENRY SEIDEL CANBY
From "Introduction" to *John Brown's Body*
1928, pp. x–xv

I t seems . . . that the Civil War was too modern in its aspects, by which I mean too much of a people's war, familiar, sordid, wide-reaching, disillusioning, to be made into literature by the old methods. It was not Shakespeare's kind of war, nor Addison's, nor Byron's, nor Tennyson's, nor Kipling's even. The age of plain people and scientific education had to pass through its naturalistic stage before Bull Run and slavery, Lincoln, Jeff Davis, and the psychology of cultures could be taken over into an intelligible literature.

And hence it is no derogation to Stephen Benét's broad and stirring saga, to say that time and events have made it possible. Neither he nor we could have known what a people's war meant before 1914–1918. A generation ago, before the United States became a Power and began to be described in terms less naïve than Manifest Destiny, it would have been impossible to make a unity of all this confusion. We did not know enough economics, could not get the rights and wrongs in perspective, would have been content either with odes on the North and pæans on the South, or with local color sketches like Stephen Crane's *The Red Badge of Courage*.

But that mid-century America is now as dead as the Past ever is. It is an Age, a Period, a Phase, still familiar but in no immediate sense Us. It is an analyzable America that might have become something different. It is heroic, wrong-headed, shameful, potent, and, like all Pasts, in a different mode from ours. It is a major premise for modern America, but active only in the results of the syllogism. We can see it now as we see the

Revolutionary fathers, acutely and sympathetically, but as something familiar, yet strange, that lived before our times. And this is a prerequisite for successful studies of the Past. It must be a real Past for the imaginative artist, where he can reconstruct according to his own interests (since the Present only is alive), remaking a Crisis according to its significance for history, which means, of course, for him and for us.

And I think also that *John Brown's Body* owes quite as much to the wave of realism in literature that has rolled up between us and that past. It is both a tribute to the climax of realism, which was naturalism, and a sign of its passing. A romantic poem, rising to heights of eloquence, and singularly rich in passages of lyric sweetness, so that, unlike any of the American poetry of the last two decades, it moves the reader to emotional enthusiasm, it is beautiful as well as intricate, and has as much pathos as excitement, as much sentiment as intellectual analysis. And yet it is as realistic as it is romantic. The Jake Diefers and the Baileys and the Shippys, the prostitutes with Confederate flags on their garters, the rough-neck business of war, and the small-town emotions; the ease with which the poet gets off his high horse when Lee has ridden past on Traveller, so that he shall get it all in, the homely with the sublime, without losing his grip on the significance of the whole;—this he has learned from naturalistic fiction, from the Zolas, the Dreisers, the Andersons, the Wellses and the Bennetts, and also from the Frosts, the Lindsays, and the Masterses that Conservatives have been deploring.

And he has taken his zig-zag continuity, where, like pictures on a screen, or memories in the consciousness, the noble and the mean, the tragic and the funny, pass and break and are picked up again and dropped, from James Joyce and the movies, from the behaviorists and the impressionists. No, this poem could not have been written twenty years ago.

I am describing *John Brown's Body* rather than analyzing it, because I cannot with any justice analyze it in a limited space and describe it too. It has been widely read, and will be still more widely read, for it is not one of your *tours de force* of intellect and technique to be admired and then tucked away on the library shelf. It is a library of story telling itself, a poem extraordinarily rich in action as well as actors, vivid, varied, and so expressive of many men and moods that prose could never have carried its electric burden. Benét has as many voices as an organ. He has the art of suspense and the gift of movement which our intellectual poets definitely lack when they try to tell a story. He has a suavity of diction, when he wants it, which is dangerous in pure lyric but indispensable to a fine narrative poem. He knows how to raise the cloud no bigger than a man's hand with his opening scene on a slaver captained by a fanatic. He has the sense for drama which chooses as his protagonist, not Lincoln who carried through, but the tough-fibred individualist, John Brown, blind to immediate consequence, a stone of fate for hammering walls, Thoreau's John Brown who had the mad courage to put his conscience against reason, a man pre-doomed to failure, whose soul went marching on. He has the broad vision of the historian of the modern type, who considers vanity, greed, ignorance, the cotton in the fields, fear, things inanimate as well as animate, until history becomes as complex as life—and much too complex for a historian to strike into a unity. And yet, as the artist must, he holds to his line of significance—not slavery, not economic rivalry, not race prejudice, but the struggle of individuals caught in karma, Lincoln and Jefferson Davis, Lee and Grant, Ellyat of Connecticut, Wingate of Georgia, Bailey of Illinois, Jake Diefer of Pennsylvania, the runaway negro, Spade, Sally Dupré, the subtle Jew Benjamin, all fighting in the irresistible tide of events sweeping through a broken dam toward chaos, all touched somewhere, somehow by great issues.

This poem, indeed, is good history, but it is also good art. I am not inclined to be apologetic with the poet for his nationalistic theme—

> So, from a hundred visions, I make one,
> And out of darkness build my mocking sun.
> And should that task seem fruitless in the eyes
> Of those a different magic sets apart
> To see through the ice-crystal of the wise
> No nation but the nation that is Art,
> Their words are just. . . .
> Art has no nations—but the mortal sky
> Lingers like gold in immortality.
> This flesh was seeded from no foreign grain
> But Pennsylvania and Kentucky wheat,
> And it has soaked in California rain
> And five years tempered in New England sleet.

We shall have passed beyond the need of national art when we shall have passed beyond nations, or rather, when the possibilities of a culture vibrant with home and traditions shall have been exhausted. Art has no nations, but it must be born somewhere, and the American must make his own his own before it can be good for others. If great events of which our own people have been part and parcel do not move us, there is little chance for a great literature built upon the Arthurian legends or the League of Nations.

Indeed it is the intense nationalism of *John Brown's Body* that is perhaps responsible for its esthetic importance, which is not equalled, I should say, by any recent American book. For Benét is writing as Shakespeare wrote in his histories, and Racine in his tragedies, and Vergil in the *Æneid*, on a great theme in which he himself has a vested interest. He cannot, and he does not, take the view of that modernistic literature from which he borrows so much in technique, that the writer should be, as a young modernist has recently said, a skilful reporter merely of phenomena whose meaning he does not pretend to understand. His poem is composed, significant, and bound together in a moral unity. For here is the inconsequentiality, the uncertainness, the mingled grossity and valor of life, the vividness of minute experience, all organized by a moral significance which in this fateful period can be shown to have given one meaning, at least, to the whole. It is the method and point of view of the great poems of the past—but this does not prove that it is wrong. His subject is a Past. On the present he does not speculate, but merely says "it is here." Perhaps only a fool expects to grasp the significance of a present, but certainly only an impressionist can write of life at all unless he tries to grasp the moral organization which makes it different from the mechanics of a coral reef.

For his poem, he has chosen a blank verse of five or six stresses, planed down almost to prose; often it is prose, and sometimes is written as such. Conservative readers have complained of this oscillation between metrical poetry, in which the rhythm is sharply marked, and the freer, rougher rhythms of prose. They have asked why *John Brown's Body*, like *The Idylls of the King*, should not have been written throughout in a regular verse form, where the lines were always scannable according to the rules of blank verse, and the tone of pure poetry was always maintained.

One might answer that the Civil War is by no means such a theme as the conflicts of King Arthur or the war between the Trojans and the Greeks. It is close to us. It is mingled high tragedy, humor, and sordidness. It is almost necessarily seen by a realistic age, like ours, in terms of realism as well as romance. There is no inherent reason why prose and verse should not be mingled or verse of high suavity with verse of a freer, rougher rhythm—especially in a dramatic poem. Shakespeare did it, and let lovers of Tennyson who complain of the drops toward prose of *John Brown's Body* imagine this work done throughout in the rather monotonous suavity of *The Idylls* and consider again their argument. Certainly Benét was well aware of what he was doing, and could very well have employed the melodious loveliness of the verse he uses in the episode of The Hiders throughout, if he had wished.

As it is, the style of his poem rises and falls with the emotions of his theme. But for his personal stories, the Georgian Wingates and Sally Dupré, Cudjo the negro butler, Ellyat the Connecticut intellectual, and the rest, there is an extraordinary variety of rhythmic movements. The versatility of his poetic style is unusual. He can do anything except the organ line in which blank verse reaches its highest powers, and perhaps for this reason the historical center of his poem is the least impressive portion, although an excellent foil for the lyric movements that surround it. Lincoln in meditation is more effective than all his accounts of Lincoln, and the silent mystery of Lee is less striking just because Lee is silent. Benét is at his best as a dramatic lyricist. Yet where most epic poets are weak, he is strong. The humorous realism of his soldiers is excellent, yet I like him best of all in those incidental narratives, touched or driven by great events yet shining with their own light of merely human interest. The Negroes are the truest I know in American poetry.

I feel that this survey of *John Brown's Body* is unusually inadequate, even for criticism which must always let so much more slip through its fingers than can be held. I should like to consider Benét's thoughtful study of Lincoln which preserves both his homeliness and his poetry, comment on his very interesting view of Jefferson Davis, the honest orator, weigh his analysis of the inner meaning of the conflict, and discuss his quite unexpected resolution of the whole tragedy into the triumph of a machine age that knows neither John Brown nor morality. Politically, it is a non-partisan poem, spiritually it is Northern. The fanaticism of the North as well as its commercialism he accepts as irrevocable; the romance of the South he makes as brittle as its charm and haunting melancholy are persuasive. The Connecticut Ellyat and the rough boys from Illinois and Pennsylvania are much more convincing than Wingate and his Black Horse Troop, because they have psychologies while the Southerners are chiefly manners and fate. This is not true of his women. Sally Dupré, next to Melora, is his best; the Northern women are shadows. The answer lies probably in his own experience and is not important. We are not far enough yet from the 1860's to view his Greeks and Trojans with even Homer's impartiality.

This poem is clearly a poem of the transition. In spite of the firm grip upon purpose and significance, it is too fluent for a classic taste, bursting out at corners, pouring and flashing and jumping and zig-zagging through wide margins, where, when we have got on top of all the fascinating new material that realism has been gathering for us, we shall be more selective, restrained, intense. There will be more in every line and less broadcast through pages. The margins of experience will be attained by sheer skill of imaginative suggestion rather than by excessive roaming back and forth in the story. But this poem could have been done successfully only this way now, and it is an immense credit to Benét that he has been able to recreate the rough and tumble, sweet and sour of an epoch with a modern imagination, and yet hold it all in one grand theme.

THOMAS BERGER

1924–

Thomas Louis Berger was born in Cincinnati on July 20, 1924. After three years in the Army, he attended the University of Cincinnati, from which he received a B.A. in 1948. While a graduate student at Columbia University in 1950, he married the artist Jean Redpath. Throughout the 1950s Berger worked as a librarian, an indexer, and an editor, both freelance and for *Popular Science Monthly*. In 1958 he published his first novel, *Crazy In Berlin*, which drew on his Army experiences. Berger continued the adventures of hapless Carlo Reinhart in *Reinhart in Love* (1962), *Vital Parts* (1970), and *Reinhart's Women* (1981).

Little Big Man, published in 1964, quickly became the totem of Berger's critical cult. This epic satire of the American West won him the Western Heritage Award and the Rosenthal Award, and was filmed in 1970. Each succeeding novel reflects a different genre and style, including science fiction in *Regiment of Women* (1973); detective fiction in *Who Is Teddy Villanova?* (1977); historical fantasy in *Arthur Rex* (1978); and a Kafkaesque tale of suburbia in *Neighbors* (1980). This last is Berger's own favorite among his own books; it was filmed in 1982.

Although he writes every day, Berger has found time to teach at the University of Kansas, Southampton College, and since 1981, Yale University. Besides his novels, Berger has written a play, *Other People* (1970), and in the early 1970's, film reviews for *Esquire*. He lives with his wife in New York.

General

Berger's books—*Crazy in Berlin, Reinhart in Love, Little Big Man*—are wild comedy, but they are not the facile, anything-goes surrealism of the black humorists. Neither are they satires, or polemics, or politically motivated gripes. They are funny in the way *Don Quixote* or Rabelais is funny—the laughter of a wise humanist, experiencing the world in all its absurdity: tolerant, pleased, saddened—and *involved*. The glory of *Little Big Man* lies in the way Berger imposes his comic view of life on a deadly accurate portrait of the Old West. I know from conversations with him that he researched the period as thoroughly as any historian, that his outlandish Cheyennes and their hilarious locutions are based on actual recorded testimony of Indian warriors. It is the truest kind of humor, a humor that derives from real situations and real people. Who can resist Berger's Cheyennes, who refer to themselves haughtily as "The Human Beings"? Or his description of the way an Indian camp smells? Or the Indians' disdain for time, schedules, anything continuous—a trait which causes them to hate the railroad?—GERALD GREEN, "Back to Bigger," *Proletarian Writers of the Thirties*, ed. David Madden, 1968, pp. 43–44

Works

Thomas Berger's ⟨*Regiment of Women*⟩ is set in a grim 21st-century New York City. Inflation has reached such proportions that the hero, Georgie Cornell, has trouble meeting the rent for a tiny Upper East Side apartment on his $1,500-a-week salary. Muggings are so common that snatch-resistent purses are obligatory. Few things work, not even toilets or traffic lights or elevators. Pollution has turned the Hudson River into a sewer and made gas masks *de rigeur*.

But all this serves mainly as a backdrop for the author's parody of current uncertainties and ambiguities about sexual roles. Thus in Berger's world men wear rouge and lipstick, dresses, stockings and garter-belts; women with close-cropped hair wear suits, ties and jackets. (Transvestism—men dressing in pants and cutting their hair short—is a serious crime punishable by detention or castration.)

Women are also the statesmen, generals and political leaders. Pregnancy has not only beeen replaced by incubators, but sexual intercourse is a Federal crime and the belief is fostered that penetration of the vagina is fatal. The picture of a child nursing at a woman's breast is considered filthy and pornographic.

The winos, perverts and rapists are women, too. Georgie Cornell lives in fear of being attacked by dildo-wearing females (especially black women who are constantly after white men), and he always misses his anal therapy sessions with his woman analyst, Dr. Prine. It is the men, naturally, who are now concerned about protecting their reputations and the women who gloat over their conquests.

One problem with *Regiment of Women* is that it is based on little more than the idea of reversal. There is something initially obvious in all satire, and therefore to be successful a unique tension must be developed between the theoretical and the concrete, the idea proposed and the life created within it. The effect of comic disproportion should be like that of a magnifying glass that focuses our attention more clearly on particular vagaries of human nature that might otherwise have been taken for granted.

Although there are glimmerings of insight into the factitiousness of outward sexual postures in Berger's futuristic fantasy, the reader is never allowed to penetrate behind the masks the author fashions. Georgie Cornell remains little more than an abstract expression of sexual opposites—passive and submissive at the beginning in women's clothes, dominant and powerful when he removes the make-up.

To a certain extent Berger's failure to go beyond clichés may stem from an unresolved question of ultimate intention. For despite its predictability, an underlying inconsistency runs throughout the work.

At the end Georgie, who has been discovering all along that he is really physically stronger and no less intelligent or capable than most women, meets up with Harriet, who is equally dissatisfied with her assigned role. The two steal the Rolls Royce of a powerful woman senator and drive north toward the Canadian wilderness, where Georgie's male dominant traits are let loose. In a moment of anger he jumps on top of Harriet, intending to kill her with his penis, only to find himself "swallowed alive by that which he would kill."

One simply is not sure what Berger is up to in this burlesque. Is his purpose to poke fun at present sociosexual trends (as in the beginning of the novel), to warn that what he envisions is in a very real sense inevitable unless mankind returns to its natural instincts, or merely to lampoon the typical escape-and-romance ending of some paperback novels?

To be sure, there is humor here that derives from a feeling of deviation, disproportion or imbalance. And it is particularly effective in Berger's description toward the end of a hefty New England woman shopkeeper with "U.S. Marines" tattooed on her biceps, and of a closemouthed pipe-smoking woman gasoline attendant. Completely missing, though, is any sense of a center, a principle of reason, nature or love to set off all the untruths, artificialities and grotesqueries in Berger's 21st century.

The conflict between conditioned roles and innate inclinations, between choice and impulse, is a genuine problem for sexuality in the modern consciousness. And no doubt it is necessary at least to start, as Berger has, with commonly held assumptions and stereotypes. Yet unfortunately, instead of opening up new areas of inquiry with its satirical treatment, the book's meticulously executed pattern serves rather to divert the author from the very questions he raises. One must be able to ascertain what are the masks and what aren't. Reading *Regiment of Women* one never quite knows.—FRANCIS LEVY, "Reversing Roles," *NL*, Nov. 12, 1973, p. 20

Who Is Teddy Villanova? is first person and extravagant, not so much a parody of Hammett and Chandler as a confident, exceedingly literary adaptation of the form, Seventies cool rather than Forties bite. Here we are, private eye and secretary, in the early pages:

> "Gawd, I'm still hungry," she said with the same righteousness as that in which Zola penned the memorable *J'accuse*. "I couldn't afford Blimpie's Best. I had to take Number One, all roll."
>
> "I haven't had the leisure for lunch, myself," said I. "I was savaged by the gigantic hoodlum you nonchalantly admitted. I called for help, but—God's blood!—you were already gone."
>
> "I don't have to take that type language," she asseverated in her fire-siren voice, her plump breasts bouncing. "My brother'd pound you to a pulp if he heard you." I didn't know to which brother she referred, the sanitation union functionary or the one who was a petty timeserver in Queens Borough Hall, sans power to fix a traffic ticket, or perhaps merely the inclination to exert it: earning him, at any rate, a deafening blow on the ear from an offended cousin at one of the Tumulty family's Thanksgiving Donnybrooks.

This may be likable, but it is hard to imagine anyone liking a whole book of it. Chandler's style was often ornate and self-conscious. To make that style only words calling attention to themselves seems more an occupation for a late-night competition among friends than for a novelist.

Some sections are tedious: an episode with cops named Calvin, Knox, and Zwingli; a yoga teacher in Greenwich Village; a Maltese Falcon, here called a Sforza figurine. But by the time I reached the figurine, late in the novel, I was unexpectedly enjoying myself, because the story is good enough to keep Berger himself interested in what he is doing. If you enjoy private-eye novels presumably you do so because you like

the mode, but what distinguishes a good from a bad one is the way the story reveals materials that in some way are being savored rather than simply used. Berger's story is nonsense. Cops and fake cops, dead bodies that reappear but were never dead, alliances that shift so frequently that at some moment everyone except the hero is or seems to be an ally or enemy of everyone else, and, governing all, Teddy Villanova, who may commit murders, or counterfeit money, or run brothels for fetishists, or sell office buildings, or deal in obscene art objects on classical themes—or, most likely, not exist at all, in which case the problem is who invented him.

What the story manages to express, however, far better than the comments on the subject made by Berger's hero, is a view of New York. When a cop says "Did you cause that man to shuffle off his mortal coil?" I feel embarrassed, as much by its inanity as coming from New York's police as by the limpness of the joke. But when the swirling tale leads the private eye from being saved from arrest by the Gay Assault Team, to sleeping all night in a Barca-Lounger left on a sidewalk in front of a brownstone, to a gunning down in Union Square, to a high-rise where a stewardess who may be a Treasury agent lives, then the motion itself expresses a decadent, improbable, fascinating wilderness that is familiar enough to be plausible and distinctive, too. The hero is beyond conspiracy theories about the city, despite the countless possible conspiracies against him, because nothing, and no one, surely, could have thought up New York.

Someone, though, is plotting against our hero, and maybe, indeed, it is his landlord, who wants only to get him to move so he can sell the office building; it might take that much to get someone out whose rent is frozen and whose funds are low. Finally, in a good last series of scenes, the plot comes back, as it should, to the original situation of a man, his secretary, and an unredeemable office building on East Twenty-third Street, expressing as it does so a piquant sense of what it takes for people to live, work, and make money in a city where everything moves but nothing works.

In this novel the first person seems fully justified. Everything the hero sees is simply out there, existing not to be understood but to be encountered, and, if possible, accepted, and everything the hero is can be said in mannered prose since he is a figure without inwardness or complexity. At the end the hero is as he was at the beginning, but given what has happened, this is an accomplishment. He is on the phone with a final claimant to the name of Teddy Villanova, and the secretary, who appears more and more full of guile as the story goes on, has just asked him if he is queer as she disappears into the bathroom:

> I had enough of this. I still had to answer Peggy's insulting question. "Well, 'Teddy,' you are a raffish fellow indeed, but my presence is required elsewhere."
>
> "If it's with those Stavrogin tots, be careful; they're police plants, old boy. If you crave green fruit, come visit me in Bavaria." He proceeded to specify certain amusements that I could not entertain even in joke.
>
> I hung up, went to the bathroom door, and cried: "No, I'm not a homosexual, nor zoophile, pederast, pedophile, flagellant, nor fetishist!"
>
> I went across the room, and in defiance, sat upon the defaced suede chair; my trousers were anyway streaked with pigeon dung.
>
> "Glad to hear that," said Peggy, opening the door and emerging in my old mulberry bathrobe.

And so to bed, the rat-tat-tat of language finally over. *Who Is Teddy Villanova?* is a good, accomplished minor novel; in these puffed up times I hope one can still offer such a judgment as genuine praise.—ROGER SALE, "Hostages," *NYRB*, May 26, 1977, pp. 39–40

Thomas Berger might be called the Green Knight of American fiction: a mysterious, protean outsider whose pose of destructiveness masks a fierce reverence for form and meaning. His best-known novel, *Little Big Man*, is a compassionate parody of the Western genre and of the American West itself; *Sneaky People*, published in 1975, is a comic masterpiece about low intrigue in a small town. *Who is Teddy Villanova?*, his last novel, simultaneously demolishes the private-eye novels of the 1940s and the allusive academic fiction of today.

Arthur Rex, a massive retelling of the Camelot legend, may be Berger's most ambitious book, at least in size and literary scale. He has forged his version of the familiar story—noble Arthur, unfaithful Guinevere, tormented Launcelot, and the dozens of familiar knights and ladies surrounding them—by drawing, as far as I can tell, on all the literary sources—the enormous body of work, dating from sixth century to the present, of Nennius, Tennyson, T. H. White, and countless others. His chief source—to which he is often surprisingly faithful—is Sir Thomas Malory, author of the massive 15th-century chronicle, *Le Morte d'Arthur*. But despite this careful scholarship, despite a prose style which borders on genius, despite many funny moments and a few painfully sad ones, *Arthur Rex*, in the end, remains less than the sum of its parts.

It begins, as one might expect, in humor and parody. Merlin quotes Freud and conjures up a tin-can telephone; Sir Kay, the Round Table's waspish headwaiter, wins honor as the inventor of the steam trolley; Sir Gawaine stars in a wickedly sexy parody of his famed adventure with the Green Knight.

Arthur himself at first seems merely a good-humored dimwit. His first act on ascending the throne is a vain attempt to close the brothel-convents flourishing behind St. Paul's cathedral. For much of the story, he eludes the malice of his enemies with the razor-edge good luck that always saved sleepwalkers teetering on high girders in silent films. Berger's version of the King's "seduction" by his half-sister Margawse (the incestuous union that produces the villainous Mordred, and, thus, the entire tragedy of the Round Table) is as funny as anything I have ever read. The enchantress comes to Caerleon with the honest purpose of killing Arthur and making off with his treasure, but finds herself—by neither her own intent nor that of the hopelessly inexperienced Arthur—somehow dizzied, disrobed, impregnated, and dismissed without a penny. In this episode, Berger's wacky diction, a mad half-parody of Malory's prose style, is at its best:

> . . . with her dexter hand [Margawse] followed the curve of the wall and felt with her dainty feet the stone treads, of which she used the broadest portion, at the maximum of their centrifugation, and the masons had laid them with such marvelous exactitude that each conformed to the rule of all, so that having found the pace, one could misstep only willfully, unless the constant revolution ever downwards agitated the humors causing vertigo. The which, in the case of this lady, came to happen. . . .

This is not the only moment in the story at which I laughed out loud. But *Arthur Rex* is not a spoof. Much of its narrative—the adulterous love of Launcelot and Guinevere, the parallel tragedy of Tristram, Isold, and Mark, Sir Gawaine's rise from

lechery and fall into vengeance—is seriously intended and often quite moving. The central tragedy in the book is that of Arthur, who attempts to found his table on pure virtue. The book's subtitle is "A Legendary Novel"; taking this term in its oldest meaning, we might consider it as the life story not primarily of a King, but of a saint. For all Arthur's goofiness, his ability to take a pratfall when the author requires it, I think Berger may intend to show Arthur as exactly that: a man who aspires to Godliness with his whole being, a seeker of selflessness who suffers the defeat of those who try for perfection.

Berger ascribes a larger role in the story to God than did the reverent but skeptical Malory. The author of *Arthur Rex* takes a dark, deeply Protestant view of life: God gives to each of us a nature, with strengths and flaws we are powerless to change. Each knight in the book struggles with a particular sin, sent by God as an individual test; but, Berger explains, "the only unforgivable sin is committed by the man who doth not use his gifts and therefore acts the coward to his own self, mocking the God who made him." The end of life is not happiness or triumph, for our sinful natures preclude these; we must simply do the best we can with what we are given, and lose. We can lose honorably or otherwise—that is our only choice.

This dark parable emerges from a 500-page narrative which is jumbled, fragmented, almost formless. Given Berger's consistent record of literacy and care, I think we can assume this is not unintentional. The Arthurian legend has always been a jumble, and Berger knows the source material in all its permutations and contradictions. Even the allusion to Freud, it turns out, is an echo of *The Once and Future King*.

One can even theorize that this jumbled effect—this deliberate splintering of character, narrative, and structure—might be Berger's mode of attack on the T. H. White novel, an attempt to erase the sanitized Camelot of *The Once and Future King* and restore the legend's mystery; to remind us that *Le Morte d'Arthur* continues to fascinate us because it is huge, redundant ("God's duty," as Dryden called it) inconsistent— in fact, not a novel in the formal sense at all.

The best characters in Berger's work continue to live in the reader's mind long after he has closed the book (I think particularly of Ralph Sandifer, the horny teenager of *Sneaky People*). Those in *Arthur Rex*, I predict, will fade. Readers will laugh at parts of this book, feel despair and grief at others; but after they have finished, it will be White's pompous, pacifistic Arthur, not Berger's doomed saint, who lingers in their minds.—GARRETT EPPS, "*Arthur Rex*," *NR*, Oct. 7, 1978, pp. 34–36

> Q: Who's Who in the East quotes your remark, "In my work I have tried to compete with that reality to which I must submit in life." How do you mean that? As opposed to showing reality up for what it is?
>
> Berger: I mean exactly what I say. My interest is in creation, not in commentary. Those who believe my intent is to criticize society, to satirize, to write spoofs and send-ups, to be that most humorless of scribblers, the so-called comic novelist, are utterly misguided. I write for the purpose of providing myself with an alternative to reality. . . . Nevertheless, be prepared to read many reviews of Neighbors that confidently announce my success or failure at holding the mirror up to suburban society and blithely ignore the truth that the book is about dying.

Berger is a writer of comedy, in the true, generic sense of the term. And as such he returns to chivalric England and to the Cheyenne of the Old West not to mock either romance or the past but because these subjects give him access to the themes that are his generic concerns. If Berger could be said to be talking about anything, beyond his formal interests, I would suggest that more basic than his coincidental satire are his (1) war with time, (2) yearning for human "rightness," that is personally and communally harmonious, and (3) a baffled love of women in uneasy tension with idealistic aspirations about manliness and realistic despair about sexual politics.

Berger goes about comedy's business choosing life, communion and order by killing time; it is difficult for him to locate this social harmony in contemporary settings. In such communal atemporality, the Indians of *Little Big Man* live naturally.

Among white men who "live in straight lines and squares," Little Big Man is prey to all the psychic dislocations of fallen man. Among Indians, he can feel, though rarely and never wholly—Berger does not romanticize primitivism—when "looking at the great universal circle" of the sky, that he is "at the center of the world, where all is self-explanatory." He has a place in the circle of the divine comedy.

Nothing could be further from that circle than the sorry cul-de-sac of suburban development where Earl Keese lives the last twenty-four hours of his never-lived life that comprise *Neighbors*, Berger's perfectly paced and inescapably disturbing tenth novel. The unneighborly way Earl's new neighbors, Harry and Ramona, treat him is as maddening as the way fate treats Jude the Obscure. They are boorish and abusive and obscene, and like characters in a Beckett or Ionesco play, talk non sequiturs with a terrible inconsequentiality that has even more terrible consequences.

Earl sees Harry thumbing through his checks, Ramona lying naked on his bed, he sees *pimp* painted on his car window. Or maybe he just thinks he does, maybe it's all an aberration of perception, maybe a dream, maybe madness—either his or Harry's and Ramona's. Earl's wife, Enid, behaves as incomprehensibly as the new neighbors; in her sealed verbal universe, she is as ineluctable to him as women always are to men in Berger novels. He suspects (as in *Sneaky People* Buddy suspects that his wife Naomi's "bland exterior" is a "mask for corrosive sarcasm") that Enid may have joined in some diabolic conspiracy to undo him. She appears to be accusing him of trying to rape Ramona, of trying to rape Harry. She appears to be in bed with Ramona. Earl's daughter appears to be in bed with Ramona. It appears that appearances are deceiving, that seeing is not believing.

Neighbors is a flawlessly crafted morality play; constructed out of the most subtle minutiae of perception and expression—as if Henry James had written *Waiting for Godot*—it must be read literally, but cannot be read realistically. Berger reminds us that the truth has very little to do with reality anyhow: King Arthur "was never historical, but everything he did was true." This is the last line of *Arthur Rex*, and, we are told, "the moral of the story." The moral of *Neighbors* is in its last line—"Earl, it could happen to anybody," Ramona says to the hero as he dies, after having finally chosen to drive off with them. In some sense, I would wager, Harry and Ramona mean death—obtrusive, unceremonial, irrational, boorish, banal and inescapable. No one will help Earl elude them, any more than Everyman's friends can help him avoid death. Against them he fights the first real fight of his life, against Ramona's seductions and Harry's brutality. But death wins in the end. Death always does. "I know I sang a different tune at first, but I was totally misguided. Actually Harry and Ramona are probably the finest people I've ever met. It just takes a while to perceive their unique quality, but once you do, you're not the same."

Without the gaiety of *Teddy Villanova* or the sweep of *Little Big Man* or the tenderness of *Sneaky People*, *Neighbors* may be easier for some to admire as a dark, brilliant artifact than to enjoy as a narrative. It is stripped of the sentiment which is essential to fictions that reach wide enough for popular success, sentiment that Berger evokes effectively in, for example, *Arthur Rex*. Besides, it is the fashion to hand the largest wreath of laurel to a large book, rather than a small perfect one like *Neighbors* or *Gatsby*, and so it seems unlikely that this book will gain Thomas Berger that nation of readers his talent deserves. *Neighbors* is his *Confidence Man*. His *Moby Dick* is still to come.—MICHAEL MALONE, "American Literature's Little Big Man," *Nation*, July 3, 1980, pp. 535–37

When Thomas Berger's *Arthur Rex* appeared in 1978, it received mixed reviews. One critic applauded its "splendid, satiric retelling of the legend of Camelot" that made Berger's "the Arthur book for our time." But another reader complained that "every episode is rife with slapstick and dirty jokes," making him long for White, Tennyson, and Malory. What was common to both reviewers was the recognition of the many changes Berger had made in the Arthurian legend in order to increase its appeal in contemporary American society. One critic liked the changes; the other did not. Anyone familiar with the historical development of the Arthurian legend knows that every author, from Geoffrey of Monmouth and Chrétien de Troyes through Malory to Tennyson and White, has made significant alterations in the legend in order to make it applicable to his own times. Unfortunately, both of the above critics fail to recognize the vitally important universal questions which are Berger's chief thematic concerns and which, far more than the matters of moment applauded or condemned by the critics, will enable *Arthur Rex* to stand the test of time as a significant contribution to the vast corpus of Arthurian literature: what is truth, Berger asks, and later, what is love? Finally, what is goodness? The answers are as ambiguous as they are difficult, but Berger seems to suggest that there *are* answers. The three themes become intertwined and culminate at the end of the novel in the enigmatic character of Sir Galahad, in whose characterization Berger most radically departs from any of his literary predecessors. . . .

Truth is sometimes only a matter of appearance in *Arthur Rex*. The appearance versus reality dichotomy, so familiar to students of literature, is presented in one form after another from the very beginning of Berger's novel. In the beginning, Merlin makes King Uther Pendragon appear to be the Duke of Cornwall so that the king can have his way with Ygraine, the duke's wife, and so beget Arthur. Later on, the whole story of Gareth presents a young nobleman who seems to be only a kitchen boy. Furthermore, in Berger's presentation of the Tristram legend, King Mark spends two nights in a closet while Tristram lies with Isold, but Mark *thinks* he is with his wife and has very real memories of her. The list is endless, but the important question is, what is Berger trying to say about the nature of reality by these incidents?

There seem to be two major points. The first is phenomenological: what matters, Berger implies, is not so much what empirically exists as what people perceive as existing, because people act upon these perceptions as much as, or more than, upon actual facts. What seems to matter is more what people *think* they are doing than what they *are* doing, because meaning comes from what people think. The scene in which Arthur first meets Guinevere is a clear example: to Arthur, Guinevere is "the most beautiful maiden in the world," but in her father's eyes, she is plain and has spots. "The truth," Berger's narrator confides, "was somewhere in between." Similarly, when Launcelot bids farewell to Elaine, he speaks to her distractedly and as if she were a child, offering to wear her token. Elaine's perception of the offer differs markedly from the spirit in which it was extended, for "the fair Elaine heard this as requital of the love she had professed" and eagerly gives him her sleeve: "Now to Elaine this was symbolic of her heart, but to Launcelot it was but the emblem of his affectionate friendship with a young girl who had brought him warm broths." It is Morgan la Fey, Arthur's evil half-sister, who best expresses the importance of human perceptions as opposed to their actions: in one of her lengthy lectures to her nephew Mordred, she asserts "'tis not the nature of the deed but rather the attitude towards it of the doer, namely the will, which determines the interest served, whether it be good or evil." . . .

Goodness is not confined by the man-made distinctions of the Christian or any other religion but is to be equated with truth, which is beyond the shaping power of human perceptions. It exists in the natural order of things. To see truth, to achieve true goodness, one must overcome the self. Berger has shown but one path to total selflessness: true love. Goodness does not come from power, nor does it seek power. It comes rather from love—true love that is a denial of self, and so a means to the truth that is beyond perceptions created by the self. That love can then grow and govern all of one's actions; Isold says it best when she tells Tristram that, because of her love of him, "now I love all the people in the world, so happy am I! And I love Mark as the King, and I love our enemies as well. For this is what love does to the soul, so saith Our Saviour Lord Jesus Christ."

The three themes of truth, power, and goodness culminate in the portrayal of Sir Galahad, whose character receives the most thorough reworking by Berger. Galahad has never been much more than a personified abstraction, the emblem of perfection as it might exist in human form, but the conception of what that perfection might look like is substantially altered in Berger's book. In Malory, for example, Galahad is introduced as one might expect the ideal to appear: "there com in twelve nunnes that brought with hem Galahad, the whych was passynge fayre and welle made, that unneth in the worlde men myght nat fynde hys macche." Launcelot, beholding him, "saw hym semely and demure as a dove, with all manner of goode fetures, that he wende of hys ayge never to have seene so fayre a fourme of a man," but in Berger, Percival finds "a youth there dressed in white velvet and with ribbons and bows, and for a moment Sir Percival did not know whether he was a boy or a maiden, for his skin was exceeding pale and his hair was long and golden." Far from the admiration manifest in Malory, Percival feels only pity for this effeminate, frail, "pale young man, who did look quite sickly to the robust Sir Percival." Galahad, in his very person, depicts the truth which lies beyond the perceptions of human beings: he really *is* the greatest knight, even though his appearance makes that possibility absurd. He is the physical demonstration of what Berger's appearance-reality theme has been leading up to all along. . . .

However, Galahad's perfection, his "goodness," is ambiguous at best. Certainly, he performs no great feats—his one great achievement, his sitting in the Siege Perilous, is done in a deserted castle, but as the ghost of Gawaine tells Arthur, "the difference between a great man and a mere entertainer is that the former doth seek to please no audience but God, and thus he goeth against the mean instincts of humanity". Galahad has not pleased anyone—he has accomplished nothing in the eyes of the world, but the eyes of the world, the perceptions

of human beings, do not see ultimate reality, truth, and so we cannot say whether Galahad pleased God or not. Galahad's one knightly deed, the slaying of his father, Launcelot, cannot be seen as a virtuous deed in human terms, but it is ambiguous: Launcelot has wanted to die from the beginning of the novel—in meeting his son he has been granted his wish. In addition, when Galahad fights Launcelot, the narrator says that he "mistakenly supposed" his father to be a "vicious enemy of virtue." Now considering Launcelot's behavior with the Queen, this supposition may not, in fact, be totally mistaken.

In any case, purpose and meaning in the last battle are ambiguous, but the novel has continually stressed that human perceptions have a way of clouding the ultimate truth in any situation. Perhaps it is appropriate that Galahad, the perfect knight, the knight of a truth beyond human perceptions, should engage in a single momentous act the meaning of which is imperceptible in human terms.

Berger seems to affirm that there *is* a truth beyond our mundane senses, that it has to do with goodness and with love, and that the way to that ultimate reality is through a denial of self, a transcending of our selfish perceptions of things. Tristram and Isold were able to attain this. Perhaps perfection, like the life of Sir Galahad, can only be fleeting. But it is worth striving for.—JAY RUDD, "Thomas Berger's *Arthur Rex*," *Crt*, Winter 1984, pp. 92–99

IHAB HASSAN
From "Conscience and Incongruity"
Critique, Fall 1962, pp. 4–15

I

Thomas Berger has written two sizable novels to date, *Crazy in Berlin*, 1958, and *Reinhart in Love*, 1962, each precisely 438 pages in the hardbound edition, both concerned with the adventures of Carlo Reinhart, a lumbering, strong-armed youth, a clowning knight errant, pure of heart—that is, a custodian of our conscience and of our incongruities. The figure of Reinhart may be one of a series of free-wheeling characters who have come into fashion since Ellison's *Invisible Man* and Bellow's *The Adventures of Augie March*. These characters testify to the openness of experience which we are attempting to recapture, the viability of the novelistic form which we are anxious to re-affirm, and the comic-absurd vision which we feel articulates our existential situation. They are, in short, ironic emblems of an age too sophisticated for piety and too vigorous for despair.

The fact remains, however, that Thomas Berger has managed to elude all critical appreciation. His talent is both ambitious and special; his manner—elliptic, extravagant, and buffoonish—repels solemnity. He is, above all, a comic and disconcerting writer, much like Bellow and a little like the more extreme Joseph Heller, author of *Catch-22*. Bellow and Heller have been widely and justly acclaimed; Berger, by some quirk of taste, remains in the shadow. Yet there is no doubt that Berger deserves more responsive readers. More novels will be forthcoming from him. We can, therefore, do no more now than begin a belated appraisal. And we can begin where he began.

II

Crazy in Berlin takes its epigraph from an old song: "*You are crazy, my child; You must go to Berlin. . . .*" Title and epigraph provide a suitable focus to the shifting and multicolor meanings of the book. Private Carlo Reinhart is barely twenty-one years old when he arrives in Berlin, singular, thoughtful, and innocent, a mammoth-sized child of life's ambiguities. He leaves the city on a medical discharge from the "psycho" ward of the Army hospital. As for Berlin itself, it is a clever cynosure of the conflicts which permeate the action of the novel. In the early days of the Occupation, Berlin stood as a premonition of all those tensions between East and West, Communism and Democracy, Power and Freedom—the rubrics of propaganda come tumbling in—which still threaten our world. With its Reichstag in rubbles, Berlin also stood—and still stands—as a symbol of an earlier terrorism, barely and extravagantly defeated, a three-cornered drama of German, Nazi, and Jew, to which no American of German descent, as Reinhart is, can remain indifferent. As if these were not complication enough, Berger, pressing his symbolism still further, makes his city the scene of a cloak and dagger story, of Intelligence and Counter-Intelligence men, *and* of Double Agents, engaged in a monstrous mummery of illusion and reality, truth and falsehood, right and wrong. Nothing is ever what it seems to be. Reinhart describes one of his experiences to the canny Army psychiatrist thus: "It is a grotesque evening, like everything in Berlin turns out to be: giants, twins who are apparently twenty years apart, blind men, would-be abortionists, experts on art, turncoats, Communists, ex-prisoners of the concentration camp, good Germans who turn out to be bad, and vice versa, and Schild and I." This is not only the nocturnal world every Berliner must know; it is also a nightmare world in which the checks and balances of our flimsy daylight existence vanish. There is no resolution to the contradictions it contains. Except, of course, the non-resolution furnished by grim irony, by that strange kind of comedy, black, satirical, gallows humor, which is indigenous to Berlin—recollections of the drawings and cartoons of *Simplicissimus* come to mind—and which qualifies the final apprehension of life in *Crazy in Berlin*. Baudelaire, Joyce, and Eliot, we recall, have chosen to define for us, in compelling, ironic forms, the nature of modern paralysis by a metaphor of the Unholy City: Paris, Dublin, and London. Moving in the same literary tradition, Berger now adds Berlin, in some ways a more grotesque symbol of conscience grappling with incongruity, of guilt and illusion running amuck under the leering sign of comedy. The book, in short, rests on the point where madness and humor meet.

The hero—despite all the ambiguities contained in the novel, Reinhart emerges a hero—is a medic affiliated with the Occupation Army. He has never fired a gun, let alone killed a man. Unusually powerful of body, he is also a slow, sentient, and irrepressible dreamer. Above all, he is a moral being, conscious of his obligations and history, yet open to experience. His moral education begins in earnest in Germany, homeland of his forbears. Back at the state university, Reinhart feels that the place, in sum, was "a flat green mall overrun with round pink faces saying 'Hi.'" It is otherwise in Berlin—here is the old theme of the American abroad once again, innocence staring experience in the face again, in the shape of Nazi horrors. The facts overreach his imagination, yet his will to understand persists. When Reinhart destroys gratuitously the lovely contents of an old German mansion, he reflects: "Yes, that was surely Nazism, that passion to destroy simply because it could be got away with. . . . Who wouldn't be a criminal if it weren't for the police?" Understanding is empathy and also identification. Thinking about his German relatives, those "blond beasts" of his own blood, Reinhart concludes: "In almost every way but the accepted idea of common decency,

he felt himself at odds with the world, a kind of Nazi without a swastika, without revolver and gas ovens, without the specific enemies—indeed, it was a crazy feeling, an apparently motiveless identification. . . ." But the identification, as Reinhart comes to realize, is not entirely above moral suspicion: it carries with it a secret and depraved pride. Reinhart, who had hitherto thought of himself as a lover and victim without portfolio, can now whisper to himself, "*once, anyway, you were not a victim.*" This is a crucial point in the moral development of the novel. For the education of Reinhart can be said to consist of this: a discovery of the real import of victimization, and the further discovery that victimization in itself is not enough. To put it more baldly: the recognition of one's guilt is the beginning rather than the end of responsibility.

The tortuous process of this recognition leads Reinhart through a gallery of odd characters who exhibit in their relations all the obscure tensions and aversions of American, German, and Russian, of Communist, Nazi, and Jew. The people closest to Reinhart are also the simplest: Marsala is portrayed as a tough, direct, and anarchic Italian-American, obtuse and devoted to the last; and Nurse Veronica Leary is characterized as a huge, bluff Venus equally devoted to Reinhart and equally senseless. These are the Healthy Americans, not so vacant as to be entirely vacuous, not so conscious as to provide guidance in the chartless terrain Reinhart is compelled to explore.

But there are other characters who bring with them greater pain and perplexity. There is Lieutenant Schild, the educated American Jew who is also a Communist, leaking military secrets to the Russians. There is Schatzi, the go-between, pock-faced, ubiquitous, and shadowy, a member of the original S. A. exterminated by Hitler, and Aryan victim of the concentration camps, who serves the Communists only to seek escape from them. There is Lichenko, naive officer of the Red Army, a deserter harbored lovingly by Schild and finally trapped by an inhuman fate. There is Bach, Lori's husband, an erudite, impuissant giant of a man, who lives with his wife in a damp cellar, discourses incomprehensibly on Oriental art, pretends to espouse anti-Semitism in the interest of the Jews themselves, and is finally shown to have saved the life of his half-Jewish wife, hiding her four years in a closet. There is Lori's twin brother, Otto Knebel, ex-Communist, a brilliant medical scientist, tortured by the Nazis, blinded, and emerging finally as an exponent of the fascist ethos, *after* the defeat of the Nazis. And there are others: faithful, handsome Lori, and her adolescent, whorish cousin, Trudschen. The mind reels at the ambiguities of human passion, the perversity of motives, the patterns of guilt and expiration. Ideologies are constantly given the lie by human realities. Nothing is simply what it purports to be.

In this elusive narrative, of comic and absurd experience, there is a superstructure of ideology, but also an underground of erotic impulses. Between the two, the existential morality of the novel defines itself in concrete and critical actions. This is the structural principle which qualifies the principle of incongruity in the book.

Ideology is a function of the intelligence behind *Crazy in Berlin*. It is the play of a mind bent both on understanding and denying itself. Hence the brilliant and unreal character—unreal because partial, abstract, and coercive—of political discourse. Schild's reflections on History, Bach's on the Jews, and Knebel's on Germany all have this scintillant, almost surreal, quality. Thus, for instance, does Bach theorize about the Jews: "The Jew does not want, and does not ask for simple understanding. He craves only total victory, and rewards anything less with corrosive hatred." The effect of Nazi tyranny, Bach continues, is to make the Jew "pure hard diamond, and his radiant leer sparkles in triumph over his fallen forge-slave." Yet the irony of Bach's irony, the queer inside-out logic of his mind, finally leads him to admit that the Jews are indeed "the chosen, the superior people." Puzzled by Bach's double somersaults—his pretense, for instance, of having been an active S. S. officer—Reinhart turns to Lori for an explanation. "Because the meaningful things are never said," she answers. "Because he (Bach) is infected with the Berliner's disease, irony and gallows humor." Similarly, the tortured political arguments of Knebel lead to one conclusion: "I have done everything. Every individual life is a questioning of the validity of all others." Ideology is finally reduced to the unique incongruity of every man.

And so is the erotic motive. There is a good deal of sex in this novel, prurient and refined, but much of it seems totally unrelated to anything else in the book. This may be precisely the point. The public concept of love has all but vanished, and sex remains a private path to sanity. Civilization—or what goes nowadays by that name—can take care of itself. Thus does Reinhart address himself: "Organize your sex life and all else followed, the phallus being the key to the general metropolis of manhood, which most of the grand old civilizations knew. . . ." His fierce relation with the masochistic Trudschen gives expression to his bestial, or "Nazi" side, while his relation to Veronica, the American nurse, restores his identity in the psycho ward. Lori remains a distant image of imagined love.

Ideology, we see, dissolves under the acid touch of irony; and love provides no occasion for responsibility. The last is defined, instead, by personal, almost quixotic, actions: Schild's concealment of Lichenko, Schild's attempt to save Reinhart's life in an unequal fight. The fight is a crucial scene in the novel. When Schild, disillusioned, balks at further "cooperation" with the Russians, they attempt to kidnap him. Reinhart is an accidental witness to this attempt, and though the fight is not his, he comes to the rescue of Schild, the American Jewish officer and the German American private having suddenly discovered friendship only a few moments ago. What ensues is a phantasmal drama of guilt and atonement, courage and sacrifice. Schild is killed; Reinhart kills one of the kidnappers, a behemoth even bigger and stronger than himself. During the following weeks, Reinhart comes slowly to realize the extent to which he wished Schild's death, and also the degree to which he was truly Schild's brother. More lucid than Millet, his psychiatrist, he answers him thus:

". . . . Was Schild my friend? On one hand, yours, no. I used him. If he hadn't been a Jew I wouldn't have given him a minute, for he was a kind of creep. I felt this definite satisfaction when he got it in the back, and it wasn't the one you spoke of. More complex than that. I felt it because, fighting for him as I was, *nobody could blame me for his death*. Well, here comes the joke: no one does but myself.

"But was he my friend? In my sense, yes. He was someone I could talk to . . . And then for another reason. When you hear it you will never let me out of Psycho, because I guess it means I really am nuts. When Schild was a boy he read the King Arthur stories. And he believed them up to the time he died."

Millet asked lazily: "What's 'nuts' about that?"

Reinhart groaned: "Because so do I. Really."

Reinhart overcomes his guilt and, in so doing, defines the human sense of responsibility, though his definition seems to have no basis except spontaneous and quixotic action. Reinhart overcomes his self-image of victim and aggressor alike. He is thus able to act once again. His last action is to betray Schatzi who had betrayed Schild to an ugly death. Is this not where freedom begins?

Standing back far enough from the novel, we can recognize that below the surface of trickery, illusionism, and incongruity lies a simple morality. Berger seems to assert, after all, that the first truth shall be the last. This ends by putting a double burden on *Crazy in Berlin*. First, it makes the moral vision of the book actually simpler than the book had led us to believe. And second, it makes the peculiarities of the form and style less than functional, since all the incongruities can be ignored, in the final analysis, by a moral fiat—the equivalent of a happy ending convention.

The criticism—and it is, I believe, a serious one—can be upheld by closer attention to the style of the novel. The central tension reflected by that style is one between absurdity and meaning. Our perceptions are constantly kept off-balance by sardonic humor, parody, twisted uses of dream and cliché. Scenes and characters are continually presented under the aspect of hyperbolic, surreal, or grotesque irony: Lichenko's first appearance, the scene with Bach in the cellar, Lovett's party, Reinhart making love to Trudschen on an office desk while he observes, with the corner of his eye, a black-market transaction between Schatzi and Pound, Schatzi and his dog following Reinhart and Veronica on their picnic, etc. There is an element of sinister buffoonery in all these scenes, sustained by a gnarled syntax, and also an element of absurdity. What we see is life caught in the gesture of self-parody, caught in its bizarre and preposterous moment. At the same time, however, the style constantly searches for meaning. It interprets heavily what it renders, even in the very act of parody. Part of the verbal energy of the book refuses to acknowledge the absurdity which the other part generates. Interpretation becomes a moral instrument, a constant, implicit point of view moving behind the shifting shapes of the characters. Even objects become endowed with a strange animate power. The fusion of these opposing impulses can be seen in the following description of an abandoned transmitting station:

As he entered, Schatzi took a noseful of the unique odor of the interior, a blend of urine, feces, damp, fire, and electrical effluvium from a transmitter that through it all—last stand, Russian plunderers, American snoopers—retained a deep, visceral stream of life. Its inexorable hum, issuing from the second floor but audible throughout, with the odor and, where the bulbs remained, the dim lights still burning in the halls from which humanity had fled and yet remained in the characteristic carpet of litter and excrement, had spent its force on Schatzi.

This is characteristic. But when the tension between meaning and absurdity fails to achieve a precarious balance, the style becomes abstract, laborious, or melodramatic. And the uneasy truce between conscience and incongruity seems an artistic accident. To put it another way: Reinhart never fully comes to terms with the harrowing ironies which the author has been at pains to create.

III

Reinhart in Love carries the *singeries* of the earlier book into civilian life. The story line is continuous, and some of the characters, like Marsala, re-appear in the later novel, which may be a warning that we have not seen the last of Reinhart.

But though the book invokes the sign of the cap and bells, it lacks the vitality of *Crazy in Berlin*. Droll it is, and the style has become less gordian and kinky; but humor and perception melt too often into triviality.

Berger is still concerned with the zany plan of appearance and reality. Once again, the reader is made witness to false pregnancies, impersonations, frauds, and protracted comedies of error. Yet the first truth is still the last. The surface of life defines reality. Splendor, a soulful quack and Negro master of prestidigitation, tells Reinhart, "The truth of life is that things are really as they appear, and symbols are the bunk." Reinhart, we quickly realize, continues to mediate between meaning and absurdity, his main resource being a monumental innocence, a radical trust in life. Power and fraud hold no final sway on him, for he is naturally a patsy, albeit one unreconciled to victimization. His aim is to *act with love*, and in the climactic scene of the novel, Reinhart does act indeed in the interests of love, though his action—ineluctable irony!—is vicarious.

Reinhart is condemned to act in a post-modern world according to the dictates of a pre-existential morality. His motto could have been the injunction of David Copperfield's aunt: "Never be mean, never be false, never be cruel." He regrets leaving the Army, for the decisions are now his to make; "he feared America, people, and life—not really but poetically, which was worse." Reinhart's progress, clownish pilgrimage, brings him to fulfill his trust, not fear, of life. His path brings him to no military or political adventures. The path runs through civic and domestic imbroglios. Reinhart first returns to his own unsentimental family—kind, passive father, violent, hard-boiled mother. He ends by establishing his own, after conquering an ogre-like father-in-law.

The plot, of course, is both simple and preposterous. In America, Reinhart's shadowy companion—again, the edge of conscience and mirror of incongruity—proves to be a Negro, not a Jew. Splendor Mainwaring, whom Reinhart remembers from his school days as a brilliant student and accomplished athlete, works in a gas station by day, and administers by night a correspondence course in Nonchemical Medicine. Reinhart becomes involved in his friend's enterprise, and is forced to preach, drunken, the gospel of the "founder," Doctor Lorenz T. Goodykuntz to a Negro crowd of whores and cutthroats. Reinhart preaches joy for man, not freedom for any singular minority. The Negro Problem can be left alone, and a man is rich, Reinhart thinks, "in proportion to the number of things he can afford to let alone." The gospel of joyous salvation leads to salvation through affluence. Reinhart works next for a crooked real estate agent, a real impressario of the improbable, and one of Berger's typically vivid and outrageous characters. In his new job, Reinhart, forever willing, attempts to reconcile the compatible vocabularies of business and romance. Romance enters bodily in the person of a secretary, Genevieve Raven, a rather prissy, pretty girl, tough-minded and firm of purpose. *"Reinhart was in love with everything."* She cons and bullies him into marrying her, though she finds him too aimless and unresolved. He falls in love; she becomes pregnant. What follows is an acute, hilarious travesty of marital life, its minor irritations and subtle conflicts. The sexual orgies of the couple do not stem Genevieve's impatience with her husband's impracticalities. "His big problem was not a career or love, but a matter of timing. His quest, of course, remained: freedom." Genevieve packs and goes back to her family, the formidable ex-Marine father, the mousy mother. But Reinhart wins her back when he is made president, and Splendor vice-president, of a phony sewage company run for graft by the mayor, chief of police, and real estate agent. Comedy and error follow in an improvised sequence of goofy incidents. Reinhart insists that the company turn honest and dig sewers; Splendor blasts a gigantic trench in the Negro section of the town, which does need sanitation, and explodes in the process a water main. Reinhart calls up his old Army friend, Marsala, to arrange for the beating of a recalcitrant contractor. The thugs beat up Reinhart instead. Finally, Reinhart goes on a two day binge in roadhouses and carnival haunts. Lurid and crazily out of joint, these scenes which make the greatest demands on our sense of order or plausibility also make their point about love. Drunk again, yet sane as the sober tarts who surround him are not, Reinhart literally turns a burlesque show into a gay orgy. He addresses the pop-eyed audience of men thus: "Your manhood is at stake, friends, and no less. What I ask of you is merely to exercise it. Do, instead of Look. Act, rather than Imagine. Move, in place of Talk. You will thank me in years to come." Reinhart, however, zips up his pants and makes well his escape by masquerading as the Law, faithful to the end to the fair Genevieve. We see him last playing touch football with his drunken father-in-law, who has been just bounced out of a dive nearby, before taking the tamed fire-eater to his home. The ending, of course, turns out to be appropriately whacky, blissful, and unexpected.

Innocence, we see, is not only preserved; it prevails. "Reinhart was really a traditional person even though he habitually frequented innovators, and nobody could say he did not keep the faith, even when to do so hardly accorded with his own welfare." The same could be said of Joseph Andrews or Don Quixote. What Reinhart contributes to the knowledge of our time is this: a more subtle sense of how Fraud and Force work to undermine our identity, of how Aggression is part of the human fundament, more damaging to commit than to endure. Of Dr. Goodykuntz' utopia, Andorra, Reinhart says: "The problem always is how to maintain the spirit while indulging the body. The Andorrans have done this by a shrewd device, having discovered that there are two kinds of people, which we may call the hurters and the hurtees. The first get their satisfaction by working their will on somebody else. The second like to be imposed upon." The aim of Reinhart, short of discovering a world from which all hurt is absent, is to neutralize the hurt by accepting his inevitable share of it, keeping the heart open to love, keeping the mind open to wonder. This is the openness of true laughter. Reinhart, playing occasionally the Lord of Misrule, proves to be a figure of comic celebration: his actions end by sustaining goodness, hope, and charity.

Whence the reader's nagging sense of dissatisfaction with *Reinhart in Love?* The writing here, though rich in texture, is less quirky than in the earlier book, and the odd humor is still effective. Berger continues to rely on irony, surprise, confusion, grotesquerie, witty interpretation, and the animation of inanimate objects for his humor. Here is an instance of the latter:

> When he opened the medicine chest above the washstand, the coiled copperhead of an enema hose sprang out and struck Reinhart at the jugular. He wrung its neck just back of the shiny black head. Ah, the atomizer! Just there behind a cartridge clip of cocoa-butter suppositories. He reached for it, but the heebie-jeebies split his vision and he saw two hands where but one was extended. The rectal bullets began to fire at him like dumdums. He seized the atomizer and, crouching below the wash-bowl, down by the gurgling gooseneck, in which was stuffed a wet rag, sent up a burst or two of ephedrine spray.

This is funny. Elsewhere, the style of the novel continues to interpret the action, though the tension between meaning and absurdity has slackened. In civilian life, the concerns of Reinhart have become a little diminished; the wildness of ideas in conflict has become somewhat domesticated. There is an essential triviality in the material that the vision has not entirely redeemed. Genevieve, the object of Reinhart's love, is not worth taking very seriously. And though this may be precisely the point Berger wants to make about the quixotic quality of love, her interests and prejudices, practical philistine, add nothing to the reach of the book. We might have reacted otherwise had Reinhart's reaction to his wife been less simple or insipid. But Reinhart shows *awareness* only sporadically. As a caricature of a certain kind of innocence, he must be denied a certain degree of consciousness. In Berger's second novel, Reinhart is physically more flabby, and also morally more bland. His expressions of love, like his expressions of sex, politics, or finance, are diffused in slapstick. The stab of truth comes through a caricature by Goya. The stab of insight comes through but rarely in *Reinhart in Love*.

IV

Two novels hardly provide an adequate basis for judgment on an author like Thomas Berger. Criticism must make allowances for its own errors just as it must allow for the unexpected turns in a writer's craft. But two novels also amount to a kind of self-declaration. The declaration, I think, is of a double import: it reveals something about Berger's singular talent, and it illuminates a new trend of American fiction.

Berger's primary concern is the individual in a world of cunning appearances and uncertified realities. Power and Fraud rule that world, distorting appearances and realities, pressing man to the limits of his sanity, and pressing on him the guilt-ridden role of victim or aggressor. But threats also contain their own answer, and shields may be fashioned of weapons. Man's response, therefore, is to adopt a stance of knowing craziness, resilient simplicity, or defensive defenselessness. These are the qualities Reinhart possesses. Nor is it an accident that his patron's day, so Berger says, is April First, Fool's Day.

The Fool and Scapegoat, from the beginning of time, have been the carriers away of death. They restore health under the guise of wit, slapstick, or chicanery. They are masters of irony and "connoisseurs of chaos." Enid Welsford, in her excellent study, *The Fool*, sees that character as "having a tendency not to focus but to dissolve events. . . . The Fool, in fact, is an amphibian equally at home in the world of reality and the world of imagination . . . " In contemporary fiction, chaos and violence—everything *inhuman*—are transformed into human use by the composite figure of the Fool and the Picaro, the Rebel and the Victim. The transformation is a comic act, and though it acknowledges the power of terror in its grim and surreal humor, it ends by affirming simplicity: the rich, incongruous surface of life.

This is why the work of Berger confirms what I consider to be a vital impulse in recent fiction. Bellow, from whom Berger has learned much, may have succeeded better. There is still too much gas, horseplay, and melodrama, too much verve *in the abstract*, in Berger's work. And the triumph of simplicity is sometimes too simply reached. But there is talent and authenticity too in the novels of Berger, and a comic use of language that has the ring of originality. Above all, there is the intent to transform the incongruities of contemporary life into a conscience for living.

LEO BRAUDY
"Regiment of Women"

New York Times Book Review, May 13, 1973, pp. 6–7

Twenty-nine-year-old Georgie Cornell, the hero of Thomas Berger's new novel, was born in 2096 and lives in New York City. The door-woman of Georgie's apartment house, "in the jungle of the East 70's," womans the front-door anti-pollution airlock with a shotgun. Georgie's psychiatrist, Dr. Prine, wears a self-adhesive nylon beard and has been treating Georgie for frigidity with a dildo, while she tells him his complaint that it hurts is merely a "defense"—as Dr. Daisy Rudin explained so well in her new book on the superiority of the anal orgasm, recently published by the giant firm where Georgie works as a secretary, unsuccessfully avoiding the attempts of his bald-headed boss, Ida Hind, to steal glances into Georgie's blouse at his newly siliconed breasts.

Through such details of satiric reversal, parallel and extension, Berger first sketches in the background of his future America. The novel's title is taken from John Knox's 1558 attack on "Bloody" Mary Tudor, *The First Blast of the Trumpet against the Monstrous Regiment of Women*, and quotations from Knox, Martin Luther, Christabel Pankhurst, Grover Cleveland, Olive Schreiner, Confucius, Virginia Woolf and others, including a final comment from Friedrich Nietzsche ("Woman was God's *second* mistake"), preface each chapter.

Georgie Cornell's America is governed entirely by women ("regiment" in Knox's title means "rule"); and in Georgie's New York men swear by Mary rather than Christ (whether Bloody or Virgin is unclear), admire Leonarda's Mono Liso, celebrate Columba's Day, and look forward patriotically to their six-month service at Camp Kilmer, where they are milked daily by sperm machines to insure the continuance of the species. (Normal intercourse in Georgie's world involves women taking men anally with dildoes, and the troubles for which Georgie is seeing Dr. Prine seem to have begun during a disastrous Junior Prom date when he was 18.)

The ruling women of 2125 haven't done very much better than the ruling men of today. The city and the society in *Regiment of Women* are basically chaotic and inefficient rather than inhumane or totalitarian. The George Washington Bridge collapsed years before into the Hudson Sewer during a rainstorm, and the general decay of 22nd-century America seeps into every part of the novel. Unlike the antiseptic dreams or nightmares of the future usually displayed in science-fiction novels, the atmosphere of "Regiment of Women" is incredibly seedy, as if Berger envisioned the world of the future as an extension of the back alleys of Dashiell Hammett and Mickey Spillane, or of Ross Macdonald's decaying southern California towns.

But *Regiment of Women* isn't merely an extended tour through a turnabout world that readers will view with disgust or approval according to their prejudices. To paste up a collage of the details of *Regiment of Women* falsifies the actual effect of the novel, which convinces almost in spite of the details. In Berger's novel *Little Big Man* Jack Crabb tells how he first couldn't stand the smell of the Indian village: "But, like anything else, living in it made it your reality, and when I next entered a white settlement, I missed the odor of what seemed to me life itself and felt I would suffocate."

Berger's imaginative power makes us live in Georgie Cornell's reality until it becomes our norm, and the arbitrary rigidity of the sex roles in Georgie's world makes us aware not of our "normality," but of our own arbitrary distinctions. There is more compassion than bitterness in *Regiment of Women*. Berger's subject is not so much the specific nature of sexual roles as the categorical severity with which roles are enforced and deviations punished. The decay of Georgie Cornell's America implies that the more politically and socially fragile a society, the more severely it attempts to police and define individual nature.

Berger's settings and characters in all his novels are plausible rather than apocalyptic. His satire refuses to make an alliance between reader and author against an oppressive, ugly "them." Paul Krassner once wrote that "the ultimate object of satire is its own audience," and Berger's integrity arranges that no reader—male chauvinist, militant feminist or in between—can emerge from *Regiment of Women* unscathed. All of Berger's main characters—Georgie Cornell here, Jack Crabb in *Little Big Man*, Carlo Reinhart in *Crazy in Berlin*, *Reinhart in Love* and *Vital Parts*—are moved more by circumstances than by some passionate belief or lack of belief. Berger's clearest outrage is reserved for anyone who presumes to sit in moral judgment on another, and his central characters are all slammed about by beings more certain than they about the location of truth.

Consequently, there is little ideological significance to Georgie's journey from New York where he is a brow-beaten secretary to the Maine lake where he discovers he can put his penis into a woman's vagina without killing her. Along the way Georgie is manipulated as much by the underground men's liberation movement as he is by the female government. "Everyone he encountered was a monomaniac of some sort, working compulsively to affect someone else: to alter their personality, change their mind, catch them out, set them straight. Everybody else always *knew better* about sex, society, history, you name it." Georgie's resolution of his problems is purely individual, the affirmation of personal identity that for Berger must precede the definition of sexual identity.

Like all great literary satirists, whose art gets at the root of imperception and self-delusion, Berger is concerned with the way language can falsify reality. ("I was never an aggressive boy," says Georgie. "I certainly don't think I could be called effeminate.") By disorienting us through its language, *Regiment of Women* indicts the society that uses language as a tool of oppression, making purely verbal differences into codes and categories—rhetoric asserting and experiencing itself as truth.

Berger's own style, with its tendency to absorb the speech rhythms of his characters and its unwillingness to stand apart from them, is especially suited for such themes. Since *Little Big Man*, especially, he has concentrated on exploring the possibilities and revealing the secrets of everyday language with a deep wit and feeling that transforms our awareness of the language we really use much more than does the flamboyance of a writer bent on asserting his personal style. *Killing Time* may be Berger's most brilliant effort to engage in this most truly poetic task of renovating the language we speak. But *Regiment of Women* is a brilliant flame from the same sources of energy.

Regiment of Women is in many ways a difficult book to talk about because, like the popular novels it imitates, it has few of the philosophical nuggets or technical tricks that professedly serious novels kindly include for the reviewer's convenience. But Berger doesn't use popular forms archly, as does, for example, Donald Barthelme. He finds in them energy, action and simple decisions that involve self-preservation rather than any abstract moral or intellectual imperatives. Berger also concocts a combination gothic-horror, science-fiction and detective story to explore and reveal a theme such works have always been fascinated by—the masculine fear of the domina-

tion of women. Berger uses these forms in the service of what I think is a compelling and finally humanizing fiction about male and female weakness perceived as human weakness, about the potential strength of individual identity which the official and underground institutions of society equally ignore.

Regiment of Women is a brilliant accomplishment by one of our best novelists. *Little Big Man*, and perhaps *Killing Time* and *Vital Parts*, are among the best novels of the past 10 years. Next to these larger achievements, *Regiment of Women*, may be more a fable, a deceptively simple romp through current prejudices. It isn't great in the way greatness has been defined by the novel since Joyce: each one a block-buster containing, as far as possible, all knowledge and experience. None of Berger's works is suitable for taking to the moon with matching toothbrush. They are novels that help you maintain a fresh response to the world around you.

With Heller and Kesey seemingly stilled—and Richard Condon plunged into self-parody—Vonnegut may be closest to Berger in style if not sensibility; but Vonnegut lacks the edge of Berger's wit and the variety of his insights. Each of Berger's novels is an expression of an esthetic presence that continues to grow in strength and importance. *Regiment of Women*, for all its exaggeration and grotesque parody, has been imagined with such ferocity and glee that we assent to it almost in spite of ourselves, celebrating with Berger that anarchic individuality that outlasts all the forms that language and society attempt to impose upon it.

JOHN W. TURNER

From *"Little Big Man*, the Novel and the Film"

Literature/Film Quarterly, Spring 1977, pp. 154–62

Ignoring the ideological components of structuralism, one can borrow the rudiments of structuralist methodologies—particularly the idea of binary opposition—to compare the principles of narrative structure in similar works of film and fiction. In analyzing the structure of Arthur Penn's *Little Big Man*, therefore, I have attempted to apply the idea of binary opposition to the question of translation from a literary text to a film. In the process, I have drawn parallels between the movie and the novel; but I have attempted to maintain a primary focus on the narrative structure of Penn's movie. I have also found it useful to comment on two earlier attempts—by Pauline Kael and Leo Braudy—to discuss the structure of Penn's movie. Both Kael and Braudy, it seems to me, ask the important questions about Penn's *Little Big Man*. But their conclusions—even when they correspond with my own—seem to rest on tenuous assumptions about the translation of novels into films.

If Arthur Penn's *Little Big Man* has an identifiable flaw, it resides in the narrative structure of the film. Leo Braudy, in perhaps the most trenchant analysis to date, argues that the problems with the movie are a result of the inadequacies of Jack Crabb as a center of consciousness. To support this assertion, with its Jamesian overtones, Braudy contrasts the film with its source, a novel by Thomas Berger. In the novel, Braudy argues, the narrative voice of Jack Crabb is sufficient to suggest an *"aura* of unity" (my emphasis), but that when events are objectified on the screen they become disassociated from any narrative voice.[1] Thus, while Braudy recognizes Penn's attempt to retain Jack as narrator by using the voice-over of the 121-year-old Crabb on the soundtrack, he concludes that the device fails and that the movie devolves into a series of un-connected vignettes.

Thomas Berger's *Little Big Man* is the story of Jack Crabb, a man who sees himself split between loyalties to both the Indian and the white world. In the course of Jack's narrative, he travels back and forth between these two worlds. Structurally, his repeated oscillations between savagery and civilization become associated with competing definitions of the self. The fundamental contrast between savagery and civilization in the novel involves differing concepts of time. The Indian measures time in terms of the cycle of nature and believes that change is as much an appearance as a reality. White men, in contrast, believe in the linear configuration of history, where progress and change are of the essence. Berger's repeated use of these contrasting notions of time warrants an interpretation of savagery and civilization as metaphors for different concepts of the self. The Indian, or circular, self involves a transcendent awareness of one's place in a timeless world; the civilized, or linear, self entails a more immediate view of one's place in a time-bound world.

When viewed as controlling metaphors in the novel, savagery and civilization define the binary opposition of the novel's structure. As *picaro*, Jack continually shifts his allegiances in the course of his adventures:

> What I had in mind on leaving the Pendrakes [he says] was of course returning to the Cheyenne. God knows I thought enough about it and kept telling myself I was basically an Indian, just as when among Indians I kept seeing how I was really white to the core.[2]

This pattern of shifting allegiances not only defines the deep structure of the novel, but provides the key to our understanding of the novel's theme of identity. What the pattern suggests is that both civilization and savagery (in the metaphoric senses) are insufficient when held in isolation. Neither the circular-spiritual self, nor the linear-social self operates independently; rather, they exist as the polar opposites by which we define the continuum of identity. This polarity explains why Jack thinks like an Indian among whites and vice versa: he requires a balance of the historical and spiritual versions of the self.

Such an extended look at the structure of Berger's novel is not irrelevant to a discussion of the film by Arthur Penn. In fact, since several reviewers have argued that Penn's central concern in the movie is the problem of identity, it seems to me essential that we understand Berger's handling of that theme and the structure that embodies it. My purpose is not to establish the novel as the standard by which to judge the film, but to present an accurate appraisal of the raw materials Penn had at his disposal in order to understand the structural difficulties involved in re-creating Berger's first-person narrative on the screen.

Fundamentally, the narrative problem that Penn faced in transferring the identity theme of the novel to the medium of film was to find a cinematic equivalent for Berger's linear and circular metaphors, because it is these tropes, and not as Braudy argues Jack's narrative voice, that define the structural principle beneath Jack's oscillations between the two worlds. That this is a specifically cinematic problem can be seen from the fact that Penn attempts to include Berger's metaphors at several points in the dialogue, but that he can find no visual equivalent to reinforce their meanings. More simply, the problem is how to create credible Indians and a tangible Indian world, so as to validate cinematically the idea that Jack defines both poles of the conflict between savagery and civilization.

Penn's decision to use Indian actors to play the roles of the Cheyenne points to a commitment in this direction. But at several points in the film, Penn's comic sense deserts him and he undermines much of the credibility that he strives to create. One example of this loss of control is the character of Little Horse, a *heemaneh*. In the voice-over narration Jack explains the role of the *heemaneh* in Indian culture: "If a Cheyenne don't believe he can stand a man's life, he ain't forced to." While Jack's comment is faithful to the novel, Penn's visualization of Little Horse is not, since he relies on movie stereotypes of the homosexual. By presenting Little Horse as an "interior decorator" in Indian clothing, the movie collapses Berger's satiric contrast between Indian and white American attitudes toward sexual roles. Certainly, Little Horse is only a minor character in both the novel and film; but this disjunction between what is said about the Indians and what we see of them is emblematic of a tendency to collapse the complex contrasts between savagery and civilization established in the novel. More than just a simplification of the novel, what we have here is a conflict in the film between its visual and auditory components, a contradiction between what it *says* and what it *is*.

While Jack's voice-over narration continually insists that we "know the Indian for what he was," the limitations of the camera make it difficult to do so. In Jack's first stay with the Cheyenne, for example, Penn tries to represent Jack's education as an Indian. In quick succession, we see Jack shooting a bow and arrow, stalking buffalo, and learning how to follow a trail. These skills, however, are only the outward manifestations of Indian life; moreover, they constitute little more than the stereotypical image of the Indian in the conventional Hollywood film. Thus they fail to communicate to the viewer what it means to do these things. The problem here, ultimately, is that what differentiates the two cultures is not what they do, but what they believe. And belief can only be limitedly represented in visual terms. As Jack says in the novel, Old Lodge Skins "taught me everything I learned as a boy *that wasn't physical* like riding or shooting. The way he done this was by means of stories" (p. 73, my emphasis). Whereas the movie can show us Jack's physical education, his psychological growth is significantly attenuated.

The difficulties of representing Indian beliefs on the screen are most apparent with respect to the Indians' faith in spiritual powers and mysteries. In the first four chapters of the novel Berger takes great pains to validate the miraculous. As with much of the novel, these mysterious incidents progress from the comic to the more serious. In the first case, Jack proves his "manly indifference to pain" by pulling his "arrow-out-of-arse trick." The hoax is very funny, but Jack points to its larger significance: "Maybe you are beginning to understand, when I pulled the arrow-out-of-arse trick, why it didn't occur to none of the children that I was hoaxing them. That is because Indians did not go around expecting to be swindled, whereas they was always ready for a miracle." Here, Jack refers indirectly to the disparity between the reader's disbelief and the Indians' absolute faith in miracles. Moreover, the comic tone provides a half-way house for the reader's acceptance of the antelope hunt in the next chapter, where Old Lodge Skins uses his "powers" to draw a magic line that brings the antelope to their destruction. Again, Berger allows Jack to mediate between the two worlds; Jack, in fact, challenges the reader's skepticism by highlighting his own doubts throughout his telling of the story. But the conviction with which he concludes carries over the reader: "If you don't like the aspect of the affair, then you'll have a job explaining why maybe a thousand antelope run towards ruin; and also how Old Lodge Skins could know this herd would be in this place, for no animal had showed a hair before he sat down on the prairie" (p. 71).

Short of trick photography, such dramatizations of the Indians' belief in man's "power to make things happen" are impossible in Penn's film. Again, this may seem like a minor limitation, but it serves to suggest the difficulty of maintaining the significant contrasts between savagery and civilization established in the novel. The Indian's sense of time, his belief in the harmony of man and nature, and his reliance on the supernatural are all aspects of a mentality alien to the "naturalism" of Penn's cinematic representation.

As a result, Penn's attempts to develop the theme of identity are circumscribed by the difficulty in generating the binary opposition between savagery and civilization that structures the novel. In the movie, Jack's oscillations between the Indians and the whites acquire little significance beyond the comic mobility of the *picaro*. What is missing from the movie's structures are the images sufficient to embody the complex cultural differences between savagery and civilization. Without those images, Penn cannot devise a structure that will fully express the identity theme.

To criticize Penn for failing to achieve the impossible, however, is not a legitimate approach to the movie. If I have done so, I stand self-accused. What I have attempted to show is that the methodology behind Braudy's criticisms of the movie rests on an insufficient theoretical base. Braudy has identified a problem in the movie, but he has misinterpreted its cause by drawing simplistic distinctions between the novel and film as narrative forms. One cannot simply assume that there are insurmountable problems involved in translating a first-person narrative to the screen. The inadequacy of this assumption is that it rests essentially on a Jamesian conception of the novel (as evidenced by Braudy's description of Jack's "inadequacies as a central consciousness"). Berger's novel, however, does not work in a Jamesian fashion: Jack Crabb is not Lambert Strether, nor was meant to be. Given the picaresque form, the novel does not center on a progressive refinement of Jack's powers of perception. Thus one is forced to question Braudy's reading of the novel, not to mention his application of that reading to the film. The problem with Penn's handling of the identity theme, therefore, is less a result of Jack's limitations as a center of consciousness than it is a product of the limited metaphoric possibilities of Penn's handling of the film.

A second reason for qualifying Braudy's criticisms of the movie is that the identity theme does not encompass all of Penn's thematic concerns, anymore than it exhausts the richness of Berger's novel. As an historical novel, *Little Big Man* dramatizes the conflict between savagery and civilization which was enacted on the American Plains and which culminated in the Battle of Little Bighorn. This story, with its epic scope, seems naturally suited for cinema, where narrative breadth is readily available. Moreover, for Arthur Penn, Berger's story of the West held particular interest because of the inherent theme of American violence. In fact, from the middle of the movie on, the historical concerns tend to displace the identity theme altogether.

Penn's handling of the history is reasonably successful, although one could quibble with his handling of a number of small details. There is, for example, no justification for changing the fact that in the novel it is the Cheyenne, and not the Pawnee as it is in the movie, who kill Jack's family. While slight, this change could be interpreted as representative of a larger tendency to sentimentalize the Cheyenne and villify the whites. Such a tendency runs counter to Berger's complex satire, where both ways of life receive a mixture of blame and praise. Nevertheless, despite these simplifications, Penn reproduces the essence of the historical theme: the acculturation of the Indian. Certainly, the single most effective scene in the movie—the massacre at Washita—vividly dramatizes the violence of the historical conflict. However, the very effectiveness of the scene has raised another set of questions about the structure of the movie.

According to Pauline Kael, Penn's portrayal of the violence of the conflict violates the form of the movie. As she sees it, the comic picaresque form cannot support the arresting violence of the massacre scene:

> For the tall tale to function as an epic form, the violence must be wry and peculiar, or surreal and only half-believable—insane, as it is in the book, and not conventionally bloody like this. . . . To be successful, the picture must deepen by comic means, and when Penn goes for seriousness he collapses the form of the movie.[3]

As with the criticism of Braudy, Kael's comment points to a structural problem in the film, but it does not provide adequate explanation. Once again, we must look more closely at both the novel and the film to interpret the formal difficulties.

Whatever else can be said, Penn handles the massacre scene extraordinarily well: sight and sound are more effectively combined in this scene than anywhere else in the movie. The setting, with its muted effect of the snow, provides the perfect visual counterpoint for the horror of the violence that follows. At the same time, the gently rising soundtrack of "Garry Owen" combines with the visual images of a dream-like advance of the soldiers to rivet the viewer's attention. We even find ourselves caught up in the visual poetry of Penn's panorama and the martial fervor of "Garry Owen," until the beauty explodes in violence. Penn's editing at this point is most expressive: by alternating shots of increasingly shorter temporal length, Penn heightens the tension of the scene, which climaxes with the death of Jack's wife, Sunshine. Jack and Sunshine hit the ground simultaneously, causing the audience to writhe with Jack in impotent horror as the visual and auditory montage culminates in the silence of Jack's agony and the stillness of Sunshine's death.

This arresting silence at the center of the Washita massacre marks the structural fulcrum of Penn's film. Significantly, the earlier identity theme coalesces with the historical theme at this point, since Jack is transformed from a passive figure into one strongly motivated by revenge. The revenge motif in the second half of the movie, in fact, is Penn's creation, because in the novel Jack remains more acted upon than active throughout the book. The problem with this change is not that it represents a violation of the sanctity of Berger's novel—because it is potentially the solution to many of the problems of translation—or even that it subverts the comic form of the first half of the movie; rather, the problem is that Penn does not accept the implications of the changes in his thematic focus.

Given the violence of the Washita scene, and given the change in Jack's character, one expects a change in the remainder of the film. If the silence at the center of the massacre is to serve as a structural fulcrum, then the movie must turn to something new. What is at issue here, therefore, is a problem of tonal control. To prevent the violence of the massacre from collapsing the structure of the movie, the comedy of the second half must be tinged with darkness. The tonal control of the rest of the movie, however, is decidedly uneven. Unfortunately, what happens is that the movie reverts too often in the second half to the comedy of Jack's earlier picaresque adventures. As a result, the underlying conception of the film becomes confused and the narrative structure collapses. The problem, then, is not so much with the scene itself (as Pauline Kael suggests), but with what follows it.

Disorienting tonal confusions occur at two significant points in the latter half of the narrative. The first of these, when Jack is down and out, is difficult to discuss, because the problem seems to reside less in Penn's conception than in the execution of the actor, Dustin Hoffman. Structurally, the design of the down-and-out sequence is perfect. The episode follows directly after Jack's failure to effect his revenge by killing General Custer. Jack's enforced recognition that "he is no Cheyenne brave" logically precipitates his despair. Yet, the despair is not maintained with any consistency.

Theoretically, the sequence should work to reinforce the structural fulcrum, since Penn contrives parallels to earlier scenes by bringing back the most important minor characters—Wild Bill Hickok, Mrs. Pendrake, and Allardyce Meriweather. But Jack's response to these visitations from the past is too reminiscent of the earlier scenes. Rather than emphasizing the difference in Jack's character after Washita (predicated in the film version), the sequence has the effect of collapsing our sense of the change. Since the potential for establishing a sense of difference is inherent in the structured parallels, one must assume that it is the limitations of Dustin Hoffman's performance that creates the confusion. One could argue, at least, that Hoffman fails to communicate the bitterness that is a requisite for the success of this narrative sequence. There is too much of the charming insouciance of the *picaro* in Hoffman for him to handle the scene with Mrs. Pendrake in the brothel. The scene needs to be filled not simply with Jack's recognition of the logical development of Mrs. Pendrake's character, but also with an emotional response that brings into play what he has lived through since his earlier experiences in the world of civilization. Hoffman's wry innocence, however, fails to convince us of the change in Jack Crabb predicated by the film's structure. Rather, the effect is to temper the importance of the revenge motif, causing the Washita massacre to seem like an anomaly in the structure of an otherwise comic tale.

While the tonal confusion here seems less a product of intention than execution, the same cannot be said of the movie's ending. Once again, given the way the massacre scene fixates our attention on the violence of the historical conflict, there is no aesthetic justification for Penn's lapse into comedy. One measure of the weakness of this comic ending is manifested in the omissions from the novel. Paralleling the earlier tendency to soften the Cheyenne character, Penn avoids any direct reference to the Indian practices of mutilating the bodies of their dead enemies. Penn also avoids the most important dramatic confrontation of the novel, which is anything but comic, between Jack and Old Lodge Skins: "Well, speak of shame, there was me. I still had not commenced to explain my presence with Custer. If indeed it could be explained, I had to try." In the movie, Old Lodge Skins inexplicably accepts Jack with open arms. And Jack does not feel compelled to explain.

But the major problem with the ending consists of the comic undermining of Old Lodge Skins. In the novel, the Indian chief wills his death. In the movie, Old Lodge Skins's gesture ends with his comic re-awakening and his statement that "sometimes the magic doesn't work." One can see parallels here with the earlier problem in the movie of handling the Indians' supernaturalism. But, more importantly, the comic ending undermines the historical sense of the movie by avoiding the ironies inherent in the Battle of Little Bighorn. Although the defeat of Custer marks the height of Indian mili-

tary success, historians have recognized that the battle also marks the beginning of the end of the Indian wars. William T. Hagan, in fact, ironically entitles his chapter on Little Bighorn, "The Warrior's Last Stand."[4] With the disappearance of the buffalo and with the renewed vigor of army operations after Custer's defeat, the Indian was forced to abandon the hope that the tide of civilization could be stemmed or that his old way of life could easily be maintained. In the novel, Berger captures this ironic sense of the Indian defeated even in victory by concluding Jack's narrative of the battle with the death of Old Lodge Skins:

> Though I was only thirty-four years of age, I felt in some ways older than I do now. Now it is only one man's life that is about to end; then it was a whole style of living. Old Lodge Skins had seen it all, up there on Custer Ridge, when he said there would never be another great battle. I didn't get his point immediately, and maybe you won't either, for there was many a fight afterward, and mighty fierce ones, before the hostile Plains tribes finally give up and come in permanent to the agencies. (p. 444)

More than simply the death of one man, the death of the old chief symbolizes the death of a mode of life.

Penn's comic ending, therefore, not only undermines the dignity of Old Lodge Skins, but also raises questions about Penn's historicism. To a great extent, Penn seems to resist the historical implications of the conflict on the Plains. By opting for a sentimental ending, Penn undermines the effectiveness of his cinematic achievement in the Washita scene, and leaves himself open to the criticisms of Pauline Kael. As we have seen, Kael is right about the massacre scene, but for the wrong reason. It is not that Penn should have excised his thematic seriousness; it is not even that "the film must deepen by comic means" alone, but that, having introduced a serious concern for history, Penn does not follow that theme to its tragic end as Berger does.

As a result, the movie lacks the closure that its story demands. Having entered the arena of history, Penn obligates himself to a narrative structure that rests on the opposition between the past and the present. Although Jack Crabb lives to tell his story, in the novel he knows that his story ended at Little Bighorn. In the movie, however, we miss that sense of an ending: Jack and Old Lodge Skins wander slowly back down the mountain, as if into the future. Their humorous discussion of sex furthers this sense of ongoing life. But the inconclusiveness of such an ending collapses the structure that Penn has striven to create. If Washita is to be the structural center of the movie, then it must mark the beginning of the end. What we have at the end, however, is an avoidance of closure, a relapse into comedy when it is least appropriate; the necessary somber note is totally absent.

The movie fails, then, despite all of Penn's admirable intentions and considerable craftsmanship, because he has not achieved a structure that will sustain the weight of his materials. Penn's reluctance to close off the movie's structure points to the weaknesses of his artistic conception. What vitiates Penn's achievement in the film is his failure to avoid romanticizing the past. As Leo Braudy puts it:

> Penn, in fact, seems torn between preserving the past through the clarity of photographic detail and preserving the past through the romantic versions of reality that are available in myth.[5]

This tension between romance and fact is nowhere more evident than in the contrast between the grim reality of Washita and the nostalgic longing of the final scene. Moreover, this conflicting attitude remains unresolved, such that the structure of the film is impaled on the horns of its own divided loyalties.

A comparison of the film and novel, therefore, is justified not because Penn either does or does not take liberties with Berger's novel, but because the comparison reveals the source of the flaws in the movie's structure. Unlike the novel, the movie fails to sustain either of the binary oppositions necessary for its structure. Understandably, Penn has minimal success establishing the savagery and civilization contrast in Berger's novel, because that opposition depends on the discursive and metaphoric aspects of language. But, less understandably, Penn also fails to maintain the separation between past and present implicit in the frame story. Without either of these oppositions to give meaning to Jack's narrative, the structure collapses.

Thus, while we cannot criticize Penn for failing to reproduce Berger's novel on the screen, we can compare the strengths and weaknesses of their respective narrative structures. Such an approach to a film version of a novel is useful because it provides the grounds for comparison without resorting to the usual criterion of fidelity to the original text. One should not expect the movie to reproduce all of the novel's complexity, or even reproduce all of its thematic concerns; but one can expect the movie to establish a viable narrative structure. And therein lies the difficulty with Penn's version of *Little Big Man*.

Notes

1. Leo Braudy, "The Difficulties of *Little Big Man*," *Film Quarterly*, 25 (Fall 1971), 3.
2. Thomas Berger, *Little Big Man* (Greenwich, Connecticut: Fawcet Publications, Inc. 1964). Further references to *Little Big Man* are cited in the text.
3. Pauline Kael, "Epic and Crumbcruncher," *Deeper Into Movies* (Boston: Little, Brown and Co., 1973), p. 213.
4. William T. Hagan, *American Indians* (Chicago: University of Chicago Press, 1961), pp. 113–142.
5. Braudy, p. 30.

JOHN BERRYMAN

1914–1972

John Berryman was born John Smith in Oklahoma in 1914. His later poems make frequent allusion of the tragedy which overwhelmed his childhood: when he was twelve years old, his father shot himself in front of his son's bedroom window. When his mother remarried, John adopted his stepfather's name, Berryman. He was educated at Columbia and Cambridge, and earned Bachelor's degrees from both universities. He taught at several universities, including Princeton and Harvard, and held a chair of English at the University of Minnesota at Minneapolis from 1955 until his death. A successful poet whose stature was widely recognized in his own lifetime, Berryman was nevertheless deeply unhappy. His battle with alchoholism forced him periodically into clinics and rehabilitation centers, and he was subject to serious depression all of his life. His psychological struggles ended in 1972, when he took his own life by jumping off of a bridge. His important works include *Poems* (1942), *The Dispossessed* (1948), *Homage to Mistress Bradstreet* (1956), *77 Dream Songs* (1964), and *His Toy, His Dream, His Rest* (1968).

Personal

⟨Berryman:⟩ In *Homage to Mistress Bradstreet* my model was *The Waste Land*, and *Homage to Mistress Bradstreet* is as unlike *The Waste Land* as it is possible for me to be. I think the model in *The Dream Songs* was the other greatest American poem—I am very ambitious—"Song of Myself"—a very long poem, about sixty pages. It also has a hero, a personality, himself. Henry is accused of being me and I am accused of being Henry and I deny it and nobody believes me. Various other things entered into it, but that is where I started.

The narrative, such as it is, developed as I went along, partly out of my gropings into and around Henry and his environment and associates, partly out of my readings in theology and that sort of thing, taking place during thirteen years—awful long time—and third, out of certain partly preconceived and partly developing as I went along, sometimes rigid and sometimes plastic, structural notions. That is why the work is divided into seven books, each book of which is rather well unified, as a matter of fact. Finally I left the poem open to the circumstances of my personal life. For example, obviously if I hadn't got a Guggenheim and decided to spend it in Dublin, most of Book VII wouldn't exist. I have a personality and a plan, a metrical plan—which is original, as in *Homage to Mistress Bradstreet*. I don't use other people as metrical models. I don't put down people who do—I just don't feel satisfied with them.

I had a personality and a plan and all kinds of philosophical and theological notions. This woman thinks the basic philosophical notion is Hegelian, and it's true that at one time I was deeply interested in Hegel. She also thinks, and so do some other people, that the work is influenced by the later work of Freud, especially *Civilization and Its Discontents*, and that is very likely. For years I lectured on the book every year here at Minnesota, so I am very, very familiar with it—almost know it word by word. But at the same time I was what you might call open-ended. That is to say, Henry to some extent was in the situation that we are all in in actual life—namely, he didn't know and I didn't know what the bloody fucking hell was going to happen next. Whatever it was he had to confront it and get through. For example, he dies in Book IV and is dead throughout the book, but at the end of the poem he is still alive, and in fairly good condition, after having died himself *again*.

The poem does not go as far as "Song of Myself." What I

mean by that is this: Whitman denies that "Song of Myself" is a long poem. He has a passage saying that he had long thought that there was no such thing as a long poem and that when he read Poe he found that Poe summed up the problem for him. But here it is, sixty pages. What's the notion? He doesn't regard it as a literary work at all, in my opinion—he doesn't quite say so. It proposes a new religion—it is what is called in Old Testament criticism a wisdom work, a work on the meaning of life and how to conduct it. Now I don't go that far—*The Dream Songs* is a literary composition, it's a long poem—but I buy a little of it. I think Whitman is right with regard to "Song of Myself." I'm prepared to submit to his opinion. He was crazy, and I don't contradict madmen. When William Blake says something, I say thank you, even though he has uttered the most hopeless fallacy that you can imagine. I'm willing to be their loving audience. I'm just hoping to hear something marvelous from time to time, marvelous and true. Of course *The Dream Songs* does not propose a new system; that is not the point. In that way it is unlike "Song of Myself." It remains a literary work.

Interviewer: Christopher Ricks has called *The Dream Songs* a theodicy. Did you have any such intention in writing the poem?

Berryman: It is a tough question. The idea of a theodicy has been in my mind at least since 1938. There is a passage in Delmore's first book, *In Dreams Begin Responsibilities*, which goes: "The theodicy I wrote in my high school days/Restored all life from infancy." Beautiful! He is the most underrated poet of the twentieth century. His later work is *absolutely* no good, but his first book is a masterpiece. It will come back—no problem. So that notion's always been with me. I can't answer the question. I simply don't know. I put my stuff, in as good condition as I can make it, on the table, and if people want to form opinions, good, I'm interested in the opinions. I don't set up as a critic of my own work. And I'm not kidding about that.

Interviewer: You once said that, among other things, a long poem demands "the construction of a world rather than the reliance upon one already existent." Does the world of *The Dream Songs* differ from the existent world?

Berryman: This is connected with your previous question. I said that *The Dream Songs* in my opinion—only in my opinion—does not propose a new system, like Whitman. But as to the creation of a world: It's a hard question to answer. Suppose I take this business of the relation of Henry to me, which has interested so many people, and which is categorically denied by me in one of the forewords. Henry both is and is not me, obviously. We touch at certain points. But I am an actual human being; he is nothing but a series of conceptions—my conceptions. I brush my teeth; unless I say so somewhere in the poem—I forget whether I do or not—he doesn't brush his teeth. He only does what I make him do. If I have succeeded in making him believable, he performs all kinds of other actions besides those named in the poem, but the reader has to make them up. That's the world. But it's not a religious or philosophical system.—JOHN BERRYMAN, Interview with Peter A. Stitt (1970), *Writers at Work*, 1976, pp. 306–9

General

At the beginning at least, Berryman could be grouped with other poets of his generation as one who, though he had moved toward passionate syntax, had not yet achieved an individual voice. Like Theodore Roethke and Jarrell before him, Berryman seems more concerned in his first volume with bringing his talent into line with a tradition than in establishing himself as an independent voice albeit, as Daniel Hughes's "The Dream Songs" (1966) suggests, the echoes may have resulted from a desire by the poet "to take on Eliot and Yeats and Auden on their own grounds, and do it better." Although Dudley Fitts was already finding the grammar of these early poems a "fanfare of ship-wrecked syntax, textbook inversions and alliterations" and "somehow without the excitement that attends the transformation of a craft into a completely realized art," Jarrell was citing the volume's most extreme dislocations of syntax— "The Nervous Songs"—as the direction the poet should be moving in. His citation of these works and the enigmatic parts of Berryman's other pieces is part of a view Jarrell derived from Auden, namely that poetry represented the Freudian ego, embodying in its realization both id and superego. This psychological part of Auden which had been pointed out by Schwartz and others is precisely what Berryman is rejecting in favor of a Yeatsian view of masks.

Yeats's masks are predicated upon not an individual memory of Freud but a racial memory akin to Carl Jung's racial unconscious and along with that a psychological typology that goes back to the Greek Stoics. By the end of Yeats's life, these masks had divided into twenty-eight phases that ranged from a nonhuman first phase to that of the fool and represented an enlargement of an early belief that masks were what people assumed to bridge the discrepancies between their own and other people's conceptions of themselves. Nowhere does Berryman publicly acknowledge an affinity with Jung, though in song 327 Henry chides Freud for having enlightened but misled others. Henry insists, in echo of James Joyce, that "a dream is a panorama/of the whole mental life" and in the next song, he refers to "his ancient brain," suggesting something like a racial recall. Berryman, however, goes only so far as to acknowledge the possibility of late Freud's having entered his work, especially *Civilization and Its Discontents* (1930). The comment follows a condescending description of a woman who sees Henry "corresponding vaguely to Freud's differentiation of the personality into superego or conscience, ego or façade or self, and id or unconscious." Berryman adds that he did not know whether or not she was right, but that he had not begun with so full-fledged a conception. *Recovery* (1973), the poet's unfinished posthumous novel, describes its autobiographical hero, Alan Severance, as having "been a rigid Freudian for thirty years, with heavy admixture however from Reich's early work," and one assumes that if the poet understood or sympathized with Jung it was mainly through an interest in Yeats.

"The Nervous Songs," which represent Berryman's clearest approximation of an acceptance of Yeatsian masks in the early poems are again realized so as to bring the Irish poet in line with the social concerns of Auden. Based as are also *The Dream Songs* on Yeats's *Words for Music Perhaps* (1933), the lyrics try to confront that twenty-eighth phase where the physical world suggests to the mind "pictures and events that have no relation to [one's] needs or even to [one's] desires; [one's] thoughts are an aimless reverie; [one's] acts are aimless like [one's] thoughts; and it is in this aimlessness that [one] finds [one's] joy." Yeats began to compose his lyrics in the spring of 1929 after a long illness; his mood was one of "uncontrolled energy and daring." He wrote Olivia Shakespear that his "songs" were "songs," "not so much that they may be sung as that I may define their kind of emotion to myself. I want them to be all emotion and all impersonal." Later he added in another letter, "Sexual abstinence fed their fire. . . . They sometimes came out of the greatest mental excitements I am capable of." "The Nervous Songs" use the same six-line stanza basic to

Yeats's pieces, but with neither his compulsion to rhyme nor his inclination to add occasional refrains. The sexual appetite of Berryman's girl in "Young Woman's Song" is not the exuberance of Crazy Jane but the result of capitalism which forces one to pay £3.10 for a hat and to turn one's body into a commodity. Similarly, the discrepancy between thinking and the world in "The Song of the Tortured Girl" results from Nazi torture methods rather than from some godly gift. If Berryman's people are to act as mediums through which new truths are made known, it will be less by any Yeatsian accident of identity than by means of an overwhelming social coercion.—JEROME MAZZARO, "John Berryman and the Yeatsian Mask," *REPP*, Dec. 1973, pp. 145–47

Love & Fame is an attempt at writing properly about the poet's own personality without the mediating device of an alter-ego. The complicated figure of Henry and his audience/conscience Mr. Bones give way to raw, unilateral self-scrutiny. There are attempts to characterise the self-obsession as a mask; Berryman dedicates the book to the memory of Tristan Corbière, saying:

> Your Mockery of the Pretentious Great
> Your Self-Revelations
> Constitute Still in Any Sunset Sky
> A Cursing Glory.

And later, in answer to imagined criticism, he claims: 'I am not writing an autobiography-in-verse, my friends. . . . It's not my life./That's occluded & lost.' To a certain extent, this is true: the 'I' of these guilt-motivated recollections is often hysterically one-dimensional, hollow, and unreal. Basically, however, Berryman has removed the 'changes and disguises' that are the sources of Freud's fore-pleasure, with disquieting results for the reader who presupposes that comfortable veil of artifice which separates 'literature' from 'life'. In *Love & Fame*, the poet has blurred the distinctions we normally expect form, persona, and tone to make between what the writer feels and what he chooses to express. Here it is the release of tension in the *writer's* mind that matters. Contrary to custom, His Majesty the Ego cries out: 'Something is happening to me' and the reader is more or less forgotten.

Berryman's work after *The Dream Songs* essentially records his efforts to identify, accommodate, conquer and expiate the devastating powers which haunted him. *Love & Fame* can be seen as a skirting manoeuvre, an attempt to neutralise his obsessions by glorifying them, as if the mere naming of these forces were the same as controlling them. In *Delusions, Etc.*, he tries to outflank his demons by appealing to a greater power for forgiveness and salvation. *Recovery*, finally, is a desperate confession. The psyche aims at liberation through purgation, in a last-ditch defence through which the writer convinces himself of his persona's progress and renewal, closing with a delirious assertion of freedom, again as if saying made it so:

> He was perfectly ready. No regrets. He was happier than he had ever been in his life before. Lucky, and he didn't deserve it. He was very, very lucky. Bless everybody. He felt—fine.

Dialectic is a basis *modus operandi* in Berryman's work. The poet establishes a tension in the poem between the narrator and a contrasting but related persona which allows him to set up a kind of conversation within himself, in which an unbridled, maniacal self is moderated and usually controlled by a projected, idealised 'other', who acts, like the girls of the *Love & Fame* poems, as a sounding-board, but also as an objectifying standard on which the reader can depend as representing the reality principle to some degree. Mr. Bones, for example, acts as Henry's super-ego in *The Dream Songs*:

> Where did it all go wrong? There ought to be a law against Henry.
> Mr. Bones: there is.

We see another version of this relationship in *Homage to Mistress Bradstreet*, and yet another in the *Sonnets*. One of the reasons *Love & Fame* seems unachieved is that this source of energy and conflict is missing from the reminiscences which make up the first part of the book. Each poem is a new, uncorrected edition of the self, incomplete and failed because unchallenged and unamplified by another point of view.—JONATHAN GALASSI, "Sorrows and Passions of His Majesty the Ego," *PN*, 1974, 118–20

Works

Who is Henry? Or perhaps, *what* is Henry? He is, variously, huffy, reluctant, somber, stricken, disordered, miserable, willful, stunned, imperishable, anarchic, lonely, longing, completely exhausted, instant, horrible, foaming, seedy. . . . He is also Henry Pussy-Cat, Henry Hankovitch, Henry of Donnybrook, Sir Henry, Henry House. He is Mr. Bones, Sir Bones. Sometimes, in my own head, I call him Calibones, or Sir Trombones, because he slides around so much. He is, in fact, the most comprehensive of souls, the very prince of picaresques, a man to whom everything happens, a man who wears his wounds openly, a man too vulnerable, a man who loves not wisely but too well. He has suffered an "irreversible loss," which we now know to have been the death of his father, by suicide, when he was still very young. He has been flung out of the garden, and in place of the tree of the knowledge of good and evil, which he has lost, he has made his own "flashing & bursting tree." He is one of the weirdest, most real, most endearing and most human inventions in modern poetry. And of course he is a persona. He is not the poet; although, as Berryman once admitted, "There is a fiendish resemblance between Henry & me." Other poets have invented personae; as Donald Justice wrote to me:

> Like others of his period he was interested in inventing and projecting a dramatic voice or voices, the lyric mode for a time having been pulled by criticism toward the dramatic. Berryman did succeed in managing this better, I think, than anyone else.

And for myself I can think of no other whose invention is both so startling and so sustained. One thinks, of course, of Prufrock—

> I grow old, I grow old,
> I shall wear the bottoms of my trousers rolled.

—and wonders what would have happened if he, not Eliot, had gone on to write the *Four Quartets*. But the fact is that Henry is quite our juiciest hero and persona.

Now the inventing of a persona is a dangerous thing for a poet. Its rewards, as in the case of Henry, are huge. But it opens him to huge dangers. And Henry is, above all, open. The first line of the whole poem "Huffy Henry hid" is, in this connection, completely ironic. But then comes the "prying open for all the world to see." The creating of a persona is for the conscious mind both unwelcome, in some sense, and a necessary extension of it. In the case of Henry, all kinds of material previously inaccessible was released and swarmed into the poems, much of it fearful, all of it *vital*. So much that previously was inexpressible could now find a voice as the whole range of invention and language widened. The width, the range, are what immediately strike one in these poems.

And with a persona one can begin to explore the furthest

reaches of one's self, as Henry does here, fiercely, single-mindedly, but without narcissism, because the uncovering of this "other" is an essential psychic task which all of us must, in some measure, undertake, whatever the dangers. And Henry does it *for* us; and that is surely part of the immense reward of these poems, the sense of both identification and release, that someone does it, and does it for us. He falls apart for us, he does his dance in front of us. No one in American poetry since Roethke, with whose *Lost Son* poems, with their gibbering language and theme of flight from the death of the father Henry has much in common, has so let down his brain, has so pried himself open.

It is, paradoxically, the basic informality of the device which seems to make possible the access to much deeper material; the vast range of tone, from high to low, seems a sort of lubrication around the subject-matter and lays the poem open to bewildering shifts and changes of direction, so that we feel we are never prepared for what might come next. The poem is left open not only to the personal circumstances of the poet's life, as Berryman said, but also to the weather of the head, with all its sudden clearings and cloudings, all its visions and frustrations. The device of dialogue brings even more space into the poems and intensifies the sense of antithesis that runs throughout the poems. Every Prospero has his Caliban, every Eliot his Sweeney, every self his shadow. And Berryman has his Henry and his Henry another name, and there is yet another voice who addresses Henry, whose name we do not know.

It is the *life* these poems have, in the person of Henry, that is perhaps the most distinctive thing about them. Often I have come away from poems feeling, "*Surely* these poems are not the measure of the experiences; surely the fires were hotter, the waters wetter; surely there was more that could have been encountered, more brought back." But Henry's poems, with their amazing range of response to experience, often with tears and laughter summoned in swift succession, do often seem to be adequate equivalents for the intensity of the emotion involved in the original experience. And the process of the poem, its speed and changes of speed, its mixtures of diction, make us feel that, yes, this is how the head works; and it is this fidelity to the process which we should note and learn from. Their language seems to be what William Meredith said of the Roethke poems, "the strange irrational language with which we talk to ourselves." And so we can identify, and so all our hidden pettinesses and shames are sucked up as into a huge updraft, into the life of the poem.

One learns, as poet, as person, not to approach any situation or experience *too narrowly*. The stock response, whether tragic or lyrical, is never adequate to the actual dimensions, often submerged, of the experience. It is the use of the persona, himself previously submerged, who helps bring these dimensions to light and immeasurably widens and intensifies the poem.—Michael Dennis Browne, "Debts to the Dream Songs," *OR*, Winter 1974, pp. 79–80

Style can be a false light to follow. The preeminent question to ask about the early Berryman is, I think, whether or not he creates a substantial number of poems that establish not so much a style as the fact of his talent and particularly that talent as it identifies itself in terms of essential subject and theme. The question is, What does the Berryman of *The Dispossessed* care about? Though he is an individual speaker of poems rather than a developed character, is there nevertheless a certain unity to his early work, does the speaker of his poems take on a

singleness of character? And to suggest the answers to these questions is naturally to anticipate his later development.

The most essential thing to say about the Berryman of *The Dispossessed* is that he offers a subjective response to the objective reality of the modern world. His early poems typically do not encounter objective reality in terms of an elaboration of the facts of that reality. He thus forgoes what we might call pure or external subject interest in favor of a focus on the individual as the individual responds to his world. It is most decidedly not an egocentric emphasis, but rather a steady and a dynamic relationship between the individual, the sensitive individual, and the world to which he *must* respond. The speaker of his early poems is typically anxious to generalize about humanity from a variety of specific experiences, but to proceed from a specific experience is not the same as to detail the specifics. The persistent concern is broad, and distinctly in the humanistic tradition. It would be fair to say that the basic character of the speaker in *The Dispossessed* is that of a sensitive and rather desperate humanist—we think too of the man who has abandoned his Catholic faith. What he cares about, broadly speaking, is our common humanity and its survival in the face of terrible threats. He cares about caring. His poetic attempt, his subject, is *how it feels* to be in a certain kind of world.

The pivot point of the world he finds himself in is World War II, the beginning of which he regards as a dark time for mankind, and as reason for feeling hatred and bitterness. It is a dark time because he finds fascism so evil and committed to destroy precious individual freedom. He sees the state as a monster of oppression, "At Dachau rubber blows forbid" ("Letter to His Brother")—this written in 1938. Or consider the terror and bitterness in these sensitive lines:

> The time is coming near
> When none shall have books or music, none his dear,
> And only a fool will speak aloud his mind.
> "The Moon and the Night and the Men"

He looks out and sees "tortured continents" ("Boston Common") and becomes inwardly tortured by what he sees. His reaction to the world of the 1930s and 1940s is to take its burdens upon himself—much as Robert Lowell was shortly to do—and, as a result, to enter into the abyss of himself, which, as Yeats remarked, may show as reckless a courage as those we honor who die on the field of battle.

The early Berryman as a speaker of poems interests us, then, as a sensitive individual meditating upon and absorbing the shocks of a grim time. His perspective is broad in the sense that besides the state he sees other threats to human freedom: materialism, for example, as he calls out, "Great-grandfather, attest my hopeless need/Amongst the chromium luxury of the age" ("A Point of Age"). In a poem called "World-Telegram" he even catalogues the ordinary events of the day, and masks his horror with this reportorial matter-of-factness:

> An Indian girl in Lima, not yet six,
> Has been delivered by Caesarian.
> A boy. They let the correspondent in:
> Shy, uncommunicative, still quite pale,
> A holy picture by her, a blue ribbon.

At the end of the same poem he speaks in desperate understatement to dramatize the condition of civilization as he sees it: "If it were possible to take these things/Quite seriously, I believe they might/Curry disorder in the strongest brain." To take upon oneself the horrors of such a world as the *World-Telegram* reports is clearly to go mad. Berryman knows that we are saved, if we can be saved, by the strength of rational awareness and perhaps a final necessary refusal to accept burdens which are beyond our capacity as individuals to endure.

The Berryman of *The Dispossessed* also emerges in the poignant terms of more personal experience, as, for example, this reference to the loss of his father: "The inexhaustible ability of a man/Loved once, long lost, still to prevent my peace" ("World's Fair"). Or the reader can look at the fine poem "Farewell to Miles" on the simple subject of saying good-bye and the "ultimate loss" which that involves. But it must be said that the pessimism, the despair, and the bitterness which characterize the early Berryman are balanced by hope and such affirmation as these lines from "Letter to His Brother": "May love, or its image in work,/Bring you the brazen luck to sleep with dark/And so to get responsible delight." And he affirms especially the life of nature, "natural life springing in May," with a healthy sense of man's mortality, "Those walks so shortly to be over" ("The Statue"). Or the reader may wish to look at another fine early poem, "Canto Amor," which tells us "Love is multiform" and sings to the end of joy.—WILLIAM J. MARTZ, "John Berryman," *Seven American Poets from Mac-Leish to Nemerov*, 1975, pp. 179–82

The most vital event of *The Dream Songs* is one which occurred long before the time of the loose "narrative frame" of the poem, but which haunts it throughout and provides its most deeply obsessive theme. Berryman was no doubt referring to it when he mentioned in his prefatory Note that Henry had "suffered an irreversible loss": the suicide of his father when the poet was only twelve years old. In his interview, Berryman recalls that he lost his childhood faith in Catholicism on that occasion: "Then all that went to pieces at my father's death, when I was twelve." Shortly after this comment in the interview, Berryman is describing his theory of what is necessary for great achievement: "Mostly you need ordeal. My idea is this: the artist is extremely lucky who is presented with the worst possible ordeal which will not actually kill him. At that point, he's in business. Beethoven's deafness, Goya's deafness, Milton's blindness, that kind of thing." His own future work, he says, will depend on his "being knocked in the face, and thrown flat, and given cancer, and all kinds of other things short of senile dementia. . . . I hope to be nearly crucified." His ordeal for *The Dream Songs* clearly was his father's suicide. For it he almost suffered crucifixion, but after writing his long poem, he could say in Song 359: "Take down the thing then to which he was nailed."

Dream Song 1 is an oblique dramatization of the event that was to become the ordeal of Berryman's life:

Huffy Henry hid the day,
unappeasable Henry sulked.
I see his point,—a trying to put things over.
It was the thought that they thought
they could *do* it made Henry wicked & away.
But he should have come out and talked.

All the world like a woolen lover
once did seem on Henry's side.
Then came a departure.
Thereafter nothing fell out as it might or ought.
I don't see how Henry, pried
open for all the world to see, survived.

What he has now to say is a long
wonder the world can bear & be.
Once in a sycamore I was glad
all at the top, and I sang.
Hard on the land wears the strong sea
and empty grows every bed.

The "departure" is his father's death; the adults, as they will, tried to mislead the boy about the death, or perhaps to tell him his father had gone to heaven. But he saw through their deceptions. From that moment he lost his faith and acquired the death consciousness that would haunt his entire life. Before, the world was like a "woolen lover," and he had sung "all at the top" in a "sycamore." But after, he is filled with a "long/wonder that the world can bear & be," living with the hard and bitter fact of transience (on "the land wears the strong sea") and death ("empty grows every bed").

It is perhaps impossible to ferret out the entire presence of this event in *The Dream Songs*. But it is easy to guess that it exists behind the guilt so brilliantly dramatized in Song 29: "There sat down, once, a thing on Henry's heart/so heavy, if he had a hundred years/& more, & weeping, sleepless, in all them time/Henry could not make good. /Starts again always in Henry's ears/the little cough somewhere, an odour, a chime." And the lost father is clearly the "journeyer" in Song 42: "O journeyer, deaf in the mould, insane/with violent travel & death: consider me/in my cast, your first son." Song 76 ("Henry's Confession"), coming near the end of 77 *Dream Songs*, is a more direct confrontation of the event than was Song 1:

Nothing very bad happen to me lately.
How you explain that?—I explain that, Mr. Bones,
terms o' your bafflin odd sobriety.
Sober as man can get, no girls, no telephones,
what could happen bad to Mr. Bones?
—If life is a handkerchief sandwich,

in a modesty of death I join my father
who dared so long agone leave me.
A bullet on a concrete stoop
close by a smothering southern sea
spreadeagled on an island, by my knee.
—You is from hunger, Mr. Bones,

I offers you this handkerchief, now set
your left foot by my right foot,
shoulder to shoulder, all that jazz,
arm in arm, by the beautiful sea,
hum a little, Mr. Bones.
—I saw nobody coming, so I went instead.

If life is an empty joke—like a "handkerchief sandwich" (no nourishment, only grief there)—then Henry might as well join his father, who "dared so long agone leave me." The resentment is still strong, the details true: the suicide occurred in Florida, near Berryman's room (and presence). The courage urged on Henry by Mr. Interlocutor—"by the beautiful sea, /hum a little"—is ironic, even bitter, and ultimately meaningless. The ambiguity of the last line suggests the weight of the knowledge Henry has had to bear alone.

In the light of this theme in *The Dream Songs*, Henry's own "death" in Book IV takes on new meaning. Songs 86 and 87 represent a plea of "Not Guilty by reason of death": the guilt linking, no doubt, with that of Song 29, and that can be traced back to the deep resentment, even hatred, of the father for committing suicide. In Book V, the last three poems (Songs 143–45) come back once again directly to the father's suicide. Song 143 is most interesting in letting Mr. Interlocutor (not Henry as Mr. Bones) give the fullest account of the suicide, revealing details that were indeed threatening for a twelve-year-old boy.—JAMES E. MILLER, "The American Bard: Embarrassed Henry Heard Himself a-Being: John Berryman's *Dream Songs*," *American Quest for a Supreme Fiction*, 1979, pp. 260–62

STANLEY KUNITZ
"No Middle Ground"
Poetry, July 1957, pp. 244–49

T he ambitiousness of John Berryman's poem ⟨*Homage to Mistress Bradstreet*⟩ resides not so much in its length—it runs to only 458 lines—as in its material and style. This is no middle flight. Despite the discrepancy in scale, the manifest intention of the poet inevitably recalls that of Hart Crane in *The Bridge*: to relate himself to the American past through the discovery of a viable myth, and to create for his vehicle a grand and exalted language, a language of transfiguration. If Berryman has been less fortunate than his predecessor in his search for a theme and a language, his failure nevertheless, like Crane's, is worth more than most successes.

The historical justification for Berryman's return to Anne Bradstreet as "a sourcing" seems clear enough. As the first woman to write verse in English in America—*The Tenth Muse, Lately Sprung up in America* appeared originally in England in 1650—she survives in the annals of our literature, companioned always by her florid title. To imagine her as the symbolic mother-muse of American poetry is, however, to stretch the point, as Berryman himself is well aware, for the mediocrity of her performance is too blatant.

> . . . all this bald
> abstract didactic rime I read appalled
> harassed for your fame
> mistress neither of fiery nor velvet verse. . . .

It is the life, the spirit, rather than the work, to which Berryman pays his homage. In a sense Anne Bradstreet prefigures "the alienated poet" with whose image we are all too familiar in our own time. The rugged environment of Massachusetts Bay, first glimpsed at eighteen, was scarcely of the kind to appeal to this fastidious, well-bred young English lady, despite her devotion to her so-much-older husband Simon, eventually governor of the colony, to whom she bore in due course eight children. "Pioneering is not feeling well." Modeling her style on DuBartas and Quarles, she sought refuge in her versifying (some 7000 lines in all) and meanwhile labored to re-create in her immediate circle some of the lost amenities of the polite tradition. Her many descendants include Oliver Wendell Holmes, Richard Henry Dana, and Wendell Phillips. Obviously, in a consideration of the American heritage, Anne Bradstreet is not to be dismissed lightly; but just as obviously she cannot easily be cast in an heroic mold. Part of the imaginative sweat of Berryman's poem is produced by his wrestle with his subject. . . .

Berryman's poem seethes with an almost terrifying activity, as must be evident even in the fragmentary phrases I have already quoted, where the peculiar energy of the language compels attention. Time and time again the medium comes powerfully alive, packed with original metaphor and galvanic with nouns and verbs that seem interchangeably charged with inventive excitement. At his best, in his moments of superlative force and concentration, Berryman writes with dramatic brilliance: "I am a closet of secrets dying," or again, ". . . they starch their minds./Folkmoots, & blether, blether. John Cotton rakes/to the synod of Cambridge." *Homage to Mistress Bradstreet*, I began by saying, is a failure, for reasons I must proceed to demonstrate, but it succeeds in convincing me that Berryman is now entitled to rank among our most gifted poets.

After at least half-a-dozen readings, in which many of the difficulties of the text and the form have been resolved, I still retain my first impression that the scaffolding of the poem is too frail to bear the weight imposed upon it. To put it in other terms, the substance of the poem as a whole lacks inherent imaginative grandeur: whatever effect of magnitude it achieves has been beaten into it. The display of so much exacerbated sensibility, psychic torment, religious ecstasy seems to be intermittently in excess of what the secular occasion requires; the feelings persist in belonging to the poet instead of becoming the property of the poem.

> I am a man of griefs & fits
> trying to be my friend. And the brown smock splits,
> down the pale flesh a gash
> broadens and Time holds up your heart against my
> eyes.

In particular, the love-duet in the central section tends to collapse into a bathos somewhat reminiscent of Crashaw's extravagant compounding of religion and sex. . . .

From the beginning of his career Berryman has been concerned with the problems of his craft. In the prefatory note to twenty of his poems first collected in *Five Young American Poets* (1940) he wrote: "One of the reasons for writing verse is a delight in craftsmanship—rarely for its own sake, mainly as it seizes and makes visible its subject. Versification, rime, stanza-form, trope are the tools. They provide the means by which the writer can shape from an experience in itself usually vague, a mere feeling or phrase, something that is coherent, directed, intelligible." In his new work, as I have already indicated, Berryman has evolved, for his language of rapture and of the "delirium of the grand depths," a dense and involuted style which in its very compression and distortion is best adapted for the production of extraordinary, not ordinary, effects. There is much that is extraordinary in his poem, often as a consequence of the magnificent conversion of the ordinary, but it is in the nature of the long poem that it must sweep into its embrace certain phenomena whose virtue is to be what they are, to resist transubstantiation—and here Berryman is tempted to inflate what he cannot subjugate. "Without the commonplace," remarked Hölderlin, "nobility cannot be represented, and so I shall always say to myself, when I come up against something common in the world: You need this as urgently as a potter needs clay, and for that reason always take it in, and do not reject it, and do not take fright at it."

A portion of Berryman's vocabulary and most of the idiosyncrasies of his technique can be traced back to Hopkins, witness such lines as these, spoken by Anne in the crisis of childbirth:

> Monster you are killing me Be sure
> I'll have you later Women do endure
> I can *can* no longer
> and it passes the wretched trap whelming me and I
>   am me
> drencht & powerful, I did it with my body!

But Hopkins, to be sure, would have known better than to let the last phrase get by. (Hysteria is not an intensity of tone, but a laxness, a giving in. By the time Anne has pressed out her child—we are spared few of the physiological details—we must be prepared to accede to the premise that never has there been such an excruciating, such a miraculous birth, and we boggle at the superfluity of the assault on our disbelief.)

In his uncompromising election of a language of artifice Berryman, like Hopkins, does not hesitate, for the sake of the emphasis and tension he aims at, to wrench his syntax, invert his word-order. The rewards of his daring are not to be minimized. The opening stanza, for example, seems to me to move with beautiful ease and dignity; the tone, the pressures, delicately controlled; the details small and particular, but the air charged with momentousness:

> The Governor your husband lived so long
> moved you not, restless, waiting for him? Still,
> you were a patient woman.—
> I seem to see you pause here still:
> Sylvester, Quarles, in moments odd you pored
> before a fire at, bright eyes on the Lord,
> all the children still.
> 'Simon . . .' Simon will listen while you read a
>   Song.

But when the dislocations have nothing to recommend them beyond their mechanical violence, the ear recoils:

> Out of maize & air
> your body's made, and moves. I summon, see
> from the centuries it.
> They say thro' the fading winter Dorothy fails,
> my second, who than I bore one more, nine.

If we examine a pair of lines from Hopkins,

> When will you ever, Peace, wild wooddove, shy
>   wings shut,
> Your round me roaming end, and under be my
>   boughs?

we can see that the older poet, however radical his deflections from the linguistic norm, keeps mindful of the natural flow and rhythms of speech, which serves him as his contrapuntal ground.

Throughout his poem Berryman handles his varied eight-line stanza, derived perhaps from *The Wreck of the Deutschland* and composed in a system of functional stressing adapted from Hopkins' sprung rhythm, with admirable assurance. Few modern poets, I think, can even approximate his command of the stanzaic structure. The alterations of pace through his juxtaposition of short and long lines are beautifully controlled; and the narrative-lyrical functions are kept in fluid relation, with the action riding through the stanza, which nevertheless preserves intact the music suspended within it.

Homage to Mistress Bradstreet can bear the kind of scrutiny that an important poem exacts. The flaws are real for me, but the work remains impressive in its ambition and virtuosity. Other poets and critics, it should be noted, have been far less qualified in their praise than I. Both Conrad Aiken and Robert Fitzgerald have not hesitated to apply the epithet "classic" to it. Robert Lowell has called it "a very big achievement". And Edmund Wilson has acclaimed it as "the most distinguished long poem by an American since *The Waste Land*".

ROBERT LOWELL
"The Poetry of John Berryman"

New York Review of Books, May 28, 1964, pp. 3–4

The poem in which everything flowers for Berryman is his long *Homage to Mistress Bradstreet*. It is wonderfully wrung and wrought. Nothing could be more high-pitched, studied and inflamed. One can read it many times, and still get lost in it; with each renewal it becomes clearer and more haunting. In part, it is a biography of Anne Bradstreet that reproduces the grammar, theology and staid decor of the period. The poet, however, heightens the action by imagining his heroine with the intensity of a seizure or hallucination. He is

in her presence, she seems inside him. In what is almost a love declaration, she speaks to him in a language that is a strange mixture of hers and his. Somehow, the story of her landing, her pious and despairing moments, the bearing of a child, the death of a daughter, and her own aging and wavering relations with her husband and family get told with a passionate fullness. Here Berryman's experiments with music and sentence structure find themselves harnessed to a subject and trial that strain them to the limit. His lovely discordant rhythms ride through every break, splutter, archaism and inversion. The old rustic, seventeenth-century, provincial simplicity survives and is greatly enriched by the jagged intellectual probing and techniques of the modern poet. *Homage to Mistress Bradstreet* is the most resourceful historical poem in our literature.

Dream Songs is larger and sloppier. The scene is contemporary and crowded with references to news items, world politics, travel, low life, and Negro music. Its style is a conglomeration of high style, Berrymanisms, Negro and beat slang and baby-talk. The poem is written in sections of three six-line stanzas. There is little sequence, and sometimes a single section will explode into three or four separate parts. At first the brain aches and freezes at so much darkness, disorder and oddness. After a while, the repeated situations and their racy jabber become more and more enjoyable, although even now I wouldn't trust myself to paraphrase accurately at least half the sections.

The poems are much too difficult, packed and wrenched to be sung. They are called *songs* out of mockery, because they are filled with snatches of Negro minstrelsy, and because one of their characters is Mr. Bones, who keeps questioning the author and talking for him. The dreams are not real dreams but a waking hallucination in which anything that might have happened to the author can be used at random. Anything he has seen, overheard or imagined can go in. The poems are about Berryman, or rather they are about a person he calls *Henry*. Henry is Berryman seen as himself, as *poète maudit*, child and puppet. He is tossed about with a mixture of tenderness and absurdity, pathos and hilarity that would have been impossible if the author had spoken in the first person.

Berryman is very bookish and also very idiosyncratic. The bookishness shows up as a fault in a certain echoing hardness, yet it tempers his quirkiness, and lets him draw on whatever models will serve his purposes. Many masters support him and are extended by his undertaking.

Here is a bit of Pound:

> I seldom go to films. They are too exciting,
>   said the honorable Possum.

Here is Stevens:

> Pleased at the worst, except with man, he shook
>   the brightest winter sun.

And here is a passage that would have pleased Cummings:

> This is the lay of Ike.
> Here's to the glory of the great white—awk—
> who has been running—cr—cr—things in recent—
>   ech—
> in the United—if your screen is black,
> ladies & gentlemen, we—I like—
> at the Point he was terrific . . .

Berryman's debt to these three authors is much deeper and more imaginative than such verbal similarities would suggest. From Pound he learned the all-inclusive style, the high spirits, the flitting from subject to subject, irreverence and humor. I say *learned*, but it is really a question of resemblance. I feel the presence of Stevens in sonorous, suggestive, nuance-like, often not quite clear, lines; in cloudy anecdotes about fanciful figures, such as *Quo*, or in the section about Clitus and Alexander the Great. Henry has much the same distance and identification with his author as Crispin in "The Comedian as the letter C." The resemblance to Cummings is in the humor, verbal contortion and pathos. There is also Joyce. . . .

Dream Songs is a hazardous, imperfect book. One would need to see the unpublished parts to decide how well it fills out as a whole. As it stands, the main faults of this selection are the threat of mannerism, and worse—disintegration. How often one chafes at the relentless indulgence, and cannot tell the what or why of a passage. And yet one must give in. All is risk and variety here. This great Pierrot's universe is more tearful and funny than we can easily bear.

JOHN BAYLEY
"John Berryman: A Question of Imperial Sway"
Contemporary Poetry in America, ed. Robert Boyers
1974, pp. 62–65

Many opinions and errors in the songs are to be referred not to the character Henry, still less to the author, but to the title of the work. . . . The poem then, whatever its wide cast of characters, is essentially about an imaginary character, (not the poet, not me) named Henry, a white American in early middleage in blackface, who has suffered irreversible loss and talks about himself sometimes in the first person, sometimes in the third, sometimes even in the second; he has a friend, never named, who addresses him as Mr. Bones and variants thereof.

(Berryman on the "I" of the *Dream Songs*)

T his of course is rubbish in one sense, but in another it is a perfectly salutary and justified reminder by the author that when he puts himself into a poem he formalizes himself. To labor the point again: Mailer is always Mailer, but Berryman in verse is Berryman in verse. That does not mean that he is exaggerated or altered or dramatized: on the contrary, if he were so the poem would be quite different and much more conventional. Berryman of course deeply admired and was much influenced by Yeats, who helped him to acquire the poet's imperial sway over himself and us, but he is not in the least concerned with Yeats's doctrine of the Masks, and with trying out contrasting dramatic representations of the self; such a cumbrous and courtly device of European poetry does not go with American directness and the new American expansiveness. Why bother to put on masks when you can make the total creature writing all the form that is needed?

Byron and Pushkin also emphasized the formal nature of their poetic device, often in facetious terms and in the poems themselves—making characters meet real friends and themselves, etc.—Berryman's gambit to emphasize a comparable formalism has a long history. None the less his comments are misleading in so far as they imply something like a dramatic relation between characters and ideas in the *Dream Songs*. The hero of Meredith's *Modern Love* would be as impossible in any other art context as Henry, but he is in a dramatic situation, and in that situation we can—indeed we are positively invited to—judge him, as we judge Evgeny Onegin. And to judge here is to become a part of. The heroes of such poems with dramatic insides to them are not taken as seriously as heroes in prose; they are unstable and frenetic, capable of all or nothing, be-

cause we do not get accustomed to them: they appear and vanish in each line and rhyme. None the less they are stable enough to be sat in judgment on, and Berryman's Henry is not. Ultimately, the formal triumph of Henry is that because he is not us and never could be, he has—like our own solitary egos—passed beyond judgment.

The paradox is complete, and completely satisfying. Clearly Berryman knew it. "These songs are not meant to be understood you understand/They are only meant to terrify and comfort" (366). But though it is not dramatic the interior of the *Dream Songs* is grippingly exciting, deep, detailed and spacious. Moreover it is not in the least claustrophobic in the sense in which the world of Sylvia Plath involuntarily constricts and imprisons: on the contrary, like the world of early Auden it is boisterously exhilarating and liberating. It has no corpus of exposition, sententiousness, or pet theory, which is why it is far more like *Modern Love* or *Evgeny Onegin* than the *Cantos*, or, say, *The Testament of Beauty*. It never expounds. Another thing in common with the Meredith and Pushkin is the nature of the pattern. Each "Number" is finished, as is each of the intricate stanzas of their long poems, but in reading the whole we go on with curiosity unslaked and growing, as if reading a serial. The separate numbers of the *Dream Songs* published in magazines could not of course indicate this serial significance, which is not sequent, but taken as a whole reveals unity.

The Russian formalists have a term *pruzhina*, referring to the "sprung" interior of a successful poetic narration, the bits under tension which keep the parts apart and the dimensions open and inviting. Thus, in *Evgeny Onegin*, Tatiana is a heroine, a story-book heroine, and a parody of such a heroine; while Evgeny is, conversely, a "romantic" hero for her, a parody of such a hero, and a hero. The spring keeps each separable in the formal art of the poem, and the pair of them in isolation from each other. I am inclined to think that Berryman's quite consciously contrived *pruzhina* in the *Dream Songs* is a very simple and very radical one: to hold in opposed tension and full view the poet at his desk at the moment he was putting down the words, and the words themselves in their arrangement on the page as poetry. When one comes to think of it, it is surprising that no one has thought of exploiting this basic and intimate confrontation before. (The weary old stream of consciousness is something quite other, being composed like any other literature in the author's head, irrespective of where he was and what he was being at the time.) The extreme analogy of such a confrontation would be Shakespeare weaving into the words of "To be or not to be," or "Tomorrow and tomorrow and tomorrow" such instant reactions and reflections as "Shall I go for a piss now or hold it till I've done a few more lines"—or—"I wonder what size her clitoris is"—or—"We must be out of olive oil." Of course there is no effect of interpretation in Berryman; but the spring does hold apart, and constantly, a terrifying and comforting image of the poet as *there*—wrestling in his flesh and in his huddle of needs—while at the same time poetry is engraving itself permanently on the page. It is this that keeps our awed and round-eyed attention more than anything else: our simultaneous sense of the pain of being such a poet, and of the pleasure of being able to read his poetry.

It is also instrumental in our not judging. The poet is not asking us to pity his racked state, or to understand and sympathize with the wild bad obsessed exhibitionist behavior it goes with. These things are simply there, as formal achievement, and Henry James, that great Whitman fan, would oddly enough, I am sure, have understood and been gratified by it.

He suggests it in the advice he gave to the sculptor Andersen about how to convey the tension and the isolation in an embracing sculptured couple.

> Make the creatures palpitate, and their flesh tingle and flush, and their internal economy proceed and their bellies ache and their bladders fill—all in the mystery of your art.

"Hard-headed Willie" in his magisterial way, and with his "blood, imagination, intellect running together," might also have given a clue; but when he says "I walk through a long school-room questioning" or—

> I count those feathered balls of soot
> The moorhen guides upon the stream
> To silence the envy in my thought.

it is well understood that he is doing no such thing. This is the rhetoric of the moment, not its apparent actuality; the thought he is silencing and the questions he asks have all been cooked up in the study afterward. His air of immediate imperiousness, with himself and us, is a bit of a fraud, and this seasons our admiration with an affectionate touch of decision. Yeats is the boss whose little tricks we can see through and like him the more for: all the same, we do judge.

And with Berryman we don't; the spring device forbids it. How judge someone who while talking and tormenting himself is also writing a poem about the talk and torment? Except that we know, deeper down, that this effect *is* a formalistic device and that Berryman's control of it is total. And this knowledge makes us watch the taut spring vibrating with even rapter attention. There is a parallel with the formalism so brilliantly pulled off by Lowell in *Life Studies*, where the poetry seemed itself the act of alienation and cancellation, as if poet and subject had died the instant the words hit the paper. The formal device or emblem above the door framing the two collections might be, in Lowell's case, a speech cut off by the moment of death: in Berryman's, a Word condemned to scratch itself eternally, in its chair and at its desk.

WILLIAM MEREDITH
"Henry Tasting All the Secret Bits of Life: Berryman's *Dream Songs*"

Wisconsin Studies in Contemporary Literature, Winter–Spring 1965, pp. 27–33

The book John Berryman published last year is only his third, but it suggests that he is one of the best American poets writing today. *77 Dream Songs* is a fine and remarkable book of poems by any standards. It can be compared for delight, I think, to the best book of Wilbur or Roethke, to *Things of This World*, say, or *The Lost Son*, or even to *Lord Weary's Castle* though it is less perfect than Lowell's book, even of its raggeder kind. It can be compared for the account it gives of some of our troubles to *The Fire Next Time*, or *Advertisements for Myself*. The latter comparisons are in Berryman's favor because he commits himself more generously than Baldwin or Mailer to a predicament he sees just as clearly. An example of this involvement can be seen in a Song about a week when the affairs of the Western World are going to hell with unusual deliberateness. Into this poem (66) Berryman interjects the following parenthesis of Eastern humility: "('All virtues enter into this world, but take one virtue, without which a man can hardly hold his own: that a man') Henry grew hot, got laid, felt bad, survived ('should always reproach himself'.)".

It is a book of powerful originality, almost of eccentricity, and it presents difficulties at first. . . . Berryman has long been famous as a poet's poet, with the contradiction that that forlorn phrase carries. This book should make him famous with everyone who uses modern poetry at all.

Two statements by the author about the Dream Songs are suggestive of how the poems are meant to be taken. Reading some of them in public two years ago he said, and has since allowed to be printed: "The poem is about a man who is apparently named Henry, or says he is. He has a tendency to talk about himself in the third person. His last name is in doubt. It's given at one point as Henry House and at other points as Henry Pussy-cat. He has a friend, moreover, who addresses him regularly as Mr. Bones, or some variation on that. Some of the sections . . . are really dialogues." In the present book he adds: "There are sections, constituting one version, of a poem in progress. . . . Many opinions and errors in the Songs are to be referred not to the character Henry, still less to the author, but to the title of the work."

In both cases the poet speaks of the poems as a single work, in spite of the fact that the eighteen-line Songs are often self-contained lyrics. And by calling attention to the dubious identity of "a man apparently named Henry" who entertains but is not accountable for "opinions and errors in the Songs," Berryman suggests that the unity of the work lies in its being the dream-autobiography of the central character. Whether this character calls himself I or it, Henry or Mr. Bones, his identity doesn't change. What does shift, with dream-like uncertainty, is the relationship of the dreamer to his dream self: am I acting this dream or watching it, or both? And who am I when I'm awake?

The discovery of Henry's whole identity, by him and by us, comprises the plot of the poem. It is a narrative poem and, as is true of a lot of literature, to discover its unity is to discover its meaning. A first reading of the poem will fasten on Songs that strike the individual reader as the most lucid and self-contained. He should not be put off by the ones that don't make any sense at first. (Some that began to shed light on and endear Henry to me were: Nos. 4, 7, 14, 18, 29, 35, 43, 62, 63, 69. Numbers in parentheses throughout refer to Songs rather than pages.)

Henry gradually emerges (to give the plot away) as a wholesome clean-cut American Proteus, a man with as many selves as our dreams confer. He commands the idiom, rhythm and experience of a jazz-man, both old-style New Orleans and hipster-junkie. He is equally at home with—or, more exactly, he can adapt himself with alcohol or Eastern philosophy to—a meeting of the Modern Language Association (35) and the role of Fulbright lecturer (out of season) on the Ganges (24, 71). He has read a lot more than I have and is more implicated in what he reads. He is generous, moral and manic, but also lecherous, alcoholic and depressive. Three songs treat directly with insanity (52–54) and half a dozen others touch on it familiarly. But through all the changes of his dreams the character and the voice remain so individual that you would no more mistake a song of Henry's, finally, than you would a meditation of Leopold Bloom's.

Henry's agonizing and beautiful energy is like that of Joyce's hero in another respect: it is profoundly, essentially humorous. The subconscious, which is chiefly what *Ulysses* and the Dream Songs record, knows no deliberate mode. It is not serious or joking, tragic or comic. It combines but doesn't rationally select, so that rational incongruity, a source of humor, is its habit:

                                                                    Two daiquiris
withdrew into a corner of the gorgeous room
and one told the other a lie. (16)

That morning arrived to Henry as well a great cheque
eaten out already by the Government & State &
other strange matters . . . (19)

Henry & Phoebe happy as cockroaches
in the world-kitchen woofed. . . . (31)

Bats have no bankers and they do not drink
and cannot be arrested and pay no tax
and, in general, bats have it made. (63)

Henry is an imaginary Negro (as the hero of Berryman's early short story is "The Imaginary Jew") and the poems draw on the several levels of humor that we owe to the Negro. Some of it runs deep and bitter, as it does in the blues, where only language and rhythm remain playful and even the word-play bites (40):

I'm scared a lonely. Never see my son,
easy be not to see anyone,
combers out to sea
know they're goin somewhere but not me.
Got a little poison, got a little gun,
I'm scared a lonely.

I'm scared a only one thing, which is me,
from othering I don't take nothin, see,
for any hound dog's sake.
But this is where I livin', where I rake
my leaves and cop my promise, this' where we
cry oursel's awake.

Wishin was dyin but I gotta make
it all this way to that bed on these feet
where peoples said to meet.
Maybe but even if I see my son
forever never, get back on the take,
free, black & forty-one.

Some of Henry's dreams are monologues and dialogues in the dialect of Negro vaudeville, a double-edged joke where the Negro plays it both cunning and obsequious, like an Elizabethan Fool, to amuse both himself and his slower-witted master. But Henry, being only an imaginary Negro, speaks mostly in a black-face parody of this, the vaudeville dialect of The Two Black Crows and Stepin Fetchit—a speech that has a rich, shrewd, rather brutal history in our national humor. Berryman refers once (72) to Henry's "burnt-cork luck." The phrase could be applied to the success with which this dialect gets at the truth in a world where the Negro's situation is both a symptom and a metaphor of our failure. The world is acutely perceived, in all its wonderful incomprehensibility, in this dialect:

—Here matters hard to manage at de best,
Mr. Bones. Tween what we see, what be,
is blinds. Them blinds on fire. (64)

But against this perception is set the cliché of rational, white man's speech and the oversimplified, disastrous culture which that speech accommodates:

There were strange gatherings. A vote would come
that would be no vote. There would come a rope.
Yes. There would come a rope.
Men have their hats down. "Dancing in the Dark"
Will see him up, car-radio-wise. So many, some
won't find a rut to park.

It is in the administration of rhetoric,
on these occasions, that—not the fathomless heart—
the thinky death consists; . . . (10)

But these Negro masks are only one of Henry's identities. It would be more accurate to describe the hero of this poem as an imaginary madman. He identifies himself easily and completely with every sort of person and situation, even some that are totally unsympathetic. He has the inability of the insane to distinguish between things that are merely alike, and it is this that charges his metaphors with so much force. They are no longer implied comparisons but terrible uncertainties of identity. Song 48 is about Christ's wild cry to God from the cross (Mark 15) and about Henry's command of tourist phrases in foreign languages, and the two confuse in an image of the Eucharist:

He yelled at me in Greek,
my God!—It's not his language
and I'm no good at—his is Aramaic,
was—I am a monoglot of English
(American version) and, say pieces from
a baker's dozen others: where's the bread?

but rising in the Second Gospel, pal:
The seed goes down, god dies,
A rising happens,
some crust, and then occurs an eating. He said so,
a Greek idea,
troublesome to imaginary Jews, . . .

In another (56) the dreamer changes abruptly into a deer, the completeness of the identification clinched by the term *two-footers* for men. Berryman's use of *tinchel* here, an obsolete Scots word meaning a ring formed by hunters to enclose deer, is unusual in its abstruseness but characteristic in its exactness:

The tinchel closes. Terror, & plunging, swipes.
I lay my ears back. I am about to die.
My cleft feet drum.
Fierce, the two-footers club. My green world pipes
a finish—for us all, my love, not some.

And often he holds to an insane accuracy of colloquial idiom and low image at moments when a sane man would be driven naturally to a more formal rhetoric:

I have been operating from *nothing*,
like a dog after its tail
more slowly, losing altitude. (54)

Madman and black-face are real identities of the "man who is apparently named Henry," who is looking for wisdom and truth along with his identity. He insists on *wording* himself and his world exactly, as though the mystery might lie in words. (Of course it's self-conscious: he is a man who sleeps and wakes in an agony of self-consciousness—he's our man.) The poems seem to escape mannerism because Berryman never takes his eye off the scene, the event, the mood of Henry's dream. A grand style, or its parody, is frequently used:

Our wounds to time, from all the other times,
sea-times slow, the times of galaxies
fleeing, the dwarfs' dead times,
lessen so little that if here in his crude rimes
Henry them mentions, do not hold it, please,
for a putting of man down. (51)

As various as they are, we learn to recognize Henry's characteristic ways of wording himself and together they make a character. Style, Frost said, is the way a man takes himself.

The form of some of the poems is very strict. Song 42 is as exact a model of the stanza as I have found: pairs of iambic pentameter lines are followed by trimeter, and these are set in units of six lines and rhymed by various schemes. Some of the lines have very memorable and conventional rhythm:

We dream of honor, and we get along. (42)

Against the strictly rhymed and scanned Songs are set some that are very free.

John Berryman's poems began appearing in magazines in the late 1930's. The first collection of them was in a New Directions volume in 1940 called *Five Young American Poets*. Six years later he published *The Dispossessed*, a book of lyrics that earned him the general regard of craftsmen in England as well as America. Among the *personae* offered by these poems are to be found recognizable fragments of the Dream Song hero and his patterns of speech. *The Dispossessed*, in fact, predicts 77 *Dream Songs* more clearly than the brilliant narrative poem, *Homage to Mistress Bradstreet* that appeared in 1956. This is a strongly eccentric work whose difficulties are not as easily resolved as those of the Dream Songs. Edmund Wilson said of it: "It seems to me the most distinguished long poem since *The Waste Land*." For many readers, it remains as inaccessible as Eliot's experiment, and they will not join Robert Lowell in placing it at the top of Berryman's accomplishments.

77 *Dream Songs* seems to me to deserve that rank. Moving forward with the intensity of vision that characterized *Mistress Bradstreet* and with the range of common experience of *The Dispossessed*, this work is free of the slight air of bookishness that hovered over Berryman's earlier work. (It is an air that hovers over all but the luckiest of modern poems.) The Dream Songs use a diction of their own, one that owes little to the familiar though flexible diction of current poetic practice. The language seems to spring naturally from the gusto (insane? holy?) with which Henry makes the human scene:

> Spry disappointments of men
> and vicing adorable children
> miserable women, Henry mastered, Henry
> tasting all the secret bits of life.   (74)

PETER STITT
"John Berryman: The Dispossessed Poet"

Ohio Review, Winter 1974, pp. 68–74

II

Berryman's earliest poetry was written during the nineteen-thirties and 'forties. Thus his sensibility would seem to have been formed in a particularly unstable and violent era, one dominated first by the threat and then by the terrible reality of the Second World War. The protagonists of these early poems are, like all men, deeply disturbed by the war. For them, however, it is an even stronger threat; as an intellectual and an artist, Berryman saw that it was the things he most loved, the things of the spirit and mind, that would suffer the most from the barbarism of war. "Conversation," written in 1938, presents a view of the modern world through the image of a fire in a fireplace. First there is a portent of war—"A snapt short log pitched out upon the hearth/The flaming harbinger come forth/Of holocausts"—and then a recognition of the probable result of that war—"the failing thought/Of cities stripped of knowledge, men,/Our continent a wilderness again." As barbarism replaces civilization, ignorance will replace knowledge, and the possibilities for meaningful art will disappear.

We find the effects of such a violent and war-torn world on a sensitive person described in other poems. Perhaps the young girl in "The Song of the Tortured Girl" could be seen as emblematic of the poetic sensibility. Through torture, the world's insanity touches her directly ("I feel them stretch my youth and throw a switch") and the result is that she slowly loses her mind. More obviously akin to the poet is the protagonist of "The Pacifist's Song," a man torn between two moral imperatives. On the one hand he recognizes the evil that exists in the world and the necessity of fighting it. On the other hand, however, the young man sees a higher necessity, that of attempting to live by the decrees of his God. Thus he feels required to wage war not in the real world but within himself, where he must fight against his basically sinful nature:

> What I try, doomed, is hard enough to do.
> We breed up in our own breast our worse wars
> Who long since sealed ourselves Hers who abides.

The point for the poet is that he, like the pacifist, also lives his life and does his work in honor of something higher than those things which impel everyday life. Poetry is in essence a thing of the spirit, a spiritual and even quasi-religious activity. Thus the poet, like the religious pacifist, is a person almost inevitably at odds with his world and his society. And it is not just the war that disturbs the sensitive person, the poet—to him the world, even in its quieter moments, appears chaotic and insane. Another of Berryman's early poems, "World-Telegram," is concerned with the effect of the news of one day on the mind of a sensitive person. Based on the May 11, 1939, edition of *The New York World-Telegram*, the poem recounts the day's events, which range from the ridiculous (a man with a tail, discovered in the jungles of Ceylon, is to be displayed at the World's Fair) to the tragic and horrifying (a father and son were crushed against a loading platform by a truck as the mother and another son looked on). In the final stanza, Berryman considers the effects:

> If it were possible to take these things
> Quite seriously, I believe they might
> Curry disorder in the strongest brain.

To be sure, Berryman's early poems are not notably strong as poetry. Yet they do show clearly the division between the sensibility of the poet and that of the world of which he is a part. The aims of the poet, largely spiritual and humane, and the aims of the rest of the world are so different as to forbid reconciliation; it is little wonder that a poet should feel himself dispossessed. As if this weren't enough, there is yet another way in which modern society dispossesses the poet—by ignoring him, by not recognizing as valid the function he thinks he serves. There was a time when poets were the only story-tellers and served society by celebrating the heroes and triumphs of the nation, as Homer and Virgil did. In Ireland, in fact, the bardic poet combined artistic, religious, and even political functions as the caretaker and transmitter of the tradition and ideals of his society. But a gradual change has taken place, and, as prose has grown in importance, poets have seen their usefulness diminish. Reflecting this, Shelley referred to poets in the early nineteenth century as "the unacknowledged legislators of the world." To the poet, the phrase still holds true; poets who are outraged by the Vietnam war and by other public acts of immorality may write protest verse in an attempt to reawaken or "legislate" a sane morality. But they are ignored, their supposed role unacknowledged.

However, the poet remains a public figure as he continues to offer, with a tremulous hopefulness, his work to the reading public. The response is not heartening. In a recent issue of *The New York Times Magazine*, Joseph Brodsky addressed himself to just this question. Brodsky is a Soviet poet who, because of severe harassment in his native land, recently emigrated to the United States. Thus he is able to see the problem from a double perspective: "The difference between the position of a writer in the East and in the West, in essence, is not too great. Both there and here he tries to knock down a rather thick wall with his forehead. In the former case the wall reacts to the touch of the smallest heads in a way threatening to the writer's physical condition. In the latter case the wall maintains silence, and this threatens one's psychological condition. To tell the truth, I do not know which is more frightening. Worst of all is when both are combined." For most modern poets, as for John Berryman, both are indeed combined; the modern poet is forced to live out his existence as a person doubly dispossessed.

III

Given this depressing situation, we might ask what it is, if anything, that sustains the modern poet and keeps him going. Hayden Carruth, among the most respected living authorities on American poetry, suggested in a review of Berryman's *Sonnets* the direction an answer to this question might take: "Once poets stood aghast before God; then before Nature. What is left? Perhaps Love, as in Berryman's sonnets. But while some poets . . . are now working to discern the primacy of love, Berryman seems to be working in the blind trauma of this third (and final?) loss." The progression of ideas here suggests that, having sometime in the nineteenth century lost the possibility of worshipping both God and Nature, the poet, should he now lose Love, will find himself with nothing to believe in, forced to face a final meaninglessness, an untimate nihilism. We must, of course, take care not to over-simplify complex issues. Berryman, like most poets living in an industrial age, wrote almost no nature poetry; and yet Frost stands as a towering exception to the rule. The question of God, too, is complex. Strangely enough, it is John Berryman who might be viewed as the modern exception, a religious poet in a distinctly unreligious age. However, because religion dominates only Berryman's last poems, we might look first at the question of love.

We can see in Berryman's use and treatment of the theme of love a movement from the positive to the negative, as love, like nature and society, comes to fail the sensitive person living in the modern world. Berryman wrote few traditional love poems; there is "Canto Amor" from his first volume, and there are the *Sonnets*, which were written in the 'forties though not published until 1967. The sonnets present an interesting case; they celebrate a woman and the poet's love for her, and they run deep. But while there is real love to be found here, we also note that the affair is adulterous on both sides, and that it ends inevitably with separation. Moreover, it is the woman, the beloved, who leaves the man; she returns to her husband, but he has only a divorce to look forward to. There is an undercurrent of betrayal in the work, as the poet turns out to be more loyal and more faithful than his mistress, and is let down by her in the end.

From the point of view of the speaker-protagonist in Berryman's works, this is the general pattern to be found—he always has more love, more loyalty, more compassion to give than he ever receives. In the later works, love itself dies out and is replaced by lust, which is the concern of some of the most enjoyable and witty of the dream songs. One begins:

> Love her he doesn't but the thought he puts
> into that young woman
> would launch a national product
> complete with TV spots & skywriting
> outlets in Bonn & Tokyo.
> I mean it,

and ends: "Vouchsafe me, Sleepless One,/a personal experience of the body of Mrs. Boogry/before I pass from lust!" However enjoyable the poem is, we must recognize that

Berryman's protagonist has given up on love; it is too painful, too risky; his chances of getting hurt are too great.

There is in Berryman's work, however, a middle stage which involves the exercise of another type of love. In *Homage to Mistress Bradstreet*, the poet goes back three-hundred years in time and, within the created realm of the imagination, attempts to seduce the first American poet, Anne Bradstreet. The burden of the poem is not sexual but cultural, for what draws Berryman to Anne is a shared situation: each of them is a poet trying to live and work within a hostile social and cultural environment. Anne lived in Puritan New England and thus operated under a double burden—not only did the Puritans think poetry was mostly a waste of time, but they also firmly believed that women belonged only in the kitchen and bedroom, that their minds were too weak for intellectual labors. And Berryman lived, of course, in the modern world already described. The key to the poem comes in these lines at the end of the second stanza:

> . . . We are on each other's hands
> who care. Both of our worlds unhanded us.

Given the nature of the world and the attitudes of society, Berryman is saying, it is essential that those who care about this fragile and spiritual thing, poetry, stick together and take care of each other.

Friendship based on the idea of a community of poets, then, is the second aspect of love in Berryman's work. Few poets have ever had so strong a sense of commitment to their calling as Berryman. As James Dickey has pointed out, Berryman was a poet-made and not a poet-born. He had to learn his craft over many years of labor, and only his fierce commitment carried him through the lean early years when he simply was not a good poet, hardly even a promising one. Part of this commitment was to poetry; the other part involved a devotion to poets, a sort of love for his co-workers and co-sufferers. And that is why so many of the strongest poems in *The Dream Songs* are elegies written in honor of other writers.

During the time Berryman was composing the songs, roughly from 1955 to 1968, many important American writers, some of them Berryman's friends, died. These, among others, appear in the songs: Wallace Stevens, Theodore Roethke, Ernest Hemingway, William Faulkner, Robert Frost, William Carlos Williams, T. S. Eliot, Sylvia Plath, Randall Jarrell, Delmore Schwartz. Henry is bitterly affected by these deaths:

> Panic & shock together. They are all going away.
> Henry took down his black four-in-hand & his black
>   bowtie
> and put away all other ties.
> . . .
> I feel a final chill. This is cold sweat
> that will not leave me now. Maybe it's time
> to throw in my own hand.

The sensitive man, the poet-protagonist, once again feels betrayed as another source of comfort and solace fails him. It is not love itself that is a fault here, of course; rather it is death that causes the trouble. Henry relies on his friends, needs them desperately, but he can only watch as one by one they are taken from him. Nature, society, love and friendship, all fade away for the poet as he searches for something to cling to and believe in. And so near the end of his life Berryman turned back to God, to the Catholicism of his childhood.

IV

There was always a religious element in Berryman's works. We have already seen a hint of it in "The Pacifist's Song," and it can be seen as well throughout the *Sonnets*, where one of the major themes is the moral rightness of the adulterous situation. In the early works religion appears only tangentially. In *The Dream Songs*, however, Henry's thoughts about and relationship with God become a primary concern. God is seen as an all-powerful watcher, the ever-present eyes beyond the clouds. In a song entitled "Henry's Programme for God," He is described as "Something disturbed, /ill-pleased, & with a touch of paranoia/who calls for this thud of love from his creatures-O." It turns out that, in Henry's eyes, there are two possible attitudes towards such a deity:

> *Our* only resource is bleak denial or
> anti-potent rage,
> both having been tried by our wisest. Who was it
>   back there
> who died unshriven, daring to see what more
> could happen to a painter with such courage?

Henry himself chooses "anti-potent rage," an attitude which, in spite of its rebelliousness, does accept the existence and power of God as fact. Henry is obsessed with God, deeply concerned about his relationship with Him.

In his last two books, Berryman turned even more directly to religion as a theme. *Love & Fame* is by and large highly secular; it is also the most confessional of Berryman's books, with all of the poems being spoken to the reader by the poet himself. There are no fictional narrators here, no middle men. The first three sections tell of the poet's dual quest for love and fame, and as we might expect the love turns out to be only lust in most cases. But in the third section a new tone seems to enter the work, one of doubt and even despair: "I am busy tired mad lonely & old. /O this has been a long long night of wrest." Going along with this, there is also a search expressed in this section ("In spite of it all, both it & me, /I'll chip away at the mystery") and even a prayer for enlightenment ("Utter, His father, one word").

The prayer is answered in the book's final section, "Eleven Addresses to the Lord." The poems here are, given the general trend of Berryman's work, astonishing. They are outwardly, traditionally, and quite seriously religious. Before the book was published, Berryman told me: "there is a grave piety in the last poems, which is going to trouble a lot of people. You know, the country is full of atheists, and they really are going to find themselves threatened by those poems." On the basis of this section, however, the underlying plan of the book comes clear; each section provides an ironic comment on the preceding section, showing a new stage of awareness that makes the earlier stage look shallow. From the perspective of the final section, the secular concern with love (lust) and fame is seen as deluded. Religious awareness turns out to be the only truly desirable state of mind.

Many things come to a climax in Berryman's final book, *Delusions, Etc.*, including the religious questions I have been discussing. It is not a simple book, however; for example, the title, which looks obvious enough, turns out to be deeply ambiguous. We might think at the outset that the word "Delusions" refers to the poet's secularity, his lust, pride, and so on. By the end of the book, however, we are forced into recognizing the possibility that it is the poet's new-found sense of grace and holiness that are the real delusions. Berryman is constantly afraid that the new goodness will not be able to cancel out the previous evil, and indeed even suggests that the new goodness isn't really very good, as some of the old habits remain. Thus we find a crucial ambiguity in many of the most important poems.

Even in the most optimistic poems here, including those in the first section, "Opus Dei," there is an undercurrent of doubt. Sometimes it is expressed openly, as in these lines from "Tierce":

> I'm not a good man, I won't ever be,
> there's no health in here. You expect too much.
> This pseudo-monk is all but at despair.

Sometimes it is more subtly expressed, as in "How Do You Do, Dr. Berryman, Sir?":

> . . . as for Henry Pussycat   he'd just as soon be dead
> (on the Promise of—I know it sounds incredible—
> if he can muster penitence enough—
> he can't though—
> glory).

It all comes down, finally, to the question of possession—the poet-protagonist of this book is possessed by demons which, try as he might, and he tries mightily, he cannot exorcise in his life. The solution which Berryman himself recognized back in the nineteen-forties ("the devil cast out may be life") now becomes a real possibility. In "No," one of the most despairing poems here, we read:

> Dust in my sore mouth, this deafening wind,
> frightful spaces down from all sides, I'm pale
> I faint for some soft & solid & sudden way out
> as quiet as hemlock in that Attic prose
> with comprehending friends attending—
> a certain reluctance but desire here too,
> the sweet cold numbing upward from my burning
>   feet,
> a last & calm request, which will be granted.

The book is finally and in the deepest sense ironic. The hope is certainly there, and very real—but it is constantly undercut by doubt, by the fear that all this may indeed be too little and too late.

Religion, like society, nature, and love, turns out to have failed the poet in his search for something meaningful to cling to in this world. We are left with a deeply despairing vision of the modern poet as a spiritual seeker in an utterly hostile environment. Everything he turns to for succor, comfort, and sustenance fails him—society and the world, which remain violent and irrational unto themselves and indifferent to the poet; nature, which is not a real possibility for most modern poets; love, which is defeated by disloyalty and death; and finally even God, religion. Berryman's body of work leads us inexorably and inevitably to the point of suicide—and not just a literary suicide. By the personal nature of his verse he has given us a clear record of what has happened to too many modern poets. As he said in one of the dream songs, "it is not a good position I am in."

ARTHUR OBERG

"John Berryman: 'The Horror of Unlove'"
Modern American Lyric
1978, pp. 57–62

I n response to the question,—"How are you?" Berryman supplies, "—Fine, fine. (I have tears unshed,") (no. 207). The response is a telling one. "Tears unshed" suggests tears still to be shed. However, by the use of parenthesis and inversion, Berryman creates an extreme metaphor of tears taken back into the body, as if in parody of the reversibility of the rain cycle arrowed in by children in early science classes.

Tears, whether shed or unshed, keep before a reader the realization that Berryman's dream songs, all 385 of them, proceed out of a lyrical center. While this center commonly acknowledges other modes (satiric, dramatic, narrative, epic), the poems in their deepest commitments are lyric. And the lyricism derives from a burden of need which depends upon love for its realization and fulfillment.

"Need" and "love" are among the most insistent words and foci in *The Dream Songs*. They are as insistent as Lear's "no"s and "nothing"s, and as pathetic as some of the later moments in that play where "need" and "love" also figure so centrally. Berryman writes:

Love me love me love me love me love me
I am in need thereof, I mean of love.
(No. 192)

Hunger was constitutional with him,
women, cigarettes, liquor, need need need
until he went to pieces.
(No. 311)

Need and love extend beyond the particular contexts to assume dimensions which are archetypal. An urgency appears in these songs which the *Short Poems* and the *Sonnets* noticeably lacked. Berryman frequently associates "needing Henry" with his protagonist's capacity as lover or would-be lover. The notes are familiar ones:

And will love last
further than tonight?
(No. 313)

& where are the moments of love?
(No. 343)

Need is never satisfied. "Enough" is meaningless.
also, also, somehow.
. . .
and needed more.
(No. 90)

too much was never enough.
(No. 351)

Such notes, if in danger of sounding trite, appear more moving in the contexts of particular poems and in the context of a life filled with impasses.

Considerations of love and need caused Berryman to raise questions that are at once abstract and intensely personal. Again, I am reminded of *King Lear*, whose set speeches and asides on "love" and "need" provide some of the more emotional and metaphysical moments in that play. By means of the many voices of Henry, Berryman is able to play not only Lear, but Cordelia with her father. In the course of *The Dream Songs*, Berryman creates more complications about matters of need and love than he can ever begin to untangle. Henry worries over relentless contradictions within and without himself. He probes the deception of need. He knows love's costs. Fears attack him regarding his capacity to love. The worries prove both private and philosophical.

Berryman shifts Henry's fear for his ability or capacity to love into third-person gossip and accusation, "They say Henry's love is well beyond Henry" (no. 269). Henry's fear nicely complicates itself. Fear or boast? Is Henry inadequate to love or does Henry's love have some kind of final, self-emptying and transcendent nature? The ironies of the line are never decided. Behind such ironies lie unending questionings, abstract disquisitions and private agonies, about Henry's and John Berryman's love. Berryman's ladder of love in *The Dream Songs* proves a complicated one. "All degrees of love" (no. 255) tax

him. "Nothing loving is alien to me," Berryman's Henry might well have sung.

The love against which Henry is measured by others measures himself, and the love toward which he aspires accounts for terrifying exactions. Christ's association with "the death of the death of love" (no. 48) intrigues Berryman. Poems that link Henry and God-as-Christ are obsessively filled with Christ, specifically as the New Testament God of Love. Such a connection leads Berryman to speculations which address contradiction and paradox at every turn, both for Henry and for Christ. How and when is sacrifice ever pure? How can one reconcile a figure of great love with situations and results which often speak of lovelessness? Berryman's painful ironies of love lie close to the heart of the poem. Out of meditative, dramatic discoursings on love and need, Berryman makes a relentless quest. In that effort as a poet, he touches on what is needed and given, wanted and returned. He does this on a scale suggestive of paranoia, a paranoia that "calls for this thud of love from his creatures-O" (no. 238).

Henry's worries regarding love continually partake of a reductive simplicity: "He wondered: Do I love?" Berryman writes in Dream Song no. 118. Yet the questions raised by the question are neither reductive nor simple. Instead, Berryman assigns to "the concept 'love'" (no. 160) a weight and an intensity that are inordinate. Such extreme burdens are placed upon love that Berryman significantly surrounds it, as word and as concept, with quotation marks. In the case of the deaths of his father and his friend, Delmore Schwartz, to whose "sacred memory" *His Toy, His Dream, His Rest* is dedicated, Berryman's love is so overwhelming in what it would give and in what it needs to be sufficient that it almost "dies" from him. The rhetoric proves to be more than a stylistic device. It represents a typical, defining movement in all of Berryman's work. Commonly, in the guise of a negative syntax or dialectic Berryman sets down his most mystical, loving words.

In his need to love and be loved, Berryman's Henry must confront the limitations of himself as a desiring man. He must also confront the limitations of that man in a world where need and realized desire seldom are one. As the dilemma of Everyman, it takes on the look of epigraph for the entire body of poems: "There ought to be a law against Henry. /—Mr. Bones: there is" (no. 4). Here, in a tellingly distanced blackface, Berryman approaches one of the informing centers of the poems. It stands as close to Berryman's sense of things as a passage in *Troilus and Cressida* stands to Shakespeare's view of the human impasse:

This is the monstrosity in love, lady, that the will is
infinite and the execution confined; that the desire is
boundless and the act a slave to limit.
(III.ii.86–90)

But epigraph need not be epitaph unless a writer chooses it to be so.

For Berryman, an acknowledgement of "overneeds," the need for "extra love" or "surplus love," causes him not to abandon man in the contradictions that surround him. Instead, Berryman begins where he can begin, with what defines man and makes him unique, his capacity for language and love. Love may not last, and need may linger on. But this does not stop Berryman from loving and "versing." Out of this situation, *The Dream Songs* proceed, like self-generated love songs or "Valentines." What the poet seeks is the creation of a community of caring friends, men and women who will share with him their talk and love.

One of the most moving moments in *The Dream Songs* occurs in no. 255, where Berryman relates the tale of the child in Henry's (his own?) daughter's kindergarten class. It is Valentine's Day and, in the classroom exchange of cards, his child receives no Valentine. In the most basic way, the entire corpus of Dream Songs is written to supply that card.

That the Dream Songs are love poems becomes most obvious in the lyric-linguistic bias of Berryman's work. In the elegies and "*Op. posth.*" pieces, Berryman insistently links the figure of poet and lover. Love and expression are one.

In *Homage to Mistress Bradstreet*, Berryman had given Anne the words, "vellum I palm."[1] Versing in *The Dream Songs* also joins the sexual to the aesthetic. Berryman's numerous memorial poems link the "heart" and "art" of love; his rhyming "heart" and "art" functions as instructively as his "need" and "seed" does in other contexts. The poet-figures Berryman eulogizes in his poems are remembered for writing well, for crafting poems as an act of love. Translators and translations also become, respectively, workers and works of love.

Berryman joins himself in *The Dream Songs* to poets like W. C. Williams and Randall Jarrell, Delmore Schwartz and Sylvia Plath. These poets, as Berryman views them, also made "a good sound" out of love. That poet-critics like Robert Lowell and William Meredith have written some of the best criticism of Berryman reveals similar connections. Such men entered into the loving, writing community which Berryman so desperately came to depend upon. The community of caring friends which Berryman established in *Homage to Mistress Bradstreet* between himself and that one poet is infinitely enlarged in *The Dream Songs* to range more freely among countries, cultures, and centuries; and this community intently seeks comfort in numbers. A majority of one ceases to be enough.

Each Dream Song makes a new attempt at expression and love. Berryman never deceives himself about the labor involved. He knows the risky attractiveness of silence and refuses to turn *The Dream Songs* into dejection odes. Although Berryman considers and names himself among the company of poets like Coleridge (no. 12), he stops short of that "last victory" dejection ode which, as Frank Kermode, writing on the English Romantic poet, points out, also "exhausts him."[2] Berryman uncannily is able to acknowledge a kinship with a poet like Coleridge without embracing that silence which has always represented for the poet, even before the Romantics, the temptation of a kind of death. But this is the Berryman of *The Dream Songs*; the later poems and books and suicide are still to come.

Notes

1. John Berryman, *Homage to Mistress Bradstreet* (New York: Farrar, Straus and Cudahy, 1956), st. 10, l. 1, n.p.
2. Frank Kermode, *Romantic Image* (London: Routledge and Kegan Paul, 1957), p. 11.

JOHN HAFFENDEN
"The Care and Feeding of Long Poems"

John Berryman

1980, pp. 43–59

By virtue of the themes of sexual treachery and recovery at the hands of a woman, muse or goddess, and by introducing fresh preoccupations—resentment at personal and professional setbacks, introspective analysis, and a certain malignity towards the father—the earliest of the Dream Songs derive

and progress from the *Eclogues*. By a logical extension into the religious sphere, Berryman's malicious and inquisitorial feelings towards his father reached also to the Heavenly Father manifested in Christ, and to the Catholic Church, his father's Faith. Since Berryman had recently endured a crisis of conscience and self-respect which included being out of work for some months, *The Dream Songs* may be seen as an attempt to resolve his problems of personal identity through the facilitation of new styles, new forms, and new areas of creativity. In a loose diary note from that time, Berryman wrote out what he called *The Argument* of the poem: 'Henry, in the face of enemies and considering his great loss, sulks, who had been a favourite and happy; suffers new losses, voluntary and not.'

Early 1958, Berryman felt that probably *The Dream Songs* would have to end with 'dreams of' death. It was not, that is to say, to end with suicide, nor in suffering, but simply in what he called 'a resigning from all this stuff', which would include 'NOT seeing POO [his son Paul] succeed'.[1] The conclusion was to be enigmatic, but not specific, since he was still making vague strivings towards a felt design. His notes exhibit a groping toward the imperceptible in structure, and sometimes even in content; he applauded the notion of 'tinkering' for 'power' and 'delicacy'—'something like the first turn in the first part of Opus III may lie ahead.'

On 4 April that year, Berryman planned a programme for *The Dream Songs*. 'When I come to write,' he devised (even though he had been fashioning the Songs for nearly three years already), 'restrict composition (as with *Anne Bradstreet*) to one every 2 days, say and spend most of that time on construction, plan-ahead.' To that end, he decided for a while to read only philosophy. All his verse fragments and notes, not only of Dream Songs, but also left-over fragments from *Homage*, could be incorporated in the new work. 'For instance,' he said, 'I don't see why there can't be flashbacks into Henry.' But, in consideration of the fact that several reviewers of *Homage* had failed readily to discern its 'plot' and 'voices' (and how, as he consoled himself by reading in H. T. Wade-Gery,[2] it took 2,000 years for the form of the *Iliad* to be recovered), he decided to have a 'clear narrative-and-meditative line', together with structural notes like those provided for the book version of *Homage*. Most of the Dream Songs written so far he already regarded as 'interludes, or fragmented'. (The language was to present just as difficult a problem as in *Homage*. One analogous usage could be seen between the archaisms in *Homage* and the 'kid-talk' in the Songs: 'This stuff (private language),' he decided in another place, 'is in fact a development from my syntax in Anne Bradstreet.')[3] The major problem outstanding in early April, 1958, was the overall organisation of what he called '*journey, action, structure*'.

Another early view of the structure of the Songs took the form of an Inferno-Purgatorio-Paradiso pattern, but only, Berryman advised himself, as a 'general' plan.[4] 'Clearly', he determined, helpless love *vis-à-vis* Mabel was to be a feature of Part I of the poem: Henry, that is to say, like Berryman himself, already had a wife. He was to get a divorce and then to marry Mabel in Part II; afterwards to have 'a Pouker'. Perhaps, he considered further, this sequence—divorce, second marriage, and the birth of a child—would be the basic action of Part II, corresponding to what was to be the basic action of Part I, a world tour. Furthermore, he felt as a conclusion to this rudimentary Dantesque plan on 5 March 1959, he would absolutely need a 'terminal date as of John Berryman/Henry'. A particular year should be such a terminal date, 'as 1300 was for Dante'.

Apart from the knowledge that Henry is still married to his

first wife in the poem 'Henry sats' (Song 5), traces of this early scheme cannot be said to have remained dominant in the complete *Dream Songs*. In fact, the only other annotation that I have been able to find in support of Berryman's plan to structure 77 *Dream Songs* as a type of *Divine Comedy* is a marginal comment on the manuscript of Song 103 (*His Toy, His Dream, His Rest*, Book V), written at the turn of the New Year 1959, which suggests that the Song might serve to conclude the *Purgatorio*, Book II of the poem, or (less likely) Book I.[5]

As an analogue of the *Inferno*, at least, *The Dream Songs* might have measured up.[6] Henry would begin in the Circle of sullenness (Circle 5), his vice of drinking would find its mark in the gluttony of Circle 3, and, for the avarice and improvidence equivalent to Circle 4, Henry would be a 'rolling stone' (an image to be used as a 'key expression', as in 'No moss! No moss!'). Henry is carnal, decidedly a heretic from Catholicism, violent towards his neighbour, treacherous—necessarily, Berryman felt—towards his kin, but not (except involuntarily) a hypocrite (Circle 8). 'Henry's Confession' might be equated with Canto 13. Despite the closeness of this parallel, it was not one that Berryman went on applying with any resolution, and he continued to look elsewhere for an exact format—perhaps, as at one time he considered doing, to creation epics (Babylonian, Amerindian, or Hindu), except for the timely awareness that the *Dream Songs* was evolving as a 'Survival-epic'.

One of the problems facing him in the poem was that of continuity, which included aspects of pace, subject, imagery, form and diction. In other words, how was he to unite the separate components into a poem that would function as a whole? It seemed clear to him that he needed Part I to be 'hard, vast, accumulating'.[7] Part II 'dark, lustful, strange' (an extreme vocabulary for what was to be the remarriage and childbirth section), but Part III was not yet clear, except for the fact that it should be 'climactic' (unlike *Homage*) and 'summary'. . . .

Recalling the fact that Delmore Schwartz used to call him 'Don Quixote',[8] Berryman saw that Henry and his friend might parallel Cervantes's heroes, an analogue which has been recently explored by Paul John Kameen:

> Is not Henry a sort of twentieth century Don Quixote out on his own bizarre quest?
>
> A close comparison between these two characters does indicate so—while it also recommends a more comic view of *The Dream Songs* than the poem is generally granted. . . . Across vast physical and mental settings their hapless adventures proceed from one courageous folly to another. The Don is insane with his visions of a loss of chivalry long since dead. Henry is insane with the loss of innocence, family and friends, all now dead. Both superimpose their own fantasies, their own dreams, over 'reality'. But in spite of their personal delusions and lack of sense, both heroes are ultimately engaging in their lunacies.[9]

Berryman himself felt that Henry's friend, or 'pal', a type of Sancho, could be characterised as 'inquisitive, reproachful, choric'.[10] This nameless interlocutor, Henry's friend, accordingly became a character in the poem, what Berryman himself called the second 'real' character—'Mabel' being the third,[11] later to be dropped. He was to be Henry's 'enemy' at the start, later his 'friend' and 'confidant', and therefore to have 'a history beginning *here*'.[12] (The 'operation' poem (Song 67) might prefigure an improved relation with the Friend, similar to that of the Don and Sancho Panza in Part II of *Don Quixote*.)[13] Like their prototypes, Mr Bones and his friend would debate their proposed adventure and its early details. By this means, the

Songs could take on a serial character, and cohere better. Although Henry is assuredly a type of Don Quixote, it does seem, however, that the idealism that accompanies the Don's suffering is not so apparent in Berryman's hero. The manifestation of what Berryman called 'humorous agony' is nevertheless common to both. Apart from that specific likeness, however, Berryman found that the details of his arrangement were still recalcitrant: 'where', he asked himself in some perplexity, 'does "Bones" stuff begin?'

For the disposition of Mr Bones and his interlocutor Berryman borrowed features from the stage pattern of minstrel show tradition, for which his source was Carl Wittke's *Tambo and Bones*, a work published in 1930. As with the structure of his 'epic' as a whole, however, the relationship between Henry and his friend is compounded of more than one paradigm. Berryman has described Henry's friend as a 'Job's comforter', a likeness which needs to be borne in mind. Henry himself, Berryman dubbed 'simple-minded. He thinks that if something happens to him, it's forever; but I know better.'[14] He added that he was more lenient with Mistress Bradstreet, in whom he had created the same dilemma (in her case, by means of her responsiveness to a sexual trial), but whom he chose to exculpate 'in ways that will allow her forgetting of it after a long period of time.'[15] Henry is absolutely unable to forget his 'irreversible loss'—that composite of father and of womb.

. . . . In April 1959, Berryman wrote: 'John Silkin's "Death of a Son" is the best poem I've read since Elizabeth Bishop's about Ezra Pound about 2 years ago ("Visits to St. Elizabeths"). This piece-meal composition of *Dream Songs* makes utterly impossible that organic kind of writing. STOP, till I can write uninterrupted.' It was clear from a comparatively early stage (77 *Dream Songs* was not published for a further five years)[16] that he should apply yet more resolute thought to structuring the poem.

By I September 1962 he had considered a fairly elementary disposition: the volume he was originally to publish as a group of 72 Songs might be divided into two parts. The first group of thirty-six Songs could be predominantly minstrel. In that section, according to the minstrel tradition that he had learned from Carl Wittke, he might include dances, jokes, superstition, fear, ballads, weird costumes, and burlesques of opera and personalities, all of which would end 'in a "walk around" of ALL'. It would seem, in fact, that the arrangement could accomodate just about every one of the Songs then written, which otherwise took on the appearance of a rag-bag.

One more searching and sophisticated plan employed a calendar framework, being measured by high days and holidays, including 4 July, Christmas, and Paul's birthday. (Thanksgiving had already been used in *Homage to Mistress Bradstreet*, and Berryman would return to it in Song 385, the last of *The Dream Songs*.) At the back of his mind, he valued the notion that, while our present civilisation celebrates birthdays, the Greeks exulted over death-days, the idea being glossed by this observation by G. R. Levy: ' . . . every hero's tomb was the scene of rites, such as still belonged to the spirits of nature, and at an earlier time to the ancestors.'[17]

Berryman was fascinated by the unity of the year, in terms of the seasons, but also as dreamlike—in the sense, it seems, that time itself is illusory. In consequence he decided late in August 1962 to try a temporal arrangement, which would be other than what he called 'fiscal or academic or calendric'. 'Huffy Henry', the first Song, would be located in 'broad summer', the season in which he first started writing Dream Songs. The Songs could then trace a single year, in a fashion analogous to Archbishop Philip Carrington's discoveries about St Mark's Gospel. In 1963 Berryman reported to A. Alvarez (in connection with Song 48, which *The Observer* was then print-ing): 'Archbishop Carrington's amazing discovery (The Prim. Xtian Calendar, and his edition of Mark since) that the struc-ture of Mk, on which Mt. and Lu wholly rely is liturgical.'[18] As Archbishop Carrington[19] interprets it, St Mark's Gospel re-formulated the events of Christ's ministry—for liturgical purposes—to the term of precisely a year. For a while Berry-man took the hint in attempting to create a blinding feature of *The Dream Songs*. To an even greater degree, however, Ber-ryman's discovery from Archbishop Carrington that St Mark's Gospel was in some sort an artifice or fiction served to confirm the metaphysical underpinning of the Songs, as the philosophi-cal thrust of his own work was both anti-Christian and anti-eschatological.

Since most critics have agreed with William J. Martz's bald pronouncement that *The Dream Songs* 'lacks plot, either traditional or associative',[20] it strikes me as important to appreciate the definition of 'plot' and 'structure' in the crucial aspect of 'coherence'. In addition to such themes as kinship and loss, a consuming interest of the *Songs* (so prevalent as to be a dominant theme) is the very nature of godhead and im-mortality. It is my contention that Berryman's disquisitions on the subjects of Christology and eschatology are so insistent and cohesive as to function as a principle of structure. He reiterates his observations about divinity and death so earnestly that he constructs a sufficiently close-knit schedule of meanings which does bring all the Songs—from the whole twelve-year span of their composition—into a relation with one another. My ob-ject is accordingly to make some answer to Jack Barbera when he observes (also in the context of estimating the poem's struc-ture):

> I suggest that any critic who proceeds by analysis of the metaphysical stance of poems cannot signifi-cantly discuss a poem such as *The Dream Songs*. Different Songs provide different stances, and it is questionable whether the whole poem's openness can be said, itself, to imply a stance.[21]

When Berryman asserted to John Plotz, 'It has no plot. Its plot is the personality of Henry as he moves on in the world',[22] he was trying manifestly to forestall criticism of the book's lack of structure. The effort seems, in fact, to have been arrant and ingenuous, a type of compensation for the fact that he had failed on his own terms to describe a narrative continuity in the work. My point is to the contrary—that the force and basic consistency of Henry's views on godhead and eschatology amount to a scheme which is ultimately ratiocinative; his 'plot' and 'structure' may be seen as the conduct of an inquiry which is coherent enough to give the poem a type of structure. Even though thematic harmony is not quite structural unity, it is not less functional.

In his search for a sound, more overt structure Berryman discovered what seemed to him a promising model outlined in Joseph Campbell's *The Hero with a Thousand Faces*.[23] Camp-bell categorises the Adventure of the Hero of myth as a three-part sequence: Departure (subdivided into five parts); Initiation (subdivided into six parts); Return (subdivided into six parts). The cycle of activities corresponds to what Berryman himself called 'out', 'into', and 'back'. Within this broad structure, Berryman tried to plot a sequence of Songs equivalent to the series of activities. . . .

Nevertheless, despite the approximations between Henry's adventures and Campbell's categorical Hero, Berryman did not adhere to this schema. It is evident from a glance at the list above that the final ordering of the Songs fell away from Camp-bell's structure.

The last and perhaps major influence on the structure of the poem was that of the *Iliad*. The three parts of the *Dream Songs* might correspond to the three grand parts of the *Iliad*.[24] In each book, there would be numerous coincidences of time and place for dealing with, in Berryman's words, 'humiliations, losses, sacrifices, loves, *fights*, triumphs, blasphemies, and magnanimities'. The hero, like a type of Achilles or King Lear, is cast out by real enemies, but he is also cast out by himself. His vulnerability is therefore self-inflicted. The quest, which is also in a sense the plot of the work, the object of the process, might not be reached or attained, because it is a self-quest. Like Job, the hero is suffering, and at war with God, but he does not know if he will survive until survival has been achieved. His friends, Job's comforters, are akin to Henry's friend: they pro-vide occasions for the study of his plights and gripes within a partially controlled environment. The hero may choose to de-termine his destiny and to undertake actions towards that end, but his choice might be void. 'Remember the three who pre-tend to be Job's friends,' Berryman apprised Richard Koste-lanetz in an interview. 'They sit down and lament with him, and give him the traditional Jewish jazz—namely, you suffer, therefore you are guilty. You remember that. Well, Henry's friend sits down and gives him the same business. Henry is so troubled and bothered by his many problems that he never actually comes up with solutions, and from that point of view the poem is a failure.'[25] Berryman regarded *Job* as a question-ing, a trial of God's justice: as of himself, the justice in question was that of his father's death. Henry combines elements of Job and Achilles, and is perhaps most like Achilles in the actuali-ties of his experience: 'Insult, unused power, loss, viciousness, generosity.' . . .

There is clearly much that is *a posteriori* about these approximations, and despite his efforts to categorise the Songs, the importance of the *Iliad* to Berryman's sense of structure remained a matter of example rather than of strict equivalence. The Achilles theme did remain with Berryman for some years, however, until Song 320, which (it is interesting to know) was probably the last of *The Dream Songs* to have been written—in 1968.

Although it might be possible to criticise Berryman on the grounds that he often seemed to be cutting and assembling the Songs according to one and then another epic format, what must be seen as more consequential are his efforts to remain fluid and flexible, to discover an artistic sequence into which the Songs might naturally fall. He needed to avoid the absolut-ist and the categorical. The internal demands of the poem, while they would not permit him to order the individual Songs *seriatim*, were not such as to allow of any similarly easy option.

Next in importance to Berryman's decision to devise di-alogues between Henry and his friend as a nexus of the plot, his desire to construe the poem by analogy with more than one epic format was fundamental. The work was to find its own integrity. The configuration of Mr Bones and his friend, which may be seen as a device similar to that of ego and id, or of *alazon* and *eiron*, is essentially a device of episodes and eventualities. More important to structure was Berryman's feel-ing for the larger movements and design of his work. Individual poems might share characteristics of temperament, psycholo-gy, and social exchange, and indeed individual poems might have won the appearance of design—simply by virtue of mass and accumulation. Berryman often feared losing control of the poem by heaping up more and more occasional verses. 'Be very careful,' he remarked, 'how I Henrify *poems*—NEVER *try* to pull into series. Lean the other way.' It was not enough for each Song to look and sound right, with Henry's characteristic tricks and tone, since there remained the danger of (to use

Berryman's own phrase) bringing any poem into line stylistically.

As early as November 1958, Berryman had wondered how seriously to take the Songs. The subject was clearly 'a man vibrating with *emotion*'.[26] What emotion? was a real question. Hatred, at imposition and insult. Fear, and anxiety. Remorse, love, a contempt for life. Doubt, especially of immortality. Grief at the loss of his father, for whom he wrote the following fragment: 'I am older than my father, Henry wept.' Finally there was, as he called it, 'rage' towards his mother. All of these emotions were relevant and indispensable: Henry is a complicated personality whose every trait and action might be articulated. Moods and behaviour patterns, particularly sullenness and weakness, prevail in the poem. The plot, the narrative, is constituted by the ways in which Henry's nature tackles the occasions of his experience, the contingencies of Berryman's own life. So too, the unity of the poem inheres in its construction as a serial, not as a series.

Berryman was tireless in seeking out all possible archetypes of his poem, to give it the credentials that he felt it needed. It was hard for him to realise that its very resistance to conventional epic overgrowth was a source not of weakness, but of strength. Rather, the integrity of the form can be found expressed by the substance of its parts. It is possible to disfavour many individual Songs, but it cannot be disputed that Berryman tried to coordinate the whole set.

Notes

1. This quotation, and all others in the paragraph, are from Unpub. DS, folder 2.
2. H. T. Wade-Gery, *The Poet of the Iliad* (Cambridge University Press, 1952).
3. Unpub. DS, folder 12.
4. Unpub. DS, folder 2. The substance of this paragraph is drawn from a note dated 5 March 1959.
5. The MS. note reads: 'poss. end of II (an assimilation of "I" and "he" as in I, I,—v. rare) *or* poss. follow w. "I am, outside" and so end II (Purg.)—*or* even I.'
6. Unpub. DS, folder 2.
7. Ibid.
8. The comment derives from Berryman's work 'Self- analysis, Record 2' (unpublished; dated 12 August 1955), p. 107.
9. Paul John Kameen, *John Berryman's Dream Songs: A Critical Introduction* (DA dissertation, State University of New York at Albany, 1976), pp. 43–4.
10. Unpub. DS, folder 2.
11. In connection with the uncollected Song 'The jolly old man', Berryman commented: ' . . . for reasons which I don't remember, I wiped Mabel out and never printed that song. For a long time after that, every now and then Ann would complain that Mabel didn't seem to be taking any part in the poem, but I couldn't find myself able to put her back in the poem, so it has no heroine.' (Stitt, 'The Art of Poetry XVI', p. 194.) Song 30 is called 'Nostalgia, Mabel' in a MS. draft, 17 May 1958.
12. Unpub. DS, folder 16.
13. Unpub. DS, folder 8.
14. Richard Kostelanetz, 'Conversation with Berryman', *Massachusetts Review*, 11 (Spring 1970), p. 341.
15. Ibid., p. 345.
16. In that connection, see a remark in Unpub. DS, folder 11, 'I won't for 5 years publish a book in the U.S.' (21 May 1958).
17. G. R. Levy, *The Gate of Horn* (London: Faber & Faber, 1948), p. 280.
18. Undated letter to A. Alvarez, cited in letter to Haffenden, n.d. (1972).
19. Philip Carrington, *According to Mark* (Cambridge University Press, 1960).
20. William J. Martz, *John Berryman* (University of Minnesota pamphlets on American Writers: University of Minnesota Press, 1969), p. 36.
21. Barbera, p. 157.
22. John Plotz et al, 'An Interview with John Berryman', *Harvard Advocate*, vol. CIII no. I (Spring 1969), p. 6.
23. Joseph Campbell, *The Hero with a Thousand Faces* (Cleveland and New York: Meridian, 1956).
24. Unpub. DS, folder 2.
25. Kostelanetz, p. 346.
26. Unpub. DS, folder 16.

AMBROSE BIERCE

1842–c. 1914

Ambrose Gwinnett Bierce was born on June 24, 1842, in Meigs County, Ohio. He attended Kentucky Military Institute and served in the Union Army during the Civil War. He later wrote graphically of his war experiences in stories and articles, some collected in *Bits of Autobiography* (1909). He became a Treasury aide in Alabama after the war, then joined an expedition through the Indian territory before settling in San Francisco. At that time Bierce began to contribute articles and sketches to California papers. His first short story, "The Haunted Valley," was published in 1871.

On Christmas Day, 1871, Bierce married Mollie Day, with whom he had two sons and a daughter. The marriage was stormy; the couple separated in 1888, and divorced in 1905. One son was killed in a duel in 1889; the other died in 1901.

In 1872 Bierce and his wife went to England, where he produced his first three books. Returning to San Francisco three years later, he took a job at the U.S. Mint, and became associate editor of *The Argonaut*. He began to write for William Randolph Hearst's *San Francisco Examiner* in 1887, and later lobbied for Hearst interests in Washington. This was his most prolific period: his vast ouput included tales, essays, fables, satiric poems, and many reviews. His vicious cynicism earned him such nicknames as "bitter Bierce," "the Devil's lexicographer," and "the wickedest man in San Francisco."

JOHN BERRYMAN

SAUL BELLOW

STEPHEN VINCENT BENÉT

AMBROSE BIERCE

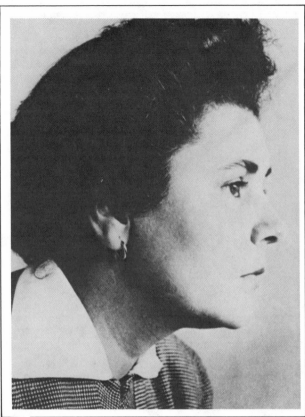

ELIZABETH BISHOP

R. P. BLACKMUR

LOUISE BOGAN

ROBERT BLY

From 1900 to 1913 Bierce lived in Washington, D.C., where he wrote for *Cosmopolitan* and published *The Cynic's Word Book* (1906), later known as *The Devil's Dictionary*. In 1908 he began the task of editing his *Collected Works*, which were published in twelve volumes between 1909 and 1912. Bierce left to travel through the South to Mexico in 1913, and vanished without a trace. It was rumored that he had been caught up in the Mexican Civil War.

Personal

It was thirty-two years ago that I first made his acquaintance; I had become friendly with his elder brother Albert (who was, like him, a Civil War veteran) a year before. Like most of our young folk of literary tastes, I was an almost abject worshipper of this yellow-haired Titan who then fulminated, from a far hill in the Napa Valley, his weekly bolts upon the small and the great. Also I had read his terrible *Tales of Soldiers and Civilians*, and was under enchantment to the magic crystals of his style. So it was with enormous interest that I awaited his visit to the camp of his brother, on a knoll on the eastern side of Lake Temescal, in the Summer of 1893.

He came at last, accompanied by several cases of Schramsberger, his favorite vintage. His visits to the lowlands were brief and infrequent, a fact due to his abiding ailment, asthma, which necessitated his living at fairly high altitudes, though, strange to say, he was seldom troubled by it afterward in the warm, close atmosphere of the eastern Summers. He came, a stalwart man a little less than six feet in height, with piercing blue eyes, over-jutted with blond shaggy brows, and with curly yellow hair and mustache. His whole personality gave the indelible impression of rugged strength and extreme vitality. Indeed, I have heard one young woman declare, "I can feel him ten feet away!" But formidable as his aspect was, he yet had about him an air of refinement, even fastidiousness, and was, in truth, the cleanest as he was the most modest of men. One would overlook an important part of his character were one to ignore those two qualities, for he was almost fanatical in his devotion to each. He would spend hours on his toilet daily, his nephew Carlton going so far as to assert that he shaved from head to foot—doubtless an exaggeration. And as to modesty, he had so high a degree of it that he was proud to boast that no woman, even his wife, had ever seen him in the buff! In witness to that, I have in mind an incident that occurred when he and I were paddling a canoe on the Russian river. We had left the swimming-pool of the Bohemian Club and I was still attired in a bathing-suit which, though somewhat abbreviated, I thought sufficient to the demands of propriety. Before long we saw a canoe coming down the river, propelled by my wife and his niece. He ceased paddling and demanded: "Do you intend to meet my niece in that costume?" "Why not?" I innocently asked. "All I have to say is," he replied, "that if you try it, I'll put a bullet through your guts."

I came perilously near to laughing but to humor him, laid aside my paddle, dived into the stream and swam back to the swimming pool. Bierce asserted afterwards, on more than one occasion, that he would have carried out his threat—and I, at the time, was his closet man-friend, perhaps!

He was able to remain but two or three days at the Lake Temescal camp, his asthma soon attacking him violently. On the first night of his stay I elected to sleep near him at the camp-fire, as even an open tent was not permitted him. And so I lay during the long night, frequently awaking, what of my lack of habit of sleeping on the bare ground. Whenever I did so, I saw Bierce lying with his face to the sky, the deep blue eyes staring up at the fainter blue of the star Lyra.

A year afterward his ailment had so lessened that he was able to take lodgings in an Oakland apartment-house, where I too had my abode. He was accompanied by his younger son, Leigh, who became one of my most frequent companions, and it was at this time that an incident occurred that threw a keen, if transient, light on the hidden tragedy of Bierce's life.

He had long been separated from his wife, and both sons had grown up to be headstrong and dissipated youths, with a full share of their father's intelligence and vitality. The elder boy, the more gifted of the two, had been murdered by a gambler in a sordid love-affair in a Northern town, several years before I made Bierce's acquaintance. The other now formed a liaison with a young woman living in the same apartment-house, and was at last summoned before his father. He left my room defiantly, well aware of his father's intention to make him give up the girl, and swearing that nothing could make him do so. In an hour he was back, broken and sobbing, his first words to me being, "My father is a greater man than Christ! He has suffered more than Christ." What tale of grief and terror lay back of his words I was never to know; but his affair with the slender, sad-eyed girl was ended with almost brutal abruptness, and in a few weeks she was dead—from measles, not blighted love. He, too, died a few years later in New York City, as the assistant editor of a newspaper there. Bierce wrote afterwards to his brother: "It is nearly a year since Leigh died; I wish I could stop counting the days."—GEORGE STERLING, "The Shadow Maker," *AM*, Sept. 1925, pp. 11–12

I had been having some correspondence with Ambrose Bierce, then the blinding light of the San Francisco *Examiner*. As far as I know he was the first of the columnists, and certainly there has never been one more brilliant. And the most fearless. Why he was never shot was one of the problems, for he spared no one, however eminent, who had a crack in his armor. His pen was dipped in vitriol and he was a master of bitter irony and wit. . . .

As he had asthma and could not stand the fogs and winds of San Francisco, he went from hotel to hotel in the country, wearing out one climate after another. At present he was living at Sunol, a hamlet in the interior. Wherever Bierce happened to be staying was a shrine to which pilgrims wended their way to offer up incense and sit at the feet of the Master. He invited me to come up and spend a day with him; it was winter and he dared not venture into San Francisco. After some hesitation I concluded to go—although I had refused to be taken to see George Meredith! I was consumed with curiosity, and after all he had been polite enough to say that he would have called upon me had it been possible.

I remember nothing of Sunol but the hotel, the station—and a pigsty.

Bierce was about forty-nine at the time, a tall man, very thin and closely knit, with curly iron gray hair, a bristling moustache, beetling brows over frowning eyes, good features and beautiful hands. His appearance did not appeal to me, however, for he looked too much like my father—what my mother would have called a typical Yank. We eyed each other rather oppugnantly when he met me at the train. I was by way of giving him to understand that although I admired his work, and had gone out of my way to meet him, I had no intention of falling down and worshipping him. What was in his own mind I never knew. I had on a very becoming blue frock, and presumably he thought I was vain and spoilt and a member of the idle rich who wrote merely to amuse herself.

The luncheon passed off well enough in that dreary fly-specked dining-room; S. S. Chamberlain, the editor of the *Examiner*, was present and he was an easy and brilliant talker. But he disappeared when the meal was over—and Bierce led me into his bedroom! He looked cynical and somewhat amused.

I did not turn a hair, however, and settled myself in the one comfortable chair, while he, with a muttered apology, lay down on the bed! Invalids have their privileges.

It was the most disagreeable afternoon I ever spent. We quarrelled incessantly. On every conceivable subject. He tore my books to rags. I had promise, but I had written nothing as yet worthy of serious consideration. This might be true, but I wasn't going to admit it to him, and I retaliated by criticizing his own work. His stories might be models of craftsmanship and style, and he had mastered the technique of horror, but they were so devoid of humanity that they fell short of true art, and would never make any but a limited appeal. He congratulated me upon the mature judgment which no doubt had made me in high demand as a critic.

We got round to authors in general. Meredith had been ignored for thirty years and should never have been "discovered" at all. Obscurity was the place for him. He could neither think straight nor write straight. His style was atrocious, and his characters as inchoate as his sentences. I was not enamoured of Meredith, but I defended him acidly. Never would I agree with that detestable man on any subject.

As for Stevenson, he was nothing but a phrase-maker; his imagination was so thin that it was all he could do to beat it out into a novel of conventional length. It was like an attenuated wire threatening to snap at any moment. No wonder he cultivated a style so artificial that it diverted what little discernment the average reader might possess from the pitiful lack of content. Novels were not worth writing anyway. The only form in which the perfection of art could be achieved, as well as the effect of totality, was that of the short story.

"The trouble with you," I said crudely, "is that you cannot write novels yourself. All short-story writers are jealous of novelists. They all try to write novels and few of them succeed. Any clever cultivated mind, with a modicum of talent, can manage the short story, even with no authentic gift for fiction—as you yourself have proved. But it takes a very special endowment and an abundant imagination to sustain the creative faculty throughout a story of novel length. *To hold it up.* Only the born novelist carries on without falling down over and over, stumbling along from one high spot to another."

And so it went. We almost spat at each other. And there would be no train until six o'clock!

Finally I thought I would change my tactics. After all the poor man was ill, and embittered through many misfortunes. He had lost his great opportunity when family obligations forced him to leave London. He was condemned to second-rate hotels in order to support an estranged wife and two children on his salary. And his eldest and favorite son—a boy of great promise—had recently been shot to death in a disgraceful fracas.

So I relented, told him I was sorry I had been so quarrelsome, for no one admired him more than I did. He was a great man and I was willing to admit it.

I might have saved myself the concession. He almost flew at me. He was not great. He wouldn't be called great. He was a

failure, a mere hack. He got so red I feared he would have an attack of asthma. He gave me some twenty reasons why he wasn't great, but I have forgotten all of them. I still think him one of the greatest short-story writers that ever lived.

The shadows were lengthening. The short winter day was drawing to a close. I rose with a sigh of relief.

"A quarter to six," I said briskly. "And I'd like a breath of fresh air before two hours in that over-heated train."

As we walked to the station his manner changed. He became almost charming. He thanked me for coming to see him and apologized for being so cantankerous, said that he had found an irresistible pleasure in arguing with me, and that I was a blue and gold edition of all the poets! ! !

The train was late. We walked about the station, conversing most amiably. It grew darker. We were in the shadows between the station and the malodorous grunting pigsty when he suddenly seized me in his arms and tried to kiss me. In a flash I knew how to hurt him. Not by struggling and calling him names. I threw back my head—well out of his reach—and laughed gayly. "The great Bierce!" I cried. "Master of style! The god on Olympus at whose feet pilgrims come to worship—trying to kiss a woman by a pigsty!"

The train steamed in at the moment. He rushed me to it and almost flung me on board. "I never want to see you again!" he barked. "You are the most detestable little vixen I have met in my life, and I've had a horrible day."

I smiled down at him from the platform. I knew my barb had gone in to the hilt, for women had spoilt him and no doubt he thought himself irresistible.

"I have only been mildly bored," I said sweetly. "And I certainly have too many pleasant places to visit to think of coming up here again to spend hours with a man in a chronic state of ill-temper—and who is so unaesthetic. . . ." The train roared out of the station.

The correspondence was renewed after a time and became almost affectionate. He took a great interest in my work and gave me much valuable advice, for which I have always been grateful. But whenever we met we both bristled with antagonism, and I never spent a pleasant hour in his company.—GERTRUDE ATHERTON, *Adventures of a Novelist*, 1932, pp. 201–6

Now Bierce had been born, as he once remarked, "to work as a peasant in the fields," and his later development was largely a consequence of this; he had not been able to escape too soon or too far from the scenes of his childhood, of which he always spoke with a certain spite. Born in 1842 on a camp-meeting site in Ohio, from which his parents had drifted to Indiana, he was known to refer with loathing to the squalor of those early days, repelled as he was by every memory of them. He alluded in one of his poems to the "scum-covered duck-pond" and the "malarious farm," he resented the religious atmosphere in which he was bathed, and his anti-fundamentalism was much like Robert Ingersoll's—it was typical of the Middle Western mentality of the time. After the Civil War, for which he volunteered at once, he never resumed relations with his parents or his home, and he could not contain his dislike of writers who were "racy of the soil," which, as he said, they rather ought to till. He scorned James Whitcomb Riley's "lyrics of the pumpkin field" along with the "corn-fed" enthusiasm of Hamlin Garland, the "language of the unlettered hind" that passed for honest dialect, the expression of "peasant instincts and pithican intuitions." The "lout of the stables" was not picturesque for him.

In every way Bierce did his best to destroy all memory of

his early life, the farm, the "unwashed savages," as he called his parents, bitter as he was about the years in which he had worked in a brickyard and learned the trade of a printer in Warsaw, Indiana. This was the town that Theodore Dreiser found so beautiful thirty years later, a "love of a place," as he described it, with its river and lakes where he lived with his hopeful, dreamy Mennonite mother, as amply nourished emotionally as Ambrose Bierce was obviously starved, driven as he was to reject these ties of blood. The personal note that one felt behind the fantasy of many of his later stories suggested the unhappiest memories and private relations, and the cruelty and coldness of the later Bierce were undoubtedly fruits of this early time when his natural instincts had been violated in one way or another. In his gruesomely facetious tales, men strangle their wives or their "sainted" mothers or hang their "dear" uncles on trees to be butted by rams, and at best the husband treats the wife with a cold contempt that suggested his own when he discarded his wife and rejected his son. No doubt his irony had been at first a protective mask for a sensitive man, as the cynicism that he flaunted in San Francisco was not wholly the result of living in this Gomorrah, this paradise of ignorance and yellowness, as he liked to call it. It had been established in him during the war and after the war and because of the romantic idealism with which he had fought. His stories revealed the horrors he witnessed and much of his feeling about them, and only an idealist could have been so disillusioned by the fraud and corruption of the regime that followed the war. Stationed as an officer in Alabama, he had been obliged to enforce the irresponsible rule of the carpet-baggers, and, observing close at hand Ben Butler's behaviour in Louisiana, he regretted the fervour with which he had fought for the North.

Bierce had entered the war, in fact, with the zeal of an anti-slavery man, and, developing a lifelong interest in strategy, he had served as a topographer and mapped a number of the most important battles. Among these were Chickamauga, Murfreesboro, Kenesaw Mountain, at which he was wounded severely, and Shiloh, his first major battle, which lasted fifteen hours and which he commemorated in several of his Civil War stories. In *Bits of Autobiography*, he recorded the intense excitement with which, as a child of the flat-lands, he had revelled in the mountains, the savage beauty of West Virginia where he and his comrades, with pure delight, had first inhaled the fragrance of spruce and pine. They stared with something like awe at the clumps of laurel, and every hill they saw they called a "peak." More than once Bierce chose hills for settings, in "A Horseman in the Sky," for instance, in which one shared his fresh feeling for lofty skylines; and countless details in other stories evoked in their verisimilitude all manner of actual memories of moments in the war. Such were the murmurs and rustlings at night in the ghostly spaces of the mountain woods, the silence in camp that was full of half-heard whispers, the cries of small animals suddenly encountering stealthy foes, the footfall of a panther in the leaves, the leap of a wood-rat. There was the line of light smoke-puffs that broke out by day on the edge of the forest and the smoke that hung in blue sheets among the branches of the trees until they were beaten into nothing by the falling rain, and there were the dead bodies lying with claylike faces in the yellow water, defiled and bespattered with mud from hoof and wheel. In their note of authenticity, Bierce's *Tales of Soldiers and Civilians*, a collection that was also called *In the Midst of Life*, resembled and rivalled the stories of Stephen Crane.—Van Wyck Brooks, "San Francisco: Ambrose Bierce," *The Confident Years*, 1952, pp. 204–7

General

The short stories and the serious critical papers of Mr. Bierce have appeared in a spasmodic and desultory way, but from first to last he has been at heart a satirist of the school of Lucilius and Juvenal, eager to scourge the follies and the foibles of mankind at large. The fact that Mr. Bierce is absolutely in earnest, that he is destitute of fear and confessedly incorruptible accounts for the oft-repeated statement that he was for years the best loved and the most hated man on the Pacific Coast. Now the ability to use a stinging lash of words is all very well in itself; it is a gift that is none too common. But to be effective it must not be used too freely. The two ample volumes of Mr. Bierce's poetical invectives form a striking object lesson of the wisdom in Hamlet's contention that unless you treat men better than they deserve none will escape a whipping. And when fresh from a perusal of the contents of *Shapes of Clay* and *Black Beetles in Amber*, one has become so accustomed to seeing men flayed alive that a whole skin possesses something of a novelty. Now there is no question that there is a good deal wrong with the world, just as there always has been, if one takes the trouble to look for it. But when any one man takes upon himself the task of reprimanding the universe, it is not unreasonable that we should ask ourselves in the first instance: What manner of man is this? What are his standards and beliefs? And, if he had his way, what new lamps would he give us in place of the old? In the case of Mr. Bierce it is a little difficult to make answer with full assurance. Somewhere in his preface he has said that he has not attempted to classify his writings under the separate heads of serious, ironical, humorous and the like, assuming that his readers have sufficient intelligence to recognize the difference for themselves. But this is not always easy to do, because in satire these different qualities and moods overlap each other so that there is always the danger of taking too literally what is really an ironical exaggeration. Here, however, is a rather significant passage taken from a serious essay entitled "To Train a Writer"; it sets forth the convictions and the general attitude toward life which Mr. Bierce believes are essential to any young author before he can hope for success—and it is only fair to infer that they represent his own personal views:

> He should, for example, forget that he is an American and remember that he is a Man. He should be neither Christian nor Jew, nor Buddhist, nor Mahometan, nor Snake Worshiper. To local standards of right and wrong he should be civilly indifferent. In the virtues, so called, he should discern only the rough notes of a general expediency; in fixed moral principles only time-saving predecisions of cases not yet before the court of conscience. Happiness should disclose itself to his enlarging intelligence as the end and purpose of life; art and love as the only means to happiness. He should free himself of all doctrines, theories, etiquettes, politics, simplifying his life and mind, attaining clarity with breadth and unity with height. To him a continent should not seem wide, nor a century long. And it would be needful that he know and have an ever-present consciousness that this is a world of fools and rogues, blind with superstition, tormented with envy, consumed with vanity, selfish, false, cruel, cursed with illusions—frothing mad!

Now this strikes the average fair-minded person as a rather wholesale indictment of what on the whole has proved to be a pretty good world to live in. In fact, it is difficult to conceive of any one honestly and literally holding so extreme a view and yet of his own volition remaining in such an unpleasant place any longer than the time required to obtain the amount of gun powder or strychnine sufficient for an effective exit. But of course Mr. Bierce does not find life half so unpleasant as he professes: in fact, he gives the impression of hugely enjoying himself by voluntarily looking out upon a world grotesquely distorted by the lenses of his imagination. He has of course a perfect right to have as much or as little faith as he chooses in any human religion or philosophy, moral doctrine or political code—only it is well when studying Mr. Bierce as a satirist and reformer to understand clearly his limitations in this respect and to discount his view accordingly. It is well, for instance, to keep in mind, when reading some of his scathing lines directed at small offenders who at most have left the world not much worse off for having lived in it, that Mr. Bierce once eulogized that wholesale destroyer of faith, Robert Ingersoll, as: "a man who taught all the virtues as a duty and a delight—who stood, as no other man among his countrymen has stood, for liberty, for honor, for good will toward men, for truth as it was given him to see it."—FREDERIC TABER COOPER, "Ambrose Bierce," *Some American Story Tellers*, 1911, pp. 339–42

Before dismissing the greater portion of Bierce's work as journalistic in gesture, it might be well to examine into it, to better understand the ironic nature of the man, and the chiseled chastity of his style. Bierce was a nihilist in this: he accepted nothing on trust; he held the venerated principles of mankind in slight esteem; he honored few men whom his contemporaries called great. Cynical he was—not the cynicism of the beaver snoozing in the mellow sunlight while his fellows worked on the dam, but the cynicism of the gaunt gray wolf running free of the pack and leaping at the throat of the bull of the herd. Injustice, dishonesty, hypocrisy, and sentimentalism caused the man to see red, and he stalked the offenders down. Once they were down, he had nothing to stand in their stead but men—and it was not for Bierce to reconstruct human nature. He caught the vision of the human race, trapped and betrayed in the wilderness of the world; but, whereas most men have the heart to fight and win, Bierce had the heart to fight and lose. The note of futility pervades his writings.—LEROY J. NATIONS, "Ambrose Bierce: The Gray Wolf of American Letters," *SAQ*, July 1926, p. 258

It requires a very special sort of sanity, I think, genuinely to appreciate the bitter satire and irony of Ambrose Bierce. Certainly he was not caviare to the general. Where he was anything, he was gall and wormwood, and it was seldom his intention to be anything else. By those who knew him and his work he was loved or hated, whichever the case may have been, with a fierceness that has been the experience of few writers in history. Yet few American writers will stand higher, I like to think, in the final appraisal of Time. When he has been compared with De Maupassant and Chekhov, in the literature of other lands, comparison is practically exhausted. In American letters he is, in his field, supreme and his books are all but unique. Perhaps he stems from Poe, but comparison is a bit inept, while other native writers of the short story, with whom comparison is possible, came after him and in most instances were influenced by him. Stephen Crane, an easy analogy for those who have read neither writer, is not to be mentioned in this connection: he was a genius in his own right and was himself unique. All this with reference to Bierce's tales by which, probably, he will be longest remembered, in spite of the Swift-like satire of his poems and essays.—VINCENT STARRETT, "Foreword" to *Ambrose Bierce: A Bibliography*, 1929, pp. 13–14

What impressed readers was the chilly disinterestedness with which Bierce, in ⟨*In the Midst of Life*⟩ and its successor, *Can Such Things Be?*, treated the most terrifying experiences. If they had looked carefully, they would have detected his secret. Bierce's stories were inhuman because their author believed that art had no relation to life. His theories of literature were as mechanical—and as false—as his theories of diction. What he was interested in was the climactic moment, for the sake of which he manipulated his puppets with little regard for psychological laws. So long as he could carry the reader with him to the unexpected dénouement, he was content. Only such situations as could be shaped to fit his theories interested him; not finding many, he wrote relatively few stories and even in those repeated himself.

Bierce came from a large family of what he later called "unwashed savages," and his boyhood must have been far from pleasant. After the Civil War, in the course of which he acquired an exhaustive knowledge of the possibilities for evil in the human race, he went to California, where he became a journalist. Essentially an idealist, he set out to attack hypocrisy and rascality wherever he found them. Already disillusioned by the war, he struck out blindly, making little effort to understand the causes of the evils he attacked, and permitting himself to be drawn into the battle of personalities that was constantly going on. Three years in London did not clarify his mind, and he returned to take up the fight precisely where he had dropped it. He was a good fighter, and he laid about him with considerable effect, but he remained a journalist, of not the finest sort.

In the midst of this pigmy warfare he wrote his two books of short stories, thus varying the literature of protest with the literature of escape. His protest was vigorous and heartfelt, but misdirected and useless. His escape was by way of a theory of literature that insists on the bizarre and surprising. For years he had been building up a philosophy that arranged human activities in various compartments, each unrelated to the others, and thus he constructed a defense against forces too strong to be met in open battle. Born of the experiences of wartime and the frustration of a youthful idealism, his conviction of the futility of life gave birth in turn to his conception, so effectively practiced, of the short story.

For cynicism to follow the defeat of early hopes is common enough and not too serious; for it never to be outgrown is tragedy. Bierce remained a sophomore, though a sophomore of talent. Personal disaster—estrangement from his wife and the loss of two sons—did nothing, of course, to lessen his bitterness. The coming of fame and the growth of a little group of disciples only made him pontifical, and he tried to rationalize the collapse of his hopes and to dignify his prejudices by calling them a philosophy. Convinced by the collapse of his own ideals that all idealism was false, he set himself up as a reactionary. To justify his own failure to abolish the evils he had fought against, he posed as an individualistic foe of all reformers. His cynicism became an affectation, but bitterness remained, and to the end it was directed quite as much against himself as against his fellowmen. In 1913 he sought Mexico and death.—GRANVILLE HICKS, *The Great Tradition*, 1935, pp. 153–54

As our planet rolls slowly or rapidly in the direction of its own eclipse, men's mind will darken with it. Losing their faith in themselves, they will look into each other's eyes with hatred, and every man's hand will rest lightly upon his dagger. Even the most sensitive will find it difficult, as the lamps go out, to draw comfort from the words of those who believe in progress. Decline and fall will be the order of the day and night. New philosophies of violence and despair will be contrived, and old nihilisms be exhumed. Among these old nihilisms that of Ambrose Bierce will take its minor place and, for all his weaknesses, he will speak to us with added vehemence.

Those weaknesses are apparent. Bierce's nihilism is as brutal and simple as a blow, and by the same token not too convincing. It has no base in philosophy and, being quite bare of shading or qualification, becomes, if taken in overdoses, a trifle tedious. Except for the skeleton grin that creeps over his face when he has devised in his fiction some peculiarly grotesque death, Bierce never deviates into cheerfulness. His rage is unselective. The great skeptics view human nature without admiration but also without ire. Bierce's misanthropy is too systematic. He is a pessimism-machine. He is a Swift minus true intellectual power, Rochefoucauld with a bludgeon, Voltaire with stomach ulcers.—CLIFTON FADIMAN, "Portrait of a Misanthrope," *SR*, Oct. 12, 1946, p. 12

The primary requirement of an artist, according to Bierce, is that he produce something interesting, and it was this very concern with "the interesting" which led Bierce to choose unusual characters and situations: "The exceptional—even 'abnormal'—person seems to me the more interesting. . . ." This concern for the exceptional and abnormal may be one of the contributing causes for his belief that a true work of literary art, whether poetry or prose, must be compressed, compact, and of narrow scope. Consequently, his interest lay not in group experience, but in the experience of the individual, and even that for only a short period of time. As Bertha Pope expressed it, "His unit of time is the minute, not the month." Quite often this minute is the last moment of life for the individual in the story, as for example in "An Occurrence at Owl Creek Bridge," "One of the Missing," "The Death of Halpin Frayser,"—a "moment" in which a great deal seems to take place. This concern with death, often death under bizarre circumstances, has led some critics of Bierce to speak of his morbid interest in the macabre, but such criticism is unjustifiable when we remember that of all experiences which men undergo in life, only two are common to all men—that moment when they enter life and that instant when they depart from it. Consequently, Bierce's representation of man's struggle against death, presented in realistic terms, could very easily arise from an impulse other than that of wanting to shock the reader's sensibilities with horrible details. The fact that many people refuse to think about death, even death in a nonviolent form, may be partly responsible for this type of misreading of Bierce. George Sterling, who knew Bierce as well perhaps as anyone knew him and whose subsequent suicide proved that death had no great terrors for him, sums up this aspect of Bierce's work fairly well:

> There was a ray [in Bierce's writing technique] that touched man only in his hour of pain, of terror, of death—a ray that revealed what we hesitate to behold and which leaves the weaker beholders ungrateful for the vision accorded.

Thus it is the fact alone that Bierce so often dealt with the moment of suffering, terror, and death, and not his lack of artistic taste, that has turned those readers who always want something cheerful against him. That he was a pessimist as far as contemporary humanity was concerned almost goes without saying, but his choice of the moment of suffering, terror, and death in the experience of the characters in his stories does not arise, as some would claim, from any diabolical strain of misanthropy in his nature which danced in unholy glee when humanity was placed on the rack. Yet he does display some of

the clinician's interest in observing the reaction of individual men under momentary stresses and in bizarre situations and in recording these reactions in a restrained, straightforward manner.—HOWARD W. BAHR, "Ambrose Bierce and Realism," *SQ*, July 1963, pp. 324–26

Works

FICTION

In Bierce, the evocation of horror becomes for the first time, not so much the prescription or perversion of Poe and Maupassant, but an atmosphere definite and uncannily precise. Words, so simple that one would be prone to ascribe them to the limitations of a literary hack, take on an unholy horror, a new and unguessed transformation. In Poe one finds it a *tour de force*, in Maupassant a nervous engagement of the flagellated climax. To Bierce, simply and sincerely, diabolism held in its tormented depth, a legitimate and reliant means to the end. Yet a tacit confirmation with nature is in every instance insisted upon.

In "The Death of Halpin Frayser", flowers, verdure and the boughs and leaves of trees are magnificently placed as an opposing foil to unnatural malignity. Not the accustomed golden world, but a world pervaded with the mystery of blue and the breathless recalcitrance of dreams, is Bierce's. Yet curiously, inhumanity is not altogether absent. Think of the episode of the deaf and dumb derelict at Chickamauga and the altogether lovable little Jo—Dickens done to life but with how much more consummate artistry.—SAMUEL LOVEMAN, "A Note" to *Twenty-one Letters of Ambrose Bierce*, 1922, p. 4

Closer to real greatness was the eccentric and saturnine journalist Ambrose Bierce, born in 1842; who likewise entered the Civil War, but survived to write some immortal tales and to disappear in 1913 in as great a cloud of mystery as any he ever evoked from his nightmare fancy. Bierce was a satirist and pamphleteer of note, but the bulk of his artistic reputation must rest upon his grim and savage short stories; a large number of which deal with the Civil War and form the most vivid and realistic expression which that conflict has yet received in fiction. Virtually all of Bierce's tales are tales of horror; and whilst many of them treat only of the physical and psychological horrors within Nature, a substantial proportion admit the malignly supernatural and form a leading element in America's fund of weird literature. . . .

Bierce's work is in general somewhat uneven. Many of the stories are obviously mechanical, and marred by a jaunty and commonplacely artificial style derived from journalistic models; but the grim malevolence stalking through all of them is unmistakable, and several stand out as permanent mountain-peaks of American weird writing. "The Death of Halpin Frayser," called by Frederic Taber Cooper the most fiendishly ghastly tale in the literature of the Anglo-Saxon race, tells of a body skulking by night without a soul in a weird and horribly ensanguined wood, and of a man beset by ancestral memories who met death at the claws of that which had been his fervently loved mother. "The Damned Thing," frequently copied in popular anthologies, chronicles the hideous devastations of an invisible entity that waddles and flounders on the hills and in the wheatfields by night and day. "The Suitable Surroundings" evokes with singular subtlety yet apparent simplicity a piercing sense of the terror which may reside in the written word. In the story the weird author Colston says to his friend Marsh, "You are brave enough to read me in a street-car, but—in a deserted house—alone—in the forest—at night! Bah! I have a manuscript in my pocket that would kill you!" Marsh reads the manuscript in "the suitable surroundings"—and it does kill him. . . .

Bierce seldom realises the atmospheric possibilities of his themes as vividly as Poe; and much of his work contains a certain touch of naiveté, prosaic angularity, or early-American provincialism which contrasts somewhat with the efforts of later horror-masters. Nevertheless the genuineness and artistry of his dark intimations are always unmistakable, so that his greatness is in no danger of eclipse. As arranged in his definitively collected works, Bierce's weird tales occur mainly in two volumes, *Can Such Things Be?* and *In the Midst of Life.* The former, indeed, is almost wholly given over to the supernatural.—H. P. Lovecraft, "The Weird Tradition in America" (1927), *Supernatural Horror in Literature*, 1973, pp. 66–70

In all Bierce's fiction, there are no men or women who are interesting as men or women—that is, by reason of their passions, their aspirations or their personalities. They figure only as the helpless butts of sadistic practical jokes, and their higher faculties are so little involved that they might almost as well be trapped animals. But Bierce does succeed in making Death play an almost personal role. His accounts of battles he took part in are among the most attractive of his writings, because here he is able to combine a ceaseless looking Death in the face with a delight in the wonder of the world, as the young man from Elkhart, Indiana, finds himself in a land where "unfamiliar constellations burned in the southern midnights, and the mocking-bird poured out his heart in the moon-gilded magnolia." As in the case of Thomas Wentworth Higginson, the enchantment that Bierce's war memories had for him was partly created by the charms of the South, so different from anything he had previously known. But eventually, in his horror stories, the obsession with death becomes tiresome. If we try to read these stories in bulk, they get to seem not merely disgusting but dull. The horror stories of Poe, with which they have been compared, have always a psychological interest in the sense that the images they summon are metaphors for hidden emotions. The horror stories of Bierce have only in a very few cases such psychological interest as may come from exploiting dramatically some abnormal phenomenon of consciousness. There is, otherwise, merely the Grand Guignol trick repeated again and again. The executioner Death comes to us from outside our human world and, capriciously, gratuitously, cruelly, slices away our lives. It is an unpleasant limitation of Bierce's treatment of violent death that it should seem to him never a tragedy, but merely a bitter jest. He seems rarely to have felt any pity for his dead comrades of the Civil War, and it is characteristic of him that he should write as if in derision, in the passage, already mentioned, of the soldiers who fell at Shiloh and who were burned, some while still alive, in a forest-fire lit by the battle. "I obtained leave," he writes, "to go down into the valley of death and gratify a reprehensible curiosity"; and then, after a description of the corpses, inhumanly swollen or shrunken, "Faugh! I cannot catalogue the charms of these gallant gentlemen who had got what they enlisted for." . . .

The best qualities of Bierce's prose are military—concision, severe order and unequivocal clearness. His diction is the result of training and seems sometimes rather artificial. The soldier commands one's respect, but the queer unsatisfactoriness of Bierce's writing is partly due to the fact that this marble correctitude is made to serve as a mask for a certain vulgarity of mind and feeling. It constitutes no real discrepancy that Neale should write about Bierce, "I should say that he was physically a perfect man," but that another of his biographers, Mr. Carey McWilliams, in remarking that "no one who ever saw Bierce could think him unimportant," notes that his features were "rather coarse." The case of Ambrose Bierce is, in this respect, the opposite of that of Mark Twain, for the homeliness of the Mississippi pilot conveys the perceptions of a sensitive man. Bierce was aware of his crudeness, and it is plain from these books about him that he resolutely struggled against it. But there was something besides the crudeness that hobbled his exceptional talents—an impasse, a numbness, a void, as if some psychological short circuit had blown out an emotional fuse. The obsession with death is the image of this: it is the blank that blocks every vista; and the asthma from which Bierce suffered was evidently its physical aspect. Mr. McWilliams points out that though, as Neale insists, Ambrose Bierce always gave the impression of possessing "the wholesome pink glow of perfect youthful health," he lived, with his periodic seizures, under a threat of suffocation. His writing—with its purged vocabulary, the brevity of the units in which it works and its cramped emotional range—is an art that can hardly breathe.— Edmund Wilson, "Ambrose Bierce on the Owl Creek Bridge" (1951), *Patriotic Gore*, 1962, pp. 622–32

Most of Bierce's mimetic tales of passion are those of ironical terror (including "An Occurrence at Owl Creek Bridge," "Chickamauga," "One of the Missing," "One Officer, One Man," and "The Man and the Snake"). In these stories, Bierce combined irony with terror in a specific way. In any terror tale, the emotional effect is basically an intense degree of fear. To this fear, Bierce adds, in these tales, an ironic twist, which rests primarily on a certain kind of relationship between plot and character, so that the reader feels an intense fear coupled with a bitter realization that it is cruelly inappropriate.

Fundamentally, this effect of ironical terror depends on a firm grasp of the connection among intellectual, emotional, and sensory factors in the human personality. In Bierce's tales of ironical terror, a character's reaction to given circumstances involves all three of these factors. First, he has an intellectual awareness of a dangerous situation—typically one which he believes threatens his life or his honor. Second, this knowledge arouses in him an emotion of fear, it deepens to terror, and frequently thence to madness. Third, this emotional involvement results in a particular kind of physical reaction—usually a tremendous heightening and acceleration of sensory perceptions, the latter often indicated by a slowing-up of subjective time.

Obviously the base of this psychology is the intellectual awareness of danger. Bierce, however, makes the intellectual awareness on which the whole psychology of his protagonist's terror rests a wrong one; hence all the emotional and sensory reactions which follow are erroneous, and the reader's perception of this gruesome inappropriateness to the real situation is what gives their peculiar distillation of horror to these tales.

Since the situation in terror stories must arouse fear, it must either be dangerous or be thought dangerous. Bierce's best tales of ironical terror can be divided into two groups: those in which the actual situation is harmful, with the protagonist conceiving it to be harmless and reacting accordingly; and those in which the actual situation is harmless, with the protagonist conceiving it to be harmful and reacting accordingly. In either of these groups, the reader may share the protagonist's misconception, not discovering the truth until the end of the story; or he may realize all along that the protagonist is wrong. What the reader's grasp of events will be is controlled by the narration.—M. E. Grenander, *Ambrose Bierce*, 1971, pp. 93–94

ESSAYS AND LETTERS

By far the greater part of this work was polemical in its nature. Journalism in the West had not yet become entirely tame, had not yet resorted to the amenities and timidities of the more cultured regions of the planet. Bierce's pen was dipped in wormwood and acid, and he being, as H. L. Mencken has justly asserted, then and to this day the keenest wit of America, his assaults were more dreaded than the bowie knife and revolver, since relegated to the eastern centers of civilization. He spared no one whom he thought deserving of his castigations. From millionaire to labor-leader, all were to know the "strength and terror" of his verbal onsets. Nor did he take refuge in words only: to my own knowledge he always carried, at least when in California, a large revolver, and was quite ready "to go farther into the matter" with such as cared to meet him on that plane! I have no memory that he was ever so challenged, though he once broke a cane over the head of a friend who had become a friend no longer.

Bierce, himself, thought that he would be remembered, if at all, as a satirist. In these days of universal tolerance and courtesy, the breed is almost extinct, but had he lived in the time of Pope he would have made that writer's work seem, by comparison, mild stuff indeed. There is little invective so terrible as that poured forth by him on California's fools and rascals—instances, in most cases, of breaking the butterfly on the wheel. But no English satirist has equaled the blistering intensity of wit that ran so easily from his pen.—GEORGE STERLING, "Introduction" to _In the Midst of Life_, 1927, pp. v–vi

Few better craftsmen in words than Bierce have lived in this country, and his letters might well have introduced him to the larger public that, even now, scarcely knows his name. A public of four hundred, however, if it happens to be a picked public, is a possession not to be despised, for the cause of an author's reputation is safer in the hands of a few Greeks than in those of a multitude of Persians. "It is not the least pleasing of my reflections," Bierce himself remarks, "that my friends have always liked my work—or me—well enough to want to publish my books at their own expense." His wonderful volume of tales, _In the Midst of Life_, was rejected by virtually every publisher in the country: the list of the sponsors of his other books is a catalogue of unknown names, and the collected edition of his writings might almost have been regarded as a secret among friends. "Among what I may term 'underground reputations'," Mr. Arnold Bennett once observed, "that of Ambrose Bierce is perhaps the most striking example." The taste, the skill and the devotion with which his letters have been edited indicate, however, that, limited as this reputation is, it is destined for a long and healthy life.

. . . ⟨W⟩hile his interests were parochial, his outlook, as these letters reveal it, was broadly human. With his air of a somewhat dandified Strindberg he combined what might be described as a temperament of the eighteenth century. It was natural to him to write in the manner of Pope: lucidity, precision, "correctness" were the qualities he adored. He was full of the pride of individuality; and the same man who spent so much of his energy "exploring the ways of hate" was, in his personal life, the serenest of stoics. The son of an Ohio farmer, he had had no formal education. How did he acquire such firmness and clarity of mind? He was a natural aristocrat, and he developed a rudimentary philosophy of aristocracy which, under happier circumstances, might have made him a great figure in the world of American thought. But the America of his day was too chaotic. It has remained for Mr. Mencken to develop and popularize, with more learning but with less refinement, the views that Bierce expressed in _The Shadow on the Dial_.

Some of these views appear in his letters, enough to show us how complete was his antipathy to the dominant spirit of the age. He disliked humanitarianism as much as he liked humanism, or would have liked it if he had had the opportunity. He invented the word peasant in Mr. Mencken's sense, as applied, that is, to such worthies as James Whitcomb Riley. "The world does not wish to be helped," he says. "The poor wish only to be rich, which is impossible, not to be better. They would like to be rich in order to be worse, generally speaking." His contempt for socialism was unbounded. Of literary men holding Tolstoy's views he remarks that they are not artists at all: "They are 'missionaries' who, in their zeal to lay about them, do not scruple to seize any weapon that they can lay their hands on; they would grab a crucifix to beat a dog. The dog is well beaten, no doubt (which makes him a worse dog than he was before), but note the condition of the crucifix!" All this in defence of literature and what he regards as its proper function. Of Shaw and, curiously, Ibsen, he observes that they are "very small men, pets of the drawing-room and gods of the hour"; he abhors Whitman, on the score equally of sentiment and form; and of Mr. Upton Sinclair's early hero he writes as follows:

> I suppose there are Arthur Sterlings among the little fellows, but if genius is not serenity, fortitude and reasonableness I don't know what it is. One cannot even imagine Shakespeare or Goethe bleeding over his work and howling when "in the fell clutch of circumstance." The great ones are figured in my mind as ever smiling—a little sadly at times, perhaps, but always with conscious inaccessibility to the pinpricking little Titans that would storm their Olympus armed with ineffectual disasters and popgun misfortunes. Fancy a fellow wanting, like Arthur Sterling, to be supported by his fellows in order that he may write what they don't want to read!

Bierce was consistent: his comments on his own failure to achieve recognition are all in the spirit of this last contemptuous remark. "I have pretty nearly ceased to be 'discovered'," he writes to one of his friends, "but my notoriety as an obscurian may be said to be worldwide and apparently everlasting." Elsewhere, however, he says: "It has never seemed to me that the 'unappreciated genius' had a good case to go into court with, and I think he should be promptly nonsuited. . . . Nobody compels us to make things that the world does not want. We merely choose to because the pay, _plus_ the satisfaction, exceeds the pay alone that we get from work that the world does want. Then where is our grievance? We get what we prefer when we do good work; for the lesser wage we do easier work." Sombre and at times both angry and cynical as Bierce's writing may seem, no man was ever freer from personal bitterness. If he was out of sympathy with the life of his time and with most of its literature, he adored literature itself, according to his lights. It is this dry and at the same time whole-souled enthusiasm that makes his letters so charming. Fortunate was the circle of young writers that possessed so genial and so severe a master.—VAN WYCK BROOKS, "The Letters of Ambrose Bierce," _Emerson and Others_, 1927, pp. 149–55

Since _The Devil's Dictionary_ is a philosophical satire, its present-day significance may be somewhat related to the philosophy which it reflects. Bierce, while well read, was no formal philosopher, and his ideas having been established in a period contemporary with Nietzsche and prior to Marx, Freud, or the moderns, may seem lacking in relation to present-day thought. On examination, however, it is interesting to note how many of these "demoniac" concepts resemble, at least incipiently, the existentialist ideas of today. Certainly this is true of Bierce's rejection of Platonic concepts and of logic unaided by intuition as a means of finding truth; his bold confrontation of death as a natural phenomenon of life and its implication of a Deity unsympathetic to human kind; and, perhaps above all, his taking refuge in the repeated phrase, "Nothing matters," when tragedy struck him in the deaths of his two sons. His distinguishing note in satire was an underlying profound grimness transformed into flippancy, laughter, and wit; if he had any peculiar contribution to make as an American or Western satirist, it is this discrepant combination, which has unusual literary implications and rates him as a writer apart.—ERNEST JEROME HOPKINS, "Introduction" to *The Enlarged Devil's Dictionary*, 1967, pp. xxiii–xxiv

AMBROSE BIERCE
From "The Short Story" (1897)
Collected Works, Volume X
1911, pp. 238–48

The art of writing short stories for the magazines of the period can not be acquired. Success depends upon a kind of inability that must be "born into" one—it does not come at call. The torch must be passed down the line by the thumbless hands of an illustrious line of prognathous ancestors unacquainted with fire. For the torch has neither light nor heat—is, in truth, fireproof. It radiates darkness and all shadows fall toward it. The magazine story must relate nothing: like Dr. Hern's "holes" in the luminiferous ether, it is something in which nothing can occur. True, if the thing is written in a "dialect" so abominable that no one of sense will read, or so unintelligible that none who reads will understand, it may relate something that only the writer's kindred spirits care to know; but if told in any human tongue action and incident are fatal to it. It must provoke neither thought nor emotion; it must only stir up from the shallows of its readers' understandings the sediment which they are pleased to call sentiment, murking all their mental pool and effacing the reflected images of their natural environment.

The master of this school of literature is Mr. Howells. Destitute of that supreme and almost sufficient literary endowment, imagination, he does, not what he would, but what he can—takes notes with his eyes and ears and "writes them up" as does any other reporter. He can tell nothing but something like what he has seen or heard, and in his personal progress through the rectangular streets and between the trim hedges of Philistia, with the lettered old maids of his acquaintance curtseying from the doorways, he has seen and heard nothing worth telling. Yet tell it he must and, having told, defend. For years he conducted a department of criticism with a purpose single to expounding the after-thought theories and principles which are the offspring of his own limitations.

Illustrations of these theories and principles he interpreted with tireless insistence as proofs that the art of fiction is to-day a finer art than that known to our benighted fathers. What did Scott, what did even Thackeray know of the subtle psychology of the dear old New England maidens?

I want to be fair: Mr. Howells has considerable abilities.

He is insufferable only in fiction and when, in criticism, he is making fiction's laws with one eye upon his paper and the other upon a catalogue of his own novels. When not carrying that heavy load, himself, he has a manly enough mental stride. He is not upon very intimate terms with the English language, but on many subjects, and when you least expect it of him, he thinks with such precision as momentarily to subdue a disobedient vocabulary and keep out the wrong word. Now and then he catches an accidental glimpse of his subject in a side-light and tells with capital vivacity what it is not. The one thing that he never sees is the question that he has raised by inadvertence, deciding it by implication against his convictions. If Mr. Howells had never written fiction his criticism of novels would entertain, but the imagination which can conceive him as writing a good story under any circumstances would be a precious literary possession, enabling its owner to write a better one.

In point of fiction, all the magazines are as like as one vacuum to another, and every month they are the same as they were the month before, excepting that in their holiday numbers at the last of the year their vacuity is a trifle intensified by that essence of all dullness, the "Christmas story." To so infamous a stupidity has popular fiction fallen—to so low a taste is it addressed, that I verily believe it is read by those who write it!

As certain editors of newspapers appear to think that a trivial incident has investiture of dignity and importance by being telegraphed across the continent, so these story-writers of the Reporter School hold that what is not interesting in life becomes interesting in letters—the acts, thoughts, feelings of commonplace people, the lives and loves of noodles, nobodies, ignoramuses and millionaires; of the village vulgarian, the rural maiden whose spiritual grace is not incompatible with the habit of falling over her own feet, the somnolent nigger, the clay-eating "Cracker" of the North Carolinian hills, the society person and the inhabitant of south-western Missouri. Even when the writers commit infractions of their own literary Decalogue by making their creations and creationesses do something picturesque, or say something worth while, they becloud the miracle with such a multitude of insupportable descriptive details that the reader, like a tourist visiting an artificial waterfall at a New England summer place of last resort, pays through the nose at every step of his way to the Eighth Wonder. Are we given dialogue? It is not enough to report what was said, but the record must be authenticated by enumeration of the inanimate objects—commonly articles of furniture—which were privileged to be present at the conversation. and each dialogian must make certain or uncertain movements of the limbs or eyes before and after saying his say. All this in such prodigal excess of the slender allusions required, when required at all, for *vraisemblance* as abundantly to prove its insertion for its own sake. Yet the inanimate surroundings are precisely like those whose presence bores us our whole lives through, and the movements are those which every human being makes every moment in which he has the misfortune to be awake. One would suppose that to these gentry and ladry everything in the world except what is really remarkable is "rich and strange." They only think themselves able to make it so by the sea-change that it will suffer by being thrown into the duck-pond of an artificial imagination and thrown out again.

Amongst the laws which Cato Howells has given his little senate, and which his little senators would impose upon the rest of us, is an inhibitory statute against a breach of this "probability"—and to them nothing is probable outside the narrow domain of the commonplace man's most commonplace experience. It is not known to them that all men and women sometimes, many men and women frequently, and some men and women habitually, act from impenetrable motives and in a way that is consonant with nothing in their lives, characters and conditions. It is known to them that "truth is stranger than fiction," but not that this has any practical meaning or value in letters. It is to him of widest knowledge, of deepest feeling, of sharpest observation and insight, that life is most crowded with figures of heroic stature, with spirits of dream, with demons of the pit, with graves that yawn in pathways leading to the light, with existences not of earth, both malign and benign—ministers of grace and ministers of doom. The truest eye is that which discerns the shadow and the portent, the dead hands reaching, the light that is the heart of the darkness, the sky "with dreadful faces thronged and fiery arms." The truest ear is that which hears

> Celestial voices to the midnight air,
> Sole, or responsive each to the other's note,
> Singing—

not "their great Creator," but not a negro melody, either; no, nor the latest favorite of the drawing-room. In short, he to whom life is not picturesque, enchanting, astonishing, terrible, is denied the gift and faculty divine, and being no poet can write no prose. He can tell nothing because he knows nothing. He has not a speaking acquaintance with Nature (by which he means, in a vague general way, the vegetable kingdom) and can no more find

> Her secret meaning in her deeds

than he can discern and expound the immutable law underlying coincidence.

Let us suppose that I have written a novel—which God forbid that I should do. In the last chapter my assistant hero learns that the hero-in-chief has supplanted him in the affections of the shero. He roams aimless about the streets of the sleeping city and follows his toes into a silent public square. There after appropriate mental agonies he resolves in the nobility of his soul to remove himself forever from a world where his presence can not fail to be disagreeable to the lady's conscience. He flings up his hands in mad disquietude and rushes down to the bay, where there is water enough to drown all such as he. Does he throw himself in? Not he—no, indeed. He finds a tug lying there with steam up and, going aboard, descends to the fire-hold. Opening one of the iron doors of the furnace, which discloses an aperture just wide enough to admit him, he wriggles in upon the glowing coals and there, with never a cry, dies a cherry-red death of unquestionable ingenuity. With that the story ends and the critics begin.

It is easy to imagine what they say: "This is too much"; "it insults the reader's intelligence"; "it is hardly more shocking for its atrocity than disgusting for its cold-blooded and unnatural defiance of probability"; "art should have some traceable relation to the facts of human experience."

Well, that is exactly what occurred once in the stoke-hold of a tug lying at a wharf in San Francisco. *Only* the man had not been disappointed in love, nor disappointed at all. He was a cheerful sort of person, indubitably sane, ceremoniously civil and considerate enough (evidence of a good heart) to spare whom it might concern any written explanation defining his deed as "a rash act."

Probability? Nothing is so improbable as what is true. It is the unexpected that occurs; but that is not saying enough; it is also the unlikely—one might almost say the impossible. John, for example, meets and marries Jane. John was born in Bombay of poor but detestable parents; Jane, the daughter of a gorgeous hidalgo, on a ship bound from Vladivostok to Buenos Aires. Will some gentleman who has written a realistic novel in which something so nearly out of the common as a wedding was permitted to occur have the goodness to figure out what, at their birth, were the chances that John would meet and marry Jane? Not one in a thousand—not one in a million—not one in a million million! Considered from a view-point a little anterior in time, it was almost infinitely unlikely that any event which has occurred would occur—any event worth telling in a story. Everything being so unearthly improbable, I wonder that novelists of the Howells school have the audacity to relate anything at all. And right heartily do I wish they had not.

Fiction has nothing to say to probability; the capable writer gives it not a moment's attention, except to make what is related *seem* probable in the reading—*seem* true. Suppose he relates the impossible; what then? Why, he has but passed over the line into the realm of romance, the kingdom of Scott, Defoe, Hawthorne, Beckford and the authors of the *Arabian Nights*—the land of the poets, the home of all that is good and lasting in the literature of the imagination. Do these little fellows, the so-called realists, ever think of the goodly company which they deny themselves by confining themselves to their clumsy feet and pursuing their stupid noses through the barren hitherland, while just beyond the Delectable Mountain lies in light the Valley of Dreams, with its tall immortals, poppy-crowned? Why, the society of the historians alone would be a distinction and a glory!

H. L. MENCKEN
"Ambrose Bierce"
Prejudices: Sixth Series
1927, pp. 259–65

The reputation of Ambrose Bierce, like that of Edgar Saltus, has always had an occult, artificial drug-store flavor. He has been hymned in a passionate, voluptuous, inordinate way by a small band of disciples, and he has been passed over altogether by the great majority of American critics, and no less by the great majority of American readers. Certainly it would be absurd to say that he is generally read, even by the *intelligentsia*. Most of his books, in fact, are out of print and almost unobtainable, and there is little evidence that his massive Collected Works, printed in twelve volumes between 1909 and 1912, have gone into anything even remotely approaching a wide circulation. I have a suspicion, indeed, that Bierce did a serious disservice to himself when he put those twelve volumes together. Already an old man at the time, he permitted his nostalgia for his lost youth to get the better of his critical faculty, never very powerful at best, and the result was a depressing assemblage of worn-out and fly-blown stuff, much of it quite unreadable. If he had boiled the collection down to four volumes, or even to six, it might have got him somewhere, but as it is, his good work is lost in a morass of bad and indifferent work. I doubt that any one save the Bierce fanatics aforesaid has ever plowed through the whole twelve volumes. They are filled with epigrams against frauds long dead and forgotten, and echoes of old and puerile newspaper controversies, and experiments in fiction that belong to a dark and expired age. But in the midst of all this blather there are some pearls—more accurately, there are two of them. One consists of the series of epigrams called *The Devil's Dictionary*, the other consists of the war stories, commonly called *Tales of Soldiers and Civilians*. Among the latter are some of the best war stories ever

479

written—things fully worthy to be ranged beside Zola's
"L'Attaque du Moulin," Kipling's "The Taking of Lungtung-
pen," or Ludwig Thoma's "Ein Bayrischer Soldat." And
among the former are some of the most gorgeous witticisms in
the English language.

Bierce, I believe, was the first writer of fiction ever to treat
war realistically. He antedated even Zola. It is common to say
that he came out of the Civil War with a deep and abiding
loathing of slaughter—that he wrote his war stories in disillusion, and as a sort of pacifist. But this is certainly not believed
by any one who knew him, as I did in his last years. What he
got out of his services in the field was not a sentimental horror
of it, but a cynical delight in it. It appeared to him as a sort of
magnificent *reductio ad absurdum* of all romance. The world
viewed war as something heroic, glorious, idealistic. Very well,
he would show how sordid and filthy it was—how stupid, savage and degrading. But to say this is not to say that he disapproved it. On the contrary, he vastly enjoyed the chance its
discussion gave him to set forth dramatically what he was always talking about and gloating over: the infinite imbecility of
man. There was nothing of the milk of human kindness in old
Ambrose; he did not get the nickname of Bitter Bierce for
nothing. What delighted him most in this life was the spectacle
of human cowardice and folly. He put man, intellectually,
somewhere between the sheep and the horned cattle, and as a
hero somewhere below the rats. His war stories, even when
they deal with the heroic, do not depict soldiers as heroes; they
depict them as bewildered fools, doing things without sense,
submitting to torture and outrage without resistance, dying at
last like hogs in Chicago, the former literary capital of the
United States. So far in this life, indeed, I have encountered no
more thorough-going cynic than Bierce was. His disbelief in
man went even further than Mark Twain's; he was quite unable
to imagine the heroic, in any ordinary sense. Nor, for that
matter, the wise. Man, to him, was the most stupid and ignoble of animals. But at the same time the most amusing. Out of
the spectacle of life about him he got an unflagging and Gar-
gantuan joy. The obscene farce of politics delighted him. He
was an almost amorous connoisseur of theology and theologians. He howled with mirth whenever he thought of a professor, a doctor or a husband. His favorites among his contemporaries were such zanies as Bryan, Roosevelt and Hearst.

Another character that marked him, perhaps flowing out
of this same cynicism, was his curious taste for the macabre.
All of his stories show it. He delighted in hangings, autopsies,
dissecting-rooms. Death to him was not something repulsive,
but a sort of low comedy—the last act of a squalid and rib-
rocking buffoonery. When, grown old and weary, he departed
for Mexico, and there—if legend is to be believed—marched
into the revolution then going on, and had himself shot, there
was certainly nothing in the transaction to surprise his acquaintances. The whole thing was typically Biercian. He died
happy, one may be sure, if his executioners made a botch of
dispatching him—if there was a flash of the grotesque at the
end. Once I enjoyed the curious experience of going to a funeral with him. His conversation to and from the crematory was
superb—a long series of gruesome but highly amusing witticisms. He had tales to tell of crematories that had caught fire
and singed the mourners, of dead bibuli whose mortal remains
had exploded, of widows guarding the fires all night to make
sure that their dead husbands did not escape. The gentleman
whose carcass we were burning had been a literary critic.
Bierce suggested that his ashes be molded into bullets and shot

at publishers, that they be presented to the library of the New
York Lodge of Elks, that they be mailed anonymously to Ella
Wheeler Wilcox. Later on, when he heard that they had been
buried in Iowa, he exploded in colossal mirth. The last time I
saw him he predicted that the Christians out there would dig
them up and throw them over the State line. On his own
writing desk, he once told me, he kept the ashes of his son. I
suggested idly that the ceremental urn must be a formidable
ornament. "Urn hell!" he answered. "I keep them in a cigar-
box!"

There is no adequate life of Bierce, and I doubt if any will
ever be written. His daughter, with some asperity, has forbidden the publication of his letters, and shows little hospitality to
volunteer biographers. One of his disciples, the late George
Sterling, wrote about him with great insight and affection, and
another, Herman George Scheffauer, has greatly extended his
fame abroad, especially in Germany. But Sterling is dead and
Scheffauer seems indisposed to do him in the grand manner,
and I know of no one else competent to do so. He liked
mystification, and there are whole stretches of his long life that
are unaccounted for. His end had mystery in it too. It is
assumed that he was killed in Mexico, but no eye-witness has
ever come forward, and so the fact, if it is a fact, remains
hanging in the air.

Bierce followed Poe in most of his short stories, but it is
only a platitude to say that he wrote much better than Poe. His
English was less tight and artificial; he had a far firmer grasp
upon character; he was less literary and more observant. Unluckily, his stories seem destined to go the way of Poe's. Their
influence upon the modern American short story, at least upon
its higher levels, is almost nil. When they are imitated at all, it
is by the lowly hacks who manufacture thrillers for the cheap
magazines. Even his chief disciples, Sterling and Scheffauer,
did not follow him. Sterling became a poet whose glowing
romanticism was at the opposite pole to Bierce's cold realism,
and Scheffauer, interested passionately in experiment, and
strongly influenced by German example, has departed completely from the classicism of the master. Meanwhile, it remains astonishing that his wit is so little remembered. In *The
Devil's Dictionary* are some of the most devastating epigrams
ever written. "Ah, that we could fall into women's arms without falling into their hands": it is hard to find a match for that
in Oscar himself. I recall another: "Opportunity: a favorable
occasion for grasping a disappointment." Another: "Once:
enough." A third: "Husband: one who, having dined, is
charged with the care of the plate." A fourth: "Our vocabulary
is defective: we give the same name to woman's lack of temptation and man's lack of opportunity." A fifth: "Slang is the
speech of him who robs the literary garbage cans on their way
to the dump."

But I leave the rest to your own exploration—if you can
find a copy of *The Devil's Dictionary*. It was never printed in
full, save in the ghastly Collected Works that I have mentioned. A part of it, under the title of *The Cynic's Word-Book*,
was first published as a separate volume, but it is long out of
print. The other first editions of Bierce are scarce, and begin to
command high premiums. Three-fourths of his books were
published by obscure publishers, some of them not too reputable. He spent his last quarter of a century in voluntary immolation on a sort of burning ghat, worshiped by his small
band of zealots, but almost unnoticed by the rest of the human
race. His life was a long sequence of bitter ironies. I believe
that he enjoyed it.

ELIZABETH BISHOP

1911–1979

Elizabeth Bishop was born in Massachusetts in 1911. She barely knew her parents: her father died before she was a year old, and before she was five, her mother was confined to a mental hospital. Brought up by maternal grandparents in Nova Scotia, and later by an aunt in Massachusetts, Elizabeth subsequently saw her mother only once. As a student at Vassar College in the early 1930's she began publishing poetry and prose in small magazines and became friends with Mary McCarthy and Marianne Moore. After graduation, she traveled and lived in New York, Europe, North Africa, Mexico, and Florida. A grant from the Amy Lowell Travel Fellowship in 1957 enabled her to go to Latin America. Although she had intended to stop in Brazil only briefly to visit friends, she ended up living there for 18 years. Most of her volumes of poetry were published during the years in Brazil, as were her translations from the Portuguese. In 1969, she returned to the United States to teach at Harvard and MIT, a task undertaken solely, she claimed, out of financial necessity. When she died in 1979, she had received numerous awards, including the National Book Award and the Pulitzer Prize, and had been elected to the American Academy of Arts and Sciences. She was also very highly regarded by fellow poets, such as John Ashbery, who called her a "writer's writer's writer," and Robert Lowell, Octavio Paz, and Marianne Moore. Her reputation rests on a relatively small body of work: *North and South*, published in 1946, *A Cold Spring* (1957), *Questions of Travel* (1965), and *Geography III* (1976).

JAN B. GORDON

From "Days and Distances: The Cartographic Imagination of Elizabeth Bishop"
Contemporary Poetry in America
1974, pp. 348–59

The course of ⟨Elizabeth Bishop's⟩ life's wanderings has a peculiar pattern. Nova Scotia, the Straits of Magellan, interior journeys into the Amazon estuary—all of these places demarcate geographical boundaries between land and sea. Whether consciously or not, Elizabeth Bishop seems fascinated by geographical *extremities*—fingers of water or land that are the sensory receptors of a larger mass. Straits, peninsulas, icebergs, radio antennas ("The Unbeliever"), wharfs and quais, capes ("Cape Breton"), and promontories are the structures of her world. These are spaces which all share the quality of near isolation; they are almost, but not quite, geologically severed as if, like Miss Bishop herself, they were being constantly pulled back to their origin. And the first poem of her 1945 volume, *North and South*, engages us in the dilemma of that layered struggle between land and sea:

> Land lies in water; it is shadowed green.
> Shadows, or are they shallows, at its edges
> showing the line of long sea-weeded ledges
> where weeds hang to the simple blue from green.
> Or does the land lean down to lift the sea from
> under,
> drawing it unperturbed around itself?
> Along the fine tan sandy shelf
> is the land tugging at the sea from under?
>
> ("The Map")

The poem itself is a mere study of a map and of the art of cartography. Musing over the color gradations that separate charted from uncharted areas, Elizabeth Bishop's introductory poem is itself a kind of map to the volume. Although the poem commences with one kind of question—does the land lie on the water or does the water lie on the land?—its conclusion involves the necessary transcendence of the epistemological:

> Are they assigned, or can the countries pick their
> colors?
> —What suits the characters or the native waters best.
> Topography displays no favorites; North's as near as
> West,
> More delicate than the historian's are the map-
> makers' colors.
>
> ("The Map")

The historical precedence of land or water has nothing whatsoever to do with the aesthetics of the "picture" beneath the glass. Maps pose the question of freedom originally encountered in the early story, "In Prison": the existence of voluntary acts would imply the possibility of choices, and to the contrary, these countries cannot elect their colors. Topography is helpless to accommodate the third dimension and hence reduces all to the flat objectivity of *necessary direction*, itself a paradox. The map which purports to guide us to a location is, from an aesthetic perspective, a neutral space where we lose rather than gain our way. Like Elizabeth Bishop herself, we are wanderers rather than travelers and the "map" is an intermediary surface between those two states of being. She has taken an object known primarily for its utility in getting us from one place to another and restored it to an existence purged of history. In the process, the aesthetic preferences of "character" or "native waters" is sacrificed to the delicacy of the mapmaker. Neither land nor water lends shape, but rather the artificial profiles of the cartographer. So obsessed with geographical boundaries, and the precise calibration of latitude and longitude, the printer nonetheless allows "the names of seashore towns [to] run out to sea." Words, whether on maps or in poems, always exceed the intersections to which they point.

But the poetic vision which imagines the most innocuous of events as "marking out maps like Rand McNally's" ("Roosters") surely embodies intriguing premises. It is a world where the poet charts—which is to say, that scale and perspective become primary considerations. Although the genre would seem to be that of the landscape, map-making is really a pseudo-landscape, enacting, to borrow from the vocabulary of Claude Lévi-Strauss, *bricolage*. She is fascinated with this activity, as the poem "Large Bad Picture" testifies:

Remembering the Strait of Belle Isle or
some northerly harbor of Labrador,
before he became a schoolteacher
a great-uncle painted a big picture.
Receding for miles on either side
into a flushed, still sky
are overhanging pale blue cliffs
hundreds of feet high,
their bases fretted by little arches,
the entrances to caves
running in along the level of a bay
masked by perfect waves.

The subject of the poem is an amateur's attempt to construct a coastal scene on canvas. As the painter becomes involved with the process of "remembering" so in the second stanza the coast line is "receding for miles on either side." There is the characteristic interiorization, followed by the quest for a sterile perfection: the "perfect waves" and later, the black birds "hanging in n's in banks." His feeble landscape lacks grandeur precisely because the painter of the "Large Bad Picture" has substituted *reconstruction* for imaginative construction: the spars of the vessels are like "burnt match-sticks" and the glassy sea resembles the middle of some "quiet floor." In order to capture that tone of the painting, Miss Bishop herself consciously resorts to the same gimmick as her great-uncle:

In the pink light
the small red sun goes rolling, rolling,
round and round and round at the same height
in perpetual sunset, comprehensive, consoling,
while the ships consider it.
Apparently they have reached their destination.
It would be hard to say what brought them there,
commerce or contemplation.

Her stanzas are artificially linked with "while" and "as" in order to establish simultaneity where none exists in the same way that the schoolteacher-painter has several objects—birds, ships, sun, and an aquatic animal—within an association which appears as a suspension. The conflict in the painting is one between "commerce or contemplation," since some objects move, while others remain static or "perpetual" in their motionlessness. Everything in the poem, like the painting, is strung together with some technique, or word, like "apparently." The terrible painting is simultaneously part cheap commercial oil painting and part the authentic product of an old man's contemplation; like its very lines, this landscape is hung between "receding" and "remembering" in stanzas one and two. And those trapped birds in "n's" above some cliff are "hanging" in Elizabeth Bishop's poem in such a way that we almost hear the "n" trapped between hard "g's." Again, like the world of her travels, everything in Miss Bishop's poetic universe is nearly severed and must be strung together with ferries or bridges or their verbal equivalents.

Like her great-uncle, Miss Bishop is always constructing when she appears to be describing, and the result is a poetry which has the quality of an engineering exercise. There is a tendency to reduce the most complicated poetic issues to "questions" that are exclusively technical in nature. Her poem "Large Bad Picture," then, is a highly self-conscious enterprise—the use of an artificially bad poem to elicit the mood of an artificially awkward oil painting. Although we marvel at the proficiency of the poem, there is something curiously absent in such mastery. The emphasis upon the coalesced perspective tends to be a substitute for any attention to the *personal*. Even though we might wish to meet the grizzled amateur painter, he will always be inaccessible, located some-

where behind his masterpiece. Behind all the present and past participles of "Large Bad Picture" lurks only a world that is somehow already *given*, never in the process of being created. One suspects that this too is part of the map-maker's vision; after all, a poetic universe that is reducible to a map might well imply that the person en route is always among the lost. Compared with so much contemporary poetry that is confessional in its detail of the loss of or dispersal of selfhood, self-negation is a point of departure in Elizabeth Bishop's craft. But it is a self-negation that the reader never records and has no way of measuring, since the loss has occurred *a priori*. For this reason, the poetry often lacks a distinctive teleology. We see no possibility of a therapeutic progression in a world so relativized that "North's as near as West" precisely because hers is at best a two-dimensional craft. There is a certain surface tension always present in Elizabeth Bishop's art that is at least partially the result of the loss of *privilege* in every sense in which we might typically use that word: the narrator's sense of an advantage to perspective; an access to secrets unknown to other protagonists in her poems; or even the subtlety of an untrustworthy vision which might confer aesthetic advantage by granting the reader the right to acknowledge a false subjectivity. She has had far more favorable response from British critics than from those in this country perhaps because the limits of her poetry prevent the kind of self-indulgence that G. S. Fraser referred to as "luxury" in his essay, "Some Younger American Poets" (*Commentary*, May, 1957). Fraser contrasted Miss Bishop's precise diction with that of her American contemporaries and came to the conclusion that she had willingly surrendered a certain polish in order that she might more clearly say exactly what her poems want to say. He equates that equation, unfortunately, with what he terms "an immense sense of responsibility toward a critically cooperative audience." Of course there is a definable responsibility in such an enterprise only when the word "responsibility" is made synonymous with a failure to take risks. The etymology of the word itself involves—as one of its primary meanings—the idea of an "answer" or a "reply," literally a "speaking again (re-spondere)." And that quality is seldom characteristic of her poetry because there is never a voice sufficiently distinctive so as to serve as a vehicle for an assumed dialogue. Responsibility seldom derives from rhetorical questions. In short, it is the responsibility of the map-maker: a world well-drawn and accurate, given the nature of current exploration, but exhibiting more and more the quality of a guidebook:

The mosquitoes
go hunting to the tune of their ferocious obbligatos.
After dark, the fireflies map the heavens in the marsh
until the moon rises.
Cold white, not bright, the moonlight is coarse-
meshed,
and the careless, corrupt state is all black specks
too far apart, and ugly whites; the poorest
post-card of itself.

("Florida")

That very ability to turn a traditional landscape into a guidebook, complete with a commentary on the state's gnarled race relations, is a peculiarly unique slant to the contemporary *paysage moralise*. Travel guides become post-cards at the end of the journey when the initiate tells the would-be traveler where to go and what to see.

But the landscape itself is altered in the process so that it always appears to the reader as if it had been reproduced rather than experienced. And the moral vision of such a universe is similarly skewed. For, as in so many twentieth-century sex manuals, occasions that we would expect to be of great intimacy are charted for us, perhaps too narrowly. If personal intercourse with the natural world is part of the mythos of the guidebook, the reader's potentiality is democratized at an enormous price. Not only does it always look easier than it is, but emotional considerations are seldom horizontal. For if the poet creates the illusion that technique alone assures mastery, then we study the craft with an idea of learning it only to discover that we have become cognizant of a world that is all surface. From the map, as from the do-it-yourself guide to auto repair, we become aware only of other surfaces. All of this is to say that Elizabeth Bishop's poetry is always an *expedition* for which preparation is needed and, though such is surely part of the Christian metaphor for life itself, her vision is peculiarly technologized since there is no authentic ground for existence in her scheme. We have the trappings of direction and guidance without the emergence, real or promised, of presence. There is no better or worse, no up or down, but only boundaries that create neutralized spaces:

> At low tide like this how sheer the water is.
> White, crumbling ribs of marl protrude and glare
> and the boats are dry, the pilings dry as matches.
> Absorbing, rather than being absorbed, . . .

> ("The Bight")

Her images are never organically related nor are they presented in any of Imagism's characteristically durational clusters. Rather her poems appear as if they were strung together, with each metaphoric "set" following the preceding one in some established order of proper priorities. The pattern involves some invisible poetic finger moving across a map and accumulating rather than creating the world: "there is this, and then this, and then this. . . ." The manner is strangely reminiscent of one of Miss Bishop's childhood favorites, Gerard Manley Hopkins, whose verse provides the epigraph to a charming little poem, "Cold Spring." As in Hopkins' progressions, a number of her poems commence *ex nihilo* followed by some highly truncated phrase: "A cold spring:/the violet was flawed on the lawn." Then the universe suddenly proliferates:

> Tufts of long grass show
> where each cow-flop lies,
> The bull-frogs are sounding,
> slack strings plucked by heavy thumbs.
> Beneath the light, against your white front door,
> the smallest moths, like Chinese fans,
> flatten themselves, silver and silver-gilt
> over pale yellow, orange, or gray.
> Now from the thick grass, the fireflies
> begin to rise:

> ("A Cold Spring")

This type of poem usually concludes with some coda that approximates the tone of Hopkins' "Praise him" in its abbreviated reduplication in emotive language of the phenomenal catalogue:

> And your shadowy pastures will be able to offer
> these particular glowing tributes
> every evening now throughout the summer.

> ("A Cold Spring")

The progression is from nothingness, through an almost incredible enumeration of the discrete, though evanescent particulars of a landscape, and then to a deliberation upon the human significance of the catalogue. We move from the distinctly non-human to the decidedly human by means of an almost imperceptible intrusion of the possessive pronoun "your" which serves to give the reader a kind of power at the very instant that he is being overwhelmed by the fertility of the scene. The use of "and" to link the human coda to the world of nature that precedes it in "Cold Spring" is one of those partial deceptions that deflect Miss Bishop's craft from a certain sincerity. As spring catches slumbering nature by surprise, so the "shadowy pastures" of the concluding lines catch the reader by surprise. Somehow, the location has been shifted, for these pastures are part of an interior landscape, part of the realm of "offer[ings]" and "tribute." At the very instant of rebirth in the book of nature, the reader is also part of the kingdom of sacrifice in the book of grace. But, like the old man's painting in "Large Bad Picture," the reader is never sure how he got there. The poem proceeds within a false *telos* punctuated by "Now, in the evening" to "Now, from the thick grass" to the "And . . . / now throughout the summer." Yet, the final "now" is not part of the world of presence, but part of the absence of sacrifice and redemption that involves the possibility of return in the future; we have entered a realm of "will be" disguised as "now." Mapmaking too is an enterprise sufficiently vicarious as to involve a similar confusion between future and present tenses. The cartographer's product is one that continually must be updated, which is yet another way of using the word "now" as a refrain.

This constant struggle with the current in Elizabeth Bishop's art is metaphorically represented as a dialectic involving natural landscape and the claims of history. But again, history in her poems appears not as chronological time nor as the presence of the past, but rather as some symbol for every failed connection. For example, the poem "Argument" from the volume *A Cold Spring* seems a lament for some lost love (one of the very few poems in Miss Bishop's canon that involves anything like intimacy), yet the rift is related in terms of a battle between distance and desire on the one hand, and days and voices on the other:

> Days that cannot bring you near
> or will not,
> Distance trying to appear
> something more than obstinate,
> argue argue argue with me
> endlessly
> neither proving you less wanted nor less dear.

> ("Argument")

History never is part of the kingdom of contiguity, but rather serves an opposite function in the dialogue with space:

> Days: And think
> of all those cluttered instruments,
> one to a fact,
> cancelling each other's experience,
> how they were
> like some hideous calendar
> "Compliments of Never & Forever, Inc."

> ("Argument")

Rather than the accumulation of experience in increments of intensity, the voice of days is merely a record of canceled hopes and fears. It is the absence rather than the presence of connection. The lines themselves are faintly derivative of the kind of emotion that Sylvia Plath wrote about with such poignancy; the female body appears as a calendar torn between the two extremes of human affections: "I *never* want to see you again" and "I shall love you *forever*." The words appear merely as another "compliment," a part of the commercial world affixed to the gift of days as an afterthought. It is something distributed free at holiday time from businesses and corporations we have never encountered in experience. For Elizabeth Bishop, history then is merely another map, a spatialization of relationships that always appears as distance. In the poem "Argument" there is no distinction whatsoever between the language of history and the language of space:

> Distance: Remember all that land
> beneath the plane;
> that coastline
> of dim beaches deep in sand
> stretching indistinguishably
> all the way,
> all the way to where my reasons end?
>   ("Argument")

Actually, the two components of this pseudo-dialogue come to participate in the life of the other. Days are related to the cancellation of experience and distance is inextricably bound to the processes of memory "stretching indistinguishably" to a point where "reasons end." Again, the poet is almost fixated by boundaries, by the extremity where each participant loses domain. It is the realm of peninsular experience, either brackish water or tidal flats, and is surely a second cousin to the terrain of the Brazilian jungle from which our map-maker continually has drawn translations throughout her poetic career. Perhaps these too are but the poetic equivalent of a mercator projection. As the solitary speaker of "In Prison" had discovered, the tiniest reduction of space nevertheless provides the occasion for the metaphoric enlargement of boundaries through psychic projection and reprojection. The recognition of imprisonment participates in and leads to the only kind of freedom to which humans have access.

SYBIL P. ESTESS
"Description and Imagination in
Elizabeth Bishop's 'The Map'"
Elizabeth Bishop and Her Art
1983, pp. 219–22

The filmmaker Michelangelo Antonioni maintains that he attempts in his movies to focus on details in order to emphasize his ways of perceiving. He writes, "I am obliged to linger ad infinitum on the details, on the repetition of the most futile gestures, in order that what I show may assume a form and a sense."[1] Joseph Conrad's statement in the preface to *The Nigger of the "Narcissus"* is now a classic one: "—My task which I am trying to achieve is, by the power of the written word, to make you hear, to make you feel—it is, before all, to make you *see*. That—and no more, and it is everything." Randall Jarrell commented on Elizabeth Bishop's first book, "All her poems have written underneath *I have seen it.*"[2] Indeed the inclination of modern and postmodern literature has long been to communicate individual vision rather than abstract truth. Bishop, like Conrad, like Antonioni, like most modern and contemporary artists, takes as her task enabling us to see as she sees. She makes description the most salient characteristic of her poetry and prose. Poems such as "The Map," "The Fish," and "The Bight," though at first glance realistic descriptions of ordinary entities, are actually much more: they are guides to her own vision of those realities. Many Bishop poems evolve toward what James Joyce thought of as an epiphanic vision.

Elizabeth Bishop seldom violates objects by imposing on them preconceived definitions, a priori interpretations, or sentimental descriptions. But even though she may seem to look at things with the exactitude and tenacity of a naturalist, Bishop necessarily creates art out of her personal life experiences, and ultimately out of her synthesized vision of whatever she

chooses to describe; her "empiricism" is not as unalloyed as it may first appear.

In the poem "The Map," Bishop offers a significant hint to her sense of how an "objective" work of art may embody the artist's subjective experience of a given reality. "The Map" embodies a way of understanding her work, for she placed it first in both *North & South* (1946) and in *The Complete Poems* (1969). On one level, the poem objectively describes an actual map: "Land lies in water; it is shadowed green." But beginning as early as the second line of the poem, Bishop's subjective kind of seeing becomes apparent. She starts to question what seems to her the various nuances of the map's configurations.

> Shadows, or are they shallows, at its edges
> showing the line of long sea-weeded ledges
> where weeds hang to the simple blue from green.

On her first look at the map, she seems to see water as surrounding and supporting land. In the following lines, however, we see the possibility that sea and land form an alliance so complementary that it is difficult to determine the exact nature of their interdependence:

> Or does the land lean down to lift the sea from
>   under,
> drawing it unperturbed around itself?
> Along the fine tan sandy shelf
> is the land tugging at the sea from under?

Bishop's map enables us to imagine myriad kinds of connections between land and sea. The land's peninsulas may seem to "take the water between thumb and finger/like women feeling for the smoothness of yard-goods." A configuration such as Norway's may appear a "hare" which "runs south in agitation." Bishop suggests in these lines that what one sees depends upon how one looks.

Is it not, then, our perspectives on the real which determine its very nature? The initial stanza of "The Map" seems to suggest that the essence of reality may be determined by our manner of seeing. Do "sea-weeded ledges . . ./hang to the simple blue from green"? "Or does the land lean down to lift the sea from under"? It all depends, Bishop first seems to say, on our chosen vantage point.

Yet reality is not merely relative to how we see it. As the poem progresses, we find that the imagination cannot create nor can it alter things as they are. A map's images can never be arbitrarily presented. As Wallace Stevens writes in what he calls an *opusculum paedogogum*: "The pears are not seen/as the observer wills" ("Study of Two Pears"). On maps, the poet's interlocutor asks of her, are countries colored "what suits the character or the native waters best"? Must reality, then, always be scrupulously and unerringly presented?

The issue at stake is that the images on maps are by definition constructions of the mind, as the mind attempts to plot the landscape in order to find its way. Though such artifacts must be "accurate," must be faithful to things as we know them, they may still be imaginatively constructed or arranged. Bishop's kind of navigational description is an invention derived not only from her empirical eye but also from her mind, as it becomes the agent which charts the various depths of the waters of her personal imagination. Such compositions are, as A. D. Hope writes, "held between the intellectual eye and the landscape."[3] Bishop seems to make a judgment in "The Map" concerning the efficacy of all "maps," of all invented, artistic images. Though the shadows of their new-found-lands may (like those of Newfoundland) appear to lie "flat and still" in comparison to real sea or land, their waters too have a strategic function: they lend the land "their waves' own conformation."

No aesthetic images, even Bishop's verisimilar kind of description, should be taken as exhaustive of reality. The maps to experience which her art provides are the result of the constant intrusion of things-as-they-are upon her particular power to come to terms with them. Bishop attempts in descriptive poems to make form and imaginative sense of what she sees. It is through her personalized, imaginative perspective that she allows us, as Stevens would have it, to "see the earth again."

As in most Bishop poems, the meaning of "The Map" extends far beyond a mere realistic description of a literal object. This poem delineates the nature of a relationship between objective reality and one's subjective and imaginative assimilation of such "facts." Bishop suggests in "The Map" that an art work may be seen as a map to an artist's particular sense of things. The analogy, of course, can be drawn further: her works—cumulations of realistic details shaped into an imaginative form—are maps to and of her own sensibility.

"Mapped waters are more quiet than the land is," the poem says. It concludes, however, "More delicate than the historians' are the map-makers' colors." Here Bishop adds to the correlation between the task of the poet and the task of the historian an even subtler dimension than did Aristotle when he claimed that "poetry is higher than history." She implies that, like the historian, the map-maker should not distort "truth"; yet she seems to know too that it is impossible to be completely objective. For just as the individual sensibility of the historian informs what he records, the artist's particular vision (with all its peculiar slants) shapes what he or she creates. Thus any poet's images are the delicate result of the imagination lending its conformation to manifestations of the real. A fragile, perhaps, yet keen and subtle sense of discrimination—"the map-makers' colors"—comprises an artist's way of seeing.

Notes

1. Michel Mardore, "Antonioni, je suis un incurable optimiste," *Les lettres française*, No. 924 (Sept 6, 1962), p. 6; cited and translated by Ted Perry in "A Contextual Study of M. Antonioni's Film *L'Eclisse*," *Speech Monographs* 37, no. 2 (June 1970), p. 92.
2. *Poetry and the Age* (1953; reprint ed., New York: Farrar, Straus and Giroux/Noonday, 1972), p. 5.
3. "The Esthetic Theory of James Joyce," in *Joyce's Portrait: Criticisms and Critiques*, ed. Thomas E. Connolly (New York: Appleton-Century-Crofts Press, 1962), p. 200.

DAVID KALSTONE
From "Elizabeth Bishop: Questions of Memory, Questions of Travel"

Five Temperaments, 1977, pp. 13–40

I

Robert Lowell, thinking back to the time before he wrote *Life Studies*, felt that Bishop's work "seemed to belong to a later century."[1] It wasn't so much a matter of experimental forms. In *North & South* (1946) there were a number of emblematic poems—"The Map," "The Monument," "The Gentleman of Shalott" among them—some in formal stanzas, some strictly rhymed. Still, from the very start, there was something about her work for which elegantly standard literary analysis was not prepared. Readers have been puzzled, as when one critic writes about "Florida": "the poet's exuberance provides a scattering of images whose relevance to the total structure is open to question. It is as though Miss Bishop stopped along the road home to examine every buttercup and asphodel she saw."[2] First of all, Bishop writes about alligators, mangrove swamps,

skeletons and shells—things exotic and wild, not prettified. More important, there is some notion of neat and total structure which the critic expects and imposes, but which the poem subverts. What makes the quoted critic nervous is a quality which becomes more and more prominent in Bishop's work—her apparent lack of insistence on meanings beyond the surface of the poem, the poem's seeming randomness and disintegration. There is something personal, even quirky, about her apparently straightforward descriptive poems which, on early readings, it is hard to identify. This is an offhand way of speaking which Bishop has come to trust and master, especially in her important book of 1965, *Questions of Travel*, and in the extraordinary poems she has published since then.

I am talking about matters of tone, the kind of authority a single voice will claim over the material included in a poem. Anyone who has heard Miss Bishop read will know how flat and modest her voice is, how devoid of flourish, how briefly she holds her final chords and cadences and allows a poem to resonate. Here is the beginning of "In the Waiting Room":

> In Worcester, Massachusetts,
> I went with Aunt Consuelo
> to keep her dentist's appointment
> and sat and waited for her
> in the dentist's waiting room.

Or another opening ("Filling Station"):

> Oh, but it is dirty!
> —this little filling station,
> oil-soaked, oil-permeated
> to a disturbing, over-all
> black translucency.
> Be careful with that match!

And this is the end of "The Bight":

> Click. Click. Goes the dredge,
> and brings up a dripping jawful of marl.
> All the untidy activity continues,
> awful but cheerful.

I have chosen the plainest and most provocative examples of the apparently random in order to raise questions common to much poetry after Wallace Stevens: how is meaning developed from individual and unamplified details? How does the observer's apparent lack of insistence, devoid of rhetorical pressure, rise to significance (if, indeed, that is the word for it)? Howard Nemerov gives us one answer: "Vision begins with a fault in this world's smooth façade."[3] But Bishop finds that fault, that break from observation into the unknown, almost impossible to locate. "There is no split," she remarks in a letter:

> Dreams, works of art (some) glimpses of the always-more-successful surrealism of everyday life, unexpected moments of empathy (is it?), catch a peripheral vision of whatever it is one can never really see full-face but that seems enormously important. I can't believe we are wholly irrational—and I do admire Darwin—But reading Darwin one admires the beautiful solid case being built up out of his endless, heroic observations, almost unconscious or automatic—and then comes a sudden relaxation, a forgetful phrase, and one feels that strangeness of his undertaking, sees the lonely young man, his eye fixed on facts and minute details, sinking or sliding giddily off into the unknown. What one seems to want in art, in experiencing it, is the same thing that is necessary for its creation, a self-forgetful, perfectly useless concentration.[4]

Heroic observation; eyes fixed on facts and minute details, sinking, sliding giddily off into the unknown; a self-forgetful, perfectly useless concentration. What she sees in Darwin, we can see in her own efforts. Take "Florida" (the poem our critic found disorganized)—a poem of almost Darwinian concentration.

The opening line is so disarming, almost trivializing, that we are in danger of taking what follows for granted: the odd changes of scale that are among this poem's secrets.

> The state with the prettiest name,
> the state that floats in brackish water,
> held together by mangrove roots
> that bear while living oysters in clusters,
> and when dead strew white swamps with skeletons,
> dotted as if bombarded, with green hummocks
> like ancient cannon-balls sprouting grass.

The scale changes as rapidly as Gulliver's: first the whole state, afloat, intact with its boundaries, the mapmaker's or aerial photographer's vision; then an organism (held together by mangrove roots), the geologist's or botanist's fanciful X ray. Her Florida is a barnacled world refined to residues. Oysters dot the mangrove roots; dead mangroves strew the swamps with skeletons. Dead turtles leave their skulls and their shells, which are themselves hosts to other growths, barnacled. The coastline is looped with seashells painstakingly and exotically named. There is sediment in the water; solvents in wood-smoke; charring on stumps and dead trees. Yet the charring is "like black velvet." The residues studding this landscape are its principal ornaments as well: artistic and historical growths, like the "tide-looped strings of fading shells" turning the "monotonous . . . sagging coast-line" to something else.

At first the description occurs in a free-floating eternal present, a series of phrases which don't commit the observer to any main verb at all. They seem if anything to exclude her, reawakening memories of geological change that stretch far before and beyond her in scale, habitually repeated historical action. The strange shifts of scale—of size and space—in a seemingly timeless, self-renewing present remind us constantly, by implication, of the frailty of our merely human observer. A descriptive poem, which in other hands, say Whitman's, appropriates landscapes and objects, here makes us aware just how, just why we are excluded from such appropriations.

Only when we get to the buzzards, two-thirds of the way through the poem, is there a form of the present tense (they "are drifting down, down, down") restricted to her particular moment of watching, a definite *now*. Here also, two strange mirrors in which we do not find ourselves. First:

> Thirty or more buzzards are drifting down, down,
>   down,
> over something they have spotted in the swamp,
> in circles like stirred-up flakes of sediment
> sinking through water.
> Smoke from woods-fires filter fine blue solvents.

And then:

> After dark, the fireflies map the heavens in the marsh
> until the moon rises.

The four elements form a self-enclosed world. Creatures of the air mirror the earth's discards (are they really there?) floating through water; and fire, as if completing the cycle, exhales fine smoke into the blue. Then again with the fireflies, air and flickering fire are reflected in the marsh, earth and water together. In other words, alternate creations dwarf or frame the poet's own: the long scale of eroding nature with its fossils and predators (buzzards, mosquitoes with "ferocious obbligatos"), and then the daily repeating creations and fad-

ings. When the moon comes up, the landscape pales. Its wonderful sounds and colors—the flashy tanagers, the pelicans gold-winged at sunset, the musical screeching—turn skeletal once more.

The world in its processes provides a delicate model for the poet's work, for art—its shells with beautiful names, its finely observed (and alliterative) oysters in clusters. But the poem continually stresses how such contrivance is made for fading and how nature's contrivances survive the artist's own. Building toward a phrase whose effect is worthy of what she admires in Darwin ("a sudden relaxation, a forgetful phrase"), Bishop sums up the impact of the scene, grasped for the fullness of her own understanding:

> Cold white, not bright, the moonlight is coarse-
>   meshed,
> and the careless, corrupt state is all black specks
> too far apart, and ugly whites; the poorest
> post-card of itself.

At the end Florida contracts to the alligator's five primitive calls ("friendliness, love, mating, war, and a warning"), and with its whimper is restored to darkness and its mysterious identity as "the Indian Princess."

Bishop exposes us to a more ambitious version of her almost toneless observer in a poem which reaches back to her Nova Scotia childhood, "At the Fishhouses." Here is the opening:

> Although it is a cold evening,
> down by one of the fishhouses
> an old man sits netting,
> his net, in the gloaming almost invisible
> a dark purple-brown,
> and his shuttle worn and polished.
> The air smells so strong of codfish
> it makes one's nose run and one's eyes water.
> The five fishhouses have steeply peaked roofs
> and narrow, cleated gangplanks slant up
> to storerooms in the gables
> for the wheelbarrows to be pushed up and down on.
> All is silver: the heavy surface of the sea,
> swelling slowly as if considering spilling over,
> is opaque, but the silver of the benches,
> the lobster pots, and masts, scattered
> among the wild jagged rocks,
> is of an apparent translucence
> like the small old buildings with an emerald moss
> growing on their shoreward walls.
> The big fish tubs are completely lined
> with layers of beautiful herring scales
> and the wheelbarrows are similarly plastered
> with creamy iridescent coats of mail,
> with small iridescent flies crawling on them.

At first, as in "Florida," a landscape seems almost without a spectator, the speaker comically unwelcome in an air which smacks of another element and which makes her eyes water and her nose run. She slowly exposes the scene, present tense, with a tempered willingness to let it speak for itself in declarative simplicity. Things *are*; things *have*. The lone fisherman, a Wordsworthian solitary, is worn into the scene, his net "almost invisible," his shuttle "worn and polished," his "black old knife" with a blade "almost worn away." The dense opening description—deliberately slow, close to fifty lines of the poem—is in all details of sight, sense and sound intended to subject us to the landscape, to draw us deeply into it. "The five fishhouses have steeply peaked roofs/and narrow, cleated gangplanks slant up": even the clotted consonants and doubling of adjectives force these words apart and force us to dwell on them, as if to carve out some certainty of vision. The reader is meant to become what the speaker jokingly claims herself to be later in this poem: "a believer in total immersion."

From this immersion a pattern gathers, unhurried but persistent: present, for example, in the odd half-rhyme of *cod-fish* and *polished*, or in the unassuming repetition of *iridescent*. The wheelbarrows are "plastered/with creamy iridescent coats of mail,/with small iridescent flies crawling on them." The crudeness and the delicacy of these details are made to appear strokes of the same master, of the landscape's age-old subjection to the sea, to the caking, the plastering, the lining, the silvering-over which turns everything to iridescence or sequins, as at the same time it rusts them and wears them away.

In its fidelity to setting—to what is both jagged and strangely jewelled—the poem accumulates the sense of an artistry beyond the human, one that stretches over time, chiselling and decorating with its strange erosions. The human enterprise depends upon and is dwarfed by the sea, just as the fishhouse ramps lead out of, but back into the water: "Down at the water's edge, at the place/where they haul up the boats, up the long ramp/descending into the water." Precisely by imagining these encircling powers, the speaker wins some authority over them. This is her largest gesture, reflected in some smaller moments of propitiation: offering a cigarette to the fisherman, and with odd simplicity singing Baptist hymns to a moderately curious seal, true creature of that "element bearable to no mortal." Behind them—or more to the point "behind us"—as if left behind in merely human history "a million Christmas trees stand/waiting for Christmas."

This "believer in total immersion," through her patient wooing or conjuring, finally wins a certain elevation of tone, a vision, in a twice-repeated phrase, of the sea "Cold dark deep and absolutely clear."

> . . . The water seems suspended
> above the rounded gray and blue-gray stones.
> I have seen it over and over, the same sea, the same,
> slightly, indifferently swinging above the stones,
> icily free above the stones,
> above the stones and then the world.
> If you should dip your hand in,
> your wrist would ache immediately,
> your bones would begin to ache and your hand
>   would burn
> as if the water were a transmutation of fire
> that feeds on stones and burns with a dark gray flame.
> If you tasted it, it would first taste bitter,
> then briny, then surely burn your tongue.
> It is like what we imagine knowledge to be:
> dark, salt, clear, moving, utterly free,
> drawn from the cold hard mouth
> of the world, derived from the rocky breasts
> forever, flowing and drawn, and since
> our knowledge is historical, flowing, and flown.

The poet returns knowledge to concreteness, as if breaking it down into its elements (dark, salt, clear). The speaker herself seems drawn into the elements: at first jokingly in the fishy air which makes the nose run, the eyes water; then in the burning if one dips one's hands, as if water were a "transmutation of fire that feeds on stones." The absorbing and magical transformations of earth, air, fire and water into one another (as in "Florida") make it impossible—and unnecessary—to distinguish *knowledge* from the *sea*, to determine what, grammatically, is "derived from the rocky breasts/forever." With a final fluency she leaves her declarative descriptions behind and captures a rhythm at once mysterious and acknowledging limitations ("flowing and drawn . . . flowing and flown").

"At the Fishhouses" makes explicit what is usually implicit, invisible and vital in Miss Bishop's poems, like a pulse: a sense of the encircling and eroding powers in whose presence all minute observations are valuably made. She is, in fact, rather like a sandpiper she describes in another poem: the bird pictured as subject to the water's roar, the earth's shaking—imagined in "a state of controlled panic, a student of Blake." He watches the sand, no detail too small ("Sandpiper"):

> The world is a mist. And then the world is
> minute and vast and clear. The tide
> is higher or lower. He couldn't tell you which.
> His beak is focussed; he is preoccupied,
> looking for something, something, something.
> Poor bird, he is obsessed!
> The millions of grains are black, white, tan, and
>   gray,
> mixed with quartz grains, rose and amethyst.

Here again are those shifts of scale which, instead of unsettling, actually strengthen our perspective. The poem is a critique of Blake's auguries of innocence: his seeing the world in a grain of sand. "The world is a mist. And then the world is/minute and vast and clear." The adjectives appear to make a quiet claim. Yet what an odd collocation—minute and vast and clear. The scales are not really commensurable; one sees the world, one sees the grain of sand, and the clarity comes in making primitive and definite distinction about what is and is not within our grasp. The bird, on the one hand, is battered and baffled by the waves, the misty "sheets of interrupting water"; on the other hand it attends and stares, is preoccupied, obsessed with the grains of sand, a litany of whose colors, minutely and beautifully distinguished, ends the poem. That is all it knows of the world.

These poems both describe and set themselves at the limits of description. Bishop lets us know that every detail is a boundary, not a Blakean microcosm. Because of the limits they suggest, details vibrate with a meaning beyond mere physical presence. Landscapes meant to sound detached are really inner landscapes. They show an effort at reconstituting the world as if it were in danger of being continually lost. It is only this sense of *precarious* possession that accounts for the way Bishop looks at the city waking up ("Love Lies Sleeping"):

> From the window, I see
> an immense city, carefully revealed,
> made delicate by over-workmanship,
>   detail upon detail,
>   cornice upon façade,
> reaching so languidly up into
> a weak white sky, it seems to waver there.
>   (where it has slowly grown
>   in skies of water-glass
> from fused beads of iron and copper crystals,
> the little chemical "garden" in a jar
>   trembles and stands again,
>   pale blue, blue-green, and brick.)

That human contrivance is frail and provisional is clear not only from the "wavering" but also from the odd, habitual changes of scale: an immense city, carefully revealed, is also a little chemical garden in a jar. That it should be seen as workmanship at all is a miracle of freshness, a confusion of proportions, part aerial vision, part closeup as of some miraculous insect civilization. Bishop triumphs in the surprising coincidence of mechanics and natural growth, fused beads of crystal, a little chemical garden—a balancing act to portray our fragile ingenuity.

The ability to see such accomplishments as provisional explains the power of one of Bishop's apparently random poems, "The Bight." It is subtitled "on my birthday," the only suggestion of much resonance beyond the impression of a tide-battered inlet—muddy at low tide, with dredges, pelicans, marl, sponge boats, sharktails hung up to dry, boats beached, some wrecked. What animates the scene this time is the observer's deliberate activity, celebrating her birthday in an off-key way with an unrelenting and occasionally mischievous series of comparisons: pilings dry as matches; water turning to gas (and which Baudelaire might hear turning to marimba music); pelicans crashing like pickaxes; man-of-war birds opening tails like scissors; sharktails hanging like plowshares. The whole rundown world is domesticated by comparisons to our mechanical contrivances, our instruments of workaday survival, enabling, in turn, an outrageous simile (stove-boats "like torn-open, unanswered letters") and an equally outrageous pun ("The bight is littered with old correspondences"). The letters wickedly enough bring Baudelaire back into the poem, merge with his "correspondences." They are unanswered letters to boot, in a poem where the author has shot off one comparison after another, like firecrackers. No wonder then that a dredge at the end perfectly accompanies this poet's activities:

> Click. Click. Goes the dredge,
> and brings up a dripping jawful of marl.
> All the untidy activity continues,
> awful but cheerful.

This is what she allows for her birthday: the pointed celebration of small-craft victories in a storm-ridden inlet.

It is no accident that much of Bishop's work is carried on at the mercy of or in the wake of the tides. There are divided and distinguished stages in her encounters: moments of civilized, provisional triumph; and then again, times when landscapes leave us behind—the northern seas of "At the Fishhouses," the abundant decay of "Florida" and later, of her adopted Brazil, magnetic poles sensed even in the title of her first volume, *North & South*. Our mortal temperate zones seem in some ways the excluded middle where we possess a language of precarious, even doomed distinctions. . . .

III

The volume *Questions of Travel* in effect constitutes a sequence of poems, its Brazilian landscapes not so much providing answers as initiating us into the mysteries of how questions are asked. It is important that the book also includes poems about her Nova Scotia childhood and the central story of that period, "In the Village." In the light of those memories, the Brazilian poems become a model of how, with difficulty and pleasure, pain and precision, we re-introduce ourselves into a world.

There are three important initiating poems: in order, "Arrival at Santos," "Brazil, January 1, 1502" and "Questions of Travel." The first is deliberately superficial, comic, sociable. We watch her straining from tourist into traveller, after the disappointments of Santos, which like all ports is like soap or postage stamps—necessary but, "wasting away like the former, slipping the way the latter/do when we mail the letters we wrote on the boat." The familiar and merely instrumental melt away and we know something more than geographical is meant by the last line: "We are driving to the interior."

We go there by means of one of Bishop's characteristic changes of scale. "Arrival at Santos"—it's not Bishop's usual practice—had been dated at the end, *January, 1952*. The next poem is "Brazil, January 1, 1502," and its first word is the generalizing *Januaries*. No longer in the "here" and "now" of

the uninstructed tourist, the poem fans out into the repeating present of the botanist and the anthropologist. Our drive to the interior is through the looking glass of natural history. There is a comforting epigraph from Lord Clark's *Landscape into Art*, "embroidered nature . . . tapestried landscape," that seems to familiarize the scene, appropriate it for European sensibilities. Yet this is a wild burgeoning tapestry, not "filled in" with foliage but "every square inch *filling in* with foliage," tirelessly self-renewing. Its distinctions of shade and color force her into relentless unflagging specificity: "big leaves, little leaves, and giant leaves,/blue, blue-green, and olive." A parade of shades: silver-gray, rust red, greenish white, blue-white. The powers of description are deliberately and delightfully taxed; it's hard for mere humans to keep up.

Then, with a bow to our desire for a familiar tapestry, Bishop draws our attention to something in the foreground. It is first identified as "Sin:/five sooty dragons near some massy rocks." The rocks are "worked with lichens" and "threatened from underneath by moss/in lovely hell-green flames." Then, in a deliberate change of scale, the little morality play turns to something wilder, more riveting, making fun of our tame exaggerations. Those dragons are, in fact, lizards in heat.

> The lizards scarcely breathe; all eyes
> are on the smaller, female one, back-to,
> her wicked tail straight up and over,
> red as red-hot wire.

Then the most daring change of all:

> Just so the Christians, hard as nails,
> tiny as nails, and glinting,
> in creaking armor, came and found it all,
> not unfamiliar.

For a moment, until we unravel the syntax, "just so" identifies the invaders with the lizards in heat. Tiny in scale, dwarfed by the scene, the settlers, after Mass, are out hunting Indian women:

> they ripped away into the hanging fabric,
> each out to catch an Indian for himself—
> those maddening little women who kept calling,
> calling to each other (or had the birds waked up?)
> and retreating, always retreating, behind it.

The tapestry—initially it seemed like a device to domesticate the landscape—instead excludes invaders from it. At the beginning we were identified with those settlers of 1502: "Nature greets our eyes/exactly as she must have greeted theirs." At the end that proves to be a dubious privilege. Nature's tapestry endures, renews itself. After our initial glimpse of order, we shrink like Alice or Gulliver—toy intruders, marvelling.

Bishop's book, then, imagines first the mere tourist, then the invader, and finally, in the title poem, faces what is actually available to the traveller. "Questions of Travel" anticipates a new submissive understanding, taking what comes on its own terms, as she does with the magical powers of "The Riverman" or the mysterious quirks of the humble squatter-tenant, "Manuelzinho." The key to this new openness and affection is in the movement of the title poem. It proceeds through a cautious syntax of questions, with tentative answers in negative clauses. The glutted, excluded observer of the two opening poems ("There are too many waterfalls here") hallucinates mountains into capsized hulls, her own sense that travel might turn into shipwreck. Her first questions are asked with a guilty air: "Should we have stayed at home and thought of here? . . . Is it right to be watching strangers in a play . . . ?"

> What childishness is it that while there's a breath of
> life

in our bodies, we are determined to rush
to see the sun the other way around?
The tiniest green hummingbird in the world?
To stare at some inexplicable old stonework,
inexplicable and impenetrable,
at any view,
instantly seen and always, always delightful?

You can hear Bishop's spirits rise to the bait of detail, the word "childishness" losing its air of self-accusation and turning before our eyes into something receptive, *childlike*, open to wonder. This is finally a less ambiguous approach than that of the traveller yearning to "look and look our infant sight away." "Questions of Travel" does not expect, as "Over 2000 Illustrations" did, that vision will add up, restore our ancient home. The yearning remains ("Oh, must we dream our dreams/and have them, too?"). But the observer is drawn very cautiously by accumulating detail, and questions themselves begin to satisfy the imagining mind. The following passage, all questions, proceeds by the method Bishop admired in Darwin ("a self-forgetful, perfectly useless concentration"):

But surely it would have been a pity
not to have seen the trees along this road,
really exaggerated in their beauty,
not to have seen them gesturing
like noble pantomimists, robed in pink.
—Not to have had to stop for gas and heard
the sad, two-noted, wooden tune
of disparate wooden clogs
carelessly clacking over
 a grease-stained filling-station floor.
(In another country the clogs would all be tested.
Each pair there would have identical pitch.)
—A pity not to have heard
the other, less primitive music of the fat brown bird
who sings above the broken gasoline pump
in a bamboo church of Jesuit baroque:
three towers, five silver crosses.
—Yes, a pity not to have pondered,
blurr'dly and inconclusively,
on what connection can exist for centuries
between the crudest wooden footwear
and, careful and finicky,
the whittled fantasies of wooden cages.
—Never to have studied history in
the weak calligraphy of songbirds' cages.

Bishop has the structuralist's curiosity. She probably enjoys Levi-Strauss, who also studies "history in/the weak calligraphy of songbirds' cages" in the Brazil of *Tristes Tropiques*. Bishop rests in doubts, proceeds by a tantalizing chain of negative questions (surely it would have been a pity . . . not to have seen . . . not to have heard . . . not to have pondered . . . etc.). The closing lines revisit the world of "Over 2000 Illustrations and a Complete Concordance" but with more abandon, more trust to the apparent randomness of travel and the state of homelessness:

"*Is it lack of imagination that makes us come*
to imagined places, not just stay at home?
Or could Pascal have been not entirely right
about just sitting quietly in one's room?

Continent, city, country, society:
the choice is never wide and never free.
And here, or there . . . No. Should we have stayed at
*   home,*
wherever that may be?"

I said earlier that details are also boundaries for Elizabeth Bishop, that whatever radiant glimpses they afford, they are also set at the vibrant limits of her descriptive powers. "In the Village" and "Questions of Travel" show us what generates this precarious state. "From this the poem springs," Wallace Stevens remarks. "That we live in a place/That is not our own and, much more, not ourselves/And hard it is in spite of blazoned days."[5] Bishop writes under that star, aware of the smallness and dignity of human observation and contrivance. She sees with such a rooted, piercing vision, so realistically, because she has never taken our presence in the world as totally real.

IV

"How had I come to be here?" Bishop asks in a recent poem, "In the Waiting Room."[6] Even more than "In the Village," "In the Waiting Room" invites us to understand Bishop's efforts in an autobiographical light. Revisiting childhood experience, less open to ecstasy than the earlier short story, "In the Waiting Room" recalls the sense of personal loss so often implied behind Bishop's observations. The poem is a melancholy visitation to a childhood world Bishop has earlier ("In the Village") described more joyfully. This time she is accompanying her aunt to the dentist's office.

while I waited I read
the *National Geographic*
(I could read) and carefully
studied the photographs:
the inside of a volcano,
black, and full of ashes;
then it was spilling over
in rivulets of fire.
Osa and Martin Johnson
dressed in riding breeches,
laced boots, and pith helmets.
A dead man slung on a pole
—"Long Pig," the caption said.
Babies with pointed heads
wound round and round with string;
black, naked women with necks
wound round and round with wire
like the necks of light bulbs.
Their breasts were horrifying.

The scream of "In the Village" is heard once again in a return to youthful memories of women in pain. But the scream, this time, is not banished.

Suddenly, from inside,
came an *oh!* of pain
—Aunt Consuelo's voice—
not very loud or long.
I wasn't at all surprised;
even then I knew she was
a foolish, timid woman.
I might have been embarrassed,
but wasn't. What took me
completely by surprise
was that it was *me:*
my voice, in my mouth.
Without thinking at all
I was my foolish aunt,
I—we—were falling, falling,
our eyes glued to the cover
of the *National Geographic,*
February, 1918.

The memory is astonishing, especially in the telling: the way in which "inside" allows us the little girl's own moment of confusion, as the cry seems to be her own. The child, entirely a spectator to others' pain "In the Village," finds unexpectedly that she is prey to it herself at the moment which sentences her to adulthood "In the Waiting Room."

Observation, the spectator's clear and lonely power, is a kind of life-jacket here. The poem is detailed and circumstantial: the child clings to details so as to keep from "sliding/ beneath a big black wave,/another, and another."

> But I felt: you are an *I*
> you are an *Elizabeth*,
> you are one of *them*.
> Why should you be one, too?

The "I" that enters this poem, bearing her very name (the first time Bishop uses it in a poem), has the same staying power, no more, no less than the furniture of the waiting room, the arctics, the overcoats, the shadowy gray knees of the adults in the waiting room—all the sad imprisoning litany of human identity, like the numbers she takes pains to mention: three days until she is seven years old; the fifth of February, 1918. These read like incantations to "stop/the sensation of falling off/the round, turning world/into cold, blue-black space." The very plainness of the poem is what saves her; she is a realist *faute de mieux*, she observes because she has to.

"In the Waiting Room," like other poems Bishop has published since her *Complete Poems* appeared in 1969, rounds a remarkable corner in her career. My impression is that these pieces, collected in *Geography III* (1976), revisit her earlier poems as Bishop herself once visited tropical and polar zones, and that they refigure her work in wonderful ways. "Poem" looks to a small landscape by what must be the same great-uncle, an R. A., who painted the "Large Bad Picture" in her first book, *North & South*. "In the Waiting Room" revisits an awakening to adulthood as seen by the child, the world of "In the Village." "The Moose" recalls the pristine wonder of her Nova Scotia poems, and "Crusoe in England" looks back at a Southern hemisphere even more exotic than her tropical Brazil. In these and other poems, returning to earlier scenes, Bishop has asked more openly what energies fed, pressured, endangered and rewarded her chosen life of travel and clear vision.

Her "questions of travel" modulate now, almost imperceptibly, into questions of memory and loss. Attentive still to landscapes where one can feel the sweep and violence of encircling and eroding geological powers, poems such as "Crusoe in England" and "The Moose" pose their problems retrospectively. Crusoe lives an exile's life in civilized England, lord in imagination only of his "un-rediscovered, un-renamable island." In "The Moose" we are city-bound, on a bus trip away from Nova Scotia, and the long lean poem reads like a thread the narrator is laying through a maze—to find her way back?

"Crusoe in England" re-creates the pleasures and the pains of surviving in a universe of one. News that a new volcano has erupted trips Crusoe's memories of his own island. His way of thinking about it is that an island has been *born*:

> at first a breath of steam, ten miles away;
> and then a black fleck—basalt, probably—
> rose in the mate's binoculars
> and caught on the horizon like a fly.
> They named it. But my poor old island's still
> un-rediscovered, un-renamable.
> None of the books has ever got it right.

The shock of birth, the secret joy of naming, of knowing a place "un-renamable"—these emotions shadow the surface, as they do for the child of "In the Waiting Room." Crusoe's whole poem is pervaded by the play of curiosity. He asks questions, concentrates and then, as Bishop says elsewhere of Darwin, one sees him, "his eye fixed on facts and minute details,

sinking or sliding giddily off into the unknown." The drifts of snail shells on Crusoe's island look from a distance like beds of irises. The next thing we know, they *are* iris beds:

> The books
> I'd read were full of blanks;
> the poems—well, I tried
> reciting to my iris-beds,
> "They flash upon that inward eye,
> which is the bliss. . . ." The bliss of what?
> One of the first things that I did
> when I got back was look it up.

No point in finishing Wordsworth's quote: *imagination* would fill the blank better than *solitude* in this case, but neither is necessary in the presence of Crusoe's joy in the homemade and under the pressure of having to re-invent the world: "the parasol that took me such a time/remembering the way the ribs should go"; the baby goat dyed red with the island's one kind of berry "just to see/something a little different"; a flute, "Homemade, home-made! But aren't we all?" The poem is crowded with fresh experience: hissing turtles, small volcanoes. Crusoe has his longings—one fulfilled when Friday appears. He also has his nightmares. When he is on the island, he dreams about being trapped on infinite numbers of islands, each of which he must in painful detail explore. Back in England the nightmare is just the opposite: that such stimulation, imaginative curiosity and energy will peter out. His old knife ("it reeked of meaning, like a crucifix") seems to have lost its numinous power. The whole poem poses a question about imagination when it is no longer felt to be intimately related to survival. Bishop seems involved with the figure of Crusoe because of the questions *after* travel, a kind of "Dejection Ode" countered by the force and energy that memory has mustered for the rest of the poem. It acts out ways of overcoming and then re-experiencing loss.

Elizabeth Bishop has always written poetry to locate herself—most obviously when she is challenged by the exotic landscapes of North and South. She now performs her acts of location in new ways—sometimes showing the pains and joys of domestication, in poems like "Five Flights Up" and "12 O'Clock News" (the imaginative transformation of the writer's desk into a war-torn landscape). More important is the relocation in time, no longer seeing herself and her characters in long geological—Northern or tropical—perspectives, but in a landscape scaled down to memory and the inner bounds of a human life. What she finds are the pleasures and the fears of something like Crusoe's experience: the live memories of naming, the sudden lapse of formerly numinous figures. Early morning "Five Flights Up," listening to an exuberant dog in a yard next door, to a bird making questioning noises, she feels alive enough to imagine

> gray light streaking each bare branch,
> each single twig, along one side,
> making another tree, of glassy veins . . .

apart enough to conclude

> —Yesterday brought to today so lightly!
> (A yesterday I find almost impossible to lift.)

In another sense the past has its sustaining surprises. "Poem" is about the feelings awakened by a small painting passed down in her family, a landscape apparently by the great-uncle responsible for the "Large Bad Picture" which Bishop approached with diffidence and only submerged affection in *North & South*. In the new poem, the painter's work is welcomed as it brings alive, slowly, a scene from her childhood.

> I never knew him. We both knew this place,
> apparently, this literal small backwater,

looked at it long enough to memorize it,
our years apart. How strange. And it's still loved,
or its memory is (it must have changed a lot).
Our visions coincided—"visions" is
too serious a word—our looks, two looks:
art "copying from life" and life itself,
life and the memory of it so compressed
they've turned into each other. Which is which?
Life and the memory of it cramped,
dim, on a piece of Bristol board,
dim, but how live, how touching in detail
—the little that we get for free,
the little of our earthly trust. Not much.
About the size of our abidance
along with theirs: the munching cows,
the iris, crisp and shivering, the water
still standing from spring freshets,
the yet-to-be-dismantled elms, the geese.

I hear in these guarded, modest, still radiant lines a new note in Bishop's work: a shared pleasure in imaginative intensity, almost as if this remarkable writer were being surprised (you *hear* the surprise in her voice) at the power over loss and change which memory has given her writing. What else is it that we hear in "The Moose," as the bus gets going through a lovingly remembered trip from salt Nova Scotia and New Brunswick, world of her childhood, toward Boston where she now lives? The fog closes in, "its cold, round crystals/form and slide and settle/in the white hens' feathers." They seem to enter an enchanted forest, and she is lulled to sleep by voices from the back of the bus, "talking the way they talked/in the old feather-bed,/peacefully, on and on." A long chain of human speech reassures her: "'Yes . . .' that peculiar/affirmative. 'Yes . . .'/A sharp indrawn breath,/half groan, half acceptance." It is almost as if this discourse and its kinship to her own powers, the storyteller's powers handed down, summon up the strange vision which stops the bus: a moose "towering, antlerless . . . grand, otherworldly"—primitive, but giving everyone a "sweet/sensation of joy." It is "homely as a house/(or, safe as houses)" like the very houses the quieting talk on the bus recalls. The moose seems both to crystallize the silence, security and awe of the world being left behind and to guarantee a nourishing and haunting place for it in memory.

In "The End of March" Bishop follows a looped cord along a deserted beach to a snarl of string the size of a man, rising and falling on the waves, "sodden, giving up the ghost. . . ./A kite string?—But no kite." It might be an emblem for these recent poems which touch on lost or slender connections. Bishop seems more explicit about that than she used to be. Where loss was previously the unnamed object against which the poems ventured forth, it is now one of the named subjects. Her poems say out very naturally: "the little that we get for free,/the little of our earthly trust. Not much." Memory is her way of bringing to the surface and acknowledging as general the experience of losing which has always lain behind her work and which the work attempts to counter. "One Art" is the title Bishop gives to a late villanelle which encourages these very connections.

> The art of losing isn't hard to master;
> so many things seem filled with the intent
> to be lost that their loss is no disaster.
>
> Lose something every day. Accept the fluster
> of lost door keys, the hour badly spent.
> The art of losing isn't hard to master.

The effort to control strong feeling is everywhere in this poem. What falls away—love, homes, dreams—is hopelessly

intertwined with the repeating rhymes which challenge each other at every turn: *master, disaster.*

> I lost my mother's watch. And look! my last, or
> next-to-last, of three loved houses went.
> The art of losing isn't hard to master.
>
> I lost two cities, lovely ones. And, vaster,
> some realms I owned, two rivers, a continent.
> I miss them, but it wasn't a disaster.
>
> —Even losing you (the joking voice, a gesture
> I love) I shan't have lied. It's evident
> the art of losing's not too hard to master
> though it may look like (*Write* it!) like disaster.

The last stubborn heartbreaking hesitation—"though it may look like (*Write* it!) like disaster"—carries the full burden, and finally confidence, of her work, the resolve which just barely masters emptiness and succeeds in filling out, tight-lipped, the form.

If Bishop's writing since *Complete Poems* still displays her tough idiosyncratic powers of observation, it also makes a place for those observations in very natural surroundings of the mind. The title *Geography III* (and its epigraph from "First Lessons in Geography") is at once a bow to her real-life relocation and a deep acknowledgment of the roots of these poems in childhood memory and loss. The time and the space these poems lay claim to are more peculiarly Elizabeth Bishop's own—less geological, less historical, less vastly natural; her poems are more openly inner landscapes than ever before.

Notes

1. Robert Lowell, "On 'Skunk Hour,'" repr. in *Robert Lowell: A Collection of Critical Essays*, ed. Thomas Parkinson (Prentice Hall, 1968), p. 133.
2. Stephen Stepanchev, *American Poetry Since 1945* (Harper and Row, 1965), p. 74.
3. Howard Nemerov, *Reflexions on Poetry & Poetics* (Rutgers University Press, 1972), p. 6.
4. Quoted in Anne Stevenson, *Elizabeth Bishop* (Twayne, 1966), p. 66.
5. *The Collected Poems of Wallace Stevens* (Alfred A. Knopf, 1954), p. 383.
6. Poems in this section are cited from *Geography III* (Farrar, Straus and Giroux, 1976).

JEROME MAZZARO
"Elizabeth Bishop's Particulars"

World Literature Today, Winter 1977, pp. 46–49

Like Marianne Moore, Elizabeth Bishop has resisted the idea that poems are important "because a / high-sounding interpretation can be put on them." In *Twentieth Century Authors: First Supplement* (1955) she expresses her opposition "to making poetry monstrous or boring," noting that "after a session with a few of the highbrow magazines one doesn't want to look at a poem for weeks, much less start writing one." Bishop, however, is not opposed to all close analysis and criticism. Rather, she believes that "no matter what theories one may have, . . . I doubt very much that they are in one's mind at the moment of writing a poem." Indeed, the course of writing a poem often appears to readers of her work as a process of questioning the value of theories of art to what she is saying. Yet she constructs "imaginary gardens" for her "real toads," and what T. S. Eliot has written of Dante can easily be applied to her: more can be learned about how to write poetry from Elizabeth Bishop than from reading the writings of most other poets. If you follow her "without talent, you will at worst be pedestrian and flat; if you follow Shakespeare or Pope without talent, you will make an utter fool of yourself." The ability of others to learn how to write from her poetry has already endeared the work to a number of writers and must in time force critics to deal increasingly with the unique properties that make imitation possible. Hopefully, in the course of their dealing with these properties, critics will not proceed "to talk the very life out of" her work.[1]

My own contact with Bishop's poetry began in the mid-fifties with the publication of *Poems: North & South/A Cold Spring* (1955). I had spent a semester at the Iowa Workshop "making an utter fool of myself" by following other models, and I was just beginning to get some sense of where my poetry might head by reading Marianne Moore's *Collected Poems* and Richard Wilbur's *The Beautiful Changes*. I was struck immediately by Bishop's direct sensuous apprehension of life—her sensitive memory. Details of "The Man-Moth," "Roosters," "The Fish," "The Bight," "At the Fishhouses," "Over 2000 Illustrations and a Complete Concordance," "The Map" and "The Imaginary Iceberg" registered long before I had any idea of what individual poems meant or that her work might submit to "close analysis and criticism." The clutter—the fresh, joyous embracing of detail—seemed far more immediately graspable than the programmatic tensions I had been taught to see in courses. Something close to what Ezra Pound identified as Dante's "precision" seemed common to the language and vision of all three poets, and for all the attention to exact observation that my background in science fostered, precision was missing in my own poetry. I had been trapped into thinking that poetry was theory, vaguenesses and iambic pentameter. I was soon trying to appropriate phrases and their attitudes of exactness into poems like "The Corporal as Puppet" (1960) and "Notes Toward an Elegy for Ben" (1961).

In 1969 I tried unsuccessfully in a review of *The Complete Poems* to deal critically with the lessons I had learned from reading Bishop's poetry. I was able to identify a quality of mapping as vital both to her own work and to my uses of it, but having a map without some assurance of the country it charted reduced me again to vagueness. I identified her variously as a scientist, historian, explorer and miniaturist, celebrating the imagination as the moment's guide to the future and concerned not so much with Deity as with worldly phenomena. Yet the very particularity of these concerns ought to have told me—much as Prince Modupe's father told him—that "maps are liars. . . . The truth of a place is in the joy and the hurt that comes from it." Subsequently my "Elizabeth Bishop and the Poetics of Impediment" (1974) dealt more honestly with joy and hurt as the bases of sensitive memory. Centering on the figure of Edwin Boomer from an early story, I divided her work into concerns about herself, about people whose lives caught her fancy and about what seemed bewilderingly inexplicable.[2] My emphasis on the experiential bases of her sensitive memory, however, did not allow my treating a second quality in the poetry: the movement from sensitive to reflective ideation often parallels a second movement from simple to complex thinking. Increasingly since *Poems: North & South/A Cold Spring*—perhaps as a matter of inclination or age—Bishop has moved her emphasis from direct apprehension to relational awareness, though, as "Night City" (1972) affirms, she is still capable of expanding a single precise image into a powerfully haunting work.[3]

"In the Waiting Room" (1971) provides an excellent illustration of the new relational emphasis.[4] The poem delineates the young poet's awareness that she is part of a general human-

ity by her growing empathy first with an aunt, then with others in the dentist's waiting room and finally with everyone on earth. Set in February 1918, shortly after the poet's departure from Nova Scotia and her grandparents' home, "In the Waiting Room" establishes almost journalistically in its opening lines the who, what, why, where and when of the event. The poet and her aunt are in Worcester, Massachusetts at a dentist's office in winter. The poet is occupying herself while the aunt is in with the dentist. The waiting room is "full of grown-up people, / arctics and overcoats, / lamps and magazines." A copy of *National Geographic* catches the young girl's attention, and she begins to read it, studying the photographs. Carefully established in this opening is the poet's isolation from her aunt, from the grown-up world and from the contents of the magazine. This isolation is soon shattered by the aunt's "*oh! of pain.*" Suddenly, the young girl realizes that it is her, her voice, in her mouth, that she is hearing in her aunt, and the waiting room becomes imagistically the world and the dentist Deity or Necessity. The poet is no longer "an island, entire of itself" but "one of *them,*" and the pronoun includes "Osa and Martin Johnson," "babies with pointed heads," "black, naked women," Aunt Consuelo and her co-waiters in "arctics and overcoats." Recovering from a dizziness that accompanies her new feeling of community, the poet regains her composure, only to have the war and weather intrude.

In the poem's development by particulars one can see something akin to the "comparison by simile to particular phenomena" that Pound finds the "vividness" of Dante dependent upon: "Dante, following the Provençal, says not 'where a river pools itself,' but 'As at Arles, where the Rhone pools itself.'"[5] For her move into adult awareness Bishop chooses the eve of her seventh birthday—the traditional date when children assume moral responsibility—and she provides for the occasion an aunt whose name means "solace." She also tampers with the February 1918 issue of the *National Geographic*, adding to it "Osa and Martin Johnson / dressed in riding breeches," the "dead man slung on a pole," "babies with pointed heads" and the "black, naked women." The particulars—so typical of what one is used to finding in a journal of that kind—echo the flowers and Traveller's Palm that Bishop asked the painter Gregorio Valdez to put in his painting of her rooming house, and it is the rare reader who will question their authenticity. This authenticity is made even more probable by the poem's calculated asides: "I could read" and "I didn't know any / word for it." Again, as in other of her works, suffering "takes place / While someone else is eating or opening a window or just walking dully along"; but here the suffering is not merely off-center, like that of Aunt Consuelo, winter and the war, but centrally life itself. The very process of defining the poem's awareness in terms of the history of their origin embraces the move from simple to complex thinking that is as much the poem's purpose as coming to an understanding of the significance of her "falling off / the round, turning world / into cold, blue-black space."

"Poem" (1972) supports this attention by readers to particulars and experience rather than to any overriding theory of art that one might try to make Bishop's poems representative of.[6] The poem centers on a small painting by the poet's uncle, George Hutchinson. The painting is "about the size of an old-style dollar bill," though it "has never earned any money in its life" and has remained for "seventy years / as a minor family relic." She identifies the painting's subject as Nova Scotia, first by the location's general characteristics and then, as the poem gains subjective power, by her own recollection of the precise place. This momentum is arrested by a history of how the poet came into possession of the painting and knowledge of its painter, but here, too, their both having known the same place, having "looked at it long enough to memorize it" so that their "visions coincided," works to force the poet from the particularities of her own personality. Just as in science, this "freedom" from personality comes with the ability to verify observations made previously and acts as what Eliot in "Tradition and the Individual Talent" (1917) calls "an escape from emotion." In expressing "a particular medium," however, Bishop does not subscribe to an Ideal Form or Platonic *Nous*. Rather, much as John Locke believed that "all our ideas come from experience" and are built upon by "the operations of the mind," she believes that art originates in things that really happened. A medium of expression can bring these experiences into complexity, but the medium should not so distort nature that one comes away feeling that art is an escape from nature or a standardizing process. Like other modernists, Bishop feels that a good work of art, like Valdez's painting of her rooming house, is an extension of nature and takes its own individual place in the world of experience; hence it should be permitted to evolve from its own impulses separately and organically.

A writer, developing as I was when I first discovered Bishop's work, is likely to be impressed most with her movement from simple to complex ideas by line construction, syntax and metaphor. "In the Waiting Room" builds on clusters of seven-syllable lines swelling at times to eight and nine syllables and subsiding to six and five. Stresses, too, vary from two in lines like "My aunt was inside" to four in "wound round and round with string," but the whole is kept "regular" by recurring words and phrases. "In Worcester, Massachusetts" opens the poem and occurs in the opening of the work's final sentence. Variants of "the *National Geographic*" occur three times and "February, 1918" twice—once in connection with Worcester and once in relation to the magazine. Thus the magazine and city are united by reference in a way which makes clear that the experiences of the one are to flow into the experiences of the other. Repetition is also used for intensity in the modulation of "waited" and "waiting room" and in the close echoing of "wound round and round with string" and "wound round and round with wire" before Bishop gives us first a deflating metaphor ("like the necks of light bulbs") and then an emotion ("Their breasts were horrifying"). But just as repetition occurs to heighten, it occurs to suggest randomness by seemingly haphazard placement. The parallelism of "The waiting room / was full of grown-up people" and "The waiting room was bright / and too hot" is obscured by the first statement's beginning in mid-line, whereas the second not only begins at the margin but also opens a stanza. Similarly, the syntactical balance of "I knew that nothing stranger / had ever happened, that nothing / stranger could ever happen" is thrown off by the way the sentence is lined.

Without Bishop's sense of syntax these repetitions and variations could founder into monotony or chaos. The lines are constructed so as not only to bring out the sense of the situation but also to make smooth transitions into metonymy and implied metaphor. Thus, in lines 8–9, "grown-up people" move among "arctics and overcoats, / lamps and magazines." Simultaneously the "inside" which comprises the waiting room will reverberate by a kind of mathematical substitution with the "inside" where Consuelo is being treated, the "inside" of the *National Geographic*, "the inside of a volcano," the "inside" of the poet's mind and finally the "inside" of life's flow, implied by her being at last "back in it." A comparable reverberation occurs with "outside." But a novice writer is likely to give less

emphasis than he ought to the flexibility that results from the poem's attention to particulars. This attention allows the moral and metaphysical speculation that goes on in the poem and at the same time helps to militate against a sentimentality that a poetics based on experience encourages. The absurdities of the world as a dentist's waiting room, the dentist as God or Necessity, dental pain as a prelude to world suffering and even the loss of control by which the poet hopes to make the poem's coming together more credible are all dependent on the reader's acceptance of a natural world; for, as her friend Flannery O'Connor rightly noted in "The Novelist and Free Will" (1961), "I think that the more a writer wishes to make the supernatural apparent, the more real he has to be able to make the natural world, for if the readers don't accept the natural world, they'll certainly not accept anything else."[7] One has, consequently, the almost journalistic opening and "factuality" carrying, so to speak, the "weight" of the poem's abstractions.

Something similar occurs in "Manners" and "First Death in Nova Scotia" from *Questions of Travel* (1965). Set in the summer of 1918, "Manners" realizes the freeing impact of formality on a child's emotions. Written in quatrains to emphasize the formalism of both the subject and the way in which the simple ideas of experience build into complexity, the poem recounts the grandfather's telling her "to always / speak to everyone you meet." A succession of meetings follows, first with "a stranger on foot," then with "a boy we knew," his crow, and lastly with automobiles, as manners extend to man, beast and machine. Finally, coming to Hustle Hill, they get down from the wagon and walk so as to make less work for their tired mare. Again, as in "In the Waiting Room," depersonalization is related to a repetition that allows the formation of the impersonal by blurring the particulars of time, place and individuals. A bit less formal, "First Death in Nova Scotia" recounts events surrounding the death of the poet's cousin Arthur. The poem explores the lies that are told children about dying: Arthur is invited "to be / the smallest page at court," but already the young poet has seen through this fiction. She knows that he resembles the dead, stuffed loon, and she questions how he can go "clutching his tiny lily, / with his eyes shut up so tight / and the roads deep in snow." Both poems establish the importance of factual tones by their negations of fictions and, as such, are perhaps not so daring as "In the Waiting Room," which accepts this negation by moving away from formal structure and poetic tradition toward a syncretic, almost aleatory structure. Yet, as if to remind her readers of her own wide range, Bishop balances this movement away from closed form with "Sestina" and, more recently, a villanelle, "One Art" (1976).[8]

In occasionally moving away from traditional structures Bishop is doing something similar to what critics of Pound say he did by moving away from iambic pentameter. Much as he opened the ear to new rhythms and new kinds of matter, she, in these nonformal, relational poems, opens the formal elements of poetry to new possibilities for seeing and tracking life. Her poetry thus challenges old codifications that tradition and theories of art place *a priori* to vision, and in keeping with the modernist biases that shape her early writing, her approach remains sensitive to exploration. The exploration exists not so much that she may "seek new human emotions to express" but that she may "use the ordinary ones" and in ways different from her contemporaries John Berryman and Robert Lowell. As they "used the language as if [they] made it" and thereby made their languages personal and inimitable, she purifies the language we all use, making it less "slushy and inexact" and less "excessive and bloated" than it was before. Writers recognize their own diction in hers and therefore can imitate her more profitably than they can follow Berryman or Lowell. It is a mark of that diction, moreover, that not only young poets learn from it. Lowell has acknowledged the impact of Bishop's diction in the reshaping of his style for *Life Studies* (1959), and in my own case, I am constantly being taught in significant ways new degrees and uses of particulars. As a poet and critic I can understand why, having unburdened herself of many of the old codifications that tradition and theories of art place on a writer's imagination, she is hesitant about embracing "art theory," "analysis and criticism" and "high-sounding interpretation." Having rid herself of one "prison," she will not rush knowingly headlong into a new one, and we are all beneficiaries of her decision.

Notes

1. Marianne Moore, "Poetry," *Collected Poems*, New York, Macmillan, 1951, pp. 40–41; "Elizabeth Bishop," *Twentieth Century Authors: First Supplement*, Stanley Kunitz, ed., New York, Wilson, 1955, pp. 88–89; T. S. Eliot, *Selected Essays*, London, Faber & Faber, 1951, p. 252.
2. Jerome Mazzaro, "Elizabeth Bishop's Poems," *Shenandoah*, 20 (Summer 1969), pp. 99–101; Jerome Mazzaro, "Elizabeth Bishop and the Poetics of Impediment," *Salmagundi*, no. 27 (Summer-Fall 1974), pp. 118–44; Prince Modupe, *I Was a Savage*, London, Museum, 1958, p. 133.
3. "Night City," *New Yorker*, 48 (16 September 1972), p. 122.
4. "In the Waiting Room," *New Yorker*, 47 (17 July 1971), p. 34.
5. Ezra Pound, *The Spirit of Romance*, London, Dent, 1910, p. 159.
6. "Poem," *New Yorker*, 48 (11 November 1972), p. 46.
7. Flannery O'Connor, "The Novelist and Free Will," *Fresco*, n.s. 1 (Winter 1961), pp. 100–101.
8. "One Art," *New Yorker*, 52 (26 April 1976), p. 40.

WILLARD SPIEGELMAN
"Elizabeth Bishop's 'Natural Heroism'"
Centennial Review, Winter 1978, pp. 28–44

In her genial invitation to Marianne Moore to come flying over the Brooklyn Bridge one fine morning for a *fête urbaine*, Elizabeth Bishop conjures up an image of Miss Moore borne aloft like the good witch of Oz, shoes trailing sapphires, cape full of butterflies, hat decked with angels. Defined by fey and glittering objects, and not quite a part of this world, Moore rises "above the accidents, above the malignant movies" of profane life, while listening to "a soft uninvented music," like Keats's spiritual toneless ditties. She floats up, "mounting the sky with natural heroism."[1] This is a curious phrase, since we are likely to think of the hero as one set apart in his superiority or struggle, and of his status as one not easily achieved. If anything, heroism and nature are antithetical. In Bishop's work, however, the "natural hero" occupies a privileged position which is unattainable by the super- or unnatural exploits of masculine achievement which the poetry constantly debunks. For Bishop, as for Stevens, "the man-hero is not the exceptional monster." This, in itself, is nothing new: ever since Wordsworth attempted to democratize the language and the subjects of poetry, his Romantic heirs have focused on ordinariness and on the self-conscious meditative habits which turn heroism inward. But Bishop goes beyond even Wordsworth's radical break with the past.[2] Her hero replaces traditional ideas of bravery with a blend of domestic and imaginative strengths. The highest value in Bishop's work is a politely

sceptical courage which neither makes outrageous demands on the world nor demurely submits to the world's own.

To understand Bishop's natural heroism, and her kinship with, yet movement beyond, Wordsworth, I wish to look at three types of poems, all tinged with her qualifying scepticism. First, there are those which trace the outline of heroic situations or devices and then negate or undercut them; second, those which internalize an encounter or conflict and, in the manner of a Romantic crisis lyric make the act of learning itself a heroic process, but which also dramatize the avoidance of apocalypse that Geoffrey Hartman has located at the heart of Wordsworth's genius;[3] and finally those in which the *via negativa* of denial or avoidance implies Bishop's positive values, poems where a dialectical struggle between two contestants is resolved by an assertion of heroic worth.

I

At her most playful, Bishop insinuates heroic, mythological allusions, often with a tentative, amused tone, so that their full impact is softened. In "House Guest," she wonders, "Can it be that we nourish / one of the Fates in our bosoms?" but Clotho is only an inept seamstress. Eros (in "Casabianca") is reduced to the obstinate boy standing on the burning deck, trying to recite Mrs. Hemans' "The boy stood on the burning deck." Hyperion-Apollo, the Romantics' fair-haired youth of morn, becomes some "ineffable creature" whose daily appearance and fall (in "Anaphora") are purposely rendered by a series of effects on his beholders, as if Bishop is too modest to describe or even name the god himself.

More important in Bishop's habitual tactic of diminution or undercutting is the way certain ideas of masculine greatness are filed down or eroded to their essential littleness. "The Burglar of Babylon" deprives its eponymous hero of his glory by recounting, in child-like ballad quatrains, his life as a petty criminal sought by a whole army of police who finally, and unceremoniously, kill him. As Ezra Pound is revealed through the expanding stanzas (modelled on "This is the house that Jack built") of "Visits to St. Elizabeth's," his simple nobility is smothered by the weakness, fragility, and insipidity of the other inmates. The stanzas enlarge, and as Pound is seen in a setting (the literal one of the hospital, the figurative one of the syntactic, grammatical units of increasing complexity) he moves from "tragic," "honored," and "brave," to "cranky," "tedious," and "wretched." The clichés of masculine conquest are exploded in "Brazil, January, 1502," and in the first half of "Roosters." In the first poem, the Portuguese invaders are no better than aroused, predatory jungle lizards. Their "old dream of wealth and luxury" provokes them to the attempted rapacious destruction of landscape and native women. In "Roosters," virility and combativeness, "the uncontrolled, traditional" virtues that create "a senseless order," are mocked by the image of the roosters as pompous, puffed-up military dictators ("Deep from protruding chests / in green-gold medals dressed") and as colorful metallic map-marking pins (the lizards and Christians in the previous poem were also hard, glinting, metallic): "Glass-headed pins, / oil-golds and copper greens, / anthracite blues, alizarins, / each one an active / displacement in perspective; / each screaming, 'This is where I live.'" Like Stevens' Chief Iffucan, Bishop's roosters virtually squawk "Fat! Fat! Fat! Fat! I am the personal," and she witnesses the "vulgar beauty" of their iridescence as well as their lunatic, pseudo-heroic fighting swagger. Even the unmilitary Gentleman of Shalott, who has been domesticated (as if Sir Lancelot, originally seen in the mirror in Tennyson's poem, has come indoors to replace the lady who died for love of him), and who is reflected in profile by the mirror, is only a shadow of his total self. Resigned and uncertain, "he loves that sense of constant re-adjustment. / He wishes to be quoted as saying at present: / 'Half is enough.'" His partner, in Bishop's first volume, is the Man-Moth, a curious creature from an imaginary bestiary, the inspiration for whose creation (a newspaper misprint for mammoth) epitomizes Bishop's metamorphosizing and whimsical imagination. As mammoth, he is literally extinct, as man-moth, confected and precarious.

It is tempting to write off these playful inhabitants of Bishop's world as cousins of Moore's fanciful animals and flowers. But even the most fragile bear weightier implications. The bravado, false heroics, and metallic sheen of the cocks, for example, as well as the speaker's scorn and patronizing amusement, are replaced in the second half of "Roosters" by a new perspective and a softer voice. No longer mock warriors, the roosters become emblems of human sin and the promise of Christian forgiveness. Peter's denial of Christ at the cock's crowing is sculpted in stone as a tangible reminder of his weakness and his master's love. Even the little rooster is "seen carved on a dim column in the travertine." If you look hard enough, in other words, the fighting cock of the first part of the poem can be seen anew. Peter's tears and the cock's call are bound together, both in action and its symbolic representation: "There is inescapable hope, the pivot: / yes, and there Peter's tears / run down our chanticleer's / side and gem his spurs." As Peter was long ago forgiven, so we still learn that "'Deny deny deny' / is not all the roosters cry." Spurs encrusted with tears mark the transformation of militancy into humility.

In the poem's last section, Bishop returns to her opening picture of daybreak, and the difference in her imagery alerts us to the distance between braggadocio and the roosters' subsequent Christian meekness. The opening was a military fanfare:

> At four o'clock
> in the gun-metal blue dark
> we hear the first crow of the first cock
>
> just below
> the gun-metal blue window
> and immediately there is an echo
>
> off in the distance,
> then one from the backyard fence,
> then one, with horrible insistence,
>
> grates like a wet match
> from the broccoli patch,
> flares, and all over town begins to catch.

The final view moves us to a slightly later stage of the dawn, gentler and tamed, as the roosters have literally ceased to crow, their threat having been figuratively replaced by the promise of forgiveness and natural harmony:

> In the morning
> a low light is floating
> in the backyard, and gilding
>
> from underneath
> the broccoli, leaf by leaf;
> how could the night have come to grief?
>
> gilding the tiny
> floating swallow's belly
> and lines of pink cloud in the sky,
>
> the day's preamble
> like wandering lines in marble.
> The cocks are now almost inaudible.
>
> The sun climbs in,
> following "to see the end,"
> faithful as enemy, or friend.

Moving as it is, "Roosters" is not typical of Bishop's work. For one thing, the vocabulary of Christian belief appears only rarely in her poetry, and her imagination is more secular than religious (in "A Miracle for Breakfast," there are mysterious hints of communion, or of the miracle of the loaves and fishes, but these are never clarified). For another, the studied symmetry, the juxtaposition of opposing views which augment one another, seems too easy. More typical is "Wading at Wellfleet," a short, early lyric which encompasses the tensions I've discussed and diminishes or deflects heroic action more subtly than "Roosters":

> In one of the Assyrian wars
> a chariot first saw the light
> that bore sharp blades around its wheels.
>
> That chariot from Assyria
> went rolling down mechanically
> to take the warriors by the heels.
>
> A thousand warriors in the sea
> could not consider such a war
> as that the sea itself contrives
>
> but hasn't put in action yet.
> This morning's glitterings reveal
> the sea is "all a case of knives."
>
> Lying so close, they catch the sun,
> the spokes directed at the shin.
> The chariot front is blue and great.
>
> The war rests wholly with the waves:
> they try revolving, but the wheels
> give way; they will not bear the weight.

The poem is deceptively simple; even its playfulness shows Bishop's ability to take a natural event (named in the title), establish it within a larger metaphoric context, and then surprise us by defusing the bomb she herself has lit. As in "Roosters," glittering danger—here in the opening military details—is evoked like a "false surmise" and then reduced, but unlike "Roosters," "Wading at Wellfleet" avoids simple dualisms. It is, instead, both neatly divided into three parts and, at the same time, seamless in its verbal repetitions and unity. The three pairs of stanzas are isolated by rhyme and subject matter. In the first, we have a backward historical glance at Biblical battles (with, I suspect, a whispered reminder of Byron's "The Destruction of Sennacherib"); in the second, the central image of the beach on Cape Cod; and in the third, a dialectical synthesis which paradoxically unites and separates the terms of the first two. The first section introduces the poem's major concept (danger) in the guise of military activity, and its first important image (sharp light) in the off-handed pun of line 2. The same wit is present in lines 5 and 6, where "rolling" sets us up for the last stanza ("revolving") and "heels" reminds us of the title ("Wading"). The second section explicitly combines the light and dazzle of the first with this day's water, and brings the Assyrian warriors into an imaginary relationship with the speaker (they become *any* warriors). The pivotal image is conditional and deliberately vague: we want to know whether any sea has ever put into action its threat, or whether the Atlantic, this particular ocean on this particular day, has been withholding its power. As it surprisingly turns out, the sea is a paper tiger, like the roosters, because it is constitutionally incapable of making real the threat which the human observer has imagined (like the scared speaker in Frost's "Once by the Pacific" who supposes that the waves "thought of doing something to the shore / That water never did to land before"). The dialectical synthesis of the last stanzaic pair, then, is imagistic only (the sea-chariot-light configuration). The waves reflect, but can never duplicate, the knife-like sharpness of the sun, itself an image of the chariot wheel (the pun in Herbert's "case of knives" suggests the same weakening of the military motifs), and their revolution is their destruction as they roll over and past the feet of the wader.

II

The frequency with which Bishop attacks and transforms military formulas, forays, and glory shows her grappling with received values and ideas, and struggling toward new ones. In "Roosters" the replacement is clear and easy, and in "Wading at Wellfleet" it is cunningly avoided by disarming the military apparatus which is the poem's unifying force without filling the void it leaves. In their dealings with large themes, these poems are relatively minor when compared with others which bring us to the very edge of imaginative revelation and then hold back. Scepticism, an unwillingness to approve either major conflicts or major revelations, is common to both groups. Heroism is undercut in the first poems, and in the next group we should not be surprised to learn that even meditative, epistemological problems (i.e., encounters between a speaker and a natural scene or object) can be subjected to the same deflating treatment. The dangers and traumas of knowledge are posed and then removed. This is, as Geoffrey Hartman has shown, the standard strategy of Wordsworth, who first plunges into some shadowy terrain within the heart or mind of man and then, when scared by what he might learn there, withdraws and calls it "nature." To raise a threat and then to dissipate it, not so much out of fear or cowardice as out of ontological scepticism (which, in "Wading at Wellfleet" and others, is disguised as polished lightheartedness) is Bishop's way as well. "Cape Breton" and "The Moose," two of her longer poems, sustain the anxieties of the shorter lyrics and build toward larger statements.[4]

Masquerading as a description of a natural scene, "Cape Breton" is a glimpse into a heart of darkness. Indeed, Bishop's vision is to Conrad's as Marlow's is to Kurtz's:

> . . . he had made that last stride, he had stepped over the
> edge, while I had been permitted to draw back my hesitating foot . . .
> perhaps . . . all truth, and all sincerity, are just compressed into
> that inappreciable moment of time in which we step over
> the threshold of the invisible.

Throughout, descriptive data are balanced by suggestions of absence, disappearance, and vacancy: "Cape Breton" is more about what is not there than what is. The opening images are negated: we see an uneven line of birds, but their backs are toward us, and we hear some sheep whose fearfulness, we are parenthetically told, causes them occasionally to stampede over the rocks into the sea. Water and mist are the salient features of this world, melting into each other, "weaving . . . and disappearing," and "the pulse, / rapid but unurgent, of a motorboat" is incorporated by the mist, while the boat's invisible body is obliterated.

The delicate beauty enfolded within and by the secret ministry of mist evinces both dissipation (". . . like rotting snowice sucked away / almost to spirit") and erosion ("the ghosts of glaciers drift / among those folds and folds of fir . . . dull, dead, deep peacock-colors"). Having set the scene in a primal, almost Gothic chill, the speaker proceeds to human, domestic details, but with the same plan of taking away with one hand what the other offers. There is a road along the coast with "small yellow bulldozers" but no activity: "without their drivers, because today is Sunday." There are "little white churches" (all the human details are deliberately dwarfed) in the hills but they, too, are vestiges of some unknown past, "like lost quartz arrowheads." The central revelation comes now and, as we might expect, it is one of human and epistemological emptiness:

> The road appears to have been abandoned,
> Whatever the landscape had of meaning appears to have been abandoned,
> unless the road is holding it back, in the interior,
> where we cannot see,
> where deep lakes are reputed to be,
> and disused trails and mountains of rock
> and miles of burnt forest standing in gray scratches
> like the admirable scriptures made on stones by stones.

The disappointment is double: the evidence of the eye leads us to nothing (we see no meaning), and the possibility of hidden truth is buried beneath hearsay ("reputed to be") and the geological palimpsests which can be seen and read only by the Kurtzes of the world. All that the speaker is able to hear these regions "say for themselves" is the song of the small sparrows, themselves too fragile to last, sustain meaning, or provide comfort: ". . . floating upward / freely, dispassionately, through the mist, and meshing / in brown-wet, fine, torn fish-nets."

The next verse paragraph looks as if it will announce a major turn in the poem, but we learn that Bishop's singular devotion to the painting of emptiness here deceives us with apparently human images. A bus, packed with people, comes into view, but once again a parenthetical afterthought reduces fullness to relative emptiness:

> (On weekdays with groceries, spare automobile parts, and pump parts,
> but today only two preachers extra, one carrying his frock coat on a hanger.)

Passing a closed roadside stand, a closed schoolhouse ("where today no flag is flying"), the bus finally emits two passengers, a man with a baby, who immediately vanish in "a small steep meadow, / which establishes its poverty in a snowfall of daisies," to return "to his invisible house beside the water." The human dimension is teasingly put into, and then erased from, the picture where even natural details are muted, softened, and so delicately and charmingly miniaturized that we might almost forget the accumulated horror that they are surely meant to convey. Indeed, as the bus itself pulls off, the birds keep on singing, normal activity, such as it is, resumes, and the poem ends like a surrealistic movie (e.g., *Blow-Up*) where, in a field, a man stands and then quite simply vanishes, as if he were never there. There remains only the mist which covers and swallows all:

> The thin mist follows
> the white mutations of its dream;
> an ancient chill is rippling the dark brooks.

Who has been dreaming, really: the mist which encompasses everything, or the human viewer who thought she saw a man on a bus? Both the landscape and its meaning have been abandoned in a cinematic sleight-of-hand that calls into question the very grounds of our knowing.

Though not as chilling in its implications, "The Moose" follows a similar course of isolating the speaker, and presenting her with the potential dangers of encounter with the unknown, but here, instead of remaining uncertain and tantalizing, the threat is destroyed. A heart of darkness, in "Cape Breton," is implied but experientially unknowable; in "The Moose," the midnight danger is tamed and domesticated, its sting removed. The poem begins as a series of farewells, as a bus moves west and south in late afternoon from Nova Scotia to Boston. The light darkens, the fog gathers round, "a lone traveller" says goodbye to family and dog. Moonlight surrounds the bus as it enters New Brunswick's forests, and the passengers sink together into their private dreams, divagations, and conversations, some overheard by others (". . . not concerning us,/but recognizable, somewhere, / back in the bus"). Two-thirds of the way through the poem, as a sense of comfort enables the travelers to succumb finally to sleep, the bus stops with a jolt, halted by a creature from the deep, dark interior:

> A moose has come out of
> the impenetrable wood
> and stands there, looms, rather,
> in the middle of the road.

But the moose is no memento of the inner depths, nor a visitor from the heart of the night. The only revelation is of the beast's harmless, almost personable curiosity as she sniffs the bus. And yet the very plainness of the beast, an emblem of the plainness of the experience of confronting it, provokes a question which Bishop refrains from answering directly:

> Taking her time,
> she looks the bus over,
> grand, otherworldly.
> Why, why do we feel
> (we all feel) this sweet
> sensation of joy?

Grand but "awful plain," the moose becomes an occasion for a shared experience, a common sense of surmounting a momentary fright (which in this case is hardly heroic) followed by the re-union, in separate contentment, of the passengers with one another.

III

Habitually, then, we see Bishop constructing situations in which disaster is averted, or at worst insinuated gently enough so as to appear harmless. We can go even further, however, to discover that active confrontation with physical or intellectual danger may yield lessons of wisdom and strength of purpose to narrators and characters in a third group of poems.

Bishop's "natural" (i.e., either automatic, "in the nature of things," or common, "universal") heroism comes clear in many of these poems, among them the terrifying "In the Waiting Room," the only one in which her own name appears. The seven-year-old Elizabeth, waiting while her aunt is in the dentist's chair, learns two primal lessons: of human pain and mortality, as she hears her aunt scream; and of unity in spite of human differences as she looks at African pictures in a *National Geographic*, and sinks into a confused semi-consciousness. She speaks her name ("you are an I, / you are an *Elizabeth*"), asserting her essential individuality, while simultaneously entertaining a nightmare vision of the universal sameness of all people: herself, Aunt Consuelo, the native African women, and the other patients in the office. This crisis lyric describes both a revelation and the joint horror and acceptance it provokes in the girl who has now, irrevocably, entered into her rational maturity. For all its differences in tone and language, it is Bishop's "Immortality" Ode, where we see the light of common day begin its irreversible movement in the child's consciousness. For Wordsworth, years bring the philosophic mind to the adult who is, at the same time, borne down by the

accumulated baggage of deadly custom and stale imitation. But where Wordsworth's manic willingness to be cheerful in the face of frost ("We in thought will join your throng") is the key to his own heroism, Bishop tentatively accepts continuity and community as bulwarks against separateness. Hence the circular structure of the poem which nakedly returns to the opening details of time and place, relocating the child after her momentary blackout in this very world, "which is," in Wordsworth's phrase, "the world of all of us." The "sweet sensation of joy" which unites the riders in "The Moose" is now replaced by an awful wonder at the fact of unity when one feels most alone:

> Why should I be my aunt,
> or me, or anyone?
> What similarities—
> . . .
> held us all together
> or made us all just one?
> How—I didn't know any
> word for it—how "unlikely."

The unlikely but perfectly natural realization that we have all of us one human heart is the crucial beginning, in Bishop's view of the self, of a transformation of isolation into community (on the egoism of the child, cf. Wordsworth's remark, "I was often unable to think of external things as having external existence"). In maturity, as opposed to childhood, it is joy that brings the separate travelers together.

It is no surprise that Bishop should instinctively be a poet of *places*, because the conditions of placement—stasis, domesticity, routine, community—compensate for her natural humility in the face of the greater "world" where she often feels estranged. The attractions of travel are its dangers ("Questions of Travel" presents the philosophical dimensions of the debate between movement and rest): hence poems like "Cape Breton" and "The Moose" which depict the avoidance of revelation of which I've written (significantly, the passengers in the bus are united by joy when the bus is stopped; when it starts up again, it leaves behind "a dim / smell of moose, an acrid / smell of gasoline"). Conversely, the domestic coziness of Bishop's Brazilian poems invokes traditional pastoral ideas of rest and also the relief that accompanies a sense of belonging in a harmonious community. In this context, the apparent oxymoron in "natural heroism" is erased: the heroic self does not stand apart from his tribe by virtue of either suffering or action (nor is he isolated like Man-Moth, Portuguese invaders, or Pound); rather, by synecdoche, he exemplifies his community.

Since he does not stand alone, the hero is usually presented as part of a group, or especially a pair. The confrontations between people in Bishop's work are sometimes ambivalent and tricky: high and low, victor and victim, master and servant, are likely to change places. The relationship of patron and tenant-farmer in "Manuelzinho" turns upon the seeming inequality between them and upon their reversal of roles, when "superior" and "inferior" lose all meaning. Manuelzinho, a blessed fool, magical and hexed, can grow nothing, and the frustrations of his employer, affectionately but exasperatingly listed, proclaim the distance between his child-like wonder and her mature sensibleness. But this distance is reduced by love, first the patronizing affection of adult for child, then gradually the accumulated sense of dependence on Manuelzinho for more than mere amusement. Figurative exaggerations become statements of fact, just as fancy begins to assume solidity:

> Account books? they are Dream Books.
> In the kitchen we dream together

how the meek shall inherit the earth—
or several acres of mine.

Colorful harlequin, aged child, and useless necessity, Manuelzinho, without his knowing it, occasions humility and warmth in his patron so that, at the poem's end, their positions have been reversed. In this quasi-feudal relationship, propriety demands courteous generosity from both, especially from the patron whose plea for understanding and forgiveness is one of those gestures in Bishop's work that reaffirm human community between equals and prove that heroism need be neither grandiose nor excessive. Having mocked Manuelzinho's ridiculous, painted hats, the speaker doffs her own to him in a kind act of homage:

> One was bright green. Unkindly,
> I called you Klorophyll Kid.
> My visitors thought it was funny.
> I apologize here and now.
> You helpless, foolish man
> I love you all I can,
> I think. Or do I?
> I take off my hat, unpainted
> and figurative, to you.
> Again I promise to try.

"I could have laughed myself to scorn to find / In that decrepit Man so firm a mind," Wordsworth's surprised response to his leech-gatherer, is equivalent to the sustenance which this speaker derives from Manuelzinho. Where Bishop surpasses Wordsworth, however, where her egoism is simply less intense, is in her continual insistence on the need for symbiosis: mutual support, rather than epiphanies wrought by otherworldly visitors, is the key to natural polity, as well as piety. Her other long poem about master and servant ("Faustina, or Rock Roses") also dramatizes "service," but through images that reflect and complement one another, it turns hierarchy into a bizarre democracy. Here it is difficult to know who is master—the white woman, shrivelled and dying, or Faustina, the black servant whose own freedom is imminent but whose current status is ambivalent. The uncertainty of the human relationship is depicted in the opening stanza:

> Tended by Faustina
> yes in a crazy house
> upon a crazy bed,
> frail, of chipped enamel,
> blooming above her head
> into four vaguely roselike
> flower formations,
> the white woman whispers to
> herself.

We must infer an initial ellipsis ("The rock roses are . . . tended by Faustina") to grasp the full, functional ambiguity of the lines: the servant is caretaker of sculptured flowers (which metamorphose into a visitor's gift of real flowers at the end of the poem) and of the white woman, equally "frail" and "chipped," lying in "white disordered sheets / like wilted roses," beside a crooked table littered with chalky powder, cream, and pills, in a room where each rag contributes "its / shade of white, confusing / as undazzling." The poem is a still life, a study in dessicated whiteness, with a human analogue. Faustina's "terms of employment" ("terms" suggesting both time and condition) are complained of, and explained to, the visitor. Her "sinister kind face" poses an unanswerable riddle of her own feelings about the mistress' approaching death and her own survival; the ambiguous antecedent of "it" is both the senora's *and* the servant's conditions:

> Oh, is it
> freedom at last, a lifelong
> dream of time and silence,
> dream of protection and rest?
> Or is it the very worst,
> the unimaginable nightmare
> that never before dared last
> more than a second?

"There is no way of telling" is the closest thing to a response as mistress and servant, polar opposites, one dying and one living, converge in the ambivalent haze of this syntax.

We do not normally think of Bishop as a poet of struggle; the tension in her poems is mostly internalized, and confrontations, when they occur, are between the self, traveling, moving, or simply seeing, and the landscape it experiences. But in "Manuelzinho" and "Faustina" we have two pairs of agonists, locked in relationships of affection and struggle from which there is no release in life. In fact, Bishop's most anthologized poem, "The Fish," is more typical of its author than we might suspect. It depicts external and internal conflict, and a heroic action which is perfectly "natural" in its motivation and accomplishment. It follows the pattern I have traced for all of Bishop's poems so far, thus making it a paradigm in her work: an action is intimated and then undercut; next, a mild revelation, hardly heralded, occurs, and then a positive reaction proves the speaker's heroism. The simple experience literally surrounds the reasons for it ("I caught a tremendous fish," line 1, "and I let the fish go," line 76). We first see deflation: the tremendous fish is caught with no struggle whatsoever, and, like the moose, turns out to be anything but dangerous: "He hung a grunting weight, / battered and venerable / and homely." It is not for the absence of a good fight, or as a testimony to the grim veteran who has struggled in the past, that the speaker releases her catch. More important to her action are the accumulated details of her revelation. These involve an anthropomorphizing of the adversary (as in "Roosters" and "The Moose") and, as a result of a camaraderie, an aesthetic epiphany which preempts and therefore obliterates the military antagonism hinted at earlier in the poem.

The description of the fish (the bulk of the poem) domesticates him (his skin is like wallpaper; there are rosettes of lime and rags of seaweed on him; the swim-bladder is peony-like), while not omitting reminders of his potential danger ("the frightening gills that can cut so badly," "his sullen face, / the mechanism of his jaw"). Stressing the fish's familiarity *and* otherness, the speaker transforms him into a veteran fighter, a survivor of many contests who wears the remnants of old fish-lines in his lower lip like battle scars or "medals with their ribbons / frayed and wavering, / a five-haired beard of wisdom / trailing from his aching jaw."

The revelation has two parts: first, the new picture which the speaker's imaginative perception has created; and second, the way this new image of the fish colors and alters her environment. For an analogue to the heroic dimension of the poem we have only to look at Wordsworth's encounters with spectral, ghastly figures (leech-gatherer, beggar, discharged soldier) who are shocking, at first, because of their sub-humanness and who subsequently chastise and instruct Wordsworth in the "unlikely" connections among us all. In his famous description, the leech-gatherer is changed from a rock into a giant sea-beast finally assuming his full human identity. Likewise, Bishop's fish undergoes a series of revisions which build to create his final symbolic weight.

The aesthetic nature of this experience, by which the fish is literally *seen* and metaphorically tamed, is the final cause of the speaker's release of him. Looking hard at her opponent, Bishop moves beyond military conquest to a "victory" in which both contestants have a part: "I stared and stared / and victory filled up / the little rented boat." The last twelve lines return us to the model of the Wordsworthian nature lyric,[5] first in their insistence on a mesmerizing vision (cf. "I gazed and gazed" in "I Wandered Lonely as a Cloud"), next in the metaphoric "wealth" which this show brings, and last, in a muted reminder of the covenant and the natural piety emblemized by a rainbow inspiring confidence and joy through a feeling of connection with the world. It is a nice detail that this feeling comes in a "rented boat" (perhaps a reminiscence of Wordsworth's stolen boat) where the speaker is a natural outsider:

> I stared and stared
> and victory filled up
> the little rented boat,
> from the pool of bilge
> where oil had spread a rainbow
> around the rusted engine
> to the bailer rusted orange,
> the sun-cracked thwarts,
> the oarlocks on their strings,
> the gunnels—until everything
> was rainbow, rainbow, rainbow!
> And I let the fish go.

Victory, then, comes with neither the catching of the fish (almost accidental) nor its release (virtually automatic) but with the conjunction of two antagonists, heroic by virtue of their endurance (the fish, like the leech-gatherer, is admirable for merely surviving), their embodiment or perception of natural beauty, and the harmony of visual detail which reflects their personal connections. For Bishop, natural heroism becomes not the elimination, or conquest, of the enemy, but the embracing, subsuming, and internalizing of him. In the largest sense, separateness is denied, and victory is earned: another name for her heroism is love.

Notes

1. References are to Elizabeth Bishop, *The Complete Poems* (New York: Farrar, Straus, and Giroux, 1969), and *Geography III* (New York: Farrar, Straus, and Giroux, 1976).
2. For a discussion of Bishop's connections with the Romantic nature lyrics of Wordsworth and Coleridge, see my "Landscape and Knowledge: The Poetry of Elizabeth Bishop," *Modern Poetry Studies*, 6 (1975), 203–24. The present essay is a continuation of certain ideas suggested and presented in the earlier one.
3. Geoffrey Hartman, *Wordsworth Poetry 1787–1811* (New Haven: Yale University Press, 1964), pp. 40–60 and passim.
4. One could examine other poems as well, such as "Question of Travel," "The Imaginary Iceberg," "Over 2000 Illustrations and a Complete Concordance," or, for the pain of knowledge, "At the Fishhouses," and "In the Waiting Room." I dealt with all of these in my first Bishop essay.
5. The best analysis of this kind of poem is M. H. Abrams, "Structure and Style in the Romantic Nature Lyric," in *From Sensibility to Romanticism*, eds. Frederick W. Hilles and Harold Bloom (New York: Oxford University Press, 1965), pp. 527–28.

HELEN VENDLER
"Elizabeth Bishop"
Part of Nature, Part of Us
1980, pp. 97–110

Elizabeth Bishop's poems in *Geography III* put into relief the continuing vibration of her work between two frequencies—the domestic and the strange. In another poet the alternation might seem a debate, but Bishop drifts rather than divides, gazes rather than chooses. Though the exotic is frequent in her poems of travel, it is not only the exotic that is strange and not only the local that is domestic. (It is more exact to speak, with regard to Bishop, of the domestic rather than the familiar, because what is familiar is always named, in her poetry, in terms of a house, a family, someone beloved, home. Ant it is truer to speak of the strange rather than of the exotic, because the strange can occur even in the bosom of the familiars, even, most unnervingly, at the domestic hearth.)

To show the interpenetration of the domestic and the strange at their most inseparable, it is necessary to glance back at some poems printed in *Questions of Travel*. In one, "Sestina," the components are almost entirely innocent—a house, a grandmother, a child, a Little Marvel Stove, and an almanac. The strange component, which finally renders the whole house unnatural, is tears. Although the grandmother hides her tears and says only "It's time for tea now," the child senses the tears unshed and displaces them everywhere—into the dancing waterdrops from the teakettle, into the rain on the roof, into the tea in the grandmother's cup.

> . . . the child
> is watching the teakettle's small hard tears
> dance like mad on the hot black stove
> the way the rain must dance on the house . . .
> . . . the almanac
> hovers half open above the child,
> hovers above the old grandmother
> and her teacup full of dark brown tears.

The child's sense of the world is expressed only in the rigid house she draws (I say "she," but the child, in the folk-order of the poem, is of indeterminate sex). The child must translate the tears she has felt, and so she "puts . . . a man with buttons like tears" into her drawing, while "the little moons fall down like tears / from between the pages of the almanac, into the flower bed the child / has carefully placed in the front of the house."

The tercet ending the sestina draws together all the elements of the collage:

> *Time to plant tears*, says the almanac.
> The grandmother sings to the marvellous stove
> and the child draws another inscrutable house.

The absence of the child's parents is the unspoken cause of those tears, so unconcealable though so concealed. For all the efforts of the grandmother, for all the silence of the child, for all the brave cheer of the Little Marvel Stove, the house remains frozen, and the bland center stands for the definitive presence of the unnatural in the child's domestic experience—*especially* in the child's domestic experience. Of all the things that should not be inscrutable, one's house comes first. The fact that one's house always *is* unscrutable, that nothing is more enigmatic than the heart of the domestic scene, offers Bishop one of her recurrent subjects.

The centrality of the domestic provokes as well one of Bishop's most characteristic forms of expression. When she is not actually representing herself as a child, she is, often, sounding like one. The sestina, which borrows from the eternally childlike diction of the folktale, is a case in point. Not only the diction of the folktale, but also its fixity of relation appears in the poem, especially in its processional close, which places the almanac, the grandmother, and the child in an arrangement as unmoving as those found in medieval painting, with the almanac representing the overarching Divine Necessity, the grandmother as the elder principle, and the child as the principle of youth. The voice speaking the last three lines dispassionately records the coincident presence of grief, song, necessity, and the marvelous; but in spite of the "equal" placing of the last three lines, the ultimate weight on inscrutability, even in the heart of the domestic, draws this poem into the orbit of the strange.

A poem close by in *Questions of Travel* tips the balance in the other direction, toward the domestic. The filling station which gives its name to the poem seems at first the antithesis of beauty, at least in the eye of the beholder who speaks the poem. The station is dirty, oil-soaked, oil-permeated; the father's suit is dirty; his sons are greasy; all is "quite thoroughly dirty"; there is even "a dirty dog." The speaker, though filled with "a horror so refined," is unable to look away from the proliferating detail which, though this is a filling station, becomes ever more relentlessly domestic. "Do they live in the station?" wonders the speaker, and notes incredulously a porch, "a set of crushed and grease- / impregnated wickerwork," the dog "quite comfy" on the wicker sofa, comics, a taboret covered by a doily, and "a big hirsute begonia." The domestic, we perceive, becomes a compulsion that we take with us even to the most unpromising locations, where we busy ourselves establishing domestic tranquillity as a demonstration of meaningfulness, as a proof of "love." Is our theology only a reflection of our nesting habits?

> Why the extraneous plant?
> Why the taboret?
> Why, oh why, the doily? . . .
> Somebody embroidered the doily.
> Somebody waters the plant,
> or oils it, maybe. Somebody
> arranges the rows of cans
> so that they softly say:
> ESSO-SO-SO-SO
> to high-strung automobiles.
> Somebody loves us all.

In this parody of metaphysical questioning and the theological argument from design, the "awful but cheerful" activities of the world include the acts by which man domesticates his surroundings, even if those surroundings are purely mechanical, like the filling station or the truck in Brazil painted with "throbbing rosebuds."

The existence of the domestic is most imperiled by death. By definition, the domestic is the conjoined intimate: in American literature the quintessential poem of domesticity is "Snowbound." When death intrudes on the domestic circle, the laying-out of the corpse at home, in the old fashion, forces domesticity to its ultimate powers of accommodation. Stevens' "Emperor of Ice-Cream" places the cold and dumb corpse at the home wake in grotesque conjunction with the funeral baked meats, so to speak, which are being confected in the kitchen, as the primitive impulse to feast over the dead is seen surviving, instinctive and barbaric, even in our "civilized" society. Bishop's "First Death in Nova Scotia" places the poet as a child in a familiar parlor transfixed in perception by the presence of a coffin containing "little cousin Arthur":

> In the cold, cold parlor
> my mother laid out Arthur
> beneath the chromographs:
> Edward, Prince of Wales,
> with Princess Alexandra,
> and King George with Queen Mary.
> Below them on the table
> stood a stuffed loon
> shot and stuffed by Uncle
> Arthur, Arthur's father.

All of these details are immemorially known to the child. But focused by the coffin, the familiar becomes unreal: the stuffed loon becomes alive, his taciturnity seems voluntary, his red glass eyes can see.

> Since Uncle Arthur fired
> a bullet into him,
> he hadn't said a word.
> He kept his own counsel . . .
> Arthur's coffin was
> a little frosted cake,
> and the red-eyed loon eyed it
> from his white, frozen lake.

The adults conspire in a fantasy of communication still possible, as the child is told, "say good-bye / to your little cousin Arthur" and given a lily of the valley to put in the hand of the corpse. The child joins in the fantasy, first by imagining that the chill in the parlor makes it the domain of Jack Frost, who has painted Arthur's red hair as he paints the Maple Leaf of Canada, and next by imagining that "the gracious royal couples" in the chromographs have "invited Arthur to be / the smallest page at court." The constrained effort by all in the parlor to encompass Arthur's death in the domestic scene culminates in the child's effort to make a gestalt of parlor, coffin, corpse, chromographs, loon, Jack Frost, the Maple Leaf Forever, and the lily. But the strain is too great for the child, who allows doubt and dismay to creep in—not as to ultimate destiny, oh no, for Arthur is sure to become "the smallest page" at court, that confusing place of grander domesticity, half-palace, half-heaven; but rather displaced onto means.

> But how could Arthur go,
> clutching his tiny lily,
> with his eyes shut up so tight
> and the roads deep in snow?

Domesticity is frail, and it is shaken by the final strangeness of death. Until death, and even after it, the work of domestication of the unfamiliar goes on, all of it a substitute for some assurance of transcendent domesticity, some belief that we are truly, in this world, in our mother's house, that "somebody loves us all." After a loss that destroys one form of domesticity, the effort to reconstitute it in another form begins. The definition of death in certain of Bishop's poems is to have given up on domesticating the world and reestablishing yet once more some form of intimacy. Conversely, the definition of life is the conversion of the strange to the familial, of the unexplored to the knowable, of the alien to the beloved.

No domesticity is entirely safe. As in the midst of life we are in death, so, in Bishop's poetry, in the midst of the familiar, and most especially there, we feel the familiar as the unknowable. This guerrilla attack of the alien, springing from the very bulwarks of the familiar, is the subject of "In the Waiting Room." It is 1918, and a child, almost seven, waits, reading the *National Geographic*, while her aunt is being treated in the dentist's office. The scene is unremarkable: "grown-up people, / arctics and overcoats, / lamps and magazines," but two things unnerve the child. The first is a picture in the magazine: "black, naked women with necks / wound round and round with wire / like the necks of light bulbs. / Their breasts were horrifying"; and the second is "an *oh!* of pain / —Aunt Consuelo's voice" from inside. The child is attacked by vertigo, feels the cry to be her own uttered in "the family voice" and knows at once her separateness and her identity as one of the human group.

> But I felt: you are an *I*,
> you are an *Elizabeth*,

you are one of *them*.
Why should you be one too?

. . .

What similarities—
boots, hands, the family voice
I felt in my throat, or even
the *National Geographic*
and those awful hanging breasts—
held us all together
or made us all just one?

In "There Was a Child Went Forth" Whitman speaks of a comparable first moment of metaphysical doubt:

. . . the sense of what is real, the thought if after all it
should prove unreal,
The doubts of day-time and the doubts of night-time,
the curious whether and how,
Whether that which appears so is so, or is it all
flashes and specks?
Men and women crowding fast in the streets, if they
are not flashes and specks what are they?

It is typical of Whitman that after his momentary vertigo he should tether himself to the natural world of sea and sky. It is equally typical of Bishop, after the waiting room slides "beneath a big black wave, / another, and another," to return to the sober certainty of waking fact, though with a selection of fact dictated by feeling.

The War was on. Outside,
in Worcester, Massachusetts,
were night and slush and cold,
and it was still the fifth
of February, 1918.

The child's compulsion to include in her world even the most unfamiliar data, to couple the exotica of the *National Geographic* with the knees and trousers and skirts of her neighbors in the waiting room, brings together the strange at its most horrifying with the quintessence of the familiar—oneself, one's aunt, the "family voice." In the end, will the savage be domesticated or oneself rendered unknowable? The child cannot bear the conjunction and faints. Language fails the six-year-old. "How—I didn't know any / word for it—how 'unlikely.'"

That understatement, so common in Bishop, gives words their full weight. As the fact of her own contingency strikes the child, "familiar" and "strange" become concepts which have lost all meaning. "Mrs. Anderson's Swedish baby," says Stevens, "might well have been German or Spanish." Carlos Drummond de Andrade (whose rhythms perhaps suggested the trimeters of "In the Waiting Room") says in a poem translated by Bishop:

Mundo mundo vasto mundo,
se eu me chamasse Raimundo
seria uma rima, não seria uma
solução.

If one's name rhymed with the name of the cosmos, as "Raimundo" rhymes with "mundo," there would appear to be a congruence between self and world, and domestication of the world to man's dimensions would seem possible. But, says Drummond, that would be a rhyme, not a solution. The child of "In the Waiting Room" discovers that she is in no intelligible relation to her world, and, too young yet to conceive of domination of the world by will or domestication of the world by love, she slides into an abyss of darkness.

In "Poem" ("About the size of an old-style dollar bill") the poet gazes idly at a small painting done by her great-uncle and begins yet another meditation on the domestication of the world. She gazes idly—that is, until she realizes that the painting is of a place she has lived: "Heavens, I recognize the place, I know it!" In a beautiful tour de force "the place" is described three times. The first time it is rendered visually, exactly, interestedly, appreciatively, and so on: such, we realize, is pure visual pleasure touched with relatively impersonal recognition ("It must be Nova Scotia; only there / does one see gabled wooden houses / painted that awful shade of brown"). Here is the painting as first seen:

Elm trees, low hills, a thin church steeple
—that gray-blue wisp—or is it? In the foreground
a water meadow with some tiny cows,
two brushstrokes each, but confidently cows;
two minuscule white geese in the blue water,
back-to-back, feeding, and a slanting stick.
Up closer, a wild iris, white and yellow,
fresh-squiggled from the tube.
The air is fresh and cold; cold early spring
clear as gray glass; a half inch of blue sky
below the steel-gray storm clouds.

Then the recognition—"Heavens, I know it!"—intervenes, and with it a double transfiguration occurs: the mind enlarges the picture beyond the limits of the frame, placing the painted scene in a larger, remembered landscape, and the items in the picture are given a local habitation and a name.

Heavens, I recognize the place, I know it!
It's behind—I can almost remember the farmer's
name.
His barn backed on that meadow. There it is,
titanium white, one dab. The hint of steeple,
filaments of brush-hairs, barely there,
must be the Presbyterian church.
Would that be Miss Gillespie's house?
Those particular geese and cows
are naturally before my time.

In spite of the connection between self and picture, the painting remains a painting, described by someone recognizing its means—a dab of titanium white here, some fine brushwork there. And the scene is set back in time—those geese and cows belong to another era. But by the end of the poem the poet has united herself with the artist. They have both loved this unimportant corner of the earth; it has existed in their lives, in their memories and in their art.

Art "copying from life" and life itself,
life and the memory of it so compressed
they're turned into each other. Which is which?
Life and the memory of it cramped,
dim, on a piece of Bristol board,
dim, but how live, how touching in detail
—the little that we get for free,
the little of our earthly trust. Not much.

Out of the world a small piece is lived in, domesticated, remembered, memorialized, even immortalized. Immortalized because the third time that the painting is described, it is seen not by the eye—whether the eye of the connoisseur or the eye of the local inhabitant contemplating a past era—but by the heart, touched into participation. There is no longer any mention of tube or brushstrokes or paint colors or Bristol board; we are in the scene itself.

. . . Not much.
About the size of our abidance
along with theirs: the munching cows,
the iris, crisp and shivering, the water
still standing from spring freshets,
the yet-to-be-dismantled elms, the geese.

Though the effect of being in the landscape arises in part from the present participles (the munching cows, the shivering iris, the standing water), it comes as well from the repetition of nouns from earlier passages (cows, iris), now denuded of their "paint" modifiers ("two brushstrokes each," "squiggled from the tube"), from the replication of the twice-repeated early "fresh" in "freshets" and most of all from the prophecy of the "yet-to-be-dismantled" elms. As lightly as possible, the word "dismantled" then refutes the whole illusion of entire absorption in the memorial scene; the world of the child who was once the poet now seems the scenery arranged for a drama with only too brief a tenure on the stage—the play once over, the set is dismantled, the illusion gone. The poem, having taken the reader through the process that we name domestication and by which a strange terrain becomes first recognizable, then familiar, and then beloved, releases the reader at last from the intimacy it has induced. Domestication is followed, almost inevitably, by that dismantling which is, in its acute form, disaster, the "One Art" of another poem:

> I lost my mother's watch. And look! my last, or
> next-to-last of three loved houses went . . .
>
> I lost two cities, lovely ones. And, vaster,
> some realms I owned, two rivers, a continent . . .
>
> the art of losing's not too hard to master
> though it may look like (*Write it!*) like disaster.

That is the tone of disaster confronted, with whatever irony.

A more straightforward account of the whole cycle of domestication and loss can be seen in the long monologue, "Crusoe in England." Crusoe is safely back in England, and his long autobiographical retrospect exposes in full clarity the imperfection of the domestication of nature so long as love is missing, the exhaustion of solitary colonization.

> . . . I'd have
> nightmares of other islands
> stretching away from mine, infinities
> of islands, islands spawning islands,
> like frogs' eggs turning into polliwogs
> of islands, knowing that I had to live
> on each and every one, eventually
> for ages, registering their flora,
> their fauna, their geography.

Crusoe's efforts at the domestication of nature (making a flute, distilling home brew, even devising a dye out of red berries) create a certain degree of pleasure ("I felt a deep affection for / the smallest of my island industries"), and yet the lack of any society except that of turtles and goats and waterspouts ("sacerdotal beings of glass . . . / Beautiful, yes, but not much company") causes both self-pity and a barely admitted hope. Crusoe, in a metaphysical moment, christens one volcano "*Mont d'Espoir* or *Mount Despair*," mirroring both his desolation and his expectancy. The island landscape has been domesticated, "home-made," and yet domestication can turn to domesticity only with the arrival of Friday: "Just when I thought I couldn't stand it / another minute longer, Friday came." Speechless with joy, Crusoe can speak only in the most vacant and consequently the most comprehensive of words.

> Friday was nice.
> Friday was nice, and we were friends.
> . . . he had a pretty body.

Love escapes language. Crusoe could describe with the precision of a geographer the exact appearances of volcanoes, turtles, clouds, lava, goats, and waterspouts and waves, but he is reduced to gesture and sketch before the reality of domesticity.

In the final, recapitulatory movement of the poem Bishop first reiterates the conferral of meaning implicit in the domestication of the universe and then contemplates the loss of meaning once the arena of domestication is abandoned.

> The knife there on the shelf—
> it reeked of meaning, like a crucifix.
> It lived . . .
> I knew each nick and scratch by heart . . .
> Now it won't look at me at all.
> The living soul has dribbled away.
> My eyes rest on it and pass on.

Unlike the meanings of domestication, which repose in presence and use, the meaning of domesticity is mysterious and permanent. The monologue ends:

> The local museum's asked me to
> leave everything to them:
> the flute, the knife, the shrivelled shoes . . .
> How can anyone want such things?
> —And Friday, my dear Friday, died of measles
> seventeen years ago come March.

The ultimate locus of domestication is the heart, which, once cultivated, retains its "living soul" forever.

This dream of eternal and undismantled fidelity in domesticity, unaffected even by death, is one extreme reached by Bishop's imagination as it turns round its theme. But more profound, I think, is the version of life's experience recounted in "The Moose," a poem in which no lasting, exclusive companionship between human beings is envisaged, but in which a series of deep and inexplicable satisfactions unroll in sequence, each of them precious. Domestication of the land is one, domesticity of the affections is another, and the contemplation of the sublimity of the nonhuman world is the third.

In this first half of the poem one of the geographies of the world is given an ineffable beauty, both plain and luxurious. Nova Scotia's tides, sunsets, villages, fog, flora, fauna, and people are all summoned quietly into the verse, as if for a last farewell, as the speaker journeys away to Boston. The verse, like the landscape, is "old-fashioned."

> The bus starts. The light
> is deepening; the fog
> shifting, salty, thin,
> comes closing in.
>
> Its cold, round crystals
> form and slide and settle
> in the white hens' feathers,
> in gray glazed cabbages,
> on the cabbage roses
> and lupins like apostles;
>
> the sweet peas cling
> to wet white string
> on the whitewashed fences;
> bumblebees creep
> inside the foxgloves,
> and evening commences.

The exquisitely noticed modulations of whiteness, the evening harmony of settling and clinging and closing and creeping, the delicate touch of each clause, the valedictory air of the whole, the momentary identification with hens, sweet peas, and bumblebees all speak of the attentive and yielding soul through which the landscape is being articulated.

As darkness settles, the awakened soul is slowly lulled into "a dreamy divagation / . . . / a gentle, auditory, slow hallucination." This central passage embodies a regression into childhood, as the speaker imagines that the muffled noises in the bus are the tones of "an old conversation":

> Grandparents' voices
> uninterruptedly
> talking, in Eternity:
> names being mentioned,
> things cleared up finally . . .
> Talking the way they talked
> in the old featherbed,
> peacefully, on and on . . .
> Now, it's all right now
> even to fall asleep
> just as on all those nights.

Life, in the world of this poem, has so far only two components: a beloved landscape and beloved people, that which can be domesticated and those who have joined in domesticity. The grandparents' voices have mulled over all the human concerns of the village:

> what he said, what she said,
> who got pensioned;
> deaths, deaths and sicknesses;
> the year he re-married;
> the year (something) happened.
> She died in childbirth.
> That was the son lost
> when the schooner foundered.
> He took to drink. Yes.
> She went to the bad.
> When Amos began to pray
> even in the store and
> finally the family had
> to put him away.
> "Yes . . ." that peculiar
> affirmative. "Yes . . ."
> A sharp, indrawn breath,
> half-groan, half-acceptance.

In this passage, so plainly different in its rural talk and sorrow from the ravishing aestheticism of the earlier descriptive passage, Bishop joins herself to the Wordsworth of the *Lyrical Ballads*. The domestic affections become, for a moment, all there is. Amos who went mad, the son lost at sea, the mother who died, the girl gone to the bad—these could all have figured in poems like "Michael" or "The Thorn." The litany of names evoking the bonds of domestic sympathy becomes one form of poetry, and the views of the "meadows, hills, and groves" of Nova Scotia is another. What this surrounding world looks like, we know; that "Life's like that" (as the sighed "Yes" implies), we also know. The poem might seem complete. But just as the speaker is about to drowse almost beyond consciousness, there is a jolt, and the bus stops in the moonlight, because "A moose has come out of / the impenetrable wood." This moose, looming "high as a church, / homely as a house," strikes wonder in the passengers, who "exclaim in whispers, / childishly, softly." The moose remains.

> Taking her time,
> she looks the bus over,
> grand, other-worldly.
> Why, why do we feel
> (we all feel) this sweet
> sensation of joy?

What is this joy?

In "The Most of It" Frost uses a variant of this fable. There, as in Bishop's poem, a creature emerges from "the impenetrable wood" and is beheld. But Frost's beast disappoints expectation. The poet had wanted "counter-love, original response," but the "embodiment that crashed" proves to

be not "human," not "someone else additional to him," but rather a large buck, which disappears as it came. Frost's beast is male, Bishop's female; Frost's a symbol of brute force, Bishop's a creature "safe as houses"; Frost's a challenge, Bishop's a reassurance. The presence approaching from the wood plays, in both these poems, the role that a god would play in a pre-Wordsworthian poem and the role that a human being—a leech-gatherer, an ancient soldier, a beggar—would play in Wordsworth. These human beings, when they appear in Wordsworth's poetry, are partly iconic, partly subhuman, as the Leech-Gatherer is part statue, part sea-beast, and as the old man in "Animal Tranquility and Decay" is "insensibly subdued" to a state of peace more animal than human. "I think I could turn and live with animals," says Whitman, foreshadowing a modernity that finds the alternative to the human not in the divine but in the animal. Animal life is pure presence, with its own grandeur. It assures the poet of the inexhaustibility of being. Bishop's moose is at once maternal, inscrutable, and mild. If the occupants of the bus are bound, in their human vehicle, to the world of village catastrophe and pained acknowledgment, they feel a releasing joy in glimpsing some large, grand solidity, even a vaguely grotesque one, which exists outside their tales and sighs, which is entirely "otherworldly." "The darkness drops again," as the bus moves on; the "dim smell of moose" fades in comparison to "the acrid smell of gasoline."

"The Moose" is such a purely linear poem, following as it does the journey of the bus, that an effort of will is required to gaze at it whole. The immediacy of each separate section—as we see the landscape, then the people, then the moose—blots out what has gone before. But the temptation—felt when the poem is contemplated entire—to say something global, something almost allegorical, suggests that something in the sequence is more than purely arbitrary. The poem passes from adult observation of a familiar landscape to the unending ritual, first glimpsed in childhood, of human sorrow and narration, to a final joy in the otherworldly, in whatever lies within the impenetrable wood and from time to time allows itself to be beheld. Beyond or behind the familiar, whether the visual or the human familiar, lies the perpetually strange and mysterious. It is that mystery which causes those whispered exclamations alternating with the pained "Yes" provoked by human vicissitude. It guarantees the poet more to do. On it depends all the impulse to domestication. Though the human effort is bent to the elimination of the wild, nothing is more restorative than to know that earth is larger than our human enclosures. Elizabeth Bishop's poetry of domestication and domesticity depends, in the last analysis, on her equal apprehension of the reserves of mystery which give, in their own way, a joy more strange than the familiar blessings of the world made human.

BONNIE COSTELLO
"The Impersonal and the Interrogative in the Poetry of Elizabeth Bishop" (1977)
Elizabeth Bishop and Her Art
1983, pp. 109–32

In Elizabeth Bishop's poetry, geography is not for adventurers looking out from a center at the horizon, nor for imperialists seeking to appropriate that horizon. Rather, it is the recourse of those hoping to discover, out of the flux of images, where they are and how to get home again. Bishop's poetry accepts our uncertain relation to other times, places, and things, suggesting we have no "self" otherwise, and no home.

It is in this context that I would like to discuss the pervasiveness of the impersonal and the interrogative in her work. I want to show that, paradoxically, for Bishop, questions are assertions. However open-endedly, they structure experience and self-awareness. Like compasses, they point to something absolute we can neither see nor get to; yet in their pointing, they show us where we are. The questions, posed to an impersonal world, turn inward when it refuses to reply. Questions about the world become, then, obliquely, questions about ourselves. While the personal begins in assumptions about the self, the impersonal usually undermines or ignores the self. But in Bishop's poetry the impersonal is not depersonalized because its form is interrogative rather than negative.

These impersonal and interrogative modes tend to promote a feeling of disunity and disorientation, but for Bishop these are precisely the conditions conducive to discovery. Not surprisingly, travel is her major metaphor. Almost every poem treats the experience of travel ambivalently, for while finalities may be static or illusory, constant change is unsettling. Bishop does not resolve this ambivalence, but she eases it by offering her characters, and her readers, fleeting but calming moments of coalescence.

In discussing the significance of the impersonal and the interrogative. I will consider the entire scope of Bishop's poetic achievement. I will focus, however, on central poems from the recent volume, *Geography III*, which most fully express the positive value of these modes. The epigraph to *Geography III*, from *First Lessons in Geography*, begins with questions and answers; but the answers are soon dropped and only the questions continue. They are, we learn, firmer and more real than the answers. Bishop was always a student of geography, but her third level of geography steps back, slightly, from all the travelling, charting, and measuring, to consider the motives and impulses behind these activities. She still asks, Where is Nova Scotia? and Where is Brazil? but in the latest work she opens up previously implicit questions: "*What is a Map?*" and "*What is Geography?*", versions of: What am I doing? and What and where am I?

Such emerging self-consciousness is present in the very earliest poems, but less explicitly. "The Map" opens *North & South* with an assertion, but characteristically calls it immediately into question, into a series of questions, and these become the mode of attention throughout as Bishop looks at a printed map.

> Land lies in water; it is shadowed green.
> Shadows, or are they shallows, at its edges
> showing the line of long sea-weeded ledges
> where weeds hang to the simple blue from green.
> Or does the land lean down to lift the sea from
> 　　under,
> drawing it unperturbed around itself?
> Along the fine tan sandy shelf
> is the land tugging at the sea from under?

Each observation leads to a new uncertainty and a new inquiry. These questions are never answered, but neither does the poem conclude as a personal complaint over the relativity and limitation of our interpretations. Instead, our curiosity persists. For all its ambiguity, the map engages our attention, draws us into a consideration of the world.

> We can stroke these lovely bays,
> under a glass as if they were expected to blossom,
> or as if to provide a clean cage for invisible fish.

We are wrong, of course; the bays will not blossom, and the glass separates us from the object of our desire, but the imagination is not repelled by these facts. We affirm the printer's excitement, even if it does "exceed its cause." There is a pleasure in inquiry and conjecture for their own sake here; we feel no great pressure to resolve the questions posed, or to define a single perspective, a legend, by which the map can be consistently translated. The poem enjoys these very shifts of focus, from landscape to map, from map to words.

If anything, it is the imagination which is explored here, rather than the landscape. Questions put impersonally to an impersonal object turn inward. Indeed, the land is to the sea as we are to both.

> These peninsulas take the water between thumb and
> 　　finger
> like women feeling for the smoothness of yard-goods.

The poem becomes, as it proceeds, an inquiry into the nature of perspective. Its conclusions are not about the land but about the map:

> Topography displays no favorites; North's as near as
> 　　West.
> More delicate than the historians' are the map-
> 　　makers' colors.

While the personal is initially preempted by the interrogative, questions do eventually lead us to an awareness of our situation.

The seven-year-old heroine of "In the Waiting Room," the first poem in *Geography III*, asks no questions at first, having little trouble knowing who or where she is:

> In Worcester, Massachusetts,
> I went with Aunt Consuelo
> to keep her dentist's appointment
> and sat and waited for her
> in the dentist's waiting room.

But wintery Worcester recedes into twilight, and the apparent hierarchy of time and space goes with it. Her aunt *seems* to be inside a long time, while she reads and studies the photographs of far-off places in the *National Geographic*. Then, the hinges of distance and duration come loose and the constructed self flaps precariously. The very layout of the magazine presses ordered differences into explosive proximity, forcing a violently widened definition of the human. The decorously English, well-protected "Osa and Martin Johnson / dressed in riding breeches, / laced boots, and pith helmets," stand side by side with the vulnerable and contagious "dead man slung on a pole," "babies with pointed heads," and "black, naked women" with "horrifying" breasts, creating a "perspective by incongruity" on humanity.

The child doesn't articulate her fascination, of course, but the very fact that she is "too shy to stop" implies that she is somehow brought home to herself here. She fixes her eyes on "the cover: / the yellow margins, the date" as a way of avoiding contact, but these form a fragile interface. The date, which should be a way of protecting boundaries, becomes rather a sign of contact between this strange world and her own. She loses her balance over the side of the cover, and in a sudden moment of undifferentiation between Aunt Consuelo and herself, a cry "from inside" the dentist's office seems to come literally "from inside" her mouth. "I—we—were falling, falling, / our eyes glued to the cover / of the *National Geographic*, / February, 1918." She clings to the cover as to the rung of a ladder which has come loose from the structure supporting it. The bits and pieces of the personal ("three days / and you'll be seven years old") no longer have much meaning.

The intensity and strangeness of the experience derive not only from the slip into undifferentiation, but from the sense of difference preserved. This is not a pure moment of symbiosis, for there is always an emphasis on how "unlikely" this likeness is. The similarity between Osa and Martin Johnson and the "black, naked women" is never expressed except in the fact of juxtaposition, although the image of the volcano forces them together by its implied threat to human life. Similarly, the difference between the child and her "foolish, timid" Aunt is preserved even while it is denied by the cry of pain. This sense of differences is especially clear in the awkwardness of the child's attempts to come to terms with the experience: "you are an *I*, / you are an *Elizabeth*, / you are one of *them*." Making self both subject and predicate, she still preserves the difference.

A shocking experience of identification, as we have seen, creates a simultaneous loss of original identity, and this loss is never overcome. The inscrutable volcano, the inside of the child's mouth, the dentist's chamber, are all figures for the abyss the child has discovered, and as she peers into it she is full of questions, another and another—why? what? how?—until she is thrown back into the exclamatory "how 'unlikely'" and it is clear they will never be answered. But the transformation of question into exclamation does create a sense of recognition, even if it is the permanently strange that is recognized. We get only a "sidelong glance," not fulfillment or total recognition. Yet, for a moment, this glance does begin to organize the dualities toward some unutterable simplicity. The questions mediate between absolute difference and undifferentiation, between stillness and total flux, and in this way, however fleetingly, accommodate the self most. The experience in the dentist's office never attains a new, more genuine orientation. But in a fundamental way, the speaker is "brought home to herself" by moving through these questions, even while they are left unanswered. Indeed, many of Bishop's characters lose themselves to find themselves. Like the speaker in George Herbert's "Love Unknown," which Bishop has juxtaposed with this poem,[1] the young Elizabeth is made "new, tender, quick" through her sudden disorientation. It serves as a kind of baptism. In one sense, then, the child experiences a traumatic leap into the impersonal, the unfamiliar. But in a more profound sense, she discovers the personal. Somehow she would have been less herself, finally, if she had picked up *Dick and Jane*, a mirror of her own complacent sense of herself, rather than the *National Geographic*. Probably both were there for her on the waiting room table. But the inquisitive mind goes toward what is not obviously of the self, and it is clear that even then, Bishop was a traveller at heart.

In Bishop's poetry, such moments of confrontation, however powerful, are always transient. The pressure of the questioning pushes the room to a volcanic limit as it grows "bright / and too hot," and the child begins "sliding / beneath a big black wave, / another, and another," as if beneath a lava flow. But when the flow subsides, finally, the world is left ashen and silent. The adult vision, the dormant volcano that the child inherits, has none of the security of her childhood world of "grown-up people, / arctics and overcoats, / lamps and magazines."

> Then I was back in it.
> The War was on. Outside,
> in Worcester, Massachusetts,
> were night and slush and cold,
> and it was still the fifth
> of February, 1918.

There is no stability in "night and slush and cold" and certainly none in war. In many ways the molten, self-annihilating questions are preferable to these dismally impersonal facts. For the adult narrator, memory is a way of reentering the charged moment of self-recognition, of escaping the bleak inheritance of certainty without security.

We have seen that Bishop constantly questions her surroundings, and inevitably in the process, questions her perspective. The usual comfort of home is, of course, that we can take it for granted, but for this very reason Bishop is never quite "at home." In the poem under discussion she is, in fact, in a "waiting room." There is certainly no place more impersonal. But precisely because she is not "at home," discovery is possible. A waiting room has very little definition as a place in itself—it is not a home or a destination, but only a transitional space where transitional time is spent. The object of those gathered there, what binds them, does not take place in the room they share but elsewhere, individually. And because it has no function in its own right, it is a place where anything can happen.

Most of the enclosed places Bishop describes are waiting rooms in one way or another (the most extreme being a wake). Her ports, islands, bights, are not microcosms of, or escapes from, history; they contain the tides of unity and discontinuity, of presence and absence, with much the same incompleteness as any wider experience of flux. But while they do not frame or displace the world, do not define us as a home does, they do become places to encounter the world in a focused way. In "The Bight" (from *A Cold Spring*), the speaker observes signs of an uncontainable amount of activity, crashing, soaring, scooping, all of it partaking in one way or another in an amorphous sky, shore and sea. The white boats are "not yet salvaged" and remind us of "unanswered letters." Pelicans dive "unneccessarily hard," "rarely coming up with anything to show for it." All the various efforts to grab hold of nature are "untidy," like the dredge which digs beneath what is seen and brings up not a neat bundle, but a "dripping jawful of marl." And yet Bishop seems to enjoy this messy business; it is "awful but cheerful." Like many of her poems this one finally affirms all endeavors to grasp and form and partake of the world, however insufficiently.

Bishop's characters never appear in places of origin or destination. Her poems are not without idealized dwellings, but these are only viewed from the outside, in a speculative attitude. The "cages for infinity" that Joseph Cornell created (described in a translation of Octavio Paz's "Objects and Apparitions") are seen from the outside, even in writing, for things "hurry away from their names." The proto-/crypto-dream-house of "The End of March" where otherness is happily contained in self-reflection, in the "diaphanous blue flame . . . doubled in the window," is "perfect" but "boarded up." The reality of the beach strollers is temporal, and so is their knowledge. Their vision of the house remains conjectural:

> a sort of artichoke of a house, but greener
> (boiled with bicarbonate of soda?),
> protected from spring tides by a palisade
> of—are they railroad ties?
> (Many things about this place are dubious.)
>
> . . .
>
> There must be a stove; there *is* a chimney,
> askew, but braced with wires,
> and electricity, possibly
> —at least, at the back another wire
> limply leashes the whole affair
> to something off behind the dunes.

The passage reveals the uncertainty with which the strollers observe this "dream house." They can only guess what it is made of, what holds it together, or how to reconstruct it for themselves. There is always "something off behind the dunes," beyond the reach of sight and insight. It seems that the whole world is "indrawn" this day, so that the possibility of contact is minimal and the imagination must make much of very little. But again, speculation is pleasurable. Since the world denies us final access to its secrets, we are left with much speculative freedom, not only about externals, but about ourselves as well. For the self is as "indrawn" in the scene as everything else. The closest the speaker gets to a stable image of herself is the house, and that is, of course, "boarded up." Similarly, in trying to find the "lion" that left the "lion-prints" on the beach, the strollers imaginatively identify him with the sun, a kind of absolute, but relative with respect to themselves, caught up in time.

Often Bishop's characters are not only displaced themselves, but disarming to others by their conspicuous vagabondage. The incorrigible Manuelzinho (in the poem of that name), "half squatter, half tenant (no rent)," works on the imagination of his mistress in spite of herself. His refusal to do as he is supposed to do—his refusal, for instance, to call a dead man dead, to respond to the conventional order of things—challenges the order she works to preserve, suggesting that she too is in some fundamental way a squatter in a world that resists human interests. All the boundaries of the personal are literally called into question. And yet in trying to incorporate the beautifully bizarre reality of Manuelzinho's gardens, his mistress' own world becomes more appealing. Similarly, the "House Guest," the "sad seamstress," challenges the "home life" to which she won't subscribe, causing us to ask, "can it be that we nourish / one of the Fates in our bosoms? . . . / and our fates will be like hers, / and our hems crooked forever?" Disturbing as the presence of the house guest is, her hosts are much more located in their sudden self-consciousness than they ever were before, within rigid boundaries of property and propriety. The guest's identity is inscrutable, "her face is closed as a nut, / closed as a careful snail / or a thousand-year-old seed," but theirs have opened in her presence, partly because she is so impenetrable.

We have been dealing with the mode of the impersonal primarily in terms of theme, setting, situation. But of course the term is most applicable to a discussion of the speaker. Personal narration is precluded by Bishop's view that the self is amorphous in an amorphous world. Instead, we get a variety of distancing techniques, which bring order to the poems without belying their vision of flux, and without lending privilege to a single perspective.

Often these homeless figures are presented by a detached, third-person narrator, who sees their familiar structures foundering but can imagine a larger womblike mystery. The "Squatter's Children" "play at digging holes," at creating roots in the wider, mysterious world which is more meaningful than the "specklike house," the shelter from which their mother's voice, "ugly as sin," calls them to come in. The description repeatedly reveals their vulnerability. Their laughter, "weak flashes of inquiry," is not answered; their "little, soluble, / unwarrantable ark" will not sustain them far. And yet their questioning, digging natures are never really criticized. The narrator intrudes to affirm and reassure their "rights in rooms of falling rain." They are, in a sense, housed in the obscurity of the storm, even as the ark of their selves founders.

Above the mist, from where this impersonal narrator views the landscape, humans look as insignificant as Brueghel's Icarus. Among other things, the impersonal mode puts

humanity in perspective. We are continually reminded of a reality that goes on quite aside from our human frame of reference. In "Cape Breton" signs of humanity are almost completely absorbed by the vaster landscape. A bus moves through the scene, but we never enter its frame, or follow the simple passenger who gets off and vanishes into the hills. In this deeply impersonal world, where the "thin mist follows / the white mutations of its dream," humanity looks slight and transient indeed. And yet, as in Brueghel's paintings, the human element is privileged, as a focus of interest if not power.

These detached narratives are among the most placid of Bishop's poems precisely because they put human confusion and loss, as well as human authority, "in perspective." By looking from above, they locate humanity in its wanderings. In a way they can be seen as acts of self-location. The tiny figures are our surrogates and thus soften our own pain in the midst of uncertainty. In "Squatter's Children" the narrator speaks directly out of a perspective from which obscurity no longer threatens. The children are safe in their unawareness, the speaker in a higher awareness. In a way all of these poems are "little exercises" through which we come to terms with our confusion by distancing ourselves from it momentarily. In fact, a poem like "Little Exercise" invites the reader directly into this special perspective. Everything in the scene is uneasy or precarious; but vulnerable as the "someone" is, his boat tied to a feeble mangrove root, he is "uninjured, barely disturbed." Little exercises like these give us a sense of ourselves in time which is much less threatening than immersion in a scene.

The impersonal, distanced narrator, then, admits a certain stability where experience is troubled. But Bishop never lets this perspective get complacently ironic. A "believer in total immersion," she continually returns to write poems from a more limited, more bewildered point of view. She enters the consciousness of characters lost in a world bigger than themselves or their ideas and lets them speak out of their limitations. We are invited into an intimacy with these speakers, but the impersonal mode is still doubly preserved. These are masks, not Bishop's own voice, or ours. And it is precisely the problem of the personal that these poems engage. In the dramatic monologues of "Rainy Season; Sub-Tropics" for instance, Bishop makes experience particular, while at the same time juxtaposing contradictory views in order to show the limits and errors of each.

"This is not my home," declares the Strayed Crab, much out of his element, not knowing how he got where he is. He has a very precise idea of his identity, but it is out of step with these new surroundings, and he is completely inflexible. "I admire compression, lightness, and agility, all rare in this loose world." For the Giant Toad and Giant Snail, too, the self is a source of both pride and discomfort. "I am too big. . . . Pity me," they cry. Each of these animals sings his own song to himself, remarking on the personal beauty that he "knows" he possesses, but at the same time bemoaning his enormous hardship and disproportion, feeling his very nature a liability in a world that does not reflect or accommodate him. Isolated as these creatures are, they continually play back a sense of themselves, inquiring, recording, and tracing their own features and sensations. The external world brushes by them, but their relationship to it is defensive rather than adaptive or communicative. They withdraw into the personal rather than asking their way home. "I keep my feelings to myself," snaps the Crab. "Withdrawal is always best," mumbles the Snail. Partly because contact is so minimal, there is a good deal of discrepancy between how we perceive the animals and how they perceive themselves. Finally, they are not only lost, but self-deceived. Since we hear only the voice of each creature, our sympathy naturally goes out to him. And yet our judgment draws back at his inflexibility and defensiveness.

We have seen how Bishop protects the reader from the disorientation she depicts, first by impersonal narration and second by a series of masks from which we feel an ironic distance. But in *Geography III* these masks are dangerously familiar. The narrative distance of "In the Waiting Room" was not between a character and a creation simply, but between the poet and a memory of her past self. There, the problem of memory became, indirectly, another aspect of the instability of time and place. Crusoe of "Crusoe in England" is the most realized of Bishop's first person narrators, and here she allows us almost no ironic distance. Because he is human, because he is less certain in his delusions, because his is the only point of view presented, we are shipwrecked with him. Self-admiring but out of proportion, cut off from his surroundings, he is like the tropical creatures, but more aware of the relativity of his own dimensions. And his attempts to find himself are inquisitive and creative, even if they don't entirely succeed. This is the longest poem in Bishop's latest volume, one that brings together a great many of the themes, motifs, and images of her other work. Here again is the shipwreck, the self and its structures foundering in an impersonal reality of empty volcanoes, waves that close in (but never completely), mist, dry rock, inscrutable cries of goats and gulls. The island is an odd combination of elements from Cape Breton, scenes in the *National Geographic*, South America, all places where characters have earlier lost themselves in order to find themselves. Here again the speaker begins by putting questions to an outer world, but turns them inward from frustration. Like other characters, Crusoe tries to construct meanings "out of nothing at all, or air" when the world won't provide them; as before, such constructs fail to satisfy or protect. But more powerfully than before the experience is affirmed, despite discomfort and struggle, because of the creative, inquiring and self-reflective attitude it provides.

Defoe's Crusoe demonstrated civilized man's victory over the grandeur of nature. But Bishop's Crusoe comes to land on an unresponsive, inscrutable but also uninspiring nature, in which he finds it impossible to place himself. The mist is not mysterious, but a confusion of "cloud-dump." The volcanoes are not majestic or threatening but "miserable, small" things, "dead as ash heaps." Crusoe, like the Giant Toad or Snail, feels his self to be an enormous burden, incongruous with his surroundings even while it is his solace. He can't seem to adjust his perspective to fit the proportions of the place, and he is left unsure whether the volcanoes are tiny or the goats grotesquely large.

What troubles Crusoe most about the place is its aridity, marked by the parched throats of the volcanoes. No rich "folds of lava" pour forth meaning. The most impressive features of the island, the "glittering" rollers, the "variegated" beaches, the "water spouts . . . sacerdotal beings of glass," invite no human association or romantic continuity. Seen as "glass," even water cannot be absorbed. All these features are "beautiful, yes, but not much company," pure abstract forms without sympathy. Even hostile otherness would be preferable to this inactive indifference, this monotonous world of white goats and gulls and oblivious lumbering turtles, of endless repetition:

> I still can't shake
> them from my ears; they're hurting now.
> The questioning shrieks, the equivocal replies
> over a ground of hissing rain

> and hissing, ambulating turtles
> got on my nerves.

Crusoe wonders if the goats think him one of their own kind, that they speak to him thus. But his mind cannot embrace these alien forms. He projects the structures of his own language onto theirs, imagining their cries as questions and replies. But they are never realized as such, for insofar as the cries are perceived in human terms, they are only echoes of his own questions, addressed only to himself. Similarly, Crusoe christens the volcano "*Mount d'Espoir* or *Mount Despair*," imposing positive and negative values on the landscape; but it will never verify any of this, as he is reminded by the blank, horizontal gaze of the goat, "expressing nothing" ("or a little malice" perhaps, since value is inevitable in human interpretation).

Crusoe tries to personalize an impersonal world, and of course his questions aren't answered. So he keeps coming back to the impersonal value-free "reality" of the landscape. But the mind cannot settle on such reductions; it seeks presence, and intersubjectivity. Since he cannot personalize his present surroundings, he infuses them with nostalgic feeling, converting the landscape to symbols of an elsewhere created more in his own image. But such symbolization remains mere simile or allegory where the distance between thing and sign is preserved. The turtles hiss like teakettles, but fail to be experienced as real teakettles just as they fail to be experienced as real turtles. The snail shells (empty vehicles) look like iris beds, and when the gulls fly up at once

> they sounded
> like a big tree in a strong wind, its leaves.
> I'd shut my eyes and think about a tree,
> an oak, say, with real shade, somewhere.

But the reality of the island keeps intruding on Crusoe's dream of home. The wish remains a pastoral one and fails as an act of self-location. Indeed, for Crusoe nostalgia adds a temporal displacement to the spatial one. Historic continuity is just as much disrupted as visual perspective. Crusoe "remembers" lines from Wordsworth, written chronologically after his lifetime. His expectation that returning to England will set things right, that he can look it up when he get home, ignores the fundamental displacement of his existence in time and space. There is no correlation between his internal sense of order and external reality.

The first theme of Crusoe, then, is that human order imposed on the landscape never "takes" as real presence. But neither does the landscape answer our questions about its objective order. (We hear in "Twelfth Morning; or What You Will": "Don't ask the big white horse, *Are you supposed / to be inside the fence or out?* He's still / asleep. Even awake, he probably / remains in doubt.") The second, related theme is that we must ask of ourselves the questions Crusoe asks: "'Do I deserve this? I suppose I must./ . . . Was there / a moment when I actually chose this? / I don't remember, but there could have been.'"

When the mind fails to find external objectifications it necessarily turns inward for its comfort. Bishop's position on such gestures is ambivalent. On the one hand they are surrenders to solipsism; on the other hand, they are all the meaning we can manage. From "Crusoe" it seems that self-explanation, achieved with self-awareness and humility, is justified. Like the Toad, Snail, and Crab, Crusoe begins explaining himself to himself; indeed, like the Snail he carries his own house around with him. But unlike the tropical creatures, he does more than complain or flatter himself; he attempts to construct a home out of the alien materials. Since his surroundings cannot be appropriated, and fail even to register his existence, he creates his own world to reflect himself in. Where love is not offered externally, he discovers self-love: "I felt a deep affection for / the smallest of my island industries." He rejoices over "homebrew" (imagination?) and his weird flute (poetry?).

But as a hero of self-consciousness, Crusoe sees the limits of his creations, and this in turn limits his ability to rejoice in them. The affection is based on an idea of free will and the autonomy and presence of the self which he cannot substantiate. "Reciting to my iris-beds," to his created, imagined correspondents (not even to the snail shells which gave rise to his metaphor), "'They flash upon that inward eye,'" he cannot finish the gesture; "'which is the bliss . . . ' The bliss of what?" The iris beds never verify his inward existence since they are projections to begin with. They never fill in the blanks of the books he reads, precisely because the answers are fundamentally subjective: " . . . of solitude." The inward eye is precisely that blank center around which all questions are formed. And as long as that primary question of the self, of solitude, remains unanswered, so do all the others. The "smallest of my island industries," but that which gives all the others their efficacy, is a "miserable philosophy" about the authority and originality of the self. The awareness that the self, too, is created ("Home-made, home-made! But aren't we all?") limits the power of all other inventions. However frustrating this may be to Crusoe, Bishop does not finally negate these inventions: by confronting an impersonal world in an inquisitive attitude, we do not verify our own values or self-images, but neither do we replace these constructions with anything else. What we gain, what is missing without this experience of disorientation, is a clearer awareness of the relative nature of our identities and our creations. Such self-consciousness is positive, though it may be disturbing in that it disrupts our notion of the genuineness and discreteness of the self. Finally, to locate ourselves in the world, we need *both* to carve out definitions and to know their limitations.

Crusoe does, in a way, experience "the bliss of solitude," but not as Wordsworth might, in communion with nature, which reveals the truth of the subjective. Experiencing a harsh isolation of things from each other ("The island had one kind of everything"), Crusoe resorts to a kind of self-doubling, a dialogue with the self, the interior version of the charity he cannot acquire elsewhere.

> I often gave way to self-pity.
>
>   . . .
>
> What's wrong about self-pity, anyway?
> With my legs dangling down familiarly
> over a crater's edge, I told myself
> "Pity should begin at home." So the more
> pity I felt, the more I felt at home.

Bishop recognizes that narcissism is an essential aspect of self-definition. Dangling over the meaningless, strange crater, Crusoe is the only familiar thing, so self-pity creates all the sense of home there is. Like "the moon in the bureau mirror" of "Insomnia," "by the Universe deserted, / she'd tell it to go to hell, / and she'd find a body of water, / or a mirror, on which to dwell."

Acts of self-creation go on throughout Bishop's poems, and though they are always incomplete, they are nevertheless affirmed steps toward self-consciousness, toward the questioning process. "Why didn't I know enough of something? / Greek drama or astronomy?" The self-splitting habit of "The Gentleman of Shalott" produces an "exhilarating" sense of "uncertainty." "He loves / that sense of constant re-adjustment."

Bishop loves it too, as the structure of human experience. Self-knowledge remains tentative and incomplete at best, like the flow created in the divided heart of "The Weed." But that flow is vital and regenerative; the Toad, Crab, and Snail, for all their beauties, do not take a questioning or creative attitude, so they are simply lost in contradiction, stuck in the phase of self-pity.

Self-pity cannot provide a certain home for Crusoe, because finally it only perpetuates the echo, the greatest source of his anxiety. Self-repetition is not much more intimate, in the long run, than the rain's "echolalia," registered formally in the repetition of lines and phrases so frequent in Bishop's poetry. Musical in moderation, the "weaving, weaving," "glittering and glittering," can become a little eerie. The hermit in "Chemin de Fer" lives in a totally self-reflexive world, and thus lives perpetually in echoes. But Crusoe does not become so static in his self-pity. Even when his efforts to partake of the larger world fail, we admire them.

Many of Bishop's poems deal with love as a way of silencing the echo. Crusoe dreams of partaking of the external world, of "food / and love," when he is not having nightmares about the endless reproduction of experience, of "frogs' eggs turning into polliwogs / of islands." And when Friday comes there is even a moment of nearly realized love. Friday offers Crusoe his only access to the external world, for "at home" in the wilderness but also human, Friday is a kind of mediator. He almost promises to end difference without repetition. But it's not a productive love; the difference isn't adequate to create a new unity out of self and objective world. "If only he had been a woman!" Indeed, interpersonal love remains a pastoral ideal in Bishop just as much as solitude does. All of the poems that raise the question of love deal with separation and loss, destruction and attachment as equal impulses. Friday dies at the end, precisely because Crusoe has drawn him into his own world; he dies of measles, a European disease.

We do not find a permanent home, then, in dates and names, not in exalted strangeness, not in nostalgia, not in self-created surroundings, not in self-pity; not even in love. Questions persist past all these closures. And yet all these failed attempts at comfort seem preferable to the permanent home offered by despair or total withdrawal. The "rescuers" take Crusoe out of a situation which ultimately proves to be the source of vitality; for vitality, it seems, is one with the struggle to survive, to find oneself, or make a place for oneself.

At the time of the narration, Crusoe is, as the title indicates, "in England," home again. We would expect that homecoming to be the subject of the poem, and yet all but three stanzas deal with Crusoe's experience of shipwreck on a strange island. The point the title makes, of course, is that England is no more "home" than the place of miserable empty volcanoes. In this version of the Crusoe story, civilization is not exalted over nature. England, the object of Crusoe's nostalgia, is familiar and thus "real" enough, but nothing like his dreams of home. Like the narrator at the end of "In the Waiting Room," Crusoe knows where he is, but now he can barely inhabit that static, barren place. Here, he desires that continual struggle he so much hated before. Once he was tormented by the endless repetition of experience, having nightmares of islands, "knowing that I had to live/on each and every one, eventually,/for ages, registering their flora,/their fauna, their geography." Now, ironically, "that archipelago/has petered out," and he is bored and dismayed, longing again for the struggle. Nostalgia persists as part of the human character, transferred now to the former center of pain. He has moved from questions of place and purpose to questions of the past, as he tries to locate himself now in terms of his former hardships.

In England the objects of his past have lost all the moisture of vitality; they are empty symbols. For Crusoe the island is "un-rediscovered, un-renamable." He feels the failure of imagination to give presence to the past: "None of the books has ever got it right." And yet the story *he* tells does become authentic, even in reviving images of desire. For all his world-weariness, Crusoe does succeed in gathering a sense of self precisely *in* images of desire.

Clearly, Bishop does not believe in settling down. We never "find ourselves" in any stable location, but rather in transit. As all her critics point out, travel is her natural, dominant metaphor for the human condition. Even dreams, which we associate with wish-fulfillment, are, in Bishop's poetry, revelations of our homeless natures. The majority of Bishop's poems deal directly with the experience of travel, and none of them posit a secure home from which the characters have departed or an ideal destination toward which they move. Perhaps this is why it took the "prodigal" "a long time/finally to make his mind up to go home." The glorious images the explorers in "Brazil, January 1, 1502" look for are already out of fashion at home. Miss Breen of "Arrival at Santos" is a retired, seventy-year-old policewoman. "Home" no longer accommodates any of them, if it ever did. Indeed, Miss Breen's "home, when she is at home, is in Glens Fall/s New York" (with a hint of The Fall, by the dropping of the s). The travel poems reinforce the point that the search for origins and ideals is our way of structuring thought, of organizing experience and thereby locating ourselves. Like questions which have no answers but nevertheless give us a point of orientation, a concept of origins and destinations shapes our personal lives which would otherwise diffuse into impersonal landscapes.

Arrivals, for Bishop, are always starting points. Either a place does not excite us as we had hoped, or it dissolves or retreats on approach. In "From the Country to the City," for instance, the solidity of the endpoint becomes instead an array of tiny lights, as the road seems interminable. Arriving at Santos, two women find not the sublime nature they had imagined, but "self-pitying mountains," and "frivolous greenery," "feeble pink" warehouses and "uncertain palms," all drearily in between the comforts of home and an exotic wilderness. Their "quest" is "answered" with the same confusion they thought they had left behind.

> Oh, tourist,
> is this how this country is going to answer you
> and your immodest demands for a different world,
> and a better life, and complete comprehension
> of both at last, and immediately,
> after eighteen days of suspension?

The arrival immediately becomes a departure as the "tender," the "strange and ancient craft," comes and they prepare for "driving to the interior," literally and figuratively.

The poem expresses a fundamental ambivalence about this quest, since the ladies, while they want the "different world," are uneasy as they climb down the ladder backwards and hope that "the customs officials will speak English . . . / and leave us our bourbon and cigarettes." And yet the poem also accepts the essential ephemerality of all domesticities; all homes are in a way only waiting rooms, or in this case ports, which leave us in suspension, where experience is not grasped but used up, like "soap, or postage stamps—/wasting away like the former, slipping the way the latter/do when we mail the letters we wrote on the boat." In one sense this makes "driving to the interior" an idle impulse, since that completely comprehended "different world" is a fiction. And yet there does seem to be something attractive about the image of these two

women moving with the natural drift of their lives, rather than resisting it.

In "In the Waiting Room," in "Crusoe," as in all the poems about travel, then, we discover not only that we are lost, but that there never *was* and never will be a home in any stable sense. Home is a fiction, a projection of an ideal state. In "Questions of Travel" Bishop both celebrates travel as leading to self-consciousness, and conversely declares there is no alternative to travel for the self-conscious person. The poem comes full circle to explain itself. In that sense it is not only a reflection on travel but a journey in its own right, like the other journeys Bishop has described.

In many ways at once, the poem "Questions of Travel" is central in Bishop's work, for it both comments on and repeats the structure of the other poems. It again deals with travel, and with the feeling of being lost, overwhelmed by change. It is structured in a series of observations that generate questions rather than answers. And again, the questions move increasingly inward, so that the quest for the external world becomes a quest for the self. The self-reflection at the end of the poem is affirmative in mood, even while it is interrogative in form.

The poem opens in complaint and regret, but as the questions push against the unfamiliar world they become more enraptured:

> What childishness is it that while there's a breath of
>   life
> in our bodies, we are determined to rush
> to see the sun the other way around?
> The tiniest green hummingbird in the world?
> To stare at some inexplicable old stonework,
> inexplicable and impenetrable,
> at any view,
> instantly seen and always, always delightful?

It is not surprising that she turns to consider what has been gained rather than what was lost, or rather, what would have been lost if they'd stayed home, since loss faces them either way. What would have been lost is not contact with nature in its pure form, but (as the examples reveal) a glimpse of human history, however blurred and inconclusive. By the end of the poem she is celebrating the inevitable. It would have been a pity "never to have had to listen to rain." Choice is no longer an issue. And what she finds in the rain is not the rain itself, but a moment of awakened self-consciousness:

> two hours of unrelenting oratory
> and then a sudden golden silence
> in which the traveller takes a notebook, writes

and the poem comes around to its original questions, with the difference that it finally asks, not only: "Should we have stayed at home" but: Where is home? Home seems to be in question, or rather, in questioning.

But travel without pause is tiring and unsatisfying. The problem of these poems becomes how to present moments of rest and coalescence which nonetheless preserve the sense that our condition is inherently restless. Bishop's solution is to create places, objects, figures representing a unity around which we collect ourselves, but at the same time symbolizing our transience. The double function of these images satisfies our ambivalence about travel. The self is kept expansive even while it experiences a needed coalescence.

The "strangest of theatres" at which the characters of "Questions of Travel" arrive, for example, reflects their own condition of motion and confusion. The "streams and clouds keep travelling, travelling,/the mountains look like the hulls of capsized ships." The waterfalls even look like "tearstains."

Surely the "strangers in a play" these travellers are watching are themselves. An early poem, "The Imaginary Iceberg," expresses this same sense of self-reflective destination especially well, for here an object in nature begins to correspond to the soul. This poem recognizes how a search for the most impersonal ideal is finally a search for the personal. Nothing could be less human than an iceberg, and yet it causes the "soul" to coalesce. We do not depart from the ship, from language, altogether at such moments, but like questions, these experiences let us look into a nonverbal center. The experience of travel toward a noncontingent endpoint is a kind of ideal condition, for the self is neither dispersed to total disorder, nor confined to static order. The imaginary iceberg, like Death, like Nature, like any absolute alterity, gives shape to the sailor's drift, just as the idea of the "Soul" gives shape to the self. Imagining an absolute other is always a way of imagining an absolute self. Perhaps this is why we are attracted in "Questions of Travel" to the "inexplicable old stonework,/inexplicable and impenetrable,/at any view,/instantly seen and always, always delightful." There is no limit here, but neither is there complete flux. Another poem, "The Fish," makes clear that these moments of sudden awareness depend upon the extension as well as the retention of difference. Here the narrator confronts, embodied in a fish she has caught, a universe of other parasitical life, and an infinite past of other similar encounters, thus locating herself in relation to other life and history.

All these are examples of the sudden feeling of home. The strange is suddenly familiar; history and change are brought into immediate focus and coherence. But of course, time and space cannot really be concentrated; the poems draw us back into extension. Though victory fills up the little rented boat in "The Fish," it is not properly ours, and we must let the fish go. "The power to relinquish what one would keep, that is freedom," wrote Marianne Moore, and it seems to be a maxim Bishop took to heart. The pain of loss and confusion is never trivialized in her poems, and yet it is overpowered by a sense of the value of process. "The art of losing's not too hard to master/though it may look like (*Write* it!) like disaster." In mastering the art of losing we master ourselves.

Possession is not the highest of goals for Bishop, but rather, engagement with the world and with one's self through inquiry, even when distance and difference result. The speaker of "Five Flights Up" may feel a certain envy for the bird or dog, without shame, without memory, their "Questions—if that is what they are—/answered directly, simply,/by day itself." In the human world distances are not so easily overcome; questions persist beyond all presences. And yet there is no preference for the nonhuman here. Acts of memory may indeed aggravate our losses, but they may also, like brief encounters with the strange, offer experiences of a sudden coalescence of feelings and associations.

"Poem" celebrates such an active concentration even while it fails to unite the self fully with the past or with others. We do not gain anything in such activities (the painting that here triggers memory may look like a dollar bill, but it is "useless and free") except perhaps self-location. The poem proceeds in a series of conjectures and questions, moments of identification and moments of separation. As a vessel of memory, the painting connects the speaker to a multiple past, not only to a scene but to those who have witnessed that scene, and even to those others through whose hands the picture has passed. None of these contacts is complete; each reach of the imagination beyond the present is curtailed by surface interruption. But at a certain juncture, the boundaries of the sign and the thing be-

come obscure; we feel at once the retention and extension of difference. Representation fails to realize the world; thought remains in questions. And yet in questioning we briefly reach an ultimate question: "life and the memory of it so compressed/they've turned into each other. Which is which?" The poem never transcends the flux of things, the distances of time and space, but in the alternation of our thought in surface and depth, in pasts and presences, there exists a certain sudden feeling of well-being: "how live, how touching. . . ."

It is just such a feeling of well-being that the bus passengers experience in "The Moose." The poem brings together all the elements—disorientation, dream, travel, sudden strange appearances, memory—which the other poems, in various combinations, introduce. All are elements that help us lose ourselves in order to find ourselves. In "The Moose," the stability of the homeland is transformed into a locus of gentle flux, and the journey begins, travel in space corresponding here to travel in time, to memory. The passengers are again surrounded by fog, by a drowsy confusion, but as the distant narrator, looking sympathetically down on them, knows, it is a homey kind of confusion, softening the "hairy, scratchy, splintery . . . impenetrable wood[s]." Out of this oblivion we overhear a conversation "in Eternity," about pain and loss, where things are "cleared up finally," where an unqualified "yes" is possible. This is not the voice of the people on the bus, nor do they hear it except in a vague dream, and yet it belongs to them as their heritage. And as the moose emerges from the wood, simple in her otherworldliness, an emblem of all that the Grandparents have accepted, the passengers do not understand the relation they have to it, and yet they are moved by it. Strange as it is, it is also "homely as a house/(or, safe as houses.)" It offers them a sudden feeling of liberation but also of placement. They coalesce for an instant around this mystery. And like the experience in the waiting room, this one is never defined but only embraced in a question the travellers ask, a question about their own natures and identities:

> Why, why do we feel
> (we all feel) this sweet
> sensation of joy?

The impersonal and the interrogative are essential and pervasive characteristics of Bishop's style, linked by their common source in her uncertain, exploratory relation to the world. Inherent in them are certain aesthetic problems with which she has had to grapple. Since these poems lack the intimacy which urges our attention in other lyrics, they risk our indifference or our disbelief. In her early poetry, Bishop tries to surmount this problem by contriving a "we," "I" and "you" who interact, but only distantly. The impersonal requires that images speak for themselves, and at times in the early work, they are too reticent. But the details that introduce "The Moose" accumulate quietly, so that even while we are taken by surprise when events suddenly lift into dream, we are not disturbed because we have been guided by a silent ordering presence. Bishop does not falsify her sense of our situation by interpreting all the details she sets adrift towards us. But neither do we feel entirely alone in the wilderness she creates.

At its weakest, the interrogative mode seems a tic, as pat as any assertion it might overturn. In "The Map" and in "The Monument," some of the questions seem contrived. But in "Filling Station," "Faustina," and "First Death in Nova Scotia," the questions emerge from a change of consciousness; in *Geography III*, they always seem genuine. We come to poetry with the desire for wholeness and order, and the poet of the interrogative mode must somehow satisfy that need without reducing experience to simple answers. When it works, this is Bishop's greatest achievement: to give us satisfaction even as she remains elusive and reticent, even as she reveals that the question is the final form. For through the impersonal mode she makes the questions our own, our most valued possessions, the very form of our identity.

Notes

1. Richard Howard, ed., *Preferences: 51 American Poets Choose Poems from Their Own Work and from the Past* (New York: Viking, 1974), pp. 27–31.

DAVID LEHMAN
"'In Prison': A Paradox Regained" (1981)
Elizabeth Bishop and Her Art
1983, pp. 61–73

Traditionally, poets have dwelled in paradoxical prisons. To enter bonds of queen and country is to affirm one's freedom, Donne seductively argued; Lovelace, equally extravagant if less playful, insisted on liberty as a function of spiritual innocence. He denied not the actuality of stone walls and iron bars, just their right to cohere into prisons and cages, in a passage that schoolchildren were presumed once upon a time to know by heart:

> If I have freedom in my love,
>   And in my soul am free,
> Angels alone, that soar above,
>   Enjoy such liberty.
>   ("To Althea, from Prison")

If Lovelace could look upon imprisonment as "an hermitage," a time to rededicate himself to a courtly ideal, Hamlet's princely mobility could scarcely preclude a bout of claustrophobia. "Denmark's a prison," he announces, and follows with a characteristic verbal gesture, robust hyperbole collapsing into poignantly prosaic understatement:

> O God, I could be bounded in a nutshell and
> count myself a king of infinite space, were it not
> that I have bad dreams.
>   (Act 2, Scene 2)

It is, as Hamlet acknowledges, a classic opposition of mind and matter. Whatever his present difficulties, he does not doubt the mind's supremacy over the world it beholds: "There is nothing either good or bad but thinking makes it so." As far as Hamlet is concerned, man's potential to breathe the infinite space of angels is, despite the narrow dimensions of his cell, still available, though not right here, not just now.

It would be interesting to determine when *despite* in that last clause turned into *because of*, when the emphasis shifted and poets actively sought a species of imprisonment because only there would the soul learn true freedom, or goodness, or the peace that passeth understanding. The argument, a recurrent one in medieval Christian theology, has in effect been rewritten, its paradox completed, by agents of the Romantic imagination. In the same spirit in which he commends duty as the "Stern Daughter of the Voice of God." Wordsworth solemnly wills a curtailment of his freedom, identifying form as a necessary jail in his sonnet on the sonnet:

> In truth the prison, unto which we doom
> Ourselves, no prison is: and hence for me,
> In sundry moods, 'twas pastime to be bound
> Within the Sonnet's scanty plot of ground;

> Pleased if some Souls (for such there needs must be)
> Who have felt the weight of too much liberty,
> Should find brief solace there, as I have found.
>   ("Nuns Fret Not at Their Convent's Narrow Room")

To Paul Pennyfeather, the beleaguered hero of Evelyn Waugh's *Decline and Fall*, prison ironically allows for the autonomy of the self, its independence from social pressures, its release from "the weight of too much liberty":

> The next four weeks of solitary confinement were among the happiest of Paul's life. . . . It was so exhilarating, he found, never to have to make any decision on any subject, to be wholly relieved from the smallest consideration of time, meals, or clothes, to have no anxiety ever about what kind of impression he was making; in fact, to be free . . . there was no need to shave, no hesitation about what tie he should wear, none of the fidgeting with studs and collars and links that so distracts the waking moments of civilized man. He felt like the happy people in the advertisements for shaving soap who seem to have achieved very simply that peace of mind so distant and so desirable in the early morning.[1]

A comic gloss on Lovelace's "To Althea, from Prison," the chapter in which this passage appears has the title "Stone Walls Do Not a Prison Make"; not surprisingly, a later chapter is called "Nor Iron Bars a Cage."

As we proceed from *despite* to *because*, we move as well from a conception of the imagination as that which redeems reality to a conception of the imagination as, in the last analysis, sufficient unto itself. A clear statement of this last analysis is found in J. K. Huysmans' *À Rebours*, which develops the logic of the prison paradox into an aesthetic principle. The protagonist of that novel ingeniously devises a means by which to travel without ever having to leave his room, secure a passport, book passage, pack bags, or say farewell—without, in short, any of the inconveniences of actuality. "Travel, indeed, struck him as being a waste of time, since he believed that the imagination could provide a more-than-adequate substitute for the vulgar reality of actual experience."[2] Two poets upon whom Elizabeth Bishop has exerted a powerful influence, James Merrill and John Ashbery, offer inspired variations on this theme of the stationary traveler. More a *récit* than a short story, Merrill's "Peru: The Landscape Game" describes a trip to the land of the Incas; the poet plans to go there, but it is his anticipation of the place that he records, a Platonic reality too good not to be true. The imagination acts, as it were, in self-defense, as it spins out an external possibility, proof against the disappointment Wordsworth experienced when he saw Mont Blanc:

> How to find the right words for a new world?
> One way would be to begin, before ever leaving home, with some anticipatory jottings such as these. Then, even if the quetzal turns out to be extinct, if sure-footed grandmothers from Tulsa overrun the ruins, and Porfirio's baby has a harelip and there are cucarachas in the Hotel Périchole, the visitor may rest easy. Nothing can dim his first, radiant impressions.[3]

Such "jottings," intended for perusal on the ride down to Lima, give new meaning to the idea of flight insurance.

Ashbery too would seem to subscribe to Verlaine's notion that "every landscape is a state of mind." From his vantage point in an office building more than a thousand miles away, the speaker of Ashbery's "The Instruction Manual" takes us on a guided tour of Gaudalajara, "City I wanted most to see, and most did not see, in Mexico!" The task of writing "the instruction manual on the uses of a new metal" serves as the launching pad for this mental flight, this enchanted product of an imagining. "How limited, but how complete withal, has been our experience of Guadalajara!" the speaker can exclaim upon his return to the desk he never had to leave.[4] Amusing as that statement is, it tells its sober truth about the poetic process. On paper the poet flies to Peru or Guadalajara not as places but as names, words, sounds; one arrives at "the imagination of the sound—a place." This is the conclusion reached by A. R. Ammons in his poem "Triphammer Bridge":

> *sanctuary, sanctuary,* I say it over and over and the
> word's sound is the one place to dwell: that's it, just
> the sound, and the imagination of the sound—a
> place.[5]

By delineating the progression from "wanted . . . to see" to "did not see" to "I fancy I see, under the press of having to write the instruction manual," Ashbery's poem makes a further point. It is as though a condition of absence were a prerequisite for the adventurous imagination. So we are directly told in another of Ashbery's early poems, "Le Livre est sur la table":

> All beauty, resonance, integrity,
> Exist by deprivation or logic
> Of strange position.[6]

The proposition that the imagination varies directly with deprivation and isolation, that imaginative need mothers invention, and that physical confinement is conducive to spiritual freedom, receives full treatment in Elizabeth Bishop's early and remarkably prescient short story (or *récit*), "In Prison."[7] This account of an ideal "life-sentence" contains the seed Ashbery would cultivate in "The Instruction Manual," even as it makes the case for creative misreading, for what Harold Bloom, like Miss Bishop a mapmaker, calls "misprision":

> I understand that most prisons are now supplied with libraries and that the prisoners are expected to read the *Everyman's Library* and other books of educational tendencies. I hope I am not being too reactionary when I say that my one desire is to be given one very dull book to read, the duller the better. A book, moreover, on a subject completely foreign to me; perhaps the second volume, if the first would familiarize me too well with the terms and purpose of the work. Then I shall be able to experience with a free conscience the pleasure, perverse, I suppose, of interpreting it not at all according to its intent. Because I share with Valery's *M. Teste* the "knowledge that our thoughts are reflected back to us, too much so, through expressions made by others"; and I have resigned myself, or do I speak too frankly, to deriving what information and joy I can from this—lamentable but irremediable—state of affairs. From my detached rock-like book I shall be able to draw vast generalizations, abstractions of the grandest, most illuminating sort, like allegories or poems, and by posing fragments of it against the surroundings and conversations of my prison, I shall be able to form my own examples of surrealist art!—something I should never know how to do outside, where the sources are so bewildering. Perhaps it will be a book on the cure of a disease, or an industrial technique,—but no, even to try to imagine the subject would be to spoil the sensation of wave-like freshness I hope to receive when it is first placed in my hands.[8]
>
> (IP, 13–14)

In Miss Bishop's later work, a quite explicit echo of this passage occurs in "The End of March" where, in a tone more wistful than whimsical, the writer describes her "proto-dream-house," a "dubious" structure that tallies in a great many particulars with her earlier version of prison as paradise:

> I'd like to retire there and do *nothing,*
> or nothing much, forever, in two bare rooms:
> look through binoculars, read boring books,
> old, long, long books, and write down useless notes,
> talk to myself, and, foggy days,
> watch the droplets slipping, heavy with light.
>
> (G, 43)

Indeed, for the way it prefigures attitudes and motifs that we encounter not only in *Geography III* but throughout the poet's career, "In Prison" commends itself to critical inspection over and beyond its intrinsic merits, considerable though these are. Here we find, at however ironic a remove, a defense of her "mentality," her faith in "the power of details" as momentary stays against confusion, her stance as a quiet non-conformist, whose individuality of style is something subtle enough to flourish within a regimented order. The insouciance of "One Art," the ironic process by which defeat turns into victory, is anticipated in the story; here is an initial statement of the dialectical tension between autobiographical disaster and artistic mastery, a tension central to the villanelle and one that lurks beneath the surface of the prose poem "12 O'Clock News" with its military metaphors for the act of writing. Moreover, "In Prison" contains information helpful for us to understand the painterly disposition of a poet who continually derived inspiration, as well as subject matter, from objects and apparitions, large bad pictures and tiny ones ("About the size of an old-style dollar bill"), and seascapes disguised as animated "cartoon[s] by Raphael for a tapestry for a Pope" (CP, 46).

The strategy for reading that Miss Bishop proffers point to the governing conceit of the story, "the pleasure, perverse, I suppose, of interpreting it not at all according to its intent"—*it* standing here for prison, which willful mis-interpretation renders to mean the inner life of the imagination, the "real life" of the soul. The narrative starts with a flip reversal of Joseph K.'s predicament in *The Trial*: like Kafka's protagonist, Miss Bishop's persona has committed no crime, but there the resemblance ends. He positively wants what Joseph K. dreads; nor is it a case, as it is for the latter, of irrational guilt seeking to justify its existence. Once arrested, Joseph K. never doubts his guilt, even while ostensibly seeking to prove his innocence; Miss Bishop's nameless character runs no risk of arrest since, in order to attain the imprisonment he "can scarcely wait for," he seems prepared to do precious little and certainly nothing criminal, unless criminality be defined in the singular way attributed to Edgar Degas in "Objects & Apparitions": "'One has to commit a painting,' said Degas,/'the way one commits a crime'" (G, 47). But if the poet adopts this position, it is without political intent or fanfare. The pun on "sentence" in the phrase "life-sentence" may get us nearer the truth; from one point of view the writer may be said to serve successive "sentences." Be that as it may, the author of "In Prison" strikes the pose of a young Hegelian, wishing literally to make a virtue of necessity. Our hero has been chosen by prison, he would say; the will is needed not to act upon this destiny but to acquiesce before it, to accept what he conceives as "necessity." Given his definition of freedom, only an attitude of passive non-resistance will do, only the passive voice will be strictly accurate. Notice the grammatical ambiguity that closes the story:

> You may say,—people have said to me—you would

have been happy in the more flourishing days of the religious order, and that, I imagine, is close to the truth. But even there I hesitate, and the difference between Choice and Necessity jumps up again to confound me. "Freedom is knowledge of necessity"; I believe nothing as ardently as I do that. And I assure you that to act in this way is the only logical step for me to take. I mean, of course, to be acted *upon* in this way is the only logical step for me to take.

(IP, 16)

Justice is beside the point. It is clear we are talking metaphorically, not about guilt and punishment, but about the self and its need to make peace with the certitude of loss. To volunteer for prison is to plan a journey into the interior, confident that in the exchange of physical liberty for imaginative freedom one has, philosophically speaking, struck a good bargain, given up the apparent, embraced the real. Like Ashbery's dreary office building, prison affords both the opportunity and the motive for metaphor, but a far more urgent task also confronts the prisoner. It will be his audacious enterprise to establish an idealized dwelling place within the least likely, least congenial, of quarters; like Crusoe on his island, he will attempt to convert an alien landscape into one that responds to his humanity. It is almost as though he (or his author) were consciously designing a test for "one" art— singular, definitive of the poet's identity—an art that feeds on what might otherwise consume it, that thrives on loss, that welcomes limits in order to transcend them. We are, in sum, solidly within the walls of a conceit, a paradox regained, a cliché renewed in surprising ways. At one point at least, prison metaphorically dramatizes the situation of the writer, any writer conscious of his belatedness. Thus, referring to the "Writing on the Wall," our would-be prisoner announces his intention to "read very carefully (or try to read, since they may be partly obliterated, or in a foreign language) the inscriptions already there. Then I shall adapt my own compositions, in order that they may not conflict with those written by the prisoner before me. The voice of a new inmate will be noticeable, but there will be no contradictions or criticisms of what has already been laid down, rather a 'commentary.' I have thought of attempting a short, but immortal, poem, but I am afraid that is beyond me; I may rise to the occasion, however, once I am confronted with that stained, smeared, scribbled-on wall and feel the stub of pencil or rusty nail between my fingers" (IP, 14). The sense of postponement here as elsewhere in the piece reinforces our impression of it as an initial statement of purpose, a warm-up for the main event yet to come, the time of confrontation, pencil stub in hand, "with that stained, smeared, scribbled-on wall" of poetic tradition.

What makes "In Prison" work so well is that, having subtly and very quickly established the figurative nature of the writing, Miss Bishop ironically becomes a literalist of the imagination, specifying the exact dimensions of the cell, describing its walls and window and the view from the window with painterly precison, ruling out such surrogates for prison as monasteries. To live, in a shabby hotel room, "as if I were in prison"? No, the narrator says, that won't do. Nor will what we now call a country-club prison, the sort of place that has temporarily housed persons of a certain class convicted of wrongdoing with relation to the Watergate burglary and cover-up. Joining the navy is likewise eliminated from consideration, though on different grounds: not so much because it would parody "my real hopes," but for the telling reason that "there is something fundamentally uncongenial about the view of the

sea to a person of my mentality" (IP, 15). Why? Because, we may infer, it is the very symbol of the lawless and limitless and as such must clash with the mentality that yearns for fixed borders; also because the sea's vastness and essential unity threaten to drown out all details, all the "slight differences" that strike the poet as inherently valuable. The sea's great expanse is a needless luxury, a point implicitly made in that portion of the story given over to a mock-review of the literature of incarceration. Oscar Wilde is rebuked for the self-pitying note that mars "The Ballad of Reading Gaol." "'That little tent of blue, Which prisoners call the sky,' strikes me as absolute nonsense. I believe that even a keyhole of sky would be enough, in its blind, blue endlessness, to give someone, even someone who had never seen it before, an adequate idea of the sky" (IP, 11). The "romantic tunnel-digging" of *The Count of Monte Cristo* is also rejected by this early spokesman for Miss Bishop's views, this hard-liner impatient with sentimental formulae. What is desired, after all, is not an escape from but an escape into, the unadorned cell of consciousness.

As in "Crusoe in England," it is a persona and not the poet who does the talking in "In Prison." To make sure we realize this, Miss Bishop takes pains to distinguish the speaker's gender from her own. (He has thought of enlisting in the armed services—and of playing on the prison baseball team.) The distance thus created between writer and text sets ironies in motion, but these seem otherwise directed than at the speaker's expense. Rather, they work to effect a delicate interplay between order and chance, limitation and space, determinism and free will, the philosophical dualities that energize the story. If one's reading consists of a single book, and that a boring one, one can multiply it by a theoretically infinite number of misreadings, magical as lies. If one's view be restricted to a bare cobblestone courtyard, framed by the window so that it takes on the aspect of a painting, its boundaries severely defined, its activity therefore rescued from disorder, it is nevertheless a series of paintings in one, and within its order there is plenty of room for chance; vagaries of weather ensure the possibility of variations galore, as Monet demonstrated with his cathedrals and haystacks, products of the changing light. The confinement, then, is meant not to eliminate dealings with the external world but to circumscribe the relations and, by doing so, to put them on an aesthetic plane. What one sees becomes an ever-changing picture, what one reads, an occasion for the imagination to roam free. If, for the aesthete's ends, what barely suffices ("a keyhole of sky") is deemed better than a surfeit, that is partially because it underscores an important truth about poetic knowledge. All that we can know are parts and fragments; by the same token, each part, each detail, acts as a synecdoche, pointing to a potential whole, a design the mind must intuit or invent. "I expect to go to prison in full possession of my 'faculties,'" the speaker says. "In fact," he adds, "it is not until I am securely installed there that I expect fully to realize them" (IP, 12–13). In short, the prison of his aspirations is nothing like a place of asylum, refuge from trouble, a rest cure; on the contrary, his sentence will tax, and reward, his powers of imagination. And one can go further: one can say too that he plots his prison itinerary for reasons similar to those that elsewhere impel Miss Bishop's "I" and fellow travellers to undertake journeys to unfamiliar places that call "home" into question. A fantasized excursion to prison can give rise to such "questions of travel" as Miss Bishop will pose in a memorable poem:

> *"Is it lack of imagination that makes us come*
> *to imagined places, not just stay at home?*

Or could Pascal have been not entirely right
about just sitting quietly in one's room?

Continent, city, country, society:
the choice is never wide and never free.
And here, or there . . . No. Should we have stayed at
     home,
wherever that may be?"

(CP, 109)

Such interrogations yield no answers, only suasions, and these subject to change. "In Prison" leans one way, *Questions of Travel* the other. But whatever the differences in their attitudes to travel, the restless geographer and the secluded inmate have an ultimate direction in common, an ultimate task in which their opposing inclinations will equally culminate—the making of the map of an identity.

As a theory of imagination which is necessarily a theory of absence, "In Prison" prepares us well for the projects of Miss Bishop's mature poetry. It is remarkable how often she turns to imagery of room, cell, cage, and box, and usually within the context of an aesthetic inquiry; she has a penchant for illustrating her sense of art by postulating constructions the shape of boxes or made of them. Take "The Monument," which traces the growth of a work of art from "piled-up boxes" to "a temple of crates." Its external appearance seems to some extent a subordinate value; it functions to safeguard "what is within," about which it is protectively reticent:

> It may be solid, may be hollow.
> The bones of the artist-prince may be inside
> or far away on even drier soil.
> But roughly but adequately it can shelter
> what is within (which after all
> cannot have been intended to be seen.)

(CP, 28)

A "crooked box," the dream house of "The End of March" is prison-like in more ways than one, a rough but adequate shelter with constraints enough to provide the stimulus, if not the necessity, for creative action. And in "Objects & Apparitions," Miss Bishop's translation of Octavio Paz's homage to the boxes of Joseph Cornell, the paradox of a nutshell's infinite space is immediately articulated:

> Hexahedrons of wood and glass,
> scarcely bigger than a shoebox,
> with room in them for night and all its lights.
>
> Monuments to every moment,
> refuse of every moment, used:
> cages for infinity.

(G, 46)

Cornell's boxes have been characterized as "monumental on a tiny scale";[9] the phrase is not without relevance to Miss Bishop's art. The impulse toward this peculiar brand of monumentality combines with the conceit of the "enormous" room most notably, perhaps, in "12 O'Clock News," in which the writer's desk and the objects on it are magnified (and mistranslated), seen as through the eyes of a Lilliputian, with results at once humorous and touching.

Paradise, as Elizabeth Bishop with tongue-biting irony conceives it, has a precedent in "The Great Good Place" Henry James described, as these sentences from James's story make clear: "Slowly and blissfully he read into the general wealth of his comfort all the particular absences of which it was composed. One by one he touched, as it were, all the things it was such rapture to be without." The tone (and much else) is different, but the sentiment the same, in "One Art." There the disaster-prone are advised to "Lose something every day" and then to "practice losing farther, losing faster" (G, 40). The

imperative seems at first purely ironic, a way to keep anguish and dread at bay, to avoid giving in to self-pity. But the ironist's supreme gesture is to mean just what she says, contrary to appearances as well as expectations. Miss Bishop does, at least in one sense, recommend that we go about losing things, not so much because this will prepare us for the major losses inevitably to follow, but because the experience of loss humanizes us; it shows us as we are, vulnerable, pathetic, and yet heroic in our capacity to endure and to continue our affirming acts amid conditions less than propitious. When Miss Bishop talks of losing as an art she does not mean losing well: it's not a matter of good sportsmanship or "grace under pressure." On the one hand, she means considerably less: it isn't hard to master what comes naturally to us: we are always losing things, from our innocence to our parents to our house keys: that is why *lose* was the perfect syllepsis for Alexander Pope. Yet "the art of losing" is a wonderfully ambiguous phrase, and the ability to reconcile its two meanings—to experience loss as itself a remedy for loss—constitutes a powerful poetic gesture, whose success may be measured by the poet's skillful handling of the villanelle's intricate form in the face of all that militates against order and arrangement.

In "The Poet," Emerson wrote that "every thought is also a prison; every heaven is also a prison." Not the least virtue of Elizabeth Bishop's poetry is that, from the start, it shows us the truth that remains when Emerson's terms are reversed.

Notes

In quoting from Miss Bishop's works, I used the following system of abbreviations:

CP   *The Complete Poems* (New York: Farrar, Straus and Giroux, 1970).
G   *Geography III* (New York: Farrar, Straus and Giroux, 1976).
IP   "In Prison," in *The Poet's Story*, ed. Howard Moss (New York: Macmillan, 1973), pp. 9–16.

Numbers following the abbreviations refer to page numbers in the cited text.

1. *Decline and Fall* (Boston: Little, Brown, 1956), p. 229.
2. *Against Nature*, trans. Robert Baldick (New York: Penguin, 1977), p. 35. Characterized by Arthur Symons as "the breviary of the Decadence," *À Rebours* made a striking impression on the hero of *The Picture of Dorian Gray*—and on Paul Valéry. A strict translation of the title of Huysman's book would give us "against the grain," "backwards," or "the wrong way."

   In *Abroad: British Literary Traveling Between the Wars* (New York: Oxford University Press, 1980), Paul Fussell refers to W. H. Davies (in *The Autobiography of a Super-Tramp*, 1908), Anthony Powell's "Waring" (in *What's Become of Waring*, 1939), and Anthony Burgess as other examples of armchair travelers who needed to take no actual journey in order to arrive at an account of time spent abroad. Fussell, it must be noted, uses the term "stationary tourist" in a rather different sense from the one I intend in this essay.

3. *Prose 2* (Spring 1971), p. 114.
4. *Some Trees* (New York: Ecco Press, 1978), pp. 14–18.
5. *Collected Poems, 1951–1971* (New York: Norton, 1972), p. 319.
6. *Some Trees*, p. 74.
7. Initially published in the *Partisan Review* (March 1938), "In Prison" was reprinted in *The Poet's Story*, ed. Howard Moss (New York: Macmillan, 1973), pp. 9–16. All page references are to the latter publication.
8. Compare with Kierkegaard's exposition of "the rotation method":

   The whole secret lies in arbitrariness. People usually think it easy to be arbitrary, but it requires much study to succeed in being arbitrary so as not to lose oneself in it, but so as to derive satisfaction from it. One does not enjoy the immediate but something quite different which he arbitrarily imports into it. You go to see the middle of a play, you read the third part of a book. By this means you insure yourself a very different kind of enjoyment from that

which the author has been so kind as to plan for you.
Either/Or, trans. David F. Swenson and Lillian Marvin Swenson (Princeton: Princeton University Press, 1971), vol. 1, p. 295.
9. John Ashbery, "Cornell's Sublime Junk," *Newsweek* (December 8, 1980), p. 111.

In an appreciation of Cornell published some years earlier, Ashbery discerns in some of the boxes a version of the theme that informs his own "The Instruction Manual." "It is likewise hard to believe that Cornell has never been in France, so forcefully does his use of clippings from old French books and magazines recreate the atmosphere of that country. Looking at one of his 'hotel' boxes one can almost feel the chilly breeze off the Channel at Dieppe or some other outmoded, out-of-season French resort. But this is the secret of his eloquence: he does not recreate the country itself but the impression we have of it before going there, gleaned from Perrault's fairy tales or old copies of *L'Illustration*, or whatever people have told us about it." "Cornell: The Cube Root of Dreams," *Art News* 66 (Summer 1967), p. 58.

DAVID BROMWICH
From "Elizabeth Bishop's Dream-Houses"
Raritan, Summer 1984, pp. 77–94

In a very striking passage of "Roosters," Elizabeth Bishop turns to address the shiny, gloating, and definitively male creatures whose cries disturb her sleep:

> each one an active
> displacement in perspective;
> each screaming, "This is where I live!"
>
> Each screaming
> "Get up! Stop dreaming!"
> Roosters, what are you projecting?

The sleeper, as she tells us in another poem, eventually recovers from these assaults and continues to inhabit "my proto-dream-house,/ my crypto-dream-house, that crooked box/set up on pilings." She has taken in enough of the roosters' admonitions to concede, "Many things about this place are dubious." But the force of her rhetorical question—"What are *you* projecting?"—suggests a reserve of personal strength. Bishop's own poems are active displacements of perspective. They too project a warning about where she lives, and they have the authority of dreams rather than awakenings.

That she was praised throughout her career for a humbler kind of success is doubtless just as well: charitable misunderstandings help an artist to go on working quietly. Yet it is worth recalling the standard terms of this praise, for they reveal how little had changed in the years that separate Bishop's first appearance from that of Emily Dickinson. Admirers of "Success is counted sweetest" (who thought it probably the work of Emerson) were replaced by encouragers of the best woman poet in English. And a sure ground of appreciation for so special a performer was taken to be her "accuracy." What did that mean? Not, evidently, that she adapted the same style to different situations, and not that she changed all the time, with a relentless originality. It was an esthetic compliment, difficult to translate into English. Similarly, Bishop was prized for her "charm." In the sense of a warm sociability, she certainly was not charming, least of all when she meant to be, as in her poems about the poor. In any other sense, charm is a tedious virtue for a poet, just as accuracy is an impracticable vice. And yet, in spite of their evasiveness, both words converge on a trait which all of Bishop's readers have felt in her poems: the presence of an irresistible self-trust. To her, art is a kind of home. She makes her accommodations with an assurance that is full

of risk, and, for her as for Dickinson, the domestic tenor of some poems implies a good-natured defiance of the readers she does not want. The readers she cares for, on the other hand, are not so much confided in as asked to witness her self-recoveries, which have the quality of a shared premise. Her work is a conversation which never quite takes place but whose possibility always beckons. . . .

To an exceptional degree in modern poetry, Bishop's work offers resistance to any surmise about the personality of the author. One reason is that the poems themselves have been so carefully furnished with eccentric details or gestures. These may seem tokens of companionability, yet a certain way into a poem the atmosphere grows a little chill; farther in, as the conversation strolls on, one senses the force field of a protective ease. Some day, a brief chapter in a history of poetry will describe Lowell's misreading of Bishop as a voice of resonant sincerity, and his appropriation for journalistic ends of her more marked traits of syntax, punctuation, and anomalous cadence. But to the reader who returns to these poems for their own sake, the question likeliest to recur is: what are they concealing? It helps, I think, to frame this as a question about a difficult passage—for example, about the pathos of some lines near the end of "Crusoe in England," in which Crusoe describes the objects that recall his years of solitude.

> The knife there on the shelf—
> it reeked of meaning, like a crucifix.
> It lived. How many years did I
> beg it, implore it, not to break?
> I knew each nick and scratch by heart,
> the bluish blade, the broken tip,
> the lines of wood-grain on the handle . . .
> Now it won't look at me at all.

Like many comparable passages of her work, the description is weirdly circumstantial. What does it mean for a poet who is a woman to write, as a man, of an object so nearly linked with masculine assertion, with this mingling of tenderness, pity, and regret?

The poetic answer, which has to do with the cost of art to life, does not exclude the sexual one, which has to do with an ambivalent femininity. The poet's own weapons in art as in life have been more dear to her than she can easily confess. The punishment for deserting them is that they refuse to return her gaze; they lose their aura, and she ceases to be a poet. A similar recognition is implied in other poems, where a wish to conquer or dominate—resisted at first, then acted on—darkens the celebration of having come through every challenge. Thus, "The Armadillo" moves from horror of a creature, quite distinct from the poet, to wonder at the same creature, which in the meantime has been implicitly identified with her. She devotes a poem to the armadillo because it is a survivor, fore-armed against any catastrophe. Like her, it watches in safety a dangerous and beautiful spectacle, the drifting of the "frail, illegal fire balloons" which at any moment may splatter "like an egg of fire/against the cliff." As for the poet herself, the poem is proof of her armor. In the same way, in "Roosters" she is a second and unmentioned crier of the morning; the poem, with its "horrible insistence" three notes at a time, announces exactly where she lives.

These identifications go deep. Such poems are not, in fact, animal-morality pieces, in the vein of Marianne Moore. They more nearly resemble Lawrence's "Fish," "The Ass," "Tortoise Shell," and "Tortoise Family Connections"—protestant inquests concerning the powers of the self, which have the incidental form of free-verse chants about animals. Bishop writes without Lawrence's spontaneous humor, and without his weakness for quick vindications. Indeed, there is something like self-reproach in a line that begins the final movement of "Roosters": "how could the night have come to grief?" By a trick of context, this phrase opens up an ambiguity in the cliché. It warns us that there has been matter for grieving during the night, before the first rooster crowed, at a scene of passion which was also a betrayal. "The Armadillo" too reveals the complicity of love with strife, in its italicized last stanza; here the last line and a half is a chiasmus, in which strength is surrounded by a yielding vulnerability.

> *Too pretty, dreamlike mimicry!*
> *O falling fire and piercing cry*
> *and panic, and a weak mailed fist*
> *clenched ignorant against the sky!*

"Weak" and "ignorant" are meant to temper the surprise of the "mailed fist clenched," and they cast doubt on those three central words: the fist, emblem of contest, is defended by weakness and ignorance, its only outward fortifications. The gesture of defiance, however, becomes all the more persuasive with this glimpse of a possible defeat. The way "The Armadillo" comes to rest has felt tentative to some readers, and yet the only question it asks is rhetorical: "See how adequately I shelter my victory?" In other poems just as surely, an elaborate craft gives away the poet as always present, at a scene she has painted as uninhabitable. The repeated line in a very late poem, "One Art," will declare her control by rhyming "disaster" with "The art of losing isn't hard to master"; as if we could expect her endurance to be taxing of course, but no more doubtful than her ability to pair the words for a villanelle.

Sexuality is the most elusive feature of Bishop's temperament—before writing any of the poems in *North & South*, she had learned to allegorize it subtly—and the reticence of her critics alone makes its existence worth noting. Like other habitual concerns, it interests her as it joins a care for what she sometimes calls the soul. This is an argument carried on from poem to poem, but its first appearance, in "The Imaginary Iceberg," is startling.

> Icebergs behoove the soul
> (both being self-made from elements least visible)
> to see them so: fleshed, fair, erected indivisible.

Until these concluding lines the poem has been a light entertainment, a "Convergence of the Twain" told from the iceberg's point of view. The lines shift our perspective on everything that came before—in effect, they translate a poem which did not seem to need translation. "Fleshed, fair, erected indivisible": the words, we see at once, belong to the human body rather than the soul. They are monstrously beautiful because they are a lie. For in the metaphor about the soul which has been perfectly built up, the comparison rightly demands instead: cold, white, immense, indestructible. This yields a pleasant description of an iceberg which, when we ponder it, is replaced by a sublime representation of the soul.

It is characteristic of Bishop's wit that she should have begun the same poem fancifully: "We'd rather have the iceberg than the ship,/although it meant the end of travel." Translating, as the poem suggests we do, this becomes: "We'd rather have the soul than the body,/although it meant the end of life." Yet for Bishop travel is not a chance metaphor. It stands for all that can divert the soul from its prospects. To hold fast to what it knows may mean for the soul to remain always "stockstill like cloudy rock"; or like a mariner, curled asleep at the top of a mast or seated with his eyes closed tight, untouchable by the charms of the voyage. This is the condition of "the unbeliever" in the poem of that title: believing only in himself, he knows "The sea is hard as diamonds; it wants to destroy us all."

With his intensity perhaps, the soul may be equal to the imaginary iceberg which "cuts its facets from within./Like jewelry from a grave/it saves itself and adorns/only itself." The phrase "from a grave," as it finally seems, is not fanciful at all but descriptive. It says that a guarding of the soul's integrity may also be a defense against death. And the sense in which this is especially true for a poet is the sense that matters to Bishop.

The titles of three of Bishop's volumes (*North & South, Questions of Travel, Geography III*) show how far she accepted—at times rather flatly—the common opinion that travel was her distinctive subject. Yet few readers are likely to know even a single region as intimately as she knew two hemispheres; and to make her geography poems interesting we have to read them as poems about something else. With this need of ours, a whole tract of her writing refuses to cooperate: poems about squatters and other half-cherished neighbors—efforts of self-conscious whimsy (like "Manuelzinho") or of awkward condescension (like "Filling Station"). I think these are the only poems Bishop ever wrote that dwindle as one comes to see them more clearly. One has to move away from these in order to learn what must have been clear to her from the first: that geography carries interest as a figure of the soul's encounter with fate (or as she puts it, with "what we imagine knowledge to be"). Occasionally, in the terms she proposes for this encounter, Bishop echoes the hero of Stevens's "The Comedian as the Letter C," who sought

> an elemental fate,
> And elemental potencies and pangs,
> And beautiful barenesses as yet unseen,
> Making the most of savagery.

But the poems I have in mind all end in a distrust of these things. In them, the dream of freedom, under the aspect of a perpetual self-renewal, is interpreted as a helpless revolt against the conditions of experience. The poet, however, offers no hope that we shall ever escape the enchantment of the dream.

"Brazil, January 1, 1502" marks the conquistadors' first step into a trap, a vast mesh of circumstance disguised as a jungle, and cozily misnamed "the new world." The poem starts off, innocuously, with an epigraph from Sir Kenneth Clark, "embroidered nature . . . tapestried landscape."

> Januaries, Nature greets our eyes
> exactly as she must have greeted theirs:
> every square inch filling in with foliage—
> big leaves, little leaves, and giant leaves,
> blue, blue-green, and olive,
> with occasional lighter veins and edges,
> or a satin underleaf turned over.

It is all, she goes on to say (confirming her epigraph) "solid but airy; fresh as if just finished/and taken off the frame." Courteously artful, we are like the conquistadors in supposing that we can make Nature over in a language we know—for them, the language of tapestry, for us that of naturalistic description. In either case we reproduce the nature prized by a Western connoisseur of art; and the poem is about how we cannot ever effect the conversion without loss. Nature will always take its revenge by drawing us still farther in, and suspending our knowledge of the thing that claims our pursuit.

So, in the next stanza, the tapestry is described as "a simple web"—a moral text, its foreground occupied by "Sin:/five sooty dragons near some massy rocks." Even after these have been naturalized as lizards, Bishop tells us "all eyes/are on the smaller, female one, back to,/her wicked tail straight up and over,/red as a red-hot wire." Between then and now, the allegorical and the natural, the poem admits no disparity—none, anyway, to compete with the similarity implied by such imperial habits of seeing. Hence the appropriateness of the poem's grammatical structure, its "As then, *so now*." This structure is completed only in the third and last stanza, which reverses the order of the comparison. As we find it now, not unfamiliar,

> Just so the Christians, hard as nails,
> tiny as nails, and glinting,
> in creaking armor, came and found it all,
> not unfamiliar:
> no lovers' walks, no bowers,
> no cherries to be picked, no lute music,
> but corresponding, nevertheless,
> to an old dream of wealth and luxury
> already out of style when they left home—
> wealth plus a brand-new pleasure.
> Directly after Mass, humming perhaps
> *L'Homme armé* or some such tune,
> they ripped away into the hanging fabric,
> each out to catch an Indian for himself—
> those maddening little women who kept calling,
> calling to each other (or had the birds waked up?)
> and retreating, always retreating, behind it.

In the light of this ending, the poem may be read as a colonial dream of all that seems infinitely disposable in the colonized.

But it is also about something that evades our grasp in every object that appeals to the human love of conquest. The Indian women, "those maddening little women who kept calling, calling to each other"—but not to their pursuers—only repeat the attraction of the female lizard, "her wicked tail straight up and over,/red as a red-hot wire." Both alike appear to beckon from behind the tapestry of the jungle fabric. They entice, and bind their spell. Another retreat will always be possible to them, since the jungle has gone opaque to the men hunting them, who believe at every point that it is transparent. This is another way of saying that the invaders have become victims of their own conquering perspective. They recreate here "an old dream of wealth and luxury"; yet the dream was "already out of style when they left home"; and the new place, as disclosed to other eyes, has seemed far from homelike. In the end their crossing of this threshhold, "hard as nails,/ tiny as nails," says most about their sense of home, which was equally marked by a failure of knowledge. What they take to be an act of possession is not, therefore, even a successful repossession, but the enactment of a familiar ritual of self-seduction.

This poem shows Bishop moving well outside the limits of the travel sketch. By itself, it is almost enough to persuade us that she exploits the genre elsewhere chiefly to break with it, from an impulse comparable to Dickinson's in revising the poem of "home thoughts." At any rate, the sketch that goes furthest to appease the worldly taste of her readers carries a suspicious title, "Over 2,000 Illustrations and a Complete Concordance," and the steady mystification of its narrative seems bent on protracting our suspicion. The poem, with an unsettling confidence, treats worldliness as a form of literal reading that is death—but the title is worth pausing over. What is a concordance? A system of reference to all the uses of every important word in the bible, or for that matter in any sacred book, including the work of a great poet. The illustrations accompanying it may be pictures—the picture-postcard atmosphere of much of the poem will toy with this—yet they are as likely to be passages longer than a phrase, which give a fuller context for the entries. When reading a concordance, we do not look at individual words to be sure of their reference, but to satisfy ourselves of a fateful pattern of choice. From the sum of an author's repetitions, we may learn a tact for whatever is

irreducible in his character. "Over 2000 Illustrations" owes its force to the propriety with which one can substitute both "reader" and "traveller" for "author," and view a place in the world as denoting a locus in a text.

The thought that troubles Bishop at the start is that the book of nature and history may not be either a clean text or an already canonical one, whether bible or secular fiction, but something more like just such a concordance, with occasional glimpses into its depths coming from the illustrations alone.

> Thus should have been our travels:
> serious, engravable.
> The Seven Wonders of the World are tired
> and a touch familiar, but the other scenes,
> innumerable, though equally sad and still,
> are foreign. Often the squatting Arab,
> or group of Arabs, plotting, probably,
> against our Christian Empire,
> while one apart, with outstretched arm and hand
> points to the Tomb, the Pit, the Sepulcher.
> The branches of the date-palms look like files.
> The cobbled courtyard, where the Well is dry,
> is like a diagram, the brickwork conduits
> are vast and obvious, the human figure
> far gone in history or theology,
> gone with its camel or its faithful horse.
> Always the silence, the gesture, the specks of birds
> suspended on invisible threads above the Site,
> or the smoke rising solemnly, pulled by threads.

The broken, randomly spliced rhythm of this opening, the discreteness of its sentences, as well as the words "often" and "always," suggest the episodic quality of the moments chronicled in the illustrations. They tell a story, apparently senseless, and in no particular order, which the poem later names the story of "God's spreading fingerprint." Only the Christians in the illustrations make a connection from place to place; and in the margin, everywhere, are faintly sinister Arabs, plotting or "looking on amused": together, these figures give it the unity it has. But as the account moves on, it grows still more oddly inconsequential: "In Mexico the dead man lay/in the blue arcade; the dead volcanoes/glistened like Easter lilies./The jukebox went on playing 'Ay, Jalisco!'" The blare of the jukebox comes in when the story's meaning appears to have been surely lost, and it signals a transition. Now, the tone of the illustrations (which somehow have become cheap guidebook images) drifts toward the hallucinatory:

> And in the brothels of Marrakesh
> the little pockmarked prostitutes
> balanced their tea-trays on their heads
> and did their belly dances; flung themselves
> naked and giggling against our knees,
> asking for cigarettes. It was somewhere near there
> I saw what frightened me most of all:
> A holy grave, not looking particularly holy,
> one of a group under a keyhole-arched stone
>   baldaquin
> open to every wind from the pink desert.

By the first five lines of this passage, every worldly fact has been rendered exchangeable with every other, and the loss is of nothing less than the history and the pathos of the things one may come to know.

Bishop is frightened "most of all" by the suddenly exposed grave in the desert because it reminds her of a life emptied of causes and consequences, with "Everything only connected by 'and' and 'and.'" The conclusion of the poem brings together author, reader, and traveller a last time, and envisions a sort of text that would return attention to something beyond it.

Everything only connected by "and" and "and."
Open the book. (The gilt rubs off the edges
of the pages and pollinates the fingertips.)
Open the heavy book. Why couldn't we have seen
this old Nativity while we were at it?
—the dark ajar, the rocks breaking with light,
and undisturbed, unbreathing flame,
colorless, sparkless, freely fed on straw,
and, lulled within, a family with pets,
—and looked and looked our infant sight away.

Much less than everything is restored by this ending.
Though the holy book, once opened, confronts us with an
ideal representation of our origins, we have to read it un-
innocently. We know how thoroughly we have revised it
already by our later imaginings, by every arrangement which
makes the end of a life or work distort its beginning. To deny
our remoteness from the scene would be to cancel the very
experience which permits us to pass through "the dark ajar."
Thus, we stand with the poet, both in the scene and outside it,
uncertain whether pleasure is the name for what we feel. Her
wishfully innocent question—"Why couldn't we have seen/
this old Nativity while we were at it?"—has the tone of a child's
pleading, "Why couldn't we *stay* there?"—said of a home, or a
place that has grown sufficiently like home. Some time or
other we say that about childhood itself. The book, then, is
hard to open because it is hard to admit the strength of such a
plea; harder still, to hear it for what it says about our relationship to ourselves. Any place we live in, savage or homely,
dream-house or rough shelter, we ourselves have been the
making of. And yet, once made, it is to be inherited forever.
Everything may be connected by "because" and "therefore,"
and every connection will be provisional. The last line accordingly yields an ambiguous truth about nostalgia: to look our
sight away is to gaze our fill, but also to look until we see
differently—until, in our original terms, we do not see at all.
The line, however, warrants a more general remark about
Bishop's interest in the eye. In common with Wordsworth, she
takes the metaphor of sight to imply the activity of all the

senses, and these in turn to represent every possibility of conscious being. Sight is reliable because it can give no account of
itself. We make it mean only when we look again, with "that
inward eye/ Which is the bliss of solitude" (words, incidentally,
which the hero of "Crusoe in England" tries reciting to himself
on the island, but can remember only after his rescue). It is in
the same poem that Wordsworth says of the daffodils, "I
gazed—and gazed"; and the action of "The Fish" turns on this
single concentrated act: "I stared and stared," and the colors of
the boat changed to "rainbow, rainbow, rainbow," and she let
the fish go.

In passing from sight to vision, or to "what is within
(which after all/cannot have been intended to be seen),"
Bishop always respects the claims of unbelievers different from
herself. Her mood is almost always optative, in its readiness to
inquire into not-yet-habitable truths; and I want to conclude
with an especially full expression of that mood, from "Love
Lies Sleeping." She writes there of a dawn in a city, with
eleven lines of a soft introductory cadence, good enough for the
opening bars of a Gershwin tune; with a memory of the waning
night and its "neon shapes/that float and swell and glare"; with
a panoramic view and a long tracking view that ends in the
window of one dwelling, where the poet asks the "queer cupids
of all persons getting up" to be mild with their captives:

for always to one, or several, morning comes
whose head has fallen over the edge of his bed,
whose face is turned
so that the image of
the city grows down into his open eyes
inverted and distorted. No. I mean
distorted and revealed,
if he sees it at all.

The words are as serious and engravable as an epitaph. At the
same time, with a doubt exactly the size of a comma, they
point to a revelation that may have occurred, and, for the sake
of its distortion as well as its truth, keep it living in surmise.

JOHN PEALE BISHOP

1892–1944

John Peale Bishop was born on May 21, 1892, in Charles Town, West Virginia. Though his earliest
vocation was that of a painter, verse written in his teens while at day school in Pennsylvania was
published in *Harper's Weekly* in 1912, and after entering Princeton University he became managing
editor of the *Nassau Literary Magazine*, then edited by Edmund Wilson. He succeeded to the
editorship the following year, and continued to sell stories and poems throughout his college years.
A volume of verse, *Green Fruit* (1912), was published shortly after he graduated.

World War I profoundly marked Bishop. During the war he served as an infantry first lieutenant, and in its aftermath commanded a company guarding German prisoners of war. Deeply
affected by what he saw as the distintegration of European civilization, he returned to New York and
took a position on the staff of *Vanity Fair*, and in 1922 collaborated with Edmund Wilson on
Undertaker's Garland, a collection of prose and poetry on the theme of death. In the same year he
married Margaret Hutchins, and they left New York to spend two years in Europe. While there he
studied French, Italian, and Provençal, concentrating on the troubador poets. Although they
returned to America in 1924, they bought a chateau in France three years later, and remained there
until 1933.

In 1931 Bishop published the prose fiction *Many Thousands Gone*, followed by the poetry collection *Now With His Love* (1933) shortly after his return to the United States. In 1935 he published his only novel, *Act of Darkness*. Deeply committed to the war effort, in 1941–42 he left his home on Cape Cod for a year in New York as Director of Publishing of the Bureau of Cultural Relations of the Council of National Defense. A year later, Archibald MacLeish offered him a position with the Library of Congress, but failing health obliged him to return home from Washington D.C. shortly after he arrived. He died on April 4, 1944, at his home on Cape Cod.

Personal

⟨Bishop⟩ was nine when his father died, and his mother soon remarried. In his last ten years it seemed to me, when we talked about such matters, as we more and more did, that he more and more took imaginatively the part of his father, of the outsider, of the *déraciné*. It was a rôle that merged very early in his life with that of the modern romantic poet. That he was fully conscious of the historical beginnings of this split in loyalty (it became later the condition of his special sensibility, liberating his powers of observation) is quite plain in the fine story "Many Thousands Gone," in which the Yankee officer occupying the Virginia town of Mordington (Charles Town) is himself a native of Mordington who has taken the side of the "enemy." He is described as having sandy hair, a small moustache, and a foxlike face. I have always seen in this portrait a caricature of Bishop himself.

. . . He had a special modesty and detachment and a generosity which people took for granted in that time of highly developed literary "personalities" and competitive literary careers. In the twenties, in Paris and New York, few people read anything, even the books which presumably had made the reputations of the writers most talked about. I am not the right person to go into this mystery of literary fashion; yet I ought to say that John Bishop was distinctly not the fashion. He had little gift for dramatizing himself as a literary personality, and I always suspected that his dandyism, a sort of social mask behind which he concealed himself, was his way of withdrawing from the literary scene, perhaps an expression of contempt for the literary *arriviste*. (This mask, of course, had its own defects; I think it limited his range as a writer.) His closest friends at that time, Hemingway, Fitzgerald, and MacLeish, were distinctly not *arrivistes*. Yet I felt that nobody in Paris quite took him seriously as a writer. The writings of all these men, and of others, including myself, would have been the poorer without his disinterested advice: he had a quick, intuitive sense of the problems involved in his friends' work.—Allen Tate, "John Peale Bishop: A Personal Memoir," *The Collected Poems of John Peale Bishop*, ed. Allen Tate, 1948, pp. xii–xv

General

Bishop's basic theme is the loss of form, the loss of myth, the loss of a pattern. The poet attempts to define the meaning of a personal experience in a world which is meaningless—"This was the time of the long war/When the old deliberated and always rose/To the same decision; More of the Young/Must die./Of them I remember and their nights/Her warmth as of a million suns." The rich sensuous personal experience has no relation at all to the public experience. Or, as in the case of many of the poems, the poet takes as his background for the same theme the days of the waning Roman empire. The public values are collapsing, and with their collapse the protagonist's world of private values cannot be sustained.

It is true that Bishop's poetry is often poetry about poetry, but then Bishop's conception of poetry is more profound than the man-in-the-street's essentially "literary" conception. The problems of writing poetry and the problems of a formless and chaotic age become at many points identical. The break-down of some of Bishop's poems, their lack of an adquate resolution for the theme, their raveling out and tailing off are indeed related to Bishop's preoccupation with his obsessive theme, but the relation is by no means a simple one. Certainly, none of Bishop's problems would be solved by his abandoning his theme in favor of one of the more "robust" themes such as have been recently recommended by Mr. Van Wyck Brooks. Or by giving up a concern for "form." Indeed, the most successful of Bishop's poems are precisely those which exploit his theme most thoroughly and which are most precisely "formed."

Sometimes the attempted resolution is too direct. Thus, "Loss in the West" ends with this rhetorical question: "And still pursues/What? Wheel of the sun/In Heaven? The west wind? Or only a will/To his destruction?" This is too flat: the last item deflates the irony of the others. Sometimes the attempted resolution is too indirect. The ending of "An Interlude," one of the Roman poems, is intentionally flat, an ironical tailing off: "We have heard the new Emperor proclaims/Our immediate deliverance . . ./In the meantime, the barbarians are back in the passes./Nothing is left but to stay devastation by tribute." But here the flatness succeeds all too well: the "poem" ends lamely—not merely the speech of *the protagonist in the poem*.

It is only fair to Bishop's achievement, however, to pause for a moment over the resolution of "The Return," a fine example of Bishop at his best.

Temples of Neptune invaded by the sea
And dolphins streaked like streams sportive
As sunlight rode and over the rushing floors
The sea unfurled and what was blue raced silver.

The temples of the seagod achieve an apotheosis and destruction together—they cease to be temples and become the sea itself. Form is overwhelmed; the god fills his temple; there are worshipers, the dolphins, though their worship is animal and unconscious. The movement of the invading sea dominates the rhythm of the stanza, overwhelms the syntax. Is it the dolphins who "as sunlight rode" or is it the "streams sportive"? Grammatically it could be either; and actually it is both, for the play of the dolphins cannot be separated from the streams in which they are immersed. And over what floors does the sea unfurl?—the marble floors of the temple? But how then are they "rushing floors"? Are they not the shifting floors of the sea itself: the invaded temple has become the sea.

But if the poem is about the triumph of content over form, it is perfectly "formed" itself—even the fluid grammar is functioning as "form" in terms of the poem. *The Selected Poems* gives us an opportunity to see how considerable a poet Bishop is. The continued omission of his work from *Modern American Poetry* remains one of the mysteries of Mr. Louis Untermeyer's editorship.—Cleanth Brooks, "Form and Content," *KR*, Spring 1942, pp. 244–46

⟨N⟩ow that the evidence is nearly all in, John Peale Bishop's place in the pantheon of American poetry seems considerably more secure than it appeared during his lifetime. We have been used to hearing the West Virginian dismissed as *too* typical, *i.e.*, too derivative, on the one hand, too immersed in class consciousness (upper level), on the other; yet his essays and poems in their progress (they are helpfully given dates by the editors) amply display an original mind and reveal the generous, passionate, humane personality finally emerging from beneath the successive masks of the "provincial," the dandy, the snob, and the ironist. "Behind the mask," as Bishop wrote in one of his "Aphorisms," "is a naked man." . . .

Bishop did not deny that his poetry was derivative; he explained rather why it was: "My imitation of other poets is in part a desire not to be myself." If we keep in mind his position as an exile in his century (he preferred the eighteenth), in his native state (his father, who stemmed from Connecticut, had been "stoned in the streets" as a Yankee), in his native land (he was an expatriate for some years), in modern civilization generally (which he admitted into his poetry only in its phases of decadence), this perhaps is explanation enough. But this is only part of the story, for it is evident that his excursions into the styles of Yeats, Pound, Eliot, and others (for example, if a collection of "Renaissance Lyrics of the Twentieth Century" were possible, Bishop's *pastiches*, with their honest sensuality, might well head the list) gave testimony of his search for a technique which might achieve that marriage of intellect and emotion needed to fulfil the aim of poetry, "the whole man."—GERARD PREVIN MEYER, "Romantic Exile," *SR*, Oct. 2, 1948, p. 24

Bishop's poetry bears profoundly the impress of his own experience. The life is more than ordinarily involved with the verse, and at the risk perhaps of seeming to shirk the tasks the poetry imposes, I intend to take up Bishop's artistic biography where it impinges most forcibly upon his writing. His verse, though little known, will make its way; yet there is, I believe, a common preconception of Bishop which would have him, like John Crowe Ransom, merely an exquisite stylist, a poet possessed of a delicate but impotent Muse, incapable of coming to terms with the bitter world. Against this preconception we can set the life and the verse which contains the man's struggle; neither, except at the creative pitch, are harrowing, but there is always a tension, lively with will and failure, between life and poetry. His technical and moral means lie in that tension. For what Bishop had said of the symbolist poets was as true for himself: "What the symbolist poets sought was not an escape from the life of their times. What they sought was life; they could only report where it failed. The poetic means which they created to that end corresponded to the exasperation of nerves which accompanied the hunt, the distraction of the mind, the extremity of the heart that came with its failure."—WILLIAM ARROWSMITH, "An Artist's Estate," *HdR*, Spring 1949, pp. 118–19

⟨A⟩s one reads the poems in chronological order, beginning with those of Bishop's Princeton days and just after, one discovers a curious fact: in the early poems there is a quite surprising inventive and prosodic vigor, and not only this, but clear, if faint, indications of that elusive essential, *poetic character*. What became of it? It looks very much as if the tadpole lost his tail to get his legs. Excellent as much of the later poetry is, even to the point of brilliance on occasion, it is a poetry without personal aroma or idiom, or when, now and then, it *has* character or idiom, these seem oddly to have a sort of vintage mark on them, as of Pound 1922, or Eliot 1918. One begins therefore to suspect that the education, for so tender a talent, was too prolonged, too diverse and too severe. The classic file ended by filing away too much. The studious and ingenious search for a kind of classic amalgam of style (and let it be said emphatically in passing that here Bishop's taste was often extremely fine) found, not a style, but a virtuosity in styles, a kind

of Alexandrianism. The poet, in the process of becoming accomplished, had somehow lost his private view.— CONRAD AIKEN, "John Peale Bishop" (1949), *Collected Criticism*, 1958, p. 135

Works

His tradition is quite evidently aristocratic. He prefers the fine, the delicate, the rare in character or in performance. Several of the poems have to do with the aristocracy of the South. I do not think, however, that one can accuse Mr. Bishop of snobbery. Through ⟨*Now With His Love*⟩ runs the realization that, regardless of preference, the time has come when the fine flower of aristocracy is decadent, that terrible though this process may be, aristocracy must now be reinvigorated by contact with more primitive and ignorant classes. The poet may greatly prefer Desdemona to the Moor, but

> The ceremony must be found
> That will wed Desdemona to the huge Moor.

The poet may find dramatic the beautiful Southern woman who has her slaves brought to her bedside and beaten, but this woman is dying. Mr. Bishop is well aware that the object studied changes as the student changes. Nor can he find any permanent value in anything. He cannot seize upon religion as a solution. But he would not separate ideal love from lust; he would merely have both present in their right proportion.

Mr. Bishop's feeling about human society is that it is, on the whole, very stupid and rather crude. He finds in literature rare people much more exciting than any broad conception of the human race. He shrinks a little from the common herd, but he does not entirely deny them.—EDA LOU WALTON, "Aristocratic Verse," *Nation*, Feb. 7, 1934, pp. 162–63

The present volume of poetry, *Now With His Love*, provokes, in one sense, a similar interest: the volume is an index, as it were, to the poetical development of the last decade or so, and a summary of its fashions. To illustrate:

> He seems to smoke a cigarette,
> And leaning on a bar of zinc
> The tired lover tries to think.
> Memory wipes away the night
> As a damp rag might smear a dirty glass.
> Above the bar he sees another face.

This passage, the conclusion of "Martyr's Hill," is early Eliot, the Eliot of "Preludes." Bishop's "Aliens" falls in the same category. The following lines from "Chateau à Vendre" show, likewise, a mechanism of wit which the early work of Eliot made current:

> The sun looks toward England
> With the old blind civilized smile
> Of Madame du Deffand
> On Horace Walpole.

And "Easter Morning," too long for quotation, shows the basic theme, the sententiousness, and something of the versification of Pound in "Gerontion."

Pound, too, has not been without influence on Bishop's verse. "Epigram" seems to be straight Pound in its technical mannerisms. "An English Lady," dated 1922, bears some relation to the portraits of Eliot and Pound, although more to those of Pound than of Eliot, in its affectation of meticulous prosiness, its oblique commentary, and its international irony. Bishop's translations, especially those from the Provençal, are done artfully in the style which Pound found so effective for the same purpose; and certain of Bishop's original pieces display the same mood and same manner—for instance, "Fiemettœ."

In several poems Bishop appears to be instructed by the practice of Yeats in his middle period. I would cite "Wish in the Daytime" and "Young Men Dead." And "Twelfth Night," a fine performance in its own right, hints at something of Yeats in another phase.

There are occasional flashes of similarity to Cummings and MacLeish, but on those occasions Bishop need concede nothing to either poet in merit. The "Return" has more than a little of the inflection of MacLeish's elaborately direct and masculine idiom, and some of the stage properties of his aborted legends and mythologies:

> . . . all of our state was down
> In fragments. In the dust, old men with tufted
> Eyebrows whiter than sunbaked faces gulped
> As it fell. But they no more than we remembered
> The old sea-fights, the soldiers' names and sculptors'.

. . . What Bishop offers, what unifies the volume, is a taste and a scrupulous technical concern. Within terms of his premises this taste is meticulous and sure; to quarrel with it is to quarrel, not with the poet, but with the age. This taste rarely fails him, and, I think, only once or twice flagrantly; as in the last two or three lines of two fine poems, "Ode" and "And When the Net Was Unwound."—ROBERT PENN WARREN, "Working Toward Freedom," *Poetry*, March 1934, pp. 343–45

ALLEN TATE
"John Peale Bishop" (1935)
On the Limits of Poetry
1948, pp. 238–47

Of the American poets whose first books were published between 1918 and 1929 not more than six or seven are likely to keep their reputations until the end of the present decade. Eliot and Pound are pre-war. Crane, Marianne Moore, Stevens, MacLeish, and Ransom are among the slightly more than half a dozen. The two or three other places may be disputed; but I take it that since 1929 there has been no new name unless it be that of a young man, James Agee, whose first volume appeared in 1934. John Peale Bishop, whose first poetry goes back to the war period but whose first book, *Now with His Love*,[1] came out in 1932, will, I believe, rank among the best poets of the last decade.

His position has been anomalous. His contemporaries made their reputations in a congenial critical atmosphere, and they have been able to carry over a certain prestige into virtually a new age. (Ages crowd upon one another in a country that has never been young.) But Bishop has lacked that advantage. The first criticism accorded him was largely of the Marxist school. Mr. Horace Gregory, shrewdly discerning the poet's technical skill, became quickly concerned about the sincerity of a man who ignored the "class struggle." Bishop was not, in fact, asked whether he was a poet but whether he expected to survive capitalism: whether given his roots in the war-generation and the prejudices of the "ruling class," he could hope to achieve the portage over to the "main stream" of American letters recently discovered by Mr. Granville Hicks.

The problems of poetry must necessarily be the same in all ages, but no two ages come to the same solutions. Happiest is that age which, like the age of Sidney and Spenser, felt no need to reduce the problems to ultimate philosophical terms: our critical apparatus is immeasurably more thorough than theirs,

our poetic performance appreciably looser. But our problems are inevitably theirs. They are the problem of language and the problem of form. The Elizabethan solution was practical, not speculative. The simple didacticism of the neo-classical Renaissance was as far as the sixteenth century got philosophically. The poets wrote better than they knew. Our knowledge is better than our performance.

In ages weak in form, such as our own age, theory will concentrate upon form, but practice upon the ultimate possibilities of language. Ages that create great varieties of forms, as the Elizabethans did in every branch of poetry, talk about language but actually take it for granted, and score their greatest triumphs with form. The powers of the language were not in the long run determined by theory, but instinctively by poets whose dominating passion was form: the language was determined by the demands of the subject. The more comprehensive the subject, the broader the symbolism, and the more profoundly relevant the scheme of reference to the whole human experience, the richer the language became. The experiment with language as such is *The Shepherd's Calendar*, and it is a failure; but even there the poet attempts only to enlarge his vocabulary with archaic words for "poetical" effect. There is no trace of that forcing of language beyond its natural limits that we find in modern verse. Propriety of diction was the problem, and it was ably discussed by Puttenham in his long *Arte of English Poesie*, a work in some respects comparable to *The Principles of Literary Criticism* by Mr. I. A. Richards, who talks not about the propriety of language but about its ultimate meaning. He thus leaves behind him language as an instrument and, by going into the *kinds* of meaning, converts the discussion into the peculiarly modern problem of form. For form is meaning and nothing but meaning: scheme of reference, supporting symbolism that ceases to support as soon as it is recognized as merely that.

Metrics as a phase of the problem of form needs attention from modern critics. It is a subject poorly understood. It is usually treated as an air-tight compartment of technical speculation. Yet surely a metrical pattern is usable only so long as it is attached to some usable form. It is a curious fact that modern metrics reflects the uncertainty of modern poets in the realm of forms. So the modern poet, struggling to get hold of some kind of meaning, breaks his head against the *impasse* of form, and when he finds no usable form he finds that he has available no metrical system either. For those fixed and, to us, external properties of poetry, rhyme and metrical pattern, are, in the ages of their invention, indeed fixed but not external. It is probable that there is an intimate relation between a generally accepted "picture of the world" and the general acceptance of a metrical system and its differentiations into patterns.

This is to say that the separate arts achieve their special formalisms out of a common center of experience. And from this center of experience, this reference of meaning, any single art will make differentiations within itself: epic, lyric, tragedy, comedy, each with its appropriate pattern of development. When the center of life disappears, the arts of poetry become the art of poetry. And in an advanced stage of the evil, in the nineteenth century and today, we get the *mélange des genres*, one art living off another, which the late Irving Babbitt so valiantly combated without having understood the influences that had brought it about. Painting tries to be music; poetry leans upon painting; all the arts "strive toward the condition of music"; till at last seeing the mathematical structure of music, the arts become geometrical and abstract, and destroy themselves.

The specialization of scientific techniques supplanting a

central view of life has, as Mr. John Crowe Ransom showed in a recent essay,[2] tended to destroy the formal arts: poetry has in turn become a specialization of aesthetic effects without formal limitations. And, as Mr. Edmund Wilson has argued,[3] the novel now does the work formerly done by epic and tragedy, forms too "limited" and "artificial" for modern minds. The novel is the least formal of the literary arts; it rose, in fact, upon the débris of the *genres*; and it has been able to drive the formal literary arts from the public interest because, appealing to the ordinary sense of reality fostered by information, science, and journalism, the novelist neither sets forth symbolic fictions nor asks the reader to observe formal limitations.

The poet then at this time must ask, not what limitations he will be pleased, after the manner of the young Milton, to accept, but whether there are any that he can get. I assume that a poet is a man eager to come under the bondage of limitations if he can find them. As I understand John Peale Bishop's poetry, he is that eager man. It is a moral problem, but that phase I cannot touch here. Bishop has no settled metrics; but that too is an aspect of the formal problem that cannot be discussed in the limited space of a note.

It has been said that Bishop has imitated all the chief modern poets. He has virtually conducted his poetical education in public. But the observation is double-edged. In our age of personal expression the poet gets credit for what is "his own": the art is not the thing, but rather the information conveyed about a unique personality. Applauding a poet only for what is uniquely his own, we lose thereby much that is good. If a poem in Yeats's manner appears in Bishop's book, and is as good as Yeats's, it is as good there as it is anywhere else.

More than most living poets Bishop has felt the lack of a central source of form. He is not the poet of personal moods and idle sensation. He constantly strives for formal structure. He has studied closely the poets of his time who, like Yeats, seem to have achieved, out of a revived or invented mythology or by means of a consciously restricted point of view, a working substitute for the supernatural myth and the concentration that myth makes possible. It is, I think, interesting to observe that in Bishop two contemporary influences, Yeats and Eliot, meet strongly, and meet only in him of all the contemporary poets whom I know anything about: Yeats for form, Eliot for the experiment in language. Only the best Yeats is better than this:

> And Mooch of the bull-red
> Hair who had so many dears
> Enjoyed to the core
> And Newlin who hadn't one
> To answer his shy desire
> Are blanketed in the mould
> Dead in the long war.
> And I who have most reason
> Remember them only when the sun
> Is at his dullest season.

It is not necessary to illustrate the early influence of Eliot, for it appears everywhere in *Now with His Love*. I will quote two poems that are harder to "place." To critics interested in poetry as private property it may be said that they are evidently his own. The poems—they must be read as carefully climaxed wholes—seem to me to be among the most successful in modern verse:

The Return

> Night and we heard heavy and cadenced hoofbeats
> Of troops departing: the last cohorts left
> By the North Gate. That night some listened late
> Leaning their eyelids toward Septentrion.

> Morning flared and the young tore down the trophies
> And warring ornaments: arches were strong
> And in the sun but stone; no longer conquests
> Circled our columns; all our state was down

> In fragments. In the dust, old men with tufted
> Eyebrows whiter than sunbaked faces, gulped
> As it fell. But they no more than we remembered
> The old sea-fights, the soldiers' names and sculptors'.

> We did not know the end was coming: nor why
> It came; only that long before the end
> Were many wanted to die. Then vultures starved
> And sailed more slowly in the sky.

> We still had taxes. Salt was high. The soldiers
> Gone. Now there was much drinking and lewd
> Houses all night loud with riot. But only
> For a time. Soon the taverns had no roofs.

> Strangely it was the young the almost boys
> Who first abandoned hope; the old still lived
> A little, at last a little lived in eyes.
> It was the young whose child did not survive.

> Some slept beneath the simulacra, until
> The gods' faces froze. Then was fear.
> Some had response in dreams, but morning restored
> Interrogation. Then O then, O ruins!

> Temples of Neptune invaded by the sea
> And dolphins streaked like streams sportive
> As sunlight rode and over the rushing floors
> The sea unfurled and what was blue raced silver.

The poem avoids the difficulty of form by leaning upon a certain violence of language. The form of "The Return" is a very general idea about the fall of Rome. The implications of the form are not wide; and it is a typical modern form in that it offers a rough parallelism with the real subject—which in this poem is modern civilization—and not a direct approach to the subject. Where shall the poet get a form that will permit him to make direct, comprehensive statements about modern civilization? Doubtless nowhere. As a feat of historical insight the "form" of "The Return" is commonplace; yet the poem is distinguished. The poet has manipulated language into painting. The line "Temples of Neptune invaded by the sea" is by no means the same as its prose paraphrase: civilizations die of an excess of the quality that made them great; we, too, shall perish when we no longer have the temple of Neptune, the form, to preserve us from the limitless energy of the sea, which the form held in check. But "Rome" is here not a symbol of anything; our inferences about modern civilization are obvious, but they are not authorized by the poem. "The poem," writes Bishop, "is a simile in which one term of the comparison is omitted." It is rather that by means of a new grasp of language, very different from the "word-painting" of eighteenth-century nature poetry, the poet achieves a plastic objectivity that to some degree liberates him from the problem of finding a structural background of idea.

What I have said about "The Return" applies with even greater force to "Perspectives Are Precipices":

> *Sister Anne, Sister Anne,*
> *Do you see anybody coming?*

>> I see a distance of black yews
>> Long as the history of the Jews

>> I see a road sunned with white sand
>> Wide plains surrounding silence. And

>> Far off, a broken colonnade
>> That overthrows the sun in shade.
> *Sister Anne, Sister Anne,*
> *Do you see nobody coming?*

A man
Upon that road a man who goes
Dragging a shadow by its toes.
Diminishing he goes, head bare
Of any covering even hair.
A pitcher depending from one hand
Goes mouth down. And dry is sand

Sister Anne, Sister Anne,
What do you see?
His dwindling stride. And he seems blind
Or worse to the prone man behind.

Sister Anne! Sister Anne!
I see a road. Beyond nowhere
Defined by cirrus and blue air.
I saw a man but he is gone
His shadow gone into the sun.

This poem I would cite as the perfect example of certain effects of painting achieved in poetry. Criticism of this kind of poetry must necessarily be tentative. Yet I think it is plain that this particular poem has not only the immediate effect of a modern abstract painting; it gives the illusion of perspective, of objects-in-the-round. Take the "road sunned with white sand"—instead of "sunlight on a sandy road," the normal word-structure for this image. Even more striking is "Wide plains surrounding silence." I leave it to the schoolmen, wherever they are, to decide whether "silence" is commonly abstract or concrete; yet it is certain that in Bishop's phrase it acquires a spatial, indeed almost sensory, value that would have been sacrificed had he written: "silence over the surrounding plains."

It is worth remarking here that the line, "Long as the history of the Jews," is the only clear example of "metaphysical wit" that I have been able to find in Bishop's verse. It is possibly a direct adaptation of a passage from Marvel:

And you should if you please refuse
Till the conversion of the Jews.

Bishop's line is the more striking for its isolation in his work, but I think it is clearly a violation of the plastic technique of the poem, and a minor blemish. The influence of Eliot, which could lead two ways, to the metaphysicals and to the symbolists, led Bishop almost exclusively to the latter. And he has perfected this kind of poetry in English perhaps more than any other writer.

It is an obscure subject: the Horatian formula *ut pictura poesis* bore fruit long before Hérédia and Gautier—as early, in English verse, as Milton. But the mixtures of the *genres* acquired a new significance after the late nineteenth-century French poets began to push the borders of one sense over into another. It was not merely that the poet should be allowed to paint pictures with words—that much the Horatian phrase allowed. It was rather that the new "correspondences" among the five senses multiplied the senses and extended the medium of one art into the medium of another. Rimbaud's absurd sonnet on the colors of the vowels was the extreme statement of an experiment that achieved, in other poets and in Rimbaud's own "Bateau Ivre," brilliant results. But the process cannot go on beyond our generation unless we are willing to accept the eventual destruction of the arts. There is no satisfactory substitute in poetry for the form-symbol.

It is on this dilemma of symbolic form or plastic form that Bishop is intelligent and instructive. He has recently written: "I am trying to make more and more *statements*, without giving up all that we have gained since Rimbaud." The difficulty could not be more neatly put. Two recent poems, "The Saints" and "Holy Nativity," are the result of this effort. The statement is form, the fixed point of reference; "all that we have gained since Rimbaud" is the enrichment of language that we have gained to offset our weakness in form.

The new experiment of Bishop's is not complete. In "Holy Nativity" the attempt to use the Christian myth collapses with a final glance at anthropology:

Eagle, swan or dove
White bull or cloud. . . .

His treatment of the supernatural, the attempt to replace our secular philosophy, in which he does not believe, with a vision of the divine, in which he tries to believe, is an instance of our modern unbelieving belief. We are so constituted as to see our experience in two ways. We are not so constituted as to see it two ways indefinitely without peril. Until we can see it in one way we shall not see it as a whole, and until we see it as a whole we shall not see it as poets. Every road is long, and all roads lead to the problem of form.

Notes

1. Bishop's first book, *Green Fruit*, a collection of undergraduate verse, appeared in 1917. See *The Collected Poems of John Peale Bishop* (New York, 1948). Bishop was born in 1892 and died in 1944.
2. "Poets Without Laurels," first published in 1935; reprinted in *The World's Body* (1938), pp. 55–75.
3. "Is Verse a Dying Technique?" *The Triple Thinkers* (1938), pp. 20–41.

R. P. BLACKMUR

1904–1965

Richard Palmer Blackmur's early life did not indicate a brilliant career as a literary critic. Born in Massachusetts in 1904, Blackmur was entirely self-educated, and never attended college. He worked initially as a book clerk in Massachusetts, and later as a freelance poet and critic. The quality of his poetry and criticism attracted the attention of the trustees of the Guggenheim Fellowship, who awarded him grants in 1936 and 1937, and the faculty of Princeton, who made him a fellow of the university in 1940. Blackmur taught at Princeton from 1940 until 1965, holding a chair of English from 1948. He was also a fellow at the Institute for Advanced Studies in Princeton during 1944–45 and at Cambridge in 1961. Other distinctions include a chair at Cambridge in 1961–62, and membership of the National Institute of Arts and Letters and of the American Academy of Arts and Sciences.

Best known for critical works such as *Language as Gesture* (1952), and A *Primer of Ignorance* (1967), Blackmur's reputation as a poet rests on *From Jordan's Delight* (1937), *The Second World* (1942), and *The Good European* (1947).

General

R. P. Blackmur died in 1965, without writing the single full-scale critical work, whether on Henry James, Henry Adams or Dostoyevsky, that would have shown all of his intellectual talents in their final integration. His several volumes of essays, particularly *Language as Gesture* (1952), remain as evidence of the best "close reader" among the New Critics. In a more diffuse sense, the image of his power in the literary world still abides, both in the realm of myth or "gossip grown old," and in the perhaps-waning prestige of literary modernism. Blackmur's judgments and prejudices are still influential, and it is a tribute to his power that his critical authority is still in the process of being overturned.

His poems, now for the first time collected, are no part of his power. Their considerable interest is founded on their comparative weakness, and their occasional poignance may be due to the vulnerable self-exposures of so daunting a power-figure. That they should be so clearly derivative, and yet so important to Blackmur himself, is of great significance in judging not only Blackmur's impressive performance as a critic, but in seeking a fair estimate as to just what was the relationship of poetry to criticism among all the New Critics.

Most of those grouped, rightly or not, as New Critics published several volumes of poetry: Eliot, I. A. Richards, William Empson, John Crowe Ransom, Allen Tate, R. P. Warren, Francis Fergusson, Kenneth Burke, Yvor Winters and others, as well as Blackmur. This is clearly a mixed grouping, as far as poetic stature is concerned. Few readers are as impressed by Richards's poetry as they are by Empson's, to cite only one instance. The line of poet-critics in English is long and impressive: Ben Jonson, Dryden, Samuel Johnson, Coleridge and Arnold are among the names that most readers would remember. Ruskin, Pater, and Wilde wrote poems in their youth, and then wisely turned to prose. Perhaps only Hazlitt, among the major critics of the past, was never inclined to verse.

Blackmur placed Yeats, Eliot and Pound foremost among the poets of this century; to some extent he helped canonize them. Toward Hart Crane and Wallace Stevens he was uneasy until the end. Though he said "that their stature is incontestable," he added that Crane "represents every ignorance possible to talent when it has genius," while Stevens "had no generalizing or organizing power." When so distinguished a critic makes judgments so clearly inadequate, a defensive anxiety seems evident.

Blackmur's own poems tend to be of two kinds, and neither is much his own. One belongs to Eliot and Pound, the other to Yeats. Here is Blackmur in "Before Sentence is Passed":

> This has become a very quiet place.
> One feels a dislocation. One tries at last
> to say only what the heart says, do only
> what the buds do: flower by conviction:
> the inward mastery of the outward act.

How could he not know that this was Eliot, rather than Blackmur? How could so acute an ear not recognize that his *Alma Venus* was not his own, but was made by Yeats?

> Looking at her there where she lies
> I see, for all the time she's run,

> There's not that beauty in her eyes
> A common woman might have earned
> Out of such seasons in love's school;
> Nor yet that look of cool
> Extravagant indifference
> A lesser spirit might have learned
> When so much adulation had been won
> And with so little violence,

Yet, in prose, he had wholly his own sensibility, stance, rhetoric. Dense and turbulent, the critical prose wins its agon against the past and against contemporaries, persuading the reader to forsake easy pleasures of apprehension. As critic, Blackmur matches his poets and novelists, compelling an energy of response that few other exegetes have evoked. Why did so powerful and agile a literary mind deceive itself as to part of its vocation?

In his posthumously published A *Primer of Ignorance*, still a vital work of criticism, Blackmur yields continually to a zest for judgment as energetic as it is ill-founded. How could so distinguished an intellect have been so wrong about Freud?

"Hysteria, which ought to be the clue to reality, becomes its creator. This we see in Freud, who began his studies with the etiology of hysteria and proceeded with its deification: as if all the gross responses uncomfortable with conduct could ordain conduct."

Blackmur's reader blinks, or should blink. Rarely has a "This we see" been such a disaster. But then Blackmur's reader may remember that "hysteria" was Blackmur's judgment upon Lawrence's poetry precisely where Lawrence was most masterful. In the sublime violence of Blackmur's late prose, some extraordinary repression is at work, and by this I mean a cultural and literary repression. Blackmur's criticism greatly dared to admit and release the Romantic energy and will to power that he tended to deprecate in Crane, Stevens and Lawrence, and that he admired, but always under other names and disguises, in Yeats and Eliot. Blackmur's verse lacks energy and power even as his critical prose carries energy and power beyond most limits. His poems are pale ghosts, shadows of other men's ecstasies.

A useful closing contrast can be provided either by Tate or by Robert Penn Warren. Tate, like Eliot, exemplifies the New Critical paradox of an anti-Romantic critic whose best poems are fiercely Romantic, as much so as those of Yeats or Crane. Warren, in the last decade, has transformed himself into our best living poet, by moving beyond Eliot's voice into an American Sublime as personal and Romantic as that of Whitman or Stevens. Blackmur, an even stronger critic than Tate and Warren, failed as a poet because he fell victim to the power of his own prose ideology. His confusion about Freud betrays the hysteria that rises when an inadequate ideology of reason confronts a larger and stronger version of reason. Freud's Romantic rationalism made no sense to Blackmur, whose prose achieved greatness in protesting the validity of its own rationalism, but only by a Romantic violence. Blackmur's poetry unfortunately waned by refusing its own ardors, and so ended as an echo, as another dying fall.—HAROLD BLOOM, "The Critic/Poet," *NYTBR*, Feb. 5, 1958, p. 9

RENÉ WELLEK
From "R. P. Blackmur Re-Examined"
Southern Review, July 1971, pp. 825–34

A friend of R. P. Blackmur told me that one of Blackmur's favorite passages came from Donne's third *Satire*:

On a high hill
Ragged and steep, Truth dwells, and he that will
Reach it, about must and about must go.

"Going about and about" seems an accurate description of Blackmur's critical method: the groping, painful struggle to describe, by circumlocution or metaphorical analogue, the experience of poetry which, he feels, is always beyond the reach of ordinary rational discourse. "There is,", he says bluntly, "finally, as much difference between words used about a poem and the poem as there is between words used about a painting and the painting. The gap is absolute" (*LG*, p. 381).[1] If this were true, Blackmur would have to conclude that descriptive criticism is a failure. Analysis cannot touch a poem; all the critic can do is "to set up clues," as there always remains a "territory of the poem which we cannot name or handle but only envisage" (*LG*, p. 264).

Still, provisionally, Blackmur defends and defines the task and limits of criticism much more coherently than his sense of the ultimate irrationality and obscurity of poetry would suggest. "Any rational approach is valid to literature and may be properly called critical which fastens at any point upon the work itself" (*LG*, p. 379) is a statement which implies an acceptance of the emphasis of the New Criticism on the text, of what I have called, after Manfred Kridl, "the ergocentric view." Certainly, Blackmur draws the consequences when he rejects the methods of extrinsic criticism: biography, psychology, Marxism, and academic historical scholarship. Blackmur had no academic education (he did not graduate from high school) and uncertain scholarly attainments (his knowledge of the classical and foreign languages, at least, was very limited), but he had—in difference, for example, from Allen Tate—no resentment or violent feelings against the English Department Establishment on public record. Actually he became a Professor of English at Princeton University by an unorthodox route, the writing program then in vogue. "Scholarship," he says, "is *about* literature," it is "without the work" (*LH*, pp. 180–1). It is useful in supplying us with facts but becomes obnoxious when it "believes it has made an interpretation by surrounding the work with facts" (*LH*, p. 181).

Marxism also remains on the periphery. Its economic insights "offer only a limited field of interest and enliven an irrelevant purpose" (*LG*, p. 374). Granville Hicks's Marxist history of American literature, *The Great Tradition*, is not "criticism at all."

Blackmur consistently has little use for the psychological schemes of Richards or Kenneth Burke. Blackmur admired Richards personally as "a warm and passionate man and a lover of poetry" (*PI*, p. 76) and grants that Richards' writings are "a preparatory school to good criticism," an "excellent aid to the understanding of poetry and its criticism" (*H&H*, III, p. 453), but that ultimately "he ought not be called a literary critic at all" (*LG*, p. 387). "A literal adoption of Mr. Richards' approach to literary criticism would stultify the very power it was aimed to enhance—the power of imaginative apprehension, of imaginative coordination of varied and separate ele-

ments" (*LG*, p. 389). Blackmur admired Richards' book *Coleridge on Imagination* for its passionate declaration of faith in poetic imagination, but felt that "he has exaggerated the bearing of his concept and made it paramount beyond practical possibility" (*The Nation*, 146, pp. 423–4).

Kenneth Burke, whose indebtedness to Richards is obvious to Blackmur (*LG*, p. 391), is "only a literary critic in unguarded moments, when rhetoric nods" (*LH*, p. 195). He "uses literature, not only as a springboard but also as a resort or home, for a philosophy or psychology of moral possibility" (*LG*, p. 392). His method, Blackmur observes acutely, "could be applied with equal fruitfulness either to Shakespeare, Dashiell Hammett, or Marie Corelli" (*LG*, p. 393). But he moves on a plane of abstract rhetoric which absorbs everything in a "methodology."

The rejection of the critical value of biography is equally emphatic. Biographical knowledge "cannot affect the poetry or our understanding of it as poetry. . . . The more life or mind, the more extraneous material of any sort, you introduce into the study of a poem as belonging to it, the more you violate the poem as such, and the more you render it a mere document of personal expression" (*KR*, I, p. 97). But this of course is not a condemnation of biography as a genre: actually Blackmur devoted a lifelong effort to an intellectual biography of Henry Adams.

Eliot was clearly the greatest influence on Blackmur. In his first early essay on Eliot, Blackmur defines "the quality which makes Eliot almost unique as a critic" as "the purity of his interest in literature as literature—as art autonomous and complete" (*H&H*, I, p. 292). This, he argues, is not sterile aestheticism. Criticism focussed on the work "without a vitiating bias away from the subject at hand" (*H&H*, I, p. 293) is the right kind of criticism. "Eliot's most remarkable criticism and his most trivial equally carry that mysterious weight of authority—which is only the weight of intelligence" (*H&H*, I, p. 317). Blackmur really drew from Eliot not only the emphasis on the autonomy of literature and the impersonality of art, but also accepted most of his decisions on matters of taste: the selection from the past, the anti-Romanticism, the interest in Dante and in symbolism. But Blackmur's reservations become articulate with Eliot's shift toward a criticism by religious criteria. "We cannot follow him" (*DA*, p. 177), he states bluntly in reviewing *After Strange Gods* in 1935. "It Is Later Than He Thinks" is the heading for a review of *The Idea of a Christian Society* (*KR*, II, pp. 235–8; also in *EG*). We are not able; it will not happen. Mr. Eliot's ideal of a Christian society . . . cannot be realised in this world and I should imagine would be unsuitable in any probable world . . . " (*EG*, p. 241). In a later article, "In the Hope of Straightening Things Out" (1951), Blackmur reviews appreciatively Eliot's key concepts of feeling, emotion, sensibility, and impersonality, but ridicules some of the effects of Eliot's criticism: Milton, Shelley, and Swinburne are not read any more. A whole literary generation sprang up whose only knowledge of Christianity was what they got by reading Eliot, and "a 'cult' for Dante spread through Bloomsbury and Cape Cod" (*LH*, p. 167). Eliot became a critical dictator unexampled in our time, but actually failed to enforce his preferences for Ben Jonson, Dryden, and Dr. Johnson. Blackmur approves of Eliot's later religious turn only insofar as it recognized that "poetry saves nobody, but shows rather the actual world from which to be saved or not . . . " (*LH*, p. 175). The "adventure of incarnating religion in poetry [,] . . . what Eliot has been up to all along" (*LH*, p. 174), failed and had to fail.

Among the Southern critics, Allen Tate is the only one with whom Blackmur sympathizes. He agrees with Tate's "battle against the Richards ideas, against any ideas not found directly in poetry itself, and in the particular poem itself, and against any positive or organized theory of literature . . . allied to one or another branch of systematic philosophy" (*PI*, p. 166). The salute to Tate ends in an oddly non-committal recitation of Tate's main notions of Incarnation, Order, Experience, Prejudice, Historical Imagination, Will, Communion, and Love, calling the list "Diplomacy on the high scale" (*PI*, p. 176). One wonders whether the term should not be applied to Blackmur's own essay.

Inevitably Blackmur discusses Ransom along with Tate. Earlier, Blackmur had seen Ransom only as a rhetorician, working with the terms "tenor," "vehicle," and "texture," ignoring, in his analysis of *Lycidas*, "the intellectual and poetic subject of the poem" (*LH*, p. 192); while, in the late essay on Tate, Ransom is criticized rather for concentrating his attention "almost exclusively on the problem of knowledge," on "epistemology and ontology." Blackmur sees Ransom as "the solipsist trying to find out how he knows the only thing he can trust in the world he creates—the formal aspects in which it appears" (*PI*, p. 169). Ontology, Blackmur knows, means a "science of Being," but he still sees Ransom as concerned only with a form and relation, not with reality. He seems, however, right in pointing to Ransom's restless experimentation: "He creates the scaffold of system after system for Tate to see through and beyond" (*PI*, p. 170), a strangely phrased conclusion which makes the teacher somehow serve the disciple.

The attitude toward Cleanth Brooks is even more negative: he "has made . . . a rhetoric of Irony and Paradox, with sub-types of Ambiguity, Attitude, Tone, and Belief." Blackmur endorses Ronald Crane's attack on Brooks's "Critical Monism." The New Criticism seems to him "impossible with Milton or Shakespeare" (*LH*, p. 192), though he recognizes the illumination of its method if applied within limits and not overruled by a thesis, "a set of principles" which, in his view, mars Brooks's *Modern Poetry and the Tradition* (*MLN*, 65, pp. 388–90).

Blackmur, with the years, set himself increasingly against the New Criticism. It "has dealt almost exclusively either with the executive technique of poetry (and only with a part of that) or with the general verbal techniques of language" (*LH*, p. 206). It seems to him "useless for Dante, Chaucer, Goethe, or Racine. Applied to drama it is disfiguring, as it is to the late seventeenth- and all the eighteenth-century poetry" (*LH*, p. 207). It has become a "methodology," a "rebirth of the old rhetoric" (*LH*, p. 189). "There was," however, "never a coherent critical position, certainly never a uniform practice . . ." (*LH*, p. 191).

The vehemence and, I think, the injustice of these later pronouncements must be due to Blackmur's reaction to his own past. Blackmur made his early reputation with analyses of modern poetry: of the techniques, forms, and meaning of Thomas Hardy, Ezra Pound, T. S. Eliot, Hart Crane, Wallace Stevens, E. E. Cummings, and Marianne Moore. He himself recognized that the accusation of criticism for criticism's sake may with point be applied to himself. But one cannot say that he recanted. If we examine his theory of criticism in its early stages we have to acknowledge a consistency throughout his career, even though his interests perceptively shifted and widened from a dominant concern with modern poetry to the novel, from purely American topics to foreign writers such as Flaubert, Thomas Mann, and Dostoyevsky, and finally to more general topics beyond the province of literary criticism

proper: to a view of our culture, to the differences between America and Europe, and even to the meaning of history and religion.

Still, the basic insight remained the same: a recognition of the central obscurity in poetry, in literature, and in life, which becomes, in the operation of the intellect, skepticism, an "unindoctrinated thinking" that harkens back to the "early Plato and the whole Montaigne" (*LG*, p. 375). He objects, for example, to the rationalism of Mortimer Adler, his ignoring of "the realm of anterior conviction (*KR*, II, p. 355), and he violently rejects the teaching of the American neo-humanists, who at the beginning of his career dominated the critical scene. In 1930, Blackmur contributed to C. Hartley Grattan's symposium, *A Critique of Humanism*, condemning its censorious attitude toward modern literature, its rigid body of arbitrary doctrine, its conception of a tradition so static and self-imitating that "they can admire only Sophocles, Dante, and Racine" (*CH*, p. 251). A later essay, "Humanism and Symbolic Imagination" (1941, in *LH*, pp. 145–61), is possibly even harsher ". . . Babbitt's mind," we are told, "operated by rote. . . ." He suffered from "some deep privation of imagination, some paucity of sympathy, some racking poverty of sensibility. . . . He never took account of the chthonic underside of things. . . ." He ". . . was interested only in the abstractable elements of literature. . ." (*LH*, pp. 146–8). Blackmur expands his criticism to condemn the whole "history of ideas" approach to literature: "To deal with literature as a current of ideas is about as rewarding . . . as dealing with the plays of Shakespeare as the current of the plots which he begged, borrowed, or invented . . ." (*LH*, p. 159). We could reach, in that way, only "the intellectually formulable order" and not the "intimate [actual] orders" which may not be "susceptible of verbalization on the intellectual level. . . (*LH*, p. 159). Intellect in general is disparaged. ". . . [It] is but the manners of the mind, and the Humanist who inadvertently makes himself, as Babbitt did, all intellect, is all manners and no man" (*LH*, p. 161).

Intellect with Blackmur is not, of course, equated with reason. He even emphatically proposed in 1948 to "evangelize in the arts . . . rational intent, rational statement, and rational technique; and I want to do it through technical judgment, clarifying judgment, and the judgment of discovery, which together I call rational judgment" (*LH*, p. 212). "Reason" is here used in a special sense as a faculty distinct from the intellect in about the way Coleridge distinguished between Reason and Understanding in a loose parallel to Kant's use. Psychology and semantics are dismissed by Blackmur as "troublemakers" which "lead to the proliferation of a sequence of insoluble and irrelevant problems so far as the critic of literature is concerned." Aesthetics is also unhelpful, as it "comprises the study of superficial and mechanical executive techniques, partly in themselves, but also and mainly in relation to the ulterior techniques of conceptual form and of symbolic form" (*LH*, p. 209). The distinctions and unusual terms are somewhat clarified by what follows. "Executive techniques" are, for example, metrical schemes or narrative or dramatic modes. "Conceptual techniques" are illustrated by examples: Dostoyevsky's *Double*, the Homeric pattern in Joyce's *Ulysses*, the phases of the moon in the later poetry of Yeats, the pattern of Christian rebirth, conversion, or change of heart in the modern novel. Blackmur defines "symbolic technique" rather obscurely as "invokable forces, or raw forces, the force of reality": it includes the creation of memorable characters such as Hamlet, Lear, Emma Bovary, and the brothers Karamazov. Blackmur conceives of these techniques as collaborating rationally: the logic, the rhetoric, and the poetic form an oddly arranged triad in which the "executive technique" is aligned with logic, "conceptual technique" with rhetoric, and "symbolic technique" with poetry. The arts "make a rationale for discovering life. . . . Through the aesthetic experience . . . we discover, and discover again, what life is, . . . we also discover what our culture is" (*LH*, p. 211). We now understand the sentence about the different kinds of judgment: the technical judgment will refer to the executive technique, to logic; the clarifying judgment to conceptual techniques, to rhetoric; and the judgment of discovery to symbolic technique, to poetry.

A slightly different classification appears in "Notes on Four Categories in Criticism" (1946). The first is that of "superficial techniques"; the second of "linguistic technique," images and tropes, as well as "idiom" which seems another term for style. The third category is "the ulterior technique of the imagination: how the mind makes its discourse in images . . . as meaningful as the original parallel experiences . . . in life" (*LH*, p. 218). Here the history of ideas, the Freudian approach, and any deterministic method as well as historical criticism belong—all considered inevitable but inadequate. Blackmur argues, in a tortuous page, that the arts exemplify the "actual," the concrete, through which the "real" shines only fitfully, as "human kind cannot *know* very much reality" (*LH*, p. 221). The theme of ultimate obscurity recurs. The artist can illuminate the mystery by the "symbolic imagination," the fourth and final category, which is exemplified only by a little scene from *Madame Bovary*: Emma on the farm, before her marriage, offering a cordial to Dr. Bovary, herself sticking her tongue into the narrow glass.

Symbolism is Blackmur's central critical concept which he tries to explain on several occasions. In the paper "Language as Gesture" (1942), which serves as the title of the third collection of his essays, all the arts are derived from a prime "gesture," a term used so broadly that it allows him to speak of gesture in architecture. A spire, a bridge, a dome, a crypt make gestures. Even sculpture is somehow "gesture": "man breeding shapes out of his brooding" (*LG*, p. 7); painting, dancing, and music derive from gesture. In poetry gesture is used as the meaning of words—the rhythm, cadence, and interval not conveyed in ordinary pedestrian writing—it appears also in repetition and culminates in symbol. "A symbol," Blackmur formulates, "is what we use to express meaningfulness in a permanent way which cannot be expressed in direct words or formulas of words with any completeness; a symbol is a cumulus of meaning" (*LG*, p. 16). The examples which follow range widely: from pithy sayings in Shakespeare such as "The rest is silence" or "Ripeness is all" to puns, synaesthesia, onomatopoeia, meter and refrain—all instances of poetic devices which abandon the traditional idea of symbol to return to "gesture," a term which seems to mean little more than any contextual meaning, any device of language deviating from the normal.

Criticism is thus for Blackmur not a science. The attempt to make it a science fails, as it "can handle only the language and its words and cannot touch—except by assertion—the imaginative product of the words, which is poetry; which in turn is the object revealed or elucidated by criticism. Criticism must be concerned, first and last—whatever comes between—with the poem as it is read and as what it represents is felt" (*LG*, p. 390), and "no amount of linguistic analysis can explain the *feeling* or existence of a poem." Nor does philosophy help: it ". . . gives criticism no power over the substance (the felt life, the behavior) which it reflects and orders" (*LH*, p. 291). Criticism ultimately leaves the reader "with the poem, with the real work yet to do" (*LG*, p. 396). Thus Blackmur can come to a modest view of criticism. It is a regrettable necessity. "Critic and scholar are go-betweens and should disappear when the couple are gotten together, when indeed there is no room left for them. That is why there are no statues to critics and scholars. That is why there is nothing deader than dead criticism and scholarship . . ." (*LH*, p. 184). This is the reason Blackmur called his second volume *The Expense of Greatness*, though only an essay on Henry Adams discusses the theme: "Failure is the expense of greatness." Criticism is ultimately a failure. Blackmur had great ambitions and real talent as a poet, and he seemed to have felt his critical writing as a *pis-aller*. But in difference from those who wrote criticism as artists *manqués*, such as Pater or Wilde, Blackmur did not want to write "creative" criticism aiming at rivaling or replacing another work of art. Rather, he modestly conceives of the "burden of criticism" as a making of bridges between society and the arts, as "The audience needs [today] instruction in the lost skill of symbolic thinking" (*LH*, p. 206). With a slightly different emphasis Blackmur phrases the perennial task of criticism as . . . "bringing the work of art to the condition of performance" (*LH*, p. 290), where performance, if I understand him rightly, must mean something like the "concretization," the right response of the reader. Criticism has a strictly mediatory task, a removal of obstacles to the wedding of reader and work—a narrow conception which forgets not only about theory but about judging and ranking.

Notes

1. I refer to Blackmur's books: *Language as Gesture* (New York, 1952) as *LG*; *The Lion and the Honeycomb* (New York, 1955) as *LH*; *Eleven Essays in the European Novel* (New York, 1964) as *EE*; *A Primer of Ignorance* (New York, 1967) as *PI*. If these fail I quote *The Double Agent* (New York, 1935) as *DA*; *The Expense of Greatness* (New York, 1940) as *EG*; *The Critique of Humanism*, ed. C. Hartley Grattan (New York, 1930) as *CH*; and a few uncollected essays in periodicals, in *Hound & Horn* as *H&H*, the *Kenyon Review* as *KR*, *Modern Language* as *MLN*.

DENIS DONOGHUE
From "R. P. Blackmur's Poetry: An Introduction"
Poems of R.P. Blackmur
1977, pp. xv–xxiii

Stevens could not have faulted Blackmur's themes; many of them are perennial like his own, the great abstractions which, to begin with, are hardly more than projects for poetry. The poems speak of loneliness, love, death, "the nightmare, If," desire, loss, "our inward beggary," terror, war, the question of sense and faith, the twist of chaos and order, the torsions of experience. As a Maine man, Blackmur turned to the sea for images of a continuity relished or feared; but those, too, are common enough. A more characteristic theme of Blackmur's is what a poem in *The Good European* calls "the shambles under the human mind," a quirky preoccupation in prose and verse. Like Stevens, Blackmur revered the mind, but he had his own special sense of the relation between mind and shambles. Many of Stevens' poems may be described as making a music of thought, showing the mind moving, turning back upon itself, charting the possible ways of seeing things. Chaos is felt as offering a problem of method rather than as a force incorrigible in its humiliation of every method. Blackmur loved thought, but he felt that it was nearly always premature.

He valued thinking rather than thought, because thinking never forgets that it is a process rather than a doctrine: thought is the mind already too much made up, congealed in conclusions. He wanted mind to regard itself as a form of feeling, or a relatively early phase in the history of its feeling; so that its discoveries would be kept fresh and scrupulous. The shambles under the mind offered a desperate situation, but at least kept the mind in a state of humility and perhaps of grace. What then of conviction, belief, principle, and knowledge itself? In *Anni Mirabiles* and elsewhere Blackmur deplored the malicious criticism of knowledge which accounted for much of modern philosophy and drove intelligence into the sand; but he did not contradict himself, the only conviction worth having was forced upon a man by a blow of experience, the only belief worth holding was inseparable from unbelief, the best principles were forced upon an honest man not as programs but as hunches, gravities, decencies. As for knowledge, it was genuine when animated by a sense of everything that lay beneath it or ranged beyond it; elusive in both capacities. What Blackmur valued, then, was the apprehensive character of mind. Many of his poems are strategies to keep the mind from becoming too fixed in its habits.

So with words. One of Blackmur's favorite citations was a sentence from Elizabeth Sewell's little monograph on Valéry: "Words are the mind's one defense against possession by thought or dreams; even Jacob kept trying to find out the name of the angel he wrestled with." Blackmur liked the sentence so much that he assumed he always quoted it accurately: not so, it often came out a little wrong as "words are the only defense of the mind against being possessed by thought or dream." But no matter, in either version it offered a justification of words, a critique of authoritarian thought, and an account of where dreams belonged. Blackmur loved every attribute of words except their fixity, and he took the harm out of fixity by giving words their head, not frivolously but experimentally. On the first page of *From Jordan's Delight* the language is encouraged to run from "boy" to "buoy" to "buoyed." Later there is serious play with "spend," "spendthrift," "spent," "unspent." It is not that Blackmur thought language wiser than any poet, but it is better in one respect, the mobility of its relations: words do not make up their minds in advance or settle prematurely upon limits. Let me revise something I have just now said. Blackmur loved words, but he loved even more the process that led to words: "chance flowering to choice," when the choice words turn out right. In "The Journeyman Rejoices," in *From Jordan's Delight*, Blackmur speaks of

> some bleak and gallant face,
> Lonely in words, but under words at home.

Later in the book he invokes "the crying out that echoes solitude," and later still

> the wordless and unsummoned sense that springs
> indifferent beneath all words?

and there is a phrase far out in the book about unhappy ripeness reaching

> from heart to groin to word
> drenching each with each.

Let these move through the poetry as mottoes, as if to say that Blackmur in loving the craft of words loved the unconscious skills and needs and cries which find in words, sometimes when luck holds, their appeasement. In *The Second World*

> One tries at last
> to say only what the heart says, do only
> what the buds do: flower by conviction:
> the inward mastery of the outward act.

It is wonderful to act upon whim and then find the whim endorsed by reason.

We often assume of poets enamored of words that they are enslaved to the sounds, the lullings and the relishes of language. They are poets more of ear than of eye. This does not necessarily mean that they are drunk with words and gone beyond the sobriety of caring what the words mean. More often than not, it means that the poet chooses among meanings those that emerge from the phonetic relations of words; a different matter, and not at all a disgrace. Blackmur more often refers to "the inward ear" and "the mind's ear" than to "the mind's eye," and he more often judges situations according to the propriety of words spoken in them than of words offered to delineate them. The propriety of the words spoken seems to reveal the grace of the relation from which they have emerged; as in 'The Cough' She says to Him

> —Words verge on flesh, and so we may,
> someday, be to ourselves the things we say.

(But I concede that the poem gives Him the last word, appealing beyond "your mere word" to "the still body.") And since we are speaking of the propriety of words, we must advert to whatever comes before the words, the quality of the silence which incites them. One of Blackmur's "Scarabs for the Living" reads thus:

> Quiet the self, and silence brims like spring:
> the soaking in of light, the gathering
> of shadow up, after each passing cloud,
> the green life eating into death aloud,
> the hum of seasons; all on beating wing.

The hum of seasons becomes, in the verse, the hum and buzz of implication; not merely sensory images but what the images have become as experiences along with other experiences not necessarily sensory at all. We are instructed to say, these days, that the relation between nature and culture has been naively represented; that, in fact, virtually nothing is nature, virtually everything culture. Let it be so. Then Blackmur's scarab has to do with the ways in which individual experience, an affair of culture through and through if you will, is amplified and enriched by forces which he calls (since their fulfilment is words) silence. "Words are the mind's one defense. . . ." I take Elizabeth Sewell's sentence to mean that the humanity of a mind possessed by dreams is an abeyance, the rift between its subconscious and its conscious life is abysmal; when possessed by thought, the same mind is congealed, transfixed by its mere contents. Either way, the true, continuous life of feeling is suppressed. Words release the human sound again by giving the mind not an official syntax but its possibility, the constituents of feeling and speech. Blackmur was not obsessed or even bemused by words; he turned to words for protection against every kind of obsession to which the mind is tempted, since words contain the experience of others as well as our own. Language is therefore to Blackmur "the country of the blue," a phrase from James' story "The Next Time" that lived in Blackmur's mind as a motif and a motive. In the third of "Three Poems from a Text" certain memories are said to be

> of the country of the blue, too far
> for capture and too near to see at once.

Blackmur thought of the country of the blue, the place which in James's story houses the artist with "a good conscience and a great idea," as "a very lonely place to be, for it is very nearly empty except for the self, and is gained only by something like a religious retreat, by an approximation of birth or death or birth-in-death." These are his terms in *A Primer of Ignorance*, but as his brooding over blueness proceeds he takes the harm out of its loneliness by making it a constituent of the work of art. The artist as a mere person is lonely: "the man fully an artist is the man, short of the saint, most wholly deprived." But the loneliness is transfigured when the artist realizes that "all the professions possible in life are mutually inclusive," that "one's own profession is but the looking-glass and the image of the others." The artist is the one who "being by nature best fitted to see the image clear is damned only if he does not." If he sees it, "his vision disappears in his work, which is the country of the blue." Let us say, then, that the country of the blue is the work of art, so far as it is an achievement of the imagination, and take for granted that the artist so far as he is a man is lonely and deprived: his art makes "the great good place," or comes upon it if the art seems natural as well. I assume that memories, to return to Blackmur's poem, are of the country of the blue, but not in it, because of the difference between memory and imagination. Only a great imagination occupies the country of the blue, and even then only on occasion and with luck. Memory knows the country but knows it as "too far for capture and too near to see at once." I have said that to Blackmur the country of the blue was Language. My authority for saying it is chiefly James' story. Blackmur's commentary upon James' story would authorize a somewhat different emphasis: if the country of the blue is the achieved work of art, it is Language only at the point and in the place where it has achieved its vocation of form. The Oxford English Dictionary is not the country of the blue. *The Tempest* is. The dictionary houses the words, but it does not provide vision or syntax, which are prerogatives of imagination. Language, to Blackmur, meant the possibility of a poem: words were meanings, but also provocations, hints, invitations.

Therefore he had favorite words, like favorite people. Mostly they are drawn from the language of natural description but used then as offering moral analogies. Silence "brims" like spring. The "radiance of wordless intimacies" between two people "brims to the flood." In "River-Walk" a friend is "friend of brimming silence." Feeling is associated with the welling-up of energy, nature offering culture a thousand good examples. "Vertigo" is used in several poems where the theme is reason in madness, matter and impertinency desperately mixed, a theme close to Blackmur's heart. Short of taking a word-count, I cannot prove that Blackmur's favorite word is "weather," but I will risk the assertion. As noun and verb it is diversely used to mean the following, and more besides: the nature of things ("weather is all"): weather as a stone weathers, or a landscape, or a house: profusion of feeling, as in "the drunken weather of the headlong heart": the hurly-burly of circumstance, time, change: weather as one weathers out a storm: and weather as a genial law of nature, a sustaining principle, a living culture, true *societas*:

> No order ripens into weather
> unless it bind and loose together
> chaos of good consuming ill,
> of lovers who search and shun God's will.

There is a famous essay in *Language as Gesture* in which Blackmur rebukes E. E. Cummings for using the word "flower" as a maid of all work. "The word has become an idea, and in the process has been deprived of its history, its qualities, and its meaning": a rebuke repeated in *Anni Mirabiles*, where Blackmur alleges that Cummings "deprives many of his words of as much as possible of *their own* meaning: so that they may take on *his* meaning." These strictures depend upon Blackmur's belief that "when a word is used in a poem it should be the sum of all its appropriate history made concrete and particular in the individual context; and in poetry all words act *as if* they were so used, because the only kind of meaning poetry can

have requires that all its words resume their full life: the full life being modified and made unique by the qualifications the words perform one upon the other in the poem." I think this principle is fulfilled, on the whole, in Blackmur's poetry. The meaning of the word "weather" is explored, revealed, its weight and density assessed; it is not used as a blank cheque, the amount to be filled in by the reader according to whim or the looseness of his emotion. "No order ripens into weather. . . ." Presumably unripe order is order prematurely arrived at and therefore insecure and therefore assertive, rigid, a formula rather than a form. What order ripens into, if it ripens, is a theoretic form for our behavior. I use Blackmur's phrases and recall his saying that "no order remains vital which has lost its intimate contact, at some point, with the disorder or the unknown order which gave it rise." It may be said that "weather" is hard-pressed to register so much, if we agree upon the meaning in these terms, but I think it passes the test. If the ripeness is all, it is because it retains a sense of the origin of order in disorders and unknown orders. "Our great delight," Blackmur says, "is when we have transformed our aspirations into behavior." Weather is that kind of behavior, order remembering its origin, and therefore bending to the rhythm of change; but bending is not breaking, and the changes are seasonal. It is by an extension of this meaning that we come upon the last of Blackmur's favorite words in a short list: eddy, eddying, and so forth. This poet is always suspicious of forces which are content with themselves, he loves to discover a misgiving, a doubt whirling within a faith to keep the faith decent. Eddy is the word he uses to mean one's strength directed against oneself:

> There in the blossoming of waywardness,
> O stalwart Lear, you eddy and confess.

—or the personal need or quirk turned against its element

> There is no shelter here, no self-warm lair,
> When every lung eddies the ocean air.

—or energy whirling off from its congenial form ("O eddying, bodiless faith") or hanging back from its fate—

> It is the coward in me will not rest,
> but eddying against the coming time
> exhausts the prayer for safety dime by dime.

—or the politics of inertia in which not even the inertia is believed in and one is identified as an eddying standstill, as in "The Dead Ride Fast." The language of eddying is natural to Blackmur's poetry, and it is no harm at all if we think he resorted to it partly under Coleridge's authority; as in Coleridge's "Dejection" ode:

> To thee do all things live from pole to pole
> Their life the eddying of thy living soul

of which I. A. Richards wrote that "*eddying* is one of Coleridge's greatest imaginative triumphs: an eddy is in something, and is a conspicuous example of a balance of forces." True; but in Blackmur's use of the word the balance is no good unless it is desperate.

PAUL A. BOVÉ
From "R. P. Blackmur and the Job of the Critic: Turning from the New Criticism"
Criticism, Fall 1983, pp. 366–70

No one has yet proposed that Blackmur's provisional and dissolving style is a heretical subversion of the rhetorics of the two dominant forms of literary criticism to be located in

America during his career. Blackmur is constantly preoccupied with the relation of orthodoxy and heresy in his writing and fears the effects of any dominant doctrine or method upon the study of literature and culture. His own strategy seems to be to subvert orthodoxy wherever possible, not by trying to escape its rhetorics, but by consciously employing them tentatively, and sometimes against themselves, with a full skepticism, in order to weaken their authority, their power as institutionalized methods, and, more broadly, to subvert any critical act which appears solely as an exercise in the will to power.

Of the two orthodoxies of literary criticism, one can be identified with Irving Babbitt and the other with Kenneth Burke; or they might be called Humanism and Rhetoric. In "Humanism and the Symbolic Imagination," a 1941 essay reprinted in *The Lion and the Honeycomb*, Blackmur offers a Nietzschean critique of Humanism as it appears in the rhetoric of Babbitt as a monumental historian. Blackmur's dissatisfaction with Humanism is essentially epistemological: "The Humanist feels that he must capture the content of literature, and as he tries to do so by intellectual means gets only an intellectual content, which naturally seems to him pretty thin; then he begins to feel that the thing would be better the other way round, that literature needs humanism in order to have any content in the sense that he can understand it, so that he rejects literature that does not declare itself immediately as humanistic. . . . Here is the radical confusion . . . into which the Humanist drives himself, whether in relation to politics or literature or religion or any great movement of the mind. He has made his Humanism absolute instead of conditional, active instead of residual, assertive instead of responsive."[1] Blackmur is objecting here not only to the vicious circularity of Humanism, that is, of a criticism which asserts itself so powerfully as to ignore altogether other types of experience or meaning which may be found, but also to its historical inappropriateness in the Modern world. Humanism is assertive and doctrinal; it aspires to complete and general applicability. Blackmur's critique demonstrates that the general goals of Humanism are obtainable only in a religious age when a controlling central presence makes possible the grand certain synthesis of intellectual discrimination. As Blackmur puts it repeatedly, the lack of grace in the Modern world fractures the facade of Humanistic knowledge so that its Tradition can only appear and function as a series of fragments, as residue, putting itself forward only tentatively, as a conditional response to something which exists now, outside that lost system of order.

Humanistic figures of speech—the dominant signs of that tradition—are empty of any meaning whenever they are employed by a Humanist. For the latter act as if they possess a "complete . . . unity" of what they see (151). But the crucial distinction for Blackmur lies in the fact that the Humanists impose rather than create order, and they do so out of their metaphysical and nostalgic belief in the continuity of the past into the present, of the past as the abode of value for the present, and of the past as the prescription for the present. Humanism, Blackmur writes, "was . . . this central attitude, the attitude that there is always an ascertainable order, very near an absolute order in the moral world, which is the only right human order" (148). "It is the circle of formula at work rather than the line of observation, is an enclosing rather than a meeting force, an agent of exclusion rather than inclusion, of shutting rather than opening" (150). In this closed form of Humanistic consciousness, the signs which belong to the tradition of the west "become laws—that is, . . . they become predictors of thought or behavior . . . [and as a result] they become mere headstones on the bodies of dead thought" (158).

Blackmur seems to be saying here that Humanism is not capable of interpretation in so far as interpretation involves an articulated response to a text. Likewise, Humanism cannot produce knowledge, because in its commitment to the tradition, it encloses Modernity within a cemetery of dead signs. Most important, however, Blackmur objects to Humanism because it is in its epistemology an exercise in the will to power over texts and experience which does not attempt to call itself into question on any level. Fundamentally, Humanists, like all those in possession of the truth, mistakenly assume that order is single and that its assertion is necessary for salvation. "Here," Blackmur writes, "is tragedy at the nub. . . . the assertion of order without imagination demolishes civilization and makes the individual impossible altogether" (149). Blackmur's concern is always for the heretic's position in confronting an orthodoxy and always suggests the link between the end of civilization and the success of orthodoxy in destroying heresy. The Humanist's values and epistemology translate themselves into an aggressive method of cultural imposition and into a style of conceptual assertion which looks on itself as the party of order.

Blackmur's rejection of Babbitt is part of a larger movement away from Humanism which is epitomized by not only T.S. Eliot's subtle critique of Babbitt's *Humanism and Democracy*, but also by Cleanth Brooks's vicious attacks on Edmund Wilson and Lionel Trilling as "general intellectuals." Historically, at least in the academic study of literature, the strongest attacks on the Arnoldian line of Humanistic criticism which moved through Babbitt to Leavis and others are made by New Critics. And for the most part, that critique, following Eliot's lead, accuses the humanist of nostalgia and of substituting art for religion.[2]

Although Blackmur's criticism often sounds like the more general one given shape by Eliot, it is substantially different from the others precisely in the emphasis to which I have pointed. To Blackmur, Humanism is dangerous because it is authoritative, epistemologically and historically naive, and stylistically self-assertive. In fact, Blackmur seems to have joined with the New Critics and Eliot in their attack out of a distaste for institutionalized orthodoxy and not out of a desire to replace Babbitt with Burke.

In the title essay of *The Lion and the Honeycomb*, written in 1950, Blackmur represents in Kenneth Burke the dangers implicit in the New Criticism. It is worth pointing out again that Blackmur has often joined forces with Burke in displacing the authority of those who would confuse literature and religion, in condemning the popularization of literature in ineffectual mass education, and in revealing the fascistic tendencies of secular Humanism. Yet, Blackmur has come to see in Burke's powerful description of the function of language in rhetorical terms the threatening spectre of another, new orthodoxy. The cultural problem posed by Burke is that "he regards poetry, philosophy, and religion as matters subordinate to rhetoric in the beginning and in the end to be transformed into rhetoric" (194). Blackmur, it must be said, is not arguing with either the truth or effectiveness of Burke's achievement, but rather with its potential threat to the heretic. It is finally of secondary importance that Burke's system is "very abstract," and owes its allegiance to Kant (194). It is of primary importance, however, that Burke's system is uninterruptable: ". . . there is nothing," Blackmur says, "to arrest him: there are no obstacles he cannot transform into abstract or reduce to neutral terms in his rhetoric" (194). The very abstraction of Burke's system depends upon and constitutes its power, its authority to overwhelm objections and to coerce any recalcitrant material into the system. Burke is a good example of the type of intimacy which Ransom recommends and which Blackmur so dislikes: "He is a very superior example indeed of the mind in which the articulate organization has absorbed the material organized" (194). Burke has mastered the material of his discipline in a manner analogous to the way in which Cleanth Brooks suggests in "The Heresy of Paraphrase" a critic must deal with a poem.[3] The critic must have so absorbed his material that he can free it from the shape in which it comes to him so that he can rearrange the parts of the text along any lines he feels are appropriate to his understanding of the poem. It is clearly this coercive ability to dissolve and rearrange a poem or novel which Blackmur has in mind when he says that Burke is the paradigm of the New Criticism and it is also clearly this coercive exercise of the will to power which Blackmur has in mind when he discloses the essence of Burke's method: "The methodology is a wonderful machine that creates its own image out of everything fed into it; nobody means what he says but only the contribution of what he says to the methodology" (194).

Blackmur assents to the temporary value of the rhetorical, but, he says, "I am certain it is no place to stay" (194). To consider all social and literary reality as merely rhetoric is, according to Blackmur, a unification in askesis, that is, the mind is reduced to merely one activity which organizes all others. The mind is left to contemplate only itself in a strangely Modern version of the sublime.

Blackmur is clearly uncomfortable in attacking Burke. He doesn't seem to think he might be wrong or unfair to his old colleague, as he describes him, but he does seem to be uncomfortable with a not-uncommon dilemma: Burke has made a major achievement in literary and linguistic study; he has helped immeasurably in breaking the hold which the old Humanism had upon Modern intellectual life, and yet, the very successes which are reason for joy make Blackmur, in his rigorous concern for the heretic, afraid. Burke has, of course, become a new orthodoxy, "today's" orthodoxy no doubt, but an institution and authority nonetheless. In Burke's own developing work—remember that this is 1950—he has already come to "substitute his account for the literature, with a general air that the account does well what the literature did badly and that the only sound use of literature is to furnish rhetoric with one of its incentives" (195). Burke's rhetorical system can be institutionalized quite easily. It consists of a set of tools and terms for analysis— despite Burke's own insistence that rhetoric is not a system and is not made of definable terms which can simply be learned and applied. Blackmur puts it this way: "I draw the inference that the characteristic risk of the 'new criticism' is that its special skills of analysis may become an omnicompetent methodology and that the risk is underlined by the rhetorical nature of the skills" (195). Rather too predictably, I am afraid, Burke's response, "Criticism as Criticism," in *Accent*, 1955, takes the form of a rhetorical analysis of Blackmur's key phrases to show that he himself blurred his terms.[4] Burke, it seems, could not have given more eloquent testimony to Blackmur's sense that nothing could arrest the rhetorical system of the New Criticism once it is put into play.

Notes

1. *The Lion and the Honeycomb* (New York: Harcourt, Brace, and Company, 1955), p. 160. Further references to this book appear parenthetically in my text.
2. T.S. Eliot, "The Humanism of Irving Babbitt," and "Second Thoughts about Humanism," *Selected Essays* (New York: Harcourt, Brace, and World, Inc., 1964), pp. 419–428 and 429–438.
3. *The Well Wrought Urn* (New York: Harcourt, Brace, and World, Inc., 1947), pp. 192–214.
4. *Accent*, 15 (1955), pp. 279–92.

ROBERT BLY

1926–

Robert Bly was born on December 23, 1926, in Madison, Minnesota. Upon graduation from high school in 1944, he enlisted in the United States Navy. It was in the Navy, oddly enough, that Bly was first introduced to poetry: "As a Navy recruit in World War II, I met for the first time a person who wrote poetry, a man named Marcus Eisenstein. . . . During a class on radar, he wrote a poem as I watched. I had somehow never understood that poems were written by human beings, and I still remember that moment with delight."

In 1950 he received an A.B. from Harvard University. He lived alone for several years in New York City writing poetry but he eventually returned to study at the University of Iowa, where he received his M.A. in 1956. It was during his time as a student in Iowa that he married Carolyn McLean.

Bly's career is indicative of his diverse interests and talents. He founded the Fifties Press, which is still in operation today as the Eighties Press. He was also one of the founders of the American Writers Against the Vietnam War. In addition to the twelve volumes of poetry he has produced, he has translated a number of Swedish, Spanish, and German poets: Georg Trakl, Pablo Neruda, and Rainer Maria Rilke, among others. In 1968 he was awarded the National Book Award for his collection *The Light Around the Body*. Bly gives frequent poetry readings at many universities and sponsors workshops and retreats for men. He remains one of the most outspoken, controversial, and challenging figures in modern North American poetry.

Personal

These occasions allow the expression of gratitude. I met Robert Bly in February of 1948, when I tried out for *The Harvard Advocate* of which he was already an editor. We have remained closest friends over the decades—through many disagreements and even quarrels, our friendship based on the bewildered but unflagging affection that opposites sometimes feel for each other. We have bickered so much—I have made many essays out of these bickerings!—that he may find it outrageous that I recommend him as a model of behavior.

As vain as anyone, and as avaricious of praise—yet among my acquaintances of poets he is the most nearly disinterested. (I refer to Keats's favorite moral idea, a word which alas loses meaning every day as people use it to mean "uninterested.") A thousand times, I have observed with amazement Bly's cordial response to negative criticism: if there is an *idea* lurking in the denunciation, he lifts the idea up to the light, examines it like a dog a bone, remarks it, wonders at it, sniffs learnedly, and then chews on it—for nourishment and to keep his teeth sharp.

Of course such behavior is only sensible—what use are the complaints against us unless we learn from them?—but most people respond to blame not with curiosity but with plots of murder. Many artists as they grow older become experts at defending themselves against taking criticism seriously. They build castles out of the praise they get from younger writers, from old students, from sycophants, and from editors seeking their names. They build moats of exclusiveness; they surround themselves with dragons and princesses. Bly on the other hand seems to look for blame, as if he were daring himself to improve.

Writers who will grow and improve through their fifties and sixties, even into their seventies and eighties, are writers who best develop dissatisfaction with themselves. Only from disappointment with one's old work can one possibly move ahead. Lately Bly has become aware that much of his work lacks sound, and lacks variety of syntax. Therefore he tries to begin again, to hear vowel and consonant sound as if for the first time.

It takes a doughty temperament. It means of course that one will never be satisfied. (To be a satisfied poet, to believe what the flatterers say . . . this is to be dead.) So one goes to the grave in labor. But the labor's end, if one is serious and persistent, is not the gratification of one's ego but a stewardship. Not long ago, when I felt discouraged, I wrote Bly a long letter; I whined to him as I would to no one else. He answered me with these words: "That the poems are useful to other people, that they are bread, that they can be eaten, and strengthen strangers, that is precisely our goal, our reward, and our vocation. . . ."—DONALD HALL, "Poetry Food," *Of Solitude and Silence*, eds. Richard Jones and Kate Daniels, 1981, pp. 31–32

Robert Bly is a cantankerous, hulking white-haired, 57-year-old poet who looks like a cross between a grizzly bear and a wizard, sort of how Marlon Brando *should* look now. He's driven by a hard-charging muse: ten books of poems (National Book Award winner, 1968); nearly forty translations (Rilke, Lorca, Neruda, others); since 1958 he has edited a crucial poetry journal called successively *The Fifties, The Sixties, The Seventies, The Eighties*. He's also blunt, a straight thinker: In 1966 he cofounded American Writers Against the Vietnam War, and recently he lectured at Esalen Institute on "New Age Bullshit." He makes money about eight months a year at a writing table in a house near Moose Lake, Minnesota (pop. 1410). He's fathered six kids.

But about four years ago Robert Bly got a mission. Nothing official, it just came up like a hunch. Bly started to focus his musing and writing on the puzzle of manhood: How do you *be a man* in the Eighties? What's it mean? He pursued this question in conferences and readings, crisscrossing the country and prodding audiences (and himself) with the basic *what's-a-man* question, retelling ancient myths about male powers and male magic, sometimes, like a witch doctor, putting on primitive, giant, man-god masks. (Poet-research methodology doesn't exactly match Mike Wallace kick-face TV journalism, but it works.) What Bly found out wasn't good. In a 1982 *New Age* magazine cover story interview he warned:

> I see the 'soft male' all over the country today. Sometimes when I look out at my audiences, perhaps half the young males are what I'd call "soft" . . . more thoughtful, more gentle . . . not interested in harming the earth, or starting wars . . . but *not* more free. [Their] amount of grief and anguish is astounding. Many are unhappy, in trouble in their marriages or relationships. Something fierce is needed—for relationships, for life.

Okay, the wound was deep. Could it be fixed? How? Bly pushed deeper, looking for the healing word, the name for what was missing. He rooted around in Jung, the Fisher King, Icarus, tales and myths, and his own bio, unsatisfied. Kept searching until . . . halfway through the *New Age* interview—a sly bull session really—he revealed his answer, the hook he'd found: past macho, past the Sensitive Male (© Marlo Thomas Productions), *past this wound*, deeper in men there was an ancient male power he named the Wildman, and this Wildman was "instinctive, sexually primitive, even frightening [but] nourishing male energy. Making contact with this Wildman," Bly declared, "is the step the Seventies male has not yet taken."—L. M. KIT CARSON, "Robert Bly wants to make a man of You," *GQ*, Oct. 1984, pp. 301–2

General

It is the characteristic Bly contract, a stipulation that in order to escape a living death, *i.e.*, a life which is no more than life in a dying body, the self must renounce its very principle of individuation, must invite death into the body not as a mere nothing at the end but as a positive force throughout, "a saviour, a home," dialectically unified with life; of course, when death and life unite in this inextricable trope, identity must be surrendered—that is what is meant when death is referred to as "the great leveller," not extinction but indistinction: going over to the majority, as the saying goes. And the terms of the contract afford the characteristic Bly music—lagging, irregular, profound, and casting about the image, the image alone, a kind of ontological glamor which leaves unattended so many other kinds of decorum, of propriety, of *keeping* which we may find, or hope to find, in poems; rhetorical splendor, rhyme, a rhythm constructed or at least contested by more than the drawing of breath, wit, elevation, even humor—none of these, but "a poetry in which the image comes forward and much more is said by suggestion . . . a poetry which disregards the conscious and the intellectual structure of the mind entirely and by the use of images, tries to bring forward another reality from *inward* experience." Robert Bly's own account of his undertaking suggests here how much he is willing to give up in order to gain what he must have even without much order, and how—by disregarding the usual congruity of the waking mind—he may even risk spoiling his finest things by an unregarded (or at least unguarded-against) intrusion of factitious material. I have twice used ellipses in the poem just quoted to indicate the omission of a line (not of a verse—Bly does not write verses, with all that the word implies of a return, a commitment to a constant; he writes *lines*, with all that the linear implies of a setting out, a movement in search of a form rather than *within* a form); in each case, the omitted line refers to the kind of specific situation which may have been the genesis of the poem, the grain of grit transcended by the pearl, but which is now irrelevant to the achieved form. In the second stanza, the elided line is "Like mad poets captured by the Moors," and in the third, "That we should taste the weed of Dillinger"—both allusions to the kind of external victimization it is Bly's special grace to refute and exceed by setting all of his poems under the sign—playful, reverent—of Jacob Boehme, who said (and Bly used the saying as the epigraph to his first book in 1962, *Silence in the Snowy Fields*) "we are all asleep in the outward man." Discarding the circumstantial husk, then, it is the inward man Bly is centrally concerned with, though it is not in fact a matter of giving up one thing for another, but rather of permitting reality and circumstance to penetrate each other.—Richard Howard, "'Like Those Before We Move to the Death We Love,'" *Alone With America*, 1980, pp. 58–59

A Russian fairy story, "The Frog Princess," published in Aleksandr Afanasyev's *Russian Fairy Tales*, describes what it's like to take up the life of an artist, especially when one doesn't know what one is doing. A father tells his sons to shoot arrows away from the house as a way to choose their brides. The older brothers get a prince's daughter and a general's daughter. The youngest son's arrow falls short and lights in a swamp, from which a frog hops, carrying the arrow in her mouth. So the youngest son has to marry a frog. When you begin to write poetry, the language doesn't behave, the line won't hold steady, the poem reveals more than you intended or something different. You feel clammy and unevolved and, moverover, your friends can tell by looking at you that you're sleeping with a frog.

It's embarrassing to bring this frog forward in public as your bride, even though you have no other. It turns out that the frog bride can slip out of her frogskin at night and do certain things your older brothers' wives can do—for example, get a shirt made, get good bread baked, and so on. But she is still a frog. Finally the crisis comes. The bride offers to appear at the king's ball for the first time as a human being, and she does, leaving her frogskin at home. Everyone is entranced with her. Without telling his wife, the man slips out of the ball early, goes home and burns the frogskin. That was a bad mistake because, as we can guess, the bride needs the frogskin. Now she has to leave, and much grief for both of them follows from the husband's secretive act.

Some rationalist inside us urges us to burn our frogskins. I don't know all that "burning the frogskin" implies, but it suggests losing something that is wet, embarrassing, precious and private. Writing a commercial novel can resemble burning a frogskin. By nature, confessional poetry, because of its lack of reserve, dries and scorches the frogskin. Publishing a book of poems when one is too young is like burning a frogskin; something is damaged. A poetry reading, when it is done to entice love, can be a public burning of your frogskin; I have done that. I have a longing for love from strangers. But Boris Pasternak gave public readings for years and retained integrity, so public readings need not damage that which should be private.

If we get rid of the frog, we lose the way back to some ancient, instinctive source. We all burn our frogskins in different ways. I have burned mine more than once, from wanting to evolve while leaving the animal behind. Pursuing the discipline of poetry then includes studying the art, experiencing grief, and keeping the frog's skin wet.—Robert Bly, "In Search of an American Muse," *NYTBR*, Jan. 22, 1984, p. 29

Works

The contrast between what I have called Romanticism and what may be called traditional verse—meaning verse that makes its first appeal to order and tradition—is suggested by the books that won the National Book Award and the Pulitzer Prize for poetry. Robert Bly's *Light Around the Body*, that won the NBA, shows a debt to surrealism and recent European and Spanish modes. . . .

In Bly's poems I am always conscious of an arranging intelligence.

Bly's ideas are clear. It is his method that is extraordinary:

> I hear voices praising Tshombe, and the Portuguese
> In Angola, these are the men who skinned Little
>   Crow!
> We are all their sons, skulking
> In back rooms, selling nails with trembling hands!

He has developed his own landscapes, inhabited by murdered Indians and Vietnamese; visions in which moles are significant and shop windows filled with terrifying objects:

> . . . a branch painted white.
> A stuffed baby alligator grips that branch tightly
> To keep away from the dry leaves on the floor.

What is true of surrealists in general is true also of Bly; his poems are moving when they are moved by a central flow, one feeling which holds all the parts together. I am aware that this can be argued against; André Breton thought that surrealism that was not automatic writing was not surrealism at all. But this made only for juxtapositions of objects, and shock became a mannerism. When surrealist poetry has been effective, as in the poems of Neruda, the images have been in the grip of that logic of the irrational which we perceive also in dreams. In certain poems by Bly I perceive a flow, and it is powerful; in other poems I do not. "The Busy Man Speaks," "After the Industrial Revolution," "Counting Small–Boned Bodies," and "Melancholia" cohere; but I do not know what connection the following images have:

> Floating in turtle blood, going backward and forward,
> We wake up like a mad sea-urchin
> On the bloody fields near the secret pass—
> There the dead sleep in jars . . .

On the other hand, these lines seem to rise out of a consciousness that is beyond the personal:

> How strange to awake in a city,
> And hear grown men shouting in the night!
> On the farm the darkness wins,
> And the small ones nestle in their graves of cold:
> Here is a boiling that only exhaustion subdues,
> A bitter moiling of muddy waters
> At which the voices of white men feed!

Bly is one of the few poets in America from whom greatness can be expected. He has original talent, and what is more rare, integrity. I think he should forget about images for a while and concentrate on music, the way things move together.—Louis Simpson, "New Books of Poems," *Harper's*, Aug. 1968, pp. 74–75

For several years I disliked what Robert Bly had done in *Silence in the Snowy Fields* (1962). Indeed, I was surprised that the book had even made it into print. His risks, I felt, were all bad ones. And his dustjacket remarks to the effect that "any poetry in the poems . . . is in the white spaces between the stanzas" offended me. I didn't expect these poems. The ones I had happened to read, in magazines and in the first selection of *New Poets of England and America*, were noisier, more ambitious. I thought that his collection was a mistake, a group of journal jottings. . . .

Silence in the Snowy Fields was like a cluster of gnats. No matter what else I did, I couldn't remain neutral about Bly's poems. It will be impossible for me to discuss my change of mind rationally, but I've come to believe that my reservations about Bly were only nigglings, that measuring the accomplishment of his work against petty objections is something like dismissing *Moby Dick* because Melville loses track of his point of view. Bly is free from the inhibitions of critical dictates many of us have regarded as truths. He manages, in fact, to write poems that are themselves suspensions of the critical faculty. The poems had to become what they are. They are quiet, unassuming. They are uninsistent, unrhetorical; they depend, often, on one another for total effect. They do not lead to the kind of intellectual pleasure (an anti-poetic pleasure) one gets from having traced down all the allusions in *The Waste Land* or from having used the unabridged dictionary to come to terms with "The Comedian as the Letter C."

In the full senses of the words these are—may I attach labels to poems that defeat labels?—"symbolic" and "mystical" poems. Yeats said that "the mind liberated from the pressure of the will is unfolded in symbols." He said that a symbol gives "body to something beyond the senses," that "Any one who has any experience of any mystical state of the soul knows how there float up in the mind profound symbols, whose meaning, if indeed they do not delude one into the dream that they are meaningless, one does not perhaps understand for years." The emotional meanings of a symbol, the meanings beyond words, can never be exhausted.

Bly's poems do not wear thin. Our inner lives speak in them, speak out from the silence and solitude of the American midwest. And there is a profound correspondence between "the man inside the body" ("Silence") and the oceans of air and water and land through which he moves. A car is a "solitude covered with iron" ("Driving toward the Lac Qui Parle River") and so is the man moving inside his struts of flesh and bone. For years I felt that Bly's poetry pointed at a mysterious and dissatisfying nothingness that was a non-subject. But he has one subject that speaks out from the spaces between lines, stanzas, and poems and unites them: The Self. But I can only attempt to express this. The most difficult sentence in *Walden* to understand is the one in which Thoreau says that he went to the woods because he wanted "to front only the essential facts of life, and see if I could not learn what it had to teach, and not, when I came to die, discover that I had not lived." My almost every action is a form and a habit. Even as I give lip-service to this recognition I realize that my almost every action is a form and a habit. I cannot begin to move inward until I can strike up a dialogue with a tree, with Whitman's leaf of grass, with Blake's grain of sand. Sons of Benjamin Franklin, sons of generations of orthodox mothers, sons driven by the furious ethic that tells us we must keep our hands and heads busy, we have, in effect, despite appearances, moved through the world with a vast disinterestedness. Bly quotes Jacob Boehme: "We are all asleep in the outward man."

The journeys in Bly's poems are journeys to the interior, as Theodore Roethke put it. Bly has stopped somewhere and is waiting for us. He can find no spiritual fathers among politi-

cians, or the rich, or the self-satisfied (hence his increasing social criticism). But the poet still has friends, a few people to share the inexplicable inner-life with. When he is with them he writes quiet, almost melancholy lines. . . .

And what Bly finds, when he is alone, when he is his own inner man, is joy. He has said that "The fundamental world of poetry is the inward world. We approach it through solitude." No matter the eerie desolation of the landscape. Happiness, a quiet beauty at the heart of things, comes through. "Alive," not asleep in the external man, "We are like a sleek black water beetle / . . . soon to be swallowed / Suddenly from beneath" ("Night"). But, for now, we have the intense pleasure of the journey, sometimes the pleasure of feeling pain, as in "Images Suggested by Medieval Music," a key poem. The hard mystery itself is the joy. . . .

Whatever the word means, in *Silence in the Snowy Fields* Bly is a Romantic. Yeats was not the last. All of our inner men are. But we think we know only what we think. The truth is that the only knowledge worth our while is our knowledge of what we feel. At the same time, it is difficult, perhaps impossible, to sort out and define our feelings. Too many things are with us at once, too many contradictory images and impulses. In "Thinking of Wallace Stevens on the First Snowy Day in December" Bly's speaker hears in the snow both the talk of virgins and concierges. This is Stevens' reality, a reality consisting of all the propositions that are made about it.

But, beyond all the contradictory evidence of the world, Whitman, for one, *knew*. And Bly knows in the same way.— WILLIAM HEYEN, "Inward to the World," *The Far Point*, Fall/ Winter 1969, pp. 42–46

The single most important word with regard to *Sleepers (Joining Hands)* is association; it is the dominant principle throughout the book. Bly has written a good deal about association in his essays; an entire issue of his magazine *The Seventies* (#1) was devoted to it. While it doesn't detract from the self-sufficiency of the poetry or the value of his stimulating essays, it is obvious that with Bly, as with Poe (and probably every other writer who has written both poetry and critical essays), a knowledge of the criticism is an important aid in getting a fuller understanding of the poetry.

When he speaks of association Bly seems to have three things in mind. First, association is a structural principle. A quotation from one of Bly's essays should make this point clear:

In Trakl a series of images make a series of events. Because these events appear out of their "natural" order, without the connectives we have learned to expect from reading newspapers, doors silently open in unused parts of the brain.

Second, association has to do with speed, the speed with which a poet is able to move from one image, feeling or idea to another, from "the known part of the mind to the unknown part and back to the known." . . . Third, association means being able to travel a long way from an initial, literal subject into subjectivity and the unconscious, and still be talking about the original subject. . . . Taken together, the result of these three ideas—the absence of connectives or "natural" order, rapid leaping, and moving the poem far from the objective world—is poetry which is demanding: the reader must be able to fly along with the poem, without the supports we rely on during most of our waking lives. The effect of this highly associative kind of poetry can be breathtaking (anyone who hasn't read it should get a copy of Shinkichi Takahashi's *Afterimages*, translated by Lucien Stryk and Takashi Ikemoto) or, if the energy doesn't flow and ignite just right, the poem can be merely busy and muddled. In *Sleepers*, there are passages near both ends of the spectrum.

The book's major poem, the title piece, is a long dream odyssey in five sections, streaming choruses of fantastic imagery, a Jungian extravaganza; it is, I suppose, about as highly associative as a poem could be. It is a poem of cumulative effect, and that effect is strong. Of the myriad images that cascade through the poem, many are excellent, evoking sudden clear pictures and quick sweeps of emotion, and suggesting dusky encounters within the psyche:

> My shadow is underneath me,
> floating in the dark, in his small boat bobbing among
>   the reeds.

An account of the movement of the spirit out of and into harmony with a Spirit, an energy, larger and older than itself, the poem is a religious work. Often its language and references are overtly religious, and there are beautiful lines resembling Biblical parables:

> For we are like the branch bent in the water . . .
> Taken out it is whole, it was always whole . . .

But when we look at the religious impulse of the poem, we also see its greatest weakness: a sort of bombastic self-consciousness which is by turns self-righteous:

> inwardness, inwardness, inwardness,
> the inward path I still walk on . . .

or rather ordinary, drifting away from simplicity toward the flatness of cliché:

> I am passive, listening to the lapping waves,
> I am divine, drinking the air.

or melodramatic with the trappings of religion:

> I walk upright, robes flapping at my heels.

In such passages there is an intensification of the ego, as it tries to dramatize itself, and, interestingly, an accompanying dissipation of imaginative power. . . .

That "Sleepers" is flawed work is obvious. But we shouldn't allow the weaknesses to blind us to what is interesting and effective in the poem, and, as I've said, in spite of its problems the cumulative effect of the poem is strong, if not entirely unmuddy. Like the book as a whole, "Sleepers" is uneven and given to excess; it is poetry that we respect for its ambitions and excellent moments and emotional drive rather than for any purity or perfection of craft or spirit. The poem shares its major problems with the collection as a whole: the tendency toward bombast and self-righteousness, images which are more bizarre than right, stumbles in the language, associative leaps that are manic rather than exciting. The strengths are the same also: images that do penetrate the psyche, leaps that do connect us with a new intuitive intelligence and release emotion, an imagination which is lavish and swift. I would like to let my comments on *Sleepers* stand there, because I want to move on to work in which Bly's talent seems to me more perfectly realized. I am thereby skipping over the whole political and social aspect of *Sleepers*, not because I think Bly's achievement in dealing with our national life is unimportant—on the contrary, I think Bly's insistence on addressing the whole question of the meaning of America in poetry is extremely important, although I don't find any of the poems in *Sleepers* as powerful as some of the darkly passionate ones in *The Light*. In any case, I think that what I've already said about "Sleepers" as poetry pertains to the political work in the book as well.—Howard Nelson, "Welcoming Shadows," *HC*, April 1975, pp. 3–6

The same smack of being spoiled by poetic success sours Robert Bly's new collection, *This Body Is Made of Camphor and Gopherwood*. Nowadays, everything Bly touches becomes a holy cause and reason for another book. Here he consecrates "the often neglected [?] medium of the prose poem." Like the snail in the book's twenty-one drawings by Gendron Jensen, Bly has crept into the shell of his own meditations and remains absorbed in Sufi poetry, Rilke, protozoa, animals, woods, and fog. The pilgrim's mecca is a small black stone, mysterious and impenetrable. One may admire such pure isolation, but the poet does not help us to share it. The result is not mysticism but solipsism, and we are left out in the cold by passages like this one from "The Pail": "So for two days I gathered ecstasies from my own body, I rose up and down, surrounded only by bare wood and bare air and some gray cloud, and what was inside me came so close to me, and I lived and died!" In earlier collections—especially *Sleepers Joining Hands*—Bly could convince us of a mystical experience by imagining and hinting at its beauty. Too often these poems are overwrought and pretentious. The one delightful piece here describes the poet's children and their friends preparing to put on a play. Except for this "Coming In for Supper," a reader would not know a family existed or, rather, mattered in the poet's hermetic world. Even the love poem that closes the volume, "The Cry Going Out over Pastures," appears to be too rhetorical to be moving, talking more about the poet than the loved one: "I first met you when I had been alone for nine days." A strange way to greet someone you love.—James Finn Cotter, "Poetry Reading," *HR*, Spring 1978, pp. 214–15

Robert Bly is a windbag, a sentimentalist, a slob in the language. Yet he is one of the half-dozen living American poets who are widely read, and of them, the one whose work is most frequently imitated by fledgling poets and students of creative writing. His success, however, is less disheartening when considered as an emblem of an age—perhaps the first in human history—where poetry is a useless pleasantry, largely ignored by the reading public. . . .

This Tree Will Be Here for a Thousand Years (forty-eight poems which had previously appeared in thirty magazines) opens with a short essay on "The Two Presences." They are, according to Bly, the poet's own consciousness, which is "insecure, anxious, massive, earthbound, persistent, cunning, hopeful," and "the consciousness out there, in creatures and plants" which (mercifully) is "none of these things," but which has "a melancholy tone." The poems, then, attempt to bridge this gap between inner and outer, and they do so by presenting an "I" whom we may assume is the poet himself, and a largely personified natural world. Not since Disney put gloves on a mouse has nature been so human: objects have "an inner grief"; alfalfa is "brave," a butterfly "joyful," dusk "half-drunk"; a star is "a stubborn man"; bark "calls to the rain"; "snow water glances up at the new moon." It is a festival of pathetic fallacy. At times, Bly's all-embracing "I," more childish than childlike, verges on the parodic: "I know no one on this train. / A man comes walking down the aisle. / I want to tell him / that I forgive him, that I want him / to forgive me." The reader longs for a new chapter to D. H. Lawrence's *Studies in Classic American Literature*. ("Oh God! Better a bellyache. A bellyache is at least specific.")—Eliot Weinberger, "Gloves on a Mouse," *Nation*, Nov. 17, 1979, pp. 503–4

Robert Bly is another poet I don't believe and never have. He explains in the preface to his new book, *This Tree Will Be Here for a Thousand Years*, that he is aware of two consciousnesses, his own and those of the "inanimate" things around him: pebbles, moons, dry grass. For my part, this is Swedenborgian nonsense, very dangerous. It saps our minds as it saps the beauty of the natural world. Distance and difference are what make us conscious, not fuzzy homologies. But let it go; Bly writes against my grain, yet in some poems he catches me, and I am not off my guard. "Sometimes when you put your hand into a hollow tree / you touch the dark places between the stars." Not many of Bly's readers have done that, I imagine, but I am a country poet, like him, and I *have* done it. I'm damned if he isn't right. I pull back. Sometimes it is good, better than good, to guard oneself and still be caught.—HAYDEN CAR-RUTH, "Poets on the Fringe," *Harper's*, Jan. 1980, p. 79

DAVID SEAL
From "Waking to 'Sleepers Joining Hands'"
Of Solitude and Silence
1981, pp. 219–32

W hat is deceptive about "Sleepers" is that it is clearly indebted to Jung. All four parts bear Jungian allusions in their titles alone. This of course brings the systematizers out in force. The briefest acquaintance with Jung reminds us that the process of individuation has four parts—persona, shadow, animus / anima, and Self—and it is clearly tempting to read the poem as a Jungian drama. This may even be the best way to begin reading the poem. As Martin Luther says, sin boldly. But it is not the proper destination. "Sleepers Joining Hands" is only apparently a Jungian drama. If we lift up the rug of in-dividuation we'll find a lot of "matter out of place" (Mary Douglas's definition of dirt). I think the poem will ultimately be read more for what Bly swept under the rug than for the pattern he wove into it.

Briefly, there is a substantial part of "Sleepers" that cannot be made sense of by Jung's individuation scheme. Further-more, this "matter out of place" is a quarrel precisely with the Jungian ideas that apparently dominate. And it seems to me that the poem is not "really" about this quarrel, but also about it. Bly consciously uses Jung, and unconsciously resists Jung. The poem, then, contains an unconscious conflict within it-self. . . .

Part One is titled, "The Shadow Goes Away." The poet begins by uttering fears of drowning, of being overwhelmed and eaten by sea monsters and predators. But these vague fears quickly reduce to a sense of loss, a loss both of a brother and of part of the self. Even in this brief tenure of the poem, we can feel the movement from all-encompassing terror through ambivalence to a dim perception of local guilt, immediate loss, the movement from anxieties known only by symptoms to the pathology of their cause. Repression is lifting. Consciousness realizes the extent of its loss, and takes its first steps in repair: it begins a search for its "shadow," and finds its signs everywhere. At first the search is directed toward the "Dark Peoples." But then the lines turn inward, to the enemies inside. The section ends with the consequences of internal troubles: hints of di-vorce, rape, incest, Napoleon's mulatto mistress framed against "the white dusk" all suggest sexual problems connected with projection, predation, religious rigidity. The huts of the "Shad-owy People" that are destroyed suggest the military's predilec-tion to project and prey upon the North America "owned" by Indians and upon Vietnam. . . .

Clearly the shadow that goes away is related to Jung's concept of shadow. Jung argues that unless our social egos, our

"personas," are connected to our unconscious energies, they dry up in routine, harden into set defensive postures. The first stage of the individuation process is the recognition that our personas cannot be purely consciously determined; that when they are, we "encounter" our unconscious as projections upon other people which we erroneously interpret as their flaws. We have collective as well as individual shadows, and this first section of the poem explores the shadow problem in both areas: the loss of the poet's shadow, the loss of the national shadow, the consequences of both. It moves from mythological to historical time, ending in the contemporary allusions to Viet-nam, with the mythological allusions abiding in the back-ground, instead of the foreground, as in the beginning.

The next section, "Meeting the Man Who Warns Me," is substantially different in mood, action, psychic landscape, from the first. It begins in a fairy tale setting: "I wake and find myself in the woods, far from the castle." The suggestion here is both that the first part's desultory search has become the more structured journey or quest, and that the wandering occurs in the unconscious, in the woods, far from the commu-nity. The context becomes more narrowly psychic, rather than domestic or political: "fragments of the mother lie open in all low places."

The poet falls asleep, and meets a man from a milder planet, Christ's. His circumcising touch is soporific. The encounter is a religious one, and the results are mixed: the fierce light of consciousness is won at the price of sexual ener-gy. Christ energy denies cock energy, and puts the speaker in a sleep within a sleep, where he dreams of the dying of the fathers. The dying religious fathers serve to put transcendental religious energy back into its chthonic "grave" where it func-tions as "great conductors / carrying electricity under the ground." In the jump in imagery characteristic of Bly, the poem moves from subterranean electrical energy to subter-ranean water moving with great force. The poet senses his shadow underneath him, and then we find a locational shift: under transforms to inside. . . .

Jung speaks of the "Wise Old Man" as an archetype which occurs when a positive father complex produces a kind of credulity with regard to authority that has, ultimately, a spir-itual cast. From this father figure decisive beliefs, prohibitions, and wise counsel emanate.[1] Furthermore, he appears when the hero "is in a hopeless and desperate situation from which only profound reflection or a lucky idea—in other words, a spiritual function or an endopsychic automatism of some kind—can extricate him."[2] This old man in the poem is obviously "the man who warns me," and the warning first produces a hesita-tion in the poet. The old man then challenges him to speak or to go back. The speaker then confesses.

This confession is crucial, both to the section and the whole poem. It begins with the line, "I am the dark spirit that lives in the dark," showing that the shadow work has been done. His confession then recounts a quest, complete with a three-day immersion in the belly of a whale. . . .

It is clear that this confession closes off the second part of the Jungian scheme, as it demonstrates that the ego can do shadow work when it follows the increasingly bright guiding light of the Self. But the confession raises some issues that it doesn't resolve. If the poet already, even if unconsciously, possesses a kind of wisdom, what is the role of the Old Man? He merely prompts the telling of the quest. What seems to be a crucial encounter is actually anti-climactic. Second, the con-fession itself is dense, dream-like, highly "poetic." The point is not only that the speaker is startled by what comes out of his mouth. In Freud's terms, the lines the speaker speaks are already "secondary revision." Something is being hidden even as something else is revealed. We'll flag this part and return to it later. The poem shows symptoms here of bulging from something not said, although it has accomplished its shadow mission satisfactorily.

"The Night Journey in the Cooking Pot," the third section, is a rebirth, told in symbols that Jung had analyzed in *Symbols of Transformation*. As Atkinson says, it is an expanded version of the trenchant story the speaker tells to the old man. The opening lines move from mythical time to real, poetic time:

> I love the snow, I need privacy as I move,
> I am all alone, floating in the cooking pot
> on the sea, through the night I am alone.

Just as snow is transformed water, with a "solidtude" of its own, the speaker is a local version of the myth, finding in winter privacy an interior time and growth that makes the myth real in his life. The poet will move from mythic time to historial time, which is not so much national, as in the first section, as autobiographical, to real poetic time, where most of this section abides. The second group of lines, set off typographically by asterisks and indentations, is a kind of immersion in poetic time, so intense that it "forgets" the form that the poem is in and takes its own. . . .

The poet in his epiphanies has pierced the earth. But he must also return to the mundane, to himself, which can even be more dangerous than the journey outside the self. At first the ecstatic energy begins to swell in the body, and the poet sings and leaps about his room, "the happy genius of my own household," as Williams would say. The culmination is a love poem:

> I am not going farther from you,
> I am coming nearer,
> green rain carries me nearer you,
> I weave drunkenly about the page,
> I love you,
> I never knew that I loved you
> until I was swallowed by the invisible,
> my black shoes evaporating, rising about
>   my head. . . .
>
> For we are like the branch bent in the water . . .
> Taken out, it is whole, it was always whole. . . .
>   (Bly's ellipses)

This is the emotional climax of the poem, not just of this section. In a moment we will see the ecstasy disintegrate, as it must for any of us fortunate enough to live it. Yet, as Kabir says in Bly's translation, "Kabir saw that for fifteen seconds, and it made him a servant for life." Ultimately the branch is whole; it will not break. . . .

The fourth section, "Water Drawn Up Into the Head," resolves in one stroke the disparagements of the previous section, and draws us back in a phrase to the new community implied in the title of the whole poem: "Now do you understand the men who laugh all night in their sleep?" This establishes more firmly the ecstatic mood, which in each of us seems so transitory and fragile, but which is an undeniable reality in the community. The prose that follows, "Once there was a man who went to a far country to get his inheritance and then returned," is a root of many fairy tales and parables, and it is now more clear that the "far country" is inside. And the lines, "I am passive, listening to the lapping waves, / I am divine, drinking the air," show us the poet beginning to enlarge his utterance, speaking not merely privately but cosmically with the voice that will soon dominate in the "Extra Joyful Chorus.". . .

"Water Drawn Up Into the Head" is unlike the previous parts of the poem. It is a congeries of argument, image-scenes, allusions, and metaphorical descriptions. There is virtually no action: no drama of discovery, no embodiment of psychic energy, no reversal of mood. That the water goes to the head and not the heart predicts argument. Some kind of mental wound has been healed by the unconscious. But while argument tends to dominate "Water Drawn Up," it is only a peroration. The pure poetry that ends the section has become an instance of the argument; it attains what the poem as a whole is aiming at. By "forgetting all that" and losing itself in the "curved energy" the poem repeats the larger drama noted by Jung in *Symbols of Transformation*: conscious attainments are sacrificed in order to let the unconscious well up and heal. By drawing upon poetic forebears, Jiménez and Kabir, Stevens and Williams, Bly is able to heal not strictly by argumentative claims but by affective metaphor. . . .

Appended to the poem, and obviously a break from the stable quaternity of sections, is "An Extra Joyful Chorus for Those Who Have Read This Far." Atkinson reminds us that the long lines of this chorus recall Whitman, even as the title of the whole poem, "Sleepers Joining Hands," reminds us of Whitman's "The Sleepers," and that both poets work within the tradition of the psychic quest. The reader is also implicated in the quest. All the Whitmanic "I am" 's that Bly borrows are not autobiographical, but typical, the kind a reader can try on, as the title encourages him to do. Bly's "I am" 's play out over not only a physical landscape, where empathy and identity become the poet's tool as in Whitman, but also over a psychic landscape, where empathy must be extended to forms of the Self. Indeed, Bly's "I am" 's have a mythological cast to them recalling the powers of Proteus and Jove to become serially the forms of Creation.

The final tercets drop the first person singular for the plural of community, but do so in lines that are clearly and beautifully Bly's:

> Our faces shine with the darkness reflected from the
>   Tigris,
> cells made by the honeybees that go on growing after
>   death,
> a room darkened with curtains made of human hair.
> The panther rejoices in the gathering dark.
> Hands rush toward each other through miles of
>   space.
> All the sleepers in the world join hands.

The Miltonic oxymoron of the first line is both part of the conceit of the whole poem and part of a poetic tradition. The poem means to explore, not the light around the body, but the light inside, a special kind of light that tumbles paradoxically into its opposite. This first line remembers the fireball floating in the corner of the Eskimo's house, the owl with blue flames, dark bodies on the horizon trailing lights, the moonlit villages of the brain, the light that makes the flax blossom at midnight. Its oxymoronic nature owes much to Milton, while the enormity of the reversal implied by the conceit, it being the product not of clever wit but of consciousness plowed under, borrows not a little from Blake. And the buried nature of the image, the fact that it is meant to work not on our wit but on our unconscious, owes much to Coleridge. . . .

If the first line in the first tercet recalls the conceit upon which the whole poem is built, the succeeding two lines reinforce by means of parallels the mood of the first line, and extend the psychic location beyond death. It might be confusing to treat the lines eschatologically, for they primarily refer to psychic phenomena: the King is dead, long live the King; the hero dies and is reborn; the ego dies to itself and is transformed. But the words "darkness," "darkened," and "dark" remind us that death at least means the absence of light, whether psychic or physical death is meant.

If the first tercet draws the curtains, the second moves behind them with joy. Some fierce but beautiful animal part of our psyche feels joy at the same time that the human part wants to share the joy. "All the sleepers in the world join hands." We may ultimately find this line to be more than a metaphor. But

for now it is enough to see what Bly had done poetically. If Stevens awakened us to the morning of a new day, Bly puts us into a special kind of sleep in the evening of a new night.

Notes

1. C. G. Jung, "The Phenomenology of the Spirit in Fairy Tales," in *Psyche and Symbol* (Anchor, 1958), p. 69.
2. Jung, pp. 72–3.

LOUISE BOGAN

1897–1970

Louise Bogan was born on August 11, 1897 in Livermore Falls, Maine. At 18 she entered Boston University but left the following year to marry Curt Alexander, an army officer. Alexander died four years later, leaving Bogan with a newborn daughter. Bogan then married a poet, Raymond Holden, who became managing editor of *The New Yorker* in 1929. Shortly after Holden's appointment, Bogan took the post of poetry editor at the same magazine, staying at the post until her death in 1970. Bogan spent most of her adult life in New York City.

Bogan published several collections of poetry, *Body of This Death* (1923), *Dark Summer* (1929), and *The Sleeping Fury* (1937). In a review of one of her later collections, *Poems and New Poems* (1941), Bogan's art was described as "compactness compacted." Bogan was a member of a group of minor poets known as the "reactionary generation" who chose to ignore contemporaries such as Ezra Pound and T.S. Eliot and maintain the 17th century English traditional use of meters. Bogan also published translations from German and French, and an anthology for children, *The Golden Journey: Poems for Young People* (1965).

Bogan received several awards and was a fellow in American Letters at the Library of Congress. She was also elected a member of the National Institute of Arts and Letters (1952) and of the Academy of Arts and Letters (1968).

In 1968, Bogan published *The Blue Estuaries*, a collection of her later poetry, which was hailed as a work of refined diction and tone. She died in New York City on February 4, 1970.

Personal

Louise Bogan was a poet who matured during the first half of this century and who embraced traditional forms, masks, and mythologies. Compared to contemporary women poets, she is neither direct, personal, nor particular. Yet buried under the metrical decorum, the masks, the symbols, and the reticence of her poetry is a person who is painfully aware of her situation as a woman, and who tries to escape it. As Adrienne Rich says of Bogan's *Blue Estuaries*, "Her work, like that of Bradstreet, Dickinson, and H.D., is a graph of the struggle to commit a female sensibility, in all its aspects, to language."

Bogan's poetic style is, in part, a reaction to her political situation. In 1941 she wrote to Morton D. Zabel that W.H. Auden "couldn't get over my obscurity; and I told him it was because I wasn't respectable." She wasn't respectable because of her stay in a mental institution, her divorce, her drinking habits, and her poverty. Her letters document an eviction, constant attempts to scrounge money to support herself and her daughter, and hours lost from poetry writing blurbs on books for *The New Yorker*. In addition to these troubles, she lacked a thriving community of women poets from which to draw strength. Bogan simply could not write in a straightforward way about the pressures male society placed upon her because male editors would not publish her and society might reject her completely. Yet Bogan would not retreat quietly as one of the

"female songbirds" she despised. She wanted to say something about the situation of women in society. And since she wanted to be published, to be heard, she had to restrain her voice. She said in a letter to Zabel, "I don't think it a virtue always to be on your guard, in any art. Reticence, yes, but not guardedness; there's a difference." The difference, of course, was that some of her anger and frustration would be expressed, but shrouded in symbols and obscurity. If we examine her poetry, we can see how she struggled with social tensions, and we can see the thematic and stylistic effects of the pressures under which she and other women poets wrote earlier in this century.

Bogan's journal entries published recently in *The New Yorker* contains a revealing parenthetical note: "(The land-locked vista: at its end that view which most nearly corresponds to peace in the heart: the horizon.)" Peace for Bogan, in this passage and elsewhere, is either distance or its polar opposite: a self-annihilation by mixing or blending herself with nature. When an object, person, or thought causes her anxiety, she retreats to a distance; but when she loves a person, landscape, or idea, she hopes to dissolve herself into it. There is no middle ground for her. Seeing anything closely, especially a human being, is very threatening. The most anxious moments in her poetry are when she meets someone face to face. This central contrast in her work, distance and a self-annihilating embrace of nature, is also revealed in her poetic techniques. She values symbolic expression because it allows her to blur her meaning so she cannot be pinned down; her masks and irony create aesthetic distance; her preference for free verse in some of her poems is an attempt to blend with the undefinable wholeness of nature and escape the objectification or "thingness" of traditional verse.—PATRICK MOORE, "The Poetry of Louise Bogan," *Gender and Literary Voice*, ed. Janet Todd, 1980, pp. 67–69

Works

Miss Louise Bogan has published three books, and with each book she has been getting a little better, until now, in the three or four best poems of *The Sleeping Fury*, she has no superior within her purpose and range: among the women poets of our time she has a single peer, Miss Léonie Adams. Neither Miss Bogan nor Miss Adams will ever have the popular following of Miss Millay or even of the late Elinor Wylie. I do not mean to detract from these latter poets; they are technically proficient, they are serious, and they deserve their reputations. Miss Bogan and Miss Adams deserve still greater reputations, but they will not get them in our time because they are "purer" poets than Miss Millay and Mrs. Wylie. They are purer because their work is less involved in the moral and stylistic fashions of the age, and they efface themselves, whereas Miss Millay never lets us forget her "advanced" point of view nor Mrs. Wylie her interesting personality.

This refusal to take advantage of the traditional privilege of her sex must in part explain Miss Bogan's small production and the concentrated attention that she gives to the detail of her work. Women, I suppose, are fastidious, but many women poets are fastidious in their verse only as a way of being finical about themselves. But Miss Bogan is a craftsman in the masculine mode.

In addition to distinguished diction and a fine ear for the phrase-rhythm she has mastered a prosody that permits her to get the greatest effect out of the slightest variation of stress.

> In the cold heart, as on a page,
> Spell out the gentle syllable
> That puts short limit to your rage
> And curdles the straight fire of hell,
> Compassing all, so all is well.

There is nothing flashy about it; it is finely modulated. . . . Miss Bogan reaches the height of her talent in "Henceforth, from the Mind," surely one of the finest lyrics of our time. The "idea" of the poem is the gradual fading away of earthly joy upon the approach of age—one of the stock themes of English poetry; and Miss Bogan presents it with all the freshness of an Elizabethan lyricist. I quote the two last stanzas:

> Henceforward, from the shell,
> Wherein you heard, and wondered
> At oceans like a bell
> So far from ocean sundered—
> A smothered sound that sleeps
> Long lost within lost deeps,
>
> Will chime you change and hours,
> The shadow of increase,
> Will sound you flowers
> Born under troubled peace—
> Henceforth, henceforth
> Will echo sea and earth.

This poem represents the best phase of Miss Bogan's work: it goes back to an early piece that has been neglected by readers and reviewers alike—"The Mark"—and these two poems would alone entitle Miss Bogan to the consideration of the coming age.

But there is an unsatisfactory side to Miss Bogan's verse, and it may be briefly indicated by pointing out that the peculiar merits of "The Mark" and "Henceforth, from the Mind" seem to lie in a strict observance of certain limitations: in these poems and of course in others, Miss Bogan is impersonal and dramatic. In "The Sleeping Fury" she is philosophical and divinatory; in "Hypocrite Swift" she merely adumbrates an obscure dramatic situation in a half lyrical, half eighteenth-century, satirical style. Neither of these poems is successful, and the failure can be traced to all levels of the performances; for example, to the prosody, which has little relation to the development of the matter and which merely offers us a few clever local effects.—ALLEN TATE, "R. P. Blackmur and Others," *SoR*, Summer 1937, pp. 190–92

Women are not noted for terseness, but Louise Bogan's art is compactness compacted. Emotion with her, as she has said of certain fiction, is "itself form, the kernel which builds outward form from inward intensity." She uses a kind of forged rhetoric that nevertheless seems inevitable. It is almost formula with her to omit the instinctive comma of self-defensive explanation, for example, "Our lives through we have trod the ground." Her titles are right poetically, with no subserviences for torpid minds to catch at; the lines entitled "Knowledge," for instance, being really about love. And there is fire in the brazier—the thinker in the poet. "Fifteenth Farewell" says:

> I erred, when I thought loneliness the wide
> Scent of mown grass over forsaken fields,
> Or any shadow isolation yields.
> Loneliness was the heart within your side.

One is struck by her restraint—an unusual courtesy in this day of bombast. The triumph of what purports to be surrender, in the "Poem in Prose," should be studied entire.

Miss Bogan is a workman, in prose or in verse. Anodynes are intolerable to her. She refuses to be deceived or self-deceived. Her work is not mannered. There are in it thoughts about the disunities of "the single mirrored against the single," about the devouring gorgon romantic love, toward which, as toward wine, unfaith is renewal; thoughts about the solace and futilities of being brave; about the mind as a refuge—"crafty knight" that is itself "Prey to an end not evident to craft"; about grudges; about no longer treating memory "as rich stuff . . . in a cedarn dark, . . . as eggs under the wings," but as

> Rubble in gardens, it and stones alike,
> That any spade may strike.

We read of "The hate that bruises, though the heart is braced"; of "one note rage can understand"; of "chastity's futility" and "pain's effrontery"; of "memory's false measure." No Uncle Remus phrase of nature, this about the crows and the woman whose prototype is the briar patch: "She is a stem long hardened. / A weed that no scythe mows." Could the uninsisted-on surgery of exposition be stricter than in the term "red" for winter grass, or evoke the contorted furor of flame better than by saying the fire ceased its "thresh"? We have "The lilac like a heart" (preceded by the word "leaves"); "See now the stretched hawk fly"; "Horses in half-ploughed fields / Make earth they walk upon a changing color." Most delicate of all,

> . . . we heard the cock
> Shout its unplaceable cry, the axe's sound
> Delay a moment after the axe's stroke.

Music here is not someone's idol, but experience. There are real rhymes, the rhyme with vowel cognates, and consonant resonances so perfect one is not inclined to wonder whether the sound is a vowel or a consonant—as in "The Crossed Apple":

> . . . this side is red without a dapple,
> And this side's hue
> Is clear and snowy. It's a lovely apple.
> It is for you.

In "fed with fire" we have expert use of the enhancing exception to the end-stopped line:

> And spiny fruits up through the earth are fed
> With fire;

Best of all is the embodied climax with unforced subsiding cadence, as in the song about

> The stone—the deaf, the blind—
> That sees the birds in flock
> Steer narrowed to the wind.

When a tune plagues the ear, the best way to be rid of it is to let it forth unhindered. This Miss Bogan has done with a W. H. Auden progression, "Evening in the Sanitarium"; with G. M. Hopkins in "Feuer-Nacht"; Ezra Pound in "The Sleeping Fury"; W. B. Yeats in "Betrothed"; W. C. Williams in "Zone." All through, there is a certain residual, securely equated seventeenth-century firmness, as in the spectacular competence of "Animal, Vegetable, and Mineral."

What of the implications? For mortal rage and immortal injury, are there or are there not medicines? Job and Hamlet insisted that we dare not let ourselves be snared into hating hatefulness; to do this would be to take our own lives. Harmed, let us say, through our generosity—if we consent to have pity on our illusions and others' absence of illusion, to condone the fact that "no fine body ever can be meat and drink to anyone"—is it true that pain will exchange its role and become servant instead of master? Or is it merely a conveniently unexpunged superstition?

Those who have seemed to know most about eternity feel that this side of eternity is a small part of life. We are told, if we do wrong that grace may abound, it does not abound. We need not be told that life is never going to be free from trouble and that there are no substitutes for the dead; but it is a fact as well as a mystery that weakness is power, that handicap is proficiency, that the scar is a credential, that indignation is no adversary for gratitude, or heroism for joy. There are medicines.—MARIANNE MOORE, *Predilections*, 1955, pp. 130–33

Louise Bogan's poetry has much in common with Miss ⟨Léonie⟩ Adams's. Here are the opening lines of three of Miss Bogan's early poems:

> In fear of the rich mouth
> I kissed the thin,—

and

> I make the old sign.
> I invoke you,
> Chastity.

and

> Now that I know
> How passion warms little.

At that point at least—and down to the Puritan marrow of Miss Wylie's bones—Miss Adams and Miss Bogan were surely sisters in the same aesthetic convent; and while I must confess that I have often wondered why that sisterhood insisted on wearing its chastity belts on the outside, poetry nevertheless remains wherever the spirit finds it. If that starting illusion was necessary to the poem, what matters is that the poems came—clean, hard, rigorously disciplined, and reaching to the nerve. Miss Bogan's capture in such an early piece as "Medusa" is enough to justify a whole burial ground of Puritan marrows.

But—speaking as one reader—if I admire objectively the poems of the first three (the earlier) sections of Miss Bogan's collection, with the poems of section four, I find myself forgetting the thee and me of it. I am no longer being objective about the excellence of a poet who leaves me shrugging down to the Neapolitan marrow of my bones. I am immediately engaged. Miss Bogan began in beauty, but she has aged to magnificence, and I find myself thinking that the patina outshines the gold stain. One has only to compare "The Dream" . . . with the poems whose openings I have already cited to see how much more truly Miss Bogan sees into herself in the late poems—and not only into herself, but deeply enough into herself to find within her that jungle—call it the Jungian unconscious if you must—that everyone has in himself. "The Dream" is not only Miss Bogan's; it is everyone's.

Beginning with the poems of section four, that it, Miss Bogan leaves the convent. She comes out of timelessness into time. Nor is this a matter of topical reference. No such thing. It is, rather, that the kind of inward perception that marks the later poems speaks not only an enduring motion of the human spirit but an enduring motion that is *toward* the timeless *from* the times. The more difficult demon has been wrestled with.— JOHN CIARDI, "Two Nuns and a Strolling Player," *Nation*, May 22, 1954, pp. 445–46

Louise Bogan is usually categorized as a poet in the metaphysical tradition or meditative mode, following Donne, Emily Dickinson, and older contemporaries like Eliot and Ransom. Yet, like so many modern poets, she is a Romantic in her rhetoric and attitudes, and her procedure at least tends towards the visionary mode, in the tradition of Blake and Yeats. Her best and most characteristic poems establish their structure by a conflict of contraries, akin to Blake's clashes of Reason and Energy and Yeats' dialogues between Self and Soul. As in Blake and Yeats, there is no transcendence of this strife in Miss Bogan's poems; it is not resolved in the traditional consolations of religious belief, or in the expectation of any permanent abiding place for the human spirit. The frequent fierceness of Miss Bogan's rhetoric proceeds from a bitterness born of the unresolved contraries, the demands of reason and energy, of limiting form and the exuberance of desire, for Miss Bogan is purely a lyrical poet, and lacks the support of the personal systems of Blake and Yeats, by which those poets were able more serenely to contemplate division in the psyche. Miss Bogan is neither a personal myth-maker in the full Romantic tradition, like her near-contemporary Hart Crane, nor an ironist in the manner of Tate, to cite another poet of her generation. The honesty and passion of her best work has about it, in consequence, a vulnerable directness.

The poems on this recording largely follow the sequence of Miss Bogan's *Collected Poems*, for that sequence hints at a kind of ordering, in which the unresolved contraries of the poet's world move towards a delicate and tentative balance. *Medusa* makes an effective introduction to the landscape of Miss Bogan's poetry. What is conveyed here is a sense of unreality pervading a desolation. The scene has a frozen-fast quality pointing towards the inner significance of the Medusa myth. The poem is altogether oblique in its presentation. What is offered is an image of the memory itself turned to stone, a hint of the theme of the rejection of nostalgia to be developed in the later poems.

Men Loved Wholly Beyond Wisdom is a gnomic parable, with overtones of the Blake of *Ah Sunflower!* and the Yeats of "Never give all the heart." The poem is a miniature dialectic, with the contrary statement rising from the sixth line onwards. The final figure of the cricket is a striking emblem akin to those of Blake's state of Experience. Lighter and still more laconic is the subtle lyric, *The Crossed Apple*, with its flavor of New England speech. Here, in a poem "about" the co-existent contraries of the freedom and necessity of choice one can observe reminders of the archetypal apple-tasting in Eden, but we recognize a humanistic emphasis:

This apple's from a tree yet unbeholden,
Where two kinds meet,—

The preceding poems are preparations for Miss Bogan's most ambitious poem, *Summer Wish*, which marks the crisis and mid-point of her work. Here the influence of Yeats is explicit and acknowledged, with the poem's epigraph being the opening of the pastoral lament for Robert Gregory, *Shepherd and Goatherd*. Two voices speak in alternation in *Summer Wish*, with the passionate soul expressing its longings, and the observant self describing the phenomena of its mutable world moving slowly towards summer, the season desired by the soul. The two voices fail consistently to heed the other, in an extended ironic vision of the divided psyche.

The first voice begins by crying out for full rebirth, rejecting the spring as a false hope. The second voice counters by calmly describing the very end of winter, the first touches of spring. The first voice reminds itself that experience denies the reality of its full, earlier yearning forwards, and categorizes love as fantasy. The second voice moves on to detail the early growth of the signs of renewal. The first voice, reproving itself yet more harshly, rejects the saving grace of memory. The second voice describes early April, and the movement towards summer. The first voice increases in bitterness, expounding the contraries of passion. The second voice, as if almost in response, describes the meeting of two figures with a gradual revelation of the man of the pair. Half in response, the first voice rejects the self-comfort to be found by the pride of one's own solitariness. The second voice now ceases to be as purely neutral in its descriptiveness, and emphasizes the sensuous beauty still to be found in the fading of the day. The first voice, again turning from refuges, rejects the mind as comfort. The second voice describes the spring planting, with a new note of purposefulness. The first voice, in its final outcry, acknowledges that earth's year begins, and responds to it, defying itself and the past with wish and laughter, and finding in rock a symbol of ultimate desperation and yet a mode of heroic consolation. The second voice completes the poem with the Yeatsian figure of the hawk's flight as an image both of acceptance and of the effort to hold oneself open to experience:

See now
Open above the field, stilled in wing-stiffened flight,
The stretched hawk fly.

Summer Wish is Miss Bogan's *Resolution and Independence*. Her later poems either celebrate the consequences of having cast out remorse, or return to a fiercer, more impatient preoccupation with the self.

Henceforth From the Mind is an exultant Romantic lyric, chanting in Yeatsian accents the greater sweetness that has flowed into the remorseless breast, and yet acknowledging with regret (as in the second stanza) the necessity for resignation to some permanent sense of loss. The Wordsworthian image of the sea-shell betokens a darker music of mature imagination, similar to the "sober-coloring" of the close of the *Intimations* ode.

The Sleeping Fury renews the Medusa image in an address to the self as the soul's dark double, "my scourge, my sister," and ends in the deliverance of a fuller awareness of both self and soul. *Putting to Sea* praises the enterprise of entering the abyss of the self, the dangerous exploration of our darkness. *The Dream* is Miss Bogan's most dramatic and convincing portrayal of the split in the self, with its renewal of the ancient myth of the appeased fury. *Song for the Last Act* is a graceful parting poem, being both a love song and a ritual of acceptance. Read at the end, it serves to round off the record of a life of humanistic craftsmanship.—HAROLD BLOOM, Jacket Notes, "Louise Bogan Reads from Her Own Works," *Yale Series of Recorded Poets*, Decca Records, 1958

FORD MADOX FORD
From "The Flame in Stone"
Poetry, June 1937, pp. 158–61

There is one word singularly useful that will one day no doubt be worn out. But that day I hope is not yet. It is the word "authentic." It expresses the feeling that one has at seeing something intimately sympathetic and satisfactory. I had the feeling acutely the other day when slipping along the east side of the Horseshoe Bend, in the long broad valley that runs down to Philadelphia. I saw sunlight, and almost in the same moment a snake fence wriggling its black spikedness over the shoulder of what in England we should call a down, and then the familiar overhanging roof of a Pennsylvania Dutch barn. It would take too long and it would perhaps be impolite to the regions in which these words will be printed to say exactly why I felt so much emotion at seeing those objects. Let it go at the fact that I felt as if, having traveled for a very long time amongst misty objects that conveyed almost nothing to my inner self— nothing, that is to say, in the way of association or remembrance—I had suddenly come upon something that was an integral part of my past. I had once gone heavily over just such fields, stopping to fix a rail or so on just such a fence, and then around the corner of just such a barn onto a wet dirt road where I would find, hitched up, the couple of nearly thoroughbred roans who should spiritedly draw over sand and boulders my buck-board to the post office at the crossroads. I had come, that is to say, on something that had been the real part of my real life when I was strong, and the blood went more swiftly to my veins, and the keen air more deeply into my lungs. In a world that has become too fluid, they were something authentic.

I had precisely the same sense and wanted to use that same word when I opened Miss Bogan's book and read the three or four first words. They ran:

Henceforth, from the mind,
For your whole joy. . . .

Nothing more.

I am not any kind of a critic of verse poetry. I don't understand the claims that verse poets make to be (compared with us prosateurs) beings set apart and mystically revered. Indeed if one could explain that, one could define what has never been defined by either poet or pedestrian: one could define what poetry is.

But one can't. No one ever has. No one ever will be able to. You might almost think that the real poet, whether he write in prose or verse, taking up his pen, causes with the scratching on the paper such a vibration that that same vibration continues through the stages of being typed, set up in print, printed in magazine, and then in a book—that that same vibration continues right through the series of processes till it communicates itself at last to the reader and makes him say as I said when I read those words of Miss Bogan's: "This is authentic." I have read Miss Bogan for a number of years now, and always with a feeling that I can't exactly define. More than anything, it was, as it were, a sort of polite something more than interest. Perhaps it was really expectation. But the moment I read those words I felt perfectly sure that what would follow would be something stable, restrained, never harrowing, never what the French call *chargé*—those being attributes of what one most avoids reading. And that was what followed—a series of words, of cadences, thought and disciplined expression that brought to the mental eye and ear, in a kind of television, the image of Miss Bogan writing at the other end of all those processes all the words that go to make up this book.

There are bitter words. But they are not harassingly bitter:

> And you will see your lifetime yet
> Come to their terms, your plans unmade—
> And be belied, and be betrayed.

There are parallel series of antithetical thoughts, but the antithesis is never exaggerated:

> Bend to the chart, in the extinguished night
> Mariners! Make way slowly; stay from sleep;
> That we may have short respite from such light
> And learn with joy, the gulf, the vast, the deep.

There are passages that are just beautiful words rendering objects of beauty:

> . . . The hour wags
> Deliberate and great arches bend
> In long perspective past our eye.
> Mutable body, and brief name,
> Confront, against an early sky,
> This marble herb, and this stone flame.

And there are passages of thought as static and as tranquil as a solitary candle-shaped-flame of the black yew tree that you see against Italian heavens:

> Beautiful now as a child whose hair, wet with rage
>   and tears
> Clings to its face. And now I may look upon you,
> Having once met your eyes. You lie in sleep and
>   forget me.
> Alone and strong in my peace, I look upon you in
>   yours.

There is, in fact, everything that goes to the making of one of those more pensive seventeenth century, usually ecclesiastical English poets who are the real glory of our twofold lyre. Miss Bogan may—and probably will—stand somewhere in a quiet landscape that contains George Herbert, and Donne and Vaughan, and why not even Herrick? This is not to be taken as appraisement. It is neither the time nor the place to say that Miss Bogan ranks with Marvell. But it is a statement of gratification—and a statement that from now on, when we think of poetry, we must think of Miss Bogan as occupying a definite niche in the great stony façade of the temple to our Muse. She may well shine in her place and be content.

W. H. AUDEN
"The Rewards of Patience"

Partisan Review, July–August 1942, pp. 336–40

"Genius has only an immanent teleology, it develops itself, and while developing itself this self-development projects itself as its work. Genius is therefore in no

sense inactive, and works within itself perhaps harder than ten business men, but none of its achievements have any exterior telos. This is at once the humanity and the pride of genius; the humanity lies in the fact that it does not define itself teleologically in relation to other men, as though there were any one who needed it; its pride lies in the fact that it immanently relates itself to itself. It is modest of the nightingale not to require anyone to listen to it; but it is also proud of the nightingale not to care whether anyone listens to it or not. . . . The honored public, the domineering masses, wish genius to express that it exists for their sake; they only see one side of the dialectic of genius, take offense at its pride, and do not see that the same thing is also modesty and humility."

So wrote Kierkegaard in 1847; he did not foresee that by 1942 the masses would have acquired such buying power that genius itself would, in many cases, be thinking of its self-development as a process of learning how to sell itself competitively to the public, that the poet whose true song, unlike that of the nightingale, continually changes because he himself changes, would be tempted to dissociate his song from his nature altogether, until the changes in the latter come to be conditioned, not by changes in himself, but by the shifting of public taste—that he would become, in other words, a journalist.

A public is a disintegrated community. A community is a society of rational beings united by a common tie in virtue of the things that they all love; a public is a crowd of lost beings united only negatively in virtue of the things that they severally fear, among which one of the greatest is the fear of being responsible as a rational being for one's individual self-development. Hence, wherever there is a public, there arises the paradox of a tremendous demand for art in the abstract, but an almost complete repudiation of art in the concrete. A demand because works of art can indeed help people along the road of self-development, and the public feels more helpless than ever; a repudiation because art can only help those who help themselves. It can suggest directions in which people may look if they will; it cannot give them eyes or wills, but it is just these eyes and wills that the public demand, and hope to buy with money and applause.

Subjectively, the situation of the poet is no less difficult. In ages when there was such a thing as a community, the self-development of which his works are the manifestation, arose, in part at least, out of his life as a member, assenting or dissenting, of and within that community; in an age when there is only a public, his self-development receives no such extraneous help, so that, unless he replaces it by taking over the task of directing his life by his own deliberate intention, his growth and hence his poetry is at the mercy of personal accidents, love-affairs, illnesses, bereavements, and so forth.

Again it was in the community that he formerly found a source of value outside himself, and unless he now can replace this vanished source by another, or at least search for it, his only standard for appreciating experience is The Interesting, which in practice means his childhood and his sex-life, so that he escapes being a journalist who fawns on the public only to become a journalist who fawns on his own ego; the selection and treatment of experience is still conditioned by its news value. In the case of much 'advanced' poetry, the public is therefore, though quite unjustifiably, quite right in repudiating it; not because, as the public thinks, it is too difficult, but because, once one has learned the idiom, it is too easy; one can translate it immediately and without loss of meaning into the language of the Daily Press. Far from being what it claims to be, and is rejected by the public for being,

The shrieking heaven lifted over men

it is, what the public demands but finds elsewhere in much better brands,

The dumb earth wherein they set their graves

A volume of good poetry, like this collection of Miss Louise Bogan's, represents today therefore a double victory, over the Collective Self and over the Private Self. As her epigraph she uses a quotation from Rilke—

Wie ist das klein womit wir ringen,
was mit uns ringt, wie ist das gross

And the poems that follow are the fruit of such a belief, held and practised over years, that Self-development is a process of self-surrender, for it is the Self that demands the exclusive attention of all experiences, but offers none in return.

The playthings of the young
Get broken in the play,
Get broken, as they should.

In the early sections Miss Bogan employs her gift in the way in which, as a rule, it should at first be employed, to understand her weakness to which it is dialectically related, for wherever there is a gift, of whatever kind, there is also a guilty secret, a thorn in the flesh and the first successful poems of young poets are usually a catharsis of resentment.

Cry, song, cry
And hear your crying lost

Poems at this stage are usually short, made up of magical lyric phrases which seem to rise involuntarily to the consciousness, and their composition is attended by great excitement, a feeling of being inspired.

Some excellent poets, like Housman and Emily Dickinson, never get beyond this stage, because the more successful the catharsis, the more dread there must be of any change either in one's life or one's art, for a change in the former threatens the source of the latter which is one's only consolation, and the latter can only change by ceasing to console. Miss Bogan, however, recognized this temptation and resisted it.

My mouth, perhaps, may learn one thing too well,
My body hear no echo save its own,
Yet will the desperate mind, maddened and proud,
Seek out the storm, escape the bitter spell.

But the price and privilege of growth is that the temptation resisted is replaced by a worse one. No sooner does the mind seek to escape the bitter spell than the lying Tempter whispers—

The intellect of man is forced to choose
Perfection of the life or of the work

The poet who escapes from the error of believing that the relation of his life to his work is a direct one, that the second is the mirror image of the first, now falls into the error of denying that there need be any relation at all, into believing that the poetry can develop autonomously, provided that the poet can find it a convenient Myth. For the Myth is a set of values and ideas which are impersonal and so break the one-one relationship of poetry to experience by providing other standards of importance than the personally interesting, while at the same time it is not a religion, that is to say, it does not have to be believed in real life, with all the effort and suffering which that implies.

Thus we find modern poets asking of a general idea, not Is It True?, but Is It Exciting? Is It Poetically useful?, and whether they are attracted to Byzantium and The Phases of the Moon, like Yeats, or to the Id or Miss History like his younger and less-talented colleagues, the motive and its motions are the same.

But the escape from the Self without the surrender of the Self is, of course, an illusion, for it is the Self that still chooses the particular avenue of escape. Thus Yeats, the romantic rebel against the Darwinian Myth of his childhood with its belief in The Machine and Automatic Progress, adopts as poetic 'organisers' woozy doctrines like The Aristocratic Mask and the Cyclical Theory of Time while remaining personally, as Eliot rather slyly remarks, 'a very sane man'; others fashion an image out of the opposites of puritanical parents or upper class education. And still the personal note appears, only now in the form of its denial, in a certain phoney dramatisation, a 'camp' of impersonality. Further the adoption of a belief which one does not really hold as a means of integrating experience poetically, while it may produce fine poems, limits their meaning to the immediate context; it creates Occasional poems lacking any resonances beyond their frame. (Cf., for example Yeats' *Second Coming* with Eliot's *East Coker*).

To have developed to the point where this temptation is real, and then to resist it, is to realise that the relation of Life to Work is dialectical, a change in the one presupposes and demands a change in the other, and that belief and behaviour have a similar relation, that is to say, that beliefs are religious or nothing, and a religion cannot be got out of books or by a sudden vision, but can only be realized by living it. And to see this is to see that one's poetic development must be restrained from rushing ahead of oneself while at the same time one's self-development must not be allowed to fall behind.

Reading through Miss Bogan's book, one realizes what is the price and the reward for such a discipline.

The hasty reader hardly notices any development; the subject matter and form show no spectacular change: he thinks— "Miss Bogan. O yes, a nice writer of lyrics, but all these women poets, you know, slight. Only one string to their bow." It is only by reading and rereading that one comes to appreciate the steady growth of wisdom and technical mastery, the persistent elimination of the consolations of stoicism and every other kind of poetic theatre, the achievement of an objectivity about personal experience which is sought by many but found only by the few who dare face the Furies.

You who know what we love, but drive us to know it;
You with your whips and shrieks, bearer of truth and
    of solitude;
You who give, unlike men, to expiation your mercy.
Dropping the scourge when at last the scourged advances to meet it,
You, when the hunted turns, no longer remain the
    hunter
But stand silent and wait, at last returning his gaze.
Beautiful now as a child whose hair, wet with rage
    and tears
Clings to its face. And now I may look upon you,
Having once met your eyes. You lie in sleep and
    forget me.
Alone and strong in my peace, I look upon you in
    yours.

In the last two sections, in poems like *Animal, Vegetable and Mineral* and *Evening in the Sanitarium* Miss Bogan turns to impersonal subjects, and here again the hasty will say: "too slight. I prefer her earlier work," because he cannot understand the integrity of an artist who will not rush her sensibility, knowing that no difficulty can be cheated without incurring punishment.

But the difficulty of being an artist in an age when one has to live everything for oneself, has its compensations. It is, for the strong, a joy to know that now there are no longer any places of refuge in which one can lie down in comfort, that one must go on or go under, live dangerously or not at all.

It is therefore impossible today to predict the future of any poet because the future is never the consequence of a single decision but is continually created by a process of choice in which temptation and opportunity are perpetually presented, ever fresh and ever unforseen. All one can say is that Miss Bogan is a poet in whom, because she is so clearly aware of this, one has complete faith as to her instinct for direction and her endurance, and that, anyway, what she has already written is of permanent value. Future generations will, of course, be as foolish as ours, but their follies like our own and those of every generation will mainly effect their judgment of their present which is always so much more 'interesting' than the silly old past.

Miss Bogan, I fancy, is then going to be paid the respect she deserves when many, including myself, I fear, of those who now have a certain news value, are going to catch it.

LÉONIE ADAMS
"All Has Been Translated into Treasure"
Poetry, December 1954, pp. 165–69

The immediate significance of ⟨*Collected Poems: 1952–53*⟩ is twofold. It provides, in an admirable arrangement and with some fine additions, work whose excellence had been recognized, but which had been for some years out of print, and it provides occasion for calling it to the attention of the wider audience it deserves.

Self-possessed, from the beginning intact, Miss Bogan's talent has never been in dispute, nor had the unhappy, often questionable merit of "eluding" definition. Since the brilliant and early beginning of *Body of This Death*, she has not stood still, nor advanced by fits and starts. After the poems in *The Sleeping Fury*, though still to bring forth those true fruits which always surprise, she could hardly exceed herself in her characteristic mode. With the publication of *Poems and New Poems*, the distinguished quality of her work had been asserted and as far as possible perhaps discriminated by some of those most competent to do this. The present reviewer feels no need for revision of their essential estimate. Indeed an old jacket reminds one that things were said of her poems in 1923 which are still, in effect, being said with perfect soundness in 1954.

What there is need of, and opportunity for, is to repeat and labor a little the estimate alluded to. The virtues of her writing which have been most often spoken of are, I should suppose, firmness of outline, prosodic accomplishment, chiefly in traditional metrics, purity of diction and tone, concision of phrase, and, what results in craft from all these, and at bottom from a way of seizing experience, concentrated singleness of effect.

The description might well delimit the classic form of the short lyric, any time, any place, abstractly, and so hold for any example, and none. Actually its elements have seldom, and never for long periods, been held in English verse in any serenity of balance, and this poet's particular management of them remains to be discussed.

Louise Bogan has not written a large body of work, nor addressed herself—though this will seem less true by concentrating on the later sections of the book—to peculiarly modern preoccupations. Just as a certain inner rhythm can be found—and some other effects of sound patterning cannot—only within freely absorbed metrical forms, a certain lyric

reduction can perhaps be reached only for recurrent norms of experience, a little beneath and apart from immediate phenomena. The evidence of the poems is that this poet has rarely written except when impelled by the strong experience of the private person. Though adhering more closely to traditional forms than many poets find will meet their case, the language of the poems is as well of now as not, their temper of mind and presuppositions perfectly so.

A large part of their moral force derives from the refusal to be deluded, or to be overborne. The learning of the unwanted lesson, the admission of the harsh fact, a kind of exhilaration of rejection, whether of the scorned or the merely implausible, the theme appears in the earliest work, and reaches maximum power in Section III. To mention some of the well known pieces there, *The Sleeping Fury*, like *The Dream*, finds an image for such admission within the self; *At a Party* situates its scene; the finely sustained *Putting to Sea* encompasses both these, the elegiac tone of innocence, and the deeper one of some inclusive mystery of survival. *Henceforth from the Mind* is the theme's more abstracted song.

Yet despite this theme's prevalence, though there are pieces which might be classified as small ironic portraits (*The Romantic, The Alchemist, Man Alone*) and even an epigram or so, the true vein of her work is not ironic in the usual sense, nor satiric, but something at once simpler and more desperately human. In the best of these poems what makes possible their strong charging of the formal balance is this: the explicit matter is unimpeded delineation; its cost, seldom adumbrated, resounds. Thus in the early *If You Take All Gold* there is some indulgence of its tonality; in *Henceforth from the Mind*, surely one of the perfect lyrics of the period, one hears its more fixed and absolute reverberation:

> Henceforward, from the shell,
> Wherein you heard, and wondered
> At oceans like a bell
> So far from ocean sundered—
> A smothered sound that sleeps
> Long lost within lost deeps,
> Will chime you change and hours,
> The shadow of increase,
> Will sound you flowers
> Born under troubled peace—
> Henceforth, henceforth
> Will echo sea and earth.

The note is present, compelling by its confinement to overtone, even where the overt scene or mood is so demoniac as in *At a Party*. *Exhortation* perhaps lacks it, and the *wholeness* of the other poems. One is reminded of Mr. Eliot's comment on the musical autonomy of Shakespeare's songs. Here, it might be said, however stringent the discipline of recognition, the sense of "All that is worth grief" remains. And to know this, though glad enough to have it, one does not need the explicit statement of *Summer Wish, Roman Fountain*, or

> Attest, poor body, with what scars you have
> That you left life, to come down to the grave.

Nor should one be surprised to find another balance, of acceptance, in some of the last lyrics in the book.

Yet the temper of being and pressure of experience just discussed is important to much of the work, to its quality of decision of style. Miss Moore has written of Louise Bogan's "compactness compacted." It is not the concentration of density, dazzling or murky, to be found in some modern work, but of rapid elucidation, and its secret is again that of the poise of elements in the poem. A few examples of the early period, in the symbolist-imagist manner, do more to develop the reserves of the image, and the last poem in the book does so magnificently; any number of phrases throughout are witness to "sensibility" for objects. "Listen but once" she oftenest tells that faculty and refuses to freight the poem with more than can be brought incisively to its light. She has always seen the use of the dramatic figure or mask, not for elaboration, but statement of the essence of a situation. (Longer pieces, like *The Sleeping Fury, Summer Wish*, are a progressive unfolding, in the same style.) Her musicianship works for what Hopkins distinguished as "candour, style" (harmony of tone) rather than "margaretting" (pearling with musical effects?). Many of her best poems should be related—for the lyric has other ancestors than the spontaneous cry—to the sort of choric lyric which speaks its comment nearest to the scene.

It is an art of limits, the limit of the inner occasion and of the recognized mode. This is part of its relevance, when writing often reminds us that there is no end to the remarks to be made, the matters to be noted; or, on the other hand, that the literary vegetation abounds less with forms, as in Mr. Stevens' phrase, than with techniques for exploitation.

Ranging only as far as may be from a personal center, this is a civilizéd poetry. Its *there* of "ordre et beauté, luxe, calme et volupté" is the humane terrain described in *After the Persian*, the "temperate threshold, the strip of corn and vine," where

> All is translucence (the light!)
> Liquidity, and the sound of water.

and

> . . . day stains with what seems to be more than the
>   sun
> What may be more than my flesh
> All has been translated into treasure.

Her eye is often on its objects, whether "currant on the branch" or "This marble herb, and this stone flame." Her voice is nearly always of it. That it is seen as approached on "mindless earth," from "the lie, anger, lust, oppression and death," and found in fragments, "continents apart," that the crisis of its access is often described in terms of the psyche, is part of the burden here of modernity.

GLORIA BOWLES

From "Louise Bogan: To Be (or Not to Be?) Woman Poet"

Women's Studies, 1977, pp. 131–35

It was difficult to be both woman and poet in the '30s and '40s in America. We know that there were women poets in this period who chose not to write about their lives as women. (Gertrude Stein, Marianne Moore are examples.)[1] But Louise Bogan could not avoid writing about her life as a woman because she believed in personal poetry. Not that she was a confessional poet. As she put it, she opted for "reticence" but not "guardedness."[2] She felt that "lyric poetry, if it is at all authentic . . . is based on some emotion—on some occasion, some real confrontation."[3] Of course, she was writing in a period which did not recognize how greatly gender affects experience. The facts of Bogan's writing life were these: that she *wanted* to write about personal experience; that she was born a woman; that the culture had little understanding of how being born woman alters experience. These facts produced in Louise Bogan great tumult, and attitudes towards her own sex full of ambivalence and contradiction.

Louise Bogan supported her mad need to write poetry by writing criticism on poetry. Early in her critical career, she refused to review women poets. She wrote to Harriet Monroe in 1929: "I have never tried to review a book of poetry by a woman contemporary."[4] In 1931: "I have found from bitter experience that one woman poet is at a disadvantage in reviewing another, if the review be not laudatory."[5] Supportiveness of the work of other women is at least one of the goals of contemporary feminist poetry; in Bogan's time, especially, women poets were in competition with each other, jealous of each other.[6] Thus, among women poets, a disassociation from their own sex set in. Women poets wished fervently not to be known as women poets. In one review she wrote, Bogan showed that she thought of feminism as a liberation from women's qualities. (It is "unfeminist to separate the work of women writers from the work of men.")[7] The liberated woman of the twenties wanted to be treated like a man: the goal was to imitate the work of the male poetic establishment, to avoid the label of sentimental, maudlin verse that was associated with women's work. This was the view of nineteenth-century American poetry by women, and the stereotype dominant in Bogan's mind when she refused in 1935 to edit a group of poems by women for an issue of the *New Republic* because "The thought of corresponding with a lot of female songbirds made me acutely ill. It is hard enough to bear with my own lyric side."[8] Here, "lyric" means "feminine lyric," that is, verse that is sentimental and sappy. In some of her criticism, Bogan says that women do have an overdeveloped feeling side and encourages women poets to bring intellect, control, craft to poetry. In a section on women poets in her book *Achievement in American Poetry, 1900–1950*, Bogan says that Elinor Wylie brought "craftsmanship" to the "feminine lyric." She praises Wylie's apprenticeship to Eliot, and to Donne, Herbert and Marvell. Bogan warns, however, that Wylie had a tendency to overcompensate for her natural feminine feeling through too great a technical virtuosity. But, Bogan says, Wylie

> . . . became more tellingly controlled as time went on, and in her last volume achieved a power that was directly structural. Although an undertone of rather inflated romanticism [*this is another word constantly associated with women poets*] was constantly in evidence, her work as a whole was far more complex than that of any feminine predecessor.[9]

Elinor Wylie succeeds because her models are male. But sometimes she becomes trapped by Crafts-Man-Ship. (Only now, in the present age, are we learning: women have to find their own poetic forms.) Bogan reviews Wylie along with other women poets; such was the tendency of the age. It seems strange to us now, for no aesthetic bound these poets together. What the critics of the period (Bogan included) seem to be telling us is that women share the same kinds of *problems* when they try to write poetry: that is, they tend to be too romantic, too feeling, too personal.

But (and here the contradictions manifest themselves) in some other reviews, Bogan praised this very feeling. Generally speaking, she was more sympathetic to her own sex in the later years, when most of her poetry was written. A belief in the unique value of the feminine experience was expressed in an essay called "The Heart and the Lyre," published in 1947—thus two years after a World War. It speaks eloquently to us today:

> The great importance of keeping the emotional channels of a literature open has frequently been overlooked. The need of the refreshment and the restitution of feeling, in all its warmth and depth, has never been more apparent than it is today, when

cruelty and fright often seem about to overwhelm man and his world. For women to abandon their contact with, and their expression of, deep and powerful emotional streams . . . would result in an impoverishment not only of their own inner resources but of mankind's at large . . . the woman poet has her singular role and precious destiny. And, at the moment, in a time lacking in truth and certainty and filled with anguish and despair, no woman should be shamefaced in attempting to give back to the world, through her work, a portion of its lost heart.[10]

I have spoken briefly of Louise Bogan's attitudes toward her own sex as reflected in her criticism and her letters. How did these contradictions, these ambivalences with regard to her womanhood affect her poetry? First, Louise Bogan published very few poems—106 in all. Her own standards were very high. But I wonder if this is not also an example of a woman poet who feels she has to be better at the game than the boys in order to succeed. Second, and most important, there is a marked movement in her poetry from a subjective to a more objective mode. With the first volume, *Body of This Death*, published in 1929, Bogan is in closest contact with her own experience: here she evokes the overpowering sense of disillusionment which a young woman, at first full of hope, feels after a failed marriage. The whole volume is "an epitaph for a romantic woman"—this is the title of one of the poems. *Dark Summer* (1929) and *The Sleeping Fury* (1937) deal in less direct ways with the events of Bogan's life: a second marriage, its failure, nervous breakdowns, love affairs, her life as a mother. As the years went on, Bogan found it more and more difficult to find subjects for her poetry. In the 21 years between 1941 and 1968, Louise Bogan was able to write only ten poems. She accepted this lack of creativity as part of her fate as a woman. She wrote (in a review of Edna St. Vincent Millay) "It is difficult to say what a woman poet should concern herself with as she grows older, because women who have produced an impressively bulky body of work are few." She continues: "Is it not possible for a woman to come to terms with herself, if not the world; to withdraw more and more, as time goes on, her own personality from her productions. . . ."[11] This is what Bogan in fact did. And because she withdrew her personality from her productions, it became harder and harder to find subjects for poetry. She wrote to her publisher in 1939 (he was begging for poems): "I shall endeavor to write a nice series of Dinggedichte (Thing poems) for you. Can you suggest any subjects?"[12] Determined to be objective, sexually neutral, Louise Bogan denied all the matter, the poetic potential, available to one who leads a life as a woman.

I do not want to leave you with the impression that Louise Bogan did not include in the collected volumes some stunning personal poems which we should read today. She did. And it is high time that this fine poet be rescued from neglect. But we should also know about the poems she didn't want us to know about—the personal poems which she published in magazines, and then decided not to use in the early volumes or those that appeared in early volumes, but never in the collected poems.[13] And some of the personal poems she did retain are puzzling because Bogan uses veiled forms to speak of very personal experience (her perverse ways of loving, for example, either her exaggerated fidelity to a man or her mad desire to betray him.) Sonnet confessionalism, we might call this. Perhaps the best path to an understanding of Bogan is to read her poems in conjunction with the newly published letters. The letters are more explicit about the life out of which the sometimes elusive poems come. Louise Bogan wanted to be subtle. But she also wanted to be understood. When she does not reach us, it is often because the age convinced her (oh so well) that it was not legitimate to value her unique experience as a woman.

Notes

1. Florence Howe, "Introduction," *No More Masks: An Anthology of Poems by Women*, eds. Florence Howe and Ellen Bass (Garden City: Doubleday, 1973), 7.
2. A letter to Sister M. Angela, August 20, 1966, p. 368 in *What the Woman Lived: Selected Letters of Louise Bogan, 1920–1970*, ed. Ruth Limmer (New York: Harcourt Brace Jovanovich, 1973). Hereafter, references to the letters will indicate recipient, date and page.
3. To Morton D. Zabel, August 10, 1936, 135.
4. To Harriet Monroe, October 12, 1929, 49. This was in regard to the poet Marjorie Seiffert.
5. To Harriet Monroe, January 17, 1930, 55. This time Bogan was refusing to review Lola Ridge's new book, *Firehead*.
6. Responding to a scholar's letter, Bogan listed among her hates "Women poets (jealousy!)" May 1, 1939, 190. The letter was written in jest and never sent; the editor of the letters does not identify the researcher.
7. "No poetesses maudites: May Swenson, Anne Sexton (1963)," *A Poet's Alphabet*, eds. Robert Phelps and Ruth Limmer (New York: Harcourt Brace Jovanovich, 1973), 431–432.
8. To John Hall Wheelock, July 1, 1935, 86. Bogan wrote about 19th-century American verse by women in an article, "Poetesses in the Parlour," *New Yorker*, December 5, 1936. Reviewing anthologies of poetry by women, Bogan looked hard to find poems that showed women not sentimental and maudlin but strong and aggressive. And she found some.
9. Louise Bogan, *Achievement in American Poetry (1900–1950)* (Chicago: Regnery, 1951), 78–79.
10. "The heart and the lyre," *A Poet's Alphabet*, 425.
11. "Edna Millay," *A Poet's Alphabet*, 298–299.
12. To John Hall Wheelock, January 29, 1939, 182.
13. The uncollected poems are "Elders," "Resolve," "Leavetaking," "To a dead lover," which appeared in the August, 1922 issue of *Poetry* but which Bogan did not include in *Body of This Death* (1923); "A letter" and "Song," which were included in *Body* but not in the later collections; "A flume," which was part of *Dark Summer* but not included in later collections; and "Hidden," published in the *New Yorker* but not in any of the volumes.

Edgar Bowers

1924–

Edgar Bowers was born in Georgia on March 2, 1924. He attended the University of North Carolina at Chapel Hill. In 1943 his studies were interrupted by military service; Bowers performed counter-intelligence activity in Germany until the end of the war. After graduating in 1947, Bowers went on to study under Yvor Winters at Stanford University, earning an M.A. in 1949 and a Ph.D. in 1953. He has taught at Duke University (1952–55), the State University of New York at Binghamton (1955–58), and the University of California at Santa Barbara.

Bowers has published three books of poetry, *The Form of Loss* (1956), *The Astronomers* (1965), and *Living Together: New and Selected Poems* (1973). Despite his lack of notoriety, he has won numerous awards, including The Swallow Press New Poetry Series Award in 1965, The Ingram Merrill Award in 1974, and Guggenheim and Fulbright Fellowships.

General

Implicit in most of Bowers' work is the attempt to understand the Judeo-Christian religious heritage from the point of view of eighteenth-century rationalism. Unlike many today, however, he regards Christian ethical values neither as conventions to be assumed for convenience nor as nostalgic vestiges to be emotionally explored and rejected, but as an emotional reality with which neither his rationalism nor any twentieth-century psychological scheme has, as yet, successfully dealt. Hence, there is a psychological uncertainty in a few poems on Christian themes, such as "Palm Sunday" (in *The Form of Loss*), that mars them. For the most part, as in the second of the "Two Poems on the Catholic Bavarians," the religious heritage never represents something irretrievably lost—and hence purely evocative—but presents a problem to be grappled with. His problem is not pride . . . but the understanding of his own nature in relation to his heritage. . . . Both the language and the experience of the poems in his second book, *The Astronomers*, constitute a remarkable development. The Romantic extremes of self and nothingness are placed in a religious context in "A Song for Rising," and the sequence "Autumn Shade" records in detail the accession to the isolated consciousness of a reality that defines and encompasses it. In this context a means for successfully handling the problem of loss, which is conceived in "Autumn Shade" in terms of personal failure, is furnished.—Helen P. Trimpi, "The Theme of Loss in the Earlier Poems of Catherine Davis and Edgar Bowers," *SoR*, Summer 1973, p. 616

Works

⟨With *The Astronomers*,⟩ Edgar Bowers now publishes his second volume since the early '50s: a collection of 14 lyrics and a ten-part autobiographical poem. Those who react with discomfort to these poems react, I imagine, less to the poems than to the human cost in terms of psychic energy to which so severely disciplined lyrics attest. From "Adam's Song": "O depth sufficient to desire, / Ghostly abyss wherein perfection hides, / Purest effect and cause, you are / The mirror and the image love provides / . . . And all your progeny time holds / In timeless birth and death. But when, for bliss, / Loneliness would possess its like, / Mine is the visage yours leans down to kiss."

The poet whose apprenticeship to the impossible results in such achieved forms is not to be construed in full retreat from the demands of sensibility. No more was Emily Dickinson abdicating life. This is not poverty of emotion but emotion more abundant than is readily borne by most, converted to enduring shape in words. So the poet "left with self-consciousness, / Enemy whom I love but whom his change / And his forgetfulness again compel, / Impassioned, toward my lost indifference, / Faithful, but to an absence. / Who shares my bed? Who lies beside me, certain of his waking, / Led sleeping, by his own dream, to the day?" All real art comes of such wakings.—Carol Johnson, *Com*, Sept. 29, 1965, p. 707

Edgar Bowers's *Living Together* is a major publication, gathering his previous poems, some of which, including "Two Poems on the Catholic Bavarians," "An Afternoon at the Beach," and "The Astronomers of Mont Blanc," are in my judgment among the best American poems, and adding new poems. The title poem defines, with ghostly and lucid agony, how an absence becomes a presence, and its masterly variation of sound and pause is essential to the defining. All the new poems, except one polemical epigram, concern solitude: human communion despaired of, at times paradoxically or briefly reached; solipsism (more precisely, philosophical problems caused by the selfhood of the observer); and the opacity and indifference of nature. In artistry Bowers is the poet furthest from the current genre, though themes overlap. The beauty of structure, rhythm, imagery, and diction of his poems belies the doubt, isolation, and valuelessness he writes of and presumes. Value, knowledge, beauty, faith—and an epistemology that makes them impossible—are his recurrent subjects, unsolved but explored with subtlety, dignity, and pain. The book ends with a magnificent image, surf riders exemplifying human presence and destiny: "Pale shadows, poised a moment on the light's/ Archaic and divine indifference."—Paul Ramsey, "American Poetry in 1973," *SnR*, Spring 1974, pp. 399–400

The poems of Edgar Bowers (in *Living Together*) are so carefully and honestly made that it is ungracious to carp at them. And yet, some of the time, I do. Consider the first two stanzas of "Two Poems on the Catholic Bavarians":

> The fierce and brooding holocaust of faith
> This people conquered, which no edict could,
> And wove its spirit stiff and rich like cloth
> That many years ago was soaked in blood.
>
> Their minds are active only in their hands
> To check and take the labor of the hills,
> To furnish nature its precise demands
> And bear its harshness as it seems God wills.

I for one have absolutely no objection to iambic quatrains. Think of Hart Crane. Of John Crowe Ransom. But these cor-

rect lines somehow do not move. Or consider all of "Chorus
for the Untenured Personnel" (and I do like the title and the
thought):

> If we are on probation, what's our crime?
> Original sin, mysterious want of grace,
> The apple that we ate in a happier time
> Of learning, friendship, courtesy, and wit—
> Our innocence! For see, the gorgon's face,
> The discipline of hatred, our true text.
> We read, in darkness visible, the X.

But what a mouthful of abstractions, and oh that saving apple,
the only solid thing to bite on! So again, in five lines of "From
William Tyndale to John Frith," we find "sweet threats,"
"malicious love," "dangerous fear of violence," "illusion's
goodness," "worldly innocence," "just persuasions' old hypocrisy." Is it too carnal of us if we remain unmoved by these airy
oxymorons? But if not moved, still admiring, since the intelligence and its expression are there.—RICHARD LATTIMORE,
"Poetry Chronicle," *HdR*, Autumn 1974, pp. 461–62

YVOR WINTERS
"The Poetry of Edgar Bowers" (1956)
Uncollected Essays and Reviews
1973, pp. 182–88

Edgar Bowers is about thirty-three years old, and this is his
first book. The book contains twenty-nine titles and
thirty-three actual poems. Six or seven of these poems could
probably be dispensed with; the rest seem to me among the best
American poems of this century, and nine or ten of them
among the very great poems.

Bowers is a Southerner, born and raised in Georgia, and
raised as a Presbyterian. He served three years or more with the
Army during World War II, the last year and a half or so with
the occupation forces in Germany, in counter-intelligence,
and he later spent a year in France on a Fulbright fellowship.
He took his Ph.D. in English at Stanford, and is now an
assistant professor of English at Harper College, in Endicott,
New York. His German, I believe, is passably good; his Latin is
good; and his French is better. His knowledge of the history of
poetry and of critical theory in both French and English is
detailed and profound. These facts may seem trivial, perhaps
merely academic; but they have a real bearing on his poetry.

Although raised a Presbyterian, Bowers appears to be no
longer a Christian. But he has a Calvinistic tendency toward
mysticism, combined with an inability, both temperamental
and intellectual, to delude himself: this is one of the important
facts to be remembered if one is trying to understand his poetry.
The words *guilt* and *deceit* recur several times as indicative of
attitudes which turn one from one's real beliefs toward something that one would like to believe, and hence toward spiritual
corruption. In the opening lines of the poem *From William
Tyndale to John Firth*, a letter supposedly written shortly before
both men were burned for heresy, one gets the theme, without
these particular words:

> The letters I, your lone friend, write in sorrow
> Will not contain my sorrow: it is mine,
> Not yours who stand for burning in my place.
> Be certain of your fate. Though some, benign,
> Will urge by their sweet threats malicious love
> And counsel dangerous fear of violence,
> Theirs is illusion's goodness proving fair—

> Against your wisdom—worldly innocence.
> And just persuasions' old hypocrisy.
> Making their choice, reflect what you become:
> Horror and misery bringing ruin where
> The saintly mind has treacherously gone
>   numb. . . .

Bowers has a somewhat un-Calvinistic sympathy for Catholic
doctrine and civilization, but he examines them from a non-
Christian position: nostalgically, at times, if you wish, but unmistakably from the outside. *The Virgin Mary* is one of the
earliest poems in this collection, but will illustrate my point,
and will exhibit Bowers' style at its most magnificent:

> The hovering and huge, dark, formless sway
> That nature moves by laws we contemplate
> We name for lack of name as order, fate,
> God, principle, or primum mobile.
> But in that graven image, word made wood
> By skillful faith of him to whom she was
> Eternal nature, first and final cause,
> The form of knowledge understood
> Bound human thought against the dark we find.
> And Body took the image of the mind
> To shape in chaos, a congruent form
> Of will and matter, equal, side by side,
> Upon the act of faith, within the norm
> Of carnal being, blind and glorified.

Bowers is involved intellectually and emotionally—and quite
consciously—in the history of western religion and philosophy,
and at the same time, for better or worse, is in the predicament
of the post-Christian intellectual. But as a post-Christian intellectual, he is not a modern provincial: quite the contrary.

Along with this feeling for western intellectual history,
goes a deep feeling for the antiquity and grandeur of western
history generally and for the evidence of decay and destruction
within that civilization in our time. *The Prince*, one of the two
or three latest poems of the volume, may be used to illustrate a
part of this theme. The poem is a monologue spoken by an old
German prince to a counter-intelligence officer. The prince
had been an anti-Nazi, in spite of his profoundly German
feelings; his son had shared his anti-Nazi principles and had
refused to serve the government, only to have his German
patriotism overcome him, with the result that he served as a spy
and was shot by the Americans. The theme is complex and
rich—psychologically, morally, socially. I quote two excerpts,
one from the middle, the other from the end, to exhibit the
beauty of the style:

> You know despair's authority, the rite
> And exaltation by which we are governed,
> A state absurd with wrath that we are human,
> Nothing to which our nature would submit.

> Such was the German State. Yet, like a fool,
> I hated it, my image, and was glad
> When he refused its service; now I know
> That even his imprisonment was mine,
> A gesture by the will to break the will. . . .
> By what persuasion he saw fit to change
> Allegiance, none need wonder. Let there be,
> However, no mistake: those who deny
> What they believe is true, desire shall mock
> And crime's uncertain promise shall deceive.
> Alas, that he was not a German soldier
> In his apostasy, but would put on
> The parody of what caprice put off,
> Enemy in disguise, the uniform
> And speech of what the sceptic heart requires—
> Ruthless the irony that is its thought.

The soldier's death should find him unaware,
The breathless air close round him as sleep falls,
Sudden with ripeness, heavy with release.
Thereby the guileless tranquilly are strong:
The man is overwhelmed, the deed remains.
Flesh of my flesh, bewildered to despair
And fallen outside the limits of my name,
Forever lies apart and meaningless.
I who remain perceive the dear, familiar
Unblemished face of possibility
Drenched by a waste profound with accident,
His childhood face concealed behind my face.
Where is the guile enough to comfort me?

Bowers' style is at once as modern and as rooted in history as his subject matter. *The Virgin*, which I have quoted, might so far as style is concerned have been written between 1595 and 1620: it offers a justification for the publisher's reference to Greville on the slipcover. But a large part of the poetry—probably the greater part—belongs to a relatively modern tradition. In the seventeenth century, the rational structure of poetry, which had characterized the work of the Renaissance and which had had its origins in medieval writing, began to disintegrate; and the ethical formulations of Shaftesbury, aided by the critical formulations of Addison and subsequent associationists, hastened the disintegration. From here onward there is less and less command of "abstract" language, that is, of precise ethical and metaphysical thought, and more and more concentration on sensory detail and on progression governed by revery. In the *Ode to Evening* things have gone so far that syntax itself has almost disappeared from about half of the poem. In the best work of the eighteenth and nineteenth centuries—for examples, in some of Blake, Mallarmé, and Rimbaud—this concentration results in a sharper and more fascinating sensory perception than one can easily find in the earlier poetry, but the gain is an insufficient compensation for the loss. However, in the nineteenth and twentieth centuries a few poets, at least a part of the time, endeavor to recover the older intellectual integrity and at the same time to retain something of the newer sensory acuteness: among the more obvious examples—and these are probably the main influences on Bowers—are Baudelaire, Leconte de Lisle, Valéry, Sturge Moore, and Stevens. The result is sensory perception not for its own sake and not in the form of the traditional metaphor or simile, but sensory perception offered as sensory perception, yet charged with perfectly explicit meaning by the total context. Bowers' poem *The Stoic*, too long to quote in full, is a clear example of the method: the protagonist, a German woman, listens to distant cannonading and bombing, regards the German Alps (the symbol of geographical antiquity and grandeur) and the rural scenes closer at hand, reflects upon "Eternal

Venice sinking by degrees Into the very water that she lights" (the symbol of the antiquity and slow decay of civilization), upon the brightness and neatness of recent civilization in pre-war Berlin, upon the lion released from his cage in Berlin by a random bomb, and upon the man killed by the lion, and then retreats into the stoicism approaching but not really reaching mysticism which is so characteristic of Bowers. The details are quiet but precise; each carries its own meaning unmistakably; the rhythmically slow release of the lion and his savage action give us one of the most effective images with which I am acquainted of the emergence of chaos from the semblance of civilization:

Remembered in Berlin the parks, the neat
Footpaths and lawns, the clean spring foliage,
Where just short weeks before, a bomb unaimed
Had freed a raging lion from its cage,
Which in the mottled dark that trees enflamed
Killed one who hurried homeward from the raid.
And by yourself there standing in the chill

You must, with so much known, have been afraid
And chosen such a mind of constant will,
Which, though all time corrode with constant hurt,
Remains, until it occupies no space
That which it is; and passionless, inert,
Becomes at last no meaning and no place.

Or one may consider this passage from an elegiac song, written in three-beat accentual verse:

Flesh old and summer waxing,
Quick eye in the sunny lime,
Sweet apricots in silence
Falling—precious in time,
All radiant as a voice, deep
As their oblivion. Only as I may,
I come, remember, wait,
Ignorant in grief, yet stay.

What you are will outlast
The warm variety of risk,
Caught in the wide, implacable,
Clear gaze of the basilisk.

These are the poems of a man between the ages of twenty-five and thirty-two, approximately. They are not perfect, at any rate not all of them. A native clumsiness sometimes shows itself, on occasions resulting in obscurity. But this does not happen often. The mind and the matter—the two are inseparable—are complex and profound, and it is small wonder that the technique occasionally falters. But it falters very seldom. The aim is mastery, not eccentricity or obscurity. And the aim is sometimes achieved.

JANE BOWLES

1917–1973

Jane Sydney Auer was born in New York on February 22, 1917. She was educated at Stoneleigh, and received private tutoring in Leysin, Switzerland, where she went to be cured of tuberculosis. As a child she had several French governesses, and learned to speak French before she spoke English. The first time she met her husband, the writer and composer Paul Bowles, she took an instant dislike to him; the second time, she decided to join him on a trip to Mexico. They were married a year later, in 1938. They traveled widely in Europe and Africa, and in 1952 settled in Tangier.

Her only novel, *Two Serious Ladies*, was published in 1943. Although it was not a popular success, it attracted an ardent group of admirers, including Alan Sillitoe, Truman Capote, Tennessee Williams (who called it his favorite book), and John Ashbery, who dubbed Bowles "a writer's writer's writer." The book was once so scarce that not even the author had a copy.

In 1954, Bowles' play *In the Summer House* was staged in New York. It received critical acclaim, but again failed to win a large audience. A short puppet play, *A Quarrelling Pair*, appeared in *Mademoiselle* in 1966. By this time *Two Serious Ladies* had been reissued, and a rediscovery of her work was underway. In the same year Bowles published *Plain Pleasures*, a collection of short stories, and *The Collected Works of Jane Bowles*, which became her last published work. In 1973, Bowles died in a Spanish convent near Tangier, after a long and debilitating illness.

Works

While it is not often that one comes across a novel which makes as little sense as ⟨*Two Serious Ladies*⟩, Jane Bowles has precedents and forerunners. In an elusive way—I make the comparison very gingerly—echoes of Firbank, Van Vechten and the lost days of Dada crop up now and again in *Two Serious Ladies*, plus an occasional reminiscence of Saroyan. To say, however, that the book is derivative would be clearly unfair. My feeling is that Mrs. Bowles has developed—and exploited—her own brand of lunacy and that she is, perhaps fortunately, unique. Certainly—to free her from the charge of plagiarism—she is nowhere near so witty as either Firbank or Van Vechten, nor do her characters, though eccentric, have the same decadent charm.

To attempt to unravel the plot of *Two Serious Ladies* would be to risk, I feel sure, one's own sanity. Obviously, however, I must identify this odd pair of heroines—one of whom is a wealthy spinster, Miss Goering, who suffers from obsessions; the other a feather-brained matron, Mrs. Copperfield. While the latter adventures down in Panama, acquiring a weird set of friends of very easy virtue, Miss Goering has her own startling experiences in her own austere home, where she is companioned by the sinister Miss Gamelon. Beyond the fact that they are casual acquaintances there is no visible connection between these two earnest ladies, nor do their deft stories dovetail in any important way.

What does, however, link both the *Two Serious Ladies* and the other characters in the book is their mad, their wayward, their bizarre aberrations, in which they indulge with so reasonable an air. Among their other eccentricities, moreover, is the naive bluntness and candor with which they all speak, the abruptness with which they move inconsequentially from one topic to another. Their world, in short, is an almost frighteningly fantastic one—the more so because its outward lineaments are so natural and so normal, because their background is so soberly realistic. Belatedly one realizes that there is hardly a character in the book who could be called really sane, unless it is the charmingly wanton and amoral Pacifica.

Two Serious Ladies is intermittently funny and certainly original, but I also felt that it strains too hard to startle and to shock and that it all too often is just merely silly. Jane Bowles undoubtedly is a clever young writer with a good deal of talent, but I feel that she has written this book with her tongue in her cheek and that it is not as irresistible as she intended it to be.—EDITH H. WALTON, "Fantastic Duo," *NYTBR*, May 9, 1943, p. 14

Surrounding Mrs. Bowles's art is an effluvium of chic despair which will alienate many readers. On the other hand, her work can easily be overvalued since it combines proud idiosyncrasy with a rather startling prescience (her novel, *Two Serious Ladies*, published in 1943, forecast the current vogue of comic gothicism). When that book first appeared here, reviewers could damn it with a clear conscience: modernism had not yet become an obligatory mass fashion. (On its first English appearance last year, the *Times Literary Supplement*, marching resolutely backward in its sensible shoes, still stomped it to bits.) Today in the United States, where the cultivated reader feels duty-bound to be affronted, Mrs. Bowles's controlled derision is likely to seem the definitive force of civilized disgust.

Surely her indictments have an easy inclusiveness. Like her husband, Paul, Mrs. Bowles writes tight little anecdotes about the pull of bestiality, an unexpected form of self-fulfillment. Like her husband's stories, hers pit the weak against the strong, the righteous against the sensual, only to record a general rout. Though her tales lack his intellectual clarity, they have greater charm.

Two Serious Ladies follows the adventures of two wacky souls. Rich Christina Goering is one of those "fanatics who think of themselves as leaders without once having gained the respect of a single human being." Seeking salvation, she makes opportunities of other people; when her needle reaches its goal on the spiritual applause meter, her goodness abruptly stops. Fluttery Mrs. Copperfield, downtrodden by a selfish husband, nevertheless has one "sole object in life . . . to be happy, although people who had observed her behavior over a period of years would have been surprised to discover that this was all."

Out of strange charitable impulses, Christina takes a female companion, a succession of male lovers, and becomes a Samaritan of polite promiscuity. Mrs. Copperfield is dragged to Panama by her husband, where she discovers in herself a fund of willfulness to match Christina's. She installs herself in a disreputable hotel and takes up with a native prostitute. Ironically, Mrs. Copperfield gets what she has always wanted. To Christina's censorious concern in the book's last scene, she replies, with her fist meanly rapping on the table:

> "True enough . . . I have gone to pieces, which is a thing I've wanted to do for years. I know I am as guilty as I can be, but I have my happiness; which I guard like a wolf, and I have authority now and a certain amount of daring, which, if you remember correctly, I never had before."

Shocked, Christina confirms her chilling logic:

> "Certainly I am nearer to becoming a saint," reflected Miss Goering, "but is it possible that a part of me hidden from my sight is piling sin upon sin as fast as Mrs. Copperfield?" This latter possibility Miss Goering thought to be of considerable interest but of no great importance.

The book's final sentence reveals that glacial disregard for "significance" which makes *Two Serious Ladies* wonderfully self-possessed, but elusive. In a novel without recognizable motivation, whose characters do not so much communicate as collide, where all interstices of life and logic are effaced, the parallels in the stories of the two women are too slight to provide the structure and carry the meaning. Nor do the parallel situations support the scrutiny they seem to invite.

To be sure, there are hints of purpose scattered about. "One must allow," Christina suggests before a tryst, "that a certain amount of carelessness in one's nature often accomplishes what the will is incapable of doing." And, as Mrs. Copperfield casually asserts on another occasion, "No one among my friends speaks any longer of character . . . what interests us most . . . is finding out what we are like." But these hints never become more than hints. Too often, Mrs. Bowles is seduced by the bizarre behavior of her characters. And our wish to find life in her shadow play finally becomes mere nervous interest.

Her play, *In the Summer House*, is more likely to attract the uninitiated—the highlighting of drama is a distinct advantage. Christina reappears as Gertrude Eastman Cuevas, a martinet who "believes in using controls," and Mrs. Copperfield becomes Mrs. Constable, a quavery-voiced sparrow with reserves of bilious clarity. Their confrontation creates a mood of tormented longing and rough-house comedy which is one of the few native expansions of theatrical emotion. On the stage, in 1954, the play worked splendidly, though the marvelous performances of Judith Anderson, Mildred Dunnock, and Jean Stapleton failed to attract large audiences.

The Collected Works also include some short stories, but most of these are mere moral muckraking. The locales are exotic, the prose is distinctive and the dialogue funny; but the plots are too familiar: repressed eccentrics acknowledging the lure of the flesh. Here too, however, there is one good piece, "A Stick of Green Candy," an "absurd" variation on the stock theme of awakening adolescence.—CHARLES THOMAS SAMUELS, "Serious Ladies," *NYRB*, Dec. 15, 1966, pp. 38–39

⟨*The Collected Works of Jane Bowles*⟩ may be the smallest volume of Collected Works since Max Beerbohm's first book. The analogy can go a shade further, for this also is a book of rare writing. It consists of one short novel, one play (produced on Broadway in 1948), and seven short stories. They could all be described as one of the characters in them describes herself, "complicated, a bit dotty, and completely original." Most of them have to do with slightly hysterical or eccentric women—

mothers, daughters, sisters, friends—and take place in exotic but uncomfortable surroundings, like tacky hotels in Panama. Everybody loves (and also eats) a great deal.

But Mrs. Bowles makes what might seem just strange into something wonderful—both haunting and witty—by her unsentimental feeling for these lost creatures, and the odd elegance of her writing. The atmosphere of almost all the works is overwrought or overheated, at times reminiscent of Tennessee Williams or even Ronald Firbank; but through all this miasma, the characters tend to speak to each other (and themselves) with the clarity and decision of people in Lewis Carroll. As you can imagine, this effect alone is extraordinary. Her writing is funny or sad or sharp or mysterious, but always arresting.—RODERICK COOK, "Books in Brief," *Harper's*, Jan. 1967, p. 98

For many women writers in our day, the old novel of sensitiveness invites parody and counterstatement. And it is in this context that one can understand the strange, funny, perverse, calculatedly unacceptable fictions of Jane Bowles. In her (one) novel, *Two Serious Ladies*, the two heroines are unaccountably innocent passersby through a totally depraved world. They are so closed off from the rest of us by being so strange, offbeat and untouchably innocent that they turn even the few male characters attending them—it is essentially a novel of women and of their journeying into places beyond their ken—into versions of singularity as strange as themselves.

In Jane Bowles all women characters become parallels to each other. Everything is dialogue, but nothing advances by dialogue, there is no natural exchange of experiences, only a mystified scratching by the characters themselves on the impenetrable surface of each other's personalities. This inability to get below the surface is a mark of the cartoon-like queerness of the women as central characters. They live in the world by not understanding it. And the unwillingness to dig for any "deeper" reality is the mark of Jane Bowles herself, who always worked with dialogue as if she were a Restoration dramatist fascinated not by the "hardness" of her characters but by their naturally closed-off state.

She, too, was a dramatized oddity; her one novel, her one play *In the Summer House*, her stories, all appeared in 1966 in one volume as *The Collected Works of Jane Bowles*, as if she were not going to write again. . . . The surfaces that her characters present to each other—they remind me of the wild collection of faces in the cartoons of George Price—are somehow summed up by Jane Bowles in the deliberately, comically deadpan surface of her work. Her characters are made original by characters that cannot open or communicate; they are total separates. Their gracious innocence in depraved joints in Panama is Jane Bowles's joke, but it is not a joke on *them*; they become fond of whores and pimps and obvious confidence men without knowing what these strangers do. Their "innocence" is indeed what interests Jane Bowles in her characters—their incommunicable queerness.

These *are* serious ladies, perhaps because the world is so plainly not serious that only the unconscious virtue of certain women can give it dignity. They are first and last untouched souls, oddities, privacies, as the women in Gertrude Stein's *Three Lives* are nothing but "characters." Although Jane Bowles's women are closer to women than to men, they do not identify with anybody at all. They are all remarkable children in literature: provisional guests in this world. Things happen to them without modifying them—that is the comedy of *Two Serious Ladies*. They just pass through the world. And such is the form of their "seriousness," their unbreakable singularity, their sweet dim inexpressiveness, their obviously privileged position, that they turn the "world" into an inconsequential background to themselves, a series of farcically tenuous stage sets—islands, country estates, tropic bordellos. These are cities not on any map, streets that do not lead into each other, islands that are *unaccountable*. The prevailing strangeness and unconnectedness of these women makes each of them a presence that just bulks over everything else. As there is no real transaction between them, so there is no action. The absurdity and intractability of being nothing but an unresisting yet untouched single "character" is all:

> "I've always been a body-worshipper," said Mrs. Copperfield, "but that doesn't mean that I fall in love with people who have beautiful bodies. Some of the bodies I've liked have been awful. Come, let's go over to Mr. Toby."
>
> The girl had the bright eyes of an insatiable nymphomaniac. She wore a ridiculous little watch on a black ribbon around her wrist.
>
> Away in the back of the room a man was bowling up a small alley all by himself; Miss Goering listened to the rumble of the balls as they rolled along the wooden runway, and she wished that she were able to see him so that she could be at peace for the evening with the certainty that there was no one who could be considered a menace present in the room.

Mrs. Bowles conceived of her fiction as an ironic extension of the old insistence, in women's fiction, that woman is the heart of a heartless world. The world in her altogether dry, vaguely jeering pages becomes even more heartless than one could have imagined it. It is literally deaf, dumb, uncomprehending, made up of characters and situations which do not flow together in the slightest, which never interact. It is a world composed somehow of silence. Since women are the point of it, it dramatizes the heroine as farcically a force, the woman who to her own mind is so original that her personality is the only weight in the story, its dominating indecipherable presence. Woman is the idiosyncrasy around which this bizarre existence is composed.—ALFRED KAZIN, "Cassandras," *Bright Book of Life*, 1971, pp. 175–78

TRUMAN CAPOTE
"Introduction" to
The Collected Works of Jane Bowles
1966, pp. v–ix

It must be seven or eight years since I last saw that modern legend named Jane Bowles; nor have I heard from her, at least not directly. Yet I am sure she is unchanged; indeed, I am told by recent travelers to North Africa who have seen or sat with her in some dim casbah café that this is true, and that Jane, with her dahlia-head of cropped curly hair, her tilted nose and mischief-shiny, just a trifle mad eyes, her very original voice (a husky soprano), her boyish clothes and schoolgirl's figure and slightly limping walk, is more or less the same as when I first knew her more than twenty years ago: even then she had seemed the eternal urchin, appealing as the most appealing of non-adults, yet with some substance cooler than blood invading her veins, and with a wit, an eccentric wisdom no child, not the strangest wunderkind, ever possessed.

When I first met Mrs. Bowles (1944? 1945?) she was already, within certain worlds, a celebrated figure: though only in her twenties, she had published a most individual and much remarked novel, *Two Serious Ladies*; she had married the gifted composer and writer Paul Bowles and was, together with her husband, a tenant in a glamorous boardinghouse established on Brooklyn Heights by the late George Davis. Among the Bowles' fellow boarders were Richard and Ellen Wright, W. H. Auden, Benjamin Britten, Oliver Smith, Carson McCullers, Gypsy Rose Lee, and (I *seem* to remember) a trainer of chimpanzees who lived there with one of his star performers. Anyway, it was one hell of a household. But even amid such a forceful assembly, Mrs. Bowles, by virtue of her talent and the strange visions it enclosed, and because of her personality's startling blend of playful-puppy candor and feline sophistication, remained an imposing, stage-front presence.

Jane Bowles is an authoritative linguist; she speaks, with the greatest precision, French and Spanish and Arabic—perhaps this is why the dialogue of her stories sounds, or sounds to me, as though it has been translated into English from some delightful combination of other tongues. Moreover, these languages are self-learned, the product of Mrs. Bowles' nomadic nature: from New York she wandered on to and all over Europe, traveled away from there and the impending war to Central America and Mexico, then alighted awhile in the historic ménage on Brooklyn Heights. Since 1947 she has been almost continuously resident abroad; in Paris or Ceylon, but largely in Tangiers—in fact, both Jane and Paul Bowles may now safely be described as permanent Tangerinos, so total has their adherence become to that steep, shadowy-white seaport. Tangiers is composed of two mismatching parts, one of them a dull modern area stuffed with office buildings and tall gloomy dwellings, and the other a casbah descending through a medieval puzzlement of alleys and alcoves and kef-odored, mint-scented piazzas down to the crawling with sailors, shiphorn-hollering port. The Bowles have established themselves in both sectors—have a sterilized, *tout confort* apartment in the newer quarter, and also a refuge hidden away in the darker Arab neighborhood: a native house that must be one of the city's tiniest habitations—ceilings so low that one has almost literally to move on hands and knees from room to room; but the rooms themselves are like a charming series of postcard-sized Vuillards—Moorish cushions spilling over Moorish-patterned carpets, all cozy as a raspberry tart and illuminated by intricate lanterns and windows that allow the light of sea skies and views that encompass minarets and ships and the blue-washed rooftops of native tenements receding like a ghostly staircase to the clamorous shoreline. Or that I remember it on the occasion of a single visit made at sunset on an evening, oh, fifteen years ago.

A line from Edith Sitwell: *Jane, Jane, the morning light creaks down again*—. This from a poem I've always liked, without, as so often with the particular author, altogether understanding it. Unless "morning light" is an image signifying memory (?). My own most satisfying memories of Jane Bowles revolve around a month spent in side-by-side rooms in a pleasantly shabby hotel on the rue du Bac during an icy Paris winter—January, 1951. Many a cold evening was spent in Jane's snug room (fat with books and papers and foodstuffs and a snappy white Pekingese puppy bought from a Spanish sailor); long evenings spent listening to a phonograph and drinking warm applejack while Jane built sloppy, marvelous stews atop an electric burner: she is a good cook, yessir, and kind of a glutton, as one might suspect from her stories, which abound in accounts of eating and its artifacts. Cooking is but one of her extracurricular gifts; she is also a spookily accurate mimic and can re-create with nostalgic admiration the voices of certain singers—Helen Morgan, for example, and her close friend Libby Holman. Years afterward I wrote a story called *Among the Paths to Eden*, in which, without realizing it, I attributed to the heroine several of Jane Bowles' characteristics: the stiff-legged limp, her spectacles, her brilliant and poignant abilities as a mimic ("She waited, as though listening for music to cue her; then, *'Don't ever leave me, now that you're here! Here is where you belong. Everything seems so right when you're near, When you're away it's all wrong.'* And Mr. Belli was shocked, for what he was hearing was exactly Helen Morgan's voice, and the voice, with its vulnerable sweetness, refinement, its tender quaver toppling high notes, seemed not to be borrowed, but Mary O'Meaghan's own, a natural expression of some secluded identity"). I did not have Mrs. Bowles in mind when I invented Mary O'Meaghan—a character she in no essential way resembles; but it is a measure of the potent impression Jane has always made on me that some fragment of her should emerge in this manner.

During that winter Jane was working on *In the Summer House*, the play that was later so sensitively produced in New York. I'm not all that keen on the theater: cannot sit through most plays once; nevertheless, I saw *In the Summer House* three times, and not out of loyalty to the author, but because it had a thorny wit, the flavor of a newly tasted, refreshingly bitter beverage—the same qualities that had initially attracted me to Mrs. Bowles' novel, *Two Serious Ladies*.

My only complaint against Mrs. Bowles is not that her work lacks quality, merely quantity. The volume in hand constitutes her entire shelf, so to say. And grateful as we are to have it, one could wish that there was more. Once, while discussing a colleague, someone more facile than either of us, Jane said: "But it's so easy for him. He has only to turn his hand. Just *turn* his hand." Actually, writing is never easy: in case anyone doesn't know, it's the hardest work around; and for Jane I think it is difficult to the point of true pain. And why not?— when both her language and her themes are sought after along tortured paths and in stony quarries: the never-realized relationships between her people, the mental and physical discomforts with which she surrounds and saturates them—every room an atrocity, every urban landscape a creation of neon-dourness. And yet, though the tragic view is central to her vision, Jane Bowles is a very funny writer, a humorist of sorts— but *not*, by the way, of the Black School. Black Comedy, as its perpetrators label it, is, when successful, all lovely artifice and lacking any hint of compassion. "Camp Cataract," to my mind the most complete of Mrs. Bowles' stories and the one most representative of her work, is a rending sample of controlled compassion: a comic tale of doom that has at its heart, and *as* its heart, the subtlest comprehension of eccentricity and human apartness. This story alone would require that we accord Jane Bowles high esteem.

JOHN ASHBERY
"Up from the Underground"
The New York Times Book Review,
January 29, 1967, pp. 5–30

Jane Bowles is a writer's writer's writer. Few surface literary reputations are as glamorous as the underground one she has enjoyed since her novel *Two Serious Ladies* was published in 1943. The extreme rarity of the book, once it went out of print, has augmented its legend. When a London publisher wanted to reprint it three years ago, even Mrs. Bowles was unable to supply him with a copy.

With the present publication of her "collected works," which comes with an introduction by Truman Capote and blurbs by Tennessee Williams ("my favorite book"), Alan Sillitoe ("a landmark in 20th-century American literature") and others, Jane Bowles has at last surfaced. It is to be hoped that she will now be recognized for what she is: one of the finest modern writers of fiction, in any language. At the same time it should be pointed out that she is not quite the sort of writer that her imposing list of Establishment admirers seems to suggest. Her work is unrelated to theirs, and in fact it stands alone in contemporary literature, though if one can imagine George Ade and Kafka collaborating on a modern version of Bunyan's *Pilgrim's Progress* one will have a faint idea of the qualities of *Two Serious Ladies*.

Her collected works are comprised of the novel, the play *In the Summer House* and seven shorter pieces. Each deals in some way with the conflict between the weak and the strong, a conflict which in Mrs. Bowles's work usually results in a draw. Her strong characters are nervous, domineering women given to ruthless but inaccurate self-analysis. They believe themselves to be idealists, and are in search of some fixed, but vague, goal. In the end they collapse, undone by their failure to take "the terrible strength of the weak" into account. The weak scarcely fare any better. They have developed organs for surviving the attacks of the strong, but, hopelessly in love with them, they rarely survive their immolation.

Sometimes a final glimmer of hope comes to them, in the form of endless vistas of despair. Mrs. Constable, alcoholic and bereft of her daughter at the end of *In the Summer House*, achieves this negative fulfillment and emerges as the only character in the play to command our negative respect: "They say that people can't live unless they fill their lives with petty details. That's people's way of avoiding the black pit. I'm just a weak, ordinary, very ordinary woman in her middle years, but I've been able to wipe all the petty details from my life . . . all of them. I never rush or get excited about anything. I've dumped my entire life out the window."

Two Serious Ladies tells the separate odysseys of two very different women: Christina Goering and Frieda Copperfield. Miss Goering, a "strong" character, decides she can achieve salvation only through divesting herself of her family mansion and living on less than a tenth of her income. She rents a small, uncomfortable house on what appears to be Staten Island and surrounds herself with a nondescript circle of friends, whom she regularly deserts to make mysterious night forays into a nearby town, where she takes up with Andy, a despondent barfly. Mrs. Copperfield reluctantly accompanies her husband on a trip to Panama, and finds herself perversely happy with Pacifica, a prostitute, in the seamy Hotel de las Palmas.

Only twice do the paths of the two heroines cross: at the beginning of the book and at the end, when they meet in a restaurant. Miss Goering now believes herself to be well on the way to the curious self-realization she has in mind. Mrs. Copperfield has taken a drunken "downward path to wisdom" like Mrs. Constable's in *In the Summer House*; she is now in love with Pacifica, who is about to marry a young man. "I can't live without her, not for a minute. I'd go completely to pieces," Mrs. Copperfield confides to Miss Goering, who replies without irony: "But you have gone to pieces, or do I misjudge you dreadfully?" . . .

Mrs. Bowles's seemingly casual, colloquial prose is a constant miracle; every line rings as true as a line of poetry, though there is certainly nothing "poetic" about it, except insofar as the awkwardness of our everyday attempts at communication is poetic. This awkwardness can rise to comic heights, and in doing so evoke visions of a nutty America that we have to recognize as ours. An old man whom Christina questions about a certain cabaret in a place called Pig Snout's Hook replies:

"'Yes . . . certain people do like that type of music and there are people who live together and eat at table together stark naked all the year long and there are others who we both know about'—he looked very mysterious—'but,' he continued, 'in my day money was worth a pound of sugar or butter or lard any time. When we went out we got what we paid for plus a dog jumpin' through burning hoops, and steaks you could rest your chin on.'"

In her later stories Mrs. Bowles has played down the picaresque local color she used to such effect in the novel.

Especially in "A Stick of Green Candy," the story which ends the book and is apparently her most recent, she achieves a new austerity that is as impressive as anything she has done. As in all her work, it is impossible to deduce the end of a sentence from its beginning, or a paragraph from the one that preceded it, or how one of the characters will reply to another. And yet the whole flows marvelously and inexorably to its cruel, lucid end; it becomes itself as we watch it. No other contemporary writer can consistently produce surprise of this quality, the surprise that is the one essential ingredient of great art. Jane Bowles deals almost exclusively in this rare commodity.

PAUL BOWLES

1910–

Paul Frederick Bowles was born in New York on December 30, 1910. His entrance to the literary world came at the age of sixteen when he had a poem published in *Transition*, but the turning point in his life came in 1931 when he met Gertrude Stein in Paris. Bowles was a composer as well as a writer, and initially Stein was more inclined to favor his musical ability than his poetry. She advised him to go to Morocco, where she thought he would discover his true vocation. Bowles followed her advice.

Bowles studied music with Aaron Copland in New York and Berlin (1930–32) and with Virgil Thompson in Paris (1933–34). In 1938 he married Jane Bowles (originally Auer), a playwright and novelist, and has said that it was when he saw her at work on her own novel that he began to think seriously of writing novels himself.

His first novel, *The Sheltering Sky* (1949), won him great critical acclaim. Since then he has published three other novels, *Let It Come Down* (1952), *The Spider's House* (1955), and *Up Above the World* (1966), but it is *The Sheltering Sky* which is the most frequently praised. In 1972 he published an autobiography, *Without Stopping*, and 1976 saw the appearance of his *Collected Stories 1939–76*. Of these Gore Vidal wrote that they are "among the best ever written by an American."

Bowles has lived in Morocco for many years, and it is the setting of most of his writing. His predominant theme has been to record the effect of an ancient and alien culture on visitors from the West, who are invariably portrayed as empty, spiritually lost ciphers whose craving for new experiences and authentic sensations masks a profound masochism and desire for annihilation.

Bowles' themes have been limited and obsessive but they have made his work chilling and unique. Bowles is responsible for an important collection of native North African music gathered for the Library of Congress, and during the last twenty years has edited and translated many texts by Mohammed Mrabet, a Moroccan storyteller.

General

There is a handful of living American novelists who have established enviable reputations on the strength of a very few books. . . . Paul Bowles is such a novelist. *The Sheltering Sky*, published in 1949, was an impressive performance; it was followed by a collection of short stories, *The Delicate Prey* (1950), and two more novels, *Let It Come Down* (1952) and *The Spider's House* (1955). This is his complete production to date, yet it has been sufficient to place him in the very first rank of American prose artists: playwright Tennessee Williams even goes so far as to place him above Hemingway and Faulkner. However one may cavil at such a pronouncement, it is difficult to deny that these four works, taken as a whole, constitute a consistent and thoughtful statement about life: they present, in Conrad's phrase, a particular "vision of life"—always the mark of a first-rate artist.

It was apparent as early as 1945, to readers of magazines like *Partisan Review* and the now defunct *Horizon*, that a remarkable new talent had emerged—a talent which, one would have been informed if he had taken the pains to glance at the "Notes on Contributors," was as much at home in musical as in literary composition. One expected and hoped to hear more from the author of such stories as "Under the Sky" and "Pages from Cold Point." That expectation and that hope have been justified: Mr. Bowles has come a long way, both as composer and author, since 1945. Serious talent deserves serious criticism, and it is time that we evaluate his literary accomplishment (since that is what concerns us here) to date.

Bowles is an obsessionist, and his obsession may be simply stated: that psychological well-being is in inverse ratio to what is commonly known as progress, and that a highly evolved culture enjoys less peace of mind than one which is less highly evolved. This is of course a romantic attitude, going back at least as far as Rousseau by way (in English literature) of Samuel Butler, D. H. Lawrence, and E. M. Forster. Lawrence is probably Bowles's strongest single influence, and it seems curious that none of the newspaper reviewers have noted this connection: Faulkner and McCullers, with much less justification, are usually pointed to, and such unlikely and dissimilar antecedents as Henry James, Frederic Prokosch, Jean Genêt, and even Elinor Glyn have all been suggested.

It is no accident that the three novels and that fifteen of the seventeen stories in *The Delicate Prey* have a foreign setting. Nor is it true, as has sometimes been charged, that Bowles is merely indulging in a pointless exoticism, for not only are the settings foreign, they are usually primitive as well. For this reason he chooses such remote locales as a small town in the Sahara, a Colombian jungle, a river boat winding painfully through the interior of an unidentified Latin-American country. And in nearly all of his work the tension arises from a contrast between alien cultures: in a typical Bowles story, a civilized individual comes in contact with an alien environment and is defeated by it. The United States is not without primitives of its own, and Bowles could perhaps have achieved something of the same effect by going to the mountains of East Tennessee or the sheep ranches of Montana—or, for that matter, by doing a little social work in his native Manhattan. The contrast, however, would not have been so great: it is important for his purpose that the language, beliefs, and psychology of his natives be as different as possible from those of his travelers, the victims of modern civilization.

There is still another reason for Bowles's choice of remote locales. Deserts and jungles are places in which people can easily get lost, and Bowles believes that modern man, if not already lost in a spiritual and moral sense, is in serious danger of becoming so. It is symbolically fitting that his civilized traveler should suffer defeat at the hands of a nature, or of a "natural" (*i.e.*, primitive) society which he has insisted upon "improving." In *The Sheltering Sky*, one is tempted to equate the Sahara with Dante's *selva selvaggia* and with Eliot's Waste Land. There is, indeed, a certain correspondence, but the difference—and an important one—is that in Dante's poem there is no connection between the symbolic forest, which has only a malevolent aspect, and a natural one; and Eliot's Waste Land has only a negative relation to nature. Bowles's desert on the other hand, is neutral—malevolent only insofar as it is prepared to destroy those who are out of tune with nature itself, of which it is the real as well as the merely formal symbol. There is nearly always a symbolic level present in Bowles's work, and he has suffered considerable injustice at the hands of popular reviewers who have insisted upon reading him at a single level.—OLIVER EVANS, "Paul Bowles and the Natural Man," *CrT*, Spring–Fall 1959, pp. 43–45

In Paul Bowles the gothic imagination had a life outside the South in the forties. Instead of the South, he used lands of primitive peoples and barren landscapes, Latin America or Arab-African civilizations, equally hospitable to the gothic. Bowles is closely related, then, to Capote, Mrs. McCullers, and Miss Welty, even though his provenance is not southern. He is also related to that nihilistic strain which we saw in the war novel, represented, for example, by Vance Bourjaily. But while these reference points help to locate him, they do not give us his unique quality. That lies, I suggest, in the intensity of his flight from the realities of the Western world. Bowles's characters are far more concerned with flight than with quest. The recognition of the failure of the West is more acute in them than their desire to find the self. It is a measure of the intensity of Bowles's nihilism that his people have, in comparison to Capote's characters, for example, so little interest and even less success in saving themselves. In an article he wrote

for the *American Mercury* in 1951, Bowles has suggested, in describing the new lost generation, what his own fiction is about. This lost generation has been learning to take dope, not to achieve self-expression but to reach a state of ecstasy related in no way to intellectual or artistic endeavor. More and more Americans, Bowles said, are coming to Tangier ". . . in passionate pursuit of one thing: an absolute detachment from what is ordinarily called reality."

Reality is defined for these Americans by Western civilization, and its bitter failure is spelled out in a variety of ways in Bowles's work. He believes, it is clear, that contemporary civilization makes for alienation from the self; the flow of one's spiritual and emotional life is frozen within the benumbed consciousness. He believes that the value systems of the West have failed. The skid into moral relativism, a tactic of compromise, cannot salvage our morality or our belief. Faith in Christianity strikes him as a ludicrous refuge. The overwhelming achievement of Western civilization is to have made victims of practically everyone, to have prepared a cage for every man to occupy. Indeed, in his pessimism, Bowles finds that finally everyone, everywhere, is a victim, in the primitive civilizations as well as in the West.

Bowles's use of African and Latin American civilizations and natural settings repudiates two recognized notions in our intellectual tradition while reinforcing his own dominant view of human experience. Bowles is absolutely contemptuous of primitivism. His underdeveloped lands are not peopled by noble savages living in a harmonious relationship with Edenic nature. Primitivism originates in a revolt against a sophisticated culture. Writers who have embraced the view in the past have used natives of one place or another as a living criticism of the West. But although Bowles rejects his own culture, he does not find noble natives in another. They are simply savage. The harder environment in which they live is not superior to the West's in its moral climate. And this assertion leads to the second idea, a related one, that Bowles repudiates. The Westerner, sick with the ills of his culture, has sometimes fled to a simpler milieu to establish life-giving relationships with elemental forces. Bowles rejects the proposition that the unsophisticated culture and a "natural" environment will revivify or save Western man. Instead, in his fiction Africa and Latin America are places where men die. Or where their spirits are finally crushed. It is an expression of his total pessimism to deny the saving possibilities in primitivism and the therapeutic values of a simple life in a simple culture. That pessimism sees that nothing endures in man but evil, no matter where he is. But Africa and Latin America make the evil more palpable, more dramatic. Bowles derives power to drive home his point partly because he frustrates the sentimental expectation of salvaging the self in a primitive land. A primitive society in a desert place awakens and encourages, in his work, the savagery and mindlessness that lie at the inner essence of human beings.—CHESTER EISINGER, "Paul Bowles and the Passionate Pursuit of Disengagement," *Fiction of the Forties*, 1963, pp. 283–85

Works

After several literary seasons given over, mostly, to the frisky antics of kids, precociously knowing and singularly charming, but not to be counted on for those gifts that arrive by no other way than the experience and contemplation of a truly adult mind, now is obviously a perfect time for a writer with such a mind to engage our attention. That is precisely the event to be celebrated in the appearance of *The Sheltering Sky*, Paul Bowles's first novel.

It has been a good while since first novels in America have come from men in their middle or late thirties (Paul Bowles is 38). Even in past decades the first novel has usually been written during the writers' first years out of college. Moreover, because success and public attention operate as a sort of pressure cooker or freezer, there has been a discouraging tendency for the talent to bake or congeal at a premature level of inner development.

In America the career almost invariably becomes an obsession. The "get-ahead" principle, carried to such extreme, inspires our writers to enormous efforts. A new book must come out every year. Otherwise they get panicky, and the first thing you know they belong to Alcoholics Anonymous or have embraced religion or plunged headlong into some political activity with nothing but an inchoate emotionalism to bring to it or be derived from it. I think that this stems from a misconception of what it means to be a writer or any kind of creative artist. They feel it is something to adopt *in the place of* actual living, without understanding that art is a by-product of existence.

Paul Bowles has deliberately rejected that kind of rabid professionalism. Better known as a composer than a writer, he has not allowed his passion for either form of expression to interfere with his growth into completeness of personality. Now this book has come at the meridian of the man and artist. And, to me very thrillingly, it brings the reader into sudden, startling communion with a talent of true maturity and sophistication of a sort that I had begun to fear was to be found nowadays only among the insurgent novelists of France, such as Jean Genet and Albert Camus and Jean-Paul Sartre.

With the hesitant exception of one or two war books by returned soldiers, *The Sheltering Sky* alone of the books that I have recently read by American authors appears to bear the spiritual imprint of recent history in the western world. Here the imprint is not visible upon the surface of the novel. It exists far more significantly in a certain philosophical aura that envelops it.

There is a curiously double level to this novel. The surface is enthralling as narrative. It is impressive as writing. But above that surface is the aura that I spoke of, intangible and powerful, bringing to mind one of those clouds that you have seen in summer, close to the horizon and dark in color and now and then silently pulsing with interior flashes of fire. And that is the surface of the novel that has filled me with such excitement.

The story itself is a chronicle of startling adventure against a background of the Sahara and the Arab-populated regions of the African Continent, a portion of the world seldom dealt with by first-rate writers who actually know it. Paul Bowles does know it, and much better, for instance, than it was known by André Gide. He probably knows it even better than Albert Camus. For Paul Bowles has been going to Africa, off and on, since about 1930. It thrills him, but for some reason it does not upset his nervous equilibrium. He does not remain in the coastal cities. At frequent intervals he takes journeys into the most mysterious recesses of the desert and mountain country of North Africa, involving not only hardship but peril.

The Sheltering Sky is the chronicle of such a journey. Were it not for the fact that the chief male character, Port Moresby, succumbs to an epidemic fever during the course of the story, it would not be hard to identify him with Mr. Bowles himself. Like Mr. Bowles, he is a member of the New York intelligentsia who became weary of being such a member and set out to escape it in remote places. Escape it he certainly does. He escapes practically all the appurtenances of civilized

modern life. Balanced between fascination and dread, he goes deeper and deeper into this dreamlike "awayness."

From then on the story is focused upon the continuing and continually more astonishing adventures of his wife, Kit, who wanders on like a body in which the rational mechanism is gradually upset and destroyed. The liberation is too intense, too extreme, for a nature conditioned by and for a state of civilized confinement. Her primitive nature, divested one by one of its artificial reserves and diffidences, eventually overwhelms her, and the end of this novel is as wildly beautiful and terrifying as the whole panorama that its protagonists have crossed.

In this external aspect the novel is, therefore, an account of startling adventure. In its interior aspect, *The Sheltering Sky* is an allegory of the spiritual adventure of the fully conscious person into modern experience. This is not an enticing way to describe it. It is a way that might suggest the very opposite kind of a novel from the one that Paul Bowles has written. Actually this superior motive does not intrude in explicit form upon the story, certainly not in any form that will need to distract you from the great pleasure of being told a first-rate story of adventure by a really first-rate writer.

I suspect that a good many people will read this book and be enthralled by it without once suspecting that it contains a mirror of what is most terrifying and cryptic within the Sahara of moral nihilism, into which the race of man now seems to be wandering blindly.—Tennessee Williams, "An Allegory of Man and His Sahara," *NYTBR*, Dec. 4, 1949, pp. 7, 38

The remarkable stories (in *Collected Stories*) are set in North America and North Africa; although the meticulously described landscape changes, the situation of Bowles' heroes remains the same.

The hero is usually a displaced person; he is suddenly, often brutally compelled to see the "heart of darkness." He is abused, violated, transformed. But Bowles refuses to allow him more than a few seconds of understanding; his broken hero disappears under "the sheltering sky."

Although we expect some final clarification of the disturbing mysteries—some "sense of an ending" (to use Frank Kermode's phrase)—we merely discover more shadows. There is no ultimate, rational solution—even after abrupt mutilations of self. It is, indeed, the sustaining axiom of these stories that the self—or the outside world—is tentative, fragile, and obscure. Bowles disdains any psychological explanation (except indirectly); he offers *moments* of ecstasy and fright—these are oddly married—and not the causes, preconceptions, or origins of the moments.

"Allal," one of the most brilliant stories in this collection of thirty-nine stories, introduces us to a youngster in North Africa. He plays alone; he works for slave wages; he enjoys little time for self-analysis. (Nor does he believe in such rationalism.) He is possessed, "primitive," dream-filled: he prefers "the sound of the wind in the trees." We are unable to understand in our "civilized," Western manner any of Allal's apparent choices. We are simply thrust into his *situation*.

Allal develops another pattern. He falls in love with snakes. He admires their delicate markings, "markings so delicate and perfect that they seemed to have been designed and painted by an artist." He decides—probably the wrong word!— to become a snake. He moves like one; he sleeps like one. Eventually he loses whatever human identity he had. He sheds his skin of self and achieves his unlimited "freedom." Before an axe severs his head, he has the pleasure of "pushing" his fangs into the bad men who pursue him.

Obviously, Bowles dislikes Allal's pursuers—civilized men who cannot recognize the beauty of madness. In "Pages from Cold Point" he gives us a narrator who is a complete, cynical rationalist. This hero, unlike Allal, refuses to submit his will. By writing his journal, he believes that he can control himself, the reader, and the "process of decay." He is, however, a divided personality—again the clinical words have little meaning in a Bowles story—because he loves chaos *even more* than the semblance of stability.

At first he devotes himself to his son, Racky, in a "normal," earnest way. But Racky is his snake—the other side. Soon it becomes impossible for father and son to act in conventional roles. They merge identities—such fluidity of reversal obsesses Bowles—and they assume mad parts in a romance.

It is, indeed, unclear whether father seduces son or vice versa. The shock, of course, is that homosexual incest occurs at Cold Point, the wonderfully named location. Here the "love" exchanged is frigid and spooky. We are chilled by the deliberate understatement of an outrageous situation. And when we read that the narrator is so insane as to believe "nothing very drastic" *has happened or will happen* to his island of contentment, we are even more astounded. The tonal coldness—which covers the emotional underground—is perfectly appropriate.

In both stories there is the sense of a spirit hovering over the landscape. And we are not surprised to see the spirit *appear as hero* in "The Circular Valley." The spirit moves in a restless way. It becomes a deer, a bee, a serpent. It overhears the love-and-struggle words of human beings. But it refuses to settle for a mere *self*. It is, if you will, an eternal, circular being—more powerful and beautiful and unpredictable than mankind.

I do not think that Bowles is a sensationalist in these stories—or, for that matter, in any of the others I have omitted from my discussion. He does not glory in his painstaking depiction of madness or destruction or mysticism. He believes firmly that life is unpredictably cruel—even to cruel heroes!—and that his accurate, intense art must *contain* the cruelty.

His style is thus stripped of prettiness. It is clear, direct, bold. Here, for example, is the last paragraph of "Allal" (and the collection): "The rage always had been in his heart; now it burst forth. As if his body were a whip, he sprang out into the room. The men nearest him were on their hands and knees, and Allal had the joy of pushing his fangs into two of them before a third severed his head with an axe." The words are almost distant; their *coolness* merely heightens the anxieties we feel because we know that without it things would really get out of hand. I am dazzled by the paragraph's complexity. (The rhythms are carefully modulated to convey the snake-like movements of Allal; the last sentence brutally severs his movements as the axe falls.) And I am convinced that the details are as "delicately marked" as snake skin.

When we read Bowles, we enter a new land. We recognize that our daily lives—our usual words—are shields against the unknowable universe. In a strange way we resemble his unwilling (?) victims. I do not mean to imply that we are Allal; I merely suggest that we suddenly appreciate how gratuitously "normality" and "abnormality" can change roles.

These stories bite and poison us—and they give us disturbing nourishment at the same time. They, like the circular spirit, will last "a long, long time—perhaps forever."—IRVING MALIN, "Abrupt Mutilations," *OnR*, Spring–Summer 1950, pp. 91–93

Paul Bowles is a man and author of exceptional latitude but he has, like nearly all serious artists, a dominant theme. That theme is the fearful isolation of the individual being. He is as preoccupied with this isolation as the collectivist writers of ten years ago were concerned with group membership and purposes. Our contemporary American society seems no longer inclined to hold itself open to very explicit criticism from within. This is what we hope and suppose to be a transitory condition that began with the Second World War. It will probably wear itself out, for it is directly counter to the true American nature and tradition, but at the present time it seems to be entering its extreme phase, the all but complete suppression of any dissident voices. What choice has the artist, now, but withdrawal into the caverns of his own isolated being? Hence the outgrowth of the "new school of decadence," so bitterly assailed by the same forces that turned our writers inward? Young men are writing first novels with a personal lyricism much like that exhibited in the early poems of the late Edna St. Vincent Millay, a comparison which is disparaging to neither party nor to the quality itself. For what is youth without lyricism, and what would lyricism be without a personal accent?

But Paul Bowles cannot be accurately classed with these other young men, not only because he is five or ten years older than most of them but because, primarily, a personal lyricism is not what distinguishes his work. His work is distinguished by its mature philosophical content, which is another thing altogether. As I noted in a review of his first novel, *The Sheltering Sky*, Bowles is apparently the only American writer whose work reflects the extreme spiritual dislocation (and a philosophical adjustment to it) of our immediate times. He has "an organic continuity" with the present in a way that is commensurate with the great French trio of Camus, Genet, and Sartre. This does little to improve his stock with the school of criticism which advocates a literature that is happily insensitive to any shock or abrasion, the sort that would sing "Hail, Hail the Gang's all Here" while being extricated, still vocally alive, from the debris of a Long Island railroad disaster.

But to revert to the opening observation in this review (of *The Delicate Prey and Other Stories*), Paul Bowles is preoccupied with the spiritual isolation of individual beings. This is not a thing as simple as loneliness. Certainly a terrible kind of loneliness is expressed in most of these stories and in the novel that preceded them to publication, but the isolated beings in these stories have deliberately chosen their isolation in most cases, not merely accepted and endured it. There is a singular lack of human give-and-take, of true emotional reciprocity, in the groups of beings assembled upon his intensely but somberly lighted sets. The drama is that of the single being rather than of beings in relation to each other. Paul Bowles has experienced an unmistakable revulsion from the act of social participation. One may surmise in him the social experience of two decades. Then the withdrawal is logical. The artist is not a man who will advance against a bayonet pressed to his abdomen unless another bayonet is pressed to his back, and even then he is not likely to move forward. He will, if possible, stand still. But Mr. Bowles has discovered that the bayonet is pointed at the man moving forward in our times, and that a retreat is still accessible. He has done the sensible thing under these circumstances. He has gone back into the cavern of himself. These seventeen stories are the exploration of a cavern of individual sensibilities, and fortunately the cavern is a deep one containing a great deal that is worth exploring.

Nowhere in any writing that I can think of has the separateness of the one human psyche been depicted more vividly and shockingly. If one feels that life achieves its highest value and significance in those rare moments—they are scarcely longer than that—when two lives are confluent, when the walls of isolation momentarily collapse between two persons, and if one is willing to acknowledge the possibility of such intervals, however rare and brief and difficult they may be, the intensely isolated spirit evoked by Paul Bowles may have an austerity which is frightening at least. But don't make the mistake of assuming that what is frightening is necessarily inhuman. It is curious to note that the spirit evoked by Bowles in so many of these stories does *not* seem inhuman, nor does it strike me as being antipathetic.

Even in the stories where this isolation is most shockingly, even savagely, stated and underlined the reader may sense an inverted kind of longing and tenderness for the thing whose absence the story concerns. This inverted, subtly implicit kind of tenderness comes out most clearly in one of the less impressive stories of the collection. This story is called "The Scorpion." It concerns an old woman in a primitive society of some obscure kind who has been left to live in a barren cave by her two sons. One of these deserters eventually returns to the cave with the purpose of bringing his mother to the community in which he and his brother have taken up residence. But the old woman is reluctant to leave her cave. The cave, too small for more than one person to occupy, is the only thing in reality that she trusts or feels at home in. It is curtained by rainfall and it is full of scorpions and it is not furnished by any kind of warmth or comfort, yet she would prefer to remain there than to accompany her son, who has finally for some reason not stated in the story decided to take her back with him to the community where he has moved. The journey must be made on foot and it will take three days. They finally set out together, but for the old woman there is no joy in the departure from the barren cave nor in the anticipation of a less isolated existence: there is only submission to a will that she does not interpret.

Here is a story that sentimentality, even a touch of it, could have destroyed. But sentimentality is a thing that you will find nowhere in the work of Paul Bowles: When he fails, which is rarely, it is for another reason. It is because now and then his special hardness of perception, his defiant rejection of all things emollient have led him into an area in which a man can talk only to himself.

The volume contains among several fine stories at least one that is a true masterpiece of short fiction—"A Distant Episode," published first in *Partisan Review*. In this story Paul Bowles states the same theme which he developed more fully in his later novel. The theme is the collapse of the civilized "Super Ego" into a state of almost mindless primitivism, totally dissociated from society except as an object of its unreasoning hostility. It is his extremely powerful handling of this theme again and again in his work which makes Paul Bowles probably the American writer who represents most truly the fierily and blindly explosive world that we live in so precariously from day and night to each uncertain tomorrow.—Tennessee Williams, "The Human Psyche—Alone," *SR*, Dec. 23, 1950, pp. 19–20

⟨*Up Above the World*⟩ is the kind of novel Malcolm Cowley and John W. Aldridge wanted to put out of business 15 or 20 years ago. That's when Truman Capote, Carson McCullers and Paul Bowles first started seeing strange things and not giving a damn. It's hard, bright and as cold as a block of ice. Gratuitous evil, upholstered innocence and insane social arrangements condemn Bowles's characters to frightful violence. They must do or be done to. Under sentence, they move inexorably toward futility and destruction. It's judgment day again in Bowles's 20th century. The judge stares into space, like Joyce's God-artist paring his fingernails, while we search his eyes for explanation of these outrages. The sin is to be alive.

Bowles's vision hasn't changed since *The Sheltering Sky* and *Let It Come Down*. His African night has fallen over the Caribbean. But it's a clearer blackness rendered as an operative nightmare. Three people are murdered during a wave of private crime in the West Indies. One of the murderers earns $100,000. The chief engineer of the bizarre electro-chemical derangement of two of the prey collects a lifetime of compensation for a lousy childhood. The victims burn up, get shot or pushed down a thousand-foot ravine. It's total dark victory. One can infer positive values only by their absence. The author's own attitude is as antimoral as a tombstone. He values situations, possibilities pushed to extreme.

Celebrating their second wedding anniversary with a trip to an obscure plantation republic, Dr. and Mrs. Slade are another pair of Bowles's displaced persons deprived of protection. Possessed by vacancy and waste, they wander through a wild landscape en route to doomsday. He is old enough to be her grandfather. She avoids the conjugal bed. The trip is a series of complaints about food, service, quarters. The tropics swarm with mysterious creatures and burst with plant life. But Day Slade can't find a copy of *Newsweek* anywhere, and Taylor Slade nervously anticipates tonight's sleeping arrangements. The air sweats and Chinese cooks dish up refried beans. The doctor is mean to kids. Mrs. Slade tells unimportant lies.

Before the existentialist talkathon we might have read Bowles's novel as a proof of the maxim Don't Speak to Strangers. Now we know hell is other people. Day Slade strikes up an acquaintance with an alcoholic old bag from Canada, Agnes Rainmantle, on her way to see her prodigal son in the island capital. For money and spite, the son, Grover Soto, has Mrs. Rainmantle syringed in the neck with curare while she sleeps. Mrs. Slade may have been a witness. Another casual meeting later, in Grover's leather-and-fur-covered apartment up above the island, and Dr. and Mrs. Slade have begun their agonizing journey to hallucination and death. They undergo systematic brainwashing—LSD, scopolamine, morphine, lights, sound effects—by Grover and his pill-popping sidekick, Thorny. But accidents do happen. Maybe the Slades remember Mrs. Rainmantle anyway. So Grover plays it safe.

The plot unwinds from a skein of weird human relationships. All are joined by sex, drugs, fantasies and the machinery of derangement. The marijuana smoke is thick enough to slice. Grover talks cut-ups to his tape recorder, dreams heavy Kafka and equips his bed with power-driven mirrors to watch what happens with his 17-year-old Cuban mistress; she paints idiot pictures to buy passage to Paris. Grover may also have something going with Thorny. Day Slade's post-coma awareness is shame in Grover's presence. After psychic castration, the final mickey comes as charity to Dr. Slade. Peel any character, strip any situation and find new sources of terror and nihilism. Control of the novel shifts from character to character as in a dream or trance.

"The 'meaning' of the book," Bowles says in a letter, "is certainly not this convoluted and improbable tale of brainwashing . . . nor is the book a *roman à thèse*, any more than was *The Sheltering Sky*. . . . A sentence from Borges should have been included in the front: 'Each moment as it is being lived exists, but not the imaginary total.'"

Agreed. As with his music the author may prefer his fiction to be as thesis-free as chords. But words form ideas. The lasting idea here is of a morally uninhabitable world, created by an artist robbed of compassion and endowed with such gifts as to make that loss seem irrelevant. Bowles's overpowering void descends on the mind and heart like a hypnotic spell.—Webster Schott, "Up Above the World," *NYTBR*, March 20, 1966, p. 4

Paul Bowles is known mainly for two books—*The Sheltering Sky* and *The Delicate Prey*—both of which appeared in the early years after the war and immediately established him as one of the best of the new crop of writers. Trained as a composer and influenced by the French symbolists and surrealists, Bowles came on the scene as a fully developed artist who was looking to revive the modernist movement. . . .

Of the writers who devoted themselves to negation and despair, Bowles was probably the most subtle as well as the most uncompromising. The stories in *A Delicate Prey* with their lucid, quiet evocation of mood and motive leading to revelations of scarifying depravity were often so powerful that they made the nihilism of the early Hemingway seem like a pleasant beery melancholy. The title story, for example, deserves to live forever in the annals of human cunning and cruelty: a tale of a desert predator and tribal fanatic who wins the confidence of three brothers traveling in a caravan, murders the two older ones after conning them into a hunt, and then, intoxicated with hashish ("carried along on its hot fumes, a man can escape very far from the world of meaning"), wounds, mutilates, rapes, and finally after many hours, kills the youngest brother. The emotional current of the story is provided by the boy's innocence which leads him to distrust his suspicions of the Moungari's treachery; distracted by the lusts and self-consciousness of youth, he is the human equivalent of the desert gazelles, the "delicate prey" that were to be hunted down. The tale concludes with the detection of the murderer whom the police turn over to the tribesmen of the three brothers. They calmly bury him up to his neck in the desert sands "to wait through the cold hours for the sun that would bring first warmth, then heat, thirst, fire, visions. The next night he did not know where he was, did not feel the cold. The wind blew dust along the ground and into his mouth as he sang."

Virtually all of the stories in *A Delicate Prey* take place in a primitive setting, usually either Central America or North Africa. The jungle and more notably the desert, the place where "all philosophical systems collapse," as a French colonial officer puts it, have provided Bowles with a natural background for narratives that are intended to crack open the standard models of reality and morality and to reveal the demonic sources of human conduct. The destructive element in which Bowles immerses his tightlaced and empty pilgrims from the modern world takes many forms: there is the incredible brutality of the Reguiba bandits who quickly reduce an anthropologist, led to them by a spiteful native guide, to a state of catatonic terror in which he functions as a kind of tribal pet; but there is also the encompassing languor of a Caribbean island into which a retired professor sinks so far that he sends his teen-age son away to a life of sybaritic perversion rather than be disturbed by his scandalous behavior.

Though most of these stories in *A Delicate Prey* still make one feel they were written with a razor, so deftly and chillingly do they cut to the bone, there was clearly more to Bowles than the desire to shock, dismay and terrorize. "Pastor Dowe at Tacate," for example, is a profoundly ironic comment on the white man's burden, a kind of "Heart of Darkness" in miniature, in which a prim missionary finds himself sliding from Christian rationality into atavism, until he finally is faced with the necessity of taking an eight-year-old girl for his wife and literally runs away in terror from the Indian village.

The abysses and furies of the human psyche; the fragile, provisional nature of the civilized instincts; the lure of the primitive and the inhuman; the sadness of deracinated people; the underground warfare of marriage and friendship; the lonely divisions between desire and behavior, between having and holding, between one hand and the other hand; the modern world's contagions of angst, dread, deadness: all these strains of the existentialist vision are dramatically presented in Bowles' earlier work and come to a classic statement in his novel, *The Sheltering Sky*, one of the most beautifully written novels of the past twenty years and one of the most shattering.

Bowles is not the philosopher that Sartre or Camus were, but he is an existentialist to his fingertips, and beside the emotional concreteness of *The Sheltering Sky*, books like *Nausea*, *The Age of Reason*, or *The Stranger* seem vague, arbitrary, imaginatively barren. Bowles' novel is a study of two American travelers, Kit and Port Moresby, and of the subtle processes between and within them that carry each to his destructive self-fulfillment in the North African desert. The epigraph of the book is Eduard Mallea's observation that "Each man's destiny is personal only insofar as it may happen to resemble what is already in his memory," the point of which is richly developed in the unfolding of Port's isolate values, his yearning to exist outside of the human community, to experience the mysteries of nothingness, which has brought him to the desert and which culminates in a series of terrible voyages into the beyond that he makes during the final stages of a fatal attack of typhoid fever. His wife, who is afflicted by a sense of dread that wars with her considerable intelligence, finally achieves the utter submissiveness she craves by falling into the hands of a young Arab merchant and undergoing a sexual enslavement that eventually drives her into madness. These parallel lines of fate, of two people consumed in accidents that minister to their deepest wishes, are drawn with a fineness and density of specification that makes the novel anything but schematic. Bowles has much the same feeling for the delicate tangibilities of character that D. H. Lawrence did and much the same powerful ability to establish the atmosphere of physical reality that reveals and conditions behavior: the squalid, sagging accoutrements of colonialism in a desert hotel; the fragments of mystery in a street wind at dusk that carries "the smell of lilies, drains, and hashish smoke"; the piles of garbage in a broken-down patio amid which lie naked scrofulous infants and pink dogs, their hairless, raw skin "indecently exposed to the kisses of the flies and the sun"; and preeminently the desert itself, with its spectacular negation of everything human except for the arid, howling void within.

In retrospect, *The Sheltering Sky* stands as the climax of Bowles' literary career: the book into which he puts his strongest image of life and his deepest knowledge about it. This image and knowledge admit of little expansion. For if, as Port says, contemplating the only book he might have written, the one absolute truth for him is that "the difference between something and nothing is nothing" and that the only interest is "in all the complicated processes that make it possible to get that result," then the novelist is doomed to rework the algebra of nihilism until he grows weary of the problem. Indeed, this has been one of the burdens of modernism, and the literary landscape of the 20th century is littered with the abandoned careers of writers who ran into the sands of alienation and found themselves unable to go on. And in recent times, fewer and fewer novelists seem able to maintain the kind of steady on-going *oeuvre*, the diversity of subject, the expansion of consciousness that once characterized the novelist's vocation.—THEODORE SOLOTAROFF, "The Desert Within," *NR*, Sept. 2, 1967, pp. 29–30

KAY BOYLE

1903–

Kay Boyle was born in St. Paul, Minnesota, on February 19, 1903, into a wealthy publishing family. Boyle's education was sporadic as a result of her family's constant moving; she attended Miss Shipley's School at Bryn Mawr for a time, and then the Cincinnati Conservatory of Music. In 1917 she began to study architecture at the Ohio Mechanics Institute, but financial troubles forced Boyle to go to work after 1919, and she enrolled in a secretarial course at night. In 1922 she moved to New York, where she worked at the magazine *Broom*, and studied creative writing at Columbia.

In 1922 Kay Boyle met and married Robert Brault. A year later the couple left on a short trip to France, which began Boyle's eighteen-year exile in France, Austria, and England. During the 1920s she became involved with the literary avant-garde, including James Joyce, Ezra Pound, Gertrude Stein, and William Carlos Williams. Boyle's work was published frequently in both Ernest Walsh's *This Quarter*, and Eugene Jolas' *transition*.

In 1929 Boyle published *Short Stories*, which appeared in the U.S. a year later under the title *Wedding Day: And Other Stories*. Boyle's first novel, *Plagued by the Nightingale*, was published in 1931. During the next ten years Boyle produced five more novels, three collections of short stories, as well as poetry, a children's book, and several translations. Her work became very popular, particularly the 1938 novel *Monday Night*. She won O. Henry prizes for two of her short stories, and in 1934 was awarded a Guggenheim Fellowship. Boyle was forced to leave Europe during World War II, and returned to America in 1941. She wrote several novels about the war; *Avalanche*, published in 1944, became required reading for the U.S. Army.

In later years Boyle's novels took an increasingly direct approach to political causes. *The Underground Woman*, published in 1975, addresses the problems of Black and Chicano women, supports the use of civil disobedience towards ending the Vietnam War, and gives a dramatic account of the dangers of depersonalizing cults. Kay Boyle continues to write and has been teaching creative writing at San Francisco State University since 1963. She has received honorary degrees from both Columbia and Skidmore colleges, and is a member of the American Academy of Arts and Letters. She has been married three times and has four children.

Personal

Kay Boyle went to live and work in Paris in the late 1920s, having moved to France earlier in the decade with her French husband, whom she had married in New York in 1922. In Paris she met many of the expatriate writers and artists then living there, including James Joyce, Samuel Beckett, Djuna Barnes, and Robert McAlmon, who wrote about them all in *Being Geniuses Together*, which Kay Boyle later reissued with her own alternating chapters. A second marriage, to Laurence Vail, ended over ideological disputes that arose from Boyle's strong position against fascism. Back in America she was blacklisted in the 1950s, when her third husband, a foreign-service officer whom she had earlier helped in obtaining a visa to leave France, was falsely accused of being a Communist. She was evidently not cowed by the experience, because she was protesting against the war in Vietnam in the 1960s and being jailed for sit-ins. "Indomitable" is the word that springs to mind.

During the course of a career that seems from the outside highly novelistic, but which Kay Boyle herself would probably shrug off as nothing out of the ordinary, she managed to produce fourteen novels and a great many short stories. Some of the latter were collected and published as *Fifty Stories* in 1980. That she is not as celebrated as she ought to be stems probably from the fact that the short story, at which she excels, has, until very recently, not been a popular genre in America. There has been an unfortunate tendency in America to judge everything by size. If one were to judge instead by accomplishment, *Three Short Novels* would have fared better in the past. Kay Boyle herself did not suffer from this confusion. "These three stories," she has said, "mean as much to me as anything I have ever done."

At first the juxtaposition seems odd. Two of these stories deal with English country life and are not overtly political; the third is a taut and harrowing account of life in the police state that was Fascist Spain. Yet the three share a central preoccupation: the workings of power. In "The Crazy Hunter" the power structure is based partly on those shadings of class distinction the English have always excelled at, balanced against the traditional power arrangements based on sex. The struggle is between husband and wife, with the daughter caught between them. "The Bridegroom's Body" also plays class against class, but the underlying power is sexual, atavistic, instinctive, and potentially tragic in its effects. This is a story whose setting may be remote but whose concerns are absolutely contemporary. The war between female and male and the aggressive and murderous competition between male and male have seldom been more potently handled. Few writers have been more skilled at conveying an underlying emotional violence imperfectly concealed by the conventional politenesses. In "Decision" again the central concern is power, but here it is the oppressive power of George Orwell's boot in the human face, the corrupting effects of a lust for power seen through their consequences. The contrast here also is between a brightly rendered surface that merely flickers and a depth in which the action takes place, monumentally, unseen.

It is the brightness of surface that is one of the hallmarks of Kay Boyle's writing. The physical observation is hard and clear, and every object observed has its own light and color; even the scenes in darkness have their own eerie glow. This is a solid world solidly described, but it is also a world in which matter is merely a form of energy. Kay Boyle's writing has sometimes been spoken of as approaching the surreal, but there is nothing of the ant-covered clock about it. What it approaches instead is the hallucinatory, or rather the moment of visionary realism when sensation heightens and time for an instant fixes and stops. If one were to pick a painter who corresponds to Boyle, it would not be Salvador Dali. One thinks rather of Brueghel, a landscape clearly and vividly rendered, everything in its ordinary order, while Icarus falls to his death, scarcely noticed, off to the side.

But to concentrate entirely on quality of vision or sureness of craft would be to miss the point entirely about Kay Boyle. It is only in North America that critics can indulge in the luxury of separating craft and politics into watertight boxes; Kay Boyle, although in many ways quintessentially American, belongs also to a wide tradition. Central to her fiction is the issue of moral choice, an issue that is as present in the family drama of "The Crazy Hunter" as it is in the much more obviously political "Decision."

"He will make his own decision," says the naïve American narrator in "Decision." She has access to papers that will save a man from the police.

"No," replies another character. "You are either every third man who is taken out and shot, or else you are not, but one is not permitted a decision. There is no choice that he can make, except the profounder choice which lies between good and evil, and that choice Jerónimo has made."

Victims of fate and circumstance Boyle's characters may be, but not entirely. Some of their destiny still rests with themselves. Although none of these stories has a resolution that suggests happiness for the protagonists, Boyle's universe is neither absurd nor hopeless. Love and its opposite, hatred, loyalty and therefore betrayal, heroism and cowardice, are all still possible within it. The *nada* that is supposed to be so central to the twentieth-century sensibility is not at its core.

"Defiance" is a word that recurs in these stories. For Boyle, it is a defiance not only of the powers ranged against the protagonists but also of easy literary fashionability. Reading Kay Boyle, one recalls Flannery O'Connor saying that novels are not written by people without hope.—MARGARET ATWOOD, "Introduction" to *Three Short Novels*, 1982, pp. vii–x

Works

Kay Boyle is the outstanding young woman member of that group of American writers who make their headquarters in Paris and whose work until recently has appeared for the most part in the pages of *transition*. This volume of short stories, ⟨*Wedding Day: And Other Stories*⟩, her first, was originally published in a special edition in Paris. Anyone who reads it and whose standards of the short story are not the standards of the correspondence school will appreciate that the work of Miss Boyle, for simple craftsmanship, is superior to most of that which is crowned annually by our anthologies. Anyone with an ear for new verbal harmonies will appreciate that Miss Boyle is a stylist of unusual taste and sensibility. It is time, therefore, to cease to regard her as a mere lower-case *révoltée* and to begin to accept her for what she is: more enterprising, more scrupulous, potentially more valuable than nine-tenths of our best-known women authors.

She is potentially valuable because it is possible—as it is so rarely possible—that she may write something that has not been written before. When we have read these few brief stories we realize that they sprang from a genuine inner necessity, that the author was helplessly obliged to communicate them with that blind honesty which is the best augury for the future. We also realize that she has an original gift. This gift is a sexual one. With the first sentence of the first story—"the

horses . . . stamping and lashing themselves with fury because she passed by them"—we are thrust into the presence of feelings which could have been generated in no other place than a woman's body. And those pages which come to life prove almost invariably to have been written either by or about desire. This is a difficult subject to handle. Miss Boyle's solution, which for the most part is mischievous, not only stakes out a new field for herself but gives the clearest evidence of her integrity. For although she has allowed herself absolute freedom on one of the most delicate of all subjects she has not written an offensive line. In fact, she has put to shame nearly every other emancipated woman writer who has attempted to deal with this subject: she is by comparison so simple, so honest, so pure. It is probable that the two stories in which she has given comic treatment to sexual themes, Episode in the Life of an Ancestor and Summer, mark the highest stage of her development.

In view of her virtues it is all the more unfortunate that her work abounds in mannerisms, that it lacks a face of its own, that it bears so continually the stamp of fashionable influences. It is unfortunate that she has expended so much of her freedom in exile toward the development of an impeccability of style which is after all but the testimony of her admiration for Hemingway, Cocteau, and others. The result of her smartness is that even her best work has its roots in nothing, being nourished by the repetition of a repetition. Surely we must all be aware by this time that we cannot hope to grow orchids in America until we have had our hardy perennials. One wonders if Miss Boyle is aware that she has only to look within herself to find strong and deep roots for her art. Does she know that she is much better when she describes a lover's kiss—"his mustache tasting of snow"—than when she repeats the jumbled password of the advance guard?—GERALD SYKES, "Too Good to Be Smart," *Nation*, Dec. 24, 1930, pp. 711–12

I picked out Kay Boyle's *Avalanche* in the hope of finding a novel worth reading, and have been somewhat taken aback to get nothing but a piece of pure rubbish.

I have heard Miss Boyle praised as a stylist, but, though there are in *Avalanche* a few fine images and gray and white mountain landscapes, I cannot see how a writer with a really sound sense of style could have produced this book even as a potboiler. One recognizes the idiom of a feminized Hemingway: "There was one winter when the blizzard got us part way up. . . . If you looked in the direction the wind was coming from, your breath stopped suddenly as if someone took you by the throat;" and a sobbing Irish lilt: "He touches my hand as if it were a child's hand, and his promise of love is given to a woman. To him it is nothing to walk into a mountain refuge and find me, and to me it's the three years without him that have stopped crying their hearts out at last." And, for the rest, there are several tricks that Miss Boyle overworks with exasperating effect. She is always giving possessives to inanimate objects, so that you have "the weather's break," "the balcony's rail," and "the mitten's pattern" all within a space of sixteen lines; and there is a formula that recurs so often in the passages of conversation that one can almost say the whole book is built of it: "'They're fiercer, more relentless,' he said, and the sound of threat was there;" "'And there is de Vaudois,' he said, and he put the mittens on;" "'You're French, partly French,' he said, and his eyes were asking the promise of her"—these are quoted from a space of less than two pages. Sometimes you get both these refrains together: "'What is the story of that?' said de Vaudois, and his eyes went suddenly shrewd beneath his hat's crisp brim."

Miss Boyle has indulged herself, also, in the bad romantic

habit of making foreign conversation sound translated. It is perhaps a part of her Hemingway heritage. A Spaniard, Arturo Barea, has sought to show, in the English review *Horizon*, that the dialogue of *For Whom the Bell Tolls* is not really a translation of Spanish but a language of Hemingway's own. So Miss Boyle—to take her at her simplest, where there is no question of special eloquence involved—will have her characters make speeches like the following:

"And Bastineau? What of Bastineau?"
"One by one they've gone from us."
"A friend come back from America is here."

Now this is certainly not colloquial English; but when you try putting it into French, you have:

"*Et Bastineau? Quoi de Bastineau?*"
"*L'un après l'autre, ils s'en sont allés de nous.*"
"*Une amie revenue de l'Amérique est ici.*"

—which is even more impossible as French. My best guess at the kind of thing you would get if the last of these thoughts, for example, were naturally expressed in French would be "*Voici une amie revenue de l'Amérique*"—of which the natural English would be "Here's a friend of ours who's come back from America." But Miss Boyle needs the false solemnity, the slow-motion portentousness, that this Never Never language gives to carry off her absurd story.

It is easy to be funny about *Avalanche*, but it has its depressing aspect. I have not read much else by Kay Boyle since her very early work, so that I do not have a definite opinion about the value of her writing as a whole; but I know from those early stories, written when she lived abroad and printed in the "little" magazines of the American *émigrés*, that she was at least making an effort at that time to produce something of serious interest. Today she is back at home, and *Avalanche* was written for the *Saturday Evening Post*, I did not see it there, but I have been haunted since I read it by a vision of *Saturday Evening Post* illustrations, in which the ideal physical types of the skin-lotion and shaving-soap ads are seen posing on snowy slopes. Nor do I doubt that this novel was constructed with an eye to the demands of Hollywood, that intractable magnetic mountain which has been twisting our fiction askew and on which so many writers have been flattened.—EDMUND WILSON, "Kay Boyle and the *Saturday Evening Post*," NY, Jan. 15, 1944, pp. 76–77

Kay Boyle has added eighteen poems from the last ten years to her earlier work in verse that culminated in the long 1944 poem *American Citizen*; these *Collected Poems* are elusive but—as always in the poetry of a writer whose characteristic achievement is in prose—they offer a reliable thematic index to Miss Boyle's preoccupations over the years: she aspires to be, doubtless is, a good European, the kind of person who knows the right café to sit in front of, the interesting wine to order, a hard ski slope to descend, an easy man to love. Her landscapes, both American and European, are made into emblems of the wild heart, the behavior of her animals likened to the actions of men. It is not entirely fair, by the way, to refer to her "earlier work in verse", since so many of these difficult pieces are experiments in mixing verse with extended prose passages; indeed, however obscure it may be, such prose is always firmer and, if not more deeply felt, then more dramatically honed than the verse, which in even the very latest poems is without much spine or spring, though Miss Boyle has spirit and to spare. The best—and last—poem of this conjugated sort, *A Winter Fable*, is a startling success; following an evocation of Salzburg, the speaker switches to an anti-scene:

. . . six old hags cast up against the wainscoting
Of Grand Central's ladies' room . . .

These women are beguiled, as are we, by a Negro confidence-woman's cat, trained to select victims who will give money to its mistress. Here Miss Boyle's prose, with its finely-tuned dialogue and extravagant imagery, works cruelly against such matter-of-fact lines as these:

The water ran into the basins
The toilets flushed and
Mrs. Morgan picked up
The dripping mop and pushed it
Across the floor.

I think that by such alternations, so carefully inflected, she has produced a really new form. Another poem I particularly like is the very last, *The Evening Grass*, a meditation on suicide that by its superb phrasing, its breathing, one might say, overcomes the lack of effective stress-pattern so noticeable in the other poems. When we hear her voice speaking just under her breath (or over it, as in certain impassioned political poems that are often more personal than her choked *intimeries*), Miss Boyle strikes the note which has sounded in her stories for so many years. Yet these poems do not define the arena of her concern distinctly enough to reveal what combats are being fought in it, and if it were not for Kay Boyle's novels and stories, I should be even more uncertain of her present focus. Yet knowing what we all know of Miss Boyle's fiction, we can readily find the values of her verse: despite the do-it-yourself punctuation, the slack and period rhythms, here is the true timbre of explicit agony, the kind of certainty-in-chaos Miss Boyle has already administered to enlarge the province of our prose. There is no odium in juxtaposing, to show the continuity of her effort, this passage from her 1938 novel *Monday Night* with one from her latest poem (1961):

"You go to sleep now, Bernie" Wilt said half aloud, and lying here sleep the deep forgetful sleep of the child, the chasm between us as well as the claim we have on each other being that we have sought all night together the flesh of our libido, you the suckler seeking the breast, I the phantasy maker seeking through fabrication the substance of his unaltered childhood dream.

                                        You ran
The jagged staircase of your grief for all
Who say tonight tonight tonight
Yes LIFE tonight to liquid ears and no
One hears it was for paintings out of frames that
Lean on warehouse walls for all
The lost engravings of the heart wild
Cardiographs of lust you wept for flesh
That did not lie upon his mouth. . . .

Miss Boyle is a maker.—RICHARD HOWARD, *Poetry*, July 1963, pp. 253–55

Kay Boyle has been one of the most elusive characters in contemporary American fiction. I say this with some feeling, because I have tried to categorize her work in every decade since the early 1930's, and each decade, it seems, I have been wrong.

She is the author of 13 novels, some of them very good, but she is not quite a major novelist. Her major medium has always been the short story and the novelette. (And it is typical of this aristocrat, whose earlier work lay in the tradition of Edith Wharton and Henry James, not to use the fashionable word, novella.) But even here, she was in the early thirties, a writer of superior sensibility—or so I thought—using a foreign scene more successfully than her native one, and belonging, in essence, both to the expatriate line of James and Wharton and to that later "lost generation" of the 1920's.

What this new collection (*Nothing Ever Breaks Except the*

Heart) of Miss Boyle's short stories and novelettes does prove is that while all of the speculation above is somewhat true, none of it is really true, or profoundly true. She has all these elements in this new collection of her mature work. But, as in the case of every first-rank writer, she rises above the disparate elements in her work or in her temperament, to become something else. What *Nothing Ever Breaks Except the Heart* proves, in short, is that Kay Boyle has at last become a major short-story writer, or a major writer in contemporary American fiction, after three decades of elusiveness, sometimes of anonymity, almost of literary "classlessness," while she has pursued and has finally discovered her true metier. It is a joy to discover such an event: not a new talent, which is rare enough, but an established and mature talent which has developed and perfected itself—and particularly in an epoch when so many false talents are proclaimed every year.

Unlike her earlier collection of *Thirty Stories*, which was arranged chronologically—and that earlier volume is fascinating now to read over and to compare with the present one—*Nothing Ever Breaks Except the Heart* is arranged topically: "Peace," "War Years" and "Military Occupation." And perhaps one should add, in the selfish concern of pure art, that nothing better could have happened for Kay Boyle than World War II and the periods of military occupation, by the German and then the Allied forces. For even in the present volume, the first section, "Peace," is less effective than the remainder of the book—and still Kay Boyle is less effective about the American than she is about the European scene. When it comes to a story like "Anschluss," dealing with a world-weary Parisian fashion-writer and a marvelously gay brother and sister in a dying Austria, she is superb.

Here, as in so many of her earlier stories and novels, her satiric strain works unrelentingly upon the German character and physique. Here, more convincingly than in earlier books, her romantic lovers are destroyed by the dissolution of a society; and here, just as in her work of the early forties, she dramatizes the pageantry of a dissolute and amoral social scene over and above the sensibilities of her characters.

In Miss Boyle's writing, there has always been a traditional sense of character—romantic, pagan at heart and best exemplified in her heroines rather than her heroes—but the European *Walpurgisnacht* of the late thirties gave her a dramatic social background that she could hardly afford to ignore. Thus, too, in her first novel, *Plagued by the Nightingale*, first published in 1931 and just recently reissued, the central theme was of an ingrown and diseased French bourgeois family, of an American heroine's struggle against this family. (Miss Boyle herself was born in St. Paul in 1903, married a Frenchman, and went to live in France in the early twenties; but her "expatriatism," as she recently wrote to me, was enforced by circumstances rather than by choice.)

The style, too, of her first novel is more precious, studied, and "literary" than her present, apparently more prosaic, and truly more beautiful style. As late as 1938, she could still turn out such a mediocre novel as *Monday Night*, a picaresque mystery, still about that "family romance" which any true novelist must have in his bones, but which, in itself, is never enough. Perhaps it was only with *Primer for Combat*, in 1942—which is curiously close to the place and theme of the "Anschluss" story—that the *larger* European scene of social and moral disintegration and corruption appeared so firmly and so incisively and so brilliantly. And it was in *Generation Without Farewell* (1960) that she added the American Occupation Forces to her Nazi conquerors, in order to prove that human debasement—the evil soul, the vicious soul, the lost soul—can

be a matter of social circumstance rather than of national origins.

Indeed, in *Nothing Ever Breaks Except the Heart*, it is a toss-up as to who the true villains are, Germans or Americans or just plain Occupiers—while the heroes, to Miss Boyle, are those who have been conquered and occupied, those who have resisted, those who have put to the acid test their property, their career and their lives. To her earlier vision of sensibility, she has added what every first-rate writer must have, a standard of human morality—and the fact that human morality is usually, if not always, related to a specific social or historical context.

It is this familiar concept, missing in so much current and "new" American fiction, that is embodied in the magnificent stories of her maturity. (For conversely, it is of no use to an artist to have a perfect sense of morality without an adequate art form to project it.) The title story of the present collection is another beauty: a Hemingway tale, so to speak, (about a pilot who is finished) but produced by an intensely feminine talent, and with an anti-Hemingway moral. (By this I mean anti-late-Hemingway, when all that remained in him was the killer pitted against a hostile menacing universe.) What is so remarkable in these late tales of Kay Boyle, by contrast, is the increased sense of sympathy in them for all the losers, all the defeated persons and peoples of contemporary history.

Here again, an earlier sense of nostalgia in her work has become an intense sense of compassion. I don't pretend to know the secrets of this fine craftsman, but I do realize how many of these stories leave you on the brink of tears. And a world in tears; since Kay Boyle has become the American writer to express the texture of European life after Chamberlain and Daladier and Munich.

There is still a final phase of writing in *Nothing Ever Breaks Except the Heart*, still another epoch of our modern history: the period of the Occupation, the black market and the reappearance of the same old people, asking for privilege and power and "deals" all over again, after the heroism, the gallantry, the selflessness of the liberation battle. No wonder that the last one of these stories describes an American State Department official returning to a McCarthyite America—ironic sequel to the war for European freedom. And no wonder that the last of these beautiful tales describes an American mother, who agrees with "a terrified race"—the French peasants of the atomic age. "'I am American,' she said to that unseen presence of people in the silent room, 'and the wrong voices have spoken out for me, and spoken loudly, and I too, I too, am terribly afraid.'"—MAXWELL GEISMAR, "Aristocrat of the Short Story," *NYTBR*, July 10, 1964, pp. 4, 16

The conflict or the relation between sensibility and habit, between the articulate surface of life and the silent reality below, between true and false dignity, between vitality and prudence, between different kinds of egotism, between love and fear, between spontaneity and feeling and the claims of tradition and society—these are all themes, reverberating with haunting overtones, which Kay Boyle handles in the earliest of the four groups of stories in this collection. Not that these stories pose these questions as questions or specifically single out opposing feelings or attitudes with a view to a dramatic confrontation. The drama is never the drama of simple conflict. For all the sharp lines of the stories the situations they project are as teasing and complex as life itself. Order is imposed, but the selection of significant detail which creates the order is so cunningly done that, while we see and are moved by the pattern, we know that it is a symbol of life's complexity rather than a schematization of life's problems. Of course art is not life, but its function is to illuminate life in its own unique way. Too much modern criticism shies away from "life" as a bad word. No one who reads these stories can doubt that the primary impulse behind them was the expression of some kind of *interest* in life, and that the virtuosity that enabled their author to find an effective way of communicating these kinds of interest existed from the beginning in the closest contact with—and indeed was in important respects determined by—the nature of the interest. It is time that it was roundly asserted that the first duty of a story is to be interesting. And the first duty of an artist is to relate his craftsmanship to his interests, to allow his sense of his medium to intermesh with his sense of life. That, indeed, is how he becomes an artist.

"Sense of life" is a vague phrase. Perhaps it can best be illustrated by examples—the brilliant combination of gaiety and pathos (and the sheer virtuosity of the gaiety) in "Friends of the Family"; the shrewd handling of incident which achieves the counterpointing of irony, comedy and pity in "Keep Your Pity"; the devastatingly realized detail of "Your Body Is a Jewel Box." Kay Boyle's stories wring from us a startled assent. We are both surprised and convinced, as in the ending of "Black Boy." The element of surprise keeps them continually lively, while the element of conviction keeps directing our imagination to the true centers of experience. . . .

Compassionate without being sentimental, moral without being didactic, contemporary without being ephemeral, *engagés* without being simply autobiographical or hortatory, these stories show one of the finest short-story writers of our time counterpointing imagination and experience in different ways as experience took on new forms and imagination shifted its role and scope to meet it.—DAVID DAICHES, "Introduction" to *Fifty Stories*, 1980, pp. 10–14

KATHERINE ANNE PORTER
"Kay Boyle: Example to the Young" (1931)
The Critic as Artist: Essays on Books 1920–1970
1971, pp. 277–81

M iss Kay Boyle's way of thinking and writing stems from sources still new in the sense that they have not been supplanted. She is young enough to regard them as in the category of things past, a sign I suppose, that she is working in a tradition and not in a school. Gertrude Stein and James Joyce were and are the glories of their time and some very portentous talents have emerged from their shadows. Miss Boyle, one of the newest, I believe to be among the strongest. At present she is identified as one of the *Transition* group, but these two books just published should put an end to that. What is a group, anyhow? In this one were included—as associate editors and contributors to *Transition*—many Americans: Harry Crosby, William Carlos Williams, Hart Crane, Matthew Josephson, Isidor Schneider, Josephine Herbst, Murray Godwin, Malcolm Cowley, John Herrman, Laura Riding—how many others?—and Miss Boyle herself. They wrote in every style under heaven and they spent quite a lot of time fighting with each other. Not one but would have resented, and rightly, the notion of discipleship or of interdependence. They were all vigorous not so much in revolt as in assertion, and most of

them had admirably subversive ideas. Three magazines sustained them and were sustained by them: *Transition*, Ernest Walsh's *This Quarter* and *Broom*. The tremendous presences of Gertrude Stein and James Joyce were everywhere about them, and so far as Miss Boyle is concerned, it comes to this: that she is a part of the most important literary movement of her time.

She sums up the salient qualities of that movement: a fighting spirit, freshness of feeling, curiosity, the courage of her own attitude and idiom, a violently dedicated search for the meanings and methods of art. In these short stories and this novel there are further positive virtues of the individual temperament: health of mind, wit and the sense of glory. All these are qualities in which the novel marks an advance over the stories, as it does, too, in command of method.

The stories have a range of motive and feeling as wide as the technical virtuosity employed to carry it. Not all of them are successful. In some of the shorter ones, a straining of the emotional situation leads to stridency and incoherence. In others, where this strain is employed as a deliberate device, it is sometimes very successful—as notably in "Vacation Time," an episode in which an obsessional grief distorts and makes tragic a present situation not tragic of itself; the reality is masked by drunkenness, evaded by hysteria, and it is all most beautifully done. "On the Run" is a bitter story of youth in literal flight from death, which gains on it steadily; but the theme deserved better treatment.

In such stories as "Episode in the Life of an Ancestor" and "Uncle Anne," there are the beginnings of objectiveness, a soberer, richer style; and the sense of comedy, which is like acid sometimes, is here gayer and more direct. In "Portrait" and "Polar Bears and Others," Miss Boyle writes of love not as if it were a disease, or a menace, or a soothing syrup to vanity, or something to be peered at through a microscope, or the fruit of original sin, or a battle between the sexes, or a bawdy pastime. She writes as one who believes in love and romance—not the "faded flower in a buttonhole," but love so fresh and clear it comes to the reader almost as a rediscovery in literature. It was high time someone rediscovered it. There are other stories, however—"Spring Morning," "Letters of a Lady," "Episode in the Life of an Ancestor"—in which an adult intelligence plays with destructive humor on the themes of sexual superstition and pretenses between men and women. "Madame Tout Petit," "Summer," "Theme" and "Bitte Nehmen Sie die Blumen" are entirely admirable, each one a subtle feat in unraveling a complicated predicament of the human heart. "Wedding Day," the title story, is the least satisfactory, displaying the weakness of Miss Boyle's strength in a lyricism that is not quite poetry.

The novel, *Plagued by the Nightingale*, has the same germinal intensity as the shorter works, but it is sustained from the first word to the last by a sure purpose and a steadier command of resources. The form, structure and theme are comfortably familiar. The freshness and brilliancy lie in the use of the words and the point of view.

It is the history of an American girl married to a young Frenchman, and living for a short period in the provinces with his wealthy bourgeois family. There is Papa, a blustering old fool, though Bridget never says it quite so plainly; Maman, a woman of energy, good will and appalling force of character; three unmarried sisters, Annick, Julie and Marthe; Charlotte the eldest sister, married to her cousin; Pierre the elder brother, a young doctor; and Nicholas, Bridget's husband. A taint in the blood causes eccentrics and paralytics to blossom like funeral wreaths in every generation. Nicholas is warned by his weakened legs that the family disease is likely to be the main portion of his inheritance. He is dependent on his people, his wife is dowerless. Charlotte's husband is little better than an imbecile, but he is wealthy. Uncle Robert, a perverse old maid of a man, is also wealthy, and amuses himself by tampering with family affairs; the victims endure him in the hope that he may give someone money sometime. First and last it is the question of money that agitates the family bosom.

The three younger daughters are waiting, each in her own way, for a proposal of marriage from Luc, an idolized young doctor, who nonchalantly enjoys the privilege of the devoted family without asking to become a member. Bridget is a vigorous personality, with powerful hates and loves, a merciless eye, and a range of prejudices which permits no offense against her secret faiths to be trivial. She has gayety and charm, and at first she is ingenuously fond of this household of persons so closely and tenderly bound, so united in their aims. Nicholas feels quite otherwise. He hates his dear good sweet people who are so warmly kind in small things, so hideously complacent and negligent in the larger essentials. He needs help, restitution really, from this family that has brought him disabled into the world. His father brutally—that is to say, with the utmost fatherly kindness—tells Nicholas that he will give him fifty thousand francs when Bridget has a child. Charlotte's five beautiful children are weak in the legs, but they are "the joy of existence" nonetheless. One's duty is to procreate for the family, however maimed the lives may be.

Bridget, caught in a whirling undercurrent of love and hatred and family intrigue, begins first to fear and then to despise these strangers as she realizes the ignoble motives back of all the family devotion. She sees her husband gradually growing hostile to her as he identifies her with his family, no longer with himself. She is confirmed in her instinctive distrust of situations and feelings sanctified by the rubber stamps of time and custom; she defends herself by mockery and the mental reservation against the blind cruelties and wrongs which are done under cover of love. Luc complicates matters by falling in love with her instead of asking for one of the sisters, but even so he does not speak until it is too late—until it is safe for him to speak, when marriage to one of the sisters is no longer the best investment he can make. And Bridget, who has wavered, been pulled almost to pieces by the tearing, gnawing, secretive antagonisms and separate aims of the family, comes to her conclusion—a rather bitter one, which in the end will solve very badly the problem. Of her own will she takes to herself the seed of decay.

This is no more than a bare and disfiguring outline of the plan of the novel. The whole manner of the telling is superb: there are long passages of prose which crackle and snap with electric energy, episodes in which inner drama and outward events occur against scenes bright with the vividness of things seen by the immediate eye: the bathing party on the beach, the fire in the village, the delicious all-day excursion to Castle Island, the scene in the market when Bridget and Nicholas quarrel, the death of Charlotte, the funeral. Nothing is misplaced or exaggerated, and the masterful use of symbol and allegory clarify and motivate the main great theme beneath the apparent one: the losing battle of youth and strength against the resistless army of age and death. This concept is implicit in the story itself, and it runs like music between the lines. The book is a magnificent performance; and as the short stories left the impression of reservoirs of power hardly tapped, so this novel, complete as it is, seems only a beginning.

HARRY T. MOORE
From "Kay Boyle's Fiction"
Age of the Modern and Other Literary Essays
1971, pp. 32–36

From the time of her first book in 1929, *Wedding Day And Other Stories,* (Kay Boyle's) fate has been occasional high praise and an occasional succès d'estime. Meanwhile, writers far less gifted have been overrated by public and critics alike. At present there are only a few books of Kay Boyle's in print; these fortunately include a hardbound edition of her novel *Monday Night* and paperbacks of *Thirty Stories* and *Three Short Novels* (the last containing one of the masterpieces of this genre in our time, *The Crazy Hunter*). Of her first novel, *Plagued by the Nightingale*, it is safe to say that it is the finest portrait of a French family by a writer from this side of the Atlantic since Henry James fixed his attention upon the Bellegardes in *The American*. Nor is it out of place to mention James here, for Kay Boyle is an important later practitioner in the area in which he worked—"the international theme." Since James, no American except Kay Boyle has concentrated so thoroughly upon that theme.

Despite the excellence of the results, however, Kay Boyle's writing career has had some severe setbacks, partly attributable to timing. She learned to write in the 1920s, when craftsmanship was important, but by the time she began turning out her full-length novels the Depression was on; instead of her subtle penetration of the behavior of Americans in Europe, readers over here wanted what seemed to be the only realities of the moment—rough stories of hunger marchers, factory slaves, or dispossessed tenant farmers. It was a time when entire social classes, rather than individuals, were of dominant interest in fiction, and it was a period when the autobiographical novel was not fashionable; consequently it didn't help Kay Boyle's cause for her to have, in most of her books, a sensitive American girl as the reflector of the action, which usually involved a group of expatriates. Now it may be seen (and I hope it will be seen) that these novels were not indulgently self-centered, not mere personal chronicles, but were rather the reworking of significant experience into fable, intensified by a prose style at once delicate and forcible. Some of these novels were well received, for there have always been intelligent readers who can look beyond the fashions of the moment, but there was no big sale and no spreading critical excitement. And now (except for *Monday Night*) Kay Boyle's fine novels of the 1930s are all out of print: besides *Plagued by the Nightingale*, these include *Year Before Last, Death of a Man, My Next Bride,* and *Gentlemen, I Address You Privately*. They deserve reprinting [and, since this review was written, *Plagued by the Nightingale* and *Year Before Last* have been reprinted in the Crosscurrents/Modern Fiction series].

Unfortunately, after her return from Europe during the Second World War, Kay Boyle began bending her high talent to the production of the fictional fudge of *Saturday Evening Post* serials, with results that were unsatisfactory from the point of view of her early admirers—and probably the readers of popular magazines were not very much pleased either, since a certain amount of subtlety remained amid the melodramatic scenes. In 1944, at a time when Edmund Wilson was exerting great influence with his *New Yorker* causeries, he came upon one of Kay Boyle's serials, *Avalanche*, published as a book, and he brought a weight of ridicule down on it. Reprinted in his brilliant volume *Classic and Commercials*, this essay has continued to damage Kay Boyle's reputation across the years. But it should have risen again with *The Smoking Mountain*, her first book about Germany, which came out in 1951. This collection of stories and sketches was certainly the finest volume of fiction written by an American, up to that time, about Europe after the war. And now, *Generation Without Farewell*, which expands several of the themes of the earlier book, is a worthy successor. Its quality is certainly far beyond the range of other novels about postwar Germany, such as Donald Davidson's *The Steeper Cliff* (1947), William Gardner Smith's *Blood of the Conquerors* (1948), or Clay Putnam's *The Ruined City* (1959)—all of them competent novels, posing moral problems in dramatic situations (Smith's book adds the Negro dilemma), but none of them more than just competent. *Generation Without Farewell* exists in a realm beyond them.

Its Germany is haunted alike by its Gothic and Nazi past and its American present. Most of the Americans in the story, whether well meaning or not, are essentially childlike. They include an army colonel who brings in his wife and college-girl daughter; a post-exchange manager whose Italian ancestry seems to offend the colonel; a sycophantic lieutenant; a marmotlike intelligence officer; and an *Amerika Haus* director named Honerkamp, whose nonconformist thinking is "dangerous"—a man who has hanging behind his office door the *Totentanz* figure of a skeleton found buried in the ruins.

The central consciousness in the story is that of a young German newspaperman, Jaeger, who has been a prisoner of war in the United States. And several of the other characters are Germans, including a young groom who watches over the white Lippizaner horses which (as in Kay Boyle's notable short story, "The White Horses of Vienna") suggest the aristocratic splendor of the past. There is also the battered young actor who presents the Wolfgang Borchert play from whose words this novel takes its title: "We are the generation without farewell. . . . We have many encounters, encounters without duration and without farewell." This applies to most of the relationships in the book, particularly to that of Jaeger and the colonel's wife. He falls in love with her and she responds, but she is abruptly sent away with her daughter, who in her quiet way has also been drawn into Germanic involvements. The colonel hustles his women off before they have a chance for farewells.

This Colonel Roberts, who is suggestively identified with the boar that is rumored to be raiding villages at night, shares a triumph with the intelligence officer when, at the end of the story, the *Amerika Haus* liberal is given dismissal orders. All such events have their parallels in the dark conflicts that take place in the forest where the colonel leads patrol parties by night to track down (ostensibly at least) the illegal hunters reported to be prowling the area in a jeep with covered-over license plates. There are violence and bloodshed in this forest but, since this is among other things a symbolist novel, the meaning of it all is not spelled out so facilely as in a popular type of book such as *The Ugly American*. Many of the same meanings that book drives toward are ultimately to be found here, however, particularly American incompetence in dealing with other nations. Colonel Roberts in this story is the embodiment of the military mind, essentially uneducated and incapable of growth, that has so often damaged America by mixing in government, for which it is untrained and temperamentally unsuited.

These points come to mind because this book is—for all its symbolic bestiary of boar, fox, and Lippizaner horse—also a political story, with politics and symbolism blending in an unusually successful way. For example, the terrible symbol of the buried man, which has a certain kinship with Honerkamp's office skeleton, is political. This "underground" man, accidentally dislodged from the ruined house where he has been immured for three years (a place stocked with food), is seen by Jaeger as he emerges:

> It moved like a spider caught in its own web, like a broken crab, clawing its way up through rusted girders and disjointed stones. . . . The rags of a *Wehrmacht* uniform clung to the figure's bones, the sleeves, the trousers hanging in shreds, slashed back and forth and up and down by outraged time.

Several men had been similarly unearthed in different parts of Germany, but to see one is a new experience for Jaeger who, in writing about the event for his paper, says that every German now "must claw his way out of the depths of what he was, letting the faded, filth-encrusted insignia fall from him, and the medals for military valor drop away." But a defeated chauvinism has been taken over by new chauvinists, and the military mind of the conquerors has no tolerance for the Jaegers or the Honerkamps, who at the last are either frustrated or defeated.

This book is not one of narrow-visioned propaganda; rather it is a later and richer chapter in Kay Boyle's continuing involvement with the international theme, which in our time has new phases. And perhaps this novel will bring her some of the recognition she deserves and will help to place her among the fine women authors of our time who do not write like men (as, say, Willa Cather does), but operate through a distinctly feminine vision (as Dorothy Richardson does), to capture and project experience in a unique and important way.

RAY BRADBURY

1920–

Ray Douglas Bradbury was born on August 22, 1920 in Waukegan, Illinois. He was an avid comic reader, circus aficionado, science fiction fan, and moviegoer, especially after his family moved to Hollywood in 1933. He published a science fiction "fanzine" in high school, then took a job as a newsboy, writing on a daily schedule (which he continues to do).

He began to sell stories to pulp magazines in 1941, and by 1945 had broken into the "slicks"—notably *The Saturday Evening Post* and *Mademoiselle*. His first collection, *Dark Carnival*, was published in 1947, the year he married Marguerite McClure. *The Martian Chronicles* in 1950 was a

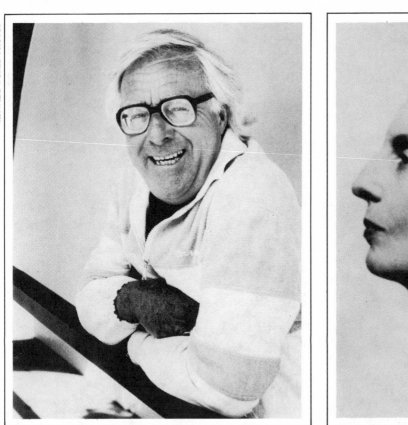

RAY BRADBURY

KAY BOYLE

PAUL BOWLES

PEARL S. BUCK

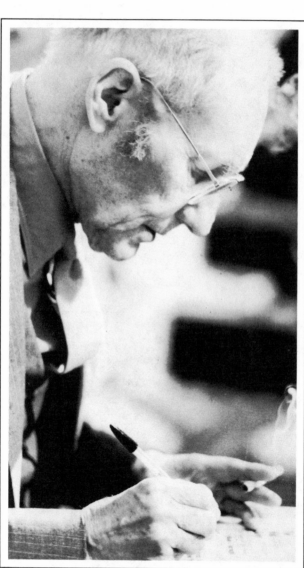

WILLIAM BURROUGHS

GWENDOLYN BROOKS

landmark: written in rich, evocative prose and emphasizing human conflicts over hardware, the book reached a much wider audience than most science fiction. It continues to sell, and was adapted into a TV mini-series in 1980.

Bradbury continued to write stories, some of which were collected in *The Illustrated Man* (1951) and *The Golden Apples of the Sun* (1953). 1953 brought his first novel, *Fahrenheit 451*, a dystopian vision of a future in which firemen burn books. Francois Truffaut filmed it in 1966. *Dandelion Wine* (1957) was not science fiction but rather sentimental tales of Bradbury's childhood in Waukegan, here renamed "Green Town." He integrated this strain in his work with his earlier dark fantasy in *Something Wicked This Way Comes*, a 1962 novel about an evil carnival in a small town.

Since then, Bradbury has concentrated increasingly on poetry and drama. He has adapted many of his stories to the stage—such as *The Wonderful Ice Cream Suit* in 1972—and published his poetry in several volumes, beginning with 1973's *When Elephants Last in the Dooryard Bloomed*. His many screenplays include *It Came From Outer Space* (1953), *Moby Dick* (1956), and the Oscar-nominated short "Icarus Montgolfier Wright" (1962). Bradbury enjoys one of the highest profiles among science fiction authors: he is a frequent talk show guest, and has won innumerable awards. He lives in Los Angeles with his wife; they have four children.

KINGSLEY AMIS
From *New Maps of Hell*
1960, pp. 105–10

B radbury is the Louis Armstrong of science fiction, not in the sense of age or self-repetition but in that he is the one practitioner well known by name to those who know nothing whatever about his field. How this has happened I am not quite sure; perhaps it was that early pat on the head he got from Christopher Isherwood; perhaps it is his tendency to fall into that particular kind of sub-whimsical, would-be poetical badness that goes straight to the corny old heart of the Sunday reviewer:

> Martin knew it was autumn again, for Dog ran into the house bringing wind and frost and a smell of apples turned to cider under trees. In dark clock-springs of hair, Dog fetched goldenrod, dust of farewell-summer, acorn-husk, hair of squirrel, feather of departed robin, sawdust from fresh-cut cordwood, and leaves like charcoals shaken from a blaze of maple-trees. Dog jumped. Showers of brittle fern, blackberry vine, marsh-grass sprang over the bed where Martin shouted. No doubt, no doubt of it at all, this incredible beast was October!

Such a poem in October would certainly appeal to the author of *This Bees Speech*, whose view it was that "article bees prime corruptor of human thinking." Another and much more unlikely reason for Bradbury's fame is that despite his regrettable tendency to dime-a-dozen sensitivity, he is a good writer, wider in range than any of his colleagues, capable of seeing life on another planet as something extraordinary instead of just challenging or horrific, ready to combine this with strongly held convictions. These last, at any rate, appear in his story "Usher II," which opens on Mars with the building of a residence after the prescription in Poe's story, great care having been taken to get the tarn "black and lurid" enough, the sedge satisfactorily "gray and ebon," etc. Inside, there are copper bats controlled by electronic beams, brass rats, robot skeletons, and phantoms. Soon the Investigator of Moral Climates, one Garrett, arrives and orders demolition, under the ordinances which have prohibited and destroyed all works of fantasy from Poe to *The Wizard of Oz*, while no films are allowed except remakes of Ernest Hemingway. There is time for one huge party, at which all the guests are members of the Society for the Prevention of Fantasy and are publicly murdered one after another by robot apes, bisected by pendulums, prematurely buried, and so on. Garrett himself is led into the catacombs by Stendahl, the owner, who mentions Amontillado and produces a mason's trowel without drawing any reaction from Garrett. The rest is soon told:

> "Garrett," said Stendahl, "do you know why I've done this to you? Because you burned Mr. Poe's books without really reading them. You took other people's advice that they needed burning. Otherwise you'd have realized what I was going to do to you when we came down here a moment ago. Ignorance is fatal, Mr. Garrett."
> Garrett was silent.
> "I want this to be perfect," said Stendahl, holding his lantern so its light penetrated in upon the slumped figure. "Jingle your bells softly." The bells rustled. "Now, if you'll please say, 'For the love of God, Montresor,' I might let you free."
> The man's face came up in the light. There was a hesitation. Then grotesquely the man said, "For the love of God, Montresor."
> "Ah," said Stendahl, eyes closed. He shoved the last brick into place and mortared it tight. "*Requiescat in pace*, dear friend."
> He hastened from the catacomb.

The suppression of fantasy, or of all books, is an aspect of the conformist society often mentioned by other writers, but with Bradbury it is a specialty. His novel *Fahrenheit 451*—supposedly the temperature at which book-paper ignites—extends and fills in the assumptions of "Usher II." The hero, Montag, is a fireman, which means that on receiving an alarm he and his colleagues pile on to the wagon and go off and burn somebody's house down, one with books in it, under the regulations of the Firemen of America, "established, 1790, to burn English-influenced books in the Colonies. First Fireman: Benjamin Franklin." In the expected central dialogue, the fire chief explains to Montag how it all came about:

> Classics cut to fit fifteen-minute radio shows, then cut again to fill a two-minute book column, winding up at last as a ten- or twelve-line dictionary resume. I exaggerate, of course. The dictionaries were for reference. But many were those whose sole knowledge of *Hamlet* . . . was a one-page digest in a book that claimed: *now at last you can read all the classics; keep up with your neighbors*. Do you see? Out of the nurs-

ery into the college and back to the nursery; there's your intellectual pattern. . . . Life is immediate, the job counts, pleasure lies all about after work. . . . More sports for everyone, group spirit, fun, and you don't have to think, eh? . . . Authors, full of evil thoughts, lock up your typewriters. . . . We must all be alike. Not everyone born free and equal, as the Constitution says, but everyone *made* equal. Each man the image of every other; then all are happy, for there are no mountains to make them cower, to judge themselves against. So! A book is a loaded gun in the house next door. Burn it. Take the shot from the weapon. . . . Ask yourself, What do we want in this country above all? People want to be happy, isn't that right? Haven't you heard it all your life? I want to be happy, people say. Well, aren't they? Don't we keep them moving, don't we give them fun? That's all we live for, isn't it? For pleasure, for titillation? And you must admit our culture provides plenty of these. . . . If you don't want a man unhappy politically, don't give him two sides to a question to worry him; give him one. Better yet, give him none. . . . Don't give [him] any slippery stuff like philosophy or sociology to tie things up with. That way lies melancholy.

One could offer plenty of objections to that, starting with the apparently small point that complacency about sociology, which Bradbury shares with his colleagues, is at least as bad as complacency about the tabloidisation of the classics, and that what we ought to want is less sociology, not more. Further, there is about Bradbury, as about those I might call the non-fiction holders of his point of view, a certain triumphant lugubriousness, a kind of proleptic *schadenfreude* (world copyright reserved), a relish not always distinguishable here from satisfaction in urging a case, but different from it, and recalling the relish with which are recounted the horrors of *Nineteen Eighty-Four* and a famous passage that prefigures it in *Coming Up for Air*. Jeremiah has never had much success in pretending he doesn't thoroughly enjoy his job, and whereas I agree with him, on the whole, in his dislike of those who reach for their revolver when they hear the word "culture," I myself am getting to the point where I reach for my ear-plugs on hearing the phrase "decline of our culture." But in this respect Bradbury sins no more grievously than his non-fiction colleagues, whom he certainly surpasses in immediacy, for *Fahrenheit 451* is a fast and scaring narrative, a virtue hard to illustrate by quotation. There are at least two good dramatic coups, one when a creature called the Mechanical Hound, constructed to hunt down book-owners and other heretics, looks up from its kennel in the fire station and growls at the hero, the other when Montag goes out on duty with the Salamander, as the fire engine is called, and finds that the alarm refers to his own house. The book emerges quite creditably from a comparison with *Nineteen Eighty-Four* as inferior in power, but superior in conciseness and objectivity. At the end, of course, Montag eludes the Mechanical Hound and joins a band of distinguished hoboes who are preserving the classics by learning them by heart.

Bradbury's is the most skilfully drawn of all science fiction's conformist hells. One invariable feature of them is that however activist they may be, however convinced that the individual can, and will, assert himself, their programme is always to resist or undo harmful change, not to promote useful change. . . . This, however, does not weaken its claim to be regarded as, some of the time and in some sense, a literature of warning, as propaganda, not always unintelligent, against the notion that we can leave the experts to work things out for us.

DAMON KNIGHT
"When I Was in Kneepants: Ray Bradbury"
In Search of Wonder:
Essays on Modern Science Fiction
1967, pp. 108–13

Ray Bradbury began writing professionally at the floodtide of the cerebral story in science fiction—in 1940, when John Campbell was revolutionizing the field with a new respect for facts, and a wholly justified contempt for the overblown emotional values of the thirties. Bradbury, who had nothing but emotion to offer, couldn't sell ⟨to⟩ Campbell.

Bradbury didn't care. He adapted his work just enough to meet the standards of the lesser markets—he filled it with the second-hand furniture of contemporary science fiction and fantasy—and went on writing what he chose.

It's curious to look back now on those first Bradbury stories and reflect how far they have brought their author. Not many of them are stories at all; most are intensely realized fragments, padded out with any handy straw. The substance of "The Next in Line," for one especially vivid example, is in a two-page description of some Mexican mummies, as relentlessly and embarrassingly horrible as any tourist photograph. The remainder—the two American visitors, the car trouble, the hotel room, the magazines—is not relevant, it merely plumps out the skeleton enough to get it into a conventional suit of clothes.

On a story-a-week schedule, Bradbury sold prodigiously to *Weird Tales, Planet Stories, Thrilling Wonder*. One day we awoke to discover that he had leapfrogged over John Campbell's head, outside our microcosm altogether: his work was beginning to appear in *Harper's*; in *Mademoiselle*; in the *O. Henry Prize Stories*; on the radio; in *Esquire, Collier's, The Saturday Evening Post*.

Outside the huge, brightly-colored bubble he had blown around himself, "serious" critics reacted with rapture:

> . . . the sheer lift and power of a truly original imagination exhilarates . . . His is a very great and unusual talent.

> (Christopher Isherwood)

Inside the bubble, we get at once a clearer and a more distorted view of Bradbury. Although he has a large following among science fiction readers, there is at least an equally large contingent of people who cannot stomach his work at all; they say he has no respect for the medium; that he does not even trouble to make his scientific double-talk convincing; that—worst crime of all—he fears and distrusts science.

. . . All of which is true, and—for our present purposes, anyhow—irrelevant. The purists are right in saying that he does not write science fiction, and never has.

To Bradbury, as to most people, radar and rocket ships and atomic power are big, frightening, meaningless names: a fact which, no doubt, has something to do with his popular success, but which does not touch the root of the matter. Bradbury's strength lies in the fact that he writes about the things that are really important to us—not the things we pretend we are interested in—science, marriage, sports, politics, crime—but the fundamental prerational fears and longings and desires: the rage at being born; the will to be loved; the longing to communicate; the hatred of parents and siblings, the fear of things that are not self. . . .

People who talk about Bradbury's imagination miss the point. His imagination is mediocre; he borrows nearly all his backgrounds and props, and distorts them badly; wherever he is required to invent anything—a planet, a Martian, a machine—the image is flat and unconvincing. Bradbury's Mars, where it is not as bare as a Chinese stage-setting, is a mass of inconsistency; his spaceships are a joke; his people have no faces. The vivid images in his work are not imagined; they are remembered.

Here is the shock of birth, in "No Particular Night or Morning":

> "Have you talked about this to the psychiatrist?"
> "So he could try to mortar up the gaps for me, fill in the gulfs with noise and warm water and words and hands touching me . . . ?"

And the death-wish, Bradbury's most recurrent theme:

> . . . When I was living I was jealous of you, Lespere. . . . Women frightened me and I went into space, always wanting them and jealous of you for having them, and money, and as much happiness as you could have in your own wild way. But now, falling here, with everything over, I'm not jealous of you any more, because it's over for you as it is for me, and right now it's like it never was.
>
> ("Kaleidoscope")

> Forty-five thousand people killed every year on this continent . . . made into jelly right in the can, as it were, in the automobiles. Red blood jelly, with white marrow bones like sudden thoughts. . . . The cars roll up in tight sardine rolls—all sauce, all silence.
> . . . You look out your window and see two people lying atop each other in friendly fashion who, a moment ago, had never met before, dead. . . .
>
> ("The Concrete Mixer")

The gulf between Bradbury and the science fiction writers is nowhere more clearly evident than in the lavish similes and metaphors that are his trademarks:

> The first concussion cut the rocket up the side with a giant can opener. The men were thrown into space like a dozen wriggling silverfish.
>
> ("Kaleidoscope")

> . . . And here were the lions now . . . so feverishly and startlingly real that you could feel the prickling fur on your hand, and your mouth was stuffed with the dusty upholstery smell of their heated pelts . . .
>
> ("The Veldt")

The aim of science-fantasy, more and more as it becomes what it has always tried to be—adult fiction—is to expand the imagination, stretch it to include things never before seen or dreamed of. Bradbury's subject is childhood and the buried child-in-man; his aim is to narrow the focus, not to widen it; to shrink all the big frightening things to the compass of the familiar: a spaceship to a tin can; a Fourth of July rocket to a brass kettle; a lion to a Teddy bear.

There is so much to say about Bradbury's meaning that perhaps too little has been said about his technique. He is a superb craftsman, a man who has a great gift and has spent fifteen years laboriously and with love teaching himself to use it. "For here was a kind of writing of which there is never much in any one time—a style at once delicate, economical and unobtrusively firm, sharp enough to cut but without rancor,

and clear as water or air." That's Stephen Vincent Benét, writing in 1938 about Robert Nathan; the same words, all but the next to last phrase, might have been written with equal justice of Bradbury. His imagery is luminous and penetrating, continually lighting up familiar corners with unexpected words. He never lets an idea go until he has squeezed it dry, and never wastes one. I well remember my own popeyed admiration when I read his story about a woman who gave birth to a small blue pyramid; this is exactly the sort of thing that might occur to any imaginative writer in a manic or drunken moment; but Bradbury wrote it and sold it.

Why Bradbury's world-line and that of the animated cartoon have never intersected, I do not know; perhaps because the result would necessarily scare the American theater-going public out of its underpants; but clearly, in such stories as "Jack-in-the-Box," Bradbury is writing for no other medium. The gaudy colors and plush textures, the dream-swift or dream-slow motion, or contrariwise, the ballooning of a face into the foreground—these are all distinctive techniques of the animated cartoon, and Bradbury uses them all.

As for the rancor, the underlying motif of much early Bradbury, the newer stories show little of it; this might be taken as a sign that Bradbury is mellowing in his thirties, and perhaps he is; I have the feeling that he is rather trying to mellow—deliberately searching for something equally strong, equally individual, less antagonistic toward the universe that buys his stories. I don't think he has yet found it. There's the wry, earthy humor of "En la Noche," the pure fancy of "The Golden Kite, The Silver Wind"; these are neutral stories, anyone might have written them. There are the moralistic tales; if you find the moral palatable, as I do in "The Big Black and White Game" and "Way in the Middle of the Air," these are sincere and moving; if you don't, as I don't in "Powerhouse" or "The Fire Balloons," there is a pious flatness about them. Then there is sentiment; and since Bradbury does nothing by halves, it is sentiment that threatens continually to slop over into sentimentality. At its precarious peak, it is a moving and vital thing: when it slops, it is—no other word will do—sickening.

It has been said of Bradbury that, like H. P. Lovecraft, he was born a century or so too late. I think he would have been a castaway in any age; if he would like to destroy airplanes, television sets, automatic washing machines, it's not because they make loud noises or because they have no faces or even because some of them kill people, but because they are grown-up things; because they symbolize the big, loud, faceless, violent, unromantic world of adults.

Childhood is after all Bradbury's one subject. When he writes of grown-up explorers visiting the sun or the Jurassic jungles, they are palpably children playing at spacemen or time-travelers. He writes feelingly and with sharp perception of young women and of old people—because, I think, he finds them childlike. But it's only when the theme becomes explicit that his song sings truest:

> The boys were playing on the green park diamond when he came by. He stood a little while among the oak-tree shadows, watching them hurl the white, snowy baseball into the warm summer air, saw the baseball shadow fly like a dark bird over the grass, saw their hands open in mouths to catch this swift piece of summer that now seemed most especially important to hold onto. . . .
> How tall they stood to the sun. In the last few months it seemed the sun had passed a hand above their heads, beckoned, and they were warm metal drawn melting upwards; they were golden taffy pulled

by an immense gravity to the sky, thirteen, fourteen years old, looking down upon Willie, smiling, but already beginning to neglect him. . . .

Learned opinion to the contrary, Bradbury is not the heir of Poe, Irving or Hawthorne; his voice is the voice (a little shriller) of Christopher Morley and Robert Nathan and J. D. Salinger. As his talent expands, some of his stories become pointed social commentary; some are surprisingly effective religious tracts, disguised as science fiction; others still are nostalgic vignettes; but under it all is still Bradbury the poet of 20th-century neurosis, Bradbury the isolated spark of consciousness, awake and alone at midnight; Bradbury the grown-up child who still remembers, still believes.

The young Ray Bradbury wrote a story called "Skeleton," about a man obsessed by the fact that he carries a horrid, white, grinning skeleton inside him. The story was raw, exuberant, gauche, pretentious, insulting to the intellect, and unforgettable. *Weird Tales* published it, and later it appeared in Bradbury's first collection, *Dark Carnival*.

The story did not soothe its readers' anxieties nor pamper their prejudices, nor provide vicarious adventure in a romantic setting. Far from solving his problem by his own courage and resourcefulness, the hero let it be solved for him by a strange little man named Munigant, who crawled down his throat, gnawed, crunched and munched away the bones which had so annoyed him, and left him lying on his carpet, a human jelly-fish.

Time passed; Bradbury got a little older, stopped running quite so hard. His stories acquired depth, smoothness, polish. Little by little he stopped writing about corpses, vampires, cemeteries, things in jars; instead, he wrote about civil rights, religion and good home cooking. The slicks, which had begun buying him as a curiosity when he was horrid, kept on buying him as a staple when he turned syrupy.

Dandelion Wine consists of sixteen loosely connected tales without a ghost or a goblin in them; they are familiar in tone and rhythm, but these stories are no longer what we mean by fantasy; they are what Hollywood means by fantasy. The setting is an imaginary Midwestern town, seen through the wrong end of a rose-colored glass. The period is as vague as the place; Bradbury calls it 1928, but it has no feeling of genuine recollection; most of the time it is like second-hand 1910.

Childhood is Bradbury's one subject, but you will not find real childhood here, Bradbury's least of all. What he has had to say about it has always been expressed obliquely, in symbol and allusion, and always with the tension of the outsider—the ex-child, the lonely one. In giving up this tension, in diving with arms spread into the glutinous pool of sentimentality that has always been waiting for him, Bradbury has renounced the one thing that made him worth reading.

All the rest is still here: the vivid images, the bombardment of tastes and sounds and smells; the clipped, faceless prose; the heavy nostalgia, the cuteness, the lurking impudence. The phrases, as before, are poignant, ("with the little gray toad of a heart flopping weakly here or there in his chest") or silly to the point of self-parody ("lemon-smelling men's room"). The characters are as lifelike as Bradbury's characters ever were: bright, pert, peppermint-stick people, epicene, with cotton-candy hair and sugar smiles.

Maybe Bradbury, like his own protagonist in "Skeleton," grew uneasy about the macabre forces in himself: or maybe success, that nemesis of American writers, was Bradbury's M. Munigant. Whatever the reason, the skeleton has vanished; what's left is recognizable but limp.

A. JAMES STUPPLE
From "The Past, the Future, and Ray Bradbury"
Voices for the Future:
Essays on Major Science Fiction Writers
ed. Thomas Clareson
1976, pp. 175–84

Anyone who has ever watched those classic "Flash Gordon" serials must have been puzzled by the incongruous meeting of the past and the future which runs through them. Planet Mongo is filled with marvelous technological advancements. Yet, at the same time, it is a world which is hopelessly feudal, filled with endless sword play and courtly intrigues. It is as if we travel deep within the future only to meet instead the remote and archaic past. This is not, however, a special effect peculiar to adolescent space operas. On the contrary, this overlapping of past and future is one of the most common features of science fiction. It is found, for example, in such highly acclaimed works as Frank Herbert's *Dune* and Ursula LeGuin's *The Left Hand of Darkness*, futuristic novels whose settings are decidedly "medieval." A similar effect is also created in such philosophical science fiction novels as Isaac Asimov's *Foundation* trilogy, Walter Miller's *A Canticle for Leibowitz*, and Anthony Burgess' *The Wanting Seed*. In each of these works a future setting allows the novelist an opportunity to engage in an historiographical analysis; in each the future provides the distance needed for a study of the patterns of the past. But of all the writers of science fiction who have dealt with this meeting of the past and the future, it is Ray Bradbury whose treatment has been the deepest and most sophisticated. What has made Bradbury's handling of this theme distinctive is that his attitudes and interpretations have changed as he came to discover the complexities and the ambiguities inherent in it.

Bradbury began to concentrate upon this subject early in his career in *The Martian Chronicles* (1951). In a broad sense, the past in this work is represented by the Earth—a planet doomed by nuclear warfare, a "natural" outgrowth of man's history. To flee from this past, Earthmen begin to look to a future life on Mars, a place where the course of man's development has not been irrevocably determined. But getting a foothold on Mars was no easy matter, as the deaths of the members of the first two expeditions show. To Captain Black's Third Expedition, however, Mars seems anything but an alien, inhospitable planet, for as their rocket lands in April of the year 2000, the Earthmen see what looks exactly like an early twentieth century village. Around them they see the cupolas of old Victorian mansions, neat, whitewashed bungalows, elm trees, maples and chestnuts. Initially Black is skeptical. The future cannot so closely resemble the past. Sensing that something is wrong, he refuses to leave the ship. Finally one of his crewmen argues that the similarity between this Martian scene and those of his American boyhood may indicate that there is some order to the universe after all—that perhaps there is a supreme being who actually does guide and protect mankind.

Black agrees to investigate. Setting foot on Martian soil, the Captain enters a peaceful, delightful world. It is "a beautiful spring day" filled with the scent of blossoming flowers and the songs of birds. After the flux of space travel it must have appeared to have been a timeless, unchanging world—a static piece of the past. But Black is certain that this is Mars and persists in his attempt to find a rational explanation. His logical mind, however, makes it impossible for him to accept any facile solutions. Eventually, though, despite his intellectual rigor, the Captain begins to succumb to the charms of stasis:

> In spite of himself, Captain John Black felt a great peace come over him. It had been thirty years since he had been in a small town, and the buzzing of spring bees on the air lulled and quieted him, and the fresh look of things was a balm to his soul.

As soon as he begins to weaken, he learns, from a lemonade-sipping matron, that this is the year 1926 and that the village is Green Town, Illinois, Black's own home town. The Captain now *wants* to believe in what he sees and begins to delude himself by theorizing that an unknown early twentieth century expedition came to Mars and that the colonizers, desperately homesick, created such a successful image of an Earth-like reality that they had actually begun to believe that this illusion *was* reality. Ironically, this is precisely what is done by Black and his crew. And it kills them.

Since by this time the Earthmen had become completely vulnerable to the seductiveness of this world of security and stasis, they now unreservedly accept "Grandma Lustig's" claim that "'all we know is here we are, alive again, and no questions asked. A second chance.'" At this point the action moves rapidly. The remainder of the crew abandons ship and joins in a "homecoming" celebration. At first Black is furious at this breach of discipline, but soon loses his last trace of skepticism when he meets Edward, his long-dead "brother." Quickly, he is taken back to his childhood home, "the old house on Oak Knoll Avenue," where he is greeted by an archetypal set of midwestern parents: "In the doorway, Mom, pink, plump, and bright. Behind her, pepper-gray, Dad, his pipe in his hand." Joyfully the Captain runs "like a child" to meet them. But later, in the apparent security of the pennant-draped bedroom of his youth, Black's doubts arise anew. He begins to realize that all of this could be an elaborate reconstruction, culled from his psyche by some sophisticated Martian telepathy, created for the sole purpose of isolating the sixteen members of the Third Expedition. Recognizing the truth too late, the Captain is killed by his Martian brother as he leaves his boyhood "home" to return to the safety of the rocket ship.

Bradbury's point here is clear: Black and his men met their deaths because of their inability to forget, or at least resist, the past. Thus, the story of this Third Expedition acts as a metaphor for the book as a whole. Again and again the Earthmen make the fatal mistake of trying to recreate an Earth-like past rather than accept the fact that this is Mars—a different, unique new land in which they must be ready to make personal adjustments. Hauling Oregon lumber through space, then, merely to provide houses for nostalgic colonists exceeds folly; it is only one manifestation of a psychosis which leads to the destruction not only of Earth, but, with the exception of a few families, of Mars as well.

On the surface, at least, Bradbury's novel, *Dandelion Wine* (1959), bears little resemblance to the classic science fiction of *The Martian Chronicles*. The setting is not Mars or some even more remote corner of the universe, but Green Town, Illinois, a familiar, snug American home town, obviously the Waukegan of the author's own childhood. The time is not the distant future but the summer of 1928. Neither are there any exotic alien characters, but instead, a cast of middle-Americans resembling more a Norman Rockwell painting than science fiction; and the novel's protagonist, rather than being a galaxy-spanning super-hero, is only Douglas Spaulding, a twelve-year-old boy more in the tradition of Tom Sawyer than Flash Gordon. In some ways, in fact, the novel seems to be anti-science fiction. A "time machine" is not, as one would

expect, a marvel of science and technology, but an old man. And a so-called "happiness machine" built by the local inventor is a failure, whereas the true happiness machine is that foundation of Green Town life, the family. But despite the fact that it cannot be called science fiction, *Dandelion Wine* closely resembles *The Martian Chronicles* and much of Bradbury's other writing in that it is essentially concerned with the same issue—the dilemma created by the dual attractions of the past and the future, of stasis and change.

In *Dandelion Wine* Bradbury uses the experiences of his adolescent protagonist during one summer to dramatize this set of philosophical and psychological conflicts. At twelve, Douglas Spaulding finds himself on the rim of adolescence. On one side of him lies the secure, uncomplicated world of childhood, while on the other is the fascinating yet frightening world of "growing up." For Doug the summer of 1928 begins with the dizzying discovery that he is "alive." With this new awareness of self comes a desire to experience as much of life as possible. To aid him in this quest, to give him the speed needed to keep up with the fast moving flow of experience, Doug buys a new pair of "Cream-Sponge Para Litefoot Shoes" which will make him so fast that, as he tells the shoe salesman, "'you'll see twelve of me.'" "'Feel those shoes, Mr. Sanderson,'" Douglas asks, "'*feel* how fast they'd make me? All those springs inside? Feel how they kind of grab hold and can't let you alone and don't like you just standing there?'" Clearly Doug is ready to move and to grow. In his new sneakers he welcomes the flux.

Soon, however, just when his shoes are getting broken in, Douglas learns that motion and change are not always good. As he is hiking with John Huff, his best friend, he is suddenly attracted by an opposite force:

> Douglas walked thinking it would go on this way forever. The perfection, the roundness . . . all of it was complete, everything could be touched, things stayed near, things were at hand and would remain.

Soon, this attraction to stasis was considerably increased when John informed Douglas that he and his family were leaving town. It is at this point that Doug comes to fully realize the dangers of movement and change:

> For John was running, and this was terrible. Because if you ran, time ran. . . . The only way to keep things slow was to watch everything and do nothing! You could stretch a day to three days sure, just by watching.

Faced now with the realization that change has a negative, destructive edge, Doug attempts to bring about stasis. The boys play "statues," a game in which the players must remain stationary until released by the player who is "it." But Douglas takes the game far more seriously than John. He attempts to use it to keep John from leaving, and when his friend protests that "'I got to go,'" Douglas snaps, "'Freeze.'" Finally John flees, leaving Doug as the statue, listening to his friend's footsteps merging with the pounding of his own heart. "'Statues are best,'" he thinks to himself. "'They're the only things you can keep on your own. Don't ever let them move. Once you do, you can't do a thing with them.'"

At this point the attractions of stasis have become greater than those of process and change. He is now drawn, with greater frequency, to "Summer's Ice House," just as he becomes more interested in the static world of his brother's statistical charts. His visits to hear the stories of olden times told by Colonel Freeleigh (himself rigidly confined to a wheelchair) become ever more frequent. And the enticements of a timeless, pastoral life become more difficult to resist, as on the day when

Doug accompanied Mr. Tridden, the conductor, on a last trolley ride to the end of the line (buses were being brought in to move people *faster*). This was a day devoid of movement, "a drifting, easy day, nobody rushing, and the forest all about, the sun held in one position. . . ." Douglas is also increasingly drawn to the local penny arcade, a place which offers him the security that only repetition and stasis can bring. This was "a world completely set in place, predictable, certain, sure." Here, the various exhibits were frozen, activated only occasionally. Here the Keystone Kops were "forever in collision or near-collision with train, truck, streetcar," and here there were "worlds within worlds, the penny peek shows which you cranked to repeat old rites and formulas."

But just as he learned of the negative aspects of change, so Douglas, in his summer of discovery, becomes aware of the dangers of stasis. His friends believe that the ice house is the abode of "the Lonely One"—Bradbury's corny personification of death. Even pastoralism held dangers. As an intensification of this pastoral world, the ravine which cut through the town was even more threatening and ominous than the ice plant. Emitting "a dark-sewer, rotten-foliage, thick green odor," this ravine goes beyond stasis, suggesting death and decay. The pastoral mode evoked a similar feeling in old Helen Loomis, a woman who had enjoyed several "long green afternoons" in her garden with Bill Forester, a young newspaperman who, like Douglas, was fascinated by stasis. Wise from her ninety-five years of life, Miss Loomis gives Forester advice which might well apply to Doug as well:

> You shouldn't be here this afternoon. This is a street which ends only in an Egyptian pyramid. Pyramids are all very nice, but mummies are hardly fit companions.

What she is telling Forester is that stasis, although alluring, leads to petrification and death, a fact which Douglas, himself, was soon to learn in the arcade.

As he sees the Tarot Witch "frozen" in her "glass coffin," Douglas suddenly shivers with understanding. He now perceives the connections between stasis and non-being. The fortune teller is actually trapped in her glass tomb, brought to life only when someone slips a coin in the slot. This creates in Douglas the awareness that just as he is alive, so "someday, I, Douglas Spaulding, must die." Seeing the similarity in his and the witch's situations, he becomes obsessed with freeing her from the spell in which she has been cast by "Mr. Black," the arcade owner. Ironically, Douglas is successful in liberating her (he shatters the case) but he, himself, falls into a spell—a deep and mysterious coma. So as the cicadas herald those late summer midwestern days when time seems suspended, Douglas' condition approaches stasis.

Bradbury seems to be reiterating what he has said in *The Martian Chronicles*—that the past, or stasis, or both, is enticing but deadly, and that Douglas, like the colonists, must forsake the past and give himself up to change and progress. But it is not so simple and clear-cut. Douglas recovers and is once again ready to grow and develop. But what brings him out of his coma is a swallow of a liquid which Mr. Jonas, the junk man, has concocted out of pieces of the past (such as Arctic air from the year 1900). With this development, Bradbury's thesis seems to fall to pieces, for Douglas is saved for the future by the past. He is liberated from a static condition by bottled stasis. The ambiguous nature of his recovery is further compounded by the strange, anti-climactic nature of the last chapters of the novel in which Bradbury indulges in a nostalgic celebration of old-fashioned family life. This conclusion so detracts from the story of Doug and his rebirth that one can only conclude that the author was confused, or more probably ambivalent, about these past-future, stasis-change dichotomies.

It is evident, then, that in *Dandelion Wine*, Bradbury began to become aware of the complexity of his subject. Where in *The Martian Chronicles* he seemed confident in his belief that a meaningful future could only be realized by rejecting the past, in this later novel he appears far less certain about the relative values of the past and stasis. Perhaps in this regard Bradbury can be seen as representative of a whole generation of middle class Americans who have found themselves alternately attracted to the security of an idealized, timeless, and static past (as the current nostalgia vogue illustrates) and the exciting, yet threatening and disruptive future world of progress and change, especially technological change. One might see in his leaving the provincial security and simplicity of Waukegan, his Green Town, as a youth and traveling cross country into the modern, futuristic setting of Los Angeles just how this conflict might have taken hold of Bradbury's mind and imagination.

But one may also go beyond these personal and sociological explanations for his obsession with this subject and place it within an aesthetic context. As a genre, science fiction (and my comments on *Dandelion Wine* notwithstanding, Bradbury is primarily a science fiction writer) must deal with the future and with technological progress. This is its lifeblood and what gives it its distinctiveness. In order to enter the future, however, if only in a theoretical, purely speculative sense, one is forced to come to grips with the past. Change and progress call for a rejection and a sloughing off. This places a great stress upon the science fiction writer, for perhaps more than any other literary genre, science fiction is dependent upon traditions—its own conventions of character, plot, setting, "special effects," even ideas. It is as stylized an art form as one can find today in America. It is therefore ironic that such a conventionalized genre should be called upon to be concerned with the unconventional—with the unpredictability of change and process. In other words, this stasis-change conflict, besides being a function of Bradbury's own history and personality, also seems to be built into the art form itself. What distinguishes Bradbury and gives his works their depth is that he seems to be aware that a denial of the past demands a denial of that part of the self which is the past. As an examination of *I Sing the Body Electric*, his lastest collection of short stories, will show, he has not been able to come to any lasting conclusion. Instead, he has come to recognize the ambiguity, the complexity, and the irony within this theme.

Of the stories in *I Sing the Body Electric* which develop the idea that the past is destructive and must be rejected before peace can be achieved, the most intense and suggestive is "Night Call Collect." In this grim little tale, eighty-year-old Emil Barton has been living for the past sixty years as the last man on Mars when he is shocked to receive a telephone call from, of all people, himself. In the depths of his loneliness Barton had tinkered with the possibilities of creating a disembodied voice which might autonomously carry on conversations. Now suddenly in the year 2097, long after he had forgotten about this youthful diversion, his past, in the form of his younger self, contacts him. Finding himself in a world peopled only by the permutations of his own self, the "elder" Barton tries desperately to break out of this electronic solipsism. He fails, however, and begins to feel "the past drowning him." Soon his younger self even becomes bold enough to warn him, "'All right, old man, its war! Between us. Between me.'" Bradbury has obviously added a new twist to his theme. Instead of the future denying the past, it is reversed: Now the past, in order to maintain its existence, must kill off the present. Young Barton now tells his "future" self that he "'had to eliminate you in some way, so I could live, if you call a transcription living.'" As the old man dies, it is obvious that Bradbury has restated his belief that the past, if held on to too tightly, can destroy. But there is an added dimension here. At the end of the story it is no longer clear which is the past, which is the present, and which is the future. Is the past the transcribed voice of the "younger" twenty-four-year-old, or is it the *old* man living at a later date in time? Or perhaps they are but two manifestations of the same temporal reality, both the "present" and the "future" being forgotten?

Of the stories in this collection one contradicts "Night Call Collect" by developing the idea that the past can be a positive, creative force. "I Sing the Body Electric" opens with the death of a mother. But, as in so many of Bradbury's writings, there is a possibility of a second chance. "Fantocinni, Ltd." offers "the first humanoid-genre minicircuited, rechargable AC-DC Mark V Electrical Grandmother." This time the second chance succeeds: the electric grandmother is the realization of a child's fantasy. She can gratify all desires and pay everyone in the family all the attention he or she wants. Appropriately, the grandmother arrives at the house packed in a "sarcaphagous," as if it were a mummy. Despite the pun, the machine is indeed a mummy, as the narrator makes clear:

> We knew that all our days were stored in her, and that any time we felt we might want to know what we said at x hour at x second at x afternoon, we just named that x and with amiable promptitude . . . she should deliver forth x incident.

The sarcaphagous in which this relic was packed was covered with "hieroglyphics of the future." At first this seems to be only another of those gratuitous "special effects" for which science fiction writers are so notorious. After further consideration, however, those arcane markings can be seen as a symbol for the kind of ultra-sophisticated technology of which the grandmother is an example. Thus, both the future and the past are incarnated within the body of this machine. The relationship between the two is important, for what the story seems to suggest is that what the future (here seen as technological progress) will bring is the static, familiar, secure world of the past.

There is one other story in this collection which is important because in it is found one of Bradbury's most sophisticated expositions of the subtle complexities of this theme. "Downwind from Gettysburg" is, once again, a tale about a second chance. Using the well-known Disneyland machine as his model, Bradbury's story concerns a mechanical reproduction of Abraham Lincoln. In itself, this Lincoln-robot is a good thing. The past has been successfully captured and the beloved President lives again, if only in facsimile. Within this limited framework, then, the "past" is a positive force. But there are complications, for just as Lincoln gets a second chance, so does his murderer. Just as John Wilkes Booth assassinated a Lincoln, so does Norman Llewellyn Booth. Thus, as Bradbury had discovered through his years of working with this theme, the past is not one-dimensional. It is at once creative and destructive. It can give comfort, and it can unsettle and threaten. Clearly, then, this story is an important one within Bradbury's canon, for it is just this set of realizations which he had been steadily coming to during two decades of writing.

GWENDOLYN BROOKS

1917–

Gwendolyn Brooks was born on June 7, 1917, in Topeka, Kansas, but grew up in Chicago. At age seven she began to write poetry, which appeared in magazines and newspapers throughout her adolescence. After graduating in 1936 from Wilson Junior College, she worked as publicity director for the NAACP Youth Council in Chicago. Brooks married Henry Blakely in 1939; they had two children, and were later divorced.

Her career took off in 1945 with the publication of her first book of poems, *A Street in Bronzeville*. Its acclaim was immediate: Brooks received a grant from the National Institute of Arts and Letters the next year, as well as a Guggenheim Fellowship. Her next book, *Annie Allen* (1949), won her the Pulitzer Prize for poetry, making her the first black Pulitzer winner. More poems followed, as well as several children's books, frequent book reviews, and the novel *Maud Martha* (1953).

In the late 1960s Brooks became increasingly concerned with black issues: she left Harper, her longtime publisher, for the black-owned Broadside Press, submitted her poetry to black-edited journals only, and edited the magazine *Black Position* and several anthologies of work by young black writers. She continues to write, and has collected numerous literary awards, including several dozen honorary doctorates. In 1969 she was named Poet Laureate of the State of Illinois. Brooks has taught at City College, the University of Wisconsin at Madison, Northeastern Illinois University, Elmhurst College, and Columbia College in Illinois. The first volume of her autobiography, *Report from Part One*, appeared in 1972. She lives in Chicago.

General

Gwendolyn Brooks does not exactly hymn "at heaven's gates," but she takes care of things below in a likable and knowing way. She has a warm heart, a cool head and practices the art of poetry with professional naturalness. Her ability to distinguish between what is sad and what is silly is unfailing, and she deals with race, love, war and other matters with uncommon common sense and a mellow humor that is as much a rarity as it is a relief. Sometimes she is overly sentimental or gets too involved with furniture and ephemera, but on the whole, ⟨*Selected Poems*⟩, which collects three earlier books, otherwise out of print, and a group of new poems, is a pleasure to read.

Good poetry describes itself best. Here are a few lines for hints: "Her affable extremes are like sweet bombs/About him . . ."; "The Mickey Mouse/However, is for everyone in the house;" "I pull you down my foxhole. Do you mind?" Not to mention whole fine poems with titles like "the white troops had their orders but the Negroes looked like men," "hunchback girl: she thinks of heaven," and "my dreams, my works, must wait till after hell."

Miss Brooks won a Pulitzer prize in 1950 and deserved it.—CARL MORSE, "All Have Something to Say," *NYTBR*, Oct. 6, 1963, pp. 4, 28

Of all Negro practitioners, only LeRoi Jones demands the same degree of poetic respect as Gwendolyn Brooks. They share a seriousness of poetic purpose, an intensely modern idiom (as opposed to Langston Hughes' "timelessness"), and a coterie audience (as opposed to his popularity). But Jones is a beatific, Blakean disbeliever in words, thrashing out raw problems of self-definition and epistemological truth in hopeless, anti-verbal expressions, all pain and incoherence. For Gwendolyn Brooks, at the other extreme, the issues, the self have all been sublimated into problems of craft, problems which she precisely and coolly solves.

What she seems to have done is to have chosen, as her handle on the "real" (often the horribly real), the other reality of craftsmanship, of technique. With this she has created a highly stylized screen of imagery and diction and sound—fastidiously exact images, crisp Mandarin diction, ice-perfect sound—to stand between the reader and the subject; to stand often so glittering and sure that all he can ever focus on is the screen. The "subjects"—racial discrimination, mother love, suffering—are dehumanized into *manerismo* figurines, dancing her meters. It is *her* intelligence, *her* imagination, *her* brilliant wit and wordplay that entrap the attention. Always, the subjects are held at arm's length away. Whoever the persona—and she is often forced to make the speakers fastidious, alienated creatures like herself—it is always her mind and her style we are dwelling in.—DAVID LITTLEJOHN, *Black on White*, 1966, pp. 89–90

The immediate occasion for her reception of the Pulitzer Prize was the publication of her *Annie Allen*, a connected sequence of poems tracing the progress to mature womanhood of a Negro girl, the counterpart, in striking ways, except for death in childbirth, of Emily of *Our Town*. . . . The life of women, particularly Negro women, and the life of Negroes, particularly those who have grown up since World War I in the North, where America's big towns are, figure prominently in Miss Brooks's poetry. . . .

Miss Brooks has assimilated, well and easily, her share of avant-garde techniques, and she uses them with no embarrassment or apparent animosity for them. Yet she seems to be a lover of old things, too. Her verse is often free. But often, too, it rhymes, in ways that poets have rhymed immemorially. And one will find that she resorts much to stanzas of the old kind, two lines or three lines or four lines, or more, in regular recurrence or a quickly discernible pattern, as poets once used to do. In *Annie Allen* even, she has sonnets, at least one of them, "First Fight. Then Fiddle," with a constantly growing circle of admirers for its exceptional qualities as a poem. . . .

Satin-Legs Smith (protagonist of *The Sundays of Satin-Legs Smith*) superficially is a creature of no consequence; and he is, indeed, the new *Lumpenproletariat par excellence*. His

Sundays are the big days of his week. On Sundays he fills (an empty word) his leisure time with diversions which express the best his world, and his conceptions of magnificence, can offer him. And what he does, like what he is, would be comic, were it all not so tragic against the background of the lost promise of the twentieth century. Her *Street in Bronzeville* and her *In the Mecca*, in all seriousness, could be used as reference works in sociology. Her *Annie Allen* quietly demonstrates the wealth of her observation of normal, not abnormal, psychology. . . . Terseness, a judicious understatement combined with pregnant ellipses, often guides the reader into an adventure which permits a revelation of Miss Brooks's capacity for sensitive interpretations of the human comedy. She never writes on "big" subjects. One finds on her agenda no librettos for Liberia, no grand excursus into history like ⟨Robert Hayden's⟩ "Middle Passage." *Annie Allen* typifies her method, the study, as it were, of the flower in the crannied wall. In such a method her genius operates within its area of greatest strength, the close inspection of a limited domain, to reap from that inspection, perhaps paradoxically, but still powerfully, a view of life in which one may see a microscopic portion of the universe intensely and yet, through that microscopic portion, see all truth for the human condition wherever it exists.—BLYDEN JACKSON, *Black Poetry in America*, 1974, pp. 81–83

Works

Two sections of ⟨*A Street in Bronzeville*⟩, including the one that gives it its title, represent rather unexciting vignettes of sentiment and character. They have, however, something of the spice and movement which many of the better Negro poets commonly lend to their work. No doubt a great bulk of the proficient and marketable poems written by poets of whatever color deal with such sure-fire or easy-mark situations as those in these groups. The good child envies the bad. Dreams are hard to sustain amid onion fumes or where red fat roaches stroll up one's wall. God must be lonely. The hunchback speculates on heaven. Yet even these sketches are somewhat safeguarded in the present case by some actuality of detail, freshness of image, dryness of angle or flexibility of tempo. Thus in *the funeral*:

> . . . The flowers provide a kind of heat. Sick
> Thick odor-loveliness winds nicely about the
>   shape of mourning.
> A dainty horror. People think of flowers upon rot—
> And for moments together the corpse is no
>   colder than they.

More interesting are several longer portraits and ballads. Thus, *The Sundays of Satin-Legs Smith*. Here the Negro's drive towards splendor, ceremony and gusto, however handicapped, is effectively evoked.

> He sheds, with his pajamas, shabby days.
> And his desertedness, his intricate fear, the
> Postponed resentments and the prim precautions.

In his closet, to chose from as he rises are

>   . . . wonder-suits in yellow and in wine,
>   Sarcastic green and zebra-striped cobalt.

and

>   Here are hats
>   Like bright umbrellas; and hysterical ties. . . .

The poem excels the others in its generality of significance. Satin-Legs is a paradigm to suggest the immitigable limitations on all such aspirations:

Below the tinkling trade of little coins
The gold impulse not possible to show
Or spend. Promise piled over and betrayed.

Equally interesting though in quite a different character is the sonnet series with a war reference, *Gay Chaps at the Bar*. Here elements of sophistication both of craft and theme are added to the volatile quality of the author's talent. And one recognizes, though not too obviously, the reading in modern poets that no doubt underlies the competence of her work. A sonnet on the inimitableness and uniqueness of each body— "Each body has its art"—suggests Hopkins' familiar angle of vision. And something of Auden's "Sir, no man's enemy" appears to underlie the unconventional prayer:

Out from Thy shadows, from Thy pleasant
        meadows,
Quickly, in undiluted light. Be glad, whose
Mansions are bright, to right Thy children's air.
If Thou be more than hate or atmosphere
Step forth in splendor, mortify our wolves.
Or we assume a sovereignty ourselves:

All in all, despite the fact that this first book has its share of unexciting verse, there are considerable resources evidenced for future work. Miss Brooks, to use one of her own phrases, "scrapes life with a fine-tooth comb." And she shows a capacity to marry the special quality of her racial experience with the best attainments of our contemporary poetry tradition. Such compounding of resources out of varied stocks and traditions is the great hope of American art as it is of American life generally.—Amos N. Wilder, "Sketches from Life," *Poetry*, Dec. 1945, pp. 164–66

Miss Brooks is a very accomplished poet indeed, often boiling her lines down to the sparsest expression of the greatest meaning, sometimes almost to a kind of word-shorthand that defies immediate grasp. Less simple and direct than the poems in her initial volume, those in *Annie Allen* give, upon careful reading, as much interest and emotional impact. The book is a mood story in varying poetic forms of a girl's growth from childhood to the age of love, marriage, and motherhood.

There are sharp pictures of neighborhoods, relatives, friends, illnesses and deaths; of big city slums, cafes, and beauty shops. To me the third section, containing about half the poems in the book, "The Womanhood", is its most effective. The qualms, the longings, the love of a poor mother for her child is here most movingly expressed:

The little lifting helplessness, the queer
Whimper-whine; whose unridiculous
Lost softness softly makes a trap for us.

And from another poem:

Life for my child is simple, and is good.
He knows his wish. . . .
Like kicking over a chair or throwing blocks out of a
    window
Or tipping over an ice box pan. . . .
But never has he been afraid to reach.
His lesions are legion.
But reaching is his rule.

The people and the poems in Gwendolyn Brooks' book are alive, reaching, and very much of today.—Langston Hughes, "Name, Race, and Gift in Common," *Voices*, Winter 1950, pp. 55–56

"She was learning to love moments. To love moments for themselves." And this tale ⟨*Maud Martha*⟩ of Maud Martha Brown's youth, marriage and motherhood is made up of the moments she loved. With a few exceptions when straightforward narrative takes over, it is presented in flashes, almost gasps, of sensitive lightness—distillations of the significance of each incident—and reminds of Imagist poems or clusters of ideograms from which one recreates connected experience. Miss Brooks' prose style here embodies the finer qualities of insight and rhythm that were notable in her two earlier books of poetry (her *Annie Allen* received the Pulitzer Prize), and gives a freshness, a warm cheerfulness as well as a depth of implication to her first novel. In technique and impression it stands virtually alone of its kind.

Her Negro heroine's life in Chicago is outwardly simple and not extraordinary: childhood, school, deaths of relatives, dates with young men, envy of her sister's beauty, and at last marriage and the slow flight of daydreams and aspirations as carefree youth flees away. What is extraordinary are Maud Martha's reactions to all this and Miss Brooks' achievement in projecting it as a novel full of living yet full of economy and restraint. After marriage to Paul Phillips, who is not exactly her ideal, Maud Martha faces disturbances which she must triumph over.

Their home is not as fine as she had hoped; Paul is not much interested in intellectual or artistic matters, and, moreover she is achingly conscious that he, much lighter in color, is faintly ashamed of her; she struggles against jealousy. But they stay together, have a baby girl, face the threat of war and its deprivations, the delicate pressure of the color line and the closing trap of near poverty. In spite of it all Maud Martha, in her "moment" that ends the book, is asking, "What, *what*, am I to do with all of this life?" For she still can feel, in an affirmation of vitality, that life is good, and people, though often ridiculous, will continue—as she puts it—to be grand, glorious and brave.—Hubert Creekmore, "Daydreams in Flight," *NYTBR*, Oct. 4, 1953, p. 4

Like ⟨John⟩ Logan and ⟨George⟩ Starbuck, Gwendolyn Brooks gives you back a part of the contemporary world. (Logan does this directly in his settings and indirectly in his presentation of a modern religious mind.) Miss Brooks writes about the Negro women (mainly) and men of Bronzeville—as she has before in *A Street in Bronzeville* and her Pulitzer prize-winning *Annie Allen*—and about the plight of the Negro today.

Her poem about Little Rock has some moving description but its burden—"They are like people everywhere"—seems trite and its conclusion—"The loveliest lynchee was our Lord"—sentimental. (Triteness damages the few pieces of social satire in the book.) Much better is *The Ballad of Rudolph Reed* about a Negro who tries to move into a white neighborhood: its literary form and language set the reality of the Negro's life against the fictions of a white culture. The shock is immediate and lasting.—Harvey Shapiro, "A Quartet of Younger Singers," *NYTBR*, Oct. 23, 1960, p. 32

In her long journey to world renown as a poet, mastery of form and technique, and versatility with the sonnet have been indispensable. Yet, in *The World of Gwendolyn Brooks*, an anthology of her works from 1945 to 1968, she has written: "Not the pet bird of poets, the sweetest sonnet/shall straddle the whirlwind." I recalled the skill with which both she and Claude McKay had handled this most Western of art forms, had managed to inject the black idiom into it, and I argued for its relevancy. . . .

"I went with the young poets to a bar," she related. "They read their poetry. The response was tremendous. I want to be able to do that." Although her movement in this direction is not complete, more recent volumes of her work (such as *In the*

Mecca, Riot and *Family Portraits*) evidence continual progression towards poetry based upon the precepts of her younger contemporaries.

The mutual concern and affection between Miss Brooks and the young black poets—demonstrated in *Jump Bad*, an anthology of their works edited by her, and in *To Gwen With Love*—are based upon the fact that they are determined to create poetry that is more meaningful to black people, poetry that speaks with the fire and determination of the first Afro-American poets, the creators of "Negro" spirituals. Those poets ("unknown bards," as James Weldon Johnson called them) were the first voices of the whirlwind, their compositions as spontaneous and remarkable as those of the moderns. They created beauty out of the anxiety and sometimes the joy of the lives about them. They searched for new and distinctive forms, founding a poetry in which "there breathes a hope—a faith in the ultimate justice of things."— ADDISON GAYLE JR., "The World of Gwendolyn Brooks," *NYTBR*, Jan. 2, 1972, p. 4

STANLEY KUNITZ
"Bronze by Gold"

Poetry, April 15, 1950, pp. 52–56

One of the things that the eponymous heroine of Gwendolyn Brooks' collection of poems tries to tell her mother is how much "just a deep and human look" means to her. The work of this young Chicago poet never fails to be warmly and generously human. In a surly and distempered age one is genuinely grateful to Miss Brooks for the lively and attractive spirit that sallies forth from her poems. In contrast to most of her contemporaries, she is neither ridden by anxiety nor self-consumed with guilt. There is in her work a becoming modesty. Though the materials of her art are largely derived from the conditions of life in a Negro urban milieu, she uses these incendiary materials naturally, for their intrinsic value, without straining for shock or for depth, without pretending to speak for a people. In reading this second volume by the author of *A Street in Bronzeville* I have been impressed by how little of the energy that should go into the building of the work has been diverted to the defence of the life.

Like many second books, this is an uneven one. In his first book, as a rule, the poet exults in his discovery that he can fly; in his second book he tests his speed and his range and possibly even begins his examination of the theory of flight. I should suppose that *The Birth in a Narrow Room* represents Miss Brooks in her most characteristic vein, or at least in the vein where what one identifies as her personality seems to express itself authentically as the genius of the form, to be communicated as a configuration of the verse:

Weeps out of western country something new.
Blurred and stupendous. Wanted and unplanned.
Winks. Twines, and weakly winks
Upon the milk-glass fruit bowl, iron pot,
The bashful china child tipping forever
Yellow apron and spilling pretty cherries.

Now, weeks and years will go before she thinks
"How pinchy is my room! how can I breathe!
I am not anything and I have got
Not anything, or anything to do!"—
But prances nevertheless with gods and fairies
Blithely about the pump and then beneath
The elms and grapevines, then in darling endeavor
By privy foyer, where the screenings stand

And where the bugs buzz by in private cars
Across old peach cans and old jelly jars.

The effect here is one of technical assurance, combined with freshness and spontaneity. The imagery, recaptured out of the world of childhood, has a particularized intensity, an almost painful luminosity of individuation, which is enhanced by devices of syntax proper to a design of separateness. In this context the wryly humorous adjective *pinchy* is a little masterpiece all by itself. At the same time the poem is deftly inwoven, as by the series of fruit images extending to the ironic artifice of the last line and, even more subtly, by the set of verbal dissolves (weeps, blurred, unplanned, winks . . . weakly winks, milk-glass) that anticipates and counterpoints the eventually achieved clarity of focus. My only dissatisfaction is with the awkward locution, "I have got not anything," and, in the thirteenth line, with the adjective "darling," which seems to me totally out of key.

In some of her poems Miss Brooks confuses simplicity with naiveté. Whenever she is self-consciously naive, as in her ballads, her sentimental lyrics of the "bronze girl," she writes badly. If there be virtues in the stereotypes of *My Own Sweet Good*, I am unable to say where:

Not needing, really, my own sweet good,
To dimple you every day,
For knowing you roam like a gold half-god
And your golden promise was gay.

Somewhere, you put on your overcoat,
And the others mind what you say
Ill-knowing your route rides to me, roundabout.
For promise so golden and gay . . . *etc.*

Furthermore, I do not believe that Miss Brooks should be encouraged to pursue her cultivation of the early Millay inflection:

By all things planetary, sweet, I swear
Those hands may not possess these hands again
Until I get me gloves of ice to wear.
Because you are the headiest of men!

In other poems Miss Brooks apostrophizes, "Oh mad bacchanalian lass"; recommends taking "such rubies as ye list"; proclaims "we two are worshippers of life," etc. The faults are not faults of incapacity or pretension: what they demonstrate at this stage is an uncertainty of taste and of direction. Another kind of uncertainty appears in her poems that touch more or less directly on problems of caste and prejudice, wherein one senses a contest between decorum and indignation for the possession of her voice:

They get to Benvenuti's. There are booths
To hide in while observing tropical truths
About this—dusky folk, so clamorous!
So colorfully incorrect,
So amorous,
So flatly brave!
Boothed-in, one can detect,
Dissect.

Miss Brooks is particularly at home in the sonnet, where the tightness of the form forces her to consolidate her energies and to make a disciplined organization of her attitudes and feelings. In the first of a sequence of five related sonnets entitled *The Children of the Poor* she writes with mature authority:

People who have no children can be hard:
Attain a mail of ice and insolence:
Need not pause in the fire, and in no sense
Hesitate in the hurricane to guard.
And when wide world is bitten and bewarred
They perish purely, waving their spirits hence

Without a trace of grace or of offense
To laugh or fail, diffident, wonder-starred.
While through a throttling dark we others hear
The little lifting helplessness, the queer
Whimper-whine; whose unridiculous
Lost softness softly makes a trap for us,
And makes a curse. And makes a sugar of
The malocclusions, the inconditions of love.

One might question "wonder-starred," "whimper-whine," and the redundant "softly," but undeniably the poem as a whole has nobility and force, with certain extraordinary developments, as in the fifth and final lines.

And yet there is better still. If only a single poem could be saved out of this book, I should speak up for the one entitled (from a witty line by Edward Young) *"Pygmies are Pygmies Still, Though Percht on Alps"*:

But can see better there, and laughing there
Pity the giants wallowing on the plain.
Giants who bleat and chafe in their small grass,
Seldom to spread the palm; to spit; come clean.

Pygmies expand in cold impossible air,
Cry fie on giantshine, poor glory which
Pounds breast-bone punily, screeches, and has
Reached no Alps: or, knows no Alps to reach.

I should vote for this brief poem because of the exquisite rightness of its scale; because, knowing its own limits, it is cleanly and truly separated from the jungle of conception and sensibility that constitutes the not-poem; because the imagery is sharp, the rhythm supple, the word-choice and word-play agreeably inventive; because the small and sequent pleasures of the verse are continually linked and at the last resolved, made one, and magnified. The concluding line is obviously triumphant in its massive concentration; among the other details that please me are the effective manipulation of the off-rhyme, the wallowing and bleating of the giants, the teasing ambiguity of "come clean"; the magical connotations of "giantshine"; the explosive irony in context of the adverb "punily."

How right Gwendolyn Brooks can be, as in projecting the crystalline neatness of—"Pleasant custards sit behind/The white Venetian blind"; or in arriving at the studied casualness of—"Chicken, she chided early, should not wait/Under the cranberries in after-dinner state./Who had been beaking under the yard of late"; or in producing on occasion the flat, slapping image—"stupid, like a street/That beats into a dead end"; or in distilling her irony into—"We never did learn how/To find white in the Bible"; or in raising her voice without shrillness to the pitch of—"What shall I give my children? who are poor,/Who are adjudged the leastwise of the land,/Who are my sweetest lepers . . ."; or in achieving the beautiful and passionate rhetoric of the lines that close her book—"Rise./Let us combine. There are no magics or elves/Or timely godmothers to guide us. We are lost, must/Wizard a track through our own screaming weed."

These are as many kinds of rightness, scattered though they be, as are tentatively possessed by any poet of her generation. To make the possession absolute and unique is the task that remains.

TONI CADE BAMBARA
From "Report from Part One"

New York Times Book Review, January 7, 1973, pp. 1–10

R eport from Part One is a seemingly chunk and hunk assemblage of photographs, interviews, letters—backward glances on growing up in Chicago and coming of age in the Black Arts Movement. It is not a sustained dramatic narrative for the nosey, being neither the confessions of a private woman/poet or the usual sort of mahogany-desk memoir public personages inflict upon the populace at the first sign of a cardiac. It is simply an extremely valuable book that is all of a piece and readable and memorable in unexpected ways. It documents the growth of Gwen Brooks. Documents that essentially lonely (no matter how close and numerous the friends who support, sustain and encourage you to stretch out and explore) process of opening the eyes, wrenching the self away from played-out modes, and finding new directions. It shows her reaching toward a perspective that reflects the recognition that the black artist is obliged to fashion an esthetic linked to the political dynamics of the community she serves.

Gwendolyn Brooks, Poet Laureate of Illinois as well as Bard of Bronzeville, was considered one of America's leading poets long before her 50th year. She is known for her technical artistry, having worked her word sorcery in forms as disparate as Italian terza rima and the blues. She has been applauded for her revelations of the African experience in America, particularly her sensitive portraits of black women in collections like *A Street in Bronzeville* (1945) and the novel *Maud Martha* (1953). Since she was first published at age 13, she has been awarded numerous poetry accolades: two Guggenheims, an American Academy of Arts and Letters grant, and a Pulitzer Prize. Yet, it was in her 50th year that something happened, a something most certainly in evidence in *In the Mecca* (1968) and subsequent works—a new movement and energy, intensity, richness, power of statement and a new stripped, lean, compressed style. A change of style prompted by a change of mind.

One need only contrast her earlier work with *Malcolm X*, any section of the "Blackstone Rangers" (*Mecca*) or any work done with Broadside Press to see a shift, for example, from the attitudes, emotions and private longings of a black woman to a focus on the ideas, perspective, preoccupations and thrust of black people of the seventies. Or, contrast her view of integration in *The Bean Eaters* with the view expressed in *In the Mecca* and other current works where she reflects the sentiment of Don L. Lee's "New Integrationist."

I
seek
integration
of
negroes
with
black
people.

Like the younger black poets, Gwen Brooks since the late Sixties has been struggling for a cadence, style, idiom and content that will politicize and mobilize. Like the young black poets, her recent work is moving more toward gesture, sound, intonation, attitude and other characteristics that depend on oral presentation rather than private eyeballing. It is important to have the poet herself assess these moves in her own way so as to establish the ground for future critical biographies. But "change" and "shift" may be too heavy-handed, somewhat misleading; for in rereading the bulk of her work, which *Report* does prompt one to do, we see a continuum.

Gwen Brooks's works have also been very much of their times. Prior to the late sixties, black writers invariably brought up the rear, so to speak, having to prove competence in techniques already laid down by mainstream critics. Jim Crow esthetics decreed that writing "negro" was not enough, not valid—not universal. In these times, however, black writers and critics are the vanguard. Black works of the Thirties and Forties reflect the "social consciousness" of the times. There was a drastic reduction in race themes as compared with the Twenties and an adoption of a "global" perspective; concern about European War II or whatever. The works of the Forties and Fifties gave credence to the shaky premise on which "protest" literature rests—that the oppressor simply needed information about grievances to awaken the dormant conscience. The works of these times, on the other hand, reflect quite another sensibility.

As Gwen Brooks says, "I knew there were injustices, and I wrote about them, but I didn't know what was behind them. I didn't know what kind of society we live in. I didn't know it was all organized." Or, assessing her appeal-to-the-Christian-heart period: "But then, I wasn't reading the books I should have read when I was young. If I'd been reading W. E. B. DuBois, I would have known." Or, "I thought I was happy, and I saw myself going on like that for the rest of my days, I thought it was the way to live. I wrote. . . . But it was white writing, the different trends among whites. Today I am conscious of the fact that my people are black people: it is to them that I appeal for understanding."

"How did you, a Pulitzer prizewinner, get turned on to the black revolution?" asks Ida Lewis, founder and editor of *Encore*, then editor of *Essence* and conducting an interview for that magazine. The question is answered throughout the book.

In 1967 Gwen Brooks attended the Second Black Writers Conference at Fisk University. Imamu Baraka, then LeRoi Jones, and Ron Milner turned the place out. It was electrifying, scarifying, bewildering. The Poet Laureate had stumbled onto something happening in black letters—a new vigor, ener-

gy and expression of writers who espoused the Black Arts ideology. When she returned home, Oscar Brown Jr. and Jean Pace invited her to a performance of *Opportunity Please Knock*, an Alley Theater Project on the South Side of Chicago that featured the talents of a gang. Poet Laureate meets Blackstone Rangers. She organized a writers workshop for the Rangers, college students, high-school students and other youth. But after several months of messing about with quatrains, she packed that up in favor of a let's-deal kind of workshop where people wrote, shared, criticized and encouraged.

Soon this erstwhile loner's house became a meeting place for young writers, dancers, choreographers, painters, musicians, anybody young and into something, something being the forging of art and politics, or more particularly the merging of the Black Arts concept and the Black Power ideology. Out of the experience came eventually the poetry anthology *Jump Bad* (Broadside, 1971). Out of the experience of hanging out with young bloods who blithely stalk into a bar and announce, "Like to lay some poetry on you," and find ready ears, out of the experience of moving into the streets for open-air recitals in front of the Wall of Respect or in the parks, came a whole new life style for Gwen Brooks. Severing ties with Harper & Row after almost 30 years for Broadside Press, she sponsored poetry competitions in elementary and high schools, traveled to Africa, began wearing a natural. She also began reordering, redefining and rethinking her position on a host of subjects:

> "I—who have 'gone the gamut' from an almost angry rejection of my dark skin by some of my brainwashed brothers and sisters to a surprised queenhood in the new black sun—am qualified to enter at least the kindergarten of new consciousness now. New consciousness and trudge-toward-progress."

PEARL S. BUCK

1892–1973

Pearl Sydenstricker Buck was born on June 26, 1892 in Hillsboro, West Virginia. The daughter of two Presbyterian missionaries, Buck grew up in the town of Chinkiang in the interior of China, where she learned to speak Chinese as her first language. Because her parents avoided the traditional missionary enclaves and lived instead among the Chinese people, Buck received most of her early education from her mother, who encouraged her to take up writing at an early age.

At the age of fifteen, Buck was sent to boarding school in Shanghai; two years later she traveled to America to earn her B.A. from Randolph-Macon Women's College in 1914. Buck returned to China shortly after, and in 1917 married a young agricultural missionary named John Lossing Buck. During the 1920s the couple lived in Nanking, where Buck taught English Literature at the university, returning to the United States long enough to receive her M.A. from Cornell University in 1926.

Pearl Buck's literary career began with the publication of *East Wind: West Wind*, in 1930, and *The Good Earth* in 1931. The latter, which chronicles the rise of Wang Lung, a destitute Chinese peasant, to a wealthy landowner, is generally regarded as Buck's greatest work, and brought her the Pulitzer Prize for Fiction in 1932, and the William Dean Howells Medal in 1935. Political tensions in China caused Pearl Buck to return to the U.S. in 1934. After obtaining a divorce from her husband, she married Richard J. Walsh, president of the John Day Publishing Company, with whom she stayed until his death in 1960. In America, Buck published biographies of her mother and father, entitled *The Exile* and *The Fighting Angel*, which brought her further critical acclaim and led to her winning the Nobel Prize for Literature in 1938.

Pearl Buck produced a steady stream of novels, children's books, plays, short stories, and essays after 1940. She became increasingly involved in struggles against injustice and racial prejudice, and founded numerous organizations. Buck received over 300 awards and honorary degrees for her humanitarian efforts throughout her lifetime. At the time of her death in 1973, her work had been translated into more languages than that of any other American author.

Before 1930 many Americans picture the Chinese only as queer laundrymen, or clever merchants like Fu Manchu, or heathens sitting in outer darkness; few believed they could greatly influence our own fate. Since then historical events have taught us otherwise—and among those "events" Pearl Buck's books might well be included. Her more than two dozen novels, translations, and non-fiction books interpreting traditional and revolutionary Asia have fully justified the early award to her of the Nobel prize in literature.

. . . ⟨*My Several Worlds*⟩ begins with the author's infant memories of China in the days of the Boxers, and carries the personal story down to her present vigorous life—she is sixty-two—as a writer, mother, educator, Bucks County farmer, and organizer of the unique Welcome House, which finds adoptive parents for foundlings of Asian American birth. It is an absorbing narrative told with warmth and humor and insight, often as moving as her best novels, with the easy grace and integrity notable in her biographies of her missionary parents. Written in modesty and humility, the book faithfully mirrors the mind and heart and strength of a truly admirable and distinguished American. For although Pearl Buck lived and studied in China forty years before she settled in Pennsylvania, it is pleasant to believe that the essence of her character—her practical human sympathy, her respect for the dignity of toil and for cultures other than her own—are part of the best in the American heritage.

Her transplantation was not an easy one. "To change countries is an overwhelming and may be a crushing experience," she says. "I have accomplished it since I left China, and my respect for all immigrants and my understanding of them have grown steadily. To move from an old-established society, and the Chinese were that and have remained so in spite of the upheavals of revolution and temporary government, into an effervescent and fluid new society, such as the American still is and must remain for many future decades or perhaps centuries, is to do more than change countries—it is to change worlds and epochs."

What she misses most about China is essentially what all Americans long exposed to a great and ancient culture are bound to feel wanting on their return. "If ever I am homesick for China, now that I am home in my own country, it is when I discover here no philosophy. Our people have opinions and creeds and prejudices and ideas but as yet no philosophy." Perhaps the search for it is part of the dynamism of America, and meanwhile Miss Buck finds many similarities between ourselves and the Chinese. "We are continental peoples, for one thing: that is, we are accustomed to think in space and size and plenty. There is nothing niggardly about either of us—there seldom is about continental peoples, possessing long sea-coasts and high mountains. We are careless, easygoing, loving our jokes and songs."

And yet our fundamental differences grew faster with intimacy, we know, than our common sympathies—despite years of pleading by people like Pearl Buck, who steadily warned of the coming catastrophe for unrepentant Western imperialism. She believes our great mistake was to assume the burdens—and hence the earned punishment—of European imperialists, whose follies we did not commit. For we shall never be able to hold our place in the world "by force of arms and government" but only by "the working of the American spirit" in policies of neighborly help and "mutual benefit and friendship"—and the fullest respect for people's rights of self-determination.— EDGAR SNOW, "Pearl Buck's Worlds," *Nation*, Nov. 13, 1954, p. 426

General

The language in which Mrs. Buck presents ⟨her Chinese novels⟩ shares the same dual character. It is English—very plain, clear English; yet it gives the impression that one is reading the language native to the characters all the time. This is very largely due, I think, to the entire absence of Chinese words in the prose. This may sound paradoxical; but is it not true that nothing makes the division between languages more obvious than to mix them? The prose which is broken by many foreign words in italics accentuates our sense of being English-speaking people reading a book written in English about an alien race. Especially is this the case when the foreign word is followed by an explanation of its meaning. Pearl Buck never uses a Chinese word, never needs to explain one. Even "Mah-Jongg," for example, is called "sparrow dominoes"—and very rightly, since that is what the Chinese word means to the Chinese. On the other hand, Mrs. Buck never, I think, uses a word for which a literal translation into Chinese could not be found. The effect of her prose is to translate what the Chinese mean into language which means that to us. That it is also exceedingly beautiful prose is just our luck, so to speak, and a remarkable instance of Mrs. Buck's skill. The grave, quiet, biblical speech, full of dignity, in which Mrs. Buck, without ever "raising her voice," is able to render both the deepest and the lightest emotions—the feelings of a mother over her dead child and the excitement of an old man over his tea—is a fine example of an instrument perfectly adapted to its task.— PHYLLIS BENTLEY, "The Art of Pearl S. Buck," *EJ*, Dec. 1935, pp. 793–94

Miss Buck's virtues are those least likely to appeal to contemporary critics; her faults must seem to them too obvious and too uninteresting to attack. She prefers to deal in human situations as close to universality as possible at a time when the special private struggle of a human mind with its interior world is a favorite subject. She subordinates her characters to her theme and approximates them, often, to types. Above all, in an intellectual world which has plunged itself into profound pessimism, whose chosen entertainments are of so grisly, so super-Gothic a nature as would cause Horace Walpole and Mrs. Radcliffe to draw back in horror and perhaps even give pause to Poe—in such a world Miss Buck is an optimist.

The meeting of East and West is her major theme. Now it is also the theme of one of the most celebrated of our new super-Gothic contrivers of tales, Paul Bowles. Mr. Bowles tells us that the twain can meet only in circumstances of the utmost squalor and personal degradation. Undoubtedly he is right in believing that they have met in this fashion many times. Miss Buck tells us that East and West can meet on the ground of affectionate understanding and that human similarities can prevail over the gulf between cultures. Undoubtedly she is right too, and there have been many instances of such meetings.

None the less, though both may be right, and only history can decide which is the righter, it is Mr. Bowles' view which is in fashion and Miss Buck's which is not. Her position has certainly suffered, in part at least, because of her bias toward morality and toward a belief in order and in generosity; toward endings which, if not vulgarly "happy," provide for the preservation of human dignity.

Should Miss Buck care that she is accounted as—and discounted as—naive among intellectual critics? Probably not. Her readership is secure. She has something to say and she says it with lucid ease. If she lacks the warmth of humor she makes up for it by the warmth of sympathy. If she has a mission she can also tell a story. She writes consistently and successfully to be read; she writes consistently; and she writes successfully. . . .

If our mores are changing in the direction of tolerance; if our knowledge of the world is broadening, it is she who is accepting the change. It is vital to communicate with this woman, for if literature has first of all the duty of reflecting life truly (I don't mean photographically), it has the second duty of presenting this reflection to as large an audience as possible. For twenty years Miss Buck has done this. It is an excellent thing that she continues to do it so well.—ELIZABETH JANE-WAY, "The Optimistic World of Miss Buck," *NYTBR*, May 25, 1952, p. 4

⟨O⟩f all she has written, her best works are her Chinese novels. According to their overall quality they should be ranked after *The Good Earth* as *Sons, Imperial Woman, Mothers, The Patriot, East Wind: West Wind,* and *Dragon Seed.* Mainly because they conform to the norms of Chinese fiction, these novels are her very best. In writing them she has tried to entertain and delight, to reach a large audience, to follow the traditional Chinese practice of emphasizing event and characterization. It is likewise true that conformation to the norms of traditional Chinese fiction is responsible for some of the shortcomings American critics detect in her work, although it may be somewhat uncritical of them to judge her fictional efforts according to artistic dogmas and aesthetic criteria she herself does not accept or attempt to emulate.—G. A. CEVASCO, "Pearl Buck and the Chinese Novel," *ASt*, Dec. 1967, pp. 449

Why do the Chinese resent her writing? The reason, I think, is one seldom stated: she violated some basic taboos, ancient and modern, about sex and childbirth. It was this, also, which helped make her a best seller in the West where she was among the first popular novelists to describe in detail childbirth and menstruation. To the Chinese she did not get at the essence of their civilization, the delicacy of human relations expressed in certain social taboos, especially in speech and writing. For example even today, one does not take a photograph of man and wife touching each other. (I tried it.) The Chinese feel Mrs. Buck degraded the dignity of Chinese women, which is ironic, since the chief appeal of her books in the West is to women. She was a maternal woman writing for women about the problems of women.

The Chinese Communists do not try to hide their poverty or the struggle against nature (locust invasions, famines) or the tragedy of peasant life under the "old society," and when Pearl Buck "speaks bitterness," they like it. It is Mao Tse-Tung, after all, who insists that the intellectuals go down among the peasants to learn the truth about them, *from* them. What the Chinese Communists *don't* like is Mrs. Buck's glorification of the worst features of the old society, especially that of the upper classes—concubinage, for instance, and the whole pattern of the old Confucian value system, the very things the Communists are trying to uproot forever. Her strongest theme—the "yearning for sons"—is what is still making it difficult to control overpopulation in China. . . .

In *The Good Earth* Wang Lung finds some treasure, becomes prosperous, takes a second wife. But he had no class consciousness, the Communists say. They look upon this as a puerile plot (which it is, of course—the poor-boy-makes-good American story, without reality for the Chinese peasant). The real Chinese peasant was often in rebellion. And in fact he did bring about the revolution in China from 1927 to 1949. He was not, the Communists say, a lump of the good earth, but a "heroic" fighter in the "class struggle."

"But," I said to my Chinese hosts, "you have to remember that Pearl Buck made more friends for the Chinese than any other influence."

"But what kind of Chinese—and what use is that if it's all based on untruth? If she had told the truth, the books would not have been popular," was the rejoinder.—HELEN F. SNOW, "An Island in Time," *NR*, March 24, 1973, pp. 28–29

⟨A⟩ factor in Pearl Buck's loss of prestige in serious literary circles stems from her optimistic, affirmative point of view. She did not lose her faith in progress, and she exalted a Rousseau-Thomas Paine, Transcendental type of belief in the basic goodness of humanity. On the other hand, bleak pessimism, subjective studies of anguish, and searing indictments of humanity are very much the fashion at the moment. Our Age of Anxiety appears attuned to a Samuel Beckett mood, and with such bleak tendencies Buck was *deliberately* out of step. She was not an escapist; she saw and understood the evils, pressures, and problems of the present era. From time to time in her personal life she experienced more than her share of poverty, peril, disappointment, and heartbreak. But she possessed an affirmative, positive, optimistic, and idealistic temperament, and she tried to put forward the more hopeful aspects of the human situation. In *American Argument* she spoke of contemporary young novelists who "write books of futility and despair," and she asserted that in their work "there is no vision, even though this is the most exciting age in human history, when the people of the whole world for the first time move with a common impulse toward a better life. Our young men and women look only at themselves and so see nothing.". . .

It is perhaps difficult not to admire Pearl S. Buck as a person. Any thoughtful and fair-minded individual must also admire the things she stands for, her viewpoints, and her humanitarianism. Once, in *American Argument*, she admitted the truth of the following statement about herself, "I am always in love with great ends." This comment is the best revelation she has given us of her mind and soul. It epitomizes her humanitarianism—in both thought and action—and is the key to her nature.

With all due admiration for Pearl Buck's humanitarian interests, one can at the same time wish that she had not written so much. Yet she had a compulsion to write, write, write, a *furor scribendi.* Even when money was not required she could not stop the flow of her pen. Writing was an obsession ("a pressure" within herself, as she called it), and she did not have the temperament or patience to check and control the flood. If she had taken more time to think out, polish, and revise many of her novels, they would probably have been vastly improved productions. One wishes, further, that she had handled her post-Nobel Prize work with greater artistry. What is truly tragic in a close perusal of the corpus of her work is that, if Buck had been reared with a higher regard for the function of the novel, she would have—in her later fiction—settled for something more than important themes combined with narrative ability. Certainly the mind was there and so too, one feels, was the talent.

Of course Pearl Buck followed the old-fashioned technique of Chinese novel writing which emphasized storytelling. Yet, as John L. Bishop has pointed out in a discussion of traditional Chinese fiction, Western novels explore much more deeply the minds of the characters than do colloquial Chinese works, resulting in more detailed and well-rounded characterization. In addition to superficial and type characters, the Chinese school of novel writing led to farfetched episodes and improbable occurrences, thus inhibiting a novel from reaching the highest levels of artistry and persuasion.

Yet judged by her own standards—"to please and to amuse . . . to entertain"—Pearl Buck must be granted considerable success. She was a born storyteller who wrote page-turner books and, at the same time, brought important social, historical, and thematic issues to the forefront.—PAUL A. DOYLE, *Pearl S. Buck*, 1980, pp. 152–53

Works

THE GOOD EARTH

The Good Earth, the first volume bearing that name, not the trilogy, is a unique book, and in all probability belongs among the permanent contributions to world literature of our times. It was the effective contradiction of Kipling's dogmatic assertion that the West and East would never meet; it was the first interpretation in English of the Chinese variety of human nature to reach and stay in the Western imagination; it was the living commentary we had all been waiting for upon the pattern of life, and particularly upon the pattern of emotion, of a great nation which, thanks to steam, electricity, and gasoline, had suddenly come to be next door to our own.

The Good Earth was built up by the imagination out of the memories of a child who had lived and thought in the Chinese pattern without losing the detachment of her Western perspective. It was a document in human nature, in which questions of style—so long as the style was adequate, and of depth—so long as the surfaces were true and significant—were not important. It did not have to be as well written as it was, in order to be distinguished.—HENRY SEIDEL CANBY, "*The Good Earth*: Pearl Buck and the Nobel Prize," *SR*, Nov. 19, 1938, p. 8

⟨I⟩f the book is not about America, it is "American" in the Pulitzer way. *The Good Earth* is the story of how Wang Lung rises from his lowly position as a poor farmer to lordship of a great house; how his rich sons are softened by the idleness to which they are bred; and how the house of Wang will sink back into the poverty from which it arose, now that the great principle of honest toil has been forsaken. Thus, despite its Chinese setting, *The Good Earth* is another ethical-moral American drama acted out against the relentless cycle of history which raises up one generation and causes the downfall of the next. Wang, despite his epicanthic eye folds, is a first cousin to Selina DeJong and Major Amberson; and Wang's sons, like the sons of these Caucasian cousins, suffer from that atrophy of initiative which, we are given to believe, accompanies inherited wealth. . . .

One can see why *The Good Earth* might have appealed to the Pulitzer jurors as it did to many other American readers in the early 1930's—before the effects of the depression went very deep or very far. There was, first of all, the escapism offered by the exotic setting of far-off China, the lavish descriptions of

poverty and famine which doubtless made the hard times at home seem a minor, transitory affair. Moreover, those inclined to seek a moral for a troubled nation did not need to probe very far below the surface of Mrs. Buck's narrative. In the rise and fall of her Chinese dynasties, one could discern the recent pattern of events at home, and perhaps one could find a guide for the future. Weren't the poverty and suffering of the 1930's a result of the extravagance of the 1920's, when America had strayed from the rocky path along which Americans had traditionally traveled, abandoning the old virtues—thrift, hard work, sobriety? As the career of Wang shows, such conduct leads to softness and moral flabbiness, and then to poverty and to hunger. One need only renounce the easy life and the primrose path, take up the hoe and shovel, and moral strength would come again, and every man would be saved. . . .

⟨I⟩n spite of its consistency and good intentions, *The Good Earth* is a childishly simple book in which good and evil are neatly labeled. Mrs. Buck always stays outside her characters, judging them sympathetically, but at the same time from a superior and somewhat patronizing altitude. The book's unity of tone is a mark of its superiority over the typical Pulitzer novel, but the pompous style by which that unity is achieved is another of the book's serious limitations. Whatever is gained in smoothness and uniformity is lost by the author's inability to make real, to dramatize thought and feeling. Its "folk poetic" or "Biblical" rhythms give the narrative a kind of factitious authority for allowing mere statement to screen psychological abysses which the author is unable to bridge. At a crucial point in the narrative, for example, when Wang is about to quit his good life as a farmer and become an idle rich man, Mrs. Buck simply says: "Then Wang Lung took it into his head to eat dainty foods. . . ." Mrs. Buck tries to make a sentence do what a better novelist would need half a novel to accomplish.—W. J. STUCKEY, *The Pulitzer Prize Novels*, 1966, pp. 90–93

The style of *The Good Earth* is one of the novel's most impressive characteristics. This style is based on the manner of the old Chinese narrative sagas related and written down by storytellers and on the mellifluous prose of the King James version of the Bible. At certain times Buck declared that her style was Chinese rather than biblical. She explained that she learned to speak Chinese and used Chinese idioms. Therefore, when she wrote about Chinese subject matter, the narrative formed itself mentally into the Chinese language, and she then translated this material into English. She asserted that her prose was based on idiomatic Chinese and that she was often uncertain about the English qualities of the style. At other times she admitted, however, the combined influences of the old Chinese sagas and the King James version. Many similarities exist between the two forms, ranging from the use of parallelism to an old-fashioned, even archaic, form of expression. The King James version of the Bible was often studied and read aloud in Pearl Buck's childhood home, and much of its phraseology remained in the young girl's mind, both consciously and subconsciously, and became a part of her stylistic forms and patterns. This double influence of the Chinese saga and the Bible, then, explains most accurately her stylistic mannerisms. . . .

Mention should be made of the haze of romanticism that hovers over and about the novel. Buck has wisely avoided the artificial romanticism and the obvious sentimentalism that marred *East Wind: West Wind*. Yet the story of *The Good Earth*, although it maintains a convincing realism, takes on a certain exotic remoteness which lends additional charm to its episodes. The strange is made familiar, and the familiar is made pleasantly strange. Indeed, certain sections of Wordsworth's preface to the *Lyrical Ballads* apply perfectly here: "The principal object . . . was to choose incidents and situations from common life . . . to throw over them a certain coloring of imagination, whereby ordinary things should be presented to the mind in an unusual aspect; and further, and above all, to make these incidents and situations interesting by tracing in them, truly though not ostentatiously, the primary laws of our nature." The faraway coloring of *The Good Earth* lights the familiar elements with new freshness and appeal. Realism and romanticism blend in just the right proportions. Life is given the glow of legend, and legend is given the aura of life.

The motto opposite the book's first page taken from Proust's *Swann's Way* alludes to the phrase from Vinteuil's sonata which had so affected Swann with truth, love, and deep feelings for humanity. This motto relates that the musician Vinteuil refused to add his own subjective feelings and emotions to the composition. He had captured life and truth in the music, and he did not wish to distort the music with his personal attitudes. This motto thus heralds the objectivity of *The Good Earth*. Buck claims that she is not inventing; she is simply transposing life to paper. William Lyon Phelps once remarked that, if *The Good Earth*'s author were unknown, a reader could not detect whether the writer was male or female, a radical or a conservative, a follower of a religious creed or an atheist. So objective and impersonal is the novel that it almost seems to exist apart from authorial composition.

Other than proclaiming the eternal cycle of birth and death, growth and decay, and continual change, the "message" of *The Good Earth* has to be inferred since it is never explicitly stated. The novel does suggest that diligent toil may achieve some satisfaction but that luxury may corrupt and ruin "the spiritual meaning of life." Certainly, too, *The Good Earth* does champion "the old American belief in hard work, thrift, ceaseless enterprise and the value of living close to the land." But, while such a "message" may be extracted from the book, such a theme is not presented as a didactic preachment. The "message" exists simply as a corollary of the movement of life itself. Even where a moral or lesson can be drawn, for example, in Wang Lung's contempt for the common people, once he himself achieves wealth and position, no exhortation or sermon is attempted. There rings in our mind only universal truth: this is the way life is; the way people are.—PAUL A. DOYLE, *Pearl S. Buck*, 1980, pp. 33–38

OTHER WORKS

To the field of biography Pearl Buck has contributed two volumes, *The Exile* (1936) and *Fighting Angel* (1936), adumbrated portraits of her missionary parents. Carie, the wife, is a genius of resourcefulness and "spunk." Her American garden under an equatorial sun in a Chinese town far up the Yangtze River is a miracle of the kind commonplace to Carie: When a daughter had diphtheria she went into a brothel to capture a dissolute doctor, pushed a strumpet off his knee, and rushed him off to administer anti-toxin. The author is harsher towards the father, Andrew, native of West Virginia, scion of "the preachingest family in Greenbrier County, with dissenting blood as strong as lye." But Andrew plainly was a rather formidable person, utterly, if not fanatically, devoted to his cause, as blind to the small results his work produced as he was oblivious to the discomfort and pain he caused his family. Joined, the books suggest that the missionary movement has hardly stimulated in the Chinese great enthusiasm for either Americans or Christianity. Mrs. Buck, critic of the movement in *Is There a Case for Foreign Missions?* (1932) for its effort at

rigid indoctrination and its lack of appreciation of native needs or culture, broke with her church on this issue. Aside from their relation to the controversy over foreign missions, Mrs. Buck's biographies reveal that her Naturalism, like that of many another Naturalist, is possibly a product of a revolt against the dogmatic discipline of her youth.—OSCAR CARGILL, *Intellectual America*, 1941, p. 153

Even the general reader will recognize biographical elements here: the association with China, the missionary and ministerial background, the divorce, the birth of a retarded child and the blossoming of the broadest, most generous of Christian interracial attitudes. Now, however, Mrs. Buck—instead of inviting us to play that not always entertaining, not always instructive game of matching fact and fiction—expects us to ponder *The Time Is Noon* as a story by itself, to consider the fate so bedeviling her heroine Joan Richards that she arrives at the prospect of a rewarding life only after years of tribulation. . . .

The parts that ordinary novelists do well stump this author, unfortunately; the parts that stump the others she handles wonderfully. Her villains are completely unbelievable—as if, in fact, she never really knew one. The minister father who steals the money hoarded by his wife, the farmer-husband and his doltish family, the scoundrel of a church organist are right out of dime novels. But her good people, customarily skimped or short-changed in fiction, often come touchingly, dramatically alive, headed by Joan herself, including even the unlikely white knight Roger Blair, who dashes to the rescue in the final pages, and including especially the batch of children surrounding Joan at the end.

As Francis and Joan found their stuffy, narrow-minded father old-fashioned in the 1920's, we find their story itself old-fashioned in the 1960's; what might once have struck us as fresh visions have staled into stereotypes. Love, religion, prejudice abide, but the frames of reference familiar then have altered beyond recognition.—W. G. ROGERS, "Pastor's Brood," *NYTBR*, Feb. 19, 1967, p. 44

MALCOLM COWLEY
"Wang Lung's Children"

The New Republic, May 10, 1939, pp. 24–25

When *The Patriot* was published this spring, I went back to read the earlier novels by Pearl Buck that compose the *Good Earth* trilogy. They bear an interesting relationship to her latest work and occupy a curious place in American criticism.

Although *The Good Earth* was among the most popular books of the 1930's—ranking just after *Gone With the Wind* and *Anthony Adverse*—and although it has received more prizes and official honors than any other novel in our history, still there are literary circles in which it continues to be jeered at or neglected. It didn't succeed in the fashion that critics regard as orthodox. They like to think that a really good novelist is discovered by those younger critics who act as scouts for the rest, and that afterwards his reputation spreads from this center in widening rings until it reaches the general public. Hemingway, Faulkner, Wolfe, Steinbeck all succeeded by this formula, but Miss Buck turned it inside out: she was discovered by the public at large while the literary scouts were looking the other way. I know that *The Good Earth* was extravagantly praised by pundits like William Lyon Phelps, but the effect in serious literary circles was merely to clinch the case against her.

On reading *The Good Earth* after all these years, I found that Mr. Phelps was right for once, and the highbrow critics mistaken. Mr. Phelps was the first, I think, to call the book a masterpiece. It is the story of Wang Lung, a poor farmer who becomes a wealthy landlord, but it is also a parable of the life of man, in his relation to the toil that sustains him. The plot, deliberately commonplace, is given a sort of legendary weight and dignity by being placed in an unfamiliar setting. The biblical style is appropriate to the subject and the characters. If we define a masterpiece as a novel that is living, complete, sustained, but still somewhat limited in its scope as compared with the greatest works of fiction—if we define it as *Wuthering Heights* rather than *War and Peace*—then Mr. Phelps has found exactly the word for *The Good Earth*.

But it wasn't intended to stand alone. "When this trilogy began to shape itself," Miss Buck wrote some years later in a foreword, "it began, not as a single book, *The Good Earth*, but as the entire span of a Chinese family rising, as nearly all great families do, out of the earth. The story told in the first book was not the story of a farmer but a man . . . who used the land as a foundation upon which to build a family. Nothing in Chinese life, and indeed in human life, is more significant than this rise and fall of families." In other words, Miss Buck planned to write three novels that would fit together and become a sort of Chinese *Buddenbrooks*.

Sons, the second novel, is a long step toward achieving this purpose. Considered by itself, I'm not sure that it isn't even better than *The Good Earth*. It deals with the three sons of Wang Lung—the first is a landlord and the second a merchant—but chiefly it deals with the third son, who becomes a warlord. Once again, the plot falls into a legendary pattern, since the career of Wang the Tiger is based on one of the oldest and most exciting stories in Chinese folklore, that of the Good Bandit. But the novel is also historical, since it describes events that are typical of Chinese life from 1900 to 1926. Thus, the legend comes face to face with modern life: Wang the Tiger is defied and morally defeated by his own son, who represents the new spirit of China. Besides this drama, the book has a quality that one doesn't associate with Pearl Buck— a rather earthy humor, most of it rising from the contrast between the traditional place of Chinese women—who are supposed to be household slaves—and the real power that they exercise over their lazy and self-indulgent husbands.

But *A House Divided* is a different story. It doesn't matter whether you judge it by itself or by what it contributes to the trilogy; in either case it is surprisingly inferior. On a second reading, I wasn't far from thinking it was the worst book ever written by a competent novelist.

Its most obvious weakness is its style. In the course of the three novels, Miss Buck has changed her setting from past to present, from an old walled city to modern Shanghai; there is even a long interlude that carries her youngest hero to an American university. Meanwhile her style has remained the same; if anything, her mannerisms out of the King James Version have become exaggerated. They seemed appropriate to Wang the Farmer and even Wang the Tiger, both figures in a legend; but they are out of place in the Shanghai drawing room of Wang the Landlord. "The chairs," she says, "were all alike, red, and very deep and soft to sit upon, and there were little tables of fine black carven wood set about here and there, and the very spittoons were not of a common sort, but were covered with bright blue painted birds and gold flowers." Of course Miss Buck intended her blue-and-gold spittoons to be funny, but not in this manner suggesting the biblical parodies that used to be popular in college papers.

And the plot of *A House Divided* is essentially even weaker than its style. Miss Buck has always had trouble constructing a novel that deals with contemporary material, partly because of her strong sense of fidelity to the events that actually happened; she refuses to rearrange them into a harmonious pattern. Her best books have been parables or legends. But even a writer used to inventing plots would have been baffled by the problem she set herself in *A House Divided*. She explains in the foreword from which I have quoted that she wanted to trace the original vigor of Wang Lung as it reappeared in his descendants. "That vigor, first found in one figure, is dissipated, as time goes on, into many sons and places. In *A House Divided* the vigor seems quite scattered." But how could anybody make a unified novel out of such material? In the last novel, the Wangs are not really a house divided, a house whose conflicts are dramatic. They are merely a prosperous Chinese family drifting on the stream of events. The result is that Chinese history becomes the real plot of the story. In the early 1930's, this was a plot that did not point toward any definite conclusion. The foreword tells us that "China is living both in the past and in the present, in ages medieval and modern. . . . Perhaps a great revolution will some day arise which will destroy one or the other, or force them into union. But that is a long way off and as yet they are not united. So the last book must end"—and notice the "must" that shows Miss Buck's almost puritanical respect for facts—"with nothing sure and nothing known." The truth is that her trilogy does not end at all. It declines into mere scaffolding, then stops in the middle like a great unfinished bridge.

When an author has written an unsuccessful book, it sometimes happens that he goes back to the same subject, either deliberately or else out of the craftsman's instinct for finishing the job. I can't be sure that this is true of Pearl Buck, yet her latest novel, *The Patriot*, is based on the same material as *A House Divided*. In both books the hero is a wavering and rather sexless Chinese liberal, with hardly anything but the names to distinguish Wang Yuan from Wu I-wan—two names that are easy to forget. In both books the hero has a Communist friend and the friend is portrayed distrustfully. Both heroes get involved in the great Shanghai conspiracy of 1927 and go abroad to escape being executed. The result is that both books are divided into three sections, beginning in China and ending there after a long foreign interlude.

From the very first, *The Patriot* seems a better novel, partly because Miss Buck is now writing modern prose, with extreme simplicity as its only mannerism, but also because of a greater subtlety and detachment in handling her material. The Wu family seems to belong in Shanghai—unlike the Wangs—and the political background is more credible. The second part of the novel, which passes in Japan, is an even greater improvement over *A House Divided*. Miss Buck does something here that very few Western novelists would even attempt: she describes the impressions of a Chinese visitor to Japan and his courtship of a Japanese woman. Without being able to pass on the ultimate truth of the picture, I found it altogether convincing.

But the third section of *The Patriot* is the one that really overcomes the weakness of the *Good Earth* trilogy. Wu I-wan has married his Japanese sweetheart, after a tender and sometimes comic love affair that is also a study in contrasting folkways. He has planned to spend the rest of his life in a little house overlooking Nagasaki Harbor. But the war has made him realize—too slowly, I think, for the pace of the novel—that his place is in China. Sent on a mission to the front, he finds his Communist friend, now commanding a division in the Eighth

Route Army, and enlists with him as a guerilla. Now the novel begins to sweep forward. Wu I-wan is planning, fighting, saving prisoners from torture, while the old China is dying before his eyes and another China is being born. Suddenly you remember what Miss Buck had said in her 1935 foreword: "Perhaps a great revolution will some day arise which will destroy one or the other or force them into union." Today the revolution has come, sooner than she expected, and history has written the climax to her trilogy.

I hope she decides to revise it. *A House Divided* is a failure

that ought to be destroyed. In its place, Miss Buck should put *The Patriot*; she would have to change the names of the characters and their family trees, but not much else. For the real end of her story is not poor Wang Yuan, standing outside the earthen house where his grandfather was born and feeling that he must always waver between the old and the new. The real end of it is the scene where Wu I-wan, the wavering liberal transformed into a soldier, stands before his general and hears the plans for a new China defended by mountains and facing southward by the Burma Road.

KENNETH BURKE

1897–

Kenneth Duva Burke was born in Pittsburgh on May 5, 1897. He briefly attended Ohio State University, where he studied with Ludwig Lewisohn and contributed poetry to the undergraduate paper, *The Sansculotte*. He also studied at Columbia, but left to become a writer before gaining his degree. Settling in Greenwich Village in 1918, he became associated with such avant-garde figures as Malcolm Cowley and Hart Crane. In 1919 he married Lillian Mary Batterham; they had three daughters.

Burke served on the editorial board of *The Dial* from 1921 to 1929, a time when he wrote much short fiction. In 1932 he published his first novel, *Towards a Better Life*. The next year he divorced his wife and married Elizabeth Batterham; they had two sons. From 1933 to 1936 he was music critic for *The Nation*, and from 1943 to 1961 he was a professor at Bennington College in Vermont. It was during the late 1930's and 1940's that he became one of the most highly regarded modern critics, publishing such volumes as *Attitudes toward History* (1937), *The Philosophy of Literary Form* (1941), *A Grammar of Motives* (1945), and *A Rhetoric of Motives* (1950).

Burke has taught at many institutions, including the New School for Social Research, the University of Chicago, the Institute for Advanced Studies, the University of California at Santa Barbara, Harvard University, and Kenyon College. He has been the recipient of the Dial Award and a Guggenheim Fellowship. He lives in Andover, New Jersey.

General

It is hard for me to write about *A Rhetoric of Motives* because the author is my oldest friend. I first met Kenneth Burke when I was three years old and he was four. At that time my father was the Burkes' family physician and he took my mother and me along with him on one of his visits. Mother used to tell me that I went around the parlor touching everything in my reach while Kenneth followed apprehensively repeating, "Don't touch. Mustn't." One is always tempted to read meanings and patterns into those childhood stories and it is true that in our high-school days I was more venturesome than Kenneth, getting into more scrapes, but afterwards our relations were reversed. As a critic he has been the one who went touching everything from floor to chandelier, while at times I have scolded him by letter for not observing the critical rules handed down by the Elders.

By touching and asking questions and taking nothing for granted he has come to be one of the few truly speculative thinkers of our time. It is not a time that encourages speculation; we have begun to speak wistfully of the past; there is a general longing for certainty or security and meanwhile our few explorations, whether intellectual or geographical, are usually made by organized groups. Even dissent, so far as it is related to Communism or anti-Communism, has become an organized and bureaucratized activity. Burke belongs to an older line, that of the individual seekers after truth; one thinks of William

James and his father, too; of C. S. Peirce, John Jay Chapman, and perhaps of Thorstein Veblen more than the others. . . .

Burke has a reputation for being difficult to read and one must admit that it is partly deserved—while adding the proviso that most Americans, including our college graduates, have been so corrupted by skimming through their newspapers and half-listening to the radio that they find any reading difficult if it deals, even in the simplest fashion, with general ideas. In so far as the difficulty can be ascribed to the author's presentation of a subject, and not to the subject itself or to the audience, I think it is largely a matter of Burke's special vocabulary, which has to be learned like a new language.

He is looking for terms that will cast new light on old situations and he finds them in unexpected places. Sometimes they are colloquial phrases like "moving in on," "slipping out from under," "cashing in" or "being driven into a corner," to which he gives a philosophical meaning. Sometimes they are technical terms that he borrows from anthropology or sociology or semantics. Sometimes they are the words of Greek philosophers or theologians carried over into English; in the present volume I noted, among others, "eristic," "chiliastic," "charismatic," "heuristic," "eschatology," "noetic." It is a good idea to have a big dictionary at hand when reading him for the first time.

Besides a special terminology, Burke also has the habits of thought that make him hard to follow. He is a dialectician who is always trying to reconcile opposites by finding that they have a common source. Give him two apparently hostile terms like poetry and propaganda, art and economics, speech and action, and immediately he looks beneath them for the common ground on which they stand. Where the Marxian dialectic moves forward in time from the conflict of thesis and antithesis to their subsequent resolution or synthesis—and always emphasizes the conflict—the Burkean dialectic moves backwards from conflicting effects to harmonious causes. It is a dialectic of reconciliation or peacemaking and not of war. At the same time it gives a backward or spiral movement to his current of thought, so that sometimes the beginning of a book is its logical ending and we have to read the last chapter before fully understanding the first.

The point I want to make is that, with a little attention, we finally understand all the chapters. Burke is one of the authors who write to be read twice, and if we give his work that second reading most of our difficulties are cleared away. A second reading is like a second journey through a recently discovered mountain pass; the trail is marked now and we no longer get lost in ravines that end at the base of a cliff. There are, it is true, a few sentences that have to be walked around like boulders in the path; but most of the second journey is easy and we make it with a sense of exhilaration, as if we had suddenly learned to be at home in a strange country. What Burke teaches us on the journey is how to interpret human experience, including literary experience, as a series of ritual dramas: initiations, penances, rebirths and castings out of scapegoats. We learn his lesson and, when we come down out of the mountains, we discern a new richness in our favorite books and a new eventfulness in the landscape of our familiar lives.—MALCOLM COWLEY, "Kenneth Burke's 'Rhetoric,'" *NR*, June 5, 1950, pp. 18–19

Mr. Burke's capacity for philosophic wonder could be named a high curiosity-quotient, and we would expect him to possess much intuition. He objects to the epithet "intuitive" only in its familiar pejorative sense. He objects to the label "idiosyncratic" in the strict sense of that term; he is the last critic in the world one would seriously want to accuse of imposing his own will, his "idiotic" private vision upon others. He has a right to squirm.

By studious labors, over many years, he has pioneered various methodological routes for the channeling of intuitions into symbol-using behavior. This strategic choice of multiple routes gives Burke a much wider range of interest than we find with most critics.

To begin with, he has written and published his own poems. He has known, from the inside, the things he had mainly been talking about. He has embodied his technical interests. Like Richards, Empson, and other modern critics, including R. P. Blackmur, he has made himself one with his formal subject of study. Also, as translator he early acquired another sort of technical skill: he made the first English translation of Mann's *Death in Venice, Tristan,* and *Tonio Kröger* (1925). He confesses to having worried, not only over Mann and Gide, but specifically and linguistically over their *German* and *French.* Such active linguistic concerns imply the two interests that lie inside the broader philosophic range, the technical and the diplomatic. As to the latter, few critics before the most recent period have done so much to bring European literature and thought home to North America. Few have gone so much "outside" their own native orb, to bring back news of foreign affairs.

Thus, as philosopher, Burke adduced classic doctrines from European tradition—in *A Grammar of Motives,* for instance, he reworked old ideas about substance and con-

substantiality, to show how the dramatic process of "identification" worked. In *The Rhetoric of Motives* he restricted the ontology of character-identity to the narrower compass of rhetoric, by whose principles human beings interact with each other as *persons,* as role-players—a move that led the argument into increasingly political areas of discourse. Politics and its consequences have always bothered Burke, and we are not surprised to find that he early encountered a most ancient paradox of symbolic action, namely the fact that while human beings may feel free individually, they can turn *en masse* into symbolically controlled slaves, working the will of demagogues. This concern gets much attention in *The Rhetoric of Motives;* it appears in specific studies elsewhere, notably his essay on *Mein Kampf,* "The Rhetoric of Hitler's Battle," where he analyzed perversions of ancient religious belief.

Only science is perpetually modern. Poetry and philosophy are both ancient—their interests recur again and again, without diminishing returns. The earliest poems we know give us the old story of passion and its troubled, troubling consequences—our suffering, which, in its most acute form leads to victimage, the dramatistic invention of the scapegoat. Techniques for symbolic survival keep changing, like styles, but the humanistic conditions for this survival seem to be constant—as well they might, considering the shortness of man's history, as compared with the "history" of our universe. Whatever the changes and refinements of technique, our projection of self through poetry and our analysis of self through philosophy seem forced to return *ad nauseam* to the oldest questions. One is impressed by Burke's continuous recourse to older thinkers. In one short recent paragraph he recently made an articulate set of moves from Occam, to Freud, to Santayana, to Morris Cohen, back to Spinoza, and on again, to Hegel. He is as much at home with Heidegger and Kierkegaard as others are with Holmby Hills and Forest Lawn. There are some philosophers who seem not to have engaged his attention, such as Wittgenstein, but I can think of very few critics who have made more active use of earlier Western thinkers. Burke is also the child of his times: he recurs to the American Pragmatists, to Bergson, to early twentieth-century thought. However, despite his own modernity, the most impressive fact is that Burke devoted his single most concentrated argument to the "rhetoric of religion," where he analyzed the ontology and epistemology of Saint Augstine, which are consequences of the ancient Hebraic-Christian theory of original creation and "origin sin."—ANGUS FLETCHER, "Volume and Body in Burke's Criticism," *Representing Kenneth Burke,* eds. Hayden White and Margaret Brose, 1983, pp. 152–54

Works

Kenneth Burke is one of the few Americans who know what a success of good writing means—and some of the difficulties in the way of its achievement. His designs are difficult, possibly offensive, at times recondite.

From the shapes of men's lives imparted by the places where they have experience, good writing springs. One does not have to be uninformed, to consort with cows. One has to learn what the meaning of the local is, for universal purposes. The local is the only thing that is universal. *Vide* Juan Gris, "The only way to resemble the classics is to have no part in what we do come of them but to have it our own." The classic is the local fully realized, words marked by a place. With information, with understanding, with a knowledge of French, a knowledge of German, I do not hear Burke calling out: Good-bye New Jersey! No place is important, words.

I know Burke would like to go to Paris if he could afford it.

He doesn't have to listen to the dialect of some big Swede or others in order to paste up a novel. Words will come to him just as they come to them, but of a different order. Writing.

This is rather negative in the way of praise, but in a starving country one might as well at least talk of food. This will be at least important to American Literature, though negatively, if there will ever be an American Literature. And when there is, that will be important to French Literature, English Literature, and so finally to the world. There is no other way. Burke seems to me to be stalled in the right place. But that doesn't finish him.

For me, his life itself is a design, gives me satisfaction enough, always from the viewpoint of an interest in writing. He is one of the rarest things in America: He lives here; he is married, has a family, a house, lives directly by writing without having much sold out.

Any cricket can inherit a million, sit in a library and cook up a complicated or crotchety style. Plenty of Americans who know the importance of the word, if it is French or British, can be taught to do smooth puttying. But damned few know it and know the reward and would rather work with the basic difficulty to what end is not apparent.

Kenneth Burke (and family, very important) found a place out in the country where they *could* live. That's all.

The White Oxen is a varied study, as any book where writing is the matter, must be. American beginnings—in the sense of the work of Gertrude Stein, difficult to understand, as against, say the continuities of a De Maupassant. It is a group of short accounts, stories, more or less. They vary from true short stories to the ridiculousness of all short stories dissected out in readable pieces: writing gets the best of him, in the best of the book: "The Death of Tragedy" and "My Dear Mrs. Wurtelbach." "Then they were all gone. They had all gone ahead, leaving the log behind them, and fresh rips in the ferns growing out of the rotten leaves, Wurtelbach had avoided the cow-flops, as well as the eyes of the girls."

Americans would prefer to be soothed, to have their wronged gentilities cold creamed, their tightened muscles massaged into relaxation after the manner of the professionals, the really understanding. This *is* literature to them.

It is hard not to have time in a rich country.

The recent "Declamations" depart further from the "story" in any form and move closer to writing as a savour of words. Burke, let us say, is now avowedly lost, in a way that is to perform brilliantly. Without question the "Declamations" are his best work. To me they offer the extraordinary rarity of plain sense as an incentive to composition. It leads to the unusual satisfaction that comes of words placed to represent—blocks, as if the lies which amuse us in romances were a conscious effort to avoid touching anything solid. There is, in the "Declamations," freedom from the effort to please, to condone, to yield to the inertia of a tide of sentences; the thought becomes the deed and stays wilfully upon the word—to have both steady against a shifting, sliding, gravitating quicksand of vulgarity.

I don't care much what he is trying to say so long as he is saying it all the time in every word.

I wish someone would start the American renaissance by publishing brochures to be sold at a low price, where writing like Burke's might be available for those who appreciate it.—WILLIAM CARLOS WILLIAMS, *Dial* 87, 1929, pp. 6–8

In one perhaps accidental symbolic act, Burke expressed his essence: he had some of his early books reissued by *Hermes* Publications. Hermes, originally a boundary stone, presently grew a face and a beard and went on to become the Roman god of boundaries, Terminus. Rising still further, he became Hermes Trismegistus, "the fabled author of a large number of works (called Hermetic books) most of which embody Neo-Platonic, Judaic, and Cabalistic ideas, as well as magical, astrological and alchemical doctrines". In other words, everything, and preferably all at once.

The dictionary from which I drew this description of Burke in his aspect as Hermes identifies him with the Egyptian scribe Thoth, who above all "created by means of words", and "appears sometimes . . . as exercising this function on his own initiative, at other times as acting as the instrument of his creator". That is a doubt one may properly have about any scribe whose *oeuvre* is imposing enough to make one wonder whether he is representing the world or proposing to replace it; Milton, for instance, invoking his heavenly muse, claims to merit the instruction by reason of his "upright heart and pure"; and yet through the intended humility I have always heard a certain obstinacy in "upright", and thought of it as comparable with another Miltonic epithet, "erected". But the doubt may be peculiarly appropriate to Burke, who "above all creates by means of words" in the special sense that he creates words, terms, terminologies—the business of Hermes. And when you ask whether he does this on his own initiative or as the instrument of his creator, you get the somewhat cryptic though certainly comprehensive reply from his address to the Logos:

> For us
> Thy name a Great Synecdoche,
> Thy works a Grand Tautology.

Schopenhauer once called the world a vast dream dreamed by a single being, but in such a way that all the people in the dream are dreaming too. A lovely figure, and in its logological translation it might do for Burke's world as well: a vast dream dreamed by a single Word, but in such a way that all the words in the dream are dreaming too.—HOWARD NEMEROV, "Everything, Preferably All At Once," *SwR*, Spring 1971, pp. 189–90

ALLEN TATE
From "Mr. Burke and the Historical Environment"
The Southern Review, 1936–37, pp. 363–72

In this brief essay I shall try to raise a few questions suggested by Mr. Kenneth Burke's able paper, "Symbolic War," published in the Summer, 1936, issue of *The Southern Review*. Mr. Burke alone of the extreme left-wing critics seems to me to possess the historical and philosophical learning necessary to the serious treatment of the literary problems of Marxism: before his "conversion" to Communism he had subjected himself to a rigorous critical discipline. Although Mr. Burke is a political partisan, he approaches the new radical literature in the spirit of inquiry, and for that reason, I suppose, he was subjected to some bitter obloquy by his colleagues at the American Writers' Congress held in New York in April, 1935. (See the volume *American Writers' Congress*, International Publishers, pp. 165ff.) At this congress Mr. Burke was attacked for describing the class-struggle as a myth competing with other myths for supremacy in the modern world: at that stage of the discussion Mr. Burke was compelled to say, "I was speaking technically before a group of literary experts, hence I felt justified in using the word in a special sense. A poet's myths, I tried to make clear, are *real*"—an effort that won only moderate success before an audience of which Mr. Granville Hicks, as a literary expert, was a member.

In "Symbolic War" Mr. Burke begins: "Poetry, I take it, is a matter of welfare—as religion and politics are matters of welfare. And welfare, in this imperfect world, is grounded in material necessities." It is true enough to be a truism, and for that reason the statement is very likely, if it mean anything, to turn out to be as false as it is true. The chief trouble is in the term "matter." The phrase "is a matter of" may mean "depends upon," "is a reflection of," or "is a way of achieving"; but these phrases all mean something different. I am not chopping Mr. Burke's logic. I am pointing out that the ablest logician in the Communist camp, when confronted with the question of the economic base of literature, is driven to subsume so much under so vague a general term that he ends up with the assumption of a "truth" that it is his business to prove. The burden placed upon "welfare" is more than it can be made to bear.

Mr. Burke goes on to say: "The dispossessed man is in a different 'environment' from the man who enjoys the fruits of the society's wealth. He has a different 'relation to the productive forces.' And in so far as this situation sharpens his fears, hopes, and conflicts, it helps to condition his 'morality.'" That is to say, under finance-capitalism we do not have a community of culture because we do not have an ordered society in which every member has an economic stake. Within the general "culture" we get the beginnings of a new "culture" that may or may not replace the old. There is thus the rise of "class-consciousness." But Mr. Burke is aware there is no one-to-one relation, in the individual person, between his economic class and his morality. "We can belong," he says, "in as many classifications as scientists or philosophers care to invent." And this fact is largely due to another fact—that our "economic environment," our specific relation to the "forces of production," is not our total environment. For Mr. Burke insists upon a distinction between the merely historical environment—an abstraction resulting from the simplification of our personal situation into a historical pattern, Marxism, agrarianism, etc.—and the "human environment"; this latter, Mr. Burke calls the "resources of the body itself" from which rise certain "superstructural counterparts," love, hate, desire for mobility, intelligence. (I cannot see mobility as coördinate with love, hate, and intelligence, but it is worth recording that Mr. Burke is the first Communist critic to come to my notice who seems to allow any autonomy to intelligence apart from the all-engrossing economic environment of the orthodox Marxist.) In some sense the relation of the superstructure of love, hate, intelligence, to the "resources of the body" corresponds to the superstructure of culture that a class erects upon its economic environment. I wish Mr. Burke had pursued this correspondence further and had isolated the dynamic factor at work in each relationship. I think we shall see in a moment that Mr. Burke is here almost a pure determinist, that the economic environment of the class and the human environment, the "resources of the body," respectively condition or perhaps actually effect the rise of their superstructures of general culture and personal experience. And it is this determinism, it seems to me, which cripples Mr. Burke's theory of literature, making it possible for him to take seriously certain modern works that merely illustrate new combinations of economic forces; I refer to such examples of "proletarian" writing as are contained in *Proletarian Literature in the United States* (International Publishers). Apart from the contributions by Edwin Seaver and Robert Cantwell, that volume seems to me to be almost worthless; and so it seems to Mr. Burke, but his own political bias commits him to the respectful consideration of

unfavorable analysis which is too often mollified by *but* and *perhaps*. Of a very bad story he writes: "Ben Field's 'Cow' is interesting as a problem in propaganda because of its vigorous attempt to combat anti-Semitism by destroying the stereotype image of the Jew and assembling a different cluster of traits in its stead. Perhaps he approaches his task a little too head on.". . .

Mr. Burke's aesthetic standards are offended by the propagandist excesses of his colleagues; but the only warning that he issues to them in "Symbolic War" is an appeal for moderation; he asks them *not to go too far*. He asks them not to mix too much of the ingredient of propaganda into the gruel of art. He does not ask them to do some fundamental aesthetic thinking that might eliminate altogether the need for compromise between the different pairs of antinomies that he describes: propaganda and imagination, historical and human environments, etc.

How far is too far? Mr. Burke must obviously be an opportunist in this, since on principle he cannot establish a point at which the poet must eschew propaganda; Mr. Burke will have to decide each case as it appears. And it seems to me that this is due to the underlying significance of his dichotomy between propaganda and imagination, between the historical and the human environments. For, in the long run, from whichever end of the dilemma the artist may begin, he is cut off, under Mr. Burke's theory, from the exercise of the critical intellect.

It is astonishing to observe that political revolutionists evince such timidity in aesthetic theory. Mr. Burke's theory of literature is the standard eighteenth-century belief in the inherent dignity of the subject: some subjects are good, some bad. It is too large a field of discussion to describe here, yet the equivalent for literature of Mr. Burke's "historical environment" is the decorous subject that from the time of Addison dominated criticism until the time of Matthew Arnold. The very use of the term "sincerity" by many Communist critics today is closely related to Arnold's notion that it is the same as high seriousness. On this point Mr. Cleanth Brooks is instructive: "If Arnold states that higher seriousness 'comes from absolute sincerity,' one remembers Coleridge's objection to the play of wit because it implied 'a leisure and self-possession incompatible with the steady fervor of a mind possessed and filled with the grandeur of its subject.' Indeed, Arnold's high seriousness amounts to little more than this *steady fervor*." The steady fervor about the Cause—Victorian morality or Marxian doctrine—cannot admit of critical examination; and, under Mr. Burke's theory, least of all can it admit of the exercise of the critical wit which tends to place all "causes" in the whole context of experience. The steady fervor cannot be fused into an integral expression of sincerity and intelligence; they come together in a mixture.

I have indicated that Mr. Burke sees in his "historical environment" the concrete reality, and in the "human environment" the wider abstract medium through which artists transcend the merely local view. Yet it is apparent that the act of transcending carries the artist over into a very thin realm of miscellaneous emotions in which Mr. Burke obviously feels very little conviction; he is aware of a vague duty to do justice to the eternal verities—love, union, hate, and the rest. They are all, of course, only a miscellany of Platonic abstractions, and although Mr. Burke calls them the "human environment" they actually have no environment at all: they were once the decorous subjects of eighteenth-century poetry and criticism. They were susceptible to the application of Coleridge's steady fervor. I need not quote exhibits of the poetic language appropriate to that zeal: criticism in the last twenty years has sufficiently described the state of the poetic vocabulary at the end of the nineteenth century. From the neo-classical belief in decorum there is a direct development of theory and practice through the Romantics and Victorians into a belief in the higher decorum, which makes the poet the "unacknowledged legislator" and, for Arnold, the Teacher.

And that is all that Mr. Burke's theory, it seems to me, allows him to be. The poet may be a purveyor of the eternal verities, and thus I suppose a capitalist poet in the "traditional" culture; or he may be concerned with the historical environment of Marxism—in which case he is still a teacher.

Mr. Burke's scheme of the two general procedures possible to the poet seems to me vulnerable at two points. First, the distinction between the human environment and the historical environment is a distinction without a difference. They are both realms of practical abstractions for the service of the will—the will of the individual prophet-teacher and the will of the radical reformer. And secondly Mr. Burke's scheme offers only a mechanical explanation of the relation of the poet to his material: in making the poet's apprehension of "ideas" explicit and self-conscious he commits himself to a theory closely resembling that of Mr. Paul Elmer More. The anomaly of this association of names disappears when one remembers that there has been no general revolution in criticism since Dryden. For, after the rise of materialism under Hobbes and Locke, the poet lost confidence in his own special function—the whole and inutile creation of the human experience—and began to compete with the scientist, until at last the poet has begun *to be* a social scientist. The practical abstraction has usurped the whole realm of the poet. Criticism for two hundred years has been based, not upon Shakespeare, for whom the "idea" has no meaning apart from the concrete experience, but upon the weaker side of Milton, upon his professed mission as Teacher and not upon his performance as a poet.

The mechanism of the abstract idea underlying Mr. Burke's theory has dominated our criticism for two centuries. Its dominion over Mr. Burke's intelligence witnesses the absence of revolutionary critical thought in a political movement whose avowed aim is revolution. If among the American Communists there were any radical thinking in literary criticism I think Mr. Burke would be aware of it, or we might expect him to supply it. Mr. Burke's case for the "proletarian" writers is persuasive, but it is not convincing on the special ground of their originality. Some of these writers are interesting, but they are interesting, from the strict critical point of view, not for their zeal in reform, but rather for whatever merit they have achieved as writers. They have most of the merits and most of the defects of other writers living within the mentality of the present age.

The test of the economics of literature is in the long run the test of time. And time here signifies not merely the stability of an economic system but the continuity of a certain way of life. Whether a Communist economic order in America—whatever it may do in Europe—can achieve a continuous pattern of life is debatable; it is debatable equally for and against. Finance-capitalism has developed on the economic side in well-defined and predictable directions; on the social, moral, and religious side there has been steady deterioration. A system of production may be made to work a high efficiency without in the least effecting for society a moral pattern durable enough for men to depend upon; without, moreover, making any sort of pattern necessary or desirable. This is indeed inevitable when men have no moral control over the method of production. And here it is difficult to see any fundamental moral

difference between the giant corporation of the present and the giant supercorporation, which is the state, of tomorrow.

Communist literature gives us no clue to such a difference. In Mr. Burke's own analysis of the situation of the American Communist writer, the novelist and the poet must be preoccupied, directly or indirectly, with the "historical environment," a picture of men abstracted into two warring classes, capitalist and worker. That is the subject of greatest "reality" to the Communist writer. Yet so far as successful works of literature are concerned the test of their reality is not the historical and political conviction of the authors, but the works themselves. It is probable that political conviction transformed into the reality of experience based upon a definite, and not merely a hoped for, order of life is the matrix of literature. There is no evidence that Shakespeare was aware, in terms of modern historical thinking, of the conflict of dying feudalism and rising capitalism. For him it was an inexhaustible subject—but not in those terms.

JOHN CROWE RANSOM
From "An Address to Kenneth Burke"

Kenyon Review, Spring 1942, pp. 219–37

I have read several times the long title essay of Kenneth Burke's book *The Philosophy of Literary Form*, and still with the sense of an adventure. It is like following the intrepid explorer who is making a path through the jungle. I indicate the range and density of the speculative field, which is poetic theory, and junglelike; and also the emancipation of Burke the explorer's mind from common academic restraints—especially from the overall cast of sobriety which he, in a cold tone, calls "neo-Aristotelian." If he suffers from a restraint, I should think it is a constitutional distaste against regarding poetic problems as philosophic ones. I suppose his feeling may be that poetry is something bright and dangerous, and philosophy is something laborious and arid, and you cannot talk about the one in the terms of the other without a disproportion, and breach of taste. Who would not understand that? Aesthetics has been the fumbling chapter of philosophy. But I believe the philosophers themselves undergo the worst fits of depression, and have to wait for courage to return before they can resume their remote speculations with the right passion.

A kind of discourse which is past the matter-of-fact competence of science to explain, falls to philosophy. I had come to think that poetry must accept this attribution, and philosophy must sharpen its tools.

Nevertheless, there are some streamlined modern "sciences" which might be persuaded to explain poetry without benefit of philosophy. Burke's procedure is to work them for all they are worth, both severally and jointly, and then to supplement them with an ingenious all-out critique of his own. He has a whole arsenal of strategies, like the German general staff, who are said to have whistling bombs if they like, and whose campaigns rest upon a highly technical and sustained opportunism.

He begins by considering the poet as a "medicine man," and the poem as the medicine by which he tries to heal or "encompass" his own difficult practical "situation." We recognize the language of anthropology. The poet is a "primitive," who tries to manage his affairs by religious rite and magic. Burke is wonderfully keen at sniffing out ritualistic vestiges in even a modern poetry—taboo, fetish, name-calling, and so on.

I wish he would consider more, though he does consider the possibility that anthropologists may have put their own bright colors on the forms of primitive religion, and that primitive men are really as various, and therefore as intelligent, as we are. Paul Radin, who spent six years with the Winnebagos but perhaps is not an orthodox anthropologist, told me that the medicine men were not magicians but philosophers, much as we assume our own best priests to be. But if they really are magicians, how does our own nicer sort of religion originate? The anthropologists do not illuminate this topic, which is discontinuous from theirs. It is striking that Burke does not permit us to confuse *him* with medicine-man mentality; is he then patronizing his poets? He is generous, and after many motions as good as concedes that primitive magic need not have much to do with poetics.

He defines the poem next as being in part a "dream," that is, a work of the unconscious; and there we have the Freudian science. The poem is not what it seems, it is not even what the author thinks it is. Freud announced the following understanding, and so far as I know never recanted from it. A poem is a discreet tract of imagery made laboriously, but without any knowing why, by editing libidinous phantasies that were in substitution for an act forbidden by the censor; the poem as it stands being such a ecstatic innocent—so excited about gray skies and little birds for example—that it is nonsense, it is unmotivated, unless it trails a lurid private history behind it. But what if the innocence is real? And how can you show it is not? There are many images not derived from libidinous phantasies; they happen every few minutes, and why not in poetry? To protract and record an innocent image seems indeed a remarkable action, it seems to be the aesthetic occasion, provoking some sort of philosophy to remark upon it; but if you have no philosophy with which to remark you are being rather arbitrary in remarking that it must be an evidence of secret guilt. Freudians have a most literal and painful version of original sin, and bank fearlessly upon it. But Burke is one of the most intelligent of writers, and has graduated with honors out of so many schools of thought that their testimonies do not tip him over but counterbalance each other. He is not too disposed to lump the guilty poetry and the innocent together, and therefore to think the Freudian strategy will work every time.

Then there is always "social science." With Burke it might be expected that this would have a "Marxist" or "class" complexion, and he is a master of Marxist "dialectic"—an analytic instrument which is acute and has made incriminating literary discoveries, as I know to my discomfiture. But he does not force it, and I wish other Marxists would learn from his moderation. Social science is much wider than Marxism. For Burke the social dimension in the poem embraces such things as "prayer" and its opposite, imprecation, on the understanding, I suppose, that what is not magical in religion is social and addressed to the poet's own community; it has a "confessional" element and an "incantatory" element, terms which are Burke's translations of Aristotle's catharsis and mimesis respectively and denote the smart way in which the poet manages to shift his own burdens onto the shoulders of society. The social aspect of the poem seems to me inflated under Burke's treatment. But this science too comes to the end of its string.

Burke is within his rights, and puts academic critics in his debt, when he turns these lively sciences upon poetry to see what they will discover. They have their powers of divination, and can find in poetry their own slightly shady materials if they are there. What they find is principally what, according to my feeling, had better not have been there. But Burke's own special approach is quite different, and worth them all put together.

He conceives of poetry as drama, whether completely realized or not. He conceives of drama as the way the poet submits some personal and limited version of the truth about a situation to its ordeal by "unending conversation," to its test of survival against competing versions. Now some poems, like *Othello*, are actual full-blown dramas; in them you can find the rights of the situation contested by the different characters in turn. You have "dialectic": it is the "social way" of obtaining the truth, or rather, since society can hardly be said to initiate anything, even a search for truth, it is the social way of correcting and refining the truth that a given character has propounded. And the competition is not merely theoretical among the cross-purposes; force, accident, the logic of events, put views to the empirical test, and if the characters do not survive to take this crucial evidence into account the spectators do, and are the wiser. And the best truth furnished by this elaborate testing may not be positive truth at all, but a critical or negative truth; for the practical disposition of the argument may be catastrophe. We may reach a terminus sufficiently "encompassing" and happy for all, or one that is only ironical and indecisive, or one that is tragic and fatal. All this is within the range of the meaning of drama.

I suppose one tends to resist good instruction, and at first I thought that Plato's dialogues, and not dramas in the technical sense, would serve as the perfect type of dialectic for Burke. But I had to observe that they lacked the evidence of the action, and the arbitrament of the event. Then I thought that prose drama would do it, and perhaps do it better than poetic drama, because it would not require that kind of incessant diversion from the argument which is basic in the poetic medium itself, and which I have been privately calling the poetic "texture." (I still venture to think so.) If the several characters are in earnest about encompassing the situation, each in the simple way that suits his own perspective, and the ways are to prove conflicting, and we are to arrive at the social solution which is the way of ways and the "perspective of perspectives," all that is serious business, and prose is the language for business. But further, extended units of literature fit Burke's dialectical purpose, but not small units; what will he make of the lyric? He considers that a Shakespeare will manage to have every sort of poetry in the plays, somewhere among the speeches. If the lyrical passages have a content not specifically taken up into the argument, and not replied to, I think he would say they could have been replied to, but in fact remain dialectically undeveloped. The independent lyrics that lie outside of formal drama are dramatic to the extent of having a "character" speaker and an imagined "setting" and "business." Lyric becomes then a bit of imperfectly realized drama, and his omnibus conception of poetry as drama has room for it. As it is the less realized, however, it must be inferior. Its truth, he says, is local and relative, and never receives the social correction which would make it "absolute." But I think its localism is exactly what makes it admired, and thought to be poetry in the strictest sense. And he has inverted the usage of relative and absolute. There is an absoluteness in lyric which is primordial, and that is what a poetic theory should make us see.

GEOFFREY HARTMAN
"The Wild Man of American Criticism"

The Washington Post, July 2, 1967

Good books, said Thoreau, are wild books, "in which each thought is of unusual daring, such as an idle man cannot read, and a timid one cannot be entertained by." One takes comfort from this when reading Kenneth Burke's *Language as Symbolic Action*. These "essays on life, literature and method" reveal a mind for which the gods seem to have decreed equal shares of fertility and futility. Burke has produced a body of literary and social criticism second only to that of Edmund Wilson, yet it has not "added up." He has been less careful of his audience than Wilson, more interested in the permutation of his ideas, more self-indulgent and obsessive in his concerns. This is only one of many paradoxes surrounding Burke, for in his writings there is constant talk of "plays" and "strategies," and his theory of dramatism, as well as that of symbolic action, implies something beyond a merely personal catharsis.

In the present collection, which ranges from Aeschylus and Shakespeare to Marshall McLuhan (via Goethe, Djuna Barnes, Poe, Emerson and others) we are offered at best "I thinking" as well as trenchant thoughts, and at worst a mind unable to let go of its ideas, catching at prodigious puns, and worrying its moods as cannily as the cat a mouse. Yet Burke has always been influential; and even if his thought is difficult to seize as a whole, its effect is as tonic as that of LSD. The Wild Man of American Criticism is being caged, moreover, by a new generation of students who are willing to read Adorno and Walter Benjamin, Sartre and Michel Foucault, and who have little to fear from him. Burke's dominant concern with the transcendence of formalism has gradually become our concern, so that his work seems almost prophetic; while his extraordinary intellectual persistence outdistances other critics who have considered art's relation to culture and society.

Burke has been asking central questions about life, literature and method for 40 years, and his first collection of essays, *Counter-Statement* (1931), published in the same year as Wilson's *Axel's Castle*, helped to prove that American criticism was as vigorous and speculative as criticism on the Continent. But the promise of the Thirties did not reach fruition. Whereas Continental thought culminated in the difficult philosophical observations of Heidegger, Adorno, Bachelard, Sartre, Merleau-Ponty and the Structuralists, American criticism was tempted to relapse into a piecemeal pragmatism and an *ad hoc* approach to theory. This is not to say that American criticism is now inferior; only that it is less theoretical, and more surrounded by implicit shibboleths. Take the relatively unexplored assumption of the *objectivity* of the work of art: for us it is the reader in his selfhood who is the problem and who needs historical, philological or other correctives (I. A. Richards' *Practical Criticism* lies entirely within that perspective), but for the Continental critic it is the objective form of the work which seems problematic and the crucial question is how to properly *violate* it so as to release its hidden subjectivity. Burke, in this respect, is European: not our subjectivity is to be feared, but our over-reaction to it, those pseudo-objective criteria which imprison both the work and ourselves.

Yet Burke, however cosmopolitan his literary interests, is not consciously in the European tradition. His thought has not gone to school except with Aristotle and Plato; his choice of sources or subjects is very personal (he writes on Kant or Heidegger when he pleases); he does not, I believe, mention Husserl, Wittgenstein or others whose concern is also with interpretation in the broadest sense—with intention, and the attributing of motives. His doctrine of symbolic action is best characterized as a response to a particular and local complex of problems: rejecting, like Richards, the idea of an "aesthetic state," yet believing with Ransom and others that art has a systematic structure of ⟨its⟩ own, Burke tried to formulate a theory of *impure* poetry. He describes poetry as pseudo-action rather than pseudo-statement, and like many others in the Thirties walks a tightrope between formalism and instrumentalism. Art is more than aesthetic; it is engaged in history, yet cannot be reduced to particular ideologies. I am uncertain whether Burke has resolved the old contradiction, but it does in a curious way dominate all his thought. His *Grammar of Motives* (1945) proposes a set of purely formal relations, while his *Rhetoric of Motives* (1950) has the obverse aim of grounding all such formalizations in the world. It is, however, this very process of unmasking, this discovery in art or science of an objective "grammar" which is then shown to have a "rhetorical" or "symbolic" aim, that constitutes his great strength.

Though Burke, then, can be an exhilarating skeptic, as tough as Gide, Sartre or La Rochefoucauld in exposing an apparent disinterest as a hidden interest, that is not his aim. His aim is to purify dialectically our notions of purity: in life, in art, in science. He creates, for example, an archeology of concepts to show that science is not as abstract as it seems. So Aristotle's "entelechy" is brought into association with the "perfect victimage" found in ritualistic societies. This may be as fanciful or unverifiable as medieval etymology, but it contains an important argument. To demystify science is not to separate it from its social context but to recognize its continuing dependence on strange universals like "victimage" or "hierarchy."

Hidden interest theories, of course, are notoriously hard to keep in bounds. In *Language as Symbolic Action* Burke is a cryptoanalyst rather than a critic, who views "faces" as a screen-word for "faeces" and occasionally seems to forget one of his own discoveries: that sex, far from being the key, is itself a "formalistic" or "rhetorical" mystification of a larger, social theme. His obsession with the "riddle of the Sphincter," his reduction of the purities of Mallarmé to sublimated scatology (*chevelure* is "joyced" to yield *ordure*), and the methodical impurity of his own style, with its Shandy-like transitions from public to private and from systematic definition to verbal clowning—these make him an interpreter in need of interpretation. Nor is the present book the *Symbolic* we have been waiting for. Burke does not advance here beyond an identification of the symbolic with the secularized, so that the religious level appears as merely another hidden interest (Djuna Barnes' *Nightwood* is characterized as "a secular variant of religious passion"). But today we need above all a critique of the anthropologically inspired and too simple concept of secularization.

If one continues to believe in Burke—in his good sense and radical good humor—it is because, however extravagant he may be in jumping from art to life, he has never attacked art in the name of life. We receive from his style, as from some aspects of his theory, a sense of that play-element which joins art to life and raises interpretation to a gay science. True, Burke does not have the lightest touch—as in Carlyle, the ludic easily becomes the ludicrous—but he does constantly startle us into new discoveries of art's deviousness. He is as vital as a satyr, and his promiscuous or "descendental" interpretations aim at nothing less than a marriage of heaven and hell, a purging away of "victimage" and "hierarchy."

WILLIAM S. BURROUGHS

1914–

William Seward Burroughs was born into a wealthy family in St. Louis, Missouri, on February 5, 1914. His grandfather is credited with the invention of the adding machine, and the revenue from it provided Burroughs with a small monthly allowance for many years.

Burroughs graduated from Harvard "without honors" and studied medicine in Vienna. He has lived in London, Paris, Mexico, Tangier, and has travelled extensively in Central America, the Amazon, and North Africa. In the United States he held a variety of jobs after the war—as a bartender, advertising executive, detective, and exterminator. He also became addicted to heroin, and was an addict for fifteen years.

All of these experiences were crucial to Burroughs' writing. His first novel, *Junkie* (1953), dealt directly with his own drug addiction. His next book, *Naked Lunch* (1959), was one of the most controversial books of its time and was the subject of an obscenity trial. The book attracted lavish praise and vitriolic criticism in equal measures, and it is still his best-known work. As an apocalyptic treatment of drug addiction, it was called by John Ciardi "a surrealistic montage of dramatic scene and dramatic hallucination." Anthony Burgess called Burroughs "the first original since Joyce." The book also revealed a satiric talent and an attentiveness to speech-patterns as acute as any in American letters.

Since then Burroughs has published many more books including *The Ticket That Exploded* (1967), *The Wild Boys* (1971), *Cities of the Red Night* (1982), and *The Place of the Dead Roads* (1984). His critical reputation, though he has become an established figure, is as volatile as it ever was. Many consider him a genius, and as many consider him a trendy charlatan. He currently divides his time between New York City and Kansas.

Burroughs was initially labelled a "beat" writer because of his friendship with Kerouac, Ginsberg, and Corso. More and more he has come to stand on his own. His recurring themes are power, addiction (as a pervasive spiritual state), and the manipulation of images. By utilizing what he calls "cut-ups" he has tried to establish "new connections between images" and to expand our range of perception. In a *Paris Review* interview he stated: "All of my work is directed against those who are bent, through stupidity or design, on blowing up the planet or rendering it uninhabitable. Like the advertising people . . . I am concerned with the precise manipulation of word and image to create an action, not to go out and buy a Coca-Cola, but to create an alteration in the reader's consciousness."

General

To speak is to lie
—William Burroughs

Some works stand in judgment on the world though the world rules their judgment invalid. Their authors cannot be punished for they have put themselves beyond any punishment the world can dispense. William Burroughs is one of these authors. "I offer you nothing. I am not a politician," Burroughs says. He offers this: the black and bodiless specter of human betrayal, the dreadful algebra of absolute need. He offers a deposition against the human race, a testimony of outrage in the metallic voice of a subtracting machine.—IHAB HASSAN, "The Subtracting Machine," *Crt*, Spring 1963, p. 4

Starting from his own experiences with drug addiction—in which one is 'fixed' by an alien power which enters and takes over one's autonomous consciousness—Burroughs has developed a whole mythology dramatizing all those malign pressures which seem bent on absorbing or exploiting the unique identity of the distinctively human individual. And instead of drawing on classical references, he has availed himself . . . of modern American materials and forms: films, cartoon-strips, science-fiction, fragmented and permeated by a 'carny world . . . a kind of midwestern, small-town, cracker-barrel, pratfall type of folklore, very much my own background'. Out of such home-products he has produced a unique version of that cycle of conditioned action which is the American hero's hell, and although his later books do suggest ways in which those enemy hands might be evaded or resisted, we may note from the beginning his insight that any freedom which may be achieved will be 'inner'.

Burroughs is an addict turned diagnostician, a victim of sickness now devoted to the analysis of diseases. That is why so many of his scenes revolve around doctors, surgeons, hospitals, sanitoriums, etc.; an image near the heart of his work is an operating-table from which the patient may perhaps one day escape. There is no question that he is concerned to issue warnings and explore the possibilities of healing, and so far from being a sensationalist writer, despite the nauseating nature of many of his scenes, he is one of the coolest, most cerebral and analytic of American writers. Eventually his scenes are not visual, and one finds oneself in a realm of abstraction close to that thin air to which he directs his readers, far removed from the terminal sewer where he is commonly supposed to have taken up permanent residence. However, his experiences of the horrors of the drug world were obviously real enough, and in the attempt to explore the nature of his vision it helps to start with his uncharacteristically traditional first novel, *Junkie*, published in 1953 under the pseudonym of William Lee (a persona he retains in later work). . . .

This idea of dope (or any other vice, or virus) as a malevolent power which can move in on you recurs on an increasing scale in his work until, in *Nova Express* (1964), it is a matter of a cosmic takeover. From the semi-hoodlum underworld of drug-trafficking which *Junkie* describes, Burroughs goes on to a war of the worlds. But if the scale has changed, the image of take-over has been there from the start. For instance, he describes a 'fag bar' as being full of puppets and ventriloquists' dummies. 'The live human being has moved out of these bodies long ago. But something moved in when the original tenant moved out.' In a similar way he describes one drug addict as having two selves: an alert, active, conscious mind, plus the other self composed of all the cells in his body inhabited by the need for junk. Need, as an all-else devouring state of body and mind, Burroughs was also to explore in later works. For need creates a shameless subservience which allows an alien substance to enter one of the many vulnerable channels of which the individual is composed. It can then drain the life out of that individual. 'Program empty body,' is the order issued by the alien invaders of his later work; 'junk takes everything and gives nothing,' he observes in *Junkie*. And the people who live off other people's needs and addictions, even in the comparatively naturalistic world of this early novel, are described as being peculiarly monstrous—animals in the walls of his prose. . . . Junk can induce an utter indifference to reality, an inertia, a flatness; at the same time it gave Burroughs horrific images of apocalypse, disintegration, and unspeakable human metamorphoses which provide part of a basic vocabulary for his later work.

Burroughs's earlier work drifts with little sense of continuity and this is a reflection of his own compulsive, seemingly purposeless travelling. Yet it was not quite purposeless. There was always the element of flight and evasion, the feeling of having to get out of the way of some gathering threat (the first words of *Naked Lunch*—'I can feel the heat closing in'). . . . And there was also the sort of inverted Holy Grail search for 'the final fix'. The last words of *Junkie* show Lee heading into South America in search of yage, in the hope that yage may be the final fix. If we look at the Yage Letters written to Allen Ginsberg in 1953, we can see once again how the necessity of moving through strange, alien territories in search of this new fix affected Burroughs's imagination. For one thing, it is inevitable that someone travelling with rather dubious motives through remote places in South America will run into a lot of trouble with all sorts of hostile bureaucracy. From these letters, it would seem that Burroughs often found himself suddenly confronted by the unpredictable powers of what he calls 'cancerous control' (another metaphor he was to develop later). This fugitive, paranoid sense of being at the mercy of malevolent powers becomes part of the larger vision of the later books. And in turn it induces what he calls a 'nightmare fear of stasis', revealed most clearly in the conclusion to his last letter in the series, from Lima.

> Everybody has gone and I am alone in a nowhere place. Every night the people will be uglier and stupider, the fixtures more hideous, the waiters ruder, the music more grating on and on like a speedup movie into a nightmare vortex of mechanical disintegration and meaningless change. . . . Where am I going in such a hurry? . . . I don't know. Suddenly I have to leave right now.

The dread of inertia and arrest, the compulsion always to move on to new places, goes deeper than the surface drama of police-dodging and drug-hunting. It is significant that when he wrote that last letter he had in fact found his yage, which proved no more of a final fix than the others. Burroughs's 'stasis horror' is really a vivid name for that common American preference for a life which is not arrested and crystallized in a

pattern. The special details of Burroughs's situation should not disguise how deeply American his particular set of responses is. What makes him unusual is where his particular movement-hunger took him. For whereas we often find the American hero vanishing or left suspended at the end of his novel, Burroughs came to a very definite halt—'at the end of the junk line'. He describes how he lived in one room in Tangier, without washing or moving—except to inject himself as he approached terminal addiction. The 'stasis horror', ironically, brought him to the horror of total stasis; the 'nightmare fear' of being 'stuck in one place' has been realized; and all that urgent evasive-questing movement has led to the dreaded state of absolute immobility. Unawares, he had been pursuing the inertia he sought to flee. And it was there, I think, that Burroughs made an important discovery. In a later interview he said, 'I suddenly realized I was not doing *anything*. I was dying. I was just apt to be finished.' And it was at this point at the end of the line that everything that had been gathering in his memory and imagination throughout his fifteen years of addiction was discharged in *Naked Lunch*. Burroughs's realization that his long roving search for junk was ultimately a death quest or 'death route'—'If all pleasure is relief from tension, junk affords relief from the whole life process'—lends an extra dimension to his use of addiction as a general metaphor for the various diseases afflicting contemporary civilization. The incredible panorama of his book reflects a world to a large extent addicted to death. Death is the final fix.—TONY TANNER, 'Rub Out the Word," *City of Words*, 1971, pp. 110–14

The world of William S. Burroughs is not a world of fantasy; it is real, it is "reality." But "reality" is defined by Western culture; it is insane, schizophrenic, and more fantastic than fantasy could ever be. It is Martin's reality film, Luce's *Time-Life-Fortune* monopoly, the machinery of visual and auditory control—"encephalographic and calculating machines film and TV studios, batteries of tape recorders." It is a reality in which the environment is objective and mechanical, and it is a reality whose machinery has come to life, like the kitchen gadgets that assault the housewife in *Naked Lunch*. Burroughs' world is one whose objects (as in Sartre's *La Nausée*) "stir with a writhing furtive life."

This is schizophrenia; objects are self-activating and living beings are inert. On a wider scale, this schizophrenia is manifest in the absolute polarization of the mechanical and the organic in Burroughs. Burroughs' vision is one in which the world has flown into two opposing principles, a labyrinthine, external, mechanical structure and a reified "organic" content. I use the word "content" in the same sense as it is used by McLuhan, who rightly sees Burroughs' origins in the Industrial Age, when "Nature" became a vessel of aesthetic and spiritual values, that is, a content. The underlying roots of this condition lie in the schizophrenic structures of thought in the West, which can only comprehend "Nature" by siphoning it off into a pure, separate space. The romantic movement, by emphasizing the "inner," the "creative," the "vital," the "natural," against the "outer," the "mechanical," the "static," etc. (see Carlyle's *Characteristics*, for example), reinforced rather than challenged those structures of thought. Its result can be seen in Burroughs, for whom the "natural" and "organic" are always shaped by the repressive nature of the "mechanical," so that their manifestations are always stained by violence and evil. The most common image of the "mechanical" and "external" in Burroughs is the City, "a labyrinth of lockers, tier on tier of wire mesh and steel cubicles joined by catwalks and ladders and moving cable cars." Maps, bureaucracies, I.B.M. punch cards, and machines are also common images of this principle, as is the recurring notion of the real world as a movie film. The most common image of the other polarity, of organic content, is protoplasm, the blob, jelly: "Some way he makes himself all soft like a blob of jelly and surround me so nasty. Then he gets wet all over like with green slime. So I guess he come to some kinda awful climax.". . .

In so many ways, Burroughs' world represents a direct attack upon the world of realism. "I have said the 'basic pre-clear identities' are now ended," he asserts in *Nova Express*, and indeed the concept of the world as "identity," and of characters as "identities," is destroyed by Burroughs. But Burroughs' destruction of reality is accomplished with the very tools of reality, not only with junk, but with scissors. The result is an object-world whose pre-confusion, whose non-identity *is* its "identity," and whose schizophrenia is precisely the accelerated schizophrenia of the real world. There is no "plot" in Burroughs' world, but its frozen space is similar, for example, to the frozen space of Fielding's world, to the extent that the permission Fielding grants the reader in *Joseph Andrews* to skip chapters, becomes in Burroughs the permission to "cut into *Naked Lunch* at any intersection point." Burroughs' novels thus become diabolical maps, maps whose surfaces have been so intersected with conflicting directions, so cut up, that they are unreadable, they are maps of Hell. Even the "conflicting directions," that is, the sense of surrealistic contradiction in Burroughs, are finally neutralized by a cutup world, a world existing in pieces which can't relate to each other enough to contradict. I should mention that this is more true of the two later novels, *Nova Express*, and *The Ticket That Exploded*, than it is of *Naked Lunch* and *The Soft Machine*. In *The Soft Machine* Burroughs makes his best use of cutups by establishing with them a dynamic rhythm of cohesion and fragmentation which becomes the experience of the novel. In the later novels, however, cutups come to seize their own space, to have less to do with other sections of the novels, except as waste bins to catch those sections when they drop. They become stagnant pools of amputated language and space through which the reader has to wade.

The amputation of language and space becomes also, at its extreme, an amputation of the body. Although the body in Burroughs is reified into two principles, an "organic" and a mechanical one, it is the mechanical which is the final condition of the body, since even purely organic life, the body as blob, eventually swallows itself, and falls into mineral existence, into death. Thus, the objectification of the body in realism becomes in Burroughs a total dismemberment of the body, an explosion of it into separate existence, into pieces whose parts are all equal to each other and equal to any other object in the vicinity. This is the final condition of realism: schizophrenic atomism, living in pieces, in a world of pieces. Burroughs' world is the "real" world broken down into the components that Democritus began "reality" with, into atoms. Cutups finally strip away all the illusions Democritus talked about, they tear objects out of any context they may have created in combination, and give their pure context back to them, so that "in *reality*" as Democritus says, "there are only Atoms and the Void."—JOHN VERNON, "William S. Burroughs," *IoR*, Spring 1972, pp. 107–23

Works

Naked Lunch belongs to that very large category of books, from Macpherson's *Ossian* to *Peyton Place*, whose interest lies not in their own qualities but in the reception given to them in their own time. In itself, *Naked Lunch* is of very small significance. It consists of a prolonged scream of hatred and disgust, an effort to keep the reader's nose down in the mud for 250 pages. Before reading it I had heard it described as pornography, but this is not the case. The object of pornographic writing is to flood the reader's mind with lust, and lust is at any rate a positive thing to the extent that none of us would exist without it. A pornographic novel is, in however backhanded a way, on the side of something describable as life.

Naked Lunch, by contrast, is unreservedly on the side of death. It seeks to flood the reader's mind not with images of sexual desire but with images of pain, illness, cruelty and corruption.

This is not in fact a very difficult thing to do, since all that is necessary is to brood on everything capable of arousing disgust and revulsion, let the images well up, and dash them down onto the paper. A book like *Naked Lunch* requires far less talent in the writer, and for that matter less intelligence in the reader than the humblest magazine story or circulating-library novel. From the literary point of view, it is the merest trash, not worth a second glance. . . .

The only writer of any talent of whom Burroughs occasionally manages to remind one is the Marquis de Sade: but if one turns to the pages of Sade after *Naked Lunch* the resemblance soon fades, since Sade, however degenerate he can be at times, has always some saving wit and irony. Burroughs takes himself with a complete, owlish seriousness: indeed, in his opening section he seems, as far as one can make out through the pea-soup fog of his prose, to be offering the book as some kind of tract against drug addiction. *"The junk virus is public health problem number one of the world to-day.* Since *Naked Lunch* treats this health problem, it is necessarily brutal, obscene and disgusting. Sickness is often repulsive details not for weak stomachs." The claim is, of course, balderdash, since the only effect of the flood of writing which takes the junkie or hipster as its central theme is to romanticize those unfortunates, as Byron and the "Byronists" romanticized a certain kind of romantic self-pity and caused it to spread throughout the world.

Altogether *Naked Lunch* offers a very interesting field for speculation, both pathological and sociological. No lover of medical text-books on deformity should miss it. The rest of us, however, can afford to spend our six dollars on something else.— JOHN WAIN, "The Great Burroughs Affair," *NR*, Dec. 1, 1962, pp. 21–23

Today men's nerves surround us; they have gone outside as electrical environment. The human nervous system itself can be reprogramed biologically as readily as any radio network can alter its fare. Burroughs has dedicated *Naked Lunch* to the first proposition, and *Nova Express* (both Grove Press) to the second. *Naked Lunch* records private strategies of culture in the electric age. *Nova Express* indicates some of the "corporate" responses and adventures of the Subliminal Kid who is living in a universe which seems to be someone else's insides. Both books are a kind of engineer's report of the terrain hazards and mandatory processes which exist in the new electric environment.—MARSHAL MCLUHAN, "Notes on Burroughs," *Nation*, Dec. 28, 1964, p. 517

According to literary legend, Allen Ginsberg, while visiting Burroughs in his Paris apartment sometime during the 1950's, found the floors littered with hundreds of sheets of paper that Burroughs had scrawled on while high on heroin. Ginsberg, it is said, gathered the papers together, read them with reverence, and put them into the form, or rather sequence, they now have. He needn't have bothered to sort them, since the book would have almost the same effect if he had shuffled the manuscript like a deck of cards.

The Naked Lunch appeared in Paris in 1959 as number 76 of The Traveller's Companion Series, those green-jacketed little volumes published by Olympia, the press to which the English-speaking world is indebted not only for an unceasing flow of well-written and clever pornography but also for keeping in print much of the work of Miller, Genet, and Sade, as well as John Cleveland's 18th-century masterpiece, *The Memoirs of Fanny Hill*. In the years between Olympia and Grove, *The Naked Lunch* dropped the definite article in its title and acquired an introduction and an appendix (informative essays on narcotics) as well as so great, notorious, and chic a reputation that if you happened to be square enough to dislike it, you immediately risked the scorn of those who were hipper than thou. Even Norman Mailer unpredictably mislaid himself long enough to write: "Burroughs is the only American novelist living today who may conceivably be possessed by genius."

Well, *Naked Lunch* is no work of genius, but the first half of it is pleasantly readable without too much skipping, and the second half of it is pleasantly skippable without too much yawning. What has given Burroughs the air of genius, aside from the up-to-date erotic passages that stud the book, and aside from having his name connected with Ginsberg, Kerouac, and Corso, is that his implications are metaphysical, almost unique in an American, and that he follows the Europeans in his abandonment of the quest for a moral position. He is the first American novelist to be not merely childishly iconoclastic about his civilization, but to have turned his back upon it totally.

Though he reminds me of other writers, he falls short by comparison. In his tireless and tiresomely intellectual use of obscenities and in his shrieks of outrage, he is like an adolescent Henry Miller. In his savage political parodies, he is like a naive George Orwell. In his brutal sexual fantasies, he is like a timid Marquis de Sade. In his overpowering belief that the mention of petroleum jelly, baboons' behinds, and contraceptives will infallibly provoke laughter, no matter how many hundreds of times repeated, he is like a senile Joey Hirsch, the boy next door to me when I was ten.

But most of all he reminds me of Lewis Carroll. Whether or not Burroughs wrote his book in a narcotic trance, his debt to *Alice in Wonderland* is enormous, and to have got himself thus indebted is so right and so brilliant that it makes me wish I liked *Naked Lunch* better than I do. In attempting to write a novel that will pull the wash-plug out of the universe, that will wither with scorn and smear with muck all the works of man and God, what could be more superb or to the point than to take as one's method the method used in the most loved story of the English language?—ALFRED CHESTER, "Burroughs in Wonderland," *Cmty*, Jan. 1963, pp. 90–91

Burroughs has, principally, two claims on the attention of serious readers: as a moralist, and as an innovator. On both counts, it seems to me, he cannot be considered as more than a minor, eccentric figure. Undoubtedly he has a certain literary talent, particularly for comedy and the grotesque, but in both precept and practice he is deeply confused and ultimately unsatisfying. *The Naked Lunch* seems to offer an appropriate epitaph on his work: 'Confusion hath—his masterpiece'.

To begin with, there is a deep confusion, not only in Burroughs but in his admirers too, on the subject of narcotics. Much of Burroughs's notoriety derives from the fact that he is a morphine addict, who has been cured, but who still writes very much out of the experience of addiction. He tells us in the Introduction to *The Naked Lunch* that it is based on notes taken during the sickness and delirium of addiction. He is our modern De Quincey; and undoubtedly this accounts for his adoption by the hipster wing of the American literary scene. Herbert Gold has called *The Naked Lunch* 'the definitive hip book' and Burroughs tells us that the title was donated by the arch-hipster Jack Kerouac. 'I did not understand what the title meant until my recovery. The title means exactly what the words say: NAKED lunch—a frozen moment when everyone sees what is on the end of every fork'.—DAVID LODGE, "Objections to William Burroughs," *CQ*, Autumn 1966, p. 205

Coleridge put the idea of balance most eloquently when he described the ideal poet as bringing the whole soul of man into activity with the faculties subordinated to each other "according to their relative worth and dignity," and "with a more than usual emotion" combined "with a more than usual order." I. A. Richards revived the idea in his early books of criticism. But what happens to it when we come up against William Burroughs and ⟨certain⟩ other authors. . . ? One side goes down kerplunk. Words like "soul" and "worth" and "dignity" become ridiculously irrelevant.

In Burroughs' *The Ticket That Exploded* the science fiction aspects are hardly coherent or amusing enough to balance the obsessively iterated sodomite fantasies, products of "masturbating afternoons." The monotony of the incomplete, mostly unconnected sentences is that of a twitching nerve. As in the Nazi atrocity pictures, or features in the *National Enquirer*, the obsession is with the human body as something to be violated, damaged, destroyed. "I caught a final glimpse of her agonized face eaten by caustic slime." In fact the novel contains many references to atrocity pictures: "glowing torture films in a land of black food," "a smell of sewage and decay breathing from years of torture films."

Since "pain and sex form flesh identity," the invaders from Venus, who want "to retain the flesh gimmick in some form" are referred to contemptuously by other cosmic groups as "terminal flesh addicts of course motivated by pornographic torture films." For Burroughs "all human sex is this unsanitary arrangement whereby two entities attempt to occupy the same three-dimensional coordinate points, giving rise to the sordid latrine brawls which have characterized a planet based on 'The Word,' that is, on separate flesh engaged in endless sexual conflict. . . . (It will be readily understandable that a program of systematic frustration was necessary in order to sell this crock of sewage as Immortality, The Garden of Delights, and LOVE)." But still there is no renunciation of the flesh. In a very narrow, literal sense the book is Reichian. Orgasms are as numerous and copious as the fountains of Rome, though hardly as various and beautiful. Much of the time *The Ticket That Exploded* sounds like Dr. Gunn's Family Medical Book rewritten by Jules Verne under the influence of heroin and haunted by "ghostly rectums."

It is easy enough to treat such a book as pathology, or to take the fact that Burroughs exists and is widely read and part of a literary movement as warning that some sort of counteraction is necessary. But this is not a literary judgment, and may be, as Sartre argued in the case of Jean Genet's early work, an inhumane one. We cannot know what the vision means unless we experience it totally, giving ourselves up to it as we do to other works of art, with suspension of disbelief and—in this instance—of distaste. We must confront Burroughs as a free being who in some sense chose to have his kind of life and write his kind of book. Our solemn, almost religious duty is to reach the bottom of his experience, take on the burden of it, see ourselves in it, temporarily *be* Burroughs. There may even be hypocrisy in pretending it is a burden. Some of the violence and filth is an expression of Swiftian disgust at the way things are. But obviously, as was true of Swift, the author delights in such imaginings. If we read the book properly we can feel the pleasure also—or learn to. Since we are also human, with the same polymorphous-perverse background, the possibility is there.—ROBERT GORHAM DAVIS, "The Perilous Balance," *HdR*, Summer 1983, pp. 281–83

William S. Burroughs is a great autoeroticist—of writing, not sex. He gets astral kicks by composing in blocks, scenes, repetitive and identical memories galvanizing themselves into violent fantasies, the wild mixing of pictures, words, the echoes of popular speech. It is impossible to suspect him of any base erotic motives in his innumerable scenes of one adolescent boy servicing another like a piece of plumbing; nor should one expect a book from him different from his others. Burroughs is the purest writer in Barney Rosset's grove, and not just because in this book he more than ever turns his obsession with cold, callous homosexual coupling into a piece of American science fiction.

The fact is, he is mad about anything that he can get down on paper. He loves, literally, being engaged in the act of writing, filling up paper from the scene immediately present to him. Composition by field, as the Black Mountain poets used to say; plus composition by frenzy and delight, and in any direction. Words, horrid isolate words, those symbols of our enslavement, are replaced by the a-b-c of man's perception of simultaneous factors—the ability to drink up the "scanning pattern." Get it down when it is still hot, vibrant and wild to your consciousness! The literary impulse is more daemonic to Burroughs than sex was to Sade, but can be just as nonconductive to onlookers.

The Wild Boys is Burroughs's fifth or sixth or seventh book. The gang of totally sadistic homosexual young Snopeses who come into the book in the last third are not important except as a culmination of the continual fantasy of boys in rainbow-colored jockstraps coldly doffing them; nor are they important to the book. Nothing here is any more important than anything else, except possibly Burroughs's unusually tender memories of adolescent sex around the golf course and locker rooms in his native St. Louis in the 1920's. But the wild boys are apaches of freedom, and so are different from the "thought-control mob," the narcotics cops and the despots of the communications monopolies who are the villains of Burroughs's other books— especially *Nova Express*. The wild boys in this book are a positive force for freedom: i.e., they have such an aversion to women (to Burroughs, women are the thought-control mob in infancy) that the boys continue the race by artificial insemination and thus, *Gott zu dank*, a "whole generation arose that had never seen a woman's face nor heard a woman's voice."

This book in texture is like Burroughs's other books— *Naked Lunch, The Soft Machine, Nova Express, The Ticket That Exploded,* and for all I know, *Skirts* and *Who Pushed Paula,* published under a pseudonym and which I have never seen. The book is essentially a reverie in which different items suddenly get animated with a marvelously unexpectable profusion and disorder. Anything can get into it, lead its own life for a while, get swooshed around with everything else. Reading it does communicate Burroughs's excitement in composition and in the arbitrarily zany rearrangements that he calls cutups. Actually, he is a cutup who writes in action-prose, kaleidoscop-

ic shifts, spurts, eruptions and hellzapoppins. But with all the simultaneous and cleverly farcical reversals, noises, revolver shots, sado-masochistic scenes on and off the high wire, the book is inescapably a reverie, the private Burroughs dream state. Whole scenes collide and steal up on each other and break away as if they were stars violently oscillating and exploding in the telescopic eyepiece of an astronomer who just happens to be gloriously soused. . . .

All stream of consciousness writing, in order to rise above the terrible fascination with itself, has to find something other than itself to love. Burroughs is mired in the excitement of writing. A book is something he doesn't really care about. He has invented an instant conduit from his mind to a TV screen before which he sits in perfect self-love. There is no end in sight; hair will grow even in the grave. But what Burroughs has never realized is that a mind fascinated by itself alone is unconsciously lonely, therefore pessimistic.

Burroughs's whole esthetic and his suspicion of every political idea are the same: let me alone! Even his endlessly fascinated, obsessive recall of homosexual intercourse says—let me alone! There is no love making, no interest in love, not even much interest in the sensation of orgasm. The emphasis is on emission as the end product. The idea is to show in how many different scenes and with how many coldly selected partners one can do it. But repetition, that fatally boring element in Burroughs's "cut-ups," turns the coupling into an obsessive primal scene that never varies in its details. The technical arrangements never vary, but they are described with such unwearied relish that the "wild boys" and their sadistic knives, scissors, gougers, castrators, etc., etc., seem like the embroidery of a cruel dream, not wickedness.

Jean Genet is a hero to Burroughs, but Genet's masturbatory fantasies were undergone in prison, and were in the service of love. Genet is indeed an addict of love, which is why his novels and plays are crowded with people. Burroughs seems to me the victim of solitude. He expresses it in the coldness with which partners are dismissed: "The boy shoved the Dib's body away as if he were taking off a garment." The comic moments in *The Wild Boys* are not situations but jokes: "Bearded Yippies rush down a street with hammers breaking every window on both sides leave a wake of screaming burglar alarms strip off the beards, reverse collars and they are fifty clean priests throwing petrol bombs under every car WHOOSH a block goes up behind them."

No situation, no line, no joke, lasts very long with Burroughs. He once noted that morphine "produces a rush of pictures in the brain as if seen from a speeding train. The pictures are dim, jerky, grainy, like old film." And Burroughs does give the impression of reliving some private scene. Everything turns in on itself. Outside, the planets and constellations reel to prove that life has no meaning, that there is not and cannot be anything else but our own sacred consciousness. Everything outside is *hell*. But as if to prove that life in the United States does imitate art, I open up the Sunday *Times* at random and find an advertisement for the *Capitalist Reporter* that cries out: "Money! Opportunity Is All Around You! . . . American treasures are all around you—attic, church bazaar, house-wrecking yards, thrift shops, etc. Old bottles, obsolete fishing lures, prewar comics. . . . names and addresses of people who buy *everything*, from old mousetraps to dirigibles to *used electric chairs* [author's italics]."—ALFRED KAZIN, *NYTBR*, Dec. 12, 1971, pp. 4, 22–23

William Burroughs's latest: a disappointing novel of uneven parts; a sketchy miscellany of short stories, scenarios, poems and fragments linked only by the slenderest threads of repetition and continuity and occasional consistencies of tone. No novelist has demonstrated less regard than Burroughs for concerns of plot and characterization; they invade his work only rarely; in no place are they sustained. And never in his fiction has there been less to supplant them than in *Exterminator!*

Since this is Burroughs, though, there are still a few things we can depend on: narratives spin in surrealist swirls; bodies are hideously transformed and giddily abused; sci-fi gadgetry abounds. The forbidden philias get short shrift; but sodomy, sadism, murder and excrement (lots of it!) find their way, often together, into his gleefully suppurating prose. And for the most part his targets—large and slightly tattered now—remain the same: American jingoism, bellicosity, bigotry, brutality, paranoia, narcissism and repression. In other words, something for everyone, including a swipe at the Queen. (Burroughs is living in England now.)

Of the novel's many parts, the first, "Exterminator!," is the simplest, the most realistic, the least pointed and, not coincidentally, the best. A brief, burly account by an exterminator of a nine-month stint at the trade, it demonstrates Burroughs's extraordinary ear for vernacular and creates, as its narrator visits the hidden corners, the basements and bottoms of things, where an exterminator presumably is always needed, a sense of hunkering menace, about to be enlarged, of dangerous thriving on the livelihood of death: "The boss has a trick he does every now and again assembles his staff and eats arsenic been in that office breathing the powder in so long the arsenic just brings an embalmer's flush to his smooth grey cheek." The story's title signals Burroughs's intentions, but it's nothing like the umbrella he intends for the various fragments of the book; they go their own refractory ways.

Several of them depend on leering, gimmicky turns; the reader of a story within a story becomes the victim of a monster he has just read about ("Wind Die. You Die. We Die."); a conspiracy to explode a train carrying nerve gas is quashed, and then the train accidentally is struck by a truck ("Twilight's Last Gleamings"); chaos mysteriously erupts around a faithful retainer, who is revealed as the evil Dr. Fu Manchu ("The Perfect Servant"). . . .

Despite occasional sparks of collision, Burroughs's satire tends to be both broad and repetitive. Too often in these pieces, it drills lamely, like a screw with stripped threads: "'The President is right. The President is always right. The laws are right. America is right. America is always right. The American way of life is the right way of life is the best way of life is the only way of life' from here to eternity."

With his severity sometimes trimmed and fringed with regret, Burroughs is mellowing in surprising ways: *Exterminator!* shelters some limp lines and carries some bulky sentimental cargo. "The 'Priest' They Called Him," a story about an old junkie who gives his last fix to a suffering young one, ends like this: "The boy was sleeping when the Priest left room 18. He went back to his room and sat down on the bed. Then it hit him like heavy silent snow, all the grey junk yesterdays. He sat there and received the *immaculate fix* and since he was himself a priest there was no need to call one."

All of which makes it a shaky trip out this time for Mr. Burroughs. The best parts of *Exterminator!*—the shards of wit, the mordant caricatures, the japing, raunchy voices, the passages of vertiginous surreality—merely echo the ferocious immediacy and originality of his earlier fiction. They underline the attenuating substance of his work. In this latest lunch, Mr. Burroughs is unflatteringly naked; the plate is close to bare.—ANDREW C. T. BERGMAN, *NYTBR*, Oct. 14, 1973, p. 14

William S. Burroughs, if not unambiguously of the Devil's party, is the author of the most sinister American novel, *Naked Lunch*, to attain the status of a classic. Nor have his books, since he published in 1959 those "detailed notes on sickness and delirium" (his description), become less sinister, or more coherent. *Port of Saints* is gamely described by its jacket copy as "the mind-boggling story of a man whose alternate selves take him on a fantastic journey through space, time, and sexuality." We are further told that the volume was written, or assembled, or whatever it is that Burroughs does with scissors and egg-beater to concoct his books, before the author's return to the United States in 1973. So we have here something of a period piece, revolving, like Marge Piercy's *Dance the Eagle to Sleep*, around a stylized struggle between a sick American society and a healthy, tribalized counterculture. In Burroughs' fantasy, the heroic outsiders are the Wild Boys, or Parries, for Paranormals—the enemy being the loathsome Norms, led by Mike Finn, if you can call it led. "Under the rule of Mike Finn it didn't pay to be good at anything. In consequence the whole structure of Western society had collapsed." . . .

Port of Saints is claptrap, but since it is murderous claptrap we feel we owe it some respect. We would like to dismiss this book but cannot, quite. A weird wit and an integrity beyond corruption shine through its savage workings, and genuine personal melancholy. . . .

Although there is a distinct autobiographical savor to *Port of Saints*, little factual is revealed. A reader might gather that the writer was born in St. Louis, inclined toward homosexuality, and had some experience of drugs and Mexico; a moment of homosexual initiation in a summer cottage recurs ever more extravagantly until this naturalistic moment of lived life is transposed into the heaven of coruscating violence where the authorial imagination finds repose. "It's all shredding away as I walk . . . cool remote toilets foghorns outside cigarette ash on a naked thigh in furnished rooms blue mist in pubic hairs crackling to dust as I walk." The "I" becomes the "we" of a triumphant army: "We are moving farther and farther out. No troops can get through the Deserts of Silence and beyond that is the Blue Light Blockade. We don't need the enemy any more. Buildings and stars laid flat for storage. The last carnival is being pulled down." Beyond the last carnival, a world's-end fair: "Xolotl Time looks like a world fair spread out in a vast square where weapons, sex and fighting techniques are displayed and exchanged." No continuous program even of nihilism develops; Burroughs' philosophy remains as mysterious as his person. Is he really in favor of all these broken necks, weapons of putrefaction, and cold-eyed boys who bare their teeth like dogs? The purposeful fragmentation of his technique even tends to conceal how much of a writer Burroughs really is. Most of the prose is simple pell-mell, and the dialogue straight from *Action Comics*. Sometimes he sounds like Kerouac or Mailer, hurriedly tossing into a sentence all that comes to mind: "Defeated and pursued, with only a handful of followers left, Audrey invokes a curse on the White Goddess and all her works, from the Conquistadores, from the Bog People to the Queen, from Dixie to South Africa. . . . " He can be funny, as when describing the drug Bor Bor: "The effect of this drug, which is held in horror by the wild boys and only used as a weapon against our enemies, is to lull the user into a state of fuzzy well-being and benevolence, a warm good feeling that everything will come out all right for Americans." But satire is not really his game; nor is propaganda, though a number of drastic programs for mass mutation and pervasive depopulation come and go. We witness in his work acts not of exhortation but of exorcism. A kind of landscape returns, as nostalgic as the windblown dunes and meadows of Winslow Homer, bathed in the unearthly green light of Maxfield Parrish illustrations, before it transmutes to extragalactic blue: "The boy did not speak. He came closer and then got on the bed kneeling. He was naked, in his eyes the cold reaches of interstellar space. Behind him Audrey could see a gleaming empty sky, a far dusting of stars." The net effect Burroughs achieves is to convince us that he has seen things beyond description.—JOHN UPDIKE, "Dark Smile, Devilish Saints," NY, Aug. 11, 1980, pp. 80–88

MARY McCARTHY
From "Burroughs' Naked Lunch"
The Writing on the Wall
1963, pp. 44–53

"You can cut into *The Naked Lunch* at any intersection point," says Burroughs, suiting the action to the word, in "an atrophied preface" he appends as a tailpiece. His book, he means, is like a neighborhood movie with continuous showings that you can drop into whenever you please—you don't have to wait for the beginning of the feature picture. Or like a worm that you can chop up into sections each of which wriggles off as an independent worm. Or a nine-lived cat. Or a cancer. He is fond of the word "mosaic," especially in its scientific sense of a plant-mottling caused by a virus, and his Muse (see etymology of "mosaic") is interested in organic processes of multiplication and duplication. The literary notion of time as simultaneous, a montage, is not original with Burroughs; what is original is the scientific bent he gives it and a view of the world that combines biochemistry, anthropology, and politics. It is as though *Finnegans Wake* were cut loose from history and adapted for a Cinerama circus titled "One World." *The Naked Lunch* has no use for history, which is all "ancient history"—sloughed-off skin; from its planetary perspective, there are only geography and customs. Seen in terms of space, history shrivels into a mere wrinkling or furrowing of the surface as in an aerial relief-map or one of those pieced-together aerial photographs known in the trade as (again) mosaics. The oldest memory in *The Naked Lunch* is of jacking-off in boyhood latrines, a memory recaptured through pederasty. This must be the first space novel, the first serious piece of science fiction—the others are entertainment. . . .

The best comparison for the book, with its aerial sex acts performed on a high trapeze, its con men and barkers, its arena-like form, is in fact with a circus. A circus travels but it is always the same, and this is Burroughs' sardonic image of modern life. The Barnum of the show is the mass-manipulator, who appears in a series of disguises. *Control,* as Burroughs says, underlining it, *can never be a means to anything but more control—like drugs,* and the vicious circle of addiction is re-enacted, worldwide, with sideshows in the political and "social" sphere—the "social" here has vanished, except in quotation marks, like the historical, for everything has become automatized. Everyone is an addict of one kind or another, as people indeed are wont to say of themselves, complacently: "I'm a crossword puzzle addict, a hi-fi addict," etc. The South is addicted to lynching and nigger-hating, and the Southern folk-custom of burning a Negro recurs throughout the book as a sort of Fourth-of-July carnival with fireworks. Circuses, with their cages of wild animals, are also dangerous, like Burroughs'

human circus; an accident may occur, as when the electronic brain in Dr. Benway's laboratory goes on the rampage, and the freaks escape to mingle with the controlled citizens of Freeland in a general riot, or in the scene where the hogs are let loose in the gourmet restaurant. . . .

The phenomenon of repetition . . . gives rise to boredom; many readers complain that they cannot get through *The Naked Lunch.* And/or that they find it disgusting. It *is* disgusting and sometimes tiresome, often in the same places. The prominence of the anus, of faeces, and of all sorts of "horrible" discharges, as the characters would say, from the body's orifices, becomes too much of a bad thing, like the sado-masochistic sex performances—the auto-ejaculation of a hanged man is not everybody's cantharides. A reader whose erogenous zones are more temperate than the author's begins to feel either that he is a square (a guilty sentiment he should not yield to) or that he is the captive of a joyless addict.

In defense, Swift could be cited, and indeed between Burroughs and Swift there are many points of comparison; not only the obsession with excrement and the horror of female genitalia but a disgust with politics and the whole body politic. Like Swift, Burroughs has irritable nerves and something of the crafty temperament of the inventor. There is a great deal of Laputa in the countries Burroughs calls Interzone and Freeland, and Swift's solution for the Irish problem would appeal to the American's dry logic. As Gulliver, Swift posed as an anthropologist (though the study was not known by that name then) among savage people; Burroughs parodies the anthropologist in his descriptions of the American heartland: ". . . the Interior a vast subdivision, antennae of television to the meaningless sky . . . Illinois and Missouri, miasma of mound-building peoples, groveling worship of the Food Source, cruel and ugly festivals." The style here is more emotive than Swift's, but in his deadpan explanatory notes ("This is a rural English custom designed to eliminate aged and bedfast dependents"), there is a Swiftian laconic factuality. The "factual" appearance of the whole narrative, with its battery of notes and citations, some straight, some loaded, its extracts from a diary, like a ship's log, its pharmacopoeia, has the flavor of eighteenth-century satire. He calls himself a "Factualist" and belongs, all alone, to an Age of Reason, which he locates in the future. In him, as in Swift, there is a kind of soured utopianism.

Yet what saves *The Naked Lunch* is not a literary ancestor but humor. Burroughs' humor is peculiarly American, at once broad and sly. It is the humor of a comedian, a vaudeville performer playing in "One," in front of the asbestos curtain of some Keith Circuit or Pantages house long since converted to movies. The same jokes reappear, slightly refurbished, to suit the circumstances, the way a vaudeville artist used to change Yonkers to Renton when he was playing Seattle. For example, the Saniflush joke, which is always good for a laugh: somebody is cutting the cocaine/the morphine/the penicillin with Saniflush. Some of the jokes are verbal ("Stop me if you've heard this atomic secret" or Dr. Benway's "A simopath . . . is a citizen convinced he is an ape or other simian. It is a disorder peculiar to the army and discharge cures it"). Some are "black" parody (Dr. Benway, in his last appearance, dreamily, his voice fading out: "Cancer, my first love"). Some are whole vaudeville "numbers," as when the hoofers, Clem and Jody, are hired by the Russians to give Americans a bad name abroad: they appear in Liberia wearing black Stetsons and red galluses and talking loudly about burning niggers back home. A skit like this may rise to a frenzy, as if in a Marx Brothers or a Clayton, Jackson, and Durante act, when all the actors pitch in. *E.g.,* the very funny scene in Chez Robert, "where a huge icy gourmet broods over the greatest cuisine in the world": A. J. appears, the last of the Big Spenders, and orders a bottle of ketchup; immediate pandemonium; A. J. gives his hog call, and the shocked gourmet diners are all devoured by famished hogs. The effect of pandemonium, all hell breaking loose, is one of Burroughs' favorites and an equivalent of the old vaudeville finale, with the acrobats, the jugglers, the magician, the hoofers, the lady-who-was-sawed-in-two, the piano-player, the comedians, all pushing into the act. . . .

The Naked Lunch contains messages that unluckily for the ordinary reader are somewhat arcane. Despite his irony, Burroughs is a prescriptive writer. He means what he says to be taken and used literally, like an Rx prescription. Unsentimental and factual, he writes as though his thoughts had the quality of self-evidence. In a special sense, *The Naked Lunch* is coterie literature. It was not intended, surely, for the general public, but for addicts and former addicts, with the object of imparting information. Like a classical satirist, Burroughs is dead serious—a reformer. Yet, as often happened with the classical satirists, a wild hilarity and savage pessimism carry him beyond his therapeutic purpose and defeat it. The book is alive, like a basketful of crabs, and common sense cannot get hold of it to extract a moral. . . .

The Naked Lunch, Burroughs says, is "a blueprint, a How-To Book. . . . How-To extend levels of experience by opening the door at the end of a long hall." Thus the act of writing resembles and substitutes for drug-taking, which in Burroughs' case must have begun as an experiment in the extension of consciousness. It does not sound as if pleasure had ever been his motive. He was testing the controls of his own mechanism to adjust the feed-in of data, noting with care the effects obtained from heroin, morphine, opium, Demerol, Yage, cannabis, and so on. These experiments, aiming at freedom, "opening a door," resulted in addiction. He kicked the imprisoning habit by what used to be known as will power, supplemented by a non-addictive drug, apomorphine, to whose efficacy he now writes testimonials. It seems clear that what was involved and continues to be involved for Burroughs is a Faustian compact: knowledge-as-power, total control of the self, which is experienced as sovereign in respect to the immediate environment and neutral in respect to others.

At present he is interested in scientology, which offers its initiates the promise of becoming "clears"—free from all hangups. For the novel he has invented his cut-out and fold-in techniques, which he is convinced can rationalize the manufacture of fictions by applying modern factory methods to the old "writer's craft." A text may be put together by two or three interested and moderately skilled persons equipped with scissors and the raw material of a typescript. Independence from the vile body and its "algebra of need," freedom of movement across national and psychic frontiers, efficiency of work and production, by means of short cuts, suppression of connectives, and other labor-saving devices, would be Uncle Bill Burroughs' patent for successful living. But if such a universal passkey can really be devised, what is its purpose? It cannot be enjoyment of the world, for this would only begin the addictive process all over again by creating dependency. Action, the reverse of enjoyment, has no appeal either for the author of *The Naked Lunch*. What Burroughs wants is out, which explains the dry, crankish amusement given him by space, interplanetary distances, where, however, he finds the old mob still at work. In fact, his reasoning, like the form of his novel, is circular. Liberation leads to new forms of subjugation. If the human virus can be treated, this can only be under conditions of asepsis: the Nova police. Yet Burroughs is unwilling, politically, to play the dread game of eugenics or euthenics, outside his private fantasy, which, since his intelligence is aware of the circularity of its utopian reasoning, invariably turns sardonic. *Quis custodet custodes ipsos?*

ADDITIONAL READING

WALTER ABISH

Knowlton, James. *American Book Review* 3 (March–April 1981): 12.

Tanner, Tony. "Present Imperfect: A Note on the Works of Walter Abish." *Granta*, September 1979, p. 65.

West, Paul. "Germany in the Aftermath of War." *Washington Post Book World*, 9 November 1980, p. 4.

HENRY ADAMS

Beach, Joseph Warren. *The Outlook For American Prose*. Chicago: University of Chicago Press, 1926, pp. 202–24.

Burke, Kenneth. *A Grammar of Motives and Rhetoric of Motives*. Cleveland & New York: Meridian Books, 1962.

Conder, John J. *A Formula of His Own: Henry Adam's Literary Experiment*. Chicago: University of Chicago Press, 1970.

Donoghue, Denis. *Connoisseurs of Chaos: Ideas of Order in Modern American Poetry*. New York: Macmillan, 1965, pp. 9–22.

Eliot, T. S. "A Sceptical Patrician." In *Major Writers of America*, Vol. II, ed. Perry Miller. New York: Harcourt, Brace & World, 1962, pp. 793–96. Reprinted from *Athenaeum*, 23 May 1919.

Hume, Robert A. *Runaway Star: An Appreciation of Henry Adams*. Ithaca: Cornell University Press, 1951.

Kirk, Russell. *The Conservative Mind*. London: Faber & Faber, 1965, pp. 338–48.

Levenson, J. C. *The Mind and Art of Henry Adams*. Boston: Houghton Mifflin, 1957.

Mane, Robert. *Henry Adams on the Road to Chartres*. Cambridge, MA: Harvard University Press, 1971.

Samuels, Ernest. *Henry Adams: The Major Phase*. Cambridge, MA: Harvard University Press, 1964.

Stevenson, Elizabeth. *Henry Adams*. New York: Macmillan, 1955.

Warren, Austin. *The New England Conscience*. Ann Arbor: University of Michigan Press, 1966, pp. 170–81.

Wilson, Edmund. "Introduction" to reprinting of Henry Adams's *Life of George Cabot Lodge*. In *The Shock of Recognition*, edited by Edmund Wilson. Garden City, NY: Doubleday, Doran, 1943, pp. 742–46.

LEONIE ADAMS

Bogan, Louise. *Selected Criticism*. New York: Noonday Press, 1955.

Roethke, Theodore. "How to Write Like Somebody Else." *Yale Review* 48 (1958–59): 336–43.

Zabel, Morton Dauwen. "A Harrier of Heaven." *Poetry* 35 (1929–30): 332–36.

RENATA ADLER

Boyd, Blanche M. "A Mannered Slouch." *Nation*, 6 November 1976, pp. 469–71.

Kornbluth, Jesse. "The Quirky Brilliance of Renata Adler." *New York*, 12 December 1983, pp. 34–40.

MacVicar, Bill. "Fuzzy Snapshots of a Failed Romance." *Maclean's*, 16 January 1984.

Simmons, Steven. *Harper's Magazine* 268 (February 1984): 76.

Todd, Richard. "Tales from Two Cities." *Atlantic Monthly* 238 (October 1976): 111–14.

Towers, Robert. "*Speedboat.*" *New York Times Book Review*, 26 September 1976, pp. 6–7.

JAMES AGEE

Barson, Alfred T. *A Way of Seeing: A Critical Study of James Agee*. Amherst: University of Massachusetts Press, 1972.

Doty, Mark A. *Tell Me Who I Am: James Agee's Search for Selfhood*. Baton Rouge: Louisiana State University Press, 1981.

Fabre, Genevieve. "A Bibliography of the Works of James Agee." *Bulletin of Bibliography* 24 (1963–66): 145–48, 163.

Kazin, Alfred. *On Native Grounds*. New York: Day, Reynal & Hitchcock, 1942.

Kramer, Victor A. *James Agee*. Boston: Twayne, 1975.

Larsen, Erling. *James Agee*. Minneapolis: University of Minnesota Press, 1971.

Madden, David, ed. *Remembering James Agee*. Baton Rouge: Louisiana State University Press, 1974.

Moreau, Genevieve. *The Restless Journey of James Agee*. Tr. Miriam Kleiger and Morty Schiff. New York: William Morrow, 1977.

Seib, Kenneth. *James Agee: Promise and Fulfillment*. Pittsburgh: University of Pittsburgh Press, 1968.

CONRAD AIKEN

"Answer to the Sphinx." *Times Literary Supplement*, 19 April 1963, pp. 257–58.

Beach, Joseph Warren. "Conrad Aiken and T. S. Eliot: Echoes and Overtones." *PMLA* 69 (1954): 753–62.

Blackmur, R. P. "Introduction" to *The Collected Novels of Conrad Aiken*. New York: Holt, Rinehart & Winston, 1964.

Blanshard, Rufus A. "Pilgrim's Progress: Conrad Aiken's Poetry." *Texas Quarterly* 1 (1958): 135–48.

Bonnell, F. W., and R. C. Bonnell. *Conrad Aiken: A Bibliography*. San Marino, CA: Huntington Library, 1982.

Edison, George. "Thematic Symbols in the Poetry of Aiken and MacLeish." *University of Toronto Quarterly* 10 (1940): 12–26.

Malin, Irving, ed. *Conrad Aiken's Prose*. Special issue of *Southern Quarterly*, Fall 1982.

Moore, Marianne. "If a Man Die." *Wake* 11 (1952): 50–56.

Peterson, Houston. *The Melody of Chaos*. New York: Longmans, Green, 1931.

Rein, David M. "Conrad Aiken and Psychoanalysis." *Psychoanalytic Review* 42 (1955): 402–11.

EDWARD ALBEE

Amacher, Richard E. *Edward Albee*. New York: Twayne, 1969.

Bigsby, C. W. E. *Albee*. Edinburgh: Oliver & Boyd, 1969.

Bigsby, C. W. E. *Edward Albee: A Collection of Critical Essays*. Englewood Cliffs, NJ: Prentice-Hall, 1975.

Corrigan, Robert W. *The Theatre in Search of a Fix*. New York: Delacorte, 1973.

Evans, Gareth Lloyd. *The Language of Modern Drama*. New York and London: J. M. Dent/Dutton (Everyman's Library), 1977.

Hayman, Ronald. *Edward Albee*. London: Heinemann, 1971.

Heilman, Robert B. *American Dreams, American Nightmares*. Carbondale: Southern Illinois University Press, 1970.

Kerr, Walter. *Thirty Plays Hath November: Pain and Pleasure in the Contemporary Theater*. New York: Simon & Schuster, 1969.

Rutenberg, Michael E. *Edward Albee: Playwright in Protest*. New York: Drama Book Specialists, 1969.

WILLIAM ALFRED

"One Saturday in Brooklyn." *The New Yorker*, 18 December 1965, pp. 42–46.

NELSON ALGREN

Beauvoir, Simone de. "An American Rendezvous: The Question of Fidelity, Part II." *Harper's* 229 (December 1964): 111–22.

Bluestone, George. "Nelson Algren." *Western Review* 22 (1957): 27–44.

Farrell, James T. "The Short Story." In *American Writers' Congress*, ed. Henry Hart. New York: International, 1935.

Fiedler, Leslie A. "The Novel in the Post-Political World." *Partisan Review* 23 (1956): 358–65.

Geismar, Maxwell. "Nelson Algren: The Iron Sanctuary." In *American Moderns: From Rebellion to Conformity*. New York: Hill & Wang, 1958, pp. 187–94.

Kazin, Alfred. "Nelson Algren on the Wild Side." In *Contemporaries*. Boston: Little, Brown, 1962.

Lipton, Lawrence. "A Voyeur's View of the Wild Side: Nelson Algren and His Reviewers." *Chicago Review* 10 (1957): 4–14.

Mailer, Norman. "Quick and Expensive Comments on the Talent in the Room." In *Advertisements for Myself*. New York: Putnam, 1959.

A. R. AMMONS

Bloom, Harold. "The Breaking of the Vessels." In *Figures of Capable Imagination*. New York: Seabury Press, 1976, pp. 209–33.

Bloom, Harold. "Emerson and Ammons: A Coda." *Diacritics* 3 (Winter 1973): 45–46.

Bloom, Harold. "In the Shadow of the Shadows: For Now." In *A Map of Misreading*. New York and London: Oxford University Press, 1975, pp. 198–203.

Davie, Donald. "Cards of Identity." *New York Review of Books*, 6 March 1975, pp. 10–11.

Donoghue, Denis. "Ammons and the Lesser Celandine." *Parnassus* 3 (1974–75): 19–26.

Holder, Alan. *A. R. Ammons*. Boston: Twayne, 1978.

Howard, Richard. "A. R. Ammons." In *Alone with America*. New York: Atheneum, 1969.

Jacobson, Josephine. "The Talk of Giants." *Diacritics* 3 (Winter 1973): 34–39.

Lehman, David. "Perplexities Embraced." *Times Literary Supplement*, 25 May 1984, p. 523.

Orr, Linda. "The Cosmic Backyard of A. R. Ammons." *Diacritics* 3 (Winter 1973): 1–12.

JON ANDERSON

Halpern, Daniel. "Letters of Song." *New Republic*, 29 March 1975, pp. 25–26.

Jaffe, Daniel. "A Shared Language in the Poet's Tongue." *Saturday Review*, 3 April 1971, pp. 31–33, 46.

Kalstone, David. "Poetry Has Made Friends with Everyone." *New York Times Book Review*, 13 February 1972, Part 2, pp. 3, 16–18.

Mills, Ralph J. "Critic of the Month: V." *Poetry* 113 (1968–69): 262–84.

Stitt, Peter. "Poets of the Inside and Out." *New York Times Book Review*, 15 April 1984.

Williamson, Alan. "The Energy Crisis in Poetry." *Shenandoah* 26 (1974): 41–53.

MAXWELL ANDERSON

Bailey, Mabel. *Maxwell Anderson: The Playwright as Prophet*. London: Abelard-Schumann, 1957.

Clark, Barrett H. *Maxwell Anderson: The Man and His Plays*. New York: Samuel French, 1933.

Cox, Martha. *Maxwell Anderson Bibliography*. Charlottesville, VA: Bibliographical Society, University of Virginia, 1958.

Downer, Alan S. "Beyond the Fourth Wall." In *Fifty Years of American Drama*. Chicago: Gateway, 1966.

Klink, William. *Maxwell Anderson and S. N. Behrman: A Reference Guide*. Boston: G. K. Hall, 1977.

Shivers, Alfred S. *The Life of Maxwell Anderson*. New York: Stein & Day, 1983.

Woodbridge, Homer E. "Maxwell Anderson." *South Atlantic Quarterly* 44 (1945): 55–68.

ROBERT ANDERSON

Adler, Thomas P. *Robert Anderson*. Boston: Twayne, 1978.

Bentley, Eric. "The Theatre." *New Republic*, 4 October 1954, p. 22.

Hayes, Richard. "The Stage: 'Tea and Sympathy.'" *Commonweal* 59 (1953): 90–91.

SHERWOOD ANDERSON

Kazin, Alfred. "The *Letters of Sherwood Anderson*." In *The Inmost Leaf: A Selection of Essays*. New York: Harcourt, Brace, 1955.

Lovett, Robert Morss. "Sherwood Anderson." In *After the Genteel Tradition: American Writers 1910–1930*, ed. Malcolm Cowley. Carbondale: Southern Illinois University Press, 1964.

Sheehy, Eugene P., and Kenneth A. Lohf. *Sherwood Anderson: A Bibliography*. New York: Kraus Reprint, 1967.

White, Ray Lewis. "Sherwood Anderson." In *The Politics of Twentieth-Century Novelists*, ed. George A. Panichas. New York: Hawthorn Books, 1971.

White, Ray Lewis. *Sherwood Anderson: A Reference Guide*. Boston: G. K. Hall, 1977.

White, Ray Lewis, ed. *The Achievement of Sherwood Anderson: Essays in Criticism*. Chapel Hill: University of North Carolina Press, 1966.

Wilson, Edmund. "Many Marriages." *The Dial* 74 (1923): 399–400.

MAYA ANGELOU

Blackburn, Regina. "In Search of the Black Female Self." In *Women's Autobiography: Essays in Criticism*, ed. Estelle C. Jelinek. Bloomington: Indiana University Press, 1980.

Cameron, Dee Birch. "A Maya Angelou Bibliography." *Bulletin of Bibliography* 36 (1979): 50–52.

Elliot, Jeffrey. "Maya Angelou: In Search of Self." *Negro History Bulletin* 40 (1977): 694–95.

Grumbach, Doris. "Fine Print." *New Republic*, 6 & 13 July 1974, pp. 30–32.

Kelly, Ernece B. *Harvard Educational Review* 40 (1970): 681–82.

Rosinsky, Natalie N. "Mothers and Daughters: Another Minority Group." In *The Lost Tradition: Mothers and Daughters in Literature*, eds. Cathy N. Davidson and E. M. Brower. New York: Frederick Ungar, 1980.

JOHN ASHBERY

Ashton, Dave. *The New York School: A Cultural Reckoning*. New York: Viking, 1973.

Auden, W. H. Forward to *Some Trees*. New Haven: Yale University Press, 1976.

Berke, Roberta. *Bounds Out of Bounds: A Compass for Recent American and British Poetry*. New York & London: Oxford University Press, 1981.

Bloom, Harold. *A Map of Misreading*. New York & London: Oxford University Press, 1975.

Bloom, Harold. *Figures of Capable Imagination*. New York: Seabury Press, 1976.

Donoghue, Denis. Review of *Rivers and Mountains*. *New York Review of Books*, 14 April 1966, p. 19.

Kermani, David. *John Ashbery: A Comprehensive Bibliography*. New York: Garland, 1976.

Kostelanetz, Richard. *The Old Poetries and the New*. Ann Arbor: University of Michigan Press, 1981.

Lehman, David. *Beyond Amazement: New Essays on John Ashbery*. Ithaca: Cornell University Press, 1980.

Molesworth, Charles. *The Fierce Embrace: A Study of Contemporary American Poetry*. Columbia: University of Missouri Press, 1979.

Perloff, Marjorie. *The Poetics of Indeterminacy*. Princeton: Princeton University Press, 1981.

Shapiro, David. *John Ashbery, An Introduction to His Poetry*. New York: Garland, 1976.

ISAAC ASIMOV

Elkins, Charles. "Isaac Asimov's 'Foundation' Novels: Historical Materialism Distorted into Cyclical Psycho-History." *Science-Fiction Studies* 3 (1976): 26–36.

Fiedler, Jean, and Jim Mele. *Isaac Asimov*. New York: Frederick Ungar, 1982.

Goble, Neil. *Asimov Analyzed*. Baltimore: Mirage Press, 1972.

Grigsby, John L. "Asimov's *Foundation* Trilogy and Herbert's *Dune* Trilogy: A Vision Reversed." *Science-Fiction Studies* 8 (1981): 149–55.

Grigsby, John L. "Herbert's Reversal of Asimov's Vision Reassessed: *Foundation's Edge* and *God Emperor of Dune*." *Science-Fiction Studies* 11 (1984): 174–80.

Olander, Joseph D., and Martin Harry Greenberg, eds. *Isaac Asimov*. New York: Taplinger, 1977.

Wilson, Raymond J. "Asimov's Mystery Story Structure." *Extrapolation* 19 (1978): 101–7.

MARGARET ATWOOD

Grace, Sherill. *Violent Duality: A Study of Margaret Atwood*. Montreal: Vehicule Press, 1980.

Trueblood, Valerie. "Conscience and Spirit." *American Poetry Review* 6 (1977): 19–20.

Wimsatt, Margaret. "The Lady as Humphrey Bogart." *Commonweal* 98 (1973): 483–84.

Wood, Susan. "The Martian Point of View." *Extrapolation* 15 (1974): 161–73.

Woodcock, George. "Margaret Atwood: Poet as Novelist." In *The Canadian Novel in the Twentieth Century*, ed. George Woodcock. Toronto: McClelland & Stewart, 1975, pp. 312–27.

LOUIS AUCHINCLOSS

Adams, J. Donald. "Louis Auchincloss and the Novel of Manners." In *Speaking of Books and Life*. New York: Holt, Rinehart & Winston, 1965.

Bryer, Jackson R. *Louis Auchincloss and His Critics*. Boston: G. K. Hall, 1977.

Kane, Patrick. "Lawyers at the Top: The Fiction of Louis Auchincloss." *Critique* 7 (1964–65): 36–46.

Long, Robert Emmet. "The Image of Gatsby in the Fiction of

Louis Auchincloss and C. D. B. Bryan." *Fitzgerald/Hemingway Annual*, 1972, p. 325–28.

Macauley, Robie. "'Let Me Tell You about the Rich . . .'" *Kenyon Review* 27 (1965): 645–71.

Newquist, Roy. "Louis Auchincloss." In *Counterpoint*. Chicago: Rand McNally, 1964.

JAMES BALDWIN

Boyle, Kay. "Introducing James Baldwin." In *Contemporary American Novelists*, ed. Harry T. Moore. Carbondale: Southern Illinois University Press, 1964.

Coles, Robert. "Baldwin's Burden." *Partisan Review* 31 (1964): 401–16.

Eckman, Fern Marja. *The Furious Passage of James Baldwin*. New York: M. Evans, 1966.

Howe, Irving. "Black Boys and Native Sons." *Dissent* 10 (1963): 353–68.

Kazin, Alfred. "The Essays of James Baldwin." In *Contemporaries*. Boston: Little, Brown, 1962, pp. 254–58.

Kinnamon, Kenneth, ed. *James Baldwin: A Collection of Critical Essays*. Englewood Cliffs, NJ: Prentice-Hall, 1974.

Paris Review. "The Art of Fiction LXXVIII" (interview with James Baldwin). *Paris Review* no. 91 (1984).

West, Anthony. "Sorry Lives." *New Yorker*, June 20, 1953, p. 85.

AMIRI BARAKA

Baraka, Amiri. *The Autobiography of LeRoi Jones*. New York: Freundlich Books, 1984.

Benston, Kimberly W. *Baraka: The Renegade and the Mask*. New Haven: Yale University Press, 1976.

Dace, Letitia. *LeRoi Jones (Imamu Amiri Baraka): A Checklist of Works by and about Him*. London: Nether Press, 1971.

Ellison, Ralph. *Shadow and Act*. New York: New American Library, 1966.

Hudson, Theodore R. *From LeRoi Jones to Amiri Baraka: The Literary Works*. Durham, NC: Duke University Press, 1973.

Littlejohn, David. *Black on White: A Critical Survey of Writing by American Negroes*. New York: Viking, 1966.

DJUNA BARNES

Burke, Kenneth. "Version, Con-, Pre-, and In-: Thoughts on Djuna Barnes' Novel, *Nightwood*." *Southern Review* NS 2 (1966): 329–46.

Eliot, T. S. "Introduction" to *Nightwood*. New York: Harcourt, Brace, 1937.

Frank, Joseph. "Djuna Barnes' *Nightwood*." In *The Widening Gyre*. New Brunswick, NJ: Rutgers University Press, 1963.

Hyman, Stanley Edgar. "The Wash of the World." In *Standards: A Chronicle of Books for Our Time*. New York: Horizon Press, 1966.

Kannenstine, Louis F. *The Art of Djuna Barnes: Duality and Damnation*. New York: New York University Press, 1977.

Messerli, Douglas. *Djuna Barnes: A Bibliography*. New York: David Lewis, 1975.

Nadeau, Robert L. "*Nightwood* and the Freudian Unconscious." *International Fiction Review* 2 (1975): 159–63.

Scott, James B. *Djuna Barnes*. Boston: Twayne, 1976.

Singer, Alan. "The Horse Who Knew Too Much: Metaphor and the Narrative Discontinuity in *Nightwood*." *Contemporary Literature* 25 (1984).

JOHN BARTH

Farwell, Harold. "John Barth's Tenuous Affirmation: 'The Absurd, Unending Possibility of Love.'" *Georgia Review* 28 (1974): 290–306.

Gerhard, Joseph. *John Barth*. Minneapolis: University of Minnesota Press, 1971.

Harris, Charles B. *Contemporary American Novelists of the Absurd*. New Haven: College and University Press, 1971.

Kiernan, Robert F. "John Barth's Artist in the Fun House." *Studies in Short Fiction* 10 (1973): 373–80.

Kyle, Carol A. "The Unity of Anatomy: The Structure of Barth's *Lost in the Funhouse*." *Critique* 13, No. 3 (1972): 31–43.

Mercer, Peter. "The Rhetoric of *Giles Goat-Boy*." *Novel* 4 (1971): 147–58.

Morrell, David. *John Barth: An Introduction*. University Park: Pennsylvania State University Press, 1976.

Noland, Richard W. "John Barth and the Novel of Comic Nihilism." *Wisconsin Studies in Contemporary Literature* 7 (1966): 239–57.

Slethaug, Gordon E. "Barth's Refutation of the Idea of Progress." *Critique* 13, No. 3 (1972): 11–29.

Tatham, Campbell. "John Barth and the Aesthetics of Artifice." *Contemporary Literature* 12 (1971): 60–73.

Tharpe, Jac. *John Barth: The Comic Sublimity of Paradox*. Carbondale: Southern Illinois University Press, 1974.

Vine, Richard Allan. *John Barth: An Annotated Bibliography*. Metuchen, NJ: Scarecrow Press, 1977.

Waldmeir, Joseph J., ed. *Critical Essays on John Barth*. Boston: G. K. Hall, 1980.

DONALD BARTHELME

Bruss, Paul. "Barthelme: The Essential Contradiction." In *Victims: Textual Strategies in Recent American Fiction*. Lewisburg, PA: Bucknell University Press, 1981.

Couturier, Maurice, and Regis Durand. *Donald Barthelme*. London: Methuen, 1982.

Donoghue, Denis. "What's Your Inner Reality?" *New York Review of Books*, 24 August 1967, pp. 12–13.

French, Warren. *Donald Barthelme*. Boston: Twayne, 1981.

Gillen, Francis. "Donald Barthelme's Cuty: A Guide." *Twentieth Century Literature* 18 (1972): 37–44.

Gilman, Richard. "Barthelme's Fairy Tale." *New Republic*, 3 June 1967, pp. 27–30.

Longleigh, Peter. "Donald Barthelme's *Snow White*." *Critique* 11, No. 3 (Summer 1969): 3–34.

McCaffery, Larry. *The Metafictional Muse: The Work of Robert Coover, Donald Barthelme and William H. Gass*. Pittsburgh: University of Pittsburgh Press, 1982.

Weixlmann, J. and S. "Barth and Barthelme Recycle the Perseus Myth." *Modern Fiction Studies* 25 (1979): 191–207.

L. FRANK BAUM

Baum, L. Frank. *The Annotated Wizard of Oz*. Edited by Michael Patrick Hearn. New York: C. N. Potter, 1973.

Bewley, Marius. "The Land of Oz: America's Great Good Place." In *Masks and Mirrors: Essays in Criticism*. New York: Atheneum, 1970, pp. 255–67.

Moore, Raylyn. *Wonderful Wizard, Marvelous Land*. Preface by Ray Bradbury. Bowling Green: Bowling Green University Popular Press, 1974.

Sale, Roger. "L. Frank Baum and Oz." In *Fairy Tales and After*. Cambridge, MA: Harvard University Press, 1978, pp. 223–43.

Wagenknecht, Edward. *Utopia Americana*. Seattle: University of Washington Book Store, 1929.

PETER S. BEAGLE

Foust, R. E. "Fabulous Paradigm: Fantasy, Meta-Fantasy, and Peter S. Beagle's *The Last Unicorn*." *Extrapolation* 21 (1980): 5–20.

Fuller, Edmund. "Unique Recluse." *New York Times Book Review*, 5 June 1960, p. 34.

Norford, Don Perry. "Reality and Illusion in Peter Beagle's *The Last Unicorn*." *Studies in Modern Fiction* 19 (1977): 93–104.

Stevens, David. "Incongruity in a World of Illusion: Patterns of Humor in Peter Beagle's *The Last Unicorn*." *Extrapolation* 20 (1979): 230–37.

ANN BEATTIE

Balliett, Whitney. "Closeups." *New Yorker*, 9 June 1980, pp. 148–54.

Goodwin, Gail. "Sufferers from Smug Despair." *New York Times Book Review*, 14 January 1979, p. 14.

Locke, Richard. "Keeping Cool." *New York Times Book Review*, 11 May 1980, pp. 1, 38–39.

Towers, Robert. "Period Fiction: 'Falling in Place.'" *New York Review of Books*, 15 May 1980, p. 32.

S. N. BEHRMAN

Bliven, Naomi. "The Smart Set." *New Yorker*, 7 December 1968, pp. 240–45.

Clurman, Harold. *New York Times Book Review*, 25 June 1972, p. 7.

Dodd, Loring Holmes. *Celebrities at Our Hearthside*. Boston: Chapman & Grimes, 1955.

Heniford, Lewis Williams. "S. N. Behrman as a Social Dramatist." Ph.D. diss.: Stanford University, 1964.

Hicks, Granville. "The Odd One." *Saturday Review*, 20 July 1968, pp. 21–22.

Levin, Milton I. "S. N. Behrman: The Operation and Dilemmas of the Comic Spirit." Ph.D. diss.: University of Michigan, 1958.

SAUL BELLOW

Adams, R. M. "Winter's Tales." *The New York Times Book Review*, 19 July 1984, p. 28.

Axthelm, Peter M. "The Full Perception: Bellow." In *The Modern Confessional Novel*. New Haven: Yale University Press, 1967.

Bayley, John. "By Way of Mr. Sammler." *Salmagundi* 30 (1975): 24–33.

Chomsky, Noam. "Bellow's Israel." *New York Arts Journal*, Spring 1977, pp. 29–32.

Clayton, John Jacob. *Saul Bellow: In Defense of Man*. Bloomington: Indiana University Press, 1968.

Dutton, Robert. *Saul Bellow*. Boston: Twayne Publishers, 1982.

Galloway, David D. *The Absurd Hero in American Fiction*. Austin: University of Texas Press, 1966.

Hall, James. "Portrait of the Artist as a Self-Creating, Self-Vindicating, High Energy Man: Saul Bellow." In *The Lunatic Giant in the Drawing Room: The British and American Novel Since 1930*. Bloomington: Indiana University Press, 1968.

Harper, Gordon Lloyd. Interview with Saul Bellow. In *Writers at Work: The Paris Review Interviews*. New York: The Viking Press, 1967.

Josipovici, Gabriel. "Herzog: Freedom and Wit." In *The*

World and The Book. Stanford: University of California Press, 1971, pp. 221–35.

Malin, Irving. *Saul Bellow and the Critics*. New York: New York University Press, 1967.

Hughes, Daniel. "Reality and the Hero: *Lolita* and *Henderson the Rain King*." *Modern Fiction Studies* 6 (1960–61): 345–64.

Nault, Marianne. *Saul Bellow: His Works and His Critics, An Annotated International Bibliography*. New York: Garland Publishers, 1977.

Rahv, Philip. "Saul Bellow's Progress." In *The Myth and the Powerhouse*. New York: Farrar, Straus, and Giroux, 1949, pp. 218–24.

Roth, Philip. "Imagining Jews." *New York Review of Books*, 3 October 1974, pp. 22–28.

Wisse, Ruth R. "The Schlemiel as Liberal Humanist." In *The Schlemiel as Modern Hero*. Chicago: University of Chicago Press, 1971.

STEPHEN VINCENT BENÉT

Fenton, Charles A. *Stephen Vincent Benét: The Life and Times of an American Man of Letters, 1898–1943*. New Haven: Yale University Press, 1958.

Kreymborg, Alfred. *A History of American Poetry: Our Singing Strength*. New York: Tudor, 1929.

LaFarge, Christopher. "The Narrative Poetry of Stephen Vincent Benét." *Saturday Review*, 5 August 1944, pp. 106–8.

Matthiessen, F. O. *The Literary History of the United States*. Vol. 2. New York: Macmillan, 1946.

Untermeyer, Louis. *American Poetry since 1900*. New York: Henry Holt, 1923.

Wiley, Paul L. "The Phaeton Symbol in *John Brown's Body*." *American Literature* 17 (1945): 231–42.

THOMAS BERGER

Bryant, Rene Kuhn. "Berger's Plastic Nostalgia." *National Review* 27 (1975): 1127–28.

Davenport, Guy. *National Review* 19 (1967): 1282.

Harris, Michael. "A Garden of Devious Delights." *Washington Post Book World*, 20 April 1975, p. 3.

Lee, L. L. "American, Western, Picaresque: Thomas Berger's *Little Big Man*." *South Dakota Review* 4 (1966): 35–42.

Mellors, John. "Squaw New World." *Listener*, 11 July 1974, pp. 61–62.

Michaels, Leonard. *New York Times Book Review*, 20 March 1977, pp. 1, 25–26.

Todd, Richard. "God's First Mistakes." *Atlantic Monthly* 232 (September 1973): 106.

Weber, Brom. *Saturday Review*, 21 March 1970, p. 42.

JOHN BERRYMAN

Arpin, Gary Q. *John Berryman: A Reference Guide*. Boston: G. K. Hall, 1976.

Arpin, Gary Q. *The Poetry of John Berryman*. Port Washington, NY: Kennikat Press, 1978.

Carruth, Hayden. "Declining Occasions." *Poetry* 112 (1968): 119–21.

Conaroe, Joel. *John Berryman: An Introduction to the Poetry*. New York: Columbia University Press, 1977.

Cott, Jonathan. "Theodore Roethke and John Berryman: Two Dream Poets." In *On Contemporary Literature*, ed. Richard Kostelanetz. New York: Avon, 1964.

Dunn, Douglas. "Gaiety and Lamentation: The Defeat of John Berryman." *Encounter* 43 (August 1974): 72–77.

Frye, Northrop. *Canadian Forum* 22 (1942): 220.

Gustafsson, Bo. *The Soul under Stress: A Study of the Poetry of John Berryman*. Stockholm: Almquist & Wiksell, 1984.

Mazzacco, Robert. "Harlequin in Hell." *New York Review of Books*, 29 June 1967, p. 12.

Shapiro, Karl. "Major Poets of the Ex-English Language." *Chicago Tribune Book World*, 26 January 1969.

Toynbee, Philip. "Berryman's *Songs*." *Encounter* 24 (March 1965): 76–78.

Wasserstrom, William. "Cagey John: Berryman as Medicine Man." *Centennial Review* 12 (1968): 334–54.

AMBROSE BIERCE

Davidson, Cathy N., ed. *Critical Essays on Ambrose Bierce*. Boston: G. K. Hall, 1982.

De Castro, Adolphe. *Portrait of Ambrose Bierce*. New York: Century, 1929.

Fatout, Paul. *Ambrose Bierce: The Devil's Lexicographer*. Norman: University of Oklahoma Press, 1951.

Fatout, Paul. *Ambrose Bierce and the Black Hills*. Norman: University of Oklahoma Press, 1956.

Hall, Carroll D. *Bierce and the Poe Hoax*. San Francisco: Book Club of California, 1943.

McWilliams, Carey. *Ambrose Bierce: A Biography*. New York: A. & C. Boni, 1929.

Neale, Walter. *Life of Ambrose Bierce*. New York: Neale, 1929.

Starrett, Vincent. *Ambrose Bierce*. Chicago: Walter M. Hill, 1920.

Woodruff, Stuart C. *The Short Stories of Ambrose Bierce*. Pittsburgh: University of Pittsburgh Press, 1964.

ELIZABETH BISHOP

Estess, Sybil. "Toward the Interior: Epiphany in 'Cape Breton' as Representative Poem." *World Literature Today* 51 (1977): 49–52.

Jarrell, Randall. "Fifty Years of American Poetry." In *The Third Book of Criticism*. New York: Farrar, Straus & Giroux, 1969.

Kalstone, David. "Conjuring with Nature: Some Twentieth-Century Readings of the Pastoral." In *Twentieth-Century Literature in Retrospect*, ed. Reuben A. Brower. Cambridge, MA: Harvard University Press, 1971.

Malkoff, Karl. "Elizabeth Bishop." In *Crowell's Handbook to Contemporary Poetry*. New York: Thomas Y. Crowell, 1973.

Mazzaro, Jerome. "Elizabeth Bishop and the Poetics of Impediment." *Salmagundi* 27 (1974): 118–25.

Perloff, Marjorie. "Elizabeth Bishop: The Course of a Particular." *Modern Poetry Studies* 8 (1977): 177–92.

Pinsky, Robert. "The Idiom of a Self: Elizabeth Bishop and Wordsworth." *American Poetry Review* 9 (1980): 6–8.

Quebe, Ruth. "Water, Windows and Birds: Image-Theme Patterns in Elizabeth Bishop's *Questions of Travel*." *Modern Poetry Studies* 10 (1979): 68–82.

Spiegelman, Willard. "Landscapes and Knowledge: The Poetry of Elizabeth Bishop." *Modern Poetry Studies* 6 (1975): 203–24.

Stevenson, Anne. *Elizabeth Bishop*. New York: Twayne, 1966.

Wylie, Diana. *Elizabeth Bishop and Howard Nemerov: A Reference Guide*. Boston: G. K. Hall, 1983.

JOHN PEALE BISHOP

Fiedler, Leslie A. "John Peale Bishop and the Other Thirties." *Commentary* 43 (1967): 74–82.

Frank, Joseph. "Force and Form." *Sewanee Review* 55 (1947): 70–107.

Frank, Joseph. "The Achievement of John Peale Bishop." In *The Widening Gyre.* New Brunswick, NJ: Rutgers University Press, 1963.

White, Robert L. *John Peale Bishop.* New York: Twayne, 1966.

Wilson, Edmund. "John Peale Bishop." In *The Bit between My Teeth.* New York: Farrar, Straus & Giroux, 1965.

R. P. BLACKMUR

Donoghue, Denis. "Poetic in the Common Enterprise." *Twentieth Century Literature* 161 (1957): 537–46.

Frank, Joseph. "R. P. Blackmur." In *The Widening Gyre.* New Brunswick, NJ: Rutgers University Press, 1963.

Hyman, Stanley Edgar. "R. P. Blackmur and the Expense of Criticism." *Poetry* 71 (1948): 259–70.

Kazin, Alfred. "Criticism and Isolation." *Virginia Quarterly Review* 17 (1941): 448–53.

Pannick, Gerald J. *Richard Palmer Blackmur.* Boston: Twayne, 1981.

Pannick, Gerald J. "R. P. Blackmur: A Bibliography." *Bulletin of Bibliography,* 31 (1974): 165–69.

Schwartz, Delmore. "The Critical Method of R. P. Blackmur." *Poetry* 53 (1938): 28–39.

ROBERT BLY

Davis, William V. "Defining the Age." *Moons and Lion's Tails* 2 (1977): 85–89.

Libby, Anthony. "Fire and Light: Four Poets to the End and Beyond." *Iowa Review* 4 (1973): 111–26.

Mersmann, James F. "Robert Bly: Watering the Rocks." In *Out of the Vortex: A Study of Poetry against War.* Lawrence, KS: University Press of Kansas, 1974, pp. 113–57.

LOUISE BOGAN

Olson, Elder. "Louise Bogan and Léonie Adams." *Chicago Review* 8 (1954): 70–87.

Peterson, Douglas. "The Poetry of Louise Bogan." *Southern Review* 19 (1983): 83–87.

Ridgeway, Jacqueline. "The Necessity of Form to the Poetry of Louise Bogan." *Women's Studies* 5 (1977): 137–49.

Tate, Allen. "Nine Poets: 1937." In *Reason in Madness.* New York: Putnam's, 1941.

Van Doren, Mark. "Louise Bogan." *Nation,* 31 October 1923, p. 494.

Whittemore, Reed. "The Principles of Louise Bogan and Yvor Winters." *Sewanee Review* 63 (1955): 161–68.

EDGAR BOWERS

Trimpi, Helen P. "Contexts for 'Being,' 'Divinity,' and 'Self in Valéry and Edgar Bowers." *Southern Review* 13 (1977): 48–82.

JANE BOWLES

Dillon, Millicent. *A Little Original Sin: The Life and Work of Jane Bowles.* New York: Holt, Rinehart & Winston, 1981.

Williams, Tennessee. "Introduction" to *Feminine Wiles.* Santa Barbara: Black Sparrow Press, 1976.

PAUL BOWLES

Aldridge, John W. "Paul Bowles: The Canceled Sky." In *After the Lost Generation.* New York: McGraw-Hill, 1951, pp. 184–93.

Codman, Florence. *Commonweal* 51 (1949–50): 346.

Davis, Robert Gorham. "A Relentless Drive toward Doom." *New York Times Book Review,* 2 March 1952, pp. 1, 17.

Hardison, O. B., Jr. "Reconsideration: Paul Bowles' *The Sheltering Sky.*" *New Republic,* 27 September 1975, pp. 64–65.

Hayes, Richard. *Commonweal* 53 (1951–52): 547.

Pritchett, V. S. *New Statesman and Nation* 44 (1952): 41.

Rolo, Charles J. "Tangier." *Atlantic Monthly* 189 (March 1952): 84–85.

Stern, Daniel. "Encounters East and West." *New York Times Book Review,* 6 August 1967, p. 24.

Thomson, Virgil. "Untold Tales." *New York Review of Books,* 18 May 1972, pp. 35–36.

KAY BOYLE

Bourjaily, Vance. "Moving and Maturing." *New York Times Book Review,* 28 September 1980, pp. 9, 32.

Burt, Struthers. "Kay Boyle's Coincidence and Melodrama." *Saturday Review,* 15 January 1944, p. 6.

Carpenter, Richard C. "Kay Boyle: The Figure in the Carpet." *Critique* 7 (1964): 65–78.

Knoll, Robert E. "Love Poems." *Prairie Schooner* 38 (1963): 176–78.

O'Hara, J. D. *"The Underground Woman."* *New York Times Book Review,* 2 February 1975, p. 4.

Rothman, Nathan L. "Foreign Legion in Colorado." *Saturday Review,* 9 April 1949, p. 13.

Rovit, Earl. "Distant Landscapes." *Nation,* 27 September 1980, pp. 286–87.

RAY BRADBURY

Attebery, Brian. *The Fantasy Tradition in American Literature.* Bloomington: Indiana University Press, 1980.

Bradford, Tom. *Chicago Review* 23 (1971): 160–66.

Indick, Ben P. *The Drama of Ray Bradbury.* Baltimore: T-K Graphics, 1977.

Johnson, Wayne L. *Ray Bradbury.* New York: Frederick Ungar, 1980.

Nolan, William F. *The Ray Bradbury Companion.* Detroit: Bruccoli Clark Books, 1975.

GWENDOLYN BROOKS

Baker, Houston A., Jr. "The Achievement of Gwendolyn Brooks." *College Language Association Journal* 16 (1972): 23–31.

Barksdale, Richard K. "Humanistic Protest in Recent Black Poetry." In *Modern Black Poets.* Englewood Cliffs, NJ: Prentice-Hall, 1973.

Lupack, Alan C. "Brooks' 'Piano after War.'" *The Explicator* 36 (1978): 2–3.

Lynch, Charles H. "Robert Hayden and Gwendolyn Brooks: A Critical Study." Ph.D. diss.: New York University, 1977.

Miller, R. Baxter. *Langston Hughes and Gwendolyn Brooks: A Reference Guide.* Boston: G. K. Hall, 1978.

Park, Sue S. "A Study of Tension: Gwendolyn Brooks's 'The Chicago Defender Sends a Man to Little Rock.'" *Black American Literature Forum* 11 (1977): 32–34.

Shaw, Harry B. *Gwendolyn Brooks.* Boston: Twayne, 1980.

PEARL S. BUCK

Brenni, Vito. "Pearl Buck: A Selected Bibliography." *Bulletin of Bibliography* 22 (1956–59): 65–69; 94–96.

Carson, E. H. A. "Pearl Buck's Chinese." *Canadian Bookman,* June-July 1939, pp. 55–59.

Henschoz, Ami. "A Permanent Element in Pearl Buck's Novels." *English Studies* 25 (1943): 97–103.

Spencer, Cornelia. *The Exile's Daughter: A Biography of Pearl S. Buck*. New York: Coward-McCann, 1944.

Walsh, Richard J. *A Biographical Sketch of Pearl S. Buck*. New York: Day, Reynal & Hitchcock, 1936.

KENNETH BURKE

Auden, W. H. "A Grammar of Assent." *New Republic*, 14 July 1941, p. 59.

Booth, Wayne C. "Kenneth Burke's Comedy: The Multiplication of Perspectives." In *Critical Understanding: The Powers and Limits of Pluralism*. Chicago: University of Chicago Press, 1979.

Brown, Merle E. *Kenneth Burke*. Minneapolis: University of Minnesota Press, 1969.

Dickey, James. "Kenneth Burke." In *Babel To Byzantium*. New York: Farrar, Straus & Giroux, 1956.

Donoghue, Denis. *The Ordinary Universe*. New York: Macmillan, 1968.

Fraiberg, Louis. "Kenneth Burke's Terminological Medium of Exchange." In *Psychoanalysis and American Literary Criticism*. Detroit: Wayne State University Press, 1960.

Frank, Armin Paul. "The Reception of Kenneth Burke in Europe." In *Critical Responses to Kenneth Burke: 1924–1966*, ed. W. H. Rueckert. Minneapolis: University of Minnesota Press, 1969.

Nemerov, Howard. "Everthing, Preferably All at Once: Coming to Terms with Kenneth Burke." *Sewanee Review* 79 (1971): 189–201.

Rueckert, William H. *Kenneth Burke and the Drama of Human Relations*. Minneapolis: University of Minnesota Press, 1963.

WILLIAM BURROUGHS

Ableman, Paul. "No Jokes." *Spectator*, 4 April 1981, p. 24.

Beaver, Harold. "Dismantling the System." *Times Literary Supplement*, 21 December 1979, p. 150.

Disch, Thomas M. "Pleasures of Hanging." *New York Times Book Review*, 15 March 1981, p. 14.

Hollinghurst, Alan. "Travelling with Kim's Gang." *Times Literary Supplement*, 4 May 1984, p. 486.

Knickerbocker, Conrad. "William Burroughs: An Interview." *Paris Review*, no. 35 (Fall 1965): 13–49.

LaHood, M. J. *World Literature Today* 55 (1981): 326.

Lodge, David. "Objections to William Burroughs." In *The Novelist at the Crossroads*. London: Routledge & Kegan Paul, 1971, pp. 161–71.

Seltzer, Alvin J. "'Confusion Hath Fuck His Masterpiece': The Random Art of William S. Burroughs." In *Chaos in the Novel: The Novel in Chaos*. New York: Schocken Books, 1974.

Tytell, John. *American Book Review* 3 (May–June 1981): 8.

ACKNOWLEDGMENTS

Advent Publishers. DAMON KNIGHT, "When I Was in Kneepants: Ray Bradbury," *In Search of Wonder: Essays on Modern Science Fiction*, copyright © 1967. Reprinted by permission.

American Imago. DANIEL WEISS, "Caliban on Prospero: A Psychoanalytic Study of the Novel *Seize the Day*," Fall 1962, copyright © 1962. Reprinted by permission of Wayne State University Press.

American Quarterly. HENRY M. LITTLEFIELD, "The Wizard of Oz: Parable on Populism," Spring 1964, copyright © 1964. Reprinted by permission.

American Scholar. EARL ROVIT, "Bellow in Occupancy," Spring 1965, copyright © 1965 by the United Chapters of Phi Beta Kappa. Reprinted by permission of the publisher.

Atheneum Publishers. RICHARD HOWARD, "A. R. Ammons: The Spent Seer Consigns Order to the Vehicle of Change," "John Ashbery: You May Never Know How Much Is Pushed Back into the Night, Nor What May Return," *Alone with America*, copyright © 1980. Reprinted by permission.

The Atlantic. JOHN ALDRIDGE, "Dance of Death," July 1968, copyright © 1968. R. P. BLACKMUR, "Conrad Aiken: The Poet," Dec. 1953, copyright © 1953. BENJAMIN DEMOTT, "Six Novels in Search of a Novelist," Nov. 1979, copyright © 1979. ALFRED KAZIN, "My Friend Saul Bellow," Jan. 1965, copyright © 1965. Reprinted by permission.

Basic Books, Inc. CONRAD AIKEN, "Poetry and the Mind of Modern Man," *Poets on Poetry*, edited by Howard Nemerov, copyright © 1966. IRVING HOWE, "Sherwood Anderson: *Winesburg, Ohio*," *The American Novel*, edited by Wallace Stegner, copyright © 1965. Reprinted by permission of Basic Books, Inc.

Beacon Press. DONALD HALL, "Poetry Food," DAVID SEAL, "Waking to Sleepers Joining Hands," *Of Solitude and Silence*, copyright © 1981 by Poetry East. Reprinted by permission of Beacon Press. LIONEL TRILLING, "Adams at Ease," *A Gathering of Fugitives*, copyright © 1956. Reprinted by permission.

Black Scholar. ROBERT CHRISMAN, "*Black Scholar* Interviews Maya Angelou," January/February 1977, copyright © 1977. Reprinted by permission.

Bowling Green University Popular Press. A. JAMES STUPPLE, "The Past, the Future, and Ray Bradbury," *Voices for the Future: Essays on Major Science Fiction Writers*, edited by Thomas Clareson, copyright © 1976. Reprinted by permission of Bowling Green University Popular Press.

Cambridge University Press. JOHN BAYLEY, "The Poetry of John Ashbery," *Selected Essays*, copyright © 1984. Reprinted by permission.

Canadian Literature. PHYLLIS GROSSKURTH, "Victimization or Survival?" Winter 1973, copyright © 1973. Reprinted by permission.

Centennial Review. WILLARD SPIEGELMAN, "Elizabeth Bishop's 'Natural Heroism,'" Winter 1978, copyright © 1978. Reprinted by permission.

Chicago Review. BEVERLY GROSS, "The Anti-Novels of John Barth," Vol. 20, No. 3 (Nov. 1968), copyright © 1968. ELDER OLSON, "Louise Bogan and Léonie Adams," Fall 1954, copyright © 1954. Reprinted by permission.

Columbia University Press. BABETTE DEUTSCH, *Poetry in Our Time*, copyright © 1952, 1956 by Columbia University Press. WERNER SOLLORS, "Early Poetry and Prose," *The Quest for a Populist Literature*, copyright © 1978. Reprinted by permission.

Commentary. PEARL K. BELL, "Marge Piercy and Ann Beattie," July 1980, copyright © 1980. RICHARD CHASE, "The Adventures of Saul Bellow: Progress of a Novelist," April 1959, copyright © 1959. JOSEPH EPSTEIN, "The Sunshine Girls," June 1984, copyright © 1984. STEVEN MARCUS, "The American Negro in Search of Identity," Nov. 1953, copyright © 1953.

Commonweal. HENRY RAGO, "Pity and Fear," Dec. 3, 1954, copyright © 1954 by the Commonweal Foundation. WILFRID SHEED, "The Twin Urges of James Baldwin," June 24, 1977, copyright © 1977 by the Commonweal Foundation. Reprinted by permission of *Commonweal*.

Contemporary Literature. DANIEL FUCHS, "Saul Bellow and the Modern Tradition," Vol. 15, No. 4 (Winter 1974), copyright © 1974. WILLIAM MEREDITH, "Henry Tasting All of the Secret Bits of Life: Berryman's Dream Songs," (Winter-Spring 1965), copyright © 1965. Reprinted by permission of the University of Wisconsin Press.

Continuum Publishing Company. HAROLD BLOOM, "The Charity of the Hard Moments," "Dark and Radiant Peripheries," "The New Transcendentalism," *Figures of Capable Imagination*, copyright © 1976 by Harold Bloom. Reprinted by permission of Continuum Publishing Company.

Cornell University Press. CHARLES BERGER, "Vision in the Form of a Task: The Double Dream of Spring," *Beyond Amazement: New Essays on John Ashbery*, edited by David Lehman, copyright © 1980. Reprinted by permission of Cornell University Press.

Critical Quarterly. KERRY MCSWEENEY, "Saul Bellow and the Life to Come," Spring 1976, copyright © 1976. Reprinted by permission of *Critical Quarterly*.

Criticism. PAUL A. BOVÉ, "R. P. Blackmur and the Job of the Critic: Turning from the New Criticism," Vol. 25, No. 4 (1983), copyright © 1983. Reprinted by permission of Wayne State University Press.

Critique. OLIVER EVANS, "Paul Bowles and the Natural Man," Spring–Fall 1959, copyright © 1959. DONALD GREINER, "Djuna Barnes' *Nightwood* and the American Origins of Black Humor," Aug. 1975, copyright © 1975. IHAB HASSAN, "Conscience and Incongruity," Fall 1962, copyright © 1962. LARRY MCCAFFERY, "Barthelme's *Snow White*: The Aesthetics of Trash," Aug. 1975, copyright © 1975. JAY RUDD, "Thomas Berger's *Arthur Rex*: Galahad and Earthly Power," Winter 1984, copyright © 1984. ALAN WILLIAMSON, "The Divided Image: The Quest for Identity in the Works of Djuna Barnes," Spring 1964, copyright © 1964. Reprinted by permission.

Diacritics. DAVID KALSTONE, "Ammons' Radiant Toys," PATRICIA A. PARKER, "Configurations of Shape and Flow," Winter 1973, copyright © 1973. Reprinted by permission of Johns Hopkins University Press.

Duke University Press. JAMES BAIRD, "Djuna Barnes and Surrealism: 'Backward Grief,'" *Individual and Community*, edited by Kenneth H. Baldwin, copyright © 1975. JOHN D. STARKS, "John Barth," *The Literature of Exhaustion: Borges, Nabokov, Barth*, copyright © 1974. Reprinted by permission of Duke University Press.

E. P. Dutton, Inc. VAN WYCK BROOKS, "San Francisco: Ambrose Bierce," *The Confident Years: 1885–1915*, copyright © 1952. Reprinted by permission.

Epoch. FORREST READ, "Herzog: A Review," Fall 1964, copyright © 1964. Reprinted by permission of *Epoch*.

Everett/Edwards, Inc. SHELDON NORMAN GREBSTEIN, "Nelson Algren and the Whole Truth," *The Forties: Fiction, Poetry, Drama*, edited by Warren French, copyright © 1969 by Warren French. Reprinted by permission.

Extrapolation. PATRICIA S. WARRICK, "The Contrapuntal Design of Artificial Evolution in Asimov's 'The Bicentennial Man,'" Fall 1981, copyright © 1981. Reprinted by permission.

The Far Point. WILLIAM HEYEN, "Inward to the World: The Poetry of Robert Bly," Fall/Winter 1969, copyright © 1969. Reprinted by permission.

Farrar, Straus & Giroux, Inc. NEWTON ARVIN, excerpts from "Introduction" to *The Selected Letters of Henry Adams*, copyright © 1951 by Newton Arvin. JOHN BERRYMAN, "A Note on *Augie*," *The Freedom of the Poet*, copyright © 1953 by Kate Berryman. TRUMAN CAPOTE, "Introduction" to *The Collected Works of Jane Bowles*, copyright © 1966 by Truman Capote. JAMES DICKEY, "Conrad Aiken," *Babel to Byzantium*, copyright © 1959, 1963, 1968 by James Dickey. EDMUND WILSON, "Prize–Winning Blank Verse," *The Shores of Light*, copyright © 1952 by Edmund Wilson. Reprinted by permission of Farrar, Straus & Giroux, Inc.

Gentleman's Quarterly. L. M. KIT CARSON, "Robert Bly Wants to Make a Man Out of You," Oct. 1984, copyright © 1984 by the Condé Nast Publications Inc. Reprinted by permission of the William Morris Agency for L. M. Kit Carson.

The Georgia Review. JEROME KLINKOWITZ, "Walter Abish and the Surfaces of Life," Summer 1981, copyright © 1981. Reprinted by permission of the *Georgia Review*.

Greenwood Press. C. W. E. BIGSBY, "The Black Poet as Cultural Sign," *The Second Black Renaissance*, copyright © 1980. Reprinted by permission.

Harcourt Brace Jovanovich, Inc. KINGSLEY AMIS, *New Maps of Hell*, 1960, copyright © 1960. HORACE GREGORY, "Léonie Adams," *A History of American Poetry*, copyright © 1946. ALFRED KAZIN, "The New Realism: Sherwood Anderson and Sinclair Lewis," *On Native Grounds*, copyright © 1942. MARY MCCARTHY, "Burroughs' *Naked Lunch*," *The Writing on the Wall*, copyright © 1966 by Encounter, Inc. Reprinted by permission of Harcourt Brace Jovanovich, Inc. VERNON L. PARRINGTON, "Henry Adams—Intellectual," *Main Currents in American Thought*, Vol. III, copyright © 1930. Reprinted by permission.

Harper's. HAYDEN CARRUTH, "Poets on the Fringe," Oct. 1980, copyright © 1979. RODERICK COOK, "Books in Brief," Jan. 1966, copyright © 1966. IRVING HOWE, "James Baldwin: At Ease in Apocalypse," Sept. 1968, copyright © 1968. Reprinted by permission of Irving Howe. HUGH KENNER, "From Lower Bellowvia," Feb. 1982, copyright © 1981. LOUIS SIMPSON, "New Book of Poems," Aug. 1968, copyright © 1968. Reprinted by special permission of Harper's Magazine Foundation.

Harper & Row, Publishers, Inc. TONY TANNER, "Rub Out the Word," "What is the Case?" "Fragments and Fantasies," *City of Words*, copyright © 1971. Reprinted by permission of Harper & Row, Publishers, Inc.

Harvard University Press. HELEN VENDLER, "Berryman, Ammons, Cummings," "Elizabeth Bishop," *Part of Nature, Part of Us: Modern American Poets*, copyright © 1980 by the President and Fellows of Harvard College. Reprinted by permission of the publishers.

The Hollins Critic. HOWARD NELSON, "Welcoming Shadows," Vol. 12, No. 2, (April 1975), copyright © 1975. Reprinted by permission of *The Hollins Critic*.

Holmes & Meier Publishers, Inc. PATRICK MOORE, "The Poetry of Louise Bogan," *Gender and Literary Voice*, edited by Janet Todd, copyright © 1980 by Holmes & Meier Publishers, Inc. Reprinted by permission of Holmes & Meier.

Holt, Rinehart & Winston. BASIL DAVENPORT, "Stephen Vincent Benét," *Selected Works of Stephen Vincent Benét*, copyright © 1942. JOHN GASSNER, "Affirmations?" *Theatre at the Crossroads*, copyright © 1960. Reprinted by permission.

Johns Hopkins University Press. ANGUS FLETCHER, "Volume and Body in Burke's Criticism," *Representing Kenneth Burke*, edited by Hayden White and Margaret Brose, copyright © 1983. Reprinted by permission of Johns Hopkins University Press.

Houghton Mifflin Company. MAXWELL GEISMAR, "Sherwood Anderson: Last of the Townsmen," *The Last of the Provincials: The American Novel 1915–25*, copyright © 1943, 1947, 1949, 1975 by Maxwell Geismar. Reprinted by permission of Houghton Mifflin Company.

House of Anansi Press Ltd. GEORGE WOODCOCK, "Bashful But Bold: Notes on Margaret Atwood as Critic," *The Art of Margaret Atwood*, edited by Arnold E. Davidson and Cathy N. Davidson, copyright © 1981. Reprinted by permission of House of Anansi Press Ltd.

The Hudson Review. WILLIAM DICKEY, "The Poem and the Moment," Spring 1971, copyright © 1971. JOHN SIMON, "Theatre Chronicle," Winter 1966–67, copyright © 1966. Reprinted by permission of the *Hudson Review*.

Indiana University Press. BRIAN ATTEBERY, *The Fantasy Tradition in American Literature*, copyright © 1980. RUBY COHN, "The Verbal Murders of Edward Albee," *Dialogue in American Drama*, copyright © 1971. STEPHANIE A. DEMETRAKOPOULOS, "The Metaphysics of Matrilinearism in Women's Autobiography," *Women's Autobiography: Essays in Criticism*, copyright © 1980. Reprinted by permission of Indiana University Press.

The Iowa Review. JOHN VERNON, "William S. Burroughs," Vol. 3, No. 2 (Spring 1972), copyright © 1972. Reprinted by permission.

Iowa State University Press. JEROME KLINKOWITZ, "Donald Barthelme's Art of Collage," *The Practice of Fiction in America*, copyright © 1980 by Iowa State University Press. Reprinted by permission of Iowa State University Press.

Judaism. HAROLD FISCH, "The Hero as Jew: Reflections on Herzog," Winter 1968, copyright © 1968. Reprinted by permission of *Judaism*.

The Kenyon Review. CLEANTH BROOKS, "Form and Content," Vol. 4, No. 2 (Spring 1942) copyright © 1942, 1970 by Kenyon College. Reprinted by permission of the publisher. RICHARD CHASE, "Sense and Sensibility," Vol. 8, No. 4 (Autumn 1951), copyright © 1951, 1979 by Kenyon College. Reprinted by permission of the publisher. HARRY T. MOORE, "Kay Boyle's Fiction," Vol. 22, No. 2 (Spring 1960), copyright © 1960. Reprinted by permission of the publisher and the author. JOHN CROWE RANSOM, "An Address to Kenneth Burke," Vol. 4, No. 2 (Spring 1942), copyright © 1942, 1970 by Kenyon College. Reprinted by permission of the publisher and the author. LIONEL TRILLING, "Greatness With One Fault In It," Vol. 4, No. 1 (Winter 1942), copyright © 1942, 1969 by Kenyon College. Reprinted by permission of the publisher and the author's estate.

Alfred A. Knopf, Inc.—Random House, Inc. ROBERT BRUSTEIN, *The Third Theatre*, copyright © 1966 by Robert Brustein. Reprinted by permission of Alfred A. Knopf, Inc. WILLIAM FAULKNER, "A Note on Sherwood Anderson," (1953), *Essays, Speeches and Public Lectures*, edited by James B. Meriweather, copyright © 1965. Reprinted by permission of Random House, Inc. RICHARD GILMAN "Chinese Boxes," *Common and Uncommon Masks: Writings on Theatre 1961–1970*, copyright © 1971 by Richard Gilman. Reprinted by permission of Random House, Inc. JOHN UPDIKE, "Dark Smiles, Devilish Saints," "Stalled Starters," (appeared as "Seeresses" in *The New Yorker*), "Draping Radiance with a Worn Veil," *Hugging the Shore: Essays and Criticism*, copyright © 1983 by Alfred A. Knopf. Reprinted by permission of Alfred A. Knopf. This material originally appeared in *The New Yorker*. GORE VIDAL, "American Plastic: The Matter of Fiction," *Matters of Fact and Fiction: Essays 1973–1976*, copyright © 1977. Reprinted by permission of Random House, Inc.

Literature/Film Quarterly. JOHN W. TURNER, "Little Big Man, The Novel and the Film," Spring 1977, copyright © 1977. Reprinted by permission.

Little, Brown and Company. ALFRED KAZIN, *Bright Book of Life: American Novelists and Storytellers from Hemingway to Mailer*, copyright © 1971, 1973 by Alfred Kazin. Reprinted by permission of Little, Brown and Company.

Louisiana State University Press. FREDERICK J. HOFFMAN, "Anderson: Psychoanalyst by Default," *Freudianism and the Literary Mind*, copyright © 1945, 1957 by Louisiana State University Press. Reprinted by permission of Louisiana State University Press.

Macmillan & Co. Ltd. (London). JOHN HAFFENDEN, "The Care and Feeding of Long Poems," *John Berryman*, copyright © 1980. Reprinted by permission.

Macmillan Publishing Co. (New York). HAROLD CLURMAN, *The Naked Image: Observations on the Modern Theatre*, copyright © 1962, 1966 by Harold Clurman. Reprinted by permission. GERALD WEALES, "Edward Albee: Don't Make Waves," *The Jumping-Off Place: American Drama in the 1960s*, copyright © 1969. Reprinted by permission.

The MIT Press. PATRICIA S. WARRICK, *The Cybernetic Imagination in Science Fiction*, copyright © 1980. Reprinted by permission of the MIT Press.

Michigan State University Press. MARTIN GARDNER, "The Royal Historian of Oz," RUSSEL NYE, "An Appreciation," *The Royal Historian of Oz and Who He Was*, copyright © 1975. Reprinted by permission.

Midstream. ROBERT ALTER, "The Stature of Saul Bellow," Dec. 1964, copyright © 1964. Reprinted by permission of Robert Alter.

Modern Fiction Studies. THOMAS M. LEITCH, "Donald Barthelme and the End of the End," Vol. 28, No. 1 (Spring 1982), copyright © 1982. CHARLES RUSSELL, "The Vault of Language: Self-Reflective

Artifice in Contemporary Fiction," Vol. 20, No. 3 (Autumn 1974), copyright © 1974. Reprinted by permission of Purdue Research Foundation.

The Nation. JOHN CIARDI, "Two Nuns and a Strolling Player," May 22, 1954, copyright © 1954. HAROLD CLURMAN, Oct. 27, 1962, copyright © 1962; Nov. 29, 1965, copyright © 1965. DOUGLAS CRASE, "Justified Times," Sept. 1, 1984, copyright © 1984. ELIZABETH FRANK, "The Middle of the Journey," April 7, 1984, copyright © 1984. GARY GIDDINS, "'Quanta, Amy Said on the Train . . .'" Feb. 18, 1984, copyright © 1984. RICHARD HOWARD, "A New Beginning," Jan. 18, 1971, copyright © 1971. STANLEY J. KUNITZ, "The Poetry of Conrad Aiken," Oct. 14, 1931, copyright © 1931. MARSHALL MCLUHAN, "Notes on Burroughs," Dec. 28, 1964, copyright © 1964. SAUL MALOFF, "Love: The Movement Within," March 2, 1963, copyright © 1963. MICHAEL MALONE, "American Literature's Little Big Man," July 3, 1980, copyright © 1980. EDGAR SNOW, "Pearl Buck's Worlds," Nov. 13, 1954, copyright © 1954. GERALD SYKES, "Too Good to Be Smart," Dec. 24, 1930, copyright © 1930. DAVID STEVENSON, "Tender Anguish," Dec. 14, 1957, copyright © 1957. ELIOT WEINBERGER, "Gloves on a Mouse," Nov. 17, 1979, copyright © 1979. Reprinted by permission of the *Nation*.

The New Leader. PEARL K. BELL, "Blacks and the Blues," May 27, 1974. FRANCIS LEVY, "Reversing Roles," Nov. 12, 1973, copyright © The American Labor Conference on International Affairs, Inc. Reprinted with permission of the *New Leader*.

The New Republic. JACK BEATTY, "Falling in Place," June 7, 1980, copyright © 1980. ROBERT BRUSTEIN, "Self-Parody and Self-Murder," March 3, 1980, copyright © 1980. MALCOLM COWLEY, "Wang Lung's Children," May 10, 1939, copyright © 1939; June 5, 1950, copyright © 1950. GARRETT EPPS, "Arthur Rex," Oct. 7, 1978, copyright © 1978. JAMES T. FARRELL, "On the Wrong Side of Town," May 21, 1956, copyright © 1956. IRVING HOWE, "Odysseus, Flat on His Back," Sept. 19, 1964, copyright © 1964. ANNE HULBERT, "Secrets and Surprises," Jan. 20, 1979, copyright © 1979. STANLEY KAUFFMAN, April 17, 1971, copyright © 1971. ROGER ROSENBLATT, "The Back of the Book," Oct. 16, 1976, copyright © 1976. DELMORE SCHWARTZ, "The Self Against the Sky," Nov. 2, 1953, copyright © 1953. THEODORE SOLOTAROFF, "The Desert Within," Sept. 2, 1967, copyright © 1967. ANNE TYLER, "End of a Love Affair," Dec. 5, 1983, copyright © 1983. JOHN WAIN, "Naked Lunch," Dec. 1, 1962, copyright © 1962. ROBERT PENN WARREN, "The Man With No Commitments," Nov. 2, 1953, copyright © 1953. Reprinted by permission of *The New Republic*.

New Statesman and Nation. FRANK KERMODE, Feb. 5, 1965, copyright © 1965. V. S. PRITCHETT, June 19, 1954, copyright © 1954. Reprinted by permission of The Statesman & Nation Publishing Company Ltd.

New York Magazine. JOHN SIMON, "Evolution Made Queasy," Feb. 10, 1975, copyright © 1975; "From Hunger Not Dubuque," Feb. 11, 1980, copyright © 1980. Reprinted by permission of *New York*.

The New Yorker. "W. A.," in "The Talk of the Town," Jan. 25, 1982, copyright © 1982. HELEN VENDLER, "Understanding Ashbery," March 16, 1981, copyright © 1981. EDMUND WILSON, "Kay Boyle and *The Saturday Evening Post*," Jan. 15, 1944, copyright © 1944. Reprinted by permission.

New York Review of Books. JOHN ASHBERY, "The American Grain," Feb. 22, 1973, copyright © 1973. ROBERT BRUSTEIN, "Everybody Knows My Name," Dec. 17, 1964, copyright © 1964. F. W. DUPEE, "James Baldwin and the 'Man,'" Feb. 1963, copyright © 1963. R. W. FLINT, "Rhapsody in Blue," Feb. 6, 1964, copyright © 1964. WILLIAM H. GASS, "The Leading Edge of the Trash Phenomenon," April 25, 1968, copyright © 1968. ROBERT LOWELL, "The Poetry of John Berryman," May 28, 1964, copyright © 1964. DARRYL PINCKNEY, "Blues for Mr. Baldwin," Dec. 6, 1979, copyright © 1979. PHILIP ROTH, "Channel X: Two Plays on the Race Conflict," May 28, 1964, copyright © 1964; "The Play That Dare Not Speak Its Name," Feb. 25, 1965, copyright © 1965. ROGER SALE, "Hostages," May 26, 1977, copyright © 1977. CHARLES THOMAS SAMUELS, "Serious Ladies," Dec. 15, 1966,

copyright © 1966. ROGER SHATTUCK, "A Higher Selfishness?" Sept. 18, 1975, copyright © 1975; "Quanta," March 15, 1984, copyright © 1984. GORE VIDAL, "The Great World and Louis Auchincloss," July 18, 1974, copyright © 1974; "On Rereading the Oz Books," Oct. 13, 1977, copyright © 1977. Reprinted by permission of *The New York Review of Books*.

New York Times Book Review. JOHN ASHBERY, "Up From the Underground," Jan. 29, 1967, copyright © 1967. Toni Cade Bambara, "Report From Part One," Jan. 7, 1973, copyright © 1973. CALVIN BEDIENT, "Sphere," Dec. 22, 1974, copyright © 1974. HAROLD BLOOM, "The Critic/Poet," Feb. 5, 1958, copyright © 1958. LEO BRAUDY, "Don Juan as a Blend of Sex and History," Sept. 10, 1972, copyright © 1972; May 13, 1973, copyright © 1973. MAXWELL GEISMAR, "Aristocrat of the Short Story," July 10, 1964, copyright © 1964. HERBERT GOLD, "After All, Who is the Enemy?" June 2, 1963, copyright © 1963. ANNIE GOTTLIEB, "Growing Up and the Serious Business of Survival," June 16, 1974, copyright © 1974. GEOFFREY HARTMAN, "A Poet as His Own Victim," July 30, 1972; "Collected Poems, 1951–71," Nov. 19, 1972, copyright © 1972. JOHN HOLLANDER, "Briefings," May 9, 1971, copyright © 1971. IRVING HOWE, Oct. 17, 1976, copyright © 1976. DAVID KALSTONE, "Uplands," May 9, 1971, copyright © 1971. ARNO KARLEN, "Hard Shell, Soft Center," Aug. 22, 1965, copyright © 1965. ALFRED KAZIN, "The Wild Boys," Dec. 12, 1971, copyright © 1971. JULIUS LESTER, "James Baldwin: Reflections of a Maverick," May 27, 1984, copyright © 1984. ABIGAIL MCCARTHY, "Tribalism, Not Feminism," Aug. 12, 1984, copyright © 1984. CHRISTOPHER MIDDLETON, "Language Woof-Side Up," June 17, 1984, copyright © 1984. ARTHUR MIZENER, "Young Lochinvar Rides to Defeat," Sept. 21, 1958, copyright © 1958. WEBSTER SCHOTT, "Up Above the World," March 20, 1966, copyright © 1966. MURIEL SPARK, "Breaking Up With Jake," Dec. 18, 1983, copyright © 1983. ROB WELLBURN, "Reviving Soul in Newark, New Jersey," Feb. 14, 1971, copyright © 1971. MICHAEL WOOD, "A Love Song to What Would Be Lost," March 6, 1983, copyright © 1983. Reprinted by permission of The New York Times Co., Inc.

New York University Press. GEORGE WELLWARTH, *The Theatre of Protest and Paradox: Developments in the Avant-Garde Drama*, copyright © 1964, 1971 by New York University. Reprinted by permission of New York University Press.

Northeastern University Press. SAMUEL J. BERNSTEIN, "'Double Solitaire' by Robert Anderson," *The Strands Entwined*, copyright © 1980. Reprinted by permission of Northeastern University Press.

Northwest Review. HOWARD NEMEROV, "A Response to the Antiphon," Summer 1958, copyright © 1958. Reprinted by permission.

Ohio Review. MICHAEL DENNIS BROWNE, "Henry Fermenting: Debts to the *Dream Songs*," PETER STITT, "John Berryman: The Dispossessed Poet," Winter 1974, copyright © 1974. Reprinted by permission.

Ohio University Press. MAX F. SCHULZ, "The Metaphysics of Multiplicity," "The Thousand and One Masks of John Barth," *Black Humor Fiction of the Sixties: A Pluralistic Definition of Man and His World*, copyright © 1973. ALLEN TATE, "John Peale Bishop," *On the Limits of Poetry*, copyright © 1948. YVOR WINTERS, "Henry Adams or The Creation of Confusion," *In Defense of Reason*, copyright © 1947. Reprinted by permission of Ohio University Press, Athens.

Ontario Review. IRVING MALIN, "Abrupt Mutilations," No. 12, Spring-Summer 1980, copyright © 1980. Reprinted by permission.

Oxford University Press. CONRAD AIKEN, "Sherwood Anderson," *Collected Criticism*, copyright © 1968. HAROLD BLOOM, "Measuring the Canon: John Ashbery's *Wet Casements* and *Tapestry*," *Agon: Towards a Theory of Revisionism*, copyright © 1982. HERBERT GOLD, "*Winesburg, Ohio*: The Purity and Cunning of Sherwood Anderson," *Modern American Fiction*, edited by A. Walton Litz, copyright © 1963. JAMES GUNN, *Isaac Asimov: The Foundations of Science Fiction*, copyright © 1982. DAVID KALSTONE, "John Ashbery: *Self-Portrait in a Convex Mirror*," "Elizabeth Bishop: Questions of Memory, Questions of Travel," *Five Temperaments*, copyright © 1977. EDMUND WILSON, "Ambrose Bierce on the

Owl Creek Bridge," *Patriotic Gore*, copyright © 1962. Reprinted by permission.

Parnassus: Poetry in Review. CAROL MUSKE, "Ourselves as History," Spring/Summer 1976, copyright © 1976 by Poetry in Review Foundation. R. B. STEPTO, "The Phenomenal Woman and the Severed Daughter," Fall 1979, copyright © 1979 by Poetry in Review Foundation. Reprinted by permission.

Partisan Review. W. H. AUDEN, "The Rewards of Patience," July–Aug. 1942, copyright © 1942, 1970. PAUL GOODMAN, Jan.–Feb. 1942, copyright © 1942. ELIZABETH HARDWICK, "A Fantastic Voyage," Spring 1959, copyright © 1959. DELMORE SCHWARTZ, "Adventure in America," Jan. 1954, copyright © 1954. STEPHEN SPENDER, "James Baldwin: Voice of a Revolution," Summer 1963, copyright © 1963. Reprinted by permission of *Partisan Review*.

Poetry. LÉONIE ADAMS, review of Louise Bogan's *Collected Poems: 1923–53*, Dec. 1954, copyright © 1954 by the Modern Poetry Association. Reprinted by permission of the editor. PAUL BRESLIN, "Warpless and Woofless Subtleties," Oct. 1980, copyright © 1980 by the Modern Poetry Association. Reprinted by permission of the editor. FORD MADOX FORD, "The Flame in Stone," June 1937, copyright © 1937. Reprinted by permission of Janice Biala Brustlein and the editor. RICHARD HOWARD, July 1963, copyright © 1963 by the Modern Poetry Association. Reprinted by permission of Richard Howard and the editor. STANLEY KUNITZ, "Bronze by Gold," April 1950, copyright © 1950; "No Middle Flight," July 1957, copyright © 1957 by the Modern Poetry Association. Reprinted by permission of Stanley Kunitz and the editor. HAROLD ROSENBERG, "Poetry and the Theatre," Dec. 1940, copyright © 1940 by the Modern Poetry Association. Reprinted by permission. VERNON SHETLEY, "Language on a Very Plain Level," July 1982, copyright © 1982 by the Modern Poetry Association. Reprinted by permission of Vernon Shetley and the editor. HELEN VENDLER, "Spheres and Ragged Edges," Oct. 1982, copyright © 1982 by the Modern Poetry Association. Reprinted by permission of Helen Vendler and the editor. AMOS WILDER, "Sketches from Life," Dec. 1945, copyright © 1945 by the Modern Poetry Association. Reprinted by permission of Amos Wilder and the editor. MORTON DAUWEN ZABEL, "The American Grain," Aug. 1936, copyright © 1936; "A Harrier of Heaven," Feb. 1930, copyright © 1930 by the Modern Poetry Association. Reprinted by permission of Alta Fisch Sutton and the editor.

Princeton University Press. DENIS DONOGHUE, "Introduction" to *Poems of R. P. Blackmur*, copyright © 1977. JAY MARTIN, "Introduction" to *Conrad Aiken: A Life of His Art*, copyright © 1962. Both excerpts reprinted by permission of Princeton University Press.

Ramparts. STEPHEN SCHNECK, "Le Roi Jones or, Poetics and Policemen, or, Trying Heart, Bleeding Heart," June 29, 1968, copyright © 1968. Reprinted by permission.

Raritan. DAVID BROMWICH, excerpts from "Elizabeth Bishop's Dream-Houses," Summer 1984, copyright © 1984. Reprinted by permission.

Review of Existential Psychology and Psychiatry. JEROME MAZZARO, "John Berryman and the Yeatsian Mask," Dec. 1973, copyright © 1973. Reprinted by permission.

Rutgers University Press. ARTHUR OBERG, "John Berryman: 'The Horror of Unlove,'" *Modern American Lyric: Lowell, Berryman, Creeley and Plath*, copyright © 1978 by Rutgers, The State University of New Jersey. Reprinted by permission.

Salmagundi. JOHN BAYLEY, "John Berryman: A Question of Imperial Sway," JAN B. GORDON, "Days and Distances: The Cartographic Imagination of Elizabeth Bishop," HYATT H. WAGGONER, "The Poetry of A. R. Ammons: Some Notes and Reflections," *Contemporary Poetry in America*, edited by Robert Boyers, copyright © 1974. Reprinted by permission.

Saturday Review. JOHN W. ALDRIDGE, "The Fire Next Time?" June 15, 1974, copyright © 1974. BENJAMIN DEMOTT, "James Baldwin on the Sixties: Acts and Revelations," May 27, 1972, copyright © 1972. HENRY HEWES, "Fair Play for Schrafft's," Feb. 10, 1968, copyright © 1968. GRANVILLE HICKS, "Portrait in Brownstone," July 14, 1962, copyright © 1962. JAMES KELLY, "Sin-Soaked in Storyville," May 26, 1956, copyright © 1956. TENNESSEE WIL-

LIAMS, "The Human Psyche—Alone," Dec. 23, 1950, copyright © 1950. Reprinted by permission.

Sewanee Review. R. P. BLACKMUR, "The Novels of Henry Adams," Vol. 51, No. 2 (Spring 1943). YVOR WINTERS, "The Poetry of Edgar Bowers," Vol. 64, No. 4 (1956), copyright © 1956. Reprinted by permission of *Sewanee Review*.

Simon & Schuster, Inc. ROBERT BRUSTEIN, "Fragments from a Cultural Explosion," "Three Playwrights and a Protest," *Seasons of Discontent: Dramatic Opinions 1959–65*, copyright © 1965 by Robert Brustein. Reprinted by permission of Simon & Schuster, Inc.

Southern Humanities Review. SIDONIE ANN SMITH, "The Song of a Caged Bird: Maya Angelou's Quest After Self-Acceptance," Fall 1973, copyright © 1973. Reprinted by permission.

Southern Illinois University Press. FREDERICK J. HOFFMAN, "The Fool of Experience: Saul Bellow's Fiction," *Contemporary American Novelists*, edited by Harry T. Moore, copyright © 1964. ANNE PAOLUCCI, "Exorcisms," *From Tension to Tonic*, copyright © 1972. Reprinted by permission of Southern Illinois University Press.

Southern Methodist University Press. W. M. FROHOCK, "James Agee— The Question of Wasted Talent," *The Novel of Violence in America*, copyright © 1957. Reprinted by permission.

Southern Review. ALLEN TATE, "Mr. Burke and the Historical Environment," Vol. 2, No. 2, copyright © 1936. Reprinted by permission of Louisiana State University Press. RENÉ WELLEK, "R. P. Blackmur Re-Examined," Vol. 7, No. 3 (Summer 1971), copyright © 1971. Reprinted by permission of *Southern Review*.

The Spectator. PETER ACKROYD, "A Little Black Magic," July 6, 1974, copyright © 1974. Reprinted by permission of the *Spectator*, London.

Stratford-Upon-Avon Studies. BRIAN WAY, "Sherwood Anderson," *The American Novel and the 1920s*, edited by Edward Arnold, copyright © 1971. Reprinted by permission of Edward Arnold Publishers.

Studies in Short Fiction. EUSEBIO L. RODRIGUES, "Koheleth in Chicago: The Quest for the Real in 'Looking for Mr. Green,'" Summer 1974, copyright © 1974. Reprinted by permission of *Studies in Short Fiction*.

TriQuarterly. GERALD GRAFF, "The Myth of the Postmodernist Breakthrough," Winter 1973, copyright © 1973. Reprinted by permission of *TriQuarterly*.

Twentieth-Century Literature. MICHAEL HINDEN, "*Lost in the Funhouse*: Barth's Use of the Recent Past," April 1973, copyright © 1973. MANFRED PUETZ, "John Barth's 'The Sot-Weed Factor': The Pitfalls of Mythopoesis," Dec. 1976, copyright © 1976. Reprinted by permission of *Twentieth-Century Literature*.

University of Chicago Press. CHESTER E. EISINGER, "Nelson Algren: Naturalism as the Beat of the Iron Heart," "Paul Bowles and the Passionate Pursuit of Disengagement," *Fiction of the Forties*, copyright © 1963. GERALD GRAFF, "Babbitt at the Abyss," *Literature Against Itself: Literary Ideas in Modern Society*, copyright © 1979. FRANK D. MCCONNELL, "Saul Bellow and the Terms of Our Contract," "John Barth and the Key to the Treasure," *Four Postwar American Novelists*, copyright © 1977. JAMES E. MILLER, "The American Bard: Embarrassed Henry Heard Himself a-Being: John Berryman's *Dream Songs*," *American Quest for a Supreme Fiction*, copyright © 1979. RUTH WISSE, "The Schlemiel as Liberal Humanist," *The Schlemiel as a Modern Hero*, copyright © 1971. Reprinted by permission of the University of Chicago Press.

University of Georgia Press. CALVIN S. BROWN, "The Poetry of Conrad Aiken," *Music and Literature*, copyright © 1948. Reprinted by permission.

University of Illinois Press. CHARLES HARRIS, "The New Medusa: Feminism and the Uses of Myth in *Chimera*," *Passionate Virtuosity: The Fiction of John Barth*, copyright © 1983. ROBERT SCHOLES, "John Barth's *Giles Goat-Boy*," *Fabulation and Metafiction*, copyright © 1959. Reprinted by permission of the University of Illinois Press.

University of Michigan Press. BONNIE COSTELLO, "The Impersonal and the Interrogative in the Poetry of Elizabeth Bishop," SYBIL P.

ESTESS, "Description and Imagination in Elizabeth Bishop's 'The Map,'" DAVID LEHMAN, "'In Prison': A Paradise Regained," *Elizabeth Bishop and Her Art*, edited by Lloyd Schwartz and Sybil P. Estess, copyright © 1983. Reprinted by permission. HARVEY GROSS, "Henry Adams," *The Contrived Corridor*, copyright © 1971. Reprinted by permission of the University of Michigan Press and Harvey Gross. MARGE PIERCY, "Margaret Atwood: Beyond Victimhood," in *Parti-Colored Blocks for a Quilt*, copyright © 1982. First appeared in a column, "From Where I Work," *American Poetry Review*, Vol. 2, No. 6 (1973). Reprinted by permission.

University of Minnesota Press. LOUIS AUCHINCLOSS, *Henry Adams*, copyright © 1970 by the University of Minnesota. WILLIAM J. MARTZ, "John Berryman," *Seven American Poets from Macleish to Nemerov*, edited by Denis Donoghue, copyright © 1969, 1975 by the University of Minnesota. CHARLES C. WALCUTT, "Sherwood Anderson: Impressionism and the Buried Life," *American Literary Naturalism: A Divided Stream*, copyright © 1956 by the University of Minnesota. Reprinted by permission of the University of Minnesota Press.

University of North Carolina Press. HOWARD M. HARPER, "James Baldwin—Art or Propaganda?" *Desperate Faith*, copyright © 1967. JAMES W. TUTTLETON, "Cozzens and Auchincloss," *The Novel of Manners in America*, copyright © 1972. Reprinted by permission of the University of North Carolina Press.

University of Washington Press. ROBERT BÉCHTOLD HEILMAN, "Anderson's *Winterset*," *Tragedy and Melodrama: Versions of Experience*, copyright © 1968. Reprinted by permission.

Viking-Penguin, Inc. Nelson Algren, interviewed by Alston Anderson and Terry Southern, *Writers at Work: The Paris Review Interviews*, edited by Malcolm Cowley, copyright © 1959. MARGARET ATWOOD, "Introduction," to *Three Short Novels* by Kay Boyle, copyright © 1982. John Berryman, interviewed by Peter Stitt, *Writers at Work: The Paris Review Interviews*, edited by George Plimpton, copyright © 1970. MALCOLM COWLEY, "Conrad Aiken: From Savannah to Emerson," *And I Worked at the Writer's Trade*, copyright © 1963, 1964, 1965, 1967, 1968, 1971, 1972, 1975, 1977, 1978 by Malcolm Cowley. Reprinted by permission of Viking-Penguin, Inc. Marianne Moore, *Predilections*, copyright © 1941, 1969 by Marianne Moore. Reprinted by permission.

Virginia Quarterly Review. JAMES M. COX, "Autobiography and America," Vol. 47, No. 2 (Spring 1971), copyright © 1971. Reprinted by permission of *Virginia Quarterly Review*.

Washington Post Book World. MARGARET ATWOOD, "Ann Beattie: Magician of Muddle," May 25, 1980, copyright © 1980. GEOFFREY HARTMAN, "The Wild Man of American Criticism," July 2, 1967, copyright © 1967. Reprinted by permission of the *Washington Post Book World*.

Whitson Publishing Co. HENRY C. LACEY, "Joseph to His Brothers," *To Raise, Destroy, and Create*, copyright © 1981. Reprinted by permission.

Women's Studies. GLORIA BOWLES, "Louise Bogan: To Be (Or Not to Be?) Woman Poet," Vol. 5 (1977), copyright © 1977. Reprinted by permission.

World Literature Today. JEROME MAZZARO, "Elizabeth Bishop's Particulars," Winter 1977, copyright © 1977. Reprinted by permission.

The Yale Review. J. D. MCCLATCHY, Vol. 64, No. 3 (March 1975), copyright © 1975. DAVID THORBURN, "Recent Novels: Realism Redux," Vol. 66, No. 4 (Summer 1977), copyright © 1977. Reprinted by permission of *The Yale Review*.

Yale University Press. ROBERT BONE, *The Negro Novel in America*, copyright © 1966. Reprinted by permission of Robert Bone. DAVID L. MINTER, "Apotheosis of the Form: Henry Adams' *Education*," *The Interpreted Design as a Structural Principle in American Prose*, copyright © 1969. Reprinted by permission of Yale University Press. RAYMOND M. OLDERMAN, *Beyond the Wasteland: A Study of the American Novel in the 1960s*, copyright © 1972. Reprinted by permission.